Handbook of General Psychology

Leon R. Pomeroy, Editorial Associate

Harry Helson

Richard S. Lazarus

Abraham H. Maslow

William J. McGuire

Consulting Editors

Handbook of

PRENTICE-HALL, Inc., Englewood Cliffs, New Jersey

General Psychology

Benjamin B. Wolman, *Editor*

Handbook of General Psychology
Benjamin Wolman, Editor

© 1973 by Prentice-Hall, Inc.
Englewood Cliffs, New Jersey

ISBN: 0–13–378141–0

Library of Congress Catalog Card Number: 74–166142

10   9   8

PRINTED IN THE UNITED STATES OF AMERICA

Prentice-Hall International, Inc., *London*
Prentice-Hall of Australia, Pty. Ltd., *Sydney*
Prentice-Hall of Canada, Ltd., *Toronto*
Prentice-Hall of India Private Limited, *New Delhi*
Prentice-Hall of Japan, Inc., *Tokyo*

In regard to human knowledge there are two questions that may be asked: first, what do we know? and second, how do we know it? The first of these questions is answered by science, which tries to be as impersonal and as dehumanized as possible. In the resulting survey of the universe it is natural to start with astronomy and physics, which deal with what is large and what is universal; life and mind, which are rare and have, apparently, little influence on the course of events, must occupy a minor position in this impartial survey. But in relation to our second question—namely, how do we come by our knowledge—psychology is the most important of the sciences. Not only is it necessary to study psychologically the processes by which we draw inferences, but it turns out that all the data upon which our inferences should be based are psychological in character; that is to say, they are experiences of single individuals. The apparent publicity of our world is in part delusive and in part inferential; all the raw material of our knowledge consists of mental events in the lives of separate people. In this region, therefore, psychology is supreme.

BERTRAND RUSSELL
Human Knowledge, Its Scope and Limits

Contents

The future historian of culture will probably call our century the Century of Psychology. The three giants of psychology, Pavlov, Freud and Piaget, and a score of brilliant and creative minds, such as Thorndike, Hull, Binet, Janet, Skinner, Anokhin, Jung, Adler, Kohler, Bykov, Lorenz, Hinde, and many others have caused a far-reaching revolution in man's knowledge of himself. It seems almost unbelievable that all this wealth of factual data and complex conceptual systems was created by this young science in such a short time. One can hardly compare the present status of psychology to its modest beginnings at the end of the last century.

Today psychology is studied and taught in all centers of human learning and applied to practically all aspects of human life. The American Psychological Association has over thirty thousand members, and tens of thousands of scholars, scientists and professionals are deeply involved in the study and application of the various branches of psychology.

To describe the present status of psychology is like painting the ocean with all its currents and undercurrents, seas and gulfs, thousands of islands, and billions of fishes. Contemporary psychology is not a single discipline any longer. It is a series of comparatively independent scientific systems dealing with human beings and animals, organisms and ideas, biochemistry of genetics and religious beliefs, child development and advertising techniques, and so on. The number of divisions of the American Psychological Association is but a partial indicator of diversity of fields, for each division unites thousands of people who do not necessarily share the same interests.

The common denominator of all these diverse psychological disciplines is the study of behavior; but the term *behavior* is as complex as the term *life*, and encompasses a multitude of overt and covert action patterns of living organisms.

My initial idea was to put together this enormous amount of knowledge and present it in a scholarly, objective, comprehensive, and precise review of psychology. It soon became obvious that no single volume can do justice to this wealth of material no matter how comprehensive it could be. Perhaps time has come for a multivoluminous *Encyclopedia of Behavior*, but the present *Handbook* had to have a more limited scope and more modest aspiration to be of service to graduate students and mature psychologists.

After a series of consultations with the consulting editors and editorial associate as well as some contributors, I have decided to call the present collective volume the *Handbook of General Psychology*. The *Handbook of General Psychology* stresses the elements common to the highly diversified special areas of psychology without pretending to cover all the common elements nor to be encyclopedic.

Perhaps the most significant element binding the various psychological disciplines is the philosophical and methodological foundations. The first three chapters of the *Handbook* review the history of psychology, analyze the present status of psychological theory and discuss the relationship between psychology and the philosophy of science. Chapters 4, 5, 6, 7, and 8 survey most of the research methods currently used by psychologists, such as statistics, psychometrics, experimental design, computer applications, and the use of mathematical models.

The second part, the Human Organism, deals with certain organic foundations of behavior, analyzing the biochemical bases of behavior, motor skills, genetics, somatological development, and psychosomatics.

Preface

Part three, Perception, is devoted to psychophysics, vision, hearing, and other sensory processes, as well as imagery, attention, and overview of theories of perception.

Learning, the subject matter of part four, starts with an introductory overview of learning theories, and continues with animal learning, classic conditioning, operant conditioning, human learning, and remembering and forgetting.

Part five, Language, Thought, and Learning, describes the processes of thinking and problem solving, speech and language, and theories of development and measurement of intelligence.

Motivation and Emotion, part six, starts with an overview of theories of motivation, analyzes aggression and some other drives, sleep and dreaming, and concludes with an analysis of feeling and emotion.

Part seven is devoted to research in Personality and describes structured personality assessment, multivariate experimental research, the humanistic approach, and personality and perception.

The last part of the *Handbook*, Selected Areas, describes four selected areas in psychology, namely, developmental, social, and industrial psychology and experimental hypnosis.

The *Handbook of General Psychology* is in more than one sense a product of collective effort. From the inception of the project, I had the benefit of wise counsel on the part of Harry Helson, Richard S. Lazarus, Abraham H. Maslow, William J. McGuire, Leon R. Pomeroy, and Richard L. Solomon. This *Handbook* couldn't have come into being without their competent, patient, and most friendly help in the choice of contributors and reading and editing of the manuscripts.

In addition to my co-editors, I sought counsel from several colleagues, among them Gordon F. Allport, John Brelsford, Leonard Carmichael, Richard DeBold, Bernard Glueck, Myman Goldstein, Edwin Kahn, William Knaus, Sigmund Koch, Daniel Lagache, Adel Mahran, George Miller, Neal E. Miller, Henry A. Murray, Karl H. Pribram, Ray Rhine, James Spizey, Philip Stone, Silvan Tomkins, and David Wechsler.

All of them have offered encouragement and advice in planning of the *Handbook* and some took part in critical evaluation of the manuscripts. The death of my dear friends Gordon Allport and Abraham Maslow saddened me and deprived all of us of two most creative and original thinkers in psychology. Most of all I am indebted to the contributors to this volume. Their generous and efficient time and efforts formed this *Handbook* into a labor of love that all of us offer to our colleagues and graduate students.

BENJAMIN B. WOLMAN

Contributors

John Calvin Armington (chapter 16), Ph.D. Brown University, is professor of psychology at Northeastern University in Boston. He was the head of the Department of Sensory Psychology at Walter Reed Army Institute of Research (1952–1966) and before that was a research associate at Brown University. Professor Armington serves on the editorial board of the *Journal of General Psychology* and is an honorary editorial advisor for *Vision Research*. His main research interest is in the area of vision and electrical recording, and he has published numerous articles and reviews in journals of physiology, optics, and experimental psychology.

Lloyd L. Avant (chapter 21), Ph.D. Kansas State University, is an associate professor of psychology at Iowa State University. He has been on the faculty of Johns Hopkins University, Kansas State University, and at the Behavioral Science Laboratory of the U.S. Army Human Engineering Laboratories in Aberdeen, Maryland. Dr. Avant's special fields of research interest are sensation, perception, learning, and memory.

Benjamin Balinsky (chapter 44), Ph.D. New York University, is professor and chairman of the department of psychology, Baruch College, City University of New York. He is co-founder and chief consultant of B.F.S. Psychological Associates (an industrial consulting organization). His main areas of interest are normal psychology, personality, interview methods, projective techniques, and executive and personnel development. Besides contributing to various professional journals, Professor Balinsky has written several books: *Counseling and Psychology* (with M.L.Blum, 1951), *The Executive Interview* (with R. Burger, 1956), and *The Selection Interview: Essentials for Management* (1962).

Theodore Xenophon Barber (chapter 45), is Director of Psychological Research at Medfield State Hospital (Massachusetts) and is Assistant Clinical Professor in the Department of Psychiatry at Boston University School of Medicine. Dr. Barber's extensive research in the areas of hypnosis, yoga, and psychedelic drugs has resulted in more than 120 articles in professional journals and numerous books. His most recent works are *Hypnosis: A Scientific Approach* (1969), *LSD, Marihuana, Yoga, and Hypnosis* (1970), and the following (edited with L. V. DiCara, J. Kamiya, N. E. Miller, D. Shapiro, and J. Stoyva): *Biofeedback and Self-Control: 1970* (1971), *Biofeedback and Self-Control: An Aldine Reader on the Regulation of Bodily Processes and Consciousness* (1971), and *Biofeedback and Self-Control: 1971* (1972).

William Bevan (chapter 20), is professor of psychology at The Johns Hopkins University and, at present, is serving as executive officer of the American Association for the Advancement of Science and publisher of *Science* magazine. In addition to attention, his areas of special interest in experimental psychology are perception and cognition.

Arnold Binder (chapter 4), Ph.D. Stanford University, has taught on the psychology faculties at Indiana University and the University of California at Irvine. He has also been a visiting professor in statistical and mathematical psychology at the University of Colorado and the University of California at Los Angeles. At the University of California at Irvine he developed a new approach in applied behavioral and life sciences, and he is now director and professor in the resulting academic unit, called the Program in Social Ecology.

Lyle E. Bourne, Jr. (chapter 28), Ph.D. University of Wisconsin, is professor of psychology at the University of Colorado. He is a consulting editor to the *Journal of Experimental Psychology*, the *Journal of Verbal Learning and Verbal Behavior*, and other scientific publications. He is a member of the Psychobiology Panel of the National Science Foundation. Professor Bourne is currently doing research on the development of logico-conceptual skills, sponsored by a National Institute of Mental Health research grant and a Research Scientist Award. He has written a book and numerous articles in professional journals on concept learning and concept identification.

B. R. Bugelski (chapter 26), Ph.D. Yale University, is Distinguished Professor of Psychology at the State University of New York at Buffalo and has previously served as chairman of the Department of Psychology. He has held a Board of Regents appointment to the Board of Examiners of Psychologists in New York State and currently serves as consultant to the Board. He was President of the Eastern Psychological Association 1969–70. Besides numerous journal publications, especially in the field of learning, Professor Bugelski is the author of several widely used textbooks: *A First Course in Experimental Psychology* (1951), *The Psychology of Learning* (1956), *An Introduction to the Principles of Psychology* (1960), and *Psychology of Learning Applied to Teaching* (revised edition, 1971).

Charlotte Bühler (chapter 42), Ph.D. University of Munich, is presently involved in private practice in Beverly Hills, California. She has held various academic positions (University of Vienna, St. Catherine College in St. Paul, Minnesota, University of Southern California) and has been visiting professor at many European and American universities. Dr. Bühler's publications are mainly in the fields of developmental psychology, psychology and human life, personality, and clinical psychology. She is co-editor of the British *Journal of Genetic Psychology* and the American *Journal for Transpersonal Psychology*, and serves on the board of editors for other journals in this country. Dr. Bühler has been president of of the Los Angeles Group Association (1958–59), the Association for Humanistic Psychology (1965–66), and in 1970 was nominated president of the First International Conference of the Association for Humanistic Psychology in Amsterdam, Netherlands.

Raymond B. Cattell (chapter 39), Ph.D. University of London, is Distinguished Research Professor and director of the Personality Laboratory at the University of Illinois. His extensive work on personality and psychometrics has resulted in some thirty books and 300 papers. Professor Cattell's most recent publications are *Meaning and Measurement of Anxiety and Neuroticism* (with I. Scheier, 1961), *Personality and Social Psychology* (1964), *The Scientific Analysis of Personality* (1965), *Objective Personality and Motivation Tests* (1967), and *The Prediction of Achievement and Creativity* (1968). His research work has developed objective measurements for small group and native culture pattern classification, discovered evidence for fluid ability concept and culture-fair intelligence tests, and has developed improved factor analytic and taxonomic methodology in personality and motivation measurement.

Norman Cliff (chapter 5), Ph.D. Princeton University, is presently professor and director of the Program in Quantitative Psychology at the University of Southern California where he has been a faculty member since 1962, except for 1969–70 when he was Distinguished Visiting Fellow at the L.L. Thurstone Psychometric Laboratory at the University of North Carolina. He has also been a research psychologist with the United States Public Health Service and Educational Testing Service.

John F. Corso (Chapter 17), Ph.D. University of Iowa, is Professor and Chairman of the Department of Psychology at the State University of New York at Cortland. He is also Visiting Research Scientist at the State University of New York Upstate Medical Center in Syracuse. Prior to this, Professor Corso taught at the Pennsylvania State University and St. Louis University, where he was Director of the Department of Psychology. He is the author of *The Experimental Psychology of Sensory Behavior* (1967), as well as many chapters in handbooks and numerous scientific articles. Professor Corso's major research interests are psychoacoustics, sensory psychology, psychophysics, and experimental methodology.

Lowell T. Crow (chapter 35), Ph.D. University of Illinois, is professor of psychology at Western Washington State College. His special research interests in psychophysiology are studying the influence of alcohol upon water-regulatory systems, behavior effects of alcohol, thirst-motivated behavior, and brain mechanisms of thirst. Professor Crow has presented his findings in various papers to professional conventions and in journals, especially *Psychological Reports, Physiology and Behavior*, and *Psychonomic Science*.

James A. Dinsmoor (chapter 25), Ph.D. Columbia University, is professor of psychology at Indiana University. He has served on the editorial boards of *Psychological Reports* and the *Journal of the Experimental Analysis of Behavior*, and he has been a member of the Council of Representatives of the American Psychological Association. Currently, Professor Dinsmoor serves on the Experimental Psychology

Research Review Committee of the National Institute of Mental Health. In his own research, he uses operant techniques to analyze behavioral processes in animal subjects. He is the author of *Operant Conditioning: An Experimental Analysis of Behavior* (1970).

David H. Dodd (chapter 28), Ph.D. University of Colorado, is a faculty member of the Department of Psychology at the University of Utah. His various professional journal publications are in the field of concept learning and language acquisition, while his current research interests are in the structure and function of language and the relation of cognitive development to, and the effects of experience on, the acquisition of language.

Stephanie Z. Dudek (chapter 13), Ph.D. New York University, is a faculty member of the Department of Clinical Psychology at the Université de Montréal. Her early research was in the areas of schizophrenia and psychosomatics. She has worked as a research psychologist at the New York Psychiatric Institute, the New York Skin and Cancer Clinic, and as a staff psychologist at Columbia Medical Center. In 1960, Dr. Dudek returned to her native Montreal as acting director of clinical psychology in the Department of Psychiatry, McGill Faculty of Medicine and in 1969 assumed her present appointment. Her collaboration with Dr. E. D. Wittkower began in 1964 and they have worked together on research in obesity and alchoholism. Her current research is in creativity with children and artists.

Howard Egeth (chapter 20), Ph.D. University of Michigan, is Associate Professor of Psychology at The Johns Hopkins University. He is a consulting editor for the *Journal of Experimental Psychology* and *Perception and Psychophysics* and serves as a reviewer for eight other professional journals. Professor Egeth has written numerous research articles; his major interests are human perception, learning, and information processing.

Jay M. Finkelman (chapter 44), Ph.D. New York University, is assistant professor in the department of psychology at Baruch College, City University of New York. He is a consultant in industrial psychology with B.F.S. Psychological Associates (an industrial consulting organization). His main areas of research and writing are industrial psychology, personnel testing and training, human factors engineering, environmental psychology, and noise control. Professor Finkelman is currently performing research, under a special City University of New York grant, in human information-processing, subsidiary task measurement, and automotive safety. He has had his work published in a variety of scientific journals and has presented papers to national and international professional societies. He is co-authoring a textbook, *Industrial and Organizational Psychology*, with Benjamin Balinsky.

Albert E. Goss (chapter 29), Ph.D. University of Iowa, is a professor of psychology at Rutgers University as a member of the Graduate Faculty of Psychology and the Department of Psychology of Douglass College. He is coordinator of the Graduate Program in Human Learning, Perception, and Cognition and Director of the Douglass Psychology Child-Study Center. Professor Goss is the author (with C.F. Nodine) of *Paired-Associates Learning: The Role of Meaningfulness, Similarity, and Familiarization* (1965), as well as several monographs, chapters in handbooks, and numerous articles for professional journals. His chief research interests are in the areas of human verbal and verbal-motor behavior and learning.

James G. Greeno (chapter 8), Ph.D. University of Minnesota, is professor of psychology at the University of Michigan. His research contributions include work on the theory of human memory, identifiability of parameters in models of learning, and analysis of statistical explanation. He is the author of *Elementary Theoretical Psychology* (1968) and (with Frank Restle) *Introduction to Mathematical Psychology* (1970).

J. P. Guilford (chapter 30), Ph.D. Cornell University, is emeritus professor of psychology at the University of Southern California. Throughout his distinguished career, Professor Guilford has published over 300 monographs and professional articles and has developed more than thirty psychological tests. Honorary degrees and professional awards for his contributions to scholarship as well as education indicate his recognition in psychology. Among Professor Guilford's most recent publications are *Personality* (1959), *The Nature of Human Intelligence* (1967), *Intelligence, Creativity, and Their Educational Implications* (1968), and *The Analysis of Intelligence* (1970).

Bruce P. Halpern (chapter 18), Ph.D. Brown University, is an associate professor in the Department of Psychology and the Section of Neurobiology and Behavior at Cornell University. He has been on the faculty in the Department of Physiology at the Upstate Medical Center of the State University of New York (1961–66) and before that was a lecturer and research associate at Cornell University. Professor Halpern's main areas of research are in neurobiology, behavior, and sensory function, and he has published numerous papers based on his recent work in gustatory responses.

Harry Helson (chapter 21), Ph.D. Harvard University, has taught at Cornell University, the University of Illinois, the University of Kansas, Bryn Mawr, Brooklyn College, the University of Texas, Kansas State University, York University (Canada), and the University of Massachusetts. He was director of the U.S. Air Force-University of Texas Radiobiological Laboratory (1952–54), and received the Howard Crosby Warren Medal of the Society of Experimental Psychologists, the Distinguished Scientific Contribution Award of the American Psychological Association, and the I.H. Godlove Award of the Inter-Society Color Council. His major research in experimental psychology is in perception and adaptation-level theory.

Marjorie P. Honzik (chapter 31), Ph.D. University of California at Berkeley, is a research psychologist at the Institute of Human Development and a lecturer in psychology. Dr. Honzik has spent most of her professional life analyzing the findings of long-term studies of normal individuals over various segments of the life span. She has also followed the mental development of a group of children undergoing open heart surgery at Pacific Medical Center in San Francisco. She is the author of *Behavior Problems of Normal Children* (with Jean W. Macfarlane and Lucille Allen, 1952) and *The Course of Human Development* (with Mary C. Jones, Nancy Bayley, and Jean W. Macfarlane, 1971), and has written more than fifty articles on aspects of mental growth, parent-child relationships, and behavioral and personality development.

E. Howarth (chapter 39), Ph.D. University of Melbourne, Australia, is professor of psychology at the University of Alberta in Edmonton, and has worked with Dr. R.B. Cattell at the University of Illinois and with Dr. H.J. Eysenck at the Maudsley Hospital, University of London. His major research interests are in multivariate applications in psychology, both pure and applied aspects, and he has recently carried out comprehensive objective and questionnaire factor projects. He is also concerned with the development of large-scale, accurate computer programs for factor-analytic work. Professor Howarth has published more than fifty articles in professional journals.

Douglas N. Jackson (chapter 38), is on the faculty of the University of Western Ontario, having previously held teaching appointments at Pennsylvania State University and at Stanford University. He has also served on the research staff of the Menninger Foundation and, recently, at the Division of Psychological Studies, Educational Testing Service as distinguished visiting scholar. He is the author of more than eighty articles and research studies, has co-edited *Problems in Human Assessment* (1967) and has prepared two personality tests, *The Personality Research Form* and the *Jackson Personality Inventory*.

Earl Jennings (chapter 7), is Associate Professor of Educational Psychology and Associate Director of the Measurement and Evaluation Center at the University of Texas at Austin. He is co-author of *An Introduction to Linear Models* (1972). His teaching and research interests are in the areas of statistics, research design, and computer applications.

Ülker Tulunay Keesey (chapter 15), Ph.D. Brown University, was born in Ankara, Turkey. She has been a research associate at Brown and a research psychologist at the University of California at Los Angeles. In 1962 she joined the faculty of the Medical School at the University

of Wisconsin where she is now an Associate Professor in the Department of Ophthalmology.

Patricia C. Keith-Spiegel (chapter 42), Ph.D. Claremont Graduate School, is associate professor of psychology at California State University at Northridge. She has published over fifty research papers and reports in professional journals and has contributed to numerous edited volumes. Professor Keith-Spiegel's current research interests are in sex-role development, the development of "femininity" and attitudes toward physical beauty and fashion, and alternative ways of raising girl children. As co-chairperson of the Committee on Social Issues in the California State Psychological Association, she is currently involved in child advocacy programs, as well as in other community-professional task force projects. Her latest publication is *Outsiders U.S.A.* (edited with D. Spiegel, forthcoming).

Albert J. Lott (chapter 43), Ph.D. University of Colorado, is professor of psychology at the University of Rhode Island. He is the author of *Negro and White Youth* (with Bernice Lott, 1963). Professor Lott's major research interests are in the fields of interpersonal attraction and prejudice and ethnic relations.

K.B. Madsen (chapter 33), Ph.D. University of Copenhagen, is Professor of General Psychology at the Royal Danish School of Educational Studies in Copenhagen. His major publications in English include *Theories of Motivation*, 4th ed. (1968) and *Modern Theories of Motivation* (forthcoming). He has also written chapters for handbooks, numerous articles for journals in English, and several textbooks in psychology published in the Scandinavian languages. His main research interest is in the meta-scientific study of psychological theories.

Howard V. Meredith (chapter 12), Ph.D. University of Iowa, is professor of child somatology, Institute of Child Behavior and Development, University of Iowa. He has published over 100 research papers and has served on the editorial boards of numerous professional journals, including the *American Journal of Physical Anthropology*, *Monographs of the Society for Research in Child Development*, *Child Development*, and *Human Biology*. Professor Meredith's principal work has been in child somatology, with emphasis on the variables influencing body size and form.

Raymond C. Miles (chapter 23), Ph.D. Ohio State University, is professor of psychology at the University of Colorado. He is the author of several articles appearing in professional journals. Professor Miles's major interest is in motivational-learning, comparative, and developmental aspects of intellectual functions. His current research includes possible behavioral effects of rearing in special environments (enriched, restricted, "random"); individual and species differences in learning ability; and effects of "arousal" upon unlearned and learned behaviors.

Robert S. Morrow (chapter 32), is chief of the Psychology Service of the Veterans Administration Hospital in the Bronx, New York. He is also a faculty member of the psychology department of the City College of New York as adjunct professor. Dr. Morrow also serves as adjunct associate professor in the departments of psychiatry and rehabilitation medicine at New York Medical College. He is a Diplomate in Clinical Psychology and a Fellow in the Clinical, Counseling, and Consulting Divisions of the American Psychological Association, a Special Examiner for the New York City Department of Personnel and the Board of Education, as well as consultant to the Department of Hospitals.

Selma Morrow (chapter 32), serves as senior psychologist of the Ethical Culture Schools in New York City and school psychologist in their lower school. She has previously been a psychologist for the New York University Testing and Advisement Center. Mrs. Morrow has served as psychologist on the Mental Retardation Study at Columbia University and has worked with Dr. Jon Eisenson on his Aphasia Study conducted at Queens College in New York.

Frederick A. Mote (Chapter 15), Ph.D. Brown University, has been a member of the Psychology Department of the University of Wisconsin since 1946, and was chairman of the department from 1955 to 1959.

He has served as an officer of the Division of Experimental Psychology and on various boards and committees of the American Psychological Association, as Secretary-Treasurer as well as Council Member of the Midwestern Psychological Association, and at present is the Secretary-Treasurer of the Psychonomic Society. For the International Encyclopedia of the Social Sciences he wrote the short account entitled "The Senses," and for the 1967 volume of the Annual Review of Psychology the chapter on "Visual Sensitivity."

Bennet B. Murdock, Jr. (chapter 27), Ph.D. Yale University, is professor of psychology at the University of Toronto. He has taught at the University of Vermont and the University of Missouri and has spent a year at the Applied Psychology Research Unit in Cambridge, England, and a year at Stanford University under National Science Foundation fellowship grants. Professor Murdock's research interests are in the field of human memory.

Gardner Murphy (chapter 1), Ph.D. Columbia University, is professor of psychology at George Washington University and a past director of research at the Menninger Foundation. Along with his lifelong dedication to teaching, Professor Murphy has explored many areas of psychology, his early interests being in social psychology and personality, with his later work focusing on perception and cognition. Throughout his career he has followed his interest in psychical research. Besides research articles and reviews, Professor Murphy has edited numerous volumes: *William James on Psychical Research* (with R.O. Ballou, 1960), *Psychological Thought from Pythagoras to Freud* (1968), and *Asian Psychology* (with Lois B. Murphy, 1968). He has written *Freeing Intelligence Through Teaching* (1961), *Challenge of Psychical Research* (1961), *Encounter with Reality* (with H.E. Spohn, 1968), and *Historical Introduction to Modern Psychology*, 3rd edition (with J.K. Kovach, 1972).

Merrill L. Noble (chapter 10), Ph.D. Ohio State University, is professor and chairman of the Department of Psychology at Pennsylvania State University. He has written numerous professional articles for the *Journal of Experimental Psychology* and the *Journal of Comparative and Physiological Psychology* and is currently consulting editor to the *Journal of Experimental Psychology*. Professor Noble has been active in research in the areas of learning, motor skill, and animal behavior and has had research grants from NIMH, NICHD, NASA, and OSR. At present he is a co-investigator for a research grant from NSF on information processing and skilled performance.

Benbow F. Ritchie (chapter 22), Ph.D. University of California at Berkeley, is a professor of psychology at the University of California at Berkeley, where he has taught since 1950. Prior to that he taught at Swarthmore College. Professor Ritchie is interested in learning, motivation, and thinking. He is the author of "The Circumnavigation of Cognition" (*Psychological Review*, 1953), and "A Logical and Experimental Analysis of the Laws of Motivation" (Nebraska Symposium on Motivation, 1954).

Joseph R. Royce (chapter 2), Ph.D. University of Chicago, is founder-director of the Center for Advanced Study in Theoretical Psychology at the University of Alberta in Edmonton, Canada. He is on the editorial boards of *Multivariate Behavioral Research*, *Psychological Record*, *Journal of Psycholinguistic Research*, and *Perspectives*. Professor Royce's scholarly and research interests are primarily theoretical and experimental. His interest in the conceptual foundations of psychology is demonstrated in his *The Encapsulated Man: An Interdisciplinary Essay on the Search for Meaning* (1964), and his editing of *Psychology and the Symbol: An Interdisciplinary Symposium* (1965), *Toward Unification in Psychology* (1971), and *The Psychology of Knowing* (with W. Rozeboom, Gordon, and Breach, 1971). Two forthcoming books, *The Contributions of Multivariate Analysis to Psychological Theory* and *A Multi-Factor Theory of Individuality* reflect his lifelong interest in factor analysis as a theoretical basis for behavior. Professor Royce's publications include over sixty journal articles on his experimental work, which deals primarily with the factor-genetic basis of emotional behavior.

Roger W. Russell (chapter 9), Ph.D. University of Virginia, is presently vice-chancellor of The Flinders University of South Australia.

He has held administrative and academic positions at the University of California at Irvine, Indiana University, the University of Canterbury (New Zealand), the University of Sidney (Australia), and the University of London, as well as other institutions. His research interests involve the areas of neuro- and psychopharmacology and his publications in these and related fields have appeared in numerous journals and edited volumes over the past thirty years.

S. Stansfeld Sargent (chapter 40), Ph.D. Columbia University, is senior psychologist at Oxnard Mental Health Center, Oxnard, California. He served for twelve years as a clinical psychologist at the Veterans Administration hospital in Phoenix, Arizona, and has held academic positions in the psychology departments of Barnard College, Columbia University, and World Campus Afloat of Chapman College. Dr. Sargent's major publications are *Basic Teachings of the Great Psychologists* (1944; revised, with K.R. Stafford, 1965), *Social Psychology* (1950; revised, with R.C. Williamson, 1958, 1966), and *Culture and Personality: Proceedings of an Interdisciplinary Conference* (edited with M.W. Smith, 1949; reprinted 1952).

J. P. Scott (chapter 34), is Regent's Professor of Psychology and director of the Center for Research on Social Behavior at Bowling Green University. He was for twenty years chairman of the Division of Behavior Studies at the Jackson Laboratory in Bar Harbor, Maine. Dr. Scott was one of the early workers in the field of animal aggression, beginning his work in the early 1940s on the fighting behavior of mice, following it up with other studies on sheep, goats, and dogs. His book, *Aggression* (1958) is a landmark in attempts to relate nonhuman animal aggression to human problems.

Jerome L. Singer (chapter 19), Ph.D. University of Pennsylvania, is professor of psychology and director of the Clinical Psychology Training Program at Yale University. He holds a certificate from the William Alanson White Institute of Psychiatry, Psychology, and Psychoanalysis and was formerly connected with Columbia University and then the City University of New York. Besides his clinical work, his research interests are in the areas of daydreaming, imagery, the stream of thought, and personality theory.

Julian C. Stanley (chapter 6), is professor of psychology at the Johns Hopkins University and was formerly director of the Laboratory of Experimental Design at the University of Wisconsin. Professor Stanley is president of the Division of Evaluation and Measurement of the American Psychological Association. He has been president of the American Educational Research Association, the National Council on Measurement in Education, and the Division of Educational Psychology of the American Psychological Association. Among his publications are *Experimental and Quasi-Experimental Designs for Research* (with Donald T. Campbell, 1966), *Statistical Methods in Education and Psychology* and *Educational and Psychological Measurement and Evaluation* (with Kenneth D. Hopkins, 1972).

Lawrence M. Stolurow (chapter 24), Ph.D. University of Pittsburgh, is professor and chairman of the department of education at the State University of New York at Stony Brook. He is the author of *Readings in Learning*, *Teaching by Machine*, *Guide to Evaluating Self-Instructional Programs*, and *Computer-Assisted Instruction in the Health Professions* (1969), plus over 100 journal articles. Professor Stolurow's major research interests are in the fields of learning, training, and educational technology, especially the uses of computers in and for instruction.

Karla Thomas (chapter 42), Ph.D. University of California at Berkeley, is an associate professor at California State University at Northridge, where she teaches comparative and developmental psychology. Previously, she has taught developmental psychology at Rhode Island College and in extension courses at the University of California at Los Angeles. Professor Thomas's special research interests are in behavior genetics and the social behavior of animals and children.

William R. Thompson (chapter 11), Ph.D. University of Chicago, is professor and head of the Psychology Department at Queen's University, Kingston, Ontario. Prior to this appointment, he was professor and chairman of the Department of Psychology at Wesleyan University,

Middletown, Connecticut. Professor Thompson has published more than 70 research and review papers, mostly in the areas of developmental genetic and psychology, and is the author of *Behavior Genetics* (with J. L. Fuller, 1960) and *Psychology: A Systematic Introduction* (1971).

Don Trumbo (chapter 10), Ph.D. Michigan State University, is professor of psychology at the Pennsylvania State University. He has published over thirty research articles and reviews in leading journals, and is a member of the editorial boards of *Organization Behavior and Human Performance, Journal of Applied Psychology*, and *Journal of Motor Behavior*. He was awarded a NATO fellowship in science in 1971 and a NATO Lectureship in 1972. Dr. Trumbo's chief research interests include skilled performance, human information processing, and applied experimental psychology.

Donald J. Veldman (chapter 7), is Professor of Educational Psychology at the University of Texas at Austin. He is also Coordinator of the Psychological Assessment Division of the R & D Center for Teacher Education. He is the author of *Fortran Programming for the Behavioral Sciences* (1967) and *Introductory Statistics for the Behavioral Sciences* (with Robert K. Young, 1965). His research interests include statistical methodology and computer applications in psychological assessment.

Paul L. Wachtel (chapter 41), Ph.D. Yale University, is associate professor of psychology at City College, City University of New York. He is a graduate of the post-doctoral training program in psychoanalysis and psychotherapy at New York University. Professor Wachtel's research and writing has focused on anxiety and attention, cognitive style, hypnosis, and psychoanalytic theory, with his most recent efforts centering on the integration of dynamic and behavioral approaches to psychotherapy.

D.M. Warburton (chapter 9), Ph.D. Indiana University, is Reader in Psychology at the University of Reading, England, and prior to that was assistant professor at the University of California at Irvine. Dr. Warburton's researches have been published in the *Psychological Review, Journal of Comparative and Physiological Psychology, Physiology and Behaviour*, and *Psychopharmacologia*, and he has also contributed a chapter to *Inhibition and Learning* (edited by R. Boakes and M. Halliday, 1972). His main interests are the biochemical control of arousal, attention, and mood.

Charles S. Watson (chapter 14), Ph.D. Indiana University, is research associate in charge of the Signal Detection Laboratory at the Central Institute for the Deaf in St. Louis, Missouri and is an associate professor in the Department of Psychology at Washington University in St. Louis. He is a Fellow of the Acoustical Society of America and serves on the editorial board of *Perception and Psychophysics* and is a member of the Committee on Hearing and Bioacoustics of the National Research Council. Professor Watson's main areas of research are in bioacoustics and perception and he has published numerous articles and reviews in professional journals, most frequently in the *Journal of the Acoustical Society of America*. His most recent researches are in vigilance and attention, recognition and discrimination of auditory patterns, psychophysical methods for laboratory and clinic, and audiology.

Wilse B. Webb (chapter 36), Ph.D. State University of Iowa, is Graduate Research Professor in the Department of Psychology at the University of Florida. He has been chairman of the department and was head of the Aviation Psychology Laboratory in the US Naval School of Aviation Medicine. Professor Webb is presently Associate Editor of *Psychological Reports* and has worked on numerous government projects for the National Institute of Health and the National Science Foundation and served on the Project Mercury Behavioral Measurement Committee. His more than 100 research papers have appeared in various professional journals in the fields of learning, motivation, and applied psychology, as well as in his special field of sleep research. He is the author of *The Profession of Psychology* (1961), *Sleep Therapy* (with R.L. Williams, 1966) and *Sleep: An Experiential Approach* (1968).

Gerald J.S. Wilde (chapter 11), Ph.D. City University of Amsterdam, Holland, is a professor of psychology at Queen's University in Kingston, Ontario. He has done research in the following fields: the methodology of twin research, personality theory and measurement, ergonomic psychology (man-machine interaction with special reference to safety problems), and the use of mass communication publicity for the promotion of road safety. He is currently interested in behavior genetics (more specifically, the study of human twins) and the psychological aspects of ergonomics.

Eric D. Wittkower (chapter 13). M.D. University of Berlin, is emeritus professor of psychiatry at McGill University and also serves as consultant psychiatrist to Royal Victoria, Montreal General, Queen Elizabeth, and Reddy Memorial hospitals in Montreal. He is editor-in-chief of *Transcultural Psychiatric Research Review*, associate editor of *Psychosomatic Medicine* (U.S.A.) and *Journal of Psychosomatic Research* (England) and is on the editorial boards of numerous journals throughout the world. Dr. Wittkower is a past president of the American Psychosomatic Society, the Canadian Psychoanalytic Society, and the American Academy of Psychoanalysis and is currently president of the International College of Psychosomatic Medicine. He is a member of the World Health Organization Expert Advisory Panel on Mental Health and a consultant to the World Federation of Mental Health and was awarded a Certificate of Honour for Outstanding Contribution to Human Understanding and Welfare by the International Association for Social Psychiatry. Dr. Wittkower is the editor of *Recent Developments in Psychosomatic Medicine* (with R.A. Cleghorn, 1954) and has written several other books, numerous book contributions, and approximately 125 scientific articles. His major research interests are psychosomatic medicine and transcultural psychiatry.

David L. Wolitzky (chapter 41), Ph.D. University of Rochester, is research associate professor of psychology, Research Center for Mental Health at New York University. He holds a Research Scientist Development Award from the National Institute of Mental Health and is a research graduate of the New York Psychoanalytic Institute. Professor Wolitzky's main research interests are cognitive style, psychoanalytic theory, and clinical judgment.

Benjamin B. Wolman (editor of the *Handbook* and author of chapter 3), is professor of psychology in the doctoral program at Long Island University and editor-in-chief of the *International Journal of Group Tensions*. Dr. Wolman has written 14 books and over 160 papers. He has co-authored and edited several collective volumes: *Contemporary Theories and Systems in Psychology* (1960), *Scientific Psychology: Principles and Approaches* (1965), *Historical Roots of Contemporary Psychology* (1968), *Manual of Child Psychopathology* (1972), and others.

Paul Thomas Young (chapter 37), Ph.D. Cornell University, spent most of his teaching career at the University of Illinois until 1960, when he became Professor of Psychology Emeritus. Professor Young received the Distinguished Scientific Contribution Award of the American Psychological Association (1965), Occidental College's distinguished alumnus award, and an honorary D.Sc. Throughout his research career, Dr. Young has specialized in studying hedonic processes in behavior and has published extensively in this and related areas of affective psychology. His work on preference showed the effect of experience in modifying acceptability; his research on need-free organisms clarified acceptance and appetitive behavior. Dr. Young's most recent book is *Motivation and Emotion: A Survey of the Determinants of Human and Animal Activity* (1961).

Handbook of General Psychology

History,
Theory,
and
Methodology

History can be conceived in terms of the broad sweep of the eye from a mountaintop, or in terms of the slow and struggling steps of those mounting an ill-defined path towards the peak. We shall attempt here the first, the panoramic method, but will offer a few paragraphs to suggest how the panoramic and the step-wise approaches may, if the reader desires, be combined.

There are renewed efforts today to make history into a science; a new attempt is evident to write "the laws of history." Arnold Toynbee, comparing many civilizations, tells us that if there is vigorous challenge to which the social group can make a response this will carry that civilization a step further; but if the challenge is too great to be borne by the social structure, the civilization fails and passes out of sight. Against all such generalizations one may still passionately reaffirm the uniqueness, the *un*repeatability of history. The issue reminds us of Gordon Allport's vivid contrast between "nomothetic" and "ideographic" studies of personality. The historian, in fact, may go so far in his struggle for lawfulness that he is concerned only with abstractions about social process, while he may go so far in the opposite direction that he becomes a chronicler of events and, in the last analysis, a student of unique personalities such as political, cultural, scientific, or other types of leaders. I have had occasion to develop this thought a little further for another audience.[1] Here I will content myself with a rather broad nomothetic view of psychological history, making rather more of movements, trends, and eras than is the usual concern of the historian, and rather less of the brilliant originators of novel conceptions. If, for example, one were to look over intellectual history and, in particular, the history of the conceptions of the mind, seeking sheer brilliance of intuitive originality, one could hardly miss the two great contemporaries Spinoza and Leibniz. But the former was so far ahead of his time and so much a unique expositor of an essentially mountaintop type of creative thinking that he left almost no dent at all upon the psychology of the period; while the latter, by virtue of his mechanics and

[1] Cf. my contribution entitled: "Is There A Science of History?" in the Jubilee Volume, 1969, for the Department of Sociology, University of Bombay, India, A. R. Desai, ed. (in press).

Gardner Murphy

Historical Review

1

mathematics, formulated a conception of perception and attention which took hold, and made a vast impact upon the psychology of the next three centuries. This is somewhat related to E. G. Boring's conception that thought must be in harmony with the *Zeitgeist*. One may, however, say simply that it is legitimate to characterize *trends*, or one may become primarily concerned with *persons*.

From this viewpoint we have to begin with general history—not political history, nor military history, nor economic history, nor scientific history, nor any other kind of special history. We have to look at our problem as Bibby (1963), for example, did in his beautiful *4000 Years Ago*, a view of the movement of human life as we know it all over the globe in the period about 2000 B.C.: the invention and use of the chariot; the audacious maritime expeditions as far as Iceland; the discovery and development of gold as an agent of trade; the development of metallurgy and of writing. All these are episodes in human history in which one can neither disentangle tribes nor assign credit for major inventions without losing the basic human perspective of what man, as an animal and as a cultural being, was discovering and applying to his individual and collective life. From this viewpoint the *history of psychology* can only begin when a stable civilization, in a rich land with a highly developed division of labor and an economic surplus, begins to turn inwards to ask about the very nature of that perceptive and reflective mind from which the social changes are being derived. This happened, for example, in China, in India, and in the Mediterranean, in the startling burst of philosophy and psychology about 500 B.C., with Lao-tse and Confucius in China, with the *Upanishads* in India, with the Greek thinkers of many city-states from southern Italy through to Asia Minor.

These were men of relatively stable societies, which had gone through periods of military and economic consolidations, who were turning to ask how reality can be known, what is the essence of mind or soul, how can life be made better. For the most part, the Chinese philosophers dealt with this question of making life better, whereas the psychologists of India generally were distrustful of this world, of our immediate intercourse with the physical realities about us, and cultivated the understanding and the discipline of the inner soul. The Greeks were concerned primarily with first principles, realities from which both the physical world and the world of the mind could be derived.

We are concerned here almost exclusively with Western psychology. In this Western picture it is worthwhile to remember that the geography of mountains, rivers, and islands leads to a punctuation, a chopping up of the activities of cities and nations —always trading, always exchanging ideas, frequently fighting, building empires which then fall apart, etc.,—into new exchanges of all sorts and new fighting or affiliation. Greek philosophy and psychology are, so to speak, choppy expressions of limited and short-term physiographic and cultural realities. The vast plains of China and India, while focussed along the seacoasts and divided by great rivers, allow easy movement over vast distances; but the tremendous chain of the Himalayas, for a good part of their history, has kept them apart. If there is greater homogeneity in Chinese than in Western philosophy, this would be part of the explanation; if there is greater homogeneity in Indian than in Western psychology (and I will grant that this is arguable, but ask for its provisional acceptance), this is because there has always been, for 5000 years or more, a recognizable Indian culture. No culture, in the same sense, has lived in the

West more than a thousand years, even if one takes Greek civilization as represented, for example by the Olympic Games from about 800 B.C. to A.D. 200, or chooses to take the Roman Empire, or even the Holy Roman Empire, as a sort of symbol of a quasi-political, quasi-cultural span of human endeavor.

Settling down, then, to a brief examination of Western psychology, we may say first of all that it began with the Greek concern with "first principles" (Russell, 1959). One man said that the first principle of all things is water; another, fire; another, number; one even said it was mind. Three conceptions took shape among the Greeks which we must specially emphasize: the Pythagorean conception that numbers are clues to the ordered structure and process of the world; Democritus' idea that tiny material particles (atoms) are combined, joined, and separated in the structure of bodies, and even minds; and the "functional" conception that souls or minds are ways of responding—or, as we should say, functions or processes of living things. All three of these conceptions were developed and systematized. Plato's conception of a soul as sharply separate from the body became important for the Christian theologian-philosophers in the third century and, later, of the Christian era, while, in time, Aristotle's conception of soul as the basic form or function of the living individual became classic and deeply reverenced in Eastern philosophy centering in Byzantium, until the fall of the city to the Turks in 1453. But after the Crusades, Western Christianity, centered at Rome, began to absorb some of the Eastern philosophy, and Aristotle's conception of the soul as form became integrated with the Christian conception of a soul separate from the body, in what became known as "scholastic philosophy."

The Crusades and the contact with the Islamic world, joined with a slow revival of learning (under Charlemagne, for example), and enhanced by the great monastic schools—and finally the establishment of universities in the twelfth century—all brought about a rearousal of modalities of thought first characteristic of Greek psychology.

From this point on, with a little less of the seven-league-boots manner of historiography, we shall attempt, working forward from the Renaissance, a view of five major trends in general science and in psychology which we can trace forward from about A.D. 1500.

1. Physical Philosophy

We begin, then, with Galileo, Professor of Mathematics at the University of Padua in northern Italy, student of Plato, mathematician and inventor of new methods. It was not his Platonism nor his mathematics that constitutes his originality, although both were fundamental in defining the cast of his experimental work. Watching a lamp swinging in the cathedral at Pisa is said to have started him thinking about the measurement of natural forces which reappeared in his studies of free-falling bodies, and the attempt to explain the action of a water pump. He was not content with the conception that light moves at an infinite speed. He attempted, with lanterns, to find actually how fast it did move. Of course, he responded positively to Copernicus' conception of the movement of the earth about the sun, as he responded likewise to the invention of the telescope; his own telescope, modeled after one in use in the Netherlands, actually showed Jupiter's moons. The world, then, could be seen through Greek eyes. It was orderly and mathematically knowable. You could actually copy nature and even separate out tiny bits of material nature and study it experimentally. In Paris, meanwhile, René Descartes, philosopher and mathematician, was drawing attention to the nature of the reflective mind in a *Discourse on Method* which gave the rational soul a place beyond, and in some ways independent of, the physiological system of the body. At the same time, in the extraordinary essay on *The Passions of the Soul*, he described the emotions "after the manner of physics," and laid the foundations for the physiological conception of reflex action. Animals were "automata," and man—except for his rational soul interacting through the body with the pineal gland—had his own physiological rooting in the principles of physics. The Englishman, Thomas Hobbes, visited both Descartes and his group in Paris and Galileo, and learned much from them. Returning to England, he injected into his systematic study of society (*Leviathan*) a materialist-atomist conception like that of Democritus. He also developed a number of ideas derived from Aristotle dealing with the association of ideas which, in combination, spelled out the doctrine that psychological events are events defined by material atomic particles interacting within the brain, all this underlying the nature of both emotion and thought. Here was modern materialistic psychology if the philosopher wanted it; and here was a reasonable physiological psychology as a working principle for the study of perception, emotion, thought, and even will. It was an extraordinarily modern-sounding conception, whether philosophically sophisticated or not.

In the meantime, the physics and the mathematics of Galileo were generating new methods in England, the Netherlands, and Germany. It is not accidental that Leibniz was both a mathematician and a philosopher of monads (particles of experience rather than particles of matter), concerned with the way in which the monad (the indivisible soul) reflects the outer world. At the same time, Newton created almost single-handed the mathematical-physical world view which gave expression to the laws of motion and to the gravitational and optical systems of what came to be called "classical physics."

It is easy to forget that the astronomy of Copernicus and Galileo, the terrestrial physics of Galileo and Newton, were of direct and enormous importance for all of modern psychology. When David Hartley (1749), in the middle of the eighteenth century, undertook to base all of psychology upon "association," he found in Newton's studies of the pendulum exactly what he wanted to provide a physical substrate. Associations were strings of vibratory activities in the "white medullary substance of the brain," which permitted each fresh sensory stimulus to trigger off a series of psychological events which had, in past experience, been connected with one another. While Newton's ideas were exercising, through Voltaire, a vast influence upon the general reading public by way of giving them an orderly physicalist universe, a "naturalist" world in which physical philosophy and mathematics were combined, Newton's physics and mathematics were likewise determining the directions in which a modern psychology could be composed. Thus when Herbart (1816), in Germany at the beginning of the nineteenth century, undertook to write about the association of ideas, he not only used the atomistic and mathematical approaches which had been defined by Newton, but he actually used the calculus in the measurement of the intensities of associative processes. Even when Newton had been arguing with

Huygens regarding the nature of light, medical men were studying the implications of physics for the living system; and at the beginning of the nineteenth century Thomas Young was suggesting how the physics of light was related to the experience of color. But the theories of "physiological optics," to which Helmholtz made massive contributions in the mid-nineteenth century, had also been taking shape largely from the work of physicians functioning as anatomists and physiologists. The physiological psychology of today is indeed still to a high degree Newtonian in its conception of the time, space, force, mass, etc. Although the new developments since 1900—quantum theory, relativity, and the uncertainty principle—have not as yet influenced psychology very much, they have begun to generate a sort of uneasiness around the fringes; and of course, the battle over logical positivism and operationism, noted elsewhere, has tended to keep psychologists constantly reminded that their science must, in some sense, be "based upon" the "basic sciences." It is not an exaggeration to say that modern psychology owes at least as much to Newton as to any of the psychological thinkers of the Renaissance period.

2. Physiology

But our second movement in general science, while still utilizing a physical substrate, is concerned with functional conceptions so different from those of Galileo and Newton that we must regard it as constituting a new scientific development. I refer to the systematic conceptions of bodily units which are both physically and physiologically capable of being compounded into the total behavioral reality of the individual. The conception of the reflex or elementary functional response unit, as developed by Descartes and his immediate followers, became fundamental for the understanding of instinct, and even of deliberate response units. To compare instinct with reflex action, and to bring habit into the circle of concepts related to reflex, had become a commonplace even before the era of William James and of German physiological psychologists such as Wundt. The reflex arc was so central in psychological thinking late in the century that John Dewey devoted a classical attack to it, with the idea that mortal thrusts with this mortal enemy offered the only conceivable basis for a new functionalism in which the integrity of the living system could be emphasized. Sherrington, at the turn of the century, was using the simple reflex as a "convenient abstraction" in the wake of which the scientific idea consistently developed that it is, after all, an *inconvenient* abstraction. The reflex, however, has not been displaced, nor is its ultimate relation to the architecture of the response system settled. Most of the struggles of elementarism and atomism on the one hand, wholism and Gestalt on the other, are related to the question of these behavioral atoms, these reflex units.

But while all these issues are rather familiar to us from our glimpses of western European psychological history, we are prone to forget that the same issues were developed brilliantly and systematically by Sechenov, in Russia, in the sixties and seventies of the last century. They had been formulated into a magnificently self-sufficient reflexological system well before the time of Bekhterev's "objective psychology" and of Pavlov's system of conditioned reflexes based upon physiologically conditioned reflex units.

Now my thesis is that in place of the atomism of Democritus, and in place of the atomism of conscious elements developed by Hobbes and Locke, there is an atomism of behavior units directly observable from the time of Descartes onwards, deriving its strength largely from the physical science background which we have just considered, but also deriving strength from the medical and zoological advances, especially as these developed in the German universities. Parallel with this came the physiological experiments and analyses of Sechenov, Bekhterev, and Pavlov. Thus one may define the shift from an introspective psychology to a behavioral psychology largely in terms of the charm and effective impact of the conception of the reflex, as it developed in more or less Cartesian terms.

3. Evolution

But we are not done with the biological sciences as background for psychology. Indeed, we have hardly begun. For the third main trend in modern psychology, as contrasted with all the psychologies of the ancient and medieval periods, is the conception of development—basically the conception of change—in the direction of diversity, differentiation, the appearance of new wholes: in short, broadly conceived, the evolutionary doctrine. There had been evolutionism among the Greeks, notably among the Epicureans, and this had been vividly Latinized by the Roman poet Lucretius, in his evolutionary poem *On the Nature of Things*. Evolutionism raised its head again in the romantic theories of change in the eighteenth century, as in Buffon's poetry, and in the geological and biological evolutionary speculations of Goethe in Germany, Erasmus, and Darwin in England. Shortly after 1800, biologists were everywhere raising the question of the development of forms of life, one from another, that is, questions about the "transmutation of species." Despite Lamarck's genius as evolutionary theorist, the evidence was not yet sufficient. But the development of a theory of evolution, together with twenty years of careful ordering of observations, made it possible for Charles Darwin, in 1859, to develop a coherent scheme of the evolution of the forms of life. This was, at the same time, background for a conception of individual growth. Francis Galton showed that a psychology of individuality could be written in these terms, and proceeded to develop experimental and statistical methods for the ordering of information about individual differences, both physical and psychological. By the end of the nineteenth century psychology was an *individualizing science*. As a matter of fact, psychiatry, as Alfred Binet reminded us in his little book of 1890, had already been developing a psychology of personality. Psychoanalysis, of course, another biological system with an evolutionary base, also became a supremely articulate individualizing type of psychology. We have, then, a picture of the development of the evolutionary way of thinking from Lucretius to Galton and Freud, fully as worthy of being regarded as a fundamental trend in psychological history as is either the Galileo-Newton physicalist trend or the Helmholtz-Sechenov-Wundt reflex action trend.

4. Impulse and Action

While almost the whole of the history of psychology—with a little stretching—could be written in cognitive terms, almost the whole of the history of *medical* thinking—with a little stretching—could be written in terms of impulse and action. From this viewpoint one could begin the history of psychology, whether Eastern or Western, with medical men. Certainly, Hippocrates and his body humors is an excellent base line figure. Medical psychology, like all of medicine, had to be concerned with the fact that the mainsprings of an evident impulse or act might be hidden both from the outside observer and from the patient-subject himself. There might be invisible reasons for feelings and for decisions; so then likewise for thoughts. The various histories of the unconscious before Freud constantly remind us of the fact that well hidden events, some called physiological and some called psychological, were always cooking up a new broth of trouble—or of creative inventiveness. Nineteenth century medicine, as L. L. Whyte (1951) has well documented, developed an elaborate array of possibilities for a psychology of the unconscious, while the philosophers, from Schopenhauer through Nietzsche to von Hartmann, provided equally appealing possibilities. When Freud, then, observed in Vienna, in Paris, in Nancy, and again, in Vienna, patterns of behaviors and patterns of thoughts which came from hidden springs, he was extrapolating a series that had begun with the medical psychology of the Greeks. Hippocrates had been an evolutionist as well as a medical psychologist; and so was Freud. In fact, there are passages in Hippocrates which are both Darwinian and Freudian. Freud, as experimental physiologist and embryologist, became Freud the psychopathologist, blending evolutionary and physiological conceptions within a broad outlook on man which is essentially Hippocratic.

5. Social Psychology

We have selected, for special attention, four massive long-term trends: (*1*) the Newtonian physicalist; (*2*) the Descartes reflexologist; (*3*) the developmental Darwinian; (*4*) the Freudian medical dynamic. It remains to consider one even broader and more pervasive: the ways in which man, in the process of meeting his life requirements and deepest intellectual, personal, and social needs, has constructed for himself a new environment both physical and social, and, in receiving feedback from this new environment, has changed himself. Richard McKeon suggests that Greek and Mesopotamian merchants, discussing business and life at large on the banks of the Tigris and the Euphrates, got to talking about all things being exchangeable for gold, as Heraclitus put it, and developing elementary ideas of continuity and conservation, as Helmholtz or Piaget would say. The money and credit system gave rise to habits of daring exchange in which both sides could gain from the transaction. Surely ideas about rationality and impulse control developed in a business world in which one could, rather than fighting it out, trade it out, plan it out, so that long-range reciprocal relations of human groups became possible. Certainly the political organization of the Greek city-state enhanced the rights of individuals and the legitimacy of group decisions restraining the scope of the despot. The same democratic individualism was taking shape in early Rome and in Hebrew society as well. Implicit ideas about human nature and the control of impulse by reason have their obscure, but challenging, story to tell about the beginnings of psychology. Surely the depression and despair of proud men who had conquered the Indian peninsula, as they observed poverty, disease, and death everywhere about them, led into a psychology which offered serenity and escape. Surely the control of the vast civilization of China by civil servants, selected on the basis of classical scholarship, had its own message to offer regarding the kind of psychology of orderliness and restraint by which a bureaucracy of this sort could give order and dignity to all in accordance with their place in the social system. Psychologies arise from philosophies that are expressions of the basic assumptions of the society, eked out, and at times brilliantly dramatized, by individuals who catch the whole spirit of the era as did Lao-tse, Confucius, Buddha, Hippocrates, Heraclitus.

James Harvey Robinson (1921) said that Greek philosophy went as far as it could go in a world dominated by the slave system because free men do not bother with things, tools, objects, but only with ideas. This is a bit overdrawn, when one thinks of the craftsmanship—for example, the armory of Hephaestus—within the Athenian city-state. But Robinson's essential point is sound and important: The way in which people do their work gives a cast to the way they think, essentially as Karl Marx had laid down this proposition. With Robinson one goes forward to see the "history of the human mind" emerging in terms of the economic, political, and military adventures which roll up on themselves like a snowball, with science as the expression of a primal curiosity found whenever there is leisure and an economic surplus. From this point of view, it was after the Greek city-state had collapsed, and indeed after slavery had begun to disintegrate as a social system, that Greek science—tool-making, tool-perfecting instrument that it was—began to shape the conception of the body and its functions as one dissected and as one looked through a lens.

After nearly 2000 years' lapse, science, in this sense—curious, tool-making, tool-using, probing into the nature of realities including the environment and man himself—took shape in the Renaissance period. From this point of view, the Commercial Revolution, as it drove against serfdom and ultimately against slavery, and as it perfected the arts, crafts, and tool-using skills of all who could inventively use them, led to growth of experimental science. To be sure, the universities played their part, despite their traditionalism, for it was the interaction of the free-lance instrumentalist and the man of thought that ultimately provided the Galilean tradition to which we have given our attention. Thus the Commercial Revolution of the thirteenth to seventeenth centuries in western Europe was more than a revolution in the ways of producing, processing, exchanging wool and wool products. It included the love of fine textiles and the prestige, power, and aesthetic satisfactions that went with this. But as the various guilds dealing with wool and other textiles, and as the bankers who facilitated these transactions, grew in power, the Commercial Revolution offered a code of rationality, calculation, personal gain, and ultimately

an individualism and democracy, to make political sense. John Locke's rationality and devotion to education and democratic principles belong to an era in which the Commercial Revolution moves on apace to erode and finally to destroy the power of the royalty and the great landowners in favor of the new commercial classes. It is not at all accidental that the discovery of the circulation of the blood and the invention of usable microscopes for medical observation went on apace in this era; for rational men, whether merchants or bankers, welcomed innovations, and indeed gladly sent their sons to the universities to imbibe, along with the classics, a little of the new experimentalism in the world of thought itself.

The new experimentalism, as far as physical objects are concerned, was expressed in James Watt's invention of the steam engine, and in the development of new shuttles and machine tools to be used in a newly invented "factory system." All these new tools and instruments increased man's power in controlling and indeed in understanding the operation of natural forces. They increased the conviction—if not in philosophical, then in very simple, everyday, practical terms—that, as La Mettrie said, man is a machine; and they created a world of "political economy" essentially machine-like, in which people and nations were to be manipulated essentially in machine terms. The great revulsion against all this was the humanistic, romantic, "storm and stress" movement of a new kind of poetry, and then the cultivation of life as the supreme value, as seen in the evolutionary principle and in the individualizing effort which came both from the romantic trend and from Darwinian evolution itself as fully understood.

We may say, then, that the socio-cultural trends epitomized in the phrases "Commercial Revolution" and "Industrial Revolution," must be understood as basic groundwork for the changing conceptions of life and mind which have taken shape in the last few centuries. This is not to say that the individual does not count. It is rather to say that the magnificent achievement of an occasional individual can best be understood if the dynamic of general history, and of scientific history within it, is fully grasped as giving context and meaning to each individual effort.

References

BIBBY, G. *4000 years ago: A panorama of life in the second millennium B.C.* New York: Knopf, 1963.

HARTLEY, D. *Observations on man, his fame, his duty, and his expectations.* 1749.

HERBART, J. *A text book in psychology.* 1816.

ROBINSON, J. H. *The mind in the making.* New York: Harper & Row, 1921.

RUSSELL, B. *Wisdom of the West.* Garden City, N.Y.: Doubleday, 1959.

WHYTE, L. L. (ed.) *Aspects of form: A symposium on form in nature and art.* New York: Pellegrini and Cudahy, 1951.

Psycho-Epistemology and the Twentieth-Century World View

I shall begin my presentation with a brief review of the state of affairs in contemporary psychology as a segment of twentieth century thought as a preliminary to a more detailed analysis of theoretical psychology per se.

Several publications (Royce, 1959, 1964; Sorokin, 1941) have pointed out that there are three basic ways of knowing: empiricism, rationalism, and metaphorism.[1] While there have been many theories of knowledge expounded in the history of philosophic thought, these three isms have been dubbed basic because of their fairly direct dependence upon varieties of psychological cognition, on the one hand, and their epistemological testability on the other hand. This view can be briefly summarized by reference to Table 2-1 below.

Table 2-1.   Three Basic Paths to Knowledge

Cognitive Processes	Corresponding Epistemologies	Epistemological Criteria
Thinking	Rationalism	Logical–Illogical
Symbolizing and Intuiting	Metaphorism	Universal–Idiosyncratic
Sensing	Empiricism	Perception–Misperception

[1]Previous publications referred to the third way of knowing as intuitionism and to the underlying psychological process as feeling. In the present text I refer to the third way of knowing as metaphorism and to the underlying psychological processes as symbolic and intuitive. The words metaphoric, symbolic and intuitive are fraught with semantic confusion. However, it was felt that the present version would focus more adequately on the epistemological criterion of universality on the one hand, and the possible underlying psychological processes on the other hand. That is, in this context we are concerned with the knowledge giving qualities which adhere to the word metaphoric—the way in which symbol systems lead to valid awarenesses of reality. The corresponding psychological processes, designated as symbolic and intuitive, imply a more imaginative-creative mode of cognition than is implied by empiricism and rationalism. Greater overtones of affectivity and unconsciousness are also implied. Additional semantic difficulty is provided by the fact that phi-

Joseph R. Royce

The Present Situation in Theoretical Psychology

2

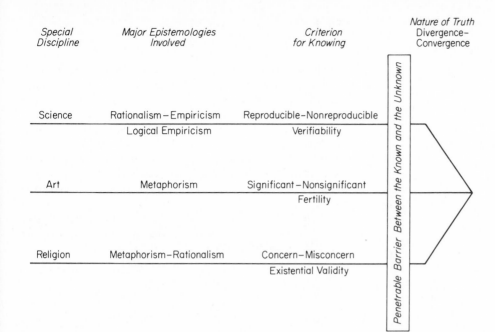

Special Discipline	Major Epistemologies Involved	Criterion for Knowing	Penetrable Barrier Between the Known and the Unknown	Nature of Truth Divergence-Convergence
Science	Rationalism–Empiricism	Reproducible-Nonreproducible		
	Logical Empiricism	Verifiability		
Art	Metaphorism	Significant–Nonsignificant		
		Fertility		
Religion	Metaphorism–Rationalism	Concern–Misconcern		
		Existential Validity		

Fig. 2-1. *Representative Special Disciplines of Knowledge. A modified version of Royce (1964, p. 20).*

The implication here is that each of these isms represents a legitimate approach to reality, but that different criteria for knowing are involved. Rationalism, for example, is primarily dependent upon logical consistency. That is, this approach says that we will accept something as true if it is logically consistent, and we will reject something as false if it is illogical. Empiricism says we know to the extent that we perceive cor-

losophers (e.g., Montague, 1928; Cassirer, 1953, 1955, 1957) have defended both intuitionism and symbolism as valid epistemologies, whereas I have shifted these terms to the psychological process side of the ledger. While these words are ambiguous as cognitive process, we can at least argue that this condition is more a function of sheer ignorance than anything else. If the present renewal of interest in cognition continues we can anticipate an eventual operational and empirical clarification of this kind of semantic ambiguity. For example, certain experimental investigations and theoretical analyses of the past decade indicate a possible bridge between the traditional behavioristic approach to cognition on the one hand, and a revitalized concern for "higher thought processes" on the other hand. Here I am thinking particularly of the introduction of the term "mediators" as exemplified in the writings of Rozeboom (1956), Mowrer (1960b), and Osgood (1957). At a more complex level, we have the emergence of psycholinguistics (e.g., see Miller, 1951; and Carroll 1953), and the psychology (i.e., beyond the traditional psychoanalytic treatment of the subject) of the symbol per se (e.g., see Werner and Kaplan, 1963; and Royce 1965a). In addition, there have been a small number of experimental studies on the nature of the intuitive process as a general psychological phenomenon (e.g., see Westcott, 1961; and Westcott and Ranzoni, 1963), as an aspect of creativity (Barron, 1965; Hitt, 1965; Hitt and Stock, 1965; Hill, 1965a, b; and Taylor, 1964), and as part of the clinician's cognitive repertoire (Meehl, 1954; Sarbin, Taft, and Bailey, 1960; Levy, 1963). Finally, I should state that I decided on the term metaphoric rather than the term symbolic for this third kind of knowledge because it is the lesser of two semantic evils—that is, there is less confusion surrounding the use of the word metaphoric than there is for the word symbolic (e.g., see Langer, 1961; Foss, 1949; and Bertalanffy, 1965). In the present context metaphoric is the larger term, a term which implies analogy, simile, and totality. It points to an indivisible unity, a gestalt which is not completely accounted for by its individual symbolic components (e.g., a drama as the metaphoric unit, in contrast to a particular character as a symbolic component).

rectly, and metaphorism says that knowledge is dependent upon the degree to which symbolic and intuitive cognitions lead us to universal rather than idiosyncratic insights. While each of these cognitive processes may lead to error, the implication is that each is also capable of leading to truth. The possibilities of intuitive error, for example, are readily apparent. Equally obvious, at least to psychologists, are the errors of perception. The errors of the thinking process are probably more subtle, but I have been led to believe that they have plagued the efforts of the logicians and mathematicians. Furthermore, we recognize that none of these psychological processes operates independently of the others. That is, one does not think independently of sensory inputs and symbolic and intuitive processes; nor do we perceive independently of intuition and thinking. In short, the correspondences indicated in Table 2-1 are oversimplified for purposes of analysis and exposition, but they represent all the known ways that man is enabled to come into contact with reality. The major point I wish to make at this juncture is that man needs to invoke all the available ways of knowing for the best possible grasp of his world, but that he tends to be partial to one or another of these cognitive approaches.

I have developed this theme at some length in a book under the title *The Encapsulated Man* (1964), the point being that men of different philosophic commitments (i.e., world views) reflect limited or encapsulated images of reality as a function of their particular epistemological profiles. This state of affairs is particularly apparent if we look at specialists in contrasting disciplines of knowledge, such as is indicated in Fig. 2-1. For our purposes I suggest we ignore the right half of this figure and focus on the left hand portion. It is understood that all three epistemologies are involved in each of the three representative disciplines of knowledge, but it is also clear that each discipline gives greater credence to one or more of them. The scientist, for example, "thinks," "intuits," "symbolizes," and "senses" as scientist, but he maximizes the rational and empirical ways of knowing and minimizes metaphoric symbolizing and intuition as final judge. Conversely, the artist, who also invokes his entire cognitive repertoire, maximizes the symbolic and intuitive processes at the expense of the thinking and sensory processes. There are, of course, wide variations in the possible permutations and combinations of epistemological profiles; this brief exposition should be taken as relative and typical rather than as absolute and general.

While my own epistemological hierarchy places rationalism at the apex, I also have strong empirical pressures. Thus, I have initiated a long range series of investigations on the adequacy of the above mentioned theoretical formulation. Although studies to date represent only a crude beginning, they fortunately tend to confirm my intuitive–rational speculations. I will now briefly summarize these findings.

Our approach was to construct an inventory, The Psycho-Epistemological Profile, as a way to measure a person's epistemological hierarchy. The ultimate goal is to construct a standardized test of fifty to one-hundred three-choice items. The choices within each item are designed so as to reflect each of the three[2] approaches to truth. *S*s task is to rank order the three choices of each item. Response preferences are scored in such a way as to reflect both ipsative and normative date.

It is impossible to specify on *a priori* grounds which items are most likely to be reliable and valid. We have, therefore, included items from several categories in the experimental version of this inventory. This means we have included items which pose hypothetical situations and ask for probable behavior; items which ask for preferences regarding activities, interests, and people; and items which relate directly or indirectly to epistemological choices. Here is an example of an epistemologically explicit item.

In attempting to ascertain the value of a new theory I am most concerned that it be:
(a) logically consistent,
(b) validated by direct experimental evidence,
(c) a new and imaginative idea.

An example of the epistemologically implicit item is as follows:

Which of the following do you think can ultimately contribute most to our lives:
(*a*) mathematics,
(*b*) art,
(*c*) biology?

The inventory has now been through several revisions, several administrations to selected and unselected samples, and several item analyses and weighting schemes. We believe the present 81-item version (Revised Experimental Form III) carries sufficient reliability and validity to be of general research use. A highly compressed summary of specific findings to date is as follows[3]:

1. It is possible to assess a person's epistemological hierarchy by way of an inventory known as the Psycho-Epistemological Profile.

2. It is estimated that the test-retest reliability coefficients of the three scales of the present 81-item version of the P.E.P. (Experimental Form III) are around .90.

3. There is preliminary evidence that the inventory is valid in the sense that it can discriminate between contrasting groups. More specifically, the data summarized in Table 2-2 show that

Table 2-2. Group Means on Empirical, Metaphoric, and Rational Scales of the Psycho-Epistemological Profile (Revised Experimental Form II)

Groups	Empirical Scale	Metaphoric Scale	Rational Scale
Chem-Bio ⟨N = 48⟩	1.223	1.141	1.337
Mu-Drama ⟨N = 50⟩	1.102	1.489	1.203
Math-Phy ⟨N = 44⟩	1.162	1.142	1.452

empiricism is the dominant characteristic of the Chem-Biology group, that metaphorism is the highest in the Music-Drama sample, and that rationalism is highest for the Math-Theoretical Physics group. This empirical confirmation of theoretical expectations is most encouraging because of the overall consistency of the data. Normative comparisons (i.e., when one compares scale performances *between* groups) turn out as predicted in all cases, and ipsative comparisons (i.e., when one compares scale performances *within* groups) turn out as predicted in all cases except one (i.e., the average scale score for the Chem-Biology group is 1.337 on the Rational Scale and 1.223 on the Empirical Scale). All but one (Math-Physics = 1.142 vs. Chem-Biology = 1.141 on the Metaphoric Scale) of the nine possible "*t*" tests are significant beyond the 5% level.

Now that minimal test construction requirements for reliability and validity have been met it should be possible to extend the application of the P.E.P. to a wide variety of empirical problems such as cultural (e.g., East vs. West) and sub-cultural (e.g., "the two cultures") differences, developmental changes, and relationships to other value commitments (such as the six values in the Allport, Vernon, Lindzey Study of Values).

A variety of other theorists have concerned themselves with issues which relate tangentially to what I have called psycho-epistemology. These include Piaget's (e.g., see Flavell, 1963) developmental cognitive studies, Festinger's (1957) theory of cognitive dissonance, Berlyne's (1960) work on epistemic curiosity, the philosopher Wallraff's (1961) analysis of knowing as an interpretation of rather than some kind of correspondence to reality, Jung's (1923) four-fold typology, the Miller, Galanter and Pribram (1960) concept of image as adapted from Boulding

[2]A fourth approach, purposely not developed in the present context, was labeled believing or authoritarianism. Although it was incorporated in an early version of the inventory as an equal-status way of knowing, we now see it as underlying the other three. That is, empiricism, metaphorism, and rationalism are the basic "truth systems" which are part of the person's total "belief system." Belief systems incorporate a variety of commitments, one of which is cognitive or epistemological in nature. One way to put this is to say we are all "believers" in something, but we make different commitments—some to empiricism, some to rationalism, and some to metaphorism. We anticipate studying the relationships between scores on a specially developed authoritarian scale, and other such measures, and scores on the empirical, rational and metaphoric scales of the P.E.P.

[3]For more details see the publications of my colleague W.A.S. Smith, graduate student associates, and myself (Jones, 1963; Royce, 1962; Smith, Royce, Ayers, and Jones, 1967). We are presently engaged in a long-range theoretical and empirical extension of these preliminary efforts under the rubric of epistemological psychology.

(1956), and Donald Campbell's (1960) evolutionary epistemology and Northrop and Livingston's (1964) anthropological epistemology. But the work most directly pertinent to the purposes of this paper is that of the Harvard sociologist P. A. Sorokin. He invokes essentially the same three epistemologies in his analysis of the shifts in the dominant values of cultures and epochs. He begins with the basic assumption of cultural cohesiveness, as follows:

Any great culture, instead of being a mere dumping place of a multitude of diverse cultural phenomena, existing side by side and unrelated to one another, represents a unity or individuality whose parts are permeated by the same fundamental principle and articulate the same basic value. The dominant part of the fine arts and sciences of such a unified culture, of its philosophy and religion, of its ethics and law, of its main form of social, economic, and political organization, of most of its mores and manners, of its ways of life and mentality, all articulate, each in its own way, this basic principle and value. This value serves as its major premise and foundation. (1941, p. 17)

Then, corresponding to the epistemologies of empiricism, rationalism, and metaphorism respectively, he analyzes culture in terms of the dominant values of sensate, idealistic, and ideational. Thus, the sensate culture is dominated by the truth of the senses, the idealistic culture focuses on the truth of reason, and the ideational culture is symbol oriented. He characterizes twentieth century Western society as a weary, sensate culture, a culture which has been dominated by empiricism since the Renaissance, but which has been disintegrating for the last four or five decades—hence, the title of his book, *The Crisis of our Age*. It should be noted that Sorokin's analyses of the rise and fall of civilizations do not follow the organic analogue of Spengler (1932) and Toynbee (1946, 1947), wherein a culture *must* die after living out its natural life span. His position is that the present crisis merely represents a decline in the sensate form of Western society, to be followed by a new integration of the various cultural facets. Let us look at the shifts in European culture since A.D. 800 as an example of Sorokin's brand of analysis.

He describes the medieval period as an ideational culture, dominated by the truth of religious symbols, a God-centered culture which was supra-sensory and supra-rational. When this theocratic culture declined around 1500, the Renaissance period ushered in the contemporary sensate culture—a culture dominated by the truth of the senses, and secular, present-moment, worldly values. Sorokin also suggests that there was a relatively short transitional period, from around 1200 to 1500, reflecting the domination of reason, an idealistic culture. Thus, while it is oversimplified and the transitional shifts are always less precise than can be diagramatically represented, I have summarized Sorokin's major value shifts in Fig. 2-2.

What Sorokin is saying about twentieth century life is that we are presently shedding our sensory world-view in favor of the other two. The exact direction we shall take is not yet clear, but his guess is that we are moving toward a more "integral" culture, one which reflects a more balanced mixture of all three major values. Sorokin's cultural analyses rarely imply complete cultural disintegration or extinction, but rather, value shifts in terms of the permutations and combinations of the three basic orientations.

The parallels between Sorokin's analysis and my own are obvious. The major world views are essentially the same, and they form the central plank for subsequent analysis. The difference is that my analysis focuses on the individual and Sorokin's unit of analysis is culture. Because of this my analysis is primarily in terms of psychological processes whereas Sorokin's analysis is primarily in terms of social change. I then turn to philosophy for valid epistemologies—ways of knowing which lead to individual survival. Sorokin then turns to history for valid cognitions—ways of knowing which lead to cultural survival. The two approaches complement one another, providing parallel analyses at the individual and cultural levels, based on the same three cognitive categories of thinking, sensing, and symbolizing-intuiting.

The point of immediate relevance is that twentieth century Western culture is clearly a sensate culture. Even if we set aside the issue of whether this will necessarily lead to the decline of contemporary civilization, it seems clear from my own analysis at the individual level, combined with Sorokin's analysis at the cultural level, that such a world view is extremely limited. Furthermore, seen in this context, it comes as no surprise that psychology, being essentially a part of twentieth century Western culture, is similarly sensate or empirically oriented. There is little doubt, in my mind at least, that contemporary psychology is suffering—stifling might be a more accurate word—from super-empiricism (Royce, 1964, 1965a, 1965c).

My argument is *not* that psychology should become *less* empirical, but rather, that it should become more *powerfully* rational and more *open* to the knowledge giving qualities of the metaphor. It seems clear that a less encapsulated discipline, one which makes the most of *all* the cognitive processes at our command, will be able to embrace the reality with which it is concerned with greater awareness. I now propose that we take a look at contemporary theoretical efforts within psychology and that we include an analysis of such efforts in terms of the three epistemologies.

An Analysis of Contemporary Theories

Theory in a field as immature as psychology cannot be expected to amount to much—and it doesn't. It is my opinion that the major reason psychology cannot point to a great man of the stature of Newton or Einstein is that it simply is not ready for the kind of grand unification which such a man can provide. A great twentieth century behavior theorist can only be expected to promote an important point of view which will

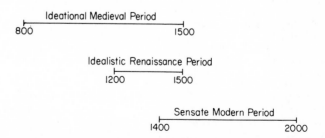

Fig. 2-2. *An Analysis of Dominant Western Cultural Values Between 800 and 2000 A.D.*

Table 2-3. The Complementary Pattern of Psychological Schools

Name of School	Structuralism	Gestalt Psychology	Functionalism		Geisteswissenschaftliche or verstehende Psychologie
			Behaviorism	Psycho-analysis	
Characteristic problem or field of research	Sensation	Perception	Learning	Motivation	Character
Temporal span of observation in typical methods	·	○	→	⟶	→ ∞
		PHYSICAL	BIOLOGICAL		SOCIAL
Conceptually allied sciences	e. g. Physics		e. g. Physiology		e. g. Sociology

Rosenzweig (1937), p. 97.

pervade broad segments of psychology, or develop a theory which covers a rather limited domain such as perception or learning, or perhaps hit the jackpot and accomplish a little of both.

During the first half of the twentieth century the major contributions to theoretical psychology have been primarily of the first type, namely, the presentation of an all-pervading point of view. The major views of this period are those of the behaviorists, the gestaltists, and the psychoanalysts. Perhaps the outstanding contribution of each of these isms to our understanding of behavior has been to point out an important approach which others had neglected—for example, the psychoanalysts' insistence that we pay attention to irrational and unconscious forces which drive the human organism. At mid-twentieth century very few psychologists find it necessary to identify themselves with one or another of these camps, as was typical of the twenties. Rather, they take the approach that each of these viewpoints is valid and important, and that they contribute to our understanding of behavior in a complementary way (see Table 2-3). It is also generally agreed that, in spite of the magnitude of their contributions, none of these viewpoints is adequate as a general theory of behavior, that they all over-generalized, were based on inadequate data, and were essentially programmatic. In short, they can be characterized more as doctrinal protests (i.e., what Rozeboom calls perspectival theory; see his category A, described in Royce [1970], p. 59) than as unifying theories.

While the efforts of neo-behaviorists such as Hull and Skinner started out as reasonably modest statements about very simple learning on the part of very simple animals such as rats and pigeons, it is unfortunately true that these authors have published volumes with such questionable titles as *Principles of Behavior* (Hull, 1943) and *The Behavior of Organisms* (Skinner, 1938). In other words, they have tended to overgeneralize in the same way as did their predecessors, although it must be admitted that the principles which have emerged from these efforts are, in general, more explicit than were those of the earlier vintage.

The tendency towards more adequate miniature theorizing which was initiated by the neo-behaviorists is a very healthy development, and it is fortunate that this tendency has continued apace. Thus, we now find perceptual theorists such as Gibson (1950) and Graham (1959) confining themselves to perceptual phenomena, and learning theorists such as Estes (1959) and Spence (1956) staying within the confines of their domain. We need more of this self-conscious concern for developing a theory to account for a relatively limited aspect of the total behavior of the organism for the simple reason that it is a goal we are more likely to reach in our present state of theoretical anarchy.

On the other hand, there are several very significant general theory efforts currently under way with an orientation radically different from the earlier vintage of general theory. In my opinion, the most promising of these efforts are those which have grown out of the concern for the unification of science and the development of scientific generalists along with the usual scientific specialists—namely, the interdisciplinary efforts of Bertalanffy's general systems theory, and the general behavior theory which is emerging from the interdisciplinary team at the University of Michigan Mental Health Research Institute under the leadership of James G. Miller. Efforts such as these are important because they are finding that methodological approaches and concepts developed in one field have relevance for other fields. For example, the methods of factor analysis, developed in psychology, have already had a significant impact on most of the social sciences, and some impact on the biological and physical sciences as well (Royce, 1965b). Similarly, the concept of homeostasis, originally developed in biology, has been shown to have a very deep and significantly unifying impact in more than one area of psychology (Royce, 1957). Thus, it would seem that much of the confusion shared by the various sciences of man is due to the barrage of special in-group terminology, and that considerable headway could be made by the simple-minded routine of translating from one technical language to the other. Furthermore, Bertalanffy has pointed out that there are important generalizations which can be made about all open systems, whether it be the psychobiological unit we call man, or the social system which exists among a species of ants or a nation of men. As long as efforts such as these are seen as they should be seen, namely, as heuristic approaches to the eventual understanding of man, and not as definitive systematic statements, there is real hope that they will eventually move us in the direction of a general theory of behavior.

Let us now take a closer look at these area and general theories. I'll begin with the area theories or "theorettes" as they have been dubbed by Krech. I propose that we analyze contemporary theorettes in terms of their underlying epistemological characteristics. Since psychology is primarily committed to the scientific Weltanschauung the analysis is cast primarily in terms of rationalism and empiricism. However, my statements occasionally carry implications regarding the relevance of symbolic and intuitive cognition, but I will return to metaphorism in the concluding section of this paper.

The essence of what I wish to say about area theories is

Table 2-4. Representative Area Theories in Contemporary Psychology

1 Primary Area of Study	2 Representative Contemporary Systems	3 Nature of Empirical Observations	4 Nature of Formalization	5 Position on the Empirical-Formalism Spectrum	6 Adequacy of Empirical-Formal Fit
Sensation	Vision, Audition	Experimental	Explanatory	Exp'l-Explanatory	Good
	Helson		Explanatory	Exp'l-Explanatory	Good
Perception	Köhler-Wallach	Experimental	Explanatory	Exp'l-Explanatory	Good
	Gibson		Descriptive	Exp'l-Descriptive	Good
Learning	Skinner		Descriptive	Exp'l-Descriptive	Good
	Mowrer	Experimental	Explanatory	Exp'l-Explanatory	Good
	Spence		Explanatory	Exp'l-Explanatory	Good
	Mathematical Models (various)		Explanatory	Exp'l-Explanatory	Fair
Motivation	Variants of psychoanalysis (i.e. Freud, Jung, etc.)	Phenomenological	Descriptive	Phenomenological-Descriptive	Minimal
	Rogers, Murray	Phenomenological	Descriptive	Phenomenological-Descriptive	Minimal
Personality	Allport, Murphy	Correlational	Descriptive	Correlational-Descriptive	Minimal
Social Behavior	Fromm	Phenomenological	Speculative	Phenomenological-Speculative	Minimal
	Lewin	Correlational	Descriptive	Correlational-Descriptive	Minimal
	Game theory	Experimental	Explanatory	Experimental-Explanatory	Fair

Table 2-5. Representative General Theories in Contemporary Psychology

1 Primary Area of Study	2 Representative Contemporary Systems	3 Nature of Empirical Observations	4 Nature of Formalization	5 Position on the Empirical-Formalism Spectrum	6 Adequacy of Empirical-Formal Fit
Individual differences	Factor analysis (Thurstone)	Correlational	Explanatory	Correlational-Explanatory	Good
Neurological (physiological)	Hebb, Krech	Experimental	Descriptive	Exp'l-Descriptive	Fair
	Rashevsky, McCulloch	Experimental	Explanatory	Exp'l-Explanatory	Minimal
Information, Cybernetics, Decision theory	Frick, Attneave, Wiener, von Neumann, Luce	Experimental	Explanatory	Exp'l-Explanatory	Fair
General systems	Bertalanffy, J. G. Miller	Various (i.e. all)	Various (i.e. all)	Empirical-Theoretical (i.e. all)	Minimal

summarized in Table 2-4. This table shows representative systems by rows and specifies epistemological characteristics by columns. For example, in the area of perception, the Köhler-Wallach theory of figural after-effects (satiation theory) is described as experimental, explanatory, experimental-explanatory, and reflects a "good" empirical-formal fit. The social behavior theory of Fromm is described as phenomenological, speculative, phenomenological-speculative, and reflecting a "minimal" empirical-formal fit. Columns 3 to 6 require brief elaboration. Column 3 refers to the mode of observation which is characteristic of the area in question. While the nature of empirical observations can best be seen as a "degree of control" continuum, ranging from the little or no control of common sense to the relatively complete control of the laboratory (Royce, 1964, pp. 50–51), we have oversimplified the task by utilizing only three terms: phenomenological, correlational, and experimental. Column 4 refers to the degree of formalized rationalization of the area theory in question, ranging from the looseness of "speculation," to the relative tightness of "explanation." The continuum here is in terms of internal consistency, the most stringent, tight system (i.e., "explanatory") being in terms of some form of mathematics or formal logic. The word descriptive is used as intermediary between speculative and explanatory. Column 5 simply refers to the particular combination of terms applied in Columns 3 and 4. It represents what Northrop (1947) refers to as an epistemic correlation. Column 6 represents my guess (and such guesses are loaded with difficulties) as to the adequacy of this epistemic correlation in terms of minimal, fair, and good, the implication being that the adequacy of conceptual-observational fit for *any* extant psychological theory is no better than "good."

A similar analysis concerning general theories is summarized in Table 2-5. What conclusions can we draw from inspection of Tables 2-4 and 2-5? I offer the following:

1. The most adequate efforts (i.e., rated good or fair) in terms of empirical-formal fit are the area theories in sensation, perception, and learning, and general theories covering individual differences and neuropsychology.

2. In general, the most successful theories are experimental-explanatory in nature.

3. However, both descriptive and correlational approaches have led to convincing theory, as in the cases of Thurstone, Skinner, and Hebb.

4. The phenomenological-speculative approach provides provocative leads, but does not eventuate in convincing theory in that form. Note, however, that it plays an important and legitimate role in the scientific enterprise.

Overall, optimal results occur when there is either high *empiricism* (i.e., sticking close to the facts), as in the case of Skinner, or relevant high *formalism* (i.e., high powered analytic models, such as an *appropriate mathematics*), as in the case of test theory and learning theory, or both, as in the cases of Thurstone and Spence, *and* when the theorist confines himself to a *relatively limited domain* rather than attempting to encompass all of behavior (i.e., figural after-effects rather than gestalt psychology, conditioning rather than behaviorism, vision rather than all the senses, etc.). This conclusion points up how difficult it is for *any* scientific endeavor to arrive at an advanced state—that is, to develop one all-encompassing theory which adequately accounts for the observed phenomena. Cases where psychological theory manifest relatively high epistemic correlations are either limited to the relatively well established domains of study (i.e., sensation, perception, learning, individual differences, and neuropsychology), or/and they are confined to a relatively limited segment of behavior (i.e., even the more successful general theories of individual differences and neuropsychology cover a relatively limited aspect of the totality of behavior). In other words, one of the conclusions we can draw from this state of affairs is that a high degree of empiricism is prerequisite to theoretical integration—that is, there must be a large number of observed facts on hand, available for meaningful conceptualization. However, it would appear that the deification of an "experimental only" brand of empiricism reflects a case of well-meaning but misguided faith. For the theoretical success of such correlational approaches as factor analysis and psychometric theory, combined with the promise of a variety of relatively simple probability models, augurs well for a more relaxed attitude toward the apparent lack of precision of psychological data. I say apparent for it is becoming more and more clear that the data of behavior, even when gathered under the "cleanest" conditions of laboratory control and precision of measurement, do not fall into the patterns of numerical invariance characteristic of the data of mechanics and other strictly nomothetic domains of study. In short, the nature of the behavioral beast is more like the weather than the motions of billiard balls, and we need to adapt our thinking and methodology to this state of affairs. On this point Egon Brunswik has been most incisive and instructive. In one of his last analytic papers, for example, he puts it this way:

So long as the organism does not develop, or fails in a given context to utilize, completely, the powers of a full-fledged physicist observer and analyst, his environment remains for all practical purposes a semi-erratic medium; it is no more than partially controlled and no more than probabilistically predictable. The functional approach in psychology must take cognizance of this basic limitation of the adjustive apparatus; it must link behavior and environment statistically in bivariate or multivariate correlation rather than with the predominant emphasis on strict law which we have inherited from physics. It is perhaps more accurate to say that the nomothetic ideology was influenced by a somewhat naive and outdated high-school type, thematic cliche of physics which some of us have tacitly carried with us in the process of developing psychology into a science. (Brunswik, 1956, p. 158)

Thus, his well known insistence that we proceed in terms of a molar-correlational-probabilism.

But even if we broaden our conception of empiricism as suggested, we will not optimally advance our understanding of behavior by an "empiricism only" approach. That is, radical empiricism can hardly pull its conceptual self up by its own bootstraps—some kind of theoretical lattice work has got to move in on the data. However, the psychologist's traditional trial and error game of importing foreign theoretical models is a mixed blessing. Most of the contemporary models being played with are mathematical in nature, ranging from the well established relevance of matrix algebra as the basis for factor theory, through the traditional differential and integral calculus and probability theory, to the provocative possibilities of group and set theory. The mathematical models have been attempted primarily in the areas of learning theory (Bush and Mosteller, 1955; Bush and Estes, 1959) and test theory, (Gulliksen, 1950) but they have also been applied to a variety of other domains. Game theory (Luce and Raiffa, 1957; Shubik, 1964) and decision theory (Thrall, Combs, and Davis, 1954; Luce, 1959) appear to be of particular relevance to choice behavior, social interaction, and value, whereas information theory (Quastler, 1955; Attneave, 1959) and cybernetics (Wiener, 1948) hold most promise as a framework for the data of cognition. Information theory currently shows signs of paying off, for it is already possible to demonstrate many human-like qualities with the use of electronic computers, such as the ability to play chess, translate languages, solve mathematical problems, and perceive. The risk in all this business is that we will forget that a model serves primarily as an analogy, and must not be taken as the thing itself. In other words, it will require a great amount of labor, much measuring, experimenting, and thinking before we can ascertain which aspects of the model to retain and which ones must be dropped. For the greatest value of an analogy is heuristic, that is, its tendency to provoke ingenious experimentation and perceptive conceptualization. It is certainly doubtful that a model from one field will be adequate in unmodified form for another field. We must, after much detailed investigation, ascertain what modifications are necessary, or we must be ready to cast aside the analogy completely if we find too few points of empirical contact. For example, early efforts at mathematizing psychology, such as that of Rashevsky (1938), made extensive use of the calculus. Beginning with a differential equation which reflected the rate of change of the neural impulse, Rashevsky introduced a variety of simplifying assumptions, derived a variety of integral equations, and eventually evolved a complete calculus of behavior which ran the gamut from neurons to war. This superstructure still stands today as a monument to formalization without empirical representation. While it is possible that a tight empirical-formal fit will eventually be found, it certainly seems to be the case that the calculus is a premature (if not actually inappropriate) mathematical model for behavior. For one thing, differentiation implies the ability to measure very minute rate changes. What aspects of behavior lend themselves to such precise measurement in mid-twentieth century? Very few. Perhaps certain aspects of physiological psychology, such as nerve conduction and the photochemical processes of the retina, and a similarly limited portion of experimental psychology, such as tracking. The point is that the calculus would be relevant only when behavioral data reflect a high degree of veridicality within the framework of a highly quantifiable system—that is, where rate of change can be measured with great precision. In other words, the Rashevsky failure is a case of an inappropriate mathematical model, or what we may refer to as mental dazzle.

Similarly, the electronic brain is probably not an adequate model for its living counterpart. But it seems worth our while at this time to pursue information theory to the limit in order to find out the extent to which this analogy will hold up. I am well aware of the fact that psychology is pirate science, and its willingness to try on the conceptual raiment of foreign systems of knowledge is well known. In fact, the claim that psychology has been *too willing* to try on the theoretical orientations of other disciplines is somewhat justified (Koch, 1959). It suggests that psychology does not know where it is going. But that is not particularly unusual in academia; it is interesting to note, for example, that the scientific field which knows best where it has been, physics, has been acting in a similar manner lately. The mathematician John von Neuman, at the time of his death, was writing a book (von Neuman, 1958) on the development of computers in terms of the latest developments in neurophysiology and neuropsychology. Here we have an example of the emergence of progress out of pooled ignorance as well as the heuristic value of the analogy in science, for we have the situation of certain men who call themselves psychologists and physiologists looking at computers as a possible model for the functioning of the brain, and another group of men who are computer experts (mathematicians and physicists) looking at men's brains as a possible model for the functioning of the computer.

What prescriptions are indicated? I suggest the following:

1. That we inductively generate, from *within* the storehouse of existing psychological data, an inventory of basic concepts, functional relationships, and principles of varying degrees of generality. Several years ago I elaborated on the need for such an inventory and gave several examples of what was called for (see Royce, 1957). Recently this kind of effort received a boost in the form of the Berelson and Steiner book, *Human Behavior: An Inventory of Scientific Findings* (1964). Although it omits large domains, such as biological correlates of behavior, it documents 1,045 such empirically based propositions of generalizations. While the adequacy of many of these concepts is questionable, and the degree of generality is limited, this extensive conceptual inventory provides an impressive basis for evolving a large number of functional relationships which are screaming to be brought into sharper focus and subsequent interrelation.

2. That we fit our research methodology to the problem at hand, rather than continue the "methodolatrous" forcing of a less appropriate approach to a given domain of study. In the case of psychology this clearly implies a greater utilization of multivariate methods of problem solving in addition to the continued use of the traditional bivariate analyses (i.e., this does *not* imply the elimination of bivariate analysis).

3. That we continue to try out a variety of conceptual schemes, both home grown and foreign, but that we screen these more critically than we have in the past in terms of their relevance to the particular area of psychological study. Let us take model building as a case in point. The history of science shows a trend away from physical analogies to empty, formal or mathematical models (Schmidt, 1957).

But many of the traditional or classical mathematical systems, such as the calculus, seem to have negligible implications for psychology. While a wide variety of mathematical models have been applied to psychology during the past decade (e.g., see Luce, Bush, and Galanter, 1963a, b), and while it is clearly too soon to assess the pay-off value of these varied efforts, my bias is that the mathematical models most relevant to the study of behavior are those which will be able to invoke an appropriate combination of the following characteristics:

(*a*) be stated in terms of probabilities.

(*b*) adequate inclusion of many variables simultaneously, as in matrix algebra.

(*c*) adequate handling of non-mensurational or qualitative data, as in topology, graph theory, and set theory.[4]

4. That we focus more on area rather than general theories of behavior, with subsequent linkages between areas as a basis for moving *toward* the eventual unification of psychology.[5] The hope of moving directly to a general behavior theory without the prior establishment of strong area theories seems to be unrealistic. The fact that no *one* theory has satisfactorily encompassed *any* discipline of study to date, including the various physical sciences, suggests that the notion of a general theory of behavior can best be thought of as an ideal toward which we should strive, but that it is probably not attainable.

[4]For coverage of the most relevant so-called modern mathematics between the covers of one book see Kemeny, Snell, and Thompson (1957). For a simplified presentation of the most relevant portion of matrix theory, see Horst (1963) or Butler (1962). For varied thumbnail sketches of applications to psychological data see Bush, Abelson, and Hyman (1956). For detailed instruction on the implementation of two probabilitistic models to social phenomena see Chapters V and VII of Kemeny and Snell (1962). For detailed instruction on the implementation of two non-metric models to behavioral data see Chapters II and VIII of Kemeny and Snell (1962). For detailed analysis of matrix theory as the underlying mathematics of factor analysis see any of several books, such as Thurstone (1947) and Harman (1967). For a provocative extension of Lewinian-type theorizing, see the monograph on graph theory by Harary and Norman (1953). For an introductory awareness of the relevance of set theory, an approach likely to be of considerable significance for psychology because it provides an analytic method for getting at patterns by way of sets and subsets of organism-environment components which relate to a given response, see Chapter 2 of Bush and Mosteller (1955). And finally, for coverage of multivariate analytic approaches which have gone beyond their traditional non-experimental domains of study see the Handbook of Multivariate Experimental Psychology (Cattell, 1966).

[5]Mowrer's recent consolidation of learning theory (1960a), and subsequent extension to symbolic processes (1960b), with necessarily (to date) vaguer asides to more complex behavior such as language, consciousness, socialization, personality, and psychopathology (i.e., primarily in the latter half of Mowrer, 1960b, and in other publications such as Mowrer, 1964), constitute a provocative example of the possibilities of moving from a hard core area theory toward a more general theory of behavior. Similar extensions of the well documented adaptation-level theory have been demonstrated by Helson (1964). My personal bias is that the approach reflected in the examples of Mowrer and Helson is more promising than the earlier isms because of the much greater accumulation of empirical evidence available for unification, the integration of earlier (sometimes apparently opposing) theoretical conceptualizations, and the general tightening up of the area theory *before* casting the nomological net abroad to include adjacent behavioral domains.

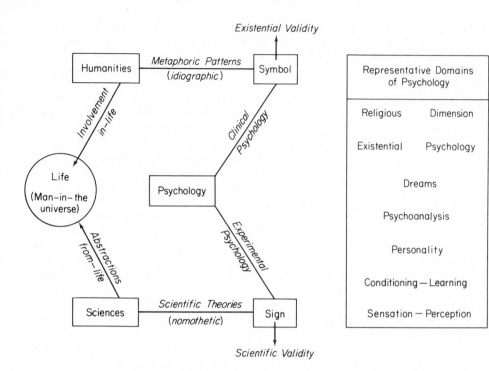

Fig. 2-3. *Psychology at the Crossroads.*

Metaphoric Knowledge and the Emergence of Humanistic Psychology

The question, How do we know? is an old and difficult one for both philosophers and psychologists. But our intuitions, perceptions, and thoughts regarding symbolic and intuitive knowing are. less adequate than our awarenesses of perceptual and rational knowing. Partly because of this, and partly because we are products of a sensate-rational culture, we tend to depreciate, or at least be wary of, the symbol and intuition. On the other hand, we recognize their pervasiveness in all the specialized disciplines of knowledge—the arts, the sciences, and the humanities—particularly when we focus on the insights of "great men" (e.g., see Havens, 1964; Royce, 1964). The discoveries of Newton and Galileo regarding gravity and the pendulum, the development of new mathematical systems such as the calculus and modern algebra, the works of art created by a Mozart, a Beethoven, or a Shakespeare, reflect a variety of combinations of symbolic and intuitive cognition. In the analysis which follows I take the position that symbolism and intuition are legitimate ways of knowing, in spite of our ignorance about how they work, that they can be brought into play at any phase of the knowing process, and that they have, in fact, manifested themselves to some extent in all domains of psychological study, but that their greatest immediate relevance lies in the present emergence of humanistic psychology. Since humanistic studies are heavily under-girded by the metaphoric epistemology (see Fig. 2-1), it follows that any alliance between psychology and the humanities would, by definition, invoke this approach to reality as primary. However, such alliances imply two-way traffic, so that we can anticipate the wedding of the empirical-rational epistemologies with the metaphoric approach in coming to grips with psychological problems of a humanistic nature. This means that the symbolic and intuitive insights typical of humanistic thought would eventually be tempered by efforts to provide

appropriate empirical tests. More importantly, however, it also implies an openness on the part of the humanistic psychologist to those metaphoric-rational awarenesses which are *not* immediately testable empirically. In another context (Royce, 1965*a*) I develop the theme that the key to the difference between scientific and humanistic psychology lies in the distinction between sign and symbol. This point can best be brought out by the diagram shown in Fig. 2-3.

The purpose of this diagram is to bring out the complementary contributions of the sciences and the humanities to the understanding of life, and particularly, to demonstrate how psychology lies peculiarly at the crossroads between the two cultures. Let us concentrate on the upper half of Fig. 2-3. Here we see the humanities as concretely involved-in-life as opposed to making abstractions *from* the phenomena of life. And, parallel to the ultimate theoretical goal of science, we see that the humanistic disciplines are also ultimately beamed at making overarching statements (i.e., metaphoric-rational) regarding man-in-the-universe. However, and this is the main point, the humanities speak through a symbolic rather than a sign language. Hence, the emerging statements take the form of metaphoric patterns or symbol systems rather than scientific theories, and the truth giving quality of such statements follows the epistemological criteria of symbols rather than signs (e.g., see Fig. 2-1 and note the "fertility" criterion of art and the criterion of existential validity for religion). As used in this context, the essence of the sign-symbol distinction is that the sign reveals a one-to-one correspondence (i.e., *A* means *B*, and *not* *C*, *D*, and *E*), whereas the symbol provides a one-to-many relationship (i.e., *A* may mean *B*, *C*, *D*, or *E*, or any combination thereof). The multiple meanings of the symbol make the task of empirical analysis extremely difficult, but they open up dimensions of reality which remain unavailable to sign language.[6] Herein

[6]For a more complete exposition of this point see Royce (1965*a*).

lies the challenge for the humanistic psychologist: to tap these symbolic dimensions of reality by invoking the knowledge giving tools of the humanistic trade on the one hand, and by doing all that is possible to provide empirical tests for whatever is so revealed on the other hand. But this must be done without the error of reductionism—that is, by throwing out as invalid those humanistic insights which are *not* amenable, or reducible, to empirical confirmation. If the reductionistic error is committed we simply will not have a humanistic psychology, for we will have reduced it to scientific (or empirical) psychology.

What might a humanistic psychology look like?

It is, of course, too early to tell, but I shall point to several possibilities. As a start I suggest we supplement the usual schematic diagram of the organism-in-the-environment (Fig. 2-4) with a diagram showing man-in-the-universe (Fig. 2-5). Such a schematic diagram allows us to cast the more philosophic aspects of man's behavior within the traditional definition of psychology as involving organism-environment interactions. The only difference is that we are now operating at the more cosmic level of man-in-the-universe. This business of painting man with such a big brush is typical of the humanistic approach, and thereby constitutes a reasonable common ground for mode of study. Also characteristic of the humanities is the effort to

unmask the universal by way of the concrete case. Our previous discussion must be kept in mind at this juncture, namely, that such universal-concrete efforts are typically conveyed symbolically rather than via signs. With this as a background we can now take a look at Fig. 2-6.

This diagram shows psychology as the study of man and his behavior rather than the science of organisms. The purpose behind this heretical, definitional shift is to legitimize symbolic and intuitive cognition (Royce, 1960, 1965a). Such a definition, which appears to be a reactionary move, is actually a forward looking suggestion in the twentieth century because it demands that we re-admit humanistic studies as a way to gain psychological knowledge. Now that we have empiricism as the core epistemology undergirding our discipline there would seem to be little danger that psychology will regress to a pre-Wundtian stage by making such a move. The solid lines indicate alliances with several humanistic disciplines (shown in solid line rectangles), the most relevant lying closest to psychology at the center. The broken lines lead to possible areas of humanistic study which are a result of such alliances. The most obvious examples of humanistic study are those indicated from an alliance with philosophy[7]: philosophy of science, operationism, logical positivism, and existential psychology (for examples of the last see Royce, 1962b, May 1961). In other words, philosophy of science and existentialism are seen as the most important currents of thought in contemporary philosophical and theoretical psychology (Royce, 1964). Similarly, the psychology of aesthetics and the psychology of religion are seen as examples of studies which have come out of alliances with the indicated humanistic-social and arts disciplines respectively.

The defense for the priority given to drama is that its action-on-a-stage (or on film, T.V., or other media) is capable of disclosing a microcosm of man living out his life in the everyday world. It is, in a very real sense, the most behavioral of the art forms. It is also one of the more time-compressed forms of artistic expression. These two points, combined with the fact that the dramatic form ordinarily involves a beginning, a middle, and an end, with a build up to a conflict which is resolved, provide the psychologist with material which simulates completed or total "lives." While similar material is also available in literature, it is not as obviously behavioral. Both forms, however, are rich in archetypal characterizations—THE HERO, tragic (e.g., Hamlet, Oedipus), Satanic (Mephistopheles in *Faust*, Iago in *Othello*), or God-like (Dion in O'Neill's *Great God Brown*); woman as GREAT MOTHER (Cybele in O'Neill's *Great God Brown*) or as GODDESS (the novel She); ANIMUS (*Wuthering Heights*)—and such universal themes as HEAVEN and HELL (*Kubla Khan, Paradise Lost*) and REBIRTH (*Job* and MacLeish's *J.B.*).

Let me be more concrete about all this by briefly analyzing William Golding's *Lord of the Flies* (1954). This is one of those cases where the now corny phrase "big allegory" (i.e., a form of metaphoric knowledge) is completely appropriate, for Golding has focused his attention on the predicament of modern man—possibly man in all time, but particularly twentieth century man. That is, he makes it clear at the beginning of the story

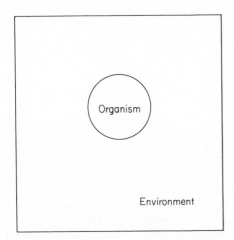

Fig. 2-4. *The Basic Schematic Definition of Psychology.*

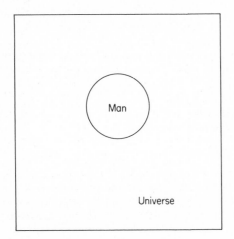

Fig. 2-5. *The Humanistic Schematic Definition of Psychology.*

[7]Greater recognition for this type of investigation is likely in the near future as the American Psychological Association has recently established a new division devoted to such study—Division 24, Division of Philosophical Psychology.

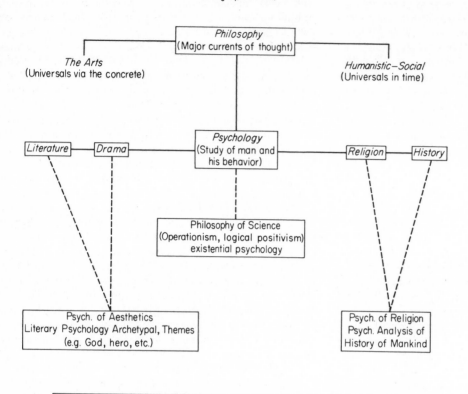

The Nature and Significance of Man
The Meaning of Man—in—the—Universe
(Idiographic man)

Philosophy
(Major currents of thought)

The Arts
(Universals via the concrete)

Humanistic—Social
(Universals in time)

Literature — Drama

Psychology
(Study of man and
his behavior)

Religion — History

Philosophy of Science
(Operationism, logical positivism)
existential psychology

Psych. of Aesthetics
Literary Psychology Archetypal, Themes
(e.g. God, hero, etc.)

Psych. of Religion
Psych. Analysis of
History of Mankind

Studies of Common Concern
Myth and Reality—Meaning of Life—Purpose of Existence—Freedom vs. Determinism

Fig. 2-6. *Psychology and the Humanities.*

that the kids isolated on the Pacific island had arrived with a cultural tradition, with an awareness of rules and custom. But in due course we observe the disintegration of order and the emergence of evil as the victor. Ralph, the Chief, says to his advisor, Piggy, "What went wrong, why did it all go wrong? We started out all right." This is the big question the story puts, and my interpretation is that the novel is primarily concerned with the forces of good and evil which are inherent in man's predicament. I see "the beast" as an externalization of potentially evil forces, and the pressure from such forces, combined with fear, fear of the unknown, as the key to what went wrong. Jack, the symbolic representative of evil, takes advantage of this fear by promising to provide protection from "the beast," thereby gaining a following. Thus, what went wrong is that fear, a very natural and necessary component for survival in the face of the unknown, dominated the situation at a time when acceptance of ambiguity was necessary. The important consideration, the rational Piggy (symbolizing the egg head) pointed out, was to be "rescued." And surely the important consideration for man, especially in a nuclear age, is for him to be "rescued." There are two clear opportunities for salvation in Golding's novel. The first one occurs when Simon comes to tell them "the truth" about "the beast" and they kill him—a rather obvious Christ symbol. The second chance comes too late at the end of the story when help arrives in the form of the British Navy. This can be taken as symbolic of the Day of Judgment, but it is too late, for all but Ralph have regressed to a savage condition by this time.

It is my view that there is considerable meat in this cosmic type of presentation for psychological analysis. Assuming for the moment that the above is an essentially correct analysis[8] of what Golding's novel is about, it seems clear that the behavior exhibited in this allegorical treatment of man must be explained.[9] I offered a brief explanation in terms of an outward projection of fear, combined with the always lurking forces of evil and man's inability to tolerate ambiguity. But I have merely

[8] Other interpretations are not only possible, but typical of metaphoric knowledge. This does *not* mean that anything goes, that any one interpretation is as good as another. A given interpretation is constrained by some combination of consistency on the one hand (i.e., external, internal, temporal, theoretical, as amplified for example in Royce, 1965a, p. 19), and the extent to which there is universal meaning as opposed to idiosyncrasy on the other hand (at this juncture the reader is reminded of our previous explication of this point, as exemplified particularly in Table 2-1, Fig. 2-1, and Fig. 2-3, and the appropriate portions of the text). Furthermore, additional valid interpretations reflect the one-to-many meanings which are characteristic of the symbol and the metaphor (see p. 16 and, for a more complete exposition, Royce, 1965a).

[9] A brief answer to the possible objection that such behavior does not have to be explained because the characters are fictional is as follows: If the literary product, such as a play or a novel, is valid (i.e., if it reaches for the universal rather than the idiosyncratic), it carries metaphoric reality or truth as a totality. That is, the play or novel says something (metaphorically or symbolically, rather than in scientific prose) "real" or "true" about the nature of man. Hence, the behavior exhibited in the literary product should (in principle) also carry metaphoric reality. The extent to which such analyses will converge with scientific analyses can be determined in individual cases.

pointed to the notion that the psychology of fear and cognition are involved. I have not offered a thorough analysis. Some of Maslow's recent work is directly relevant here, particularly his thinking on what he calls "being cognition." In an entirely different context, he says, for example:

Sometimes the safety needs can almost entirely bend the cognitive needs to their own anxiety-allaying purposes. The anxiety-free person [e.g., Simon in Lord of the Flies] *can be more bold and more courageous . . . anxiety kills curiosity and exploration . . . . It seems quite clear that the need to know, if we are to understand it well, must be integrated with fear of knowing, with needs for safety and security.* (1962, pp. 62–64)

I see the possibility for a long range dialogue between the literary picture of man presented by Golding in his provocative novel and the picture of man painted by a traditional scientific psychology. It seems to me that complete psychological analyses of literary products such as *Lord of the Flies*, analyzed and empirically investigated à la Maslow and others, could not help but provide valid insights about man and his behavior patterns, and that the ensuing dialogue between the scientific and humanistic approaches would further provoke an eventual synthesis, thereby leading to greater understanding.

Mythic patterns such as those cited above have recurred throughout recorded history and have transcended geographical and cultural boundaries as well. Continuing failure in the name of scientific purism on the part of psychologists to study such a rich storehouse of psychologically laden material borders on the foolhardy. Furthermore, the typical sexual reductionism of Freudian psychoanalysis is simply not up to the requirements of the task, and while Jungian analysis may be more promising, contemporary psychologists have not yet given serious thought and effort to the possibilites at hand. For example, of the 4,500 items listed in Kiell's (1963) recent bibliography on psychology and literature, practically all of them involve some kind of psychoanalytic interpretation, and further, possibly as many as one third of the drama listings deal with Hamlet. The majority of the references to psychology per se are in terms of a very prosaic analysis of audience response to some dramatic productions, such as radio, T.V., or films—i.e., a problem in the measurement of public opinion and/or attitude change. There is very little indication that standard approaches, such as content analysis or projective testing, have been adapted for study in this domain, or that new techniques of analysis, appropriate to the available material, have been developed. There is, in short, a sad lack of imaginative inquiry in what we might refer to as literary psychology.

A similar concern for the symbolic is required for investigation in the psychology of religion, for here we are focusing on the ultimate commitments of man, those commitments around which the meaning of one's existence is built. Penetrating analyses of value, myth, and that which is existentially "real" are all necessary for vital investigation in this area. The typical psychological studies in this area are concerned with such matters as how many people attend church on Sunday and the number of conversions recorded for various denominations as a function of age. Such studies seem to bypass religion almost completely. A humanistic psychology of religion would not lose Tillich's depth dimension; it would not lose the heart of that which is religious in the name of ease of observation and meas-

urement. In short, contrary to the present dominant positivistic Zeitgeist, the humanistic-psychological study of religion would deal in whatever way it can with the subjective meaning of life—with that which is existentially valid. Such an approach would begin with ontological anxiety, for example, rather than focusing on the easier neurotic anxiety. It takes more courage "to be" (Tillich, 1952) in the face of ontological as opposed to neurotic anxiety for the simple reason that there is no illusion of "cure" in the case of the former variety. The traditional scientific approach to the psychological study of religion, one of the most important and ubiquitous characteristics of mankind, has not yet penetrated very deeply—it seems to me that the humanistic approach is more likely to probe the "inner man"[10] because of its greater willingness to deal with the fullness of subjective experience via an all-encompassing phenomenology as opposed to a narrow, albeit more rigorous, empiricism.

If we assume, as it seems reasonable to do, that the events of human history are a result of the interdependence between the individual and the culture of his time, then it follows that a more explicit psychological analysis of history is required than has been manifested to date. Due to the overwhelming complexities of life scholars in all fields oversimplify their domains of study in order to get launched. This approach, however, eventually reveals its simplistic inadequacies. Thus, the study of history has not been of a psycho-cultural order, but rather, it has been dominated by a kind of abstract analysis of political, economic, and military events—"as if" there were no human organisms generating these changes. There are indications that a psycho-historical alliance would lead to a more complete understanding of the evolution of the human psyche on the one hand, and a better understanding of man through time on the other hand. Toynbee, for example, brings psychology to bear in his analyses of the rise and fall of civilizations. A central plank in his approach is the importance of the symbol and the myth as unconscious manifestations of the human spirit. At this juncture his thinking merges with Jung's in their claim that "progress" is crucially dependent upon the validity of symbolic commitments—especially those carrying religious implications. For example, in his concept of "challenge and response" Toynbee indicates that the response to a challenge must eventually become a religious one if the civilization is to survive. Further, Toynbee takes this analysis to the level of the individual personality, particularly the "creative minority" (i.e., the leading artists, scientists, and thinkers of a given epoch), as the source of new values for meeting the challenge of continued existence.

A psychological history is potentially the most empirical of the several humanistic alliances briefly described above, for it can be studied more easily than any of the others within the context of social psychology. However, it does suffer from the fact that behavior as such cannot be observed directly, only reconstructed from the records and artifacts of the past. Nevertheless, the recent book by Zevedei Barbu (1960) speaks well for the mutual enrichment which should follow the union of the two disciplines.

[10]For a provocative entree to the implied possibilities see the interdisciplinary roundtable discussion edited by Havens (1968).

Summary and Conclusions

Briefly recapitulating, what I have tried to do is assess the present situation in contemporary theoretical psychology in terms of underlying epistemologies (i.e., empiricism, rationalism, and metaphorism). Because of twentieth century encapsulation within the epistemology of empiricism, contemporary man finds it difficult to be open to symbolic and intuitive cognition. Psychology, as part of the contemporary sensate culture, and psychologists, as part of the contemporary cultural Zeitgeist, can also be characterized as super-empirical, somewhat at the expense of the rational, and almost completely at the expense of the metaphoric, approach to reality.

An analysis of contemporary scientific theories was made in terms of the degree of epistemic correlation between empiricism and rationalism. This analysis revealed that the most adequate theoretical efforts have been made in the domains of sensation, perception, learning, individual differences, and neuropsychology. While the most successful theories are experimental-explanatory in nature, descriptive and correlational approaches have also led to convincing theory. The phenomenological-speculative approach provides provocative leads, but does not eventuate in convincing theory in that form. Overall, optimal results occur when there is high empiricism, high relevant formalism, or both, *and* when the theorist confines himself to a relatively limited domain.

Prescriptions for action include: (*1*) That we inductively generate, from within the storehouse of existing psychological data, an inventory of basic concepts, functional relationships, and principles of varying degrees of generality. (*2*) That we make greater use of multivariate methods of problem solving in psychology on the grounds that these are, in general, more appropriate than the more traditional bivariate analysis. (*3*) That we continue to try out a variety of conceptual schemes, both home-grown and foreign, but that we screen these more critically than we have in the past in terms of their relevance to the particular area of psychological study (e.g., appropriateness of certain physical and mathematical models). (*4*) That we focus more on area rather than general theories of behavior, with subsequent extensions of well established theorettes and linkages between areas as a basis for moving toward the eventual unification of psychology.

While intuition is involved at all phases of the scientific enterprise it is minimized as final judge in science. However, metaphoric knowledge is crucial in the humanistic disciplines and it would assume a dominant position in a humanistic psychology. The possibilities for the evolution of such a development within an expanded definition of psychology were pointed to but not elaborated in detail. Priority was given to alliances with the humanistic disciplines of philosophy, drama, religion, literature, and history.

Acknowledgements. This paper was presented as a Distinguished Visiting Lecturer Address, Educational Testing Service in September 1965. The last section appeared under the title "Metaphoric Knowledge and Humanistic Psychology" in J. F. T. Bugental (ed.), *Challenges of Humanistic Psychology* (New York: McGraw-Hill, 1967); and the entire chapter prereleased in J. R. Royce (ed.), *Toward Unification in Psychology* (University of Toronto Press, 1970); reprinted by permission of the publisher.

References

ATTNEAVE, F. *Applications of information theory to psychology.* New York: Holt-Dryden, 1959.

BARBU, Z. *Problems of historical psychology.* New York: Grove Press, 1960.

BERELSON, B., and G. A. STEINER. *Human behavior: An inventory of scientific findings.* New York: Harcourt Brace Jovanovich, 1964.

BERLYNE, D. E. *Conflict, arousal, and curiosity.* New York: McGraw-Hill, 1960.

VON BERTALANFFY, L. On the definition of the symbol. *In* J. R. Royce (ed.), *Psychology and the symbol: An interdisciplinary symposium.* New York: Random House, 1965, pp. 26–72.

BOULDING, K. E. *The image.* Ann Arbor: University of Michigan Press, 1956.

BRUNSWIK, E. Historical and thematic relations of psychology to other sciences. *Scientific Monthly,* 1956, *83,* 151–161.

BUSH, R. R., R. P. ABELSON, and R. HYMAN. *Mathematics for psychologists: Examples and problems.* New York: Social Science Research Council, 1956.

BUSH, R. R., and W. K. ESTES (eds.). *Studies in mathematical learning theory.* Stanford, Calif.: Stanford University Press, 1959.

BUSH, R. R., and F. MOSTELLER. *Stochastic models for learning.* New York: Wiley, 1955.

BUTLER, L. E. *Basic matrix theory.* Englewood Cliffs, N.J.: Prentice-Hall, 1962.

CAMPBELL, D. T. Blind variation and selective retention in creative thought as in other knowledge processes. *Psychological Review,* 1960, *67,* 380–400.

CARROLL, J. B. *The study of language.* Cambridge, Mass.: Harvard University Press, 1953.

CASSIRER, E. *The philosophy of symbolic forms* (3 vols.). New Haven, Conn.: Yale University Press, 1953–1957.

CATTELL, R. B. (ed.) *Handbook of multivariate experimental psychology.* New York: Rand-McNally, 1966.

COWARD, H. A conceptual survey of symbolizing and intuiting as the psychological processes of metaphorism. (Unpublished Master's Thesis, University of Alberta, 1969.)

ESTES, W. K. The statistical approach to learning theory. *In* S. Koch (ed.), *Psychology: A study of a science,* Vol. 2. New York: McGraw-Hill, 1959, pp. 380–491.

—— Component and pattern models with Markovian interpretations. *In* R. R. Bush and W. K. Estes (eds.), *Studies in mathematical learning theory.* Stanford, Calif.: Stanford University Press, 1959, pp. 9–52.

FESTINGER, L. *A theory of cognitive dissonance.* Evanston, Ill.: Row, Peterson, 1957.

FLAVELL, J. H. *The developmental psychology of Jean Piaget.* Princeton, N.J.: Van Nostrand, 1963.

FOSS, M. *Symbol and metaphor.* Lincoln: University of Nebraska Press, 1949.

GIBSON, J. J. *The perception of the visual world.* Boston, Mass.: Houghton Mifflin, 1950.

GOLDING, W. *Lord of the flies.* London: Faber & Faber, 1954.

GRAHAM, C. H. Color theory. *In* S. Koch (ed.), *Psychology: A study of a science,* Vol. 1. New York: McGraw-Hill, 1959, pp. 145–287.

GULLIKSEN, H. *Theory of mental tests.* New York: Wiley, 1950.

HARARY, F. and R. Z. NORMAN *Graph theory as a mathematical model in social science.* Ann Arbor, Mich.: Institute for Social Research, 1953.

HARMAN, H. H. *Modern factor analysis.* Chicago: University of Chicago Press, Revised edition, 1967.

HAVENS, J. (ed.) *Psychology and religion: A contemporary dialogue.* Princeton: van Nostrand, 1968.

HEBB, D. O. *The organization of behavior.* New York: Wiley, 1949.

HELSON, H. *Adaptation-level theory.* New York: Harper & Row, 1964.

HORST, P. *Matrix algebra for social scientists.* New York: Holt, Rinehart & Winston, 1963.

HULL, C. L. *The principles of behavior.* New York: Appleton-Century, 1943.

JONES, B. The psycho-epistemological profile: Its scoring, validity and reliability. (Unpublished Master's thesis, University of Alberta, 1963.)

History, Theory, and Methodology

JUNG, C. G. *Psychological types* (trans. by H. G. Baynes). London: Routledge & Kegan Paul, 1923.

KEMENY, J. G., and J. L. SNELL. *Mathematical models in the social sciences.* Boston, Mass.: Ginn, 1962.

—— and G. L. THOMPSON. *Introduction to finite mathematics.* Englewood Cliffs, N.J.: Prentice-Hall, 1957.

KIELL, N. *Psychoanalysis, psychology, and literature: A bibliography.* Madison: University of Wisconsin Press, 1963.

KOCH, S. (ed.) Epilogue. In *Psychology: A study of a science,* vol. III. New York: McGraw-Hill, 1959, pp. 729–88.

KOHLER, W., and H. WALLACH, Figural after-effects. *Proceedings of the American Philosophical Society,* 1944, *88,* 269–357.

LANGER, S. K. On a new definition of "symbol." In *Philosophical Sketches.* Toronto: New American Library of Canada, 1964, pp. 53–61.

LEVY, L. H. *Psychological interpretation.* New York: Holt, Rinehart & Winston, 1963.

LUCE, R. D. *Individual choice behavior.* New York: Wiley, 1959.

—— R. R. BUSH, and E. GALANTER (eds.) *Handbook of mathematical psychology,* vols. 1 and 2. New York: John Wiley & Sons, 1963*a.*

—— *Readings in mathematical psychology,* vols. 1 and 2. New York: John Wiley & Sons, 1963*b.*

LUCE, R. D. and H. RAIFFA, *Games and decisions.* New York: John Wiley, 1957.

MASLOW, A. H. *Toward a psychology of being.* Princeton: Van Nostrand, 1962.

MAY, R. (ed.) *Existential psychology.* New York: Random House, 1961.

MEEHL, P. *Clinical versus statistical prediction.* Minneapolis: University of Minnesota Press, 1954.

MILLER, G. A. *Language and communication.* New York: McGraw-Hill, 1951.

—— E. GALANTER, and K. H. PRIBRAM. *Plans and the structure of behavior.* New York: Holt, 1960.

MONTAGUE, W. P. *The ways of knowing.* London: Allen & Unwin, 1928.

MOWRER, O. H. *Learning theory and behavior.* New York: John Wiley 1960*a.*

—— *Learning theory and the symbolic processes.* New York: John Wiley, 1960*b.*

—— *The new group therapy.* Princeton: Van Nostrand, 1964.

VON NEUMANN, J. *The computer and the brain.* New Haven, Conn.: Yale University Press, 1958.

NORTHROP, F. S. C. *The logic of the sciences and the humanities.* New York: Macmillan, 1947.

—— and H. H. LIVINGSTON (eds.) *Cross-cultural understanding: Epistemology in anthropology.* New York: Harper & Row, 1964.

OSGOOD, C. E., G. J. SUCI, and P. H. TANNENBAUM. *The measurement of meaning.* Urbana: University of Illinois Press, 1957.

QUASTLER, H. (ed.) *Information theory in psychology.* Glencoe, Ill.: Free Press, 1955.

RASHEVSKY, N. *Mathematical biophysics.* Chicago: University of Chicago Press, 1938.

ROSENZWEIG, S. Schools of psychology: A complementary pattern. *Philosophy of Science,* 1937, *4,* 96–106.

ROYCE, J. R. Toward the advancement of theoretical psychology. *Psychological Reports,* 1957, *3,* 401–10.

—— The search for meaning. *American Scientist,* 1959, *47,* 515–35.

—— Heretical thoughts on the definition of psychology. *Psychological Reports,* 1960, *8,* 11–14.

—— Studies of value and psycho-epistemological hierarchies. *In* S. Cook (ed.), *Research plans in religion, values, and morality.* New York: Religious Education Association, 1962*a,* pp. 85–88.

—— Psychology, existentialism, and religion. *Journal of General Psychology,* 1962*b, 66,* 3–16.

—— *The encapsulated man: An interdisciplinary essay on the search for meaning.* Princeton, N.J.: Van Nostrand, 1964.

—— (ed.) *Psychology and the symbol: An interdisciplinary symposium.* New York: Random House, 1965*a.*

—— A bibliography of factor analytic studies in the fields other than psychology. (Unpublished manuscript, University of Alberta, 1965*b.*)

—— Pebble picking versus boulder building. *Psychological Reports,* 1965*c, 16,* 447–50.

—— (ed.) *Toward unification in psychology.* Toronto: University of Toronto Press, 1970.

—— and W. A. S. SMITH. A note on the development of the psycho-epistemological profile (P.E.P.). *Psychological Reports,* 1964, *14,* 297–98.

ROZEBOOM, W. W. Mediation variables in scientific theory. *Psychological Review,* 1956, *63,* 249–64.

SARBIN, T. R., R. TAFT, and D. E. BAILEY. *Clinical inference and cognitive theory.* New York: Holt, Rinehart & Winston, 1960.

SCHMIDT, P. F. Models of scientific thought. *American Scientist,* 1957, *45,* 137–49.

SHUBIK, M. (ed.) *Game theory and related approaches to social behavior.* New York: John Wiley, 1964.

SKINNER, B. F. *The behavior of organisms.* New York: Appleton-Century, 1938.

SMITH, W. A. S., J. R. ROYCE, D. AYERS, and B. JONES. The development of an inventory to measure ways of knowing. *Psychological Reports,* 1967, *21,* 529–35.

SOROKIN, P. A. *The crisis of our age.* New York: Dutton, 1941.

SPENCE, K. W. *Behavior theory and conditioning.* New Haven, Conn.: Yale University Press, 1956.

SPENGLER, O. *The decline of the west.* London: Allen & Unwin, 1932.

TAYLOR, C. W. *Creativity: Progress and potential.* New York: McGraw-Hill, 1964.

THRALL, R. M., C. H. COOMBS, and R. L. DAVIS. *Decision processes.* New York: Wiley, 1954.

THURSTONE, L. L. *Multiple factor analysis.* Chicago: University of Chicago Press, 1947.

TILLICH, P. W. *The courage to be.* New Haven, Conn.: Yale University Press, 1952.

TOYNBEE, A. J. *A study of history* (2-vol. abridgement). Cambridge: Oxford University Press, 1946 & 1947.

WALLRAFF, C. F. *Philosophical theory and psychological fact.* Tucson, Ariz.: University of Arizona Press, 1961.

WERNER, H., and B. KAPLAN. *Symbol formation.* New York: Wiley, 1963.

WESTCOTT, M. R. On the measurement of intuitive leaps. *Psychological Reports,* 1961, *9,* 267–74.

—— and J. H. RANZONI. Correlates of intuitive thinking. *Psychological Reports,* 1963, *12,* 595–613.

WIENER, N. *Cybernetics.* New York: Wiley, 1948.

1. Philosophy of Science

The term "science" has two connotations: the search for knowledge and the results of the search. Traditionally, all knowledge was called "philosophia" or the love of wisdom. Wisdom meant knowledge in contradistinction to stupidity which meant ignorance. Wise man have always had an edge, for the more one knows the better his chances in the struggle for survival and in competition with other men.

In the *Republic* Plato suggested the rule of wise men called "philosophers." This suggestion conveyed what has been common practice: the proverbial wise men have always walked in light, while the ignorant have groped in darkness. In Ancient Egypt the knowing priests ruled the entire society, and in Karl Marx's theory those who know should rule the masses.

THE DECLINE OF PHILOSOPHY

Philosophy was the queen of knowledge in Ancient Greece, and in the Middle Ages it continued its role of alleged omniscience for centuries to come, prescribing rules for human knowledge. However, scientific progress in Modern Times bypassed both philosophy and theology. Technicians, engineers, physicians, sailors, explorers, and adventurers produce more knowledge than learned monks and armchair philosophers. Science was created by men who *needed it* for their trade, craft, and pleasure, and mostly by those who actively sought to find the facts. Laboratories and scientific expeditions have discovered more factual knowledge in the last three centuries than ever was invented by meditation and speculation.

Only one branch of knowledge remained for a long period of time under the tutelage of the old queen of knowledge. "Know thyself" remained the pastime of armchair philosophers, and Kant's speculation on the nature of the *absoluter Geist* came one hundred years after Galileo, Harvey and Newton.

Psychology could have remained the asylum for meditating

Benjamin B. Wolman

Concerning Psychology and the Philosophy of Science

3

philosophers forever if not for the revolutionary ideas of evolution and the great discoveries in neurophysiology which broke the artificial barriers between man and the rest of nature. Philosophers and theologians have taken humanity out of the context of nature but biology, physiology, neurology, and modern psychology view men as part and parcel of the organic world. Meditations on the nature of the soul, the psyche, the mind and so on, have been replaced by observations and experiments concerning the behavior of living organisms, including human behavior.

The breaking away of psychology from speculative philosophy was spectacular and complete.

Philosophy of Science

With the breaking away of psychology, philosophy lost its last subject matter and its membership card to the family of sciences. Today, anyone seeking knowledge must turn to a particular branch of science. The great philosophical theories of the past are no longer judged on a true-false scale because they are considered irrelevant meditations concerning a variety of real and imaginary problems.

Modern philosophy seems to have accepted the inevitable verdict and abdicated its prerogatives to the expanding sciences. Instead of serving the past queen of science, many contemporary philosophers have eagerly accepted the role of useful servicemen of science who analyze the procedures of scientific research.

An analysis of scientific behavior can go in many directions. It can be a study of the development of scientific concepts (Piaget 1949, 1950, 1960, 1965); it can be a study of the scientists' behavior (Naess 1936, 1965); it can be a history of science; it can also be a *philosophy of science*.

Philosophers of science are not philosophers in the traditional sense and have little to do with world-embracing metaphysical systems. Modern philosophers of science such as Reichenbach, Schlick, Kotarbinski, Carnap, Nagel, Hempel, Bergmann, Maxwell, Feigl, Scriven, Sellars and others do not pretend to know more than the scientists whose work they study. Philosophers of science do not discover or communicate any knowledge concerning astronomy, physics, biology, and psychology, but rather analyze the works and words of astronomers, physicists, biologists, and psychologists. Their particular job is the study of sciences. In this study the philosophers have become exceedingly useful by developing methods of a formal analysis of scientific work.

Formal Science

These modern "scientists of science" are engaged in critical analysis of the work of the respective scientists. Scientists produce knowledge in more than one way; some of them proceed cautiously, some daringly formulate far-fetched theories. They use a variety of research tools and apply highly diversified systems of symbols, but as a rule, the empirical scientists *do not study symbols and signs*. Symbols and signs are *used* in scientific research in an intuitive manner, e.g., French-born scientists analyze their data and report their findings in the same words and phrases as the French butcher, baker and candlestick maker. Scientists as scientists strive for objectivity and precision, but as members of a particular culture they use the traditional forms of expression that have developed in the nurseries, marketplaces, and political meetings of France, Italy, the U.S.A., and any other country.

Small wonder that the analysis of signs and symbols became one of the main issues in the philosophy of science, for the studies of mathematical models, semantics, semiotics and other symbols and signs are of utmost importance for scientific inquiry.

Every science, such as physics, astronomy, zoology or psychology, can be viewed as a system of statements or propositions, that is a system of signs that communicate knowledge. Obviously there are other systems of communication, such as musical tones and melodies. All systems of signs, however, must be constructed in a manner that facilitates precise communication.

Thus scientists need an auxiliary science that scrutinizes their procedures and communications. This is hardly a science in the traditional sense, for it does not discover or communicate any information concerning objects or facts. This auxiliary science is called the science of science or the philosophy of science. The philosophy of science is a *formal science* for it sets the rules for the formal aspects of empirical sciences. Moreover, while all other sciences seek knowledge and are, therefore, empirical, the philosophy of science studies the conditions that facilitate such a search and permit a proper communication of the findings. Some philosophers of science, such as Bertrand Russell (1948) and Rudolf Carnap (1931, 1937), have stressed the importance of analysis of the propositions whether they are coated in linguistic or mathematical symbols.

Ultimately, *every scientific system is a system of propositions that convey knowledge*. When the philosophy of science studies these propositions irrespective of their content, such as $p \supset q$ (whenever p, then q) or $p = q$ (p equals q) it is called formal logic. Where modern logic uses mathematics it is called mathematical logic and logistics. When the philosophy of science studies the connection between the scientific propositions and the empirical data they report, it is called epistemology. When the philosophy of science analyzes the correspondence between the propositions and their meaning and contrast, it is called logical syntax, semantics, and semiotics. Philosophy of science that analyzes research procedures and theory foundation is called methodology of science.

Synthetic and Analytic Propositions

The difference between formal and factual sciences can be easily ascertained by comparison of what they say. One may distinguish two types of propositions or statements.

Synthetic propositions are descriptive, empirical statements that report facts such as, "My office is on the seventeenth floor," or "George Washington was the first president of the U.S.A.," or "All birds have wings." These propositions describe objects (the term objects includes bodies, animals, people, and facts)—that is, what is going on with the objects. Synthetic propositions are either true or false, that is either they do or do not agree with what they intend to describe. For instance, such propositions as "Cows have wings," or "My office is in Tokyo," or "Kennedy was the first president of the U.S.A.," are not true.

It is a matter of scientific inquiry to find out whether a synthetic proposition is true or false. Scientists go about finding the truth in more than one way, but the common denominator of all scientific inquiry is *observation*. There are several types of observation, ranging from the naturalistic to highly sophisticated methods using powerful microscopes, telescopes and other precision instruments.

The following chapters of this Handbook describe in detail the highly sophisticated research methods called experimentation. When research workers set the conditions of observation, isolate the facts to be observed, manipulate the observational variables, and check and control the relevant factors, in short, when they observe facts under conditions set and controlled by themselves, they are performing experiments. The findings of empirical sciences are usually reported in synthetic propositions.

Analytic propositions (also called definitions) are not related to facts. They are true or false irrespective of any factual information they may convey. Take, for instance, such a statement: "If my office is on the seventeenth floor and there is a desk in that office, this desk is on the seventeenth floor." The following sentences are also analytic: "If all birds have wings and canaries are birds, canaries have wings" and "Today is Tuesday or it is another day."

Analytic propositions can be either true or false. The above propositions are true; they report the obvious, thus they are called *tautologies*. The following analytic propositions are not true and are called *contradictions*: "When it rains, it does not rain," or "If all birds have wings and canaries are birds, then canaries do not have wings."

The empirical or factual sciences can operate with both synthetic and analytic propositions (Carnap 1953). Formal sciences use analytic propositions only. Synthetic or descriptive propositions are true when what they say agrees with the facts; for instance, the statements, "My office is on the seventeenth floor," or "Bodies enlarge when exposed to heat" are true if what they say corresponds to what is. Thus, a synthetic statement such as "The earth is flat" is untrue. The agreement between statement and fact is called *transcendent truth* and the task of all empirical sciences is to discover such a truth and make truthful statements. Formal sciences make statements that are free from inner contradiction. The freedom from inner contradiction is called the *immanent truth* (Bergmann 1958, p. 26; Wolman 1960, chap. 14).

SCIENTIFIC DISCOVERY

Not all scientific discoveries have been a product of carefully elaborated research methods derived from the works of logicians and philosophers of science. History of science is full of anecdotic stories, such as Archimedes' discovery that his body weighed less in a bathtub than on the surface of the earth, and the apple that inspired Newton's discovery of gravity. Even contemporary research does not necessarily follow the rules of logic and methodology. E.g., Pavlov's and Thorndike's systematic studies eschewed experimental controls; Freud made his most significant discoveries by listening to an accidental but non-randomized sample of mental patients and by analyzing his own dreams; Piaget's observations and investigations did not follow rigorous experimental procedures. Several highly important scientific discoveries such as Darwin's theory of evolution and Galileo's and Copernicus' discoveries did not start as a result

of careful, systematic and precise observation or experimentation, but rather as an "unsupported speculation" (Feyerabend 1963, p. 5). The history of psychology is not just a history of a particular science, and the history of science is a history of how certain human beings observed, reasoned, abstracted, tried, and erred. Obviously, all of these actions belong to psychology and all of them are part of cognitive behavior; and logic and scientific methods are intertwined with the psychology and cognitive processes of certain human beings.

There is no reason to ascribe superhuman intellectual powers to a Plato, Spinoza, Newton, Darwin, Lavoisier, or Einstein; all were members of the human race driven by curiosity and ambition, vanity and altruism, and other human motives. All scientists were brought up in a certain cultural tradition and were faced with problems presented by their ancestors and contemporaries.

Philosophy of science was never a midwife of scientific discoveries nor did it inspire scientists in their creative work. Kessel's statement that "the intuitive apprehension of a reality as yet undiscovered, the altering of fundamental presuppositions by the creative act—these are all crucial elements in the progress of science . . ." (Kessel 1969, p. 1004), is correct within the framework of history of science, but it has nothing to do with the tasks of the philosophy of science. Philosophy of science was not supposed to stimulate, encourage, or otherwise guide the works and lives of scientists any more than the theory of music inspired great composers. The philosopher of science like the philosopher in Molière's "Bourgeois Gentilhomme" reminds scientists that they speak prose and makes them aware of what they are trying to do and say.

DISCOVERY AND EVIDENCE

Reichenbach (1938) suggested the distinction between scientific discovery, which is a psychological act, and the adduction of evidence, which belongs to the formal philosophy of science. This distinction is, however, rather tenuous. Both discovery and proof can be viewed from either point of view for they are parts of behavior as well as systems of procedures and signs. A comparison with language might shed light on this issue, for language can be studied as a behavioral pattern and as a system of signs, according to one's perspective.

The distinction between psychology and the philosophy of science is therefore not a matter of the area under scrutiny but the approach. Both discovery and justification are acts of human beings, thus both of them belong to psychology (Naess 1965; Polanyi 1964) and to some extent also to the history and sociology of scientific behavior (Merton 1969). Archimedes' and Newton's discoveries are as legitimate topics for psychological, historical, and sociological inquiry as Clark Hull's and Niels Bohr's detailed and elaborate experimental procedures aimed at adducing evidence of their theorems, as long as one views the discoveries and the evidence as actions of certain human beings. However, the statements related to discovery and evidence can be analyzed as statements, and such analysis belongs to the philosophy of science.

Philosophers of science neither observe nor experiment; neither can they make the observation and experimentation of others more precise or more reliable. It is the business of the scientists and the technicians to improve their tools and techniques. Scientists and technicians have developed precision instruments in laboratories and factories with little if any assistance from philosophical lecture halls and libraries. Newton, Lavoisier, Darwin, Pasteur, Einstein, Palov and others developed their research techniques irrespective of the ideas expressed by Spinoza, Schopenhauer, and Bergson.

Philosophy of science has not broken any new paths in scientific inquiry, but it has followed the inquiry and helped the scientist in a critical evaluation of his work. The famous dictum of Hegel's *Minerva's Eule kommt an Dämmerung* (Minerva's owl comes at sunset) applies to the philosophy of science. Philosophers of science are not pioneers or path-breakers of science; they come after the work has been done, analyze it and examine it critically. Thus the philosophy of science is as useful as experts who check old houses, condemn those that are uninhabitable, and recommend rehabilitation whenever it is possible. They also may guide in the repair work and supply logical tools to make the houses of science habitable.

2. Between Science and the Philosophy of Science

SPECULATIVE PHILOSOPHY

Speculative philosophy reached its peak with Kant's distinction between *noumena*, nature-as-it-is (*Ding an sich*, usually translated as "thing-in-itself"), and *phenomena*, nature as perceived. In a truly anti-Copernican revolution Kant set the perceiving mind above nature as if human beings existed outside the scope of living matter. According to Kant, laws of nature were not a part of nature but abstract terms of time, space, quantity, causation, etc., allegedly embedded in the *absoluter Geist* and prescribed to the universe (Cassirer 1923; Kant 1929; Wolman 1968*b*).

When in the *Prolegomena of Any Future Metaphysics* (1783) Kant outlined the prerequisites for future metaphysicists, he was unaware of the fact that soon physics would make metaphysics superfluous and obsolete. Most of the nineteenth century was dominated by Kantians and neo-Kantians. Hegel (1902) dictated his didactic logic to the universe and ascribed dialectic laws to human history assuming that whatever happens, happens in a trilogy of thesis, antithesis, and synthesis. When Hegel's highly biased and distorted historical presentation was criticized as full of factual errors and his theory blamed for distortion of reality, Hegel's famous reply was *Desto schlimmer für die Wirklichkeit* (It's too bad for reality). Schopenhauer has shown even less respect for reality. In his solipsism he pictured the world as an act of will and representation (*Die Welt als Wille und Vorstellung*), reducing reality to a product of individual wishes and ideas. The universe is a mere representation, an idea created by a perceiving mind; but I am (my will is) a thing-in-itself. "The will is the thing-in-itself, the inner content, the essence of the world," Schopenhauer wrote. "Life, the visible world, the phenomenon, is only the mirror of the will." (Schopenhauer, 1923, Bk. 4, p. 254).

Though several German philosophers modified Kant's ideas and even opposed them, the complete rejection of Kant's epistemology is connected with the names of the French philosopher, Auguste Comte, and the British philosopher, Herbert Spencer. Comte and Spencer initiated the new role of philosophy by demanding that philosophy abdicate its status as the queen of knowledge and accept the role of a serviceman of science. Comte's system of positive philosophy and Spencer's search for a synthesis of science are the two pillars of the new philosophy of *positivism*. Comte's *Cours de philosophie positive* (1833) contains no systematic exposé of epistemology.

EMPIRICISM VS. RATIONALISM

The problem the modern logical positivists tried to solve has historical roots in the old controversy between sensualist empiricism and rationalist speculation. Wrote R. Descartes, "Our inquiries should be directed not to what others have thought, not to what we ourselves conjecture, but to what we can clearly and perspiciously behold and with certainty deduce; for knowledge is not won in any other way..." (1931, vol. I, Rule III). According to Descartes only mathematics succeeds in producing "evident and certain" reasons (1931, vol. I, p. 93). Descartes believed that "the power of forcing a good judgement and of distinguishing the true from the false... is by nature equal in all men" (1931, vol. I, p. 81). Hence Descartes logically deduced his own existence (*Cogito ergo sum*) and the existence of God and universe without referring to empirical evidence.

J. Locke was critical of Descartes and other "scholastic men." He rejected innate ideas and ridiculed "remote speculative principles" that are "like curious imagery men sometimes see in the clouds..." (in Bourne, 1876, vol. L, p. 224). "All ideas come from sensation or reflection," wrote Locke. "Our observation employed either about external sensible objects, or about the internal operations of our minds perceived and reflected on by ourselves, is that which supplies our understanding with all the materials of thinking. These are the two fountains of knowledge..." (Locke 1894, II, 11, p. 1). Our sensory apparatus is the sole source of information: *Nihil est in intellectu quod in sensibus non fuerat* (There is nothing in our intellect that was not in our senses), stressed Locke.

The controversy became more involved with the progress of science and mathematics. Descartes was "revised" by Spinoza; Locke was "reformed" by Hume. Galileo's application of mathematics enchanted Spinoza, who developed a system of definitions, axioms, and propositions deduced therefrom. Spinoza's system was a deductive system of propositions related to empirical data. His philosophy was rationalistic, his evidence speculative, his reasoning mathematico-deductive. Spinoza believed that his first premises were self-evident "adequate ideas" that needed no proof (1919, Pt. II, Prop. vii).

Hume distinguished between impressions and sensations such as hearing, seeing, etc., and ideas. Ideas are derived from impressions. Hume pointed to the fact that since "external objects as they appear to the senses, give us no idea of power or necessary connection, by their operation in particular instances, let us see, whether this idea be derived from reflection on the operations of our own minds and be copied from any internal impressions" (1894, III, ii, 1).

One may see in Spinoza a radical version of Descartes', and in Hume a radical version of Locke's philosophy; certainly empiricism and rationalism do not blend easily. The rationalists believed that knowledge is a system of a priori propositions; the empiricists sought a posteriori observations. Kant's *Critique of the Pure Reason* rejected both points of view and offered a solution that weighed heavily upon any later analysis of the problem.

Kant wrote:

Though all our knowledge begins with experience, it does not follow that it all arises out of experience. For it may be that even our empirical knowledge is made up of what we receive through impressions and of what our own faculty of knowledge (sensible impressions serving merely as the occasion) supplies from itself. If our faculty of knowledge makes any such addition, it may be that we are not in position to distinguish it from the raw material. . . . This, then, is a question which at best calls for closer examination, and does not allow of any offhand answer: whether there is any knowledge that is thus independent of experience and even of all impressions of the senses. Such knowledge is entitled a priori, *and is distinguished from the empirical, which has its sources* a posteriori, *that is, in experience."* (1929, p. 1)

Thus Kant agreed with the empiricists that sensations are the source of knowledge. But, Kant stated, this sensory knowledge is a knowledge of mere phenomena perceived in a manner determined by the nature of the human mind. The mind perceives things in terms of time and space and the categories of relation, quantity, quality and modality.

These terms of knowledge are a priori and independent of any experience. The only true science is, therefore, mathematics, for its propositions are non-empirical, synthetic, and a priori. The world of objects-in-themselves is inaccessible to empirical sciences; what the empiricists grasp are not the things as they are, but appearances, phenomena perceived in terms of the transcendental mind.

PHENOMENOLOGY

As mentioned before, Kant's *Prolegomena* put the perceiving transcendental mind in the center of the universe. In this truly anti-Copernican revolution the world began to revolve around the cognizant mind that prescribed to nature time and space, causality and quality. Empirical sciences were reduced to a study of mere appearances and mathematics was the only true science (Wolman, 1968*b*).

Those philosophers and scientists who preferred to remain empirical but could not break the spell of Kant's heritage sought various ways out. One of the leading currents was *phenomenalism.* Phenomenalists rejected Kant's idea that phenomena are mere appearances of real objects. To the contrary, one may doubt the existence of things-in-themselves, but human perceptions of objects cannot be doubted. Subjective processes of perception became the only true foundation of knowledge. As Husserl (1931) put it, everything else can be doubted except the fact that humans have *experiences.* Phenomenology, despite its opposition to Kant, preserved the Kantian notion that the perceiving or experiencing subject was the center of the universe.

A most influential brand of phenomenalism was developed by Ernst Mach. Mach (1920) rejected Kant's idea of the thing-in-itself, and refuted the mind–matter dualism. The only thing we know, he wrote, is our sensory perception of the world. The so-called physical and mental phenomena presumably outside our experience are sheer metaphysical concepts. Science deals with observables, but the only observables are our own sensations. "Pure experience" is the sole foundation of science.

Mach opposed Kant and leaned toward Hume; he is often believed to be a logical successor of Auguste Comte. However, I believe his system is a direct continuation of the radical idealistic metaphysics of George Berkeley. Wrote Berkeley in 1710:

As several of these (ideas) are observed to accompany each other, they come to be marked by one name, and so to be reputed as one thing. Thus, for example, a certain color, taste, smell, figure and consistence having been observed to go together, are accounted one distinct thing, signified by the name apple. Other collections of ideas constitute a stone, a tree, a book, and the like sensible things. (1901, Pt. I, p. 1)

Berkeley influenced Mach, Avenarius, Pearson, and Bridgman by questioning the existense of things that are not perceived:

The table I write on I say exists; that is, I see and feel it; and if I were out of my study I would say it existed, meaning thereby that if I was in my study I might perceive it, or that some other spirit actually does perceive it. . . . For as to what is said of the absolute existence of unthinking things, without any relation to their being perceived, that is to me perfectly unintelligible. Their esse *is* percipi; *nor is it possible they should have any existence out of the minds or thinking things which perceive them.* (1901, Pt. I, p. 3)

To Berkeley, *esse est percipi* (to be is to be perceived); things that are not perceived by the perceiver are outside the scope of human knowledge.

Mach "insisted on the direct discussion of observations and regarded scientific laws as the description of observations in the most economical way. . . . Mach missed the point that to describe an observation that has not been made yet is not the same thing as to describe one that has been made; consequently he missed the whole problem of induction." (Jeffreys 1957, pp. 15–16)

Actually Mach implied that observation of the observer himself (of his own activities, perceptions, etc.) is more valid than the perception of outer phenomena. When a scientist perceives a rock, the existence of the rock can be questioned: but the fact that he perceives cannot be questioned . . .

Mach's philosophy is closely related to Wundt's psychology based on introspection. Sensations, perceptions, etc. are directly, immediately given "inner experience" and cannot be doubted. Psychology, wrote Wundt (1874), has to investigate "internal experience," such as sensations, thoughts, feelings, etc., in contradistinction to objects of "external experience"; that belongs to natural sciences.

Psychology has long abandoned belief in the infallibility of the "inner experience" but, for a while, this phenomenalistic approach dominated European philosophy.

According to Mach:

The world consists of colors, sounds, temperatures, pressures, spaces, times, and so forth, which now we shall not call sensations nor phenomena, because in either term an arbitrary, one sided theory is embodied, but simply elements. *The fixing of the flux of these elements, whether mediately or immediately, is the real object of physical research.* (1960, p. 208 ff.)

Mach continued:

Nature is composed of sensations as its elements. Primitive man, however, first picks out certain compounds of these elements—those namely that are relatively permanent and of greater importance to him. The first and older words are names of "things".... No inalterable thing exists. The thing is an abstraction, the name of a symbol.... Sensations are not signs of things; but, on the contrary, a thing is a thought-symbol for a compound sensation of relative fixation. Properly speaking, the world is not composed of "things" as its elements, but of colors, tones, pressures, spaces, time, in short what we ordinarily call individual sensations. (1960, p. 482 ff.)

Scientific procedure should be limited to three steps. First, the sensory perceptions, for they are the only valid elements of knowledge. Logical operations and connections between the empirical observations are the second step. In the third step the scientist formulates a simple and economical hypothesis that permits precise description and prediction.

Scientific theory should be directly derived from observational data. Wrote Mach in 1872:

In the investigation of nature we have to deal only with the knowledge of the connection of appearances with one another. What we represent to ourselves behind the appearances exists only in our understanding.... (1911, p. 49) *If the hypotheses are so chosen that their subjects never appeal to the senses and therefore also can never be tested ... the investigator has done more than science, whose aim is facts, required of him—and this work of supererogation is evil.... In a complete theory, to all the details of the phenomena details of the hypothesis must correspond, and all rules for these hypothetical things must also be directly transferable to the phenomena.* (1911, p. 57)

Similar ideas to those of Mach have been espoused by R. Avenarius in his *Kritik der reinen Vernunft* (1888–1890) and K. Pearson in his *Grammar of Science* (1911). Pearson was more radical than Mach, and insisted that it is impossible to assume the existence of anything outside our sense impressions. Pearson's version of phenomenology assumed that the only things that exist are our sense-impressions. Thus Pearson (1911), after Mach, rejected the idea of things-in-themselves:

There isn't a necessity, nay, there is want of logic, in the statement that behind sense-impressions there are "things-in-themselves" producing *sense impression.* (p. 62) *There is no better exercise for the mind than the endeavor to reduce the perception of "external things" to the simple sense-impressions by which we know them. ...* (p. 60) [Furthermore] *atom and molecule are intellectual conceptions by aid of which physicists classify phenomena and formulate their relationships between their sequences .... [These conceptions] do not ... represent direct sense-impressions.* (p. 95) [*The laws of motion in the science of mechanics*] *solely attempt to describe as completely and simply as possible the repeated sequences of our sense-impressions.* (p. 115)

In other words, science is a science of sense-impressions and intellectual conceptions that formulate the relationships between these impressions.

THE LOGICAL POSITIVISM

The spectacular development of the physical sciences in our century has forced philosophers to reexamine their conceptual tools. A group of philosophers and scientists including Moritz Schlick, Rudolf Carnap, Otto Neurath, Herbert Feigl, Philipp Frank, and Kurt Goedel was formed in Vienna in the early twenties and called themselves *Der Wiener Kreis* (The Vienna Circle). Their contemporaries in Britain such as Bertrand Russell and Ludwig Wittgenstein and later Susan Stebbing, R.R. Braithwaite, A.J. Ayer; in Poland, Tadeusz Kotarbinski, Kazimierz Ajdukiewicz, J. Lukasiewicz, and later A. Taitelbaum-Tarski; and in Germany, Hans Reichenbach, Richard von Mises, and later Carl Hempel, have formed the movement of logical positivism, joined by several scholars the world over.

The spiritual fathers of logical positivism were Hume and Mach. Wrote Hume:

When we run over to libraries, persuaded of these principles what move must we make? If we take in our hand any volume of divinity or school metaphysics, for instance, let us ask, Does it contain any abstract reasoning concerning quantity and number? No. Does it contain any experimental reasoning concerning matter of fact and existence? No. Commit it then to the flames: for it can contain nothing but sophistry and illusion." (1894).

This was the battle cry of the new philosophical movement. According to the logical positivists all statements were either empirical-synthetical that conveyed information about bodies and facts or formal-analytical definitions. Everything else was sheer nonsense (Kotarbinski 1929; Ayer 1959). Most of the problems of yesterdays' philosophy were declared pseudo-problems. The development of microphysics, the discovery of quanta and relativity made metaphysical theories sound like obsolete ramblings that could no longer be taken seriously. Science was surging ahead notwithstanding old philosophers, and the new positivists have joined arms with the positive sciences. Following in the footsteps of Wittgenstein's *Tractatus Logico-Philosophicus* (1921) they have emphasized the importance of logical analysis of language. In the foreword to his book *Logical Syntax of Language* (1937) Carnap wrote:

Philosophy is to be replaced by the logic of science—that is to say by the logical analysis of the concepts and sentences of the sciences, for the logic of science is nothing other than the logical syntax of the language of science.

Apparently Wittgenstein, Carnap, and their disciples believed that truthful elementary statements are descriptions of observable events as experienced by the perceiving subject. They are his "sense-data." Thus the language of science advocated by the logical positivists is a system of "protocol sentences," a term synonymous with "observation sentences."

In 1932 Carnap wrote:

We may ignore entirely the question concerning the content and form of the primary sentences (protocol sentences) which has not yet been definitely settled. In the theory of knowledge it is customary to say that the primary sentences refer to "the given"; but there is not unanimity on the question what it is that is given. At times the position is taken that sentences about the given speak of the simplest qualities of sense and feelings (e.g. "warm," "blue," "joy" and so forth); others incline to the view that basic sentences refer to total experiences and similarities between them; a still different view has it that even the basic sentences speak of things. Regardless of this diversity of opinion it is certain that a sequence of words has a meaning only if its relations of deducibility to the protocol sentences are fixed, whatever the characteristics of the protocol sentences may be; and similarly, that a word is significant only if the sentences in which it may occur are reducible to protocol sentences.

Since the meaning of a word is determined by its criterion of application (in other words: by the relations of deducibility entered into by its elementary sentence-form, by its truth-condition by the method of verification), the stipulation of the criterion takes away one's freedom to decide what one wishes to "mean" by the word. If the word is to receive an exact meaning, nothing less than the criterion of application must be given; but one cannot, on the other hand, give more than the criterion of application for the letter is sufficient determination of meaning. The meaning is implicitly contained in the criterion; all that remains to be done is to make the meaning explicit. (1959, p. 63)

But such an assumption easily leads to a barren solipsism resembling Schopenhauer's, a view that was summed up in the famous statement that the meaning of a proposition is its method of verification:

The assumption behind this slogan was that everything that could be said at all could be expressed in terms of elementary statements. All statements of higher order, including the most abstract scientific hypotheses, were in the end nothing more than shorthand descriptions of observable events. But this assumption was very difficult to sustain. It was particularly vulnerable when the elementary statements were taken to be records of the subject's immediate experiences: for a while it has sometimes been maintained that for statements about sense-data, no such translation has ever been achieved: there are indeed good grounds for supposing that it is not feasible. Moreover, this choice of a basis raised the question of solipsism: the problem of making the transition from the subject's private experiences to the experiences of others and to the public world. (Ayer 1959, p. 13)

Thus the logical positivists reduced the problem of science to a task of constructing some sort of simplistic language comprised of protocol-sentences. Such a "physicalistic" language represented to them a cure-all for all the past ills of metaphysics and the present-day ills of philosophy of science (Neurath 1931, 1932–1933, 1934).

Obviously the logical positivism of the *Wiener Kreis* was a continuation of Mach's philosophy. Their "physicalism" was a new version of Machism, and their allegedly objective language of "elementary terms" or "observational terms" was an intersubjective language of introspective reports of sensory perceptions (Frank 1949, 1956; Mises 1951). Moreover, according to Nagel,

Such an autonomous language of bare sense contents actually does not exist, nor is the prospect bright for constructing one. As a matter of psychological fact, elementary sense data are not the primitive materials of experience out of which all our ideas are built like houses out of initially isolated bricks. On the contrary, sense experience normally is a response to complex though unanalyzed patterns of qualities and relations; and the response usually involves the exercise of habits of interpretation and recognition based on tacit beliefs, and inferences, which cannot warrant by any single momentary experience. Accordingly, the language we normally use to describe even our immediate experiences is the common language of social communication, embodying distinctions and assumptions grounded in a large and collective experience, and not a language whose meaning is supposedly fixed by reference to conceptually uninterpreted atoms of sensation.

It is indeed sometimes possible under carefully controlled conditions to identify simple qualities that are directly apprehended through the sense organs. But the identification is the terminus of a deliberate and often difficult process of isolation and abstraction, undertaken for analytic purposes; and there is no good evidence to show that sensory qualities are apprehended as atomic simples except as the outcome of such a process. Moreover, though we may baptize these products by calling them sense data and may assign different labels to different classes of them, the use and meanings of those names cannot be established except by the way of directions instituting processes involving overt bodily activities. Accordingly, the meanings of sense-data terms can be understood only if the distinctions and assumptions of our commerce with the gross objects of experience are taken for granted. In effect, therefore, those terms can be used and applied only as part of the vocabulary of the language of common sense. In short, the "language" of sense data is not an autonomous language, and no one has yet succeeded in constructing such a language. However, if there is indeed such a language, the thesis that all theoretical statements are in principle translatable into the language of pure sense contents is questionable from the onset. (1961, pp. 121–22)

OPERATIONISM

Bridgman's operationism represents, in a way, another version of Mach's philosophy. What is an operational definition? "In general, we mean by any concept nothing more than a set of operations; the concept is synonymous with the corresponding set of operations" (Bridgman 1927, p. 5). Thus a concept which cannot be defined by an operation has no place in science. Newton used the concept of absolute time in his physics; since there is no way to perform an operation in physics which will display the meaning of this concept, Newton's concept of absolute time must be banished from physics because it is a meaningless concept. Bridgman was also critical of Einstein's theory for its failure to use operational terms (Bridgman 1936, 1959).

Bridgman's argument started with the following reasoning:

The new attitude toward a concept is entirely different: We may illustrate by considering the concept of length: What do we mean by the length of an object? We evidently know what

we mean by the length if we can tell what the length of any kind of object is, and for the physicist nothing more is required. To find the length of an object, we have to perform certain physical operations. The concept of length is therefore fixed when the operations by which length is measured are fixed; that is, the concept of length involved as much as and nothing more than a set of operations; the concept is synonymous with the corresponding set of operations. (1927, p. 5)

But what are precisely the operations? What is then, an operationally defined measurement? To measure, says *Webster's New Collegiate Dictionary*, is an "act of process of ascertaining the extent, dimensions, quantity, degree, capacity, or the like of a thing." The extent and dimension are ascertained by measurement. What is measurement? Ascertaining of extent, length, etc. Now, how can length be defined by measurement, if the definition of measurement includes extent, length, or the like? Some psychologists did not notice the circularity of operational definitions. What is intelligence? That which is measured by intelligence tests, and the tests are the yardsticks used to measure intelligence.

Consider measuring length. But what does it mean, in operational terms, to measure? To use a yardstick? What is, operationally speaking, a yardstick? The standard yardstick is determined by the Bureau of Weights and Measures in Washington, D.C., which is under the control of the U.S. Congress.

OPERATIONISM AND THE PHILOSOPHY OF SCIENCE

Einstein was undoubtedly indebted to Mach the physicist, but not to Mach the philosopher. Einstein wrote in 1916, "Mach recognized the weak spots of classical mechanics and was not very far from requiring a general theory of relativity half a century ago. . . . Mach's considerations about Newton's bucket experiment show how close his way of thinking was to the search for relativity in a general sense" (p. 103).

However, Einstein rejected Mach's idea

that the fundamental concepts and postulates of physics were not in the logical sense free inventions of the human mind but could be deduced from experience by "abstraction"—that is to say by logical means. . . . The fictitious character of the fundamental principles is perfectly evident from the fact that we can point to two essentially different principles, both of which correspond with experience to a large extent. . . . This proves that every attempt at a logical deduction of the basic concepts and postulates of mechanics from elementary experience is doomed to failure." (1934, p. 35)

Einstein emphatically stated that

In order to be able to consider a logical system as physical theory it is not necessary to demand that all of its assertions can be independently interpreted and tested operationally; de facto this has never yet been achieved by any theory and cannot at all be achieved. (1959, p. 679)

While many psychologists (Skinner 1945; Stevens 1935, 1939; Tolman 1936) enthusiastically accepted operationism,

physicists were rather cautious and critical, for no physical theory could fit into Bridgman's requirements (Hesse 1952). E.g., Bridgman noticed that quantum theory may give the impression of being an operational theory thanks to "labelling some of the mathematical symbols 'operations,' 'observables,' etc. But in spite of the existence of a mathematical symbolism of that sort, the exact physical manipulations are . . . obscure, at least in the sense that it is not obvious how one would construct an idealized laboratory apparatus for making any desired sort of measurement" (1936, p. 189).

Bridgman like Mach believed in the value of familiarity. Uncommon things were "perplexing and astonishing" to Mach. Only "uniform and constantly reappearing" elements can have names that have meanings. When elements constantly reappear, wrote Mach, "we are no longer surprised, there is nothing new or strange to us in the phenomena, we feel at home with them; they no longer perplex us, they are *explained*" (1960, p. 7). Bridgman concurred: "Explanation consists merely in analyzing our complicated systems into simpler systems in such a way that we recognize in the complicated system the interplay of elements already so familiar to us that we accept them as not needing explanation" (1936, p. 63). Yet, as Nagel amply pointed out, explanation often refers the familiar to the unfamiliar (1961, p. 46). E.g., theories of physical and mental disorders usually explain the familiar symptoms by unfamiliar concepts.

Consider operational definitions in geometry. What is a straight line? How can one produce a straight line? By stretching a cord? But can one know that this line is straight? Let us assume one measures it and finds it is shorter than many other lines between two points. If one says it is "the shortest line," what is the operational definition of "shortest line"? Apparently, one cannot form an operational definition of length unless one has already a concept of length before he starts measuring length (see Frank, 1957, p. 313; Plutchik, 1963, p. 236).

For a while operationism was more popular among philosophers of science (especially amongst the logical positivists), but soon its solipsistic nature discouraged even its most ardent followers. Carnap, for instance, favored operationism for a while, but in 1956 he wrote "that the requirement of testability and of operationism exclude some empirically meaningful terms, can be easily seen" (p. 56).

Bridgman's demand that theories be stated in operational terms was reputed by Einstein, rejected by physics, and abandoned by most logicians and philosophers of science. Bridgman's operationism does not clarify epistemology but leads it back into the solipsistic version of Kantianism (Wolman 1960, chap. 14).

Kant put the perceiving, transcendent mind in the center of the universe. Kant's rules of the mind became the laws of nature, leaving no room for empirical science: truth was transcendental, determined a priori. Consider Kant's conception of space: "Space does not represent [things] in their relation to one another. . . . It is, therefore, solely from the human standpoint that we can speak of space, of extended things, etc." (1929, p. 26).

Kant's world was limited to his ideas, Mach's world to parts of his brain, Bridgman's world to his hands (for he told scientists to look at their hands and tools). If you describe a triangle, you are not scientific: Only if you describe how you draw a triangle on a blackboard, you are a genuine, operational scientist. Kant, Mach, and Bridgman seem to believe that observation of the observer is more valid, more scientific, than the observation of the observed object.

ELEMENTARY IDEAS

The logical positivists have been influenced by three principles borrowed from Kant's philosophy. The first was the belief in unusual powers of the observer to observe himself; this belief eventually led to operationism. The second was the belief in the special status of the allegedly self-evident a priori propositions, which led to Wittgenstein's "elementary statements." The third was Kant's adoration of mathematics.

According to Ayer the prevailing view amongst the logical positivists was that these "elementary statements" report the subjects' introspective or sensory experiences. Like Russell and Berkeley, the logical positivists believed that perceiving physical objects should be analyzed in terms of having sensations, or as Russell defined it, of sensing sense-data.

Though physical objects might be publicly accessible, sense-data were taken to be private. There could be no question of our literally sharing one another's sense-data, any more than we can literally share one another's thoughts or images or feelings. The result was that the truth of an elementary statement could be directly checked only by the person to whose experience it referred. And not only was his judgement sovereign; in most favorable cases, it was held to be infallible. One can indeed be mistaken about the experiences that one is going to have in the future, or even about those that one has had in the past; it is not maintained that our memories cannot deceive us: but if one sets out merely to record an experience that one is actually having, then, on this view, there is no possibility of error. Since one can lie, one's statement may be false; but one cannot be in doubt or mistaken about its truth. If it is false one knows it to be so. A way in which this point is sometimes put is by saying that statements of this kind are "incorrigible."

This conception of elements of statements was exposed to attack on various grounds. . . . The most serious difficulty lay in the privacy of the objects to which the elementary statements were supposed to refer. If each one of us is bound to interpret any statement as being ultimately a description of his own private experiences, it is hard to see how we can ever communicate at all. Even to speak of "each one of us" is to beg a question; for it would seem that on this view the supposition that other people exist can have no meaning for me unless I construe it as a hypothesis about my own observations of them, that is, about the course of my own actual or possible experiences.

Because of such difficulties, Neurath and subsequently Carnap, rejected this whole conception of elementary statements. They argued that if elementary statements were to serve as the basis for the intersubjective statements of science, they must themselves be intersubjective. They must refer, not to private incommunicable experiences, but to public physical events. More generally, statements which ostensibly refer to experiences or to "mental states" or processes of any kind, whether one's own or anybody else's, must all be equivalent to "physical statements": for it is only this way that they can be publicly intelligible. This is the thesis of physicalism. (Ayer 1959, p. 20)

One can easily trace the difficulties faced by both the solipsistic and the physicalistic brands of logical positivists to their inability to free themselves from the pseudo-problems created by Berkeley and Kant. Kant took the perceiving mind away from the realm of nature and invented its imaginary categories. Kant subordinated real events that take place in the universe to the artifacts of the human mind; Berkeley made existence of the world dependent upon the perceiver; Mach reduced science to a cluster of sensations; and the logical positivists fell into the trap of self-contradictory statements they tried to avoid.

There has been, however, a significant opposition to this introspectionistic self-involvement of the logical positivists. Not all members of the *Vienna Circle* adhered to the sole rule of *immanent truth* believing that the only criterion of scientific truth is the inner consistency of scientific propositions. Carnap (1928) tried to deduce all empirical concepts from any arbitrarily chosen solipsistic statements (but changed his view in 1938). Schlick (1925) and the Warsaw School (Kotarbinski, 1929, 1965; Lukasiewicz, 1934; and others) insisted on correspondence between the propositions and empirical data described by them. This principle of *transcendent truth* was modified in 1935 by Karl Popper (1958) who proved that erroneous empirical propositions can be disproved by testing them against reality, and redefined Kotarbinski's version of radical epistemological realism as the guidepoint of empirically oriented philosophy of science (Wolman 1965a).

Also the Kantian idea of the supremacy of mathematics has caused serious controversy in the conceptual work of the logical positivists. Whitehead and Russell (1910–1913), and Russell (1903, 1919) deviated from Kant's ideas, and, approaching Wittgenstein's set of concepts, proved that mathematics is reducible to logic and its propositions are formal-analytic. Thus mathematics became an ideal, complete, system perfectly representing the principle of immanent truth. However, in 1931 Kurt Goedel showed beyond doubt that an axiomatic system is either consistent or complete and it cannot be both as Whitehead and Russell believed it to be. In any mathematical system there are arithmetic theorems that cannot be derived from the basic axioms, and if all theorems are derived from the axioms, then they are inevitably self-contradictory (Goedel 1931; Bunge 1962; Nagel and Newman 1958; Gunther 1968).

SCIENCE AND THE PHILOSOPHY OF SCIENCE

The main opposition to logical positivism came not from fellow philosophers but from scientists. Philosophers argued back and forth the dead issues of introspection, solipsism, and private events and tried to prove that words and sentences are all that counts in scientific inquiry, but these arguments did not carry much weight in scientific laboratories. Philosophical analysis of scientific work was of service to the scientists, provided the philosophers were fully acquainted with the problems scientists had to cope with. Experimentalists and theoreticians in physical sciences proceeded boldly in developing new and ingenious research techniques while paying little attention to the philosophical discussions of rationalists, idealists, pseudo-empiricists, old Kantians, and new phenomenologists.

Modern theoretical physics broke off with the empirical tradition as represented by philosophers, old and new. This change in scientific methodology is described by Northrop in a preface to Heisenberg's *Physics and Philosophy: The Revolution in Modern Science.*

Newton left the impression that there were no assumptions in his physics which are not necessitated by the experimental data. This occurred when he suggested that he made no hypotheses and that he had deduced his basic concepts and laws from the experimental findings. Were this conception of the relation between the physicist's experimental observations and this theory correct, Newton's theory would never have required modification, nor could it ever have implied consequences which experiment does not confirm. Being implied by the facts, it would be as indubitable and final as they are.

In 1885, however, an experiment performed by Michelson and Morley revealed a fact which should not exist were the theoretical assumptions of Newton the whole truth. This made it evident that the relation between the physicists' experimental facts and his theoretical assumptions is quite other than what Newton had led many modern physicists to suppose. When, some ten years later, experiments on radiation from black bodies enforced an additional reconstruction in Newton's way of thinking about his subject matter, this conclusion became inescapable. Expressed positively, this means that the theory of physics is neither a mere description of experimental facts nor something deducible from such a description; instead, as Einstein emphasized, the physical scientists only arrive at this theory by speculative means. The deduction in his method runs not from facts to the assumptions of the theory but from the assumed theory to the facts and the experimental data. Consequently, theories have to be proposed speculatively and pursued deductively with respect to their many consequences so that they can be put to indirect experimental tests. In short, any theory of physics makes more physical and philosophical assumptions than the facts alone give or imply. For this reason, any theory is subject to further modification and reconstruction with the advent of new evidence that is incompatible, after the manner of the results the Michelson-Morley experiment, with its basic assumptions. (1958, pp. 3–4).

Theoretical physicists, among them Niels Bohr, De Broglie, Arthur Eddington, Albert Einstein, Werner Heisenberg, James Jeans, Max Planck, and Erwin Schrödinger, are today's leading philosophers of the physical science. They do not share the beliefs of Mach and Wittgenstein; Max Planck (1931) was highly critical of the logical positivists; Einstein's conception of science was based on the particular needs of physics irrespective of the ideas developed by Carnap and Ryle (Einstein, 1936, 1940; Northrop, 1959; Ryle, 1949). Einstein's epistemological system is not a continuation of logical positivism; it is a logical result from physical research and theory.

Physical scientists have developed their own tools of critical thought. Wrote Heisenberg:

Coming now to the comparison of Kant's doctrines with modern physics, it looks in the first moment as though his central concept of the "synthetic judgements a priori" had been completely annihilated by the discoveries of our century. The theory of relativity has changed our views of space and time, it has in fact revealed entirely new features of space and time, of which nothing is seen in Kant's a priori forms of pure intuition. The law of cau-

sality if no longer applied in quantum theory and the law of conservation of matter is no longer true for the elementary particles. (1958, p. 88)

Obviously Kant could not have foreseen the new discoveries. It seems that some philosophers have used obsolete psychological concepts in their effort to solve complex scientific problems. What seemed obvious to a Locke, Hume, Kant, Wittgenstein, and Ryle was not necessarily acceptable to Einstein, Schrödinger, and De Broglie. Ever so often philosophers use common sense notions, counterposing time and space, mind and matter, and so on, but scientists endeavor to reach beyond such philosophical concepts as "innerly given," "self-evident" and others derived from common sense or yesterday's sciences. Pre-Copernican philosophers religiously believed that the earth was flat, and prior to Harvey no philosopher dreamed of blood circulation. Nineteenth-century, and to a certain extent contemporary philosophy as well, have operated on the assumptions of the early associationism, and even today it may be hard to divest oneself from the idea that matter is a collection of individual entities called atoms (Schrödinger 1952, p. 17ff.). Philosophers have always assumed continuity of observation following their common sense experience, but contemporary physics can hardly share this assumption.

We assume—following a habit of thought that applies to palpable objects—that we could have kept our particle under continuous observation, thereby ascertaining its identity.

This habit of thought we must dismiss. We must not admit the possibility of continuous observation. Observations are to be regarded as discrete, disconnected events. Between them there are gaps which we cannot fill. There are cases where we should upset everything if we admitted the possibility of continuous observation. That is why I said it is better to regard a particle not as a permanent entity but as instantaneous event. Sometimes these events form chains that give the illusion of permanent beings— but only for an extremely short period of time in every single case. (Schrödinger 1952, pp. 27–28)

Apparently in modern physics the facts of observation cannot be reconciled with a continuous description in space and time of something, "but we do not claim that this something is observable or observable facts; and still less we do claim that we thus describe what nature (matter, etc.) really *is*" (Schrödinger 1952, p. 40).

Contemporary philosophy of science is produced either by scientists familiar with philosophical analysis or by philosophers who have acquired a thorough familiarity with the particular branch of science they study. Einstein, Planck, Schrödinger, Bohr, Nagel, Northrop, Margenau and many others are the new brand of philosophers who analyze the problems faced by the particular science. Nagel's *The Structure of Science* (1961), which is divided into several philosophies of distinct sciences, analyzes soberly distinct issues related to specific branches of knowledge.

Russell's words (1921) might well serve as concluding remarks on the relationship between science and philosophy:

Philosophy, from the earliest times, has made greater claims, and achieved fewer results, than any other branch of learning.

...The one and only condition, I believe, which is necessary in order to secure for philosophy in the near future an achievement surpassing all that has hitherto been accomplished by philosophers, is the creation of a school of men of scientific training and philosophical interests, unhampered by the tradition of the past, and not misled by the literary methods of those who copy the ancients in all except their merits.

Russell's statement concerning all sciences applies also to psychology. However, as described in the following pages, the prolonged union between metaphysical philosophy and psychology, as well as the particular nature of the subject matter of psychology, makes the relationship between psychology and the philosophy of science more complicated.

3. Between Psychology and the Philosophy of Science

Psychological data is reported in sentences or, as logicians prefer to call them, propositions. As long as psychology was a part of metaphysics, psychological propositions were analytic. The psychological propositions of Plato and Aristotle, St. Thomas Aquinas, and "faculty" philosophers were analytic. They did not convey factual information; they were mere definitions. Plato wrote in the *Republic*, Book vii, that knowledge is related to unchanging objects; when we really know something we can't go wrong; perception therefore cannot give us knowledge (Peters 1953, p. 66). Plato *assumed* all that, and *defined* knowledge as related to things that do not change. As stated above, analytic propositions are true or false irrespective of any factual information they convey. Accordingly, if knowledge pertains to unchanging objects, perception does not give knowledge.

"Memory is, therefore, neither perception not conception, but a state of affection of one of these, conditioned by lapse of time," wrote Aristotle in the treatise *On Memory and Recollection*. Aristotle concluded, "Hence not only human beings and the beings which possess opinion or intelligence, but also certain other animals possess memory. Whenever one actually remembers having seen or heard or learned something, he includes in this act (as we have already observed) the consciousness of 'formerly' and the distinction of 'former' and 'latter' in a distinction of time" (Dennis 1948, pp. 1 and 2).

Aristotle's proposition is true irrespective of whether it does or does not convey factual information. Its logic is irrefutable. If memory is based on distinction of time, and animals have the distinction of time, then animals have memory. One may reverse the order of reasoning and say, "Since animals have memory, they must have perception of time."

As long as psychology was a "philosophy of mind," we could make such statements. Consider Descartes' following statement, taken from his *Meditations*: "I have often shown that the mind can work independently of the brain; for clearly there can be no use of the brain for pure intelligence, but only for imagination and sensation" (Peters 1953, p. 355).

J.F. Herbart was the last psychologist who operated with analytic propositions and developed a dogmatic system which was not related to empirical research. But Herbart's psychology was also the last metaphysical psychology.

The first steps of psychology toward an empirical science are associated with the name of Wilhelm Wundt (1832–1920), his *Principles of Physiological Psychology* (first published in German in 1873), and his founding of the first psychological laboratory in 1879 in Leipzig. In the preface to the first edition Wundt wrote:

The work which I have presented to the public is an attempt to mark out a new domain of science. I am well aware that the question may be raised whether the time is yet ripe for such an undertaking. The new discipline rests upon anatomical and physiological foundations which in certain respects, are themselves very far from solid; while the experimental treatment of psychological problems must be pronounced, from every point of view, to be still in its first beginnings. (Dennis 1953, p. 248)

It was not an easy task to transform the old "mental philosophy" into a natural science. Natural sciences used observation and experimentation; they observed their subject-matter, as it were, from without. Wundt's psychology was supposed to study observable stimuli and responses, but there was so much that was unobservable in psychology. Wundt tried to solve this problem by assuming that the subject matter of psychology was the "inner experience."

As strange as it may seem from the perspective of almost a whole century later, Wundt's decision took psychology out of the realm of metaphysics and created an empirical science. Metaphysics dealt with body and soul; Plato, Aristotle, Thomas Aquinas, Descartes, and even the materialist Herbart described "the nature of the soul." For better or worse, Wundt expelled the soul from psychology and dealt with "experiences." The mind, said Wundt, is not an object, it is a process. It is something that goes on in us and we are aware of. The true subject matter of psychology is the being-aware-of (*Bewusst sein* in German means "being aware of." As one word, *Bewusstsein* is a noun and it is translated into English as awareness, consciousness, conscious.)

All other sciences use naturalistic observation and controlled observation under conditions created by the observer. The latter type of observation is called experimentation. In the preface of the fifth edition of Wundt's *Principles of Physiological Psychology* translated by E.B. Titchener and published in 1910, Wundt succinctly described the main problems of the new science:

As an experimental science, physiological psychology seeks to accomplish a reform in psychological investigation comparable with the revolution brought about in the natural sciences by the introduction of the experimental method. From one point of view, indeed, the change wrought is still more radical: for a while in natural science it is possible, under favourable conditions, to make an accurate observation without recourse to experiment, there is no such possibility in psychology. It is only with grave reservations that what is called "pure self-observation" can properly be termed observation at all, and under no circumstances can it lay claim to accuracy. On the other hand, it is the essence of experiment that we can vary the conditions of an occurrence at will and, if we are aiming at exact results, in a quantitatively determinable way. Hence even in the domain of natural science, the aid of the experi-

mental method becomes indispensible whenever the problem set is the analysis of transient and impermanent phenomena, and not merely the observation of persistent and relatively constant objects. But conscious contents are at the opposite pole from objects; they are processes, fleeting occurrences, in continual flux and change. In their case, therefore, the experimental method is of cardinal importance; it and it alone makes a scientific introspection possible. For all accurate observation implies that the object of observation (in this case the psychical process) can be held fast by the attention, and any changes that it undergoes attentively followed. And this fixation by the attention implies, in its turn, that the observed object is independent of the observer. Now it is obvious that the required independence does not obtain in any attempt at a direct self-observation, undertaken without the help of experiment. The endeavour to observe oneself must inevitably introduce changes into the course of mental events,—changes which could not have occurred without it, and whose usual consequence is that the very process which was to have been observed disappears from consciousness. The psychological experiment proceeds very differently. In the first place, it creates external conditions that look towards the production of a determinate mental process at a given moment. In the second place, it makes the observer so far master of the general situation, that the state of consciousness accompanying this process remains approximately unchanged. The great importance of the experimental method, therefore, lies not simply in the fact that, here as in the physical realm, it enables us arbitrarily to vary the conditions of our observations, but also and essentially to further the fact that it makes observation itself possible for us. The results of this observation may then be fruitfully employed in the examination of other mental phenomena, whose nature prevents their own direct experimental modification.

Wundt opened the Pandora's box of modern psychology. If the factual data of psychology are given in *inner* experience in contradistinction to the data of all other sciences, than introspection is the choice method. Such self-observation affects the conscious processes of the observed-observer, and therefore it cannot be objective. According to Wundt experimentation is superior to introspection, for the experimenting observer is a "master of situation."

This "mastery" led to a great many problems in psychological inquiry which will be discussed later. But at this point, let us try to understand why psychology had to break away from introspection and follow the lead of the physical sciences.

METHODOLOGICAL REDUCTIONISM

Reductionism is probably an infantile disease common to all young sciences. Perhaps it is not a disease but a temporary and much needed phase of infantile dependence on older sciences.

Pavlov did not believe that the psychology developed by Wundt as a "science of consciousness" and a study of "subjective states" could ever become an independent science (1928, p. 219). Perhaps psychology could some day become sort of a "superstructure" to physiology.

J.B. Watson was more optimistic about the future of psychology, provided psychology would join the community of the physical sciences. Watson wrote in 1913:

Psychology as the behaviorist views it is a purely objective experimental branch of natural science. Its theoretical goal is the prediction and control of behavior. Introspection forms no essential part of its methods, nor is the scientific value of its data dependent upon the readiness with which they lend themselves to interpretation in terms of consciousness. The behaviorist, in his efforts to get a unitary scheme of animal response recognizes no dividing line between man and brute. The behavior of man, with all of its refinement and complexity, forms only a part of the behaviorist's total scheme of investigation.

The time seems to have come when psychology must discard all reference to consciousness; when it need no longer delude itself into thinking that it is making mental states the object of observation. We have become so enmeshed in speculative questions concerning the elements of mind, the nature of consciousness (for example, imageless thought, attitudes, and Bewusssteinlage, etc.) that I, as an experimental student, feel that something is wrong with our premises and the types of problems which develop from them. There is no longer any guarantee that we all mean the same thing when we use terms now current in psychology.

Psychology, as the behaviorist views it, is a purely objective, experimental branch of natural science which needs introspection as little as do the sciences of chemistry and physics. It is granted that the behavior of animals can be investigated without appeal to consciousness. Heretofore the viewpoint has been that such data have value only in so far as they can be interpreted by analogy in terms of consciousness. The position is taken here that the behavior of man, and the behavior of animals must be considered on the same plane; as being equally essential to a general understanding of behavior. It can dispense with consciousness in a psychological sense. The separate observation of "states of consciousness" is, on this assumption, no more a part of the task of the psychologist than of the physicist.

A few years later Watson restated his position:

Psychology as a science of consciousness has no community of data. The reader will find no discussion of consciousness and no reference to such terms as sensation, perception, attention, image, will and the like. . . . I frankly do not know what they mean nor do I believe that anyone can use them consistently. (1919, p. xii)

With Pavlov and Watson psychology has become an objective and experimental science. The question of whether the analytic proposition that conveyed the conclusions reached by behaviorists and learning theorists was true or false, cannot be adequately dealt with here, but it must be said that is beyond the scope of doubt that psychology has accepted the research methods and conceptual system of the physical sciences, thus practicing methodological reductionism.

PSYCHOLOGY AND THE LOGICAL POSITIVISM

This uncritical and enthusiastic acceptance of the methods of physical sciences created unpredicted difficulties. Pavlov's study of the "Higher Nervous Processes" introduced five mechanistic laws of excitation, inhibition, irradiation, concentration, and induction. Pavlov declared that he was deeply and irrevocably convinced that the objective physiological study will ultimately bring "the knowledge of the mechanism and laws of human nature" (1928, p. 41).

Watson, too, expressed optimism concerning the future of the new psychology. He wrote, "In a system of psychology completely worked out, given the stimuli the response can be predicted" (1913).

Watson did not do justice to the complexities of psychological research and theory formation. Watson uncritically adopted Pavlov's system, but more sophisticated researchers, such as C.L. Hull, B.F. Skinner, E.C. Tolman, K.W. Spence and others felt that Pavlov's and Watson's pioneering work requires further elaboration and methodological sophistication.

Watson's and Pavlov's philosophy of science was, implicitly, related to the materialistic tradition of the nineteenth century and to the positivistic philosophies of A. Comte, H. Spencer, C. Darwin, and pre-Einsteinian physicists. Watson's mechanistic determinism corresponded to yesterday's physics, and Pavlov's inductive empiricism was a straight continuation of simple generalizations of Helmholz, Ludwig, and Sechenov (Anokhin, 1968).

Meanwhile modern physics abandoned the eighteenth and nineteenth century empiricism and developed bold hypotheses that trangress the traditional forms of Aristotelian logic and mathematics. New systems of mathematics and mathematical logic have been developed. For instance, the so-called irrational number i ($\sqrt{-1}$) found its place in scientific research and contemporary philosophers of science have become deeply involved in the development of new conceptual and linguistic tools to fit the spectacular development of physical sciences; the insistence on the use of J. S. Mill's inductive method is no longer general.

The Viennese logical positivists embarked upon a new and fascinating enterprise of developing a new "logic of science" assuming that the logic of science is actually a "logical system" of the language of science (Carnap 1937). The logical positivists planned to develop a "physicalistic language" hoping that their analysis of the language of definitions (analytic propositions) will be of great help in the formation of scientific concepts.

However, as described above, the overemphasis on the principle of *immanent truth* (inner consistency), which was applicable to the formal sciences such as logic and mathematics did not help in answering the questions raised by empirical research in physics, nor was logical positivism able to offer adequate "correspondence rules" that could mediate between the empirical data and the non-empirical theories, though there has been a great deal of communication between theoretical physicists and logical positivists (Ayer 1959; Feigl 1951, 1958; Einstein 1936; Frank 1957; Reichenbach 1938; Russell 1948; Schrödinger 1951).

Small wonder that psychologists have been enchanted by logical positivists. The writings of logical positivists, and especially of H. Feigl, had a considerable influence on the thinking of post-Watsonian behaviorism and post-Pavlovian learning theory. An excellent exposé of this trend of thought is found in Stevens's (1939) paper on "Psychology and the Science of Science." The common theme of the logical positivists, Stevens wrote, "is probably to be esteemed as a truly great advance in the Philosophy of Science of the Science of Philosophy." This new movement

has proved disastrous for metaphysics, challenging for logic and salutary for science. Philosophers and scientists in essential agreement are astonishing enough, but here we have them pleading for a common method. In this strange harmony we are witnessing the birth of a new discipline: the Science of Science. It is a triumph for self-consciousness. The science-makers are asking themselves how they make science and are turning on that problem the powerful empirical weapons of science itself; while at the same time a tough-minded outcropping among the philosophers is carefully combing the metaphysics out of logic in order to investigate more easily the common linguistic structure of science.

We shall see how this movement concords with "behavioristics" which is a behavioristic psychology tuned up to keep pace with a fast-moving logical criticism. And finally, we shall see what the impact of this movement means for some specific problems in psychology, and what is indicated as the future role of psychology in this scheme.

In this paper Stevens described the birth of the logical positivism and operationism, stressed the connection between these two approaches, and strongly recommended both of them.

Perhaps we are too close to this young Science of Science either to judge its value or see clearly how it came to be. We shall forego the value-judgement, since it would merely disclose the author's particular prejudice (already clear, no doubt), but an observation about the movement's immediate ancestry is not entirely out of order. It now appears, in retrospect, that the Science of Science emerged as the reasonable outcome of revolutions in the three major fields; physics, psychology, and philosophy. These revolutions occurred almost independently, but a general community of spirit among them led directly to extensive cross-fertilization. Operationism as a revolution against absolute and undefinable concepts in physics, behaviorism as a revolution against the absolute and dualistic mentalism in psychology, and logical positivism as a revolution against rational metaphysics in philosophy were the three forces whose convergence into a common effort is effected by the Science of Science.

This new frontier was expanded in two different directions by two outstanding psychologists who developed two new scientific systems. Both Hull and Skinner accepted the fundamental principles of the logical positivists but applied them in two wholly different directions.

Hull developed a bold mathematico-deductive system. Very few psychologists had such a broad knowledge of philosophy of science, formal logic, and mathematics, combined with rigorous experimentalism and superb reasoning power. Hull's approach to the problems of research in psychology corresponds to the logical positivist critique of naive empiricism. There have been three methods of scientific procedures, Hull wrote (1943a, p. 2ff.). The first is unplanned observation; the second, planned observation; the third, experimental testing of unrelated hypotheses. All three methods, especially the third one were quite useful and led to empirical generalizations and an inductive formation of theories.

However, only mathematical and formal logical analytic propositions can be absolutely true according to the principle of immanent truth. According to Hull, a theory is nothing else but "a systematic deductive derivation of secondary principles of observable phenomena from a relatively small number of primary principles or postulates much as the secondary principles or theorems of geometry are ultimately derived" (1943a, p. 20).

Hull introduced the following steps in theory formation:

1. *Definitions and postulates:* Hull suggested four rules as the first steps of his theory. The definitions and postulates which are clearly analytic propositions, must be bound by the principle of immanent truth (inner consistency), clarity of language (logical syntax), few (parsimony). These definitions and postulates must permit the formation of *theorems*, that is they must be of heuristic value. In short, immanent truth, logical syntax, parsimony, and heuristic considerations were the guideposts in Hull's work. Hull's definitions and postulates, like Einstein's theories, are not necessarily related to empirical data. The theorems form the link between theory and facts, between the analytic and synthetic propositions.

2. *Theorems:* The theorems must be *deduced* from definitions and postulates, by implications and inferences. This formal logical procedure must be clear, detailed, and stated explicitly, thus permitting "observational determination" of the truth conveyed by the theory. The observational validation implied experimental testing of the theorems. The observational validation seeks agreement between the primary principles and the observable data, thus it applies the principle of *transcendent* truth necessary in empirical sciences.

Hull spent all his indefatigable life checking and rechecking his theorems, striving toward rigorous quantification of data (1952), and developing an entire new school in psychology. His followers include a host of prominent psychologists, among them J. Dollard, C.I. Hovland, G.A. Kimble, N.E. Miller, H.O. Mowrer, K.W. Spence and others, some of whom have developed their own systems. And yet, despite the wealth of empirical data, rigorous experimentation, and logical clear thinking, neither Hull's theory nor any of its offshoots has gained clear victory over any of the competing psychological theories, as was eloquently explained by several authors participating in the collective volumes edited by S. Koch (1959–1963) and B.B. Wolman and E. Nagel (1965). The analysis of problems of theory formation in psychology must be delayed to the last section of this study, but it must be stated here that the way Hull developed his theory fits exactly the description given by Carnap:

Would it be possible to formulate all laws of physics in elementary terms admitting more abstract terms only as abbreviations?

But it turns out . . that it is not possible to arrive in this way at a powerful and effective system of laws. (In contemporary physics) the construction begins at the top and then adds lower and lower levels. (1937, p. 64)

Hull's theory construction followed the same pattern.

DESCRIPTION VS. EXPLANATION

As mentioned before, the logical positivists have perpetuated certain aspects of Mach's philosophy. Mach's brand of phenomenology sounded more Humeian and thus more empirical than any other kind of empiricism. Opposed to any statement in the physical sciences that went beyond data derived from observation, Mach substituted description for explanation,

mathematical functions for causation. Mach's idea that "the world consists of colors, sounds . . . simply elements" (1920, p. 208) and that "nature is composed of sensations as its elements" (1960, p. 482) enchanted B.F. Skinner.

Following in Mach's footsteps, Skinner (1931) suggested that the terms cause and effect must not be used in scientific inquiry. "The terms which replace them, however refer to the same factual core. A 'cause' becomes a 'change in an independent variable' and an 'effect' 'a change in a dependent variable.' The new terms do not suggest 'how' a cause causes its effect; they merely assert that different events tend to occur together in a certain order" (1953, p. 23). Psychology must accept the "more humble view of explanation and causation which seems to be first suggested by Mach." Explanation should be "reduced to description" and "the notion of function substituted for that of causation." (1938, p. 44). One could quote Mach at this point: "In the investigation of nature, we have to deal only with knowledge of the connection of appearances with one another" (1911, p. 49).

Skinner's radical empiricism has made him a staunch supporter of Bridgman's operationism.

OPERATIONISM

In their enthusiasm for a physical-type concept formation, many psychologists embraced the methodological proposals brought forward by Bridgman. As stated above, Bridgman's operationism was not too well accepted by physicists and philosophers of science. It was apparent to them that no theory could be coated in operational terms (Einstein, 1959, p. 189), for no theory was a result of empirical operations. Certainly a theory should be open to empirical test, but even on that issue above described objections have been raised by Carnap who wrote, "that the requirement of testability and of operationism exclude some empirically meaningful terms" (1956, p. 65).

Bridgman's influence on psychology (Skinner 1945; Stevens 1935, 1939) represents one of the most interesting curiosities in the history of human thought. As mentioned above, Bridgman's reasoning is almost a replica of Mach's. Mach was deeply indebted to Kant, Berkeley, and Schopenhauer, and introspection was one of the fundamental principles of his system (Mach 1920). Everything could be doubted except self-observation. The only unquestionable elements of knowledge were the sensory data of the self-observing observer. Bridgman, following in Mach's footsteps, believed that observation of the activities of the observer were more valid than the observation of all other objects and activities.

For Pavlov, Bekhterev, Thorndike, Watson, Guthrie, Hull, Skinner and many others, psychology became "objective" and independent of introspectionistic data. And here, through the backdoor of operationism, self-observation came back. Operationists assume that the observation of one's own observations and actions is more valid and more objective than observation of experimental subjects or any other observation. An operationist doubts the validity of his observations of animal and human behavior; the only valid observation is the observation of the operations of the observer and the experimenter.

Kant told the observers to observe not the world but their own observing minds; Bridgman ordered them to observe their operations of observing. Psychologists who study human behavior probably know more about observation than Kant and

Bridgman, yet they have accepted the guidance of the incompetent and, for a while, almost every research paper has started with an "operational" definition of its terms and endeavored to report the findings and explanations in the language of "operations" performed by the research worker.

In 1936 Bridgman switched to solipsism. Because science reports the operations of a particular research worker, it is impossible to make meaningful statements not derived from these particular operations: scientific concepts that come from any other source are meaningless. Bridgman arrived at a logical conclusion that science, defined in terms of *my* scientific operations, is private. "In the last analysis science is only my private science" (1936).

Psychologists could not accept solipsism, but they did not abandon operationism. Stevens (1939) tried to solve the issue by suggesting "public and verifiable" procedures, as if Sullivan's "consensual validation" could serve as a guarantee for objective evidence.

For thirty years operationally minded psychologists tried to formulate their theories in operational terms, not realizing that theories cannot be wholly formulated in terms of experimental data, nor can they be directly proven by experimentation (Ritchie, 1965). This fact was realized by theoretical physicists a long time ago, but only recently have psychologists begun to realize that theoretical concepts cannot be defined in terms of operations.

Lately we have been witnessing a growing criticism of Machism and operationism. "The punctiform sensations of Mach were discredited by the failure of introspectionism and were replaced by Russell's 'perspectives' and 'aspects' of things, and more recently by Carnap's 'thing language' and Neurath's 'language of daily life'," wrote Postman and Tolman (1959, p. 506).

The reaction against operationism comes from various sources (Adler 1947; Bergmann 1958; Plutchik 1963). "In personality theory and in social psychology, however, concepts like ego strength, defense mechanisms, role systems, and role conflict are so remote from their measurement that they have no single clearly required set of operational measures," wrote Katz and Scotland (1959, vol. III, p. 471).

Let us quote a recent criticism of operationism in regard to conditioning:

It is frequently argued that the phrase "conditioned response" is merely a label denoting the particular animal behavior which is elicited under specific conditions or by equivocally defined experimental "operations"....

Biologists, says the operationalists, should not be concerned with such meaningless Aristotelian concepts as the "essential nature" of a phenomenon, for to do so would commit them to a statement about the nature of what exists. He feels they should only be concerned with a careful description of what they did to the animal and what the animal did as a consequence.

The claim of the operationalist, that he only uses the term "conditioned response" to denote some particular aspect of an animal's behavior under specific experimental conditions, cannot be accepted as an accurate description of his actual practice. In practice operationistic epistemology is never rigorously followed, even by the most devout operationalist, and it could not be.

In proof, it is only necessary to observe the operationalist in action. He uses the term "conditioned response" to denote some

particular aspect of a dog's behavior (salivation in response to a bell) which occurred following a uniquely specific set of experimental operations. He also uses the term "conditioned response" to describe the tears which certain poems, motion pictures, and patriotic symbols evoke in men. By what particular principle does the operationalist decide that the three sets of responses should all be called the "conditioned response" if he has denied himself, and others, the use of a unifying, non-operational concept? (Efron 1966, pp. 510–11).

THEORETICAL REDUCTIONISM

Methodological reductionists assume that the science to be reduced must accept methods of the science it is being reduced to. Theoretical reductionism assumes that the subject matter and findings of one science can be presented in terms of the science to which it is being reduced. Many psychologists practice both types of reductionism.

One hundred and twenty-five years ago, Emile du Bois-Reymond, Ernest Bruecke (who was Freud's teacher), Herman Helmholtz, and Karl Ludwig, all four students of Johannes Mueller, united in a pact for the interpretation of biological phenomena by reducing them to the laws of physics and chemistry. The reductionistic pact has impressed all psychological studies since, and especially those of Pavlov and Freud. This was the stage of psychology and it was probably necessary for the emerging science to break away from mother philosophy and join empirical sciences of physics, chemistry, and physiology. Even Wundt, whose introspectionistic theory stood with one foot in Kantianism, called his main work *The Principles of Physiological Psychology*. Since then many psychologists have expressed the idea that ultimately all psychology could be reduced to neurophysiology.

The belief that human behavior can be reduced to physico–chemical factors is representative of the *theoretical reductionism*. The theoretical reductionism in psychology represents one of the following possibilities: (*1*) radical reductionism maintains that psychological data can now be presented in terms of the subject matter of another science, for example neurophysiology; (*2*) future research may discover that such a reduction is feasible; or (*3*) the scientific propositions and theories derived from empirical studies in psychology could and should be presented as logical consequences of scientific propositions of other sciences. The subject matter of psychology is reduced to biochemical processes related to nutrition.

Not all psychologists share the belief that such a reduction is possible at the present time, and some oppose radical reductionism on methodological grounds; yet they share the belief that such a reduction may become possible in the future. This belief, which we shall call "hoped-for reductionism," is widely accepted in psychology.

A third alternative is to deal with the problem on a formal basis. Logical reductionism tries to reduce the formal logical propositions derived from empirical studies and conceptualization of psychological theory to scientific propositions of other sciences.

The radical reductionists assumed that the so-called mental phenomena must be reduced to phenomena known from more basic sciences. The sole difference between psychology and physiology, as Watson saw it (1919, p. 20), was that physiology dealt with separate physiological functions whereas psychology dealt with functions of the organism as a whole. "The findings of psychology become the functional correlates of structure and lend themselves to explanation in physico-chemical terms" (Watson 1913). The Russian reflexologist Bekhterev believed that consciousness is a state of physical energy related to central inhibition and resistance in cortical processes (1913, p. 45ff.). Hebb (1949) described "the kind of activity throughout the cerebrum which we call consciousness" (p. 29), and maintained that the "interest or motivation" can be "provisionally translated into the stability and persistence of the phase sequence" in nerve cells (p. 223). Pratt (1948) wrote that psychology would become a truly scientific system when it would "resolve" itself into a basic science such as physiology.

Radical reductionism has invited criticism from diverse sources. For instance, Skinner (1950) wrote that in modern science "the picture which emerges is almost always dualistic ...." The study of human behavior need not be described in physiological terms. There is no reason to relate behavior to "events taking place somewhere else, at some other level of observation, described in different terms, and measured, if at all, in different dimensions."

Some psychologists, although renouncing "here-and-now" radical reductionism, have not abandoned the idea that ultimately psychological propositions can and will be presented in terms of the physico-chemical sciences. In fact, such a hoped-for reductionism is very much in vogue in contemporary psychology.

Freud's hope for an ultimate victory of reductionism was clearly stated in his last work where he wrote that "the future may teach us how to exercise a direct influence, by means of particular chemical substances, upon the amount of energy and their distribution in the apparatus of mind" (1949, p. 79). Also the ethologists, as Hinde summarized the situation, held that "analysis down to physiological level is a desirable, but not at present usually attainable aim" (1959, p. 565).

Pavlov dealt with behavior from a neurological point of view and his data were derived from observation and experimentation with the nervous system; Pavlov's theory operated with neurological terms. If it was speculative (cf. Wolman 1960, pp. 62ff.), it was a speculation regarding the functioning of the nervous system. Yet Pavlov expressed the hope that some day psychology would be built as a "superstructure" on physiological foundations.

Hull's theory likewise belongs to the category of hoped-for reductionist systems. Hull believed that at the present time psychology must be a molar theory, dealing with behavior as a whole. "Students of the social sciences are presented with a dilemma of waiting until the physico-chemical problems of neurophysiology have been adequately solved before beginning the elaboration of behavior theory" (1943a). Hull did not wait, and developed a theory independent of neurophysiology with the hope that some day the reduction would take place.

The efforts to reduce psychology to other sciences are in full swing. At the present, neurophysiological propositions are largely interpreted in terms of physics and chemistry. Should psychology be reduced in neurophysiology, it could *eo ipso* join the physicochemical kingdom of pure science. The methodological advantages of such a reduction cannot be overestimated.

Several workers are driving toward this goal, and serious efforts are being made in the direction of reducing psychology

to neurophysiology and behavior to brain. Pribram (1954), for example, has tried to solve this problem by experimental manipulation of both the central nervous system and the environmental conditions in their interaction with behavior of the organism in the hope that such a procedure would eventually lead to a science of neuropsychology.

Several research workers, concerned with psychosomatic disorders, also have attacked the problem of reductionism. Yet, despite the most thorough research work, reported by F. Alexander (1950), F. Deutsch (1953), Grinker and Robins (1954), and many others, we are not any closer to "reduction" of mental processes.

Another version of reductionism, the logical reductionism, does not assume synonymity of psychological and nonpsychological terms. Its aim is to interpret theoretical propositions derived from observation and experimentation in terms of theoretical propositions of another science. As Nagel put it:

The objective of the reduction is to show that the laws or general principles of the secondary science are simply logical consequences of the assumptions of the primary science (the reducing science). However, if these laws contain expressions that do not occur in the assumptions of the primary science, a logical derivation is the explicit formulation of suitable relations between such expressions in the secondary science and the expressions occurring in the premises of the primary discipline. (1953, p. 541)

According to Nagel, it is necessary to find logical connections between empirically confirmed propositions of the two sciences, the one that has to be reduced and the one that will "incorporate" the reduced science. However, even "the reduction of chemical laws to contemporary physical theory would not wipe out or transform into a mere appearance the distinction between the two sciences" (Nagel 1953, p. 459; 1961, Chap. 11).

Let us apply this reasoning to reductionism in psychology. Logical reductionism does not prove that mental and somatic process are "the same," but it suggests that the propositions presenting psychological theories could be inferred from formal propositions of other sciences (cf. Feigl 1958; Nagel 1961).

The problem of reductionism was also discussed by the Soviet psychologist Rubinstein as follows:

The discovery of the biochemical nature of physiological phenomena has not resulted in the disappearance of those as specific phenomena.... However far-reaching the discoveries of biochemical regularities controlling the formation of cortical connections, reflexes will not cease to be reflexes.... Since psychic phenomena obey the physiological laws of higher nervous activity they appear as the effect of the operation of chemical laws. But physiological processes represent a new, unique form of manifestation of chemical laws, and it is precisely the discovery of these new specific forms of manifestation that is covered by the laws of physiology. In the same way, the physiological laws of neurodynamics find psychic phenomena a new unique form of manifestation which is expressed in the laws of psychology. In other words, psychic phenomena remain psychic phenomena, even though they appear as a form of manifestation of physiological laws; just as physiological phenomena remain physiological though as an outcome of biochemical investigation they also appear as a form of manifestation of the laws of chemistry. Such, in general, is the interrelationship of the laws governing the lower and higher forms of movement of matter, the relationship between "lower" and "higher" regions of scientific investigation. The fact that the more general laws governing the lower regions spread to the more specialized regions does not exclude the necessity of discovering the specific laws of these higher regions (1957, pp. 268–69)

TRANSITIONISM

Were it possible to explain behavior in push-and-pull terms or by neurons and metabolism, a logical reductionism would be justified. For example, when a wave hits a rock, a physicochemical interpretation of the phenomenon is wholly justified. When a human organism fights infections, a biochemical interpretation is possible. But when a man hits a man, his aggressive behavior can be explained in no other terms than his mental processes. Assuming that the assailant was intoxicated, alcohol, a chemical agent, was an additional factor of his behavior; assuming that the assailant was upset by his own misconduct and developed psychosomatic symptoms, there was an additional organic effect of his guilt feeling.

Transitionism assumes that mental processes are a continuation of and have developed out of the biochemical process, just as the latter developed out of the lower-level and more universal physicochemical processes. There is a triple connection between mental and other biological processes: (*1*) phylogenetic evolution, (*2*) ontogenetic evolution, and (*3*) intra-organic processes.

Transitionism is a theory of *continuous transition of organic life from one developmental stage to another*. Each species represents a part of the evolution; *A* developed into *B*, *B* into *C*, *C* into *D*, and so on. Once a species has developed into something new, it is no longer what it was before. Organic life (Oparin, 1957) developed out of inorganic life, but once it developed, it was no longer inorganic. Thus, instead of *unity* and *identity*, transitionism proposes *unity of continuity*.

The principle of transitionism expands Einstein's formula, $E = mc^2$, into a general theory of physics, physics being seen as the most general science. Biology is a peculiar, "higher level" branch of physics-chemistry, that is, a science that deals with organic matter. New processes require new scientific formulations. Whatever is old in the new processes, can be reduced; whatever is new, cannot be reduced.

The unity of the universe does not contradict the diversity of singular events and bodies. Assuming that all nature is a series of energy fields, the fact remains that each field is different. When field A_1 receives an additional load of energy, it becomes field A_2. Field A_2 is different from field A_1, and so on. The fact that quantum theory does not prove such a continuum is probably, as Einstein wrote, because quantum theory "offers no useful point of departure for future development" (1959, p. 87).

Transitionism applies to ontogenetic processes. A tree develops out of a seed via sapling, yet a tree is neither sapling nor seed. A man *was* an infant but he is an infant no more. The fact that there are amoebas, apes, and men, supports the idea of the *continuity* of nature. Organic life started from the inorganic but cannot be reduced to the inorganic life; humans stem from lower animals yet their behavior cannot be interpreted in terms of white rats; an adult was a child, yet his actions cannot

be interpreted in terms of infancy. Could we chop a tree up to find the seed that started the tree?

Mental processes start in prenatal life. The earliest reflex responses in humans have been reported between the seventh and eighth weeks, measured from the last menstruation (Hooker 1954). There is a difference between histological and functional nervous development, and between nervous development and mental development. When the nervous cells mature, how many of them are in operational condition? How many of them accept stimuli and discharge responses? Does mental life start at once at a certain point? Does it start before the embryonic cells for the nervous system separate from the cells for muscle, bones, and so on, or after that separation? (Sperry, 1958).

Genes are mainly composed of deoxyribonucleic acid (DNA), and heredity is to large extent an interaction between ribose sugar molecules and DNA (Crick, 1961). We may hypothesize that, at a certain point of ontogenetic development, genetic, prenatal, or natal physicochemical factors *cause* mental symptoms. Causation, however defined, is one of the possible modes of transition.

Yet such a causal soma-psyche connection cannot be proven for a great many, indeed for the majority of mental disorders. At present, only certain mental disorders are known to be produced by chemical factors. A majority of mental disorders is most probably caused by interaction with the social environment.

Transitionism tries to reduce whatever can be reduced. There is no reason to force a radical, here-and-now reduction at the empirical level. On a formal logical level, transitionism seeks to develop a set of constructs in psychology that would enable us to present mental phenomena not as logical derivative but as a *continuation* of the other organic processes. A programmatic and imaginary formula would, more or less, represent *O* (organic phenomena) that can in certain conditions of *k* (conditions of transition) turn into *M* (mental phenomena) and vice-versa. Thus (1) $O_k \longrightarrow M$ and (2) $M_{k1} \longrightarrow O$ (Wolman 1965*b*, *c*).

4. Toward a Psychological Philosophy of Science

THE NATURE OF PSYCHOLOGICAL DATA

The discussion of theoretical reductionism has pointed to the possible irreducibility of psychological data to data obtained by other sciences. There have been several approaches to the problem of specificity of the subject matter of psychology, even after psychology ceased to be a study of the immortal soul, spirit and the like. Twenty-one years after Wundt's classic *Principles of Physiological Psychology*, Windelband (1894), a prominent neo-Kantian, came out with a division of sciences into natural and historical sciences. According to Windelband and Rickert (1899) the natural sciences are not concerned with single events, they study necessary, general occurrences and seek the universal rules and laws of nature, and thus they are *nomothetic*.

In contradistinction to the natural sciences, the cultural or historical sciences are concerned with individual events and unique, unrepeatable *idiophenomena*.

Natural sciences try to assess not a particular case of

change but "the changeless form of change," while historical sciences seek out the individual facts and the individual changes (Windelband 1894).

Similar ideas to those of Windelband's were expressed by Rickert in 1899 and Dilthey in 1883 and 1894, and the division of sciences into *Naturwissenschaften* (natural sciences) and *Geisteswissenschaften* (humanities) has influenced the thinking of generations of German, British, and American psychologists. In the programmatic essay called *Ideas Concerning a Descriptive and Analytical Psychology* (1894) Dilthey wrote:

We know natural objects from without through our senses. However we may break them up or divide them, we never reach their ultimate elements in this way. We supply such elements by an amplification of experience. Again, the senses, regarded from the point of view of their purely physiological function, never give us the unity of the object. This exists for us only through a synthesis of the sense-stimuli which arises from within. . . . How different is the way in which mental life is given to us! In contrast to external perception, inner perception rests upon an awareness (Innewerden), a lived experience (Erleben), it is immediately given. Here, in sensation or in the feeling of pleasure accompanying it, something simple and indivisible is given to us (1924).

Natural sciences observe from without and they explain (*erklären*) what they see. Psychological data are given in inner perception: they are lived experiences of the human mind and they do not need explanation. Psychology must instead try to understand the mind as a whole.

In understanding we start from the system as a whole, which is given to us as a living reality (der uns lebending gegeben ist), *to make the particular intelligible to ourselves in terms of it . . . . The apprehension of the whole makes possible and determines the interpretation of the particular part . . . . (1924).*

Dilthey maintained that the main task of psychology is to understand human nature as a whole. Windelband wrote that psychology as practiced by Wundt and Ebbinghaus was a nomethetic science, but that a study of individual human beings, their individual life histories, and their unrepeatable life-events, belongs to the historical, *idiophenomenological* sciences (1894). Rickert maintained that natural sciences study causes while cultural sciences are concerned with cultural values. Brentano (1874) introduced the concept of *act*; all mental processes are acts and are therefore intentional. Furthermore, Brentano suggested a distinction between perception and observation. All sciences observe and perceive their subject matter, but mental processes cannot be observed; they are only perceived (Sullivan 1968).

Spranger (1928) developed a psychological system based on the premise of Dilthey, Windelband, Rickert, and Brentano. Spranger stressed understanding versus description, the molar approach versus molecular, the individual case versus generalization, purposefulness versus causation, and based his psychology on values.

The discussion concerning the nature of psychological phenomena as compared to physical phenomena is still much alive. One way out was suggested by Skinner's staunch opposition to any theoretical reductionism. Skinner saw no reason to relate psychological observable data to the data of other science. Why should psychology interpret its solid observation in terms of other sciences "which appeal to events taking place somewhere else, at some other level of observation, described in different terms, and measured, if at all, in different dimensions" (Skinner, 1950).

Many psychologists have been quite concerned with the particular nature of psychological phenomena; Windelband's ideas have influenced Spranger, Stern, Allport, Gestalt psychologists, Lewin, Adler and many others. And the issue of idiophenomena has intrigued several psychologists—Allport (1942, 1961), Holt (1962), Wolman (1960, 1965c) and others, leading to a quite important use of the case study methods.

Yet it seems that Windelband's division of science into idiographic and nomothetic branches is not at all justifiable. Unless one assumes the "realist" position in the Platonic sense and ascribes existence to general concepts, the entire issue of idiophenomena seems to rest on a misunderstanding. Whatever happens, happens once; whatever happens "for a second time" is no longer what it was before. Not only are historical events idiophenomena, but every drop of rain, every fall of a rock, and every motion of air are idiophenomena. The idiophenomenon, that is, the single case, is the raw material of science. The work of science starts with single cases. Sciences compare, abstract, generalize, and classify single cases using a common denominator. No science can exhaust all cases; Newton did not experiment with all falling bodies, nor did Darwin and Mendel study all biological species or cases.

Every experiment is, in a sense, a case study. Psychology, like any other science, uses generalization; the individual case study is only the first step, which must lead to classification and generalization. Psychological phenomena are more complex than those phenomena studied by physics and biology, for a human being is a physical body, a living organism, and a personality, all of them at the same time, and psychological generalizations are more complex.

The great monotheistic religions superimposed man on nature by ascribing to him an immortal soul. Kant, Schopenhauer, Windelband, Dilthey, Stern, Lewin, Adler, Fromm and many others counterposed man to nature. Darwin, Pavlov, Watson, Freud, and still others viewed man as a part of nature. Psychology as the study of human behavior has become a part of the biological sciences that deal with living organisms and life processes. Thus, if there is any reason for a methodological reductionism, it should lean to biology rather than physics; and whenever psychological models are necessary, they should resemble animate rather than inanimate nature.

Observation. The problem of methodological reductionism has broad implications. Consider the concepts of time and space. Observations of time and space are as irreconcilable with the concepts of modern physics as the observation of sunrise and sunset is with astronomy. In order to solve the problem encountered by physicists in their endeavor to formulate an uninterrupted description of time and space, Bohr and Heisenberg suggested "that the [*observed*] object has no existence independent of the observing subject . . . . Recent discoveries in physics have pushed forward to the mysterious boundary between the subject and the object which thereby has turned out not to be a sharp boundary at all. We are to understand that we never observe an object without it being modified or tinged by our activity in observing it" (Schrödinger, 1952, pp. 50–51).

Such a hypothesis might be necessary for research in quantum mechanics. However, like any other hypothesis, this one is also open to criticism, and it is doubtful that astronomers and chemists who do not deal with microphysics would accept this hypothesis of quantum theorists. Moreover, there is no reason to assume that whenever a psychologist observes rats in mazes or human subjects through a one-way screen, the "mysterious boundary" between observer and observed break down. Psychologists do not encounter the problems arising from research in quantum mechanics and have no reason to borrow someone else's headaches.

Apparently, physicists and philosophers of physical science cannot solve the problem concerning the observer and the observed. Consider the following statement from a prominent theoretical physicist who questions the validity of Bohr and Heisenberg's assumption:

Physical action is always inter-*action, it always is mutual. What remains doubtful to me is only just this: whether it is adequate to term one of the two physically interacting systems the "subject." For the observing mind is not a physical system, it cannot interact with any physical system.* (Schrödinger 1952, p. 53.)

Psychology and Physics. Psychophysical data may serve here as a case in point. A double increase in physical electro-chemical energy acting upon a particular sensory receptor does not necessarily produce twice as much reaction. The human sensory apparatus is not subject to the laws of electromagnetic waves, and our perception of paintings and symphonies is not controlled by the laws of electromagnetic radiation.

There is a definite relationship between physical stimuli and the human sensory and perceptual experience; this relationship is the subject matter of psychophysics, which is sort of a go-between science. The awareness of a dire need for building bridges proves that a deep gulf separates physics and psychology and that these two discplines are ruled by two separate sets of laws. The fact that the subject matter of psychology, which is the behavior of living organisms, is part and parcel of the physical universe cannot justify a simple and uncritical application of physical laws to psychology. Certainly living organisms are subject to the fundamental laws of gravitation, osmosis, and electrodynamics, but these laws account for but a fraction of behavior (Field 1960). For instance, if John Doe jumped from the seventeenth floor to commit suicide, a physicist, knowing the weight of John's body and all other physical variables, could predict how much time it will take till John's skull will hit the pavement. No physicist can explain why John committed suicide and why he did what he did at a particular time and place. In short, physics is of no help in predicting and interpreting John's behavior. *An entirely new set of scientific tools is needed for the study of behavior.*

Such tools cannot be borrowed from physics. In fact, contemporary psychology has developed highly sophisticated methods of observation, measurement, and experimentation unheard of in physics. One way screens, clinical techniques, socio-psychological and longitudinal studies, questionnaires, case studies, surveys, mental tests, projective techniques, mazes, obstacle boxes and thousands of other ingenious devices have been developed by psychologists independently of philosophers of science and physicists. Tolman's concepts of intervening variable, Skinner's box, Hathaway's MMPI, Rorschach ink-blots, to mention only a few techniques, bear witness to the methodological sophistication and independence of contemporary psychology, though the tendency to carry borrowed hats is still much in vogue in psychology (Wolman 1972).

Between the Observer and the Observed. The above quoted passage from Schrödinger applies to research in physics, but psychologists cannot dismiss a somewhat similar problem they face in their own research. As early as in the first years of Wundt's experimental work psychologists had become aware of the impact of the experimenter's ideas and techniques on the outcome of the experiments. Why, for instance, did Guthrie's and Rock's experimental animals learn on a single trial, but Thorndike's need several trials and errors? Why do some experimental subjects waste time in mazes while others display orienting reflex (Platonov), and cognitive maps (Tolman)?

What is the impact of the experimental design? The extent to which the ideas or even the personality of the experimenter influence the results of a research, is a question that deserves careful study, and the diversity of opinions amongst the most conscientious research workers might be at least partially related to the impact of their particular approach and research technique (Amsel 1965; Ritchie 1965; Miller 1959).

Ethological research and especially the experiments with imprinting are another case in point. Imprinting is believed to be a natural and innate behavioral pattern or, at least, if it is related to learning, it definitely depends on innate potentialities and occurs in certain biologically determined "critical moments." However, new born chicks and ducks can be imprinted upon by the experimenter and the entire imprinting process can be delayed and modified by experimental procedures. Would the ingenious experiments of Harlow and associates (1959, 1966) have yielded different results if the wire and the surrogate mothers had been differently constructed?

Or consider the studies of frustration. In the Dollard et al's famous research (1939), frustration led to aggression. In Barker, Dembo, and Lewin's study (1941) frustration led not to aggression but to regression, and there have been lately several hypotheses concerning aggression.

Apparently, the question of the unwitting influence exercized by the research worker on the results of his work is of utmost importance in clinical and social psychology. Consider the differences in data reported by Freud and Sullivan concerning schizophrenia. Not only their interpretations but even the mere descriptions were completely different.

The reclining position of the patient and the sparse communication from the silent psychoanalyst facilitated transference phenomena. Freud made transference the cornerstone of his therapeutic method. However, when psychotic patients were asked to recline with the psychoanalyst sitting behind the couch and watching, silence was perceived as a rejection and the invisible analyst became a threatening figure. The patients withdrew even more and did not dare to communicate their true feelings. Such behavior gave the impression of narcissistic withdrawal and lack of transference feelings (Freud 1946).

Sullivan worked with patients moving back and forth and acting out their feelings. He saw patients in interpersonal relations, and he did not fail to notice the socially induced changes in their behavior. The interaction became the clue to the understanding of the psychotic's personality (Sullivan 1953). Most probably what has been observed in participant observations was not the patient as an isolated entity but the patient in interaction with the therapist, a *psychosocial* field situation.

Epistemology or Perceptology. Perhaps the question about whether we actually perceive what we perceive, which tradionally formed the epistemology branch of philosophy, could be dealt with more successfully by the science that studies human perception. Were, indeed, Hume, Kant, Nagel, Schopenhauer, Mach, and Ryle better prepared to find out how we perceive than let us say, Békésy (1967), Corso (1967), Gibson (1966), Gregory (1966), and Helson (1964, and in this Handbook)? Why should one assume that someone sitting at his desk knows more about the moon than people who landed there? Since all human beings are equipped with sensory apparatus, what is the reason to assume that people who never saw microbes know more about them than those who study microbiology with the help of powerful tools? And how do epistemological essays compare to experimental studies in sensation and perception?

The fundamental laws of neurophysiology exclude the possibility of a one-to-one relationship between the external physical stimulus and its perception (Hodgkin 1964). When a stimulus reaches an axon's ending, it either produces a nerve impulse or fails to do so, depending on whether it was strong enough to reach the sensitivity threshold of a particular neuron in a particular time. This "all or none" reaction of neurons already limits the possibility of a simple one-to-one reaction, because the exact same stimulus may produce an impulse in a resting neuron, and fail when the neuron is in an absolute refractory state. The intensity of stimuli is translated by the nervous system into a frequency code, but the precision of the translation depends on the nervous system. Thus, in a somewhat oversimplified way one can say that we do not react in the same way to the same stimuli: our perception of the outer world is *selective* and depends upon the state of our receptors, conveyors, etc.

Moreover, once the stimulus reaches the threshold of a neuron, the magnitude of the stimulus has little to do with the magnitude of the nerve impulse. The struggle of an impulse produced in a particular axon is constant; it either fires or does not fire, according to the *all or none law*. The firing releases all the electric energy available in the axon, irrespective of the struggle of the stimulus, just as a cannon discharges all its fire power irrespective of the struggle in the muscles of the artillerist.

While some stimuli are reacted upon irrespective of their strength, provided they are strong enough to fire the axon, stimuli acting upon the dendrites cause a reaction proportioned to their strength, but their strength is not carried faithfully to the brain. According to the law of decremental conduction, part of it gets lost, and sometimes the loss is so heavy that the carrier arrives empty-handed at the brain. Since we receive all information about the outer world and our own organism through the nervous system, and the nervous system reacts in at least the three above mentioned different ways, we may receive three different pictures of the outer or inner environment, when (*a*) the threshold of an axon is momentarily heightened or lowered, (*b*) the axon reacts with the same impulse to a strong and a weak stimulus, and (*c*) the dendrites lose part of the message (Eccles 1964; Field 1960, Hodgkin 1964; and others).

No epistemological speculations, whether developed in philosophical studies or borrowed from the most precise research in nuclear physics, can solve these problems. The solution of the problems of cognition must come out of research in psychology proper, in its study of neurophysiological and sensory, perceptual, and other behavioral processes. A psychologist who seeks inspiration in philosophy or physics resembles a millionaire who asks his poor relatives for a loan to pay the mortgage on his paid-in-full mansion. For if there is to be found a solution for the perennial "philosophical" problems of how and what we perceive, of perception and reality, perceiver and perceived, it must be sought in the realm of psychology as the science that studies behavior (including the truth seeking behavior called scientific research). Psychology deals with those who perceive and whose behavior cannot be reduced to physics and biochemistry.

CAUSATION

It would require a separate volume to trace the history of the causal principle and its relationship to behavioral science (MacIver 1942; Wolman 1938, 1948). In the framework of the present chapter it will suffice to say that most of the discussion concerning causation in psychology has been borrowed from contemporary physics.

Nineteenth century physics followed in the footsteps of Newton's conceptual framework and assumed that whatever happens is caused by physical forces. The difficulties of causation in modern physics stem from two sources; namely, the quantum theory, which cannot present its data in a cause-effect continuum, and the relativity theory, which has undermined the concept of temporal sequence. Thus, at least in microphysics, the concept of causation has become useless and its transcendent truth questionable (Bergmann 1929; Braithwaite 1942; Cassirer 1956; Duhem 1954). "Observation," wrote Dingle, "in Humeian fashion teaches us only the facts of invariable succession. There cannot be any doubt that quantum theory has rendered the causal principle useless. The elaborate structure that the nineteenth century science has built seems to be dismantled and reduced to a pile of bricks" (1931, p. 88).

Yet several contemporary physicists maintain that the causal principle is still the leading principle of natural science. Wrote Planck, "Physical science together with astronomy and chemistry and mineralogy are all based on the strict and universal validity of the principle of causality" (1932, p. 147). And further on, "The last goal of every science is the full and complete application of the causal principle" (p. 158). Einstein also took a definite stand on causation, assuming that its validity had not been finally abolished by the recent developments in theoretical physics.

All attempts to represent the particle and wave features displayed in the phenomena of light and matter, by direct course to a space-time model, have so far ended in failure.... At the present, we are quite without any deterministic theory directly describing the events.... For the time being, we have to admit that we do not possess any general theoretical basis for physics, which can be regarded as its logical foundation (1940, p. 147).

Contemporary physics cannot present its data in a deterministic continuum, but some physicists, among them Einstein himself,

cannot believe that we must abandon, actually and forever, the idea of direct representation of physical reality in space and time; or that we must accept the view that events in nature are analogous to a game of chance (1940, p. 147).

It is a matter of fact that contemporary physics has substantial difficulties with the concept of causality. However, there is no reason for importing these difficulties into other research areas. The time sequence is a clearly definable issue in behavior, and there is a definite beginning for every human life and an irrevocable dead end to it. Whatever goes on between conception and death can be presented in temporal sequence as intrauterine, childhood, adolescence, infancy, middle age, and old age. There cannot be any doubt that human behavior is a series of *temporal sequences*, notwithstanding the relativity and quantum theories.

The causal relationship has never been questioned in any field of psychology. If one doesn't feed experimental rats, they become food deprived. When parents don't love their children, the children become love deprived. No research worker, whether his name was Thorndike, Pavlov, Freud, Hull, Spence, Binet, Skinner, Piaget, Harlow, or Newcomb has ever operated with loosely connected psychological events.

The concept of cause and effect has been derived from human behavior and extended to inanimate nature—to the dismay of Hume who introduced the distinction between succession and production. Hume (1874, 1894) fought against the Newtonian idea of "forces" that allegedly produce changes in nature. Nature cannot be interpreted in terms of human behavior that *produces* tools and weapons, and it smacks of *anthromorphism* to ascribe human behavioral patterns to inanimate nature. But it smacks of *reimorphism* to deprive human behavior of human traits and prescribe laws of physics to human actions.

Modern theoretical physics operates with the time-space four dimensional model, and is unable to determine temporal sequences in quanta. These difficulties do not exist in human behavior. Human behavior is full of unmistaken cause and effect relationships. Human actions *produce* results: consider agriculture, industry, and creative writing; consider sexual behavior, fertilization and heredity. Biology and behavioral sciences do not need to follow microphysics (Kaganov and Platonov 1961; Sarris 1968).

Explanation in psychology reads as follows: A psychological datum is *explained* when the datum is known and the *causes* of this datum are discovered. A psychological datum is *predicted* when the causes of an unknown datum are known and the *effects* are discovered. Explanation proceeds from the known effects to the unknown causes; prediction proceeds from the unknown causes to the unknown effects. Explanation and prediction are two parts of the interpretive process; the first looks to the past, and the second looks toward the future.

Explanations and predictions in psychology are never perfect, but probability calculus is not a substitute for causation; it merely interpolates the inevitable gaps in our knowledge. Predictions of the future and explanation of the past are hampered by the inadequate knowledge of the present and the inability to assess all factors that may produce the future, Probability does not necessarily mean an abrogation of determinism; probability is a useful method of *approximation* to truth because the ultimate truth is inaccessible (Poincaré 1902; Reichenbach 1949; Wolman 1948). Laplace wrote:

We ought to regard the present state of the universe as the effect of its antecedent state and as the cause of the state that is to follow. An intelligence knowing all the forces acting in nature at a given instant, as well as the momentary position of all things in the universe, would be able to comprehend in one single formula the motions of the largest bodies as well as the lightest atoms in the world, provided that its intellect were sufficiently strong to subject all data to analysis: to such an intellect nothing would lack certainty, and both the future and the past will become present in its eyes.... All the efforts of the human mind in the search for truth tend to move toward such imagined intelligence mentioned above. Yet it will forever stay remote from such an intelligence (1820).

An imaginary omniscient intellect could interpret empirical data with precision and accuracy but knowledge produced by human beings must use ancillary methods, such as probability, correlations, levels of confidence, and so on, being aware of the deterministic rationale of all these methods.

THE NATURE OF PSYCHOLOGICAL PROPOSITIONS

The argument for specificity of psychology as science has been supported by a great variety of reasons. Allport (1942, 1961), Lewin (1936, 1944), Merton (1969), Sargent (1971), and others stressed the specific nature of psychological phenomena, mainly related to human efforts, strivings, uniqueness, and purposefulness. Lewin saw human behavior as a sequence of tensions, locomotion and equilibrium; this sequence is equivalent to need-activity-relief sequence, and counterposed "psychological field" to "physical field." Though enchanted by modern physics, Lewin was as opposed to theoretical reductionism as Skinner was.

From the formal logical point of view, psychological propositions certainly display particular characteristics (Bergmann 1958; Kotarbinski 1965; Scriven 1956; Wolman 1965c). These propositions can be divided into several classes.

1. Synthetic propositions describing *directly observable behavior*, such as overt acts of love, violence, learning, and so on.
2. Synthetic propositions describing *introspectively observable behavior*, such as feelings of attachment, planned genocide, contemplated suicide, and so on. Despite the opposition

to Wundt's and Titchener's reliance on introspection, psychology cannot afford to exclude covert behavior from its realm of study.

3. Synthetic propositions describing *inferable unconscious behavior,* such as hidden displacements of fear, repressed incestuous desires, and so on. Unconscious phenomena are not easily accessible, yet their existence cannot be denied, and empirical sciences deal with all that exists whether it is visible or not.

4. The above-mentioned types of propositions could apply to group, classes, and categories of behavior, thus becoming synthetic propositions conveying *empirical generalizations.* These generalizations were called by Feigl (1951) "empirical laws" and by Nagel (1961) "experimental laws."

Actually empirical statements are not "laws" but mere inductive generalizations. Consider such statements as "Hereditary traits are carried by genes," "Newborn children can suck," "The average age of menarche in American females is 13," "Most manic-depressives harbor suicidal thoughts," "Dreams apply pictorial symbolism" and so on.

Empirical generalizations can be arrived at by naturalistic observation, measurement, surveys, statistical studies, and experimentation. Empirical generalizations in psychology may not be as simple as they seem to be. Take, for example, the following cases:

"Whenever you hit a window pane with a hammer, you break the glass." Whenever p, then q, or $p \supset q$; p stands for the first proposition, q for the second. Now substitute "iron door" for "window pane." Apparently "iron" would not break. Thus, whenever p, then not q, or $p \supset q'$; p stands for the proposition, "A hammer hit the iron door," and q' stands for "The iron door did not break."

Now let us substitute a person for the "window pane." So far as physiology and anatomy are concerned, the issue might be presented as follows: "The skin was bruised, there was some bleeding, swelling, and eventually damage to a bone."

What happens to people when they are hit by someone? Were a man a simple organism, his reaction would be fight or flight. But people react in different ways. One may start a verbal fight, rationalize, negotiate, forgive, plan revenge, blame himself, and take several courses of action. Thus general statements such as "Hurt men cry," "Hurt men blame themselves," are not true if "men" means "all men." It may be true in regard to "some men," but even the same man may react in different ways.

Small wonder that psychologists turn to stochastic models and probability calculus. Inductive generalizations inevitably lack precision. Refined statistical and mathematical models not only increase the level of precision but also make psychologists aware of the degree of precision attained in their research (Busch and Estes 1959; Busch and Mosteller 1955; see also the following chapters in this Handbook).

5. The fifth type of psychological propositions is neither synthetic nor analytic. Consider the following examples:

"The dashboard in a car needs *light for safe driving";"A personnel director* should *be tactful"; "A factory foreman* must *give clear directions and allow questions"; "A psychoanalyst* need not *disclose to his patients any information concerning his personal life." These statements do not describe any facts or define anything, but they say what* ought to be done. *These statements are* praxeological *for they deal with rules and norms, and they represent branches of psychology applied to industry, treatment of patients, and so on.*

These propositions deal with what *ought to be* and I call them *praxeologic.*

THEORY FORMATION IN PSYCHOLOGY

The last group of propositions is related to psychological theory. Not all theoretical propositions are synthetic, nor are all of them necessarily a product of empirical generalizations. For example, Hull's (1943, 1952) theory is a system of analytic propositions worded as postulates and definitions and Freud's (1949, 1962) theory is comprised of several theoretical constructs, hypotheses, and models (Horwitz 1963; Wolman 1960).

Not all psychologists form theory formation and explanatory hypotheses. Skinner (1950, 1953) maintained that the business of science is to describe *what* is going on and *how*, leaving out the question *why.* Skinner was opposed to interpretations of behavior that went beyond observable data. What is to be studied are the facts: whether stimuli produce certain reactions, how they are brought about, and to what extent. Psychology has no business going beyond public and observable events. For example, Skinner used the term "drive" merely as a convenient way of refering to "the effects of deprivation and satiation and of other operations which alter the probability of behavior in more or less the same way" (1953, p. 144). Skinner was also opposed to looking "inside the organism," and refused to deal with the "private" events.

Lewin believed that conceptualization and theory formation are synonymous terms. According to him (1936, 1944), a theory is a system of concepts related to observable facts in such a way that the empirical facts may be derived from the concepts. A system of concepts forms a theory. The concepts fill the gap between one observable fact and another. Lewin quoted Tolman's statement that "behavior cannot be derived from behavior." One has to introduce "intervening concepts," or, as Tolman calls them," intervening variables." These concepts should fit the logical structure of psychological phenomena. No science can be purely empirical; empirical laws are functional relationships of observable data, and they have to be related to dynamic laws which are functional relationships of concepts. A system of concepts and dynamic laws forms a theory, and a theory should be constructed in such a manner that the empirical data are the logical outcome of the concepts and laws.

According to Lewin scientific theories must apply two types of concepts. Those of the "first order" are mathematical. They "represent the logical structure of empirical relationships." Thus, the selection of a proper mathematical system is of greatest importance in theory construction. It is imperative to choose the mathematical concepts that will suit the nature of a given science and by "coordinating definitions" to establish the rules of their application. Lewin believed that psychology should apply geometrical concepts, and he introduced the topological–geometrical system into psychology. Lewin paid more attention than most psychologists to the technique of theory construction. He wrote: "Logical form and content are closely interwoven in any empirical science. Formalization should include the development of constructs every one of which is considered from the start both as a carrier of formal implication and as an adequate representation of empirical data . . . ."

According to Lewin there are four kinds of functional interrelation between constructs (called "dynamic" facts) and observable facts: (*1*) logical interdependence between the constructs; (*2*) empirical interdependence between the constructs; (*3*) measurement of the constructs by observable facts; and (*4*) functional interrelation between observable facts.

Most psychologists seem to believe that there are three main levels in scientific inquiry. The first is the ascertainment of facts and empirical proof of them; the second is abstraction, classification, and empirical generalizations; the third is interpretation of facts or formation of a theory. A theory without facts is mere speculation, said David Hume. But science is not a collection of facts, just as a house is not a pile of bricks, said Henri Poincaré.

Having accumulated a great many detailed observations pertaining to behavior, psychologists try to develop a system of hypotheses that interpret why things happen the way they happen. A theory of behavior, as any other theory, explains facts and predicts them as well.

As any other theory, a theory of behavior must be free of inner contradiction. Explanations of facts must fulfill logical requirements and apply consistently the rules of implication and inference. A theory can be accepted or rejected or modified, but a self-contradictory theory cannot be truthful and, therefore, is a priori unscientific. The principle of inner contradiction of a scientific system is called the principle of *immanent truth*.

The principle of immanent truth suffices in formal sciences such as logic and mathematics, but not in empirical sciences. Explanatory theories in empirical sciences must not contradict factual evidence. This agreement with empirical facts is the principle of *transcendent truth*. If a theory is to be used as an instrument of explanation and prediction, it must somehow be linked with observable materials (Nagel 1961, p. 93).

Moreover, a scientific theory has to be heuristically *useful*. Each theory or system of hypotheses should be helpful in the future search for truth. A scientific theory may not be able to offer a final explanation of the empirical data, but it has to be formulated in a manner that facilitates search for additional evidence. Whether a theory is composed of tentative hypotheses or of more positive explanations, room has to be left for future research and further elaborations.

Theories can be formed in several ways. They may evolve out of empirical data in cautious induction; they also may be deduced from arbitrarily set definitions and postulates. Validity of a theory does not depend upon the way it was arrived at but the way it serves empirical science. As the logical positivists noticed, a theory can be formed in any possible way and manner. Since theories use constructs and models, a theory, as Einstein (1959) stressed, can not be coated in operational terms. Deductive theories are comprised of "empirically unobservable, purely imaginative or intellectually known, theoretically designated factors, related in very complicated ways to the purely empirically given" (Northrop 1959, p. 389).

Consider the psychoanalytic theory. Its statement that anxiety is a state of tension created by a conflict between the ego and the superego, or the ego and the id, cannot be experimentally or observationally validated. This statement is neither true nor false, because ego and superego are not observable data but hypothetical constructs. Likewise drive, habit, irradiation, and concentration are not empirical facts but hypothetical constructs. Hypothetical constructs cannot be directly validated; there is no shortcut between these and empirical generalizations; special "correspondence rules" must be established. These rules can be formulated in several ways, depending on the nature of the empirical data (cf. Cohen and Nagel 1934; Nagel 1961, pp. 97 ff.).

An important step in the conceptual development of psychological theory was introduced by Tolman. According to Tolman all the observable factors set by the experimenter should be put together as the "independent variables," and the resulting behavior of the experimental subjects are the "dependent variables." Intervening variables "are to behavior as electrons, curves, or whatever it may be, are to the happenings in inorganic matter" (1932, p. 414).

MacCorquodale and Meehl (1948) distinguished between intervening variables and "hypothetical constructs." They believed hypothetical constructs are more elaborated than intervening variables. Feigl (1951) called the hypothetical constructs "existential hypotheses." Existential hypotheses "fill out" the space assigned to intervening variables and should be introduced on the basis "of some new and heterogenous area of evidence."

The differences are probably related to differences in language. When one talks about experimental procedures, the proper terms are "independent variables" and "intervening variables." Whenever one deals with theoretical propositions, the terms to be used are "theoretical constructs" or "hypothetical constructs." Freud's ego and libido are not empirical facts but theoretical constructs. They could serve as a variable if one could design an experiment in which these constructs could be interpolated between the independent and dependent variables in experimental design.

The increased sophistication in psychology has led to diversified approaches to theory formation. Perhaps the credit of bold pioneering and experimentation should go to Kurt Lewin, but the last two decades witnessed the appearance of several new and original ideas concerning theory formation, such as brought forward by Estes (1957), Lachman (1960), Rapaport (1960), Turner (1967), and several others. The collective works edited by Feigl and Scriven (1956-), Koch (1959–1963), Marx (1963), Wolman and Nagel (1965), and others prove the increased concern of psychologists with philosophy of science related to their particular field of research.

Summary

I. PHILOSOPHY

1. Philosophy, as started in Ancient Greece, was both an all-encompassing system of knowledge and at the same time a system of rules for cognitive processes. In the first role, philosophers developed metaphysical systems, and, in the second, epistemological and logical systems.

2. In modern times physics gradually replaced metaphysics, and empirical research rendered obsolete any speculations about the nature of the universe. However, some philosophers (e.g. Leibniz) continued building speculative systems.

3. The emphasis in philosophy has gradually shifted from the "content" of knowledge (metaphysics) to the techniques of acquiring knowledge. Formal logic, epistemology, and methodology of science played a most important role in a critical analysis of scientific inquiry in the eighteenth and nineteenth centuries.

4. This new role found an outstanding expression in Kant's philosophy. The main source of Kant's impact was his critical epistemology. Kant's *Prolegomena* has influenced a host of philosophers and scientists by making epistemological considerations a prerequisite for knowledge.

5. Kant's disciples, such as Hegel and Schopenhauer, went to extremes in stressing the role of the cognizant mind, and some of them took the even more radical viewpoint of Berkeley.

6. A radical opposition to Kant's philosophy and the alleged supremacy of epistemology started with A. Comte and H. Spencer.

7. The twentieth century has brought a spectacular revolution in the physical sciences. This revolution made Kantian and nonKantian ideas of time, space, causation and so on, obsolete.

8. A group of philosophers called neo-positivists tried to develop a new philosophy of science, hoping to keep pace with modern physics. Operationism is one of the offshoots of this movements.

9. Contemporary physicists could hardly accept this new philosophy and instead began to develop their own conceptual tools closely connected to research and theory formation of their new science.

II. PSYCHOLOGY

1. Psychology, as the study of man himself, was the last science to break away from philosophy, and as late as the nineteenth century J. F. Herbart developed a psychological theory as a part of his metaphysical system.

2. It was difficult for psychology to break away from philosophy for an additional reason. When philosophy turned into a formal science of logical procedure, it overlapped with the psychology of perception and reasoning. John Dewey's *How We Think* is an example of the overlap between logic and philosophy, and James' psychology is partly epistemology.

3. The rebellion against philosophy started perhaps with Wundt and Ebbinghaus, but it came to its full expression with Pavlov and Watson.

4. As psychology developed highly specialized and sophisticated research techniques and discovered complex relationships, it could not continue its progress without careful examination of its methods and concepts. Hull, Tolman, Skinner, Lewin and many others sought an appropriate philosophy of science that could help them scrutinize their empirical studies and theory formation.

5. It is quite natural that psychologists embraced various aspects and versions of neo-positivism and operationism. Feigl, Bridgman and others exercised considerably influence

on psychology in the fourth, fifth, and sixth decades of our century.

6. The conceptual system of the neo-positivists has, however, created several problems for psychology. Borrowing conceptual systems and methods from other fields (methodological reductionism) has not proved successful, and we are witnessing an interest in developing a philosophy of science particularly suited for psychology. K. Lewin was a forerunner of this idea, though the pattern he developed in theory formation did not attract too many.

7. However, Lewin's experience sheds light on the nature of the problems psychology faces. K. Lewin has inherited Dilthey's and Spranger's division of science into the nomothetic and ideographic and, like G. W. Allport, he was plagued by this division. Actually, all sciences deal with ideophenomena and all of them generalize and classify, thus all are nomothetic.

8. The nature of psychological observations is another problem that must be solved by philosophers of science versed in psychology or by psychologists versed in the philosophy of science. The problems of perspective raised by the relativity theory of physics have hardly any bearing on psychological research, but there is an undeniable impact of observers on observed subjects in ethological research and of experimental design on the results of experimentation.

9. To present psychological data in operational terms may increase the risk of bias of the observer and experimenter. Operationism comes close to Kant's and Berkeley's subjectivism and even Schopenhauer's solipsism.

10. In several areas of research, notably in perception (e.g., H. Witkin, Ames, etc.), social psychology (Asch and others), and certainly the clinical area, the observer and the experimenter may interact with their subjects creating a veritable psychological field.

11. The problems of validity of observation belong traditionally to the realm of epistemology. The question could be raised whether the modern psychology of sensation and perception must rely on epistemological speculations. Perhaps empirical psychological research can replace epistemological speculations, just as the physical science replaced metaphysics.

12. This issue leads to the problem of *theoretical reductionism* that endeavors to reduce psychological data to the data of other, allegedly more basic, sciences such as neurophysiology, biochemistry, etc. Psychologists are split on this issue; some of them, like Hebb, defend radical reductionism, while, at the other extreme, Skinner refutes any reduction at all.

13. Possible solutions to this problem have been introduced by Freud, Pavlov, Hull, and others. Another possibility is to view the matter and mind dichotomy in an evolutionary continuum of transitional states.

14. The causal principle had been rendered invalid in modern quantum theory, and Einstein's conceptualization of time and space has reduced the usability of causation in physics. Psychology need not be affected by the misfortunes of the causal principle in physics for whatever psychologists study has a distinct beginning, a deadly end, and an irrefutable temporal sequence.

15. Causality could serve as the guiding principle in theory formation in psychology. *Explanation* is derivation of causes from known results, and *prediction* is deduction of future effects from known causes.

16. Theory formation in psychology is an exercise in formal science involving formal logic, semantics, and syntax. An analysis of psychological propositions, formulation of hypotheses, and other procedures must be geared to the specificity of psychological data.

References

ADLER, F. Operational definitions in sociology. *American Journal of Sociology*, 1947, *52*, 438–44.

ALEXANDER, F. *Psychosomatic medicine*. New York: Norton, 1950.

ALLPORT, G. W. *Pattern and growth in personality*. New York: Holt, Rinehart & Winston, 1961.

——— The use of personal documents in psychological science. *Social Science Research Council Bulletin*, 1942, No. 49.

AMSEL, A. On inductive versus deductive approaches in neo-Hullian behaviorism. *In* B. B. WOLMAN and E. NAGEL (eds.) *Scientific psychology: Principles and approaches*. New York: Basic Books, 1965.

ANOKHIN, P. K. Ivan P. Pavlov and psychology. *In* B. B. WOLMAN (ed.), *Historical roots of contemporary psychology*. New York: Harper, 1968.

AVENARIUS, R. *Kritik der reinen Vernunft* (2 vols.). Leipzig: Barth, 1888–1890.

AYER, A. J. (ed.) *Logical positivism*. Glencoe, Ill.: Free Press, 1959.

BARKER, R. G., T. DEMBO, and K. LEWIN. Frustration and regression: An experiment with young children. *University of Iowa Studies in Child Welfare*, 1941, *18*, 1–314.

BÉKÉSY, VON G. *Sensory inhibition*. New York: Van Nostrand Reinhold, 1967.

BEKHTEREV, V. M. *Objektive Psychologic Reflexologie*. Leipzig: Teubner, 1913.

BERGMANN, G. *Philosophy of science*. Madison: University of Wisconsin Press, 1958.

BERGMANN, H. *Der Kampf um das Kausalitaetsprinzip in der juengsten Physik*. Leipzig: Barth, 1929.

BERKELEY, G. *Principles of human knowledge*. Oxford: Oxford University Press, 1901.

BOURNE, FOX, H. R. *The life of John Locke* (2 vols.). New York: Harper, 1876.

BRAITHWAITE, R. B. *Scientific explanation*. Cambridge: Cambridge University Press, 1942.

BRENTANO, F. *Psychologie vom empirischen Standpunkte*. Leipzig: Duncker & Humblot, 1874.

BRIDGMAN, P. W. Einstein's theories and the operational point of view. *In* P. A. SCHILPP (ed.), *Albert Einstein: Philosopher-Scientist*. New York: Harper, 1959.

——— *The logic of modern physics*. New York: Macmillan, 1927.

——— *The nature of physical theory*. Princeton, N.J.: Princeton University Press, 1936.

BUNGE, M. *Intuition and science*. Englewood Cliffs, N.J.: Prentice-Hall, 1962.

BUSH, R. R., and W. K. ESTES *Studies in mathematical learning theory*. Stanford, Calif.: Stanford University Press, 1959.

BUSH, R. R., and F. MOSTELLER *Stochastic models for learning*. New York: Wiley, 1955.

CARNAP, R. *Der logische Aufbau der Welt*. Berlin: Welkreis-Verlag, 1928.

——— *Die physikalische Sprache als Universalsprache der Wissenschaft*. *Erkenntnis*, 1931, *2*, 432–65.

——— Psychologie in physikalischer Sprache. *Erkenntnis*, 1932–1933, *3*.

——— *Logical syntax of language*. New York: Harcourt Brace Jovanovich, 1937.

——— Formal and factual science. *In* H. FEIGL and M. BROBECK (eds.), *Readings in the philosophy of science*. New York: Appleton-Century-Crofts, 1953.

——— The elimination of metaphysics through logical analysis of language. *In* A. J. AYER (ed.), *Logical positivism*. Glencoe, Ill.: Free Press, 1959.

——— The methodological character of theoretical concepts. *In* H. FEIGL and M. SCRIVEN (eds.), *Minnesota studies in the philosophy of science*, vol. 1. Minneapolis: University of Minnesota Press, 1956.

CASSIRER, E. *Kant's Leben und Lehre*. In *Kant: Werke*, vol. XI. Berlin: Cassirer, 1932.

——— *Determinism and indeterminism in modern physics*. New Haven, Conn.: Yale University Press, 1956.

COHEN, M. R., and E. NAGEL *An introduction to logic and scientific method*. New York: Harcourt Brace Jovanovich, 1934.

COMTE, A. *Cours de philosophie positive*. Paris: Bailliere et fils, 1864.

CORSO, J. F. *The experimental psychology of sensory behavior*. New York: Holt, Rinehart & Winston, 1967.

CRICK, F. M. DNA. *In* L. I. GARDNER (ed.), *Molecular genetics and human disease*. Springfield, Ill.: Charles C Thomas, 1961.

DE BROGLIE, L. *New perspectives in physics*. New York: Basic Books, 1962.

DENNIS, W. (ed.) *Readings in the history of psychology*. New York: Appleton-Century-Crofts, 1948.

DESCARTES, R. *Philosophical works* (2 vols.). Cambridge: Cambridge University Press, 1931.

DEUTSCH, F. (ed.) *The psychosomatic concept in psychoanalysis*. New York: International Universities Press, 1953.

DILTHEY, W. Einleitung in die Geisteswissenschaften (1883). In *Gesammelte Schriften*. Leipzig: Teubner, 1924.

DINGLE, W. *Science and human experience*. London: William and Norgate, 1931.

DOLLARD, J., L. W. DOOB, N. E. MILLER, D. H. MOWRER, and R. R. SEARS. *Frustration and aggression*. New Haven: Yale University Press, 1939.

DUHEM, P. *The aim and structure of physical theory*. Princeton, N. J.: Princeton University Press, 1954.

ECCLES, J. C. *The physiology of synapses*. New York: Academic Press, 1964.

EFRON, R. The conditioned reflex: A meaningless concept. *Perspectives in Biology and Medicine*, 1966, *9* (4), 4488–4514.

EINSTEIN, A. Ernst Mach. *Physikalische Zeitschrift*, 1916, *17*, 101–4.

——— *The world as I see it*. New York: Friede, 1934.

——— Physik und Realität. *Journal of the Franklin Institute*, 1936, *221*, 313–47.

——— The fundaments of theoretical physics. *Science*, 1940, *91*, 487–92.

——— Remarks on the essays appearing in the collective volume. *In* P. A. SCHLIPP (ed.), *Albert Einstein: Philosopher-Scientist*. New York: Harper, 1959.

ESTES, W. K. Of models and men. *American Psychologist*, 1957, *12*, 609–17.

FEIGL, H. Principles and problems of theory construction in psychology. *In* W. DENNIS (ed.), *Current trends in psychological theory*. Pittsburgh, Pa.: University of Pittsburgh Press, 1951.

——— The "mental" and the "physical." *In* H. FEIGL, M. SCRIVEN, and G. MAXWELL (eds.), *Minnesota studies in the philosophy of science*, vol. 2. Minneapolis: University of Minnesota Press, 1958.

——— and M. SCRIVEN, (eds.) *Minnesota studies in the philosophy of science*, 3 vols. Minneapolis: University of Minnesota Press, 1956–1962.

FEYERABEND, P. K. How to be a good empiricist—a plea for tolerance in matters epistemological. *In* B. BAUMRIN (ed.), *Philosophy of science: The Delaware Seminar*, 2 vols. New York: Wiley, 1963.

FIELD, J. (ed.) *Handbook of physiology*. Baltimore, Md.: Williams and Wilkins, 1960.

FRANK, P. *Modern science and its philosophy*. Cambridge, Mass.: Harvard University Press, 1949.

——— (ed.) *The validation of scientific theories*. Boston, Mass.: Beacon Press, 1956.

——— *Philosophy of science*. Englewood Cliffs, N.J.: Prentice-Hall, 1957.

FREUD, S. Three essays on the theory of sexuality (1905). *The Standard Edition of the Complete Psychological Works of Sigmund Freud*. London: Hogarth Press, 1962.

——— On narcissism: An introduction (1914). *Ibid.*, vol. 4, 1946.

——— *An outline of psychoanalysis.* New York: Norton, 1949.

GIBSON, J. J. *The senses considered as perceptual systems.* Boston: Houghton-Mifflin, 1966.

GOEDEL, K. Ueber formal unentscheidbare Saetze der *Principia Mathematica* und verwandter Systeme. *Monatshefte fuer Mathematik und Physik*, 1931, *28*, 173–98.

GREGORY, R. L. *Eye and brain: The psychology of seeing.* New York: McGraw-Hill, 1966.

GRINKER, R. R. and ROBINS, E. P. *Psychosomatic casebook.* New York: McGraw-Hill, 1954.

GRIZE, J. B. Genetic epistemology and psychology. *In* B. B. WOLMAN and E. NAGEL (eds.), *Scientific psychology: Principles and approaches.* New York: Basic Books, 1965.

GUNTHER, P. A. The philosophy of science: Its functions. *Main Currents in Modern Thought*, 1968, *24* (3), 68–74.

HARLOW, H. F. and M. K. HARLOW. Learning to love. *American Scientist*, 1966, *54*, 244–72.

HARLOW, H. F. and R. R. ZIMMERMAN. Affectional responses in the infant monkey. *Science*, 1959, *130*, 421–32.

HEBB, D. O. *The organization of behavior.* New York: Wiley, 1949.

HEGEL, G. W. F. *Philosophy of history.* New York: Colonial Press, 1902.

HEISENBERG, W. *Physics and philosophy.* New York: Harper, 1958.

HELSON, H. *Adaptation level theory.* New York: Harper, 1964.

HESSE, M. Operational definition and analogy in physical theories. *The British Journal of Philosophy of Science*, 1952, *2*, 282–94.

HINDE, R. A. Some recent trends in ethology. *In* S. KOCH (ed.), *Psychology: A study of a science*, vol. I. New York: McGraw-Hill, 1959.

HODGKIN, A. L. *The conduction of the nervous impulse.* Springfield, Ill.: Charles C Thomas.

HOLT, R. R. Individuality and generalization in the psychology of personality. *Journal of Personality*, 1962, *30*, 377–404.

HOOKER, D. Early human fetal behavior with a preliminary note on double fetal stimulation. *Proceedings of the Association for Research in the Nervous Diseases*, 1954, *33*, 98–113.

HORWITZ, L. Theory construction and validation in psychoanalysis. *In* M. H. MARX (ed.), *Theories in contemporary psychology.* New York: Macmillan, 1963.

HULL, C. L. The problem of intervening variables in motor behavior theory. *Psychological Review*, 1943a, *50*, 273–91.

——— *Principles of behavior.* New York: Appleton-Century-Crofts, 1943b.

——— *A behavior system.* New Haven: Yale University Press, 1952.

HUME, D. *A treatise on human nature.* London: Longmans, 1874.

——— *An enquiry concerning the human understanding.* Oxford: Clarendon Press, 1894.

HUSSERL, E. *Ideas: General introduction to pure phenomenology.* London: Allen and Unwin, 1931.

JEFFREYS, H. *Scientific inference* (2nd ed.). London: Cambridge University Press, 1957.

KAGANOV, V. M. and G. V. PLATONOV. *The problem of causality in contemporary biology.* Moscow: USSR Academy of Sciences Publishing House, 1961.

KANT, I. *Critique of pure reason.* London: Macmillan, 1929.

——— *Prolegomena to any future metaphysics* (1783). New York: Liberal Arts Press, 1950.

KATZ, D. and E. STOTLAND. A prelimary statement to a theory of attitude structure and change. *In* S. KOCH (ed.), *Psychology: A study of science.* New York: McGraw-Hill, 1959.

KESSEL, F. S. The philosophy of science as proclaimed and science as practiced: "identity" or "dualism"? *American Psychologist*, 1969, *24*, 999–1005.

KOCH, S. (ed.) *Psychology: A study of science* (6 vols.). New York: McGraw-Hill, 1959–1963.

KOTARBINSKI, T. *Elements of the theory of knowledge, formal logic and methodology of sciences* (Polish). Lwow: Atlas, 1929.

——— Psychological propositions. *In* B. B. WOLMAN and E. NAGEL (eds.), *Scientific psychology: Principles and approaches.* New York: Basic Books, 1965.

LACHMAN, R. The model in theory construction. *Psychological Review*, 1960, *67*, 113–29.

LAPLACE, P. S. *Theorié analytique des probabilités.* Paris: 1820.

LAZARSFELD, P. F. Logic, methodology and philosophy of science. *In* NAGEL, E., P. SUPPES, and A. TARSKI (eds.), *Logic, methodology and philosophy of science.* Stanford, Calif.: Stanford University Press, 1962.

LEWIN, K. *Principles of topological psychology.* New York: McGraw-Hill, 1936.

——— Constructs in psychology and psychological ecology. *University of Iowa Studies in Child Welfare*, 1944, *20*, 1–29.

——— *Field theory in social science.* New York: Harper, 1951.

LOCKE, J. *An essay concerning human understanding.* Oxford: Oxford University Press, 1894.

LUKASIEWICZ, J. *On science.* (Polish) Lwow: Atlas, 1934.

MAC CORQUODALE, K. and MEEHL, P. E. On a distinction between hypothetical constructs and intervening variables. *Psychological Review*, 1948, pp. 55, 95–107.

MACH, E. *History and root of the principle of the conservation of energy.* La Salle, Ill.: Open Court, 1911.

——— *Erkenntnis und Irrtum* (4th ed.). Leipzig: J. H. Barth, 1920.

——— *The science of mechanics.* Chicago: Open Court, 1960.

MACIVER, R. M. *Social causation.* Boston: Ginn, 1942.

MARX, M. H. *Theories in contemporary psychology.* New York: Macmillan, 1963.

MERTON, R. K. Behavior patterns of scientists. *American Scholar*, 1969, *38*, 197–225.

MILLER, N. E. Liberalization of basic S-R concepts: extensions to conflict behavior, motivation and social learning. *In* S. KOCH (ed.), *Psychology: A study of a science*, Vol. 2. New York: McGraw-Hill, 1959.

MISES, R. VON *Positivism: A study in human understanding.* Cambridge, Mass.: Harvard University Press, 1951.

MORGENBESSER, S. (ed.). *Philosophy of science today.* New York: Basic Books, 1967.

NAESS, A. *Erkenntnis and wissenschaftliches Verhalten.* Oslo: Jacob Dybwad, 1936.

——— Science as behavior. *In* B. B. WOLMAN and E. NAGEL (eds.), *Scientific Psychology: Principles and approaches.* New York: Basic Books, 1965.

NAGEL, E. Reduction in natural science. *In* P. P. WIENER (ed.), *Readings in the philosophy of science.* New York: Scribner, 1953.

——— *The structure of science.* New York: Harcourt Brace Jovanovich, 1961.

——— and J. R. NEWMAN. *Goedel's proof.* New York: New York University Press, 1958.

NEURATH, O. Physicalism: The philosophy of the Viennese circle. *Monist*, 1931, *41*.

——— Protokollsaetze. *Erkenntnis*, 1932–33, *3*, 204–14.

——— Radicaler Physikalisms und "Wirkliche Welt." *Erkenntnis*, 1934, *4*, 346–62.

NORTHROP, F. S. C. Preface. *In* W. HEISENBERG, *Physics and philosophy.* New York: Harper, 1958.

——— Einstein's conception of science. *In* P. A. SCHLIPP (ed.), *Albert Einstein: Philosopher-scientist.* New York: Harper, 1959.

OPARIN, A. I. *The origin of life on earth.* New York: Academic Press, 1957.

PAVLOV, I. P. *Lectures on conditioned reflexes.* New York: Loveright, 1928.

PEARSON, K. *The grammar of science.* London: Everyman, 1911.

PETERS, R. S. *Brett's history of psychology.* London: Allen & Unwin, 1953.

PIAGET, J. *Traité de logique.* Paris: Colin, 1949.

——— *Introduction a l'épistémologie génétique* (3 vols.). Paris: Presses Universitaires de France, 1950.

——— Problèmes de la construction du nombre. *Etudes d'Epistémologie Générale*, 1960, *11*, 1–68.

PLANCK, M. *Positivismus und reale Aussenwelt.* Leipzig: Akademische Verlagsgesellschaft, 1931.

——— *Where science is going?* New York: Norton, 1932.

PLUTCHIK, R. A. Operationism as methology. *Behavioral Science*, 1963 *8*, 234–41.

POINCARÉ, H. *La science et l'hypothese.* Paris: Flammation, 1902.

POLANYI, M. *Science, faith and society.* Chicago: University of Chicago Press, 1964.

POPPER, K. *The logic of scientific discovery*. London: Hutchinson, 1958.

POSTMAN, L. and E. C. TOLMAN. Brunswick's probabilistic functionalism. *In* S. KOCH (ed.), *Psychology: A study of science*, Vol. 1. New York: McGraw-Hill, 1959, pp. 502–564.

PRATT, C. C. *The logic of modern psychology*. New York: Macmillan, 1948.

PRIBRAM, K. H. Toward a science of neuropsychology. *In* R. A. PATTON (ed.), *Current trends in psychology and the behavioral sciences*. Pittsburgh: University of Pittsburgh Press, 1954.

RAPAPORT, D. The structure of psychoanalytic theory: a systematizing attempt. *Psychological Issues*, 1960, No. 6.

REICHENBACH, H. *Experience and prediction*. Chicago: University of Chicago Press, 1938.

———— *The theory of probability* (2nd ed.). Los Angeles: University of California, 1949.

RICKERT, H. *Kulturwissenschaft und Naturwissenschaft*. Tübingen: 1899.

RITCHIE, B. F. Concerning an incurable vagueness in psychological theories. *In* B. B. WOLMAN and E. NAGEL (eds.), *Scientific psychology: Principles and approaches*. New York: Basic Books, 1965.

RUBINSTEIN, S. L. Questions of psychological theory. *In* B. SIMON (ed.), *Psychology in the Soviet Union*. Stanford, Calif.: Stanford University Press, 1957.

RUSSELL, B. *The principles of mathematics*. Cambridge: Cambridge University Press, 1903.

———— *Our knowledge of the external world*. Chicago: Open Court, 1914.

———— *Introduction to mathematical philosophy*. London: Allen & Unwin, 1919.

———— *The analysis of mind*. London: Allen and Unwin, 1921.

———— *Human knowledge, its scope and limits*. New York: Norton, 1948.

RYLE, G. *The concept of mind*. London: Hutchinson, 1949.

SARGENT, S. S. Humanistic approach. *In* B. B. WOLMAN (ed.), *Handbook of General Psychology*. Englewood Cliffs, N.J.: Prentice-Hall, 1972.

SARRIS, V. Zum Problem der Kausalität in der Psychologie: Ein Diskussionsbeitrag. *Psychologische Beiträge*, 1968, *10* (2), 173–86.

SCHLICK, M. *Allgemeine Erkenntnislehre* (2nd ed.). Berlin: Julius Springer, 1925.

SCHOPENHAUER, A. *The world as will and idea*. New York: Scribner, 1923.

SCHRÖDINGER, E. *Science and humanism*. London: Cambridge University Press, 1952.

SCRIVEN, M. A possible distinction between traditional scientific disciplines and the study of human behavior. *In* H. FEIGL and M. SCRIVEN (eds.), *Minnesota studies in the philosophy of science*, Vol. I. Minneapolis: University of Minnesota Press, 1956.

SKINNER, B. F. The concept of the reflex in the description of behavior. *Journal of General Psychology*, 1931, *5*, 427–58.

———— *The behavior of organisms*. New York: Appleton-Century-Crofts, 1938.

———— The operational analysis of psychological terms. *Psychological Review*, 1945, *52*, 270–77, 291–94.

———— Are theories of learning necessary? *Psychological Bulletin*, 1950, *57*, 193–216.

———— *Science and human behavior*. New York: Macmillan, 1953.

SPERRY, R. W. Physiological plasticity and brain circuit theory. *In* H. F. HARLOW and C. N. WOOLSEY (eds.), *Biological and biochemical bases of behavior*. Madison: University of Wisconsin Press, 1958.

SPINOZA, B. *Ethics*. London: Bell, 1919.

SPRANGER, E. *Types of men*. Halle: Niemyer, 1928.

STERN, W. *Person und Sache: System der philosophischen Weltanschauung*. Leipzig: Barth, 1906–1924.

STEVENS, S. S. The operational definition of psychological concepts. *Psychological Review*, 1935, *42*, 517–27.

———— Psychology and the science of science. *Psychological Bulletin*, 1939, *36*, 221–63.

SULLIVAN, J. J. Franz Brentano and the problems of intentionality. *In* B. B. WOLMAN (ed.), *Historical roots of contemporary psychology*. New York: Harper, 1968.

SULLIVAN, H. S. *Conceptions of modern psychiatry*. New York: Norton, 1953.

TOLMAN, E. C. *Purposive behavior in animals and men*. New York: Appleton-Century-Crofts, 1932.

———— Operational behaviorism and current trends in psychology. *Proceedings of the 25th Anniversary Celebrating the Inauguration of Graduate Studies*. Los Angeles: University of Southern California Press, 1936.

TURNER, M. B. *Psychology and the philosophy of science*. New York: Appleton-Century-Crofts, 1967.

WATSON, J. B. Psychology as the behaviorist sees it. *Psychological Review*, 1913, *20*, 158–77.

———— *Psychology from the standpoint of a behaviorist*. Philadelphia: Lippincott, 1919.

WHITEHEAD, A. N. and RUSSELL B. *Principia Mathematica* (3 vols.). Cambridge: Cambridge University Press, 1910–1913.

WINDELBAND, W. *Geschichte und Naturwissenschaft*. Tübingen: 1894.

WITTGENSTEIN, R. *Tractatus logico-philosophicus*. London: Kegan Paul, 1922.

WOLMAN, B. B. The chance: A philosophical study. Tarbitz, *Hebrew University Quarterly* (Hebrew), 1938, *10*, 56–80.

———— *Prolegomena to sociology: A study of methods* (Hebrew). Jerusalem: Kiryath Sefer, 1948.

———— The theory of history. *Journal of Philosophy*, 1949, *46*, 342–51.

———— *Contemporary theories and systems in psychology*. New York: Harper, 1960.

———— Psychoanalysis as an applied science. *American Imago*, 1964, *21*, 153–64.

———— Clinical psychology and the philosophy of science. *In* B. B. WOLMAN (ed.), *Handbook of clinical psychology*. New York: McGraw-Hill, 1965b.

———— Principles of monistic transitionism. *In* B. B. WOLMAN and E. NAGEL (eds.), *Scientific psychology: Principles and approaches*. New York: Basic Books, 1965c.

———— Toward a science of psychological science. *In* B. B. WOLMAN and E. NAGEL (eds.), *Scientific psychology: Principles and approaches*. New York: Basic Books, 1965a.

———— History of psychology in perspective. *In* B. B. WOLMAN (ed.), *Historical roots of contemporary psychology*. New York: Harper, 1968a.

———— Immanuel Kant and his impact on psychology. *In* B. B. WOLMAN (ed.), *Historical roots of contemporary psychology*. New York: Harper, 1968b.

———— and E. NAGEL (eds.) *Scientific psychology: Principles and approaches*. New York: Basic Books, 1965.

———— Does psychology need its own philosophy of science? *American psychologist*, 1971, *26*, 877–86.

WUNDT, W. *Principles of physiological psychology* (2 vols.). London: Macmillan, 1874.

One conspicuous aspect of recent treatments of statistical methods for psychologists has been their increase in sophistication in terms of probability theory and associated mathematical models. Prior to the present trend, the ultimate in reader taxation required following the purely algebraic derivation of the least squares regression line or the decomposition of sums of squares in the analysis of variance. Textbooks of this latter sort typically devoted only a few pages to probability which applied only to outcomes that were equally likely. In that context, probability could be defined as the ratio of the number of ways in which a success could occur over the total number of ways both successes and failures could occur.

One cannot, of course, accomplish very much in the area of statistical methods in a chapter the size of this one. Among the alternatives available to a writer are the provision of (1) a listing, with accompanying brief descriptive material, of the statistical tools and methods available to the investigator in the behavioral sciences; (2) a summary of statistical methods that have recently been developed in the journal literature but have not yet appeared in the textbooks; or (3) a succinct overview of the basic concepts and definitions in order that a clearer picture of the entire statistical structure may be obtained.

I have decided against the first alternative since very thorough catalogues of statistical methods (with accompanying descriptive material much more thorough than can be presented here) are available in recent treatments of experimental design for the behavioral sciences (Winer 1971; Myers 1966). The second alternative has been ruled out because such surveys are provided in the *Annual Review of Psychology* which is updated on a yearly basis. (See, for example, the excellent review by Hays in the 1968 *Annual Review*.) I have therefore adopted the third approach, and not solely on the basis of exclusion. I think a succinct, yet comprehensive, picture of the logical and mathematical basis of statistical methods will be of value to the experienced investigator whose statistical training preceded the current more sophisticated trend as well as to those who are not widely experienced but need an introduction to the field. Obviously there are some for whom this approach will be use-

The Statistical Method

4

less. But that would be the case no matter which of the three alternatives I adopted and I think the set will be of minimum size with the one chosen.

Science and Statistics

The Place of Statistics in Psychological Investigations

The typical psychological investigation has three phases which may be called (1) experimentation or environmental evaluation and measurement, (2) statistical analysis, and (3) interpretation. The middle phase exists only as a bridge between the first and the third phases; it has no independent status. While many writers of statistical texts and editors of journals have tried to elevate statistics from servant to master, the overwhelming tendency at the present time is in the reverse direction. But we shall have more to say about that later.

In the phase of experimentation or environmental analysis and measurement, the investigator makes his observations. Usually the experiment or study involves operations of measurement which result directly in collections of numbers. On the other hand, the observations sometimes lead to classifications that are not obviously numerical. Even in this case, however, the results can always be summarized by some arrangement of numerals. For example, suppose patients in a hospital are classified as schizophrenic or not schizophrenic. If one assigns the numeral 1 to schizophrenics and 0 to non-schizophrenics, then the numerical average is equal to the proportion of schizophrenics in a group. One can then perform the usual tests involving means and make meaningful interpretations in terms of relative frequencies.

After the data have been collected they must be organized, summarized, and generally put into a form from which interpretations may be made. This is the phase of statistical analysis. Statistical methods provide a systematic group of techniques for organizing collections of numbers and analyzing them so as to emphasize their important features and suppress unimportant details. They also provide methods for making generalizations. In the process of summarization and generalization the investigator may wish to ask any of a number of questions. Sometimes, for example, he may have a single collection of numbers arising from measurements made on only a few subjects, and he may desire to infer on the basis of his data involving only a few subjects what may be said about all subjects similar to the ones he has actually observed. On another occasion he may have two or more collections of numbers arising from two or more groups of subjects and he may ask whether the individual collections differ from one another in any important way. The conclusions he reaches in the application of statistical methods are, of course, based upon the collections of numbers he has obtained and will consist of statements made about the collections of numbers. Generalizations and inferences that apply to real world phenomena represented by the numbers involve the phase of interpretation.

Scientific investigations, no matter how elaborate their data collection methods and complex their numerical analyses, are directed toward answering questions about phenomena rather than about numbers. A psychological investigation is aimed at answering questions that have psychological import.

The phase of interpretation is, therefore, the return link between conclusions about collections of numbers and decisions about empirical phenomena. This interpretation must take into account all aspects of experimental design, measurement techniques and data analysis, since it is only when certain interpretations have been ruled out by the proper application of experimental and statistical controls that a single interpretation can be accepted as an answer to some psychological question. Although the phase of interpretation is obviously based directly on the statistical analyses, it goes far beyond the issues raised in these analyses.

It is perfectly clear that in actual practice these three phases are very much intertwined and interdependent. The investigator starts with a question or certain questions. Then he imagines a situation which he can arrange and manipulate or perhaps merely study in order to obtain measurements relative to the questions. In most cases he will simultaneously plan how to analyze his data statistically in order to determine the meaning of his measurements. He may vary the design of his experiment or the method of measurement in accord with the necessities of the statistical methods. Finally, considering how his statistical analysis may turn out he formulates how his statistical conclusions may be translated into an answer to his original questions. At this point he surveys carefully what the overall picture is in order to foresee alternative interpretations of his data which may prohibit a clear answer to the questions with which he started. If he finds such an alternative interpretation he may start anew with the aim of revising his imagined situation to rule out the unwanted alternative.

The primary purpose of this chapter is, of course, to survey the concepts and definitions underlying statistical analysis. But because of the very close ties to the other phases of the investigatory process, bridges will be erected frequently between the statistical phase and the world of design and measurement at one end and the interpretation of statistical results in terms of empirical phenomena at the other.

A Survey of Statistics

In the previous section repeated reference was made to sets (or collections) of numbers since a set of numbers is one of the basic concepts of statistics. Sets of numbers may be designated in various ways, as, for example, 16, 93, 8, 47, 1041, or the even integers, or all the numbers between 0 and 1. The goal of statistics is to make statements and inferences about sets of numbers of a great variety of forms. In this process, one may feel perfectly free to rearrange or tabulate the numbers or plot graphs based on them, and to make any kind of algebraic manipulation upon the members of the set in order to make various characteristics of the numbers more apparent and consumable in the reasoning process.

Two types of sets of numbers of critical importance in statistical inference are referred to as population and sample. The set of numbers of prime interest in a given investigation is called a population, while the set of numbers actually at hand for the purpose of drawing generalizations and conclusions is called a sample. In non-technical usage, the terms sample and population are used to refer to collections whose members are not necessarily numbers. For example, we speak of populations of children or pupils or cattle and many statistical texts use the terms in an inconsistent and occasionally confusing manner. When one refers to a sample of children, for example, in an investigatory context involving intelligence, one is referring to the set of intelligence quotients measured in some fashion. Similarly, one could be referring to their heights or their weights or their performances on a list of paired-associates. The particular numerical reference is usually clearly understood in the context. However, since in the statistical phase we begin with numbers and end up with statements about numbers, it aids clarity of communication to restrict the use of the terms population and sample to numbers exclusively.

The sample or set of numbers at hand may be selected from the population by some formal sampling procedure or it may be available because of some extraneous or even fortuitous factors. It is clear that when the investigator has at hand all numbers of interest to him, the sample and the population coincide. It seems worth mentioning that the restriction of the use of the terms population and sample to numbers is relevant when a formal sampling procedure is used. That is, in a strict sense, one does not sample students or children but, rather, one samples IQ's, or learning scores. If one were interested in a random sample, one might sample quite differently if one were interested in intelligence as opposed to yearly parental income.

With this distinction between population and sample in mind, let us consider some of the statements that may be made about numbers. For convenience these statements may be put into three categories. In the first category are statements which refer only to the properties of samples. Statements of this sort are categorized as descriptive statistics. The remaining two categories apply to the case where the sample is necessarily only part of the population. They both involve statements about the population which are inferred from properties of the sample. In the first of these two categories we have statistical estimation which refers to the procedures for estimating properties of the population from what is observed in a sample or samples. The second of these latter categories is called hypothesis testing. In the procedure of this category certain statements are made about the population called statistical hypotheses; one then proceeds to see whether the data in the sample or samples are consistent with these statements. The term statistical inference refers to the process and procedure whereby inferences are drawn about a population from data in a sample. It includes both statistical estimation and statistical hypothesis testing.

The Statistical World and Its Relationship to the Empirical World

There are two broad domains of endeavor to which the term statistics is applied. In the first, statistics is a purely mathematical discipline consisting of sets of primitive terms, definitions, and axioms, from which (together with theorems of other mathematical disciplines) other theorems may be deduced. This branch of statistics is called mathematical statistics.

Let us illustrate the process of mathematical deduction within the statistical arena by a simple example. Suppose the terms variable, distribution, mean (μ), and variance (σ^2) had been defined in discussions prior to the miniature model with which we now deal. We introduce the following additional definition: the variable X is normally distributed if its distribution is

$$f(x) = \frac{1}{\sqrt{2\pi}\sigma} e^{-(1/2)[(x-\mu)/\sigma]^2}, \quad -\infty \leq x \leq \infty.$$

The single axiom in our system is remarkably simple and, concomitantly, general: $f(y)$ is any distribution of the variable Y that has mean, μ, and finite variance, σ^2.

Suppose a sample of size n is drawn from $f(y)$ and $\bar{Y}_n$ is the mean of the sample; that is

$$\bar{Y}_n = \frac{y_1 + y_2 + y_3 + \cdots + y_n}{n}.$$

Using the above axiom as well as the preceding and concurrent definitions, one can apply mathematical logic to deduce the following theorem: the distribution of $\bar{Y}_n$ approaches normal with mean μ and variance σ^2/n as n increases infinitely. This is the well-known and extremely important central limit theorem.

The second major domain of statistics is experimental statistics. This is the world of the consumer of the products of the mathematical statistician. The empirical scientist using statistical models attempts to find a correspondence between the formal system and his empirical area of interest. In this process, the scientist substitutes specific expressions and constants for the free terms of the formal model. Thus, the random variable X might become a set of intelligence quotients with their associated probabilities of occurrence. If the axioms are valid with these substitutions, he has an interpretation of the formal system within his empirical domain. He may then take advantage of all the theorems which were deduced on the basis of the mathematical model for the analysis and interpretation of his data.

The assumptions of which we typically speak in psychology are the axioms of certain mathematical models. Thus when it is necessary to assume that a certain psychological variable is normally distributed, there is an axiom in the corresponding formal system that states the random variable is normally distributed. The theorem in which we may be interested in is the one stating that if X is normally distributed with mean zero and unit variance, then X^2 has a χ^2 distribution with one degree of freedom. Obviously the theorem will only apply if the axiom is valid, but it frequently happens that if the axioms are violated somewhat the theorems hold approximately. Thus, if the distribution of a certain variable differs from the normal by a moderate amount, the distribution of its square may be approximately of χ^2 form. The more statistical theorems are insensitive to violations of the axioms, the more *robust* they are said to be.

The deductions of the statistical model are then valid for the real world interpretation to the extent that the assumptions are satisfied. When so satisfied we can perform the algebraic transformations specified by the model in its applicable theorems. A theorem may state that a certain random variable is distributed as t, or that the probability is .95 that a certain confidence bound encompasses the parameter, or that the ratio of two sums of squares multiplied by a constant is distributed as F.

The above discussion should certainly not be interpreted as implying that the axioms of statistical models must be satisfied for the results of algebraic computations upon data to be meaningful. As discussed in the preceding section, an investigator may perform computations upon data for descriptive purposes as well as for inferential purposes. For example, various statements may be made about a set of numbers on the basis of knowledge of the median or the standard deviation or the correlation coefficient. These statements are based, although indirectly, upon the mathematical model underlying ordinary algebra. Clearly when the usual statistical assumptions are met, such as normality and independence, many more powerful and important interpretative statements can be made. Descriptions or descriptive interpretations are limited to statements about the characteristics of the actual data at hand while generalizations or inferential interpretations refer to the population from which the data at hand are a subset.

A Survey of the Theory of Probability

THE ROLE OF PROBABILITY

A common feature across scientific as well as applied disciplines is the variability of the results of observation. Even when external conditions are controlled as carefully as the capabilities of the investigator permit, he cannot be sure he will obtain the same result on two separate occasions. Empirical processes that produce variability in observational results are called *random phenomena*.

From a formal perspective, probability is a mathematical discipline that deals with random phenomena. Since it is a mathematical discipline, probability incorporates random phenomena into a logical structure containing defined and undefined terms, axioms, and the various theorems deduced from other parts of the structure. Probability theory is without empirical content but may be interpreted in terms of the random phenomena of any empirical area. In fact, it is this detached, yet relevant, position that probability maintains with respect to empirical disciplines that puts it in the category of a mathematical model. As stated in the preceding section, a mathematical axiom system is said to be a model of a class of empirical phenomena if there is some way of translating the concepts and axioms of the mathematical system into the terms and relationships of the empirical domain. The empirical system provides an interpretation of the mathematical system and the theorems of the model may be retranslated in order to arrive at empirical conclusions. In the preceding section we illustrated the interpretation of statistical models in an empirical domain by the use of such concepts as normality and chi square. In the case of the probability model, such concepts as points, events, space, probability as a numerical quantity, Bernoulli trial, and binomial theorem have comparable roles. These roles will be discussed in detail in the following sections, but the broad features of the formal-empirical relationship may be illustrated by the game of drawing a single card from a deck of 52 cards. Each of the 52 possible empirical outcomes is equated with a point in probability theory and, assuming a well-shuffled deck, the probability value of 1/52 is assigned to each point. But the probabilities assigned to each of the points need not be equal; it is only required that they be numerical values between 0 and 1 and that they sum to 1. If we consider an event like "the occurrence of a picture card," the theorems of probability theory may be used to compute its probability.

Let us start with the intuitive notion of what is meant by a set of points. The set may consist of a single point, three points, ten points, forty-seven points, a hundred million points, or even an infinite number of points.

Given two such sets it is frequently useful to relate them by the concept of function. Let A be one set of points and B another. A function from A to B is defined as a grouping of correspondences such that with each point in A there is associated one and only one point in B. We shall use the letter f to represent a function. The set A is called the domain of definition of the function. If we let f(a) be the point in B corresponding to the point a in A (as specified by the function), f(a) is called the value of the function at point a and the set of all values is called the range.

To illustrate the concept of function imagine a point associated with each adult (18 and older) in the city of Los Angeles. The set of all these points is set A. Suppose set B consists of a point for each integer between 18 and 150. The statement, "a person's age at his last birthday," would then be a function since it consists of a set of correspondences such that each adult (point in A) has one and only one age (point in B). The ages are the values [f(a)] of the function.

We say that two sets are in a one-to-one correspondence for a particular function, f, if (1) different points in A have different values in B, and (2) if for every point, b, in B, there is one point, a, in A such that b is the value of $a[b =$ f(a)]. For example, the dots . . . . are in a one-to-one correspondence with the integers 1, 2, 3, 4 by the function specifying that, starting from the left, each dot is assigned the integer corresponding to its position (the first dot is assigned 1, the second 2, etc.). Obviously, different dots have different numbers and every number is the value of one dot.

Actually, a function relating the points in a set to the positive integers provides a method of specifying the number of points in the set. For a positive integer n, let I_n be the set whose points are the integers 1, 2, 3, 4, . . . , n. In addition, let I be the set of all positive integers—that is, the integers obtained by counting 1, 2, 3, 4, 5, and so on forever. If a set A can be put into one-to-one correspondence with some I_n, it is said to be finite (and, in fact, of cardinal number n). Otherwise set A is infinite (except for the set consisting of no points which is considered finite). If set A can be put into a one-to-one correspondence with I, it is countably infinite. A is non-countable if it is neither finite nor countably infinite.

An example of non-countability is the set of points lying on a line drawn between any two points.

In probability and statistics, a set of points used for purposes of analysis is most frequently referred to as a sample space. The use of the term sample space reflects the method whereby mathematical and empirical worlds are associated. That is, as we shall later discuss in detail, each point in the basic set of points is equated with one of the possible outcomes for the experiment in question, and the outcomes are frequently obtained as samples.

A sample space is often called discrete if it contains a finite or countably infinite number of points. On occasion one also sees references to continuous sample spaces, but this particular use depends on the intuitive notion of a continuum of points and is not formally defined.

In the discussion that follows we shall restrict our attention to discrete sample spaces because of the many complications associated with non-countability. But the basic concepts are the same so that understanding of the discrete space puts one a long way toward understanding the nondiscrete.

Any grouping of points in a sample space is called an event. An event may contain only a single point or as many as the entire set of points in the sample space. In addition, there is one other event called the null event or the empty event which is the set containing no points. It may seem intuitively unreasonable to include an event like the null event since it contains no points, but the use of the concept is quite important and comparable to such definitions as any number to a zero power is one and 0! is one. One is forced into such definitions by the need to maintain consistency in the system.

Consider the roll of a single die as an example. The observer might be interested in such outcomes of the single roll as the number of times the die rolls over or the number of times it bounces off the table before stopping or even the location on the table where it comes to rest. However, it is almost always the case that in an experiment involving the roll of a die, that the experimenter or gambler, as the case may be, is interested in the number of pips that are visible looking downward on the die when it comes to rest. But it should be emphasized that the results that are observed and recorded are determined entirely by the interests of the experimenter. The mathematical model has no empirical meaning independent of the particular phenomena the experimenter chooses to observe and the method of equating the mathematical and empirical worlds. Let us assume that the experimenter chooses to observe the number of pips on top of the die that has come to rest and nothing else. There are, thus, six possible outcomes. The sample space representing this empirical experiment would then contain six points; one point corresponding to the occurrence of a single pip on top of the die, another point corresponding to two pips, a third point to three pips, and so forth. We could define an event in the sample space by combining the points corresponding to one pip, three pips, and five pips into a subset. This event could then be conveniently labeled as "an odd number of pips."

The events which contain only single points are most often called elementary or simple events. The simple events in the above example are, of course, the events containing the single point for one pip, the single point for two pips, the single point for three pips, etc. A distinction is made between a point and the event which contains only that point because of differences in the rules for relating and manipulating points and events.

The event which contains all of the points in the sample space is called the *universal event*.

The expression "event X has occurred" derives its meaning from the association of points in the sample space and empirical outcomes. Thus, if a given set of points is in event X and one of the experimental outcomes associated with these points occurs, we say that event X has occurred. In the example of the die given above we say that the event "an odd number" has occurred if the experimental outcome of one pip up, three pips up, or five pips up has resulted from the throw of the die.

Suppose intelligence is measured by a standard intelligence test and the subjects are students in a certain school district. The IQ of each individual in the district will be represented by a point in the sample space. One event might be "an IQ of 110." This event will contain all points representing individuals who achieve an IQ of 110 on the test. If we sample one individual from our group of students in the district and his IQ is 110, we say that the event "an IQ of 110" has occurred. The number of points in this event in the sample space will be precisely the number of students who have IQ's of 110.

THE AXIOMS OF PROBABILITY

Probability was previously defined in terms of a mathematical system that served as the formal framework for the operation of empirical random phenomena. But the quantity (between 0 and 1) assigned to the point corresponding to an empirical outcome, and reflecting such empirical phenomena as relative frequency and subjective feeling of likelihood, is also called probability. The context usually makes it quite clear which use is intended and so no distinction will be made here.

Before discussing the axioms of probability, it is desirable to introduce various terms and concepts that will facilitate that discussion. These deal with the relationships between events and the operations that may be performed upon events to produce new events.

The first relationship of interest is that of inclusion. Event A is said to be included in event B if every point in A is also in B; this relationship is symbolized as $A \subset B$. Two events, A and B, are said to be mutually exclusive or disjoint if they have no points in common—that is, if a point is in A it is not in B and if a point is in B it is not in A.

To refer to all points not contained in a given set we use the term complementary event. All points in the sample space that are not in event A are said to be in the complement or complementary event of A, which is designated by the symbol $\bar{A}$. Obviously the events A and $\bar{A}$ are mutually exclusive since they contain no common points. Moreover, it is clear that every point in the sample space is in either A or $\bar{A}$.

The two principal operations on sets are those of union and intersection. The union of two sets, $A \cup B$, is a new set which contains all the points in A and all the points in B. That is, if a point is in A alone or in B alone or in both A and B then the point is in the union of A and B. The intersection of events A and B, $A \cap B$, contains only those points which are in both A and B. If A and B are mutually exclusive events their intersection contains no points, or in other words, the event which is the intersection of two mutually exclusive events is the null event.

Let us illustrate each of the above by the experiment consisting of a single draw from a deck of 52 playing cards. Let event A contain the points corresponding to each of the four threes, event B to the points red threes (that is, three of hearts and three of diamonds), event C to the points corresponding to all black cards (that is, spades and clubs), event D to the points corresponding to spades, and event E to the four points derived from the four kings. It is apparent that event B is included in event A ($B \subset A$); that events A and E are mutually exclusive;

that the complement of event C ($\bar{C}$) is an event that contains the points corresponding to the red cards; that the union of events A and D ($A \cup D$) consists of an event containing points corresponding to the thirteen spades plus the three of hearts, the three of diamonds, and the three of clubs; and that the intersection of A and C ($A \cap C$) consists of the three of spades and the three of clubs.

The operations of union and intersection may be extended to any number of sets. Thus, if we have the sets A, B, C, D, E, F, their union is the event

$$A \cup B \cup C \cup D \cup E \cup F$$

which contains all the points unique to any of the events or common to any grouping of them. Similarly their intersection is the event

$$A \cap B \cap C \cap D \cap E \cap F$$

which contains only those points common to all the events.

The concepts are represented for a countable infinity of events by

$$A \cup B \cup C \cup D \ . \ . \ . \ . \ . \ .$$

and

$$A \cap B \cap C \cap D \ . \ . \ .$$

Finally, a given grouping of events is said to be exhaustive if their union contains every point in the sample space.

With the notation provided by the above discussion we are now ready to return to probability. A probability function on a sample space occurs if each of the following three axioms is satisfied:

Axiom 1. To every event, A, in the sample space there corresponds a certain number called the probability of A, designated by the symbol $P(A)$, which satisfies the inequality

$$0 \leq P(A) \leq 1.$$

Axiom 2. The probability of the universal event (the event containing all points in the space) is 1. That is, if we use the symbol S to designate the universal event, $P(S) = 1$.

Axiom 3. The probability associated with the union of a finite or countably infinite union of mutually exclusive events equals the sum of the probabilities of the separate events. That is

$$P(A_1 \cup A_2 \cup \ldots \cup A_n) = P(A_1) + P(A_2) + \ldots + P(A_n)$$

and

$$P(A_1 \cup A_2 \cup A_3 \cup \ldots) = P(A_1) + P(A_2) + P(A_3) + \ldots$$

A sample space with associated numbers that satisfy these three axioms is called a probability space.

Let us illustrate the reasonableness of these axioms in terms of the relative frequency interpretation of probability used in gambling games. There are six points in the sample space associated with the experiment of throwing a single die when interest lies in the number of pips on top. Except for the universal event, the axioms of probability do not tell us specifically what

numbers to assign to the events. They only specify the relationships that must exist among the numbers that are assigned. Unless there is contrary information, we assume that a die is unbiased, which means that each side has an equal probability of appearing topmost; in other words, over an extended array of throws of the die we would expect each of the six surfaces to appear on top one-sixth of the time. Each of the elementary events (events with only one point) is thus assigned a probability of one-sixth. The event "the occurrence of four or fewer pips" is the union of the four mutually exclusive events: "the occurrence of one pip," "the occurrence of two pips," and so on. This union event is assigned a probability of four-sixths which is equal to one-sixth plus one-sixth plus one-sixth plus one-sixth. Other mutually exclusive events have similarly assigned probabilities. The universal event is, of course, composed of all six points and one of these points must occur on each throw and so the universal event has a probability of 1.

The definition of probability as a function is in accord with our earlier specification of function. Thus, corresponding to each event (which may be represented by a point in a new set of points) in our sample space there is one and only one number out of a set of possible numbers assigned in such a manner than the three axioms are satisfied.

It is probably useful to deduce a simple theorem within the system in order to illustrate the use of these axioms.

Theorem: Given any event A and its complement, $\bar{A}$,

$$P(\bar{A}) = 1 - P(A).$$

Proof

1. Rewrite the equation in the more convenient form

$$P(A) + P(\bar{A}) = 1.$$

2. By definition of complementary event,

$$A \cup \bar{A} = S.$$

and the events A and $\bar{A}$ are mutually exclusive and exhaustive. That is, every point in the sample space is in A or $\bar{A}$, but not in both.

3. By axiom 2,

$$P(S) = 1,$$

and therefore, because of step 2, above,

$$P(A \cup \bar{A}) = 1.$$

4. By axiom 3, since A and $\bar{A}$ are mutually exclusive,

$$P(A \cup \bar{A}) = P(A) + P(\bar{A}).$$

5. And finally we establish the proof by combining steps 3 and 4

$$P(A) + P(\bar{A}) = P(A \cup \bar{A}) = 1.$$

CONDITIONAL PROBABILITY

Conditional probability has assumed a place of increased significance in the scientific and statistical literature because of approaches like information theory and Bayesian inference. The latter shall be discussed later.

Within the mathematical system, conditional probability is a purely defined concept. More particularly, if $P(B/A)$ is the probability that event B will occur given that event A has occurred and $P(A)$ is not zero,

$$P(B/A) = \frac{P(A \cap B)}{P(A)}.$$

That equation provides the full definition for the term "$(P(B/A)$" just as an unabridged dictionary provides the definition for the term "motherhood." But the choice of that definition for $P(B/A)$ is certainly not arbitrary, as may be seen in the following example.

Imagine a sample space in which there is a point corresponding to each worker in a certain factory. Suppose we sample one worker from the factory and that every worker has an equal probability of being sampled. That is, if there are N workers in the factory each one has a probability $1/N$ of being selected. If there are N_G workers in the factory with gray hair and N_O who weigh more than 180 pounds, the probability that our selected man will have gray hair is N_G/N and the probability that the man will weigh more than 180 pounds is N_O/N. Now, suppose a man has been selected and we have some knowledge about one of his characteristics and would like to use that knowledge to determine the probability of his having another characteristic. For example, suppose we know that the selected man has gray hair and wish to determine the probability that a gray-haired man in the factory weighs more than 180 pounds. One may consider this problem from the point of view of a new sample space which contains points only for those men in the factory who have gray hair. The number of points in this new sample space is, of course, N_G. If N_{OG} is the number of points in this reduced sample space corresponding to men who are over 180 pounds in weight (they, of course, also have gray hair since the points in this space represent only men with gray hair), the probability that a man with gray hair is also over 180 pounds is N_{OG}/N_G. Since it is known that the man in question has gray hair and N_{OG}/N_G is the probability that he weighs over 180 pounds conditional upon that fact (that is, only men with gray hair are considered), the ratio N_{OG}/N_G has historically been called a conditional probability. Let us now modify the ratio without changing its value.

Dividing numerator and denominator by N gives us $N_{OG}/N \div N_G/N$. Since N_{OG} is the number of men who are gray-haired and also over 180 pounds, N_{OG}/N represents the probability of drawing a man who is both gray-haired and over 180 pounds, or

$$\frac{N_{OG}}{N} = P(O \cap G).$$

Similarly,

$$\frac{N_G}{N} = P(G).$$

Therefore,

$$\frac{\frac{N_{OG}}{N}}{\frac{N_G}{N}} = \frac{P(O \cap G)}{P(G)},$$

and the last expression was defined above as $P(O/G)$.

What we have shown is that for the special case of a sample space with equal probabilities over the simple events, the conditional probability, $P(B/A)$, is

$$P(B/A) = \frac{P(A \cap B)}{P(A)}.$$

But this relationship is made more general in applying to all sample spaces, and hence we have conditional probability as the defined concept given earlier.

INDEPENDENCE

At an intuitive level, we may think of independent events as those which do not affect each other in the sense that the likelihood of one occurring is the same whether or not the other has occurred. In formal terms this may be written as

$$P(A/B) = P(A)$$

and

$$P(B/A) = P(B).$$

The first of these states that the probability of A occurring given that B has occurred is precisely the same as the probability of A without any knowledge regarding the occurrence of B. Actually, both of these equations are not necessary since if either one holds the second necessarily follows. To show this, suppose

$$P(A/B) = P(A).$$

Using the definition of conditional probability,

$$P(A/B) = \frac{P(A \cap B)}{P(B)}$$

and our supposition that $P(A/B) = P(A)$ gives

$$P(A) = \frac{P(A \cap B)}{P(B)},$$

so that

$$P(A \cap B) = P(A)P(B).$$

Using the definition again

$$P(B/A) = \frac{P(A \cap B)}{P(A)},$$

and substituting for $P(A \cap B)$ on the basis of the equality derived immediately above gives

$$P(B/A) = \frac{P(A)P(B)}{P(A)} = P(B),$$

which is what we wished to show.

The remainder of the proof would require showing that if $P(B/A) = P(B)$ then $P(A/B) = P(A)$, but that deduction is precisely the same as the above except for the substitution of letters.

The expression

$$P(A \cap B) = P(A)P(B)$$

is used to define the independence of events A and B. That is, if the expression holds for two events, they are said to be independent; otherwise they are dependent (or nonindependent).

The above proof may be extended to show that if

$$P(A/B) = P(A)$$

or

$$P(B/A) = P(B)$$

then

$$P(A \cap B) = P(A)P(B).$$

And if

$$P(A \cap B) = P(A)P(B)$$

then

$$P(A/B) = P(A)$$

and

$$P(B/A) = P(B).$$

That is to say, independence may be defined by a form like

$$P(A/B) = P(A)$$

or by

$$P(A \cap B) = P(A)P(B)$$

since they are logically equal.

In concluding this section on probability, it would seem desirable to mention references for more detailed coverage. The most thorough treatments of probability are by Feller (1957) and Parzen (1960), but a briefer, and quite respectable, discussion of sets, functions, and probability aimed at behavioral scientists may be found in Chapters 1–5 in Hays (1963).

Statistical Inference

As stated previously, statistical inference refers to the process of drawing conclusions about populations on the basis of samples that are randomly drawn subsets from the populations. Before discussing the classical theory (Neyman-Pearson) as well as considering the newer approaches of decision theory and Bayesian inference, it is again desirable to introduce terms, concepts, and relationships that are necessary for the exposition.

RANDOM VARIABLE

Typically, when an experiment is conducted or a study made, one assigns numbers in accord with the particular config-

urations of results. When two dice are thrown, for example, in the game of craps, interest lies in the total number of pips on top. In other words, with each configuration of possible pip arrays resulting from the throw of the dice a number is associated which is the sum of the number of pips on the dice. In a similar fashion one might sample a single person from a larger group and have interest in his height or his weight or his intelligence quotient as measured by a standard test. In each case, interest lies not in the spatial configuration of the individual or his hair color or his attitude toward religion, but only in the specific number of interest. More explicitly, if height or weight or IQ are considered variables, then the experimenter is interested in the particular value of the variable which is associated with the individual who is selected.

In each of these cases, there is an operation or a rule that assigns to each possible configuration resulting from the conduct of an experiment a numerical value. But a set of correspondences of that sort is precisely what is defined as a function earlier in this chapter. That is, with each point that represents an outcome (or a potential configuration of experimental results) in the space of all possible experimental outcomes, there is associated one and only one numerical value or point in the set of all possible numerical values. The set of possible outcomes is thus the domain of the function and the set of numerical values the range.

Although it would seem natural to think that the term random variable refers to the numerical values in the range, that is not the case. Instead, the term has been associated with the function itself and thus refers to the set of correspondences. The reason for this use stems from the desirability of using the term random variable only for a set of values where there are probabilities associated with the values. The functional concept of random variable provides the correspondence between value and probability by associating value with point in probability space which in turn is the point in an elementary event that has an assigned probability. One could equivalently, as many have done, define a random variable as a range of number events each with an associated probability. But the functional definition has certain deductive advantages. Thus it is possible to associate with the same probability space two or more random variables.

In accord with the notational form that has become relatively standard we shall most often use capital letters, like X, to refer to a random variable and small letters, like x, to one of its values. When a Greek letter is used to designate a random variable, a subscript will be used to specify one of its values; thus if θ is a random variable, θ_i is a value.

PROBABILITY DISTRIBUTIONS

Suppose we have a finite probability space with a random variable defined over the points of the space. Since only one value is associated with each elementary event in the sample space (but there may be any number of elementary events in the sample space associated with a given value) the number of values which the random variable may assume is necessarily finite. Although it may be a nuisance in some cases, one could provide a list of the possible values of the random variable and their associated probabilities. One would accomplish this for a given value by adding up the probabilities associated with the array of elementary events that are paired with that particular

History, Theory, and Methodology

value by the random variable. For example, suppose there are 52 points in a sample space corresponding to the 52 playing cards and suppose the value of the random variable associated with a given elementary event is the number of the card if it lies between one and ten. The number eleven is associated with Jacks, the number twelve with Queens, and the number thirteen with Kings. The experiment consists of drawing a single card after the pack is thoroughly shuffled. The probability corresponding to a four would then be 4/52 since there are four elementary events in the sample space associated with the value four and each has a probability 1/52.

That sort of listing of values of the random variable and their associated probabilities is an example of a probability distribution for a random variable with finite possible values. For the particular example presented above, the probability distribution (or, simply, distribution) consists of a listing of the numbers between one and thirteen together with the probability of 4/52 for each of the values.

The essential ingredients of a distribution are possible values of a random variable and associated probabilities of occurrence. In addition to a simple listing these may be given in a mathematical form like

$$P(X = x) = \binom{25}{x}\left(\frac{3}{5}\right)^x\left(\frac{2}{5}\right)^{25-x}, \text{ if } x = 0, 1, \ldots, 25$$
$$= 0 \text{ otherwise,}$$

or in the form of some kind of bar graph. In the case of the mathematical equation, the values that the random variable may assume are given to the right and the probability associated with each value is obtained by inserting the particular value into the form and reducing it to a single number.

One could use a similar method to define a probability distribution in cases where the random variable may assume a countably infinite number of values. But it is not possible to define it in this manner where the values of the random variable are noncountable in number, as, for example, any value between 0 and 500. One can, however, provide a direct pairing of values and probabilities by associating probabilities not with individual values of the random variable but with all values equal or less than some specified value x. This provides a cumulative distribution function. We have, then, a formal definition of the expression *cumulative distribution function*: Given the random variable X the cumulative distribution function of X is that function F whose values are

$$F(x) = P(X \leq x).$$

That is, the cumulative distribution function gives for each real number x the probability of a value for X equal or less than this particular x. Where X takes on only discrete values

$$F(x) = \sum_j P(X = x_j),$$

where the sum is taken over all $x_j \leq x$. As in the case of a probability distribution, the cumulative distribution may be given in tabular, graphical, or mathematical equation form.

From the cumulative distribution in the noncountable case one may derive a probability distribution which is similar in form to the probability distribution of the discrete case expressed as an equation. But the distribution for noncountable values does not provide the probabilities of individual values (only of intervals containing a noncountable number of values), and so the two types of distribution are almost always distinguished by verbal labels. The term probability function is used for discrete values and probability density function for noncountable possible values.

POPULATIONS, PARENT DISTRIBUTIONS, SAMPLING DISTRIBUTIONS

It has been said that the theory of probability allows one to infer the probable characteristics of a sample on the basis of population characteristics, whereas statistics allows one to infer the characteristics of a population on the basis of sample characteristics. This statement is not completely accurate for a number of reasons, but it does properly stress the distinction between the basic deductive process leading from primitive terms, axioms, and definitions to theorems specifying probable sampling results and the inductive process of statistical inference where the properties of the basic model are inferred from experimental data. Consequently, the inductive process by which inferences are drawn is understandable only within the context of the deductive system; mathematical theory has been discussed in the preceding sections to provide the framework. Now we are ready to put the theory into more specific terms with reference to the particular issues of statistical inference.

The population is the set of numbers in the empirical world about which we would like to infer characteristics on the basis of the methods of statistical inference. These values of the empirical world are idealized in the mathematical world by means of a random variable defined on an appropriate probability space. The associated probabilities reflect the likelihoods of occurrence of the population values in an experimental sampling scheme or by some other equivalent selection procedure. We shall refer to the probability distribution of the random variable reflecting the population values of the empirical world as the population distribution or the parent distribution.

The procedure in statistical inference is to draw a sample of size n from the population and then compute some summary characteristic of the values in the sample (called a statistic). The mean of a sample,

$$\bar{X} = \sum_{i=1}^{n} x_i,$$

is such a statistic. Obviously, any one of a large array of different values could have been obtained for a given statistic depending upon the particular sample that had resulted from a sampling process; that is, $\bar{X}$, for example, could equal 5 or 12 or 26.3 or 109.7. And with each value there is a certain probability of its occurrence. This probability would be a function of the probabilities associated with the population values as well as of the particular sampling scheme.

Again, there is a parallel in the mathematical world to this set of potential values of statistics and their associated probabilities. The probability distribution associated with the corresponding random variable, defined on an appropriate sample space, is called the derived sampling distribution. The random variable and its derived sampling distribution, which parallel the possible values of the statistic and their probabilities of occurrence, are the critical elements in statistical inference.

Once an obtained value for a statistic is at hand we can feed the information into our mathematical conceptual framework to determine the likelihood that this outcome resulted from a given distribution or to estimate some characteristic of the population distribution or to determine some range which will include the value of some population distribution characteristic with a certain probability. We shall summarize each of these procedures a bit later.

It should be emphasized that all populations consist of a finite number of possible values. That is clearly the case in measurements on human beings. But even measuring a variable like time necessarily produces only a finite number of alternate possible values no matter how accurate the chronometer. We might measure time to tenths of a second or hundredths of a second or thousandths of a second or even millionths of a second. But in any event there is clearly some limit to the precision of our measurements, and this leads to a set of obtained or possible measurements of time that is necessarily finite.

Even though populations and the resulting values of statistics derived from sampling a set n from the population are necessarily finite, we frequently use population distributions and derived sampling distributions (with their associated random variables) that are of the continuous type. This is done because continuous random variables and distributions frequently provide excellent approximations for finite value sets and probabilities and are at the same time very tractable in terms of their power for mathematical deduction.

Consider an illustrative sample. Suppose our interest lies in the IQ's of the children in a certain school district. Our population is then the set of IQ's of the children in that school district. If our sampling scheme is such that each student has an equal probability of being drawn in a sample, the probability associated with each IQ would be the number of students in the district who have that IQ divided by the total number of students. In our mathematical world we could have a random variable whose values are identically the values in the population and whose probability distribution is the finite probability function identical in form to that of the real world. But it has been found repeatedly that IQ's and their associated probabilities may be very well approximated by a continuous random variable with the following probability distribution (probability density function)

$$f(x) = \frac{1}{\sqrt{2\pi}\sigma} e^{-(1/2)[(x-\mu)/\sigma]^2}, \infty < x < \infty,$$

which is the normal distribution. And the normal distribution has enormous deductive power. In fact, it has been so central in statistical inference that it is not much of an exaggeration to say that for many years normal distribution theory was statistical inference.

Let us extend that example to illustrate a derived sampling distribution. Suppose we sample a hundred children from the school district, which is saying the same as suppose we sample a hundred IQ's from the population. And suppose the statistic or sample characteristic in which we have interest is the mean of the hundred IQ's in the sample. Each possible sample mean has a certain probability of occurring. Now, corresponding to the set of possible mean IQ's in a sample of size hundred and the associated probabilities are a random variable and its probability distribution in the mathematical world. This derived sampling distribution would reflect the probabilities of the various possible means in the given sample. One important property of the normal distribution is relevant in this context. If a parent population is normal then the derived sampling distribution of the means of samples from this population distribution is normal.

POINT ESTIMATION

As implied above, statistical inference falls into certain classes in accord with the nature of the conclusion that the experimenter desires. One such class is estimation. In the case of point estimation one desires to infer the value of a characteristic of a population probability distribution called a parameter. A parameter is a variable or rule that occurs in the mathematical equation of a probability distribution, such as μ or σ in the normal distribution. Another form of estimation is interval estimation. In interval estimation the goal is to state a range which includes the value of a certain parameter with a given probability. While an interval estimate is less precise in form than a point estimate, it has the advantage of enabling one to accompany the estimate with a probability statement as to its accuracy.

The statistic used in the process of point estimation of a parameter is called an estimator. The question arises as to which of the many available statistics one uses as the estimator. Some choices would seem intuitively obvious, like the use of the mean of a sample to estimate the mean of a population distribution. But there are many cases in which the choice is not intuitively obvious and, besides, as any experienced observer will testify, that which is intuitively obvious is not always logically sound.

The theory of point estimation consists of two aspects. In the first, there are certain specified criteria for what is considered a good estimator. One must have an estimation procedure at hand; one then examines the estimation procedure in the context of the various criteria and decides on the relative adequacy of the procedure on the basis of whether the criteria are or are not satisfied. In aspect two, on the other hand, certain methods of proceeding are specified whereby one will get a relatively good estimate of a parameter if the procedure is followed.

Consider aspect one, the criteria for a good estimator. First, a comment on notation: a caret is used over the symbol for a parameter to designate the sample function used to estimate the parameter. Thus, if the parameter is θ its estimator is $\hat{\theta}$.

An estimator is unbiased if its average value over a very large number of samples is equal to the parameter value. For example, the mean of a sample, $\bar{X}$, is an unbiased estimator of the mean of the population, μ, since, if a very large number of samples are drawn from the population and a mean computed each time, as $\bar{X}_1$, $\bar{X}_2$, $\bar{X}_3$, $\bar{X}_4$, etc., where the subscript indicates the sample number, the average of a very large number of these $\bar{X}$'s is equal to μ.

A consistent estimator is one that tends, in a probabilistic sense, to get closer and closer to the value of the parameter as the sample size increases. That is, with a consistent estimator one can be sure that the estimate will be close in value to the parameter if a large enough sample is drawn. Letting $\hat{\theta}_i$ be a value for the estimator and $|\hat{\theta}_i - \theta|$ be a discrepancy from the parameter's value, a consistent estimator is one for which the probability is 1 that this discrepancy is equal or less than any small value (say ϵ) for large enough sample size.

The third property applies only to the class of unbiased estimators of θ. Among all unbiased estimators of θ, the one that has the smallest variance is called the minimum variance, unbiased estimator of θ. In other words, for a given sample size n, a minimum variance estimator will tend to have a value closer to the parameter than any other unbiased estimator. The unbiased estimator with the minimum variance is sometimes called the efficient estimator.

An estimator $\hat{\theta}$ is a sufficient estimator of the parameter θ if $\hat{\theta}$ contains all the information in the sample about θ. In other words, if one has a sufficient estimator all the information about the parameter in the sample has been exhausted, and further knowledge of sampling results does not help the estimating process. More formally, $\hat{\theta}$ is sufficient if the conditional distribution of sample variables, given $\hat{\theta}$, is independent of the parameter θ.

We turn now to the second aspect of point estimation which involves the specification of procedures that lead to good estimators. The first of these procedures is called the principle of maximum likelihood estimation. It depends upon a concept called the likelihood function. Let the likelihood function be designated by L. If X is a discrete random variable and $P(X = x_i) = p_i$, then, for a sample of size n, where x_1 is the first value in the sample, x_2 the second, and so on,

$$L = p_1 p_2 p_3 \ldots p_n.$$

In this case, L is the probability of obtaining the particular sample of n values in the designated order.

On the other hand, if X is a continuous random variable with probability density function $f(x)$, then

$$L = f(x_1)f(x_2) \ldots f(x_2).$$

For the continuous case, L is not the probability of obtaining the particular sample, but it is clearly of a form that reflects the likelihood of the sample, as for discrete X.

To illustrate, suppose an urn contains m red balls and n green balls and suppose a sample of 4 balls is drawn with replacement (a ball drawn on a particular trial is replaced in the urn prior to the next trial). The urn is well-shaken prior to each draw, and so we set the probability of a red ball

$$p_r = \frac{m}{m+n}$$

and the probability of a green ball

$$p_g = \frac{n}{m+n} = 1 - p_r.$$

The probability space contains two points, one representing a red draw with probability p_r, and one representing a green draw with p_g. Although this step is frequently omitted because it doesn't contribute much to the solution of simple problems, we shall create a random variable by assigning the value 0 to the elementary event containing the point for a red outcome and a 1 for a green outcome. The possible samples (and their probabilities) are: 0 0 0 0 (p_r^4), 0 0 0 1 $(p_r^3 p_g)$, 0 0 1 0 $(p_r^3 p_g)$, $\ldots$, 1 1 1 0 $(p_r p_g^3)$, 1 1 1 1 (p_g^4). The probabilities given in parentheses are the values of the likelihood function (called likelihoods) for the particular sampling results. Clearly the magnitude of each likelihood is a function of the values of p_r or p_g (either one since $p_r + p_g = 1$). And, in general, a likelihood for a given sampling result will be more or less, depending upon the value of the parameter or parameters that enter into the probability distribution.

In the case of a normal distribution the likelihood function for an independent sample of size 4 is

$$L = \frac{1}{\sqrt{2\pi}\sigma} e^{-(1/2)(x_1-\mu)^2/\sigma^2} \cdot \frac{1}{\sqrt{2\pi}\sigma} e^{-(1/2)(x_2-\mu)^2/\sigma^2}$$
$$\times \frac{1}{\sqrt{2\pi}\sigma} e^{-(1/2)(x_3-\mu)^2/\sigma^2} \cdot \frac{1}{\sqrt{2\pi}\sigma} e^{-(1/2)(x_4-\mu)^2/\sigma^2}$$

which is obviously a function of μ and σ.

Let us now see how the likelihood function may be used in estimation. Returning to our example of the urn, consider two different values for the parameter p_r, say, p_{r_1} and p_{r_2}. Suppose that inserting these parameters in the likelihood function produces a higher value when p_{r_1} is used than when p_{r_2} is used. This may be symbolized

$$L(p_{r_1}) > L(p_{r_2}).$$

To illustrate by a numerical example, let $p_{r_1} = 1/2$ and $p_{r_2} = 1/3$, and suppose our sample produced the result 0001. Then

$$L(p_{r_1}) = (\tfrac{1}{2})^3(\tfrac{1}{2}) = \tfrac{1}{16}$$

and

$$L(p_{r_2}) = (\tfrac{1}{3})^3(\tfrac{2}{3}) = \tfrac{2}{81}.$$

If one had to choose between these values as an estimate of the parameter p_r for that particular sample, surely the choice would be p_{r_1} or, in the numerical example, 1/2.

The essential feature of the principle of maximum likelihood estimation is that it leads to that estimate of the value of the parameter for which the value of the likelihood function is a maximum. In the discrete case it chooses that estimate which if substituted for the the value of the parameter in the probability function will lead to a higher probability for the obtained sample than all other possible values. The methods of calculus permit a search over all possible values for the parameter and the choice of that particular value that leads to the highest value of the likelihood function. Where it is desired to estimate two or more parameters, the likelihood function is a function of all of them and the maximum likelihood estimators for all parameters will be those numbers that lead to the maximum value of the likelihood function.

Maximum likelihood estimation has a good deal of intuitive appeal. That is, it says that when we are faced with the task of deciding what is the value of a parameter, we choose the one that leads to the highest prior probability for the obtained result. We are, in essence, betting on the value associated with the highest probability for the obtained result. In addition to this intuitive appeal, maximum likelihood estimators have a number of very desirable properties. In fact, under quite general conditions, maximum likelihood estimators are consistent, asymptotically efficient and a function of sufficient estimators when they exist. In addition, the distribution of a maximum likelihood estimator approaches normality as the sample size gets larger and possesses the quite important invariance property. By invariance property we mean the following: The maximum likelihood estimator of a monotonic function of the parameter is simply that function of the maximum likelihood estimator of the parameter. That is, let $\hat{\theta}$ be the maximum likelihood estimator of θ. If $G(\theta)$ is a monotonic function of θ, then the maximum likelihood estimator of $G(\theta)$ is $G(\hat{\theta})$.

Another frequently used estimation procedure is the method of least squares. This method has been used most widely to estimate the parameters in the process of fitting a line to observed data. Suppose we have the scores on a college entrance examination as well as grade point averages for a number of college seniors. And suppose we hypothesize that there is a linear relationship between college entrance examination score and grade point average. A linear relationship between grade point average and test score would be represented by the equation

$$Y = \alpha + \beta X + \epsilon,$$

where α and β are the parameters that are to be estimated; ϵ is an error term that allows for random and unpredictable components that affect the magnitude of Y. It is assumed that the expected value of ϵ is 0 and its variance, for all values of X, is σ^2. If, as is customarily done, we let a be the estimate of α and b the estimate of β, the line derived from the estimation process is

$$Y = a + bX + e,$$

where e reflects the discrepancies between obtained observations and the points on the line. Points on the line are usually shown by the form

$$Y' = a + bX,$$

where Y' is called the predicted value.

In the estimation process it is clearly desirable to arrive at an a and a b that define a line passing most closely through the points on a plot of examination scores by grade point averages. One approach is to choose that line (by choosing a line we mean choosing a and b) which for each x minimizes the squared discrepancies between the observed values and the points on the line. In other words, choose that value for a and that value for b that minimizes

$$\sum (Y - Y')^2 = \sum (e^2).$$

The procedure of choosing the line that minimizes the sum of these squared discrepancies is called the method of least squares. This is certainly a reasonable way to produce a best fitting line. In addition, the method of least squares may be used even where the model is nonlinear. For example, one may obtain the estimates of the parameters in a quadratic function by the method of least squares.

Other estimation procedures are the method of moments, the Bayes' procedure, and the minimax principle. Discussion of these procedures will not be attempted.

Interval Estimation

It is obvious that in all but the rarest of cases a point estimate differs from the parameter value. But by how much and with what probability, we cannot say. The method of interval estimation overcomes this shortcoming by providing an estimated range of values within which the parameter lies with a certain probability. The length of a confidence interval will tend to be long or short as the variance of the derived sampling distribution is large or small.

Suppose the derived sampling distribution is normal with variance σ^2 and suppose we desire a .95 level of confidence that our interval does indeed include the parameter mean value. We know that for a normal distribution the probability of a value in the range -1.96σ to $+1.96\sigma$ about μ is .95. In other words, when sampling from a normal distribution, ninety-five times in a hundred a value between -1.96σ and $+1.96\sigma$ about μ will be obtained. This characteristic may be used to set up confidence intervals. Assume that the estimator is unbiased.

Imagine that we subtract 1.96σ from each possible value of the derived sampling distribution of the sample mean, and also add 1.96σ to the value. Associated with each value of the derived sampling distribution will be an interval that starts at 1.96σ below the value and goes up to 1.96σ above the value. By this procedure we are setting up a functional relationship between possible values of our statistic and intervals. These intervals are of the form

$$\hat{\theta}_i - 1.96\sigma \text{——} \hat{\theta}_i + 1.96\sigma.$$

Let us return for a moment to consideration of the derived sampling distribution of the mean. Take the value that is precisely 1.96σ below θ in the distribution. Clearly, the interval derived from this value will include the parameter (if only at its end point) because the interval is derived at its upper limit by adding 1.96σ to $\hat{\theta}_i$. In a similar fashion, the interval derived from the point in the distribution exactly 1.96σ above θ will include the parameter because the lower end of the interval is derived by subtracting 1.96σ from the obtained $\hat{\theta}_i$. All points between 1.96σ below θ and 1.96σ above θ will a fortiori lead to intervals that include θ. However, all points smaller than 1.96σ below θ and larger than 1.96σ above θ will lead to intervals that do not include θ. Finally, we have the fact that the probability of a value between 1.96σ below θ and 1.96σ above θ is .95. Therefore, we can state that if we subtract 1.96σ from each $\hat{\theta}_i$ and add 1.96σ to it, we will have intervals with a probability of .95 that they will cover the parameter θ. The probability of .95 in this case means that ninety-five times in a hundred the desired result of covering the parameter will be achieved. Symbolically, the confidence interval is written in the following form

$$P[\hat{\theta}_i - 1.96\sigma \leq \theta \leq \hat{\theta}_i + 1.96\sigma] = .95.$$

The choice of the .95 confidence interval was, of course, arbitrary. If, for example, one had chosen the .99 confidence interval, one would use 2.58σ rather than 1.96σ since the probability of a value, in the normal distribution, between 2.58σ below the mean and 2.58σ above the mean is .99. In general, the $1 - \alpha$ confidence interval is

$$p[\hat{\theta}_i - k_{(1-\alpha)}\sigma \leq \theta \leq \hat{\theta}_i + k_{(1-\alpha)}\sigma] = 1 - \alpha$$

where $k_{(1-\alpha)}$ is the value of the normal distribution such that the probability of a value between $-k_{(1-\alpha)}\sigma$ and $+k_{(1-\alpha)}\sigma$ is $(1 - \alpha)$.

History, Theory, and Methodology

In testing a statistical hypothesis, one plays a game in which he pretends that a certain state of affairs is, in fact, true. He then looks at certain features of his sampling results and deduces the likelihood of their occurrence, given the state of affairs which he has accepted as true. If the likelihood of the outcome is sufficiently low, given the accepted state of affairs, the experimenter concludes that it may not be reasonable to accept the truth of the state of affairs upon which his deductive logic was based. If the likelihood is not that low, he concludes that the outcome of the experiment is in accord with the state of affairs as postulated.

As in all uses of statistics in drawing conclusions about empirical matters, there is a mathematical component or model that parallels an empirical system. For the moment, our attention will be directed to the formal or mathematical aspects.

The state of affairs referred to in the first paragraph above consists of two portions: the assumptions and the hypothesis. These together form the axioms of the mathematical system forming the framework of the deductive system. The assumptions are not subject to verification by the empirical test, only the hypothesis is.

We consider an example to illustrate the process of hypothesis testing. The assumptions are that the parent distribution is normal and it has a standard deviation of 5. The hypothesis to be tested is that the mean of this parent distribution is equal to 63. We know from statistical theory that if our parent distribution is normal with $\sigma = 5$ and $\mu = 63$, the sampling distribution of means is normal with

$$\sigma_{\bar{x}} = \frac{\sigma}{\sqrt{n}} = \frac{5.0}{\sqrt{n}}$$

and

$$\mu_{\bar{x}} = \mu = 63.0.$$

Suppose the sample size is 100. We are now in a position, accepting the assumptions and hypothesis—which were previously referred to as the state of affairs—as true, to deduce the likelihood of any particular sample mean. Suppose the sample produces

$$\bar{x} = 64.3.$$

To determine the likelihood of this outcome given the accepted state of affairs, we compute

$$z = \frac{\bar{x} - \mu}{\sigma_{\bar{x}}} = \frac{64.3 - 63.0}{.5} = 2.6.$$

And then, using tables of the normal distribution, we determine that the probability is less than 1 in a hundred of getting a deviation as large as 2.6 in either direction with the distribution specified by the assumptions and hypothesis. This, of course, is a highly unlikely outcome. But highly unlikely outcomes do occur, and so it is possible that our assumptions and hypothesis provide an accurate description of the population distribution of concern. Surely it is easy to imagine, however, a point being reached where the probability of a certain outcome, given assumptions and hypothesis, is so low that an observer questions the reasonableness of his specified state of affairs. For example,

almost anyone would question the specified state of affairs if it led to an outcome with probability of less than one in ten billion if the state of affairs is true. As one moves from a probability of the order of one in ten billion to one of the order of one in a hundred, there would, of course be less widespread agreement in calling the state of affairs into question. One might, therefore, require an extremely low probability figure to justify questioning the state of affairs were it not for another consideration to which we shall turn shortly.

Before doing so, however, let us see what questioning the state of affairs means explicitly. As stated previously, in playing the game of testing a statistical hypothesis, the assumptions are not subject to challenge when the state of affairs is questioned. Therefore, all doubt is focused upon the hypothesis. Questioning the state of affairs is synonymous with doubting the truth of the hypothesis. In the accepted jargon of statistics, when the probability of an outcome is so low given a specified state of affairs that one has serious doubts about the accuracy of the hypothesis, we say that the statistical hypothesis is rejected. Rejecting an hypothesis has no implications other than this questioning of its accuracy on the basis of the low probability of an outcome deduced from a state of affairs of which the hypothesis is a component.

If the specified state of affairs does not provide an accurate description of our population distribution, then clearly some other state of affairs is accurate. Remembering that the assumptions may not be called into question, an alternate state of affairs consists of these same assumptions plus a different hypothesis. Therefore, an alternate state of affairs is referred to as an alternate hypothesis. In playing this game, the observer is never sure as to which hypothesis is true. In the Neyman-Pearson theory of hypothesis testing, either the hypothesis or an alternate hypothesis is true, and the investigator formulates his testing procedure in these terms. When he rejects the hypothesis he is in effect accepting the alternate hypothesis and, conversely, when he accepts the hypothesis, he is rejecting the alternate hypothesis. The procedure is symmetrical except for the fact that the probability level for rejection of the hypothesis falsely is specified in advance and the probability of rejecting the alternate hypothesis, if it is true, is made as small as possible.

In the preceding example, suppose the alternate hypothesis is that μ is equal to 65. Therefore, our decision to reject the hypothesis that μ is equal to 63.0 is equivalent to a decision to accept the hypothesis that μ is equal to 65.0. And this is entirely reasonable since the obtained result of $\bar{x} = 64.3$ deviates so little from 65.0 in standard deviation units. In fact, we may determine

$$z = \frac{64.3 - 65.0}{.5} = -1.4.$$

A deviation as large or larger than 1.4 (in a positive or negative direction) has a probability of .15.

Most usually, the alternate hypothesis doesn't designate a point as in the preceding example. Typically it is a hypothesis expressed in a form like "μ is not equal to 63.0" or "μ is larger than 63.0." This will be considered in more detail later.

In the Neyman-Pearson theory, there are two types of error, a type I error which is the rejection of the hypothesis when it is, in fact, true, and a type II error which is the erroneous rejection of the alternate hypothesis. The probability of rejecting the hypothesis (or, in other words, accepting the alternate hypothesis) when the alternate is true is called the power of the test. Obviously,

Power $= 1 - P$[type II error].

A few words about terminology may be in order at this point. In the literature of the behavioral sciences the hypothesis is most frequently referred to as the null hypothesis. This term stems from the testing theory of Fisher and is of that particular form because of its frequent reference to the lack of difference between two groups being compared. It certainly makes no difference whether we use the expression null hypothesis or simply hypothesis so long as we are well aware of the phenomena to which we are referring. There is nothing sacrosanct about the null hypothesis; it is simply that hypothesis for which we control the probability of erroneous rejection, that is, the probability of a type I error. The word size is frequently used in place of the more cumbersome probability of a type I error. It is used in the form "size of the test." If the probability of a type I error in a particular case is .05, for example, we say that the size of the test is .05. Finally, the term critical region refers to the set of values which leads to a rejection of the hypothesis. That is, the probability of a value occurring in the critical region is the probability of a type I error if the hypothesis is true and the power of the test if the alternate hypothesis is true.

The initial step in testing a statistical hypothesis is to determine the desired size of the test. This is almost always .05 or .01 or .001. The specific value chosen is a compromise resulting from the joint concern of type I and type II errors. As one makes the probability of a type I error smaller and smaller, one increases the probability of a type II error or, in other words, decreases the power of the test.

We have been discussing testing statistical hypotheses with almost exclusive attention to the statistical model. But the goal of the procedure is to draw conclusions about phenomena in the empirical world. Corresponding to the assumptions and hypotheses of the statistical model are assumptions and hypotheses about numbers in the empirical world. The assumption of normality in the statistical world, for example, corresponds to an empirical assumption that a population of numbers may be well approximated by a normal distribution. The extent to which conclusions arrived at by statistical deduction apply to empirical phenomena again depends on how closely empirical and statistical statements correspond.

Once the significance level or size of the test is chosen, one chooses that critical region involving the smallest probability of type II error. This has been accomplished for the experimenter by the mathematical statistician. In the cases with which most experimenters are familiar, the critical region is chosen at one or both tails of the distribution in question. The use of one or two tails depends upon the nature of the alternate hypothesis.

In most investigations, one does not have a specific alternate hypothesis like $\mu = 65.0$, but rather a range or set of alternate values, all of which compose the alternate hypothesis. When there are a number of different possible values in a hypothesis, we have what is called a composite hypothesis. For a formal definition, it is easier to start with the contrasting hypothesis that is called a simple hypothesis. The simple hypothesis is one which specifies completely the parent distribution. For example, both the hypothesis and the alternate hypothesis in the example above were simple since they specified μ as 63.0 and 65.0, respectively, which specified the distribution completely when taken in conjunction with the assumptions of normal distribution with $\sigma = 5$. An example of a composite alternate hypothesis would be $\mu > 63.0$. Still other examples are $65.0 < \mu < 68.5$ and $\mu \neq 63.0$. In each of these examples, if the hypothesis is $\mu = 63.0$, we would be testing a simple hypothesis against a composite alternate hypothesis. One could, of course, have a composite hypothesis but one usually does not because of certain difficulties in arriving at the statistical test.

When a composite alternate hypothesis specifies values on one side of the null hypothesis, one establishes the critical region on that side. For example, if the hypothesis is $\mu = 63.0$ with the assumptions specified above and the alternate hypothesis $\mu > 63.0$, the critical region would be toward the righthand tail of the hypothesized distribution. That is, a vertical line would divide the range of possible outcomes into a lefthand portion which is the region of acceptance and a righthand portion which is the critical region in such a way that the area to the right of this vertical line under the distribution specified by the hypothesis would be equal to the significance level of the test. This is called a one-tailed test. On the other hand, if the composite alternate hypothesis specified merely that $\mu \neq 63.0$, that is, that it could lie in either direction, the critical region would lie both to the left and to the right of the distribution specified by the hypothesis. In this case there would be two vertical lines with the region of acceptance between them and the critical region in two portions to the left and to the right of these lines. In this case, the sum of the areas under the distribution specified by the hypothesis in both tails would be equal to the significance level or size of the test. A one-tailed test may be to the right or to the left depending upon whether the alternatives are to the right or to the left, respectively.

The procedure sketched above is used even when a hypothesis is in a much more complicated form like the statement that the means of two distributions are equal, or even where the means of many distributions are equal. One merely deduces from this hypothesis a characteristic or characteristics of a single distribution. And a statement regarding this characteristic or these characteristics becomes the statistical hypothesis actually under test. To illustrate, suppose the empirical hypothesis is that the mean learning score for Group A is equal to the mean learning score for Group B. One must resort to sampling procedures if Groups A and B are so large as to make it impossible or impractical to determine the learning scores of all relevant individuals in the groups. If the populations are assumed normally distributed with known variances, the statistical hypothesis takes the form

$$H_0 : \mu_A = \mu_B,$$

where μ_A is the mean of the population distribution based on Group A, and μ_B has a similar meaning.

Since distributions A and B are normal we know that the distributions of $\bar{X}_A$, $\bar{X}_B$, and of $\bar{X}_A - \bar{X}_B$ are normal. The respective standard deviations of these distributions are

$$\sigma_{\bar{X}_A} = \frac{\sigma_A}{\sqrt{n_A}},$$

$$\sigma_{\bar{X}_B} = \frac{\sigma_B}{\sqrt{n_B}},$$

and

$$\sigma_{\bar{X}_A - \bar{X}_B} = \sqrt{\sigma_{\bar{X}_A}{}^2 + \sigma_{\bar{X}_B}{}^2},$$

where n_A is the sample size from Group A, n_B the sample size from B, and independence of samples is assumed.

For purposes of the statistical test, one works with the distribution of the difference between the sample means from Groups A and B. The random variable is

$$\bar{X}_A - \bar{X}_B.$$

This random variable is normal with variance under the assumptions

$$\sigma_{\bar{X}_A}{}^2 - \sigma_{\bar{X}_B}{}^2,$$

and the hypothesis takes the form

$$\mu_A - \mu_B = 0.$$

Under the assumptions and hypothesis therefore

$$Z = \frac{(\bar{X}_A - \bar{X}_B) - (\mu_A - \mu_B)}{\sqrt{\sigma_{\bar{X}_A}{}^2 + \sigma_{\bar{X}_B}{}^2}}$$

is normally distributed with mean 0 and variance 1. Consequently, if a deviation is obtained which is as large or larger than the value established by the desired significance level, the hypothesis

$$\mu_A - \mu_B = 0$$

is rejected, otherwise it is accepted.

Those interested in further reading in the area of classical statistical inference will find the best treatments in Mood and Graybill (1963) and Hogg and Craig (1959). Those who have not had calculus will undoubtedly prefer the good, but lesser, treatments of Hays (1963) and Stillson (1966).

STATISTICAL DECISION THEORY

This approach is predicated upon the notion that the goal of statistics is to guide the investigator in deciding upon a course of action. It is usable in the classical contexts of point estimation and hypothesis testing.

Suppose appropriate action depends upon an unknown parameter, θ, which completely specifies some distribution. We assume three spaces: one containing a point for each possible value the parameter can assume, another containing a point for each possible sampling result, and the third a point for each possible action or decision. There are, respectively, the parameter, the sampling, and the decision spaces.

A decision rule is a function from the sampling space to the decision space. For example, in point estimation the decision rule is precisely what has previously been called an estimator, while in hypothesis testing the parameter may lie in one or two subspaces (one for null and one for alternate hypothesis) and the decision rule specifies accept or reject hypothesis on the basis of an observed statistic.

Since there are obviously many different functions that can

be used as the decision rule, decision theory aims at developing good rules and the methods of evaluating them. To evaluate the consequences resulting from the decisions of a particular rule, a loss function $L(d_j, \theta_i)$ is used, where d_j is a specific decision and θ_i is a parametric value. The values of the loss function are non-negative and reflect the loss in making decision d_j when θ_i is the parameter. It is usually taken to be zero when the correct decision is made.

The average loss over repeated uses of a given decision rule, d, for θ_i is called the risk, designated by $R(d, \theta_i)$. The goal of statistical inference is to select that decision rule that minimizes the risk. Unfortunately, the decision rule leading to minimum risk depends upon the value of the parameter. There are various alternative solutions to this difficulty: among them to minimize the maximum risk and to minimize the weighted average of the risks over the θ_i's. The latter is called the Bayes solution for the decision problem. If $P(\theta)$ denotes the *a priori* probability over the parameter space, the average risk over the θ's is

$$B(P, d) = \sum_{i=1}^{k} R(d, \theta_i) P(\theta_i),$$

where there are k parameter values in the space. The *a priori* probability over the parameter space is of course not a crystal clear concept but one must think of it in terms of the likelihood that each parameter value is the true one—the subjective probability of the Bayesians, as we shall see, is one approach.

Consider the following examples that illustrate the decision theory approach. Suppose we have a normal distribution with mean μ and variance 1 and we wish to estimate μ from a sample of n observations. In decision-making situations of this sort, a loss function with many desirable properties is

$$L = (\hat{\theta}_j - \theta_i)^2$$

where $\hat{\theta} = d(x_1, x_2, \ldots, x_n)$ is the estimator. According to this function, the loss is zero when $\hat{\theta}_j = \theta_i$ and increases the more $\hat{\theta}_j$ and θ_i differ.

Assuming that the *a priori* distribution of μ's is normal with mean 0 and variance 1, the Bayes estimator for μ is

$$\frac{\sum x_i}{n + 1}.$$

In general, it can be shown that the Bayes estimator differs little from the maximum likelihood estimator.

In the case of hypothesis testing, there are two possible decisions, d_n and d_a, corresponding to acceptance of the null and alternate hypothesis. Assume that these hypotheses divide the parameter space into two sets ω_n and ω_a; in which case decision d_n is preferred if the parameter is in ω_n and d_a if it is in ω_a. Accordingly,

$$L(d_n, \theta_i) = 0, \text{ if } \theta_i \text{ is in } \omega_n$$

and

$$L(d_a, \theta_i) = 0, \text{ if } \theta_i \text{ is in } \omega_a.$$

Assuming a simple hypothesis (ω_n consists of a single point which is designated θ_n) and a simple alternate hypothesis (ω_a consists of a single point designated θ_a), the risk function is

$$R(d, \theta_n) = L(d_a, \theta_n)\alpha$$

for θ_n, and

$$R(d, \theta_a) = L(d_n, \theta_a)\beta$$

for θ_a, where α and β are the probabilities of type I and type II errors, respectively. For this case, the Bayes solution leads to acceptance of the hypothesis if the likelihood of the sample under the hypothesis $\theta = \theta_n$ is more than k times larger than the likelihood of the sample under the alternate $\theta = \theta_a$. It leads to rejection if the opposite is true and to a random choice between the hypotheses if the ratio of the two likelihoods is equal to k. If $k = 1$, one simply chooses the hypothesis, θ_n or θ_a, that leads to the highest likelihood for the sample.

A thorough, but non-calculus, coverage of decision theory may be found in Chernoff and Moses (1959). Mood and Graybill (1963) provide discussion of the decision approach at a somewhat more sophisticated level mathematically.

Bayesian Inference

The essence of the Bayesian approach to statistical inference is the use of observations to change the beliefs of investigators. The method is based on a relationship between conditional probabilities which may be developed in a straightforward manner.

Suppose a probability space is divided into two sets such that every point is in one of the two sets but not in both. If H is one of the sets, it would be natural to call the other $\bar{H}$. But to facilitate communication, we will refer to the sets as H_1 and H_2 rather than H and $\bar{H}$. Similarly, suppose the space is divided into a different pair or sets in the same manner; in place of D and $\bar{D}$ in this case we shall use D_1 and D_2.

By the definition of conditional probability

$$P(H_1 \mid D_1) = \frac{P(H_1 \cap D_1)}{P(D_1)}$$

and

$$P(D_1 \mid H_1) = \frac{P(H_1 \cap D_1)}{P(H_1)}.$$

Using the relationship

$$P(H_1 \cap D_1) = P(D_1 \mid H_1)P(H_1)$$

from the second of these definitions and substituting for $P(H_1 \cap D_1)$ in the first gives

$$P(H_1 \mid D_1) = \frac{P(D_1 \mid H_1)P(H_1)}{P(D_1)}.$$

Since all points in the space are in H_1 or H_2, and $H_1 \cap D_1$ and $H_2 \cap D_1$ are mutually exclusive, it is obvious that

$$P(D_1) = P(H_1 \cap D_1) + P(H_2 \cap D_1).$$

Again using the relationships

$$P(H_1 \cap D_1) = P(D_1 \mid H_1)P(H_1)$$

and the similar

$$P(H_2 \cap D_1) = P(D_1 \mid H_2)P(H_2)$$

we get

$$P(D_1) = P(D_1 \mid H_1)P(H_1) + P(D_1 \mid H_2)P(H_2).$$

Finally, substituting this gives

$$P(H_1 \mid D_1) = \frac{P(D_1 \mid H_1)P(H_1)}{P(D_1 \mid H_1)P(H_1) + P(D_1 \mid H_2)P(H_2)}$$

or, equivalently

$$P(H_1 \mid D_1) = \frac{P(D_1 \mid H_1)P(H_1)}{\sum\limits_{k=1}^{2} P(D_1 \mid H_k)P(H_k)}.$$

This is Bayes' theorem in its simplest form.

To illustrate its meaning, suppose there are two urns, one containing two red balls and eight green balls and the other containing five of each color. The experiment consists of choosing one of the urns and a ball within the chosen urn. And suppose H_1 refers to the 8-2 urn, H_2 to the 5-5 urn, D_1 to the occurrence of a red ball, and D_2 to the occurrence of a green ball. We can think of a sample space containing 20 points, each point designated by urn and color. Suppose, finally, that the probability of choosing the urn designated H_1 is .7 and that the balls in the selected urn are well-shaken before a ball is randomly pulled from it. We have, then,

$$P(H_1) = P(\text{selecting urn } H_1) = .7,$$
$$P(H_2) = P(\text{selecting urn } H_2) = .3,$$
$$P(D_1 \mid H_1) = P(\text{drawing a red ball given that}$$
$$\text{urn } H_1 \text{ has been selected}) = 2/10,$$
$$P(D_1 \mid H_2) = P(\text{drawing a red ball given that}$$
$$\text{urn } H_2 \text{ has been selected}) = 5/10.$$

If a person knows only the end-product of this experiment—that is, whether a red or a green ball occurred—Bayes' theorem will allow him to determine the probabilities that it came from each of the urns. The letters H and D were chosen because in scientific situations the urns correspond to alternate hypotheses generating data—in this case balls colored red or green—with certain probabilities. Given a hypothesis we know the probabilities of various possible experimental results, but the inferential task is to decide among the hypotheses on the basis of results; that is where Bayes' theorem comes in. In this example,

$$P(H_1 \mid D_1) = \frac{(.2)(.7)}{(.2)(.7) + (.5)(.3)} = .48.$$

That is, knowing the result that a red ball occurred, the probability it was chosen from urn H_1 is .48. If no result were available, this probability would be .7, which is the unconditional probability of H_1.

If one regards H_1 and H_2 as referring to alternative scientific hypotheses and D_1 and D_2 as alternative sets of data resulting from an experiment, it is easy to see how Bayes' theorem may be used to draw theoretical conclusions on the basis of observed

History, Theory, and Methodology

data. Unfortunately, however, a major problem arises because of the occurrence of $P(H_k)$, for all k, in the theorem. $P(H_k)$ is the *a priori* probability of the kth hypothesis. One can readily see the difficulty by imagining that hypothesis H_1 designates the mean of a certain IQ distribution as 115 while H_2 designates it as 138. What meaning does one attach to the probabilities of these hypotheses?

One answer came from a book published by Savage (1954) which has become the Bible of Bayesian inference. He used the concept of subjective probability defined as a measure of the confidence a person has in the truth of a position, hypothesis, or theory. It is accepted that different people have different belief systems; may have different degrees of confidence in hypotheses like H_1 and H_2 above; $P(H_k)$ is personal.

In addition to the use of subjective probability in the context of Bayes' theorem (rather than probability as relative frequency) another distinguishing characteristic of the full Bayesian is his tendency to use the language and concepts of decision theory.

Let us illustrate the Bayesian method by an example from the work of Mosteller and Wallace (1964). At issue in their research was the authorship of the disputed essays of *The Federalist* papers published in 1787–88. The question of whether the author of twelve of the papers was Hamilton or Madison has been a hot item of controversy among historians. Using the relative frequencies of words as data, Mosteller and Wallace determined the odds favoring Hamilton or Madison.

In one of their examples they counted occurrences of the word "also." The distributions of use of the word by both Hamilton and Madison could be approximated. An illustration of expected counts in a paper of 2000 words follows (0, .538, .262), (1, .334, .351), (2, .103, .235), (3, .0214, .105), and (4, .00331, .0352).*

Suppose "also" occurs four times in a 2000 word paper and we wish to determine the odds that Hamilton wrote the paper. Let hypothesis H_h be that Hamilton wrote the paper and H_m be that Madison wrote it. And let $P(i_h)$ be the probability of i occurrences of the word given that Hamilton wrote the paper; $P(i_m)$ is similarly defined. Finally, the *a priori* subjective probabilities that hypotheses H_h and H_m are true are designated p_h and p_m. Bayes' theorem is, then,

$$P(H_h|i) = \frac{P(i|H_h)P_h}{P(i|H_h)P_h + P(i|H_m)P_m}.$$

The authors argue that certain computational and intuitive advantages result from the use of odds rather than probabilities. The odds for H_h relative to H_m are given by the ratio of the relevant probabilities. Accordingly

$$\text{Odds}(H_h \text{ to } H_m|i) = \frac{P(H_h|i)}{P(H_m|i)} = \frac{P(i|H_h)P_h}{P(i|H_m)P_m}$$

$$= \left(\frac{P_h}{P_m}\right)\left(\frac{P(i|H_h)}{P(i|H_m)}\right)$$

$$= (a \text{ priori odds}) \times (\text{ratio of likelihoods}).$$

Returning to the example above in which $i = 4$, if we

*The numbers in parentheses are, respectively, frequency, probability of that frequency by Hamilton, and probability of that frequency by Madison.

initially thought the authorship was a toss-up between Hamilton and Madison, the final odds would be

$$\text{Odds}(H_h \text{ to } H_m|4) = \frac{.5}{.5} \cdot \frac{.00331}{.0352},$$

or about 10 to 1 in favor of Madison. On the other hand, if we were initially quite sure that Hamilton was the author, say with $P_h = .999$ and $P_m = .001$, we have

$$\text{Odds}(H_h \text{ to } H_m|4) = \frac{.999}{.001} \cdot \frac{.00331}{.0352} \cong \frac{100}{1}.$$

In this case the observation of four uses of "also" (an event more likely by Madison than by Hamilton) has reduced our subjective odds favoring Hamilton from about (1000 to 1) to (100 to 1).

As final comments on Bayesian inference, it should be pointed out that Bayesians are particularly unhappy with the significance testing procedure whereby the size α is chosen relatively arbitrarily and then a decision rule chosen that maximizes power. They argue that loss considerations and prior (subjective) probabilities must enter into the decision rule explicitly. While Bayesians allow point estimation in the manner described above under "Decision Theory," they reject the Neyman-Pearson method of confidence intervals since the procedure depends upon the concept of relative frequencies over infinite replications.

Initial thrust for the current Bayesian emphasis came from the monograph of Savage (1954). Broader coverage of the methods may be found in Schlaifer (1961) and Raiffa and Schlaifer (1961), with the latter being considerably more mathematical than the former. A quite comprehensive treatment of Bayesian methods was written by Lindley (1965) who, among other things, translates various classical statistical methods into Bayesian terms. Summaries for behavioral scientists have been contributed by Edwards, Lindman, and Savage (1963) and by Binder (1964).

References

BINDER, A. Statistical theory. *Annual Review of Psychology*, 1964, *15*, 277–310.

CHERNOFF, H., and L. E. MOSES. *Elementary decision theory.* New York: Wiley, 1959.

EDWARDS, W., H. LINDMAN, and L. J. SAVAGE. Bayesian statistical inference for psychological research. *Psychological Review*, 1963, *70*, 193–242.

FELLER, W. *An introduction to probability theory and its applications.* (2nd ed.). Vol. I. New York: Wiley, 1957.

HAYS, WILLIAM L. *Statistics for psychologists.* New York: Holt, 1963.

——— Statistical theory. *Annual Review of Psychology*, 1968, *19*, 417–36.

HOGG, R., and A. CRAIG. *Introduction to mathematical statistics.* New York: Macmillan, 1959.

LINDLEY, D. V. *Introduction to probability and statistics from a Bayesian view point: Pt. 1, Probability; Pt. 2, Inference.* London: Cambridge University Press, 1965.

MOOD, A. M. and F. A. GRAYBILL *Introduction to the theory of statistics* (2nd ed.). New York: McGraw-Hill, 1963.

MOSTELLER, F. and D. L. WALLACE, *Inference and disputed authorship: The Federalist.* Reading, Mass.: Addison-Wesley, 1964.

MYERS, JEROME L. *Fundamentals of experimental design.* Boston: Allyn and Bacon, 1966.

PARZEN, E. *Modern probability theory and its applications.* New York: Wiley, 1960.

RAIFFA, H., and R. SCHLAIFER. *Applied statistical decision theory.* Boston: Harvard University Press, 1961.

SAVAGE, L. J. *The foundations of statistics.* New York: Wiley, 1954.

SCHLAIFER, R. *Introduction to statistics for business decisions.* New York: McGraw Hill, 1961.

STILLSON, D. W. *Probability and statistics in psychological research and theory.* San Francisco: Holden-Day, 1966.

WINER, B. J. *Statistical principles in experimental design.* (2nd ed.) New York: McGraw Hill, 1971.

Introduction

Very generally, measurement may be defined as the classification of observations into categories according to specific rules. The categories may be said to possess quantitative characteristics if they can be shown or assumed to behave according to certain mathematical principles. In psychology, the ways in which the classification should take place and the methods for quantifying the category scheme have not been immediately obvious. The field of psychometrics is concerned with how best to make the observations, classify them, and go from the manifest categories themselves to quantitative scales.

To a large extent, its prime concern is with the latter function. This is because the primary level of classification of observations in psychology is often either one of simply counting the number of times a given event, such as a bar-press or the correct response to a problem, occurs, or of a measurement in physical units, such as the number of microamps of current in a circuit or the number of grams of food provided. Often, neither of these more or less directly measured kinds of quantities is felt to reflect directly the relevant psychological quantities. Rather, it is felt necessary to go from them to psychological variables that are in some sense more valid through varying degrees of processing in accordance with certain specific models for the observations. The main focus of psychometrics is on the development of quantitative models for certain kinds of data and of procedures for applying the models. The emphasis is not primarily on the verification of the model as such, but rather with its use for the purpose of attaching numbers to stimuli and persons.

In general and certainly as discussed here, psychological measurement, psychometrics, concentrates on "software," ways of manipulating the observations that have been gathered, rather than upon instrumentation for the actual gathering of the data. The tasks of controlling stimuli to be presented and recording of responses made are left to the experimental psychologist or the test construction specialist, albeit the same person may appear in both the role of experimenter and psychometrician.

It may be useful to mention in this introductory section the

Norman Cliff

Psychometrics

5

relation between psychometrics and statistics. Here, it must be admitted that the situation is rather curious. Despite the fact that most of the data of psychometrics is statistical in nature rather than deterministic, statistical considerations of the inferential, sampling theory kind are often treated only secondarily. The data are often treated as if they were deterministic, and the models proposed are the same. It is often only at later stages in the development of a given model that sampling considerations come into play; indeed, as late as the 1950's population quantities and sample estimates were almost routinely treated interchangeably in psychometrics. Fortunately, there is an increasing tendency to formulate the models in explicitly statistical frameworks, but there are still large gaps where there are only the most informal, subjective methods of testing the appropriateness of a psychometric model for a given kind of data.

Psychometrics is typically divided into three subfields: scaling, test theory, and factor analysis. Of the three, scaling is the most central; in fact, from some points of view the other two could be subsumed under it. For the present discussion, however, only topics that arise out of problems of attaching numbers to stimuli (stimuli being defined very broadly) will be included there. Test theory, on the other hand, is concerned with the attachment of numbers (scores) to people or to their responses. Factor analysis, often thought of as simply concerned with finding out what tests measure, may more generally be looked on as the application of a certain set of models to certain kinds of observations in order to simultaneously attach numbers to both stimuli and people. There are interconnections among the areas, and certain concepts and methods developed in one have been found to have application in another, but for the most part we will discuss the three separately. In addition to the three separate areas, there are some principles and concepts in measurement that cut across all three. These will be briefly discussed in the first of the following sections.

Measurement, Relations, and Models

The Nature of Measurement

S. S. Stevens (1959b) has defined measurement as "the assignment of numerals to objects or events according to rule —any rule." While most measurement theorists would agree with this definition, it has been criticized (Ellis 1966) as being too inclusive. Doubtless all theorists, including Stevens, would agree that not all procedures fitting this definition are *desirable* forms of measurement. One would at least want to add the condition that the procedure be reliable, leading to highly similar classifications for the observations if the process of measurement is repeated. One would also want it to be communicable, so that interested or skeptical persons can try the measurement procedures for themselves.

A further characteristic of good measurement is relevance. A given set of measurements (a classification scheme) should relate to other sets of measurements. In fact, Ellis (1966) uses the number and the simplicity of the relationships entered into by a measurement scheme as the indicators of its value. Taking into consideration this criterion and those above, we might define good measurement as the use of rules, that are readily communicable and can be reliably applied, for the assignment of numbers to observations in such a way that these numbers are related as

simply as possible to as many other sets of measurements as possible.

Measurement and Relations

To say that a science has quantitative laws is to say that there exist in that field quantitative *variables* which display mathematical relations to each other when combined in certain ways. That is, there are verifiable mathematical models. There is, though, always the proviso that the relations hold only if the observations are made in certain ways and, often, only if they are subjected to certain kinds of preliminary mathematical processing. Making the observations and processing them in the prescribed ways are necessary steps in measurement. The variables used in the laws are what in psychology we refer to as scales. One does not know that he has correctly identified the variables in an area and measured them appropriately unless he observes relations among them. Once relationships among variables do become empirically established, we are wise to make use of some of these relations to check on the validity of our measurements whenever we are attempting to measure the same variables in any new context or way.

We may illustrate these concepts by considering the familiar example of physical length, by which we mean the straight-line distance between two points as measured according to certain operations. One such way of measuring length is the foot ruler method in which we lay the ruler down, mark where its ends lie, lay it down again so that one of its ends is on one of the marks, and so on, counting the number of times we lay the ruler down. If we make a number of observations on length, and, are able to satisfy certain conditions such as ensuring that the successive positions for the ruler lie in a straight line, we might be able to infer relations among lengths, such as that defined by the 3–4–5 right triangle, and other empirical geometric principles, but we would not be able to demonstrate them very exactly because this is not a very accurate way to measure distance, being subject to errors of various kinds. We would seek other methods of measuring distance that agreed approximately with our foot-rule method but which demonstrated the relationships more accurately. The exactness and the variety of the relations are more important underpinnings for the measurement methods than is their agreement with the foot-rule method.

Relationships among variables are important in another way: they may lead to redefinition of the variables. For example, a number of physical relations are specifiable using measurements of the physical variable *weight*, which is measurable in a number of familiar, straightforward ways. Experience has shown, however, that the important variables actually are *mass*, time, and distance, and that weight, as we ordinarily understand it, is specifiable only in terms of all three, the confusion of weight with mass arising from the fact that under a number of different methods of measurement and in a wide but limited class of situations, measurements of weight are equivalent to measurements of mass. The non-equivalence, though, is detectable through the occasional failure of weight to enter into the appropriate kinds of relationships with other variables, thus leading to a changeover from using weight as a variable to using mass. Perhaps even more striking is the effect of relativity theory on the variable of distance. Distance (and time) were replaced as separate variables by space-time in order to simplify relationships. Thus not only are methods of measurement dependent for their status as methods upon the way they can be used in systems of mathematical relationships, but the very variables themselves rely for their existence upon their ability to enter into as many relationships as possible as simply as possible.

MEASUREMENT AND MODELS

Systems of mathematical relations have a second, perhaps equally important function in psychological measurement. This is due to the importance of what is often called "derived" as opposed to "direct" measurement. That is, the number of items right on a test, which itself is a perfectly valid example of measurement since it uses an unequivocal way of classifying observations, is assumed not to be the variable of interest. Further processing, utilizing a particular mathematical model in order to yield a trait score or a factor score, is assumed to be necessary in order to achieve valid measurement. The same is true of such a datum as the proportion of times a given object is preferred to another one. Again, this could be looked upon as being itself a perfectly valid example of measurement. The practice is, however, to subject several data of this kind to analysis according to a mathematical model of a particular kind to yield "measurements" of the objects that are held to be more important, valid, or useful than the more direct observations. It is implicitly assumed that the operation of the underlying (derived) quantities leads, according to specific relationships among them, to the observations themselves. Therefore, the latter must be analyzed in accordance with the model in order to enable us to uncover or derive the "true" variables.

This may not actually be as far from the situation with physical measurement as is sometimes assumed. For example, when voltage is "measured" with an ordinary pointer-type voltmeter, what we actually observe is distance, the distance the pointer travels when the switch is closed. It happens that there is a theory or model that relates that distance to voltage and it happens that the model is a linear one. This allows us to translate centimeters of traverse into volts, provided the voltmeter has been manufactured and calibrated accurately enough.

Models are, however, almost ubiquitous in psychological measurement. Hardly any measurement takes place without resort to them. In fact, the field of psychometrics may be said to primarily consist of the study of these models and the search for models that will lead from the direct observations to derived quantities which will in some way prove more useful than the observations from which they are derived.

Scaling

Psychological scaling, in the form of Fechner's psychophysics, is the oldest study in the field of empirical psychology, dating back over a century. The objective of scaling may be said to be the quantification of stimuli or of the psychological reactions to them, where it is to be understood that by "stimuli" we mean any objectively specifiable events, including words and other symbolic stimuli. For the most part, scaling is accomplished by means of the analysis of *judgments*, or other kinds of subjective reports, but it is not limited to processing this kind of data. Responses of other kinds are also used, but judgments are usually the most efficient source of data to analyze to yield scale values for the stimuli.

In its earliest form, scaling was considered to be the study of the relation between psychic quantities and physical values, and it relied upon the subject's explicitly introspective observation of his internal states. The rise of the behavioristic view which became dominant during the present century, in addition to certain contradictions which arose in the data of psychophysics itself, resulted in a change in the view of scaling. The judgment came to be treated as a response much like any other, and the field of psychophysics came to be subsumed under the general stimulus-response paradigm.

On the part of workers in the field of scaling, however, there has always been a strong tendency to think in terms of intervening variables. Guilford (1954) distinguished three continua: the stimulus continuum (in physical units), the internal response continuum, and the overt response continuum, which he called the judgment continuum. Only the first and last of these are directly observable, but the relation between them was described by recourse to the middle one.

Until recently, scaling has focussed almost exclusively upon the attempt to quantify the typical organism's response to particular stimuli—stimuli which were specified in terms of their objective characteristics. Certain kinds of mathmatical models were used as an aid in this quantification, and to relate the observed responses to internal continua. The idea was that the stimuli, whether monochromatic lights, line drawings, names of political parties or different brands of soap, could be labeled with their scale values. This is also a primary purpose in many current studies, but the view of scaling has lately been broadening.

SCALING AND MODELS

In particular, it has been placed more explicitly in the context of modeling psychological processes. For example, a common application of scaling is in preference studies where the data consist of the proportion of times a given object is preferred to another. Treating this as a scaling problem, we attempt to attach scale values to the stimuli. However, we do this through recourse to a model, say the Bradley-Terry-Luce (Luce 1959a; Bradley and Terry 1952). This states that for stimuli A, B, . . . there are corresponding numbers $x(A)$, $x(B)$, . . . and the probability that A is preferred to B, $\Pr(AB)$ depends on these numbers according to the following rule:

$$\Pr(AB) = \frac{x(A)}{x(A) + x(B)} \qquad [1]$$

This implies a series of equations relating observed proportions to the scale values, and these can be solved to yield the scale values. The point we wish to emphasize here is that this is also a straightforward *model* for preference behavior, and the data can be used not only to scale the stimuli but also to test the model. This would routinely be done, and different preference models can be tested on the same set of data. (See Morrison 1963; Hohle 1966; Burke and Zinnes 1965 for this kind of research on this or closely related problems.)

The converse, using what is primarily a behavioral model to scale some things can also take place. For example, a stochastic learning model can be used to scale the difficulty of situations. Equation **2** gives the probability of making a response G in a certain situation when it is reinforced with probability p of $n - 1$ trials (Atkinson, Bower, and Crothers 1965, p. 363).

$$\Pr(G_n) = p - [p - \Pr(G_1)][1 - \theta]^{n-1} \qquad [2]$$

$\Pr(G_n)$ refers to the probability that G occurs on trial n. The parameter θ is a "learnability" parameter which may vary from situation to situation or task to task, so if the model is found to hold for a variety of conditions, the value of θ may be determined for each, and thus the situations can be scaled. This reverse kind of application is rare, but if models are to be taken seriously we must expect it to be more frequent.

Except in the trivial cases of scaling by fiat, scales do not have an existence independent of a model for describing relations among observations. In fact, scale values are often arrived at through the employment of a model, at least implicitly. Now, in many applications of scaling, such as in the familiar case of rating scales, no explicit use is made of a model or theory. The numbers furnished by the subject are simply "believed." The view presented here is that this procedure is not justified except in the cases where, in the past, it has been found that such a procedure does yield quantities which reflect, fairly directly, a variable which does have a place in a model. Thus, the magnitude estimation procedures of Stevens (Stevens 1957) have by now been sufficiently verified in the study of sensory magnitude that they can be used for this purpose rather directly without any elaborate investigation of whether the relevant model—the power law—holds. It is of course necessary that all the appropriate experimental safeguards be observed. A second example might be the rating scale. What justification is there for using the mean rating by subjects of a particular stimulus as a scale value? Here the relation to a model is more distant. It has been found, however, that a model for categorical ratings can be verified; this is the successive categories or successive intervals model (Torgerson 1958). It is also found that the mean ratings of the stimuli agree fairly closely with their scale values as obtained by the successive intervals method, although the relation is often curvilinear. Moreover, when mean ratings are, for appropriate data, analyzed by multidimensional scaling procedures, such as are discussed below, a certain kind of model can be verified. Thus the use of rating scales as bona fide variables is grounded on their reflecting, at least under some circumstances, variables of models which can be verified. This support is only suggestive, however, in any given use of rating scales. For example, the assumption that ratings reflect the subject's attitude toward a concept in an experiment studying an attitude change model may be only very approximately correct. A better justified, albeit much more unfamiliar and perhaps difficult approach, would be to use the attitude change model itself to scale the ratings, building in sufficient redundancy to allow for a check on the validity of the model.

In any application of scaling, however, the emphasis is on the outcome of the scaling, rather then upon the model, itself, provided that the model has been found appropriate in the past.

The purpose of scaling is usually thought of as the attachment of numbers to stimuli, primarily through the analysis of judgments. Countless studies have shown, however, that objective events (stimuli) have permanent, determinate psychological scale values in at best a very limited sense. The scale value of a stimulus depends on the context in which it is judged (e.g., Parducci 1963; Sutcliffe and Bristow 1966; Ross and DeLollo 1968) or who is doing the judging (e.g., McGill 1960). It seems more appropriate to think of the scale value as characterizing an internal state of an organism at a particular time. It is these internal states that can presumably be related to each other and to overt responses.

An interesting recent development in scaling is the attempt to show how scale values obtained by different methods or in different contexts can be related to each other and to other responses. The results seem to be consistent with the notion that a set of scale values for stimuli obtained by judgment methods is one representation of an S's internalized schema for those stimuli and that other scale values and responses are additional representations of the same schema. Often different representations are derivable from each other or from the same (conjectured) schema by simple mathematical transformations. This is one approach to the problem of the same stimulus having different scale values which reduces the lack of parsimony.

Some progress has also been made in dealing with the problem of individual differences short of treating each subject separately. Tucker and Messick (1963) present a method for essentially finding subgroups of subjects whose judgments are relatively homogeneous; weighted averages of the responses of these groups are used rather than either the responses of the individual subject, with their large measurement error, or the overall mean of a heterogeneous group which does not characterize the responses of more than a small proportion of its members.

Our attempt in this introductory section has been to provide a general framework for scaling. The next section consists of brief considerations of the main problems and methods of scaling.

METHODS FOR DETERMINING SENSITIVITY

Classical methods. In its earliest form, Fechner's law, the scaling of stimulus magnitudes was tied to sensitivity through the Weber constant, and consequently there was considerable focus on methods for determining the organism's sensitivity to different levels of stimulus input for various sensory modalities and various stimulus forms. These methods for determining the absolute and differential thresholds, *AL* and *DL*, are what are referred to as the classical methods of psychophysics. As described in such standard works as Guilford (1954), Woodworth and Schlosberg (1954), and Torgerson (1958), the models and experimental procedures are still in use, although methods of analyzing the resulting data have become more sophisticated (viz., Jones and Bock 1968). These models and methods now seem to be in the process of being replaced by those deriving from signal detection theory.

For *DL* determination, the classical methods generally employ numerous presentations of a standard stimulus and a comparison stimulus. The subject indicates whether or not the stimuli appear equal, and sometimes the direction of the difference. The data are then treated by one of several alternative statistical methods to yield the *DL*. Basically, *DL* is defined as the difference in *physical* units between the standard and comparison stimulus which is reported as different a specified percentage of the time. The term *DL*, defined in this sense, is used as equivalent to "just noticeable difference" or jnd. The methods are made to yield a "scale" for the stimuli through the doctrine that "just noticeable differences are equal"; therefore, they may be added up to yield a scale value for any given stimulus since with sufficient data it can be found to be a certain number of DL's from zero as defined by the absolute limen.

Fechner's law follows from this when the (approximate) empirical fact of Weber's law is introduced. Weber's law states that the DL is proportional to the physical intensity of the stimulus; Fechner's principle states that the DL's are equal. If the DL is taken as a mathematical differential, we have Weber's law as a differential equation, which, on integration, yields Fechner's law:

$$\psi = k \log \phi, \qquad\qquad [3]$$

which states that the psychological magnitude ψ is proportional to the log of the stimulus magnitude ϕ; k is the Weber constant. It has been pointed out (Luce and Edwards 1958) that the integration is not legitimate, although this problem can be patched up (Eisler 1963). Taken at its face value, though, Fechner's law states that the psychological scale value of a stimulus can be determined simply from its physical value.

Signal detection theory. There has come to be increasing dissatisfaction with the classical psychophysical methods themselves as methods for determining sensitivity. The principal problem grows out of the fact that in the classical methods the sensitivity of the subject is confounded with his criterion for response. How certain does the subject have to be that he heard a tone or noticed a difference before he reports it? A whole new psychophysics, called signal detection theory (TSD), has grown up in an attempt to separate out the influence of the subject's criterion for response, although Treisman and Watts (1966) have shown that the classical methods could also be adapted for this purpose.

TSD was first developed for electronics engineering (Peterson, Birdsall, and Fox 1954) but soon found application to problems in psychophysics and sensory functioning (e.g., Tanner and Swets 1954; Swets, Tanner, and Birdsall 1961; Green 1960). In a typical TSD experiment for the determination of sensitivity, i.e., an AL study, the subject is presented stimuli (signals) of various intensities *including zero* (i.e., noise only).

The theory recognizes that the subject may respond positively when there is indeed a signal (stimulus) or when there is none (noise only). It relates the probabilities of positive response to two variables which are points on the internal response continuum. One of these, d', is the mean of the distribution of (internal) response to the signal, and the other, β, is the criterion, the point on the continuum which, if exceeded, will result in a positive response. The criterion's position on the continuum will vary, presumably depending on the utilities of hits, false alarms, and misses. The placement of the criterion is assumed to be rather analogous to deciding on a significance level in hypothesis testing through the assessment of the relative costs of Type I and Type II errors. These analogies are not necessary to the formal properties of the model, however.

TSD analysis has served quite well in the function for which it was developed, the determination of sensitivity independently of response bias. It also serves as a model for responding under uncertainty and has been found useful in this respect although there are others that can be applied. Luce (1963) offers an alternative, for example. TSD constitutes a method for scaling stimuli because one of its variables, d', is assumed to characterize the stimuli. Thus one may perform a study to determine the *detectability* of various stimulus intensities. One strong source of support for the model is that the scales are reasonably invariant over various experimental methods for getting the responses (Swets 1961; Markowitz and Swets 1967). Green and Swets (1966) is a good text and sourcebook, and Egan and Clark (1966) provides a good introduction.

UNIVARIATE JUDGMENT METHODS

For present purposes, it seems efficient to lump together all those methods based on the subject's judgment of the intensity, magnitude, or degree to which stimuli possess a single given quality, regardless of whether the judgments are ordinal or numerical and of whether the stimuli are presented singly or in pairs or larger groups. That is, in this section we will consider all those methods based on *judgments* of *how much*. Included here are the method of pair comparisons and its generalizations, the ubiquitous rating scale methods, the ratio judgment methods, and the models associated with each.

Pair comparisons. In the method of pair comparisons the subject is presented two stimuli and asked which one is louder, smellier, more desirable, etc. The result is an ordering or dominance relation on the pair for which we will use the symbol $\geq$. When this is done it is found that if $A \geq B$ and $B \geq C$, then much more often than not $A \geq C$, but not always. Both aspects, the transitivity and its stochastic nature, are interesting empirical facts. The attempt to account for them in all their details has led to the development of several models for pair comparison judgments and the concomitant methods for scaling the stimuli.

The two most prominent models are the Bradley-Terry-Luce cited earlier (Bradley and Terry 1952; Luce 1959*a*), and the Thurstone (Torgerson 1958; Thurstone 1959), the latter principally in its "Case V" form. This states that

$$z_{AB} = S(A) - S(B) \qquad\qquad [4]$$

where z_{AB} is the normal deviate corresponding to Pr(AB), and $S(A)$ and $S(B)$ are scale values of A and B. The models are presumed to describe the behavior of individual subjects, but in practice Pr(AB) usually refers to the proportion of subjects judging $A \geq B$.

Both models are usually reasonably consistent with a given set of data, although if enough data are gathered, Mosteller's test (Mosteller 1951) will usually show that it significantly departs from the model. The two models are very difficult to distinguish empirically, making highly similar predictions about the relations among all the $1/2n(n-1)$ proportions. Studies evaluating their relative validity have been inconclusive, but perhaps tend to favor Bradley-Terry-Luce (Burke and Zinnes 1965; Sutcliffe and Bristow 1966; Hohle 1966).

A drawback of the method of pair comparisons is its inefficiency as a data-gathering device. Coombs (1964) has presented a variety of generalizations of it, pointing out that one can not only ask for the dominant one in a set of two, but also the dominant two in a set of five, etc. In fact, the general case is when there are n stimuli presented k at a time; from each subset of k, the r brightest, most valuable, etc., are selected and these r are ordered. A limiting case is the ranking of all n stimuli at once, $r = k = n$.

In evaluating any scaling method, it is important to ask what the scale values represent. In the case of pair comparison models, this is what might be called a stochastic dominance scale; given scale values for two stimuli, A and B, one can attach a probability to A being judged greater than B. One can summarize the $1/2n(n-1)$ probabilities with the n scale values. Whether or not these scale values have any broader application depends on the accumulation of evidence that they are related to other behaviors. While there is not much hard evidence of this kind, one gets the impression that a dominance scale developed by a pair comparison model has application to other dominance relations among the same stimuli, although the scale is used rather roughly. One can and should, raise the question of the generalizability of scale values obtained by any method, but those methods that employ essentially introspective procedures are most easily questioned.

Numerical judgments. Most "scaling" is done by simply presenting the stimuli to subjects and having them attach numbers to the stimuli. Then the judgments are replicated either across or within subjects and the mean or median judgment of a stimulus is used as its scale value. Within this framework, there are a variety of different scaling methods, depending on how the subject assigns the numbers, how the stimuli are presented, and how the judgments are processed.

Undoubtedly the most common such task of this kind is the rating scale method. The subject is given a fixed series of numbers (e.g., one through nine) or a fixed number of categories. Provided the numbers are taken literally or the categories are treated as if they were equally spaced, and mean or median judgments are taken, an equal-appearing interval scale is the result. The methods, while among the most simple for the subject and efficient for data-gathering, suffer from two weaknesses. First, they are subject to certain obvious kinds of instability. There are context and order effects (Helson 1964; Parducci 1963), and different subjects tend to use the scales differently. These defects can be reduced by the use of careful instructions, anchor stimuli to define the different points on the scale, and a stratified-random stimulus order. Conceptually, such scales' lack of support from any underlying model is more damaging. The intervals are equal only by fiat, and if subjects are instructed to make them equal, that merely shifts the grounds of the objection. The lack of a model for the data can be remedied if the data are analyzed by the method of successive intervals or categories (Torgerson 1958; Jones and Bock 1968).

The other common class of numerical methods is the ratio class (ratio estimation, magnitude estimation). In these methods, the subject is not limited to a fixed interval of the number scale to use for his responses, and he is not instructed to attempt to keep intervals equal. Rather, the key instruction is that his numerical responses are to be chosen in such a way that they reflect the ratios between the magnitudes of the sensations produced by the stimuli. Often, the subject is provided with a modulus stimulus, and his responses are to reflect the ratio between the modulus and the other stimuli. The responses of the subject, or the mean or median responses of several subjects, are treated directly as ratio scales.

We have emphasized here the importance of *relationships* in defining scales, and the relationship that gave the initial

impetus to ratio scaling was "power-law psychophysics." It was found (Stevens 1957, 1958; Stevens and Galanter 1958) that on a large number of perceptual continua the psychophysical relation was the power law

$$\psi' = c\phi^a \qquad [5]$$

where ψ' is the psychological scale, ϕ is physical magnitude, and c and a are constants, c depending on the details of the scaling method and a being a characteristic of the perceptual continuum.

The ratio methods have enjoyed rather wide popularity since the publication of a number of studies using them (Stevens 1957, 1958; Stevens and Galanter 1957). Validation of the scales takes place by comparing the scales resulting from using different modulus stimuli, and by the use of cross-modality matching (Torgerson 1958; Stevens 1959a). In the latter, S is required to match a stimulus ratio in one modality with a stimulus ratio in another. While ratio scaling methods have been found to be useful and effective, some of the initial enthusiasm for them has worn off. They have been found to be sensitive to the choice of modulus and to the range of stimuli judged; also, subjects appear to differ in the number ranges they prefer to use in their responses (Engen and Levy 1955; Kunnapas 1960; Ekman and Sjoberg 1965; Mashour and Hosman 1968).

THE PSYCHOPHYSICAL LAWS

Two psychophysical laws have been presented here, Fechner's law (Equation 3) and Stevens' law (Equation 5), and considerable controversy has arisen over which is "correct." The former is obtained if discrimination methods such as a Thurstonian comparison model is used, and, as noted above, Equation 5 summarizes the results if ratio scaling methods are used. A glance at the two equations shows that the two psychological scales ψ and ψ' should be related logarithmically, and indeed this has been found to be the case in several empirical instances (e.g., Ekman and Kunnapas 1962; Galanter and Messick 1961). Ekman (1964) presents an interesting hypothesis to account for this relation, pointing out that, psychologically, the continuum of number itself obeys something akin to Weber's law, and suggesting that the subject takes this into consideration in his ratio judgments. This means that he uses a sort of equiprecision rule when he gives his ratio judgments. This hypothesis is consistent with the results of the cross-modality matching studies.

The issue of the relation between the two types of scales is somewhat clouded, however, when it is noted (Eisler, 1965) that in almost all recent published data using discrimination methods intra- and interindividual variability have been confounded, and that generally group averages have been used for the ratio scale studies (N.B., Kunnapas 1967), whereas any psychological law must apply to the individual.

Recently, a rather complex solution to the psychophysical law controversy has been offered (Eijkman, Thijssen, and Vendrik 1966; Thijssen and Venrik 1968). These authors presented data to show that the basic fact of psychophysics, Weber's law, did not hold if the range of comparison stimuli were made narrow enough! Using a combination of signal detection and classical psychophysical methods, these workers were able to separate the effect of noise in the neural system from that of the transducer function that changes the input to a neural signal. They concluded that the magnitude of noise does not change with stimulus intensity, and that the apparent loss of discrimination occurs through the operation of a "multi-range meter" mechanism that adjusts the intensity of the internal signal to a more or less constant level before the noise enters in. They also concluded that over limited ranges Equation **5** holds, but that the exponenet decreases with increasing stimulus intensity. This approach seems to be a highly sophisticated one, both experimentally and mathematically, and it will be interesting to see if it gains additional support.

From the point of view expressed here, the important grounds for an answer to the question of which psychophysical law, if either, is "correct" are those of the relations that the scale values enter into. In the case of both methods there is a consistent form of relation with the physical continuum. In both cases at least a certain amount of consistency in the judgments can be demonstrated. Given two stimuli, Fechnerian psychophysics is a summary statement of how discriminable they will be, and Stevensian tells us the relation to expect between their apparent magnitudes. As usually determined, neither system may reflect anything very profound about the internal workings of the nervous system if the research reported in the previous paragraph is assumed to be valid. For general psychological purposes, however, scale values derived by either may be useful.

MULTIDIMENSIONAL SCALING

The methods and issues discussed to this point have all derived from observations of dominance or order relations among stimuli. In the present section we discuss methods developed around a fundamentally different relation, that of distance (or differentness) or its complement, proximity (or similarity). The distinction between order and proximity is one of the three fundamental differentiators among kinds of data emphasized by Coombs (1964). Formally, the proximity relation differs from dominance in being symmetric rather than antisymmetric and in not being necessarily transitive. It can be made to have a sort of analogue of transitivity through the introduction of stronger conditions such as the triangle inequality.

Multidimensional scaling as treated here is the analysis of data consisting of the proximity of or distance between stimuli. It began as a procedure for analyzing the Euclidean distances among a set of points to find the coordinates of the points on underlying dimensions. Procedures for doing this were described by Young and Householder (1938) and Richardson (1938), and these methods were later improved (e.g., Torgerson, 1952) and expanded (e.g., Ross and Cliff, 1964). These methods follow from the definition of Euclidean distance:

$$d^2 = \sum_m x_{jm}^2 + \sum_m x_{km}^2 - 2 \sum_m x_{jm} x_{km}, \qquad [6]$$

for the squared distance between points j and k. It states the relation between the squared distance and the coordinates x_{jm}, x_{km} of points j, k on dimensions m. The key term is the last one which indicates that distance depends on the sum of products of coordinates, just as in the fundamental equation of factor analysis (see below); therefore, the methods of factor analysis could be adapted to the recovery of coordinates from distances.

The next problem is how the "distances" among the stimuli are derived. The simplest paradigm to describe is that in which the stimuli are presented in pairs and the subject gives a direct judgment of their similarity. Often, a Thurstone-based method for analyzing such judgments is used to derive the distance scale (see Torgerson 1958). However, other behavioral measures can be used. For example, Shepard (1958) employed a rationally derived transformation of the proportion of times one response was substituted for another as an error in paired associates learning. He (Shepard 1960) suggests several other possibilities.

As a model Equation **6** derives much of its force from the requirement that relatively few dimensions be required to account for the data. Now, behaviorally, it is often the case that proximity is defined only ordinally (or at best with an unknown zero point). There have been a series of developments in psychometric theory which allow the Euclidean model, together with the requirement of low dimensionality, to define the transformation that changes behaviorally defined proximity into Euclidean distance. Messick and Abelson (1956) took the first step by using the Euclidean model to define a zero point for what is initially only an interval scale of distance. Then Helm (1960) used the model to determine the optimum value of parameters for an exponential transformation of judged distance. It remained for Shepard (1962a, b) to see the generality of the process. He showed that the behavioral data could be used to define the distance simply ordinally, and that the Euclidean model could then find the specific case of the ordinal scale that was most consistent, as a distance, with the hypothesis that the stimuli were points in a space of a given number of dimensions. Thus the Euclidean model as interpreted by Shepard can be used to transform ordinal information about proximity into a higher order scale, just as Luce's and Thurstone's do for dominance data.

There is now a substantial body of evidence that indicates that a structure revealed by multidimensional scaling represents a sort of cognitive map of the stimuli, and that S uses this structure to determine a variety of his responses to the stimuli. For example, a number of workers (e.g., Carroll and Chang 1967; Doelert and Hoerl 1967; Green and Carmone 1968; Cliff 1969) have related individuals' preference functions for stimuli, products, or concepts to their perceptual spaces for the same stimuli. Cliff and Young (1968) found that a variety of univariate judgments about stimuli could be related to their positions in multidimensional space. Cliff (1968) found evidence supporting the conjecture that the individuals' responses to a personality inventory could be related to their perceived position of the items in a multidimensional space. Thus it appears that multidimensional scaling could be an important tool in the understanding of how the individual responds to stimuli of a particular class in particular situations. It should be admitted, however, that while the advent of the high speed computer has permitted the solution of the problem of analyzing proximity data, methods for gathering it are still cumbersome, since they involve getting estimates of the distance between all or almost all possible pairs of stimuli.

There has been considerable interest in whether psychological distance is Euclidean or measured in some other type of geometry. For distance measurement, the key property of Euclidean space is that it is measured the same way in any direction. This is in contrast to a "city block" space (Attneave 1950) in which distance must be measured "down streets and across avenues." Shepard (1964) and Torgerson (1965) have found that for stimuli with obvious and distinct dimensions, the Euclidean model is not completely descriptive. Hyman and Well (1967) concluded that a whole range of spatial models may be appropriate, depending not only on the nature of the stimuli but the subjects doing the judging. It still tends to be true, though, that a Euclidean map can often be an adequate picture of a non-Euclidean psychological space, just as a flat road map is an adequate picture of the non-Euclidean space defined by the surface of a globe.

Limitations of space have precluded the discussion of certain methods such as Ekman's (1954, 1963) scalar product approach and multidimensional unfolding (Coombs 1964; Bennett and Hays 1960). Also omitted are those procedures such as the Semantic Differential (Osgood, Tannenbaum, and Suci 1957) which are really ratings on a number of single scales.

MEASUREMENT THEORY

The general nature of measurement has been briefly discussed in the chapter's introductory section, emphasizing the importance of relations among measurements and the importance of substantive models and theories to measurement. In the present brief section some empirical results and conceptual developments which are important to the status of psychological measurement and of particular methods will be mentioned.

Defining scale types through allowable transformations. Since the publication of Stevens' historic paper (1951), the characteristic that distinguishes different kinds of scales has been the kind of arbitrary transformation of them that could be made without disturbing empirical relations. Originally, Stevens (1951) distinguished four scale types: nominal, ordinal, interval, and ratio. If the data are on a *nominal* scale, then we may transform the scale by any one-to-one transformation without losing any information. If *ordinal*, any strictly monotonic transformation is legitimate. An *interval* scale allows only for general linear $(ax + b)$ transformation, while the only transformation allowable of *ratio* data is multiplication by a positive constant. This classification scheme was later expanded slightly by Stevens (1957) and Torgerson (1958) and appreciably by Coombs (1952). It was designed to serve psychology as a replacement for the system of Campbell (1920) which was based upon the empirical operations that could be performed in measurement process. The Stevens system of basing measurement theory on the kind of transformations that are allowable currently appears to be being replaced by a view given impetus by conjoint measurement theory (Luce and Tukey 1964), that the kind of measurement that takes place depends on the kind of relations that are observed.

Scale type theory, to say nothing of ratio judgment methods, received considerable impetus from the publication of Luce's (1959b) startling paper which appeared to show that if there were a psychophysical law relating a physical ratio scale to a psychological one, the relation *must be* a power function (Equation 5). Rozeboom (1962) showed that this followed primarily from the innocuous assumption that legitimate transformations of one scale should lead to legitimate transformations of the other without changing the form of the relation. He showed

that Luce's seeming restriction can be circumvented by reducing the laws to dimensionless form. Luce (1962) replied that this leads to some loss of elegance and does not occur in the most coherent areas of physical science theory. Ellis (1966) has a rather extensive discussion of this and related problems.

In this context, it is interesting to note that the most general form of the power law (Stevens 1961, p. 44),

$$\psi' = c(\phi - \phi_0)^a$$

amounts to an illegitimate transformation of the physical scale, translation of the origin as if *it* were an interval scale, but note that this is done to simplify a relationship.

Helm's study (1964) may be used to illustrate the importance of data relations in defining the nature of a scale. He had subjects give ratio estimates of the dissimilarity of color chips, and treated these as distances between the colors. A Euclidean multidimensional scaling analysis of the data yielded a very satisfactory fit in two dimensions, as was anticipated from the colors' positions in the Munsell system. This strongly reinforces the view that the judgments really are on a ratio scale since any transformation of it, except multiplication by a positive constant, would disturb the fit of the Euclidean model.

Data relationships can also be used to define the zero point on what is otherwise an interval scale. Temperature is frequently cited as an example of an interval scale, the choice of Fahrenheit or centigrade being arbitrary. Many years ago, though, certain observed relationships gave compelling reason for defining the zero point on the temperature scale, and thus the Kelvin scale is *the* temperature scale, the others being useful for everyday purposes. In a more limited form, the same thing can happen with psychological scales. Cliff (1959) showed that relations among the scale values of adverb-adjective combinations required the definition of a zero point on what was initially only an interval scale. Similarly, we have seen how the assumption of the Euclidean model can be used to change an ordinal scale of proximity into a ratio scale of distance. Thus, we would emphasize, as Ellis (1966) does, that the nature of the scale is determined by the kinds of relations it enters into.

Scales and statistics. Concern about the type of scale their data was on has had a substantial influence on experimenters' use of statistics, largely accounting for the rise in the use of non-parametric methods. It is difficult to defend most psychological data as being on an interval scale, but the latter is an assumption of most parametric statistics. The continued use of parametric statistics can be justified on grounds which are based on the view that the important thing is the validity of the *conclusions from* a statistical analysis. This is emphasized by Adams, Fagot, and Robinson (1965).

The initial concern of the investigator is that, if the data are only on an ordinal scale, it would be possible to make a monotonic transformation of it which would lead to different conclusions. A straightforward defense against this possibility is simply to confine the conclusions to the *particular* form of the scale on which the analysis took place. If this is considered overly restrictive, then in most cases a more general ground may be used. This defense is in the finding by Abelson and Tukey (1959) that a monotonic transformation is unlikely to change the statistical significance of a result or the size of a correlation coefficient very much anyway, especially if the extremity of the monotonic transformation is limited mildly, such as by saying that if two intervals are equal in the original form of the scale, one of them can be made no more than, say, ten times larger than the other in the transformed version. In most instances the investigator may be prepared to defend this kind of restriction. It is also important that the number of degrees of freedom not be too small.

It can be noted that there is one clear kind of exception to this generally comforting conclusion. This occurs when the empirical question revolves around differences of differences, where, say, A's are hypothesized to change more than B's with respect to some variable. Clearly, if the initial levels are different then the conclusions may change radically with monotonic changes in the scale. This problem could occur, for example, in the measurement of the galvanic skin response because the latter is a *change* in an electrical measure. This measure can be either resistance or conductance, and the conclusions could depend on which was used. If reasonable care is taken, however, difficulties of this kind can be avoided.

The probability statements made on the basis of statistical analyses are rarely exact in a literal, numerical way anyway, so one may well prefer the additional amount of uncertainty introduced by weaknesses of the scale to the complications in the descriptions of the data relationships that would arise from treating the scale as only ordinal. Against this consideration may be set the fact that ordinal statistics are nearly as powerful as parametric ones, and may be more so if the assumptions of the latter are departed from.

Axiomatic systems. What might be called the "allowable transformation" approach to measurement theory in psychology now appears to be being replaced by a more deductive, axiomatic approach. Here, the theorist starts from a set of relations that are, or ideally could be, satisfied by a set of data or observations, and uses these, together with some auxiliary assumptions and definitions, to form an axiomatic system. Whether or not the observations can then be formed into a scale having interval or ratio properties depends on whether these properties can be deduced from the system of axioms, not upon any *assumed* equality of ratios or intervals.

The most important aspect of this development has been the demonstration that the existence of certain kinds of ordinal data relations can be used to imply the existence of scales with very strong measurement properties. While the approach may have its origin in Coombs's (1952) system and bears some relation to Weitzenhoffer's (1950) interesting early paper, the approach may be said to have reached an important new stage with the development of conjoint measurement theory. The important papers here include Luce and Tukey (1964), Krantz (1964), Roskies (1964) and Tversky (1967).

These authors show that where there are two or more independent variables, each with a large number of categories on it, certain kinds of ordinal relations among the observations on the dependent variable can be used to derive interval scales for all three variables. Various approaches to doing this are possible; we will sketch here Luce and Tukey's (1964). Their contribution was especially important because it showed the way around the difficulty imposed by the fact that additivity, or concatenation, of measurements of the literal kind routine in physical systems is not possible in psychology.

The combining of changes of levels on two variables serves much the same purpose in conjoint measurement in defining the scale that combining levels of one variable does in physics.

Moreover, it is fairly easy to introduce the notion of a zero point, thus making the scales ratio scales.

Early axiomatic views of measurement theory (e.g., Weitzenhoffer 1950; Cliff 1959) took a somewhat naive view in which "the" axioms of the real number system were to be listed and those which seemed to be satisfied by a given kind of data noted. Conjoint measurement theory has made use of the fact that the set of possible axioms for a number system is large, and certain subsets may be logically equivalent to other different ones. Therefore quite different sets of axioms can be used to evolve systems which have many of the same properties, including many very powerful properties of the number system (see especially Krantz 1964). In any event, defining scales in terms of the axioms they satisfy rather than in terms of transformations which are "allowable" provides a more powerful and general system.

Conclusion

As presented here, scales are variables in models, models which can come from a variety of contexts, not just human judgments. The important recent developments revolve around the development of methods for building mathematically strong structures from the observation of a large number of individually weak relations, such as ordinal or proximity relations. These structures may then provide verification, as substantive theories, of the models employed; they may also, especially in the case of proximity analysis, provide useful "maps" of how the subjects view the stimuli. These developments should help scaling to be an integral part of the general field of psychological research.

Test Theory

Classical Test Theory

As noted in the introductory remarks, the second problem in psychological measurement is the measurement of characteristics of individuals. The fact that such measurements contain a substantial amount of error necessitates the development of a set of software for dealing intelligently with error-filled measurements. The first system developed for handling such measurement was classical test theory, which is a small model for the behavior of measurements which are not error-free.

In classical test theory, the problem may be approached from either of two directions which turn out to be equivalent. First, we may begin from a definition of the properties of *error*. The model states that the observed score X is the sum of a true score T plus an error E:

$$X = T + E \qquad [7]$$

and makes several assumptions about the statistical charactristics of true and error scores.

The other approach follows from a definition of *true* score and its properties. It starts from the notion of a population of tests where T_i the true score of individual i may be interpreted as in Equation **8**:

$$T_i = \lim_{k \to \infty} \frac{1}{k} \sum_{g}^{k} X_{ig} \qquad [8]$$

in which X_{ig} is his score on test g. It is also assumed that all of the parallel tests have equal means, variances, and covariances. This set of assumptions can be used to prove the assumptions of the previously mentioned approach.

Either approach may be used to derive a number of useful formulas; mainly these are concerned with the relations among test reliability (defined as the correlation between parallel measures), true variance, error variance, and observed variance, and the correlations among true, error, and observed scores. Some of the more important of these are the following:

$$\sigma_e^2 = \sigma_g^2(1 - r_{gh});$$ [9]

error variance is proportional to the complement of r_{gh}, the reliability or correlation between parallel measures. Also,

$$r_{ex} = \sqrt{1 - r_{gh}};$$ [10]

the correlation between observed score and error also depends on the complement of the reliability, and

$$r_{gh} = \sigma_t^2/\sigma_x^2;$$ [11]

reliability is the ratio of true variance to error variance. It may be noted that several of these formulas are somewhat analogous to some in linear regression analysis with the reliability replacing the squared correlation between dependent and independent variables. Gulliksen (1950) presents a coherent development of the main results and Novick (1966) puts the theory on a more rigorous axiomatic base.

The definition of parallel measures as those having equal means, variances, and covariances, together with some simple uses of the definition of correlations between two variables when the variables are sums of other variables, leads to the development of other formulas. The most important of these are the well-known Spearman-Brown and Kuder-Richardson formulas. The former is used in various applications to predict the reliability of a test whose length is altered by a factor of K through the addition to it of K tests which are strictly parallel to a given test (or through the deletion of strictly parallel subsections of it). Equation **12** is the general form of the Kuder-Richardson Formula:

$$r_{GH} = \frac{Kr_{gh}}{1 + (K-1)r_{gh}}$$ [12]

where r_{GH} is the (predicted) reliability of the test altered in length, K is the factor by which the length will be altered, and r_{gh} is the known reliability of the test in its present form.

The KR-20 is the most important of the Kuder-Richardson formulas. While it is used as a "reliability estimate," it is actually also a prediction, in this case the prediction of the correlation between an available test and a hypothetical parallel test. It is used where the test consists of a number of separate items, and its basis is the assumption that the average covariance between the items in the available test and those in the hypothetical test will be the same as the average covariance among the items of the available test. This should be approximately true where tests can be formed of items selected from a pool of items. This assumption leads to the following reliability formula

$$r_{gh} = \left(\frac{n}{n-1}\right)\left(1 - \frac{\sum_{i}^{n} \sigma_i^2}{\sigma_g^2}\right)$$ [13]

where n is the number of items in the test, σ_i^2 is the variance of item i, and σ_g^2 is the variance of the test.

Also important in classical test theory is a series of formulas giving the effect of selection of Ss on various test statistics, particularly reliabilities and correlations with other variables. They rest on assumptions concerning the linearity of regressions and homogeneity of the variances around the regression lines. They, too, are given in some detail in references such as Gulliksen (1950), Guilford (1954, 1965), Ghiselli (1964), Horst (1966), and Rozeboom (1966), but will not be presented here. They are referred to as "corrections for restriction in range."

The fact that both the reliability of the test and the heterogeneity of the group tested affect the correlations it has with other variables leads to the use of corrections on correlation coefficients for these effects. The *correction* for attenuation as given in Equation **14** attempts to estimate what the correlation between two variables would be if they could be made perfectly reliable:

$$r'_{gp} = \frac{r_{gp}}{\sqrt{r_{gh}r_{pq}}}$$ [14]

where r_{gp} is the observed correlation between g and p, the two terms in the denominator are their respective reliabilities, and r'_{gp} is the estimated correlation if they were perfectly reliable. It is an aid in deciding whether a test should be improved or dropped. It is perhaps superfluous to insert the caution that any significance test should be made using the observed correlations rather than any "corrected" values.

FURTHER DEVELOPMENTS IN TEST THEORY

While simple conceptually and useful practically, the classical test theory models are empty ones in the sense that either the assumptions made are true by definition, or they cannot be checked directly. The assumptions are convenient rather than interesting in themselves, and the theorems are relatively straightforward algebraic consequences of them. A disadvantage of such a system is that it is relatively poor in predictive or explanatory power, and it is somewhat limited in its applicability. Consequently, there have been efforts to make test theory into a stronger system, one which would give a richer description of the behavior of test data, be more general in applicability, or incorporate other concepts of psychological measurement.

In the present discussion we will attempt to sketch three aspects of the more recent developments in test theory. These we will refer to as Strong True Score Theory, which seeks additional power by more explicit assumptions about the distributions of true scores and particularly the conditional distributions of error scores on true scores, Traceline Theories, which attempt to specify the relation between observed scores and true scores more exactly, and Generalizability Theory, which attempts to extend the ideas of parallel measurement so as to include both reliability and construct validity within the same framework.

Strong true-score models. As outlined by Lord (1965), a strong true-score theory attempts to use assumptions about the form of the distribution of errors of measurement and, sometimes, the distribution of true scores, in order to yield useful predictions about univariant and bivariate test score distributions and to equate tests.

Instead of a model for *scores*, Lord focuses on the *distribution* of scores. His basic equation is quite a general one, describing the distribution of observed scores $\phi(x)$ in terms of the distribution of true scores $g(t)$ and the conditional distribution of observed scores $h(x|t)$:

$$\phi(x) = \int_0^1 g(t)h(x|t)\,\mathrm{d}t \qquad [15]$$

This theory distinguishes between true scores on the test and the score on the underlying trait. The latter can range from $-\infty$ to ∞. The true score t is this variable mapped monotonically into the 0, 1 interval. While this general formulation can be used to prove some very general theorems (Lord and Novick 1968; Lord 1967), specification of the nature of $g(t)$ and $h(x|t)$ is necessary for practical applications. These specifications, however, can take a general form.

The ones which so far seem to be the most satisfactory start from a transformation of x and t into proportions. The model is mainly concerned with cases where the test consists of n items, so that scores run from 0 to n in discrete steps. Consequently, the symbol t here stands for a proportion, the "true proportion right," being defined so as to have

$$E(x/n|t) = t \qquad [16]$$

which parallels saying that the expected value of the difference between true and observed scores is zero, and that the regression is linear. The difference $x/n - t$ corresponds to an error of measurement. The proportion-right approach enables the model to more explicitly incorporate the characteristics of test scores as they actually occur: the range is not infinite but bounded.

As actually applied, the model assumes that $g(t)$ is a four-parameter beta distribution (Kendall and Stuart 1963, pp. 150–51; Lord 1965) in which the limits are free parameters rather than being specified as zero and unity. The distribution of errors of measurement, the conditional distribution $h(x|t)$, is taken to be a "compound" binomial function of t, simplifying to an ordinary binomial if all the items are of equal difficulty. The true score t is the "proportion" parameter of this binomial distribution.

This dependence of the distribution of errors of measurement upon the true score level is one of the most interesting results in modern test theory because it means that ordinarily the standard error of measurement is smallest at the extremes and largest in the middle of the score distribution. This fact has been empirically verified (Lord 1960a).

Application of the model to actual test data has required some ingenuity and persistence in the search for explicit solutions for the equations involved, particularly since empirical estimates of a number of parameters are necessary. Fairly satisfactory solutions have been found to most of these problems, however, and this approach can usually do an accurate job of describing univariate and bivariate test score distributions. The accuracy with which bivariate distributions of tests of the same trait can be predicted from characteristics of their univariate distributions has been remarkable, particularly for a number of cases where the regression of the two tests was markedly nonlinear and non-homoskedastic.

Strong true score theory has relatively little in the way of direct consequences for the scores of individuals except that it has some utility for comparing the performance of individuals who have taken different tests. For a single group, however, the estimated true score of an individual is simply a nonlinear (but presumably monotonic) function of his number-right observed score (Lord 1960b). Its primary utility would seem to be for large-scale test users who wish to be able to control their score distributions and test reliabilities and equate different test forms. The modern development discussed next, traceline theories, has somewhat more to say about inferring true scores.

Traceline theories. Traceline theories are directly concerned with the problem of locating the individual on the latent continuum which is believed to underlie and account for the individual's behavior with respect to the test items. While its roots can undoubtedly be traced deeper, for present purposes its origin is in the development during World War II of *latent structure analysis* as a theoretical foundation for attitude questionnaire responses (see Lazarsfeld 1950, 1954).

In latent structure theory, the first assumption is that there is a function relating p_i, the probability of passing (or agreeing with, endorsing, etc.) each item, to a position on the latent continuum:

$$p_i = f(s) \qquad [17]$$

where s is the latent continuum, analogous to the true score scale of classical test theory or the trait score of strong true score theory. The other basic assumption is that items are locally independent; by this is meant that for a fixed level of s, the probability of passing one is independent of the probability of passing the other:

$$p_{ij(s)} = p_i(s)p_j(s) \qquad [18]$$

Detailed treatments of the concepts and equations basic to latent structure analysis are given by McDonald (1962a), Meredith (1965), and Lazarsfeld and Henry (1968).

Equation **18** furnishes a means of verifying the fact that one has correctly located individuals on the latent continuum, but does not go far toward showing how they should be so located. As is the case with many models some further specification of the nature of the function in Equation **17** is necessary in order to do this. A variety of approaches have been suggested.

One is to assume that the latent continuum is not continuous but discrete. Thus the individuals all fall in a finite number of distinct classes, and for each item the individual's probability of a positive response depends on his class. The discovery of the classes and the probabilities of response within classes is *latent class analysis*. The solutions employ the joint probabilities of occurrence of responses to two or more items, up to the limiting case of using the probability of each complete response pattern. Green (1951) gives a factor-analytic approach to solving for the latent parameters, and Lazarsfeld and Henry (1968) present others, including a maximum likelihood solution. The solutions are approximate and/or iterative, however, and require large numbers of subjects since the proportion of Ss displaying various response patterns becomes small rapidly if more than two or three responses are considered. Obviously, this limits application to cases where there are relatively few items and latent classes.

A second group of approaches to latent structure analysis are the true traceline methods. Here, it is assumed that the function of Equation **17** is (or may be approximated by) a continuous function of some simple nature. The analytic problem then becomes one of identifying the parameters of the function for each item; these may then be used in conjunction with the individual's responses to scale him on the latent continuum.

Lazarsfeld and Henry (1968) describe methods for solving for the parameters of the traceline for several special cases, including those where the function is a power function or a general polynomial. The solutions seem to be cumbersome and they sometimes suffer from a kind of non-uniqueness similar to that which is introduced into factor analysis by the possibility of rotation.

There are two other traceline approaches which bear mention. These are the logistic method of Birnbaum (1968) and the mathematically related but simpler method of Rasch (1960). Birnbaum's assumption about the nature of the traceline is that it is a logistic function of the latent continuum. This makes the probability of a correct response an ogive-shaped function, similar to that which would obtain if correct response were a normal curve function of the latent continuum. Such a normal model has in fact been investigated (Tucker, 1955a). Logistic functions have the practical advantage over normal models of explicit integrals whereas the integral of the normal curve must be approximated.

The basic Birnbaum formula for the probability of correct response is given below.

$$p_i = c_i + \frac{1 - c_i}{1 + \exp{(-Da_i(s - b_i))}} \qquad [19]$$

This gives the probability of passing the item as a function of the latent continuum s. There are three parameters (D is a known constant), reflecting the main characteristics which can be observed about items. The parameter a_i reflects the discriminatory power of item i; b_i, the point on the continuum where maximum discrimination occurs; and c_i the difficulty for persons at the lowest ability levels. Birnbaum (1968) and Lord (1967) give methods for estimating these parameters; they are largely reflected by the relation between score on the item and score on the test.

In Birnbaum's model, the individual's score on the test is not simply a monotonic function of his total raw score; rather, the items are weighted by the parameters a_i. Such differential weighting may not have important practical consequences in a given application since such scores are likely to have high correlations with total score (Gulliksen 1950, pp. 355–56; Cliff 1960). It does mean, however, that the model has stronger implications for the scaling of the individuals than does Strong True Score theory.

Ross (1966) and Lord (1967) report applications of the model to data. It seems to fit the data for well-constructed tests quite well.

Rasch (1960) presents a model for test scores that is related to Birnbaum's but somewhat simplified. It states that the probability that person a gets item j correct, p_{aj}, depends in a simple fashion on two parameters, the ability of the person, s_a, and the easiness of the test b_j:

$$p_{aj} = \frac{s_a}{s_a + b_j} \qquad [20]$$

This formula is equivalent to a simplification of Equation **19** in which the discrimination and lower-asymptote parameters are not included. This simple model is surprisingly effective as a descriptor of the behavior of tests, in which case p_{aj} is taken as the proportion of items on test j which person a gets correct. Rasch (1960) and Keats (1967) cite evidence to this effect.

Keats (1967) presents an interesting formulation whereby he uses Rasch's model as a bridge between modern test theory and the theory of conjoint measurement mentioned earlier in the context of scaling (Luce and Tukey 1964). In order for p_{aj} to have an empirical counterpart it must be a proportion. It could be the proportion of items on test j which person a gets correct, the proportion of persons in group a who get item j correct, or a combination of both, provided groups of items and or persons are homogeneous enough. If such information is available and is arranged in groups by tests matrix, we would expect it to be possible to arrange the groups and items in an order such that the proportions always increased as one moved to the right in a given row, and as one moved down in a given column. The data might well obey the somewhat more restrictive assumption imposed by conjoint measurement. In that event, it must be possible to establish interval scales of ability and item difficulty. If the Rasch model holds, for example, these interval scales must be the s and b variables of Equation **20**. Thus there is hope that in test theory as well as in scaling there is the possibility of using a large number of ordinal relations to arrive at interval scales for the tests and persons. The notion of ordinal measurement will be returned to briefly later.

In evaluating these extensions of classical test theory, one cannot help but admire the mathematical elegance of many of them and the ingenuity that has gone into making abstract systems of equation amenable to empirical verification. Along with Keats (1967) one can hardly avoid the temptation to deplore the fact that they have not had wider application, while at the same time feeling that the reason that they have not been applied more widely is that their relevance is not generally appreciated by the test user, and feel that to some extent this is due to the fact that they are most relevant to large-scale testing programs and publishers. Part of the problem may well be however, that much of the most relevant material is scattered through a variety of rather obscure sources. The recent publication of authoritative books (e.g., Lord and Novick 1968; Lazarsfeld and Henry 1968) may help to remedy this situation and furnish these modern test theories with the kind of feedback from application that is so important for the growth of a scientific field.

GENERALIZABILITY THEORY

As mentioned earlier, classical test theory can be based either on a set of axioms involving the existence and behavior of true scores and error scores or around the existence of a universe of potential "parallel" measures. The extensions discussed in the immediately preceding section derive primarily from the true score approach. Perhaps equally important is a series which derives from the parallel measures approach. These developments are largely the work of Cronbach and his collaborators (Cronbach 1951; Cronbach and Azuma 1962; Gleser, Cronbach, and Rajaratnam 1965; Cronbach, Gleser, and Rajaratnam 1963; Rajaratnam, Cronbach, and Gleser 1965). It builds on earlier papers by Hoyt (1941) and Jackson and Ferguson (1941).

As originally formulated, the parallel form approach

appears extremely restrictive in its axioms, assuming as it does the existence of an infinite universe of tests all of which have equal means, variances, and covariances. Its corresponding advantage is the attractiveness of the notion of looking upon the available observed score of the individual as a sample observation from which one is to make generalizations about the universe from which it is sampled.

The recent developments are able to reduce the unrealistic appearance by loosening some of the restrictive assumptions while at the same time clarifying the nature of the conclusions that are being made under a variety of methods of estimating "reliability." It does this by making explicit the universe which is being generalized to in various cases, largely through application of the analysis of variance paradigm.

The relevant analysis of variance is based on a matrix of data which is *persons* by *measures*. The measures are not necessarily parallel in any sense beyond that in which the investigator might want to generalize from scores on one to scores on the others. Then, in the simplest form of the theory, the unreliability of the average score is the ratio of persons by measures interaction mean square to that of persons. Reliability then becomes the same as the intraclass correlation:

$$r_{gg} = 1 - \frac{MS_I}{MS_p} \qquad [21]$$

Cronbach (1950) showed that in the special case of dichotomous items this was equivalent to the KR-20, and opened the way for the use of his generalization, coefficient α, in a wide variety of situations. The important aspect is that the measures themselves need not be parallel; it need only be possible to look on those at hand as a sample from a larger universe of possible measures.

In later papers, the methods were extended to stratified sets of measures (Rajaratnam et al. 1965) and to a unification of various kinds of reliability (test retest, parallel form) with construct validity (Cronbach et al. 1963; Gleser et al. 1965). "Construct validity" is displayed when high correlations are shown between different measures which are thought to reflect the same trait (cf. Cronbach and Meehl 1955). This would occur, for example, if a paper and pencil test of anxiousness correlated with magnitude of galvanic skin response. What Cronbach et al. (1963) showed was how the various kinds of reliability, and the various reliability coefficients, reflected the magnitude of various mean squares in an analysis of variance in which the factors were persons, occasions, samples of measures, methods of measurement, etc. They thus provided an extremely important link between test theory and the kinds of measurement concerns voiced by Campbell and Fiske (1959).

THE NATURE OF MEASUREMENT OF THE INDIVIDUAL

Abstract consideration of the nature of measurement has occurred much less frequently in the context of the measurement of the individual than it has in the context of measurement of the stimuli. It may be worthwhile to make one or two points with respect to this problem before closing our overview of test theory.

The conceptual framework provided by Coombs (1964) can be used as a base. Observation of the individual's performance on a test item (i.e., whether or not he gives the keyed response) yields a kind of relation on the person-item pair. Typically, this is considered an ordering or dominance relation on the pair. This is defensible, however, not simply on the basis of an arbitrary decision on the part of the test constructor, but rather only if one can show that such relations have, for sets of persons and items, some semblance to the properties of the order relation. The focal property is perhaps that of transitivity, which involves consistency in the relations among three or more of the entities to be ordered. In the case of test data, the relations among sets of three entities inevitably involve two items and a person or vice versa, and one cannot directly observe the relation between the two items or two persons as is required if the transitivity is to be verified through consistency in the relations. How then can transitivity be empirically established so that our order relation can be established other than arbitrarily?

The answer may be more or less as follows. Recall that transitivity can be formulated as "$X*Y$ and $Y*Z$ implies *not* $Z*X$," where X, Y, Z are entities and $*$ is a relation possessing transitivity. In the case of persons a, b and items i, j, the analogue to this is "$a*i$ and $l*b$ implies not $b*j$ and $j*a$." Guttman (1950) was a leader in emphasizing the importance to test theory and practice of observing this kind of consistency, items for which it holds exactly defining the familiar Guttman scale. In practice, of course, sets of items and persons for which the relation holds for all quadruples a, b, i, j are very rare and typically small. Here as well as in the case of stimuli, what is observed in practice is a kind of stochastic transitivity of the relations, with "implies" being modified by "usually." The point to be emphasized here is that this kind of consistency need not necessarily occur. Also, there are whole domains of items for which the above relation is inappropriate, but which display a different kind of consistency.

The above kind of relation applies quite naturally in the domains in which test theory was first developed, ability and achievement testing, where a person gets an item correct if he has "enough" of the required knowledge or skill. It applies less readily to certain kinds of attitude and personality items; here, very often S would seem to be responding positively to an item if it is close enough to his self-concept or to his beliefs, and negatively if it diverges too far in either direction. In Coombs's (1964) scheme, this is an example of a *proximity* relation on the item - person pair. A parallel to the transitivity property which would allow us to verify that we are dealing with a proximity relation is rather difficult to formulate, but its formulation deserves attention.

The lack of such a formulation may account for Keats (1967) saying that "the application of (test) theory to personality tests is by no means straightforward." This is not to say that the methods and indices of classical test theory cannot be applied to any system of measurements whatsoever, and, with a little care, have the conclusions be valid. There is, however, an uneasiness which arises from the greater degree to which the individual can exert control over his own scores in the case of personality inventories and similar instruments. The degree to which the scores are the result of such seeming irrelevancies as response styles (Jackson and Messick 1962) is also bothersome. Part of the problem would appear to arise, however, from a suspicion that in the case of a number of personality-measurement situations we are dealing with proximity rather than dominance relations. This means that we cannot conclude if a person gets an item wrong (does not endorse it) he will also get most of the easier (more popular) items wrong. Thus, the kinds of inferences we would like to make are not always possible. The invention and employment of models that explicitly take into account the likely cognitive processes involved may be a more fruitful approach to attitude and personality testing.

The Assimilation of the Computer

Psychologists and statisticians concerned with testing were quick to exploit the development of the stored-program computer. Their use of it, however, has been almost entirely as a device for scoring traditionally administered tests and processing the scores on them, including performing the extensive computations in some of the modern models. Involvement of the computer in the testing process itself has been relatively rare, quite in contrast to the interest in computer-aided instruction.

The most obvious use to which the computer could be put would be as a device for selecting the questions to ask the individual, initially on the basis of some known information about him, but as the testing progressed increasingly on the basis of his responses to earlier items. Clearly, there is little to be gained from presenting an item to which we are 98 per cent sure of the response. This scheme is incorporated in a crude fashion in a number of available testing procedures, several individually administered intelligence tests, for example. The computer would seem to offer an opportunity to do this much more efficiently. This is perhaps widely recognized, but attempts to implement the notion are relatively rare and for the most part very tentative. The work of Starkweather (1965) and of Cleary, Linn, and Rock (1966) represent steps in this direction. Lord (1967) gives some quite explicit suggestions concerning computer-aided testing when Birnbaum's model is used as a basis for analyzing the responses. It would seem, however, that there is perhaps some validity to the notion that current test theory models grew up on the basis of the technology available as of World War II, and a radical change in the overall view may be necessary before efficient use of the computer can be made.

Conclusion

In this chapter, the view that measurement takes place only or at least primarily through the application of some mathematical model has been taken as a focus. The models in test theory focus around the kinds of conclusions about individuals' characteristics that can be made on the basis of their responses to a particular set of stimuli, the test. One might say that the main result of an application of the classical test model was a cautionary one. Conclusions were drawn about the reliability of a measurement with a view toward the worth of steps taken to increase it. More recent developments might be said to focus on characteristics of tests and the distributions of scores on them through the attempt to relate the observed score scale to an underlying trait scale which is not linearly related to it. The results seem mainly useful to large-scale testing applications. Assimilation of the computer into the testing situation may in the near future result in better application of testing to inferences concerning the individual, but such developments are not expected to be forthcoming in the next year or two.

Factor Analysis

Origins and Purposes of Factor Analysis

As we will discuss it here, factor analysis consists of the use of a small number of models designed to discover the stimulus dimensions which lead to consistent variation in the behavior of individuals. It began in the attempt to analyze coefficients of correlation between tests to discover whether human intelligence was one single continuum or had many facets, and has evolved into a set of procedures for estimating the loadings of variables upon the underlying hypothetical trait constructs called factors. In studying the problem, it was discovered that concepts from matrix algebra could be used for these purposes, and recognition of the related mathematical properties in other settings, for example those of multidimensional scaling, has led to the application of techniques developed in factor analysis to other problems. Also, the methods of factor analysis have nearly reached the status of a generally applicable multivariate technique. It is felt, however, that the factor analysis model is best understood and applied in the context of the general substantive area for which it was developed. This is particularly necessary since in its general form the model is general enough to serve as a model for any set of data and only gains power as an explanatory device through the addition of substantive content considerations specific to the area studied.

The Basic Factor Analysis Models

General model. All of the aspects of factor analysis discussed here are based on data matrices consisting of the scores of a number of individuals on a number of measures. For the most part, the methods may *loosely* be said to look for clusters of measures on which all individuals have more or less parallel scores. The measures that cluster together are then assumed to depend on or reflect the same underlying dimension or factor. A more exact statement, however, is that the methods attempt to discover, for the measures, the underlying dimensions that account for the degree to which they cluster together. The approach we have introduced and the one on which we will concentrate throughout, is generically called R technique. Among several alternatives the principal one is Q technique, which attempts to use the same kind of data to discover a typology of persons rather than of measures. (See Cattell 1966a; Coan 1961; and Tucker 1966 for more complete discussions of the various possibilities.)

The factor analysis models attempt to account for the scores of N S's on n measures with k underlying factors. It is further assumed that the generalizable or systematic parts of the scores can be accounted for with only p factors, where p is less than n. The basic equation is a linear one

$$x_{aj} \doteq \sum_{m=1}^{k} f_{am} a_{jm} \qquad\qquad [22]$$

in which x_{aj} is the score of individual a on measure j; f_{am} is his score on factor m; and a_{jm} is the loading of test j on factor m, the degree to which m is involved in j. Most commonly, of course, x_{aj} represents scores on tests, but they can also be scores on attitude questionnaires, judgments of stimuli, numbers of correct responses in blocks of trials, scores on single test items, or various objective or physical characteristics of the subjects.

It is convenient to express most equations in factor analysis in matrix form, in which case Equation 22 becomes

$$X = FA' \qquad [23]$$

Here, X is N persons by n tests matrix of the x_{aj}; F is N by k; and A is n by k (A' is the transpose of A), the latter containing the f_{am} and a_{jm}, respectively.

Particular forms of the basic equation. Equation 23 (or 22) is a trivial statement in the sense that if $k = n$ (or N, whichever is smaller) it is always possible to find values of F and A which make it true. Substantive value for it is achieved in two different ways. First, it is stated that X should be *almost* accounted for by p factors where p is considerably less than n, and second, certain restrictions are placed on the nature of the entries in A. We will refer to the various aspects of the first of these as the *small rank hypothesis.* The most common kind of restriction on the nature of A is that it contains a large number of zero or near-zero entries, implying that any given factor is involved in only a minority of measures and that most measures depend on only a few factors. This is the *simple structure hypothesis.*

In factor-analytic research, a distinction is made between *exploratory* and *confirmatory* studies, the distinction reflecting the degree to which the investigator believes he can specify the factor structure of the measures. The small rank and simple structure hypotheses are most appropriate in the case where the investigator can predict the major sources of variation with some degree of confidence, but is not able or willing to predict the factor loadings of each measure exactly. The two hypotheses are unlikely to hold with any degree of stringency in the initial exploration of an area. On the other hand, once an area does become extremely well worked out, the factor model should take this knowledge into account, either through the use of "Procrustes" procedures (Mosier 1939; Cliff 1966; Schönnemann 1966) or through the even more specific procedure of Jöreskog (1967a). Simple structure and small rank should be reasonable requirements for situations falling between these extremes.

For some special kinds of data, a particular form of Equation 22 is either expected on theoretical grounds or is suggested by the patterns in the correlation matrix. Guttman (1954, 1955) suggests particular forms of the latter, notably the simplex, the circumplex, and elaborations on them. Empirical examples are presented by Guttman (1957) and Hoepfner, Dunham, and Guilford (1968). Cliff (1962) presents methods for dealing with some kinds of theoretical specification of the exact nature of Equation 23.

When factor analysis is used, the importance of doing studies following the full range from exploratory to explicitly confirmatory cannot be overemphasized. The factor loading is a dependent variable, and the ability of the experimenter to predict and control it through manipulation of the stimulus material is as important in factor analysis as elsewhere in psychology. There is evidence (e.g., Guilford 1967) that this is possible in the case of factor loadings, at least to a degree.

Estimating factor loadings. Most applications of factor analysis are on data where the small rank and simple structure hypotheses are expected to hold approximately but where the exact nature of the loadings is not specifiable by hypothesis. Here, the empirical problem in factor analysis is posed in the form of estimating the factor loadings in such a way as to make the two hypotheses as nearly true as possible (in particular quantitative senses). Making the small-rank hypothesis as nearly true as possible will be referred to as the problem of "extracting" factors, and the use of the simple structure hypothesis will be called the "rotation" problem.

There are two general approaches to the extraction problem, both taking into account the fact that the small rank hypothesis will not hold exactly with a given set of data, but doing so in rather different ways. One, the components approach, emphasizes accounting for the *score* matrix with the factors, while the other, the *common factor* approach, focuses on accounting for the covariances or correlations among the variables.

The components approach. The components approach uses a special case of Equation 22 which can be expressed as Equation 24:

$$x_{aj} = \sum_{m=1}^{p} f_{am} a_{mj} + e_{aj} \qquad [24]$$

Here, the idea is that it should be possible to make the e_{aj} have small variances compared to those of the x_{aj} with p a relatively small number, and that the e_{aj}, which are considered "error" scores, are to be uncorrelated with the f_{am}. Several approaches are possible, but the most important one is as follows. It is well-known (Eckart and Young 1936) that the total sum of squares of the e_{aj} is minimized through the use of the principal components (Hotelling 1933). The equation is:

$$\mathbf{X} = \mathbf{VGW'} + \mathbf{E} \qquad [25]$$

In the equation, N is the sample size; V is an N by p matrix of the normalized eigenvectors of $(1/N)\mathbf{XX'}$; $\mathbf{G}$ is a diagonal matrix containing the square roots of the p largest eigenvalues of $(1/N)\mathbf{X'X}$; and $\mathbf{W'}$ is a p by n matrix of the corresponding eigenvectors. $\mathbf{E}$ is the N by n matrix of errors. The matrix $\mathbf{V}$ is an example of an F matrix, and $\mathbf{UG}$ is a matrix of factor loadings, an $\mathbf{A}$.

Very often, the investigator wants to decide how large p should be from the sample data. This is generally done on descriptive or heuristic grounds (Cattell 1966b; Linn 1968; Guttman 1954b; Gollob 1968), although there is a significance test (Bartlett, 1950).

Some authorities (e.g., Horst 1965) argue that the components approach should be the main one to computing factor loadings. The validity of this contention would appear to depend on the accuracy with which $\mathbf{X}$ can be reproduced with a small number of components. If it can, then this model's formal simplicity offers advantages over that described next. Unfortunately, where $\mathbf{X}$ consists of scores on mental tests it may not be possible to approximate it adequately with a small value for p.

Common factor analysis. The second model, common factor analysis, focuses on describing the correlations between the variables rather than on the score matrix itself. This was the original approach in factor analysis, and it forms the main concern of several of the important texts and sourcebooks (e.g., Thurstone 1947; Harman 1967; Cattell 1966c).

The basic equation of this model might be said to be

$$r_{jk} = \sum_{m=1}^{p} a_{jm} a_{km} \qquad j \neq k \qquad [26]$$

where r_{jk} is the correlation between tests j and k; and a_{jm} and a_{km} are the loadings of tests j and k on factor m. The point of the model is that the factors should be such as to reproduce the off-diagonal entries of the correlation (or covariance) matrix as exactly as possible.

A key concept in this model is that of *communality*, that part of its variance which is due to common factors, factors shared with other variables rather than unique to the given test. The remainder of the test's variance, its uniqueness, is attributed to a factor specific to the test and to error of measurement. The resulting matrix formulation of Equation **26** is

$$\mathbf{R} = \mathbf{AA'} + \mathbf{U} \qquad [27]$$

where $\mathbf{R}$ is the correlation or covariance matrix, $\mathbf{A}$ is again n tests by p factors, and $\mathbf{U}$ is a diagonal matrix with u_{jj} the uniqueness of test j. Note that the diagonal of $\mathbf{AA'}$ will contain the test's sum of squared factor loadings, its communality. If the uniquenesses (or the communalities) were known, it would be relatively simple, provided p is enough smaller than n, to solve Equation **27** for the matrix of factor loadings. The fact that it is not known has necessitated the use of considerable ingenuity.

The most common approach is to use estimated communalities, thus eliminating $\mathbf{U}$ from Equation **27**, even though only approximately, and then solve for $\mathbf{A}$ in such a way as to make the residual correlations, i.e., the difference between the observed correlation and that reproduced from the factor loadings, as small as possible. Currently, the most common practice is to compute the principal components of the correlation matrix with estimated communalities substituted for the diagonal (in this case the resulting factors are called principal factors rather than principal components). Prior to the advent of the electronic computer, various compromise methods were developed, such as the centroid, multiple group, and diagonal (see Harman 1967, Chaps. 8, 11) which sacrificed some of the accuracy with which a given correlation matrix could be reproduced in exchange for computational ease. Guttman (1944) provides a general matrix theory for these methods. With any method the goal is to solve for an $\mathbf{A}$ which will make Equation **28** hold as nearly as possible; the value of p is typically decided on from the data, although it may be dictated in some cases by theoretical considerations.

There are various methods for estimating communalities. These include the variable's squared multiple correlation with all the other variables, which has been shown to be theoretical lower bound for the true communality (Guttman 1954b), and each variable's highest correlation with another. Currently, it is rather common to iterate the communalities, starting from an estimate, using the obtained factor loadings to revise the estimate, factoring again, and so on until (hopefully) the process converges. This was originally suggested by Thomson (1934) and elaborated by Browne (1968).

A second approach to the communality problem is to involve it explicitly in the solution for the factor loadings. Prominent here are the maximum likelihood methods of Lawley (1940), Lawley and Maxwell (1963), Rao (1955), and Jöreskog (1963, 1967b), and the Minres method of Harmon and Jones (1966). The computational requirements of these methods are substantial even by current standards, but the methods can expect to see wider application as computational science advances even further.

An undesirable property of the common factor model is the fact that the factor scores are not empirically obtainable in any direct sense. This is because of the model for observed scores that is used. We can still refer to Equation **25** as the basic equation, but the e_{aj} term is to be interpreted differently and an additional restriction is made on it. The e_{aj} are now the scores of the individual on the *unique* factor of test j. We also require that these scores be uncorrelated not only with the f_{am} but with each other. With these interpretations, Equation **24** is a model for common factor analysis, and Equation **27** is easily derived as a consequence. The problem that now arises, though, is that we now have $p + n$ factor scores that are to be uncorrelated with each other whereas we have only n tests. This means that there is no empirically obtainable $\mathbf{F}$ matrix of common factor scores that both are uncorrelated and can be used in conjunction with the matrix of factor loadings to reproduce the correlation matrix, a fact that is found disturbing by some, although in many applications the problems can be circumvented.

The nature of the factor score matrix together with the difficulties introduced by the communality concept detract from the common factor model in comparison to the components approach. Against this must be set the fact that a given number of common factors will always reproduce the *correlations* between the variables more closely than will the same number of component factors. Also, better simple structure can be obtained using common factors than using component factors.

These considerations lead the present author to feel that the one which should be used will depend on the main interest of the investigator. If his main concern is with reproducing the data matrix, he should use the component model; if he is mainly concerned with explaining the correlations between variables, he should use common factor analysis. The former concern will often be paramount when he is simply interested in summarizing n measures with fewer variables, or when he wishes to be able to compute factor scores on his factors, or when the amount of specificity and measurement error in his data is expected to be small. The latter may often be the case in applications to non-test data. Also, it can be used when the number of factors is only a small fraction of the number of variables, since communalities will then have little influence on the solution even if they are computed.

On the other hand, it is probably better to use common factor analysis in problems where the main interest is in trait variables as constructs underlying mental test scores. Here, the factor scores are not so important, and the estimation of communalities may lead to a substantially more parsimonious description of the variables.

Nonlinear models. The factor analytic model is one in which the manifest data are described as conforming to a model of linear regression on p underlying variables. It may often be that actually there are fewer than p latent variables but the manifest variables are non-linearly dependent on them.

Non-linearity can arise from a number of sources, some of them artifactual.

An unfortunate difficulty with non-linearity is that it is often hard to detect and often even harder to interpret. Since a basic tenet of factor analysis is parsimony in the number of variables postulated, it would nevertheless appear to be important to identify such instances. McDonald (1962, 1965, 1967) has made important contributions to the solution of this problem. Preventive measures in the form of controlling the measurement properties and distributions of the variables would seem to be equally important.

Nonmetric factor analysis. The models employed by factor analysis described so far are algebraic, treating the data as if it had interval or ratio scale properties. Earlier, the recent developments for treating only the ordinal properties of data were mentioned in the context of multidimensional scaling. Somewhat the same approach can be employed in factor analysis. In particular, a variable's correlation with another can be taken as an ordinal measure of their closeness in a Euclidean space. The methods of Shepard (1962*a*, *b*) and Kruskal (1964*a*, *b*) could then be applied, but methods have been designed to deal explicitly with this kind of data (Guttman 1967; Lingoes and Guttman 1967; Lingoes 1968). It is consistent with the ordinal orientation to use rank-order rather than Pearson correlations, and this feature can be incorporated.

The non-metric approach has the advantage of not requiring the kind of assumptions about the scale properties of the data that are often felt to be unrealistic with psychological measures. They have the additional advantage in the factor analysis context of avoiding complicated factor solutions that can arise with certain kinds of data where Guttman's (1954) radex concepts can apply. One can expect that an increasing proportion of studies will use these methods in preference to either the component or common factor models.

The Rotation Problem

All of the factor analytic models described in the previous section are indeterminate in the sense that there are an infinite number of factor loading matrices and/or factor scores that can be used to account equally well for the observed data or covariance matrix. The reason for this is that the factor loadings and scores are described in terms of a particular coordinate or basis system (these two defining systems often being confused in the models), and since these latter may be readily transformed, the factor loadings and scores are correspondingly transformed.

The difficulty can readily be seen from Equations 25 and 27. If

$$\mathbf{X} = \mathbf{FA'} + \mathbf{E} \qquad [28]$$

where F and A are defined as in Equations 25 and 26, then one can also have

$$\mathbf{X} = \mathbf{GB'} + \mathbf{E} \qquad [29]$$

where $\mathbf{X}$ and $\mathbf{E}$ are the same as in Equation 28, but $\mathbf{G} = \mathbf{FT}$ and $\mathbf{B} = \mathbf{AT}$, where $\mathbf{T}$ is an orthogonal transformation. (A similar relation can hold if $\mathbf{T}$ is not orthogonal, but now $\mathbf{G} = \mathbf{FT'^{-1}}$.) Correspondingly, wherever a solution A of Equation 27 is computed, we could have instead

$$\mathbf{R} = \mathbf{BB'} + \mathbf{U} \qquad [30]$$

where $\mathbf{B} = \mathbf{AT}$ ($\mathbf{T}$ orthogonal) or

$$\mathbf{AA'} = \mathbf{BTQT'B'} \qquad [31]$$

if $\mathbf{T}$ is not orthogonal. It should be noted that this does not mean that one can have any set of factor loadings he wants. Rather, it means that a large set of possibilities (often including none that one wants) are equally good numerical fits to the data at this level.

It should be admitted at this point that the principal component (or principal factor) and maximum likelihood methods yield factor loadings that are unique in their particular mathematical senses. On the other hand, once determined, the solutions can be transformed in the ways noted above while still giving an overall fit to the data that is just as good as that of the untransformed factors. The difference is that, somewhat artificially, these methods define the dimensions in the factor space in decreasing order of importance.

Criteria for determining the location of the axes. Additional principles must be invoked if the factor solution is to be determinate in any but a narrow, statistical sense which is a function of the particular data at hand. As noted earlier, the different kinds of additional constraints are either those resulting from considerations imposed by theories or expectations or of simplicity.

A substantive theory may predict the data with varying degrees of explicitness. A theory may require a particular mathematical function, in which case the methods of Tucker (1958) and Cliff (1962) are appropriate. Alternatively, it may predict the pattern of loadings in the factor matrix; here, the methods of Browne (1967) or Horst (1941) are used if the transformation is not required to be orthogonal, while those of Cliff (1966) or Schönnemann (1966) are used if it is. Also, Jöreskog (1967) provides a rather general procedure for fitting a factor matrix to hypotheses of varying degrees of specificity. Theory may guide the transformation even less explicitly, simply defining a stopping point for the process when a solution is judged to be "meaningful" in terms of the preconceptions of the investigator.

It is safe to say that by far the majority of studies utilizing factor analysis more often employ the concept of simplicity than theory to define the final form of the factor matrix. That is, the principle of parsimony is applied to the rotation process as well as to the factor extraction process. Generally stated, this requirement is that there should be as many near-zero entries in the factor matrix as possible, but there are a variety of ways in which this is made more specific. Thurstone (1935) formulated a set of criteria for "simple structure," but in practice, the criteria may be unattainable with a given set of data or attainable in many different ways. Consequently the usual practice is to seek the "best" solution, that one in which all factors are defined by at least a few high loadings but in which there are as many near zero ones as possible.

If the matrices for transforming the original factor loadings are orthogonal, the uncorrelatedness property of the factors in the model is retained. If oblique transformations are allowed, the common factors or component factors in the model are then correlated.

Rotation methods. Operationally, there are two quite distinct approaches to achieving simple structure. Originally (Thurstone 1935, 1948), the procedure was to plot pairs of columns of the factor matrix against each other and visually seek ways of rotating the axes of the figures so that the loading patterns would be simpler. Despite some simplifications in technique (e.g., Zimmerman 1946), the method is exceedingly tedious, cumbersome, and difficult for more than about five factors. There have been attempts to adapt it to the electronic computer (Tucker 1955b; Cattell and Muerle 1960), but the most commonly used computer rotation methods take a somewhat different tack.

The second approach to simple structure is to develop a numerical analogue of it. This yields the "analytic" rotation methods. Here, the paradigm is to define functions of the factor loadings that should reflect the degree of simple structure and then attempt to find the transformation that maximizes it. There is not sufficient space available here to develop the rationale completely, but it can be argued very reasonably that the degree of simple structure in a factor matrix should be reflected by the kurtosis of the distribution of factor loadings, and the currently most common methods of rotation attempt to maximize this parameter. There are a number of variations.

The earliest one started from the premise that the loading pattern of the *variables* should be simplified. Here, several different paths were taken to essentially the same mathematical solution (Carroll 1953; Neuhaus and Wrigley 1954; Saunders 1953) and the method is now generally referred to as the *quartimax* since it maximizes the sum of the fourth powers of the loadings. Alternatively, one may attempt to simplify the loadings on the factors. The method which seems to most successfully incorporate this consideration is *varimax* (Kaiser 1958). Saunders (1962) showed that the criterion functions in the case of quartimax and varimax were special cases of the same general function of the loadings. Certain terms in the function receive particular weights in these methods, but there are a wide variety of alternative sets of weights, each of which would define a rotation procedure. Thus the set of possible analytic rotation methods was extended.

These methods restrict the transformation matrix to orthogonality; there are analytic procedures for oblique rotation as well. Carroll (1953 1957) presented a series of formulations of the problem and solutions to it, arriving, as did Saunders in the orthogonal case, at a family of functions which could serve as the criterion to be maximized, different members of the family corresponding to special cases. Empirically, different oblique solutions tend to differ in the degree of correlation between the factors that they typically induce.

All of the analytic rotation methods are iterative, typically rotating the factors pairwise until no further improvement in the value of the criterion occurs. For all but very small numbers of factors they require the use of an electronic computer.

After more than a decade of experience with analytic rotation methods it is safe to say that they are frequently very useful but not universally successful. Where the simplicity of the structure is very great, they usually find an acceptable solution, but often one which is not the most esthetically pleasing possible. As the structure becomes more complex, they have increasing difficulty in finding the optimum position for the axes. Generally speaking, the orthogonal methods are more successful than the oblique, with quartimax less successful than varimax

and its derivatives. Harman (1967, chaps. 14, 15) gives an extensive discussion to which we would add the note that a combination of Procrustean and analytic methods may represent a more optimum approach. Since computational cost no longer inhibits the investigator from using large batteries of measures (in large problems, an optimum computer configuration can now turn out factor loadings for about two cents each, starting from a magnetic tape of the score matrix), so his curiosity and obsessiveness will more often than not lead him to do so. Consequently, he will very likely employ some kind of analytic procedure.

SAMPLING CONSIDERATIONS

The nature of the statistical problem. As was noted in the introductory remarks, psychometric theory, while largely based on stochastic data, for the most part followed an algebraic approach rather than explicitly incorporating the concepts of statistics into its initial models. These observations hold true in factor analysis as well as the other branches. There are some exceptions, especially in the most recent developments, but as originally formulated the factor problem is one of solving, say, Equation **28** for *the* set of factor loadings; sampling was not considered. Currently, there is a much stronger concern for sampling questions, although sometimes this is expressed only to the extent of saying that the assumed model is descriptive of the population, and methods for solving that would work with the population data will be employed in the sample. A number of developments do attempt to explicitly incorporate optimum sampling properties into factor methods and there is some interest in investigating the sampling characteristics of methods that are in widespread general use. Although some approaches to factor analysis emphasize the sampling of tests (e.g., Kaiser and Caffrey 1965), it is more consistent with the other applications of inferential statistics in psychology to attempt to assess the degree to which results of a factor analysis rest on person sampling.

In modern statistics, whether classical or Bayesian, statistical inference is attacked through the evaluation of the likelihood of the data conditional on a hypothesis about the value of population parameters. There is some awkwardness in translating this concept into factor analysis, but there are two main ways in which sampling notions have been brought to bear, both revolving around the model of common factor analysis. These two are the maximum likelihood and the Monte Carlo approaches.

Maximum likelihood methods and the number of factors. Here, the common factor model is assumed to hold in a population where the factor scores are normally distributed, and estimates of the parameters (common factor loadings and uniquenesses) which maximize the likelihood function are sought. The resulting equations can be solved, at least in principle. A necessary part of the methods is a hypothesis concerning the number of common factors, but a statistical test of the hypothesis that the given number of factors satisfactorily accounts for the covariances among the variables is usually included. Important contributions to the maximum likelihood methods were made by Lawley (1940, 1953), and Rao (1955), and more recently by Jöreskog (1963, 1967).

Guttman (1958) contends that the null hypothesis is stated in the wrong direction since the rejection of the null hypothesis there implies that more factors are necessary. He contends that the null hypothesis should be that there are many common factors rather than only a few. In justification of the maximum likelihood methods it may be stated that if there are many common factors the estimates of loadings on them will contain a large proportion of error. One can contend that one does not simply want to know if the null hypothesis is false, but how it is false. The number of significant maximum likelihood factors might be interpreted as those whose loadings can be estimated sufficiently free of sampling error.

The maximum likelihood methods provide what seems to be the only rigorously derived methods for deciding on the number of "significant" factors. A number of others have been proposed on heuristic grounds, depending on the relative sizes of the eigenvalues of the correlation matrix (Cattell 1966b) or through the use of artificially generated auxiliary data (Horn 1965; Linn 1968). The rules provided by Kaiser (1960) are based on the sampling of variables rather than of persons.

Sampling stability of loadings. Maximum likelihood methods have in some instances provided sampling variances for the factor loadings (e.g., Jöreskog 1963), and McNemar (1941) proposed that factor loadings have the same sampling characteristics as the correlation coefficients on which they are based. These are not fully satisfactory, however, so much of the information on the stability of factor loadings under sampling has come from Monte Carlo sampling studies.

Answers to this question are complicated by the fact that the methods used to estimate the loadings must be specified. Cliff and Hamburger (1967) argue that the degree of stability of principal factor loadings may vary greatly, depending on the relative sizes of the factors, but it seems that the stability may in some cases approach that of the correlation coefficient (cf. Browne 1968). The only data with respect to analytically rotated loadings is provided by Hamburger (1964), who concluded that sampling variances of loadings were about $1/N$ in cases where the simple structure was well defined. The largest amount of data is from studies where the obtained sample factors are rotated to a best fit with the population factors (Cliff and Pennell 1967; Pennell 1968). Here, the data indicate quite clearly that ideally the sampling variances of loadings are

$$\sigma_a^2 = \frac{1 - a^2}{N} \qquad [32]$$

where a is the size of the loading in question. This limit will be approached as the communalities are well estimated, the factors all have substantial independent variance on them, and the sample size is large. This degree of stability is quite consistent with the typical practices in interpreting loadings, but indications are that the sampling situation may deteriorate if the ideal is departed from too far.

Investigations, empirical and theoretical, into sampling questions in factor analysis may never be fully satisfactory in the sense that the investigator may not be able to attach probability statements to his results in all applications. To some extent this is inherent in the exploratory and descriptive nature of factor analyses. The indications are, though, that where the state of knowledge of the factors underlying scores on the measures reaches a high level, there it may be possible to statistically evaluate the conformity of the data to a detailed hypothesis.

Conclusions

In a sense, factor analysis is a set of related models for scaling stimuli, using the degree to which they lead to individual differences as the basis for scaling the stimuli on dimensions. The nature of these underlying dimensions must be inferred from the measures that "go together" on the factors, subject to verification by studies involving other measures, especially newly developed ones. As such it is not a method suited for one-shot studies, but rather one which can be one of several used in programmatic projects.

A persistent problem with factor analysis is the degree to which the basic data are not themselves sufficient to define the solution, but rather the investigator is given latitude to intrude himself into the process. We have seen that there have been attempts, such as through the simple structure concept, and through the use of statistical tests, to introduce a greater degree of objectivity into the process. As in the case of all other models, it is well to remember that the factor loadings of the variables are determined only in the context of the model invoked to arrive at them, and are valid only insofar as the model is appropriate. In many of its forms, factor analysis may not have enough psychological content to yield, in itself, final information about the variables.

On the favorable side, one should call attention to the fact that factor analysis can contribute to the understanding of many psychological problems. Perhaps most important here is its usefulness to the study of human cognitive functioning and the nature of its development, primarily through showing that different tasks behave differently. For example, the methods of the study by Durham, Guilford, and Hoepfner (1968) provide unique and useful information on the nature of human concept learning. The methods of factor analysis have also found application to a wide spectrum of areas other than the study of individual differences. Here, in addition to the previously noted applications to multidimensional scaling (Tucker and Messick 1963) and learning (Tucker 1960), one may also cite its use in neurophysiology (John 1967).

Concluding Remarks

Psychometrics has been described here as consisting primarily of a series of models for analyzing data in order to derive measurements of subjects and stimuli on psychologically relevant variables. The foundation of any measurement has been taken to rest on a theoretical system formulation or model for a class of observations; measurement does not exist in the abstract, but rather measurements owe their status to the demonstration that when appropriately entered as variables into models, the resulting system has an explanatory power and conceptual simplicity. The foregoing holds true even when the observations have what are apparently direct numerical interpretations, as is the case with the most familiar kinds of physical measurements. It might further be argued that their apparent directness is the result of centuries of verification of their involvement in readily verifiable systems.

In all fields, very many examples of measurement are those in which there is a model intervening between the observation, such as of how far a pointer moves, to the quantity measured, such as a voltage. An aspect which is perhaps more important for psychology is the degree to which a large number of observations, each of which individually has only weak quantitative properties rather than the strong ones of the numbers, can be used collectively to define measurement scales that have virtually all of the properties of the real number system itself. Thus measurement is the process of going, with varying degrees of directness, from the observations themselves to more general variables assumed to underlie them.

In psychology, measurement concentrates on the quantification of stimulus properties and of the characteristics of individuals. Parallel to the recent movement in psychology away from the view of the stimulus as externally definable, stimulus measurement might currently be more properly defined as the attempt to quantify the internal response to an objective situation, and perhaps with the quantification of the relations among internal responses. We defined this area as the field of scaling. Some of the main problems with which scaling models have been designed to deal were described here, emphasizing again the degree to which measurement was tied to the particular model used.

The other two major subfields of psychometrics, test theory and factor analysis, concern themselves with the measurement of characteristics of individuals. Actually, test theory concentrates on the characteristics of good measuring devices and on the degree to which manifest observations reflect the underlying attribute. The aspects of the models which are concerned with going between the observation and the attribute are fairly straightforward in all but the most recent developments. The psychological content of test theory models is meager but increasing; their main concern is with the behavior of test scores rather than of people, but the traceline models represent at least some departure from this.

The models of factor analysis are at least somewhat more psychological than those of test theory. Factor analytic models are rather primitive and weak ones which attempt to define the dimensions of stimuli which are most relevant to the existence of individual differences. The very indeterminateness of the factor model in its most general form necessitates the addition of some psychological principles in order to make the factor solution other than the outcome of haphazard circumstances.

To date, psychometrics has provided a set of methods which have proved useful for a number of scientific and practical purposes. It showed that stimuli and individuals could be "measured" in ways that were relevant to psychology as a whole. Currently, psychology is changing in a number of ways which are relevant to the place of psychometrics in psychology. One of the ways is through the development of specific mathematical models for psychological processes. The continuing development of psychometrics should lead from a field focusing on the measurement of *the* psychological characteristics of stimuli and persons to one focusing more generally on the quantification of variables in these models.

References

ABELSON, R. P., and J. W. TUKEY. Efficient conversion of nonmetric information into metric information. *Proceedings of the Social Statistics Section, American Statistical Association*, 1959, pp. 226–30.

ADAMS, E. W., R. F. FAGOT, and R. E. ROBINSON. A theory of approximate statistics. *Psychometrika*, 1965, *30*, 99–127.

ATKINSON, R. C., G. H. BOWER, and E. J. CROTHERS. *An introduction to mathematical learning theory*. New York: Wiley, 1965.

ATTNEAVE, F. Dimensions of similarity. *American Journal of Psychology*, 1950, *63*, 516–56.

BARTLETT, M. S. Tests of significance in factor analysis. *British Journal of Mathematical and Statistical Psychology*, 1950, *3*, 77–85.

BENNETT, J. F., and W. L. HAYS. Multidimensional unfolding: Determining the dimensionality of ranked preference data. *Psychometrika*, 1960, *25*, 27–43.

BIRNBAUM, A. Some latent trait models and their use in inferring an examinee's ability. *In* F. M. LORD and M. R. NOVICK, *Statistical theories of mental test scores*. Reading, Mass.: Addison-Wesley, 1968.

BOCK, R. D., and L. V. JONES. *The measurement and prediction of judgment and choice*. San Francisco: Holden-Day, 1968.

BRADLEY, R. A., and M. E. TERRY. Rank analysis of incomplete block designs: I. The method of paired comparisons. *Biometrika*, 1952, *39*, 324–45.

BROWNE, M. W. On oblique Procrustes rotation. *Psychometrika*, 1967, *32*, 125–32.

——— A comparison of factor analytic techniques. *Psychometrika*, 1968, *33*, 267–334.

BURKE, C. J., and J. L. ZINNES. A paired comparison of pair comparison. *Journal of Mathematical Psychology*, 1965, *2*, 53–76.

CAMPBELL, D. N., and D. W. FISKE. Convergent and discriminant validation by the multitrait multimethod matrix. *Psychological Bulletin*, 1959, *56*, 81–105.

CAMPBELL, N. R. *Physics, the elements*. Cambridge: Cambridge University Press, 1920. [Republished as *Foundations of science*. New York: Dover, 1957.]

CARROLL, J. B. An analytical solution for approximating simple structure in factor analysis. *Psychometrika*, 1953, *18*, 23–38.

——— Biquartimin criterion for rotation to oblique simple structure in factor analysis. *Science*, 1957, *126*, 1114–15.

CARROLL, J. D., and J. CHANG. Relating preference data to multidimensional scaling solutions via a generalization of Coombs' unfolding model. (Paper read at meeting of Psychometric Society, Madison, Wisconsin, 1967.)

CATTELL, R. B. The data box: Its ordering of total resources in terms of possible relational systems. *In* R. B. CATTELL, ed., *Handbook of multivariate experimental psychology*. Chicago: Rand McNally, 1966, pp. 67–128. (*a*)

——— The meaning and strategic use of factor analysis. *Ibid.*, 1966, pp. 174–243. (*b*)

———, ed. *Handbook of multivariate statistical psychology*. Chicago: Rand McNally, 1966. (*c*)

———, and J. L. MUERLE. The "maxplane" program for factor rotation to oblique simple structure. *Educational and Psychological Measurement*, 1960, *20*, 569–90.

CLEARY, T. A., R. L. LINN, and D. A. ROCK. An exploratory study of programmed tests. *Research Bulletin 66–44*. Princeton: Educational Testing Service, 1966.

CLIFF, N. Adverbs as multipliers. *Psychological Review*, 1959, *66*, 27–44.

——— Analytic rotation to a functional relationship. *Psychometrika*, 1962, *27*, 283–96.

——— Orthogonal rotation to congruence. *Psychometrika*, 1966, *31*, 33–42.

——— Adjective check list responses and individual differences in perceived meaning. *Educational and Psychological Measurement*, 1968, *28*, 1063–1077.

——— Liking judgments and multidimensional scaling. *Educational and Psychological Measurement*, 1969, *29*, 73–85.

——— and C. D. HAMBURGER. The study of sampling errors in factor analysis by means of artificial experiments. *Psychological Bulletin*, 1967, *68*, 430–45.

——— and R. PENNELL. The influence of communality, factor strength, and loading size on the sampling characteristics of factor loadings. *Psychometrika*, 1967, *32*, 309–26.

——— and F. W. YOUNG. On the relation between unidimensional judgments and multidimensional scaling. *Organizational Behavior and Human Performance*, 1968, *3*, 269–85.

CLIFF, R. The effect of unlike distributions on the weights of variables. *Educational and Psychological Measurement*, 1960, *20*, 305–10.

COAN, R. W. Basic forms of covariation and concomitance designs. *Psychological Bulletin*, 1961, *58*, 317–24.

COOMBS, C. H. A theory of psychological scaling. *Bulletin No. 34*, 1952, Engineering Research Institute, University of Michigan.

—— *A theory of data*. New York: Wiley, 1964.

CRONBACH, L. J. Coefficient alpha and the internal structure of tests. *Psychometrika*, 1951, *16*, 297–334.

——, and H. AZUMA. Internal-consistency reliability formulas applied to randomly sampled single-factor tests: An empirical comparison. *Educational and Psychological Measurement*, 1962, *22*, 645–65.

——, and P. E. MEEHL. Construct validity in psychological tests. *Psychological Bulletin*, 1955, *52*, 281–302.

——, N. RAJARATNAM, and G. C. GLESER. Theory of generalizability: A liberalization of reliability theory. *British Journal of Statistical Psychology*, 1963, *16*, 137–63.

DOELERT, D. H., and A. E. HOERL. Finding the preferred regions in a multidimensional space. (Paper read at meeting of Psychometric Society, Madison, Wisconsin, 1967.)

DUNHAM, J. L., J. P. GUILFORD, and R. HOEPFNER. Multivariate approaches to discovering the intellectual components of concept learning. *Psychological Review*, 1968, *75*, 206–21.

ECKHART, C., and G. YOUNG. The approximation of one matrix by another of lower rank. *Psychometrika*, 1936, *1*, 211–18.

EGAN, J. P., and F. R. CLARKE. Psychophysics and signal detection. *In* J. B. SIDOWSKI, ed., *Experimental methods and instrumentation in psychology*. New York: McGraw-Hill, 1966, pp. 211–46.

EIJKMAN, E., J. M. THIJSSEN, and J. A. H. VENDRIK. Weber's law, power law and internal noise. *Journal of the Acoustical Society of America*, 1966, *40*, 1164–73.

EISLER, H. Magnitude scales, category scales, and Fechnerian integration. *Psychological Review*, 1963, *70*, 243–53.

—— The connection between magnitude and discrimination scales and direct and indirect scaling methods. *Psychometrika*, 1965, *30*, 271–89.

EKMAN, G. Dimensions of color vision. *Journal of Psychology*, 1954, *38*, 467–74.

—— A direct method for multidimensional ratio scaling. *Psychometrika*, 1963, *28*, 33–41.

—— Is the power law a special case of Fechner's law? *Perceptual and Motor Skills*, 1964, *19*, 730.

—— and T. KÜNNAPAS. Scales of aesthetic value. *Perceptual and Motor Skills*, 1962, *14*, 19–26.

——, and L. SJOBERG. Scaling. *Annual Review of Psychology*, 1965, *16*, 451–74.

ELLIS, B. *Basic concepts of measurement*. Cambridge: Cambridge University Press, 1966.

ENGEN, T., and N. LEVY. The influence of standards on psychophysical judgment. *Perceptual and Motor Skills*, 1955, *5*, 193–97.

GALANTER, E. H., and S. MESSICK. The relation between category and magnitude scales of loudness. *Psychological Review*, 1961, *68*, 363–72.

GHISELLI, E. E. *Theory of psychological measurement*. New York: McGraw-Hill, 1964.

GLESER, G. C., L. J. CRONBACH, and N. RAJARATNAM. Generalizability of scores influenced by multiple sources of variance. *Psychometrika*, 1965, *30*, 395–418.

GOLLOB, H. F. A statistical model which combines features of factor analytic and analysis of variance techniques. *Psychometrika*, 1968, *33*, 73–116.

GREEN, B. F. A general solution for the latent class model of latent structure analysis. *Psychometrika*, 1951, *16*, 151–66.

GREEN, D. M. Psychoacoustics and detection theory. *Journal of the Acoustical Society of America*, 1960, *32*, 1189–1203.

——, and J. A. SWETS. *Signal detection theory and psychophysics*. New York: Wiley, 1966.

GREEN, P. E., and F. J. CARMONE. Advertisement perception and evaluation: An application of multidimensional scaling. [Philadelphia, Marketing Science Institute, University of Pennsylvania, 1968. (Multilithed report.)]

GUILFORD, J. P. *Psychometric methods*. New York: McGraw-Hill, 1954.

—— *Fundamental statistics in psychology and education* (4th ed.). New York: McGraw-Hill, 1965.

—— *The nature of human intelligence*. New York: McGraw-Hill, 1967.

GULLIKSEN, H. *Theory of mental tests*. New York: Wiley, 1950.

GUTTMAN, L. General theory and methods for matrix factoring. *Psychometrika*, 1944, *9*, 1–16.

—— The basis for scalogram analysis. *In* S. A. STOUFFER et al., eds., *Measurement and prediction*. Princeton: Princeton University Press, 1950.

—— A new approach to factor analysis: The radex. *In* P. F. LAZARSFELD, ed., *Mathematical thinking in the social sciences*. Glencoe, Ill.: Free Press, 1954, pp. 216–348. (*a*)

—— Some necessary conditions for common factor analysis. *Psychometrika*, 1954, *19*, 149–61. (*b*)

—— A generalized simplex for factor analysis. *Psychometrika*, 1955, *20*, 173–92.

—— Empirical verification of the radex structure of mental abilities and personality traits. *Educational and Psychological Measurement*, 1957, *17*, 391–407.

—— To what extent can communalities reduce rank? *Psychometrika*, 1958, *23*, 497–515.

—— The development of nonmetric space analysis: A letter to Professor John Ross. *Multivariate Behavioral Research*, 1967, *2*, 71–83.

HAMBURGER, C. D. Factorial stability as a function of analytic rotation method, type of factor pattern, and size of sample. (Unpublished doctoral dissertation, University of Southern California, 1965.)

HARMAN, H. H. *Modern factor analysis* (2d ed.). Chicago: University of Chicago Press, 1967.

——, and W. H. JONES. Factor analysis by minimizing residuals. *Psychometrika*, 1966, *31*, 351–68.

HELM, C. E. A successive intervals analysis of color differences. [Princeton: Educational Testing Service, 1960. (Multilithed report.)]

—— Multidimensional ratio scaling analysis of perceived color relations. *Journal of the Optical Society of America*, 1964, *54*, 256–62.

HELSON, H. *Adaptation-level theory*. New York: Harper, 1964.

HOEPFNER, R., J. L. DUNHAM, and J. P. GUILFORD. Simplex components. *Multivariate Behavioral Research*, 1968, *3*, 161–72.

HOHLE, R. H. An empirical evaluation and comparison of two models for discriminability scales. *Journal of Mathematical Psychological Psychology*, 1966, *3*, 174–83.

HORN, J. L. A rationale and test for the number of factors in factor analysis. *Psychometrika*, 1965, *30*, 313–22.

HORST, P. A non-graphical method for transforming an arbitrary factor matrix into a simple structure factor matrix. *Psychometrika*, 1941, *6*, 79–99.

—— *Factor analysis of data matrices*. New York: Holt, Rinehart and Winston, 1965.

—— *Psychological measurement and prediction*. Belmont, Calif.: Wadsworth, 1966.

HOTELLING, H. Analysis of a complex of statistical variables into principal components. *Journal of Educational Psychology*, 1933, *24*, 417–41.

HOYT, C. Test reliability estimated by analysis of variance. *Psychometrika*, 1941, 6, 153–60.

HYMAN, R., and A. WELL. Judgments of similarity and spatial models, *Perception and Psychophysics*, 1967, *2*, 233–48.

JACKSON, D. N., and S. MESSICK. Response styles and the assessment of psychopathology. *In* S. MESSICK and J. ROSS, eds., *Measurement in personality and cognition*. New York: Wiley, 1962.

JACKSON, R. W. B., and G. A. FERGUSON. *Studies in the reliability of tests*. Bulletin 12. Toronto: Department of Educational Research, University of Toronto, 1941.

JOHN, E. R. *Mechanisms of memory*. New York: Academic Press, 1967.

JÖRESKOG, K. G. *Statistical estimation in factor analysis*. Stockholm: Almquist and Wiksell, 1963.

—— A general approach to confirmatory maximum likelihood factor analysis. Research Bulletin 67–48. Princeton: Educational Testing Service, 1967. (multilith.) (*a*)

—— Some contributions to maximum likelihood factor analysis, *Psychometrika*, 1967, *32*, 443–82. (*b*)

KAISER, H. F. The varimax criterion for analytic rotation in factor analysis. *Psychometrika*, 1958, *23*, 187–200.

—— The application of electronic computers to factor analysis. *Educational and Psychological Measurement*, 1960, *20*, 141–51.

KEATS, J. A. Test theory. *Annual Review of Psychology*, 1967, *18*, 217–38.

KENDALL, M. G., and A. STUART. *The advanced theory of statistics* (2nd ed.), vol. I. New York: Hafner, 1963.

KRANTZ, D. H. Conjoint measurement: The Luce-Tukey axiomatization and some extensions. *Journal of Mathematical Psychology*, 1964, *1*, 248–77.

KRUSKAL, J. B. Multidimensional scaling by optimizing goodness of fit to a nonmetric hypothesis. *Psychometrika*, 1964, *29*, 1–27. (*a*)

—— Nonmetric multidimensional scaling: A numerical method. *Psychometrika*, 1964, *29*, 115–29. (*b*)

KÜNNAPAS, T. Scales for subjective distance. *Scandinavian Journal of Psychology*, 1960, *1*, 187–92.

—— Note on ratio estimation. *Scandinavian Journal of Psychology*, 1967, *8*, 77–80.

LAWLEY, D. N. The estimation of factor loadings by the method of maximum likelihood. *Proceedings of the Royal Society of Edinburgh*, 1940, *60*, 64–82.

—— A modified method of estimation in factor analysis and some large sample results. *Uppsala symposium on psychological factor analysis*. Uppsala: Almquist and Wiksell, 1953, pp. 35–42.

——, and A. E. MAXWELL. *Factor analysis as a statistical method.* London: Butterworth, 1963.

LAZARSFELD, P. F. The logical and mathematical foundation of latent structure analysis. *In* S. A. STOUFFER et al., eds., *Measurement and prediction.* Princeton: Princeton University Press, 1950, pp. 362–412.

—— A conceptual introduction to latent structure analysis. *In* P. F. LAZARSFELD, ed., *Mathematical thinking in the social sciences.* Glencoe, Ill.: Free Press, 1954, pp. 349–87.

——, and N. W. HENRY. *Latent structure analysis.* New York: Houghton Mifflin, 1968.

LINGOES, J. C. The multivariate analysis of qualitative data. *Multivariate Behavioral Research*, 1968, *3*, 61–94.

——, and L. GUTTMAN. Nonmetric factor analysis: A rank reducing alternative to linear factor analysis. *Multivariate Behavioral Research*, 1967, *2*, 485–505.

LINN, R. L. A Monte Carlo approach to the number of factors problem. *Psychometrika*, 1968, *33*, 37–72.

LORD, F. M. An empirical study of the normality and independence of errors of measurement in test scores. *Psychometrika*, 1960, *25*, 91–104. (*a*)

—— Inferring the examinee's true score. *In* H. GULLIKSEN and S. MESSICK, eds., *Psychological scaling: Theory and applications.* New York: Wiley, 1960, pp. 97–108. (*b*)

—— A strong true-score theory with applications, *Psychometrika*, 1965, *30*, 239–70.

—— Estimating true-score distributions in psychological testing (an empirical Bayes estimation problem). Princeton: Educational Testing Service, 1967. (Multilithed report.)

——, and M. R. NOVICK. *Statistical theories of mental test scores.* Reading, Mass.: Addison-Wesley, 1968.

LUCE, R. D. *Individual choice behavior.* New York: Wiley, 1959. (*a*)

—— On the possible psychophysical laws. *Psychological Review*, 1959, *66*, 81–95. (*b*)

—— Comments on Rozeboom's criticism of "On the possible psychophysical laws." *Psychological Review*, 1962, *69*, 548–51.

—— Detection and recognition. *In* R. D. LUCE et al., eds., *Handbook of mathematical psychology.* New York: Wiley, 1963, pp. 103–91.

——, and W. EDWARDS. The derivation of subjective scales from just noticeable differences. *Psychological Review*, 1958, *65*, 222–37.

——, and J. W. TUKEY. Simultaneous conjoint measurement: A new type of fundamental measurement. *Journal of Mathematical Psychology*, 1964, *1*, 1–27.

MARKOWITZ, J., and J. A. SWETS. Factors affecting the slope of empirical ROC curves: Comparison of binary and rating responses. *Perception and Psychophysics*, 1967, *2*, 91–97.

MASHOUR, M., and J. HOSMAN. On the new "psychophysical law": A validation study. *Perception and Psychophysics*, 1968, *3*, 367–75.

MCDONALD, R. P. A note on the derivation of the general latent class model. *Psychometrika*, 1962, *27*, 203–6. (*a*)

—— A general approach to nonlinear factor analysis. *Psychometrika*, 1962, *27*, 397–414. (*b*)

—— Difficulty factors and nonlinear factor analysis. *British Journal of Mathematical and Statistical Psychology*, 1965, *18*, 11–23.

—— Numerical methods for polynomial models in nonlinear factor analysis. *Psychometrika*, 1967, *32*, 77–112.

MCNEMAR, Q. On the sampling errors of factor loadings. *Psychometrika*, 1941, *6*, 141–52.

MEREDITH, W. Some results based on a general stochastic model for mental tests. *Psychometrika*, 1965, *30*, 419–40.

MESSICK, S., and R. P. ABELSON. The additive constant problem in multidimensional scaling. *Psychometrika*, 1956, *21*, 1–17.

MORRISON, H. W. Testable conditions for triads of paired comparisons choices. *Psychometrika*, 1963, *28*, 369–90.

MOSIER, C. I. Determining simple structure when loadings for certain tests are known. *Psychometrika*, 1939, *4*, 149–62.

MOSTELLER, F. Remarks on the method of paired comparisons: III. Test of significance for paired comparisons when equal standard deviations and equal correlations are assumed. *Psychometrika*, 1951, *16*, 207–18.

NEUHAUS, J. O., and C. WRIGLEY. The quartimax method: An analytical approach to orthogonal simple structure. *British Journal of Mathematical and Statistical Psychology*, 1954, 81–91.

NOVICK, M. R. The axioms and principal results of classical test theory. *Journal of Mathematical Psychology*, 1966, *3*, 1–18.

OSGOOD, C. E., G. J. SUCI, and P. H. TANNENBAUM. *The measurement of meaning.* Urbana: University of Illinois Press, 1957.

PARDUCCI, A. Range-frequency compromise in judgment. *Psychological Monographs*, 1963, *77*, (2, Whole No. 565).

PENNELL, R. The influence of communality and N on the sampling distributions of factor loadings. *Psychometrika*, 1968, *33*, 423–440.

PETERSON, W. W., T. G. BIRDSALL, and W. C. FOX. The theory of signal detectability. *IRE Transactions*, 1954, *PGIT-4*, 171–212.

RAJARATNAM, N., L. J. CRONBACH, and G. C. GLESER. Generalizability of stratified-parallel tests. *Psychometrika*, 1965, *30*, 39–56.

RAO, C. R. Estimation and tests of significance in factor analysis. *Psychometrika*, 1955, *20*, 93–111.

RASCH, G. *Studies in mathematical psychology, I. Probabilistic models for some intelligence and attainment tests.* Copenhagen, Denmark: Danish Institute of Educational Research, 1960.

RICHARDSON, M. W. Multidimensional psychophysics. *Psychological Bulletin*, 1938, *35*, 650–60.

ROSKIES, R. A measurement axiomatization for an essentially multiplicative representation of two factors. *Journal of Mathematical Psychology*, 1965, *2*, 266–76.

ROSS, J. An empirical study of a logistic test model. *Psychometrika*, 1966, *31*, 325–40.

——, and N. CLIFF. A generalization of the interpoint distance model. *Psychometrika*, 1964, *29*, 167–76.

——, and V. DILOLLO. A vector model for psychophysical judgment. *Journal of Experimental Psychology*, 1968, 77 (Monograph Supplement, No. 3).

ROZEBOOM, W. W. The untenability of Luce's principle. *Psychological Review*, 1962, *69*, 542–47.

—— *Foundations of the theory of prediction.* Homewood, Ill.: The Dorsey Press, 1966.

SAUNDERS, D. R. An analytic method for rotation to simple structure. Research Bulletin 53–10. Princeton: Educational Testing Service, 1953. (Multilith.)

—— Trans-varimax: Some properties of the ratiomax and equamax criteria for blind orthogonal rotation. *American Psychologist*, 1962, *17*, 395–96 (abstract).

SCHÖNEMANN, P. H. A generalized solution of the orthogonal Procrustes problem. *Psychometrika*, 1966, *31*, 1–10.

SHEPARD, R. N. Stimulus and response generalization: Tests of a model relating generalization to distance in Psychological space. *Journal of Experimental Psychology*, 1958, *55*, 509–23.

—— Similarity of stimuli and metric properties of behavioral data. *In* H. GULLIKSEN and S. MESSICK, eds., *Psychological scaling: Theory and methods.* New York: Wiley, 1960, pp. 33–43.

—— The analysis of proximities: Multidimensional scaling with an unknown distance function: I. *Psychometrika*, 1962, 125–40.

—— The analysis of proximities: Multidimensional scaling with an unknown distance function: II. *Psychometrika*, 1962, *27*, 219–46.

———— Attention and the metric structure of the stimulus space. *Journal of Mathematical Psychology*, 1964, *1*, 54–87.

STARKWEATHER, J. A. Computest: A computer language for individual testing, instruction, and interviewing. *Psychological Reports*, 1965, *17*, 227–37.

STEVENS, S. S. Mathematics, Measurement, and Psychophysics. *In* S. S. STEVENS, ed., *Handbook of Experimental Psychology*. New York: Wiley, 1951, pp. 1–49.

———— On the psychophysical law. *Psychological Review*, 1957, *64*, 153–81.

———— Problems and methods of psychophysics. *Psychological Bulletin*, 1958, *54*, 177–96.

———— Cross-modality validation of subjective scales for loudness, vibration, and electric shock. *Journal of Experimental Psychology*, 1959, *57*, 201–9. (*a*)

———— Measurement, psychophysics, and utility. *In* C. W. CHURCHMAN, and P. RATOOSH, eds., *Measurement: Definition and theories*. New York: Wiley, 1959, pp. 18–63. (*b*)

———— Toward a resolution of the Fechner-Thurstone Legacy. *Psychometrika*, 1961, *26*, 35–48.

————, and E. H. GALANTER. Ratio scales and category scales for a dozen perceptual continua. *Journal of Experimental Psychology*, 1957, *54*, 377–411.

SUTCLIFFE, J. P., and R. A. BRISTOW. Do rank order and scale properties remain invariant under changes in the set of scaled stimuli? *Australian Journal of Psychology*, 1966, *18*, 26–40.

SWETS, J. A. Detection theory and psychophysics: A review. *Psychometrika*, 1961, *26*, 49–63.

————, W. P. TANNER, JR., and T. G. BIRDSALL. Decision processes in perception. *Psychological Review*, 1961, *68*, 301–40.

TANNER, W. P., and J. A. SWETS. A decision-making theory of visual detection. *Psychological Review*, 1954, *61*, 401–9.

THIJSSEN, J. M., and A. J. H. VENDRIK. Internal noise and transducer function in sensory detection experiments: Evaluation of psychometric curves and ROC curves. *Perception and Psychophysics*, 1968, *3*, 387–400.

THOMSON, G. H. Hotelling's method modified to give Spearman's g. *Journal of Educational Psychology*, 1934, *25*, 366–74.

THURSTONE, L. L. *The vectors of mind*. Chicago: University of Chicago Press, 1935.

———— *Multiple factor analysis*. Chicago: University of Chicago Press, 1947.

———— *The measurement of values*. Chicago: University of Chicago Press, 1959.

TORGERSON, W. S. Multidimensional scaling: I. Theory and method. *Psychometrika*, 1952, *17*, 401–19.

———— *Theory and methods of scaling*. New York: Wiley, 1958.

———— Multidimensional scaling of similarity, *Psychometrika*, 1965, *30*, 379–94.

TREISMAN, M., and WATTS, R. R. Relation between signal detectability theory and the traditional procedures for measuring sensory thresholds: Estimating d' from results given by the method of constant stimuli. *Psychological Bulletin*, 1966, *66*, 438–545.

TUCKER, L. R. Some experiments in developing a behaviorally determined scale of vocabulary. Research Memorandum 55–10. Princeton: Educational Testing Service, 1955. (*a*)

———— The objective definition of simple structure in factor analysis. *Psychometrika*, 1955, *20*, 209–25. (*b*)

———— Determination of parameters of a functional relationship by factor analysis. *Psychometrika*, 1958, *23*, 111–37.

———— Determination of generalized learning curves by factor analysis. ONR Technical Report. Princeton: Educational Testing Service, 1960. (Multilith.)

———— Some mathematical notes on three-mode factor analysis. *Psychometrika*, 1966, *31*, 279–311.

————, and S. MESSICK. An individual differences model for multidimensional scaling. *Psychometrika*, 1963, *28*, 333–67.

TVERSKY, A. A general theory of polynomial conjoint measurement. *Journal of Mathematical Psychology*, 1967, *4*, 1–20.

WEITZENHOFFER, A. M. Mathematical structures and psychological measurements. *Psychometrika*, 1951, *16*, 387–406.

WOODWORTH, R. S., and H. SCHLOSBERG. *Experimental psychology* (rev. ed.) New York: Holt, Rinehart and Winston, 1954.

YOUNG, F. W., and ROGER J. PENNELL. An IBM system/360 program for points of view analysis. *Behavioral Science*, 1967, *12*, 166.

YOUNG, G., and A. S. HOUSEHOLDER. Discussion of a set of points in terms of their mutual distances. *Psychometrika*, 1938, *3*, 19–22.

ZIMMERMAN, W. S. A simple graphical method for orthogonal rotation of axes. *Psychometrika*, 1946, *11*, 51–55.

This chapter focuses on the design of psychological experiments, with only incidental attention to the ensuing statistical analysis. It deals more with logic and taxonomy than with mathematics. Of course, one cannot separate design from analysis fully, though they can be discussed somewhat apart. Good design is the *sine qua non* for rigorous analysis. It is possible to have a well-designed and well-executed experiment, and yet analyze the resulting data improperly; but it is scarcely possible to have a poor design and excellent analysis. If one brings the statistical consultant a bucketful of data gathered without much attention to principles of experimental design, about all the statistician can do is to perform an autopsy to see what the data died of. This statement may seem a bit extreme, but it is meant to drive home a warning against thinking that an experimental design can be imposed suitably on already-gathered results. This is not to say that researchers cannot make any sense out of "nature's experiments," such as evolution or cigarette smoking. Darwin did and medical researchers do, but not quickly or easily. Later we shall see some of the pitfalls such persons encounter because their data do not come from controlled experiments, and how they surmount them.

Principles of experimental design are based on simple but uncommon logic—the same kind of logic that enables some persons to detect fallacies in advertising. It seems to be composed of approximately two parts skepticism, two parts relevant information, and three parts deductive and inductive reasoning. (Even bright graduate students and professors within a field such as psychology appear to vary greatly in this respect.)

Take a familiar statement such as "Our group had 20 percent fewer [dental] cavities," made by an attractive child on television. Just what does that mean? The statement may be supported by an experiment; if so, the full technical report of that experiment should be studied. The reader needs to ask several questions, among them the following: Fewer than what other groups? How were they treated? With the worst possible tooth-paste, or even with no brushing at all? How were the various groups chosen or formed? Were they all equally susceptible to cavities? Were the groups large enough so that a

Julian C. Stanley

Designing Psychological Experiments

6

20 percent difference in favor of one is not due to chance? Was just one comparison of "our" group with the other group(s) made, or did the toothpaste company commission a large number of comparisons and then report just those findings favorable to its product? For many splendid examples of the need for this type of alertness and caution when reading advertisements or even the daily newspaper, see Wallis and Roberts (1955).

Four Kinds of Experiments

We shall consider four kinds of experiments: *controlled, quasi-, natural,* and *pseudo-*. Most of our attention will be given to *controlled experimentation,* because where applicable it is the preferred type of psychological research, well represented in most of the journals published by the American Psychological Association, and particularly in the *Journal of Experimental Psychology*. It will be defined and discussed in the next section and thereafter.

Quasi-experiments, like fully controlled experiments, are systematically managed attempts to manipulate certain aspects of the research environment, even though other aspects are intractable (Campbell 1957). (Here the prefix "quasi-" means "almost" or "nearly.") Campbell and Stanley define quasi-experiments as follows:

There are many natural social settings in which the research person can introduce something like experimental design into his scheduling of data collection procedures (e.g., the when *and to* whom *of measurement), even though he lacks the full control over the scheduling of experimental stimuli (the* when *and to whom of exposure and the ability to randomize exposures) which makes a true experiment possible. Collectively, such situations can be regarded as quasi-experimental designs. One purpose of this [volume] is to encourage the utilization of such quasi-experiments and to increase awareness of the kinds of settings in which opportunities to employ them occur. But just because full experimental control is lacking, it becomes imperative that the researcher be thoroughly aware of which specific variables his particular design fails to control. It is for this need in evaluating quasi-experiments, more than for understanding true experiments, that the check lists of sources of invalidity [see pp. 104–5, below] . . . were developed. (1966, p. 34)*

A governor or a police commissioner conducts an experiment when he cracks down on highway speeders or on thieves (Campbell 1969). Does he thereby reduce highway fatalities or stealing? Scholarships and favorable publicity go to winners of national talent searches. Do such awardees do better in college that they would have without the financial aid and news coverage? Graduate students in psychology achieve high scores on the Miller Analogies Test. Has studying psychology made them more test-wise than, say, graduate students in history? It is not likely that we will find experimental results for questions of this type, but it is important that we seek more than merely impressionistic answers to them. As we shall see much later in this chapter, principles exist for *designing* quasi-experiments, and for determining their relevance and validity as well.

Natural experiments occur without explicit man-made design. In the above examples of quasi-experimentation we noted intervention by the governor, police commissioner, scholarship agency, and psychology teacher. Here persons other than the individuals affected attempted to manipulate variables. Contrast this with a study of the effect of divorce of parents on the divorce rate of their children, which is an example of a "natural" experiment. Do the children of divorced parents tend to be more divorce-prone themselves *because* their parents did not remain together? It is difficult to determine just what question is being asked, much less how to answer it.

A less complicated example was a large investigation conducted by Rice (1897) before the days of *t*-tests and the analysis of variance. He wanted to know whether the length of time elementary school children spent in studying spelling affected their spelling ability. Fortunately, Rice realized that a survey of spelling as taught and learned in various schools would not automatically answer his causal inquiry. By considering various plausible alternative interpretations of his data (for instance, that the ablest students were taught spelling the shortest length of time and the least able students the longest), and by seeking subgroups within the data with which to test these hypotheses, he managed to make a surprisingly good case for the futility of teaching spelling many minutes per day by the methods then used. Rice did not *manipulate* the experimental variable, i. e. length of time spelling was studied by a given child each day. "Nature" (i.e., the various school systems) manipulated the variable for him, but in the process may have confounded it with various characteristics of the pupils and the schools.[1] More about this problem later. The distinction between quasi-experiments and natural experiments is not always sharp, because when the researcher intervenes to study outcomes of a natural experiment he usually gains some control over the scheduling of data-collection procedures.

Pseudo-experiments constitute a vaguer, more heterogeneous category than do controlled, quasi-, or natural experiments. Much of advertising at least loosely implies causation ("Smoke Open Country cigarettes and [by implication] become a virile man, irresistible to beautiful women in the cool forest"). This is deliberate, of course, and not meant to be scientific. On the other hand, quite a few would-be researchers unknowingly adopt designs that are foredoomed to yield inconclusive or misleading results because of inherent defects in the logic underlying the design. Stanley (1966a) has written in detail about one common design of this type. For example, does brain damage at birth affect arithmetic-reasoning ability at age 14? It is virtually impossible to answer this question satisfactorily by taking brain-damaged 14-year-olds and comparing them on arithmetic-reasoning tests with non-brain-damaged 14-year-olds. The chief difficulty is that one cannot be sure the brain-damaged youths would have had the same arithmetic achievement as the non-damaged ones even if they had not suffered the brain damage. Nature does not seem to assign brain damage at random to the newborn, without regard to their family background or personal characteristics.

Complete Two-Factor Factorial Designs

Following the above brief discussion of the last three of the four kinds of experiments we turn to the first, i.e. controlled,

[1]For further discussion of Rice's pioneering comparative study, see Stanley (1965, 1966c).

variable-manipulating experimentation. Before defining it, however, we shall need to consider certain terms.

The first of these is the *sampling unit*. This may be an individual person or infrahuman organism, a classroom, a county, a cage of rats, a bag of wheat, etc.—who- or whatever is used in the experiment.

The next concept is that of a *factor*, which in the experimental-design sense is *not* the same as the "factor" in what psychometrically oriented psychologists call "factor analysis" (for that, see Harman, 1967.) As we shall use the word, *a factor is merely one of the bases for structuring the experimental design.* A factor may be defined by levels—e.g., 0%, $33\frac{1}{3}\%$, $66\frac{2}{3}\%$, and 100% knowledge of results for a reinforcement factor. This happens to be a factor whose levels are *ordered*—here, they are equally spaced on a percentage continuum stretching from 0 to 100%. Three different ways to teach a topic in general psychology would define a "method of teaching" factor at three *unordered* or nominal levels. Physicians, lawyers, architects, physicists, and psychologists would constitute five "levels" of the unordered *classificatory* (i.e., not manipulated) factor, occupation. Physiological sex (male, female) is a two-level unordered classificatory factor; small, average, and large classes would be a three-level ordered classificatory factor.

Note that the experimenter does not have control over the levels of a classificatory factor. There are as many different populations of experimental subjects as there are levels of the classificatory factor—physicians, for instance, are a different population from lawyers. The experimenter does not assign occupation or sex to a given experimental subject, but instead takes them as they occur. However, in an experiment with manipulated factors, e.g., three different ways of teaching psychology, he can assign levels at random to students from a single population. With classificatory factors, groups of subjects probably differ from each other appreciably *before* the experiment begins, but for manipulated factors their differences are not statistically significant. This distinction becomes quite important when one is interpreting the results of experiments.

To recapitulate: A factor used in an experimental design may have two or more levels. Levels may be *nominal* (i.e., unordered, just naming each level, such as Method A, Method B, and Method C) or ordered. Some factors may be manipulated by the experimenter as he assigns the various levels randomly to the units used in the experiment—30 pupils to each method, for example. Other factors may be classificatory, not manipulated, such as "took Latin in Grades 9-10 versus did not take Latin then."

FACTOR-LEVEL COMBINATIONS

There may be more than one factor of the sorts discussed above in one experiment. For example, the four levels of reinforcement might occur in conjunction with the three methods of teaching. If every level of the reinforcement factor occurs with every level of the methods factor, a complete *crossed*-factors design with $4 \times 3 = 12$ *factor-level combinations* results. To each of these combinations a certain number of the available sampling units (say, classrooms) would be assigned *at random*. At least 24 classrooms would be needed in order to *replicate* the design—i.e., have at least two classrooms per factor-level combination. It would be simplest and most efficient to have the same number of classrooms for each factor-level combination. For a schema of the two-factor *factorial design* see Table 6-1.

Table 6-1. General Schema for a Two-Factor Factorial Design

Levels of the Row Factor	Levels of the Column Factor					
	1	*2*	...	*C*	...	$\mathscr{C}$
1	X_{111} X_{112} · · · $X_{11n_{11}}$	X_{121} X_{122} · · · $X_{12n_{12}}$	...	X_{1C1} X_{1C2} · · · $X_{1Cn_{1C}}$	...	$X_{1\mathscr{C}1}$ $X_{1\mathscr{C}2}$ · · · $X_{1\mathscr{C}n_{1\mathscr{C}}}$
2	X_{211} X_{212} · · · $X_{21n_{21}}$	X_{221} X_{222} · · · $X_{22n_{22}}$	...	X_{2C1} X_{2C2} · · · $X_{2Cn_{2C}}$	...	$X_{2\mathscr{C}1}$ $X_{2\mathscr{C}2}$ · · · $X_{2\mathscr{C}n_{2\mathscr{C}}}$
· · ·	· ·	· ·	·	·	·	· ·
R	X_{R11} X_{R12} · · · $X_{R1n_{R1}}$	X_{R21} X_{R22} · · · $X_{R2n_{R2}}$	...	X_{RC1} X_{RC2} · · · $X_{RCn_{RC}}$	...	$X_{R\mathscr{C}1}$ $X_{R\mathscr{C}2}$ · · · $X_{R\mathscr{C}n_{R\mathscr{C}}}$
· · ·	· ·	· ·	·	·	·	· ·
$\mathscr{R}$	$X_{\mathscr{R}11}$ $X_{\mathscr{R}12}$ · · · $X_{\mathscr{R}1n_{\mathscr{R}1}}$	$X_{\mathscr{R}21}$ $X_{\mathscr{R}22}$ · · · $X_{\mathscr{R}2n_{\mathscr{R}2}}$	...	$X_{\mathscr{R}C1}$ $X_{\mathscr{R}C2}$ · · · $X_{\mathscr{R}Cn_{\mathscr{R}C}}$	...	$X_{\mathscr{R}\mathscr{C}1}$ $X_{\mathscr{R}\mathscr{C}2}$ · · · $X_{\mathscr{R}\mathscr{C}n_{\mathscr{R}\mathscr{C}}}$

This table is more general than is needed this early in the chapter, so please do not pore over it *unduly* now. We shall refer to it several more times later. The $R \times C$ portion, set off by double vertical and horizontal lines within the table, illustrates the two-factor factorial design we have been considering, which is a special case of the more general $\mathscr{R} \times \mathscr{C}$ design that, as set forth here, will accomodate a number of variations to be discussed later. At least, though, read the following three paragraphs of explanation *carefully* once so that you will begin to understand the symbolism.

The table shows X_{rci} notation, where X is the outcome measure (i.e., the observation of the dependent variable) for the rth row, cth column, and ith sampling unit nested within that rcth factor-level combination. The rcth cell contains n_{rc} observations. For instance, the number of observations for the factor-level combination resulting from the intersection of the 2nd row and the 1st column is n_{21}. For a given experiment n_{21} has a certain value; it may be 0 *or* 1 *or* 2, 3, 4, etc.

There are just two factors in this design. Their levels cross each other. The row factor has two or more levels. Let any one of them be the rth level, so that $r = 1, 2, \ldots, R, \ldots, \mathscr{R}$. R represents the number of levels of the row factor actually used in a particular experiment. The number of levels of the row factor *that exist in the target population* of levels for that factor is symbolized in the table by the script letter $\mathscr{R}$. For example, the factor that defines rows might be "style of printing type." If there are 57 different styles of type in the population of styles *that the experimenter plans to sample*, then $\mathscr{R} = 57$. If the experimenter draws, say, 10 styles randomly from the 57 and uses those 10 in his experiment, then $R = 10$. If, instead, he uses all 57 in his experiment, then $\mathscr{R} = R = 57$. Although R may exhaust the target population of levels and therefore equal $\mathscr{R}$, obviously it cannot exceed $\mathscr{R}$.

A similar rationale holds for the levels of the column factor. The double vertical and horizontal lines within the table bound off the results of a particular experiment, which involves R row levels and C column levels.

A factor-level combination *involving experimenter-manipulated factors* is called a *treatment*. If, for example, a design involves four levels of a manipulated reinforcement factor crossed with three levels of a manipulated methods factor and with two levels of the classificatory sex factor, there are $4 \times 3 = 12$ treatments within each of the two sexes, but a total of $4 \times 3 \times 2 = 24$ factor-level combinations.

THE EXPERIMENT VERSUS THE STATUS STUDY

We now have the terminology with which to specify what operations produce an experiment. There must be at least one *manipulated* factor in the design, and the sampling units must be assigned in some *random* way to the levels of that manipulated factor. If there is more than one manipulated factor in the design, the sampling units must be assigned at random to all the factor-level combinations involving those factors (i.e., at random to all the treatments). Of course, random assignment is a necessary but not sufficient condition for a controlled experiment; other types of control must also be exercised.

If none of the factors in the design are manipulated, a *status study* rather than an experiment results. Consider, for example, a crossed design with four occupations, three marital conditions (single, married, formerly married), and two sexes (male, female) for which the *dependent variable* (i.e., the "out-come" variable being analyzed) is annual income. There are $4 \times 3 \times 2 = 24$ factor-level combinations; i.e., 24 populations of individuals. One can perhaps carry out the same type of analysis that would be used if these were manipulated factors, but the results must be interpreted in associative rather than causal terms. ["Causation" is never easy to establish even by controlled experimentation, as Lerner (1965) and others have shown, but the status study affords far less opportunity for getting at it directly than an experiment does.] This is not to deny, of course, that valuable descriptive and inferential data can be generated in a crossed-factors status study, even though no individual was assigned at random by the experimenter to any treatment.

For example, from the results of the above status study we could not say directly that unmarried male lawyers earn less than married male lawyers *because* clients and society favor married males. *Perhaps* unmarried men who are lawyers are younger, more poorly trained, or less hard-working than are married men who are lawyers. Certainly we would have to investigate those three plausible alternative hypotheses, and many others, before concluding that unmarried male lawyers are discriminated against financially *because* they are unmarried.

SIMPLE VERSUS RESTRICTED RANDOMIZATION

One cannot overstress the importance of assigning the sampling units *at random* to all of the treatments. This may be done quite simply, for instance by giving a random half of the available experimental subjects Treatment A and the other random half Treatment B. With more complex designs, the randomization may be restricted in various ways. For example, if there are two sexes and three levels of a manipulated factor in the design, one can assign one-third of the males at random to each of the three treatments, and one-third of the females at random to each treatment. Sex of the subject, a non-manipulated organismic characteristic, dictates that one does not assign one-third of the total sample of males and females, without regard to sex, at random to each of the treatments. Physiological sex is a "nest," and individuals of a particular sex are "nested" within it because they cannot cross the sex boundary into the other nest.

This brings out the difference between an actually manipu*lated* factor and a potentially manipul*able* factor. Physiological sex is somewhat manipulable (by such drastic measures as sex-changing surgery), but not usually manipulated by a psychological researcher. So is the two-level factor "studied psychology versus did not study psychology." An experimenter could, in principle, ask a random half of his experimental subjects to study psychology and ask the other half not to do so, but seldom does he have enough control of the situation to accomplish this.

If, instead of sex or "studied psychology," one had two manipulated levels of awareness of results crossed with the three levels of the other manipulated factor, the experimenter would assign one-sixth of his subjects randomly to each of the six factor-level combinations. This is simple, unrestricted assignment of units.

WHY RANDOMIZE, AND HOW?

One *must* assign the sampling units at random to the treatments in order (*a*) to avoid biasing comparisons of the effectiveness of the various treatments and (*b*) to provide a valid basis for testing the significance of treatment differences statistically. Let us consider each of these two points in turn.

If the psychological experimenter were to assign his experimental subjects to the various treatments judgmentally, rather than in a completely mechanical random fashion, he might put potentially better performers into one treatment group than into another. That particular treatment would then have an advantage over the others. It would not be readily possible to ascertain how much of the observed difference in outcome is due to superiority of the treatment itself and how much of it is due to pre-treatment bias in assigning subjects to treatment groups. Human beings are not good randomizers.

The other reason for randomization is that modern statistical theory and practice is based squarely on probability theory. Judgmental assigning of experimental subjects to treatments, however unbiased it might *happen* to be, cannot provide a sound mathematical basis for assessing the amount of sampling error of the treatment means (i.e., fluctuation of sample means in successive *random* sampling). For the factorial design, variation among observations within factor-level combinations is usually the basis for computing the "error" term, but this figure will be appropriate only if the sampling units were assigned at random to the various treatments.

How does one randomize? Tossing an unbiased coin or rolling a fair die appropriately may be adequate for some designs. Trying to randomize via a deck of playing cards is to be avoided unless one has an excellent mechanical shuffler, because cards shuffled—even repeatedly—by a person are quite unlikely to be arranged randomly with respect to their former order. By far the best way is to use a table of random numbers or the *equivalent* in an electronic computer. (In the late 1960s some computer randomizing that had been thought to be random provoked considerable controversy among computer scientists.) Most statistics books provide short tables of random numbers that are useful for many types of designs and sizes of experiments and explain how to use them.[2]

SOURCES OF VARIATION

The design depicted in Table 6-1 yields outcome data that provide three sets of means: of rows, of columns, and of factor-level-combination cells. Actually, only the row and column means reflect the main effects in which the experimenter is interested. If the cell means "agree" with the row and the column means in a sense we shall discuss soon, then variations among them can be disregarded. They may not agree, however, and this makes the interpretation of results less simple.

Three *sources of variation* in the data are important. These are variation among row means, variation among column means, and variation among cell means after they have been "adjusted" for their respective row and column means. Essentially, one computes the variance (a statistical measure of dispersion) of the row means, the variance of the column means, and the variance of the cell means after their respective row and column means have been subtracted. In symbols, one is concerned essentially with the variance of the R $\bar{X}_r$'s, the variance of the $C \bar{X}_c$'s, and the variance of the $R \times C$ ($\bar{X}_{rc} - \bar{X}_r - \bar{X}_c + \bar{X}$)'s (i.e., *interaction residuals*),[3] where for instance $\bar{X}_c$ represents the mean ($\bar{X}$) of the cth column.

From the three sources of variation among means, plus (usually) the within-group variation to provide the "error" term, one estimates the *main effect* of each row level and of each column level, and the *interaction* effect for each cell. A main effect is the difference between the population mean of the row (or of the column) and the population grand mean. Of course, the actual main effects are unknown, because one has sample rather than population values, but they can be estimated from the outcome data of a properly designed experiment. Interaction effects will be discussed in the next section.[4]

The Concept of Interacting Factor Levels

If one factor interacts with another, then the interpretation of the effect of one level of the first factor depends on the particular level of the second factor that defines the cell under consideration. If there is no interaction, then every cell mean in the population is determined by its row and column means in the following manner:

$$\mu_{rc} = \mu_r + \mu_c - \mu,$$

where the μ's represent population means. If this equality holds

for every cell, all of the $R \times C$ interaction effects are zero, and we say that the row and column effects are *additive*. If the equality does not hold for all cells, the row and column effects are said to be *nonadditive*. Of course, one cannot know the population means, but must estimate them from the data yielded by the experiment.

Figure 6-1 illustrates, with hypothetical data on reading speed, three kinds of interaction: zero, *ordinal*, and *disordinal*. Figure 6-1*a* shows that girls are equally superior to boys on all three types of reading material. Figure 6-1*b* shows that girls are superior to boys on all three types, but most so on fashion and least so on sports. Figure 6-1*c* shows that girls greatly excel on fashion, are equal to boys on American history, and are greatly excelled by boys on sports questions.

Statistically significant interaction may occur in either the presence or the absence of significant main effects, because if the n_{rc}'s are equal for every rc the three sources of variation (among row means, among column means, and among adjusted cell means) covary zero with each other. Then the three sources of variation must sum to the total of the sources of variation, so in another sense than the above they are additive. Thus main effects do not themselves drag interaction effects up or down.[5]

Significant interaction can be illustrated in a four-reinforcements by three-methods design by noting that the factor-level combination formed by the most effective reinforcement level combined with the most effective method may yield a cell mean smaller (or larger) than one would expect on the basis of the respective row and column means. Interaction may be ordinal or disordinal. The former is less bothersome than the latter, because ordinal interaction means that although a particular level of one factor is differentially effective at various levels of the other factor, that level of the first factor maintains its rank order of effectiveness at all levels of the second factor. For example, 100% reinforcement may be relatively better with Method A than with Methods B and C, but it is better than 67% reinforcement with all methods—though not equally better.

Disordinal interaction means that whether one level of the first factor is more effective than another level of that factor depends on which level of the second factor is being considered. E.g., one psychology instructor performs considerably better with Method A, whereas another is much more effective using Method B. (It would probably be desirable to let the former use Method A and the latter Method B.)

Statistically significant interaction is best studied graphically, by plotting the means.[6] Keep in mind that interaction effects are as real as main effects and must be considered care-

[2]See Edwards (1968), Kirk (1968), and Myers (1966); for larger tables, see RAND Corporation (1955). Also consult your data-processing center for up-to-date information about randomizing via computer, especially if your randomizing task is likely to be complex or tedious.

[3]The constant $\bar{X}$ does not affect the variance of a particular set of interaction residuals.

[4]*It is not the province or purpose of this chapter to deal much with statistical analysis,* other than to indicate that a given design implies a given analytical procedure. Readers who have not completed two semesters or more of statistics courses may wish to read a short treatment of the analysis of variance, such as Stanley (1968), or to study a textbook, such as Edwards (1968) or Glass and Stanley (1970).

[5]The sources of variation (more strictly, the anova "sums of squares") will also be additive if $n_{rc} = n_r n_c / N$ for every rc, where

$$N = \sum_{r=1}^{R} \sum_{c=1}^{C} n_{rc}.$$

See Scheffé (1959, p. 119). Statisticians disagree among themselves about the validity of the model for such *proportional-subclass-frequency* designs, however, so the psychological researcher will usually want his n_{rc} constant—i.e., the same n for every factor-level combination—or as nearly so as feasible. Procedures and computer programs for analyzing disproportional-subclass-frequency designs exist. See, for example, Bock (1963) and Finn (1967).

[6]Stanley (1969) discusses four ways to do this. Most statistics textbooks treat the topic at length—e.g., see Campbell and Stanley (1966, pp. 27–29), Edwards (1968, pp. 212–15), Kirk (1968, pp. 177–78), and Glass and Stanley (1970, pp. 406–411).

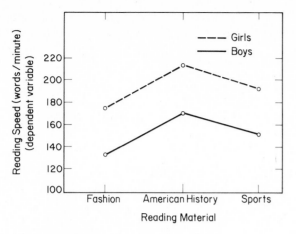

(a) No Interaction

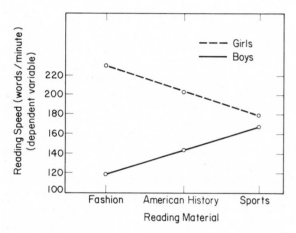

(b) Ordinal Interaction

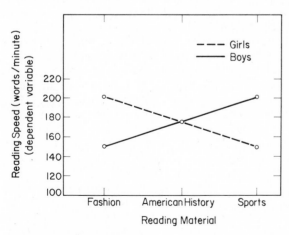

(c) Disordinal Interaction

Fig. 6-1. *Graphic representation of the mean reading speed scores for boys and girls on three types of reading material.* [Adapted from Glass and Stanley, 1970, pp. 407, 409.]

fully when one is interpreting the results of an experiment. Terminology points up the resemblance. Main effects are sometimes called zero-order interactions. Two-factor interactions are called *first-order* interactions, three-factor interactions are second-order, etc.

As Vale and Vale (1969) stress, in some studies interactions may be more interesting and important than main effects. For instance, Stanley (1961) found that the political party of raters interacted strongly with the political party of their ratees, and that there was also a significant (but weaker) three-factor interaction of party of rater with party of ratee with trait rated. E.g., Democrat raters tended to consider national Democrat leaders more intelligent, honest, friendly, and generous than Republican raters did, but this bias varied somewhat from trait to trait. For another interesting triple interaction in a status study, see Jensen (1969).

Significant interactions may be classified as *transformable* versus *nontransformable*. Box and Cox (1964) and Box (1967, pp. 94–95, 98–99) show that some interactions can be removed by mathematical transformation of the dependent variable and others cannot. In informal discussion Box said:

For instance, suppose two effects are multiplicative (there are many physical laws defining such effects); then they will be additive in their logs. If you used the original metric, you would have an interaction, but in the logs there would be no interaction. There are other types of interaction where no matter what transformation you make, the effects will not be additive. If an interaction can be eliminated by just changing the metric, then perhaps you weren't measuring the response on the right scale to begin with. An untransformable interaction is a more basic thing. . . . It seems most desirable to do the analysis in the metric in which the assumptions are all most nearly satisfied, and then to express the answers in whatever metric is most easily understood (1967, pp. 94–95).

One other comment about interactions seems desirable at this point. If an experimenter uses *all* the levels of each factor that are of interest to him (i.e., the entire target population of levels), his interpretation of significant interaction and of significant main effects will be somewhat different than if he samples levels randomly from a target population of levels. This distinction, suggested in the footnote to Table 6-1, will be considered in the next several sections.

Analysis-of-Variance Models: Fixed, Random, and Mixed

The appropriate mathematical model underlying an analysis of variance is determined by the operations performed and the nature of the effects.[7] A highly useful general scheme, from which three more customary models flow as special cases, is the *finite-effects model* (see Brownlee, 1965, pp. 489–501). For this model, the number of levels of the factor that are used in the experiment is an appreciable percentage of the number of levels in the *target population*—i.e., in the population of levels to which the experimenter plans to generalize his results (see the footnote to

[7]See Cornfield and Tukey (1956), Stanley (1968), or Glass and Stanley (1970).

Table 6-1). There are two target populations of factor levels in Table 6-1. The experimenter uses some or all of the levels in his study. For example, the three methods he actually chooses for his experiment may be all the methods in which he is interested, and therefore he has exhausted *his* target population of three methods levels. That other methods exist is not relevant for defining the population of levels to which *he* wishes to generalize from a given experiment. The ratio of the number of levels he uses to the number of levels in *his* target population of levels is important, however.

If the ratio is 1, as with methods above—i.e., if he uses in the experiment all the levels of a factor that are of interest to him—that is said to be a *fixed-effects factor*. If the experimenter replicated the experiment, he would use the *same* levels the second and subsequent times. He is trying to estimate the population means of the dependent variable for just *those* levels and no others. Thus, he is interested in the relationship among fixed constants, the population means of those particular levels. Levels he used would not vary from experiment to experiment, so he is *not* trying to estimate the variance among a larger number of levels from the variance among the levels he uses in his experiment. Most factors that the experimental psychologist employs are of this fixed-effects sort, so typically he works with the *fixed-effects model*, often called *Model I*. Fortunately, this is by far the most-investigated and best-understood model.

However, if the number of factor levels drawn randomly from a target population of levels is quite small relative to the number of levels in that population, so that the percentage approaches 0, that is said to be a *random-effects factor*. For example, the experimenter might draw 25 twin pairs at random from all the twins less than 21 years of age in the United States, or 20 raters randomly from a target population of 100,000 raters; he might choose at random 100 ways from among the 3,628,800 possible ways to permute 10 books on a bookshelf, or twelve 10×10 Greco-Latin squares (defined later) from among the enormous number of such squares that can be created. From the small number drawn *randomly* he plans to estimate the variance of the means of all levels in the target population.

If both of the factors involve random effects, one has a *components-of-variance model*, sometimes called *Model II*, and can estimate three *components of variance* (or *variance components*): the population variance of the means of all levels of one factor; the population variance of the means of all levels of the other factor; and the population variance of the interaction residuals. Components of variance are additive, so that a component of variance can be expressed as a percentage of the sum of the components. This percentage supplements the usual tests of statistical significance, which do not tell how strong the effects are, but instead whether or not they are probably due merely to fluctuations in random sampling. Also, one can set up an approximate confidence interval for a variance component or an exact confidence interval for the ratio of an effects variance component to the corresponding error variance component.

It is easy to confuse *sources* of variation with *components* of variance. They are related, but the former applies to the analysis of the actual data from the experiment by computing *mean squares* that reflect the underlying variance components plus random sampling error, whereas the latter are free of sampling error. For example, in symbols the variance component for the row factor is, at its simplest,

$$E_r(\mu_r - \mu)^2;$$

$E_r(\ )$, the expectation operator, is the arithmetic mean, over the infinite number of levels of the row factor, of the squared differences between the *population* mean of a given level and the grand mean of *all* the levels.

Controlling or Randomizing Extraneous Factors

In our brief exposition above the reader may have sensed that two different types of populations were involved: the population of sampling units, usually considered infinite, and the target population of levels of a given factor incorporated into the design, which can vary from two to infinity, depending on what number of levels are of interest to a particular researcher.

If there is just one level of a factor in the target population (such as only males, or requiring every experimental subject to record his responses rather than having some subjects record while others consider them mentally), the experimenter is choosing to hold that factor constant at one level. In any actual experiment a virtually infinite number of factors are held constant at one level; e.g., all subjects are human beings, all subjects participate in the experiment in the same room, city, state, college, etc. Where a factor is not introduced *explicitly* into the experiment at two or more levels (e.g., using both males and females, or four levels of reinforcement) or held constant at one level, it must be randomized out. If, for example, an experiment is run at several times of the day, it would be poor design to run one treatment early in the morning, another at noon, and so on, because such factors as temperature, humidity, and fatigue might vary systematically throughout the day and thereby confound the interpretation of differences found between treatments. Depending on the nature of the experiment, it may be possible and desirable to randomize the assignment of experimental subjects to time of day. If the statistical *power* (to be discussed later) of the experiment with such randomizing is likely to be low, however, and/or if one wishes to ascertain whether time of day interacts with treatments, it may be better to introduce time of day as an explicit classificatory factor. This requires carrying out all treatments at each time of day, unless a reduced design (to be discussed later) is employed.

Much more randomization is required for sound experimentation than is usually done. Not only should the sampling units be chosen randomly from the population of such units to which generalization is sought and the factor levels chosen randomly from the target population of factor levels, but also the order in which subjects are tested should usually be random, even *within* a factor-level combination. The exact set of factorializing and randomizing operations to be used in the experiment should be considered carefully, because this set determines the statistical analysis that must be used. *Design dictates analysis. By the time the design is complete on paper, the experimenter can and should know just how he will analyze the outcome data.* This requirement means that much more time and thought must be given to designing an experiment expertly than the typical experimenter seems to feel necessary, but that when an experiment is completed the experimenter should know, within the limits of fidelity of execution of the experiment, how to analyze his data. *Having to search for a suitable analysis when the data are already in hand is symptomatic of poor initial planning*, or at least of bad luck in carrying out the study.

As explained later, certain types of restricted or stratified randomization will often be more effective than simple randomization.

Mixed Models

If the design involves some combination of fixed-effects factors, random-effects factors, and finite-effects factors, the underlying structure for the experiment is a *mixed-effects model*. Usually, this term is restricted to designs that include some fixed-effects factors and some random-effects factors, but a finite-effects factor (where the percentage of the target-population levels of a factor used is appreciably greater than zero and appreciably less than one) is also an intermediate consideration. Mixed-model designs present more difficulties in analysis than do fixed or random models.[8] Central to the estimation of variance components are expressions called *expected mean squares* that show the variance-component structure of the hypothetical long-term average mean square for a particular factor or interaction of factors. [These are explained in most statistics textbooks that treat the analysis of variance, e.g., Glass and Stanley (1970).]

Blocking, Stratifying, and Leveling

The conceptually clearest factorial design occurs when all the factors involved have fixed effects, are fully crossed (i.e., every level of each factor occurs with every level of each other factor), and are manipulated by the experimenter—i.e., assigned at random to the sampling units. As we have noted already, however, classificatory factors may also be used. They may reduce random variation within factor-level combinations. For example, if girls have a different mean from that of boys for a given treatment, the variability of observations *within* sexes is likely to be smaller than for the total group.

Also, classificatory factors enable the experimenter to determine whether his findings hold across the levels of the classificatory factor—e.g., does sex interact with treatment? If so, results must be viewed as contingent on sex. Perhaps 100% reinforcement works relatively better for girls than for boys, or psychogalvanic response under induced stress is relatively greater for ego-involved boys than for ego-involved girls. *Non-significant interaction of classificatory factors with treatment factors indicates generalizability of the treatment findings across the levels of the classificatory factors.* Experimental psychologists have not been concerned much with classificatory factors (particularly little with individual-difference factors) in the past, but the article by Vale and Vale (1969), among others, makes it seem likely that many of them will move in this direction during the coming years.

[8]For discussion of this model, see Stanley (1956), Scheffé (1959), Edwards (1968), and Glass and Stanley (1970).

The first systematically studied experimental design involving crossed classifications was the *randomized-block design* suggested in 1923 by the father of modern experimental statistics, Sir Ronald A. Fisher, in a letter to a statistician named William Gosset who published under the pseudonym "Student" (see Stanley, 1966b). This design is illustrated by the present author's study of the performance of 35 rats on a T-maze (see Jenkins and Stanley, 1950). The design was 7×5, with 7 classificatory blocks and 5 levels of a manipulated reinforcement-ratio factor. Each block consisted of 5 male littermates—i.e., all 5 had the same mother and father and were born in the same litter. (Note that sex was held constant at a single level, male. One has no *statistical* warrant for generalizing the findings of this experiment to female rats, though vast experience with rats may give us confidence in doing so. Also, type of animal— i.e., Norway gray rat—was held constant at one level, as were many other factors.)

This randomized-block design yielded three sources of variation: between blocks, between treatments, and interaction of blocks with treatments. If the littermate classificatory blocking procedure had not been used, there would have been just two sources of variation, between treatments and within treatments. The "within treatments" sum of squares was partitioned into "between blocks" and "blocks × treatments." Precision of estimating population characteristics and statistical power of significance tests were improved if the mean square for blocks × treatments was appreciably smaller than the mean square within treatments, which is to say that the mean square for blocks should be large. Unless littermates perform more like each other than like rats in other litters, the blocking effort has been wasted. Note that in the randomized-block design one cannot test the blocks × treatments mean square for statistical significance, because there is no "error" mean square against which to test it. (Also, for fixed-effects treatments, one cannot without bias test the mean square for blocks for significance.)

Thus, the randomized-blocks design can improve precision and statistical power, compared with the simple-randomized design, but it cannot extend generalizability by showing that interaction of the classificatory and treatment factors is statistically non-significant or weak (but see Tukey 1949). Probably an experimenter has little interest in the littermate blocking factor, which here is *considered* to be a random-effects factor even though the five litter-blocks were not actually drawn at random from any virtually infinite population of male littermates. Justification for so considering it is given by Cornfield and Tukey (1956, pp. 912–14). Generalization is made to an infinite population of male littermates "like these," of which these are considered conceptually to be a random sample. In that sense this randomized-block design has an underlying mixed model—random-effects blocks and fixed-effects treatments.

Note carefully that each of the 35 rats was independent of every one of the other 34, though sets of 5 rats had a common-litter bond. This keeps the design from involving *repeated measurements* on the same sampling units. Some psychologists tend to confuse this nonrepeated-measurement blocking design with seemingly similar ones in which individuals are measured more than once. They are different, and require different scrutiny of results, even though the formal analysis may seem identical. We shall consider repeated-measurement designs later. Good examples of randomized-blocking factors in psychology are not plentiful. Twin pairs, brothers or sisters, and even blocking of units by committee qualify. For example, one might ask a state school supervisor to block the high schools in his state by threes according to the average socioeconomic level of the parents of the children who attend them. If his information and judgment are good, this may reduce sampling variability in a three-treatment experiment considerably.

In the next three sections let us extend the concept of classificatory factors by considering three kinds: blocking, stratifying, and leveling.

Nominal-Scale Classificatory Factors (Blocking)

The littermate blocks are on an unordered (nominal) scale. Not only randomized blocks but also other classificatory variables such as male versus female and occupational groups are on a nominal scale. It would be possible to use sex as a *blocking factor* by, say, assigning *one* male to each of the five treatments and *one* female to each of the five, but this would provide too little precision and statistical power and, even worse, this would not produce a usable "error" term for testing the statistical significance of the treatment effects because physiological sex can hardly be considered a random-effects factor. Thus one would use *at least* two males and two females per treatment. This would provide an estimate of within-factor-level-combination variability (i.e., within sex-treatment groups), and would also at least double the number of sampling units used. Sex is a nominal-scale classificatory factor, but the sex × treatment replicated design (i.e., the basic 2 × 5 design with 20 sampling units) is not the randomized-block design of agricultural-research fame. Similar considerations apply to occupational groups that are intrinsically unordered; occupation could be a random-effects factor, though, because it is *possible* to draw a few occupations at random from a large target population of occupations.[9] If it is, the mean square for treatments should be tested against the mean square for the interaction of occupations with treatments. The within-occupation-treatment variation serves to test the main effects of occupations and the interaction of occupations with treatments.

Interestingly, when there are just two categories to a nominal-scale variable such as sex, they can be given order arbitrarily, such as 1 for male and 0 for female. If there are three or more categories, say physicians, lawyers, and architects, that simple *dummy-variable* scheme is not feasible. Instead, each sampling unit is given a 0 *or* 1 for *each* of the three categories, a 1 for the category to which it belongs, and a 0 for each of the other two categories. [Mathematical statistics textbooks treat linear regression analysis, including the analysis of variance, in this way. See Williams (1968) or Graybill (1961).]

Ordinal-Scale Classificatory Factors (Stratifying)

There are some factors whose levels are crudely ordered on what Stevens (1958) has termed an "ordinal" scale of measure-

[9]Often, occupational categories are considered ordered, e.g., by mean income, socioeconomic status, or educational requirements.

ment. Five levels of socioeconomic status or ten occupational levels illustrate this kind of *stratifying factor*. Quite likely, each of these two factors will be considered to have fixed effects; the experimenter is hardly likely to have drawn socioeconomic levels or occupational levels randomly from a larger target population of either. Therefore, replication within factor-level-combinations is essential. For an $R \times C$ design of this sort there will be nRC sampling units, with n greater than 1. (Schemes where n_{rc} varies from cell to cell can be handled, but in order to simplify discourse we shall not consider them. From the standpoints of efficient design and simple analysis, it is usually desirable to have n the same for every cell; see footnote 5, above).

Interval-, Ratio-, or Absolute-Scale Classificatory Factors (Leveling)

A great number of variables that might be used as classificatory factors are ordered with approximately equal intervals (e.g., Fahrenheit or Centigrade temperature); equal intervals and a real zero point (e.g., linear distance); or equal intervals, a real zero, non-negative numbers, and meaningful units (e.g., number of children in the family). Each of these *leveling factors* is likely to constitute a fixed-effects factor, so again replication is required. In addition, it may be desirable to study the trend of the outcome measures from level to level of the classificatory factor. For that purpose, it is preferable to space the levels of the classificatory factor equally far apart on the outcome measures or on a transformation (e.g. square root or logarithm) of them. *Trend analysis* is discussed by Edwards (1968), Kirk (1968), Winer (1971), and others. For ordered variables (which need not be classificatory—cf. the levels of reinforcement) a careful study of interactions is especially important.

Organismic variables such as height or weight, response measures such as reading score, IQ, summed responses to a personality inventory, or ecological variables such as socioeconomic status or distance to the nearest college may be rather powerful classificatory factors because the regression of the outcome measures of the experiment on them may be strong. It is important, of course, to base classificatory factors on variables that are likely to be related highly to the dependent-variable measure of the experiment. Otherwise, time will be wasted in classifying and incorporating them into the experiment. Even worse, in small experiments one may lose considerable precision and statistical power if the classificatory factor is ineffective; randomized blocking, in particular, will cost as many as 50% of the degrees of freedom for the error term if the number of treatments is small. This caution merely means that the experimenter must know his problem area well enough to be rather sure what the most suitable classificatory variables are, and he must *plan* his experiment to yield the precision he needs.

Repeated Measurements

Up to now, we have considered only experimentally independent observations. A sampling unit appeared just once in the design, there being only one observation (measurement, rating, count, etc.) for each sampling unit used. The basic factorial design does not permit a sampling unit to be used two or more times, either within a factor-level combination or across it. Many designs favored by psychologists involve *repeated measurements*, however, as when the same experimental subject is run under two or more different treatments or is run more than once under the same treatment. This repeated measurement of the same sampling unit (we might say that each observation of a particular sampling unit is made on an *experimental unit*) can produce difficulties in the statistical analysis and the interpretation of data, as Myers (1966, pp. 152–73) points out. His discussion (especially on p. 172) or an equivalent one should be consulted by persons planning to use repeated measurements. We can, however, sketch some of the problems here.

Consider a simple experiment in which half the experimental subjects hear Hawaiian music for 30 minutes and then classical music for the next 30 minutes each day for two weeks, and the other half hear classical music before Hawaiian. This is a repeated-measurement *counterbalanced* (or *crossover* or *switchover*) design, the statistical analysis for which is discussed in Stanley (1955). Listeners are nested within orders, because each sampling unit is exposed to only one of the two orders, and considered a random-effects factor. Listeners cross the treatment factor, because each sampling unit is exposed to both types of music. Every day at the end of each 30 minute period each listener is asked to rate his liking for the music on a carefully devised 7 point rating scale. Thus at the end of the experiment each sampling unit has 10 scores for Hawaiian music and 10 scores for classical music, so another factor (day) at 10 levels can be considered in the design (unless the experimenter chooses to sum the 10 scores for a given person on each type of music to give him just two scores).

How likely do you think it is that the results of this experiment would agree with those secured with a non-repeated-measurement design wherein a random half of the experimental subjects heard only Hawaiian music 60 minutes per day and the other random half heard only classical music? It seems probable that in the two-exposure situation the carryover effects from the first type of music to the second might be great, different from person to person, and different for Hawaiian followed by classical music versus classical followed by Hawaiian music. Even if Hawaiian music were distinctly preferred to classical music in the repeated-measurements experiment, a factory manager might hesitate to play only Hawaiian music an hour each day because under those conditions, without the diversion and contrast provided by classical music, it might grow monotonous to the workers.

With only two treatments the purely statistical problems are minimized, but the two types of experiments (with and without repeated measurement) do not seem likely to answer equally well a single question, "If one plays classical *or* Hawaiian music 60 minutes per day for two weeks, which will be preferred?" The repeated-measurement experiment seems aimed instead at two questions about the pattern of music: (a) "If every day for two weeks one plays Hawaiian music 30 minutes followed immediately each day by 30 minutes of classical music, which type of music will be preferred?" (b) The same question, but with the order of the types of music reversed.

If the music factor in the repeated-measurement experiment had three levels instead of the two mentioned above, it would be highly desirable to have all six orders represented in the experiment by setting up equal-size order groups (one-sixth

of the sampling units assigned randomly to each) or by assigning orders at random to each sampling unit. For a large number of sampling units the two procedures would differ little; the former method guarantees equal order-group size, whereas the latter doesn't. However, the former provides more explicit sources of variation than the latter does, such as the interaction of order with treatment. The simple randomizing procedure minimizes the effects of correlated errors and thereby helps provide a valid significance test for the treatment effects—i.e., for the ratings given the three types of music. It cannot, however, remove the effect of context on the ratings.

The situation is more seriously affected statistically when, for example, one is trying to ascertain the effects of successive trials whose order cannot be randomized within each subject— Trial 1 must always precede Trial 2, etc. Under this condition the covariances among trials are likely to be heterogeneous and thereby to increase the apparent statistical significance of the trials factor spuriously. For further discussion of this and other relevant points see Winer (1971) and Myers (1966).

If repeated measurement is so fraught with logical and statistical hazards, why do psychological experimenters continue to use it? Because a sampling unit that serves as a control for itself is almost certain to result in less sampling fluctuation (i.e., sampling "error") than do independent sampling units for the various treatments, and sometimes a great deal less. For example, some raters in the types-of-music experiment will have little liking for any kind of music played while they work, whereas others will have moderate liking for any kind, and others considerable liking. Also, some are generally high raters on almost any rating scale, whereas others tend to be low raters.

Such tendencies may result in substantial positive correlation between ratings of the types of music, and because correlated means fluctuate less in successive random sampling than do the means of independent groups, one usually can get greater precision with a given number of repeatedly measured sampling units than with that number of sampling units not repeatedly measured. One hundred persons exposed to both types of music will usually provide more precision than 50 persons who hear one type and 50 who hear the other. In addition, the persons are already available for one treatment, so often it is economical of time and money to give them two or more. Incidentally, non-zero correlation is the effective principle of the randomized-block design, too, but there no repeated measurement of a sampling unit occurs. The formal statistical analysis (but not the interpretation of results) of the two types of experiments— repeated measurements and randomized-block design—is identical, when each of the manipulated factors has just two levels. For more than two levels, repeated-measurement analyses may require special techniques.

Nested Repeated Measurements

A rather common design for psychological experiments is groups × manipulated factor, with groups being a classificatory factor within which individuals repeatedly measured across the treatments are nested. The grouping factor may be nearly any of the classificatory variables mentioned earlier. It might, for example, be strain of rat, as when albinos, hooded rats, and Norway gray rats are used and each rat is run under all treatment conditions. If the order of treatments is randomized separately for each rat, and if enough time elapses between treatments for the rat to "regain its composure" (i.e., to dissipate at least the stronger carry-over effects), then an analysis into the following sources of variation can be made with some assurance: between groups, between treatments, between individuals nested within groups, groups × treatments, and individuals nested within groups × treatments. This is a "degenerate" groups × individuals × treatments design; groups cannot interact with individuals because individuals do not "cross" groups. A rat is *either* albino *or* hooded *or* gray; it does not change during the experiment. Therefore, the three-factor interaction, of groups with individuals with treatments, is also missing.

Here, groups is a fixed-effects factor. Individuals within groups are considered a random-effects factor. Treatments may be either fixed-effects or random-effects (or even finite-effects), depending on the target population of treatments. [For an analysis of this and other nested designs see Millman and Glass (1967) or Cronbach *et al.* (1972).]

Some nested designs are hierarchical and do not involve repeated measurement. They are essentially sampling schemes with which to estimate variance components via the random-effects model. Suppose one has available a huge number of trucks. In each truck a huge number of boxes is nested. Within each such box a huge number of smaller boxes is nested, and within each such box a huge number of aspirin tablets is nested. Choose at random a small number of trucks. Choose at random from each truck a small number of large boxes. Choose at random from each large box a few of the small boxes. Choose at random from each of the small boxes a few aspirin tablets. Determine the purity of each tablet. This is four-stage sampling, in hierarchical genealogical-tree fashion. It is a random-effects model with four factors, none of which are crossed. Thus there are no interactions, but only main effects. There is no repeated measurement unless two or more determinations of purity per tablet are made. [For statistical details see Brownlee (1965, pp. 482–89).]

Various modifications of the hierarchical design can be made, as when, say, there are only a few manufacturers of a certain drug (manufacturers being a fixed-effects factor) but their inventories are huge and can be sampled randomly. [For expected mean squares under such mixed-model circumstances, see Millman and Glass (1967).]

Reducing Error Variance

The variance of sample means in successive random samples each of size n from a parent population is the variance of the measures in that population divided by n. One can reduce sampling fluctuation of means by reducing the variance of the measures and/or by increasing n, the sample size. Where the variance is of observations within a certain factor-level combination, it consists of true differences among the sampling units plus errors of measurement, errors of technique, etc. One can reduce the true-difference variation by restricting the range of the sampling units used, but of course this also reduces the generalizability of the experiment. Errors of measurement can be reduced by increasing the quality of the measuring process; experimenters and their assistants can be more careful and better trained, tests used can be made more reliable, etc. Technical errors can be controlled by better calibration of equipment, by using more sensitive and accurate equipment, and the like.

Aside from eliminating serious technical errors and sloppy running of experimental subjects, the most powerful way to reduce the sampling variance of means is to increase n, the number of observations per cell. This reduces both true-score variability and error-of-measurement variability, whereas making measurements more error-free reduces only the latter. One must be careful, however, not to let his experiment get out of hand as n increases, because then the error per observation and technical errors might increase the sampling variance of means faster than increasing n reduces it.

Sampling error of means in experiments may be reduced by holding one or more factors such as time of day or experimenter constant at a single level—i.e., conducting the experiment at just one time of day or with a single experimenter, where variation across times of day or experimenter would otherwise be thrown into the within-experimental-combinations error term. However, this may undesirably limit generalization to that one time or that one experimenter, so usually it is better to incorporate several times of day and/or several different experimenters explicitly as factors in the design.

ANALYSIS OF COVARIANCE

We have already seen that blocking, stratifying, and leveling classificatory variables can reduce variability within treatments. It is also possible to do so by making adjustments during the statistical analysis of the results, rather than by structuring the design with one or more ordered classificatory variables during the planning phase. The adjustment procedure is known as the *analysis of covariance* (*ANCOVA*) (see McNemar, 1969). ANCOVA is closely related to the analysis of variance (*ANOVA*). It involves having in hand, before the experiment begins, measurements or scores for one or more prior variables on which the dependent variable of the experiment is likely to regress fairly strongly linearly. (In language more often used in psychology, the correlation of the *antecedent variables* with the dependent variable should be high.) Such antecedent variables are called *covariables* or (especially the actual values they take) *covariates*. It is crucial to have the covariates on hand *before* the experiment begins, and to avoid considering them when assigning sampling units to treatments, which should be done randomly in the usual way.

In effect, one uses the antecedent measurements to estimate, by least-squares linear regression, the outcome measurements and then performs an anova of the differences between the actual outcome measurements and the outcome measurements estimated from the antecedent measurements. Thus one is performing an analysis of variance of the errors of estimation, which are likely to be less variable than are the actual outcome scores within factor-level combinations unless the experimenter chose antecedent variables largely unrelated to the outcome measures.

Regression of the outcome variable on the covariables should be linear, and each within-experimental-level-combination regression slope should be the same (in the population of sampling units) as any other such slope. Therefore, ANCOVA is a rather delicate technique, compared with the randomized-block design. Where either would be appropriate, the latter is often preferable (see Cox, 1957, and Elashoff, 1969). Often, a replicated stratifying or leveling design such as was discussed earlier will be better than either.

In addition, ANCOVA can accommodate two or more covariates readily, whereas trying to use more than one classificatory variable for creating randomized blocks may force one to throw out a considerable number of sampling units because it is difficult to secure low-high and high-low subjects but much easier to find them for the concordant groups (e.g., high-high, average-average, and low-low). This can be a particularly acute problem with highly correlated covariates, leading either to judgmental weighting schemes for combining covariates or to restricted generalizability because many sampling units are discarded from the experiment.

A solution is to use the most relevant antecedent variable to create a randomized-blocking (or other explicit-classificatory-factor) design and the other antecedent variables as covariates. Interpretation of the results from such designs may be somewhat complex, however, because if the covariates correlate appreciably with the blocking or leveling variable, ANCOVA will tend to "partial out" the block and block × treatment effects. This may be an advantage, however, especially when blocks do not constitute a random-effects factor and hence the blocks × treatments mean square is not the correct error term for testing the treatment mean square unless one can assume that the block × treatment component of variance is negligible. [When treading in these waters, one is well advised to seek help from statisticians and publications such as Edwards (1968), Kirk (1968), McNemar (1969), Myers (1966), Snedecor and Cochran (1967), and Stanley (1967b)].

PRECISION AND STATISTICAL POWER

The statistical concept of *precision* is implied in several discussions so far in this chapter. If one can cut down sampling-error variance, the width of confidence intervals will shrink so that one can set up, more precisely, bounds within which a parameter such as the population mean is likely to lie.

A related concept is that of statistical *power*, which applies to the testing of hypotheses. If the probability of making an *error of the second kind* (i.e., of failing to reject a false null hypothesis) is symbolized by β, then power is $1 - \beta$. Usually one controls α, the probability of making an *error of the first kind* (i.e., of rejecting a true null hypothesis), explicitly by operating at a certain level of significance, typically .05 or .01. Beta is often allowed to run wild, however; without the experimenter's suspecting, it may become rather large, e.g. .25 or .50. This makes power for testing the null hypothesis small, biasing the experiment in the direction of failing to reject null hypotheses that are untrue.

Power-function equations involve a number of parameters, only a few of which can be mentioned here. Other aspects being constant, the more stringently the level of statistical significance, α, is set, the larger β becomes. Power varies directly with n and inversely with within-factor-level-combination variability. The larger the effects one is trying to detect, the higher the power of a particular design for detecting them. The careful experimenter will take such considerations into account in planning his study. He may even choose to set both α and β and decide how large his experiment must be in order to have them at those values.

Multivariate Analysis of Variance (MANOVA)

The analysis of variance is multivariate in its independent variables (i.e., there may be more than one factor in a design) but univariate in its dependent variable (i.e., only one dependent variable is used in a given ANOVA). Often, however, several dependent variables characterize the outcome of an experiment better than one dependent variable does, e.g., running time and number of errors. In recent years, especially since high-speed electronic digital computers have become rather widely available for tedious computations, an extension of ANOVA known as the *multivariate analysis of variance (MANOVA)* is beginning to be used, though not yet by many psychologists. Rationale and computations for MANOVA are not easy to understand. The diligent, quantitatively apt psychologist can turn to Bock (1963) for a rather comprehensive treatment or ask his computer consultant about a suitable MANOVA program and the interpretation of it, such as Finn (1967).

Incomplete Designs

Please look back at the footnote to Table 6-1 and note again that n_{rc}, the number of sampling units used for the treatment defined by the intersection of the rth row with the cth column, was permitted to be 0—i.e., some vacant cells could occur in the crossed design. If not all $R \times C$ cells contained observations, one would have an incomplete factorial design. By arranging the "holes" in certain *balanced* ways, researchers in agriculture, chemistry, and elsewhere have effected considerable economies in experimentation while getting the information they needed. Those systematically incomplete layouts are called *fractional factorial designs*. The experimenter uses 1/2, 1/4, 1/8, 1/16, or even fewer of the total possible number of factor-level combinations. [For an elementary introduction to such designs and to the somewhat related *balanced incomplete block designs*, see Cox (1958, esp. pp. 219–68). See also Kirk (1968) and Cochran and Cox (1957).]

THREE TYPES OF SQUARES

A special class of fractional designs consists of Latin squares, Greco-Latin squares, and hyper-squares. The Latin-square design and its applications to agriculture are quite old. It is used in psychology fairly frequently for controlling order effects (Edwards 1968, pp. 171–99). Consider a small part of a field arranged into R rows and R columns. On each of the *plots* formed by the intersection of a row with a column, one of R different varieties of wheat is to be planted. The order of the varieties is set restrictively such that each variety occurs once in each row and once in each column. The rows are randomized blocks and so are the columns.

Table 6-2 depicts one of many possible 5×5 Latin squares. Note that Variety A occurs on 5 different plots, as does each other variety. The design replicates the treatments 5 times, using 5 plots for each treatment. In a narrow sense, it is a $5 \times 5 \times 5$ factorial design (rows × columns × levels of the manipulated variable) collapsed to a 5×5 design. However, the design is not intended as a "poor man's substitute" for a regular three-factor factorial design, but instead to be used in special cases

Table 6-2. A 5 × 5 Latin Square Showing the Latinization of Five Treatments Within the Row-Column Framework

Row	Column				
	1	2	3	4	5
I	A	B	C	D	E
II	B	C	D	E	A
III	C	D	E	A	B
IV	D	E	A	B	C
V	E	A	B	C	D

such as the agricultural example, where control of fertility gradients in the soil is effected by setting up the plots and assigning the treatments to them *randomly* in the balanced way dictated by the Latin-square-design principle. Latin squares are useful for such special purposes, but they are more fraught with hazards than are complete factorial designs and must therefore be used cautiously. Most psychological-statistics textbooks include discussions of their advantages and limitations.

Greco-Latin squares consist of one Latin square superimposed onto another Latin square of the same size orthogonally so that each of two letters per cell occurs once in each row, once in each column, and once with each other-type letter. Table 6-3 illustrates the smallest possible Greco-Latin-square

Table 6-3. A 3 × 3 Greco-Latin Square

Row	Column		
	1	2	3
I	Aa	Bc	Cb
II	Bb	Ca	Ac
III	Cc	Ab	Ba

design, a 3 × 3. There, three levels of one manipulated factor occur with three levels of another manipulated factor, so that each plot contains a *different* one of the 9 possible factor-level combinations. The capital letters might represent varieties of wheat, and the lower-case letters three different amounts of fertilizer. Note that for this basic design 9 plots (i.e., sampling units) are required, so there is no replication of the basic 9-treatment design; only one observation is produced for each treatment.

For a century and a half it was thought that Greco-Latin squares of side $4k + 2$, where $k = 0, 1, 2, \ldots$, could not exist. This is obviously true for $k = 0$, because a 2 × 2 square cannot be constructed, and was finally shown by enumeration to be true for the 6 × 6 square (i.e., for $k = 1$). What about $k = 2$, the 10 × 10 Greco-Latin square? In recent years, with the aid of computers and an algorithm for generating such squares, it was shown that a large number of them exist. The same situation was found for 14 × 14, 18 × 18, etc. squares.

One can extend the Latinizing principle indefinitely. For instance, it is possible to construct a 4 × 4 square in which the letters A, B, C, and D appear in the 16 cells in combination with the letters a, b, c, and d and the letters α, β, γ, and δ, each letter appearing once in each row, once in each column, and once with any other letter. Unlike the Greco-Latin square, in

which each possible combination of the levels of the manipulated factors must be used, in the hyper-squares where three or more variables are Latinized not all possible treatments can occur. For the 4 × 4 square above there are $4 \times 4 \times 4 = 64$ possible treatments to be Latinized, but only $4 \times 4 = 16$ of them can be used in any one such square. Thus, this hyper-square is a 1/4th fractional factorial with respect to its treatments, or a 1/64th fractional factorial if the row factor and the column factor are considered (Cochran and Cox 1957, pp. 274–75).

The basic Latin, Greco-Latin, and hyper-squares are not widely used in psychology as the entire design for an experiment, but instead as part of a larger design. (Even in agricultural research replication of such squares is rather common.) Much has been written about whether, and how, one should replicate Latin squares. For example, should one draw at random a single Latin square and then use *n* sampling units in each of its cells, or should one draw a number of Latin squares at random from the population of Latin squares of that size and assign only one sampling unit (or just a few units) to each cell of a given square? One has to be careful about the model for his design and the expected mean squares that it dictates. *Ingenuity in designing an experiment must be matched by competence in analyzing the results it generates.*

Edwards (1968, p. 172) gives a simple example of a Latin square used to control days (rows) and hours within days (columns). There were 5 days, 5 hours, and 5 treatments. Five different experimental subjects were run each day, so in all 25 subjects participated in the experiment. Sources of variation were between treatments, between days, between hours, and error (the remaining variation). Only the treatment effects are of substantive interest to the experimenter. He has freed error variability of between-day and between-hour variability, analogously to what one does for a single blocking variable in a simple randomized-block design.

REPEATED MEASUREMENT IN LATIN SQUARES

In some designs for psychological experiments sampling units are used to define rows of the Latin square—e.g., one person may have all the entries in the first row, another all those in the second row, etc. This is repeated measurement, of course. Table 6-4 contains a design of this sort, a 3 × 3 Latin square in

Table 6-4. A Latin Square Where Rows Are Repeatedly-Measured Persons

Person	Treatment Taken		
	1st	2nd	3rd
1	B	A	C
2	C	B	A
3	A	C	B

which the first person is given treatments in the order B, A, C. The second person has the order C, B, A. The third person has the order A, C, B. The persons are not ordered ("person" here is a nominal variable), so one may permute the row freely. (One could not do this with the row fertility gradient, because those blocks of ground have a definite, fixed spatial relationship to each other.) Therefore, one can use three more individuals with orders ABC, BCA, and CAB to construct a second Latin square and with the two squares exhaust the six possible permutations of the letters ABC. There would be one person per order. The two Latin squares could be analyzed, or instead one might replicate the orders (i.e., use at least 12 persons, 2 assigned randomly to each of the 6 different orders of treatments) and analyze the design differently (see recent textbooks and Stanley, 1955). The usual logical and statistical problems with repeated measurements apply to these designs, too.

An alternative procedure, which is simpler but probably gives less control of sampling error, is to assign the order of treatments randomly to each person, without regard to the order any other person gets. A persons × treatments design results; the random-effects persons × treatments mean square is the error term for testing the statistical significance of treatment effects. One still has repeated-measurement pattern problems with which to contend, of course.

Sampling Units Not Drawn Randomly

The linear-hypothesis model that underlies the analysis of variance specifies that the sampling units used in an experiment must be drawn at random from an *infinite* population of such units. In psychological experiments this is usually quite untrue. The researcher is fortunate to lure out of Psychology 1 enough "handcuffed volunteers" to do the experiment at all, much less to draw his units randomly from even that small group. How, then, can he estimate variance components and test hypotheses statistically? This was a difficult-to-answer question for most researchers until Cornfield and Tukey (1956) provided a strong rationale based on an urn-sampling model. The justification can be given simply, as follows.

Capture a "grab group" of N potential experimental subjects, such as those students you can secure from the general psychology course. Assign $N/2$ of them *randomly* to one of your treatments, and the other $N/2$ to the other treatment. Conduct the experiment and gather measures of the dependent variable. Record these and compute the mean for each treatment. Then find the difference between the two means. Now list on a tag each of the N measures that the experiment generated. Shuffle them thoroughly. Put two wastebaskets, one labeled "Treatment A" and the other "Treatment B," at your feet. Toss $N/2$ of the tags randomly into Basket A, and put the rest into Basket B. Compute the mean for Basket A, and subtract from it the mean for Basket B. This procedure yields one random-sampling difference between means based on just those measures actually resulting from the experiment itself. Reshuffle the N tags, and then repeat the random tossing into baskets to generate a second difference, mean of A minus mean of B. Repeat the process until you have a large number of mean differences. The mean of these random differences between means will be very nearly zero.

Where in the randomly generated distribution of differences does the difference you found in your experiment lie? Is it close to zero, or near one tail or the other of the mean-difference distribution? If a difference as large as yours, or larger, occurs infrequently in the distribution, then your difference is statistically significant *for the grab group you used.*

This process can of course be done much more efficiently by computers (via "Monte Carlo" methods) than in the heuristic way described. For small N an exhaustive tabulation of all possible partitionings of N into two sets of $N/2$ measures each will be feasible. Extensions to more than two levels of one manipulated factor and to more than one factor are readily envisioned. Fortunately, results of the urn-sampling procedure are often well approximated by the ordinary t or F tests.

The possible difficulty, of course, is that one's finding of a significant difference in favor of a particular treatment cannot be generalized *probabilistically* from the grab group used to any other sampling units whatsoever, because the population that one "sampled" is only of size N—namely, consists only of those sampling units used in the experiment. This limitation may not be as lethal as it seems, however, because one needs to worry only about *interactions* of characteristics of his experimental subjects with levels of the manipulated factor(s) employed in the experiment. For example, if the experimenter was comparing the effect of fixed-ratio reinforcement with variable-ratio reinforcement, did peculiarities of his experimental subjects cause variable-ratio reinforcement to be superior, when for other types of subjects fixed-ratio would excel? It does not matter that he used only albino rats *if* there is no appreciable tendency for type of rat (albino vs. non-albino, say) to interact with type of reinforcement ratio. Logically and empirically, such interaction may seem unlikely to the experimenter, so that he feels reasonably confident that he would have secured essentially the same *difference* (but not necessarily the same treatment means) had he used gray rats instead.

On the other hand, if good distance vision was more important for one treatment than for the other, it might matter a great deal whether one used only albino rats, or only pigmented rats.

If his subjects are end-of-semester, slow-to-volunteer sophomores at Eastern Subnormal University, would his findings hold for first-of-semester eager volunteers at Classic U? Perhaps the two groups differ greatly in ability, ethnic background, and psychological sophistication. Replication of the experiment at other institutions is highly desirable; failing that, the researcher must try to decide, on the basis of the known characteristics of the group he used and their probable relationship to the treatments employed, how tentative he should be in reporting his findings. Differences in characteristics between the various potential sets of subjects are not the point of concern. *Interactions* of these characteristics with treatment effects are; and although such interactions have been found to be far less common than the differences themselves, they can occur. They may explain why some studies fail to replicate; but, more likely, in a number of them it was not possible to replicate the experimental operations themselves. Detailed study of the replication process, perhaps including the devising of a taxonomy of operations, seems needed. [For more on interactions, see Vale and Vale (1969), and Edgington (1966).]

Variable-Manipulating Experiments Versus Natural Experiments

We noted earlier that "nature" is a prodigious experimenter but a messy one. She abhors randomization, preferring to confound a number of variables in ways that make them extremely difficult to untangle. She cheerfully leaves large gaping holes in our Table 6-1, with no attention to creating a balanced design. As Willems (1967) points out in an important article, she may seldom or never employ certain treatments that the experimenter with his crossed factor levels creates. This causes researchers to ask questions in the laboratory that may have no counterpart in the "real world." For some purposes that may be desirable, but for others it will be impractical. For example, what happens to a certain type of person when he is given power experimentally that he never attains otherwise? Suppose that a boy who pitches a baseball badly is allowed to pitch for three innings in a game with much abler players. How do he and they react? Nature rarely, if ever, performs such an experiment, but a social scientist might do so. Nature does highly applicable research, but it is not very rigorous. The careful researcher is rigorous, but sometimes the generality of his findings may be doubtful. [For illuminating points about this topic, see Chapanis (1967).]

The psychological researcher may arrange contingencies that nature doesn't, but more often he is forced to study natural experiments in which events occur that he would prefer to control himself but cannot. For example, he can hardly conduct long-term controlled experiments concerning smoking versus not smoking with human beings, and must therefore fall back on the gigantic smoking "experiment" that nature conducts continuously. So cleverly has nature confounded the variables, however, that the ablest and most diligent investigators must struggle for years to wrest convincing causal inferences from her.

Sometimes it is possible to combine naturalistic observation with manipulating important variables. For example, Webb *et al.* (1966) have pointed out how a researcher might manipulate the location of items or exhibits in a museum and then collect certain "unobtrusive measures" such as amount of wear on a carpet or floor to ascertain the effectiveness of one location versus another. Campbell and Stanley (1966), too, argue for capitalizing more fully on certain controllable features of the environment, as we noted earlier. In the next section we shall examine some of the sources of invalidity they point out as threatening the soundness of causal inferences.

Causes of Biased Comparisons Within Research Studies

Campbell and Stanley (1966, p. 5) list eight factors jeopardizing the internal validity of a comparative study. All of these are avoided when sampling units are assigned at random to the various factor-level combinations. (This is not to say, of course, that the conclusions of experiments escape argument and reinterpretation, but merely that experimentation provides a mechanism for eliminating sources of bias in ascertaining the effects of treatments.) Nonexperiments are more subject than controlled experiments to what Campbell and Stanley call "plausible alternative hypotheses," i.e., ways of accounting for the results, other than the ones favored by the researcher, that make the study inconclusive. ("It's not cigarette smoking that causes lung cancer, but living in those dirty cities and breathing that foul air.") The eight different classes of variables extraneous to the direct conduct of an investigation that threaten its *internal validity* are as follows:

1. *History*, the specific events occurring between the first and second measurement in addition to the experimental variable
2. *Maturation*, processes within the respondents operating as a function of the passage of time per se (not specific to the particular events), including growing older, growing hungrier, growing more tired, and the like
3. *Testing*, the effects of taking a test upon the scores of a second testing
4. *Instrumentation*, in which changes in the calibration of a measuring instrument or changes in the observers or scorers used may produce changes in the obtained measurements
5. *Statistical regression*, operating where groups have been selected on the basis of their extreme scores
6. Biases resulting in differential *selection* of respondents for the comparison groups
7. *Experimental mortality*, or differential loss of respondents from comparison groups
8. *Selection-maturation interaction*, etc., which in certain of the multiple-group quasi-experimental designs . . . is confounded with, i.e., might be mistaken for, the effect of the experimental variable

The above eight factors may be used, judiciously and tentatively, as a check list in evaluating the proposed or actual design of a study. In the glare of its scrutiny, many supposed "designs" will be found to be as weak as what Campbell and Stanley (1966, p. 8) term the one-shot case study, the one-group pretest-post-test design, and the static-group comparison.

Factors That Restrict Generalizability of Findings

Unless one can rule out the eight sources of internal invalidity listed above, any generalizing of the results of the study is likely to be based on fallible conclusions. Even if the study is impeccable internally, however, the following factors (Campbell and Stanley 1966, pp. 5–6) may jeopardize its *external validity* or *representativeness*:

9. The *reactive* or *interaction* effect of testing, in which a pretest might increase or decrease the respondent's sensitivity or responsiveness to the experimental variable and thus make the results obtained for a pretested population unrepresentative of the effects of the experimental variable for the unpretested universe from which the experimental respondents were selected
10. The *interaction* effects of *selection* biases and the *experimental variable*
11. *Reactive effects of experimental arrangements*, which would preclude generalization about the effect of the experimental variable upon persons being exposed to it in nonexperimental settings
12. *Multiple-treatment interference*, likely to occur whenever multiple treatments are applied to the same respondents, because the effects of prior treatments are not usually erasable

You will recognize most of the above points from discussions earlier in the chapter. Even well-controlled experiments may be subject to some of these four threats to generalizability. Of course, one tries to guard against them while designing the experiment or other type of study, rather than waiting until after the data are analyzed. Campbell and Stanley (1966) devote most of their short book to consideration of "patched-up," quasi-experimental designs that help protect researchers against the 12 sources of invalidity. For an extension of their approach see Bracht and Glass (1968).

Causal inference is just one mode of psychological inquiry. Descriptive and classificatory studies are highly important, too, and nothing in this chapter is meant to assign them low status. As the brilliant physicist-philosopher Bridgman said, "The scientific method, as far as it is a method, is nothing more than doing one's damndest with one's mind, no holds barred" (1945, p. 45). Vale and Vale (1969) call for rapprochement of the associational and experimental approaches to gaining psychological knowledge, in part by having more designs in which both classificatory and manipulated factors appear.

Suggestions for Further Study

In this brief chapter we have been able to consider only a few of the more verbal aspects of experimentation. Hopefully, they will motivate some of you to examine books and articles about experimental design and causal analysis [esp. Lerner (1965)]. You might be wise to begin by scanning the first classic, Fisher (1935 *et seq.*). Then shift to Edwards (1968), which first appeared in 1950. It is clearly written and invites *study*. Go from there to Lindquist (1953), a landmark. Lindquist (1940) first got psychology and education a bit conscious of Fisherian experimental design. The definitive handbook of designs and their analysis since it first appeared in 1950 is Cochran and Cox (1957). McNemar (1969) has been serving statistics classes for psychologists and others with comprehensive fare since 1949. Also see the big books by Winer (1971), Hays (1963), Brownlee (1965), Kirk (1968), and Glass and Stanley (1970). Myers (1966) is smaller but helpful.

A high-level book by mathematical statistician Kempthorne (1952) has influenced specialists in design and some of the more mathematically trained researchers. If you really want a good, determinedly verbal approach to experimental design, rather than chiefly to statistical analysis, few books are available. Foremost among these are Cox (1958) and Lindquist (1953). Ray (1960) is less inclusive than they but worth perusing. And finally, don't overlook the agricultural-research classic that has bailed many of us psychologists out of statistical dilemmas since 1934, Snedecor and Cochran (1967).

Throughout the chapter a number of articles have been mentioned. It may be well here to put some of them and others into a sequence recommended for your scanning. They vary in difficulty, rigor, and inclusiveness. You can judge which of them are worth how much of your effort. Sometimes reading the same things presented in several different ways promotes more understanding than avoiding redundancy would.

Boring (1954) reviewed the nature and history of experimental control. The present writer (Stanley 1967a, 1971) offered two elementary introductions to experimental design that might usefully supplement this chapter. For a brief survey of the design of experiments by the leader in that area see Cochran (1968). His treatment, though somewhat more statistical and technical than Stanley's two articles, is probably the best single short introduction to this topic available. Stanley's (1966b) comments about the history and progress of Fisherian principles may clarify certain concepts further. His expository article (Stanley, 1968) about the analysis of variance may provide background for beginning detailed study of that technique or an overview for those persons already exposed to ANOVA. Chapanis (1967) provided support for his contention that "one should generalize with extreme caution from the results of laboratory experiments to the solution of practical problems" (p. 557). Argyris (1968) discussed possible effects on the rigorousness of psychological studies of asymmetrical relationships between researchers, research assistants, and subjects.

Anderson (1969) used lessons in high school biology to illustrate and explain comparative field experimentation. Campbell's (1969) "Reforms as Experiments" article contains much wisdom about quasi-experimentation and some excellent examples of it. Willems (1967) defended and espoused naturalistic research methods. Vale and Vale (1969) urged a blending of experimentation and associational analysis.

For relatively simple explanations of specific topics in experimental design and statistical analysis see the subject index of the *International Encyclopedia of the Social Sciences* (Sills, 1968). E.g., multiple comparisons among means, not treated in this chapter, are covered well by Nemenyi (1968); see also Marascuilo and Levin (1970). Other reviews of design and analysis appear in the *Annual Review of Psychology* and the *Review of Educational Research*. Abstracts of many relevant articles and books appear in the monthly *Psychological Abstracts*. Several statistical journals have articles on experimental design from time to time. Perhaps *Biometrics* contains the most material that would be understandable to psychologists, but highly important articles for researchers are published by such technical periodicals as the *Journal of the American Statistical Association*, the *Annals of Mathematical Statistics*, *Technometrics*, *Biometrika*, and *Psychometrika*. Within the field of psychology itself is the *Psychological Bulletin*, which frequently contains expository reviews of statistical topics. Occasionally the *Psychological Review* does, too. Some relevant articles appear in *Educational and Psychological Measurement*, the *American Educational Research Journal*, and the *Journal of Educational Measurement*.

Illustrations of experimental designs used in psychological investigations can be found in the *Journal of Experimental Psychology* and also in virtually all the other substantive journals of psychology. Of course, the quality of design and analysis will vary greatly both between and within journals, though those with alert editors and well-functioning refereeing arrangements for manuscripts submitted will keep most of the more egregious errors from getting into print.

Many excellent resources for designing experiments well exist, but of course they must be sought and used. Properly designing an experiment requires *far* more time, effort, and thought than most researchers realize. There are no shortcuts to designing an experiment optimally, but time and effort spent in the design phase may be saved at the analysis stage—not to mention the frustration avoided, the "face" saved, and the greater research contributions made.

Acknowledgements. I would like to thank Gerry F. Hendrickson, Roger E. Kirk, Samuel A. Livingston, Carol A. Vale, and Jack R. Vale for helpful comments. [*J.C.S.*]

References

ANDERSON, R. C. The comparative field experiment: An illustration from high school biology. In *Proceedings of the 1968 Invitational Conference on Testing Problems.* Princeton, N.J.: Educational Testing Service, 1969.

ARGYRIS, C. Some unintended consequences of rigorous research. *Psychological Bulletin,* 1968, *70,* 185–97.

BOCK, R. D. Programming univariate and multivariate analysis of variance. *Technometrics,* 1963, *5,* 95–117.

BORING, E. G. The nature and history of experimental control. *American Journal of Psychology,* 1954, *67,* 573–89.

BOX, G. E. P. Bayesian approaches to some bothersome problems in data analysis. Chap. 2 (pp. 61–101) in Julian C. Stanley (ed.), *Improving experimental design and statistical analysis.* Chicago: Rand McNally, 1967.

———, and DAVID R. COX. An analysis of transformations. *Journal of the Royal Statistical Society, Series B,* 1964, *26,* 211–52.

BRACHT, G. H., and G. V. GLASS. The external validity of experiments. *American Educational Research Journal,* 1968, *5,* 437–74.

BRIDGMAN, P. W. The prospect for intelligence. *Yale Review,* 1945, *34,* 444–61.

BROWNLEE, K. A. *Statistical theory and methodology in science and engineering* (2nd ed.). New York: Wiley, 1965.

CAMPBELL, DONALD T. Factors relevant to the validity of experiments in social settings. *Psychological Bulletin,* 1957, *54,* 297–312.

——— Reforms as experiments. *American Psychologist,* 1969, *24,* 409–29.

———, and J. C. STANLEY. *Experimental and quasi-experimental designs for research.* Chicago: Rand McNally, 1966.

CHAPANIS, A. The relevance of laboratory studies to practical situations. *Ergonomics,* 1967, *10,* 557–77.

COCHRAN, W. G. Experimental design I: The design of experiments. In DAVID L. SILLS (ed.), *International encyclopedia of the social sciences,* vol. 5. New York: Macmillan and Free Press, 1968, 245–54.

———, and GERTRUDE M. COX, *Experimental designs* (2nd ed.). New York: Wiley, 1957.

CORNFIELD, J., and J. W. TUKEY. Average values of mean squares in factorials. *Annals of Mathematical Statistics,* 1956, *27,* 907–49.

COX, DAVID R. The use of a concomitant variable in selecting an experimental design. *Biometrika,* 1957, *44,* 150–58.

——— *Planning of experiments.* New York: Wiley, 1958.

CRONBACH, LEE J., G. C. GLESER, H. NANDA, and N. RAJARATNAM. *The dependability of behavioral measurements.* New York: Wiley, 1972.

EDGINGTON, E. S. Statistical inference and nonrandom samples. *Psychological Bulletin,* 1966, *66,* 485–87.

EDWARDS, ALLEN L. *Experimental design in psychological research* (3rd ed.). New York: Holt, Rinehart and Winston, 1968.

ELASHOFF, J. D. Analysis of covariance: A delicate instrument. *American Educational Research Journal,* 1969, *6,* 383–401.

FINN, JEREMY D. *Multivariance Fortran program for univariate and multivariate analysis of variance and covariance.* Buffalo 14214: Dept. of Educational Psychology, School of Education, State University of New York at Buffalo, May 1967.

FISHER, R. A. *The design of experiments.* New York: Hafner, 1935, 1937, 1942, 1947, 1949, 1951, 1960.

GLASS, G. V., and J. C. STANLEY. *Statistical methods in education and psychology.* Englewood Cliffs, N. J.: Prentice-Hall, 1970.

GRAYBILL, F. A. *An introduction to linear statistical models,* vol. 1. New York: McGraw-Hill, 1961.

HARMAN, H. H. *Modern factor analysis* (2nd ed.). Chicago: University of Chicago Press, 1967.

HAYS, W. L. *Statistics for psychologists.* New York: Holt, 1963.

JENKINS, W. O., and J. C. STANLEY. Partial reinforcement: A review and critique. *Psychological Bulletin,* 1950, *47,* 193–234.

JENSEN, A. R. Intelligence, learning ability, and socioeconomic status. *Journal of Special Education,* 1969, *3,* 23–35.

KEMPTHORNE, O. *The design and analysis of experiments.* New York: Wiley, 1952.

KIRK, R. E. *Experimental design: Procedures for the behavioral sciences.* Belmont, Cal.: Brooks/Cole, 1968.

LERNER, DANIEL (ed.). *Cause and effect.* New York: Free Press, 1965.

LINDQUIST, E. F. *Statistical analysis in educational research.* Boston: Houghton Mifflin, 1940.

——— *Design and analysis of experiments in psychology and education.* Boston: Houghton Mifflin, 1953.

MCNEMAR, Q. *Psychological statistics* (4th ed.). New York: Wiley, 1969.

MARASCUILO, L. A., and J. R. LEVIN. Appropriate post-hoc comparisons for interaction and nested hypotheses in analysis of variance designs: The elimination of Type IV errors. *American Educational Research Journal,* 1970, *7,* 397–421.

MILLMAN, J., and G. V. GLASS. Rules of thumb for writing the ANOVA table. *Journal of Educational Measurement,* 1967, *4,* 41–51.

MYERS, J. L. *Fundamentals of experimental design.* Boston: Allyn and Bacon, 1966.

NEMENYI, P. Linear Hypotheses III: Multiple comparisons. *In* DAVID L. SILLS (ed.), *International encyclopedia of the social sciences,* vol. 9. New York: Macmillan and Free Press, 1968, pp. 337–51.

RAND CORPORATION. *A million random digits with 100,000 normal deviates.* Glencoe, Ill.: Free Press, 1955.

RAY, W. S. *An introduction to experimental design.* New York: Macmillan, 1960.

RICE, J. M. The futility of the spelling grind, I and II. *Forum,* 1897, *23,* 163–72; 409–19.

SCHEFFÉ, H. *The analysis of variance.* New York: Wiley, 1959.

SILLS, D. L. (ed.). *International encyclopedia of the social sciences.* New York: Macmillan and Free Press, 1968.

SNEDECOR, G. W., and W. G. COCHRAN. *Statistical methods* (6th ed.). Ames: Iowa State University Press, 1967.

STANLEY, J. C. Statistical analysis of scores from counterbalanced tests. *Journal of Experimental Education,* 1955, *23,* 187–207.

——— Fixed, random, and mixed models in the analysis of variance as special cases of the finite model. *Psychological Reports,* 1956, *2,* 369.

——— Analysis of a doubly nested design. *Educational and Psychological Measurement,* 1961, *21,* 831–37.

——— Quasi-experimentation. *School Review,* 1965, *73,* 197–205.

——— A common class of pseudo-experiments. *American Educational Research Journal,* 1966, *3,* 79–87. (*a*)

——— The influence of Fisher's *The Design of Experiments* on educational research thirty years later. *American Educational Research Journal,* 1966, *3,* 223–29. (*b*)

——— Rice as a pioneer educational researcher. *Journal of Educational Measurement,* 1966, *3,* 135–39. (*c*)

——— Elementary experimental design—an expository treatment. *Psychology in the Schools,* 1967, *4,* 195–203. (*a*)

——— Problems in equating groups in mental retardation research. *Journal of Special Education,* 1967, *1,* 241–56. (*b*)

——— Linear hypotheses II: Analysis of variance. *In* DAVID L. SILLS (ed.), *International encyclopedia of the social sciences,* vol. 9. New York: Macmillan and Free Press, 1968, pp. 324–36.

——— Plotting ANOVA interactions for ease of visual interpretation. *Educational and Psychological Measurement,* 1969, *29,* 793–97.

——— Design of controlled experiments in education. *In* LEE C. DEIGHTON (ed.), *The encyclopedia of education,* Vol. 3. New York: Macmillan and Free Press, 1971, pp. 474–83.

STEVENS, S. S. Mathematics, measurement, and psychophysics. *In* SMITH S. STEVENS (ed.), *Handbook of experimental psychology* (2nd ed.). New York: Wiley, 1958, pp. 1–49.

TUKEY, J. W. One degree of freedom for non-additivity. *Biometrics,* 1949, *5,* 232–42.

VALE, JACK R., and CAROL A. VALE. Individual differences and general laws in psychology: A reconciliation. *American Psychologist,* 1969, *24,* 1093–1108.

WALLIS, W. A., and H. V. ROBERTS. *Statistics made easy.* Glencoe, Ill.: Free Press, 1955.

WEBB, E. J., D. T. CAMPBELL, R. D. SCHWARTZ, and L. SECHREST. *Unobtrusive measures: Nonreactive research in the social sciences.* Chicago: Rand McNally, 1966.

WILLEMS, EDWIN P. Toward an explicit rationale for naturalistic research methods. *Human Development,* 1967, *10,* 138–54.

WILLIAMS, EVAN J. Linear hypotheses I: Regression. *In* DAVID L. SILLS (ed.), *International encyclopedia of the social sciences,* Vol. 9. New York: Macmillan and Free Press, 1968, pp. 310–24.

WINER, B. J. *Statistical principles in experimental design* (2nd ed.). New York: McGraw-Hill, 1971.

Just as man's brain is the most significant aspect of his evolutionary development, the computer may be viewed as the most significant tool developed by man in his accelerating extension of knowledge and control over his environment—and himself. This analogy is based on properties common to the human brain and the modern computer: generality and adaptability. What makes man's cognitive system uniquely powerful is not its overall superiority, but its ability to handle a tremendous range of problem situations. In fact, there are few human perceptual-cognitive abilities, considered separetely, that one or another lower form of life does not possess in superior form. The same sort of generality/adaptability is what makes the computer man's most useful tool.

Language can be viewed as the *vehicle* for this uniquely human capability; it is the coding system as well as the primary form of cognitive expression. From one viewpoint, computers can be seen as tools for extending man's language—his data-processing capabilities. The modern digital computer is actually misnamed; the term "computer" implies that the machines are suited only to calculation with quantitative data. In fact, the modern digital computer is an *information processing* device, in the most general sense of the term. A fundamental assumption of information theory is that all information can be represented by series of binary choices. The term "binary" implies two possible states: on–off, yes–no, 0–1. Thus, the smallest, (elementary) unit of information is a single binary choice, which in quantitative terms is a binary digit, abbreviated "bit." A sequence of bits can be interpreted as a numerical quantity in the binary (base 2) number system, but it can also represent a series of choices. Sets of bits can stand for larger units of information, and sequences of the sets for still larger units. Ultimately, therefore, any factual (static) or process (dynamic) information can be coded in terms of bits.[1]

Because most digital computers are binary machines, which store and manipulate binary-coded data, a digital computer

D. J. Veldman

& E. Jennings

[1]Distasteful though it may seem to some, "The light that lies/In woman's eyes" can, at least in theory, be represented as information by a cold, hard, magnetic storage device.

Computer Applications in Psychology

7

can theoretically achieve any information manipulation process that can be completely specified. Therefore any cognitive process of a human brain, which is consistent and fully understood, can be duplicated by a computer—often with greater speed and precision. When asked by a friend whether machines could think, a scientist once replied, "I compute so."

Why then have not the computers been programmed to do our most difficult thinking for us? The answer is that they have—to the extent that our thought processes are understood. It is one of the goals of psychological science to extend knowledge of man's cognitive behavior, and as we will see later in this chapter, the computer itself has become one of the most powerful tools of the cognitive psychologist. Although it has often been noted that the information storage capacity of the human brain far exceeds that of the largest computer systems, this fact does not explain the inability of psychologists to adequately duplicate the brain's cognitive abilities with computers. The essential reason is that we know so very little about the way humans process information. Realization of the primitive state of our knowledge prompted one cognitive theorist to call his model "Pandemonium" and to describe its elements as "demons" which "shriek" at each other (Selfridge 1959). Even if we had a machine as big and as fast as the human brain, we wouldn't know how to duplicate all the informational processes of which humans are capable.

Of course, *some* cognitive processes of the human mind are easily duplicated by computers, usually with much greater precision and speed. For instance, arithmetic calculation is something that humans do according to the same set of conventions that can be programmed into a computer. Putting a list of words in alphabetic order is also easily programmed, because the process can be completely specified. Consider, however, the process a personnel officer goes through in deciding which of a number of job applicants to hire. Given the information on the candidates' application forms and their test scores (assuming no interview), we could program a computer to form a regression equation to predict the human's decisions. We could get the human to verbalize the steps he goes through in making the decision, and then program the machine to follow the same process. We could also program to represent a theory of human decision making, and then test it with the available data. All three of these procedures would be called "simulation" by some computer scientists. We will consider a variety of the actual applications in all three areas later in this chapter. The important point here is that none of the "simulations" will be entirely accurate, because even when we use the human's description of his own behavior, we will almost certainly be dealing with an incomplete analysis of the actual process. Although we will further discuss the point later in this chapter, it is important to note here that most computer simulations of human processes probably do not even resemble the actual working of human brains, even when the products of the two systems are indistinguishable.

In this chapter we will first consider the nature of modern computer hardware (the machines) and software (the programs of instructions). Then we will review the field of psychological applications under three broad headings: (1) data acquisition and process control, (2) statistical analysis, and (3) simulation. Some readers may be surprised by the variety of ways in which psychologists have already used computers to extend and speed their research. Others may be disappointed by the dearth of

genuine breakthroughs that have so far resulted from applications of computers in psychological research. By acquainting the reader with the field, we hope to stimulate his imagination and interest in following fruitful applications, and at the same time offset some of the ignorance and wild optimism that is often encountered in articles written for the general public.

Hardware: The Machines

The term "computer" may be considered a substitute for "stored-program digital information-processing system." There are two basically different types of computers in use: analog and digital. We will discuss their differences shortly, but the digital computer is by far the most common and most general in its applications—particularly in the field of psychology. The term "system" implies the fact that modern computers consist of a number of semiautonomous machines interconnected and centrally controlled. The term "stored-program" indicates the essential reason for the speed and efficiency of a modern computer: the fact that the sequence of instructions that controls its operations is stored in the same memory unit that holds the data to be manipulated, thus permitting the machine to modify its own instructions during the execution of the program. This feature sets the computer apart from other machines used by man. We have already commented on the significance of the term "information-processing" in our definition of a computer; any kind of information can be coded as binary sequences and processed by computers. The main reason that the first and most common applications were with quantitative data is that the processes for manipulating numbers are completely specified, and many important questions involve numerical analysis too tedious and complex to be done any other way.

Analog vs. Digital Machines. These terms refer to two essentially different ways of representing quantitative values. *Analog* devices, such as the thermometer and the slide rule, register quantities as the physical states of some medium that can vary continuously over a range of values. The precision of the representation is ultimately limited by the physical device used. *Digital* devices, such as a light switch and the abacus, represent numerical values in discrete units. Some digital machines have multi-state units; the common desk calculator, for instance, uses a series of geared number wheels to represent digits in the decimal number system. Each wheel, however, has only ten possible states or positions. Digital computers store data in series of binary units. Unlike analog devices, the accuracy with which a value can be represented is limited only by the length of the string of units employed, and can be extended quite practically beyond the limits of any analog device. Furthermore, in a sequence of quantitative operations, device errors of analog units tend to accumulate, whereas they can be made to cancel each other in a digital machine.

Some hybrid machines are in use in certain kinds of psychological research. Usually these machines collect data from analog recording devices and transform them into digital form for analysis. A thermostat is an example of a simple analog to digital converter, changing the continuous information of a thermometer to the binary signal needed by the furnace, which is either on or off at any given moment. Analog machines are used by psychologists almost exclusively to process physiological data. A detailed description of methods of analog-to-digital data conversion may be found in a recent book by Uttal (1967).

Computer System Components. There are four basic types of components in any computer system. The heart of the system is the *processing control* unit which executes the instructions of the program. It receives both instructions and data from *storage* devices, and sends modified instructions and the results of data manipulations back to the storage units. Almost all computer systems have a central storage unit, often called the "memory," to which the processing control unit has very rapid access. Other larger but slower storage devices are also parts of most computer systems, and may be used to hold programs waiting to be executed and output information waiting to be handled by other devices.

Input to the system may be from a variety of units employing different media. Probably the most common type of input is still the punch or tab card, which is "read" by a unit that senses the pattern of punched holes by means of wire brushes or photoelectric cells. Other types of input are magnetic tapes on which magnetized spots serve the same function as the holes in tab cards. Although such devices have been used experimentally for many years, machines have recently been marketed commercially which permit data to be entered directly from a keyboard onto a magnetic tape. Time-shared systems, which will be discussed later, can simultaneously service large numbers of remote terminals, which consist of keyboard and sometimes a TV-like display screen, allowing direct and immediate communication between the computer and the user. At some installations punched paper tape can also be used as an input medium. Such tapes are prepared by other machines, such as a Flexowriter or a specialized data-acquisition device. Occasionally, a computer will receive input over a common phone line directly from the memory of another computer, but such networks are at present quite rare.

Output from a computer system is most often in the form of printed pages; speeds of up to 1000 lines per minute are quite common. Magnetic and paper tapes can be generated by computer programs, as well as punched cards. Graphic plots of output data can be produced on paper, on microfilm, or on CRT (cathode ray tube) display screens. Most computers have at least one electric typewriter connected to the system, by which the operator monitors, and occasionally controls, the operation of the machine. Some computer systems use a CRT-keyboard terminal for this purpose. Some progress has been made in research on speech recognition and generation, and at least one computer system provides spoken stock market quotations over telephone circuits. Recognition of human verbalizations, however, has proved to be an extremely difficult problem.

Off-line Machines. Almost every computer installation, and many other organizations which do not have their own computers, operate card-processing machines. Of course, "key-punch" machines are needed to transfer data from source documents to punch cards. Figure 7-1 shows a typical tab card, punched with codes for a commonly used character set. Each column of the card has 12 punching positions, and will hold the code for one alphameric character. Codes for decimal numerals, plus and minus signs require only one punch; alphabetic characters require two; and other characters require three punches in a column. One card can hold 80 characters, which may be subdivided in many ways into fields representing specific pieces of information. The key-punch machine that is used to prepare these cards operates very much like a typewriter.

Another useful card-handling machine is called the "sorter." It separates a card deck into bins by examining the punches in a single column. There are also machines called "collators" which will match cards from two decks and merge or select them on the basis of a series of card columns. Also found in most installations that prepare data cards is a machine called the "reproducer," which will rapidly punch a duplicate of any deck

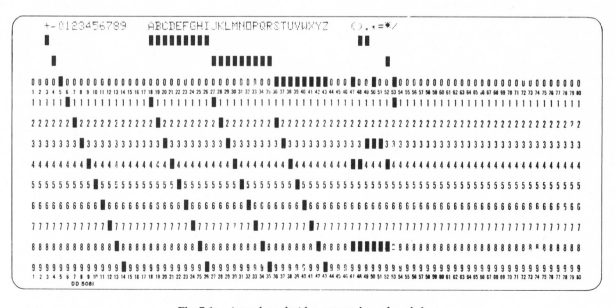

Fig. 7-1. *A punch card with a commonly used symbol set.*

of cards. A printer is also frequently available to make printed listings from a deck of cards.

By careful planning, a substantial amount of statistical summary and analytic work can be carried out with these "off-line" machines, without resorting to the use of computer programs. As the number of subjects and variables and complexity of the statistics increases, however, the efficiency of card-handling machines rapidly gives way to that of the computer.

Time-Shared Systems. The most recent major development in computer hardware has been the introduction of systems which are designed to service a number of remote terminals simultaneously. Since the fastest part of any computer system is the central processing unit, as much as 70% of the time in older systems was spent waiting for input/output functions to be completed. Time-shared systems automatically switch control from one to another terminal as it needs central processing, thus accomplishing far more effective utilization of the system's capabilities.

From the viewpoint of the user at a remote terminal, he has the whole machine to himself and gets almost immediate replies to his requests, which may involve computation, searching of central files, or instructional material. The cheapest and simplest kind of terminal is the teletype machine, which operates like a typewriter. Terminals with a display screen instead of paper printout are more expensive, but better adapted to many applications. Some terminals also include audio tape recorders and slide projectors under control of the central computer. The simpler typewriter terminals may be located at any distance from the controlling computer, connected over ordinary phone lines; terminals with display screens generally require more complex direct lines.

Academia. Almost every medium and large institution of higher learning in the United States now owns or rents a large-scale digital computer and the necessary offline machines to support research applications. Many large universities have established departments of computer science which grant undergraduate and graduate degrees in this academic specialty. In some institutions the computer center is operated by an organization independent of any of the traditional disciplines; in other places, departments of mathematics or electrical engineering may be responsible for providing computing services. Research institutes associated with many universities maintain their own computer installations, also. With the advent of time-shared systems a few consortiums of small schools have been formed to obtain computer services over telephone lines from a central installation. In addition to large-scale central computing service centers, many academic departments have found it useful to maintain smaller computers suited to the particular educational and research needs of their students and faculty members, particularly where analog-to-digital conversion of data is necessary for pre-processing of experimental results.

Software: The Programs

Without programs a computer is as useless as a vehicle without a driver. Computers execute instructions in sequence;

the set of instructions which accomplish a specific purpose is known as a "program." Although most machines operate entirely in terms of binary information—instructions and data—the user fortunately does not have to prepare either in this form. The computer can call upon already available programs to "translate" the user's instructions and data from other forms into that which it can use directly. The data punched in tab cards, for instance, are not in binary-coded form, but are converted automatically as they are input through the computer's card reader.

The programs of instructions to the computer also may be written in a variety of "languages" which the machine then translates automatically into specific operational codes that it can use. The programs which do this language translation are called "compilers" because they compile series of specific machine instructions from each of the much more general statements in the higher-order language. By far the most widely used of these general languages is FORTRAN, which stands for "FORmula TRANslation." Although originally developed by IBM to simplify the programming of mathematical procedures, it has proved to be extremely versatile as a vehicle for many other applications. Other general languages have been developed which

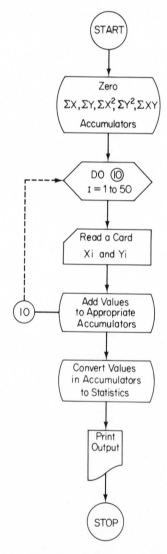

Fig. 7-2. *Flow chart for computing a correlation coefficient.*

are somewhat more elegant and convenient, but none has achieved much acceptance in the United States. ALGOL, for example, is widely used in Europe and widely praised by many computer scientists in this country. The main reasons for the increasing ubiquity of FORTRAN seem to be the continually increasing investment of users in programming effort with this language, and the fact that relatively few programmers attempt to become proficient in more than one language.

Flow Charts. Although attempts have been made to declare various sets of standard symbols and arrangements for flowcharting of procedures, no one set of conventions has been universally accepted. A flowchart should be judged on an empirical basis: does it communicate the nature of the procedure without ambiguity? Flowcharts may also be constructed at various levels of specificity, depending on the purposes for which they are intended.

To illustrate flowcharting and programming, we have chosen the computation of the correlation coefficient. The mathematical formula for this statistic is:

$$r_{xy} = \frac{\sum\limits_{i=1}^{N} X_i Y_i / N - \mu_x \mu_y}{\sigma_x \sigma_y}$$

where

$$\mu_x = \sum_{i=1}^{N} X_i / N$$

and

$$\sigma_x = \sqrt{\sum_{i=1}^{N} X_i^2 / N - \mu_x^2}$$

Now, from these formulas one might reasonably assume that the first thing to do would be to read all of the X and Y scores into the computer memory, and then to set about the process of computing the means, sigmas, and the correlation coefficient. The problem could be solved in this way, but as is often the case in computer programming, a somewhat different approach turns out to be more economical. Figure 7-2 illustrates the steps in the process which is expressed as a computer program in Figure 7-3.

To use this program we would proceed through the following steps:

1. *Punch the program*: Each line in the program would be keypunched into a single tab card.
2. *Punch the data:* The rather cryptic notation of statement

```
PROGRAM COR

XM = 0

YM = 0

XS = 0                          Zero Accumulators

YS = 0

R  - 0

DO 10 I = 1, 50

READ 5, X, Y

5 FORMAT (10X, F2.0, 1X, F2.0)

XM = XM + X

YM = YM + Y

XS - XS + X**2

YS = YS + Y**2                  Add Values to Accumulators

10 R = R + X * Y

XM = XM / 50.0

YM = YM / 50.0

XS = SQRT (XS / 50.0 - XM**2)   Compute Statistics

YS = SQRT (YS / 50.0 - YM**2)

D = XS * YS

IF (D.GT.0.0) D= 1.0 / D

R = R/50.0 - XM * YM) * D

PRINT 15, XM, YM, XS, YS, R

15 FORMAT ( // 5F10.4)

END
```

Fig. 7-3. *FORTRAN program to compute a correlation coefficient.*

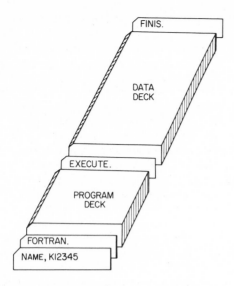

Fig. 7-4. *Input deck arrangement for program COR.*

The first thing the program does is to store zero values in memory locations called *XM*, *YM*, *XS*, *YS*, and *R*, which are going to hold accumulated sums, sums of squares, and cross products. Then, using an index variable I to keep track, the program orders the reading of each data card in turn into memory locations *X* and *Y*, and the addition of the appropriate values to the five accumulator locations. When statement 10 has been completed 50 times (I=50), the "DO loop" is finished and the program proceeds to calculate the means, sigmas, and finally the correlation coefficient. These values are then printed and the "FINIS" card turns control of the computer back to the monitor system. Note that the sigma-product denominator in the correlation formula is computed in a way that avoids possible division by zero, which is not allowed in most computer systems. It is best to anticipate such difficulties in writing general programs.

Some computer systems allow the punching of the binary language program by the compiler, to avoid the necessity of compiling the program every time it is run. Other systems allow the user to store the compiled version of the program on tape for later use.

number 5 in the program indicates that each of 50 subjects' *X* and *Y* scores are to be punched as two-digit numbers in columns 11–12 and 14–15, respectively, of 50 separate data cards. Other data on the cards will be ignored by the program.

3. *Assemble the input deck*: The cards in front of the program deck, between the program and data decks, and after the data are called "system" control cards (see Figure 7-4). Even though this FORTRAN program and data could be run on almost any computer in the country, each computer system has somewhat different requirements for the cards which control the operation of the "monitor" which decides what is to be done with the input.

4. *Process the input deck*: In most installations the psychologist-user would turn over his deck to the computation center staff and return later to pick up his deck and the output produced by the processing. The computer system would read the cards in the order in which they are stacked. After recording the user's name and problem number, it would encounter the "FORTRAN" card which it would interpret as a request for the use of the FORTRAN compiler program, which it would bring into central memory from one of its peripheral storage units, such as a magnetic tape. This compiler program would then take control of the computer, read and translate each of the FORTRAN statements into the specific binary-coded instructions implied, and store the resulting machine-language version of the program in its central memory. All FORTRAN compiler programs include many tests of the statements being processed to insure that the programmer has not inadvertently erred in writing the program. Passing these tests, however, is no guarantee of correct answers from the program, since such mistakes as doing the right things in the wrong order cannot be detected by the compiler.

When the "EXECUTE" card is encountered, the compiler realizes it has finished the program, and it turns control of the computer over to the machine-language program it has just produced (providing no errors have been detected so far).

Subroutine Libraries. One of the most powerful features of the FORTRAN level languages is the fact that frequently needed procedures can be separately programmed and then called into operation by single statements or references in other programs. For instance, the term "SQRT" in our example calls into operation a standard subroutine which computes the square root of the value enclosed in the parentheses which follow the term. The value computed within the parentheses in this case is the variance, the square root of which is the sigma (standard deviation) needed in the computation of the correlation coefficient. The value in parentheses is called the "argument" to the subroutine.

All FORTRAN compilers have a variety of standard mathematical subroutines available to them automatically. Most manufacturers also provide subroutines for various complex mathematical operations such as matrix multiplication, and most university computer centers have also developed additional subroutines for the convenience of their users. The individual user is also free to devise subroutines for particular procedures that he frequently wishes to employ. The wider the variety of subroutines available to the programmer, the simpler he will find the chore of programming to be, since most of the work of constructing a particular procedure may already be completed. Some of the sources for statistical routines will be described later in this chapter.

Learning a Language. There are two major reasons for a psychologist to seriously consider investing the time and energy necessary to learn a programming language such as FORTRAN. In the first place, even though standard statistical subroutines are available locally to carry out most of the procedures he may wish to use in his research, these subroutines have to be called into operation by some sort of "driver" program written in FORTRAN. Even if the driver programs are already set up for him, they often need to be modified slightly to fit special cases. The second reason for learning how to program is that many important kinds of data processing cannot be adequately cast in the form of general purpose programs. The psychologist who is able to write his own routines may be able to save months of clerical work with a few minutes of programming effort. If he has to depend on someone else to do this for him, he will find inevitably that no one either understands or cares about his problem as much as he does—a situation that has led many a researcher to exasperation in attempting to complete a large-scale project.

Learning FORTRAN is very much like learning any "foreign" language. The vocabulary is very small, however, and the grammar is entirely consistent. Most students of the language quickly realize that the difficulty of programming lies in the analysis and organization of the problem-solving procedure, and not in the actual coding of the operations in FORTRAN statements. As is the case in learning any language, the more one uses it in a realistic context, the more fluent he becomes. Also, he has the benefit of an impartial judge, since the machine will either reject faulty statements completely, or will generate nonsensical replies with them. Programming in FORTRAN is not really difficult, and every year it is becoming a more significant skill for a research worker in the behavioral sciences.

Although FORTRAN reference manuals for specific computers are important for reference purposes, such manuals are usually not as valuable for learning the language as are instructional texts, such as those by McCracken (1961. a general text), Plumb (1961, a "programmed learning text"), Lehman and Bailey (1968, a general introduction for behavioral scientists), and Veldman (1967, emphasizing statistical programming in the behavioral sciences).

Data Acquisition and Process Control

Most of the techniques to be described here are types of "real-time" applications. This means that the computer is programmed to process data *during* the experiment, and in some cases even to control the procedure itself. Applications of time-shared computers with remote terminals, in which a human interacts directly with the computer, are also real-time processes. One might consider some of these methods as "simulation" of a human experimenter by the computer, but this seems to stretch the usual definitions of simulation too far, since the focus here is on the data collected, rather than on the collector's behavior.

Another distinguishing feature of this class of applications is the analogy that anthropomorphizes the computer as a clerk, rather than as a mathematician or statistical assistant. The clerk's behavior is no more sensible than the instructions given to it, but its speed and precision far exceed the capabilities of human beings. Some critics have felt that this somehow debases humanity, but the opposite argument seems more valid: human minds are freed to function at a more complex and creative level when computers can be programmed to take over the simple mechanical tasks.

Generation of Stimuli. Preparing stimulus materials for psychological experiments is a tedious clerical chore for which a computer can easily be programmed. Printing lists of randomly arranged nonsense syllables, or lists of words matched for certain characteristics, or even complete stimulus sentences are rel-

atively simple programming problems. Green (1963) describes a variety of such applications in research on human learning.

When a computer is programmed to generate stimulus materials and to present them to the experimental subjects in real-time, many elaborate variations are possible. The most interesting of these involve contingent scheduling of the materials to be presented, using the subject's own previous responses to determine automatically which stimulus to present next.

Visual patterns and auditory stimuli can also be prepared and presented by computers. In fact, many recent studies of pattern perception could not have been conducted without the aid of the computer in constructing the extremely complex stimulus materials. White (1962) surveys a variety of studies of visual and auditory perception involving computer-generated stimuli. Probably the most generally useful piece of hardware in these applications is the cathode-ray display screen. Systems are now in use which use an ordinary TV set with an attached keyboard as a computer terminal. As the costs of such devices settle into reach of the average family, we may expect far-reaching changes in the way "education" enters our lives.

Experiment Control. There is nothing novel about the use of machines to systematically present stimuli to experimental subjects and to record their responses. When these procedures are extended to the use of a general-purpose computer, however, the possibilities are tremendously increased. Special-purpose devices have been constructed in many laboratories to present stimuli systematically, or to record responses such as reaction times. Off-line card processing machines such as the reproducer (summary punch) have also been adapted to present stimuli and record responses on punch cards automatically. Machines such as the Flexowriter have been modified to allow coding of videotaped behavior by human judges to be recorded on punched paper tape for later analysis (Fuller 1970).

In their survey of computer-controlled experiments, Miller, Bregman, and Norman (1965) note that a wide variety of new experimental designs becomes possible when the computer is used to provide continuous feedback to the experimenter of trends in his data as they are collected. This area has been explored only superficially so far, however.

We have already mentioned the presentation of stimuli by typewriters and cathode-ray displays. Since a computer can control any relay-actuated instrument, a wide variety of standard stimulus devices, such as slide projectors, can be automatically handled as well. Most computers have internal real-time clocks, and these signals can be utilized by the programmer to sequence stimuli and to record temporal response measures.

Responses of the subjects to keyboards or other relay devices are easily recorded by the computer, and more complex instruments may be used to abstract certain indices of the subjects' behavior, such as variation in voice quality. Some CRT display screens allow use of a "light-pen" by the subject to "point" to particular places on the screen. The signal is then returned to the computer memory for storage and/or use by the controlling program. Generally, the computer can act on the subjects' behavior far more quickly than a human experimenter, and with error-free decisions based on extremely complex aspects of the responses.

Theoretically, a computer with remote terminals could schedule subjects, run the experiment, analyze the data, and write the report while the experimenter took a vacation. One might expect experimental subjects to resent being manipulated by a machine, but many psychologists have reported markedly greater subject interest and cooperation when a computer has been used to control the experimental procedure.

On-Line Monitoring. These applications are very similar to the computer-controlled experimentation just discussed, but the purposes are quite different. The behavior of a body organ, a person under observation, or even a group of people interacting is continuously recorded by the computer, which analyzes the data in real time and reports regularly, or on special conditions, to some human supervisor. Of course, such continuous recording is a crucial part of many physiological experiments, but here we are interested in the applications where the computer looks only for "red flag" conditions.

Such computer applications in the field of medicine are obviously an important advance in patient care. Collen, Ruben, and Davis (1965) described an automated system for screening patient data from $2\frac{1}{2}$ hour multiphasic battery of clinical tests in a very large clinic. The system not only signals medical personnel when additional tests are indicated, but also prepares summary reports on individual patients and the clinic population. Baruch (1965) also discussed applications of time-shared computers in hospital automation. Hon (1965) reported a much more specific use of on-line computer monitoring: the detection of distress signs in the unborn fetus. Various physiological measures are continuously recorded during labor and birth; the data are immediately available to the attending physician, and are recorded for later analytic research.

In an entirely different context, Cooley (1964) has advocated the use of computers to continuously monitor student performance in academic settings. He compared present test-scoring and grade reports to the calibrated oil-pressure gauges once standard in automobiles. Far more useful is the now-common flashing red light that automatically comes on when oil pressure gets too low. The point is not that a psychologist/counselor cannot interpret test data adequately, but that he does not have time to scan the mass of data so as to head off serious problems by dealing with them in their early stages. Cogswell (1966) has described the development of computer-based student record systems which could easily serve as the basis for such a monitoring arrangement. As we will see later, this type of monitoring is inherent in many computer programs designed for instruction, also.

Data Reduction. The massive amounts of digital data generated by physiological recording devices must be reduced to manageable summary form before an experimenter can use them effectively. The computer can do this kind of reduction with relative ease, as fast as the data are collected in many cases. Adey (1965) has surveyed the use of computers for such purposes in neurophysiological research, and Brazier (1965) discussed their use specifically in the analysis of EEG records. Pipberger (1962) considered comparable techniques as they have been applied to ECG data. Of particular interest is his report that automated computer analysis of 134 patient records led to the correct diagnosis in all cases, while conventional methods missed 22%.

Of course, if a computer terminal is used to present test items and record subject responses, it can easily score the items for various scales immediately, and even feed back the interpretations to the subject for comment (Veldman 1967). In any case, item data need not be retained as permanent records when the only interest is in summary scores. Veldman and Menaker (1968) have reviewed the many computer applications in the field of psychological assessment and counseling.

One of the most interesting applications of computers in data reduction is exemplified by the work of Stone and his colleagues (1966). Their *General Inquirer* system automatically carries out content analysis of verbal productions, and has been used to study and compare such diverse materials as suicide notes, political speeches, and therapy interviews. The data are entered as straight text from punch cards or magnetic tape, and are reduced to counts of salient features preselected by the researcher. Borko (1967) has reviewed a variety of studies of this type, as well as the widely publicized use of computers to determine authorship of such things as the Federalist Papers and the Pauline Epistles.

Assessment-Diagnosis. Any decision-making process that is fully specified, and for which the necessary data can be obtained in unambiguous form, can be programmed for computer processing. Lusted (1965) has surveyed the field of computer applications in medical diagnosis. These are of three general types: (1) use of the computer as an aid to the physician in flagging unusual symptoms or syndromes, (2) differential diagnostic research based on multivariate statistical analysis, and (3) training/assessment of the medical student in differential diagnostic procedures. The later applications have the appearance of game-playing programs, but the students take them with deadly seriousness. The computer acts the role of a supervising physician, who evaluates the appropriateness of each successive test requested and decision made by the student as he approaches his final diagnosis of the hypothetical patient. In some ways these programs resemble some of the simulation techniques to be discussed later in this chapter.

With regard to the efficacy of human vs. computerized diagnosis, data reported by Goldberg (1968) and by Meehl (1954) rather convincingly demonstrate the superior results of capitalizing on the objectivity of the computer procedures. The evidence also strongly suggests that clinical lore about the necessity of complex configural (interactive) diagnostic rules may be largely unfounded. In both a medical and a psychological setting, Goldberg found that a simple regression equation produced more accurate diagnoses than human experts using their best subjective judgement based on the same data, and that complex configural equations yielded no significant improvement in predictive efficiency.

Many personality inventory scoring procedures have been adapted to computers, and then extended to provide verbal interpretations of the numerical-score profiles. Rome and his colleagues (1965) have reported on the development of such a system for the *Minnesota Multiphasic Personality Inventory*, which is routinely administered to all patients entering the Mayo Clinic. Other interpretive services of this kind are available on a commercial basis from various organizations such as the Roche Psychiatric Institute. The senior author of the present chapter, in collaboration with S. L. Menaker and R. F. Peck, has developed computer-based systems for deriving numerical scores for various personality constructs from verbal responses to the *One-Word Sentence Completion* instrument (Veldman, Menaker, and Peck 1969).

Information Retrieval. The clerical powers of a large-scale computer system are enormous, and a great deal of research by linguists and others has been invested in developing methods for maximizing the effectiveness of storage and retrieval of information with machines. Books by Borko (1967) and by Becker and Hayes (1963) provide comprehensive surveys of this type of application of computers. Of particular interest because of their relevance to psycholinguistics are those programs designed to answer natural-language questions by appropriate retrieval of stored information (Simmons 1962, 1967). These applications are also naturally relevant to computer-assisted instruction.

Much of the work on computer applications in student appraisal and guidance is based on the initial establishment of a comprehensive machine storage/retrieval system for student data. A recent innovation in the field of guidance is a commercial service to graduating high school seniors which resembles the ubiquitous "computer dating" services more than anything else. The students' characteristics are matched against a large file of descriptive data on colleges in the United States, and a written report is prepared for the student on each of the few colleges which seem most compatible with his characteristics, aspirations, finances, and so forth.

Reorganizing and storing data from any institution is an expensive, complex, and tedious process, but once it is accomplished, the benefits resulting from machine-based files more than offset the initial costs. Academic and medical institutions have generally lagged in making this kind of conversion, probably because accounting in terms of unit costs is so ambiguous. What is the definition of a "unit" of education or medical care? Without the stimulus of such evaluation, an institution is less motivated to maximize its efficiency. A recent book by Weed (1969) convincingly documents the need for massive re-orientation of medical records systems to facilitate such evaluations, and offers realistic proposals for such changes.

Instruction. One of the few innovations in education that has any hope of significantly improving the quality of instruction in the public schools of this country is computer-assisted instruction (CAI). Initially, computer systems were used only as simple "teaching machines," which afforded few advantages over the programmed workbooks originated by B.F. Skinner and others.

Only recently have the computer manufacturers begun to invest heavily in developing hardware and software especially designed for instructional uses. A number of research centers have been established at universities, where materials are being designed to capitalize on the flexibility of real-time computers with remote terminals. Uttal (1967) and Loughery (1966) have provided detailed surveys of this area.

Ordinary programmed learning materials are structured for sequential presentation of small amounts of information, each followed by a simple test question. Gradually, the student accumulates a body of knowledge with a maximum of positive reinforcement. Although students seem to learn as much by this approach as by conventional instruction, some of them find it excruciatingly dull—an attitude that may generalize beyond the particular facts they learned.

The computer adds both variety and efficiency to the teaching procedure. Auditory and graphic materials may be used as well as verbal text. Complex answer-recognition techniques can be used to relax the constraints on student responses. Diagnostic pretests can be employed to shift the student to appropriate speeded or remedial tracks.

From another viewpoint, the basic advantage of computer-assisted instruction is that it takes account of individual differences in students. Although research has only begun in this regard, it is logically feasible to design instructional materials which vary not only in difficulty, but in other respects as well. It may be, for instance, that some students would learn material faster if it was presented in an auditory rather than a visual mode. Pretesting could automatically assign students to the particular instructional programs that best suited their needs.

When a whole classroom or school is organized to make maximum use of the advantages of CAI facilities, individualization of instruction becomes far more than a cant phrase. Traditional structures based on lock-steps through grade levels become virtually meaningless; each student progresses through the curriculum at his own pace. Teachers devote almost all of their time to supervision, planning, and dealing with truly unique learning problems. It may be decades before the full impact of this technological development is realized; computers are expensive, and our massive public education program will require massive new funding before the conversion is complete. Many knowledgeable educators think the benefits will more than justify the cost; Oettinger (1968), however, warns against false optimism in this area.

Statistical Analysis

Psychologists have been among the earliest and most enthusiastic users of computers (Wrigley 1957). By the mid-50's psychologists at the University of Illinois under the leadership of Charles Wrigley and Raymond Cattell were using the ILLIAC machine extensively for statistical analysis. Due in part to the early emphasis on the use of computers for statistical analysis and in part to the fact that computers are much more easily programmed to deal with quantitative data, psychologists have probably used computers more for this than for any other purpose.

During the late 50's even quantitative data processing posed formidable problems for psychologists, who had to write their own programs with the then-primitive languages, or else develop a vocabulary to communicate with someone who could program. Most of the early programs were written in machine-level languages and, due to rapid obsolescence and/or saturation of old computer systems and the introduction of new ones, it was not uncommon for a relatively extensive library of routines to become useless overnight. The development of algorithmic compiler languages solved the problem of rapid obsolescence of programming effort in large part, and by the early 60's it became possible for a user to modify his entire library to fit a new machine in a reasonable period of time. Among the compiler languages, FORTRAN holds an unrivaled position of popularity.

Compiler languages greatly reduced the tedium and intricacy of programming, and many psychologists were encouraged to write their own routines. Moreover, it is a simple job to modify an existing program written in FORTRAN to suit a particular problem, whereas the modification of a program written in machine language by someone else is, in most cases, a very formidable assignment.

In terms of ease of use, the major advantage of a compiler language is the simplicity and flexibility of input/output operations and the conversion to and from different internal representations of values and symbols. In this context, it is difficult to overestimate the impact that variable data formatting has had on statistical analysis. Variable format enables the user to describe the arrangement of the data on his cards or tape at the time he is ready to perform an analysis. The net result is that the same data base can be processed by a variety of routines without program modification.

Statistical Routines. Computers have been used for almost every type of statistical analysis that a psychologist can imagine. Space does not allow an extensive discussion of all of them. The interested reader is referred to the journals *Behavioral Science* and *Educational and Psychological Measurement*, which contain special sections on the use of computers. Borko (1962) edited one of the earliest texts of special interest to psychologists, and Green (1963) followed shortly thereafter. Cooley and Lohnes (1962) produced the first widely available exposition of multivariate statistical procedures through the use of FORTRAN. Their book includes examples of multiple correlation, canonical correlation, analysis of variance and covariance, factor analysis, and discriminant analysis.

Despite the tremendous amount of activity in the field, the Cooley and Lohnes book remained relatively unique in the field until 1967 when a text by Alluisi and another by Veldman appeared. Covered in these volumes are examples of test scoring, standard score generation, frequency distributions, simple and multiple correlation and regression routines, factor analysis, analysis of variance, discriminant analysis, canonical analysis, scaling, hierarchical grouping, chi square, and the treatment of non-numeric data.

During the period from 1962–1967, most psychologists either wrote their own routines or obtained them through informal borrowing arrangements. An extensive set of statistical routines called the BIMED programs (Dixon 1962) achieved wide distribution during this period. The most recent version, referred to as BMD (Dixon 1968), includes a number of routines for descriptive and tabulating purposes, factor analysis, canonical analysis, discriminant analysis, regression analysis, analysis of variance and covariance, general linear hypothesis, and Guttman scaling procedures. Included in most of the BMD routines are provisions for what is called "transgeneration," whereby input data values can be transformed in interesting and useful ways. Ward (1967) accomplished the same purpose in a more general way by incorporating a subroutine "call" after each input command. The user writes his own transformation instructions into this subroutine, which returns the desired values to the calling program.

Also of interest to many psychologists is the BCTRY system for cluster and factor analytic procedures, which was described by Tryon and Bailey in the first issue of *Multivariate Behavioral Research* (1966). Horst's definitive book on factor analysis (1965) also contains many Fortran routines.

Using Statistical Routines. Despite the availability of comprehensive software, the novice user will still encounter problems when attempting to perform some types of statistical analysis on a computer. In the first place, when the data base is not large and the analysis is not complicated, many problems can be solved on a desk calculator in less *human* time than that required to learn how to use a program. Moreover, the load is so heavy at many computing installations that the output for a job that requires only seconds may not be returned for hours or even days. The increasing availability of time-shared systems with "conversational" computer languages such as APL (Iverson 1966) will probably alleviate this condition to some degree. APL (A Programming Language) has one tremendous advantage over a compiler language such as FORTRAN. Although FORTRAN is an exceedingly simple language, one has to know at least a little about a great number of things before he can do much useful work. Many psychologists are not willing to invest the time and effort required to reach the "take-off point." With APL, on the other hand, one can use a remote terminal much as he would a desk calculator after a few minutes of instruction. Greater motivation then exists to explore the *uses* of the language. For example, a user can write a function for computing a mean with less than 10 symbols, store it in his file space in the computer system, and call for it whenever he needs it.

For some time, however, most psychologists probably will continue to do their statistical analysis in "batch mode", where the user submits a program and data to the computing installation and returns later to retrieve his output. The users' jobs are stacked one after another, and a batch of jobs are fed into a card reader together.

In a typical computing center, the software available to a prospective user is so extensive as to be dismaying. If he plans to write his own program, he may be forced to choose among a number of languages. If he wishes to use a program available at the installation, he may find, for example, ten different multiple regression programs with (1) no documentation, (2) documentation so brief as to be of value only to the original programmer, or (3) documentation so voluminous that it may be faster to reprogram than to read the documentation. One of the major advantages in learning FORTRAN is that one can often learn how to use a program more easily from a source listing than from a writeup.

Assuming that a psychologist has managed to locate a program whose title appears to be relevant to the analysis he is contemplating, he will generally find that in addition to providing his data, he must also prepare a number of other "control" cards which are required in addition to those containing the data. Most programs require the user to provide a card or cards containing identification or comments; these are frequently called "title cards" in the writeup. Another type of required card contains control information such as the number of variables, number of cases, number of groups, etc. Most programs also require that the user describe his data-card format on one or more cards. Almost all statistical programs will require these three types of cards, which generally precede the data cards. Some require (or allow) other control cards which give the user additional flexibility in applications of the program.

If a program has only a limited number of functions, generally the user will have little difficulty. As a program increases in versatility and flexibility, the number of options which the user must specify proliferate, and sometimes interact in bewildering ways. Finn (1968) has produced an excellent program for multivariate analyses in which over twenty different types of control cards are either required or allowed. For a program such as Finn's, the investment in time is worthwhile if one is likely to use a substantial number of the options at one time or another. Unfortunately, this cannot be claimed for all programs. Good programs generally include default parameters whenever possible so that a user does not have to specify all of the options. In this way, different levels of documentation can be made available. As a result, even a very complicated program can be used with a minimum of difficulty for a limited purpose.

As programming languages become more user-oriented and thus easier to learn and apply and as documentation becomes more standardized with a corresponding increase in comprehensibility, another trend has been operating in the opposite direction. As computers have grown larger and faster, the number of ways in which they can be used has also grown. The result has been an increase in the complexity of the monitors which control the mix of jobs to be performed. Logically, a monitor operates on different jobs much in the same way that a statistical program operates on its data. Just as the more complex statistical routines require more control and option cards, the more complex monitors require more control information to properly schedule and perform jobs. This control information is generally provided by means of a "job control language." In the Fortran example described earlier, the cards containing NAME, FORTRAN, EXECUTE, and FINIS are examples. Job control languages are not very well standardized at the present time and the documentation is sometimes quite technical.

One of the major problems that developers of statistical routines have had to solve is the choice between ease of use and flexibility. Generally speaking, a program which is very easy to use is not very flexible and a very flexible program frequently requires quite a bit of time to understand. One way of avoiding this dilemma is to generate a higher order language that enables the user to write a special-purpose program that is easy to use, yet sufficient for a particular purpose. In some cases this higher order language is basically an integrated set of FORTRAN subroutines (Ward, 1967; Buhler, 1966). In much the same way that the FORTRAN statement:

$$\text{ANSWER} = (A + B)/\text{SQRT}(C)$$

is much easier for the coder to write and understand than the corresponding instructions coded in a machine-level language, a subroutine CALL statement of the form

CALL CORREL (NOBS, NVAR, R, XBAR, SIG),

which enables the user to compute a correlation matrix, is much easier to write than the corresponding series of FORTRAN statements.

As many statistical procedures can be expressed in terms of matrix operations, subroutine systems that are matrix-oriented are quite common and almost every computing installation will have a fairly extensive library. Computer manufacturers frequently supply a set of statistical routines along with system software and some person or group at almost every university will make routines available for others to use (e.g., Clyde *et al.*, 1966).

Some efforts have been made to develop higher order

languages that can be driven by a set of control cards. Golden (1965) gives an example of the way such a language might be developed in FORTRAN. Another example can be found in a book by Hilsenrath *et al.* (1966).

Cautions and Prospects. The widespread availability of programs for statistical data processing has not been an unmixed blessing for the psychologist. On the positive side, it has relieved him of a great deal of the drudgery in statistical analysis. Also, it has encouraged some to become familiar with procedures that, in the absence of computers, would have been ignored as impractical. On the other hand, there can be little doubt that analyses which might have been more meaningful have been abandoned because a less appropriate analysis could be handled with an available program. Moreover, the tendency of some to attribute to statistical methodology the power to overcome unreliable data or design problems has been heightened. A correlation coefficient reported to eight decimal digits by a five-million-dollar computer somehow *seems* more impressive than a two-place coefficient calculated by hand.

Before computers became available, psychologists rarely attempted statistical analyses without formal training or at least some independent self-study. The temptation to "do" a factor analysis is almost overwhelming when it only takes five minutes to keypunch some control cards. One of the most disheartening experiences an enthusiast of both statistical methods and computers can endure is to have a student or colleague enter his office with a request to "run his cards through the computer," or even worse, armed with six pounds of computer printout, inquire in effect, "Here are my answers; what are my questions?"

Fortunately, this problem may be greatly alleviated in the future by a different type of educational approach, and a book by Lohnes and Cooley (1968) may be its harbinger. In this book, elementary statistical procedures are taught by running computer-controlled Monte Carlo studies on the sampling distributions of various statistics. This should make the basic foundations of statistical inference much more understandable and at the same time initiate students to the use of computers.

In addition to enhancing understanding for those with minimum mathematical backgrounds, Monte Carlo methods can also be used creatively to acquire new knowledge about statistical methods that are mathematically intractible. Examples of this can be found in Bradley (1968) and Pennell (1968). Elementary introduction to the use of Monte Carlo methods can be found in Golden (1965), Sprowls (1966), and Dorn and Greenberger (1967).

As indicated by Hotelling (1940) in a discussion of the teaching of statistics, statistical methodology infiltrated many applied areas in such a way as to become little more than high level arithmetic taught in "cookbook" courses. By and large this procedure was defended on the grounds that there simply was not time to give students both a good grounding in statistical theory *and* teach him how to compute the answers. In order to be "practical" the arithmetic was employed at the expense of theory. Many current texts in the area of correlation theory, for example, give different computing expressions for a typical correlation coefficient, phi coefficient, and a point-biserial coefficient. Many treatments of experimental design leave a student feeling that "main effects" and "interactions" are standard in the analysis of variance, whereas other comparisons of interest have somewhat different status. Although the thesis is arguable, there is reason to suspect that typical presentations are guided in large part by computational convenience at the expense of clarity. Although the situation has probably improved somewhat in almost three decades, Neyman (1960) recently expressed the opinion that Hotelling's thesis was still relevant.

The creative and imaginative use of computers to handle the arithmetic of statistical analysis (e.g., Greenberger et al., 1965) should free both the teacher and the student from a great deal of drudgery; more importantly, it also promises to lead to the development of pedagogical strategies that are much less constrained by computational considerations.

Simulation

The dictionary definition of simulation is "to assume or have the appearance of." Psychologists, being concerned with behavior, would paraphrase this: "to act or seem to act like." The appearance of the behavior is of concern here, and not the structure of the behaving entity.

Simulation research usually fits this sort of definition, in that no implication is intended that human beings are actually structured internally like computers. Rather, the computer serves as a vehicle for constructing a process model, a mechanism that processes information the same way that human beings do.

An ultimate test of simulation models was once proposed by A. M. Turning (1963). A computer and a human would answer questions from behind a screen. If an observer could not distinguish the two, the simulation was perfect. It should be quite obvious, however, that a mechanism capable of perfect simulation need not necessarily duplicate the structure of that which is modeled, any more than efficient prediction necessarily implies theoretical knowledge.

Any operational model of a process consititutes a testable theory regarding that which is modeled. In many fields of psychology, recent efforts to construct computer models of human information processing have had very important heuristic effects, in that the rather pathetic ambiguity of many so-called psychological theories has been made painfully evident to those who attempted to convert them into computer programs. In other cases, computer models of human processes have duplicated the behavior of human subjects with surprising accuracy. Research of this type began about 1948, and has increased very rapidly since 1957.

Most of the efforts at simulation have been concerned with neural activity and pattern recognition models, cognitive processes and decision making, and personality characteristics. A few efforts have been made toward simulating social groups and large organizations, also. Probably the most fruitful efforts so far have been in the simulation of cognitive behavior, where theoretical models are somewhat more precise and comprehensive than is the case with personality or neural organization. Leonard Uhr (1965) provides a thoughtful general discussion of models and computer simulation.

Neural Activity. Neurophysiologists had described models of neurons and nerve networks long before computers were available to put them into operational form. Some of these models were based on partial differential equations, while others have attempted to make more direct use of the binary nature of computer memories in duplicating the all-or-none characteristics of neuron firing. Most of the models have been concerned with the manner in which the character of the network adapts to particular kinds of stimuli, which is assumed to be the fundamental process of learning. Green (1963) has reviewed a variety of studies in this area, Farley (1965) describes in detail the development of a model of the EEG, and Ashby (1962) discusses the broad requirements of any adequate model of the brain.

Pattern Recognition. Very similar to the models of nerve networks are those which simulate pattern recognition processes. The most researched of these models is Rosenblatt's "perceptron," which is described by Daly, Joseph, and Ramsey (1965). A perceptron is a neutral unit larger than the neuron, but much smaller than a brain. It is a convenient unit for modeling neural systems, but has no known or necessary physical counterpart.

The simplest pattern recognizers simply compare input configurations with a variety of standards until a sufficiently close match is noted. More complex models analyze the input for its essential properties, which then lead to the decision. When pattern recognition models are built to include the ability to change decision rules automatically from feedback, we approach the simulation of cognitive processes. Green (1963) has reviewed a variety of pattern-recognition studies, concerning such stimuli as Morse code, handwritten letters, and vowels in human speech.

Ledley (1962) discusses the pattern recognition problem in a quite different context—that of medical diagnosis. Given a set of symptoms and a set of possible diseases, the task is to select the disease which has a symptom pattern most like the input. Psychological assessment, to a limited degree, can also be cast in these terms. The real breakthrough, not yet achieved, would be a computer model that would learn to make successively more accurate diagnoses as it acquired experience with greater numbers of cases.

Cognitive Processes. This has been the most active area of psychological research involving computer simulation techniques. Newell, Shaw, and Simon (1958) pioneered this field by building a program called the *Logic Theorist* which proved theorems in elementary symbolic logic. One way of approaching such problems has been called the "British Museum Alogorithm." This name is based on the old story about monkeys at typewriters being able—eventually—to write all of the books in the British Museum by chance. Newell, Shaw, and Simon estimated that 50 million possible proofs would have to be tried to find a desired one, if this procedure were used on their problem. Needless to say, the *Logic Theorist* employed shortcut principles or *heuristics* which vastly reduced the searching procedure.

More recent work in this field has attempted not simply to model the outcome of cognition, but also the steps of the process human problem-solvers take in moving toward a goal. Data are collected from human subjects who have been instructed to "think out loud" as they try to solve a problem, and then a computer routine is constructed to parallel the process. Using a program called the *General Problem Solver*, Newell, Shaw, and Simon were able to simulate a wide variety of human problem-solving procedures and outcomes (Newell and Simon 1963).

History, Theory, and Methodology

Feldman (1962, 1963) has described in detail the simulation of binary-choice behavior, illustrating the construction of a program to duplicate a subject's "thinking-out-loud" procedure, as well as methods of assessing the degree to which the computer model matches actual human behavior.

Newell, Shaw, and Simon designed a complete computer programming language called IPL-V (Newell 1961) for their simulation work. This classic "list-processing language" has been used by these authors and many others as the vehicle for implementing a wide variety of problem-solving and game-playing models. Other list-processing "languages" have been devised which are more elegant and flexible. At least one is designed as a series of subroutines embedded in the structure of FORTRAN, which has a variety of advantages for the user.

One particular type of cognitive simulation has received an inordinate amount of publicity: the game-playing programs. Because of the challenge, chess has been a favorite. Newell, Shaw, and Simon's program is the more sophisticated of the various routines that have been devised; it has been characterized as "a competent amateur." More recently, a program designed by Greenblatt (1967) was awarded honorary membership in the United States Chess Federation, and is reputed to be the best of the current "players."

In another area, Feigenbaum (1963) developed a model of verbal learning behavior called EPAM, for Elementary Perceiver and Memorizer. It simulates the learning of paired-associate nonsense syllables. The model in operation shows many of the well-established features of human performance on such a task.

Efforts have been made by other investigators to construct computer-based models of concept-formation and attitude change under controversy. Theoretically, of course, any cognitive process could be approached through simulation. At present, however, relatively few psychologists possess the necessary sophistication in computer programming.

Assessment. One rather specialized form of human cognition, the psychological assessment or decision process, has received some research attention. Whenever a psychologist interprets test data and reaches conclusions or makes decisions on the basis of them, he is engaging in an activity that could be simulated with a computer program. There are three rather different ways of approaching this problem: (1) The program can use mathematical models (e.g. regression analysis) to "capture" the decision-making strategy of a particular human. Ward (1962) has described such a procedure in the context of personnel selection. Such studies often reveal a startling degree of inconsistency in the behavior of some human decision makers. (2) The program can be constructed to duplicate the "think-aloud" procedures which reflect the assessor's understanding of his own decision-making methods. Kleinmuntz (1963) has used this technique with considerable success in duplicating human judgement of MMPI protocols. (3) The computer program can be constructed to embody principles of an a priori theory of the assessment process. The work of Rome and his colleagues (1965) exemplifies this approach to the interpretation of MMPI profiles in terms of various configural scoring rules which have accumulated from years of empirical research with the instrument.

So far, none of the computer models which have been constructed to simulate the assessment behavior of a psychologist have incorporated any adaptive-learning mechanisms. A model which profited from experience, and built up its own non-mathematical assessment rules, might eventually surpass the accuracy of regression equations, which now appear to operate as well or better than human assessors. Another potentially promising approach, mentioned by Veldman, Menaker and Peck (1969) in their discussion of machine interpretation of sentence-completion data, is an interactive assessment procedure involving the unique advantages of machine normative analysis and human interpretation of rare, but frequently crucial, responses.

The procedure mentioned earlier for training and assessing the diagnostic behavior of medical students may also be viewed as a form of simulation. The computer program simulates the patient, the hospital's laboratory facilities, and a supervising physician. It is against this "reality" that the student must apply his abilities and knowledge to arrive at a correct diagnosis with maximum efficiency. McGuire and Babbott (1967) discuss one such program, as well as some of the problems of determining the validity of such performance measures as those provided by this type of assessment of competence.

Personality. The attempts which have been made to devise computer programs that model human behavior in terms of personality constructs have been much less rigorous than those in the area of cognitive processes. The reason is the vagueness of most theories of personality, and the major contribution of these attempts has been heuristic. With a computer model of a theoretical network of constructs, the hidden inconsistencies and gaps in the theory become glaringly obvious.

Many critics have attacked the early attempts to model this aspect of human behavior, but most have misunderstood the purpose of the modeling, as Samuel Messick pointed out in his resume of a conference on computer simulation of personality (Tomkins and Messick 1963).

In these terms, then, to criticize, for example, a simulation of a neurotic process *because it does not simulate a* neurotic person *may be to lament its incompleteness or to question its realism or relevance to therapy, but it is not a criticism of the simulation as a circumscribed model.*

In a more recent book, Loehlin (1968) considers the general problems of building computer models of personality, and describes in detail four important examples of this activity. His own model, called ALDOUS (because his is a "Brave New World"), is perhaps the most entertaining, if not the most significant or complex. The original version of the program was written for a very small computer, and emphasizes the fact that many important models of theoretical networks do not demand much in the way of hardware. Aldous "recognizes situations, reacts to them emotionally, acts, and learns (or fails to learn) from his experience." This is all accomplished in very schematic form with a memory of less than 1500 cells.

Although the changes in Aldous' "personality" with various kinds of "experience" are intriguing, the studies which allow *two types* of Aldous to interact with each other are utterly fascinating as analogues of marital and therapeutic relationships, for example.

Colby (1965) has approached the simulation of neurotic thought processes from a somewhat different angle, basing his model on the concept of a "belief matrix." In this structure concepts such as *I*, *father*, and *people*; verbs such as *love* and *hate*; and modifiers such as *should*, *did*, and *sick* are organized to represent such belief statements as *I love father* and *father hates sick people*. The model operates according to general principles of psychoanalytic theory as they predict the results of belief conflicts.

The program is written so that the belief structure of a particular person may be represented by the model, which Colby has done for one patient that had been seen for hundreds of therapy hours. The potential advantage to the therapist of being able to explore in simulation the probable consequences of various approaches to a patient is perhaps the most important practical aspect of Colby's work.

Social-Organizaional Behavior. There has been relatively little research into the potential of the computer as a vehicle for modeling the behavior of social groups and large organizations, although a number of writers have suggested that this might be a valuable avenue toward a comprehensive theory of group interaction. Abelson (1968), who has been very active in this field himself, has written a comprehensive and detailed survey of the field of computer simulation in social psychology which is both reasonable and readable.

Computers have been used to apply matrix algebra to the identification of clique and communication structures within extant groups. We are concerned here, however, with attempts to construct operational computer models of organizations. Rome and Rome (1962) described a model called *Leviathan* which simulates a hypothetical organization that deals with the communication of symbolic material. Benson (1962) reviewed a variety of simulation approaches to the study of international politics and diplomacy. He describes in detail his own programming of a simulation that permits study of the consequences of various kinds of actions by states upon themselves as well as other states.

A more specific application is reported by Cogswell (1966), who developed a dynamic computer model of a real or proposed school organization which incorporates descriptors of the characteristics of both the school and its student population. The program has been used to simulate an actual school involved in an experimental arrangement which allows students to progress at their own individual rates through the curriculum.

An even more specific kind of social simulation model, which could also be viewed as an extension of personality simulation, is HOMUNCULUS, which was developed by John and Jeanne Gullahorn (1963). It permits the study of the progress of interactions between two persons or among three individuals. Actions are represented by Bales' 12-category scheme, and attitudes are developed within individuals during the simulation. Because of the greater feasibility of collecting empirical data for comparison with simulations, this type of research appears to hold particular promise for further investigation.

Summary

In this chapter we have discussed the nature of computer hardware and software, and have surveyed the wide variety of basic and applied research uses to which computers have been put by psychologists and other behavioral scientists. By now, the reader should be convinced that the potential of the computer as a research tool extends far beyond calculation of statistical indices. Although statistical analysis was the earliest, and is still the most common use made of computers by psychologists, the recent studies utilizing computers as tools for simulation of psychological processes promise much more for the field in the years ahead.

We have cited particular articles from a number of excellent books of readings in the field of computer applications. For the benefit of the reader who wishes to explore this topic further, we would particularly recommend the following sources:

Green (1963), *Digital Computers in Research*, in addition to providing a general introduction to the logic of computer hardware and software, includes a very readable survey of behavioral science applications.

Uttal (1967), *Real-Time Computers*, concentrates on recent "on-line" applications, but builds his discussion on thoroughly detailed explanations of hardware principles.

Borko (1962), *Computer Applications in the Behavioral Sciences*, although somewhat dated, includes a number of topics not adequately covered in more recent works.

Feigenbaum and Feldman (1963), *Computers and Thought*, the best single reference for classic papers on computer simulation of cognitive processes.

Stacy and Waxman (1965), *Computers in Biomedical Research*, includes a variety of articles concerning physiological and psychiatric applications.

Loughery (1966), *Man-Machine Systems in Education*, provides one of the few book-length surveys of educational applications of computers.

Tomkins and Messick (1963), *Computer Simulation of Personality*, edited this unique series of papers concerning some of the more imaginative modeling-simulation applications.

Ralston and Wilf (1960, 1967), *Mathematical Methods for Digital Computers*, (two volumes) offer rigorously thorough presentations of many basic statistical procedures employed by behavioral scientists.

It is tempting to end this discussion with some extravagant predictions about the future of computers in psychology, since the development has been even more rapid than many expected ten years ago. However, we feel that the pace is slowing, the more obvious possibilities have been explored, and a stage of deliberate consolidation and organization has begun. We expect a steady increase in the number of universities which expect their psychology graduates to be competent in computer methods as well as statistics. We also expect a steady increase in the regular use of computer-assisted instruction by public school systems. Increasing use of objective computer-based techniques of psychological assessment also appears quite certain. Because of the high degree and varieties of skills needed, it is difficult to predict the future of simulation-modeling of psychological theory. The potential is there, but the researchers capable of genuine innovations are few and far between.

Acknowledgements. The authors wish to thank Professor John Loehlin for his helpful comments on a preliminary draft of this paper.

References

ABELSON, R. P. Simulation of social behavior. *In* G. LINDZEY and E. ARONSON, eds. *The Handbook of Social Psychology*, 2nd ed., vol. 2. Reading, Mass.: Addison-Wesley, 1968, 274–356.

ADEY, W. R. Computer analysis in neurophysiology. *In* R. W. STACY and B. WAXMAN, eds. *Computers in Biomedical Research*. 1965, pp. 223–64.

ALLUISI, E. *Basic Fortran for Statistical Analysis*. Homewood, Ill.: Dorsey, 1967.

ASHBY, W. R. Simulation of a brain. *In* H. BORKO, ed. *Computer Applications in the Behavioral Sciences*. Englewood Cliffs, N.J.: Prentice-Hall, 1962, pp. 452–67.

BARUCH, J. J. Hospital automation via computer time-sharing. *In* R. W. STACY and B. WAXMAN, eds. *Computers in Biomedical Research*. 1965, vol. II, pp. 291–314.

BECKER, J. and R. M. HAYES. *Information Storage and Retrieval*. New York: Wiley, 1963.

BENSON, O. Simulation of international relations and diplomacy. *In* BORKO, ed. *Computer Applications in the Behavioral Sciences*. 1962, pp. 574–95.

BORKO, H., ed. *Computer Applications in the Behavioral Sciences*. Englewood Cliffs, N.J.: Prentice-Hall, 1962.

——— *Automated Language Processing*. New York: Wiley, 1967.

BRADLEY, J. V. *Distribution-Free Statistical Tests*. Englewood Cliffs, N.J.: Prentice-Hall, 1968.

BRAZIER, M. A. B. The application of computers to electroencephalography. *In* STACY and WAXMAN, eds. *Computers in Biomedical Research*. 1965, pp. 295–318.

BUHLER, R. *PSTAT: Statistical Analysis of Social Science Data*. Princeton, N.J.: Princeton University Computing Center, 1966.

CLYDE, D. J., E. M. CRAMER, and R. J. SHEVIN. *Multivariate Statistical Programs*. Coral Gables, Fla.: Biometric Laboratory, University of Miami, 1966.

COGSWELL, J. F. Computers in student appraisal and educational planning. *In* J. W. LOUGHERY, ed. *Man-Machine Systems in Education*. 1966, pp. 157–67. (*a*)

——— Systems technology in education. *In* J. W. LOUGHERY, ed. *Man-Machine Systems in Education*. New York: Harper and Row, 1966, pp. 45–68. (*b*)

COLBY, K. M. Computer simulation of neurotic processes. *In* STACY and WAXMAN, eds. *Computers in Biomedical Research*. 1965, pp. 491–504.

COLLEN, M. F., L. RUBEN, and L. DAVIS. Computers in multiphasic screening. *In* STACY and WAXMAN, eds. *Computers in Biomedical Research*. 1965, 339–52.

COOLEY, W. W. A computer-measurement system for guidance. *Harvard Educational Review*, 1964, *34*, 558–72.

——— and P. R. LOHNES. *Multivariate Procedures for the Behavioral Sciences*. New York: Wiley, 1962.

DALY, J. A., R. D. JOSEPH, and D. M. RAMSEY. Perceptrons as models of neural processes. *In* STACY and WAXMAN eds. *Computers in Biomedical Research*. 1965, pp. 525–46.

DIXON, W. J. *BIMED: A Series of Statistical Programs for the IBM 709, Part 1. Behavioral Science*, 1962, 7, 264–67.

——— *BMD: Biomedical Computer Programs*. Los Angeles: University of California Press, 1968.

DORN, W. S. and H. J. GREENBERG. *Mathematics and Computing with Fortran Programming*. New York: Wiley, 1967.

FARLEY, B. G. A neural network model and the "slow potentials" of electrophysiology. *In* STACY and WAXMAN, eds. *Computers in Biomedical Research*. 1965, vol. I, 265–94.

FEIGENBAUM, E. A. The simulation of verbal learning behavior. *In* FEIGENBAUM and FELDMAN, eds. *Computers and Thought*. 1963, pp. 297–309. (*a*)

———, and J. FELDMAN. *Computers and Thought*. New York: McGraw-Hill, 1963. (*b*)

FELDMAN, J. Computer simulation of cognitive processes. *In* BORKO, ed. *Computer Applications in the Behavioral Sciences*. 1962, pp. 337–59.

——— Simulation of behavior in the binary choice experiment. *In* FEIGENBAUM and FELDMAN, eds. *Computers and Thought*. 1963, pp. 329–46.

FINN, J. D. *Multivariance: Univariate and Multivariate Analysis of Variance, Covariance, and Regression*. Buffalo, N.Y.: Faculty of Educational Studies, State University of New York, 1968.

FULLER, F. F. Fair System Manual: Fuller Affective Interaction Records. *In* A. SIMON and E. GIL BOYER, eds. *Mirrors for Behavior* vol. IX. Philadelphia, Pa.: Research for Better Schools, 1970.

GOLDBERG, L. R. Simple models or simple processes? Some research on clinical judgments. *American Psychologist*, 1968, *23*, 483–96.

GOLDEN, J. T. *Fortran IV Programming and Computing*. Englewood Cliffs, N.J.: Prentice-Hall, 1965.

GREEN, B. F. *Digital Computers in Research*. New York: McGraw-Hill, 1963.

GREENBERGER, M., M. M. JONES, J. H. MORRIS, and D. N. NESS. *On-line Computation and Simulation: The OPS-3 System*. Cambridge, Mass.: M.I.T. Press, 1965.

GREENBLATT, R. D., D. E. EASTLAKE, and S. D. CROCKER. The Greenblatt chess program. *Proceedings of the AFIPS 1967 Fall Joint Computer Conference*, 1967, *31*, 801–10.

GULLAHORN, J. T. and J. E. GULLAHORN. A computer model of elementary social behavior. *In* FEIGENBAUM and FELDMAN, eds. *Computers and Thought*. 1963, pp. 375–86.

HILSENRATH, J. et al. *Omnitab: A Computer Program for Statistical and Numerical Analysis*. U.S. Dept. of Commerce, National Bureau of Standards Handbook 101, 1966.

HON, E. H. Computer aids in evaluating fetal distress. *In* STACY and WAXMAN, eds. *Computers in Biomedical Research*. 1965, pp. 409–38.

HORST, P. *Factor Analysis of Data Matrices*. New York: Holt, Rinehart, and Winston, 1965.

HOTELLING, H. The teaching of statistics. *Annals of Mathematical Statistics*, 1940, *11*, 457–70.

IVERSON, K. E. *A Programming Language*. New York: Wiley, 1966.

KLEINMUNTZ, B. Personality test interpretation by digital computer. *Science*, 1963, *139*: 416–18.

LEDLEY, R. S. Advances in biomedical science and diagnosis. *In* H. BORKO, ed. *Computer Applications in the Behavioral Sciences*. 1962, pp. 490–521.

LEHMAN, R. S., and D. E. BAILEY. *Digital Computing: Fortran IV and its Applications in Behavioral Science*. New York: Wiley, 1968.

LOEHLIN, J. C. *Computer Models of Personality*. New York: Random House, 1968.

LOHNES, P. R., and W. W. COOLEY. *Introduction to Statistical Procedures: with Computer Exercises*. New York: Wiley, 1968.

LOUGHERY, J. W. ed. *Man-Machine Systems in Education*. New York: Harper, 1966.

LUSTED, L. B. Computer techniques in medical diagnosis. *In* STACY and WAXMAN, eds. *Computers in Biomedical Research*. 1965, pp. 319–38.

MCCRACKEN, D. D. *A Guide to Fortran Programming*. New York: Wiley, 1961.

MCGUIRE, C. H., and D. BABBOTT. Simulation technique in the measurement of problem-solving skills. *Journal of Educational Measurement*, 1967, *4*: 1–10.

MEEHL, P. E. *Clinical Versus Statistical Prediction: A Theoretical Analysis and a Review of the Evidence*. Minneapolis: University of Minnesota Press, 1954.

MILLER, G. A., A. S. BREGMAN, and D. A. NORMAN. The computer as a general purpose device for the control of psychological experiments. *In* STACY and WAXMAN, eds. *Computers in Biomedical Research*. 1965 pp. 467–90.

NEWELL A. ed. *Information Processing Language-V Manual*. Englewood Cliffs, N.J.: Prentice-Hall, 1961.

——— J. C. SHAW, and H. A. SIMON. The elements of a theory of human problem solving. *Psychological Review*, 1958, *65*, 151–66.

——— and H. A. SIMON. GPS, a program that simulates human thought. *In* FEIGENBAUM and FELDMAN, eds. *Computers and Thought*. 1963, pp. 279–96.

NEYMAN, JERZY. Harold Hotelling, a leader in mathematical statistics. *In* I. OLKIN et al., eds. *Contributions to Probability and Statistics*. Stanford, Calif.: Stanford University Press, 1960.

OETTINGER, A. G. The myths of educational technology. *Saturday Review*, May 1968, 760.

PENNELL, R. The influence of communality and N on the sampling distributions of factor loadings. *Psychometrika*, 1968, *33*: 423–39.

PIPBURGER, H. V. Computer analysis of the electrocardiogram. *In* STACY and WAXMAN, eds. *Computers in Biomedical Research.* pp. 377–408.

PLUMB, S. C. *Introduction to Fortran.* New York: McGraw-Hill, 1961.

RALSTON, A., and H. S. WILF, eds. *Mathematical Methods for Digital Computers.* New York: Wiley, 1960, 1967.

ROME, S. C., and B. K. ROME. Computer simulation toward a theory of large organizations. *In* BORKO, ed. *Computer Applications in the Behavioral Sciences.* 1962, pp. 522–55.

ROME, H. P. et al. Automatic personality assessment. *In* STACY and WAXMAN, eds. *Computers in Biomedical Research.* 1965, pp. 505–24.

SELFRIDGE, O. G. Pandemonium: a paradigm for learning. *Proceedings of the Symposium on Mechanization of Thought Processes.* London: H. M. Stationery Office, 1959.

SIMMONS, R. F. Synthex: toward computer synthesis of human language behavior. *In* BORKO, ed. *Computer Applications in the Behavioral Sciences.* 1962, pp. 360–93.

—— Answering English questions by computer. *In* BORKO, ed. *Automated Language Processing.* 1967, pp. 253–91.

SPROWLS, R. C. *Computers: A Programming Problem Approach.* New York: Harper, 1966.

STACY, R. W., and B. WAXMAN, eds. *Computers in Biomedical Research* (2 vols.). New York: Academic Press, 1965.

STONE, P. J., D. C. DUNPHY, M. S. SMITH, and D. M. OGILVIE. *The General Inquirer.* Cambridge, Mass: M.I.T. Press, 1966.

TOMKINS, S. S., and S. MESSICK. *Computer Simulation of Personality.* New York: Wiley, 1963.

TRYON, R. C. and D. E. BAILEY. The BC TRY computer system of cluster and factor analysis. *Multivariate Behavioral Research*, 1966, *1*: 95–111.

TURING, A. M. Computing machinery and intelligence. *In* FEIGENBAUM and FELDMAN, eds. *Computers and Thought.* 1963, pp. 11–35.

UHR, L. Complex dynamic models of living organisms. *In* STACY and WAXMAN, eds. *Computers in Biomedical Research.* 1965, vol. I, 15–32.

UTTAL, W. R. *Real-time Computers.* New York: Harper, 1967.

VELDMAN, D. J. Computer-based sentence completion interviews. *Journal of Counseling Psychology*, 1967, *14*: 153–57. (*a*)

—— Fortran Programming for the Behavioral Sciences. New York: Holt, Rinehart and Winston, 1967. (*b*)

——, and S. L. MENAKER. Computer applications in assessment and counseling. *Journal of School Psychology*, 1968, *6*: 167–76.

——, and R. F. PECK. Computer scoring of sentence completion data. *Behavioral Science*, 1969, *14*: 501–7.

WARD, J. H. Multiple linear regression models. *In* BORKO, ed. *Computer Applications in the Behavioral Sciences* (op. cit.), 1962, pp. 204–37.

——, J. BUCKHORN, and K. HALL. *Persub Reference Manual.* San Antonio, Texas: Personnel Research Laboratory, Lackland AFB, 1967.

WEED, L. L. *Medical Records, Medical Education and Patient Care.* Cleveland: Case Western Reserve Press, 1969.

WHITE, B. W. Studies of perception. *In* BORKO, ed. *Computer Applications in the Behavioral Sciences.* 1962, pp. 280–307.

WRIGLEY, C. Electronic computers and psychological research. *American Psychologist*, 1957, *12*, 501–8.

That a chapter called "Mathematical Models" should be included in this handbook indicates that quantitative theory has achieved considerable importance in several areas of psychological research. It also indicates that quantitative theory is in an early stage of its development in psychology. For from the point of view of psychology, mathematical models are not subjects of study, interesting in themselves. This is not to say that mathematical research is improper for psychologists; like any craftsman, a theorist in psychology can profit from improvements in his tools, and mathematical questions frequently arise about structures that are useful in psychological theory. But for a psychologist, mathematical research is instrumental, serving the goal of increased understanding of psychological processes.

Mathematical models in psychology are hypothetical descriptions of specific processes. There are models of memorizing, and concept identification, and perception, and choice and decision, and other processes. Thus, the contents of this chapter are all borrowed from the psychological territory discussed in other chapters. On the other hand, mathematical psychology is an identifiable subfield of psychology. The mathematical structures that are developed to deal with problems in one area often are applicable to other substantive problems, and a number of scientists have contributed to quantitative theory in several areas of psychological study. Mathematical psychologists have acquired the appurtenances of a scientific community; we attend specialized scientific meetings and write articles for a specialized journal, and we teach courses and conduct doctoral training programs in mathematical psychology. Nevertheless, the topics that have been analyzed by mathematical psychologists are diffuse, and at the present stage of development, the topics surveyed here have a greater unity of style than of subject matter.

No review of an active scientific field is easy, but mathematical psychology presents some special problems. The literature of the field has literally exploded during the 1960s. Nearly every issue of the *Journal of Mathematical Psychology* contains

J. G. Greeno

Preparation of this chapter was aided by the U.S. Public Health Service under Grant GM-1231 to the University of Michigan.

A Survey of Mathematical Models in Experimental Psychology

8

the development of quantitative theory for some new psychological topic. Thus, in addition to omissions from this review that are my own responsibility, new areas of study are almost sure to develop between the time of writing and publishing. This chapter, then, cannot be interpreted as an exhaustive review of important developments in mathematical psychology. What I have tried to do is to present a variety of topics and theoretical methods to communicate an impression of the breadth of subject matter and technique that characterize mathematical models in experimental psychology at this time.

The main focus of this chapter will be on models that include explicit assumptions about psychological processes, and that have been used in the analysis of experimental data. Large segments of mathematical psychology involving computer models, as well as the methods used in psychological testing and scaling, have been largely omitted. This selection reflects my own interests and competence, but it is also justified by the inclusion of chapters specifically dealing with psychometric methods and computer applications in this handbook. Less defensible omissions include models of reaction time and perceptual-motor performance, and models of social interaction. The main reason for these omissions was my inability to prepare the material during the time available to me for writing this chapter.

Regarding the models included in the restricted scope of this chapter, I have tried to present the main ideas and a few sample results of applying models to experimental data. I have not tried to present any of the technical details regarding parameter estimation or statistical evaluation of the models. Readers interested in these technical matters should consult the original sources, and introductory discussions regarding techniques of derivation, estimation, and statistical evaluation are included in texts by Atkinson, Bower, and Corthers (1965), by Coombs, Dawes, and Tversky, (1970), and by Restle and Greeno (1970).

1. Problem Solving

The psychological processes involved in solving problems are thought by many to be among the most complex that have been studied by psychologists. Despite this, the mathematical models that have been applied and tested in problem-solving experiments are among the simplest that we have. In a sense, this condition reflects the relative lack of experimental data regarding problem solving. We have simple models partly because we do not have the kind of data needed to guide detailed theorizing. But in another way, simple models of problem solving reflect an important feature of theorizing in psychology as well as other sciences. The complexity of a model need not correspond to the complexity of the system being modeled in any direct way. Often we make considerable progress in understanding a process because we have a general description that increases our understanding of some important aspects of the process, even if it ignores other important aspects.

A familiar illustration of this principle is the simple model of planetary motion in the solar system that we learned as school children. In a simple form, the model specifies only the orbits of the planets and their periods of rotation. This ignores the revolutions of the planets and the existence of satellites, as well as an enormous amount of detail about the planets' atmospheres, temperatures, and chemical makeup. Nonetheless, the model incorporates a good number of important general principles, such as the inverse square law of gravity, the classical first law of motion, and centrifugal force. A person who understands the simple model of planetary motion certainly has some important, albeit partial, knowledge about astronomy and physics.

Concept Identification

An experiment in concept identification is most often conducted using a large set of stimuli, generated by varying the values of several dimensions such as size, shape, color, and number of figures. In principle, any number of values can be used for each dimension, but many experiments have used only two values per dimension. For example, the values of the dimensions listed above might be small and large, triangle and circle, red and blue, two and three. Then one of the stimuli would be two small red triangles; another example is three small blue circles. If there are n binary dimensions, and all the combinations of values are used as stimuli, there are a total of 2^n stimuli.

The experimenter decides on a rule for classifying the stimuli, usually into two categories. For example, the categories might be labled "A" and "B" and the rule might be "circles are A, triangles are B." More complicated rules are possible (for example, "red circles are A, other stimuli are B") but this discussion will be restricted to experiments involving one-dimensional rules. In the experiment, the subject sees stimuli one at a time. When he sees a stimulus, he indicates which category he thinks the stimulus belongs in. Then the experimenter tells the subject which category the stimulus belongs in, and then presents the next stimulus. The subject's task is to discover the correct rule for classifying the stimuli, using the trial-to-trial information about the categories of individual stimuli. The experimenter infers that the correct rule has been discovered when the subject gives a long series of consecutive correct responses, such as ten or fifteen correct classifications in a row.

There is a simple model of problem solving in concept identification, given by Restle (1962). According to the model, the subject has a set of hypotheses about what might be the correct rule. He samples from the set of hypotheses, then rejects hypotheses that are inconsistent with the information he receives, and if his sample of hypotheses includes the correct rule, he can solve the problem. If the initial sample did not include the correct rule, or if he makes an error by using an hypothesis in the sample that is incorrect, he selects another sample and starts again.

It is easiest to understand this model if we begin by considering the special case where the subject's sample of hypotheses contains only a single hypothesis. Then on any trial, the subject is either using the correct rule (and thus has solved the problem) or he is using an incorrect hypothesis. Assume that for any incorrect hypothesis, the probability that the hypothesis leads to a correct response is a constant p, and let $q = 1 - p$. And assume that each time the subject chooses a new hypothesis, there is probability c that he will choose the correct hypothesis.

The model involving one hypothesis at a time can be expressed in the form of a Markov chain with three states. One of the states, State L, describes a subject after he has selected the correct rule. The other two states, State E and State C, apply when the subject is using any incorrect hypothesis. State E applies on trials when the incorrect hypothesis leads to an incorrect response. State C applies on trials when the incorrect hypothesis leads to a correct response. The probabilities of transitions among the states are

$$P = \begin{array}{c} \\ L_n \\ E_n \\ C_n \end{array} \begin{array}{|ccc|} L_{n+1} & E_{n+1} & C_{n+1} \\ \hline 1 & 0 & 0 \\ c & (1-c)q & (1-c)p \\ 0 & q & p \end{array} \qquad [1]$$

According to the model, when the subject has an incorrect hypothesis if he happens to give a correct response, he continues to use the same hypothesis. Thus, he will be in either State C or State E on the next trial, depending on the stimulus that is shown. But after an error he selects another hypothesis, with probability c of selecting the correct hypothesis. Thus, the occasions on which learning can occur are the presentations of information following subject's errors. It is assumed that the subject starts either in State E or State C on the first trial, before he has any information, on the basis of a guess.

The model of Eq. 1 was used by Bower and Trabasso (1964) in the analysis of data from several experiments. A number of theorems were derived, showing properties of data that are implied by the model. The predictions include a formula for the relative frequency distribution of the number of errors made by the individual subjects before they solved the problem. Let T be the number of errors that a subject commits. Then

$$P(T = k) = c(1 - c)^{k-1}. \qquad [2]$$

Equation 2 is the geometric distribution, with the learning rate c as the parameter. Bower and Trabasso presented their data in the form of the cumulative distribution, which has the formula

$$P(T < k) = 1 - (1 - c)^k. \qquad [3]$$

In one of their experiments, Bower and Trabasso estimated that the value of c was .048. Fig. 8-1 shows the theoretical distribution calculated using the estimate in Eq. 3, compared with the data from 66 subjects. The theory apparently is in good agreement with the data.

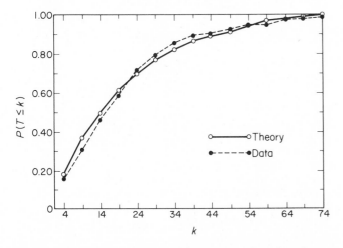

Fig. 8-1. *Theoretical and empirical distributions of number of errors by individual subjects in solving a concept identification problem.* [From Bower and Trabasso (1964)]

It should be noted that the method of estimating parameters uses the mean number of errors, so that the theory is bound to agree with the empirical mean of this distribution. However, the test of the theory compares the complete distribution of data with a theoretical prediction. There is no a priori reason for expecting good agreement with the whole distribution. An idea of the situation may be gained by considering the standard deviation of this statistic. The geometric distribution has a high variance; the standard deviation has the same order of magnitude as the mean. With an obtained mean of 20.8 errors, the predicted standard deviation was 20.3. The obtained standard deviation was 18.5. Experimenters commonly observe that their data are highly variable, and often they express negative feelings about this fact. In this case, the use of an appropriate quantitative model gives an explanation of the amount of variability in the data, and uses it to help make inferences about the nature of the process.

Another feature of the geometric distribution is that it is strongly skewed; the theoretical frequency of the number of errors is a monotonically decreasing function. Statistical procedures in common use are based on a model that assumes normally distributed scores, and investigators frequently transform scores so that analyses can be carried out using numbers that are approximately normally distributed. It seems preferable to use a model that gives distributions that are in approximate agreement with the data to start with.

Bower and Trabasso's (1964) analyses were based on the version of Restle's model involving one hypothesis at a time. A later series of studies by Trabasso and Bower (1968) used a more general version of the model, in order to analyze the results of experiments where more than one rule can be used to classify the stimuli. For example, if the stimulus dimensions were size, shape, color, and number an experimenter might decide to set up a problem where the subject could correctly classify the stimuli using either the shapes of the figures or their colors. This would not work with the whole set of stimuli, but it would if one-half of the possible stimuli were omitted from the experiment; for example, the stimulus set might include only blue circles (with size and number varying) and red triangles (also with size and number varying). Then the experimenter could use the rule, "Blue circles are A, red triangles are B." In this example, shape and color are redundant because certain combinations of stimulus values are not included in the set of stimuli. And they are both relevant, in that the subject can correctly classify all the stimuli using either the shapes or the colors of the stimuli. Trabasso and Bower's analysis mainly dealt with the solution of problems using redundant relevant cues, and with performance on various tests and transfer tasks given after such problems had been solved.

The general model deals with the relative salience or weight of the various dimensions of stimulus variation. The attention value or salience of the ith dimension is represented by a quantity w_i, and its relative weight in a problem with dimensions 1, 2, $\ldots, N$ is

$$a_i = \frac{w_i}{\sum\limits_{j=1}^{N} w_j} \qquad [4]$$

When the subject selects a sample of hypotheses, he may include more than one representation of the same hypothesis among the s elements in his sample. It is assumed that the sample is obtained by s independent selections, where on each selection the probability of choosing the ith hypothesis is a_i. Let x_i be the number of representations of the ith hypothesis in a sample. The probability of some number j of representations of the ith hypothesis in a sample is

$$P(x_i = j) = \binom{s}{j} a_i^j (1 - a_i)^{s-j}.$$

When we deal with problems involving redundant relevant cues, we consider the probability of including some number, j, of representations of the first relevant hypothesis, and another number, k, of representations of the other relevant hypothesis. Let the relevant dimensions be numbered 1 and 2. The probability we want is part of the multinomial distribution

$$P(x_1 = j, x_2 = k)$$
$$= \frac{s!}{j! k! (s - j - k)!} a_1^j a_2^k (1 - a_1 - a_2)^{s-j-k} \qquad [5]$$

and the expected numbers of representations are

$$E(x_1) = a_1 s, \quad E(x_2) = a_2 s. \qquad [6]$$

When a stimulus is presented, the subject may have some hypotheses in his sample leading to one response, and some to another. For example, his sample might have the two hypotheses, "circles are A" and "large figures are A." If the presented stimulus has small circles, then one of the hypotheses in the sample says that it belongs in category A, but the other says that the stimulus belongs in category B. It is assumed that the probability of a response to a stimulus is equal to the proportion of hypotheses in the subject's sample that leads to the response.

If the subject's response is correct, he removes hypotheses from his sample that would have led to an error on that trial. The hypotheses that were consistent with the correct response are kept in the sample. If the subject makes an error, it is assumed that he has to start again by taking a new sample of s hypotheses. Further, it is assumed that the probabilities of sampling the correct hypotheses remain constant throughout the experiment.

These assumptions imply several interesting properties. First, the data generated by this system will have all the properties of all-or-none learning implied by the model of Eq. 1. Restle (1962) showed that treating s, the size of the hypothesis sample, as a free parameter does not change the empirical implications of the model. When the subject takes a larger sample, there is a higher probability of including one or more representations of a correct hypothesis, but there is also a higher probability of making an error due to irrelevant hypothesis that may also be included in the sample.

A second property is that the value of c, the probability of solving following any error, is equal to the relative weight of the relevant dimension or dimensions. If there are N dimensions and dimension 1 is relevant but the others are irrelevant, then

$$c_1 = a_1 = \frac{w_1}{\sum\limits_{j=1}^{N} w_j} \qquad [7]$$

If dimensions 1 and 2 are made relevant with the remaining $N - 2$ dimensions irrelevant,

$$c_{12} = a_1 + a_2 = \frac{w_1 + w_2}{\sum\limits_{j=1}^{N} w_j}. \qquad [8]$$

This property, called additivity of cues, was also shown by Restle (1962) although his model differed from Trabasso and Bower's in the details of how a sample of hypotheses is selected by the subject.

The last property to be presented here deals with the nature of the solutions that various subjects will achieve in a problem with relevant redundant cues. As mentioned above, a subject can solve such a problem using either of the relevant dimensions. Also, if the sample of hypotheses includes more than a single element, it is possible that the subject will solve using both of the relevant cues. Let p_1 be the probability that the solution involves dimension 1, given that a solution is found. Let p_2 be the probability that the solution involves dimension 2, given that a solution is found. And let p_{12} be the probability that the solution involves both of the relevant dimensions, given that the problem is solved. Trabasso and Bower (1968) showed that

$$p_1 = \frac{a_1}{a_1 + a_2}(1 - a_2)^{s-1}, \quad p_2 = \frac{a_2}{a_1 + a_2}(1 - a_1)^{s-1}$$
$$p_{12} = 1 - \frac{a_1(1 - a_2)^{s-1} + a_2(1 - a_1)^{s-1}}{a_1 + a_2} \qquad [9]$$

Trabasso and Bower conducted an experiment testing the implications of cue additivity and the proportions of solutions of various types. Three groups had five dimensions; (1) the shape of a figure (circle or triangle), (2) the position of a dot (above or below the figure), (3) the color (red or blue), (4) the number of lines in a figure (one or two) and (5) the position of a gap in the figure (left or right side). Group 12 had both of the first two dimensions relevant and the others irrelevant. Group 1 had shape relevant and the other four dimensions irrelevant. Group 2 had the position of the dot relevant and the other dimensions irrelevant. A fourth group, Group 1′, had shape relevant and no dots were used; dimensions 3, 4, and 5 were irrelevant. Group 2′ had the position of the dot relevant, but all the figures were squares, eliminating dimension 1; dimensions 3, 4, and 5 were irrelevant.

In testing the predictions involving additivity of cues, Trabasso and Bower used the data from Groups 1′ and 2′ to estimate two parameters;

$$r_1 = \frac{w_1}{w_3 + w_4 + w_5} = \frac{c_{1'}}{1 - c_{1'}};$$
$$r_2 = \frac{w_2}{w_3 + w_4 + w_5} = \frac{c_{2'}}{1 - c_{2'}} \qquad [10]$$

which can be derived from Eq. 7. The values of c_1, and c_2, estimated from the data were .114 and .173, giving

$$r_1 = .129; \quad r_2 = .209.$$

It is easy to show that Eqs. 7 and 8 imply that the remaining learning rates should be

$$c_1 = \frac{r_1}{1 + r_1 + r_2}, \quad c_2 = \frac{r_2}{1 + r_1 + r_2}, \quad c_{12} = c_1 + c_2$$
$$= \frac{r_1 + r_2}{1 + r_1 + r_2}. \qquad [11]$$

Substituting the estimated values in Eq. 11 gives predictions of .096, .157, and .253, which were very close to the obtained values of .094, .164, and .239.

Following the learning phase, subjects in Group 12 were tested to assess the kinds of solutions they found. Two tests were given: First, series of test cards were given to the subject, and he was asked to classify them but was not given any feedback. Sixteen of the cards were like those given in training to Group 1′, so that if a subject had solved using shape, he could sort these test cards correctly. The test deck also included 16 cards like those given in training to Group 2′, so that if a subject solved using the position of the dot he could sort these test cards correctly. If a subject solved the problem using both of the relevant dimensions, he could sort all 32 of these cards correctly. After this test, subjects were asked how they solved the orginal problem. The proportions of subjects who appeared to solve using shape, dot, and both were practically identical by both measures. The estimated number of subjects in the three categories were 31, 45, and 13 respectively. Theoretical quantities corresponding to these data were obtained using Eq. 9, with values of a_1 and a_2 estimated from the learning data, and with s estimated as 2. The theoretical frequencies were 28.8, 49.3, and 10.9, in good agreement with the data.

I have described this study from Trabasso and Bower's monograph in some detail, because it illustrates an important feature of mathematical theorizing that is beginning to be common. Mathematical modeling is often characterized as a self-fulfilling enterprise. The simple structures used whenever possible in quantitative theories are inconsistent with the data of many experiments. Often, special conditions have to be created in order to generate data that satisfy the predictions of models like the one expressed by Eq. 1. In many cases, the achievement involved when data agree with a model involves a large element of creating an appropriate experiment for the model, as well as success in finding an appropriate model for the experimental situation.

This is not necessarily an undesirable development; it certainly is not a trivial one, in terms of the amount of effort, skill, and good luck that are required to bring it about. It often happens that a mathematical model describes a simple structure that apparently incorporates important general features of a process in a particularly simple and lucid way. A successful model can then serve as a base-line description against which to compare the results of more complicated experiments in order to discover further features of the process that are not explicitly considered in the original model. Numerous studies have been carried out investigating the kinds of information obtained by subjects from specific stimuli and other details that are not dealt with in the simple model.

But in addition to providing a stimulus and a set of analytical tools for more detailed analysis, a mathematical model can also provide the basis for the measurement of interesting psychological quantities associated with the processes described by the model. Trabasso and Bower's work illustrates this, in that they used the concept identification model to measure the relative attention values of various dimensions of stimulus variation in their experiment. Thus, the model not only provides a description of the process of problem solving in their situation, but also gives a method of measuring the values of a psychological variable, in this case attention, that is relevant to the process that is described by the model. Note,

too, that these measurements are made in the context of specific assumptions about how the auxiliary process is involved in the structure that is described by the model, and these assumptions are testable in appropriate experimental situations. In the case discussed here, explicit assumptions about the role of attention in problem solving were stated and worked out in mathematical form, and this permitted tests of the adequacy of the assumptions by comparison of learning rates among different experimental groups, and by the results of special tests given after solution of a special problem.

MULTISTAGE PROBLEMS

The analysis of problem solving in concept identification experiments, given above, is based on the idea of an all-or-none process. In the experiment, the time taken to solve the problem is measured in discrete trials. An analysis of solution times for a variety of different problems, given by Restle and Davis (1962) extends this general line of theorizing in two ways. First, it allows for processes of finding solutions that involve more than a single stage; in fact, a main focus of the analysis is on the estimation of the number of stages involved in solving the various problems. Secondly, the process of solution occurs in continuous time rather than over discrete trials.

In an experiment by Davis (1961) subjects solved three problems. In one problem, subjects had to explain how a prisoner escaped from a tower. He had a rope that was half long enough to allow him to reach the ground. He divided the rope in half and tied the two halves together and escaped. (Answer: he divided the rope lengthwise.) Another problem was called Word Tangle: "If the puzzle you solved before you solved this one was harder than the puzzle you solved after you solved the puzzle you solved before you solved this one, was the puzzle you solved before you solved this one harder than this one?" (Answer: yes.) And the remaining problem was called Gold Dust: The subject was told that he had containers of 163, 14, 25, and 11 ounces, and he was to obtain exactly 77. [Answer: $163 - 2(25) - 14 - 2(11)$ or $163 - 25 - 2(14) - 3(11)$]

The theory used by Restle and Davis is a simple one. It is assumed that a given problem requires some number of stages to solve, and that the achievement of each stage is an all-or-none process. This implies that the distribution of times needed to achieve a single stage is the exponential,

$$f(t; \lambda) = \lambda e^{-\lambda t}, \tag{12}$$

where λ is a parameter of the distribution. When several stages are required to solve a problem, if each stage is an all-or-none process and all have the same parameter λ, the distribution of the total time will have the gamma distribution,

$$g(t; \lambda, k) \frac{\lambda}{(k-1)!} e^{-\lambda t} (\lambda t)^{k-1} \tag{13}$$

where k is the number of stages. The mean and variance of the gamma distribution are

$$\mu = k/\lambda, \quad \sigma^2 = k/\lambda^2. \tag{14}$$

Equation 14 can be used to estimate the number of stages and the value of λ.

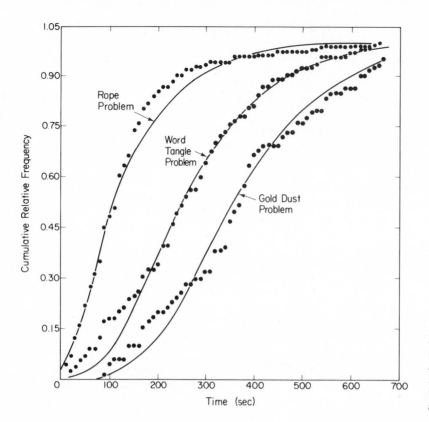

Fig. 8-2. *Theoretical (lines) and empirical (dots) cumulative distributions of time to solve three problems.* [From Restle and Davis (1962), p. 524. Copyright 1962 by the American Psychological Association and reproduced by permission.]

Restle and Davis analyzed measures of time taken to solve the three problems described earlier. Subjects who failed to solve a problem and subjects who gave wrong answers were omitted from the analysis, and a constant reading time estimated from subsidiary measurements was substracted from each subject's total time to solution. From the means and variances of the resulting scores, it was estimated that the numbers of stages were 1.3 for the rope problem, 3.0 of Word Tangle, and 5.0 for Gold Dust. These estimates agree rather well with the intutive judgments that one might make about the relative complexity of the problems. In addition, the actual distributions of solution times agreed quite well with the theoretical distributions. These are shown in Fig. 8-2, in the form of cumulative distributions.

The final example of models for problem solving to be given here is an analysis given by Bjork (1968). In an experiment, Bjork's subjects sat in front of a circular display containing the digits 0, 1, . . . , 9, with a light next to each of the digits. Subjects were told that lights would appear in a numerical sequence and that their task was to discover the scheme or system underlying the sequence. They were told that each new member of a sequence would be obtained by adding or substracting some number from the previous one, and that multiplication or division would never be used. On each trial, the subject announced his prediction, and the experimenter turned on the correct light. In one of the sequences, the first number was 2, then 7 (5 to the right of 2), then 6 (1 to the left), 1 (5 to the right), then 9 (2 to the left), then 4 (5 to the right), then 1 (3 to the left), then 6 (5 to the right), then 2 (4 to the left), and so on. The sequence of moves can be abbreviated +5, −1, +5, −2, +5, −3, +5, −4, and so on.

Each of the sequences used by Bjork consisted of some number of rules, applied in successive order. In the example described above, one of the rules is "add 5," and the other is "subtract one more than last time." Every rule either involved a constant to be added (or subtracted) or an advancing number. The other property of a rule involved its period: it was either applied on every trial (period 1) or every other trial (period 2) or every third trial (period 3) or every fourth trial (period 4). Bjork used 12 different sequences, and each subject learned all 12 sequences in a fixed order.

The overall learning of each sequence was quite a complicated process, but Bjork was able to analyze the learning process into subunits that were learned in an all-or-none fashion. According to Bjork's analysis, each subrule (e.g., "add 5") constituted an element of the total process of solving the problem, and the learning of each individual subrule was an all-or-none process. The different subrules were not all equally difficult; for example, constant rules with period 3 showed a learning rate of .71, while advancing rules with period 1 showed a learning rate of .48. Bjork tested the predictions of the all-or-none hypothesis for subrule learning by examining distributions of statistics such as the total number of errors made at times when a given subrule applied. The predictions were in satisfactory agreement with the data.

Bjork's analysis illustrates an important use of quantitative models in the analysis of relatively complex tasks. By identifying the relevant subunits of the problem, Bjork was able to provide an elegant and comprehensible analysis of the problem-solving process. This is basically what analyses like those of Restle and Davis (1962) provide, but in Restle and Davis' situation, the stages of problem solving have to be treated as hypothetical processes. In the situation studied by Bjork, the subprocesses of problem solving were observable in a more direct way, and properties of their learning could be examined more directly.

2. Memorizing

The ability to study and reproduce verbal materials is an important human attribute, and rote memorizing has been studied extensively by psychologists for many years. An experiment with an attractively simple structure is paired-associate memorizing, where subjects study a list of pairs, then are tested by presentation of the first member of each pair and try to remember the second. Traditionally, it was assumed that the subject's memory of an association depended on the strength of a connection between the two members of the pair, and that the strength increased gradually over trials. Results obtained by Rock (1957) suggested that the formation of an association occurred in an all-or-none fashion. This led to further experimental and theoretical analysis by Estes (1960), and in 1961, Bower published a formal model incorporating the all-or-none hypothesis.

All-or-None Memorizing

The mathematical structure of Bower's model is a two-state Markov chain. The model describes the course of learning for an individual item. In the first state, the item is unlearned, and there is some probability g that the correct response will be given, presumably by guessing. In the second state the item is learned, and only correct responses occur. The transition from the unlearned state to the learned state occurs in a single trial, and there is a fixed probability c that this transition will occur on any trial. Once learning has occurred, it is assumed that there is no forgetting within the context of the experiment—that is, the learned state is an absorbing state. The learning assumption can be represented by a matrix of transition probabilities, Eq. 15.

$$P = \begin{array}{c} L_n \\ U_n \end{array} \begin{array}{|cc} L_{n+1} & U_{n+1} \\ \hline 1 & 0 \\ c & 1-c \end{array} \qquad [15]$$

If a test trial is given at the beginning of the experiment, when the subject must guess before seeing the correct answer, the initial probabilities of the chain are

$$P(L_1, U_1) = (0, 1). \qquad [16]$$

Finally, let 0_n denote a correct response on Trial n and let 1_n denote an error on Trial n. The performance assumptions of the model are represented in the equations

$$P(0_n \mid U_n) = g; \ P(0_n \mid L_n) = 1.0. \qquad [17]$$

The assumptions imply a number of statistical properties of data that can be used to test the model. Two that are commonly used are the trial of the last error per item and the number of errors per item. It is an elementary exercise in probability theory to calculate the probability distributions of these and

other statistics. The formula for the trial of the last error is

$$P(L = k) = \begin{cases} \dfrac{gc}{1 - g + gc} & k = 0 \\ (1 - c)^{k-1}(1 - g)\dfrac{c}{1 - g + gc} & k \geq 1. \end{cases} \qquad [18]$$

And the distribution of the number of errors per item is

$$P(T = j)$$
$$= \begin{cases} \dfrac{gc}{1 - g + gc} & k = 0 \\ \left(\dfrac{(1 - c)(1 - g)}{1 - g + gc}\right)^{k-1} \dfrac{c(1 - g)}{(1 - g + gc)^2} & k \geq 1. \end{cases} \qquad [19]$$

Theoretical distributions are calculated by substituting estimates of g and c into formulas like Eqs. 18 and 19, and the results are compared with the empirical frequency distributions.

The data used by Bower were from an experiment in which each subject memorized a list of pairs with bigrams as stimuli. The response for each item was either the number 1 or 2. Thus, the value of g was .50, and Bower estimated that c was about .33. Figs. 8-3 and 8-4 present the theoretical and empirical distributions of the statistics whose formulas are given as Eqs. 18 and 19. The agreement was obviously very good.

Many investigators have obtained results that are inconsistent with predictions derived from the simple all-or-none model. An important feature of quantitative theories is that they are specific enough so that they can be falsified by data. It should not be surprising that a structure as simple as the one described in Eqs. 15–17 is inconsistent with the results of many experiments. The surprising fact is that conditions were found in which the data are consistent with such a simple structure. It may be that all-or-none learning provides a kind of ideally simplified case of learning, much as a frictionless gas serves as an ideally simplified case of gaseous substance in physics. If the model does correspond to a simple case of memorization, then it reveals important general principles that are clouded by other factors in more complex situations. However,

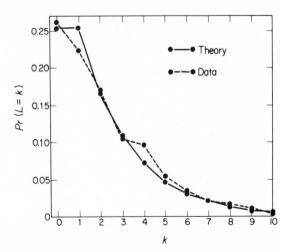

Fig. 8-3. *Theoretical and empirical distributions of trial of last error for individual paired-associate items.* [From Bower (1961)]

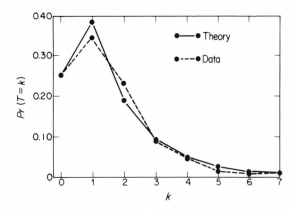

Fig. 8-4. *Theoretical and empirical distributions of number of errors for individual paired-associate items.* [From Bower (1961)]

the mere demonstration that it is possible to obtain data consistent with the all-or-none model does not establish it as the appropriate basis of a general theory of memorizing. This takes a good deal more, and one of the important steps in this more complicated procedure involves developing more complex models, incorporating the simple model, but dealing with additional factors that are present in situations where data are inconsistent with the all-or-none model.

SHORT-TERM RETENTION

One important aspect of human retention is that if an item is presented and then tested immediately or within a few seconds, the subject will recall it with a probability that is considerably higher than his probability of recall after a longer time. This phenomenon of short-term retention is ignored in the all-or-none model described above, but it has been the subject of quantitative theories. One interesting model that focuses on short-term retention was developed by Atkinson and Shiffrin (1967). In Atkinson and Shiffrin's model it is assumed that there is a short-term memory system, analogous to an input buffer in a computer system. The short-term buffer holds a fixed number of items, the number being a free parameter that presumably depends on the nature of the materials being presented and possibly on other variables. During the time that an item is held in the short-term buffer, information about it is transferred to long-term memory.

The model has been applied to the results of a number of experiments, but its characteristics are easiest to describe in relation to a continuous paired-associate experiment using a few stimuli and a relatively large number of responses. After the first few trials of the experiment, when a stimulus is presented the subject's task is to give the response that was most recently paired with that stimulus. After the subject responds, the stimulus is presented with a new response for a few seconds, during which the subject is to study the pair. That stimulus will be presented on a test trial at some later time. Its test may follow its study presentation immediately (lag 0) or it may follow a test and study interval of one other item (lag 1) or two test and study intervals (lag 2), and so on.

Let r be the number of paired-associate items that can be held in the short-term buffer. When an item is presented, the subject makes a decision whether to place it in the buffer. With probability α he decides positively. In that case the item is placed in the buffer, and one of the items residing in the buffer is dropped out. Now suppose that the next item is different from any that are in the buffer. With probability α this new item is placed in the buffer, and the new item placed in the buffer just previously may be dropped out, or it may remain. The selection of an item to be dropped out is assumed to be random, so the probability that a given item is dropped out is $1/r^2$. These assumptions imply that when an item is in the buffer and another item is presented that is not in the buffer, the probability that the first item will be dropped out is α/r.

Another possibility is that an item is presented for testing while it is still in the buffer. It is assumed that the subject can always give the correct response in this case, and that he then replaces the item in the buffer so that other items are not dropped out.

The number of trials that an item resides in the buffer is a random variable. There is probability $1 - \alpha$ that an item will not be placed in the buffer at all. If an item x is placed in the buffer, then there will be some number of times that another item not in the buffer is presented, but item x will not be dropped out. Call this number s. The probability distribution of s is

$$P(s = i) = \begin{cases} 1 - \alpha & i = 0 \\ \alpha(1 - \frac{\alpha}{r})^{i-1}(\frac{\alpha}{r}) & i \geq 1 \end{cases} \qquad [20]$$

In addition, while item x is in the buffer, there will be some number of times that an item will be presented that is already in the buffer. Call this number n. The value of n will depend on s and on the experimental procedure—if items are frequently presented for test after relatively short intervals, n will be larger than if most tests occur after relatively long delays. The total number of intervals that an item remains in the buffer will be $s + n$, with s distributed according to Eq. 20, and n varying with experimental conditions.

It is assumed that information about an item is transferred to long-term memory at a constant rate θ, as long as the item remains in the buffer. Thus, the amount of information transferred about an item is a random variable with a value proportional to the value of $s + n$; specifically, it equals $(s + n)\theta$. After the item has been dropped from the buffer, the information about it in long-term memory is assumed to decay exponentially. Suppose that the item is to be tested after a lag of k items following its presentation, and that it resided in the buffer for $s + n$ intervals where $s + n < k$. Then the amount of information about the item in long-term memory at the time of the test is $(s + n)\theta(\tau^{k-s-n})$, where τ is the rate of decay.

The final assumption of the model deals with the probability of retrieving an item from memory on a test. If the item is still in short-term memory, it is assumed that it will be retrieved with probability one. If it is not in long-term memory, the probability of retrieval depends on the amount of information about the item in long-term memory. Specifically,

---

[2]In more complex versions of the model, the new item tends to replace the older items in the buffer, more than those that have entered more recently. Let item 1 be the oldest item in the buffer, and item r the newest. The probability that an entering item will replace item j is $\delta(1 - \delta)^{j-1}/[1 - (1 - \delta)^r]$, where δ is a free parameter. The model described above with random dropout is the limiting case of the general model as δ approaches zero.

$$P(\text{retrieval} \mid s + n = i) = \begin{cases} 1 & \text{if } i \le k \\ 1 - e^{[-i\theta(\tau^{k-i})]} & \text{if } i > k \end{cases} \qquad \text{[21]}$$

The probability of retrieval on a test is

$$P(\text{retrieval}) = \sum_{i=0}^{k} P(s + n = i)P(\text{retrieval} \mid s + n = i) \qquad \text{[22]}$$

where k is the number of intervals between the study of an item and its test.

The application of the theory is illustrated in an experiment by Atkinson, Brelsford, and Shiffrin (1967). Subjects were run in three conditions. In all the conditions, the paired-associate responses were the 26 letters of the alphabet. The stimuli were two-digit numbers. The three conditions differed in the number of different stimuli that were used: four, six, and eight. The idea of the experiment was that with fewer stimuli, the presented item would more frequently be in the buffer, and this would result in better performance. A single set of parameters was estimated for all three conditions: $r = 2$, $\alpha = .39$, $\theta = .40$, $\tau = .93$. The results of the experiment, along with the theoretical predictions, are shown in Fig. 8-5. The theory and the data seem to be in quite good agreement.

Atkinson and Shiffrin's model gives a detailed hypothetical description of a mechanism that could underlie the phenomena of short term retention. The model has been applied to a substantial variety of experimental results, with notable success. However, the purpose of this chapter is to survey a variety of theories, rather than to provide detailed empirical evaluations. And another line of theorizing has been followed, exploring the role of short-term retention in memorizing in a different way.

A model given by Atkinson and Crothers (1964) and analyzed further by Greeno (1967) is a simple extension of the all-or-none model described earlier. Learning is an all-or-none event, with a constant probability. But while an item is still unlearned, it may be recalled on a test due to its being in short-term memory. Thus, an item can be in any of three states: L (learned), U (unlearned), or H (held in short-term memory). The model has been applied to experiments using the anticipation procedure; that is, each trial has a test where the subject tries to give the correct response followed by a study trial. There is a fixed list of paired-associate items. The experiment consists of repeated cycles of anticipation trials, and in each cycle all the trials in the list are presented with the order of items varying from one cycle to the next. On a test, the subject gives a correct response if the item is in State L or State H. If the item is in State U, the subject guesses and gives a correct response with probability g. It is assumed that an item will not move to a different state as a result of a test trial.

Following the test, a study interval occurs. There is some probability that an item will be learned during the study interval, and that probability may depend on whether the item was in short-term memory at the beginning of the trial. Then the effect of the study interval is described by a transition matrix

$$P_s = \begin{array}{c} L \\ H \\ U \end{array} \begin{array}{c} \begin{array}{ccc} L & H & U \end{array} \\ \left[\begin{array}{ccc} 1 & 0 & 0 \\ c & 1-c & 0 \\ d & 1-d & 0 \end{array} \right] \end{array} \qquad \text{[23]}$$

Equation 23 includes the assumption that an item that is not learned on a study trial will be placed in short-term memory. This is a questionable assumption, especially in the light of Atkinson, Brelsford, and Shiffrin's result, mentioned above, where the probability of placing an unlearned item in short-term memory was estimated as $\alpha = .39$. On the other hand, with a fixed list of items to memorize, the value of α might be higher than when there is a continually changing set of items. And in any case, changing the model to include a free parameter corresponding to α would not change its empirical implications, for a reason that will be mentioned below.

After an item is presented for study, a number of other items are tested and studied before the item is tested. During this interval between its presentations, the item may reside in short-term memory for a time and the processing that occurs may result in the item's being transferred to the learned state. Even if the item is not transferred to the learned state, it may

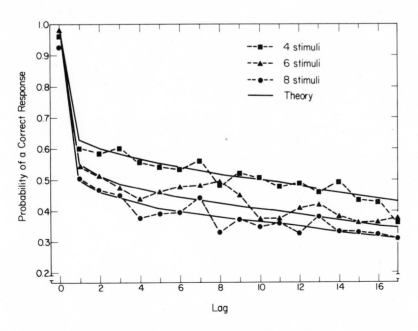

Fig. 8-5. *Theoretical and empirical probabilities of correct response as a function of lag in continuous paired-associate memorizing with different numbers of stimuli.* [From Atkinson, Brelsford, and Shiffrin (1967)]

remain in short-term memory until its test in the next cycle. These possibilities are expressed in a transition matrix describing the effect of the interval between trials of an item.

$$P_B = \begin{array}{c} \\ L \\ H \\ U \end{array} \begin{array}{|ccc} L & H & U \\ \hline 1 & 0 & 0 \\ a & (1-a)h & (1-a)(1-h) \\ 0 & 0 & 1 \end{array} \qquad [24]$$

The value of h is the probability of holding an item in short-term memory until its next presentation, given that it was not transferred to long-term memory. The value of a is the probability of transferring the item to the learned state during the interval between presentations. If one wished to allow for the possibility that an unlearned item was not placed in short-term memory after a study trial, then a would be interpreted as the probability that an item placed in the buffer was then transferred to the learned state, and $(1-a)h$ would be the probability that an item placed in the buffer was not transferred to State L, but held in the buffer until the item's next presentation.

Information about the state of an item is obtained only on test trials. Thus, the separate effects of study intervals and intervals between presentations cannot be separately studied in an ordinary experiment. The combined effects of these two kinds of interval are described by a transition matrix which is a product of P_S and P_B, given in Eqs. 23 and 24. The probabilities of transitions occurring between test trials are

$$P_T = P_S \times P_B$$

$$= \begin{array}{c} \\ L \\ H \\ U \end{array} \begin{array}{|ccc} L & H & U \\ \hline 1 & 0 & 0 \\ c+(1-c)a & (1-c)(1-a)h & (1-c)(1-a)(1-h) \\ d+(1-d)a & (1-d)(1-a)h & (1-d)(1-a)(1-h). \end{array}$$

$$[25]$$

Equation 25 is the statistical structure that can be applied to data[3], based on the assumptions about the effects of study trials and intervals between presentations of an item.

The model given in Eqs. 23–25 deals with the same processes as Atkinson and Shiffrin's model, described earlier. But it is simpler in a number of ways. For one thing, in the more detailed model, the transfer of information to long-term memory is treated as a graded process, with the amount of information transferred depending in a specified way on the length of time that the item resides in short-term memory. In the simpler model, the transfer of an item to the learned state is an all-or-none process, and details of the relationship between transfer and length of residence in short-term memory are ignored.

On a given trial, either there is enough information transferred to long-term memory to ensure correct responding up to the experimental criterion of learning, or there is not. And if it is not then it is assumed that any information that is transferred does not help the subject on later trials. A second feature of the detailed model that is ignored in the simpler model is the decay of information from long term memory. In the simpler model,

the learned state is an absorbing state, and any loss of information from the long-term memory is assumed to be negligible. The more detailed model, being more complex and general, probably is closer to the truth than the simpler model. On the other hand, it may be that in many experiments the effects of graded information transfer and decay from long-term memory may not be important enough to affect the experimental results substantially. The simpler model has numerous advantages in making the analysis of effects of repeated trials manageable. And if it supplies an adequate approximation to the memorizing process in a variety of experiments, it can be used as the basis for investigating additional aspects of the process of memorizing.

TRANSFER OF TRAINING

One analysis that was based on this model dealt with positive transfer of training (Greeno and Scandura 1966). The task studied involved verbally mediated concepts. The materials to be memorized were paired associates, with nonsense syllables used as responses. The stimuli were words, and subsets of the stimuli were related through common associations to descriptive adjectives. (For example, "wheel," "barrel," and "doughnut," are members of the same concept category, namely, "round.") First, each subject memorized a list of pairs containing a single member of one concept category, two members of a second category, and four members of a third. All the stimuli that were taken from any one category were paired with the same response. After the first list had been memorized, the subject learned a second, or transfer, list containing six new pairs. The same responses were used in both lists. Three of the stimuli in the transfer list were members of the concept categories represented in the initial list, and three were control words, unrelated to any of the concepts.

After a subject learned an association involving a response and one or more words from a concept category, the task of learning to associate that response with another word from the same concept category should have been facilitated. This facilitation or positive transfer was the process studied in the experiment. It turned out to be a surprisingly simple process, especially when it is described in terms of the model of memorizing given here as Eq. 25. First, consider the fact that subjects probably knew the correct response for some of the items in the transfer list when they were presented for the first time. (If "wheel" and "barrel" went with the response "mur," then "doughnut" should also go with "mur.") As we saw earlier in the discussion of transfer from one concept identification problem to another, this kind of initial knowledge can be described in terms of the initial vector of a Markov model. Let t be the proportion of items that are known at the start. Then the initial probabilities of the states in Eq. 12 are

$$P(L_1, H_1, U_1) = (t, 0, 1-t). \qquad [26]$$

For simplicity, let the matrix of transition probabilities be

$$P = \begin{array}{c} \\ L \\ H \\ U \end{array} \begin{array}{|ccc} L & H & U \\ \hline 1 & 0 & 0 \\ c' & (1-c')h & (1-c')(1-h) \\ d' & (1-d')h & (1-d')(1-h) \end{array} \qquad [27]$$

---

[3]Due to statistical factors that are too complicated to go into here, data that agree with this model do not provide enough information to estimate all of its parameters. A discussion of this problem, and some data bearing on the relative values of the three learning parameters c, d, and a, are presented by Greeno (1967).

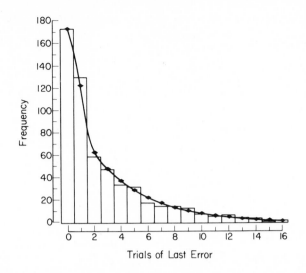

Fig. 8-6. *Theoretical (diamonds) and empirical (bars) distributions of trial of last error for paired-associate items in a transfer experiment.* [From Greeno and Scandura (1966)]

The first question to ask is whether the data from this experiment were in approximate agreement with predictions that are implied by the model. Equations for distributions of statistics are similar in form to those given earlier for the all-or-none model (Eqs. 18 and 19) although they are somewhat more complicated to state, due to the additional parameters that relate to short-term retention. Values of the parameters were estimated and used to calculate predictions. Empirical and theoretical distributions of the trial of last error and the number of errors, are given for transfer and control items combined in Figs. 8-6 and 8-7. The agreement appears to have been satisfactory.

If it is accepted that the model agreed with the data to a satisfactory approximation, then we can use the model to ask questions about the process of transfer. One question is whether

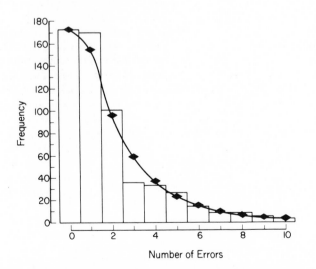

Fig. 8-7. *Theoretical (diamonds) and empirical (bars) distributions of number of errors for paired-associate items in a transfer experiment.* [From Greeno and Scandura (1966)]

transfer is simply a process of recognition that occurs on the first trial, or whether there are continuing opportunities for transfer to occur during the learning trials on the new items. According to the hypothesis of first-trial recognition, the critical trial for transfer is the first presentation of a new item in the transfer list. If the subject recognized the relationship between the new item and other items learned previously, transfer should have occurred. But if the relationship was not recognized on the first trial, then the new item had to be learned in the way that it would have, had the earlier items not been learned. According to this hypothesis, the difference between transfer and control items should be entirely in the value of t, the initial probability of State L. According to the continuing-opportunities hypothesis, the subject could transfer the response from a previously learned item to a new similar item as long as the new item remained unlearned. In this case, control and transfer items would differ in the values of the learning parameters c' and d', as well as in the values of t.

The hypotheses can be compared using standard statistical procedures. We need to test two null hypotheses: First, we ask whether t can hold constant across transfer and control items. Secondly, we ask whether the transition probabilities can be held constant across transfer and control items. The hypothesis of a single value of t is rejected in these data; a test statistic that would be distributed as $\chi^2(1)$ under the null hypothesis had the value of 59.60. But the hypothesis of equal values for the transition probabilities could not be rejected. A test statistic that would be distributed as $\chi^2(2)$ under the null hypothesis had the value 1.92.

These results support an hypothesis about learning and transfer that is attractively simple. The agreement between the data and the all-or-none learning model support the idea that in simple learning tasks, memorizing is approximately an all-or-none process. And the additional results about transfer suggest that in the simplest case, positive transfer occurs on the basis of all-or-none recognition of relationships between new items and materials that were learned previously.

Two-Stage Memorizing

We have now considered extensions of the all-or-none model of memorizing that describe the role of short-term retention and positive transfer of training in memorizing. But in both of these extensions, the basic process of memorizing an item is characterized as an all-or-none process. Of course, memorizing is not always all-or-none. But the interesting question is not whether memorizing can involve more than one stage, but rather what the stages of memorizing are.

An hypothesis given by Kintsch and Morris (1965) applies when memorizing has two stages. The situation studied was free recall memorizing, where a list of words is read to a subject, and he tries to repeat as many of them as he can. Then the list is repeated in a different order, the subject tries to remember the words again, and this continues until the subject can give all the words in the list. Kintsch and Morris' idea was that memorizing an item might consist mainly of two stages; a first stage in which the subject learns to recognize the item, and a second stage in which the subject learns to recall the item. An alternative terminology for virtually the same idea is that in the first stage the subject stores the item in memory, and in the second stage he learns to retrieve it from memory. Kintsch and Morris used a statistical model that had been given earlier by Bower and Theios (1964) and generalized and analyzed in more detail by Greeno (1968). The model is a generalization of the all-or-none model, and assumes that learning requires two discrete steps, each occurring in an all-or-none fashion. A graphical representation of the process is shown in Fig. 8-8. This model can be applied when only errors occur in the initial state (State 0), and there is a constant probability of a correct response, $p = 1 - q$, in the intermediate state (State 1). Since the two-stage process is more complex than the all-or-none process, the calculations involved in deriving predictions are somewhat more complicated. An example of the predictions made by the two-stage model is the distribution of total errors. Equation 28, given below, was calculated assuming that $b = c$, and that the first observation comes after a single trial where all items are in State O on that trial.

$$P(T = j) = \frac{(1-a)^{j+1} - \left(\frac{q(1-c)}{q+pc}\right)^{j+1}}{(1-a)\left(\frac{q(1-c)}{q+pc}\right)} \frac{ac}{q+pc} \qquad [28]$$

Predictions like Eq. 28 differ from predictions derived from the all-or-none model in some general ways. The difference is illustrated in Fig. 8-9, showing theoretical distributions of error derived from the all-or-none and the two-stage models. The all-or-none model was used in a somewhat simpler version than those used earlier; it was assumed that the initial guessing trial, included in the earlier calculations, was omitted from the experiment. Using the representation of Eq. 27, the parameters used in the calculation were $c' = d' = .25$, $g = .25$, $h = .067$. Note that when the initial guessing trial is omitted, the all-or-none model gives a predicted distribution in which the mode is zero errors and the predicted frequency decreases monotonically with the number of errors. Parameters were selected for the two-stage model that give the same mean number of errors as did the all-or-none model. (A two-stage process does not necessarily occur more slowly than an all-or-none process.) The values chosen were $a = b = c = .40$, $p = .60$. Note that in the two-stage model, the predicted frequency of one error is as high as the predicted frequency of zero errors. In general, theoretical distributions derived from the two-stage model are less skewed and have lower variance than comparable theoretical distributions derived from the all-or-none model.

Kintsch and Morris investigated their idea about learning to recognize and then learning to recall by examining both recognition and recall learning in separate groups. According to the hypothesis, learning to recognize should be an all-or-none process, and learning to recall should be a two-stage process. The first hypothesis was tested by a group in which a list of 15

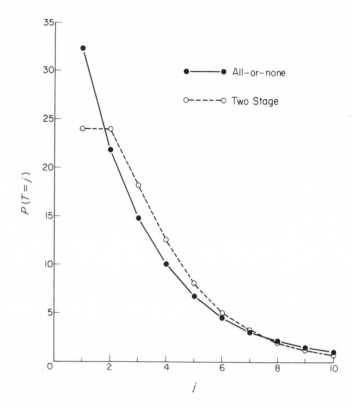

Fig. 8-9. *Theoretical distributions of errors derived from assumptions of all-or-none and two-stage learning. Parameter values were chosen to equalize the mean number of errors.*

nonsense syllables was presented for study, then presented along with 15 new items and the subject said "yes" or "no" to each item, indicating whether he thought he had seen it before or not. This procedure was repeated until the subject gave only correct responses on three complete recognition tests. The data obtained with this procedure agreed with predictions derived from the all-or-none model. For example, the predicted standard deviations of the distributions of errors per item and trial of last error were .92 and 2.45. The obtained values of these statistics were .89 and 2.14.

A second group memorized a list of 10 nonsense syllables in a free recall procedure. The items were presented and the subject recalled as many as he could, with the procedure repeated until there were three consecutive complete recalls of the list. These data were consistent with the two-stage model: the predicted standard deviations of number of errors and trial of last error were 1.9 and 3.1; the obtained values were 1.7 and 2.7.

The main test of Kintsch and Morris' hypothesis was given by a third group. This group learned to recall a set of 10 nonsense syllables, but the learning task was separated into two phases; first the subjects learned to recognize the items, and then they had the same items in a list that they learned to recall. The data in the recognition phase agreed with the all-or-none model, as expected. But the important question involved the data in the recall phase. According to Kintsch and Morris' hypothesis, the process of learning to recognize constitutes the first stage of the two-stage memorizing process that ordinarily occurs in free recall. Thus, a group learning to recall items that they have already learned to recognize should accomplish this in an all-or-none fashion. The data were consistent with this

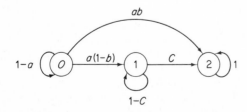

Fig. 8-8. *Graphical representation of a two-stage learning process.*

expectation. Predicted standard deviations of errors and trials of last error were 1.01 and 1.39, compared with obtained values of 1.00 and 1.45.

The idea that free recall learning of an item has the two all-or-none stages of storing in memory, or learning to recognize, followed by learning to recall or retrieve the item from memory, is intuitively satisfying, and it has support in Kintsch and Morris' data. An analysis by Restle (1964), and an experiment by Polson, Restle, and Polson (1965) gives a similar proposal for paired-associate memorizing. According to Restle's idea, the first stage of memorizing a paired-associate item is the learning of an association between the stimulus and response. This, like Kintsch and Morris' first stage, can be described as storage of the item in memory. In some cases, this accomplishment is sufficient to count as "learning," but in other situations there is an additional requirement. This would happen if the subject had difficulty in retrieving stored items from memory as, for example, when the stimuli are quite similar and the subject has difficulty in learning to discriminate between different stimuli.

In Polson, Restle, and Polson's experiment, there were 16 stimuli; 8 were very distinctive, the other 8 consisted of 4 pairs of stimuli similar to each other, but very different from all the other stimuli. Five responses were used, assigned randomly to the stimuli except that twinned stimuli never had the same response, and different pairs of twinned stimuli could not have the same pair of responses.

The application of Restle's idea to the experiment is straightforward. The items with distinctive stimuli should be easy to retrieve from memory, once the responses have been associated with them (or, once the stimulus-response pairs have been stored in memory). Thus, only one stage of learning should be needed to memorize the distinctive items; learning should be all-or-none. However, after a twinned item has been stored in memory, retrieval errors are still likely because of confusions between similar items. Thus, the process of memorizing twinned items should have two stages. However, during the second

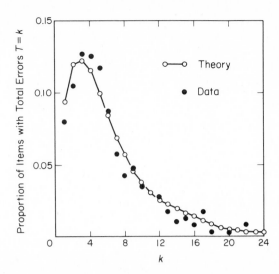

Fig. 8-11. *Theoretical and empirical distributions of number of errors for twinned paired-associate items.* [From Polson, Restle, and Polson (1965), p. 52. Copyright 1965 by the American Psychological Association and reproduced by permission.]

stage the errors that are made on any twinned stimulus should be restricted to the response paired with its twin. Therefore, it is interesting to perform an analysis on the nonconfusion errors—the three incorrect responses that are not paired with the twin of an item. Since these nonconfusion errors should occur only in the first stage, the distribution of nonconfusion errors should agree with the all-or-none model.

The data agreed with these expectations. Fig. 8-10 shows the distribution of number of errors for distinctive items; the theoretical distribution is the familiar distribution implied by the all-or-none model, and the data agree with it closely. Fig. 8-11 shows the distribution of total errors for the twinned items.

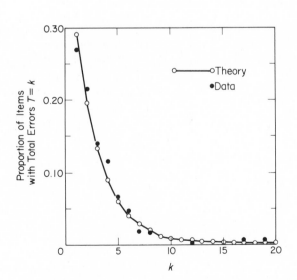

Fig. 8-10. *Theoretical and empirical distributions of number of errors for distinctive paired-associate items.* [From Polson, Restle, and Polson (1965), p. 51. Copyright 1965 by the American Psychological Association and reproduced by permission.]

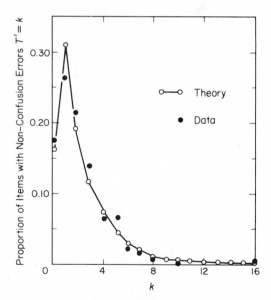

Fig. 8-12. *Theoretical and empirical distributions of number of nonconfusion errors for twinned paired-associate items.* [From Polson, Restle, and Polson (1965), p. 53. Copyright by the American Psychological Association and reproduced by permission.]

This theoretical distribution is typical of two-stage processes. The first-stage parameters of this model were set equal to the values estimated for the distinctive items, and only the second-stage learning parameter was estimated from the data of twinned items. The data again seem in quite good agreement with the predicted distribution. Finally, Fig. 8-12 shows the distribution of nonconfusion errors for twinned items. This theoretical distribution was calculated from the parameters estimated from the distinctive items, with an adjustment for the fact that only three responses were counted as errors. Again, the data and the theory agree well.

MEMORIZING CATEGORIZED ITEMS

In the models described above, the subject's memory of an item is treated in a unitary way, and the models are applied to data in which only the subject's success or failure on each item is recorded. A model by Cowan (1966) dealing with free recall memorizing considers some relationships among items in the list, and thus begins to describe some organizational properties of memory.

Cowan's model applies to lists in which the items can be classified into some number of categories. Cowan worked out implications of the model and applied them to an experiment with two categories. Thirty words were presented: ten connected with food called C_1 (e.g., "apple," "eat," "kitchen") and 20 miscellaneous words called C_2 (e.g., "bible," "hammer," "spear"). The main concept of the model is the idea of associative strength between items within the two categories, and between items in the different categories. The first word is assumed to be recalled on the basis of a process not dealt with in the model, but presumably involving recency of presentation. After the first word is recalled, further recall is assumed to be governed by measures of intra- and inter-category associative strengths, denoted as $m(C_i \rightarrow C_j)$, such that the probability of giving a word from C_j following a word from C_i is

$$P(C_j \mid C_i) = \frac{m(C_i \rightarrow C_j)}{m(C_i \rightarrow C_1) + m(C_i \rightarrow C_2)} \qquad [29]$$

The relevant measures of associative strength will not be constant throughout recall. Suppose that a total of c_1 words from category C_1 and c_2 words from C_2 are recalled. Let a_1 and a_2 be measures of total interitem association within categories C_1 and C_2, respectively, and let b be the measure of interitem association between the categories. At any time while the subject is recalling words, the word just recalled is either from C_1 or from C_2, and there have been some number r_1 words from C_1 and r_2 words from C_2 recalled before. The measures mentioned in Eq. 29 are assumed to be

$$m(C_i \rightarrow C_j) = \begin{cases} \left(\dfrac{a_i}{c_i}\right)\left(\dfrac{c_i - r_i - 1}{c_i - 1}\right) & \text{for } i = j, \\[2ex] \left(\dfrac{b}{c_i}\right)\left(\dfrac{c_i - r_j}{c_j}\right) & \text{for } i \neq j. \end{cases} \qquad [30]$$

In general, the measure of association decreases as more words from the category are recalled. The difference between the cases where $i = j$ and $i \neq j$ is due to the fact that the previous word came from category C_i, and is therefore not available as a response.

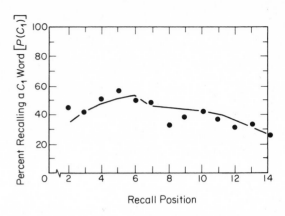

Fig. 8-13. *Theoretical and empirical percentages of words from category C_1 of words at varying ordinal positions in recall list.* [From Cowan (1966)]

Cowan analyzed an experiment in which the 30-item list was presented three times for study, and then tested once. He used the parameter values $c_1 = 6$, $c_2 = 10$ (the mean numbers of items actually recalled from the two categories), $b = 7.5$, $a_1 = 89.0$, $a_2 = 48$. (b and a_1 were obtained from free association data, and are the numbers of free associates common to two or more words in C_1 and between C_1 and C_2, respectively, adjusted to correspond to the empirical values of c_1 and c_2. a_2 was estimated from the data of the experiment.) The final empirical parameter was $P(C_1)$, the probability of giving a C_1 word first, estimated to be .275.

Cowan's data compared with predictions derived from his model, are in Figs. 8-13, 8-14, and 8-15. Apparently the model gives a reasonably accurate description of the structure of recall, as indicated by positions of words in the recall protocols, and by first-order sequential properties.

RETENTION OF COMPLEX ITEMS

The final model to be presented in this section also deals with the organization of memory structures. Bower (1967) considered the organization of complex memory traces that

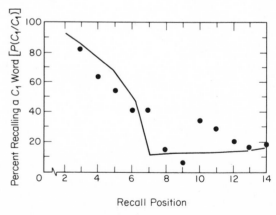

Fig. 8-14. *Theoretical and empirical percentages of words from category C_1 recalled at varying ordinal positions in recall lists where the first recalled word was from category C_1.* [From Cowan (1966)]

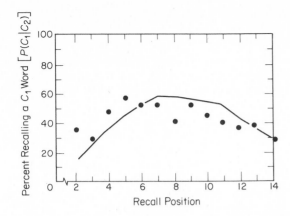

Fig. 8-15. *Theoretical and empirical percentages of words from category C_1 recalled at varying ordinal positions in recall lists where the first recalled word was from category C_2.* [From Cowan (1966)]

represent the individual items studied by a subject. The analysis is applied to a number of experimental situations, including recognition and recall. One of the simplest and most illustrative analyses used a special form of paired-associate memorizing.

Bower assumed that when a paired-associate item is presented, a memory record is stored containing a number of components. The stored record represents both the stimulus and response members of the pair. On a test, the subject is assumed to scan the contents of memory and compare the presented stimulus with the stimulus members of his stored memory records. If he still has the item stored in memory, he will find a match and then he performs the response stored with the stimulus. In general, he can fail to give the correct response either because he has lost information about the stimulus and thereby fails to find a memory record to match the presented stimulus, or because he has lost information about the response and cannot perform it, at least not completely.

An experiment was run using paired associates with high-frequency common nouns as stimuli. The subject faced a panel of buttons, and was to try to remember which button was correct for each stimulus. The novel feature of the experiment was the arrangement of the response display. The buttons were in a horizontal line, but strips of tape were placed on the panel to suggest an hierarchical relationship among the responses. The arrangement used for eight responses is shown in Fig. 8-16. For each stimulus, the light above one of the buttons signalled the correct response. In this case the response could be represented by a vector with three elements, each standing for a

left vs. right side distinction at one of the levels of the hierarchy. For example, suppose that one of the stimuli was "house," and its correct response was the fifth button from the left in Fig. 8-16. Then the item could be represented in memory by the vector (house, right, left, left). During the experiment, each subject was run in four conditions, varying in the number of response alternatives. The various conditions used two, four, eight, and 16 button responses. With two and four alternatives, the response displays had one and two-level hierarchies. With 16 alternatives, there were two eight-item displays like Fig. 8-16, placed one above the other. The idea of the experiment was that subjects would store the information about responses in vectors with the number of components in the vectors depending on the number of response alternatives. Theoretically, there should be one component for the two-alternative situation, two components for the four-alternative situation, three for the eight-alternative situation, and four components when there were 16 alternatives.

The main concept of Bower's theory is the idea that forgetting involves loss of information about the material studied, and this loss can be represented by losses of components from the stored vectors. The simplest kind of loss involves independent forgetting of components.[4] Suppose that in the situation examined in the experiment, the stimulus component of each vector is always retained, but the information about the responses is subject to forgetting. Let t be the amount of time between presentation of an item and its test. There is some probability $r(t)$ that any given component is retained at the time of the test. Then the number of components retained at the time of the test is a random variable with distribution

$$P(R(t) = i) = \binom{N}{i} r(t)^i [1 - r(t)]^{N-i} \qquad [31]$$

where N is the number of components in the stored vector that are subject to forgetting.

Equation 31 was used to derive a formula for the probability of a correct response. It was assumed that if a component had been lost, the subject would guess about its content, and he would have probability $g = .50$ of inserting the correct component by chance. A correct response occurred only if all the components were correct—either because they were retained or because of correct guessing about them. Then the probability of a correct response on the test is

$$C(t) = [r(t) + (1 - r(t))g]^N. \qquad [32]$$

In the experiment, four different intervals between study and test were used. Each interval contained a number of study or test presentations of other items, and each of these events took 2.5 sec. The intervals used were one, three, five, seven, and nine intervening items. A value of $r(t)$ was estimated from the data for each value of t; the estimates were .88, .60, .58, .54, and .45, respectively. Values of N were set at 1, 2, 3, and 4, for the conditions varying in number of response alternatives.

---

[4]Bower also considered a more complex forgetting rule, where forgetting occurs first for the least important components; in this case, the components corresponding to the last decision made in generating the response. Application of this hierarchical rule of forgetting required special assumptions about the forgetting process not required in using the independent-loss scheme, and was more complicated in some other ways as well.

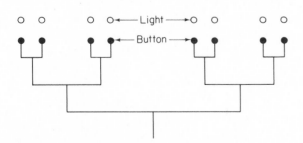

Fig. 8-16. *Arrangement of lights and buttons in the eight-response display from Bower's (1967) experiment.*

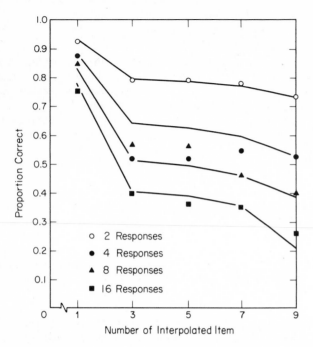

Fig. 8-17. *Theoretical (lines) and empirical (symbols) retention curves for groups with varying number of responses arranged as in Fig. 8-16.* [Data from Bower (1967)]

Fig. 8-17 shows the data and the theoretical predictions based on Eq. 32. The success of the analysis is encouraging for the idea that analysis of the organization of memory traces is a reasonable undertaking, and that Bower's model provides a promising basis for such analyses.

The models discussed in this section have dealt almost entirely with paired-associate and free recall memorizing. This omits a substantial body of theorizing about recognition memory. Some of the ideas that have been developed about recognition will be presented later; they have been deferred because they involve interactions between memory and decision process, which will be introduced in Section 4.

3. Choice and Decision

The study of motivation has occupied many psychologists and many informal theories have been developed in the attempt to understand the nature of human motives, the differences among individuals' motivational tendencies, and the changes that occur in individuals' motives as a result of maturation and experience. At the present time, systematic data concerning the traditional problems in the psychology of motivation are not available in enough detail to permit the development of rigorous theories. On the other hand, there is a large body of quantitative theory relating to the way that people make choices and decisions. In these theories, the motives and values of people are treated as free parameters. The models then serve the double function of any quantitative model in psychology; measurement and description. In this case the models provide the basis of measurement of individuals' motives and values, and they propose hypothetical descriptions of the process in which motives and values operate along with other factors when people make choices.

An early model of choice was given by Thurstone (1927), and served as the dominant model of choice behavior for over 30 years, providing the basis for much of the theory underlying psychological scaling (e.g., Torgerson 1958; Bock and Jones 1968). This model of choice was used by Hull (e.g., 1943, 1952) in his general behavior theory. It is called the classical strength theory by Restle and Greeno (1970) and that label will be used here.

The model is based on the idea that any object or action that is available to an individual as a choice alternative corresponds to a response strength. As an example, a graduate student in psychology might have to choose between (1) a course in mathematical models and (2) a course in operant conditioning. According to the model, the student would have a response strength v_1, representing the attractiveness to him of choosing the course in mathematical psychology, and a strength v_2, the attractiveness of the course in operant conditioning. According to the classical strength theory, the individual chooses whichever alternative has the higher strength.

If the response strength in the classical theory were constant, the model of choice behavior would be extremely simple. However, for many reasons it is more realistic to assume that the response strength for choosing an alternative is a random variable. It is customary to assume that a response strength v_i has the normal distribution with mean μ_i and standard deviation σ_i. Then when an individual chooses between two alternatives, v_1 is a sample value taken from the distribution of its values, and v_2 is also a sample value. The situation is shown in Fig. 8-18, where the upper panel shows hypothetical distributions of

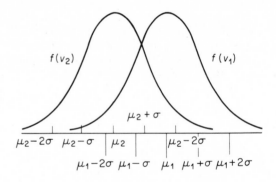

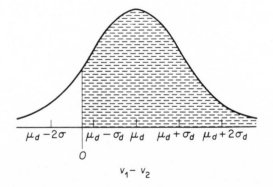

Fig. 8-18. *Hypothetical distributions of response strength for two alternatives (upper figure) and of difference between response strengths (lower figure).*

v_1 and v_2. If the momentary value of v_1 is higher than the momentary value of v_2, the individual will choose the first alternative; thus, the probability of choosing the first alternative, denoted $P(1, 2)$, is just the probability that v_1 exceeds v_2.

$$P(1, 2) = P(v_1 > v_2) = P(v_1 - v_2 > 0). \quad [33]$$

If v_1 and v_2 are normally distributed, then their difference is also distributed normally. This distribution of differences has mean and standard deviation

$$\mu_d = \mu_1 - \mu_2; \sigma_d = \sqrt{\sigma_1^2 + \sigma_2^2 - 2r_{12}\sigma_1\sigma_2} \quad [34]$$

The model is almost always used with the special simplifying assumptions of equal variances and zero correlation between the variables. In that case,

$$\sigma_d = \sigma\sqrt{2} \quad [35]$$

This case was used to draw the lower panel of Fig. 8-18. The shaded portion of the distribution corresponds to the probability that $v_1 - v_2$ exceeds zero; that is to $P(1, 2)$.

An alternative theory of choice was given by Luce (1959). Luce's model also uses the idea of a response strength corresponding to each choice alternative. However, while the classical strength theory considers the response strength as a random variable with choices produced deterministically by the momentary strengths, Luce assumed that the response strengths were fixed quantities and that choices are produced probabilistically. Again, letting v_1 and v_2 stand for the response strengths, Luce's theory is based on the assumption

$$P(1, 2) = \frac{v_1}{v_1 + v_2} \quad [36]$$

One of the advantages of Luce's model is that it can easily be applied to choices involving more than two alternatives. Let $P(i; A)$ be the probability of choosing alternative i from a set of alternatives called A. In general,

$$P(i; A) = \frac{v_i}{\sum_{j \in A} v_j} \quad [37]$$

The ideas in the two choice models can be compared and illustrated in data from experiments where subjects choose between pairs of alternatives. It is important to have a sizable number of observations, so hypothetical alternatives are used, as they typically are in any psychological test of attitudes or values, and a number of different sets of alternatives are presented to each of the subjects. Data collected by Estes were used by Atkinson, Bower, and Crothers (1965) to illustrate the application of Luce's model. The classical strength model will also be used here for Estes' data, to show the similarity of the two theories.

Estes presented pairs of names of four famous people to 117 college students and for each pair, a subject was to indicate which person he would prefer to talk with for an hour about a topic of the subject's choice. The names were Dwight Eisenhower (E), Winston Churchill (C), Dag Hammarskjøld (H), and William Faulkner (F). All six possible pairings of the four names were used, and the empirical proportions of choice were

$$P(E, C) = .57, P(E, H) = .80, P(E, F) = .82,$$
$$P(C, H) = .76, P(C, F) = .80, P(H, F) = .60. \quad [38]$$

In applying the classical strength theory, we assume that all the distributions of strength are normal and have the same variance. The value of σ_{dif} is an arbitrary parameter; assume that $\sigma_{dif} = 1$. We can also set one of the means arbitrarily; assume that $\mu_F = 1$. Then the data of Eq. 38 lead to the estimates

$$\mu_E = 1.98, \mu_C = 1.86, \mu_H = 1.16. \quad [39]$$

These parameters lead to the predictions

$$P(E, C) = .54, P(E, H) = .79, P(E, F) = .84,$$
$$P(C, H) = .76, P(C, F) = .82, P(H, F) = .60. \quad [40]$$

The theoretical probabilities in Eq. 40 are quite close to the data, indicating that the classical strength model gives a reasonably good account of the choices.

The Luce model can also be applied to data from paired comparisons. When the data of Eq. 38 are used to estimate response strengths in Luce's model, the numbers that are obtained are different. The value of one of the strengths can again be set arbitrarily; assume that $v_F = 1$. Then the data yield the estimates

$$v_E = 5.07, v_C = 4.02, v_F = 1.34, \quad [41]$$

which lead to the predictions

$$P(E, C) = .55, P(E, H) = .79, P(E, F) = .84,$$
$$P(C, H) = .75, P(C, F) = .80, P(H, F) = .57. \quad [42]$$

The predictions based on Luce's model use ratios of estimated response strengths, and also seem to be in good agreement with the data. But a more important fact is that the two models give almost identical predictions about the data. This is a general property of the two-choice models. Any set of paired-comparison data that fits one of the models will fit the other to a very close approximation. (See Burke and Zinnes 1965; Luce and Suppes 1965.)

As was mentioned above, Luce's choice model can be applied easily to choices made from sets of more than two alternatives. Estes' experiment included choices from two sets of three alternatives each: $A = [E, C, H]$ and $B = [C, H, F]$. Using Eq. 38 and the estimates of response strength given in Eq. 41, the predictions derived from Luce's model are

$$P(E; A) = .49, P(C; A) = .39, P(H; A) = .12,$$
$$P(C; B) = .63, P(H; B) = .21, P(F; B) = .16. \quad [43]$$

The data obtained from the three-alternatives choices were

$$P(E; A) = .51, P(C; A) = .36, P(H; A) = .13,$$
$$P(C; B) = .65, P(H; B) = .20, P(F; B) = .15, \quad [44]$$

which are satisfactorily close to the theoretical probabilities.

Estes' data, analyzed above, were obtained from a large group of students, each of whom gave one choice for each combination of alternatives in the experiment. The models of choice behavior used in carrying out the analyses are intended as descriptions of choice processes of individuals, and the procedure of pooling across individuals introduces unknown distortions in the data. On the other hand, it is difficult, if not impossible, to obtain appropriate data with individual subjects for testing choice models of this kind. Estimates of choice probabilities are unreliable if they are based on small numbers of observations. And if a subject is asked to give a large number of choices for the same sets of alternatives he will soon come to remember many of his previous responses and therefore the process of choice probably will be confounded by factors of memory and efforts to perform consistently.

Studies using lower animal subjects seem to offer a chance to obtain evidence relevant to the hypotheses of probabilistic choice models that at least lessens the difficulties encountered when human subjects are used. An animal subject can be kept in a restricted environment for a long period of time, and therefore, his behavior can be observed with a relatively constant set of choice alternatives. An experiment conducted by Premack (1963) was of this kind, and Greeno (1968, chap. 2) analyzed the results in relation to Luce's choice model.

A monkey named Chicko was tested during one-hour periods at the same time each day to measure the attractiveness of several toys. Each of the toys was attached to the front of Chicko's cage during the test period, and the amount of time that Chicko spent playing with the toy was measured. Complete choice data were presented for three toys: (1) a handle, (2) a door, and (3) a plunger. In latter sessions, pairs of these toys were presented simultaneously. The analysis using Luce's model used the data from the single-toy test to predict the results obtained when pairs of the toys were presented.

In the single-toy test, Chicko had a continuous choice involving the toy and a miscellaneous variety of other responses, including eating, drinking, climbing about the cage, grooming, and so on. The proportion of time spent playing with the toy can be used to measure the attractiveness of the toy relative to the miscellaneous responses, called M. The single-toy data led to the estimates

$$v_1/v_M = 0.28, \; v_2/v_M = 0.18, \; v_3/v_M = 0.05, \qquad \text{[45]}$$

In the two-toy tests, the miscellaneous alternatives were available, along with the two presented toys. Then, letting i and j denote the toys, the proportion of time spent playing with one of the toys should be

$$P(i) = \frac{v_i}{v_i + v_j + v_M} = \frac{v_i/v_M}{v_i/v_M + v_j/v_M + 1} \qquad \text{[46]}$$

The predictions obtained using the estimates of Eq. 45 are shown, along with the data from the two-toy tests, in Table 1. The

Table 8-1. Predicted and Obtained Proportions of Time

Alternative	Predicted	Obtained
Handle	.19	.19
Door	.12	.10
Handle	.21	.24
Plunger	.04	.04
Door	.15	.14
Plunger	.04	.05

Data from Premack (1963).

predictions seem acceptably close, especially considering that no data from the two-toy tests were used in estimating the response strengths.

The data of Premack's experiment have to be analyzed in less detail using the classical strength theory, since the situation involves many alternatives. However, an analysis of the relative strengths of the choices to play with the toys is possible. For this analysis, the relative strengths can be estimated using the single-toy data. These numbers indicate Chicko's tendency to play with a specific toy, given that he chooses to play rather than to do something else. The estimated values were .44, .17, and −.60 for the handle, door, and plunger. This gives theoretical values of $P(1, 2)$, $P(1, 3)$ and $P(2, 3)$ of .61, .85, and .78, which are identical to the theoretical values obtained for these probabilities from Luce's theory. The empirical value of $P(i, j)$ is the amount of time spent playing with toy i, divided by the amount of time spent playing with either toy i or toy j in a two-toy test. The empirical values were .64, .86, and .74.

An extension of the classical strength theory has been given by Coombs (1964). Often, a set of choice alternatives can be ordered on some dimension. An example, studied by a number of investigators including Coombs and Pruitt (1960) is a set of fair gambles with equal probabilities of winning but with differing stakes. An example of such a set is (50¢, 1/3, 25¢), (80¢, 1/3, 40¢), ($1.40, 1/3, 70¢) where the first number is the amount that the person might win, the second number is the probability of winning, and the third number is the amount that the person might lose. The gambles differ in what is called the variance of the gamble, and variance probably relates to some extent with the subjects' feelings about the riskiness of the bets. Another example, studied by Coombs (1958), used a set of gray patches varying in brightness.

In Coombs' model, it is assumed that the subject has some ideal value on the dimension. For example, some shade of gray is most pleasing to him, or for fair bets with a fixed probability of winning he has some preferred level of variance or risk. The location of this most-preferred point is assumed to vary from time to time, so there is a distribution $g(b)$ of the position along the dimension which the subject considers best. In addition, the subject's judgments of the positions of the alternatives on the dimension vary, so there are distributions $f(x_1)$, $f(x_2)$, . . . associated with the judged positions of the alternatives. Given a pair of alternatives i and j, the subject will choose the alternative whose momentary position is closer to the momentary location of his ideal point. Using the terminology introduced earlier, the response strength for choosing alternative i decreases as the absolute difference between x_i and b increases, and the probability of choosing i rather than j is

$$P(i, j) = P(|x_i - b| < |x_j - b|) \qquad \text{[47]}$$

Fig. 8-19 shows hypothetical distributions for two alternatives, with an hypothetical distribution for the ideal that happens to be between the two alternatives, on the average. Given these distributions, we would expect $P(1, 2) > .50$, since it is likely that x_1 would be closer to b than x_2. The four displays below the hypothetical distributions show different sample values that would result in a choice of alternative 1 rather than alternative 2.

One use of Coombs' model is to measure the location of b, the most favored position on the dimension. This is a property

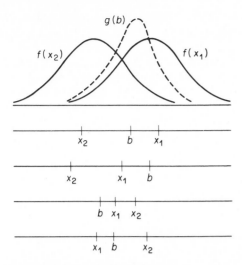

Fig. 8-19. *Hypothetical distribution of judgments about two objects, x_1 and x_2, and of subject's ideal, b (figure at top). Positions of marks at bottom show four ways in which sampling from the three distributions can lead to preference of alternative 1.*

of an individual, and in appropriate experimental conditions with sufficient data the alternative closest to each individual's value of b can be estimated. In Coombs and Pruitt's study (1960) the data from about two-thirds of the subjects showed that their most preferred gambles were either near or below the lowest variance bet or were near or above the highest variance bet (involving, in the case of a 1/3 probability of winning, a chance to win $14.20 or lose $7.20). The remaining one-third of the subjects' data indicated that their most preferred gambles were bets with intermediate variance.

On the other hand, the model also provides an hypothetical description of a process of making choices. Coombs (1958) tested a prediction of the model in the experiment involving gray patches. The prediction involves a relationship among choices for different pairs, called transitivity. According to the model, when there are three alternatives, say i, j, and k, such that $P(i, j) > .50$, and $P(j, k) > .50$, then the true value of $P(i, k)$ should be greater than either $P(i, j)$ or $P(j, k)$. This property is called strong stochastic transitivity. However, the relationship may or may not appear in data, because of the randomness in the choice process. The number of violations of transitivity should depend on the amount of variability in the choice process. A violation of transitivity is a kind of inconsistency in the choices of a subject, and there should be more inconsistencies if the choice process is more variable.

In Coombs' model, variability comes from two sources: variability in the judgments about alternatives, and variability in the location of the ideal point. Variation in the ideal will influence choices between some pairs, but not others. If two alternatives are on the same side of the ideal, changes in the position of the ideal do not change the relationship between the alternatives. But for alternatives on opposite sides of the ideal, changes in the position of the ideal change the choice probabilities. For example, if i is to the right of the ideal, and j is to the left, then a change in the ideal toward the right makes i closer to the ideal, and j farther from the ideal. Thus, we expect more inconsistency in choice between pairs that are on opposite sides of the ideal than between pairs that are on the same side.

Now recall that the property of transitivity involves triples of alternatives. Three kinds of triples can be distinguished: unilateral triples, where all three alternatives are on the same side of the ideal, bilateral split triples where $P(i, j)$ and $P(j, k)$ are both greater than .50 and where i and k are on the same side but j is on the other side of the ideal, and finally bilateral adjacent triples where $P(i, j)$ and $P(j, k)$ are greater than .50 and where i and j are on one side of the ideal and k is on the other. Transitivity is confirmed if $P(i, k)$ is greater than either $P(i, j)$ or $P(j, k)$, so we expect the largest number of violations in the case of bilateral adjacent triples. This prediction was nicely supported in the data. In the data of four subjects, there were 116 unilateral triples, of which 13 violated strong stochastic transitivity. There were 134 bilateral split triples, none of which violated strong stochastic transitivity. And there were 230 bilateral adjacent triples, of which 120 violated strong stochastic transitivity.

A generalization of Luce's choice model also has been given. Restle (1961) presented a model in which choice alternatives are represented as sets of valued aspects. Then two alternatives a and b are represented as in Fig. 8-20. Restle proposed that in choosing between a and b, a person should be unaffected by those aspects that are shared by a and b, since these are obtained in either case. The amount of attraction for an alternative is the measure of its valued aspects, but the probability of choice is

$$P(a, b) = \frac{m(A) - m(A \cap B)}{m(A) + m(B) - 2m(A \cap B)} \qquad \textbf{[48]}$$

Restle's model has many of the properties of Luce's model, except that it allows for the effects of similarity between alternatives. In general, probabilities of choice between similar alternatives should be closer to one or zero than might be expected on the basis of choices between those alternatives and others.

Restle's (1961) monograph contains analyses of several situations involving choice and judgment, including an analysis of the situation studied by Coombs (1958), described above. In effect, Restle showed that an analysis in terms of similarity leads to the same expectations about violations of transitivity as Coombs' model. The reason is that alternatives on the same side of the ideal are more similar to each other than are alternatives on opposite sides of the ideal; thus subjects should be more consistent in their choices between alternatives on the same side of the ideal, just as we expect from Coombs' model.

Another feature of Restle's model involves choices between different quantities of the same valued thing, such as money. Suppose an individual were offered a choice between $100 and $101. We would expect an individual to choose the larger

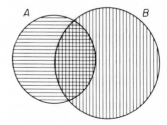

Fig. 8-20. *Representation of two choice alternatives as sets, as in Restle's (1961) model. The probability of choice depends on aspects that are not in the intersection (Eq. 48).*

amount with probability one, unless some special circumstances were involved. However, if we analyze the situation in terms of Luce's theory, considering only the attractiveness of each alternative, we would expect the response strength for choosing $101 to be only a little higher than for choosing $100. Thus, Luce's model leads us to expect choice probabilities near .50 in situations where we are confident they will be near one or zero. However, Restle's model includes consideration of similarity, and notes that the person receives $100 regardless of which alternative he chooses. The person's choice then depends only on the attractiveness of the extra dollar, which should be positive in most situations.

ANALYSIS OF CHOICE BASED ON UTILITY

The models described above deal with choices between different amounts of valued things offered in the same situation. The conclusion of Restle's analysis that a person will always prefer the larger amount seems reasonable for the direct comparison of amounts, but it cannot be generalized to situations where different amounts of, say, money are involved in choices made in different situations. The problem of measuring the attractiveness or utility of different amounts of money has been studied by economists for many decades, because of its importance in theories about prices, wages, and other economic variables. However, questions about the utility of money are really psychological questions and psychologists have worked toward theories of choice and decision that give reasonable descriptions of individuals' utility functions.

A large body of theory has been developed applying to choices made under conditions of uncertainty, (see, e.g., Edwards, Lindman and Phillips 1965). Many decisions have to be made with incomplete knowledge about the outcome. For example, when a person buys stock in a company, he cannot foresee whether the market price of his stock will increase or decrease, although he can often assign probabilities to various outcomes. This leads to the idea of subjectively expected utility. Let a be an action that a person is considering. (In general, there will be alternative actions a, b, . . .) And let $o_1, o_2, \ldots o_n$ be a set of outcomes which the person thinks may be possible results of his action. The person has a utility $u(o_j)$ corresponding to the attractiveness of each possible outcome. Another important factor is his expectation or subjective probability of the likelihood of each outcome if he chooses a, $s(o_{j,a})$. The person's attraction to choosing a will not be affected as much by possible outcomes that he thinks are unlikely as it will be outcomes for which he has stronger expectations. Then the overall attraction of action a is called the subjectively expected utility, or SEU(a),

$$\text{SEU}(a) = \sum_{j=1}^{n} s(o_{j,a})u(o_j) \qquad [49]$$

an average of the utilities of the outcomes, weighted by their subjective probabilities. (This quantity might correspond to the response strength for a, used in the theories described earlier, although this presents some problems when SEU turns out to be negative.)

With several alternatives, each with a value of SEU, there are a number of possible ways in which a choice might be made.

The simplest rule is to choose the alternative that has the highest subjectively expected utility. This would correspond to having response strengths in the classical strength theory equal to SEU values. The rule of maximizing SEU would also correspond to Restle's model, if it were assumed that the quantities of SEU affect choices in the same way as quantities of money or other things, so that when two alternatives differ in SEU the subject can obtain the smaller amount of SEU regardless of his choice, and then the decision is like a choice between the extra amount of SEU and nothing.

A number of experiments have been carried out to test the assumptions of the SEU model of choice uncertainty and use it to measure utilities for amounts of money. A recent study by Tversky (1967) will be described here to illustrate the use of the model.

In Tversky's experiment, the materials were four sets of hypothetical gambles. On any trial, the subject was presented with a situation where he could win or lose some amount x, with a specified probability. The probabilities were indicated by the number of black spots on a wheel of fortune that had ten spots in all. The probabilities ranged from .1 to .9 and the amounts to win or lose ranged from 15¢ to $1.35. On each trial the subject's response was an amount of money that he would take in exchange for the chance to play the gamble (or in the case of negative outcomes, an amount he would pay in order to avoid having to play the gamble). The subjects were 11 inmates at a state prison. At the end of each session, each subject actually played two gambles (or received his selling price) but the data are entirely from the hypothetical gambles.

Tversky's analysis, based on the SEU model, depends on the assumption that when the subject gives a selling price for a gamble, he equalizes two subjectively expected utilities. One, the SEU of the gamble, is given by

$$\text{SEU}(g) = s(p)u(x) + s(1 - p)u(0).$$

There are two possible outcomes, winning or losing x and winning or losing nothing. The subject will win (or lose) with probability p, and $s(p)$ represents the subjective probability or expectation that the wheel of fortune will land on one of the black spots. (It should be close to p, but not necessarily exactly equal to p.) $u(x)$ is the positive (or negative) subjective value of winning (or losing) the specified amount of money. $u(0)$ was arbitrarily set at zero.

The other subjectively expected utility is simpler. When the subject sets a selling price, he is prepared to receive (or pay) his set amount rather than play the gamble. And if he sells the gamble, there is no uncertainty. In the case of a positive gamble he receives the amount of money he states, and in a negative gamble he pays his set amount. Let $M(x, p)$ be the subject's selling price for a gamble involving the amount x and the probability p. Then

$$u[M(x, p)] = \text{SEU}(g) = s(p)u(x).$$

Tversky tested the hypothesis that the utilities are related to amounts of money by a power function:

$$u(x) = x^{\theta} \qquad [50]$$

where θ can have different values for positive and negative

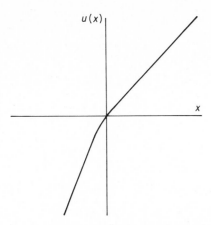

Fig. 8-21. *Utility function u(x) for different amounts of money, x, inferred from a subject's judgments of the values of gambles. This subject had* $\theta_+ = 1.01, \theta_- = 1.20$. [From Tversky (1967), p. 31. Copyright 1967 by the American Psychological Association and reproduced by permission.]

values of x. This leads to the prediction

$$m(x, p)^\theta = s(p)x^\theta, \log M(x, p) = \log x + \frac{1}{\theta} \log s(p).$$

The model assumes that $s(p)$ depends only on p, and thus is independent of the value of x involved in a gamble. If this is true, and if Eq. 50 is a correct description of the relationship between amounts of money and utility, then it should be possible to arrange the values of $\log M(x, p)$ as the scores of a factorial design, with x and p as the factors. The analysis of variance should not show a significant interaction between amounts of money and probability. The analyses were run separately for each subject and each set of gambles, and the prediction was confirmed in 40 of the 44 analyses. Thus, the data were generally consistent with the hypothetical description of the process of choice.

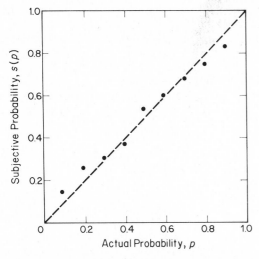

Fig. 8-22. *Inferred subjective probabilities for events with varying actual probabilities based on one subject's judgments of the values of gambles.* [From Tversky (1967), p. 32. Copyright 1967 by the American Psychological Association and reproduced by permission.]

Used as a measurement device, the model permits estimates of the values of θ for positive and negative gambles (θ_+ and θ_-) for each subject. The values of θ_+ were close to one (ten were between .97 and 1.06; one was .77) indicating that the utilities of positive amounts between 15¢ and $1.35 were approximately proportional to the amounts of money involved. Most of the values of θ_- were greater than one (ranging from .94 to 1.43 with a mean of 1.21), corresponding to a utility function that is concave upward. The utility function for a typical subject is given in Fig. 8-21.

The model also permits measurements of the subjective probabilities corresponding to each value of p for each subject. Most of the subjects showed subjective probabilities that were very close to the actual probabilities but some showed systematic tendencies to overestimate low probabilities (i.e., behave as though the low probabilities were not quite as low as they really were) and to underestimate high probabilities. The estimates of subjective probability for a typical subject are shown in Fig. 8-22.

THEORIES OF LEARNING EXPECTATIONS

The psychological theory of choice involves two main variables; one is response strength or value or utility, and the other is expectation or subjective probability. Both of these are almost certainly influenced by an individual's experience, and a complete theory of choice should include a description of the ways in which response strengths and expectations change as a result of events. There has been little or no systematic research on changes in response strength in the context of choice theory, although it probably is possible to consider the large literature on conditioning in ways that are relevant to choice theory.[5] On the other hand, two lines of theorizing have dealt with the question of how expectations or subjective probabilities depend on the individual's experience.

Beginning with an article by Estes and Straughan (1954), a substantial body of experimental literature was developed using a situation called probability learning. A sizable number of studies, along with other applications of the theory that is sketched below, have been collected by Neimark and Estes (1967). In the simplest version of the experiment, the subject sits in front of a panel containing two response switches with a light above each switch. On each trial the subject tries to predict which light will go on, and he indicates his prediction by pressing the appropriate switch. The sequence of lights is preprogrammed by the experimenter. Here we will consider only the simplest kind of sequence, where the sequence of lights is random and independent of the subject's responses. The lights are designated E_1 and E_2, and each has a specified probability of occurrence on each trial,

$$P(E_1) = 1 - P(E_2) = \pi.$$

The theory, called stimulus sampling theory, deals with the subject's probability of predicting E_1. Denote the responses as

[5] This line of theorizing was developed to some extent by Greeno (1968, chap. 3), but the development has to be largely speculative since only a few experimental studies of conditioning have provided data appropriate for quantitative analysis. Some quantitative models of conditioning will be presented in a later section.

A_1 and A_2; then the main theoretical analysis focuses on the quantity $P(A_{1,n})$, the probability of response A_1 on trial n. Here we will interpret $P(A_{1,n})$ as an indication of the subjective probability of event E_1.[6]

According to stimulus sampling theory, the effective stimulus on a trial is a sample from a population of stimulus elements. The population S includes a large number of potential properties. Let N be the number of elements in S. It is assumed that θN is the number of stimulus properties or elements that are active or effective on any trial.[7] The probability of response A_1, interpreted here as the subjective probability of event E_1, is the proportion of elements in the effective sample that are conditioned to response A_1. It is assumed that the sample is selected randomly from trial to trial, so the average value of $P(A_{1,n})$ is equal to the proportion of elements in S that are conditioned to response A_1 on trial n.

At the beginning of a probability learning experiment the subject has no reason to expect that one light is more likely than the other, that is, $P(A_{1,1}) = .50$. On any trial, the subject makes a response, and then one of the lights goes on. It is assumed that if E_1 occurs, the sampled stimulus elements (the effective stimuli on that trial) become conditioned to A_1. If E_2 occurs, then the sample stimulus elements become conditioned to A_2. Thus, the occurrence of E_1 increases $P(A_1)$, and the occurrence of E_2 decreases $P(A_1)$. Since E_1 occurs with probability π,

$$\begin{aligned} P(A_{1,n+1}) &= \pi[(1-\theta)P(A_{1,n}) + \theta] \\ &\quad + (1-\pi)(1-\theta)P(A_{1,n}) \\ &= (1-\theta)P(A_{1,n}) + \pi\theta. \end{aligned} \quad [51]$$

Eq. 51 gives the value of $P(A_{1,n+1})$ as a function of $P(A_{1,n})$. This difference equation can be solved to obtain an explicit expression for $P(A_{1,n})$. With $P(A_{1,1}) = .50$,

$$P(A_{1,n}) = \pi - (\pi - .50)(1-\theta)^{n-1}, \quad [52]$$

and since $(1 - \theta) < 1$,

$$\lim_{n \to \infty} P(A_{1,n}) = \pi. \quad [53]$$

That is, the subjective probability of E_1 will eventually match the actual probability of E_1.

Many sets of data have been analyzed using the model described above, including detailed analyses of response-event sequences that are omitted from this discussion. One experiment, reported by Friedman et al. (1964) used a sequence with $\pi = .80$ followed by a sequence with $\pi = .50$. These trials had been preceded by extended training to familiarize the subjects with the situation and to decrease biases to respond to particular patterns of event sequences. Their data are shown in Fig. 8-23, along with the curve calculated using Eq. 52.

[6]This interpretation is not the one found in most of the literature on probability learning, since the experiment is most commonly considered as a study of a kind of conditioning. However, a number of writers have interpreted the experiment in roughly the way that I do here (e.g., Siegel 1959; Luce and Suppes 1965).

[7]Two versions of the theory that have been analyzed extensively. In one version, called the linear model, N is considered a very large number, so the probability of response is a continuous variable. In another version, called the N-element pattern model, N is considered finite, and it is assumed that a single pattern operates on each trial which means $\theta = 1/N$. Either version is compatible with the brief presentation given here.

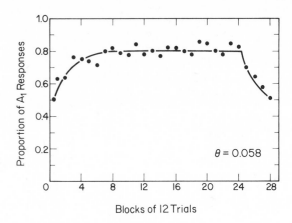

Fig. 8-23. *Theoretical and empirical proportions of A_1 choices during probability learning.* [From Friedman et al. (1964)].

Another line of theoretical work related to the learning of subjective probabilities has dealt with a somewhat different situation. In the probability learning experiment, the subject usually receives very little information about the possible ways in which the sequence of events may have been generated. An alternative is to explain to the subject that two random systems exist, and his task is to decide which system is actually generating the sequence that he is experiencing. In one version of the experiment, (Edwards, Lindman and Phillips 1965), subjects were shown two bookbags and were told that one contained 70 red and 30 blue poker chips, and the other contained 70 blue and 30 red chips. One of the bags was chosen randomly with equal probabilities for the two bags. Then the experimenter randomly drew chips from the selected bag, and after each draw the subject judged the odds that the bookbag was the one containing mostly red chips, rather than the bag containing mostly blue chips.

Theory applied by Edwards et al. (1965) is based on an elementary principle of probability theory known as Bayes' Theorem. In the present case, there are two hypotheses: that the selected bookbag has mostly red chips (H_R) and that it has mostly blue chips (H_B). Since the two bookbags have equal probability of being selected at the start, the two hypotheses have equal probability before any chips are drawn. That is,

$$P(H_R \mid D_0) = P(H_B \mid D_0) = .50.$$

The odds for H_R are expressed as a likelihood ratio,

$$\Omega_0(H_R, H_B) = \frac{P(H_R \mid D_0)}{P(H_B \mid D_0)} = 1.0,$$

at the beginning.

After a chip is drawn, the odds change. If a red chip is drawn, the odds for H_R increase, since it is more likely that a red chip would be drawn from the bag containing mostly red chips. If a blue chip is drawn, the odds for H_R decrease. In general, if there are two hypotheses, Bayes' Theorem is

$$\begin{aligned} P(H_R \mid D_1) &= \frac{P(H_R \cap D_1)}{P(D_1)} \\ &= \frac{P(H_R)P(D_1 \mid H_R)}{P(H_R)P(D_1 \mid H_R) + P(H_B)P(D_1 \mid H_B)} \end{aligned} \quad [54]$$

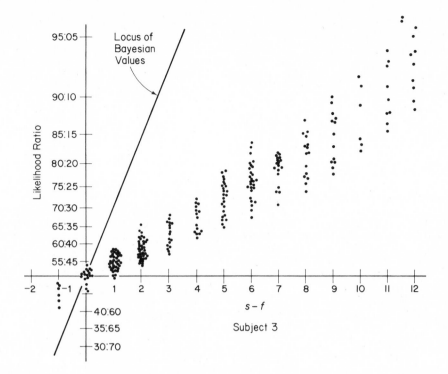

Locus of Bayesian Values

Likelihood Ratio

s − f

Subject 3

Fig. 8-24. *Judgments of likelihood ratio (dots) compared with actual likelihood ratios calculated from Bayes' Theorem.* [From Edwards, Lindman, and Phillips (1965) in *New Directions in Psychology*, Vol. II, by Frank Barron, William C. Dement, Ward Edwards, Harold Lindman, Lawrence Phillips, and James and Marianne Olds. Copyright © 1965 by Holt, Rinehart and Winston, Inc.; reprinted by permission of Holt, Rinehart and Winston, Inc.]

A similar expression can be given for $P(H_B \mid D_1)$. Then the new odds are

$$\Omega_1(H_R, H_B) = \frac{P(H_R)P(D_1 \mid H_R)}{P(H_B)P(D_1 \mid H_B)}. \qquad [55]$$

Since $P(H_R)/P(H_B)$ is just the initial likelihood ratio,

$$\Omega_1(H_R, H_B) = \Omega_0(H_R, H_B)\frac{P(D_1 \mid H_R)}{P(D_1 \mid H_B)}. \qquad [56]$$

In the experimental example described above, suppose that the first chip drawn is red. Then $P(D_1 \mid H_R) = .70$, $P(D_1 \mid H_B) = .30$, and since $\Omega_0(H_R, H_B) = 1.0$, $\Omega_1(H_R, H_B) = 7/3 = 2.33$.

Equation 56 is stated in terms of a single draw. Its form is general and applies to any sequence of draws. Suppose that after a number of draws there have been n blue chips and $n + j$ red chips. Then

$$\begin{aligned}\Omega_{2n+j}(H_R, H_B) &= \Omega_0(H_R, H_B)\frac{P(D_{2n+j} \mid H_R)}{P(D_{2n+j} \mid H_B)} \\ &= (1.0)\frac{.70^{n+j}.30^n}{.30^{n+j}.70^n} = \left(\frac{.70}{.30}\right)^j \end{aligned} \qquad [57]$$

Equation 57 shows that in the kind of situation described, the odds for an hypothesis depend only on the difference between the number of draws favoring the hypothesis and the number of draws against the hypothesis. A convenient form of Eq. 57 involves the logarithm of the odds.

$$\log \Omega_{2n+j}(H_R, H_B) = \log \Omega_0(H_R, H_B) = j \log (.70/.30), \qquad [58]$$

for the case in which the proportions of red chips in the two bookbags are .70 and .30.

Fig. 8-24 shows data from an experiment described above. The dots show the subject's estimates of the odds in situations during the experiment where j had the values given on the abscissa. Note that the subject's estimated odds were systematically lower than those given on the basis of Bayes' Theorem. This kind of result is typical, although in some experiments the estimated odds approach the actual (Bayesian) odds more closely or even exceed the actual odds. The Bayesian model, unlike most of the other models described in this chapter, gives a normative rule for behavior. In the data of Fig. 8-24, and in most of the data obtained in experiments of this kind, the model does not give a very accurate description of what subjects do. Even so, the model is useful in providing a basis of comparing subjects' performance with a rational ideal, and experimentation can be directed toward determining the conditions under which subjects can use information more efficiently.

4. Perception and Recognition

THEORIES OF DETECTION

A classical problem in the psychology of perception is the measurement and analysis of the sensitivity of perceptual systems. For many years it was assumed that sensitivity was determined by sensory thresholds, and experimentalists developed a variety of psychophysical methods designed to measure these thresholds. These methods consisted of variants of a basic experimental task in which the subjects were asked to detect weak stimuli or to detect small differences between stimuli. One of the major contributions of mathematical models in psychology has been the development of new and sophisticated analyses of performance in detection experiments, including hypotheses about the interaction between sensory and decision processes.

The theory of detection that has been developed most extensively and applied in the largest number and variety of experiments is called the theory of signal detectability. (See Swets, Tanner, and Birdsall 1961; Green and Swets 1966). The theory includes a detailed physical analysis of acoustic signals, which will be omitted in this discussion. The main effort in this chapter will be to present the main outline of the theory, especially the relationship that is hypothesized between sensory and decision factors in detection.

The theory has its simplest application in an experimental situation known as yes–no detection. The subject's task on each trial is to judge whether or not a pure tone signal was presented. Whether or not there is a signal, the subject hears a background of white noise on each trial. The ratio of signal energy to noise energy is low enough so that the subject cannot perform perfectly—in fact, it would be impossible to tell whether the signal was present or absent on all trials even from a complete physical description of the stimuli.

According to the theory, the subject is able to use information in the stimulus to make a judgment corresponding to the likelihood that the stimulus was produced by a combination of signal plus noise, rather than by noise alone. This is expressed in the theory as the likelihood ratio,

$$\Omega(SN, N) = \frac{\ell(x \mid SN)}{\ell(x \mid N)},$$ [59]

where x denotes the stimulus.

Consider a large set of trials on which the signal is present with the noise. Because of the variability of the noise input, there will be some trials in which the signal can be heard quite clearly. In those cases, $\ell(x \mid SN)$ will be high and $\ell(x \mid N)$ will be low, leading to a high value of $\Omega(SN, N)$. On other trials the signal will be masked by the noise, leading to a low value of $\ell(x \mid SN)$ and a high value of $\ell(x \mid N)$, or a low value of $\Omega(SN, N)$. More specifically, there will be a distribution of values of $\Omega(SN, N)$, and when white noise with energy N_0 per unit of bandwidth is used as a background for a pure tone signal, with energy E, $\log \Omega(SN, N)$ will be distributed normally with mean E/N_0 and standard deviation $\sqrt{2E/N_0}$. Similarly, there will be a distribution of values of $\Omega(SN, N)$ applying to trials on which noise is presented alone; the mean of this distribution will be $-E/N_0$ and the standard deviation will also be $\sqrt{2E/N_0}$. These specific properties of the distribution of $\log \Omega(SN, N)$ assume that all the physical properties of the stimulus are used in arriving at a value of $\Omega(SN, N)$. If part of the stimulus information is not available or is not used, as with a human subject, the difference between the means of the distributions will be smaller than $2E/N_0$, and the shapes of the distributions will not necessarily be normal.

The description of the stimulus situation given by the theory of signal detectability is closely related to the classical strength theory of choice, described in the previous section of this chapter. The subject is asked to give a response on each trial, whether he thinks there was a signal or not. Each of these responses has some strength, and the strength might correspond to the likelihood of each possibility. One possibility is that the subject will respond "yes," indicating a judgment that a signal was present, whenever $\ell(x \mid SN) > \ell(x \mid N)$, that is, whenever $\Omega(SN, N) > 1$, or $\log \Omega(SN, N) > 0$. This will happen on some fraction of the trials when the signal is presented, though not always. And it

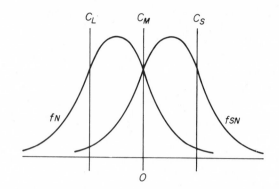

Fig. 8-25. *Hypothetical distributions of log likelihood ratio generated on trials with signals (f_{SN}) and on trials without signals (f_N). The vertical lines correspond to relatively strict, medium, and relatively lax decision criteria.*

will also happen on some fraction of the trials when only the noise is presented, though there will be more trials with noise alone when the value of $\log \Omega(SN, N)$ is less than zero.

The situation is described graphically in Fig. 8-25, where f_{SN} and f_N represent the distributions of $\log \Omega(SN, N)$ on trials with and without the signal, respectively. The case in which the subject responds "yes" whenever $\log \Omega(SN, N) > 0$ corresponds to a criterion C_M, shown as a vertical line in the figure. The probabilities of response correspond to areas under the distribution functions to the right of C_M. The area under f_{SN} to the right of C_M is the probability of saying "yes" on trials when the signal is present, $P(\text{yes} \mid SN)$, and the area under f_N to the right of C_M is the probability of saying "yes" when only the noise is presented, $P(\text{yes} \mid N)$. Note that if the distributions were farther apart, $P(\text{yes} \mid SN)$ would be larger and $P(\text{yes} \mid N)$ would be smaller. In general, the difference between the distributions represents the detectability of the stimulus, so that if a stimulus is easy to detect the distributions of $\log \Omega(SN, N)$ are relatively widely separated.

The paragraph above dealt with a special situation where the subject says "yes" whenever $\log \Omega(SN, N) > 0$. This is a suitable strategy under some conditions, but there are conditions in which it is better to select a criterion for saying "yes" that is somewhat above or below zero. The selection of a criterion depends on two factors; the relative frequency with which signals are presented, and the payoffs and costs for correctly or incorrectly saying "yes" and "no". Let c be an arbitrary criterion, such that the subject says "yes" whenever $\log \Omega(SN, N) > c$. Further, let $F_{SN}(c)$ be the area under f_{SN} that is to the left of c, and let $F_N(c)$ be the area under f_N that is to the left of c. Finally let $P(SN)$ be the probability that a signal is presented on a trial. When the subject sets a criterion, he is committed to a strategy that will lead to probabilities of four events:

$$\begin{aligned}
P(SN \ \& \ \text{"yes"}) &= P_1 = P(SN)[1 - F_{SN}(c)] \\
P(SN \ \& \ \text{"no"}) &= P_2 = P(SN)F_{SN}(c), \\
P(N \ \& \ \text{"yes"}) &= P_3 = [1 - P(SN)][1 - F_N(c)], \\
P(N \ \& \ \text{"no"}) &= P_4 = [1 - P(SN)]F_N(c).
\end{aligned}$$ [60]

Outcomes for the subject can be adjusted so that some of these events are more important than others. For example, it may be very important not to miss any more than a very small number of signals. This could be accomplished by imposing a very high cost whenever the event (SN & "no") occurred. In general, these are outcomes o_1, o_2, o_3, o_4 determined by the experimenter. (Ordinarily, o_1 and o_4 would be positive, since they are payoffs for correct responses, while o_2 and o_3 would be negative and used as costs for errors.) We can use the theory of subjectively expected utility, developed in the preceding section. Here we consider the subjectively expected utility for the entire task as a function of the criterion, c,

$$\text{SEU} = \sum_{i=1}^{4} P_i u(o_i)$$
$$= P(SN)\{[1 - F_{SN}(c)]u(o_1) + F_{SN}(c)u(o_2)\}$$
$$+ [1 - P(SN)]\{[1 - F_N(c)]u(o_3) + F_N(c)u(o_4)\}. \quad [61]$$

Now, if we assume that the subject will select a value of c that maximizes SEU for the task, we can obtain the result

$$c = \log\left(\frac{1 - P(SN)}{P(SN)}\right) + \log\frac{u(o_4) - u(o_3)}{u(o_1) - u(o_2)} \quad [62]$$

where c is a value of $\log \Omega(SN, N)$. Equation 62 says that the subject should adopt a higher value of c (a stricter criterion) if the signals are unlikely, and if the difference in outcome following his "no" responses is great, (that is, the importance of outcomes of saying "no" is relatively great). Note that in a symmetric situation with $P(SN) = .50$ and $u(o_4) - u(o_3) = u(o_1) - u(o_2)$, the best value of c turns out to be zero, the case used as an introductory example earlier.

In one kind of yes–no detection experiment, the energy levels of the signal and noise are kept constant, but variables are manipulated that should affect the subject's criterion. This can be done either by explicitly varying costs and payoffs or $P(SN)$, or more simply by merely asking the subject to use different criteria (e.g., "very strict," "strict," "medium," "lax," "very lax") at different times in the experiment. If the experimenter succeeds in having the subject vary c, then the result will be to get measurements of detection of the same signal with varying decision factors. Each criterion determines two performance quantities; $P(\text{yes}\,|\,SN)$, the hit rate, and $P(\text{yes}\,|\,N)$, the false-alarm rate. For a lax criterion (low value of c) both $P(\text{yes}\,|\,SN)$ and $P(\text{yes}\,|\,N)$ will be relatively high. For a stricter criterion, $P(\text{yes}\,|\,SN)$ and $P(\text{yes}\,|\,N)$ will be lower. It is common practice to plot the values of $P(\text{yes}\,|\,SN)$ and $P(\text{yes}\,|\,N)$ obtained with different criteria in the form shown on the right in Fig. 8-26, and the curve is called the receiver operating characteristic (ROC). Some data, reported by Swets, Tanner and Birdsall (1961) are in Fig. 8-27. The curves represent theoretical functions of the kind shown in Fig. 8-26. The assumption here is that the two distributions may not have equal variance. The numbers shown beside the theoretical functions are indicies of difference between the distributions, called d', where

$$d' = \frac{\mu_{SN} - \mu_N}{\sigma_N}$$

In one sense, the theory of signal detectability is a normative model, analogous to the Bayesian model of learning subjective probabilities that was discussed in the previous section. Given an exact physical description of the stimuli, the distributions of likelihood ratios can be derived and used in the model to specify optimal performance. The model can then be used

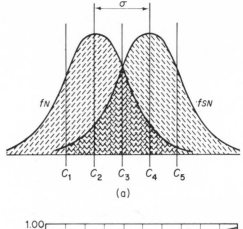

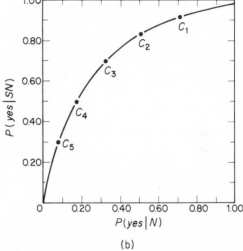

Fig. 8-26. *Hypothetical distributions of log likelihood ratio, with difference between means of 1σ, and the receiver operating characteristic (ROC).*

as a baseline for performance, and experimental manipulations can be used to test hypotheses about the kinds of stimulus information that human observers can use, and about the factors that cause performance to be less than optimal.

One of the controversial assumptions in the theory of signal detectability is the idea that the sensory information used by the subject in making judgments is strictly continuous. This assumption disagrees with the traditional idea that when a stimulus is presented, the subject is in one or the other of two states; either the subject detects the stimulus, or he does not. This discrete-state theory uses the idea of a sensory threshold—an amount of effective stimulation that must be exceeded for the subject to detect a stimulus.

Krantz (1969) has given a model of detection using the idea of a sensory threshold and extending earlier theoretical work by Luce (1963), Norman (1964a) and others. In Krantz' model, two thresholds are assumed. One is a low threshold, which can sometimes be exceeded by a stimulus consisting only of the background or noise. The other is a high threshold, which is never exceeded when noise is presented alone. Thus, Krantz postulates three states that can result from presentation of a signal: $\bar{D}$, failure to detect; D, detection; and D^*, detection

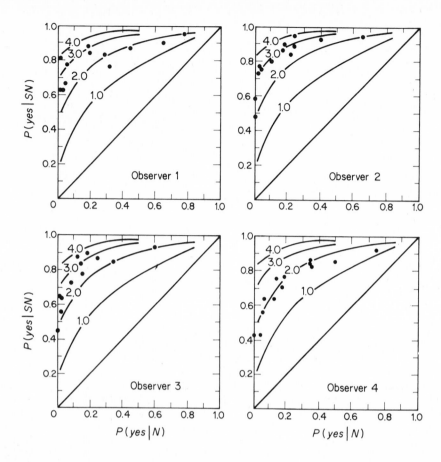

Fig. 8-27. *Theoretical (curves) and empirical (dots) ROC's obtained from four subjects.* [From Swets, Tanner, and Birdsall (1961), p. 319. Copyright 1961 by the American Psychological Association and reproduced by permission.]

with certainty. $\bar{D}$ and D can result from the presentation of noise. The situation can be expressed as a matrix of conditional probabilities:

$$P = \begin{array}{c|ccc} & \bar{D} & D & D^* \\ \hline N & 1-q & q & 0 \\ SN & p_0 & p_1 & p_2 \end{array} \qquad [63]$$

Krantz assumed that the subject always says "yes" when the sensory state is D^*. His responses in the other states depends on the setting of a criterion corresponding to a probabilistic division of responses in State D or in State $\bar{D}$. The subject could decide to say "yes" with probability b whenever he is in State D, and always say "no" in State $\bar{D}$. Or he could decide to say "yes" whenever he is in State D and say "yes" with probability a in State $\bar{D}$. Then the probabilities of saying "yes" are

$$P(\text{yes} \mid SN) = p_2 + bp_1 + ap_0,$$
$$P(\text{yes} \mid N) = bq + a(1-q),$$

where $0 \le b \le 1$, $a = 0$; or $b = 1$, $0 \le a \le 1$. In Fig. 8-28, data from four subjects, presented by Swets, Tanner and Birdsall (1961) are shown along with families of theoretical ROC's calculated from Krantz' model.

A number of other workers have proposed models of detection, including Atkinson (1963), whose model shares a number of important features with Krantz' model, sketched above. In Atkinson's model, a signal trial may produce a detection or a state where the subject is uncertain, and a noise trial may pro-

duce a state where the subject recognizes the absence of a signal or a state where the subject is uncertain. The probabilities of these states are assumed to be variable during the experiment, depending on information that is given to the subject about the presence or absence of signals. If the subject is in the uncertain state, he responds "yes" or "no" with probabilities that depend on the subjective probability of a signal. Atkinson assumed that the subject learns a subjective probability through the process described by stimulus sampling theory (presented in Section 3). Atkinson's model has been used to analyze detailed properties of performance in detection and recognition experiments, especially sequential dependencies in response.

Recent work in the theory of detection has included the development of detailed hypotheses about sensory mechanisms. For example, Jeffress (1968) has developed an electrical model of hearing. An important feature of the model is the inclusion of a band-pass filter, which represents an hypothesis that the subject is especially attentive to stimulus inputs with frequencies in the neighborhood of the signal. The circuit also includes a half-wave rectifier and a leaky integrator. The circuit mimics a number of the features of human monaural detection. Jeffress' investigation included using the output of the electrical model to develop hypotheses about the distributions of Ω (SN, N) on trials with noise alone and with a signal combined with noise. In the original version of the theory of signal detectability, discussed above, the assumption was that the distributions were normal. Jeffress' results suggest that the distributions are noncentral chi, a distribution that is similar but not identical to the normal.

Sperling and Sondhi (1968) have given a model of photopic

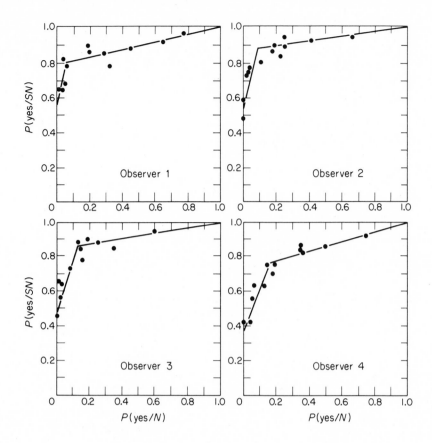

Fig. 8-28. *Data of Swets, Tanner, and Birdsall (1961) compared with theoretical ROC's derived from a model postulating two thresholds.* [From Krantz (1969), pp. 320–21. Copyright 1969 by the American Psychological Association and reproduced by permission.]

vision which is worked out in mathematical detail. The hypothesis is that the visual system has properties like those of an electrical circuit containing three main kinds of components. The simplest kind of component is a low-pass filter p stages. This determines the upper limit on the speed of response in the system, and thus represents a limit of temporal resolution. The output of the jth stage of this filter depends on the input of the preceding stage according to the formula

$$\tau_p \frac{d}{dt} v_j(t) + v_j(t) = v_{j-1}(t),$$

where $v_{j-1}(t)$ and $v_j(t)$ are the outputs of the $j-1^{st}$ and j^{th} stages of the filter, and τ_p is the time constant of the filter.

A second kind of component in Sperling and Sondhi's model is a parametric-feedback filter with n stages. This component has the property that the transformation that it imposes on its input depends on its current output. Its main function in the system is to compress the dynamic range of the inputs. Sperling and Sondhi observe that the dynamic range of photopic stimuli is on the order of 10^7, but the physiological mechanisms of the visual system (neuron spike rates and propagated neuron potentials) have a range on the order of 10^3. A compression in range from 10^7 to 10^3 would be accomplished by a system containing a parametric-feedback filter with two stages.

If n is the number of stages, the output of each stage depends on the output of the preceding stage and the output of the nth stage according to

$$\frac{d}{d\lambda}(v_j)\lambda + v_j(\lambda)[1 + v_n(\lambda)] = v_{j-1}(\lambda),$$

where $\lambda = t/\tau_F$. Sperling and Sondhi report that a parametric-feedback filter has properties that are related to the power law (Eq. 73). The amplitude of transient responses and steady-state responses of the feedback filter, and the speed of response and the sensitivity of the filter all approach power functions of the input as the input stimulus increases in magnitude.

A third kind of component in the model is a delayed feedback filter. The effect of the component is to spread out the input signal in time. After the stimulus has been transformed by the feedforward filter, its magnitude no longer depends on the absolute magnitude of the stimulus, but depends on the magnitude of the input compared to the time-average of recent inputs. Thus, the inclusion of a delayed feedforward filter makes the model a Weber-law system; that is, it is sensitive to the ratio of an input relative to a steady baseline. The output of the filter is governed by the equations

$$\frac{d}{d\lambda} v_1(\lambda) + v_1(\lambda)[1 + v_0'(\lambda)] = v_0(\lambda),$$

$$\frac{\tau_0}{\tau_F d\lambda} \frac{d}{d\lambda} v_0'(\lambda) + v_0'(\lambda) = v_0(\lambda).$$

The final component of the model is a threshold detector. It is assumed that there is a threshold ϵ, and the output of the threshold detector is either one or zero, depending on whether the output of the system exceeds ϵ. Let Y be the output of the threshold detector.

$$Y = \begin{cases} 1 \text{ if } |v| > \epsilon, \\ 0 \text{ if } |v| \le \epsilon. \end{cases}$$

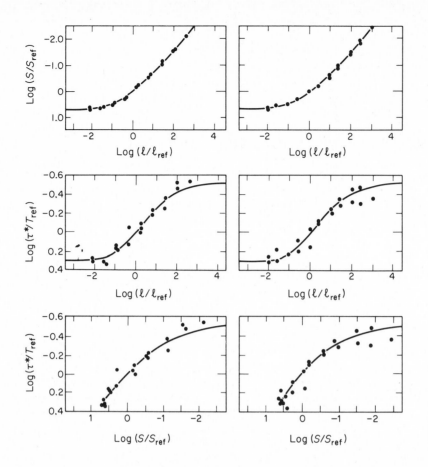

Fig. 8-29. *Relationships between sensitivity S, critical duration τ*, and luminance ℓ, for data obtained by Herrick (1956), left panels, and by Graham and Kemp (1938), right panels. Data include varying durations of increment and decrement pulses. Solid lines represent theoretical functions.* [From Sperling and Sondhi (1968), p. 1137]

Sperling and Sondhi analyzed data reported by Graham and Kemp (1938) and by Herrick (1956) on luminance discrimination. They assumed that the feedback filter has two stages, and the low-pass filter has six stages. The data were reported in terms of three variables: S, the sensitivity or reciprocal of threshold energy; τ^*, a critical duration such that for $t < \tau^*$ detection depends on the product of luminance and duration; and the independent variable ℓ, the luminance of the flash. Fig. 8-29 shows the relationships between the three variables, compared with theoretical functions obtained from the model.

DECISION FACTORS IN RECOGNITION

The ideas developed in the theory of signal detectability have been extended and applied to the analysis of recognition memory. One model of recognition memory was given by Wickelgren and Norman (1966). They analyzed an experiment in which lists of three-digit numbers were pronounced by the experimenter at the rate of one per second. In different sessions, lists of different lengths were used, with list-length ranging from two to seven. After a list was presented, a single three-digit number was presented, and the subject was asked whether this item had been in the list. The subject also rated his confidence in whether his response was correct on a five-point scale.

Wickelgren and Norman considered a variety of models about the processes involved in the experiment. According to the model that was most favored by the data, the presentation of an item in the kth position produces a trace in memory with

strength a_k. Then when each succeeding item is presented, the strength of the trace decays to a constant fraction f of its preceding strength. Let L be the number of items in the list. After the last item is presented, the strength of the kth item is

$$d(k, L) = a_k f^{L-k}. \qquad \textbf{[64]}$$

The strength given in Eq. 64 is assumed to be the mean of a distribution of trace strengths, and the distributions are all assumed to be normal with a variance arbitrarily set at one. New items are assumed to have strengths distributed with mean zero.

By collecting confidence ratings, Wickelgren and Norman were able to obtain several points on the operating characteristic without repeating the experiment using different motivational conditions. However, we will consider only one aspect of the data; the probability of giving a correct "yes" response for old items that have been presented at different positions in lists of different lengths. Fig. 8-30 shows the data along with predicted functions obtained by estimating two values of a (one for the first position, and a single value for the other positions) and a value of f for each subject. The agreement between the data and the theory demonstrates that it is appropriate to analyze recognition memory in terms of a concept of trace strength, and that there is an orderly relationship between this hypothetical variable and the number of items studied between the presentation of an item and its test.

A somewhat different approach to the analysis of recognition memory was used by Bernbach (1967), who assumed that there are only two underlying distributions of strength, f_o and f_n, with means differing by an amount d^*. In Bernbach's model,

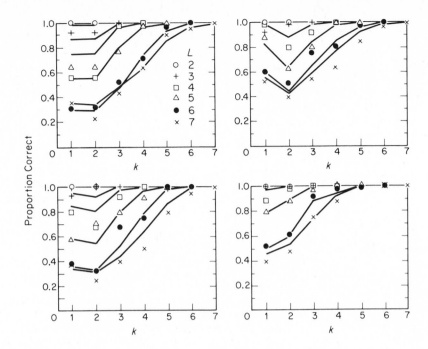

Fig. 8-30. *Proportions correct recognition of items presented in position* k *in lists of length* L, *for four subjects.* [From Wickelgren and Norman (1966)]

any new item has a strength consisting of a sample value taken from f_n. When an item is presented, it receives a strength consisting of a sample value of f_o. During the time between study and test forgetting may occur, so at the time of a test, the distribution of strengths for old items is a mixture of strengths taken from f_n and f_o. If b is the probability of forgetting, then the difference between old and new items will be

$$d' = (1 - b)d*. \qquad [65]$$

Thus, if there are two conditions and one of them has more forgetting, then that condition will produce poorer recognition. However, the theoretical reason for the difference is not a more-or-less uniform decay of strength of all the traces, but rather an all-or-none loss of strength of some proportion of the items.

An analysis similar to Bernbach's (1967) was given by Kintsch (1967). Kintsch's model also postulates two underlying distributions of trace strength, but there is a threshold strength which separates old items into two states; a state of temporary or short-term memory from which forgetting can occur, as in Bernbach's model, and a state of permanent memory from which forgetting does not occur under the conditions of the experiment. Transitions from the unlearned state (where strengths have distribution f_n) occur to the two memory states (where strengths have distribution f_o) on presentation trials. And transitions from the short-term state to the unlearned state occur when other items are being presented. The result is a model with discrete states corresponding to those of the Markov model presented in Section 2, but with corresponding distributions of trace strength to permit analyses of variables like confidence ratings that require assumptions of a continuous dimension of trace strength.

TEMPORAL VARIABLES IN PATTERN RECOGNITION

A common experimental method for studying properties of perceptual processing involves presenting material briefly and measuring the amount that an observer can perceive. The obvious result is that with longer periods of exposure an individual can perceive more. But given that, it is useful to examine the exact functional relationships between exposure time and perceptual accuracy under varying conditions to guide the development of theories about the way that perception occurs in real time.

In recent years, a number of experimental innovations have led to new hypotheses about the process of visual pattern recognition. The main ideas have been introduced in a number of articles, including Sperling (1967), Wolford, Wessel, and Estes (1968), and Ericksen (1966). A number of concepts have been brought together and given a precise formulation by Rumelhart (1970).

In Rumelhart's model, the process of pattern recognition is basically a process of extracting features from a visual display. The number of features that can be extracted in a given time is a random variable, and a pattern is recognized if a sufficient number of its features are extracted. Let T be the amount of time that the display is present. During the interval (O, T) it is assumed that features are extracted at a constant average rate so that

$$\lim_{\Delta t \to 0} \frac{\Delta p(t)}{\Delta t} = v \qquad (0 \leq t \leq T) \qquad [66]$$

where $\Delta p(t)$ is the probability that a feature is extracted during a small interval of time Δt. After the display is taken away, it is assumed that the visual information does not immediately go away, but is stored in the sensory system for a time. On the other hand, the visual information decays—probably quite rapidly—and it is assumed that this decay follows an exponential function. Further, the removal of the target display may coincide with the presentation of other material, so there may be an immediate degradation of the visual information by some amount a. The combination of these factors is expressed by a formula for the average rate of extracting features after the visual display is removed.

$$\lim_{\Delta t \to 0} \frac{\Delta p(t)}{\Delta t} = ave^{-(t-T)/u} \qquad (t > T) \qquad \text{[67]}$$

One set of data analyzed by Rumelhart was collected by Sperling (1960), who measured the number of letters that could be correctly reported after a 50 msec. flash with a varying number of letters in the display. Rumelhart assumed that the subject divides his attention equally among the N letters, so that when a feature is extracted, the probability that it comes from any given letter is $1/N$. A letter is reported correctly if c of its features are extracted. Rumelhart derived a formula for the mean number of reported letters $E(R)$ as a function of the number of displayed letters, N.

$$E(R) = N \sum_{k=c}^{\infty} \frac{\left[\frac{v}{N}(T+u)\right]^k}{k!} \exp\left[-\frac{v}{N}(T+u)\right] \qquad \text{[68]}$$

(In this situation, it was assumed that $a = 1$.)

In a second set of conditions, Sperling showed a matrix of letters, and then sounded a tone indicating which of the rows the subjects should try to report. In this partial report procedure, subjects were able to give a higher proportion of the letters. In Rumelhart's model, this occurs because the subject is able to restrict his attention to processing the visual information about the n letters in the cued row. For the data to be considered here, the cue was presented immediately upon the offset of the visual display. Sperling reported his data using a measure of "letters available," the average number of letters from the cued row of n, multiplied by N/n, where N was the total number of letters in the display. The formula for the expected value of this measure derived from Rumelhart's model is

$$E(A) = N \sum_{k=c}^{\infty} \frac{\left[v\left(\frac{T}{N} + \frac{u}{n}\right)\right]^k}{k!} \exp\left[-v\left(\frac{T}{N} + \frac{u}{n}\right)\right] \qquad \text{[69]}$$

Parameters were estimated separately for five subjects. Values of c ranged from 1.45 to 2.50; v ranged from .025 to .090; and u ranged from 106 to 399. The data for the five subjects, along with the theoretical functions calculated from Eqs. 68 and 69, are given in Fig. 8-31.

Another set of data that Rumelhart analyzed in detail was obtained by Estes and Taylor (1964). Displays of varying sizes were presented to subjects for brief periods, as in the Sperling study. In one condition, subjects, were asked to report as many of the letters as they could. In another condition, subjects were asked only to say whether the display contained a "B" or an "F." The proportion of correct detections was multiplied by the number of elements in the display and called the "number of elements processed." Rumelhart assumed that processing in both conditions would be carried out according to the assumptions leading to Eq. 69, but that c would be higher for the report condition than for the detection condition. He estimated a single value of $v(T + u) = 16.4$; the estimates of c were 1.92 and 1.15 for the report and detection conditions, respectively. His theoretical functions, along with Estes and Taylor's data, are shown in Fig. 8-32.

The last of Rumelhart's analyses to be presented here is an application of his model to backward masking. In a parametric experiment Thompson (1966) presented one of three letters for 18.7 msec., followed by a 100 msec. flash of .039, .067, .102, or .200 foot lamberts, with delay of 0, 5, 10, 25, 50, or 75 msec. between the offset of the letter and the onset of the flash. The equation from the model for proportion correct is

$$P(R) = \sum_{k=c}^{\infty} \frac{m^k}{k!} e^{-m}$$

where

$$m = v(T + u) - (1 - a)vu \, e^{-(\tau - T)/u}. \qquad \text{[70]}$$

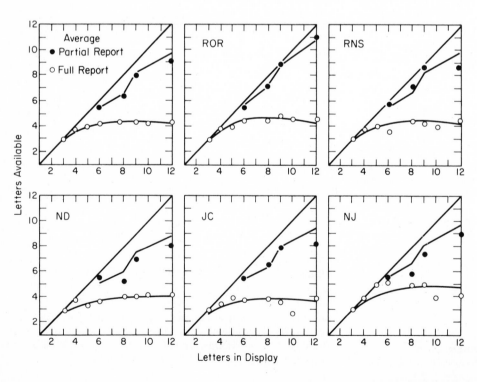

Fig. 8-31. *Data from Sperling's (1960) experiment on tachistoscopic recognition, compared with theoretical functions.* [From Rumelhart (1970)]

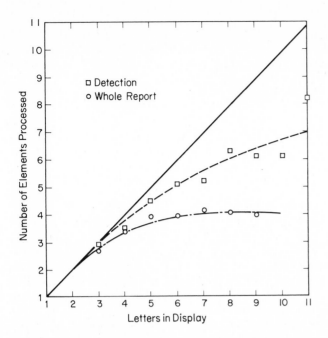

Fig. 8-32. *Data from Estes and Taylor's (1964) experiment on tachistoscopic recognition and detection, compared with theoretical functions.* [From Rumelhart (1970)]

The value of τ is the delay between the target and the masking flash, and a is a parameter which depends on the intensity of masking.

Rumelhart estimated a single value for each of the parameters c, v, T, and u, obtaining the values 1.99, .08, 2.4, and 47.8, respectively. The values of a for the four intensities were .58, .40, .17, and .00. The theoretical functions are presented

along with the empirical proportions of correct responses obtained by Thompson in Fig. 8-33.

An interesting problem involving temporal properties of recognition was studied by Sternberg (1966). Suppose that a subject sees a small set of items, such as digits, and then sees another item. His task is to decide whether the last item was a member of the set. Sternberg used sets of from one to six digits, and showed each digit for 1.2 seconds. Then there was a 2.0 second delay, after which a warning signal was given and then the test digit appeared. The subject had two levers; one was for positive responses, indicating that the test stimulus was in the study set, the other was for negative responses. The subjects gave correct responses on nearly all trials (98.6%), and the data of interest are the times taken to respond. The results are in Fig. 8-34.

First, consider the latencies of positive responses, shown as filled circles in Fig. 8-34. The data agree very well with a straight line that has a slope of about 38 milliseconds per symbol. In other words, if the size of the set is increased by one symbol, there is a constant addition to the amount of time that it takes to decide that a given symbol was in the set. Sternberg used this fact to draw an interesting conclusion about the process of recognizing an item as being in the set. He concluded that when a test item was shown, the subject scanned the set of items he had memorized in a serial fashion. If all of the items were available simultaneously so that comparisons could be made in parallel, there would not have been a linear relationship between set size and time to respond. (The simplest kind of parallel comparison process would give a function with zero slope. However, if it were assumed that the process involved comparisons taking random amounts of time, then there should be increased time with increased set size but the function should not be linear. The dashed line in Fig. 8-34 shows the upper bound on the amount of increase to be expected from a parallel process.)

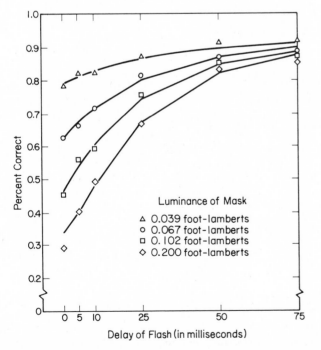

Fig. 8-33. *Data from Thompson's (1966) backward masking experiment compared with theoretical functions.* [From Rumelhart (1970)]

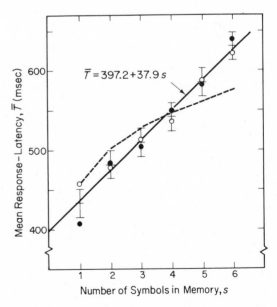

Fig. 8-34. *Mean latency of positive responses (filled circles) and negative responses (open circles) as a function of the number of items in memory, s.* [From Sternberg (1966), Fig. 1; copyright 1966 by the American Association for the Advancement of Science.]

A second aspect of the data led Sternberg to conclude that the comparison with memorized items was exhaustive—that is, the subject scanned the contents of memory by examining one member at a time, and went through the entire set before initiating a response. The data bearing on this comparison involve comparing positive and negative responses. If the comparison process were serial and exhaustive, then the slope of the function should be equal for positive and negative responses, as it apparently was, especially if we consider mainly the cases involving set sizes two through six. However, consider an alternative process, where the subject terminates his search when he finds a positive comparison. In a self-terminating process, the subject would have to go through the entire set before initiating a negative response, but on the average, positive responses could be initiated when about one-half of the set members had been examined. In that case, the slope of the latency function for positive responses would be about one-half as great as for negative responses, a result that clearly is inconsistent with the data. Thus, Sternberg's data support the idea that when a set of items is held in immediate memory and a new item is shown, the decision whether the new item is a member of the set is made by scanning the elements in the memory set one by one, with the entire set examined before a response is initiated.

JUDGMENTS OF STIMULUS MAGNITUDE

In addition to processes of detecting and recognizing stimuli, the psychology of perception includes analyses of judgments about quantitative properties of stimuli. One of the classical problems in psychophysics is the determination of functional relationships between the physical magnitudes of a set of stimuli and the judgments that subjects give in response to the stimuli. An experiment about judgments that has a simple structure, called magnitude estimation, has a subject who gives a numerical response J for each stimulus. Stevens (1957) has shown that these judgments often are in approximate agreement with a power-law relationship with physical magnitude, H. That is,

$$J = cH^p,$$ [73]

where p is an empirical parameter and c is an arbitrary constant.

An hypothesis that is consistent with Stevens' result is that subjects perceive stimulus magnitudes in the form of ratios. A necessary and sufficient condition for the power law to hold is that for all pairs of stimuli i and k,

$$\frac{J_i}{J_k} = \left(\frac{H_i}{H_k}\right)^p,$$

for some constant p. Thus, Stevens' finding of a power-law relationship between physical and judged magnitudes makes it reasonable to assume that judgments are based mainly on ratios of physical magnitude. On this assumption, judgments are relative, depending on the relationship of the judged stimulus to other stimuli, rather than on the absolute physical magnitude of the stimulus.

The idea of perceptual relativity, depending on perception of ratios, is the basis of a model given by Helson (1964) for judgments stimulus magnitudes. The central notion in Helson's model is the idea of an adaptation level or reference point for judgments. The judgment of any stimulus depends on the ratio of its magnitude to the adaptation level, A.

$$J = H/A.$$ [74]

The value of A represents a combination of the subject's experience with stimuli of different magnitudes. In Helson's formulation, A is a weighted geometric mean of stimulus magnitudes

$$A = (H_1^{w_1} H_2^{w_2} \cdots H_n^{w_n})^{1/\sum_{i=1}^{n} w_i},$$

$$\log A = \frac{\sum_{i=1}^{n} w_i \log H_i}{\sum_{i=1}^{n} w_i}$$ [75]

The weight w associated with a stimulus is a measure of its contribution to the subject's frame of reference. Thus, w should be large if a stimulus is perceptually salient, and if it is presented frequently in the situation, or if it has been presented recently, rather than in the distant past.

A frequent use of Helson's adaptation level theory is in the analysis of experiments where stimulus backgrounds are manipulated systematically. An illustration is provided by an experiment by Restle, reported by Restle and Greeno (1970). Subjects judged the lengths of lines having squares of various sizes at the ends. The lines subtended visual angles of 12, 16, 20, 24, and 28 min. The sides of the squares subtended visual angles of 8, 12, 16, 20, 24, and 28 min. On each trial, the subject

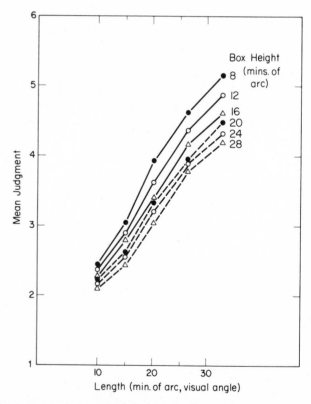

Fig. 8-35. *Judged length of a line, as a function of actual length, for lines displayed between boxes of varying size.* [From Restle and Greeno (1970)]

judged the length of the line and indicated his judgment by pushing one of six buttons. Fig. 8-35 shows the mean judgment plotted against physical line length, with box size as the parameter. This merely shows that the experimental variable had orderly effects on the judgments, with judgments tending to be smaller when box size was larger.

The overall effect of box size is in the direction expected by adaptation-level theory. With a large box, A will be larger than it is with a smaller box. Then, by Eq. 74, the value of J will be smaller with larger boxes than with smaller boxes. For a precise analysis, assume that on any trial, A depends on the line length X, the box size B, and other factors K that include the dimensions of the experimental room and the effects of previous trials, which are assumed to be relatively constant. Then

$$\log A = \frac{x \log X + b \log B + k \log k}{x + b + k}.$$

For abbreviation, let

$$x' = \frac{x}{x + b + k}, \qquad b' = \frac{b}{x + b + k}.$$

Then

$$\log A = x' \log X + b' \log B + (1 - x' - b') \log K.$$

Using Eq. 74, the judgments should agree with the formula

$$\log J = (1 - x') \log X - b' \log B + C, \qquad [76]$$

where C is a constant.

The data gave estimates of the parameters $x' = .054$, $b' = .108$. The data are replotted in Fig. 8-36, in the form of logarithms of log J plotted as a function of log X (averaged over

log B) and also as a function of log B (averaged over log X). The data apparently agree with the prediction of linear function, implied by the adaptation level assumptions.

The general problem dealt with in adaptation-level theory is understanding the appearances of stimuli. The theory of adaptation level can be applied in situations where the dimensional structure of both the physical and the subjective appearances is simple, involving a single dimension of variance. Krantz (1968) has given an analysis that is more general, using the idea that structural properties of the appearances of stimuli can be inferred from changes in appearance that are produced by changes in context. Krantz' analysis uses a number of technical properties of abstract algebra, which will not be developed in this discussion. However, a special case of his analysis gives some of the basic ideas.

The major substantive idea of Krantz' analysis is the invariance of transformations across contexts. Consider two different contexts S and T. An example would involve two of the box sizes used in Restle's experiment, described above. Now consider two different stimuli X and Y (line lengths in the example) which appear the same when they are shown in the different contexts. If stimulus X in context T appears the same as stimulus Y in context S, denote

$$J_T(X) = J_S(Y).$$

Now consider a transformation of stimulus X. With stimuli that can be described using simple quantities, a transformation might be the addition of a certain quantity to stimulus X or multiplication of the magnitude of X by a certain quantity. Denote the transformation of X by $f(X)$. Now suppose that we fix a transformation f, and we find stimuli X, Y, and Z, such that

$$J_T(X) = J_S(Y), \text{ and } J_T[f(X)] = J_S(Z). \qquad [77]$$

That is, Y and Z are stimuli that are judged the same as X and $f(X)$, respectively, when X and $f(X)$ have context T and Y and Z have context S. Finally, given the situation described by Eq. 77, suppose that we can find transformations g and h to apply to stimuli Y and Z, respectively, so that

$$J_S[g(Y)] = J_S[h(Z)]. \qquad [78]$$

That is, we find ways to change Y and Z so that they are judged the same in context S. In fact, there should be a family of pairs of pairs of transformations (G, H) that will satisfy Eq. 78.

The idea of invariance of transformations over contexts is that a transformation like f, operating on stimuli in one context, can be represented by a family of differences between transformations like (g, h), operating in another context. This requires that in case Eqs. 77 and 78 hold for transformations f, g, and h, applied to stimulus X and the stimuli Y and Z that match X and $f(X)$, then Eqs. 77 and 78 should hold regardless of our selection of X, for all pairs of transformations g and h in the family (G, H).

Krantz' analysis can be illustrated using the theory of adaptation level, in the situation used by Restle and described above. Consider two contexts consisting of boxes of size B_S and B_T. Now select any line length X. If a line of length X is judged with a box of size B_T, the judged length of X will be

$$J_T(X) = X^{1 - s'} B_T^{-b'} K^{-(1 - s' - b')}.$$

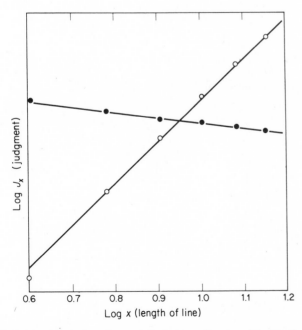

Fig. 8-36. *Logarithm of mean judgment as a function of log line length (open circles) and of log box size (filled circles). The linear relationships agree with Eq. 76.* [From Restle and Greeno (1970)]

Now let Y be the length of a line judged with a box of size B_S.

$$J_S(Y) = Y^{1-s'}B_S - b'K^{-(1-s'-b')}.$$

For X and Y to be judged equal, $J_T(X) = J_S(Y)$. Then

$$Y = X\left(\frac{B_T}{B_S}\right)^{b'/(1-s')}. \qquad [79]$$

Now, consider a transformation of X,

$$f_A(X) = X + a,$$

the addition of a specified magnitude to the length of X. A stimulus in context S that matches $f_A(X)$ would be

$$Z = (X + a)\left(\frac{B_T}{B_S}\right)^{b'/(1-s')}.$$

The question is whether we can produce changes in Y and Z that will produce stimuli that are judged equal in context S. Clearly, an appropriate family of transformations exists.

$$g(Y) = Y + v, \quad h(Z) = Z + v - a\left(\frac{B_T}{B_S}\right)^{b'/(1-s')},$$

since these transformations will produce identical stimulus magnitudes. Now, consider another transformation of X,

$$f_M(X) = mX, \quad m \geq 0.$$

In this case, the magnitude of Y is unchanged from Eq. 79, but a stimulus that matches $f_M(X)$ would be

$$Z = (mX)\left(\frac{B_T}{B_S}\right)^{b'/(1-s')},$$

and transformations that produce equivalent stimuli in S are

$$g(Y) = mu\,Y, \quad h(Z) = uZ, \quad u \geq 0.$$

In systems that agree with adaptation-level theory, the transformations of adding a fixed quantity or multiplying by a non-negative number are both invariant across contexts, in Krantz' sense. However, the multiplicative transformation is simpler in that it does not depend on the particular contexts that are considered. This relates to the fact, mentioned earlier, that adaptation-level theory is based on the assumption that perceived quantities depend on ratios of physical magnitude.

Krantz' analysis is more interesting and significant in cases where stimuli are not described simply as unidimensional quantities. As an example, Krantz cited results of experiments on matching of colors in different surrounds. An appropriate description of a colored stimulus is a vector of values referring to three hypothetical physiological systems. The transformation used was addition of colored lights, which was represented as vector addition. The results supported the idea that additive transformations of energy distributions are invariant across certain kinds of change in context. The application of Krantz' analysis can lead to systematic descriptions of the structure of perceptual relationships among complex systems, and to inferences about the processes underlying these perceptions.

The preceding discussion has dealt with judgments of single stimuli. Often, information about an object is not received all at once, and the person must integrate several pieces of infor-

mation received in a sequence. Anderson (1968) has given a simple model of information integration. Anderson's model asserts that the overall impression formed about an object or set of objects is a weighted average of values of separate pieces of information. If there are n pieces of information, the overall judgment is

$$J = \frac{\sum_{i=1}^{n} w_i s_i}{\sum_{i=1}^{u} w_i}, \qquad [80]$$

where s_i is the scale value or judgment of the ith piece of information, and w_i is the contribution of the ith piece of information. The different pieces of information may be in the form of items presented in a sequence, as in the example below, or in the form of different aspects of a single stimulus, such as the weight and volume of an object (Anderson 1970).

In one experiment, Anderson (1967) presented different series of weights of 2 and 6 oz. Each series had six weights, but the first two, the second two, and the last two were always the same. For example, the series HLH had the 6-oz weight presented twice, then the 2-oz weight twice, and then the 6-oz weight twice. After all six weights were lifted, the subject judged the overall weight of the series on a 20-point scale. Anderson hypothesized that each of the two stimuli would have a scale value, and the contribution of each stimulus would vary with the position in the series. Thus, the analysis involves four parameters, s_H, s_L, and two parameters determining the relative contributions

$$w_1' = \frac{w_1}{\sum_{i=1}^{3} w_i}, \qquad w_2' = \frac{w_2}{\sum_{i=1}^{3} w_i}.$$

For example, the judgment for the series LHL should be

$$J = w_1's_L + w_2's_H + (1 - w_1' - w_2')s_L.$$

Table 8-2 shows Anderson's data, compared with theoretical values of J obtained with the estimates $s_H = 19.23$, $s_L = 2.11$, $w_1' = .29$, $w_2' = .32$. The agreement between predicted and obtained values is quite satisfactory.

Table 8-2. **Theoretical and Empirical Judgments of Series of Weights**

Series	Theoretical	Empirical
HHH	19.2	19.6
HHL	12.6	12.4
HLH	13.8	13.8
LHH	14.3	14.1
HLL	7.1	7.0
LHL	7.6	7.6
LLH	8.8	8.4
LLL	2.1	2.4

Data from Anderson (1967).

5. Conditioning

For at least two decades, from 1940 to 1960, systematic theory in psychology was predominately concerned with the problem of finding relationships between performance and outcome-contingencies in the experimental environment. Changes in performance related to these contingencies were definitionally equated with learning by the major theorists (see Hilgard and Bower, 1966). The experimental situations used to study learning, in this sense, involved various forms of conditioning which were thought to reveal principles of behavior modification in its simplest form. Studies of conditioning in animals were especially popular, presumably because the study of subhumans permitted observation of behavior change that was not influenced by verbal mechanisms. It is an interesting historical fact that the simplest structures that are apparently needed to give quantitative analyses of conditioning are comparable to the most complex models that were described earlier in discussing human problem solving and memory. This, of course, does not imply that the processes of human cognition are simpler than those of conditioning. It may be that the greater simplicity that has been achieved in models of human cognition results from greater experimental control that is possible when one human being communicates directly with another about the nature of a task.

Aversive Conditioning in Rats

A few sample results will be presented from the work of Theios and his associates on aversive conditioning. In addition to the sources to be mentioned, a summary and discussion of the work has been given by Theios (1969).

In a standard avoidance-conditioning experiment, a rat is placed in a compartment with a metal grid floor. Each trial begins with the presentation of a warning signal, at which time the rat can move from the compartment to another part of the apparatus. At a fixed short time after the warning signal, an electric current is passed through the floor, so if the rat has not moved away he receives a shock. A successful avoidance of the shock is a correct response; failure to avoid is counted as an error.

In a model given by Theios and Brelsford (1966) it is assumed that learning to avoid the shock involves two discrete stages. The first stage involves establishing a connection between the warning stimulus and the response of running out of the compartment, mediated permanently. However, the connection between the warning stimulus and the emotional response may only be stored in temporary memory.

The second stage of learning involves storing the connection between the warning stimulus and the emotional response in permanent memory. This permanent storage may occur on the trial when the connection is first established; this has probability b. If the stimulus-arousal connection is only stored in temporary memory, there is probability p that the subject will perform an avoidance response on the next trial. On each trial when the connection is in temporary memory, there is probability c that it will be stored in permanent memory.[8] If it is not stored in permanent memory, it is reinstated in temporary memory, so that the probability of an avoidance response on the next trial again is p.

[8]Theios and Brelsford actually assumed that there was probability c of permanently storing the connection only if the subject made an error. However, the empirical implications of the model are not different from the version described here.

The structure of this conditioning model is the same as that of the two-stage model for memorizing described in Section 2 (recall Fig. 8-8). Theios (1969) presented data from a number of experiments, showing that the model agrees with the results of many experiments. This is important in itself, but more significant results were obtained by comparing the estimated values of the model's parameters in different experimental conditions. Theios and Brelsford (1966) had one group of subjects run in the standard way, and another group of subjects that were trapped and not permitted to escape if they failed to run before the shock. According to the assumptions described above, the procedure of trapping the subjects would be expected to retard the process of forming a connection between the stimulus and the instrumental response of running, and thus reduce the value of a, the probability of completing the first stage of learning. This is what happened, and the two groups did not differ significantly in the values of parameters b, c, and p. This result supports the idea that the second stage of learning involves fixing the classically conditioned connection between the warning stimulus and arousal.

Another interesting set of experiments was carried out by Brelsford (1967). First, Brelsford ran a study in which he omitted the shock after a subject's first avoidance response. Brelsford's hypothesis was that some proportion of subjects would make no errors after the first avoidance, but the others who eventually would make an error would make only errors until they received another shock. Then there would be a proportion of subjects with no more errors, but the remaining subjects would again make an error eventually and continue to make errors until a shock was given. The experiment succeeded; Brelsford obtained the predicted runs of errors following a failure to avoid, and the performance of the extinction group was successfully predicted using parameters estimated from a control group.

In a second experiment Brelsford gave 20 classical conditioning trials involving pairings of the warning stimulus and shock before the subjects were allowed to escape or avoid the shock. The hypothesis of this experiment was that the pretraining trials would establish a permanent connection between the warning stimulus and emotional arousal, so that after avoidance training was started only the instrumental running response would have to be connected to the arousal state. This idea was supported by the results, since the pretrained subjects made only an average of 1.1 errors during the avoidance conditioning trials.

Brelsford's third experiment involved presenting a brief shock along with the warning stimulus on each trial. A control group was used to show that the brief shock by itself was not sufficiently strong to produce the running response. But Brelsford hypothesized that the shock would ensure memory of a connection between the warning stimulus and arousal, after that connection had been established. This idea implies that subjects receiving a brief shock along with the warning stimulus should not make errors after the first avoidance response, and this strong prediction was confirmed by the performance of 65 of Brelsford's 70 subjects.

Human Eyelid Conditioning

Another conditioning situation that has been given quantitative analysis is human eyelid conditioning. The analysis was carried out by Prokasy and Harsanyi (1968), using the model given by Norman (1964b) with estimation techniques developed by Theios (1968). Like the model described above for avoidance conditioning, the model for eyelid conditioning assumes that there are two main stages of learning. However, there is a nonzero probability of response in the initial stage, and the final probability of response is less than one. Also, instead of having just one intermediate level of performance, performance is assumed to change gradually from the initial level to the final level.

There is some trial k on which the first stage of learning is achieved. On trials 1 through k, the subject's performance is constant. After trial k, performance improves in a regular fashion, approaching an asymptote. The learning process is described by four parameters; p_0, the initial probability of response; k, the trial before the first change in response probability; θ, the rate of change in response probability after trial k; and p_∞, the asymptotic response probability. Let p_n be the probability of response on trial n. According to the model,

$$P_n = \begin{cases} p_0 \text{ for } n < k, \\ p_\infty - (p_\infty - p_0)(1 - \theta)^{n-k} \text{ for } n > k. \end{cases}$$

Prokasy and Harsanyi (1968) carried out an eyelid conditioning experiment where the conditioned stimulus was presented by turning on a light which the subject saw through a red cutglass jewel. One-half second after the light went on, a puff of nitrogen was delivered to the subject's eye. The air puff lasted for 50 milliseconds, and had different pressures for subjects in different groups; 100, 150, and 200 ml of mercury.

The experiment used a series of 280 trials following an adaptation sequence, giving enough data to permit separate estimates of the parameters for individual subjects. The model was tested by using a computer to simulate the performance of groups of subjects having the parameter values estimated for the experimental subjects; the agreement between the simulated performance and the data was generally good. The average values of the parameters for subjects in the different experimental conditions were calculated and these means permit inferences about the way in which intensity of the unconditioned stimulus influenced the learning process.

The values of p_0 for the three groups were .09, .09, and .10; this merely shows that the groups were comparable at the beginning. A second parameter, θ, also did not differ systematically among the groups. The means of the estimates of θ were .16, .20, and .17 for the groups receiving unconditioned stimuli having 100, 150, and 200 mls of pressure. Values of k and p_∞ apparently were influenced by the experimental variable. The means of the estimates of k were 25.7, 10.6, and 10.0, indicating that the first stage of learning took longer to accomplish when the unconditioned stimulus was weak. And the means of the estimates of p_∞ were .69, .74, and .84, indicating that stronger unconditioned stimuli produced higher levels of asymptotic performance.

An important use of mathematical models is illustrated by Prokasy and Harsanyi's analysis. An experimental variable—in this case, the intensity of the unconditioned stimulus—presumably affects some aspects of the process being studied and not others. In this analysis, the effect seems to have involved the rate of completing the first stage of learning and the terminal level of performance, but not the rate of learning in the second

stage. This fact in itself is not sufficient to support any detailed hypotheses about the nature of conditioning, but as analytic methods are developed and applied to a variety of experimental manipulations, it seems likely that the results will permit development of specific hypotheses about the processes involved in conditioning.

ANIMAL DISCRIMINATION LEARNING

Investigators interested in animal conditioning have been particularly concerned with discrimination learning, where the animal subject has to learn an appropriate response to a specific aspect of the stimulus situation. In a common type of experiment, called simultaneous discrimination, a rat is placed in front of two alleys or doors and the choices are associated with several stimulus differences. Obviously, one difference is position—one is on the left and the other is on the right. Other differences are introduced, such as color (one alley black and the other white), or the size of a circle painted on each door (one large and the other small), or the orientation of a bar painted on each door (one horizontal and the other vertical). One of the stimulus dimensions is chosen by the experimenter as the relevant dimension, and if the rat chooses the positive value of that dimension (also chosen by the experimenter) he gets fed after his choice. From trial to trial the combinations of values on the various dimensions are changed. For example, on the first trial, there might be a black door with large circle and horizontal bar on the left (so that white, small, vertical would be on the right). Then on the second trial, the white door with a large circle and vertical bar might be on the left (with black, small, horizontal on the right). The experimenter might decide to use the circlesize as the relevant dimension, and feed the subject for choosing the large circle. Then in the example mentioned above, food would be on the left side on both of the trials described.

Lovejoy (1968) has given a model of simultaneous discrimination learning. According to Lovejoy's model, learning occurs at two levels. At one level, animals learn which of the stimulus dimensions to attend to, so that after a large number of trials, subjects attend primarily to the relevant stimulus dimensions. The other learning process involves the choice of a response, conditional on attending to a given stimulus dimension, so that after a large number of trials animals will choose the positive value of the relevant dimension.

Each stimulus dimension has a distinctiveness value which has a fixed component D_i. If a dimension has a high value of D, it will get a relatively large amount of attention. In addition, there is an amount of directable distinctiveness which is divided among the cues. On each trial each cue has some amount of this directable distinctiveness $d_{i,n}$, and the total amount of directable distinctiveness is

$$\sum_{i=1}^{N} d_{i,n} = 1,$$

where N is the number of stimulus dimensions.

For each dimension there is a response strength for choosing each of the two alternative values. The strength for choosing value 1 of dimension i is $V_{i,n}$ and the strength for choosing value 2 is $1 - V_{i,n}$. Lovejoy assumed that on each trial, the subject's response is controlled by a single dimension. There is a control strength C for each dimension, depending on the dimension's distinctiveness, and the relative strengths of the responses for that dimension,

$$C_{i,n} = \frac{D_i + d_{i,n}}{V_{i,n}(1 - V_{i,n})}.$$

The probability of being controlled by dimension i is

$$P(\text{control by } i) = \frac{C_{i,n}}{\sum_{j=1}^{N} C_{j,n}}.$$

Given control by dimension i, the probability of choice depends on V_i. Lovejoy assumed that there is a parameter m such that the probability of choosing value 1 is zero if $V_{i,n}$ is less than m, and the probability of choosing value 1 is one if $V_{i,n}$ is greater than $1 - m$. The formula relating V_i to response probability is

$$P(\text{choose value 1} \mid \text{control by } i)$$
$$= \begin{cases} 0 & \text{if } V_{i,n} < m \\ \dfrac{V_{i,n} - m}{1 - 2m} & \text{if } m \leq V_{i,n} \leq 1 - m \\ 1 & \text{if } V_{i,n} > 1 - m. \end{cases}$$

After a choice occurs, the animal either receives a reward or he does not. With probability r, he remembers what dimension he used for control of choice, and learns about that cue. With probability $1 - r$, he forgets which dimension he used, and resamples at random, with the probability of learning about a dimension proportional to the distinctiveness of the cue, $D_i + d_{i,n}$. The learning that takes place about a dimension consists of changing the response strengths for the alternatives on that dimension. If the animal receives a reward, the strength of the chosen response increases, and if the animal is not rewarded, the strength of the chosen response decreases. Keep in mind that the strength that is changed is for the dimension that controlled the choice if the animal remembers which dimension controlled the choice, otherwise it is for a randomly selected dimension. If the animal chose value 1 and was rewarded,

$$V_{i,n+1} = 1 - a_1(1 - V_{i,n}).$$

If value 2 was chosen and the animal was rewarded,

$$V_{i,n+1} = a_1 V_{i,n}.$$

If the animal chose value 1 and was not rewarded,

$$V_{i,n+1} = a_2 V_{i,n}.$$

And if value 2 was chosen and the animal was not rewarded,

$$V_{i,n+1} = 1 - a_2(1 - V_{i,n}).$$

Finally, Lovejoy assumed that on trials when the animal remembers which dimension was used to control the choice, the detectable distinctiveness of the dimensions changes. If the animal used cue i, and remembers that he used cue i, and was rewarded,

$$d_{i,n+1} = 1 - a_3(1 - d_{i,n}),$$
$$d_{j,n+1} = a_3 d_{j,n}, \qquad \text{for } j \neq i.$$

If the animal was not rewarded,

$$d_{i,n+1} = a_4 d_{i,n} + (1 - a_4)d_{i,1}, \qquad \text{for all } i.$$

On trials when the animal forgets which cue controlled the choice there are no changes in the directable distinctiveness.

Lovejoy did not fit his model to data from specific experiments. However, the assumptions of his model were carefully developed in relation to known facts about discrimination learning in rats, and he carried out computer simulation to show that a number of empirical findings are consistent with the assumptions of the model. For example, an experiment was simulated involving two dimensions: (1) color and (2) position. Parameter values for the simulation were $D_1 = .25$, $D_2 = 1.50$, $a_1 = .80$, $a_2 = .98$, $a_3 = a_4 = .97$, $r = .70$, $m = .20$. Forty sequences were simulated—simulation was carried out until a stat-rat met a criterion of 18 correct responses in 20 trials. Then each sequence was continued in two ways—a reversal was simulated, with the previously correct value of the relevant color dimension made incorrect, and also overtraining trials were simulated followed by reversal. Lovejoy reported several features of the simulation that agree with observations that often are obtained in experiments. First, the number of trials required for learning was highly variable—one stat-rat met the criterion after 51 trials, another took 245 trials. Secondly, position preferences appeared in the simulated data—31 of the 40 sequences contained at least one run of 10 or more consecutive choices of the same side, 20 of the sequences had a run of 30 or more, and there was one run of 150 choices to the same side. Thirdly, the choice made after a position run usually was correct—80 of the 91 position runs of 10 or more were terminated by choice of the positive stimulus. Finally, simulated reversal learning was faster for the sequences that had overtraining than the sequences where reversal commenced immediately after the learning criterion was achieved. In the sequences with overtraining, reversal learning was accomplished in an average of 158 trials, an average of 229 trials was required for reversal in the sequences without overtraining. This last finding, corresponding to an overtraining reversal effect, is found in some experiments but not consistently, especially when discrimination is easy. Among Lovejoy's several simulations he included a condition involving easy discrimination ($D_1 = 2.00$, $D_2 = 1.00$, and the same values of the other parameters listed above) and this condition failed to show an overtraining reversal effect.

ROLE OF INCENTIVES IN ANIMAL DISCRIMINATION

Lovejoy's model, discussed above, deals with the process of learning to respond appropriately when stimulus values are easily discriminated, but when two or more dimensions are varied so that the animal must learn which to use. A different but related problem involved asymptotic behavior, where the animal has learned to use the relevant stimulus dimension but the values are hard to discriminate. Boneau and Cole (1967) have given a model based on ideas from statistical decision theory. The model makes predictions very similar to those of signal detectability theory, discussed in Section 4, but the ideas are developed differently.

The situation considered by Boneau and Cole involves presentations of different stimuli, varying along a single dimension. The model was applied where the dimension was the wavelength of light illuminating a key. The subjects were pigeons, who were trained to peck the key to obtain food. During the experiment, 10 different wavelengths were used, varying from 530 mμ to 539 mμ in steps of 1 mμ. On trials when one of the five highest wavelengths was present, there was a fixed probability (.03) that the pigeon would receive food if he pecked the key. On trials when any of the five lowest wavelengths was present, the pigeon received no food, whether he pecked or not.

Following Thurstone (1927), Boneau and Cole assumed that the psychological effect of stimulation can be represented on a dimension corresponding to the dimension along which the stimuli are varied, but the effects of presenting a given stimulus are not always the same. If a certain stimulus is presented many times, the perceived hues of the stimulus have a distribution, and it is assumed that the distribution is normal. To simplify analysis, it is assumed that all of the stimuli have distributions with the same variance, and means that are equally spaced along the dimension. The perceived hue that describes the effective stimulus on a trial is called h, and the distribution of h associated with presentations of stimulus S_i is called $f(h \mid S_i)$.

Boneau and Cole's main assumption was that the pigeon in this situation stores information corresponding to the relative frequency of rewards following pecks to particular perceived hues. This information is built up over many experiences, where the pigeon perceives a particular hue, pecks, and then either receives food or does not. Let $P(R \mid h)$ be the probability of a reward for a peck when the perceived hue is h. $P(R \mid h)$ depends on the probability of reward for positive stimuli, as well as on the frequencies of the perceived hue h associated with the positive and negative stimuli. Specifically, for the conditions of the experiment,

$$P(R \mid h) = \frac{.03 \sum_{i=6}^{10} f(h \mid S_i)}{\sum_{i=1}^{10} f(h \mid S_i)} \qquad \textbf{[81]}$$

where stimuli $S_1, \ldots, S_5$ are the negative stimuli, and stimuli $S_6, \ldots, S_{10}$ are the positive stimuli.

Boneau and Cole assumed that there is a positive utility $u(R)$ for the reward, and a negative utility $u(N)$ for pecking when there is no reward. The pigeon's decision whether to peck on a trial is determined by the subjectively expected utility of pecking, given the perceived hue on that trial. That is

$$\text{SEU(peck} \mid h) = u(R)P(R \mid h) + u(N)[1 - P(R \mid h)],$$

with $P(R \mid h)$ given in Eq. 81.

Since positive stimuli were the ones with higher wavelengths, the value of $P(R \mid h)$ will be greater for the higher values of h. This means that SEU(peck$\mid h$) will tend to increase with h, being negative for very low values and positive for very high values. Boneau and Cole assume that the pigeon will decide to peck on exactly those where SEU(peck$\mid h$) is greater than zero. There is some value of h, h_c, where SEU(peck$\mid h_c$) is zero. For values of h below h_c, SEU(peak$\mid h$) will be positive, and the pigeon will peck. The value of h_c satisfies the equation

$$\frac{-u(N)}{u(R)} = \frac{(.03) \sum_{i=6}^{10} f(h_c \mid S_i)}{\sum_{i=1}^{5} f(h_c \mid S_i) + (.97) \sum_{i=6}^{10} f(h_c \mid S_i)} . \qquad \textbf{[82]}$$

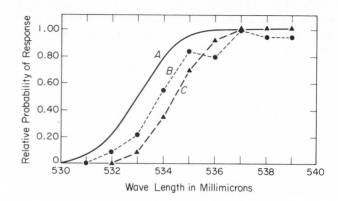

Fig. 8-37. *Empirical probability of response. B: strong hunger (first 500 trials); C: less hunger (next 1000 trials). Curve A is a normal ogive with standard deviation of 1 mμ.* [From Boneau and Cole (1967), p. 134. Copyright 1967 by the American Psychological Association and reproduced by permission.]

The observable data are proportions of pecking to the different stimuli. For each stimulus, the probability of pecking is the probability that the perceived hue is above h_c. That is,

$$P(\text{peck} \mid S_i) = \int_{h_c}^{\infty} f(h \mid S_i) \, dh.$$

This probability will increase as the wavelength of S_i increases, giving a psychophysical function. Under the assumption that all the $f(h \mid S_i)$ are normal with equal variances, $P(\text{peck} \mid S_i)$ should be a normal give when it is plotted against the wavelengths of the stimuli.

According to Boneau and Cole's model, the effects of a change in motivation should be to change the value of h_c. For example, if the pigeon becomes less hungry this would change the value of $u(R)$, decreasing the ratio $-u(N)/u(R)$, and thus increasing the value of h_c that satisfies Eq. 82. An implication of this is that the psychometric functions obtained under different motivational conditions should be displaced to the right or left from each other. Boneau and Cole presented data consistent with this implication, shown in Fig. 8-37.

6. Conclusion

A reader who has searched this chapter for simple, unifying characteristics of mathematical theory in psychology will probably have failed. There is no single methodology that is shared by all of the contributions that have been discussed, and there is no simple characterization of the way in which mathematical work has contributed to the theoretical developments. It is true that most of the contributions included in this survey are applications of a single branch of mathematics—probability theory—but there are exceptions even to this mild generalization, and the exceptions become the rule when one considers areas of mathematical psychology such as computer models and theory of measurement that were omitted from this chapter. But in my opinion the only feature of real significance that is shared by all mathematical models is also a feature that they share with all ideas in psychology. Each represents an attempt to understand as clearly and as deeply as possible some aspect of an important psychological process.

Because of the way in which I have presented the various

models in this survey, a reader may have the impression that a mathematical psychologist typically develops a model that represents his idea about a process, and then looks for data either in the literature or in new experiments to test the model. This sequence of events does sometimes occur, but it is reversed at least as often. And most frequently there is no clear precedence for either theoretical or empirical results. Virtually every successful theoretical analysis is developed through a process of successive approximations, including consideration of some empirical findings, development of a tentative hypothesis that may or may not be very formal, checking one or more aspects of the hypothesis against data, revising the hypothesis or making it more rigorous, and so on. In short, the question "Does theory guide experiment, or do experimental results guide theory?" has the answer, "Yes," since each aspect of the analysis guides the other.

Finally, a remark about contemporary history. We have already reached a point where the literature referred to as "mathematical models" is too large and diverse to be surveyed conveniently in a single chapter. It seems certain that in future handbooks of psychology, the material included in this chapter will be dealt with in a number of chapters, each encompassing a more manageable domain of subject matter. There may be three or four chapters titled "Mathematical Models of ..." in future handbooks of psychology. But another possibility is that in the future, quantitative theories of psychological processes will be merged with the other existing theories, so that material of the kind described in this chapter will appear in the regular subject-matter chapters of handbooks and other texts. One hopes that the latter possibility is the one that will be realized, and the current literature in mathematical psychology, which is increasingly focused on substantive psychological questions, provides reasons for optimism.

References

ANDERSON, N. H. Application of a weighted average model to a psychophysical averaging task. *Psychonomic Science*, 1967, *8*: 227–28.

——— A simple model for information integration. *In* R. P. ABELSON, E. ARONSON, W. J. MCGUIRE, T. M. NEWCOMB, M. J. ROSENBERG, and P. H. TANNENBAUM (eds.), *Theories of cognitive consistency: a source book*. Chicago: Rand-McNally, 1968, pp. 731–43.

——— Averaging model applied to the size-weight illusion. *Perception and Psychophysics*, 1970, *8*: 1–4.

ATKINSON, R. C. A variable sensitivity theory of signal detection. *Psychological Review*, 1963, *70*: 91–106.

———, G. H. BOWER, and E. J. CROTHERS. *An introduction to mathematical learning theory*. New York: Wiley, 1965.

ATKINSON, R. C., J. W. BRELSFORD, JR., and R. M. SHIFFRIN. Multi-process models for memory with applications to a continuous presentation task. *Journal of Mathematical Psychology*, 1967, *4*: 277–300.

ATKINSON, R. C., and E. J. CROTHERS. A comparison of paired-associate learning models having different acquisition and retention axioms. *Journal of Mathematical Psychology*, 1964, *1*: 285–315.

ATKINSON, R. C., and R. M. SHIFFRIN. Human memory: a proposed system and its control processes. *In* G. H. BOWER and J. T. SPENCE (eds.) *The psychology of learning and motivation, advances in research and theory* (vol. 2). New York: Academic Press, 1967, pp. 90–197.

BERNBACH, H. A. Decision processes in memory. *Psychological Review*, 1967, *74*: 462–80.

BJORK, R. A. All-or-none subprocesses in the learning of complex sequences. *Journal of Mathematical Psychology*, 1968, *5*: 182–95.

BOCK, R. D., and L. V. JONES. *The measurement and prediction of judgment and choice*. San Francisco: Holden-Day, 1968.

BONEAU, C. A., and J. L. COLE. Decision theory, the pigeon, and the psychophysical function. *Psychological Review*, 1967, *74*: 123–35.

BOWER, G. H. Application of a model to paired-associate learning. *Psychometrika*, 1961, *26*: 255–80.

——— A multicomponent theory of the memory trace. *In* K. W. SPENCE and J. T. SPENCE (eds.) *The psychology of learning and motivation: advances in research and theory*, (vol. 1). New York: Academic Press, 1967, pp. 230–321.

———, and J. THEIOS. A learning model for discrete performance levels. *In* R. C. ATKINSON (ed.) *Studies in mathematical psychology*. Stanford: Stanford University Press, 1964, pp. 1–31.

BOWER, G. H., and T. R. TRABASSO. Concept identification. *In* R. C. ATKINSON (ed.) *Studies in mathematical psychology*. Stanford: Stanford University Press, 1964, pp. 32–94.

BRELSFORD, J. W., JR. Experimental manipulation of state occupancy in a Markov model for avoidance conditioning. *Journal of Mathematical Psychology*, 1967, *4*: 21–47.

BURKE, C. J., and J. L. ZINNES. A paired comparison of pair comparisons. *Journal of Mathematical Psychology*, 1965, *2*: 53–76.

COOMBS, C. H. On the use of inconsistency of preferences in psychological measurement. *Journal of Experimental Psychology*, 1958, *55*: 1–7.

——— *A theory of data*. New York: Wiley, 1964.

———, R. M. DAWES, and A. TVERSKY. *Mathematical psychology: an elementary introduction*. Englewood-Cliffs, N. J.: Prentice-Hall, 1970.

———, and D. G. PRUITT. Components of risk and decision making: probability and variance preferences. *Journal of Experimental Psychology*, 1960, *60*: 265–77.

COWAN, T. M. A Markov model for order of emission in free recall. *Journal of Mathematical Psychology*, 1966, *3*: 470–83.

DAVIS, J. H. Models for the classification of problems and the prediction of group problem-solving from individual results. (Doctoral dissertation, Michigan State University, 1961.)

EDWARDS, W., H. LINDMAN, and L. D. PHILLIPS. Emerging technologies for making decisions. In *New directions in psychology II*. New York: Holt, Rinehart and Winston, 1965, pp. 261–325.

ERICKSEN, C. W. Temporal luminance summation effects in backward and forward masking. *Perception and Psychophysics*, 1966, *1*: 87–92.

ESTES, W. K. Learning theory and the new "mental chemistry". *Psychological Review*, 1960, 67: 207–23.

———, and J. H. STRAUGHAN. Analysis of a verbal conditioning situation in terms of statistical learning theory. *Journal of Experimental Psychology*, 1954, *47*: 225–34.

ESTES, W. K., and H. A. TAYLOR. A detection method and probabilistic models for assessing information processing from brief visual displays. *Proceedings of the National Academy of Sciences*, 1964, 52: 446–54.

FRIEDMAN, M. P., C. J. BURKE, M. COLE, L. KELLER, R. B. MILLWARD, and W. K. ESTES. Two-choice behavior under extended training with shifting probabilities of reinforcement. *In* R. C. ATKINSON (ed.) *Studies in mathematical psychology*. Stanford: Stanford University Press, 1964.

GRAHAM, C. H., and E. H. KEMP. Brightness discrimination as a function of the duration of the increment in intensity. *Journal of General Physiology*, 1938, *21*: 635–50.

GREEN, D. M., and J. A. SWETS. *Signal detection theory and psychophysics*. New York: Wiley, 1966.

GREENO, J. G. Paired-associate learning with short-term retention: mathematical analysis and data regarding identification of parameters. *Journal of Mathematical Psychology*, 1967, *4*: 430–72.

——— *Elementary theoretical psychology*. Reading, Mass.: Addison-Wesley, 1968a.

——— Identifiability and statistical properties of two-stage learning with no successes in the initial stage. *Psychometrika*, 1968b, *33*: 173–215.

———, and J. M. SCANDURA. All-or-none transfer based on verbally mediated concepts. *Journal of Mathematical Psychology*, 1966, *3*: 388–411.

HELSON, H. *Adaptation-level theory*. New York: Harper and Row, 1964.

HERRICK, R. M. Foveal luminance discrimination as a function of the duration of the decrement or increment in luminance. *Journal of Comparative and Physiological Psychology*, 1956, *49*: 437–43.

HILGARD, E. H., and G. H. BOWER. *Theories of learning.* 3rd ed. New York: Appleton-Century Crofts, 1966.

HULL, C. L. *Principles of behavior: an introduction to behavior theory.* New York: Appleton-Century-Crofts, 1943.

—— *A behavior system.* New Haven: Yale University Press, 1952.

JEFFRESS, L. A. Mathematical and electrical models of auditory detection. *Journal of the Acoustical Society of America,* 1968, *44*: 187–203.

KINTSCH, W. Memory and decision aspects of recognition learning. *Psychological Review,* 1967, *74*: 496–504.

——, and C. J. MORRIS. Application of a Markov model to free recall and recognition. *Journal of Experimental Psychology,* 1965, *69*: 200–206.

KRANTZ, D. H. A theory of context effects based on cross-context matching. *Journal of Mathematical Psychology,* 1968, 5: 1–48.

—— Threshold theories of signal detection. *Psychological Review,* 1969, *76*: 308–24.

LOVEJOY, E. *Attention in discrimination learning, a point of view and a theory.* San Francisco: Holden-Day, 1968.

LUCE, R. D. *Individual choice behavior: a theoretical analysis.* New York: Wiley, 1959.

—— A threshold theory for simple detection experiments. *Psychological Review,* 1963, *70*: 61–79.

——, and P. SUPPES. Preference, utility, and subjective probability. *In* R. D. LUCE, R. R. BUSH, and E. GALANTER (eds.) *Handbook of mathematical psychology,* (vol. 3). New York: Wiley, 1965, pp. 249–410.

NEIMARK, E. D., and W. K. ESTES. *Stimulus sampling theory.* San Francisco: Holden-Day, 1967.

NORMAN, D. A. Sensory thresholds, response biases, and the neural quantum theory. *Journal of Mathematical Psychology,* 1964, *1*: 88–120 (a).

NORMAN, M. F. A two-phase model and an application to verbal discrimination learning. *In* R. C. ATKINSON (ed.) *Studies in mathematical psychology.* Stanford: Stanford Univ. Press, 1964, pp. 173–87 (b).

POLSON, M. C., F. RESTLE, and P. G. POLSON. Association and discrimination in paired-associates learning. *Journal of Experimental Psychology,* 1965, *69*: 47–55.

PREMACK, D. Rate differential reinforcement in monkey manipulation. *Journal of Experimental Analysis of Behavior.* 1963, *6*: 81–89.

PROKASY, W. F., and M. A. HARSANYI. Two-phase model for human classical conditioning. *Journal of Experimental Psychology,* 1968, *78*: 359–68.

RESTLE, F. *Psychology of judgment and choice: a theoretical essay.* New York: Wiley, 1961.

—— The selection of strategies in cue learning. *Psychological Review,* 1962, *69*: 329–43.

—— Sources of difficulty in learning paired associates. *In* R. C. ATKINSON (ed.) *Studies in mathematical psychology.* Stanford: Stanford Univ. Press, 1964, pp. 116–72.

——, and J. H. DAVIS. Success and speed of problem solving by individuals and groups. *Psychological Review,* 1962, *69*: 520– 36.

——, and J. G. GREENO. *Introduction to mathematical psychology,* Reading, Mass.: Addison-Wesley, 1970.

ROCK, I. The role of repetition in associative learning. *American Journal of Psychology,* 1957, *70*: 186–93.

RUMELHART, D. E. A multicomponent theory of the perception of briefly exposed visual displays. *Journal of Mathematical Psychology,* 1970, 7: 191–213.

SIEGEL, S. Theoretical models of choice and strategy behavior: stable state behavior in the two-choice uncertain outcome situation. *Psychometrika,* 1959, *24*: 306–16.

SPERLING, G. The information available in brief visual presentations. *Psychological Monographs,* 1960, *74*: 1–29.

—— Successive approximations to a model for short-term memory. *Proceedings of the Eighteenth International Congress of Psychology.* Amsterdam: North-Holland Publish. Co., 1967.

——, and M. M. SONDHI. Model for visual luminance discrimination and flicker detection. *Journal of the Optical Society of America,* 1968, *58*: 1133–45.

STERNBERG, S. High-speed scanning in human memory. *Science,* 5 August 1966, *153*: 652–54.

STEVENS, S. S. On the psychological law. *Psychological Review,* 1957, *64*: 153–81.

SWETS, J. A., W. P. TANNER, JR., and T. G. BIRDSALL. Decision processes in perception. *Psychological Review,* 1961, *68*: 301–40.

THEIOS, J. Finite integer models for learning in individual subjects. *Psychological Review,* 1968, *75*: 292–307.

—— Mathematical models for aversive conditioning. *In* F. R. BRUSH (ed.) *Aversive conditioning and learning.* New York: Academic Press, 1969.

——, and J. W. BRELSFORD, JR. Theoretical interpretations of a Markov model for avoidance conditioning. *Journal of Mathematical Psychology,* 1966, *3*: 140–62.

THOMPSON, J. H. What happens to the stimulus in backward masking? *Journal of Experimental Psychology,* 1966, *71*: 580–86.

THURSTONE, L. L. A law of comparative judgment. *Psychological Review,* 1927, *34*: 278–86.

TORGERSON, W. S. *Theory and methods of scaling.* New York: Wiley, 1958.

TARBASSO, T., and G. H. BOWER. *Attention in learning: theory and research.* New York: Wiley, 1968.

TVERSKY, A. Utility theory and additivity analysis of risky choices. *Journal of Experimental Psychology,* 1967, *75*: 27–36.

WICKELGREN, W. A., and D. A. NORMAN. Strength models and serial position in short-term recognition memory. *Journal of Mathematical Psychology,* 1966, *3*: 316–47.

WOLFORD, G. L., D. L. WESSEL, and W. K. ESTES. Further evidence concerning scanning and sampling assumptions of visual detection models. *Perception and Psychophysics,* 1968, *3*: 439–44.

The Human Organism

During recent years biological scientists from a variety of different disciplines have focused more and more of their attention upon interactions between behavior and biochemical events. Why has this trend developed? From the most general of views, the answer lies in man's attempts to systematize knowledge about living organisms by describing them in terms of certain basic properties: anatomical, biochemical, electrophysiological and behavioral. Clearly, no living biological system can adequately be characterized by any one of these properties alone. Observing such a system over even a short period of time establishes the fact that dynamic interactions between properties are continuously in progress and that an understanding of how the system functions as a whole depends upon knowledge about the nature of the interactions. Against this general background there are developing "interactive models" to describe dynamic relations between two, and sometimes three, and even all four of the basic properties. It is with such dynamic relations when behavior and its biochemical substrates are involved that the present discussion is concerned.

Before examining the converging lines of theory and research which have led historically to the knowledge and methodology upon which present developments in the field depend, the point should be made that the strong intellectual appeal of basic research on biochemical bases of behavior has been paralleled by the equally strong attraction of the possible uses to which knowledge about such relations could be put. Primary among the potential uses have been applications in the treatment of behavior disorders, of mental illnesses. These prospects were envisaged as early as the hippocratic writings (ca: 460–370 B.C.) in which normal behavior was said to occur when the four humors—blood, phlegm, black bile and yellow bile—were present in the brain in the correct proportions. Abnormal behavior resulted from an imbalance and could, supposedly, be cured by administering treatments which had selective actions on the various humors. During the years between then and now the search for biochemical factors in behavior disorders has waxed and waned with developments in the disciplines of biochemistry, pharmacology, psychology, and psychiatry. It

R. W. Russell
& D. M. Warburton

Biochemical Bases of Behavior

9

is still true that the search has more prospects than definitive knowledge. Firm information is available for certain disorders, e.g., the "organic" psychoses, but very little is yet known about biochemical bases of others, e.g., schizophrenia. Yet, as Hippocrates predicted, selective treatments using drugs as tools, pharmacotherapies, are now in wide use, based upon empirical evidence of their efficacies even though satisfactory theoretical underpinnings are still lacking.

History

An historian studying the development of knowledge about biochemical substrates of behavior would attribute the fallow period of some 2,000 years during which Hippocrates' ideas were advanced little, if at all, to the lack of new conceptualization and of methods by which behavioral and biochemical variables could be observed and measured. By the middle of the last century, signs of change began to appear. Techniques for the assay of nervous tissue were applied in attempts to determine differences in the chemical composition of the brains of normal and mentally disturbed patients. In *A Treatise on the Chemical Composition of the Brain*, Thudichum (1884), the founder of modern neurochemistry, stated the basic concept of the role of "toxic" substances in interactions between biochemical systems and mental disorders.

The possibility that transmission of nerve impulses across synaptic junctions between fibers might be chemically mediated added a strong stimulus to the further development of chemical and bioassay procedures. In 1904 Elliott suggested that nerve impulses released epinephrine at the smooth muscle junctions of sympathetic nerves, and two years later Dixon (1906) hypothesized the release of a chemical at parasympathetic junctions, which was later (Loewi 1921) identified as the substance now known to be acetylcholine. The power of these new concepts and methodologies was later redirected from the peripheral to the central nervous system, where the technical problems of observation and measurement are of another order of magnitude.

This was an era during which the pace of scientific discovery generally was quickening at an amazing rate. It was during the early years of this period that modern experimental psychology began to ask new kinds of questions about the behavioral property of living organisms and to suggest that behavioral variables were legitimate subjects for study using the logics of scientific method. As Boring (1950) has expressed it: "The big event of the nineteenth century for psychology was the discovery of scientific men that the mind can be brought to tune by the methods of natural science." The effects of analysis and measurement in other areas of the biological sciences showed themselves in changes of attitudes among psychologists toward the relevance to their science of hypotheses about relations between behavior and other properties of living organisms. The controversies between molar and molecular views about behavioral theory gave way to the generally accepted position that psychology has a place for both. Leaders in the development of psychological theories whose views were as different as those of Hull and Tolman distinguished between the characteristics of molar behavior and those of other properties of living organisms while agreeing that the former ". . . are presumably strictly correlated with, and, if you will, dependent upon, physiological motions"

(Tolman 1932). Hull (1943) agreed and was concerned about the constraints which present levels of knowledge and technique placed upon the study of such dependencies: ". . . any theory of behavior is at present, and must be for some time to come, a molar theory. This is because neuroanatomy and physiology have not yet developed to a point such that they yield principles which may be employed as postulates in a system of behavior theory. . . ." The situation has now changed and the psychologist is hard-pressed to keep abreast of major developments in other biological sciences which are most relevant to his primary interest in behavior.

As Lashley (1950) foresaw in his dramatic midcentury review of the state of affairs in the "search for the engram" of learning, dynamic events within the organism, biochemical and electrophysiological, are now much more in prominence than they have been at any other time in the history of physiological psychology. Research results strongly suggest that the change in behavioral variables as an organism adjusts to its continually altering environment may better be understood in terms of the dynamics of somatic events than in terms of the more static features of its anatomical property. Recent developments in techniques have made it possible for researchers to measure and to alter, experimentally, biochemical events at the level of neurohumoral systems involved in nerve conduction and even at the level of changes in the synthesis and in the configuration of macromolecular components of individual neurons. Knowledge from the use of such techniques has led to the development of theoretical models which are stimulating new directions in research.

To these trends of development in biochemistry and psychology must be added advances in pharmacology. Drugs serve as the most important tools by which a research worker may produce the systematic variations in biochemical events required by an experimental approach to the study of biochemical events—behavior interactions. Like its sister sciences discussed earlier, pharmacology has come a long way during the past century: "Thus emanating from a background of mystery and magic, from folklore and empiricism, the medical science of pharmacology came coincidental with the turn of the century" (Krantz and Carr 1961). Pharmacology is the study of how living organisms respond to chemical stimuli. As stimuli, drugs have their direct effects by modifying biochemical processes which are already present in the organism. Kety (1961) has stated ". . . a very important principle of pharmacology, which to the best of my knowledge has never been breached. . . . We cannot expect drugs to introduce anything new into the mind or into behavior, but merely to accentuate or to suppress functions in behavior which are already present." Thus, drugs may become the "tools" of the experimenter seeking to study interactions between biochemical events and behavior by varying the former. To be used properly, the characteristics of a tool must be understood. It has been to the task of defining the characteristics of drugs that modern pharmacology has directed much of its attention.

This historical background emphasizes the convergence of effort in three areas of scientific investigation toward the study of "biochemical substrates of behavior." As would be expected, at such an interface there are occurring construction of new theoretical models, discovery of new areas of problems to be solved, reports of new empirical observations which enable a stalled attack upon important familiar problems to move forward once again, development of new integrations of existing knowledge. To describe the full thrust of these activities, it is important to be familiar with research strategies and tactics in the field and with the nature of the variables studied.

Research Methods

Operationally the definition of the phrase, "relation between a biochemical event and behavior," is in terms of *concomitant variation* between these two classes of variables. In their generalized forms current hypotheses about the nature of such interactions conceive of biochemical events and behavior as being reciprocally related. It has been claimed that changes in biochemical events may produce concomitant changes in behavior and that changes in behavior may be reflected in persisting modifications of biochemical events. Two types of research approaches have been used to test such hypotheses. The first, "correlated variation," is nonexperimental in the usual sense of that term; methodologically it requires determination of the degree to which individual differences in some measure of behavior are correlated with individual differences in some biochemical event. The second, which John Stuart Mill referred to as "concomitant variation," demands experimental manipulation of a biochemical event and measurement of consequent changes in a measure of behavior or manipulation of behavior with measurement of changes in the biochemical event. These general approaches must be translated into specific research tactics in which the variables are specified, independent variables are manipulated and dependent variables measured.

BIOCHEMICAL VARIABLES

Two directions of development in biochemistry have had major influences upon the specification of those biochemical variables chosen for study. The first has been the momentous discoveries relating to the chemical coding of genetic information. Genetic information is conveyed from parental cells to their progeny by way of nucleic acids, which are constituents of the chromosomes in plants and animals. The information which determines the inherited characteristics of the offspring is encoded in the sequences of bases in one type of nucleic acid, deoxyribonucleic acid (DNA). The chemical structure of a section of the DNA molecule and its double helix configuration are shown in Figure 9-1. Important to its role in storing genetic information is the capability of such molecules to reproduce themselves at each cell division. As would be expected if genetic information within a species is to be transmitted over countless generations, as it is, DNA molecules, once formed, must be very stable, resistant to change in their physical and chemical environments. The read-out of information so coded involves a second type of nucleic acid, ribonucleic acid (RNA), in *the process of protein synthesis*. DNA imposes some part of its pattern upon RNA molecules synthesized in the nucleus of the cell. Each of these messenger RNAs, then, is a copy of a DNA sequence, serving as a short-lived template in specifying the sequence of amino acids along the chain of the protein being synthesized. Transfer RNAs, each specific to one amino acid, localize amino acids from the surrounding chemical environment at their proper

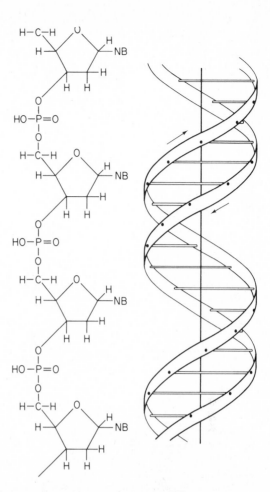

Fig. 9-1. *Diagrammed on the left is the chemical structure of a small section of deoxyribonucleic acid (DNA). Illustrated on the right is the double helix form of the nucleic acid molecule.*

places on the chain, which is finally formed on the ribosomal particles in the cell. The order in which amino acids are lined up determines the special characteristics of the protein synthesized; even very slight differences in structure may result in very significant differences in their effects on the anatomical, electrophysiological, and behavioral properties of the organism. Unlike DNA, RNA and the protein synthesis process may be widely influenced by the physicochemical conditions of the environment. Their production in nerve cells is at a rate which follows neuronal activity: actively secreting cells contain nuclei which are larger in volume than those of nonsecreting cells, due primarily to differences in amounts of protein. The superficial analogy between the storage of genetic information and possible chemical storage of "memory" has combined with new knowledge about techniques for systematically varying protein synthesis to stimulate an extensive search for relations between the process of protein synthesis and behavior.

Even before this dramatic turn in microbiology occurred, psychobiologists had been searching for relations between behavior and primary features of *neurohumoral transmitter systems*. Much earlier work had pointed to the nervous system as being the general site of action for biochemical events involved in the dynamics of behavior. The diagram in Figure 9-2 outlines

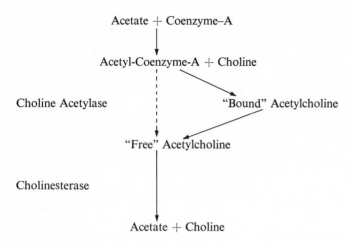

$$\text{Acetate} + \text{Coenzyme-A}$$

$$\downarrow$$

$$\text{Acetyl-Coenzyme-A} + \text{Choline}$$

Choline Acetylase   "Bound" Acetylcholine

$$\text{"Free" Acetylcholine}$$

Cholinesterase

$$\downarrow$$

$$\text{Acetate} + \text{Choline}$$

Fig. 9-2. *Diagram of the step reactions involved in the synthesis and later inactivation of the transmitter substance, acetylcholine (ACh).*

the typical step reactions involved in the synthesis and later inactivation of a neurohumoral transmitter substance. The cholinergic system, to which the greatest amount of research attention has so far been given, serves as a prototype. Existing presynaptically are quantities of the transmitter's precursors, acetyl-coenzyme-A + choline, and of the synthesizing enzyme, choline acetylase. Catalyzed by the enzyme, the transmitter, acetylcholine (ACh), is synthesized and stored in "bound" form in morphological units, synaptic vesicles (Figure 9-3), concentrated in close relationship to the synaptic membrane. Following stimulation, the presynaptic impulse releases "free" ACh, which diffuses across the synaptic cleft combining with free postsynaptic receptors to form a transmitter-receptor complex and initiating a postsynaptic potential. The inactivating enzyme, acetylcholinesterase (AChE), catalyzes the dissociation of the newly formed complex to the free receptor and the metabolic products, acetate + choline. Uptake of some of the choline occurs as part of the synthesis of new transmitter chemical. The enzymes, which serve as biocatalysts controlling the velocities of the chemical reactions involved, are long-chain protein molecules whose syntheses are genetically determined by the process described above. During the years since the chemical hypothesis of nerve transmission was formally proposed, ample support has been obtained for the basic role of ACh as a transmitter substance in the peripheral nervous system (PNS). However, it was only in the early 1950s that the possibility of electrical transmission in the central nervous system (CNS) was ruled out by intracellular recording of the synaptic delay. Since then most

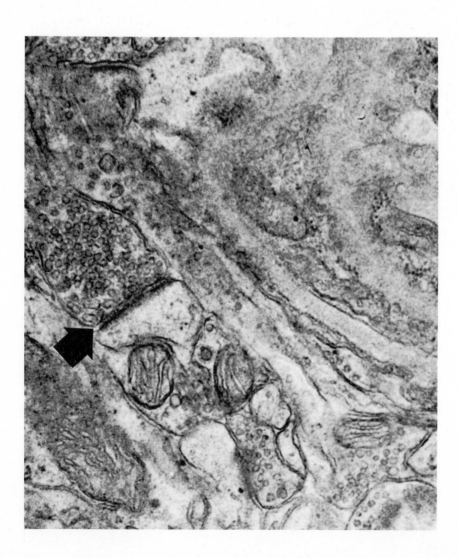

Fig. 9-3. *Electron-micrograph of a synapse in a rat's cortex, $\times$ 8000. The arrow indicates the synaptic cleft with synaptic vesicles located presynaptically above the arrow.* [Cotman, unpublished electron-micrograph].

studies of the biochemical bases of behavior have assumed that the known PNS transmitter substances are homologous with those mediating central neural transmission. Drugs can act selectively at any stage in such neurohumoral transmitter systems to change normal functions and, therefore, may be used selectively as tools in studying, experimentally, relations between a particular system and behavior.

Whether it is serving as an independent or as a dependent variable, quantitative assessment of the biochemical event under study is essential in order that its state may be related to the corresponding state(s) of behavioral variable(s) during the time frame of the same treatment. The general protocol for conduct of a biochemical assay may be outlined briefly as follows. The animal is painlessly sacrificed by decapitation and, if the rate of metabolism of the target biochemical is rapid, the head is frozen immediately in liquid nitrogen (Takahashi and Aprison 1964). The frozen head is thawed until it can be separated into parts corresponding to the major anatomical regions to be studied separately. Each brain part is then homogenized and the target compound extracted. Refinement of extraction techniques has enabled acetylcholine, norepinephrine, serotonin, and dopamine to be extracted from the same sample (Fleming, Clark, Fenster, and Towne 1965). Acetylcholine has traditionally been assayed with bioassay procedures, but more recently chemical methods have started to be developed (Jenden, Hanin, and Lamb 1968). Spectrophotofluorometric methods have been used for the determination of norepinephrine, serotonin, and dopamine due to the fluorescent properties of the indole nucleus. At the present time, these analyses have been confined to measures of the total amount of compound recovered from the homogenate. Evidence now exists that some transmitter substances are present in at least two states: "free" and "bound." In the inactive form, it is stored presynaptically by being bound tightly to protein molecules and then released as the "free," active form by the presynaptic potential. Studies of radioactively labeled norepinephrine in the brain have disclosed that the bound norepinephrine disappears from the brain in a multiphasic fashion indicating that there may be at least two bound forms: a large, rapidly released store and a small, more firmly bound store (Glowinski, Kopin, and Axelrod 1965). As yet biochemical techniques have not been devised that will separate the "free," the "rapidly released" and the "firmly bound" forms, and it is possible that behavior will only be correlated with one or two of these, probably the "free" and "rapidly released" forms.

These assay techniques have shown that there is not a uniform distribution of compounds throughout the brain. In fact, transmitters are distributed along specific pathways (Hillarp, Fuxe, and Dahlstrom 1966; Shute and Lewis 1966). Norepinephrine is widely distributed, but is particularly concentrated in the older parts of the brain, especially the hypothalamus and limbic system. Dopamine is located mainly in the neostriatum (basal ganglia) and limbic system, while serotonin is exclusively located in the lower brain stem. Acetylcholine is widely distributed like norepinephrine, but located along specific fiber pathways. In all cases, the highest concentrations are at the synaptic regions. In some cases, the same nuclei have synapses of more than one type, suggesting the possibility of differential chemical coding, i.e., distinction between two types of neural information at the same site on the basis of different transmitter substances.

There are many neural networks which have the same neurotransmitter. Acetylcholine is known to be involved with many types of behavior, including transmission at the motor end plate (del Castillo and Katz 1954), transmission in the retina (Glow and Rose 1964), transmission in both sympathetic and parasympathetic nervous systems, central control of water intake (Miller 1965), and in the storage of information in the cortex (Krech, Rosenzweig, and Bennett 1954). Thus, not only does there seem to be biochemical separation of function, but there seems to be localization of function. This does not mean that there are centers in the phrenologist's sense, rather there are integrated networks with an interplay between areas of the brain in the form of reciprocating pathways. Thus, drugs circulating in the blood plasma may influence many systems to a greater or lesser degree.

Behavioral Variables

Specification of behavioral variables also has its set of requirements. The wealth of different behavior patterns from which to choose those to be measured in any specific study presents problems of selection. While we cannot argue that an investigator should not select a particular behavior pattern because of his empirical interest in it *per se*, we can raise the question of what generalizations he can make from his observations. It is logically inaccurate to generalize from single measures of behavior, e.g., on a rotorod or in a pole-climbing test, to "behavior" with a capital "B." The research literature shows two approaches to more systematic selection.

One of these is based upon *a priori classification of behavior* and involves the selection of behavior patterns which are "representative" of one or more of the classes. Typical of this approach are studies of relations between the cholinergic system and the processes of "learning," "memory," and "motivation." Each of these is a label for a theoretical construct: learning is not observed directly; rather, it is said to have occurred when measures of behavior show systematic modification under certain specified conditions. The number of specific behavior patterns which can show such modification is great. Investigators interested in learning choose one or, if they are wise, several representatives from among these many possibilities.

The second approach begins with some *systematic model of behavior*. A present favorite is derived from models in communication theory and analyzes behavior in terms of such processes as sensory input, central fixation and storage, central retrieval or read-out, and motor output. The task for the investigator using this approach is to select measures of behavior which differentiate among these various processes.

Selection of behavior patterns to be studied is only the first step. Measures of these patterns must be developed which meet the requirements of sound scientific measuring instruments. Each measure must have *validity*, i.e., it must measure the behavior it is supposed to measure, and it must be capable of being applied consistently, i.e., it must have *reliability*. Because of the special problems they face, behavioral scientists have given particular attention to application of psychometric techniques in the development of behavioral measures. They have shown on innumerable occasions that measures purported to measure the same behavior are not highly correlated and that lack of reliability results in variability of measurement which masks existing relations. The search for interactions between neurochemical and behavioral variables still suffers greatly from inadequate attention to behavioral measures and from unwarranted generalizations from them. One of the most serious of the latter offenses is to treat what in fact are different measures of behavior as if they were the same; this offense is made most noticeably by investigators who generalize to "learning" and "memory" after observing effects of changes in a neurochemical system on only one of the multitude of specific behavior patterns which may be included under each of these broad theoretical constructs.

Clearly, to analyze the configuration of behavioral effects following a neurochemical change requires the use of multiple behavior measures.

Much effort in the search for relations between biochemical events and behavior has been directed toward the study of behavior patterns which have been acquired and well-stabilized through repetition. Such patterns provide highly consistent pre-treatment baselines against which to evaluate effects of altering biochemical events. It is also clear that such behavioral baselines are inappropriate when the search is for relations between a biochemical event and the modification of behavior during acquisition, extinction, fatigue, sensory adaptation, etc. Again the issue is one of specifying behavior patterns to be measured in accordance with the demands of the hypothesis under test.

Although it would be of interest if manipulation of a particular biochemical event affected all measurable behavior patterns, information provided by *selective or differential effects* can be more helpful in mapping biochemical substrates of behavior. For example, evidence that decrease in AChE activity below a certain level in some way interferes with behavior under conditions of extinction but not of acquisition or maintenance (Russell, Watson, and Frankenhaeuser 1961; Glow and Rose 1966) provided a direction to the study of cholinergic "control" of behavior. Careful specification of behavioral measures can maximize the chances of discovering differential effects, as, for example, when a response pattern which is learned slowly is selected rather than one learned rapidly in studying biochemical changes believed to facilitate acquisition, the former providing fuller opportunity for measurement of facilitation effects. The selective nature of effects may be evidenced in the *direction of change* of a behavioral variable(s), as well as in the pattern of change among several variables. The use of a quantitative scale in measuring a variable under observation permits change along a continuum which has dimensionality, so long as the initial measures of the variable are intermediate on the scale.

There is one further technical issue in need of consideration at this point. This is the general problem of measuring both neurochemical and behavioral variables in the same subjects. Measurement of neurochemical variables would have to follow measurement of behavioral variables if samples of brain tissue must be taken to carry out the former. But, since the interaction between neurochemical events and behavior are dynamic and reciprocal, an organism may not be the same neurochemically after a behavioral test as it was before. In any event, most research designs require repeated measures over time, making the use of the same subject for both neurochemical and behavioral assay an impossible procedure. The logical alternative is to use matched groups of subjects, different groups being sacrificed for neurochemical assay at different stages of the research design, with the requirement that all groups progress through identical procedures to the time of assay. There are few, if any

investigators who have been this rigorous in their efforts. The more usual procedure has been to carry out the neurochemical assay as a separate experiment. There appears to have been no empirical checks on the comparability of data collected in these two ways. As successive approximations lead to increasing demands for precision, such determinations will have to be made.

MANIPULATION OF VARIABLES

A basic requirement of both the research strategies described earlier, correlated variation and concomitant variation, is that a variable of one class, biochemical event or behavior, must change in some parameter. If a variable in the other class is altered concomitantly although no other relevant circumstance has changed, then the two variables are said to be related (Wolf 1948). The major difference between the two strategies rests in the fact that concomitant variation demands experimental manipulation of an independent variable, while correlated variation seeks to measure variations, i.e., individual differences, as they may be found "in nature."

Illustrative of the approach via *correlated variation* are studies during the early period of the extensive Berkeley program (Rosenzweig, Krech, and Bennett 1960), which have motivated interest and debate in the general area of neurochemical bases of behavior. Research began with the proposition ". . . that variation in brain chemistry is a major determinant of variation in adaptive behavior among normal individuals. . . ." The method of correlated variation was chosen and a basic procedure established, using rats as subjects, which involved the measurement of (a) "adaptive behavior" as evidenced in such standardized situations as the Krech hypothesis apparatus, the Lashley-III maze and the Hebb-Williams maze, and the Dashiell maze; and (b) the activity level of the enzyme, ChE, in various regions of the cerebral cortex and of the subcortex. Selective breeding techniques were also used to maximize the range of individual differences in the neurochemical variable. The investigators reported higher levels of the ChE activity in subjects who altered their behavior in adapting to changes in their experimental environments when compared with the levels of those who did not. Although the differences were replicated in several experiments, they were relatively small in magnitude, approximately 5%, a magnitude which seemed puzzling in view of the large margin of safety associated with ChE activity in the brain. This was not the only problem in interpreting the results. Logically, neurochemical and behavioral variables may be related in three basic ways: (a) behavioral variables may follow temporally changes in neurochemical variables; (b) behavioral variables may initiate a chain of events which leads to changes in neurochemical variables; and (c) the variables may be correlated because they are consequents of some event(s) common to them both. Even a highly significant association obtained by the method of correlated variation provides no basis for distinguishing among these. Difficulties of these kinds led the Berkeley group to shift their research strategy after stating: "Obviously it is hazardous to argue from correlations to existence of a causal relation . . . the traditional procedure in seeking (such relations) . . . would be to manipulate experimentally the biochemical variable and observe whether . . . performance changed. . . ." in a manner appropriate to the hypothesis being tested.

With development of the modern science of pharmacology,

there continues to come knowledge about the modes of action of drugs which enables their selective use as tools to alter biochemical events. For example, let us return for a moment to the diagram in Figure 9–2 of the step reactions involved in the synthesis and later hydrolysis of the transmitter, ACh. Drugs can act at any stage in this system to change the normal course of events. "Depletors," e.g., hemicholinium-3, interfere with either the synthesis or release of the transmitter. A "membrane blocker," e.g., pentobarbital sodium, prevents the presynaptic impulse from reaching neuronal terminal. Cholinomimetics, e.g., carbamylcholine chloride, mimic the action of ACh, combining with the postsynaptic receptor to initiate a postsynaptic potential. A "receptor blocker," e.g., the cholinolytic, atropine sulfate, prevents the transmitter from reaching the receptor by forming a blocker-receptor complex, temporarily preventing depolarization. Other receptor-blockers, e.g., decamethonium, combine with the receptor to produce prolonged depolarization. Inactivating enzyme inhibitors ("anticholinesterases") of several varieties decrease the level of AChE activity, some reversibly, e.g., physostigmine, and some irreversibly, e.g., DFP and other organophosphorus compounds. The fuller the knowledge about the modes of action of such drugs, the more powerful they become as tools to manipulate selectively those biochemical events which may be substrates for behavior.

As a tool, a drug may be described in terms of certain characteristics, which determine the effects it produces in the biochemical system(s) it affects. Brodie (1962) has discussed the general nature of these characteristics as falling into two classes: characteristics which permit the drug to reach its site of action in adequate concentration and characteristics which determine the drug's "intrinsic activity." To reach its loci of action, a centrally-active drug administered by a peripheral route must cross several hurdles, including the blood-brain barrier, boundaries of various tissue cells, and even intracellular barriers. If it reaches its site of action in sufficient concentration, the duration of its action depends upon such factors as the degree of its localization at the site, its biotransformation in reacting with other chemical substances within the body, and the interrelation of its absorption and excretion (Schanker 1966).

Because of its great importance to the pharmacology of the CNS, the *blood-brain barrier* has received special attention. This barrier is hypothesized to be a lipid membrane in the CNS, perhaps in the capillary walls. Lipid soluble compounds administered peripherally readily pass this barrier by simple diffusion. Ions, on the other hand, are lipid insoluble; the rate of passage of an ionized agent is dependent upon its degree of ionization (Schanker 1966). Thus, strong bases like the quaternary compounds, scopolamine methyl bromide and atropine methyl bromide, do not readily pass the barrier. By contrast, weak bases such as the teritiary compounds, atropine sulfate and scopolamine hydrochloride, are lipid soluble at pH 7.4 and rapidly pass into the CNS. By suitable selection of their forms, effects of drugs on neurochemical events in the PNS alone can be compared with effects of similar compounds acting on both the PNS and the CNS. There are certain circumstances in which drugs which do not normally pass the blood-brain barrier can act upon neurochemical events in the CNS. First, the blood-brain barrier is not always fully developed in the neonatal animal and, therefore, does not function as in the more mature organism. For example, in day-old chicks, norepinephrine produced behavioral and electrocortical sleep, whereas in the

adult with a mature blood-brain barrier, the same drug elicited behavioral and electrocortical arousal (Dewhurst and Marley 1964). Second, lesions in the brain produce changes in the blood-brain barrier which result in increased penetration of chemicals into the CNS (Lahja 1962). Third, certain chemicals, e.g., iproniazid, increase the permeability of the blood-brain barrier, changing the normal pharmacological mode of action of other drugs. Fourth, drugs can be injected directly into specific sites in the CNS. Quaternary compounds injected in this fashion appear to have similar effects as peripheral injections of their tertiary equivalents (Khavari and Maickel 1967).

The history of the search for relations between neurochemical systems and behavior shows a progressive trend toward increasing anatomical localization in the experimental manipulation of neurochemical events. In the early stages of an investigation highly localized injection may not be required and administration into the cerebrospinal fluid may answer some of the problems raised. The cerebrospinal fluid is produced by the choroid plexes in each of the lateral ventricles, but also by plexes in the third and fourth ventricles. It flows through the center of the brain and is absorbed from the subarachnoid space by the meningeal pockets, so that a subarachnoid injection only bathes the cortex with the chemical administered. Feldberg (1963) has reported special techniques using this general approach which allow certain conclusions to be drawn about the localization of effects. However, for more precise analysis, drugs must be injected into specific sites by means of cannulae implanted using coordinates obtained from one of the stereotaxic atlases. An atlas contains anatomical diagrams corresponding to a series of cross-sections of the brain, enabling important structures to be specified in three dimensional coordinates using extracerebral landmarks, e.g., bregma, on the skull or the interaural line as reference points. In the young of some species a hypodermic needle may be inserted through the skull case and into the brain tissue. However, in older animals a trephine hole must be made in the skull, the skin sewn over, and, later, injection made through the skin and hole. Under these circumstances, the preferred technique is to insert, sterotaxically via the trephine hole, a microcannula into the desired brain site; the microcannula can be permanently attached to the skull using dental cement, thus providing a route for multiple administrations. Even when constraints of this kind are imposed, the possibility of diffusion from the initial site and of the activation of excitatory and/or inhibitory circuits spreading from the site must be considered.

The choice between introducing drugs as solids, e.g., crystals, or solutions depends on the aims of the investigation. MacLean (1957) and Grossman (1960) have discussed the disadvantages of injection in solution and have concluded that the main problem is uncontrolled spread of the solution from the specific injection site, thus preventing precise identification of site of action. The problem with introducing chemicals in solid form into the brain is the difficulty in determining the quantity introduced and, therefore, of obtaining exact doses. In addition, the high concentration of drug in the extracellular fluid at the tip of the cannula tends to produce tissue changes. Glial cells tend to form a pad around the top of the crystal cannula, interfering with the direct action of the drug, and certain drugs, e.g., epinephrine and norepinephrine, accentuate these tissue changes. For these reasons, injections in solution have some advantages for the more thorough investigation of dose-response relations (Miller, Gottesman, and Emery 1965); it is the best method for intraventricular injection when rapid and widespread distribution of the injected compound is required (Warburton and Russell 1968). Any investigation of the properties of neurochemically coded pathways in the brain must consider the symmetrical structures within the CNS. In the drinking circuit of the rat brain, both unilateral stimulation (Grossman 1962; Fisher and Coury 1962) and bilateral stimulation (Miller, Gottesman and Emery 1965; Khavari and Russell 1966) will trigger the system and drinking will occur. Russell (1966) compared the two kinds of stimulation and found that the peak amount of drinking per unit time was identical, but the total amount drunk was greater and the latency lower for bilateral stimulation. The comparison of unilateral and bilateral stimulation could be carried further by comparing incompatible stimulation (Levitt and Fisher 1967), hemispheric dominance and lateralization as suggested by Khavari, Feider, Warburton, and Martin (1967), and by comparing different intensities of stimulation in each hemisphere (Russell 1966).

The concept of concomitant variation places particular demands upon two pharmacological characteristics, the effective concentration of the drug at its site of action and the duration of its action, as means for systematically varying biochemical events. A logical assumption is that, when other conditions are controlled, the extent of changes induced in a biochemical system will be some function of the dose level of the drug producing the change. Such assumptions inevitably need to be tested as one of the preliminaries to proper use of a drug as a tool. Proper research design in the search for biochemical substrates of behavior provide for data from which *dose-response relations* may be determined. Variation of a target biochemical event also occurs over time following administration of a drug adequate to produce its change. When such an event is sensitive to a particular dose of a drug, measures at different times after administration can be expected to vary in magnitude from pre-drug base-line to peak effect and, eventually, to a recovery base-line level. If a measure is taken too soon in relation to the peak effect time, there may appear to have been no behavioral effect, even though a relation does, in fact, exist; the same misperception may result if observation is delayed too long. Thus, provision for the study of *time-response relations* is another important requirement in manipulating variables during research of the kinds we are discussing.

It can be seen that by the appropriate use of drugs, neural transmission can be modified. Obviously changes will only occur at synapses dependent on the transmitter system sensitive to the drug, so that only some parts of the nervous system will be affected. Biological activity, including behavior, depends on the total pattern of activity within the nervous system, and thus, on transmission at synapses. Each synapse is a choice point, either transmitting or not transmitting the neural impulse. In the brain there appears to be an enormous amount of *redundancy* with no single synapse, and thus no single neuron, essential for normal functioning. With so many neural pathways in parallel, there is considerable tolerance for malfunctioning and disruption in the neural networks. In addition, at a single synapse there appears to be considerable "redundancy" in the biochemistry. For example, there is a reserve supply of transmitter sufficient for 10,000 impulses in the sympathetic ganglia, while there is also a large margin of safety in level of activity of the inactivating enzyme (Aprison 1962). Drug-induced changes in behavior occur as increasing doses of drug progressively change neural function.

As a result, the dose-response curve has two portions: subthreshold, where redundancy is still protecting the behavioral system, and suprathreshold, where behavior changes as some function of dose. Behavior is altered from its pre-drug state as long as the effective level of the drug at its site of action is sufficient to overcome the redundancy in the system.

Experience has focused the attention of investigators upon these several theoretical and methodological issues. How they come to light in the practical action of putting hypotheses to test will be apparent in the discussions to follow. These discussions take a new tack: they look at the present state of knowledge about relations between behavior and biochemical events at the levels of enzyme systems and of protein synthesis.

Cholinergic Mechanisms in Behavior

In view of the attention it received during the early history of research on neurohumoral transmission, it is not surprising that the cholinergic system (Figure 9-2) is involved in the most detailed example of the search for biochemical substrates of behavior. The story which follows does not attempt to review the relevant literature in full, but rather to show how research efforts have led to increasing precision in our knowledge about differential relations between particular features of the cholinergic system and particular aspects of behavior.

GROSS CHANGES IN THE CHOLINERGIC SYSTEM

Early experiments (Russell 1954, 1958) were based upon no more specific goals than the search for general empirical relations between ChE activity and behavior. ChE activity was reduced by administration of an organophosphorus agent (OO-diethyl-S-ethylmercaptoethanol thiophosphate) and, since there was no idea how behavior might be affected, a wide variety of standarized behavior patterns was studied. Initial results indicated that, although the acquisition of new response patterns appeared not to be affected by the reduction, extinction of responses once established was slower for experimental than for control animals. Extinction is defined operationally in terms of withdrawing the reinforcement present during the acquisition of a response. Other aspects of behavior seemed not to be affected. Further investigation (Russell, Watson and Frankenhaeuser 1961) confirmed the differential effects between conditioning and extinction when the same operant response was involved. Dose-response functions showed that the relation between ChE activity and extinction was not a linear one. There was a "critical level" between 40 and 50% of normal ChE activity below which speed of extinction was inversely related to ChE activity. A consistent tendency was found for the efficiency of responding to increase at levels of ChE activity between this critical level and normal, but the effect was never sufficiently great to be statistically significant. These characteristics of the overall biphasic relation have interesting analogies with results of research on relations between ChE activity and variables other than behavior. Metz (1958) has described a crossover from potentiation to decline in a respiratory reflex at about 40% of normal brain ChE activity. This critical level is in the range where Aprison (1962) has reported the enzyme to lose control of its substrate, ACh content in brain tissue analyzed increasing rapidly below this level. It is also about this level that a sharp drop in nerve conductance begins to occur (Wilson and Cohen 1953).

The general nature of these results has been confirmed and extended in a series of studies by Glow and his collaborators (Glow and Rose 1966; Glow, Rose, and Richardson 1966) at the University of Adelaide in Australia, using several different behavior patterns. Acute as well as chronic reduction in ChE activity was found to be related to slower extinction. As in the earlier experiments, the effect occurred when ChE activity was reduced below 40 to 45% of normal. Glow and Rose (1966) confirmed by bioassay of brain tissue under their conditions for varying ChE activity that there occur "... runaway, or out of control, increases in ACh after acute ChE reduction to below 40% ..." of normal. They also provided further evidence that, on the behavioral side, the resistance to extinction could not be explained in terms of motivational or performance factors.

These relations between behavioral extinction and the state of the cholinergic system could be interpreted in terms of control of the system over "competing responses." Observation of behavior under even the most restricted environmental circumstances shows that an array of different responses are initially available to the organism, the majority of which soon cease to appear as they fail to be reinforced. That the latter have not been "destroyed" can be demonstrated by altering some feature of the situation; the effect is to reinstate some or perhaps all of the original array, indicating that during exposure to the situation competing responses had merely been suppressed. If reduction in ChE activity were to enhance their suppression, competing responses would not be as readily available to interfere with the dominant, reinforced behavior and hence, the latter would be more resistant to extinction; cholinolytics would be expected to have an opposite effect. Such an interpretation would be consistent with views expressed a few years ago by Carlton (1963)

and summarized in this statement: "... there are inferential grounds for supposing that a cholinergic system selectively antagonizes the effect of activation on certain behavior and that the basis of this selectivity is the extent to which that behavior is unrewarded." In the majority of experiments cited by Carlton in support of this hypothesis, behavioral effects of the administration of cholinolytic agents were interpreted as attenuating the usual effects of nonreinforcement. Data provided by Giarman and Pepeu (1964) show that, at the dose levels administered, brain ACh levels are significantly reduced, but that no gross behavioral toxicity can be observed.

In other experiments (Banks and Russell 1967), summarized in Figure 9-4, the effect of chronic reductions of ChE activity below the critical level of 40 to 50% was to increase errors in serial problem solving, presumably by interfering with suppression of competing responses when new problems were presented. As the level of ChE activity decreased, changes in behavior followed a course similar to the changes in brain ACh reported by Aprison (1962). The operation of such a mechanism could result under some circumstances in the appearance of stereotyped behavior patterns resistant to wide variations in the organism's environment. Stereotyped responding has been described by Feldberg and Sherwood (1954) following intraventricular injections of physostigmine, DFP, and ACh into cat brain. The possibility that the extreme stereotypy of human patients suffering from catatonic schizophrenia might be altered by intraventricular administration of ChE has been tested by Sherwood (1952), who reported marked but temporary relief of the major symptoms. Callaway and Stone (1960) have described effects of the cholinolytic agent, atropine, on the behavior of human subjects, who, following injection, "... are more than ordinarily susceptible to interference from peripheral stimuli, yet they perform more efficiently than do control subjects when apparently irrelevant stimuli actually serve a useful function." Observations of these kinds are consistent with the results of research on infrahuman animal subjects. They also suggest the hypothesis that relations between the cholinergic system and behavior, possibly through control of competing responses, may be involved in human behavior disorders (Russell 1965).

A number of data from a variety of different sources appear to have coherence when viewed in terms of a simple concept of relations between the cholinergic system and behavior. Such concepts are still too brash to be considered as other than general hypotheses, but they serve the useful purpose of helping to organize available empirical information and to suggest ways of putting new ideas to test.

LOCALIZED CHANGES IN THE CHOLINERGIC SYSTEM

These series of studies was consistent in suggesting the existence of a relation between certain states of the cholinergic system and the behavioral processes of extinction or competing responses. But the experiments had been relatively crude and, consequently, had left many questions unanswered. For example, in the first studies the anticholinesterase had been administered orally and, therefore, had reduced ChE activity wherever the enzyme occurred in the body; assays of the activity had been carried out on whole-brain homogenates only. Quite rightly questions were asked about how the results should be interpreted. The Adelaide group, Glow and Rose (1966), approached

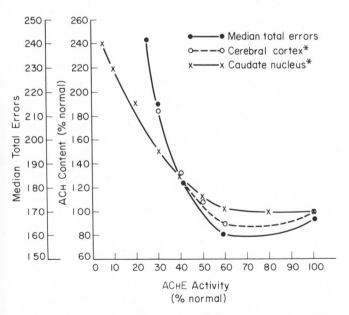

Fig. 9-4. *The curve for median total errors in a serial problem-solving situation shows that error scores increase significantly with decreasing ChE activity below a critical level between 40% and 50% of normal. The other curves show that at this level ChE loses control of its substrate, ACh.*

greater specificity of interpretation by studying peripheral vs. central ChE reduction. Behavior of animals in which whole-body reduction had been induced by intramuscular injection of the organophosphate, DFP, was compared with behavior of others receiving concurrent administration of DFP plus a potent reactivator of phosphorylated ChE (1, 3 bis, 4-hydroxyiminomethylpyridinium) which does not readily pass through the blood-brain barrier. Their report on the effectiveness of the procedure showed that, although there was some peripheral reduction in subjects receiving the combined treatment, the activity level of those without protection was lower by a factor of two, reaching 30% of normal during the first 24 hours after administration; brain ChE activity reached the same level of approximately 30% normal after 24 hours following both treatments. In later experiments in our laboratory injections have been made centrally via cannulae implanted in the lateral ventricle and effects of peripheral administration of tertiary and quaternary compounds, the latter passing through the blood-brain barrier with difficulty, have been compared. Our findings so far support the conclusion that extinction is a central process with very little peripheral component, if any.

Examination of the behavioral data from these experiments within the general context of communication models suggested three hypotheses about the possible nature of the behavioral mode of action by which the empirically observed relations are produced. First, the effect of altering the cholinergic system may be to interfere with or to retard the input of information relevant to the change in conditions of reinforcement which define the extinction procedure; second, changes in the cholinergic system may affect the encoding of information following input; and, third, the information, once encoded, may not be put to use. To test these hypotheses Warburton (1969) selected a lever-pressing situation in which rats were reinforced for making 10 lever presses whenever a light signal was presented; presses during the interval between trials postponed the onset of the next trial. In one set of experiments the cholinergic system was altered by intraventricular injection of the anticholinesterase, physostigmine, or the cholinolytic, atropine, at the point when the response pattern had stabilized. The behavioral situation was changed so that only alternate trials were reinforced. The results were subjected to a fuller analysis than had been possible in the experiments described earlier by using a mathematical model of learning, the single operator model of Bush and Sternberg (1959). This analysis, summarized in Figure 9-5, showed that the effect of both drugs had been to delay the onset of extinction of the nonreinforced alternate responses, but not to affect the rate of the subsequent extinction process. The same effect was also found in later experiments using the more conventional procedure of withholding reinforcement on all trials.

A second set of related experiments studied effects of the drugs on the maintenance of the alternation behavior after it was established. It was found that both atropine and physostigmine disrupted stable single alternation behavior, but the increase in nonreinforced responding produced by atropine was much more marked than the increase produced by physostigmine. Thus, both drugs interfered with ongoing and already extinguished responding. In addition the results of the acquisition experiment contradicted the third hypothesis. This hypothesis predicted that, if the information had been encoded, but could not be used, then, when the cholinergic system recovered, a decrease in errors would occur and the rate of decline would be faster than that of the saline-injected animals. No changes in rate were observed, suggesting that both atropine and physostigmine impaired either the input or encoding of information about the changed situation. This interpretation is consistent with the recent experiments of Carlton (1968) and Bohdanecký and Jarvik (1967). The latter study confirmed the similarities in the behavioral effects of cholinolytics and anticholinesterases.

One explanation for these behavioral similarities can be given in terms of the neuropharmacological actions of the two drugs. McLennan (1963) pointed out that both drugs can produce a functional blockade of synapses. Atropine sulfate blocks the cholinergic receptors directly, while physostigmine sulfate produces an excess of the ACh, which induces a depolarization block of the receptors. Excess ACh is produced when physostigmine inhibits AChE above a critical level and AChE loses control of its substrate ACh. The critical AChE activity level for both neural and behavioral changes appears to be about 45% of normal (Russell 1966, 1969). Behaviorally, reduction of the activity to this level or below is evidenced by a failure of subjects to withhold responding; the opposite effects have been reported at activities between the critical level and normal where there

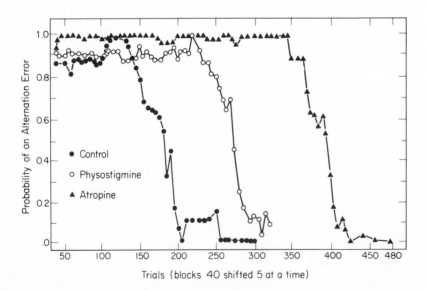

Fig. 9-5. *Acquisition of single alternation by three subjects injected intraventricularly with either normal saline, physostigmine sulfate, or atropine sulfate.*

seems to be a decrease in the variety of behavior patterns i.e., in the appearance of the stereotyped behavior discussed above, which is resistent to wide variations in the organism's environment.

The use of implanted microcannulae, which make it possible to reach into those sites where cholinoceptive cells are known to exist, has led to a series of studies involving cholinergic stimulation of the hippocampus (Warburton and Russell 1969). Up to 50% of neurons of the hippocampal cortex, including pyramidal and possibly basket cells, have been found to be sensitive to ACh and to cholinomimetics. Histochemical and microassay studies have shown the presence of both ACh's synthesizing and inactivating enzymes at the terminals of septohippocampal fibers reaching the pyramidal cells of the ventral hippocampus (Lewis, Shute, and Silver 1964). These fibers terminate in excitatory synapses on the pyramidal dendrites (Anderson, Blackstad, and Lömo 1966) and are believed to initiate the theta rhythm in the hippocampus (Stümpf 1965). Cholinergic drugs modify theta activity and a relation has been found between these changes and disruptions of a class of behavior patterns labelled "passive avoidance" (Bureš, Burešová, Bohdanecký, and Weiss 1964). Direct injection of the cholinolytic, atropine sulfate, into the hippocampal formation has been reported as producing an increase in previously inhibited responding (Khavari and Maickel 1967) while the cholinomimetic, carbamylcholine chloride, impaired responses to noxious stimuli and treated animals were generally unresponsive except for momentary escape reactions (McLean 1957). The response pattern used in the new experiments is a stable behavioral baseline, single alternation, which provides three response measures: responding when the response is proper, responding when it should be inhibited, and responding during the intertrial interval. Results, illustrated in Figure 9-6, from the experiments showed significant differential effects of cholinomimetics and cholinolytics on these measures: atropine greatly increased responding when no response should have been given, but had a much smaller effect on responding during the interval between trials; carbamylcholine chloride had the opposite effects. These results

provide another example of predictable relations between stimulation of a cholinoceptive area and changes in behavior. They are consistent with results reported by other investigators that intraseptal administration of a cholinomimetic decreased avoidance responding (Grossman 1964; Sepinwall 1966), while a cholinolytic reliably increased it (Grossman 1964) and that stimulation with the former in the midbrain reticular formation also decreased avoidance behavior, but increased appetitive responding (Grossman and Grossman 1966). These behavioral effects have been interpreted as resulting from changes in level of general reactivity which affect irrelevant response tendencies. Interpreted in this way, the results appear to support the concept of a pathway ascending from the reticular formation to the septal nuclei and hence to the hippocampal formation which is cholinoceptive and may mediate nonreinforcement as postulated by Carlton (1963).

CHRONIC CHANGES IN THE CHOLINERGIC SYSTEM

The emphasis in the research discussed above has been upon changes in the cholinergic system induced by acute administration of various drugs as tools. Recently studies of chronic changes in the system resulting from repeated administration of the anticholinesterase, DFP, have begun to suggest new concepts about the feature of the system which may be of basic importance in the cholinergic "control" of behavior.

The literature on anticholinesterases contains a number of references to the fact that behavioral adjustments may occur under conditions of chronic exposure (e.g., Sumerford, Hayes, Johnston and Spillane 1953). Glow and Rose (1966) reported similar observations during the course of some of their studies, which have been described above. The general class of observations may be described briefly in these terms: initially the behavioral changes induced by chronic administration are similar to those produced by acute administration; however, as ChE continues to remain at a reduced level, ±30% in the Glow et al. studies (1966), behavior recovers, often to the extent of not being discernably different from pretreatment levels. Clearly it is not the absolute activity level of ChE that exerts "control" over the behavior.

In order to take advantage of the new cues suggested by these almost incidental observations, we have recently undertaken a series of chronic studies in our laboratory in which we have measured behaviors of several varieties and have obtained more quantified descriptions of the phenomena reported earlier. The behaviors measured were water intake, food intake, continuous avoidance, discrete trial appetitive lever pressing, and single go-no go alternation responding. Food intake, continuous avoidance, and discrete trial responding recovered their baseline levels within 12 days, whereas water intake and single alternation were disrupted for over 18 days. The dynamics of this recovery are illustrated in Figure 9-7, where two processes are clearly observable. An anti-ChE, DFP, was administered intramuscularly every third day. Short-term recovery occurred during the periods between injections. A slower process of increased tolerance, shown by the dashed line, took place with repeated administration.

These data confirm that the behavioral effects produced could not be dependent solely upon the absolute level of activity of ChE per se. The initial changes can be related, directly or in-

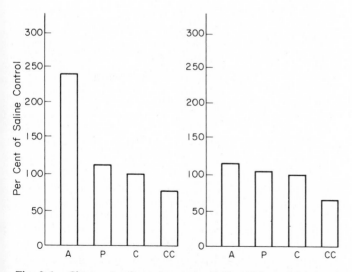

Fig. 9-6. *Changes in alternation errors (left) and intertrial interval (ITI) responding (right) following intrahippocampal injection of atropine (A), physostigmine (P), normal saline control (C) and carbachol (CC).*

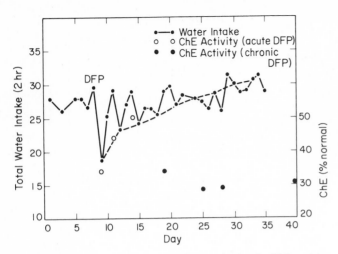

Fig. 9-7. *Effects on drinking of chronic reduction in ChE activity. Solid line shows short-term recovery of behavior during periods between administrations of DFP (every third day). Dashed line follows slower process of increased tolerance taking place with repeated administrations. Open and filled circles indicate levels of ChE activity following acute and chronic injections of DFP, respectively.*

directly, to this biochemical variable; they were similar to changes observed in many acute studies reported in the literature. But some other event(s) must be involved to account for the "recovery" of behavior during a period when ChE activity remained low. The most parsimonious view would seem to take advantage of knowledge about "feedback control" mechanisms which keep enzymes from being produced unnecessarily (Platt 1962). The general hypothesis is that experimental reduction of the ChE activity would provide feedback to the mechanism controlling ACh synthesis; the activity of choline acetylase would be altered by the processes of activation or inactivation or those of stimulation or inhibition (Pardee and Wilson 1963). The effect would be to change the quantitative relation between ACh and ChE, which had been distorted as a result of the administration of DFP, returning it eventually to its normal ratio. Presumably this process would be reflected in the recovery of behavioral measures to their predrug levels, as noted empirically in our experiments. Although the research has not yet been done, this hypothesis is testable now that techniques for the chemical analysis of ACh content in small amounts of tissue are available (Jenden et al. 1968).

EFFECTS OF DIFFERENCES IN BEHAVIOR

At several points in the earlier discussion the proposition has been stated that the relation between the cholinergic system and behavior is reciprocal in the sense that changes in behavior may be reflected in persistent neurochemical modifications, as well as changes in cholinergic events giving rise to concomitant differences in behavior. The evidence for this is now very convincing. Since it adds further support to our present theme, biochemical substrates of behavior, some typical lines of evidence will be explored very briefly.

The communications-theory model of behavior depicts behavior patterns as comprised of a series of processes, the first of which is sensory input. If relations exist between the cholinergic system and behavior, they might be observable as changes

resulting from sensory stimulation. Research reported by Liberman (1962) illustrates the search for the nature of such changes. In order to vary the amount of stimulation, one of two groups of age-matched rats was reared for 17 weeks in total darkness; the other under normal light-dark conditions. Assay of the retinas at the end of the period showed the total AChE activity of the former to be very significantly lower than that of the latter. Presumably the lower level of stimulation under the dark conditions resulted in less ACh being released in the retina; the lower AChE activity of the dark-raised rats would be explained if the synthesis and maintenance of AChE were dependent upon the level of ACh. The specificity of the effects was indicated by the fact that the activity levels of other ChEs were not affected. De Robertis and Franchi (1956), using electron microscopy, have observed a sharp decrease in the size of synaptic vesicles after even nine days in complete darkness. The facts that the retina is an embiological outgrowth from the diencephalon and is capable of neural integrating functions suggest the possibility that central enzyme activity and substrate concentration may also be affected by processes of sensory input which constitute one basic component of behavior.

This possibility has been the basis for a series of studies in the second period of the Berkeley group's search for relations between the cholinergic system and behavior (Bennett, Krech, and Rosenzweig 1964; Diamond, Krech, and Rosenzweig 1964; Krech, Rosenzweig, and Bennett 1964; Rosenzweig, Bennett, and Krech 1964). The standard procedure has been to assign littermate animals to two groups, which, from time of weaning, live in markedly different environments for 80 days, after which they are sacrificed and regional assays of brain tissue carried out. Cortical AChE activity per unit weight has been reported to decrease, while the less specific cortical ChEs increased as a function of experience; in other brain structures there were no changes in ChE, while AChE activity increased. No consistent effects upon serotonin were observed. Norepinephrine and dopamine also responded to the differential effects of the experimental environments, the changes varying in magnitude in different brain areas, thus indicating that the behavioral effects were not specific to the cholinergic system.

This brief story of interactions between the cholinergic system and behavior illustrates many of the theoretical and methodological issues discussed in the opening section of this chapter. It also provides some examples of progress in knowledge based upon successive approximations. Biochemical systems other than the cholinergic have received similar treatment, although not yet in as great depth. One related group of such systems are the monoamines.

Cerebral Monoamines

There are three major monoamines in the central nervous system—dopamine (dihydroxyphenylethylamine), norepineprine, and serotonin (5 hydroxytryptamine) whose distribution has been determined by means of fluorescent methods (Hillarp, Fuxe, and Dahlstrom 1966). The precision of this technique has enabled extensive and accurate mapping of the neuronal pathways containing these amines. In the reticular formation, two groups of norepinephrine neurons have been found: one set descends in the spinal cord while the second ascends in the medial forebrain bundle and terminates in the hypothalamus, neocortex and parts of the limbic forebrain including the septal area and hippocampal formation. Parallel to these neurons are others with serotonin-bearing axons whose cell bodies are in the mesencephalon and end in the neocortex, hypothalamus and limbid forebrain. The major differences in distributions are the higher concentrations of norepinephrine in the medial and rostral parts of the hypothalamus and the higher concentrations of serotonin in the caudate nucleus and putamen. Dopamine is found primarily in the basal ganglia with lower concentrations in other regions; it is, as shown in Figure 9-8, the precursor of norepinephrine. The basic features of the serotonin system are summarized in Figure 9-9. By means of electron microscopy, the intraneuronal distribution of the amines has been found to be highly characteristic. The soma and axons have low concentrations, whereas the synaptic terminals have 50 to 100 times more of the amine in the form of granules. These granules are believed to be stores of the inactive, or bound, amine.

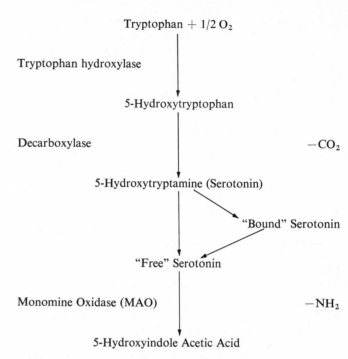

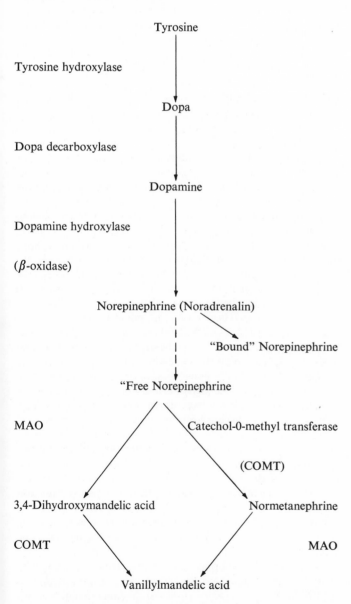

Fig. 9-8. *Diagram of the synthesis and later inactivation of the transmitter substance, norepinepherine (NE).*

Fig. 9-9. *Diagram of the synthesis and later inactivation of the transmitter substance, serotonin.*

Any unbound norepinephrine or serotonin occurring intraneuronally is deaminated by the enzyme, monoamine oxidase, regulating the tissue levels of free norepinephrine and serotonin. Neural impulses release the free amine into the synaptic cleft to reach the postsynaptic receptors. Within the cleft, both norepinephrine and serotonin are removed from the active site by enzymatic inactivation, by diffusion and by dilution. However the main mechanism for terminating the action of these transmitters appears to be active reuptake into the neuron. These processes have been worked out in the peripheral nervous system, but circumstantial evidence exists to suggest that the same principles apply to the central nervous system.

The similarities in the biochemistry of norepinephrine and serotonin, as shown in Figures 9-8 and 9-9, have made difficult attempts to correlate behavioral changes with specific biochemical systems. The separation of function of norepinephrine and serotonin has been made possible by differences in the rate and mechanism of synthesis of the two amines. Differences in rate of synthesis give different time courses for recovery for the two amines and so behavioral time-response curves can be compared with the biochemical time-response curves. In addition drugs have been discovered which act on the mechanism of synthesis of only one amine and, as a result, the function of monoamines in the central nervous system has become clearer.

EFFECTS OF INCREASED NOREPINEPHRINE RELEASE ON BEHAVIOR

Present evidence suggests that the amphetamines release free norepinephrine from the endogenous stores in the neurons and block the inactivation of norepinephrine by cellular reuptake (Glowinski and Axelrod 1966). As a result of action of the extraneuronal enzyme, catechol-0-methyl transferase, inactivating free norepinepherine, large doses of amphetamines (e.g., 10 mg/kg of amphetamine sulfate) deplete the cerebral concentration of norepinepherine while increasing serotonin and changing dopamine very little (Smith 1965). It must be remembered that these estimates of concentration represent static measures taken at specific times. On the other hand, changes in behavior are believed to be the result of the dynamic processes of norepinephrine release that result in the depleted concentrations (Scheckel and Boff 1964). This distinction must be borne in mind when interpreting all studies correlating behavior with brain amines. For example, a comparison has been made of the effects of amphetamine on locomotor activity of rats tested in groups of five and on concentrations of brain amine (Smith 1965). The results showed dose-response relations for locomotor activity were poorly correlated with changes in the concentration of the brain amines—norepinephrine, serotonin and dopamine— measured after the activity test. This experiment has a number of problems which plague research in this area. Very important is the fact that the biochemical analyses were made only after the behavioral measures were completed; thus, concomitant relations of the two classes of variables during the period of dynamic changes in the amines could not be determined. Secondly, it has been found that group interaction, i.e., aggregation, enhances norepinephrine release after amphetamine (Moore 1963): this effect is a potential source of bias affecting the biochemical variables in research designs of the kind employed by Smith in the study just described. A third type of bias may also have occurred in this study, affecting the behavioral dependent variable: aggregation results in social exploration which is enhanced by amphetamine (Chance and Silverman 1964) and there is an inverse relation between the amount of social exploration and locomotion. Contamination by such sources of bias makes difficult the interpretation of the low correlation between measures of the dependent variables, behavioral and biochemical.

The finding of increased activity associated with release of norepinephrine by amphetamine is not obtained in all behavioral situations with all doses. Responding in aversive situations has been shown to be facilitated by much lower doses of amphetamine, e.g., 0.56 mg/kg i.p. (Heise and Boff 1962). Improved performance in such situations has been explained in terms of a decrease in the competing response of "freezing" behavior (Hearst and Whalen 1963). At higher doses, e.g., there is a reversal of effect so that lever-pressing rates decrease giving a "U" shaped dose-response curve (Weissman 1959). By contrast, another form of behavior, general activity, increases over the same range of doses. This suggests that the decline in lever pressing may be due to interference by the general increase in activity. Anorexic effects of the amphetamines are well known and, in general, behavior reinforced by food is decreased by methamphetamine (Heise 1964). However, again the relation is not simple for, if the food-motivated response has a low probability of occurrence due to the characteristics of the schedule, the responding is increased by amphetamines, e.g., DRL (Kelleher and Cook 1959). Similar evidence has been obtained from thirst-motivated behavior (Hearst 1961). Electrical self-stimulation of the brain has been used in efforts to interpret this paradoxical effect. The data support the finding that low rates of responding are increased proportionally more than higher rates (Stein 1964b; Olds and Olds 1964) and that sometimes high rates are decreased (Olds and Olds 1964). In summary, the release of norepinephrine by amphetamine results in an increase in the

probability of occurrence of the measured response, but there are two confounding factors. First, in appetitive situations, there appear to be anorexic and adipsic effects tending to decrease responding and, second, there is evidence of a tendency for high-probability responses to decrease in frequency. This second paradoxical finding will be considered later in the discussion of the theory of reward thresholds.

While the amphetamines result in a decrease in cerebral norepinephrine, the monoamine oxidase inhibitors produce a rise in the brain levels of both serotonin and norepinephrine by inhibiting monoamine oxidase inactivation. Generally speaking, no behavioral effects in normal animals have been reported even when large elevations of the levels of the amines are produced. It is hypothesized that this lack of behavioral effect is due to the restriction of inactivation to within the neuron. When the increased intraneuronal norepinephrine is released extraneuronally, e.g., by administration of amphetamine, there is a marked increase in the rate of continuous avoidance responding (Heise and Boff 1960; Segal, Cox, Stern and Maickel 1967). This hypothesis that behavioral changes occur only when norepinephrine is released extraneuronally is supported by most of the available information. However, recent results by Poschel and Ninteman (1964) reporting facilitation of self-stimulation following i.p. administration of several monoamine oxidase inhibitors and current studies of consummatory behavior in our own laboratory raise questions about its universality.

EFFECTS OF DECREASED NOREPINEPHRINE RELEASE

One method of reducing the quantity of norepinephrine released is by depletion of the intraneuronal stores. It is believed that both reserpine and tetrabenazine interfere with the binding of monoamines resulting in the free intraneuronal amines being deaminated by monoamine oxidase (Kopin 1964). In this system, there appears to be a wide margin of safety for depletion and very little behavioral effect is found until the brain monoamines are reduced to 10% of normal. When effects do occur there is a marked correlation between the behavioral measures and the reduction of amines (Haggendal and Lindquist 1964).

From the early research it was not clear whether the behavioral changes were related to the depletion of norepinephrine or serotonin. However disulfiram, which inhibits norepinephrine synthesis, was found to prolong the depressant effects of reserpine on continuous avoidance (Scheckel and Boff 1966), showing that norepinephrine depletion was more important. In addition administration of the catecholamine precursor, dopa, prevented depletion of norepinephrine and the resulting behavioral depression, while serotonin's precursor, 5-hydroxytrytophan, did not (McGeer, McGeer and Wada 1963). In research on the relation between brain chemistry and behavior, few drugs are completely specific in their action at all doses. In most cases the relation must be elucidated by eliminating known alternatives. In the example just described the system of importance was found by using a second agent which had specific action on only one precursor.

An alternative approach to the problem of disentangling multiple drug actions is available when two biochemical systems show different time-response curves to the same chemical agent. Thus, in an experiment by Scheckel and Boff (1964), a single dose of 500 mg kg of alpha-methyl meta-tyrosine (α-MMT) produced a decrease in NE maximal at six hours but lasting for more than 72 hours, and a small decrease in dopamine and serotonin, maximal within three hours and returning to control within 48 hours. The first dose of α-MMT has been shown to increase responding in continuous avoidance, but a second dose, after considerable recovery of dopamine and serotonin but before NE recovery, had no effect. Thus, the changes in responding followed the time course of the NE release; increased responding was only observed when NE was available for release and bore no relation to the concentration of serotonin. This finding is relevant to one of the earliest theories of monoaminergic function and behavior, the ergotropic-trophotropic theory of Brodie and Shore (1959).

ERGOTROPIC-TROPHOTROPIC THEORY

The theory was based on Hess's description of two opposing functional systems in the diencephalon: the cerebral representations of the sympathetic, or ergotropic, system and of the parasympathetic, or trophotropic, system. These systems were thought to be active antagonists although one or the other might be predominant. Brodie and Shore (1959) postulated that diametrically opposed neuronal systems in the same area of the brain should require different neurohormonal transmitters. They identified the ergotropic transmitter as norepinephrine and the trophotropic transmitter as serotonin, thus putting forward one of the first theories of the chemical coding of behavior. Changes in behavior produced by some chemical agents were considered as changes in the relative excitability of the two systems as a result of the agents influencing transmission at the synapses. Thus, heightened behavioral arousal resulted from an increased activity in norepinephrine neurons relative to the activity of serotoninergic neurons, while sedation resulted from the opposite change. As a result, predominance of one system could be produced by chemical agents which either stimulated that system or blocked the antagonistic one. Behavioral arousal occurred with ergotropic predominance resulting from ergotropic stimulation by amphetamine or with trophotropic blocking by d-lysergic acid (LSD). In contrast, trophotropic predominance with its lowered responsiveness resulted from either trophotropic stimulation by reserpine or ergotropic blocking by chlorpromazine (Brodie and Shore 1959).

Since this formulation, further research has not confirmed that serotonin is an essential part of the stimulation-depression system. Earlier evidence was presented showing that reserpine-induced sedation was probably the result of norepinephrine depletion rather than the presence of free serotonin in the brain. It also appears likely that LSD has an action similar to that of amphetamine, as well as being a serotonin blocker. These findings are not incompatible with the theory, but in the absence of direct evidence for a serotonergic system, it has become more parsimonious to explain the behavioral changes in terms of norepinephrine alone. Chemical agents, which deplete or inactivate norepinephrine centrally, induce a decreased responsiveness; while drugs, which increase or potentiate norepinephrine release, produce increased responsiveness. Because the former drugs are used clinically in the treatment of pathological depression and the latter are used for the treatment of agitation, one version of this theory (Schildkraut and Kety 1967) states that clinical depression results from a deficiency of norepinephrine at functionally important receptor sites in the brain, whereas agitation

may be associated with an excess of this amine. In apparent contradiction to this hypothesis are a number of studies, summarized by Mandell and Spooner (1968), which demonstrated that norepinephrine injected directly into the brain produces behavioral depression. At the present time it is not clear whether these findings apply to all doses or only the relatively high doses used in the studies so far reported. As Schildkraut and Kety (1967) make clear, a catecholamine hypothesis of affective disorders can only be confirmed by a direct demonstration of a biochemical imbalance in the naturally occurring illness. Meanwhile the theory provides a framework for further work on the biochemistry of agitation and depression. The catecholamine theory of normal and abnormal behavior was based on pharmacological evidence and describes behavior only in terms of stimulation and depression. A closely related theory has been developed from behavioral studies and its frame of reference is psychological (Olds 1962; Stein 1962, 1964a & b, 1969).

THEORY OF REWARD THRESHOLDS

Like the theory of Brodie and Shore (1959), the theory of reward thresholds postulates two diencephalic systems, but these are no longer identified with the ergotropic and trophotropic systems of Hess (Olds 1962). The reward system, which facilitates ongoing operant behavior, is localized in the median forebrain bundle while the punishment system, which inhibits ongoing operant behavior, is mediated by a periventricular system. Each system has a threshold of operation which must be exceded before behavior is affected. As the two systems are assumed to be mutually inhibitory, they jointly determine the net effect on operant behavior. Thus, increased responding can result from both a lowering of the reward threshold or an increase in the punishment threshold. Conversely, decreased responding occurs with either a rise in the reward threshold or a decrease in the punishment threshold.

The model proposes that the functioning of the reward system depends on norepinephrine. For support of this notion, a number of drugs have been tested for their effects on the threshold for self stimulation (Stein 1962). In the early training each lever press delivered trains of current of fixed intensity to the posterior hypothalamus; after stable rates were obtained, threshold training was begun. Each press then produced a train of current and also reduced the intensity by a small step. A second lever was available which reset the current at its original intensity. In this way the animal reset the current when it was at a non-rewarding level i.e., subthreshold. The thresholds were found to be stable and could be obtained reliably during testing over many months. Using this preparation, Stein (1962) found that amphetamine lowered the threshold, whereas reserpine and chlorpromazine produced increases, supporting the proposal that norepinephrine was involved in the function of the reward system.

In an operant situation many responses occur prior to the culminating sequence of approach, press and release of the lever that delivers reinforcement. It would be predicted that the stimuli associated with all of these responses would have a tendency to activate the hypothalamic reward system; those that had been remote from reinforcement would have less tendency than those closely associated with reward (Stein 1964a). A decrease in the reward threshold by drugs would increase the tendency for all stimuli to activate the reward system, but remote stimuli would be increased proportionally more. As a result of testing these hypotheses, the frequency of occurrence of previously low probability responses was found to be augmented proportionally more than high probability responses during the increased release of norepinephrine by amphetamine (Stein 1964*b*; Olds and Olds 1964). This could have been the mechanism involved in the facilitation of avoidance rates reported by Hearst and Whalen (1963) which occurred when the probability of "freezing" responses was decreased by augmentation of the relatively lower probability lever pressing. High lever-pressing rates tend to be decreased as competing responses increase, giving the U-shape found in many situations (Weissman 1959).

THEORY OF PATHOLOGICAL AGITATION AND DEPRESSION

It has been proposed that agitation and depression arise from an imbalance between the two reward and punishment systems (Olds and Travis 1960; Stein 1962). Agitation results from pathological hyperactivity of the reward system, while depression results from hypoactivity in the system although the environmental input is normal (Stein 1962). In support of this theory are studies in which drugs, e.g., reserpine, used therapeutically to control psychotic agitation, increase reward thresholds (Stein 1962), while depressant drugs which are not specific for agitation, such as meprobamate, decrease self-stimulation responding very little (Olds and Olds 1964). Drugs that are therapeutically effective against depression, such as amphetamine and pargyline enhanced self-stimulation responding (Stein 1962; Poschel and Ninteman 1964). This theory is closely related to the catecholamine hypothesis of affective disorders discussed earlier and it has not been possible either to confirm or reject it on the basis of clinical data obtained so far.

MONOAMINERGIC THEORIES OF SLEEP

While norepinephrine appears to be important in levels of behavioral excitation, serotonin has been implicated in the occurrence of slow wave sleep (Jouvet 1967). Lesions in the serotonergic pathway ascending from the midbrain raphé result in marked increases in wakefulness (Jouvet 1968). Injections of parachlorphenylalanine, a serotonin depletor, decreased the amount of slow wave sleep (Koella, Feldstein and Czicman 1968). In contrast, an increase in serotonin by injections of the serotonin precursor, 5-hydroxytrytophan, produce an increase in the proportion of slow wave sleep (Jouvet 1969). Although serotonin plays a role in slow wave sleep it is not yet clear what biochemical systems are involved in paradoxical sleep. Some evidence suggests serotonin, acetylcholine and norepinephrine may all play some part (Jouvet 1969).

Protein Synthesis

Repeatedly in this discussion it has been necessary to refer to the primary role of protein synthesis in all the biochemical systems suspected of involvement in control of behavior. Since there are dynamic systems whose *in vitro* velocities depend upon the biocatalytic action of enzymes, that is, as stated at the very

introduction of our story, entirely to be expected. In the readout of genetic information from the DNA codes, transcription into RNA structure and translation into amino acid sequences find expression in the synthesis of specific enzymes. These in turn, acting in precisely defined temporal and spatial manners, presumably control the construction of other cell constituents and, eventually, the specialized structures and functions of the living organism. Relations of these kinds make very understandable the recent livening of interest in protein synthesis as a potential source of substrates for behavior.

The hypothesis that information storage might be accomplished by protein synthesis was part of Zeitgeist of the late 1940 s. Biologists had long stressed the similarity between the storage of memory and of genetic information. Following the advances in biochemical genetics, biochemists, neurophysiologists and psychobiologists carried the analogy further. The immense coding possibilities of the protein macromolecules were recognized; the number of "bits" of information held in the human memory would require molecules, like polymers of nucleic acids, sufficiently rich in patterns to hold such information (Katz and Halstead 1950; Gerard 1960). Except for the nucleic acids, it seems that proteins may be the only chemical structures capable of forming a molecular code of any complexity. As advances in molecular biology occurred, attention focused upon DNA and RNA molecules as the possible basis of the memory code. RNA with its enormous turnover would give a unique site for an interaction between the organism's genetic potential and its environmental experiences, but other macromolecules have not yet been discarded from among the candidates (Gaito 1966a and 1966b; Humphrey and Coxon 1963).

Empirical tests of hypotheses at this level have become possible as knowledge has led to the invention of suitable techniques for observing, measuring and manipulating the biochemical events involved. The result has been rapidly increasing efforts in research of three kinds:

Class 1. Experimenters have manipulated the learning experiences of the organism as the independent variable. Chemical analysis of brain tissue extracts have provided measures of the dependent variable.

Class 2. Frequently referred to as "transfer" experiments, these studies begin by exposing subjects to learning experiences. The subjects are then sacrificed and some form of biochemical extract made from brain tissue. This extract is then injected into an untrained, "naive" subject of the same or different species. The behavioral effect of the injection is measured as the dependent variable.

Class 3. Specific events at the macromolecular level within the organism have been manipulated by means of drugs as tools. The effect of systematic changes in these independent variables are measured behaviorally.

Class 1. *Learning-Produced Biochemical Changes:* In reviewing this group of studies, discussion will consider only those experiments which have manipulated learning as the independent variable and examined changes in the protein precursors as the dependent variables. A number of experiments have been performed in the U.S.S.R.; and two of particular interest were described by Palladin and Vladmirov in 1956. In the first experiment, rats received an electric shock paired with a neutral stimulus according to the usual Pavlovian conditioning paradigm. Before the acquisition of the conditioned defense reaction, they received intraperitoneal injections of radioactive phosphorus, P^{32}; after conditioning, the animals were sacrificed and the rate of incorporation of the radioactive phosphorus into brain RNA examined. Rats that had learned showed increased incorporation of radioactive phosphorus into the brain RNA, suggesting that learning had been correlated with increased synthesis of RNA. A second experiment by Kreps (quoted by Palladin and Vladmirov 1956) showed that pairing a neutral stimulus with food produced increased incorporation of radioactive phosphorous in the primary sensory cortex associated with the neutral stimulus. These studies suggest that sensory stimulation in a learning situation produces increased RNA synthesis, which appears to be localized in that part of the sensory cortex associated with the particular stimulus involved. Unfortunately, the brief reports in Palladin and Vladmirov do not provide adequate evidence as to whether appropriate controls were performed to distinguish sensory stimulation from learning.

A second group of studies (Hydén 1959, 1961) examined effects of learning and of sensory stimulation upon glial- and nerve-cell RNA and upon the proportions of the four bases in the RNA of these cells, i.e., adenine, guanine, cytosine and uracil. In addition Hydén and his co-workers have examined the purine and pyrimidine base ratios in the nerve cells of rats that have learned (Hydén and Egyházi 1962, 1963). Rats learned to balance and walk up a steel wire inclined at 45° to reach food. The rats were sacrificed and the RNA from the lateral vestibular nucleus, Deiter's neurons, and the surrounding glial cells analysed and compared with corresponding material from control rats who were merely stimulated by rotation. In the rats that learned, the adenine-uracil ratio increased significantly and there was also an increased amount of RNA per nerve cell. In a later experiment, rats were trained to use their non-preferred paw to reach for food in a narrow tube e.g., right-handed rats were trained to use their left paw. Analysis was made of the base ratios of RNA extracted from the fifth and sixth cortical layers of the right somatosensory cortex; earlier studies had demonstrated that lesions in these areas prevent transfer of handedness, indicating that this area of the cortex is involved in mediating this form of behavior. A significant increase in amounts of RNA and changes in the base ratios were found in this area, using the comparable area in the left cortex as a control. In still more recent studies Hydén and Lange (1968) have found that labeled leucine was incorporated into the hippocampal cells as the result of training on the transfer of handedness task. The trend was for higher incorporation to occur in cells contralateral to the paw used.

Many of the experiments demonstrating changes in RNA metabolism have involved prolonged training. However, Zemp, Wilson, Schlesinger, Boggan and Glassman (1966) have reported that 15 minutes training in a discriminated avoidance situation is sufficient to produce increased incorporation of radiouridine into the RNA of whole mouse brain. In contrast there were no consistent changes in the incorporation of uridine into the liver RNA of trained mice. Yoked control animals, that received the same treatment escept for the escape contingency, did not show any consistent changes. The marked and consistent changes in the trained animals suggest that there is either an RNA change in many parts of the brain or there is a large change in the specific area as the result of training.

These are but a few among the increasing number of experiments designed to discover whether macromolecular changes are concomitant with changes in behavior, e.g., with learning. Of all three classes of research approaches, this type of design could give the most straightforward answer to the general questions which are motivating the investigations. But there are many serious technical problems yet to be solved before the requirements of the design can be fully satisfied. For example, a recurring problem is selection of proper research groups to control for nonspecific effects of the behavioral change; ideally it is essential to have subjects treated in *identical* ways, yet some learning and some not. There are difficulties in specifying that a particular macromolecule detected in such an experiment is *unique* to the behavioral processes involved (Machlus and Gaito 1968). From the brief illustrations given above it is apparent that these technical problems are recognized and that ingenuity is being called upon to solve them.

Class 2. *"Transfer" Experiments:* In experiments of this type some brain extract from a trained subject is introduced into a naive subject and some "savings" is sought in measures of the latter's performance of the behavior for which the donor had initially been trained. Among the very early attempts to carry through this type of design were an extensive series of experiments using planaria, flatworms, as subjects (McConnell 1966). Planaria were subjected to a classical conditioning paradigm; they were then cut in pieces and fed to "hungry cannibals," naive as far as the conditioned response was concerned. A day later, the latter were found to be significantly more responsive to the conditioned stimulus than were control subjects fed earlier on untrained planaria (McConnell 1962). As can readily be imagined, these reports caused much excitement, although considerable controversy about methodological issues followed (e.g., Jensen 1965). There were reports of failures to replicate results (Bennett and Calvin 1964) and rebuttals (McConnell 1966). Regardless of the final outcome, these studies were important in suggesting and refining the "transfer" type of research design in the search for macromolecular substrates of behavior.

As might have been anticipated, studies of planaria stimulated an interest in examining the "transfer" phenomenon in more complex organisms, the rat becoming a favorite subject. In an early experiment (Jacobson, Babich, Bubash and Jacobson 1965) two groups of rats were trained to approach a food cup when a discriminative stimulus, a light or click, was presented. When this training was completed the trained animals were sacrificed and a portion of the brain removed. RNA was extracted from the tissue and eight hours later injected intraperitoneally into a food-deprived test rat. A research design was used whereby the experimenters were unaware of which extract, i.e., from animals trained to click or light, the test rat had received. Responses of the rats to magazine clicks were counted. It was found that, on the average, rats injected with 'click' RNA tended to approach the food cup significantly more often after the magazine click than rats receiving injections of "light" RNA. These differential response tendencies were attributed to differences in the RNA extract injected and were considered as evidence for memory transfer.

These intriguing results have been followed up by many investigations with attempts to replicate and extend these findings. While some positive results have been reported (e.g., Rosenblatt, Farrow and Herblin 1966; Ungar 1966 and 1968;

Ungar and Irwin 1967), extensive work in some other laboratories have failed to replicate the phenomenon using intraperitoneal, intracisternal and intraventricular injections of RNA extracts (Byrne and 22 others 1966). An alternative explanation of the positive transfer experiment was offered by Halas, Bradfield, Sandlie, Theye and Beardsley (1966), who were unable to transfer a differential response tendency, but found a change in level of general activity. They suggested that this change in behavior may well have been dependent upon the presence of some stimulating contaminate in the RNA extract. Whatever the merits of this explanation, it has been shown that in the normal animals, P[32] labeled RNA does not pass the blood-brain barrier (Luttges, Johnson, Buck, Holland and McGaugh 1966), indicating that positive results obtained in some experiments were not the result of unmetabolised RNA entering the brain and carrying encoded information.

An interesting variation on the usual transfer paradigm, which attempts to come to grips with this problem, has been described by Albert (1966). Rats were trained in a passive avoidance situation with one hemisphere blocked with spreading depression induced by potassium chloride applied cortically. The medial cortex of the trained hemisphere was then removed, abolishing the avoidance behavior. An extract of the nuclei of these cortical cells was obtained and injected intraperitoneally into the same animal. This injection resulted in a savings in acquisition by the remaining portions of the cortex. The savings was found only when the following conditions held: with injections of nucleoli of the medial cortex, nuclear material from the animal itself, nuclear material removed several hours after a retest in the same situation. These data suggest that very specific transfer of information was mediated by nuclear material. Albert cites evidence from Lajtha (1962) that lesions increase the permeability of the blood-brain barrier and permit larger molecules than normal to enter the brain. Thus, in his experiment, large molecules in the extracted material may have reached the CNS.

It is interesting that early in the search for macromolecular substrates of behavior, RNA played the role of leading candidate. Encouraged by reports from Hydén's laboratory that learning might result in changes in RNA synthesis and base ratios and by some of the studies of planaria (Corning and John 1961), many "transfer" studies began with the assumption that RNA was involved and therefore prepared their brain extracts accordingly. The techniques for extraction have often been questioned. Furthermore, the evidence presented above that RNA does not normally pass the blood-brain barrier (Luttges et al. 1966) raises serious issues as to whether active components of extracts, even when they appeared to affect behavior, were acting peripherally or whether the effective component(s) was in fact a metabolite(s) of the extracts. These questions have seemed particularly appropriate when injections of brain extracts have been given peripherally, most often intraperitoneally, and the opportunity for biotransformation has been great. Not all investigators have started with the RNA assumption. Reports by Rosenblatt, Farrow and Herblin (1966) and by Ungar and Irwin (1967) suggest that peptides or proteins are involved as active components in the "transfer" process. It will be well at this point to recall a point emphasized in the opening paragraph of this section in which the close, dynamic relations between the roles of DNA, RNA, and amino acid sequences in the process of protein synthesis was emphasized. Basically all must be involved in any "transfer" process of the kind we have been discussing.

Class 3. Experimental Manipulation of Protein Synthesis: The third class of investigations have been concerned with manipulations of specific macromolecular events involved at some step in protein synthesis and with measuring concomitant changes in behavior. One subclass has attempted to facilitate the learning process and another to examine impairment of learning.

Early among these were clinical studies by Cameron and Solyom (1961) which examined the effects of RNA supplements, administered both orally and intravenously, on the memory performance of geriatric patients suffering from organic memory defects. It was found that RNA improved performance on a standardized test of memory, i.e., the Wechsler Memory Scale counting test, and on conditioning of the galvanic skin response. In addition, the patients were more generally alert. The change in alertness suggests that the RNA may have enhanced attention due to the dietary improvement which itself facilitates nerve cell regeneration. The nutritional improvement hypothesis is supported by both the wide range of doses need to facilitate the test behaviors, i.e., 30–1482 gms., and the fact that facilitation was accompanied by a gain in body weight. These results obtained within a clinical setting were paralleled by Cook, Davidson, Davis, Green and Fellows (1963) in the animal research laboratory. They administered RNA intraperitoneally to rats and examined the acquisition and extinction of a pole-climbing response in a discriminated avoidance situation. In this experiment, it was found that the RNA-treated group had a significantly faster rate of acquisition compared with a saline-injected control group. As in Cameron's experiments, extinction appeared slower for the RNA group, but since their initial performance was better no exact comparison is possible. Cook et al. (1963) were very conservative in their conclusions, suggesting that they had not yet eliminated the possibility of an interaction of RNA with some of the parameters of the behavioral situation, e.g., motivation due to increased sensitivity to shock.

One approach to solving poblems arising from the compounding of drug effects on learning with the drug's nonspecific effects has been to use *post-trial injections:* learning trial; injection of drug; and tests of comparative performances of drug- and placebo-injected control subjects. In a series of experiments with strychnine, which has been shown to increase the concentration of brain RNA (Carlini and Carlini 1965), McGaugh and his co-workers (McGaugh 1966) have shown that a variety of tasks is facilitated by injections of strychnine up to 30 minutes after training. These data suggest that permanent registration of information can be improved by injections of a drug which increases brain RNA.

Among the earliest of the studies designed to manipulate protein synthesis experimentally were some which involved *production of fraudulent ribonucleotides.*

Dingman and Sporn (1961) examined the effects of an RNA antimentabolite 8-azaguanine, injected intracisternally in very small amounts, 136 gamma, on the acquisition of a water maze. 8-azaguanine acts as an analog of the purine base, guanine, and produces fraudulent ribonucleotides which in turn produce non-replicating messenger RNA. Although the control and drug groups were matched on their performance on two other mazes, the 8-azaguanine-injected animals made a significantly greater number of errors on the test maze. An examination of the results shows that the greatest differences between groups in mean errors were found during the first five trials and that the most marked difference was on the first trial. But trial 1 cannot validly be considered as demonstrating learning, and after the first few trials learning curves were essentially parallel for both groups. When the scores on each trial are considered as percentages of the first trial, the Vincent curves for the two groups overlap to a great extent and the drugged animals, when equated for "exploratory" activity, show no impairment in learning. The hypothesis that the experimental treatment affected exploratory activity is supported to some extent by the results of the experiment reported in the same paper (Dingman and Sporn 1961) where rats were tested for recall after 8-azaguanine and it was found that the mean number of "errors" made by the drug group was double the control, although the variance was so large as to affect tests of significance. One approach to this problem of nonspecific effects is to use an experimental design which enables separate assessment of the general effects of the drug's effects on performance from those on learning as well as controlling for the irreversibility of the learning experience. Warburton and Russell (1968) studied behavioral effects of 8-azaguanine using an experimental design described by Cox (1954). The design was developed for situations where a subject can be used as its own control, but the treatment order cannot be reversed. Using this design, it was possible to shown that 8-azaguanine injected intraventricularly delayed the acquisition of a new temporal discrimination response when rats trained on one continuous avoidance schedule were changed to a second. The period of this delay was consistent with that for the inhibition of protein synthesis by 8-azaguanine reported by Dingman and Sporn (1961). In their study Warburton and Russell (1968) used a staining technique to demonstrate that intraventricular injection of 8-azaguanine inhibited protein synthesis in the hippocampus, concomitantly with which the impairment in learning occurred.

In the mid 1950 s biochemical pharmacologists developed a group of drugs, as antibiotics and anticancer agents, whose biochemical mode of action involved *inhibition of protein synthesis*. Some of these have been used as tools for the experimental manipulation of protein synthesis in studies of behavioral effects. For example, the puromycin molecule is an analogue of the soluble RNA-amino acid complex and thus interferes with the final stage of protein synthesis. Puromycin has been used by Flexner and his colleagues in an extensive series of experiments. In their early studies (Flexner, Flexner, and Stellar 1963; Flexner, Flexner, Stellar, Roberts, and de la Haba 1964) they found that, although there was 83% inhibition of protein synthesis after a subcutaneous injection of puromycin, acquisition of a shuttle-box avoidance response or a discriminated avoidance response in a Y maze was not impaired. The most marked effect on protein synthesis was found in the hippocampus, and injections directly into this site and into the caudal cortex one to three days after learning impaired retention. The most convincing demonstration of this phenomenon used a reversal procedure. The animals were trained to run into one side of a Y maze, and then 21 days after the original learning the position habit was reversed. The day following the reversal training the animals were given bilateral injections of puromycin into the hippocampus and adjacent cortex. When retested the following day, the reversal was abolished and the animals performed consistently in accordance with the habit learned three weeks previously. These results supported the view that the functional integrity of the hippocampus is important for either the storage of information or retrieval during the retention test.

Biochemical studies of other inhibitors of protein synthesis have shown modes of action to involve different components of the process. Barondes and Jarvik (1964) have taken advantage of the fact that actinomycin D in a specific inhibitor of DNA-dependent RNA synthesis to inhibit RNA synthesis in the cortex. Intracerebral injections of actinomycin into the brains of mice in doses sufficient to produce marked inhibition of RNA synthesis did not interfere with the learning of a simple passive avoidance response. These results are in contrast to those of Agranoff, David, Casola and Lim (1967) who have reported that in goldfish, actinomycin "blocks formation of memory" in shock-avoidance training. Discrepancies of this kind may be due to constraints of the behavioral measure used, e.g., responding is truncated as a subject approaches zero responses in the passive avoidance situation, or to differences in time after training that retention is measured and the test species used.

Acetoxycycloheximide exerts its action by impairing the transfer of amino acids from the transfer RNA to the polypeptides preventing the formation of peptide bonds. Intracerebral injection of acetoxycycloheximide does not impair the retention of memory when tested three days after learning, despite a large inhibition of protein synthesis (Flexner and Flexner, 1966). This inhibition occurs with a decrease in the rate of decay of messenger RNA. By comparison, injection of puromycin does not prevent the formation of peptide bonds and so messenger RNA decays without replacement; as stated above, such injection directly into certain CNS sites resulted in impairment of retention. These contrastive data suggest that messenger RNA may be important for the preservation of the encoded information. In addition to such uses of acetoxycycloheximide in the search for differential relations between behavior and the various components of protein synthesis, investigators have studied the drug's effects upon retention when administered at various times before and after training (Flexner, Flexner, and Roberts 1967; Barondes and Cohen 1968). Although the results are adding significantly to knowledge about biochemical bases of behavior, there are still important problems of interpretation, among which is the pervading question of whether specific or nonspecific effects are involved. For example, Cohen and Barondes (1967) have demonstrated that intrahippocampal injection of puromycin, but not of acetoxycycloheximide, increased the susceptibility of animals to develop seizures. Divergent effects of the two drugs upon retention could thus be due to differences in their effects upon seizure acivity rather than directly to different mechanisms in the inhibition of protein synthesis.

In order to determine the time that puromycin must be present in the brain to disrupt previous training, Flexner (1968) used a *saline washout technique*. Saline injected four to twenty hours after puromycin partly alleviated the disruptive effects of the antibiotic. However, saline injections between two and sixty days also resulted in some recovery of memory. The saline wash was effective in restoring memory when the puromycin was injected one or more days after the training session, but was relatively ineffective when puromycin was injected either before or immediately after, i.e., four to eight minutes, the session (Flexner and Flexner 1968). Thus puromycin appears to interfere with both the registration and retrieval of information, but not with retention; saline injections can partly reverse the retrieval block. This retrieval block could be due to impairment of synaptic functions by the abnormal peptides synthesized.

The first *theoretical models of the biochemical basis of memory* suggested that information was stored as changes in nucleoprotein. One theory of how this might be accomplished, proposed by Hydén (1959), is based on the fact that DNA controls the production of cytoplasmic proteins through the mediation of RNA. Neuronal RNA may change as the result of the pattern of neural impulses. These impulses affect the ionic equilibrium of the cytoplasm, change the stability of one or more bases of the RNA, and result in an exchange with another base in the intraneuronal pool. The specification of the RNA is completed if the new bases were stable under the influence of the new pattern of neural impulses. The specified RNA with its novel sequence of bases then controls the production of a new protein. Subsequent stimulation activates the previously specified protein, which releases a transmitter substance and transmits an impulse to the next neuron. This model accounts for the changes in base ratios reported by Hydén and his co-workers. It would also explain the disruptions observed with protein synthesis inhibitors. At the present time there is no very good evidence to support this type of instruction of RNA. Evidence against specification of novel protein has been put forward by Briggs and Kitto (1962), who have pointed out that changes in the genetically determined RNA would disrupt normal cellular metabolism and that the novel protein synthesised would elicit a foreign protein reaction.

A model not subject to these criticisms is the gene expression theory of Flexner and his co-workers (Flexner et al. 1967). According to this model, protein molecules are believed to be the final storage molecule and their synthesis is controlled by a species of m RNA. Training is believed in some way to trigger the transcription of specific species of m RNA by particular genes, i.e., from DNA. Thus, the essential biochemical change in memory storage is not modification of molecule, but increased production of already available species of m RNA. The "memory molecule" synthesised is the outcome of a change in the pattern of gene expression produced during training. The newly synthesised proteins are thought to modify the characteristic of synapses to facilitate future neural transmission. In addition, the proteins or their products act as inducers of their specific m RNA, maintaining the concentration of the inducer proteins above the critical level for further gene induction. When this model was proposed, it was argued that puromycin, by preventing the formation of protein, interfered with the permanent registration of information by the formation of fraudulent polypeptides and also led to the decay of the m RNA and thereby to loss of information. Acetoxycycloheximide prevented permanent encoding but also delayed decay of m RNA so that recovery from inhibition found persisting m RNA still capable of serving as the "memory Molecule." Actinomycin, although inhibiting RNA synthesis, did not interfere with the permanent storage, whereas 8-azaguanine which produced fraudulent RNA did interfere. Thus, blocking a step in the protein synthesis process did not prevent permanent encoding, although this might be delayed until recovery from the inhibitor, whereas when the process proceeded but resulted in nonreplicating molecules, there was loss in this storage of information.

It is not feasible here to review the several other theoretical models which have been proposed to account for the kinds of empirical results reported earlier in this section (Landauer 1964; Dingman and Sporn 1964; Gaito 1966; Ungar 1968). The brief descriptions above provide a general view of the form such models now take. Clearly, new research results will lead to refinements in present conceptions and probably to different forms than have yet been considered.

The Road Ahead

Throughout the preceding discussion has run the view, based upon both the phylogenetic and ontogenetic genealogies of each individual, that the biochemical property of living organisms has a kind of historical priority when compared with other properties. It has also been emphasized that biochemical events share with behavior the characteristic of frequent change over time. Thus, in a very general sense, we might expect to find interactions between these two properties, both of which are dynamic and one of which is clearly the temporal antecedent of the other. This expectation is rapidly becoming a reality. What lies in the road ahead?

Clearly, the trend toward the use of more precise techniques for specifying the nature and the laws of changes induced by experimental manipulations of biochemical variables must continue as a matter of highest priority. As developments of knowledge and methodology occur in biochemistry, pharmacology, and neurophysiology, it will be possible to direct attention toward the search for much greater specificity than is now possible in defining the biochemical bases of behavior.

It is also very apparent that increasing care must be taken in selecting behavioral variables to be studied and in insuring that their measurement involves techniques which meet the criteria of all good measuring instruments. Investigators must use multiple measures, rather than depend upon single measures whose behavioral significance may be difficult to interpret.

Since relations between biochemical events and behavior are complex in nature, particular attention must be given to research design. The concept of concomitant variation, which is basic to the search for such relations, requires that the independent variable be systematically altered in several quantitative steps. To do this, investigators have most often used a randomized groups design in which n subjects are assigned at random to one of k treatments and results analyzed by analysis of variance. The advantages of using the same subjects for repeated treatment have led a few researchers to employ some variation of the latin square design. We have referred in the preceding pages to still more sophisticated approaches which will support economy of research effort and permit more effective analyses of complex interactions among the variety of behavioral, biochemical, and pharmacological variables characteristically present in experiments of the kind we are discussing.

Recently there has begun to appear a use of mathematical models in terms of which parameters of behavior can be identified and defined with greater quantitative precision. Such models will be helpful in suggesting new hypotheses. Their appearance means that this field of research is moving in a direction which has characterized increasing maturity in scientific development generally.

It is probably true that in so complex an area of biological relationships no single *experimentum crucis* can be designed to answer any major question. Instead we can expect that new principles will develop by the convergence of results from a number of related experiments: knowledge will become systematized by a series of approximations. Success will be contingent upon new ideas and solutions of technological problems in the basic disciplines which will continue to be involved in the search for biochemical bases of behavior; it will be particularly dependent upon the ingenious melding of concepts and methods from all.

References

AGRANOFF, B. W., R. E. DAVIS, L. CASOLA, and R. LIM. Actinomycin D blocks formation of memory of shock-avoidance in goldfish. *Science*, 1967, *158*: 1600–1601.

ALBERT, D. J. Memory in mammals: evidence for a system involving nuclear ribonucleic acid. *Neuropsychologia*, 1966, *4*: 79–92.

ANDERSON, P., T. W. BLACKSTAD, and T. LÖMO. Location and identification of excitatory synapses on hippocampal pyramidal cells. *Experimental Brain Research*, 1966, *1*: 236–48.

APRISON, M. H. On a proposed theory of the mechanism of action of serotonin in the brain. *Recent Advances in Biological Psychiatry*, 1962, *4*: 133–46.

BANKS, A., and R. W. RUSSELL. Effects of chronic reductions in acetylcholinesterase activity on serial problem solving behavior. *Journal of Comparative and Physiological Psychology*, 1967, *64*: 262–67.

BARONDES, S. H., and H. D. COHEN. Memory impairment after subcutaneous injection of acetoxycycloheximide. *Science*, 1968, *160*: 556–57.

———, and M. E. JARVIK. The influence of actinomycin-D on brain RNA synthesis and on memory. *Journal of Neurochemistry*, 1964, *11*: 187–96.

BENNETT, E. L., and M. CALVIN. Failure to train planarians reliably. *Neurosciences Research Program* Bulletin, 1964, *2*: 3–24.

———, D. KRECH, and M. R. ROSENZWEIG. Reliability and regional specificity of cerebral effects of environmental complexity and training. *Journal of Comparative and Physiological Psychology*, 1964, *57*: 440–41.

BOHDANECKÝ, Z., and M. JARVIK. Impairment of one-trial passive avoidance learning in mice by scopolamine, scopolamine methylbromide, and physostigmine. *International Journal of Neuropharmacology*, 1967, *6*: 217–22.

BORING, E. *A history of experimental psychology*. New York: Appleton-Century-Crofts, 1950.

BRIGGS, M. H., and G. B. KITTO. The molecular basis of memory and learning. *Psychological Review*, 1962, *69*, 537–41.

BRODIE, B. B. Difficulties in extrapolating data on metabolism of drugs from animal to man. *Clinical Pharmacology and Therapeutics*, 1962, *3*, 374–80.

———, and P. SHORE. Mechanism of action of psychotropic drugs. In *Psychopharmacology Frontiers*. Proceedings of the Psychopharmacology Symposium of the Second International Congress of Psychiatry. Boston, Mass.: Little, Brown and Co., 1959.

BUREŠ, J., O. BUREŠOVA, Z. BOHDANECKÝ, and T. WEISS. The effect of physostigmine and atropine on the mechanism of learning. *In* H. STEINBERG, A.V.S. DE REUCK, and J. KNIGHT, (eds.) *Animal behavior and drug action*. London: Churchill, 1964.

BUSH, R. R., and S. H. STERNBERG. A single operator model. *In* R. R. BUSH and W. K. ESTES (eds.) *Studies in mathematical learning theory*. Stanford: Stanford Univ. Press, 1959.

BYRNE, W., and 22 others. Memory transfer. *Science*, 1966, *153*: 658–59.

CALLAWAY, E., and G. STONE. Re-evaluating focus of attention. *In* L. UHR and J. G. MILLER (eds.) *Drugs and behavior*. New York: Wiley, 1960.

CAMERON, D. E., and L. SOLYOM. Effects of ribonucleic acid on memory. *Geriatrics*, 1961, *16*: 74–81.

CARLINI, G. R. S., and E. A. CARLINI. Effects of strychnine and cannabis sativa (marijuana) on the nucleic acid content in the brain of the rat. *Medicina et Pharmacologia Experimentalis*, 1965, *12*: 21–26.

CARLTON, P. L. Cholinergic mechanisms in the control of behavior by the brain. *Psychological Review*, 1963, *70*: 19–39.

——— Brain acetylcholine and habituation. *In* P. B. BRADLEY and M. FINK, *Anticholinergic drugs and brain functions in animals and man*. Amsterdam: Elsevier, 1968.

CHANCE, M. R. A., and A. P. SILVERMAN. The structure of social behavior and drug action. *In* H. STEINBERG, A.V.S. DE REUCK, and J. KNIGHT (eds.) *Animal behavior and drug action*. London: Churchill, 1964.

COHEN, H. D., and S. H. BARONDES. Puromycin effect on memory may be due to occult seizures. *Science*, 1967, *157*: 333–34.

COOK, L., A. B. DAVIDSON, D. J. DAVIS, H. GREEN, and E. J. FELLOWS. Ribonucleic acid: effect on conditioned behavior in rats. *Science*, 1963, *141*: 268–69.

CORNING, W. C., and E. R. JOHN. Effect of ribonuclease on retention of conditioned response in regenerated planarians. *Science*, 1961, *134*: 1363.

COX, D. R. The design of an experiment in which certain treatment arrangements are inadmissible. *Biometrika*, 1954, *41*: 287–95.

DE ROBERTIS, E., and C. M. FRANCHI. Electron microscope observations on synaptic vesicles in synapses of the retinal rods and cones. *Journal of Biochemical and Biophysical Cytology*, 1956, *2*: 307–18.

DEL CASTILLO, J., and B. KATZ. The membrane change produced by the neuromuscular transmitter. *Journal of Physiology*, 1954, *125*: 546–65.

DEWHURST, W. G., and E. MARLEY. Differential effect of sympathomimetic amines on the central nervous system. *In* H. STEINBERG, A.V.S. DE REUCK, and J. KNIGHT, (eds.) *Animal behavior and drug action*. London: Churchill, 1964.

DIAMOND, M. C., D. KRECH, and M. R. ROSENZWEIG. The effects of an enriched environment on the histology of the rat cerebral cortex. *Journal of Comparative Neurology*, 1964, *123*: 111–19.

DINGMAN, W. and M. B. SPORN. The incorporation of 8-azaguanine into rat brain RNA and its effect on maze learning by the rat: An inquiry into the biochemical basis of memory. *Journal of Psychiatric Research*, 1961, *1*: 1–11.

——— Molecular theories of memory. *Science*, 1964, *144*: 26–29.

DIXON, W. E. Vagus inhibition. *British Medical Journal*, 1906, *2*: 1807.

FELDBERG, W. *A pharmacological approach to the brain from its inner and outer surfaces*. London: Arnold, 1963.

———, and S. L. SHERWOOD. Behavior of cats after intraventricular injections of eserine and DFP. *Journal of Physiology* (London), 1954, *125*: 488–500.

FISHER, A. E., and J. N. COURY. Cholinergic tracing of a central neural circuit underlying the thirst drive. *Science*, 1962, *138*: 691–93.

FLEMING, R. M., W. G. CLARK, E. D. FENSTER, and J. C. TOWNE. Single extraction method for the simultaneous fluorimetric determination of serotonin, dopamine, and norepinephrine in brain. *Analytical Chemistry*, 1965, *37*: 692–96.

FLEXNER, L. B. Dissection of memory in mice with antibiotics. *American Scientist*, 1968a, *56*: 52–57.

———, and J. B. FLEXNER. Intracerebral saline: effect on memory of trained mice treated with puromycin. *Science*, 1968b, *159*: 330–31.

———, and R. B. ROBERTS. Memory in mice analysed with antibiotics. *Science*, 1967, *155*: 1377–83.

FLEXNER, J. B., L. B. FLEXNER, E. STELLAR. Memory in mice as affected by intracerebral puromycin. *Science*, 1963, *141*: 57–59.

———, G. DE LA HABA, and R. B. ROBERTS. Inhibition of protein synthesis in brain and learning and memory following puromycin. *Journal of Neurochemistry*, 1962, *9*: 595–605.

——— Loss of recent memory as related to regional inhibition of cerebral protein synthesis. *Proceedings of the National Academy of Science*, 1964, *52*: 1165–69.

GAITO, J. Molecular psychobiology: A chemical approach to learning and other behavior. Springfield, Ill.: C. C Thomas, 1966.

——— (ed.) *Macromolecules and behavior*. New York: Appleton-Century-Crofts, 1966.

GERARD, R. W. Neurophysiology: An integration. *In* J. FIELD (ed.) *Handbook of Neurophysiology* (Vol 3) Washington, D. C.: American Physiological Society, 1960.

GIARMAN, J. J., and G. PEPEU. The influence of centrally acting cholinolytic drugs on brain acetylcholine levels. *British Journal of Pharmacology*, 1964, *23*: 123–30.

GLOW, P. H., A. RICHARDSON, and S. ROSE. Effects of acute and chronic inhibition of cholinesterase upon body weight, food intake, and water intake in the rat. *Journal of Comparative and Physiological Psychology*, 1966, *61*: 295–98.

———, and S. ROSE. Effects of light and dark on the acetylcholinesterase activity of the retina. *Nature*, 1964, *202*: 422–23.

——— Cholinesterase levels and operant extinction. *Journal of Comparative and Physiological Psychology*, 1966, *61*: 165–72.

GLOWINSKI, J., and J. AXELROD. Effects of drugs on the disposition of H³ norepinephrine in the rat brain. *Pharmacological Review*, 1966, *18*: 775–86.

———, I. KOPIN, and J. AXELROD. Metabolism of H³-norepinephrine in the rat brain. *Journal of Neurochemistry*, 1965, *12*: 25–30.

GROSSMAN, S. P. Eating and drinking elicited by direct adrenergic or cholinergic stimulation of the hypothalamus. *Science*, 1960, *132*: 301–20.

——— Effects of adrenergic and cholinergic blocking agents on hypothalamic mechanisms. *American Journal of Physiology*, 1962, *202*: 1230–35.

——— Effect of chemical stimulation of the septal area on motivation. *Journal of Comparative and Physiological Psychology*, 1964, *58*: 194–200.

———, and L. GROSSMAN. Effects of chemical stimulation of the midbrain reticular formation on appetitive behavior. *Journal of Comparative and Physiological Psychology*, 1966, *61*: 333–38.

HAGGENDAL, J., and H. LINDQUIST. Disclosure of labile monoamine fractions in brain and their correlation to behavior. *Acta Physiological Scandinavica*, 1964, *60*: 351–57.

HALAS, E. S., K. BRADFIELD, M. E. SANDLIE, F. THEYE, and J. BEARDSLEY. Changes in rat behavior due to RNA injection. *Physiology and Behavior*, 1966, *1*: 281–83.

HEARST, E. Effects of d-amphetamine on behavior reinforced by food and water. *Psychological Reports*, 1961, *8*: 301, 309.

———, and R. E. WHALEN. Facilitating effects of d-amphetamine on discrimination avoidance and performance. *Journal of Comparative and Physiological Psychology*, 1963, *56*: 124–28.

HEISE, G. A. Animal techniques for evaluating anorexigenic agents. *In* S. H. NODINE and P. E. SIEGLER (eds.) *Animal and clinical techniques in drug evaluations*. Chicago: Year Book Medical Publishers, 1964.

———, and BOFF, E. Behavioral determination of time and dose parameters of monoamine oxidase inhibitors. *Journal of Pharmacology and Experimental Therapeutics*, 1960, *129*: 155–62.

——— Continuous avoidance as a baseline for measuring behavioral effects of drugs. *Psychopharmacologia* (Berlin), 1962, *3*: 264–82.

HILLARP, N-A., K. FUXE, and A. DAHLSTROM. Demonstration and mapping of central neurons containing dopamine, noradrenaline, and 5-hydroxytryptamine and their reactions to psychopharmace. *Pharmacological Review*, 1966, *8*: 727–42.

HULL, C. L. The problem of intervening variables in molar behavior theory. *Psychological Review*, 1943, *50*: 273–91.

HUMPHREY, G., and R. U. COXON. *The chemistry of thinking*. Springfield, Ill.: C. C Thomas, 1963.

HYDÉN, H. Biochemical changes in glial cells and the nerve cells at varying activity. *In* F. BRÜCKE (ed.) *Biochemistry of the Central Nervous System*, New York: Pergamon, 1959.

——— Satellite cells in the nervous system. *Scientific American*, 1961, *205*, No. 6, 620–70.

———, and E. EGYHÁZI. Nuclear RNA changes of nerve cells during a learning experiment in rats. *Proceedings of the National Academy of Science*, 1962, *48*, 1366–73.

——— Glial RNA changes during a learning experiment with rats. *Proceedings of the National Academy of Science*, 1963, *48*: 618–24.

———, and P. W. LANGE. Protein synthesis in the hippocampal pyramidal cells of rats during a behavioral test. *Science*, 1968, *159*: 1370–73.

JACOBSON, A. L., F. R. BABICH, S. BUBASH, and A. JACOBSEN. Differential approach tendencies produced by injection of RNA from trained rats. *Science*, 1965, *150*: 636–37.

JENDEN, D. J., I. HANIN, and S. I. LAMB. Gas chromatographic microestimation of acetylcholine and related compounds. *Analytical Chemistry*, 1968, *40*: 125–28.

JOUVET, M. Biogenic amines and the states of sleep. *Science*, 1909, *163*: 32–41.

——— Neurophysiology of the states of sleep. *In* G. C. QUARTON, T. MELNECHUK, and F. O. SCHMITT (eds.) *The neurosciences: a study program*. New York: Rockefeller University Press, 1967.

——— Insomnia and decrease of cerebral 5-hydroxytryptamine after destruction of the raphé system in the cat. *Advances in Pharmacology*, 1968, *6B*: 265–79.

KATZ, J. J., and W. C. HALSTEAD. Protein organization and mental function. *Comparative Psychology Monographs*, 1950: 201–11.

KELLEHER, R. T., and L. COOK. Effects of chlorpromazine, meprobamate, d-amphetamine, mephenesm, or phenobarbital on time discrimination in rats. *Pharmacologist*, 1959, *2*: 51.

KETY, S. S. Chemical boundaries of psychopharmacology. *In* S. M. FARBER and R. H. L. WILSON (eds.) *Control of the mind*. New York: McGraw-Hill, 1961.

KHAVARI, K. A., A. FEIDER, D. M. WARBURTON, and R. A. MARTIN. Bilateral cannulae for central administration of drugs in rats. *Life Sciences*, 1967, *6*: 235–40.

KHAVARI, K. A., and R. P. MAICKEL. Atropine and atropine methyl bromide on behavior of rats. *International Journal of Neuropharmacology*, 1967, *6*: 301–6.

KHAVARI, K. A., and R. W. RUSSELL. Acquisition, retention, and extinction under conditions of water deprivation and of central cholinergic stimulation. *Journal of Comparative and Physiological Psychology*, 1966, *61*: 333–39.

KOELLA, W. P., A. FELDSTEIN, and J. S. CZICMAN. The effect of parachlorophenylalanine on the sleep of cats. *EEG. Clinical Neurophysiology*, 1968, *25*: 481–90.

KOPIN, I. J. Storage and metabolism of catecholamines: Role of monoamine oxidase. *Pharmacological Review*, 1964, *16*: 179–91.

KRANTZ, J. C., and C. J. CARR. *The pharmacologic principles of medical practice*. Baltimore: Williams & Wilkins, 1961.

KRECH, D., M. R. ROSENZWEIG, and E. L. BENNETT. Chemical and anatomical plasticity of brain. *Science*, 1964, *146*: 610–19.

LAJTHA, A. The brain-barrier system. *In* K. A. C. ELLIOTT, J. A. PAGE, and J. H. QUASTEL (eds.) *Neurochemistry*. Springfield, Ill.: C. C Thomas, 1962.

LANDAUER, T. K. Two hypotheses concerning the biochemical basis of memory. *Psychological Review*, 1964, *71*: 167–79.

LASHLEY, K. S. In search of the engram. *Symposium of the Society for Experimental Biology*, 1950, *4*: 454–82.

LEVITT, R. A., and A. E. FISHER. Anticholinergic blockade of centrally induced thirst. *Science*, 1967, *154*: 520–21.

LEWIS, R. R., C.C.D. SHUTE, and A. SILVER. Confirmation from choline acetylase analyses of a massive cholinergic innervation to the hippocampus. *Journal of Physiology* (London) ,1964, *172*: 9–10P.

LIBERMAN, R. Retinal cholinesterase and glycolysis in rats raised in darkness. *Science*, 1962, *135*: 372–73.

LOEWI, O. Über humorale Übertragbarkeit der Herznervenwirkung. *Pfügers Archiv.*, 1921, *189*: 239–42.

LUTTGES, M., T. JOHNSON, C. BUCK, J. HOLLAND, and J. MCGAUGH. An examination of "transfer of learning" by nucleic acid. *Science*, 1966, *151*: 834–37.

MCCONNELL, J. V. Memory transfer through cannibalism in planarians. *Journal of Neuropsychiatry*, 1962, *3*, 542.

——— Comparative physiology: Learning in invertebrates. *Annual Review of Physiology*, 1966, *28*, 107–136.

———, A. L. JACOBSON, and D. P. KIMBLE. The effects of regeneration upon retention of a conditioned response in the planarian. *Journal of Comparative and Physiological Psychology,* 1959, *52*: 1–5.

MCGAUGH, J. L. Time-dependent processes in memory storage. *Science*, 1966, *153*: 1351–58.

MCGEER, P. L., E. G. MCGEER, and J. A. WADA. Central aromatic amine levels and behavior. *A.M.A. Archives of Neurology*, 1963, *9*: 81–89.

MACLEAN, P. D. Chemical and electrical stimulation of hippocampus in unrestrained animals, I and II. *A.M.A. Archives of Neurology and Psychiatry*, 1957, *78*: 113–42.

MCLENNAN, H. *Synaptic Transmission*. New York: Saunders, 1963.

MACHLUS, B., and J. GAITO. Detection of RNA species unique to a behavioral task. *Psychonomic Science*, 1968, *10*: 253–54.

MANDELL, A. J., and C. E. SPOONER. Psychochemical research studies in man. *Science*, 1968, *162*: 1442–53.

METZ, B. Brain acetylcholinesterase and a respiratory reflex. *American Journal of Physiology*, 1958, *192*: 101–5.

MILLER, N. E. Chemical coding of behavior in the brain. *Science*, 1965, *148*: 328–38.

———, K. S. GOTTESMAN, and N. EMERY, Dose response to carbachol and norepinephrine in rat hypothalamus. *American Journal of Physiology*, 1964, *206*: 1384–88.

MOORE, K. E. Toxicity and catecholamine releasing actions of d- and l- amphetamine in isolated and aggregated mice. *Journal of Pharmacology and Experimental Therapeutics* 1963, *142*: 6–12.

OLDS, J. Hypothalamic substrates of reward. *Physiological Review*, 1962, *42*: 554–604.

———, and R. R. TRAVIS. Effects of chlorpromazine, meprobamate, pentobarbital and morphine on self–stimulation. *Journal of Pharmacology and Experimental Therapeutics*, 1960, *128*: 397–404.

OLDS, M. E., and J. OLDS. Pharmacological patterns in subcortical reinforcement behavior. *International Journal of Neuropharmacology*, 1964, *2*: 309–25.

PALLADIN, A. V., and G. E. VLADMIROV. The use of radioactive isotopes in the study of the functional biochemistry of the brain. In *First international conference on peaceful uses of atomic energy* (vol. 112). New York: United Nations, 1956.

PARDEE, A. B., and A. C. WILSON. Control of enzyme activity in higher animals. *Cancer Research*, 1963, *23*: 1483–90.

PLATT, J. R. A "book model" of genetic information—transfer in cells and tissues. *In* M. KASHA, and B. PULLMAN (eds.) *Horizons in biochemistry*. New York: Academic Press, 1962.

POSCHEL, B. P. H., and F. W. NINTEMAN. Excitatory (antidepressant?) effects of monoamine oxidase inhibitors on the reward system of the brain. *Life Sciences*, 1964, *3*: 903–10.

ROSENBLATT, F., J. T. FARROW, and W. F. HERBLIN. Transfer of conditioned responses from trained rats to untrained rats. *Nature*, 1966, *209*: 46–48.

———, J. T. FARROW, and S. RHINE. The transfer of learned behavior from trained to untrained rats by means of brain extracts, II. *Proceedings of the National Academy of Science*, 1966, *55*: 787–92.

ROSENZWEIG, M. R., E. L. BENNETT, and D. KRECH, Cerebral effects of environmental complexity and training among adult rats. *Journal of Comparative and Physiological Psychology*, 1964, *57*: 438–39.

———, D. KRECH, and E. L. BENNETT. A search for relations between brain chemistry and behavior. *Psychological Bulletin*, 57: 476–92 (1960).

RUSSELL, R. W. Effects of reduced brain cholinesterase on behavior. *Bulletin of the British Psychological Society*, 1954, No. *23*, b.

——— Effects of "biochemical lesions" on behavior. *Acta Psychologica*, 1958, *14*: 281–94.

——— Biochemical factors in mental disorders. *In* B. B. WOLMAN (ed.) *Handbook of clinical psychology*. New York: McGraw-Hill, 1965.

——— Biochemical substrates of behavior. *In* R. W. RUSSELL (ed.) *Frontiers of Physiological Psychology*. New York: Academic Press, 1966.

——— Behavioral aspects of cholinergic transmission. *Federation Proceedings*, 1969, *28*: 121–31.

———, R. H. J. WATSON, and M. FRANKENHAEUSER. Effects of chronic reductions in brain cholinesterase activity on acquisition and extinction of a conditioned avoidance response. *Scandinavian Journal of Psychology*, 1961, *2*: 21–29.

SCHANKER, L. S. Passage of drugs into and out of the central nervous system. *Antimicrobial Agents and Chemotherapy*, 1966: 1044–50.

SCHECKEL, C. L., and E. BOFF. Behavioral stimulation in rats associated with a selective release of brain norepinephrine. *Archives Internationales Pharmacodynamie*, 1964, *152*: 479–90.

——— Pharmacological control of behavior. *Proceedings of the XVIII international congress of psychology*. Moscow: Soviet Psychological Society, 1966.

SCHILDKRAUT, J. J., and S. S. KETY. Biogenic amines and emotion. *Science*, 1967, *156*: 21–30.

SEGAL, D. S., R. H. COX, W. C. STERN, and R. P. MAICKEL. Stimulatory effects of pemoline and cyclopropylpemoline on continuous avoidance behavior: Similarity to effects of d-amphetamine. *Life Sciences*, 1967, *6*: 2567–72.

SEPINWALL, J. Cholinergic stimulation of the brain and avoidance behavior. *Psychonomic Science*, 1966, *5*: 93–94.

SHERWOOD, S. L. Intraventricular medication in catatonic stupor. *Brain*, 1952, *75*: 68–75.

SHUTE, C.C.D., and P. R. LEWIS. Cholinergic and monaminergic pathways in the hypothalamus. *British Medical Bulletin*, 1966, *22*: 221–26.

SMITH, C. B. Effects of d-amphetamine upon brain amine content and locomotor activity of mice. *Journal of Pharmacology and Experimental Therapeutics*, 1965, *147*: 96–102.

STEIN, L. Effects and interactions of imipramine, chlorpromazine, reserpine, and amphetamine on self-stimulation: Possible neurophysiological basis of depression. *In* J. WORTIS (ed.) *Recent advances in biological psychiatry*. New York: Plenum Press, 1962.

——— Reciprocal action of reward and punishment mechanisms. *In* R. G. HEATH (ed.) *The role of pleasure in behavior*. New York: Harper, Row, 1964a.

——— Self-stimulation of the brain and the central stimulant action of amphetamine. *Federation Proceedings*, 1964b, *23*, 836–50.

——— Chemistry of purposive behavior. *In* J. TAPP (ed.) *Reinforcement and the control of behavior*. New York: Academic Press, 1969.

STÜMPF, C. Drug action on the electrical activity of the hippocampus. *International Journal Neurobiology*, 1965, *8*: 77–138.

SUMERFORD, W. T., W. J. HAYES, J. M. JOHNSTON, K. WALKER, and J. SPILLANE. Cholinesterase response and symptomatology from exposure to organic phosphorus insecticides. *A.M.A. Archives of Industrial Hygiene*, 1953, 7: 383–98.

TAKAHASHI, R., and M. H. APRISON. Acetylcholine content of discrete areas of the brain obtained by a near-freezing method. *Journal of Neurochemistry*, 1964, *11*: 887–98.

THUDICHUM, J. W. L. *A treatise on the chemical composition of the brain*. London: Tindall & Cox, 1884.

TOLMAN, E. C. *Purposive behavior in animals and man*. New York: Appleton-Century-Crofts, 1932.

UNGAR, G. Chemical transfer of acquired information. *Proc. C.I.N.P. Vth International Congress, Washington, D. C.*, 1966.

——— Molecular mechanisms in learning. *Perspectives in Biology and Medicine*, 1968, *11*: 217–32.

———, and L. N. IRWIN. Transfer of acquired information by brain extracts. *Nature*, 1967, *214*: 453–55.

UNGAR, G., and C. OCEGUERA-NAVARRO. Transfer of habituation by material extracted from brain. *Nature*, 1965, *207*: 301–302.

WARBURTON, D. M. Behavioral effects of central and peripheral changes in acetylcholine systems. *Journal of Comparative and Physiological Psychology*, 1969, *68*; 56–64.

———, and RUSSELL, R. W. Effects of 8-azaguanine on acquisition of a temporal discrimination. *Physiology and Behavior*, 1968, *3*: 61–63.

——— Some behavioral effects of cholinergic stimulation in the hippocampus. *Life Sciences*, 1969, *8*: 617–27.

WEISSMAN, A. Differential drug effects upon a three-ply multiple schedule of reinforcement. *Journal of the Experimental Analysis of Behavior*, 1959, *2*: 271–88.

WILSON, I. B., and M. COHEN. The essentiality of acetylcholinesterase in conduction. *Biochemical and Biophysica Acta*, 1953, *11*: 147–56.

WOLF, A. *Textbook and logic*. London: Allen & Unwin, 1948.

ZEMP, J. W., J. E. WILSON, K. SCHLESINGER, W. O. BOGGAN, and E. GLASSMAN. Brain function and macromolecules, I. Incorporation of uridine into RNA of mouse brain during short-term training experience. *Proceedings of the National Academy of Science*, 1966, *55*: 1423–31.

The initial problem in a chapter on motor skill is to describe the area of discourse. Frequently, the term "motor has skill" been used as nearly synonymous with "non-verbal behavior," even though verbalization is obviously motoric and probably involves as precise coordination as can be found anywhere, while many so-called skill tasks have not required the precision of execution usually associated with skilled performance. Thus, studies cited in the motor skill literature have included button pressing, toggle switching, maze running and other tasks requiring any muscle system save that involved in vocalization. As often as not, either response precision has not been a task requirement, or performance measures have not been chosen which reflect the precise temporal-spatial organization of the motor behavior.

It may be, as Irion (1966) suggested in his historical review of research on skill acquisition, that researchers in the area would show a great deal of agreement in dichotomizing the literature into skill and non-skill research, based on a common "feel" for what constitutes "skill," but formal definitions are not easy to come by. However, Bilodeau and Bilodeau (1961), Fitts et al. (1959), Fitts (1964), Irion (1966), Poulton (1966), and Underwood (1966) have offered some helpful suggestions toward a definition of motor skill. The Bilodeaus (1961), in their review of motor skills learning, distinguished motor skills ("the hand holds and moves some physical apparatus") from verbal learning and perceptual learning and concluded that, ". . . a simpler way to say about the same thing is to distinguish areas according to the relative importance of the hand, tongue and eye. Also implicit in motor skills learning is the emphasis on learning to make R, rather than to select R on cue . . ." (p. 243).

This last statement by the Bilodeaus provides a significant point in the classification of motor skill. That is, motor skill research emphasizes the *execution* of the response, rather than the *selection* of the response, on cue, from a set of response alternatives. This emphasis has broad implications for the choice of tasks and response measures appropriate to the study of skill. Irion (1966) has suggested that motor skill tasks are generally low in response availability and low in response

D. Trumbo
& M. Noble

Motor Skill

10

selection requirements as contrasted with verbal learning or selective learning (C. Noble 1966), tasks which are high in both response availability and response selection requirements. Learning to swim, play the piano, or drive a golf ball are cited by Irion as examples of tasks low in response availability and response selection requirements.

If by *availability*, one means the ability to produce the response readily and with great precision, then Irion's examples are certainly valid. On the other hand, the *classes* of responses in these examples are quite available to normal human subjects. That is, most anyone can swing a golf club, depress a piano key, or move his arms and legs in the swimming motions. What is not available, it would appear, is the temporal-spatial patterning of responses in a highly precise and consistent manner. Furthermore, if response *selection* is taken to mean choosing among a finite set of discrete response alternatives, then it is true that skill tasks have a low requirement. On the other hand, skill tasks frequently involve the selection of a response from continuous gradients with respect to amplitude, force, direction, and rate. In this sense skilled responses place by far the heaviest demands on the subject for response selection. Fitts et al. (1959) have incorporated this aspect of motor skill in their concept of *response constancy*, the ability of the skilled performed to select a graded response appropriate to both input and feedback signals at the moment.

Given these considerations, it appears more fruitful to differentiate skill from non-skill research on the basis of the relative emphasis placed upon response execution as compared with response selection. This emphasis on process rather than outcome also implies that motor skill research is apt to utilize performance measures which reflect the time-varying pattern of behavior. Skill research might well involve the tongue, the eye, the hand, or any voluntary muscle system, providing tasks and measures are used which permit observation of the organization of temporal-spatial patterning in the execution of responses.

Poulton (1966) has made this point well. If the term "motor skill" is substituted for "tracking," the following quotation provides a basis for identifying skill research which is consistent with the emphasis in the present report:

All behavior can be said to involve deciding what to do and then doing it . . . the study of selective motor learning [See: C. Noble, 1966] is concerned mainly with deciding what to do. For example, the man may have to decide which one of four buttons to press, or in which of four directions to move a lever. The excellence of his performance is assessed in terms of time taken and whether the response selected is the correct one or not. The button or lever has simply to moved sufficiently far to make an electrical contact. The exact distance it moves, and the exact force on it by the man, are not considered.

In contrast, the study of tracking is concerned more with the execution of the response. Here performance is assessed in terms of the distance moved or the force exerted. Typically the man is supplied with only one control; he does not have to choose between controls as he often does in selective motor learning. Thus selective motor learning and tracking emphasize different aspects of motor behavior. (p. 362)

Similarly, in discussing this statement by Poulton, Underwood (1966) wrote:

He [Poulton] pointed out that we rarely study the learning of the skill to execute a particular verbal response. Learning to give the proper pronunciation to words in a foreign language would be an illustration. Or suppose we required our subjects to respond with a particular frequency and intensity in paired-associate learning in addition to responding to the appropriate stimulus. Under these circumstances we would be more nearly studying skill learning. As it is, we merely use the vocal response as an instrumental response to demonstrate associative learning, and the vocal characteristics of the response that we will accept as correct are very broadly defined. (Underwood; 1966, p. 495)

Finally, in 1959, Fitts and his associates (Fitts *et al.*, 1959) characterized skill in terms of (a) the spatial-temporal patterning of behavior, involving (b) the interplay of receptor and effector processes, and (c) modifiable by experience. Spatial-temporal patterning of behavior was seen by Fitts to be dependent on response constancy, timing and anticipation, and feedback information, Five years later Fitts defined a skilled response as ". . . one in which receptor-effector-feedback processes are highly organized, both spatially and temporally. The central problem for the study of skill learning is how such organization or patterning comes about" (Fitts 1964, p. 244).

The study of the temporal-spatial organization of behavior, which is so explicit and observable in motor skills, was seen by Fitts as a proper approach to the understanding of more complex, less explicit cognitive processes. In this respect, he was in agreement with Bartlett (1958) and Woodworth (1958) who, among others, have advocated the study of motor behavior as the appropriate basis for understanding organization in thinking, reasoning, and other cognitive processes.

Our focus in the remainder of this paper shall be on organization in the execution of motor behavior and the conditions of feedback, timing and anticipation, and other task conditions which affect the temporal-spatial patterning of motor behavior.

Historical Perspectives

The study of motor responses has, quite reasonably, been in the service of learning theory or general behavior theory more frequently than in the search for explanations of skilled performance. Thus, Irion (1966) in a recent historical review, pointed out that the period prior to 1927 was devoted largely to procedural variables, particularly distribution of practice and the part-whole problem. Perhaps in part because of this focus, researchers were concerned almost exclusively with outcome measures of performance and gave little attention either to task variables or to response execution and organization.

A few important exceptions are apparent in this early period, however. Notable among these are the works by Woodworth (1899) and by Bryan and Harter (1899). Woodworth (1899), in his studies of the accuracy of voluntary movements, anticipated by about 50 years some of the implications of more recent studies of motor skill from the viewpoint of feedback theory. Later (1958) Woodworth extended his earlier views to include the notion that motor behavior can best be understood in terms of "two-phase motor units." Woodworth described the first phase as *preset*, the preparatory or readiness phase of the response; the "hauling off" to throw a punch, the "cocking" of a bat to hit a ball, the backstroke of a golf club or a hammer.

The significance of the preset phase is that it may be viewed as the time during which response programming occurs. That is, in cocking the arm, one is selecting the appropriate force, amplitude, direction, and rate as demanded by the external situation, or as "intended" to meet external or self-instructions. The question of whether the "feel" of the preset is cued entirely by kinesthetic feedback or in part from direct information about the magnitude of the innervation itself will be discussed at a later point.

Woodworth's concepts of biphasic response and preset provide the first four terms of his $S_1 R_1 S_2 R_2 — R_x$ model. The R_x term is attributed to Troland (1928) and refers to his concept of "retroflex." As Woodworth (1958) stated, the end of the S–R (or S–O–R) sequence is not the effective response (R_2), but the information feedback (R_x) as to the effects of R_2 on the environment. Thus, Woodworth and Troland appear to have anticipated both the current concepts of response feedback and the preprogramming of responses.

Probably the most oft quoted research in motor skills was reported by Bryan and Harter (1897, 1899). They were among the few investigators who were concerned with changes in skill performance as a function of training, rather than with the testing of hypotheses derived from conditioning, discrimination, or rote verbal learning. They observed the development of skilled performance in two telegraph operators and described "plateaus" in the learning curves. Although the plateau phenomenon is now suspect (Keller 1958), Bryan and Harter's explanation of it as a period in which lower-order habits were becoming automated, but were not yet sufficiently free of attention requirements to permit the development of higher-level habits, is in some way similar to current thinking about some aspects of the development of hierarchies and "plans" in skilled behavior (Miller, Galanter, and Pribram 1960).

The second period (1927–1945), as identified by Irion (1966), showed a continuation of interest in distribution of practice and a growing interest in transfer of training. As with the distribution of practice research, however, the transfer studies focused on the amount of transfer as reflected in summary performance measures, and little if any attention was given to the analysis of the transfer of component processes.

While both theoretical and methodological advances were made with respect to the procedural variables (McGeoch and Irion 1952), distribution of practice theories (Wheeler and Perkins 1932; Doré and Hilgard 1937; Snoddy 1935) were not concerned with other important aspects of skilled performance, e.g., the execution and temporal-spatial organization of the responses, or in the standardization of tasks and apparatus (Ammons 1955). However, some interest in such matters was evident in the work of Hartson (1939), who expanded on the earlier work of Stetson and McDill (1923) in classifying movements, as *slow tension* and *ballistic* movements.

Similarly, interest in transfer of training, particularly bilateral transfer or cross-education (e.g.: Cook 1933, 1936), naturally led to the selection of motor tasks. These tasks were, for the most part, convenient vehicles for the study of the broader issues. Just *what* was transferred, or *how* skilled performance was benefitted in the transfer task were not the issues, however.

Problems of the forgetting and retention of skill, which had been of some interest in the earlier period (Bean 1912; Book 1925; Hill 1914; Swift 1905, 1906, 1910; Tsai 1924) were again evident in the 1930 s. Since the earlier work had usually shown little or no loss in the retention of motor tasks, even after more than a year of no practice, it was generally accepted that retention was better for motor than for verbal material. These results were usually attributed to greater overlearning and less interference from subsequent learning for the motor tasks. Thus, comparing mazes and nonsense syllables, and controlling for overlearning, McGeoch and Melton (1929) found no appreciable differences in retention after one week. Freeman and Abernethy (1930) found superior retention for a typing task as compared with a letter coding task after eight weeks, but not after the briefer two-week period. These findings were replicated (Freeman and Abernethy 1932) using independent groups at each retention test. Van Tilborg (1936) compared a 20-choice maze with 20 pairs of nonsense syllables and found no differences in retention after 50 days. Leavitt and Schlosberg (1944) compared the retention of pursuit rotor and nonsense syllables and supported the classical finding of superior retention of the motor habit, using savings scores as a criterion. They concluded that the motor task was more integrated, and that this integration, or organization, was the basis for superior retention. No attempt was made in this earlier research to analyze the changes which occurred in motor performance to account for losses in outcome latency, error, or time-on-target scores.

Differential psychologists were also active during this middle period. Most notable was the work of Woodrow and his students (Kintzle 1946, 1949; Woodrow 1938a b, c, 1939a, b, 1940, 1946). Woodrow was perhaps the first to take note of the fact that when trial scores are inter-correlated the correlation coefficients systematically decrease with the distance between trials, and as practice continues the coefficients between adjacent trials increase. Thus, in the inter-trial correlation matrix, moving across the rows or up the columns is accompanied by a regular decrease in the magnitude of the coefficients. This pattern, which Marshall Jones (1962) subsequently labeled the "super-diagonal form," and which has been observed repeatedly by others (e.g.: Adams 1953; Fleishman 1953a; Fleishman and Parker 1959; Greene 1943; Houston 1950; Melton 1947a; Reynolds, 1952a, b) was the basis for Woodrow's (1938c) speculations about changes in factor structure as practice continues, and reflected directly in current correlational and factor analytic work, particularly in that of Fleishman and his associates (Fleishman 1966).

A second body of correlational work has dealt with attempts to predict performance on motor tasks, particularly in skilled occupations. This research has used both performance tests (which, in one form, become "job sample" tests) and paper-and-pencil tests; the latter with the assumption that underlying aptitudes or abilities involved in the acquisition rate and/or final level of skilled performance may be measured by non-motor tests.

Much of the early work on the use of apparatus tests in the prediction of performance in skilled tasks, or in occupations which include skilled tasks, has been summarized by Melton (1947a, b). It is sufficient at this point to note that personnel selection research has seldom been concerned with the analysis of skilled performance beyond identifying skill requirements at a functional level ("eye-hand coordination," "finger dexterity," etc.) then has hurried off to determine whether tests designed to measure these skills yield practically significant correlations with global job performance criteria. This critique does not apply to the factor analytic work (Seashore 1951; Fleishman 1953b, 1966) which *has* been concerned with analyzing the structure of skilled performance.

The period since 1945 in motor skill research has shown the clear influence of World War II and the concurrent growth of engineering psychology and systems engineering concepts on the one hand, and the era of comprehensive behavior and learning theories—particularly Hullian Theory (Hull 1943)—on the other hand.

Among other things, WW II led to an emphasis upon task variables, rather than procedural variables, in skill performance. As indicated earlier, little attention had been given prior to 1945 to the task itself—the input rate, coherence, complexity, modality, intensity or form. Man-machine systems created a demand for information about human capabilities and error tolerance as a function of a wide range of input conditions. Frequently, the demands were highly specific and problem-oriented and the research, often in unique simulators or in the context of highly specific task parameters, frequently did not lead to many generalizations about human behavior. As Taylor and Birmingham (1959) have pointed out, performance measures of the output of complex man-machine systems may hopelessly confound man and machine contributions to that performance when systems variables are manipulated.

The pressing problems of World War II also resulted in a renewal of interest in the psychometric or correlational approach to skill. Attempts to develop test batteries predictive of success in training and practice for pilots and other skilled operators received new priorities. In addition, attempts at skill analysis and task classification through the factor analyses of both performance and paper-and-pencil tests were given new emphasis (Adams 1953; Fleishman 1953a, b, 1954, 1956).

Finally, both engineers and psychologists came to recognize the need for continuous, time-varying methods of measurement and analysis. The engineer was accustomed to deriving describing functions relating the output of a system component to the input, and it should come as no surprise that he approached the man component in the same way—as a black box, the dynamics of which could be described in terms of a transfer equation. This approach focused on task variables; viz., writing the describing function when the input is, for example, a step-function, a sinusoid, or a ramp function (cf.: Elkind 1956; Ellson, 1949, 1959; McRuer and Krendal, 1957, 1959; McRuer, Graham, Krendal, and Reisner, 1965; Senders, 1959).

Engineering psychologists also became involved in the applications of servotheory concepts to man-machine systems, viewing man as a processor of information in a feedback loop. From this point of view, it was possible to describe the transformation which the operator had to perform on the error information in order to null out the system error. By manipulating the control dynamics and by performing transformations (amplification, differentiation, or integration) on the error data, the perceptual and motor requirements of the operator were manipulated. Man's performance as a manual controller could then be systematically viewed as a function of the information-processing requirements of the task, with the requirements described in mathematical-engineering terminology. For example, the progression and regression hypotheses describe changes in the human operator's transfer function in terms of the number of derivative terms required. Thus, man is seen to progress from

a "zero"-order controller (responding to error magnitude only) through first-order (responding to error rate—the first derivative) and second-order (responding to error acceleration—the second derivative) control with continued practice. Conversely, the practiced operator may regress from second-order to first- or to zero-order control under conditions of increased stress. (Fitts, *et al.* 1959; Fuchs 1962; Garvey 1960; Garvey and Mitnick 1957).

While engineering considerations gave impetus to research on task variables, learning theory stimulated further research on procedural variables. Thus, Hullian theory gave rise to a flurry of research on distribution of practice and reminiscence in a quest for reactive (Ir) and conditioned (sIr) inhibition (e.g., Adams and Reynolds 1954; Ammons and Willig 1956; Bilodeau 1954; Digman 1959).

Learning theory also gave rise to a further interest in transfer of training and the related problems of part-whole learning during this period. Yet, despite a determined effort, Lewis and his associates (e.g.: Barch and Lewis 1954; Lewis, McAllister, and Adams 1951; Lewis and Miles 1956; McAllister and Lewis 1951) at Iowa had to conclude that motor performance was relatively impervious to both transfer and interference effects.

In the period between 1945 and 1960, two programs of research contributed a good deal to current trends in motor skills research. One began in 1950 under the direction of Paul Fitts at The Ohio State University and culminated in 1959 in a two-volume technical report (Fitts *et al.* 1959). The contents of this report include empirical findings and theoretical discussions of such topics as: the nature of skilled performance, the taxonomy of tasks, servotheory, communications theory and information models of skilled performance, stimulus-response compatibility effects, models for proprioceptive feedback, and two chapters on the quantification of skilled performance. Much of this latter section has been reviewed in a chapter by Bahrick and Noble (1966).

A second somewhat more diversified program was conducted in England at The Applied Psychology Research Unit at Cambridge. It has made a number of significant contributions to theory and knowledge of skilled performance, including such issues as the psychological refractory phase, information processing, anticipation in skilled tasks, dual-task performance, aging and skill performance, memory, and other cognitive processes. As Adams (1961a) pointed out, this work has been directed in an important way toward specifying ". . . the response classes which intervene between the displayed stimuli and the measured motor response" and to the investigation of such issues as whether the apparently smooth and continuous responding observed in continuous control (tracking) tasks is fundamentally intermittent.

Finally, recent workers have shown a renewed interest in the retention of skill (Naylor and Briggs 1961), turning from the pursuit rotor and time-on-target scores to more analytic measures, and from questions of relative amounts of forgetting of motor and verbal material to issues of task organization and integration (Naylor and Briggs 1963, a, b; Noble, Trumbo, Ulrich, and Cross 1966; Trumbo, Noble, Cross, and Ulrich 1965), warm-up phenomena (Adams 1952, 1961), and, most recently, to questions of short-term memory (Adams and Dijkstra 1966; Posner and Konick 1966) for skilled movements. Some efforts have also been directed toward analyzing just what changes occur over the retention interval in the overall temporal-spatial pattern of behavior (Noble et al. 1966; Trumbo et al. 1965)

In summary, it appears that after the early interests of Woodworth and Bryan and Harter in the development and execution of motor skill, research using skill tasks was largely influenced by questions arising in learning theories with a functionalistic interest in the effects of procedural variables on performance outcomes. Little interest was shown in analyzing changes in the response processes by which the performance outcomes were achieved, or in assessing the fate of various component processes in retention or transfer research. With the advent of engineering psychology and servotheory, skill tasks were used to test the efficacy of certain systems configurations and control dynamics for systems performance. Again, the orientation was functional rather than analytic, in large part, although the interest in control dynamics and the transformation of information, as well as the concern with task variables and the development of time-varying response measures, have resulted in renewed interest in response processes. Most recently skilled tasks have been used as vehicles in the investigation of information handling, decision making and other cognitive processes. At the same time, interest in the execution and organization of the temporal-spatial patterns of behavior which are the essence of motor skill has been revived together with a resurgence of research on the components of skill; timing and anticipation, proprioceptive feedback, and movement control. A small but active group of psychologists continues to measure individual differences in skill performance and to describe the factor structure and changes in factor structure with practice.

The Measurement of Abilities and Structure

Interest in individual differences and the correlational, factor analytic approach to motor skill has paralleled experimental work in the area. Perhaps in no other area of psychology have the same researchers more freely "crossed lines" and combined both experimental and correlational approaches, as evidenced by the work of Adams (1953; 1957), Bilodeau (1952), Fitts et al. (1959), and particularly, Fleishman and his associates (Fleishman 1966).

As indicated earlier, the more basic and systematic approach to skill using correlational and factor analytic method can be traced to Woodrow and his students, beginning in the late 1930 s (Woodrow 1938a, b, c, 1939a, b, 1940, 1946; Kientzle 1946, 1949). These studies were concerned with accounting for and predicting subject variance, identifying factors in skilled performance, and describing changes in factor structure which occur with practice. This period also saw the beginnings of research on the interrelationships of scores from different skill tests (Buxton 1938; Buxton and Humphreys 1935; Seashore, Buxton, and McCollom 1940).

The work of Woodrow and Kientzle was largely concerned with the correlations between trials on the same task, rather than between scores on different tests or tasks. Jones (1966) credited Perl (1934) with the first correlational analysis of practice. However, Woodrow was the first to give systematic attention to the fact that inter-trial correlation matrices showed some consistent regularities; viz., coefficients decrease as a function of a distance between trials, but the coefficients between successive trials increase from early to late practice.

Woodrow attempted to explain these regularities in terms of changes in the abilities required as practice continued, with abilities which were initially important falling off as practice continued, and other abilities, important at later stages of practice, increasing in importance. If the abilities were independent, then the correlation between initial and final performance would be zero, as Woodrow (1938a) noted. Conversely, the lower the correlation between initial and final performance, the greater the change in the ability pattern.

In what may be an early demonstration of the value of the correlational approach for explaining phenomena identified experimentally, Kientzle (1946, 1949) showed that inter-trial correlations were dependent on the ordinal number of trials, but not on the length of rest intervals in a distribution of practice paradigm, thus demonstrating, as Irion (1966) has pointed out, that ". . . the effects of rest and the effects of practice represent separate entities" (p. 20).

An extension of Woodrow's work is to be seen in the studies of the 1950 s which were concerned, in part, with identifying predictors of performance at various stages of practice (Reynolds 1952; Adams 1953, 1957). The results were conflicting: reference tests (Fleishman 1966) showed decreased predictive power with practice for Reynolds (1952), suggesting that ability requirements might become more task-specific with practice. On the other hand, reference tests developed to measure presumed underlying abilities (as identified by factor analytic studies) have frequently been more predictive of final performance than were early performance scores on the task itself (Adams 1957; Fleishman and Hempel 1955). Other evidence, however, supports the notion of increased task specific factor loadings with continued practice (Fleishman and Hempel 1955; Jones 1966). Fleishman and Rich (1963) have shown that groups of subjects stratified on the basis of reference tests may either converge or diverge as a function of practice, depending upon the abilities tested. These findings support the view, stated by Woodrow (1938), that: "If the goodness of the scores be regarded as determined by a set of cooperating but independently variable abilities, then practice may be regarded as a change in the conditions under which various constituents of this set of abilities operate" (p. 227). This statement is nearly identical with the conclusion stated by Fleishman and Hempel (1955) and by Fleishman (1966), arrived at after nearly 30 years of intervening research. However, other contributions and refinements have been added to the correlational literature which will be discussed shortly.

In 1951, Seashore reviewed much of the earlier literature on correlational and factor analytic studies of motor performance. He distinguished between *gross* and *fine* motor coordinations on the basis of the extent of muscular involvement and strength in the former, and the timing and spatial precision requirements in the latter, as well as the evidence of near-zero correlations between tests designed to measure the two classes of performance. He also distinguished between *single* and *serial* action, the latter including both serial and continuous responses.

Seashore's (1951) principal intervening or explanatory concept was *aptitude* which he defined as ". . . any structural or functional asset that gives a man a head start in the acquisition of a given skill, and conversely, a low degree of aptitude may be thought of as a handicap" (p. 1344). Reviewing the evidence, much of it from his own research, (Seashore 1940; Seashore and Seashore 1941; Seashore et al. 1940), for the effects of sense modality, musculature, and patterns of movement, he concluded "... the sense employed is of moderate significance, the musculature employed is of very slight significance, and the pattern of movements involved is likely to be the most important factor" (p. 1345). This conclusion coincided with his concept of *work methods*, the notion:

that individual differences in any human ability (not just motor skills) are attributable to three groups of factors: (1) the physical constants of the various organs (especially sense organs, nervous system, and musculatures) employed, (2) the general qualitative pattern of component actions involved, and (3) the refinement of these component actions with respect to both strength and timing so as to produce an optimal pattern of action, [but that the evidence indicated that superior performance is usually the result of]... hitting upon qualitative patterns of action, or work methods, that make the work easier. (p. 1353)

Thus, in Seashore's view, skilled performance is seldom limited by sensory or effector mechanism, but more often by inadequate patterning or sequencing of actions.

Seashore dismissed the possibility of any *general* ability factor on the grounds that measures of many human abilities are not correlated, but concluded in favor of six *group factors* which he labeled "speed of single reaction," "finger, hand, and forearm speed in restricted oscillatory movement," "forearm and hand speed in oscillatory movements of moderate extent," "steadiness," "skill in manipulating spatial relations," and a residual factor. He concluded that specific factors very frequently had a high degree of task specificity. Finally, Seashore concluded that motor skills are developed largely by trial and error learning without much aid from verbal instructions, coaching, or other cognitive mediators; that is, work methods are "... hit upon rather than carefully thought out or even recognized afterward" (p. 1354).

Much of the research and theorizing since Seashore's review has been concerned with the changes in factors or abilities which accompany practice. Jones (1966) has stated that there is concensus among researchers that the inter-trial correlation regularities (the "superdiagonal form") indicates that the number of abilities involved in performance decreases with successive trials. However, the major issue concerns the interpretation of this concensus. Jones' own hypothesis—"the simplicial hypothesis"—(Jones 1959, 1962, 1966) states that one process governs the effects of practice reflected in the inter-trial correlation matrix. This process is one of simplification, the dropping out of factors (or "composites of differential elements") as practice proceeds. The factors which are present on early trials, but then drop out, are seen as more general than those which remain. Thus, Jones sees the simplicial model as consistent with the evidence cited earlier that reference tests relate more highly to early than to later performance on a task; they are related through the more general factors. When these have dropped out, the correlations between the more dissimilar reference tests and the task scores go down. Tests of the simplicial hypothesis involve generating theoretical correlation matrices and factor structures and comparing them with obtained data to determine the goodness of fit. Thus, the approach is seen by its proponents (Jones 1962) as more deductive and hypothesis-testing than the traditional inductive factor-analytic approach.

Fleishman has differentiated "ability," the more general

trait of individuals inferred from intertask correlations, from "skills," the more task-specific concepts. He starts with the assumption that skills can be described and related in a logical manner in terms of the more basic abilities. Abilities are seen as relatively constant and enduring in the adult, a fact which Fleishman attributes to overlearning. In contrast, skill levels and learning rates can change markedly in adults, although they are limited by the underlying abilities.

Fleishman (1953b, 1954) began by attempting to develop a taxonomy of perceptual-motor abilities. Building on previous factor-analytic evidence, he conducted a major study with over 40 psychomotor tests designed to sharpen and more adequately define the perceptual-motor abilities and to test the usefulness of printed tests for predicting performance test variance. Additional studies were concerned with the analysis of more specific classes of motor behavior: fine manipulations (Fleishman and Hempel 1954, Fleishman and Ellison 1962), gross physical actions (Hempel and Fleishman 1955; Nicks and Fleishman 1962; Fleishman, Kremer, and Shoup 1961; Fleishman, Thomas, and Munroe 1961; Fleishman 1963; Fleishman 1964), positioning movements and static reactions (Fleishman 1958a). Perhaps the most important series of studies by Fleishman and his associates, as viewed from the context of the present report, dealt with tasks requiring precision and control in continuously adjustive movements (Fleishman 1956; Fleishman 1958b; Fleishman and Parker 1962). The latter reference will be discussed further because it uniquely combines experimental and correlational methods.

The taxonomy of the more important abilities resulting from this programmatic research is briefly described by Fleishman (1966):

Control precision: This factor is common to tasks which require fine, highly controlled, but not overcontrolled, muscular adjustments, primarily where larger muscle groups are involved...

Multilimb coordinations: This is the ability to coordinate the movements of a number of limbs simultaneously...

Response orientation: This ability factor...appears to involve the ability to *select* the correct movement in relation to the correct stimulus, especially under highly speeded conditions.

Reaction time: This represents simply the speed with which an individual is able to respond to a stimulus when it appears...

Speed of arm movement: This represents simply the speed with which an individual can make a gross, discrete arm movement where accuracy is not the requirement...

Rate control: This ability involves the making of continuous anticipatory motor adjustments relative to changes in speed and direction of a continuously moving target or object...

Manual dexterity: This ability involves skillful, well-directed arm-hand movements in manipulating fairly large objects under speed conditions...

Finger dexterity: This is the ability to make skill-controlled manipulations of tiny objects involving, primarily, the fingers...

Arm-hand steadiness: This is the ability to make precise arm-hand positioning movements where strength and speed are minimized; the critical feature, as the name implies, is the steadiness with which such movements can be made . . .

Wrist, finger speed: This ability has been called "tapping" in many previous studies . . .

Aiming: This ability appears to be measured by printed tests which provide the subject with very small circles . . . The subject typically goes from circle to circle placing one dot in each circle as rapidly as possible. (pp. 152–56)

There is little doubt that these factors represent the most carefully defined, thoroughly researched description of the structure of psychomotor abilities produced to date. Measures of these factors, which have been refined as part of the same research program, are used as the reference tests for determining the loadings of trial scores on a criterion task at different stages of practice. (Fleishman 1960; Fleishman and Hempel 1954a, 1955). The results of these studies are summarized by Fleishman (1966):

In general, these studies, with a great variety of practice tasks, show that (a) the particular combination of abilities contributing to performance changes as practice continues; (b) these changes are progressive and systematic and eventually become stabilized; (c) the contribution of "nonmotor" abilities (e.g., verbal, spatial), which may play a role early in learning, decreases systematically with practice, relative to "motor abilities"; and (d) there is also an increase in a factor specific to the task itself. (p. 159)

Fleishman (1966) agrees with Jones and, perhaps with Seashore's "work methods" hypothesis, that performance is increasingly a function of habits and skills specific to the task, but argues that abilities also play a role and interact in important ways with task learning. Probably the best illustration of this sort of interaction is the evidence that kinesthetic ability factors play an increasing role while spatial-visual abilities play a decreasing role with increased practice on a motor task (Fleishman and Rich 1963). This study, which compared task performance of subjects stratified on the ability measures, is exemplary of the combined use of individual differences and experimental variables for which Cronback (1957) appealed.

The study by Fleishman and Parker (1962) is another example of the fruitful combination of subject and experimental variables. This study was designed to evaluate retention of a complex motor skill for periods up to 24 months. Retention losses on this continuous control task were essentially zero, regardless of the retention interval, but retention performance was highly correlated with individual differences at the end of original learning. Furthermore, because ability measures were available, it was possible to conclude that the predictive relationship between learning and retention scores was not a function of pretask abilities, but could be attributed to differences in ". . .specific habits acquired in practicing the original task" (Fleishman 1966, p. 164). These results extend the notion, stated 15 years earlier by Seashore (1951), that patterns of movement, or "work methods," developed in the context of practice on a given task, account for superior performance.

A final correlational approach has been directed at the evaluation of various indicants taken from performance on a single task (Fitts *et al.* 1959). A total of 17 indicants, including integrated-error scores, time-on-target and target-zone scores,

zone-transition scores, and indicants from the autocorrelation function of the error record, from a compensatory tracking task were factor analyzed. Skill, as reflected by an overall (RMS) error criterion, was accounted for principally by three factors: (1) Factor I, which appeared close to being a G factor, was associated with the avoidance of very large errors apparently as a function of detecting and compensating for the statistical regularities (periodicities) in the target course. (2) Factor II appeared to involve the ability to handle smaller-amplitude, high-frequency components of the input and was labeled the "fine tuning" factor. (3) The third factor was labeled the "correction-speed factor" and was associated with high-frequency corrections. Additional factors were obtained on which the criterion error score did not have high loadings; (4) a factor reflecting the frequency characteristics of tracking skill; (5) a positioning skill factor; (6) a factor primarily identified with the rotary pursuit task, and two factors which were not readily interpreted.

The authors, (Fitts et al. 1959) in summarizing the results just described, provide a fitting summary of this section of the present report:

The principal purpose of previous studies is that of identifying human abilities common to a variety of motor tasks; the main purpose of the present analysis is to develop better understanding of performance measurement in a particular task. Yet the present findings show an important relation to earlier findings. Seashore, in summarizing results of earlier studies (1951, p. 1345) concludes that changes of musculature or sense modality are only moderately important variables underlying individual differences, but changes in the pattern of movement are very important variables. Although the present analysis is concerned primarily with performance of a single task, differentiation among the factors becomes possible through the identification of individual differences of movement patterns by means of analytic scores. Such scores are capable of differentiating patterns of motion which remain undifferentiated on the basis of the RMS criterion or any other single indicant of tracking skill derived from the amplitude distribution alone. (p. 6.46.)

Timing and Anticipation

Helson was one of the first to describe anticipatory behavior in skilled tasks. In the Foxboro studies (1949) of hand-crank tracking, he identified two strategies used to overcome the reaction-time handicap: anticipation and averaging. Anticipation was most evident with a low-frequency, simple sine wave input. At higher frequencies, subjects continued to anticipate, but undershot the peak amplitudes in order to keep in phase. However, with increased input complexity they developed an averaging strategy. That is, subjects continued to anticipate, but because they could not accurately predict amplitudes, they apparently used the statistical properties of the input to produce a "least square error" type of output. Trumbo, Noble, Cross, and Ulrich (1965) have also described an averaging strategy for pursuit tracking of irregular step-function inputs.

During the 1950's, research on anticipation was contributed, in the main, by British investigators. Prominent in this area was the work of Poulton (1950a, b, 1952a, b), Bartlett (1951), and Leonard (1953). In an early study, Poulton (1952a) compared anticipatory responding in pursuit and compensatory tasks with varied levels of input complexity. Increased complexity on the compensatory ("one-pointer") task did not appreciably increase tracking error, suggesting that the redundancies of the simpler course did not increase beneficial anticipations. However, with practice, subjects showed improvement in anticipatory responding for both simple and complex inputs. Meanwhile, improvement in pursuit tracking was not attributed to improved timing, since response time distributions did not change with practice, but to changes in dexterity and subjects' reduced error tolerances. It was concluded that practice improved anticipation on the compensatory, but never to the level of proficiency obtained with the pursuit task.

Poulton then (1952b) sorted out the effects of speed cues and course cues by varying intermittency in a pursuit task. He found the sharpest reduction in error under that condition of intermittent viewing where subjects first reported they were obtaining speed cues. Knowledge of course characteristics was ascertained by having subjects predict future course positions while tracking. Relatively accurate predictions were made for 3/4 cycle with the simple course, but for only 1/2 cycle on the more complex course. The amount of course which could be predicted, rather than the input rate or the time span of the prediction, was found to be the principal determinant of tracking accuracy.

By adding a course indicator to the compensatory display, providing unconfounded information about the track, Poulton (1957a) demonstrated significant tracking improvement, although comparable information about the control output did not yield reliable improvement, presumably because the latter information was redundant with response-produced cues. Poulton suggested that the principal deficiency of the compensatory task was that control movements could not be apprehended directly in relation to the target movements.

In further studies of advance information as the basis of anticipation, Poulton (1957b) introduced intermittency into the display of target, cursor, and both target and cursor information. Continuous information for both target and cursor resulted in the best performance, but intermittency of cursor (response) information was less detrimental than intermittency of target information. In one experiment tracking with the eyes closed was as good as visually guided tracking for periods up to 5.0 seconds with a high-frequency sine wave input.

One outcome of Poulton's work (1957c) was his conceptualization of three types of anticipation:(1) *effector anticipation*, or predicting the amount of muscle activity necessary to achieve a desired control output; (2) *receptor anticipation*, resulting from advance information (preview) of the target course; and (3) *perceptual anticipation*, based on knowledge of the course obtained through practice or stimulus pre-training. Effector anticipation, like Woodworth's "preset" (1899), appears to describe the preprogramming of the appropriate innervation requirements, whereas receptor anticipation is the provision of advance information about forthcoming movement requirements and should also facilitate innervation programming. Perceptual anticipation should provide the same sort of advance information though the latter depends on long-term memory and imagery, while receptor anticipation requires only short-term storage. In this connection, Wagner, Fitts, and Noble (1954) found that performance improved with preview up to about 1.0 second, but that additional preview did not yield appreciable gains, indicating either that subjects did not read ahead by more

than two seconds, or, if they did, it did not facilitate further accuracy in programming of movements. The latter interpretation is supported by Fitts and Peterson (1964), who found that increasing preparation time did not affect movement accuracy in a positioning task.

Adams and Xhignesse (1960) defined as *beneficial anticipations* those responses initiated within ±133 milliseconds of target events in step-function tasks. The significance of this indicant of timing behavior is that it identifies responses which are optimal in that they overcome the reaction-time handicap, but which do not result in large lead errors. Adams and his associates have demonstrated the sensitivity of this indicant for tasks varied in track coherency, pretraining for advance information, and interstimulus intervals (Adams and Xhignesse, 1960; Adams and Creamer, 1962a, b). It should be noted that the proportion of beneficial anticipations may be predicted from the root mean squared (RMS) error, assuming normality of the error distribution.

The role of task coherency in anticipatory responding was further evaluated by Trumbo et al. (1965) using step-function tracking tasks. In addition to coherent and non-coherent (random) sequences of target events, intermediate degrees of coherence were obtained by degrading the coherent sequence by replacing some proportion of the events (every second, third, or fourth event) with new events randomly selected on each trial. As expected, the coherent task yielded a more rapid decrease in error and increase in anticipations than the noncoherent task. However, the sequences with low intermediate coherence resulted in even fewer anticipations than the non-coherent (random) task. On the other hand, a task with a coherent (RLRL) directional pattern, but with random amplitudes, produces a high level of anticipatory responding, and, consistent with Helson's (1949) results, an averaging strategy in the amplitude predictions. Thus, uncertainty with respect to both amplitude and direction for a proportion of the events (the intermediate tasks) was more deterimental to anticipations than uncertainty about the amplitudes of all events, given a coherent directional pattern (the RIRL sequence). In this study, spatial accuracy was sacrificed to timing, especially by subjects with the best tracking performance. Their strategy was to anticipate even though cognitive learning of the pattern was impossible or incomplete, and spatial accuracy actually declined except under rather extended practice (Noble et al. 1966).

In two experiments on the tracking of temporal patterns, the coherence of a sequence of target *durations* was varied from coherent to random in a manner analogous to that used in the prior experiments on event uncertainty (Trumbo, Noble, Fowler, and Porterfield 1968). Under these conditions, subjects developed an averaging strategy, anticipating on the events of longer duration and lagging the shorter durations. This "range effect" was relatively independent of task coherence or sequence length, although coherence was associated with greater anticipation of the longest dwell times.

The effects of combinations of temporal and spatial uncertainty on tracking performance were investigated by Cross (1966), using stepfunction inputs. He combined coherent and random directional, temporal, and amplitude patterns so that zero to three of these task dimensions were coherent. With only one dimension coherent, tracking was no better than on the random task. However, with two of the three dimensions coherent (time and direction of direction and amplitude) tracking was better than on the random task. While error scores were similar, response strategies were clearly different for the tasks with two coherent dimensions. Subjects with coherent amplitude and direction patterns anticipated about 50% of all target events, while those with coherent timing and direction patterns anticipated only 20% of the events. Amplitude accuracy was essentially identical for the coherent and random tasks in this study, despite the fact that subjects anticipated nearly 100% of the coherent task events but less than 20% of the random task events. Thus, anticipatory responses had the same amplitude accuracy as responses made after the target events occurred.

In a further study of task coherence, Trumbo, Noble, and Quigley (1968) varied the sequential dependencies among target events. Each of six target positions was followed by one of two of the remaining positions, with probabilities from .50-.50 to .90-.10 for different tasks. Anticipatory responding was positively related to task redundancy, although the least redundant two-choice tasks were not clearly superior to the random (five-choice) control. Of greater interest, however, were the strategies which the subjects developed to cope with task uncertainties. When sequential alternatives were in the same direction, trained subjects anticipated 85–90% of the events, but with alternatives in opposite directions anticipations fell to 70–75%. Furthermore, response strategies were different for amplitude and directional choices. With alternatives in *opposite* directions, anticipatory responses *matched* the probabilities of the two alternatives. However, with alternatives in the *same* direction, subjects *averaged* the amplitudes required by the two alternatives, moving to a position proportionately near the high probability alternative.

Taken together, these studies indicate that temporal and spatial coherence of the input is used to organize responses and to beneficially anticipate target events, although low levels of coherence do not appear to increase anticipatory responding or to improve task performance. In fact, low partial task coherence appeared to result in a more conservative level of anticipation than non-coherence in some instances ((Trumbo et al. 1965; Noble et al. 1966).

TIMING

The previous section focused on variables which affect the availability of advance information for receptor or perceptual anticipation. Course preview, redundancy, and complexity were found to affect the probability of anticipatory responding. It should be evident, however, that the precision of anticipatory behavior, its accuracy and consistency, depend upon time estimation. Even with preview, subjects must deal with the time differential between the advance information and response requirements.

The central question for skilled performance has to do with the means by which one can judge the interval between events so as to accurately anticipate. Mechanisms posited as bases of time-keeping are many and varied, as indicated in Michon's recent review (1967). In attempting to account for the data, particularly the optimal interval, many of these models propose a quantum of time. However, neither Michon nor earlier researchers appear to have found clear evidence for a universal quantum.

Among the more recent theories of timing is that of Adams

(Adams and Creamer 1962a, b, c), which proposes kinesthetic feedback as the basis of time-keeping in serial responding. That is, when two responses define the interval to be timed, kinesthetic feedback from the first response leaves a decaying memory trace which bridges the interval. The subject learns to discriminate the time-varying characteristics of the trace as the basis of time-keeping. Assuming a negatively accelerated decay function, the theory predicts finer discriminations and, therefore, better time estimates, for shorter intervals. With the further assumption that more intense stimulation will produce more discriminable traces, it also predicts increased accuracy of timing with increases in either amplitude or force of the cueing response. Consistent with these predictions, Adams and Creamer (1962b) demonstrated that timing was enhanced with shorter intervals and a spring-loaded control, but failed to show either that movement amplitude improved timing accuracy or that the effects of these variables were additive in improving timing.

Starting with the evidence that movement-filled intervals are timed more accurately than empty ones (Goldfarb and Goldstone 1963; Grose 1964), Ellis, Schmidt, and Wade (1968) varied force and amplitude requirements of movements which filled the interval to be timed. Timing was improved for the greater amplitude, but not for the greater force conditions. Ellis (1969) then found improved timing with movement-filled as compared with unfilled intervals, particularly when force requirements varied with movement velocity or acceleration (i.e., with viscous-damped or mass-loaded controls). Nevertheless, accuracy did not vary directly with force requirements in the movement-filled conditions, thus failing to support the notion that timing depends on the *amount* or level of feedback available during the interval. However, with minimal movement-produced cues (unfilled intervals or low-tension movements), timing was enhanced by spelling words during the interval, presumably as a function of proprioception rather than verbal feedback, which was masked.

At first blush, the results of Adams and Ellis appear contradictory. However, while Adams dealt with feedback from responses which *initiated* the interval, Ellis manipulated conditions for movements which *filled* the interval to be timed. For Adams, the mediator is a proprioceptive memory trace; for Ellis it is the level and consistency of proprioceptive input during the interval. It is quite possible that both positions are correct: when intervals are unfilled, memory traces of prior movements may serve as timing cues, but when movement fills the interval, current level of feedback determines timing accuracy. This does not account for the discrepant results with respect to the variables of amplitude and force, but the comparison is further complicated by the fact that the Ellis paradigm confounds mechanical and proprioceptive effects. That is, Ellis measures the accuracy of moving a control through a constant distance in a fixed time under a variety of control dynamics. Thus, his task is one of rate discrimination and control, and, significantly, those dynamics which presumably enhance velocity and acceleration cues (i.e., viscous damping and mass) yielded the greatest timing accuracy.

Schmidt (1968) shifted the proprioceptive feedback cues to the left arm in an attempt to separate proprioceptive and mechanical effects. Enhancing proprioception increased beneficial anticipations but did not reduce error or intravariance. Furthermore, it appeared that timing responses by the right hand were cued by the amount of movement of the left hand, and, since the condition for optimal timing presumably enhanced rate and acceleration of these movements, Schmidt's task may also be viewed as one of rate control rather than timing, *per se.*

Research involving proprioceptive cues or memory traces has other methodological difficulties as Bahrick (1957) has pointed out. It is difficult to manipulate proprioceptive and tactual cues independently, and, succeeding at this, one is still hard-pressed to measure the intensity and time-varying distribution of proprioceptive stimulation. Nevertheless, it is an intuitively satisfying approach, particularly when taken together with the proprioceptive theory of the spatial control of movements to be discussed in the next section. (Bahrick 1957; Bahrick, Bennett, and Fitts 1955; Bahrick, Fitts, and Schneider 1955).

Feedback and Movement Control

A major question with respect to motor skill is how information about the time course and the outcome of responses can be utilized to control the movement and lead to the development of increased response precision. Information about responses may be available through a variety of sensory channels and may include both information intrinsic to the task (e.g., via visual monitoring and proprioceptive cues) and extrinsic information (e.g., cumulative error scores, time-on-target, etc). The latter, of course, may be transformed to any arbitrary scale and be made as specific or general as the experimenter chooses (I. McD. Bilodeau 1966). Similarly, both exteroceptive and interoceptive feedback may be enhanced, degraded, distorted, or delayed by a variety of manipulations of display and control conditions.

In an ideal servo-system, output information would be fed back without delay, compared to intended or desired output, and the resulting information (error) used to modify the input and consequently reduce the output error to zero. Without delays in the transmission, comparison, or correction processes, the system would be error-free. It is obvious, however, that real systems are not error-free because delays do occur at one or more of these points in the utilization of feedback information (Conklin 1957; Warrick 1949). Furthermore, in the case of human systems, lags will vary depending on the sensory channel, the coding of the information, and the response system involved. One thing seems certain, however; feedback information will be information about prior responses or responses segments, and, because of processing delays, it can be used to modify future responses only.

While the foregoing may seem all too obvious, it is the factual basis for some fundamental questions of movement control, movement modification, and the development of skilled performance. For example, with rapid biphasic positioning movements, the movement itself may be completed in less time than is required to process feedback information and thus appears to be an open loop system with amplitude, force and direction dependent solely on the preprogrammed innervation to the muscle system. If one surprises the subject by moving the target as the response is being initiated, the response is appropriate to the original target and a correction occurs only after some delay (e.g., McLaughlin 1967).

A second question has to do with the rapid sequencing of responses. The traditional S–R explanation has leaned heavily on the notion that response-produced stimuli become cues for subsequent responses in the chaining process. The difficulty, of course, is to account for sequences as rapid as sixteen responses per second, as Lashley (1951) pointed out. Even with reaction times of 110–120 msec. to kinesthetic feedback (Chernikoff and Taylor 1952), which are considerably faster than current estimates of reaction times of 190–230 msec. to visual feedback (Keele and Posner 1968) it is difficult to see how feedback cues could be utilized in such rapid sequences.

VISUAL FEEDBACK

In a majority of tasks, information is available through exteroceptors as to the course of movement with respect to some goal, or desired outcome within the receptor field of the subject. Thus, if one is attempting to follow an irregular pattern while guiding a board through a jigsaw, the outline of the pattern is the external standard for evaluating the course of the saw blade, and a discrepancy between these two visible tracks is the basis for correcting one's output by applying more pressure in a particular direction by one hand or the other. The discrepancy between the desired outcome (the pattern outline) and the perceived outcome (the saw cut)—the error—is the basis for response modification aimed at error nulling. Furthermore, with preview of the pattern course, the operator can "read ahead," anticipate required modifications, and prepare larger response segments in the way an automobile driver does upon entering a curve in the roadway (Leonard 1953). Still, it would appear, he must monitor his momentary course, at least intermittently, though the sampling rate may decrease as a function of practice (Adams and Chambers 1962; Fitts 1964; Schmidt 1968).

In the preceding example, visual information about the effect of one's movement was used to control the graded response, and preview provides the advance information necessary to overcome the reaction time handicap. However, in this relatively slow, self-paced task some of the issues with respect to movement control do not become apparent. When movements are either rapid and discrete or in rapid sequences, visual information is apparently not used, since practiced subjects do as well with eyes closed as with eyes open (Woodworth 1899; Vince 1948). In a recent report, Pew (1966) found that the modal time to initiate a corrective response when the display was blanked out was 300–350 msec. after the display was again visible. Pew, Duffendack, and Fensch (1967) also reported that corrective responses were made about 190–220 msec. after feedback delay in a sine-wave tracking task.

DEGRADATION AND ENHANCEMENT OF VISUAL FEEDBACK

A rather substantial body of literature has dealt with variations in the displayed information which provides feedback about discrepancies between the goal and the response in motor tasks. Although this research has not always been addressed to questions of feedback, it is possible to review it from this point of view.

Pursuit and Compensatory Displays. A major area of investigation has involved the comparison of tracking performance in pursuit and compensatory display conditions, much of which has been reviewed recently by Poulton (1966) and Briggs (1966). In pursuit tracking, independent information is provided about the courses of the target and of the follower, or response indicator, by two display indicators. The course of the target indicator is determined solely by whatever energy source programs it, while the course of the follower is determined solely by the responses of the operator acting on a control device. In a compensatory display, on the other hand, one element, the null indicator, is stationary, while the second element, the error indicator, displays the error obtained when the operator attempts to compensate for changes in the input source which drives the error indicator from the null position. For example, the automobile driver engages in compensatory tracking when he attempts to maintain a constant speed by accelerating and decelerating to compensate for input variations introduced by changes in the grade of the roadway.

Pursuit and compensatory displays present equivalent information about the error under comparable conditions of display gain. However, the pursuit display almost universally has yielded superior tracking performance, presumably because (1) regularities and statistical properties of the target course can be more directly observed and utilized to anticipate response requirements, (2) information about responses is unconfounded and can be used to modify subsequent responses, and (3) error can be unambiguously attributed to either modifications of the target course or of the control movements (Poulton 1966). Thus, with respect to feedback, the two display modes differ, not in terms of error information, *per se*, but rather with respect to the ambiguity which the information conveys for the modification of responses.

Other Display Variables. Feedback information has been modified by manipulating the size of the display ("display magnification"), its continuity ("intermittent displays"), and its noise level ("noisy displays"). The "U"-hypothesis with respect to system variables (Helson 1949) appears to hold for display magnification: performance is improved up to some optimal display size, then declines for greater magnifications (Battig, Nagel, and Brogden 1955; Hartman and Fitts 1955).

The effects of display intermittencies depend upon the predictability, complexity, and rate of the task and, for pursuit displays, on whether target or response information or both are being interrupted (Poulton and Gregory 1952; Poulton 1957b). Practiced subjects can do relatively well without a response marker, but loss of the stimulus course usually results rather quickly in performance decrements. However, the addition of high frequency, low amplitude, noise to the display, although it degrades performance, does not appear to affect the rate of learning (Briggs, Fitts, and Bahrick 1957). Subjects appear to learn to "track through" the noise, suggesting that "degrading" of information by filtering out high frequencies may well result in better performance. (In effect, the practiced driver integrates the input information by "reading ahead" and ignoring minor perturbations in feedback information.)

Feedback Delays and Distortions. The functional differences between intrinsic feedback and extrinsic or cumulative feedback information are most apparent in the research on feedback

delay. Even very brief delay of feedback in continuous control tasks usually has proven detrimental to performance. Such delay normally takes the form of a lag between control action and the display of the effects of such action. The lag may be a simple delay (transmission lag) or, as frequently is the case in real world systems, the displayed effects are some exponential or sigmoidal function of the control action. In contrast, delays in the feedback of response outcome information do not appear to be effective for performance (Bilodeau and Bilodeau 1958; Denny, Allard, Hall, and Rokeach 1960). Rather, the effective variable appears to be interference from response events occurring during the delay interval. This, of course, could account for the detrimental effects of lags in continuous control situations: the lag interval is filled with interfering response events.

An impressive amount of research on feedback delay, spatial inversion, and angular displacement of feedback information has been conducted by K. U. Smith and his associates (e.g.: McDermid and Smith 1964; Smith 1962, 1963, 1966; Smith, Wargo, Jones, and Smith 1963). This research leaves little doubt as to the significance of feedback loops for response execution, the detrimental effects of delays and displacements, and the functional non-equivalence of response-produced feedback and experimenter-produced knowledge of results, or "reinforcements." It is unfortunate, as Attneave (1966) pointed out, that this research has not dealt more with the time-varying characteristics of behavior as a function of feedback manipulations, rather than with summary outcome scores which discard this information.

Control Order and Gain. A zero order, or positional control, provides the most direct feedback information about response effects. With the positional control there is a direct and usually linear relationship between the displacement of the control and the displacement of the controlled element (the "follower" in a pursuit display). In higher order controls (rate, acceleration, or Δ acceleration), however, control displacement is reflected in the display as a change in rate (or acceleration, or Δ acceleration) and the processes of evaluating the effects of responses from the feedback data become more complex. The complexity is increased if the higher order dynamics also involve lags, as is frequently the case in real-world systems. Furthermore, the response requirements become more complex with higher order controls. Thus, with a rate control, one movement is required to put in the desired rate and another counter movement to remove it. It is not surprising, therefore, that the positional control is best suited to human capabilities (Poulton 1966).

KINESTHETIC FEEDBACK

Evidence for the role of kinesthetic feedback in movement control is not as clearcut as might be expected. There are several reasons for this, not the least of which are the difficulties (a) of controlling and measuring the intensity of stimulation to kinesthetic receptors and (b) of isolating the kinesthetic sense from confounding with tactual and other sensory data. In addition, manipulations may so alter the mechanical aspects of the task as to confound behavioral effects with systems performance (Bahrick 1957). For example, increasing the mass constant of a control could, at the extreme, produce a control with such inertia that Ss could not achieve any but the slowest acceleration rates.

Keele (1968) identified four approaches to the evaluation of kinesthetic feedback in movement control. The first approach looks for loss of control corresponding to the blocking or loss of kinesthetic cues through ischemia (Lazlo 1966, 1967) or local anesthetics (Provins 1958). As Keele points out, however, ischemia may involve efferent as well as afferent loss, and local anesthetics do not eliminate kinesthetic cues from muscles and tendons.

A second approach looks for evidence that kinesthetic cues are being utilized. For example, Gibbs (1965) found response correction times as short as .11 seconds, and, since these were considerably shorter than known reaction times to visual feedback, concluded that kinesthetic cues were being used.

A related body of research has attempted to degrade or enhance kinesthetic information by manipulating the physical control constants. A few studies (Burke and Gibbs 1965; Gibbs 1954; North and Lomnicki 1961) have compared tracking performance using pressure controls and free-moving stick controls. The results, which generally favored the pressure control, have been interpreted as demonstrating the importance of kinesthetic feedback in movement control. However, as Keele has noted, this evidence is not unambiguous. Movement amplitudes required with the two controls (as well as control-display ratios) differed; thus, movement time may have favored the pressure control. Furthermore, unless one is operating within the optimal (or comparable) ranges of the pressure and amplitude dimensions, no legitimate comparisons could be made. In fact, when force characteristics are comparable (elasticity, viscous damping, and inertia) a movable (amplitude) control results in better performance that an isometric (pressure) control (Notterman and Page 1962). Briggs et al. (1957) found superior tracking with control conditions requiring relatively high amplitude and force. While these conditions apparently enhanced kinesthetic feedback information, they were also confounded with modifications in the mechanical characteristics of the control and the control-to-display ratio and therefore do not clearly indicate the use of or the importance of kinesthetic information.

Finally, attempts have been made to evaluate the role of kinesthetic feedback by relating performance in skilled tasks to independent measures of kinesthetic acuity. Fleishman and Rich (1963) found that a kinesthetic acuity measure was positively related to performance in a two-hand coordination task, the relationship increasing with practice. A measure of visual (spatial) acuity also correlated positively with performance, but this relationship decreased with practice. These results indicate not only that both visual and kinesthetic feedback information may be important for movement control, but also that the relative importance of these two feedback channels may be a function of the skill level attained. The implication that a high level of skill depends upon discrimination of kinesthetic information should not be surprising in view of the evidence cited earlier for faster reaction times to kinesthetic than to visual feedback information.

A Kinesthetic Feedback Theory of Movement Control. A kinesthetic feedback theory has been developed by Bahrick (1957) which predicts relative accuracy of position, rate, and acceleration control as a function of the control system dynamics. Assuming kinesthetic feedback to be roughly proportional to the force requirements, the theory essentially predicts accuracy in the discrimination of movement amplitude to the extent that force requirements change with control position, accuracy in the discrimination of movement *rate* to the extent that force requirements change with control velocity, and accuracy in the discrimination of movement *acceleration* to the extent that force requirements change with control acceleration. The statement of force requirements, $F(t)$, for moving a mass M is:

$$F(t) = KX + B\,dx/dt + M\,d^2x/dt^2$$

where X, dx/dt, and d^2x/dt^2 represent the position, velocity, and acceleration of the control, respectively, and K, B, and M represent the spring-loading, viscous damping, and mass constants of the control system. The theory predicts, therefore, that discrimination (and control) of movement amplitude, rate, and acceleration should vary directly with the absolute and relative magnitude of K, B, and M, respectively. In this connection, Poulton (1966) has made the following predictions about movement control:

If Bahrick is correct, two combinations of control resistance and control-system dynamics are suitable for constant-velocity tracts: a spring-centered rate control, and a positional control with viscous resistance. And three combinations are suitable for constant-acceleration tracks: a spring-centered acceleration control, a rate control with viscous resistance, and a positional control with inertial resistance. It is not known which combination is in fact the easiest to handle. (p. 383)

Evidence for this feedback theory of movement control has been summarized by Fitts et al. (1959). In general, the evidence from a number of studies is consonant with the theory (Bahrick 1957; Bahrick et al. 1955a; Bahrick et al. 1955b; Helson and Howe 1943; Howland and Noble 1953). The manipulations of spring-loading, viscous damping, and mass constants have usually resulted in predicted effects on amplitude, rate, and acceleration control of movements. However, as indicated earlier, a number of methodological problems hamper clearcut tests of the theory, including the inaccessibility to direct manipulation and measurement of the proximal stimuli, and the confounding of mechanical effects in the control system with the changes in force requirements.

MOTOR COMMANDS AND MOVEMENT CONTROL

The control of movements on the basis of feedback information could be accomplished by changes in the amount or in the rate and duration of innervation outflow, or in some motor program which controls innervation to the effector system. This model represents an *inflow* theory of control and the evidence for the role of kinesthetic and exteroceptive feedback information tends to support the inflow position. However, because of the delays involved in utilizing feedback information and the evidence of movement control which appears to exceed the feedback limitations, the *outflow* position has gained recent attention. Basically, this position involves the notion of the monitoring of the innervation outflow via a central feedback loop. The outflow is compared with some internalized image, or standard, representing the "intended" innervation, or "efference copy" (von Holst 1954).

Keele (1968), after reviewing the evidence, argued for a central feedback loop whereby the *rate* and *duration*, rather than the *amount*, of innervation are monitored and modified on the basis of discrepancies from the intended, or programmed, innervation. Presumably, such a central feedback loop would have a very short lag time and could account for rapid corrections and rapid sequencing of movements.

A detailed review of the outflow-inflow controversy which dates back to Helmholtz (1925) and James (1950) is beyond the scope of this chapter. Festinger and Cannon (1965) have recently reviewed the literature most central to this issue as background for an experiment which provided some evidence as to the role of innervation in information about spatial location. Crucial to Festinger and Cannon's interpretation is the following rationale:

Let us be specific. If it is true, as seems likely, that we know the position of the eye mainly in terms of knowing where the eye was directed to go, then it should be possible to show that when the eye is directed to go to a specific location, a subject knows where his eye is more accurately than if the eye arrives at the same position without directions concerning this specific location ever having been issued. (Festinger and Cannon, 1965, p. 376)

The two conditions required to test this statement were obtained by comparing subjects who tracked a light source to a terminal position with those who made a discrete movement to the terminal position with respect to their accuracy in locating the terminal position. The results provided some support for the outflow theory; subjects who could program a discrete eye movement were better able to locate the terminal position than subjects who tracked the target to that position with no opportunity to pre-program a discrete response.

MOTOR PROGRAMS

The notion of a motor program, or efference copy, or some mechanism to serve as an internal standard, is critical to an outflow or innervation monitoring, central control loop notion. The converse is not true; concepts of motor programs may or may not include central feedback loops directly monitoring the outflow. In one sense, the model of a "motor program" (Keele 1968), or "plan" (Miller et al. 1960) or "subroutine" (Fitts 1964) which runs its course (perhaps as an open-loop system) until it is modified by feedback information, provides an alternative to the innervation-monitoring concept. That is, if the program, or plan, is seen as running its course without modification; but subject to program modifications on the basis of outcome information, then the need for an outflow-monitoring mechanism is not as evident. Such programs or plans are seen not only as modifiable on the basis of outcome information, but also subject to increasing complexity and increasing autonomy from attention and feedback control as a function of practice. Thus, a highly overlearned movement pattern may be run off on command; that is, on the basis of internalized cues,

with only occasional monitoring of the output, as implied in the term "automatization" of responses (Adams and Chamber 1962; Fitts 1964; Keele 1968; Schmidt 1968).

Fitts (1962, 1964), using computer concepts as his model, likened the development of sequences of skilled movements to the integration of subroutines under the monitoring of a master or executive routine. Thus, as the skill develops, the subroutines, representing portions of the total movement pattern, were seen as becoming more automated and more autonomous with respect to monitoring by the executive routine. The executive routine was seen by Fitts as a sort of master program of the intended outcome of the behavior and as such presumably modified by information about error provided by exteroceptive and proprioceptive feedback.

Fitts's model may suggest a basis for reconciling the two alternative explanations of apparently open-loop movements. If one assumes that the "subroutines," or motor programs, have central feedback loops monitoring the innervation outflow, while the executive routine or master plan, within which the subroutines are integrated, monitors the output and, in turn, is modified by sensory feedback, then a rational basis emerges to account both for response feedback and for central loop information about innervation. That is, information about the amount (or rate and duration) of innervation may be compared with the intended innervation, or internal reference level, (Adams 1968) with relatively rapid adjustments in outflow to null the discrepancy, while feedback from both exteroceptor and interoceptor loops serves to modify and increase the precision of the reference level, or motor program. Such a notion suggests that both perceptual and response learning is taking place in the development of movement control.

Adams (1967, 1968) has recently stated a closed-loop theory of learning in which he hypothesizes that two habit states are developed. The first is the conventional S-R habit, the association between a response and its eliciting stimulus. In Adams's scheme, this is the memory trace. The second habit involves establishing a perceptual trace, ". . . the image of conditioned sensations as the representation of stimuli which impinge on the subject and become its reference level" (Adams 1968, p. 497). Learning and forgetting are seen as the strengthening and weakening of either or both of these traces and,

Being a function of stimuli, perceptual traces are laid down by environmental stimuli as well as response-produced stimuli, and a perceptual trace is considered the reference for recognizing an environmental stimulus when it is presented at a later time. Thus, stimulus recognition and response recognition become a function of the same mechanism. (Adams, p. 497)

Space does not permit a more adequate development of Adams's theory, which includes a concept of subjective reinforcement, resulting from the comparison of feedback information and the internal reference. The theory does not include a central feedback mechanism monitoring innervation outflow. In fact, Adams appears to dismiss the Helmholtz "outflow" position. However, most of the research cited by Adams involves behavior which emphasizes the *selection* rather than the execution of responses (animal learning studies, verbal learning, and "selective learning"). With such behavior, the need for monitoring of outflow is less apparent that under conditions of continuous control where reaction times to feedback appear to be altogether too long to permit the precision so frequently observed. Modifications in the *selection* of responses may well be handled on the basis of cumulative feedback information from prior responses; modifications in the *execution* of ongoing responses, however, may require a mechanism which effectively monitors the outflow as the response is being executed.

AMPLITUDE, SPEED, AND ACCURACY OF MOVEMENTS

Conflicting results are reported in the literature with respect to the relationship between movement amplitude and movement duration. Early investigators concluded that duration of rapid movements was essentially constant over a fairly wide range of amplitudes (Bryan 1892; Freeman 1914; Hartson 1939; Stetson and McDill 1923). However, as Fitts (1954) noted, most early research dealt with ballistic movements, free of visual control or terminal accuracy requirements. Woodworth (1899) found that for quick visually controlled movements error increased with increases in either amplitude or speed, and more recent investigators have shown that movement time increases with amplitude when the task requires precision of response amplitudes. (Brown and Slater-Hammel 1949; Craig 1949; Hick and Bates 1950; Searle and Taylor 1948). Therefore, the discrepancy of findings with respect to amplitude and duration of movements appears to be a function of the presence or absence of an accuracy requirement in the task.

Given this background, Fitts (1954) hypothesized a constant information transmission rate for the motor system. Specifically, he predicted a speed-accuracy trade-off wherein the accuracy demands of the task were stated as a ratio of target width (W) to movement amplitude (A). The information content, or index of difficulty (Id) for a movement was given as:

$$Id = -\log_2 \frac{W}{2A},$$

and movement time (MT) was predicted to be a linear function of the information content of the movement:

$$MT = a + b \log_2 \frac{W}{2A}, \text{ or } MT = a + b(Id)$$

The constant information rate is reflected in the statement: $Id/MT = C$. Fitts' (1954) data supported this prediction; the rate of information was nearly constant at about 10 bits per second for three different tasks and several values of movement amplitude and target width. Subsequent research (e.g. Annett, Golby, and Kay 1958) also supported what has come to be known as Fitts Law.

Fitts and Radford (1966) demonstrated that increasing the monetary payoff for speed resulted in faster performance, but with a proportionate decrease in accuracy, and Fitts and Peterson (1964) showed that reaction time (RT) and movement time (MT) were independent, i.e., while MT increased with the index of difficulty, RT did not. Furthermore, the amount of preparation time prior to movement initiation did not affect movement accuracy.

Keele (1968) reanalyzed data from a number of studies and found them generally consistent with Fitts's Law. He also demonstrated that Fitts's Law could be derived from feedback theory, as well as from information theory, by assuming (a) the time required for each initial and each corrective movement is constant, and (b) the *relative* accuracy of each movement is constant.

In addition to amplitude and terminal precision requirements, movement time depends upon direction of movement. In the horizontal plane, right-handed movements to the upper right and lower left are both faster (Schmidtke and Stier 1960) and more accurate (Briggs, Thompson, and Brogden 1954; Corrigan and Brogden 1949). This means, of course, that direction affects the information transmission rate. Furthermore, movement time is affected by the type of manipulation required at movement termination (Harris and Smith 1954; Simon and Smader 1955; Wehrkamp and Smith 1952). These latter results might well be found consistent with Fitts's Law if the information content of the terminal manipulations was specified.

In contrast to the Fitts and Peterson (1964) data which showed that MT, but not RT, increased with the information content of the movement, a number of studies manipulating S–R and R–R compatibility have demonstrated predictable effects on RT. *Compatibility* refers to the empirical evidence that different ensembles of stimulus and response elements result in different levels of performance. Fitts and Seeger (1953) found that performance was a function of the combination of stimulus and response codes (the ensemble) and that there was no one best stimulus or response code for all conditions. Fitts and Deininger (1954) then demonstrated that different pairings of S and R elements had the greatest effects when the original ensemble was the most compatible (i.e., two-dimensional spatial correspondence of S and R elements). Brainard, Irby, Fitts and Alluisi (1962) also found RT to decrease with increases in compatibility of S–R arrangements. Keele (1966) showed compatibility effects on response times in a serial response task which apparently combined RT and MT, while Cross, Noble, and Trumbo (1964) and Trumbo, Rogers and Avant (1967) found S–R effects on both total response times and response initiation (RT) times, but failed to find clear-cut evidence of R–R, of S–R–R compatibility effects. (The latter effects were tested by comparing combinations of clockwise and counterclockwise movements of the two hands together with three different codes of the stimulus information). Fitts and his associates (Fitts et al. 1959) outlined a theory of compatibility effects, based upon the utilization of population stereotypes, the utilization of familiar concepts and sets in the mapping of S and R elements, ambiguity of figure-ground and error-command signals, the number of information transformations, and the utilization of systematic search procedures.

The fact that compatibility of S–R arrangements as well as stimulus uncertainty (e.g., Hick 1952; Keele 1966) affect RT, while factors determining the information content of the response (response amplitude, terminal accuracy, and terminal manipulation requirements) affect MT is consistent with the assumption that RT and MT are independent and probably relate, respectively, to response selection and response execution phases of information processing. Incompatible S–R arrangements and/or stimulus uncertainty should interfere with anticipation and selection of responses, but once these processes are complete, the execution of the responses would appear to be governed primarily by precision demands of the task.

References

ADAMS, J. A. Warm-up decrement in performance on the pursuit-rotor. *American Journal of Psychology*, 1952, *65*, 404–14.

—— The prediction of performance at advanced stages of training on a complex psychomotor task. USAF *Human Resources Research Center Bulletin*, 1953, No. 53–49.

—— The relationship between certain measures of ability and the acquisition of a psychomotor criterion response. *Journal of General Psychology*, 1957, *56*, 121–34.

—— Human tracking behavior. *Psychological Bulletin*, 1961*a*, *58*, 55–79.

—— The second facet of forgetting: a review of warm-up decrement. *Psychological Bulletin*, 1961*b*, *58*, 257–73.

—— *Human Memory*. New York: McGraw-Hill, 1967.

—— Response feedback and learning. *Psychological Bulletin*, 1968, *70*, 486–504.

——, and CHAMBERS, R. W. Response to simultaneous stimulation of two sense modalities. *Journal of Experimental Psychology*, 1962, *63*, 198–206.

ADAMS, J. A., and L. R. CREAMER. Anticipatory timing of continuous and discrete responses. *Journal of Experimental Psychology*, 1962*a*, *63*, 84–90.

—— Proprioceptive variables as determiners of anticipatory timing behavior. *Human Factors*, 1962*b*, *4*, 217–22.

—— Data processing capabilities of the human operator. *Journal of Engineering Psychology*, 1962*c*, *1*, 150–58.

ADAMS, J. A., and S. DIJKSTRA. Short-term memory for motor responses. *Journal of Experimental Psychology*, 1966, *71*, 314–18.

——, and B. REYNOLDS. Effect of shift in distribution of practice conditions following interpolated rest. *Journal of Experimental Psychology*, 1954, *47*, 32–36.

——, and L. V. XHIGNESSE. Some determinants of two-dimensional tracking behavior. *Journal of Experimental Psychology*, 1960, *60*, 391–403.

AMMONS, R. B. Rotary pursuit apparatus: I. Survey of variables. *Psychological Bulletin*, 1955, *52*, 69–76.

——, and L. WILLIG. Acquisition of motor skill: IV. Effects of repeated periods of massed practice. *Journal of Experimental Psychology*, 1956, *51*, 118–26.

ANNETT, J., C. W. GOLBY, and J. KAY. The measurement of elements in an assembly task. The information output of the human motor system. *Quarterly Journal of Experimental Psychology*, 1958, *10*, 1–11.

ATTNEAVE, F. Cybernetic theory and analysis of learning. *In* E. A. BILODEAU (ed.), *Acquisition of Skill*. New York: Academic, 1966.

BAHRICK, H. P. Analysis of stimulus variables influencing proprioceptive control of movements. *Psychological Review*, 1957, *64*, 324–28.

——, W. F. BENNETT, and P. M. FITTS. Accuracy of positioning responses as a function of spring loading in a control. *Journal of Experimental Psychology*, 1955*a*, *49*, 437–44.

——, P. M. FITTS, and R. SCHNEIDER. The reproduction of simple movements as a function of factors influencing proprioceptive feedback. *Journal of Experimental Psychology*, 1955*b*, *49*, 445–54.

——, and M. E. NOBLE. Motor behavior. *In* J. B. Sidowski (ed.), *Experimental Methods and Instrumentation in Psychology*. New York: McGraw-Hill, 1966.

BARCH, A. M., and D. LEWIS. The effect of task difficulty and amount of practice on proactive transfer. *Journal of Experimental Psychology*, 1954, *48*, 134–42.

BARTLETT, F. C. Anticipation in human performance. *In* G. EKMAN et al. (eds.), *Essays in Psychology*. Uppsala: Almquist & Wiksells, 1951.

—— *Thinking*. London: Allen & Unwin, 1958.

BATTIG, W. F., E. H. NAGEL, and W. J. BROGDEN. The effects of error magnification and marker size on bidimensional compensatory tracking. *American Journal of Psychology*, 1955, *68*, 585–94.

BEAN, C. H. The curve of forgetting. *Archives of Psychology*, 1912, *3*, No. 21.

BILODEAU, E. A. Transfer of training between tasks differing in degree of physical restriction of imprecise responses. USAF *Human Resources Research Center Research Bulletin*, 1952, No. 52–40.

—— Rate recovery in a repetitive motor task as a function of successive rest periods. *Journal of Experimental Psychology*, 1954, *48*, 197–203.

——, and I. MCD. BILODEAU. Variation of temporal intervals among critical events in five studies of knowledge of results. *Journal of Experimental Psychology*, 1958, *55*, 603–12.

—— Motor-skills learning. *Annual Review of Psychology*, 1961, *12*, 234–80.

BILODEAU, I. MCD. Information feedback. *In* E. A. BILODEAU (ed.), *Acquisition of Skill*. New York: Academic, 1966.

BOOK, W. F. *The psychology of skill*. New York: Gregg, 1925.

BRAINARD, R. W. ET AL. Some variables influencing the rate of gain of information. *Journal of Experimental Psychology*, 1962, *63*, 105–10.

BRIGGS, G. E. Tracking behavior: comments on Dr. Poulton's paper. *In* E. A. BILODEAU (ed.), *Acquisition of Skill*. New York: Academic, 1966.

——, P. M. FITTS, and H. P. BAHRICK. Effects of force and amplitude cues on learning and performance in a complex tracking task. *Journal of Experimental Psychology*, 1957, *54*, 262–68.

——, R. F. THOMPSON, and W. J. BROGDEN. The effect of angle of tilt upon the trigonometric relationship of precision and angle of linear-pursuit movements. *American Journal of Psychology*, 1954, *67*, 475–83.

BROWN, J. S., and A. T. SLATER-HAMMEL. Discrete movements in the horizontal plane as a function of their length and direction. *Journal of Experimental Psychology*, 1949, *39*, 84–95.

BRYAN, W. L. On the development of voluntary motor ability. *American Journal of Psychology*, 1892, *5*, 125–204.

——, and N. HARTER. Studies in the physiology and psychology of the telegraphic language. *Psychological Review*, 1897, *4*, 27–53.

—— Studies on the telegraphic language: the acquisition of a hierarchy of habits. *Psychological Review*, 1899, *6*, 345–75.

BURKE, D., and C. B. GIBBS. A comparison of free-moving and pressure levers in a positional control system. *Ergonomics*, 1965, *8*, 23–29.

BUXTON, C. E. The application of multiple factorial methods to the study of motor abilities. *Psychometrika*, 1938, *3*, 85–95.

——, and L. G. HUMPHREYS. The effect of practice upon intercorrelations in motor skills. *Science*, 1935, *81*, 441–42.

CHEVNIKOFF, R., and F. V. TAYLOR. Reaction time to kinesthetic stimulation resulting from sudden arm displacement. *Journal of Experimental Psychology*, 1952, *43*, 1–8.

CONKLIN, J. E. Effect of control lag on performance in a tracking task. *Journal of Experimental Psychology*, 1957, *53*, 261–68.

COOK, T. W. Studies in cross-education: I. Mirror tracing the star-shaped maze. *Journal of Experimental Psychology*, 1933, *16*, 144–60.

—— Studies in cross-education: V. *Theoretical Psychological Review*, 1936, *43*, 149–78.

CORRIGAN, R. E., and W. J. BROGDEN. The trigonometric relationship of precision and angle of linear pursuit movements. *American Journal of Psychology*, 1949, *62*, 90–98.

CRAIG, D. R. Effect of amplitude range on duration of responses to step function displacements. *USAF Technical Report*, 1949, No. 5913.

CRONBACH, L. J. The two disciplines of scientific psychology. *American Psychologist*, 1957, *12*, 671–84.

CROSS, K. D. Discrete tracking proficiency as a function of temporal, directional, and spatial predictability. Unpublished doctoral dissertation, Kansas State University, 1966.

——, M. NOBLE, and D. TRUMBO. On response-response compatibility. *Human Factors*, 1964, *6*, 31–37.

DENNY, M. R. ET AL. Supplementary report: Delay of knowledge of results, knowledge of task and intertrial interval. *Journal of Experimental Psychology*, 1960, *60*, 327.

DIGMAN, J. M. Growth of a motor skill as a function of distribution of practice. *Journal of Experimental Psychology*, 1959, *57*, 310–16.

DORÉ, L. R., and E. R. HILGARD. Spaced practice and the maturation hypothesis. *Journal of Psychology*, 1937, *4*, 245–59.

ELKIND, J. I. Characteristics of simple manual control systems. MIT Lincoln Laboratory: *Technical Report*, No. 111, 1956.

ELLIS, M. J. Control dynamics and timing a discrete motor task. *Journal of Motor Behavior*, 1969, *1*, 119–34.

———, R. A. SCHMIDT, and M. G. WADE. Proprioceptive variables as determinants of lapsed time estimation. *Ergonomics*, 1968, *11*, 577–86.

ELLSON, D. G. The application of operational analysis to human motor behavior. *Psychological Review*, 1949, *56*, 9–17.

——— Linear frequency theory as behavior theory. *In* S. KOCH (ed.), *Psychology: A study of a science*. Vol. 2. New York: McGraw-Hill, 1959.

FESTINGER, L., and L. K. CANON. Information about spatial location based on knowledge about efference. *Psychological Review*, 1965, *72*, 373–84.

FITTS, P. M. The information capacity of the human motor system in controlling the amplitude of movement. *Journal of Experimental Psychology*, 1954, *47*, 381–91.

——— Skill training. *In* R. GLASER (ed.), *Training Research and Education*. Pittsburgh: University of Pittsburgh Press, 1962.

——— Perceptual motor skill learning. *In* A. W. MELTON (ed.), *Categories of Human Learning*. New York: Academic, 1964.

——— ET AL. Skilled performance. *USAF WADC Final Report*, 1959.

———, and R. L. DEININGER. S-R compatibility: correspondence among paired elements within stimulus and response codes. *Journal of Experimental Psychology*, 1954, *48*, 483–92.

———, and J. R. PETERSON. Information capacity of discrete motor responses, *Journal of Experimental Psychology*, 1964, *67*, 103–12.

———, and B. K. RADFORD. Information capacity of discrete motor responses under different cognitive sets. *Journal of Experimental Psychology*, 1966, *71*, 475–82.

———, and C. M. SEEGER. S-R compatibility: spatial characteristics of stimulus and response codes. *Journal of Experimental Psychology*, 1953, *46*, 199–210.

FLEISHMAN, E. A. A factor analysis of intra-task performance on two psychomotor tests. *Psychometrika*, 1953a, *18*, 45–55.

——— Testing for psychomotor abilities by means of apparatus tests. *Psychological Bulletin*, 1953b, *50*, 241–62.

——— Dimensional analysis of psychomotor abilities. *Journal of Experimental Psychology*, 1954, *48*, 437–54.

——— Psychomotor selection tests: research and application in the United States Air Force. *Personnel Psychology*, 1956, *9*, 449–67.

——— An analysis of positioning movements and static reactions. *Journal of Experimental Psychology*, 1958a, *55*, 13–24.

——— Dimensional analysis of movement reactions. *Journal of Experimental Psychology*, 1958b, *55*, 438–53.

——— Abilities at different stages of practice in Rotary Pursuit performance. *Journal of Experimental Psychology*, 1960, *60*, 162–71.

——— Factor analyses of physical fitness tests. *Educational and Psychological Measurement*, 1963, *23*, 647–61.

——— *The Structure and Measurement of Physical Fitness*. Englewood Cliffs, New Jersey: Prentice-Hall, 1964.

——— Human abilities and the acquisition of skill. *In* E. A. BILODEAU (ed.), *Acquisition of Skill*. New York: Academic Press, 1966.

———, and G. D. ELLISON. A factor analysis of fine manipulative tests. *Journal of Applied Psychology*, 1962, *46*, 96–105.

———, and W. E. HEMPEL, JR. The relation between abilities and improvement with practice in a visual discrimination reaction task. *Journal of Experimental Psychology*, 1955, *49*, 301–12.

———, S. J. KREMER, and G. W. SHOUP. *The dimensions of physical fitness—a factor analysis of strength tests*. ONR, Contract Nonr 609 (32), *Technical Report*, 2, Yale Univ., 1961.

———, and J. F. PARKER. Prediction of advanced levels of proficiency in a complex tracking task. USAF *WADC Technical Report*, 1959, No. 59–255.

——— Factors in the retention and relearning of perceptual-motor skill. *Journal of Experimental Psychology*, 1962, *64*, 215–26.

FLEISHMAN, E. A., and S. RICH. Role of kinesthetic and spatial-visual abilities in perceptual-motor learning. *Journal of Experimental Psychology*, 1963, *66*, 6–11.

———, P. THOMAS, and P. MUNROE. The dimensions of physical fitness—a factor analysis of speed, flexibility, balance, and coordination. ONR, Contract Nonr 609 (32), *Technical Report*, 3, 1961.

FREEMAN, F. N. Experimental analysis of the writing movement. *Psychological Monographs*, 1914, *17*, No. 4 (whole No. 75).

———, and E. M. ABERNETHY. Comparative retention of typewriting and of substitution with analogous material. *Journal of Educational Psychology*, 1930, *21*, 639–49.

——— New evidence of the superior retention of typewriting to that of substitution. *Journal of Educational Psychology*, 1932, *23*, 331–34.

FUCHS, A. H. The progression-regression hypothesis in perceptual-motor skill learning. *Journal of Experimental Psychology*, 1962, *63*, 177–82.

GARVEY, W. D. A comparison of effects of training and secondary tasks on tracking behavior. *Journal of Applied Psychology*, 1960, *44*, 370–75.

———, and L. L. MITNICK. An analysis of tracking behavior in terms of lead-lag errors. *Journal of Experimental Psychology*, 1957, *53*, 372–78.

GIBBS, C. B. The continuous regulation of skilled response by kinaesthetic feedback. *British Journal of Psychology*, 1954, *45*, 24–39.

——— Probability learning in step-input tracking. *British Journal of Psychology*, 1965, *56*, 233–42.

GOLDFARB, J. and S. GOLDSTONE. Proprioceptive involvement, psychophysical method and temporal judgement. *Perceptual and Motor Skills*, 1963, *17*, 286.

GREENE, E. B. An analysis of random and systematic changes with practice. *Psychometrika*, 1943, *8*, 37–53.

GROSE, J. E. Timing control in finger, arm, and whole body movements. *Research Quarterly*, 1967, *38*, 10–21.

HARRIS, S. J., and K. U. SMITH. Dimensional analysis of motion: VII. Extent and direction of manipulative movements as factors in defining motions. *Journal of Applied Psychology*, 1954, *38*, 126–30.

HARTMAN, B. O., and P. M. FITTS. Relations of stimulus and response amplitude to tracking performance. *Journal of Experimental Psychology*, 1955, *49*, 82–92.

HARTSON, L. D. Contrasting approaches to the analysis of skilled movements. *Journal of General Psychology*, 1939, *20*, 263–93.

HELMHOLTZ, H. VON. *Treatise on physiological optics* (3rd Ed.) P. C. Southall, ed. and trans. Vol. 3. Menasha, Wisconsin: Optical Society of America, 1925.

HELSON, H. Design of equipment and optimal human operation. *American Journal of Psychology*, 1949, *62*, 473–97.

———, and W. H. HOWE. Inertia, friction, and diameter in handwheel tracking. *OSRD Report*, 1943, No. 3454. (PB406114)

HEMPEL, W. E., JR., and E. A. FLEISHMAN. A factor analysis of physical proficiency and manipulative skill. *Journal of Applied Psychology*, 1955, *39*, 12–16.

HICK, W. E. On the rate of gain of information. *Quarterly Journal of Experimental Psychology*, 1925, *4*, 11–26.

———, and J. A. BATES. *The human operator of control mechanisms*. London: Ministry of Supply, 1950.

HILL, D. S. Minor studies in learning and relearning. *Journal of Educational Psychology*, 1914, *5*, 375–86.

HOUSTON, R. C. An evaluation of the predictive properties of measures of variability of performance on three psychomotor tasks. Unpublished doctoral dissertation, University of Maryland, 1950.

HOWLAND, D., and M. E. NOBLE. The effects of physical constants of a control on tracking performance. *Journal of Experimental Psychology*, 1953, *46*, 353–60.

HULL, C. L. *Principles of Behavior*. New York: Appleton-Century-Crofts, 1943.

IRION, A. L. A brief history of research on the acquisition of skill. *In* E. A. BILODEAU (ed.), *Acquisition of Skill*. New York: Academic, 1966.

JAMES, W. *Principle of Psychology*, vol. 2. New York: Dover, 1950.

JONES, M. B. Simplex theory. *USN School Aviation Medicine Monograph*, 1959, No. 3.

——— Practice as a process of simplification. *Psychological Review*, 1962, *69*, 274–94.

——— Individual differences. *In* E. A. BILODEAU (ed.), *Acquisition of Skill*. New York: Academic 1966.

KEELE, S. W. An analysis of S-R compatibility. Unpublished doctoral dissertation, University of Wisconsin, 1966.

——— Movement control in skilled motor performance. *Psychological Bulletin*, 1968, *70*, 387–403.

———, and M. I. POSNER. Processing of visual feedback in rapid movements. *Journal of Experimental Psychology*, 1968, *77*, 155–58.

KELLER, F. S. The phantom plateau. *Journal of the Experimental Analysis of Behavior*, 1958, *1*, 1–13.

KIENTZLE, M. J. Properties of learning curves under varied distributions of practice. *Journal of Experimental Psychology*, 1946, *36*, 187–211.

―――― Ability patterns under distributed practice. *Journal of Experimental Psychology*, 1949, *39*, 532–37.

LASHLEY, K. S. The problem of serial order in behavior. *In* L. A. JEFFRESS (ed.), *Cerebral Mechanisms in Behavior*. New York: John Wiley, 1951.

LAZLO, J. I. The performance of a simple motor task with kinesthetic sense loss. *Quarterly Journal of Experimental Psychology*, 1966, *18*, 1–8.

―――― Training of fast tapping with reduction of kinesthetic, tactile, visual and auditory sensations. *Quarterly Journal of Experimental Psychology*, 1967, *19*, 344–49.

LEAVITT, H. J., and H. SCHLOSBERG. The retention of verbal and motor skills. *Journal of Experimental Psychology*, 1944, *34*, 404–17.

LEONARD, J. A. Advance information in sensori-motor skills. *Quarterly Journal of Experimental Psychology*, 1953, *5*, 141–49.

LEWIS, D., D. E. MCALLISTER, and J. A. ADAMS. Facilitation and interference in performance on the Modified Mashburn Apparatus: I. The effects of varying the amount of original learning. *Journal of Experimental Psychology*, 1951, *41*, 247–60.

LEWIS, D., and G. H. MILES. Retroactive interference in performance on the Star Discrimeter as a function of the amount of interpolated learning. *Perceptual and Motor Skills*, 1956, *6*, 295–98.

MCALLISTER, D. E., and D. LEWIS. Facilitation and interference in performance on the modified Mashburn Apparatus: II. The effects of varying the amount of interpolated learning. *Journal of Experimental Psychology*, 1951, *41*, 356–63.

MCDERMID, C., and K. U. SMITH. Compensatory reaction to angularly displaced visual feedback in behavior. *Journal of Applied Psychology*, 1964, *48*, 63–68.

MCGEOCH, J. A., and A. L. IRION. *The psychology of human learning* (2nd ed.). New York: Longmans, Green, 1952.

MCGEOCH, J. A., and A. W. MELTON. The comparative retention values of maze habits and of nonsense syllables. *Journal of Experimental Psychology*, 1929, *12*, 392–414.

MCLAUGHLIN, S. C. Parametric adjustments in saccadic eye movements. *Perception and Psychophysics*, 1967, *2*, 359–62.

MCRUER, D. T. ET AL. Human pilot dynamics in compensatory systems: theory, models, and experiments with controlled elements and forcing function variations. AFFDL–TR–65–15, 1965.

MCRUER, D. T., and E. S. KRENDEL. Dynamic responses of human operators. WADC, TR 56–524, 1957.

―――― The human operator as a servo system element. *Journal of the Franklin Institute*, 1959, *267*, No. 56.

MELTON, A. W. (ed.) *Apparatus tests*. Washington, D.C.: U. S. Government Printing Office, 1947a.

―――― (ed.) *Apparatus tests* (supplement). Washington, D.C.: U.S. Government Printing Office, 1947b.

MICHON, J. A. *Timing in temporal tracking*. Soesterberg, The Netherlands: Institute for Perception RVO–TNO, 1967.

MILLER, G. A., E. GALANTER, and K. H. PRIBRAM. *Plans and the structure of behavior*. New York: Holt, Rinehart & Winston, 1960.

NAYLOR, J. C., and G. E. BRIGGS. Long-term retention of learned skills: a review of the literature, U.S. Air Force. *ASD Technical Report*, 1961, 61–390.

―――― Effects of task complexity and task organization on the relative efficiency of part and whole training methods. *Journal of Experimental Psychology*, 1963a, *65*, 217–24.

―――― Effect of rehearsal of temporal and spatial aspects on the long-term retention of a procedural skill. *Journal of Applied Psychology*, 1963b, *47*, 120–126.

NICKS, D. C., and E. A. FLEISHMAN. What do physical fitness tests measure? A review of factor analytic studies. *Educational and Psychological Measurement*, 1962, *22*, 77–95.

NOBLE, C. E. Selective learning. *In* E. A. BILODEAU (ed.) *Acquisition of Skill*. New York: Academic, 1966.

NOBLE, M. ET AL. Task predictability and the development of tracking skill under extended practice. *Journal of Experimental Psychology*, 1966, *72*, 85–94.

NORTH, J. D., and Z. A. LOMNICI. Further experiments on human operators in compensatory tracking tasks. *Ergonomics*, 1961, *4*, 339–53.

NOTTERMAN, J. M., and D. E. PAGE. Evaluation of mathematically equivalent tracking systems. *Perceptual and Motor Skills*, 1962, *15*, 683–716.

PERL, R. E. An application of Thurstone's method of factor analysis to practice series. *Journal of General Psychology*, 1934, *11*, 209–12.

PEW, R. W. Acquisition of a hierarchical control over the temporal organization of a skill. *Journal of Experimental Psychology*, 1966, *71*, 764–71.

―――, J. C. DUFFENDACK, and L. K. FENSCH. A quantitative description of the effects of delayed feedback on motor performance. Paper presented at meetings of the Psychonomic Society, 1967.

POSNER, M. I., and A. F. KONICK. Short-term retention of visual and kinesthetic information. *Organizational Behavior and Human Performance*, 1966, *1*, 71–86.

POULTON, E. C. Perceptual anticipation and reaction time. *Quarterly Journal of Experimental Psychology*, 1950a, *2*, 99–112.

―――― Perceptual anticipation in tracking. *Applied Psychology Unit Report*, No. 118. Cambridge, England, 1950b.

―――― Perceptual anticipation in tracking with two-pointer and one-pointer displays. *British Journal of Psychology*, 1952a, *43*, 222–29.

―――― The basis of perceptual anticipation in tracking. *British Journal of Psychology*, 1952b, *43*, 295–302.

―――― Learning the statistical properties of the input in pursuit tracking. *Journal of Experimental Psychology*, 1957a, *54*, 28–32.

―――― On prediction in skilled movements. *Psychological Bulletin*, 1957b, *54*, 467–78.

―――― On the stimulus and response in pursuit tracking. *Journal of Experimental Psychology*, 1957c, *53*, 189–94.

―――― Tracking behavior. *In* E. A. BILODEAU (ed.), *Acquisition of Skill*. New York: Academic, 1966.

―――, and R. L. GREGORY. Blinking during visual tracking. *Quarterly Journal of Experimental Psychology*, 1952, *4*, 57–65.

PROVINS, K. A. The effect of peripheral nerve block on the appreciation and execution of finger movements. *Journal of Physiology*, 1958, *143*, 55–67.

REYNOLDS, B. The effect of learning on the predictability of psychomotor performance. *Journal of Experimental Psychology*, 1952, *44*, 189–98.

SCHMIDT, R. A. Anticipation and timing in human motor performance. *Psychological Bulletin*, 1968, *70*, 631–46.

SCHMIDTKE, H., and F. STIER. Der aufbau komplexer bewegungsabläufe aus elementar bewegungen, *Forschungsberichte des landes Nordrhein-Westfalen*, 1960, No. 822, 13–32.

SEARLE, L. V., and F. V. TAYLOR. Studies in tracking behavior: I. Rate and time characteristics of simple corrective movements. *Journal of Experimental Psychology*, 1948, *38*, 615–31.

SEASHORE, R. H. Experimental and theoretical analysis of fine motor skills. *American Journal of Psychology*, 1940, *53*, 86–98.

―――― Work and motor performance. *In* S. S. STEVENS (ed.), *Handbook of experimental psychology*, New York: John Wiley, 1951.

―――. C. E. BUXTON, and I. N. MCCOLLOM. Multiple factorial analysis of fine motor skills. *American Journal of Psychology*, 1940, *53*, 251–59.

SEASHORE, S. H., and R. H. SEASHORE. Individual differences in simple auditory reaction times of hands, feet and jaws. *Journal of Experimental Psychology*, 1941, *29*, 342–45.

SENDERS, J. W. Survey of human dynamics data and a sample application. WADC *Technical Report*. 59–712 (1959).

SIMON, J. R., and R. C. SMADER. Dimensional analysis of motion: VIII. The role of visual discrimination in motion cycles. *Journal of Applied Psychology*, 1955, *39*, 5–10.

SMITH, K. U. *Delayed sensory feedback*. Philadelphia: Saunders, 1962.

―――― Sensory feedback analysis in medical research: I. Delayed sensory feedback in behavior and neural function. *American Journal of Physical Medicine*, 1963, *42*, 228–62.

―――― Cybernetic theory and analysis of learning. *In* E. A. BILODEAU (ed.), *Acquisition of Skill*. New York: Academic, 1966.

―――― ET AL. Delayed and space-displaced sensory feedback and learning. *Perceptual and Motor Skills*, 1963, *16*, 781–96.

SNODDY, G. S. *Evidence for two opposing processes in mental growth*. Lancaster, Pa.: Science Press, 1935.

STETSON, R. H., and J. A. MCDILL. Mechanisms of the different types of movement. *Psychological Monographs*, 1923, *32*, No. 3: 18–40.

SWIFT, E. J. Memory of a complex skillful act. *American Journal of Psychology*, 1905, *16*, 131–33.

────── Memory of skillful movements. *Psychological Bulletin*, 1906, *3*, 185–87.

────── Relearning a skillful act: an experimental study of neuromuscular memory. *Psychological Bulletin*, 1910, *7*, 17–19.

TAYLOR, F. V., and H. P. BIRMINGHAM. That confounded system performance measure—a demonstration. *Psychological Review*, 1959, *66*, 178–82.

TROLAND, L. T. *The fundamentals of human motivation.* New York: Van Nostrand Reinhold, 1928.

TRUMBO, D. ET AL. Task predictability in the organization, acquisition, and retention of tracking skill. *Journal of Experimental Psychology*, 1965, *70*, 252–63.

TRUMBO, D. ET AL. Motor performance on temporal tasks as a function of sequence length and coherence. *Journal of Experimental Psychology*, 1968, *77*, 397-406.

TRUMBO, D., M. NOBLE, and J. QUIGLEY. Sequential probabilities and the performance of serial tasks. *Journal of Experimental Psychology*, 1968, *76*, 364–72.

TRUMBO, D., S. ROGERS, and L. L. AVANT. Compatibility effects in a two-hand cranking task. *Journal of Applied Psychology*, 1967, *51*, 35–38.

TSAI, C. A comparative study of retention curves for motor habits. *Comparative Psychology Monographs*, 1924, *2*.

UNDERWOOD, B. J. Motor-skills learning and verbal learning: some observations. *In* E. A. BILODEAU (ed.), *Acquisition of Skill.* New York: Academic, 1966.

VAN TILBORG, P. W. The retention of mental and finger maze habits. *Journal of Experimental Psychology*, 1936, *19*, 334–41.

VINCE, M. A. Corrective movements in a pursuit task. *Quarterly Journal of Experimental Psychology*, 1948, *1*, 85–103.

VON HOLST, E. Relations between the central nervous system and the peripheral organs. *British Journal of Animal Behavior*, 1954, *2*, 89–94.

WAGNER, R. C., P. M. FITTS, and M. E. NOBLE. Preliminary investigations of speed and load as dimensions of psychomotor tasks. USAF *Personnel Training Research Center Technical Report*, 1954, No. AFPTRC—TR–54–45.

WARRICK, M. J. Effect of transmission-type control lags on tracking accuracy. *ASAF WADC Technical Report No. 5916*, 1949.

WEHRKAMP, R., and K. U. SMITH. Dimensional analysis of motion: II. Travel-distance effects. *Journal of Applied Psychology*, 1952, *36*, 201–6.

WHEELER, R. H., and F. T. PERKINS. *Principles of mental development.* New York: Thomas Y. Crowell, 1932.

WOODROW, H. The relation between abilities and improvement with practice. *Journal of Educational Psychology*, 1938a, *29*, 215–30.

────── The effect of practice on groups of different initial ability. *Journal of Educational Psychology*, 1938b, *29*, 268–78.

────── The effect of practice on test intercorrelations. *Journal of Educational Psychology*, 1938c, *29*, 561–72.

────── Factors in improvement with practice. *Journal of Psychology*, 1939a, *7*, 55–70.

────── The application of factor analysis to problems of practice. *Journal of General Psychology*, 1939b, *21*, 457–60.

────── Interrelations of measures of learning. *Journal of Psychology*, 1940, *10*, 49–73.

────── The ability to learn. *Psychological Review*, 1946, *53*, 147–58.

WOODWORTH, R. A. *Dynamics of Behavior.* New York: Holt, Rinehart & Winston, 1958.

WOODWORTH, R. S. The accuracy of voluntary movement. *Psychological Review Monograph Supplement*, 1899, Whole No. 13.

It is well known that certain breeds of dog such as setters and pointers or labradors respond quickly and eagerly to training for hunting—that is, location of game-birds and, when necessary, their retrieval. Other breeds, such as dobermans, alsatians, or mastiffs are much better adapted to guarding functions; still others—the working breeds—are most adept at handling large groups of domestic animals such as sheep or cattle. These obvious differences have been achieved through many generations of deliberate breeding for sets of traits or behaviors that are considered useful or desirable. Particularly in the case of the *Canidae*, there is a tremendously wide range of characteristics that are under direct genetic control (Colbert 1958; Ginsburg and Slatis 1962).

Such facts as these have been known to dog fanciers and animal breeders for centuries. But it is only relatively recently that they have come under the formal scrutiny of the sciences of biology and psychology. Within the last few decades, there has emerged a large literature dealing directly with the study of the relationships between genetic factors and behavior. The discipline concerned with these problems has been variously labelled "Psychogenetics" (Hall 1951; Broadhurst 1960), "Behavior Genetics" (Fuller and Thompson 1960) and "Behavior Genetic Analysis" (Hirsch 1967a). Although there are some who insist that the nuances of meaning between these terms are of considerable importance (see Hirsch 1967b), we do not feel that they are worth arguing about at this point. Since the first comprehensive survey of the field was published under the title of *Behavior genetics* (Fuller and Thompson 1960)—and also because of obvious personal biases—we will use this descriptive term here.

The formal goals of Behavior Genetics may be summarized as follows:

1. estimation of the extent of effects of hereditary factors or genes on behavior and their mode of operation;
2. specification of the genetic, biochemical, and physiological pathways by which such effects are mediated;
3. analysis of the manner in which genetic factors relate to

W. R. Thompson
& G. J. S. Wilde

Behavior Genetics

11

behavioral characteristics of populations and the manner in which these relationships both reflect and influence evolutionary change.

To give examples of each of these: the first goal may be represented by an experiment aimed at demonstrating whether it is possible to select high and low intelligence strains from a base population of rats. The second goal would be involved in a subsequent attempt to locate the immediate biochemical effects (e.g., cholinesterase activity) of the genes known to be mainly responsible for high or low intellectual ability. The third goal would call for studies attempting to show that intelligent behavior had, in certain ecological circumstances, some survival value or perhaps some relevance to mating patterns in rat societies.

With human subjects similar kinds of questions can be asked. Due to the greater difficulties of control at this level, however, different methodologies are required and more modest conclusions usually must be accepted. The basic goals, of course, are still the same.

It would be well to emphasize at this juncture that the area of investigation we are describing is an empirical one that makes no prior commitment as to the relative importance of heredity or environment in the determination of behavioral differences between individuals. In the past, genetics has been prostituted by different political systems in directions both overplaying and underplaying hereditary components in the makeup of man. The proper scientific attitude must be of a more provisional character. Thus a question of the kind—"Is schizophrenia inherited?"—is an empirical one that cannot be settled before all the data are in. It certainly does not reflect any kind of prejudice or bias to ask it in the first place; but it does reveal a prejudice to deny that it is permissable to ask it at all.

The History of Behavior Genetics

With Darwin, biology turned away from the descriptive taxonomy of Linnaeus toward the historical problem of lineage and the transmission of characters through animal generations. Darwin's major interest was initially in the morphological aspects of the species he studied, for example, in the plumage colors of the various groups of finches he observed in the Galapagos. Mendel, likewise, worked out the laws of classical genetics from observations of discrete, all-or-none characters in plants, particulary flower color in garden peas. Gradually there grew up, in the 19th century, an appreciation of the importance of behavioral traits in the study of inheritance. Darwin himself came to this realization, and his work *Expression of the emotions in man and animals* (1872) is devoted precisely to showing the psychological continuities that appear in phylogeny.

It is Darwin's half-cousin, Francis Galton, however, who deserves, perhaps, more than anyone else, to be called the founder of the field of behavior genetics. Taking his cue from Darwin, he set out with vigor and imagination to explore hereditary influences in a variety of human traits—genius and scholarly aptitudes, statesmanship, clerical abilities, athletic skills such as rowing and wrestling, and many others. He concluded from the study of numerous pedigrees that these qualities were strongly dependent on nature rather than on nurture. Galton was quite well aware that families passed on not only genes but also attitudes, motives, and opportunities for special learning, but he did not accord to these very great importance. This work of Galton and Darwin represents the first phase in the history of behavior genetics.

The next phase saw two major advances in methodology. One of these was the derivation by Karl Pearson of a statistical expression for degree of similarity between variables. By means of his product-moment correlation, it became possible to make statements concerning extent of likeness between related individuals, in respect to psychological traits. This set the stage for the development of quantitative genetics in which the notions of correlation, covariation, and regression figure importantly. Later, Ronald Fisher and Sewell Wright were major contributors in this regard.

Coordinately, there arose in England, France, and the United States a strong interest in the problem of measurement and testing. The kinds of psychological tests devised and used by Galton in his studies represented a good beginning. But there was still much to be done, and it was left to such men as Spearman, Binet, Cattell, and Thurstone to develop, in a sophisticated way, notions of reliability, validity, and scaling, as well as the idea of basic factors of intelligence and personality. So armed with new statistical techniques and well-standardized tests, many investigators set out to study the influence of heredity in the determination of likeness within family groups, including especially monozygotic and dizygotic twin pairs.

At this time, work on learning in animals in a laboratory setting was also on the increase, thanks to the initial efforts of such men as Thorndike, Watson, Harvey Carr, and Lashley. Accordingly, an interest arose in applying to this section of the field the principles and methods of genetics. Yerkes, Dawson, Vicari and others studied behavioral differences between strains of mice, and selection experiments were carried out by Tolman and Tryon for maze-ability, by Rundquist for activity-level, and by Hall for emotionality (cf., Fuller and Thompson 1960).

During this period, work both on humans and animals was of a very empirical character and was concerned with the basic problem of simply establishing the extent of hereditary determination of various behavioral characters. By and large, very few attempts were made to go beyond this and inquire into the modes of transmission involved or the nature of the pathways from genes to behavior.

Such questions arose naturally in the third historical phase of behavior genetics. Starting around the late 1930's and 1940's, and continuing into the 1960's, applications of sophisticated variants of classical Mendelian models to behavioral data increased at a steady rate. For example, genetic analyses were made of human intelligence (Burt 1958); of schizophrenia and manic-depression (Kallman 1938, 1954); various forms of mental defects such as phenylketonuria (Jervis 1939); activity-levels in mice (Thompson and Fuller, 1957; McClearn 1961); audiogenic seizures in mice (Fuller, Easler and Smith 1950); and emotionality in the rat (Broadhurst and Jinks 1966). During this period, also, four major texts in the field of behavior genetics appeared: *Behavior genetics* by Fuller and Thompson (1960); *Genetics and the social behavior of the dog* by Scott and Fuller (1965); *Methods and goals in human behavior genetics*, edited by Vandenberg (1965); and *Behavior-genetic analysis*, edited by Hirsch (1967a).

Thus, as of the 1960's, the field had become a well-established part of biological psychology. Today it is represented at numerous important centers in many countries and constitutes a fruitful meeting-ground for psychologists and biologists. Where its future lies is difficult to say, and before we attempt to make guesses it will be appropriate to review some of the basic methods used and some of the empirical conclusions it has so far reached.

Basic Methods

The methods of genetics deal both with all-or-none and with continuous variables. The classical principles of segregation and assortment were, of course, worked out using characters of the first type, but it is generally assumed that the principles involved are applicable to those of the second type which are presumably transmitted by multiple minor genes rather than by a few or even single major genes. Thus syndromes like phenylktonuria or galactosemia are phenotypically dramatic and show relatively simple modes of genetic transmission. Differences between individuals falling within the normal range of intelligence, however, are by comparison far less striking and are probably dependent on systems of polygenes.

Since most behavioral characters are continuous, it is important to indicate how Mendelian principles can be so adapted as to throw light on the genetic mechanisms underlying their expression. We will illustrate these methods first with reference to experimental and then natural populations.

Experimental Populations

The following model illustrates a simple case of quantitative inheritance between two parental types, each homozygous for two different alleles at unlinked autosomal loci. The genes are symbolized by letters. Those represented by capitals are assumed to produce a unit increment in the trait. Those represented by small letters produce no change.

If the action of the genes in this case is assumed to be additive, the parents and their F1 hybrids will yield the scores shown in parentheses:

P1   P2
AABB   ×   aabb
(4)   (0)
        F1
       AaBb
        (2)

A cross between F1 hybrids will produce the combinations shown in Table 11-1.

It will be seen that of the sixteen genotypes resulting from the cross, 1/16 have a score of 4, 1/16 a score of zero, 4/16 a score of 3, 6/16 a score of 2, and 4/16 a score of 1. This will yield for the whole F2 population a mean phenotypic score of 2.

In the foregoing example, the effects of each allele are independent and additive. That is to say, $A = B = 1$ and $AB = 2$; $a = b = 0$, and $ab = 0$. Very often, however, there may occur both allelic and nonallelic interactions, these being called dominance and epistatic effects respectively. With domi-

Table 11-1

Fl Male gamete

		AB	Ab	aB	ab
Fl Female gamete	AB	ABAB (4)	AABb (3)	AaBB (3)	AaBb (2)
	Ab	AABb (3)	AAbb (2)	AaBb (2)	Aabb (1)
	aB	AaBB (3)	AaBb (2)	aaBB (2)	aaBb (1)
	ab	AaBb (2)	Aabb (1)	aaBb (1)	aabb (0)

nance, we may have, in the case of two gene loci, a situation as follows:

$$A = B = 1, a = b = 0$$

But

$$AA = Aa = 2$$
$$BB = Bb = 2$$
$$aa = bb = 0$$

In this case the F1 hybrids will all have a score of 4 and the mean of the F2 will be 3.0—that is, it will be skewed towards the value of the high-scoring parents.

With epistasis, we might have the following:

$$A = 1$$
$$a = b = 0$$
$$AB = 2, aB = 0$$

Here, the B allele has a positive effect only if an A gene is present and not otherwise. In other words, the genotype AaBB will have a value of 3. But the genotype aaBB will have a value of zero. The mean of the F1 population will then turn out to be:

$$AaBb = 2$$

The mean of the F2 works out to be 1.75.

It will be obvious that F1 and F2 variances, as well as means, will differ from parental variances and means, depending on which model is applicable. This means essentially that having estimated these statistical parameters from actual data obtained from parental and hybrid crosses, we can make inferences about the kind of model which best fits these data. The same will hold if we have multiple loci rather than only two as in the cases described above. In fact, procedures are available for estimating the number of allelic pairs underlying continuously distributed characters (Wright 1952). It is only possible, however, with many genes operating, to estimate *average* amount of dominance or epistasis without reference to specific loci. This information can be interesting and useful, particularly in connection with selection programs, since the outcomes in specific cases will be quite different (Fuller and Thompson 1960; Falconer 1960).

Many extensions and refinements of the above methods have been made (cf. Broadhurst and Jinks 1961; Bruell 1962, 1967; McLearn 1967; Roberts 1967). Special mention must be given to one of them—the diallel cross method described and applied to behavior genetic problems by Broadhurst (cf. Broadhurst 1967; Broadhurst and Jinks 1966). This appears to hold special promise, not only on account of its greater economy experimentally, but also on account of the power it has to answer some of the more important and subtle problems in behavior genetics. Basically, it involves an analysis of components of variance and covariance in a matrix made up of all possible F1 crosses between *n* strains. These include those between like parents and also reciprocal hybrid crosses. A simple example is shown in Table 11-2. Provided the data meet certain scaling

Table 11-2. Diagram of a Diallel Table, with an Indication of the Genetic Constitution of the F_1 Offspring of which it is Comprised

			Strain of Father			
		A	B	C	D	E	F
	A	AA	AB	AC	AD	AE	AF
	B	BA	BB	BC	BD	BE	BF
Strain of	C	CA	CB	CC	CD	CE	CF
Mother	D	DA	DB	DC	DD	DE	DF
	E	EA	EB	EC	ED	EE	EF
	F	FA	FB	FC	FD	FE	FF

criteria, they may be statistically analyzed to yield a great deal of useful genetic information. One such piece of information (in common with other methods) is an estimate of heritability of the trait being studied. This latter concept is defined broadly as the proportion of trait variance in a specified population which is determined by *additive* genetic causes. It is written as follows:

$$h^2 = \frac{V_A}{(V_A + V_{NA} + V_E)} \qquad [1]$$

Where h^2 = heritability estimate

$(V_A + V_{NA} + V_E)$ = total phenotypic variance (V_P)

V_A = trait variance due to additive genetic effects

V_{NA} = variance due to nonadditive (e.g., dominance or epistatic interaction) causes

V_E = variance due to environmental causes

A rather similar but looser estimate of relative genetic influences is given by *the degree of genetic determination* (Roberts 1967). This is written simply as V_G/V_P, where the terms have the same meaning as above.

In addition to furnishing an estimate of heritability, the diallel cross method allows a separation to be made between variation due to genes and that due to prenatal maternal effects.

This is provided by a comparison between reciprocally crossed animals having the same genetic make-up. Sex linkage can also be assessed in this comparison. Thirdly, an estimate of average dominance or lack of it in all strains taken together can be made and also the proportion of dominant to recessive genes in each of the parental strains. This is exceedingly important information and has implications for the theory of the evolution of behavior (Broadhurst and Jinks 1966). Later on we will discuss an example of one of the applications that has been made of it.

Genetic methods of the kind just summarized are applicable only in cases where we have good experimental control over the genotypes of the subjects. With strains of animals which are inbred (e.g., mice) and therefore relatively homozygous, this is entirely feasible. But with natural free-breeding populations (such as humans) it is usually quite impracticable. Consequently, the methods we must use are different and the questions they allow us to ask are more limited in scope. We will now briefly summarize some of these methods.

NATURAL POPULATIONS

In research on behavior genetics using natural populations, we generally have these kinds of goals: (a) determination of the mode of genetic transmission of unitary all-or-none traits; (b) determination of the heritability of quantitative traits, for example, intelligence; (c) assessment of the manner in which genotype and environmental influences interact to produce a certain phenotype.

With *common* traits of qualitative sort the usual methodology involves simply counting frequency of occurrence of the trait within families and comparing this with its frequency as predicted by a particular genetic hypothesis. Such a comparison is usually made by reference to the so-called Hardy-Weinberg law. This states the relative frequency of certain gene combinations in a randomly breeding population, given the frequency of occurrence of a gene and its allele. Thus if we have a gene A with a frequency p, its allele, A′, must have a frequency of $1 - p$, or q. If A and A′ combine at random, then the proportions of each genotype at equilibrium will be:

$$p^2AA + 2pqAA' + q^2A'A'$$

In a cross between two pure breeding lines—for example, plants with white and plants with red flowers—p and q will be equal; that is $p = q = 0.50$. In such a case, the proportions of genotypes in the F2 will fit the familiar Mendelian ratios: 0.25AA, 0.50AA′ and 0.25A′A′. However, in a population that is relatively isolated reproductively, a particular allele may have a very high or very low frequency. Accordingly, the proportions at equilibrium will be different.

Now of course, in human populations, we cannot directly estimate gene frequencies. All we can do is to identify, with greater or less accuracy, persons who have the trait and persons who do not. The latter may also carry a gene for the trait if the condition is dependent on recessive genes. For different genetic hypotheses, we can then set up predictions concerning the theoretical incidence of the trait in offspring resulting from marriages of all possible types, i.e., trait-bearers × trait-bearers, two non-trait-bearers, and trait-bearers × non-trait-bearers. Approximation of observations to estimates will, or course, give support to a particular model.

A good example is the genetics of taste-blindness—that is, the inability to taste phenylthiocarbamide (PTC)—as reported by Snyder (1932). Marriages of two tasters were found to yield 87.7% taster and 12.3% nontaster offspring; between tasters and nontasters, 63.4% taster and 36.6% nontasters; and between two nontasters, 2.1% taster and 97.9% nontaster offspring. These figures very closely approximate estimates based on the hypothesis that PTC blindness is carried by a single auto-somal recessive gene. Deviations from the expected proportions can be explained by such factors as incorrect diagnoses, illegitimacy of offspring, or incomplete penetrance of the gene in some cases.

The above methods have been applied to the study of many other traits, notably Huntington's chorea, epilepsy, and handedness (Fuller and Thompson 1960).

When a qualitative trait is rare, there are obvious difficulties in finding enough instances of mating types to allow an analysis of the kind described above. In such cases, it is necessary to work from known *index cases* (also called *propositi* or *probands*) and study both the lineal and collateral relatives of these. By the very fact of their rarity, the genes underlying the trait are usually recessive. Consequently, trait-bearers will usually come from phenotypically normal parents both of whom are heterozygous for the gene. Many such parents will not, of course, produce any double recessive offspring and are therefore not readily distinguishable from normal parents—that is, those homozygous for the normal allele. Another problem lies in the fact that for certain conditions (e.g., schizophrenia) morbidity rate varies with age. To cope with these and other technical problems, various statistical methods have been devised by a number of investigators (Fuller and Thompson 1960). Some of these have applied to the genetic analysis of such traits as schizophrenia, enuresis, and dyslexia.

The above methods cannot readily be applied in the case of continuous traits in natural populations. Attempts have been made by such workers as Burt (1958) and Burt and Howard (1956) to draw inferences about the genetics of such traits as human intelligence; but in most studies the major goal has been the more modest one of establishing estimates of heritability. Methods used are variations of those described already in the case of experimental populations. Perhaps the most common is one based on a comparison between monozygotic, or one-egg, twins and dizygotic, or two-egg, twins. The main advantage of using twins is that it can more safely be assumed that environmental effects on trait variance for monozygote pairs are approximately equal to those on trait variance for dizygotic pairs. The phrase "*more safely*," it should be pointed out, is used advisedly. This is an assumption which, though reasonable, need not always hold true and is not readily verifiable.

If the variance within MZ pairs (σ_{WMZ}) arises from environmental sources only, while the variance within DZ pairs (σ^2_{WDZ}) reflects both environmental and genetic influences, then the difference between these variances must indicate the amount of genetic contribution, thus:

$$V_G = \sigma^2_{WDZ} - \sigma^2_{WMZ} \qquad [2]$$

The contribution of the genetic variance is, however, usually

expressed as a coefficient H' (Newman, Freeman, and Holzinger 1937), which reads:

$$H' = \frac{\sigma^2_{WDZ} - \sigma^2_{WMZ}}{\sigma^2_{WDZ}} \qquad [3]$$

This formula gives an estimate of the genetic contribution to phenotypic variance *within families* and H', therefore, underestimates the genetic contribution in the population h^2 as in equation (1). This is due to the fact that DZ twins on the average share 50% of their genes and have therefore more genetic communality than unrelated persons. It should also be noted that the use of equation (3) is justified only if the between-pair variances for MZ and DZ twins are equal ($\sigma^2_{bDZ} = \sigma^2_{bMZ}$). The concordance rates in twins are often expressed in intra-class correlation coefficients r_{MZ} and r_{DZ}. As $r_{DZ} = 1 - \sigma^2_{WDZ}/\sigma^2_{bDZ}$, $r_{MZ} = 1 - \sigma^2_{WMZ}/\sigma^2_{bDZ}$ and assuming that $\sigma^2_{bMZ} = \sigma^2_{bDZ}$, equation (3) can be written as

$$h^2 = \frac{r_{MZ} - r_{DZ}}{1 - r_{DZ}} \qquad [4]^1$$

Slightly different formulas have been suggested by Nichols (1966) and Jensen (1967); the former includes an automatic correction for attenuation due to unreliability in the variables measured. Some disadvantages associated with the use of h^2 have been pointed out by Vandenberg (1966). Following Clark (1956), Vandenberg advocates the use of the familiar F ratio to assess the significance of the difference between concordance rates:

$$F = \frac{\sigma^2_{WDZ}}{\sigma^2_{WMZ}} \qquad [5]$$

Vandenberg also shows the straightforward relationship between F and H' according to equation (3):

$$H' = 1 - \frac{1}{F}, \qquad \text{and} \qquad [6]$$

$$F = \frac{1}{1 - H'} \qquad [7]$$

An important advantage of the analysis of variance approach is that it yields confidence limits for H' (Partanen, Bruun, and Morkkonen 1966). These are given as:

$$1 - \frac{1 - H'}{F_{05}} \text{ and } 1 - \frac{1 - H'}{F_{95}} \qquad [8]$$

In view of the assumption made that $\sigma b^2_{MZ} = \sigma b^2_{DZ}'$ the sensitivity of variance estimates to non-normality of distributions, and the observation of skewed distribution of within-pair differences, some others, however, have argued that non-parametric evaluation of concordance differences may be preferable (Stafford 1965a; Wilde 1964). When discrete traits are investigated a heritability estimate H*, derived from the concordance percentages (C) in MZ and DZ twins is sometimes used:

[1]In twin research the symbol h^2 is frequently used interchangeably with H', but it should be understood that this h^2 regards within family heritability only and does not equal h^2 according to equation (1).

$$H^* = \frac{C_{MZ} - C_{DZ}}{100 - C_{DZ}} \qquad [9]$$

In an ingenious attempt to obtain heritability estimates for psychological trait variation in the population rather than within families, Cattell (1960) developed his *multiple abstract variance analysis* (MAVA). Another important feature of this method is that the covariance between heredity and environment does not have to be assumed to be zero. On the contrary, this term, an example of which would be a positive correlation between heredity for schizophrenia and being brought up in a schizophrenogenic environment, can be estimated both within and between families. The values of the abstract variances can be derived from the observed variances, according to a number of postulated equations. As there are more unknowns in these equations than can be solved, certain assumptions must be made to arrive at "nature-nurture" ratios. Unfortunately, the practicality of the MAVA method is limited by the fact that many different groups of subjects are needed, such as MZ and DZ twins reared together, MZ twins reared apart, siblings reared together and apart, unrelated children reared together and apart, half-siblings reared together and apart, etc.

Other recent developments in twin research designs include the multivariate analysis procedure as presented by Vandenberg (1965) and Loehlin and Vandenberg (1966). When some phenotypic variables have been found to show considerable genetic contributions, the question arises whether these variables can be grouped into a smaller number of genetic pathways. If differences between MZ twins are due to environmental variations only, then the intercorrelations of these differences can be investigated factor-analytically to assess the number of environmental factors responsible for these differences. In a similar manner the number and nature of factors in partly genetically determined variables can be ascertained by subtracting the matrix intercorrelations of trait difference in MZ twins from the corresponding matrix obtained from DZ twin differences. The actual analysis is carried out on covariance matrices, as correlation matrices do not take the generally larger variances in DZ twin differences into account. If K_{MZ} is the covariance matrix of differences in MZ twins, and K_{DZ} the corresponding matrix for DZ twins, then

$$|K_{DZ} - \lambda K_{MZ}| = 0 \qquad [10]$$

Solving for λ yields the number and lengths of the latent roots, that is the number of independent components and the amount of variance explained by each. According to Vandenberg, this may reveal the number of genes of groups of linked genes responsible for the heritable variance of the traits in question. But, as has been pointed out by Thompson (1966), there are other possible explanations for such trait intercorrelations than in terms of genetic communality, namely environmental communality, gametic communality, and chromosomal communality.

The discussion above should be sufficient to acquaint the reader with the basic rationale behind some of the methods most commonly used in the field of behavior genetics. Let us now look at examples of some of the substantive conclusions that have been reached by workers in the area, as well as some of the difficulties commonly encountered.

Results from Animal Studies

SIMPLE RESPONSE PATTERNS

In lower animals especially, we find a great variety of relatively simple patterns of response. These include fixed action patterns (FAP's), instinctive behaviors, taxes, and kineses. Each of these terms has a slightly different connotation, but for our purposes here we may lump them under one broad category. Some of them may be studied as unitary traits, being either present or absent; others may be studied as continuous variables showing, in a population, a distribution of values.

An interesting example of the first case is afforded by the work or Rothenbuhler (1958, 1964a, 1964b, 1967) on "hygienic behavior" in bees.

A common disease among bee colonies is known as American foulbrood. The agent is a bacillus which attacks and kills the larvae in their cells. Colonies differ widely in their response to foulbrood, some being highly susceptible to it, others being resistant. What occurs in any particular case appears to depend on the behavior of the adults in respect to the dead larvae. Resistant bees uncap the cells containing the dead larvae and then eject them from the hive. This has been called *hygienic behavior*. Susceptible bees show this only to a minimal degree. Rothenbuhler selected two lines for this nest-cleaning activity— a Brown hygienic line and a Van Scoy non-hygienic line. An F1 cross between the two lines yielded all non-hygienic bees. This suggested that the trait (hygienic) was a recessive. A test back-cross between F1's and the recessive parental line (F1 drone × hygienic Queen) yielded twenty-nine new colonies. Of these, six displayed typical hygienic behavior; nine would uncap the cells but did not remove the larvae, and fourteen were non-hygienic. This suggested the operation of two genes, one concerned with uncapping (*u*), the other with removal (*r*). The genetic hypothesis is as shown in Figure 11-1. Evidently one of these lines $u/+$, r/r would be expected to remove the larvae if the uncapping was done for them. An appropriate experiment gave fairly strong support to this notion.

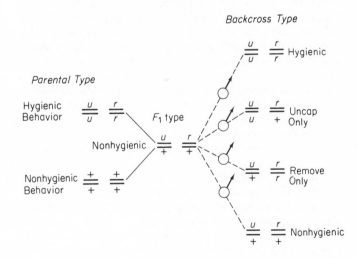

Fig. 11-1. *Genetic hypothesis offered in explanation of different responses to American-foulbrood-killed brood observed in 63 colonies of bees.* [Rothenbuhler 1964b].

The work of Hirsch and his colleagues on *Drosophila* (Hirsch 1967*a*) illustrates the genetic study of simple traits as continuous variables. Phototactic and geotactic preferences were measured by means of multiple unit mazes in which animals were allowed a series of free choices between higher or lower values of the trait in question. The method is very similar to that of Brown and Hall (1936) for measuring phototaxic in drosophila and that used by Herter (1936) for measuring choice of thermotactic optima in mice. In all cases, there is a free selection on the part of the subjects of the value of the trait (temperature, gravity, light intensity) which it reliably prefers. Hirsch used a number of "tester" stocks in which the presence of particular chromosomes could be identified by marker genes. He attempted to relate these chromosomes to distribution and level of phototactic and geotactic performance by comparing animals from unselected, selected, and various hybrid stocks. Results indicated a strong relationship between behavior and presence or absence of particular chromosomes or combinations of chromosomes.

Although the picture is not as clear as it might be, there seems little question that, particularly in the case of traits which are polygenic, the use of chromosomes rather than individual genes as units of analysis may be profitable. There are a great many genes in a genonome but relatively few chromosomes. The informational content of the latter may turn out to be quite adequate to the problem of explaining much of the variation in behavior. This is certainly true in the case of some of the grosser abnormalities in human beings. A good example is Down's syndrome (Mongolism) which is dependent on trisomy—that is, the presence of an extra chromosome due to non-disjunction during gametogenesis (Jacobs et al. 1959). It is possible that, for many normal traits, chromosomal architecture might be equally critical.

A third class of relatively simple behavior which has been studied fairly intensively by behavior geneticists has been sexual behavior in insects, particularly in *Drosophila* and in two types of the Hymenoptera—that wasp, *Habobracon*, and the honey-bee, *apis mellifera*. Although there seem to be no instances in *Drosophila* (unlike *Apis*) in which particular genes are directly responsible for some qualitative form of behavior, single mutants, whose effect is most obviously morphological, can influence behavior quantitatively. One example, is the *yellow* gene. Bastock (1956) has divided the courtship behaviour of *drosophila Melanogaster* into four basic patterns. These are:

1. *Orientation*, in which the male approaches close to female;
2. *Vibration*, in which the male rapidly vibrates the wing proximal to the female;
3. *Licking*, involving licking of female's genitalia;
4. *Attempted copulation*, or mounting behavior.

The presence of the yellow gene does not alter the sequence of occurrence of these components, but it does reduce the intensity of the third and fourth. The total effect is that the male's courtship is considerably less "stimulating."

Manning (1963) has further shown that mating speed is highly responsive to selection. After seven generations, his slow mating line took thirty minutes or more to mate, whereas the fast maters took as little as three minutes. The difference was most pronounced in males. Interestingly enough, slow maters

were intensely active in all but sexual responses. Just the opposite held true for members of the fast mating line.

These studies, together with other work on sexual behavior in insects and its evolutionary significance, have been summarized by Fuller and Thompson (1960), and by Manning (1967). Analogous work with mammals has been undertaken by a number of investigators, including especially McGill (1962) and Young and Grunt (1951). At this phylogenetic level, of course, the behavior involved is usually not as fixed and stereotyped as it is in many of the insect forms.

Examples of other simple types of response patterns that have been studied include: dancing behavior, flight activity, nectar and pollen collection, brood rearing and defensive behavior in bees, courtships patterns in fish, silk-spining in meal-worms, and geotaxis in young rats (Fuller and Thompson 1960; Hirsch 1967*a*).

COMPLEX BEHAVIOUR

Learning and Intelligence. At least three major studies have shown that it is possible to select for maze-brightness and maze-dullness in rats. Tryon (1942), following up a preliminary experiment by Tolman (1924), and using an automated multiple-unit T maze, selected animals over a long period of time. By the eighth generation there was virtually no overlap between the brights and dulls. There is no doubt that the trait being selected was complex rather than unitary. Tryon himself (1940) was aware of this and educed data to show that ten components of maze-ability were operating. Wherry (1941), using a somewhat different mode of analysis, suggested three major factors whose relative contribution to maze performance varied with degree of training. These he identified as "forward-going," "food-pointing," and "goal-gradient." Searle (1949) similarly showed that Tryon's brights and dulls differed not only on maze-ability but on a great many other measures as well, including other maze-tests. Consequently, selection must have been operating on many traits whose particular combinations in the brights and dulls yielded good and poor scores respectively on the original criterion test.

Since Tryon, two other workers have successfully selected for maze-learning ability. Heron (1935, 1941) obtained, over 16 generations, a 20% reduction of error in the bright line and almost a 100% increase of errors in the dull line. However, fluctuations of mean scores for the generations in between were considerable. These may have been due to changing environmental conditions. Thompson (1954) reported a rapid response to selection for "brightness" and "dullness" on the Hebb-Williams maze test of intelligence. By generation six there was virtually no overlap between the two lines. Data are shown in Figure 11-2.

Two studies with negative results have also been reported by Rhine and McDougall (1933) and by Kuppusawny (1947). In both of these studies, learning ability was measured by means of performance in a water-maze—a fact which may or may not have significance.

Besides the method selection, many investigators have examined differences between groups of animals known to be genetically different in the first place—for example, breeds or strains. Bagg (1916, 1920) and Vicari (1929) demonstrated rather

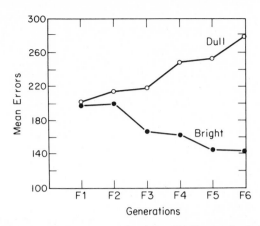

Fig. 11-2. *Mean error scores of 'bright' and 'dull' rats selectively bred on the Hebb-Williams maze over six filial generations.* [Fuller & Thompson 1960] Reprinted by permission of John Wiley & Sons, Inc.

Table 11-3. A Comparison of Hereditary and Environmental Effects on the Intelligence of Rats (Thompson 1954)

	Error Score on Hebb-Williams Maze
Hereditary dull	279.5
Environmental restriction	238.2*
Hereditary bright	142.8
Environmental free	137.3*

*Scores based on data of Forgays and Forgays (25) and Hymovitch (50).

complex differences between various mouse strains on several measures. A good deal later, Royce and Covington (1960) and Collins (1964) reported significant strain effects from performance on an avoidance learning task. An extensive replication was carried out by Schlesinger and Wimer (1967) using a rather superior testing apparatus. They found differences between seven inbred mouse strains on both acquisition rate and extinction. Four F1 hybrid groups were superior in performance to the average of the parental strains. This result was considered by the investigators to be a heterotic effect (heterosis = hybrid vigor).

Dog breeds have also been studied extensively. Most of this work has been done by Scott, Fuller, and their colleagues at the Jackson Laboratory, Bar Harbor, Maine (see Scott and Fuller 1965). These workers have concentrated mostly on five breeds—shetland sheep dogs, wire-haired fox terriers, basenjis, beagles, and cocker spaniels. These were compared on a large battery of tests including seventeen which aimed at measuring intellectual performance. Marked differences were found between the breeds, but these varied a good deal with the test used. Beagles and wire-haired fox terriers were superior on most tests of discrimination, for example. But cockers were the best on a test of spatial orientation. In the end, one must concede that it is quite meaningless to attempt a ranking of breeds on some hypothetical unitary trait of intelligence. Each breed has been selected for a particular configuration of abilities that is maximally adaptive in certain situations. It is pointless to call one configuration "better" than another.

Two final points may be made. The first concerns the stability of inherited intelligence. While there is no question that this trait, as reflected in many measures, depends on genetic factors, it is equally true that environment is very important. In fact, "dull" or "bright" phenotypes as extreme as those resulting from selection can be produced quite as readily by differential rearing conditions. This point is illustrated in the data presented in Table 11-3. Rats from a random population reared in enriched conditions are as bright as those selected for brightness. Those reared in restriction, on the other hand, are as dull as those selectively bred for dullness. It is also true that a rich environment can greatly improve maze-performance in genetically "dull" animals and, conversely, a restricted rearing

condition can lower performance in genetically "bright" rats (Cooper and Zubek 1958).

The second point concerns the mechanisms involved in the genetic transmission of intelligence. Very little work has been done on this problem. It is certainly likely that a polygenic system is involved and that inheritance is intermediate. But we can say little beyond this. The one study by Tryon (1940) in which crosses were made between bright and dull rats yielded an F1 population with a variance as large as that of the F2. This made further analysis impossible. Whether this effect (sometimes labelled the "Tryon effect") is a genuine one, perhaps due to behavioral heterosis, or a spurious one, due to lack of homozygosity of the parental populations, is not entirely clear. More work is needed on this important problem.

Emotionality, Temperament, and Social Behavior. Several workers have successfully selected low and high emotional strains of rats. The first of these, Calvin Hall (1938, 1951) used defecation and urination in an open field as the criterion measures. Selection was rapid for the low-emotional strain (maximal in G1) but more gradual in the high-emotional line. Broadhurst (1960, 1967) has obtained similar results also using defecation as an index of "reactivity" and "non-reactivity" (Maudsley strains).

Summary of his results is shown in Figure 11-3.

Finally, Bignami (1965) and Bignami and Bovet (1965) selected two lines (Roman strains) on the basis of speed of acquisition and retention of a conditioned avoidance response

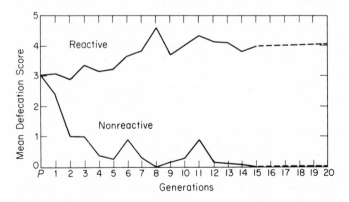

Fig. 11-3. *Progress of selection for high and low emotional defecation in the rat—the Maudsley Emotionally Reactive and Nonreactive Strains. The ordinate shows the mean number of fecal boluses deposited per trial in the open field and the abscissa the successive generations. After S_{15} selection was suspended for five generations (dashed line). Measurement resumed at S_{20} shows little evidence of reversion to the foundation population score.* [Broadhurst 1966].

(CAR). Broadhurst (1966) has shown that the traits involved in each study are independent genetically, in that although the Maudsley strains also differ on a CAR measure, the Roman strains do not differ in respect to open-field defecation. Thus phenotypic correlations computed between different measures of emotionality are likely to vary considerably between strains and also to vary in respect to the extent to which they are dependent on genetic or environmental causes.

Numerous instances of differences between strains and breeds have been reported (Broadhurst 1960; Fuller and Thompson 1960; McClearn 1965; DeFries 1967). Mouse and rat strains, dog breeds, and a variety of other species have been used as subjects in studies of temperament. The following traits represent a partial list of those for which heritable variation has been found: activity level and exploratory behavior, urination and defecation in an open field, eating behavior, hoarding, wildness and aggressive behavior, dominance and territoriality, approach-avoidance behavior, responsiveness to stimuli, responsiveness to handling, running speed, wariness, and escape-avoidance conditioning.

Thus one can hardly avoid the conclusion that emotionality —however it may be assessed—is strongly dependent on genetic factors.

Little is known about the modes of genetic transmission of emotionality. Several studies have attempted analyses of it, using various measures (Broadhurst and Jinks 1961, 1963). These have demonstrated a moderate degree of heritability and shown the operation of multiple genes often with strong dominance components (Fuller and Thompson 1960). However, they cannot be regarded as having yielded very conclusive or even very fruitful information. Two most important problems still remain. The first of these concerns the relationships between the different measures that are commonly used to test the domain; the second, the stability of these measures over time. Both must be examined and answered in reference to genetic and environmental sources of variation. Obviously, these two questions can be asked of other behavioral domains as well, for example, intelligence and abnormal behavior. However, we raise them here because the work relevant to them has, in fact, involved the domain of emotionality.

The first we have already touched on above. It seems clear that the many measures that have been developed to assess emotionality may correlate or not depending on the genotypes of the subjects being tested and the environmental circumstances in which they have developed. Any phenotypic correlation can be partitioned into genetic (r_g) and environmental (r_e) components and the relative size of these will depend ultimately on the heritability of the traits involved. As we have already indicated, this value will be particular to the population in which it is assessed. Consequently, the kinds of data reported by Broadhurst (1966) on the Maudsley and Roman strains are entirely reasonable.

The second point, concerning the stability of measures of emotionality, has been examined in a most original manner by Broadhurst and Jinks (1966). By applying diallel analysis to measures repeated over trials, they were able to show that heritability values changed with each trial, and that the relative contribution to phenotypic variance of environmental, additive, and dominance components also altered. In the case of elimination scores, there occurred over several days of testing a proportional increase in dominance variation which, in turn, mainly

underlies low scoring on this test. On the other hand, ambulation tested over days showed a drift to intermediate values, this level also being mainly controlled by dominant genes. Broadhurst and Jinks suggest that this phenotypic plasticity is highly adaptive in that it allows, with repeated exposure to a situation, the expression of genetically based responses having maximal survival value. Their argument is a subtle one and too complex to discuss in full in this chapter. But whatever its validity, its focus on the problem of trait "stability" (Thompson 1966, has used the term "fluidity") represents a major forward step in the field of behavior genetics.

Miscellaneous Traits. A great many different forms of behaviour are not readily classifiable under the two categories so far discussed. We will present a few examples of these. Rundquist (1933) selected two lines of rats for high and low scores in activity wheels. There was a faster and greater selection response for inactivity than for activity particularly among male animals. Brody (1942) later made two series of crosses (F21 and F22) between the lines in an effort to identify the genetic mechanisms involved. She claimed that the evidence suggested the operation of a single locus, with one allele being dominant for low activity in males and the allele for high activity being dominant in females. As Fuller and Thompson have pointed out, however, (1960, pp. 264–65), the data do not by any means unambiguously support this hypothesis. Rescaling of the data she used might well have produced different results. If her two series and male and female groups are all pooled together, the mean values of parents and hybrids fall into a clear linear order (P1, BX1, F1 and F2, BX2, P2) that suggests the operation of polygenes. Transformation of scores in order to correct for correlation between means and variances might well have improved the approximation to a polygenic model. Broadhurst and Jinks (1963) reanalyzed Brody's data (without rescaling) using the methods of Mather. They estimated that a minimum of 1.95 interacting factors were operating and that these also interacted with the environment.

A second behavioral character of considerable importance is susceptibility to sound-produced convulsions. This has been intensively investigated by behavior geneticists. In rats, seizure-proneness appears to be carried by polygenes (Fuller and Thompson, 1960). In mice, however, there has been some debate as to its mode of transmission. Witt and Hall (1949) crossed two strains—susceptible (DBA's) and non-susceptible (C57BL's). Seizure incidence in F1, F2, and three back-crosses approximated percentages expected on the basis of a single Mendelian dominant determining susceptibility. However, there were some crosses in which the fit—if the one locus model is really applicable—should have been perfect and not merely approximate. On account of this ambiguity, Fuller, Easler, and Smith (1950) repeated the study and found an even less satisfactory fit. They therefore proposed that convulsing was a threshold character controlled by a polygenic system. Their model is shown in Figure 11-4. What it implies is that by manipulating test conditions or the physiological state of the animal, seizure-risk in parents and hybrid groups will shift markedly and may yield observed values that will mimic the operation of a single factor. The hypothetical case shown in the second graph involves values that might suggest a single dominant. The cogency of the threshold model is indicated, first, by the fact that seizure susceptibility in mice

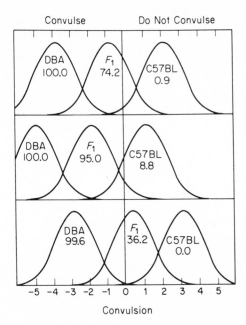

Fig. 11-4. *Changes in convulsive risk on first trial (figures under curves) associated with conditions shifting physiological susceptibility by one standard deviation. The abscissa is a scale of physiological susceptibility. Each genotype is assumed to vary normally about some point on this scale. The convulsive risk is dependent upon the proportion of the curve to the left of an arbitrary threshold.* [Fuller & Thompson 1960]. Reprinted by permission of John Wiley & Sons, Inc.

is readily alterable by various procedures, for example, by prestimulation; and, secondly, by the fact that successive back-crossing of susceptible F1's into the nonsusceptible parent stock yields a gradual reduction in number of reactors. Under a single factor dominance model, however, this should not be possible; rather the proportion of reactors should remain constant at 50%.

If a polygenic system is involved, at least two relevant loci have been tentatively identified. Ginsburg and Miller (1963) have shown that one of them, *A*, is associated with hippocampal adenosine triphosphatase; the other, *B*, regulated response to glutamic acid—a compound that can markedly affect susceptibility to seizures. Both of these genes in combination control seizure incidence in a manner that depends on total genetic background. Thus the final relation between behavioral phenotype and genes is a highly complex one mediated via a number of biochemical pathways (Ginsburg 1967).

Another behavioral character on which a good deal of work has been done is the disposition to consume alcohol. Williams, Berry, and Beerstecher (1949, 1950) originally proposed that alcoholism is due to a gene-controlled defect in production of enzymes relevant to metabolism of certain essential nutritive substances, with an ensuing compensatory intake of alcohol. He reported (Williams, Petton, and Rogers 1955), in a test of this hypothesis, that rats put on a vitamin-deficient diet did drink more alcohol solution than controls. Others have argued, however, that drinking alcohol is a response only to a caloric deficiency and that the consumption of alcohol corrects this deficiency (Richter 1941).

There is little question but that, in mice and rats at least, the propensity to consume alcohol is under genetic control. Mardones, Segovia, and Hederra (1953) were successful in selecting

strains of rats showing differential voluntary consumption rates. Likewise, there is known to be a marked variation in alcohol preference between different inbred mouse strains. For example, the C57BL strain shows a high preference, C3H an intermediate to low, and BALB's, DBA's and A strains a low preference. The mode of inheritance is still not fully known. However, there is some indication of polygenic inheritance (McClearn and Rodgers 1961; Fuller 1964). Bruell (1967), in discussing these data, has put forward the view that the intermediacy of preference in F1 hybrids is due to balanced dominance rather than to additive effects. He has further suggested that such a genetic situation is likely to accrue in the case of a trait that has not been exposed to selection.

The biochemical pathway by which gene effects are mediated appear to relate to liver alcohol dehydrogenase (ADH) activity (Rodgers et al. 1963). Thus ADH activity is found to be higher in C57BL mice than in DBA animals. Forced consumption produces increments in ADH activity in both strains about equally, however (McClearn et al. 1964). These results show generally that animals which can metabolize alcohol most easily also have the highest preference for it.

The precise conditions which may bring out an "addiction" are still unknown. Exposures to alcohol during the gestation period or early in life do not appear to be important. Nor does exposure during the "high acceptance" period that seems to occur in some strains (BALB's) during maturation have any lasting consequences (Kakihana and McClearn 1963). However, Rodgers (1967) has reported that with high-preference mice (C57BL) continued exposure to alcohol over a fairly long period of time does lead to a condition at least resembling alcoholism in human beings; that is a high level of voluntary intake with attendant nutritional defects, liver cirrhosis, and symptoms of behavioral discoordination. Work in this important area promises to yield large "pay-offs" in the not too distant future.

Besides activity-level, seizure susceptibility, and alcohol preference, many other traits have been studied by genetic methods. Since we cannot discuss them in this chapter the reader is referred to general reviews by other authors (Fuller and Thompson 1960; McClearn 1963; 1965; Krushinski 1962; Hirsch 1967*a*).

Results from Genetic Studies of Human Behaviour

We will now turn to the question of genetic aspects of human personality differences. To make the transition from animal to human studies is quite a formidable task; and perhaps even more so in the domain of personality than in, for instance, the areas of conditioning and perception. This is partly due to the generally lesser degree of control of both environmental and genetic variables in the investigations of humans. But in addition, more essential questions concern the generalizability of animal research results to human behavior. First, is a trait such as maze-brightness the same or similar to what is called intelligence in humans? Can emotionality, as measured by increased mobility, frequent defecation, and micturition in rats or mice, be equated with emotionality, anxiety-proneness, or neuroticism, in the human situation? Secondly, besides questions of comparable *content*, there are *structural* differences between the notion of personality in humans and the individual differences measured in animals. By means of the general psychological premise B = f (O, S) (behavior is a function of the organism and the situation), the characteristic nature of personality can readily be specified. First of all, we are interested in differences in behavior caused by organismic, and not by situational variations. Of the many variations between organisms we are more interested in relatively permanent ones, rather than in transient psychological states such as pain, hunger, or anxiety. Some of these more permanent variations relate to specific psychological objects as is the case with attitudes and interests; others determine behavior differences only in specific situations, as in the case with roles. The notion of personality, however, postulates generality across psychological objects and trans-situational consistency, and has therefore a much wider scope than the study of individual differences on specific variables in animals or humans for that matter. Personality differences are reflected in *groups* of variables showing functional unity as substantiated by high intercorrelations for instance. These personality differences, frequently called dimensions or traits, however, may be assessed by means of single measurement variables if these have good validity for the common variance to the group of variables concerned (Wilde 1969a).

Table 11-4 gives an example of a personality dimension, Introversion-Extraversion, and the variables in which it is

Table 11-4. Showing the Great Heterogeneity of Variables (Morphological, Cognitive, Motor, Social, Learning, Perceptual, Physiological, etc.) that Reflect the Personality Dimension Introversion-Extraversion

	Introversion	*Extraversion*
Neurotic syndrome	Dysthymia	Hysteria: Psychopathy
Body build	Leptomorph	Eurymorph
Intellectual function	Low IQ/Vocabulary ratio	High IQ/Vocabulary ratio
Perceptual rigidity	High	Low
Persistence	High	Low
Speed	Low	High
Speed/Accuracy ratio	Low	High
Level of aspiration	High	Low
Intra-personal variability	Low	High
Sense of humour	Cognitive	Orectic
Sociability	Low	High
Repression	Weak	Strong
Social attitudes	Tender-minded	Tough-minded
Rorschach test	M% High	D High
T.A.T.	Low productivity	High productivity
Conditioning	Quick	Slow
Reminiscence	Low	High
Figural after-effects	Small	Large
Stress reactions	Overactive	Inert
Sedation threshold	High	Low
Perceptual constancy	Low	High

After Eysenck (1960)

reflected. Inspection of this table shows such a striking heterogeneity of variables that have extraversion as a common factor, that one wonders whether such a multifaceted trait can be learned in all its aspects. Although not impossible, it would necessitate quite a theoretical effort to try to fit all aspects into a single environmental agent. It might be more appropriate to hypothesize the action of a number of environmental factors that happen to be correlated. An alternative way, however, to explain the origin of such personality traits is to look for a possible biological basis. This seems particularly plausible as there are several innate conditions that encompass a considerable variety of characteristics. Down's syndrome (mongoloid idiocy),

for instance, is based upon a chromosomal aberration involving the presence of three instead of the normal two of the No. 21 chromosome, the extra chromosome being responsible for such diverse characteristics as stunted growth, small round neck, upward-slanted eyes set wide apart, short squat nose, deep tongue tissue, protruding underlip, broad stubby hands, short little finger, under-developed genitals, and considerable mental deficiency.

BEHAVIOR ANOMALIES ASSOCIATED WITH CHROMOSOMAL ABERRATIONS

Recently, especially due to the technical improvements in microscopy (Tjio and Levan 1956), *chromosomal studies* have contributed greatly to the understanding of genetic mechanisms in discorders involving behavior pathology. *Down's syndrome* is a case of autosomal trisomy (Lejeune, Turpin, and Gautier 1959; Jacobs et al. 1959). It is due to non-disjunction before polarization of the chromosome pair No. 21 (the number indicating the rank order in size) during meiosis (reduction division) when the female gamete (ovum) is formed. The effects on intelligence have been described by Gottesman (1962). The chances of birth of affected children increases distinctly with advancing age of the mother, from a frequency of less than 1 : 1500 among mothers under age 30 to 1 : 60 among mothers aged 45 and over. There is no such relation to the father's age (Redding and Hirschhorn 1968). In some cases, called *mosaicism*, trisomy is found in one-half of the body cells, the other half counting 45 chromosomes (monosomy). Sometimes trisomic, monosomic, and normal cells are found to be distributed 1 : 1 : 2 in an individual's body cells. This condition is found to be associated with severe or mild mental retardation (Polani 1962). Another chromosomal aberration involving chromosome No. 5, has been observed. The syndrome has been called "cri du chat" because the infant's crying reminds one of a cat's cry and is due to a partial deletion of chromosome No. 5. Another group of chromosomal aberrations involves autosomal translocations, due to junction of chromosomal material of nonhomologous chromosomes (chromosomes belonging to different pairs) resulting in two abnormal chromosomes. Autosomal aberrations are frequently lethal and are often found in stillbirths (Sergovich 1967). Trisomy as well as polysomy of sex chromosomes also have major implications for behavior pathology. Male individuals characterized by two or more female chromosomes—*Klinefelter's syndrome*—tend to be below average in intelligence. According to Forsmann and Hambert (1967) there is a definite statistical connection between *antisocial behavior* and extra female or male chromosomes in males and too many or too few female chromosomes in females. They attribute the behavioral consequences of the abnormal numbers of sex chromosomes to cerebral abnormality of the type known as minimum brain damage leading to restlessness, lack of concentration, and aggressiveness, all impairing favorable adjustment. Various authors have suspected an increased incidence of chromosomal deviation in schizophrenia. Small positive trends have been observed by Raphael and Shaw (1963) but others (Böök, Nichtern, and Gruenberg 1963; Judd and Brandkamp 1967) found no significant or constant chromosomal abnormalities in schizophrenic patients. They conclude that if genetic factors are present in the etiology of schizophrenia, they cannot be elicited by current cytogenetic methods. Because of the very marked abnormal features that have been found to be associated with chromosomal accidents, it seems doubtful that such mechanisms will have major implications for normal personality variations.

Phenylketonuria, Huntington's Chorea, and Schizophrenia in Families

Much older than the microscopic investigation of chromosomes is the *pedigree methods*. It consists of the study of the genealogical record of a family with particular emphasis upon the incidence of individuals with a specific condition or trait. The point of departure in such a study is an affected individual or proband. It is with this type of investigation that the genetic mechanism in Huntington's chorea and such inborn disorders of metabolism as phenylketonuria (PKU) has been established. Hungington's chorea, manifested by jerky movements of the head, trunk, arms and legs, and progressive intellectual and adaptive deterioration, affects men and women to the same extent and shows an average age of onset at about 35. The physical basis of disease is the premature decay of nerve cells in the cortex and basal ganglia of the cerebrum. Personality changes take the form of increased irritability and aggressiveness, unreliability, lack of control, "sloppiness," and delinquency. The prevalence has been estimated by Pleydell (1954) at 2000 manifest cases in England and Wales plus perhaps twice as many destined to develop the condition. Unlike Huntington's chorea, *phenylketonuria* becomes manifest shortly after birth. The disease is due to a deficiency of the enzyme needed to metabolize the amino acid *phenylalanine* which leads to brain impairment through a number of chemical processes. It can be controlled partially, however, if the affected individual is given a phenylanine-restricted diet (Hsia, Knox, Quinn, and Paine 1956; Moncrieff and Wilkinson 1961). The frequency in the population has been estimated at 6 per 100,000 (Hsia, 1967). A particular feature of the pedigree method is that it allows certain conclusions regarding the mode of inheritance. Huntington's chorea and PKU are typical examples of respectively dominant and recessive gene action as has been shown with methods as described in the section dealing with natural populations. Heterozygous carriers of the PKU gene, although not overtly deviant, show a limited tolerance for large amounts of phenylalanine as compared to normals and they can thus be detected (Hsia 1967). As can be shown with a variation of the pedigree method in which samples of consanguineous individuals and their ancestors as well as descendants are studied, the incidence of PKU is much greater in such related persons. Between 5 and 10% of the parents of PKU patients were found to be first cousins, against an expectation of approximately .5 percent in the average population (Munro 1947; Ferris 1954).

The pedigree method has shown to be very fruitful in the discovery of genetic mechanisms of abnormalities in which environmental factors have only limited influence. The method also allows investigation of sex-linkage in particular conditions, as has been hypothesized in some cases of *mental retardation* in view of its being more common in males than in females (Dunn et al, 1963). If, however, there is reason to assume that environmental factors play an important part—as it must do in behavior pathology and personality—the method is less useful, since it does not permit a clear disentanglement of hereditary and experiential variables. If children are not brought up by their own parents, but in institutions or adoptive homes, as were the schizophrenic cases studied by Heston (1966), the basis for genetic conclusions becomes considerably firmer. It is necessary, however, to assume or else to insure that the foster children constitute a representative sample of all children of the subpopulation of propositi and that there is no correlation between the phenotypic characteristics of the true and foster parents. Heston compared 47 adults born to schizophrenic mothers with 50 matched controls, all subjects having been separated from their natural mothers from the first few days of life. Assessment by means of psychological tests, life records, and psychiatric interviews showed that schizophrenia, mental deficiency, neurotic personality disorders, and sociopathic personality disorders were significantly more often found in those persons born from schizophrenic mothers. Quite interestingly, it was also observed that among the unaffected individuals born to schizophrenic mothers there was a relatively large proportion of conspicuously successful adults. They possessed artistic talents and demonstrated imaginative adaptations to life which were uncommon in the control group. This finding offers some support for the suggestion that there may be biological advantages associated with heterozygosity for the pathogenic gene or genes. Osmond and Hoffer (1966) also point out that schizophrenic patients may have certain physiological characteristics that provide them with some biological advantage.

Another variation of the family method, involving the calculation of *parent-child test score correlations* has been applied in order to cast light on genetic hypotheses, especially in the area of cognitive abilities. Such correlations, of course, can be expected to be highly sensitive to environmental effects, as is frequently the case in pedigree studies, but under certain conditions a unique pattern of family correlations may occur. If the transmission of a trait is determined by a gene on the X chromosome, no correlation between father and son would be expected, as the father can only pass on his X chromosome to his daughter. Consequently, a high correlation between father and daughter would be predicted, and likewise, a correlation of equal magnitude between mother and son. Because of the presence of two X chromosomes in women, mothers and their daughters should yield a somewhat lower correlation. Eight cognitive variables were investigated along these lines by Stafford (1965). The resulting patterns of correlations suggested a sex-linked recessive transmission for two of the eigth traits: spatial visualization and mental arithmetic. As the possibility of environmental transmission cannot be excluded, however, Stafford emphasized the need for including foster children in such studies in order to obtain more conclusive empirical data.

Heritability of Abnormal and Normal Trait Variation as Suggested by Twin Research

In another effort to obtain better control of the environmental action upon phenotypic differences, the *twin method* has been frequently applied in the genetic study of physical disease, mental disease, intellectual abilities, and normal personality variation. Our practical and ethical inability to manipulate genetic variables in man as is done in animals is partly compensated by the experimental manipulation provided by nature itself. With very few exceptions (Darlington 1963; Allen 1965) all MZ twins are genetically identical, DZ twins being genetically no more similar than ordinary sibs. In the study of concordance or discordance (phenotypic similarity or dissimilarity) of individual twin pairs for particular traits, it is important to bear in mind that MZ twins may be genetically different, due to the possibility that one may lose a chromosome, or to the asymmetrical division of the cytoplasm. DZ twins may be genetically very similar due to positive assortative mating (like marrying or like homogamy) and consanguinuity in the ancestors. There has been some speculation on the possible existence of a third type of twin, supposedly originating from one ovum and two spermatozoids. Zygosity tests would classify such pairs as DZ, but according to Allen (1965) they would have major consequences only for the estimation of genetic and environmental components of variation in a very precise analysis. In order to classify twins into DZ and MZ, zygosity tests nowadays usually consist of serological procedures (Smith and Penrose 1955) and dermatoglyphics (Cummins and Midlo 1961) and no longer by means of the polysymptomatic method (Siemens 1924), which compares the appearance of both twins in a pair on a large number of physical characteristics. The latter method is considered to be too subjective. On the basis of similarity or dissimilarity in various blood groups and finger and palm prints the probability of a twin pair being DZ or MZ is calculated, and 95 percent certainty is accepted as sufficient for reliable diagnosis. In some cases errors may be made on statistical grounds, and some instances of incongruence between the serological diagnosis and the dermatoglyphic diagnosis have been recorded (Connell et al. 1962). The certainty of twin diagnosis is considerably increased if the blood-groups and prints of the parents are also obtained or if skin transplanation tests are carried out (Bain and Lowenstein 1964). However, these added procedures are usually not feasible for practical reasons.

If the twin method is applied to *discrete* conditions, concordance ratios for MZ twins and DZ twins can be calculated and tested for statistical difference in order to establish whether there is a genetic contribution to the development of the behavior or not. Discrete classification as opposed to continuous measurement is applicable when it is possible to establish whether an individual possesses a particular characteristic or not (e.g., having committed suicide). Neuroticism and intelligence are examples of continuous variable; assessment takes the form of establishing degree or extent, not whether the individual has the trait or does not have it. Psychiatric diagnosis of behavior pathology has traditionally applied discrete classification of disease entities. There have been many criticisms of this procedure (Eysenck 1960) which emphasize the unsatisfactory nature of psychiatric classificatory systems as indicated by the low rate of diagnostic agreement between psychiatrists when they assess patients independently. The major results of a number of studies of concordance rates in MZ and DZ twins regarding a variety of psychogathological conditions have been condensed in Table 11-5. The heritability coefficients have also been calculated. Although some of the discrepancies between the studies may be attributable to diagnostic variations and unreliability, the heritability estimates of *schizophrenia*, for instance, differ so much from study to study that only tentative conclusions can be drawn regarding the contribution of genetic variance. A publication by Gottesman and Shields (1966) has offered an

elaborate discussion of the relevant findings. Among other things, they found that concordance rates tend to be higher in females than in males, higher in severe schizophrenia than in milder cases, higher when the diagnosis is made in a long-stay rather than a short-stay hospital, higher in some geographical areas and lower in others, the Scandinavian countries in particular. Criticisms of the conclusions drawn from twin studies in schizophrenia have also been made by Rosenthal (1959, 1960, 1961, 1962a, 1962b, 1966, 1968) and Jackson (1960) (see Rosenthal and Kety 1968).

As the twin method does not allow any inferences in regard to the *mode* of inheritance, the method has sometimes been combined with the study of pedigrees and consanguineous individuals. An example of this procedure, called the *twin-family method*, is presented in Table 11-6. The frequency of *schizophrenia* in persons of varying degree of blood relationship to the proband are corrected for age (as there is a statistical relation between age and probability of onset and presence of the disease), and therefore show the risk or expectancy rates of schizophrenia. It can be seen from this table that there is a definite increase of risk with closer consanguinity of the affected individual (N equals 953 schizophrenic index cases). Inspection of the table also shows that *environmental closeness* increases the morbidity risk. These findings seem to indicate recessive inheritance of autosomal nature, since no relationship between sex of the affected parent and the affected child has been observed. In a recent paper, Gottesman and Shields (1967) described a polygenic theory of schizophrenia, the manifestation of which would depend upon the number of pathogenic genes present as well as the amount of environmental stress. Children of two schizophrenic parents must be homozygous, but not all develop the condition (about 70% do). It has, therefore, been inferred that the penetrance of the genotype, that is the rate of manifestation when the necessary genetic material is available, can be estimated at this percentage. Similar research regarding *manic-depressive psychosis* has suggested dominant inheritance with around 30% penetrance (Slater 1938; Kallman 1950; Stenstedt 1952). Limited penetrance may be due to environmental variables that have a rather wide action range, or to the masking or compensating effects of other (non-allelic) genes (epistasis). Concordance rates in MZ twins can only provide an upper limit for penetrance estimation (Allan 1965), since complete concordance in such twins is compatible with low penetrance in the population. This is because both genetic and environmental conditions which influence gene penetration are very similar in MZ twins. In an investigation with regard to *normal personality variation*, Cattell, Stice, and Kristy (1957) applied the MAVA method as mentioned in a previous section of this chapter. Eleven personality traits as measured by the Junior Personality Quiz were involved. Difficulties associated with the estimation of sampling error and the rather low reliabilities of the questionnaire variables, as well as with regard to selectivity in the placement of the adopted children, make any conclusions with regard to the genetics of personality rather tentative. However, two rather consistent and quite remarkable observations were made. Deviations due to heredity tended to correlate negatively with deviations due to environment, especially in respect to between-family comparisons. It might be hypothesized that environment forces the genetically deviant to adjust to the average and, accordingly, Cattell (1965) has postulated his "law of coercion to the biosocial mean." In other words,

Table 11-5. Heritability Estimates (H*) of Various Pathological Behaviours Derived from Concordance Rates in MZ and DZ Twins (largely after Shields and Slater 1960)

Condition	Total	Number of Pairs Mono-zygotic	Dizygotic	Percentage Positively Concordant * = corrected for age Mono-zygotic	Dizygotic	Heritability Estimates H*
Mental deficiency (institutionalized cases)						
Rosanoff et al. (1937)	366	126	240	91	53	.84
"Endogenous" cases only	189	60	129	100	58	1.00
Juda (1939) All cases	220	71	149	97	56	.93
Schizophrenia						
Luxenburger (1928)	81	21	60	67	3	.66
Rosanoff et al. (1934)	142	41	101	67	10	.63
Essen-Möller (1941)	35	11	24	71	17	.65
Slater (1953)	156	41	115	68 / 76*	11 / 14*	.64 / .73*
Kallmann (original report 1946)	691	174	517	69	10	.66
Kallmann (latest report 1953)	953	268	685	86*	15*	.83*
Kallmann and Roth (1956): childhood schizophrenia	52	17	35	71	17	.65
Inouye (1963)	72	55	17	76*	22*	.65
Tienari (1963)	37	16	21	0	5	.00
Kringlen (1964)	20	8	12	25	17	.10
Harvald and Hauge (1965)	42	9	33	29	6	.24
Gottesman and Shields (1966)	47	24	33	65*	17*	.58
Kringlen (1966)	145	55	90	39	10	.32
Manic-depressive psychosis						
Luxenburger (1942, cited by Gedda, 1951)	139	56	83	84	15	.81
Rosanoff et al. (1935)	90	23	67	70	16	.69
Kallmann (1950)	75	23	52	96	26*	.95
Kallmann (1953)	85	27	58	100*	26*	1.00
Slater (1953): Endogenous affective disorder	38	8	30	50 / c.57*	29*	.39*
Da Fonseca (1959): Endogenous affective disorder	60	21	39	75	38	.60
Involutional depression						
Kallmann (1950)	96	29	67	61*	6*	.59
Senile psychosis						
Kallmann (1950)	108	33	75	43*	7*	.38
Epilepsy						
Rosanoff et al. (1934)	107	23	84	70	24	.61
Conrad (1935): Idiopathic	161	22	97	86	4	.85
Symptomatic		8	34	13	0	1.00
Lennox and Jolly (1954): Without brain damage	173	51	47	88	13	.86
With brain damage		26	49	35	12	.26
Other behaviour disorders						
Male homosexuality (Kinsey Scale, 3 or more): Kallmann (1952)	63	37	26	100	12	1.00
Adult crime: Lange (1931), Rosanoff et al. (1934), Kranz (1936), Stumpfl (1936), Borgstroem (1939)—combined results	216	103	113	68	35	.51
Juvenile delinquency: Rosanoff et al. (1934, 1941)	67	42	25	85	75	.40
Childhood behavior disorder, etc.: Rosanoff et al. (1934, 1941): Behaviour disorder	107	47	60	87	43	.77
Kranz (1937): Juveniles with personality disorder requiring institutionalization	14	11	3	71	0	1.00
Shields (1954): Behavior disorder or marked neurotic traits (based on 62 unselected pairs of twin-school-children)	41	23	18	74	50	.48
Hysteria: Stumpfl (1937)	18	9	9	33	0	1.00
Neurosis, Psychopathic personality: Slater (1953)	37	8	29	25	14	.13

Table 11-5. (Cont.)

Condition	Number of Pairs			Percentage Positively Concordant * = corrected for age		Heritability Estimates
	Total	Mono-zygotic	Dizygotic	Mono-zygotic	Dizygotic	H*
Neurosis, Psychopathic personality: Slater and Shields (1955): New series, provisional	70	38	32	53	25	.37
Alcohol addiction: from series of 201 twin-pairs whose drinking habits were studied (After Kaij, 1957). See also Partanen et al. (1966)	82	26	56	65	30	.50
Suicide: Kallmann and Anastasio (1947)	56	28	28	4	4	.00

Table 11-6. Risk of Schizophrenia for Relatives of Schizophrenics

Class	Percentage Risk of Schizophrenia
Children of two non-schizophrenic parents (general population)	0.85
Relatives of adult schizophrenic index cases	
Not consanguineous: Step-sibs	1.8
Spouse	2.1
First cousins	2.6
Nephews and nieces	3.9
Grandchildren	4.3
Half-sibs	7.1
Parents	9.3
Full-sibs	14.2
Dizygotic co-twins	14.5
Dizygotic co-twins of same sex	17.6
Children with one schizophrenic parent	16.4
Children with two schizophrenic parents	68.1
Monozygotic co-twins	86.2
Monozygotic co-twins living apart for at least 5 years	77.6
Monozygotic co-twins not so separated	91.5

After Kallmann (1946, 1950), Shields and Slater (1960), and Rainer (1966)

these findings were contrary to the frequently assumed positive heredity-environment correlation.

Six subtests of Thurstone's Primary Abilities Test (verbal, space, number, reasoning, word fluency, and memory) were included in studies by Vandenberg (1965) and by Loehlin and Vandenberg (1966) who used his method involving covariance matrices of MZ and DZ twin differences (see equation 10). He concluded from the results that there were four genetically independent variables in twin tests. In a study of hereditary components in alcoholism, personality traits, and intelligence, Partanen, Bruun, and Markkanan (1966) applied a similar analysis. Their results indicated that there was a common hereditary basis for amount of drinking and the tendency to lose control, whereas the genetic contribution to *frequency* of drinking was to some extent independently inherited. Intelligence variables were also included in this study, and like Vandenberg, the authors concluded that four independently inherited dimensions were operative.

In 1950, it was suggested by Eysenck that personality type items such as those used in personality questionnaires might be analyzed with heritability as a criterion. First, the items are to be investigated along item analytic lines, in order to divide them into a category of items with high MZ and low DZ concordance and a category with equal concordance rates in both types of twins. Each set of items is subsequently factor analyzed. Items from the Thurstone Temperament Survey and the Cattell Junior Personality Quiz were analyzed in this way by Loehlin (1965). Each subgroup (high and low heritability) yielded four factors. In both groups of items, factors associated with introversion-extraversion, neuroticism and physical activities were extracted. Loehlin observed a slightly different emphasis between the high and low heritability factors, the former reflecting more or less private activities of the subject and the latter appearing to be more focused on his reaction to social environments.

Most results obtained so far, regarding the heritability of cognitive and personality traits, however, have been gathered by more traditional methods using equations 4 and 5. Tables 11-7, 8, and 9 present major empirical findings in personality, while Figure 11-5 summarizes the results of as many as 52 studies of the heritability of intelligence, involving 99 groups of subjects of various degrees of genetic and environmental commonality.

Table 11-7. Heritability F-ratios ($F = \sigma_{WDZ}^2/\sigma_{WMZ}^2$) Observed in Three Twin Studies of the Minnesota Multiphasic Personality Inventory

	Gottesman (1963)	Gottesman (1965)	Reznikoff et al. (1966)	Combined Data
Hypochondriasis	1.19	1.01	2.33*	1.21
Depression	1.81*	1.82*	1.62	1.53**
Hysteria	.86	1.43	2.70*	1.27
Psychopathic Deviate	2.01*	1.63*	1.54	1.39*
Masculinity-Femininity	1.18	1.41	2.37*	1.10
Paranoia	1.05	1.61*	1.78	1.27
Psychasthenia	1.58	1.46	.82	1.52**
Schizophrenia	1.71	1.49*	1.40	1.36*
Hypomania	1.32	1.15	1.65	1.21
Social Introversion	3.42**	1.49*	2.02	1.59**
Number of MZ twins	34	68	18	120
Number of DZ twins	34	82	18	132

After Vandenberg (1966b)
*p < .05
** p < .01

Table 11-8. Heritability F-ratios $(F = \sigma^2_{W\,DZ}/\sigma^2_{W\,MZ})$ Observed in Three Twin Studies of the High School Personality Questionnaire

	Cattell (1955)	Vandenberg (1962)	Gottesman (1963)	Combined Data
I, tenderminded vs. toughminded	1.47	.97	1.07	1.23
Q_4, nervous tension	1.56*	2.08*	.53	1.23
C, general neuroticism	1.60*	3.20	1.03	1.71**
Q_3, will control	1.08	1.87*	1.53	1.38*
D, impatient dominance	1.35	.93	.62	.91
A, cyclothymia vs. schizothymia	1.08	1.30	1.11	1.26
H, adventurous cyclothymia vs. withdrawn schizothymia	1.34	.90	1.60	1.42*
K, socialized morale vs. boorishness	1.39	1.06	—	—
E, dominance vs. submissiveness	.90	.97	1.44	1.26
J, energetic conformity vs. quiet egocentricity	1.57*	1.56	1.41	1.58**
F, surgency vs. desurgency	1.47	1.45	2.29**	1.96**
Number of MZ pairs	52	45	34	131
Number of DZ pairs	32	37	34	103

After Vandenberg (1966a)
*p < .05
**p < .01

Table 11-9. Heritability Estimates (h^2) of the Personality Traits, Neuroticism and Introversion-Extraversion, Obtained in a Variety of Studies Using Mainly Personality Inventories

	No. of Pairs MZ	DZ	r_{MZ}	r_{DZ}	h^2	Authors
Neuroticism						
Inventory						
Bernreuter	55	44	.63	.32	.45	Carter (1935)
Thurstone	45	35	.36	.08	.31	Vandenberg (1962)
Eysenck	26	26	.77	.03	.77	McLeod (1954)
Wilde, N-Scale	88	42	.53	.11	.47	Wilde (1964)
NS-Scale	88	42	.67	.34	.50	Wilde (1964)
Bruun	157	189	.28	.21	.07	Partanen et al. (1966)
Woodworth	52	52	.56	.37	.30	Newman et al. (1937)
Factor scores	25	25	.85	.22	.81	Eysenck & Prell (1951)
Introversion-Extraversion						
Thurstone	45	35	.50	−.06	.47	Vandenberg (1962)
Bernreuter	55	44	.57	.41	.22	Carter (1935)
Factor scores	26	26	.50	−.33	.50	Eysenck (1956)
Comrey	111	90	(F = 1.94)		.48	Vandenberg (1966b)
Stern	50	38	(F = 1.54)		.35	Vandenberg (1966b)
Wilde	88	42	.37	.35	.03	Wilde (1964)
Bruun	157	189	.51	.26	.41	Partanen et al. (1966)
Meyer-Briggs	40	27	(F = 1.84)		.46	Vandenberg (1966b)

Observed Characteristics of Identical and Fraternal Twins as Individuals and as Pairs

Conclusions from twin research have been frequently criticized by authors who disputed that the following conditions were fulfilled: (1) zygosity diagnosis should be accurate, (2) twin samples should be representative for the total twin population, (3) the total twin population should be genetically and environmentally representative for the population at large, (4) the within-pair environmental variance in MZ and DZ pairs should be equal on the average, (5) heritability estimates of particular traits should be reliable across different investigations.

Numerous empirical findings do indeed cast doubt on these assumptions. The probability of twinning has been shown to be positively related with age and parity of the mother (Scheinfeld and Schachter 1963; Allan 1965; Russell 1961). Twin births have been found to be significantly higher in illegitimate maternities (Erikson and Fellman 1967) and more frequent in the lower social classes (Lilienfeld and Pasamanick 1955; Smith 1965). Twins are more often born prematurely and their birth weight is considerably below average while mortality rate is higher until the third year (Zazzo 1960). Rosanoff, Handy, and Plesset (1935, 1937), Judd (1939), Munro (1965), and Reitman, Linnstaedter, and Pokorny (1964) found evidence that schizophrenia, depressive mental illness, and mental retardation (Allan and Kallmann 1955) are more prevalent or more pronounced among twins than in the general population. The same was found to be true for cerebral palsy and minor forms of brain damage (Russell 1961). Some of the factors mentioned affect MZ and DZ twins to different extents. Both Eysenck and Prell (1951) and Wilde (1964) found low neuroticism scores in British and Dutch samples of twins. Such samples, moreover, very frequently show a preponderance of female over male pairs, and a larger proportion of MZ twins than would be expected on the basis of their frequency in the population (e.g., Osborne and DeGeorge 1959; H. Koch 1966). Greater differentiation in social dominance and social skills were found in MZ pairs by Zazzo (1960) and Von Bracken (1936), and in DZ pairs by Partanen, Bruun, and Markkanen (1966), who also observed that MZ twins are more concordant in marital status and live longer together than DZ twins. Lower average IQ in twins as compared to singletons has frequently been reported (Day 1932; Davis 1937; Rosanoff, Handy, and Plesset 1937;

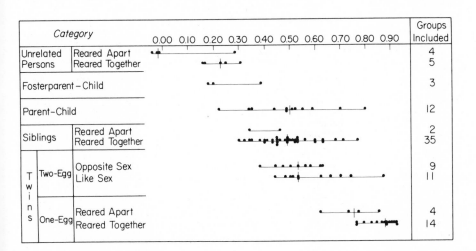

Fig. 11-5. *Intelligence test score correlations between groups of persons of different degrees of environmental and genetic commonality. The correlations are derived from 52 studies, involving a total of 89 subject groups. Both ranges and median values of the coefficients have been marked in the figure.* [After Erlenmeyer-Kimling and Jarvik 1963, Fig. 1]

Benton 1940; Allan and Kallman 1955; Drillien 1964; Husén 1960, 1963; Zazzo 1960; Koch 1966). This difference tends to be more pronounced in MZ than DZ twins. Similar observations have been made regarding slower language development (Day 1932; Davis 1937; Koch 1966; Zazzo 1960). On the other hand, no differences between MZ twins, DZ twins, and the general population in IQ were found in a study involving twins between 60 and 90 years of age (Jarvik, Kallman, and Falek 1962).

In a sociometric study by Pire (1966) male MZ twins were found to be more popular than their classmates, whereas no such difference was found for DZ twins, and the within-pair variability in this respect was found to be less in MZ than DZ twins. Closer bonds of attachment in MZ twins were observed by Shields (1954) and more similar treatment by their parents by Jones (1955). Smith (1965) found greater similarity in such behaviors as "studying together," "being dressed alike," "eating between meals," "sharing the same close friends," "dietary habits," and others. According to some authors (e.g., Wilson 1934) the effects of such conditions "must be attributed ultimately to the influence of their heredity which led, or forced them to 'select' more similar environments." But, according to Zazzo (1960), twins are developmentally so atypical that the meaningfulness of quantitative heritability coefficients is greatly reduced. As Vandenberg (1966, p. 330) has stated, "it may reflect as much of an experimental bias to attribute the final differences to environment alone as it would to attribute them to heredity alone." He suggests that "for the purposes of ranking variables with respect to the importance of heredity, this dilemma may be left unsolved." Such a ranking of variables, however, necessitates the crucial assumption that all traits will tend to lead to the selection of certain environments or to particular environmental repercussions to the same extent. As the human environment is more responsive to some traits than to others, this assumption does not seem very likely. In addition, some individual traits such as introversion may lead to the selection of particular environments, but it is difficult to see that such traits as visual acuity, perceptual rigidity, tapping speed, or critical flicker fusion frequency would do so to the same extent. Loehlin (1969) has recently suggested a method to estimate the quantity of the biasing effect of greater environmental within-pair similarity in MZ twins upon heritability estimates. Unfortunately, however, this procedure must assume that the bias is roughly constant for a range of traits. An interesting alternative procedure has been presented by Sandra Scarr (1966), who compared concordance rates in MZ twins correctly identified by their mothers as identicals and MZ twins misclassified by their mothers as fraternals with correctly and incorrectly classified DZ twins.

Because of the interpretative ambiguity of twin research results due to the above-mentioned factors, it has frequently been suggested that the use of twins reared apart would provide more control over environmental variables. From a sampling point of view, however, such twins would hardly seem to provide a remedy, since not only are they hard to find, but also they constitute a rather unrepresentative sample of individuals. That the environments of twins placed in different foster homes are indeed fundamentally different needs to be assured, moreover, as Lewis (1966) has pointed out in a critical comment on Burt's (1966) research on IQ in MZ twins reared together and apart. Johnson (1963) and Vandenberg and Johnson (1966) found that

MZ twins separated early after birth were more similar in IQ than those subjects separated at a later age. In a study of achievement test performance, Husén (1963) noticed greater concordance in MZ pairs in Grade 6 than in Grade 4, despite the expected progressively increasing environmental variance. Shields (1962) observed greater MZ concordance for extraversion in MZ twins separated shortly after birth than in pairs grown up together. In a study of five personality traits by Wilde (1964), it was found that DZ twins who had been separated for at least five years were more concordant than DZ twins living together. A comparison between predominantly DZ twins and regular siblings was carried out by Portenier (1939). In the majority of personality and interest variables involved, twins were found to resemble one another less than the siblings despite the age differences between the latter. Partanen, Bruun, and Markkanen (1966) have also reported that DZ pairs tend to exhibit more variation than ordinary same-sexed siblings. Other disturbing findings involve the not infrequent observation of negative intraclass correlations in DZ twins, whereas the corresponding correlations for MZ twins are positive and sometimes rather high (Carter 1935; Gottesman 1963; Eysenck 1956). Even when such correlations differ significantly from one another, the interpretation that the trait is inherited is to some extent contradicted by the very fact that the DZ intraclass correlation was found to be negative. If the trait were inherited, the latter correlation should, of course, be positive since DZ twins are genetically more similar than unrelated persons. As might be expected from findings such as the above, MZ as compared to DZ twin pairs were found to display a greater tendency to mutually conform and to overestimate actual similarity in an experimental study derived from Milgram's (1961) procedure for the assessment of yielding to social cues (Wilde 1969b).

We will finally discuss the question of reliability of heritability estimates. Some of the discrepancies in findings between different studies may be attributable to the use of different measurement variables and, therefore, we will consider only those studies in which the same assessment variables were involved. Estimates for h^2 for the same scale obtained in different studies might be compared to see to what extent their confidence limits overlap, but because of the limited interpretability of absolute magnitudes of h^2, it may be more meaningful to focus upon the *ranking* of heritabilities, as has been emphasized by Vandenberg (1966). Rank order correlations of trait heritabilities may thus be run across the traits measured between older and younger twins and between male and female twins in the same study, and between different twin samples comparing a number of studies. The results of these consistency checks are presented in Tables 11-10 and 11. None of the correlations reached significance, and several of them were found to be negative. Not only absolute magnitudes of h_2 but also their relative values seem to justify limited confidence according to this observation.

In a longitudinal study by Rutter, Korn, and Birch (1963) of infant twins and siblings, the children were rated for various "primary reaction patterns" at the age of one year and one and two years later. Concordance for activity level, regularity, approach to or withdrawal from novel stimuli, adaptability, response intensity, threshold of responsiveness, and quality of mood, were calculated at each age level. Greater MZ than DZ concordance was found at all three age periods for adaptability, activity, and approach to new stimuli, and from the four remaining behavioral traits in two out of three age periods. The behav-

Table 11-10. Consistency of $F = \sigma^2_{W\text{DZ}}/\sigma^2_{W\text{MZ}}$ Rankings of Personality Traits across Sex and Age (expressed in rank-order correlation coefficients)

Across sex of twins
(1) Stern High School Activities Index:
   30 scales, Vandenberg (1966)   = .14
   Stern High School Activities Index:
   12 factor and 4 area scores, Vandenberg (1966)   = .09
(2) California Psychological Inventory:
   20 scales, Gottesman (1966)   = .06
(3) Comrey Personality and Attitude Factors;
   12 scales, Vandenberg (1966)   = .23
(4) Minnesota Vocational Interest Inventory;
   21 scales and 9 factor scores, Vandenberg et al. (1966) = .26
(5) MMPI, Gottesman (1963); 10 scales   = .19
   Gottesman (1965); 10 scales   = .04
(6) HSPQ, Gottesman (1963); 14 scales   = .08

Across age of twins
(1) Partanen et al. (1966): 15 intelligence, personality,
   and drinking variables, older versus younger twins   = .18
(2) Wilde (1964): 5 personality measures, comparing twins
   living separately with twins living together   tau   = .20

Table 11-11. Consistency of $F = \sigma^2_{W\text{DZ}}/\sigma^2_{W\text{DZ}}$ Rankings of Personality Traits across Different Studies (expressed in rank-order correlation coefficients)

(1) Cattell's HSPQ; 10 scales
   Cattell et al. (1955) vs. Vandenberg (1962)   = .45
   Cattell et al. (1955) vs. Gottesman (1963)   = −.45
   Vandenberg (1962) vs. Gottesman (1963)   = −.45
   Cattell vs. Vandenberg vs. Gottesman:
   Kendall's W = .26 (.70 > P > .50)
(2) MMPI; 10 scales
   Gottesman (1963) vs. Gottesman (1965)   = .54
   Gottesman (1963) vs. Reznikoff et al. (1967)   = −.58
   Gottesman (1965) vs. Reznikoff et al. (1967)   = −.52
   Gottesman vs. Gottesman vs. Reznikoff et al.:
   Kendall's W = .20 (.90 > P > .80)
(3) California Psychological Inventory; 20 scales
   Nichols (1966) vs. Gottesman (1966)   = −.22 (males)
                                                    = −.24 (females)

---

iors were also investigated for their stability over time. According to the authors, "Perhaps one of the most striking findings was that those categories (activity and approach) in which the evidence for a genetic basis was strongest were also those showing the greatest instability over time. Further, the two most stable categories (threshold and regularity) were those in which the evidence for a genetic basis was least strong." No evidence was found for a possible genetic basis of instability over time. The authors concluded that ". . . it is essential that one avoids the sterile genetic versus environmental categorization in developmental research. Clearly, effective environment representing those features of the surround which may influence developmental course is the result of the selective sensitivity and capacities for response of the organism."

EVALUATION OF HERITABILITY STUDIES OF HUMAN BEHAVIOR TRAITS

If one reconsiders the evidence and implications presented in the foregoing paragraphs a considerable variety of reactions seems possible. One might argue out that some of the biases tend to increase heritability estimates, whereas other factors tend to lower them and that both kinds of influences tend to

cancel out one another especially when samples are large. But can one strengthen a chain with several weak links by making it longer? One might point out that heritability estimates can not be expected to be consistent across sex or across different samples, since it follows from $h^2 = v_G/v_G + v_E$ (see equation 1) that an increase in environmental variance lowers h^2. This consideration perhaps may apply to the observed inconsistency across the sexes or between samples especially if they come from different regions or different countries. Some of the differences between the Scandinavian estimates of heritabilities for mental illness and those obtained in the United States may be due to greater environmental variance (v_P) impinging upon individuals in countries that were, for instance, subject to German occupation in World War II than in other generations or in other countries that were not. Homogeneity of school experiences in some samples may be greater than in other subjects whose experiences are based upon more flexible educational contents and techniques matched to their individual preferences and capabilities. If samples are drawn from more or less the same social class, their child-rearing experiences tend to be more similar than when they are drawn from different social strata. Numerous other factors might be mentioned, and they may act to different extents upon different traits. The parents of some samples of twins may have emphasized their individuality, whereas those in other samples may have treated their children very similarly; this tendency, in turn, may covary more with zygosity in some cases than in others, and because of yet other factors some twin pairs may react more pronouncedly to this than others. One might assert that human variety is so overwhelming that matching of samples is an impossible task. Such considerations would greatly reduce the meaningfulness of calculating heritability estimates. And even if it were justifiable, the problem of genetic and environmental representativeness of twins for the population at large would still have to be faced.

Any study in which the kind of conclusions drawn can reflect the experimenter's opinion or assumptions on which others do not necessarily agree is certainly most undesirable in scientific research. More unambiguous methods are necessary. If the problem of general representativeness of twins is disregarded, most of the disagreements between studies as well as the various paradoxical observations can be attributed to the lack of control over environment. In other words, the twin method that was developed because of the environmental contamination in the pedigree method is not completely successful for the very same reasons. Apart from his many criticisms of the twin method, Rosenthal (1968) has made a number of constructive suggestions that may help remedy the problem. One of these involves the careful selection of parents for certain traits, the study of the parent-child interaction, and the measurement of the children's responses. Another consists of studying adopted children in a way that is similar to the aforementioned investigation by Heston (see page 217). Rosenthal also emphasizes the importance of specifying the particular environmental variables that interact with a particular genotype, since environment has commonly been conceptualized in too broad terms whose specific stimulus parameters are not known.

In addition to these procedures a greater amount of control over environmental variables in studies involving *twins* may be obtainable. In a less direct way this can be accomplished by follow-up studies of twins who are placed in different classrooms as is done in Denmark by Juel-Nielsen (1965). More direct control over environmental variables was exercised by McNemar (1933) and Brody (1937), who investigated the effects of *practice* in consecutive trials on motor tasks and on a task of mechanical ability upon the concordance in performance of MZ and DZ twins. In a similar way, as Broadhurst and Jinks (1963) have done with regard to data collected by Vicari (1929) on maze learning by mice, we have calculated the values for h^2 in consecutive trials in the data gathered by McNemar and Brody. Two contrasting examples are presented in Figures 11-6 and 7. As can be seen from Figure 11-6, r_{MZ} for mechanical ability increased more than r_{DZ} over the six consecutive trials with one to five minute intervals. The value for h^2 at the first trial is insignificant; the value obtained for the sixth trial is significant at the .01 level. If, therefore, measurements had been obtained at the first trial only, the "instant picture approach," which is common in usual twin research designs, would have led to under-

estimation of the heritability of the trait. An entirely different pattern is seen in Figure 11-7 regarding a motor skill test. In the first trial, heritability of the trait is suggested, but it approaches zero as more experience with the task is obtained because the DZ twins became more concordant in their performance and eventually as concordant as the MZ twins. In this case, the "instant picture approach" would have overestimated the heritability of the trait, but the process of interaction between experience and trait shows otherwise. The initial difference between MZ and DZ concordance in this case might have been due to greater common experience of MZ twins prior to the experiment. It seems, therefore, quite possible that the "moving picture approach" that studies heritability as a function of controlled ongoing experience will remove many of the difficulties encountered in twin research that were discussed in the preceding paragraphs. However, the procedure used by McNemar and Brody would need some improvement. The twins should be given the same environmental stimulation over time, but independently of one another, so that their social interaction during the experiment may be reduced to a minimum. Secondly, it would be preferable to take all subjects up to *asymptotic performance* so that the upper or lower limits of h^2 may be calculated. In a case such as illustrated in Figure 11-7 this obviously cannot be achieved, since the performance, intraclass correlations, and heritability estimates are still rather unstable in the later trials.

If this *experimental-psychometric twin research design* is used in order to obtain limits for the value of h^2, a number of assumptions have to be made. The most important ones are that the asymptotic concordance with increasing experience in MZ and DZ twins is not limited by differential environmental variance between DZ and MZ pairs or between DZ and MZ as individuals *prior* to the experiment. It would not matter, however, if such distracting factors operated in the earlier trials of the investigation. Moreover, the magnitude of the eventual behavioral changes brought about by the experimental manipulation as compared to the pre-experimental variance or the variance in trial one can be empirically assessed, and the relationship between the pre-experimental within-pair differences and final performance differences can be calculated.

A number of possible patterns of MZ and DZ intraclass correlations as a function of controlled experience have been presented in Figure 11-8. Each would lead to different conclusions in regard to the heritability of the trait under investigation. Limited space precludes the theoretical elaboration of these patterns. It may be noted, however, that the finding of Husén of greater heritabilities of certain scholastic tasks in Grade 6 than in Grade 4 (see page 222) seems to fit pattern No. 13 of our present model and might be explained in terms of greater expressivity of relevant genes as a result of appropriate environmental stimulation. Brody's findings regarding mechanical ability also seem to follow pattern No. 13 or perhaps No. 16. In contrast, McNemar's observations based upon a spool-packing test may be more in agreement with pattern No. 5. Expanding the suggested procedure to the twin family method could give further insight into the mode of inheritance, heredity-environment correlation, and gene-environment interaction. Of course, it may be argued that this method can say very little about the magnitude of the genetic component of a particular phenotypic trait as it actually occurs in the general population since h^2 is taken in terms of unknown amounts of environmental

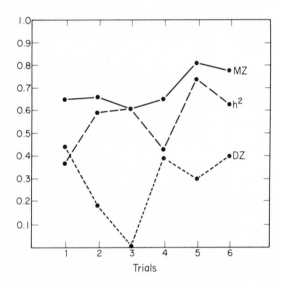

Fig. 11-6. *Changes in h^2 as a function of practice in a test for mechanical ability.* [After Brody 1937]

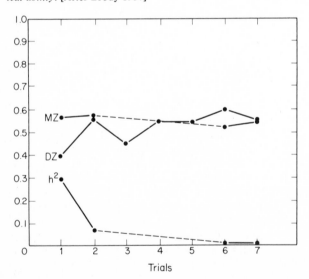

Fig. 11-7. *Changes in h^2 as a function of practice in a test for motor skills.* [After McNemer 1933]

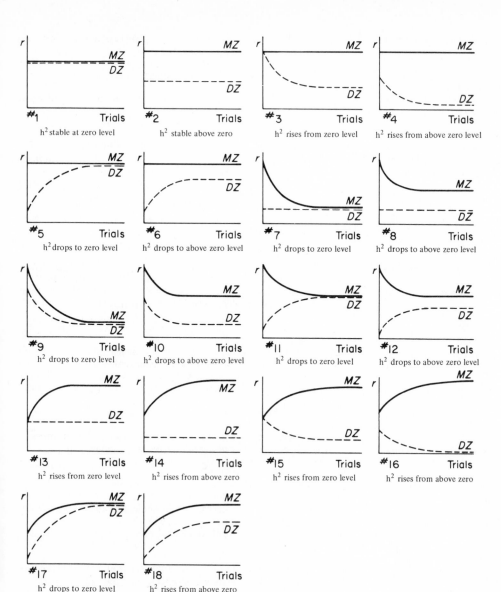

Fig. 11-8. *Patterns of r_{mz} and r_{dz} and effects upon the heritability coefficient h^2 as a function of practice or experimental manipulation running from trial one to asymptotic performance. Fictitious data.*

exposure or manipulation. Moreover, we do not know to what extent increases or decreases in environmental variables as they actually occur in the population would modify the values of h^2. In view of the rather disappointing empirical observations with regard to heritability estimates of personality traits, the low consistency across the sexes, across different studies, and across twins of different ages, however, this problem may be of less consequence. We may anticipate, therefore, that applications of the experimental-psychometric twin method will prove to be applicable to cognitive, perceptual, and motor tasks as well as to personality variables and that it may throw more light on the operation of those genetic and environmental factors which produce phenotypic variations between human beings.

Acknowledgements. This manuscript was prepared with the aid of grants from the National Research Council of Canada, the Alcohol and Drug Addiction Research Foundation of Ontario, the Canada Council, and Queen's University Arts Research Committee.

References

ALLAN, G. Twin research: problems and prospects. *In* H. G. STEINBERG and H. G. BEARN, *Progress in medical genetics.* New York: Grune & Stratton, 1965.

———, and F. J. KALLMANN. Frequency and types of mental retardation in twins. *American Journal of Human Genetics,* 1955, 7, 15–20.

BAGG, H. J. Individual differences and family resemblances in animal behavior. *American Naturalist,* 1916, *50,* 222–36.

——— Individual differences and family resemblances in animal behavior. *Archives of Psychology,* 1920, *6,* 1–58.

BAIN, B., and L. LOWENSTEIN. Genetic studies on the mixed leucocyte reaction. *Science,* 1964, *145,* 1315–16.

BASTOCK, M. A gene mutation which changes a behaviour pattern. *Evolution,* 1956, *10,* 421–39.

BENTON, A. L. Mental development of prematurely born children, a critical review of the literature. *American Journal of Orthopsychiatry,* 1940, *10,* 719–47.

BIGNAMI, A. Selection for fast and slow avoidance conditioning in the rat. *Bulletin of the British Psychological Society,* 1965, *17* (abstr.)

———, and D. BOVET, Experience de selection par rapport à une reaction conditionnée d'évitement chez le rat. *Comptes Rendus des Sciences de L'Academie des Sciences, Paris,* 1965, *260,* 1239–44.

BÖÖK, J. A., S. NICHTERN, and E. GRUENBERG. Cytogenetical investigations in childhood schizophrenia. *Acta Psychiatrica Scandinavica*, 1963, *39*, 309.

BORGSTROEM, C. A. Eine Serie von Kriminellen Zwillingen. *Archive für Rassenkunde und Geschlechtsbiologie*, 1939, *33*, 334–43.

BRACKEN, H. V. Verbundenheit und ordnung in Binnenleben von Zwillingspaaren. *Zeitschrift für pädagogische Psychologie*, 1936, *37*, 65–81.

BROADHURST, P. L. Experiments in psychogenetics; applications of biometrical genetics to the inheritance of behavior. *In* H. J. EYSENCK (ed.), *Experiments in personality*, vol. 1, *Psychogenetics and psychopharmacology*. London: Routledge & Kegan Paul, 1960.

———— Experiments in psychogenetics. *In* H. J. EYSENCK (ed.), *Experiments in personality*. London: Routledge & Kegan Paul, 1960.

———— Behavioral inheritance: past and present. *Conditional Reflex*, 1966, *1*, 3–15.

———— An introduction to the diallel cross. *In* J. HIRSCH (ed.), *Behavior-genetic analysis*. New York: McGraw-Hill, 1967.

————, and J. L. JINKS. Biometrical genetics and behavior; analysis of published data. *Psychological Bulletin*, 1961, *58*, 337–62.

———— The inheritance of mammalian behavior re-examined. *Journal of Heredity*, 1963, *54*, 170–76.

———— Stability and change in the inheritance of behaviour in rats: a further analysis of statistics from a diallel cross. *Proceedings of the Royal Society, Series B*, 1966, *165*, 450–72.

BRODY, D. Twin resemblances in mechanical ability, with reference to the effects of practice on performance. *Child Development*, 1937, *8*, 207–16.

BRODY, E. G. Genetic basis of spontaneous activity in the albino rat. *Comparative Psychology Monographs*, 1942, *17*, No. 5: 1–24.

BROWN, F. A., JR., and B. U. HALL. The directive influence of light upon Drosophila melanogaster and some of its eye mutants. *Journal of Experimental Zoology*, 1936, *74*, 205–21.

BRUELL, J. H. Dominance and segregation in the inheritance of quantitative behaviour in mice. *In* E. L. BLISS, (ed.), *Roots of behavior*. New York: Harper & Row, 1962.

———— Behavioral heterosis. *In* J. HIRSCH, (ed.), *Behavior-genetic analysis*. New York: McGraw-Hill, 1967.

BURT, C. The inheritance of mental ability. *American Psychologist*, 1958, *13*, 1–15.

———— The genetic determinations of differences in intelligence: a study of monozygotic twins reared together and reared apart. *British Journal of Psychology*, 1966, *57*, 137–53.

————, and M. HOWARD. The multifactorial theory of inheritance and its application to intelligence. *British Journal of Statistical Psychology*, 1956, *9*, 95–131.

CARTER, H. D. Twin similarities in emotional traits. *Character and Personality*, 1935, *4*, 61–78.

CATTELL, R. B. The multiple abstract variance analysis equations and solutions: for nature-nurture research on continuous variables. *Psychological Review*, 1960, *67*, 353–72.

———— *The scientific analysis of personality*. Baltimore: Penguin, 1965.

————, D. B. BLEWETT, and J. R. BELOFF. The inheritance of personality. *American Journal of Human Genetics*, 1955, 7, 76–93.

CATTELL, R. B., G. F. STICE, and N. F. KRISTY. A first approximation to nature-nurture ratios for eleven primary personality factors in objective tests. *Journal of Abnormal and Social Psychology*, 1957, *54*, 143–59.

CLARK, P. J. The heritability of certain anthropometric characters as ascertained from measurement of twins. *American Journal of Human Genetics*, 1956, *8*, 49–54.

COLBERT, E. H. Morphology and behavior. *In* A. ROE, and G. G. SIMPSON (eds.), *Behavior and evolution*. New Haven, Conn.: Yale University Press, 1958.

COLLINS, R. L. Inheritance of avoidance conditioning in mice: a diallel study. *Science*, 1964, *143*, 1188–90.

CONNELL, G. E. ET AL. Phenylketonuria in one of twins. *University of Toronto Medical Journal*, 1962, *39*, 257–64.

CONRAD, K. Erbanlage und Epilepsie. *Zeitschrift der Gesellschaft für Neurologie und Psychiatrie*, 1935, *153*, 271–326.

COOPER, R. M., and J. P. ZUBEK. Effects of enriched and restricted early environment on the learning ability of bright and dull rats. *Canadian Journal of Psychology*, 1958, *12*, 159–64.

CUMMINS, H., and C. MIDLO. *Finger prints, palms and soles; an introduction to dermatoglyphics*. New York: Dover, 1961.

DA FONSECA, K. F. *Analise heredoclinica das perturbacoes afectivas atraves de 60 pares de gémeos*. Oporto: Faculdade de Medicina, 1959.

DARLINGTON, C. D. Psychology, genetics and the process of history. *British Journal of Psychology*, 1963, *54*, 293–98.

DARWIN, C. *The expression of the emotions in man and animals*. London: John Murray, 1872.

DAVIS, E. A. Linguistic skill in twins, singletons with siblings and only children from age five to ten years. *University of Minnesota Institute for Child Welfare Monograph Series*, 1937, No. 14.

DAY, E. The development of language in twins. Comparison of twins and single children. *Child Development*, 1932, *3*, 179–99.

DEFRIES, J. C. Quantitative genetics and behavior: overview and perspective. *In* J. HIRSCH (ed.), *Behavior-genetic analysis*. New York: McGraw-Hill, 1967.

DRILLIEN, C. M. *The growth and development of the prematurely born infant*. Baltimore: Williams & Wilkins, 1964.

DUNN, H. G. ET AL. Mental retardation as a sexed-linked defect. *American Journal of Mental Deficiency*, 1963, *67*, 827–48.

ERIKSON, A. W., and J. FELLMAN. Twinning in relation to marital status of the mother. *Acta Genetica et Statistica Medica*, 1967, *17*, 385–98.

ERLENMEYER-KIMLING, L., and L. F. JARVIK. Genetics and intelligence: a review. *Science*, 1963, *142*, 147–79.

ESSEN-MOLLER, E. Psychiatrische Untersuchungen an eine Serie von Zwillingen. *Acta Psychiatrica* (Copenhagen), 1941, Suppl. 23.

EYSENCK, H. J. Criterion analysis: an application of the hypothetico-deductive method to factor analysis. *Psychological Review*, 1950, *57*, 38–53.

———— The inheritance of extraversion-introversion. *Acta Psychologica*, 1956, *12*, 95–110.

———— Classifications and the problem of diagnosis. *In* H. J. EYSENCK (ed.), *Handbook of abnormal psychology*, London: Pitman, 1960.

————, and D. B. PRELL. The inheritance of neuroticism. *Journal of Mental Science*, 1951, *97*, 441–65.

FALCONER, D. S. *Introduction to quantitative genetics*. Edinburgh and London: Oliver & Boyd, 1960.

FORSMANN, H., and G. HAMBERT. Chromosomes and antisocial behavior. *Excerpta Criminologica*, 1967, *2*, 113–17.

FULLER, J. L. Measurement of alcohol preference in genetic experiments. *Journal of Comparative and Physiological Psychology*, 1964, *57*, 85–88.

————, C. EASLER, and M. E. SMITH. Inheritance of audiogenic seizure susceptibility in the mouse. *Genetics*, 1950, *35*, 622–32.

FULLER, J. L., and THOMPSON, W. R. *Behavior genetics*. New York: John Wiley, 1960.

GEDDA, L. *Studio dei Gemelli*. Rome: Ediz. Orizzonte Medico, 1951.

GINSBURG, B. E. Genetic parameters in behavioral research. *In* J. HIRSCH (ed.), *Behavior-genetic analysis*. New York: McGraw-Hill, 1967.

————, and D. S. MILLER. Genetic factors in audiogenic seizures. *Colloque International, Centre National de Recherches Scientifiques* (Paris), 1963, No. 112: 217–25.

GINSBURG, B. E., and H. SLATIS. The use of purebred dogs in problems in genetics. *Proceedings Animal Care Panel*, 1962, *12*, 151–56.

GOTTESMAN, I. I. Genetic aspects of intelligent behavior. *In* N. R. ELLIS (ed.), *Handbook of mental deficiency*. New York: McGraw-Hill, 1963a.

———— Heritability of personality: a demonstration. *Psychological Monographs*, 1963b, 77, (9): Whole No. 572.

———— Personality and natural selection. *In* S. G. VANDENBERG (ed.), *Methods and goals in human behavior genetics*. Chicago: Aldine, 1965.

———— Genetic variance in adaptive personality traits. *Journal of Child Psychology and Psychiatry*, 1966, 7, 199–208.

————, and SHIELDS, J. Contributions of twin studies to perspectives on schizophrenia. *In* B. A. MAHER (ed.), *Experimental personality research*. New York: Academic, 1966.

———— A polygenic theory of schizophrenia. *Proceedings of the National Academy of Science*, 1967, *58*, 199–205.

HALL, C. S. The inheritance of emotionality. *Sigma Xi Quarterly*, 1938, *26*, 17–27.

——— The genetics of behavior. *In* s. s. STEVENS (ed.), *Handbook of experimental psychology*. New York: John Wiley, 1951.

HALVARD, B., and M. HAUGE. Hereditary factors elucidated by twin studies. *In* J. V. NELL, M. W. SHAW, and w. J. SCHULL (eds.), *Genetics and the epidemiology of chronic diseases*. Washington, D.C.: U.S. Dept. of Health, Education and Welfare, 1965.

HERON, W. T. The inheritance of maze-learning ability in rats. *Journal of Comparative Psychology*, 1935, *19*, 77–89.

——— The inheritance of brightness and dullness in maze-learning ability in the rat. *Journal of Genetic Psychology*, 1941, *59*, 41–49.

HERTER, K. Das thermotaktische optimum bei Nagetieren, ein mendelndes Art-und Rassenmarkmal. *Zeitschrift für vergleichende Physiologie*, 1936, *23*, 605–50.

HESTON, L. L. Psychiatric disorders in foster home reared children of schizophrenic mothers. *British Journal of Psychiatry*, 1966, *112*, 819–25.

HIRSCH, J. (ed.). *Behavior-genetic analysis*. New York: McGraw-Hill, 1967*a*.

——— Behavior-genetic or "experimental" analysis: the challenge of science versus the lure of technology. *American Psychologist*, 1967*b*, *22*, 118–30.

HSIA, D. Y. Y. The hereditary metabolic diseases. *In* J. HIRSCH (ed.), *Behavior-genetic analysis*. New York: McGraw-Hill, 1967.

———, K. V. QUINN, and R. S. PAINE. A one-year controlled study of the effect of low-phenylalaline diet on phenylketonuria. *Pediatrics*, 1958, *21*, 178–202.

HUSÉN, T. Abilities of twins. *Scandinavian Journal of Psychology*, 1960, *1*, 125–35.

——— Intra-pair similarities in the school achievements of twins. *Scandinavian Journal of Psychology*, 1963, *4*, 108–14.

INOUYE, E. Similarity and dissimilarity of schizophrenia in twins. *Proceedings of the Third World Congress of Psychiatry*, vol. 1. Montreal: University of Toronto Press, 1963.

JACKSON, D. D. A critique of the literature on the genetics of schizophrenia. *In* D. D. JACKSON (ed.), *The etiology of schizophrenia*. New York: Basic Books, 1960.

JACOBS, P. ET AL. The somatic chromosomes in mongolism. *Lancet*, 1959, No. 7071: 710.

JARVIK, L., F. J. KALLMAN, and A. FALEK. Intellectual changes in aged twins. *Journal of Gerontology*, 1962, *17*, 289–94.

JENSEN, A. R. Estimation of the limits of heritability of traits by comparison of monozygotic and dyzygotic twins. *Proceedings of the National Academy of Science*, 1967, *58*, 149–56.

JERVIS, G. A. The genetics of phenylpyruvic oligophrenia. *Journal of Mental Science*, 1939, *85*, 719–62.

——— Phenylpyruvic Oligophrenia (Phenylketonuria). *Research Publications of the Association for Mental and Nervous Disease*, 1954, *33*, 259–82.

JOHNSON, R. C. Similarity in IQ of separated identical twins as related to length of time spent in same environment. *Child Development*, 1963, *34*, 745–49.

JONES, H. E. Perceived differences among twins. *Eugenics Quarterly*, 1955, *2*, 98–102.

JUDA, A. Neue psychiatrisch-general ogische Untersuchungen an Hilfsschulezwillingen und ihren Familien: I Die Zwillingsprobanden und ihre Partner. *Zeitschrift der Gesellschaft für Neurologie und Psychiatrie*, 1939, *166*, 365–452.

JUDD, L. J., and W. W. BRANDKAMP. Chromosome analyses of adult schizophrenics. *Archives of General Psychiatry*, 1967, *16*, 316–24.

JUEL-NIELSEN, N. *Individual and environment*. Copenhagen: Munksgaard, 1965.

KAIJ, L. Drinking habits in twins. *First International Congress on Human Genetics*, Part 5, *Acta Genetica*, 1957, *7*, 437–41.

KAKIHANA, R., and G. E. MCCLEARN. Development of alcohol preference in BALB/C mice. *Nature*, 1963, *199*, 511–12.

KALLMAN, F. J. *The genetics of schizophrenia*. New York: J. J. Augustin, 1938.

——— The genetic theory of schizophrenia. *American Journal of Psychiatry*, 1946, *103*, 309–22.

——— The genetics of psychoses: an analysis of 1,232 twin index families. *Rapports du Congrés International de Psychiatrie*, vol. 6. Paris: Hermann, 1950, pp. 1–27.

——— Comparative twin studies on the genetic aspects of male homosexuality. *Journal of Nervous and Mental Disorders*, 1952, *115*, 283–98.

——— *Heredity in health and mental disorder*. New York: Norton, 1953.

——— Genetic principles in manic-depressive psychoses. *In* P. H. HOCH and J. ZUBIN (eds.), *Depression*. New York: Grune & Stratton, 1954.

———, and M. M. ANASTASIO. Twin studies on the psychopathology of suicide. *Journal of Nervous and Mental Disorders*, 1947, *105*, 40–45.

KALLMAN, F. J., and M. ROTH. Genetic aspects of preadolescent schizophrenia. *American Journal of Psychiatry*, 1956, *112*, 599–606.

KOCH, H. *Twins and twin relations*. Chicago: University of Chicago Press, 1966.

KRANZ, H. *Lebensschicksale krimineller Zwillinge*. Berlin: Springer, 1936.

——— Untersuchungen an Zwillingen in Fürsorgeerziehungsanstalten. *Z. indukt. Abstamm. Vererbungslehre*, 1937, *73*, 508–12.

KRINGLEN, E. Schizophrenia in male monozygotic twins. *Acta Psychiatrica Scandinavica*, 1964, *40*, Suppl. 178.

——— Twin study in schizophrenia. *Excerpta Medica International Congrès des Sciences*, 1966, No. 124, *Proceedings 1st International Congress Academy Psychosomatic Medicine*, Palma de Mallorca.

KRUSHINSKI, L. V. *Animal behavior: its normal and abnormal development* (Basil Haigh trans.) New York: Consultants Bureau, 1962.

KUPPUSAWNY, B. Laws of heredity in relation to general mental ability. *Journal of Genetic Psychology*, 1947, *36*, 29–43.

LANGE, J. *Crime as destiny*. London: Allen & Unwin, 1931.

LEJEUNE, J., R. TURPIN, and M. GAUTIER. Le mongolisme, premier example d'aberration autosomique humaine. *Annales Génétiques*, 1959, *2*, 41–49.

LENNOX, W. G., and D. H. JOLLY. Seizures, brain waves and intelligence tests of epileptic twins. *Research Publications of the Association for Nervous and Mental Disorders*, 1954, *33*, 325–45.

LEWIS, D. G. Commentary on "the genetic determination of differences in intelligence: a study of monozygotic twins reared together and apart" by Cyril Burt. *British Journal of Psychology*, 1966, *57*, 431–33.

LILIENFELD, A., and B. PASAMANICK. A study of variations in the frequency of twin births by race and socio-economic status. *American Journal of Human Genetics*, 1955, *7*, 204–17.

LOEHLIN, J. C. A heredity-environment analysis of personality inventory data. *In* S. G. VANDENBERG (ed.) *Methods and goals in behavior genetics*. New York: Academic, 1965.

——— Psychological genetics, from the study of human behavior. *In* R. B. CATTELL (ed.), *Handbook of modern personality theory*. Chicago: Aldine, 1969.

———, and S. G. VANDENBERG. *Genetic and environmental components in the covariations of cognitive abilities: an additive model*. Research report from the Louisville Twin Study, Child Development Unit, Department of Pediatrics, University of Louisville, 1966.

LUXENBURGER, H. Demographische und psychiatrische untersuchungen in der engeren biologischen Familie von Paralytikerehegatten. *Z. ges. Neurologie Psychiatrie*, 1928, *112*, 331–491.

——— Das zirkulare Irresein. *In* A. GUTT (ed.) *Handbuch der Erbkrankheiten*, vol. 4. Leipzig: Thieme, 1942.

MCCLEARN, G. E. Genotype and mouse activity. *Journal of Comparative and Physiological Psychology*, 1961, *54*, 674–76.

——— The inheritance of behavior. *In* L. POSTMAN (ed.), *Psychology in the making*. New York: Knopf, 1963.

——— Genotype and mouse behaviour. In *Genetics today*, 3, Proceedings of the 11th International Congress on Genetics, The Hague. Oxford: Pergamon, 1965.

——— Genes, generality and behavior research. In Hirsch, J. (ed.), *Behavior-genetic analysis*. New York: McGraw-Hill, 1967.

——— ET AL. Alcohol dehydrogenase activity and previous ethanol consumption in mice. *Nature*, 1964, *203* (4946): 793–94.

MCCLEARN, G. E., and D. A. RODGERS. Genetic factors in alcohol preference of laboratory mice. *Journal of Comparative and Physiological Psychology*, 1961, *54*, 116–19.

MCGILL, W. B. Sexual behavior in three inbred strains of mice. *Behaviour*, 1962, *19*, 341–50.

MCLEOD, H. *An experimental study of the inheritance of introversion-extraversion.* (Ph. D. thesis, University of London Library, 1954.)

MCNEMAR, Q. Twin resemblances in motor skills and the effect of practice thereon. *Journal of Genetic Psychology*, 1933, *42*, 70–79.

MANNING, A. Selection for mating speed in drosophila melanogaster based on the behavior of one sex. *Animal Behavior*, 1963, *11*, 116–20.

—— Genes and the evolution of insect behavior. *In* J. HIRSCH (ed.), *Behavior-genetic analysis.* New York: McGraw-Hill, 1967.

MARDONES, R. J., N. M. SEGOVIA, and A. D. HEDERRA. Heredity of experimental alcohol preference in rats. II. Coefficient of heredity. *Quarterly Journal of Studies on Alcohol*, 1953, *14*, 1–2.

MILGRAM, S. Nationality and conformity. *Scientific American*, 1961, *205*, 45–51.

MONCRIEFF, A., and R. H. WILKINSON. Further experiences in the treatment of phenylketonuria. *British Medical Journal*, 1961, *5228*, 763–67.

MUNRO, T. A. Phenylketonuria. Data on 47 British families. *Annales Eugenics*, 1947, *14*, 60–88.

—— Depressive illness in twins. *Acta Psychiatrica Scandinavica*, 1965, *41*, 111–16.

NEWMAN, H. H., F. N. FREEMAN, and K. J. HOLZINGER. *Twins: a study of heredity and environment.* Chicago: University of Chicago Press, 1937.

NICHOLS, R. C. The resemblance of twins in personality and interests. *National Merit Scholarship Corporation Research Reports*, 1966, *2*, No. 8: 1–23.

OSBORNE, R. H., and F. V. DEGEORGE. *Genetic basis of morphological variations: an evaluation and application.* Cambridge, Mass: Harvard University Press, 1959.

OSMOND, H., and A. HOFFER. A comprehensive theory of schizophrenia. *International Journal of Neuropsychiatry*, 1966, *2*, 302–9.

PARTANEN, J., K. BRUUN, and T. MARKKANEN. *Inheritance of drinking behaviour: a study of intelligence, personality and use of alcohol of adult twins.* Helsinki: Finnish Foundation for Alcohol Studies, 1966.

PIRE, G. Application des techniques sociometriques à l'étude des jumeaux. *Enfance*, 1966, *1*, 23–48.

PLEYDELL, M. J. Huntington's chorea in Northamptonshire. *British Medical Journal*, 1954, *2*, 1121–28.

POLANI, P. E. Chromosome abnormalities as a cause of defective development. *In* D. RICHTER ET AL. (eds.), *Aspects of psychiatric research.* London: Oxford University Press, 1962.

PORTENIER, L. Twinning as a factor influencing personality. *Journal of Educational Psychology*, 1939, *30*, 542–47.

RAINER, J. D. The contributions of Franz Josef Kallman to the genetics of schizophrenia. *Behavioral Science*, 1966, *11*, 413–37.

RAPHAEL, T., and M. SHAW. Chromosome studies in schizophrenia. *Journal of the American Medical Association*, 1963, *183*, 1022.

REDDING, A., and K. HIRSCHHORN. Guide to human chromosome defects. *Birth defects original articles series*, 1968, 4, No. 4. New York: The National Foundation, March of Dimes.

REITMAN, E. E., A. LINNSTAEDTER, and A. D. POKORNY. Developmental analysis of schizophrenia in identical twins. *Archives of General Psychiatry*, 1964, *10*, 131–37.

REZNIKOFF, M., and M. HONEYMAN. MMPI profiles of monozygotic and dizygotic twin pairs. *Journal of Consulting Psychology*, 1967, *31*, 100. *See* Vandenberg, 1966 (research report) for quantitative data.

RHINE, J. B., and W. MCDOUGALL. Third report on a Lamarckian experiment. *British Journal of Psychology*, 1933, *24*, 213–35.

RICHTER, C. P. Alcohol as food. *Quarterly Journal of Studies on Alcohol*, 1941, *1*, 650–62.

ROBERTS, R. C. Some concepts and methods in quantitative genetics. *In* J. HIRSCH (ed.), *Behavior-genetic analysis.* New York: McGraw-Hill, 1967.

RODGERS, D. A. Paper in symposium. *The mouse as a model.* Washington: American Psychological Association, 1967.

—— ET AL. Alcohol preference as a function of its caloric utility in mice. *Journal of Comparative and Physiological Psychology*, 1963, *56*, 666–72.

ROSANOFF, A. J. ET AL. The etiology of so-called schizophrenic psychoses with special reference to their occurrence in twins. *Journal of Nervous and Mental Disorders*, 1959, *129*, 1–10.

ROSANOFF, A. J., L. M. HANDY, and I. R. PLESSET. The etiology of manic-depressive syndromes with special reference to their occurrence in twins. *American Journal of Psychiatry*, 1935, *91*, 225–362.

—— The etiology of mental deficiency with special reference to its occurrence in twins. *Psychology Monographs*, 1937a, *48*, No. 216.

—— The etiology of mental deficiency. *Psychology Monographs*, 1937b, *216*, 1–137.

—— The etiology of child behavior difficulties, juvenile delinquency and adult criminality, with special reference to their occurrence in twins. *Psychiatry Monographs*, Dept. of Institutions, Sacramento, 1941.

ROSANOFF, A. J., L. M. HANDY, and J. A. ROSANOFF. Etiology of epilepsy with special reference to its occurrence in twins. *Archives of Neurological Psychiatry, Chicago*, 1934a, *31*, 1165–93.

—— Criminality and delinquency in twins. *Journal of Criminal Law and Criminology*, 1934b, *24*, 923–34.

ROSENTHAL, D. Some factors associated with concordance and discordance with respect to schizophrenia in monozygotic twins. *Journal of Nervous and Mental Disorders*, 1959, *129*, 1–10.

—— Comparison of identity and the frequency of schizophrenia in twins. *Archives of General Psychiatry*, 1960, *3*, 297–304.

—— Sex distribution and the severity of illness among samples of schizophrenic twins. *Journal of Psychiatric Research*, 1961, *1*, 26–36.

—— Problems of sampling and diagnosis in the major twin studies of schizophrenia. *Journal of Psychiatric Research*, 1962a, *1*, 116–34.

—— Familial concordance by sex with respect to schizophrenia. *Psychological Bulletin*, 1962b, *59*, 401–21.

—— The offspring of schizophrenic couples. *Journal of Psychiatric Research*, 1966, *4*, 169–88.

—— The genetics of intelligence and personality. *In* D. C. GLASS (ed.), *Genetics.* New York: Rockefeller University Press, 1968.

——, and S. S. KETY (eds.). *The transmission of schizophrenia.* London: Pergamon, 1968.

ROTHENBUHLER, W. C. Genetics of a behavior difference in honey bees. *Proceedings of the 10th International Congress on Genetics*, Montreal, 1958, *2*, 242.

—— Behaviour genetics of nest cleaning in honey bees. I. Response of four inbred lines to disease-killed brood. *Animal Behaviour*, 1964a, *12*, 578–83.

—— Behaviour genetics of nest cleaning in honey bees. IV. Response of F_1 and backcross generations to disease-killed brood. *American Zoologist*, 1964b, *4*, 111–23.

—— Genetics and evolutionary considerations of social behavior of honey bees and some related insects. *In* J. HIRSCH (ed.), *Behavior-genetic analysis.* New York: McGraw-Hill, 1967.

ROYCE, J. R., and M. COVINGTON. Genetic differences in the avoidance conditioning of mice. *Journal of Comparative and Physiological Psychology*, 1960, *53*, 197–200.

RUNDQUIST, E. A. The inheritance of spontaneous activity in rats. *Journal of Comparative Psychology*, 1933, *16*, 415–38.

RUSSELL, E. Cerebral palsied twins. *Archives of Disease in Childhood*, 1961, *36*, 328–36.

RUTTER, M., S. KORN, and H. G. BIRCH. Genetic and environmental factors in the development of "primary reaction patterns." *British Journal of Social and Clinical Psychology*, 1963, *2*, 161–73.

SCARR, S. *Environmental bias in twin studies.* (Paper read at the Second International Conference on Human Behaviour Genetics, Louisville, 1966.)

SCHEINFELD, A., and J. SCHACHTER. Bio-social effects upon twinning incidences. *Proceedings of the 11th International Congress on Human Genetics*, 1963, Vol. 1.

SCHLESINGER, K., and R. WIMER. Genotype and conditioned avoidance learning in the mouse. *Journal of Comparative and Physiological Psychology*, 1967, *63*, 139–41.

SCOTT, J. P., and J. L. FULLER. *Genetics and the social behavior of the dog.* Chicago: University of Chicago Press, 1965.

SEARLE, L. V. The organization of hereditary man-brightness and mouse-dullness. *Genetic Psychology Monographs*, 1949, *39*, 279–325.

SERGOVICH, F. R. Cytogenetic practice in a mental retardation clinic. *Canadian Psychiatric Association Journal*, 1967, *12*, 35–52.

SHIELDS, J. Personality differences and neurotic traits in normal twin school children. *Eugenics Review*, 1954, *45*, 213–45.

—— *Monozygotic twins brought up apart and brought up together.* London: Oxford University Press, 1962.

SIEMENS, H. W. *Die Zwillingspathologie.* Berlin: Springer, 1924.

SLATER, E. Zur Erbpathologie des manisch-depressiven Irreseins: die Eltern und Kinder von Manisch-Depressiven. *Zeitschrift der Gesellschaft für Neurologie und Psychiatrie,* 1938, *163,* 1–47.

—— Psychotic and neurotic illnesses in twins. *Medical Research Council, Special Report* Series No. 278. London: HMSO, 1953.

——, and J. SHIELDS, Relation of genetics to population studies. *Nature,* 1955, *176,* 532–33.

SMITH, R. T. A comparison of socioenvironmental factors in monozygotic and dizygotic twins, testing an assumption. *In* S. G. VANDENBERG (ed.), *Goals and methods in behavior genetics.* New York: Academic, 1965.

SMITH, S. M., and C. S. PENROSE. Monozygotic and dizygotic twin diagnosis. *Annals of Human Genetics,* 1955, *19,* 273–89.

SNYDER, L. H. The inheritance of taste deficiency in man. *Ohio Journal of Science,* 1932, *32,* 436–40.

STAFFORD, R. E. New techniques in analyzing parent-child test scores for evidence of hereditary components. *In* S. G. VANDENBERG (ed.), *Methods and goals in behavior genetics.* Chicago: Aldine, 1965a.

—— *Nonparametric analysis of twin data with the Mann-Whitney U Test.* Research report from the Louisville Twin Study, Child Development Unit, Department of Pediatrics, University of Louisville School of Medicine, 1965b.

STENSTEDT, A. A study in manic-depressive psychosis. *Acta Psychiatrica* (Copenhagen), 1952, Suppl. 79.

STUMPFL, F. *Die Ursprünge des Verbrechens dargestellt am Lebenslauf von Zwillingen.* Leipzig: Thieme, 1936.

THOMPSON, W. R. The inheritance and development of intelligence. *Proceedings of the Association on Research on Nervous and Mental Disease,* 1954, *33,* 209–31.

—— Multivariate experiment in behavior genetics. *In* R. B. CATTELL (ed.), *Handbook of multivariate experimental psychology.* Skokie, Ill.: Rand McNally, 1966.

——, and J. L. FULLER. The inheritance of activity in the mouse. *American Psychologist,* 1957, *12,* 433.

TIENARI, P. Psychiatric illnesses in identical twins. *Acta Psychiatrica Scandinavica,* 1963, *39,* Suppl. 171.

TJIO, J. H., and A. LEVAN. The chromosome member in man. *Hereditas,* 1956, *42,* 1–6.

TOLMAN, E. C. The inheritance of maze learning in rats. *Journal of Comparative Psychology,* 1924, *4,* 1–18.

TRYON, R. C. Studies in individual differences in maze ability. VII. The specific components of maze ability and a general theory of psychological components. *Journal of Comparative and Physiological Psychology,* 1940, *30,* 283–335.

—— Individual differences. *In* F. A. MOSS (ed.), *Comparative psychology.* Englewood Cliffs, N.J.: Prentice-Hall, 1942.

VANDENBERG, S. G. The hereditary abilities study; hereditary components in a psychological test battery. *American Journal of Human Genetics,* 1962, *14,* 220–37.

—— Innate abilities: one or many? *Acta Geneticae Medicae et Gemellologiae,* 1965, *14,* 41–47.

—— Contributions of twin research to psychology. *Psychological Bulletin,* 1966a, *66,* 327–52.

—— *Hereditary factors in normal personality traits (as measured by inventories).* Research report from the Louisville Twin Study, Child Development Unit, Department of Pediatrics, University of Louisville, 1966b.

—— (ed.). *Methods and goals in human behavior genetics.* New York: Academic, 1965.

—— ET AL. *The Louisville twin study.* Research report from the Louisville Twin Study, Child Development Unit, Department of Pediatrics, University of Louisville, 1966.

VANDENBERG, S. G., and R. C. JOHNSON. *Further evidence on the relation between age of separation and similarity in IQ among pairs of separated identical twins.* Research report from the Louisville Twin Study, Child Development Unit, Department of Pediatrics, University of Louisville, 1966.

VICARI, E. M. Mode of inheritance of reaction time and degree of learning in mice. *Journal of Experimental Zoology,* 1929, *54,* 31–88.

WHERRY, R. J. Determination of the specific components of maze-ability for Tryon's bright and dull rats by means of factorial analysis. *Journal of Comparative Psychology,* 1941, *32,* 237–52.

WILDE, G. J. S. Inheritance of personality traits: an investigation into the hereditary determination of neurotic instability, extraversion, and other personality traits by means of a questionnaire administered to twins. *Acta Psychologica,* 1964, *22,* 37–51.

—— Trait description and measurement by personality questionnaires. *In* R. B. CATTELL (ed.), *Handbook of modern personality theory.* Chicago: Aldine, 1969a.

—— An experimental study of mutual person perception and behavioral conformity in monozygotic and dizygotic twins. (Paper presented at the First International Symposium on Twin Studies, Rome, September, 1969b.)

WILLIAMS, R. J., L. J. BERRY, and E. BEERSTECHER JR. Individual metabolic patterns, alcoholism, genotropic diseases. *Proceedings of the National Academy of Sciences, Washington,* 1949, *35,* 265–71.

—— The concept of genotropic disease. *Lancet,* 1950, *258,* 287–89.

WILLIAMS, R. J., R. B. PELTON, and L. L. ROGERS. Dietary deficiencies in animals in relation to voluntary alcohol and sugar consumption. *Quarterly Journal of Studies on Alcohol,* 1955, *16,* 234–44.

WILSON, P. T. A study of twins with special reference to heredity as a factor determining differences in environment. *Human Biology,* 1934, *6,* 324–54.

WITT, G. M., and C. S. HALL. The genetics of audiogenic seizures in the house mouse. *Journal of Comparative and Physiological Psychology,* 1949, *42,* 58–63.

WRIGHT, S. The genetics of quantitative variability. *In* E. C. R. REEVE and C. H. WADDINGTON (eds.), *Quantitative inheritance.* London: Her Majesty's Stationery Office, 1952.

YOUNG, W. C., and J. A. GRUNT. The pattern and measurement of sexual behavior in the male guinea pig. *Journal of Comparative and Physiological Psychology,* 1951, *44,* 492–500.

ZAZZO, R. *Les Jumeauz, le couple et la personne* (2 vols.). Paris: Presses Universitaires de France, 1960.

Somatological development names an area of knowledge no less extensive than psychological development. It encompasses ontogenetic and phylogenetic changes of organisms in regard to anatomical and physiological variables. Many comparative zoologists investigate evolutionary elaborations and simplifications of structures and functions from unicellular species, through primitive fishes and generalized reptiles to placental mammals. Many human zoologists study modifications of biological components and processes from formation of the zygote, through childhood and adolescence, to senescence.

The vast quantity of available ontogenetic research on *Homo sapiens* deals with innumerable facets of development including (1) physiological changes associated with placentation, transition from prenatal to postnatal life, puberty, and menopause, and (2) anatomical sequences of alteration in body size, body form, body composition, number of structural units, and position of structures. The space limits of a unitary chapter on somatological development necessitate great selectivity of content respecting breadth and depth of the topics discussed.

In the main, the present chapter treats human anatomical development during the first twenty years of ontogeny. Little attention is given to gerontological, phylogenetic, or physiological matters beyond reference in the next section to illustrative modifications during adulthood and old age, followed later in the chapter by discussions of change in body size during the last century, and variation in the time of first menstruation.

Human Anatomical Ontogenesis

Human anatomical ontogenesis comprises all of the structural changes that human organisms undergo between the beginning of prenatal life and the close of senility. Although an immense amount of knowledge falls within this province, it cannot be claimed that every variety of structural change has been identified and studied. There is considerable accumulated evidence of changes occurring in the size, form, kind, number, position, and composition of cells, tissues, and organs.

H. V. Meredith

Somatological Development

12

Changes in Kind. The life span of a human individual commences with the merging of two cells of different kinds. Following constitution of the zygote, there are many changes in kind. Embryonic ectoderm is replaced by nerve cells, epidermis, nail tissue, and tooth enamel. Mesenchyme is replaced by muscle tissue, cartilage, bone, and tooth dentin. The face region acquires eyes and ears, nose and lips, tongue and teeth, eyebrows and eyelashes. The trunk region acquires heart and stomach, liver and lungs, shoulders and hips, and outgrowths of upper and lower limbs (Arey 1965).

Some kinds of structural components are found at most stages of ontogeny. Nerve cells are present from the first month, bone cells from the second month, and nail cells from the third month. The heart is present from the first month, limbs from the second month, and body hair from the fourth month.

Other kinds of structural components are transitory. Gill arches appear near the end of the first month and are present for no more than three weeks. Between the second and fourth months an external tail emerges and is submerged. In the period from the third to fifth months touch pads on the fingers are acquired and lost. At birth the umbilical cord is discarded, in childhood the deciduous dentition is shed, and during adolescence and early adulthood the cartilaginous metaphyses of the skeleton are replaced with bone (Watson and Lowrey 1967).

Changes in Number. In its earliest ontogenetic state the human being is a unicellular zygote; by adulthood it has become an organism of several trillion cells.

Some cells are stable for long periods, others are highly transient. For nerve cells there is rapid increase in number during early prenatal life; little numerical change during the first four decades of postnatal life; and cellular decrease exceeding 20 percent during late adulthood and senility (Shock 1962). Numerical increase of striated muscle cells during fetal life, with stability from infancy into adulthood, is a close variant of the pattern for nerve cells. In contrast, the outer layer of human skin is renewed about once a month (Medawar 1957). There is similar transience for blood cells; from the first month of prenatal life until death, blood cell count is the product of simultaneous cell production and dissolution, with a given red blood corpuscle living about four months.

During the middle third of the prenatal period taste receptors increase in number on the tongue, tonsils, palate, and parts of the esophagus. In late prenatal life and early childhood there is decrease in the number of taste receptors to the extent that usually none remain except on the tongue. There is increase in the number of developing teeth from the embryonic period into childhood; around five years of age the child's dentition consists of 48 to 52 teeth in varying stages of development. A decade later the 20 deciduous teeth have been discarded, and with the passing years there is further numerical reduction. The number of bone masses does not gradually progress to some maximum, rather there is staggered bone formation and coalescence such as to produce overall increase for the period from the second prenatal month to puberty and decrease thereafter. At puberty the count of bone masses approximates 350; in early adulthood it is near 200.

Changes in Position. During ontogeny cells or portions of cells often move to new sites, and organs or parts of organs frequently tilt, rotate, or shift locations (Moscona 1961). At the cell level, examples are the essentially migratory blood cells, and the nerve fibers that extend out to muscles and skin of the fingers and toes.

At the organ level, there are movements in many directions. Initially the heart lies in the vicinity of the lower part of the face. Its positional changes include downward and backward migration, counterclockwise rotation, and oblique tilting from right to left. When the stomach first is identifiable, it is situated high in the trunk. Its repositionings include movement to a lower level, rotation clockwise, and oblique tipping from left to right. In early prenatal life the stomach has a vertical orientation, in early childhood it lies almost transversely, and in late childhood it returns to a predominantly vertical orientation.

The teeth first travel deeply into the jaws, then reverse directions and erupt into the oral cavity. Combined with these largely vertical excursions there are tooth rotations, lateral movements, and migrations in oblique paths (Brodie 1934). The ribs are formed in a nearly horizontal plane and subsequently tilt downward at the front. The ovaries move from their original vertical orientation into a transverse position; they also revolve about the uterine tubes and come to rest below them. There is migration of the testes from the abdomen, through the pelvic cavity, into the scrotum. A gradual shift occurs in the positional relations of the vertebral column and larynx; the level of the cricoid cartilage approximates the top of the fourth cervical vertebra in the newborn, the bottom of the fifth cervical vertebra in early adulthood, and the top of the seventh cervical vertebra in late adulthood.

In the prenatal period, both pairs of limbs undergo torsion of 90 degrees; for the upper limbs there is turning at the shoulders so that the elbows are rotated from an outward position to a posterior position, for the lower limbs there is turning at the hips so that the knees are brought to the front. The feet first lie along the same axes as the shafts of the legs; during the last half of the second prenatal month they turn out of the leg planes and approach a right-angle relationship with the legs. When the great toes are individuated, each diverges from the four other toes and has its plantar surface turned toward them; gradually each moves to a position parallel with the other toes and rotates sufficiently to bring its plantar surface into the plane of the soles.

Changes in Size. During the first few days after formation of the zygote no increase occurs in the size of the organism; the number of cells increases without any enlargement of overall size (Streeter 1937). There follow a great variety of size changes in respect to direction, rate, and duration.

Increase in size is too apparent to require illustration. By contrast, decreases in size are either unfamiliar or overlooked to the degree that a listing of examples is appropriate. The external tail becomes progressively smaller during the last half of the second prenatal month. A short time later there are decreases in the size of the Mullerian ducts in boys and the mesonephric ducts in girls. During the last third of the prenatal period, Hunter's gubernacula shorten in boys by 75 percent, pulling the testes down into the scrotum.

Body weight decreases by about six percent during the first few days after birth. There also are neonatal decreases in size of the suprarenal glands, mammary glands, and female genitalia.

Thickness of the subcutaneous adipose tissue on the thorax and calf decreases in the period between the middle of the first postnatal year and the sixth year. Deciduous teeth undergo reduction in length for many months prior to being shed. There are decreases in the size of the thymus gland from late childhood through adolescence, and in the size of the pharyngeal tonsil in early adulthood. Later adulthood brings shrinkage of cerebellar fibers, and reduced cross-sectional area of head hairs. In senility there are decreases in thickness of the skin, volume of the striated muscles, weight of the liver, and size of the corpus callosum (Scammon 1930; Watson and Lowrey 1967).

Some trends of change in size are complex. Size of the female uterus increases in the fetal period, decreases during the first month after birth, remains almost stationary throughout infancy and early childhood, increases in late childhood and adolescence, enters a fairly stable period except for fluctuations with pregnancies, and decreases following the menopause. The alveolar processes of the jaws increase in height preceding and during eruption of deciduous teeth, remain fairly constant in height over the period they are supporting these teeth, show regional decreases as deciduous teeth are exfoliated, increase again with permanent tooth eruption, and decrease markedly with loss of the latter.

Frequently when anatomic structures change in size there is increase in one region and decrease in another. The lower jaw changes in its breadth by deposition on the lateral surfaces and absorption along its mesial surfaces. For the shaft of the thigh bone, the interplay of increase at the periphery and decrease at the center is such that its inner cavity in adulthood is as large as the entire shaft at birth.

Changes in Form. Two weeks after fertilization the human organism has the shape of an ovoidal disc, the widest part being toward one end. Roughly 65 percent of the disc is the head region and 35 percent the trunk region. Three weeks later the organism has become cylindroid, with a large head flexed far forward and a thorax that is 50 percent greater in depth than in breadth. Aspects of body configuration at the end of the second prenatal month are: breadth of head greater than breadth of shoulders or hips, face and nose each broad and short, almost circular thorax, and length of the limbs shorter than distance from shoulders to hips.

Lower limb length increases from 37 percent of trunk length at the end of the second prenatal month to 87 percent by the middle of the prenatal period. This relation remains almost constant during the last half of the prenatal period, but during infancy and childhood the index rises again. Research on white children has shown that around 12 years of age lower limb length approximates 150 percent of trunk length. Between this time and early adulthood predominance of the lower limbs decreases, the index declining to less than 145 percent (Meredith 1939*a*).

During infancy the cervical and lumbar curvatures of the back become more pronounced, the hands and feet lesss tubby, the nose more elongated and high-bridged. In childhood the abdomen attains a less protruding contour, and the limbs become progressively more slender (Meredith and Sherbina 1951). At adolescence the aperture of the male larynx becomes strongly elliptical, and the aperture of the female pelvis decreases in ellipticity (Greulich and Thoms 1944).

Changes in shape or form are no less varied at the cell and organ levels. Cells elongate, flatten, invaginate, and branch; internal organs bulge, bend, loop, and convolute. The stomach, which undergoes a comparatively simple sequence of alterations in shape, begins as a swelling of one portion of the digestive tube, passes from this capsular form to a configuration resembling a cow's horn, and then changes toward a "J" shape (Arey 1965).

Changes in Composition. Many human tissues and organs exhibit ontogenetic change in texture, resilience, and color. These modifications usually reflect quantitative change in such variables as calcium, protein, water, or pigment.

The iris of the eye is blue or violet in the neonate and, as a result of increasing density of pigment, darkens during the childhood years. In senility there is decrease in the ratio of pigment-carrying cells to pigment-free cells, and eye color becomes lighter. During infancy and childhood there is darkening in skin color; this holds for Negroid as well as non-Negroid persons. Negro infants show rapid increase in skin pigmentation during the first few months after birth, and slower increase thereafter. The hair of the head darkens over the childhood years and lightens (grays) with advancing adulthood. During adult life pigmentation occurs in the dentate nucleus of the cerebellum, and with advanced age the muscle fibers of the heart become densely pigmented.

Underlying the fact that subcutaneous adipose tissue is less resistant to compression in infancy than in childhood, there are reductions in both extracellular water and proportion of oleic acid. Compositional changes in striated muscle between birth and early adulthood include declines of water and chloride content, and a rise in nitrogen content.

During the fetal and infancy periods, the human body undergoes dehydration; the typical decline in total body water is from near 90 percent in the young fetus, through about 73 percent at birth, to around 60 percent at the end of the first postnatal year. During childhood and adolescence there is moderate increase in total body calcium (Forbes 1952).

The inorganic iron content of the liver rises during the fetal and neonatal periods, drops precipitously during the last half of the first postnatal year, remains fairly constant during the second year, then gradually rises throughout childhood. During the adult years the kidneys show an increase in calcium and iron deposits. Changes with age in the composition of the skeleton include a decrease in water content, an increase in nitrogen content, and increases in calcium, phosphorous, and total ash. In old age the brittleness of many bones attests a decrease in the ratio of organic to inorganic components.

Compositional change is a forefront research interest. Present activity ranges from studying changes in bone, muscle, and fat components of the body during the childhood years (Malina and Johnston 1967; Maresh 1961; Tanner 1965) to investigating lessening suppleness of the arteries and declining resiliency of the heart valves over the adult years (Birren 1959; Shock 1962).

Weight and Stature of Fetus, Child, and Adolescent

Average Weight. Human body weight increases from less than one-thousandth of an ounce at the end of the first prenatal month, through approximately one-fourteenth of an ounce at the end of the second month, to about fourteen ounces at the middle of prenatal life (age 19 weeks). Average weight at birth, on full-term North American white infants, regardless of sex, is 7.5 pounds. For birth order subgroups, body weight increases with order of birth; the average first-born neonate is 10 ounces, or 9 percent, lighter than the average fifth-born neonate (Meredith 1950). Typically, newborn white boys are nearly 5 ounces, or 4 percent, heavier than newborn white girls (Aicardi and Rugiati 1965; Štukovský 1963).

Means for body weight on present-day North American white males approximate 7.7 pounds at birth, 44 pounds at age 5 years, 75 pounds at age 10 years, 133 pounds at age 15 years, and 156 pounds at age 20 years. Eighty years ago the average North American white male was lighter in weight by 5 pounds at age 5 years, 13 pounds at age 10 years, fully 30 pounds at age 15 years, and 15 pounds at age 20 years (Meredith 1963). The relation of corresponding secular trends for females is similar, with differences becoming larger from infancy to age 13 years, and declining markedly in late adolescence and early adulthood.

Recent studies of body weight for adolescent girls age 13 years have obtained means (1) below 80 pounds on Burmese, Chinese, and several African Negro samples, and (2) above 100 pounds on British, Czechoslovakian, Norwegian, and American Negro samples (Foll 1958; Lin 1957; Rauh, Schumsky, and Witt 1967; Sundal 1957). Similarly for adolescent boys age 15 years, means below 100 pounds have been found on Bantu, Egyptian, Indian, and Mayan Amerindian samples, in contrast to means above 120 pounds on samples of white boys living in Australia, Sweden, and the United States (Abramson and Ernest 1954; Méndez and Behrhorst 1963; Meyers 1956).

On the average, body weight of North American Negro and white persons is three times greater at age 1 year than at birth, ten times greater at age 10 years than at birth, and 18 times (girls) to 20 times (boys) greater at age 20 years than at birth. Throughout the elementary and secondary school years, averages for body weight in the United States are similar for American Negro and white children (Altman and Dittmer 1962), and two to four pounds higher for children whose fathers are in professional and managerial positions than those whose fathers are unskilled or semiskilled workmen (Meredith 1951).

Increase in human body weight takes place at velocities that decline during infancy and early childhood, remain fairly constant during middle childhood, rise during early adolescence, and decline again during late adolescence. Average age of the adolescent acceleration is later for boys than girls by a biennium (Tuddenham and Snyder 1954).

Individual Differences in Weight. Normal full-term white infants vary in weight at birth from approximately 5 pounds to 11 pounds. At older ages, individual variations in weight among normal United States Negro or white children extend from 30 pounds to 60 pounds at age 5 years, and from 50 pounds to 105 pounds at age 10 years. It follows that among healthy present-day children of a given age, the body weight of one child may be twice that of another.

The typical body weight of today's United States white girl, age 13 years, is near 105 pounds. The lightest 10 percent of these girls weigh less than 82 pounds and the heaviest 10

percent more than 132 pounds. Since the lightest one-tenth fall 24 pounds or more below the typical weight, whereas the heaviest one-tenth fall 28 pounds or more above the typical weight, the weight distribution is "skewed positively." Distributions of human body weight on groups homogeneous for sex, race, and generation are skewed to the right at all ages beyond infancy, the asymmetry increasing from mild manifestation in early childhood to pronounced manifestation during adolescence (Keyfitz 1942; Blommers and Lindquist 1960).

During the first twenty years of postnatal life there are appreciable shifts in individual rankings for body weight and weight velocity. Instances of low positive correlation (r's between 0.2 and 0.4) are as follows: weight at birth with weight at age 5 years, weight at birth with weight in early adulthood, gain in weight between ages 6 years and 9 years with gain between ages 9 years and 18 years, and weight at age 9 years with gain in weight from age 9 years to age 18 years. Higher associations that involve a quadrennium or more include r's between 0.5 and 0.7 for (a) weight at age 5 years with gain in weight from this age to age 9 years, and (b) weight at age 9 years with weight in early adulthood; and r's approximating 0.8 for (a) weight at age 6 years with weight at age 11 years, and (b) weight at age 14 years with early adult weight (Meredith 1965).

Average Stature. Stature is the general term for a measurement of the extended human body from the top of the head (vertex) to the soles of the feet. It is customary to refer to stature measured in the erect position as standing height, and in the recumbent position as vertex-soles length.

During the first month of prenatal life the human organism does not have lower limbs. In the early part of the second month the limbs develop rapidly, and by the close of this month the feet have formed and turned to positions almost at right angles with the legs.

Average stature approximates 1.5 inches at the end of the second prenatal month, 9.5 inches at the middle of the prenatal period, and 19 to 20 inches at birth. The averages for vertex-soles length at birth are (1) somewhat lower for Chinese and Indian infants than white infants of Europe and North America, (2) slightly higher for boys than girls, and (3) a little less for first-born infants than infants of later birth orders (Ghosh and Beri 1962; Meredith 1943; Millis 1954).

Today, the typical stature of North American white males is 20 inches at birth, 41 inches at age 4 years, 51 inches at age 8 years, 66 inches at age 15 years, and 69 inches at age 20 years. Eighty years ago North American males, on the average, were similar in stature at birth; and shorter by 2 inches at age 4 years, 3 inches at age 8 years, 5 inches at age 15 years, and less than 2 inches at age 20 years (Meredith 1963).

At age 8 years, boys presently living in China, India, Japan, New Guinea, Kenya, and the Congo have average statures between 46 inches and 48 inches; while averages between 49 inches and 51 inches typify boys living in Czechoslovakia, Germany, Great Britain, the Netherlands, Poland, Scandinavia, and Switzerland (Chang et al. 1963; Heimendinger 1964). Corresponding averages at age 15 years vary from 58 inches to 63 inches for boys indigenous to the African and Asian regions indicated, and from 64 inches to 67 inches for boys residing in different parts of northern and central Europe (Inoue and Shimizu 1965; Sundal 1957). North American Negro children and youth are similar in height to those of white ancestry, but taller than North American groups of Japanese, Chinese, Navaho Amerindian, and Mexican descent (Altman and Dittmer 1962).

Increase in stature takes place at (1) declining velocities throughout fetal life, infancy, and childhood, (2) rising velocities in early adolescence, and (3) declining velocities in late adolescence. The first rate decline is illustrated by the progressively longer times taken for stature to double itself; average status doubles in the third month of prenatal life, in the last half of the prenatal period, and for North American Negro and white children, in the period between birth and age 4 years. Average increase in stature approximates 50 percent from birth to age 1 year, and 16 percent between ages 1 year and 2 years. By late childhood the average annual increment has declined to less than 4 percent. In no year of adolescence does the average increase reach 5 percent, and rarely does an individual youth gain as much as 8 percent in one adolescent year. After ages 15 years (females) and 17 years (males), average yearly increment in stature falls below 1 percent.

Individual Differences in Stature. Healthy newborn white infants vary in vertex-soles length from slightly less than 18 inches to approximately 22 inches. Individual variations in height among older North American white children and youth extend from 36 inches to 46 inches at age 4 years (both sexes), from 47 inches to 59 inches at age 9 years (both sexes), from 52 inches to 66 inches at age 12 years (females), and from 55 inches to 72 inches at age 14 years (males). The distribution of human stature (within groups homogeneous for age, sex, race, and generation) closely approximates the Gaussian or normal frequency model. On present-day North American white persons of each sex, standard deviations for stature approximate 0.8 inch at birth, 1.3 inches at age 2 years, 2.2 inches at age 6 years, 3.0 inches at 12 years (females), 3.4 inches at 14 years (males) and, at age 20 years, 2.3 inches and 2.5 inches for women and men, respectively (Kasius et al. 1957; O'Brien, Girshick, and Hunt 1941).

Knowledge of an individual's stature at birth is of little value for predicting either his stature five years later or his stature in early adulthood. In both instances there is low positive relationship near $r = 0.3$ (Meredith 1965).

Changes in stature ranking are most marked in infancy, and progressively stabilized in early childhood. In the period between middle and late childhood the stature ranks of children are highly stable (r's on each sex exceed 0.9 for height at ages 5 years and 9 years). During adolescence, as a consequence of individual differences in the timing and intensity of accelerated growth, stature rankings change considerably. In practical terms, healthy children of average stature in middle childhood sometimes become tall or short as adolescents, and conversely, children tall or short in middle childhood sometimes shift ranks in the adolescence period to near average (Meredith 1939b). Whether a child is tall or short in middle childhood, the adolescent spurt can occur early or late; frequencies are slightly greater for tall children accelerating early and short children late. There is no association between the age at which the adolescent spurt occurs and height in adulthood (Meredith 1965).

Components of Stature. Distance from the vertex of the head to the soles of the feet can be regarded as a composite measurement including length of head and neck, length of trunk, and length of lower limbs. Growth rates are different for the three segments.

At the end of the second prenatal month stature is about 45 percent head and neck length, 33 percent trunk length, and 22 percent lower limb length. By the middle of the prenatal period lower limb length has become equal with head and neck length, each of these components constituting 32 percent of stature. At birth, stature is about 25 percent head and neck length, 39 percent trunk length, and 36 percent lower limb length.

During childhood and adolescence head and neck length continues to increase less rapidly than either trunk or limb length. Its contribution to stature declines to slightly less than 19 percent by age 14 years, and remains practically constant thereafter. Lower limb length increases to 48 percent of stature at age 12 years for white females, and 49 percent of stature at age 14 years for white males. There follows a gradual percentage decline, so that in early adulthood this component of stature approximates 47 percent and 48 percent for females and males, respectively. The decline reflects faster growth during late adolescence in trunk length than in lower limb length (Meredith 1939a).

The different components of stature are not highly correlated. One child may have short lower limbs and be average in lengths of head, neck, and trunk; a second may have long lower limbs and be short in lengths of head, neck, and trunk; a third may have a long trunk and be average in lengths of head, neck, and lower limbs; and a fourth may have a short trunk, long lower limbs, and be average in head and neck length. A few children are long, average, or short in all segments. Throughout childhood and adolescence, r's at any given age approximate 0.3 for trunk length with head and neck length, 0.4 for lower limb length with head and neck length, and 0.5 for trunk length with lower limb length (Meredith 1939a).

Distance from the vertex to the lower end of the trunk is known as the sitting height or stem length. Comparative studies at ages 1, 4, 8, and 15 years have shown that stem length in percentage of stature varies in different races. Chinese and Japanese children and youth have long body stems relative to lower limb length, whereas African Bantu children and youth have long lower limbs relative to stem length (Meredith 1968, 1969a, 1969b, 1970).

Height Weight Interpretation Charts. Charts for interpreting height and weight records on United States Negro and white elementary and secondary school children are available from the National Education Association or the American Medical Association. Sample copies can be secured from either source by requesting a "Height Weight Interpretation Folder for Girls" and a "Height Weight Interpretation Folder for Boys." The folders discuss how to measure height and weight, how to transfer pupils' records to the charts, and how the charts can be used (1) to depict somatological development and (2) as an aid in health appraisal.

The chart for a given sex enables teachers, school nurses, physicians, or others to determine, at ages from 4 years to 18 years, whether individual pupils are "short" (below the tenth centile), "moderately short" (between centiles 10 and 30), "average" (between centiles 30 and 70), "moderately tall" (between centiles 70 and 90), or "tall" (above the ninetieth centile). Through the same statistical procedure, the chart provides for describing body weight as light, moderately light, average, moderately heavy, or heavy.

The charts are serviceable for both description and screening (Meredith 1955). In addition to providing a graphic portrayal of height and weight status and progress, they can be used to select individuals who deviate sufficiently in their height-weight ranks, or growth rates, to warrant special study. This second function recognizes the reciprocal roles of somatological screening and health exploration. The charts do not evaluate health; instead, they provide school health personnel with objective leads on *possible* departures from sound health. For example, screening identifies and selects a child of "average height" and "light weight" for intensive examination. The physician, nutritionist, and physical educator then determine whether this child is best appraised as a satisfactorily healthy individual of slender physique, or as an "underweight" child in need of medical therapy, dietary changes, or a modified activity program.

Size and Form of Body Segments

Head and Face. The human head increases in size at a rapid rate in the embryonic period, less rapidly during infancy, and at a slow rate throughout childhood and adolescence. For the average white child, disregarding sex differences, head circumference approximates 1.5 inches two months after formation of the zygote, 7.0 inches near the middle of the prenatal period, 18.2 inches at the end of the first postnatal year, 19.8 inches at age 4 years, and 21.0 inches near age 11 years (Meredith 1966). Averages smaller by 0.5 inches than corresponding averages on white individuals have been obtained from Melanesian and Polynesian infancy studies in Oceania, and from an Indian childhood study in Bombay (Currimbhoy 1963; Malcolm 1952; Malcolm and Massal 1955). Compared with the typical girl, the typical boy is larger in head girth by 0.3 inches at birth and 0.4 inches at all ages beyond infancy. The normal spread of variation among individuals of a given age, sex, and racial group approximates 3.0 inches, i.e., 1.5 inches above and below the mean (Meredith 1946b; Nellhaus 1968).

Average head width is approximately 0.5 inches at age 2 months and 2.0 inches at the middle of prenatal life. This early increments of 300 percent in 2.5 months slows to an increment of less than 5 percent for the entire second decade of life (Meredith 1953). Racial differences are indicated at age 8 years by means of 6.0 inches for Buryat children in Siberia, 5.7 inches for white children in northern and central Europe, and 5.3 inches for Italian and Hutu children in Sardinia and Ruanda, respectively. There is a moderate inverse relation between averages for head width and head depth (distance from forehead to back of head); head width at age 8 years expressed in percentage of head depth is 72 on Sardinian and Hutu children and 89 on Buryat children (Meredith 1969a).

Face width of the typical North American white child approximates 1.3 inches at the middle of the prenatal period, 2.9 inches at birth, and 4.1 inches at the end of the second postnatal year (Meredith 1954; Scammon and Calkins 1929). The 120 percent increase during the last half of prenatal life is far greater than the total increase postnatally after age 2 years; between 2 years and early adulthood face width increases 1.1 inches, or 26 percent, for the average white female, and 1.2 inches, or

31 percent, for the average white male. Typically, males have wider faces than females by 1 percent at birth, 2 percent at age 2 years, 3 percent at age 10 years, and 6 percent in early adulthood. Children of a given sex and racial group increase in face width at differing velocities; during the period between ages 3 years and 15 years, one child may gain as little as 0.7 inches and another as much as 1.1 inches (Meredith 1954; Woods 1950). Width of face increases in relation to width of head. Values for face width in percentage of head width are 69 at the middle of the prenatal period, 78 at birth, 84 at age 10 years, and 90 in early adulthood.

Face height, for North American white people, averages 0.9 inches at the middle of prenatal life, 2.0 inches at birth, 3.4 inches at age 3 years, 4.1 inches at age 10 years, and 4.6 inches in early adulthood (Krogman and Johnston 1965; Smyth and Young 1932). Sex differences increase with age; on the average, males have longer faces than females by less than 0.1 inches at birth and by 0.4 inches in early adulthood (Haataja 1963; Low 1950). Facial form becomes more elongated during childhood and adolescence; relative change is from face height approximately 70 percent of face width at birth, to face height 87 percent of face width in early adulthood (Meredith 1966). At age 5 years, individual differences are distributed from face height two-thirds to nine-tenths of face width. Study of variations across time, over the sexennium from 5 years to 11 years, shows that although increase in the facial index is usual, there are instances of no change. Examples include individuals with face height near 80 percent of face width at each age, and individuals for whom face height relative to face width increases from 81 percent at 5 years to 89 percent at 11 years (Meredith 1960).

Body Trunk. Chest girth, which approximates 50 percent of head girth at age 2 months and 80 percent near the middle of prenatal life, becomes equal with head girth in infancy, and reaches 120 percent of head girth by late childhood or early adolescence. Averages for chest girth at age 1 year fall between 19.0 inches and 18.5 inches for North European and North American white infants, near 18.0 inches for Sardinian infants, and at or below 17.5 inches for Japanese infants and infants living on islands of the New Hebrides and Bismarck Archipelago. At age 8 years, mean chest girth approximates 24.0 inches for United States white children, and is between 23.0 inches and 22.5 inches for children residing in India, in Japan, and on the East Indies island of Timor. Throughout childhood, the circumference of the trunk in the mid-thoracic region averages more than its circumference at the abdominal level. Among the groups discussed at age 8 years, mean abdomen girth in percentage of mean chest girth varies from 88 on Japanese children to 98 on United States white children (Meredith 1969a, 1970).

At the end of the second month of prenatal life, width of shoulders approximates one-third inch and width of hips one-fifth inch. Between this time and the middle of the prenatal period shoulder width increases 500 percent and hip width 700 percent. For United States white children, increases of 500 percent and 600 percent occur from the middle of prenatal life to age 8 years, bringing average shoulder and hip widths at this age to 11.1 inches and 8.0 inches, respectively. Hip width means between 6.0 inches and 7.0 inches have been obtained at age 8 years on Hutu and Tutsi children in Ruanda, Wadigo children in Kenya, and Toda children in India (Meredith 1969a). Hip width in percentage of head width increases from near 40 at age 2 months, through 80 at the middle of prenatal life and 125 at age 2 years, to 165 at age 10 years and around 185 in early adulthood (Boynton 1936; Meredith 1935; Scammon and Calkins 1929). On 15-year-old white males, shoulder width relative to hip width averages 139 percent and varies in different individuals from less than 125 percent to more than 150 percent (Trim and Meredith 1952).

Upper and Lower Limbs. For the typical North American white individual, upper limb length (distance from acromion of shoulder to tip of middle finger) is roughly 4.0 inches at the middle of the prenatal period, 14.0 inches at age 2 years, 24.0 inches at age 11 years and, in early adulthood, 28 inches and 31 inches on males and females, respectively (Meredith 1947). Compared with the mean of 21.3 inches for North American white children at age 8 years, North American Negro children have longer upper limbs by 0.8 inches and Japanese children have shorter upper limbs by 1.5 inches (Meredith 1969a). At age 15 years, individual differences in upper limb length among North American white boys extend from 24.5 inches to 34.5 inches (Newcomer and Meredith 1951).

Averages for arm girth of North American white people are 1.6 inches at the middle of the prenatal period, 6.0 inches at age 1 year, 7.6 inches at age 8 years and, at age 15 years, 9.4 inches and 10.2 inches for females and males, respectively (Meredith and Boynton 1937; Newcomer and Meredith 1951). Means between 6.0 inches and 6.5 inches have been obtained at age 8 years on contemporary groups of Egyptian, Hutu, Tutsi, and Mayan Amerind children (Meredith 1969a). Over the period from age 12 years to early adulthood, average thickness of the adipose tissue between the skin and muscles of the arm decreases 20 percent in males and increases 20 percent in females (Boynton 1936; Fry et al. 1965; Reynolds 1950).

In regard to average upper limb form, arm girth approximates 40 percent of upper limb length at the middle of prenatal life, increases to 45 percent in early infancy, and decreases through 40 percent near age 3 years to 35 percent in adolescence (Meredith and Sherbina 1951). Among North American white males age 15 years, arm girth relative to upper limb length varies from 28 percent to 46 percent (Trim and Meredith 1952).

Marked change in human form is indicated by comparison of the lower limb segment of stature with the head and neck segment. In relation to average distance from the vertex to the level of the shoulders, average lower limb length is 70 percent less at age 2 months, equal at the middle of the prenatal period, around 45 percent greater by the end of the first postnatal year and, for North American white males, more than 150 percent greater in early adulthood (Meredith 1939a). In absolute terms, means for lower limb length on North American white children are 10.6 inches at age 1 year, 17.3 inches at age 4 years, 23.1 inches at age 8 years, and 32.1 inches at age 15 years (Meredith 1968, 1969a, 1969b, 1970). Compared with North American white children, means are (1) higher for North American Negro children by 0.4 inches at age 1 year, and 1.2 inches at age 8 years, and (2) lower for Japanese children by 0.2 inches at age 1 year, and 2.9 inches at age 8 years. Individual differences in lower limb length among North American white males age 15 years are distributed from approximately 28 inches to 37 inches (New-

comer and Meredith 1951; Spurgeon, Young, and Meredith 1959).

Averages for leg (calf) girth on North American white persons approximate 4.5 inches at birth, 7.7 inches at age 1 year, 10.4 inches at age 8 years and, on males, 13.7 inches at age 15 years (Kasius et al. 1957; Meredith 1969a, 1970; Newcomer and Meredith 1951). Sex differences are slight prior to late adolescence; at ages 15 years to 20 years means are about 0.5 inches less for females than males (Knott 1963; Meredith and Boynton 1937). Comparative study of means at age 8 years shows leg girth of North American white children to exceed that of Egyptian, Japanese, Hutu, and Tutsi children by 1.2 inches. The lower limbs, like the upper limbs, become stockier between the middle of prenatal life and early infancy, then continually slenderize throughout childhood (Meredith and Sherbina 1951). At age 15 years, individual differences among white males spread from leg girth 30 percent of lower limb length to leg girth 50 percent of lower limb length (Spurgeon, Young, and Meredith 1959; Trim and Meredith 1952).

Tooth Agenesis, Eruption, and Loss

Eruption and Loss of Deciduous Teeth. The first set of teeth is designated the primary, or deciduous, dentition; usually it consists of 20 teeth. Moving from the center of each jaw outward and backward the primary teeth are named: central incisor, lateral incisor, canine (cuspid), deciduous first molar, and deciduous second molar.

Eruption of the primary dentition into the mouth ordinarily occurs in the period between early infancy and age 3 years. Typically, the first tooth emerges (pierces the gum tissue) approximately 7 months after birth. Most children erupt their first tooth sometime between 4 months after birth and age 1 year; in rare instances tooth emergence commences prior to birth or as late as 16 months following birth (Lysell, Magnusson, and Thilander 1962; Meredith 1946a).

The characteristic eruption sequence for the primary dentition is as follows: lower central incisors, upper central and lateral incisors, lower lateral incisors, deciduous first molars, canines, and deciduous second molars. Individual differences include several variations in sequence (Meredith 1946a).

At age 1 year, normal infants vary in tooth emergence from none to the full deciduous complement; 50 percent of infants have between 4 and 8 erupted teeth; and the average number of erupted teeth is 6, usually 2 lower central incisors and 4 upper incisors (Falkner 1957; Meredith 1946a). Emergence of the deciduous dentition may be completed before age 1 year or after age 3 years; on the average it is completed by 2.5 years (Haataja 1963; Pyle and Drain 1931). Different individuals erupt their 20 deciduous teeth within periods varying from less than 9 months to approximately 3 years.

In the period between ages 4 years and 6 years the roots of most primary teeth begin to show reduction in size. Usually three-fourths of a tooth's root is resorbed before the tooth is shed (Knott and O'Meara 1967). Average ages of shedding approximate 6.5 years for lower central incisors, 7 to 8 years for other incisors, and 10 to 11 years for canines and deciduous molars (Hellman 1923). Rarely is a deciduous tooth shed prior to age 5 years (Pyle and Drain 1931).

Eruption of Permanent Teeth. Thirty-two teeth usually comprise the second, or permanent, dentition. Nomenclature is the same as for the primary dentition except that the five teeth in each jaw behind the canine are, successively, first and second premolars (bicuspids) and first to third permanent molars.

Permanent teeth pierce the gum tissues at the following average ages: first permanent molars and lower central incisors, between 6 years and 6.5 years; upper central and lower lateral incisors, between 7 years and 8 years; upper lateral incisors, between 8 years and 9 years; canines, premolars (the teeth that replace the deciduous molars), and second permanent molars, between 10 years and 12.5 years; and third permanent molars, near age 20 years (Cattell 1928; Fanning 1962; Hellman 1936; Knott and Meredith 1966; Lee, Low, and Chang 1965). There are marked individual variations (Haataja 1963; Knott and Meredith 1966). At age 6 years, one child may have a full deciduous dentition, with no erupted permanent teeth; another child may have shed his deciduous incisors, and erupted 8 permanent incisors plus 4 permanent first molars. At age 12 years, one child may have 24 erupted teeth, 12 deciduous and 12 permanent; another child may have 28 erupted permanent teeth (Klein and Cody 1939). Eruption of all permanent teeth except the third molars is found sometimes by age 10 years and sometimes not until age 17 years (Shuttleworth 1939).

Permanent tooth eruption in the individual child commences with the permanent first molars and central incisors; continues with the lateral incisors; shows high sequence variation for the canines, premolars, and permanent second molars; and terminates with the permanent third molar. More than 20 different sequences occur, none being common to more than 30 percent of children. Two of the commonest sequences are: (1) first molar, central incisor, lateral incisor, first premolar, canine, second premolar, second molar, third molar, and (2) central incisor, first molar, lateral incisor, canine, first premolar, second premolar, second molar, and third molar (Knott and Meredith 1966).

Although the deciduous dentition manifests no tendency for girls to erupt teeth erlier than boys (Falkner 1957; Lysell, Magnusson, and Thilander 1962; Meredith 1946a), this tendency is found for canine and premolar teeth of the permanent dentition (Cattell 1928; Knott and Meredith 1966). The permanent lower canine shows the greatest sex difference; girls typically erupt this tooth almost a year earlier than boys. Permanent incisor and canine teeth in the lower jaw tend to erupt earlier than corresponding teeth in the upper jaw (Hellman 1923; Knott and Meredith 1966).

After piercing the gum tissues, a tooth proceeds toward contact with teeth of the opposing jaw, moving rapidly at first and then more slowly. One-half of this movement takes place within four months after a tooth's emergence, and nine-tenths of the migration is completed within two years (Giles, Knott, and Meredith 1963).

Congenital Absence of Teeth. Although any tooth may not develop, agenesis is commonest for the permanent third molars. Fully 20 percent of white persons lack at least one third molar while in 3 percent all four of these teeth are missing (Dahlberg 1945; Hellman 1936). Frequencies of absence are higher for Eskimo than white persons, lower for Negro than white persons, and higher for females than males. Agenesis in white persons occurs at frequencies near 2 percent for the permanent upper lateral incisor and the lower second premolar. There is a tendency for one or more of these teeth to be absent in association with missing third molars (Garn and Lewis 1962).

Puberal Changes and Relations

Termination of childhood is signified by increase in the growth rates for size of breasts, ovaries, and uterus in the female; size of testes, scrotum, and penis in the male; and, in both sexes, size of trunk, limbs, and total body mass. Other puberal changes include beginning menstruation by the adolescent girl, voice change and growth of facial hair by the adolescent boy, and development by both sexes of moderately coarse pigmented hair in the armpit and groin regions. On the average, those puberal changes common to both sexes begin a biennium earlier in females than males.

Size Changes and Hair Growth in Girls. The typical female has an "adolescent spurt" in body height that begins shortly after age 10 years and reaches its crest approximately at age 12 years; there follows a sharp velocity decline, so that by age 14 years, height is increasing much more slowly than in late childhood (Meredith 1939b). Similarly timed "humps" characterize mean velocity curves for trunk length, hip width, arm girth, leg girth, and body weight (Boynton 1936; Shuttleworth 1937). In individual girls, these puberal changes commence, fairly simultaneously, at any age from 8 years to 13 years and, on rare occasions, both earlier and later (Meredith 1939b; Shuttleworth 1939).

Average age of beginning breast enlargement is approximately 10.5 years, individual girls commencing enlargement at ages from 2.5 years earlier to 2.5 years later (Bryan and Greenberg 1952; Lee, Chang, and Chan 1963). Length of time from beginning enlargement to full breast development is about three years (Nicolson and Hanley 1953; Reynolds and Wines 1948).

Somatological changes in female size during adolescence do not all classify under moderate acceleration (stature and hip width) or marked acceleration (volume of uterus and breasts). There are no puberal spurts in size of the central nervous system, pineal body, or adenoid mass (Scammon 1930; Todd 1936). Although a mild spurt occurs in external width of hips, there is considerable resorption at the rim of the pelvic inlet involving marked bone loss along the sides of this skeletal aperture.

White girls typically show first appearance of a few pigmented hairs in the pubic region near age 11 years, and in the axillary regions shortly after age 12 years (Hansman and Maresh 1961; Nicolson and Hanley 1953). Individual variations normally extend below and above these averages approximately 3 years for beginning growth of pubic hair, and more than 3 years of beginning growth of axillary hair. Instances are known of pubic and axillary hair development in early childhood (Montagu 1946; Seckel, Scott, and Benedict 1949). The time from first appearance of some pigmented pubic (or axillary) hair to attainment of a fairly full density is roughly three years. Compared with the average white girl, growth of pigmented pubic and axillary hair in the average Chinese girl commences somewhat later and is more sparse (Lee, Chang, and Chan 1963).

In relation to first appearance of pigmented pubic hair, breast enlargement may begin 2 years earlier, simultaneously, or 2 years later (Reynolds and Wines 1948). Beginning growth of pigmented axillary hair occasionally precedes beginning growth of pigmented hair (Priesel and Wagner 1931).

Menarche and its Relationships. A century ago, the average age of the first menstrual cycle for white girls was 14.5 years or later (Bowditch 1877; Montagu 1946; Tanner 1962). Recent studies on large samples of British, Hungarian, Israeli, and Polish girls indicate that today the average age at which white girls reach menarche is approximately 13 years (Bottyán et al. 1963; Scott 1961; Shilloh and Goldberg 1965; Zukowski, Kmietowicz-Zukowska, and Gruska 1964). Averages from menarche records collected in the period 1955–1965 on non-white girls are near age 13 years for Assamese, Burmese, Japanese, and Southern Chinese, near age 14 years for Ibo in Eastern Nigeria and Mayan Amerindian in Guatemala, and near age 15 years for South African Bantu and Siberian Buryat (Burrell, Healy, and Tanner 1961; Foll 1961; Inoue and Shimizu 1965; Lee, Chang, and Chan 1963; Oettle and Higginson 1961; Sabharwal, Morales, and Méndez 1966; Tanner and O'Keeffe 1962; Vlastovsky 1966).

Among present-day white girls, variations in age of menarche are as follows: 50 percent between ages 12 and 14 years, 80 percent between ages 11.5 and 14.5 years, 95 percent between ages 10 and 16 years, and 2 percent each at ages 8 to 10 years and 16 to 19 years (Bottyán et al. 1963; Heimendinger 1954; Nicolson and Hanley 1953; Scott 1961). Menarche variations for North American Negro girls are similar to those for white girls (Michelson 1944). Instances are on record of menarche occurring before school age and later than age 20 years (Montagu 1946).

In different individuals, breast and pubic hair development may commence any time from more than 4 years before to shortly after menarche; velocity increase in height may reach its crest at times from more than 3 years before to 1 year after menarche; and pigmented axillary hair may begin to appear from 4 years before to 2 years after menarche (Hansman and Maresh 1961; Lee, Chang, and Chan 1963; Meredith 1967; Pryor 1936; Shuttleworth 1937).

Attempts have been made to discover ways of predicting menarche. Moderately strong associations (*r*'s 0.75 to 0.80) have been found for age at menarche with (1) age at beginning breast enlargement and (2) age at beginning ossification of a small sesamoid bone near the lower end of the thumb (Flory 1935; Nicolson and Hanley 1953; Reynolds and Wines 1948).

The typical amount of increase in height after menarche is 2.5 inches, with only 1 girl in 7 increasing 4 inches or more (Fried and Smith 1962). Rarely does a girl have the ability to procreate at menarche; commonly there is a puberal sterility interval of 3 or more years between onset of menses and fertile ovulation (Mills and Ogle 1936; Montagu 1946).

Genital, Hair, and Other Changes in Boys. Usually the earliest externally observable indication of puberal change in boys is increase in size of the testes. On the average, puberal enlargement of the male genitalia commences shortly before age 12 years for the testes, and near age 12.5 years for the penis.

Individual differences in age at onset of these changes extend from 9.5 years to 14.5 years for the testes, and from 10 years to 15 years for the penis (Greulich et al. 1942; Kubitschek 1932; Schonfeld 1943; Stolz and Stolz 1951). The typical periods of time between initial increase in velocity and attainment of maximum size approximate 5 years for the penis and 7 years for the testes; in most individuals the period of puberal testicle increase commences before and continues after that of penis increase. Quantitatively, average length of the penis almost doubles from ages 12.5 years to 17 years, and average volume of the testes increases more than tenfold from ages 12 years to 19 years (Schonfeld 1943).

The findings reported in the foregoing paragraph are for white males. Findings on penis development for Chinese males are as follows: average age of beginning puberal increase near 13 years; variation in time of beginning increase from 11 years to 16 years; and average interval between puberal onset and full size less than four years (Chang et al. 1966).

The male puberal velocity increase for body height typically starts near age 12.5 years and reaches its peak shortly after age 14 years; rapid reduction in velocity ensues, and by age 16 years, height is increasing more slowly than in late childhood. Individuals vary from 10.5 years to 16 years in age at onset of their height spurt, and from below 12 years to near 17 years in age at attaining peak velocity (Meredith 1939*b*; Shuttleworth 1939; Stolz and Stolz 1951). Maximum gain in height of an adolescent boy during the year extending from 6 months before to 6 months after peak velocity approximates 5 inches, or 8 percent. This increase is large in comparison with maximum gain for an individual during the year before puberal change begins (3 inches, or 5.5 percent), and small in comparison with average gain during the first year after birth (10 inches, or 50 percent).

Average age at which a few pigmented pubic hairs are first observable in white boys approximates 13 years; normal variability is from age 10 years to age 16 years, with 80 percent of boys showing this stage of development at ages from 11 years to 15 years (Bryan and Greenberg 1952; Dimock 1937; Schonfeld 1943). Pigmented pubic hair is not seen in the typical Chinese boy before age 14 years, and some Chinese boys do not develop pigmented pubic hair until after age 16 years (Chang et al. 1966). Pubic hair growth is rapid in some adolescent boys, slow in others: one boy may remain at the stage of a few pigmented hairs near the base of the penis for a period of 2 years, another may take less than 6 months in passing from first appearance of any pigmented hair to a moderately dense growth (Stolz and Stolz 1951). The average time from beginning pigmented hairs to a dense growth is about 3 years.

A few males exhibit sparse development of pigmented axillary hair by age 11 years, a few not until after age 17 years, and most between ages 12 years and 16 years. Approximately 14 years is the average age for (1) first appearance of pigmented axillary hair, (2) initial development of pigmented hair near each end of the upper lip, (3) puberal voice unevenness and huskiness, and (4) the puberal velocity apex for body height (Chang et al. 1966; Jerome 1937; Kubitschek 1932; Nicolson and Hanley 1953; Richey 1937; Schonfeld 1943; Stolz and Stolz 1951).

Puberal changes in males include small to moderate amounts of breast enlargement. A node of firm tissue, sometimes exceeding 0.5 inch in diameter, develops under each nipple. Nodes are present in a few boys by age 11 years and in most boys at age 15 years; by late adolescence, they frequently become too small to palpate (Jung and Shafton 1935; Schonfeld 1943; Stolz and Stolz 1951).

Relative to onset of the puberal spurt in size of testes, the spurt in penis size may commence near the same time in one individual and 2 years after in another; relative to time at which full size of testes is reached, approximate full size of penis may have been attained 2 years earlier in one boy and only a few months earlier in another. Beginning development of pigmented pubic hair before noticeable increase in testicle size occurs in about 25 percent of boys. In rare instances, there is some growth of pigmented axillary hair prior to any appearance of pigmented pubic hair. When boys reach the apex of the puberal velocity hump in height, they vary in amount of pigmented pubic hair from lack of any to practically a full density. Perceptible voice change occurs sometimes before penis acceleration or the presence of any pigmented pubic or axillary hair, and sometimes following full penis size, dense growth of pubic hair, and moderately dense growth of axillary hair. The combination of fully developed testes, scrotum, penis, pubic hair, and axillary hair may be attained by age 15 years, or may not be attained before age 20 years (Chang et al. 1966; Greulich et al. 1942; Priesel and Wagner 1931; Schonfeld 1943; Stolz and Stolz 1951).

Prediction of puberal changes has been investigated less extensively for males than females. The relation between height in middle childhood (e.g., age 6 years) and age of maximum puberal velocity in height is too low for use in forecasting (Meredith 1965). There is moderate positive association (r near 0.65) between age at beginning enlargement of the testes and age at reaching maximum puberal velocity in height (Nicolson and Hanley 1953).

No puberal spurt occurs in volume of the brain, weight of the eyeballs, size of the bones of the inner ear, or number of erupting teeth (Knott and Meredith 1966; Scammon 1930). There is gradual decrease throughout adolescence in weight of the cortex and medulla of the thymus, and in thickness of subcutaneous adipose tissue on the male arm and leg (Boyd 1936; Boynton 1936; Fry et al. 1965; Meredith 1935; Reynolds 1950). There also is loss of head hair, causing indentation of the male hair line on each side of the upper forehead (Schonfeld 1943).

References

ABRAMSON, E., and E. ERNEST. Height and weight of schoolboys at a Stockholm secondary school, 1950, and a comparison with some earlier investigations. *Acta Paediatrica*, 1954, *43*, 235–46.

AICARDI, G., and S. RUGIATI. Osservazioni sul peso dei neonati a Sassari dal 1933 al 1963. *Minerva Pediatrica*, 1965, *17*, 936–42.

ALTMAN, P. L., and D. S. DITTMER (eds.). *Growth, including reproduction and morphological development*. Washington, D.C.: Federation American Societies Experimental Biology, 1962.

AREY, L. D. *Developmental anatomy* (7th ed.). Philadelphia: Saunders, 1965.

BIRREN, J. E. (ed.). *Handbook of aging and the individual*. Chicago: University of Chicago Press, 1959.

BLOMMERS, P., and E. F. LINDQUIST. *Elementary statistical methods*. Boston: Houghton Mifflin, 1960.

BOTTYÁN, O. ET AL. Age of menarche in Hungarian girls. *Annales Historico-Naturales Musei Nationalis Hungarici Pars Antropologica*, 1963, *55*, 561–72.

BOWDITCH, H. P. The growth of children. *Eighth Annual Report, Massachusetts State Board of Health*, 1877, 273–324.

BOYD, E. Weight of the thymus and its component parts and number of Hassall corpuscles in health and in disease. *American Journal of Diseases of Children*, 1936, *51*, 313–35.

BOYNTON, B. The physical growth of girls between birth and eighteen years. *University of Iowa Studies in Child Welfare*, 1936, *12*, No. 4.

BRODIE, A. G. Present status of knowledge concerning movement of the tooth germ through the jaw. *Journal of American Dental Association*, 1934, *21*, 1830–38.

BRYAN, A. H., and B. G. GREENBERG. Methodology in the study of physical measurements of school children. *Human Biology*, 1952, *24*, 117–44.

BURRELL, R. J. W., M. J. R. HEALY, and J. M. TANNER. Age at menarche in South African Bantu schoolgirls living in the Transkei Reserve. *Human Biology*, 1961, *33*, 250–61.

CATTELL, P. Dentition as a measure of maturity. *Harvard Monographs in Education*, 1928, No. 9.

CHANG, K. S. F. ET AL. Height and weight of Southern Chinese children. *American Journal of Physical Anthropology*, 1963, *21*, 497–509.

——— Sexual maturation of Chinese boys in Hong Kong. *Pediatrics*, 1966, *37*, 804–11.

CURRIMBHOY, Z. Growth and development of Bombay children. *Indian Journal of Child Health*, 1963, *12*, 627–51.

DAHLBERG, A. A. The changing dentition of man. *Journal of American Dental Association*, 1945, *32*, 676–90.

DIMOCK, H. S. *Rediscovering the adolescent: a study of personality development in adolescent boys*. New York: Association Press, 1937.

FALKNER, F. Deciduous tooth eruption. *Archives of Disease in Childhood*, 1957, *32*, 386–91.

FANNING, E. A. Third molar emergence in Bostonians. *American Journal of Physical Anthropology*, 1962, *20*, 339–45.

FLORY, C. D. Predicting puberty. *Child Development*, 1935, *6*, 1–6.

FOLL, C. V. Physical development of schoolgirls in upper Burma. *Archives of Disease in Childhood*, 1958, *33*, 452–54.

——— The age at menarche in Assam and Burma. *Archives of Disease in Childhood*, 1961, *36*, 302–4.

FORBES, G. B. Chemical growth in infancy and childhood. *Journal of Pediatrics*, 1952, *41*, 202–32.

FRIED, R. I., and E. SMITH. Postmenarcheal growth patterns. *Journal of Pediatrics*, 1962, *61*, 562–65.

FRY, E. I. ET AL. The amount and distribution of subcutaneous tissue in Southern Chinese children from Hong Kong. *American Journal of Physical Anthropology*, 1965, *23*, 69–80.

GARN, S. M., and A. B. LEWIS. The relationship between third molar agenesis and reduction in tooth number. *Angle Orthodontist*, 1962, *32*, 14–18.

GHOSH, S., and S. BERI. Standard of prematurity for North Indian babies. *Indian Journal of Child Health*, 1962, *11*, 210–15.

GILES, N. B., V. B. KNOTT, and H. V. MEREDITH. Increase in intraoral height of selected permanent teeth during the quadrennium following gingival emergence. *Angle Orthodontist*, 1963, *33*, 195–206.

GREULICH, W. W. ET AL. Somatic and endocrine studies of puberal and adolescent boys. *Monographs of the Society for Research in Child Development*, 1942, 7, No. 3.

GREULICH, W. W., and H. THOMS. The growth and development of the pelvis in individual girls before, during, and after puberty. *Yale Journal of Biology and Medicine*, 1944, *17*, 91–104.

HAATAJA, J. *Cephalic, facial and dental growth in Finnish children*. Helsinki: Center for Study of Child Growth and Development, 1963.

HANSMAN, C. F., and M. M. MARESH. A longitudinal study of skeletal maturation. *American Journal of Diseases of Children*, 1961, *101*, 305–21.

HEIMENDINGER, J. Die ergebnisse von körpermessungen an 5000 Basler kindern 2–18 jahren. *Helvetica Paediatrica Acta*, 1964, *19*, Suppl. 13.

HELLMAN, M. Nutrition, growth and education. *Dental Cosmos*, 1923, *65*, 34–49.

——— Our third molar teeth: their eruption, presence and absence. *Dental Cosmos*, 1936, *78*, 750–62.

INOUE, T., and M. SHIMIZU. *Physical and skeletal growth and development of Japanese children*. Tokyo: Japan Society for Promotion of Science, 1965.

JEROME, E. K. Change of voice in male adolescents. *Quarterly Journal of Speech*, 1937, *23*, 648–53.

JUNG, F. T., and A. L. SHAFTON. The mammary gland in the normal adolescent male. *Proceedings, Society for Experimental Biology and Medicine*, 1935, *33*, 455–58.

KASIUS, R. V. ET AL. Maternal and newborn nutrition studies at Philadelphia Lying-in Hospital: V. Size and growth of babies during the first year of life. *Milbank Memorial Fund Quarterly*, 1957, *35*, 323–72.

KEYFITZ, N. *A height and weight survey of Toronto elementary school children, 1939.* Ottawa: Department of Trade and Commerce, Dominion Bureau of Statistics, 1942.

KLEIN, H., and J. F. CODY. Graphic charts which depict the variations in numbers of erupted permanent teeth in grade school children. *Journal of American Dental Association*, 1939, *26*, 609–11.

KNOTT, V. B. Stature, leg girth, and body weight of Puerto Rican private school children measured in 1962. *Growth*, 1963, *27*, 157–74.

────── and H. V. MEREDITH. Statistics on eruption of the permanent dentition from serial data for North American white children. *Angle Orthodontist*, 1966, *36*, 68–79.

KNOTT, V. B., and W. F. O'MEARA. Serial data on primary incisor root resorption and gingival emergence of permanent successors. *Angle Orthodontist*, 1967, *37*, 212–22.

KROGMAN, W. M., and F. E. JOHNSTON. *The physical growth of Philadelphia white children, age 7–17 years.* Philadelphia: Center for Research in Child Growth, 1965.

KUBITSCHEK, P. E. Sexual development of boys with special reference to the appearance of secondary sex characteristics and their relation to structural and personality types. *Journal of Nervous and Mental Disease*, 1932, *76*, 425–51.

LEE, M. M. C., K. S. F. CHANG, and M. M. C. CHAN. Sexual maturation of Chinese girls in Hong Kong. *Pediatrics*, 1963, *32*, 389–98.

LEE, M. M. C., W. R. LOW, and K. S. F. CHANG. Eruption of the permanent dentition of Southern Chinese children in Hong Kong. *Archives of Oral Biology*, 1965, *10*, 849–61.

LIN, C. Anthropometric measurements of Shanghai students and preschool children in 1954. *Chinese Medical Journal*, 1957, *75*, 1018–23.

LOW, A. *Growth of children: sixty-six boys and sixty girls.* Aberdeen: University of Aberdeen Press, 1952.

LYSELL, L., B. MAGNUSSON, and B. THILANDER. Time and order of eruption of the primary teeth. *Odontologisk Revy*, 1962, *13*, 217–34.

MALCOLM, S. Nutrition investigations in the New Hebrides: results of research carried out during 1951. *Commission du Pacifique Sud, Technique Paper*, 1952, No. 23.

────── and E. MASSAL. Études sur la nutrition et l'alimentation dans les établissements français de l'océanie. *Commission du Pacifique Sud, Document Technique*, 1955, No. 85.

MALINA, R. M., and F. E. JOHNSTON. Relations between bone, muscle and fat widths in the upper arms and calves of boys and girls studied cross-sectionally at ages 6 to 16 years. *Human Biology*, 1967, *39*, 211–23.

MARESH, M. M. Bone, muscle and fat measurements of the extremities during the first six years of life. *Pediatrics*, 1961, *28*, 971–84.

MEDAWAR, P. B. *The uniqueness of the individual.* New York: Basic Books, 1957.

MÉNDEZ, J., and C. BEHRHORST. The anthropometric characteristics of Indian and urban Guatemalans. *Human Biology*, 1963, *35*, 457–69.

MEREDITH, H. V. The rhythm of physical growth: a study of eighteen anthropometric measurements on Iowa City white males. *University of Iowa Studies in Child Welfare*, 1935, *11*, No. 3.

────── Length of head and neck, trunk, and lower extremities on Iowa City children aged seven to seventeen years. *Child Development*, 1939a, *10*, 129–44.

────── Stature of Massachusetts children of North European and Italian ancestry. *American Journal of Physical Anthropology*, 1939b, *24*, 301–46.

────── Physical growth from birth to two years: I. Stature. *University of Iowa Studies in Child Welfare*, 1943, *19*, 1–255.

────── Order and age of eruption for the deciduous dentition. *Journal of Dental Research*, 1946a, *25*, 43–66.

────── Physical growth from birth to two years: II. Head circumference. *Child Development*, 1946b, *17*, 1–61.

────── Birth order and body size: II. Neonatal and childhood materials. *American Journal of Physical Anthropology*, 1950, *8*, 195–224.

────── Relation between socioeconomic status and body size in boys seven to ten years of age. *American Journal of Diseases of Children*, 1951, *82*, 702–9.

────── Growth in head width during the first twelve years of life. *Pediatrics*, 1953, *12*, 411–29.

────── Growth in bizygomatic face breadth during childhood. *Growth*, 1954, *18*, 111–34.

────── Measuring the growth characteristics of school children. *Journal of School Health*, 1955, *25*, 267–73.

────── Changes in form of the head and face during childhood. *Growth*, 1960, *24*, 215–64.

────── Change in the stature and body weight of North American boys during the last 80 years. *In* L. P. LIPSITT and C. C. SPIKER (eds.), *Advances in child development and behavior*, vol. 1. New York: Academic 1963.

────── Selected anatomic variables analyzed for interage relationships of the size-size, size-gain, and gain-gain varieties. *In* L. P. LIPSITT and C. C. SPIKER (eds.), *Advances in child development and behavior*, vol. 2. New York: Academic, 1965.

────── Body size and form in childhood, with emphasis on the face. *In* S. L. HOROWITZ and E. H. HIXON (eds.), *The nature of orthodontic diagnosis*. St. Louis: C. V. Mosby, 1966.

────── A synopsis of puberal changes in youth. *Journal of School Health*, 1967, *37*, 171–76.

────── Body size of contemporary groups of preschool children studied in different parts of the world. *Child Development*, 1968, *39*, 335–77.

────── Body size of contemporary groups of eight-year-old children in different parts of the world. Monographs of the Society for Research in Child Development, 1969a, *34*, No. 1.

────── Body size of contemporary youth in different parts of the world. Monographs of the Society for Research in Child Development, 1969b, *34*, No. 7.

────── Body size of contemporary groups of one-year-old infants studied in different parts of the world. Child Development, 1970, *41*, 551–60.

────── and B. BOYNTON. The transverse growth of the extremities: an analysis of girth measurements for arm, forearm, thigh, and leg taken on Iowa City white children. *Human Biology*, 1937, *9*, 366–403.

MEREDITH, H. V., and P. R. SHERBINA. Body form in childhood: ratios quantitatively describing three slender-to-stocky continua: on girls four to eight years of age. *Child Development*, 1951, *22*, 275–83.

MEYERS, E. S. A. Height-weight survey of New South Wales school children. *Medical Journal of Australia*, 1956, *1*, 435–53.

MICHELSON, N. Studies in the physical development of Negroes: IV. Onset of puberty. *American Journal of Physical Anthropology*, 1944, *2*, 151–66.

MILLIS, J. Gain in weight and length in the first year of life of Chinese infants born in Singapore in 1951. *Medical Journal of Australia*, 1954, *1*, 283–85.

MILLS, C. A., and C. OGLE. Physiological sterility of adolescence. *Human Biology*, 1936, *8*, 607–15.

MONTAGU, M. F. A. *Adolescent sterility.* Springfield, Ill.: Charles C Thomas, 1946.

MOSCONA, A. A. Tissue reconstruction from dissociated cells. *In* M. X. ZARROW (ed.), *Growth in living systems*. New York: Basic Books, 1961.

NELLHAUS, G. Head circumference from birth to eighteen years: practical composite international and interracial graphs. *Pediatrics*, 1968, *41*, 106–14.

NEWCOMER, E. O., and H. V. MEREDITH. Eleven measures of body size on a 1950 sample of 15-year-old white schoolboys at Eugene, Oregon. *Human Biology*, 1951, *23*, 24–40.

NICOLSON, A. B., and C. HANLEY. Indices of physiological maturity: derivation and interrelationships. *Child Development*, 1953, *23*, 3–38.

O'BRIEN, R., M. A. GIRSHICK, and E. P. HUNT. *Body measurements of American boys and girls for garment and pattern construction*. Washington, D. C.: United States Department of Agriculture, Bureau of Home Economics, Miscellaneous Publication No. 366, 1941.

OETTLE, A. G., and J. HIGGINSON. The age of menarche in South African bantu (Negro) girls: with a comment on methods of determining mean age at menarche. *Human Biology*, 1961, *33*, 181–90.

PRIESEL, R., and R. WAGNER. Gesetzmässigkeiten im auftreten der extragenitalen sekundären geschlechtsmerkmale bei mädchen. *Zeitschrift für Konstitutionslehre*, 1931, *15*, 333–52.

PRYOR, H. B. Certain physical and physiological aspects of adolescent development in girls. *Journal of Pediatrics*, 1936, *8*, 52–62.

PYLE, S. I., and C. L. DRAIN. Some conditions in the dentition of preschool children. *Child Development*, 1931, *2*, 147–52.

RAUH, J. L., D. A. SCHUMSKY, and M. T. WITT. Heights, weights, and obesity in urban school children. *Child Development*, 1967, *38*, 515–30.

REYNOLDS, E. L. The distribution of subcutaneous fat in childhood and adolescence. *Monographs of the Society for Research in Child Development*, 1950, *15*, No. 2.

————, and J. V. WINES. Individual differences in physical changes associated with adolescence in girls. *American Journal of Diseases of Children*, 1948, *75*, 329–50.

RICHEY, H. C. The relation of accelerated, normal and retarded puberty to the height and weight of school children. *Monographs of the Society for Research in Child Development*, 1937, *2*, No. 1.

SABHARWAL, K. P., S. MORALES, and J. MÉNDEZ. Body measurements and creatinine excretion among upper and lower socio-economic groups of girls in Guatemala. *Human Biology*, 1966, *38*, 131–40.

SCAMMON, R. E. The measurement of the body in childhood. *In* J. A. HARRIS ET AL. *The measurement of man*. Minneapolis: University of Minnesota Press, 1930.

————. and L. A. CALKINS. *The development and growth of the external dimensions of the human body in the fetal period*. Minneapolis: University of Minnesota Press, 1929.

SCHONFELD, W. A. Primary and secondary sexual characteristics, study of their development in males from birth through maturity, with biometric study of penis and testes. *American Journal of Diseases of Children*, 1943, *65*, 535–49.

SCOTT, J. A. *Report on the heights and weights (and other measurements) of school pupils in the County of London in 1959*. London: County Council Publication No. 4086, 1961.

SECKEL, H. P. G., W. W. SCOTT, and E. P. BENDITT. Six examples of precocious sexual development. *American Journal of Diseases of Children*, 1949, *78*, 484–515.

SHILLOH, A., and R. GOLDBERG. A study of the menarche among Tel Aviv school girls. *Harefuah*, 1965, *68*, 161–63.

SHOCK, N. The physiology of ageing. *American Scientist*, 1962, *206*, 100–10.

SHUTTLEWORTH, F. K. Sexual maturation and the physical growth of girls age six to nineteen. *Monographs of the Society for Research in Child Development*, 1937, *2*, No. 5.

———— The physical and mental growth of girls and boys age 6 to 19 in relation to age at maximum growth. *Monographs of the Society for Research in Child Development*, 1939, *4*, No. 3.

SIMMONS, K., and W. W. GREULICH. Menarcheal age and the height, weight, and skeletal age of girls age 7 to 17 years. *Journal of Pediatrics*, 1943, *22*, 518–48.

SMYTH, C., and M. YOUNG. Facial growth in children, with special reference to dentition. *Medical Research Council, Special Report Series*, 1932, No. 171.

SPURGEON, J. H., N. D. YOUNG, and H. V. MEREDITH. Body size and form of American-born boys of Dutch ancestry residing in Michigan. *Growth*, 1959, *23*, 55–71.

STOLZ, H. R., and L. M. STOLZ. *Somatic development of adolescent boys*. New York: Macmillan, 1951.

STREETER, G. L. Prenatal growth of the child. *Carnegie Institution of Washington, News Service Bulletin*, 1937, *4*, 127–32.

ŠTUKOVSKÝ, R. The offspring of "old" mothers: influence of parity upon weight, length, bodybuild and sex of the newborn. *Acta Facultatis Rerum Naturalium Universitatis Comenianae, Anthropologia*, 1963, *8*, 469–94.

SUNDAL, A. *The norms for height and weight in healthy Norwegian children from birth to 15 years of age*. Bergen: Griegs Boktrykkeri, 1957.

TANNER, J. M. *Growth at adolescence*. Oxford: Blackwell Scientific Publications, 1962.

———— Radiographic studies of body composition in children and adults, In *Human body composition: approaches and applications*. Oxford: Pergamon, 1965.

————, and B. O'KEEFFE, Age at menarche in Nigerian school girls, with a note on their height and weights from age 12 to 19. *Human Biology*, 1962, *34*, 187–96.

TODD, T. W. Integral growth of the face: I. The nasal area. *International Journal of Orthodontics and Oral Surgery*, 1936, *22*, 321.

TRIM, P. T., and H. V. MEREDITH. Body form in Homo sapiens: a study of five anthropometric ratios on white boys fifteen years of age. *Growth*, 1952, *16*, 1–14.

TUDDENHAM, R. D., and M. M. SNYDER, Physical growth of California boys and girls from birth to eighteen years. *University of California Publications in Child Development*, 1954, *1*, 183–364.

VLASTOVSKY, V. G. The secular trend in the growth and development of children and young persons in the Soviet Union. *Human Biology*, 1966, *38*, 219–30.

WATSON, E. H., and G. H. LOWREY. *Growth and development of children*. (5th ed.). Chicago: Year Book Medical Publishers, 1967.

WOODS, G. A. Changes in width dimensions between certain teeth and facial points during growth. *American Journal of Orthodontics*, 1950, *36*, 676–700.

ZUKOWSKI, W., A. KMIETOWICZ-ZUKOWSKA, and S. GRUSKA. The age of menarche in Polish girls. *Human Biology*, 1964, *36*, 233–34.

The concept of psychosomatic medicine represents one of the major breakthroughs of twentieth-century medicine. Its roots may be found in the mind-body problem of antiquity. Warren (1914) described the mind-body problem as "the Wandering Jew of Science. It is ever reappearing when other issues are dead and buried."

The histories of Greek, Egyptian, Chaldean and Indian medicine refer to the mind-body relationship but the emphasis is primarily on the somato-psychic aspect. Hippocrates (460–375 B.C.) and his school established the rationalistic, mechanistic approach which has prevailed, with intercurrent lapses into demonology, until the twentieth century. He also left records showing an appreciation of the role of adaptive factors in health and disease, with a stress not only on the importance of the environment but also on the relationship between physician and patient. It was Galen (131–201 A.D.), however, who emphasized adaptive biology. Galen's philosophy prevailed throughout the medieval period. The causes of disease were claimed to be disturbances of the natural harmony of the body, especially of the four humors. An excess of any of the four humors had to be removed whereas a deficiency had to be corrected by diet. The Galenic tradition was so well integrated into Western culture that it was not until the fifteenth century that it began to be questioned. The observation that emotions had profound effects on the body had been dealt with by many scientific thinkers. These attempts to introduce the psyche into biology made little progress until the end of the nineteenth century when Charcot and later Freud demonstrated the undeniable importance of psychological factors in the development of disease. However, the psychosomatic attitude was not accepted by classical medicine as a scientific principle until the contributions of Hughlings-Jackson, Sherrington and Cannon made their impact. The publication of Dunbar's book (1935) *Emotions and Bodily Changes* registered the fact that the psychosomatic approach had become a formalized and accepted attitude in modern medicine. World War II gave strong support to the psychosomatic approach. It was impossible to deny the importance of emotional factors when it became clear that thousands

E. D. Wittkower
& S. Z. Dudek

Advances in Neurophysiological
and Conceptual Models

Psychosomatic Medicine: The Mind-Body-Society Interaction

13

of soldiers were debilitated by symptoms of psychological stress.

However, traditional medicine was not without strong resistance to the psychosomatic approach. It could not easily accept a reversal of the classical tenets of the organic approach, and a strictly organic attitude is still being advocated in many sectors. According to the new approach, Virchow's principle which specifies that disease produces alteration in structure had to be changed to state that as a result of emotional factors, altered function may lead to alteration of structure, and thereby to disease. Traditional medicine could neither accept emotional cause of disease nor was it willing to consider that emotions could be objectively studied by science. In the thirty years that followed the publication of Dunbar's book, enormous advances in scientific knowledge have taken place and considerable research has accumulated to make a strictly organic approach no longer possible.

SCIENTIFIC DISCOVERIES ESSENTIAL TO EMERGENCE OF PSYCHOSOMATIC MEDICINE

Although the unity of the body had been seriously proposed as a basic concept by many scientific thinkers, it was necessary for several important developments in independent fields of science to merge in the twentieth century in order to make the emergence of the psychosomatic attitude inevitable. More specifically it was necessary to establish that (1) the organism functions as a whole, and that there is a mind-body unity; (2) that emotions can be unconscious and nevertheless exert a profound psychological effect on the body; (3) that they can be scientifically measured and studied.

UNITY OF THE BODY

The discoveries of the physiologists and neurologists, especially the work of Hughlings-Jackson, Sherrington, and Cannon were of major importance to psychosomatic medicine. That disease of the CNS can result in regression of the CNS to earlier levels of function added a new insight into the altered functioning of traumatized or diseased tissue. The realization that the altered functioning is as much the result of the healthy tissue that remains as of diseased or lost tissue made a startling difference in the treatment and management of emerging symptoms. Not only did Sherrington's and Cannon's work result in a new awareness of the unity of the organism but it also provided methods for research into the mind-body relationship. Sherrington's demonstration of the fact that even the simplest reflex arc is subject to continuous alteration and even to reversal under the influence of the activities of the CNS indicated the ways in which the external stimulus could be enhanced or distorted beyond its objective reality by cognitive aspects. This further emphasized the importance of psychological factors—i.e., learning, early traumata, etc.—in the control of behavioral discharge, and it described dramatically the psychological continuity of the organism. It was the contribution of Cannon, however, which provided psychosomatic medicine with its basic conceptual model. Cannon's experimental work challenged the James-Lange Theory of emotions which states that perception of visceral discharge constituted the emotional experience. Cannon proposed a thalamic theory which maintains that the discharge of a pattern of excitation in the thalamus, when communicated to the cortex, gives rise to the experience of emotion. Emotions to Cannon were energizers. The nervous system, particularly the sympathetic part of the autonomic nervous system, plays an important role in the preparation of the organism for emergency function, i.e., for mobilizing the resources of the organism for action. In situations evoking fear and rage to which the characteristic responses are fight or flight, important changes take place in the body in preparation for action. These changes are inhibition of salivation, gastric motility, secretion of gastric juices and peristalsis, thus stopping or retarding the digestive process, acceleration of heartbeat, redistribution of the blood to the musculature and brain stem from the viscera, and increase in blood pressure; all of these prepare the body for vigorous muscular activity. Cannon's elaboration of the complicated interaction between the ductless and endocrine glands and the vegetative functions helped to elaborate how emotional tension could be conducted to any part of the body via corticothalamic and autonomic pathways. When this emotional tension becomes chronic or excessive it results in functional alteration and eventually in structural damage and disease. This new emphasis on emotional factors left the door wide open for psychotherapy to enter the medical field.

Cannon's most valuable contribution was this elaboration of the concept of homeostasis. The notion that excitation of the sympathetic nervous system together with adrenalin secretion is an emergency reaction led him to trace the interlocking mechanisms by which the organism maintains a dynamic equilibrium despite environmental changes. He maintained that it was the sympathetic nervous system which counteracts every kind of environmental pressure, while the parasympathetic system builds up bodily resources. The various bodily changes during emotion, as well as the reactions to heat and cold, are brought about by the sympathetic nervous system and act as homeostatic mechanisms. The emergency emotions such as fear and anger are signs of disturbance and signal the fact that equilibrium has to be restored after the emergency is over.

Cannon's concept of homeostasis was extended by the work of Selye (1946; 1950). Selye clarified the role of the emotions by showing how the pituitary adrenocortical system responds to both physical and emotional stress by a release of ACTH into the bloodstream for the purpose of stimulating the adrenal cortex to secrete various hormones. He showed how animals, exposed to stress of various kinds, secreted not only more adrenalin but also larger quantities of cortical hormones in order to counteract the damage of stress. He coined the term *general adaptation syndrome* for the organized pattern of biological reaction to stress which he inevitably observed. It was obvious to him that excessive adaptive reactions can cause disease.

TOOLS FOR RESEARCH

Pavlov's conditioned reflex method provided an unexpected tool both for induction of stress and for measurement of emotions as correlates of physical stress. The conditioned reflex method has been extensively used in psychosomatic research, particularly in the U.S.S.R., where it is known as Viscerocortical Medicine. Freud's exhaustive elaboration of the mechanisms of unconscious dynamic factors in the development of disease, both psychic and/or somatic, provided the necessary theoretical framework for psychosomatic medicine, while development of a method by which the unconscious could be made conscious provided an essential experimental tool.

Psychosomatic medicine now had a psychological as well as a neurophysiological model of the unity of the organism; it had tools for measurement of emotions, and tools for access to repressed or unconscious contents. It could very well launch forth as a scientific method of studying disease. The publication of Dunbar's book (1935) summarized the scattered observations on the psychosomatic relationships observed up to that time. The establishment of the Psychosomatic Society in 1939 was the official announcement the Psychosomatic Medicine had become an established scientific attitude.

IMPORTANCE OF PSYCHOSOMATIC ATTITUDE

The need for a psychosomatic approach lies in the fact that somatic medicine is still unable to say what the causes of disease are. According to Jores (1961), the reasons for this may be that the cause of disease is not located in the domain of external reality, i.e. the domain accessible to the research methods of natural science. According to him, medicine today offers only symptomatic treatment, despite its isolation of bacilli, etc. Before our clinical methods indicate the presence of a pathological process, a long period of development, not accessible to clinical methods, has already taken place. According to Lériche, a famous French surgeon, today's medicine is in the position of a visitor to a theatre in which the first two acts took place in darkness, with the stage lights not switched on before the third act. The first act may very well have been played in childhood with no apparent sequelae. Then a certain life situation or crisis turns up, and complaints set in—the third act begins. It would be erroneous, says Jores, to assume that nothing has happened in the somatic domain. It is more probable that the alterations which had already ensued were merely not accessible to present methods of investigation.

Hopefully, the gap between the first and third acts may be bridged by the psychological approach. Lashley (1928) stated that neurophysiology offers few principles from which we may predict normal organization of behavior, whereas the study of psychology furnishes a mass of factual material to which the laws of nervous action in behavior must conform. It is therefore more expedient to apply the more subtle and differentiated methods of psychology and of psychotherapy to the psychosomatic problem. Psychotherapy has been shown to provide not only symptomatic cure but at times to restore complete health.

Irving Heller, a noted Montreal neurologist, has expressed the same position in evaluating the findings of strictly somatic techniques. In referring to neurological techniques for diagnosing organic brain damage, he stated that machines have no inherent intelligence. They merely present data; only the clinician can make interpretations and he must ask the patient relevant questions about his actual functioning in order to decode the mechanical findings, otherwise one might find oneself in the ridiculous position of treating the abnormal EEG pattern of a clinically normal subject.

LOGIC OF THE PSYCHOSOMATIC APPROACH

The definition of Psychosomatic Medicine in Vol. 1 of the *Journal of Psychosomatic Medicine*, January 1939, described it as "the endeavour to study in their interaction the psychological and physiological aspects of all normal and abnormal bodily functions and thus to integrate somatic therapy and psychotherapy" (Alexander, 1939). This definition implies that psychosomatic medicine is a way of looking at biological phenomena. It is not a specialty or a division of medicine. As an approach it relies on the standard methodological procedures of any scientific approach, i.e., (1) operational definition, (2) precise observation, (3) objective measurement, and (4) experimental procedure.

A psychosomatic disorder may be defined as one in which the etiological factors may be traced back to the emotions. Oskar Guttman (1966) defines it as follows:

Such a psycho-physiological syndrome, called by some "organ neurosis" could have the meaning of a manifestation of a deep-seated unconscious, neurotic conflict, with the value of an unconscious gratification. In some cases it may appear only as a physiological vegetative corollary of psychoneurotic disturbances, as an "affect equivalent" as Fenichel calls "a state in which the mental content of the affect has been warded off, whereas the physical concomitants of the affect do take place." (p. 282)

What does this mean in (a) physiological, (b) psychological terms? Normal functioning implies that the organism is able to make adequate adjustment to the short- and long-term demands of his environment and is therefore able to carry on without prolonged somatic or mental distress. When, however, environmental pressures or internal resources are such that adaptation cannot be maintained without disorganization of behavior, the organism will react to the pressures or stresses by developing a neurotic, psychotic or psychosomatic reaction. Which manner of response will be favored depends on a great many factors, constitutional as well as environmental. A neurotic may be characterized by behavior that is maladaptive and that to a large extent is accompanied by retreat into fantasy instead of being reality-oriented. That is, either the organism performs the wrong actions, thus gaining some discharge of tension but increasing reality problems, or he withdraws from action into symbolic (fantasy) activity. In both cases, a vicious circle begins, but the control is predominantly on the symbolic level, i.e. within the central nervous system. A psychosomatic breakdown on the other hand implies that appropriate action is either impossible or the discharge of excitation is inadequate, and the excess floods the central nervous system or the vegetative system. Because adequate discharge is impossible, the organ system remains chronically innervated, "excited." If this condition persists long enough, or if there is some constitutional weakness in the organ system, a somatic breakdown occurs and new adjustments must ensue. According to our present knowledge, a psychosomatic disorder implies that the following necessary events must be present: (1) emotional factors must antedate the actual outbreak of psychosomatic disease; (2) emotional factors are generally presumed to be unconscious or at least inhibited; (3) the psychosomatic resolution implies a breakdown of previous coping defenses; (4) the innervation of the CNS must be chronic with chronically impaired functioning; (5)

psychosomatic breakdown will occur if there is a constitutional or acquired weakness of an organ system. Additional but not unequivocal components are: (6) psychosomatic illness implies psychological as well as physiological regression and occurs in persons who are less mature; (7) some life crisis is the precipitant for somatic breakdown, activating available pathological mechanisms which have been conditioned early in life.

NECESSARY CONDITIONS.

1. The emotional factors or sources of stress must antedate outbreak of the somatic condition by some period of time. The emotional response of distress and disorganization cannot be transitory—as is the case in normally distressing situations. The total amount of time the disturbance must persist prior to somatic breakdown will depend on a large number of constitutional as well as environmental factors. This does not imply that emotions cause disease. It means simply that the emotional distress is generally overtly perceived before the somatic condition becomes apparent. However, both the emotional and the somatic changes occur at the same time.

2. The emotional factors underlying the somatic breakdown are generally presumed to be unconscious, i.e. repressed. This does not imply that conscious components are absent or irrelevant. However, if they are not unconscious, total or partial awareness of the emotion must be coupled with inability to act, i.e. to discharge the emotion in sufficient quantities to relieve the stress; or inability to alter the frustrating life situation which maintains the affects in a chronically elevated and disturbed state.

3. The organism has adjusted to his life situation at the expense of normal physiological and possibly mental functioning as well. How he has achieved this, that is, whether he does this by repressing the unacceptable affects into the unconscious, inhibiting them, substituting patterns of reaction formation, projecting or displacing them, or paralyzing their function, will determine the nature of the physical symptoms. Thus different defense mechanisms may be tied up with different physiological systems (conversion symptoms are motor and sensory organ neuroses which rely on the vegetative system).

Originally it was believed that the symptom was the symbol language of the patient and expressed both the instinctual wish and the defense against it, e.g. in paralysis of an arm in conversion hysteria. Later, when discharge of affects into the vegetative system was demonstrated, symbol language had to be modified. The symptom was seen as the physiological response to the wish, which could be expressed symbolically or as a defense reaction, e.g. the sympton of an ulcer patient was presumed to be expressing passive dependent needs—a basic wish to be fed and cared for: the gastric oversecretion was the physiological response to these dependency wishes. His habitual behavior, however, was inconsistent with this; while he professed by word and by deed how independent he was, the behavior of his stomach revealed a different underlying attitude. The ulcer was the end result of the chronically frustrated dependency need combined with the chronic compensating activity which did not allow sufficient expression or gratification of dependency needs. Once the ulcer develops, new adjustments must be made both by the patient and by those involved with him.

4. The innervation of the nervous system must be chronic, with chronically impaired functioning, and beyond the voluntary control of the subject; this will eventually lead to morphological changes in tissue structure and therefore to the development of a disease process. The disease is the point at which a new line of adjustment is reached—the point at which previous defenses and adaptations break down and a new set of communications and interactions set in. There is considerable evidence for the mechanism of tissue breakdown as a result of chronic innervations in laboratory experiments and in nature's experiments on the human level.

5. The final condition for which more and more evidence is accumulating is that stressful emotional conditions will lead to somatic breakdown only if there is some constitutional weakness in an organ system—whether as a result of heredity or traumatization, physical or emotional, at some point in life. This was Alexander's original position.

Less evident but prevailing assumptions about the factors necessary for psychosomatic breakdown are the following:

6. There is a strong opinion that psychosomatic illness occurs in persons who are less mature in psychological development or who have regressed from higher levels of ego development to lower levels. This position has been elaborated by Jurgen Ruesch (1948). His main point is that immaturity in psychological development precludes adequate communication on the symbolic level and requires expression in organ language. Some schools (Grinker) go so far as to say that psychosomatic illness is a physiological regression to primitive vegetative patterns. However, the concept of immaturity of development does not necessarily involve the notion of physiological regression.

7. Life history crisis activates available pathological somatic mechanisms (e.g. hypertensive) which have been conditioned early in life and possibly maintained by the organism's coping mechanisms at a subliminal level. Life situations are experienced as stressful because of unresolved emotional conflicts. Each personality type will have his specific conflict which in a crisis situation will activate his specific physiological mechanism. This may then be elaborated in idiosyncratic patterns of somatic breakdown.

THE PROBLEM OF SPECIFICITY

The theory that specific personality types develop specific psychosomatic disease has had very little support. It originated with Dunbar's study of personality profiles for each disease process. While some data exists linking greater incidence of certain personality types with certain psychosomatic diseases, as a whole this theory is untenable as a psychosomatic principle. Most of the specificity theories were replaced by Alexander's theory of psychosomatic causality in which he suggests that specific unconscious conflicts result in specific disease because specific emotional reactions have specific autonomic-organ innervations.

Continuing research is bringing more and more evidence to indicate that the conflicts in all diseases appear to be highly similar: dependency, repressed aggression, grief over object loss. There is increasing experimental support for the nonspecificity theoretical approaches (Wolff, Selye). The basic assumption here is that visceral response to personality stress follows a general pattern much like the GAS of Selye and the differences as well as similarities are more the result of the organ choice than of specific conflict. The animal experimentalists (Grant, Liddell) have produced psychosomatic symptoms in animals by inducing stressful situations and conflicts. The latter, one would assume, have little resemblance to the specific conflicts in man. The non-specificity theorists maintain that it is enough to postulate that disease symptoms result where psychological defenses cease to be adequate or cannot be established. Although the original specificity theories have been discredited, the problem of why and how specific organs break down under the onslaught of chronic stress has not been successfully answered. There is considerable evidence to suggest that a constitutional weakness of heredity, or acquired early in life is responsible for this. Mirsky et al. (1958) have isolated higher pepsinogen levels in adults who later developed ulcers under stress conditions. Higher pepsinogen levels have also been found at birth in infants, thus presumably predisposing them to respond to situational stress by hypersecretion. Lability of blood sugar levels in diabetes and the lability of the skin in wheal formation have been demonstrated in subjects who break down under emotionally stressful conditions. Malmo and Shagass (1949) have shown that under emotional pressure specific symptoms show stressful response quickly. Shipman et al. (1970) were also able to show response specificity among muscular and autonomic variables. This indicates that there is specificity of response to stress once this specificity has been established. The problem now centers around what defines a stressful situation for the individual concerned.

Conceptual Models

Freud provided the basic conceptual model for psychosomatic medicine in his outline of the psychodynamics of anxiety hysteria. Since that time, theorizing has ranged far from the original scheme and there are many models of disease. One rough division is into psychoanalytic and non-psychoanalytic models. However, there are so many non-psychoanalytic models that these deserve an independent elaboration.

PSYCHOANALYTIC MODELS

These comprise: (1) Models according to which psychosomatic symptoms are symbolically meaningful—i.e., are due to genital or pregenital conversion (e.g. Freud, Ferenczi, Garma); (2) models according to which psychosomatic symptoms have no symbolic meaning but are affect concomitants resulting from blocking of emotional expression (Dunbar, Alexander); and (3) models according to which no single factor specificity exists but the disease is attributable to emotional states: (a) states of hopelessness (Engel, Greene, Schmale); (b) lack of capacity to use fantasy causing a failure in the integration of conflicts in the psychic sphere (D'Uzan); (c) stress-determined regressive resomatization of stimulus response (Mitscherlich's regressive revival of infantile somatic correlates of excitation); and (d) a stress-determined regressive physiological de-differentiation of adult responses concomitant with a psychological regression (Margolin, Grinker).

NON-PSYCHOANALYTIC MODELS

Non-analytic models of psychosomatic disease include H. Wolff's "adaptational theory"; Ruesch's model based on communication theory, von Weizsacker's and von Gebsattel's approach of anthropological medicine, Binswanger's and Medard Bos's existential approach, the socio-psychological and sociocultural approaches of Halliday, Mead and Pflanz, and the corticovisceral approach of Russian scientists.

FREUD, FERENCZI, KLEIN, GARMA

The first psychosomatic formulation was Freud's elaboration of conversion hysteria. His conceptual model of psychosomatic conditions requires the concept of a permanent intrapsychic memory trace of somatic and environmental stimuli. The original stimuli, now memory traces, have both physical and mental components. The organism as a functioning unit is open to a stream of somatic energy converging onto the sensory end of the reflex arc. Whether this energy finds motor discharge or is repressed depends on the mental evaluative system of the individual subject. According to Freud's instinctual theory, each emotion represents a definite charge of instinctual energy seeking discharge. If discharge is not possible, some of this energy is channelled off into fantasy or thinking. If this does not result in sufficient substitute gratification or problem solution, the instinctual energy will be repressed from the conscious mind and remain in a state of tension, or attempt to find other channels of discharge. If this is also impossible, a compromise between the repressed unconscious and the repressing force is achieved and a hysterical conversion symptom results. For instance, if the wish to strike a parent is unacceptable and repressed, the undischarged energy might find discharge in a paralysis of the arm—in this way effecting both discharge of energy and a defense against action. Thus, a repressed instinctual drive gains expression at a somatic level, leading to a symptom with a meaningful symbolic relationship to the psychic event. Ferenczi (1926) was one of the first theoreticians in this field to fuse Freud's conceptual model to explain vegetative dysfunction. Klein (1948) accepted Freud's model as far as it went but differed from Freud in postulating that the first part of the mental mechanism, functional dominance, was not predominantly concerned with the discharge of libidinal energy but with release of aggressive energy. Super-ego conflict could therefore occur at the level of the oral and anal stages of psychosomatic development directly. She therefore felt that a pregenital conversion could occur in the form of an organ neurosis. Garma (1950) went a step further than Klein and postulated that regression might occur not only in the sphere of psychic events but also at the level of physiological events. For example, by means of a mental mechanism such as introjection, anxiety about an internalized aggressive mother could, through regressive phantasies in the psychic sphere, find symbolic expression at the level of gastro-intestinal function. This would lead to a physiological regression in which earlier embryological structures could again become active.

DUNBAR, ALEXANDER

Both Dunbar and Alexander followed essentially Cannon's flight-fight model and Freud's original formulations of a conversion hysteria model. However, they both extended Freud's theories by adding that psychic energy could be discharged down the vegetative system of the body and thus lead to impairments of visceral function. Dunbar (1947) further felt that the excess psychic energy, which could not be discharged at the psychic level, needed to be constantly inhibited, and it was this constant overactivity of the nervous and hormonal pathways connected with the reflex patterns of fight or flight that led to specific psychosomatic illness. Dunbar used a personality profile method to correlate specific character traits with specific psychosomatic illness.

Like Dunbar, Franz Alexander (1939, 1950) believed that specific emotions are accompanied by special innervation patterns of the sympathetic or parasympathetic branch of the vegetative nervous system affecting selected organs and causing specific psychosomatic disturbances. In the course of his studies, Alexander came to believe that the fundamental conflicr was not fight-flight, but the desire to take in and retain versus the desire to give or to expel. He felt that for specific emotions there are appropriate vegetative patterns. If emotions were suppressed from overt expression, chronic tension resulted with chronic concomitant vegetative innervations. In the end, as a result of this, morphological changes in tissue occurred and disease set in. However, Alexander did not subscribe to a monistic concept of causality. He listed nine etiological categories from heredity to later life. He also believed that constitutional vulnerability inherited, or acquired in early life, was necessary to the development of a psychosomatic disorder.

GRINKER, MARGOLIN

Both these scientists start with the undifferentiated boundary-less homeostatic biological field of the human organism which slowly differentiates as the child matures. The original primordial psychosomatic mother-child unit extends and differentiates by means of transactional reactions of parts of the self with the whole and with the environment. "In my opinion the central core of the psychosomatic problem is the period of differentiation from total hereditary to individual learned factors and their integration into a new personal system" (Grinker 1953). The undifferentiated infantile patterns of hypersecretion, hypermotility and hyperemia are substituted by neural control methods—but of course the earlier mechanisms are not extinguished. "Multiple psychosomatic systems respond to alleviate need, overcome obstacles or adjust to frustration. They prepare for and participate in emergency action and disintegrate functionally if the anxiety and the called-for responses of excessive alertness or action persist in time or in quantity. These processes are always transactional among many systems which represent nodes created by the focus of the observer" (p. 180). The transactional system grows more and more complex with age, and the homeostatic mechanism becomes more rigid so that it is more easily disturbed. When this happens, a breakdown or differentiation occurs and the organism regresses to an earlier psychosomatic unity in which the somatic participation is primary. Regression is never complete. The picture is of a sick person in various stages of regression and maturity with various levels of integrity as well as dissociation.

RUESCH, WOLFF

Ruesch, Wolff, and their co-workers focus strongly on the meaning of the life situations and the total culture in precipitating disease. According to Wolff (1950), stresses arise not only from the biological and physical environment but also from symbols of danger learned in past experience as well as from cultural pressures. Stressful life situations all call out a generalized defensive reaction—swelling, redness, hypersecretion, and hypermotility. The stress is symbolized and culture largely determines which organ will represent which symbol. The somatic symptom serves the purpose of adaptation to the particular life stress.

Ruesch (1948) developed a more precise formulation of life situations according to communication theory. He maintains that the somatizing individual never developed an adequate system of communication and feels uneasy with higher level symbolization and has to rely on his body for expression. Disease disturbs the instruments of communication, and likewise inability to communicate may result in disease. Ruesch felt that psychosomatic patients communicate best at a pre-verbal level, i.e. in order to maintain communication they use more primitive channels which are more difficult for others to read, and which ultimately lead to hyperfunction of the vegetative autonomic nervous system and to pathological change.

KUBIE

Kubie's publications (1943, 1953, 1956, 1965, 1968) offer one of the most original and challenging conceptual formulations of the psyche-soma interaction. He has combined the psychoanalytic approach with that of the biological sciences to produce a theoretical framework which is large enough to encompass the findings of the experimentalists as well as the psychoanalysts. His formulation is complex; and reference to the original articles is necessary for a comprehensive appraisal. To explain the correlation of events in the external environment and the psychic and somatic spheres of the individual, Kubie (1953) has grouped the body involvements in psychological conflicts under four categories. (For the purposes of this summary he has revised the original formulation to bring it in harmony with his current thinking.)

1. *Organs which implement our relationships to the external environment.* These are essentially the organs of ego functions, all of which occupy a clearly defined place both in the continuous stream of preconscious processing of experience and in the sampling of this stream which receives conscious symbolic representation. Disorders of these functions are classified as conversion hysterias.

2. *The organs of internal economy.* These lie within the interior of the body and are consequently hidden from the individual's capacity for direct conscious symbolic knowledge of himself. Therefore conscious symbolic representation of these is limited. These disorders are spoken of as "organ neuroses." They are one of the sources of the continuous subliminal (preconscious) afferent bombardment.

3. *The organs of instinctual function.* These have direct apertural connections to the outside world (organs for intake and output of food, air, excrement, the swallowing mechanism, genital function and thermal stability). These are the organs whose needs when synchronized are represented by the body's appetites.

4. *The involvement of the body-image as a whole.* This is obviously not confined to any one organ group. The individuals whose disturbances fall into this group are the so-called neurasthenics and the chronic invalids.

Emotional tensions are normally expressed through symbolic processes of speech, language and sensory imagery. They "can also be expressed through the 'language of the body,' that is through disturbance of sensation, or of somato-muscular or vegetative functions, or through distorted combinations of these processes" (1953, p. 4). It does not follow however that disturbances are expressed either in body language alone or in symbolic language alone. The two expressions may be concurrent, "because symbolic representatives of every conceptual process are rooted inevitably both in the body and in the outside world" (p. 4). Kubie calls the world of internal somatic sensations the "I" world and the world which is external to the boundaries of the body the "non-I" world; even though the latter includes some of the elements of the body image. Thus every conceptual unit is rooted simultaneously both in the "I" and "non-I" worlds. There probably is also a third link, that of the intermediate or communicating world. Kubie believes that "the symbolic processes with their multipolar conscious, preconscious and unconscious linkages provide us with projective pathways for language and for distance imagery at the one end, and introjective pathways for somatic dysfunction at the other" (p. 5). The neuroanatomical and neurophysiological representation of this multipolar function of symbolic processes is mediated by the limbic system or "visceral brain" (1956).

Kubie's (1968) present position remains basically unchanged; but he adds:

today I would give greater emphasis to the preconscious, (the "imageless") processing of experience; and to that subliminal, to wit, preconscious input from the body which is constantly being processed by our brains without the participation of any conscious processes at all. This is what the Wurzburg School called "imageless thought"; and I have come to realize that it is the dominant central activity, whereas our conscious processes are in reality only a weighted and fragmentary sampling of the preconscious stream, with unconscious processes exercising largely a limiting and distorting influence on this conscious symbolic sampling process.

THE ROCHESTER SCHOOL: ENGEL, SCHMALE, GREENE

The Rochester School concentrates on object loss as the precipitating factor of psychosomatic disease. Failure of defenses has been accepted as a sine que non for the development of a psychosomatic disease. Whether the cause of this is repressed affects, aggression, or what, is not clear. In any case, "the psychological factors associated with a whole range of organic diseases are preceded by affective states described as 'despair,'

depression, giving up, grief; all indicating a sense of irresolvable loss or deprivation" (Engel and Schmalle 1967). The authors feel that failure to accomplish the work of grief after object loss leads to a personality state of hopelessness and helplessness. He describes the emotional condition as one of "giving up—given up" and states, "It should be regarded as neither necessary nor sufficient for, but only as contributing to, the emergence of somatic disease, and then only if the necessary predisposing factors are also present." The organ choice may be caused by primary constitutional traumatic defects.

Engel's (1962) opinion is that "no linear concept of etiology is appropriate, but that rather the pathogenesis of disease involves negative and positive feedbacks with multiple simultaneous and sequential changes potentially affecting any system of the body" (p. 268). The biological, psychological, social and cultural parameters are always operating in the field of the organism. The biological factor includes intracultural mother-child interactions. "At some point the somatic system involved comes to exert a specific influence on psychic development, sometimes in the form of derivatives of bodily language, sometimes through erotization processes, and sometimes through involvement in the process of object relating or drive discharge. They also ensure a further measure of specificity in respect to the circumstances that prove psychologically stressful and the sequence of ego responses that culminate ultimately in the appearance of specific somatic lesion."

CORTICOVISCERAL MEDICINE

In Eastern Europe, particularly in the U.S.S.R., the psychosomatic attitude is represented by corticovisceral medicine. The emphasis in the East is on corticovisceral discharge, whereas in the West it is on the relevance of emotional conflicts to vegetative dysfunction. The Pavlovian School has dominated the research in the East, and a considerable amount of experimentation has concentrated on interoceptive conditioned reactions in the production of disturbed somatic functioning. Much of the research has been on animals, although more recently the conceptual models derived from animal experiments have been successfully applied on the human level. Myasnikov (1954), Cernoruckij (1949), and Bulatov (1963) have successfully shown the applicability of cortico visceral interactivity in hypertension, peptic ulcers and bronchial asthma respectively.

Researchers have also made important advances with exteroceptive conditioning on the human level in the production of psychosomatic "neuroses." Thus Psonik (1961) was able to produce a vascular neurosis in his experimental subjects by a disruption of a conditioned pattern of an interoceptive conditioned stimulus and equally successfully by disruption of verbal conditioning. Corticovisceral medicine differs from psychomatic medicine in proposing a unitary etiological concept of neurosis and psychosomatic diseases. The focus of corticovisceral research is mainly on how psychophysiological disturbances occur, not why or to whom. Thus neurophysiological and neuroendocrine mechanisms are explored. Clinical, i.e. introspective, studies with humans have received little investigation although they seem to be in the ascendance at present. The importance of constitution and acquired predisposition are accepted as basic for the choice of organ in the development of disease. According to Bykov (1957), interoceptive impulses are even more important than exteroceptive stimulation for organ choice and explain more convincingly by their ubiquitous, unconscious, readily conditionable nature, the chronic character of corticovisceral illness.

Wittkower et al. (1967) have described—

three discernable tendencies in cortico-visceral medicine: (1) to demonstrate the relevance of temperamental types (choleric, sanguinic, phlegmatic, melancholic) to the nature and course of psychophysiological disturbance. (2) To show that the pathophysiology of nervous breakdown, i.e. forced collision or overstraining of excitation and/or inhibition, is responsible for malfunctioning of internal organs; and (3) to stress the role of peripheral factors. The protective, compensatory influence of the cortex is not disputed, but a concomitant "locus minoris resistantiae" is implicated in the choice of organ pathology.

Anthropological Medicine (von Gebsattel, von Weizsacker, van der Horst)

The term anthropological is used not in the American sense but in the sense of "anthropos"; the study of man and of the essential meaning and characteristics of being human. Von Weizsacker (1951) believes in replacing the dualism of Psyche and Physis by "the polar unity of subject and object." "But the subject is not a stable property; one has to continuously acquire it in order to possess it." It is only noticed in a "crisis" when one is threatened with losing it. "In so far as a living being through its movement and perception integrates itself into an environment, these movements and perceptions form a unit, a biological act." Von Weizsacker refutes the concept of causality in psychosomatic disease as too narrow and problematic. He believes that symptoms often represent "a fragment of unlived life," a response of unconscious mind-body patterns to disturbing life situations. The significance of an illness has its specific meaning in the life of the patient. Biography is the key to understanding of illness. However, von Gebsattel (1954) cautions that the time has not yet come for philosophical anthropology.

Existential Approach (Biswanger, Bos)

This model is centered around the phenomenological works of Husserl and the philosophy of Heiddeger. Like the anthropological approach, it rejects scientific medicine and with it experimental medicine. The research of the existential approach is concerned with the understanding of the patient's life history as a modification of his being in the world. Nervous diseases are regarded as changed existential processes. The relationship between doctor and patient is one of encounter, in which the goal is to make the patient experience how he has failed to realize the fullness of his humanity and to open up new structures for the battered existential processes. The approach is always to the *whole* man.

Socio-Psychological and Socio-Cultural Models (Halliday, Mead, Pflanz, Leighton)

The concept of social sickness became the focus of Halliday (1943), a public health expert. He implied that the entire society

itself could be considered as ill under certain circumstances. He felt that mechanistic aetiology provides no direct guidance about measures that will keep people from becoming ill. The biological viewpoint, on the other hand, is concerned with the organism and his environment. Illness is not a fault but a reaction or mode of behavior. He elaborated that economic stress and altered value systems were among the many factors which had greatly altered the mother-child relationship, which he considers of vital importance in the development of disease. He felt that medical action should be concerned primarily with measures designed to alter or prevent characteristics of the person known to be causal and to alleviate or remove factors of the environment known to be causal. Margaret Mead (1947) maintained:

It is necessary to realize that every individual born into a society is from birth—and in all probability from before birth—subjected to a progressive moulding by the culture, mediated through all those with whom he comes in contact, so that the cultural pattern is built into his whole personality in one process in which no dualism exists, so that the temper tantrums, the tightened muscles, the change in the manufacture of blood sugar, and the verbal insults hurled at an offending parent, all become patterned and integrated. Then we see that every individual, and not merely every patient, may be viewed from the psychosomatic point of view, within which individuals who show definite organ neuroses are merely extreme and special developments of one potentiality of the total personality. And we further see that there is no basic human personality but that every individual must be seen against the cultural base line, that he is a special idiosyncratic variant of one of many culturally unique ways in which human personality is developed. (p. 68)

Transcultural Psychosomatics (Wittkower)

According to Wittkower, disease can be viewed from various angles—from the genetic, biological, psychological, social and cultural viewpoints. Each of these approaches is of necessity segmental. To gain a wider perspective of the patient, he must be viewed as a person acting within and interacting with his total socio-cultural environment. Transcultural psychosomatics interprets observed phenomena in cultural terms. At present this is mainly an area for research. The questions that are asked are aimed at an evaluation of differences in value orientation, family structure, role and status of women, urbanization, political change, social institutions, etc., as these relate to and influence the frequency and incidence of psychosomatic disorders. Wittkower indicates that there are two approaches to cultural and transcultural psychosomatics; the clinical (predominantly psychiatric) and the social science point of view.

Methodologies of transcultural psychosomatic research consist of application of the same investigative technique to persons and situations in contrasting cultures either by the same observers or by different observers. The investigative tools comprise (1) clinical interviews, (2) field surveys, (3) hospital records, (4) psychological tests, and (5) questionnaires. Team cooperation is an essential aspect of this type of research. Wittkower's own approach most clearly resembles that of Alexander. However, he places much greater emphasis on the contribution that culture makes on the choice and symbolic elaboration of the symptom. Wittkower's basic assumption is that cultural measures and stresses may predispose to, precipitate and maintain, mental and psychosomatic illness. He believes that some cultures are more stressful than others, with the consequent result that the modal personality in some cultures is more susceptible to stress than in others.

The Autonomic Nervous System and Control of Behavior

Research demonstrating the original psychosomatic hypothesis that chronic autonomic neuroendocrine innervation leads to altered function and structural tissue change has been voluminous, productive and convincing. The physiological mechanisms of how this occurs have been intensely studied by viscerocortical medicine in the U.S.S.R. and more recently in the U.S.A., and some of the intricate dynamics appear to be emerging.

It has been demonstrated that electrical stimulation of parts of the brain controlling somatic mechanisms involved in various psychosomatic diseases will result in somatic breakdown of the precise type that occurs in psychosomatic disease. Experiments with animals with direct stimulation of the hypothalamus to produce ulcerative lesions in the stomach (French et al. 1957) and with sham feeding (Silbermann 1927) both have successfully demonstrated that excessive stimulation of the areas involved by one method or another resulted in tissue breakdown. A more sophisticated experiment by Brady (1958) with "executive monkeys" (in which the responsible monkey developed ulcers as a result of the need to avoid an electric shock situation, on a 6 hours off – 6 hours on schedule) has demonstrated that emotional factors and not purely physical stress (ECT) are responsible for the development of lesions.

The discovery of the reward and aversion drive zones in the hypothalamus by electrical stimulation of the brain through implanted electrodes in animal brains has broadened understanding of avoidance behavior and anxiety. Areas in the posterior hypothalamus which lead to avoidance behavior stimulate the pituitary adrenal axis and the release of autonomic and neuroendocrine changes which are normally associated with flight-fight responses. Presumably chronic emotional stress will result in structural damage in the same way that prolonged electrical stimulation does. Henry et al. (1967) have offered new and highly convincing evidence that prolonged social stress in animals continuing over 12 months will result in psychosomatic breakdown. Sines (1962) has pointed out that rats selectively bred for stomach lesion development under stress show some characteristics suggesting that they may be "functionally sympathectomized."

On the human level, considerable evidence exists to indicate the contribution of continual stress to the production and maintenance of all the major psychosomatic illnesses. Thus stress in experiments involving observation of subjects with fistulas in natural surroundings, psychoanalytic studies, observation of subjects in stressful laboratory and real life situations have produced convincing evidence of the importance of emotional stress in psychosomatic breakdown.

However, why one organism under stress will respond with psychosomatic mechanisms whereas another one with similar organ involvement under similar stress is able to use successful fight of flight coping mechanisms and a third develops neurotic or psychotic adjustment patterns is not at all clear. There is an emerging body of research to indicate the importance of both genetic and constitutional factors on the one hand and of early experience or conditioning on the other hand in the predisposition to symptom choice; but there has been little convincing "proof" that "organ inferiority" under traumatic or prolonged stress must inevitably result in somatic disease. It is logical to infer that conditions which are not self-limiting, which in fact might be self-stimulating through a feedback system, must be terminated one way or another. This intervention might logically take the form of somatic breakdown, thus altering the present maladaptive pattern of physiological as well as psychological adaptation. However, it may also be effected by a psychotic breakdown or by medical intervention as well as by environmental change.

Recent research has focused on several new directions. One of the these has been emphasis on constitutional differences as these relate to conditioning and to disease; another is emphasis on cognitive factors in the structuring of, and response to, the disease process; another is emphasis on the life crisis situation and on the importance of social stresses in the precipitation of disease. A fourth area which has begun to emerge is a new awareness of the "unconscious" in both the induction and maintenance of psychological mechanisms.

Constitutional Differences in ANS Reactivity—and Conditioning

Genetic or constitutional predisposition has been postulated as one of the factors in autonomic nervous system regulation which is important in the development of psychosomatic disease. There is now an impressive body of data to indicate that marked differences between individuals in CNS excitability exist at birth. Thus, types of foetal activity (Jost and Sontag 1944) have been related to nature of behavioral response at nursery-school age. Marked differences in autonomic functioning at birth have been shown by Richmond and Lustman (1955); Grossman and Greenberg (1957); Greenberg, Cepan, and Loesch (1963). Grossman and Greenberg found that homeostatic regulation in infants was not necessarily uniformly deficient as was postulated by Cannon. The authors found that in using any single index of ANS function, a given group of newborn infants will show a normal distribution with graduations from "rigidity" to "lability." The same individuals may show reversed degrees of homeostasis when another index of CNS is used. The authors felt that "lability" or instability may be constitutionally characteristic for only a single or few components of the CNS, and it would require the fortuitous concomitant of an available "vulnerable" segment with the "proper psychopathology" for a psychosomatic disorder to occur.

Lang (1966) has demonstrated that the effect of autonomic activation on perceptual behavior decreases with age, whereas the external features of stimuli increase with age. Lipton et al. (1966) in a study of cardiac control in infants at birth to five months of age, demonstrated significant changes between infancy and $2\frac{1}{2}$ months of age. By $2\frac{1}{2}$ months the cardiac pattern had changed significantly, characterized by faster reaction, attenuated initial rise in rate, and generally greater return to below pre-stimulus level. Readings at $2\frac{1}{2}$ months and 5 months showed significant correlations demonstrating increasing stability after the newborn period. Extent and precursors of lability at infancy and for the first few months is not certain, but it is clear from the emerging research that there is lability in one or more systems, and maturational changes in the direction of greater control do occur in the first few months of life. On the basis of this evidence, the early period may be regarded as sufficiently labile and unstable to warrant the theoretical formulations of Mandler that pervasive conditioning might take place.

The Cognitive Control of Response

Experiments by Schachter and Singer (1962) with adrenaline are of considerable theoretical importance for psychosomatic medicine. The experimenters invited a student to participate in an experiment, presumably to study "drug effects on perception." The student was told that the effects of the drug would be tremor, increased heart rate, and a flushed face. After the injection of the drug, the student was asked to wait in a waiting room in order to let the drug take effect. He found another student there who, unknown to the subject, was a stooge. The stooge soon began to behave in a very mad fashion. The stooge made and flew paper planes around the room, played basketball with some scrap paper and generally behaved in a riotous manner. He invited the experimental subject to join in but was met with a terse refusal, and soon after this the experiment was concluded. Schachter repeated the experiment with a second volunteer student, except that this time the student was informed that the transitory effects of the drug would be numbness in the feet, a slight headache, and itching sensations, i.e. misinformation about drug effects. In the waiting room the student met the same stooge as had his predecessor. The stooge went through the same antics but this time the volunteer student joined in the fun and carried on as madly as the stooge. Asked later how he felt, he said he had experienced a feeling of madness, happiness and euphoria. The results of the experiment using a total of 183 subjects, including controls, were as Schachter had predicted. "Given a state of physiological arousal for which an individual has no immediate explanation, he will label this state and describe his feelings in terms of the cognitions available to him." Whereas when the individual has an appropriate explanation, he is relatively free of environmental manipulation and describes his feelings as he experiences them or to the extent that he experiences them. Schachter and Singer conclude that "cognitive factors are major determinants of the emotional labels we apply to a common state of sympathetic arousal" (p. 397).

This experiment not only calls attention to the importance of cognitive factors but also indicates how diffuse the visceral discharge may be, despite the specific activity of the injected substance. The innervations which are appropriate to fear and rage can equally well evoke affects which can also be experienced by the subject as euphoric or happy. Bovard (1959) has also pointed out that psychological stress has no invariant effect.

The essential difference between psychological and physical stress is that the former, necessarily mediated by the CNS, has no invariant effect. Whether a given psychological stimulus (making a public speech) triggers a protein catabolic response is a function of the previous conditioning and present level of reactivity of the nervous system. The effect of purely physical stress, such as cold, can be considered far more invariant and unavoidable for both

rat and man. Since the pituitary-adrenal response to the psychological stress can be considered maladaptive, the fact that the latter has to be mediated by the CNS permits us to intervene and prevent triggering of this protein catabolic response, by altering activity of the nervous system. From the psychological point of view, this means influencing the early and present experience of the organism. (p. 268)

The importance of cognitive preparation in determining the nature of the physiological response has also been pointed out by Grings, Carlin and Appley (1962). They showed that subjects could be led to report they had received a shock and to give galvanic skin responses reflecting this, even when no shock was administered. This happened under conditions in which a series of unrelated expectancies were consistently confirmed and the subject could certainly expect shock to be given in the situation. Berkun et al. (1962) found that real life (military training) stresses were very effective if the subjects perceived them as such and were completely ineffectual if they did not perceive them as stressful.

Arnold (1960), Appley and Trumbull (1967), Pepitone (1967), and Lazarus (1966), have all stressed the process of appraisal in the production of emotion. Lazarus identified cognitive processes as the precursors in the stress reaction. He pointed out that if the appraisal of the stress situation is altered there will be a correspondingly altered stress response. Furthermore, cognitive processes underlie not only perception of threat but the form of coping which the individual will select (fight or flight) "All indicators of psychological stress are subject to individual response and stimulus specificity" (1967, p. 154). Appley (1967) subdivides appraisal as it relates to the perception of stress into three dimensions. He points out that an individual's perception of stress depends first on his appraisal of task requirements and of his own competence to deal with the stressful situation. Secondly, appraisal of his own role in relation to task performance and, thirdly, appraisal of environmental constraints— i.e., reality testing. Appley feels that a similar analysis must be made for coping behavior. Here the dimensions of competence, relevance, consequence and significance (physical, social and psychological) must be evaluated. "I would go further to suggest the notion that stress is a complex *residual* of the processes resulting from appraisals of threat, of danger, and of the effectiveness of coping" (1967; p. 171). He underlines the need to perceive stress not as if it were a binary on-or-off process, but as a continuum involving successive thresholds in which instigation, action, frustration, and stress is the logical step progression.

I am suggesting a graded increase from mild distress or mild discomfort—which leads to or instigates change in behavior— to a state of frustration and a beginning of worry about the self and self-threat, possibly accompanied by psychosomatic change, to a more active disturbance which we are calling stress. To complete the picture it would be fair to speak of an exhaustion threshold, *or point of helplessness or hopelessness, in which ego defensive behaviors and the enervating physiological changes give way to energy-conserving inactivity or to disordered behavior. (1967, p. 171)*

The final pattern is the product of this interaction of personality and physiological process and will certainly carry personal-specific characteristics.

In the face of the above analysis, how does one account for the fact that there is nevertheless considerable stimulus specificity or as Lacey (1967) has more recently preferred to call it, situational stereotypy? This refers to physiological mechanisms which can be counted on to occur as a function of specific types of behavior. Lacey points out that there are a large number of psychophysiological experiments which demonstrate that different stimulus situations produce different patterns of somatic response, e.g. anger directed outwards, anger directed inwards (Ax 1953). Another of these *patterns* is that "attentive observation of the external environment is productive of cardiac deceleration, cardiac stabilization and either blood pressure decrease or a marked diminution of pressure increase. These results occur simultaneously with other procedures, such as vasocostriction and palmar conductance increase" (Lacey 1967, p. 33). Lacey summarizes a series of experiments demonstrating the above principle and concludes, "We heuristically interpreted these results to mean that depression-decelerative processes facilitated environmental intake and that pressor-accelerative responses tended to filter out irrelevant stimuli that have distraction value for the performance of internalized cognitive elaboration" (p. 34). Obrist (1963) confirmed these findings. The conclusion which can be drawn from this again is that there are physiological, relatively stable patterns of response for general classes of behavioral function, e.g. such as cognitive or externalized attending, that impose a specific or stereotyped, i.e. non-idiosyncratic control behavior which will dominate the behavioral pattern if they are dominant factors in the response. To the extent that cognitive or attentional factors are involved, they "can diminish, cancel, or convert cardiac acceleration and blood pressure increases 'caused' by suitable behaviors," (Lacey 1967, p. 35) and cardiac activity in turn exercises considerable control of the central nervous system—more specifically the cardiovascular system—has control of the bulbar inhibitory areas which have a capacity to decrease cortical electrical activity. It is obvious that "cortical and subcortical systems and peripheral mechanisms can control at early stages in the transmission process the very nature and kind of signals that are allowed to be transmitted, and can even determine the variable nature of the transmission process itself" (Lacey 1967, p. 33; Galin 1964). It has also been obvious that there are different patterns within the sympathetic nervous system and that these are related to the stimulus characteristics (Lacey 1959; Engel 1960).

This recent research points out again the amazing unity of the body as well as the importance of both the environmental and physiological factors to which the organism is responding. While the physiological patterns follow a stereotype laid down by the nature of the system involved, cognitive factors may play a large part in determining which stereotype will take over and why. Thus, intention and direction would become extremely important factors in the possible explanation of symptom choice in psychosomatic medicine. It is obvious that the "psyche" aspect of the psychosomatic equation cannot be ignored although much more research is needed before we understand the mechanisms of this complex interaction.

Studies with hypnotically induced blindness, deafness, and vasomotor, metabolic, and gastrointestinal functions indicate that physiological changes in all these organ systems can be produced both by hypnosis and often without it in some subjects. Ullman and Dudek (1960) effected 67 percent cure of warts by hypnosis in adults, and Dudek (1967) was able to demonstrate 50 percent cure of warts in children without use of hypnosis. A number of researchers have shown a rise in blood sugar level in hypnotized diabetic subjects under the instructions to relax and to increase blood sugar level. It is a fact that blood glucose level is excessively labile in diabetics. Hinkle and Wolff (1953) and Mirsky (1948) have shown that diabetics tend to show more extreme alterations in bood sugar content during arousal. On the other hand, hypnotic suggestion could effect no change in the blood sugar level in non-diabetic subjects. Induction of blisters (Borelli 1953) was only possible in the small group of persons with a physiological predisposition to blister or wheal formation. Heyer (1925; cited in Barber 1961) was able to induce secretion of gastric juice within 10 to 15 minutes after hypnotic suggestion to the effect that the subject was eating a meal; and the acidity and proteolytic activity appeared to vary with each food suggested. However, similar effects could be achieved in nonhypnotized subjects merely by suggestion. Berman, Simonson and Heron (1954), using 14 susceptible hypnotic subjects with normal EKG, found that during hypnotically induced fear and anxiety, two subjects showed elevation and five showed depression or inversion of T waves. However, some persons who have not been given "hypnotic induction" show similar EKG alterations during emotional stimulation. Barber concludes his review of the physiological effects of hypnosis with the statement that "a group of so-called hypnotic phenomena, e.g. production of blisters, cure of warts, alteration of blood glucose levels, production of tachycardia or cardiac bloc, can apparently be elicited without an 'hypnotic induction' in a small number of individuals who possess a specific lability of the physiological systems involved" (1961, p. 415).

INSTRUMENTAL CONDITIONING AND THE POTENTIAL CONTROL OF BEHAVIOR

It was evident early in psychosomatic research that the autonomic nervous system could be readily conditioned to all kinds of stimuli by means of classical conditioning (Bykov 1957). However, more recently instrumental conditioning has been able to achieve the same results, and there is a substantial body of published research in this area. Much of the research has focused on heart rate changes both in animals and humans (Chevine 1970) and some of this work will be cited. The theoretical significance of this research lies in the potential it holds for understanding of mechanisms of behavioral control on the psychosomatic level. Di Cara and Miller (1968a) in a series of experiments with curarized rats, have shown that heart rate, peripheral vasomotor responses, gastrointestinal motility, and urine production can be modified by brain stimulations or by the effect of painful electric shock as reinforcement. In order to rule out mediation of visceral responses by respiratory change and/or overt skeletal responses, the rats were paralyzed by *d*-tubocurarine and maintained on artificial respiration. In a recent experiment of instrumental learning of systolic blood pressure responses (Di Cara and Miller 1968b), curarized rats were again used. Each rat was yoked to a control rat. The experimental animal would avoid shock to the tail by learning to elevate (one group) or decrease (another group) systolic blood pressure. The control group could do nothing to avoid the shock. The experimenter obtained highly significant results for diastolic heart pressure while heart rate and temperature remained within normal range, i.e. the general pattern of activation did not change. The yoked animals did not show any significant change in blood pressure. The conditionability of blood pressure levels suggests that "abnormal cardiovascular and other responses may be learned as psychosomatic symptoms and contribute to the development of atypical profiles of autonomic reactivity to stress and cardiovascular renal pathology. The instrumental learning of blood pressure responses has interesting therapeutic possibilities for clinical medicine since it may be possible to teach hypertensives to permanently lower their blood pressure levels" (p. 494). Citing the work of Carmona, Di Cara further states that "it is also conceivable that in some cases the responses reflected in abnormal EEG activity can be modified by learning" (p. 493).

Shapiro et al. (1970) were able to demonstrate significant heart rate conditioning in humans in a single session without concomitant effects on systolic blood pressure. The authors conclude that their data "demonstrate that instrumental fractionation of closely related visceral behavior is possible in man, and support the possibility of a behavioral therapy for autonomically-mediated disorders" (p. 423). Weiss and Engel (1971) were able to teach successful long-term control of heart rate in patients with premature ventricular contractions by means of operant conditioning.

The complexity of the problem in assessing the determinants of physiological and behavioral changes has been lucidly and incisively reviewed by Malmo and Belanger (1967). They cite their own work as well as that of others in this field to demonstrate, as Lacey has done, the importance of the stimulus side of ANS in an analysis of conditioning. In experiments on the effects of water deprivation upon heart rate and instrumental activity in the rat, Belanger and Feldman (1962) demonstrated that animals showed heart rate increase when they found themselves before the dish containing water. The subsequent experiments of O'Kelly et al. (1965) with water-deprived rats in which they found no heart rate changes when the animals were presented with an empty dish served to demonstrate that an interaction between internal condition (organic need) and appropriate environmental cue was required for measurable physiological change to manifest itself. Malmo and Belanger cite the above experiments to support their own multiple factor theory of motivation. "The environmental stimulating conditions under which the heart rate changes were measured must in every case be kept in mind" (p. 295). They also cite experiments by Ducharme (1962) which demonstrate "that cues other than those of adequate unconditioned reinforcement can produce heart rate acceleration in the animal 'sensitized' by deprivation" (p. 298). Ducharme has made it clear that "the conditioned" cues can be even more effective than the "unconditioned cues" in effecting behavioral change. The interoceptive experiments of the Soviet scientists have led to the same conclusions (Razran 1961).

We may hypothesize about the potential effects of con-ditioned autonomic mechanisms of childhood in the induction and maintenance of disease in adulthood. Moreover, the Soviet research on interoceptive conditioning suggests that autonomic responses condition readily and are more "fixed" than skeletal responses once they have been established. If this proves to be the case, considerably more involuntary and unconscious conditioning of the autonomic nervous system, on a contiguity basis, probably occurs both in infancy and adulthood than has been previously suspected. This may also help to account for some of the idiosyncrasies in physiological patterning when the expected stimulus specificity either does not occur or when it cannot be explained by the obvious external S–R connections which are evident to the observer. This emphasis does not reduce the subjective peripheral-evaluation-aspect of experience. It merely adds another level of complexity to the analysis of both physiological and emotional patterning.

ANTICIPATION IN THE STRUCTURING OF SOMATIC RESPONSE

Obrist (1968) has hypothesized that

the direction and magnitude of the anticipatory cardiac response will be, to a significant degree, determined by whether the organism initiates or inhibits somatic motor activity preparatory to the UCS. Thus, the influence of the effective and motivational processes initiated by the CS on heart rate will be determined in part by whether an organism initiates or inhibits activity in coping with the anticipated UCS. The type of activity would seem to be a function of several variables such as the species of the organism, and the nature of the conditions. For example, where flight or fight appear possible, activity might increase; where a recourse to activity is not possible then a cessation of activity is resorted to, e.g. an animal freezing. (p. 191)

Obrist cites Engel (1950) who suggested that in certain stress situations, where inhibitory effects over cardiac and somatic responses are considerable, vasopressor syncope may occur "during the experience of fear when action is inhibited or impossible." The work of Bonvallet and Allen (1961); Engel (1950); Lacey (1967); Obrist (1968), suggests that it may be valid to extrapolate similar homeostatic effects (reinforcement or inhibition of response) to other organ systems. This brings us full circle to the problem of cognitive appraisal in the structuring and control of behavioral responses.

INSTRUMENTAL CONDITIONING AND THE SICK SOCIETY

The effects of socially stressful situations have been shown to result in marked somatic reactions in experimental animals. For example, the social aspects of living conditions, like crowding versus isolation (Thiessen 1963), unexpected change of cage environment (Friedman 1966), interference with sexual and protective reflexes (Miminoshuili 1960), competition for territory (Christian 1964; Barnett 1963) have resulted in significant changes in behavior (increase in aggressive fighting), weight loss, neurogenic hypertension, and changes in adreno-cortical function. Brain norepinephrine levels were found to be lower in grouped rather than in isolated mice (Welch and Welch 1965). Ulcers are more common in isolated as compared to aggregated mice (Stern et al. 1960).

On the human level, Scotch's (1957) interesting finding that social groups with high blood pressure exhibit greater social tensions and conflicts than groups with normal pressures offers suggestive evidence of the importance of the social environment in the pathogenesis of disease much as Halliday maintained in *The Sick Society*. Beginning with the hypothesis that in human populations increase in systolic pressure with age is a response to repeated stressful symbolic stimuli arising from the social environment, Henry et al. (1967) attempted to simulate real life stressor conditions in experimental animals "by playing on their inborn drives for territory, survival, and reproduction." Four techniques for social stimulation were used: (1) mixing adult males which had never previously been in contact, (2) submitting male and female mice to chronic threats from a predator, (3) reducing the floor space available until animals were so closely aggregated that the fur was in contact, and (4) exposing males and females to an interconnecting box system, leading to chronic territorial conflict. The experiments were continued for 6 to 12 months. The experimenters summarized their findings as follows:

1. All methods resulted in a sustained elevation of systolic arterial pressure of the order of 160 mg Hg in the males. There was elevation to 140–150 mg Hg in the females, and the aggregation of male castrates showed only minimal blood pressure effects.

2. Histologic examination of the kidneys in controls and in the less affected experimental groups showed no abnormality which would account for the blood pressure changes, but interstitial nephritis was found in the severely hypertensive group.

3. On returning the mice to a less stimulating situation, the pressures usually subsided toward the baseline control value of 126 ± 12 mm Hg.

4. Early experience proved to be important. If the aggregated animals or those in the interconnected boxes were kept together from birth, the pressure elevations were less severe, while isolation from weaning to maturity exacerbated the blood pressure effects of the conflict for territory.

5. The sustained blood pressure elevations persisted despite ether anesthesthesia but fell to normal with reserpine administration.

6. The results support current hypotheses that in a constant external environment the systemic arteriolar pressure of a group is a measure of the symbolic stimuli received during social interaction and that early experience plays a role in determining the arousal value of the stimuli received.

The authors point out that the fact that blood pressure tends to return to normal values after cessation of noxious stimulation is consistent with findings on the human level (Smirk 1957). This was obviously no longer true for animals in whom interstitial nephritis had developed.

Bovard (1958) has presented evidence for the beneficial effects of social stimuli from which we may infer that the potential for a healthy society is as much inherent in man as the potential for a sick one. In his review, Bovard (1959, p. 269), cites a number of studies to indicate the supportive effect of the small group under stress.

Titmuss (1950) showed that separation from the family and evacuation from London appeared more stressful for London children than did enduring the blitz with their family. Combat studies have suggested the effectiveness of the small group (platoon, bomber crew) in sustaining members under severe battle stress (Mandlebaum 1952). Marshall (1951) found that battle stragglers during a retreat were relatively ineffective when put back into the line with new units, but that units that had been able to stay together fought courageously and well when put back into the line as units. Research at Boston Psychopathic Hospital (1955) has shown that lysergic acid diethylamide (LSD) taken in a group situation results in less anxiety, interpersonal distortion, and inappropriate behavior than when taken individually. These and other studies suggest that the presence of others, particularly others with whom one has previously interacted, has a protective effect under stress.

THE UNCONSCIOUS—INFERRED AND OBSERVABLE

Another area which is crucial to an understanding of the aetiology of psychosomatic disorders and for which there is as yet insufficient experimental evidence is the influence of unconscious affects and fantasies in the precipitation and maintenance of emotional stress. Mirsky et al. (1948) and Margolin (1951) have shown that where no observable stimulus is evident in producing a specific somatic reaction its genesis can be explained by the presence of unconscious affects; more recently attempts to correlate conscious and unconscious anxiety with autonomic response (Lacey, Smith & Green 1955) showed very different physiological patterns in subjects who were aware of the conditioning procedures and as opposed to subjects who were unaware and presumably developed "unconscious anxiety" following the experimenters' successful manipulation of the conditioning procedures. The spread of anxiety, as measured by generalization curves, appeared to be greater in subjects functioning under unconscious anxiety. Subjects who were aware of the experimental design prior to the experiment developed a strong emergency response following the designated stimulus words, and this response showed a gradual adaptation. Lisina (in Razran 1961) also demonstrated that if a subject is made fully conscious of the conditioned connection, this connection could be radically altered.

Allied to the problem of the unconscious is the relatively new area of research on "unconscious" control of affect expression. Experiments on the inhibition versus the expression of affect as a factor in physiological response under stress were undertaken by Oken et al. (1962). The authors measured two groups of subjects on the basis of free expression of affect versus low expression of affect. Findings were in opposite directions to the hypothesis that emotionally expressive subjects would give lower physiological responses for heart rate, systolic blood pressure, skin resistance, calf-muscle blood flow and respiratory rate. The only variables which showed greater physiological response in the inhibited group of subjects were diastolic and finger blood flow, and skin temperature. The authors interpreted their findings to mean that suppression of feelings was linked to development of essential hypertension. The problem with this experiment lies in the fact that it is impossible to determine whether feelings were inhibited unconsciously or were of a low order of response for other reasons, such as defective or initially low hypothalamic excitability.

The problem of the "unconscious" has been highlighted by a relatively recent survey of experimental work on conditioning in the Soviet Union, entitled: "The Observable Unconscious and the Inferrable Conscious in Current Soviet Psychophysiology," by Razran (1961) which has indicated exciting theoretical implications for psychosomatic medicine. There has been considerable research on interoceptive conditioning in the Soviet Union since 1928. This class of conditioning is one in which the CS or the US are both delivered directly to the mucosa of some specific viscus. It represents a condition in which the milieu interieur acquires the function of a signalizer, or initiator, or conveyer of the acquired conditioned information. The conditioning has been done on both animals and humans, predominantly by use of fistulas in situ and also by surgical exteriorization. The main significance of this research has been summarized by Razran (1961). He points out that the conditioning of interoceptive stimulation which leads to readily obtainable conditioned responses is by its very nature largely unconscious in character. By nature, interoceptive kinds of stimulation are "much more recurrent periodic and organism bound, making interoceptive conditioning an almost built-in function that is constantly generated and regenerated in the very process of living and acting" (p. 97). While interoceptive conditioning is slower in formation than exteroceptive, it is much more fixed and irreversible once it has been conditioned. In situations where equal and opposing interoceptively and exteroceptively produced reactions are juxtaposed, the interoceptive reactions dominate over the exteroceptive. The result is that the exteroceptive stimuli become conditioned stimuli for the succeeding interoceptive. Finally, when conditioned interoceptive and exteroceptive stimuli of the same conditioned reaction are juxtaposed, a certain amount of conflict and loss of conditioning strength is the result. This is in contrast to what happens when similar exteroceptive stimuli of different modalities are juxtaposed.

Relevance of interoceptive conditioning for both Freudian theory and psychosomatic medicine is profound. Interoceptive conditioning involves the modification of functions of the vital organs. It is accomplished unconsciously and has marked effects on the functioning of vital organs and concurrently on the emotional response of the organism, whether the response be in terms of free floating anxiety or the activation of hypertensive mechanisms experienced, etc. "Not only may feelings of anxiety, or its unconscious visceromotor accompaniments become conditioned stimuli for the production of, let us say, constipation, but also unconscious rectal distention, or sensations of constipation, may equally be conditioned to bring about conscious and unconscious anxiety, or bring about abnormal bile secretion or gout, or asthma, dyspnoea, hypertension, angina pectoris, or any other functional disturbance" (Razran 1961, p. 99). Razran points out that introceptive conditioning may well hold the key to an analysis of the effects of the unconscious on conscious life, much in the way that Freud postulated it.

Razran's survey includes a section on verbal conditioning, and its relevance to visceral response is intriguing. One of the experiments on verbal conditioning involves an experiment on conditioning of reduction in time of blood coagulation to the sound of a metronome (Markosyan 1958). After CR was established, these CR transferred from the sound of the metronome to the sound of the word metronome, and to phonetographically related words.

In another experiment, Shvarts (1960) conditioned vasoconstriction to the words *dom* (home) and *doctor* (doctor). CR transfers occurred to phonetographically related words *dym* (smoke), and *diktor* (announcer), and to the semantically related English word home (since the subjects knew the English language) and the Russian word *Vratch* (physician). The CR transfers to phonetographic words disappeared after CR had become well established (after 25 trials) but reappeared again after the subject was administered chloral hydrate, i.e. *at lower levels of organic functioning*.

Razran summarizes his review of somatic conditioning experiments with the statement that it demonstrates the ability of

a vast realm of experimentally separable meaning-units continually entering in complex functional relationships with each other and with non-meaningful units, existing both in and out of consciousness, and normally, whether conscious or unconscious, forming controlling rather than controlled systems. Small wonder that the significance of semantic conditioning extends to such varied fields as: the psychology and thinking, ranging from unbewusste Bewusstseinlagen of the Würzburg School to modern views of cognition as a high level, controlling mechanism of which we may not be aware. Freud's symbolism, secondary processes, and conscious-unconscious ego relations; cultural anthropology; clinical observations on aphasia and agnosia; practical problems in psychotherapy; general linguistics; general similarities; and such applications as education techniques and the psychology of advertising and of propaganda. (p. 108)

It is evident that many lines of research can be merged to elaborate both the psychological and the neurophysiological mechanisms of the psychosomatic development. Whatever the stimulation and whatever the locus of symptom development, the pathways always merge in the cerebral cortex and two concurrent responses, one psychic and one somatic, inevitably emerge. The logic of body-mind unity appears to be inescapable.

PSYCHOSOMATIC AND NEUROPHYSIOLOGICAL EXPLANATIONS IN DIFFERENT PSYCHOSOMATIC CONDITIONS

Research methods may focus more on one level than another but it is impossible to deal with the somatic component without affecting the psychological and vice versa. Oscar Guttmann (1966) has elaborated the problem as follows. An emotional disturbance will be accompanied by:

(1) A break in the balance of the vital rhythm causing dysrythmia and inadequate energy utilization in our inner economy, (2) a varying degree of upset on the central symbolic representation of the body image, and (3) a threat to disrupt the intrinsic cohesiveness of the organization of the personality .The dysrythmia disturbs a harmonious antagonism between the two main vegetative nervous systems. Thus one or the other of these systems or both in varying degrees, may receive a hyperactive continuous overstimulation which can cause morphological changes in the effected organs. (p. 285)

The emphasis is on concurrent disturbance on two levels—psychological and physiological. The early concepts of psychosomatic medicine were mainly concerned with the psychodynamic level, but in the 30-odd years of research which followed the formulation of psychosomatic conceptual models, some of the intricate mechanisms of the neurophysiological basis have gradually emerged.

The Psychosexual Stages and Disease

The oral phase has only temporarily a relative primacy in the physiological development of the child. In terms of awareness, the child makes contact with reality first by oral, later by sensori-motor, and still later by symbolic and conceptual models. Development of secondary process thinking indicates the need for greater and greater renunciation of direct instinctual gratification. While the oral phase may lay the groundwork for the kind of conceptual models of reality which the child will develop, it is probably no more important for the psychosomatic model than any other developmental phase. The reason for this has already been pointed out—namely, that the conditioning of the autonomic nervous system begins early and is not dependent on psycho-sexual stages. In terms of the autonomic nervous system, the infant's first need is more for air and regular heart rhythm and kidney function than it is for food. The built-in neurological feeding pattern is no more and no less important than any of the other reflexive behaviors. The need-searching, tension reduction orientation of the infant is indiscriminately externally oriented. The most important feature of the maintenance of his homeostatic equilibrium is the mother and therefore, in a sense, his relationship to her is more important than anything else. The kind of conditioning which begins to take place in terms of breathing, touching, dropping, holding, feeding, washing, etc., is likely to determine greatly his autonomic nervous system balance and integrity. In the differentiation that begins in his transactions with the external world—the mother will determine whether he will be conditioned in terms of pleasure or anxiety, i.e., in terms of sympathetic or parasympathetic functioning. The child's contribution in this early transaction with the world is his constitutional inheritance and his somatic response. The somatic response is the only language by which he can communicate need as well as satisfaction. As he matures, somatic language gives way to symbolic and determines whether under stress he is likely to break down in terms of neurosis, psychosis, or psychosomatic illness.

Constitution, Conditioning and the Psychosomatic Development—A Reappraisal.

The psychosomatic research literature of the last decade has clearly indicated that all manner of psychological conflicts can be carried by every organ system. The early theories of specificity, e.g., that passive receptive and dependency problems would be expressed solely by organ systems involved with gratification of oral needs, were an oversimplification. The physiological response of the organism to any specific need will depend on the manner in which that need will be perceived by the organism and how it will attempt to express itself, e.g. oral needs may be accepted or rejected by the organism. They may be expressed directly or indirectly, passively or aggressively; they may involve higher and lower levels of symbolization. Biting, spitting, screaming, mutism, oral fantasy, overeating, not eating at all, may equally well express oral needs. Persistence

of oral needs may also express itself in overambitiousness, constant sense of frustration, hypersexuality, alcoholism, drug addiction, etc. The same is true for impulse expression on every level of psychological development. The early theories of specificity did not do justice to the complexity of the problem. The mechanism at the disposal of the child for the somatic expression of his problems may have been conditioned within the first 6 weeks of his life or at any time during his physiological maturation and may have originally been determined partly by accident, partly by constitutional weakness, partly by deliberate parental conditioning and/or various other methods. It has been established that the autonomic nervous system of the infant is labile in the first few weeks of life and shows rather extreme signs in a variety of organ systems. Heart rate may vary from 50 to 200 beats per minute; respiration and other organ systems also show considerable variability. Cannon maintained homeostatic regulation is established slowly by the infant, although according to Grossman and Greenberg (1957) it does not appear to be uniformly deficient. Mandler suggests that pairing of stimuli in the environment with such a labile and variable state of the organism may well be the basis of the kind of conditioning that is necessary to produce diffuse visceral discharge. The same applies for stimuli which discharge adrenalin into the blood. It is also possible that considerable spread of conditioning occurs from organ to organ and over large blocks of visceral activity going on at the same time. It is possible that early conditioning of this nature is the basis for stereotyped or fixed patterns of response both adaptive and maladaptive. A child experiencing problems in feeding may unwittingly condition a hypertensive mechanism rather than or as well as a gastrointestinal one, depending both on his own physiological system and on the nature of his transaction with his environment at the time. Although the instrumental conditioning experiments suggest how pathological mechanisms may be induced, little is actually known about how psychosomatic mechanisms get established and how they are maintained.

However, experiments with animals are highly suggestive. Hofer and Reiser (1969), Hofer and Weiner (1971) showed how cardiac rate regulation may occur in pre-weanling rats. They were able to show that not only the presence of the mother but the feeding experience as such was crucial in the maintenance of sympathetic tone and of cardiorespiratory rate control in pre-weanling rats. They suggest a critical period hypothesis for the conditioning of different control mechanisms. Blizzard (1971), also working with rats, concludes that autonomic reactivity, as measured by heart rate, is partially dependent on infantile experience. To what extent these may be generalizable to the human level only future research will tell.

Anxiety as a factor in the infant's early transaction with his environment probably plays a considerable role in the conditioning of psychosomatic mechanisms. While the effects of sympathetic discharge are not experienced with displeasure, even small doses of adrenalin significantly increase the "alerting" mechanism in both humans and animals (Black 1957). In an elaboration of the child's experience of his instincts, Freud maintains that one of the traumas which the child may experience is to be flooded by greater amounts of excitation from his nervous system than he is ready to assimilate at the time. Thus massive autonomic discharge would result in severe discomfort, i.e., anxiety. Schachter and Singer have made the same claim (1962). However, they have suggested that perhaps strong visceral activity may not itself be noxious but that the direction of the discharge will determine whether it is to be experienced pleasantly or as anxiety. That is, if the final activity is to be avoidance or escape rather than approach, the visceral experience will be one of anxiety and unpleasure. The direction of final discharge will to a large extent be determined by the nature of the child's early transactions with his environment. Support for this statement comes from an experiment by Kulka et al. (1966). The authors have demonstrated a high degree of parallel rises and falls in EKG and EMG recordings in the mother-infant interaction.

Selye has stressed that the general adaptation syndrome follows a universal pattern. The reaction of the body to stress is hyperemia, hypermotility and hyperactivity. On the psychological level we have stressed the psychological condition of the organism prior to and at the outbreak of disease rather than his immediate response to the disease process. This general precipitating condition has been variously described as a generalized feeling of helplessness and hopelessness signalling a breakdown of previously functioning defenses, mainly of defenses in the face of grief over loss of a loved object. While the feelings of helplessness and hopelessness seem to antedate the overt outbreak of disease, in actual fact, somatic breakdown occurs at the same time that emotional distress emerges. It could not be otherwise, according to the logic of psychosomatic medicine. We are simply more easily alerted by one or the other side of the psychosomatic coin depending on our conceptual framework and on our tools for detection of physiological or psychological disorder. Analyses of psychodynamic formulations, underlying specific disease process appear to suggest that it matters little which disease organ system we examine. The basic problems are generally dependency, hostility, frustration of sexual needs, grief over loss of love object. One psychological conflict situation may be more obvious in one disease type, e.g., dependency in ulcers, whereas another conflict situation may be more obvious in another disease complex, e.g., ambition and repressed hostility in hypertension. The recent emphasis on constitutional factors indicates that at a certain point, generally early in life, the constitution of the developing organism must play its part in shaping personality development. This may explain the similarity of personality types in certain disease categories. For example, the organism's tendency to respond primarily with hypertensive mechanisms to stress is probably conditioned much earlier in life than has been suspected—"the first dark act" in the psychosomatic drama—and makes its subtle contribution from that time onward to the development of a certain type of personality. If gastro-intestinal mechanisms are the ones conditioned early in life, a different type of personality will emerge.

HELPLESSNESS, HOPELESSNESS—A BEHAVIORISTIC HYPOTHESIS

Engel first delineated a depression withdrawal reaction in his study of the infant Monica with gastric fistula. In this depressive reaction immobility and hypoteomia were marked features. He further elaborated his position by stating that there are two opposite CNS patterns of response to a need: one involving fight-flight reaction, and directed toward activity and energy expenditure, and the other a conservation-withdrawal system directed toward inactivity, energy conservation and withdrawal from the environment. He believed that each of these is an inborn system with its own underlying mediating neural organization. Both Hess (1954) and Riss (1967) have provided neurophysiological evidence consistent with this hypothesis, in a situation involving separation or object loss, much as is experienced in separation of infant from its mother. In the seventh month after birth, the infant reacts with intense distress for a while and then subsides into a state of profound withdrawal—the conservation response—during which period the organism presumably has an opportunity to recuperate and following this to search again for replacements for the object loss. The grief reaction in response to object loss in the adult is synonymous with this state of withdrawal. Engel has described it as a "disease." This state of grieving has also been called the helplessness-hopelessness syndrome, and it is this condition which Engel associates with psychosomatic breakdown.

The distress response to separation is highly specific and has been very clearly demonstrated on both the human and animal level. The distress response of infant animals to separation from the mother is initially identical to that of humans. In an experiment of separation of infant monkeys, Kaufman and Rosenblum (1967) have generalized, "In line with the thesis that much of behavior is organized around a comfort-distress dimension and that the mother's presence is primarily comforting while her absence is distressing, the reaction to separation is seen as a distress reaction. Its stages appear to represent successive efforts at adaptation based on available response systems, involved for their selective advantage, or developed ontogenetically, especially through dominance—hierarchial regulatory influences; at an undifferentiated level these response systems seem common to man and monkey" (p. 672).

The authors point out that fortunately the infant monkey seems to be better equipped than the human infant to survive without its mother (by virtue of its greater locomotor ability). The infant monkey is better able to find substitute comfort-producing stimulation. In the human infant and the adult as well, failure to find a substitute mother results in the helplessness-hopelessness syndrome.

Many researchers have drawn attention to the fact that the infants between the ages of 6 months and one year show general reactions of distress when the mother leaves the room for an appreciable length of time, or when a stranger enters the room. The presence of the mother, however, appears to be an inhibitor to distress. The fact that the fear of strangers, as well as the acute distress reaction to mother-infant separation, is only evident after a 6-month period of mother-child relating indicates that the meaning of the mother as an inhibitor of distress is learned. Mandler has pointed out that certain activities such as sucking and rocking are highly successful at inhibiting expressions of distress. These two activities are distinctly at the upper end in the hierarchy of mother-child interactions. Mandler has suggested that the mother figure, as a person who has been consistently paired with sucking and rocking activity, acts as the principle inhibitor to distress of any kind. Kaufman and Rosenblum's formulation is stated in more positive terms, but also implies that the comfort reaction is conditioned or learned on the "basis of the mother's biotaxic effects such as temperature, visual, olfactory, auditory, and gentle contactual stimuli." They suggest that in higher organisms psychotaxic processes arise and the mother soon acquires a meaning. Presence of the mother is therefore comforting—or according to Mandler's (1962) formulation, presence of mother is an inhibitor of distress. Distress inhibition is also suggested by the recent work of Gordon and Foss on the role of stimulation in the delay of crying in the newborn infant in which offering positive stimulation during quiet periods delayed the onset of crying (the researchers postulated crying as a search for stimulation). Experiments on swaddling also indicate a decreased level of H.R. response and physiological responses generally in keeping with greater stability of autonomic responsiveness, i.e., swaddling appears to act as an inhibitor to discomfort and overactivity (Lipton et al. 1960). Harlow's studies of infant monkeys with surrogate mothers have established the importance of biotaxic stimuli (clinging need) as well as the importance of the surrogate mother in inhibiting distress reactions in a novel environment.

Bovard (1959) cites a number of human and animal experimental studies: (Titmuss 1950; Mandelbaum 1952; Marshall 1951; Liddell 1950; Davitz and Mason 1955; Conger Sawrey and Turrell 1957) to support the position that the activity of the posterior hypothalamus can be dampened by the presence of another person or by the presence of an animal of the same species and thus reduce and even eliminate defensive responses (fear and rage).

The presence of, and interaction with, another member of the same species has been shown to have a protective effect on the vertebrate organism under stress. This effect is accounted for in terms of dampening of the pituitary-adrenal cortical and sympathetico-adrenal medullary responses to stress, through inhibition of the posterior hypothalmic centers that, in the general case, trigger these reactions. Such inhibition is hypothesized to result from stimulation of anterior hypothalamic activity by the social stimulus. (p. 275)

The above evidence suggests that the presence of the mother and the presence of increased stimulation as a factor of proximity may act more as inhibitors to discomfort than as elicitors of pleasure; or at best, they may elicit pleasure by inhibiting discomfort. We can make the further generalization that once mother acquires meaning, her meaning as an inhibitor of discomfort or an elicitor of pleasure can be conditioned or generalized to other important people in the environment. It has often been observed that both children and older adults feel vaguely restless until they are back in their comfortable surroundings with comfortable people. The loss of a significant object relationship elicits a profound response of grief. It is also possible to say that loss of an important object relationship releases or disinhibits the distress response, because the primary inhibitor of distress is gone. It is possible to speculate further that if the loss is perceived as irreplaceable, the helplessness-hopelessness syndrome may emerge and psychosomatic breakdown may be likely to follow as a possible adaptation to an unbearable situation.

Overview: Psychosomatic Medicine 1935 to Present

1935–1959

At the beginning of the psychosomatic movement which officially began with the founding of the Psychosomatic Society in 1939, the primary focus was on conceptualization of the psychosomatic attitude and on theoretical formulations of the development of psychosomatic disease. The research methods at this time consisted mainly of anmnestic and therapeutic studies. As time went on, laboratory and clinical experimental studies increased. Although the psychosomatic attitude implied a multiple combined approach to disease, the lion's share of psychosomatic research fell to the psychiatrist and particularly the psychoanalyst. By the late 50's internists had practically abandoned the field. However, psychologists increasingly entered psychosomatic research and the focus turned from clinical observations to basic research. By the late 50's psychologists were making very large contributions to all areas of psychosomatic medicine. During the years 1935 to 1959 the important discoveries in the fields of neuroanatomy, neurophysiology, and neuro-endocrinology were incorporated and contributed to the understanding of the intricate relationships involved in visceral regulation. Areas covered during this research period include: (1) the role of the hypothalamus as part of a feedback system which mediates and regulates neural impulses concerned with emotions and neuro-endocrine activity; (2) the visceral system which, according to Maclean, mediates visceral rather than ideational functions; (3) the differentiation of non-adrenaline from epinephrine; (4) the role of the adrenals and importance of corticoids in the defense against trauma; (5) the effect of adrenergic hormones in mobilizing their defense; and (6) last, but not least, the revelance of emotional factors in the etiology of so-called psychosomatic disorders.

1959 TO THE PRESENT

In accordance with the trend toward the objectifiable and measurable, psychiatrists and psychologists; much of the research was carried out jointly.

Psychologists, on the other hand, contrary to expectations and predictions, lost interest in validating psychoanalytic concepts in their application to psychosomatic problems. Instead, they showed an increasing tendency towards isolating and qualifying objectively measurable variables of personality and opened up new areas of laboratory and experimental research. Animal studies have been on the ascendance.

Content-wise, more than in previous years, psychiatrists devoted interest to such situational problems as antecedents of asthmatic attacks, to such somatopsychic problems as the psychological effects of mitral surgery and to problems arising from doctor-patient relationships. There is a remarkable lack of psychopharmacological studies in psychosomatic disorders. A double-blind study by Wittkower et al. (1962), regarding the effect of phenotropic drugs on skin disorders is one of the few examples. A few epidemiological studies have been carried out which, however, have been exposed to severe criticism on methodological grounds. Laboratory and experimental studies recently carried out include a revival and application to novel problems of hypnotic experimental techniques, conditioning of biological functions in humans and investigations concerning the psychophysiological effects of sleep deprivation and of sensory input.

Much interest has been shown in patterns of autonomic responses—in normals and in patients suffering from psychosomatic disorders, at rest and under emotional stress. Stress was induced by hypnotic suggestion, by interviews, by staged situations, by psychomotor performance tests, by projective tests, by conditioned stimuli, by movies and by total or partial perceptual isolation. Physiological variables studied include skin potential, skin temperature, finger pulse volume, rate of respiration, heart rate, blood pressure and muscle activity. Individual differences, differences with various emotional states and differences on comparison of various psychosomatic disorders have been noted.

More frequently than during the previous period surveyed, conditioning experiments demonstrating the deleterious effects of anxiety elicited by conditioned stimuli have been carried out in humans and in animals, by psychologists and by neurophysiologists. Experimental lesions of the gastrointestinal tract in primates have been inadvertently induced by intense conditioning stress techniques, and deliberately in the cat by hypothalamic stimulation and in the rat by restraint and shock. Advances in neurophysiology and neuro-endocrinology have made it possible to carry out critical manipulation on the nervous system and to obtain depth recording of classical events associated with brain and pituitary adreno-cortical function. Electrodes have been implanted in critical areas of the brain.

In the testing area, attempts have continued to identify personality variables either typical of certain psychosomatic disorders or of prognostic significance. Comparisons have been carried out between patients suffering from different psychosomatic disorders and between patients and healthy subjects. As regards theory, there has been a marked falling off in publications of articles of a theoretical or speculative nature by psychiatrists and psychologists.

DIFFERENTIAL DEVELOPMENTS OF PSYCHOSOMATIC MEDICINE.

Three countries have been selected—Germany, Japan, and Russia—to illustrate contrasting developments of psychosomatic medicine (Wittkower et al. 1969). In two of these countries, special journals devoted to the subject are published.

Germany. Eminent German internists have been in the avant-garde of those recognizing the relevance of emotional factors to the etiology of organic disease. But despite their observations and despite some experimental psychophysiological research, largely under hypnosis, previous to the initiation of the psychosomatic concept, psychosomatic medicine and psychosomatic research have fought a hard uphill struggle for acceptance in Germany. Reasons for the delay in the developing of this branch of medicine, according to Pflanz and Von Uexkull, Görres, Heiss and Thomä, have been the deeply rooted organic tradition of German medicine, the reluctance of German psychiatrists in academic positions to concern themselves with psychotherapy and especially the opposition in academic circles to the teachings of Sigmund Freud. This opposition to psychoanalysis was reinforced on ideological grounds during the national socialistic era. Consequently, though during the postwar period interest in psychotherapy and psychosomatic medicine grew in Germany, progress has been slow, internists rather than psychiatrists played a leading role, and a fragmentation of concepts often impeding communication is noticeable. There is a small enthusiastic group of workers who have rallied under the banner of Freudian psychoanalysis, and there are representatives of the Jungian approach, of a neoanalytical approach which has not spread beyond Germany, of existentialism, of anthropological medicine and of the "organismic" approach. Adlerian psychology and behavior therapy are not represented in Germany. There is a grave shortage of academic teachers in psychotherapy and psychosomatic medicine in Germany for the reasons given. It is a major concern of various German writers, e.g., Görres, Heiss, Thomä, to establish facilities for training in these areas which at present takes place almost exclusively outside the universities.

Japan. It has been pointed out that Japanese physicians, more than others, are receptive to psychosomatic concepts because a holistic approach to diseased individuals is deeply rooted in oriental thought and especially in the tenets of Buddhism. Japanese psychosomatic medicine assumed its present systematized form after World War II when the impact of American and European research in this field, and especially that of the psychoanalytic approach, made itself felt. However, despite imported concepts, it retained its national characteristics owing to the influence of Morita's teachings on psychiatric theory and practice. Attempts are under way to integrate the psychoanalytic approach of the West with the various psychotherapies of the East, and especially with the principles laid down by Morita.

After some preliminary moves dating back to 1950, the Japanese Psychosomatic Society came into being in 1960 and its official journal a year afterward. The Japanese Psychosomatic Society is the largest in the world. It has over one thousand members and is composed of internists, psychiatrists, other medical specialists, neurophysiologists, sociologists, social workers and educators. A majority of its members consists of internists and of other non-psychiatric specialists. Its objectives are to combine features of the American Psychosomatic Society and of the Academy of Psychosomatic Medicine, i.e., it is both research- and practice-oriented. It has been stressed that Japanese physicians think in terms of a psychosomatic (holistic, comprehensive) approach to diseased individuals rather than in terms of specific psychosomatic disorders. In line with the other developments named has been the setting up of the first and only institute of Psychosomatic Medicine at Kyushu University in 1963, where an elaborate intensive and extensive teaching program has been developed.

To begin with, as elsewhere, the introduction of psychosomatic medicine met resistance on the part of tradition-bound physicians, but as time went on, more and more medical specialists expressed lively interest in the new field. Meanwhile, within the short span of a little over one decade, a substantial body of clinical and experimental psychosomatic research data has been accumulated. Difficulties still encountered include delay in the acceptance of the psychosomatic approach by general practitioners and by the public at large, shortage of research workers qualified and willing to participate in multi-disciplinary teams, and scarcity of psychoanalytic-oriented psychiatrists. As regards treatment, handicaps in existence are reluctance on the part of patients to undergo psychotherapy and on the part of practitioners to embark on this time-consuming procedure in view of the very low fees paid. Generally, the psychotherapeutic orientation is eclectic. Psychoanalytic orientation assumes an ever increasing role. Other forms of psychotherapy include dynamically oriented hypnotherapy, autogenic training, existential therapy and, as mentioned before, Morita therapy.

Russia. In Russia, endeavors to integrate psychology and medicine were initiated by Sechenov's book, *The Reflexes of the Brain* published in 1863. Sechenov spoke of "dark feelings" arising from the internal organs and influencing both cognitive and affective states. Later on, Botkin, a teacher of Pavlov, introduced the concept of nervism. Pavlov, with the discovery of the conditioned reflex, gave not only a research tool but also a conceptual model for exploration of the interrelationship between external and internal events in animals and disease. An outgrowth of these developments, i.e., arising from laboratory research with animals, was the concept of corticovisceral medicine.

Corticovisceral medicine represents no doubt the most comprehensive attempt to demonstrate the effect of neural processes upon body function. Its weakness lies in its failure to come to grips with the complexity and variety of human experience—the predominant focus of psychosomatic medicine. Today, the two-way connection between cerebral cortex and viscera is uniformly accepted in the Soviet Union as the basis for understanding a group of somatic diseases and even as a new orientation in medicine.

Investigators differ, however, in the emphasis they place on central (cortical) or peripheral (visceral) factors, to the extent that they postulate a different etiology, for corticovisceral diseases and for neuroses.

As stated before there are three discernible tendencies in corticovisceral medicine: (1) to demonstrate the relevance of temperamental types (choleric, sanguinic, phlegmatic, melancholic) to the nature and course of psychophysiological disturbances; (2) to show that the pathophysiology of nervous breakdown, i.e. forced collision or overstraining of excitation and/or inhibition, is responsible for malfunctioning of internal organs; and (3) to stress the role of peripheral factors. The protective, compensatory influence of the cortex is not disputed, but a concomitant "locus minoris resistantiae" is implicated in the choice of organ pathology.

At present, the theory of corticovisceral medicine is taught on all levels of medical education, in physiology as well as in clinical subjects. Over the last twenty years, the knowledge gained in animal experimentation has to some extent permeated the realm of clinical practice and has been employed (a) in establishing important etiological factors and (b) in the treatment of what we would call psychosomatic disorders. However, the bulk of the research in this area is still carried out by neurophysiologists. As regards therapeutic measures, different forms of sleep therapy are applied in the treatment of gastric ulcer, hypertensive disease, hyperthyroidism and different dermatological conditions; conditioned reflex therapy to nocturnal enuresis and alcoholism. Psychotherapy based upon the Pavlovian theory, which considers speech as a second signalling system, is practiced in a problem solving, re-educative manner and as hypnotherapy.

COMMENTS

It is evident that the concept of psychosomatic medicine as we know it in North America is not internationally accepted. The degree to which it is accepted varies from nation to nation; the basic theoretical orientation toward psychophysiological disturbances is subject to cultural variations; the investigators in this field are in some countries, e.g., Germany, predominantly internists, in others, e.g., Russia, predominantly neurophysiologists and in still others, e.g., the United States, predominantly psychiatrists and psychologists. On comparison of different countries considerable differences in the forms of psychosomatic research exist. The impression is obtained that the differences noted are related to differences in national character, in prevailing ideologies, in the medical specialities and disciplines involved and in the prominence of national investigators—Freud versus Pavlov.

Research Literature

It is evident that with the passage of time the focus of scientific interest in any given field of research changes, and that the use of new and refined methodologies opens new problems and vistas, offering possibilities to answer questions which previously could not be answered. Since the beginning of psychosomatic research many new lines of research have been opened, and there is at present a voluminous research in all areas of psychosomatic medicine. Alexander and Flagg have presented an excellent and comprehensive survey in B. B. Wolman's the *Handbook of Clinical Psychology* (1965). Several other surveys exist (Friedman and Kaufman's *Comprehensive Psychiatry*, 1967; Wittkower and Cleghorn's *Recent Advances in Psychosomatic Medicine*, 1954; Arieti's *Handbook of Psychiatry* (*Vols. II* [1959] *and III* [1966]), *Psychosomatic Specificity* by Alexander et al., 1968. The present review will not attempt to duplicate this work. Some of the recent literature indicating new advances in knowledge have been cited in the elaboration of the psychosomatic thesis. We will attempt to add only a brief survey of current trends and directions.

Research concerning the etiological relevance of emotional factors has been extended to neurological conditions such as multiple sclerosis (Mei-Tal 1970), to infectious diseases, such as pulmonary tuberculosis, and to malignant diseases such as cancer and leukemia. The importance of psychological factors in the etiology of TB was emphasized as early as 1949 by Wittkower. Fain and Marty (1954), Kissen (1962), and Begoin (1965) have demonstrated similar findings.

CANCER AND LEUKEMIA

Miller and Jones (1948) first indicated that psychological factors are operative in the development of leukemia. Since then many researchers have confirmed the importance of psychosocial stress in leukemia and other forms of cancer (Greene 1954, 1956; Baltrusch 1961, 1964; Aleksandrowicz et al. 1964; Oo et al. 1963; Kissen 1962, 1963; Nemeth and Mazel 1963; LeShan and Worthington 1956; Booth 1961; Coppen and Metcalfe 1964; Bahnson and Bahnson 1964; Paloucek and Graham 1959). LeShan and Worthington (1956) described the cancer patient as a highly dependent personality lacking autonomy and highly limited in ability to relate to others. He felt that loss of desire to live, resulting from the loss of an object who had become the central axis of their lives, precipitated neoplastic development. Bahnson et al. (1971) were unable to verify the hypothesis of recent loss by death but found ego-defensive denial and high commitment to social norms to be striking features of cancer patients.

Object loss and depression as precipitating causes are stressed again and again (LeShan 1956, 1963; Meerloo 1954; Kowal 1955; Reznikoff 1955; Schmale and Iker 1966). LeShan has more recently stressed not only antecedent depression but despair in the existential meaning of the word.

Object loss has been variously identified as due to death, divorce, etc. Greene et al. (1956) have indicated that instead of reacting with grief, the patients denied it and identified with, and introjected, the lost object. Bahnson and Bahnson found that the personality of cancer patients was characterized by bleakness, depletion and lack of emotional meaning. They have maintained that this flattening is not necessarily related to depression but is a syndrome of ego defenses of repression and denial. They felt that it is the nature of the defensive mechanism rather than the depression which is potentially related to malignant development. They felt that use of these defense mechanisms necessitated regression to archaic physiological discharge patterns. The patients are described as leading a double existence—with a socially adequate but empty and meaningless facade and a tragic, tormented and explosive unconscious self. Using a psychosociological and anthropological approach, Aleksandrowicz et al. were unable to corroborate the above findings on 100 leukemic patients. Their leukemic patients were of lower socioeconomic status in contrast to the American samples of higher class situatus; loss of an important person was not evident in the five years prior to the discovery of the illness. The personality of the patients was described as conscientious, affectionate, sensitive, yielding, caring for others, and not outwardly depressed. Problems of family and work conflicts were not more evident in the leukemic than in the control group. Their main finding was that each type of leukemia appeared to occur in a specific constitutional type. Inconsistencies between American and European findings may perhaps be partially explicable on the basis of differences in class status, in conceptual model, and in level of psychological investigation. Alexandrowicz et al. appear to have been observing more the "facade" characteristics of their population (cf. Bahnson et al. 1971). A deeper level analysis of leukemic children by Baltrusch described the children as involved in vicarious object relationships. They appeared to be strangulated by maternal overcare, overprotection, and overanxiety, the mother revealing deep-lying unconscious death wishes against the children. Baltrusch (1964) hypothesized that the child unconsciously seeks a way out of this symbiotic relationship with the mother by means of slow extinction. He speculates that leukemia may occur as a "physiologic response to certain patterns of withdrawal-conservation and that severe ego regressions may lead to ultimate somatic states of disorganization and exhaustion on a cellular level. Leukemia in this sense appears as a physiological pattern of decompensation in which the psychical state of decomposition has become expressed" (p. 180).

THERAPEUTIC CLUES

Other investigators attempted to identify psychological variables which might help predict the course of tuberculosis and cancer (Wittkower et al. 1955). They studied patients with tuberculosis and noted that those who displayed a greater pressure of dependent needs and a tendency to seek attention, submit to authority, and avoid responsibility, were likely to have an unfavorable course. Conversely, patients characterized by greater maturity and less conflict over dependency had a favorable course. These findings were confirmed by Calden (1960).

Observations similar to the above have been made in cancer patients. Renneker and Cutler (1952) reported that patients with breast cancer with metastases who survived for long periods were characterized by self-confidence, in contrast to the short-lived patients who were incapable of expressing outwardly aggressive or sexual impulses. Blumberg et al. (1954) noted that male patients with terminal cancer who presented the facade of calm in the presence of inner anxiety had a generally shorter life span. There is accumulating evidence that good ego strength and ability to express basic drives and affects in an adaptively modulated manner are psychological characracteristics which increase host resistance to a wide variety of organic illnesses including cancer (Katz et al. 1970). If these hypotheses are corroborated by further research, they may provide important predictive and even therapeutic clues.

ANIMAL RESEARCH ON CANCER

Animal experimental research on cancer investigating factors of importance in host resistance to implanted tumors has been productive and suggestive. Solomon (1968), Newton, Bly and McCrary (1962) report in a series of experiments on handling and training of rats by splitting litters that early handled animals showed significantly greater resistance to tumor growth. Another experiment by Newton et al. (1963) indicates that early stimulated groups of animals who received forced exercise in an electrically driven wheel, both prior and following innoculation with tumor suspension, appeared to be best able to resist cancer growth surviving longest; while the group of rats receiving no early stimulation and no exercise fared worst (no rats surviving on the 33rd day following transplant). Newton suggests that "an individual's level of physical activity, as conditioned by psychological experience and contact with early environmental stressors, may prove a salient variable increating high resistance to cancer development" (p. 78). An infantile stimulation experiment with mouse pups by Levine and Cohen (1959) revealed opposite results to that of Newton et al. The early manipulated mice showed a shorter survival time. Dennenberg and Karas (1959) replicated the findings for both rats and mice. Research on individual differences in tumor susceptibility have suggested that there may be tumorestatic substances in the body which inhibit tumor growth (Hoffman et al. 1962; Szent-Gyorgyi et al. 1963). Karetsky et al. (1966) found that they could increase the number of precancerous alveolar nodules by making C_3HA mice experimentally neurotic. La Barba (1970) summarizes the current literature in this area.

INTERPERSONAL INTERACTION

An area of clinical research which has immediate practical implications for the medical practice as a whole is that of doctor-patient relationship. Hackett and Weisman (1960) studied the importance of the doctor-patient relationship in the practice of surgery and discussed ways in which a psychiatric consultant can intervene therapeutically in the cases of emotional disturbances preceding or following an operation. A crisis in the relationship between a patient and his surgeon may express itself in the development of such manifestations as aberrant somatic symptoms, complaints about the hospital, refusal to undergo an operation, disregard for ward routine, etc. Such behavior may seriously interfere with effective management of the patient's illness and is often an expression of fear or despair regarding the impending surgical intervention and its expected effects. In the setting of a trustful relationship with the treating physician and free communication between him and the patient, distressing affects and consequent disturbing behavior are less likely to occur. Other studies of interpersonal interacting between two or more individuals (Malmo 1957: muscle tension; Di Mascio et al. 1957: heart rate; Nowlin et al. 1968 and Kaplan et al. 1964: GSR) reported a "physiologic co-variation" between subjects who had either positive or negative (but not neutral) feelings toward each other. Williams et al. (1971) suggest that the interpersonal interaction is more important than the content of the interview in determining diastolic blood pressure.

SURGERY AND EMOTIONS

Still another area of psychosomatic research has been the study of the emotional consequences of certain therapeutic procedures, such as cardiac surgery. On the basis of their studies in this area, Kennedy and Bakst (1966) conclude that the psychological condition of the patient has significant influence on morbidity and mortality in cardiac operations. The best overall therapeutic results were shown by patients who had strong and unambivalent motivation to live and be healthy. These patients also tended to have less anxiety regarding the risks of surgery and its possible complications. On the other hand, patients with marked secondary gains from their chronic illness as well as those displaying overwhelming fear of the operation or lacking a desire to live, tend to suffer from more medical and psychiatric postoperative complications and have a higher mortality rate. Combination of strong anxiety with weak motivation for recovery was found to be associated with poorest prognosis. Kimball (1968) carried out a prospective study of heart surgery patients dividing them into (1) adjusted (2) symbiotic (3) anxious and (4) depressed groups. The adjusted group showed greatest improvement whereas the depressed group had highest mortality (80 percent). Tufo and Ostfeld (1968) in a prospective study of open-heart surgery found 100 percent mortality in their preoperatively severely depressed group whereas preoperative anxiety bore no relationship to postoperative course.

SENSORY DEPRIVATION

Various physiological changes have been noted in response to isolation and sensory deprivation. Decreases in frequency in electroencephalographic traces from the parieto-occipital (Heron 1961) and from the occipital area (Zubek 1963) were noted as the period of isolation progressed. Following termination of isolation, the mean frequency increased only gradually.

Other changes observed in response to isolation and sensory deprivation are an increase in urinary adrenaline and noradrenaline secretion (Mendelson et al. 1961) as well as changes in skin resistance, finger pulse volume, respiratory rate and tissue catechol excretion (Cohen et al. 1962). Persky et al. (1966) have demonstrated that both perceptual and social isolation result in significant arousal relative to normal unconfined life situations (Zuckerman et al. 1968).

EVERYDAY LIFE STRESSES

Other new developments in psychophysiological research have been studies of the effects of spontaneous stresses of everyday life (by telemetry) and of the effects of dreaming. It has been shown that during non-dreaming sleep, autonomic function remains at a low level, while during dreaming sleep an autonomic "storm" occurs. This activation of the autonomic nervous system during dreaming is probably part of an invariable biological rhythm, but there is good reason to believe that the extent of such an activation is related to dream content. Fisher (1965) noted that the degree of penile erection is inversely related to the anxiety content of dreams. Moreover, it has been demonstrated that electrocardiographic changes (Nowlin et al. 1965) and the degree of fat mobilization (Gottschalk et al. 1966) during dreaming are probably related to the affects of the dreamer. Lester et al. (1967) showed that pre-sleep states (stress) increased EEG and GSR activity.

PSYCHOENDOCRINE RESEARCH

As regards physiological accompaniments of *disturbing emotions of psychiatric patients*, much attention has been paid to hormonal changes and especially to the effects of adrenal cortex and medulla function.

One current emphasis in *psychoendocrine research* appears to be on effectiveness of ego defenses. Fox et al. (1968) demonstrate this trend in a study on individual personality characteristics and relatively enduring patterns of pituitary-adrenocortical function. In a study of 20 pairs of monozygotic twins, they found that the twins' 17-KS level could be predicted with considerable accuracy (intra-class correlation of 0.88). On the personality level, they found differences between subjects with high as compared to low steroid levels. Subjects with high levels for 17-KS excretion had forceful, aggressive drives, expressed or indicated by active defenses against them. Subjects with low levels were correlated with well-established inhibition of impulses resulting in less conscious awareness of conflict. Subjects with high 17-OHCS were emotional, responsible and vulnerable, while subjects with low 17-OHCS used denial, isolation, or highly organized neurotic defenses. Henry et al. were able to demonstrate that the changes observed 3 years later corresponded to their tentative psycho-physiological hypotheses. Rossler et al. (1963) in a study of ego strength and physiological responsivity found that individuals with greater responsivity to experimentally induced stimulation demonstrated significantly greater ego strength.

Levitt et al. (1964) have shown that the adrenal cortex in anxious subjects under stress reacts in a similar way to that of normals. However, radioactive cortisol has a higher turnover rate in those with anxiety than in normals, indicating that cortisol is produced in larger amounts and metabolized faster in anxious subjects. In these subjects, corticosteroid levels correlated positively and significantly with measures of anxiety. Corticosteroid levels also correspond with the severity of depressive illness (McHugh and Gibbons, 1963), but are relatively low during manic states. Thus, it has been inferred that when the ego defense of denial is operative, adrenal cortical activity is held in check. This conclusion has been further documented by C. T. Wolff et al. (1964) who found that parents of fatally ill children who defended themselves most effectively against experiencing the loss had lower 17-OHCS levels than those immersed in their grief.

Teece et al. (1965) also studying parents of leukemic children found higher 17-OHCS levels in parents scoring high on the K (defensiveness) Scale of the MMPI. They interpreted their findings to mean that elevated levels of adrenocortical activity were related to curtailment of verbal expression and anxiety. Poe et al. (1967) found 17-OHCS to be related to the effectiveness of ego defenses in recruits during basic training.

DEPRESSION AND HORMONES

McClure (1966a) was able to show good correlation between severity of clinical depression and levels of plasma cortisol. He hypothesized that cortisol may be responsible for early morning awakening in psychotic patients. In a subsequent study (McClure 1966b) on antidepressant medication in depressed psychotic patients, he found that clinical improvement was accompanied by a fall in cortisol values. In cured cases, cortisol values had returned to normal. Mendels and Ewing (1967) and Doig et al. (1966) replicated the latter finding in hospitalized depressives. Doig et al. also found higher cortisol levels at 6 a.m. in depressives.

A psychoendocrine study of the psychotherapy of reactive depression by Sachar et al. (1968) revealed interesting psychosomatic implications. The disturbances in adrenal cortical activity which were noted were marked enough to have somatic repercussions. The highest individual as well as mean corticosteroid levels occurred during the psychotherapeutic confrontation of object loss. In the case of the adrenal medulla, most attention has been focused on the relationship between emotional states and catecholamine levels. It has been established that in the manic phase of manic-depressive disease, catecholamine excretion is higher than during the depressive phase (Bunney et al. 1965). The emphasis in the past on the association between elevated catecholamine levels and unpleasant emotional states is complicated by the finding that adrenaline output may increase in states of joy. However, using an indirect measure of catecholamine secretion (plasma-free fatty acids), Gottschalk et al. (1965) found a precise association between anxiety and plasma FFA in response to stress, but no such association could be established in the case of experimentally aroused hostility.

It is evident from the brief review given, that there has been considerable development in the scope of psychoendocrine research. However, "how the hormones in the body act together as a group to accomplish homeostatic regulation of physiological processes is one of the major unsolved problems in endocrine physiology." (Mason 1968, p. 800). Mason suggests the concept of "overall" hormonal balance as the key to endocrine organiza-

tion. Psychological factors are evidently highly implicated. There is little "physical stress" (Bush), unless there is an emotion-provoking situation. This problem is posed by Mason as follows: "Does the widely occurring pituitary adrenal cortical response, then, reflect a 'general adaptive' or 'nonspecific' endocrine response to many 'nocuous' stimuli or does it reflect a specific response to a *single* type of stimulus (psychological) which these various unpleasant situations share in common" (1968, p. 800). In his 1970 presidential address Mason goes further. In analyzing what is common to the skeletal-muscular system, the autonomic nervous system, and the endocrine systems he states "it also appears that the central nervous system exerts a continuous tonicity on these effector systems and that the tonic level of excitation through the three systems can be either raised or lowered by psychologic mechanisms" (Mason 1970, p. 430).

DENTISTRY AND PSYCHE

The psychosomatic aspects of dentistry were acknowledged as early as 1944 (Weiss 1964). There is at present a sizeable body of literature in this area. Landa (1953) has written about the psychological foci of infection and has stressed the contribution of psychogenic factors to tooth decay, some diseases of periodontal tissues, Vincent's infection, malocculusion and tempero-mandibular joint and muscle pain. Harvey Rosen, noted Montreal dental surgeon, attributes the etiology of both bruxism (gnashing and clenching of teeth) and tempero-mandibular joint pain to the interaction of occlusal interference and to hypertonicity of the jaw muscles resulting from psychic tension. On the basis of his experience, he feels that in some cases of tempero-mandibular joint pain, the pain persists even after occlusion therapy because it is maintained by subconscious jaw movements induced by psychic tension.

Rumfjord and Ash (1966) have pointed out that the "psychic component of repressed aggression, emotional tension, anger and fear, has been stressed by many writers as the most important sole factor in the aetiology of bruxism" (p. 100). Lipke and Posselt (1960) have suggested that patients with muscle hypertonicity and bruxism, as well as patients with myalgias, may have a malfunction of proprioceptive and sensory muscles as well as of the reflect activity within the muscles.

SOCIOCULTURAL FACTORS

Finally, still another experiment of nature which has been subjected to investigation is the effect of socio-cultural factors on the frequency and distribution of psychosomatic disorders. Research in this area is fraught with methodological difficulties. Evidence obtained suggests the following:

(a) Peptic ulcer of the stomach (Doll and Jones 1951) and probably also other psychosomatic disorders, such as essential hypertension and obesity (Pflanz et al. 1956) differ markedly in frequency among different branches of industry and different echelons of employment.

(b) There is little support for the belief that psychosomatic disorders are more common in urban areas than in agricultural workers and in primitive peoples (Platanov 1958). Thyrotoxicosis and coronary thrombosis appear to be rare in the African bush.

(c) Westernization and social disintegration, e.g., in Africa, India and the Far East, result in a rising rate of psychosomatic disorders (Collomb 1964; Gaitonde 1958; Leighton et al. 1963; Seguin 1956; Yap 1951).

(d) The rarity of psychosomatic disorders in some primitive peoples, e.g., of Africa, living in cultural isolation may be attributed to supportive group cohesion (Collomb 1964).

(e) Depressive illness is common to all cultures. A cross-cultural study of depression by Murphy, Wittkower and Chance (1967) indicated that there appears to be a basic depressive disorder which exhibits the same few primary symptoms in all cultures. Other symptoms such as thought retardation and self-depreciation appear to be culturally determined.

ANIMAL RESEARCH ON ULCERS

The importance of animal experimentation in the exploration of the mechanisms of neurophysiological involvement in the development of psychosomatic disorder cannot be overstressed. In the experimental induction of cancer, of asthma, of ulcers, of cardiovascular disease, the main advances in knowledge, since 1958, both for the neurophysiology and for the relevance of social variables, have come from animal laboratory research. The research on ulcers will be cited as an example of the nature and relevance of animal experimentation to human psychosomatics.

The role of conflict in the genesis of ulcers was demonstrated by Sawrey and Weisz (1956). They were able to produce ulcers in rats as a result of a conflict situation, combined with restraint and exposure to shock. This was an ambiguous situation since variables other than conflict were involved.

Brady (1958) attempted to show that emotional conflict and not effects of shock was the cause of ulcer development in animals. He trained monkeys to avoid shock. The animal could avoid the shock if it pressed a lever at least once in every 20-second interval. Monkeys were exposed to this procedure over a prolonged period of time. To exclude the possibility that the cumulative effect of shock alone was responsible for the ulcer, Brady designed his experiment so that two monkeys were placed in yoked chairs in which both monkeys received shocks but only one monkey had access to the lever which could prevent shock for himself and his partner. The control monkey's lever was a dummy. Both animals received the same number of shocks. The animals were placed on a continuous schedule of alternative period of shock-avoidance and rest. An arbitrary interval of 6 hours was chosen for each period. The "executive" monkey soon learned to press the lever to the cue of a red light at a rate of between 15 to 20 times a minute. After 23 days of continuous six hours on, six hours off of shock, the executive monkey died and autopsy showed a large perforation in the wall of the duodenum. Microscopic analysis revealed both acute and chronic inflammation. The control monkey was sacrificed and autopsy showed no evidence of ulcer or any other gastrointestinal abnormalities. Several follow-up experiments replicated the original findings (Rice 1963).

Conger et al. (1958) and Sawrey and Sawrey (1966) were able to demonstrate the importance of social factors in the production of gastric ulcers in hooded rats. They found that animals placed in a conflict situation alone were more prone to get ulcers than animals placed with other animals in the same conflict situation. This appears to be the case on the human level as well. Age of separation from the mother (Ader et al. 1960) as well as early experience and differential housing (Ader 1965, 1970) have been shown to be related to greater susceptibility to ulcer development in male rats. Sawrey (1962) also noted strain and sex differences. McMichael (1961) demonstrated the effects of pre-weaning shock and gentling on later susceptibility to stress. Some behavior characteristics, e.g. emotionality, as well as strain differences were also related to greater ulcer susceptibility by Mikhail and Broadhurst (1965).

Ader, Beels and Tatum (1960) were able to relate blood pepsinogen to the production of ulcers in both male and female rats in immobilization situations. Since no erosions were found in the stomachs of control animals with high pepsinogen levels, they concluded that a high pepsinogen level, per se, is not indicative of the presence of gastric erosions but appears rather to be indicative of susceptibility to gastric erosion (cf. Mirsky 1958). The immobilization procedure resulted in erosions confined to the lower, glandular portion of the rats' stomach, whereas in the conflict situation, ulcers were confined almost exclusively to the lumen of the rat's stomach. In two later studies, Ader (1964, 1967) found that rats subjected to a six-hour period of immobilization were more susceptible to the development of gastric erosions if the immobilization was imposed during the peak rather than the trough of the animal's 24-hour rhythm.

In a series of experiments on selective breeding for stress ulcer susceptibility, Sines hypothesized (1962) that such animals show some characteristics suggesting that they may be functionally sympathectomized. In later experiments (1965, 1966) he found that the selectively bred rats were characterized by significantly elevated levels of motor activity, increased responsiveness to extraneous stimulation, increased intestinal peristalsis under stress, and more rapid learning of an active avoidance response. Sines (1966) attempted to integrate these findings under the theoretical premise of generalized level of activation, maintaining that the prime characteristic of the ulcer-susceptible rat was higher activation level.

The importance of level of activation in the evaluation of characteristics of disease-prone individuals has been receiving considerable attention in recent years. Ploski et al. (1966) have found significant relationships between activation level and voluntary movement impairment, and between low activation levels and personality rigidity in Parkinson's disease.

Research progress on the human level in ulcers has also been maintained. Engel's extensive study (Engel et al., 1956) of an infant with gastric fistula aged 15 months, which not only established that gastric secretion varies with different emotions but also identified a pattern of depression withdrawal of hyposecretion in response to object loss, has been replicated in every detail twelve years later by Coddington (1968) on an infant with gastric fistula and her normal twin. In keeping with the depression-withdrawal hypothesis, Kehoe and Ironside (1963) were also able to demonstrate a pattern of hyposecretion in response to a helplessness-hopelessness attitude induced by hypnosis. Their experiment dealt with five categories of affects.

PERSONALITY AND DISEASE

In contrast to the exciting advances on the neurophysiological level, the personality and psychological causality studies appear on superficial glance to have produced a large number of negative findings. An analysis of both the positive and negative studies, however, permits a different picture. It has been evident that some of the earlier studies suffered from premature and overenthusiastic generalization. As soon as replication of findings on more representative population samples was attempted, the phenomenon of the normal curve intruded to undermine the early simplistic explanations. It also became evident that homogeneity of population samples could not be assumed. As research continued variables of age, sex, intelligence, education, duration of disease, socioeconomic and cultural variables emerged as highly relevant in the symbolic elaboration of a specific disease process, and in the attitudinal characteristics developed as a function of these variables. And finally, methodological differences were seen to determine the type of conclusions which could be safely generated by the data. Depth interviews versus superficial personality inventories could result in a different and superficially inconsistent picture of the personality in a specific disease process.

THE ULCER PERSONALITY

For example, while the original picture of the ulcer personality presented itself as passive and dependent, evidence of a second type was equally convincingly presented; this was the active, aggressive, go-getter type of personality. Closer analysis of the pattern indicated that both types of behavior descriptions were equally valid and could be explained by the same underlying dynamics. That is, both ulcer groups were passive, dependent people with basic conflicts centering around the need to be cared for and loved. However, one type of patient gave in to dependency needs while the other overcompensated. As early as 1942, Rubin and Bowman presented EEG findings demonstrating two types of alpha patterns in ulcer patients. The group with alpha rhythms of low frequency appeared to be aggressive, outgoing and independent, whereas the group with high-frequency alpha were found to fit the picture of passive and dependent personality. Karush et al. (1968) has identified two types of ulcerative colitis patients—an active group who are relatively independent and controlling, and a passive group who see themselves as helpless victims of others.

ASTHMA, ALLERGY, AND PERSONALITY

Studies of asthma personality yielded highly ambiguous results until Block et al. (1964) suggested that the asthma population was far from homogeneous and that contradictions in the previous literature might result from inadvertently mixing together subjects who had a high allergenic component in the disease; Block et al. found that these two groups of subjects (children) were clinically significantly different. She found that children who scored low on allergy tests showed significantly more psychogenic factors in the precipitation of asthma than children who scored high. Both Jacobs et al. (1966, 1967) and Freeman et al. (1967) corroborated these findings with adults. Freeman et al. found marked psychological differences between weak and strong reactors to skin allergy tests. The weak reactors were far more unhappy. They characterized themselves as depressed, uneasy, withdrawn and incompetent. The strong

reactors presented a more normal picture. Mathé and Knapp (1971) found an anxiety-depression-guilt-shame syndrome in adult asthmatics. The focal conflict appeared to be inhibition of aggressive impulses.

CORONARY PERSONALITY

A review of the literature on the coronary personality (Mordkoff and Parsons 1968) from 1935 to 1967 produced no consistent support for a unique configuration of personality traits characterized by "excessive competitive drive, persistent desire for recognition, advancement and achievement, and persistent inclination for multiple vocational and avocational involvements on the one hand, and of chronic immersion in 'deadlines' on the other hand" (Friedman and Rosenman 1963). Nor did they find consistent support for the focal conflicts attributed to the coronary personality, i.e. strongly aggressive tendencies that have been totally repressed. Clinical studies, in contrast to the experimental, show a fair degree of unanimity in the description of personality traits associated with CHD, but these generally early studies lack control groups. Mordkoff and Parsons feel that in addition to methodological differences between clinical and experimental studies, biases in the studied populations such as age, sex, socio-economic status and chronicity may account for the discrepant findings. Taking these factors into account, Syme et al. (1964) and Bruhin and Chandler (1965) found that factors such as educational and occupational mobility distinguished coronary men from matched controls. Brandt et al. (1964) suggest that the low incidence of CHD in an Italian-American community in Pennsylvania may be related to the way of life of the community.

It is generally agreed that psychological stress is implicated in CHD. However, the general conclusion is that the validity of the coronary personality configuration needs to be more carefully evaluated with especial reference to socio-cultural factors. Rosenman et al. (1968) encountered Mordkoff and Parsons' critique by indicating that some of their interpretations of the studies which they review were overly subjective. They cited further support for the type A behavior pattern of the CHD patient (characterized by enhanced aggressiveness, ambitiousness, drive, competitiveness and time urgency) in a prospective study undertaken by Jenkins et al. and in 1960 on 3,524 men (published in 1967). They found significantly higher incidence of new coronary disease in men assessed at intake (in 1960) as type A pattern compared to men who did not possess these behavioral characteristics. The authors maintain that type A behavior is as indicative of CHD as any of the classical risk factors, such as serum lipids, etc. Rosenman et al also make the point that the pattern profile of the CHD patient is highly related to environmental challenge and could not be expected to show up in a patient group hospitalized, for example, for acute myocardial infarction.

More recent studies have attempted to focus on relevant socio-cultural variables with rewarding results. Wardwell et al. (1968) studied 87 white male CHD patients matched on physiological variables known to be related to coronary disease, such as obesity, smoking and dietary fat. They found that Protestants and Jews showed higher incidence of CHD than Catholics. Social mobility was also found to be associated with high incidence of CHD. Inability to relax after a hard day's work was consistent with findings pertaining to social background. They interpret their findings in the following way. Inability to cope realistically with anxiety and tension except by compulsive planning, higher drive for occupational achievement, anxiety over and defense against the expression of unacceptable drives, and the compelling need to organize and control masterfully one's total environment appear to be factors related to high incidence of CHD.

Thus, it would appear that more recent research with better controlled population samples, incorporating socio-cultural variables, is beginning to provide some explanations for the contradictions which existed in the earlier literature; and it is also revealing the complexity of the variables involved and the increasing necessity to focus on the interaction of biological, psychological and sociological factors.

In a survey of main currents of psychiatric development, Havens (1968, p. 288) has summed up the status of modern psychiatry in the following quotation which we believe applies equally well to psychosomatic medicine. "The time considered relevant to an understanding of the patient and his condition has expanded from the immediately observable present to encompass past, future and, finally, the entire lifetime. Psychiatric phenomena have been ordered according to the faculty or psychological system affected. Psychiatric thought has moved inward to explore individual subjective experience and outward, to take in relationships—of the individual to family and society, and of symptoms to total personality. Overall, the attitude toward patients has shifted from viewing the patient as an object to the patient as a person."

THE BODY-MIND-SOCIETY INTERACTION AND CONTROL OF BEHAVIOR

The most exciting advances in knowledge about the mechanisms of psychosomatic development under stress have come from experimental research on ANS reactivity, on instrumental conditioning of heart rate and other physiological responses, and on the experimental induction of pathological somatic (and psychic) mechanisms in both human and animal subjects. The most striking feature of this research is the potential which it appears to open up for the more efficient control of pathology on the psychosomatic as well as the social levels. For example, Razran's (1961) summary of experiments in the U.S.S.R. demonstrates the mechanisms of experimental "doing and undoing" on a physiological level. Psonik (1961) demonstrated the development of vascular neurosis after the disruption of a chain of CRs (dynamic stereotype). Conditioned vasodilation was forced into collision with conditioned vasoconstriction. Postulating a similar underlying mechanism, Levitin showed that a clash between a CR formed to the injection of acetylcholine, and the unconditioned response to I.V. epinephrine led to paroxysmal tachycardia observed in his experiments. In these experiments, as well as in experiments utilizing classical conditioning, the underlying mechanism was outside awareness. Lisina (1961) showed that if the subject was made aware of the conditioned connection, this connection could be radically altered. In one experiment, reinforcement was contingent upon the subject's response and when he became fully conscious of this connection a stress-induced vasoconstriction was transformed to vasodilation.

In the U.S.A. the instrumental conditioning experiments of Di Cara and Miller (1968, 1970) have indicated not only how pathological mechanisms can be conditioned but also how they may be extinguished. Carmona's (1967) work with conditioned EEG changes, Kamiya's (1961), and Hart's (1967) conditioning of human subjects to recognize and control alpha rhythms by informational feedback, indicate therapeutic possibilities for learned control of pathological brain activity (e.g. in epilepsy).

Barber's recent investigations (1968) of the differential effectiveness of different types of hypnotic suggestion in the removal of, and interference with, instrumentally conditioned responses is exciting from the point of view of learning more efficient methods for the extinction of pathological responses. The experiments with hypnotic control of behavior and the even more impressive findings that the same type of results can be effected by suggestion alone (without hypnosis) in some individuals also indicates the high degree of control over physiological functions which is inherent in the human organism under certain conditions.

THE SOCIAL CONTRIBUTION

There is an emerging important body of research literature which not only demonstrates the unity of the mind and body but which underlines clearly the inescapable intertwining of mind–body–society. Experiments on interactional monitoring in the neonate (Sander and Julia 1966) indicate how quickly the physiological rhythms of the child begin to respond to the interaction as a function of temporal fit between care-taking activity and infant activity, and, one may also infer, as a function of the personality characteristics of the mother. The studies on "physiologic covariations" (Kaplan et al. 1964; Nowlin et al. 1968, Williams et al. 1971) indicate the marked physiological effects of social stimuli on behavioral response. Wolman's recent article (1967) on sociopsychosomatic determinants of schizophrenia is another attempt to single out environmental forces as the starting point in the process of schizophrenic disbalance of cathexis. "The disbalance of *inter-individual cathexes* (social) inevitably affects the balance of intra-cathexes (psychological)" (p. 377). The relevance of experimentally induced psychosocial factors in the induction of hypertension in mice (Henry et al. 1967) and of ulcers in mice (Conger et al. 1958; Sawrey and Sawrey 1966) the demonstration by Scotch (1957) of the higher incidence of hypertension in human societies living under greater social pressures, and Bovard's (1959) demonstration of the effectiveness of social stimuli in alleviating human distress suggest interesting directives for a more comprehensive analysis of social stresses and conditions. We may perhaps infer that such an analysis may lead to the possibility of the drafting of a programme for a more "healthy" organization of social institutions.

The present survey has attempted to point out the relevance of cognitive controls in the functioning of the body and in the shaping of behavior. On the basis of the research surveyed and the current trends examined, the inevitable conclusion is to admit the reality of the "psyche" in health and disease in both its conscious and its unconscious counterparts. The effects of "cognitive appraisal," "externalized attending," "conservation-withdrawal," "unconscious instrumentally conditioned modification of the functioning of vital organs" on ANS reactivity in the psychosomatic elaboration of disease cannot be ignored. The problem today is to determine whether there is sufficient evidence to regard the psyche as a biological system like other systems of the body. The dilemma in which modern medicine finds itself has been recently expressed by the Seminar Group of Mt. Sinai hospital (Los Angeles). "The problem of modern medicine in regard to the organismic point of view is whether or not the *psychic system is acceptable as a system* in the sense of cardiovascular, central nervous, or enzyme systems. There is no difficulty in conceptualizing and experimentally demonstrating the interrelationship of all somatic systems to each other. As a matter of fact, it is difficult to conceive of any point of view in modern medicine which would run contrary to such an acceptance of interaction. When the psychic system is involved, the old dichotomies seem to enter into the picture. . . . In relation to sensory modalities no difficulties exist. It is when one deals with thought processes, fantasies, and especially unconscious mentation that this begins to act as a stumbling block toward the acceptance of the psychic system at the same level as the others. Once this system is viewed from the same frame of reference, the difficulties should disappear" (Kaufman and Heiman 1964, pp. 97–98).

The massive body of research on instrumentally conditioned physiological responses, the important research on cognitive appraisal, the recent strategies in the study of consciousness by conditioned control over EEG rhythms (Stoyva 1968) and the suggested reformulation of Cannon's theories by Hastings and Obrist (1967), focusing on the relatively constant alertness of parasympathetic and sympathetic nervous systems, suggest that the formulation of the Mt. Sinai study group merits experimental consideration.

References

ADER, R. Gastric erosions in the rat: Effects of immobilization at different points in the activity cycle. *Science*, 1964, *145*: 406–7.

———. Effects of early experience and differential housing on behavior and susceptibility of gastric erosions in the rat. *Journal of Comparative and Physiological Psychology*, 1965, 60: 233–38.

———. Behavioral and physiological rhythms and the development of gastric erosions in the rat. *Psychosomatic Medicine*, 1967, 29: 345–53.

———. Effects of early experience and differential housing on susceptibility to gastric erosions in lesion-susceptible rats. *Psychosomatic Medicine*, 1970, *32*: 569–80.

———, C. C. BEELS and R. TATUM. Social factors affecting emotionality and resistance to disease in animals: Age of separation from the mother and susceptibility to gastric ulcers in the rat. *Journal of Comparative and Physiological Psychology*, 1960, 53: 446–54.

ADER, R., and M. PLAUT. Effects of prenatal maternal handling and differential housing on offspring: Emotionality, plasma corticosterone levels, and susceptibility to gastric erosions. *Psychosomatic Medicine*, 1968, 30: 277–86.

ALEKSANDROWICZ, J. ET AL. Psychosociological and anthropological analysis of leukaemia patients. *In* D. M. KISSEN, and L. L. LESHAN (eds.), *Psychosomatic aspects of neoplastic disease*. Philadelphia: Lippincott, 1964, pp. 63–70.

ALEXANDER, F. Emotional factors in essential hypertension. *Psychosomatic Medicine*, 1939, *1*: 173–79.

———. *Psychosomatic medicine: Its principals and applications*. New York: Norton, 1950.

———, and W. FLAGG. The psychosomatic approach. *In* B. B. WOLMAN (ed.), *Handbook of clinical psychology*. New York: McGraw-Hill, 1965, pp. 885–947.

ALEXANDER, F., T. M. FRENCH, and G. H. POLLACK (eds.) *Psychosomatic specificity*. Vol. 1. *Experimental study and results*. Chicago: University of Chicago Press, 1968.

APPLEY, M. H., and R. TRUMBULL (eds.). Psychological stress. In *Issues in research*. New York: Appleton-Century-Crofts, 1967.

ARNOLD, M. B. *Emotion and personality* (2 vols.). New York: Columbia University Press, 1960.

AX, A. The physiological differentiation between fear and anger in humans. *Psychosomatic Medicine*, 1953, *15*: 433–42.

BAHNSON, C. B., and M. B. BAHNSON. Denial and repression of primitive impulses and of disturbing emotions in patients with malignant neoplasms. *In* D. M. KISSEN, and L. L. LESHAN (eds.), *Psychosomatic aspects of neoplastic disease*. Philadelphia: Lippincott, 1964a, pp. 42–62.

———. Cancer as an alternative to psychosis: A theoretical model of somatic and psychologic regression. *In* D. M. KISSEN, and L. L. LESHAN (eds.), *Psychosomatic aspects of neoplastic disease*. Philadelphia: Lippincott, 1964b, pp. 184–202.

———, and W. I. WARDWELL, A psychological study of cancer patients. *Psychosomatic Medicine*, 1971, 23: 466–7 (abstract).

BALTRUSCH, H. J. F. Psyche-Nervensystem-neoplastische Prozess: ein altes Problem in neuer Aktualität. *Zeitschrift für Psychosomatische Medizin*, 1963, 9.

———. Problems of research strategy in the psychosomatic approach towards malignant hemic disease. *In* D. M. KISSEN, and L. L. LESHAN (eds.), *Psychosomatic aspects of neoplastic disease*. Philadelphia: Lippincott, 1964, pp. 170–83.

BARBER, T. X. Physiological effects of hypnosis. *Psychiatric Bulletin*, 1961, *58*: 390–419.

———. Psychological effects of "hypnotic suggestions": A critical review of recent literature, 1960–64. *Psychological Bulletin*, 1965, *63*: 201–20.

———, and K. W. HAHN. Effects of hypnotic procedures and suggestions of deafness on a cardiac response that has been conditioned to an auditory stimulus. Paper presented at the Convention of the American Psychosomatic Society, Boston, 1968.

BARNETT, S. A. *The rat: A study in behavior*. Chicago: Aldine, 1963.

BEGOIN, J. Tuberculose pulmonaire et problèmes psychosomatique. *Revue de Medicine Psychosomatique*, 1965, 7: 159–95.

BELANGER, D., and S. M. FELDMAN. Effects of water deprivation upon heart rate and instrumental activity in the rat. *Journal of Comparative and Physiological Psychology*, 1962, 55: 220–25.

BERKUN, M. M. ET AL. Experimental studies of psychological stress in man. *Psychological Monographs*, 1962 (15), 76.

BERMAN, R., E. SIMONSON, and W. HERON. Electrocardiographic effects associated with hypnotic suggestion in normal and coronary sclerotic individuals. *Journal of Applied Physiology*, 1954, 7: 89–92.

BLACK, A. H. Cardiac conditioning in curarized dogs: The relationship between heart rate and skeletal behavior. *In* W. F. PROKASY (ed.), *Classical Conditioning*. New York: Appleton-Century-Crofts, 1965.

BLIZZARD, D. A. Individual differences in autonomic responsivity in the adult rat: Neonatal influences. *Psychosomatic Medicine*, 1971, *33*, 445–57.

BLOCK, J. ET AL. A possible relationship between psychological factors and human cancer. *Psychosomatic Medicine*, 1954, *16*: 307–20.

BLUMBERG, E. M., P. M. WEST, and F. W. ELLIS. A possible relationship between psychological factors and human cancer. *Psychosomatic Medicine*, 1954, *16*: 277–86.

BONVALLET, M., and M. B. ALLEN, JR. Prolonged spontaneous and evoked reticular activation following discrete bulbar lesions. *Electroencephalography Clinical Neurophysiology*, 1963, *15*: 1133–34.

BOOTH, G. Communication to International Psychosomatic Cancer Study Group. Paper presented at the Second International Meeting of the International Psychosomatic Cancer Study Group, Paris, 1961.

BORELLI, S. Psychische Einflüsse und reactive Hauterscheinungen. *Münchener Medizinische Wochenschrift*, 1953, 95.

BOSTON PSYCHOPATHIC HOSPITAL. Experimental psychoses. *Scientific American*, 1955, *192*(6), 34–39.

BOVARD, E. W. The effects of early handling on viability of the albino rat. *Psychological Review*, 1958, 65: 257–71.

———. The effects of social stimuli on the response to stress. *Psychological Review*, 1959, 66: 267–77. Copyright by the American Psychological Association; reproduced by permission.

BRACKBILL, Y. ET AL. Differences in autonomic and somatic conditioning of infants. *Psychosomatic Medicine*, 1968, *30*: 193–201.

BRADY, J. V. Ulcers in "executive monkeys." *Scientific American*, 1958, *199*: 95–104.

BRANDT, E. N. ET AL. Coronary artery disease in Roseto, Pennsylvania and among Italians and non-Italians in nearby communities. Paper presented at the First International Conference on Preventive Cardiology, Burlington, Vermont, 1964.

BRUHN, J. G. and D. CHANDLER. Social characteristics of patients with myocardial infarctions. Unpublished manuscript 1965; cited in Mordkoff and Parsons, 1968.

BULATOV, P. K. The higher nervous activity in persons suffering from bronchial asthma. In *Questions of the interrelationship between psyche and soma in psychoneurology and general medicine. Tr. Inst. Behterova (Leningrad)*, 1963, 29.

BUNNEY, W. E., JR., E. L. HARTMAN, and J. W. MASON. Study of a patient with 48-hour manic depressive cycles. *Archives of General Psychiatry*, 1965, *12*: 611–18.

BYKOV, K. M. *The cerebral cortex and the internal organs*. New York: New York Chemical Publishing Company, 1957.

CALDEN, G. ET AL. Psychosomatic factors in the rate of recovery from tuberculosis. *Psychosomatic Medicine*, 1960, *22*: 345–55.

CARMONA, A. Trial-and-error learning of the voltage of the cortical EEG activity. (Unpublished doctoral dissertation, Yale University, 1967.)

CERNORUCKIJ, M. V. The etiopathogenesis of peptic ulcers. In *Cortico visceral pathology*. Moscow: Publishing House of the U.S.S.R. Academy of Medical Science, 1949.

CHRISTIAN, J. J. Physiological and pathological correlates of population density. Proceedings of the Royal Society of Medicine, 1964, 57 (169), 169–74.

CODDINGTON, R. D. Study of an infant with a gastric fistula and her normal twin. *Psychosomatic Medicine*, 1968, *30*: 172–92.

COHEN, S. I., A. J. SILVERMAN, and B. M. SHMAVONIAN. Psychophysiological studies in altered sensory environments. *Journal of Psychosomatic Research*, 1962, *6*: 259–81.

COLLOMB, H. Psychosomatic conditions in Africa. *Transcultural Psychiatric Research Review*, 1964, *1*: 130–34.

CONGER, J. J., W. L. SAWREY, and E. S. TURRELL. An experimental investigation of the role of social experience in the production of gastric ulcers in hooded rats. *American Psychologist*, 1957, *12*: 410. (Abstract)

——— The role of social experience in the production of gastric ulcers in hooded rats placed in a conflict situation. *Journal of Abnormal and Social Psychology*, 1958, *57*: 214–20.

COPPEN, A. J., and M. METCALFE. Cancer and extraversion. In D. M. KISSEN, and L. L. LESHAN (eds.), *Psychosomatic aspects of neoplastic disease*. Philadelphia: Lippincott, 1964, pp. 30–34.

DAVITZ, J. R., and D. J. MASON. Socially facilitated reduction of a fear response in rats. *Journal of Comparative and Physiological Psychology*, 1955, *48*: 144–55.

DENENBERG, V. H., and G. G. KARAS. Effects of differential infantile handling upon weight gain and mortality in the rat and the mouse. *Science*, 1959, *130*: 629–30.

DI CARA, L. V., and E. MILLER. Changes in heart rate instrumentally learned by curarized rats as avoidance responses. *Journal of Comparative and Physiological Psychology*, 1968a, *65*: 8–12.

——— Instrumental learning of systolic blood pressure responses by curarized rats: Dissociation of cardiac and vascular changes. *Psychosomatic Medicine*, 1968b, *30*: 484–94.

DI MASCIO, A., R. W. BODY, and M. GREENBLATT. Physiologic correlates of tension and antagonism during psychotherapy. *Psychosomatic Medicine*, 1957, *19*: 99–104.

DOIG, R. J. ET AL. Plasma cortison levels in depression. *British Journal of Psychiatry*, 1966, *112*: 1263–67.

DOLL, R., and A. JONES. Peptic ulcer in industry. *Medical Research Council Special Report Series*, 1951, 276.

DUCHARME, R. Inanition et activation: Leur influence sur l'activité instrumentale. (Unpublished doctoral dissertation, Université de Montréal, 1962.)

DUDEK, S. Z. Suggestion and play therapy in the cure of warts in children. *Journal of Nervous and Mental Disease*, 1967, *145*: 37–42.

DUNBAR, F. *Emotions and bodily changes* (3rd ed.). New York: Columbia University Press, 1947.

ENGEL, G. L. *Fainting, Physiological and psychological considerations.* Springfield, Ill.: Charles C Thomas, 1950.

———. A unified concept of health and disease. *Perspectives in Biology and Medicine*, 1960, 3.

———. *Psychological development in health and disease.* Philadelphia: Saunders, 1962.

———, F. REICHSMAN, and H. L. A. SEGAL. A study of an infant with a gastric fistula. I. Behavior and rate of total hydrochloric acid secretion. *Psychosomatic Medicine*, 1956, *17*: 374–98.

ENGEL, G. L. and A. H. SCHMALE. Psychoanalytic theory of somatic disorder: Conversion, specificity, and the disease onset situation. *Journal of the American Psychoanalytic Association*, 1967, *15*, 344–65.

FAIN, M., and P. MARTY. Notes sur certains aspects psychosomatiques de la tuberculose pulmonaire. *Revue française de Psychanalyse*, 1954, *2*: 244–75.

FERENCZI, S. *Further contributions to the theory and technique of psychoanalysis*. London: Hogarth Press, 1926.

FISHER, C., J. GROSS, and J. ZURCK. Cycle of penile erection synchronous with dreaming. *Archives of General Psychiatry*, 1965, *12*: 29–45.

FOX, H. M. ET AL. Psychophysiological correlation of seventeen ketysteroids and seventeen hydrocorticosteroids in twenty-one pairs of monozygotic twins. *Psychosomatic Medicine*, 1968, *30*: 548 (Abstract).

FREEMAN, E. H. ET AL. Personality variables and allergic skin reactivity: A crossvalidation study. *Psychosomatic Medicine*, 1967, *29*: 312–22.

FRENCH, J. P. ET AL. Experimental gastroduodenal lesions induced by stimulation of the brain. *Psychosomatic Medicine*, 1957, *19*: 209–20.

FRIEDMAN, M., and R. H. ROSENMAN. Behavior patterns, blood lipoids and coronary heart. *Journal of the American Medical Association*, 1963, 35.

FRIEDMAN, S. B., and L. A. GLASGOW. Psychologic factors and resistance to disease. *Pediatric Clinics of North America*, 1966, *13*: 315–35.

GAITONDE, M. R. Cross-cultural study of the psychiatric syndromes in outpatient clinics in Bombay, India, and Topeka, Kansas. Paper presented at the 14th Meeting of the American Psychiatric Association, San Francisco, 1958.

GALIN, D. Effects of conditioning on auditory signals. *In* W. S. FIELDS and B. R. ALFORDS (eds.), *Neurological aspects of auditory and vestibular disorders*. Springfield, Ill.: Charles C Thomas, 1964.

GARMA, A. On the pathogenesis of gastric ulcer. *International Journal of Psychoanalysis*, 1950, 31.

GEBSATTEL, V. E. *Prolegomena einer medizinischen Anthropologie.* Berlin: Springer, 1954.

GOTTSCHALK, L. A., and W. STONE. Anxiety levels in dreams, relation to changes in plasma free fatty acids. *Science*, 1966, *153*: 654–57.

GOTTSCHALK, L. A. ET AL. Studies of relationships of emotions to plasma lipids. *Psychosomatic Medicine*, 1965, *27*: 102–11.

GREENBERG, N. H., P. CEPAN, and J. G. LOESCH. Some cardiac rate and behavioral characteristics of sucking in the neonate. *Psychosomatic Medicine*, 1963, *25*: 492.

GREENE, W. A., JR. Psychological factors and reticuloendothelial disease: I. Preliminary observations on a group of males with lymphomas and leukemias *Psychosomatic Medicine*, 1954, *16*: 220–30.

———, L. E. YOUNG, and S. N. SWISHER. Psychological factors and reticuloendothelial disease. II. Observations on a group of women with lymphomas and leukemias. *Psychosomatic Medicine*, 1956, *18*: 284–303.

GRINGS, W. W., S. CARLIN, and M. H. APPLEY. Set, suggestion and conditioning. *Journal of Experimental Psychology*, 1962, *63*: 417–22.

GRINKER, R. R. *Psychosomatic research*. New York: Norton, 1961.

GROSSMAN, H. J., and N. H. GREENBERG. Psychosomatic differentiation in infancy. I. Autonomic activity in the newborn. *Psychosomatic Medicine*, 1957, *19*: 213–306.

GUTTMANN, O. Psycho-physiological conditions and psychotherapy. In *The collected award papers*. New York: Gralnick Foundation, 1966, pp. 279–90.

HACKETT, T. P., and A. D. WEISMAN. Psychiatric management of operative syndromes: I. The therapeutic consultation and the effect of noninterpretive intervention. *Psychosomatic Medicine*, 1960a, *22*: 267–82.

————. Psychiatric management of operative syndromes: II. Psychodynamic factors in formulation and management. *Psychosomatic Medicine*, 1960*b*, 22: 356–72.

HALLIDAY, J. L. Concept of a psychosomatic affection. *Lancet*, 1943, 2: 692–96.

HART, T. H. Auto control of EEG alpha. Paper presented at the Meeting of the Society for psychophysiological Research, San Diego, California, 1967.

HASTINGS, S., and P. A. OBRIST. Heart rate during conditioning in humans: Effect of varying the interstimulus (CS-UCS) interval. *Journal of Experimental Psychology*, 1967, 74: 431–42.

HAVENS, L. Main currents of psychiatric development. *International Journal of Psychiatry*, 1968, 5: 288–310.

HENRY, J. P., J. P. MEEHAN, and P. M. STEPHENS. Use of psychosocial stimuli to induce prolonged systolic hypertension in mice. *Psychosomatic Medicine*, 1967, 29: 408–32.

HERON, W. Cognitive and physiological effects of perceptual isolation. *In* P. SOLOMON ET AL. (eds.), *Sensory deprivation.* Cambridge: Harvard University Press, 1961, pp. 6–33.

HESS, W. R. *The functional organization of the diencephalon.* New York: Grune and Stratton, 1954.

HEYER, G. H. Psychogene Functionsstorungen des Verdauungstraktes. *In* O. SCHWARZ (ed.), *Psychogenese und Psychotherapie korperlicher Symptome.* Wien: Springer, 1925.

HINKLE, L. E., JR., and S. WOLFF. A summary of experimental evidence relating life stress to diabetes mellitus. *Journal of the Mount Sinai Hospital, New York*, 1953, 19: 537–70.

HOFER, M. A., and M. F. REISER. The development of cardiac rate regulation in pre-weanling rats. *Psychosomatic Medicine*, 1969, 31: 372–88.

————, and H. WEINER. Development and mechanisms of cardiorespiratory responses to maternal deprivation in rat pups. *Psychosomatic Medicine*, 1971, 33: 353–62.

HOFFMAN, S. A. ET AL. The influence of exercise on the growth of transplanted rat tumors. *Cancer Research*, 1962, 22: 597–99.

JACOBS, M. A. ET AL. Incidence of psychosomatic predisposing factors in allergic disorders. *Psychosomatic Medicine*, 1966, 28: 679–95.

————. Interaction of psychologic and biologic predisposing factors in allergic disorder. *Psychosomatic Medicine*, 29: 572–85.

JENKINS, C. D. ET AL. Reproducibility in rating the coronary-prone behavior pattern. *Journal of Chronic Diseases*, 1967, 20: 371–79.

JORES, A., and H. FREYBERGER. *Advances in psychosomatic medicine.* New York: R. Brenner, 1961.

JOST, H., and L. W. SONTAG. The genetic factors in autonomic nervous system. *Psychosomatic Medicine*, 1944, 6: 308–10.

KAMIYA, J. Behavioral, subjective and physiological aspects of drowsiness and sleep. *In* D. W. FISKE, and S. R. MADDI (eds.), *Functions of varied experience.* Homewood, Ill.: Dorsey, 1961, pp. 145–74.

KAPLAN, H. B., N. R. BURCH, and S. W. BLOOM. Physiological covariation and sociometric relationships in small peer groups. *In* P. H. LEIDERMAN, and D. SHAPIRO (eds.), *Psychobiological approaches to social behavior.* Stanford, Cal.: Stanford University Press, 1964, p. 92.

————. Physiologic (GSR) activity and perceptions of social behavior in positive, negative and neutral pairs. *Journal of Nervous and Mental Disease*, 1965, 140: 457–63.

KARUSH, A. ET AL. The response to psychotherapy in chronic ulcerative colitis. I. Pretreatment factors. *Psychosomatic Medicine*, 1968, 30: 255–76.

KATZ, J. L. ET AL. Psychoendocrine aspects of cancer of the breast. *Psychosomatic Medicine* 1970, 32: 1–18.

————. Stress, distress, and ego defenses: The psychoendocrine response to impending tumor biopsy. *Archives of General Psychiatry*, 1970, 23: 131–42.

KAUFMAN, I. C., and L. D. ROSENBLUM. The reaction to separation in infant monkeys: Anaclitic depression and conservation-withdrawal. *Psychosomatic Medicine*, 1967, 29: 648–75.

KAUFMAN, R. M., and M. HEIMAN. *Evolution of psychosomatic concepts. Anorexia nervosa: A paradigm.* New York: International Universities Press, 1964.

KAVETSKY, R. E. ET AL. On the psychological mechanism of the organism's resistance to tumor growth. *Annals of the New York Academy of Science*, 1966, 125: 933 ff.

KEHOE, M., and W. IRONSIDE. Studies on the experimental evocation of depressive responses using hypnosis: II. The influence of depressive responses upon the secretion of gastric acid. *Psychosomatic Medicine*, 1963, 25: 403–19.

KENNEDY, J. A., and H. BAKST. The influence of emotions on the outcome of cardiac surgery: A predictive study. *Bulletin of the New York Academy of Medicine*, 1966, 42.

KIMBALL, C. P. The experience of open-heart surgery: Psychological responses to surgery. Paper presented at the Annual Convention of the American Psychosomatic Society, Boston, 1968.

KISSEN, D. M. *Emotional factors in pulmonary tuberculosis.* London: Tavistock Publications, 1958.

————. Personality characteristics in males conducive to lung cancer. *British Journal of Medical Psychology*, 1963, 36: 27–36.

KISSEN, D. M., and H. J. EYSENCK. Personality in male lung cancer patients. *Journal of Psychosomatic Research*, 1962, 6: 123–27.

KLEIN, M. *Contributions to psychoanalysis.* London: Hogarth Press, 1948.

KOWAL, S. J. Emotions as a cause of cancer. *Psychoanalytic Review*, 1955, 42: 217–27.

KUBIE, L. S. The basis of a classification of disorders from the psychosomatic standpoint. Paper presented at the Joint Meeting of the Section of Neurology of the New York Academy of Medicine and the New York Neurological Society, New York, 1943.

————. The central representation of the symbolic process in psychosomatic disorders. *Psychosomatic Medicine*, 1953, 15: 1–7.

————. Influence of symbolic processes on the role of instincts in human behavior. *Psychosomatic Medicine*, 1956, 18: 189–208.

————. The struggle between preconscious insights and psychonoxious rewards in psychotherapy. *American Journal of Psychotherapy*, 1965, 19: 365–71.

————. Personal communication, 1968.

KULKA, A. M., R. D. WALTER, and C. FRY. Mother-infant interaction as measured by simultaneous recording of physiological processes. *Journal of the American Academy of Child Psychiatry*, 1966, 5: 496–503.

LA BARBA, R. C. Experiential and environmental factors in cancer. *Psychosomatic Medicine*, 1970, 32: 259–76.

LACEY, J. I. Psychophysiological approaches to the evaluation of psychotherapeutic process and outcome. *In* E. A. RUBINSTEIN, and M. B. PARLOFF (eds.), *Research in Psychotherapy.* Washington, D.C.: National Publishing Company, 1959, pp. 160–208.

————. Somatic response patterning and stress: Some revisions of activation theory. *In* M. H. APPLEY, and R. TRUMBULL (eds.), *Psychological Stress.* New York: Appleton-Century-Crofts, 1967.

LACEY, J. I., R. SMITH, and A. GREEN. Use of conditioned autonomic responses in the study of anxiety. *Psychosomatic Medicine*, 1955, 17: 208–17.

LANDA, J. S. *The dynamics of psychosomatic dentistry.* New York: Dental Items of Interest Publishing Company, 1953.

LANG, A. Perceptual behavior of 8 to 10 week old human infants. *Psychonomic Science*, 1966, 4: 203–4.

LASHLEY, K. S. Experimental analysis of instinctive behavior. *Psychological Review*, 1928, 46.

LAZARUS, R. S. *Psychological stress and the coping process.* New York: McGraw-Hill, 1966.

————. Cognitive and personality factors underlying threat and coping. *In* M. H. APPLEY, and R. TRUMBULL (eds.), *Psychological Stress.* New York: Appleton-Century-Crofts, 1967.

LEIGHTON, A. H., ET AL. *Psychiatric disorder among the Yoruba.* Ithaca, New York: Cornell University Press, 1963.

LESHAN, L. Loss of a cathexis as a common psychodynamic characteristic of cancer patients. An attempt at statistical validation of a clinical hypothesis. *Psychological Reports*, 1956, 2: 183–93.

————. Some observations on the problem of mobilizing the patient's will to live. *In* D. M. KISSEN, and L. L. LESHAN (eds.), *Psychosomatic aspects of neoplastic disease.* Philadelphia: Lippincott, 1964, pp. 109–20.

————, and R. E. WORTHINGTON. Personality as a factor in the pathogenesis of cancer. A review of the literature. *British Journal of Medical Psychology*, 1956, 29: 49–56.

LESTER, B. K., N. R. BURCH, and R. C. DOSSETT. Nocturnal EEG, GSR profiles: The influence of pre-sleep states. *Psychophysiology*, 1967, 3: 23–28.

LEVENE, H. I. ET AL. Differential operant conditioning of heart rate. *Psychosomatic Medicine*, 1968, *30*: 837–45.

LEVINE, S., and C. COHEN. Differential survival to leukemia as a function of infantile stimulation in DBA/2 mice. *Proceedings of the Society of Experimental Biology and Medicine*, 1959, *102*: 53–54.

LEVITT, E. E., H. PERSKY, and J. P. BRODY. *Hypnotic induction of anxiety*. Springfield, Ill.: Charles C Thomas, 1964.

LIDDELL, H. Some specific factors that modify tolerance for environmental stress. *In* H. G. WOLFF, S. G. WOLFF, JR., and C. C. HARE (eds.), *Life stress and bodily disease*. Baltimore: Williams and Wilkins, 1950.

LIPKE, D., and V. POSSELT. Parafunctions of the masticatory system (Bruxism). *Western Society Periodontology Journal*, 1960, 8.

LIPOWSKI, Z. L. Review of consultation psychiatry and psychosomatic medicine. III. Theoretical issues. *Psychosomatic Medicine*. 1968, *30*: 395–422.

LIPTON, E. L., A. STEINSCHNEIDER, and J. B. RICHMOND. Autonomic function in the neonate. II. Physiologic effects of motor restraint. *Psychosomatic Medicine*, 1960, *22*: 57–65.

———. Autonomic function in the neonate: IV. Individual differences in cardiac reactivity. *Psychosomatic Medicine*, 1961, *23*: 472–84.

———. Autonomic function in the neonate: VII. Maturational changes in cardiac reactivity. *Child Development*, 1966, *37*: 1–16.

LISINA, M. I. (Cited in Razran). The observable unconscious and the inferable conscious in current Soviet psychophysiology: Interoceptive conditioning, semantic conditioning, and the orienting reflex. *Psychological Review*, 1961, 68.

LIVINGSTON, R. B. Central control of afferent activity. *In* H. H. JASPER ET AL. (eds.), *Reticular formation of the brain*. Boston: Little, Brown, 1958, pp. 741–60.

MCCLURE, D. J. The diurnal variation of plasma cortisol levels in depression. *Journal of Psychosomatic Research*, 1966a, *10*: 189–95.

———. The effects of anti-depressant medication on the diurnal plasma cortisol levels in depressed patients. *Journal of Psychosomatic Research*, 1966b, *10*: 197–202.

MCHUGH, P. R., and J. L. GIBBONS. Interrelationships between the endocrine system and neuropsychiatry. *International Review of Neurobiology*, 1963, 5.

MCMICHAEL, R. E. The effect of preweaning shock and gentling on later resistance to stress. *Journal of Comparative and Physiological Psychology*, 1961, 54.

MALMO, R. B., and D. BELANGER. Related physiological and behavioral changes: What are their determinants. *Research Publications of the Association for Research in Nervous and Mental Disease*, 1967, *45*: 288–318.

MALMO, R. B., T. J. BOAG, and A. A. SMITH. Physiological study of personal interaction. *Psychosomatic Medicine*, 1957, *19*: 105–19.

MALMO, R. B., and C. SHAGASS. Physiologic study of symptom mechanisms in psychiatric patients under stress. *Psychosomatic Medicine*, 1949, *11*: 25–29.

MANDLEBAUM, D. G. *Soldier groups and Negro soldiers*. Berkeley: University of California, 1952.

MANDLER, G. EMOTION. In *New Direction in Psychology*. New York: Holt, Rinehart & Winston, 1962, pp. 267–343.

MARGOLIN, S. G. The behavior of the stomach during psychoanalysis: A contribution to a theory of verifying psychoanalytic data. *Psychoanalytic Quarterly*, 1951, *20*: 349–73.

MARKOSYAN, A. A. The interaction of signal systems in the process of blood coagulation. *Zhurnal Vysskei Nervnoi Deiatel'nosti imeni I. P. Pavlova*, 1958, 8.

MARSHALL, S. L. A. *Men against fire*. Washington, D. C.: Combat Forces Press, 1951.

MASON, J. W. The "over-all" hormonal balance as a key to endocrine investigation. *Psychosomatic Medicine*, 1970, *32*: 427–39.

———. Strategy in psychosomatic research. Presidential address. *Psychosomatic Medicine*, 1970, *32*: 427–39.

MATHE, A. A., and P. H. KNAPP. Emotional and renal reactions to stress in bronchial asthma. *Psychosomatic Medicine*, 1971, *33*: 323–40.

MEAD, M. The concept of culture and the psychosomatic approach. *Psychiatry*, 1947, *10*: 57–76.

MEERLOO, J. A. M. Psychological implications of malignant growth: A survey of hypotheses. *British Journal of Medical Psychology*, 1954, *27*: 210–15.

MEI-TAL, V. ET AL. The role of psychological process in a somatic disorder: Multiple sclerosis. *Psychosomatic Medicine*, 1970, *32*: 67–68.

MENDELS, J., and J. A. EWING. Fractionation of urinary 17-ketosteriod in depressed patients. *Psychosomatic Medicine*, 1967, *29*: 544. (Abstract).

MENDELSON, H. H. ET AL. Physiological and psychological aspects of sensory deprivation—a case analysis. *In* P. SOLOMON ET AL. (eds.), *Sensory deprivation*. Cambridge: Harvard University Press, 1961, pp. 91–114.

MIKHAIL, A. A., and P. L. BROADHURST. Stomach ulceration and emotionality in selected strains of rats. *Journal of Psychosomatic Research*, 1965, *8*: 477–79.

MILLER, F. R., and H. W. JONES. The possibility of precipitating the leukemic state by emotional factors, *Blood*, 1948, *3*: 880–84.

MIMINOSHVILI, D. I. Experimental neurosis in monkeys. *In* I. A. UTKIN (ed.), *Theoretical and practical problems of medicine and biology in experiments on monkeys* (U.S.S.R. Academy of Medical Science). New York: Pergamon, 1960.

MIRSKY, I. A. Physiologic, psychologic, and social determinants in the aetiology of duodenal ulcer. *American Journal of Digestive Diseases*, 1958, *3*: 285–314.

MIRSKY, I. A., ET AL. Uropepsin excretion by man. I. The source, properties and assay of uropepsin. *Journal of Clinical Investigation*, 1948, 27.

MORDKOFF, A., and O. PARSONS. The coronary personality: A critique. *International Journal of Psychiatry*, 1968, *5*: 413–26.

MURPHY, H. B. M., E. D. WITTKOWER, and CHANCE, N. A. Crosscultural inquiry into the symptomatology of depression: A preliminary report. *International Journal of Psychiatry*, 1967, *3*: 6–22.

MYASNIKOV, A. L. *Hypertension*. Moscow: Medgiz, 1954.

NEMETH, G., and A. MAZEL. Personality traits of cancer patients compared with benign tumour patients on the basis of the Rorschach Test. *In* D. M. KISSEN, and L. L. LESHAN (eds.), *Psychosomatic aspects of neoplastic disease*. Philadelphia: Lippincott, 1964, pp. 12–17.

NEWTON, G. Early experience and resistance to tumour growth. *In* D. M. KISSEN, and L. L. LESHAN (eds.). *Psychosomatic aspects of neoplastic disease*. Philadelphia: Lippincott, 1964, pp. 71–79.

NEWTON, G., C. G. BLY, and C. MCCRARY. Effects of early experience on the response to transplanted tumor. *Journal of Nervous and Mental Disease*, 1962, *134*: 522–27.

NOWLIN, J. B. ET AL. The association of nocturnal angina pectoris with dreaming. *Annals of Internal Medicine*, 1965, *63*: 1040–46.

———. Physiologic response to active and passive participation in a two-person interaction. *Psychosomatic Medicine*, 1968, *30*: 87–94.

———. Heart rate and psycho-motor coupling during classical aversive conditioning in humans. *Journal of Experimental Psychology*, 1968, *77*: 180–93.

OBRIST, P. Cardiovascular differentiation of sensory stimuli. *Psychosomatic Medicine*, 1963, *25*: 450–59.

O'KELLY, L. I. ET AL. Water regulation in the rat; heart rate as a function of hydration, anesthesia and associated with reinforcement. *Journal of Comparative and Physiological Psychology*, 1965, *59*: 159–65.

OKEN, D. ET AL. Relation of physiological response to affect expressions including studies of autonomic response specificity. *Archives of General Psychiatry*, 1962, *6*: 336–51.

OO, M., J. CSIRSZKA, and J. HEGEDUS. Psychological tests in leukemia patients. *In* D. M. KISSEN, and L. L. LESHAN (eds.), *Psychosomatic aspects of neoplastic disease*. Philadelphia: Lippincott, 1964, pp. 18–29.

PALOUCEK, F. P., and J. B. GRAHAM. Precipitating factors in cancer of the cervix. Unpublished paper presented at the Annual Convention of the American College of Surgeons, Atlantic City, New Jersey, 1959.

PEPITONE, A. Self, social environment and stress. *In* M. H. APPLEY, and R. TRUMBULL (eds.), *Psychological stress*. New York: Appleton-Century-Crofts, 1967, pp. 182–208.

PERSKY, H. ET AL. Psychoendocrine effects of perceptual and social isolation. *Archives of General Psychiatry*, 1966, *15*: 499–505.

PFLANZ, M., E. ROSENSTEIN, and TH. VON UEXKÜL. Socio-psychological aspects of peptic ulcer. *Journal of Psychosomatic Research*, 1956, *1*: 68–74.

PLATONOV, K. *The word as a physiological and therapeutic factor; the theory and practice of psychotherapy according to I. P. Pavlov.* (trans. and ed. D. A. Myshne). Moscow: Foreign Languages Publishing House, 1959.

PLOSKI, H. A., E. LEVITTA, and M. RIKLAN. Impairment of voluntary movement in Parkinson's Disease in relation to activation level, autonomic malfunction and personality rigidity. *Psychosomatic Medicine*, 1966, *28*: 70–77.

POE, R. O., R. M. ROSE, and J. W. MASON. Multiple determinants of 17 hydroxy-cortico-steroid excretion in recruits during basic training. *Psychosomatic Medicine*, 1970, *32*: 369–78.

PSONIK, A. T. (cited in Razran) The observable unconscious and the inferable conscious in current Soviet psychophysiology: Interoceptive conditioning, semantic conditioning and the orienting reflex. *Psychological Review*, 1961, 68.

RAZRAN, G. The observable unconscious and the inferable conscious in current Soviet psychophysiology: Interoceptive conditioning, semantic conditioning, and the orienting reflex. *Psychological Review*, 1961, *68*: 81–147.

RENNEKER, R., and M. CUTLER. Psychological problems of adjustment to cancer of the breast. *Journal of the American Medical Association*, 1952, *148*: 833–38.

REZNIKOFF, M. Psychological factors in breast. *Psychosomatic Medicine*, 1955, *17*: 96–108.

RICE, H. K. The responding-rest ratio in the production of gastric ulcers in the rat. *Psychological Records*, 1963, *13*: 11–14.

RICHMOND, J. B., and S. L. LUSTMAN. Autonomic function in the neonate. I. Implications for psychosomatic theory. *Psychosomatic Medicine*, 1955, *17*: 269–75.

RISS, W., and F. SCALIA. *Functional pathways of the central nervous system.* Amsterdam: Elsevier, 1967.

ROESSLER, R. ET AL. Ego strength and physiological responsivity: 1. The relationship of the Barron Es scale to skin resistance finger blood volume, heart rate, and muscle potential responses to sound. *Archives of General Psychiatry*, 1963, *8*: 142–54.

ROSENMAN, R. H. ET AL. Is there a coronary-prone personality? *International Journal of Psychiatry*, 1968, *5*: 427–29.

RUBIN, S., and K. W. BOWMAN. Electroencephalographical personality correlates in peptic ulcer. *Psychosomatic Medicine*, 1942, *4*: 309–18.

RUESCH, J. The infantile personality—the core problem of psychosomatic medicine. *Psychosomatic Medicine*, 1948, *10*: 134–44.

RUMFJORD, S. P. Bruxism—a clinical and electromyographic study. *Journal of the American Dental Association*, 1961, 62.

RUMFJORD, S. P., and M. ASH. *Occlusion.* Philadelphia: Saunders, 1966.

SACHAR, E. J. ET AL. Corticosteroid responses to the psychotherapy of reactive depressions. *Psychosomatic Medicine*, 1968, *30*: 23–44.

SANDER, L. W., and H. L. JULIA. Continuous monitoring in the neonate. *Psychosomatic Medicine*, 1966, *30*: 822–35.

SAWREY, T. M., and W. L. SAWREY. Age, weight and social effects on ulceration rate in rats. *Journal of Comparative Physiological Psychology*, 1966, *61*: 464–66.

SAWREY, W. L., and D. H. LONG. Strain and sex differences in ulcers in the rat. *Journal of Comparative Physiological Psychology*, 1962, 55.

SAWREY, W. L., and J. D. WEISZ. An experimental method of producing gastric ulcers. *Journal of Comparative Physiological Psychology*, 1956, *49*: 269–70.

SCHACHTER, S., and J. E. SINGER. Cognitive, social and physiological determinants of emotional state. *Psychological Review*, 1962, *69*: 376–79.

SCHMALE, A. H., and H. P. IKER. The affect of hopelessness and the development of cancer. *Psychosomatic Medicine*, 1966, *28*: 714–21.

SCOTCH, N. A. An anthropological study of essential hypertension in three societies. Ph. D. Thesis. Pub. 23543, Chicago: Northwestern University, 1957.

SEGUIN, C. A. Migration and psychosomatic disadaptation. *Psychosomatic Medicine*, 1956, *18*: 404–9.

SELYE, H. The general adaption syndrome and the diseases of adaption. *Journal of Clinical Endocrinology and Metabolism*, 1946, *6*: 117–230.

———. *Physiology and pathology of exposure to stress.* Montreal: Acta Press, 1950.

SHAPIRO, D. ET AL. Differentiation of heart rate and systolic blood pressure in man by operant conditioning. *Psychosomatic Medicine*, 1970, *32*: 417–23.

SHIPMAN, W. G., H. A. HEATH, and D. OKEN. Response specificity among muscular and autonomic variables. *Archives of General Psychiatry*, 1970, *23*: 369–77.

SHVARTS, L. A. Conditioned reflexes to verbal stimuli. *Voprosy Psikhologie*, 1960, 1.

SILBERMANN, I. S. Experimentalle magenduodenalulcus-erzeugung durch scheinfüttern nach Pavlov. *Zeitblatt Chirurge*, 1927, *54*: 2385.

———. Referred to in The Psychosomatic Approach. *In* B. B. WOLMAN (ed.), *Handbook of clinical psychology.* New York: McGraw-Hill, 1965.

SINES, J. O. Strain differences in activity, emotionality, body weight, and susceptibility to stress-induced stomach lesions. *Journal of Genetic Psychology*, 1962, *101*: 209–17.

———. Pre-stress sensory input as a non-pharmacologic method for controlling restraint-ulcer susceptibility. *Journal of Psychosomatic Research*, 1965, *8*: 399–403.

———. Elevated activation level as a primary characteristic of the restraint-stress-ulcer-susceptible rat. *Psychosomatic Medicine*, 1966, *28*: 64–69.

SMIRK, F. H. *High arterial pressure.* Springfield, Ill.: Charles C Thomas, 1957.

SOLOMON, F. Conference report: Psychophysiological aspects of cancer. II. *The Sciences*, 1968, 8.

STERN, J. A. ET AL. The effects of group vs. individual housing on behavior and physiological responses to stress in the albino rat. *Journal of Psychosomatic Research*, 1960, *4*: 185–90.

STOYVA, J., and J. KAMIYA. Electrophysiological studies of dreaming as a prototype of a new strategy in the study of consciousness. *Psychological Review*, 1968, *75*: 192–206.

SYME, S. L., M. HYMAN, and P. E. ENTERLINE. Some social and cultural factors associated with the occurrence of coronary heart disease. *Journal of Chronic Diseases*, 1964, *17*: 277–89.

SZENT-GYORGYI, A. HEGYELI, and J. A. MCLAUGHLIN. Cancer therapy: A possible new approach. *Science*, 1963, *140*: 1391–92.

TEECE, J. J., S. B. FRIEDMAN, and J. W. MASON. Anxiety, defensiveness and 17 hydrocorticosteroid excretion. *Journal of Nervous and Mental Disease*, 1965, *14*: 549–54.

THIESSEN, D. D. Varying sensitivity of C57BL/Crgl mice to grouping. *Science*, 1963, *141*: 827–28.

TITMUSS, R. M. *Problems of social policy.* London: H. M. Stationary Office, and Longmans, Green, 1950.

TUFO, H. M., and A. M. OSTFELD. A prospective study of open-heart surgery. Paper presented at the Annual Meeting of American Psychosomatic Society, Boston, 1968.

ULLMAN, M. and S. DUDEK. On the psyche and warts: II. Hypnotic suggestion and warts. *Psychosomatic Medicine*, 1960, *22*: 68–76.

WARREN, H. C. The mental and the physical. *Psychological Review*, 1914, 21.

WEINER, H., ET AL. Etiology of duodenal ulcer. I. Relation of specific psychological characteristics to rate of gastric secretion. (Serum Pepsinogen). *Psychosomatic Medicine*, 1957, *19*: 1–10.

WEISS, E. Psychosomatic aspects of dentistry. *Journal of the American Dental Association*, 1964.

WEISS, T. and B. T. ENGEL. Operant conditioning or heart rate in patients with premature ventricular contractions. *Psychosomatic Medicine*, 1971, *33*: 301–21.

WEIZSÄCKER, F. *Der Kranke Mensch.* Stuttgart: Koehler, 1951.

WELCH, B. L., and A. S. WELCH. Effect of grouping on the level of brain norepinephrine in white Swiss mice. *Life Sciences*, 1965, 4.

WILLIAMS, R. B. ET AL. The influence of varying interpersonal interaction and direction of attention on diastolic blood pressure. *Psychosomatic Medicine*, 1971, *33*: 465–66 (Abstract).

WITTKOWER, E. D. *A psychiatrist looks at tuberculosis.* (The National Association for the Prevention of Tuberculosis) London: Tavistock House, 1949.

———. Perspectives of transcultural psychiatry. *International Journal of Psychiatry*, 1969, *8*: 811–24.

———, and J. AUFREITER. Psychosomatic concepts in psychoanalytic education. Paper presented at the Boston Psychoanalytic Institute, Boston, 1962.

WITTKOWER, E. D., H. B. DUROST, and W. A. D. LAING. Psychosomatic study of the course of pulmonary tuberculosis. *American Review of Tuberculosis*, 1955, 77.

WITTKOWER, E. D., and L. SOLYOM. Models of mind-body interaction. *International Journal of Psychiatry*, 1967, *4*: 225–233.

WITTKOWER, E. D. ET AL. A global survey of psychosomatic medicine. *International Journal of Psychiatry*, 1969, *7*: 499–516.

WOLFF, C. T. ET AL. Relationship between psychological defenses and mean urinary 17-hydroxy-corticosteroid excretion rates. *Psychosomatic Medicine*, 1964, *27*: 576–91.

WOLFF, H. G. *Life stress and bodily disease—a formulation. In* H. G. WOLFF and C. C. ITASE (eds.), *Life stress and bodily disease.* Baltimore: Williams and Wilkens, 1950.

WOLMAN, B. B. The sociopsychosomatic theory of schizophrenia. *Psychotherapy and Psychosomatics*, 1967, *15*: 373–87.

YAP, P. M. Mental diseases peculiar to certain cultures: A survey of comparative psychiatry. *Journal of Mental Science*, 1951, *97*: 313–27.

ZUBEK, J. P., G. WELCH, and M. G. SAUNDERS. Electroencephalographic changes during and after 14 days of perceptual deprivation. *Science*, 1963, *139*: 490–92.

ZUCKERMAN, M. ET AL. Experimental and subject factors determining responses to sensory deprivation, social isolation, and confinement. *Journal of Abnormal Psychology*, 1968, *73*: 183–94.

Perception

C. S. Watson

Psychophysics has been defined so broadly by some that it encompasses all objective measurement in psychology, and so narrowly by others that it is restricted to the topics of the scaling of sensations, or to the measurement of the discriminability between stimuli. The arbitrary, but perhaps defensible, bases for choosing subjects for inclusion in this chapter have been, first *to attempt to maintain continuity with the previous psychophysical tradition(s) represented in the theories and research of Helmholtz, Wundt, and Fechner; of Müller, Urban, Titchener, Boring, and Thurstone; and more recently, of Stevens and his many students and co-workers.* Second, *although recognizing the influence of psychophysics on many theories and methods outside the field of sensory psychology, especially in the areas of psychometrics and learning, the major developments of psychophysics have dealt with the relations between immediate sensory input and behavior. This emphasis is reflected in the chapter, even though many of the topics do have obvious relevance to non-sensory issues.* Third, *the selection of material has been made in an attempt to describe contemporary methods and theories as they* are, *rather than as we might propose that they ought to be. While "prediction is a dangerous game," an attempt has also been made to stress areas that appear most likely to generate future scientific activity. Exclusions are most often founded in the lack of adequate space to cover the enormous range of researches that are generically* psychophysics, *particularly those specific to one sensory modality. Finally, it cannot be claimed that this is an updating of other chapters, as the two most recent handbooks in psychology (in English) in one case failed to allot any space to this subject (Murchison 1934), and in the other devoted the discussion of psychophysics to the development of a major theoretical position (Stevens 1951).*

The intent of this chapter, in summary, is to bring the reader, especially the graduate student or the non-psychophysically oriented researcher, up to date on those topics that most experimental psychologists now call psychophysics, within the limits suggested above. It amounts to an autopsy on yesterday's Zeitgeist, *with a few attempts at predicting tomorrow's.*

Psychophysics

14

I. Introduction

Psychophysics is a branch of experimental psychology to which there has been diverse contributors, including brilliant innovators, plodding followers, rustic empiricists, philosophers of science, and critics and chroniclers of the works of others. It is small surprise that eleven decades after the founding of psychophysics by Fechner its boundaries incorporate a great variety of theories, methods, and subjects of experimental investigation. Tying the loose ends of psychophysics together would betray its reality, and therefore the reader is cautioned against expecting to find cohesive unity in what follows. This chapter can only review some representative, though widely distributed, regions of the field and add a few hints to stimulate the student reader to learn through the study of more complete sources how it became as it is.

Following general introductory remarks in Section I, Section II presents an organization of the tasks of sensory psychophysics into two major divisions, the measurement of *sensory capability* and the establishment of *response proclivities*. Section III deals with classes of theories which currently generate research in psychophysics, with examples ranging between functional conceptions of the organism as "black box," and theories oriented by modern neurophysiological descriptions of the peripheral sensory receptors. Section IV reviews some considerations pertinent to the choice of psychophysical methods, with special attention to methods appropriate to the separate studies of capability and proclivity. The final section (V) contains two precautionary suggestions for the psychophysical novice, included at the risk of offending old hands in sensory psychology. This last section, and also many similarly flavored digressions throughout the text, were included in an attempt to make some of the useful but generally private folklore of psychophysics a little more public.

Origins of Psychophysics. The *Elemente der Psychophysik* was published by Fechner in 1860. In this single volume he laid out a program by which the contemporary methods of science were to be directed toward determining, once and for all, the relation between the mental and physical realities. The introduction to the *Elements* (from the first English translation, published only recently) set both the scientific style and the modest goals of the new discipline.

As an exact science, psychophysics, like physics, must rest on experience and the mathematical connection of these empirical facts that demand a measure of what is experienced, or, when such a measure is not available, a search for it . . . One cannot build a house without bricks; and, when even the plan for the house has yet to be drawn, one cannot have everything right on the first try and get it all to fit together. Every subsequent attempt of this kind is bound on the one hand to be more complete and on the other to be briefer and more precise.

The trail of psychophysics, from Fechner and Wundt, through Plateau, Müller, and Urban, and significantly for American psychology, to Titchener, has been traced with wit and elegance in the writings of the late E. G. Boring. Boring's monumental volumes on the *History of Experimental Psychology* (1929, 1950) and on *Sensation and Perception in the History of Experimental Psychology* (1942) are classics, and the student of modern psychophysics is urged to turn to these works, especially since he may thereby avoid the embarrassment of "new" conceptions of problems that were well known to Warner Brown, or Jastrow, or Cattell. (For a review of the first fifty years of psychophysics, see Titchener 1905.)

CLASSICAL PROBLEMS IN PSYCHOPHYSICS

As Boring has pointed out, the classical problems of psychophysics were five: (1) the absolute *limen*, or threshold: the sensitivity of an observer to a particular form of stimulus energy; (2) the differential *limen*, or difference threshold: the sensitivity of the observer to an increment in the stimulus; (3) equivalents: the stimuli that are judged to be equal, generally in the intensive dimension of subjective judgment; (4) sense-distance: the differences between two pairs of stimuli that are judged to be equal; and (5) sense-ratios: those stimuli that are judged to stand in particular ratios to each other. In this influential chapter on "Mathematics, Measurement, and Psychophysics," Stevens (1951) added two additional problems to this list: (6) stimulus order: the determination of the ranking, or order, into which observers place particular sets of stimuli; and (7) stimulus rating: the determination of the precision with which observers can estimate the true physical values of stimuli.

SOME DIVERGENT VIEWS

These seven problems seem straightforward enough, until they are viewed in the context of several generations of debate over the proper methods by which they might be approached, and a longstanding doubt by some schools that sensory experience is at all subject to quantification.[1]

One of the issues that raised serious concern was that of the possibility of scaling whatever mental events might be correlated with points along a stimulus dimension. Attempting to construct such scales was ultimately accepted by some scientists via a logical justification derived from behaviorism and operationism: that the verbal report is as properly subject to scientific description as any other physical event. This view has been developed and defended by Stevens (1935), who, with Boring, is responsible for much of the continuing vigor of psychophysics in modern American psychology.

An alternative position to that of Stevens has been that psychophysics can exist without reliance on verbal report, or at least without great concern for the idiosyncratic interpretations of particular response words by particular observers. Sensory psychologists with a pure behavioristic inclination accomplished this goal by restricting the domain of psychophysics. Where it had once been set up to expose the totality of the relations

---

[1] There did seem to be general agreement about one issue: that psychophysics in practice was a tedious business, as the often-quoted remark by William James demonstrates: "*Within a few years what one may call a microscopic psychology has arisen in Germany, carried on by experimental methods, asking of course every moment for introspective data, but eliminating their uncertainty by operating on a large scale and taking statistical means. This method taxes patience to the utmost, and hardly could have arisen in a country whose natives could be bored. Such Germans as Weber, Fechner, Veirordt, and Wundt obviously cannot; . . .*" (W. James, *Principles of Psychology*, 1890, p. 192).

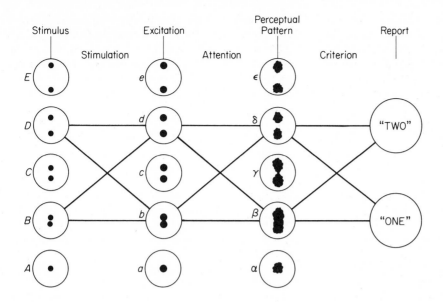

Fig. 14-1. *A model psychophysical situation, as described by Boring ("The Stimulus Error," 1921). The experiment considered here was a determination of the "limen of dual impression upon the skin."*

between mental and physical events, the non-verbal psychophysics would determine only the sensitivity and the resolving power of an observer's sensory systems. Concurrent developments in the psychology of learning, especially in animal learning where "anthropomorphizing" was viewed as a chief evil, made the development of such an "objective" psychophysics very much a part of the *Zeitgeist*.

In the older psychophysics another related controversy concerned exactly what the observer, in a psychophysical experiment, should be attempting to do. Should he be trying to outguess the experimenter by describing the *source* of the energy to which he is exposed? Or should he be a skilled scientific observer looking inward, describing the actual *sensations* without concern for the source of the physical energy that elicited them?[2] Figure 14-1, taken from Boring (1921), shows an insightful concep-

[2]There is far too little space here to devote to one more long discussion of the meaning of the terms *sensation* and *perception*. But, any use of these words must reflect, even if unknowingly, the position of the writer on some hoary questions. Since the point of view of this chapter is meant to be that of contemporary psychophysics, it would be appropriate to simply ignore those issues, but it would be a disservice to the reader. The changing use of these terms can best be understood by reading Boring (1942) and short of this, by considering a very few highlights from his discussion: Thomas Reid, who originally made the distinction, conceived of sensations as simpler, yet more difficult to have, than perceptions. The perception, to Reid, was the conclusion that a particular sense-object was in the environment (thus the stimulus-error, of Titchener), while the sensation (only for the sentient being) is the difficult-to-achieve awareness of the individual sensory qualities on which the sensation depends. Reid's ideas were modified and complicated by many writers over the next two centuries, emerging from storms of controversy over the bases of perceptions in the native character of mind or in the learned associations between stimulus and response, until sensation finally became, for the student of elementary psychology, "the irreducible elements of which perceptions are formed." The process of this terrible oversimplification, in addition to losing most of the sensible ideas concerning the interpretation of information about the environment by living creatures, ideas which could have been subjected to rigorous experimental tests, finally resulted in the restriction of most sensory research to analyses of those stimulus-response relations that might yield information about the peripheral sensory mechanisms. In a chapter read diligently by most of the current generation of sensory psychologists, Graham noted that,

tualization of this issue. The symbols *A–E* represent various separations of the stimuli in an experimental determination of the two-point limen (the minimal separation of two sharp points that can be distinguished from a single point, on the surface of the skin). Patterns of neural excitation, *a–e* are assumed to elicit the perceptual patterns, *α–ε*. The observer may respond by either describing these patterns as "sharp point, blunt point, oval, long oval, dumbbell, or two points," or he may respond with his best guess about the source of the stimulation, with the perceptual reports "one" or "two." Exactly *where* the point of demarcation between the stimuli that lead to a "one" and those that lead to a "two" will occur was recognized to be in part a function of variables other than the immediate stimuli or the resulting neural excitation patterns. Boring described this limen-like point of separation between the perceptual reports as a complicated variable, which he labeled *criterion* in the figure, and which he proposed would be influenced, among other things, by the degree of attention, fatigue, and the incentive to do well. Two brands of psychophysics arose from these con-

From the point of view of behavior, a specification of what a subject does when he analyzes "sensation" and what he does when he perceives is not now available and probably will not be available for a long time. In any case it is doubtful if such specialized behavior would be of great interest . . . . In general it seems that the term sensation has been applied to those discussions for which some relevant sense organ theory exists, and the term perception to those for which no such theory exists. No basis for differentiation exists in the psychological functions obtained.

This restricted point of view is characteristic of many, if not most, contemporary research workers who are concerned with the senses. Not only, as Boring commented, has "operationism eaten sensation and had it too," but modern rustic empiricism and anti-mentalism has succeeded so well that most 20th-century psychophysics excludes all but the relations between the physical dimensions of the immediate stimulus and the simplest discrimination responses from the realm of acceptable scientific problems. Whether this is as it should be depends on the importance placed on the variables so often left out: learning, motivation, genetic differences, and the experimental context. To the student of peripheral receptor systems these topics are reasonably excluded from experimental consideration, but to the psychologist such exclusions surely result in an incomplete analysis of the relations between sensory information and behavior.

siderations: one that studied the relations between stimuli and perceptual patterns by training observers until they could reliably describe the patterns; and a second that restricted its attention to the final responses ("one" or "two" in the figure).

The separation between the "mental events" associated with the different stimuli could be estimated from either of these procedures. In the case of the perceptual-pattern responses the observers could report *how much more* dumbbell-shaped one pattern is than another. In the case of stimulus-description responses, however, the observer was not trusted to make such a subtle judgment. Instead, what Stevens (1961*a*) has termed "indirect" measurement was resorted to, scaling the separation between the effects of stimuli in units derived from the variance in the responses, i.e., from the apparent stimulus confusability, or *discriminability*.

That discrimination is somehow basic to nearly all behavior, and that stimuli could be scaled in terms of their pairwise discriminability began to be accepted by many psychologists in the 1920s and 1930s. Even Stevens (1939), who later opposed the use of discriminability as the basis of scales of sensation, when commenting on another topic said,

When we attempt to reduce complex operations to simpler and simpler ones, we find in the end that discrimination or differential response is the fundamental operation. Discrimination is prerequisite even to the operation of denoting or "pointing to," . . .

The assumption that the discriminability between stimuli could be used to define the steps of a subjective scale much earlier had been the basis of Fechner's integration of Weber's law, to form the law bearing his own name, but in 1942 Thurstone formalized a similar scaling procedure, as the *law of comparative judgment*. Basically, this "law" assumes that there is a psychological continuum along which a particular pair of stimuli are compared, and that each stimulus gives rise to a distribution of responses on this continuum. These distributions, or *discriminal dispersions* are assumed to be normal, and the difference between the effects of the two stimuli is measured by the separation between the means of their two distributions of responses, scaled in units of the standard error of the difference (see Torgerson [1958] for a discussion of the five versions of the law of comparative judgment). While the applicability of his law to psychophysics was quite clear to Thurstone, its main use came in other fields, such as personality, where it could be used to assess the discriminability of opinions, or other variables difficult to compare by other forms of measurement.

In psychophysical research the standard procedures for establishing subjective scales were greatly influenced by Stevens' arguments that the *indirect* procedure of adding up equidiscriminability units end-to-end simply does not produce a scale which can predict the stimulus value an observer will call twice as loud, or bright, or voluminous, as another. A *direct* procedure, somewhat akin to asking the observer to describe the various perceptual patterns in Figure 14–1, was to inquire of the observer exactly the information which the theory was later to be required to describe: "In what ratio do you judge the stimulus *A* to be to *E*? To *D*?," etc. The success of this experimental procedure was considerable, because estimates of loudness predict estimates of loudness more accurately than do intensity-discrimination data. But, of course, magnitude estimation did not produce data on questions of sensitivity or resolving power,

and in the confusion that so often surrounds heated discussion some basic considerations seemed to be either forgotten or ignored when procedures were labeled "direct" or "indirect." Now that an historical perspective is available, it seems clear that methods are direct or indirect, not in any absolute sense, but in relation to the problem at hand. In the next section it is argued that two major divisions of problems and appropriate methods in psychophysics are those, on the one hand, for which discrimination and discriminability are direct measures, and on the other, those which can only be approached directly through subjective judgments.

II. Basic Issues in Modern Sensory Psychophysics

SENSORY CAPABILITY AND RESPONSE PROCLIVITY

Despite the variety of questions, methods, and theories now included under the heading of psychophysics, it remains a field with recognizable structure. The structure of a science is jointly determined by the questions which it was originally intended to answer and by the habits shared by most of its practitioners. The main direction of sensory psychophysics has been given by our basic curiosity about the ways that behavior is (partly) determined by immediate sensory input. Dividing the question into two parts, psychophysics has attempted to answer, first, "What *can* we do with our senses?," and second, "What *do* we do with them?" Answers to the first question amount to the determination of *sensory capability*, or the limits of sensitivity and resolving power of sensory systems. Answers to the second question are less easily defined, but they amount to the measurement of *response proclivities*.

By a response proclivity is meant merely an observed systematic tendency to respond to a particular sensory event, or sequence of events, in a particular way, even though other responses are clearly within the capability of the organism. For example, we are capable of calling many different intensity ratios a ratio of 2:1 in loudness, but one may be characteristically chosen. The selection of that particular ratio may be based in the nature of the sensory nervous system, or it may reflect our previous experience with sounds and with words, or it may be determined in an interaction between "nature" and "nurture." Preconvictions about the bases of response proclivities may allow us to skirt knotty problems but seldom helps to solve them. In any case, sensory capabilities *and* response proclivities are both real characteristics of organisms, and the task of psychophysics has been to establish them as rigorously as possible. The next-order problem, not necessarily in time but on a parallel track in normal scientific sequence, is the elucidation of those features of the organism that account for whatever capabilities and proclivities we discover. Naturally, these are to be found in the organism's genetic or environmental history.

Table 14–1 shows an organization of some of the problems of classical psychophysics into these categories of sensory capability and response proclivity. The measurements of absolute and differential sensitivity are the primary experimental determinations of sensory capability, with stimulus identification an important, although derived, third member of this class. Response proclivities here include many common psychophysical measures, those of stimulus values called "equal" along some instructionally defined continuum, or pairs of stimuli called

Table 14-1. Classes of Psychophysical Problems and Some Appropriate Experimental Methods

Class	Problems	Examples of Some Appropriate Methods	Measures
SENSORY CAPABILITY (The measurement of the sensitivity and resolving power of an organism.)	*Absolute sensitivity.* Ability to discriminate between presence and absence of some stimulus, or more accurately, between stimulus-plus-ambient background and only that (specified) background. When background is parametrically manipulated this is the special case called *masking*.	Forced-choice (spatial or temporal), with m-alternatives. Single-interval methods, with binary decisions (yes-no), or with confidence ratings.	Per cent correct. d' or other index of detectability. $P(C)_{max}$.
	Sensitivity to differences. Ability to discriminate between stimuli, each of which is discriminable from the ambient background.	Paired comparisons. Rating, or binary decisions of the sameness or differentness of stimulus pairs, AA, AB, or BB. Identification of third stimulus in sequence ABX.	Per cent correct. d' or other index of discriminability.
	Stimulus identification. The ability to assign a different response to each stimulus from a set of n stimuli. A special case of differential sensitivity, in which the ability to make all possible pairwise discriminations, and the absolute sensitivity for each stimulus must be considered.	Identification, generally using a pre-learned response associated with each stimulus, thus providing the data for a confusion matrix (n-stimuli-by-n-responses).	Constant error. Standard error or other measure of dispersion. Information transmitted. d' matrix.
	Effective stimulus magnitude. The magnitude of a stimulus, scaled in units derived from measurement of a sensory capability.	Measurement of effective stimulus intensity in terms of equi-discriminable units.	Stimulus values (range) called equal on some specified per cent of the judgments.
RESPONSE PROCLIVITIES (The measurement of characteristic responses to particular stimuli, or stimulus sequences, when the stimuli are clearly discriminable from each other and from the ambient background.)	*Equality.* The determination of those stimuli called equal along some instructionally defined continuum, as distinct from a determination of the ability to discriminate between the stimuli.	Method of adjustment. Paired comparison, with "equal" judgment allowed. Constant method. Limits.	Average and dispersion of stimuli called equal on specified per cent of the judgments.
	Equality of Differences. The determination of those stimulus pairs reported to have the same differences along an instructionally defined continuum, as distinct from the determination of the ability to discriminate between the differences.	Method of adjustment. Paired comparison, with "equal" judgment allowed. Constant method.	Average and dispersion of stimulus differences called equal on specified per cent of the judgments.
	Sense Ratio. The determination of those stimuli that are reported to stand in particular ratios to one another along an instructionally defined continuum.	Method of adjustment. Magnitude estimation.	Average and dispersion of stimulus ratios reported as standing in ratio required by instructions.
	Stimulus ranking. The determination of the rank order into which stimuli are placed on an instructionally defined continuum.	Rating, ranking, or sorting of individual stimuli. Paired comparison.	Means and dispersions of ranks. Separation between ranks in terms of stimulus confusability. Mean stimulus values in various classes.

"equally different," or standing in an "equal ratio" to each other. The common element in this second class of experiment is that the continuum, or "dimension" of interest is defined for the observer through instructions. Although the determination of points along such instructionally defined dimensions can be made with great experimental rigor, it is important that they be expressed without assertions about the *capability* of the observer to process information. That is, the central tendency shown in measures of response proclivity cannot be considered a measure of sensory capability, even though the variability of these judgments is certainly capability-limited. In fact, the variability of proclivity measurements can be of considerable interest, since it is on this basis that one instructionally defined continuum may prove of considerable scientific interest, while another is less so. If, for example, observers are able to rate members of a set of sounds by the "purpleness" of each, with good reliability, then this would be of interest to the psychophysicist. On the other hand, if they could make reliable rank-

ings, in terms of "loudness" but not of "purpleness," then the purpleness of sounds would be of less interest and the loudness of more. Whether a *construct* such as "loudness" is validated through the low variability of judgments seems a matter best left to one's personal philosophy of science; whatever its epistemological status it reflects an orderly behavioral pattern and the psychophysicist is responsible for discovering the relation between such behavior and the physical stimulus.

The primary requirement of the *methods* used in establishing sensory capability is that they allow the conclusion that a particular pattern of judgments could not be achieved by the observer unless he is able to discrimate between certain stimuli. If, for example, there is a statistically significant correlation between a sequence of *yes* and *no* responses, and a sequence of tone- and no-tone trials, then there can be no question that the listener is sensitive to these tones. This, of course, is no demonstration that he "heard" the tones. The listener may claim that he heard nothing at all, as sometimes happens in experiments in which a randomly chosen half of the trials include tones, and when people are admonished to say yes half the time. By such an instruction the problem of the *criterion*, as shown in Figure 14–1, can be circumvented, although in the process certain useful information is obviously lost.

The determination of the response proclivity called the *behavioral threshold* has been one of the major problems of psychophysics. By this is meant the level of a stimulus above which an observer will *admit* that he is sensitive, i.e., that he sees, or hears, or smells, or feels it. But measured proclivity, such as the threshold, while closely related to sensitivity measurements, are not identical to them. For purposes of clinical convenience the high correlation between behavioral thresholds and sensitivity measures, for most observers, permits the more simply obtained threshold to be used as a reasonable index of a patient's ability to see or hear. But, where feasible in terms of time and the demands of adequate experimental design, studies that claim to measure sensory capability should literally *do just that*. Many scientists have wasted much valuable time criticizing studies that could have shown a desired effect through a sensitivity measurement, but settled for a more quickly obtained measure of response proclivity. Replication of such studies seldom changes the observed effect, but the fact that it *can* makes every such unreplicated investigation slightly suspect.

One final distinction between measures of sensory capability and those of response proclivity is the difference between the interpretations which may be made of each. Within the generality permitted by a particular experimental design, a measure of response proclivity yields an *exact* (stimulus) *value*, the validity of which is given by definition. That is to say, the level of a stimulus which a listener asserts he can hear *is* his behavioral threshold, within the variability of the experimental procedure. The measure of sensory capability, however, only establishes a lower bound in the sensitivity domain. The correlation discussed above, between a sequence of stimuli and a sequence of responses, showed that a listener had *at least* a measured level of sensitivity; we are always prepared to learn that he is even more sensitive when tested under some other procedure. In general, a measure of response proclivity is valid by definition; a measure of sensory capability is more valid than another such measure when it demonstrates greater sensitivity. An organism is obviously at least as sensitive as is shown by the "most sensitive measure of sensitivity."

ATTRIBUTES OF SENSATIONS, OR INSTRUCTIONALLY DEFINED "DIMENSIONS"

One of the most complex problems in psychophysics has been the rationale for selecting certain instructionally defined dimensions for special emphasis in studies of response proclivity. As suggested earlier, the major basis of selection seems to have been that certain "dimensions" are used reliably by both individuals and whole populations of observers (*loudness* of sounds), while others lead to less orderly judgments (*purpleness* of sounds). When a particular adjective such as loud, bright, or purple is used in such a way that it clearly is primarily determined by a single feature of the physical stimulus, then psychophysicists have tended to speak of this feature as an *attribute*. But what is not always clear in such discussions is that

the attribute must be a characteristic of the observer's interaction with the stimulus, not of the stimulus itself. Osgood (1953, p. 124) for example defined an attribute as a feature of a sensation that has, (a) physical dependence, (b) a relation to differential neural activity within a modality, and (c) independence of other attributes. The last requirement does not appear valid because of the strong likelihood that any stimulus can be judged along the "dimension" associated with any adjective, and that there will be some degree of non-random order in the resulting judgments. The empirical criteria which may assist in selecting certain adjectives for sensational scaling must therefore go beyond a list like that proposed by Osgood. The fact that most people judge stimuli within a given class by using certain words (sounds are loud, have pitch, volume, density; lights have brightness, hue, saturation, etc.) is a useful additional criterion for including adjectives in a list of attributes. However, we are still skeptical of lists of subjective dimensions, such as those used by some amateur wine tasters, if there is no clear demonstration of the relation between the dimensions and the stimuli.

Possibly the best practical solution to the problem of which attributes should profitably be considered in psychophysical research may be found in the techniques developed by Osgood (1952) for another purpose (development of the semantic differential). Osgood proposed that the determination of the number of meaningful dimensions associated with a set of stimuli be made by simply allowing observers to rate the stimuli according to the degree that they possess each of a very large number of instructionally defined characteristics. Thus the wine tasters might judge a number of samples for aroma, fragrance, bouquet, "nose," acidity, bitterness, mellowness, nuttiness, and-so-on. If it may be shown, perhaps through factor analysis, that only four variables account for most of the relation between the wines and the judgments, then these four might as well be called the attributes of the beverage. Failing to say that they are the attributes of the beverage-taster interaction is a convenience that the psychophysicist might adopt, so long as he knows better.

III. Theories and Models as Generators of Psychophysical Research

It can reasonably be argued that there are few modern theories that are peculiar to psychophysics, but rather that theories from several other disciplines yield predictions about psychophysical performance. These predictions are tested through psychophysical methods and the results then become a part of the research literature of those other disciplines. In this section four different kinds of theories are examined. *Functional theories*, or "black-box" hypotheses from sensory psychology, are closest to being literally psychophysical theories. *Structural theories* are based in the neurophysiology or neuroanatomy of the sensory systems. *Physical theories* are oriented by a detailed (waveform) consideration of the physical stimulus and are often based on the concept of "ideal observers." Finally, *evolutionary theories* grow out of ethology, or from a consideration of the evolutionary pressures on sensory systems. The arguments of proponents of these various theories sometimes suggest that one or the other is based in a more logically valid approach to science. However, the differences between these approaches can best be understood by paying very little attention to such claims, and noting instead that scientists trained in neurophysiology find much of the variance in psychophysical performance accounted for in the structure of the system, those from physics and electrical engineering associate it with the stimulus, while those schooled in the mathematical modeling of behavior find it quite closely linked to a probabilistic view of nature.

FUNCTIONAL THEORIES IN PSYCHOPHYSICS

The theories which have been most clearly the product of experimental psychology are those founded in observations of typical relations between sensory input and whole-system, or behavioral, responses. The input in this class of theories is sometimes described in less elaborate detail than in the stimulus-oriented, or "ideal observer" theories discussed in a later section. For example, it may be specified only as the presence or absence of a "signal," with only slight regard for the manner of physical specification of this stimulus. Likewise the response may be described in these models as the presence or absence of a behavioral event, without consideration of the underlying neural relations. This contrasts with theories which attempt physiological or physical relevance. The response is typically regarded as a button press, the statement of a number, or some other such behavioral unit. Somewhat finer grain has been introduced by the observers being allowed to squeeze a handgrip, but in the treatment of data this is equivalent to a numerical magnitude response. In two examples discussed here, one functional model is generally based in data from studies of response proclivities using the scales derived from magnitude estimation. The second is designed to describe data from studies of sensory capability using discrete-state, or "choice" models.

Scaling of Sensational Attributes. The topic of scaling is a difficult one to touch on briefly. In its broadest sense scaling includes the results of any operation that can be called measurement. Measurement is defined by some authors as *any* procedure that associates numbers with objects or events, and by others as any *systematic* procedure that accomplishes this result. The difference between these views is that the second disallows random assignment, and thus removes "nominal" scaling from consideration. The subtleties of measurement theory and, indirectly, of scaling have been described at length in the classical texts by Campbell (1920) and Russell (1938), and more recently in a pair of influential works, a chapter by Stevens (1951) and a book by Torgerson (1958). A very up-to-date survey of the literature of scaling has been written by Zinnes (1969), which is remarkable both for its thoroughness and its close adherence to a strict mathematico-deductive view of the nature of science. A broader view is presented in discussion by Ekman and Sjöberg (1965). The general topic of measurement in psychology has been discussed in elaborate detail in a text by Coombs (1964).

An example of the standardization of measurements in psychological units is readily available in the field of acoustics. The following definitions have been adopted by the American Standards Association (1960) as standard acoustical terminology:

2.6. *Sound Pressure Level.* The sound pressure level, in decibels, of a sound is 20 times the logarithm to the base 10 of the ratio of the pressure of this sound to the reference pressure. The reference pressure shall be explicitly stated.

12.3. *Loudness.* Loudness is the intensive attribute of an auditory sensation, in terms of which sounds may be ordered on a scale extending from soft to loud.

12.4. *Sone.* The sone is a unit of loudness. By definition, a simple tone of frequency 1000 cycles per second, 40 decibels above a listener's threshold, produces a loudness of 1 sone. The loudness of any sound that is judged by the listener to be n times that of the 1-sone tone is n sones.

12.6. *Loudness Level.* The loudness level of a sound, in phons, is numerically equal to the median sound pressure level, in decibels, relative to 0.0002 microbar, of a free progressive wave of frequency 1000 cycles per second presented to listeners facing the source, which in a number of trials is judged by the listeners to be equally loud.

12.7. *Phon.* The phon is the unit of loudness level as specified in definition 12.6.

12.15. *Level Above Threshold.* (Sensation Level). The level above threshold of a sound is the pressure level of the sound in decibels above its threshold of audibility for the individual observer or for a specified group of observers.

(In the following section the numbers refer to items in the terminology list.) This set of definitions is of interest, both because it helps demonstrate the development of a practical scale of sensation, and also because it is a rare case of an "officially" adopted definition of a subjective phenomenon.

In moving from a physical measurement of intensity to a sensational scale, the first step is obviously to establish a physical unit. In the case of acoustics the unit is 20 times the logarithm of a pressure ratio, as described in (2.6), and the psychophysical operation of threshold determination establishes thresholds for each stimulus frequency, defined in these units. The *Sensation Level* of a particular tone (SL) is established by measuring, in these same (decibel) units, the ratio between the pressure of the sound and the threshold pressure at that same frequency. The sensation level scale thus depends on a psychophysical judgment, but only for its endpoint. Next the *Loudness Level* can be determined by a matching operation, the match being made between SL and a 1000-Hz tone, the intensity of which is varied until it is called equal *in loudness* to the sound. By definition, the loudness level of the sound is then said to be the sound pressure level (relative to 0.0002 microbar) of the equally loud 1000-Hz tone. The loudness levels of all frequencies except 1000 Hz thus depend on psychophysical judgments at every sound pressure level, not merely at the endpoint of the scale, as in the case of sensation level.

The Loudness-Level scale is useful for communicating how loud a sound is in a meaningful way, or for comparing the loudness of one sound with that of another, but it is not a scale that truly represents the "growth of loudness" in the sense that a sound that is twice as loud has twice the Loudness Level, or half as loud, half the Loudness Level. The most straightforward way to determine such a response proclivity as calling one sound twice as loud as another is by requiring observers to do exactly that, in an experimental context. Stevens (1936) named the modal unit, the loudness of a forty-phon, 1000-Hz tone, as one *sone*. The forty-phon level of any frequency is thus the "one-sone loudness" (not *level*, since by convention this word is reserved for measurement in decibels), two sones is twice as loud as one, one-half sone half as loud, and so on. The applicability of this technique for the establishment of a scale of the subjective effects of sound on yet another instructionally defined continuum has been demonstrated by Kryter (1959). Kryter used the procedure established by Stevens in arriving at the sone scale of loudness, but he required observers to match sound stimuli in *noisiness*, or *acceptability* (in the case of aircraft sounds) if the observer was to hear the sound "in your home 20 or 30 times during the day and night." The resulting scale of "noisiness" has the unit *noy*, defined as the perceived *noisiness* of the band of random noise from 910–1090 Hz, at a sound pressure level of 40 dB re 0.0002 microbar. The noy scale is thus an excellent example of the practical utility of a systematically measured response proclivity.

General Laws of the Growth of Sensation. Weber's law, so named by Fechner, was the first general rule relating the growth of sensation to increases in the magnitude of physical stimuli. The form of this law most familiar to psychologists states that the size of an *increment* in stimulation that is just noticeable, or detectable, is a constant proportion of the standard stimulus. That is, $\Delta S/S = K$.

A common finding in studies of sensory discrimination has been that Weber's law provides a good description of just-noticeable differences (j.n.d.) in stimuli, over the central portions of the ranges to which the human is sensitive. At the extremes of sensory ranges the predictions often underestimate the amount that the stimuli must be changed for the increment to be noticed. Table 14–2, abstracted from a study of the difference limen for

Table 14-2. Predicted and Obtained Values of the *J.N.D.* for Tonal Frequency

Frequency	Predicted j.n.d.	Obtained j.n.d.	Obtained/Predicted
250	.625	.900	1.44
500	1.250	2.000	1.60
1000	2.500	3.200	1.28
2000	5.000	4.100	0.82
4000	10.000	10.200	1.02
8000	20.000	18.500	0.92
16000	40.000	176.000	4.40

Predictions based on $\Delta f/f = .0025$, all values in Hz.
After Shower and Biddulph, 1931

tonal frequency (Shower and Biddulph 1931), illustrates these generalizations about Weber's law. The observed values of the j.n.d.'s between 500 and 8000 Hz are fairly well described by $\Delta S/S = 0.0025$. The average ratio of obtained-to-predicted values over this frequency range is 1.18, not too bad as behavioral predictions go. On the other hand, the prediction of 40 Hz at 16,000 Hz is quite a departure from the obtained value of 176 Hz.[3]

[3]In a more modern determination of the ability of the human listener to detect differences in tonal frequency, Henning (1966) showed that the resolving power is even worse at 8000 and 16,000 Hz than was indicated in the data of Shower and Biddulph. Apparently, if the human listener is allowed to do so, he discriminates tones at high frequencies on the basis of loudness rather than by subjective

Fechner noted that the Weber fraction seemed to tell us something about the relation between stimulus magnitude and the size of the associated sensation, but only in the limited sense of specifying the stimulus for the j.n.d.—the smallest possible sensation, for the early psychophysics. If the relation were still more general, the magnitude of the resulting sensation might be predicted for any stimulus. Fechner therefore postulated a small change in sensation (ΔR) that might be associated with the small change in stimulation (ΔS) with the same constant proportionality specified by Weber's law, $R = C \cdot \Delta S/S$. He underscored the primacy of this relation by calling it the *Fundamentalformel*. Substituting, under the apparent assumption that the small increments would be of constant size, the delta's were made derivative notation and the expression was integrated to yield

$$R = C \cdot \log_e S + B, \qquad [1]$$

where C is the same constant of proportionality and B is a constant of integration.[4] The constants could be eliminated by noting that the threshold level of the stimulus (So) is presumably associated with zero sensation, so that Equation 1 must be valid when

$$O = C \cdot \log_e(So) + B,$$

and rewriting,

$$B = -C \cdot \log_e(So).$$

pitch. In support of this phenomenological interpretation Henning showed that the j.n.d. increases by a factor of 4-5, at these high frequencies, when the tones to be compared are varied in *intensity* by some randomly selected amount, as compared to the earlier results for constant-intensity stimuli. Henning's method demonstrates a useful dictum for the measurement of sensory capabilities: the observer, when led to be "right" as often as possible, will use any cues that he can to accomplish this goal. This is to the advantage of the experimenter, but only if he manages to preclude the possibility of correct decisions being based on features of sensory processing other than the one which he has set out to study. This point again illustrates the difference between the psychophysics which is oriented by the concept of sensory capability and that which had its foundations in the idea of perceptual awareness, or consciousness. These two approaches have treated issues like the discrimination of wave length in fundamentally different ways, both in their experimental methods and in the interpretation of data. From a perceptual point of view one may ask whether two wave lengths are discriminated by an observer through differences in hue, or are they distinguishable only in terms of brightness? Approached in terms of sensory capability the question would be merely, how well can visual stimuli be discriminated *only* by their wavelengths? There are certainly valid reasons for using either approach to the study of sensory behavior. But it is vital that the experimenter correctly identify the nature of his own question and choose a method that is adequate to answer it.

[4]Woodworth and Schlosberg (1954, p. 237) derived a Fechnerian scale without resorting to the assumption that ΔS may be equated to dS, by considering the number of perceptual steps (n) separating two stimuli, S_o and S. If r is the quantity $(1 + \Delta S/S)$, then

$$S = S_o \cdot r^n,$$

and solving this equation,

$$n = (l/\log r) \cdot (\log S - \log S_o).$$

If n is considered a measure of sensational magnitude, and the stimulus S is scaled in units of threshold size (S_o), then this amounts to Fechner's law, $n = K \cdot \log (S)$, with K equal to $(S + \Delta S)/S$.

Substituting in Equation 1,

$$R = C \cdot \log_e S - C \cdot \log_e (So),$$

or

$$R = C \cdot \log_e S/So,$$

which Fechner called the *measurement formula*. Finally, if a new constant is substituted for C, and the stimulus is measured in threshold-size units (So), the measurement formula may be rewritten as $R = K \cdot \log_{10} S$, the version called Fechner's law. This rule allows the production of a scale of sensations, not only for the case of the j.n.d., but also for stimuli of any size relative to the threshold. From such a scale we could estimate how much to increase in stimulation would be required for one sound to be twice as loud, or half as bright, or seven times less dense than another. Unfortunately, although correct in their general direction, the predictions made by Fechner's law fail badly at the extremes.

Stevens (1961*a*) has argued that the indirect procedure of reasoning from the size of a just-noticeable increment to the amount of a stimulus required for "fifty units of sensation" is too great a theoretical step to have much hope of success. He proposed that a more direct approach to this problem would be to ask observers to judge the size of a particular stimulus in relation to some other standard stimulus, as was done in the development of the *sone* scale. Here the observer gives the judgmental response in numerical, or other, units of subjective magnitude. Such judgments are typically elicited by telling the observer that a standard stimulus has the size "one," or "one hundred" and that he should assign numbers to other stimulus values in a manner consistent with these modal values. Stevens (1961*a*) has shown that data obtained by this procedure are described fairly well by power functions of the form, $\psi = \phi^m$, where ψ is the magnitude of the sensation and ϕ is the size of the physical stimulus, in arbitrary units. Stevens suggests this relation for *prothetic* continua, those for which the judgment is one of *how much*, e.g., loudness, brightness, etc., while other functions may have to be derived for the *metathetic* continua associated with judgments of *what kind* or *where*, e.g., pitch, localization, etc. The data from the magnitude estimation procedure are often displayed on double logarithmic coordinates, where m is then

Table 14-3. Representative Exponents of the Power Functions Relating Psychological Magnitude to Stimulus Magnitude on Prothetic Continua

Continuum	Exponent	Stimulus Conditions
Loudness	0.6	Binaural
Loudness	0.54	Monaural
Brightness	0.33	5° target—dark-adapted eye
Brightness	0.5	Point source—dark-adapted eye
Lightness	1.2	Reflectance of gray papers
Smell	0.55	Coffee odor
Smell	0.6	Heptane
Taste	0.8	Saccharine
Taste	1.3	Sucrose
Taste	1.3	Salt
Temperature	1.0	Cold—on arm
Temperature	1.6	Warmth—on arm
Vibration	0.95	60 Hz—on finger
Vibration	0.6	250 Hz—on finger
Duration	1.1	White-noise stimulus
Repetition rate	1.0	Light, sound, touch, and shock
Finger span	1.3	Thickness of wood blocks
Pressure on palm	1.1	Static force on skin
Heaviness	1.45	Lifted weights
Force of handgrip	1.7	Precision hand dynamometer
Autophonic level	1.1	Sound pressure of vocalization
Electric shock	3.5	60 Hz, through fingers

After Stevens, 1961*a*.

the slope of the subjective magnitude function. Table 14-3 shows the values of m for a large variety of stimuli, and Figure 14–2 shows experimental results fitted by the power functions, both after Stevens (1961*a*). The data of Figure 14–2 were obtained by matching the force with which the observers squeezed a handgrip to various criterion stimuli, a procedure intended to reduce the dependence on numerical estimates.

While there is near universal agreement that "Stevens' law" is an effective descriptive summary of magnitude estimation data, there remain a number of questions about the proper interpretation of the law as a general description of the growth of sensation, and even about the basic incompatibility of a power law with the logarithmic law of Fechner. Each of the arguments has been expounded at length by one or more authors, and they are only briefly summarized here.

1. There are differences in the estimated ratios between two stimuli that are related to the range of stimuli used in the

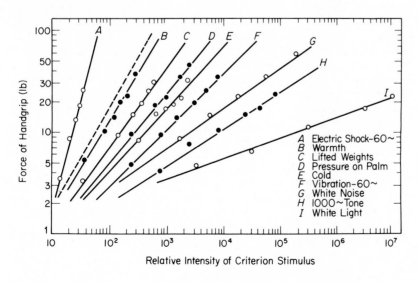

Fig. 14-2. *Equal-sensation functions produced by instructing the observer to match the stimulus with a correspondingly intense "squeeze" of a handgrip.* [Stevens 1961]

total set, perhaps reflecting an adaptation-level type of dependence of sensation magnitude on stimulus context. Engen and Levy (1955), for example, showed reduced slopes for power functions when a wider range of stimuli was employed.

2. Whether the numerical magnitude estimate is of fundamental enough importance to warrant its use as "the" measure of sensation has been questioned, with the alternative suggestion raised by Ekman (1964) that the numerical response itself may bear a Fechnerian relation to true sensational magnitude. If this is the case, then the sensations would perforce have a Fechnerian (logarithmic) relation to stimulation, given the observed exponential relation between stimulus and numerical response.

3. A similar argument to that above is that the relation between sensory stimulation and the particular behavior called *magnitude estimation* may not be of any unique significance, and in fact may tend to obscure relations that reflect more about the processing of sensory information (Graham, 1958).

4. Garner (1958) has demonstrated greater resistance of scales based on discriminability than scales based on magnitude estimation to stimulus context effects, and has raised a variety of other reasons for preferring the "indirect" scales to the "direct" one supported by Stevens. The use of *direct* and *indirect*, although puzzling to one author (Zinnes 1969), reflects only the difference between scales of the growth of sensation based in observers' judgments of their own sensations (a measure of response proclivity), when instructed to do so, as compared to scales based in judgments obtained when the observers are attempting to do something else, as discriminate between pairs of stimuli (a measure of sensory capability). This seems a simple enough distinction, although the case might be biased a little less if it were put in terms of more-or-less *face validity*, which is what it amounts to. Face validity, of course, is of less consequence as more experimental evidence is available.

5. It might be expected that magnitude estimation would be subject to the effects of an observer's past experience in the same way as any other behavior. Warren (1963) has proposed a systematic basis for predicting the growth of sensational magnitude, called the physical correlate theory. Under this theory loudness, for example, should be determined by the typical interaction between listener's and sound sources. Since most sound sources emit a constant intensity, most of our experience with differential intensity has been associated with moving closer to, or farther from, the sources of sound. Therefore, Warren proposes that twice loudness should be reported for the change of intensity normally experienced when we move twice as close to a sound source, half loudness for the intensity change associated with doubling the distance, and so on. While this is not the typical result of magnitude estimation experiments, Warren believes that loudness judgements made by observers wearing earphones in a laboratory may not be a sufficient basis on which to discount the effects of experience when judging sounds in our normal environment. Warren's extension of Berkeley's *New Theory of Vision* and Helmholtz's doctrine of "unconscious inference" probably

warrants further investigation, despite its failure to describe a large number of experimental results.

Perceptual Geometry. Another form of scaling has been under development during the past decade. Several papers have appeared in which the similarity of stimuli is scaled by procedures which both convert "similarities" into distance measures and also determine the best fitting (Euclidian) space. Shepherd (1962) has demonstrated such a procedure by computer-simulation experiments, in which "true" similarities are recovered from similarity-judgment data. Kruskal (1964) has shown good agreement between the distance measures obtained with such a model and those from other multidimensional scaling procedures for experimental data. Although we may be unduly influenced by the sophisticated mathematical treatments involved in these methods, they seem to promise a scaling calculus that will be free from some of the problems of the procedures mentioned earlier in this section.

Choice Models, Discrete-State Models. Due to the number of topics to be touched upon in this chapter it will not be possible to do justice to the rich assortment of models and theories that fall under the rubrics of *choice* and *discrete states*. Instead, one of the simple examples will be demonstrated, and the reader is urged to refer to the works of Luce (1959a, b, 1963a, b), and of Atkinson (1963) for other versions of the basic idea.

Before launching the discussion of a particular mathematical model, the basic orientation of the mathematical modeler must be considered. The product of mathematical modeling has been often misunderstood by scientists whose attitudes toward psychophysics originate in considerations of the sensory nervous system, of the phenomenal facts of "sensation," or of the information content of a waveform and the means by which an ideal device might extract this information. In contrast to the theories of these last three, the builders of mathematical models have approached psychophysics with an array of intentional oversimplifications, based on the idea that one way to make a terribly comlex set of problems manageable is to define many of them out of existence, at least for the moment. What this may mean in practice is that a set of inputs to a system, which are multidimensional in character, and for which several of the dimensions have previously been shown to be individually, systematically related to behavior, are treated as though they are homogeneous in their effects. Similarly the output of the system, although it may have been shown previously to be potentially rich in a vocabulary that describes many features of the input, may be assumed to be restricted to, say, binary choices. Thus a psychophysical experiment in which a puls of a sinusoidal acoustic event is mixed with a random noise clearly leads to a vast array of possible inputs to an earphone, and we have long known that many of these inputs can be discriminated, one from the other. If the listener were allowed to use an appropriate vocabulary (say, including confidence ratings, judgments of pitch, or loudness, or some other scales), he could order the stimuli with fair reliability along these dimensions, in the sense that physical measurements would, *a posteriori*, indicate that a physical ordering was accomplished by the subjective judgments. But for the purpose of devising a hypothetico-deductive model, this sort of experimental problem may be simplified by assuming there to be only two classes of input (noise, and signal-plus-noise) and that the listener can make only a binary (yes-no) response. The model that is then constructed, and which may describe the data of the binary-decision experiment very well indeed, is a model of the results of this experimental procedure, and *only* of this procedure. The advantages of such seemingly unrealistic restrictions are that the pared-down models can be completely described and comprehended by the model builder, and that as they are refined until they fit as well as possible (i.e., that they come as close as possible to describing the data from the relevant experimental procedure), they can tell us how much of the results *could* be accounted for by a simple system such as the one they postulate. The difficulty in communication between scientists, beginning with differing views on the proper origins of theories, arises in the area of *just what is a valid test of such a model.* The builders of hypothetico-deductive models insist that it is of no relevance to demonstrate that the postulates of a model are incorrect. Thus, it is of no significance that the observer, described as being restricted to binary decisions by the model, can in fact increase the amount of information in his responses by using a rating scale rather than a binary decision. This latter fact relates to the nature of the responding organism, or system, but it says nothing about the excellence with which the behavior of the system can be described by a particular simplified model. An analogy might be made with a technique for fitting a linear equation to a set of two-dimensional data, which we are convinced actually originate in a systematic curvilinear relationship. Determination of which of several procedures for fitting a linear equation to the data yields the minimum errors in prediction may be a useful accomplishment, and one that is in no way thrown into disrepute by a demonstration that the data are in fact better fitted by, say a quadratic. The additional characteristics of a data-generating system that are ignored by such models are seldom mathematical features, as might be implied by this analogy. More frequently they are, as in the previous discussion, characteristics such as the ability to judge the loudness of stimuli along a finely grained scale, or of the nervous system to be constructed primarily in such a way that information is almost certainly *not* grouped into gross, homogeneous categories at an early stage. It is to be expected that models constructed with such strong, simplifying assumptions should describe the results of the particular experiment to which they are relevant more accurately than general models which are constrained by attempts to incorporate details of the nature of the responding system and of the "grain" of the stimuli. Whether the postulates of a simple hypothetico-deductive model are consistent with reality is not considered a measure of its excellence. Likewise the accurate description of a restricted range of experimental results should not be the sole measure of a general theory. As simple as this point seems, recent controversies in psychophysics have been generated by failure to understand it.

In summary, psychophysical theories may be constructed with an eye toward incorporating as many empirical relations as possible, including relevant sense-organ information as well as psychophysical results. Or they may be constrained to describe only the results of a single experimental paradigm, even for a specific observer. Considerations favoring each approach have been expounded by various partisans (including this writer, e.g., Watson and Bourbon 1965), and they are related to a variety of issues in the philosophy of science, including classical arguments over hypothetical constructs versus intervening variables as the proper building blocks of a theory. The approach selected by any individual scientist must be a function of the long-range goals of his work, whether it be to describe the functioning of a sensory system, to establish the interrelations between various response patterns within the confines of one experiment, or (most often) some combination of these. Luce (1963b) has argued that models should first be constructed to describe the relations between responses, and that the stimulus-response relationships that have been the major domain of psychophysics might best be studied after this has been at least moderately well accomplished. "There is precious little point, however, in trying to establish such relations until the response-response theory has been rather carefully tested." (p. 147) This attitude is reminiscent of another one that is rather prominent among modern learning theorists: that the day will come when it is worthwhile to consider the neurophysiological relations underlying certain behavioral observations . . . but that time is not yet, and that it will not be until behavior has been far more thoroughly examined.

A simple example of a discrete-state psychophysical model is the two-state threshold model proposed by Luce (1959a). The experimental paradigm for which this model is designed is one in which a trial consists of the presentation of one of two classes of input, signal-plus-background-noise (SN), or only the background noise (N), to an observer. The observer enters state D (detect) whenever his threshold is exceeded by the input (either by SN or N). If the input fails to exceed his threshold he enters state $\bar{D}$. Either state may be entered as a result of the presentation of either stimulus, although presumably the threshold is exceeded more frequently by SN than by N. The observer may also respond either "yes" or "no," and may do so when in either state, although he is more likely to respond *yes* when in the state D. The special constraints of this model are: (1) Stimuli are considered to be effectively indistinguishable, except inasmuch as they lead to either D or $\bar{D}$. (2) The observer *must* respond either "yes" or "no" on each trial. (3) It is apparently assumed that *if* the observer says yes less than 100 percent of the time in state D, then he never says yes in $\bar{D}$; and similarly, that if he says yes at all when in $\bar{D}$, that he always says yes in D. This last constraint seems plausible when stated in terms of logical assumptions about what the observer might be attempting to accomplish by failing to respond part of the time when he is in fact in the 'detect' (D) state. He is probably adopting a conservative strategy, since the occurrence of both D and $\bar{D}$ states as a result of either SN or N inputs means the unavoidability of false positive responses, as well as failures to detect signal occurrence. Thus the conservative strategy might take the form of restricting the number of yes responses—even when in the D state—in order that false positives be held at some low value, lower than the number of N trials that lead to the D state.

Table 14–4 shows the performance of this model, in terms of the predicted conditional response probabilities, $p(y|SN)$ and $p(y|N)$ (the rates of correct detections and false positive responses), for an experimental condition in which the threshold is exceeded (i.e., state D is entered) by 60 percent of the signal-

Table 14-4. Predicting the Results of a Yes-No Detection Experiment with a Two-State Model: Effects of Variation in the Criterion.

Assume: $p(D) = 1 - p(\bar{D})$; $p(D|SN) = 0.6$ and $p(D|N) = 0.2$

Strategies:	$p(Y\|D)$ $[p(Y\|\bar{D}) = 0.0]$	$p(Y\|SN) =$ $p(D\|SN)p(Y\|D)$	$p(Y\|N) =$ $p(D\|N)p(Y\|D)$
	0.0	0.00	0.00
	0.1	0.06	0.02
"STRICT"	0.3	0.18	0.06
	0.6	0.36	0.12
	0.9	0.54	0.18
	1.0	0.60	0.20
	$p(Y\|\bar{D})$ $[(p(Y\|D) = 1.0]$	$p(Y\|SN) =$ $p(D\|SN) + (1 - p(D\|SN))p(Y\|\bar{D})$	$p(Y\|N) =$ $p(D\|N) + (1 - p(D\|N))p(Y\|\bar{D})$
	0.1	0.64	0.28
	0.3	0.72	0.44
"LAX"	0.6	0.84	0.68
	0.9	0.96	0.92
	1.0	1.00	1.00

plus-noise trials, and by 20 percent of the noise-alone trials. From the third constraint it was clear that the conditional probabilities would have to be computed differently, depending on the observer's strategy to be "strict" (respond yes sometimes when in the D state and never in the $\bar{D}$ state), or to be "lax" (respond yes whenever in the D state, and sometimes when in the $\bar{D}$ state). Further, there are varying degrees of laxness or strictness, indicated by the particular value of $p(y|D)$, or $p(y|\bar{D})$.

No mention has been made of computing the probabilities of *no* responses, for the simple reason that, as indicated by the second constraint, if the observer does not say "yes," he must say "no," and statistics associated with the "no" responses bear no information beyond that contained in the "yeses." This being the case, a simple way to display the predictions about a yes-no experiment is to plot the two conditional probabilities from Table 14-4, $p(y|SN)$ against $p(y|N)$. The resulting graph, termed an isosensitivity curve by Luce (1963*a*), is shown in Figure 14–3. This relation between the "hit" and "false-alarm" rates is better known as a receiver-operating characteristic, or *ROC curve*, a name used in the Theory of Signal Detectability, and in

the context of which it has become an influential tool in modern psychophysics (as discussed in a later section). The simple two-state model may, as Luce has commented, have many other features "grafted onto it." But as shown here it is a good example of an input-output model based in a drastic, and intentional, simplification of the ingredients of a psychophysical experiment. The stimulus is treated as being of only two possible types, *SN* or *N*, and any further subdivision is considered to be "probabilistic." That this is clearly an incomplete assessment of the stimulus is not of importance to the testing of the model, even though it can be shown that there are actually measurable differences in stimuli (for example in the amount of "signal-like" energy) from trial to trial, and that these trial-by-trial differences have been shown to be related to the performance of the listener. The model also deals severely with the response capabilities of a human observer, since it rules out the possibility that the human is able to increase the information content of his yes and no judgments by tagging them with estimates of his own certainty that he is correct. But again this fact has no bearing on the excellence of the simple model, for of it we only ask a circumscribed set of questions. How well does it describe the overall results of the relevant experiment? What systematic deviations are there, in experimental data, from the predictions of the model? Does the "elbow" that the model fits to data, that is, the point of intersection of the two lines shown in Figure 14–3, occur systematically above or below the negative diagonal?

Among the features that have been grafted onto models like this one are assumptions about the effects of variability in the response criterion and about the effects of progressive changes in the proportions of *SN* and *N* trials that evoke the states D and $\bar{D}$, i.e. assumptions about *learning* in the course of a psychophysical procedure. Questions about learning have been notably lacking in most modern psychophysical research, and it is this aspect of discrete-state models which represents their potential value to our understanding of human sensory performance.

Procedure-Specific Models. A third class of input-output model in psychophysics includes theories which are oriented by some frequently observed result of a particular experimental procedure. The potential generality of such models seems greatest when a procedure yields similar results in two or more sensory modalities, an example of which is the reduction in performance

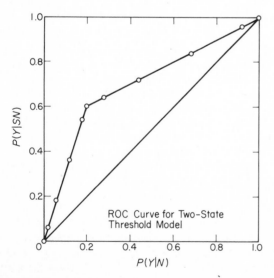

Fig. 14-3. *Iso-sensitivity curve for theoretical psychophysical data of Table 4.* [after Luce 1963]

that is sometimes noticed when a monitoring task is continued for a long period, called the "vigilance decrement." Some authors have questioned the validity of this observation, on the grounds that it may represent a shift of response strategy over time, rather than a change in sensitivity (Broadbent and Gregory 1963). However, others have reported such a decrement only in loosely coupled tasks, that is, those from which you can look away. Thus Loeb and Binford (1968) showed the sensitivity decrement on a visual task, but only a gradual change in strategy on a corresponding auditory task.

Psychophysical observations which appear to be specific to particular experimental procedures are also included in the wealth of facts gathered by investigators in the Gestalt tradition. These experiments have demonstrated special sensitivity to complex stimuli, which could not readily be predicted from the psychophysical features associated with the individual elements of the complexes. Thus there appears to be a tendency in perceptual responses to emphasize points of change, or discontinuity, in time, or space, or in any one of several other physical dimensions of stimuli. Much contemporary research is concentrated around two features of these "perceptual" experiments; first, the possibility that the peculiar organizing properties may, in some cases, be the result of processing at more peripheral neural levels than was previously theorized, and second, that some results which were first demonstrated through the psychophysics of response proclivity might be demonstrable via the techniques developed for measuring sensory capability. Some early examples of the use of standard psychophysical procedures to investigate "perceptual" phenomena were given some years ago in a text by Postman and Egan (1949), in which the authors described classroom demonstration experiments for quantification of brightness-, size-, and color-constancy.

A well developed theoretical position that has depended very strongly on a few standard experimental procedures, is Adaptation Level Theory (Helson 1964). The fundamental observation on which AL theory rests is that the responses of observers are based not only in the immediate sensory stimulus, but also, in a systematic way, in the previous temporal sequence of stimuli to which they have been exposed, or "adapted." Most generally, the sensitivity of observers is said to increase to stimuli that are the complement of the adapting stimuli, and to decrease to the stimuli close, along some continuum, to the adapting one. Among other implications of such a theory is the very clear one that AL effects might sharply decrease the generality of psychophysical findings, when those findings are not assessed in light of the total stimulus context of an experimental procedure. There may eventually be some degree of closure between the analyses of AL theory, and other current theoretical positions that have also concerned themselves with sequential phenomena within psychophysical investigations (especially the mathematical-model oriented psychophysics discussed in the previous section) but at this time there is too little communication between the adherents of these various positions. Since Professor Helson has prepared a chapter for the present book, no further comments will be attempted here on AL theory, except to offer this author's suspicion that it is an area that should become a more significant part of sensory science in the next decade. There is a renewed interest in the psychophysics of complex stimuli, and it may be that AL theory can provide both some appropriate methods and also point to the

importance of some frequently ignored variables. The usefulness of one procedure adapted from AL theory has been demonstrated in two recent experiments, in which "special" trials were inserted in the course of psychophysical sequences. When all of the trials except a few are homogeneous (the signal is the same frequency, or the motivation level is constant) the observer may be considered to be in a constant condition (level of adaptation). If the signal frequency is slightly changed (Greenberg and Larkin 1968), or if the level of motivation is different (Watson and Clopton 1969) on a few trials that are interpolated into the sequence, then these interpolated trials may be viewed as the test stimuli, while the remaining trials are the context, or "frame." The performance on test trials is examined for systematic relations to the characteristics of the context, and by inference, to the effect of this context on the state of the listener. For example, in the studies cited above: when a listener is trained to detect a 1000-Hz tonal signal in noise and an occasional signal is interpolated with a slightly different frequency, 1010 Hz, or 990 Hz (and when the observer is *unaware* of the change), the detection performance is reduced significantly, even though it has been demonstrated that all the signal frequencies are equally detectable on separate tests. Similarly, when a listener is trained under standard instructions to do as well as he can on a psychophysical task, if an occasional trial is interpolated on which there is the threat of electric shock for an incorrect response, detection performance is slightly enhanced—but may remain at its typical level on the context trials. This last result is of interest since it has also been shown that strong increases in motivation, over the usual psychophysical instruction to "Do as well as you can," have little or no effect on performance in the same task, when they are introduced for entire sequences of trials (Swets and Sewall 1963).

Physiological Models and Psychophysical Research

Some investigators design their psychophysical experiments with one ear (or eye) cocked toward the neurophysiology laboratory. This is slightly more true of people who work with animals, perhaps because in conjecturing about the results of psychophysical investigations with animals it is more likely that the relevant sensory physiology will be available, or at least obtainable. Many theories in the history of psychophysics have rested in some general convictions about the nature of the relevant physiological mechanisms. For example, the neural-coincidence detector proposed by Jeffress (1948) which has inspired many experiments in binaural hearing was a logical extension of Boring's (1933) "physiological" concept that all discrimination must ultimately be spatial in the nervous system.

The neurophysiological theories, or generalizations, discussed in this section were selected because of the number of psychophysical experiments which they have influenced. In each case they represent a basic modification of our conception of the organizational properties of the sensory nervous system, and, naturally enough, psychophysical research has turned to the task of discovering what whole-system features of sensory capability or of response proclivities might also reflect the newly discovered facts of sensory physiology. Although the philosophers of science have occasionally decried the practice, when a new structure, set of elements, or system of interconnections is

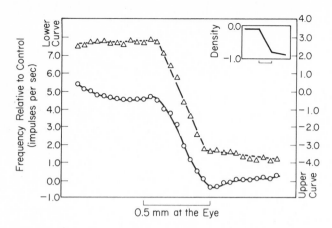

Fig. 14-4. *The response of a single receptor cell (ommatidium) of the limulus eye to a simple gradient of light moved across its receptive field. The upper curve shows the response when only stimulation of the single cell was allowed, by means of a mask. The lower curve shows recordings from the same cell under simultaneous illumination of adjacent receptors, leading to lateral-inhibitory effects.* [Ratcliff & Hartline 1959]

recognized, many of us still ask ourselves, "If it is there, it must have a role in processing information . . . what is it?"

Lateral Inhibition and Receptor Processing. Research in vision, audition, and also in the "minor" senses (a useful distinction which tends to reduce some students of tactile and thermal sensitivity, taste, olfaction, etc., to inarticulate rage) has begun, in the past ten to fifteen years, to emphasize the role of specialized processing by complexes of receptor cells working together, so that sensitivity is enhanced for particular classes of stimuli. Much of this work has been influenced by the pioneering research of Hartline and Ratliff (1957) and others in vision (see especially the excellent summaries by Ratliff, 1962, 1965), and corresponding research in other senses has been described in a recent book by von Békésy (1967). The basic phenomenon is demonstrated in Figure 14–4, taken from Ratliff and Hartline (1959). The interaction of complexes of receptor cells might have been ideally studied by implanting an electrode in each of several cells within a small spatial region of the *limulus* retina. The impossibility of this procedure, in the current state of the neural-recording art, led to the design of an almost equivalent experiment. A single electrode is implanted, and then a stimulus gradient is moved across its receptive field (the receptive field, for a particular range of stimuli, is defined as that region of the retina which seems functionally related to changes in the output of nerve impulses, at a particular level of the nervous system). In Figure 14–4, the gradient was produced by a linear-density-gradient filter, which was moved across the retina (between it and a light source) so that the successive records from the single electrode were approximations of what would have been obtained from several cells located along the gradient. The upper curve shows the effect of the changing intensity when a mask was interposed between the retina and the filter, so that only a pinpoint of light actually stimulated the sensitive cell, and it shows that under this condition the change in receptor output is a close approximation of the intensity gradient of the stimulus, as shown in the insert. When the pin-hole mask is removed, however, and cells all along the stimulus gradient

are illuminated simultaneously, the lower recording is obtained. In the lower recording enhanced response at the top of the steep gradient and the inhibited response at the bottom have been interpreted as a "neural sharpening" or "funneling" (von Békésy 1959, 1967). This effect very soon became an *a la mode* topic, first in vision and, later, in other modalities. The surge of investigations was supported by the fact that adequate neurophysiological theories were generated to describe and interrelate the findings at about the same rate as new results were generated. The basic theory is simply that each receptor element has both excitatory effects directed toward the higher-order nuclei and also *lateral inhibitory* connections to cells at the same neural level. With properly selected combinations of inhibition and excitation, neural "nets" can be devised which have high sensitivity to all sorts of special stimulus parameters, for example, to stimuli moving in a particular direction (Barlow, Hill, and Levick 1964), or for a frog, to an object the size of an edible bug, at striking distance (Lettvin, Maturama, McCulloch, and Pitts 1955). That these theories and physiological results may influence psychophysical research is suggested both by the nature of some of the oldest puzzles in sensory science, and because the peculiar sensitivity of certain complexes of cells may be reflected in whole-system sensitivity (the frog *does* perform rather well in catching bugs). Dilemmas that have long been bothering sensory researchers include many instances of the acuity of the senses being somewhat greater than can be easily accounted for, if the initial stage in the system is no more than a mosaic of passive receptor elements. An example is the difficulty in understanding the ability to discriminate between two pure tones, when they are separated by only a few hertz, and when the mechanical activity associated with either tone is spread along the basilar membrane over a range that (according to place theory) is twenty to fifty times greater, in hertz, than the clearly discriminable difference between the two frequencies. Figure 14–5 shows the results of a psychophysical demonstration by Carterette, Friedman, and Lovell (1969) of the neural sharpening, or funneling, effect shown in Figure 14–4, but this time the stimulus was a narrow band of (computer-generated) noise. Their experiment consisted of a determination of the amount of masking (the difference between the "threshold" in the quiet and that obtained in the presence of the masking noises) at various frequencies below, within, and above the band of masking noise. The results show some indications, particularly at medium levels of the masker, of edge effects, or sharpening, and the authors interpreted several earlier studies, in which similar effects had been obtained but ignored, as other instances of lateral inhibition affecting the results of investigations in psychoacoustics. It is likely that a great deal more attention in psychophysical studies will be paid to the phenomena of sharpening or funneling in the next decade now that it is clear that the effects can be obtained in behavioral investigations. Mach himself, after describing the bands that bear his name, suspected that they could not be studied by psychophysical methods. As Ratliff has observed (1965), time has proven Mach wrong (a rare event) on this point, and innumerable psychophysical studies of the bands have appeared in recent years. The reason for suspecting that they could not be so investigated was that the presence of an investigatory stimulus (a "probe") was thought to reduce, or even abolish the contour enhancement. However, various ways around the interference between probe and generating stimuli have been discovered, including the simple

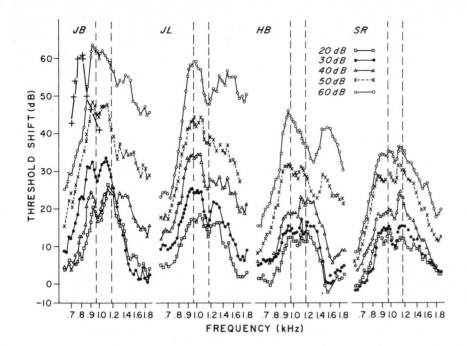

Fig. 14-5. *Masking of tones (labeled "threshold shift") for four listeners, resulting from a steep-sided synthetic noise band 100-Hz in width, centered at about 1060 Hz. The discontinuities associated with the edges of the noise bands may be compared to those of the lower curve of Fig. 14-2.* [Carterette, Friedman & Lovell 1969]

expedient of presenting the probe to the opposite eye and asking the observer to make a psychophysical judgment about the relation between probe brightness and the brightness on either side of a contour (Fiorentini and Radici 1957, as cited by Ratliff 1967). The new direction suggested by this work is more than a physiological foundation for some ideas that have long existed in Gestalt psychology, but it is certainly partly that.

Efferent Control of the Peripheral Receptor. A second hypothesis, partially supported by some anatomical and physiological observations, is that the "passive" receptors may not only have specialized sensitivity as suggested in the previous section, but they may *also* be subject to variable tuning, or to changes in their transmission characteristics, by control from points more central in the nervous system. That this is *grossly* possible has long been obvious; we can clearly blink our eyes, animals can intentionally close the external auditory meatus, and the tension on the ossicular chain can be modified via the *tensor tympani* and the stapedius muscle, in somewhat the same way that the amount of light striking the retina may be modified by adjustment of the pupillary aperture. But recent versions of this principle have postulated the possibility of more direct control of the receptor outflow, achieved perhaps in a manner similar to the contour enhancement described in the previous section, except that the inhibitory influences might be supplied from a remote point, rather than from the action of the current stimulus on an adjacent cell. A great deal of conjecture has gone on in this area, and it is worth a brief digression to list some of the firmer facts of the matter. The existence of an auditory efferent supply to the cochlea was demonstrated by Rasmussen in 1942, and the pertinent bundle of fibers bears his name. Subsequent anatomical and physiological investigations have shown the efferent connections to the ear (cochlea) to consist both of fibers originating in the nuclei of the same side (uncrossed, or ipsilateral fibers) and also of fibers from the opposite side of the brain (crossed, or contralateral)—giving

rise to conjecture about the possibility of reduction of the sensitivity of one ear by introducing a sound into the other. Some physiological properties of these fibers have been demonstrated. For example, stimulation of the bundle of Rasmussen can lead to a reduction of as much as 80 percent of the amplitude of the action potential on the VIIIth nerve (Desmedt 1962), even when all possibility of the effects being mediated by the intra-aural muscles has been avoided (Fex 1962). These demonstrations have led to certain presumptions of the behavioral significance of the efferent sensory connections. It is easy to move from the observation that these connections exist, and that when directly stimulated they modify the output of receptors, to the idea that they may provide the mechanism for all sorts of whole-system functions. These functions might include habituation, adaptation, and the effects of motivation on perception. However, the demonstrations of such behavioral changes have been quite infrequent, at least when accompanied by direct evidence of efferent impulses acting upon the receptors. The initial evidence on which a great deal of theorizing has been based included experiments by Hernández-Peón, Scherrer, and Jouvet (1956) and by Galambos, Sheatz, and Vernier (1956), in which the output of the cochlea was shown to change when the animal's attention was attracted by some non-auditory event (fish odors, the sight of a mouse). The decade since these observations has failed to produce the revolution of sensory theory that they appeared to presage, but their effect on psychophysics lingers on. The reasoning is basically that some processes that we formerly believed to be accomplished at the higher levels of the nervous system actually may be complete at the periphery. The intrigue of this possibility stems in part from its being so great a departure from the old practice of relegating anything that seemed to require complex processing to higher reaches of the nervous system, and partly because of the prospect that some of the neural bases of "perception" might be vulnerable to investigation by contemporary physiological techniques.

A model system in which the role of efferent connections is clear is the muscle spindle receptor. As Granit (1955) has described them, neural activity of the gamma efferent fibers connecting to muscle bundles elicits no contraction response, but rather acts to modulate the afferent outflow of the muscle spindle receptors. Even in the absence of true contraction-eliciting stimulation, the gamma fiber activity serves to modify the spontaneous discharge of the receptors. Whether this control scheme is typical of other receptors, especially the ear or the eye, remains to be determined, but it raises the question of an interesting mode of operation, whereby the effective dynamic range of a sensory system might be quite broad, despite limitations imposed by maximum obtainable rates of neural discharge. One application of psychophysics in investigating these possibilities may be through studies of the temporal limits of sensitivity to stimuli with wide dynamic ranges.

Some other psychophysical models that are partly founded in assumptions about the sensory nervous system are the neural quantum (NQ) model of Stevens, Morgan, and Volkmann (1941) and Stevens (1961a), a model by Triesman (1964) in which Weber's law may be derived from assumptions about the distributions of neural impulses, and McGill's (1967) neural counting model. While apparently profound in their implications, none of these theories are reviewed here because of space limitations and because they are thus far only loosely related to neurophysiological evidence.

"All-or-None Law." Perhaps one of the more significant concepts from older neurophysiology, from the view of psychophysics, has been the all-or-none law of neural conduction. This "law" has occasionally been used as an introduction to a scientific non sequitur, in that it has been hinted that the threshold of psychophysics is its version of the all-or-none law; that at some level of the nervous system (generally unspecified) the just-noticeable increment in a stimulus is associated with the firing of *an* impulse. On careful thought it is doubtful that anyone would have seriously accepted this interpretation, and the error would not be worth pointing out in a section intended for physiologically sophisticated readers. But in an era of controversy between threshold and non-threshold theories (discussed in the following sections) some good may come of mentioning this particular bit of illogic. The pertinent fact is quite simple: the information carried along an axon is *never* determined by the presence or absence of a neural impulse, but rather by the distribution of neural impulses over time. This fact was nicely demonstrated by Fitzhugh (1957), who showed overlapping distributions of neural output from retinal ganglion cells, for levels of visual illumination of zero, below behavioral threshold, and above behavioral threshold. Elias (1961) has provided a valuable comment in noting that the coding of information into neural impulses is not an example of a digital code. It may be a pulse-operated feature of the nervous system, but to be digital means that the pulse sequence could be represented, with no loss of information, by a series of zero's and one's. When the times at which events may occur are distributed continuously in time, then such a digital transformation is not possible in the same sense that it is if the events can only occur at certain fixed times (as when the clock pulse occurs in a digital computer). Thus the mode of neural information transmission is, in itself, no barrier to the nervous system carrying a continuous rather than a discrete transform of the stimulus.

PSYCHOPHYSICAL THEORIES BASED ON THE CONCEPT OF AN "IDEAL OBSERVER"

One of the most recent trends in psychophysics has been the analysis of performance in terms of the accuracy with which a particular psychophysical task could be accomplished by the best possible system, i.e. by an *ideal observer*. This orientation to psychophysics is primarily appropriate to the study of sensory capabilities, although questions of response proclivities might also be considered in these terms inasmuch as favored response patterns must fall within the realm of the observer's capability.

Ideal Observers Derived from the Nature of the Stimulus. Stimuli that are of interest to psychophysics often consist of variations in the pressure of a conducting medium over time, and are thus subject to description by the modern tools of waveform analysis. The application of waveform analysis to psychophysical theory construction was begun as the result of interaction between a group of engineers (Peterson, Birdsall, and Fox 1954) and psychologists, the latter headed by Wilson P. Tanner, Jr., at the University of Michigan in the mid-1950's (Tanner and Swets 1954). In the following fifteen years the approach to psychophysics that has grown out of this interaction, called the "Theory of Signal Detectability" (TSD) has had a widespread influence, raising controversies, generating research, and in general provoking a renewed interest in many worked-over areas of psychophysics. There have been several excellent summary articles and chapters on TSD, including Swets, Tanner, and Birdsall (1961); Clarke and Bilger (1963); Egan and Clarke (1966); and Tanner and Sorkin (1969), and the publication of a collection of significant research articles (Swets 1961), and of a general textbook devoted to the theory (Green and Swets 1966), so there will be no attempt here to review the details that are so well described in these sources. Instead the major features of the theory are presented in a way that will hopefully give some understanding of the impact that TSD has had on modern sensory research.

The simple words, "modern tools of waveform analysis," in the previous paragraph describe a large body of knowledge, and one for which most sensory psychologists lack the appropriate training in physics and engineering-oriented mathematics. Egan (1967) has done a valuable service for those who would try to acquire a background in these subjects; he has prepared a topical bibliography of TSD covering the related papers in physics and engineering theory and also including applications of TSD to problems in psychophysics.

The significance of detection theory has been obscured for some readers by its details. Most generally, it can be divided into two sections, the theory of the nature of signals, and a theory of the nature of detection systems. The signal is typically multidimensional; the detecting system is pictured as making a statistical decision along a unidimensional decision axis. This axis can be compared to the one described by Thurstone, on which he displayed the distributions of responses called "discriminal dispersions." In TSD this axis is given an interpretation more consistent with the statistical distributions of two classes of to-be-discriminated stimuli, by assuming that any stimulus is associated with a single point, x, having the coordinates: x_1, $x_2, \ldots x_n$, in the n-dimensional coordinate system required

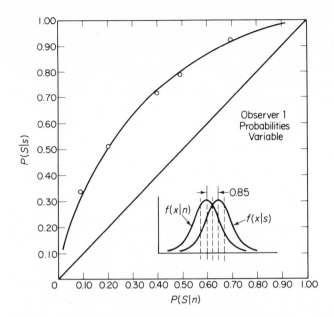

Fig. 14-6. *Empirical ROC curve, with inset showing theoretical distributions on a decision axis. Dashed vertical lines represent decision criteria corresponding to the points on the ROC curve.* [Green & Swets 1966; data from Tanner, Swets & Green 1956]

to completely describe that stimulus. For example, if a sample of a waveform of duration t and bandwidth w requires $2wt$ independent amplitude samples for an exact specification, then it can be said that we are dealing with a $2wt$-dimensional stimulus. If either of two sources of stimulation can potentially give rise to any point (x) in this space, then the decision of which source has in fact been sampled on one trial in a psychophysical sequence is clearly a statistical one. Such a decision can be made if the point x has a different probability of occurrence, given a sample from one source than if the sample is from the other. The likelihood ratio $(l(x))$ associated with that point is the ratio of two conditional probabilities, $l(x) = p(x \mid SN)/p(x \mid N)$, and represents the relative likelihood that x originated in signal-plus-noise rather than in background noise alone. Thus, each point in the multidimensional space used to describe the input can be mapped down to a unidimensional decision axis, namely, likelihood ratio.

The distributions of log $[l(x)]$, for the case of a signal whose starting time and amplitude are exactly known, are normal (for tonal signals presented in broad-band noise), and of equal variance for SN and N, as shown in the inset of Figure 14–6, from Green and Swets (1966).

Decisions based on likelihood ratios have been shown to be optimal for a variety of decision goals (Green and Swets 1966), including maximizing the expected value of a decision, maximizing the percentage of correct decisions, and maximizing the number of correct detections of the signal, while maintaining a constant rate of false positive responses (the goal of the Neyman-Pearson observer). More importantly perhaps, any monotonic rescaling of the entire decision axis has no effect on the degree to which decisions based on likelihood achieve any of these goals.

The decision points shown in Figure 14–6 are indicated as specific criterion values along the decision axis, although some

prefer to discuss the criterion as the interval to the right of a particular value. In either case, the establishment of a criterion for responding clearly divides the decision axis into two segments of correct judgments and into two corresponding segments associated with the familiar Type I and Type II errors. As noted in the section dealing with mathematical models, if the form of the distributions of responses on the decision axis are known, (or are assumed), all of the response information is given by one area from each distribution, if these areas are each relative to the same criterion. The areas usually selected for analysis are those associated with a positive response, i.e., are to the right of a criterion value. The progressive change in one of these statistics, $p(y \mid SN)$ with variations in the other $p(y \mid N)$ is often displayed as a Receiver Operating Characteristic as shown in Figure 14–6. Several points along the ROC curve are obtained by having observers adopt different criteria in each of several experimental sessions, or by having them respond with confidence-scale judgments rather than simple yeses and noes. An ROC plotted from confidence ratings is shown in Figure 14–7 (Watson, Rilling, and Bourbon 1964), along with a fitted curve, based in the assumption of overlapping normal distributions on the decision axis. In this case, as is frequently observed, a better description of detection data is provided when the generating distributions are assumed to have a ratio of standard deviations between the SN and N distributions of approximately 1.33 (Green and Swets 1966, p. 96).

The index of sensitivity used by TSD, d', is the separation between the means of the generating distributions, in units of the standard deviation of the noise-alone distribution. When this index is not calculated from data under the assumption of equal-variance, normal generating distributions, one of several alternative indices must be used, each of which has the same general interpretation as d' (Green and Swets 1966). The chief advan-

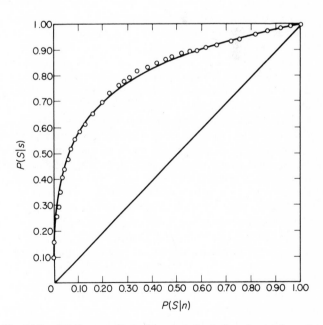

Fig. 14-7. *ROC curve obtained by a mechanical analog to the rating scale, fitted by a curve based on the assumption of normal distributions on the decision axis.* [Green & Swets 1966, data from Watson, Rilling & Bourbon 1964]

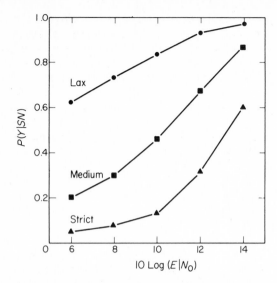

Fig. 14-8. *The effects of instructions to adopt strict, medium, or lax criteria, on the results of a psychophysical method of constant stimuli.* [Data are previously unpublished, from an experiment by Emmerich, Viemeister & Egan 1966; used by permission of the authors.]

tage that has been claimed for TSD as a basis of psychophysical methods is the ability to separately estimate sensitivity (d'), and response bias (β) for a given observer in a given task. Psychophysical performance is always the joint result of these two variables, and methods which fail to recognize this fact are incapable of precise interpretation. In practice, if a normal human observer (no obvious pathology of senses or personality) asserts that he can see, hear, or feel a stimulus above some intensity and cannot when it is reduced below that intensity, it is unlikely that the particular criterion that he has adopted will account for a large part of the variance between him and humans with *sensory* difficulties. However, it is also true that the difference *between* observers, who are called "normal" as the result of simple screening tests, are about as likely to be the result of differences in criterion as of differences in sensory capability. Figure 14–8 shows the average performance of four "normal" human listeners tested by the method of constant stimuli (data collected by Emmerich, Viemeister, and Egan at the Hearing and Communication Laboratory of Indiana University 1966, see Egan 1971), when three different instructions were given to the group. The abscissa in this figure, labeled E/N_o, is a measure of the ratio of signal energy (E) to noise power per unit bandwidth (N_o), a useful variant of signal-to-noise ratio common to stimulus-oriented psychophysics. The data labeled *medium* were produced when they were told, "Say yes when you hear the tone;" those labeled *strict*, when they were told, "Say yes when you are quite certain the tone was presented;" those labeled *lax*, when they were told, "Say yes when you think the tone might have been presented." The separation between the psychometric functions for each of the instructional conditions varies with the observer's interpretation of the instructions. But it is clear that criterion problems should be given serious consideration whenever a psychophysical experiment is designed. As suggested in earlier sections, the awareness of the criterion problem is not new in psychophysics, but systematic *valid* methods of dealing with it are.

One result of signal detection research has been a great

deal of discussion of the validity of the threshold concept. This is probably not nearly as important an issue as many writers have made it seem. But, as this author has said elsewhere, "that the statistical decision model predicts threshold-less performance has provoked some unhappiness on the part of those accustomed to classical methods, but they should consider that detection theory, especially as presented by these authors [Green and Swets] makes no claim as to the existence of a 'hard' threshold for real observers. It is only suggested that an ideal detector would not have such a threshold, that real observers *may or may not*, and that the psychophysical methods we use should not reflect blindness to either possibility. Inasmuch as the statistical decision model, with its estimates of both the response strategy adopted by the observer and of his sensory capability, should be sensitive to either threshold or threshold-less performance, and as it enables us to discriminate between the two, the evidence they present favors the latter alternative" (Watson 1967).

The predictions of TSD are actually assertions about the ideal observer, but they raise questions about the real human observer as well. Thus, if an ideal detector must have a particular bandwidth in its initial detection stage, and a perfect memory, and an ability to perfectly estimate the consequences of his decisions in terms of the values and costs associated with particular outcomes, then one can ask about the degree to which the human listener is deficient in any of these. An experimental method of asking such questions involves the intentional introduction of uncertainty into the stimulus. Thus, although the ideal observer performs considerably better in a detection task when the starting phase of the signal is known, the human does equally well when the starting phase is random as when it is fixed. Conclusion: this form of information is not usable by the human (in monaural listening).

Ideal Observers Conceived in Terms of Realizable Hardware. A somewhat different type of model from that based on the stimulus waveform is a model that is actually simulated in electronic, or other, hardware. Examples of such sensory models over the past half century have included Meyer's (1931) hydraulic model of the cochlea, Békésy's models of the basilar partition, various computer-oriented visual models, and the electronic models that will be discussed here.

It is one thing to suggest that the ear, for example, acts as a low-pass filter, a rectifier, and an integrator, but it is quite another to put together such a set of components with any hope that their output will bear some resemblance to the psychophysical responses of a human listener. Such attempts have been made by several researchers, however, including Jeffress (1964, 1967), Sherwin, Kodman, Kovaly, Prothe, and Melrose (1956), and Nichols (1966). Others, including Watson (1962), Pfafflin and Mathews (1966), and Ahumada (1967) have simulated the ear in a variety of other ways, and compared the output of the simulation to the responses of human listeners. The basic difference between some of this research and general psychophysical experimentation is that the attention is to characteristics of the stimulus which are measured on a trial-by-trial basis. In an experiment discussed earlier, a tonal signal was presented in a gaussian noise background and listeners were asked to discriminate between instances of signal plus noise and equal-duration samples of noise alone. If listeners are considered as sorting many samples of *SN* and *N* into those sets that sound signal-like and those that they judge to be only noise (or, by rating, those that sound more and less signal-like), then a useful *a posteriori* analysis may be performed on the sets of stimuli. The samples in which a signal has actually been presented, and which are judged signal-like, will have those physical characteristics that denote "signal-likeness" to a listener *plus* whatever other features are associated with signal energy. Samples of the noise, however, that are judged signal-like have only those characteristics that bear information for the human sensory system, and *a posteriori* examination of the stimuli in this set may be a way to learn what these characteristics are. Very little of this form of "molecular" psychophysics has been done, in comparison to the "molar" psychophysics that examines only the average response to the average stimulus (Green 1964), perhaps because of the technical difficulties involved in trial-by-trial sorting and examination of waveforms. But the arrival of the small computer in many laboratories will certainly make research on molecular issues in psychophysics far simpler to accomplish.

Informational Analysis as a Form of Ideal-Observer Theory[5]. For centuries people have pondered the way in which *meaning* is communicated through various forms of symbolic representation. The history of this question, as traced by Cherry (1966), culminated in the development of *information theory* (see especially Shannon 1948). In its most familiar form to experimental psychologists, information theory is a method of analyzing the amount of uncertainty that can be resolved by the correct reception of a message. If the circumstances surrounding the reception of a particular sensory event are such that only one possible symbol *could* have been transmitted, then the amount of information conveyed by the correct identification of that symbol (or message) is zero. If the message is one chosen from two equally likely alternatives then the amount of information acquired through a correct reception of it is one *bit*, or one binary decision's worth. The general formula is that the (average) amount of information potentially in a message, *H*, is given by,

$$H = -\sum_{i=1}^{n} p_i \log (p_i),$$

where there are *n* possible messages in a set, from which the *i*th one may be randomly chosen, with a probability p_i.

The use of information theory in psychophysics has waxed

[5]It might seem that information theory belongs in the section of this chapter dealing with *functional* theories in psychophysics, rather than in this section on theories based on the concept of ideal performance, or on ideal observers. While the decision to discuss information theory here was somewhat arbitrary (a fair case could be made for the other alternative), this approach to communication does have much in common with other ideal-observer based theories. Most importantly, informational analysis allows a comparison between observed and possible performance in terms of the capacity of the channels over which the information is carried, whether these channels be band-limited components of actual electronic hardware, or merely similar units postulated in an organic sensory system. In the psychologist's use of information theory, dealing normally with the probabilities of discrete stimulus and response events, it is easy to forget that the general theory of information may be equally well applied to the information content of a continuous waveform. These matters are thoroughly discussed by Cherry (1966, p. 189–98).

and then waned since the last *Handbook* was published (Stevens 1951) in the field of psychology. This approach to the processing of sensory information by the observer had a natural appeal that led some researchers to apply informational analysis when there was no real reason to do so (Cronbach 1955). The view that stimulus configurations are "information bearing," as systematically related to the size of the stimulus set from which they are a sample is, however, an example of a psychophysical problem that might not have been conceived without the concepts of information theory (Miller, Heise, and Lichten 1951). Use of information theory in psychophysical research has been common in experiments with speech as the sensory stimulus (Pollack 1959). It has also provided a useful means of determining the benefits to be gained by allowing an observer to use more than a binary decision in psychophysical tasks, as in experiments with rating-scale responses or confidence judgments (Garner and Hake 1951). Garner (1962) has surveyed a great many applications of information theory to problems in psychology in an excellent text, in which the modern research on judgmental response time is also especially well presented.

An example of discrimination and identification problems that have been productively attacked by the information-theory approach is the determination of the critical factor involved in a decrease in recognition or identification performance as the size of the set of stimuli, and thus the average information content of a single stimulus item, is increased. In a series of experiments, Pollack has shown that the decrease in performance occurs mainly because of *response* rather than *stimulus* uncertainty. Figure 14–9 shows the major result of one of Pollack's (1959) experiments in which this distinction was demonstrated. The experimental procedure was that of intelligibility testing. On each trial the listeners were asked to identify a single bisyllabic word, presented in a noisy background. The listener's attention was directed to the set of alternative stimuli from which the word had been drawn, and he was required to select the most likely stimulus from that set. As in previous experiments, when the set size was increased in steps from two to sixty-four words, the probability of a correct response was systematically reduced. This reduction is shown by the connected filled circles in Figure 14–9. Fifteen seconds after the presentation of the word the listener was asked to make a second selection, this time from two alternatives. One of the two was in fact the word which had been presented. The choice from two alternatives had a uniform probability of being correct, independent of the size of the original stimulus set, as shown by the connected open circles in Figure 14–9. Thus it could be concluded that performance is mainly degraded by response uncertainty and is much less affected by stimulus uncertainty. A further interpretation might be that there is no "setting up" of the input stages of the sensory nervous system to be especially receptive to particular stimuli. Rather the limitation in information transmission occurs at the stage of response encoding, where the neural representation of a stimulus must be compared to each of the items in the response set. For complex stimuli this appears to be a valid generalization, but possibly not for very simple stimuli, such as the pure tones used by Greenberg and Larkin (1968). These authors trained observers to detect a faint, brief tonal signal in a noisy background. When the signal frequency was slightly changed from that on which the observers had been trained, they showed a large reduction in their ability to detect it. This was true even when the procedure was two-alternative

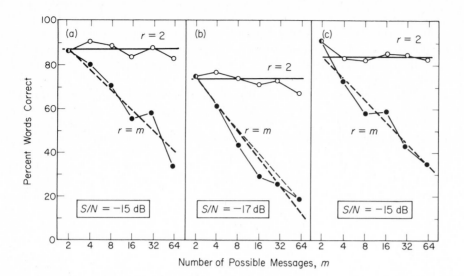

Fig. 14-9. *Results of an experiment by Pollack (1959) comparing the effects of* response *and stimulus* uncertainty. *The open circles show results when listeners were told, after hearing a word in noise, that it was one of two particular words. The filled circles show results when the permissible response could be any item in the message set.*

forced choice, the change in frequency was as small as from 1000 to 1010 Hz, and the observers were unaware that there had been any change in the stimulus. In this type of experiment the uncertainty does seem to be in regard to the stimulus, for the response set remained constant. Thus it may be that observers can "set up" their sensory systems to be acutely sensitive to particular simple stimuli, while no such pre-tuning can be accomplished for more complex stimuli. Considerably more research is needed before this hypothesis can be given the status of a psychophysical fact.

PERFORMANCE-ORIENTED, OR "EVOLUTIONARY," MODELS IN PSYCHOPHYSICS

Psychophysical theories have generally been framed with almost total disregard for the particular relevance of stimulus patterns to the responding organisms. Theories of *perception*, on the other hand, have been carefully tailored to include features of the "meaningfulness," or "appropriateness," of particular stimuli to particular species. Thus, while it is assumed that higher organisms have enhanced sensitivity only for broad stimulus categories, such as changing or moving stimuli, Thorpe (1956, p. 134) asserts that "Over and above these primary or basic instincts, it has been biologically advantageous for many animals, which have to live in and deal with a relatively restricted environment, to develop innate powers of recognition to respond to much more complex and specialized patterns of stimulation."

This point of view has been reflected, in the past decade, in several studies of sensory neurophysiology, including the one cited earlier by Lettvin et al. (1959), in which certain receptor-cell complexes in the frog retina seem particularly attuned to respond to the image of a fly-flying-at-fly velocity, and at striking distance for the frog. Similarly, a species of moth has been demonstrated to be especially sensitive to the cry of a moth-eating bat that inhabits the same regions (Roeder 1966). These are simple and appealing facts to anyone convinced that sensory systems evolve as a result of the ecology of a given organism. Whether the same kind of interpretation may be given to complex human perceptual phenomena, such as the studies by

Gibson and Walk (1960) in which kittens, young goats, and human infants were all shown to have similar tendencies to avoid regions that appear to be abruptly lower than that in which they are located (i.e., "visual cliffs"), is not clear. However, the future of psychophysics, in addition to including more research on sensitivity to complex stimuli, may also bring studies in which stimuli are selected for their relation to naturally occurring sensory events, and perhaps even a reexamination of the advantages of *representative design*, that name given by Brunswik (1956) to the creation of experiments in the normal ecological surround of the organism. Experiments by J. J. Gibson (1959) on the perception of texture are of this sort. Representative designs are more obviously directed toward the establishment of response proclivities than toward measuring sensory capability, although their use with objective psychophysical methods might demonstrate relations between experimental context and measures of sensitivity or resolving power. There is no logical reason that psychophysical methods which provide separate indices of response bias and sensitivity should not eventually provide a means of distinguishing between those stimuli to which the evolution of an organism has made it peculiarly sensitive and those stimuli that it *characteristically* seeks or avoids, even though it is no more sensitive to them than to others with similar physical values. Naturally, the dictum that psychophysical investigations can *never* yield neural, or physiological data must be kept in mind here because of the temptation to promote (depending on one's theoretical biases), either the *sensorium* or the receptor systems as responsible for any peculiar sensitivities. If future research were to show the human to be particularly sensitive to shifts in the frequency of an auditory stimulus that are similar to those bearing information in speech, it would remain to be determined whether this special sensitivity were a feature of the cochlea, the auditory cortex, structures in between, or a complex interaction of all of these. The types of stimuli, and of stimulus processing, that are relevant to this section are those that have been so frequently studied under the rubric of *perception* rather than *sensation*. Some theorists, especially those emphasizing the natural integrity of certain stimulus complexes, may have been too ready to assume that "perceptual" phenomena are logically resistant to investigation by precise psychophysical methods.

Choosing Specific Methods for Psychophysical Research

For details of specific psychophysical methods the reader is advised to check two prime sources. These are the survey chapters on psychophysical methods in the texts by Woodworth and Schlosberg (1954) (for classical methods), and by Green and Swets (1966) (for detection-oriented methods). Robinson and Watson (1972) reviewed a variety of considerations in the use of single- and multiple-interval procedures for detection research. Perhaps a more efficient method of finding the best procedure for any given problem is a critical reading of the recent experimental literature related to that problem.

The suggestions for selecting a psychophysical method in this section are mainly devoted to techniques by which meaningful measures of performance can be obtained for specified stimulus conditions. Commonly the experimenter will want, as his final product, a summary of all those stimulus conditions that lead to a specified performance. Figures 14–10 and 14–11 show the steps in arriving at such a summary for one type of experimental procedure (Watson, Franks, and Hood 1967). The psychophysical method was two-alternative, temporal forced choice, with a to-be-detected stimulus presented in one of the two intervals, on every trial. The stimulus in every case was a 100-msec tonal signal presented without external masking noise. The top panel in Figure 14–10 shows the percent of correct

judgments in 100-trial blocks, as a function of the signal level of the tone, for a single listener, at six test-tone frequencies. A psychometric function was fitted to the data for each frequency. In this experiment the function used was $d' = m(E/N_o)K$, although a normal ogive would be a more common function. See Green and Swets (1966) for further discussion of the selection of appropriate equations for fitting forced choice data. The center panel shows the fitted psychometric functions for each of twelve listeners, and (dashed line) the mean-slope, mean-intercept function. The lower panel shows the mean-slope, mean-intercept functions for the same twelve listeners at each of the six frequencies. To summarize these results in a form that could be readily compared to other tests of auditory sensitivity, the psychometric functions in the lower panel were evaluated at each of six performance levels (defined as values of the detection index, d', ranging from 0.1 through 4.0). Figure 14–11 shows the final transformation of the data into iso-detectability contours, by which a comparison could be made with previous standard measures of sensitivity. In the particular case illustrated in Figure 14–11, the results of an experiment using the forced-choice methods appropriate to the direct measurement of sensory capability could thus be compared to response-proclivity based estimates of auditory sensitivity. The curves labeled "*ASA*" and "*ISO*" represent values of audiometric zero accepted by the American Standards Association and the International Audiometric Zero (Davis and Kranz 1964). Treatment of

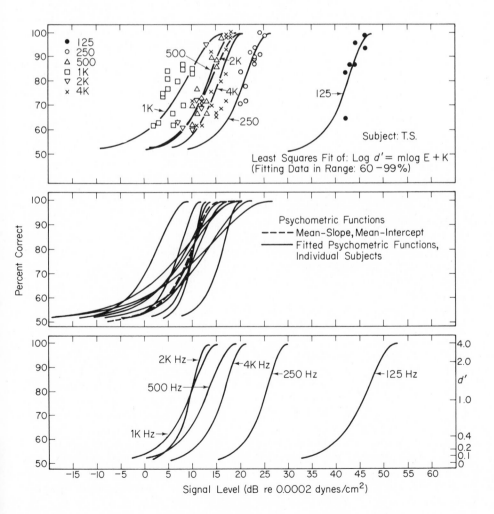

Fig. 14-10. *The top panel shows data for a single listener detecting a tonal signal in the quiet. Each data point represents a 100-trial block. Middle panel shows fitted psychometric function for twelve listeners, each for 1000 Hz. Lower panel shows mean-slope, mean intercept fitted functions for all twelve listeners. [Watson, Franks & Hood 1967]*

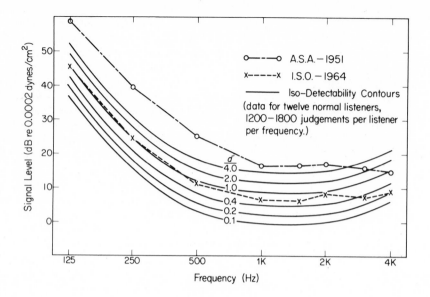

Fig. 14-11. *Iso-detectability contours constructed from data shown in Fig. 14-9, by evaluating fitted psychometric functions each of six performance levels.* [Summary of data from Watson, Franks & Hood, "Detection of Tones in the Absence of External Masking Noise."]

psychophysical data in this way allows comparison between the results of different methods and emphasizes the information of major interest to the sensory psychologist.

The choice of a particular psychophysical method is very much a product of the investigator's theoretical biases and of the particular variables that he wishes to investigate in a given experiment. If there is a single warning that should be kept in mind during the design of every experiment, it is the normal one for all scientific work: that the method must be adequate to the conclusions that the investigator hopes to be able to draw from his data. The following discussion belabors this point at some length.

METHODS FOR THE STUDY OF RESPONSE PROCLIVITIES

The response proclivity discussed most frequently in earlier sections of this chapter was that of determining a particular stimulus that is called twice (or half) as strong, loud, bright, etc. as another. In this psychophysical scaling problem there is clearly no "right" answer, except that it is generally expected that the observer will *rank* the stimuli about as they are ranked in physical intensity, so long as they are discriminably different in intensities. The relations between the intervals on the subjective scale and those on the physical scale are only of general interest inasmuch as the observer is allowed to give the judgments that he would in his normal sensory environment. A case in point is a study by Kikuchi (1957), in which the "objective" and "subjective" median planes were located, for binaural stimulation. In the subjective portion of the experiment the observer adjusted the time delay of a sound to one ear, relative to the arrival time of the same sound at the other ear, and the data consisted of the distribution of times that were judged to correspond to the auditory image being reported at subjective center (on the median plane). In the "objective" portion of the experiment, the variable delay could be permuted from one ear to the other, and the observer alternately adjusted the delay, and then permuted the two sounds at a rapid rate between his two ears (i.e. switched the delay from one ear to the other), until he could no longer hear a change when the permuting

occurred. The results, in Figure 14–12, show a great reduction in the variance of the distribution of time delays established by the "objective" procedure as compared with the "subjective." Even more significantly, there is virtually no constant error under the objective procedure. At first inspection, this might have been viewed as the discovery of a far more precise method of locating the median plane, but this is not the case. The "objective" method achieves only (a) an identification of the point at which the arrival times of the signal at the two ears are physically equal (a determination which might be better made with an oscilloscope), and (b) a measure of the minimum value of permuted interaural delays that a listener is able to detect (from the dispersions of the judgments). The moral is that the *median plane*, defined as a subjectively identified relation between the arrival times of stimuli at the two ears, can *only* be established by a method which allows the observer either to set up, or to choose, the specific stimulus condition that he prefers to label "median plane." Thus, response proclivity psychophysics is basically a semantic/sensory science. An important implication of this fact is that it is generally inappropriate to use "right" and "wrong" feedback in experiments on response proclivity. There clearly is no right and wrong response in such experiments, only "favored" ones, and anything the experimenter does to shape the judgments can be interpreted as improperly biasing his results.

METHODS FOR THE STUDY OF SENSORY CAPABILITY

Perhaps the best single dictum that can be suggested for the study of sensory capability is that "Anything goes!" That is to say, the observer may, in fact *should*, be given every bit of information that can assist him in making a sense-based discrimination, except that one vital bit that enables him to make the correct choice on a single trial. Psychophysics should not be in the business of creating guessing games for observers, when it claims responsibility for determining the precision with which observers can use a particular sensory system. Methods should be avoided which tax the memory, the ability to decide on a correct response out of a large and stimulus-incompatible

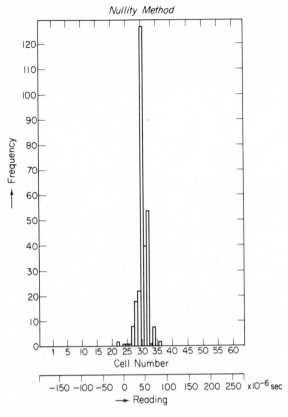

Nullity Method

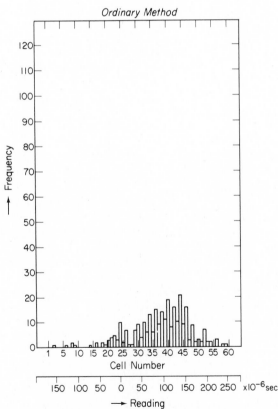

Ordinary Method

Fig. 14-12. *Distributions of judgments of inter-aural time disparity, from Kikuchi (1957). The lower panel represents a median-plane localization, made by the method of adjustment; the upper panel shows the results of an "objective" method* [see text].

catalog, or which mislead or fail to inform the observer about some feature of the stimulus display. Special care may fruitfully be taken to let the observer know the *a priori* probability of individual stimulus items. Naturally there are many experiments on questions other than sensory capability where each of these non-stimulus parameters may be of interest, and in which they may be systematically varied. To recapitulate, there is no reason, if sensory capability is at issue, that the observer should not be carefully informed of every feature of the experimental routine, with the exception of what stimulus is to be presented at what time. (One problem has been that observers do not fully comprehend the nature of a random sequence and therefore persist in various versions of the "gambler's fallacy," thus appearing to do less well than they can in processing the sensory information. Careful instruction can reduce this problem considerably.) Finally, where sensory capability is at issue, extreme care to bar the effects of learning from psychophysical results is appropriate. The phrase, *the highly trained observer*, should generally mean that the experimenter can prove that his subjects have reached asymptotic performance prior to collecting his primary data.

Temporal Forced-Choice Procedures. If the question of immediate concern is the discriminability of two stimuli, and the response biases (criteria) discussed earlier are not of special interest, then some form of forced-choice procedure is probably the best selection. Thus, if the discriminability of stimuli *A* and *B* is to be determined, one can present the random sequence of pairs, *AB, BA, AB, AB, BA . . . BA*, pausing after each pair to ask the observer whether the sequence was *AB* or *BA*. Such a simple paradigm may appear without potential contamination, and relative to many other methods it is so, but there *are* some built-in problems. These include: (a) the observer may have a *response proclivity* for saying *AB* more often than *BA*, and thus his overall percentage of correct judgments may be reduced below what he could achieve with a neutral response bias; or (b) the observer may be less sensitive to one stimulus than to the other and may base his judgments entirely in the "absolute" judgment of which interval includes the more "*A*-like," or "*B*-like" of the inputs. The first of these problems can be handled most easily by instructing the observer that the two sequences are in fact equally likely, and perhaps by demonstrating the truth of this claim by informing him of the actual sequence following each response. It should be noted that the use of feedback *can* reduce the overall percentage of correct judgments for the highly trained observer, which makes theoretically good sense if the effect of feedback is to produce variability in the criterion—equivalent to reducing the sensory acuity (Schoeffler 1966). The second problem is automatically resolved if the only question of interest is, "How discriminable are the two inputs, *A* and *B*?" But it is often of interest to know that the observer requires both stimuli for his judgments and not just one or the other. One way to rule out the possibility that the observer is simply judging the presence of one of the stimuli is through additional experiments in which *A* and *B* are each discriminated from the ambient background, and another is to use a "roving standard." A third problem in the temporal forced-choice procedure is one recognized by early psychophysicists, that the stimuli may be more discriminable in one sequence than in the other. If, for example, stimuli differ slightly in intensity ($I_A < I_B$) and the sensory system has slightly reduced sensitivity following any single stimulus presentation, then the *AB* sequence might be described by the observer as two sounds of almost equal loudness, whereas the *BA* sequence would be called two very different "loudnesses." For the study of response proclivities this is a real problem, but in terms of sensory capability it is not. The two sounds certainly are described as being very order-dependent in their subjective effects, but the sequential decrease in sensitivity is part of the discrimination process, and the experimenter is free to describe the results of such a procedure without recourse to questions of subjective interpretation. If a strong sequential effect is suspected (and it will be discovered quickly, if the experimenter acts as his own "pilot" subject in every task that he sets up), then separate control procedures can readily be instituted to estimate its magnitude and time course. The experimental question of how well you can discriminate *AB* from *BA* does not depend on such a subjective issue.

When the discriminability of one stimulus from the ambient background is of major interest, then temporal forced-choice procedures with more than two alternatives are often used. Green and Swets (1966) discuss the logic and analysis of the general *m*-alternative temporal forced-choice methods. In visual or tactile experiments, similar procedures may be used with the alternatives being displayed spatially, rather than temporally.

Single-Interval Procedures. In some experiments it may be difficult or impossible to present stimuli in a forced-choice paradigm, either spatial or temporal, or the subject of study may in fact be the systematic relation between correct detection responses and false positive responses. In either case the appropriate procedure is one in which a single observation interval is defined for the observer, and he is instructed to decide which stimulus was presented during that interval (this is clearly a case of comparison with a remembered standard, and questions of both short- and long-term memory may be of importance in such procedures).

In single-interval procedures a variety of different responses may be allowed by the observer. In cases where only two stimuli are used, the responses are either binary decisions (yes-no, or *A-B*) or ratings of the certainty that each stimulus is *A* or *B*. In the case of stimulus sets containing more than two stimuli (as in studies of speech intelligibility) the responses are most often identifications of the particular stimulus which the observer believes was presented, although a confidence rating may also be usefully coupled with an identification.

The major difficulty in interpreting the results of single-interval psychophysical procedures is the one so often discussed in the context of signal detection theory. The probability that an observer will identify stimulus *A* correctly is jointly determined by his ability to discriminate between *A* and *Ā* (other stimuli than *A*) and by his criterion, or the required degree of *A*-ness that he insists on before calling a stimulus an "*A*." As many experiments have now shown, an observer's ability to make a given sensory discrimination is much less influenced by instructions than is his criterion. By instructions to be "strict" or "lax" in his requirement that a stimulus be *A*-like before thus identifying it, the experimenter can manipulate the observer's probability of making a correct identification, as illustrated in Figure 14–8. The range of stimulus values associated with different criteria may be fairly small for observers given typical psychophysical instructions to, "Say *A* when you think *A* may

have been presented," or, "Only say *A* when you are *sure A* was presented." However, this is *not* a valid excuse to discount the variance contributed by the observer's interpretation of instructions. This component of variance can be as great as that associated with casual, as compared to careful, calibration of laboratory equipment, and few experimenters would advocate a relaxed attitude toward that source of experimental error. (The theoretical range of stimulus values associated with criterion shifts is, of course, infinite. That this is not totally unrealistic can be readily shown by suggesting to an observer that he will be awarded a few dollars for each correct identification of *A*, but must sacrifice an arm following a false positive response.)

Table 14–5a is included to help familiarize the reader with the relation between *d'* and variations in the hit and false report rates. While his table is too coarse to be useful for actual research purposes, its size allows easy assessment of the effects of even large changes in one probability, while the other is held constant. The irregular line through the body of the table separates values of *d'* that are greater and less than 1.0. While there is no special theoretical significance to this value, it is roughly the level of detectability which highly trained listeners call their threshold. This relation is particularly clear in Figure 14–11, in which the international Standard Audiometric Zero (Davis and Kranz 1964) can be compared to the signal level for *d'* = 1.0. Table 14–5b shows the values of the criterion, β, which are associated with each value of *d'* in Table 14–5a. The criterion is equal to the slope of the *ROC* curve at the *operating point*. It may be calculated as the ratio of the probability density associated with the presence of a signal, to the corresponding density for noise alone, as displayed on a decision axis. One experiment can thus lead to a measure of sensory capability (*d'*), taken from Table 14–5a, and an independent measure of a response proclivity (β) from Table 14–5b.

Solutions to the criterion problem are quite simple in theory, even discounting the unsupported claim that the highly trained observer keeps a fixed and experimentally suitable criterion. Campbell (1968) found that observers given neutral instructions select as "threshold" signals levels at which they can achieve 99-100 percent correct in a forced-choice task. In practice the criterion is evaluated by knowing, or assuming, the relation between the rate of correct identifications and the rate of false positive responses. For example, a pair of observed probabilities, $p("A"|A)$ and $p("A"|\bar{A})$, can be adjusted to some standard values, $p_s("A"|A)$ and $p_s("A"|\bar{A})$, exactly as "corrections for guessing" involve the transformation of an observed score into a "true score" plus an error component, by evaluating *g*, a guessing rate. Such corrections are valid, however, only to the degree that their assumptions actually describe the relation between "hit" and "false-alarm" rates. It is worth repeating the observation made by Swets (1961), that the correction-for-guessing procedure yields predictions that simply do not agree with data. This shortcoming is now well recognized in psychophysics, and although this author is not aware whether the well-known "*T + E*" model of psychometrics currently enjoys the popularity that it once had, such theories should be viewed with caution no matter what their application. Failures of models or theories which compare the human to a roulette wheel or other random generator may occur because the human is basically an *information processing system*, and that no matter how sparse the input, he may constantly attempt to generate response patterns that are related to it.

Table 14-5a* Reduced Table of d' for Single-Interval Procedures

$$d' = \frac{\bar{x}_{SN} - \bar{x}_N}{\sigma_N}$$

(for case: $\sigma_{SN} = \sigma_N$)

$P(Y|SN) = $ Probability of a Hit;
$P(Y|N) = $ Probability of a false alarm.

$P(Y\mid SN)$		0.00	0.05	0.10	0.15	0.20	0.25	0.30	0.35	0.40	0.45	0.50	0.55	0.60	0.65	0.70	0.75	0.80	0.85	0.90	0.95	1.00
	0.00	0.00																				
	0.05	∞	0.00																			
	0.10	∞	0.36	0.00																		
	0.15	∞	0.61	0.25	0.00																	
	0.20	∞	0.80	0.44	0.19	0.00																
	0.25	∞	0.97	0.61	0.36	0.17	0.00															
	0.30	∞	1.12	0.76	0.51	0.32	0.15	0.00														
	0.35	∞	1.26	0.90	0.65	0.46	0.29	0.14	0.00													
	0.40	∞	1.39	1.03	0.78	0.59	0.42	0.27	0.13	0.00												
	0.45	∞	1.52	1.16	0.91	0.72	0.55	0.40	0.26	0.13	0.00											
	0.50	∞	1.64	1.28	1.04	0.84	0.67	0.52	0.39	0.25	0.13	0.00										
	0.55	∞	1.77	1.41	1.16	0.97	0.80	0.65	0.51	0.38	0.25	0.13	0.00									
	0.60	∞	1.90	1.53	1.29	1.09	0.93	0.78	0.64	0.51	0.38	0.25	0.13	0.00								
	0.65	∞	2.03	1.67	1.42	1.23	1.06	0.91	0.77	0.64	0.51	0.39	0.26	0.13	0.00							
	0.70	∞	2.17	1.81	1.56	1.37	1.20	1.05	0.91	0.78	0.65	0.52	0.40	0.27	0.14	0.00						
	0.75	∞	2.32	1.96	1.71	1.52	1.35	1.20	1.06	0.93	0.80	0.67	0.55	0.42	0.29	0.15	0.00					
	0.80	∞	2.49	2.12	1.88	1.68	1.52	1.37	1.23	1.09	0.97	0.84	0.72	0.59	0.46	0.32	0.17	0.00				
	0.85	∞	2.68	2.32	2.07	1.88	1.71	1.56	1.42	1.29	1.16	1.04	0.91	0.78	0.65	0.51	0.36	0.19	0.00			
	0.90	∞	2.93	2.56	2.32	2.12	1.96	1.81	1.67	1.53	1.41	1.28	1.16	1.03	0.90	0.76	0.61	0.44	0.25	0.00		
	0.95	∞	3.29	2.93	2.68	2.49	2.32	2.17	2.03	1.90	1.77	1.64	1.52	1.39	1.26	1.12	0.97	0.80	0.61	0.36	0.00	
	1.00	∞	∞	∞	∞	∞	∞	∞	∞	∞	∞	∞	∞	∞	∞	∞	∞	∞	∞	∞	∞	—

*Line through table separates values above and below $d' = 1.0$.

Table 14-5b. Criterion (β) for Equal-Variance Normal Distributions on Decision Axis

$$\beta = \frac{f_{SN}(x)}{f_N(x)}$$

$P(Y\mid SN)$		0.00	0.05	0.10	0.15	0.20	0.25	0.30	0.35	0.40	0.45	0.50	0.55	0.60	0.65	0.70	0.75	0.80	0.85	0.90	0.95	1.00
	0.00	1.00																				
	0.05		1.00																			
	0.10		1.70	1.00																		
	0.15		2.26	1.33	1.00																	
	0.20		2.72	1.60	1.20	1.00																
	0.25		3.08	1.81	1.36	1.14	1.00															
	0.30		3.37	1.98	1.49	1.24	1.09	1.00														
	0.35		3.59	2.11	1.59	1.32	1.18	1.07	1.00													
	0.40		3.75	2.20	1.66	1.38	1.22	1.11	1.04	1.00												
	0.45		3.84	2.26	1.70	1.41	1.25	1.14	1.07	1.02	1.00											
	0.50		3.87	2.27	1.71	1.42	1.26	1.15	1.08	1.03	1.01	1.00										
	0.55		3.84	2.26	1.70	1.41	1.25	1.14	1.07	1.02	1.00	0.99	1.00									
	0.60		3.75	2.20	1.66	1.38	1.22	1.11	1.04	1.00	0.98	0.97	0.98	1.00								
	0.65		3.59	2.11	1.59	1.32	1.18	1.07	1.00	0.96	0.94	0.93	0.94	0.96	1.00							
	0.70		3.37	1.98	1.49	1.24	1.09	1.00	0.94	0.90	0.88	0.87	0.88	0.90	0.94	1.00						
	0.75		3.08	1.81	1.36	1.14	1.00	0.91	0.86	0.82	0.80	0.80	0.80	0.82	0.86	0.91	1.00					
	0.80		2.72	1.60	1.20	1.00	0.88	0.81	0.76	0.72	0.71	0.70	0.71	0.72	0.76	0.81	0.88	1.00				
	0.85		2.26	1.33	1.00	0.83	0.73	0.67	0.63	0.60	0.59	0.58	0.59	0.60	0.63	0.67	0.73	0.83	1.00			
	0.90		1.70	1.00	0.75	0.63	0.55	0.50	0.47	0.45	0.44	0.44	0.44	0.45	0.47	0.50	0.55	0.63	0.75	1.00		
	0.95		1.00	0.59	0.44	0.37	0.32	0.30	0.28	0.27	0.26	0.26	0.26	0.27	0.28	0.30	0.32	0.37	0.44	0.59	1.00	
	1.00	1.00	0.00	0.00	0.00	0.00	0.00	0.00	0.00	0.00	0.00	0.00	0.00	0.00	0.00	0.00	0.00	0.00	0.00	0.00	0.00	1.00

One method for determining the validity of an assumed relation between hit and false-alarm rates is the obvious empirical one. That is, if a single-interval experiment is to be conducted with stimuli, or for an observer, for which the relation is not known, then one can vary the criterion by instructions and learn what it is. This is a long, but safe, procedure which enables the experimenter to correctly interpret subsequently gathered single-interval data. But since such a tedious empirical process may be an impediment to accomplishing any other research, the relation is often assumed to be the simplest case treated in signal detection theory. This is the assumption of overlapping, equal-variance, normal distributions on the decision axis (as tabled by Elliott, in Swets 1964), and it has been demonstrated to give a good, though not perfect, description of the results of many experiments in which the criterion was actually manipulated. Perhaps the least time-consuming method of determining the relation between hit and false-alarm rates is the confidence rating procedure, although its use also depends on an assumption: that the observer who categorizes inputs by assigning confidence ratings is *ordering* those inputs as he would if he adopted different binary-decision criteria in each of several experimental sessions. Egan, Schulman, and Greenberg (1959) have demonstrated the similarity of data gathered with the binary-decision and with the rating procedures and Watson, Rilling, and Bourbon (1964) showed the correspondence between the predictions of the overlapping-normal-distribution model and the data gathered with a continuous (analog) rating procedure, as shown in Figure 14–7. The detailed resolution of the relation between hits and false reports that seems to be provided by rating procedures requires a precautionary comment. The data shown in Figure 14–7 were gathered in an experimental procedure designed to maximally stabilize the rating criteria. This means that *very* highly trained and motivated listeners (the authors) were employed, who were tested in sessions lasting two to three hours, and with the entire experiment completed in a two-day span. Experiments with less well-trained observers, shorter sessions, or that extend over several weeks or months have produced considerably "noisier" results in this writer's laboratory. This problem with rating variability has been ascribed to the difficulty in maintaining a constant criterion, but further direct investigation is required, possibly by the techniques of molecular psychophysics. Psychophysics must continue to investigate the observer's ability to include more information in his response than that in a binary decision. The use of confidence ratings in signal detection research is an example of the way that this can be done in the context of rigorous psychophysical procedures. Responses other than binary decisions were once rejected because they forced the experimenter to depend on the observer's meaning of particular words. Now it is clear that the same (criterion) problem exists in the case of binary decisions as in the interpretation of the observer's use of any other responses. The answer to the old question of yes-no *versus* yes-maybe-no as proper psychophysical responses seems to be that a three-category rating scale can transmit significantly more information than a two-category scale.

Procedures Using the Intelligibility Testing Paradigm. When more than two stimuli are used in a psychophysical experiment, as in the case of tests of speech intelligibility, problems of the observer's criterion must again be faced. The methods of "correcting" the data are more complex than with only two stimuli. Several authors have developed analyses based in the reasoning outlined above for the case of two-stimuli sets. In one of the most general theories of word recognition, Nakatani (1968) has expanded earlier developments by Egan (1957), Pollack (1959), Clarke (1957), and Broadbent (1967), among others, in applying decision theory to the interpretation of data displayed in a confusion matrix. The confusion matrix is simply a matrix showing the probability of each identification response to each stimulus, generally with one response defined as correct for each stimulus.

A few rules describe a great many experimental results in the history of intelligibility testing, with spoken, or visually presented, words as the stimuli. The probability of a response being correct is increased as (1) the speech-to-noise ratio is increased, (2) there are fewer messages in the set from which the stimulus is drawn, and that set is known to the observer, and (3) the messages, or words, are presented in a context which heightens their predictability as compared to their presentation in isolation. Message recognition is reduced as the physical

Table 14-6. Master Matrix and Submatrix, Obtained Probabilities and Predictions from Constant-Ratio Rule

Master Matrix

		—Responses—					
		/pa/	/ta/	/ka/	/fa/	/θa/	/sa/
	/pa/	0.405	0.242	0.162	0.128	0.048	0.015
	/ta/	0.293	0.319	0.233	0.085	0.045	0.025
	/ka/	0.208	0.440	0.240	0.023	0.057	0.032
—Stimuli—	/fa/	0.097	0.015	0.015	0.660	0.163	0.050
	/θa/	0.058	0.050	0.040	0.315	0.340	0.197
	/sa/	0.012	0.078	0.050	0.035	0.282	0.543
	p(R)	0.179	0.191	0.123	0.208	0.156	0.144

Submatrix, Obtained Probabilities and Predictions from Constant-Ratio Rule

		—Responses—		
		/pa/	/ta/	/ka/
	/pa/	0.555	0.224	0.221
		(0.501)*	(0.299)	(0.200)
—Stimuli—	/ta/	0.362	0.324	0.314
		(0.347)	(0.378)	(0.276)
	/ka/	0.235	0.430	0.335
		(0.234)	(0.495)	(0.270)

After Clarke, 1957.
*Entries in parentheses were calculated from the master matrix, using the constant-ratio rule.

similarity between the messages in the set is increased. Finally, there is a reciprocal relation between the probability of a correct identification of any single message and the probability of correctly identifying other messages in the set, when the observer responds more often with one response than with others. While rules like these have been developed primarily from experiments with verbal stimuli, the experimental paradigms and related theories may be appropriate to any psychophysical problem involving the identification of multiple stimuli, as opposed to simple pairwise discrimination.

Although there is not enough space in a general chapter like this one to describe the details of either the stimulus identification paradigm or the various theories associated with it (some of which are presented in the references included in the previous paragraphs), one example will help to understand the class of problems to which these theories and procedures are appropriate. The Constant-Ratio Rule devised by Clarke (1957) is a procedure by which the confusability within a subset of stimuli may be predicted from the confusions observed with the total set. In one of Clarke's experiments the total stimulus set consisted of the consonant-vowel pairs, *pa, ta, χa, fa, θa,* and *sa.* Table 14–6 shows the confusion matrix produced when listeners made 150 judgments of each of these speech sounds, as they were spoken in random sequence, with a noisy background. Each entry in the table is the conditional probability of giving a particular response to a particular stimulus (as $p(\text{"ta"} | ta)$ is the probability of the correct response to item *ta*). Clarke's question was whether the results of experiments with smaller sets, or subsets, such as the presentation of only *pa, ta,* and *ka* (with the listeners aware of the reduced set size) could be predicted from the data of Table 14–6. An empirical rule that Clarke found to describe the results of the reduced experiments quite well is that the *ratio* between any two entries in the reduced matrix would be equal to the ratio between the corresponding two entries in the master matrix. Thus Table 14–6 shows the predicted new matrix for the reduced stimulus set suggested above, and also the obtained values when the reduced experiment was actually conducted. While the correspondence between predicted and obtained probabilities is quite good with the constant-ratio rule, it should be noticed that it side-steps the whole problem of response bias. Clearly, as shown by the last line of the master matrix in Table 14–6, the listeners in Clarke's experiment did not use the responses equally often, as for example they seem to have much stronger tendencies to identify the stimuli as *ta* or *fa* and a much lower probability to report a *ka*. The response biases reflected in the response probabilities are simply transferred intact into the predictions of the reduced experiments by the constant-ratio rule, but this rule offers no procedure for predicting the results of such experiments if the observers adopt different response biases. In the case of stimulus sets of size two it is clear that the response bias can be treated exactly as in the preceding section on single-interval experiments. Nakatani (1968) developed a general theory utilizing axioms like those of Luce's (1959a) choice models that handle the response bias problem quite elegantly, although a somewhat simpler procedure is described in a recent report by Eguchi and Hirsh (1969). In the latter report it is assumed that the pairwise discriminability between all stimuli pairs in a confusion matrix can be described by the overlapping normal distribution model of detection theory. The discrimination index, d', for each pair may thus be determined from a constant-ratio-rule-derived two-by-two matrix for that pair. The average value of d' for a given stimulus is then an estimate of its discriminability within that particular stimulus set, which is relatively free of the effects of response bias.

Adaptive Psychophysics. All of the methods discussed in the sections on forced-choice and single-interval psychophysical methods have been concerned with stimuli presented at a single level of detectability, or discriminability. These methods are typically used to establish sensory capability by separately determining the discrimination performance for each of several values of a stimulus, or of a stimulus difference. The selection of stimulus values is made so that performance will be maintained in a meaningful psychophysical range. That is to say, stimuli are selected which lead to behavior in the range between near-chance and near-perfect performance. Stimulus values above those which lead to near-perfect performance or below those which lead to near-chance performance obviously do not produce readily interpreted psychophysical measurements.

The selection of stimulus values may be made prior to an experiment, allowing the experimenter to lay out a well counter-balanced experimental design. But in many cases too little is known about the sensory problem under study for such pre-selection to be possible, or the requirement of rapid or "single-shot" testing may preclude such preliminary work. Adaptive psychophysical procedures are ideally suited to problems such as these. These methods initially introduce stimuli at high levels of discriminability and then automatically reduce them when the judgments of the observer demonstrate that they are not within the "meaningful psychophysical range."

Békésy audiometry. Although this section is primarily devoted to psychophysical methods which are used to measure sensory capability, Békésy's (1947) audiometric technique for tracing the behavioral threshold should be mentioned as one of the first, and probably still the most common, adaptive method. In it a listener is instructed to respond by pressing a button whenever he can "hear a sound." Pressing the button causes the sound to be automatically attenuated at a fixed rate in decibels per second; when it is released the attenuator is run in the opposite direction. A graphic record of the sound levels achieved in this manner is, in effect, a tracing that moves up and down across the level that the listener has selected as his threshold. The threshold is estimated by either averaging the extreme values of the tracing, or by drawing a line that visually fits midway between these extremes. The drawback with this procedure, in spite of its proven clinical usefulness, is that it offers no way to discriminate between the effects of criterion and response bias. The magnitude of the stimulus swings between maxima and minima is also affected by the instructions to the listener. For example, "Press the button when you hear it," and, "Press *promptly* when you hear it and release *promptly* when you can no longer hear it," yield different records in that the latter instruction results in the listener producing a lower-amplitude tracing. This is of more than passing interest, as the trace amplitudes have been given clinical interpretation (Jerger 1960). Although the results of this method are closely related to true sensitivity measurements, the earlier discussion of the problems of interpreting criterion-confounded measures should make its drawbacks as a research procedure clear.

Forced-choice adaptive procedures. Campbell (1963) and Taylor and Creelman (1967) have developed adaptive psychophysical methods based in the two-alternative, forced-choice psychophysical procedure. These methods typically begin with the signal level adjusted for easy discriminations, and use formal rules for modifying the level so that the observer will perform at a particular percentage (L_t) of correct judgments. For example, the rules suggested by Taylor and Creelman are based in the sequential-likelihood-ratio test developed by Wald (1947). These rules operate by determining, after each trial, whether the sequence of correct and incorrect responses at the current level has a probability $p(C)$, of less than some preselected value of being from a population, the mean of which is at the preselected performance level (L_t). The method described by Taylor and Creelman has been dubbed PEST, for "Parameter Estimation by Sequential Testing." If the $p(C)$ is above or below the selected value, the signal level is either raised or lowered, as appropriate, using a set of empirically determined rules to progressively decrease the size of the steps. With a target probability of 75–80 percent correct, in a simple auditory detection task, these authors report that they typically stop the test when a step of 0.5 *dB* is called for. Using this criterion for run-ending, runs begun with 4-*dB* steps take 20–80 trials, with an average of about 45 trials. With a typical spacing of about three seconds per trial this means the collection of a usable psychophysical datum in less than 2.5 minutes.

In addition to the development of the PEST method, Creelman and Taylor also derived an index of efficiency for general psychophysical methods. As suggested earlier, the goal of most methods can be seen as the determination of the stimulus value associated with a preselected level of performance, and thus a measure of efficiency is the number of trials required to reach this goal, or to approximate it to some preselected degree of accuracy. A more formal index, the "sweat factor," was defined as the ratio of the number of trials required for a psy-

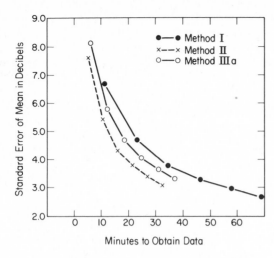

Fig. 14-13. *Comparison between three adaptive psychophysical procedures, in terms of the standard error achieved in a specified amount of experimental time.* [Miller, Watson & Covell 1963]

chophysical method to achieve a particular target level to that required by an ideal method. A related analysis is illustrated in Figure 14–13 from Miller, Watson, and Covell (1963), which shows a comparison between three adaptive psychophysical methods. Each data point in this figure represents a single threshold determination, with the determinations requiring the least time under Method I and the most under Method II. By the criterion of *number* of determinations to achieve a particular value of the standard error Method I might clearly have been selected. However, the size of the standard error achieved in a brief testing session favored Method II. (As a matter of fact, the authors actually chose Method III, using other criteria peculiar to their particular experimental demands.)

TEMPORAL UNCERTAINTY AND PSYCHOPHYSICS WITHOUT DEFINED OBSERVATION INTERVALS

In terms of both theory and method, perhaps the most complex problem in the study of sensory capability is that of psychophysical measurements made without defined observation intervals. In each of the methods discussed earlier in this section, the observer is instructed that the times at which a stimulus may occur will be clearly marked for him, generally by a signal presented in a sensory modality other than that of the to-be-detected stimulus (lights in the case of auditory detection, sounds in the case of visual detection, etc.). The signal defining the observation interval may either be presented co-temporally with that interval, or it may be presented before or after it, depending on the demands of the experiment. But however the observation time is defined, this definition accomplishes two goals: (a) the observer knows the temporal portion of the incoming energy on which his decision should be based, and (b) the experimenter is able to compute conditional response probabilities on the basis of discrete trials, each consisting of one stimulus configuration and one response. The effects of additional temporal uncertainty can be studied within a defined-trial paradigm, as Egan, Greenberg, and Schulman (1961a) demonstrated by simply using a long observation light to define

their intervals, and by then injecting a brief signal at a random time, within (half of) the intervals. Use of various durations of observation intervals allowed these experimenters to conclude that about two seconds of temporal uncertainty (with 0.5 second signals) led to near maximum depression of performance, as compared to the minimum-temporal-uncertainty case in which the signal (when present) was co-temporal with the observation interval.

It is the second accomplishment of trial definition, that of allowing the calculation of stimulus-response probabilities, however, that is vital to most psychophysical methods. Figure 14–14 shows the design of an experiment which was conducted with and without defined observation intervals (Watson and Nichols 1966). The top line shows observation intervals (initially defined by lights) which were presented at randomly selected instants in time. By a second randomization, auditory signals were introduced in half of these observation intervals (line 2). When observers had been tested under the defined-interval procedure, the observation lights were deleted and the listeners were told to respond whenever "they thought they heard a signal." The data available for analysis from such a procedure are two temporal records, one of stimuli occurring at random points in time, and one of responses, with the latter often appearing to be only slightly related to the former. The obvious relation to be discovered is which response should be associated with which stimulus for purposes of analysis, and it is equally obvious that there is no unequivocal answer to this question. A common solution has been to define any response that occurs within some arbitrarily selected time after a stimulus, a response to that stimulus, and then to describe the performance of the observer in terms of his percentage of "correct" judgments. Such an analysis, however, has two shortcomings. First, it offers no means of separately evaluating the response bias and the actual ability to discriminate the stimulus from its background. Second, the use of an arbitrary latency criterion for discriminating between "true" responses and responses to something other than the signal must produce measures of performance that are strongly dependent on the particular latency criterion adopted. One method of dealing with these two problems, the Method of Free Response, was developed by Egan, Greenberg, and Schulman (1961b), and it is a revision of this method that was described above (Figure 14–14). In the revised Method of Free Response, both signal and noise-alone intervals are defined (from the vantage point of the experimenter, not for the observer), and the latencies of first responses following each type of observation interval are separately tallied. For any arbitrary criterion latency, this method then allows computation of the

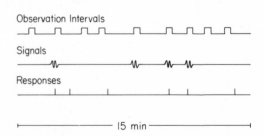

Fig. 14-14. *Paradigm for study of detection without defined observation intervals. Top line shows "observation intervals" used by experimenter as points from which response latencies were measured, but not displayed, for the observers.*

four entries in a typical discrimination matrix ($p(y|SN)$, $p(y|N)$, $p(n|SN)$, and $p(n|N)$). By assuming a particular relation between hit and false-alarm rates, as for example the common assumption that they may be generated by overlapping normal distributions on the decision axis, the index of discriminability, d', can then be computed. Having dealt in this way with the criterion problem, the remaining issue, that of the arbitrary definition of the latency that distinguishes between responses to signals and those to some other temporal portion of the input, can be partially solved by varying the latency criterion over a large range of values. Figure 14–15 shows the values of d' associated with the range of criterion latencies shown on the abscissa for the experiment by Watson and Nichols (1966). The detectability index reaches a maximum at a particular criterion latency, but this latency is different for each observer. Thus, if one compares the performance of the observers for a latency criterion of 0.6 seconds, subject *SM* has a value of d' of 1.5, while other observers fell below 0.8. With a criterion of two seconds, however, subject *HB* appears to be the most accurate of the group. The solution is to select, as the measure of sensory capability, the maximum value of d' achieved by each observer, independent of the latency criterion. Unfortunately, this manner of treating the data from experiments without defined observation intervals, while allowing fairly valid comparisons between observers and between stimulus conditions, does not provide a theoretical base by which comparisons may be made between values of d' for the non-defined trial case, and those computed in a defined-trials procedure. Such a theory has been proposed by Egan et al., but in it the false-alarm rate is estimated from the overall response density, which may not reflect the waxings and wanings of the response probabilities. Green and Luce (1967) have been working toward a general model of detection without defined observation intervals, as has Cronholm (1968), but no completely viable model has yet been proposed. Solution of this problem will be a significant development in psychophysics, as it will open the way to detection and identification paradigms that are much more closely related to the demands placed on our senses in normal human activities than are the defined-trial procedures. After all, the sound of an oncoming vehicle is seldom preceded by a light that says, "If you are to be hit, it will be now!"

The specific topic in which psychophysical methods without defined trials have been most frequently used has been that of vigilance (prolonged monitoring of signals presented with moderate-to-low temporal density). The most unique finding in this application of the methods has been that of the *vigilance decrement*, a progressive decrease in the probability of a positive response to a signal as a function of "time on watch." Hopefully, if it is not completely obvious without them, the preceding discussions will lead to the question, "Is the reduction of $p(y|SN)$ over time associated with any significant changes in the false-alarm rate?" A recent review by Swets and Kristofferson (1970) presents both negative and positive responses to this question. The bulk of the evidence, gathered by experimenters accustomed to working with defined-trial procedures, seems to show that the decrement is related to a gradual tightening of the criterion rather than to a change in sensitivity. In contrast to this view is research, such as that by Taylor (1966) showing that the index of detectability, d', falls linearly as the square root of "time on the task." There is enough conflicting data on this subject that it looks suspiciously as though there must be certain conditions under which a real sensitivity decrement occurs and others under which it does not.

Animal Psychophysics. The modern developments in chronic electrode implantation and other long-term animal preparations, coupled with concern about the physiological nature of the *behaving* animal have led to renewed interest in animal psychophysics. This is a fortunate reversal of a tendency to assume that stimuli that are shown to elicit neural activity at some level (even at the peripheral receptor) are thereby "sensed" by the animal. The special methods of animal psychophysics are intimately related to the characteristics of the species to be tested. Thus the species that are more amenable to training by positive rewards, especially the primates, are tested very much as are human observers, while less readily trained species (e.g., felines) are often tested under shock-avoidance procedures. The procedures for testing animals are, thus, far less uniform than those with humans and they are certainly too numerous to catalog here. Instead the following general comments are offered:

1. The difficulty in predicting the degree of effectiveness of motivational variables upon animals makes the need to distinguish between response bias and sensitivity, if anything, more crucial than for human observers.
2. The considerable differences in operant rates observed between animals, even within a single testing group, might be handled effectively by decision-theory statistical procedures.
3. Automated testing of animals, under operant conditioning procedures, may make forced-choice psychophysical methods feasible, where the large number of trials required by these methods have been prohibitive under "handtesting" methods.

One special method of testing animals on sensory tasks which is worth individual comment is the "Blough Technique," under which an operant-conditioning paradigm is used to establish behavior in the animal which is similar to that described

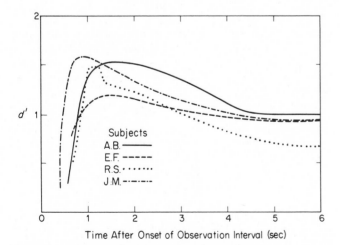

Fig. 14-15. *The detectability index,* d', *determined for various latency criteria (latencies shorter than which a response was called correct). No single latency criterion can be selected which will measure the maximum detection capability of each listener.*

earlier as Békésy audiometry. That is, Blough (1961) managed to have animals track their thresholds in an automated psychophysical procedure (see earlier section on "Adaptive Psychophysics"). Rilling and McDiarmid (1965) demonstrated that a similar method could fulfill the requirements for measuring sensory capability.

Two Final Comments

THE PHYSICS IN PSYCHOPHYSICS

What distinguishes rigorous psychophysics from other experimental work in psychology is partly the degree of attention to the definition and control of the physical stimulus. The worker in psychophysics has traditionally become an *expert* in the calibration and use of the apparatus used to produce lights, sounds, tactile vibrations, and so on. Nothing less is good enough. All his conclusions must first depend on the precision with which the stimulus is described and the constancy with which it is maintained.

THE RELATION BETWEEN SENSE PHYSIOLOGY AND PSYCHOPHYSICS

General Principle. No property of a subsystem can be established *only* by knowledge of the functional character of the larger system of which it is a part. (E.g., the filter-like properties of the cochlea cannot be *established* by masking experiments, nor by frequency discrimination data, nor by any other psychophysical results.) The converse is also true. (E.g., the ability to detect a faint tone, or a complex of tones, cannot be *established* from cochlear microphonic recordings, nor from the response of the eighth (auditory) nerve, nor from any other purely physiological evidence.) However, the history of the study of sense physiology and of psychophysics is one of vigorous and fruitful reciprocal generation of hypotheses and experiments, in one discipline by the other. Often the interaction has taken place within the same laboratory, or even within the same scientist. For example, see the remarkable sequences of studies by long-time leaders in the field of hearing (e.g., Georg v. Békésy and Hallowell Davis). The relation between psychophysics and studies of the anatomy and physiology of sensory systems is fairly compared to research on a radar. Assuming that someone else has designed and installed the device and neglected to leave the operating-and-maintenance manual, an engineer would first study it by detecting and identifying signals, and then by tinkering with its components until after moving back and forth between sub- and total-systems, he could write a new manual. *Reductionism*, from this point of view, is obviously an acceptable approach to science.

Acknowledgments. Preparation of this chapter was supported in full by a U. S. Public Health Service, Department of Health, Education, and Welfare research grant from the National Institute of Neurological Diseases and Stroke to the Central Institute for the Deaf. The author wishes to express his appreciation to James P. Egan for his detailed criticism and advice, which has added significantly to the value of this chapter. Thanks are also due Donald H. Eldredge, Ira J. Hirsh, James D. Miller, Donald E. Robinson, and Donald A. Ronken for their helpful comments on preliminary versions of the manuscript.

References

AHUMADA, A. *Detection of tones masked by noise: a comparison of human observers with digital-computer-simulated energy detectors of varying bandwidths. Tech. Rept. No. 29*, Los Angeles, California, Human Communication Laboratory, University of California at Los Angeles, 1967.

AMERICAN STANDARDS ASSOCIATION. *American standard acoustical terminology*. New York: American Standards Association, 1960.

ATKINSON, R. C. A variable sensitivity theory of signal detection. *Psychological Review*, 1963, *70*: 91–106.

BARLOW, H. B. The physical limits of visual discrimination. *In* A. C. GIESE (ed.), *Photophysiology* (2 vols.). New York: Academic Press, 1964, *2*: 163–202.

BARLOW, H. B., R. M. HILL, and W. R. LEVICK. Retinal ganglion cells responding selectively to direction and speed of image motion in the rabbit. *Journal of Physiology*, 1964, *173*: 377–407.

BÉKÉSY, G. VON. A new audiometer. *Acta-Otolaryngologica*, 1947, *35*: 411–22.

—— Neural funneling along the skin and between the inner and outer hair cells of the cochlea. *Journal of the Acoustical Society of America*, 1959, *31*: 1236–49.

—— *Sensory inhibition.* Princeton, N. J.: Princeton University Press, 1967.

BLOUGH, D. S. Experiments in animal psychophysics. *Scientific American*, 1961, *205*: 113–22.

BORING, E. G. The stimulus-error. *American Journal of Psychology*, 1921, *32*: 449–71.

—— *A history of experimental psychology.* New York: Appleton-Century-Crofts, 1929.

—— *The physical dimensions of consciousness.* New York: The Century Co., 1933.

—— The relations of the attributes of sensation to the dimensions of the stimulus. *Philosophy of Science*, 1935, *2*: 236–45.

—— *Sensation and perception in the history of experimental psychology.* New York: Appleton-Century-Crofts, 1942.

BROADBENT, D. E. Word-frequency effect and response bias. *Psychological Review*, 1967, *74*: 1–15.

BROADBENT, D. E., and M. GREGORY, Vigilance considered as a statistical decision. *British Journal of Psychology*, 1963, *54*: 309–23.

BRUNSWIK, E. *Perception and the representative design of psychological experiments.* Berkeley: University of California Press, 1956.

CAMPBELL, N. R. *Physics, the elements.* Cambridge: Cambridge University Press, 1920.

CAMPBELL, R. A. Detection of a noise signal of varying duration. *Journal of the Acoustical Society of America*, 1963, *35*: 1732–37.

CAMPBELL, R. A., and L. L. MOULIN. Signal detection audiometry: an exploratory study. *Journal of Speech and Hearing Research*, 1968, *11*: 402–10.

CARTERETTE, E. C., M. P. FRIEDMAN, and J. D. LOVELL. Mach bands in hearing. *Journal of the Acoustical Society of America*, 1969, *45*: 986–98.

CHERRY, C. *On human communication.* (2nd ed) Cambridge, Mass.: MIT Press, 1966.

CLARKE, F. R. Constant-ratio rule for confusion matrices in speech communication. *Journal of the Acoustical Society of America*, 1957, *29*: 715–20.

CLARKE, F. R., and R. G. BILGER. The theory of signal detectability and measurement of hearing. *In* J. JERGER (ed.), *Modern developments in audiology.* New York: Academic Press, 1963.

COOMBS, C. H. *A theory of data.* New York: John Wiley, 1964.

CRONBACH, L. J. On the non-rational application of information measures in psychology. *In* H. QUASTLER (ed.), *Information theory in psychology.* New York: Free Press, 1955.

CRONHOLM, J. N. *A stochastic model of signal detection under conditions of temporal uncertainty. Rept. No. 782*, U. S. Army Medical Research Laboratory, Fort Knox, Kentucky, 1968.

DAVIS, H., and F. KRANZ. International audiometric zero. *Journal of the Acoustical Society of America*, 1964, *36*: 1450–54.

DESMEDT, J. E. Auditory-evoked potentials from cochlea to cortex as influenced by activation of the efferent olivocochlear bundle. *Journal of the Acoustical Society of America*, 1962, *34*: 1478–96.

DEVALOIS, R. L. Behavioral and electrophysiological studies of primate vision. *In* W. D. NEFF (ed.) *Contributions to sensory physiology.* New York: Academic Press, 1965.

EGAN, J. P. *Message repetition, operating characteristics and confusion matrices in speech communication, Tech. Report No. AF 19 (604)-1962.* Bloomington, Indiana: Hearing and Communication Laboratory, Indiana University, 1957.

—— *Signal detection theory and psychophysics: a topical bibliography.* Washington, D. C.: National Academy of Sciences, National Research Council, Committee on Hearing and Bioacoustics, 1967.

EGAN, J. P. Auditory masking and signal detection theory. *Audiology,* 1971: *10,* 41–47.

EGAN, J. P., and F. R. CLARKE. Psychophysics and signal detection. *In* J. B. SIDOWSKI (ed.). *Experimental methods and instrumentation in psychology.* New York: McGraw-Hill, 1966.

EGAN, J. P., G. Z. GREENBERG, and A. I. SCHULMAN. Interval of time uncertainty in signal detection. *Journal of the Acoustical Society of America*, 1961a, *33*: 771–78.

—— Operating characteristics, signal detectability, and the method of free response. *Journal of the Acoustical Society of America,* 1961b, *33*: 993–1007.

EGAN, J. P., A. I. SCHULMAN, and G. Z. GREENBERG. Operating characteristics determined by binary decisions and by ratings. *Journal of the Acoustical Society of America*, 1959, *31*: 768–73.

EGUCHI, S., and I. J. HIRSH. Development of speech sounds in children. *Acta Oto-Laryngologica, Supplementum 257,* 1969.

EKMAN, G. Is the power law a special case of Fechner's law? *Perceptual and Motor Skills,* 1964, *19*: 730.

EKMAN, G., and L. SJÖBERG. Scaling. *Annual Review of Psychology,* vol. 16. Palo Alto, California: Annual Reviews Inc., 1965, 451–74.

ELIAS, P. A note on the misuse of 'digital' in neurophysiology. *In* W. E. ROSENBLITH (ed.), *Sensory communication.* New York: John Wiley, 1961.

ELLIOTT, P. B. *Tables of d'. Tech. Rept. No. 97.* Ann Arbor: Electronics Defense Group, University of Michigan, 1959. *Reprinted in* J. A. SWETS (ed.), *Signal detection and recognition by human observers: contemporary readings.* New York: John Wiley, 1964, pp. 651–84.

ENGEN, T., and N. LEVY. The influence of standards on psychophysical judgment. *Perceptual Motor Skills,* 1955, *5*: 193–99.

FECHNER, G. T. *Elements of psychophysics.* (Trans. H. E. Adler) New York: Holt, Rinehart & Winston, 1966.

FEX, J. Auditory activity in centrifugal and centripetal cochlear fibers in a cat. A study of a feed-back system. *Acta Physiologica Scandinavia,* 1962, *55*: 1, Suppl. 189.

FIORENTINI, A., and T. RADICI. Binocular measurements on a field presenting a luminance gradient. *Atti della Fondazione "Giorgio Ronchi,"* 1957, *12*: 453–561.

FITZHUGH, R. The statistical detection of threshold signals in the retina. *Journal of General Physiology,* 1957, *40*: 925–48.

FLETCHER, H., and W. A. MUNSON. Loudness, its definition, measurement, and calculation. *Journal of the Acoustical Society of America,* 1933, *5*: 82–108.

GALAMBOS, R., G. SHEATZ, and V. VERNIER. Electrophysiological correlates of a conditioned response in cats. *Science,* 1955, *123*: 376–77.

GARNER, W. R. Advantages of the discriminability criterion for a loudness scale. *Journal of the Acoustical Society of America,* 1958, *30*: 1005–12.

—— *Uncertainty and structure as psychological concepts.* New York: John Wiley, 1962.

GARNER, W. R., and H. W. HAKE. The amount of information in absolute judgments. *Psychological Review,* 1951, *58*: 446–59.

GIBSON, E. J., and R. D. WALK. The "visual cliff." *Scientific American,* 1960, *202*: 64–71.

GIBSON, J. J. Perception as a function of stimulation. *In* S. KOCH (ed.), *Psychology: A study of a science,* vol. 1. New York: McGraw-Hill, 1959, pp. 456–501.

GRAHAM, C. H. Visual perception. *In* S. S. STEVENS (ed.), *Handbook of experimental psychology.* New York: John Wiley, 1951.

—— Sensation and perception in an objective psychology. *Psychological Review,* 1958, *65*: 65–76.

GRANIT, R. *Receptors and sensory perception.* New Haven, Conn.: Yale University Press, 1955.

GREEN, D. M. Consistency of auditory detection judgements. *Psychological Review,* 1964, *71*: 392–407.

GREEN, D. M., and R. D. LUCE. Detection of pulsed sinusoids presented at random times. *Perception and Psychophysics,* 1967, *2*: 441–50.

GREEN, D. M., and J. A. SWETS. *Signal detection theory and psychophysics.* New York: John Wiley, 1966.

GREENBERG, G. Z., and W. D. LARKIN. Frequency-response characteristics of auditory observers detecting signals of a single frequency in noise: the probe-signal method. *Journal of the Acoustical Society of America,* 1968, *44*: 1513–23.

GUILFORD, J. P. *Psychometric methods.* New York: McGraw-Hill, 1936.

HARTLINE, H. K., and F. RATLIFF. Inhibitory interaction of receptor units in the eye of *Limulus. Journal of General Physiology,* 1957, *40*: 357–76.

HELSON, H. *Adaptation-level theory.* New York: Harper & Row, 1964.

HENNING, R. B. Frequency-discrimination of random-amplitude tones. *Journal of the Acoustical Society of America,* 1966, *39*: 336–39.

HERNÁNDEZ-PEÓN, R., H. SCHERRER, and M. JOUVET. Modification of electric activity in cochlear nucleus during "attention" in unanesthetized cats. *Science,* 1956, *123*: 331–32.

JAMES, W. *Principles of psychology.* New York: Henry Holt, 1890.

JEFFRESS, L. A. A place theory of sound localization. *Journal of Comparative and Physiological Psychology,* 1948, *41*: 35–39.

—— Stimulus-oriented approach to detection. *Journal of the Acoustical Society of America,* 1964, *36*: 766–74.

—— Stimulus-oriented approach to detection reexamined. *Journal of the Acoustical Society of America,* 1967, *41*: 480–88.

JERGER, J. Békésy audiometry in the analysis of auditory disorders. *Journal of Speech and Hearing Research,* 1960, *3*: 275–87.

KIKUCHI, Y. Objective allocation of sound-image from binaural stimulation. *Journal of the Acoustical Society of America,* 1957, *29*: 124–29.

KRUSKAL, J. B. Multidimensional scaling by optimizing goodness of fit to a nonmetric hypothesis. *Psychometrika,* 1964, *29*: 1–27.

KRYTER, K. D. Scaling human reactions to the sound from aircraft. *Journal of the Acoustical Society of America,* 1959, *31*: 1415–29.

LETTVIN, J. Y., H. R. MATURAMA, W. S. MCCULLOCH, and W. H. PITTS. What the frog's eye tells the frog's brain. *Proceedings of the Institute of Radio Engineers,* 1959, *47*: 1940–51.

LOEB, M., and J. R. BINFORD. Variation in performance on auditory and visual monitoring tasks as a function of signal and stimulus frequencies. *Perception and Psychophysics,* 1968, *4*: 361–67.

LUCE, R. D. *Individual choice behavior.* New York: John Wiley, 1959a.

—— On the possible psychophysical laws. *Psychological Review,* 1959b, *66*: 81–95.

—— A threshold theory for simple detection experiments. *Psychological Review,* 1963a, *70*: 61–79.

—— Detection and Recognition. *In* R. D. LUCE, R. R. BUSH, and E. GALANTER (eds.), *Handbook of mathematical psychology.* New York: John Wiley, 1963b.

MACCORQUODALE, K., and P. E. MEEHL. On a distinction between hypothetical constructs and intervening variables. *Psychological Review,* 1948, *55*: 95–107.

MCGILL, W. J. Neural counting mechanisms and energy detection in audition. *Journal of Mathematical Psychology,* 1967, *4*: 351–76.

MEYER, M. Salient features of the functioning of the cochlea with demonstrations of a transparent hydraulic model. *Journal of the Acoustical Society of America,* 1931, *3*: 7-(A).

MILLER, G. A., G. A. HEISE, and W. LICHTEN. The intelligibility of speech as a function of the context of the test materials. *Journal of Experimental Psychology,* 1951, *41*: 329–35.

MILLER, J. D., C. S. WATSON, and W. P. COVELL. Deafening effects of noise on the cat. *Acta Oto-Laryngologica, Suppl. 176,* 1963.

MURCHISON, C. (ed.), *A handbook of general experimental psychology.* Worcester, Mass.: Clark University Press, 1934.

NAKATANI, L. H. *A confusion-choice stimulus recognition model applied to word recognition. Tech. Rept. No. 31.* Los Angeles: Human Communication Laboratory, University of California at Los Angeles, 1968.

NICHOLS, T. L. Detection performance and two parameters of the auditory stimulus. Ph.D. dissertation, The University of Texas, 1966.

OSGOOD, C. E. The nature and measurement of meaning. *Psychological Bulletin*, 1952, *49*: 197–237.

—— *Method and theory in experimental psychology*. New York: Oxford University Press, 1953.

PETERSON, W. W., T. G. BIRDSALL, and W. C. FOX. The theory of signal detectability. *Trans. Institute of Radio Engineers Professional Group on Information Theory*, 1954, *PGIT-4*: 171–212.

PFAFFLIN, S. M., and M. V. MATHEWS. Detection of auditory signals in reproducible noise. *Journal of the Acoustical Society of America*, 1966, *39*: 340–45.

POLLACK, I. Message uncertainty and message reception. *Journal of the Acoustical Society of America*, 1959, *31*: 1500–1508.

POSTMAN, L., and J. P. EGAN. *Experimental psychology*. New York: Harper & Row, 1949.

RASMUSSEN, G. L. An efferent cochlear bundle. *Anatomical Record*, 1942, *83*: 441.

RATLIFF, F. Interrelations among sciences in studies of vision. *In* S. KOCH (ed.), *Psychology: a study of a science*, vol. 4. New York: McGraw-Hill, 1962.

—— *Mach bands: quantitative studies on neural networks in the retina*. San Francisco: Holden-Day, 1965.

RATLIFF, F., and H. K. HARTLINE. The response of *Limulus* optic nerve fibers to patterns of illumination on the receptor mosaic. *Journal of General Physiology*, 1959, *42*: 1241–55.

RILLING, M., and C. MCDIARMID. Signal detection in fixed-ratio schedules. *Science*, 1965, *148*: 526–27.

ROBINSON, D. E., and C. S. WATSON. Application of signal detection theory. *In* J. V. TOBIAS (ed.), *Foundations of modern auditory theory*, vol. II. New York: Academic Press (in press, 1972).

ROEDER, K. D. Auditory system of noctuid moths. *Science*, 1966, *154*: 1515–21.

RUSSELL, B. *Principles of mathematics* (2nd ed.). New York: Norton, 1938.

SCHOEFFLER, M. A. Theory for psychophysical learning. *Journal of the Acoustical Society of America*, 1965, *37*: 1124–33.

SHANNON, C. E. A mathematical theory of communication. *Bell System Technical Journal*, 1948, *27*: 379–423, 623–56.

SHEPHERD, R. N. The analysis of proximities: multidimensional scaling with an unknown distance function, I and II. *Psychometrika*, 1962, *27*: 125–40, 219–46.

SHERWIN, C. W., R. KODMAN, JR., J. J. KOVALY, W. C. PROTHE, and J. MELROSE, Detection of signals in noise: a comparison between the human detector and an electronic detector. *Journal of the Acoustical Society of America*, 1956, *28*: 617–22.

SHOWER, E. G., and R. BIDDULPH. Differential pitch sensitivity of the ear. *Journal of the Acoustical Society of America*, 1931, *3*: 275–87.

STEVENS, S. S. The operational basis of psychology. *American Journal of Psychology*, 1935, *47*: 323–70.

—— A scale for the measurement of a psychological magnitude: loudness. *Psychological Review*, 1936, *43*: 405–16.

—— Psychology and the science of science. *Psychological Bulletin*, 1939, *36*: 221–63.

—— Mathematics, measurement, and psychophysics. *In* S. S. STEVENS (ed.), *Handbook of experimental psychology*. New York: John Wiley, 1951.

—— On the psychophysical law. *Psychological Review*, 1957, *64*: 153–81.

—— The psychophysics of sensory function. *In* W. A. ROSENBLITH (ed.), *Sensory Communication*. New York: MIT Press and John Wiley, 1961a, pp. 1–33.

—— Is there a quantal threshold? *In* W. A. ROSENBLITH (ed.), *Sensory communication*. New York: MIT Press and John Wiley, 1961b.

—— To honor Fechner and repeal his law. *Science*, 1961c, *133*: 80–86.

—— The basis of psychophysical judgments. *Journal of the Acoustical Society of America*, 1963, *35*: 611 (L).

STEVENS, S. S., C. T. MORGAN, and J. VOLKMANN. Theory of the neural quantum in the discrimination of loudness and pitch. *American Journal of Psychology*, 1941, *54*: 315–35.

SWETS, J. A. Is there a sensory threshold? *Science*, 1961, *134*: 168–77.

SWETS, J. A. (ed.), *Signal detection and recognition by human observers*. New York: John Wiley, 1964.

SWETS, J. A., and A. B. KRISTOFFERSON. Attention. *Annual Review of Psychology*, Palo Alto, California: Annual Reviews, Inc., 1970, *21*: 339–66.

SWETS, J. A., and S. T. SEWALL. Invariance of signal detectability over stages of practice and levels of motivation. *Journal of Experimental Psychology*, 1963, *66*: 120–26.

SWETS, J. A., W. P., TANNER, JR., and T. G. BIRDSALL. Decision processes in perception. *Psychological Review*, 1961, *68*: 301–40.

TANNER, W. P., JR., and R. D. SORKIN. Theory of signal detectability. *In* J. V. TOBIAS (ed.), *Foundations of Modern Auditory Theory* Vol. II. New York: Academic Press, 1972.

TANNER, W. P., JR., and J. A. SWETS. The human use of information: I. Signal detection for the case of the signal known exactly. *Transactions of the Institute of Radio Engineers Professional Group on Information Theory*, 1954, *PGIT-4*: 213–221.

TANNER, W. P., JR., J. A. SWETS, and D. M. GREEN. Some general properties of the hearing mechanism. *University of Michigan: Electronics Defense Group, Technical Report No. 30*, 1956.

TAYLOR, M. M. The effect of the square root of time on continuing perceptual tasks. *Perception and Psychophysics*, 1966, *1*: 113–19.

TAYLOR, M. M., and C. D. CREELMAN. PEST: efficient estimates on probability functions. *Journal of the Acoustical Society of America*, 1967, *41*: 782–87.

THORPE, W. H. *Learning and instinct in animals*. Cambridge, Mass.: Harvard University Press, 1956.

THURSTONE, L. L. A law of comparative judgment. *Psychological Review*, 1927, *34*: 273–86.

TITCHENER, E. B. *Experimental psychology*. New York: Macmillan, 1905.

TORGERSON, W. S. *Theory and methods of scaling*. New York: John Wiley, 1958.

TREISMAN, M. Noise and Weber's law: the discrimination of brightness and other dimensions. *Psychological Review*, 1964, *71*: 314–30.

WALD, A. *Sequential analysis*. New York: John Wiley, 1947.

WARREN, R. M., and R. P. WARREN. A critique of S. S. Stevens' "New Psychophysics." *Perceptual and Motor Skills*, 1963, *16*: 797–810.

WATSON, C. S. Measurement of individual stimuli in a signal detection task. *Journal of the Acoustical Society of America*, 1964, *36*: 1042 (A).

—— Signals, noise, discriminations and decisions. Review of D. M. Green and J. A. Swets, *Signal detection theory and psychophysics*. *Contemporary Psychology*, 1967, *12*: 386–88.

WATSON, C. S., and W. T. BOURBON. Rating scales and two-state threshold models. *Journal of the Acoustical Society of America*, 1965, *38*: 667–81.

WATSON, C. S., and B. M. CLOPTON. Motivated changes of sensitivity in a simple detection task. *Perception and Psychophysics*, 1969, *5*: 281–87.

WATSON, C. S., J. A. FRANKS, and D. C. HOOD. Detection of tones in the absence of masking noise. *Journal of the Acoustical Society of America*, 1967, *42*: 1194 (A).

WATSON, C. S., and T. L. NICHOLS. Replication and revisions of Egan's method of free response. *Journal of the Acoustical Society of America*, 1966, *39*: 1247 (A).

WATSON, C. S., M. E. RILLING, and W. T. BOURBON. Receiver-operating characteristics determined by a mechanical analog to the rating scale. *Journal of the Acoustical Society of America*, 1964, *36*: 283–88.

WOODWORTH, R. S., and H. SCHLOSBERG. *Experimental psychology*. New York: Holt, Rinehart & Winston, 1954.

ZINNES, J. L. Scaling. *Annual Review of Psychology*, Palo Alto, California: Annual Reviews, Inc., 1969, *20*: 447–78.

Some Basic Phenomena

The light which serves as the stimulus for vision is radiant energy from a narrow range, the visible region, of the radiant energy (electromagnetic) spectrum. Light energy is characterized as having two aspects: as an energy particle, or photon, and as a wave.[1] Most commonly the wave aspect is used to refer to visual stimuli; thus "white" light as ordinarily seen is usually said to result from the combination of many wave lengths distributed throughout the visible spectrum, whereas to see "colored" light is generally understood to mean stimulation by wave lengths from restricted spectral regions. The visible wave lengths are very short and are expressed in nanometers (abbreviated nm, 1 nm $= 10^{-9}$ meter), a new name recently adopted to replace the old name, millimicron, for the same unit. The range of visible wave lengths is often stated to be from 400 to 700 nm, but these limits are known to be only approximate since, if the radiant energy is increased, visual responses can be evoked throughout the range from 365 nm to 1050 nm.

A schematic illustration of the gross anatomy of the right eye in horizontal section is shown in Figure 15–1. The sclerotic coat is a tough, fibrous, white enveloping tissue. In the front it is continuous with the protruding segment of the eyeball, the cornea, which is transparent and serves as the main refracting part of the eye. (The lens gives additional refraction, performing its function by means of changes in its shape so as to bring objects at different distances into focus.) The choroid coat is a dark, pigmented tissue, largely composed of blood vessels.

The retina is the receiving, integrating, and transmitting part of the eye. It is a complex stratified structure, some of its layers of neural tissue being organized so as to form a chain of three neurons, as shown in Figure 15–2. Starting from the back and going toward the front of the eye, these are: the primary receptor cell layers, the rods and the cones, which make up the first-order neurons; next the layers forming the bipolar cells, the second-order neurons; and finally the layers constituting the

---

[1]The terms "photon" and "quantum" are used synonymously in this chapter.

F. A. Mote
& Ü. T. Keesey

The Psychophysics of Vision

15

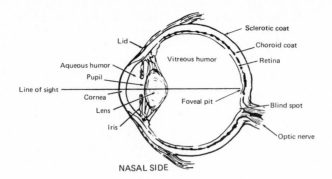

Fig. 15-1. *Schematic drawing of the structures of the eye.* [Mueller 1965; reprinted by permission]

ganglion cells, the third-order neurons. The ganglion cell axons are the optic nerve fibers. They come from all parts of the retina to a point about 15° of arc nasally from the fovea where they leave the eyeball. This location is the optic disk, or blind spot, because there are no receptors where the retina is pierced for the exit of the optic nerve.

The duplicity theory is one of the basic concepts in the field of vision. It assumes there are two types of receptors, the rods and the cones, which differ in a variety of ways, all contributing to their difference in function.

A basic functional difference is displayed in Figure 15–3, which shows the logarithm of the relative amounts of radiant energy in the 400-700 nm range required to evoke a constant visual response at two locations in the retina, one in the periphery and the other at the fovea. The lower curve shows the results obtained in the periphery, using a procedure in which the subject adjusted the energies of a series of wave lengths, taken one at a time, to match the brightness of a white light of constant intensity and so dim as to be near the absolute threshold. A value of 10 was assigned to the wave length requiring the least energy for the match and the energies of the others expressed relative to it. At such low intensity levels only the rods respond, and visual activities are said to be carried out under scotopic, or dim, visibility conditions. The upper curve displays the foveal measurements and shows that for wave lengths shorter than about 625 nm considerably higher intensities are required than for the periphery. At these intensities visual functions take place under conditions of photopic, or bright, visibility. The position of the curves with respect to each other as they are shown in the figure indicates that, as a general statement, the thresholds of the rods

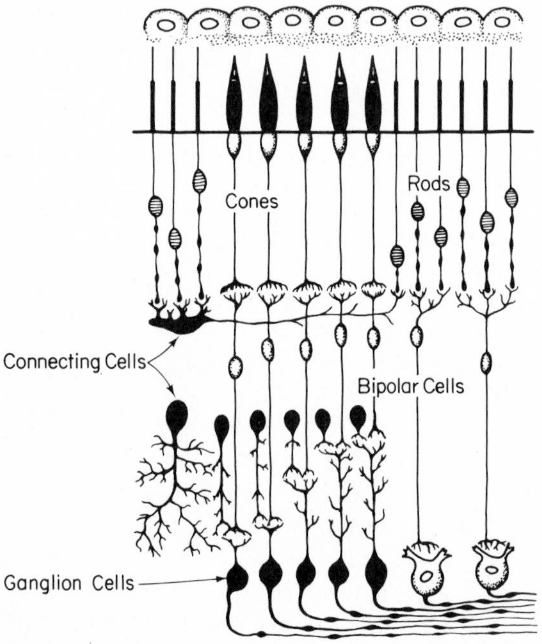

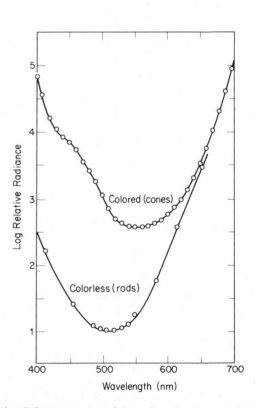

Fig. 15-3. *Relative response of the rods and cones to radiant energy as a function of wave length.* [Hecht and Hsia, after Graham 1965; reprinted by permission of John Wiley & Sons, Inc. and the Journal of the Optical Society of America]

Fig. 15-2. *Structure of the retina.* [Detweiler, after Mueller 1965; reprinted by permission]

and cones most nearly coincide in the long wave length end of the spectrum; however, more precise specification of the form of the curves and their relationship to each other depends upon the particular conditions of the experiment.

At both retinal locations high relative energy is needed to evoke a response at short wave lengths, less and less being called for as wave length increases until, at about 510 nm for the periphery and around 555 nm for the fovea, the energy is at a minimum; beyond these wave length regions the energy required increases out to the long wave length limits. This difference between the periphery and the fovea with respect to the wave lengths at which minimum energy is required is known as the Purkinje shift.

In addition to the quantitative differences in response of the two retinal regions, there is also a qualitative one: a stimulus of given wave length at threshold in the periphery is seen as colorless, whereas at the fovea it is colored. For example, a stimulus of 500 nm is seen as a very dim white light at the scotopic threshold; as its energy is increased the stimulus simply becomes brighter until the photopic threshold is reached, the energy now being about one hundred times the scotopic threshold level, according to the data shown in Figure 15–3. The stimulus is now green. Thus, both the brightness and the color aspects of stimuli can be seen at photopic intensity levels, but only the brightness aspect at scotopic levels. The area between the curves is known as the photochromatic, or colorless, interval, the vertical height of the ordinate separating them at any wave length representing the approximate value of the factor by which the energy must be multiplied to bring about the change from colorless to colored light. The magnitude of the multiplying factor at a given wave length will depend upon the conditions of the experiment.

For both the rods and the cones the event that initiates the visual response is the absorption of radiant energy by a photosensitive substance. In the rods this is rhodopsin, which is located in their outer segments. The electron microscope shows this part of the rod to be a laminated structure consisting of hundreds of layers of very thin dark disks containing rhodopsin, each layer alternating with lighter non-photosensitive material, all being oriented transversely to the receptor axis and looking like a pile of different colored poker chips stacked within the outer segment. When light energy acts upon rhodopsin, a series of breakdown processes occur that Wald, in his Nobel prize award lecture (1968), pictures as follows: rhodopsin → pre-lumirhodopsin → lumirhodopsin → metarhodopsin I → metarhodopsin II → retinal + opsin. Some of the retinal converts to vitamin A, the amount depending primarily upon the intensity and duration of the light stimulus. As these processes go on, color changes also take place: rosy-red rhodopsin bleaches to pale yellow retinal and on to colorless vitamin A; these are "visual yellow" and "visual white," the names that have often been used to refer to the stages of rhodopsin breakdown. A supply of rhodopsin must be maintained if rod visual activity is to go on—and the only way this can be done is for it to be regenerated. There are two avenues of regeneration. One is direct, via the spontaneous combination of retinal and opsin. The other is indirect, the vitamin A converted from retinal, with the addition of new vitamin A which derives ultimately from the blood stream, combines with opsin to reform retinal and this, in turn, combines with opsin to bring about the regeneration. The cycle of breakdown and regeneration continues as long as light acts upon the rods; in the dark,

regeneration proceeds until all the retinal and opsin has been used—the concentration of rhodopsin is then at its maximum.

Only the radiant energy it absorbs can bring about a reaction in a photosensitive material. A great amount of work on the absorption of rhodopsin with respect to wave length has been done, most of it spectrophotometric measurements on rhodopsin in solution. When radiant energy falls upon a solution, part of it is absorbed and part transmitted. If the percentage absorbed at various wave lengths is plotted as a function of wave length, the graph is an absorption spectrum. Studied in this way rhodopsin is, of course, *in vitro*. Measurements *in vivo* have also been carried out using instruments which operate on the principle of the opthalmoscope. Light of known wave length and intensity is sent into the eye, and the portion reflected back outside is picked up. Basically the method used is the same as with a spectrophotometer, except that the light falls upon the living eye, and allowance must be made in the measurements for its having traversed the retina twice, once as the incident beam and again as the beam reflected from the tissues behind the retina. Usually the optical density of rhodopsin is determined. This is a measure of transmittance, the ratio of transmitted to incident radiation, and in the form it is usually employed, optical density is defined as the negative common logarithm of transmittance:

$$D = -\log_{10} (I_t)/(I_i),$$

or

$$D = \log_{10} (I_i)/(I_t)$$

If the optical densities for various wave lengths are plotted against wave length, a density spectrum (also known as extinction spectrum) is generated. Recently microspectrophotometric techniques have been developed so that the absorbing and transmitting characteristics of single rod cells in small pieces of freshly dissected retinas can be measured.

It has generally been accepted that rhodopsin absorption accounts for the relationship between wave length and visual response when the visual stimulus is at scotopic luminance levels and falls upon the rods. For the purpose of comparing them with the absorption spectrum and the density spectrum of rhodopsin, the behavioral data are presented in the form of a luminosity curve (also known as visibility curve, spectral sensitivity curve, and by other names). Here the reciprocal of the energy value at the wave length requiring least energy for threshold, a brightness match, etc., is taken as 100 percent (or unity), and the reciprocals of the values at other wave lengths expressed relative to it. Plotting these against wave length gives the luminosity curve. These data are for energy incident at the cornea, and they must be corrected before the comparison can be made with the rhodopsin spectra. One correction involves the relationship between radiant energy and wave length. The necessary stimulus for rhodopsin activation is the absorption of photons. The energy, E, of a photon and wave length, λ, are related by

$$E = h(c/\lambda)$$

where h and c are constants. The relationship is inverse, so that if radiant energy is the same at the two wave lengths, there are only two-thirds as many photons at 400 nm as at 600 nm; hence any comparisons should be made for equal numbers of photons absorbed and not on the basis of equal radiant energies. It is

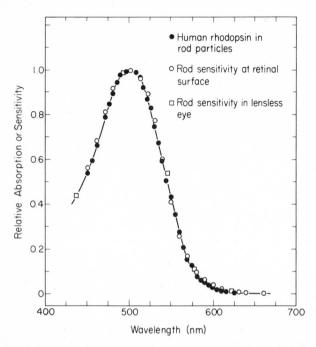

Fig. 15-4. *Density spectrum of human rhodopsin compared with the scotopic function for a lensless eye. Such an eye lacks one of the main energy absorbing media for which it is necessary to make a correction when the same comparison is made for the normal eye.* [data from Wald & Brown, "Human Rhodopsin," *Science* 1958, *127:* 222–26 and reprinted in Alpern, *Sensory Processes* (Belmont, Calif.: Brooks-Cole Publishing Co., 1967); reprinted here by permission]

also necessary to correct for the transmission of the ocular media since the eye is far from being transparent. Ocular transmission varies as a function of wave length—from less than 10 percent at 400 nm to over 60 percent at 620 nm, according to the measurements most often referred to. A third correction is needed to take into account the absorption of rhodopsin in the retina. There are several ways that have been used to obtain an estimate of this, among them the microspectrophotometric and ophthalmoscopic methods already mentioned. When the corrections are made, the behavioral data agree with the density and absorption spectra of rhodopsin as shown in Figure 15–4. The correspondence is considered to support the view that the response to wave length at scotopic luminance levels in the periphery is determined by the photon-catching characteristics of rhodopsin.

In a now classic experiment Hecht, Shlaer, and Pirenne (1942) determined the energy required at the absolute threshold of human vision. So that the measurements could be obtained under circumstances of maximum sensitivity, the study was carried out under optimum experimental conditions. The eye was dark-adapted for 30 minutes before any stimuli were given. The stimulus of 510 nm wave length was presented as a circular patch of 10′ diameter in flashes of 1 msec duration at a location 20° temporally from the fovea on the horizontal meridian of the eye. The psychophysical method of constant stimuli was used and the magnitude of the stimulus at the 60 percent value taken as the threshold. The energy measurements were made with a thermopile, which showed the number of photons falling upon the eye varied between 54 and 148. However, all these were not represented in the photochemical action, since some corrections for losses are necessary in order to arrive at the number involved in the threshold reponse. Reflection at the

cornea accounts for about 4 percent loss, and there is a further 50 percent loss in transmission through the ocular media at 510 nm. Finally they estimated that no more than 20 percent of the photons reaching the retina were absorbed. These corrections lead to the calculation that about one out of every ten photons incident at the cornea could have been photoactive. The approximately 500 rods within the stimulus area were considered to be a population so large that there was a negligibly small chance of one rod absorbing more than one photon. Since it was assumed that one molecule of rhodopsin is activated by one photon, the data indicate that the absorption of one photon by one molecule of rhodopsin in each of only 5 to 14 rods within 1 msec is all that is required to initiate the threshold response in the human visual system.

According to these findings the number of photons involved at the absolute threshold is remarkably small. Indeed, it appears that so few are needed that, as a check on their results, Hecht, Shlaer, and Pirenne used another—entirely different—method of evaluation. Photons are discrete entities and their absorption by the retina represents random and independent events. The Poisson, an appropriate distribution when small numbers of discrete and independent events are involved, can be used to give an estimate of the number of photons absorbed. If a is the mean number of photons in a stimulus flash of any intensity, the probability, p_n, that n or more photons will be absorbed at a single flash is given by

$$p_n = a^n/(e^n n!)$$

where e is the base of natural logarithms. There are tables of values of p_n for various values of a and n. Graphs constructed from the tables that show the probability of n or more events as a function of log a reveal that the slope of the curve becomes steeper as n increases. For small values of n the slopes are so different that a set of data points can be fitted to the curve for a particular value by visual inspection. The results of the Hecht, Shlaer, and Pirenne study were graphically presented as percent flashes seen as a function of $\log_{10} a$. The three authors were among the subjects, and their data, along with the best-fitting Poisson distribution for each, are presented in Figure 15–5. This shows an estimate of around 5 to 7 photons, which is in such good agreement with the physical measurements that they consider the Poisson method of evaluation satisfactorily accounts for their data.

It has long been known that for many reactions involving light, a constant amount of energy is necessary in order to bring about a constant effect. In photochemistry the quantitative expression of this relationship is the well known Bunsen-Roscoe law, $Lt = C$, where L is the luminance, t is the duration, and C is a constant. The law is a statement of temporal integration (also known as temporal summation). Whenever the luminance-duration reciprocity is strictly fulfilled, there is complete temporal integration, which is to say, the constant effect has been achieved —whether by a low luminance acting for an extended duration or by a high luminance for a short duration.

There are many visual responses, among them the absolute threshold and brightness matching, which exhibit complete temporal integration for small areas of stimulation, but only up to a limiting time, known as the critical duration, t_c; beyond this, time is no longer a variable and it is simply the luminance that seems to determine the response. Thus, $Lt = C$, where $t \leq t_c$;

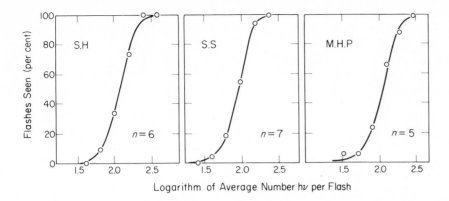

Fig. 15-5. *Average number of photons as determined by Poisson distribution curve fitting to the frequency of seeing data for Hecht, Shlaer, and Pirenne.* [Hecht, Shlaer, and Pirenne, after Graham and Ratoosh 1962]

when $t > t_c$, $L = C$. The results of experiments on the luminance-duration relationship are usually presented graphically as plots of log Lt as a function of log t. For example, Figure 15–6 shows data for the absolute threshold gathered by Karn (1936).

As this figure shows, as long as there is complete integration the data fall on a straight line of zero slope; the values for times longer than the critical duration tend to describe another straight line with a slope of approximately one. The reciprocity relationship in human vision is known as Bloch's law, since Bloch was the first to propose (1885) that for brief flashes the effect is determined by the product of intensity and time. Brindley (1952) demonstrated complete temporal integration for extremely brief flashes, some of them as short as 4×10^{-9} seconds, when he showed such stimuli could be matched in brightness to longer, low luminance flashes.

In experiments using brief flashes, care is taken to insure very rapid onset and cessation of the luminance, so that it may be considered to have a constant value throughout the time of presentation; in other words, its wave form is essentially rectangular. It has been shown that this is not a necessary stimulus condition at the absolute threshold. Long (1951) studied the wave form of the light pulse, using different patterns of rise and decay time, and Davy (1952) used rectangular pulses, but varied their number from 1 to 5. The findings were the same in both experiments: it is the total quantity of energy presented during a period less than the critical duration that determines the constant effect; the time characteristics of its delivery have no influence.

The critical duration is not a constant; its magnitude depends upon such factors as the region of the retina stimu-

lated, the visual task, and others. In the usual case, its value for a particular experiment is an estimate obtained by locating on the log t axis the duration at which the lines fitted to the $Lt = C$ and $L = C$ points on the graph intersect. For the data shown in Figure 15–6 this procedure gives a value of around 125 msec, but there are other results showing a critical duration of about one-half this amount. From measurements of the latent period of the first impulse after the stimulus onset, and other response features in the single optic nerve fiber of Limulus, Hartline (1934) demonstrated that its individual photoreceptor exhibits complete temporal integration for short flashes. The results show the shift from $Lt = C$ to $L = C$ is more abrupt than is usually found for human measurements. Almost without exception the human subject in a luminance-duration relationship experiment is instructed to respond "Yes" ("I see it," or "It matches," etc.) or "No" ("I don't see it," or "It doesn't match," etc.). Hartline pointed out that in such experiments, in which there is no measurement of the receptor cell activity, the duration at which the data show an abrupt shift may be considered to indicate the time of the criterion event leading to the subject's language response. Activity subsequent to the critical duration may occur, but it is of no significance for the criterion event—obviously, once this event has happened, nothing that takes place afterward can influence it.

At the level of the absolute threshold for small areas in both the fovea and the periphery, there is an interaction between the luminance and the area of the stimulus which turns out to be the same as the luminance-duration relation. This is Ricco's law: $LA = C$, where L is the luminance, A is the area, and C is a constant. Over the range for which there is strict reciprocity—up to areas on the order of 20 minutes of arc—there is complete spatial integration. For somewhat larger areas another expression, Piper's law, $L\sqrt{A} = C$, is an approximation. For large areas there is no relation and $L = C$. Among the many studies of this area-luminance relationship—referred to as the area-intensity effect for nearly a century—most, such as the 1936 study of Karn, have been concerned with the absolute threshold, but the effect can also be shown in data on dark adaptation, brightness discrimination, and other visual functions.

Just as complete temporal integration specifies the conditions under which an increase in duration may compensate for a decrease in luminance, complete spatial integration expresses the compensatory trade-off between area and luminance. When both types of integration are taken into account, it is clear that the luminance, the duration, and the area are all involved in specifying the situations in which a constant amount of energy is needed to evoke a constant visual effect.

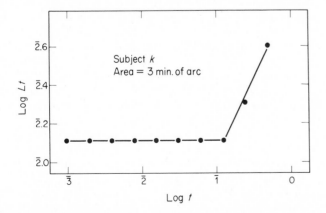

Fig. 15-6. *Luminance-duration relationship for a small area in the fovea.* [Data from Karn 1936]

In a well-known experiment, Graham and Margaria (1935) studied the relations among luminance, time, and stimulus areas for white light at a region 15° from the fovea. They determined the threshold luminance for durations from a fraction of a msec to more than 500 msecs, and for areas with diameters of 2 and 16 minutes and 1° and 3° of arc visual angle. The results showed strict reciprocity up to about 100 msecs for the smallest area, but only to around 2 msecs for the largest. Baumgardt and Hillman (1961) carried out a similar experiment with red and blue-green lights at 20° in the periphery for durations from about 3 to 1000 msecs, and areas having diameters of 3.43 minutes and 1°, 3°, and 8° visual angle. The data showed complete spatial integration up to 100 msecs for both colors and all areas, findings considerably different from those obtained by Graham and Margaria. The reasons for such contradictory results are not known and the situation is unclear. Some aspects of both sets of results are supported by the measurements of Sperling and Jolliffe (1965). In their study both light and dark stimulus target surrounds, both foveal and peripheral regions were stimulated, and red and blue stimuli were used. All were found to be factors influencing the results.

In Figure 15–7 are shown the results of the Graham and Margaria experiment. The dashed lines in each panel represent the $Lt = C$ and $L = C$ conditions, and they intersect at the same value on the log t axis, that is, at the same critical duration. The progressive reduction in the value of log Lt as area increases is an expression of the area-luminance effect: the greater the area, the less the luminance needed for the threshold response.

The most prominent feature of the figure is the relationship between the area of the stimulus and the critical duration. For the smallest area the critical duration is longest, and the curve resembles Hartline's results for the Limulus single receptor. As area increases the critical duration gets shorter and shorter and the transition from $Lt = C$ to an approximation of $L = C$ becomes more and more gradual. This finding is attributed to neural interaction, which is presumed to have a greater opportunity to manifest itself in larger retinal areas since more receptors are involved and there is a greater chance for interconnecting neurons to influence responses. The Graham and Margaria experiment has been influential because it called attention to the importance of neural interaction effects in the psychophysics of vision. The topic of neural activity in vision is too extensive to take up here, and only some aspects of interaction as it relates to spatial summation will be considered.

Estimates of the numbers of receptor cells in each eye vary, but they are usually given as 5–7 million for the cones and 75–150 million for the rods. It is estimated the number of optic nerve fibers is about one million. In view of these estimates it is obvious that there cannot be a one-to-one ratio of receptor cells to optic nerve fibers. Furthermore, the distribution ratio is uneven. In the central fovea it seems to be one-to-one, but in the periphery the ratio is much higher and varies from one location to another. Hence, although their numbers might lead to the expectation of an average receptor-fiber ratio in the periphery, perhaps on the order of about 140 to 1, this is not the case. In some locations it may be several thousand to one. This means that a convergence system—many receptors connected with one bipolar cell, and many bipolars with one ganglion cell—must prevail over much of the retina.

Such an organization provides a way whereby neighboring

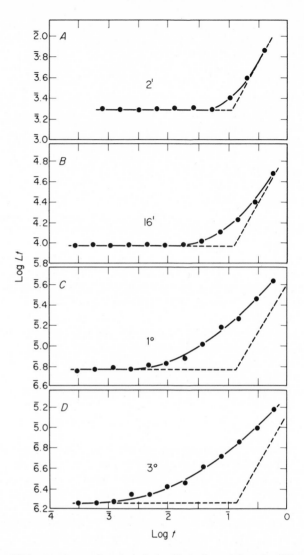

Fig. 15-7. *Luminance-duration relationship in the periphery for different stimulus sizes.* [Graham and Margaria, after Woodworth and Schlosberg 1954]

receptors, each subliminally stimulated, may pool their activities and together evoke a response in an optic nerve fiber when no individual receptor could do so. In addition, however, there are neurons, referred to as "connecting cells" in Figure 15–2, which also contribute to summative reactions. Those shown lying between the receptor cells and the bipolars are the horizontal cells, and those between the bipolars and the ganglion cells are the amacrine cells. It is clear that provision for spatial summation exists at the level of the retina. This is not surprising in view of the fact that ontogenetically the retina has derived from the brain and is a true higher nervous center.

The receptive field of a single optic nerve fiber refers to the area on the retina from which responses in the fiber can be evoked by a small exploring spot of light. In the receptive fields of the frog, Hartline (1940) demonstrated spatial integration and also that when they were stimulated together, subliminal excitation of several small areas within the field could bring about a discharge in the fiber. Bartlett (1965) points out that

Ricco's law may be considered an adequate description of peripheral spatial integration for small retinal areas served by a single optic nerve fiber.

The Ricco and Piper equations are simple mathematical descriptions which have no theoretical foundation in any theory about visual activity from which rational equations predicting the area-luminance relationship could be derived. A theoretical formulation based upon interaction effects in the retina has been proposed and subjected to experimental test by Graham, Brown and Mote (1939) and Graham and Bartlett (1939). The basic notion of the hypothesis is that an evenly illuminated stimulus sets up in the retina a gradient of excitation which is maximal at the center and falls off toward the boundary. It is assumed that the excitation contributed by any small elemental area to the excitation at the center is inversely proportional to some power of its distance from the center. If E is the excitation needed for the threshold response at the center, the excitatory contribution, dE, of each elemental area is $(1/r^p)$, where r is its distance from the center and p is a constant. Letting e be the excitatory effect of each elemental area and summing these for the total area, an expression for E can be derived. By making certain approximations and substitutions, equations in forms suitable for comparison with experimental results were obtained. In both experiments data gathered from the fovea and the periphery were satisfactorily fitted by the equations.

Dark Adaptation

Dark adaptation is the process of adjustment of the visual system to reductions in the level of illumination in the environment. For many changes of level, for example that which occurs upon going from outdoor daylight indoors, there is a very rapid sensitivity shift to the reduced level, and most visual tasks can continue to be carried on with no loss in efficiency. Since the shift is so rapid, on the order of a fraction of a second, it is considered to be predominantly determined by neural processes; hence it is known as *neural dark adaptation* (also as *field adaptation*). However, when there is a large change in illumination level, for example the change between outdoor daylight and movie interiors, neural adaptation does not suffice to bring about the necessary adjustment and a further stage of adjustment must occur before optimum sensitivity is achieved. The time required for this to take place may be half an hour or longer, and it is considered to be the result of receptor-neural processes and interactions which go on when the bleached photochemical materials in the receptors are regenerated during the time in darkness. This is *photochemical dark adaptation*, and it is the conditions and variables influencing this type of sensitivity adjustment, and the hypotheses proposed to explain it, which have received most of the attention devoted to dark adaptation.

In the typical dark adaptation experiment there are two periods, the first, a time during which the eye is exposed to a given luminance for a fixed duration, a preadapting exposure, which establishes light adaptation. When this terminates, the eye is in darkness, and the second period, dark adaptation, begins. Threshold measurements that trace out the course of recovery from loss of visual sensitivity are taken from time to time during this period. Since the luminance required for threshold detection decreases during the time in the dark, the sensitivity of the visual system increases. Therefore, visual sensitivity in dark adaptation is defined as the reciprocal of the threshold.

Figure 15–8 shows the course of dark adaptation following a preadapting exposure to a white light of 2250 mL luminance, presented for 4 minutes, and covering an area of 35° visual angle. The 2° testing stimulus was also white and presented at 1 or 2 minute intervals in flashes lasting 0.2 seconds. Both preadapting and testing stimuli were centered 7° temporally from the fovea. The data show the usual course of dark adaptation when measurements are taken at a peripheral location on the retina. The whole curve consists of two segments which meet at a point of transition. The upper segment represents the cone phase of dark adaptation. Here, for the first 2 to 3 minutes the threshold drops rapidly, then declines more slowly to a plateau which is interrupted after about 6 to 7 minutes. During this time the threshold has fallen about 1.5 log units. The interruption at the transition marks the beginning of the rod phase; the thresholds again descend, now over about 2 log units, until at around 30 to 35 minutes since the end of the preadaptation, an essentially stable dark-adapted threshold level is reached. Since the total range of threshold values is about 3.5 log units, more than a thousand-fold change in sensitivity has taken place. Had testing been continued for another hour or more, the threshold would probably have gradually fallen another 0.3–0.5 log units, a negligible sensitivity change compared to that taking place during the first 35 minutes.

In this experiment (and the same situation holds true for most experiments on dark adaptation), the subject was in darkness after the preadaptation. The course of dark adaptation, therefore, represents the increase in sensitivity resulting from a reduction in light from the preadaptation value to zero. If the shift is from the preadaptation luminance value to some lower luminance, so long as the difference is too great for neural dark adaptation to serve as the mechanism of adjustment, the subject does not see the light, and dark adaptation proceeds until the time at which the sensitivity reaches such a level that the light is seen. From this time on, the threshold does not change.

Since the fovea contains cones only, in order to obtain information about their dark adaptation without any intrusion or complication brought about by rod responses, the procedure is to preadapt the central region of the retina and use a small

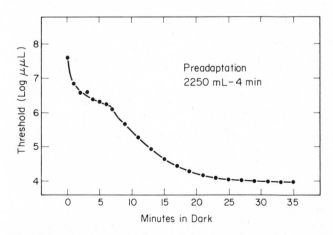

Fig. 15-8. *A representative human dark adaptation curve for a peripheral region.* [Unpublished data of Mote]

testing stimulus, 1° visual angle or less, which stimulates only the fovea. The dark adaptation curves will be similar to the first segment of Figure 15–8. When the preadaptation conditions are varied, certain features of cone adaptation change. If its duration is about 2 minutes, a high luminance preadaptation may bring about 2 or 3 log units elevation of the threshold above the dark-adapted threshold level, and the time required for dark adaptation may be 10–12 minutes. A low luminance may raise the threshold only 0.6–0.8 log units, and dark adaptation is complete in 2–3 minutes.

In the normal eye there is no region outside the fovea which does not contain both rod and cone receptors; hence the method employed for gathering information about cone response cannot be used if it is desired to measure exclusively rod dark adaptation. However, some individuals who are completely colorblind, and who therefore are presumed to have no cone receptors, have been studied. Figure 15–9 shows the dark adaptation measurements obtained by Hecht, Shlaer, Smith, Haig and Peskin from such a person along with comparison data from a normal subject. Following preadaptation to 1600 mL for 4 minutes, the data for the normal subject show both cone and rod responses, the range of thresholds for the cones extending about 2 log units and about 3 log units for the rods. The total time for dark adaptation is more than 30 minutes. For the same preadaptation conditions the data for the colorblind subject show no evidence of cone response, the range of threshold values is less than 3 log units, and dark adaptation is essentially all over in 10 minutes. The data for the normal subject show no indication of rod dark adaptation during the cone adaptation phase. What is involved here is probably not so simple a matter as mere delay; even if it were possible to avoid the intervention of cone dark adaptation

in the normal subject, his rod dark adaptation most likely would not be the same as that of the colorblind for the same conditions of preadaptation. Although the extent of the rod portion of the data for the normal is about the same as for the colorblind subject, his rate of dark adaptation is much slower; whereas his 3 log unit drop in threshold requires about 20 minutes, the comparable drop for the colorblind takes less than 10. Further experimentation showed that the preadaptation exposure for the normal subject must be reduced tremendously, to 10 mL or less, in order to obtain data which show an elevation of the threshold and rapidity of dark adaptation comparable to that found for the colorblind at 1600 mL exposure. It seems reasonable to consider that there are factors more complex than merely a delay resulting from the cone adaptation which is affecting the rod adaptation in the normal subject.

When the same preadapting and testing conditions are used, but their retinal location is varied, it is to be expected that different dark adaptation curves will be obtained. Centering the preadaptation on the fovea and using a small testing stimulus, about 2° visual angle, should provide data similar to the cone segment of Figure 15–8 and very little, if any, rod segment should appear. However, when the preadaptation and testing areas are located at regions farther and farther away from the fovea, the participation of the rods should become more and more evident, with the result that the data more and more nearly resemble Figure 15–8. Such an experiment was carried out by Hecht, Haig, and Wald (1935) who used the same preadaptation stimulus, centering it at 0° (the fovea), and at 2.5°, 5°, and 10° in the periphery. The testing stimulus was 2° visual angle. At 0° only the cone phase was present, the range of the thresholds was about 1.0 log unit, and dark adaptation was complete in a few minutes. When the testing was carried out at the more peripheral locations, the rod phase appeared earlier and became more prominent until, at 10°, it was the predominant aspect of the curve. The thresholds for this segment extended over a range

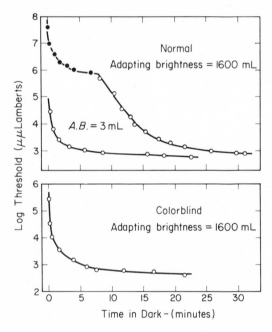

Fig. 15-9. *Comparison of the dark adaptation of a normal and a colorblind subject. Following the same preadaptation condition as for the normal, the data of the colorblind show no evidence of cone adaptation. To approximate the data of the colorblind after 1600 millilamberts for 4 minutes preadaptation, the normal subject requires only about 3 millilamberts for 4 minutes.* [Hecht, Shlaer, Smith, Haig and Peskin 1948]

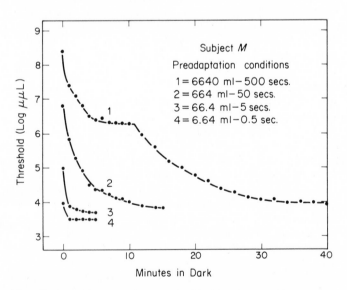

Fig. 15-10. *Peripheral dark adaptation following preadaptation to different luminances and durations. Recovery of sensitivity proceeeds more rapidly as luminance and duration decrease. At the lowest luminance and shortest duration preadaptation condition recovery is complete in about one minute.* [Mote and Riopelle 1953; copyright 1953 by the American Psychological Association and reprinted by permission]

of about 2.0 log units, and dark adaptation was not complete until around 40 minutes.

Also in this experiment, data were gathered again after the same preadaptation conditions, but using preadapting and testing stimuli of different sizes: 2°, 3°, 5°, 10°, and 20° visual angle, all centered upon the fovea. Thresholds were measured for 30 minutes. For the 2° field, cone adaptation lasted for about 12 minutes, the data showing some suggestion of rod participation during the remainder of the testing period. For the other sizes, the rod segments of the curves became more and more prominent and their thresholds descended to lower and lower values as the area increased. For the 3° area, the thresholds for this segment dropped about 0.5 log units; for the 20° area, however, they descended over 2.0 log units and were still slowly falling at the end of the 30 minute testing period.

Over a wide range of values of these variables, the luminance and duration of the preadapting exposure are important determiners of the subsequent dark adaptation. In one typical experiment concerned with these factors (Mote and Riopelle 1953), a peripheral region of the retina was exposed to luminances ranging from 6.64 to 6640 mL and durations from 0.5 to 500 seconds. A portion of the data is shown in Figure 15–10. At the highest luminance and longest duration the dark adaptation curve has both cone and rod segments. Only the rod segment appears in the other three curves. For these, the lower the luminance and the shorter the duration, the lower is the value of the initial threshold, the more rapid the descent of the threshold, and the shorter the time required to reach the final level of dark adaptation.

The results of this experiment indicate something of a reciprocal relationship between preadaptation luminance and duration, as long as their product is not too large. For example, the dark adaptation curves for 6640 mL times 0.5 seconds, 664 mL times 5 seconds, and 66.4 mL times 50 seconds could all be superimposed, and similar results were found for lower products of luminance times duration. This was not the case for higher products; for example, the 6640 mL times 50 seconds and 664 mL times 500 seconds preadaptations did not have the same effect upon subsequent dark adaptation. It has also been found for cone dark adaptation that a similar reciprocal relationship between preadapting luminance and duration can be demonstrated.

The durations employed in these preadapting exposures are too long for their mutual interrelationships to be considered as manifestations of Bloch's reciprocity law, which is usually considered to hold for durations less than approximately 0.1 second. However, Crawford (1946) found this reciprocity relation to hold for dark adaptation in the fovea and parafovea for durations of the order of 1 second.

Hecht (1934, 1937) gave a detailed and quantitative exposition of a photochemical theory to explain several basic visual functions. According to the theory, the events taking place in dark adaptation are the result of photochemical breakdown and regeneration processes, the concentration of photosensitive material present determining the level of visual sensitivity at a given moment. The course of dark adaptation is the manifestation of the regeneration process. After the preadapting exposure, the concentration of material is low, hence sensitivity is low, and the threshold is high; as regeneration proceeds, sensitivity increases with the increasing concentration, and the threshold declines until, when all the material has been regenerated, sensitivity is maximum and the final dark-adapted threshold has been reached. Sensitivity and threshold are inversely related, the reciprocal of the threshold luminance, $1/L$, being a measure of sensitivity, but since threshold and the concentration of material are also inversely related, $1/L$—or some function of it—is also a measure of concentration. Hecht was able to fit several sets of data obtained in typical dark adaptation experiments with quantitative expressions derived from his theory.

The procedures used in most experiments do not permit the first threshold measurement to be taken immediately following the preadapting exposure, but only after a delay of several seconds. Baker (1963) showed that the threshold of a human subject may drop as much as 1.7 log units in less than a second after the termination of preadaptation. Dowling (1963) measured the b-wave of the electroretinogram of the rat and the amount of rhodopsin bleached at various luminances, finding that no measurable amount of bleaching occurred until the luminance was more than 4 log units above that required to elicit the b-wave. He also measured dark adaptation, taking a constant magnitude of the b-wave as the threshold measure, and found that, over the range of preadapting luminance for which there was no bleaching, the initial threshold drop was precipitous. The loss of sensitivity resulting from the preadapting exposure (as indicated by the rise in threshold) and the recovery of sensitivity (as indicated by the very rapid and extensive threshold drop immediately upon the cessation of exposure) depend almost entirely upon the conditions of preadaptation and not upon the amount of photosensitive material bleached. If these changes in visual sensitivity occur because of rapid neural adjustments, as is generally considered to be the case, they are not accounted for by Hecht's theory, which considered dark adaptation only in terms of a photochemical regeneration process. It should be pointed out, however, that he came to realize his theoretical account of dark adaptation was an oversimplification and he abandoned it.

It has been found that a preadapting exposure which bleaches a small amount of photosensitive material can result in a large elevation of the threshold. Wald (1954) carried out an experiment in which the visual threshold of a dark-adapted human subject was compared with the amount of bleaching of rhodopsin contained in a glass cell, the preadaptation conditions being the same in both situations. The data showed that an exposure which bleached less than 1 percent of the rhodopsin raised the threshold 3300 times. To account for this result, Wald proposed an hypothesis based upon a conception of the receptor as a compartmented structure which can respond compartment by compartment in a stepwise fashion. Each compartment contains many molecules of rhodopsin, any one of which discharges the compartment and excites the receptor when one quantum is absorbed. The compartment has then made its whole contribution to the excitation, for although the other molecules in the compartment can absorb more quanta, they are ineffective to evoke a further response—the compartment cannot excite the receptor again until all the molecules have been restored. This hypothesis accounts for a small amount of bleaching as a consequence of a small number of quantum absorptions. But even though this is the case and bleaching is minimal, the threshold is elevated, since if all the compartments in each of many receptors absorb only one quantum, the threshold testing stimulus can excite only those receptors with no discharged compartments or those with compartments still undischarged. Thus, the visual threshold is not related in any simple way to the concentration of photosensitive material, but instead to the number of undischarged compartments.

The measurements obtained by Rushton, Campbell, Hagins, and Brindley (1955), using the method of retinal densitometry, showed that following a preadapting exposure which bleached almost all the photosensitive material, the time required for regeneration in the cones is about 5–8 minutes and in the rods 30–40 minutes, times which are about the same as required for their dark adaptation. The measurements show that at around 7 minutes about one-half of the rhodopsin has regenerated. According to the assumption that the visual threshold and concentration of the photosensitive material are related in one-to-one fashion, the threshold luminance at 7 minutes should be twice that required after all the material has regenerated; actually the luminance required is hundreds of times greater. A later experiment by Rushton (1961) in which only measurements of the rods were involved showed that, for more than a million-fold range of threshold values, the logarithm of the threshold during dark adaptation is proportional to the amount of rhodopsin still in the bleached state.

Crawford (1947) found that the values of the threshold during dark adaptation are about the same as the values of the brightness increment threshold when these are measured for a wide range of background luminances. This result is the basis for the idea of an "equivalent luminance," a concept which Rushton (1961, 1963) uses in his theory of visual adaptation.

In the retina clusters of rods, each cluster consisting of perhaps as many as several thousand individual rod receptors, are connected to a single optic nerve output. Rushton's theory proposes that when a molecule of rhodopsin absorbs a quantum of light, the molecule breaks down—it bleaches—and a signal is released which goes to a "summation pool." Signals from all the rods in a cluster go to the same pool and—via its output—contribute to the sensation of light. As long as the molecule remains in the bleached condition, a weak but steady signal continues to be transmitted to the pool. The output from the pool is fed back to it in such a way as to constitute an automatic gain control so that the summation pool is continually being reorganized. According to this hypothesis, it is not the receptor threshold but the state of the summation pool that determines the visual threshold. During dark adaptation the molecules bleached by previous exposure to light keep up the flow of signals to the summation pool, which continues to be reorganized by way of the feedback mechanism; however, since there is no light present, there is no further bleaching, and the signal flow decreases as more and more of the bleached molecules regenerate. These "black light" signals affect the threshold the same as if the dark adaptation test stimulus were projected, not against darkness, but against an illuminated background, an equivalent luminance, which is decreasing with time. Thus, the threshold during dark adaptation is analogous to the brightness increment threshold for background fields at the equivalent luminance.

In the dark, blackness is not the visual sensation, but rather that of seeing an extremely dim, turbulent, foggy background. One assumption about the origin of this sensation is that it is a manifestation of retinal "noise" brought about by spontaneous breakdown of material in the receptors. Barlow and Sparrock (1964) point out that this can be thought of in terms of dark light and that the hypothetical equivalent luminance background resulting from a preadapting exposure may be considered as an increase in this dark light. The exposure increases retinal noise, and the decline in the visual threshold during dark adaptation is an expression of the decrease in dark light as the bleached material in the receptors regenerates. In considering this hypothesis, Barlow and Sparrock raise the question of why the subject is not dazzled by the effects of the preadapting exposure, that is, by its positive afterimage, at the beginning of dark adaptation. There are such afterimages which follow light stimulation, but these usually soon fade, and after a few minutes nothing is seen. Barlow and Sparrock used a stabilized image technique in their experiment, a method they found to be effective for maintaining the positive afterimage through the course of dark adaptation. By using an appropriate experimental arrangement, they induced a stabilized afterimage of a photoflash preadapting exposure whose brightness the subject could match by varying the luminance of a light reflected into the eye from a white surface in the form of an annulus, and which was also kept stabilized so as to be concentric with the afterimage. The subjects were able to make matches during the 40 minutes of dark adaptation. After each matching judgment, the dark adaptation threshold was determined. In another part of the experiment, brightness increment thresholds were obtained for real background luminances over a range equal to the range of the afterimage matching luminances. The thresholds for the afterimage in dark adaptation were comparable to the brightness increment thresholds for the matching real luminances, as they should have been according to the hypothesis, since the dark adaptation threshold is an increment threshold against the afterimage equivalent background brightness. It is their conclusion that the bleached material in the receptors does not make them unresponsive; it makes them noisy.

Dowling (1967) has proposed an interaction between neural elements in the retina which may function as an inhibitory feedback system and which could thus constitute the feedback proposed by Rushton. From his work on the rat, in which the b-wave of the electroretinogram was used as the measure, he finds two phases of dark adaptation, one rapid, the other slow. As has been pointed out previously, since no measurable amount of rhodopsin bleaching is associated with the elevation and subsequent drop of the threshold occurring when the eye is exposed to low and moderate luminances, these changes are attributed to neural mechanisms which function so as to control the gain—or sensitivity—of the visual system. The slow phase is obtained when measurable amounts of rhodopsin are bleached by higher preadapting exposures, and the greater the amount of bleaching, the longer is the time required for dark adaptation to run its course. Although the fast and slow phases appear to be the result of different processes, one neural and the other photochemical, Dowling considers this is not the case, and he proposes an hypothesis that assumes a common origin for both.

Since the course of change in the b-wave and the course of threshold change in psychophysical experiments are similar, Dowling believes that processes taking place at the locus of origin of the b-wave determine dark adaptation. The evidence indicates that the source of the b-wave is the inner nuclear layer of the retina, a region containing bipolars, the cells from which the b-wave may arise. His histological studies indicate synaptic connections between a bipolar cell and an amacrine cell process and a ganglion cell dendrite which lie in contact with it, the direction of polarity being from the bipolar to the amacrine and the ganglion cell. A short distance away from the synaptic location is another synaptic connection between the bipolar and the amacrine process. Such a reciprocal arrangement could serve as the basis for a feedback system on the bipolar cell. If it is assumed that stimulation of the amacrine cell process by the bipolar results in an inhibitory synaptic feedback upon the bipolar, reducing its gain in proportion to the amount of its excitation, this interaction could constitute a way to control bipolar cell sensitivity.

Flicker and Intermittent Stimulation

The visual system, as well as being able to resolve spatial variations in light, is capable of detecting flicker, that is, temporal variations in luminance. The temporal resolving power of the eye has been the subject of a great many experiments which have been reviewed by Landis (1954).

The general method in most flicker experiments requires that the subject report the presence or absence of flicker. A target, usually circular, is illuminated intermittently by means of rotating a sectored disk in front of a steady beam of light. The shape and the relative width of the open and closed sectors control, respectively, the waveform and the duration of light and dark portions within one cycle of variation. The speed of rotation controls the number of full cycles per unit time; thus frequency of flicker is expressed as cycles/second or in Hertz (Hz). In an experimental situation, the speed is increased from a value at which the observer clearly sees flicker to the value at which he sees the light as steady. Then the procedure is reversed, and speed of rotation is decreased from above fusion to a point where flicker is visible. Upon many repetitions, a frequency of flicker can be determined that represents a criterion percentage, 50 or 75 percent of "no flicker" judgments. This is called critical fusion frequency (CFF), and is assumed to be a measure of the temporal resolving power of the eye.

One of the most general phenomena of flicker perception is that, at CFF and above, the brightness of the flickering field matches that of a steady field whose luminance is equal to the time-average luminance of the flickering field. If, for example, the flickering stimulus is composed of light and dark periods of equal duration, when fused it will match in brightness a steady field whose luminance is one half that of the individual light period. Talbot, and later Plateau, formulated a general expression for this relationship, and the Talbot-Plateau "law" is widely used in flicker photometry as a method whereby the luminance of two different wave lengths can be matched. (See Hecht and Verrijp 1933b, for a discussion of the Talbot-Plateau law.)

The parameters which influence the frequency at which fusion occurs are numerous, some of the more important ones being: (1) luminance of the interrupted light; (2) area of the flickering field; (3) region of the retina stimulated; (4) stimulus surround; (5) adaptation state; (6) temporal patterning, that is, the ratio of light and dark portions within a cycle, and the waveform. In addition, monocular or binocular presentation and wave length are also factors which change CFF. The age of the observer and his metabolic state have been shown to influence CFF to such a degree that on occasion it has been used as a clinical tool (Landis 1954).

Among these parameters, the luminance, the size of the retinal area, and the retinal location are the most important and most closely interrelated variables. Their combined effect can be summarized by a synopsis of some representative early studies.

Granit and Harper (1930) investigated mainly the effect of area on CFF. They used disks ranging between 21′ and and 6° visual angle and found that for a given luminance CFF increases approximately linearly with log area. This relation is known as the Granit-Harper law and is expressed in the form $CFF = b \log A + d$, where A is the area, and b and d are constants. It appears to hold true for foveally fixated as well as peripherally located stimuli and is applicable with minor variations for a large range of luminances.

Hecht and Smith (1936) studied systematically the relations of area and luminance in determining CFF. They employed fields ranging from 0.3° to 19° visual angle located in a 30° surround. The surround was matched to the Talbot level (time-average luminance) of the flickering fields. Foveal fixation was used. A typical result is shown in Figure 15–11.

It is seen that for all stimulus areas there is a portion of the function over a medium range of luminances at which cones are responding where CFF increases linearly with the logarithm of target luminance. This relation is known as the Ferry-Porter law and has the form $CFF = a \log I + b$. The data show that at high luminance levels the Ferry-Porter law does not hold, since CFF does not change as luminance increases. Another feature of the results is that with large areas of 6° and 19° visual angle, the CFF curves extend into the low luminance region where flicker could not be determined with the small foveal fields. Here, over a restricted range, CFF shows a linear increase with the logarithm of the target luminance and then becomes asymptotic. The dual nature of the CFF luminance curves found only for the larger stimuli attests to the increasing contribution of rods brought in with an increase in the size of retinal area stimulated.

Hecht and Verrijp (1933a) studied the interrelation of the retinal position of the stimulus and its luminance on CFF. Their target was a 2° field in a 10° steadily illuminated surround, located at the fovea and 5° and 15° above it. As seen in Figure 15–12, the CFF-intensity relationship just discussed holds true for all retinal locations. The dual nature of this relationship becomes evident with greater displacements of the target from the fovea. This effect is similar to that found by enlarging the

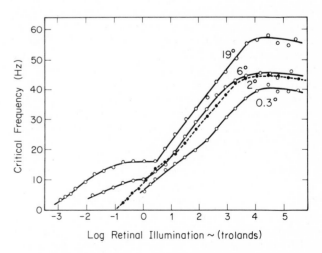

Fig. 15-11. *CFF as a function of log retinal illuminance for different target areas, all centrally fixated.* [Hecht and Smith 1936]

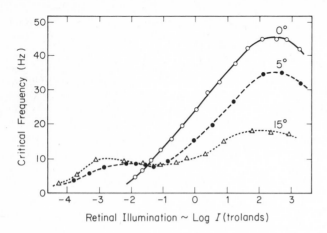

Fig. 15-12. *CFF as a function of log retinal illuminance for three retinal locations: at the fovea, and at 5° and 15° above the fovea.* [Hecht and Verrijp 1933a]

size of the target to encompass the rods outside the fovea and again can be attributed to the capability of the rods to function at low levels of luminance.

Figure 15–12 also shows that for the 2° field, CFF is higher in the fovea than in the periphery at high luminance, but the opposite is true at low luminance. Conflicting results relating retinal locus to CFF have been obtained by different investigators. Hylkema (1942), for example, found that fields larger than 1° at all luminance levels gave consistently higher CFF in the periphery than in the fovea. This may be due to the failure of the investigators to use uniform conditions of pupil diameter, surround, and adaptation state of the eye. Alpern and Spencer (1953) have been able to mimic the decrease in CFF as a function of retinal location by decreasing pupil size, even when retinal location was not changed. They also show that, if a constant pupil size is used, a 0.9° field will produce a very sharp drop in CFF when it is moved 3° from the fovea; using the natural pupil, on the other hand, will produce the opposite effect.

The importance of surround and the adaptation state of the eye on CFF can be exemplified by the results of an experiment by Lythgoe and Tansley (1929). The presence of a steadily illuminated surround which is matched in luminance to the Talbot level of the flickering target will insure that the area surrounding the flickering field is subject to the same level of stimulation, minimizing any spatial contrast effect on CFF which may result from any boundary effects between the flickering and surround fields. Lythgoe and Tansley investigated target luminances ranging from 0.003 to 7 mL and found that indeed CFF is influenced by surround luminance. They also found that CFF changes with light and dark adaptation. In general, light adaptation tends to increase and dark adaptation to decrease CFF, both in the fovea and the periphery.

The effect of the temporal distribution of light within a full cycle of variation has been investigated and found to be a major variable controlling CFF. Most of the work in flicker has been done with a rectangular wave form, the light and dark portion within a cycle of alternation being equal. Lengthening or shortening the duration of the light pulse will increase or decrease respectively the time-average, that is, the Talbot level of luminance. Therefore, the adaptation level of the eye will fluctuate as a result of changes in the light-time fraction. However, if compen-

sations are made at the light source by amounts appropriate to the relative duration of the light pulse within the cycle, average luminance can be held constant for any light-time fraction. Lloyd and Landis (1960) studied the effect of light-time fraction on CFF for a wide range of basic luminance values. The results indicated that when the average luminance is held constant, fusion will occur at lower frequencies as the light pulse becomes longer relative to the dark portions of the cycle. That is to say, at a given repetition rate, if a short light pulse produces flicker, lengthening it will produce fusion, provided the luminance of the pulse is decreased to hold the average amount of light within a cycle constant. The results are generally different when the luminance of the light pulse is held constant. In this case, an increase in the relative duration of the light pulse will first produce fusion, a further increase will reinstate flicker, and the longest pulse within a cycle will produce fusion once again. As would be expected, the area, the luminance of the stimulus, and its retinal location interact with the effect of light-time fraction in determining fusion.

Fusion frequency is also influenced by the shape of luminance variation. For example, Ives found that CFF was highest for square wave, lower for triangular, and lowest for sinusoidal variations.

Any waveform which regularly repeats itself can be considered [to be composed of] a fundamental frequency and a series of harmonics [which can be] analyzed into sinusoidal components, whose amplitude and phase relations can be calculated by the Fourier analysis technique. Ives applied the principles of Fourier analysis to flicker in 1922. In his experiments he used several waveforms and analyzed each into various sinusoidal components, showing that for a given average luminance, flicker will occur when the fundamental sinusoidal component reaches a certain level. Ives (1922) and Cobb (1934) urged the use of sinusoidal wave forms in the study of flicker mainly because, unlike other wave forms, sinusoids are composed of one frequency; but it was not until the 1950's that the pioneering work of deLange (1958) described the conditions under which a sinusoidally modulated light appears to flicker. This type of light variation is now widely used in flicker research.

Sinusoidal modulation is represented schematically in Figure 15–13. Light intensity, L, varies by amount, a, at a frequency, f, around an average level, L_o. Despite changes in the amplitude, a, and frequency, f, of variation, L_o remains a constant. Modulation, m, is expressed as a percentage of L_o; for example, in Figure 15–13 two values of m, 50 percent and 75 percent, are shown.

In flicker experiments using sinusoidal modulation, the rate of flicker is usually held constant, and m is adjusted by the subject until he can detect or no longer see flicker. What is changed, then, is not frequency, as was the situation in older studies, but the amount of light variation. This procedure is repeated at different frequencies and the threshold amount of light variation for flicker detection is plotted as a function of frequency. The resulting curves are called temporal modulation transfer functions, or flicker sensitivity curves.

Figure 15–14 represents deLange's data showing typical flicker sensitivity curves for various L_o levels obtained with a 2° field centrally located in a very large 60° steadily illuminated surround whose luminance matched the average luminance, L_o, of the flickering field. It seems that the ability of the visual system to detect temporal variations in light depends both on

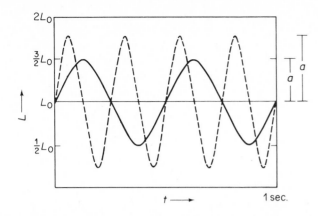

Fig. 15-13. *Schematic representation of sinusoidally modulated light. L varies by an amount, a, always around an average level, L_o, which remains constant despite changes of a and of frequency, f. Modulation, m, is expressed as a percentage of L_o, $m = a/L_o \times 100$. The solid line shows sine wave modulation of $f = 2 Hz$, $m = 50$ percent; and the broken line, $f = 4 Hz$, $m = 75$ percent.*

the amount and the frequency of variation. For example, in viewing 1 Hz flicker, more than 1 percent variation of the 100 troland (a measure of retinal illuminance) light is necessary to detect flicker, while at a rate of 10 Hz, only 0.5 percent variation

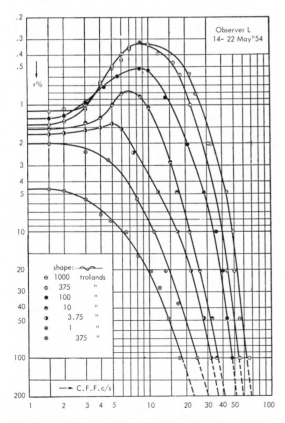

Fig. 15-14. *Flicker sensitivity curves for $L_o = 0.375$ to 1000 trolands.* [de Lange 1958]

is sufficient to see the field as flickering. At higher frequencies threshold modulation increases rapidly; that is, sensitivity decreases until at some frequencies even 100 percent modulation is not enough to detect the flicker. Figure 15–14 also illustrates how the average luminance, L_o, influences flicker response. It shows that the total range of frequencies to which the visual system is sensitive becomes narrower as L_o approaches very low levels.

Many of the data obtained by varying the frequency of square wave flicker have been reworked in terms of the results obtained with sinusoidally modulated light. As an example, Kelly (1964) takes the data of Bartley and Nelson (1961) on the effect of light-time fractions on CFF, and he attempts to show how the results would have been predicted by transforming the square wave stimulus with different light-time fractions to its sine wave equivalent.

DeLange (1961) compared flicker sensitivity to sinusoidally modulated light with sensitivity to square wave modulation. He found that, for frequencies above 10 Hz, the amount of variation needed to see flicker was the same regardless of the waveform. It can be inferred from this that the visual system does indeed respond to the fundamental frequency of a waveform. His experiments also show that at frequencies below 10 Hz a smaller percentage of variation is needed to see flicker if a square wave rather than a sinusoidal variation is used. It would appear, therefore, that at low frequencies flicker detection with any waveform depends not only on the fundamental frequency, but also on the higher order harmonics.

The low frequency portion of the flicker sensitivity curve is especially subject to the effects of size of the field and other spatial characteristics of the stimulus. It has been shown, for example, that if the field is large enough to include most of the peripheral retina, sensitivity to low frequencies is markedly depressed while sensitivity to high frequencies is somewhat elevated. The amount of variation needed to detect low frequency flicker in small foveal fields can also be manipulated by the presence or absence of a surround or a dark edge between the flickering field and the surround (Levinson 1964). It appears that the spatial distribution of light on the retina controls sensitivity to low frequency flicker.

Various models (Levinson 1968) have been put forth to account for both the low and high frequency portions of the flicker sensitivity curves. Most of them have regarded the visual system as analogous to a series of electronic filters which pass low frequencies unchanged but attenuate high frequencies. The results of experiments pose difficulties for these models, because it has been shown that under most conditions low frequencies are attenuated also. Complicated models have been proposed to account for the low frequency behavior, and electronic networks have been built which simulate neural networks and which can reproduce the psychophysical data.

It is very clear that the visual system limits its response to frequency of light variation at some location. Some earlier formulations were based on the breakdown of photosensitive material during the light cycle and the photosynthesis which takes place during the dark cycle. Accordingly fusion would occur when the decrease in concentration of the photosensitive products is offset by its increase in the dark phase (Hecht and Verrijp 1933b). Yet the very strong effect of spatial interactions on response to flicker argues for the existence of a neural component, perhaps retinal, in determining CFF. However, ERG and

Mote & Keesey

cortical-evoked potential studies in man do not clarify the question of location, for electrical responses from both the eye and the occipital region of the skull can be recorded which show the same frequency as the frequency of the flickering light up to the subjective CFF. (See *Documenta Ophthalmologica*, Volume XVIII, 1964, for a recent account of related studies.) There are some electrophysiological findings from acute animal preparations which indicate that the visual system up to the cells of the lateral geniculate body will respond to higher frequencies of stimulation than the cortical cells (Grüsser and Saur 1960). This would argue for a cortical limitation of the flicker response. In summary, the question of the basis of flicker response has not yet been clearly answered.

Brightness Discrimination

Brightness discrimination, when it is considered broadly as a property of the visual system, has to do with the recognition of luminance differences in the environment. However, it is the determination of the least luminance difference, the differential luminance threshold, which is posed as the experimental problem. The situation may be described in general terms as follows: for a field of given luminance, L_1, what must be the luminance, L_2, of another field in order that the luminance difference, ΔL, can just be detected? The L_1, or simply L, field is known as the adapting field, the one at L_2 as the test, or ΔL, field. In the limiting case where the adapting field has zero luminance, the value of the test field is the absolute threshold. When the adapting field is above zero, the test field luminance may be greater or less than that of the adapting field; in the latter case ΔL is the just detectable decrement. Almost always, however, it is the value of the ΔL increment which is sought.

In most experiments the adapting and test fields are similar in shape and are presented to the same region of the retina. A configuration commonly used is that in which the adapting field is circular and a smaller concentric test field is superimposed upon it. This arrangement is used not only for investigations using field sizes that are maintained constant throughout the experiment, but also for many studies which seek to determine how variations in the areal interrelationships of the two fields affect the differential threshold. In another arrangement, the bipartite configuration, the adapting field is circular and the semicircular test field is superimposed on one half.

The measurements obtained in brightness discrimination experiments are the luminance values of the test field, which increase as the adapting field luminance increases. However, by reason of its historical significance in connection with Weber's law, as well as because of its theoretical significance, the ratio of ΔL and L, $\Delta L/L$, is important. This ratio is usually considered an index of discrimination sensitivity: when $\Delta L/L$ is small, discrimination is fine ("good"); when it is large, discrimination is gross ("poor").

The Weber relationship is $\Delta L/L = C$. In most experiments, since the range of adapting luminance is large, $\Delta L/L$ is plotted as a function of log L. This is the form in which König and Brodhun (1889) presented the results of their classic experiment, which are displayed in Figure 15–15. This graph, and most others are similar to it in their form, shows that $\Delta L/L$ is large at low levels of adapting luminance; it then decreases and for a considerable range it is nearly horizontal to the log L axis.

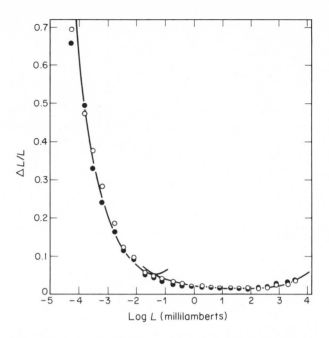

Fig. 15-15. *The relation between $\Delta L/L$ to log L. Only over the range from about -0.5 to 2.5 on log L axis does the Weber law, $\Delta L/L = C$, hold approximately true.* [König and Brodhun, after Hecht 1934]

Such data provide the basis for the statement often seen that throughout the high luminance range Weber's law holds, but it is clear that when the whole range of adapting luminance is considered, the most obvious feature of the graph is that $\Delta L/L$ is not constant; for these data it varies by a factor of about 40. A similar result has been found in almost every brightness discrimination experiment in which an extensive range of adapting luminance was used.

If the luminance range is large and the ΔL test field falls upon retinal areas containing both rods and cones, the graph of the data plotted as log $\Delta L/L$ versus log L forms a segmented curve such as the one in Figure 15–16. The finding that the curves have two branches is taken as support for the duplicity theory. The left-hand segment, which extends over only the

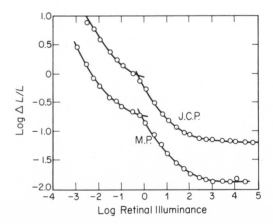

Fig. 15-16. *Brightness discrimination curves for two subjects showing division into rod (left hand) and cone (right hand) segments.* [Hecht, Peskin, and Patt, after Graham 1965; reprinted by permission of John Wiley & Sons, Inc. and the Journal of the Optical Society of America]

lower luminance range, shows that discrimination is gross and represents rod activity; the right-hand segment, encompassing the higher luminances, indicates finer discrimination and represents cone function. If only cones are stimulated, as is the case when the stimulus is confined to the fovea, the data obtained will tend to fall along the right-hand segment only.

The influence of size of test field upon brightness discrimination has often been studied using the concentric adapting and test field configuration. The results usually show that as the size of the test field increases, $\Delta L/L$ decreases; that is, discrimination improves. In many of the investigations the adapting field size is kept constant, and the threshold for various test field sizes is determined at different values of adapting field luminance. There are drawbacks when this procedure is used. For one thing, as the test field size is increased, the surrounding area of the adapting field is necessarily decreased, so that it may not be simply the variation in the test field area, but also interactions between changing test field-adapting field areas, which influence the results. Also, when a centrally fixated adapting field is large enough to include populations of both rods and cones, as the test field size increases from small to larger sizes, at first only cones—but then more and more rods—are brought into play as the boundary of the adapting field is approached. Further, sensitivity varies throughout any region of the retina of appreciable size, and this must be considered when the effect of test field size upon brightness discrimination is explored.

Graham and Bartlett (1940) avoided some of these complications by confining their stimuli to the fovea and taking measurements for circular adapting and test fields of equal size. After the S had adapted to an adapting field of a given size and luminance, the method of limits was used to determine the differential threshold for a concentric test field of the same size, presented in flashes of 30 msec duration. This procedure was repeated for the same fields at another adapting field luminance—and so on throughout that session—until the nearly 5 log units range of adapting field luminance was covered. At the next session measurements were taken for fields of a different size. The stimuli were small, ranging from 4 to 56 minutes visual angle. Their results agree with those of other studies on the influence of test field size upon brightness discrimination in showing that the product of area and luminance is approximately constant. For areas of the order of 30 minutes visual angle and smaller, this $LA = C$ relationship, Ricco's law, has been found to hold for stimuli at the absolute threshold. By making certain modifications of a formulation proposed to account for the absolute threshold data, Graham and Bartlett derived a quantitative expression which fits their brightness discrimination results reasonably well.

A part of Hecht's (1934, 1935) general theory of visual functions concerns brightness discrimination, for which he proposed an hypothesis and, later, another somewhat different one. The earlier one involves the establishment of two photostationary states. The luminance of the adapting field causes the breakdown of a photosensitive material in the receptors into its photoproducts; this is a "forward" reaction, whose rate depends upon the concentration of material and the value of the luminance. There is also a reverse, or "back" reaction, by which the photoproducts combine to reform the material as soon as they are produced. The two reactions proceed simultaneously until the overall rate of reaction approaches an equilibrium condition. This is the photostationary state. The crucial feature of this

hypothesis is the assumption that for any adapting field luminance, the differential threshold is determined by the value of the test field luminance which establishes a constant difference in the amount of photoproducts in the two fields.

Hecht's quantitative formulation of this hypothesis is as follows: Let L be the luminance, a the initial concentration of photosensitive material, x_1 and x_2 the concentrations of the breakdown products of the adapting and test stimuli respectively, m and n constants which refer to the orders of the reactions, and constants k_1 and k_2 the reaction rates. Upon the presentation of the adapting luminance, the forward reaction is

$$dx/dt = k_1 L(a - x_1)^m$$

The back reaction, which is independent of luminance, is

$$-dx/dt = k_2(x_1)^n$$

where the minus sign indicates that this one is opposite in sense to the forward reaction. In time the reactions approach the equilibrium condition so that the overall reaction rate will be

$$dx/dt = k_1 L(a - x_1)^m - k_2(x_1)^n = 0$$

Letting $K = k_1/k_2$, and rearranging, gives

$$KL = (x_1)^n/(a - x_1)^m = 0$$

This is the photostationary state equation. The test field luminance leads to the same condition, the expression for its photostationary state being

$$K(L + \Delta L) = (x_2)^n/(a - x_2)^m$$

The assumption that the differential threshold is reached upon the establishment of a constant difference in the amounts of photoproducts formed by the adapting and test field luminances is expressed by

$$\Delta L = x_2 - x_1 = C$$

By using appropriate values for the constants and for $x_2 - x_1$, Hecht derived expressions for $\Delta L/L$ which fit the data of König and Brodhun, among others. In these studies it is assumed that the adapting and test fields were presented for durations long enough to bring about complete adaptation to their luminances. To account for the results of studies in which this situation does not prevail, for example, when the adapting field is of long duration and the test field is a briefly presented added luminance, he proposed the second hypothesis. As before, in the adapting field there are both forward and back reactions and a photostationary state is established. The different feature of this hypothesis is that the differential threshold is determined by a critical rate of photochemical breakdown by the luminance of the test field at the moment it is presented. The equation for this condition is

$$dx/dt = k_1 \Delta L(a - x)^m$$

He found that the values for $\Delta L/L$ derived from this expression fit results obtained in experiments using test field presentations of short duration.

Graham and Kemp (1938) point out that such a formulation, which involves initial photochemical events, brings up the problem of how it may be related to the Bunsen-Roscoe law. They proposed a modification of Hecht's equation into the form

$$\Delta x / \Delta t = k_1 \, \Delta L (a - x)^m$$

where the increase in x, Δx, through a small but finite time, Δt, is proportional to the concentration of photochemical material at the photostationary state. Taking Δt as equal to the duration, t, of the test field leads to

$$\Delta x = k_1 \, \Delta L \cdot t (a - x)^m$$

If the Δx increment is assumed to be constant for any value of adapting luminance, the expression becomes

$$k_1 \, \Delta L \cdot t (a - x)^m = C$$

In this equation the duration of the test field is a variable. At a given adapting luminance, if the Bunsen-Roscoe law holds, $\Delta L \cdot t = C$ up to a critical duration, t_c, whose value depends upon the experimental conditions. For durations at and beyond t_c the relation changes to $\Delta L \cdot t_c = C$, which means the constant increment is determined within the limits of t_c.

In their experiment, Graham and Kemp investigated foveal brightness discrimination for a 5 log unit range of adapting field luminance and for test field durations extending from 2 to 500 msec. As seen in Figure 15–17, at a given adapting luminance, for durations of 2, 5, 13, and 30 msec, the value of log $\Delta L/L$ is highest at the shortest durations and decreases as duration increases. This is not the case for the 80, 200, and 500 msec durations; for all these the value of log $\Delta L/L$ is approximately the same at a given adapting luminance. The data show that up to a critical duration, which varies with the adapting luminance, $\Delta L \cdot t = C$ at all adapting luminances. For durations at and beyond the critical duration, time is no longer a variable and $\Delta L = C$. This does not mean the Bunsen-Roscoe law fails for long test field durations but that the event which determines the differential threshold is completed within a time shorter than the critical duration.

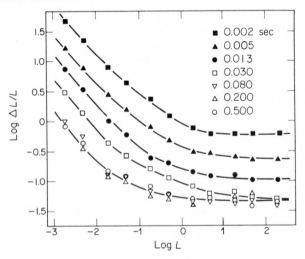

Fig. 15-17. *The relationship between $\Delta L/L$ for various durations of the ΔL stimulus, and at different adapting luminances.* [Graham and Kemp, after Graham and Ratoosh 1962]

Some formulations of brightness discrimination have been proposed which consider it as analogous to conditions of message transmission involving the detection of signals in the presence of background noise, where the test field increment is the "signal" to be discriminated and the adapting field, the "noise." The Poisson distribution is frequently used to describe the variability in the number of quanta absorbed from the increment and from the adapting field. In some experiments one of the approaches used by Hecht, Shlaer, and Pirenne (1942) in their measurement of the absolute threshold has been employed; that is, the psycho-physical method of constant stimuli has been used to measure the differential threshold at various levels of adapting field luminance and the obtained frequency of seeing curves compared to Poisson distribution curves. The value of the mean associated with the Poisson curve, which the frequency of seeing curve fits best, is taken to be the number of quanta required for the differential threshold. Mueller (1950) appraised several of these formulations and experiments and (1951) shows how some of their assumptions are not supported by the results of an experiment which he carried out for the purpose of testing them. In this study he determined the differential threshold by the method of constant stimuli at 9 values located throughout a 5.9 log units range of adapting field luminance. Some quantum theories require a linear relationship between log $\Delta L/L$ and log L; this he finds is not upheld by his results. Others suggest that the slope of the frequency of seeing curve is independent of the adapting field luminance. Mueller calculated the slopes for all his curves and found that they were approximately constant at the higher but decreased at the lower luminance levels. The number of quanta emitted from the adapting field during a given time is distributed according to a Poisson distribution, hence also the number, n_1, of quanta absorbed. The same holds true for the number, n_2, absorbed during the test field presentation. In some experiments it has been assumed that the difference, $n_2 - n_1$, is distributed as a Poisson variable. Mueller points out that this assumption is invalid: the distribution of differences from two Poisson variables is not a Poisson distribution. He also demonstrates that estimating the number of quanta for the differential threshold by comparing frequency of seeing curves to the Poisson distributions they best fit is equivalent to assuming that the ΔL increment is subject to quantum fluctuations but that the adapting field is not.

Cornsweet and Pinsker (1965) measured brightness discrimination with a stimulus configuration consisting of a small fixation light centered on the fovea and two circular test fields, each 50' in diameter, one located 1° above, the other 1° below, the fixation light. In one experiment the subject adapted to the fields, both at luminance L; one was then increased to $(L + \Delta L)$ for 3.6 msec, and back to L. The results usually found when this procedure is used were obtained: the Weber relationship did not hold true; the ratio $\Delta L/L$ was high for low values of L and did not become constant until L was several log units above the absolute threshold. In one of the other experiments, the eye was always in the dark-adapted state, with the exception that every 2 minutes the fields were presented for 4.5 msec in the L and $(L + \Delta L)$ configuration. In the third experiment the subject was adapted to the luminance L for both fields; these were then darkened for 5 seconds and re-illuminated, one at L, the other at $(L + \Delta L)$, for 4.5 msec, and after 3 seconds both returned to L. In these experiments the Weber law was found to hold from a luminance just above the absolute threshold up to the maximum attainable with the apparatus, a luminance range of about 5 log units. In two of the experiments the retina was adapted photochemically at the luminance level L, except for the period of 5 seconds darkness preceding the test flashes in the third experiment, a time considered too short for any appreciable photochemical change but long enough for any neural activity from the adapting luminance to cease so that the retina was in a relatively inactive state. The results obtained under these two conditions were different. However, when the retina was inactive—in one case because the eye was dark-adapted, in the other case because the illumination was turned off before the test flashes were presented—the Weber relationship was found to hold. The authors conclude that it is the state of neural activity of the retina, and not its state of photochemical activity, that determines whether or not Weber's law holds true.

Recently, as a result of his investigation of activity in the lateral geniculate body, Jacobs (1964, 1965) has proposed a neurophysiological hypothesis to account for brightness discrimination. Electrical recordings from this neural center show that there are two classes of cells which change their rate of firing when the luminance changes from the level to which the eye is adapted. One class, the "broad band excitators," shows an increase in rate when the luminance is raised, and a decrease when it is lowered. The response of the other class, the "broad band inhibitors," is just the opposite. Jacobs measured the responses of these cells to luminance increments and decrements around adapting luminances of 1, 2, 3, and 4 log units below 21.1 cd/m^2. The data indicate that there are systematic differences in the firing rate when adaptation to a given luminance level has taken place and that these differ for the two classes of cells. A cell exhibits good differentiation over a range of about ± 1 log unit around the adapting luminance, the magnitude of the change in firing rate being roughly proportional to the logarithm of the luminance change. One way the data were treated was to determine, for both classes of cells and for each adapting level, the luminance increment or decrement required to evoke a shift in firing rate of 3 per second, and this luminance value was taken as the ΔL. A plot of log $\Delta L/L$ versus log L produced curves similar in form to the usually obtained psychophysical functions for brightness discrimination. Jacobs considers two possible bases for brightness coding. One assumes that the summed total activity of both classes of cells to a given luminance shift provides the coding mechanism. The other, which he considers a more likely hypothesis, depends upon the character of the two classes of cells. A luminance shift, either incremental or decremental, evokes a shift in the firing rate of both types of cells, so that an excitator-inhibitor rate difference is established, and the greater the shift, the larger the rate difference. This hypothesis assumes that the coding of brightness change, and the magnitude of the change, is related to the magnitude of the firing rate difference.

Visual Acuity

Visual acuity is generally described as the capability of the eye to resolve detail. It is a visibility threshold which is specified in terms of the angle, or the reciprocal angle, subtended at the eye by the just discriminable critical feature of the object. This general description implies that there may be as many measures

of acuity as there are objects around us. Indeed, even under identical conditions of observation, the resolving power of the eye depends largely on the target used; that is, discrimination of a single dark line on a uniformly illuminated background constitutes a different acuity than the discrimination of alternate light and dark bars, both in the threshold value obtained and the type of judgment made.

A successful classification of acuity, advocated by Riggs (1965), is based on both the type of visual target and the judgment to be made about it. The vernier test target (see Figure 15–18a), for example, is composed of a line broken in the middle; the task of the observer is to localize correctly, to some percentage criterion, the direction of the displacement. Under the best conditions, vernier displacements of 2 to 3 seconds of arc can be just identified. Another type of acuity requires that the observer report the presence or absence of a single object on a uniform background, such as a single dark line or a spot on a bright background, or a single luminous line or spot on a dark background (Figure 15–18b). The best estimate of the just detectable single dark line is 0.5 second of arc. There is no limit in terms of angular size when the test object is luminous against a dark background, since in this case the acuity measurement is actually a determination of the absolute threshold.

The class of targets most generally used in acuity research are gratings consisting of alternate dark and light bars of equal width (Figure 15–18c). The observer is required to resolve the grating and sometimes to report the orientation of the bars. The critical dimension is the thickness of the black bar or, more correctly, the distance from the center of a black bar to the adjoining light bar. The best estimates of resolution are values as low as 40 to 50 seconds of arc. Two closely spaced bars or dots and checkerboard patterns also belong to this group of resolution targets.

Yet another type of acuity task depends upon the recognition and naming of a test object. The Snellen letters used in the clinic for over a century to evaluate the refractive power of the eye are the most familiar test targets in this category. The test chart is composed of progressively smaller letters which have lines and serifs whose thickness is one-fifth the height or width of the letter. The observer is required to identify the smallest letter he can see. Another test pattern used in the clinic, and sometimes in experimental studies of acuity, is the Landolt C, which is a circle having a gap equal to its thickness, which in turn is one-fifth the diameter of the circle (Figure 15–18d). The observer is required to indicate the direction of the gap; the acuity task, therefore, is a complex one requiring both recognition and resolution.

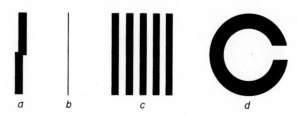

Fig. 15-18. *Acuity targets for the tasks of (a) localization, vernier off-set; (b) detection, single line; (c) resolution, square-wave grating; (d) recognition, Landolt C.*

Any of the psychophysical methods used in the measurement of acuity is limited to observers who can make a subjective judgment and articulate it. There have been some efforts made toward developing an objective measure of acuity which can be used for testing animals and very young children. A method called arrestovisiography induces pursuit movements of the eye by moving a large patterned target. These movements can be arrested by suddenly presenting an acuity target, a grating, for example, in the middle of the moving pattern. It has been found that if the grating cannot be resolved, the pursuit movements continue. Even if gratings finer than the arresting grating can be resolved under ordinary conditions, it appears that acuity measured by the Snellen chart shows a strong positive correlation to acuity measured by arrestovisiography (Vorpio and Hyrarinen, 1966). Another objective method which is being developed for the measurement of acuity had its origin in studies undertaken to determine the correlation between the electrical activity of the visual system and the subjectively determined visibility thresholds. In a typical experiment scalp electrodes are attached to the occiput and a proper reference site in order to record activity associated with the visual cortex. With proper electronic equipment many potentials can be averaged, a technique which brings out the small cortical response from the random background activity. When the observer is presented with a patterned light stimulus, for example, a checkerboard pattern, an averaged occipital potential is evoked with certain waveform and time course characteristics. It has been demonstrated recently that the amplitude of the late components of the evoked occipital potential are very sensitive to both the size of the checks in the pattern and the sharpness of focus of the pattern on the retina (Harter and White, 1968). Riggs (1969) has developed a new method whereby the bars making up the grating target can change position at regular intervals, thus eliciting a very small electroretinogram (ERG). It is found that the amplitude of the ERG diminishes as the stimulus contrast is lowered. These are two promising approaches which may lead not only to the development of an objective measure of acuity but also to the study of some of the physiological factors underlying the resolving power of the whole visual system.

There are a great many variables determining acuity which can be conveniently classified under two headings: (1) the physiological variables of the observer, and (2) field variables.

1. The image-formation properties of the eye and the characteristics of the retinal receptors, their size, and distribution are the major factors contributing to the resolving power of the whole visual system.

Excellent visual acuity does not mean that the optical system of the eye is perfect. The image on the retina bears little relation to the target in the object space since not only do the optical media scatter and absorb most of the light that is passed through the pupil, but sharp transitions from light to dark are lost because of the aberrations and refractive defects of the optical components of the eye. The diffraction pattern of the image as a function of pupil size has been known for a long time and now actual measurements of the retinal image are available (Figure 15–19a and b). These show that thin dark lines or bright lines in object space are imaged on the retina as a gradient of intensities covering many receptors. Similarly, a grating target with light and dark bars is imaged as a series of sinusoidal gradients. Using Fourier theory as applied to optics, image profiles of a great many targets can be derived, and it has been found that the optical performance of the eye is best with small pupils of

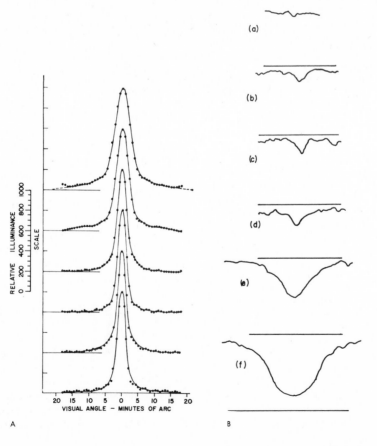

Fig. 15-19. *The left-hand column, A, shows light distribution in the image reflected from the retina formed by black bars of various widths. A 5 mm artificial pupil was used. From top to bottom, records show dips in light distribution caused by bars of width 1.0; 1.4; 2.4; 3.5; 7.5; and 21 minutes of arc.* [Westheimer and Campbell 1962.] *The right-hand column, B, shows reconstructed retinal images of a bright vertical line 1.6 minutes of arc wide for various pupil diameters, from top to bottom, 8, 7, 6, 5, 4, and 3 mm.* [Krauskopf 1962]

approximately 2 to 5 mm, which is also the range of pupil diameters for best acuity.

It has been known for a long time that acuity is best at the very center of the fovea where the small slender cones are packed very closely together and the center-to-center distance between two adjacent cones is about 25 seconds of arc. About 10 minutes of arc outside the center of the fovea, the density of the cones falls off by approximately 25 percent, and there is a similar reduction in acuity. As the retinal image falls farther and farther away from the center of the fovea, acuity becomes progressively poorer. The extraordinarily high acuity in the central fovea may be attributed to the low ratio of cones to optic nerve fibers in this region, whereas in the periphery, where rods predominate, the ratio of receptors to optic nerve fibers is much higher.

2. There are many field variables which influence acuity. For example, better acuity measures are obtained with long as compared to short exposure times. It has also been found that vernier acuity is finer when the lines that make up the target are long. The most important target parameter is perhaps luminance. It has been known since the late nineteenth century that acuity measured by a recognition task improves with increasing luminance (see Figure 15–20). Although the quantitative aspects differ for each acuity task—for example, there is a 3 log unit increase in detection acuity for a 7 log unit increase in luminance, whereas over the same range of luminances, acuity for gratings increases

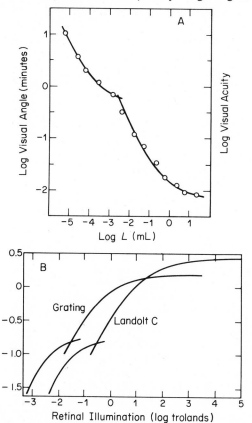

Fig. 15-20. *Relation of visual acuity to logarithm of retinal illuminance. A. Acuity is expressed as log visual angle subtended by the just detectable line. Threshold angle decreases, that is, detection acuity improves as illuminance is increased. [Hecht and Mintz 1939.] B. Acuity is expressed as the reciprocal of the log threshold visual angle. Both resolution acuity (grating targets) and recognition acuity (Landolt C) improve as a function of illuminance. [Shlaer 1937]*

by only 1.5 log units, and for the Landolt C by 2 log units—the shapes of the curves relating acuity to target luminance remain similar. The curves show, for the normal human eye which contains both rods and cones, a range of poor acuity for the rods, which function at the low luminance levels, and a range of progressively better acuity as luminance increases, signifying cone activity. In order to account for the relation of acuity to luminance, Hecht (1928) theorized that there is a normal distribution of thresholds within each group of receptors. As more and more light is available to the eye, a greater number of receptors become active, thereby providing a finer retinal mosaic for the discrimination of detail.

A later interpretation of the acuity-luminance relation depends on the quantum hypothesis of visual thresholds and the concept of receptive field size (Pirenne 1962). In a simplified version, this hypothesis can be summarized by stating that at low levels of illumination large receptive fields are operative because their size makes the probability of their catching the minimum number of quanta necessary for excitation greater than for the smaller receptive fields. Thus, at low luminance levels only large details can be discriminated. As luminance is increased, the probability of catching quanta in the smaller receptive fields improves, making resolution of fine details possible.

There is a large quantity of data gathered by electrophysiological methods in subhuman retinas which give unequivocal evidence for the existence of receptor fields. Such data reveal the immense summative properties of the receptors and show that one ganglion cell may be the final retinal conductor for the activity of thousands of rods. This kind of convergence is absent in the cone portion of the retina. Another important finding of electrophysiological studies is that at high levels of luminance the receptive field organization changes, so that the central summation region becomes surrounded by an inhibitory zone, effectively reducing the size of the summation area at high luminance levels (Barlow, Fitzhugh, and Kuffler 1957).

Much of the recent evidence for spatial summation and inhibition in the human visual system comes from Westheimer's work (1967). Perhaps the most important finding of his studies for visual acuity is that the area over which summation occurs is smaller in the cone portion of the retina than in the rod portion. There are also psychophysical data showing that in the human eye the summation region becomes smaller as luminance is increased. This evidence supports a receptive field hypothesis as the basis for the acuity-luminance relationship.

The effect of exposure duration on acuity follows the well-known intensity-time relationship which has already been discussed. Acuity improves as duration increases, up to a critical duration, t_c, which appears to be about 0.2 second in the Keesey experiments (Figure 15–21). For longer durations there is no improvement, and the determining factor is luminance.

The effect of target-to-background contrast on acuity can be simply expressed by saying that, at a given luminance level, acuity improves as contrast increases. Recently, the problem has received renewed attention and is being investigated by the use of spatial modulation transfer functions, or spatial contrast sensitivity curves. In order to obtain a contrast sensitivity curve, the spatial dimension of the test object is held constant and its contrast with the background increased or decreased until the subject can discriminate the object. A target frequently used is one in which the alternation in luminance of the grating from maximum to minimum varies sinusoidally, as in Figure 15–22.

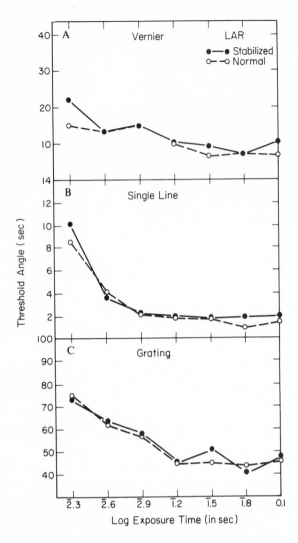

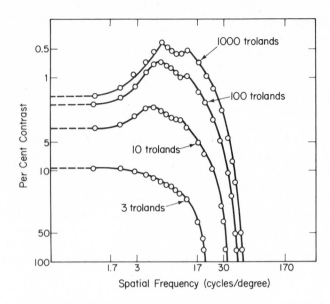

Fig. 15-23. *Contrast sensitivity curves. Contrast necessary for resolution of sinusoidal gratings for different mean retinal luminances, L_o, and spatial frequencies.* [After Patel 1966]

Fig. 15-21. *Effect of exposure duration of target and image stabilization on visual acuity, for the vernier (A), fine line (B); and grating targets (C). Acuity is expressed in terms of threshold visual angle of the critical aspect of the target. The broken lines depict acuity under viewing conditions when the normal motions of the image were allowed; the solid lines represent acuity under optical conditions which render the image stationary with respect to the retina.* [Keesey 1960]

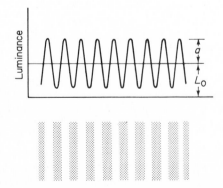

Fig. 15-22. *Sine wave grating and a plot of modulation. L_o, the average level of luminance, remains constant, while a varies around it. Percent contrast, or m, can be measured by one of the various formulas, for example, $a/L_o \times 100$. Spatial frequency in this figure is 9 cycles/degree.* [Fender and Gilbert 1966]

The number of cycles per unit distance along the grating is the measure of its frequency. The observer's task, for each spatial frequency, is to adjust the contrast by varying a around a constant luminance level L_o, until the grating can just be seen. The logarithm of the threshold contrast is then plotted as a function of the logarithm of the spatial frequency. Usually, threshold contrast is plotted as increasing downwards, so that the highest point designates maximum sensitivity. Figure 15-23 shows a typical contrast sensitivity function. It is seen that sensitivity to spatial distribution of light increases; that is, progressively less contrast is needed to see a grating, as spatial frequency increases. Beyond a maximum, however, smaller separations between the maxima and the minima of light distribution require more contrast in order to be resolved. Figure 15-23 also shows the effect of L_o on contrast sensitivity. A reduction in average luminance appears to reduce sensitivity; that is, the contrast needed to resolve a grating increases as average luminance decreases.

Although contrast sensitivity does not have to be measured by sinusoidal targets, those which have sharp transitions between light and dark are degraded by the optics of the eye into a blur on the retina, whereas a sinusoidal distribution of light in object space remains sinusoidal in retinal space, a situation which makes it easier to speculate about factors determining spatial resolution. In addition, according to the principles of Fourier analysis, the response, for example, the contrast sensitivity curve to all waveforms, can be synthesized from the response to the sinusoidal waveform, provided the criteria for linearity are met. It should be emphasized, however, that these criteria are not always satisfied, limiting the predictive value of sinusoidally distributed patterns.

The problem of how the visual system utilizes a blurred image on the retina so as to achieve a sharp and clear perception of targets has given rise to various theories of acuity.

Human visual acuity appears to be extraordinarily fine when the optical qualities of the eye and the dimensions of the retinal mosaic are considered. For example, a single line whose width is no more then one-fortieth the diameter of a cone can be

326   Perception

detected. Hecht and Mintz (1939) took diffraction into account and proposed that a target will be detected if its retinal image has enough of a "dip," or contrast (Figure 15–19a) to provide for the differential responding of the receptors. They calculated that the contrast contained in the retinal image of an object subtending 0.5 second of arc, which is the limit of detection acuity, provides a 1 percent difference in luminance between the central dip and the surrounding area, as shown in Figure 15–19a. They point out that 1 percent is also the limit of luminance difference for intensity discrimination. In its broadest interpretation, this theory states that acuity, for the detection task at least, is limited by the contrast in the retinal image and the differential thresholds of the receptors. It treats acuity as a special case of intensity discrimination, a point of view that has proved valid.

Hecht's theory belongs to the general class known as static theories of acuity, which are so named because no consideration is given to the movement of the image on the retina. The dynamic theories of acuity (Marshall and Talbot 1942), on the other hand, are based on the uncontrollable small continuous motions of the eye that are present even under conditions of concentrated fixation. The result of these motions is that the blurred retinal image is effectively moved over a retinal area of 10 minutes of arc and, in a typical 4–5 seconds of fixation, the image stimulates approximately 30 receptors (Riggs, Armington, and Ratliff, 1954). These movements are extremely important to vision, for when they are absent the perceptual experience is that the target fades and finally disappears (Riggs, Ratliff, Cornsweet and Cornsweet 1953). The main hypothesis of the dynamic theories of acuity is that the receptors lying under the steepest part of the image gradient are subjected to large temporal variations in luminance and, because of this, develop a stronger response than the receptors surrounding them. The theory also involves higher neural centers where further sharpening of the response occurs. However, in an experiment (Ratliff 1952) where eye movements were measured during short exposures of a grating target, correct identifications of grating orientation were found to be associated with the least amount of eye movements. In a later study, Keesey (1960), using an optical method developed by Riggs et al. (1953) and by Ditchburn and Ginsborg (1952) that renders the image stationary on the retina, obtained measures of fine line, grating, and vernier acuity. Exposure durations were short so as to avoid fading. Acuity measures were also obtained under normal conditions in which image movements were permitted. The results (Figure 15–21) show that acuity in the absence of retinal image movements has the same values for each exposure as acuity in the presence of image motions. The data do not support the hypothesis that the neural mechanisms for sharpening the image depend on temporal changes in stimulation over the receptors. Instead, it was proposed that a contrast-sharpening mechanism based on lateral inhibition forms the basis of acuity. This view stems from the findings of Ratliff (1965) on the Limulus eye, which show that neighboring receptors exert an inhibitory influence upon each other, the magnitude of the influence depending chiefly on the luminance differential on adjacent receptors and the separation between them. As a consequence of this situation, the response of the receptors in the transition zone between the evenly illuminated portion of the retinal image and the gradient will be most subject to inhibition; and the sum total of the response of the affected receptors will reflect in an exaggerated fashion the differences in retinal illuminance.

This neural interaction hypothesis can be used also to explain resolution acuity. It is possible by the use of a double slit pupil (Byram 1944), or interference fringes produced by coherent light sources, to bypass the diffraction errors of the eye and cast upon the retina diffraction-free square wave or sinusoidal gratings of any linear dimension (Campbell and Green 1965). Acuity for such a diffraction-free image, as measured by the smallest discriminable bar size, was found to be approximately 21 seconds of arc (Byram 1944). This value is close to the diameter of a single cone in the central fovea, and considerably lower than the value obtained with a normal diffracted image. Therefore, the ultimate limit of resolution acuity may appear to be the size of the elements in the retinal mosaic. Campbell and Green (1965) compared two contrast sensitivity curves, one obtained with an aberration-free sinusoidal pattern directly imaged on the retina, the other obtained with a sinusoidal grating imaged through the dioptrics of the eye, to get an estimate of loss of sensitivity due to the errors of diffraction and aberration. They found at high spatial frequencies the diffracted image contributed only approximately 25 percent of the reduction in contrast sensitivity. Their conclusion is that the quality of the optics of the eye is better than that indicated by ordinary methods and that the major factor determining resolution is the neural transmission network. Under normal conditions, however, both the dioptrics of the eye and the neural make-up of the retina must contribute to the resolving power of the visual system.

It has already been seen (Figure 15–23) that, at some medium spatial frequency, the contrast necessary to resolve the lines of a grating is minimal. The relative insensitivity of the eye to high spatial frequencies can be accounted for partly by the degradation of the image by the optical system and partly by the limitations of the neural network. However, contrast thresholds for resolution rise again for spatial frequencies lower than 5 cycles/degree. In this case, the optics of the eye cannot be responsible, because at these frequencies the loss of target contrast through the optical media is minimal. Fender and Gilbert (1966) suggest that at low frequencies the reduction in resolution may be because the stimulus pattern falls on retinal regions having wider interreceptor spacings. The widely spaced luminance maxima and minima in the target image may also bring inhibitory influences into play. The interpretation that inhibitory interactions are responsible for the decline in contrast sensitivity finds support in the experiments of Patel (1966) and Nachmias (1967) who showed that at low levels of luminance (Figure 15–23) and short exposure durations, there is no such decline. As has been pointed out, animal electrophysiology indicates that high levels of luminance are needed to bring out inhibitory effects. There are also data showing that inhibitory effects take a longer time to develop; therefore, any such influence would be expected to be minimal at short exposure durations (Ratliff 1965).

Vernier acuity has been more difficult to treat theoretically than either detection or resolution acuity. Perhaps the most successful formulation uses the concept of "mean local signs" (Weymouth, Andersen, and Averill 1923). Here the assumption is that each cone has a local sign, and that stimulation of adjacent receptors would shift the local sign to an average position, making it possible to distinguish very small differences in the position of two blurred lines on the retina. The stimulation of a great number of cones is the basis of this theory, and the fact that longer lines yield better vernier acuity is taken as corroborative evidence. Movements of the retinal image, resulting in the stimulation of more cones, are also necessary factors. Keesey (1960) showed that temporal factors are relatively unimportant for all acuities, including vernier. Therefore, it is reasonable to assume that, as for detection and resolution acuity, spatial interrelationships among receptors must also be important for vernier acuity.

References

General

DAVSON, H. (ed.). *The eye.* Vol. 2, *The visual process.* New York: Academic Press, 1962.

GRAHAM, C. H. (ed.). *Vision and visual perception.* New York: John Wiley, 1965.

Specific

ALPERN, M. Vision. In *Sensory Processes, Basic Concepts in Psychology Series.* Belmont, Calif.: Brooks-Cole Publishing Co., 1967.

ALPERN, M., and R. W. SPENCER. Variation of critical fusion frequency in the nasal visual field. *Archives of Ophthalmology*, 1953, *50*: 50–63.

BAKER, H. D. Initial stages of dark and light adaptation. *Journal of the Optical Society of America*, 1963, *53*: 98–103.

BARLOW, H. B., R. FITZHUGH, and S. W. KUFFLER. Change in the organization in the receptive fields of the cat's retina during dark adaptation. *Journal of Physiology*, 1957, *137*: 338–54.

BARLOW, H. B., and J. M. B. SPARROCK. The role of afterimages in dark adaptation. *Science*, 1964, *144*: 1309–14.

BARTLETT, N. R. Thresholds dependent on some energy relations and characteristics of the subject. In C. H. GRAHAM (ed.), *Vision and visual perception.* New York: John Wiley, 1965.

BARTLEY, S. H., and T. M. NELSON. A further study of pulse-to-cycle fraction and critical flicker frequency. A decisive theoretical test. *Journal of the Optical Society of America*, 1961, *51*: 41–45.

BAUMGARDT, E., and B. HILLMANN. Duration and size as determinants of peripheral retinal response. *Journal of the Optical Society of America*, 1961, *51*: 340–44.

BLOCH, A. M. Expériences sur la vision. *Comptes Rendus de la Société de Biologie*, 1885, *37*: 493–95.

BRINDLEY, G. S. The Bunsen-Roscoe law for the human eye at very short durations. *Journal of Physiology*, 1952, *118*: 135–39.

BYRAM, G. M. The physical and photochemical basis of visual resolving power. II. Visual acuity and the photochemistry of the retina. *Journal of the Optical Society of America*, 1944, *34*: 718–38.

CAMPBELL, F. W., and D. G. GREEN. Optical and retinal factors affecting visual resolution. *Journal of Physiology*, 1965, *181*: 576–93.

COBB, P. W. Dependence of flicker on the dark-light ratio of the stimulus cycle. *Journal of the Optical Society of America*, 1934, *24*: 107–13.

CORNSWEET, T. N., and H. M. PINSKER. Luminance discrimination of brief flashes under various conditions of adaptation. *Journal of Physiology*, 1965, *176*: 294–310.

CRAWFORD, B. H. Photochemical laws and visual phenomena. *Proceedings of the Royal Society, B*, 1946, *133*: 63–75.

——— Visual adaptation in relation to brief conditioning stimuli. *Proceedings of the Royal Society, B*, 1947, *134*: 283–302.

DAVY, E. The intensity-time relation for multiple flashes of light in the peripheral retina. *Journal of the Optical Society of America*, 1952, *42*: 937–41.

DE LANGE, H. Research into the dynamic nature of the human fovea-cortex systems with intermittent and modulated light. I. Attenuation characteristics with white and colored light. *Journal of the Optical Society of America*, 1958, *48*: 777–84.

——— Eye's response at flicker fusion to square wave modulation of a test field surrounded by a large steady field of equal luminance. *Journal of the Optical Society of America*, 1961, *51*: 415–21.

DITCHBURN, R. W., and B. L. GINSBORG. Vision with a stabilized retinal image. *Nature* (London), 1952, *170*: 36–37.

DOWLING, J. E. Neural and photochemical mechanisms of visual adaptation in the rat. *Journal of General Physiology*, 1963, *46*: 1287.

——— The site of visual adaptation. *Science*, 1967, *155*: 273–79.

FENDER, D., and D. S. GILBERT. Temporal and spatial filtering in the human visual system. *Science Progress, Oxford*, 1966, *54*: 41–59.

GRAHAM, C. H. Some fundamental data. In C. H. GRAHAM (ed.), *Vision and visual perception.* New York: John Wiley, 1965.

GRAHAM, C. H., and N. R. BARTLETT. The relation of size of stimulus and intensity in the human eye: II. Intensity thresholds for red and violet light. *Journal of Experimental Psychology*, 1939, *24*: 574–87.

——— The relation of size of stimulus and intensity in the human eye: III. The influence of area on foveal intensity discrimination. *Journal of Experimental Psychology*, 1940, *27*: 149–59.

GRAHAM, C. H., R. H. BROWN, and F. A. MOTE. The relation of size of stimulus and intensity in the human eye. I. Intensity thresholds for white light. *Journal of Experimental Psychology*, 1939, *24*: 555–73.

GRAHAM, C. H., and E. H. KEMP. Brightness discrimination as a function of the duration of the increment in intensity. *Journal of General Physiology*, 1938, *21*: 635–50.

GRAHAM, C. H., and R. MARGARIA. Area and the intensity-time relation in the peripheral retina. *American Journal of Physiology*, 1935, *113*: 299–305.

GRAHAM, C. H., and P. RATOOSH. Notes on some interrelations of sensory psychology, perception, and behavior. In S. KOCH (ed.), *Psychology: A study of a science.* Study II. *Empirical substructure and relations with other sciences.* New York: McGraw-Hill, 1962.

GRANIT, R., and P. HARPER. Comparative studies on the peripheral and central retina: II. Synaptic reactions in the eye. *American Journal of Physiology*, 1930, *95*: 211–27.

GRÜSSER, O.-J., and G. SAUR. Monoculare und binoculare Lichtreizung einzelner Neurone im Geniculatum laterale der Katze. *Pflügers Archiv für die gesamte Physiologie*, 1960, *271*: 595–612.

HARTER, R. M., and C. T. WHITE. Effects of contour sharpness and check-size on visually evoked cortical potentials. *Vision Research*, 1968, *8*: 701–11.

HARTLINE, H. K. Intensity and duration in the excitation of single photoreceptor units. *Journal of Cellular and Comparative Physiology*, 1934, *5*: 229–47.

——— The nerve messages in the fibers of the visual pathway. *Journal of the Optical Society of America*, 1940, *30*: 239–47.

HECHT, S. The relation between visual acuity and illumination. *Journal of General Physiology*, 1928, *11*: 255–81.

——— Vision: II. The nature of the photoreceptor process. In C. MURCHISON (ed.), *Handbook of general experimental psychology.* Worcester, Mass.: Clark University Press, 1934.

——— A theory of visual intensity discrimination. *Journal of General Physiology*, 1935, *18*: 767–89.

——— Rods, cones and the chemical basis of vision. *Physiological Review*, 1937, *17*: 239–90.

HECHT, S., S. SHLAER, E. L. SMITH, C. HAIG, and J. C. PESKIN. The visual functions of the complete colorblind. *Journal of General Physiology*, 1948, *31*: 459–72.

HECHT, S., C. HAIG, and G. WALD. The dark adaptation of retinal fields of different size and location. *Journal of General Physiology*, 1935, *19*: 321–39.

HECHT, S., and Y. HSIA. Dark adaptation following light adaptation to red and white lights. *Journal of the Optical Society of America*, 1945, *35*: 261–67.

HECHT, S., and E. U. MINTZ. The visibility of single lines at various illuminations and the retinal basis of visual resolution. *Journal of General Physiology*, 1939, *22*: 593–612.

HECHT, S., J. C. PESKIN, and M. PATT. Intensity discrimination in the human eye. II. Relationship between $\Delta I/I$ and intensity for different parts of the spectrum. *Journal of General Physiology*, 1938, *22*: 7–19.

HECHT, S., S. SHLAER, and M. H. PIRENNE. Energy, quanta, and vision. *Journal of General Physiology*, 1942, *25*: 819–40.

HECHT, S., and E. L. SMITH. Intermittent stimulation by light. VI. Area and the relation between critical frequency and intensity. *Journal of General Physiology*, 1936, *19*: 979–91.

HECHT, S., and C. D. VERRIJP. Intermittent stimulation by light. III. The relation between intensity and critical fusion frequency for different retinal locations. *Journal of General Physiology*, 1933a, *17*: 251–65.

——— Intermittent stimulation by light. IV. A theoretical interpretation of the quantitative data of flicker. *Journal of General Physiology*, 1933*b*, *17*: 266–86.

HYLKEMA, B. S. Examination of the visual field by determining the fusion frequency. *Acta Ophthalmologica*, 1942, *20*: 181–93.

IVES, H. E. Critical frequency relations in scotopic vision. *Journal of the Optical Society of America*, 1922, *6*: 254–68.

JACOBS, G. H. Single cells in squirrel monkey lateral geniculate nucleus with broad spectral sensitivity. *Vision Research*, 1964, *4*: 221–31.

——— Effects of adaptation on the lateral geniculate response to light increment and decrement. *Journal of the Optical Society of America*, 1965, *55*: 1535–40.

KARN, H. W. Area and the intensity-time relation in the fovea. *Journal of General Psychology*, 1936, *14*: 360–69.

KEESEY, Ü. T. Effects of involuntary eye movements on visual acuity. *Journal of the Optical Society of America*, 1960, *50*: 769–74.

KELLY, D. H. Sine waves and flicker fusion. *Documenta Ophthalmologica*, 1964, *18*: 16–35.

KÖNIG, A., and E. BRODHUN. Experimentelle Untersuchungen ueber die psychophysische Fundamentalformel in Bezug auf den Gesichtssinn. *Sitzungsberichte Preuss Akademie Wissenschaft, Berlin*, 1889, *27*: 641–44.

KRAUSKOPF, J. Light distribution in human retinal images. *Journal of the Optical Society of America*, 1962, *52*: 1046–50.

LANDIS, C. Determinants of the critical flicker-fusion threshold. *Physiological Review*, 1954, *34*: 259–89.

LEVINSON, J. Z. Nonlinear and spatial effects in the perception of flicker. *Documenta Ophthalmologica*, 1964, *18*: 36–55.

——— Flicker fusion phenomena. *Science*, 1968, *160*: 21–28.

LLOYD, V. V., and C. LANDIS. Role of the light-dark ratio as a determinant of flicker fusion threshold. *Journal of the Optical Society of America*, 1960, *50*: 332–36.

LONG, G. E. The effect of duration of onset and cessation of light flash on the intensity-time relation in the peripheral retina. *Journal of the Optical Society of America*, 1951, *41*: 743–47.

LYTHGOE, R. J., and K. TANSLEY. The relation of the critical frequency of flicker to the adaptation of the eye. *Proceedings of the Royal Society (London)*, 1929, *105B*: 60–92.

MARSHALL, W. H., and S. A. TALBOT. Recent evidence for neural mechanisms in vision leading to a general theory of sensory acuity. *In* H. KLÜVER (ed.), *Biological symposia*, Vol. 7, *Visual mechanisms*. Lancaster, Pa.: Jacques Cattell, 1942.

MOTE, F. A. Unpublished data.

MOTE, F. A., and A. J. RIOPELLE. The effect of varying the intensity and the duration of pre-exposure upon subsequent dark adaptation in the human eye. *Journal of Comparative and Physiological Psychology*, 1953, *46*: 49–55.

MUELLER, C. G. Quantum concepts in visual intensity discrimination. *American Journal of Psychology*, 1950, *63*: 92–100.

——— Frequency of seeing functions for intensity discrimination at various levels of adapting intensity. *Journal of General Physiology*, 1951, *34*: 463–74.

——— *Sensory psychology. In* R. S. LAZARUS (ed.), Foundations of modern psychology series. Englewood Cliffs, N. J.: Prentice-Hall, 1965.

NACHMIAS, J. Effect of exposure duration on visual contrast sensitivity with square wave gratings. *Journal of the Optical Society of America*, 1967, *57*: 421–27.

PATEL, A. S. Spatial resolution by the human visual system. The effect of mean retinal luminance. *Journal of the Optical Society of America*, 1966, *56*: 689–94.

PIRENNE, M. H. Visual acuity. *In* H. DAVSON (ed.), *The eye*, Vol. 2. New York: Academic, 1962.

RATLIFF, F. The role of physiological nystagmus in monocular acuity. *Journal of Experimental Psychology*, 1952, *43*: 163–72.

——— *Mach bands: Quantitative studies on neural networks in the retina.* San Francisco: Holden-Day, 1965.

RIGGS, L. A. Visual acuity. *In* C. H. GRAHAM (ed.), *Vision and visual perception.* New York: John Wiley, 1965.

——— Progress in the recording of human retinal and occipital potentials. *Journal of the Optical Society of America*, 1969, *59*: 1558–66.

RIGGS, L. A., J. ARMINGTON, and F. RATLIFF. Motions of the retinal image during fixation. *Journal of the Optical Society of America*, 1954, *44*: 315–21.

RIGGS, L. A., RATLIFF, F., CORNSWEET, J. C., and CORNSWEET, T. The disappearance of steadily fixated visual test objects. *Journal of the Optical Society of America*, 1953, *43*: 495–501.

RUSHTON, W. A. H. Rhodopsin measurement and dark-adaptation in a subject deficient in cone vision. *Journal of Physiology*, 1961, *156*: 193–205.

——— Increment threshold and dark adaptation. *Journal of the Optical Society of America*, 1963, *53*: 104–109.

——— The Ferrier Lecture, 1962: Visual adaptation. *Proceedings of the Royal Society, B*, 1965, *162*: 20–46.

RUSHTON, W. A. H., CAMPBELL, F. W., HAGINS, W. A., and BRINDLEY, G. S. The bleaching and regeneration of rhodopsin in the living eye of the albino rabbit and of man. *Optica Acta*, 1955, *1*: 183–90.

SHLAER, S. The relation between visual acuity and illumination. *Journal of General Physiology*, 1937, *21*: 165–88.

SPERLING, H. G., and C. L. JOLLIFFE. Intensity-time relationship at threshold for spectral stimuli in human vision. *Journal of the Optical Society of America*, 1965, *55*: 191–99.

VORPIO, H., and L. HYRARINEN. Objective measurement of visual acuity by arrestovisiography. *Archives of Ophthalmology*, 1966, *75*: 799–802.

WALD, G. On the mechanism of the visual threshold and visual adaptation. *Science*, 1954, *119*: 887–92.

——— Molecular basis of visual excitation. *Science*, 1968, *162*: 230–39.

WALD, G., and P. K. BROWN. Human rhodopsin. *Science*, 1958, *127*: 222–26.

WESTHEIMER, G. Spatial interaction in human cone vision. *Journal of Physiology*, 1967, *190*: 139–54.

WESTHEIMER, G., and F. W. CAMPBELL. Light distribution in the image formed by the living human eye. *Journal of the Optical Society of America*, 1962, *52*: 1040–45.

WEYMOUTH, F. W., E. E. ANDERSEN, and H. L. AVERILL. Retinal mean local sign; a new view of the relation of the retinal mosaic to visual perception. *American Journal of Physiology*, 1923, *63*: 410–11.

WOODWORTH, R. H., and H. SCHLOSBERG. *Experimental psychology* (rev. ed.). New York: Henry Holt, 1954.

There are many aspects to the visual stimulus, but color has always been one of the most striking. It has attracted the interest of men since the beginning of history. Even primitive man colored his drawings, and the technology of color rendition has advanced with the major civilizations of the world. However, man has only recently begun to understand color vision and the processes which contribute to it. Quantitative study of color vision took its origin with the researches of Newton who, using simple prisms, noted that a beam of white light can be split into a rainbow of colors and that these can be reconstituted to form white. He also discovered that if only two of the prism's colors are combined, a mixture having a color different from either may be obtained.

Analysis of color processes has since advanced at an ever-increasing pace. There was a rapid evolution of the psychophysics of color during the nineteenth century. The names of Young, Maxwell, Grassman, Helmholtz, Hering, Ladd-Franklin, and many others became well known. This evolution, continued into the twentieth century, has given rise to a variety of color theories, and the rapid advance of physiological techniques has made it possible to test the physiological basis of these more or less directly.

Definition. Because of the multidisciplinary concern with color, it is difficult to find a definition which provides a complete description of all of its meanings. The layman often equates color with hue, but the specialist is more likely to think of colors in terms of their hue, brightness, and saturation. Thus, the spectral composition of the stimulus and its luminance are of prime importance in psychophysical investigations of color and in color specification. It must be recognized, however, that almost any dimension of the visual stimulus can have some influence. An exact physical specification of a colored patch of light will seldom be sufficient to describe its appearance. Colors which are adjacent to one another either in space or in time will have a mutual effect on one another. All of the factors which influence color also condition the definition given to it. Since the word "color" is apt to be used in different senses by different researchers, published

J. C. Armington

Color Vision

16

reports must always be read carefully to see which meaning is implied. This chapter deals with some of the topics which are generally considered to fall under the heading of color vision.

Spectral Sensitivity

The visual literature is replete with curves and graphs which describe the actions of the eye under a variety of conditions. If one is to have a good understanding of vision, either from a practical or from a theoretical point of view, he must have a clear understanding of the commoner forms of data presentation as well as the experimental methods used to obtain them. This and the following sections will cover several of the major topics in color vision, giving particular attention to methodology and data presentation.

Spectral sensitivity curves are fundamental to color specification. They show how the sensitivity of the eye changes with the wavelength of a monochromatic stimulus. A quantitative indication of sensitivity is given by the reciprocal of the change in stimulus energy required to produce a constant visual effect. In general, any phenomenon can be described by a variety of measures, any of which can be taken as an index of sensitivity. The absolute threshold, or stimulus energy required to just be seen with the dark-adapted eye, is often taken as an index of visual sensitivity. Determinations may be made at different wavelengths because all stimuli close to threshold except those of long wavelength appear colorless when the eye is dark adapted. The scotopic spectral sensitivity curve is a plot of the reciprocal of threshold energy against stimulus wavelength. An example is given in Figure 16–1. Scotopic response has been shown to be governed by a single mechanism having its greatest sensitivity at about 500 nm.

If thresholds are measured for test flashes presented against a lighted background of moderate luminance, the eye's sensitivity, again defined by the reciprocal of the energy increment which can just be seen, will be lower. The maximum of sensitivity for the light-adapted or photopic eye will be found near 550 nm. A spectral sensitivity curve comparable to a threshold curve for the photopic condition also is shown in Figure 16–1. The difference between the maxima of the curves in Figure 16–1 provides an indication of the magnitude of the Purkinje shift.

The ordinate of a spectral sensitivity curve may be scaled in either linear or logarithmic units. However, logarithmic ones are to be preferred in many applications because the sensitivity scale covers a wide range of values, and a logarithmic presentation permits a better study of the ranges where general sensitivity is low.

There is one very important difference between photopic and scotopic spectral sensitivity curves that is not apparent in Figure 16–1. The visual effect produced by stimuli close to threshold is not the same in the dark- and in the light-adapted eye. Under scotopic conditions all threshold stimuli appear colorless and alike. Under photopic conditions they are colored. Thus, even though photopic thresholds are constant in the sense that their luminance is barely sufficient for detection, their effect is not the same in other regards. Stimuli above the threshold of the light-adapted eye can be distinguished on the basis of their hue. The photopic sensitivity curve only describes one aspect of the visual stimulus, its luminance. Changes in hue should not be regarded merely as hindrances to accurate measurement. The fact that

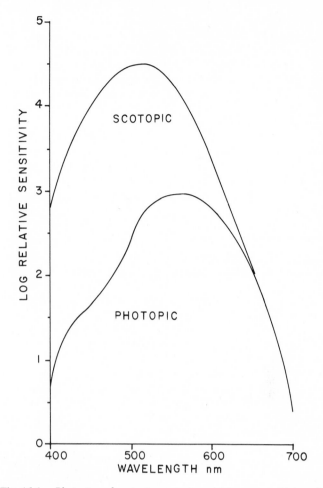

Fig. 16-1. *Photopic and scotopic spectral sensitivity curves.* [Adapted from Hecht and Hsia 1945]

different hues are seen along the photopic curve must mean that different processes contribute to it. It is a composite representation of several contributing receptor activities. One of the major tasks of color research is to identify and describe the processes which mediate photopic vision.

Other Procedures of Measurement. A wide variety of other methods, in addition to those described above, have been used for investigating photopic spectral sensitivity. It will be convenient to consider the methods examined here under three headings: (1) heterochromatic brightness matching, (2) flicker photometry, and (3) incremental threshold. Each has been developed with some specific purpose in mind; each offers its own problems of measurement; each provides results which differ to some degree from those of another.

Differences in hue and saturation can be a serious problem when measuring photopic spectral sensitivity, as has already been seen. This is especially true of heterochromatic matching. Heterochromatic matching typically makes use of two adjacent stimulus fields. One field, the standard, is fixed constant in luminance and in spectral composition. The wavelength and the radiance of the other, the comparison field, can be varied. The investigator sets the comparison stimulus to wavelengths spaced at intervals throughout the visible spectrum. The task of the observer is to find the luminance at each of these wavelength settings which equals that of the fixed field. To do this the observer must disregard the difference in hue of the two fields and base his judgment only on their brightness, a task which is not at all easy. The problem of hue difference may be overcome by using a step-by-step procedure of brightness matching. In this case the wavelength of the standard field is also adjustable. The first measurement is made with the wavelengths of the two fields close together so that there is only a small difference between them. Then, the standard is set to the same luminance and wavelength as that of the comparison; the comparison wavelength is advanced a small amount, and a second reading is made. These operations are cascaded until the end of the visible spectrum is reached. Ideally, the steps should be taken at very small progressive intervals along the wavelength scale so the differences in hue between the two fields never becomes detectable. This is not possible in practice because the eye is very sensitive to small differences. An extremely large number of steps would have to be taken. A compromise is made by using intervals which are close enough to keep hue differences from being too striking, but large enough to permit completion of the procedure in a reasonable length of time. The difficulty of the subject's task may be reduced by suitably arranging the stimulus field. If the standard and comparison stimuli are presented as a pattern of interlaced stripes, their difference in hue is less disturbing.

The method of flicker photometry reduces the problem of chromatic differences. It makes use of coincident standard and comparison fields which are alternated with one another so that the appearance is that of a single flickering field. The flicker rate must be carefully adjusted. It should be rapid enough so that the stimulus appears to flicker rather than alternate, but it must not be rapid enough to approach fusion. When the two fields are equal in luminance they differ only in hue and saturation so that flicker is at a minimum. The luminance of the standard is held constant while the spectral curve is being determined. The comparison field is set to various wavelengths, and the observer attempts to reduce the flicker by adjusting its luminance. Luminances of different wavelengths which yield a minimum flicker are deemed equal. They may be taken as a sensitivity index.

With simple threshold procedures the subject is required to detect a stimulus in the absence of any other visual input. They cannot be easily applied to many problems, however. Hence, the incremental method is often used to study photopic vision. It is a threshold procedure in which the subject is required to detect a test flash against a background field. Threshold test flashes of different wavelengths are taken to have the same luminance.

Figure 16–2 compares spectral curves made by three measurement procedures. The forms of each are similar, but significant differences remain. The spectral sensitivity curve determined by the threshold method is somewhat broader. The irregularities, humps, and shoulders which appear on all of the curves are more pronounced for the threshold method. These differences in form may result from differing involvements of the underlying mechanisms.

Luminosity and Abney's Law. The word "luminosity" is often used when reference is made to the spectral sensitivity of the eye. Luminosity may be defined as the reciprocal of the energy required to produce a constant brightness. It is clear that the form of the photopic luminosity curve varies depending upon the method used for its measurement, the luminance level at which

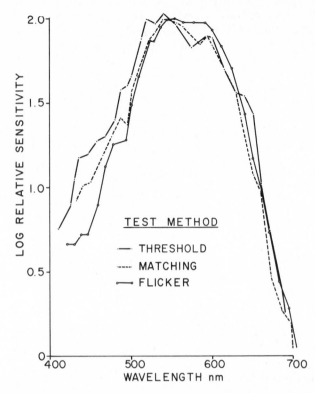

Fig. 16-2. *Photopic spectral sensitivity curves based upon three different testing procedures: flicker photometry, heterochromatic brightness matching, and absolute threshold.* [Redrawn from Sperling and Lewis 1959]

it is measured, and other factors. Nevertheless, the spectral sensitivity curve is sufficiently stable so that for many quantitative purposes it is convenient to regard it as a single function. An average curve based upon measurements from several laboratories has been adopted to permit a standardized specification of light and color. It is called the CIE (Commission Internationale de l'Éclairage) photopic luminosity function. Using this, it is possible to express the luminance of a visual stimulus by

$$L = k \int V_\lambda e_\lambda d\lambda \qquad [1]$$

where L is the luminance of the stimulus, V_λ is the luminosity function, e_λ is the energy distribution of the source, λ is wavelength and k is a constant which controls the units. This formulation says, in effect, that the luminance of the stimulus is the summation throughout the visual spectrum of the product of the eye's sensitivity at each wavelength and the energy available in the stimulus.

An important assumption behind this formulation is that of Abney's law. Abney's law states that the luminance of a mixture of two or more lights of different color is equal to the sum of their luminances. In other words, the law implies that the luminance contributions of component wavelengths to a total luminance are directly additive. Experimental investigations have not provided Abney's law with complete support. When, however, the component luminances which contribute the total luminance expressed by formula (1) are determined by matches based upon flicker photometry and when other conditions are met, Abney's law may show a reasonable degree of validity (Sperling 1958).

Components of the Spectral Curve. Although the luminosity curve often appears to be quite smooth and stable, some testing procedures bring shoulders and humps like those in Figure 16–2. Advantage may be taken of these in attempts to isolate component color processes. For example, several studies have shown that working at low luminance levels and using foveal stimuli of small angular subtense will bring out a strong secondary maximum in the red part of the spectrum. The delicacy of the procedure is clear because the wavelength at which the maximum appears varies from one study to another. That of Wright (1946) puts it near 600 nm while that of Sloan (1928) puts it at 580 nm. Conversely, in some cases very high energy levels may also bring out humps on the luminosity curve.

Relative spectral sensitivity is not uniform across the retina. There is a gradient of blue sensitivity across the retina, and it even extends within the fovea. Standard luminosity curves such as the photopic CIE function describe the central visual field. Relative blue sensitivity is higher in the peripheral regions. Measures made here, as in the example of Figure 16–3, exhibit a blue process of considerable prominence.

Perhaps the most pronounced alternation of the photopic spectral curve may be seen by measuring it against colored backgrounds. One of the most elegant results has been obtained by Stiles (1953) who proceeded by determining the incremental thresholds of colored test stimuli superimposed upon colored adaptation fields. A wide range of test and adaptation wavelengths was used. Although the fundamental data were families of curves relating differential thresholds to adaptation luminances, the analysis of these yielded spectral curves of the mechanisms which underlie color vision. Examples of these are shown in Figure 16–4. The first analyses carried out with this two color threshold technique revealed three cone processes, one of which is more sensitive to red, one to green, and one to blue light. More recent experiments have suggested a greater complexity.

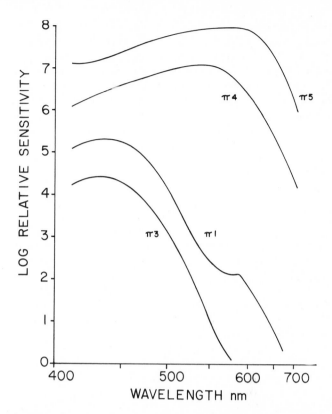

Fig 16-4. *Spectral sensitivity of color mechanisms.* [Adapted from Stiles 1953]

There are three blue mechanisms which have been given the noncommittal names of π_1, π_2, and π_3. The mechanism sensitive to the middle green part of the spectrum has been named π_4, and that whose sensitivity extends into the red, π_5. One of the blue mechanisms, π_2, is not shown in Figure 16–4 because its details have not yet been established, but it may be similar to π_1 and π_3 below 500 nm.

Several procedures have been developed for investigating spectral sensitivity under dynamic conditions while the eye is changing its state of color adaptation (Auerbach and Wald 1955; Boynton 1956). These also have demonstrated the compound nature of the photopic luminosity function.

Importance of Spectral Curves. It is difficult to provide a simple summary statement that encompasses all of our knowledge of photopic spectral curves. A significant property, however, is their remarkable stability under many testing conditions. Relative spectral sensitivity is so consistent, in fact, that a smooth average luminosity curve, the photopic CIE curve, has been adopted. It is of value in many practical situations. Individual spectral curves are seldom completely smooth. They are overlaid with several humps. Although some of these may reflect filtering exerted by colored substances in the ocular media, it is often assumed that the photopic spectral curve is compounded of at least three separate underlying processes. These may be brought out by a variety of testing procedures. The nature of these underlying processes and the manner in which they interact are fundamental to any understanding of color vision.

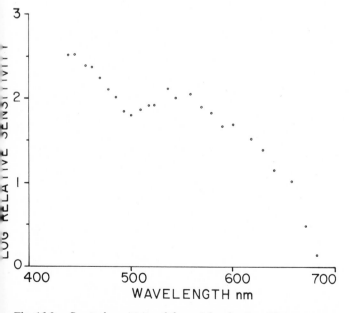

Fig. 16-3. *Spectral sensitivity of the peripheral retina. These measurements were made for test stimuli that were 45° away from the fovea.* [Redrawn from Weale 1953]

Color Addition

When scientists speak of color mixture, they usually refer to color addition of the sort discovered by Newton. He noted that beams of colored light may be combined to produce light having a color which is entirely different from either. His observations and those of subsequent investigators were later formalized into a system of laws of color mixture by Grassman. The essential nature of these may be understood by considering the arrangement for adding colors shown in Figure 16–5a. Three projectors throw superimposed red, green, and blue spots of light onto a reflecting screen. The light from these is identified as S_R, S_G, and S_B. For the moment, assume that the light projected by each is monochromatic, or at least highly saturated, and that the illumination produced by each can be adjusted independently. A fourth projector, S_U, produces a patch of light which is to one side of the patch produced by the others. The spot it produces is also colored but not of such a high saturation. Now, if the luminances of S_R, S_G, and S_B are adjusted appropriately, the spot of light they produce will be indistinguishable from that of S_U. Although the physical make-up of the two patches of light is completely different, they look exactly the same. The equality

produced may be expressed by the following equation:

$$L_U(S_U) \equiv L_R(S_R) + L_G(S_G) + L_B(S_B) \qquad [2]$$

This formulation states that L_U units of light S_U match the sum of L_R units of S_R, L_G units of S_G and L_B units of S_B. The identity sign, $\equiv$, signifies a complete match. The lights, S_R, S_G, and S_B, can be regarded as primaries, suitable proportions of which will match any of a range of colors. They can thus be used to provide a specification of a color whose properties are otherwise unknown.

Good matches will not be very frequent if the primaries are not well saturated for their combination will be too pale to match most stimuli. Furthermore, if S_U is a highly saturated monochromatic light, the arrangement shown in Figure 16–5a cannot produce a perfect match no matter how saturated the primaries may be. The combination they produce may be adjusted to resemble S_U in hue, but it will not be sufficiently saturated. Nevertheless, if the primary projectors are free to move so that their light can be mixed with S_U, it will be possible to produce two mixed patches of light which appear the same. Assume, for example, that the unspecified color is a rich blue-green such as would be produced by monochromatic light of 510 nm. A blue-green of like hue but lower saturation can be produced by adding the green and blue primaries together in the proper amounts. Now, if the red projector is turned so that its light is coincident with the unknown light, S_U, the latter can be desaturated so that it appears equal to the mixture of the green and blue primaries (Figure 16–5b). Of course, the luminances of the primaries must be adjusted appropriately to achieve a perfect match. This particular arrangement can be described as follows:

$$L_U(S_U) + L_R(S_R) \equiv L_B(S_B) + L_G(S_G) \qquad [3]$$

The red primary cannot be used to desaturate all colors. In some cases the blue or green primary would be needed. Provided that no one of the primaries can be produced by a mixture of the other two, however, it will always be found possible to match a combination of some two of them with a mixture of the unknown and the remaining one.

When red is used as a desaturating light, as in the example above, Equation 3 may be rewritten as:

$$L_U(S_U) \equiv -L_R(S_R) + L_B(S_B) + L_G(S_G)$$

Except for the minus sign, this is the same as Equation 2. Thus, Equation 2 may be used to describe color addition for all situations provided it is understood that algebraic addition is implied, and that one of the primaries on the right-hand side may assume a negative value. The often cited statement that any color may be matched by a suitable mixture of three primaries is incorrect, unless this qualification is taken into account.

Equation 2 is one of the most important formulations to be found in the field of vision. It states that any photopic stimulus can be described in terms of only three variables, and thus it implies that color information must be transmitted through a three-channel track at some level of the receptor system. The operations of color addition which it summarizes stand behind much of the speculation and experimentation of color vision.

Color Subtraction. Almost everyone is familiar with the techniques used by artists in mixing paints and pigments to

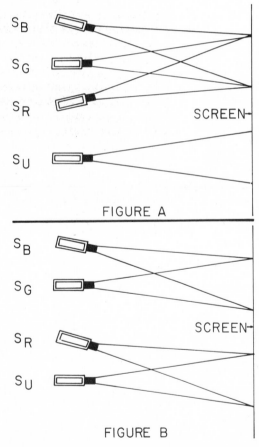

Fig. 16-5. *Arrangements of light projectors for producing additive color mixtures. In the upper half of the figure the rays from three projectors, S_B, S_G, and S_R, converge to produce a single patch of mixed light on the screen. It can be matched with the patch produced by projector S_U. In the lower half of the figure, projector S_R has been turned so that its light adds to that of S_U to produce a match as explained in the text.*

Perception

produce new colors. The rules which govern pigment mixture are not the same as those of color addition because a new principle, that of color subtraction, is involved. Pigments attain their color by absorbing light from some portions of the spectrum and reflecting other portions. The light reflected to the eye determines the pigment's color. When two pigments are mixed, a part of the light which is not absorbed by one may be absorbed by the other. Light of some wavelengths may not be appreciably absorbed by either. This light produces the resultant color. In color subtraction colors are removed from the light through selective absorption. The color of a pigment mixture is determined by the light which remains unabsorbed.

Chromaticity. The simple operations of color addition expressed by Equation 2 may lead to rather complicated mathematical formulations and scale transformations. Many of these are of great value both for theoretical and practical applications. An example is given by chromaticity, a concept used to refer to the hue and saturation of stimuli when their brightness is held constant. Chromaticity may be quantified with coefficients which give the *relative* proportions of the three primaries required to match a color. It is not the custom to apply the coefficients of Equation 2 directly. All of its terms are written with the same units of luminance, but this is not necessary. In practice, it is convenient to measure the primaries each with its own individual scale of luminance units. When this is done the number of units in the red, green, and blue primaries are called tristimulus values and are denoted by C_R, C_G, and C_B. The conversion factors which relate the tristimulus values to standard luminance units, such as foot-lamberts or millilamberts, depend upon the particular scales adopted. In general, they will not be the same from one study to another. Addition of the tristimulus values for the three primaries produces a resultant tristimulus value which is designated C_S.

$$C_S = C_R + C_G + C_B \qquad [4]$$

The units of C_S depend upon those of each of the tristimulus values.

The relative amount of each primary can be expressed as a fraction of the total luminance as follows:

$$c_1 = \frac{C_R}{C_S}, \qquad c_2 = \frac{C_G}{C_S}, \qquad \text{and} \qquad c_3 = \frac{C_B}{C_S} \qquad [5]$$

Adding these together algebraically, it is found that

$$c_1 + c_2 + c_3 = 1 \qquad [6]$$

These values, c_1, c_2, and c_3, are the proportions of the primaries needed to match or to produce any given stimulus. Thus, they describe its chromaticity and are known as chromaticity coordinates or as trichromatic coefficients. Because their sum is unity, only two are needed for stimulus specification. The third value is completely determined by the other two.

Since chromaticity can be specified by two coefficients alone, the third being entirely determined by them, all colors produced by simple stimulus mixture can be located within the bounds of a two-dimensional figure. An example for one set of primaries is given in Figure 16–6. The surface is enclosed by a curved triangular line known as the spectral locus because the colors of the

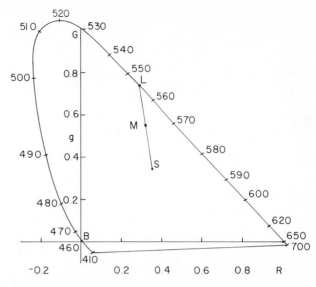

Fig. 16-6. *Chromaticity diagram. Spectral colors are located on the perimeter of this figure. Purples lie on the straight line joining the points at 410 and 700 nm.* [Adapted from Wright 1946]

spectrum are arranged in order along its path. It marks the chromaticity coordinates for the spectral colors. Purples are formed from mixtures of red and blue stimuli. Saturated purples lie on a straight line joining the violet and red ends of the spectral locus. All desaturated colors lie within the limits set by the curve. White light is located at point S near the center of the figure. The more saturated colors are, the closer they lie to the spectral locus; the less saturated they are, the nearer they lie to point S at the center. Colors whose coordinates lie outside of the spectral locus are more saturated than the spectral colors. They may be seen when there is color contrast.

Dominant Wavelength and Excitation Purity. Results from experiments with color mixture are conveniently expressed on the chromaticity diagram. For example, if the points representing two colors are plotted on the diagram, the color which results from their mixture will be located at some place between on the straight line which joins them. The diagram also makes it clear how any color can be described in terms of its dominant wavelength and purity. Suppose that one wishes to find these for the color represented by point M in the figure. A straight line is extended through M and point S to the spectral locus. The dominant wavelength is given by their intersection. The farther a stimulus is from point S, the more colored it will appear to be. Hence, its distance from white is a measure of the color's purity. The ratio of this distance to that of its dominant spectral wavelength from white SM/SL is defined as excitation purity.

In many cases an experimenter knows the spectral energy distribution of a stimulus and needs to calculate its chromaticity coordinates. The distribution coefficients, defined by the following formulae, make it possible to do this:

$$\bar{c}_1 = \frac{c_{1\lambda}V_\lambda}{I_\lambda}, \qquad \bar{c}_2 = \frac{c_{2\lambda}V_\lambda}{I_\lambda}, \qquad \text{and} \qquad \bar{c}_3 = \frac{c_{3\lambda}V_\lambda}{I_\lambda} \qquad [7]$$

In these equations the terms $\bar{c}_1$, $\bar{c}_2$, and $\bar{c}_3$ are the distribution coefficients. V_λ is the relative luminosity function, I_λ is a function which depends upon the luminous units involved and $c_{1\lambda}$, $c_{2\lambda}$ and $c_{3\lambda}$ are the chromaticity coordinates required to match monochromatic light of wavelength λ. Thus, the distribution coefficients are a transformation of the tristimulus values for monochromatic lights in which the relative spectral sensitivity of the eye is taken into account. A plot of distribution coefficients against wavelength is given in Figure 16–7a.

There is no unique solution for the distribution coefficients. Their value depends upon the primaries involved. The distribution coefficients merely describe the light mixtures which are required to match the spectrum in terms of the units and system under consideration.

There are many systems of coordinates, each based upon a particular set of primaries and units and each having its own merits. Thus, it is fortunate that data based on any given set of primaries and units can be transformed by calculation to another. Otherwise, it would be difficult to compare the results of different experimental studies. In fact, it is even possible to obtain systems based upon primaries which have no real physical existence. Although it may seem surprising, primaries which lie outside of the spectral locus are often useful in colorimetry. They make it possible to derive distribution coefficients which are not negative in any part of the spectrum. Based upon various considerations, one may adopt primaries whose distribution coefficients presume to describe the spectral response of the receptor mechanisms. When plotted against wavelength they yield the hypothesized spectral sensitivities of the color receptors. An example of fundamental curves is shown in Figure 16–7b. Note that unlike the curves in Figure 16–7a, they are positive at all wavelengths.

The methods of color addition and colorimetry have led to many sophisticated analyses, but it might almost be said that they are often more descriptive of the stimulus than of the visual system. The range of conditions examined is certainly limited.

The subject's principal contribution is that of a null detector, and the behavior of the visual system away from conditions of equilibrium is not usually considered. Furthermore, colorimetric observations are generally conducted with small stimuli which are centrally fixated and of relatively low luminance. Nevertheless, as already emphasized, the fact that successful measurements can be made using a system of three variables is of considerable importance. It leads to the nearly inescapable conclusion that all color information must travel through a three-channel filter at some level of its visual system. If this were not so, our color experience should be much richer than, in fact, it is. Many have postulated that the restriction is at the receptor level, and hence, much of the work in color vision has been a search for the spectral sensitivities of three fundamental cone processes.

Wavelength Discrimination. The accuracy of color measurement is closely tied to the ability of the eye to detect differences in hue. This ability may be measured in a variety of ways. One of the more common is that of asking the subject to compare two adjacent fields of monochromatic light. The experimenter sets one field at some fixed wavelength; the subject adjusts the other so that it is just barely different in color. The wavelength difference between the two fields is the difference threshold. Because colored stimuli are multidimensional, this procedure must be followed with care. It is important that the two fields be of identical luminance. Otherwise, the subject may inadvertently respond to a difference in brightness rather than hue. For this reason some of the published data, especially that of older studies, is inaccurate. With good control, results such as those given in Figure 16–8 are seen. The threshold for hue discrimination is low. Although not uniform it is less than 2 nm over most of the spectral range. The curve has definite minima in the

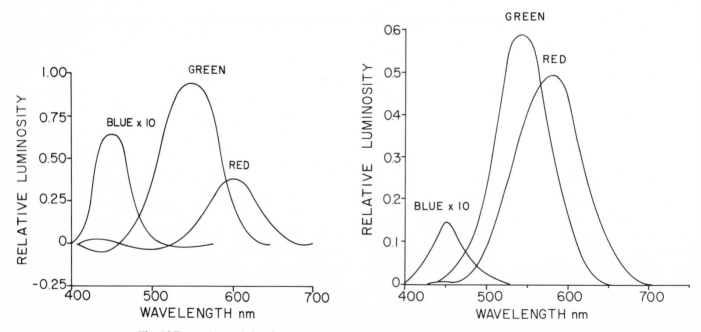

Fig. 16-7. *a. Spectral distribution curves in terms of monochromatic primaries at 650 nm, 530 nm, and 460 nm.* [Redrawn from Wright 1946.] *b. Fundamental response curves.* [Redrawn from Pitt 1944.]

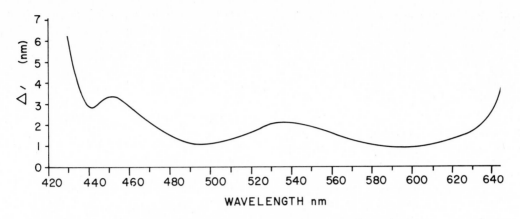

Fig. 16-8. *Hue discrimination curve.* [Redrawn from Pitt 1944].

spectral regions of optimal discrimination near 440–450, 490–500, and 580–600 nm.

Saturation. Excitation purity does not provide the only means of dealing with saturation. Several scales have been developed for its specification. Saturation being a complicated dimension, these scales are generally based upon different operations and are not isomorphic with one another. A mixture of monochromatic and white light is often used in experimental studies. In such cases it is convenient to describe the results in units of colorimetric purity. Colorimetric purity may be defined by the following expression:

$$P_c = \frac{L_\lambda}{L_w + L_\lambda} \qquad [8]$$

where L_λ is the luminance of the monochromatic light, L_w is the luminance of a white light which has been added to the monochromatic light, and P_c is the colorimetric purity. Colorimetric purity is thus the ratio of the luminance of the monochromatic light in a mixture to the total luminance. When the amount of monochromatic light added to the white light is barely enough to produce a result which is just noticeably different from white, the value given by P_c is known as the least colorimetric purity. This measure may be used to show that light in the yellow part of the spectrum is the least saturated of all monochromatic lights.

Color Appearances

Although color appearances are not completely disregarded, they tend not to be emphasized in classical psychophysics. The subject's manipulation of the stimuli rather than their reported appearance is of prime concern. There is a literature in visual perception which deals with color appearance. For example, the color constancies and color contrast have been studied extensively from this point of view. A good review of these topics may be found in Graham (1966). Two particular phenomena will be reviewed here: the altered appearance of small spots of light and the effectiveness of two primary projection systems.

An impoverished experience of color is produced by small spots of light, and it becomes extremely so when they are present-ed as threshold flashes of brief duration. In one experiment (Krauskopf and Srebro 1965) the subject was given repeated presentations of a brief pinpoint of light having a wavelength of 570 nm. Light of this wavelength usually appears yellow. The brief foveal exposures used here, however, never gave this result. The subject's responses indicated that the flashes appeared green on some presentations and red on others. One interpretation of the result is that the fovea only possesses red and green receptor mechanisms. There are no yellow ones. A small, short flash of light containing just a few quanta activates only one of the two mechanisms, and it is capable of eliciting only its fundamental response regardless of stimulus wavelength. Thus, either red or green is perceived. The data from small spot experiments may be analyzed for spectral sensitivity of the foveal red and green mechanisms. Spectral curves resulting from such an analysis show good agreement with several sets of fundamental response curves as well as with recent physiological evidence reviewed later in this chapter.

Two-color Projection. Any person who has attempted to make colored paintings or drawings will have noticed the profound changes which occur in the appearances of pigments as they are taken from the pallet and transferred to the canvas. The color of a stimulus is strongly dependent upon the context in which it is viewed. Land (1959) has developed a series of demonstrations which draw attention to important relational factors between different patches of light in a complex stimulus field. In one experiment, two photographic positives of a natural scene are projected upon a screen on top of one another and in register. One positive was originally photographed with a green glass in front of the camera lens; the other with a red. To produce the demonstration, the picture which was taken through the red filter is projected with red light. The other is projected with white. Thus, a picture is produced on the screen with a projection system having just two primaries, a red one and a white one. It might be expected that the resulting picture would appear in tones of desaturated pink, but this is not the case. The scene appears in nearly natural colors which are quite similar to those of the original. Land (1959) has suggested that his experiments, which certainly can be said to have generated a greatly renewed interest in color appearance, show that the classical laws of color mixture conceal the great basic laws of color vision. According to Judd (1960), on the other hand, the experiments provide a vivid demonstration of principles which have long been well-known, such as those of color contrast and constancy, certain effects produced by chromatic illumination, and a phenomenon which Helson (1943) has named "color conversion."

Colorblindness

It is not unusual to encounter someone who selects clothing of peculiar color or who has difficulty in distinguishing traffic lights. Approximately eight percent of the male population and a much smaller percentage of the female population are unable to distinguish colors in a normal manner. Some forms of colorblindness are acquired as a result of disease within the eye, but those which have held the most interest for theorists are inherited. Colorblindness is seldom total. Most colorblind persons retain some ability to distinguish lights on the basis of their spectral composition. Several forms of colorblindness are recognized. These may be classified according to the kinds of behavior exhibited in color mixing situations. A person with normal vision requires three primaries in order to match all of the possible colors as described above. Such a person is called a normal trichomat. Many colorblind subjects require only two primaries for color matches. Such persons are called dichromats. Dichromats can still discriminate differences in hue, but their ability is limited. A few subjects have such a severe difficulty that they cannot distinguish hue at all. These subjects, known as monochromats, can match any color with a single primary and presumably make use of only one fundamental response system. Thus, a basic separation of the colorblind may be made in terms of the number of primaries required to match colored stimuli.

This division can be carried further. According to the types of confusions made, dichromats may be classified as protanopes, deuteranopes, or tritanopes. There are several bases for this, but it will be convenient here to regard dichromatism as a reduced form of vision with an absence of one of the tristimulus fundamentals. According to this point of view, protanopes lack the first or red fundamental; deuteranopes lack the second or green fundamental; and tritanopes lack the blue. Recent evidence has given this idea good credence (Hsia and Graham 1957). The evidence is in the form of spectral sensitivity curves such as those shown in Figure 16–9 for protanopes and deuteranopes. Compared with a normal, the protanope has a low luminosity in the red part of the spectrum suggesting an absence of the red fundamental. The deuteranope is less sensitive in the middle and short wavelength range having lost the green process. Tritanopia is a rare form of color blindness, and the changes it produces are less well documented. Nevertheless, there is some evidence for reduced blue sensitivity in tritanopia (Wright 1952). Furthermore, all normal eyes are essentially blue-blind in the fixation area of the fovea. Wald (1967) has described the lowered blue sensitivity of this retinal area.

There is not complete agreement on the nature of deuteranopia. Most of the older measures show little difference between the luminosity curves of deuteranopes and normals. It used to be the custom, however, to normalize spectral data and to plot it in linear units of sensitivity. These procedures could conceal differences between normal and deuteranopic eyes. Willmer (1955) has suggested that there are two forms of deuteranopia, one of which shows a loss of luminosity as exemplified in Figure 16–9 and another in which there is no loss in luminosity even

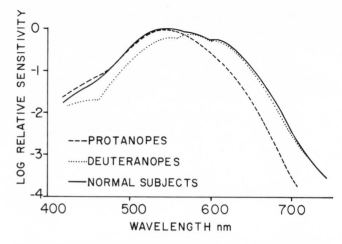

Fig. 16-9. *A comparison of the spectral sensitivity of the protanope and of the deuteranope with that of the normal eye.* [After Hsia and Graham 1957.]

though the subject still has difficulty in distinguishing red from green stimuli. This latter form could be called fusion deuteranopia.

Some colorblind subjects require three primaries for color matching as do normal subjects, but the proportions of the primaries they use are distinctly abnormal. Such subjects are said to be color-weak or color-anomalous. Anomalous subjects can be fitted into the same system of classification as can dichromats. Thus, three types of anomaly depending upon the specific character of the subject's weakness can be recognized. These are known as protanomaly, deuteranomaly, and tritanomaly.

Of course, colorblindness is an extremely complicated topic of itself. There is some evidence for defects that do not fit in with the scheme given here. For this reason other methods of classification are occasionally used, but none of these has found the same general usefulness either in practical or theoretical context.

Color Theory

During its long history, color vision research has produced an extensive collection of carefully worked out quantitative data. It is, therefore, no wonder that there have been many attempts to fit the data into a comprehensive theory. The number of approaches which have been attempted of itself provides a sufficient demonstration of the complexity of the task. Various models have been made, and each has given an account of some—but not of all—of the features of color vision. One of the first tasks presented to any color theory is to determine the number and the spectral properties of the mechanisms whose simultaneous action results in chromatic vision. Then the question arises as to whether these represent the spectral sensitivity of the receptors directly or some form of their interaction.

Color theories can be arranged according to the number of fundamental color mechanisms they postulate. The trichromacy of color mixture has led many theorists to three factor models. In fact, any theory of color vision must take color mixture into account. Most three-factor theories incorporate the following hypotheses:

1. Color vision is mediated by three receptor processes. Each of these has its own spectral sensitivity curve, total response of a process being defined by

$$J_i = k \int j_i P_\lambda d\lambda \qquad [9]$$

where J_i is the total response output of the mechanisms i; λ stands for wavelength; j_i describes the relative spectral sensitivity of the mechanisms; P is the energy distribution of the source and λ is wavelength; and k is a constant.

The spectral sensitivities of the three processes are the fundamental response curves. Mathematical transformation may be made between the primaries which are used in any given experiment and these curves.

2. The color of a stimulus depends upon the relative values of the three response outputs, J_1, J_2, and J_3.

3. Brightness depends upon some additive combination of the three response outputs. If Abney's law is assumed, as is often the case, linear addition is implied.

Three-factor theories have a number of desirable features. They provide a good, quantitative account of the results of color combination and can be related to data on wavelength discrimination and saturation. They point to hypotheses which can be tested using physiological procedures. The shoulders often seen on relative luminosity curves can be related to the fundamentals. The theories can also account for colorblindness. Protanopia and deuteranopia may be postulated to result from an absence of the red and green fundamentals, respectively. Thus, trichromatic theories can be compatible with data of the sort shown in Figure 16–9. They can be designed to give an account for fusion deuteranopia. This is done with the aid of the Fick hypothesis which proposes that the red fundamental and the green fundamental of the deuteranope are united within the same receptors.

Hering theory. Three-color theories have not yet given a complete account of all color vision phenomena. For instance, many observers report that yellow has a unitary, distinctive quality similar to that of red, green, and blue. Trichromatic theory fails to recognize this uniqueness of yellow light. It also has difficulty in accounting for the fact that the hue of monochromatic light shifts with luminance and in explaining some of the color perceptions experienced by the colorblind. These problems, particularly that of yellow's unique appearance, are partially met by the Hering theory. The theory proposes four distinct types of color response: red, yellow, green, and blue. It also postulates two achromatic types of sensitivity: white and black. These are arranged in three opposing pairs as follows: a red-green, a yellow-blue, and a white-black. The Hering theory may be classed as a four-factor theory because it postulates four chromatic processes. In another sense, however, it is trichromatic because there are three pairs of processes whose actions are mutually antagonistic.

The colors of the Hering system may be interpreted in terms of a color solid (Figure 16–10). The four chromatic responses are located at opposite points on the circumference of the solid in the manner of a color wheel. An axis in the third dimension is perpendicular to the plane of the wheel and passes through the center. It defines the degree of blackness or whiteness of a

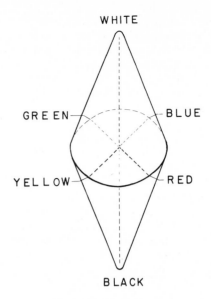

Fig. 16-10. *A color solid.*

stimulus. Colors of maximum saturation are found on the surface. Colors of lower saturation are found in the interior, the lowest saturation being closest to the center. Neutral gray is located at the very center of the structure. The color systems used to classify paints and pigments frequently can be traced back to such a color solid.

The location of colors such as yellow and blue or red and green on opposite sides of the surface helps account for the cancellation or neutralization of hue which occurs when they are mixed together. The theory states that the three pairs of response mechanisms produce actions which antagonize one another. The perceptions of white, red, and yellow are considered the result of dissimilative, breakdown processes, while blue, green, and black are assimilative, buildup processes. When opposed colors are mixed together in the proper proportions, the buildup and breakdown processes cancel one another and neither one is experienced.

The Hering theory does not have a long history of exact formulation. Because of this it has not been subjected to the same critical evaluation that has been given three-factor theory. This does not mean that specific quantitative statements of the Hering theory are not possible. One has, in fact, recently been formulated by Jameson and Hurvich (1955, 1956). Their detailed model is based upon careful experimental observations and will undoubtedly receive continuing attention in the future.

Trichromatic theory has been found of advantage in accounting for some color effects and Hering theory for others. Systems have evolved which incorporate features of both. These, known as zone or stage theories, state that trichromatic action is descriptive of vision at some level of the response system but that four-factor opponent function is more typical of others.

Retinex Theory. Color appearances in natural context have not been the major concern of most theories. Although most of the phenomena of color perception have long been recognized, they have not been easily fitted into a single experimental framework. Land's demonstrations have convinced some workers that new theoretical approaches are needed to deal with the phenomena of color appearance. The retinex theory, currently under development (Land 1965, 1967), is being formulated to meet this purpose. It stresses the importance of the relations between the patches of light that make up the entire visual field. It notes that the color of a patch of light in a complex array does not depend so much upon its energy and upon its spectral composition as it does upon its relations with other patches within the field. The retinex approach to vision assumes that there are three or more independent light-sensitive systems, each starting with a set of receptors peaking respectively in the long, middle, and short wave parts of the spectrum. Each system forms a separate "image" of the world. The images are never mixed but, instead, are compared, the comparison being between regions that, in the geometry of the outside world, are geographically corresponding. Since a complete account of the retinex theory is not yet available, an evaluation is not possible. In some respects it appears to be merely a restatement of the Helson-Judd color conversion principle. Nevertheless, it is likely to have considerable influence upon future work dealing with color perception.

Physiology of Color Vision

So far this discussion has been concerned with the results of psychophysical studies and the theories they have produced. Enormous advances have been made in the electrophysiology and photochemistry of the retina during the last two or three decades. These are beginning to make direct tests of color theory possible. Attention will now turn to the consideration of relevant physiological evidence.

Electrophysiological Methods: The Electroretinogram. A variety of electrical signals may be obtained from the visual system. These may be classed according to their time course as either slow wave or as fast (unit) responses. Alternately, they may be classed according to recording techniques as gross electrode or microelectrode responses. Each type of electrical response provides its own unique kind of information.

Since interest in color centers around the vision of man, it is a distinct advantage to be able to obtain electrical data from the human eye. The electroretinogram provides a way of doing this. This response is easily picked up with a gross electrode supported in a contact lens. Its complex waveform is produced by the combination of several components. Experimental procedures, which isolate components associated with photopic retinal activity from scotopic components, facilitate study of color phenomena. For example, when a single flash of red light is used to elicit the electroretinogram and when the eye's adaptation is carefully adjusted, a response like that shown in Figure 16–11 is obtained. An initial downward deflection, known as the A wave and signifying negativity of the lens electrode, is followed by two positive waves. Being relatively large and easy to measure, the positive waves are more easily subjected to experimental examination. The first positive wave, often called the X wave, is a result of photopic activity. The second, the scotopic B wave, is released by activity of the rods. There are several methods for obtaining isolated photopic components. One of the most effective is to use a recurrent stimulus flickering at a rate of 20 flashes per second or more (Dodt 1951;

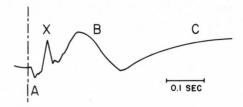

Fig. 16-11. *Components of the electroretinogram. The vertical dashed line marks the time of stimulus onset.*

Armington 1955). It produces a train of X waves alone since the scotopic response is more sluggish and has too long a time course to repeat itself at this rate.

The photopic nature of the X component may be proven by comparing its spectral sensitivity with the photopic luminosity function as has been done in Figure 16–12. But having established its photopic nature, the problem still remains of identifying underlying processes which may contribute to it. Electroretinal spectral curves may be overridden with humps and shoulders as are many psychophysical curves, and as with psychophysical curves, they do not provide unambiguous measures of the underlying color mechanisms of themselves. Special maneuvers must be taken to isolate color components. One of the more obvious has not been completely successful. It is the procedure of measuring the spectral sensitivity of the response under conditions of strong chromatic adaptation. In one experiment (Armington and Biersdorf 1956), the eye was exposed to a steady, strong red adaptation stimulus during the entire recording session. Responses were elicited by flickering test flashes spaced at intervals along the visible spectrum. These were always super-

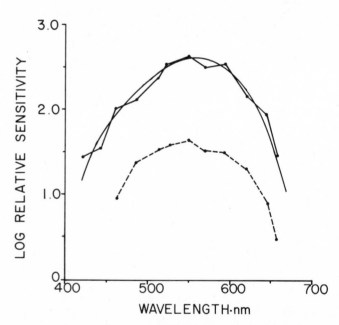

Fig. 16-12. *A comparison of psychophysical spectral sensitivity with that of the electroretinogram. Flickering stimuli were used to elicit the ERG. The smooth curve is a plot of Wald's (1945) psychophysical measures of the peripheral cones. Straight lines connect the points which describe the ERG. The lower dashed lines show the spectral sensitivity of the electroretinogram in the presence of a strong red adaptation field.* [Adapted from Armington and Biersdorf 1956.]

imposed upon the red background, the supposition being that the responsiveness to red test flashes would be reduced while that to light of other colors would be left relatively intact. A large selective depression of spectral sensitivity was expected, but not obtained (Figure 16–12). Red adaptation of high luminance produced a decrease in sensitivity uniformly throughout the spectrum. At best, small change in the sensitivity to long wavelengths relative to that of others could be discerned. The experiment was repeated with other adaptation colors, and none produced a marked selective depression of sensitivity. Recent experiments using modern response averaging procedures show that chromatic adaptation stimuli can produce small but definite selective reductions of spectral sensitivity (Padmos and van Norren 1971). Thus, this method may prove useful for isolating color processes in the future.

A more successful approach is to use stimulus fields having alternating stripes of color (Riggs, Johnson, and Schick 1966). The electroretinogram is not produced by flashing the stimulus on and off but rather by interchanging adjacent stripes. The stripes can be made to differ only in hue and saturation but not in luminance. The response is then elicited by the hue change alone. By using different sets of stripes covering a range of colors, rather detailed data can be obtained on the chromatic properties of the electroretinogram. An analysis indicated that the photopic human ERG can be best interpreted in terms of a trichromatic model. It has been found that the response can be described in terms of three coefficient functions which in some ways are similar to the trichromatic coefficients of psychophysics (Figure 16–13).

Another successful approach has been to investigate the ERG of color-blind individuals. Electroretinal spectral sensitivity curves of protanopes and deuteranopes show distinct changes from those of normal subjects. Protanopes have a loss of sensitivity in the red part of the spectrum and deuteranopes in the green. Thus, electroretinal spectral curves may be obtained which are comparable to the psychophysical ones for colorblind subjects shown in Figure 16–9 (Armington 1952; Copenhaver and Gunkel 1959; Dodt 1964).

There is every indication that improved methods for electrophysiological study of human color phenomena will continue to be developed in the future. For example, routine recordings of the human visually evoked cortical response may now be made using external scalp electrodes. Although this response which arises within the visual cortex tends to be quite erratic with present-day techniques, it is likely that improved procedures will appear in the future. Its spectral sensitivity has been determined and found to agree with the photopic luminosity function (Armington 1966; DeVoe, Ripps, and Vaughan 1968). There also is evidence that the response waveform depends upon the color of the stimulus. Its waveform may be different in subjects with various types of color-blindness (Shipley, Jones, and Fry 1968). Although much of the current work is of a qualitative nature, detailed accounts of color processes at the evoked response level are to be anticipated soon.

S-*potentials.* Electroretinograms and evoked potentials, when recorded as described above, are of considerable value for investigating the electrophysiology of color. These methods are of advantage because they can be used both in human and animal subjects without requiring any surgery and because they provide information regarding the action of rather large masses of neural tissue. Nevertheless, there are limitations to the information they can provide. Other techniques are required for obtaining detailed accounts of action within specific levels and structures of the visual system. Using surgical procedures it is possible to insert tiny needle-like recording electrodes, known as microelectrodes, within the retina or the brain. Although these electrodes are obviously limited to use with animal subjects, they do make it possible to record activity arising in small local retinal regions.

Microelectrode technique owes much to the pioneering work of Granit and Svaetichin (1939) who developed it for fast, spike potentials from single neurons. Subsequent research has shown that microelectrodes also may be used to investigate local slow potentials. One type of slow retinal response is called a graded

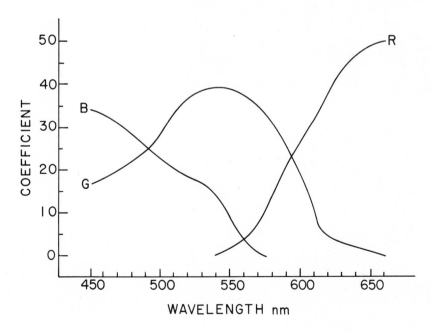

Fig. 16-13. *Coefficient curves which may be used to determine the relative magnitudes of electroretinograms elicited by changes in stimulus color.* [Redrawn from Riggs, Johnson, and Schick 1966.]

potential. The S-potential, named after its discoverer, Svaetichin, is a photopic graded potential having considerable interest for color theorists. This step-like response may be obtained from fish retinas. It appears as a steady potential which is maintained as long as the stimulus light remains on (Svaetichin and MacNichol 1958). Although the exact sites of origin of the S-potentials have not been determined, they are believed to arise in "compartments" near the outer plexiform layer and in the bipolar layers of the retina. Three types of compartments have been distinguished on the basis of their functional performance, their electrical polarity, their wavelength sensitivity, and their depth within the retina. These are the luminosity compartment, the red-green compartment, and the yellow-blue (also termed green-blue) compartment.

The interesting behavior of the S-potentials may be understood by first considering the responses from a red-green compartment. These have an electrical sign which depends upon stimulus wavelength as may be seen in Figure 16–14. Long wavelength stimuli give a hyperpolarizing negative response; short wavelengths give a depolarizing positive one. Yellow-blue compartments respond in an opposite manner. They give depolarizing responses to long wavelengths and hyperpolarizing responses to short wavelengths. The performances of these color compartments are not just mirror images of one another. The maxima of response amplitude are not obtained at the same wavelengths. The largest short wavelength response of the red-green compartment occurs near 500 nm; that of the yellow-blue is near 450 nm. The third kind of compartment does not reverse its electrical sign. It hyperpolarizes to light of all colors and has a single sensitivity maximum. In a sense it is more complicated than the color compartments because it receives signals from all of the types of cones. All of these properties are appropriate to its designation as the luminosity compartment.

It is tempting to compare the performance of the S-potential with Hering color theory. Because one type of color compartment shows responses of opposed polarity to red and green while the other shows opposed responses to blue and yellow, their action appears to be that of the opponent mechanisms called for by the theory. The action of the luminosity compartment seems to account for the black-white axis of the color solid. However, the comparison should be made with caution. Psychophysical theory states that the wavelength loci of the four pure hues are independent of luminances, but the wavelength at which there is a transition from positive to negative responses in the S-potential does not seem to be independent of luminance. The compartments of any given type have similar, but not identical, spectral properties. Furthermore, it must also be remembered that the retinal organization of the fish producing these responses may be quite different from that of men.

Receptor Potentials. An exciting event has been the recent development of a technique for "harpooning" single cones of the carp retina with microelectrodes (Tomita et al. 1967; Kaneko and Hashimoto 1967). This makes it possible to record the response of a single retinal cone. Although the electrical waveform of cone responses are similar to those of S-potentials, the former is easily distinguished because it is smaller, always responds with the same sign, and is found at more peripheral depths within the retina. Only three types of cones having sensitivity maxima at 467 nm, 529 nm, and 611 nm have been identified with this recently developed method. This result suggests that fish have some form of trichromatic vision.

A second recent development has also attracted much attention. It has been found that a signal, known as the early receptor potential, can be recorded from the retinas of many species using gross electrodes and very intense light flashes (Cone 1964). A study of its spectra properties in the frog eye indicates that it, too, will be useful in analyzing color vision (Goldstein 1967).

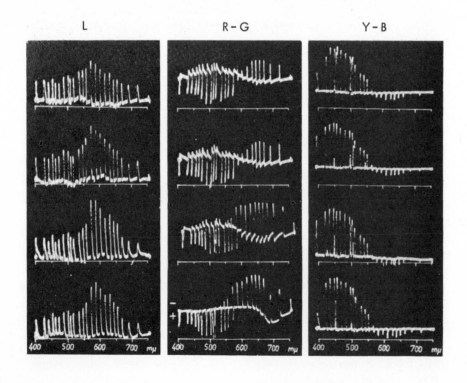

Fig. 16-14. *S potentials from the three types of compartments. The figures show the amplitude of the response as a function of wavelength. Each pulse is an S potential produced by briefly switching light of the specified wavelength on and off. Its square waveform does not show with this type of presentation. Only total response amplitudes are indicated, not their change with time.* [After Svaetichin 1956.]

Single-Unit Recording

Microelectrodes are useful for recording local slow wave responses, but they find their chief application in isolating unit potentials from single cells. An active neuron gives rise to electrical impulses which are transmitted along its axon membrane. Because all color information which travels from the eye to the brain must be encoded in this form, Granit's development of microelectrode techniques for retinal recording marked a real step forward in the electrophysiology of color. In early studies (Granit 1947), impulses were obtained from single ganglion cells by placing the electrode tip close to their body. The cells were tested in a variety of animal species to see how they responded to stimuli of different wavelengths and intensities. The results pointed to a complexity of retinal action that had hardly been anticipated. A bewildering variety of spectral curves were obtained. A partial understanding of their function was obtained by classifying them as modulators and dominators. Dominators had broad response curves which seemed related to the photopic or scotopic luminosity function for the species in question (Figure 16–15). The modulators, on the other hand, had narrow spectral response curves, thus seeming to be related to specific color mechanisms. Modulators were found with spectral maxima at a good many different positions in the spectrum depending upon species under examination and other factors. Granit made an attempt to arrange these into three categories which were assigned the names of red, green, and blue. However, other groupings could have been made as easily.

More sophisticated methods have since been applied to the collection and analysis of data from single retinal ganglion cells (Wagner, MacNichol, and Wolbarsht 1963). These studies have emphasized the fact that the message sent by any cell does not depend upon color alone. Adaptational factors, stimulus size, luminance, and other variables all exert their influence upon the response. A ganglion cell responds to stimuli falling anywhere within a limited retinal area called a receptive field. Some ganglion cells have fields which are said to have "on" centers. These cells produce a burst of impulses when a small stimulus imaged in the center of their receptive field is switched on. If the stimulus is moved to the edge of the field, an opposed action

is seen; the cell responds when the stimulus is switched off. Other cells have receptive fields with "off" centers and "on" surrounding areas. The antagonism of the center and the surround becomes even more evident with colored stimuli. The center of the receptive field is maximally sensitive to light of one wavelength and the surround to that of another. For example, a field may have an on center which is most responsive to red light and an off surround which favors green, or there may be an opposition between other pairs of colors. If stimuli are used which are large enough to fall on the center and the surround at the same time, both color processes will affect the response. The first investigations of ganglion cells did not take these interactions into account. Thus, they produced spectral curves which are not easily related to simple receptor processes.

The same microelectrode can be used to pick up slow potentials (local electroretinograms) of specific retinal areas and accompanying single spike discharges. The spectral sensitivities of both may then be determined and compared to see whether they offer the same information. One study indicated that these two responses have similar spectral sensitivities (Chapman 1962). Both were capable of providing nearly the same information. There were, however, small but significant differences in spectral detail.

Primate Vision. The visual structure and function of the monkey approaches that of man, with some species such as the macaque appearing even to have normal trichromatic sensitivity. Thus, they make unusually good subjects for comparison of electrophysiological and behavioral color vision data. They are intelligent enough to provide good psychophysical data, and they also can be subjected to physiological and surgical procedures that could not be safely attempted in humans. In an impressive series of studies, DeValois (1965) and his associates have collected extensive data relating single unit activity of the lateral geniculate body to color function. Broad-band cells and spectral opponent cells have been identified. Broad-band cells either show an increase (excitatory cells) or a decrease (inhibitory cells) in firing rate to stimuli of all wavelengths. They are believed to mediate brightness vision. Opponent cells show

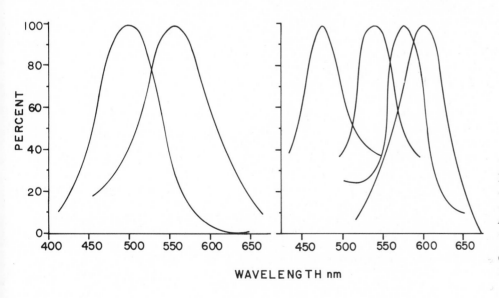

Fig. 16-15. *Dominator and modulator curves from the frog. The dominator curves shown on the left are for scotopic and photopic units. The modulator curves shown to the right are for blue, green, and two types of red units. [Adapted from Granit and Svaetichin 1939, and Granit 1947.]*

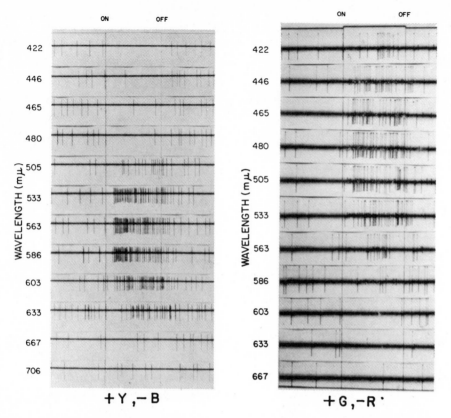

Fig. 16-16. *Examples of unit response from a +Y-B and a +G-R cell.* [After DeValois 1966.]

excitation at some wavelengths and inhibition at others. Two types of opponent cells have been discerned. One is facilitory to long wavelength stimulation and inhibitory to short, while the other is inhibitory to long wavelengths and facilitory to short. Examples of these which in some respects are like the opponent ganglion cells of the retina are shown in Figure 16–16. The spectral sensitivity of the broad-band units is quite similar to the human photopic luminosity curve. This supports the conclusion that they mediate brightness sensitivity. The opponent cells, on the other hand, do not respond as much to changes in luminance as they do to changes in wavelength (DeValois, Abramove, and Jacobs 1966). Thus, they seem to mediate color sensitivity. An analysis of the properties of the opponent cells permits derivation of curves resembling human psychophysical functions such as those for wavelength discrimination. Modern methods of animal psychophysics also permit direct comparison of physiological and behavioral data from the same species.

As in the retina, the response of single units at the geniculate body may be governed by several stimulus parameters acting together. For example, the same unit may be sensitive to changes in wavelength, luminance, and the size and shape of the stimulus field. If all stimulus dimensions are taken into account, description of color sensitive cells in the geniculate body becomes quite complicated (Wiesel and Hubel 1966). A distinction must still be made at this level of the visual system between the central area of a receptive field and its more or less annular adjacent area because here, too, the center and the surround are often opposite in their response characteristics. Wiesel and Hubel describe several types of cells having antagonistic center-surround arrangements. Some cells increase their firing rate when stimulated with white stimuli of small diameter centered upon their receptive field but decrease their rate when presented with larger stimuli extending into the antagonistic surrounding area.

The spectral sensitivity of the center and the surround of a receptive field are not the same. The opponent color action of a cell depends upon the distribution of light within its receptive field.

Interpretation of single unit data is difficult not only because a multitude of variables exert their influence but also because many different kinds of units are seen. Only small samples of each of these cell types have been examined. Yet, there is sufficient evidence to indicate that some form of opponent activity is present within the nervous system. In fact, Daw (1967) has shown that center-surround relations exist even at the retinal level of the goldfish, a finding that could explain color contrast. Since electrophysiology is in an early stage of development and since it is inherently more complicated than psychophysics, most available data are not sufficiently systematic to be used in a detailed test of color theory. Nevertheless, the results which are available do suggest that color function can be described in some form of trichromatic model at the early stages of the receptor process. This information is then recoded in terms of complex opponent mechanisms at higher levels.

Photopigments. Vision is initiated through the absorption of light energy by photopigments contained within the receptors. In the case of scotopic vision, the absorption process is quite well understood. A light-catching pigment known as visual purple is contained within the rods. When visual purple is bleached by light, the rods are activated. Visual purple can be extracted from the outer rod segments using well-known biochemical procedures and subjected to experimental study in the test tube. Since human vision is trichromatic, there must be at least three other pigments in the cones. Since these pigments have never been extracted, their identity and properties are less clear. Yet there are procedures which make it possible to gain information regarding their behavior. Recently, two optical methods have been developed which permit spectral study of cone pigments within the receptors. These are known as reflection densitometry and microspectrophotometry. These methods provide a complement to the recording procedure of Tomita et al. mentioned above.

The method of reflection densitometry, developed through the efforts of Rushton and Campbell (1954) and of Weale (1953a, 1959), permits measurement within the intact living eye and can thus be used with human subjects. A measuring light is directed through the pupil and imaged upon the receptors of the fovea. There, a fraction is absorbed by the photopigments within the cones. The rest is either reflected or it goes through the receptors without being caught. The actual amount of light absorbed by the photopigment depends upon the degree of its bleaching. A small proportion of the non-absorbed light is reflected through the pupil back out of the eye. This proportion, which may be detected with an elaborate array of optical and electronic devices, is not fixed; it depends upon the amount absorbed by the receptors. More light is absorbed by an unbleached than by a bleached photopigment. Thus, if one compares the amount of light that is reflected from the fovea when it is dark-adapted with the amount reflected when the pigments have been bleached away through light adaptation, he can obtain an indication of the pigments' absorption. Furthermore, if monochromatic measuring lights are used, spectral determinations may be made. Two foveal cone pigments have been identified. One is a pigment sensitive to long wavelengths and known as erythrolabe. The other is a middle wavelength or green sensitive pigment known as chlorolabe. A third pigment, cyanolabe, is believed to exist in some of the cones of the human retina, but the method of retinal densitometry has not been adequate for revealing its properties.

Spectral curves of erythrolabe and chlorolabe are given in Figure 16–17. It is interesting to note that these pigments are obtained in isolation in dichromats (Rushton 1963, 1965). Deuteranopes, lacking the green sensitive pigment, show the foveal spectral sensitivity curve of erythrolabe. Spectral sensitivity of the protanope is that of chlorolabe. A comparison may be made between these photochemical spectra and some of those of psychophysics. The spectrum of erythrolabe agrees fairly well with Stiles' π_5 mechanism. That of chlorolabe provides a reasonable match with the green sensitive π_4 mechanism.

Microspectrophotometry. The method of microspectrophotometry is not suitable for use with living eyes, but it does permit measurement with single cones. With this method the retina is removed from the eye, and the transmission of single receptor cones or of a small cluster of them is measured before and after bleaching of the photopigment. Just as in reflection densitometry, the difference in spectral transmission provides a measure of the spectral absorption of the photopigment which has been bleached away. It is a technical feat of first magnitude to be able to make measurements in this way. The receptors have extremely small dimensions, and the quantities of pigment involved are not great. Since the measuring light produces some receptor bleaching of itself, delicate care is required and data collection must be followed by a rather sophisticated analysis. Thus, data which is available today must be regarded rather tentatively. Despite this, the method is providing results. Eyes of several species, including those of monkeys and of man, have been examined (Marks, Dobelle, and MacNichol 1964; Brown and Wald 1964). Spectral curves obtained from a population of primate and human cones seem to cluster into three groups (Figure 16–18). One group has a spectral sensitivity close to that of erythrolabe; the second has a spectrum like that of chlorolabe; and the third provides the only clear-cut photochemical demonstration of cyanolabe. Its spectrum is reasonably similar to that of Stiles' π_1 or π_3 mechanism.

Electrophysiology and photochemistry both seem to provide a good basis for trichromatic theory at the receptor level. The spectra revealed by microspectrophotometry agree well with the electrophysiological measurements made by Tomita and his associates on single cones. Despite some uncertainty in the existing data, no method has yet revealed more than three receptor processes. Thus, although our present knowledge may be modified in the future, today it is reasonable to conclude that there are three cone pigments, cyanolabe, chlorolabe, and erythrolabe. These pigments are not mixed, but they likely inhabit separate

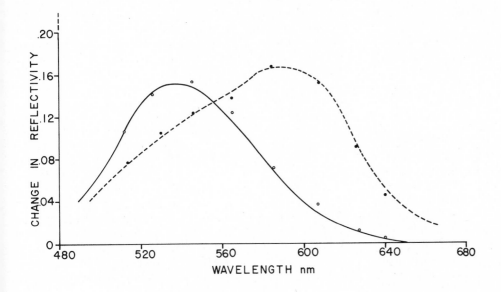

Fig. 16-17. *Spectral curves for erythrolabe and chlorolabe.* [Redrawn from Rushton 1962]

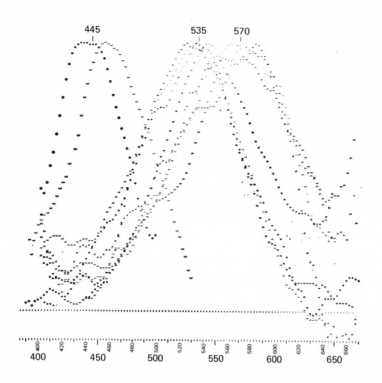

Fig. 16-18. *Spectral curves for ten individual primate cones based upon measures made with a recording microspectrophotometer.* [From Marks, Dobelle, and Mac-Nichol 1964.]

cones. If a fourth receptor type is discovered, a considerable revision of current theoretical ideas will necessarily follow.

Summary

This chapter has attempted to draw attention to some of the principal data of color vision and to the theories which are used to account for them. In reality, color vision is an interdisciplinary study including a vast range of subtopics and areas of interest. It is interesting to note that the contributions made by visual psychophysiologists in many of these areas have set the pattern for the physiological investigations which followed. Observations of early investigators indicated that color vision has three degrees of freedom. The implication was that color information must be restricted to three channels at some stage in the visual process. It seemed most reasonable to hypothesize three types of cone receptors, each with its own distinct photopigments and spectral process. Other psychophysical data pointed to more complex phenomena. It suggested that color information is channeled into a four variable color system together with at least one additional channel for mediating brightness information at higher neural levels. Although the first histological investigations as well as those of photochemistry and physiology failed to provide any foundation for the psychophysiological theories of color vision, this is no longer true. Electrophysiology has demonstrated a number of parallels between neural function and psychophysical indices of visual processes. It points to three receptor processes. These give rise at higher levels of neural action to much more complex, opposed color systems whose characteristics are influenced by many stimulus parameters in addition to those of wavelength. Recent photochemical methods also seem to have identified three photopigments each of which exists in a separate type of cone as predicted by psychophysical theory.

The effort of relating psychological, anatomical, physiological, chemical, and physical data is not an easy one. It is the one, however, which is likely to produce solutions to the problems of color in the future. The predictions and models made by the psychophysiologists did not provide unique determinations of the fundamental response curves. The data we have today are still in need of additional physiological support. Although there has been a great advance in our understanding of color vision, much still remains to be done. In fact, research with color naming and appearances has convinced many workers that the real problems of color vision are just being recognized. Perhaps the most significant experiments still lie in the future.

Acknowledgment. The preparation of this manuscript was supported in part by PHS Research Grant No. 5R01 NB07529-02 from the National Institute of Neurological Diseases and Blindness.

References

ARMINGTON, J. C. A component of the human electroretinogram associated with red color vision. *Journal of the Optical Society of America*, 1952, *42*: 393–401.

——— Amplitude of response and relative spectral sensitivity of the human electroretinogram. *Journal of the Optical Society of America*, 1955, *45*: 1058–64.

——— Spectral sensitivity of simultaneous electroretinograms and occipital responses. *Vision Research*, 1966, Supplement 1, 225–33.

ARMINGTON, J. C., and W. R. BIERSDORF. Flicker and color adaptation in the human electroretinogram. *Journal of the Optical Society of America*, 1956, *46*: 393–400.

AUERBACH, E., and G. WALD. The participation of different types of cones in human light and dark adaptation. *American Journal of Ophthalmology*, 1955, *39*, No. 2, Part II, 24–40.

BOYNTON, R. M. Rapid chromatic adaptation and the sensitivity functions of human color vision. *Journal of the Optical Society of America*, 1956, *46*: 172–79.

BROWN, P. K., and G. WALD. Visual pigments in single rods and cones of the human retina. *Science*, 1964, *144*: 45–52.

CHAPMAN, R. M. Spectral sensitivities of neural impulses and slow waves in the bullfrog retina. *Vision Research*, 1962, *2*: 89–102.

CONE, R. A. Early receptor potential of the vertebrate retina. *Nature*, 1964, *204*: 736–39.

COMPENHAVER, R. M., and R. D. GUNKEL. The spectral sensitivity of color-defective subjects determined by electroretinography. *American Medical Association Archives of Ophthalmology*, 1959, *62*: 55–68.

DAW, N. W. Goldfish retina: Organization for simultaneous color contrast. *Science*, 1967, *158*: 942–44.

DEVALOIS, R. L. Behavioral and electrophysiological studies of primate vision. *In* W. D. NEFF (ed.), *Contributions to sensory physiology*, I. New York: Academic, 1965.

DEVALOIS, R. L., I. ABRAMOVE, and G. H. JACOBS. Analysis of response patterns of LGN cells. *Journal of the Optical Society of America*, 1966, *56*: 966–77.

DEVOE, R. G., H. RIPPS, and H. G. VAUGHAN, JR. Cortical responses to stimulation of the human fovea. *Vision Research*, 1968, *8*: 135–47.

DODT, E. Cone electroretinography by flicker. *Nature*, 1951, *168*: 738–39.

—— Ergebnisse der Flimmer-Elektroretinographie. *Experimentia*, 1954, *X/8*: 330–32.

—— Elektrophysiologie der Netzhaut. *Bericht über die 66. Zusammenkunft der Deutschen Ophthalmologischen Gesellschaft in Heidelberg*, 1964, *66*: 14–22.

GOLDSTEIN, E. B. Early receptor potential of the isolated frog (*Rana pipiens*) retina. *Vision Research*, 1967, *7*: 837–46.

GRAHAM, C. H. (ed.), *Vision and Visual Perception*. New York: John Wiley, 1966.

GRANIT, R. *Sensory mechanisms of the retina*. London: Oxford University Press, 1947.

GRANIT, R., AND G. SVAETICHIN. Principles and technique of the electrophysiological analysis of color reception with the aid of microelectrodes. *Upsala Läkareförenings Förhandlingar*, 1939, *65*: 161–77.

HECHT, S., and Y. HSIA. Dark adaptation following light adaptation to red and white lights. *Journal of the Optical Society of America*, 1945, *35*: 261–67.

HELSON, H. Some factors and implication of color constancy. *Journal of the Optical Society of America*, 1943, *33*: 555–67.

HSIA, Y., and C. H. GRAHAM. Spectral luminosity curves of protanopic, deuteranopic and normal subjects. *Proceedings of the National Academy of Science*, 1957, *43*: 1011–19.

HURVICH, L. M., and D. JAMESON. Some quantitative aspects of an opponent-colors theory. II. Brightness, saturation, and hue in normal and dichromatic vision. *Journal of the Optical Society of America*, 1955, *45*: 602–16.

JAMESON, D., and L. M. HURVICH. Some quantitative aspects of an opponent-colors theory. I. Chromatic responses and spectral saturation. *Journal of the Optical Society of America*, 1955, *45*: 546–52.

—— Some quantitative aspects of an opponent-colors theory. III. Changes in brightness, saturation, and hue with chromatic adaptation. *Journal of the Optical Society of America*, 1956, *46*: 405–15.

JUDD, D.B. Appraisal of Land's work on two-primary color projections. *Journal of the Optical Society of America*, 1960, *50*: 254–68.

KANEKO, A., and H. HASHIMOTO. Recording site of single cone response determined by an electrode marking technique. *Vision Research*, 1967, *7*: 847–51.

KRAUSKOPF, J., and R. SREBRO. Spectral sensitivity of color mechanisms: Derivation from fluctuations of color appearance near threshold. *Science*, 1965, *150*: 1477–79.

LAND, E. H. Color vision and the natural image. Part II. *Proceedings of the National Academy of Science*, 1959, *45*: 636–44.

—— The retinex. *In* A. V. S. DE REUCK, and JULIE KNIGHT (eds.), *Colour vision: Physiology and experimental psychology*. Boston: Little, Brown, 1965.

—— Retinex theory of color vision. *Journal of the Optical Society of America*, 1967, *57*: 1428.

MARKS, W. B., W. H. DOBELLE, and E. F. MACNICHOL, JR. Visual pigments of single primate cones. *Science*, 1964, *143*: 1181–83.

PADMOS, P. and D. VAN NORREN. Cone spectral sensitivity and chromatic adaptation as revealed by human flicker-electroretinography. *Vision Research*, 1971, *11*: 27–42.

PITT, F. H. G. The nature of normal trichromatic and dichromatic vision. *Proceedings of the Royal Society of London*, Series B., 1944, *132*: 101–17.

RIGGS, L. A., E. P. JOHNSON, and A. M. L. SCHICK. Electrical responses of the human eye to changes in wavelength of the stimulating light. *Journal of the Optical Society of America*, 1966, *56*: 1621–27.

RUSHTON, W. A. H. The cone pigments of the human fovea in colour blind and normal. *In Visual problems of colour* (symposium held at the National Physical Laboratory on September 23, 24, and 25, 1957). London: Her Majesty's Stationery Office, 1958.

—— Visual pigments in man. *Scientific American*, 1962, *207*: 120–32.

—— A cone pigment in the protanope. *Journal of Physiology*, 1963, *168*: 345–59.

—— A foveal pigment in the deuteranope. *Journal of Physiology*, 1965, *176*: 24–37.

RUSHTON, W. A. H., and F. W. CAMPBELL. Measurement of rhodopsin in the living human eye. *Nature*, 1954, *174*: 1096–97.

SHIPLEY, T., R. WAYNE JONES, and AMELIA FRY. Spectral analysis of the visually evoked occipitogram in man. *Vision Research*, 1968, *8*: 409–32.

SLOAN, LOUISE L. The effect of intensity of light, state of adaptation of the eye, and size of photometric field on the visibility curve. *Psychological Monographs*, 1928, *38*, No. 173.

SPERLING, H. G. An experimental investigation of the relationship between colour mixture and luminous efficiency. In *Visual Problems of Colour* (symposium held at the National Physical Laboratory on September 23, 24, and 25, 1957). London: Her Majesty's Stationery Office, 1958.

—— Prediction of relative luminous efficiency from fundamental sensation curves. *Vision Research*, 1961, *1*: 42–61.

SPERLING, H. G., and W. G. LEWIS. Some comparisons between foveal spectral sensitivity data obtained at high brightness and at absolute threshold. *Journal of the Optical Society of America*, 1958, *49*: 983–89.

STILES, W. S. Further studies of visual mechanisms by the two colour threshold method. *Coloquio Sobre Problemas Opticos de la Vision. I. Conferencias Generales*. Madrid: Union International de Physique Pure et Appliquée, 1953, 65–103.

SVAETICHIN, G. Spectral response curves from single cones. *Acta Physiologica Scandinavica*, 1956, 39 suppl. *134*: 19–46.

SVAETICHIN, G., and E. F. MACNICHOL, JR. Retinal mechanisms for chromatic and achromatic vision. *Annals of the New York Academy of Science*, 1958, *74*: 385–404.

TOMITA, T. ET AL. Spectral response curves of single cones in the carp. *Vision Research*, 1967, *7*: 519–31.

WAGNER, H. G., E. F. MACNICHOL, JR., and M. L. WOLBARSHT. Functional basis for "on"-center and "off"-center receptive fields in the retina *Journal of the Optical Society of America*, 1963, *53*: 66–70.

WALD, G. Human vision and the spectrum. *Science*, 1945, *101*: 653–58.

—— Blue blindness in the normal fovea. *Journal of the Optical Society of America*, 1967, *57*: 1289–1301.

WEALE, R. A. Photochemical reactions in the living cat's retina. *Journal of Physiology*, 1953a, *122*: 322–31.

—— Colour vision in the peripheral retina. *British Medical Bulletin*, 1953b, 9: 55–67.

—— Photo-sensitive reactions in foveae of normal and cone-monochromatic observers. *Optica Acta*, 1959, *6*: 158–74.

WIESEL, T. N., and D. H. HUBEL. Spatial and chromatic interactions in the lateral geniculate body of the rhesus monkey. *Journal of Neurophysiology*, 1966, *29*: 1115–56.

WILLMER, E. N. A physiological basis for human colour vision in the central fovea. *Documenta Ophthalmologica*, 1955, *9*: 235–313.

WRIGHT, W. D. *Researches on normal and defective colour vision*. London: Kimpton, 1946.

—— The characteristics of tritanopia. *Journal of the Optical Society of America*, 1952, *42*: 509–21.

Introduction

As a sensory process, hearing may be considered from two broad points of view: psychophysics and neurophysiology. Narrowly defined, psychophysics deals with relationships between discriminatory responses and specifiable properties of the stimulus, whereas neurophysiology is concerned with the effects of physical stimulation upon the electrical activity of the nervous system. Thus, hearing involves the study of variables in three major disciplines—physics, physiology, and psychology.

The primary emphasis of this chapter is on the psychological variables of hearing and their interrelationships within contemporary theories of hearing. This material is presented against a background on the physical characteristics of sound and the anatomy and physiology of the auditory system. The material on sound, however, is limited; it is intended only to provide a brief review of some major concepts which are useful in understanding the experimental literature. Extended coverage of this topic is readily available in other sources, e.g., Hirsh 1952; C.M. Harris 1957; Corso 1967a.

The anatomy and physiology of the auditory system, however, is treated in greater detail. An understanding of the physiological properties of the mediating sensory system should serve to facilitate the comprehension of the facts, principles, and theories covered in this chapter. Also, the present state of knowledge on neurophysiological functions requires that theories of hearing, among others, must be formulated within the restrictions imposed by physiological findings and must be consistent with extant knowledge in that area.

Briefly stated, this chapter presents a general survey of recent developments in the field of hearing. Major consideration is given to the experimental literature on human hearing and to those studies which appear most relevant to the critical appraisal of contemporary theories and concepts. Material is included on both normal hearing and clinical abnormalities, although the latter is included to a lesser extent; speech perception is considered briefly and only in relation to auditory pathology. As appropriate throughout the presentation, reference is made to

J. F. Corso

Hearing

17

recent advances in research instrumentation and to improved techniques in the laboratory and clinic. In general, the chapter covers the current trends in the study of human hearing and describes the most prominent theories in the contemporary literature on audition.

Experimental Variables of Sound

In hearing, as in other areas of psychology, there are two major objectives of research. Studies may be performed (1) to determine whether the independent variables (acoustic stimuli presented to subjects) are capable of producing experimental effects as measured by the dependent (hearing) variables, and (2) to establish the form of the functional relationships which obtain between the two classes of variables.

PHYSICAL BASIS FOR THE SPECIFICATION OF ACOUSTIC STIMULI

The physical stimulus for hearing is sound; sound is an oscillation in the pressure, particle displacement, or particle velocity of an elastic medium, such as air or water. The magnitude of these quantities is ordinarily represented as a function of time with respect to a particular reference. For instantaneous acoustic pressure, the magnitude is alternately greater and smaller than the reference, corresponding respectively to the portions of compression and rarefaction in the sound wave. Although the air particles which are set into oscillation by the vibrating source travel only short distances to and fro, the changes in air pressure which they produce are propagated rapidly through the medium. In dry air at 0°C, the velocity of the wave is approximately 1088 ft/sec and increases about 2 ft/sec for every degree rise in temperature.

Regardless of the physical complexity of the sound, there are two basic ways of describing an acoustic wave and specifying its dimensions in quantitive terms: waveform and spectrum. The use of each is facilitated by laboratory techniques which make it possible to convert acoustic signals into electrical signals and vice versa.

Waveform. Whenever an electroacoustic system initially at rest is activated for a prolonged period, two distinct effects are produced in the waveform of the sound. The first effect consists of a series of initial oscillations or transients which fade away more or less rapidly depending on the resonant properties of the system; the second effect occurs after the transients have faded and consists of a steady state response.

The electrical analog of the acoustic waveform is conventionally displayed on a cathode-ray oscilloscope, with time on the horizontal axis and instantaneous amplitude on the vertical axis. The maximum value that the instantaneous amplitude attains is called the peak amplitude, and it is this value which is ordinarily read from the oscilloscope. This procedure provides an analysis of the signal which describes how the amplitude of the pressure wave varies in time.

A variety of waveforms may be observed on the oscilloscope depending upon the particular source of the sound and its duration. Sounds of short duration, such as clicks or pulses, do not attain a steady state and are characterized by transient waveforms; sounds of longer duration do attain a steady state which may or may not be repetitive in waveform.

Spectrum. The second method of classification involves the designation of the frequency content of sound. The specific laboratory procedure which is used in this approach will depend upon the particular sound being analyzed, i.e., whether the waveform of the sound is repetitive or nonrepetitive. If repetitive, as in the case of musical tones, the analysis may be performed mechanically, mathematically, or electronically by means of a harmonic wave analyzer. The components which are contained in the resulting spectrum will have three dimensions: frequency, amplitude, and phase. If the sounds are continuous but nonrepetitive, the analysis must be made in a different manner; this usually involves some type of electronic noise analyzer.

The results of the analysis of a repetitive waveform are represented graphically in the form of a line spectrum. The components are discretely located on the horizontal axis at appropriate frequencies and their relative amplitudes are shown on the ordinate, with phase angle as the parameter. The resolution of a sound with a nonrepetitive waveform produces a continuous spectrum, i.e., one in which the components are continuously distributed over a fairly wide frequency region. Thus the spectrum with its three dimensions (frequency, amplitude, and phase) completely describes a sound wave, as does the waveform with its two dimensions (amplitude and time). Which of these methods is selected for representing a particular soundwave in a given situation will depend upon the form of the analysis which more clearly delineates the characteristics of the stimulus under consideration.

MAJOR CLASSES OF SOUNDS

The results of a time analysis and a corresponding frequency analysis of a typical set of acoustic stimuli are shown in Figure 17–1. These analyses by waveform and by spectrum provide a physical basis for classifying auditory stimuli into four major categories: (1) pure tones, (2) complex tones, (3) noise, and (4) speech.

Pure Tones. The most elementary type of waveform is that of a simple (pure) tone, as shown in Part A of Figure 17–1. A pure tone is a sound wave in which the instantaneous sound pressure is a sinusoidal function of time. The term sinusoidal refers to the class of simple harmonic motions which can be represented by a trigonometric function; of these, the sine wave and cosine wave are the most familiar examples. In each case, the functions are periodic, repeating their trigonometric values in multiples of 360 degrees.

Any sinusoidal wave may be described in terms of three variables: frequency, maximum amplitude, and phase. The frequency is the number of complete repetitions (cycles) of the function per unit time; the time interval is usually taken as 1 sec, and the frequency is specified in Hertz (Hz), i.e., cycles per second. The maximum amplitude of the wave is given by the maximum displacement of the function from the zero position. Phase is specified as an angular measurement in relation to an arbitrary origin at a selected instant in time. In the waveform

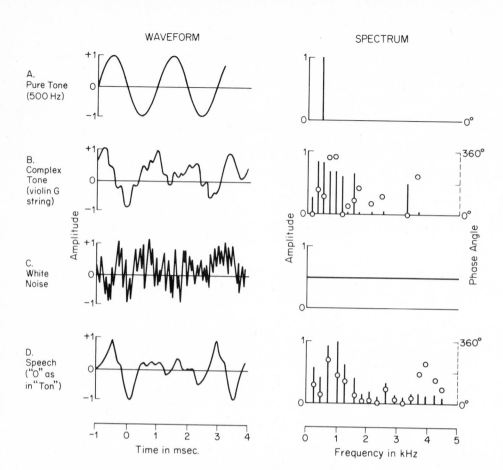

WAVEFORM   SPECTRUM

A. Pure Tone (500 Hz)

B. Complex Tone (violin G string)

C. White Noise

D. Speech ("O" as in "Ton")

Amplitude

Amplitude

Phase Angle

Time in msec.

Frequency in kHz

Fig. 17-1. *Representation of acoustical stimuli by waveform and spectrum. The waveform at the left shows amplitude as a function of time; the spectrum at the right shows both amplitude and phase angle as functions of frequency. In each of the pairs of diagrams, the waveform provides exactly the same information as the spectrum. The waveform graphs should be considered as extending indefinitely in both directions; the spectrum graphs, only to the right. Amplitude is specified in arbitrary units; phase angle is given in degrees.*

representation of a sinusoid, the arbitrary origin is usually taken as the last previous passage of the function through zero from the negative to positive direction.

Complex Tones. A complex tone is a sound wave with a repetitive waveform which contains simple sinusoidal components of different frequencies, as shown in Part B of Figure 17–1. The fundamental frequency of a complex tone is the rate at which the waveform is repeated per unit time. The reciprocal of the fundamental frequency is the period of the wave, i.e., the smallest time interval for which the function repeats itself. The components of a complex tone are called partials, which are usually integral multiples of the fundamental frequency. The fundamental frequency—or simply fundamental—is designated as the first partial or first harmonic. The component with a frequency twice that of the fundamental is called the second partial or second harmonic, etc. If the frequency of a component in a complex tone is not a multiple (or submultiple) of the fundamental, it is called an inharmonic partial.

Noise. Noise is defined physically as a sound with an irregular waveform, i.e., one which shows no repetition of a periodic pattern as in Part C of Figure 17–1. Consequently, noise does not have a fundamental frequency; although noise contains many sinusoids, these are not integrally related.

Two kinds of noise are often used in psychoacoustic experiments: random noise and white noise. Random (Gaussian) noise

is a particular kind of noise in which the distribution of instantaneous amplitudes of the waveform as a function of time follows the normal (Gaussian) probability distribution. White noise consists of a wide range of audible frequencies, all of which are uniform in maximum amplitude and different in phase. White noise sounds like the rush of air or steam released under pressure.

Speech. Speech sounds have traditionally been divided into two classes: vowels and consonants. The vowels are of longer duration and resemble complex tones whose partials are reinforced or diminished by the resonant properties of the vocal system. The consonants, particularly the voiceless consonants and fricative consonants, are of shorter duration and resemble noise. The plosive consonants are complicated acoustic transients. In general, the vowels have spectral components which are lower in frequency than those of the consonants and their steady states are longer. Part D of Figure 17–1 shows the waveform of a common vowel and its associated spectrum.

GENERATION, MEASUREMENT, AND CONTROL OF ACOUSTIC VARIABLES

Research and clinical work in hearing have been facilitated tremendously by the development of electroacoustic devices for the generation, measurement, and control of acoustical variables. Transducers, such as earphones and loudspeakers, have acoustical outputs which quite accurately represent the electrical input.

Thus, rather than working directly with acoustical measures, investigators in this field have often used electrical analogs of physical variables in their experimental manipulations.

Frequency

Pure tones. Pure tones are generated by means of commercial audio-oscillators or by pure tone audiometers. The signals from either source may be presented to the listener by means of earphones or a loudspeaker. Although tuning forks are still used in some routine clinical tests of hearing, pure tone audiometers are now standard equipment for general diagnostic purposes. There are three basic units in a pure tone audiometer: (1) an electronic oscillator for generating alternating electric currents of fixed or variable frequency; (2) an amplifier with an attenuator for altering the output level of the signal by known amounts; and (3) a transducer for applying the sound to the listener's ear via air conduction or bone conduction.

Although the tuning dials of commercial oscillators and audiometers are calibrated in frequency, these are nominal values only and the frequency must be accurately measured if a precise value is required. The simplest method is to feed the electrical signal into a frequency meter; this device counts the number of successive waves in a fixed period of time and displays the measured frequency directly on a counter. If a frequency meter is not available, the measurement may be made by an auditory comparison (method of beats) (Hirsh 1966) or by a visual comparison on an oscilloscope (Lissajous' figures) (Beranek 1949).

Complex tones. Complex tones are produced by numerous sound sources, such as musical instruments, electronic tone synthesizers, the human voice, and industrial machines which produce sounds with pitch-like characteristics. The fundamental frequencies of musical tones (vocal and instrumental) are easily and quickly measured by means of a chromatic stroboscope (Young and Loomis 1938). The spectra of individual speech sounds are provided in the instantaneous graphic recordings of the sound spectrograph (Pierce and David 1958). Although the apparatus required for analyzing and synthesizing musical tones is technically elaborate, such systems are now available for research purposes. The most versatile involve electronic computers which not only perform these functions (Risset and Mathews 1969), but also compose simple melodies and generate speech (Schroeder 1969).

Noise. For laboratory purposes, noise may be generated by various models of commercially available electronic noise generators. These generators produce high-level, broad-band electrical noise which is converted to acoustic noise by means of a loudspeaker or earphone. If a narrow band of frequencies is desired, the output can be filtered electronically to provide a band that is tunable over the audio range. The location of the band may be specified by its lower and upper cut-off frequencies, or by its geometric center frequency and bandwidth.

Since noises contain numerous components which are not integrally related and the waveform is continually changing, the method for specifying the frequency composition of noise differs from that for complex tones. A common procedure is to pass the noise of unknown spectrum through a set of filters in an octave-band noise analyzer. This provides a measurement of the amount of energy which is present in each of the octave-bands within the frequency limits of the analyzer; ordinarily ten bands are used to cover the audible range for human hearing. In an octave-band analysis, the filters pass a band of frequencies such that the highest frequency in the band is twice the lowest. A finer analysis may be obtained by using filters whose passbands are one-half octave, one-third octave, or less.

Intensity

Sound pressure and decibels. Intensity may be considered as a generic term which includes three alternative ways of specifying a physical property of sound. These correspond to three quantities which are associated with a sound wave and vary with time: particle displacement, particle velocity, and instantaneous pressure. By convention, the measure of intensity that is in common use is pressure (or energy, which under certain circumstances is proportional to the square of pressure).

The unit of sound pressure is dynes per square centimeter, or microbars. (One microbar is equal to 1 dyne/sq cm, since normal atmospheric pressure is approximately 1 bar or 10^6 dynes/sq cm.) Sounds with pressure values on the order of .0001 microbar are inaudible in human hearing, whereas sounds on the order of 1,000 microbars produce pain. In present-day practice, this large range of pressure values has been compressed into a logarithmic scale in which the sound pressure is expressed as a ratio rather than an absolute magnitude. The unit of measurement on this scale is the decibel (dB) and the range of human hearing covers approximately 120 dB.

Since the decibel scale is a ratio scale of sound pressure, the denominator of the ratio must always be explicitly stated. The most frequently used reference for sound pressure level (SPL) is 0.0002 microbar, which approximates the absolute threshold of hearing at 1000 Hz. The equation for computing SPL in dB is:

$$dB_{SPL} = 20 \log_{10} \frac{P_x}{0.0002 \text{ microbar}},$$ [1]

where P_x is the root mean square (rms) sound pressure of a given sound. (The rms value is the square root of the arithmetic mean of the squares of the instantaneous sound pressures.) For example, if the rms sound pressure of a given sound is 0.02 microbar, its SPL is 40 dB above 0.0002 microbar.

This is a convenient formula, since the instruments which are used in auditory studies measure the intensity of sounds in terms of acoustical sound pressure or corresponding electrical voltage. The decibel applies to both, although there is no standard reference for voltage. One volt or a submultiple is often used for convenience, and some voltmeters are provided with a dB scale. If a dB voltmeter is not available, actual calculations can be avoided by using published tables that provide dB values for given voltage ratios, and vice versa (Peterson and Gross 1963).

Measurement and Control. The sound pressure level of acoustic stimuli is measured typically in two widely different situations. In one case, the measurement is made in free space at a known distance and direction from the sound source. The source might be, for example, a loudspeaker or an industrial machine. Measurements of this type are most often made by a sound level meter (which indicates the overall SPL of complex, wide band sounds; for a detailed description of the SPL values of noise in various frequency bands, a noise analyzer must be used (Beranek 1949).

If the sound is from a point source, i.e., one which radiates sound equally in all directions from an apparent center, and if the source is far from any object including the ground, the sound pressure will be the same in every direction at equal distances from the source. Furthermore, the sound pressure will vary inversely as the distance from the source. Thus, if the distance from the source is doubled, the sound pressure is halved and the SPL will be decreased by 6 dB. The sound field produced under these idealized conditions is called a free sound field, or simply a free field. In practice these conditions do not exist, since sound waves are reflected from room surfaces and nearby objects. By the proper design and application of acoustic absorbing material, however, an anechoic (echo free) chamber may be constructed which possesses the essential characteristics of a free field over a wide range of frequencies (Berger and Ackerman 1956; Ingersleev et al. 1968).

For accurate readings in many kinds of acoustic and psychoacoustic studies, measurements should be made in such an environment. A typical situation involves Minimum Audible Field (MAF) measurements in which the threshold sound pressure is specified in terms of the sound field at the listener's ear. The elimination of sound reflections is also critically important in other studies, such as the spatial localization of sound sources.

In addition to point sources of sound, there are directional sources which radiate more sound in some directions than others. The sound field in this case must be specified by taking many SPL measurements at given distances and in different directions from the source. From these measurements, sound pressure contours may be graphically constructed to show the general pattern of the sound field. This is an important consideration in the measurement of sound pressure levels produced by industrial machines or other noise sources.

An alternate method for measuring SPL must be employed when the sound under consideration is radiated from an earphone. Ordinarily this involves a complicated electroacoustical system which includes a small coupler. This coupler is a device which has a specified arrangement of acoustic elements and a 6 cc volume that simulates the characteristics of the normal human ear. The earphone is placed firmly on the coupler and the sound pressure generated in the cavity of the coupler is carefully measured by refined reciprocity techniques involving a calibrated condenser microphone (Beranek 1949). Threshold sound pressure values which have been obtained from an earphone calibrated in this manner are called Minimum Audible Pressure (MAP) measurements.

Although this procedure provides reliable measures of sound pressure in the coupler, other techniques must be used to determine the precise values which are generated by the same earphone on a listener's ear. By inserting a small probe tube in the ear canal under the earphone, intra-aural measurements may be made at the entrance of the external canal or near the eardrum. Transfer tables have been prepared, however, so that it is possible to convert a single set of sound pressure measurements into any other (Pollack 1949). Also, for the specification of hearing thresholds, response curves are available which permit the transfer of coupler pressure values among five different earphones (Shaw 1966a).

Anatomy and Physiology of the Human Auditory System and Related Functions

The human auditory system consists of six major parts: (1) the external ear, (2) the middle ear, (3) the inner ear, (4) the acoustic nerve and nuclei of afferent fibers, (5) the auditory cortex, and (6) the pathways and nuclei of efferent fibers. The physiological structures included in the first three of these are shown in Figure 17–2.

EXTERNAL AND MIDDLE EAR: SOUND CONDUCTION PROCESSES

External Ear

Pinna. The external ear consists of the pinna and the external auditory canal. Airborne sound waves strike the pinna and are then channeled into the external canal, at the end of which is located the eardrum or tympanic membrane. Experimental findings indicate that in the absence of head movements, the presence of the pinna is the critical factor for auditory localization (Fisher and Freedman 1968). This confirms the electronic demonstrations of Batteau (1967) and his pinna theory of auditory localization (Batteau 1968). According to this theory, the three-dimensional asymmetry of the pinna acts upon the incoming wavefront and sets up a series of delayed replications which are fed into the external canal. Directionality is encoded in the pattern of delay intervals formed by the directly received pulse and its reflections. The delay paths measured for the structural features of a single pinna show that they can be mapped on a coordinate system ranging from 0–80 μsec for azimuth and 100–300 μsec for elevation. The theory is mathematically stated and is capable of explaining both monaural and binaural localization. Further support for the theory is found in the report that, at least under laboratory conditions, monaural localization can be as accurate as binaural localization (Fisher and Freedman 1967).

External canal. The external auditory canal is an irregularly shaped opening about 2.5 cm in length, with a diameter of about 7 mm and a cross section of about 30 to 50 sq mm; the canal has a volume of about 1 cc and a natural resonant frequency of about 2.4 kHz (Shaw 1966b). The skin of the outer portion of the canal secretes a protective dark yellow wax (cerumen).

The tympanic membrane is a slightly oval structure with the larger diameter being about 9.2 mm and the smaller about 8.5 mm. The area of the membrane is approximately 69 sq mm. The tympanic membrane is not stretched flat across the end of the canal but is cone-shaped and points inward and upward due to its oblique orientation, with an included angle of about 135°. The membrane is thin, tough, and fibrous; however, the edges are flexible and permit the large central portion to move in a unified manner for tones below about 2500 Hz; the membrane vibrates in segments at higher frequencies.

Middle Ear

Ossicular chain. The middle ear is located within the temporal bone beyond the tympanic membrane. It is a boxlike cleft of one or two cc which contains three small bones (malleus,

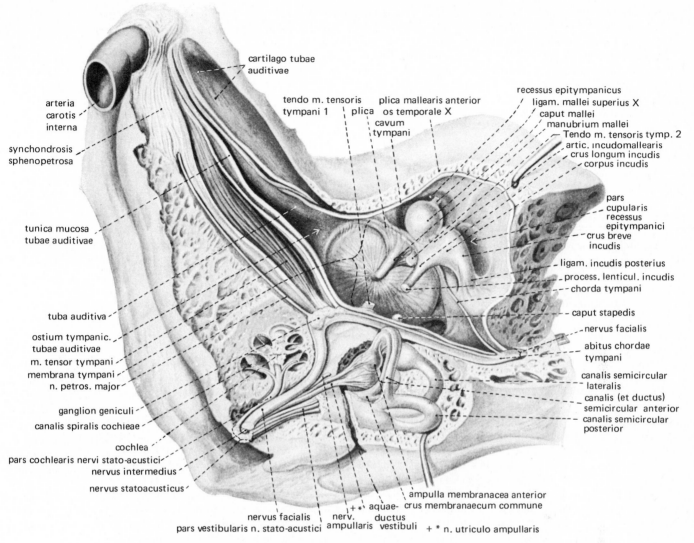

Fig. 17-2. *A dissection of the right temporal bone, showing the middle ear and inner ear with associated structures. The bone was decalsified and the cranial part of the petrous portion was removed. The facial (VII) and vestibulocochlear (VIII) nerves were dissected to show their relation to the labyrinth and middle ear cavity. The walls of the cavity were separated to expose the structures of the middle ear.* [From Sobotta 1963]

incus, and stapes) that arch upward and medially across the cavity. The handle of the malleus is firmly attached to the interior surface of the tympanic membrane and the footplate of the stapes (3.2 sq mm) is set into the oval window of the inner ear. The incus, situated between the other two bones, is firmly interlocked with the head of the malleus and articulates with the head of the stapes. At the cat's threshold of hearing for 1000 Hz, the handle of the malleus shows a peak displacement of 10^{-10} cm and for 5000 Hz about 10^{-11} cm (Tonndorf and Khanna 1967).

When sound waves strike the tympanic membrane, the membrane is set into vibration such that its inward and outward displacements produce turning movements of the ossicular chain. This results in a rocking motion of the stapes at the oval window which converts the mechanical vibrations of the ossicles into fluid pressure waves in the inner ear. For moderate sounds, the stapes rotates lengthwise about a vertical axis at its posterior end, whereas for intense sounds it rotates sidewise about an anteroposterior axis, i.e., its long axis (Békésy 1939). The interaction of the ossicles serves as a mechanical lever system with a ratio of 2.2:1 from malleus to stapes for frequencies below 1000 Hz. This reduces the amplitude of vibration from the tympanic membrane, while increasing the pressure exerted at the footplate of the stapes. Depending on the frequency, the pressure per unit of area at the footplate may be more than 20 times that at the membrane (Davis 1957a).

Middle ear muscles. Under certain conditions the action of the ossicular chain is modified by small muscles which enter the middle ear cavity: (1) the tensor tympani muscle (25 mm), which is attached to the handle of the malleus and is innervated by the mandibular branch of the trigeminal (Vth cranial) nerve; and (2) the stapedius muscle (6.3 mm), which is attached to the neck of the stapes and is innervated by a branch of the facial

(VIIth cranial) nerve. One of the current questions is whether both ear muscles are involved in the acoustic reflex which is induced by intense acoustic stimulation.

Although a number of different methods have been employed to study the characteristics of the acoustic reflex, many studies now use the Zwislocki acoustic bridge (Zwislocki 1963). This allows a direct measurement of both ear canal volume and impedance at the eardrum (Feldman 1967a) and appears to be a reliable technique (Nixon and Glorig 1964).

When this method was used for several cases in which the stapedius muscle was inoperative due to pathological or post-surgical procedures, the acoustic reflex was not observed; however, in other patients with sectioned tensor tympani muscles, a normal reflex was elicited (Feldman 1967b). Pure-tone stimulation from 65–115 dB above threshold (Sensation Level, SL) was found to usually produce only a stapedius reflex, while stimuli at high intensities (115–140 dB SPL) elicited a tensor tympani contraction which seemed to be part of the startle-related cochleo-palpebral reflex (Djupesland 1964). These and other studies indicate that the reflex measured by an acoustic bridge is actually a stapedius reflex, although others disagree (e.g., Weiss 1963).

The threshold for the stapedius reflex to pure tones at 2 and 4 kHz is approximately 81 dB SL; for third-octave noise in the same frequency region and for white noise, it is much lower at approximately 62 dB SL (Deutsch 1968). Repeated stimulation reduces the threshold for white noise and narrow band noise very slightly (about 2 dB). The latency of the stapedius reflex is dependent on the intensity of the stimulus; the greater the intensity, the shorter the latency. For a 1-kHz tone at 100 dB SL, the latency in human subjects varies from 15 to 42 msec (Neergaard and Rasmussen 1966), but values as low as 10 msec have been reported (Djupesland 1965; Fisch and Schulthess 1963).

The stapedius contraction of the acoustic reflex does not demonstrate any short-term adaptation or fatigue for very intense stimuli, at least for 2 min (Dallos 1964). This supports the hypothesis that the reflex serves as a protective mechanism against intense sounds for the middle and inner ears. Since the reflex produces a stiffening of the tympanic membrane and the ossicular chain, there is an increase in the natural period of vibration which reduces the efficiency of sound transmission, particularly for low frequency tones. This reduction is probably on the order of 10 or 15 dB for continuous sounds of moderate intensity (Neergaard et al. 1964). For impulsive sounds, however, the latency of the reflex is sufficiently long so that a sharp wavefront will pass before the muscular contractions can occur. In this situation, protection may be offered by slippage which occurs between the incus and malleus at the incudomallar joint (Tonndorf and Khanna 1967).

Other functions of the acoustic reflex have also been postulated. Since the acoustic reflex is activated immediately before vocalization and persists until after it has ceased, the hypothesis is offered that the reflex serves to eliminate self-induced noise, including the sounds of chewing and head movement (Simmons 1964; Djupesland 1965). It has also been suggested that the reflex reduces the masking of speech by noise, since the muscles act as a highpass filter eliminating more low frequencies than high (Liden, Nordland, and Hawkins 1964). Finally, the acoustic reflex has been related to the activity of the reticular formation; when the reticular activity is depressed, the reflex threshold is increased (Giacomelli and Mozzo 1965).

Round window and cochlear microphonics (CM). The round window is located in the medial wall of the middle ear just below the oval window; it is an opening into the inner ear that has an area of about 2 sq mm and is closed by a flat, thin membrane. When the ossicular chain is activated by sound striking the eardrum, the movements of the stapes are transmitted via the oval window to the fluid of the inner ear; the fluid in turn is moved and the round window is displaced accordingly. It is during this sequence of events that the sensory structures of the inner ear (cochlea) are stimulated.

If an electrode is placed on the round window and another is located anywhere on the tissues of the neck or head, an electrical (ac) potential can be measured between the two electrodes when the ear is stimulated. The changes in potential are called cochlear microphonics (CM) and have been studied, among other purposes, in terms of the nonlinear distortion in the ear.

This distortion is of three basic forms: frequency distortion, phase distortion, and amplitude distortion (Wever and Lawrence 1954). Frequency distortion occurs when a system responds differentially to various frequencies, so that some frequencies are passed more efficiently than others. Evidence for frequency distortion in the human ear is found in the curve for the threshold of hearing which shows maximal sensitivity between 1000 and 2000 Hz and minimal sensitivity at either end of the audible frequency range. Phase distortion is produced when different degrees of time delay occur in the transmission of different frequencies through a system, resulting in altered phase relations among the components of a complex sound. For tones up to 5000 Hz, the middle ear of the cat produces a moderate phase shift up to 74°, and is usually less than 40° (Wever and Lawrence 1954). At frequencies below 50 Hz, the phase of the malleus leads that of the stapes (Tonndorf and Khanna 1967).

Amplitude distortion is the most serious form of distortion in a system and occurs when there is a variation in the efficiency of sound transmission which depends upon the intensity of the input. Numerous studies of the ear have shown that for sounds of low or moderate intensity, the magnitude of the potentials recorded from the round window are proportional to the sound pressure of the input signal; but, as the intensity is increased, the proportionality gradually ceases and the auditory system is considered to be overloaded. In the cat this occurs at a sound pressure of one microbar for 1000 Hz (Wever and Bray 1938). The overloading of the system produces two primary effects: (1) some of the energy in the overloaded transmission system is transformed to higher frequencies (harmonics) which are integral multiples of the input frequency, producing harmonic distortion; and (2) if more than one frequency is present in the input, new frequencies of vibration will be produced in the form of combination tones (Wever and Lawrence 1954). In this case the output will correspond to the primary frequencies and their multiples and all combinations of these frequencies in terms of their sums and differences. The harmonics and combination tones are generated in the cochlea beyond the middle ear (Wever, Bray, and Lawrence 1940).

Subharmonics have also been recorded from CM potentials at high stimulus intensities; these represent energy at frequencies that are 1/2, 1/5, 2/3, 3/4, etc., fractions of the input frequency. The one-half submultiple is typically detected in the CM and occurs in guinea pigs primarily above 2500–3000 Hz at 120 dB SPL (Dallos and Linnell 1966). The distortion components of even-order subharmonics appear to be radiated by the non-linear vibration of the eardrum. In chinchilla ears, odd-fractional sub-harmonics occur between 1000 and 3000 Hz and are attributed to a mechanical distortion process in the cochlea of the inner ear (Dallos 1966).

Eustachian tube. The Eustachian tube connects the middle ear cavity with the back of the nasal cavity called the nasopharynx. The Eustachian tube is normally closed, but opens momentarily during certain movements such as swallowing, yawning, sneezing, or coughing. This action provides a means of equalizing the air pressure between the external auditory canal and the middle ear cavity. Differential atmospheric pressure between these two regions may be produced by changes in altitude or by the gradual absorption of oxygen and hydrogen from the air bubbles in the middle ear cavity.

INNER EAR: GENERATION OF ELECTRICAL POTENTIALS

Anatomy. The inner ear, as shown in Figures 17–2 and 17–3, is located in the bony labyrinth lying deep within the petrous portion of the temporal bone in the base of the skull. Within the bony labyrinth there is suspended a corresponding series of membranous tubes and sacs called the membranous labyrinth. The membranous labyrinth has three major divisions: the semicircular canals (superior, posterior, and lateral), the otolith organs (utricle and saccule), and the cochlea. Of these, only the cochlea relates to hearing and will be considered in further detail.

Figure 17–4 is a drawing based on a photomicrograph of a cross-sectional preparation of the cochlea. The cochlea is a coiled structure of approximately 2 5/8 turns and contains a series of canals which start at the base and extend about 35 mm in length to the apical end. A spiral shelf of bone (osseous spiral lamina) protrudes from the inner wall of the cochlea so as to partially divide it into an upper and lower chamber: the scala vestibuli and the scala tympani which are both filled with perilymphatic fluid. A fibrous but flexible membrane (basilar membrane) completes the division of the two chambers by extending from the lower edge of the bony shelf to the spiral ligament attached to the outer wall of the cochlea. Since this partition does not extend the full length of the cochlea but lacks one or two millimeters, the two chambers are joined in the apex of the cochlea at the helicotrema. This opening has an area of about 0.25 to 0.40 sq mm.

The specialized sensory cells for hearing and their supporting structures are located in a third canal within the cochlea (the scala media or cochlear duct). The scala media is filled with endolymphatic fluid and is separated from the scala vestibuli by a thin partition (Reissner's membrane); at the helicotrema, the scala media terminates as a closed tube. The complex organ of Corti (see Figure 17–4) is situated within the scala media and rests on the surface of the basilar membrane. The basilar membrane is about 32 mm long, but is not uniform in width; it is narrowest (about 0.05 mm) at the base of the cochlea near the oval window and increases to its maximum width (about 0.50 mm) near the apex.

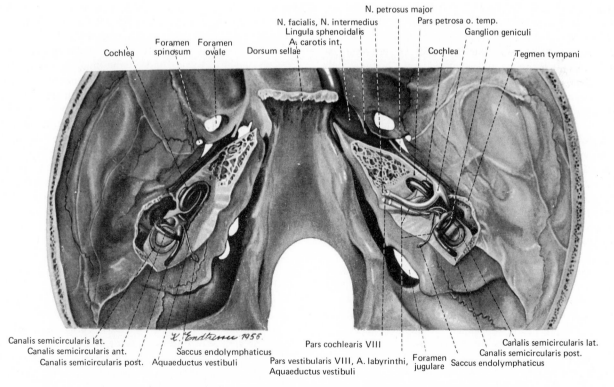

Fig. 17-3. *A cross-sectional view of the bony labyrinth and associated structures for the right and left ears. The labyrinth lies in the petrous part of the temporal bone and the top of the pyramid has been chiseled from both sides. Cast of the labyrinth.* [from Pernkopf 1963]

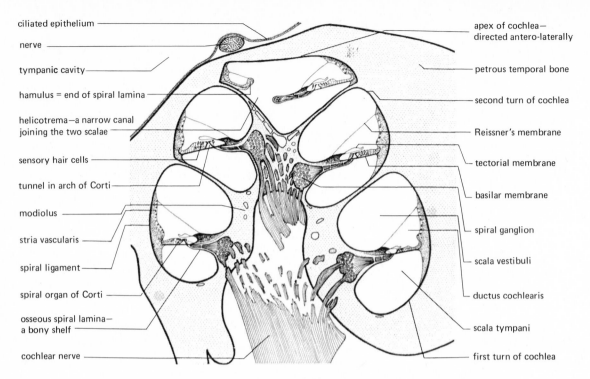

ciliated epithelium

nerve

tympanic cavity

hamulus = end of spiral lamina

helicotrema—a narrow canal joining the two scalae

sensory hair cells

tunnel in arch of Corti

modiolus

stria vascularis

spiral ligament

spiral organ of Corti

osseous spiral lamina— a bony shelf

cochlear nerve

apex of cochlea— directed antero-laterally

petrous temporal bone

second turn of cochlea

Reissner's membrane

tectorial membrane

basilar membrane

spiral ganglion

scala vestibuli

ductus cochlearis

scala tympani

first turn of cochlea

Fig. 17-4. *Drawing based on a photomicrograph of a cross-sectional preparation of the human cochlea. The intact cochlea is a continuous coil of approximately two to five-eighth turns.* [From Freeman and Bracegirdle 1967.]

A schematic representation of the neuroanatomy of the cochlea is shown in Figure 17–5. The sensory cells of the organ of Corti are called hair cells and are arranged in lengthwise rows on each side of the rods (pillars) of Corti. One row lies inward of the rods and contains the inner hair cells; on the opposite side are located the outer hair cells. In the lower half of the basal coil there are three parallel rows of outer cells arranged more or less regularly; in the upper half of the basal coil there is an incomplete fourth row. In the second and apical coils many of the outer hair cells are missing from the first three rows, but incomplete fourth and fifth rows are always found (Johnsson and Hawkins 1967).

It is estimated that the cochlea of the human foetus (24 wks) contains about 3,400 inner hair cells and 13,400 outer hair cells. Each outer hair cell is about 8 microns in diameter; the inner hair cells are slightly larger. The inner hair cells are uniformly distributed from the base to the apex, but the density of the outer hair cells per unit surface area is maximal at the base of the cochlea and decreases to nearly half at the apex (Bredberg 1968).

The free surface of the outer and inner hair cells is bounded by a fairly stiff plate (reticular lamina) from which the hairs protrude. The lower ends of the outer hair cells rest on the cup-shaped body of the outer phalangeal (Deiter's) cells while the inner hair cells are nearly surrounded by the inner phalangeal cells. When the hairs of each outer and inner cell are examined in cross section, they are found to be arranged in a W pattern, with the base of the W facing the cells of Hensen. In the basal turn of the cochlea there are about 142 hairs in a single outer sensory cell; the hairs in the peripheral rows of the W are larger than those of the inner row (Kimura 1966).

It has been found that the stereocilia from the first two rows of outer hairs cells are in contact with the main body of the tectorial membrane. Also, the margin of the membrane is in contact with hairs from the outer cells of the third row in the basal coil of the cochlea; in the upper coils, "finger-like projections" of the membrane reach out to the scattered cells of the fourth and fifth rows. Hairs of the inner row of sensory cells have also been found attached to the membrane (Hawkins and Johnsson 1968), but not by all investigators (Kimura 1966).

A method for "the perfusion into the labyrinth of all agents required for preparation and optimal preservation of the tissues of the membranous labyrinth for light, phase contrast, and electron microscopic studies" has been described (Kirchner 1968); the method offers a mathematical means for the quantitative assessment of the morphological effects of the critical technical steps and a computer program is provided in Fortran IV language (McCormick and Salvadori 1964) for organizing the results of the analysis into three types of data: anatomical, processing, and ultrastructural.

Cochlear Innervation

Afferent fibers. The primary afferent fibers of the cochlear division of the auditory (VIIIth cranial) nerve originate in bipolar ganglion cells which lie in irregular clusters in the bony spaces of the modiolus (Mahon and Igarashi 1968). The dendritic processes of these cells travel outward to innervate the hair cells of the organ of Corti and their axons travel inward to the axis of the coiled cochlea to form the trunk of the cochlear nerve. (See Figures 17–2 and 17–4.) In man, the total number of afferent

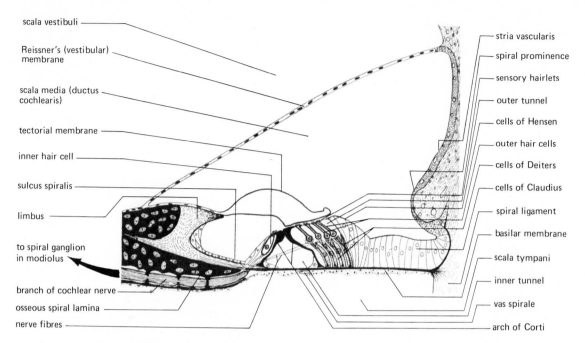

Fig. 17-5. *Schematic representation of the cochlear duct and the neuroanatomy of the human organ of Corti.* [From Freeman and Bracegirdle 1967]

auditory fibers is estimated to be about 25,000 to 30,000; the fibers are myelinated and of moderate, uniform size (3 to 5 μ in diameter) (Davis 1961). The fibers acquire their myelin sheaths, however, only after they leave the hair cells and pass through the openings along the tympanic lip of the spiral lamina near the inner pillars of Corti's arch (habenula perforata).

The peripheral distribution of the cochlear portion of the auditory nerve (of the guinea pig) shows four types of fibers: (1) the inner radial bundle, in which each fiber innervates two or three adjacent inner hair cells and each cell is related to a small number of fibers; (2) the outer radial fibers, which innervate the outer hair cells in a manner like the inner radial fibers, but are less orderly and fewer in number; (3) the external spiral fibers, which cross the tunnel of Corti with each fiber innervating many outer hair cells and often including cells in different rows; and (4) the internal spiral fibers, which form part of the efferent system (Fernandez 1951).

Efferent fibers. Recent evidence indicates that there is an enormous amount of efferent innervation of the cochlear receptors (Smith and Rasmussen 1963; Spoendlin 1966). In the cat, the estimated number of efferent fibers at the level of the outer hair cells is eighty times greater than the number of primary (olivo-cochlear) fibers. At the level of the outer hair cells, the efferent fibers show a predominantly radial distribution; in the inner spiral plexus, the fibers present a wide spiral extension. The radial fibers make synaptic contacts almost exclusively with outer sensory cells, while the spiral fibers contact afferent dendrites. The efferent fibers have only occasional direct contact with the inner hair cells. The efferent and afferent fibers in the organ of Corti also appear to have a different ultrastructure. It has been suggested that the complex arrangements and interrelationships between afferent dendrites and efferent fibers offer the possibility of spatial and temporal summation, and they may explain the difference in sensitivity between the inner and outer hair cells (Spoendlin 1968).

Cochlear Mechanics. It is now well established that the cochlea serves as a mechanical analyzer of acoustic stimuli, although not in accordance with the classical resonance principle. Békésy (1948) showed that the basilar membrane, the key structure in the analytic function, is not under tension and that any tension which may exist is unimportant in the process of analysis. However, the basilar membrane does vary in stiffness by a hundred-fold from one end to the other, with its greatest stiffness at the basal end of the cochlea. When such a system, characterized by a stiffness gradient along its length and by longitudinal coupling between its elements, is driven by a periodic force, the movements produced in the system give rise to a traveling wave. This has been demonstrated in mechanical models and in the cochlea (Békésy 1960) and has been confirmed by a variety of techniques in numerous studies.

The movement of the traveling wave along the basilar membrane is shown in Figure 17–6. The waves move from the narrower, stiffer end at the base of the cochlea toward the broader, more flexible part of the apex. The amplitude of the traveling wave increases as it approaches the resonant region of the basilar membrane, reaches a peak, and then declines rather abruptly. As the frequency of the sound input is increased, the maximum of the amplitude envelope moves progressively towards the basal end of the membrane, as shown in Figure 17–7. It takes a traveling wave about 5 msec to move from the stapes to the helicotrema.

For a low frequency tone, about 50 Hz, the basilar membrane vibrates as a whole; for other frequencies, there is a difference in phase angle between the movement of the stapes and a given point on the basilar membrane at a particular instant in time. The phase of the traveling wave changes progressively in its movement along the membrane.

Several models of cochlear mechanics have been developed (e.g., Flanagan 1962; Klatt and Peterson 1966) which involve a set of differential equations that relate pressure and displace-

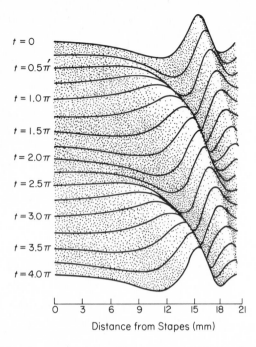

Fig. 17-6. *Sequences of traveling waves at 2000 Hz obtained by computer simulation. Solid curves show the instantaneous displacement of the basilar membrane over a 2-cycle period, at intervals of 1/8 cycle.* [From Khanna, Sears, and Tonndorf 1968; reprinted by permission of the Acoustical Society of America]

ment in the inner ear. To implement the models for experimental use, equivalent computer networks have been built and tested. The significance of the models lies in their potential use for determining how the output of the computer will be affected by changes in the input parameters, thereby providing predictions of wave motion in the inner ear.

Electrical Potentials

Terminology. The term electrical potentials embraces a number of different concepts associated with electrical effects within the auditory system. When the system is not activated by sound, resting dc potential differences can be recorded between

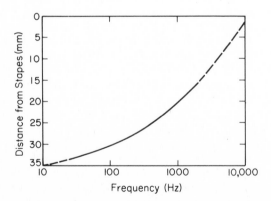

Fig. 17-7. *Curve relating the place of maximum amplitude of vibration on the basilar membrane to the frequency of a pure tone.* [From Khanna, Sears, and Tonndorf 1968; reprinted by permission of the Acoustical Society of America]

different parts of the cochlea. One of these indicates the internal resting negative potential of particular cellular elements in the cochlea; the other indicates the extra-cellular positive potential difference between the endolymph and perilymph and is called the dc endolymphatic potential or, simply, EP. When an acoustic wave enters the normal ear, the cochlea generates two primary electrical responses: (1) the ac cochlear microphonic potential (CM) which can be recorded at the round window and at other parts of the auditory system, and (2) the nerve action potential (AP) which is propagated along the auditory (VIIIth cranial) nerve. If the CM is recorded from the round window or from the scalae with a dc amplifier, a third effect is also noted. As the ac response follows the frequency of the input signal, the mean dc potential level of the CM is displaced for the duration of the stimulus; this is identified as the summating potential (SP) and may be positive or negative, depending on several factors.

Endolymphatic potential (EP). The EP appears to be limited to the endolymphatic space bounded by Reissner's membrane, the stria vascularis, and the reticular lamina; this excludes the basilar membrane and the organ of Corti (Tasaki, Davis, and Eldredge 1954). Although it has been suggested that the endolymphatic potential is generated by the hair bearing end of the hair cells, there is some evidence which indicates that the changes in EP reflect variations in the output of dc generators located on the basilar membrane (Butler and Honrubia 1963). The hypothesis is that these generators produce a positive potential when the basilar membrane is displaced toward the scala tympani and a negative potential, toward the scala vestibuli. Also, the EP is believed to be involved in the generation of CM (Butler 1965), but some doubt it (Dohlman 1960).

Cochlear microphonics (CM). The classical view of the origin of CM (Stevens and Davis 1938) postulated that when the hair cells were deformed by the application of pressure, they acted like an inorganic crystal such as quartz and produced a piezo-electric effect. More recent information, however, argues against this hypothesis. Not only is the mechanical energy available at the threshold of hearing extremely small, but there is no relation between the mechanical work done by a needle in displacing the basilar membrane and the resultant electrical output (Békésy 1950). These considerations, coupled with the data on the dc resting potential in the scala media, seem to indicate that the mechanical movement of the basilar membrane modulates some undetermined source of power, rather than providing the energy directly.

Several hypotheses have been proposed on how this might be done. One idea is that the bending of the hairs produces a change in resistance across the cuticular layer of the hair cell which then modulates EP (Davis 1957b). However, several experiments offer counter-evidence since, during asphyxia, the EP is absent but CM can be detected (Rice and Shinabarger 1961; Butler 1965). Another hypothesis states that the bending or deflection of hairs produces the CM due to the tangential shearing action between the tectorial membrane and the organ of Corti (Békésy 1953, 1967), but a new proposal argues that the adequate stimulus for the CM is the direct pressure exerted by the tectorial membrane upon the hair cells (Mygind 1966). The data on cochlear mechanics, however, seem to favor the first alternative.

The cochlear system has also been considered as a spatially distributed envelope-detection system in which the excitation of hair cells is based on the mechanical impact of the cochlear hairs against the tectorial membrane (Crane 1966). The theory requires the absence of any actual or functional connections between the hair cells and the tectorial membrane, but this assumption appears untenable (Hawkins and Johnsson 1968). Also, no signs of impact have been found in the tectorial membrane (Kimura 1966).

Summating potential (SP). Like the CM, the origin of SP is still undetermined although several hypotheses have been proposed. SP does not appear to arise simply as a result of nonlinearity of the CM generators, thereby producing a rise in the dc component (Butler and Honrubia 1963). Neither does it seem to be produced by the longitudinal shearing of the inner hair cells (Davis, Fernandez, and McAuliffe 1950), since the SP is found in the pigeon which does not have the mammalian differentiation of inner-outer hair cells (Stopp and Whitfield 1964).

Another hypothesis has suggested that SP is due to the nonlinear vibration of the basilar membrane (Whitfield and Ross 1965), but the measurements of odd and even harmonics in the CM do not conform to the predictions from this particular hypothesis (Engebretson and Eldredge 1968). However, the data do support the hypothesis that SP is the product of an asymmetrical nonlinearity; the locus of the nonlinearity is not specified, but the model contains a simple nonlinear network with asymmetrical peak-clipping. The model is consistent with the requirements of a traveling wave theory (Nieder and Nieder 1968).

Nerve action potential (AP). All the information passing from the ear to the brain must funnel through the auditory nerve. There are about 30,000 individual fibers in the auditory nerve and each fiber upon activation transmits neural impulses in an all-or-none manner to the brain. The pattern of impulses in the auditory nerve represents a particular pattern of mechanical vibration of the basilar membrane and its associated hair cells. The two basic questions which must be resolved are (1) the identification and description of the transducer mechanism or process which is activated by the mechanical vibration of the basilar membrane and "triggers" the discharge of auditory nerve impulses; and (2) the analysis of the encoding process whereby the information contained in the parameters of the stimulus are transformed into the space-time pattern of neural responses.

The general contention is that the extremely minute vibrations of the basilar membrane are converted into CM; these in turn are somehow involved in the initiation of the action potentials in the auditory nerve. Evidence on these processes in the vestibular system shows that there is an inverse relationship between the CM and the discharge rate of the associated sensory nerve (Trincker 1962).

Some of the chemical factors which influence the electrical potentials of the cochlea have been determined, but there is little direct evidence on the mechanism of nerve stimulation within the organ of Corti. If the calcium concentration in the perilymph of the scala tympani is increased, AP is depressed while CM and SP are augmented (Moscovitch and Gannon 1966). AP is abolished immediately, but not EP or CM, when the Na+ solution is replaced (Konoshi and Kelsey 1967). One proposal is that CM may stimulate the hair cells to release a chemical agent (acetylcholine) which then participates in the generation of the nerve impulse (Gannon, Laszlo, and Moscovitch 1966).

Many experiments have been performed on guinea pigs, cats, and other animals in which the AP of the auditory nerve

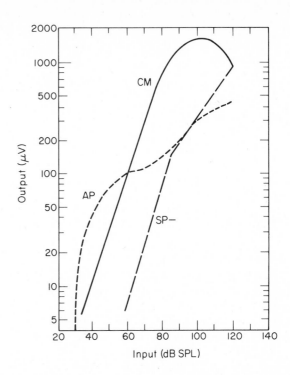

Fig. 17-8. *Typical input-output functions for the cochlear microphonic (CM), action potential (AP), and summating potential (SP) recorded by intracochlear electrodes from the basal turn of a guinea pig for 7-kHz tone bursts with 1-msec rise time.* [From Davis 1961; reprinted by permission of the MIT Press and John Wiley & Sons, Inc.]

was measured as a function of different characteristics of the stimulus. To measure AP satisfactorily, it is necessary to eliminate the unwanted CM from the recorded potential by a suitable laboratory technique. Figure 17-8 shows how AP, CM, and SP vary as the intensity level of the input signal (7 kHz) is increased from about 30 to 120 dB SPL. The latency of the initial AP response (N_1) decreases considerably from 10 to 20 dB; the amplitude of the response increases very rapidly at low intensity levels, then more slowly at medium levels, and finally climbs rapidly at the higher levels. At about 120 dB SPL, N_1 has an amplitude of about 1 millivolt and it is estimated that this represents about five or six nerve fibers per microvolt of peak voltage (Davis 1961).

AFFERENT AND EFFERENT NEURAL PATHWAYS AND THE AUDITORY CORTEX

Schematic Representation of Neural Pathways. The structures of the afferent and efferent pathways of the auditory system connecting the inner ear and the brain have been extensively studied and reported (e.g. Galambos and Davis 1943; Gross and Thurlow 1951; Galambos 1952; Hilali and Whitfield 1953; Katsuki et al. 1958; Katsuki, Watanabe, and Maruyama 1959; Whitfield 1967). Some of the relevant points on neural pathways can be obtained from inspection of Figure 17-9 which shows the connections for the afferent (centripal) and efferent (centrifugal) portions of the auditory system. Caution should be exercised in utilizing this figure, however, since the auditory system may be more complex than shown in this simplified diagram.

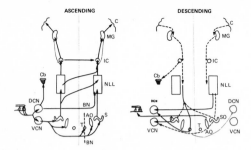

Fig. 17-9. *Diagram of the neural connections and synapses in both the ascending (afferent) and descending (efferent) pathways of the auditory nervous system. Pathways are shown for only half of the binaural system; ascending from one ear, descending to the other.* [From Whitfield 1967]

Electrical Responses at Different Levels of the Auditory Tract. The recording of electric responses of single auditory neurons to airborne sounds has provided information on different levels of activity in experimental animals. In the cat, recordings have been made from the cochlear nerve, the dorsal and ventral cochlear nuclei, the trapizoid body, the inferior colliculus, the medial geniculate body, the cerebral primary and secondary auditory areas, and the ascending reticular system (Katsuki 1961).

In the peripheral regions of the auditory tract, the frequency of neural discharge increases with an increase in sound intensity. However, the higher the level of neural structure, the lower the rate of increase. The sigmoidal relation between frequency of impulses per second and sound intensity in dB is found only at the lower levels. Also, all neurons at the periphery respond to both continuous and brief sounds, whereas in the upper brain structures many neurons respond only to brief sounds.

With sounds of sufficient intensity, each neuron responds continuously over a wide range of input frequencies; but as the intensity is decreased, the neuron responds less and less. In the asymmetrical type of primary neuron, the response to low frequencies is diminished while the upper limit remains essentially unchanged; in the symmetrical type, the responses are reduced for both high and low frequencies. Thus, in both cases there is a narrowing of the frequency range of response with decreased intensity.

The neurons of the ascending reticular system in the region of the midbrain and thalamus have high thresholds for sound intensity and most do not respond solely to specific frequencies. Inhibitory interactions of responses occur in the auditory tract as well as in the reticular system. An electrical potential of neural origin which reproduces both the frequency and waveform to the stimulus has recently been observed in recordings from the central pathway up to the level of the inferior colliculus (Marsh and Worden 1968). At a stimulus intensity of 80 dB SPL, the response has a frequency range of 500–5000 Hz, and it has been suggested that the potential may be involved in frequency discrimination.

Recordings from single neurons have failed to show tonotopic localization at the auditory cortex (Evans, Ross, and Whitfield 1965). While there is a general grouping of low, medium, and high frequency tones, tonotopic localization is better along the auditory tract, but a precise arrangement occurs only at the cochlea.

With the advent of the average response computer, renewed interest has developed in the continuous electrical activity of the human brain as measured from electrodes placed on the top of the head at the vertex (Davis 1968). Responses are recorded as the stimulus is repeatedly presented and the computer establishes the common characteristics of these responses for a block of trials, while averaging out towards zero all of the miscellaneous random activity which is not time-locked to the stimulus. The recorded vertex (V) potential in response to auditory stimuli shows a small positive wave with its peak at about 50 msec, followed by a strong negative wave at 100 msec and then a large positive wave at 175 msec (Davis 1965a). The V potential does not arise from the auditory projection area of the temporal lobe and can be elicited by visual and tactile stimuli, as well as auditory.

The Psychophysics of Hearing

THRESHOLD OF AUDIBILITY

Absolute Thresholds

Sonic frequencies. The absolute threshold, or stimulus limen, is defined as the intensity at which a particular sound is just discriminable from silence on a given percentage of trials. The kinds of stimuli, the psychophysical testing procedure, the psychological characteristics of the subject, the testing environment and other factors have a marked effect on threshold values. In general, threshold studies may be classified as laboratory studies or field studies, depending upon the degree of control of the relevant variables in the testing situation. The threshold curves for laboratory studies (e.g., Sivian and White 1933, Corso 1958b) are, therefore, usually lower (more sensitive) than those obtained in field studies or mass audiometric surveys (e.g., U.S. Public Health Service 1938; Glorig et al. 1957).

A comparison of the threshold curves obtained in some typical studies is presented in Figure 17–10. The laboratory data indicate that the lowest threshold values occur in the region of 1 to 2 kHz; additional data show that for air conducted sounds the frequency limits of hearing extend from about 5 Hz (Corso 1958a) to 23 kHz (Corso 1967a).

The values of the absolute threshold for a given set of testing conditions may be influenced by practice effects which are reflected in measures of inter- and intra-subject variability. Both of these increase at the higher frequencies, but at a given frequency the intersubject standard deviation is about two or three times larger. Repeated threshold measurements at 125 Hz on the same subjects showed a 4 dB decrease over ten trials in a single testing session (Corso and Cohen 1958). Three tests administered over a 10-day period show significant intersubject variability, but not intrasubject variability, regardless of frequency.

Ultrasonic frequencies. A few studies have been conducted to determine whether the frequency limits of hearing can be extended by bone conduction. In this mode of stimulation, the test tone is presented by means of a transducer pressed firmly against the skull, usually on the mastoid bone. Preliminary observations indicated that the upper limit of hearing could be extended by bone conduction (Pumphrey 1950; Deatherage, Jeffress, and Blodgett 1954) and a threshold curve was later obtained for frequencies up to 100 kHz (Corso 1963a). Other investigators have obtained bone-conduction thresholds at these

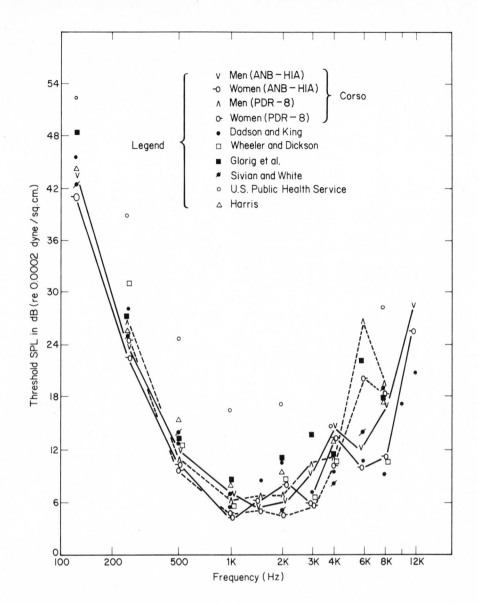

Fig. 17-10. *Determinations of the threshold of audibility in audiometric surveys and in laboratory studies.* [From Corso 1958b; reprinted by permission of the Acoustical Society of America]

frequencies (Haeff and Knox 1963) and up to 225 kHz (Sagalovich and Melkumova 1967). Also, the audibility function of the Common Seal in water has been found to extend to 180 kHz (Møhl 1968), with the slope of the function approximating that reported earlier (Corso 1963a).

The significance of these findings in relation to auditory theory and clinical practice remains to be determined. However, in children with a congenital loss of hearing, an ultrasound of 62.5 kHz could be perceived if some evidence of cochlear function was present; otherwise it could not (Belucci and Schneider 1962).

Reference Level for Audiometers. The clinical assessment of hearing sensitivity involves the use of an audiometer which, at each frequency, generates a signal of known intensity with a given setting of the attenuator dial. The sound pressure produced by the particular earphone associated with the audiometer is calibrated in a standard coupler, such as the National Bureau of Standards coupler 9-A commonly used in the United States. In 1951, the American Standards Association (ASA) specified

the zero reference level for diagnostic audiometers to conform to the threshold of hearing in "normal" ears as measured in the 1935–36 United States Public Health Survey (Beasley 1938).

Since that time other studies have appeared which have shown that the 1951 American standard is too lenient; young normal ears have thresholds which are lower than the prescribed values. Consequently, the British Standards Institute adopted another set of data (Dadson and King 1952) as the British zero reference for audiometers, thereby producing a dual set of standards for different parts of the world.

In 1955, therefore, the International Organization for Standardization (ISO) started to examine carefully and critically all of the published data on thresholds of normal hearing. Finally, fifteen studies from five different countries (France, Germany, Russia, United Kingdom, and the United States) were selected as meeting stringent criteria and formed the basis for the 1964 proposed revision of audiometric zero reference (Weissler 1968). Four of the studies were from the United States (Harris 1954; Glorig et al. 1956; Albrite et al. 1958; and Corso 1958b).

The 1951 ASA curve and the 1964 ISO curve are shown in Figure 17–11. The smallest difference between the two curves is

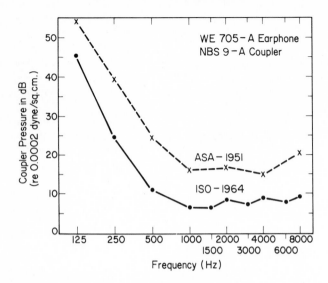

Fig. 17-11. *Comparison of the present zero reference level for audiometers of the American Standards Association (ASA-1951) with the curve recommended by the International Standards Organization (ISO-1964).* [From Davis and Kranz 1964; reprinted by permission of the Acoustical Society of America]

6 dB (Davis 1965b). In America the medical and paramedical professional associations involved with the measurement of hearing have all adopted the ISO values, but the ASA has not as yet. Some investigators have argued for a basic physical reference zero rather than one derived from statistical studies of audiometric data (Riley et al. 1965).

TEMPORAL INTEGRATION

Within certain time limits, stimulus duration (t) can be exchanged for stimulus intensity (I) to produce a given sensory effect (Bloch's law). In hearing, as the duration is decreased below this value, the intensity must be increased correspondingly for the sound to reach a threshold value (k). This effect is known as temporal summation or temporal integration; in its simplest form, $It = k$.

Since this relationship does not hold for very short or very long durations, several alternative formulations have been proposed. One of these is the diverted input hypothesis (Garner and Miller 1947) as labelled by Licklider (1951):

$$t(I - I_o) = k, \qquad [2]$$

where k is the threshold constant, t is effective stimulus duration, I is the overall power of the signal in watts/sq cm, and I_o is a constant portion of the stimulus input that is diverted from the auditory excitation process and is not integrated. Data on tone pips of 100 Hz with gradual rise-fall times have confirmed the appropriateness of Equation 2 (Dallos and Olsen 1964), as have data for different frequencies and for white noise (Olsen and Carhart 1966).

Miskolczy-Fodor (1959) has provided the equation:

$$k = n - a \log (T_o/T), \qquad [3]$$

in which k is the threshold constant, n is the threshold change

in dB, T_o is the adjusting time of the auditory mechanism with an assigned value of 150 msec, a is the threshold change (8.92 dB) for a tenfold decrease in pulse duration below 150 msec, and T is the actual pulse duration. By appropriate substitutions in Equation 3, an expression can be derived from which the amount of shift in threshold (in dB) may be calculated for any pulse duration (T) between 3 and 300 msec. The value for the amount of predicted threshold shift has been confirmed (Goldstein and Kramer 1960).

A complete theory of temporal auditory summation has been developed and applied to the threshold of audibility for various temporal patterns of pulses and pure tones (Zwislocki 1960). The ear is considered as a power integrator with a time constant of 200 msec, and the locus of integration is placed at a level above the neurons of the first order. For pulses, threshold depends upon the repetition rate and, up to 0.5 sec, the duration of stimulation. Threshold data for the detection of tones of various durations in narrow-band noise show good agreement with predicted values (Zwicker and Wright 1963).

Other data, however, support the theoretical formulation of Plomp and Bouman (1959). In this development, the functional relationship between the intensity level I of a tone pulse and the pulse duration t for a threshold response k is given by:

$$k = aI(1 - e^{-t/\tau}), \qquad [4]$$

where a is the constant of proportionality and τ is the constant of temporal summation. The value of τ varies from about 375 msec at 250 Hz to about 150 msec at 8 kHz.

The principle of temporal summation has been extended to the clinical setting for the differential diagnosis of auditory disorders (Wright 1968).

SIGNAL DETECTION AND DISCRIMINATION

The material in the foregoing section on auditory thresholds may be considered to fall within the framework of classical psychophysical theory. Other approaches, such as signal detection theory (TSD), information theory, and adaptation level theory, provide alternative ways of conceptualizing traditional problems and offer new experimental possibilities (Corso 1967b).

Detection Studies Related to TSD. One of the features which distinguishes signal detection theory experimentally is that the observer is usually required to detect the presence of a sinusoidal signal in a background of noise from an external source. Signal detection studies, therefore, typically involve noise; however, no consideration will be given in this chapter to those studies involving noise which are primarily methodological in nature. Attention will be directed to those studies which advance the understanding of auditory processes, not decision processes in general.

Stimulus parameters. In studies of temporal summation the usual approach has been to determine the intensity and duration of stimulation required for an observer to make a positive report. Since the report is based on a threshold value, the stimulus conditions may be considered to yield constant detectability. In signal detection, detectability is permitted to vary as the amplitude and duration of a pure tone are experimentally manipulated in the presence of a masking random noise. Data supporting the diverted input hypothesis have been obtained with this technique from about 15 to 150 msec; also, equations with three parameters have been developed which show how the index of detectability (d') changes for different signal durations. The general form of the equations indicates that detection varies as a function of signal power times a function of signal duration (Green, Birdsall, and Tanner 1957).

From judgments of equal loudness, detectability functions for signals of different durations and intensities have been determined (Creelman 1963). The form of the intensity-duration function for a constant loudness has been found to agree with the intensity function for a constant level of detectability (d').

A number of studies have reported a pedestal effect in the detection of sinusoids in noise. When tone pulses are delivered as in-phase additions to a continuous standard tone (pedestal) that is embedded in a steady background noise, audibility is greater than when the pulses are delivered in noise alone. For example, given a constant level of detectability of 75 percent correct responses, a 1000 Hz tone requires less intensity when presented with the pedestal than without, regardless of its duration (Leshowitz and Raab 1967). In terms of the intensity-reciprocity factor for constant detectability, a simple detection task shows a 10 dB change per log unit of time, while the more sensitive pedestal studies show 14 dB.

The discrimination of phase is another classically investigated variable which has been reexamined within the context of TSD. Given a complex signal composed of a fundamental (525 Hz) and a second partial (1050 Hz) that was altered in six relative phase positions, the observer was forced to choose in which of four noise bursts the signal appeared. As the relative phase relationship increased from 0° to 120°, the number of correct responses also increased (Fricke 1968). This confirms the classical studies which indicated that phase can be discriminated (Chapin and Firestone 1934; Lewis and Larsen 1937).

Signal detectability theory has been continually revised to accommodate new experimental situations. It is now possible to predict the level of monaural detection of a pure tone in noise by solving a series of equations (Mulligan et al. 1968), to apply TSD to matching procedures (Sorkin 1962), and to develop rating scales (Watson, Rilling, and Bourbon 1964).

Detectability theory can also be used to reexamine earlier theoretical positions. The issue of sensory differential thresholds has been reopened through the study of two models: a discrete model—the neural quantum theory; and a continuous model—signal detectability theory (Norman 1963). Data on the discrimination of a 1000-Hz tone which was varied briefly in amplitude seem to support the existence of a low differential threshold, but the evidence was insufficient to permit a definite conclusion about the validity of the neural quantum theory. However, a reanalysis and a reinterpretation of the data favored the TSD model, without threshold (Taylor 1964). Thus, the sensory continuity-noncontinuity issue seems to be no nearer a resolution than when last reviewed (Corso 1956a, 1963c); nevertheless, significant advances in theories and methodology have been achieved since that time.

Observer-related determinants. One concern which continually appears in psychophysical research is whether there are trial-by-trial dependencies of responses on previous responses or stimuli, i.e., whether the data show sequential dependencies. Earlier reviews of this problem are available (Senders and Soward 1952; McGill 1957). Among other factors, information feedback is considered to be a variable which may directly affect the dependencies of responses and, accordingly, the level of performance. Without feedback, the sequential effects are primarily determined by the observer's prior responses; with feedback, the response on a given trial is related in a complex manner to the stimulus, response, and outcome on the previous trials.

On an easy task of auditory discrimination, no knowledge of results (no feedback) is better than partial or complete feedback, but feedback after each trial is better on a difficult task (Carterette, Friedman, and Wyman 1966). The data suggest that the observer changes his criterion following a trial in which his response did not agree with the feedback.

In an auditory recognition task (as distinguished from detection) the observer's hits and false alarms were found to be markedly influenced by the response and signal events on the preceding trial, even though the task was arranged so that there was no trial-to-trial feedback nor any other information regarding the relative frequencies of the two tones to be recognized (Tanner, Haller, and Atkinson 1967). The sequential effects appear to be stronger when trial by trial feedback is omitted than when it is given (Tanner, Rauk, and Atkinson 1970). The data indicate that the observer repeats his previous response on approximately 70 percent of the two-choice trials (Green 1964).

The effects of monetary motivation and practice have also been studied in the TSD context. The general conclusion seems to be that increased motivation of this type has very little effect on the detection of a sinusoid in noise; also, the effects of practice are limited to the first session and are not appreciable at 1000 Hz (Swets and Sewall 1963). When the data are analyzed on a trial by trial basis, the observer tends to show a slow drift in attention over time which is not stimulus specific (Sorkin 1969).

CRITICAL BANDWIDTH, CRITICAL RATIO, AND MASKING

The concepts of critical bandwidth, critical ratio, and masking are of fundamental importance in psychoacoustics, both theoretically and experimentally, and are closely interrelated.

Pure Tone Masking. Masking is the process by which the threshold of audibility for a given sound is raised by the presence of another (masking) sound. The amount of masking is the difference between the absolute threshold of the signal in the presence of the masking sound (masked threshold) and the absolute threshold of the signal alone; the unit customarily used to express the amount of masking is the dB.

The classic experiment on pure-tone masking (Wegel and Lane, 1924) shows that (1) tones of adjacent frequencies produce greater masking than widely separated frequencies; (2) low tones mask higher frequency tones considerably better than high tones mask lower frequencies; and (3) when the intensity of the masking tone is increased, masking also increases, but at a rate dependent upon the frequency of the masked tone.

The locus of the masking effect—whether peripheral or central—has been given some theoretical consideration. At the peripheral level, some believe that masking results because the hair cells or nerve fibers which are activated by the masking sound are not available to contribute to the loudness of a simultaneous tone. The lack of available neural elements requires that the intensity of the signal be increased to effect a change in the level of neural activity; this corresponds to an increase in the auditory threshold.

Others (e.g., De Boer 1966) offer a statistical basis for masking and consider that the internal noise of the observer interferes with the auditory process of measuring the average intensity of the signal presented during a certain period of time. Within this framework, there are those who consider that masking has both peripheral and central components. When the auditory system is modeled as a tuned narrow band filter, much of the narrow band character of the system can be attributed to the transducer operation of the end organ, but data on the efficiency of performance (η) in a monaural vs. dichotic amplitude discrimination task indicate that filter effects may occur at higher centers (Sorkin 1966).

Masking of Tones by White Noise: Critical Ratio. The concept of critical bandwidth was developed to account for pure tone masking data and other data in which pure tones were masked by noise (Fletcher 1940). The concept involves two assumptions: (1) the masking of a pure tone by noise is in effect produced by a narrow band of frequencies around the tone so that the masking produced by the frequency components of the noise outside this band can be ignored; and (2) when the masked tone is just audible in the given noise, the acoustic power of the tone is equal to the acoustic power of the noise components contained within the masking band of frequencies.

If both of these assumptions are accepted, the size of the masking band can be calculated from the masked threshold for a pure tone in white noise, since (1) the intensity of the masking noise is known and white noise contains all audible frequencies at equal intensity, and (2) the intensity of the masked threshold is also known. The size of the band which is centered at the frequency of the masked tone and contains the same amount of energy as the masked tone is, by definition, the width of the masking band.

Stated in a different way, the width of the masking band can be calculated by taking the ratio of the intensity of the masked tone to the intensity per cycle of the masking white noise. For example, at 2000 Hz the level per cycle of white noise is 20 dB below the masked monaural threshold of the pure tone (Hawkins and Stevens 1950). A value of 20 dB corresponds to a power ratio of 100:1; therefore, since the intensity in each one-cycle band of noise is 1/100 the intensity of the masked tone, a band of frequencies 100 cycles wide will have a total intensity equal to that of the masked tone. The width of the masking band is, therefore, 100 cycles at 2000 Hz. Since there are alternate ways of arriving at the width of the masking band, the value of the masking band determined in this manner is called a critical ratio. (Notice that the critical ratio can be expressed either in dB or in number of cycles.) The critical ratio does not change as a function of the level of the masking noise; however, the critical ratio is different at different center frequencies of the band.

Other studies have been performed in which pure tone thresholds have been measured in the presence of bands of white noise of different widths (Fletcher 1940; Greenwood 1961). This procedure provides a direct measure of the width of the masking band. The data indicate that a pure tone masked by white noise becomes more difficult to detect as the bandwidth

of the noise is increased and approaches the value of the masking band. When the bandwidth of the noise is increased beyond the masking band, the masked threshold is no longer affected.

When the masking noise reaches 80 dB SPL, a remote masking is observed at frequencies which are considerably below the bandwidth of the noise. As the noise level is increased up to 120 dB SPL, remote masking increases in an accelerating manner; beyond this level, deceleration is observed (Bilger and Hirsh 1956).

It has also been shown that if a pure tone is followed by a burst of noise after a silent interval up to 25 msec, the threshold of the pure tone will be elevated. This is called backward masking (Pickett 1959); the tone to be detected occurs before the masking noise. As the level of the noise burst is increased, there is a progressive increase in the elevated threshold. However, increasing the duration of the masking noise stimuli from 25 to 100 msec produces no differences in backward masking (Elliott 1964).

Critical Bandwidths. The significance of the concept of a masking band as measured by the critical ratio is that it leads to the concept of a critical bandwidth, or simply critical band. This is a very useful concept theoretically since it receives empirical support from four different kinds of experiments: the abso-

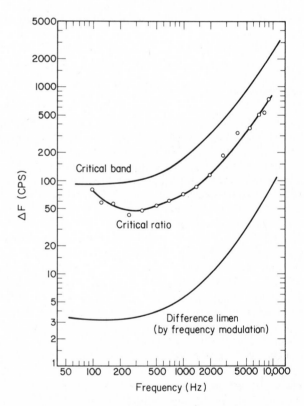

Fig. 17-12. *Comparison of the curves for critical bandwidth and critical ratio. The top curve was derived from four kinds of experiments (see text) and shows the width (ΔF) of the critical band as a function of the center frequency of the band derived from the masking of tones by noise. The bottom curve shows the difference limen for frequency discrimination with a signal which was sinusoidally modulated in frequency at a rate of 2 cycles per sec. (Shower and Biddulph 1931). [From Zwicker, Flottorp, and Stevens 1957; reprinted by permission of the Acoustical Society of America]*

lute threshold of complex tones, the masking of narrow band noise by two pure tones, the detection of phase differences by the comparison of amplitude modulated tones (AM) vs. frequency modulated tones (FM), and the measurement of the loudness of complex sounds as a function of bandwidth. Summaries of this evidence have been provided (Zwicker, Flottorp, and Stevens 1957; Scharf 1961).

The evidence supports a critical band which is a function of frequency, although the band by the four kinds of experiments is about 2.5 times that of the critical ratio. The two curves are compared in Figure 17–12. The differences between the widths of the bands in the two curves may be directly related to the differences in the assumptions which are made in the various kinds of experiments (Swets, Green, and Tanner 1962).

Other functions of frequency (the mel scale of pitch and the difference limen for frequency) also reflect the critical band function. The key underlying this commonality seems to lie in the basilar membrane. It has been proposed that the basilar membrane may be represented by 24 or 25 equal sized segments, with each segment corresponding to a critical band; in this view the critical band corresponds to a constant distance of about 1.3 mm along the basilar membrane (Feldtkeller and Zwicker 1956).

The notion of a fixed critical band, however, is being altered by results from TSD experiments. Mounting evidence favors some form of an adjustable bandpass model. This means that observers are able to vary the characteristics of their receptive systems to match the signals to be detected (Green 1958; Creelman 1961; Van Den Brink 1964).

DIFFERENTIAL THRESHOLDS

The differential threshold (or difference limen, DL) is defined as the smallest difference between two stimuli that can be judged correctly by an observer in a specified percentage of test trials.

Frequency. The most extensive recent study on frequency discrimination is that of Harris (1952) who compared his findings using the method of constant stimulus differences with the classical results of Shower and Biddulph (1931) and several other investigators. The comparison is shown in Figure 17–13 for values of the relative differential threshold ($\Delta F/F$) at a sensation level of 30–40 dB. The relative DL varies as a function of frequency and has a minimal value in the region of 1 to 2 kHz.

Frequency sensitivity also varies as a function of loudness level in phons. (The Loudness Level, LL, of a sound expressed in phon units is numerically equivalent to the dB sound pressure level of an equally loud 1000-Hz tone.) Loudness level up to 30 phons has little effect on the absolute DL for tones of low frequency (below about 500 Hz), although the absolute DL uniformly decreases with frequency, regardless of loudness level; for higher frequencies, the absolute DL is very large at low loudness levels but decreases rapidly as loudness level is increased.

If the relative differential threshold (Weber ratio) is taken as the index of sensitivity, the function relating sensitivity to loudness level is essentially constant at the higher levels for both air and bone conduction (Corso and Levine 1965a). Up to 4000 Hz, the relative DL at 20 phon LL is approximately .004; beyond that it increases sharply for both modes of transmission. At all frequencies, sensitivity is significantly greater for bone conduction.

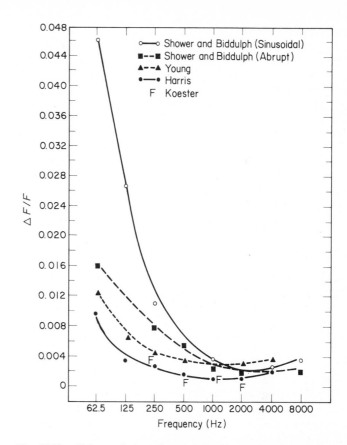

Fig. 17-13. *Values of the relative difference limen for frequency discrimination ($\Delta F/F$) obtained by various investigators. Data were collected at approximately 30 to 40 dB above the threshold of audibility.* [From Harris 1952; reprinted by permission of the Acoustical Society of America]

The duration of the tonal stimulus has also been varied to determine its effect on frequency discrimination. For tone pulses of gradually shortened duration, there is a reduction in differential sensitivity and a decision-theory model has been evolved to show how the ear can "trade" frequency for duration in order to maintain a constant probability of error in discrimination (Sekey 1963). This finding lends further support to the view that the auditory system is capable of adapting its parameters to the stimuli to be detected.

Finally, it has been determined that frequency discrimination is not affected by aural harmonics (Henning 1965) and that it is not better for a diotic tone than a monotic one (Grisanti 1965). Frequency discrimination is absent in the perception of ultrasonic frequencies presented via bone conduction (Corso and Levine 1963).

Intensity. The standard reference work on intensity discrimination is that of Riesz (1928). The results of this study are shown in Figure 17–14. At a given frequency the relative DL approaches a constant value for intensities above 50 dB Sensation Level (SL); as the SL is reduced towards the absolute threshold for that frequency, the relative DL increases very rapidly. The relative DL is a minimum at about 2500 Hz. These data have been confirmed (Harris 1963) and under optimal conditions of judgment, the DL value is found to be less than 1.5 dB regardless of frequency or loudness level; the most acute value is about 0.5 dB.

A significant problem on intensity discrimination has

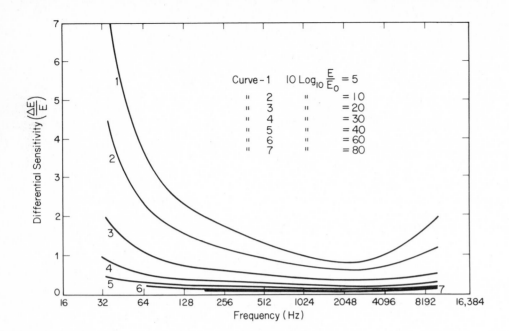

Fig. 17-14. *Values of the relative difference limen for intensity discrimination* ($\Delta E/E$) *as a function of frequency for various levels of intensity. The intensity parameter is* $10 \log_{10} (E/E_o)$ *where the reference* E_o *is the threshold value for a given frequency.* [From Riesz 1928.]

recently been noted which has important theoretical implications. Suppose two separate experiments produce the same amount of masking of a gated sinusoidal signal; but, in one experiment the masking is produced by adjusting the level of continuous noise, while in the other by adjusting the level of a sinusoid. Now consider that the noise and sinusoid are combined. How much must the level of the signal be increased to attain the same level of masking effectiveness as in the initial condition? Theoretically, the signal should be increased by only 3 dB; the problem is that this result is not typically obtained.

One explanation is that an increment greater than 3 dB indicates that the processing of a signal when masked by noise differs from that when masked by a pure tone (Green 1967). Another explanation has been offered after a restatement of the problem in terms of the masking function (McGill and Goldberg 1968). In this model intensity discrimination for pure tones is described as an energy detection process; this provides a single rationale which can then account for the kinds of masking functions which have been obtained for both pure tones and noise.

DURATION

This section will consider some studies in which the observer's task was related primarily to the estimation of the duration of an auditory stimulus or of an interval bounded by auditory cues. Material on time as a variable in temporal integration and masking is contained in earlier sections of this chapter.

It has been found that the estimated duration of an auditory stimulus depends upon its particular characteristics and the psychophysical conditions of judgment. When an observer is required to produce a designated duration up to 6 sec, the intervals appear shorter when a 1000-Hz tone increases or decreases in intensity over a range of 22 dB than when the intensity is held constant (Danziger 1965). With an intermodality matching of visual and auditory signals, the visual modality produces

overestimates of duration relative to hearing (Tanner, Patton, and Atkinson 1965).

The conditions of judgment for the paired comparison of tonal duration are optimal when the time interval between the standard stimulus and the comparison stimulus is sufficiently long to permit the observer to identify the first stimulus in the pair (McGavren 1965). When the interval is shorter than 0.4 sec, short tonal durations (between 0.4–0.6 sec) are underestimated; for greater interstimulus time intervals, they are overestimated. Longer tonal durations are underestimated for all intervals tested (Faroqi and Parameswaran 1966).

The repetition rate of acoustic clicks has been found to significantly affect the direct magnitude estimation of duration (Jones and Maclean 1966). In this study, the clicks ranged from 0 to 10 clicks/sec and the durations to be estimated ranged from 8 to 250 msec. The estimates obtained were almost perfect linear functions of physical duration. As the repetition rate increased up to 1.5 clicks/sec, the estimated durations increased somewhat; for higher rates, they decreased slightly.

Some interest has been shown in the perception of temporal order for auditory stimuli. When pairs of tones are monaurally presented and differ in pitch, type of sound (noise, clicks), or duration, an observer can report the "twoness" of events at intervals of only 2 msec, but an interval of approximately 17 msec was required for 75 percent correct judgment of temporal order (Hirsh 1959). Plomp (1964) found that the just-noticeable time interval between two noise pulses of equal intensity, presented monaurally, was essentially constant at 3 msec from 30 to 75 dB SL; for lower sensation levels, the interval increased rapidly to approximately 30 msec at 10 dB SL.

However, when clicks are presented dichotically between 12 and 20 msec, the correct judgment of temporal order is dependent on the subjective loudness of the clicks at the two ears; as the clicks are judged more often as equal in loudness, the percent correct judgment of temporal order decreases. Thus, the cue of relative loudness must be considered as a significant factor in judging the temporal order of auditory stimuli (Babkoff and Sutton 1963).

A model of some temporal relations has recently been developed which describes the synchronized structure of human behavior in the time domain. The model is based on information processing and shows how research on timing and the conceptualization of the human "time sense" can be handled within a common framework (Michon 1968).

BINAURAL PHENOMENA

Within the last few years, several papers have been published in this area which provide comprehensive coverage of binaural hearing (Rosenzweig 1961; Deatherage, 1966; Green and Henning 1969).

Sound Localization. The data on sound localization in a free field appear to support the duplex theory of Stevens and Newman (1936). The theory maintains that nontransient tones are localized through two sets of cues: for low frequencies, temporal cues are dominant; for high frequencies, intensive cues are dominant. In the midrange, neither cue is effective and localization errors occur. For complex sounds like noise and impulses, both cues operate simultaneously.

However, these cues are not effective in localizing sound in a nonfree field. In this case, head movements provide cue information (Wallach 1940); without movement, the time of arrival of the initial transients in the wavefront provides a reliable indicant of location when compared to the second (echo) transient (Wallach, Newman and Rosenzweig 1949). The research on lateralization (i.e., "locating" the sound image within one's head when the sound is presented diotically with earphones) has indicated that time and intensity cues are both operative in a complementary manner.

Masking Level Difference. The masking level difference (MLD) is another phenomenon which indicates that the auditory system can perform a binaural analysis of incoming sounds. This effect can be demonstrated by putting noise into binaural earphones and then adding a signal to one of the phones. The signal is easier to hear in this situation than having either (1) a single phone with signal and noise or (2) adding the signal in phase to both phones. The presence of noise alone in one ear produces an effect in the other ear which separates the signal from the same noise waveform, thereby decreasing the masking effectiveness of the noise.

Two major explanations have been advanced to account for MLD: (1) the time difference model (Jeffress 1965) and (2) the model of equalization and cancellation (Durlach 1960). In the Jeffress model, there is "a set of two filter systems, one for each ear. The incoming acoustic waveform is filtered by a set of bandpass filters. Each successive filter is tuned to a lower frequency and the action is designed to mimic the filtering accomplished in the cochlea and first-order neural structures. The width of each filter might be about the size of a critical band" (Green and Henning 1969, p. 121).

In the Durlach model, "the waveforms presented at the two ears are first filtered, then amplified and attenuated, and then shifted in time. The amount of attenuation or time shifting depends on the nature of the task. Finally, the scaled and perhaps

time-shifted signals from each ear are either added or subtracted in a cancellation device. In all cases the specific mode of operation or parameter value is chosen to optimize the signal-to-noise ratio" (Green and Henning 1969, p. 122).

The major differences between the two theories are (1) that the time-difference model can be more readily interpreted physiologically and (2) that the equalization and cancellation model is more specific and generates direct quantitative hypotheses.

INFORMATION PROCESSING

The use of information theory in psychology seems to have declined considerably in recent years, except for work in England on short-term memory (e.g., Baddeley 1968). Several general reviews of information theory as applied to psychology are available (Miller 1956; Alluisi 1957; Broadbent 1958; Attneave 1959; Garner 1962; Corso 1967a). The material in this section is intended to provide a perspective of the kinds of studies performed, rather than a complete review of the literature.

Transmission of Information. In an early study dealing with the single auditory dimension of pitch (Pollack 1952a), it was found that, on the average, observers can transmit a maximum of only 2.3 bits of information, given a set of eight alternative tones ranging in frequency from 100 to 8000 Hz. This is equivalent to perfect discrimination for about five categories of frequency. Furthermore, the spacing of the stimuli on the frequency continuum had very little effect on discrimination; increasing the spacing of the eight tones from the range 100–1500 Hz to 1000–8000 Hz increased transmission by less than 0.5 bit. Practice over several weeks can lead to some improvement if there is a sufficiently large separation in frequency among the alternative stimuli (Hartman 1954).

In loudness discrimination for a 1000-Hz tone, observers were presented with 4 to 20 stimuli covering the intensity range from 15 to 110 dB (re 10^{-16} watt/sq cm) (Garner 1953). The information transmission, averaged for several subjects, was approximately 2.1 bits, or the equivalent of perfect discrimination between 4 to 5 tones.

For auditory duration, tones ranging from 0.5 to 5.0 sec provide 2.77 bits of transmitted information (between 6 and 7 categories), but shorter intervals between 0.1 to 1.0 sec provide only 2.04 bits (between 4 and 5 categories) (Murphy 1966).

When absolute judgments are made in a multidimensional auditory task, the amount of transmitted information is increased over that for a single dimension. Given 20 different tones obtained by combining five frequencies in equal logarithmic steps between 125 and 7000 Hz and five intensities between loudness levels of 20 and 90 phons, the information transmission for the simultaneous pitch and loudness cues was 3.1 bits. However, these same stimuli presented in a unidimensional task yielded 1.8 bits for frequency and 1.7 bits for intensity—a total of 3.5 bits. Thus, when two dimensions are used, there is an increase in the total amount of information transmitted, but at a decrease in the amount per dimension (Pollack 1953). If the stimulus dimensions are independent, the stimulus confusion to multidimensional stimuli can be predicted from the responses to unidimensional stimuli (Corcoran 1966).

The upper limit of auditory information transmission with

tones and noise is reached when eight dimensions are used simultaneously. This yields 7.0 bits, or about 128 absolutely discriminable auditory signals (Pollack and Ficks 1954). In certain practiced situations, frequency seems to be the most effective dimension (Mudd 1965).

Some estimates have been made on the theoretical limits of the rate of information transmission in the auditory system (Jacobson 1951). On the basis of some rather tentative assumptions, the maximum capacity for the human ear is calculated to be 8000 bits/sec for random sound and 10,000 bits/sec for loud sounds. Spoken English is estimated maximally as about 50 bits/sec, given a 150,000 word vocabulary and a speaking rate of 300 words/min; musical listening gives a maximum transmission rate of approximately 70 bits/sec. It is estimated, therefore, that the brain can process less than one percent of the information that the ears can pass. With about 29,000 ganglion cells per ear and a maximum capacity of 10,000 bits/sec, the average rate of information transfer over a single nerve fiber is estimated to be about 0.3 bits/sec.

Auditory Pattern Perception. Few studies have been published in this area, if studies related to speech perception are excluded.

In the recognition of nonverbal material, Royer and Garner (1966) had listeners press a key in synchrony with auditory patterns formed by two different stimuli arranged in sequences of eight items each. The results show that those patterns with fewer alternative modes of combining the stimuli were more easily perceived.

Corso (1957a) had college musicians make absolute judgments of equally tempered tonalities (key name and mode). Three series of piano tones were used for each of the twelve major and twelve minor keys: (1) eight-tone ascending diatonic scales, (2) the same eight tones arranged in random order, and (3) sequences of four chords. With 4.58 bits of information presented for each series, the information transmitted was 1.02, 0.37, and 0.77 bits, respectively; for judgments of the two modes, (major and minor) the information transmitted was 0.47, 0.03, and 0.37 bits, respectively, for the three series. When the listeners were required to judge only mode (omitting key names), performance improved somewhat, but the results confirm that absolute judgments of musical tonality impose a difficult perceptual task.

Theoretical Positions. Data from numerous studies support the position that information theory may be appropriately used in conceptualizing certain aspects of auditory processes. In general, the evidence favors the hypothesis of a limited capacity system for hearing (Broadbent 1958). In such a system it is assumed that there are multiple input lines which converge onto a switch (or selective filter) which can select any one incoming message while holding the messages from the other lines in short-term storage. Beyond the switch there is a channel with a limited capacity. Some view the channel more-or-less anatomically (Broadbent 1958); others view it functionally in terms of a filter mechanism which precedes certain stages of analysis of the stimulus input (Triesman 1964).

However, a modification of the concept of limited channel capacity has recently been proposed (Moray 1967). Specifically, it is hypothesized that there is not a limited channel capacity in the sense of a transmission line, but rather a central processor with a limited capacity; the organization of this processor can be altered flexibly by some internal selfprogramming. Unlike the transmission line which passively carries messages, the central processor receives, transforms, and generates messages so that from moment to moment the size of the processing channel may appear to vary.

ATTRIBUTES OF AUDITORY PERCEPTION

Pitch. Pitch is that attribute of auditory sensation in terms of which sounds may be ordered on a psychological scale extending from low to high. Given a sound of sufficient duration and intensity, pitch appears to depend upon two physical parameters: frequency spectrum and time pattern. Each of these gives rise to a particular kind of pitch or, more specifically, each involves a different mechanism for mediating pitch perception. (1) The pitch parameter which depends on the frequency spectrum is controlled by the location of maximum excitation along the basilar membrane and is called place pitch. Different frequencies produce vibrations whose amplitude is maximum at different places along the membrane; these maxima differ from the excitation maxima due to time delays and neural inhibition. (2) The pitch associated with the time pattern or periodicity of the acoustic stimulus is not directly dependent on the locus of maximal stimulation and is called periodicity pitch. Both of these mechanisms appear to be needed to account theoretically for the pitch data currently available on normal and pathological ears (Carhart 1967).

The case for place pitch is now firmly established and the earlier experimental and clinical evidence has been summarized by Wever (1949). This material shows the regions of frequency over which localization of response occurs in the cochlea and the degree of specificity which obtains. Stated broadly, the findings from numerous lines of evidence indicate that low frequency tones are localized towards the apical end of the cochlea; high frequency tones, towards the basal end. Mechanical differentiation of acoustic spectra occurs, then, in the form of peripheral spatial patterning of vibrations along the cochlear partition.

However, a simple tonotopic or place theory of pitch perception appears inadequate. The patterning along the cochlear partition provides relatively broad maxima of amplitude, particularly for frequencies below 500 Hz; thus it seems reasonable to consider that sharpening must occur to permit frequency differentiation as acute as that obtained in discrimination studies. The contemporary theoretical issue concerns the nature of the sharpening mechanism and its locus, whether peripheral or central. Two hypotheses regarding a peripheral mechanism are: (1) that sharpening occurs due to changes in the axis of displacement between the tectorial and basilar membranes in the region where the traveling wave has its maximum amplitude (Davis 1957b), and (2) that the localization of response is sharpened neurologically through the inhibitory effects of the neural network of the inner ear associated with the delay in the time of arrival of stimulation at different sections of the basilar membrane (Békésy 1960).

Others have proposed that sharpening occurs in the central nervous system and involves the time pattern of the responding neural units. Since the excitation of an individual unit in the acoustic nerve occurs at a particular instant when stimulated by different frequencies, a train of "time-locked" neural spikes is generated as in the volley-place theory; it is hypothesized that this train is then decoded by the nervous system at the level of the cochlear nucleus, and possibly also at higher levels (Carhart 1967).

A second difficulty with the place theory is found in the results of studies on periodicity pitch. In several kinds of experiments, a definite pitch is heard which does not correspond to a component that is present in the Fourier analysis of the stimulus. These experiments include the residue phenomenon (Schouten 1962). Given Fourier-components that are too narrowly spaced in frequency to be separately resolved and perceived, e.g., 1800, 2000, and 2200 Hz, a pitch is heard which corresponds approximately to the spacing of the components, e.g., 200 Hz, or to the periodicity of the harmonics. This type of low pitch occurs for clusters of high frequency harmonics up to about 5000 Hz and numerous studies have shown that the residue phenomenon can be elicited at low signal intensities, so that it is not an artifact of mechanical distortion in the ear. The low subjective pitch continues to be heard even when the low frequency elements of the peripheral sensorineural system are activated by random masking noise.

A second line of studies has also shown that a definite pitch can be heard when there is no energy in the stimulus spectrum at the corresponding frequency. Given a periodically interrupted tone, subjects can perceive two pitches; one pitch corresponds to the pitch of the tone as if there were no interruptions, while the other corresponds to the frequency of interruptions. If white noise or a pulse train is used as the signal and is periodically interrupted, a distinct pitch is again heard corresponding to the interruption rate. This shows that differential perception of the frequency of interruption can occur even when the signal produces equally distributed disturbances along the basilar membrane, provided the rates of interruption are low. It appears that periodicity pitch (which includes residue pitch) is dependent upon the periodicity of the envelope waveform or the pulse repetition rate of the stimuli (Rosenberg 1965).

The experimental data on pitch discrimination and on the electrophysiological responses of individual units of the auditory nerve suggest that (1) only a "time-locked" mechanism for pitch operates below about 300 Hz, (2) only a place sensitive mechanism operates above about 5000 Hz, and (3) between these two limits there is an overlapping and graded operation of the two mechanisms.

These findings have led to several hypotheses on pitch-extracting mechanisms responsive to information in the time domain. The most detailed explanation is that of Licklider (1959) who proposed a triplex theory in which the acoustic patterns delivered to the two ears are subjected to a mechanical frequency analysis in the cochlea according to the traditional place hypothesis; the products of that analysis are then subjected to a twofold correlational analysis in unspecified centers of the nervous system. One of these analyses mediates sound localization, while the other exposes periodicities that may have appeared only in the envelope and not in the waveform, per se, of the acoustic stimulus. The third stage of the theory involves certain self-organizing functions of the auditory neuronal network. The extension of the theory (Licklider 1962) shows how various transformation systems can allocate incoming temporal information to specific neural locations in the afferent pathways, starting with the cochlear nuclei.

Other investigators, while accepting periodicity pitch, do not agree that the analyzing function is performed by a special mechanism or one that is central to the cochlea. Tonndorf (1962) holds to a modified place concept in which a time/frequency analysis is performed on the place patterns induced along the cochlear partition, but some evidence argues against this (Campbell 1963). Békésy (1963) has reinterpreted some of the periodicity findings in terms of place theory and doubts that the periodicity principle alone is sufficient to determine the pitch of a sound. He has pointed out that a band of low frequency noise gives rise to a pitch corresponding to its upper and lower edges, even though there is no periodicity to account for these pitches. Thurlow (1963) believes that there is no precise time analyzing system for determining low pitch and that low pitch is related to a mediating vocal response for musically trained subjects.

Relatively little work has been performed in recent years on matters of place pitch. The mel scale of Stevens, Volkmann, and Newman (1937) relating pitch to pure-tone frequency has been replicated (Siegel 1965), except at frequencies above about 5000 Hz. Corso and Levine (1965a) have shown that pitch discrimination ceases near the upper frequency limit of audibility.

The pitch-intensity function has also been reexamined. In the original study (Stevens 1935), it was found that the pitch of low tones seems to decrease for increasing sound levels, whereas the opposite occurs for high frequencies. These findings have been replicated, but the magnitude of the shifts is very small (Cohen 1961). The pitch of low frequency tones is also shifted downward by masking wide band noise, upward for high frequency tones (Steiner and Small 1966). In addition, masking tends to accelerate the mel function (Richards 1968).

A series of experiments has been performed to determine whether the pitch of complex tones is based on the fundamental frequency or on its periodicity (Plomp 1966). For fundamental frequencies beyond 1400 Hz, the pitch follows the fundamental; but, for lower frequencies, the pitch follows the periodicity of the harmonics. This holds for tones with harmonics of equal amplitude and for tones with harmonics which decrease in amplitude by 6 dB/octave.

The pitch of complex tones was found to possess two distinguishable attributes (Shepard 1964): (1) tone height, which is a monotonic function of frequency and is measured in mels; and (2) tonality (musical pitch or chroma), which is cyclical (or circular) with a period of slightly more than a physical octave. Except for individuals with absolute pitch, tonality is a relative property. A given tone can be heard to be the same or different from another in tonality, but it does not seem to have a subjectively unique quality that can be identified absolutely. Corso (1957a) has shown that this same principle applies to complete diatonic scales and chord progressions in major and minor keys.

Loudness. Loudness is the intensive attribute of an auditory sensation in terms of which sounds may be ordered on a psychological scale extending from soft to loud. Loudness is not the perception of intensity and the decibel is not a unit of loudness. As an auditory dimension, loudness is measured on a psychological scale; as generally adopted, the scale is that derived by Stevens (1936), with the sone as the unit of measurement. One sone is the loudness of a 1000-Hz tone at 40 dB SL, listened to binaurally. The loudness of any sound which is judged by the listener to be *n* times that of the l-sone tone is said to have a loudness of *n* sones.

The relation between loudness and physical intensity has been studied by numerous investigators, using both direct and indirect scaling methods (Torgerson 1958). Stevens' law states that the loudness of a 1000-Hz tone increases as a power function of sound pressure. That is,

$$L = k(p - p_o)^{0.6} \qquad [4]$$

where L is loudness, p is sound pressure, k is a constant that depends upon units, and p_o is the threshold value (Stevens 1955). The loudness of white noise grows at the same rate, except at levels lower than approximately 40 dB SL.

A scale of loudness derived from the data of twelve different investigations differs very little from the Stevens' scale (D.W. Robinson 1957). Also, cross-modality matches have been made between loudness and ten other perceptual continua; all matching functions are power functions, but the data indicate that the loudness exponent may be about 0.64 (Stevens 1966). The loudness function has recently been extended to low frequencies and weak intensities (Hellman and Zwislocki 1961, 1968). In general, the lower the frequency, the more rapidly loudness grows as a function of stimulus intensity, at least below 100 dB SPL.

Since loudness is a function of frequency as well as intensity, equal loudness (isophonic) contours have been derived by several investigators. The contours typically show sound pressure level plotted as a function of frequency, with loudness level (LL) in phons as the parameter (Robinson and Dadson 1956). The curves are shown in Figure 17–15. Above 1000 Hz, the shapes are complex, probably due to distortion effects of the sound field around the head. Below 500 Hz, low frequency tones increase in loudness by a greater amount than high frequency tones for equal increments in intensity.

Equal loudness contours for bone-conducted sounds are similar in form to those for air conduction, but loudness may extend to higher frequencies under bone conduction (Corso and Levine 1965b). Equal-loudness contours are also available for narrow bands of random noise (Pollack 1952b). For a given wide-band noise spectrum, the loudness in sones need not be determined experimentally but may be calculated by a variety of methods and converted into loudness level in phons (Stevens 1961).

In addition to frequency and intensity, loudness is a function of stimulus duration. From 50 to 500 msec, the loudness of a 1000-Hz tone increases as a logarithmic function of duration (Ekman, Berglund, and Berglund 1966). Loudness also is the product of two other auditory attributes: volume (apparent size) and density (apparent compactness or concentration) (Stevens 1965).

Electrophysiological studies on recorded impulses from single nerve cells have provided experimental evidence on the manner in which intensity information is carried within the auditory system. For a given stimulus, the intensity is encoded in terms of the total number of nerve impulses delivered to the cortical centers per unit time. If the intensity is increased, the total number of impulses may be increased in two ways: (1) by increasing the rate of neural firing in the active fibers and (2) by activating additional fibers with different intensity thresholds. The change in discharge rate is probably important at the lower neural level. There are some indications that the auditory cortex does not need to be involved in normal intensity discrimination.

Timbre. Timbre is that attribute of auditory sensation in terms of which a listener can judge that two sounds are dissimilar even though they have the same pitch and loudness. Timbre,

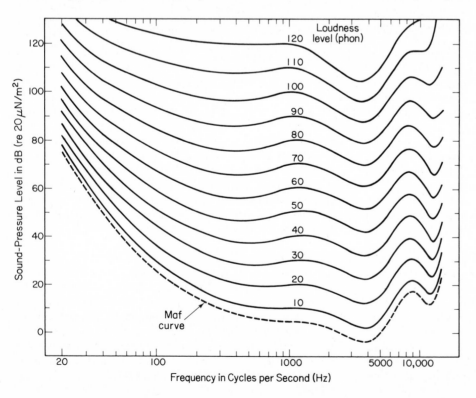

Fig. 17-15. *Equal loudness contours for pure tones by free field measurements. The number on each curve is the sound pressure level of the equally loud 1000-Hz tone used for comparison for that curve.* [From Robinson and Dadson 1956; Crown Copyright, National Physical Laboratory (England)]

like pitch and loudness, is a psychological dimension of complex tones, but is far less understood.

There are two prevalent theories of timbre. The classical harmonic-structure theory modified from von Helmholtz holds that timbre is a function of the frequency, relative amplitude, and phase relations among the partials of a tone. In this view, the primary determinant of timbre is the acoustic spectrum as revealed by the cross-sectional analysis of a tone in the momentary duration of one cycle.

An alternative (or supplement) to the classical theory is the formant theory of musical quality. The theory holds that the characteristic tone quality of an instrument is due to the relative strengthening of whatever partials lie within a fixed or relatively fixed region of the musical scale.

This region is called a formant of that tone, and any tone may have more than one formant. The partials nearest this region or regions are those that are strengthened in intensity. The strengthening may be due to the resonance of some part of the musical instrument or to the body of air enclosed within the instrument. Thus, the frequencies in the formant region do not need to be harmonically related to the fundamental of the tone.

In contrast to the classical theory which requires a fixed spectrum for tones from a particular musical instrument, the formant theory relies upon changes in the spectrum of a tone to produce constancy of timbre. Also, the formant theory can explain the fact that the tonal quality of a musical instrument tends to be simplified as the fundamental frequency is increased throughout the range of the instrument. This occurs as a given formant is eliminated from the complex tone when the fundamental reaches that particular frequency region.

A third theoretical explanation for timbre has recently been proposed (Plomp 1966). The explanation stems from the classical view of harmonic structure and proposes that timbre is determined by the relative sound levels within successive critical bands. This gives the vibration pattern along the basilar membrane an important role in mediating timbre judgments. The critical-band timbre hypothesis is extended to cover nonperiodic sounds as well as periodic sounds.

Experimental data on these three positions are, unfortunately, very limited. Timbre judgments for ten musical instruments failed to yield unequivocal support for either the classical or formant theory (Saldanha and Corso 1964). However, it was found that initial transients and a vibrato tone are important determiners of timbre; also, it was suggested that the temporal gradients of the appearance and disappearance of the partials during the beginning and ending of a tone may provide additional cues.

Other evidence seems to indicate that timbre is correlated with movement of the formants of the stimulus (Jenkins 1961). It is suggested that in terms of cochlear functions the total acoustic stimulus undergoes a differential filtering action along the cochlear partition which is brought about by the resonant characteristics of the cochlear structure.

The response of a segment of the partition will show first-order and second-order time envelopes. The aggregate of the repetition rates of the first-order time envelopes is said to elicit the perception of pitch; the second-order envelope defines a function over the entire cochlear partition which purportedly elicits the perception of timbre.

Clinical Aspects of Hearing

HEARING DISORDERS AND AUDIOMETRY

The practical benefits to be derived from an understanding of the functioning of the human auditory system are related to problems of deafness and hearing loss. Deafness refers to a total loss of hearing or the inability to communicate in terms of everyday speech; hearing loss is a general designation for impaired hearing or the processes which produce it. The measurement of hearing ability is through audiometry which includes a variety of tests to determine: (1) auditory sensitivity for pure tones, (2) the recognition of pitch, (3) the discrimination of pitch, loudness, and speech, and (4) the tolerance for high intensity sound. Thus, deafness and hearing loss extend beyond simple tests of sensitivity; the other impairments are classed under the more general heading of dysacusis.

Varieties of Dysacusis. There are two major categories of hearing impairment: peripheral and central. A peripheral impairment involves the poor conduction of sound to the cochlea or an abnormality in the auditory structures up to the cochlea and its associated cranial nerve; central dysacusis involves an impairment in the central nervous system beyond the cochlea or auditory nerve.

Peripheral hearing loss is usually subdivided into conductive and sensorineural classifications to designate more specifically the nature or locus of the disorder. If a peripheral impairment in a given person includes both conductive and sensorineural aspects, the term mixed hearing loss is commonly used. Central dysacusis may be subdivided into three types: (1) aphasia, the failure to understand the meanings of words which are clearly heard; (2) phonemic regression, the impairment of speech perception in the aged; and (3) functional or psychogenic deafness due to personality disorders (Ventry and Chaiklen 1965). The distinction between conductive and sensorineural hearing loss is important since it implies different causal factors, prognosis, and treatment.

Forms of Audiometry. In clinical practice, two types of audiometry are routinely used: pure tone audiometry and speech audiometry.

Within pure tone audiometry there are numerous kinds of pure tone audiometers, each with certain advantages for particular situations: (1) screening audiometers vs. monitoring audiometers vs. diagnostic audiometers, which, respectively, yield results in terms of a pass-fail test, a limited number of tested frequencies, and a complete audiogram; (2) individual vs. group audiometers; and (3) manual vs. semiautomatic vs. fully automatic audiometers.

The pure tone test on a diagnostic audiometer provides a measure of auditory sensitively at different frequencies, usually within the range of 250 to 8000 Hz, with the tones presented by air conduction through earphones. The results are presented in the form of an audiogram which shows the number of decibels that a person's threshold of hearing is above or below the standard zero reference of the audiometer for that particular frequency. The term hearing level is used to designate the status of hearing as measured in decibels on the audiometer; the term threshold shift refers to any change in the hearing level. The audiogram is extremely valuable in the classification of hearing disorders.

Pure-tone audiometers are also provided with a bone-conduction receiver so that tests may be made to determine the individual's sensitivity to bone-conducted sounds. Comparison of air-conduction and bone-conduction thresholds provides useful diagnostic information on the nature of auditory impairments. The principle is that in a conductive loss, hearing by air conduction is impaired, but hearing by bone conduction is essentially normal; in a sensorineural loss, hearing by both modes is ordinarily equally affected. The mechanism of bone conduction has recently been reported in a revised theory (Tonndorf et al. 1966) and considerable progress has been made in establishing a normal reference level for bone conduction (Studebaker 1967).

In the automatic audiometry category, the Békésy audiometer (Békésy 1947) is among the most widely used. The subject controls the intensity by pressing and releasing a switch while the frequency is slowly but gradually increased or decreased as predetermined by the experimenter, or the frequency may remain fixed. Also, the tone may be continuous or interrupted. A graphical record is automatically traced showing the subject's threshold as a function of frequency. Numerous studies have been performed to determine the effects of testing time, signal attenuation rate, direction of frequency sweep, tone pulsing, and other variables on the auditory threshold (e.g., Corso 1955; Corso 1956b; Corso and Wilson 1957; Epstein 1960; Harbert and Young 1966; and Wright 1968). The results have also been shown to be related to the personality variables of anxiety and depression (Shepherd and Goldstein 1968).

Speech audiometry is ordinarily used to measure two aspects of hearing ability: (1) the threshold for speech, which is the intensity level at which speech must be presented in order that the listener may respond correctly to 50 percent of the test items; and (2) speech discrimination, which is denoted in the form of an articulation curve showing the percentage of words from a specified list that are correctly identified as a function of intensity. Discrimination loss for speech is the difference between 100 percent and the percentage of words of a phonetically balanced (PB) list which a listener repeats correctly when the list is presented at an intensity so high that a further increase will not improve his score.

The material used in speech audiometry is presented from records or by live voice and ordinarily consists of standard items of the following form: (1) spondees, familiar words with equal stress on each syllable, e.g., baseball, (2) two-digit numbers, e.g., six four, (3) lists of monosyllabic words that are phonetically balanced, (4) lists of sentences with certain key words, and (5) lists of questions which must be answered. The purpose of the tests is to measure hearing impairments which are not detected in pure tone audiometry and to provide an index of the individual's social adequacy of hearing.

For young adults with no otological impairments, the threshold of speech for spondaic words presented monaurally is 18.5 dB SPL (Corso 1957b); the mean value for the maximum articulation score on phonetically balanced word lists presented at 78 dB SPL is about 98 percent (Corso 1957c).

Another form of audiometry receiving considerable current emphasis is electroencephalic audiometry (EEA), sometimes called evoked response audiometry (ERA). The method depends on the amplification of small electroencephalographic potentials recorded from the vertex (V) of the head and the improvement of the signal-to-noise ratio by averaging or summing many time-locked responses, while an auditory signal is being presented (Davis and Niemoller 1968). Typically the responses to 50–64 stimuli are averaged, with an interstimulus interval of about 1 sec. The writeout from the computer provides a graphical record of the V potential from which the threshold is estimated in dB.

Validation studies of ERA on children from four to ten years of age show that the group mean thresholds for V potentials are within about 2 dB of the values obtained from conventional clinical audiograms (Davis et al. 1967). The method has also been used successfully with infants unable to understand language or instructions and with clinical patients who were unable or unwilling to respond appropriately to conventional audiometric procedures. Additional research is being conducted to establish the method as a diagnostically useful technique in assessing hearing disorders (McCandless 1967) and for auditory work with animals (Henderson et al. 1969).

Other innovations in audiometry are related to electrodermal techniques (I.E. Watson 1968); cortical conditioning (Pollack 1967); signal detection theory (Campbell and Moulin 1968); brief tone audiometry (Sanders 1967); and high-frequency methods (Harris and Harris 1969).

NOISE EXPOSURE

Temporary Threshold Shift (TTS). When the ear is stimulated by sound, the effects which occur can be divided into two general classes: (1) perstimulatory phenomena, those which are observed during exposure, and (2) poststimulatory phenomena, those which are measured following exposure. Each of these classes contains numerous specific effects, measured physiologically or psychophysically.

One effect which has received much attention in the current literature is the poststimulatory temporary threshold shift (TTS). TTS is defined as the difference in the threshold of audibility for a given tone measured before and after an individual has been exposed to sounds with known physical characteristics. The amount of shift is conventionally measured 2 min after the given exposure is terminated. TTS is a transitory phenomenon in which the absolute threshold that has been elevated by noise exposure returns to its preexposure level in the absence of noise, usually within a matter of hours or days.

Studies have been conducted to determine the effects of duration, intensity level, repetition rate, and acoustic spectrum on TTS for pure tones (Ward, Glorig, and Sklar 1958). Equations have been developed which show that TTS is a linear function of the logarithm of exposure time; also, the growth of TTS is approximately proportional to the fraction of time that the noise is presented and increases with noise intensity. The recovery curves for TTS are linear functions of the logarithm of time following the cessation of stimulation; the rate of recovery is proportional to the amount of TTS produced by the exposure conditions.

Noise Induced Permanent Threshold Shift (NIPTS). The practical significance of TTS lies in its possible relationship to hearing losses produced by exposure to noise. It has definitely been established that noise exposure can produce permanent hearing impairments, and damage-risk criteria have been specified in terms of TTS (Kryter et al. 1966). For different spectra, the criteria indicate the maximal levels and durations of sounds that can be tolerated without endangering hearing. Recent data indicate that in some respects these criteria may be too stringent (Cohen and Jackson 1969). As a general rule, any exposure to sound which produces TTS approaching or exceeding 40 dB is imminently capable of producing a permanent loss. Any condition of stimulation which produces TTS that is completely recovered prior to the next day's exposure is not likely to produce a hearing impairment, even after long time periods.

It should not be assumed, however, that a person's resistance to TTS for a particular set of exposure conditions can be used to predict his resistance to a permanent loss for noise in general. Such a relationship has not been established (LaBenz, Cohen, and Pearson 1967); there is even some question whether "susceptibility to a NIPTS from a particular source can be predicted from knowledge of susceptibility to TTS from the same noise" (Ward 1967). Noise-induced hearing loss is now considered to be a major health hazard in American industry. Noise level measurements on new tractors and thirteen other types of farm machinery have also indicated a potential NIPTS for the agricultural worker (Jones and Oser 1968).

A typical set of data on NIPTS is shown in Figure 17–16 for airport inspectors. This figure compares the mean hearing level of noise-exposed workers with that of nonexposed groups of the same age and sex (male). As the length of service in increased from 0–5 years to 16–20 years, the differences between the two groups become more marked. Note also that the curves for the nonnoise exposed groups show hearing losses from the baseline (0 dB); these curves reflect losses due to aging (presbycusis). Both kinds of impairments develop gradually over the years.

For military pilots, aging seems to have a greater influence on permanent threshold shift than exposure to aircraft noise during flying time (Schulthess and Huelsen 1968). Small but statistically significant hearing losses at 2000 to 4000 Hz have been obtained for women in a textile fiber manufacturing plant (Pell and Dickerson 1966).

The audiometric curve in noise-induced hearing loss has a characteristic threshold dip at 4000 and 6000 Hz and rises again at 8000 Hz, but not to the normal level. Hearing losses appear first in the region of 3000 to 6000 Hz, with the greatest loss usually at 4000 Hz. There is little disturbance at the speech frequencies below 3000 Hz in the early stages of loss so the impairment often remains undetected for long periods of time.

Recent data show that noise has the same deleterious effects from 10 to 14 kHz as it has at 4000 and 6000 Hz (Sataloff, Vassallo, and Menduke 1967). Also there appears to be no interaction between the effects of noise and age; this implies that the hearing loss for the two factors is combined in an additive manner.

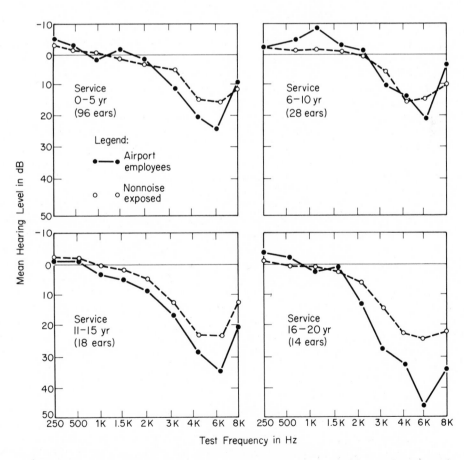

Fig. 17-16. *Comparison of mean hearing levels for airport inspectors and for non-noise exposed groups equated by age and sex. Each graph provides a comparison for different lengths of service.* [From Cohen 1965.]

Another form of hearing disorder resulting from noise is acoustic trauma. This is an injury due to a single or limited number of brief exposures to high intensity sounds, such as the impulse noise of gunfire in military activities or sports and rock-and-roll music. Acoustic trauma may manifest itself by tinnitus, hearing loss, changes in pitch perception, or pain. If the degree of acoustic trauma is not severe, recovery may occur over a few hours or days, otherwise the threshold shift is permanent.

In the case of noise-induced hearing loss and in severe acoustic trauma, the impairment is sensorineural in character. Irreversible damage occurs to the hair cells of the cochlea which do not regenerate; this produces a form of hearing impairment for which remedial therapy is not available. The need for hearing conservation programs and noise abatement in industry, military services, sports, and daily activities must be recognized and implemented if human hearing is to be preserved.

AGING

The pathologies which occur in aging produce a decrease in hearing sensitivity and suggest four kinds of presbycusis (Schuknecht 1964): (1) sensory presbycusis, in which there is epithelial atrophy in the basal end of the organ of Corti that produces an abrupt hearing loss for high frequency tones; (2) neural presbycusis, in which there is a loss in neuron population in the auditory pathways that produces a loss in the ability to discriminate speech; (3) metabolic presbycusis, in which there is atrophy

of the stria vascularis in the cochlea that produces a fairly uniform pure tone loss, and (4) mechanical presbycusis, in which there is a stiffening of the basilar membrane that produces an increase in the amount of hearing loss at higher frequencies. In individuals over 75 years of age, there is also a reduction in the population of afferent nerve cells in the cerebral cortex which leads to impaired hearing and the inability to communicate effectively (Sataloff 1965).

Extensive data have been published on presbycusis in men and women by Corso (1963b); these data and the results from seven other studies have been combined to yield a set of threshold curves for men and women from 25 to 85 years of age (Spoor 1967). The values of presbycusis for the combined studies are shown in Figure 17–17 for men and in Figure 17–18 for women. The curves indicate that for frequencies up to 1000 Hz, the increase in hearing level is less than 5 dB up to 50 years and, regardless of age and sex, is almost independent of frequency. For frequencies above 1000 Hz, hearing level increases with frequency for all age groups, except 8000 Hz for the younger age group. At ages up to 50 years, the highest hearing level is obtained at 4000 and 6000 Hz; above this age, the highest level is at 8000 Hz. Also, with advancing age, the curves begin to drop at progressively lower frequencies.

In general, the hearing level for men is higher than that for women, age held constant, for 2000 Hz and above. At and below 1000 Hz, the hearing level of women is generally slightly higher than that for men. Although caution must be used in interpretation, it is interesting that the hearing of the Maabans of the

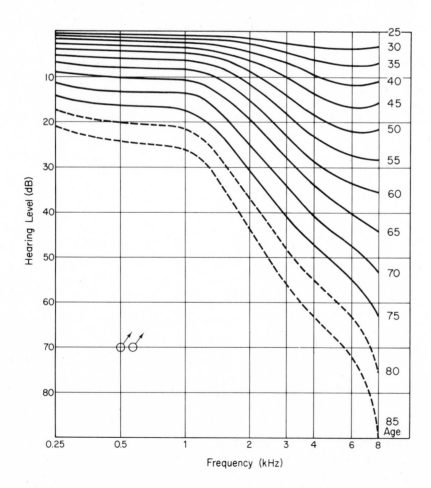

Fig. 17-17. *Curves showing the relation between hearing level and frequency for men at different ages according to data calculated from eight published studies.* [From Spoor 1967.]

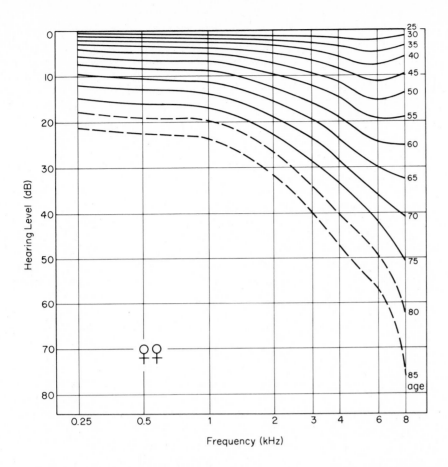

Fig. 17-18. *Curves showing the relation between hearing level and frequency for women at different ages according to data calculated from eight published studies.* [From Spoor 1967.]

Sudan (Rosen et al. 1962) and the Todas of South India (Kapur and Patt 1967) does not show the marked deterioration with age found in the United States and Europe.

ILLNESS AND DISEASE

Conductive Deafness. Illness and disease are frequent causes of hearing loss. The incidence of conductive deafness is high in infectious diseases such as typhoid fever, smallpox, mumps, and cases of riboflavin and nicotinic acid deficiencies (Kapur 1966). The most frequent condition leading to conductive deafness is otitis media; this is an infection in the middle ear that usually develops from a cold. The acute condition of otitis media produces only a temporary impairment; but a chronic infection may lead to a permanent hearing loss.

Otosclerosis is a common disease that leads to a conductive loss. This disease is estimated to occur in about 12 percent of white women and about 6 percent of white men. It produces a soft long growth at the stapes in the region of the oval window which prevents the normal movement of the stapes in the transmission of sound to the cochlea. Otosclerosis is a hereditary disease but, fortunately, hearing impairment is produced in only about 10 percent of the cases in which it occurs.

The treatment of otosclerosis may involve fenestration (the opening of a new path for sound conduction to the cochlea via the round window), stapes mobilization (direct mechanical manipulation and freeing of the stapes), or a plantinectomy operation (in which the footplate of the stapes is replaced by a small piece of vein from the back of the hand). More recent

techniques utilize the replacement of the stapes by one of stainless steel (M. Robinson 1965) and the possible application of a laser beam to irradiate the stapedial footplate (Sataloff 1967). The commonality of these and other surgical procedures for otosclerosis depends inevitably upon the mobilization of the perilymph; no operation can restore hearing until the cochlear fluids are set in motion by incoming sound.

Sensorineural Impairments. While some diseases produce conductive hearing losses predominantly, they may sometimes produce sensorineural impairments; such diseases include typhoid fever, chicken pox, and small pox. Mumps and vitamin B deficiency cases do not ordinarily lead to sensorineural losses. About 35 percent of patients with multiple sclerosis show a pure tone hearing loss, but there is no characteristic pattern (Dayal, Tarantino, and Swisher 1966). Ménière's disease, which involves a dilution of the endolymphatic system, leads to a loss at high frequencies often accompanied by severe tinnitus and dizziness. Among others, two new causes of sensorineural impairment have been identified as German measles (rubella) during the first three months of pregnancy and Rh-incompatibility. Of all cases of congenital deafness, about one-third to one-half seem to be due to hereditary factors, with an incidence between 1 in 2000 to 1 in 6000 births (Proctor and Proctor 1967).

DRUGS

Sensorineural deafness may also be produced by certain antibiotic drugs, such as dihydrostreptomycin, kanamycin, streptomycin, framycetin, and polymyxin B. The effects of some of these drugs may not be detected for two or three months after medication; in other cases it is more immediate. Eleven grams of neomycin administered orally over two days produced deafness which was detected in eight days (Ruben and Daly 1968). Antibiotic drugs should not be administered without audiometric control to ensure that no impairment of hearing will occur as a result of medical treatment.

COMMENT ON ELECTRICAL STIMULATION OF THE AUDITORY SYSTEM

For years the exciting possibility of direct electrical stimulation of the auditory nerve in patients with cochlear impairment has been entertained as a method of restoring hearing. Unfortunately, the evidence from an exhaustive study indicates that while it is possible to connect small electrodes to the human auditory nerve without severe tissue reactions, infections, or nerve fiber degeneration, the patient cannot learn to identify specific words or phrases. Thus, the chances are extremely remote that direct electrical stimulation of the auditory nerve can provide a unique means of useful communication (Simmons 1966).

More recently, however, bipolar electrodes have been inserted into the scala tympani of the human cochlea after the round window has been removed under local anesthesia. The electrodes make contact with the first turn of the basilar membrane and terminate in a tiny amplitude modulation radio receiver placed beneath the skin. The receiver derives its power from radio frequency energy transmitted across the skin barrier from an antenna placed on the skin surface overlying the receiver. Thus, from externally applied sound, it is possible to generate an audio-electric field that replaces the cochlear microphonic.

Tests on human subjects with severe sensorineural hearing loss indicate that in some cases nearly normal pitch and loudness discrimination can be obtained with this method. Békésy audiometry can be repeatedly and consistently performed without difficulty. While information transmission is low, speech recognition is immediate and certain speech tasks can be performed above the chance level (Michelson 1971). While these findings are not conclusive, they are sufficiently encouraging to warrant further exploration of this technique.

References

ALBRITE, J. P. ET AL. Research in normal threshold of hearing. *Archives of Otolaryngology*, 1958, *68*: 194–98.

ALLUISI, E. A. Conditions affecting the amount of information in absolute judgments. *Psychological Review*, 1957, *64*: 97–103.

ATTNEAVE, F. *Application of information theory to psychology: a summary of basic concepts, methods, and results.* New York: Holt, Rinehart & Winston, 1959.

BABKOFF, H., and S. SUTTON. Perception of temporal order and loudness judgments for dichotic clicks. *Journal of the Acoustical Society of America*, 1963, *35*: 574–77.

BADDELEY, A. D. How does acoustic similarity influence short-term memory? *Quarterly Journal of Experimental Psychology*, 1968, *20*: 249–64.

BATTEAU, D. W. The role of the pinna in human localization. *Proceedings of the Royal Society*, 1967, *168*, No. 1011, Series B, 158–80.

——— Role of the pinna in localization: theoretical and physiological consequences. *In* A. V. S. DEREUCK and J. KNIGHT (eds.), *Hearing mechanisms in vertebrates.* Boston: Little, Brown, 1968.

BEASLEY, W. C. National Health Survey, Hearing Study Series, Washington: U.S. Public Health Service, 1938, Bull. 5.

BÉKÉSY, G. VON. Über die mechanish-akustishen vorgänge bein hören. *Acta Oto-Laryngologica*, 1939, *27*: 281–96, 388–96.

——— A new audiometer. *Acta Oto-Laryngologica*, 1947, *35*: 411–22.

——— On the elasticity of the cochlear partition. *Journal of the Acoustical Society of America*, 1948, *20*: 227–41.

——— DC potentials and energy balance of the cochlear partition. *Journal of the Acoustical Society of America*, 1950, *22*: 576–82.

——— Description of some mechanical properties of the organ of Corti. *Journal of the Acoustical Society of America*, 1953, *25*: 770–85.

——— *Experiments in hearing* (E. G. Wever, trans. and ed.). New York: McGraw-Hill, 1960.

——— Hearing theories and complex sounds. *Journal of the Acoustical Society of America*, 1963, *35*: 588–601.

——— *Sensory Inhibition.* Princeton, N.J.: Princeton University Press, 1967.

BELUCCI, R. J., and D. E. SCHNEIDER. Some observations on ultrasonic perception in man. *Annals of Otology*, 1962, *71*: 719–26.

BERANEK, L. L. *Acoustic measurements.* New York: John Wiley, 1949.

BERGER, R. L., and E. ACKERMAN. The Penn State anechoic chamber. *Noise Control.* 1956, *2*, No. 5, 16–21.

BILGER, R. C., and I. J. HIRSH. Masking of tones by bands of noise. *Journal of the Acoustical Society of America*, 1956, *28*: 623–30.

BREDBERG, G. Cochlear structure and hearing in man. *In* A. V. S. DE REUCK and J. KNIGHT (eds.), *Hearing mechanisms in vertebrates.* Boston: Little, Brown, 1968.

BROADBENT, D. *Perception and communication.* London: Pergamon Press, 1958.

BUTLER, R. A. Some experimental observations on the dc resting potentials in the guinea pig cochlea. *Journal of the Acoustical Society of America*, 1965, *37*: 429–33.

BUTLER, R. A., and V. HONRUBIA. Responses of cochlear potentials to changes in hydrostatic pressure. *Journal of the Acoustical Society of America*, 1963, *53*: 1188–92.

CAMPBELL, R. A. Frequency discrimination of pulsed tones. *Journal of the Acoustical Society of America*, 1963, *35*: 1193–1200.

CAMPBELL, R. A., and L. K. MOULIN. Signal detection audiometry: an exploratory study. *Journal of Speech and Hearing Research*, 1968, *11*: 402–10.

CARHART, R. Probable mechanisms underlying kernicteric hearing loss. *Acta Oto-Laryngologica*, 1967, Supplement 221, 1-41.

CARTERETTE, E. C., M. P. FRIEDMAN, and M. J. WYMAN. Feedback and psychophysical variables in signal detection. *Journal of the Acoustical Society of America*, 1966, *6*: 1051–55.

CHAPIN, E. K., and F. A. FIRESTONE. The influence of phase on tone quality and loudness. *Journal of the Acoustical Society of America*, 1934, *5*: 173–80.

COHEN, A. Further investigation of the effects of intensity upon the pitch of pure tones. *Journal of the Acoustical Society of America*, 1961, *33*: 1363–76.

——— U.S. Public Health Service field work on the industrial noise hearing loss problem. *Occupational Health Review* (Ottowa, Ontario), 1965, *17*: 3–10, 27.

COHEN, A., and E. JACKSON, JR. Threshold shift in hearing as a function of bandwidth and mode of noise exposure. RR-10. Bureau of Occupational Safety and Health, U. S. Department of Health, Education and Welfare, Cincinnati, Ohio, 1969.

CORCORAN, D. W. J. Prediction of responses to multidimensional from responses to unidimensional stimuli. *Journal of Experimental Psychology*, 1966, *71*: 47–54.

CORSO, J. F. Evaluation of operating conditions on a Békésy-type audiometer. *Archives of Otolaryngology*, 1955, *61*: 649–53.

——— The neural quantum theory of sensory discrimination. *Psychological Bulletin*, 1956a, *53*: 371–93.

——— Effects of testing methods on hearing thresholds. *Archives of Otolaryngology*, 1956b, *63*: 78–91.

——— Absolute judgments of musical tonality. *Journal of the Acoustical Society of America*, 1957a, *29*: 138–44.

——— Confirmation of the normal threshold for speech on C. I. D. Auditory Test W-2. *Journal of the Acoustical Society of America*, 1957b, *29*, 368–70.

—— Confirmation of normal discrimination loss for speech on C. I. D. Auditory Test W-22. *Laryngoscope*, 1957c, *67*: 365–70.

—— Absolute thresholds for tones of low frequency. *American Journal of Psychology*, 1958a, *71*: 367–74.

—— Proposed laboratory standard of normal hearing. *Journal of the Acoustical Society of America*, 1958b, *30*: 14–23.

—— Bone-conduction thresholds for sonic and ultrasonic frequencies. *Journal of the Acoustical Society of America*, 1963a, *35*: 1738–43.

—— Age and sex differences in pure tone thresholds. *Archives of Otolaryngology*, 1963b, *77*: 385–405.

—— A theoretico-historical review of the threshold concept. *Psychological Bulletin*, 1963c, *60*: 356–70.

—— *The experimental psychology of sensory behavior.* New York: Holt, Rinehart & Winston, 1967a.

—— Sensory processes: systematic developments and related data. *In* H. HELSON and W. BEVAN (eds.), *Contemporary approaches to psychology*. New York: Van Nostrand Reinhold, 1967b.

CORSO, J. F., and A. COHEN. Methodological aspects of auditory threshold measurements. *Journal of Experimental Psychology*, 1958, *55*: 8–12.

CORSO, J. F., and M. LEVINE. The pitch of ultrasonic frequencies heard by bone conduction. *Proceedings of the Pennsylvania Academy of Science*, 1963, *37*: 22–26.

—— Pitch-discrimination at high frequencies by air- and bone-conduction. *American Journal of Psychology*, 1965a, *78*: 557–66.

—— Sonic and ultrasonic equal-loudness contours. *Journal of Experimental Psychology*, 1965b, *70*: 412–16.

CORSO, J. F., and J. F. WILSON. Additional variables on the Békésy-type audiometer. *Archives of Otolaryngology*, 1957, *66*: 719–28.

CRANE, H. D. Mechanical impact: a model for auditory excitation and fatigue. *Journal of the Acoustical Society of America*, 1966, *40*: 1147–59.

CREELMAN, C. D. Detection of complex signals as a function of signal bandwidth and duration. *Journal of the Acoustical Society of America*, 1961, *33*: 89–94.

—— Detection, discrimination, and the loudness of short tones. *Journal of the Acoustical Society of America*, 1963, *35*: 1201–5.

DADSON, R. S., and J. H. KING. A determination of the normal threshold of hearing and its relation to the standardization of audiometers. *Journal of Laryngology*, 1952, *66*: 366–78.

DALLOS, P. J. Dynamics of the acoustic reflex: phenomenological aspects. *Journal of the Acoustical Society of America*, 1964, *36*: 2175–83.

—— On the generation of odd-fractional subharmonics. *Journal of the Acoustical Society of America*, 1966, *40*: 1381–91.

DALLOS, P. J., and C. O. LINNELL. Even-order subharmonics in the peripheral auditory system. *Journal of the Acoustical Society of America*, 1966, *40*: 561–64.

DALLOS, P. J., and W. O. OLSEN. Integration of energy at threshold with gradual rise-fall tone pips. *Journal of the Acoustical Society of America*, 1964, *36*: 743–51.

DANZIGER, K. Effect of variable stimulus intensity on estimates of duration. *Perceptual and Motor Skills*, 1965, *20*: 505–8.

DAVIS, H. The hearing mechanism. *In* C. M. HARRIS (ed.), *Handbook of noise control*. New York: McGraw-Hill, 1957a.

—— Biophysics and physiology of the inner ear. *Physiological Review*, 1957b, *37*: 1–49.

—— Peripheral coding and auditory information. *In* W. A. ROSENBLITH (ed.), *Sensory communication*. Cambridge, Mass.: MIT Press, 1961, and New York: John Wiley, 1961 Pp. 119–41.

—— Slow cortical response evoked by acoustic stimuli. *Acta Oto-Laryngologica*, 1965a, *59*: 179–85.

—— The ISO zero-reference level for audiometers. *Archives of Otolaryngology*, 1965b, *81*: 145–49.

—— Slow electrical responses of the human cortex. *Proceedings of the American Philosophical Society*, 1968, *112*: 150–56.

DAVIS, H. ET AL. Further validation of evoked response audiometry (ERA). *Journal of Speech and Hearing Research*, 1967, *10*: 717–32.

DAVIS, H., C. FERNANDEZ, and D. R. MCAULIFFE. Excitatory process in cochlea. *Proceedings of the National Academy of Science, U.S.A.*, 1950, *36*: 580–87.

DAVIS, H., and F. KRANZ. International audiometric zero. *Journal of the Acoustical Society of America*, 1964, *36*: 1450–54.

DAVIS, H., and A. F. NIEMOELLER. A system for clinical evoked response audiometry. *Journal of Speech and Hearing Disorders*, 1968, *33*: 33–37.

DAYAL, V. S., L. TARANTINO, and L. P. SWISHER. Neuro-otologic studies in multiple sclerosis. *Laryngoscope*, 1966, *76*: 1798.

DEATHERAGE, B. H. Examination of binaural interaction. *Journal of the Acoustical Society of America*, 1966, *39*: 232–49.

DEATHERAGE, B. H., L. A. JEFFRESS, and H. C. BLODGETT. A note on the audibility of intense sound. *Journal of the Acoustical Society of America*, 1954, *26*: 582.

DE BOER, E. Intensity discrimination of fluctuating signals. *Journal of the Acoustical Society of America*, 1966, *40*: 552–60.

DEUTSCH, L. J. *The threshold of the stapedius reflex to selected acoustic stimuli in normal human ears.* U.S. Naval Submarine Medical Center, Groton, Conn., Rept. No. 546, *24 September 1968*.

DJUPESLAND, G. Middle ear muscle reflexes elicited by acoustic and non-acoustic stimulation. *Acta Oto-Laryngologica*, 1964, Supplement 188, 287–92.

—— Electromyography of the tympanic muscles in man. *International Audiology*, 1965, *4*: 34–41.

DOHLMAN, G. F. Histochemical studies of vestibular mechanisms. *In* G. L. RASMUSSEN and W. F. WINDLE (eds.), *Neural mechanisms of the auditory and vestibular systems*. Springfield, Ill.: Charles C Thomas, 1960.

DURLACH, N. I. Note on the equalization and cancellation theory of binaural masking level differences. *Journal of the Acoustical Society of America*, 1960, *32*: 1075–76.

EKMAN, G., B. BERGLUND, and U. BERGLUND. Loudness as a function of the duration of auditory stimulation. *Scandinavian Journal of Psychology*, 1966, *7*: 201–8.

ELLIOTT, L. L. Backward masking: different durations of the masking stimulus. *Journal of the Acoustical Society of America*, 1964, *36*: 393.

ENGEBRETSON, A. M., and D. H. ELDREDGE. Model for the nonlinear characteristics of cochlear potentials. *Journal of the Acoustical Society of America*, 1968, *44*: 548–54.

EPSTEIN, A. Variables involved in automatic audiometry. *Annals of Otology, Rhinology, and Laryngology*, 1960, *69*: 137–41.

EVANS, E. F., M. F. ROSS, and I. C. WHITFIELD. The spatial distribution of unit characteristic frequency in the primary auditory cortex of the cat. *Journal of Physiology*, 1965, *179*: 238–47.

FAROQI, M. A., and E. G. PARAMESWARAN. Effect of the interval between signals on temporal judgment. *Canadian Journal of Psychology*, 1966, *20*: 12–17.

FELDMAN, A. S. Acoustic impedance studies of the normal ear. *Journal of Speech and Hearing Research*, 1967a, *10*: 165–76.

—— A report of further impedance studies in the acoustic reflex. *Journal of Speech and Hearing Research*, 1967b, *10*: 616–22.

FELDTKELLER, R., and E. ZWICKER. Das ohr als nachrichtenempfänger. Stuttgart: Hirzel, 1956. Cited by Scharf, B., in Complex sounds and critical bands. *Psychological Bulletin*, 1961, *58*: 205–17.

FERNANDEZ, C. The innervation of the cochlea (guinea pig). *Laryngoscope*, 1951, *61*: 1152–72.

FISCH, U., and G. V. SCHULTHESS. Electromyographic studies on the human stapedial muscle. *Acta Oto-Laryngologica*, 1963, *56*: 287–97.

FISHER, H. G., and S. J. FREEDMAN. Localization of sound during simulated unilateral conduction hearing loss. Paper presented to Psychonomic Society, Chicago, October 1967.

—— The role of the pinna in auditory localization. *Journal of Auditory Research*, 1968, *8*: 15–26.

FLANAGAN, J. L. Computational model for basilar-membrane displacement. *Journal of the Acoustical Society of America*, 1962, *34*: 1370–76.

FLETCHER, H. Auditory patterns. *Review of Modern Physics*. 1940, *12*: 47–65.

FREEMAN, W. H., and B. BRACEGIRDLE. *An atlas of histology* (2 ed). London: Heinemann Educational Books, 1967.

FRICKE, J. E. Monaural phase effects in auditory signal detection. *Journal of the Acoustical Society of America*, 1968, *43*: 439–43.

GALAMBOS, R. Microelectrode studies on medial geniculate body of cat, III. Response to pure tones. *Journal of Neurophysiology*, 1952, *15*: 381–400.

—— Some recent experiments on the neurophysiology of hearing. *Annals of Otology, Rhinology, and Laryngology*, 1956, *65*: 1053–59.

GALAMBOS, R., and H. DAVIS. The response of signal auditory-nerve fibers to acoustic stimulation. *Journal of Neurophysiology*, 1943, 6: 39–57.

GANNON, R. P., C. A. LASZLO, and D. H. MOSCOVITCH. The effect of physostigmine on the latency of the cochlear potentials. *Acta Oto-Laryngologica*, 1966, 61: 536–46.

GARNER, W. R. An informational analysis of absolute judgments of loudness. *Journal of Experimental Psychology*, 1953, 46: 373–80.

GARNER, W. R., and G. MILLER. The masked threshold of pure tones as a function of duration. *Journal of Experimental Psychology*, 1947, 37: 293–303.

GARNER, W. R. *Uncertainty and structure as psychological concepts.* New York: Wiley, 1962.

GIACOMELLI, F., and W. MOZZO. An experimental and clinical study on the influence of the brainstem reticular formation on the stapedial reflex. *International Audiology*, 1965, 4: 42–44.

GLORIG, A. ET AL. Determination of the normal hearing reference zero. *Journal of the Acoustical Society of America*, 1956, 28: 1110–13.

GLORIG, A. ET AL. *1954 Wisconsin state fair hearing survey*, Subcommittee on Noise in Industry of the American Academy of Ophthalmology and Otolaryngology, Los Angeles, 1957.

GOLDSTEIN, R., and J. KRAMER. Factors affecting thresholds for short tones. *Journal of Speech and Hearing Research*, 1960, 3, No. 3, 249–56.

GREEN, D. M. Detection of signals in noise and the critical band concept. University of Michigan Technical Report No. 82, 1958.

——— Consistency of auditory detection judgments. *Psychological Review*, 1964, 71: 392–407.

——— Additivity of masking. *Journal of the Acoustical Society of America*, 1967, 41: 1517–25.

GREEN, D. M., T. G. BIRDSALL, and W. P. TANNER, JR. Signal detection as a function of signal intensity and duration. *Journal of the Acoustical Society of America*, 1957, 29: 523–31.

GREEN, D. M., and G. B. HENNING. Audition. *In* P. H. MUSSEN and M. R. ROSENZWEIG (eds.), *Annual Review of Psychology*, 1969, 105–28.

GREENWOOD, D. D. Auditory masking and the critical band. *Journal of the Acoustical Society of America*, 1961, 33: 484–502.

GRISANTI, G. L'audition binaurale et al discrimination de fréquence. *International Audiology*, 1965, 4: 56–58.

GROSS, N. B., and W. R. THURLOW. Microelectrode studies of neural auditory activity of cat, II. Medial geniculate body. *Journal of Neurophysiology*, 1951, 14: 409–22.

HAEFF, A. V., and KNOX, C. Perception of ultrasound. *Science*, 1963, 139: 590–92.

HARBERT, F., and I. M. YOUNG. Amplitude of Békésy tracings with different attenuation rates. *Journal of the Acoustical Society of America*, 1966, 39: 914–19.

HARRIS, C. K., and J. D. HARRIS. Comparison of seven systems for air conduction audiometry from 8–20 KC/S. U.S. Naval Submarine Medical Center Report No. 567. Groton, Conn., 1969.

HARRIS, C. M. (ed.). *Handbook of noise control.* New York: McGraw-Hill, 1957.

HARRIS, J. D. Pitch discrimination. *Journal of the Acoustical Society of America*, 1952 24: 750–55.

——— Normal hearing and its relation to audiometry. *Laryngoscope*, 1954, 64: 928–57.

——— Loudness discrimination. *Journal of Speech and Hearing Disorders*, Monograph Supplement II, 1963.

HARTMAN, E. B. The influence of practice and pitch-distance between tones on the absolute identification of pitch. *American Journal of Psychology*, 1954, 67: 1–14.

HAWKINS, J. E., JR., and L. G. JOHNSSON. Light microscopic observations of the inner ear in man and monkey. *Annals of Otology, Rhinology, and Laryngology*, 1968, 77: 608–28.

HAWKINS, J. E. JR., and S. S. STEVENS. The masking of pure tones and of speech by white noise. *Journal of the Acoustical Society of America*, 1950, 22: 6–13.

HELLMAN, R. P., and J. ZWISLOCKI. Some factors affecting the estimation of loudness. *Journal of the Acoustical Society of America*, 1961, 33: 687–94.

——— Loudness determination at low sound frequencies. *Journal of the Acoustical Society of America*, 1968, 43: 60–64.

HENDERSON, D. ET AL. A comparison of chinchilla auditory evoked response and behavioral response thresholds. *Perception and Psychophysics*, 1969, 5: 41–45.

HENNING, G. B. Effect of aural harmonics on frequency discrimination. *Journal of the Acoustical Society of America*, 1965, 37: 1144–46.

HILALI, S., and I. C. WHITFIELD. Responses of the trapezoid body to acoustic stimulation with pure tones. *Journal of Physiology*. 1953, 122: 158–71.

HIRSH, I. J. *The measurement of hearing.* New York: McGraw-Hill, 1952.

——— Auditory perception of temporal order. *Journal of the Acoustical Society of America*, 1959, 31: 759–67.

——— Audition. *In* J. B. SIDOWSKI (ed.), *Experimental methods and instrumentation in psychology.* New York: McGraw-Hill, 1966.

INGERSLEEV, F. ET AL. The anechoic chambers at the Technical University of Denmark. Brüel and Kjaer Technical Review, 1968, 2: 1–29.

JACOBSON, H. Information and the human ear. *Journal of the Acoustical Society of America*, 1951, 23: 463–71.

JEFFRESS, L. A. Binaural signal detection: vector theory. Defense Research Laboratory Acoustics Report No. 245. University of Texas, 1965.

JENKINS, R. A. Perception of pitch, timbre, and loudness. *Journal of the Acoustical Society of America*, 1961, 33: 1550–57.

JOHNSSON, L. G., and J. E. HAWKINS, JR. A direct approach to cochlear anatomy and pathology in man. *Archives of Otolaryngology*, 1967, 85: 599–613.

JONES, A., and M. MACLEAN. Perceived duration as a function of auditory stimulus frequency. *Journal of Experimental Psychology*, 1966, 71: 358–64.

JONES, H. H., and J. L. OSER. Farm equipment noise exposure levels. *American Industrial Hygiene Association Journal*, 1968, 29: 146–51.

KAPUR, Y. P. Hearing and infectious tropical and nutritional diseases. *Laryngoscope*, 1966, 76: 418–57.

KAPUR, Y. P. and PATT, A. J. Hearing in Todas of South India. *Archives of Otolaryngology*, 1967, 85: 400–406.

KATSUKI, Y. Neural mechanism of auditory sensation in cats. *In* W. A. ROSENBLITH (ed.), *Sensory communication.* New York: John Wiley, 1961.

KATSUKI, Y. ET AL. Electrical responses of auditory neurons in cat to sound stimulation. *Journal of Neurophysiology*, 1958, 21: 569–88.

KATSUKI, Y., T. WATANABE, and N. MARUYAMA. Activity of auditory neurons in upper levels of brain of cat. *Journal of Neurophysiology*, 1959, 22: 603–23.

KHANNA, S. M., R. E. SEARS, and J. TONNDORF. Some properties of longitudinal shear waves: a study by computer simulation. *Journal of the Acoustical Society of America*, 1968, 43: 1077–84.

KIMURA, R. S. Hairs of the cochlear sensory cells and their attachment to the tectorial membrane. *Acta Oto-Laryngologica*, 1966, 61: 55–72.

KIRCHNER, F. R. Introlabyrinthine perfusion. *Laryngoscope*, 1968, 78: 2049–2118.

KLATT, D. H., and G. E. PETERSON. Reexamination of a model of the cochlea. *Journal of the Acoustical Society of America*, 1966, 40: 54–61.

KONOSHI, T., and E. KELSEY. Effect of sodium deficiency on cochlear potentials. *Journal of the Acoustical Society of America*, 1967, 43: 462–70.

KRYTER, K. D. ET AL. Hazardous exposure to intermittent and steady-state noise. *Journal of the Acoustical Society of America*, 1966, 39: 451–64.

LABENZ, P., A. COHEN, and B. PEARSON. A noise and hearing survey of earth moving equipment operators. *American Industrial Hygiene Association Journal*, 1967, 28: 117–28.

LESHOWITZ, B., and D. H. RAAB. Effects of stimulus duration on the detection of sinusoids added to continuous pedestals. *Journal of the Acoustical Society of America*, 1967, 41: 489–96.

LEWIS, D., and M. J. LARSEN. The cancellation, reinforcement, and measurement of subjective tones. *Proceedings of the National Academy of Science*, 1937, 23: 415–21.

LICKLIDER, J. C. R. Basic correlates of auditory stimulus. *In* S. S. STEVENS (ed.), *Handbook of experimental psychology.* New York: John Wiley, 1951.

——— Three auditory theories. *In* S. KOCH (ed.), *Psychology: A study of a science*, Vol. 1. *Sensory, perceptual, and physiological formulations.* New York: McGraw-Hill, 1959.

——— Periodicity pitch and related auditory process models. *International Audiology*, 1962, *1*: 11–36.

LIDÉN, G., B. NORDLUND, and J. E. HAWKINS. Significance of the stapedius reflex for the understanding of speech. *Acta Oto-Laryngologica*, 1964, Supplement No. 188, 275–79.

MAHON, R. G., and M. IGARASHI. Comparative histological study of the tympanic ganglion. *Laryngoscope*, 1968, *78*: 334–43.

MARSH, J. T., and F. G. WORDEN. Sound evoked frequency-following responses in the central auditory pathway. *Laryngoscope*, 1968, *78*: 1149–64.

MCCANDLESS, G. A. Clinical application of evoked response audiometry. *Journal of Speech and Hearing Research*, 1967, *10*: 468–78.

MCCORMICK, J. M., and M. G. SALVADORI. *Numerical methods in Fortran.* New York: Columbia University Press, 1964.

MCGAVREN, M. Memory of brief auditory durations in comparison discriminations. *Psychological Record*, 1965, *15*: 249–60.

MCGILL, W. J. Serial effects in auditory threshold judgments. *Journal of Experimental Psychology*, 1957, *53*: 297–303.

MCGILL, W. J., and J. P. GOLDBERG. Pure-tone intensity discrimination and energy detection. *Journal of the Acoustical Society of America*, 1968, *44*: 576–81.

MICHELSON, R. P. Electrical stimulation of the human cochlea. *Archives of Otolaryngology*, 1971, *93*, 317–23.

MICHON, J. A. A model of some temporal relations in human behavior. *Psychologische Forschung*, 1968, *31*: 287–98.

MILLER, G. A. The magical number seven, plus or minus two: some limits on our capacity for processing information. *Psychological Review*, 1956, *63*: 81–97.

MISKOLCZY-FODOR, F. Relation between loudness and duration of tonal pulses. I. Response of normal ears to pure tones longer than click-pitch threshold. *Journal of the Acoustical Society of America*, 1959, *31*: 1128–34.

MØHL, B. Auditory sensitivity of the common seal in air and water. *Journal of Auditory Research*, 1968, *8*: 27–38.

MORAY, N. Where is capacity limited? A survey and a model. *Acta Psychologica*, 1967, *27*: 84–92.

MOSCOVITCH, D. H., and R. P. GANNON. Effects of calcium on sound-evoked cochlear potentials in the guinea pig. *Journal of the Acoustical Society of America*, 1966, *40*: 583–90.

MUDD, S. A. Experimental evaluation of binary pure-tone auditory displays. *Journal of Applied Psychology*, 1965, *49*: 112–21.

MULLIGAN, B. D. ET AL. Prediction of monaural detection. *Journal of the Acoustical Society of America*, 1968, *43*: 481–86.

MURPHY, L. E. Absolute judgments of duration. *Journal of Experimental Psychology*, 1966, *71*: 260–63.

MYGIND, S. H. Functional mechanism of the labyrinthine epithelium. III. Consequences of my own theory, theoretical and practical; refutation of objections. *Archives of Otolaryngology*, 1966, *83*: 3–9.

NEERGAARD, E. B. ET AL. Experimental studies on sound transmission in the human ear. III. Influence of the stapedius and tensor tympani muscles. *Acta Oto-Laryngologica*, 1964, Supplement 188, 280–86.

NEERGAARD, E. B., and P. E. RASMUSSEN. Latency of the stapedius muscle reflex in man. *Archives of Otolaryngology*, 1966, *84*: 173–80.

NIEDER, P., and I. NIEDER. Studies of two-tone interaction as seen in the guinea pig microphonic. *Journal of the Acoustical Society of America*, 1968, *44*: 1409–22.

NIXON, J. C., and A. GLORIG. Reliability of acoustic impedance measures of the eardrum. *Journal of Auditory Research*, 1964, *4*: 261–67.

NORMAN, D. A. Sensory thresholds and response bias. *Journal of the Acoustical Society of America*, 1963, *35*: 1432–41.

OLSEN, W. O., and R. CARHART. Integration of acoustic power at threshold by normal hearers. *Journal of the Acoustical Society of America*, 1966, *40*: 591–99.

PELL, S., and T. H. DICKERSON. Changes in hearing acuity of noise-exposed women. *Archives of Otolaryngology*, 1966, *83*: 207–12.

PERNKOPF, E. *Atlas of topographical and applied human anatomy*, Vol. 1, H. Ferner (ed.). Philadelphia: Saunders, 1963.

PETERSON, A. P. G., and E. E. GROSS, JR. *Handbook of noise measurement.* West Concord, Mass.: General Radio Co., 1963.

PICKETT, J. M. Backward masking. *Journal of the Acoustical Society of America*, 1959, *31*: 1613–15.

PIERCE, J. R., and E. E. DAVID, JR. *Man's world of sound.* Garden City, N. Y.: Doubleday, 1958.

PLOMP, R. Rate of decay of auditory sensation. *Journal of the Acoustical Society of America*, 1964, *36*: 277–82.

——— *Experiments on tone perception.* Soesterberg, The Netherlands: Institute for Perception, RVO-TNO. National Defense Research Organization TNO, 1966.

PLOMP, R., and M. A. BOUMAN. Relation between hearing threshold and duration for tone pulses. *Journal of the Acoustical Society of America*, 1959, *31*, 749–58.

POLLACK, I. Specification of sound pressure levels. *American Journal of Psychology*, 1949, *62*: 412–17.

——— The information of elementary auditory displays. *Journal of the Acoustical Society of America*, 1952a, *24*: 745–49.

——— The loudness of bands of noise. *Journal of the Acoustical Society of America*, 1952b, *24*, 533–38.

——— The information of elementary auditory displays. II. *Journal of the Acoustical Society of America*, 1953, *25*: 765–69.

POLLACK, I., and L. FICKS. Information of multidimensional auditory displays. *Journal of the Acoustical Society of America*, 1954, *26*: 155–58.

POLLACK, K. C. Electroencephalic audiometry by cortical conditioning. *Journal of Speech and Hearing Research*, 1967, *10*: 706–16.

PROCTOR, C. A., and B. PROCTOR. Understanding hereditary nerve deafness. *Archives of Otolaryngology*, 1967, *85*: 23–40.

PUMPHREY, R. J. Upper limit of frequency for human hearing. *Nature*, 1950, *166*: 571.

RICE, E. A., and E. W. SHINABARGER. Studies on the endolymphatic dc potential of the guinea pig's cochlea. *Journal of the Acoustical Society of America*, 1961, *33*: 922–25.

RICHARDS, A. M. The perception of pitch in a white noise mask. U.S. Naval Submarine Medical Center, Report Number 548, Groton, Conn., 1968.

RIESZ, R. R. Differential intensity sensitivity of the ear for pure tones. *Physics Review*, 1928, *31* (2nd Series), 867–75.

RILEY, E. C. ET AL. Critique on the concept of audiometer zero. *Archives of Otolaryngology*, 1965, *81*: 139–44.

RISSET, J. C., and M. V. MATHEWS. Analysis of musical-instrument tones. *Physics Today*, 1969, *22*: 23–30.

ROBINSON, D. W. The subjective loudness scale. *Acustica*, 1957, *7*: 217–33.

ROBINSON, D. W., and R. S. DADSON. A re-determination of the equal-loudness relations of pure tones. *British Journal of Applied Physics*, 1956, *7*: 166–81.

ROBINSON, M. A four-year study of the stainless steel stapes. *Archives of Otolaryngology*, 1965, *82*: 217–35.

ROSEN, S. ET AL. Presbycusis study of a relatively noise-free population in the Sudan. *Annals of Otology*, 1962, *71*: 727–43.

ROSENBERG, A. E. Effect of masking on the pitch of periodic pulses. *Journal of the Acoustical Society of America*, 1965, *38*: 747–58.

ROSENZWEIG, M. R. Development of research on the physiological mechanisms of auditory localization. *Psychological Bulletin*, 1961, *58*: 376–89.

ROYER, F. L., and W. R. GARNER. Response uncertainty and perceptual difficulty of auditory temporal patterns. *Perception and Psychophysics*, 1966, *1*: 41–47.

RUBEN, R. J., and J. F. DALY. Neomycin ototoxicity and nephrotoxicity. *Laryngoscope*, 1968, *78*: 1734–37.

SAGALOVICH, B. M., and G. G. MELKUMOVA. New data on the spectrum of sound and ultrasound frequencies producing sound effect in man. *Bulletin of Biological Medicine*, 1967, *9*: 12–15.

SALDANHA, E. L., and J. F. CORSO. Timbre cues and the identification of musical instruments. *Journal of the Acoustical Society of America*, 1964, *36*: 2021–26.

SANDERS, J. W. Brief tone audiometry. *Archives of Otolaryngology*, 1967, *85*: 83–91.

SATALOFF, J. Otolaryngologic problems. *In* J. I. FREEMAN (ed.), *Clinical features of the older patient.* Springfield, Ill.: Charles C Thomas, 1965.

——— Experimental use of laser in otosclerotic stapes. *Archives of Otolaryngology*, 1967, *85*: 58–60.

SATALOFF, J., L. VASSALLO, and H. MENDUKE. Occupational hearing loss and high frequency thresholds. *Archives of Environmental Health*, 1967, *14*: 832–36.

SCHARF, B. Complex sounds and critical bands. *Psychological Bulletin*, 1961, *58*: 205–17.

SCHOUTEN, J. F. The residue phenomenon and its impact on the theory of hearing. *International Audiology*, 1962, *1*: 8–10.

SCHROEDER, M. R. Computers in acoustics: symbiosis of an old science and a new tool. *Journal of the Acoustical Society of America*, 1969, *45*: 1077–88.

SCHUKNECHT, H. F. Further observations on the pathology of presbycusis. *Archives of Otolaryngology*, 1964, *80*: 369–82.

SCHULTHESS, G. V., and E. HUELSEN. Statistical evaluation of hearing losses in military pilots. *Acta Oto-Laryngologica*, 1968, *65*: 137–45.

SEKEY, A. Short term auditory frequency discrimination. *Journal of the Acoustical Society of America*, 1963, *35*: 682–90.

SENDERS, V., and A. SOWARD. Analysis of response sequences in the settings of a psychophysical experiment. *American Journal of Psychology*, 1952, *65*: 358–74.

SHAW, E. A. G. Ear canal presssure generated by circumaural and supra-aural earphones. *Journal of the Acoustical Society of America*, 1966a, *39*: 471–79.

——— Ear canal pressure generated by a free sound field. *Journal of the Acoustical Society of America*, 1966b, *39*: 465–70.

SHEPARD, R. N. Circularity in judgments of relative pitch. *Journal of the Acoustical Society of America*, 1964, *36*: 2346–2453.

SHEPHERD, D. C., and R. GOLDSTEIN. Intrasubject variability in amplitude of Békésy tracings and its relation to measures of personality. *Journal of Speech and Hearing Research*, 1968, *11*: 523–35.

SHOWER, E. G., and R. BIDDULPH. Differential pitch sensitivity of the ear. *Journal of the Acoustical Society of America*, 1931, *3*: 275–87.

SIEGEL, R. J. A replication of the mel scale of pitch. *American Journal of Psychology*, 1965, *78*: 615–20.

SIMMONS, F. B. Variable nature of the middle-ear muscle reflex. *International Audiology*, 1964, *3*: 136–46.

——— Electrical stimulation of the auditory nerve in man. *Archives of Otolaryngology*, 1966, *84*: 24–76.

SIVIAN, L. J., and S. D. WHITE. On minimum audible sound fields. *Journal of the Acoustical Society of America*, 1933, *4*: 288–321.

SMITH, C. A., and G. L. RASMUSSEN. Recent observations on the olivo-cochlear bundle. *Annals of Otology, Rhinology, and Laryngology*, 1963, *72*: 489–506.

SOBOTTA, J. *Atlas of human anatomy.* (Vol. III, Part II, 8th English ed.), F. H. J. Figge (ed.), New York: Hafner, 1963.

SORKIN, R. D. Extension of the theory of signal detectability to matching procedures in psychoacoustics. *Journal of the Acoustical Society of America*, 1962, *34*: 1745–51.

——— Temporal interference effects in auditory amplitude discrimination. *Perception and Psychophysics*, 1966, *1*: 55–58.

——— Attention mechanisms in auditory signal detection. Paper presented at the 19th International Congress of Psychology, London, July 1969.

SPOENDLIN, H. The organization of the cochlear receptor. In *Advances in Oto-Rhino-Laryngology*, Vol. 13. New York: Karger, 1966.

——— Ultrastructure and peripheral innervation pattern of the receptor in relation to the first coding of the acoustic message. *In* A. V. DEREUCK and J. KNIGHT (eds.), *Hearing mechanisms in vertebrates.* Boston: Little, Brown, 1968.

SPOOR, A. Presbycusis values in relation to noise induced hearing loss. *International Audiology*, 1967, *6*: 48–57.

STEINER, S. J., and A. M. SMALL, JR. Pitch shifts of tones in wide-band noise. *Journal of the Acoustical Society of America*, 1966, *40*: 912–13.

STEVENS, S. S. The relation of pitch to intensity. *Journal of the Acoustical Society of America*, 1935, *6*: 150–54.

——— A scale for the measurement of a psychological magnitude: loudness. *Psychological Review*, 1936, *43*: 405–16.

——— The measurement of loudness. *Journal of the Acoustical Society of America*, 1955, *27*: 815–29.

——— Procedure for calculating loudness: Mark VI. *Journal of the Acoustical Society of America*, 1961, *33*: 1577–85.

——— Loudness, a product of volume times density. *Journal of Experimental Psychology*, 1965, *69*: 503–10.

——— Matching functions between loudness and ten other continua. *Perception and Psychophysics*, 1966, *1*: 5–8.

STEVENS, S. S., and H. DAVIS. *Hearing: Its Psychology and Physiology.* New York: John Wiley, 1938.

STEVENS, S. S., and E. B. NEWMAN. The localization of actual sources of sound. *American Journal of Psychology*, 1936, *48*: 297–306.

STEVENS, S. S., J. VOLKMANN, and E. B. NEWMAN. A scale for the measurement of the psychological magnitude of pitch. *Journal of the Acoustical Society of America*, 1937, *8*: 185–90.

STOPP, P. E., and F. C. WHITFIELD. Summating potentials in the avian cochlea. *Journal of Physiology*, 1964, *175*: 45–60.

STUDEBAKER, G. A. The standardization of bone-conduction thresholds. *Laryngoscope*, 1967, *77*: 823–35.

SWETS, J. A., D. M. GREEN, and W. P. TANNER, JR. On the width of critical bands. *Journal of the Acoustical Society of America*, 1962, *34*: 108–13.

SWETS, J. A., and S. T. SEWALL. Invariance of signal detectability over stages of practice and levels of motivation. *Journal of Experimental Psychology*, 1963, *66*: 120–26.

TANNER, T. A., JR., R. W. HALLER, and R. C. ATKINSON. Signal recognition as influenced by presentation schedules. *Perception and Psychophysics*, 1967, *2*: 349–58.

TANNER, T. A., JR., R. M. PATTON, and R. C. ATKINSON. Intermodality judgments of signal duration. *Psychonomic Science*, 1965, *2*: 271–72.

TANNER, T. A., JR., J. A. RAUK, and R. C. ATKINSON. Signal information as influenced by information feedback. *Journal of Mathematical Psychology*, 1970, *7* (2): 259–74.

TASAKI, I., H. DAVIS, and D. H. ELDREDGE. Exploration of cochlear potentials in guinea pigs with a microelectrode. *Journal of the Acoustical Society of America*, 1954, *26*: 765–73.

TASAKI, I., H. DAVIS, and J. P. LEGOUIX. The space-time pattern of the cochlear microphonics (guinea pig), as recorded by differential electrodes. *Journal of the Acoustical Society of America*, 1952, *24*: 502–19.

TAYLOR, M. M. Comments on "Sensory thresholds and response bias." *Journal of the Acoustical Society of America*, 1964, *36*: 599–600.

THURLOW, W. R. Perception of low auditory pitch: a multicue, mediation theory. *Psychological Review*, 1963, *70*: 461–70.

TONNDORF, J. Time/frequency analysis along the partition of cochlear models: a modified place concept. *Journal of the Acoustical Society of America*, 1962, *34*: 1337–50.

TONNDORF, J., ET AL. Bone conduction: studies in experimental animals; a collection of seven papers. *Acta Oto-Laryngologica*, 1966, Supplement 213, 1–132.

TONNDORF, J., and S. M. KHANNA. Some properties of sound transmission in the middle and outer ears of cats. *Journal of the Acoustical Society of America*, 1967, *41*: 513–21.

TORGERSON, W. S. *Theory and methods of scaling.* New York: John Wiley, 1958.

TRIESMAN, A. M. The effect of irrelevant material on the efficiency of selective listening. *American Journal of Psychology*, 1964, *77*: 533–46.

TRINCKER, D. The transformation of mechanical stimulus into nervous excitation by the labyrinthine receptors. *Symposium of the Society of Experimental Biology*, 1962, *16*: 289–317.

U.S. Public Health Service. *National health survey (1935–1936).* Preliminary reports, hearing study series, Bulletins 1–7. Washington, D.C.: U.S. Public Health Service, 1938.

VAN DEN BRINK, G. Detection of tone pulse of various durations in noise of various bandwidths. *Journal of the Acoustical Society of America*, 1964, 1206–11.

VENTRY, I. M., and J. B. CHAIKLIN (eds.). Multidiscipline study of functional hearing loss. *Journal of Auditory Research*, 1965, *5*: 179–272.

WALLACH, H. The role of head movements and vestibular and visual cues in sound localization. *Journal of Experimental Psychology*, 1940, *27*: 339–68.

WALLACH, H., E. B. NEWMAN, and M. R. ROSENZWEIG. The precedence effect in sound localization. *American Journal of Psychology*, 1949, *52*: 315–36.

WARD, W. D. Adaptation and fatigue. *In* A. B. GRAHAM (ed.), *Sensorineural hearing processes and disorders.* Boston: Little, Brown, 1967.

WARD, W. D., A. GLORIG, and D. L. SKLAR. Dependence of temporary threshold shift at 4 kc on intensity and time. *Journal of the Acoustical Society of America*, 1958, *30*: 944–54.

WATSON, C. S., M. E. RILLING, and W. T. BOURBON. Receiver operating characteristics determined by a mechanical analog to the rating scale. *Journal of the Acoustical Society of America*, 1964, *36*: 283–88.

WATSON, J. E. Utilization of compound stimuli in electrodermal audiometry. *International Audiology*, 1968, *7*: 200–204.

WEGEL, R. L., and C. E. LANE. The auditory masking of one pure tone by another and its probable relation to the dynamics of the inner ear. *Physics Review*, 1924, *23*: 266–85.

WEISS, H. S. The normal human intra-aural muscle reflex in response to sounds. *In* J. L. FLETCHER (ed.), *Middle ear function seminar*. U.S. Army Medical Research Laboratory, Fort Knox, Ky., Rept. No. 576, 1963.

WEISSLER, P. G. International standard reference zero for audiometers. *Journal of the Acoustical Society of America*, 1968, *40*: 264–75.

WEVER, E. G. *Theory of hearing*, New York: John Wiley, 1949.

WEVER, E. G., and C. W. BRAY. Distortion in the ear as shown by the electrical responses of the cochlea. *Journal of the Acoustical Society of America*, 1938, *9*: 227–33.

WEVER, E. G., C. W. BRAY, and M. LAWRENCE. The origin of combination tones. *Journal of Experimental Psychology*, 1940, *27*: 217–26.

WEVER, E. G., and M. LAWRENCE. *Physiological acoustics*. Princeton, N.J.: Princeton University Press, 1954.

WHITFIELD, I. C. *The auditory pathway*. London: Edward Arnold, 1967.

———— and H. F. ROSS. Cochlear-microphonic and summating potentials and the outputs of individual hair-cell generators. *Journal of the Acoustical Society of America*, 1965, *38*: 126–31.

WRIGHT, H. N. Comparison of Békésy audiometric thresholds obtained with 200–millisecond, 500–millisecond, and continuous tones. Technical Report No. 5. State University of New York Upstate Medical Center, Syracuse, 1968.

YOUNG, R. W., and A. LOOMIS, Theory of the chromatic stroboscope. *Journal of the Acoustical Society of America*, 1938, *10*: 112–18.

ZWICKER, E., G. FLOTTORP, and S. S. STEVENS. Critical band width in loudness summation. *Journal of the Acoustical Society of America*, 1957, *29*: 548–57.

ZWICKER, E., and H. N. WRIGHT. Temporal summation for tones in narrow-band noise. *Journal of the Acoustical Society of America*, 1963, *35*: 691–99.

ZWISLOCKI, J. Theory of temporal auditory summation. *Journal of the Acoustical Society of America*, 1960, *32*: 1046–60.

———— An acoustic method for clinical examination of the ear. *Journal of Speech and Hearing Research*, 1963, *6*: 303–14.

Humans appear to be most often aware of the sights and sounds of their external environment. This predominance of hearing and vision results in the relegation of all other environmental energy forms to a minor, nebulous category: the *other senses*. This dichotomy is a self-fulfilling prophecy. Since we choose to (or are able to) attend to only two classes of the many aspects of the environment, we have little vocabulary with which to describe all other sensory experience. Then, since we are unable to speak with great precision or to convey much information about our non-visual or non-auditory sensory experiences, it follows that they are not worth great investigation or study. We then cite the relative paucity of knowledge of these other senses as evidence of their limited interest and value. Finally, we often naively assume that the total environment of all living creatures is organized by our own sensory systems. Understanding our world is difficult under any circumstances and is made into a near hopeless task when pure tones, narrow wave lengths, etc. are taken to be the basic information in all animal-environment transactions. There is little likelihood that auditory and visual stimuli of this type or indeed of any more natural type are the sole, or even the dominant, environmental energy factors for many of our co-inhabitants of this planet.

A meaningful analysis of sensory systems requires that the stimuli considered be appropriate to the evolutionary history of the organisms under study. Thus, for the sensory systems which will be briefly discussed in this chapter, *chemoreception* and *somesthesis*, the sources of stimulation would ideally consist of the foods, pheromones, and alomones that are present in the ecosphere of the animal involved. Similarly, the sources of somesthetic stimuli would be the surfaces and objects that are normally encountered and manipulated. The argument is often made that using such complex "stimuli" would prevent an analysis of a sensory system. This argument is then used to justify the so-called "simple" stimulus sources, such as single pure chemicals for chemical senses, and isolated cutaneous deformations, joint movements or bursts of thermal radiation for somesthesis. Three assumptions underlie the substitution of "simple" for natural stimulus sources: a) the natural stimulus

B. P. Halpern

The Other Senses

18

sources are composed of combinations of the simple sources; b) the natural combinations have no unique properties in and of themselves; and c) if a receptor system responds to a particular stimulus source, then that source must be a natural stimulus for that sensory system (a qualification is commonly added that the energy levels involved must be "low" or "reasonable"). These three assumptions are not really adequate and can actually prevent an understanding of sensory function.

The first two assumptions, that responses to natural sources can be constructed *post hoc* from responses to "simple" sources indicates, for example, that pure tones should be a suitable probe for analyzing the functional properties of the auditory system. However, experiments have repeatedly demonstrated that many auditory neurons which are unresponsive to pure tones or which give a very slight and phasic response become either responsive or greatly increase their responsiveness when F. M. modulated tones are used (Whitfield 1967). This effect, which is observed in a number of mammals, seems reasonable in view of the types of sounds actually produced (the natural stimulus sources) by the animals under study. A similar uniqueness of natural sources is apparent in vision (Maturana et al. 1960; Hubel and Wiesel 1968).

The third assumption, that a functional analysis of a sensory system is possible by presentation of "reasonable" intensities of various physical energies (simple stimulus sources) is questioned in many instances. For example, a receptor structure found in cartilaginous fish, the ampullae of Lorenzini, was shown to be a sensitive thermal receptor and sensitive mechano-receptor (Murray 1962). Temperature changes which would affect this receptor are not often encountered in the environment in which the fish in fact lives and therefore would not be available from natural stimulus sources. The ampullae of Lorenzini is in fact an electroreceptor which enables these animals to detect changes in electromagnetic fields in the conductive medium in which they live and move (R. W. Murray 1965). Electroreception might seem to be an unreasonable choice, since it represents a receptor system not present in our species and, therefore, could not be anticipated. However, there are other sensory systems which humans are either only slightly equipped with, such as sensitivity to ultraviolet light (Kay 1969) or polarized light (Carthy 1965) or totally unequipped with, such as highly sensitive and directional infrared detectors found in the pit organs of certain snakes (Bullock and Barrett 1968). Thus, sensory systems with which humans are not equipped are a common situation, rather than an unusual deviation.

A possibly less obvious class of meaningless sensory responses are those in which a "simple" stimulus source can readily activate a receptor system if it gains access, but, under normal circumstances, its energy output never reaches the receptors. This situation is exemplified by such cases as the absence of human responses to UV due to absorbing properties of the lens of the eye (Fry 1959), or the elimination of all movement except transients by the macroscopic laminated structure of the pacinian corpuscle (Loewenstein 1965). In both these instances, an obvious accessory structure blocks access by certain energies. However, in other situations, the stimulus filtering is not done by an accessory structure directly related to the receptor. For example, thermal stimuli applied to olfactory receptors of frogs will readily elicit responses (M. M. Mozell, personal communication), but in man, at least, inspired air is

equilibrated to a constant temperature before it reaches the olfactory epithelium on the superior turbinates (Stone, 1963).

Whenever senses are studied, the permissible intensity of the stimulus sources must be considered. Unless the experimental subjects are humans, the assumption of human thresholds as a useful source of intensity criteria is quite dubious. For example, in our fellow mammal, the cat, responses to skin stimulation from radiant sources, excluding the face area, occur only at the same intensity levels at which avoidance responses to the stimuli also occur (Kenshalo 1964, 1967). This does not happen with a radiant source in humans. Similarly, human behavioral taste thresholds to the presence of certain chemicals, such as quinine hydrochloride, are considerably lower than thresholds found for the hamster or the rabbit (Pfaffmann 1959; Carpenter 1956). On the other hand, the sensitivity of some insects to vapor phase chemical stimulation seems to be several orders of magnitude greater than that present for any known stimulus in humans (Schneider 1966).

The reasonable deduction from the foregoing long list of caveats is that the experiments which will be considered in this very brief chapter will use only natural, ecologically relevant stimulus sources, presented at intensity levels that are behaviorally meaningful for the animal under study. If this were the case, the chapter would be nonexistent rather than very brief, since few such studies exist in either chemoreception or somesthesis. Consequently, the majority of the information to be presented was elicited by "simple" stimulus sources with all the attendant problems.

Behavioral responses to the natural stimulus sources of an environment indicate not merely an ability to discriminate between various environmental energy patterns, but more importantly, a grouping of various energy patterns into meaningful modalities. Depending on the particular sensory system, these groupings may have various degrees of overlap and interdependence. It is generally assumed, and occasionally demonstrated, that single, consistent, systematic relationships exist between change in behavioral and/or neural responses to environmental stimulus sources and change in a physically measurable characteristic of the environmental sources. Furthermore, it is commonly assumed that these changes occur along parallel stimulus dimensions or stimulus continua. In some cases such dimensions can be specified for both "simple" and natural stimulus sources. Thus, with reference to sound, the frequency of sound pressure waves is related to human experiential reports of pitch and also relates in a systematic manner to behavioral changes in other vertebrates. In addition, at least some of the physical characteristics of speech sounds can be systematically related to human reports of these sounds (Whitfield 1967).

The chemical senses are particularly poorly understood in regard to physical classification of stimulus sources. The relationships between individual molecules, groups of different molecules, natural sources, and responses of chemoreceptors, and the occurence of behaviors dependent upon them, are very unclear (Pfaffmann 1959; Amerine, Pangborn, and Roessler 1965; Sato and Kusano 1960), although attempts to relate some classifications of chemical stimuli to physical properties of chemicals have been made (Pfaffmann 1959; Amerine, Pangborn, and Roessler 1965; Shallenberger and Acree 1969). The commonly accepted four-category classification of taste stimulus sources for humans, which has often been extended to other species, finds no support in this chapter. A general strategy for predicting, discovering, and understanding modalities and the stimulus continua of senses has been described (Erickson, 1968). In this view, the senses are considered to be separable into two modality groups, topological or non-topological. For topological modalities, stimulus quality is represented by the locations on the receptor surface which is activated. Examples are hearing, visual localization, and cutaneous localization. For both visual localization and cutaneous localization, the receptor sheet itself is more or less directly and discreetly affected by spatially localized environmental events. In audition, sound frequencies are converted by the cochlea of the inner ear into a pattern of activity across the auditory receptor sheet. In each of these cases, the specific receptor cells activated change when the stimulus quality, that is, stimulus location, changes. This change, in which few receptors of the entire array are activated, is a major component of the change in stimulus quality. In contrast, non-topological modalities such as color vision, and perhaps olfaction and taste, use the same small set of receptors to respond to all stimulus dimensions of the modality. In this case, each receptor of this set has a similar but somewhat different sensitivity characteristic, and, therefore, the output of the set produces unique patterns for relatively small differences in the energy output of natural stimulus source. Thus, if stimulus quality must be fully represented at all locations on the receptor surface, broadly tuned receptors must be present. The nature of the modality is not specified by the receptors, however, since the topographic modality of visual localization and the non-topographic modalities of color vision, contour orientation, speed, etc., are constructed from the output of the same set of receptors.

References

AMERINE, M. A., R. M. PANGBORN, and E. B. ROESSLER. *Principles of Sensory Evaluation of Food.* New York: Academic, 1965.

BULLOCK, T. H., and R. BARRETT. Radiant heat receptors in snakes. *Communications in Behavioral Biology,* 1968, A, *1*: 19–29.

CARPENTER, J. A. Species differences in taste preferences. *Journal of Comparative and Physiological Psychology,* 1956, *49*: 139–44.

CARTHY, J. D. *The Behavior of Arthropods.* San Francisco: W. H. Freeman, 1965.

DZENDOLET, E. A structure common to sweet-evoking compounds. *Perception and Psychophysics.* 1968, 3(1B): 65–68.

ERICKSON, R. P. Stimulus coding in topographic and non-topographic afferent modalities. *Psychological Review,* 1968, 75: 447–64.

FRY, G. A. The image-forming mechanism of the eye. *In* J. FIELD (ed.), *Handbook of Physiology. Section I: Neurophysiology. Vol. I.* Washington, D.C.: American Physiological Society, 1959.

HUBEL, D. H., and T. N. WIESEL. Receptive fields and functional architecture of monkey striate cortex cells. *Journal of Physiology,* 1968, *195*: 215–43.

KAY, R. E. Fluorescent materials in insect eyes and their possible relationship to ultraviolet sensitivity. *Journal of Insect Physiology,* 1969, *15*: 2021–38.

KENSHALO, D. The temperature sensitivity of furred skin of cats. *Journal of Physiology,* 1964, *172*: 439–48.

—————— Thresholds for thermal stimulation of the inner thigh, footpad, and face of cats. *Journal of Comparative and Physiological Psychology,* 1967, *63*: 133–38.

LOEWENSTEIN, W. R. Facets of a transducer process. *In* L. FRISH (ed.), *Sensory Receptors. Cold Springs Harbor Symposia on Quantitative Biology,* 1965, *30*: 29–43.

MATURANA, H. R., ET AL. Anatomy and physiology of vision in the frog. *Journal of General Physiology,* 1960, No. 6, Part 2, *43*: 129–71.

MURRAY, R. W. Temperature receptors in animals. *In* J. W. L. BEAMENT (ed.), *Biological Receptor Mechanisms. Symposia of the Society for Experimental Biology,* 1962, *16*: 245–66.

MURRAY, R. W. Receptor mechanisms in the ampullae of Lorenzini of elasmobranch fishes. *In* L. FRISCH (ed.), *Sensory Receptors. Cold Spring Harbor Symposia on Quantitative Biology,* 1965, *30*: 233–43.

PFAFFMANN, C. The sense of taste. *In* J. FIELD (ed.), *Handbook of Physiology. Section I: Neurophysiology. Vol. I.* Washington, D.C.: American Physiological Society, 1959.

SATO, M., and K. KUSANO. Electrophysiology of gustatory receptors. In *Electrical Activity of Single Nerve Cells.* Tokyo: Iga Kushoin, Hongo, 1960.

SCHNEIDER, D. Chemical sense communication in insects. In *Nervous and Hormonal Mechanisms of Integration.* New York: Symposia of the Society for Experimental Biology, 1966.

SHALLENBERGER, R. S., and T. E. ACREE. Molecular structure and sweet taste. *Journal of Agricultural and Food Chemistry,* 1969, *17*: 701–3.

STONE, H. Influence of temperature on olfactory sensitivity. *Journal of Applied Physiology,* 1963, *18*: 746–51.

WHITFIELD, I. C. *The Auditory Pathway.* London: Edward Arnold, 1967.

Imagery is a feature of man's behavioral repertory which is at once so private and close to the self as to belie effective scientific scrutiny in an age of operationalism. While the properties and implications of imagery were regarded by pre-behaviorist psychologists as being central issues in psychology (witness the vigor of the "imageless thought" controversy at the turn of the century), there was a period of almost fifty years in which almost no research in this field appeared (Holt, 1964). Today, emboldened by advances in neurophysiology, by the findings of sensory deprivation and dream research, and by the new look at man as an information-processing organism brought on by computer theory, psychologists are again ready to study the phenomena which have been so much a part of them all along. The image represents man's duplication of the structure of physically measurable objects or events in his environment by an as yet not understood neural process. A percept involves a response to an object that continues to be within the physical scanning capacity of the sense organs for at least a second or so. If the original source of stimulation is further removed in time from the observer but is nevertheless described as present or experienced in some form as a part of the subject's consciousness, we are dealing with an image. It does not matter for the first step in definition whether the observer believes the object to be there still (hallucination) or whether he knows it is not and can reproduce it at will (memory image). The critical issue is the presence or absence in the physical environment of an object or wave pattern that allows measurement or description by other than the observer. The image thus represents man's capacity to duplicate environmental information in the absence of the persistence of external signals.

Another distinction that must be made at the outset in approaching the subject of imagery is between sensation-based imagery and the more centrally controlled processes. The afterimage is an interesting phenomenon and has been studied exten-

J. L. Singer

Imagery and Daydreaming

19

sively by early students of sensation and perception. Essentially, however, it is a response tied to the properties of the visual mechanism at the end-organ level. Thus, unlike the eidetic image which stays in place while the eyes of the imager move, the after-image is rooted to the eyeball and moves with it. Other phenomena which seem essentially products of the very operation of the optic nerve endings are the phosphenes, those kaleidoscopic lights and shapes which leap into view when we shut our eyes. While the phosphenes probably can be used by some people as pleasant ways of relaxing—a kind of abstract film one can watch in private—they are either almost unnoticed by many people or perhaps somewhat frightening to a few. It is possible that some visual hallucinations are triggered by persons becoming suddenly aware of these dancing lights and odd shapes that seem to appear on the eyelids (Horowitz 1969).

Of much greater interest are the images that seem to stem from central processes. It is essential, however, that one take a position about perception itself before describing the mechanism of imagery. Neisser (1967) has argued effectively that perception itself must be viewed as a construction. The eyes scan only bits of any external stimulus field in a given second. One must view the percept as built up over a period of time—measured in milliseconds perhaps, but nevertheless not grasped all at once. In this sense, the ocular motility becomes an essential feature of the integrative process of perception. The closeness of the motor system to the perceptual process urged long ago by Werner (1945) has been recently reaffirmed for perception and imagery by Neisser (1969) and Hebb (1968). The eye movements are essential parts of a feedback process, although in imagery they need not directly follow the outline of the image as they do in perception (Hebb, 1968). For those rare cases of children with true eidetic imagery, uncovered in the important recent reexamination of this problem by Haber and Haber (1964), the projection of an image is so vivid that scanning does occur. More typically, however, the image is a much vaguer reconstruction with only fleeting oculo-motor accompaniment.

Hebb (1968) has attempted a speculative but intriguing theory of the neural basis of imagery by an effort to demonstrate that certain vivid imagery such as the eidetic children report is based on first-order cell assemblies. Thus, the eidetic image may be monocular if formed with one eye open, and disappearing when that eye is closed and the other eye opened. Second-order assemblies (which are involved in binocular activities or more complex imagery) show the characteristics of greater generalizability and interchangeability of structure. In this sense, the extreme vividness of imagery of the eidetic child may actually be a handicap, a symptom of mild brain defect (Siipola and Hayden 1965). Neisser (1969) has suggested that it is the flexible utilization of imagery that is the key to the cognitive adaptive implications of the process rather than sheer *vividness*. If anything, extreme vividness may hinder other ongoing processes in the same modality (Segal 1971). A capacity to rely on imagery, however, clearly aids memory according to Paivio and Madigan (1968). Concrete images lead to better paired-associates recall than abstract nouns. Indeed, even in clinical efforts at uncovering personality complexes, an experimental study by Reyher and Smeltzer (1968) has demonstrated the superiority of visual imagery over verbal associations. Visual imagery yielded higher GSR activity and more material associated with drives or "primary processes." A series of investigations summarized by Neisser (1969) have made it clear that sheer vividness of imagery as a

characteristic individual difference has few significant correlates in other cognitive or personality functions.

Important methodological advances in the study of imagery have been made by Segal (1971) and Sheehan (1966). Sheehan, for example, developed both questionnaire and apparatus methods for eliciting information on the vividness and other dimensions of visual imagery. Using a procedure by which *S*, having examined a picture of an object, then projected it mentally onto a screen, the imager then manipulated a projector light for color, intensity, and shape to come as close as possible to his own image. Sheehan was able to ascertain how effective memory images were in producing something comparable to an original stimulus object. He was also able to study the differential imagery-producing properties of the original stimuli.

Segal (1971) has been exploring the parameters of the Perky phenomenon in a very careful series of experiments. Originally Perky, a student of Titchener, reported that if *S*'s were instructed to imagine the projection of an object such as a red tomato upon a screen, they could not detect the fact that *E* was surreptitiously projecting an *actual* image of the object thereon. Segal has been able to replicate the Perky effect, the failure to detect a "real" from a mentally projected image, and has studied assimilation effects, individual differences, familiarity and unfamiliarity of the "actual" image, and methods of reporting. Her results make it clear that some profound mechanism of screening out "external" stimulation is operative when *S*'s are engaged in the production of mental images.

What is increasingly clear from a review of recent research trends in imagery is that as Holt (1964) put it, "the ghost is out of the closet." Psychologists are confronting more and more the fact that man is best viewed not so much as a machine responding to external wavelengths, but rather a complex feedback information system whose outputs are not only motor responses but also images. Indeed, even the so-called behavior modification methods of psychotherapy that have been yielding dramatic effects of late have resorted increasingly to the power of self-generated imagery in producing systematic reductions in anxiety.

Daydreaming and Fantasy Processes

SOME DEFINITIONS AND RESTRICTIONS

Whereas imagery involves a cognitive response or conscious experience rather close in time to the occurrence of an external stimulus source, daydreams or fantasies represent much more complex processes, the heaping up of images often in several modalities and far removed in time from the original external stimuli which they duplicate. Indeed, the danger in attempting any scientific approach to a phenomenon such as daydreaming is that it is so ubiquitous a human experience and so complexly intertwined with the entire problem of human thought that it suffers from a plethora of popular labels all essentially based on somewhat different formulations of private experiences.

The vividness and hallucinatory quality of nightdreaming has made for greater popular as well as scientific interest in the nocturnal imagery we experience. The daydream and related phenomena such as the interior monologue or other manifestations of the stream of thought take place in a setting of relative wakefulness with complex information processes actively involved. Hence men are often less sensitive to the degree to which they are indeed carrying on extensive internal glosses or commentaries on the perceptual phenomena of their environment, getting lost in well-learned trains of memory sequences, or developing novel combinations of associative material into elaborate and often creative fantasies. The dream has considerably more figural quality while the daydream tends more often to be part of the background in the conscious experience because of the urgency of processing new external stimulus material.

It is not surprising then that there has been so little formal study of daydreaming. Although James' famous chapter on the Stream of Thought (1890) called attention to the problem and a school of writing grew up addressed to capturing the stream of consciousness in literary form (Humphrey 1958), almost no studies of daydreaming were carried out by psychologists. The Structuralist school led by Titchener carried on considerable research on associations to directly presented stimuli, but very little attention was paid to their own spontaneous fantasy processes by the practitioners of that introspective group. In England, in the 1920s, Green (1923) collected accounts of children's daydreams, and in the mid '30s, Jersild, Markey, and Jersild (1933) and Shaffer (1936) made efforts to obtain samples of daydream content in various categories from children and young adults. With the emergence of projective techniques in the early 1940s, considerable normative data and some experimental studies were available using certain scores or content categories on the Rorschach or TAT as examples of daydream or fantasy tendencies.

Naturally, Sigmund Freud turned his attention early to the daydream and waking fantasy. Indeed, the essence of his revision of the theory of infantile sexuality was built around his recognition that many so-called childhood seductions were based upon children's daydreams rather than upon actual encounters with adults.

The psychoanalytic technique as developed by Freud and continued to this day by the various schools of clinicians still relies heavily on the use of daydreams, nightdreams, and other fantasy processes for information of the motivations and transference distortions of the patient. The emphasis in psychoanalytic theory and practice has largely been placed upon the *content* of dreams or daydreams, and less attention has been paid to what might be termed the structural characteristics of these phenomena, e.g., their functional role in the economy of the personality, their relation to cognition and perceptual processes, the range of individual differences in style or form of daydreaming. In two early but seminal papers, Freud did indeed speculate on the psychological significance of the daydream and stressed the fact that the conscious product of the fantasy represented essentially a compromise between a partially repressed conflictual wish and a more socially acceptable resolution. His view of fantasy was essentially rooted in his theory that all thought grew out of deprivation or conflict, a position which has been only fairly recently modified with the emergence of ego psychology and Hartmann's consideration of fantasy as an autonomous ego function (Freud 1908, 1911; Hartmann 1958).

Although Freud (1908) was inclined to define daydreaming as a diversion from task-oriented thought, few early investigators paid special attention to careful definition. This has left terms such as daydreaming, reverie, fantasy, etc. subject to a vague popular terminology. In approaching some reasonable definition which can serve as a basis for suitable research, it may be best to consider daydreaming to be a form of thought that represents a diversion from an ongoing physical, perceptual, or mental task. More technically, still, we might call it a form of *stimulus-independent mentation*.

The distinction raised at the outset of this paper for image and percept in terms of the continued presence of the external stimulus source is clearly relevant here, too. A daydream in its narrowest form would be a simple fleeting association to an object in the environment, "That chair reminds me of the one my father used to sit in." It could be a far more extensive unrolling of an elaborate memory as in the famous description by Proust in "*Swann's Way*" of the effects of tasting the cookie crumbs steeped in the tea which calls up the vivid scenes of a childhood in Combray. Or it could involve an elaborate make-believe vacation in the South Sea Islands which a student conjures up while presumably listening to a boring lecture. Whether daydreams represent wish fulfillments or are adaptive in any sense should be the object of research, not something built into definition. In the balance of this chapter we shall concentrate on explicating some of the major methodological approaches to studying this ephemeral phenomenon and indicating some of the major research findings to date (Richardson 1969; Klinger 1971).

INTROSPECTIVE APPROACHES

Since stimulus-independent mentation is essentially a private experience, all approaches to studying the phenomena of daydreaming eventually involve some form of introspection. The scientific approach calls for a system of organizing the essentially introspective material into a form that is replicable and reasonably measurable. This was, of course, the goal of the "introspectionist" school of Titchener with its emphasis upon careful training of experimentalists in examining their imagery. From our present vantage point it would appear that Titchener's students, in their efforts to avoid the "stimulus error" and to hew as closely as possible to the sensation-pole in their attention to their experiences, threw out the most interesting data, their own idiosyncratic associations, memories, fears, and wishes. By contrast, Freud, in analyzing his own dreams, gave free rein to his associations and was able to discover the vast implications of these nocturnal phenomena for understanding the nature of human conflicts, memories of childhood, resistances, the role of processes such as condensation and displacement in all types of mental activity and creative art, etc. Freud carried this further in his great work on everyday slips or memory lapses, but he did not concentrate especially on his daydreams.

Early applications of the introspective method to a careful study of daydreaming were carried out by Silberer (1951) and Varendonck (1921). Silberer developed an ingenious technique for studying the nature of the symbolism in his fantasy during reverie states. Relaxing himself in a state just prior to sleep, he attempted to maintain in consciousness a fairly formidable mental problem, e.g., comparing Schopenhauer's and Kant's theories of time. Silberer reported the occurrence, after a brief period, of clear images which often translated the abstractions of the theory into vivid allegorical or metaphorical scenes. Modifications of this technique have been used subsequently by Rapaport (1967) and by Singer (1966).

Some examples of how introspective methods can be employed to study ongoing mentation in a fashion susceptible to systematic study and formal statistics are provided in Singer (1966). For example, one question raised about daydreaming might be whether spontaneous imagery is more intrusive when someone is engaged in a mental task reconstructing well-known events from memory or when planning some new steps for the future. Or one might ask whether extraneous imagery intrudes more if the task assigned is personal or impersonal, or simple or complex. By establishing in advance a series of mental tasks to which S must attend for a period of time such as 5 or 10 minutes and having S's report immediately afterward on relative frequency of extraneous imagery, vividness of such imagery, content, etc., formal experimental data can be obtained either for a single individual or for groups. Randomizing order and type of task and using counterbalancing techniques assures control comparable to that attainable in most factorially designed experiments in which a perceptual judgment is obtained. Thus, one clear finding from an experiment performed on a single subject and then repeated with a group was that a memory task ("How did you spend last summer?") unrolled itself in the 5 minutes with a minimum of extraneous fantasy intrusion and was rated as involving far less physical strain. By comparison, planning a future vacation was occasioned by more extraneous imagery and sense of strain.

It seems likely that psychologists will never be completely satisfied with an introspective technique as a *sole* basis for drawing conclusions in an area so private as fantasy experience. Nevertheless, the time seems ripe to employ the advanced technology of experimental design in studies of individuals and in experiments in which verbal reports can be obtained systematically under conditions that allow for effective estimation of error variances and appropriate statistical analyses. Perhaps, too, we need not be ashamed to return to use of trained introspectionists in this area as long as we take into account the effect of the training on the variable under question. It seems likely that just as many people are relatively unaware of dreaming until instructed by a psychoanalyst to bring in dreams; so too, many of us are oblivious of our ongoing stream of thought until our attention is called to it. Indeed, it is intriguing that both psychoanalysis and its current rival, behavior therapy, place great emphasis on the subject's ability to control and generate fantasies.

PROJECTIVE METHODS FOR THE STUDY OF DAYDREAMING

The emergence of the projective techniques in psychology during the late 1930s excited considerable interest in the mental health professions as well as among personality researchers because it seemed that at last methods were available for obtaining relatively objective data about the more private inner experiences of man. The Rorschach inkblots and Thematic Apperception Test pictures seemed (as the most famous and widely used of the projectives) to offer psychologists insights into S's daydreams or affective tendencies without having to rely upon direct questioning. Especially relevant to the subject of this chapter are the results obtained from studies of imaginative tendencies in children and adults obtained through the use of the Human Movement response to the Rorschach inkblots. In his early efforts to explore psychopathological and personality patterns

through associations to inkblots, the Swiss psychiatrist Hermann Rorschach (1942) began to observe certain consistencies between overt behavior and the pattern of response to form, movement, and color. He noticed, for example, that persons who often reported that the inkblots looked like humans in action, e.g., "two people dancing," "clowns playing pattycake," etc. also tended to be rather imaginative, inner-oriented persons and at the same time somewhat more motorically awkward or inhibited. This relationship of inhibited overt motility, perception of motion on the inkblots, and considerable "movement in the mind's eye" became one of the focal points of Rorschach's psychodiagnostic method. The importance of the Human Movement response (M) in the study of personality, and more specifically imagination, was confirmed by all of the leading clinicians who pioneered the development of the Rorschach method: Samuel Beck, Bruno Klopfer, Zygmunt Piotrowski, and Ernst Schachtel.

The great developmental psychologist, Heinz Werner, saw in Rorschach's linkage of motion perception to inhibited motility and imagined motion an opportunity to test his own theory of a sensory-tonic system which linked overt muscular activity to perception via the medium of body tonicity. He performed some experiments which supported Rorschach's linkage of M responses to inhibited or controlled motility (Werner 1945). This opened the way to a whole series of experiments which have sought to explore the behavioral correlates of the M response (Singer 1960, 1968). For example, it has been consistently found that children and adults, normal or pathological, who show more M responses on the Rorschach are less likely to move around rapidly or restlessly in waiting rooms, write more slowly in "slow writing" tasks, are more deliberate in Porteus Maze Test performance, less likely to use physical gestures if called upon to define verbs like "twist," "spiral," "interwine." At the same time on measures of imagination such as in storytelling, High M subjects do better than those who show few M. High M responders were shown to have greater interpersonal sensitivity and awareness (King 1960). Writers or sedentary, literary-minded college students gave more M responses than did ballet dancers or college athletes (Singer 1968; Dudek 1968). Goldberger and Holt (1961) found that persons in a sensory deprivation situation who showed the capacity for extended thought about topics *other* than the immediate experimental situation also gave considerably more M responses on the Rorschach test.

Of special relevance to daydreaming was a finding by Page (1957). He developed a questionnaire listing a variety of daydreams. S's who indicated a greater frequency of daydreaming also proved to be significantly higher in producing Rorschach M responses. Schonbar (1965) found Rorschach M related positively to the recall of dreams as well. It seems clear that the perception of Human Movement on inkblots does indeed bear a correspondence to the tendencies to see people and events in the mind's eye. Obviously there are differences between a response to inkblots and the actual ongoing stream of thought. Nevertheless, for research purposes where direct inquiry about daydreams or the use of questionnaire or laboratory techniques are precluded, the availability of the projective measure of daydreaming has obvious value for the investigator. Some further examples of the use of Rorschach M responses in estimating imaginative predisposition in children will be described below.

The Thematic Apperception Test has also been extensively employed to obtain estimates of the daydream patterns of adults and children especially as these bear on the motivational trends in the personality. The literature on the use of TAT or related picture-story methods to estimate achievement, aggression, or affiliation motivation is too extensive to be summarized here and is described in detail in a variety of reviews (Atkinson 1958; Singer 1968; Rabin 1968). If we regard the general imaginativeness of stories told to TAT-type pictures as an indicator of daydreaming tendencies in general, then there is some evidence that supports this notion, at least insofar as Rorschach *M* and various TAT-derived measures of fantasy are concerned (Singer 1960; Dudek 1968; Singer 1968). On the other hand, the question of whether specific TAT fantasies are related to actual reported daydreams of *S*'s is more difficult to answer. Some studies have even suggested a negative relationship between the TAT themes and the themes of reported daydreams (Page 1956); others have been inconclusive (Singer 1966). A really thorough examination of the relationship of self-reported daytime fantasies can be sure that thematic fantasy is the same as the ongoing daydreaming activities of subjects.

The major limitation of the projective methods for the study of daydreaming is the fact the instruments are essentially intermediate procedures, subject to various psychometric complexities which require several additional steps in the assumptive process before we can be sure we are talking of the same thing as the ongoing daydreams of the waking state. It would appear more reasonable that for a research approach to daydreams some fairly direct questioning of *S*'s ought to be more fully explored as well.

Questionnaire Studies

Although there is indeed some cultural inhibition about discussing daydreams (an obvious reason why projective methods have flourished), it has seemed to some investigators that more direct approaches, especially with normal persons, were worth trying. Shaffer (1936), for example, drew up a series of categories of daydream types and administered them to college students to establish patterns of sex differences. Later, Seeman (1951), using a comparable system, felt that the pattern of responses from normal adults supported the Freudian wish-fulfillment theory. Page developed a much more detailed list of very specific daydreams which he also administered to college students and correlated with the Rorschach method. His results (described above) are the major basis for linking Rorschach *M* and daydreaming frequency.

Another questionnaire similar to Page's was developed by Singer (1966) and various collaborators, and administered in various studies to hundreds of subjects, mainly college-educated or middle-class high school students. Data from this questionnaire have been employed to estimate general frequency of daydreaming in normal adults, age changes in reported frequency of daydreaming, background and familial factors associated with reported frequent and infrequent daydreaming, sociocultural variations in content and frequency of daydreaming for American-born *S*'s as well as sex differences in daydream patterns (Singer 1966; Singer and McCraven 1961; Singer and McCraven 1962; Singer and Schonbar 1961; Wagman 1967). In order to relate questionnaire-derived daydream patterns to other relevant personality variables, a factor analytic study was carried out by Singer and Antrobus (1963) employing interview data as well as a variety of other cognitive and personality instruments. The findings of this latter study have led to the development of a new instrument (Singer and Antrobus 1972) which is now the basis for a further large scale exploration of the interrelations of frequency and content of daydreaming to patterns of repressive style, motoric or ideational orientation, and various other personality characteristics.

Space permits only a very brief summary of some of the major findings derived from questionnaire usage in this field. It should be stressed that employment of an inventory leads inevitably to many of the same considerations of response-set, reliability, and other technicalities of questionnaire construction. These have been dealt with in various fashions (Singer and Antrobus 1963). For example, an obvious question is whether response to such a questionnaire, which includes very personal or bizarre daydreams, is simply a function of the social desirability orientation of the respondents. A check for this was included in the Singer-Antrobus (1963) factor analysis and recent data have indicated that social desirability is not a major element in the response of *S*'s to this type of daydream questionnaire.

Among the main findings from questionnaire studies are the following: Most people report some daydreaming every day, especially in periods of solitary waiting or just prior to going to sleep (Singer and McCraven 1961). While there are no marked differences in reported daydream frequency between men and women, specific types of daydreaming obviously related to cultural sex role expectations, as well as early psychological differences in treatment of boys and girls, do seem to emerge (Singer 1966; Wagman 1967; Pytkowicz, Wagner, and Wechsler 1969). Daydreaming seems to be at a peak in late adolescence and drops off very gradually in the next three decades (Singer and McCraven 1961), but there is evidence of persisting daydreaming even in the very aged (Bakur 1967).

While factors such as education (in middle-class *S*'s) or marital status do not seem significantly related to frequent daydreaming, the sociocultural background of *S*'s seems to relate both to frequency of reported daydreaming and to content. For example, Singer and McCraven (1962) found that American-born adults coming from Negro, Jewish, or Italian cultural backgrounds reported more frequent daydreaming than *S*'s whose parents were of Irish, German, or Anglo-Saxon background. Similarly, early relationships with parental figures seemed to be associated with frequency of daydreaming. *S*'s who reported greater closeness to their mothers than to their fathers, or who described their fathers as more discrepant from their own ideal selves, also reported more frequent daydreaming (Singer and McCraven 1961; Singer and McCraven 1962; Singer and Schonbar 1961). Self-reports of daydreaming frequency were also associated significantly with measures of self-awareness and anxiety (Singer and Schonbar 1961; Singer and Rowe 1962). Although there is no clear evidence as yet that daydreaming is associated with specific pathological tendencies, some differences in patterns of daydreaming between hospitalized psychiatric patients and medical inpatients (Pytkowicz, Wagner, and Wechsler 1969) or between schizophrenics and normals (Cazavelan and Epstein 1966) have been reported using questionnaires of the type described above.

The whole issue of individual differences in daydreaming

is still in its beginning stages. It may be that there exists a general personality style of self-awareness (Singer and Schonbar 1961) or openness to inner experiences (as Rorschach data on *M* responders would suggest); this self-awareness may perhaps be related to other stylistic variables described in the personality literature such as *tolerance for unreal experience* (Klein, Gardner, and Schlesinger 1962), or the dimension of *ego-closeness ego-distance* as developed by Voth and Mayman (Voth and Mayman 1963; Voth, et al. 1968). The latter dimension measured by perception of autokinetic movement as well as by a variety of interview and Rorschach measures suggests a kind of introversion-extroversion dimension in which the *ego-close S*'s are emotionally labile, highly responsive to external stimuli, while ego-distant *S*'s are characterized as possessing more detachment from the environment and more sensitivity to their own inner experiences. In several studies, *S*'s rated high for Daydreams, Reflectiveness, and Thoughtfulness, in general loaded positively on the ego-distance factor. A factor analytic study of daydreaming patterns carried out by Singer and Antrobus (1963) also revealed evidence for a second-order general factor of inner responsiveness with more fanciful daydreaming at one pole and more controlled thoughtfulness at another. A very clear-cut extroversion factor with no daydreaming proclivities evident also emerged in that study. The trend of all of this literature is toward a revival of attention to the introversion-extroversion dimensions defined by Guilford in relation to inner experience as well as to a further examination of this notion in relation to Eysenck's more behaviorally-oriented I-E dimension.

DEVELOPMENTAL STUDIES

Although Green (1923) and Jersild, Markey, and Jersild (1933) made some early collections of children's daydreams, there have been surprisingly few efforts to examine how daydreaming, fantasy styles, or introspective tendencies develop in the normal child. Piaget had long ago pointed to the way in which the egocentric speech of the child gradually becomes internalized and persists, he felt, as inner fantasy. Similar observations or descriptive accounts came from other workers (see Singer 1966). The Rorschach studies of successive age samples suggested that there is in general an increase in Rorschach *M* responses with some suggestion of spurts at the beginning of school age and in adolescence. Relatively little direct attention has been paid to the individual differences in imaginative play which characterize children although such differences in *content* of fantasy are widely used for diagnostic purposes by clinicians.

Direct interviews with children about their fantasy lives are of course difficult to carry out, especially with very young children. In one study (Singer 1961), children aged 6–9 were indeed asked a series of questions about their daydreaming and fantasy play patterns. Those who gave positive responses to items such as "Do you have pictures in your head?" or "Do you have make-believe playmates?" were contrasted with others who reported minimal inner activity or whose spontaneous play was oriented to games of skill or direct experience rather than toward introduction of make-believe elements. These High and Low Fantasy groups were then observed in experimental situations. It was found, for example, that High Fantasy children were able to sit quietly for a longer period in a simulated space capsule. Their spontaneous storytelling was rated as more

creative by judges unfamiliar with the experimental groupings. They showed more personality characteristics associated with obsessional personality structure than did Low Fantasy children whose behavior was rated by a clinician as more like a hysterical personality type. High Fantasy *S*'s chose more cool than warm colors to draw with and were more achievement-oriented. They came from homes in which there were fewer siblings, had close relationships with one parent, and experienced more interaction with that parent around storytelling or actually playing of fantasy games.

A subsequent study employing somewhat similar procedures examined the role of the visual modality in providing children with the stimulus nutriment that forms the basis for a differentiated fantasy life. Congenitally blind and sighted children were interviewed and given opportunities to tell of their daydreams and dreams. The relative imaginativeness of the protocols were rated. It was found that on the whole the sighted children showed a much greater variety and complexity in their fantasy productions, whereas the blind children were more inclined to describe incidents very close to their direct experiences (Singer and Streiner 1966).

An attempt to explore the role of imaginative predisposition in spontaneous play of 5-year olds as well as the role of the degree of structure in toys was carried out by Pulaski (1968). Children rated as High and Low in Imaginative Predisposition based on interview, drawing, and Rorschach *M* responses were observed in playrooms in which the available toys were either highly structured or minimally structured. In general the results indicated that the more imaginatively predisposed children played longer and more creatively with the toys irrespective of structure and were also more flexible in being able to shift patterns in relation to experimental demands. Evidence of clearly different styles of play for the two groups emerged in this study.

Working with older children, Gottlieb (1968) divided her *S*'s into High and Low Imaginative Predisposition groups using inkblot *M* responses, a measure of preferences for thoughtful or physical activities, and a Torrance measure of imagination. The intent of this study was to examine whether children or adolescents would show some imitative effects of the imaginative responses of an adult model. Abstract movies were shown the children followed by a talk by an adult female who presented either a literal, fairly realistic, or highly imaginative account of the film. Following another abstract film, the children were required to write their own stories about the film. In general, the children did indeed tend to present stories along the lines observed in the model—not direct imitations of content but structurally comparable. The imitation effect was stronger for the younger (elementary school) children, while for the older children (junior high school), the imaginative predisposition effect was more prominent, i.e., the children's stories at this age followed the lines of their own imaginative inclinations rather more than what they had seen presented by the model. In general these studies suggest that children are indeed responsive to environmental factors in their imaginative tendencies, e.g., toy content or adult influence, but that predisposition to imaginative play or fantasy is early established and fairly pervasive.

Work in an area of this sort seems just in its beginnings. We have little knowledge of the changes with age in imaginative play or whether children early inclined to play "make-believe" games go on to become more frequent daydreamers or internally sensitive persons in later life. Some retrospective reports (Singer 1966) do suggest that persons rated as creative or imaginative adults do report more childhood daydreaming, but ongoing studies of children remain to be done. There are some suggestions that children's imaginative play can be increased by modeling or by similar techniques (Marshal and Hahn 1967), but systematic efforts at modification of play styles remain to be carried out. This seems especially important if we are to attempt increasing enrichment techniques with children from poverty groups. The relation of imaginative play or daydreaming tendencies to the more general dimension of "playfulness" studied by Lieberman (1965, 1966) or to the cognitive style of reflection-impulsivity examined by Kagan (1966) remains to be studied.

EXPERIMENTAL STUDIES OF DRIVE, AFFECT, AND DAYDREAMING

A significant series of experimental approaches to the study of the adaptive role of fantasy processes has stemmed from the implications of Freud's view of the nature of imagination. For Freud, the origin of fantasy lay in its relation to the period of delay between arousal of a drive and the arrival of the gratification (e.g., the mother with milk for a hungry infant). In the interim after arousal, the infant hallucinated the image of the gratifier, and this image partially reduced the quantum of drive energy, permitting the child to hold out longer before being suffused with anxiety. As elaborated by Rapaport (1960) and other investigators, the theory implies that fantasy can partially reduce drive pressure. This notion forms the basis for the widely held popular view (as well as widely practiced clinical technique) that imaginative responses have a cathartic effect on aroused drives such as aggression, sex, or hunger.

Common experience such as the use by people of specific fantasies to *arouse* desire or the advertising industry's emphasis on stimulating needs for products by encouraging fantasies (of sex by a girl in the car or of power by a tiger in its tank) suggests that drive enhancement may also be a consequence of fantasy. Especially telling criticisms of the drive-reduction theory of fantasy have come from recent re-evaluations of the nature of energy constructs in psychoanalysis (Kubie 1948; Rubinstein 1967; Holt 1964) and the serious questioning of the whole notion of drive-reduction in learning theory and motivation (Tomkins 1962; Scott 1958; Miller 1963).

Tomkins, for example, has shown that the specificity of drives and their localized satisfaction capabilities can scarcely deal with the great range of behaviors which organisms acquire. One must instead postulate a centrally mediated reward-punishment system of relatively differentiated affects or emotions which amplify the drive signals or other stimuli to produce directed behavior. Thus a great deal of the organism's so-called drive-induced behavior can be understood better as motivated by the efforts to increase positive affects such as "interest" or "joy" and to avoid negative affects such as "anger" or "distress," or else to establish control over affects. This conception, related of course to physiological studies of centrally mediated reward-punishment and feedback processes, has won support in significant papers on dreaming by Breger (1967), preemptory ideation (Klein 1967) and memory (Paul 1967), all sophisticated scholars of psychoanalytic theory.

An important starting point for experimental research on the drive-reducing theory of fantasy came in the work of Feshbach (1955). Feshbach found that experimentally angered S's showed less subsequent aggressive tendencies towards the person who had insulted them if they were given an opportunity to engage in writing TAT stories following the initial insult. A control group of insulted S's who were given a non-fantasy task showed no comparable reduction in expression of aggression in their ratings. A non-insulted control group who also wrote TAT stories were the least aggressive in comments suggesting that the fantasy opportunity was indeed partially drive-reducing. An unpublished study by Estess using cowboy movies indicated some reduction in anger in boys frustrated by unsolvable math problems. Later Feshbach used movies of a prizefight as the aggressive fantasy technique and again found support for a reduction in aggressive reactions to the experimenter (Feshbach 1961).

Studies by deCharms and Wilkins (1963), Kenny (1952), and an investigation of fantasy play in children by Feshbach (1956) provided evidence that aggressive response could actually be increased subsequent to a fantasy experience. Indeed, the bulk of experimental evidence from studies with children who view aggressive behavior in movies or on television suggests that what they observe is carried over fairly directly into aggressive play (Bandura and Walters 1963). We have had all too much tragic evidence in recent years of the way in which the communication media's focus on violence and death makes available fantasy material that seems to crystalize the aggressive intentions of lonely, embittered people.

It may be more useful to regard daydreaming as one recourse for people which, under certain circumstances, can change the prevailing affective state (rather than affecting the drive level). In one study, Singer and Rowe (1962) arranged to have instructors administer surprise midterm examinations in a number of college classes. Immediately afterwards some students were given an opportunity to daydream while others filled out opinion questionnaires. The S's who daydreamed showed, if anything, an *increase* in self-reports of test anxiety. They showed less anger, however, than the control S's. The daydreaming in one situation seemed to keep S's in the psychological field since they could reminisce about the test, remember their wrong answers, etc. The greatest anxiety was for those S's who had had essay exams and were less certain what a good answer would be and how well they did.

In another study, Rowe (1963) examined the physiological manifestations in young men, wired up and expecting to receive electric shock. Those given an opportunity to daydream showed lowered heart rate while those given a simple but compelling cognitive task showed a continued elevation and increase in heart rate from the originally aroused level. In the shock situation as set up, the impending shock was clearly coming, and the S's were reminded of this periodically. Those with free opportunity to fantasize were able to distract themselves by shifting away from thoughts of what was coming and lowered their general arousal level. For the control S's engaged in busy work, what thoughts they could sneak were generally related to the shock, and so they stayed in a high state of activation. Of interest in this study, too, was the finding that S's predisposed to considerable daydreaming were in general less prone to autonomic arousal.

A rather complex study by Pytkowicz, Wagner, and Sarason (1967) should also be mentioned here. These investigators used Feshbach's approach and insulted groups chosen as High and Low in daydreaming predisposition, based on an early version of our Daydream Questionnaire (Singer and Antrobus 1966). After insult, some *S*'s had opportunity to daydream, while others wrote TAT stories. Results indicated that a reduction in expressed aggression was obtained following both fantasy methods, but this effect was chiefly observed for *S*'s already *predisposed* to engage in fantasy. In addition, they could not support a hydraulic notion since the *S*'s who showed the reduction in anger after the daydreaming proved to be more inclined to be intropunitive and self-critical rather than merely showing a reduction of a certain quantity of an aroused drive.

If the issue is one of drive, then, one must anticipate very specific effects. A Freudian model would predict that the fantasy must be fairly directly related to the aroused drive even if cast in symbolic form. On the other hand, if one adopts a cognitive-affective model, one could argue that any fantasy activity which yielded a change in the stimulus field for the *S* by distraction or by the recall of familiar positive events or by anticipation of positive outcomes could lead to some experiences of moderate joy. These could in effect lower the high persisting level of what Tomkins calls "density of neural firing" and generally change *S*'s mood. A study addressed to this point has recently been completed by Paton (in preparation). *S*'s angered by a series of insults were shown pictures either specific to aggression (Vietnam battle scenes) or relatively benign in content. Evidence suggests that fantasy responses to the neutral material yielded more reduction in the anger thus supporting an affect rather than a drive-specific model. For those persons already skilled in daydreaming, that is, those who have learned that one can manage to process internal material without slipping too far from reality, fantasy becomes a resource for whiling away boring trips, changing one's mood under adversity or also gaining some perspective on a situation.

In this connection, daydreaming comes close to humor as a resource. Indeed, although the literature does indicate some support for a model of aggressive humor that has cathartic implications (Singer 1968; Levine 1969), there are also indications that neutral humor or playful fantasy may also reduce anger. Dworkin and Efran (1967), for instance, found aggressive motivation was reduced after *S*'s listened either to aggressive or neutral humorous recordings. Often a fantasy, when elaborated, can provide a number of opportunities to reexamine a situation and to change a mood.

INFORMATION PROCESSING AND PSYCHOPHYSIOLOGICAL APPROACHES

As one looks even more deeply into the nature of daydream processes, it becomes clear that these fantasy mechanisms are largely indistinguishable from the ongoing stream of consciousness. If one defines daydreaming as stimulus-independent mentation removed in time from the original external stimulus, one finds that inquiry yields reports of ongoing mental activity unrelated to a specific task at hand almost all the time for most adult *S*'s. A series of experiments by Antrobus and Singer have examined the problem of increasing or suppressing spontaneous imagery by changing the rate of externally derived information-processing, by making task more complex, by increasing financial penalties for errors, etc. While space prevents description of the specific experiments, they may be described as applications of the methods of vigilance and signal detection tasks to studies of ongoing task-irrelevant imagery or interior monologues. *S*'s sit in relatively sensory restricted chambers. They are required to process fairly simple auditory or visual signals presented at rapid rates. Periodically, reports of irrelevant mentation are obtained in a carefully systematized fashion. While the ultimate data are *S*'s' reports of either content or of frequency or of occurrence-nonoccurrence of stimulus-independent thought (as well as of accuracy of external signal detections), it can be shown that these reports follow lawful patterns and come about as close as one can to the ongoing inner stream of consciousness.

Some of the major results of these experiments are the following.

1. Varied internal cognitive activity such as free associative thought is able to maintain arousal more effectively than restricted inner cognitive activity during long vigilance watches. If, however, arousal is maintained artificially, e.g., by loud music, then *S*'s accuracy in detections is greater if they restrict inner cognitive activity (to counting, for example) rather than permit it to range widely (as in free associative thought) (Antrobus and Singer 1964).

2. Although increasing speed of signal presentation, or demands for *S* to rely upon short-term memory for accurate processing, does significantly reduce reports of task-irrelevant mentation, a sizable amount of such mentation persists even when signals come as fast as one every 0.5 seconds. Financial reward can increase *accuracy* and *reduce* task-irrelevant mentation reports; sudden new information about escalation of the Vietnam conflict can *increase* task-irrelevant mentation reports (leading to fantasies of being drafted or losing loved ones, etc.), but without drastic effects upon accuracy of detections (Antrobus, Singer, and Greenberg 1966). The reports of ongoing fantasy in the face of varied presentation-rates and information loads of signals for processing can be shown to be predictable from an information-theory model (Antrobus 1968). A recent study has shown that processing of internal material and of external signals can apparently be carried on in parallel fashion during high rates of signal presentation but that as pressure lessens, the person moves to a sequential processing system shifting back and forth rapidly between internal and external stimulus sources (Antrobus and Goldstein in preparation). Apparently, some type of self-pacing schedule is set up by most people so that they anticipate in a given situation how much time they will have to shift back and forth to processing material from long-term memory, their fantasies, hopes, doubts, etc., as well as the new information coming in from the environment. Indeed, Drucker (1969) found that only when *S*'s were presented with signals in random rhythms, i.e., unpredictable sequences, did reports of ongoing fantasy disappear almost completely.

3. Individual differences in fantasy predisposition do also play a role in these experiments. Antrobus, Coleman, and Singer (1967) found that persons High in Daydream frequency and thoughtfulness (as measured by questionnaires), were significantly more likely to report task-irrelevant mentation than *S*'s Low in Daydreaming predisposition. Similarly, Singer, Auster, and Antrobus (in preparation) found that persons who, given a choice, preferred sitting in silence for long periods in a sensory-restricted booth rather than have external auditory stimulation also produced more complex, imaginative, and

positive affective content in their spontaneous reports of stimulus-independent mentation.

4. Studies of ocular motility during ongoing fantasy suggest that unlike night-dreaming, waking fantasy with eyes open, or with eyes covered, is characterized by *minimal* eye-movement. Attempted suppression of a mental image, however, is usually associated with spurts of rapid eye movement (Singer and Antrobus 1965; Antrobus, Antrobus, and Singer 1964). Engaging in fantasy with eyes open, for example, means that *S* must suppress ocular motility to avoid having to process additional information which would interfere with the ongoing fantasy. A striking demonstration of this has come in a study by Greenberg (1969). *S*'s engaging in daydreaming while in a room in which the only visual stimulation consisted of a band of moving stripes showed a dropping out of the optokinetic reflex, i.e., they blocked out the powerful reflex of eye movement while concentrating on inner cognitive activity.

This series of studies, and others still in progress, have suggested in general that daydreaming and fantasy processes are best viewed as part of the brain's ongoing processing and reprocessing of stored material. The adaptive function of fantasy lies not in the drive-reducing quality at first attributed to it, but rather in its role as part of the ongoing organization and reorganization by the brain of the unfinished business of the organism. One might propose, as a tentative model, the notion that the active brain (even in the less deep phases of sleep) is involved in constant reverberatory restructuring of stored material. If one withdraws from active processing of *new* material from *outside*, one at once becomes aware of these ongoing inner processes which may be viewed as competing stimulus sources for the limited channel space of consciousness. For some persons, the shift to attention to inner material is better developed or preferred, and such introverted types (Broadbent's long-processors) learn to pace themselves so as not to bump into too many external objects while steering themselves through their environments. By and large, all of us do some such shifting most of our waking lives and the internal processing serves to reconstruct and reorganize our past as well as our future by making available new integrations and new schemas, or (in the terms of Tomkins or Miller, Galanter, and Pribram) new images and plans by which to steer ourselves through life.

References

ANTROBUS, J. S. Information theory and stimulus-independent thought. *British Journal of Psychology*, 1968, *59*: 423–30.

ANTROBUS, J. S., J. S. ANTROBUS, and J. L. SINGER. Eye movements accompanying daydreaming, visual imagery, and thought suppression. *Journal of Abnormal and Social Psychology*, 1964, *69*: 244–52.

ANTROBUS, J. S., R. COLEMAN, and J. L. SINGER. Signal detection performance by subjects differing in predisposition to day-dreaming. *Journal of Consulting Psychology*, 1967, *31*: 487–91.

ANTROBUS, J. S., and J. L. SINGER. Visual signal detection as a function of sequential variability of simultaneous speech. *Journal of Experimental Psychology*, 1964, *68*: 603–10.

ANTROBUS, J. S., J. L. SINGER, and S. GREENBERG. Studies in the stream of consciousness: experimental enhancement and suppression of spontaneous cognitive processes. *Perceptual and Motor Skills*, 1966, *23*: 399–417.

ATKINSON, J. (ed.). *Motives in fantasy, action and society.* New York Van Nostrand Reinhold, 1958.

BAKUR, M. The relationship of internal cognitive processes to adjustment in the older adult. Unpublished master's thesis, City College, City University of New York, 1966.

BANDURA, A., and R. H. WALTERS. *Social learning and personality development.* New York: Holt, Rinehart & Winston, 1963.

BREGER, L. Function of dreams. *Journal of Abnormal Psychology Monograph*, 1967, 72 (Whole No. 641).

BROOKS, L. R. The suppression of visualization by reading. *Quarterly Journal of Experimental Psychology*, 1962, *19*: 289–99.

CAZAVELAN, J., and S. EPSTEIN, Daydreams of female paranoid schizophrenics. *Journal of Clinical Psychology*, 1966, *22*: 27–32.

DECHARMS, R., and E. J. WILKINS. Some effects of verbal expression of hostility. *Journal of Abnormal and Social Psychology*, 1963, *66*: 462–70.

DRUCKER, E. Temporal uncertainty and the suppression of task-irrelevant imagery during signal detection performance. Unpublished doctoral dissertation, City University of New York, 1969.

DUDECK, S. Z. M: an active energy system correlating Rorschach M with ease of creative expression. *Journal of Projective Techniques and Personality Assessment*, 1968, *32*: 453–61.

DWORKIN, E., and J. EFRAN. The angered: Their susceptibility to varieties of humor. *Journal of Personality and Social Psychology*, 1967, *6*: 233–36.

ESTESS, B. D. The cathartic effect of two kinds of fantasy aggression on aggressive behavior. Unpublished honors thesis, Smith College, 1960.

FESHBACH, S. The drive-reducing function of fantasy behavior. *Journal of Abnormal and Social Psychology*, 1955, *50*: 3–11.

——— The catharsis hypothesis and some consequences of interaction with aggressive and neutral play objects. *Journal of Personality*, 1956, *24*: 449–62.

——— The stimulating versus cathartic effects of a vicarious aggressive activity. *Journal of Abnormal and Social Psychology*, 1961, *63*: 169–75.

FREUD, S. Creative writers and daydreaming. (1908). *In* J. STRACHEY (ed.), *The Standard Edition of the Complete Psychological Works of Sigmund Freud.* London: Hogarth, 1962, Vol. XII.

——— Formulation on the two principles of mental functioning. (1911). *In* J. STRACHEY (ed.), *The Standard Edition of the Complete Psychological Works of Sigmund Freud.* London: Hogarth, 1962, Vol. XII.

GOLDBERGER, L., and R. R. HOLT. A comparison of isolation effects and their personality correlates in two divergent samples. WADD Technical Report, Wright Air Development Division, Wright Patterson Air Force Base, Ohio, March 1961.

GOTTLIEB, S. Modelling effects on fantasy. Unpublished doctoral dissertation, City University of New York, 1968.

GREEN, G. H. *The daydream: A study in development.* London: University of London Press, 1923.

GREENBERG, S. Optokinetic nystagmus during fantasy and directed thought. Unpublished doctoral dissertation, City University of New York, 1969.

HABER, R. N., and R. B. HABER. Eidetic imagery: I. Frequency. *Perceptual and Motor Skills*, 1964, *19*: 131–38.

HARTMANN, H. *Ego psychology and the problem of adaptation.* New York: International Universities Press, 1958.

HEBB, D. O. Concerning imagery. *Psychological Review*, 1968, *75*: 466–77.

HOLT, R. R. Imagery: The return of the ostracized. *American Psychologist*, 1964, *19*: 254–64.

HOROWITZ, M. Image-formation and cognition. New York: Appleton-Century-Crofts, 1971

HUMPHREY, R. *Stream of consciousness in the modern novel.* Berkeley: University of California Press, 1958.

JAMES, W. *The principles of psychology.* (1890). New York: Dover, 1950.

JERSILD, A. T., F. V. MARKEY, and C. L. JERSILD. Children's fears, dreams, wishes, daydreams, likes, dislikes, pleasant and unpleasant memories. *Child Development Monographs*, No. 12. New York: Teachers College, Columbia University, 1933.

KAGAN, J. Reflection-impulsivity: The generality and dynamics of conceptual tempo. *Journal of Abnormal Psychology*, 1966, *71*: 17–24.

KENNY, D. T. An experimental test of the catharsis hypothesis of aggression. Unpublished doctoral dissertation, University of Washington, 1952.

KING, G. F. An interpersonal conception of Rorschach human movement and delusional content. *Journal of Projective Techniques*, 1960, *24*: 161–63.

KLEIN, G. Preemptory ideation structure and force in motivated ideas. *In* R. R. HOLT (ed.), Motivation and thought: Psychoanalytic essays in honor of David Rapaport. *Psychological Issues*, 1967, *5*, Monograph 18–19.

KLEIN, G. S., R. W. GARDNER, and H. J. SCHLESINGER. Tolerance for unrealistic experiences: A generality study. *British Journal of Psychology*, 1962, *53*: 41–55.

KLINGER, E. *Structure and function of fantasy.* New York; Wiley, 1971

KUBIE, L. Instincts and homeostasis. *Psychosomatic Medicine*, 1948, *10*: 15–30.

LEVINE, J. *Motivation in humor.* New York: Atherton, 1969.

LIEBERMAN, J. N. The relationship between playfulness and divergent thinking at the kindergarten level. *Journal of Genetic Psychology*, 1965, *107*: 219–24.

——— Playfulness: An attempt to conceptualize a quality of play and of the player. *Psychological Reports*, 1966, *19*: 1278.

MARSHALL, H. R., and S. C. HAHN. Experimental modification of dramatic play. *Journal of Personality and Social Psychology*, 1967, *5*: 119–21.

MILLER, N. Some reflections on the law of effect produce a new alternative to drive reduction. *In* M. R. JONES (ed.), *Nebraska Symposium on motivation.* Lincoln, Nebraska: University of Nebraska Press, 1963.

NEISSER, U. *Cognitive psychology.* New York: Appleton-Century-Crofts, 1967.

——— Visual imagery as process and as experience. *In* J. S. ANTROBUS (ed.), *Cognition and affect: The City University of New York Symposium.* New York: Little, Brown, 1969.

PAGE, H. Studies in fantasy-daydreaming and the TAT. *American Psychologist*, 1956, *11*: 392.

——— Studies in fantasy-daydreaming frequency and Rorschach scoring categories. *Journal of Consulting Psychology*, 1957, *21*: 111–14.

PAIVIO, A., and S. A. MADIGAN. Imagery and association value in paired-associate learning. *Journal of Experimental Psychology*, 1968, *76*: 35–39.

PAUL, I. H. The concept of schema in memory theory. *In* R. R. HOLT (ed.), Motivation and thought: Psychoanalytic essays in honor of David Rapaport. *Psychological Issues*, 1967, *5*, Monograph 18–19.

PULASKI, M. A. The effects of highly structured and minimally structured playthings on children's fantasy production. Unpublished doctoral dissertation, City University of New York, 1968.

PYTKOWICZ, A. R., N. N. WAGNER, and I. G. SARASON. An experimental study of the reduction of hostility through fantasy. *Journal of Personality and Social Psychology*, 1967, *5*: 295–303.

PYTKOWICZ, A. R., N. N. WAGNER, and J. C. WECHSLER. The effects of sex, illness and hospitalization on daydreaming patterns. *Journal of Consulting Psychology*, 1969, 33: 218–24.

RABIN, A. I. *Projective Techniques in Personality Assessment.* New York: Springer Publishing company, 1968.

RAPAPORT, D. On the psychoanalytic theory of motivation. *In* M. R. JONES (ed.), *Nebraska Symposium on motivation.* Lincoln, Nebraska: University of Nebraska Press, 1960.

——— States of consciousness. *In* M. GILL (ed.), *The collected papers of David Rapaport.* New York: Basic Books, 1967.

REYHER, J., and W. SMELTZER. Uncovering properties of visual imagery and verbal association: A comparative study. *Journal of Abnormal Psychology*, 1968, *73*: 218–22.

RICHARDSON, A. *Mental imagery.* New York: Springer, 1969.

RORSCHACH, H. *Psychodiagnostics.* Berne: Hans Huber, 1942.

ROWE, R. The effects of daydreaming under stress. Unpublished doctoral dissertation, Teachers College, Columbia University, 1963.

RUBINSTEIN, B. B. Explanation and mere description: A metascientific examination of certain aspects of the psychoanalytic theory of motivation. *In* R. R. HOLT (ed.), Motivation and thought: Psycho-

analytic essays in honor of David Rapaport. *Psychological Issues*, 1967, *5*, Monograph 18–19.

SCHONBAR, R. Differential dream recall frequency as a component of "life style." *Journal of Consulting Psychology*, 1965, *29*: 468–74.

SCOTT, J. P. *Aggression.* Chicago: University of Chicago Press, 1958.

SEEMAN, W. The Freudian theory of daydreams: An operational analysis. *Psychological Bulletin*, 1951, *48*: 369–82.

SEGAL, S. J. (ed.) *Imagery.* New York: Academic Press, 1971.

SHAFFER, L. F. *The psychology of adjustment.* Boston: Houghton Mifflin, 1936.

SHEEHAN, P. Accuracy and vividness of visual images. *Perceptual and Motor Skills*, 1966, *23*: 391–98.

SIIPOLA, E. M., and S. D. HAYDEN. Influencing eidetic imagery among the retarded. *Perceptual and Motor Skills*, 1965, *21*: 275–86.

SILBERER, H. Report on a method of eliciting and observing certain symbolic hallucination phenomena. *In* D. RAPAPORT (ed.), *Organization and pathology of thought.* New York: Columbia University Press, 1951.

SINGER, D. L. Aggression arousal, hostile humor, catharsis. *Journal of Personality and Social Psychology*, 1968, Monograph Supplement 8.

SINGER, J. L. The experience type: Some behavioral correlates and theoretical implications. *In* M. R. RICKERS-OVSIANKINA (ed.), *Rorschach psychology.* New York: John Wiley, 1960.

——— Imagination and waiting ability in young children. *Journal of Personality*, 1961, *29*: 396–413.

——— *Daydreaming.* New York: Random House, 1966.

——— Research applications of projective methods. *In* A. I. RABIN (ed.), *Projective techniques in personality assessment.* New York: Springer Publishing Company, 1968.

——— Drives, affects and daydreams: The adaptive role of spontaneous imagery or stimulus-independent mentation. *In* J. S. ANTROBUS (ed.), *Cognition and affect: The City University of New York Symposium.* Boston: Little, Brown, 1969.

SINGER, J. L., and J. S. ANTROBUS. A factor-analytic study of daydreaming and related cognitive and personality variables. *Perceptual and Motor Skills Monograph Supplement*, 1963, 3, Vol. 17.

——— Eye movements during fantasies. *AMA Archives of General Psychiatry*, 1965, *12*: 71–76.

——— Daydreaming, imaginal processes and personality: A normative study. P. W. SHEEHAN (ed.), *The function and nature of imagery.* New York: Academic Press, 1972.

SINGER, J. L., and V. MCCRAVEN. Some characteristics of adult daydreaming. *Journal of Psychology*, 1961, *51*: 151–64.

——— Patterns of daydreaming in American subcultural groups. *International Journal of Social Psychiatry*, 1962, *8*: 272–82.

SINGER, J. L., and R. ROWE. An experimental study of some relationships between daydreaming and anxiety. *Journal of Consulting Psychology*, 1962, *26*: 446–54.

SINGER, J. L., and R. SCHONBAR. Correlates of daydreaming: A dimension of self-awareness. *Journal of Consulting Psychology*, 1961, *25*: 1–7.

SINGER, J. L., and B. STREINER. Imaginative content in the dreams and fantasy play of blind and sighted children. *Perceptual and Motor Skills*, 1966, *22*: 475–82.

TOMKINS, S. S. *Affect, imagery, consciousness.* New York: Springer-Verlag, 1962, Vol. I.

VARENDONCK, J. *The psychology of daydreams.* New York: Macmillan, 1921.

VOTH, H. M., ET AL. Autokinesis and character style: A clinical-experimental study. *Journal of Psychiatric Research*, 1968, *6*: 51–65.

VOTH, H. M., and M. MAYMAN. A dimension of personality organization: An experimental study of "ego-closeness-ego-distance." *Archives of General Psychiatry*, 1963, *8*: 366–80.

WAGMAN, M. Sex differences in types of daydreams. *Journal of Personality and Social Psychology*, 1967, *7*: 329–32.

WERNER, H. Motion and motion perception: A study on vicarious perception. *Journal of Psychology*, 1945, *19*: 317–27.

Introduction

The purpose of this chapter is to provide the reader with an up-to-date account of the empirical and theoretical status of the concept of attention. More specifically, the emphasis in this review is on the selective and intensive properties of attention that are manifested in studies of human perceptual processes. This means that some large areas of current interest have been neglected, such as the role of attention in learning, the nature of the orientation reaction, the physiological correlates of attention, and the study of attention as an expression of cognitive style. The reader interested in pursuing any of these other lines of research is directed to Appendix I, where a short set of relevant references has been compiled.

A BRIEF HISTORY

It is possible to find discussions of attention that date back to the Golden Age of Greece. However, it was not until the nineteenth century that attention became the subject of experimental inquiry and began to be accorded an important place in psychological thought.

For the introspective psychologists such as Wundt and Titchener, attention was defined in terms of conscious clarity. In Wundt's analysis the field of consciousness was likened to the field of vision in that it contained a point where impressions were clear and distinct (the *Blickpunkt*) that was surrounded by a region where impressions were fuzzy and indistinct (the *Blickfeld*). Wundt's student, Titchener, carried the Structuralist's psychology of content to its logical extreme when he relegated attention to the status of an attribute of sensory experience, which he called attensity.

In contrast to the Structuralist point of view, there stands James's (1890) emphasis on the functional significance of the act of selective attention. He pointed out that a multitude of items are available to the senses that never properly enter into one's experience. They fail to register because they lack interest

Howard Egeth
& William Bevan

Attention

20

for the subject. In short, experience is what one agrees to attend to; without selective interest, experience would be an utter chaos.

By the early 1900s a great deal was known about attention, and interest in the subject was rather keen. The interested reader will find an encyclopedic discussion of the early work on attention in Pillsbury's (1908) highly readable book. However, in the years following the publication of Pillsbury's book the concept of attention fell on hard times. In America, the rise of Radical Behaviorism led to the abandonment of attention. As Hebb (1949) has pointed out, Behaviorism was predicated on the complete sensory control of behavior and there was no room in this system for mentalistic concepts such as set or attention that seemed to imply some degree of central autonomy from sensory dominance. In Germany, the rise of Gestalt psychology proved to be equally uncongenial to the concept of attention. The neurological model underlying Gestalt psychology was very different from the Sherringtonian nervous system of the Behaviorists, but again there was the assumption of complete sensory dominance of behavior.

It is interesting to note that although the theoretical status of attention may have been questionable from the 1920s through the 1940s, interest in attention on the empirical level never quite died (see, e.g., Paschal's 1941 review). This fact points up a long-lasting historical dilemma very clearly; psychologists have generally recognized the existence and importance of attention-like phenomena, but they haven't known how to incorporate them into their theoretical structures. However, the years since World War II have seen a period characterized both by a heightened concern with attention and by a better understanding of its place within general theories of behavior. Many factors have been important in this renaissance. For one, there has been a marked decline in the prominence of the great "schools" of psychology, with an attendant broadening and liberalization of conceptual approaches.

A second factor was the emergence of a new neurology with emphasis on the continuous nature of cerebral activity (e.g., Jasper 1937). If the brain is always active, then afferent excitation must be superimposed on an already existent excitation and thus behavior cannot be solely under the control of immediately given stimuli. The relevance of this new conception of neural activity to attention became even more obvious with the discovery of the reticular activating system (e.g., Lindsley 1951), and afferent neuronal interaction (e.g., Hernández-Peón Scherrer, and Jouvet 1956).

A third factor of considerable importance was that psychologists active in human factors work during the war had forced on them the practical significance of the fact that the human nervous system is quite limited in its capacity to process information. An analysis of the capacity for selective attention became essential for a proper understanding of the possibilities for man-machine interaction.

The result of the concatenation of all of these favorable factors is that there is at present a great deal of exciting work being performed on the many aspects of attention. It is to this research that we now turn.

The Selective Properties of Attention

At the very outset it will be helpful to draw a distinction between the concepts of set and selective attention since these two terms have often been used interchangeably, with much attendant confusion. In this paper *set* will be used in a very general sense to refer to adjustments of the cognitive apparatus caused by factors such as instructions, expectancy, context, value, and familiarity. By contrast, *selective attention* will be used to refer to one of the consequences of set. Specifically, it will be used to describe any mode of information processing that permits a subject to respond on the basis of a limited portion of the available stimulus information. It may be useful to clarify this distinction with a concrete example. Bruner and Minturn (1955) showed that a particular pattern was perceived as a 13 when presented in the context of a series of numbers and as a B when presented in the context of a series of letters. Presumably, in both conditions subjects saw, and responded on the basis of, all of the features of that particular pattern and thus selectivity was not the point at issue in this experiment. Rather, it was a study of the effects of context on the interpretation of ambiguous figures. Such judgmental effects will be discussed briefly, but they are not the main focus of this chapter.

Partly in an effort to impose some structure on a large, heterogeneous body of literature, a further distinction has been made between two phenotypically different kinds of selective attention. The first results when a subject is able to limit the simple physical features or attributes on the basis of which he is to respond. The second kind may occur even when the object of a subject's attention is specified only by meaning or by inclusion in an ill-defined category. This second kind of selectivity is somewhat speculative, and fuller discussion of it will be deferred until the discussion of the first kind is completed.

SELECTIVE ATTENTION MEDIATED BY PHYSICAL FEATURES

Vision. Since Külpe's (1904) seminal experiments on abstraction there have been many investigations of the ability of humans to respond selectively on the basis of specified attributes of complex displays. Külpe demonstrated that when complex stimuli were presented tachistoscopically to his subjects, accuracy of report for stimulus attributes they had been instructed to observe was greater than for incidental attributes. Subsequent investigators have been concerned with interpreting this finding, and, in particular, with assessing the locus of the selective effect (i.e., perception, memory, response selection).

The locus of selective attention. A study by Yokoyama (Boring 1924) will serve to illustrate the methodology of the early experiments in this field. Subjects were shown, very briefly, pairs of lighted rectangles which could differ slightly in either length or brightness. In a given block of trials they were asked to compare the rectangles with respect to one or the other of the two dimensions of variation. Occasionally, shortly after the stimulus had been flashed, the experimenter asked for a judgment about the other dimension. Thus in a block of trials devoted to length judgments, on about two per cent of the trials the experimenter would ask, "What about brightness?" Accuracy of report was substantially lower on the incidental dimension than on the primary one. Following Külpe, this result was interpreted to mean that the instructional set accentuated perception of the crucial aspects of the display and inhibited perception of the incidental aspects.

The Yokoyama study and others which supposedly showed the effects of preparatory set on perception were criticized on methodological grounds by several writers (e.g., Wilcocks 1925). The major flaw in these studies was that subjects were asked for their judgments on incidental attributes only after they rendered their report on the primary attribute. Thus, inferiority of report on the unemphasized attributes might be due simply to the additional time this information was held in memory, and not to impoverished perception. In fact, Wilcocks showed that accuracy of report was strongly related to the delay between stimulus and response, and that this was true even for emphasized dimensions.

In an attempt to circumvent the problem of forgetting, Chapman (1932) made use of a slightly more complex design than had previously been used. He reasoned that if instructions can influence perception they ought to be effective only if presented before the stimulus is presented. However, if the effect of instructions is due to the selective reporting of the contents of memory, then instructions given shortly after the stimulus ought to be as effective as instructions given before the stimulus. In his experiment, accuracy of report for a particular dimension was consistently higher when the to-be-reported dimension was specified before rather than after stimulus presentation. Thus, Chapman concluded, the effect of instructional set was at least partly perceptual in origin.

Despite the plausibility of Chapman's argument there were still skeptics who thought it unlikely that a perceptual process could be modified by a cognitive factor such as verbal instructions. Indeed their reservations seem justified; looking at Chapman's research it *is* clear that he had only reduced the memory factor, but did not wholly eliminate it. Specifically, in the After conditions there must have been at least a .25 sec delay between the offset of the flashed material and the subject's reception of the instructions specifying what aspect of the display to report (*cf.* Egeth 1967, for more details). In the light of recent evidence (e.g., Sperling 1960), .25 sec is clearly enough time for a substantial amount of information to be lost from immediate visual memory. Thus, in the Before condition, subjects could attempt to process the primary attribute immediately upon stimulus reception; however, in the After condition, by the time they had received report instructions, the stimulus from which this information was to be abstracted was considerably impoverished. Pursuing this weak point in the Before-After design Lawrence and La Berge (1956) and Brown (1960) argued that the effects of preparatory instructions could be interpreted in terms of established principles of learning and memory without recourse to any concept of perceptual modification. Lawrence and La Berge claimed that the effects of instructions emphasizing one attribute rather than others was simply a manifestation of an order-of-report effect. In their study the stimuli varied along the attributes of color, form, and numerosity. Two conditions are of particular importance for this discussion. In the Emphasis condition, subjects were told to pay especially close attention to one of the dimensions, but to report on all three after the tachistoscopic stimulus presentation. They were asked to imagine that they would receive $100 for every correct report of an emphasized dimension but only $1 for each correct report of an unemphasized dimension. In the Ordered condition subjects were asked to pay equal attention to all three attributes at the time of presentation; however, the order in which they were to be reported was specified only after stimulus exposure. These subjects were asked to imagine a $34 bonus for every correct report. The results of the Emphasis condition confirmed the earlier findings of Külpe, Yokoyama, and others: Emphasized dimensions were reported significantly more accurately than unemphasized ones. The main point of the study, however, was established by the finding that in the Ordered condition the difference in accuracy between the first dimension reported and the average of the other two dimensions was equal to the difference found between the emphasized and unemphasized dimensions of the other condition. This suggested to the investigators that the effect of emphasis instructions is to determine the order in which dimensions are reported, and that it is this order which dictates the accuracy of report. Although this conclusion has been criticized elsewhere (Egeth 1967), we may accept it as essentially correct for the purposes of this analysis.

Brown's (1960) strategy was to circumvent the forgetting problem by comparing the effect of a preparatory (Before) instruction with that of a nonpreparatory (Simultaneous) instruction that arrived before there could be any substantial amount of forgetting. The instructions were auditory signals that told the subject what subset of a complex display he was to report. In the Before condition these instructions preceded the tachistoscopic display by 2 sec while in the Simultaneous condition they arrived at the same time. The subject's task in this experiment was different enough from the standard task used by previous investigators to warrant full description. Stimulus cards bearing eight symbols were displayed for .09 sec. The symbols were arranged in two rows of four symbols each. The four comprising the extreme left and right members of each row were designated the "outer" set and the remaining four were designated the "inner" set. On a given trial, the members of a particular set were either all red or all black and were either digits or consonants, depending on the condition. Thus, it was possible for the experimenter to ask the subject to report, say, the identity of the four red symbols, or of the four letters, or of the four inside symbols, etc. Note that in the previous experiments on abstraction the subject's instruction would specify a dimension, e.g., color, and the subject would then be asked to specify the color(s) of the displayed objects. Brown's task might more appropriately be called conditional-abstraction since the instructions specified a single value on an attribute and the subject's task was to identify all of the symbols that were of that value.

The gist of the results was that Before instructions resulted in superior performance than Simultaneous instructions only when the instructions specified the class of symbols to be named (letters vs. numbers). For color and location instructions there was no significant effect due to time of presentation of instructions. However, in view of the serial nature of the subject's responses and in view of some of his earlier work in selectivity in memory, Brown was unwilling to conclude that the effect was perceptual in origin in this experiment. He felt it more parsimonious to describe the results in terms of the principles of learning and memory.

The fundamental assumption underlying Brown's experiment was that if instructions can modify perception at all, they will be able to do so only if given prior to stimulus presentation. This was, of course, the same assumption made by Chapman and by Lawrence and La Berge. It seems now that this assumption is wrong, and thus, that Brown's experiment was actually inappropriate to the study of visual selectivity. The critical point is that perception is an active process, the duration of which may outlast the offset of a briefly exposed stimulus.

Evidence of this assertion comes from the studies of Averbach and Coriell (1961) and Sperling (1960) on what has variously been called short term sensory storage, immediate visual memory, and iconic storage. What these investigators demonstrated was that following a brief display of a matrix of letters, subjects had available to them a rather large amount of information, but that this information was lost rapidly (within about a second) except for that portion which the subject had time to encode verbally. Since the duration of iconic storage is dependent upon sensory factors such as illumination level and figure-ground contrast, it seems reasonable to conceive of this storage process as part of the overall perceptual system, rather than what has traditionally been construed as memory. This usage is consistent with the phenomenal reports of subjects in these experiments who think that they are still "seeing" the letters after they have been removed. Actually, the Sperling, and Averbach and Coriell experiments may themselves be considered as experiments on selective attention mediated via the physical cue of spatial location. A description of Sperling's experiment will clarify this point. He showed rectangular arrays of letters, three rows of three letters each. When such an array was displayed for 50 msec, subjects could typically report between four and five letters (the ordinary span of apprehension). However, Sperling then contrived to signal the subject to report the contents of only a single row. The signal was high, medium, or low tone, the pitch being correlated with the row to be reported, i.e., the high pitch tone indicating the top row, etc. The tone was brief and could be presented before the visual display, simultaneous with its offset, or at some time after its offset. When the subjects were told 1 sec before the onset of the display which row to report, they averaged over 90 percent correct. However, even when the cue was delayed the subjects still performed at a level indicating that they had substantially more letters available than they could identify using the whole-report method. One plausible description of these results is that the cue results in selective attention by increasing the rate of acquisition of information from the relevant portions of the visual field (*cf.*, Sperling 1967, pp. 290–91).

In the light of these data Brown's experiment can now be seen as corroborating the efficiency of readout when a partial report is directed by a post stimulus cue that comes on with hardly any delay at all. A recent experiment by von Wright (1967) makes this point very clearly. His stimuli were letter matrices, and his method was an extension of the partial report technique. However, as in Brown's study, the letters were distinguishable on several criteria. In the various conditions of the experiment the letters differed in: hue, lightness, size, or orientation (upright vs. 45° tilt). The efficiency of selectivity on each of these criteria was assessed by comparing the results of the whole report method with partial reports. The tonal cue was delayed by only 5 msec in all conditions. The data indicated that hue, lightness and size were all useful bases for selection since the partial-report data was consistently superior to the whole report for those conditions. However, orientation was not useful. When subjects were instructed to report only the tilted letters or only the upright letters, they were no better than when they were simply asked to report *any* letters. The explanation for this negative finding given by von Wright is instructive. He suggested that letters may have to be identified before their orientation can be determined since lettershapes contain a variety of differently oriented parts. Alternatively, he suggested

that analysis of orientation may be a more complex process than analysis of color or size. In support of this interpretation, he mentions Sperling's (1960) finding that when his subjects were cued to report the digits or the letters contained in alphanumeric displays by means of his partial report technique, there was little improvement in performance over the whole report technique. The fact that Brown found that partial performance was superior on letter vs. number identification with a 2 sec pre-cue than with a simultaneous cue is not inconsistent with von Wright's argument; the result may simply mean that complex perceptual analyses must be readied before stimulus onset to ensure that they can begin working quickly, before much decay sets in.

The description of the preceding experiments suggests that selective visual attention under conditions of tachistoscopic exposure is the result of directing the readout from iconic storage, i.e., of selective encoding of the visual input. Material that is not encoded for further storage decays and becomes unavailable within a matter of seconds, at the most. This encoding hypothesis was developed, tested, and confirmed in the important experiment of Harris and Haber (1963, replicated by Haber 1964). These investigators noticed a discrepancy between the conclusions of the studies by Wilcocks (1925) and Lawrence and La Berge (1956). The latter writers had maintained that manipulation of order-of-report of stimulus attributes after the presentation of a complex stimulus could completely mimic the manipulation of attention instructions given prior to the stimulus presentation. However, Wilcocks, who had also manipulated order-of-report after the stimulus presentation had found that for any given ordinal position within a report, including the first, an emphasized dimension would be reported more accurately than an incidental attribute. Wilcocks's observation, in conjunction with observations of subjects in their own laboratory suggested to Harris and Haber that the order in which information was reported might not be as important as the order in which information was put into storage. It should be made clear that by "storage" these authors did not mean iconic storage; they were referring to the transfer of information from inconic storage to a longer-term, essentially verbal, memory storage.

The stimuli were essentially the same as those used by Lawrence and La Berge (1956), having also been selected from the Wisconsin Sorting Cards. Pairs of cards were presented for .10 sec, after which 20 sec were allowed for the subject to report what he had seen. As in the Lawrence and La Berge study there was an Emphasis condition in which the value of a correct report about one particular dimension was enhanced relative to the other two by an imaginary point system. There was also an Equal condition in which all three dimensions were to receive equal attention. In both Emphasis and Equal situations the order-of-report was specified only after the brief presentation of the stimulus cards. So far, this experiment sounds just like the Lawrence and La Berge study. However, Harris and Haber added an important new twist. By dint of fairly extensive preliminary training they created two groups of subjects that differed in the strategy with which they approached the experimental task. One group of subjects, the Objects coders, were trained by being given practice in which they described pairs of Wisconsin Sorting Cards as two sets of objects, e.g., three blue squares, two red circles. The other group of subjects, the Dimensions coders, were taught to describe the cards by dimensions, e.g., three, two; blue, red; square, circle. The expectation underlying this study was that during the experimental session the subjects would tend to encode the stimuli implicitly in the same manner that they had been trained to describe them explicitly.

The key finding of the Harris and Haber experiment was that the coding used by a subject determined whether or not his accuracy of report was influenced by attention instructions. Dimensions coders were able to give preferential treatment to emphasized dimensions by encoding them before the unemphasized dimensions, whereas the Objects coders did not have this flexibility, presumably because to do so they would have to go against long-standing verbal habits. Since order-of-report was controlled here, the conclusion seems inescapable that the crucial factor was the order in which the dimensions were extracted from the visual image and stored for recall. Presumably, this factor could be operative in any perceptual task as long as the order-of-encoding required by emphasis instructions is not incompatible with the "natural" or stereotyped way of describing the stimulus objects.

Although the coding response theory seems to be quite general in its application, at least within the purview of tachistoscopic identification experiments, there is evidence that it does not always provide an appropriate description of results. One weakness of the model is the emphasis that it places on serial, verbal encoding. There are several recent experiments on multidimensional stimulus identification which cast doubt on the generality of the hypothesis that information is withdrawn one dimension at a time from a briefly displayed stimulus. Tulving and Lindsay (1967) made a direct test of the hypothesis that simultaneously presented stimuli are examined sequentially. On the basis of this hypothesis they predicted that if visual and auditory stimuli were presented simultaneously and briefly, then subjects might be able to render accurate absolute judgments about one of these stimuli but would not have time to switch attention from one to the other and thus should not be able to accurately identify both stimuli. However, at durations long enough to permit the switching of attention from one of the stimuli to the other, subjects ought to be able to identify both accurately. They used durations of .02, .05, and 2.0 sec and found that unidimensional judgment was superior to multidimensional judgment at all three durations and, most importantly, that the degree of superiority was equal at all three durations. Thus, they were led to reject the sequential processing model. Egeth and Pachella (1969) used the three visual dimensions of color, ellipse size, and ellipse eccentricity and performed essentially the same analysis as Tulving and Lindsay, with the same results. In addition, Egeth and Pachella performed another test of the serial processing model. In their experiment they controlled each subject's order-or-report. If it is assumed that dimensions are encoded in the same order that they are to be reported (*cf.* Harris and Haber 1963), then at very short durations there ought to be a substantial order-of-report effect reflecting an underlying order-or-encoding effect. However, as exposure duration is increased, the relative advantage of the first dimension reported ought to be diminished. One obvious reason for expecting a reduced advantage is that with a long-lasting stimulus even the later dimensions can be encoded from the icon before decay begins. In other words, the serial processing argument leads to the prediction that there ought to be an interaction between the effects of order-of-report and stimulus

duration. However, Egeth and Pachella found this interaction to be insignificant.

The difference between the results of the absolute judgment experiments (of Tulving and Lindsay and Egeth and Pachella) and the more common kind of recognition experiment (e.g., Lawrence and La Berge and Harris and Haber) is probably due to differences in the stimulus materials. In the two former studies the values along each stimulus dimension were not highly discriminable from one another and the associations between these values and their corresponding response labels were not highly learned. For example, in the Egeth and Pachella study the color dimension consisted of six shades of "orange." By contrast, on the Wisconsin Sorting Cards used by Lawrence and La Berge, and Harris and Haber, the color dimension consists of red, green, blue, and yellow. These stimuli are highly discriminable and the responses are highly overlearned. A serial naming strategy may make sense with such easy stimuli, but would not necessarily be appropriate with the difficult stimuli. Indeed, all of the existing evidence points to essentially parallel processing in the more difficult absolute judgment task.

Factors affecting selectivity. The picture that we have sketched of selective attention has been based on the results of experiments in which complex stimuli were exposed for controlled, usually very brief, durations. Almost all of the preceding experiments were quite specifically oriented toward the theoretical problem of specifying the locus (or loci) of the selective effects underlying the abstraction paradigm. Since an effect can't be localized unless it occurs, it is understandable that in these experiments little effort was made to manipulate factors that would make the task of filtering difficult. Unfortunately, this emphasis is liable to give a distorted view of the human capacity for efficient abstraction. It turns out that there are, in fact, many ways to make abstraction difficult and it is to a description of such factors that we now turn. We will find this information to be of both theoretical and practical interest.

The experiments to be described below fit into a common formal framework which is most easily described by means of a hypothetical two-dimensional example. Imagine a set of stimuli defined by the joint values of two dimensions or attributes, X and Y. In a control condition, performance in discriminating among values of X is determined with variable Y held constant. Performance may be measured in terms of any of a number of variables; latency, accuracy, information transmission, etc. It is best, though not always necessary, to measure performance at several different levels of Y. But for any particular determination of performance on X-discrimination, Y must be held constant. In the experimental condition, both X and Y vary from trial-to-trial but the subject is instructed to base his response only upon X. By fiat, X is made relevant, Y irrelevant. Since we are not here interested in the effects of redundancy, we must also specify that the X and Y be uncorrelated over trials. To the extent that performance is poorer in the experimental condition we may say that variation in Y from trial-to-trial interferes with performance on X. More colloquially, the subject is distracted by Y. Actually, this description of the abstraction is somewhat simplified. It has recently been pointed out (Egeth and Pachella 1969) that performance decrements in an abstraction experiment may result in part from perceptual interaction between X and Y. Although such effects are interesting in their own right, they fall outside the scope of the present chapter. The distracting effects of strong stimuli such as loud noises and bright, flashing lights will also be ignored here. The reason for doing so is partly strategic; it seems that a description of the process underlying distraction caused by subtle cues may be capable of explaining the gross effects of very conspicuous stimuli.

The effects of variation along irrelevant dimensions have been studied in quite a few experiments. Several of these studies have reported essentially zero distraction (e.g., Archer 1954; Fitts and Biederman 1965; Imai and Garner 1965; Morin, Forrin, and Archer 1961) whereas others have reported substantial interference effects (e.g., Egeth 1966; Gregg 1954; Morgan and Alluisi 1967; Stroop 1935).

What are the causes of distraction? We suggest that the most plausible explanation of distraction is the competing-response hypothesis which may be stated in the following way: variation in an irrelevant attribute will be distracting to the degree that the values of that attribute are associated with responses incompatible with the responses associated with the relevant attribute. Perhaps the strongest support for this hypothesis comes from research on the Stroop color-word test (e.g., Stroop 1935; Klein 1964; Pritchatt 1968). In Stroop's experiment subjects were presented with sheets on which color-names were printed, each name in an ink that was a different color than the one named by the word. For example, the word "blue" might be printed in red, green, or yellow ink. The task was simply to name the ink-colors in which the words were printed. In a control task subjects had to name the colors in which rectangles were printed; there was no irrelevant verbal information. The results were very clear and have proven to be easy to replicate—both speed and accuracy were much lower with the color-word stimuli than with the rectangles. Furthermore, in conditions where the subjects had to read the color names they were just about as fast when these words were colored incompatibly as when they were all in ordinary black type. The usual explanation that is given for these findings is that in the color naming conditions the verbal content of the word list gave rise to responses that were in conflict with the responses that were to be made to the ink-colors. This explanation is completely consistent with the subjective reports of participants in these experiments. They indicate that it is extremely difficult to keep from reading and responding to the printed words. Of course, in the control condition there is no such conflict. By the same token, in the word reading conditions, reading is such a highly overlearned and unequivocal response that the tendency to name colors was completely overshadowed and thus interference was very slight.

Subsequent research on the Stroop test has both confirmed and extended this analysis. Undoubtedly the most important of these later studies is that of Klein (1964) who showed that essentially any kind of verbal material can produce some degree of interference with color-naming in addition to color-words themselves. In the various conditions of his experiment Klein presented irrelevant verbal information in the form of: nonsense syllables, rare English words, common words not associated with color (e.g., put, take), common words that implicated colors in the meaning (e.g., grass, sky), common words of the same response class as the named colors (e.g., tan, purple), and the standard color names of the Stroop task (e.g., red, green). The data showed that interference increased in the same order as the conditions that have been listed. In a similar vein, Rouse and Maas (1961) showed that increasing amounts of

familiarity training with a set of nonsense syllables were used in the color naming task. Although there is no definitive evidence yet available, these two studies suggest the possibility that two different sources of interference are operative. First, familiarity may tend to increase the tendency to read the word in which a color is printed. Second, over and above an increased tendency to read a word, similarity of *meaning* between the word and the set of responses appropriate to the relevant attribute (hue) may cause competition among vocal response tendencies.

The rather considerable success of attempts to explain distraction in the Stroop test by means of response competition has led, naturally enough, to efforts to explain other instances of distraction in the same way. To get ahead of the discussion for a moment, it seems fair to say that these efforts have not been unambiguously successful. For example, Hodge (1959) and Montague (1965) both attempted to experimentally build in competition between primary and secondary dimensions and then examine performance for evidence of distraction. Unfortunately, both studies are flawed by a confounding of degree of response competition with degree of task complexity. The subjects who were supposedly faced with a high degree of response competition were also found with quite a complex cognitive task rather than a straightforward filtering task, and so it is not surprising that they fared poorly in comparison with control subjects. Thus, these two attempts to make a direct test of the competing-response hypothesis must be considered inadequate.

If the competing-response hypothesis is correct, we would expect to be able to produce some indirect support for it by showing that in situations in which there is no distraction there is also little reason to expect, a priori, the existence of competing responses. Fitts and Biederman (1965) provide just such a demonstration. In their Filtering condition subjects were instructed to respond with a key press on the basis of the attributes of shape (square vs. circle) but to ignore the number of presented shapes, i.e., one square or two squares received one response, while one circle or two circles received the other response. In the Conservation condition only single forms were presented and so there was no irrelevant number information. The data indicated no differences in either information transmission rate or median reaction time between the two conditions. Since number was never relevant to the key press response for the Filtering subjects, there is no reason to think that the number information should have caused any response competition.

In contrast to the Fitts and Biederman findings which are not inconsistent with the competing-response hypothesis, there are the data of Imai and Garner (1965) which seem to be clearly contradictory to that hypothesis. These investigators compared performance in conditions that either did or did not present irrelevant information, and they found no distraction due to the presence of irrelevant attributes. What is especially important about these data is that they used a completely within-subject design in which all three of their stimulus attributes were relevant during some parts of the experiment but irrelevant during other parts. Moreover, subjects were run in each of the various parts of the experiment several times during the course of five experimental sessions. It would seem that this would have been a situation ideally suited to the development of competing responses, however, if they did develop they did not result in distraction. This experiment was well conceived and presents a fairly massive amount of data comparing filtering with nonfiltering conditions. However, as has been pointed out elsewhere (Egeth 1967) this experiment lacked a truly appropriate control group. The constant switching of conditions in this experiment might have instilled in the subjects a pervasive filtering strategy so that they "tried" to filter even in conditions in which this was unnecessary. Thus, it might be more appropriate to conclude that nonfiltering performance was as *bad* as filtering performance rather than that filtering performance was as *good* as nonfiltering performance.

Perhaps the most suggestive support for the competing-response hypothesis outside of the research on the Stroop test comes from a study by Gregg (1954). In this study there were four independent groups of subjects each of which was given practice on one of four different simple discriminations. The response mode was the same for all subjects, viz., the left-right movement of a joystick; however, the stimulus dimensions were selected to ensure that the stimulus-response compatibilities (Fitts and Deininger 1954) of the four tasks were quite different from one another. The most compatible task was to indicate whether a dot displayed on a CRT was left or right of center by moving the joystick in the appropriate direction, and the least compatible task was to indicate the brightness of the dot, again with a specified left or right movement. When the simple discriminations were complicated by the addition of irrelevant information (i.e., variation along dimensions that were relevant for *other* groups of subjects), performance was impaired. What is especially interesting is that the degree of impairment increased as the compatibility of the primary task decreased. Unfortunately this result must be considered more suggestive than conclusive because the compatibilities of the relevant and irrelevant dimensions were confounded. For example, when the primary task was discrimination of the left-right location of the dot, the irrelevant dimensions were, of necessity, less compatible with the response. An extension of this research is clearly called for.

It is interesting to note that some of the effects of manipulating stimulus parameters such as discriminability or distinctiveness (Imai and Garner 1965; Morgan and Alluisi 1967) may be explicable in terms of the competing-response hypothesis. This is because stimulus discriminability is one of the determinants of degree of association. For example, the elements of a set of barely discriminable stimuli simply cannot have very strongly developed associations to specific responses.

A final comment on response competition. Although a strong case can be made for the competing response hypothesis, it clearly does not provide a complete description of the data on distraction. It should be noted that this hypothesis is, after all, an attempt to account for "selective attention" solely in terms of postperceptual processes. Such a simple model did not fit the data of the tachistoscopic recognition experiments cited earlier. Furthermore, there are the data of the Imai and Garner (1965) study. It may be that the conclusions drawn in that paper would still hold even if the control condition that we have suggested were used. Finally, some recent work using materials similar to the Stroop color-word test indicates that interference may not occur even when the opportunity for overt response conflict exists. For example, Egeth, Blecker, and Kamlet (1969) have found that when subjects had to count the number of times a color was used on a sheet, they were just as fast and accurate when the colors appeared in the form of numerals as when the colors appeared simply as Xs. It would seem that the presence of the irrelevant numerals could have interfered with

the counting task in the same way that color-words interfere with the task of naming colors, but this was not the case.

Audition. The investigation of selective processes in hearing has been every bit as productive and interesting as its visual counterpart although the auditory research got off to a much later start. The first major theoretical contribution to this field was Broadbent's (1958) book, *Perception and Communication*, and most of the work on selective listening since then has its roots in this work.

Cherry (1953) introduced the technique of "shadowing," which has become the most widely used tool in the investigation of selective listening. In this procedure speech messages are presented dichotically (one to each ear) to listeners, and the subject is asked to repeat back word-by-word the one that is designated as the target, keeping as close to the designated message as possible. The unattended message has sometimes been explicitly described to the subject as a source of distraction that ought to be ignored, although in other experiments the investigator has requested the subject to voluntarily divide his attention between the two messages. In either case it should be made clear that the purpose of the shadowing task is to allow control over the subject's attention.

Although shadowing has achieved the status of the classic procedure in its field, it should not be assumed that the technique is without fault. In particular, it is difficult to assess the degree to which the required shadowing response interferes with performance. It is likely that subjects must actually divide their attention among three sources: the two messages and the stream of speech produced while shadowing. To avoid this problem some recent investigators have required the subject to shadow covertly and to make an overt response only when a specified target item is detected. However, even in this situation it is difficult to be sure of what the subject is really doing while he is shadowing. For these reasons one should exercise considerable caution in interpreting the following studies.

One of the important findings of Cherry's original report was that this method allows almost perfect selectivity since subjects were able to repeat the target message with a very low error rate. We may take Cherry's results as a demonstration of the efficacy of the factor of spatial separation in permitting selective attention to be paid to one message rather than another. In addition to Cherry's work there have been other demonstrations that simple physical differences between messages allow a subject to listen selectively to a designated one of several simultaneous messages. Broadbent (1954) showed that differences in spatial location much less extreme than Cherry's left-ear right-ear difference also permitted quite effective selectivity. Differences in phase, intensity, and frequency range have also been shown to be useful, although in some of these experiments the "message" has only been a tone to be detected against a background of white noise (Egan, Carterette, and Thwing 1954; Hirsh 1950; Licklider 1948). What was especially important about Cherry's experiment was the raising of a new question: What is the fate of the rejected message? This question came up because in addition to demonstrating perfect selectivity the subjects also showed virtually no knowledge of the contents of the rejected message. During the course of a trial the experimenter changed the nature of the material coming over the rejected ear. At the beginning and end of a trial the rejected message was ordinary speech, but during the middle portion the message was changed in several ways. For some subjects the language of the message was changed from English to German although it was spoken in the same voice; for other subjects the voice was changed from male to female; while still others were presented with reversed speech or a pure tone. After the session all of the subjects were asked to describe the message that had come over the rejected ear. All of the listeners who were subjected to a change from speech to a pure tone noticed the change and almost all of the subjects for whom the voice changed from male to female recalled noticing this change. However, very few subjects recalled noticing the change to German or the change to reversed speech. What do these results mean? As we shall see, essentially the same problem faced the students of selective listening as faced Külpe and the other early workers in visual selectivity: it was necessary to determine whether attention was a process operating during perception, memory, or response organization and execution.

The locus of selectivity. In Broadbent's (1958) discussion of Cherry's results he pointed out that subjects only perceived changes in the gross physical characteristics of the unattended messages and that they failed to notice even radical semantic and syntactic changes, changes that would, presumably, require a rather high level of information processing to be detected. It was further noted that the gross physical cues that were noticed when they were changed were precisely the sort of cue that can serve to distinguish one message from another in a selective listening task.

To account for the existing data on a selective listening (as well as short-term memory) Broadbent proposed an information processing model which relied heavily on the concept of attention. This model specified the existence of a large-capacity immediate memory store. As we have seen in our discussion of the work of Averbach and Coriell (1961) and Sperling (1960) such a system seems necessary in vision. From this immediate storage system information may be passed by a selective filter for more permanent storage or, presumably, for further elaboration. This filter is the mechanism of attention, and its purpose is to protect the limited capacity information-processing channel that follows it from overload. The filter does not reject information randomly; the selection is made on the basis of physical cues such as spatial location, voice, intensity, etc. These physical cues specify what Broadbent called *channels* of input. Since a message coming over an unattended channel would be stopped by the filter, a listener ought to be quite unaware of the content of the verbal content of the message, just as Cherry found.

As would be expected in any field of science Broadbent's theory was soon the victim of critical attack. The gist of the criticism was that the verbal content of a rejected message could, in certain circumstances, be identified and thus that it is wrong to think that the filter operates prior to the full perceptual analysis of signals. The evidence on which these criticisms were based was presented in three separate experiments. Moray (1959) showed that instructions delivered over the unattended ear in a shadowing task were more likely to be noticed if they were preceded by the subject's name. Oswald, Taylor, and Treisman (1960) reported that brain wave recordings taken from sleeping subjects showed significantly larger disturbances when a subject's name was spoken than when other names were spoken. Treisman (1960) manipulated the transition

probabilities between words on the attended and unattended channels and made the very important observation that when a word in the unattended ear happened to fit into the concurrent context of the attended message, the subject was likely to switch channels and momentarily shadow the wrong message. All three of these studies clearly indicated that the filter was not perfectly effective in screening out unwanted messages. The Treisman study is especially important because it shows that the filter is not bypassed by only a very few "special" signals, but by essentially any word if the circumstances are right.

Since Broadbent's original conception of attention was clearly unable to account for the identification of the verbal content of rejected messages, Treisman (1960) proposed a modification of the filter model that was designed to handle this problem. She assumed the existence of a filter that *attenuated* the informational content of a rejected channel without eliminating it entirely. It was further assumed that all inputs, attenuated or otherwise, are subjected to the usual processes of recognition and identification, and that these processes are hierarchical (e.g., Neisser 1967, chap. 3). Unattended inputs, being attenuated, will very frequently lack the information necessary to pass even low-level tests in the hierarchy, and it is in this way that selective attention reduces the subject's information processing load. In order to account for recognition of unattended material, it is useful to conceive of outcomes of tests in the recognition hierarchy as being based on simple statistical decisions (e.g., Swets, Tanner, and Birdsall 1961), and thus being susceptible to criterion shifts. On the basis of the data that we have already considered it is apparent that if this conception is appropriate, then certain tests are permanently biased (e.g., those leading to the recognition of one's name) whereas others are only temporarily biased (e.g., those that fit the current context). The theoretical virtue of this conception is that even an attenuated message may carry enough information to result in recognition if the tests that it is subjected to have had their criteria lowered.

Is Treisman's model sensible? It seems that there are at least three key points that deserve examination: (1) there is the conception of the filter as an attenuator rather than an all-or-none switch; (2) the assumption that perception is a hierarchical process; (3) the assumption that the tests involved in perceptual recognition can be biased in favor of certain outcomes. The second and third assumptions are discussed in some detail in the section of this chapter on selection mediated by meaning; suffice it to say here that they both seem reasonable. We may turn now to consideration of the first and probably most important assumption of Treisman's model. There are several experimental findings consistent with her assertion that there is a perceptual filter that attenuates stimulus information without completely blocking it. Broadbent and Gregory (1963b) examined the perceptual consequences of division-of-attention. (In a division-of-attention task the subject is informed that there are messages on two or more channels that he must respond to, although the channels are not necessarily of equal "importance.") To one ear they presented six digits at the rate of 2 per second while white noise was presented to the other ear. On some trials a .5-sec tone burst was added to the noise. In one condition the subject was instructed to pay undivided attention to the ear receiving noise and to report, immediately after the trial, whether or not a tone had been presented on that trial. In the divided attention condition, subjects were told that at the end of each trial they were to repeat back the six digits and then report on the presence or absence of the tone. The results indicated that there was a difference in performance between these two conditions. Specifically, there was a decrease in detectability of the tone (d') rather than a change in decision criterion (β) as a result of division-of-attention. A reduction in detectability is precisely the kind of data needed to support the attenuation argument. A similar result has more recently been reported by Moray and O'Brien (1967). In that experiment subjects had to listen for the presence of letters in a stream of digits. They found that d' was significantly higher for the attended ear than the unattended one.

As has been pointed out elsewhere (Egeth 1967) the Broadbent and Gregory study (and several others like it) suffers from a methodological defect: report about the critical signal was delayed in the divided attention condition. Specifically, in the Broadbent and Gregory study the detection response came after the recall of the digits and thus the performance decrement may have been due to forgetting. The problem caused by delay of report has not been insurmountable, however, and there are now studies available that can provide a clearer picture of the perceptual consequences of divided attention.[1]

Eriksen and Johnson (1964) examined the storage and decay of a briefly presented unattended tone for delays varying from 0 up to 10.5 sec. Their manipulation of attention was rather unusual for laboratory research in that they told each subject to bring an absorbing novel to the laboratory where they served for two-hour stretches. Their main task was simply to read the novels. At random intervals during the session the 1000 Hz tone was presented; it was at a level such that it gave rise to 100 percent detection when subjects paid attention to it. In order to test memory for the tone, an alerting stimulus was provided by the turning-off of one of the subject's two reading lamps. When this cue was given, the subject was to report whether or not a tone had been sounded at any time within the past 10-15 sec. To assess false alarm rates the alerting cue was sometimes given when no tone had recently been sounded. The result of key interest to us is that subjects failed to report tones on about 50 percent of the trials that tested at zero delay, which seems to be a clear indication that auditory perception was impaired by the act of attending to the novel. The most recent research on this question (Norman 1969) had essentially the same outcome. In one condition of Norman's study subjects paid primary attention to a message that they had to shadow, while only secondary emphasis was placed on the task of remembering six two-digit numbers presented to the other ear. In another condition subjects were asked only to remember the numbers and disregard the verbal message. When recognition memory for the numbers was tested at zero delay, the subjects in the shadowing condition performed substantially more poorly than the memory-only subjects. This performance difference was especially pronounced for the last (sixth) serial position, the only serial position that could actually be tested with a nearly zero delay. Since little memory loss could have occurred between the presentation and the test for the last serial position, we are left with the alternative that it was the

perception of the numbers that was somewhat impaired by the simultaneous shadowing task.

One further study deserves mention in this context. Treisman and Riley (1969) had subjects shadow one of two lists of synchronized digits. They were also asked to listen for letters that would occasionally be presented to either ear. As soon as they heard a letter, they were to tap with a ruler and stop shadowing. The target letters, when they did occur, were in either the same (male) voice as the digits or a different (female) voice. The results were very clear. When the letters were in the same voice as the digits, subjects detected many more in the shadowed than the unshadowed list (76 percent vs. 33 percent). When the letters differed from the digits in the physical characteristic of voice, about 99 percent accuracy was attained with both lists. These data are clearly consistent with the notion that the informational content of an unattended message is attenuated and that a simple physical difference, which would require less complex analysis, may be detected even on an unattended channel if the difference is large enough.

More on the locus of selectivity. Treisman's modification of Broadbent's filter theory was required to make that model capable of predicting the occasional intrusion of meaningful material from an unattended message. However, the discrepant data that led Treisman to propose an attenuator instead of an all-or-none switch have led some other theorists in quite a different direction. Deutsch and Deutsch (1963) reasoned that if the filter proposed by Broadbent was passing signals on the basis of their meaning (e.g., Moray 1959), then these signals must have been analyzed at the highest levels of the nervous system. In their words (p. 83), "... a message will reach the same perceptual and discriminatory mechanisms whether attention is paid to it or not ..." Thus, the selectivity of attention must be subsequent to the perceptual analysis of inputs, possibly at the level of response selection. This logical analysis of attention has recently been incorporated into Norman's (1968, 1969) model of information processing. In Norman's model it is assumed that every sensory input is analyzed, which implies that each excites its representation in memory. At the same time it is assumed that an analysis of previous signals is being performed and that this analysis determines a class of inputs that are deemed to be *pertinent* to the current context. (Presumably some inputs such as one's name are permanently pertinent.) Thus every location in memory receives two simultaneous inputs, based upon the analysis of sensory information and the other based upon the analysis of pertinence level. It is the combined value of the sensory and pertinence data that determines what stimulus information will be attended to. Although Norman's model seems quite different from Treisman's, these two formulations actually lead to many of the same predictions. Indeed, there are not yet any data that would lead to the unambiguous rejection of one or the other of these models, and the decision between them must await further research.

Even if it is assumed that all sensory inputs are not analyzed equally thoroughly, it is still possible to raise a very fundamental question about the validity of Treisman's model, viz., is a filter necessary at all? (A model like Norman's obviously does not require a filter.) For example, suppose that attention were a finely divisible resource of which a human possessed a fixed amount at any moment. If a large amount of attention is deployed on one channel, then there must be less available for

---

[1]Among these studies must be counted a replication of the original Broadbent and Gregory experiment (Broadbent, personal communication, 1969) in which judgment about the tone was made immediately, with report of the digit following. The results were essentially the same as before except that the change in d' was numerically smaller.

other channels and so perception of stimuli would be impaired on those other channels (except for simply physical cues which require relatively little attention for their analysis). On this model the mechanism of attention consists simply of the concentration of cognitive resources on a particular input source. This description of attention was presented by Neisser (1967) as an integral part of his model of information processing. To put the issue somewhat differently, we may ask if it is not possible to account for the phenomena of attention strictly in terms of attending, without bringing in the concept of ignoring? There is very little research on this fundamental question. Perhaps the most germane data come from another experiment by Treisman (1964). She used a selective listening task with three spatially distinct message sources. One spoken message appeared at the right ear, one at the left, and one at both (such a binaural message is subjectively localized in the center of the head). The subject was told to attend to and shadow the message on the right ear but to ignore the other two messages. Shadowing accuracy was markedly lower in this condition than when the same two irrelevant messages were played through a single channel, either the center one or the left one.

Neisser (1967) has argued that Treisman's data are embarrassing to any view of perceptual selectivity in which attention consists of some special processing of relevant inputs. The following quote (p. 213) explains the embarrassment. In Neisser's model of perception, preliminary passive receptive process are

. . . normally supplemented by an active process of analysis-by-synthesis in which the listener produces "inner speech" (at some level of abstraction) to match the input. I suggest that this constructive process is itself the mechanism of auditory attention. On this hypothesis, to "follow" one conversation in preference to another is to synthesize a series of linguistic units which match it successfully. Irrelevant, unattended streams of speech are neither "filtered out" nor "attenuated"; they fail to enjoy the benefits of analysis-by-synthesis.

If this formulation is correct, it would seem that it should not matter to a subject whether irrelevant information is being sent over one or two separate channels. Since Treisman's (1964) data do not support this contention, they would seem to require a process that includes active ignoring or irrelevant inputs.

Although Neisser's argument is appealing, it may be possible to account for Treisman's (1964) data without recourse to the concepts of filtering and ignoring. The crucial point is that when two messages are sent over a single channel, their intelligibilities are considerably reduced. The result is something of a babble and there is little reason to expect a babble to interfere with reception of a prose message coming over another channel. However, when the two irrelevant messages are sent over separate channels, both remain intelligible and thus both of them can serve as sources of interference with the relevant message. We must conclude that there is not yet sufficient evidence to decide whether or not a filter is a necessary concept.

SELECTIVE ATTENTION MEDIATED BY MEANING

We have considered the behavioral consequences of attending to inputs that share some physical feature such as hue or spatial location. "Meaning" has been introduced only as one of the sources of distraction that occurs in the filtering paradigm. We turn now to a direct consideration of how selectivity itself can be based upon the meaning of a stimulus or upon its inclusion in an ill-defined category (for simplicity we shall use meaning to refer to both of these bases of selection).

A mechanism that can permit selectivity based on meaning has already been adumbrated in the discussion of Treisman's model for selective listening. What seems to be required is a recognition or categorization process that is organized hierarchically. The primary example of such a system is Selfridge's (1958) model for pattern recognition: Pandemonium. According to a recent version of this model (Neisser 1967) the first step in the recognition or categorization of an input is the segregation of a figure from its background by means of low-level preattentive processes. Subsequently, the isolated stimulus is subjected to the simultaneous scrutiny of a large number of elementary feature analyzers. The outputs of these feature analyzers are then fed into a set of intermediate-level analyzers that combine and weight the data they receive from the feature analyzers. The outputs of the intermediate analyzers are in turn fed into a set of "cognitive" analyzers each of which evaluates the likelihood that the stimulus is an exemplar of the particular category of object to which it is attuned. The analyzer that achieves the highest likelihood is the one that determines the interpretation to be placed on the external stimulus. In order to incorporate the fact that categorization can be influenced by cognitive factors such as context, it seems necessary to introduce some refinements into this model. In particular, it seems necessary to include some means of manipulating the likelihood calculations performed by the cognitive analyzers so that probable or important stimuli can be detected with less sensory information than improbable or unimportant stimuli. This kind of bias in the operation of the cognitive analyzers is completely analogous to the concept of the variable criterion in signal detection theory (Swets, Tanner and Birdsall 1961).

This analysis of set effects has two important implications for behavior. First, it suggests a mechanism whereby selective attention may in certain circumstances result from genuine perceptual selectivity, quite apart from selective response or selective encoding of the contents of iconic storage. This would occur when performance can be based upon less than a full hierarchical analysis of an input. Second, in situations where a full (albeit biased) analysis is performed it seems inappropriate to speak of selective attention, since there is no substantial reduction in the amount of information processing effected by this mode of analysis. Not only does there not seem to be any important economy introduced by criterion biasing, but whatever effects there are would seem to be judgmental rather than perceptual, although this is admittedly a difficult distinction to draw.

In support of the first suggestion there is the work of Neisser and his colleagues on visual search (Neisser 1963, 1964; Neisser, Novick, and Lazar 1963). In these experiments subjects scanned from top to bottom through vertical lists, each consisting of fifty lines, to find the single target embedded in the list. The nature of the targets varied from condition to condition. In some instances the target might be a single letter, e.g., Z, in which case each line would consist of 5 or 6 alphanumeric characters in some meaningless combination. In other instances the target might be a word, in which case each line contained a single word. There was only one target in each list.

The methodological point which made this method so useful was the consistent finding that, for any given kind of list, search time was a linear function of the serial position of the target within the list. The slope of this function gives a measure of the speed with which subjects can examine an item and determine that it is not a member of the target class. It is a measure of decision time without reaction time, since it is the intercept of the function that includes factors such as starting and stopping time.

Subjects attained a fairly stable level of performance after several daily practice sessions. There are several characteristics of their asymptotic behavior that are important for the purposes of this discussion. (1) Introspectively, subjects did not "see" the nontarget items; they were passed over in a blur while the target item seemed to jump out at them. (2) Subjects did not demonstrate any memory for the nontarget items in a later recognition test. (Unfortunately, this part of this research was not described in detail.) (3) In certain conditions Neisser contrived to put a "target," e.g., a Z, in every line but one, and the subjects were requested to find the line that did *not* contain a Z. Comparison of search rates in this task with rates in the usual task indicated that search *for* a given target is faster than search for its absence. (4) The similarity of the target to the nontargets had a pronounced effect on search rate. For example, it was easy to find a Q when all of the other letters in the list were angular (X, V, W, etc.) but difficult when the nontarget letters were rounded (O, G, C, etc.).

All of these results are consistent with the hierarchical model of recognition described by Selfridge (Selfridge 1959; Selfridge and Neisser 1960). The key to understanding these phenomena in the context of a hierarchial model is that it is possible to know what a stimulus is not, more quickly than to know what it is. For example, if low-level analyzers detect a set of features that is inappropriate to the target of a particular search, it should be possible to proceed to the analysis of the next input without subjecting obviously inappropriate features to the relatively sophisticated scrutiny of the cognitive analyzers. Of course, in a task involving words as targets it would probably be impossible to reject an input at as low a level as has just been described, but in a hierarchical system there are opportunities for rejection at higher levels as well. If this conception is correct, it is easy to understand why subjects would feel that they had not really seen the nontargets and why they could not remember them. Furthermore, search for the line that does not contain a target letter requires that the full depth of the recognition hierarchy be engaged once on every line, which ought to result in slower processing than search for a given target since that requires full analysis only when the single target is finally found. Finally, if the similarity of the targets and nontargets is high, then it will generally not be possible to reject a nontarget simply on the basis of a rudimentary analysis and thus this situation ought to result in fairly slow search rates.

It was suggested above that even when a full analysis is performed on a sensory input it is possible for set to influence recognition, although it would seem inappropriate to call such an effect selective attention. It was further asserted that such high-level set effects could more properly be considered judgmental than perceptual. Although the issue is still being argued, it seems that a fair case can be made to support this claim. There is, of course, an extensive literature on the topic of "perceptual" set (e.g., Dember 1960; Haber 1966; Steinfeld 1967); however, we shall take only a limited and highly selective look at this literature.

Lawrence and Coles (1954) performed one of the classic experiments on perceptual selectivity. They were interested in determining the extent to which preparatory set could influence perception rather than memory or response processes. Their stimuli were pictures of common objects and the subject's task was to indicate what was shown to him by selecting one of a set of four alternative verbal labels that the experimenter provided him with. The logic of their experimental design followed Chapman's (1932). They reasoned that perception must be richer and more detailed than memory. Consider, then, the possible effects of giving alternatives either before or after the tachistoscopic presentation of the stimulus picture. If these alternatives are quite different from one another, then even the relatively crude memory trace of the picture ought to contain enough information to enable the subject to select the label that matches the picture. Thus, it should not make much difference if distinctive alternatives are presented before rather than after the picture is presented. However, if the alternatives are similar to one another (i.e., denote rather similar objects), the memory trace may well lack the essential information for accurate discrimination if these alternatives are only presented after the picture. If the alternatives are presented before the picture, *and* if there is a mechanism of perceptual selectivity, then it may be possible for this mechanism to be tuned to the fine details that can discriminate between the similar alternatives. Presumably, this mechanism could only be used if it were readied before the stimulus picture were shown. Therefore, the hypothesis of perceptual selectivity leads to the prediction of an interaction between time of presentation of alternatives (Before vs. After) and the similarity of these alternatives to one another.

In the Lawrence and Coles experiment the hypothesized interaction failed of significance (indeed there was not even a main effect of Before vs. After instructions) and so the authors concluded that perceptual selectivity had not been demonstrated. This conclusion seems eminently reasonable on the basis of the analysis of set that has been offered in this paper. After all, just how could a set of verbal labels have influenced the organization of perception since these labels only specified generic classes of objects, the exemplars of which may *look* radically different from one another. In contrast to the Lawrence and Coles experiment there is the similar study of Egeth and Smith (1967) in which the alternatives as well as the stimulus objects were pictorial. Thus, instead of presenting the four (similar) verbal responses of church, school, house, and cabin, a picture of a specific exemplar of each category was shown to the subject, and the stimulus was a particular one of the four alternatives. In all other essential respects this study was a replication of the one by Lawrence and Coles. Egeth and Smith found the crucial interaction to be significant, thus implying the existence of perceptual selectivity. Again, this result is quite understandable. With pictorial alternatives subjects in the Before conditions had an opportunity to examine the alternatives and find critical features that could serve to distinguish among the four possible answers. The Before conditions permitted the tuning of relevant analyzers (or the attenuation of irrelevant ones). In other words, by using specific pictorial alternatives rather than generic verbal labels Egeth and Smith converted the set experiment of Lawrence and Coles into a selective attention experiment.

Although judgmental or interpretive set may not affect forced-choice accuracy (as in the Lawrence and Coles experiment), this is not to suggest that it has no behavioral consequence. Indeed, if the present analysis has any merit, we ought to be able to demonstrate substantial set effects when the task permits behavior to change as response criterion varies. A very important demonstration of just such an effect has been given by Broadbent (1967) in his recent discussion of the word frequency effect. There has long been a controversy over the locus of the apparently enhanced perceptibility of common as opposed to uncommon words. As Dember (1960) has pointed out, a familiarity effect may be considered due to implicit set based upon the subject's past experience. In his research Broadbent tried to distinguish among four possible sources of the word frequency phenomenon and concluded that his data were consistent with only one of them—systematic criterion biases in favor of frequent words. In other words, the results indicated that subjects were biased in their analysis of sensory data. They required less evidence to conclude that a particular input was a high-frequency rather than a low-frequency word.

Future Directions. The evidence that has been reviewed here concerning the behavioral consequences of set and selective attention suggest some directions for further research.

If we consider selective attention to be a useful means of overcoming the effects of stimulus impoverishment, then it becomes important to determine just what kinds of impoverishment it can overcome. Tachistoscopic exposure is apparently one, as shown by the Egeth and Smith paper. However, if stimuli are blurred or made noisy, selective attention may not be an effective perceptual strategy since critical features may themselves be rendered indistinct by such procedures. Indeed, a careful reading of two studies that used relatively long exposures of very unclear stimuli supports this conjecture (Long, Reid, and Henneman 1960; Long, Henneman, and Garvey 1960). Specifically, in terms of the Lawrence and Coles criterion for perceptual selectivity, the interaction between time of presentation of alternatives and similarity of alternatives was in the wrong direction in these studies.

It also seems to be important to pursue further the analysis of the mechanisms that underlie set and attention phenomena. We have suggested that in the Egeth and Smith study subjects given Before instructions were able to selectively attend to critical visual features in the flashed stimulus picture. However, there is an alternative explanation that has not yet been thoroughly examined, viz., that recognition is mediated by visual memory in this kind of experiment. There is no evidence yet that directly supports this alternative; however, there are some suggestive leads in the literature. For example Epstein and Rock (1960) have demonstrated that the perception of an ambiguous figure is determined by which unambiguous alternative the subject saw last, rather than by which alternative the subject expected to see. In that study, recency only operated over a delay of about 1 sec, and thus it is quite plausible to think that visual memory was the effective determinant of which alternative was seen in the ambiguous picture. It seems clear that a more systematic exploration of the role of visual memory is called for in set research. A recent finding that gives even greater urgency to this program of research is the observation that there may be conditions in which subjects can translate a *verbal*

(acoustic) instruction into a *visual* code (Posner, Boies, Eichelman, and Taylor, 1969). If this is right, then it should not be difficult to demonstrate selective attention following verbal instructions (as Lawrence and Coles attempted to do) in situations where the subject can transform the instructions into fairly specific visual forms.

The Intensive Properties of Attention

In addition to its selective nature, attention is intensive in character. Just as the focus of attention varies, so does its vigor. It has been traditional to divide the study of the phenomena related to the intensive aspects of attention into two topical areas, short-term and long-term. The study of short-term effects includes such topics as attention span, fluctuations of attentiveness, and distractibility. The study of long-term effects is concerned chiefly with the vigilance decrement, i.e., the decline in signal detection observed during long periods of watch-keeping.

SHORT-TERM PHENOMENA

The literature on short-term effects is, for the most part, the literature of an earlier period. Bibliographic listings dealing with fluctuations and shifts of attention, attention span, and distraction in the *Psychological Abstracts* during the past 15 years total only about 60 items and many of these are developmental or clinical papers and thus fall outside the scope of the present chapter.

Fluctuations of Attention. As our discussion of selectivity implies, the overriding characteristic of attention is that it is constantly changing. In some situations, e.g., reading, the pattern of shifts is highly regular and easily predicted. When, however, the stimulus is a complex visual array, the characteristics of the viewing pattern will depend on the spatial arrangement and the complexity of the display. Buswell's (1935) now classic study of how people look at pictures clearly revealed that the fixation point shifts from area to area within the visual field, following a course that bears no relationship to the order of the elements that make up the picture. This yields a series of overlapping retinal images, of which only the focal points of attention are registered in fine detail. These fixation periods have a modal duration of about 230 msec. If subjects, however, are asked to attend to a particular point they may do so for as long as five seconds (Billings 1914). A variety of phenomena— the fading in and out of stimuli at threshold, retinal rivalry, figure-ground reversals—have been classed as shifts in attention. However, this is quite probably a misnomer. For one thing, the rate at which these phenomena shift is many times slower than the shifts associated with reading or viewing a visual display (e.g., Guilford 1927; Glen 1940). Furthermore, in the case of sensory fluctuations, their periodicity varies with modality and cannot be attributed to a common central mechanism. Recently, Cesaric and Nilsson (1963, 1964) have related figure-ground reversals to general alertness or tension level through correlations with blood pressure values and the amplitude of the finger plethysmogram.

Attention Span. The span of attention for adults varies from 6 to 11 objects and averages about 8 (Woodworth and Schlosberg 1954, p. 94). When random arrays of stimuli are presented tachistoscopically, one or another of three processes underlies the subject's report of the number presented: counting, subitizing, and estimating. Counting occurs when the number of stimuli is small, and probably depends on the persistence of what Neisser (1967, chap. 2) calls *iconic memory*. Indirect evidence in support of the counting operation is found in an increase in response latencies with an increase in the number of stimuli in the display from 1 to 10 (Saltzman and Garner 1948). At the same time, there are occasions when the numbers appear to the subject to be immediately given or to occur so quickly as to preclude counting. Furthermore, these impressions are highly accurate with up to 5 or 6 stimuli. This fact prompted Kaufman, Lord, Reese, and Volkmann (1949) to introduce the term *subitizing* for these rapid responses. Neisser (1967, p. 42) has suggested that subitizing may involve the subject using the shape of the spatial array as a cue to number. He points out, for example, that three stimuli usually make a triangle and four a quadrangle. Similarly, Freeman (1916) observes that the objective grouping of stimuli facilitates the correct identification of numbers. Thus if 25 stimuli are arrayed in 5 groups of 5 dots each in the manner of the spots on a playing card, most subjects will correctly report the 25. And if a stimulus is omitted from any of the groups, its omission is usually detected. When the number of stimuli in random array exceeds 6 to 8 (Taves 1941; Kaufman, Lord, Reese, and Volkmann 1949), the process underlying report becomes one of estimation. This is readily detected as a discontinuity in the function relating the reported to the actual number of stimuli. Furthermore, if the judge is given knowledge of his performance, errors are quickly reduced in size (Minturn and Reese 1951).

The span of attention for displays of up to 12 dots varies with both the illumination of the field and the duration of the stimulation and remains constant for a constant $I \times t$ product, in the manner of the Bunsen-Roscoe law (Hunter and Sigler 1940). It also is influenced by the density of the array and the range of stimuli used (Reese et al. 1953) and by the size of the stimuli (Miller and Baker 1968). The influence of context is seen in an experiment of Bevan and Turner (1964). Subjects were shown random arrays of dots on a gray background and asked to estimate their number. The experimental conditions involved surrounding each array with either a large or a small square frame and instructing the subject to consider the array and frame together as focal stimuli or to think of them separately, the dots as focal stimuli and the frame as part of the background. When the frame was large relative to the area occupied by the dots and when the instructions were to treat dots and frame as one, the numerical estimates of the dots were enhanced as the number of dots displayed increased from 21 to 336. When the frame was small and tightly enclosed the display, the "figure" instructions were associated with an underestimation of the dots. With instructions to consider dots as figures and frames as background, the large frame was associated with a reduction in the numbers estimated while the small frame produced a trend of overestimation.

Properties of the span have been elucidated with letters and words as well as with simple geometrical forms. Glanville and Dallenbach (1929) report it to be 6.9 for letters to be read, while Sperling (1960) estimates the limit for the correct identification of letters to be from 3.8 to 5.2. Miller (1956) in his provocative paper on the magical number seven, noting the close correspondence in size between the span of attention, the number of categories typically used in absolute judgment and the span of immediate memory, tentatively identified the first with limitations in the human capacity for information processing. Imae and Takeuchi (1959), using series of words or syllables constructed in accordance with Shannon and Miller's guessing technique, found that the span of attention increased with the order of approximation to language. Similarly Hoffman (1927) reported that in school children attention span for familar words increased with grade level from 1 to 8 (5 to 20 words), but that span for jumbled consonants remained low and changed hardly at all (3 to 5 letters). Warrington, Kinsbourne, and James (1966) have studied the span with stimulus ensembles of various sizes which included letters and digits and found that when letters and digits were presented as mixed sequences, the span was reduced in proportion to the number of letter-digit juxtapositions. The span also varied with the serial position at which a single juxtaposition occurred and was greatest when this was near the midpoint of the array. The experimenters attribute their findings to the higher transitional probabilities in the real world between items of the same class as compared to different classes and the greater ease of grouping such items. Neisser (1967, p. 42), a decade after Miller, concludes that span of attention does indeed depend on the span of immediate memory and explains the fact that the former is generally shorter than the latter because a high rate of stimulus encoding is normally required in attention-span experiments.

Distraction. The literature on distraction spans most of the years of modern psychology. It consists largely of studies empirically oriented toward questions of performance efficiency and the outcomes have been varied. At the turn of the century Todd (1912) reported that reaction time to a light was lengthened if it was preceded by either a tone or an electric shock, and Evans (1916) showed that the greatest effect of a distraction occurs when it is presented to the same modality as the stimulus. Dallenbach and Cassell (1918) examined the effect of both continuous and intermittent distractors and found the latter to be more interfering. However, subjects could adapt to either type. In a relatively recent study Fried (1959) found an increase in detection time for geometric patterns when subjects were exposed to continuous visual noise with performance decrement paralleling the intensity of the interference. In an early report MacDougall (1903) found reaction time to sounds increased by varying degrees of visual input, the greater effect being produced by the stronger light. When the distraction consisted of varied talking or repetitive counting, Antrobus and Singer (1964) found that the detection of a brightness difference was adversely affected. When the task studied involved the reception of a visually and auditorily presented message, auditory presentation was found to be superior to visual presentation in its resistance to distraction (Henneman, Lewis, and Matthews 1953).

Among the earliest studies relating to the question of distractors was Bowditch and Warren's (1890) observation that the clenching of the fist .4 seconds or sooner before the activation of the patellar reflex facilitated this simple motor response presumably by release of the reflex from voluntary control. But the classic study of the effect of distraction on perceptual-motor performance remains that of Morgan (1916). The subject was given a code substitution test and was required to respond by pressing appropriate keys on a keyboard. The distractors were an assortment of auditory stimuli. Performance initially was suppressed in the fact of these stimuli but then returned to normal and in some cases actually exceeded baseline performance. This was accomplished at the expense of extra effort as indicated by the increased pressure with which the response keys were pressed. A similar experiment by Ford (1929), which included physiological measures of effort, yielded similar results. Measures of metabolic rate of typists while working under quiet and distracting conditions indicated an increase of 20 percent in the latter over the former (Laird 1929). Subjects may not only adapt to distracting stimuli, but they may also become totally insensitive to them. Murphy recently (1959), found no evidence that orally presented series of random numbers had any effect upon performance in a card-sorting task. On the other hand, when the distractor was in the same modality as the signal, Howell and Briggs (1959) found that tracking performance was degraded. Error was lower for the simpler of the two tracking courses, with noise having less effect when it appeared on the cursor, than on the target, the cursor and target together, or on a compensatory display. Similarly, Kerstin and Eysenck (1965) found that when distraction was associated with a second task (selective pedal pressing), pursuit rotor performance was always degraded, even with a very slow signal rate. Indeed, performance decrement was related in linear fashion to signal rate. A further study (Eysenck and Thompson 1966) revealed that the degrading effect of distraction was reflected in performance but not learning. Half of the subjects were presented a distracting task during a rest period while the other half simply rested and there was no evidence that the consolidation processes presumed to be operative during rest experience any degradation. Meanwhile, Grings (1953) has described a detrimental effect of distraction on nonsense syllable learning. Distraction consisted of flanking the stimulus display with small, brightly colored discs and presenting an intermittent 1000-cycle tone. Both free and controlled recall were adversely affected by this procedure through an increase in the number of irrelevant responses given. On the other hand, Hovey (1928), in a frequently cited study of the effect of an array of both visual and auditory noises upon intelligence test performance, failed to find any significant interference and Smith (1951) in a similar experiment with intermittent bursts of loud noise and several paper and pencil tasks obtained similar outcomes. Fendrick (1937) reports music to have an adverse effect on reading comprehension while Henderson, Crews, and Barlow (1945) found less evidence for a detrimental effect.

These differences in experimental results, especially where higher-order tasks are involved, underline the importance of subjective variables. Cason (1938), and, more recently, Kerstin and Eysenck (1965), have pointed out the importance of individual differences in distractability and Baker (1937) has demonstrated the importance of attitude. Subjects were given an arithmetic task to perform, sometimes in noise and sometimes in quiet. Some of the subjects were led to expect a detrimental effect of noise, others a beneficial effect and performance changed accordingly. Broverman (1960) reports that "conceptually-dominant" subjects were less distracted than "perceptual-motor dominant" subjects in doing a difficult arithmetic task, that "perceptual-motor dominants" were less affected than "conceptually-dominant" subjects when tracing a difficult pattern, and that subjects who more readily adapted to automatic tasks were less affected than less readily adapted subjects when tracing a straight line. Similarly, Lofchie (1955) has found that persons scoring high on the Perceptual Maturity Index of the Rorschach were less distracted during psychomotor performance than those who score low.

Long-Term Phenomena: Vigilance

Unlike the literature on the short-term intensive properties of attention, the literature that bears most directly on intensive changes over long periods of time is of relatively recent origin. Although interest in the problem of vigilance began with the studies of watch-keeping during World War II (cf., e.g. Ditchburn 1943; Lindsley 1944), conceptually-focused work dates from the appearance of the Mackworth monograph (1950) which introduced the term. Mackworth borrowed the word *vigilance* from Sir Henry Head and used it to refer to a state of response readiness reflected in the efficiency with which the observing organism detects weak, infrequent and irregularly occurring signals. Certain conventions have been widely observed in the design of vigilance experiments. While signals may be complex, they most frequently are simple—a weak pip on the face of a cathode ray tube, a short tone presented through a headset, or the double jump of the hand on the face of an instrument dial. Although occasionally negative signals—e.g., the absence of a pip or a tone—are used, signals more commonly are positive. Except in a very small number of experiments, the modalities involved have been either vision or hearing or a combination of these two sense avenues. The duration of the vigil is at least an hour, frequently is several hours, and may be as much as 24 hours long. The interval between signals varies from a few seconds to a matter of 10 minutes or more but usually averages about two minutes in length. Performance is expressed in terms of errors or response latency. In the latter instance, the experimental paradigm differs from the traditional reaction-time experiment in that no premonitory cue is used to alert the subject to the onset of the signal. In the former, two kinds of errors are involved—errors of omission and of commission, although the greatest attention has been paid to errors of omission. Typically, errors of omission increase during the first 15 to 30 minutes of the vigil and then performance levels off, although an end spurt may also be observed (Bergum and Lehr, 1963b). The causes of this performance decrement have been the central preoccupation of investigators throughout the short history of systematic work on vigilance, first for practical reasons but later from an awareness that the question of the time course of detectability embodies the essence of the vigilance problem.

There are now some 1300 papers on vigilance and related matters in the literature most of which have appeared in the past decade. While the recent heightened interest in arousal has inevitably meant a consideration of vigilance in arousal terms, even to the formulation of an arousal theory of vigilance (Deese 1955; Scott 1957), at the same time, the fundamental connection between attention and vigilance is readily apparent from a catalogue of the kinds of independent variables that have figured prominently in the vigilance literature: sensory modality; signal duration, intensity, and rate; single versus multiple channels; single versus multiple tasks; the effect of distraction on performance; the statistical properties of the schedule; the complexity of the response requirements, etc.

Vigilance and the Physical Properties of the Signal. Relatively few experiments have been concerned with vigilance as a function of the physical properties of the signal. However, as might be expected, there are data to indicate that better performance is associated with increases in signal intensity, signal duration, and signal-to-noise ratio (Mackworth 1950; Adams 1956; Jenkins 1958; Baker 1963). Meanwhile a more recent study by Gulian (1966) suggests a curvilinear relationship between detection and background noise level, the best performance being associated with intermediate levels. The few studies that have dealt with the question of modality suggest that auditory and visual signals do not differ systematically in ease of detection (Baker, Ware, and Sipowicz 1962*a*; Cheney and Eaton 1968). Thus, Binford and Loeb's finding (1963) that an increment in a steady noise was easier to detect than the double jump of a clock hand is probably more a matter of a difference in task difficulty than it is of modality. At the same time Loeb and Hawkes (1961, 1962) have reported that auditory vigilance is superior to that for cutaneous signals.

Vigilance and the Temporal Structure of the Schedule of Signals. Of greater interest has been the temporal properties of the vigil. As already has been pointed out, the practical implications of the vigilance decrement have lead to the early and continuing investigation of this phenomenon. Most laboratory studies have involved vigils of one or two hours. Mackworth (1964*a*) observed a linear relationship between the decrement and the square root of task duration. Webber and Adams (1964) studied monitoring in a complex visual task over a six-hour period and found performance to be essentially the same as for sessions of two or three hours duration. On the other hand, Baker, Ware and Sipowicz (1962*b*) have found that when the signal was the brief interruption of a continuous light source, performance showed a gradual decline throughout a 24-hour vigil, reaching its nadir after 16 to 18 hours of watch. Furthermore, the control group showed a steeper gradient than an experienced group of watch keepers, a finding the experimenters regard to be in conflict with Jerison's (1958) conclusion that expectation of a short vigil reduces the magnitude of the decrement. Consistent with Jerison is the Bergum and Lehr (1963*b*) observation that knowledge of task duration induces end spurt. While decrements are commonly observed within sessions, the general picture of performance across sessions is one of no change or improvement. Adams, Humes, and Stenson (1962) had subjects monitor a complex visual display for nine consecutive days with a tenth session following after about a week and obtained no statistically reliable between-sessions effect. In a second study, which extended the first by employing a heavy visual load, Adams, Humes and Sieveking (1963) obtained a reliable decrement within sessions but observed improvement over sessions, a result suggestive of learning. In an earlier study, O. S. Adams and Chiles (1961) had observed poorer performance for consecutive daily sessions during a fifteen-day confinement study. Here the adverse between-sessions effect is probably due to the circumstances of confinement rather than to the properties of the vigilance process itself.

The question of the temporal properties of the vigil also involves questions of signal rate, the inter-signal interval, the ratio of signals to non-signals, and matters of signal uncertainty. Generally, performance improves as signal rate is increased. For example, Deese and Ormond (1953) report a positive correlation between rate and the quality of performance with rates of 10 to 40 per hour and Johnston, Howell, and Goldstein (1966) with rates of 36 and 90. Furthermore, Stern's results (1966) suggest that subjects at lower rates make not only relatively fewer correct detections but a greater number of false alarms than at higher rates. Meanwhile, Martz (1967), using a latency measure of vigilance with signal rates of from 2.5 to 120 per hour, has concluded that a rate of 15 per hour is most efficient and that the frequency of false alarms is unrelated to signal rate. The relation of the duration of the interval between two successive signals has come in for special attention. When this is defined as the time between signal presentations, no relationship is apparent (Deese and Ormond 1953). However, when it is defined as the time between detections, the relationship is negative (Jenkins 1958). Furthermore, a series of related studies (Harabedian, McGrath and Buckner 1960; McGrath 1960; Buckner and McGrath 1961) indicate that the probability of detection decreases with positively skewed and increases with rectangular distributions of intervals. Boulter and Adams (1963), while they found no significant relation between the range of interval durations and response latency, found a significant interaction between range and interval duration. When the trial sequence involved nine different durations ranging from 15 to 900 seconds, latency increased with interval duration. However, when the intervals 120, 220 and 270 seconds were involved, the relationship was reversed. A number of investigations with randomly ordered variable schedules (Baker 1959*a*; Hardesty and Bevan 1965; Bevan, Avant and Lankford 1966; Johnston, Howell, and Goldstein 1966) have indicated that latencies are shorter at the mean than at the extreme interstimulus intervals. Indeed, when range and mean are held constant, the shape of the frequency distributions of intervals as a determinant of response latency is irrelevant (Bevan, Avant, and Lankford 1966). Of course, response latencies for variable interval schedules are, on the average, longer than for comparable constant-interval schedules (Bevan, Hardesty, and Avant 1965). All of which suggests that vigilance behavior reflects the extent to which the monitor can comprehend and then predict the temporal pattern of signals. However, a recent experiment by Taub and Osborne (1968) adds a complicating dimension. In a task where the signal was the double jump of a clock hand, signal rate (30, 60, 120 per hour), the rate of signals and stimuli not classed as signals (single jumps) combined (1800 and 3600 per hour), and signal probability were all examined in their relation to detection frequency. Results indicate that signal rate and signal probability are less important to performance than total stimulation rate, poor performance being associated consistently with the faster rate of stimulation. This, Taub and Osborne suggest, indicates that detection performance is directly related to observing responses which are, in turn, dependent upon the various signal rates.

Vigilance and Task Complexity. In recent years, increased interest has been directed toward the various aspects of task complexity—signal load and the use of false signals, multiple channels, multiple displays, and multiple tasks—as determinants of vigilance. It has been widely observed that when the task is simple detection, performance improves as the signal frequency increases. For example, Kidd and Micocci (1964) report that the number of omissive errors decreases as signal frequency increases from one signal every six minutes to one per minute. However, performance decreases with an increase in the number of different signals to be detected. Thus Robey and Roazen (1963) found that performance was best when a single signal was used, poorer when two were involved, and poorest with three. However, as just noted, Taub and Osborne (1968) have presented evidence to indicate that the total number of stimuli may be more important than signal frequency in influencing the number of correct detections. When multiple channels (signal locations) are involved, performance may deteriorate, although this variable is less important than signal load. Robey and Roazen (1963) report some increase in error probability with an increase from one to three locations. Adams, Stenson, and Humes (1961), comparing performance with six and thirty-six locations in a simulated air defense surveillance task, obtained 99 and 97 percent correct responses respectively when the task requirement was detection and 95 and 89 percent when the task required evaluation of the signals. Similarly, Gould and Schaffer (1966) observed that subjects monitoring alphanumeric displays made over 95 percent correct detections with up to 8 channels and 80 percent or more with up to 16. When performance with a single display has been compared to that with multiple displays, it usually is better with the single display. For example, Jerison and Wallis (1957) had subjects monitor clock hands for double jumps and found that they did better with a single clock than with three. After decrement, the former leveled off at 50 percent while the latter never reached more than 30 percent. Wiener (1964) obtained the same results with a voltmeter display: no difference between groups watching two and three meters, but superior performance with a group monitoring only a single meter. As far as multimodal presentations are concerned, it generally may be concluded that at least when signals are synchronized, performance is facilitated (Loveless 1957; Buckner and McGrath 1961; Osborn, Sheldon, and Baker 1963; Gruber 1963). In addition, Gruber has reported that alternation between modalities is an effective strategy for maintaining alertness. When vigilance tasks are performed in conjunction with other tasks, he result is usually poorer performance. Alluisi and Hall (1963) had subjects do auditory monitoring along with two other passive tasks (probability and warning-light monitoring) and three active tasks (arithmetic computation, pattern discrimination, and code-lock solving) and found a vigilance decrement in the target task. However, Hall, Passey, and Meighan (1965), in a second study with these same tasks, found that when the passive tasks alone were involved, performance was better than when they were combined with the active tasks. Even when a time-sharing strategy was imposed, the interpolation of active task (mental arithmetic) was found to adversely affect vigilance in a voltmeter-monitoring task (Wiener, Poock and Steele 1964). On the other hand, Smith, Lucaccini, Groth, and Lyman (1966) report that the interpolation of periods of work in a "compatible" task did not produce an adverse effect on vigilance.

Vigilance and the Detection Criterion. When one has arrived at a consideration of such matters as task compatibility,

one finds oneself viewing situational determinants of vigilance behavior less in terms of the physical characteristics of the setting and more in terms of the psychobiological properties of the responding organism. Thus Jerison and Pickett (1963) point to attention as a necessary antecedent of signal detection and emphasize the importance of the observing response to an understanding of vigilance. They note (1964) that this response may be elicited by regularly occurring events that occasionally become signals. Accordingly, they varied the overall rate of stimulus presentation while holding signal rate constant and found that the monitor missed about 10 percent of the signals at a low stimulus rate in contrast to about 70 percent with a higher stimulus rate. These results were extended (Jerison, Pickett and Stenson 1965) and led to a suggestion of three types of observing behavior: alert, blurred, and distracted. These three types may be distinguished in terms of the signal detection measures d', which indicates the observer's sensitivity to the signal, and beta, which reflects the subject's judgmental criterion. Alert observing reflects perfect attentiveness (both "true" d' and beta), while "blurred" observing refers to a less effective condition (low d', "true" beta) and distraction to no observation at all. In the 1965 study just mentioned there was a greater performance decrement with the faster stimulus rate; this occurred with no change in d' but a systematic change in beta suggested an increase in caution with the passage of time on watch. Meanwhile, J. Mackworth (1964a) has observed reliable decrements in d' with subjects monitoring jumps of a clock hand. Binford and Loeb (1966) report that with an auditory detection task, d' decreased slightly during sessions but increased slightly over sessions, while beta increased both within and over sessions. Meanwhile, a study of the value of hits and the cost of misses (Levine 1966) suggests that a significant performance decrement is associated with an increasing cost for misses and false detections. Since d' did not change with time, increasingly poor performance appeared to be due to an increasingly strict criterion for the presence of the signal. A similar conclusion has been reached by Broadbent and Gregory (1965).

Vigilance and Reinforcement. This shaping of the detection criterion points to the importance of reinforcement to vigilance behavior, something which is born out by a variety of empirical results. Deese (1957) early recognized detection as a reinforcing event and thus successfully predicted more efficient performance with higher than with lower signal rates. Holland (1958) identified observing responses as the reinforcing events and, using the paradigm of the operant conditioning experiment, demonstrated a decrease in these responses following detection. Conventional rewards and punishments influence vigilance performance. Money for correct detections, withdrawal of reward, blast of a truck horn, and electric shock for errors all facilitate performance (Pollack and Knaff 1958; Bergum and Lehr 1963a; Bevan and Turner 1965). In an experiment which combined rewards for correct detection and punishment for missed signals or false alarms, Smith, Lucaccini, and Epstein (1967) found that some combinations of reward and punishment facilitated performance while others did not and subjects who were punished for missed signals did better than those punished for false alarms. Bevan and Turner (1965) shifted from coins for correct detections to shocks for errors at the midpoint of the test session and obtained better performance throughout the session than with either reward or punishment alone. Since the subject was led in his initial instructions to expect the shift, it is apparent that preparatory set is an important ingredient in determining performance level. Similarly, subjects instructed to regard monitoring as a challenging task did better than others told to view it as a boring affair (Lucaccini, Freedy, and Lyman 1968).

Vigilance and Knowledge of Results. Knowledge of results is a form of reinforcement that has been of continuing interest to vigilance researchers. Knowledge of results, even partial knowledge of results, generally facilitates performance. Johnson and Payne (1966) had subjects perform a simple visual monitoring task with either 0, 25, 50, 75, or 100 percent knowledge of results. Significant differences occurred between the 0 and 25 percent groups and the 25 and 50 percent groups, but not among the 50, 75 and 100 percent groups. Similarly Antonelli and Karas (1967) obtained their best performance with 100 percent KR, poorer performance with 50 percent KR and still poorer with 20-30 percent KR. When information in an earlier study about missed signals was provided by means of signal lights, there was a reliable reduction in the number of false responses given. In contrast, when KR was for correct detections, there was a decrease in the proportion of missed signals. Finally, when the subject received information about false responses, there was both a significant increase in reaction time on correct detections and a decrease in the number of false responses (Chinn and Alluisi 1964). Meanwhile, Ware and Baker (1964) have reported that when KR was presented verbally, it made no difference whether it was for hits or for misses. When the KR was non-verbal, knowledge of missed signals was more effective than knowledge of detected signals. Overall, verbal KR was more effective than nonverbal, and auditory KR was more effective than visual. Hardesty, Trumbo, and Bevan (1963) found this last relationship to hold even when the experimenter was not physically present but delivered KR over an intercom system. Furthermore, verbally presented KR probably was more effective in the form of evaluative comments than as quantitative information (Hardesty and Bevan 1964).

And false KR is better than no KR at all. Weidenfeller, Baker, and Ware (1962) had reported that a group receiving false KR did as well as one receiving correct information and both did better than a control group and J. Mackworth (1964b), while she found KR to be more effective than false KR, also found both to be superior to no KR at all. When response latency was the measure under consideration, Antonelli and Karas (1967) found no difference between KR and false KR, although when knowledge of results had to do with speed of response itself, true KR was more effective than false KR in preventing the common increase in latency that occurs over the course of a vigil (Loeb and Schmidt 1963). KR may also be combined with monetary reward to facilitate performance (Montague and Webber 1965). And an enchancement of the verbal reinforcement effect can be produced by introducing a change from KR for hits to KR for errors or vice versa during the course of the vigil (Bevan and Turner 1966). Meanwhile, several studies indicate the effects of KR appear to be limited to the periods during which it is applied (Montague and Webber 1965; Colquhoun 1966), although others suggest a carry over to periods when none is available (Wiener 1963; Mackworth 1964b).

As is the case with short changes in the intensive character of attention, the literature on vigilance indicates the influence of a variety of constitutional factors: age (Thompson, Opton, and Cohen 1963; Surwillo and Quilter 1964; Neal and Pearson 1966; Tune 1966a and 1966b); sex (Neal and Pearson 1966); intelligence (Kappauf and Powe 1959; Holcomb and Kirk 1965); general activity level (Baker 1959b), and temperament (Bakan 1959; Holcomb and Kirk 1965; Tune 1966b).

THEORIES OF VIGILANCE

Theories of vigilance, after almost twenty years, continue to be, for the most part, rather broadly drawn thematic statements. Their prime instigation has been the explanation of some particular aspect of a complex of phenomena and, as Broadbent (1964) has observed, none accounts for all of the data. As is the case with conceptualizations in many areas of psychology, they can be categorized into two general classes: S-R theories and cognitive theories. The former were prominant in the earlier period of theory-making while those currently competing for attention are largely of the cognitive type.

The earliest theory of vigilance was N. Mackworth's (1950) Pavlovian explanation of the vigilance decrement. The deterioration of performance over time Mackworth associated with internal inhibition. The rapid recovery of performance following interruption he attributed to disinhibition. A major difficulty of this early formulation was that it associated greater performance decrements with high rather than low signal rates, a prediction denied by the facts. Furthermore, it is difficult to accept task interruptions as bona fide disinhibitors.

Another early attempt to explain vigilance is found in Broadbent's filter theory (1953). According to this approach, the monitor is conceived of as a system for selecting stimuli, with selection criteria being related to the physical intensity of stimuli, their biological importance, and their novelty. Decrement is explained in terms of reduced novelty. Recovery following the interpolation of stimuli is accounted for in the same terms. The failure of the decrement to appear in the performance of complex tasks is associated with shifts in stimulus priority and the maintenance of novelty. But as Frankmann and Adams (1962) have observed, many of Broadbent's explanations of specific data associated with this point of view appear to be *ad hoc* formulations rather than deductions from filter theory.

McCormack (1962), meanwhile, has advanced an inhibition-motivation theory of vigilance. His initial concern was to account for the performance decrement associated with the withholding of knowledge of results. To achieve this he assumed the operation of three intervening variables: inhibition that develops in the absence of reinforcement, drive level, and constitutional factors. Response to a signal depends both upon the strength of excitatory processes associated with the latter two variables and upon the strength of the former. The development of a decrement in response latency with time in the vigil reflects the growth of the former. The reduction of latency with the interpolation of rest or other activity is identified as the dissipation of inhibition and shorter response latencies with fixed interval schedules are attributed to an assumed increase in drive level associated with these schedules. In a reexamination of his formulation after a period of five years, McCormack (1967) advances the view that it may be extended to include data on signal detection as well, if one confines the approach to studies involving visual signals occurring at infrequent intervals over periods of up to 3 hours. Stable performance, he reiterates, depends upon the availability of knowledge of results. When it is absent, inhibition builds up. Furthermore, he assumes knowledge of results to have motivational as well as informational properties, so that even when the withdrawal of KR induces decrement, overall performance may remain high.

Bergum and Klein (1961), dissatisfied with the inability of classical conditioning theory to accommodate motivational variables, have taken recourse to Spencian learning theory to explain vigilance. Vigilance behavior is conceived of as chains of serially dependent responses and fractional responses, with each serving as the stimulus for the next in the sequence. When any component in the series is not reinforced, there is a tendency toward inhibition of the fractional responses with a resultant reduction in response probability or a generalization of inhibition from the fractional responses to the responses. In addition, performance reflects differences in both the magnitude and frequency of reinforcement.

Interest in the activation theory of vigilance has persisted and grown in recent years as part of a wider interest in the role of brain stem mechanisms in arousal. It was first suggested by Deese (1955) and developed by Scott (1957). It associates vigilance with the monitor's general level of alertness, a condition related by theorists to variations in sensory input. Invariant input, a condition that characterizes the vigil, leads to adaptation and a reduction in vigilance. This is how the decrement occurs. In contrast, when multiple tasks are involved, as when active tasks are used to break the vigil into shorter periods, the decrement is expected to be reduced or even removed. In an early study, Adams, Stenson, and Humes (1961), found a slight decrement in response latency for a simple vigilance task but none for a complex task. On the other hand, Adams and Boulter (1962) induced head and leg movements during monitoring and obtained no reduction in the decrement. But again, in contrast, Kirk and Hecht (1963) have described an improvement of performance in the presence of variable intensity ambient noise. Meanwhile, Bakan and Manley (1963) have reported better performance in an auditory vigilance task by blindfolded subjects than by subjects with normal opportunities for visual stimulation. And Alluisi and Hall (1963) obtained a vigilance decrement even though their subjects were simultaneously engaged in six different tasks. Similarly, Wiener, Poock, and Steele (1964) found no difference between a control group in a visual monitoring task and groups monitoring in the face of random noise or monitoring while performing mental arithmetic. Meanwhile, Gulian (1966) has reported a greater number of errors of omission in auditory vigilance under conditions either of quiet or of loud intermittent noise than under other conditions of background stimulation. Background noise also produces an increase in response latency (Gulian, 1967), the extent of the effect depending more on the type of noise than its intensity. In contrast, Smith, Myers, and Murphy (1967) describe superior auditory vigilance during four days of quiet, dark sensory deprivation. Zuercher (1965) had subjects stand, stretch, and breathe deeply or converse with the experimenter during a 48-minute vigil, and he observed that performance improved under both of these conditions.

In an attempt to clarify these contradictions, Bevan, Avant, and Lankford (1967) had subjects perform a simple detection task under conditions of both interpolated activity and inactivity. In addition to a control group, there were groups that engaged in vigorous physical exercise for five minutes every 30, others that solved anagrams, still others that were subjected to sensory restriction. Unlike the control, all of the experimental groups performed the vigilance task at a high level, and with no decrement, throughout. What the three experimental conditions had in common, in contrast to the control, is that they represented a change in what was otherwise an invariant and relatively monotonous routine. Thus, in considering the relation between alertness and performance one does well to think less in terms of energy levels and more in terms of monotony, less in terms of variety and more in terms of change. Specifically relevant is Gruber's (1964) observation that the alternation of visual and auditory signals led to better performance than either type alone or even both together. After a thoughtful examination of the activation concept and certain studies representative of it, Jerison (1967) has concluded that it is so broadly and vaguely stated that it can be made to accommodate almost any data that confronts it. This state is worsened by the uncritical and vague way it has been interpreted by investigators who have sought to apply it. Thus, Jerison points out that it is important to recognize that vigilance, like other behavioral functions, consists of multiple phases and one must consider the role of arousal in the light of these phases. For example, he ventures the view that the activation system has no effect on the purely sensory aspects of the vigilance task. On the other hand, aspects of the detection-indicating response are quite probably affected by activation level and more discriminating experiments continue to be in order.

When Broadbent (1964) observed that no theory of vigilance accounts for all vigilance phenomena, he also identified signal detection theory as the most likely candidate for future success. Indeed, Jerison and Pickett (1963) had already identified signal detection theory as a means of verifying the importance of observing responses in vigilance. This optimism about signal detection theory stems as much from its methods as from its conceptual orientation, for it allows the experimenter to differentiate between basic sensitivity and response criteria as determinants of the decrement. As indicated earlier, a number of investigators (Broadbent and Gregory 1963a, and 1965; Colquhoun and Baddeley 1964; Loeb and Binford 1964; Loeb, Hawkes, Evans, and Alluisi 1965; Jerison, Pickett, and Stenson 1965) all point to an increasing strictness in the detection criterion, as measured by beta, rather than decreasing sensitivity, as measured by d', as the basis for the decrement. Meanwhile, others (J. Mackworth and Taylor 1963; J. Mackworth 1964a, 1965a, 1965c) also report a significant decrement in d' over time. J. Mackworth (1968) speculates that this discrepancy in results is due to the rate at which background events occur. Her view is supported by the finding that d' displayed a decrement with a rapid but not with a slow event rate (J. Mackworth 1965b). The evidence of Taub and Osborne (1968) suggests that stimulus rate is more important for vigilance than either signal rate or signal probability. Meanwhile, there is evidence of actual improvement in d' over sessions (Binford and Loeb 1966; Colquhoun, 1966). However, Taylor (1967) cautions that signal detection measures must be used with care. He points out that in vigilance experiments the ROC curve will be markedly skewed, causing *d'* and beta both to be elevated with the result that any correlation between the two should be interpreted only in the context of the curve itself.

The beginnings of the cognitive approach to vigilance are represented by the work of Deese (1955) and Baker (1959a). In the earlier formulation Deese recognized two classes of independent variables: activation level and expectancy. Reference already has been made to the former. In the case of the latter, it is shaped by the pattern of the monitor's task-related experiences and in turn constitutes the set of assumptions that orients him in future encounters with the task. This approach predicts a higher rate of signal detection with fast than with slow rates, a fact borne out by a number of studies in the literature, and a better level of performance with regular than with irregular schedules, a relationship confirmed by Bevan, Hardesty, and Avant (1965). Baker (1959a) has extended the expectancy approach to include five classes of variable: average signal rate, regularity of intersignal interval, knowledge of results, knowledge of signal location, and signal intensity. For example, he (1962) has confirmed the fact that detection efficiency is greatest when the signal occurs after the mean interval duration and is poorer as the intersignal interval is greater or less than this value, a relationship also confirmed for response latency by Hardesty and Bevan (1965). It, therefore, was a small step for Bevan (1967) to suggest a further formalization of the expectancy approach to vigilance in terms of the model of adaptation-level theory. This approach through AL theory involves a two-factor model in which both arousal and expectancy are viewed as the product of the interaction of focal, background, and residual stimulation. Except for one experiment on activity level and vigilance (Bevan, Avant, and Lankford, 1967), the experimental test of this approach has been directed toward the relationship between expectancy and response latency. The paradigm for all experiments has been a modification of one devised by Mowrer, Rayman, and Bliss (1940) for their study of the central locus of set. In this the subject is exposed to an invariant sequence of signals followed without notice by a critical or test signal introduced under some condition of variation.

In an initial experiment, Hardesty and Bevan (1965) presented their subjects with brief flashes on one of three fixed-interval schedules followed by a single flash at one of five test intervals. When the difference between response latency on the test trial and average response latency for the adaptation sequence (ΔRL) was plotted against test-interval duration, it did not differ perceptibly from zero when the test interval coincided with the duration of the series intervals but increased in monotonic fashion as the test interval was either shorter or longer. In a second experiment, the fixed-interval adaptation sequences were replaced by variable-interval sequences with the interval durations on the average equal to those of the fixed-interval schedules. Results were the same. The experimental strategy was then changed slightly in a third experiment. All subjects received a schedule of intersignal intervals having a different mean, mode, and mid-range duration, with a third of the subjects receiving a test interval at each of these values. Since Adaptation Level Theory assumes an integrative process, it predicts that ΔRL will be shortest when test duration coincides with the average duration for the adaptation sequence. Simple expectancy theory, based on probabilistics, predicts a minimal ΔRL for the modal duration. Finally, if the monitor's strategy is to minimize

error in his prediction of interval duration for a randomly ordered variable sequence, then the midrange provides a reasonable standard. When ΔRLs were compared for these three test conditions, those associated with the mean intervals were significantly shorter than those for mode and midrange, which, in turn, did not differ from each other.

Bevan, Avant, and Lankford (1966) then examined the pooling strategy further by varying the shape of the frequency distribution of intervals in the adaptation sequence while mean duration, range of durations, and number of interval sizes involved were held constant. Their results indicated no relationship between the statistical shape of the schedule and ΔRL, an outcome which again emphasized the role of pooling in the establishment of the response norm.

Having been convinced that the pooling model of adaptation-level theory can competently describe the role of expectancy in determining response latency to simple signals, Bevan, Bell, and Taylor (1966) undertook an examination of ΔRL when the test trial represented variation in a substantive property of the signal. This involved a replication of the three experiments just described with change in pitch of the test signal as the independent variable. Results were consistent with those of the previous series; ΔRL increased as the discrepancy between the pitch or average pitch of the adaptation sequence and that of the test tone increased. In addition, however, it was found that when the discrepancy exceeded a certain magnitude, ΔRL dropped back to zero. This reversal, Bevan, Bell, and Taylor suggest, may have resulted from a change in the monitor's assumptions about the nature of the experimental task. When the test pitch was too widely discrepant to be identified as a member of the to-be-pooled class of pitches, the monitor may have resolved this cognitive dissonance by redefining the task as one of responding to tones rather than to pitches.

From the study of the mechanism of expectancy in terms of the "when" and "what" of signals as sequelae, Bevan and his colleagues more recently have turned to a consideration of the "where" of signals. In an experiment (Bevan and Avant 1969) involving the paradigm of the Bevan, Avant, and Lankford (1966) experiment, subjects were presented a horizontal line of five lights and asked to respond to a momentary brightening at one or the other of the several locations. Test signals appeared either at the middle or at one or the other of the two end positions. In line with expectation, ΔRL was lower for the middlemost (mean) position than for either extreme. A second experiment employed the design of Experiment Three of the Hardesty and Bevan (1965) sequence. All subjects received a skewed distribution of signal locations with mean differing from the midrange position and with the modal position at a third location. When test signals were arranged at each of these three average positions, ΔRL for the mean location was shorter than for either of the other two.

Recent research by Kagan (1968) on the maintenance of attention in very young children bears on this same point. Four-month-olds looked longer at the photographs of a face, regular or disfigured, then at randomly generated shapes, a difference in performance not present at birth. Furthermore, when stimuli of increasing irregularity were shown to verbalizing children of different ages, the older children devoted longer attention to the more discrepant stimuli than did the younger. A regular face or body elicited the longest fixation in one-year-olds while a "scrambled" face or body provoked the longest fixation in three-year-olds. In still another experiment three-month-old children were exposed at home to a mobile almost daily for about a month and then taken to the laboratory where they were shown the original mobile plus three transformations they had never seen. Cardiac deceleration was used as the measure of attention and the magnitude of deceleration was greater for the transformations than for the original stimulus and maximal for second and third order transformations. The development of these attentional mechanisms Kagan relates explicitly to the principle of Adaptation Level.

Summary

It should be evident to the reader that probably no integrative summary can be written yet for the literature that has been discussed in this chapter. One major reason for this is that there has been relatively little cross-fertilization of ideas among workers in the various areas that have been covered. Indeed, there is little conceptual communality from one area to another. For example, attention probably does not mean the same thing to a researcher in vigilance that it does to one in selective listening. Underlying this diversity of method and theory is the very serious problem that much of the scientific meaning of the word "attention" has devrived from the common language usage of the word. It is a catchall phrase that is so vague as to permit a great variety of interpretations to be placed on it. Until this semantic problem is resolved in such a way as to allow more exact definition of terms, the field of attention will continue to be a hodgepodge.

Acknowledgment. Work on this chapter was supported by grants from the National Science Foundation (GB-5287) and the Office of Education (OEG-3-9-300284-0037(010), and by Contract N00014-67-A-0163-001 between The Johns Hopkins University and the Physiological Psychology Branch, Office of Naval Research. The authors would like to thank Donald Broadbent, Neville Moray, Donald Norman, and George Sperling for their thoughtful comments on portions of this paper. The section on the selective properties of attention is chiefly the responsibility of H. E., while the section on the intensive properties of attention is chiefly the responsibility of W. B. The literature review was completed in May, 1969.

Appendix I

The following references will provide the interested reader with an introduction to some areas of research that were not covered in the present chapter.

ATTENTION IN LEARNING

KAMIN, L. "Attention-like" processes in classical conditioning. *In* JONES, M. R. (ed.), *Miami symposium on the prediction of behavior 1967: Aversive stimulation.* Coral Gables, Fla.: University of Miami Press, 1968.
MACKINTOSH, N. J. Selective attention in animal discrimination learning. *Psychological Bulletin*, 1965, *64*, 124–50.

TRABASSO, T., and G. H. BOWER *Attention in learning: Theory and research.* New York: John Wiley, 1968.

PHYSIOLOGICAL CORRELATES OF ATTENTION

HERNÁNDEZ-PEÓN, R., H. SCHERRER, and M. JOUVET. Modication of electric activity in cochlear nucleus during "attention" in unanesthetized cats. *Science*, 1956, *123*, 331–32.
——— Recticular mechanisms of sensory control. *In* W. A. ROSENBLITH (ed.), *Sensory communication*, pp. 497–520. New York: John Wiley, 1961.
HORN, G. Physiological and psychological aspects of selective perception. *In* D. S. LEHRMAN, R. A. HINDE, & E. SHAW (eds.), *Advances in the study of behavior*, vol. 1, pp. 155–215. New York: Academic Press, 1965.
WORDEN, F. G. Attention and auditory electrophysiology. *In* E. STELLER, and J. M. SPRAGUE (eds.), *Progress in physiological psychology*, pp. 45–116. New York: Academic Press, 1966.

ORIENTATION REACTION

LYNN, R. *Attention, arousal and the orientation reaction.* New York: Pergamon Press, 1966.
SOKOLOV, E. N. *Perception and the conditioned reflex.* New York: Macmillan, 1963.

ATTENTION AS AN EXPRESSION OF COGNITIVE STYLE

Chapters 77, 78, 79, 80 on selective exposure to information. *In* ABELSON, R. P.; ARONSON, E.; MCGUIRE, W. J.; NEWCOMB, T. M.; ROSENBERG, M. J.; and TANNEBAUM, P. H. (eds.), *Theories of cognitive consistency: a sourcebook.* Chicago: Rand McNally, 1968.
GARDNER, R. W.; HOLTZMAN, P. S.; KLEIN, G. S.; LINTON, H.; and SPENCE, D. P. Cognitive control: A study of individual consistencies in cognitive behavior. *Psychological Issues*, 1959, *1*, No. 4.
WACHTEL, P. L. Conceptions of broad and narrow attention. *Psychological Bulletin*, 1967, *68*, 417–29.

References

ADAMS, J. A. Vigilance in the detection of low-intensity visual stimuli. *Journal of Experimental Psychology*, 1956, *52*, 204–8.
——— and BOULTER, L. R. An evaluation of the activationist hypothesis of human vigilance. *Journal of Experimental Psychology*, 1962, *64*, 495–504.
ADAMS, J. A.; HUMES, J. M.; and SIEVEKING, N. A. Monitoring of complex visual display: V. Effects of repeated sessions and heavy visual load on human vigilance. *Human Factors*, 1963, *4*, 385–89.
ADAMS, J. A.; HUMES, J. M.; and STENSON, H. H. Monitoring of complex visual displays: III. Effects of repeated sessions on human vigilance. *Human Factors*, 1962, *4*, 149–58.
——— Monitoring of complex visual displays: II. Effects of visual load and response complexity on human vigilance. *Human Factors*, 1961, *3*, 213–21.
ADAMS, O. S., and CHILES, W. D. Human performance as a function of the work-rest ratio during prolonged confinement. *USAF ASD Technical Report.*, no. 61–720, 1961.
ALLUISI, E. A., and HALL, T. J. Declines in auditory vigilance during period of high multiple-task activity. *Perceptual and Motor Skills*, 1963, *16*, 739–40.
ANTONELLI, D. C., and KARAS, G. G. Performance on a vigilance task under conditions of true and false knowledge of results. *Perceptual and Motor Skills*, 1967, *25*, 129–38.
ANTROBUS, J. S., and SINGER, J. L. Visual signal detection as a function of sequential variability of simultaneous speech. *Journal of Experimental Psychology*, 1964, *68*, 603–10.

ARCHER, E. J. Identification of visual patterns as a function of information load. *Journal of Experimental Psychology*, 1954, *48*, 313–17.

AVERBACH, E., and CORIELL, A. S. Short-term memory in vision. *Bell System Technical Journal*, 1961, *40*, 309–28.

BAKAN, P. Extroversion-introversion and improvement in an auditory vigilance task. *British Journal of Psychology*, 1959, *50*, 325–32.

—— *Attention.* Princeton: Van Nostrand, 1966.

—— and MANLEY, R. Effects of visual displays during a vigilance task: I. Biasing attention. *British Journal of Psychology*, 1963, *54*, 115–19.

BAKER, C. H. Toward a theory of vigilance. *Canadian Journal of Psychology*, 1959a, *13*, 35–41.

—— Attention to visual displays during a vigilance task: II. Maintaining the level of vigilance. *British Journal of Psychology*, 1959b, *50*, 30–36.

—— Probability of signal detection in a vigilance task. *Science*, 1962, *136*, 46–47.

—— Signal duration as a factor in vigilance tasks. *Science*, 1963, *141*, 1196–97.

BAKER, K. H. Pre-experimental set in distraction experiments. *Journal of General Psychology*, 1937, *16*, 471–78.

BAKER, R. A., WARE, J. R., and SIPOWICZ, R. R. Vigilance: A comparison in auditory, visual and combined audio-visual tasks. *Canadian Journal of Psychology*, 1962a, *16*, 192–98.

—— Sustained vigilance I: Signal detection during a 24-hour continuous watch. *Psychological Record*, 1962b, *12*, 245–50.

BERGUM, B. O., and KLEIN, I. C. A survey and analysis of vigilance research. *HumRRO Research Report* no. 8, 1961, 1–56.

BERGUM, B. O., and LEHR, D. J. Vigilance as a function of task and environmental variables. *HumRRO Research Report* no. 11, 1963a, 1–32.

—— Endspurt in vigilance. *Journal of Experimental Psychology*, 1963b, *66*, 383–85.

BEVAN, W. Behavior in unusual environments. In H. HELSON, and W. BEVAN (eds.), *Contemporary Approaches to Psychology*, pp. 409–11. Princeton: Van Nostrand, 1967.

——, and AVANT, L. L. Serial reaction-time and the changing location of successive signals. Unpublished manuscript. Johns Hopkins University, 1969.

——; and LANKFORD, H. G. Serial reaction-time and the temporal pattern of prior signals. *American Journal of Psychology*, 1966, *79*, 551–59.

—— Influence of interpolated periods of activity and inactivity upon the vigilance decrement. *Journal of Applied Psychology*, 1967, *51*, 352–56.

BEVAN, W.; BELL, R. A.; and TAYLOR, C. Changes in response latency following shifts in the pitch of a signal. *Journal of Experimental Psychology*, 1966, *72*, 864–68.

BEVAN, W.; HARDESTY, D. L.; and AVANT, L. L. Response latency with constant and variable interval schedules. *Perceptual and Motor Skills*, 1965, *20*, 969–72.

BEVAN, W., and TURNER, E. D. Assimilation and contrast in the estimation of number. *Journal of Experimental Psychology*, 1964, *67*, 458–62.

—— Vigilance performance with a qualitative shift in reinforcers. *Journal of Experimental Psychology*, 1965, *70*, 83–86.

—— Vigilance performance with a qualitative shift in verbal reinforcers. *Journal of Experimental Psychology*, 1966, *71*, 467–68.

BILLINGS, M. L. The duration of attention. *Psychological Review*, 1914, *21*, 227–51.

BINFORD, J. R., and LOEB, M. Monitoring readily detected auditory signals and detection of obscure visual signals. *Perceptual and Motor Skills*, 1963, *17*, 735–46.

—— Changes within and over repeated sessions in criterion and effective sensitivity in an auditory vigilance task. *Journal of Experimental Psychology*, 1966, *72*, 339–45.

BORING, E. G. Attributes and sensation. *American Journal of Psychology*, 1924, *35*, 301–4.

BOULTER, L. R., and ADAMS, J. A. Vigilance decrement, the expectancy hypothesis, and intersignal interval. *Canadian Journal of Psychology*, 1963, *17*, 201–9.

BOWDITCH, H. P., and WARREN, J.W. The knee-jerk and its physiological modifications. *Journal of Physiology*, 1890, *11*, 25–64.

BROADBENT, D. E. Classical conditioning and human watch-keeping. *Psychological Review*, 1953, *60*, 331–39.

—— The role of auditory localization in attention and memory span. *Journal of Experimental Psychology*, 1954, *47*, 191–96.

—— Perception and Communication. London: Pergamon Press, 1958.

—— Vigilance. *British Medical Bulletin*, 1964, *20*, 17–20.

—— Word-frequency effect and response bias. *Psychological Review*, 1967, *74*, 1–15.

——, and GREGORY, M. Vigilance considered as a statistical decision. *British Journal of Psychology*, 1963a, *54*, 309–23.

—— Division of attention and the decision theory of signal detection. *Proceedings of the Royal Society* (B), 1963b, *158*, 222–32.

—— Effects of noise and of signal rate upon vigilance analyzed by means of decision theory. *Human Factors*, 1965, 7, 155–62.

BROVERMAN, D. M. Dimensions of cognitive style. *Journal of Personality*, 1960, *28*, 167–85.

BROWN, J. Evidence for a selective process during perception of tachistoscopically presented stimuli. *Journal of Experimental Psychology*, 1960, *59*, 176–81.

BRUNER, J. S. and MINTURN, A. L. Perceptual identification and perceptual organization. *Journal of General Psychology*, 1955, *53*, 21–28.

BUCKNER, D. N., and MCGRATH, J. J. A comparison of performance on single and dual sensory mode vigilance tasks. Human Factors Research, Los Angeles, *Technical Report* No. 8, 1961.

BUSWELL, G. T. *How people look at pictures.* Chicago: University of Chicago Press, 1935.

CASON, H. The influence of attitude and distraction. *Journal of Experimental Psychology*, 1938, *22*, 532–46.

CESAREC, Z., and NILSSON, L. Level of activation and figure-ground reversal: Inter-individual comparisons. *Psychological Research Bulletin*, 1963, *3*, (6), 1–11.

—— Level of activation and figure-ground reversal: Intra-individual comparisons. *Psychological Research Bulletin*, 1964, *3* (7), 1–16.

CHAPMAN, D. W. Relative effects of determinate and inderminate *Aufgaben. American Journal of Psychology*, 1932, *44*, 163–74.

CHENEY, C., and EATON, P. Visual and auditory signal detection. *Psychonomic Science*, 1968, *10*, 301–2.

CHERRY, E. C. Some experiments on the recognition of speech with one and two ears. *Journal of the Acoustical Society of America*, 1953, *25*, 975–79.

CHINN, R. M., and ALLUISI, E. A. Effect of three kinds of knowledge-of-results information on three measures of vigilance performance. *Perceptual and Motor Skills*, 1964, *18*, 901–12.

COLQUHOUN, W. P. Training for vigilance: A comparison of different techniques. *Human Factors*, 1966, *8*, 7–12.

——, and BADDELEY, A. D. Role of pretest expectancy in vigilance decrement. *Journal of Experimental Psychology*, 1964, *68*, 156–60.

DALLENBACH, K. M., and CASSELL, E. E. The effect of auditory distraction upon the sensory reaction. *American Journal of Psychology*, 1918, *29*, 129–43.

DEESE, J. Some problems in the theory of vigilance. *Psychological Review*, 1955, *62*, 359–68.

—— Changes in visual performance after visual work. *WADC Technical Report.* No. 57–285, 1957.

——, and ORMOND, E. Studies of detectability during continuous visual search. *WADC Technical Report* No. 53–8, 1953.

DEMBER, W. N. *The psychology of perception.* New York: Holt, Rinehart, & Winston, 1960.

DEUTSCH, J. A., and DEUTSCH, D. Attention: Some theoretical considerations. *Psychological Review*, 1963, *70*, 80–90.

DITCHBURN, R. W. Some factors affecting efficiency of work of lookouts. Admiralty Great Britain, Rep. no. APL/RI/84.46/0, 1943.

EGAN, J. P.; CARTERETTE, E. C.; and THWING, E. J. Some factors affecting multi-channel listening. *Journal of the Acoustical Society of America*, 1954, *26*, 774–82.

EGETH, H. Parallel versus serial processes in multidimension stimulus discrimination. *Perception and Psychophysics*, 1966, *1*, 245–252.

—— Selective attention. *Psychological Bulletin*, 1967, *67*, 41–57.

——; BLECKER, D. L.; and KAMLER, A. S. Verbal interference in a perceptual comparison task. *Perception and Psychophysics*, 1969, *6*, 355–56.

EGETH, H., and PACHELLA, R. Multidimensional stimulus identification. *Perception and Psychophysics*, 1969, *5*, 341–46.

———— and SMITH, E. E. Perceptual selectivity in a visual recognition task. *Journal of Experimental Psychology*, 1967, *74*, 543–49.

EPSTEIN, W., and ROCK, I. Perceptual set as an artifact of recency. *American Journal of Psychology*, 1960, *73*, 214–28.

ERIKSEN, C. W., and JOHNSON, H. J. Storage and decay characteristics of nonattended auditory stimuli. *Journal of Experimental Psychology*, 1964, *68*, 28–36.

EVANS, J. E. The effect of distraction on reaction time. *Archives of Psychology*, 1916 (whole no. 37) 1–106.

EYSENCK, H. J., and THOMPSON, W. The affects of distraction on pursuit rotor learning: performance and reminiscence. *British Journal of Psychology*, 1966, *57*, 99–106.

FENDRICK, P. The influence of music distraction on reading efficiency. *Journal of Educational Psychology*, 1937, *31*, 264–71.

FERÉ, C. S. *Sensation et mouvement*. Paris: F. Alcan, 1899.

FITTS, P. M., and BIEDERMAN, I. S-R compatibility and information reduction. *Journal of Experimental Psychology*, 1965, *69*, 408–12.

FITTS, P. M., and DEININGER, R. L. S-R compatibility: Correspondence among paired elements within stimulus and response codes. *Journal of Experimental Psychology*, 1954, *48*, 483–92.

FORD, A. Attention-automatization: an investigation of the transitional nature of the mind. *American Journal of Psychology*, 1929, *41*, 1–32.

FRANKMANN, J., and ADAMS, J. A. Theories of vigilance. *Psychological Bulletin*, 1962, *59*, 257–72.

FREEMAN, F. N. *Experimental education*. Boston: Houghton-Mifflin, 1916.

FRIED, C. A study of the effects of continuous wave jamming on the detection of antiaircraft operations center symbols. *USA Ordinance Human Engineering Laboratory Technical Memo*, Nos. 59–9, 1–27, 1959.

GLANVILLE, A. D., and DALLENBACH, K. M. The range of attention. *American Journal of Psychology*, 1929, *41*, 207–36.

GLEN, J. S. Ocular movements in reversibility of perspective. *Journal of General Psychology*, 1940, *23*, 243–81.

GOULD, J. D., and SCHAFFER, A. Visual monitoring of multi-channel displays. *IEEE Transactions on Human Factors in Electronics*, 1966, *72*, 69–76.

GREGG, L. W. The effect of stimulus complexity on discriminative responses. *Journal of Experimental Psychology*, 1954, *48*, 289–97.

GRINGER, W. W. Some effects of distraction in rote learning. *American Journal of Psychology*, 1952, *65*, 594–96.

GRUBER, A. Sensory alternation and performance in a vigilance task. *USAF ESD Technical Document Report* No. 63–605, 1963.

GULIAN, E. Effects of noise on an auditory vigilance task. *Revue Roumaine des Sciences Sociales*. Série de Psychologie, 1966, *10*, 175–86.

———— Effects of noise on reaction time and induced muscular tension in an auditory vigilance task. *Revue Roumaine des Sciences Sociales*. Série de Psychologie, 1967, *11*, 33–45.

GUILFORD, J. P. "Fluctuation of attention" with weak visual stimuli. *American Journal of Psychology*, 1927, *38*, 534–83.

HABER, R. N. A replication of selective attention and coding in visual perception. *Journal of Experimental Psychology*, 1964, *67*, 402–4.

———— The nature of the effect of set on perception. *Psychological Review*, 1966, *73*, 335–50.

HALL, T. J.; PASSEY, G. E.; and MEIGHAN, T. W. Performance of vigilance and monitoring task as a function of work load. *USAF AMRL Technical Report* No. 65–622, 1965.

HARABEDIAN, A.; MCGRATH, J. J.; and BUCKNER, D. N. The probability of signal detection in a vigilance task as a function of inter-signal interval. Human Factors Research, Los Angeles, *Technical Report* No. 3, 1960.

HARDESTY, D., and BEVAN, W. Forms of orally-presented knowledge of results and serial reaction time. *Psychological Record*, 1964, *14*, 445–48.

———— Response latency as a function of the temporal pattern of stimulation. *Psychological Record*, 1965, *15*, 385–92.

HARDESTY, D.; TRUMBO, D.; and BEVAN, W. Influence of knowledge of results on performance in a monitoring task. *Perceptual Motor Skills*, 1963, *16*, 629–34.

HARRIS, C. S., and HABER, R. N. Selective attention and coding in visual perception. *Journal of Experimental Psychology*, 1963, *65*, 328–33.

HEBB, D. O. *Organization of behavior*. New York: John Wiley, 1949.

HENDERSON, M. T.; CREWS, A.; and BARLOW, J. A study of the effect of music distraction on reading efficiency. *Journal of Applied Psychology*, 1945, *29*, 313–17.

HENNEMAN, R. H.; LEWIS, P.; and MATTHEWS, T. L. The influence of the sensory requirements of the distracting task. (The first of a series of reports on auditory and visual message presentation under distracting task conditions.) *USAF, WADD Technical Report* No. 53–309, 1953, 1–20.

HERNÁNDEZ-PEÓN, R.; SCHERRER, H.; and JOUVET, M. Modification of electrical activity in cochlear nucleus during "attention" in unanesthetised cats. *Science*, 1956, *123*, 331–32.

HIRSH, I. J. The relation between localization and intelligibility. *Journal of the Acoustical Society of America*, 1950, *22*, 196–200.

HODGE, M. H. The influence of irrelevant information upon complex visual discrimination. *Journal of Experimental Psychology*, 1959, *57*, 1–5.

HOFFMAN, J. Experimentell-psychologische Untersuchungen über Leseleistungen von Schulkindern. *Archiv für die gesamte Psychologie*, 1927, *58*, 325–88.

HOLCOMB, G. G., and KIRK, R. E. Organismic variables as predictors of vigilance behavior. *Perceptual and Motor Skills*, 1965, *21*, 547–52.

HOLLAND, J. G. Human vigilance. *Science*, 1958, *128*, 61–63.

HOVEY, H. B. Effects of general distraction on the higher thought process. *American Journal of Psychology*, 1928, *40*, 585–91.

HOWELL, W. C., and BRIGGS, G. E. The effects of visual noise and locus of perturbation on tracking performance. *Journal of Experimental Psychology*, 1959, *58*, 166–73.

HUNTER, W. S., and SIGLER, M. The span of visual discrimination as a function of time and intensity of stimulation. *Journal of Experimental Psychology*, 1940, *26*, 160–79.

IMAE, K., and TAKEUCHI, Y. Perception and recall of the series of approximation to Japanese. *Japanese Journal of Psychology*, 1959, *30*, 166–77.

IMAI, S., and GARNER, W. R. Discriminability and preference for attributes in free and constrained classification. *Journal of Experimental Psychology*, 1965, *69*, 596–608.

JAMES, W. *Principles of psychology*. New York: Henry Holt, 1890.

JASPER, H. H. Electrical signs of cortical activity. *Psychological Bulletin*, 1937, *34*, 411–81.

JENKINS, H. M. The effect of signal rate on performance in visual monitoring. *American Journal of Psychology*, 1958, *71*, 647–61.

JERISON, H. J. Experiments on vigilance, duration of vigil and the decrement function. *USAF WADC Technical Report* No. 58–369, 1958.

———— Activation and long term performance. *Acta Psychologica*, 1967, *27*, 373–89.

————, and PICKETT, R. M. Vigilance: a review and reevaluation. *Human Factors*, 1963, *5*, 211–38.

———— The importance of the elicited observing rate. *Science*, 1964, *143*, 970–71.

JERISON, H. J. and STENSON, H. H. The elicited observing rate and decision processes in vigilance. *Human Behavior*, 1965, *7*, 107–28.

JERISON, H. J., and WALLIS, R. A. Experiments on vigilance: II. One-clock and three-clock monitoring. *WADC Technical Report* No. 57–206, 1957.

JOHNSON, E. M., and PAYNE, M. C. Vigilance: Effects of frequency of knowledge of results. *Journal of Applied Psychology*, 1966, *50*, 33–34.

JOHNSTON, W. A.; HOWELL, W. C.; and GOLDSTEIN, I. L. Human vigilance as a function of signal frequency and stimulus density. *Journal of Experimental Psychology*, 1966, *72*, 736–43.

JOHNSTON, W. A.; HOWELL, W. C.; and ZAJKOWSKI, M. M. Regulation of attention in complex displays. *Journal of Experimental Psychology*, 1967, *7*, 481–82.

KAGAN, J. On cultural deprivation. *In* GLASS, D. C. (ed.). *Environmental Influences*, pp. 211–250. New York: Rockefeller University Press, 1968.

KAPPAUF, W. E., and POWE, W. E. Performance decrement on an audio-visual checking task. *Journal of Experimental Psychology*, 1959, *57*, 49–56.

KAUFMAN, E. L.; LORD, M. W.; REESE, T. W.; and VOLKMAN, J. The discrimination of visual number. *American Journal of Psychology*, 1949, *62*, 498–525.

KERSTIN, S., and EYSENCK, H. J. Pursuit rotor performance as a function of different degrees of distraction. *Life Science*, 1965, *4*, 889–97.

KIDD, J. S., and MICOCCI, A. Maintenance of vigilance in an auditory monitoring. task. *Journal of Applied Psychology*, 1964, *48*, 13–15.

KIRK, R. E., and HECHT, E. Maintenance of vigilance by programmed noise. *Perceptual and Motor Skills*, 1963, *16*, 553–60.

KLEIN, G. S. Semantic power measured through the interference of words with color-naming. *American Journal of Psychology*, 1964, *77*, 576–88.

KÜLPE, O. Versuche über Abstraktion. Bericht über den Ie Kongresz für Experimentale Psychologie, 1904, 56–58.

LAIRD, D. A. Experiments on the physiological cost of noise. *Journal of the National Institute of Industrial Psychology*, 1929, *4*, 254–58.

LAWRENCE, D. H., and COLES, G. R. Accuracy of recognition with alternatives before and after the stimulus. *Journal of Experimental Psychology*, 1954, *47*, 208–14.

LAWRENCE, D. H., and LABERGE, D. L. Relationship between recognition accuracy and order of reporting stimulus dimensions. *Journal of Experimental Psychology*, 1956, *51*, 12–18.

LEVINE, J. M. The effects of values and costs on the detection and identification of signals in auditory vigilance. *Human Factors*, 1966, *8*, 525–37.

LICKLIDER, J. C. R. The influence of interaural phase relations upon the masking of speech by white noise. *Journal of the Acoustical Society of America*, 1948, *20*, 150–59.

LINDSLEY, D. B., (ed). Radar operator fatigue: The effects of length and repetition of operating periods on efficiency of performance. *Office of Scientific Research Development*, Report No. OSRD-3354, 1944.

—— Emotion. *In* S. S. STEVENS (ed.), *Handbook of Experimental Psychology*, pp. 473–516. New York: John Wiley, 1951.

LIVINGSTON, R. B. Brain mechanisms in conditioning and learning. *Neuroscience Research Progress Bulletin*, 1966, *4*, 235–347.

LOEB, M., and BINFORD, J. R. Vigilance for auditory intensity changes as a function of preliminary feedback and confidence level. *Human Factors*, 1964, *6*, 445–58.

LOEB, M., and HAWKES, G. R. The effect of rise and decay time on vigilance for weak auditory and continuous stimuli. *USA Medical Research Laboratory Report* No. 491, 1961.

—— Detection of difference in duration of acoustic and electrical cutaneous stimuli in a vigilance task. *Journal of Psychology*, 1962, *54*, 101–11.

LOEB, M.; HAWKES, G. R.; EVANS, W. O.; and ALLUISI, E. A. The influence of d-amphetamine, benactyzine and chlorpromazine on performance in an auditory vigilance task. *Psychonomic Science*, 1965, *3*, 29–30.

LOEB, M., and SCHMIDT, E. A. A comparison of the effects of different kinds of information in maintaining efficiency on an auditory monitoring task. *Ergonomics*, 1963, *6*, 75–81.

LOFCHIE, S. H. The performance of adults under distraction stress: A developmental approach. *Journal of Psychology*, 1955, *39*, 109–16.

LONG, E. R.; HENNEMAN, R. H.; and GARVEY, W. D. An experimental analysis of set: The role of sense modality. *American Journal of Psychology*, 1960, *73*, 563–67.

LONG, E. R.; REID, L. S.; and HENNEMAN, R. H. An experimental analysis of set: Variables influencing the identification of ambiguous visual stimulus objects. *American Journal of Psychology*, 1960, *73*, 553–62.

LOVELESS, N. E. Signal detection with simultaneous visual and auditory presentation. Air Ministry, London, Flying Personnel Research Committee, Report No. 1027, 1957.

LUCACCINI, L. F.; FREEDY, A. F.; and LYMAN, J. Motivational factors in vigilance: Effects of instructions on performance in a complex vigilance task. *Perceptual and Motor Skills*, 1968, *26*, 783–86.

MCCORMACK, P. D. A two-factor theory of vigilance. *British Journal of Psychology*, 1962, *53*, 357–63.

—— A two-factor theory of vigilance in the light of recent studies. *Acta Psychologica*, 1967, *27*, 400–9.

MACDOUGALL, R. On the influence of varying intensities and qualities of visual stimulation upon the rapidity of reactions to auditory stimuli. *American Journal of Physiology*, 1903, *19*, 9, 116–21.

MCGRATH, J. J. The effect of irrelevant environmental stimulation on vigilance performance. Human Factors Research, *Los Angeles, Technical Report* No. 6, 1960.

MACKWORTH, J. F. Performance decrement in vigilance, threshold determinations, and high speed perceptual motor tasks. *Canadian Journal of Psychology*, 1964a, *18*, 209–23.

—— The effect of true and false knowledge of results on the detectability of signals in a vigilance task. *Canadian Journal of Psychology*, 1964b, *18*, 106–17.

—— Decision interval and signal detectability in a vigilance task. *Canadian Journal of Psychology*, 1965a, *19*, 111–17.

—— Deterioration of signal detectability during a vigilance task as a function of background event rate. *Psychonomic Science*, 1965b, *3*, 421–22.

—— The effect of amphetamine on the detectability of signals in a vigilance task. *Canadian Journal of Psychology*, 1965c, *19*, 104–10.

—— Vigilance, arousal, and habituation. *Psychological Review*, 1968, *75*, 308–22.

——, and TAYLOR, M. M. The d' measures of signal detectability during vigilance-like situations. *Canadian Journal of Psychology*, 1963, *17*, 302–25.

MACKWORTH, N. H. Researches on the measurement of human performance. *Medical Research Council. Special Report* No. 268. London: H. M. Stationery Office, 1950.

MARTZ, R. L. Auditory vigilance as affected by signal rate and inter-signal interval variability. *Perceptual and Motor Skills*, 1967, *24*, 195–203.

MILLER, A. L., and BAKER, R. A. The effects of shape, size, heterogeneity, and instructional set on the judgment of visual number. *American Journal of Psychology*, 1968, *81*, 83–91.

MILLER, G. A. The magical number seven, plus or minus two: Some limits on our capacity for processing information. *Psychological Review*, 1956, *63*, 81–97.

MINTURN, A. L., and REESE, T. W. The effect of differential reinforcement on the discrimination of visual numbers. *Journal of Psychology*, 1951, *31*, 201–31.

MONTAGUE, W. E. Effect of irrelevant information on a complex auditory-discrimination task. *Journal of Experimental Psychology*, 1965, *69*, 230–36.

——, and WEBBER, C. E. Effects of knowledge of results and differential monetary reward on six uninterrupted hours of monitoring. *Human Factors*, 1965, *7*, 173–80.

MORAY, N. Attention in dichotic listening: Affective cues and the influence of instructions. *Quarterly Journal of Experimental Psychology*, 1959, *11*, 56–60.

——, and O'BRIEN, T. Signal-detection theory applied to selective listening. *Journal of the Acoustical Society of America*, 1967, *42*, 765–772.

MORGAN, B. B., JR., and ALLUISI, E. A. Effects of discriminability and irrelevant information on absolute judgments. *Perception and Psychophysics*, 1967, *2*, 54–58.

MORGAN, J. J. B. Overcoming of distractions and other resistances. *Archives of Psychology*, 1916 (whole no. 35) 1–84.

MORIN, R. E.; FORRIN, B.; and ARCHER, W. Information processing behavior: The role of irrelevant stimulus information. *Journal of Experimental Psychology*, 1961, *61*, 89–96.

MORUZZI, G. Synchronizing influences of the brain stem and the inhibitory mechanisms underlying the production of sleep by sensory stimulation. *In* JASPER, H. A. and SMIRNOV, G. D. (eds.). Moscow Colloquium on electroencephalography of higher nervous activity. *EEG and Clinical Neurophysiology*, suppl. no. 13, 1960.

——, and MAGOUN, H. W. Brain stem reticular formation and activation of the EEG. *EEG and Clinical Neurophysiology*, 1949, *1*, 455–73.

MOWRER, O. H.; RAYMAN, N.; and BLISS, E. L. Preparatory set (expectancy)—an experimental demonstration of its central locus. *Journal of Experimental Psychology*, 1940, *26*, 357–61.

MURPHY, R. E. Effects of threat of shock, distraction and task design on performance. *Journal of Experimental Psychology*, 1959, *59*, 134–41.

NALVEN, F. B. Relationship between digit space and distractability ratings in emotionally disturbed children. *Journal of Clinical Psychology*, 1967, *23*, 466–67.

NEAL, G. L., and PEARSON, R. G. Comparative effects of age, sex, and drugs upon two tasks of auditory vigilance. *Perceptual and Motor Skills*, 1966, *23*, 967–74.

NEISSER, U. Decision time without reaction time: Experiments in visual scanning. *American Journal of Psychology*, 1963, *76*, 376–85.

——— Experiments in visual search and their theoretical implications. Paper read at Psychonomic Society, Niagara Falls, October 1964.

——— *Cognitive psychology*. New York: Appleton-Century-Crofts, 1967.

———; NOVICK, R.; and LAZAR, R. Searching for ten targets simultaneously. *Perceptual and Motor Skills*, 1963, *17*, 955–61.

NORMAN, D. A. Toward a theory of memory and attention. *Psychological Review*, 1968, *75*, 522–36.

——— *Memory and attention: An introduction to human information processing*. New York: John Wiley, 1969.

——— Memory while shadowing. *Quarterly Journal of Experimental Psychology*, 1969, *21*, 85–94.

OSBORN, W. C., SHELDON, R. W., and BAKER, R. A. Vigilance performance under conditions of redundant and nonredundant signal presentation. *Journal of Applied Psychology*, 1963, *47*, 130–34.

OSWALD, I.; TAYLOR, A.; and TREISMAN, M. Discrimination responses to stimulation during human sleep. *Brain*, 1960, *83*, 440–53.

PASCHAL, F. C. The trend in theories of attention. *Psychological Review*, 1941, *48*, 367–82.

PILLSBURY, W. B. *Attention*. New York: Macmillan, 1908.

POLLACK, I., and KNAFF, P. R. Maintenance of alertness by loud auditory signal. *Journal of the Acoustical Society of America*, 1958, *30*, 1013–16.

POSNER, M. I.; BOIES, S. J.; EICHELMAN, W. H.; and TAYLOR, R. L. Retention of visual and name codes of single letters. *Journal of Experimental Psychology Monograph*, 1967, *79*, no. 1, part 2.

PRITCHATT, D. An investigation into some of the underlying associative processes of the Stroop Colour Effect. *Quarterly Journal of Experimental Psychology*, 1968, *20*, 351–59.

REESE, E. P.; REESE, T. W.; VOLKMAN, J.; and CORBIN, H. H., eds. *Psychophysical research; summary report, 1946–1952*. U.S.N. Special Devices Center Technical Report No. SDC-131-1-5, 1953, 1–194.

ROBEY, T. B., and ROAZEN, H. Signal and channel load in vigilance tasks. *Perceptual and Motor Skills*, 1963, *16*, 641–47.

ROUSE, R. O., and MAAS, J. B. Interference with color naming as a function of degree of practice on the color bearing materials. Paper presented at the meeting of the Eastern Psychological Association, 1961.

SALTZMAN, I. J., and GARNER, W. R. Reaction-time as a measure of span of attention. *Journal of Psychology*, 1948, *25*, 227–41.

SCOTT, T. H. Literature review of the intellectual effects of perceptual isolation. *Defense Research Board of Canada*, report no. HR66, 1957.

SELFRIDGE, O. G. Pandemonium: A paradigm for learning. In *The mechanisation of thought processes*. London: H. M. Stationery Office, 1959.

———, and NEISSER, U. Pattern recognition by machine. *Scientific American*, August 1960, *203*, 60–68.

SMITH, K. R. Intermittent loud noise and mental performance. *Science*, 1951, *114*, 132–33.

SMITH, R. L.; LUCACCINI, L. F.; and EPSTEIN, M. H. Effects of monetary rewards and punishments on vigilance performance. *Journal of Applied Psychology*, 1967, *51*, 411–16.

SMITH, R. L.; LUCACCINI, L. F.; GROTH, H.; and LYMAN, J. Effects of anticipatory alerting signals and a compatible secondary task on vigilance performance. *Journal of Applied Psychology*, 1966, *50*, 240–46.

SMITH, S.; MYERS, T. I.; and MURPHY, D. B. Vigilance during sensory deprivation. *Perceptual and Motor Skills*, 1967, *24*, 971–76.

SPERLING, G. The information available in brief visual presentations. *Psychological Monographs*, 1960, *74* (11, whole no. 498), 1–29.

——— Successive approximations to a model for short term memory. *Acta Psychologica*, 1967, *27*, 285–92.

STEINFELD, G. J. Concepts of set and availability and their relation to the reorganization of ambiguous pictorial stimuli. *Psychological Review*, 1967, *74*, 505–22.

STERN, R. M. Performance and physiological arousal during two vigilance tasks varying in signal presentation rate. *Perceptual and Motor Skills*, 1966, *23*, 691–700.

STROOP, J. R. Studies of interference in serial verbal reactions. *Journal of Experimental Psychology*, 1935, *18*, 643–61.

SURWILLO, W. W., and QUILTER, R. Vigilance, age, and response-time. *American Journal of Psychology*, 1964, *77*, 614–20.

SWETS, J. A.; TANNER, W. P., JR.; and BIRDSALL, T. G. Decision processes in perception. *Psychological Review*, 1961, *68*, 301–40.

TAUB, H. A., and OSBORNE, F. H. Effects of signal and stimulus rates on vigilance performance. *Journal of Applied Psychology*, 1968, *52*, 133–38.

TAVES, E. H. Two mechanisms for the perception of visual numerousness. *Archives of Psychology*, 1941, *27* (whole no. 245), 1–47.

TAYLOR, M. M. Detectability theory and the interpretation of vigilance data. *Acta Psychologica*, 1967, *27*, 390–99.

THOMPSON, L. W.; OPTON, E., JR.; and COHEN, L. D. Effects of age, presentation speed, and sensory modality on performance of a "vigilance" task. *Journal of Gerontology*, 1963, *18*, 366–69.

TODD, J. W. Reactions to multiple stimuli. *Archives of Psychology*, 1912 (whole no. 25), 1–65.

TREISMAN, A. M. Contextual cues in selective listening. *Quarterly Journal of Experimental Psychology*, 1960, *12*, 242–48.

——— The effect of irrelevant material on the efficiency of selective listening. *American Journal of Psychology*, 1964, *77*, 533–46.

———, and RILEY, J. G. A. Is selective attention selective perception or selective response? A further test. *Journal of Experimental Psychology*, 1969, *79*, 27–34.

TULVING, E., and LINDSAY, P. H. Identification of simultaneously presented simple visual and auditory stimuli. *Acta Psychologica*, 1967, *27*, 101–9.

TUNE, G. S. Age difference in errors of commission. *British Journal of Psychology*, 1966a, *57*, 391–92.

——— Errors of commission as a function of age and temperament in a type of vigilance task. *Quarterly Journal of Experimental Psychology*, 1966b, *18*, 358–61.

VON WRIGHT, J. M. Selection in visual immediate memory. *Quarterly Journal of Experimental Psychology*, 1968, *20*, 62–68.

WARE, J. R., and BAKER, R. A. Effects of method of presentation, modes and response category, knowledge of results and detection performance in a vigilance task. *Journal of Engineering Psychology*, 1964, *3*, 111–16.

———, and SHELDON, R. W. Effect of increasing signal load on detection performance in a vigilance task. *Perceptual and Motor Skills*, 1964, *18*, 105–6.

WARRINGTON, E. K.; KINSBOURNE, M.; and JAMES, M. Uncertainty and transitional probability in the span of apprehension. *British Journal of Psychology*, 1966, *57*, 7–16.

WEBBER, C. E., and ADAMS, J. A. Effect of visual display mode on six hours of visual monitoring. *USAF School of Aviation Medicine Technical Document Report*, no. 64-34, 1964.

WEIDENFELLER, E. W.; BAKER, R. A.; and WARE, J. R. Effects of knowledge of results (true and false) on vigilance performance. *Perceptual and Motor Skills*, 1962, *14*, 211–15.

WIENER, E. L. Knowledge of results and signal rate in monitoring: A transfer of training approach. *Journal of Applied Psychology*, 1963, *47*, 214–22.

——— Multiple channel monitoring. *Ergonomics*, 1964, *7*, 453–460.

WIENER, E. L.; POOCK, G. K.; and STEELE, M. Effect of time-sharing on monitoring performance: Simple mental arithmetic as a loading factor. *Perceptual and Motor Skills*, 1964, *19*, 435–40.

WILCOCKS, R. W. An examination of Külpe's experiments on abstraction. *American Journal of Psychology*, 1925, *36*, 324–40.

WOODWORTH, R. S., and SCHOLSBERG, H. *Experimental Psychology*. New York: Holt, 1954.

ZUERCHER, J. D. The effects of extraneous stimulation on vigilance. *Human Factors*, 1965, *7*, 101–6.

Introduction

The importance of theories of perception can hardly be over-estimated for the position taken with regard to basic issues in this area are often decisive with respect to all other problems in psychology. Theories of perception have served as cornerstones in most systems of psychology. Witness the central importance of treatments of perception in structuralism, in Gestalt psychology, in sensory-tonic theory, in Hebb's system, and in the transactional approach, to name but a few. The importance of perception lies not so much in the fact that it was historically first made amenable to experimental and quantitative treatment but in its role as the prime determiner in all forms of behavior. The senses as the gateways to the central nervous system furnish the primary data of our knowledge of the external world and serve as feedback mechanisms to tell us how well we are adjusting to the physical, geographical, and social aspects of the world in which we live.

It is almost a truism in present-day psychology to say that how we react depends on the way we perceive. With modern extensions of the concept of perception it has now become a basic topic not only in normal, individual human psychology, but also in developmental, social, personality and clinical psychology, as a glance at almost any textbook in these areas will show. Accordingly, it is important to know what the basic ideas are in the various approaches to this subject. As will be seen from reading this chapter (and others in this book) the topic of perception has many facets and many implications. The difficulties and complexity of perception, as shown by the enormous accumulation of facts in vision, hearing, and the other senses, are somewhat mitigated by approaching them through a consideration of the main theories, which help to understand and order the critical data.

In this chapter we shall use the terms sensation and perception with the understanding that, as will be shown later, sensations are only limiting cases, or constructs. We assume that perception is always involved when responses are directly or indirectly linked with, or dependent upon, the activities of sense

Lloyd L. Avant & Harry Helson

Theories of Perception

21

organs. Consonant with this view is the proposition that perceptions differ in complexity or degree of differentiation; when only a single attribute like quality or intensity of a stimulus is the focus of interest, we can speak of sensations or simple perceptions. This position makes the difference between sensation and perception a matter of degree and manner of approach and not a matter of kind (cf. Graham 1958).

There are many important topics in the field of perception that will not be explicitly treated here because they cannot yet be considered general theories although they contribute importantly to an understanding of certain areas of perception. Instead we shall concentrate on a number of theories that have generated experimental research and have had implications for a number of other areas of psychology.

Structuralism

The importance of the Wundt-Müller-Titchener structural approach to perception, although largely historical, still has relevance for more modern points of view. Most subsequent theories of perception arose as reactions against analytical introspective analysis, which was the main tool of the structuralists' approach. According to the proponents of this school as exemplified in the late E. B. Titchener's views, the task of science is to describe in terms of the elements into which original, complex data can be resolved. The models for this, the first experimentally oriented approach to mental life, were the older, better established sciences of physics and chemistry. From chemistry the structuralists inherited the notions of analysis of complexes into elements and from physics the notion of dimensions.

The tasks of science are to tell us the what, how, and why of its data (Titchener 1910, pp. 36ff.). What a complex mental state is is determined by introspective analysis. This procedure enables us to analyze into elements; these elements were at first thought to be sensations aroused by stimuli impinging on receptors, images that were fainter copies of sensations, and feelings that were ultimately reduced to simple states of pleasantness and unpleasantness. However, even the feelings lost their status as elements and were said to be sensations of light and dull pressures (Nafe 1924). Thus, in Titchener's system, all mental life was reduced to sensory components. The attributes or dimensions of the elementary units were quality (red, sour, pitch, pressure, pain, etc.), intensity, protensity (duration), extensity (spatiality), and attensity (degree of clearness).

The second task of science, to tell how complexes arise from their elements, is the task of synthesis. Sensations are organized through the laws governing attention—"even the simplest kind of perception . . . implies the grouping of sensations under the laws of attention . . . the process-attended-to becomes clearer and more distinct than the rest of consciousness. The processes-attended-from are rendered less clear and distinct" (Titchener 1901, p. 110). Besides the grouping of stimuli according to their degrees of clearness there are other characteristics of attention such as its range, conditions favoring it (suddenness, movement, repetition, etc.), degree of attention, and accommodation and inertia phenomena of attention. These should be contrasted with the Gestalt laws of grouping given below.

We are now ready to consider the theory of perception that emerges from the general point of view underlying Titchener's

scientific credo. Since sensations are meaningless by definition (science according to Titchener does not deal with meanings that involve logic and value, only with pure existences or scientific facts) the question arises: How do we perceive such things as forms, melodies, the quality of lemonade and so on? Titchener's answer was that while sensations, considered as independent units of analysis and description, are meaningless, in context they acquire meaning. Hence meaning arises from context. When there are two or more sensations or a sensation and an image, or two images (ideas?), then there is meaning. Perception carries meaning because it consists of a primary core of sensations aroused by the stimulus and a context of secondary sensations and/or images provided (in the main) by past experience. This is Titchener's context theory of perception (1910, pp. 364ff.).

It is at once evident from the above account of perception how different individuals both agree and disagree in their reactions to identical stimuli. Thus two individuals looking at a pencil both agree on its color, size or length, and other sensory properties, assuming both have normal color and spatial vision. The cores of their perceptions are sufficiently alike to elicit agreement on the dimensional aspects of their experience. But the meaning of the pencil is different for the two observers: to one it is "my pencil" and to the other it is "his pencil" because the context aroused by the stimulus is different owing to prior experience with the pencil.

Perceptions are also subject to changes with changes in any of their dimensions. The chief dimension responsible for changes in perception of objects is clearness. Thus certain illusions, particularly illusions of reversible perspective, were regarded as springing from fluctuations in clearness of various parts of the figures. Solution of puzzles requiring discovery of hidden figures was explained in terms of the greater clearness of the figure when it is finally seen. The brain-babies figure given by Titchener in his textbook (1910, p. 277) illustrates his use of the concept of clearness to explain changes in perception. At first sight the drawing seems to delineate the convolutions of the human brain, but upon closer inspection it turns out to be a mass of intertwining naked babies. According to Titchener's account, when the picture is seen as a brain, the babies are unclear, and when the babies are seen "the diagram becomes fairly alive with them, and the brain-perception is reduced to a very bare and vague schema. . . . Suddenly you find what you are looking for . . . the picture of the brain drops clean away from the upper level: the concealed outlines stand out with all imaginable clearness, and the form of the brain is no clearer than the feel of the book in your hand" (1910, p. 278).

The atomistic logic of the context theory appears even more clearly in Titchener's accounts of color constancy and the perception of wholes when incomplete figures are the stimuli. Lightness constancy, the tendency of a white sheet of paper to appear white in full illumination and in shadow and when the quality (spectral energy) of the light falling on it changes radically, was ascribed by Titchener to the operation of "memory color," a concept he took from Hering: we remember how the paper looked in daylight and memory color leads us "to overlook in great part the actual variation of lights and colors . . . " (1923, p. 62). Similarly, when a complete form or figure is perceived from incomplete parts, the perception of the whole pattern is said to arise from a "tied image," that is, the sensations are supplemented by images.

The third task of a scientific psychology, the explanation of mental processes, takes us outside the domain of the observable to the physiological processes underlying the data of introspection. It is a well-known fact that content drops out with repetition although meaning may be preserved. Experiments in both perception and thinking have shown that very familiar stimuli arouse few or no secondary sensations or images to carry their meaning. To explain this paradoxical situation Titchener invoked the concept of "brain habit" as the carrier of meaning when content drops out or is impoverished. Titchener preferred to explain in terms of the nervous system even though "reference to the body does not add one iota to the data of psychology, to the sum of introspections ... it does enable us to systematize our introspective data" (1910, p. 40). This solution seems to contain a tacit admission that structuralist existentialism, a psychology dealing only with introspectable, palpable data, cannot give a complete account of mental processes.

An attempt to remedy the difficulties of structuralism, especially in the light of the criticisms made by the Gestalt psychologists, was made by Boring (1933). The doctrine of conscious elements, attributes, or dimensions as direct objects of observation is given up, for "one makes them up and uses them as phenomenological exigencies require" (Boring 1933, p. vii). The ideal is to get away from conscious dimensions to physical dimensions. Thus the "sensation is no longer regarded as actual but as a systematic construct" (Boring 1933, p. 6). Whereas Titchener had earlier met Rahn's criticism (1914) of the static nature of sensation by saying essentially what Boring says here, and by even going further in granting that experience is dynamic, a process, and not a thing, it appears that Boring was willing to abandon the concept of anything mental whether it be sensation, psychological dimension, or conscious attribute. The dualism of physical and mental is abandoned, leaving the physical as the only reality.

We shall return to other difficulties in the structuralists' approach in our discussion of Gestalt psychology but before leaving this theory let us remind ourselves of its many positive contributions. As pointed out above, structuralism made possible the new experimental science of mental life by specifying the receptor and the stimulus correlates of identifiable aspects of experience. Methods of quantifying were developed and laws relating magnitude of stimulus and sensory experience were formulated, paving the way for measuring learning, memory, and intellectual capacities. That a beginning science had to narrow its sights in order to get started was indisputable; that it would burst its original, self-imposed limitations was inevitable. But we should not forget that the earlier study of sensory processes furnished a standard and still serves as a corrective to the molar approaches that now tend to dominate thinking about perception. Let us now turn to one of the first reactions against structuralism—Gestalt psychology—and then to some other approaches to appreciate the fascinating complexity of perceptual processes.

Gestalt Psychology

In advancing its thesis that perception is always of wholes, forms, configurations, the Gestalt psychologists attacked the atomism of the structural school saying that perception of a friendly face is not merely a sum of visual sensations, for both the form and the friendliness are as immediately given as are the sensory dimensions of hue, brightness, and saturation. In rejecting sensory elements as the ultimate units, the Gestalt psychologists also rejected the method of introspective analysis and attentive isolation, claiming these are highly artificial procedures with no verisimilitude to everyday ways of experiencing objects.

To understand the Gestalt approach we must recall the work of some of their precursors while granting that the great leap forward remained to be taken by Wertheimer (1912). Also opposed to the Wundtian program was Franz Brentano (1874), who rejected introspection because one cannot introspect mental states at the moment of their appearance. Sensory contents are merely signs of the way the mind works, not data of psychology in and for themselves. Brentano still accepts psychology as the science of the mental, but what is mental? Not tones, not visual, taste, and olfactory data—it is the *acts* of seeing, hearing, tasting, etc., and of thinking and feeling that are mental. And in every mental act an object of some sort is intended. Thus for psychology there is no real landscape, only a landscape that I see, that dwells in (*inwohnt*) my perception. This was the doctrine of intentional inexistence that was to stimulate Meinong, Husserl, Stumpf and many others. While banishing objects along with sensations from psychology, Brentano laid the basis for the phenomenological philosophy of Husserl and its adaptation to problems of perception by Rubin (1921), the Gestalt psychologists, and by the Graz school led by Meinong (cf. Helson 1925, 1926).

Concentrating on the intended objects of Akt psychology, Meinong developed a theory of objects (*Gegenstandstheorie*) and Husserl developed an even more radical view known as phenomenology. For Meinong, sensory data furnish the ground or fundament for objects of higher order. Thus four lines at right angles are the ground on which a rectangle, an object of higher order, is perceived. Such objects require higher psychic activities called production processes. Less psychological and more philosophical, Husserl took the radical step of asserting that the real or unreal, physical or mental status of perceived objects is irrelevant to their intrinsic meaning—an imagined tree has as much "treeness" as a tree perceived in ordinary ways. We have here the basis for the insistence by the Gestalt psychologists that properties of wholes are as real as, if not more real than, the properties of the parts. But of this more later!

The unique properties of wholes had been stressed by Mach (1886) and von Ehrenfels (1890), the former a famous physicist with a keen sense for psychological reality, the latter a philosopher-psychologist who made several important contributions. Mach pointed out that a square on its side had quite different perceptual properties from one on a corner, the latter having a diamond shape that was later shown to yield a quite different type of gamma movement from that of the square. Von Ehrenfels, starting from Mach, asked a decisive question: If among n individuals each hears one of n tones, do the n individuals have the melody? The answer was "No" for two reasons: (1) there must be a common carrier for the n tones; and (2) the melody is more than a sum—it must contain at least $n + 1$ elements. Thus a melody in different keys composed of entirely different elements is more like itself than another tonal sequence built upon the same elements. Therefore, the particular elements in a whole do not matter and this leads to von Ehrenfels' third criterion of what he was to call a form-quality (*Gestaltqualität*): the properties of form-qualities are transposable; they do not depend upon specific elements. In addition, von Ehrenfels recognized temporal form-qualities, requiring time for their completion like melodies, and non-temporal form-qualities like spatial configurations. Any change in a definite direction such as a rise in scale, blushing, blanching, or growing bluer can be apprehended as a unitary and independent thing and hence becomes a form-quality (von Ehrenfels 1890).

Both Mach and von Ehrenfels failed to take the decisive step to initiate a radically new approach to perception. For Mach asserted that to recognize a figure, that is, to apprehend figural properties, required "mechanical and intellectual operations" over and above sensory processes, thus giving a dualistic interpretation to facts of perception. This approach was also adopted by the Graz configurationists (Meinong, Benussi, and others as pointed out by Helson 1925, 1926). Von Ehrenfels' position regarding the origin and nature of form-qualities was rejected by Wertheimer because it was couched in terms of "ideational contents" composed of separable elements and because it was dualistic in that some form-qualities, like perception of relations, require the activity of a subject to be brought into being.

What, then, did the Gestalt psychologists add or change in prevailing ways of regarding perception when they came on the scene (cf. Helson 1969)? First, Wertheimer rejected the notion that wholes are synthesized out of parts whether by attention, synthetic production processes or by the classic laws of association. Following Wertheimer's rejection of the logic of atomistic compounding of wholes out of parts, Köhler said: "For it cannot be assumed that sensations of color and tone, and meanings of single words, are to be considered as 'parts' of space-forms, melodies and higher thought processes; since the exact impression of a visual figure or of the specific character of a musical motif, and the meaning of an intelligible proposition, contain more than a sum of patches of color, tone sensations, and individual word meanings" (Köhler 1920, p. ix). And Koffka went even further in asserting that the child learns to recognize the "friendly" face before it has any perception of its colors as such (Koffka 1924). Mental elements are therefore not the real or natural data in perception.

Gestalt psychology thus made the perception of forms, segregated units in space, and extended units in time a fruitful and legitimate object of scientific study. The perception of objects like trees, tables, and human faces had been banished as such from psychology by the Wundt-Müller-Titchener school of introspection and by Brentano in his emphasis on acts. The structuralists reduced perception of objects first to complexes of sensations and images and later to mere aggregates of dimensional attributes while Brentano kept only the dynamic act as psychically existential. The Gestalt psychologists, on the other hand, made organization the fundamental postulate of their psychology: organized wholes are immediately intuited as a result of dynamical self-distribution of processes in central and peripheral neural mechanisms.

It is evident that having made immediately intuited wholes, structures, or configurations primary in perception, it then devolved on the Gestalt psychologists to formulate laws governing the appearance and behavior of such totalities. Here the procedure was to derive principles based on phenomenological properties of observed Gestalten, and a large number of generalizations ensued (Helson 1933) that can be reduced to a few statements as follows:

1. Wholes are primary and appear before their so-called parts (Law of Primacy).
2. To perceive and react to wholes is more natural, easier, and occurs earlier than perception of parts.
3. Wholes tend to be as complete, symmetrical, simple, and good as possible under prevailing conditions (Law of Prägnanz).
4. Wholes tend to be governed by internal rather than external factors (Law of Autonomy).
5. Parts derive their properties from their place or function in the whole.

In accordance with the fundamental place assigned to whole properties, various problems in perception, learning, and thinking assume new forms and are given new solutions. Thus the detection of a hidden face or form in a puzzle picture is a matter of restructuration, of the emergence of a new figure against the background, or even, as in the case of the Rubin reversible vases-faces figure, a reversal of figure and ground so that what was ground becomes figure. Such phenomena, say the configurationists, involve the creation of new wholes, new objects, which are not adequately explained in terms of attention, association or assumed higher mental activities acting on fixed sensory contents.

There are also conditions favoring the grouping of parts into wholes. Among them are nearness, similarity, and good continuation or common fate. Parts form wholes when the conditions for wholeness are present, not optionally, or mechanically, or senselessly.

Stated as more or less formal propositions, the Gestalt laws may seem abstract and mere arm-chair assertions but they were all buttressed by solid experimental or factual data. Space does not permit presentation of the evidence supporting the various generalizations, but it is now a well-known part of psychology and can be found in elementary texts as well as in special treatises (cf. Asch 1968). Moreover, the principles discovered operative in perception were shown to hold also for learning and thinking (Wertheimer 1959; Koffka 1935); for social psychology (Heider 1958); for art (Arnheim 1954); for animal behavior (Köhler 1917); and for numerous other applications.

It would be surprising if there had not been progress in the study of Gestalten during the last fifty years. The concept of Gestalt as a primitive, unanalyzable datum has been shown to be amenable to experimental and quantitative analysis quite different from the type of analytical introspection rejected by Wertheimer, Koffka, and Köhler. Only a few of the advances can be discussed here but they will serve to show that the field of Gestalt perception is still an interesting one to study. Thus while certain lines of evidence support generalizations regarding the tendency of forms to be as simple, complete, and "good" as possible (Fehrer 1935; Mowatt 1940), there are others that limit their applicability. For example, different geometric figures were not found to have significantly different absolute thresholds, and the circle, supposedly the most perfect form, did not come out as the best figure according to a number of different criteria under threshold conditions (Helson & Fehrer 1932).

Progress, especially in the study of visual forms, has been great, utilizing the informational approach of Shannon (1948). Information theory is based essentially on the extent to which ignorance is replaced by knowledge and possible alternatives are reduced as a result of added knowledge. Measurement of information is in "bits," a bit representing reduction of possibilities by one-half. Thus if candy is concealed in one of eight jars and the child is told that the correct jar is among the four on the right, one bit of information has been conveyed to the child, since the eight possibilities have been reduced to four. Three bits of information are necessary to pick the right alternative from eight and, in general, the number of bits is the logarithm of the number to the base two, or the power to which two must be raised to equal the number. One of the most important concepts in information theory is that of redundancy, which refers to the amount of surplus information in any situation. Thus a structured pattern is more redundant than a random pattern and a meaningless pattern has less redundancy than a meaningful one. Information theory thus provides an initial quantitative account of meaning, one of the most vexing problems in psychology and psycholinguistics (cf. Garner 1962).

In a recent article Garner (1970) has summarized a number of studies by himself and by coworkers that show how an information approach to the study of visual forms can be analytical without destroying their originally given phenomenological properties. Garner seeks and proposes an answer to the question: What makes a *good* form or pattern? Briefly, "the good patterns are the redundant patterns, because the whole is so highly predictable from any part, while the poor patterns, being unpredictable from any part, are not redundant" (p. 34). Contrary to the Gestalt theorists' habit of illustrating configurational principles concerning "good Gestalt" by appeals to single examples, Garner points out that "a stimulus is a member of a set of meaningfully related stimuli, and from any set we can form various meaningful subsets. . . . redundancy as a *quantitative* concept is directly related to the size of subsets, not to the individual stimulus itself" (p. 34). Garner then goes on to show with concrete examples that the best figures maintain their properties under rotation and reflection (which relate to the property of symmetry). Furthermore, good patterns are associated with fewer alternative patterns than are poor patterns and hence are "more unique." This helps explain why circles and squares are good patterns: there are very few ways in which these can be made, as contrasted with the many ways in which inkblots (poor patterns) can be made. For the application of information theory to temporally extended patterns, the reader is referred to Garner's article and others cited by him.

It must not be inferred from the above that quantification of form perception is limited to the informational approach, fruitful as it has been. As Michels and Zusne (1965) point out, quantification has passed beyond the limits of information theory and there are many measures of physical form. Their list includes linearity of contour, area, elongation, dispersion (defined as perimeter squared, divided by area), sizes and relations among angles, curvature, area overlap, ratios of angles, and various relations of parts within figures and contours, in addition to the properties noted earlier. Attneave and Arnoult (1956) have shown that 87 percent of the variance in responses to forms can be accounted for by the number of independent sides, angular variability, symmetry, and the ratio of perimeter squared to area.

Problems still remain regarding the perception of forms. It is necessary to reconcile findings under conditions of tachistoscopic exposure, threshold illuminances, discriminability under various conditions, accuracy of recognition and reproduction with what is known concerning good forms from the Gestalt and informational approaches. Contrary to popular belief, a good theory is not necessarily one that answers all questions, leaving nothing more to be done in a field, but rather it is one that opens up new problems and new avenues of investigation Judged from this point of view, Gestalt theory has been and continues to be a most fruitful and stimulating approach to perception. On the other hand, perception has so many facets it is unlikely that any one theory can cover them all, and in the succeeding sections we shall see how still other approaches have contributed to our knowledge of this fertile topic.

The New Look: Perception Viewed as Instrumental Activity

Proponents of what Krech (1949) called the New Look in psychology objected to theories that treat perception as a self-sufficient process in and of itself. Klein and Schlesinger (1949) claimed that such theories made no room in perception for the perceiver. Bruner and Postman (1949a) contrasted such Formal theories with their Functional theory in which the concept of need or adjustment was the central theme. According to Bruner and Postman (1948) a comprehensive theory of perception has to explain not only the organism's receptivity at its sensitive surfaces and the organizational properties of its physiology; the task has to include an identification and explanation of the mechanisms that involve in each percept such central processes as the individual perceiver's needs, motives, predispositions, and past learnings.

THE THEORY

The emphasis in the New Look is upon the extent to which perception is determined by the organism's directive state, that state depending upon its current biological needs, its need for or value of portions of the impinging stimulus configuration, the social stress of the moment, the emotional tone of the stimulus, the organism's prevailing set to perceive something in particular in the stimulus, and the extent to which given percepts have been previously reinforced in that perceptual situation. The unit of behavioral analysis is the *hypothesis*, a term that "denotes the attempt to perceive a stimulus configuration in a certain way, for a given purpose, or with a given meaning" (Postman & Bruner 1948, p. 314). Determinants of hypothesis strength and utilization changed as the theory developed. In the early statements (Bruner & Postman 1948, 1949a), hypothesis sounded very much like *unbewusster Schluss* or James' preperceptions, while the later statements (Bruner 1951; Postman 1951) presented six determinants of hypothesis strength and described a cognitive process by which hypotheses are faced with stimulus information and either confirmed or infirmed.

To the extent that stimulus ambiguity permits other than autochthonous factors to operate, the perceptual mechanism is sensitive to the organism's directive state. In early statements of the theory (e.g., Bruner & Postman 1948), operation of the perceptual mechanism was governed by such principles as the Principles of Resonance, Defense, and Vigilance. Given some diversity among the percepts possible with an ambiguous stimulus, the perceptual mechanism, in response to the organism's directive state, would select the percept most *resonant* with the organism's inner condition, accentuating and vivifying aspects of that percept and at the same time, it would *defend* the individual against percepts of stimulus objects that are inimical to the individual's state. The defensive function fails if the stimulus material is *too* threatening or *too* exacting; instead, the mechanism becomes extremely *vigilant* and meets such material with "utmost alertness and speed."

The task of ensuing research was to discover other such governing principles, and "primitivation" of perceptual responses (increases in recklessness and aggressive elements in prerecognition hypotheses caused by social stress) promised to be the next formally presented principle. Luchins (1950, p. 75) was able to abstract from the New Look according to McGinnies (1949) the mechanisms of sensitization, defense, value resonance, vigilance, and primitivation, while Bevan (1958, pp. 47-48) suggested that Bruner and Postman would add to the Gestalt' principles of closure, symmetry, proximity, similarity, and good continuation the New Look principles of accentuation, fixation, vigilance, defense, and selectivity.

In their 1949 statement, Bruner and Postman (1949*a*) modified their earlier position somewhat, conceding that the Formal theorists had contributed to New Look goals. They suggested, for example, that accentuation might be a special case of Helson's (1948) more general principle of adaptation level. They also saw in the Gestalt treatment of the interaction between stimulus processes and memory traces some cognizance of central directive determinants. However, they claimed, as Gestalt's error, their failure to be influenced by Koffka's (1935) conception of the ego. What appeared to be necessary was a theory which met three objectives. First, the theory should avoid what Krech (1949) termed the "perceptual imperialism" of Hochberg and Gleitman's (1949) claim that motivational processes could be subsumed under perceptual processes. Second, the theory should not eliminate, as Postman (1951) claimed Krech's (1949) "dynamic systems" did, the separation between formal and instrumental by translating instrumental variables into formal processes. Finally, the theory should not, as had Brunswik (1947), mitigate the formal-instrumental dichotomy by focusing almost entirely upon instrumental achievement. The New Look of 1951 was offered to meet these objectives.

Bruner's (1951) was a theory of perception while Postman's (1951) was a theory of cognition: both presented the same model. The crucial intervening construct for both is the concept of hypotheses, and the model is a three-step process of hypothesis-information-confirmation. Noticeably absent are the principles of resonance, defense, and vigilance that earlier governed a unitary perceptual process, and in their stead, a cognitive *process* is more clearly stated. As before, the organism is, in the sense of Woodworth (1947), *eingestellt* to receive a limited range of *information* from the stimulus, and the hypotheses it brings to any stimulating situation comprise the first phase of the three-step process. The second step in the process is the input of information from the environment via the distance receptors and the somatic senses. The third step is a checking or confirmation procedure in which the stimulus information serves to either (1) broaden or narrow the range of hypotheses or (2) confirm or infirm specific hypotheses. Confirmation of a perceptual hypothesis results in a stable perceptual organization, and failure of

confirmation means the continuation of the trial-and-check procedure until a successful hypothesis shift occurs, confirmation is obtained, and the percept stabilizes. Subjective certainty sufficient to terminate the trial-and-check process varies with the subject's task, the strength of the hypotheses, and the opportunities for trial-and-check in the given situation.

Hypothesis strength is provisionally defined in terms of the amount of appropriate information necessary to confirm or infirm it. The small amount of information available in ambiguous stimuli is sufficient to confirm a very strong hypothesis whereas the weaker hypothesis may not be confirmed when a considerable amount of information is available. Hypothesis strength is determined by the following six factors (Postman, 1951).

1. *Frequency of past confirmation.* The more frequently an hypothesis has been confirmed in the past, the smaller the amount of appropriate information required for confirmation on subsequent occasion.

2. *Number of alternative hypotheses.* Monopolistic hypotheses (that a single event will occur) require a minimum amount of appropriate stimulus information for confirmation or denial. The relative slowness of disjunctive reaction time shows the behavioral effects of arousing multiple hypotheses.

3. *Motivational support.* Instrumental hypotheses are stronger than non-instrumental ones, and they may as well be reality-oriented as oriented toward wish fulfillment. For example, hypotheses related to *means* (e.g., fork, plate) may become stronger than hypotheses related to the *end* (e.g., actual foods) as hunger need progresses past the peak hunger condition of the normal eating cycle.

4. *Cognitive support.* The greater the extent to which an hypothesis is an integral part of a larger cognitive organization of hypotheses, the smaller the amount of appropriate information needed to confirm it and the more resistant will it be to infirming information. For example, a reversed *s* is less readily detected in tachistoscopic exposures of *plaster* than in similar exposures of *nlrsthl* (Postman, Bruner, & Walk, 1950). There is an evident similarity between cognitive support and Gestalt principles of organization.

5. *Dominance of hypotheses in the absence of appropriate information.* The less the adequacy of the presented stimulus information, the greater is the determination of the perceptual organization by the dominant hypothesis. For example, if gray paper is cut in the shape of a tomato and placed against a blue background, the match to its induced contrast color requires more red in a matching red-yellow matching disc while a similar gray shaped like a lemon requires more yellow (Bruner, Postman, & Rodrigues, 1950); the *shape* of the gray patch arouses a dominant hue hypothesis.

6. *Consensual validation.* As stimulus ambiguity increases, so does the capacity of group consensus for validation of an hypothesis. Postman (1951, p. 263) claims that the socialization process for a child consists of building into him the "system of hypotheses which will prepare him to perceive and know his environment in the ways which his culture favors."

Within Postman's (1951) theory of cognition, memory consists of a hypothesis trace-confirmation cycle that parallels the perceptual hypothesis-information-confirmation cycle. Remembering occurs as a current perceptual process activates a trace system, built by prior perceptual processes, which arouses an hypothesis. Trial and check of this hypothesis is against appropriate *trace* information rather than appropriate stimulus information. Determinants of hypothesis strength in memory are the same as those which determine perceptual hypotheses.

The Research

A representative sample of the research upon which the theory was built may be most appropriately summarized under the following headings: (1) biological needs, (2) positive and negative reinforcement, (3) stress, (4) emotionality, (5) set or expectancy, and (6) need and value.

Influence of Biological Needs upon Perception. Several investigators have found increases in hunger to be accompanied by increases in the number of food-related responses to ambiguous stimuli. Sanford (1936, 1937) presented subjects words for association and ambiguous pictures for interpretation and found that the number of food responses increased as the deprivation period was extended to the close of the normal eating cycle, and only slightly more food responses occurred as the deprivation period was extended to twenty-four hours. Levine, Chein, and Murphy (1942) similarly found that the number of food responses to poorly focused pictures of food objects, meaningless drawings, and household items increased to about the sixth hour of food deprivation. McClelland and Atkinson (1948) projected dim patches of light, or sometimes shadows, informed their subjects that they were seeing pictures projected under low illuminances, and asked for reports of stimulus content, ratings of the strength of these content impressions, and comparative size judgments of objects suggested in various pictures. They found that as time since eating increased, the number of food-related instrumental responses (fork, plate, etc.) increased but the number of food responses (names of actual foods) did not. Also, the size judgments of the food-related objects (hamburger, plate) suggested in some pictures increased relative to the neutral objects suggested in other pictures. Atkinson and McClelland (1948) obtained similar results when they asked for responses to TAT type pictures from subjects who had been deprived of food for varying lengths of time.

While in the early statements of directive state theory (e.g., Bruner & Postman 1948, pp. 87ff.), these studies were used to illustrate the operation of the principles of resonance, defense, and vigilance, Postman (1951, pp. 256-57) employed them to show how perceptual hypotheses function in perception. The data revealed the motivational support for instrumental over non-instrumental hypotheses. And, the importance of going beyond a wish-fulfillment theory of perception appeared in the shift from non-instrumental (food object) hypotheses to instrumental (food-related) ones.

Influence of Positive and Negative Reinforcement on Perception. Early studies (e.g., Braly 1933; Djang 1937; Henle 1942), stimulated by Gottschaldt's (1926) demonstration that at least some stimulus configurations resist modification by experience, were used by Postman (1951, pp. 252-53) as partial support for the proposition that perceptual organization is a function of past reinforcements. That experience exhibits itself in perception is certain, as has been shown by more recent work (Bell & Bevan 1968; Helson & Avant 1967; Turner & Bevan 1964).

The data marshalled in defining the New Look emphasis on reinforcement were collected by Proshansky and Murphy (1942), Shafer and Murphy (1943), and Postman and Bruner (1949b). Proshansky and Murphy positively reinforced subjects when they judged lines to be long, when they judged weights to be heavy, and when they reported a spot of light in a dark room to move to the right; opposite judgments were negatively reinforced. Relative to unreinforced control subjects who showed no pre- and post-training differences, reinforcement of length and weight judgments produced the hypothesized effect while results with autokinetic movement were equivocal.

Shafer and Murphy (1943) showed subjects a reversible figure that could be seen as a profile looking either right or left and they gave a money reward for seeing one profile but not the other. Reward or punishment was given twenty-five times for each face, and of the sixty-seven perceptions reported on test trials, fifty-four were of the profile that had been rewarded.

Postman and Bruner (1949b) found that children judged three-inch toy figures to be taller than control blocks of equal height, and with experimental subjects who were promised they could keep the toys, a further increase in judged size accompanied the experimenter's broken promise and later removal of the toys.

Influence of Stress on Perception. The influence of tension and tension release upon perception was studied by Bruner and Postman (1947) who compared estimates of the size of pink plastic discs before, during, and after shock accompanied handling of the discs. While their subjects were under the tension of receiving shock, size judgments decreased but not significantly. When subjects were informed that no further shock would be given, size judgments showed a reliable increase of from 6 to 14 percent overestimation of disc size.

After determination of recognition thresholds for three-word sentences with control and experimental subjects, Postman and Bruner (1948) presented complex pictures to both groups. Controls were allowed enough time to see the pictures, while the experimentals were presented the pictures too briefly for adequate response and were severely criticized for failing. Post-harassment determination of thresholds for the three-word sentences showed a learning effect in lowered thresholds in the control group; this effect was absent in the experimental subjects whose responses were more reckless and contained more aggressive elements.

Influence of Emotionally Loaded Stimuli on Perception. The most notable study of the effect of emotionally loaded stimuli upon perception was reported by McGinnies (1949) who found that college students required longer tachistoscopic exposure of such socially taboo words as raped, whore, penis, and bitch before correct response to them than was the case for words that were emotionally neutral. Also, when exposures were too brief to permit correct report, the emotionally loaded words prompted greater galvanic skin responses than did the neutral stimuli. This study, along with its implication of a defensive function within the perceptual mechanism *per se*, has been the most criticized of the New Look studies, and it remains a spur to research (see, e.g., Goldstein, Himmelfarb, & Feder 1962; Natsoulas 1965).

Influence of Set or Expectancy on Perception. Although interest in the effects of instructions, set, and expectancy did not originate in the New Look (see Gibson 1941 for review of earlier work), several studies were generated by the emphasis on directive states. Postman and Bruner (1949a) investigated the difference between single and multiple sets, and Blake and Vanderplas (1950) studied auditorily aroused hypotheses, but the New Look emphasis will be illustrated here with Bruner and Postman's (1949b) study of responsivity to regular and altered playing cards. Altered cards were printed in reversed colors (e.g., black three of hearts, red two of clubs). Exposure durations for the cards ranged up to 1,000 msec, and verbal responses, as well as their latencies, were recorded. Recognition times for altered cards (114 msec) were reliably higher than for regular cards (28 msec), and four categories of responses to the altered cards were observable. In *compromise* responses, color was incorrectly reported; the red six of spades would be reported as a purple six of hearts. In *dominance* responses, either color or form dominated, and the non-dominant characteristic was incorrectly reported. Some responses showed *disruption*; subjects failed to achieve a coherent organization in the card and reported that they did not know what it was. Other responses showed *recognition of incongruity* in which the subject reported the objective situation.

Influence of Needs and Values on Perception. Among the better known studies of the influence of personal needs and values on perception are those reported by Bruner and Goodman (1947) and by Postman, Bruner, and McGinnies (1948). In the former study, ten rich children from a progressive school near Boston, ten poor children from a Boston slum settlement house, and ten "control" children (no economic status given) initially adjusted a variable size disc of light to match their memory image of a penny, a nickel, a dime, a quarter, and a half-dollar. Following this, both rich and poor children again matched the disc to coin size with the coins in hand while the control children matched the light disc to cardboard discs of sizes equal to the coins. With coins absent, memory image for all children was an overestimate of coin size, the estimates varying with coin value up to, but not including, the half-dollar. Also, with coins present the poor children's overestimates were reliably greater than those of the rich children. With coins absent, the poor children overestimated less, while no difference between coin-present and coin-absent conditions was observed for the rich children. For Bruner and Goodman, these findings evidenced the poor children's greater subjective need for money.

Postman, Bruner, and McGinnies (1948) defined personal value systems in terms of individual profiles on the Allport-Vernon scale of values. They established such profiles for twenty-five subjects, and tachistoscopically presented to these subjects six words representing each of the six value areas. Beginning at .01 sec, exposure duration was increased in .01 sec steps until words were correctly reported; recognition times and all prerecognition responses were recorded. They found that, with indi-

viduals' value scores ranked from 1 to 6, recognition of rank 1 words occurred at significantly shorter exposure durations than did either rank 5 or rank 6 words. Prerecognition responses were categorized as *covaluant* (in the same value area), *contravaluant* (in an opposite or antagonistic area), *nonsensical* (not a word), *structural* (based on structural characteristics of the stimulus word), or *unrelated* (the residual category). Mean frequency of occurrence for each of these categories was calculated for subjects' high (ranks 1, 2, and 3) and low (ranks 4, 5, and 6) value areas. Covaluant responses occurred more frequently for high value words and both contravaluant and nonsense responses occurred more frequently for low value words.

RESPONSES TO THE NEW LOOK

Rebuttal to the New Look position began almost immediately after the initial statements of the theory (e.g., Bruner & Goodman 1947; Bruner & Postman 1948), and, by and large, consisted of responses to the developing theory rather than to the more nearly finished theoretical product offered by both Bruner and Postman in 1951. The issues addressed by the proponents and opponents of the theory, both in theoretical debate and in empirical research, are quite complex, and resolution of the issues has not been achieved in all cases. The present discussion will present only samples of this rather extensive literature.

Investigators have responded to the New Look predictions with regard to the influence of reinforcement, needs and values, and the emotional loading of words upon perception. With regard to the influence of reinforcement, Rock and Fleck (1950) repeated the Shafer and Murphy (1943) study on reinforcing the perception of one of two possible face profiles and obtained negative results. However, Smith and Hochberg (1954) supported the Shafer and Murphy finding by successfully decreasing the tendency for one of the faces to be perceived after perception of that face had been accompanied by electric shock.

The thesis that needs and values determine perceptual responses drew a number of responses. Carter and Schooler (1949), for example, retested the Bruner and Goodman (1947) finding that coins appear larger to poor than to rich children, and found the influence of need for money relatively limited to estimates of the memory images of coin sizes; they attributed the earlier findings with direct perception to Bruner and Goodman's small sampling of poor children. Similarly, Solomon and Howes (1951) noted the positive correlation between threshold measures for words representing personal values and the frequency with which such words occur in ordinary language, and they re-examined the findings reported by Postman, Bruner, and McGinnies (1948). Employing a procedure similar to that of the earlier study, they predicted that differences in thresholds for high and low value words would be smaller than differences in threshold for frequently and infrequently occurring words. Results confirmed their prediction, and only with infrequently occurring words was the difference between high and low value words reliable. Postman and Schneider (1951) confirmed these findings, but claimed support for the New Look position in the findings on the influence of values with infrequently occurring words.

Certainly the liveliest controversy instigated by the work on inner determinants of perception came from McGinnies's (1949) finding of higher thresholds for taboo than for neutral words.

The issue of perceptual defense is of considerable theoretical importance and may not be thoroughly handled in the present condensed discussion; the reader is directed to other sources (e.g., Garner, Hake & Eriksen 1956; Bruner 1957; Bevan 1964; Natsoulas 1965, 1968; Garner & Morton 1969) for fuller discussion of the issues related to the question of perceptual defense.

The initial McGinnies finding has been variously interpreted to be a function of frequency of word usage (e.g., Howes & Solomon 1950), withholding of responses by subjects (e.g., Lazarus & McCleary 1951), and of information processed from subliminal exposures (e.g., Bricker & Chapanis 1953). Natsoulas (1965) has evaluated much of the recent relevant literature and has concluded that none of the data are immune to interpretation in terms of a "stimulus effect hypothesis," which refers to "defense instigated by a stimulus but occurring in the response system" (p. 394). Meanwhile, Garner and Morton (1969) have concluded that "the concept of perceptual independence is not a unitary concept and cannot be studied as such" (p. 258).

The most nearly convincing evidence of perceptual defense was reported by Worthington (1964) who found that, with dark-adapted males, the mere presence of light projected through slides was detected earlier if the slides were photographs of neutral words than if the photographed words were taboo. But alas, as with earlier apparent demonstrations of perceptual defense, Worthington's finding failed replication in a later, well controlled study by Weintraub and Krantz (1968).

The theoretical cleavages separating the motivational approach from other positions have been addressed by various writers. Murphy (1949), for example, pointed out the need for a theory yielding specific predictions for concrete cases and criticized the dichotomy drawn between formalists and functionalists. Hochberg and Gleitman (1949) noted that the motivational approach lends itself to *ad hoc* explanatory hypotheses, and they pointed out that the New Look position pays too little attention to factors of organization and to existing laws within perception proper. Luchins (1950, 1951) took proponents of the motivational approach most severely to task for their criticisms of the configurationism of Gestalt psychology. Luchins claimed that the directive state theorists had not understood Gestalt, else they would not have criticized Gestalt in their emphasis upon dynamic theory. Indeed, Gestalt psychology had provided a corrective for the lack of dynamics in contemporary theory; Wertheimer's studies of stroboscopic movement were important in introducing dynamic concepts into the study of psychological phenomena. Dynamics in Gestalt psychology refers to stresses and strains in a field of force of which the organism's inner condition is certainly a part; it should not then be criticized for lacking the psychoanalytic orientation of the New Look. Similarly, the claim that Gestalt neglected the influence of past experience revealed a misunderstanding; Gottschaldt's (1926) often-referenced studies were not intended to disclaim the influence of past experience, but, instead, to show that past experience, as sheer repetition, fails in some situations to modify perceptual organization. Effects of past experience should be studied, but the emphasis should be on determining whether the operation of past experience is to be best understood in terms of field principles or, instead, as an essentially piecewise, arbitrary matter. Other criticisms were made by Luchins, and the reader is directed to his two papers for fuller discussion.

Finally, Helson (1953, pp. 33-34) noted that, like classical associationism, the New Look theory tended to grow by accretion of new hypotheses for each new finding, such that the theoretical superstructure tended to overrun the bases on which it supposedly rests.

The general tenor of the most nearly reasonable response from the New Look to its critics came from Postman (1951, 1953). His claim was that the theory was still developing, its development evident, for example, in his rejection of the notion of perceptual defense in favor of an interpretation of the previous data in terms of the dominance of strong alternative hypotheses. Regrettably, the theory has not since specified how any particular hypothesis develops, how it relates to others in memory, how it relates to expectancy in a given concrete situation, or the precise nature of the stimulus input that confirms or infirms it in a particular situation.

Brunswik's Probabilistic Functionalism

According to Postman and Tolman (1959, p. 504), "Brunswik's systematic contribution represents a productive blend of philosophy of science, historical analysis, experimental methodology, and a functionalist theory of perception and cognition." Brunswik insisted that psychology share with other disciplines in science the objectivity of methodological physicalism; its basis must be in physical measurement of stimuli and response to them. It should not, however, seek universal behavioral laws within analysis of elemental units of sensations or reflexes so as to reduce behavioral analysis to the laws of more "fundamental" disciplines such as physiology, physics, or chemistry. Rather, "psychology has to focus its description on what the organisms have become focused on" (Brunswik 1963, p. 231), which is veridical perceptual and cognitive achievement of objects in the environment. Since objects do not present invariant, totally trustworthy cues at the organism's sensitive surfaces, psychology's account of behavior must be in terms of the organism's adjustment to an uncertain environment, which is proximally mediated by probabilistic cues. This recommends an experimental methodology which examines the organism's functional achievement of representative samples of objects from its environment.

THE THEORY

According to Brunswik, psychology's concern should be the organism's "distal focusing" in its achievement of the environment. With two exceptions, the study of the perceptual thing-constancies (e.g., Brunswik 1944) and molar behaviorism (e.g., Tolman 1932), the discipline has restricted the focus of its inquiry to stimulation at the boundaries of the organism and the central states—conscious content or sensations—corresponding to that stimulation. This is an error inherent in the nomothetic bias accompanying adherence to the aims and procedures of physics, and the cost of the error to psychology has been a lack of emphasis upon the relationship between central states (perceptual and cognitive responses) and distal stimuli. The latter relationship indexes the organism's maintenance of a stable perceptual environment in spite of varying proximal mediation.

The formal features of Brunswik's *probabilistic functionalism* are those of a double convex lens (Brunswik 1952) that highlights distal achievement and the vicarious functioning of proximal stimuli. The features of the model are perhaps clearest in its application to an analysis of the perceptual thing-constancies. Light rays emanating from an initial focus are brought back to convergence at a terminal focus. A measured physical property of a distal stimulus is represented as the initial focus, and the rays ("process details") emanating from this stimulus represent energy modifications produced by the source. These process details give rise to a pattern of proximal effects on the sensory surface of the organism (the lens surface) that function as cues to the distal stimulus and initiate a series of processes within the organism (again, "process details") that mediate the final perceptual response. This response constitutes the organism's achievement with regard to the distal stimulus, and it is represented as the terminal focus in the model.

Analysis of the thing-constancies in terms of this model emphasizes the three functional relationships in terms of which the organism's adjustment is best understood. These relationships are those between (1) distal variable and proximal effects, (2) proximal effects and perceptual response, and (3) distal variable and perceptual response. The strengths of these relationships, each indexed by a constancy ratio or a correlation coefficient, reflect, respectively, the ecological validity of a proximal cue with respect to a distal property, the extent to which the organism's utilization of cues matches their ecological validities, and the functional validity of the perceptual response.

Indexing the relationship between distal variables and proximal effects is essential because the presence of any given distal property assures no certain pattern of proximal effects. To illustrate: "It is easily seen that not even the so-called primary depth cues, such as binocular disparity, are foolproof in our ecology. For example, binocular disparity is present in the stereoscope, yet depth is absent in the underlying reality; in viewing reality through a camera, binocular disparity is absent while depth is present in the chain of causal ancestry" (Brunswik 1955, pp. 199-200). And so it is with all proximal cues to shape, size, and distance; some have, in the real world, high ecological validity (e.g., retinal disparity) while others (e.g., linear perspective) have lower validities.

Given such an uncertain array of proximal mediators, the organism's necessary strategy is to weight and combine cues so as to derive the likeliest perceptual inference about the distal object. Adjustment requires flexibility in the utilization of cues, and maximal success in adjustment comes with weighting different cues in accordance with their ecological validities. Utilization is indexed by determining the ecological validities of different cues and ascertaining the organism's weighting of these cues.

The correlation indexing the relationship between distal variable and perceptual response measures the functional validity of the perceptual response. The perceptual thing-constancies demonstrate that functional validity is normally high, but not perfect. Perfect attainment of the distal object is, in principle, impossible for an organism that must depend upon proximal cues, and the major portion of perceptual error is a function of undependable object-cue relationships rather than inefficiency in the organism's utilization of cues.

Though Brunswik's system developed largely within analysis of the thing-constancies, its applicability to behavioral as well as perceptual attainment was stressed by Brunswik, particularly in his later work (e.g., Brunswik 1955). In such application, some condition of the organism, for example, hunger, becomes the

initial focus, and the habit hierarchy associated with this condition is formally analogous to the pattern of proximal stimuli in the constancy situation. For the given situation, the organism differentially weights alternative actions so as to maximize the probability of attaining satisfaction of the need state. A feedback loop in the lens model allows modification of action combinations until a weighting of actions appropriate to attainment results. This account of behavioral attainment is harmonious with Tolman's (1932) presentation of purpose in terms of goal attainment by persistent but docile behavior.

THE METHOD

The combined errors of adhering to the nomothetic bias of physics and concentrating on proximal-central relations has saddled psychology with classical systematic design, with the ideal of "the rule of one variable," as its methodology. Even though modern trends in psychology are toward multivariate designs that offer possibilities of handling context effects, analysis of the organism's achievement is not really possible within the strictness of experiments based on the rigorous control and isolation of variables. Systematic design is inadequate because (1) it is difficult to know which, and how many, variables should be permitted to vary in a given situation, (2) the values of the variables selected usually cover a restricted range and are spaced in even, discrete steps that do not represent the function of the variable under normal conditions of behavior, and (3) controlling variation of individual variables necessarily determines the nature of the covariation among variables.

Control of covariation is accomplished by artificially tying variables, artificially interlocking variables, or artificially untying variables (Brunswik 1956, pp. 8-10). For example, in the experimental arrangement for the classical measurement of length discrimination, in which the subject is asked to equate the standard and comparison lengths presented side by side, the distal variable of physical length and the proximal variable of retinal length are artificially tied by holding a third variable, the difference in distance between standard and comparison lines, constant at zero. It thus becomes impossible to determine the extent to which perceptual achievement is individually related to the distal and proximal variables. The use of diacritical design in the experiment, that is, setting the distance between standard and comparison lengths at some value other than zero, artificially interlocks the distal and proximal variables. With this arrangement, retinal projections must differ when physical lengths are equal, and physical lengths must differ when retinal projections are equal. With a constant separation between standard and comparison lengths, only two retinal lengths are possible for a given physical length, and there can be only two physical length correlates of any given retinal projection. The two variables are separated by this "crucial experiment," and the reduction in the extent of covariation between the variables to less than unity is a step toward greater representativeness, but results from the experiment must be considered contingent upon the specific choices of sizes, distances, and other conditions. Brunswik's (1956, p. 27) study of social perception illustrates artificial untying of variables. In this study, personality traits were judged from photographs of subjects identically dressed and posed. This sameness of dress and pose eliminated from personality trait judgments the influence of attitudes attributable to clothing and posture, but this control destroyed the correlation between personality traits and habits of dress and posture that are likely to exist outside the experiment.

Systematic design will not reveal universal laws of behavior since it is not possible to diacritically oppose each significant variable to each other possibly influential variable. Basically, it fails of behavior-research isomorphism; it is not conceptually focused on what the organism is focused on, viz., adjustment to an uncertain environment. It should, therefore, be replaced by *representative design*, which aims at accurately indexing the probabilistic nature of environmental supports for behavior and quantitatively exhibiting the full range of the organism's ability to incorporate environmental contingencies. In representative design, one measures the organism's responses to representative samples of situations from its natural-cultural habitat. The universe of situations that the organism is likely to encounter in daily living constitutes its ecology, the definition of which is in terms of objective measurement of the stimulus objects offering behavioral support, independent of the organism's responses to them. Since relationships between distal variables and between distal and proximal variables are inherently probabilistic, psychology's proper focus is in the employment of representative design to measure an individual's responses to representative samples of "variate packages" from his environment that are otherwise left undisturbed. This achieves behavior-research isomorphism.

Probabilistic relationships prompt the principle of perceptual compromise. In adjustment, the individual does not perfectly attain either the distal or the proximal stimulus; perceptual responses are a compromise between the two. The naive-realist attitude, favoring distal attainment, is normal for the observer, but attitude can be directed to the proximal stimulus, and emphasis on either "pole-of-intention" correspondingly improves attainment. Intraindividual observational reliability in distal attainment may be indexed in an individual's responses to repeated random samples from the environment, and interindividual reliability is revealed in the agreement among responses of different individuals to the same sample of situations. Statistical significance of observed correlations is evaluated by conventional procedures, with the important modification that N refers to number of sampled objects and n to the number of respondents.

THE RESEARCH PROGRAM

In the research stimulated by Brunswik's position, attention has generally been given to (a) the diversity of the situations in which an understanding of behavior requires analysis in terms of the constancy of distal attainment, (b) the variety of perceptual and cognitive functions influencing both the pole of attainment focus and the degree of attainment, and (c) the relative merits of systematic and representative design.

The Generality of Distal Focus. The research initiated by Brunswik's position has most often concerned the attainment of distal object *size*. In the classic example of representative design (Brunswik 1944), a female graduate student was accompanied in her daily activities by an experimenter who periodically asked her to judge the linear dimensions of the objects she was observ-

ing at the moment. Judged and measured size correlated .987 when judgments were made with the "naive-realist" attitude of attaining object size, while estimated and calculated retinal sizes correlated .85 when the judging attitude was the "painter's attitude" of attaining retinal or photographic size. Perceptual compromise was evident in the judgments from both "poles-of-intention," and the bias favored distal achievement. The large sample of objects judged lends ecological generality to these results, and responses from the experimenter, who judged the sizes of the same objects, indicates their "responder generality." Judged distal sizes (naive realist attitude) from the two individuals correlated .976, and the functional validity of the experimenter's judgments under the same conditions reached .993. Confirmation of the responder generality of Brunswik's data has been reported by Dukes (1951) and by Bolles and Bailey (1956). Dukes's subject, a six-year-old boy, judged the sizes of selected objects by indicating five other objects, at varying distances, that were of equal height; the functional validity of his judgments was .991. The college students in Bolles and Bailey's study judged objects in or around a home, first while they were blindfolded and then without blindfolds. On the average, nonvisual judgments correlated .988 with measured physical size, and with visual cues, the correlation increased to .994. The high functional validity of the nonvisual judgments was taken to indicate that object names or other descriptive sounds are as legitimate cues for distal attainment as are visually mediated cues. Similar contributions to distal attainment from such cognitive factors as familiarity and suggestion have been shown by Hastorff (1950) and by Hochberg and Hochberg (1952).

Brunswik insisted (1956, p. 25) that evaluation of the contribution of individual cues to perceptual achievement be initiated with all cues available to the observer so as to note the loss to behavioral adjustment as individual cues are successively removed. Holaday (1933) and Holway and Boring (1941) employed this technique in studies of size constancy. Holaday's subjects employed both binocular and monocular vision and judged the sizes of cubes distributed about the floor of a large auditorium. As viewing conditions varied from normal lighting and normal head movements to a darkened room and fixed head position, constancy ratios for the binocular condition decreased from .88 to .67; with monocular vision, the ratios went from .88 to .15. The successive omission technique was particularly useful in evaluating the cue of retinal disparity; only under the most restricted condition of the experiment was the difference between binocular and monocular vision (.67 vs. .15) of considerable magnitude.

Holway and Boring's (1941) subjects adjusted the size of a circular patch of light located 10 feet away to apparent equality with a second patch as the latter was moved from 10 to 120 feet away while maintaining a retinal projection of 1-degree of visual angle. Judgments were made in darkened corridors, and other cues were successively removed by reducing binocular to monocular vision, then monocular vision through an artificial pupil, and finally vision through an artificial pupil and a reduction tunnel. The slope of the function relating size judgment and object distance showed, for the respective conditions, these ratios: 1.09, .98, .44, and .22. The bias of perceptual compromise toward distal attainment was indicated by the error of "superconstancy" (the error of overestimating distal object size) produced by the cue of binocular disparity.

Although the problem of size constancy has received the

greatest amount of attention, investigations of constancy in the perception of shape, loudness, weight, and density have been reported. Klimpfinger (1933a) found that training improved attainment of either the distal or the proximal stimulus shape using, respectively, the naive-realist and the painter's attitude. Mohrman (1939) found that visual cues functioned, as did the naive-realist attitude, to improve judgments of the intensity of a sound at its source; similarly, the lack of visual cues served, like the proximal pole-of-intention, to aid judgment of sound intensity at the ear. While the constancy ratios are generally lower than those observed with visual or auditory perception, some constancy in the tactile-kinesthetic perception of weight and density has been reported by Izzet (1934), and Schreiber (1935) found some degree of constancy in the perception of the weight, speed, and force of impact of balls dropped into the hand. Trends in the acquisition of cues for size, lightness, and shape constancy have been investigated, respectively, by Beyrl (1926), Brunswik (1928), and Klimpfinger (1933b) whose subjects ranged in age from two or three years to adulthood. All three trends reached a peak during the early teens and either leveled or dropped off after that age.

Perception of Social Objects.   The study of distal attainment is most difficult when the objects of perception are other persons. Such traits as intelligence, energy, and likeability were termed covert distal variables by Brunswik; in addition to proximal mediation at the perceiver's receptors, they must be mediated by distal physical features of the perceived person. The difficulties of studying such variables were evident in studies by Brunswik (1956, pp. 26-39) and by Brunswik and Reiter (1937). In the former study judgments of such traits as intelligence were made from photographs of the faces of the persons to be judged, distal attainment being measured against intelligence test scores for the judged individuals. The ecological validities of facial features were uniformly low, and functional validities of the judgments were correspondingly low. There were also high correlations among intertrait judgments, indicating the extreme difficulty of obtaining judgments of single isolated traits. Methodological difficulties were further highlighted in Brunswik and Reiter's (1937) study of the perceptual impressions prompted by schematized faces. These investigators selected five variable facial features for which schematized faces were drawn as stimuli to accommodate a $3 \times 3 \times 3 \times 3 \times 3$ factorial study of the relationships between single facial features and individual covert variables. In executing this design, they found that two very unrealistic combinations of facial features thwarted their subjects' judgmental attitude and could not be included in the study, thus complicating the statistical analysis of the data and demonstrating that multi-variate designs are not likely to meet the requirements of representativeness.

Contributions of Perception and Thinking to Behavioral Achievement.   Brunswik maintained that perception, which is "uncertainty geared," and thinking, which is "certainty geared," make distinctly different contributions to behavioral achievement. The distinction is evident, for example, in Holaday's (1933) report that when subjects went through the rational *thought* process of "making a bet" on judgments made with the naive-realist and analytical *perceptual* attitudes, the constancy ratio for naive-realist judgments increased from .86 to .94 while the ratio for judgments under the analytical attitude decreased from .39 to .25.

Judgmental errors also discriminate between perception and thinking. Gross errors are unlikely in perception because it functions with probabilistic cues, none of which is likely to have, at the same time, an extremely low ecological validity and an extremely high weighting by the organism so as produce a large judgmental error. Achievement in thinking, however, is provided in the application of general physical laws, and making a single false assumption in applying such laws may be sufficient to shunt the entire intellectual process into grossly incorrect judgments; if no incorrect assumptions are made, the solution should be precisely correct. This hypothesized distinction was observed in a study of size judgments when Brunswik (1956, pp. 89-93) presented to some subjects, in an examination setting preceding the size judgments, sufficient information about the physical situation to permit precisely correct distal judgments while other subjects judged sizes under the naive-realist attitude without benefit of information about the physical situation. About half the judgments of distal size from the informed group were precisely correct, while a majority of the incorrect responses exactly attained the proximally correct value—a correct solution to the wrong problem. Judgments under the naive-realist attitude were normally distributed about the correct distal value, showing the usual perceptual compromise.

The resistance of perceptual responses to influence from intellectual insight has been demonstrated by Fieandt (1936). He employed the concealed shadow technique to investigate the acquisition of cues to lightness constancy. No lightness constancy obtained when a shadow covered only the disc in the centered opening of a screen of the same albedo. With extensive training he was able to obtain an apparent lightening of the shadowed disc with successively smaller sections of the screen shadowed simultaneously with the disc, but the conditioning was tenuous and easily extinguished; intellectual understanding that disc and screen were of the same albedo failed to reliably modify the perceptual response. In its contribution to behavioral attainment, Brunswik (1956, p. 92) has termed the perceptual system somewhat "stupid" because it utilizes uncertain cues in a rather stereotyped, superficial manner.

THE RESPONSE TO BRUNSWIK

With the possible exception of Krech (1955), all of Brunswik's critics acknowledge a debt for his insistence upon sampling situations as well as subjects and his emphasis upon studying behavior under natural conditions. However, few have been persuaded to relinquish a nomothetic bias in favor of probabilistic functionalism, and representative design has not gained a preference over systematic design in general usage.

In defense of systematic design, Postman (1955) pointed out that the less-than-unity stimulus-response correlations stressed by Brunswik are derivable from the explanatory premises, stated as universals, that emerge from laboratory investigations. Further, Postman claimed that Brunswik's "achievement" denotes an a priori evaluation of the organism's performance that limits the scope of inquiry—this limit evident, for example, in Brunswik's apparent lack of concern with the motivational factors in perception stressed by those of the New Look persuasion. In addition, Postman maintained that Brunswik's equation of nomothetic bias with microscopic mediational processes was unjustified, pointing to Skinner, McGeoch, Melton, Tolman, and Spence as scientists with a nomothetic bias who had deliberately deferred the problems of microscopic mediation. Postman's claims for the systematic experiment are (1) that it serves to determine functional relationships, and failure in extrapolation simply indicates the need for further research, (2) it permits testing of implications of a theoretical position, and (3) it permits the limited generalizations upon which miniature systems are built prior to attack on large-scale problems. Correspondingly, representative design has its weaknesses. Determination of what is the universe that is to be sampled is difficult, particularly with regard to what its units are. In the study of some aspects of behavior, representative sampling is difficult; sampling representatively among learning behaviors is an example. Finally, with the loss of control in representative design, an investigator may have to forego the possibility of measuring the nature and amount of interactions among variables.

Hilgard (1955) termed correlation "an instrument of the devil," and cautioned against "working backward from after-analysis." He also noted that very high functional validity coefficients may obscure large errors in detail; the size estimates made by Brunswik's graduate student and the accompanying experimenter were sometimes in error by a 3:1 ratio even when judged and measured size correlated .99.

Krech's (1955) position was completely opposite to Brunswik's. Krech was committed to the discovery of a neurological basis for universal laws of behavior; he would have us "become unified scientists by consciously espousing the 'microscopic' approach" (p. 231). He claimed that Brunswik took a methodological criticism and made of it a cosmology. Feigl (1955) similarly disallowed Brunswik's system the status of a theory since "his enterprise limits the subject matter of psychology to the study of certain (statistically certifiable) teleological relations between environmental and achievement variables" (p. 233).

The essential features of the rebuttal to the above criticisms (see Brunswik 1955; Postman & Tolman 1959) can be given the following summary. There is no basic incompatibility between the emphasis upon universal laws and Brunswik's probabilism. In principle, one may accept the existence of universal laws and yet maintain that, in the propositions of a science, only probabilistic relationships may be adequately represented. In accounting for actual behavior, first priority must be given to "correlational achievement mapping of generalized functional arcs at the top of a hierarchical pyramid; this is followed by the macromediational analysis of vicarious attainment strategy" (Brunswik 1955, p. 237). Priority may then be given to reductive study of micromediational tactics, so long as analysis is accomplished under firm commitment to the above two functional aims and does not overlook, or by-pass, the organism's "grand strategy." Reduction must be "from above," from the high-complexity functional units of behavior represented in the lens model. In view of the breadth of emphasis in the above assignment of priorities and the breadth of the behavioral situations to which the lens model is applicable, both Krech's and Feigl's complaints about the limits of Brunswik's position appear unjustified. A similar response is appropriate for Postman's concern about motivational variables in Brunswik's system; as psychologically relevant variables, they are included in the demands of representative design.

In accounting for behavior, the psychologist meets the empirical fact that features of the ecology accessible to the organism are, to a significant degree, unpredictable. In order to adjust, the organism must behave as an intuitive statistician in utilizing cues. However, Brunswik avoided Helmholtzian reasoning and unconscious inference as the universal model of behavior. Perceptual inferences were not for Brunswik, as they had been for Helmholtz, "automatized versions of processes which had been originally conscious." (Postman and Tolman 1959, p. 554) Nor were perceptual inferences essentially rational; Brunswik's research consistently pointed out the different contributions from perception and intellectual processes to distal achievement.

Perception as Transaction

Bevan (1958) has noted, as will the reader of this chapter, that the transactional point of view contains elements which are similar in some respects to some of the other theories presently under consideration. Similarities to Helmholtz's unconscious inferences, New Look hypotheses, Brunswik's probabilism, and Helson's adaptation level all appear in the transactional position; the uniqueness of the approach resides in the concept of the continuous transaction between an individual and all aspects of the environment.

According to Kilpatrick (1952) any discussion of perception from the transactional point of view necessarily does violence to that view because one cannot isolate perception, as a chemist might isolate a pure chemical, from the total experience of living, the "enormously complex evolving process which includes space and time and environment, as well as the organism in an indissoluble whole" (p. 88). Any time segment of that process constitutes a transaction that occurs because of and through all participants in the process, the individual as well as all aspects of the environment. Transactional theory has been distilled as follows by Kilpatrick (1952, p. 89):

By perception, then, is meant that part of the transactional process which is an implicit awareness of the probable significance for action of present impingements from the environment, based on assumptions related to the same or similar impingements from the environment. By assumption is meant that generally unconscious aspect of the transactional process which may be described as a weighted average of past experience in dealing with those portions of the impingements from the environment to which it is related. Assumptions function as probabilities which are builtup by action, checked by action, and modified by action as the consequences of these actions are registered in relation to purposes. Taken altogether, our assumptions form our "assumptive world" which we bring to every occasion and on which our perceptions are based; therefore, the only world we know is determined by our assumptions. The assumptive world is conceptualized as that complex set of internalized, interrelated generalizations or standards which are not dependent for their effectiveness on any given reference point in space or in time. It thus provides whatever constancy there is in our environment, and whatever continuity there is in our experience.

As that part of the process of living through which each

individual creates for himself the world that provides his experiences, the perceptual process is characterized in terms of four major aspects (Ittelson 1962). The first of these is that it is transaction; to be understood it must be studied within the total situation of a transaction. In addition, it links, within this process, the experience of inner and outer events; in perceiving, the individual externalizes certain aspects of experience in the creation of his world while he also internalizes, so as to recognize them as his own subjective experience, other aspects of the perceptual process. Thirdly, each perceptual experience is carried through within a process of weighting the various assumptions comprising the individual's assumptive world; each assumption is included in the weighting process with "a weight determined on a probability basis adjusted in terms of its previous importance to the individual and its relationship to the immediate transaction" (Ittelson 1962, p. 679). Each experience provides the situation for revision of the weights assigned within an existing framework of assumptions as well as an opportunity for perceptual relearning and the acquisition of totally new assumptions. Finally, perceptions are prognostic directives for action which verifies or modifies the subjective probability assigned to assumptions.

That perception is of one's environment rather than of that portion of the environment that is seen or felt at the moment was pointed out in Ames' (1953) distinction between "stimulus" and "ultra-stimulus" perception. Perception provides not only the writer's experience of his typewriter, which he sees and feels, but also the wastepaper basket behind him; action toward the latter, which usually occurs with the object out of view, assures its position within the assumptive world.

As is the case with all the theories considered in this chapter, a thorough review of the research stimulated by transactional theory exceeds presented limitations and the reader is directed to other sources for fuller discussion (e.g., Kilpatrick 1952, 1961; Ittelson 1952, 1962; Ittelson & Cantril 1954). Generally, the research strategy has been to present subjects stimulating situations that appear to be the same as, but are different from, the environment that is normally experienced; responses to these situations reveal the assumptions normally operative as well as the process of changing assumptions when the subject runs into a "hitch" and finds his assumptions incorrect.

Probably no research in psychology is as widely known as the demonstration with Ames' distorted rooms and the rotating trapezoidal window. Several different distorted rooms have been constructed such that, when they are viewed from specified positions under specified lighting conditions, the distortions present the visual cues accompanying normal cubical rooms (see Ittelson & Kilpatrick 1961). In one, for example, the floor slopes downward to the left, the ceiling slopes upward to the left, and the rear wall slopes leftward from near to far while all dimensions of the room, as well as its windows and the objects placed in the room, are such as to specify to the eye a normal room containing objects of usual dimensions. Upon viewing this room, subjects see it as cubical, and faces of persons appearing in the differently sized rear windows appear much larger or much smaller than normal depending on which window they appear through. Similarly, persons appear to grow from dwarf size to giant size as they walk from the left to the right side of the room, and they appear to shrink again to dwarf size as they walk from right to left. Marbles rolled from right to left in a leftward-sloping trough appear to roll uphill. A revised appearance of the room occurs as a result of action taken with regard to the room; when asked to touch a certain spot on the rear wall with a stick, the subject finds his actions inadequate initially, and as he learns to appropriately modify his actions, his perception of the room changes, and he sees it as distorted. These demonstrations are interpreted as indications that individuals approach each situation from an assumptive world, that assumptions are prognostic directives for action, and that weighting of assumptions or total revision of frameworks of assumptions occur in perceptual experience. Forced to unconsciously choose to distort either room size or face size, subjects distort the faces. That the extent of the distortion depends upon the stability of assumptions about the persons viewed in the room was indicated by Wittreich's (1952) report that marital partners appear less distorted than do strangers.

Equally dramatic was Ames's (1951) demonstration with the rotating trapezoidal window. The window was constructed as a trapezoid, but with mullions and shadows painted so as to make it appear, when viewed monocularly under certain light conditions, to be a window viewed obliquely. As the window is made to rotate, it appears to the viewer to be oscillating through an arc of about 100 degrees. At the same time, a small cube attached to its longer vertical side appears to be circling in space, leaving the window and floating through space during that portion of the window's apparent oscillation that is in the direction opposite to the movement of the cube. A tube placed through the window openings appears to either slice through the window or bend to accommodate the mullions as the window apparently reverses its direction of movement from that of the tube, and the appearance of the tube depends upon whether the subject is told it is a steel rod or a rubber rod. In addition, when a rectangular window and the trapezoidal window are rotated, one above the other, about the same vertical shaft, the difference in apparent movement is accompanied by apparent shifts in the sizes of the two windows. It would seem that this situation reveals several assumptive worlds simultaneously, one appropriate to each of the seeming conflicts among the actions of the several viewed objects, and this perceptual experience is not easily modified by intellectual insight into the objective situation. Similarly difficult of intellectual modification is the experience of near-far movement of two balloons that are equally distant from the viewer but appear to either advance or recede as one is made larger than the other or is more brightly illuminated than the other; the perceptual experience of "chairness" also obtains whether the "chair" is objectively comprised of strings and a piece of cardboard or is, rather, a jumble of strings and a painted diamond (Kilpatrick 1961).

The gradualness with which the assumptive world is modified is illustrated by Ames's (1946) observations on the effects of aniseikonic lenses and Engel's (1956, 1958) studies of binocular resolution of structurally dissimilar figures presented independently to the two eyes. The general observation with aniseikonic lenses, which selectively distort various dimensions of visual space, is that the subject wearing the glasses can observe the development of the distortion once he has put the glasses on. And observed distortion is greater in some situations than in others; paved streets are less distorted than is the "leaf room," a room in which the walls are covered with leaves, apparently because the subject's assumptions about the former are more stable than his assumptions about the latter.

Engel's evidence indicates that binocular resolution can be

influenced by meanings and past experience. He found that when upright pictures of two different male faces were presented stereoscopically, the two faces were resolved into a compromise having characteristics that were not directly derived from either face, and that the compromise was particularly pleasing and attractive. If one of the faces was upright while the other was inverted, the upright face dominated the perception. Engel also noted work by others that showed that emotionally or socially acceptable material presented to one eye would prevail over unacceptable material presented to the other eye. Similarly, a face initially presented under greater illumination persists even as the illumination for a second face increases beyond that of the first. These findings are consistent with the report from Ittelson and Ames (1950) that accommodation of the eye corresponded to apparent rather than objective distance.

While the studies generated from the transactional point of view rightfully demand attention for the transactional view, the theory lacks the quantitative specification of its claims and phenomena desirable in an adequate theory, and Hochberg (1962, p. 311) has noted that "What such demonstrations cannot do, no matter what their ingenuity, is prove that we can perceive space *only* because of what we have learned by experience." Meanwhile, Klein (1951) noted the relevance of the transactional research to the emphasis on inner determinants of perception, but correctly termed the transactional approach only a starting point for a theory of personality.

Sensory-Tonic Field Theory

This theory had its origins in experiments concerned with the interaction of various sense modalities such as hearing, tactile-kinesthetic, and electrical stimulation with visual perception. It was then extended to include the interplay of cognitive (meaning) and emotional systems with sensory systems. Contrary to classical psychophysics, which Werner and Wapner (1949) rightfully assert ruled out the organism in its approach to sensory processes, these authors stress the interplay of tonic and other afferent input with visual perception and argue for greater recognition of interaction between the sensory and motor areas of the brain. As is true of almost all perceptual theories since Wertheimer (1912), this theory enlarges the sphere of Gestalt, or the concept of interaction, by recognizing that to account for what is perceived in a single sense modality, other modalities and cognitive-emotional systems must also be included in the explanation.

Stated tersely, Werner and Wapner maintain that perception is sensory-tonic, that is, factors contributing to perception are tonic as well as sensory. Tonus is used in its wide connotation as a state of organismic tension as evidenced by visceral and somatic (muscular-skeletal) activity (1949, p. 91). Interaction is assumed as a postulate that implies that analysis of perceptual processes into sensory and tonic factors does not mean that perception is a mere combination of these.

Perception exhibits the following four main characteristics according to sensory-tonic theory:

1. Interaction among sensory systems whereby the input of a system subsidiary to the one in the focus of attention has an important influence on the latter. The input of the former is referred to as extraneous stimulation.

2. Functional equivalence between sensory systems whereby extraneous stimulation under certain circumstances produces "analogous" results in focal perception.

3. Organic activity exhibits vicariousness, by which is meant that the energy available at any given time may be released through different channels. There may also be vicarious channelization as will be shown later.

4. Finally, perception is always projective in nature, not merely when unstructured material such as ink blots are in question, but also under what we may call "neutral" conditions: "cognitive and conative organismic states are an [intimate] part of perception" (Werner & Wapner 1952, p. 324).

Let us now consider some of the experimental data supporting the basic assumptions and generalizations of sensory-tonic field theory. Almost all the experiments by Werner and Wapner and their co-workers demonstrate interaction and the potency of extraneous stimuli. They also show the functional equivalence of different sensory systems. Three experiments are especially noteworthy. In the first by Wapner, Werner, and Chandler (1951), Ss had to adjust a luminous rod in a dark room to appear vertical while electrical stimulation was applied to either side of the neck via the sternocleido-mastoid muscle. It was found that electrical stimulation on one side resulted in visual displacement of the rod to the opposite side; thus functional equivalence of electrical stimulation presumably affecting tactile-kinesthetic or postural systems in addition to the visual system was demonstrated. While the results were not so clear-cut for women as for men in this first experiment, later replication gave statistically significant directional effects for two separate groups of twenty women Ss.

Similar effects of extraneous stimulation were found with body tilt on perception of the visual vertical (Werner, Wapner, & Chandler 1951): the apparent visual vertical shifts in a direction opposite to body tilt; unsupported tilt resulted in greater shift of the apparent vertical, presumably due to greater muscular strains, than did supported bodily tilt. In the third study of this series (Wapner, Werner, & Morant 1951), labyrinthine stimulation was used as the extraneous stimulus affecting perception of the visual vertical. Ss adjusted a luminous rod attached to a rotating chair in a dark room while being accelerated or decelerated in clockwise (CW) or counter-clockwise (CCW) direction. The results showed that under CW acceleration the apparent visual vertical shifted to the left of the control while under CCW acceleration it shifted to the right of the control. Under deceleration from CW rotation, the apparent vertical was shifted to the right of the control and under deceleration of CCW rotation it was shifted to the left of control. Thus deceleration in one direction functions like acceleration in the opposite direction.

This last study may be regarded as the converse, in some respects, of an earlier study by Wapner and Witkin (1950) who found that maintenance of body balance on an unstable platform on which Ss stood grew progressively worse as the visual field was reduced to obliteration by blindfold and in the unstable condition where the visual field was moved. Women showed greater dependence on the visual field than men because they had poorer balance when the field became unstable. There were also marked individual differences throughout for both men and women.

The third principle, the vicariousness of energy channelization, is demonstrated in an experiment by Krus, Werner, and Wapner (1953). Here Ss were shown figures suggesting motion such as a train, a man on skis, etc., after exerting pressure on a pushboard for 20 seconds. These Ss gave fewer reports indicating active motion than did the controls who viewed the figures without previous muscular involvement. The introduction of motor involvement had the effect of decreasing perceived movement in the visual materials thus supporting the hypothesis of vicariousness of channeling.

The projective nature of perception, the fourth principle, was demonstrated in two studies, one on effects of danger on space localization (Wapner, Werner, & Comalli 1956) and the other on success and failure as it affected space localization (Wapner, Werner, & Krus 1957). In the first study, Ss were placed on the edge of a platform with a sharp drop either on the right or the left, and since the Ss were made aware of this, there was a pull to that side that was counteracted by muscular strains toward the opposite side. The Ss task was to adjust a luminous rectangle so that it appeared straight ahead. The results were that with dangerous edge on the left, the apparent median plane was shifted to the right (6.4 cm.) compared with dangerous edge on the right (.3 cm). Variants of this procedure confirmed the conclusion that the apparent median plane shifts in a direction opposite to the location of the danger.

In the experiment on success-failure by Wapner, Werner, and Krus (1957) it was assumed that "success" has a spatial upward connotation and that "failure" has a downward connotation. After being told they received an A (success) or an F (failure) in an examination taken previous to the experimental session, Ss were required to indicate where a black line would appear against a luminous background in a dark room. The success Ss gave significantly higher upward shifts in their horizons, the failure group significantly lower shifts. This result confirms Rosenblatt's finding (quoted by the authors) that the apparent horizon was located significantly higher by an elated group than by a depressed group, while a normal group fell between the other two groups.

Still other studies showed effects of cognitive (meaning) induced sets on perception (Comalli, Werner, and Wapner 1957) and effects of other conditions also—age, for example (Wapner and Werner 1957; Comalli, Wapner, and Werner 1959). It is thus seen that sensory-tonic field theory has much in common with other approaches to perception such as Gestalttheorie, the New Look approach, and adaptation-level theory, to name but a few. That various approaches to perception have much in common is a sign of the maturity and the scientific character of the theories, for the more advanced a science is, the more do the pieces it studies hang together. Had sensory-tonic field theory evaluated the relative contributions of the various interactions in perception that it has so strikingly demonstrated, such concepts as functional equivalence and vicarious channelization could have been elevated to quantitative status. Similarly the demonstrations in sensory-tonic field theory of the interaction of asymmetrical extent and directional dynamics, which cannot be discussed here for lack of space (cf. Kaden, Wapner, & Werner 1955; Werner & Wapner 1954), bear replication by future workers with a view toward parametric formulations with all the added power that accrues to quantification of scientific data.

Hebb's Neuropsychology

THE PROBLEM

As Hebb saw it (1949, p. xvi), the central problem in behavior theory is, for the psychologist, the problem of thought, and for the physiologist, the problem of the transmission of excitation from sensory to motor cortex. Before Hebb's, no theory had met the requirement of showing how behavior relates directly to the activity of individual neurons.

Several lines of evidence indicated that a new model of cortical processes was needed. Selectivity in responses had long required the concept of attention (see review by Gibson 1941) which had no adequate physiological account. Hebb had found that rather extensive removal of frontal lobe cortex had little influence upon intelligence as measured by Binet-type tests (Hebb 1939, 1942, 1945; Hebb & Penfield 1940). Evidence from numerous investigators made it clear that central nervous system cells fire spontaneously and, thus, that cortical firing is not directly controlled by sensory input (see review by Jasper 1937). And, Lashley (e.g., Lashley 1941, 1942a, 1942b) had shown convincingly that "visual discriminations do not depend upon any direct or specific transcortical connections (of visual cortex) with other regions of the neopallium" (1942a, p. 219).

The transcortical reflexes of simple connectionism had no defense against the onslaught of such lines of evidence; it was similarly defenseless against the Gestalt insistence upon configurational determinants in perception (see, e.g., Köhler 1929; Brown & Voth 1937). The Gestalt counterproposal that "perceptual work" is performed by autochthonous cohesive and restraining forces (see, e.g., Koffka 1935, pp. 138ff) failed to convince the neurophysiologist. In Gestalt theory, the brain appeared to be a statistically homogeneous medium having "all the finer structure of a bowlful of porridge" (Hebb 1949, p. xvii). Lashley's (1942b) irradiating waves of excitation and their interference patterns improved matters little, if at all.

Hebb's task was, then, the development of a "comparatively simple formula of cortical transmission, . . . a conceptual system . . . which relates the individual nerve cell to psychological phenomena, a bridge . . . across the great gap between the details of neurophysiology and the molar conceptions of psychology" (Hebb 1949, p. 101). The task required a conceivably true theory that accommodates the facts of perceptual generalization while postulating a memory trace that is in some way structural and static. With Milner's (1957) modification, the system proposed by Hebb is such that "the model of the brain which it presupposes is in line with current data" (Wilson & Wilson 1967, p. 66).

THE THEORY

Hebb explains psychological processes in terms of a central semiautonomous process comprised of cell assemblies and phase sequences. Sensory events are centrally registered as cell assemblies. Motor components or correlates of sensory input are similarly registered, and the associations between assemblies provide the structure within which sensory input initiates motor activity. Phase sequences are temporally consolidated series of cell assemblies, and they correspond to events in perception and thought. Selectivity in stimulus input and/or responses resides within the continuous, partly autonomous, activity of the brain.

Lorente de No's (1938) reverberating circuits, groups of neurons arranged in closed, self-exciting loops, are the physiological basis for Hebb's cell assemblies. Such circuits provide a transient, unstable "immediate memory" of the initiating stimulus. Hebb adds to this physiological evidence the fundamental assumption that when a neuron is repeatedly instrumental in firing another, a structural change develops at the synapse that reduces synaptic resistance and increases the first cell's efficiency as one of the cells firing the second. Considerations of the number of synaptic connections possible for a single cell (Forbes 1939, estimated 1300 synaptic knobs on a single anterior horn cell), the convergence of multiple impulses upon single cells within the diffusity of connections among sensory, association, and subcortical areas, and the probabilities of synchrony in firing relations among interconnected neurons permit Hebb the demonstration that such circuits may reverberate long enough to accommodate the gradual development of the assumed structural change. The change might be either a chemical change or the growth of microscopic synaptic knobs (Hebb 1958, p. 103).

Hebb (1958, p. 105) summarizes the development of the cell assembly in terms of four assumptions. The first assumption is that the assembly gradually develops, usually in infancy, as a result of a repeated, particular kind of sensory event. He next assumes that several assemblies that are repeatedly active at the same time will form a single assembly—for example, the several assemblies corresponding to the angles and sides of a triangle, along with their motor components, combine to form the "t" assembly corresponding to perception of the triangle as a distinctive whole. If the several assemblies are active at different times, they will remain separate, but associated, systems, and the firing of one by another will require collaboration with a third assembly. The next assumption is that most assemblies have motor components; visual assemblies produce eye movements, somesthetic assemblies produce hand or foot movements, and so forth. Finally, each assembly is assumed to correspond to a relatively simple sensory input—a pressure pattern on a given skin area, a particular vowel sound, a particular optical contour, or perhaps the common property (hardness, smoothness) of a series of tactual stimulations. "In short, the assembly activity is the simplest case of an *image* or an *idea*" (Hebb 1959, p. 628).

Milner (1957) noted the weakness of Hebb's recruitment of some neurons, and loss of others by fractionation, in a developing and changing assembly (Hebb 1949, pp. 76-77, 97) which depends largely upon changing frequency characteristics of the assembly. With each cell firing only other excitatory cells, excitation would rapidly snowball, and a seizure rather than a cell assembly would result. Milner's most important corrective assumptions were that inhibitory cells are also fired when excitatory cells are fired and that the inhibitory fibers that are fired by a particular neuron have connections with excitatory neurons other than the one that fires them. Milner's modification is a more convincing means for containing excitation within an assembly as well as a means for excitation to pass among independent, but associated, assemblies.

The mechanism of association is the connection formed among assemblies, and a temporally integrated series of assembly activities forms a phase sequence, which "amounts to one current in the stream of thought" (Hebb 1959, p. 629). Each assembly in the sequence may be excited sensorily, by other assemblies, or in both ways; the latter is the usual occurrence in a perceptual event or in other organized behavioral sequences. Thus, momentary control of behavior is a joint function of the demand characteristics of current sensory input and the ongoing central activity.

THE EVIDENCE: STUDIES OF PERCEPTION

While Hebb intends a general theory of behavior, the strongest recommendations for his system have come from studies of perception. It was Senden's (1960) compilation of cases of congenital blindness corrected by cataract removal in adulthood, together with Riesen's (1947) work with dark-reared chimpanzees, which initially convinced Hebb that his theoretical notions merited serious consideration. More recently, Hebb (1963) has interpreted the stabilized retinal images data as the clearest support for his theory. Haber (1967) has also sought, in Hebb's theory, an account for his finding that repeated brief stimulus exposures increases the probability that the stimulus will be perceived.

In Senden's (1960) report of the first vision of newly sighted adults, Hebb observed the distinctions among (a) primitive unity, (b) nonsensory figure-ground organization, and (c) figural identity in perception. These distinctions, particularly that between (a) and (c), were not made in Gestalt theory, and the theory appeared to negate learning in basic perceptual organization (the appearance is illusory—see Luchins 1951).

The primitive unity of a figure is "that unity and segregation from the background which seems to be a direct product of the pattern of sensory excitation and the inherited characteristics of the nervous system on which it acts" (Hebb 1949, p. 19). It is, in other words, the primitive separation between figure and ground, and the separation appears to be a native capacity of the organism; it is evident in the normal person, in the first vision of the newly seeing adult (Senden 1960), in the normal rat (Lashley 1938), and in the first vision of rats reared in darkness (Hebb 1937).

Nonsensory figure-ground organization does not depend upon luminosity gradients in the visual field, but rather "occurs in perception whenever the subject responds selectively to a limited part of a homogeneous area in the visual field" (1949, p. 21). This occurs, for example, only after one has learned to discriminate the "middle" of a line from its remainder. The influence of learning in perception is even more apparent on the more frequent occasions when the perceived entity is a function of both sensory and nonsensory factors. Such, for example, is the case with Boring's (1930) "Wife and Mother-in-law" ambiguous figure; the figure presents the option of at least two figural boundaries, and figural organization may be lastingly determined by the perceiver's earlier experience.

Figural identity refers to "the properties of association inherent in a perception" (1949, p. 26). Within a figure's identity reside its immediately experienced similarity and dissimilarity with other figures and its ease of association with other objects or with some action. Figural identity is a matter of degree, is influenced by experience, and is to be kept carefully distinct from the figure's "unity" as well as its "meaning." The notion bears a resemblance to Gibson's (1950a) account of perceptual learning, and perhaps its readiest illustration is the learning, by a Caucasian, of the distinctiveness of individual Oriental faces.

Since primitive unity is common to species ranging from rat to man, while the perceptual generalization of figural identity is quite limited in the lower species (Gellerman 1933), Hebb proposes that unity and identity have separate physiological bases. The structure of the visual apparatus provides the innate capacity for primitive unity, across species, but the capacity for developing figural identity is limited in the lower mammals. Figural identity develops, over many repetitions of particular stimulus configurations, in terms of cell assemblies and phase sequences. Hebb supposes that the infant learns to perceive through a process similar to that evident in the cases of newly sighted adults compiled by Senden (1960). With such persons, primitive unity is evident in first vision, but recognition and naming of simple forms in various contexts occurs only after a lengthy and arduous learning process. During early vision, such patients must painstakingly count corners to distinguish between a triangle and a square. Once training has progressed far enough for such a patient to recognize a triangle with relative quickness, the recognition may be cancelled if the form is turned around to reveal its differently colored back side. In the cases reported, approximating normal perception of simple forms required, at a minimum, about a month of training, and recognition failed after a year's training in some cases. Miner (1905) reported that an intelligent patient failed visual recognition of two persons following a month of daily conferences with them; two years after cataract removal she recognized only four or five faces.

Riesen's (1947) work with dark-reared chimpanzees also suggests that normal visual perception in higher mammals presupposes a long learning period. Even the eyeblink appears to be learned. At about three months of age, normally reared chimpanzees blink in response to an object approaching the face; for the animal reared twenty months in the dark, the response subsequently develops gradually with visual experience. Hebb suggests (1949, p. 108) that connections between afferent and efferent systems are being formed during the development period.

Some of the more recently investigated effects of stabilizing images on the retina (see review by Heckenmueller, 1965) support the cell assembly notion while others deny it. The disappearance and regeneration of stabilized images is fragmented; parallel lines of a square disappear and reappear as a unit, BEER may alternately appear to be BEEP, PEER, BEE, etc., and meaningful objects remain visible longer than meaningless ones. Moreover, both Krauskopf and Riggs (1959) and Cohen (1961) have shown the effect to be central rather than retinal. These phenomena are entirely consistent with the digital activity of cell assemblies as Hebb proposed. The difficulties for Hebb are that stabilized solid squares disappear gradually from the center toward the corners, sections that increase the "goodness" (in the Gestalt sense) of irregularly shaped figures may appear to replace portions of the stabilized figure, and the completions for missing portions of simple forms are often less than substantial.

Haber and associates (e.g., Haber 1967; Haber & Hershenson 1965; Sales & Haber 1968) have recently shown that when words are presented for very brief intervals such that no letters can be discriminated on the first trial, repeated presentations of the words at this same exposure duration increases the probability of correct report of all letters by the end of 10-15 trials. The finding appears not to be a function of such obvious variables as word length or familiarity. Along with other theoretical possibilities, Haber (1967) has considered Hebb's model applicable to his data, the repetition effect being due to such variables as (a) stimulus adequacy (intensity, discriminability), (b) extent of initial organization of particular cell assemblies, and (c) degree of assembly arousal. Haber has yet to show, however, how his use of the model to account for the repetition effect in adults with normal vision *does not* conflict with Hebb's statement (1963, p. 21) that "the theory makes perception the digital activity of cell assemblies and does not provide for analogical processes within them."

OTHER MEDIATING FUNCTIONS IN THE SYSTEM

The semiautonomous nature of cell assembly and phase sequence activities provides an account of other central processes that share a selective interaction with stimulus input. Wilson and Wilson (1967, pp. 64-66) have quite briefly and lucidly presented Hebb's treatment of these mediating processes, and the present summary is drawn from that discussion.

Attention is the excitation from a previously active assembly that impinges upon, and assists in the firing of, an assembly that is being activated by a sensory event. *Meaning* exists in the interconnections among a set of assemblies that can maintain activity within the set longer than in any of its components. A complete perceptual event resides in the rapid serial excitation of the cell assemblies comprising a phase sequence. *Thinking* occurs through complex and extended phase sequences, and the component assemblies of the thought pattern may be determined by external stimuli, by central facilitation as in the attention process, or by both. Reverberation within the neural network assures a transient representation, or *immediate memory* of a stimulus idea or object beyond its point of entry into the thought process. *Permanent memory* is accounted for in the formation of the structural changes postulated in cell assembly development.

Hebb discusses developmental and species differences in terms of the distinction between perceptual and associative learning. In the human, the autonomous slow-wave activity of the normal resting cortex predominates until a history of sensory stimulation develops. First learning is *perceptual learning*, the slow and continuous process of organizing this ongoing activity into cell assemblies and phase sequences that can then be easily activated by a sensory event. Later learning occurs in associating already organized systems into higher-order ones, increasing the probability that one assembly will excite others in the association. Phylogenetic differences are similarly accounted for. Lower species have less association cortex with which to organize higher-order systems; thus initial learning should take less time, and complexity of final learning should be of a lesser degree than in man, for whom perceptual learning is slower and in whom the species capabilities for more complex learning are realized less rapidly.

Within Hebb's system, *motivation* is based on the assumed behavioral role of the diffuse activating systems of the brain. To an extent generally proportional to sensory input, the brain is aroused by diffuse bombardment through these systems, and this is assumed to be analogous to drive state since utilization of the cue value of specific stimuli depends upon activation. The slow-wave, hypersynchronous brain activity characteristic of sleep occurs when the arousal system is not functioning. A moderate amount of diffuse stimulation facilitates cortical function, but intense stimulation disrupts assembly systems, and the cue function of a sensory event is lost. This is *emotional disruption* in Hebb's theory.

Ongoing activity in the brain may not influence the assembly aroused by a sensory event. Hebb defines as *intention* central guidance of behavior by an enduring system that maintains its independence despite sensory input. When incompatible phase sequences are excited by sensory and central states, the result is the disruption of behavior by *conflict*. Arousal of a phase sequence by central facilitation prior to its arousal by a sensory event is *expectancy*, and facilitation of the same sequence by the sensory event provides confirmation, or *cognitive reinforcement* of the expectancy. Expectation, set, and current stimulation control voluntary behavior. *Recall* is arousal by central facilitation of a sequence that has been aroused before by a sensory event. Thus, memory and perception involve the same kinds of activity; recognition is necessarily involved in perception.

In summary, Hebb's theory deals with the specifics of how stimulus-response relationships are formed; they are associations formed among systems and circuits rather than discrete sensory and motor elements. And, with these systems and circuits, Hebb has the physiological mechanism for the plasticity of behavior evident in perception, learning, motivation, emotion, memory, attention, reinforcement, expectancy, voluntary behavior, and sleep. The theory is nonetheless convincing by postulating all these as particular aspects of the central semiautonomous process.

Gibson's Psychophysical Theory of Perception

ORIENTING HYPOTHESES

Gibson's concern is with the process by which an organism maintains "contact" with its environment. His formula appears simple: "perception is a function of stimulation and stimulation is a function of the environment; hence perception is a function of the environment" (1959, p. 459). The theory is focused on veridical perception, consideration of the environment is at the level of ecology rather than at the level of molecules or continents, and concern with stimulation from the environment is in its excitation of entire sense organs rather than single receptors. Maturation and learning function to increase the organism's ability to discriminate the details of information resident in the energy distributions stimulating receptive surfaces (Gibson & Gibson 1955; E. J. Gibson 1969).

Gibson's explicit hypothesis is that "for every aspect or property of the phenomenal world of an individual in contact with his environment, however subtle, there is a variable in the energy flux at his receptors, however complex, with which the phenomenal property would correspond if a psychophysical experiment could be performed" (1959, p. 465). The hypothesized stimulus variables differ from the classically considered sensations of color, sound, touch, taste, and smell, and a reformulation of the problems of perception accompanies the change in the concept of stimulation. The above hypothesis incorporates, as the causally chained variables leading to perception, the ecology of the environment, the orders and patterns of energy distributions at the body surface, the sensory equipment (organs, not individual receptors) of the perceiver, and neural transmission through the projection centers of the cerebral cortex.

The central fact of perception, for Gibson, is that potential information about surrounding objects and events resides within the array of energy at the organism's receptive surface, and the perceptual mechanism functions to obtain the information that provides contact with the environment. Explaining this fact requires a reconsideration of the nature of perception and stimulation and of the relationship between stimulation and perception on the one hand, and on the other, that between stimulation and the environment.

For all perceptual systems, stimulation is always energy, and it is not to be confused with its source in the environment. Neither is it to be confused with excitation; stimulation has reference backward to the environment while excitation has reference forward to the organism. Stimulation for a receptive cell is not the same thing as stimulation for an animal, and perception is a function of the variables of adjacent and successive order in the energy which stimulates the animal. A stimulus is never a replica or a representation of the object or event perceived; the only necessity is that it be specific to its source. Stimulation is *not* elemental sensations of color, sound, taste, touch, and smell that the perceptual mechanism compounds, by sensory organization or learned association, into a resulting percept. Such supposedly irreducible data of sensory experience are the occasional symptoms of perception, not its cause; they are the products of introspection. Introspection informs us that awareness of the world has an objective and a subjective pole, that proprioception and interoception necessarily accompany exteroception, and that the phenomenal world is continuous in both adjacent and successive order. In introspection, a cultivated naiveté about what the world *does* look, feel, and sound like provides necessary directives for research, but introspection to ferret out the essential sensory qualities in perception is misdirected. In vision, sensory qualities are evident in the visual *field* but not the visual *world* (see Gibson 1950a, chap. 3; 1952b; Boring 1952a, 1952b). One can experience the visual field by ferreting out the sensory qualities of the patchwork of color and brightness in the view afforded by a particular fixation of the eyes, and the more one observes the patchwork, the less one *sees the objects* in the world. However, the objects, as well as the sensory qualities, are specified in the optical stimulation; they simply depend on higher *orders* of stimulation.

Perception applies equally to behavior and to consciousness, neither of which is necessarily prior; it occurs in either reacting to or contemplating the environment, and no mediating processes for explaining the conversion of sensory data into percepts are needed in the theory. Gibson's central hypothesis disclaims the classical notion that remembering, as the arousal of memory images, is essential for veridical perception. Recalling and imagining occur, and they are important, but they are a function of something other than stimulation as Gibson defines it—"a flowing sea of energy in which the organism is immersed," whose variations of order constitute considerably more potential stimuli than any one observer is likely to respond to. The energy flux provides multiple concomitant variables of stimulation that can yield, and guarantee the validity of, the same quality of experience; such is the case with various gradients in the array of energy specifying visual depth in their registration at the retina. The theory does not claim that perception is innate, nor does it deny that perception is limited by the sensory equipment of the species or that it is influenced by attention. Rather, it claims that perceptual learning is increasing awareness of the detail in stimulation, that perception is not a mental act necessitated by poor sensory equipment, and that differences attributed to attention reflect differences in the stimulus variables attended to. Since the theory is mainly concerned with veridical perception, misperception in general is not addressed, although Gibson's discussion of the geometrical illusions in vision (1966, pp. 312-15) resembles Gregory's (1963) account of these phenomena as instances of misapplied constancy scaling.

THE INFORMATION AVAILABLE IN STIMULATION

Though Gibson intends a general theory of perception (see, e.g., Gibson 1962, 1963 on touch; Gibson 1966 for discussion of auditory, haptic-somatic, taste, and smell perception), the theory has been most thoroughly elaborated for visual perception. The considerations given vision would, with appropriate modification, extend to other perceptual domains as well as the interactions among perceptual systems.

The initial consideration of electromagnetic energy is what Gibson terms the optic array (1961, pp. 254–57). Such an array "is the light converging to any position in the transparent medium of an illuminated environment insofar as it has different intensities in different directions. . . . Geometrically speaking, it is a pencil of *rays* converging to a point, the rays taking their origin from textured surfaces and the point being the nodal point of an eye" (1961, p. 255). The important fact about the array is that it has pattern and structure—fine structure at the level of seconds of arc, coarse structure at the level of minutes, and gross structure at the level of degrees. Varying structures and transitions in structures are specific to the regularities and irregularities of the surfaces, edges, and corners of objects reflecting light, and these differences in patterns are the natural stimuli for all animals. The array's fundamental variables would be such as the following (1961, p. 260):

1. Abruptness of transition, or the "sharpness" of boundaries ranging from an edge to a penumbra.
2. Amount of transition, measured as a ratio or fraction of adjacent intensities.
3. Shape of a boundary, e.g., rectilinear, curved, or pointed.
4. Closure or non-closure of a boundary.
5. Density of transitions, or number per unit angle of the array.
6. Change in the density of transitions; also the "gradient" or rate of change in density of transitions.
7. Motion of a boundary relative to others.
8. Presence or absence of transitions within a closed boundary of the array.

Such variables function by laws (see Gibson 1961, p. 260) to specify the phenomenal properties of determinant surfaces (see Gibson 1950b, pp. 368–69) and various types of perceived forms (see Gibson 1951, pp. 405–8). The following types of information, as well as their importance to the active process of seeing the world, are present in the light stimulus (Gibson 1960):

1. Presence or absence of texture. Lack of texture in a region of the array specifies an unobstructed medium of air; texture specifies a relatively solid surface. When texture is absent in the downward direction, it means loss of support and falling. Coarse texture identifies an optically near surface while denser and smaller texture identifies an optically far surface as evidenced by the refusal of Walk, Gibson, and Tighe's (1957) rats to descend from an elevated runway to that side of the visual cliff with denser texture.
2. Pattern or form depends on the spacing and regularity of transitional elements; texture may be grainy, pebbled, mottled, aligned, irregular, or sinuous.
3. Closed contours with internal texture specify solid objects; closed contours with external texture identify holes in the environment such as openings into caves.
4. Shape and size of abstract forms. The shape of a closed contour which is without motion and has neither internal nor external texture identifies the family of abstract forms which could produce that array.
5. Gradients of density of the same texture yield impressions of distance. Finer textures appear more distant in accordance with the law of visual angle, and stepwise increases in density correspond to edges.
6. Projective transformations of both contours and surfaces correspond to movement of the organism; they provide guidance and control of locomotion.
7. Forms and patterns remain invariant with perspective transformations, i.e., the array specifies an object throughout motion of the perceiver as well as transformations from bidimensional to tridimensional projections. This latter property redefines, and recommends the solution to, the problem of constancy and the stability of the phenomenal environment in spite of changes in the retinal image.

Gibson (1950b, 1952a, Gibson & Cornsweet 1952) distinguishes the dimensions of slant and tilt from the usual spatial directions of up-down, forward-backward, and near-far. Tilt depends upon clockwise or counterclockwise rotation of the optic array with respect to the up-down axis of the retina or the gravitational vertical. Gibson (1952a) found that veridical perception occurs when the optic array corresponds to the gravitational vertical, and misalignment of these two produces an unnatural situation for perception. Slant derives from gradients of texture that become finer and finer as the eye travels from near to far. The gradient may become finer in the down-up, up-down, right-to-left or left-to-right direction. Artificially produced texture gradients in each of these directions converging toward the center of the field of view produce the impressions of surface, solidity, recession, distance, and parallel-sidedness of Gibson, Purdy, and Lawrence's (1955) optical pseudo-tunnel. Gibson and Cornsweet (1952) distinguish between geographical and optical slant; a desert plane may be geographically flat, but an individual looking across the plane into the distance sees an optical slant of increasing fineness from himself to the horizon. Data from Gibson and Cornsweet indicate geographical and optical slant to be functionally and phenomenally different. Meanwhile, Gibson (1950b) has found correspondence between visual and tactual perception of slant.

Gibson has shown (1962, 1963) that many of the spatial properties of vision are also to be found in tactile-kinesthetic perception. He distinguishes between the impressions and information yielded by active, searching touch and by passive touch. Active touch is like ocular scanning in that it obtains information about the shape of objects over and above momentary transient sensations. In active touch, which involves joints and tendons in addition to tactile components, the perceived qualities are referred to the felt object rather than to the skin; the form of the object remains invariant in spite of changing tactile sensations. Also, new perceptual qualities such as rough-smooth, soft-hard, and such "solid geometry" qualities as curvature, planarity, parallelity of surfaces, edges, angles, and corners are yielded by active touch. Gibson's phenomenological approach also points out distinctions among the kinds of sources of touch stimulation. Brief deformations of the skin yield pressure, push, pat, slap, prick, and tap; prolonged deformations without displacement yield vibration, stretching, kneading, and pinching; prolonged deformations with displacement yield scratching, scraping, rubbing, sliding, brushing, and rolling.

It is Gibson's claim (1963) that the sense of touch provides the clearest examples of the invariance of perception with varying sensations. The increase in sensation that comes with pressing or squeezing an object specifies its *rigidity*; its *unity* prevails although feeling it with two fingers provides separate cutaneous sensations; the *stability* in its protuberances overrides the changes in sensation as one's finger passes over and beyond the irregularities; its *weight* remains invariant in spite of the differences in sensation from the receptors of the finger joints, wrist joints, and arm joints; and its *shape* remains the same whether the object is specified by a photograph or by active touch (Caviness & Gibson 1962).

Gibson notes (1959, pp. 497–98) that his theory still needs adequate accounts of selective attention, of the problem of illusions and errors in perception, of the problem of the perception of meaning, of the role of interoceptive stimulation in perception, and of the problem of perceptual neurophysiology. There is also an obvious need for the development of psychophysical methodology adequate to the investigation of Gibson's higher-order variables. Gibson (1963, p. 14) suggests that "the first problem in perceptual physiology is not how the brain responds to form as such, unvarying form, but instead how it responds to the invariant variables of changing form." The need is for a physiological theory of object perception rather than picture perception.

Adaptation-Level Theory

We have seen how the Gestalt psychologists made the problem of organization primary not only for perception but for all types of behavior. Their solution to the problem was to make whole-qualities a postulate, thereby removing it from further question. Granting that organization is perhaps the most important problem in all psychology, we cannot rest content with the mere ascription of various findings to organization. Moreover, we now realize that the segregated units (Gestalten) of the configurationists are not completely autonomous or self-determined. Each unit, in addition to its own figure-ground organization, depends for its properties in large measure on internal norms that must be included in any account of perceptual processes.

The perception of objects is envisaged in adaptation-level theory as part of the broader problem of perceiving and cognizing classes of objects. Thus we see a man not only as a segregated unit but as a member of the class of men having various attributes. Any given man is perceived as tall or short, kind or cruel,

intelligent or stupid, and so on through all the attributes men possess. Adaptation-level theory deals with such properties by starting from some obvious and commonly observed facts. If a number of individuals are asked to order a representative set of stimuli varying along some dimension such as loudness, lightness, or pleasantness, some stimuli will be classed as loud, light, or pleasant, some as soft, dark, or unpleasant with one or more as medium, neutral, or indifferent. Furthermore, the stimuli dividing the bipolar continua will be found to vary with the composition of the stimuli, with the background against which they are perceived, and from individual to individual. The stimuli perceived as dividing the stimuli into bipolar opposites and called medium or indifferent denote the adaptation level underlying the individual judgments. In general, the adaptation level (AL) has been found to be a weighted log mean of focal, background, and residual stimuli.

It follows from the definition of AL that stimuli above or on one side of the indifferent zone (AL) have properties opposite to stimuli below or on the other side of the neutral zone. The way in which stimuli are ordered (organized) with respect to any given attribute depends upon their relations to prevailing AL. A sound heard against the background noises of a busy street is hardly heard but against the stillness of night it is very loud; a gray that appears light on a black background is perceived to be dark on a white background; and a weight that is judged heavy by a college student is reported as light by a truck driver. These cases represent changes in perception of identical stimuli that spring from differences in AL either as a result of variations in accompanying stimuli or as a result of different prior experience. Differences in AL thus account for different reactions by the same individual to identical stimuli under different ancillary conditions and for different reactions by individuals to the same constellation of stimuli.

Let us examine the concept of AL a little more closely in order to see more clearly its implications. According to the weighted log mean definition, AL is the pooled effect of all stimuli constituting an observable class or set. Not only is there interaction or pooling of perceived properties of objects as wholes, there is also interaction among the various dimensions or attributes in the establishment of any given level. Thus, as Helson and T. Kozaki have shown (1968), the AL for apparent size is affected by duration of exposure both of stimuli being judged and anchor stimuli. Similarly, frequency of presentation also affects the extent to which given stimuli influence prevailing level. In short, *all conditions within the stimulus constellation and in the perceiving organism enter into the determination of AL.* When only one dimension of stimulation is in question and conditions such as frequency, duration, area, instructions and other factors are the same for all stimuli, then the weighted log mean formula for AL need take only the dimension under consideration into account, otherwise special parameters must be included to provide for special weighting factors. Thus, for the unidimensional case where a set of visual stimuli (X_i) are judged against a background (B), the formula would read:

$$A = (\bar{X}_i^p \cdot B^q \cdot R^r)^{1/p+q+r}$$

where A is the AL, $\bar{X}_i$ is the log mean of the reflectances being judged for lightness, B is the background reflectance, R is a reflectance denoting the effects of residual stimulation, and p, q, and r are weighting coefficients that must be determined experimentally (Michels & Helson 1949). The greater area of the background is taken into account by making the weighting coefficient, q, greater than p for the usual viewing situation. The coefficient r is determined by designing experiments so as to yield data for its evaluation (cf. Michels & Helson 1949). Other examples of differential weighting are to be found in Helson (1964) and Helson and T. Kozaki (1968).

Reference has been made to the fact that not all stimuli have equal weight in determining AL. Particularly important are stimuli that differ in recency, frequency, intensity, area, duration, and in higher order attributes such as meaningfulness, familiarity, or ego-involvement. So far AL theory has been concerned largely with variation in sensory dimensions, but it is not limited in principle to these as is shown by a number of studies in interpersonal relations, attitude and trait scaling, words and phrases having quantitative denotations, and transposition and learning (see Helson 1964, for discussion and references to these and other studies in various areas).

Three broad classes of stimuli have been identified as contributing to prevailing AL and within these it is useful to distinguish between series, predominant, anchor or background, and standard stimuli. When a set of stimuli varying along some dimension such as luminance, loudness, or weight is presented, we refer to them as series stimuli, the members of the series furnishing a context for every other member. If one of the series stimuli is emphasized by longer exposure than the others or by calling attention to it in the instructions given subjects, we refer to such stimuli as predominant stimuli. If a given stimulus, either inside or outside the series, is repeated or emphasized very strongly, for example, the background against which a series of colors is viewed, or a 900 gm weight which is presented before each member of a series of weights from 200 to 400 gm, we speak of it as an anchor or background stimulus. Finally, if series stimuli are judged with respect to an anchor we speak of the anchor as a standard stimulus. It has been found that effects of stimuli on AL increase progressively from being series or contextual stimuli, to predominant, to anchor, to standard stimuli, and the weighting coefficients must be increased accordingly in the weighted log mean definition of AL.

With the development of various functions embodying AL as a parameter it is now usual to determine AL by least squares fits to experimental data and then to use the weighted log mean definition to determine the relative contributions of focal (series), background (anchor) or standard, and residual stimuli to AL (Helson 1948; Michels & Helson 1949; Helson 1964; Restle & Merryman 1968; Restle 1970). It is thus evident that AL theory provides a means for quantifying the factors responsible for organization in its many behavioral manifestations. We are now prepared to discuss some concrete applications of AL theory to a number of crucial problems in perception.

One of the most difficult, and in some ways mysterious, problems of the psychology of perception and judgment has been the so-called time-order error (TOE). It springs from the fact that when a series of stimuli is compared with a standard, usually the middle stimulus in the series, the standard is not judged equal to itself. Various explanations of this phenomenon have been shown to be inadequate and the reason is not hard for us to see: so long as it is assumed that only the standard and the stimulus being judged are concerned in the judging process, such ad hoc explanations as fading images, physiological traces, and the like, will not work. Only recognition of the fact

that all the stimuli affect the judgment has yielded a satisfactory quantitative theory of TOE (Michels & Helson 1954). If we admit that, in addition to the standard, the other stimuli enter into the judgment, we are saying that the effective standard is not merely the stimulus designated as such but the pooled effect of all the stimuli and this is simply the AL.

Attempts have been made to explain away effects of context as mere semantic changes having no basis in the sensory data or as artifacts to be eliminated in various ways. These arguments seem plausible when verbal category ratings (very loud, soft, etc.) are used in judging stimuli, but effects of anchors on series stimuli are equally great when judgments are in numbers (Helson & A. Kozaki 1968) and in Stevens' type "magnitude" estimates. Thus in magnitude estimations where a modulus is provided and numerical judgments are used, the obtained scale values of stimuli (exponents of the power function) are affected by range and distance of stimuli from threshold, position of the standard, distance of the first variable, size of the modulus, and whether fractional or multiple types of estimates are made (Poulton 1968; Poulton & Simmonds 1963). Even an unjudged part of the stimulus-constellation, such as reflectance of background against which visual stimuli are scaled, has been shown to influence the shape of the psychophysical function (Egeth, Avant, and Bevan 1968). For AL theory context and anchor effects are not errors to be explained away or ignored; they are important indicators of the way the organism adjusts. Such effects are now known to be orderly and predictable and enter into the explanation of many otherwise unresolved problems (cf. Bevan 1968). Let us consider some of them.

Among the most interesting and puzzling perceptual phenomena have been the visual illusions. It has been known, for example, that various factors within figures such as the Müller-Lyer, Zöllner, Wundt, Hering, and Necker figures determine the amount or potency of these illusions. In addition, factors within the organism, such as prior experience, are also known to affect perception of figural properties (Bell & Bevan 1968). That pooling of parts making up the various figures is responsible for the illusions they produce has been known for a long time but only recently within the framework of AL theory have the relative contributions of focal, contextual, and residual stimuli been quantitatively evaluated as in a recent study of an illusion of extent, wherein the perceived length of a line is influenced by the size or area of boxes tangent to the ends of the line (Restle & Merryman 1968). In this study observers were presented lines of 4, 6, 8, 10, and 12 units in length with boxes either 4, 6, 8, 10, or 12 units on a side. The Os were asked to denote the apparent length of the center line by pressing one of six keys of which the extreme left denoted "quite short" and the extreme right "quite long" with the intermediate keys denoting intermediate lengths. The results show the larger the boxes at the ends of the lines the shorter do the lines appear to be, except for the two shortest lines which do not suffer any illusory shortening. Our interest extends beyond the phenomenological facts; we, like the authors, are interested also in the analysis leading to a quantitative evaluation of figural and organismic factors responsible for the illusion.

Using a simple linear hypothesis, Restle and Merryman assume that the perceived length of the line J_A, is a function of the ratio of the line, L, to the AL, A, or:

$$J_A = L/A \qquad \text{[1]}$$

A is a weighted mean of line length, box size (B), and residuals, R, so that we have:

$$A = (L^p \cdot B^q \cdot R^r)^{1/p+q+r} \qquad [2]$$

p, q, and r are weighting coefficients that can be normalized to equal 1.0 so that the exponent in Eq. 1 becomes 1.0. We can now write Eq. 1 as follows by substituting the value of A from Eq. 2:

$$J_A = L/A = L^{1-p} \cdot B^{-q} \cdot R^{-r} \qquad [3]$$

The least squares solution for the values of the weighting coefficients turn out to be 0.082 for line length, 0.138 for box size, and 0.593 for residual or organismic factors.

It is noteworthy that the largest contribution to the magnitude of the illusion is the residual and this argues against the Gestalt law of autonomy in so far as it places the main emphasis on purely figural properties as the source of whole qualities. Another important result of this study by Restle and Merryman is methodological: by using the method of so-called absolute judgment, or single stimuli, there was no bias introduced into the judgments by the presence of an anchor or standard. We have an example here of a type of analysis that keeps figural or whole properties intact yet the factors responsible for them have been isolated and measured.

Using similar procedures, Avant and his co-workers (Avant and Kent 1970; Wagner and Avant 1970; and Avant, Wagner, and Kent, in preparation) have investigated the influence of lines *outside* the Müller-Lyer figure on the M-L illusion, and conversely, the influence of the M-L figure employed as a contextual stimulus on the perceived length of lines. Other illusions were also studied (Titchener's area illusion and the Zöllner illusion in one of its variants) and the authors conclude that: (1) spatial ALs may be established as quickly as chromatic ALs, which may occur practically instantaneously; (2) the responses required of Os make the ascription of these phenomena to other than perceptual processes highly unlikely; and (3) lawful relations govern the various phenomena when analyzed from the point of view of AL theory.

STIMULUS GENERALIZATION, TRANSPOSITION, AND EQUIVALENCE

Contrary to nativistic and intuitional theories of perception there is development and learning in this function as well as in motor and higher intellectual activities. We have already noted that objects are perceived as members of classes and we must now ask how this is brought about since the new-born child can hardly be presumed to come into the world with pre-established internal norms. At least the beginnings of a new approach to the development of perception have been made in treatments of transposition, stimulus generalization, and stimulus equivalence from the point of view of AL theory.

In the matter of transposition of perceptual discrimination, AL theory differs from both pattern and elementaristic theories as the following experiments by Helson and Kaplan (1950) and Campbell and Kral (1958) demonstrate. In the experiment by the first-named authors Ss were shown five gray squares mounted on a black background arranged in random order and were asked to choose one. They were then informed whether their choice was right or wrong. The grays had reflectances of 15, 20, 28, 50, and 62 percent. The reflectance of 28 percent was called the correct stimulus, and after Ss made 10 correct choices in succession, the same stimuli were then presented on a white background. The first choice of the correct stimulus on the new background constituted the test of transposition of the discrimination. According to element theories, the gray having 28 percent reflectance should have been chosen from among the five grays on the white background because it was identical with the training stimulus; and according to pattern theories it should have been chosen because it occupied the same position in the lightness pattern on the white background as it did on the black background. If, however, transfer is based on similarity, that is, on the same gradient of excitation with respect to AL, then the stimulus of 50 or 62 percent reflectance should be chosen on the white background since these stimuli had approximately the same lightness on the white background as the training stimulus had on the black background. Of the 62 Ss, 53 percent chose the stimulus of 50 percent reflectance; 8 percent chose the stimulus of 62 percent reflectance; 32 percent chose the stimulus of 28 percent reflectance, and the remaining 7 percent chose the stimulus of 20 percent reflectance. Hence 61 percent of the Ss chose in accordance with relation to prevailing AL in transfer trials.

An even more striking confirmation of AL theory was found by Campbell and Kral using parakeets as Ss. In their experiment six birds were taught to eat from a food dish over which a card was placed having a lightness value of 3, and to avoid dishes with cards having lightness values of 1 and 5. Training was given with background lightness of value 4. After 20 correct choices in the training trials, food dishes with covers having values of 1 and 3 were presented on a background having a lightness value of 2. In the 20 transposition trials, the birds chose the dish with the card of value 1 rather than the card of value 3, the percentages being 85, 80, 70, 85, 90, and 45. Campbell and Kral maintain that the animals transferred by similarity since the card of value 1 on the background of value 2 was most nearly equivalent to the card of value 3 on background of value 4. Thus in two experiments, one with human and the other with animal Ss, transposition occurred in accordance with predictions from AL theory. That the birds behaved more in accordance with AL theory than the humans was probably due to the fact that 20, rather than only 1, transfer trials were made in the test of transfer. Still other applications of the AL model to transfer have been made with considerable success by James (1953), Zeiler (1963), and Capehart and Pease (1968).

Closely bound up with the problem of transposition is that of stimulus generalization. Here again context effects have been largely neglected in S-R theories of stimulus generalization, it being assumed that the generalization gradient decreases symmetrically on both sides of the specific stimulus originally learned. An experiment by Thomas and Jones (1962) with spectral stimuli showed that the maximal frequency with which a stimulus was chosen from a number of stimuli as the learned stimulus depended upon the series of stimuli containing the learned stimulus, contrary to elementaristic theories. Repeating this experiment with squares of differing sizes, Helson and Avant (1967) verified the earlier findings: after a 3-inch square had been "learned," it was presented among five different sets of squares in which it occupied the top, next to the top, middle, next to the bottom, and bottom positions in size compared with other members of the series. Again the stimulus chosen as the previously learned one depended upon the test series, the maximal frequency shifting toward the center of the test series.

The adequacy of a theory is often better tested by its ability to explain results in apparent conflict with it than by its ability to account for results expected from it. A case in point is a study by White (1965) in which the maximum frequency of response was to the learned stimulus: the generalization gradient decreased unidirectionally, thus showing no context effect to speak of. Hebert and Capehart (1969), surmising that White's results were due to "overpresentation" of the original training stimulus, devised an experiment with lifted weights in which the training stimulus was presented to independent groups either equally often or five times as often as the test stimuli. The results showed their surmise was correct: overpresentation of the training stimulus yielded the unilateral generalization gradient while normal presentation (equally often) yielded the shift toward the center of the test series. Since, as noted above, frequency of presentation affects AL, both the White and the Hebert and Pease results find explanation within a single theory.

Transposition and stimulus generalization have been subsumed to the problem of stimulus equivalence by Capehart, Tempone, and Hebert (1969). In transposition and generalization, stimuli are essentially being responded to as the same or similar. Following Helson (1964) and Murdock (1960), these writers pointed out that the farther stimuli are from AL, the more distinctive they are, and hence the more readily are they categorized. In the experiments cited above by Capehart and Pease (1968) and by Hebert and Capehart (1969), latencies were longest for stimuli at or near AL, and decreased with distance from AL, a fact supporting the contention that stimuli farther from AL are categorized more easily. As Capehart, Tempone, and Hebert point out, two types of gradients are implied by their AL model, one based on similarity and the other on category responses in the conditional discrimination situation. The latter should be investigated further, they suggest, "because it may be of great interest in exploring the limits of class or category responding" (1969, p. 417). The problem of stimulus equivalence raises questions concerning the pooling process for it is by pooling that frames of reference or internal norms are formed. Pooling is by no means a simple and indiscriminate process and an understanding of what will and will not pool is important for the understanding of the categorizing process. Let us, therefore, consider some of the salient features of the pooling process.

SOME CHARACTERISTICS OF THE POOLING PROCESS

The tendency for "impressions" to fuse was noted long ago and, to paraphrase William James, everything fuses that can fuse and what doesn't, fuses as well as it can! That pooling is greatest within a sense modality or dimension and decreases across modalities or dimensions is to be expected and indeed has been shown experimentally. Behar and Bevan (1961) found that although anchors had greater effects within the same sensory mode when visual or auditory time intervals were judged, the cross-modal interactions (vision on audition and vice versa) were highly significant. Even more surprising, perhaps, is the simultaneous induction of multiple anchor effects on some dimensions while others remain unaffected as shown in a study by Turner and Bevan (1962). In this study three groups of Ss

were presented rectangles with anchor stimuli that deviated (1) in size and shape from the series stimuli while their color was the same; or (2) in color and shape with size neutral, that is, equal to the middle member of the series; or (3) in color and size with shape neutral, that is, intermediate with regard to length and breadth. All Ss judged the size, shape, and color of the series stimuli. The results showed clear anchor effects on the two dimensions of the anchor that differed markedly from the series stimuli while the dimension on which the anchor was neutral showed no effect. Hence while there is pooling within and across dimensions and modalities, there is also independent variability. The pooling process is therefore not an all-or-none affair.

If the pooling mechanism can extend across sensory modalities, it is not surprising to find interactions between different bodily members and between cognitive and sensory systems. One illustration of each is enough to show that James' statement referred to above is even more general than he probably realized. Dinnerstein (1965) found that anchors of 20 or 320 gm held in the left hand affected comparisons of a series of weights ranging from 70–90 gm with a standard of 80 gm hefted with the right hand. Here the sensory areas in two different hemispheres must interact, a fact supported by Adams and Helson (1966) who found that the two-point threshold was smaller when the points were applied across the midline of the body than on one side of the body.

Pooling involving judgments of size as affected by color-coding demonstrates the interaction of cognitive and sensory systems in a study by Helson and T. Kozaki (unpublished data). In this study Ss judged the size of 10 squares ranging from 20 to 150 mm on a side in terms of a rating scale from very, very small through medium to very, very large. Five of the squares were colored green and five were orange. The green squares were 20, 27, 36, 48 and 64 mm on a side while the orange squares were 48, 64, 84, 110, and 150 mm on a side. The stimuli were presented in random order yet the two series were grouped into distinct classes according to their color. Both the slopes of the two curves fitted to the judgments of the green and orange stimuli as well as the judgments of the two stimuli common to the green and orange series (48 and 64 mm squares) were significantly different. The 48 and 64 mm squares were judged larger in the green series than in the orange series. After this experiment was completed, it was found that a similar experiment had been performed by Brown and McBride at the University of California at Berkeley some years earlier but with lifted weights (communicated by W. Köhler to one of the authors, L. L. A.). In their experiment, Ss judged weights of 200, 300, 400, 500, and 600 gm colored green and another series, 500, 600, 700, 800, and 900 gm colored red. Thus the 500 and 600 gm weights were common to the two series. After several rounds of judgments, the Ss judged a test weight of 550 gm colored red or green. As in the experiment by Helson and T. Kozaki, the test stimulus colored green was judged heavier than the one colored red. In discussing this experiment the late Professor Köhler attributed the difference in judgment to the fact that the weights belonged to different organizations when differently colored, thus using organization as an explanatory concept.

An AL explanation, however, attributes the different organization to the fact that different ALs are involved: in the green series the 48 and 64 gm weights are *above* AL and, therefore, are judged heavy while in the orange series, they are *below* AL and are, therefore, judged to be light. We regard organization as derivative from AL since the way in which stimuli are perceived depends upon their relation to prevailing ALs.

A critical issue for theories of perception is the way they handle, or do not handle, effects of subliminal stimulation. Existential and phenomenological theories like structuralism and Gestalttheorie cannot account for the fact that stimuli that are not perceived as such may nevertheless have profound influence on what is perceived because their explanations are couched only in terms of phenomenal data. The doctrine of traces, advanced by Koffka (1935) for the influence of memory and residuals of perception on present experience, does not apply to subliminal stimulation because it is present and hence cannot be considered as a trace. A number of studies have shown that subliminal stimuli, interpolated between supraliminal stimuli, can alter the perceived quality and magnitude of the latter. Thus Bevan and Pritchard (1963*b*) showed that subliminal sounds raised judgments of supraliminal sounds; Black and Bevan (1960) showed the same was true with shock stimuli; and Boardman and Goldstone (1962) found that subliminal visual figures affected the perception of supraliminal form judged for size. However, it must not be inferred from these results that subliminal stimuli are always effective in perception, at least in a direct way. It has long been known that overtones determine the timbre of musical sounds without being heard as such, and the timbre is not merely a reflection of the pitch of the component partials. But we should not assume that the limit of effectiveness of stimuli is reached at the absolute threshold in view of the pervasiveness of pooling in perceptual processes (cf. Bevan 1964).

We can now face the question: When is an object included among a given class of objects so that it is categorized as having such and such qualities? This question concerns the problem of what will pool in forming internal norms. The problem of relevance was first raised explicitly by Brown (1953) following its recognition by Helson (1947) who restricted pooling to attributes or objects within given universes of discourse. There are many examples from everyday life showing that objects are assigned to different classes when they exceed the usual limits of members of the class. Thus men in fairy stories far outside normal limits of height are called giants, and beings with extraordinary powers and immortality were called gods by the ancient Greeks and Romans. Ubiquitous as pooling is, there are limits to the interaction of stimuli, and we now have considerable experimental evidence bearing on this question. We have already seen that various dimensions interact within given sense modalities and that different senses interact—for example, vision and hearing. Much of the work by the sensory-tonic field theorists was concerned with interaction of various sense modalities as well as with interaction of postural, emotional, and cognitive (meaning) systems with vision.

In view of the many instances and types of pooling, it is nevertheless a process that has limits as pointed out earlier in this section. It has been suggested that the limits are set by the relevance of stimuli, particularly anchor stimuli, to the stimuli being judged. Following Brown's demonstration that a tray weighing the same as, but different in shape from, an anchor stimulus had less effect than the latter on judgments of lifted weights (1953), Bevan and Pritchard (1963*a*) found that introduction of a circular stimulus having the same area as a rectangular anchor had no effect on perception of squareness of series

stimuli. Similarly, anchors having the same shape but one-fourth or four times as large an area as an effective anchor failed to exert anchor effects. The same was true of an anchor equal in area but differing in color from an effective anchor. These writers conclude that "Effective anchors must possess the criterial attributes of the stimuli whose judgments they influence" (1963*a*, p. 159).

We are still left with the problem of what makes for relevance. The concept of relevance implies similarity, nearness, effectiveness, pertinence, and so on. We seem to be in a vicious circle for if a stimulus modifies perception of other stimuli, we say it is relevant to them, and if it is relevant, it should affect them. It is obvious we cannot accept relevance as an undefined term and must seek its underlying factors. A study by Helson, Bevan, and Masters (1966) has thrown additional light on such factors. In this study *S*s judged the sizes of five circles that ranged from 9.0 to 15.0 in. in diameter following preadaptation to sets of small circles that ranged from 1.5 to 7.5 in. in diameter. Thirteen groups of *S*s were each presented different variants of the small circles in a preadaptation period. These varied in degree of likeness to the large, standard set of circles. One set consisted of empty, outline circles exactly like the test circles except for size; the other twelve sets contained angles varying in size and length of sides, and positively, negatively, or not correlated with the size of circles. In addition, some sets consisted of open circles (unenclosed angles); others were closed. The response language was also varied in some of the conditions.

It was found that while similarity of the preadapted stimuli to the standard ones was important, it was not the most important factor determining the effect of preadaptation on succeeding perception of the standard set. The preadaptation set of stimuli exerting greatest effect on judgments of the standard set was not the most similar set but the set containing enclosed angles with sizes of angles positively correlated with sizes of circles. Apparently the enclosed angles accentuated "smallness" of the preadapting circles to a greater extent than did any of the other twelve conditions. This set resulted in the lowest AL and highest judgments of size of the standard circles. It thus appears that anything that focalizes or lends greater weight to stimuli, whether or not it is similar to them, tends to increase their role in the pooling process and thus to modify internal norms.

We are thus able to account for the various cases of pooling discussed above as well as perceptual involvement in transposition and learning. The classical conditioning paradigm, for example, can thus be regarded as a process of focalizing a stimulus so that it modifies an internal norm that it would otherwise not do. In short, what stimuli we perceive to belong together depends on their relation to prevailing norms. Almost any stimulus may be perceived to relate to another if it enters into the formation of a common level for both. Something of this sort must underlie the types of perception and behavior characteristic of maladjusted and deviant personalities.

Many facts in everyday life are elucidated by what has been learned about the role of internal norms in perception and judgment. To take but one example, we venture the hypothesis that much of the unrest in our society springs from the perceived contrasts between various groups and strata. The contrast of super-abundance in some segments of society with poverty in others, of billions for a far-off war with lack of funds for slum clearance, hospitals, and medical care, and the many other contrasts that are perceived almost daily through modern media of communication accentuate the disequilibria that exist and are felt by so many of our people today. AL theory has shown that relative, not absolute, quantities determine our perceptions. This is true of the perception of socio-economic conditions as well as the perception of simple, psychophysical data. Perceptual theory is thus not unrelated to the facts and problems of everyday life.

References

ADAMS, C. K., and HELSON, H. Two-point threshold as a function of position in the dermatome. *Journal of Comparative and Physiological Psychology*, 1966, *62*, 314–16.

AMES, A., JR. Binocular vision as affected by relations between uniocular stimulus patterns in commonplace environments. *American Journal of Psychology*, 1946, *59*, 333–57.

—— Visual perception and the rotating trapezoidal window. *Psychological Monographs*, 1951, *65*, No. 14 (Whole No. 324).

—— Reconsideration of the origin and nature of perception in situations involving only inorganic phenomena. In S. RATNER (ed.) *Vision and action.* New Brunswick, N.J.: Rutgers University Press, 1953, pp. 251–74.

ARNHEIM, R. *Art and visual perception.* Berkeley: University of California Press, 1954.

ASCH, S. E. Gestalt theory. *International encyclopedia of the social sciences.* New York: MacMillan and Free Press (David Sills, editor), 1968, *6*, 158–75.

ATKINSON, J. W. and MCCLELLAND, D. C. The projective expression of needs. II. The effect of different intensities of the hunger drive on thematic apperception. *Journal of Experimental Psychology*, 1948, *38*, 643–58.

ATTNEAVE, F. and ARNOULT, M. D. The quantitative study of shape and pattern perception. *Psychological Bulletin*, 1956, *53*, 452–71.

AVANT, L. L. and KENT, M. Anchoring stimuli and the Müller-Lyer illusion. (Paper presented at the meeting of the Midwestern Psychological Association, Cincinnati, May, 1970.)

AVANT, L. L., WAGNER, K., and KENT, M. Helson's pooling model and the geometrical illusions in vision. (In preparation, 1970.)

BEHAR, I. and BEVAN, W. The perceived duration of auditory and visual intervals: cross-modal comparison and interaction. *American Journal of Psychology*, 1961, *74*, 17–26.

BELL, R. A. and BEVAN, W. The influence of anchors upon the operation of certain Gestalt organizing principles. *Journal of Experimental Psychology*, 1968, *78*, 670–78.

BEVAN, W. Perception: Evolution of a concept. *Psychological Review*, 1958, *65*, 34–55.

—— Subliminal stimulation. *Psychological Bulletin*, 1964, *61*, 81–99.

—— The contextual basis of behavior. *American Psychologist*, 1968, *23*, 701–14.

BEVAN, W. and PRITCHARD, J. F. The anchor effect and the problem of relevance in the judgment of shape. *Journal of General Psychology*, 1963a, *69*, 147–61.

—— Effect of "subliminal" tones upon the judgment of loudness. *Journal of Experimental Psychology*, 1963b, *66*, 23–29.

BEYRL, F. Über die Grössenauffassung bei Kindern. *Zeitschrift fur Psychologie*, 1926, *100*, 344–71. Cited in Brunswik, E., *Perception and the representative design of psychological experiments.* Berkeley: University of California Press, 1956, p. 83.

BLACK, R. W. and BEVAN, W. The effect of subliminal shock upon the judged intensity of weak shock. *American Journal of Psychology*, 1960, *73*, 262–67.

BLAKE, R. R. and VANDERPLAS, J. M. The effect of prerecognition hypotheses on veridical recognition thresholds in auditory perception. *Journal of Personality*, 1950, *19*, 95–115.

BOARDMAN, W. K. and GOLDSTONE, S. Effects of subliminal anchors upon judgment of size. *Perceptual and Motor Skills*, 1962, *14*, 475–82.

BOLLES, R. C. and BAILEY, D. E. Importance of object recognition in size constancy. *Journal of Experimental Psychology*, 1956, *51*, 222–25.

BORING, E. G. A new ambiguous figure. *American Journal of Psychology*, 1930, *42*, 444–45.

—— *The physical dimensions of consciousness.* New York: Appleton-Century-Crofts, 1933.

—— Visual perception as invariance. *Psychological Review*, 1952a, *59*, 141–48.

—— The Gibsonian visual field. *Psychological Review*, 1952b, *59*, 246–47.

BRALY, K. W. The influence of past experience in visual perception. *Journal of Experimental Psychology*, 1933, *16*, 613–43.

BRENTANO, F. *Psychologie vom Empirischen Standpunkte.* Leipzig: Duncker and Humboldt, 1874.

BRICKER, P. D. and CHAPANIS, A. Do incorrectly perceived tachistoscopic stimuli convey some information? *Psychological Review*, 1953, *60*, 181–88.

BROWN, D. R. Stimulus-similarity and the anchoring of subjective scales. *American Journal of Psychology*, 1953, *66*, 199–214.

BROWN, J. F. and VOTH, A. C. The path of seen movement as a function of the vector-field. *American Journal of Psychology*, 1937, *49*, 543–63.

BRUNER, J. S. Personality dynamics and the process of perceiving. In R. R. BLAKE and G. V. RAMSEY (eds.), *Perception: An approach to personality.* New York: Ronald Press, 1951, pp. 121–47.

—— On perceptual readiness. *Psychological Review*, 1957, *64*, 123–52.

BRUNER, J. S., and GOODMAN, C. C. Value and need as organizing factors in perception. *Journal of Abnormal and Social Psychology*, 1947, *42*, 33–44.

BRUNER, J. S. and POSTMAN, L. Tension and tension release as organizing factors in perception. *Journal of Personality*, 1947, *15*, 300–308.

—— An approach to social perception. In W. DENNIS (ed.), *Current trends in social psychology.* Pittsburgh: University of Pittsburgh Press, 1948, pp. 71–118.

—— Perception, cognition, and behavior. *Journal of Personality*, 1949a, *18*, 14–31.

—— On the perception of incongruity: A paradigm. *Journal of Personality*, 1949b, *18*, 206–223.

BRUNER, J. S., POSTMAN, L., and RODRIGUES, J. S. Stimulus appropriateness and ambiguity as factors in judgment. (Paper read at Eastern Psychological Association, 1950.)

BRUNSWIK, E. Entwicklung der Albedowahrnehmung. *Zeitschrift fur Psychologie*, 1928, *109*, 40–115. Cited in Brunswik, E. *Perception and the representative design of psychological experiments.* Berkeley: University of California Press, 1956, p. 83.

—— Distal focusing of perception: Size-constancy in a representative sample of situations. *Psychological Monographs*, 1944, No. 254.

—— *Systematic and representative design of psychological experiments.* Berkeley: University of California Press, 1947.

—— The conceptual framework of psychology. *International encyclopedia of unified science*, 1952, *1*, No. 10.

—— Representative design and probabilistic theory in a functional psychology. *Psychological Review*, 1955, *62*, 193–217.

—— *Perception and the representative design of psychological experiments.* Berkeley: University of California Press, 1956.

—— The conceptual focus of systems. In M. H. MARX (ed.), *Theories in contemporary psychology.* New York: Macmillan, 1963, pp. 226–37.

—— and REITER, L. Eindrucks-Charaktere schematisierter Gesichter. *Zeitschrift fur Psychologie*, 1937, *142*, 67–134. Cited in Brunswik, E., *Perception and the representative design of psychological experiments.* Berkeley: University of California Press, 1956, pp. 42ff, 100ff.

CAMPBELL, D. T. and KRAL, T. P. Transposition away from a rewarded stimulus card to a nonrewarded one as a function of shift in background. *Journal of Comparative and Physiological Psychology*, 1958, *51*, 592–95.

CAPEHART, J. and PEASE, V. An application of adaptation-level theory to transposition responses in a conditional discrimination. *Psychonomic Science*, 1968, *10*, 147–48.

CAPEHART, J., TEMPONE, V. J., and HEBERT, J. A theory of stimulus equivalence. *Psychological Review*, 1969, *76*, 405–18.

CARTER, L. F. and SCHOOLER, K. Value, need, and other factors in perception. *Psychological Review*, 1949, *56*, 200–207.

CAVINESS, J. A. and GIBSON, J. J. The equivalence of visual and tactual stimulation for the perception of solid forms. (Paper read at the meeting of the Eastern Psychological Association, Atlantic City, April, 1962.)

COHEN, H. B. The effect of contralateral visual stimulation on visibility with stabilized retinal images. *Canadian Journal of Psychology*, 1961, *15*, 212–19.

COMALLI, P. E., JR., WAPNER, S., and WERNER, H. Perception of verticality in middle and old age. *Journal of Psychology*, 1959, *47*, 259–66.

COMALLI, P. E., JR., WERNER, H., and WAPNER, S. Studies in physiognomic perception: III. Effect of directional dynamics and meaning-induced sets on autokinetic motions. *Journal of Psychology*, 1957, *43*, 289–99.

DINNERSTEIN, D. Intermanual effects of anchors on zones of maximal sensitivity in weight-discrimination. *American Journal of Psychology*, 1965, *78*, 66–74.

DJANG, S. The role of past experience in the visual apprehension of masked forms. *Journal of Experimental Psychology*, 1937, *20*, 29–59.

DUKES, W. F. Ecological representativeness in studying perceptual size-constancy in childhood. *American Journal of Psychology*, 1951, *64*, 87–93.

EGETH, H., AVANT, L. L., and BEVAN, W. Does context influence the shape of a perceptual scale? *Perception and Psychophysics*, 1968, *4*, 54–56.

VON EHRENFELS, C. Ueber Gestaltqualitäten. *Vierteljahres-schrift für wissentschaftliche Philosophie und Soziologie*, 1890, *14*, 249–92; *15*, 285ff.

ENGEL, E. The role of content in binocular resolution. *American Journal of Psychology*, 1956, *69*, 87–91.

——— Binocular fusion of dissimilar figures. *Journal of Psychology*, 1958, *46*, 53–57.

FEHRER, E. V. An investigation of the learning of visually perceived forms. *American Journal of Psychology*, 1935, *47*, 187–221.

FEIGL, H. Functionalism, psychological theory, and the uniting sciences: Some discussion remarks. *Psychological Review*, 1955, *62*, 232–35.

FIEANDT, K. V. Dressurversuche an der Farbenwahrnehmung. *Archives fur die Gesampt Psychologie*, 1936, *96*, 467–95. Cited in Brunswik, E., *Perception and the representative design of psychological experiments*. Berkeley: University of California Press, 1956, pp. 124–26.

FORBES, A. Problems of synaptic function. *Journal of Neurophysiology*, 1939, *2*, 465–72.

GARNER, W. R. *Uncertainty and structure as psychological concepts.* New York: John Wiley, 1962.

——— Good patterns have few alternatives. *American Scientist*, 1970, *58*, 34–42.

GARNER, W. R., and MORTON, J. Perceptual independence: Definitions, models, and experimental paradigms. *Psychological Bulletin*, 1969, *72*, 233–59.

GARNER, W. R., HAKE, H. W., and ERIKSEN, C. W. Operationism and the concept of perception. *Psychological Review*, 1956, *63*, 149–59.

GELLERMAN, L. W. Form discrimination in chimpanzees and two-year-old children: I. Form (triangularity) *per se. Journal of Genetic Psychology*, 1933, *42*, 3–27.

GIBSON, E. J. *Principles of perceptual learning and development.* New York: Appleton-Century-Crofts, 1969.

GIBSON, J. J. A critical review of the concept of set in contemporary experimental psychology. *Psychological Bulletin*, 1941, *38*, 781–817.

——— *The perception of the visual world.* Boston: Houghton Mifflin, 1950a.

——— The perception of visual surfaces. *American Journal of Psychology*, 1950b, *63*, 367–384.

——— What is a form? *Psychological Review*, 1951, *58*, 403–12.

——— The relation between visual and postural determinants of the phenomenal vertical. *Psychological Review*, 1952a, *59*, 370–75.

——— The visual field and the visual world: A reply to Professor Boring. *Psychological Review*, 1952b, *59*, 149–151.

——— Perception as a function of stimulation. *In* S. KOCH (ed.), *Psychology: A study of a science, Vol. 1.* New York: McGraw-Hill, 1959.

——— The information contained in light. *Acta Psychologica*, 1960, *17*, 23–30.

——— Ecological optics. *Vision Research*, 1961, *1*, 253–62.

——— Observations on active touch. *Psychological Review*, 1962, *69*, 477–91.

——— The useful dimensions of sensitivity. *American Psychologist*, 1963, *18*, 1–15.

——— *The senses considered as perceptual systems.* Boston: Houghton Mifflin, 1966.

GIBSON, J. J., and CORNSWEET, J. The perceived slant of visual surface—optical and geographical. *Journal of Experimental Psychology*, 1952, *44*, 11–15.

GIBSON, J. J. and GIBSON, E. J. Perceptual learning: Differentiation or enrichment? *Psychological Review*, 1955, *62*, 32–41.

GIBSON, J. J., PURDY, J., and LAWRENCE, L. A method of controlling stimulation for the study of space perception: The optical tunnel. *Journal of Experimental Psychology*, 1955, *50*, 1–14.

GOLDSTEIN, M. J., HIMMELFARB, S., and FEDER, W. A. A further study of the relationship between response bias and perceptual defense. *Journal of Abnormal and Social Psychology*, 1962, *64*, 56–62.

GOTTSCHALDT, K. Uber den einfluss der erfahrung auf die Wahrnehmung von Figuren. *Psychologische Forschung*, 1926, *8*, 261–317. (Translated and condensed as "Gestalt factors and repetition" in Ellis, W. D., *A source book of Gestalt psychology.* New York: Harcourt, 1938, pp. 109–35.

GRAHAM, C. H. Sensation and perception in an objective psychology. *Psychological Review*, 1958, *65*, 65–76.

GREGORY, R. L. Distortions of visual space as inappropriate constancy scaling. *Nature*, 1963, *199*, 678–80.

HABER, R. N. Repetition as a determinant of perceptual recognition processes. *In* W. WATHEN-DUNN, J. MOTT-SMITH, H. BLUM, and P. LIEBERMAN (eds.), *Models for the perception of speech and visual form.* Cambridge: MIT Press, 1967, pp. 202–10.

HABER, R. N., and HERSHENSON, M. The effects of repeated brief exposures on the growth of a percept. *Journal of Experimental Psychology*, 1965, *69*, 40–46.

HASTORF, A. H. The influence of suggestion on the relationship between stimulus size and perceived distance. *Journal of Psychology*, 1950, *29*, 195–217.

HEBB, D. O. The innate organization of visual activity: II. Transfer of response in the discrimination of brightness and size by rats reared in total darkness. *Journal of Comparative Psychology*, 1937, *24*, 277–99.

——— Intelligence in man after large removals of cerebral tissue: Report of four left frontal lobe cases. *Journal of General Psychology*, 1939, *21*, 73–87.

——— The effect of early and late brain injury upon test scores, and the nature of normal adult intelligence. *Proceedings of the American Philosophical Society*, 1942, *85*, 275–92.

——— Man's frontal lobes: A critical review. *Archives of Neurology and Psychiatry*, 1945, *54*, 10–24.

——— *The organization of behavior.* New York: John Wiley, 1949.

——— *A textbook of psychology.* Philadelphia: Saunders, 1958.

——— A neuropsychological theory. *In* S. KOCH (ed.), *Psychology: A study of a science, Vol. I.* New York: McGraw-Hill, 1959, pp. 622–43.

——— The semiautonomous process: Its nature and nurture. *American Psychologist*, 1963, *18*, 16–27.

HEBB, D. O., and PENFIELD, W. Human behavior after extensive removal from the frontal lobes. *Archives of Neurology and Psychiatry*, 1940, *44*, 421–38.

HEBERT, J. A. and CAPEHART, J. E. Generalization of a voluntary response as a function of presentation frequency of the training stimulus in testing. *Psychonomic Science*, 1969, *16*, 315–16.

HECKENMUELLER, E. G. Stabilization of the retinal image: A review of method, effects, and theory. *Psychological Bulletin*, 1965, *63*, 157–69.

HEIDER, F. *The psychology of interpersonal relations.* New York: John Wiley, 1958.

HELSON, H. The psychology of Gestalt. *American Journal of Psychology*, 1925, *36*, 342–70; 494–526; 1926, *37*, 25–62; 189–223.

——— The fundamental propositions of Gestalt psychology. *Psychological Review*, 1933, *40*, 13–32.

——— Adaptation-level as frame of reference for prediction of psychophysical data. *American Journal of Psychology*, 1947, *60*, 1–29.

——— Adaptation-level as a basis for a quantitative theory of frames of reference. *Psychological Review*, 1948, *55*, 297–313.

——— *Perception and personality: A critique of recent experimental literature.* Report No. 1, Project No. 21-0202-0007, USAF, School of Aviation Medicine, Randolph Field, Texas, 1953.

———— *Adaptation-level theory: An experimental and systematic approach to behavior.* New York: Harper & Row, 1964.

———— Why did their precursors fail and the Gestalt psychologists succeed? Reflections on theories and theorists. *American Psychologist*, 1969, *24*, 1006–11.

HELSON, H., and AVANT, L. L. Stimulus generalization as a function of contextual stimuli. *Journal of Experimental Psychology*, 1967, *73*, 565–67.

HELSON, H. and FEHRER, E. V. The role of form in perception. *American Journal of Psychology*, 1932, *44*, 79–102.

HELSON, H. and KAPLAN, S. Effects of background reflectance on transposition of lightness discrimination. (Unpublished study, 1950.)

HELSON, H. and KOZAKI, A. Anchor effects using numerical estimates of simple dot patterns. *Perception and Psychophysics*, 1968, *4*, 163–64.

HELSON, H. and KOZAKI, T. Effects of duration of series and anchor stimuli on judgments of perceived size. *American Journal of Psychology*, 1968, *81*, 291–302.

HELSON, H., BEVAN, W., and MASTERS, H. G. A quantitative study of relevance in the formation of adaptation levels. *Perceptual and Motor Skills*, 1966, *22*, 743–49.

HENLE, M. An experimental investigation of past experience as a determinant of visual form perception. *Journal of Experimental Psychology*, 1942, *20*, 1–21.

HILGARD, E. R. Discussion of probabilistic functionalism. *Psychological Review*, 1955, *62*, 226–28.

HOCHBERG, J. E. Nativism and empiricism in perception. *In* L. POSTMAN (ed.), *Psychology in the making.* New York: Knopf, 1962, pp. 255–330.

HOCHBERG, J. E. and GLEITMAN, H. Towards a reformulation of the perception-motivation dichotomy. *Journal of Personality*, 1949, *18*, 180–91.

HOCHBERG, C. B. and HOCHBERG, J. Familiar size and the perception of depth. *Journal of Psychology*, 1952, *34*, 107–14.

HOLADAY, B. E. Die Grössenkonstanz der Sehdinge. *Archives fur die Gesampt Psychologie*, 1933, *88*, 419–86. Cited in Brunswik, E., *Perception and the representative design of psychological experiments.* Berkeley: University of California Press, 1956, pp. 22f, 63f.

HOLWAY, A. H. and BORING, E. G. Determinants of apparent visual size with distance variant. *American Journal of Psychology*, 1941, *54*, 21–37.

HOWES, D. N. and SOLOMON, R. L. A note on McGinnies' "Emotionality and perceptual defense." *Psychological Review*, 1950, *57*, 229–34.

ITTELSON, W. H. *The Ames demonstrations in perception.* Princeton, N.J.: Princeton University Press, 1952.

———— Perception and transactional psychology. *In* S. KOCH (ed.), *Psychology: A study of a science, Vol. 4*, New York: McGraw-Hill, 1962, pp. 660–704.

ITTELSON, W. H., and AMES, A., JR. Accommodation, convergence, and their relation to apparent distance. *Journal of Psychology*, 1950, *30*, 43–62.

ITTELSON, W. H. and CANTRIL, H. *Perception, a transactional approach.* New York: Doubleday, 1954.

ITTELSON, W. H. and KILPATRICK, F. P. The monocular and binocular distorted rooms. *In* F. P. KILPATRICK (ed.), *Explorations in transactional psychology.* New York: New York University Press, 1961, Chapter 8.

IZZET, T. Gewicht und Dichte als Gegenstände der Wahrnehmung. *Archives für die Gesampt Psychologie*, 1934, *91*, 305–18. Cited in Brunswik, E., *Perception and the representative design of psychological experiments.* Berkeley: University of California Press, 1956, pp. 74–76.

JAMES, H. An application of Helson's theory of adaptation level to the problem of transposition. *Psychological Review*, 1953, *60*, 345–52.

JASPER, H. H. Electrical signs of cortical activity. *Psychological Bulletin*, 1937, *34*, 411–81.

KADEN, S. E., WAPNER, S., and WERNER, H. Studies of physiognomic perception: II. Effect of directional dynamics of pictured objects and of words on the position of the apparent horizon. *Journal of Psychology*, 1955, *39*, 61–70.

KILPATRICK, F. P. Statement of theory. *In* F. P. KILPATRICK (ed.), *Human behavior from the transactional point of view.* Hanover, New Hampshire: Institute for Associated Research, 1952, Chapter 7.

———— The nature of perception: Some visual demonstrations. *In* F. P. KILPATRICK (ed.), *Explorations in transactional psychology.* New York: New York University Press, 1961 Chapter 2.

KLEIN, G. S. The personal world through perception. *In* R. R. BLAKE and G. V. RAMSEY (eds.), *Perception: An approach to personality.* New York: Ronald Press, 1951, pp. 328–55.

KLEIN, G. S., and SCHLESINGER, H. J. Where is the perceiver in perceptual theory? *Journal of Personality*, 1949, *18*, 32–47.

KLIMPFINGER, S. Ueber den Einfluss von intentionaler Einstellung und Uebung auf die Gestaltkonstanz. *Archives fur die Gesampt Psychologie*, 1933a, *88*, 551–98. Cited in Brunswik, E., *Perception and the representative design of psychological experiments.* Berkeley: University of California Press, 1956, p. 22.

———— Die Entwicklung der Gestaltkonstanz vom Kind zum Erwachsenen. *Archives fur die Gesampt Psychologie*, 1933b, *88*, 599–628. Cited in Brunswik, E., *Perception and the representative design of psychological experiments.* Berkeley: University of California Press, 1956, p. 83f.

KOFFKA, K. *The growth of the mind: An introduction to child psychology.* (Translated from the German by R. M. Odgen.) New York: Harcourt Brace Jovanovich, 1924.

———— *Principles of Gestalt psychology.* New York: Harcourt Brace Jovanovich, 1935.

KÖHLER, W. Die Farbe der Sehdinge beim Schimpansen und beim Haushuhn. *Zeitzchrift für Psychologie*, 1917, *77*, 248–55.

———— *Die physischen Gestalten in Ruhe und im stationären Zustand.* Erlangen: Weltkreisverlag, 1920.

———— *Gestalt psychology.* New York: Liveright, 1929.

KRAUSKOPF, J. and RIGGS, L. A. Interocular transfer in the disappearance of stabilized images. *American Journal of Psychology*, 1959, *72*, 248–52.

KRECH, D. Notes toward a psychological theory. *Journal of Personality*, 1949, *18*, 66–87.

———— Discussion: Theory and reductionism. *Psychological Review*, 1955, *62*, 229–31.

KRUS, D. M., WERNER, H., and WAPNER, S. Studies in vicariousness: Motor activity and perceived movement. *American Journal of Psychology*, 1953, *66*, 603–608.

LASHLEY, K. S. The mechanism of vision: XV. Preliminary studies of the rat's capacity for detail vision. *Journal of General Psychology*, 1938, *18*, 123–93.

———— Patterns of cerebral integration indicated by the scotomas of migraine. *Archives of Neurology and Psychiatry*, 1941, *46*, 331–39.

———— The mechanism of vision: XVII. Autonomy of the visual cortex. *Journal of Genetic Psychology*, 1942a, *60*, 197–221.

———— The problem of cerebral organization in vision. *Biological Symposia*, 1942b, *7*, 301–22.

LAZARUS, R. S. and MCCLEARY, R. A. Autonomic discrimination without awareness: A study of subception. *Psychological Review*, 1951, *58*, 113–22.

LEVINE, R., CHEIN, I., and MURPHY, G. The relation of the intensity of a need to the amount of perceptual distortion: A preliminary report. *Journal of Psychology*, 1942, *13*, 283–93.

LORENTE DE NO, R. Analysis of the activity of the chains of internuncial neurons. *Journal of Neurophysiology*, 1938, *1*, 207–44.

LUCHINS, A. S. On an approach to social perception. *Journal of Personality*, 1950, *19*, 64–84.

———— An evaluation of some current criticisms of Gestalt psychological work on perception. *Psychological Review*, 1951, *58*, 69–95.

MACH, E. *Analysis of sensations.* Chicago: Open Court, 1914. (German ed. Jena, 1886.)

MCGINNIES, E. Emotionality and perceptual defense. *Psychological Review*, 1949, *56*, 244–51.

MCCLELLAND, D. C. and ATKINSON, J. W. The projective expression of needs. I. The effect of different intensities of the hunger drive on perception. *Journal of Psychology*, 1948, *25*, 205–22.

MICHELS, K. M. and ZUSNE, L. Metrics of visual form. *Psychological Bulletin*, 1965, *63*, 74–86.

MICHELS, W. C. and HELSON, H. A reformulation of the Fechner law in terms of adaptation-level applied to rating-scale data. *American Journal of Psychology*, 1949, *62*, 355–68.

———— A quantitative theory of time-order effects. *American Journal of Psychology*, 1954, *67*, 327–34.

MILNER, P. M. The cell assembly: Mark II. *Psychological Review*, 1957, *64*, 242–52.

MINER, J. B. A case of vision acquired in adult life. *Psychological Review Monograph Supplement*, 1905, *6*, No. 5, 103–18.

MOHRMANN, K. Lautheitskonstanz im Entfernungswechsel. *Zeitschrift fur Psychologie*, 1939, *145*, 146–99. Cited in Brunswik, E., *Perception and the representative design of psychological experiments*. Berkeley: University of California Press, 1956, pp. 70f.

MOWATT, M. H. Configurational properties considered "good" by naive subjects. *American Journal of Psychology*, 1940, *53*, 46–69.

MURDOCK, B. B. The distinctiveness of stimuli. *Psychological Review*, 1960, *67*, 16–31.

MURPHY, G. Discussion. *Journal of Personality*, 1949, *18*, 51–55.

NAFE, J. P. An experimental study of the affective qualities. *American Journal of Psychology*, 1924, *35*, 507–44.

NATSOULAS, T. Converging operations for perceptual defense. *Psychological Bulletin*, 1965, *64*, 393–401.

———— Interpreting perceptual reports. *Psychological Bulletin*, 1968, *70*, 575–91.

POSTMAN, L. Toward a general theory of cognition. *In* J. H. ROHRER and M. SHERIF (eds.), *Social psychology at the crossroads*. New York: Harper & Brothers, 1951, pp. 242–72.

———— On the problem of perceptual defense. *Psychological Review*, 1953, *60*, 298–306.

———— The probability approach and nomothetic theory. *Psychological Review*, 1955, *62*, 218–25.

POSTMAN, L., and BRUNER, J. S. Perception under stress. *Psychological Review*, 1948, *55*, 314–23.

———— Multiplicity of set as a determinant of perceptual organization. *Journal of Experimental Psychology*, 1949a, *39*, 369–77.

———— Satisfaction and deprivation as determinants of perceptual organization. (Paper read at Eastern Psychological Association, 1949b.)

POSTMAN, L., BRUNER, J. S., and MCGINNIES, E. Personal values as selective factors in perception. *Journal of Abnormal and Social Psychology*, 1948, *43*, 142–54.

POSTMAN, L., BRUNER, J. S., and WALK, R. D. The perception of error. (Paper read at Eastern Psychological Association, 1950.)

POSTMAN, L. and SCHNEIDER, B. H. Personal values, visual recognition, and recall. *Psychological Review*, 1951, *58*, 271–84.

POSTMAN, L. and TOLMAN, E. C. Brunswik's probabilistic functionalism. *In* S. KOCH (ed.), *Psychology: A study of a science, Vol. I*. New York: McGraw-Hill, 1959, pp. 502–64.

POULTON, E. C. The new psychophysics: Six models for magnitude estimation. *Psychological Bulletin*, 1968, *69*, 1–19.

POULTON, E. C. and SIMMONDS, D. C. V. Value of standard and very first variable in judgments of reflectance of grays with various ranges of available numbers. *Journal of Experimental Psychology*, 1963, *65*, 297–304.

PROSHANSKY, H. and MURPHY, G. The effects of reward and punishment on perception. *Journal of Psychology*, 1942, *13*, 294–305.

RAHN, C. L. The relation of sensation to other categories in contemporary psychology. *Psychological Monographs*, 1914, *16*, No. 67, pp. vi, 131.

RESTLE, F. Moon illusion explained on the basis of relative size. *Science*, 1970, *167*, 1092–96.

RESTLE, F. and MERRYMAN, C. T. An adaptation-level theory account of a relative-size illusion. *Psychonomic Science*, 1968, *12*, 229–30.

RIESEN, A. H. The development of visual perception in man and chimpanzee. *Science*, 1947, *106*, 107–108.

ROCK, I. and FLECK, F. S. A re-examination of the effect of monetary reward and punishment on figure-ground perception. *Journal of Experimental Psychology*, 1950, *40*, 766–76.

RUBIN, E. J. *Visuell wahrgenommene Figuren*. Copenhagen: Gyldendalske, 1921.

SALES, B. D. and HABER, R. N. A different look at perceptual defense for taboo words. *Perception and Psychophysics*, 1968, *3*, 156–60.

SANFORD, R. N. The effects of abstinence from food upon imaginal processes. *Journal of Psychology*, 1936, *2*, 129–36.

———— The effects of abstinence from food upon imaginal processes: A further experiment. *Journal of Psychology*, 1937, *3*, 145–59.

SCHREIBER, L. Perceptual attainment of weight, speed, and kinetic energy of falling bodies, 1935. Reported in Brunswik, E., *Perception and the representative design of psychological experiments*. Berkeley: University of California Press, 1956, pp. 73f.

SENDEN, M. V. *Space and sight*. New York: Free Press, 1960.

SHAFER, R. and MURPHY, G. The role of autism in figure-ground relationships. *Journal of Experimental Psychology*, 1943, *32*, 335–43.

SHANNON, C. E. A mathematical theory of communication. *Bell System Technical Journal*, 1948, *27*, 379–423; 623–56.

SMITH, D. E. and HOCHBERG, J. E. The effect of "punishment" (electric shock) on figure-ground perception. *Journal of Psychology*, 1954, *38*, 83–87.

SOLOMON, R. L. and HOWES, D. H. Word frequency, personal values and visual duration thresholds. *Psychological Review*, 1951, *58*, 256–70.

THOMAS, D. R. and JONES, C. G. Stimulus generalization as a function of the frame of reference. *Journal of Experimental Psychology*, 1962, *64*, 77–80.

TITCHENER, E. B. *Experimental psychology*. New York: Macmillan, 1901, Vol. 1, Pt. 1.

———— *A textbook of psychology*. New York: Macmillan, 1910.

———— *A beginner's psychology*. New York: Macmillan, 1923.

TOLMAN, E. C. *Purposive behavior in animals and men*. New York: Century, 1932.

TURNER, E. D. and BEVAN, W. Simultaneous induction of multiple anchor effects in the judgment of form. *Journal of Experimental Psychology*, 1962, *64*, 589–92.

———— Patterns of experience and the perceived orientation of the Necker Cube. *Journal of General Psychology*, 1964, *70*, 345–52.

WAGNER, KATHLEEN and AVANT, L. L. Anchoring stimuli and Titchener's illusion. (Paper presented at the meeting of the Midwestern Psychological Association, Cincinnati, May, 1970.)

WALK, R., GIBSON, E. J., and TIGHE, T. The behavior of light-and dark-reared rats on a visual cliff. *Science*, 1957, *126*, 80–81.

———— *Perceptual development*. Worcester, Massachusetts: Clark University Press, 1957.

WAPNER, S., WERNER, H., and CHANDLER, K. A. Experiments on sensory-tonic field theory of perception: I. Effect of extraneous stimulation on the visual perception of verticality. *Journal of Experimental Psychology*, 1951, *42*, 341–45.

WAPNER, S., WERNER, H., and COMALLI, P. E., JR. Space localization under conditions of danger. *Journal of Psychology*, 1956, *41*, 335–46.

WAPNER, S., WERNER, H., and KRUS, D. M. The effect of success and failure on space localization. *Journal of Personality*, 1957, *25*, 752–56.

WAPNER, S., WERNER, H., and MORANT, R. B. Experiments on sensory-tonic field theory of perception: III. Effect of body rotation on the visual perception of verticality. *Journal of Experimental Psychology*, 1951, *42*, 351–57.

WAPNER, S. and WITKIN, H. A. The role of visual factors in the maintenance of body-balance. *American Journal of Psychology*, 1950, *63*, 385–408.

WEINTRAUB, D. J. and KRANTZ, D. H. Non-differential rates of dark adaptation to "taboo" and "neutral" stimuli. *Psychological Record*, 1968, *18*, 63–69.

WERNER, H. and WAPNER, S. Sensory-tonic field theory of perception. *Journal of Personality*, 1949, *18*, 88–107.

———— Toward a general theory of perception. *Psychological Review*, 1952, *59*, 324–38.

———— Studies in physiognomic perception: I. Effect of configurational dynamics and meaning induced sets on the position of the apparent median plane. *Journal of Psychology*, 1954, *38*, 51–65.

WERNER, H., WAPNER, S., and CHANDLER, K. A. Experiments on sensory-tonic field theory of perception: II. Effect of supported and unsupported tilt of the body on visual perception of verticality. *Journal of Experimental Psychology*, 1951, *42*, 346–50.

WERTHEIMER, M. Experimentelle Studien über das Sehen von Bewegung. *Zeitschrift für Psychologie*, 1912, *61*, 161–265.

———— *Productive thinking*. New York: Harper & Row, 1959 (enlarged edition, edited by Michael Wertheimer).

WHITE, S. H. Training and timing in the generalization of a voluntary response. *Journal of Experimental Psychology*, 1965, *69*, 269–75.

WILSON, W. A., JR. and WILSON, M. Physiological psychology: Neuropsychology. *In* H. HELSON and W. BEVAN (eds.), *Contemporary approaches to psychology*, Princeton: Van Nostrand Reinhold, 1967, pp. 35–89.

WITTREICH, W. J. The Honi phenomenon: A case of selective perceptual distortion. *Journal of Abnormal and Social Psychology*, 1952, *47*, 705–12.

WOODWORTH, R. S. Reinforcement of perception. *American Journal of Psychology*, 1947, *60*, 119–24.

WORTHINGTON, A. G. Differential rates of dark adaptation to "Taboo" and "Neutral" stimuli. *Canadian Journal of Psychology*, 1964, *18*, 257–65.

ZEILER, M. D. The ratio theory of intermediate size discrimination. *Psychological Review*, 1963, *70*, 516–33.

Learning

Remarkable techniques have been developed for the purpose of collecting data about the behavior of animal organisms under rigorously controlled conditions and for assessing these by elaborate statistical procedures. In this way a large mass of scientifically impeccable evidence has been built up and the pile is daily augmented. We cannot call it an edifice. For in spite of the general agreement about the method of making bricks, there is no accepted way of putting them together. There is no concord among psychologists about what the facts they have accumulated are evidence for. This does not mean that they are merely in disagreement about the edifice they wish to erect; they have not even decided what constitutes a building. That is, not only do they disagree about the explanation of their findings, but they are not clear about what would explain them.

J. A. Deutsch
The Structural Basis of Behavior.

During the past 20 years untold millions of dollars have been spent in support of research devoted to the study of learning in both animals and men. This expenditure has produced a tremendous mass of facts about a wide variety of behavioral phenomena. Some of these facts will be described and discussed in the six chapters that follow this one. This brief chapter will, I hope, prepare the reader to evaluate the various theories that purport to explain these facts. For the reader who wants to compare the various rival theories with each other, there are several fine surveys devoted to such comparison (*cf.*, Goldstein, Krantz, and Rains 1965; Hilgard, and Bower 1966; Hill 1963; Marx 1963; and Melton 1964). In this chapter we shall not be concerned with such comparisons. Instead, we shall concern ourselves with what seems to be a more fundamental issue. We shall try to understand the logical and empirical problems that face any attempt to explain behavioral phenomena.

Before we seek to understand how psychologists theorize about behavior, it will help if we try to answer two important questions.

1. What must we know, or at least think we know, before we are prepared to explain some phenomenon?

Benbow F. Ritchie

The Facts You Need Before
You Explain the Facts

Theories of Learning:
A Consumer Report

22

2. How are our explanations or theoretical beliefs corrected and made more precise by our experimental research?

In order to answer the first question let us begin with some common explanation for the difference in behavior of two organisms, *A* and *B*. Let us suppose that both *A* and *B* are litter mates of the same sex from some genetically pure strain, that they have received identical treatment and training, and that during this training they have responded alike (e.g., at the same rate). However, now we test them both and discover that *A* responds at a higher rate than *B*. We ask for an explanation of this difference, and we are told that *A* responds at a higher rate than *B* because *A* is hungrier than *B* during this test. If this explanation is to be regarded as relevant, and thus possibly true, we must know, or at least think we know:

1. that in this test *A* was hungrier than *B*; and
2. that the hungrier organism will always respond at a more rapid rate than a comparable less hungry one.[1]

If, on the other hand, we doubt either or both of these propositions, the proposed explanation must be rejected as either inconclusive or irrelevant.

Let us consider then the grounds for believing that *A* was hungrier than *B* during these behavioral tests. Clearly we beg the question if we take *A*'s faster response rate as evidence that *A* was hungrier than *B*. We need some evidence that is logically independent of this response rate. Suppose, then, that we give a second test to both *A* and *B*. We measure the amount of food consumed by both *A* and *B* before they stop eating and discover that *A* eats more than *B*. Such a fact is commonly taken to mean that prior to this second test, *A* was hungrier than *B*. If this is what "hungrier-than" means in the proposed explanation, then we must have the results of such a second test before we can have grounds for believing that *A* was hungrier than *B* during the first test. Without such evidence for *A*'s greater hunger, the proposed explanation must be rejected as inconclusive.

Let us now consider the grounds for believing that the hungrier organism will *always* respond at a more rapid rate than a comparable less hungry one. We can believe this proposition only if we know of *no* exception to it. If we know of a single instance in which the hungrier organism failed to respond more rapidly than a comparable but less hungry one, the proposition is false, and therefore cannot be believed. As long as we cannot believe this second proposition, the proposed explanation must be rejected as irrelevant.

Because behavioral scientists have usually misunderstood this point, they have usually ignored it. Let us examine the argument closely. Suppose first that we know that the second proposition is false, that is, we know of at least one exception to it. As a result, the most we can assert is that the hungrier organism will respond more rapidly in most but not in all instances. Suppose next that we discover an organism that, after several days of responding at a stable rate, shows on the following day an increase in response rate. Finally, let us suppose that in our search for an explanation of this surprising increase in response

[1]By "a comparable but less hungry organism" I mean one that is believed to be similar to the organism with which it is compared in all relevant respects (i.e., in genetic constitution, in past history, and in present environment) except that it is believed to be less hungry at the moment its behavior is tested.

rate, we discover clear evidence that on this last day the organism was hungrier than he was on all the preceding days. I suspect that some readers would be tempted to accept this last fact as the explanation of the increase in response rate, but they would be wrong to do so. As long as we know that sometimes an increase in hunger fails to produce an increase in response rate, we cannot be sure that this was not one of the times when it failed to do so. The fact that the response rate *did* increase tempts us to believe that this could not have been one of the rare exceptions. But such evidence proves nothing except that something caused the increase in response rate. It is just as reasonable to suppose that the increased rate was the result of some undetected fortuitous cause such as a sudden increase in fear, a sudden anticipation of greater reward, a sudden removal of some source of inhibition, and so on. Of course, we can exclude some of these alternative explanations by providing evidence that the animal was not frightened, or did not anticipate greater reward, and so on. But because we cannot list *all* the alternative possible causes of this effect, we cannot prove by exclusion that this increase in response rate must have been the effect of the increase in hunger.

This argument shows, I think, that unless we base our explanations upon behavioral laws that admit of no exceptions, we cannot present an explanation of any behavioral phenomenon that is any more plausible than a host of alternative explanations. The reader will discover as he studies the following six chapters that in the field of learning there are no theoretical explanations that are not challenged by many equally plausible alternative explanations. The reason for this state of confusion is, I believe, that none of the proposed explanations are based upon behavioral laws that admit of no exceptions.

Now at this point many of my readers will cry "Stop!" It is hopeless, they will say, to search for such behavioral laws, because the most we can hope to discover are statistical generalizations from which we can estimate the probability that a certain kind of event will produce a certain kind of effect. We know, the argument goes, that sometimes an increase in hunger increases the response rate, and that sometimes it does not. We can do no more than study the frequency with which this cause is followed by this effect and then summarize our findings in a statistical generalization that describes the probability of such a rate increase whenever the hunger increases.

We shall shortly consider the merits of this argument, but at this point let us suppose the claim is sound and ask what hope we have, in this event, of discovering the explanation of any behavioral phenomenon. Suppose that after prolonged empirical study, we summarize all of our data in the following three statistical generalizations:

1. in 7/10 cases a rate-increase follows an increase in hunger;
2. in 3/10 cases a rate-increase follows an increase in fear; and
3. in 9/10 cases a rate-increase follows an increase in fear and in hunger.

Now let us suppose we come upon a case in which both the animals' fear and hunger increased and these changes were followed by an increase in response rate. How are we to explain this rate-increase? Many will perhaps be tempted to conclude that this effect must be explained by the joint influence of the fear and hunger increases. But why? As long as we know that in 1/10 cases joint fear-and-hunger-increases fail to produce this effect, and as long as we have no ground for believing that this is not one of these exceptional cases, we have no reason to prefer this explanation to the two other explanations or to an indefinite number of other possible explanations as yet unspecified.

In elementary probability theory, it is stressed that one cannot estimate the probability of a single case, and that one can only estimate the probability of a particular kind of case within a larger class of cases. Some readers may be tempted to apply the same sort of argument to our present problem and conclude that explanations cannot be given for single cases, but only for long-term trends. Now if we are to do justice to this point, we must be careful to distinguish the unique case from the single case. The unique case, which by definition cannot be repeated, can, of course, never be explained by any sort of generalization which by its logical form assumes the possibility of an indefinite repetition of instances. We can explain Caesar's crossing of the Rubicon only if we consider this event as one repeatable case in which, for example, a Roman general decided to ignore the laws of the Roman Senate, and if we have some generalization describing the conditions that cause Roman generals to make such decisions. [Although Caesar crossed the Rubicon only once, the event viewed in this way—like any event so viewed—is unique, our explanation of this single case must view this case as a kind of event that can be repeated.] Thus, although no explanation can be given of the unique case, the explanation of single cases is an essential part of the research in all the physical sciences. The student of physical astronomy tries to explain why a particular star exploded; the student of physical optics tries to explain why a particular light ray is bent in a certain way, and so on. Only in the behavioral sciences do we hear the claim that the single case cannot be explained, and this claim is based, it seems, upon the premise that in the study of behavior the most we can hope to discover are long-term statistical generalizations.

It is time now to consider the grounds for this extraordinary premise. Kaplan (1964) has, I think, very cogently disposed of all the common metaphysical arguments purporting to prove that it is impossible to discover laws of behavior. At the end of his discussion of these views, he presents his own view which he calls *methodological determinism*. This view "states only that laws are worth looking for here (e.g., in the realm of behavior) and not that they surely exist here, and surely not that they necessarily exist always and everywhere." (p. 124). Because this view seems wholly reasonable to me, I shall adopt it as my basic methodological premise. Now once this view is adopted, the question of whether we can hope to find behavioral laws becomes an empirical question.

In the hopes of arriving at a better understanding of what it is to search for a behavioral law, I shall now return to the other question I raised at the beginning of this chapter. How are our explanations or theoretical beliefs corrected and made more precise by our experimental research? Now those familiar with the evidence will agree that *in general* it is true that increases in hunger produce increases in response rate. They will also agree that our research should provide us with facts that increase our confidence in such beliefs. The point where confusion and disagreement arise is the point at which we start to consider how our research facts increase the credibility of our beliefs.

Common sense, with its blind heedless faith in inductive generalizations, assumes that the purpose of research is to accumulate a larger and larger mass of positive instances in agree-

ment with some hypothesis. So if an experiment shows that response rate is greater in every instance when the animal is hungrier, the way to increase our confidence in this generalization is to replicate this same experiment and thus increase the N of the tested subjects. But most behavioral scientists believe that, beyond a certain point, little is to be learned by further replications of the same experiment. Instead of this, they prefer to test the generalization under as wide a variety of conditions as the terms of the generalization will allow. Clearly, the more frequently we find positive instances in such tests, the more confident we are that *in general* increases in hunger produce increases in response rate. But what of the negative instances? As long as we find such negative instances from time to time, how can we hope to rid ourselves of the qualification: "in general it is true that—"? These are the questions that must be faced if we are to understand not only how our research corrects our beliefs, but also what sorts of research must be done if we are to discover whatever behavioral laws are there to be discovered.

The methodology of the behavioral sciences, particularly in the field of learning, has, for various historical reasons, found itself saddled with the common sense view that the purpose of research is to discover evidence that confirms (i.e., is consistent with) our hypothesis. Thus research, according to this view, is directed towards piling up positive instances and little interest is taken in what can be learned from the negative instances. Indeed, the craving for positive instances often becomes so strong that we are tempted to increase the vagueness of our basic ideas (e.g., of reward, drive, habit, etc.) so that we can protect ourselves from discovering anything but positive instances (B.F. Ritchie 1923). But when we yield to this temptation, we open ourselves to the serious charge that our theoretical ideas have been so stripped of content that they are consistent with, and thus are confirmed by, every possible fact. It is this dilemma of the orthodox methodology that leads us to ask once again: What is the purpose of experimental research? Clearly no one experiment nor any set of experiments can ever prove a hypothesis true, because we can never escape the possibility that some further experiment will yield results that once and for all prove it false.

And here we have the crucial and pivotal point. Although experiments can never verify our hypotheses, they can give us one bit of certain knowledge. If it is true first that this animal when tested was hungry, and second that this animal responded at a rate no greater than that of a comparable but less hungry animal, then it is certain that the hypothesis, "All hungry animals respond at higher rates than comparable but less hungry animals," is false. The matter is settled once and for all, provided we remain convinced that this animal was indeed hungry and that he failed to respond at a higher rate than his comparable but less hungry mate. Viewed in this way, the sole purpose of all experimentation is to provide those comparisons that will tell us when our hypotheses are false. It is only from the negative instances that we can gain any certain knowledge. Once we accept this point, we begin to see how research helps us to correct our beliefs and make them more precise, and how through such research we can look for behavioral laws. We know that sometimes an increase in hunger appears to produce an increase in response rate, and sometimes it does not. The purpose of properly designed research is to discover from these negative instances exactly what is the scope and what are the limits of this generalization.

Toulmin (1960) argues this point with great clarity in his

discussion of the logical and empirical character of natural laws. To illustrate his argument, he considers the various stages in the study of the refraction of light leading to Snell's law: "Whenever any ray of light is incident at the surface which separates two media, it is bent in such a way that the ratio of the sine of the angle of incidence to the sine of the angle of refraction is always a constant quantity for these two media." Once this law has been formulated on the basis of a few empirical observations, research is then directed towards discovering all those conditions in which this law fails to apply, that is, those conditions in which the evidence contradicts the law. Each such experiment with a negative outcome serves, then, to help specify the scope and limits of this law. "Very soon," says Toulmin, "indeed as soon as its fruitfulness has been established—the formula in our hypothesis comes to be treated as a law, i.e., as something of which we ask not 'Is it true?' but 'When does it hold?'" (p. 79). In this analysis the statement of any natural law is sharply distinguished from the statements (1) of all those conditions in which this law is believed to hold without exception, and (2) of all those conditions in which it is known not to hold.

To every law [says Toulmin] there correspond a set of statements of the form "X's law has been found to hold or not to hold for such-and-such systems under such-and-such circumstances." Further in order to find how far this range of substances and circumstances, i.e., the "scope" of the law, can be extended, a great deal of routine research is undertaken, research which can in no way be said to call in question the truth or acceptability of the law itself (p. 78).

Now at last we can understand the significance of the so-called negative instances. From them and only from them can we discover the conditions under which some law holds without exception, and only when we have discovered this, do we know enough to explain certain phenomena when they occur under these specified conditions.

So much then for the crucial importance of negative instances in our search for natural laws. From this analysis, I hope it is now possible to see clearly the kind and the amount of research that must be done in order to transform our crude behavioral generalizations into exact behavioral laws. Let us return once more to our well-worn example: increases in hunger tend to increase response rate. Our first job (and perhaps the most difficult of all) is to come to grips with the few individuals in each experiment whose behavior deviates from that of the great majority (e.g., those few individuals who, despite their greater hunger, fail to respond more rapidly). How are we to deal with these deviates? Sidman's (1960) distinction between "intrinsic variability" and "imposed variability" suggests that our first task is to discover whether these deviations are intrinsic to the individuals. To do this we need only repeat the test several more times and ask whether or not it is the same individuals on each test that deviate from the majority. If the individuals that deviate from the majority vary from test to test in an unpredictable way, we know that these deviations are not intrinsic to the individuals but must somehow result from uncontrolled influences in our testing procedure. Our task in this case, as Sidman emphasizes, is to change our experimental procedures in such a way as to eliminate these influences. Such discrepancies in the phenomena of refraction were what led experimenters to insist upon the homogeneity of the media through which the light rays were passed. Thus in the search for behavioral laws, we must begin by devising apparatus and testing procedures that reduce all such chance discrepancies to a minimum. Now, if after we have done this, we still find a minority of individuals who consistently deviate from the majority, our next task is to discover in what *other ways* these individuals differ from the majority. Once we know this we can begin to specify the scope and limits of our behavioral law—it holds for such-and-such sorts of animals, but not for such-and-such other sorts of animals.

Now, when we have successfully dealt with the problem of the deviates, we have, as Toulmin puts it, demonstrated the fruitfulness of our formula. That is, we have brought the phenomenon under experimental control in the sense that we now know one set of conditions to which the formula applies. At this point our research expands. We test animals of different species, strains, ages, and so on. We test animals with different habits, in different physiological states, and drawn from different environments. In this way we discover the exact scope and limits of this law. Although it may seem easy to state in this abstract way what needs to be done, doing it is by no means easy. The job requires great skill and knowledge, great imagination, and great amounts of that ingredient so essential to all important creative enterprises, luck. "The process of scientific discovery, of finding natural laws. . .is an art. . . .It is quite impossible to lay down rules knowing which anybody can write poems like Shelley or make statues like Praxiteles. So also it is impossible to lay down rules which will enable anybody to make discoveries like Faraday or Pasteur" (A.D. Ritchie 1923). The most we can do is to describe the sorts of discoveries that must be made. But how to make them must always remain an art.

We have by now, I hope, a better understanding of what sorts of facts we need to know before we can explain some phenomenon as an instance of some natural law. Now before we can begin to understand what psychologists have meant by a theory of learning, we must consider a second sort of scientific explanation. Perhaps the simplest way to distinguish this new sort of explanation from the sort we have been talking about is to show that it is designed to answer a new sort of question. Such explanations try to show why it is that a particular natural law holds in some conditions but not in others. Why is it, for example, that Snell's law holds for light rays that pass through many transparent media, but not for those that pass through certain crystalline substances? To answer this question, the physicist tries to imagine first the structure of these critical crystalline substances and second how light rays would travel through such an imagined structure. In this way the physicist tries to explain why Snell's law fails to hold in these cases. Such an answer to such a question is a physical theory. Physical theories, like the kinetic theory of gases, Einstein's special theory of relativity, and so on, are all designed to explain why certain physical laws hold in some conditions but not in others. Now it should be apparent from all we have said so far that until we have discovered some behavioral laws and have determined their exact scopes and limits, there is no use in behavioral science for such theories as these.

However, behavioral scientists and in particular the learning theorists are only beginning to understand this important point. Between 1935 and 1950, when most of the traditional learning theories were first formulated, it was widely assumed that such learning theories were to be, in principle at least, essentially like the various theories in physics. Because physical theories all based their explanations on some hypothetical analysis of the structural properties of the material substances underlying the phenomena to be explained, the learning theorists assumed almost uncritically that their theories must begin with some similar hypothetical analysis of the internal structures of the organisms whose behavior they sought to understand. Some like Lashley (1929), Hebb (1949), Sperry (1961), Pribram (1965), and others tried to provide a neuro-physiological analysis of the organism's structure that would *somehow* lead to an explanation of certain behavioral phenomena. Others like Tolman (1932), Hull (1951), Deutsch (1960), and Tinbergen (1951) tried to provide a functional analysis of the organism's structure in which the elements in the structure were not identified anatomically, but instead were specified by the function they perform in dealing with sensory input and motor output. Fascinating as such speculations often are, they are, I fear, both inconclusive and uncalled for.

They are inconclusive because even if we had a complete and accurate description of the organism's neuroanatomy, we could deduce nothing from this description about the organism's behavior unless we also knew all the laws that govern the behavior of all the elements in this structure. Consider, for example, the kinetic theory of gases. No proposition about the behavior of gases follows directly from a molecular analysis of such gases. Only when we add to this analysis the premise that such gas particles are governed by the laws of mechanics can any proposition about the behavior of gases be deduced. So, until we know the electro-biochemical laws that govern the behavior of all the parts of the organism, we shall be unable to deduce any proposition concerning the behavior of this organism. In this sense, all such structural theories of behavior are inconclusive, and presumably will remain inconclusive for some time to come.

Not only are such theoretical speculations inconclusive, they are also uncalled for. The reason for this is that as yet we have no facts to explain. Take the phenomenon we have already discussed, the tendency for response-rate to increase when hunger increases. Only when our research has determined the precise scope and limits of this "law," will it be reasonable to speculate about why an increase in hunger has this effect in some conditions and not in others. Until we know at least this much about the phenomenon, it is pointless to try to explain it.

In recent years, interest in such ambitious theories has almost disappeared. Although behavioral scientists continue to give lip service to the grand old theories of Tolman, Hull, Hebb, and others, their research is beginning more and more to reflect a new interest. The mathematical learning theorists (Atkinson et al. 1965; Bush and Mosteller 1955; Luce 1959; Restle 1961), the information-processing theorists (Feigenbaum and Feldman 1963; Sayre and Crosson 1963; Yovitts and Cameron 1960), and many of the new generation of neurophysiologists (Delafresnaye 1961; Field et al. 1960; Kimble 1965; Konorski 1967; Wooldridge 1963; Young 1964) are starting to reconsider the basic empirical premises of learning and to ask how we can make these premises more sensitive to experimental tests. This, as I have argued, is what we must do to make a fresh start. We all know that rewards *tend* to strengthen and maintain habits. But if we are to move from such common sense knowledge into the realm of scientific law, we must begin by sharpening the meanings of our key concepts like reward and habit so that we can begin to deal with the problem of the deviates and thus establish the

fruitfulness of this law by bringing the phenomena under exact experimental control. When, finally, we have exactly determined the scope and limits of this law, we shall for the first time be able not only to explain certain instances of learning, but also to speculate meaningfully about why rewards have these effects under certain conditions but not under others.

The list of half-truths that we call "empirical premises" or "general principles" is a long one. In the chapters that follow you will come upon many such principles in the fields of classical conditioning, operant conditioning, discrimination learning, cognitive learning, verbal learning, and thinking. Two features make them easy to recognize. *They tend to be printed in italics and they tend to use the word "tend."* If you are to understand the research in these fields, you must train yourself to recognize such principles and to ask of each one you recognize: Under what conditions does it apply and under what conditions does it fail to apply? If it appears that there are no conditions under which it fails to apply, suspect it of hidden vagueness. But do not stop here. Track down the vagueness to its source and then see what you can do to remove this vagueness so that you can clearly detect the conditions in which it fails to apply. Only if you do this can you begin to understand the research in the field of learning, and only if you do this can you help to transform our vague common sense half-truths into behavioral laws by helping to discover the scope and limits of these vague but important ideas.

Appendix

Vagueness in the idea of reinforcement has made many hypotheses about learning untestable. Here we examine the roots of this vagueness and suggest a radical change in the meaning of this concept.

A. HOW LEARNING THEORIES TRY TO UNDERSTAND LEARNING

All psychologists who study learning begin by assuming that learned changes in behavior can be understood only if we take into account the effects which this behavior produces. Consider the case of an animal that stops making certain responses to its environment and begins to make a different response. To understand this change in behavior we all assume that we must begin by discovering how the effects produced by this new response differ from those produced by the old. Thus, implicit in all our learning theories is the assumption that certain sorts of response-produced effects have the power to support the response that produces them, and that other sorts of response-produced effects do not. Thus, to understand any learned change in behavior we must, according to this assumption, demonstrate that the effects produced by the new response have this power, whereas the effects produced by the old response do not. On this point, I think, all psychologists who study learning agree.

Psychologists often disagree about what name should be given to some abstract idea. Psychologists have given various names to this relationship between performance and response-produced effects. Many call the relationship "reinforcement"; others call it "confirmation," or "contiguity" or "association."

For the purpose of my argument, the name we choose is not important because my argument is solely concerned with clarifying what is meant by saying that such effects support performance. However, because "reinforcement" is the name used most widely for this relationship, and also because this name is likely to strike a responsive chord in most readers, I have chosen it. Finally, I believe there is an important issue here in making this relationship intelligible and I doubt that it can be escaped by choosing a different name.

Not only do psychologists disagree about what name to give to this idea, but they also disagree about what they call "the mechanism of reinforcement." From the very first, psychologists have tried to give some rule of thumb to distinguish those response-produced effects that have the power to support performance from those that do not. Thus Thorndike suggested that pleasant or satisfying changes in stimulation in contrast to indifferent or unpleasant changes had this power. Pavlov had a different suggestion. For him stimuli that evoke a strong reflexive reaction (either conditioned or unconditioned), in contrast to stimuli that evoke little or no reflexive action, were the ones that had the power to support performance. Hull had two other suggested rules of thumb: (1) need-reducing stimuli, and (2) drive-reducing stimuli were the ones that support performance, in contrast to stimuli that reduce neither needs nor drives. Recently Premack (1965) has suggested a new rule of thumb. For him, an rps (e.g., food) that evokes a response (e.g., eating) of a certain probability in a free-operant situation, will reinforce any response (e.g., bar pressing) with a lower probability in the same free-operant situation. Many such rules of thumb have been suggested and called "mechanisms of reinforcement," and although psychologists continue to disagree about which, if any, are useful hypotheses, we need not concern ourselves about this, because we have a different problem to solve.

Our task is to make clear in exactly what sense a response-produced change in stimulation (hereafter called an "rps") supports the performance of the response that produces such an rps. Only after this idea has been made so clear and so exact that we can determine which rps have this power and which do not, can we begin to speculate fruitfully about a rule of thumb that will distinguish reinforcers from nonreinforcers. In short, I am here concerned with clarifying what has commonly been called "the empirical law of effect," the assumption that the performance of any learned response is partly controlled by the rps that are contingent upon this response. Kimble and others have argued that "at this empirical level there is no important dispute about the validity of the principle of reinforcement, and there is no such thing as a nonreinforcement theorist" (1961, p. 203).

Perhaps it is just because there have been no important disputes about the validity of this idea that the current interpretation of this empirical law has never been critically examined. I shall try to demonstrate in what follows that the current empirical conception of reinforcement is so vague that we cannot distinguish those rps that have this power from those that do not. As a result the current conception is worthless. In the place of this vague conception, I want to suggest another empirical interpretation of reinforcement which seems to be both exact and practical. In fact, I believe that if this new interpretation is adopted, we shall for the first time be able to find decisive answers to a variety of questions which have plagued students of learning since Thorndike's early puzzle box experiments.

B. How the Pop-Op Definition Fails to Define (i.e., to Set the Limits of) the Idea of Reinforcement.

Skinner was the first to suggest what has since become a popular operational definition of reinforcement. This Pop-Op definition says:

Any rps that increases the probability of the response it follows is (by definition) a reinforcing stimulus.

"There is no circularity about this," says Skinner. "Some stimuli are found to produce the change, others are not, and they are classified as reinforcing and non-reinforcing accordingly" (1938, p. 62). Meehl (1950) amplified Skinner's claim that this definition did not, as Postman (1947) had suggested, make the law of effect circular or tautological. Meehl argued that once we discover that some rps, like food, increases the probability of bar pressing in a Skinner box, we can say that this food is a reinforcer for bar pressing, but we cannot infer from this that this food will act as a reinforcer in any other situation. The law of effect, says Meehl, asserts that some and perhaps all reinforcers are transituational, that is, they will increase the probability of any response that produces them. Whether or not this law is true cannot be decided simply by an appeal to this definition, it must be decided by an appeal to the facts. Thus, says Meehl, the law of effect (all or some reinforcers are transituational) is not logically derivable from the Pop-Op definition of reinforcement. After the publication of Meehl's paper, the Pop-Op definition began to be widely adopted, until today it is virtually universal. Consider the following 10 variants on this single theme:

S. A. Barnett: A positive reinforcer may be defined as a stimulus which increases the strength of a response (1963, p. 167).

D. E. Broadbent: Anything we do to an animal which makes its immediately preceding action more probable, can be regarded as a reward (1961, p. 164).

W. K. Estes: A class of outcomes which produce increments in probability of response A is represented by element E in the set of "reinforcing events" (1959, p. 459).

G. A. Kimble: A reinforcer is an event which, employed appropriately, increases the probability of occurrences of a response in a learning situation (1961, p. 203).

S. A. Mednick: Operationally defined, a reward is an event that immediately follows a response and increases the likelihood of that response (1964, p. 22).

George A. Miller: Reinforcement: strengthening. In discussions of conditioning, a reinforcement is any outcome of an act that tends to increase the likelihood of that act under similar circumstances in the future (1962, p. 352).

N. E. Miller: I have defined rewards as events empirically found to have the effect of strengthening cue-response connections (1959, p. 240).

James Olds: Reward: a positive response selector; anything which increases the frequency of a response or response series which it follows (1955, p. 75).

Murray Sidman: Any event, contingent upon the response of the organism, that alters the future likelihood of that response, is called a *reinforcement* (1960, p. 396).

K. W. Spence: Environmental events exhibiting this property of increasing the probability of occurrence of the responses they accompany constitute a class of events known as reinforcers (1956, p. 32).

I conclude from this list that on no other question in psychology can we find more widespread agreement. The Pop-Op definition of reinforcement is the one and only orthodox definition of this idea. And yet when we understand what this definition means, we shall discover that it is too vague to be of any use.

We can begin by asking how we are to test the following simple statement: *This rps improves the performance of response R.*[2] The first point to notice about this statement is that it is elliptical, that is, it fails to include the various conditions that must be met before we can begin to test the statement. Thus the statement should read, "This rps improves, etc., under conditions *a, b, c, . . . , n.*" These conditions include specifications of the animal's deprivation, of the test environment, and so on. Although it may be difficult in some cases to specify all the restricting conditions or to meet the conditions we have specified, I am not concerned here with these difficulties, and I shall assume for the purpose of argument that we can in most, if not all, cases find a satisfactory solution to them.

The question I want to raise is this: Does this statement mean that under these specified conditions the rps *always* improves the performance of R, or does it merely mean that these rps *sometimes* improves the performance of R?

Before I try to answer this question, let me briefly explain what I think is required in an empirical test of any statement. In such a test, a controlled situation is set up in which several alternative outcomes are possible. To make sure that we have set up a situation that fairly tests our statement, we must show that among the sentences describing the alternative outcomes there is at least one that contradicts the statement we are testing. If the outcome of the test forces us to believe such a sentence, then the statement we have tested is false. If, on the other hand, the outcome of the test does not force us to believe such a sentence, then the statement we have tested has been corroborated, that is to say, it has been tested and not falsified.

Now consider again the testing of the statement: *This rps improves the performance of response R.* It seems clear that this statement can be tested and either falsified or not only if we take it as meaning that this rps always has this effect under the specified conditions. If we should take it to mean merely that the rps sometimes has this effect and we did not exactly specify the times when it *always does*, then there is no possible outcome of any test that would falsify this statement. And if the statement cannot be falsified, then it makes no sense to say that it can be corroborated because to say *that* is simply to say that the statement has been tested and not falsified.

It follows from all this that unless our Pop-Op definition says that the rps is *sufficient* to produce this effect under the specified conditions, we shall never be able to distinguish those rps that are reinforcers from those that are not. I conclude then that the Pop-Op definition must be refined as follows:

Any rps that is sufficient (under the specified conditions) to improve the performance of the response it follows is (by definition) a reinforcer of that response.

[2]Because there is a maximal value for probability I have changed the phrase "increase the probability" to "improve the performance," by which I designate whatever measures of performance like frequency, speed, and so on, are appropriate.

But now that we have revised the Pop-Op definition so that we can distinguish exactly between reinforcers and nonreinforcers it turns out that this definition is practically worthless because there are *in fact* no rps that are sufficient to improve the performance of the responses they follow. Take any rps you like, and specify any test conditions you wish, and I can point to three different sorts of facts that prove that these rps are not sufficient to improve performance.

1. The performance of the critical response does not improve after each training trial. Often there is no improvement after the first trial, and throughout training there are always trials in which the performance fails to improve.
2. After extended training the performance always reaches a stable maximum, and although each instance of the critical response continues to be followed by this rps, the performance no longer improves.
3. In virtually every learning experiment, there is a small number of subjects who have to be discarded after several training sessions because their performance fails to improve, although the rps follows each instance of the critical response.

Although such facts are commonplace enough, and although we are quite familiar with various explanations of why performance fails to improve in each of these cases, the brute fact remains that performance did *not* improve, and we cannot escape concluding that such rps are *not* sufficient to improve performance. Finally, if we refuse to part with the Pop-Op definition, we are forced to conclude that no rps is a reinforcer.

Now this argument is, of course, rejected by all those who believe that a sharp distinction can still be made if only we ignore those exceptions. Those who seek to save the Pop-Op definition argue that these exceptions can be disregarded provided we can give a reasonable explanation of why performance fails to improve in these cases. But all this theoretical ingenuity is wasted, because even if we had the one and only true explanation of why performance fails to improve, we cannot conclude from this that performance did improve. Thus we are faced with a cruel choice. We must either conclude that we know of no rps that is a reinforcer (we know of none sufficient to improve performance) or we know of no rps that is *not* a reinforcer (all may at sometime or other improve performance). Such a dilemma illustrates the basic weakness of the Pop-Op definition. No interpretation of this definition provides us with a practical distinction between reinforcers and nonreinforcers.

We can now understand what I meant when I said that the current empirical definition of reinforcement is not exact enough to allow us to answer questions about reinforcement with decisive experiments. It is fashionable in many quarters today to pooh-pooh this idea of designing experiments to answer such questions and to imply that our past failures were the result of an excessive concern for theoretical rigor and precision. Certainly Hull, Spence, and others of the neobehaviorist camp had an admirable concern for precision in their ideas and statements, but their failure to settle these questions by experiments came not from the fact that their ideas were too precise but from the fact that they were not precise enough. To determine whether performance will improve without reinforcement, for example, our idea of reinforcement must be exact enough so that we can be certain that the rps that follows the critical response is *not* a reinforcer. Unfortunately, no one directed his analytical skill to this kind of primary problem. The ideas of reinforcement, of stimulus, of response, of habit, and of drive were never given the kind of careful analysis they require. Instead these ideas were vaguely illustrated by some experimental demonstration that was called an operational definition. But what about the distinctions between those rps that are *reinforcers* and those that are not; between those physical energies that are *stimuli* and those that are not; between those corporeal reactions that are *responses* and those that are not; between those customary acts that are *habits* and those that are not; and between those preparatory dispositions that are *drives* and those that are not? Although all these distinctions are crucial for any empirical study of behavior, the so-called operational definitions failed to provide any practical ways of making these distinctions. As a result, all the most interesting and important questions about behavior and learning remained unanswered. The failure to provide these distinctions is, I think, the reason for the distrust of learning theory that in recent years has swept through academic psychology.

Thus, what most needs to be done today is to create definitions for these elementary ideas that will furnish us with the kinds of practical distinctions we need to test our beliefs about behavior. In the next section of this appendix, I shall propose a new definition of a reinforcer which I hope captures what was interesting and important in the old idea of reward, but escapes the vagueness of the Pop-Op concept of a reinforcer.

C. A New and Improved Definition of Reinforcement.

Let us begin by trying to agree about the conditions that must be met by a satisfactory definition of reinforcement.

1. The definition must provide us with an exact distinction between two classes of response-produced stimulation: the reinforcers and the nonreinforcers. Only if this distinction is exact can we test statements about the effects of reinforcers on behavior. If the distinction is so vague that frequently we cannot decide whether or not a certain rps is a reinforcer, then the definition must be rejected as unsatisfactory.
2. This distinction not only needs to be exact but it also needs to be practical in the sense that both classes of rps (the reinforcers and the nonreinforcers) must *in fact* have members. Because there are *in fact* no rps that are sufficient to improve performance, the distinction between those rps that are sufficient and those that are not is exact but wholly impractical.
3. The distinction must not only be exact and practical but it must also be relevant to the rough common sense distinction between rewards and non-rewards which it seeks to replace. This rough common sense distinction regards rewards as rps that somehow are sufficient to support the performance of the responses that produce them. Thus, a satisfactory definition must specify in what sense reinforcers support such performance.

Before the idea of reinforcement became a common one in psychology, the idea of reward served much the same purpose. In Thorndike's hand this latter idea was rather broad and loose. Like the idea of reinforcement it included all those effects of

a response that improve the performance of the response (i.e., that strengthen this S-R bond). But it also included those effects of a response that maintain the performance of a well-established habit (i.e., that prevent the extinction of this S-R bond).

I want now to propose a new way of distinguishing reinforcers from nonreinforcers that is based on this second property of rewards. I propose then the following distinction: *all those effects of a response that prevent its extinction* (i.e., all those rps that are sufficient to maintain the performance of this response) *are reinforcers of this response*. On the other hand, *all those effects of a response that fail to maintain the performance are nonreinforcers of this response*. In short, a reinforcer is an rps that prevents the extinction of a well-established habitual response.

This proposal presumes that we could, if we troubled to, determine the operant level for any habit in any individual under any specified and controlled testing conditions. This is the stable rate at which this response is repeated under these testing conditions when the contingent response-produced changes in stimulation are reduced to a minimum. When the individual responds at a stable rate that is higher than his operant level, then the rps for this response are *reinforcers*.[3] Whenever the animal's stable rate is no greater than the operant level, then the rps for this response are *nonreinforcers*.

One way to better our understanding of a new idea is to consider how this new idea changes our view of certain traditional problems or questions.

The Question of Transsituational States. In describing the history of the Pop-Op definition, we considered Meehl's (1950) argument against the view that this definition made the Law of Effect tautological. A key point in this argument was that experiment and only experiment can determine whether a particular rps that reinforces one response, in one individual, in one test situation will or will not reinforce any other responses, in any other individuals, in any other test situations. Meehl's conclusion was that the Law of Effect asserts that all, or at least many reinforcers are transsituational (i.e., will reinforce all other responses, in all other individuals, in all other test situations). But after Meehl's paper no experiments were done to test this assertion. Instead, we seemed to accept the Law of Effect as a kind of self-evident first principle. Perhaps the reason for our failure to challenge this principle and follow this obviously important new line of research was that we secretly doubted that the Pop-Op definition provided the kind of practical distinction between reinforcers and nonreinforcers that was required for such research. As a result, today, 20 years after Meehl's paper, we still know no more about the transsituational generality of various reinforcers than we knew then. But with our new and improved definition of reinforcement we can, for the first time, turn directly to this problem. In fact, none of the remaining problems concerning reinforcement can be effectively attacked until we have determined the transsituational status of each rps that has the power to maintain some established habit in some particular situation and individual.

[3]Because the operant rate is sometimes higher after training than before, it is best to compare the post-training rates when (1) the contingent rps are minimal (operant rate) and (2) the test rps is contingent upon the habitual response.

The Problem of Synthesizing New Reinforcers. Once we have discovered the transsituational status of some of the more common reinforcers, we can begin research designed to create new reinforcers of greater power and generality. To do this we must analyse the stimulus components of each rps, and then ask which, if any, of these components is irrelevant to maintaining the habit. Once we have discovered how to remove these irrelevant components, we shall have synthesized a new reinforcer, one with greater power and generality. It seems obvious that such research promises to tell us something important about how reinforcers work and promises to provide us with new more powerful tools for the study of learning and performance.

The Problem of Estimating the Reinforcing Powers of Various rps. It is obvious that we cannot long discuss the concept of reinforcement without implicitly, at least, assuming that it is sensible to speak of varying amounts of reinforcing power. Because the Pop-Op definition failed to provide an exact distinction between reinforcers and nonreinforcers there was no obvious way of estimating the reinforcing powers of different rps. But with our new and improved definition of reinforcement we have an obvious and simple way of estimating reinforcing power. If, under identical testing conditions, an rps maintains a certain habitual response at a higher supraoperant level than another rps then surely the first rps has more reinforcing power than the second. This suggests that the reinforcing power of an rps can be estimated from the level at which it maintains a habit. On the other hand, the fact that this level is also determined by the reinforcement schedule proves that we cannot measure reinforcing power directly by this method. The most we can expect from this method is the order of the various reinforcers ranked by their power to maintain a certain habit under specified and controlled testing conditions. We must discover much more about the interaction of reinforcement schedules and reinforcing power before we shall be able to devise a method of measuring reinforcing power (i.e., so that this power can be represented by a single number).

The Problem of How and When Reinforcers Influence the Acquisition of New Habits. Once we know the transsituational status of certain reinforcers and are able to estimate their various reinforcing powers, we are ready to consider how such reinforcers influence the acquisition of new habits. As we have repeatedly pointed out, we do not as yet know of any rps that is sufficient to improve the performance of a new response. If we are to discover when and how reinforcers produce such improvement, we must, of course, have some way of identifying a reinforcer that is logically independent of its effect upon new responses. It is just on this point that the inadequacy of the Pop-Op interpretation of reinforcement is most apparent. The new and improved definition of reinforcement, on the other hand, provides us with just such a way of identifying reinforcers. Thus it enables us to discover through our experiments (1) those reinforcers that are responsible for such improvement, and (2) those conditions that are necessary for such improvement to occur. Eventually, I think, such a program of research will isolate those reinforcers and conditions that are sufficient to produce improvement in the performance of new responses.

Before we end this discussion of reinforcement let me consider the two criticisms this proposal most frequently arouses in the reader.

1. Some readers will ask: But how does this proposed new and improved idea differ from what we have always meant by a reinforcer? Surely, they will go on, we have always believed that when a habit extinguished, the reinforcement for it must have somehow been withdrawn.

2. Other readers will ask: But how is this proposed new and improved idea in any way relevant to what we have always meant by a reinforcer? The idea of reinforcement, they will go on, was introduced to help explain learning, that is, the improved performance of a new response through practice. The proposed new interpretation of reinforcement seems totally irrelevant to this important problem.

The fact that this proposal arouses such contrary criticisms suggests to me that the amount of confusion and vagueness in the accepted idea of reinforcement is perhaps even greater than we have so far supposed. When faced with two critics so clearly at cross-purposes, it is tempting to suggest that the critics settle the matter between themselves. But I will resist this temptation and, instead, try to settle the kinds of doubts that appear to give rise to these criticisms.

There can be little question that we psychologists of learning have, for a long time, continued to use the word "reinforcement" in much the same way that Thorndike used to use the word "reward." On the other hand, whenever our usage was under critical attack, we usually turned our back on this loose usage and pledged our support to the Pop-Op interpretation of the idea. In this sense it is quite true that we have implicitly assumed for years that reinforcers have the power to maintain established habits and prevent extinction. Thus, all that our present proposal does is to make this implicit meaning explicit, and to plan a program of research that enables us to discover which rps have this power and which do not. Only in this sense does our proposal make a radical change in the interpretation of this crucial concept.

The second criticism is harder to answer because it is based on the curious assumption that a proper definition of this idea will somehow explain how learning occurs. In the main body of this paper we considered at length the sorts of facts we must know if we are to explain any behavioral fact. If, as I hope, those arguments were sound ones, then it is quite clear that no definition or distinction by itself can explain any phenomenon. On the other hand, it is equally evident that any explanation of learning will have to take account of the role played by the rps of the favored learned response. Thus, it seems, we must begin our analysis of behavior by distinguishing those rps that somehow support the behavior that produces them. The accepted Pop-Op interpretation failed to provide a way of distinguishing such rps, simply because we know of no rps that is sufficient to support (i.e., to improve) the behavior that produces it. On the other hand, we can distinguish those rps that are sufficient to maintain (i.e., to prevent the extinction of) the behavior that produces them. This, I think, is a first necessary step in the search for those rps that influence the acquisition and maintenance of new habits. In this sense, then, our proposed new interpretation of this idea is directly relevant to research that will someday lead to the facts that can explain the various phenomena of learning.

References

ATKINSON, R. C., BOWER, G. H., and CROTHERS, E. J. *Introduction to mathematical learning theory.* New York: John Wiley, 1965.

BARNETT, S. A. *The rat: A study in behavior.* Chicago: Aldine, 1963.

BROADBENT, D. E. *Behavior.* New York: Basic Books, 1961.

BUSH, R. R., and MOSTELLER, F. *Stochastic models of learning.* New York: John Wiley, 1955.

DELAFRESNAYE, J. F. (ed.). *Brain mechanisms and learning.* Oxford: Blackwell, 1961.

DEUTSCH, J. A. *The structural basis of behavior.* Chicago: University of Chicago Press, 1960.

ESTES, W. K. The statistical approach to learning theory. In S. KOCH (ed.), *Psychology: A study of a science,* vol. 2. New York: McGraw-Hill, 1959.

FEIGENBAUM, E. A., and FELDMAN, J. *Computers and thought.* New York: McGraw-Hill, 1963.

FIELD, S., MAGOUN, H. W., and HALL, V. E. (eds.). *Handbook of Physiology,* vol. 3. Washington, D. C.: American Physiological Society, 1960.

GOLDSTEIN, H., KRANTZ, D. L., and RAINS, J. D. *Controversial issues in learning.* New York: Appleton-Century-Crofts, 1965.

HEBB, D. O. *The organization of behavior.* New York: John Wiley, 1949.

HILGARD, E. R., and BOWER, G. H. *Theories of learning.* 3d ed. New York: Appleton-Century-Crofts, 1966.

HILL, W. F. *Learning: A survey of psychological interpretations.* San Francisco: Chandler, 1963.

HULL, C. L. *Essentials of behavior.* New Haven, Conn.: Yale University Press, 1951.

KAPLAN, A. *The conduct of inquiry: Methodology for behavioral science.* San Francisco: Chandler, 1964.

KIMBLE, D. P. (ed.). *Learning, remembering, and forgetting,* vol. 1. *The anatomy of memory.* Palo Alto, Calif.: Science and Behavior Book, 1965.

KIMBLE, G. A. *Hilgard and Marquis's conditioning and learning,* 2d ed. New York: Appleton-Century-Crofts, 1961.

KONORSKI, J. *Integrative activity of the brain.* Chicago: University of Chicago Press, 1967.

LASHLEY, K. S. Learning: Nervous mechanisms in learning. In C. MURCHISON (ed.), *The foundations of experimental psychology.* Worcester, Mass.: Clark University Press, 1929.

LUCE, R. D. *Individual choice behavior.* New York: John Wiley, 1959.

MARX, M. H. *Theories in contemporary psychology.* New York: Macmillan, 1963.

MEDNICK, S. A. *Learning.* Englewood Cliffs, N.J.: Prentice-Hall, 1964.

MEEHL, P. E. On the circularity of the law of effect. *Psychological Bulletin,* 1950, *47,* 52–75.

MELTON, A. W. *Categories of human learning.* New York: Academic, 1964.

MILLER, G. A. *Psychology: The science of mental life.* New York: Harper & Row, 1962.

MILLER, N. E. Liberalization of basic S-R concepts: Extensions to conflict behavior, motivation and social learning. In S. KOCH (ed.), *Psychology: A study of a science,* vol. 2. New York: McGraw-Hill, 1959.

OLDS, J. Physiological mechanisms of reward. In M. R. JONES (ed.), *Nebraska symposium on motivation.* Lincoln: University of Nebraska Press, 1955.

POSTMAN, L. The history and present status of the law of effect. *Psychological Bulletin,* 1947, *44,* 489–563.

PREMACK, D. Reinforcement theory. In M. R. JONES (ed.), *Nebraska symposium on motivation: 1965.* Lincoln: University of Nebraska Press, 1965.

PRIBRAM, K. H. Proposal for a structural pragmatism: Some neuropsychological considerations of problems in philosophy. In B. B. WOLMAN and E. NAGEL (eds.), *Scientific psychology.* New York: Basic Books, 1965.

RESTLE, F. *The psychology of judgment and choice.* New York: John Wiley, 1961.

RITCHIE, A. D. *Scientific Method.* New York: Harcourt, 1923.

RITCHIE, B. F. Concerning an incurable vagueness in psychological theories. In B. B. WOLMAN and E. NAGEL (eds.), *Scientific psychology.* New York: Basic Books, 1965.

SAYRE, K. M., and CROSSON, F. J. *The modeling of mind.* Notre Dame, Ind.: University of Notre Dame Press, 1963.

SIDMAN, M. *Tactics of scientific research.* New York: Basic Books, 1960.

SKINNER, B. F. *The behavior of organisms: An experimental analysis.* New York: Appleton-Century-Crofts, 1938.

SPENCE, K. W. *Behavior theory and conditioning.* New Haven, Conn.: Yale University Press, 1956.

SPERRY, R. W. Cerebral organization and behavior. *Science,* 1961, *133,* 1749–57.

TINBERGEN, N. *The study of instinct.* Oxford: Clarendon Press, 1951.

TOLMAN, E. C. *Purposive behavior in animals and men.* New York: Appleton-Century-Crofts, 1932.

TOULMIN, S. *The philosophy of science.* New York: Harper & Row, 1960.

WOOLDRIDGE, D. E. *The machinery of the brain.* New York: McGraw-Hill, 1963.

YOVITTS, M., and CAMERON, S. (eds.). *Self-organizing systems.* New York: Pergamon, 1960.

YOUNG, J. Z. *A model of the brain.* Oxford: Clarendon Press, 1964.

Historical Perspective

Although there now are thousands of published experiments on animal learning, the scientific study of learning in animals has a relatively short history. Prescientific speculation ascribed rudimentary or virtually no learning capacity to animals. General intellectual processes such as foresight, judgment, and even the ability to profit from experience were almost always viewed as characteristics unique to man. Animals were presumed to be rather mechanically guided and controlled by "instincts," the general implication being that certain inherited proclivities inclined or directed an organism toward particular behavioral outcomes, e.g., nest building, maternal behavior, etc. (Beach 1955). Thus, it was assumed that there was a clear dichotomy between animals and man and that only man had the capacity to learn, i.e., to modify behavior as a result of previous experience.

This outlook was significantly changed by the gradual acceptance of Darwin's theory of evolution. Acceptance of evolutionary theory led to the view that the behavior of man and of animals evolved from a common natural background and that adaptive capacities, such as the ability to profit from experience, were selectively propagated. It appeared that human and animal intellectual functions had a great deal in common (Darwin 1871).

In the absence of a tradition of laboratory experimentation, early animal learning data frequently were obtained from casual observations of behavioral phenomena believed to be of special significance. Such an anecdotal approach is analogous to the compiling of a series of miniature case histories, a method which makes it rather difficult to clearly separate observations from interpretations (Romanes, 1906). The growth of a systematic and repeatable body of animal learning data awaited the development of more formal laboratory methodology. Early animal learning procedures usually required the subject to behave in a certain way in some apparatus in order to escape shock or to obtain reward. Although conscientious efforts were made to collect objective data, most relevant variables were as yet un-

Raymond C. Miles

Animal Learning: An Overview

23

specified; as a result, many early experiments did no more than demonstrate that animal subjects were capable of learning when certain procedures were used (Warden et al. 1936). Lack of standardization among procedures and apparatuses resulted in such a diversified array of data that it was difficult to deduce common learning principles. A few established principles were anticipated, but most early interpretations of learning data did not endure.

Thorndike (1911) placed animal subjects in problem boxes in which certain behavioral acts, such as releasing a latch or pulling a string, were required in order to escape from the box. When escape time was plotted on a graph, a gradual improvement in performance as a function of trials became apparent. It also appeared that the subjects ceased to make "abortive" responses which were unrelated to or interfered with problem solution. These observations suggested to Thorndike that animal learning was a somewhat blind, trial-and-error process. Of more enduring significance was Thorndike's suggestion of a principle defined behaviorally as the "law of effect." The modern conceptualization of reinforcement actually is a more precise definition of this original principle:

"Of several responses made to the same situation, those which are accompanied or closely followed by satisfaction to the animal will, other things being equal, be more firmly connected with the situation, so that, when it recurs, they will be more likely to recur" (p. 244).

The behavioristic viewpoint initiated by J. B. Watson (1914) contributed to learning methodology by its strong emphasis on objective response measures. Although Watson insisted that animal learning be cast in a restrictive, nonmentalistic mold, wherein complex behavior was typically viewed as mere chains of reflexes, two factors were emphasized which anticipated principles which have since become well established. A *frequency* principle, stating that the behaviors during learning which eventually became predominant are those which occur most often, has been experimentally demonstrated many times with various learning procedures and many animal species. With increasing practice, there occurs an increment in some criterion of learning (usually an increase in response magnitude or response probability). The second factor was a *recency* principle which stated that, if other variables are relatively constant, the behavior which becomes predominant is the most recent response. This phenomenon, which was never thoroughly investigated by Watson, has been demonstrated by the results of many subsequent learning experiments. There now is ample evidence that the behavioral act immediately preceding reinforcement is the response which is most strengthened and that even a short delay of reinforcement adversely affects rate of learning (Kimble 1961).

Among investigators of animal learning, it was Clark Hull who perhaps was most responsible for the initiation of current research techniques. In addition to demonstrating the merits of carefully controlled procedures, he asked research questions which contributed significantly to the understanding of the learning process. Although Hull fell short of his goal of formulating a generally accepted, all-encompassing theory of learning, there is no doubt that his careful sifting of variables led to the demonstration of functional relationships which previously had

been vaguely defined or unknown. Hull (1943) emphasized that the behavioral changes referred to as "learning" came about because of a reduction in some basic physiological drive state such as hunger, thirst, or pain stimulation. Thus, the capacity to modify behavior as a result of experience (i.e., learning) was included among other adaptive biological mechanisms. Behavior which reliably results in escape from pain or a decrease in hunger or thirst is strengthened.

Other learning theories of broad scope also were developed during this period. Tolman's (1932) proposal and investigation of mentalistic ("cognitive") constructs countered to some extent a tendency for the study of animal learning to become overly structured and narrow. Rather than attributing the modification of behavior to one or to a very few principles, Tolman argued in favor of the possibility of several different basic types of animal learning (Tolman 1949). Although he included Hull's principle of drive reduction, he emphasized a cognitive theory of "field expectancy" learning which proposed that animals learn as they become aware of sequential stimulus events ("signs") and of the general topography of their surroundings. Drive reduction was considered to be sufficient but not necessary; an organism also could learn merely by being exposed to or exploring an environment, thereby gaining knowledge and even making inferences about the external world.

Careful observations of cats in the process of solving a puzzle box problem provided the basis for an ingenious reductionistic learning theory developed by Guthrie (1935). He noted that cat subjects tended to repeat in a somewhat stereotyped manner the behavior which preceded escape from the puzzle box. Guthrie deduced that the act preceding escape was contingent upon a particular stimulus complex (i.e., the interior of the box) which changed markedly when the subject moved from the inside to the outside of the box. Recurrence of the within-box stimuli again induced the same behavioral act. Thus, Guthrie assumed that an animal learns an association between the stimulus complex and a behavioral act after only one experience. He suggested that the reason numerous trials often are required for the demonstration of learning is that associative learning conditions have not been sufficiently controlled. Consequently, repeated trials are not actually duplications and the subject must learn to respond to a number of similar but not really identical stimulus complexes. Only after several associations have been formed will the behavioral criterion of learning be achieved.

These briefly sketched early attempts to formulate comprehensive theories of learning were optimistically expanded by subsequent investigators to account for a wide range of learning phenomena. A flurry of research activity undertaken to test the relative merits of various learning theories gradually brought about a mood of general scepticism. It became apparent that a particular theory might account very well for the data upon which it was based, but that the generality of any one theory was limited. There then evolved a trend away from comprehensive learning theories toward careful and detailed accounts of a more circumscribed range of phenomena.

Skinner (1938) strongly emphasized the necessity for the gathering of systematic and reliable learning data unhindered by the influence of any preconceived theoretical position. His system, which studiously excluded formal postulates and inferential or deductive constructs, was developed on the basis of a methodology whereby an unrestrained animal actually generated its own learning functions. For example, a rat subject was placed in a box equipped with a lever. While freely exploring the box, the subject would press the lever, and this act would result in the automatic delivery of a small pellet of food. Each lever press was recorded by the upward step of a pen drawing on a paper which moved from right to left at a slow and constant rate. Thereby the subject generated a continuous record which duplicated the actual course of acquisition and learned performance of the lever pressing response. This descriptive approach proved to be a very valuable method for investigating the temporal course of behavioral changes which develop as a result of different reinforcement and discrimination learning schedules. Ingenious adaptations of the method have made it applicable to the study of a wide variety of behavioral phenomena. The system begun by Skinner has remained a dominant method for studying animal learning, perhaps because it is unrestricted by theoretical boundaries and because its highly objective and precise analysis of learned behavior has led to some useful and significant practical applications (Skinner 1953).

Laboratory demonstrations of animal learning are by now almost innumerable. Typical procedures for investigating the acquisition of a learned response are designed to determine the increase in response strength as a function of repeated stimulus-stimulus, stimulus-response, or response-response occurrences followed by reinforcement. Reinforcement usually consists of the presentation of some drive-reducing agent, such as food or water.

Basic Processes

The term "learning" often is defined as a relatively permanent change in behavior which occurs as a result of practice. When human subjects are used in a learning experiment, it is possible to instruct them to repeatedly and consistently practice some formally structured task. With animal subjects a fairly strong reinforcer must be used to induce the subject to repeatedly perform the designated behavioral act. A positive reinforcer is defined as an environmental event (or "stimulus") which strengthens behavior when it is presented. The ongoing behavior (or "response") which precedes the reinforcing stimulus increases in frequency and probability. For example, a hungry rat placed in an enclosure will exhibit a variety of behaviors (e.g., sniffing, locomoting, face washing, standing up on hind legs, turning, etc.). One behavioral act, such as standing up in the left front corner of the enclosure, is selected as the response to be strengthened, and a reinforcing stimulus (e.g., a small food pellet) is immediately presented whenever this act occurs. The typical finding is that the reinforced response occurs more and more often while other behaviors gradually diminish. The same method also can be applied to determine whether a particular stimulus is reinforcing. In the preceding example, the fact that delivery of the food pellet strengthened the immediately preceding behavioral act showed that food presentation was a reinforcing event. Once it has been empirically established that a given stimulus is a reinforcer, it can be used to systematically investigate how learning is affected by manipulation of other variables (e.g., delay of reinforcement, quantity of reinforcement, level of hunger, etc.).

CLASSICAL CONDITIONING

The behavior of many organisms is almost constantly being modified by a process referred to as *classical conditioning*. This type of learning was first discovered and investigated by Ivan Pavlov (1927). Pavlov, a physiologist, was initially interested in studying the reflex secretions of certain glands involved in the process of digestion. A *reflex* is defined as a response or responses which occur automatically when some signal is presented. The environmental event responsible for the occurrence of a reflex is called an *eliciting stimulus*. This stimulus does not force the organism to make the response but functions as a "trigger" which automatically elicits the reflex, either a glandular or a muscular reaction. Using dogs as subjects, Pavlov devised an arrangement to collect and measure salivary gland secretions. A natural stimulus, such as meat powder or weak acid, was used to elicit the salivary reflex. As these investigations continued, Pavlov noticed that some salivation seemed to occur prior to presentation of the natural eliciting stimulus. Research efforts then were concentrated upon the systematic investigation of this new type of "psychic" reflex.

Classical conditioning occurs when a "neutral" stimulus, one which does not naturally elicit a given reflex, is repeatedly paired with a stimulus which does elicit the reflex. For example, in Pavlov's investigations, the ringing of a bell (a neutral stimulus) occurred just before presentation of the meat powder elicited salivation. After a number of paired presentations of bell and meat powder, a new reflex became evident. Salivation was elicited by the ringing of the bell. Conventional terminology refers to the original eliciting stimulus (in this case, the meat powder) as the *unconditioned stimulus* (US); salivation in response to the unconditioned stimulus is called the *unconditioned response* (UR). An originally neutral stimulus (e.g., ringing of the bell) which elicits a response after pairing with a US is referred to as a *conditioned stimulus* (CS), and the response to it is called a *conditioned response* (CR).

By recording either the magnitude of a CR or the frequency with which it is elicited by the CS, it is possible to graphically represent the acquisition of a learned response. Results of most investigations reveal a monotonic growth function, i.e., a conditioned "habit" becomes stronger by progressively smaller increments as a function of the number of conditioning trials. A conditioned response gradually diminishes in strength when the CS is repeatedly presented in the absence of the US. This process is referred to as experimental extinction. The extinction process appears to be the reverse of acquisition in that response strength decreases as a function of repeated trials.

After a response has become reliably conditioned, it can be shown that the behavioral control acquired by the CS is shared by other stimuli. Presentation of another stimulus similar to the CS will often elicit the CR, but usually with a lower probability of occurrence or of a lesser magnitude (Anrep 1923). Behavioral equivalence of the two stimuli is a function of their degree of similarity, and this phenomenon is referred to as *stimulus generalization*.

By means of the process of classical conditioning, a wide variety of environmental events are potential conditioned stimuli. It should be noted that an organism does not acquire new responses through the process of classical conditioning but that the variety of stimuli which can come to elicit a given reflex is almost limitless. Classical conditioning apparently gives an animal a significant adaptive contact with its environment. A *CR* is essentially a preparatory reaction to the *US* and is strengthened in proportion to the number of consistent experiences. The response is generalized along a similarity dimension to other stimuli, and nonoccurrence of the *US* results in extinction of the *CR*. Consequently, the behavior of the organism is constantly being modified by environmental contingencies.

OPERANT (INSTRUMENTAL) CONDITIONING

Although classical conditioning became recognized as a highly significant learning phenomenon, it was not universally accepted as the prototype of all animal learning. Thorndike (1911), in his previously mentioned experiments in which animal subjects learned to escape from problem boxes, obtained learning functions without using the classical conditioning procedure. When escape time was recorded as a measure of learning, it was evident that the subjects experienced considerable difficulty in solving this apparently simple problem but that there was a slow and gradual improvement in performance as training continued.

This type of simple trial-and-error learning later was thoroughly explored by Skinner (1938). His careful observations of animal subjects revealed that they often engaged in some type of behavior which acted upon the environment. Activity of this type was descriptively classified as *operant* behavior. Because there were no specifiable eliciting stimuli, it was said that the behavior was *emitted*, and the investigation of operant behavior necessarily concentrated on changes in responding rather than stimulus-response associations.

The operant (or instrumental) conditioning procedure consists of strengthening a response which already is a part of an organism's behavioral repertoire by means of the presentation of a reinforcing stimulus. In the typical demonstration of operant conditioning, a hungry rat is placed in a chamber which has a lever protruding from one wall. When the lever is pressed, a small food pellet is automatically delivered to the subject. The behavioral consequence of this reinforcing event is that the immediately preceding operant response (lever pressing) increases in frequency and probability. After a number of reinforcements, the effect becomes obvious—the reinforced act occurs repeatedly, while there is a pronounced decrease in the occurrence of other emitted responses. The importance of reinforcement in the operant conditioning process is clearly shown by the automatic strengthening of whatever response(s) happens to immediately precede presentation of a reinforcer. After an operant has become conditioned, it is possible to demonstrate experimental extinction by discontinuing delivery of reinforcement. Rate of emission of the conditioned operant response gradually decreases until the response almost never is emitted.

Operant discrimination learning can be demonstrated by arranging conditions so that a response is followed by reinforcement only when it occurs in the presence of a particular environmental stimulus (S^D). When this stimulus is absent, the subject is free to make the response but reinforcement does not occur. For example, after a subject has learned to press a lever for food reinforcement, contingencies are changed so that lever pressing is reinforced only when a light is turned on (the positive, S^D condition). When the light is out (the negative, S^D condition),

lever pressing is not followed by reinforcement. With repeated exposures to these conditions, the response undergoes many successive extinctions and reconditionings. The subject at first will press the lever equally often under both conditions; then, as discrimination training continues, the response becomes partially extinguished during S^Δ periods and reconditioned when the S^D condition occurs. These two processes take place more and more rapidly until the lever pressing response almost never is made during S^Δ periods. After thorough training, the S^D condition controls the behavior so effectively that it seems as if the conditioned operant response is "turned on" by presentation of the discriminative stimulus (Skinner 1938).

When a discrimination has become well established, it can be demonstrated that the effect generalizes to other stimuli which are similar to the S^D. It is possible to generate a stimulus generalization gradient like that obtained by means of classical conditioning procedures.

INSTRUMENTAL ESCAPE AND AVOIDANCE LEARNING

Most examples of animal learning in the preceding sections of this chapter described behavioral changes which occur as a consequence of "positive" reinforcement, i.e., as a result of stimulation which strengthens behavior by its presentation. There is a contrasting type of reinforcement which is referred to as "negative." A negative reinforcer is a stimulus which strengthens behavior by its cessation or withdrawal. Some common examples of negative reinforcers are shocks, burns, pinches or blows, unpleasant odors and tastes, etc. Aversive stimuli such as these act as a *US* that elicits a *UR*, such as pain or nausea.

Instrumental *escape* learning can be demonstrated by using escape from shock as reinforcement. Assume that a subject is placed on a grid and receives a shock which continues until the subject presses a lever, whereupon the shock is terminated for a short period of time. After repeated exposure to this situation, the time (or latency) before the subject emits the lever-pressing escape response becomes shorter and shorter until the response occurs almost immediately upon onset of shock.

A type of learning referred to as instrumental *avoidance* can be shown by presenting a neutral stimulus shortly before the onset of an aversive *US*. An experiment by Solomon and Wynne (1954) provides a good illustration of this type of learning. A dog subject was placed in one compartment of a two-unit shuttle box with a shock-grid floor and a hurdle separating the two compartments. A buzzer was sounded for 10 sec, after which an electric shock (the *US*) was turned on and remained on until the subject emitted the escape response of jumping over the hurdle into the other compartment. After a subject had experienced several such trials, the latency of the escape response became shorter and shorter until some avoidance responses began to occur, i.e., the subject sometimes jumped over the hurdle when it heard the buzzer rather than waiting for shock to occur. After a relatively few training trials, the subjects almost always avoided shock.

This procedure actually incorporates both classical and operant conditioning processes. The buzzer first becomes a *CS* which induces fear because it is repeatedly paired with a *US* (shock). At first, emission of the designated operant response (hurdle jumping) is reinforced by escape from the naturally aversive stimulus, but hurdle jumping soon begins to occur in the presence of the *CS* before the shock is turned on. Some theorists assume that the buzzer becomes a strong conditioned aversive stimulus and that avoidance responses are reinforced by a reduction in a conditioned fear reaction (Mowrer 1939).

The experiment by Solomon and Wynne (1954) is an example of what is sometimes called *active* avoidance learning because an animal must perform a specific act in order to avoid aversive stimulation. Another type of avoidance learning procedure does not require the emission of any specified response (Mowrer 1960). In *passive* avoidance learning experiments the subject is free to emit a wide variety of responses but must avoid the source of aversive stimulation. McCleary (1961) permitted cat subjects to move freely about a room and go into an open feeding box to obtain food. After many such feeding experiences, the grid floor of the feeding box was electrified and the subject had to retreat from the box in order to escape shock. Thereafter, the subjects very rarely or never entered the feeding box. It can be seen that no particular response was required to avoid shock; the subjects were free to perform a variety of behavioral acts (e.g., grooming, stretching, exploring, etc.), and no aversive stimulation was encountered so long as they did not enter the feeding box.

Reinforcement Schedules

There are many circumstances in which a particular response is reinforced intermittently rather than every time it occurs. Intermittent reinforcement can have marked effects upon the rate of emission of a learned response. When an animal has become thoroughly familiar with a particular pattern of reinforcement, the reinforcement schedule rather than the total number of reinforcements achieves predominant control over the operant behavior (Ferster and Skinner 1957). Following are brief descriptions of four commonly used intermittent reinforcement schedules:

The *fixed-interval* (*FI*) schedule is periodic with respect to time. During a specified (e.g., 2 min) period, a particular operant response is not reinforced. Reinforcement is delivered immediately following the first occurrence of the response after termination of the fixed interval, and this event marks the beginning of another 2-min interval which must transpire before the response is again reinforced. The schedule is automatically programmed so that it occurs over and over again. When a subject has become adapted to a fixed-interval schedule, records of responding during the interval indicate the formation of a temporal discrimination. Response rate is relatively slow early in the interval and then progressively increases until, at the end of the interval, the response is followed by reinforcement. The overall rate of responding of trained subjects is lower when the fixed interval is long and higher when the interval is shorter.

With a *fixed-ratio* (*FR*) schedule, reinforcement is contingent upon the emission of a specified number of responses. After one response has been followed by reinforcement, a fixed number of responses must be emitted before the response is again reinforced. A pattern of reinforcement whereby every tenth response is rewarded would be referred to as a *FR-10* schedule. As a subject becomes adapted to a *FR* schedule, a high overall rate of responding usually develops. Unless the fixed-ratio is unusually large, responding begins soon after

reinforcement and there is a tendency for response rate to increase with the approach of the next reinforcement. When the ratio is very large, pauses in responding ("time-outs") often occur, especially immediately following the occurrence of reinforcement.

The *variable-interval* (*VI*) schedule is arranged so that the occurrence of reinforcement is variable, rather than fixed, with respect to the passage of time. Length of the interval during which a response is not reinforced changes unsystematically within a predetermined range. For example, intervals of 60, 90, 120, 150, and 180 sec might be programmed to occur in an unpredictable sequence; at the end of each scheduled interval, the next response is reinforced and the succeeding interval begins. Because the average interval length in this example is 2 min, the pattern of reinforcement would be referred to as a *VI-2* schedule. The unpredictability of reinforcement with a *VI* schedule produces effects which are different from the temporal response pattern found when a *FI* schedule is used. Subjects usually develop a steady and persistent rate of responding.

With a *variable-ratio* (*VR*) schedule, reinforcement is delivered following a variable, rather than a fixed, number of responses. For example, after one response has been followed by reinforcement, the emission of either 10, 15, 20, 25, or 30 responses could be required before the response is again reinforced. The schedule is programmed so that the number of required responses between reinforcements is unpredictable. Because the mean number of required responses in this case is 20, this would be called a *VR-20* schedule. *VR* and *VI* schedules are similar in that reinforcement is an unpredictable event; the important difference is that a rapid rate of responding under a *VR* schedule results in the significantly earlier delivery of reinforcement and more reinforcements per unit time. When subjects become thoroughly adapted to a *VR* schedule, they exhibit a steady and rapid rate of responding. If the variable ratio is gradually made larger, response rate tends to become even faster, as if the subject has learned that more rapid responding results in more reinforcement. However, if the ratio should be made very large, even a well-trained subject will refrain from responding, take "time-outs," for fairly long periods of time. These "time-outs" seem to occur most often immediately following the delivery of reinforcement.

The effects of more complicated schedules, some consisting of the sequential occurrence of the different kinds of common reinforcement schedules, have also been investigated. One significant contribution of this research has been the clear demonstration of a new dimension of behavioral control, a powerful kind of control which evolves from the sequential pattern of reinforcement and overshadows the effect of number of reinforcements *per se*.

Secondary Reinforcement

In the preceding examples of learning procedures, the modification of behavior was almost always attributable to a kind of reinforcement which is commonly referred to as biological or *primary*. Responses followed by a reduction in some physiological drive state (e.g., hunger, thirst, pain, etc.) are strengthened. There is another kind of reinforcer, referred to as *secondary*, which acquires reinforcing properties by being consistently associated with a stimulus which is a fairly strong

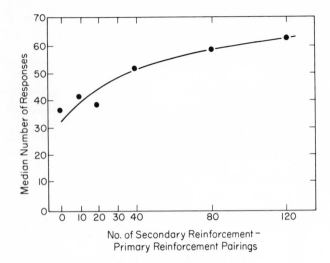

Fig. 23-1. *Median number of lever-pressing responses as a function of number of pairings of a secondary reinforcer with a primary reinforcer* [Bersh 1951].

primary reinforcer. The following procedure can be used to demonstrate acquired reinforcing effects of a secondary reinforcer: Hungry subjects are trained to press a lever for food reinforcement and the sound of a buzzer occurs with each lever press and before delivery of the food pellet. After the subjects have experienced a series of such acquisition trials, food reinforcement is discontinued and degree of learning is measured during an extinction session. By comparing groups which undergo extinction with and without the sound of the buzzer, it can be shown that more lever pressing responses occur during extinction when the response is followed by the familiar sound of the buzzer.

In an experiment by Bersh (1951), five groups of rats received either 10, 20, 40, 80, or 120 reinforcements during conditioning of a lever pressing response. Delivery of the food pellet was preceded by the brief presentation of a light stimulus. A control group earned 120 reinforcements without the light stimulation. After initial conditioning, all groups experienced an extinction session during which neither food nor light was presented. This session was planned to reduce the strength of lever pressing, without the secondary reinforcer, to about the same level in all groups. During the final phase of the experiment, each lever press was followed by presentation of the light stimulus. The results, illustrated in Figure 23–1, show that a greater number of lever presses were emitted in proportion to the number of times the light had been paired with reinforcement during training.

HABITUATION

There also have been many demonstrations of a type of behavioral modification which occurs due to stimulation without the occurrence of any reinforcing event. Following placement in an unfamiliar environment or a change in stimulation, an animal shows an initial high level of activity, or "exploratory" behavior, which decreases with the passing of time (Harris 1943). There appears to be a close parallel between this phenomenon, referred to as "reaction decrement," and habituation.

The typical demonstration of habituation consists of introducing a novel stimulus to a subject in a familiar environment and continuing to present the stimulus over a period of time. The novel stimulation at first arouses the subject and elicits certain orienting reactions (e.g., head turning, ear erection, sniffing, etc.); then as the stimulus is repeated, these reactions decrease in intensity and frequency and eventually no longer occur (Sokolov 1960). Habituation is somewhat specific to the particular stimulus which produced the phenomenon. After a certain repeated stimulus no longer elicits orienting reactions, the introduction of another novel stimulus often will cause these reactions to again occur. The probability of this happening is related to the degree of difference between the new stimulus and the stimulus that previously produced habituation (Thompson and Spencer 1966).

Results of both reaction decrement and habituation research have established that organisms become aroused by novel stimuli in the environment and that this heightened level of activity gradually diminishes with repeated or continual exposure to the stimulation. Occurrence of this phenomenon has apparent adaptive significance in that it prevents an organism from continuing to react to stimulation which has proved to be inconsequential. If the situation is changed so that reinforcement is presented in the presence of the repetitive stimulation, arousal reactions will reappear.

Toward Complexity

Experimental procedures described up to this point are those which have been used to demonstrate basic learning phenomena common to a wide variety of species. We will now explore some extensions of these basic procedures and other methods which have produced systematic, although sometimes subtle, behavioral changes.

EXTINCTION-RECONDITIONING

A relatively uncomplicated extension of the common conditioning and extinction procedures consists of presenting a subject with successive extinction and reconditioning trials. With this extinction-reconditioning procedure, a response is conditioned during one training session and then immediately extinguished until the response rate drops to almost zero. The subject then experiences a series of similar daily sessions during which the response is again conditioned until the level of responding appears to be about equal to that of the first sessions and then is extinguished. The typical finding is that both reconditioning and extinction occur more and more rapidly as a function of number of successive reconditioning-extinction sessions. This phenomenon has been demonstrated with both classical (Brogden et al. 1938) and operant (Bullock and Smith 1953) conditioning procedures. It is particularly noticeable when the behavioral measure of response strength consists of the number of operant responses emitted during successive extinction periods.

In one such experimental demonstration (Wickens and Miles 1954), rat subjects experienced a series of 30 reconditioning-extinction sessions during which they received 15 reinforcements of a lever-pressing response and then underwent

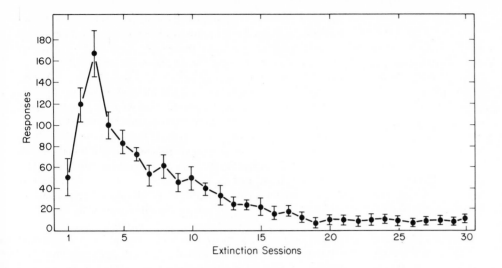

Fig. 23-2. *Median number of extinction responses during successive extinction sessions following interspersed reconditioning* [Wickens and Miles 1954].

extinction for one hour. The obtained function is illustrated in Figure 23–2. Although number of extinction responses increased from session to session early in the series, extinction responding then began to decrease rapidly until almost no responses were emitted following the first nonoccurrence of reinforcement in each session. Furthermore, the same phenomenon was observed during the last five sessions when the sequence of reconditioning and extinction periods was randomly determined. It also has been shown that strength of extinction responding is no longer positively related to number of reconditioning reinforcements after a subject has experienced a long series of reconditioning-extinction sessions (Miles 1965). Even when number of reinforcements varied from 3 to 160, there was no reliable difference in number of emitted extinction responses.

These data indicate that repeated conditioning and extinction of an operant response in animals produces a type of learning function which is different from the simple relationship between number of reinforcements and extinction response strength. The occurrence or nonoccurrence of reinforcement apparently comes to achieve fairly strong discriminative control over behavior. This type of learning, of course, is quite obvious in the behavior of human adults. We usually quit making a response when a desired and previously consistent outcome no longer occurs. Responses to nonfunctioning water fountains, vending machines, radios, etc., are almost immediately extinguished.

SUCCESSIVE REVERSALS

Another sequential learning procedure is referred to as the method of successive reversals. A subject first is trained on a simple discrimination problem in which a particular positional response (e.g., a right vs. a left turn in a maze) or a response to a given stimulus (e.g., a white vs. a black door) is "correct," i.e., is followed by reinforcement. After initial training, reinforcement contingencies are reversed so that the previously correct choice is now incorrect, and reinforcement can be obtained only by choice of the initially incorrect alternative. When the subject has learned this reversal, reinforcement contingencies are switched again so that the initially correct

choice is again reinforced. This procedure continues until a subject has experienced a sequence of successive reversals.

Results of an experiment by Pubols (1957) illustrates the typical reversal learning function. Ten rat subjects were trained on a positional discrimination problem in a one-unit Y-maze. Each time a subject attained the learning criterion (chose the correct arm of the Y on nine out of ten trials), reinforcement contingencies were reversed for the next session. All subjects experienced a sequence of 10 successive reversals. Figure 23–3 shows a slight decrease in mean number of correct responses after the first reversal; performance then progressively improved until all subjects made the correct choice after only one reversal trial. It appears that the non-reinforcement of a particular choice had acquired sufficient cue value to result in an immediate switch to the other alternative.

Use of the method of successive reversals results in a type of learning function which is similar to that produced by the extinction-reconditioning procedure. As an animal experiences a series of successive reversals, the reinforcement outcome of each single problem becomes less and less significant until behavior eventually is predominantly controlled by the more subtle but consistent problem-to-problem contingencies.

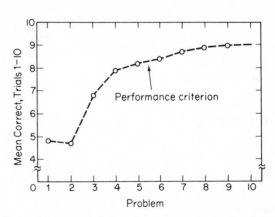

Fig. 23-3. *Mean number of correct responses on the first ten trials of each of ten successive discrimination reversals.* [Adapted from Pubols 1957].

A simple technique used to increase the difficulty of many learning tasks is the imposition of a temporal delay between a response and delivery of reinforcement. Assume that various groups of subjects experience different periods of delay (e.g., 5, 10, 15, or 20 sec) between lever pressing and reinforcement during the acquisition of a lever-pressing response. The average amount of time before there is evidence of learning would increase with increasing length of the delay period.

Perhaps this phenomenon is best illustrated by the results of an experiment by Grice (1948) in which rat subjects, while learning a black-white discrimination problem, experienced various delays of reinforcement after making the correct choice. A trial consisted of allowing the subject to approach a right-left choice point and make a response toward either a black or a white stimulus; after making a correct response, various groups were detained in a delay chamber for either 0, .5, 1.2, 2.0, or 5.0 sec prior to delivery of reinforcement. The learning function illustrating the effect of length of delay (Fig. 23–4) shows that difficulty of the problem increased disproportionately until there was little evidence of learning when reinforcement was delayed by 2.0 sec or more.

Another delay procedure which has often been used to investigate the learning capacity of various animal species was introduced by Hunter (1913). Early studies using this procedure had a philosophical overtone because the procedure was designed to determine if animals were capable of "imagery." It was proposed that if an animal responded appropriately after an environmental cue signifying food had been removed (e.g., a light turned off), the behavioral act might be controlled by a mental representation ("image") of the absent signal. Animal subjects were trained to look at four identical doors, each of which had a light bulb directly above it. On each trial one of the four bulbs was turned on and a screen was raised so that the subject could approach the illuminated door and obtain reinforcement. After the subjects had learned to consistently approach whichever door was illuminated, a delay interval was interposed by turning off the signal light for a short period of time before raising of the screen permitted the subject to make the approach response. Because the environmental cue was absent when the response occurred, it was assumed that a correct selection indicated the presence of some short-term memory trace or "image." With the development of objective data language, most investigators of animal learning ceased to speculate about imagery or other inferred mental states. This general delayed-response procedure has remained in use, however, because it has produced systematic behavioral data.

A current standardized version of the delayed-response technique makes use of an experimental arrangement typified by the Wisconsin General Test Apparatus (WGTA). The apparatus, illustrated in Figure 23–5 (Harlow 1949), consists of two compartments, one to house the animal during testing and the other equipped with a movable tray with two small indentations (foodwells) over which stimulus objects can be placed. A row of vertical bars and a movable opaque screen separate the two compartments. Each delayed-response trial consists of the following sequence of events: With the tray retracted so that the subject in the housing compartment cannot reach it, the experimenter raises the opaque screen, extends a morsel of food over the tray, and conspicuously places the food in one of the two foodwells. He then covers the foodwells with two identical stimulus objects, e.g., small wooden cubes. After a designated period of delay, the tray is pushed forward and the subject is permitted to displace one of the objects. If a correct selection is made, the subject obtains the food reinforcement from the foodwell; the tray is immediately retracted after an incorrect selection.

This simple delayed-response procedure has been used as a means of estimating the comparative learning ability of several different animal species. Delayed-response learning by marmosets and rhesus monkeys was investigated in an experiment by Miles (1957). The marmoset, with its relatively smooth cortex, clawlike nails, and small size, is representative of the lower phylogenetic ranks in the primate order. The rhesus monkey, which has long been a favorite subject in animal learning experiments, is viewed as having a fairly advanced phylogenetic rank among primates. To assure that all subjects had the same test experience over an equivalent number of trials, the test procedure was arranged so that each subject

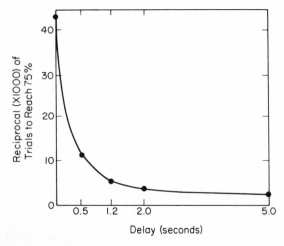

Fig. 23-4. *Rate of learning as a function of delay of reward* [Grice 1948].

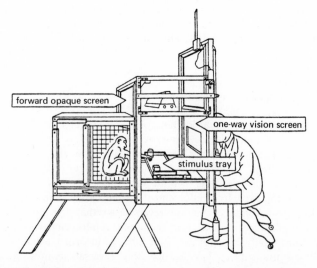

Fig. 23-5. *Wisconsin General Test Apparatus* [Harlow 1949].

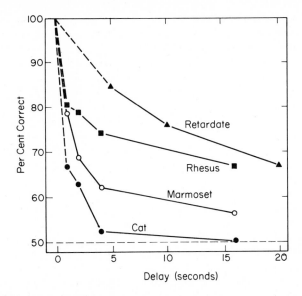

Fig. 23-6. *Comparative delayed-response performance as a function of length of delay.*

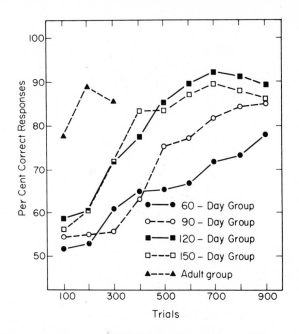

Fig. 23-7. *Performance of four infant groups and one adult group of rhesus monkeys on 5-sec. delayed response* [Harlow et al. 1960].

experienced all delay conditions (1, 2, 4, and 16 sec) within each daily test session. Another experiment (House and Zeaman 1961) investigated delayed-response learning by 33 mentally defective children (ranging in mental age from 2 to 5 years) with the same general procedure but slightly longer delays. Delayed-response learning by domestic cats was studied in an experiment by Meyers et al. (1962). The comparative performance of subjects in all three experiments is illustrated in Figure 23-6. First, it can be seen that the problem became noticeably more difficult for all species as a function of increasing length of delay interval. Comparisons among the four species show that their performances were reliably different and consistent with estimated phylogenetic rank. Young humans, even though mentally retarded, performed better than rhesus monkeys; the rhesus monkeys were definitely superior to the marmosets; and the marmosets in turn outperformed domestic cats.

The delayed-response procedure also has been used to compare learning ability at different age levels within species (Harlow et al. 1960). In this investigation, the performances of 60-, 90-, 120-, and 150-day-old and adult rhesus monkeys were compared using a procedure which included a 0-sec (no delay) and a 5-sec delay condition. All subjects experienced 900 delayed-response trials. There occurred a general improvement in performance as a function of age, Figure 23-7.

Both comparative and developmental data indicate that delayed-response learning represents a distinctive type of learning process. This notion receives further support from the fact that lesions of the frontal cortex, which do not interfere with simple discrimination learning, do produce impaired performance or complete lack of ability to learn delayed-response problems even when the delay is relatively short (Warren and Akert 1964). In an investigation by Miles and Blomquist (1960), six squirrel monkeys received 500 training trials during which they experienced delay intervals of 1, 3, and 9 sec; equal experience with all lengths of delay was insured by arranging the sequence of conditions so that all delay lengths occurred before any one

occurred again. After completion of this delayed-response training, the frontal granular cortex was removed from the lateral surface of both hemispheres in all subjects. Figure 23-8, which shows percent correct responses when performances under all delay conditions were combined, summarizes the results of this experiment. In the preoperative phase of the investigation, all subjects learned the problem with little difficulty and achieved a learning criterion of more than 80 percent correct responses by the end of the series of 500 training trials. Percentage of correct responses was markedly lower during the 1000-trial postoperative phase of the experiment. This effect suggests that lesions of the frontal cortex interfere with some "immediate memory" process which is necessary for delayed-response learning. There are data indicating that an inclination toward greater distractibility may contribute to the behavioral deficits exhibited by frontal subjects. Delayed-response performance of frontal animals improved moderately when the subjects were calmed by a sedative (Wade 1947). Grueninger and Pribram (1969) found that increased response latencies due to an unexpected "distracting" stimulus were significantly longer for frontal than for normal rhesus monkeys.

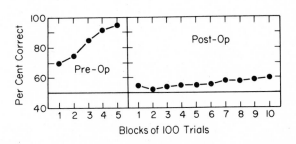

Fig. 23-8. *Delayed-response performance of squirrel monkeys before and after extirpation of frontal granular cortex* [Miles and Blomquist 1960].

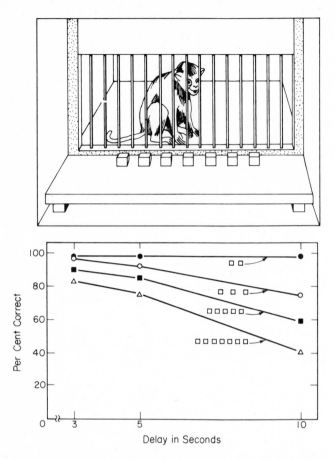

Fig. 23-9. *The test situation and performance of squirrel monkeys according to delay intervals and number of alternatives as indicated by the number of squares* [Rumbaugh 1968].

Although the conventional delayed-response procedure has proven to be a useful comparative tool in animal learning investigations, the upper difficulty range is so limited that the procedure cannot be used to investigate the comparative learning ability of normal human children and adults. Humans make so few errors on these simple two-choice problems that results reveal very little or no behavioral differentiation. A technique which has been used to extend the difficulty range of delayed-response problems is to vary both length of delay and number of response alternatives. This procedure was first used with squirrel monkey subjects in an investigation by Miles summarized in Rumbaugh (1968). Four subjects were extensively trained to observe placement of reinforcement under one of several identical stimulus objects and, after a designated period of delay, to attempt to select the correct object. Illumination in the apparatus was turned off after placement of reinforcement and turned on when it was time for the subject to make an object selection. Figure 23–9 summarizes the performance of well-trained squirrel monkeys as a function of length of delay and number of response alternatives; each point illustrates percent correct choices during the last 100 test trials under the designated combination of delay and response alternative conditions. It can be seen that both independent variables had a significant effect upon performance. When confronted with a two-choice problem, the subjects could "hold" the event of reward placement with virtually no loss throughout a 10-sec

period of delay. A rather marked increase in difficulty level became evident as the number of response alternatives increased from 2 to 3 to 5 to 7.

DOUBLE ALTERNATION

Another method for investigating comparative learning ability is referred to as the double alternation procedure. This technique was introduced by Hunter (1920) in an investigation designed to determine if animals could learn to respond appropriately to sequential cues in the absence of any environmental signal. To solve the problem a subject was required to make two consecutive selections of an object or position located to the right and then two consecutive responses to the left. This correct response sequence (*RRLL*) occurred repeatedly during each test session. (The procedure can be simplified by requiring single [*RLRL*] rather than double alternation of responses.) The alternation method is similar to the delayed-response procedure in that the subject is faced with two identical stimulus objects and receives consistent reinforcement only by recalling recent events, in this case by remembering which position was selected on the previous trial(s) and whether reinforcement occurred.

Results of early research suggested that the ability to solve double alternation problems was related to phylogenetic rank. Most of these studies, however, used such small groups of subjects that the effects of within-species variance could not be estimated. Subsequent investigators have tested 17 rhesus monkeys (Warren and Sinha 1959), 5 rhesus monkeys (Livesey 1969), 10 rabbits (Livesey 1964), 7 raccoons (Johnson 1961) 9 rats and 8 cats (Livesey 1965), and 21 cats (Warren 1961) with a standardized double alternation procedure. After considerable training, all species showed a progressive improvement in performance. In contrast to the results of delayed-response experiments, however, within-species variability was so great that it is impossible to infer any clear hierarchical differences among the species. There was some indication that rats were the poorest performers. It also appeared that rhesus monkeys, once they had learned a *RRLL* response sequence, could learn to solve problems consisting of 8 or even 12 sequential responses, an accomplishment which appeared to be impossible for the cat and raccoon subjects.

The type of frontal lesions which produces a delayed-response deficit also disrupts performance on double alternation problems. In an experiment by Leary et al. (1952), rhesus monkeys with extensive bilateral lesions of the frontal cortex performed more poorly than did normal animals on a series of 150 alternation problems, each consisting of 8 sequential responses (*RRLLRRLL* or *LLRRLLRR*). Results of other similar investigations substantiate the finding that the performance of normal animals is superior to that of subjects with frontal lesions (Warren and Akert 1964).

CONDITIONAL DISCRIMINATION

The difficulty of discrimination learning has been increased by the use of the conditional discrimination procedure. With the conventional two-choice discrimination technique, a subject is presented with two distinctively different stimulus objects (e.g., a red triangle vs. a blue square); selection of one of the objects is consistently reinforced, and reinforcement never occurs when the other object is selected. The strategy for solution of this problem has been referred to by Levine (1959) as a "win-stay, lose-shift hypothesis." Defined behaviorally, this means that the subject learns to select the reinforced object and not select the nonreinforced object even though the right-left position of the objects changes unsystematically from trial to trial. There are data indicating that solution of discrimination problems by some animal subjects may depend upon extinction of unlearned response tendencies and/or preferences for certain types of stimulus objects (Menzel 1962). Also, it appears that some invalid "hypotheses" as to response outcomes may accidentally receive periodic reinforcement during the course of discrimination training and that these must be extinguished before the correct response becomes consistently predominant. Such fortuitous reinforcement of irrelevant response tendencies has been recognized and discussed by Harlow (1950) and by Spence (1936). One example of reinforcement ambiguity occurs when a subject selects the correct one of a pair or stimulus objects on the first trial of a discrimination problem. Because reinforcement is associated both with the object itself and with its spatial (right or left) location, more trials in which the object shifts from one location to the other are necessary in order for the subject to learn that the location of the object is irrelevant to solution of the problem.

With the conditional discrimination method, conditions are arranged so that reinforcement ambiguity is a planned aspect of the procedure. A pair of distinctively different stimulus objects is presented, but the reinforcement outcome of the selection of a particular object is not consistent. Additional cues are presented to signify which one of the two objects is correct on a given trial, i.e., the reinforcement outcome of object selection is conditional and depends upon the presence of some additional cue. An experiment by Thompson (1953) exemplifies the use of a conditional discrimination procedure. Different paired combinations of a set of three stimulus plaques were repeatedly presented to five chimpanzee subjects. The reinforcement outcome of selecting a given plaque was dependent upon which one of the other two plaques it was paired with. For example, a red plaque was correct when paired with a striped plaque but incorrect when presented with a blue stimulus; in turn, the blue stimulus became incorrect when paired with the striped plaque. Thus, the reinforcement outcome of selecting any particular stimulus was ambiguous, and a subject could receive consistent reinforcement only by responding appropriately to the different paired combinations of stimuli. This type of problem proved to be rather difficult for the chimpanzee subjects. More than 700 trials were required before they reached the learning criterion of 90 percent correct responses within a block of 60 trials.

It has been found that rats can learn a conditional discrimination when a simpler version of the procedure is used (North et al. 1958). The animals were trained to jump toward an upright triangle and not toward an inverted triangle when the stimuli were placed against a black background and to make the opposite selection when the background was striped. Results indicated that this type of problem is very difficult for rats. Even when a few subjects which showed no evidence of learning were eliminated from the group, the remaining subjects required an average of 868 trials to achieve the learning criterion (19 correct responses out of 20). Results of this study and of Thomp-

son's experiment with chimpanzees indicate that conditional discrimination problems are considerably more difficult than simple discriminations. The solution of conditional discriminations apparently is dependent upon more complex types of learning processes which may approximate a higher mental function.

LEARNING-SET FORMATION

The formation of discrimination learning sets is another example of an apparently more complicated type of learning process. The first comprehensive investigation of learning-set formation was carried out by Harlow (1949). After rhesus monkeys had been trained on many different object-quality discriminations, Harlow noticed a progressive increase in the speed with which the subjects learned to solve new but similar discrimination problems. With the object-quality discrimination procedure, each problem consists of the presentation of a pair of stimulus objects which differ along a number of dimensions (e.g., height, shape, color, texture, etc.). The test apparatus used by Harlow was the same as the one which is used in delayed-response experiments. It consisted of two compartments, one to house the subject and the other equipped with a movable tray with two small foodwells, separated by vertical bars and an opaque screen. At the beginning of each trial the experimenter placed a bit of food in either the right or the left foodwell and covered the foodwells with the two stimulus objects specified for that particular problem. The opaque screen then was raised so that the subject could view the two objects, and the tray was pushed forward to permit the subject to displace one of the objects. If the correct object was selected, the subject obtained the food reward from the underlying foodwell; the tray was immediately retracted after an incorrect selection. Right-left position of the objects changed unpredictably from trial to trial so that the only consistent information upon which to base a correct choice was whether or not the selection of a particular object had been reinforced on preceding trials. Each discrimination problem consisted of six trials. Thus, as the subjects learned a long series of different discriminations, each with its unique pair of stimulus objects, they experienced many problems which were independent of each other but were similar in that they all belonged to the same general class, i.e., were discriminations based upon object quality.

The results of this original learning-set investigation, in which 8 rhesus monkeys were trained on a series of 344 independent discrimination problems, are illustrated in Figure 23–10. The functions were obtained by combining data into problem blocks as follows: first 32 discriminations (blocks of 8 problems), next 200 discriminations (blocks of 100 problems), and final 112 discriminations (blocks of 56 problems). The increases in per cent correct choices from Trial 1 through Trial 6 represent the learning of independent discrimination problems. Of more significance was the gradual and continuous development of another type of learning function—the progressive increase in rate of learning successive problems until experience on just one trial of a new problem was sufficient to produce nearly perfect performance. Harlow referred to the improvement in performance as a function of trials within problems as "intra-problem" learning; the improvement due to number of problems experienced was referred to as "interproblem" learning, or the

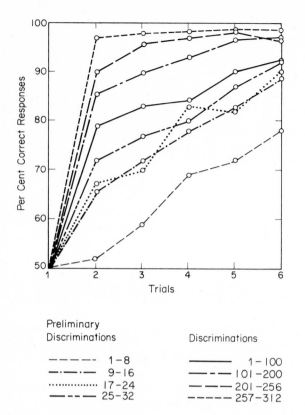

Fig. 23-10. *Discrimination learning curves on successive blocks of problems* [Harlow 1949].

formation of a learning set. It should be noted that the difference between intraproblem learning functions early and late in the series is considerable. The functions illustrating early learning show the continuous improvement in performance typical of simple discrimination learning, whereas the function representing performance on the last block of 56 problems is discontinuous and reveals a marked increase in percent correct choices after only one presentation of a new pair of stimulus objects.

The learning-set procedure has proven to be one of the most effective methods for assessing the comparative learning ability of various animal species. In fact, with the exception of experiments in which the previously described delayed-response procedure was used, most comparative investigations before the introduction of the learning-set method revealed no reliable and systematic phylogenetic ordering of species (Maier and Schneirla 1935). The formation of learning sets by various species has been studied by many investigators during the past decade. Because the learning-set performance of rhesus monkeys had been so thoroughly investigated, these data became a standard against which the learning ability of other species was compared. Subjects in experiments using the standard learning-set procedure (presentation of a series of independent object-quality discrimination problems, each consisting of six trials) include rats and tree squirrels (Warren 1965), domestic cats (Meyers et al. 1962), marmosets and rhesus monkeys (Miles and Meyer 1956), and squirrel monkeys (Miles 1957). The discrimination efficiency of subjects in all these experiments increased as a function of both trials within problems and experience in solving successive independent discriminations. Because the reinforcement outcome of the first trial of each problem provides sufficient information for the latter type of learning (i.e., the formation of a learning set), performance on the second trial is the most sensitive index of comparative learning ability. Comparative differences in performance are striking (Figure 23–11). Among the primates the rhesus monkey is clearly superior and is followed in turn by the squirrel monkey and the marmoset. The learning ability of domestic cats, which are next in rank, is probably underestimated because of their extremely poor color vision (Meyer and Anderson 1965). There is evidence from the results of research with primates (Warren 1954) that color is the dominant cue dimension in the solution of object-quality discriminations, and the relative inability of cats to perceive color would make it much more difficult for them to discriminate between the stimulus objects. The comparatively very poor performance of rats and tree squirrels can be plainly seen; even after these subjects has experienced 1800 problems (10,800 trials), they only achieved a level of approximately 63 percent correct choices.

An overall comparison of the functions in Figure 23.11 reveals that these species were clearly differentiated both by rate of learning and terminal performance level and that, at least

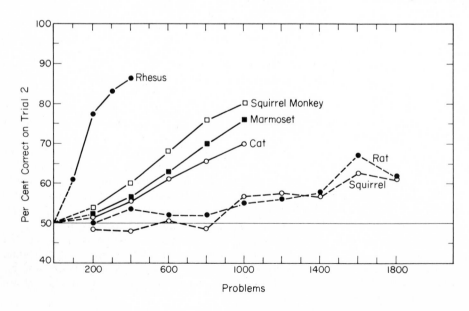

Fig. 23-11. *Learning-set formation by primates, carnivores, and rodents* [Schrier 1965].

for the species included in these experiments, the ability to form a learning set increases with phylogenetic rank. Other species which have been tested with the learning-set procedure include cebus and spider monkeys (Shell and Riopelle 1958), orangutans, gorillas, and chimpanzees (Rumbaugh and Rice 1962), gorillas (Fischer 1962), and tree shrews (Leonard et al. 1966). Although the procedures used by the various investigators were not identical, they were similar enough to permit speculation regarding comparative learning ability. With but few exceptions, a comparison of the results of these experiments indicates that learning-set proficiency is positively correlated with phylogenetic standing. The difficulty of this type of problem for most animal species, the slow but progressive development of a "learning-to-learn" function which is different from simple discrimination learning, and the systematic phylogenetic differences in ability all imply that some higher mental process is involved in the formation of learning sets.

Results of an extensive learning-set investigation with young rhesus monkeys as subjects (Harlow et al. 1960) indicate that there also is a positive relationship between ability to form a discrimination learning set and chronological age. Learning-set performance of various age groups during a series of 600 six-trial discrimination problems is illustrated in Figure 23–12. The extreme difficulty of this type of problem for the younger monkeys is most apparent: The 60- and 90-day-old groups showed virtually no interproblem increase in percentage of correct choices on the second trial; the performance of 120- and 150-day-old subjects was somewhat better but improved at a very slow rate. It appears that rhesus monkeys must be almost a year old before they show any appreciable ability to form a learning set. The fact that young rhesus monkeys are capable of simple discrimination learning implies that learning-set formation represents a more complex learning process which requires the attainment of a certain maturational level.

In contrast to the effect of frontal lesions upon delayed-response learning, lesions of the frontal cortex do not seriously interfere with learning-set formation. By the use of special procedures or meticulous trial-by-trial analyses of data, however, it is possible to demonstrate that the response pattern of subjects with frontal lesions is more stereotyped than that of normal subjects. This perseverance is reflected in more consecutive selections of a preferred stimulus despite the reinforcement outcome of selecting that particular object (Warren and Akert 1964). Primates with lesions which are posterior to the somesthetic area and anterior to the primary visual area perform with almost normal proficiency on delayed-response and alternation problems but usually show a deficit in discrimination learning ability (Warren and Akert 1964). There is evidence that the deficit is smaller when the subjects are experienced (Warren and Harlow 1952b) and that it is most severe when they are required to discriminate between patterned stimuli (Riopelle et al. 1951) or when cue differences are minimal (Warren and Harlow 1952a).

Temporal lesions (which usually are anterior to the primary visual area, below the posterior cortical region, and extend to the temporal lobe) seem to interfere with the retention of a previously learned discrimination and apparently also have some adverse effect upon relearning and upon learning new discrimination problems (Brown 1963; Chow 1954; Mishkin 1954, Pinto-Hamuy et al. 1957). Results of an experiment by Riopelle et al. (1953) indicate that temporal lesions interfere with the ability to form discrimination learning sets. Four normal rhesus monkeys showed progressively better performance on successive object-quality discrimination problems, while the performance of four temporal subjects showed little interproblem improvement. It appears that the severity of the learning-set deficit may be influenced by the subject's learning history prior to the temporal operation. Chow (1954) found no deficit in the performance of temporal subjects which had received pre-operative learning-set training, and results of a study by Meyer (1958) revealed that rhesus monkeys which had been trained on either a single color discrimination or a learning-set series before a temporal operation showed better post-operative performance on that task which they had experienced before surgery. Although the latter two investigations suggest that previously untrained subjects show more severe learning deficits, it should be mentioned that there was at least one atypical subject in each experiment. Minor inconsistencies in the results of temporal research are not surprising in that behavioral effects could be influenced by variations in the nature of the learning task, prior experience, degree of training, and in the location and size of the lesion (Harlow and Woolsey 1958).

CONCEPT FORMATION

Another type of learning which is difficult for animal subjects is generally defined as concept formation. Concept learning depends upon the classification of objects or events, and appropriate categorization usually depends upon recognizing some relationship among stimuli rather than the physical features of a particular stimulus display. A description of this relationship serves to define the concept, and the formation of a concept is demonstrated behaviorally when a subject is able to solve problems with sets of stimuli which are physically different from problem to problem but which have the same relationship in common. A representative example of concept formation by animal subjects is the learning of an oddity discrimination problem. The test apparatus is the same as that used in delayed-response and object-quality discrimination experiments except that there are three foodwells in the movable tray. Of the three stimulus objects which are presented, two are

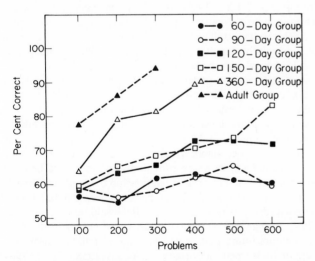

Fig. 23-12. *Trial 2 performances of various age groups of rhesus monkeys as a measure of learning-set formation* [Harlow et al. 1960].

identical and one is different, and the principle common to all problems is that selection of the odd member of the set is always reinforced. The procedure is similar to that used in learning-set investigations in that a subject experiences many independent problems, each with a unique set of stimulus objects. Improvement in performance within each problem produces intra-problem learning curves, and an interproblem learning function evolves as the subject experiences a series of oddity discriminations.

Levine and Harlow (1959) tested seven rhesus monkeys with a technique which differed from the usual oddity discrimination procedure in that each set of three stimulus objects (i.e., each problem) was presented only once. Thus, Figure 23–13, in which each point represents percent correct responses within blocks of 432 problems, illustrates the learning of an oddity concept. The fact that the subjects made only slightly more than 60 percent responses after experiencing many (1624) problems indicates that learning to ignore physical features of stimuli and respond on the basis of an abstract oddity concept is much more difficult than simple discrimination learning. Results of a study by Harlow et al. (1951), in which all of the rhesus monkey subjects had previously experienced extensive learning-set training, indicated that cortical lesions anterior to the primary visual area did not produce a deficit in oddity learning but that lesions of the frontal cortex did interfere with ability to form an oddity concept.

Problems which required the formation of a number concept also are very difficult for animal subjects (French, 1965). Hicks (1956) trained adolescent rhesus monkeys on a visual discrimination in which solution of the problem was contingent upon the concept of "three-ness." The test stimuli were various sets of geometric figures mounted on square cards. The correct stimulus card always had three figures on it and was paired with an incorrect card with either one, two, four, or five figures. In the early stages of training, subjects learned that various sets of three specific figures were correct; then, as training progressed, irrelevant cue dimensions (e.g., size, color, configuration, etc.) were varied unsystematically so that solution of a problem was entirely dependent upon a "three-ness" concept. Percent correct responses decreased as more and more specific features of the stimuli were changed, but performance level remained significantly above chance. These data show that the subjects were able to acquire a number concept but that this type of learning is very difficult for rhesus monkeys.

Motivational Factors

Numerous animal learning experiments during the past twenty years have investigated the effects of manipulating motivational variables such as drive level and type of reward (or "incentive"). The resulting data have led to an empirical distinction between learning and performance. In many studies in which hungry subjects worked for food reinforcement, the experimental designs called for differences in degree of hunger (i.e., in drive level). Results of these investigations indicated that, when number of training trials was constant, differences in hunger drive during training had little bearing on the degree of learning but that drive level at the particular times when the response was performed did affect behavioral strength (Cofer and Appley 1964).

A systematic research program conducted by Hull (1952) led to the development of a theory which differentiated between degree of learning (habit strength, $_sH_R$) and the expressed strength of the learned response (performance strength, $_sE_R$) when activated by motivational variables. Hull's final formulation proposed that habit strength increases incrementally as a function of number of reinforced trials (N) and that performance strength is dependent upon both the degree of learning and the motivational effects of drive (D) and incentive magnitude (K). The proposed relationship among variables was expressed by the following formula:

$$_sE_R = {}_sH_R \times D \times K.$$

Most experimenters who have investigated the effects of variation in drive have found that a higher drive level, if not extreme, facilitates learned performance (Bolles 1967; Cofer and Appley 1964; Hall 1966). This relationship is most consistently revealed by the results of experiments which have used time-dependent measures of performance strength, e.g., time to traverse a maze or runway (Barry 1958) or number of responses emitted during extinction (Perin 1942). An experiment by Corman and Miles (1966) illustrates the facilitative effect of drive upon performance. Five male rat subjects were trained to displace a lever and go to the opposite end of the test chamber for food reinforcement. After thorough training and adaptation to a 24:1 fixed-ratio schedule, the subjects experienced repeated 55-min test sessions under a wide range of drive conditions (i.e., after 0-, 2-, 6-, 22-, and 44-hr food deprivation). A markedly higher response rate as a function of increasing deprivation clearly illustrates a behavioral "energizing" effect attributable to drive level, Figure 23–14.

On the other hand, results of experiments using time-independent (e.g., response probability) measures of behavior have not revealed a consistent relationship between performance strength and drive level. Better performance as a function of increased drive was reported by Buckwald and Yamaguchi (1955), Eisman (1956), and Eisman et al. (1956), while other investigators found that drive level had no reliable effect upon strength of learned performance (Armus 1958; Coate 1964; Hillman et al. 1953; Lachman 1961; Meyer 1951; Miles 1959; Teel 1952). Thus, although Hull's theory has been sup-

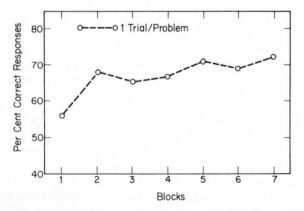

Fig. 23-13. *Performance on successive blocks of 1-trial oddity problems; each point is the mean per cent correct responses for 7 Ss during a block of 432 problems.* [Adapted from Levine and Harlow 1959].

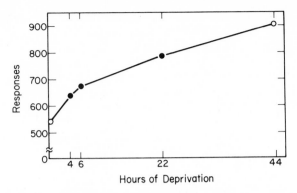

Fig. 23-14. *Median number of lever presses as a function of increasing food deprivation* [Corman and Miles 1966].

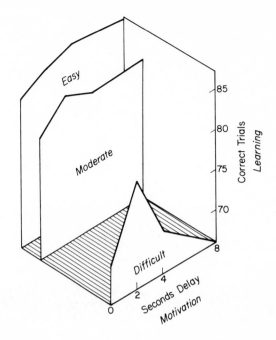

Fig. 23-15. *A three-dimensional surface showing the relationship between discrimination learning and (a) degree of air deprivation, and (b) level of difficulty of the discrimination task* [Broadhurst 1957].

ported by results of experiments using time-dependent measures of performance strength, it appears that the theory must be modified to account for the effects of drive upon time-independent behavioral measures.

Some early studies found that high drive levels actually disrupted discrimination learning and performance (Hall 1966). Most of these experimenters varied drive level by varying the strength of aversive stimulation and used what is referred to as a "correction" procedure (i.e., after making an incorrect choice, the subject was immediately permitted to switch over and choose the correct alternative). The typical finding was that acquisition and performance of relatively difficult discriminations were enhanced by a moderate level of drive but were disrupted as drive level increased beyond a certain point. Results of an early study by Yerkes and Dodson (1908), in which mice were tested on black vs. white discrimination problems of three levels of difficulty, indicated that effects of drive level were related to the difficulty of the discrimination task. Percent correct responses on the easiest discrimination problem increased as a function of shock intensity. On the most difficult discrimination, percent correct choices increased with shock intensity up to a point and then progressively decreased as intensity became greater. The data indicated that there was a certain level of shock which was optimal for learning at each difficulty level and that the optimal intensity became lower as problem difficulty increased. This functional relationship is referred to as the "Yerkes-Dodson law."

The Yerkes-Dodson law is clearly illustrated by the results of an experiment by Broadhurst (1957) in which drive level was varied by manipulating degree of air deprivation. Rat subjects were submerged in water for either 0, 2, 4, or 8 sec before being allowed to swim underwater down the stem of a Y-shaped tank and choose either the right or the left alley. Doors at the ends of the alleys were differentially illuminated. By approaching the brighter door, the subjects could enter a goal chamber and arise to the surface for air; if they chose the darker door, they found it locked and were forced to turn around and swim to the lighter one. Three levels of difficulty were produced by varying the difference in the brightness of the two doors. Results of this 3 × 3 factorial design are illustrated in Figure 23–15. Increasing air deprivation resulted in an increase in percent correct choices on the easiest discrimination problem. This function changed as the task became more difficult, indicating that a moderate increase in air deprivation enhanced learning

but that further increases in drive level resulted in a decrease in percent correct choices.

Several other investigators (Cole 1911; Denenberg and Karas 1960; Dodson 1915; Hammes 1956) have obtained similar results. The fact that practically all experimenters who have found that high drive disrupts discrimination learning and performance have used aversive stimulation suggests that the effect of increasing drive may be described by two different functions, one applicable to appetitive drives such as hunger and thirst and the other applicable to drive produced by aversive stimulation. This conclusion should await further evidence, however, since there are other methodological differences which could have affected the behavioral functions. All such experiments using aversive stimulation have also used a correction procedure so that the subject could withdraw from an incorrect choice and experience a reduction in aversive stimulation (i.e., obtain reinforcement) by choosing the other alternative. Since subjects can obtain reinforcement either by making a correct choice or by withdrawing from an incorrect choice and switching to the correct alternative, it seems reasonable to assume that a correction procedure would promote the development of competing response tendencies. The number of times that the "switching choice" response is reinforced would be directly proportional to the difficulty of the discrimination; thus, it would seem that the incorrect response would become stronger as a function of discrimination difficulty. Also, the use of aversive stimulation, especially of high intensity, could conceivably induce conditioned or unconditioned escape behavior which might interfere with the correct response and thereby reduce the efficiency of discrimination performance.

Results of numerous experiments indicate that an increase in incentive magnitude has little if any effect upon learning but that it does facilitate the performance of a learned response (Pubols 1960). It has been found that performance strength is an

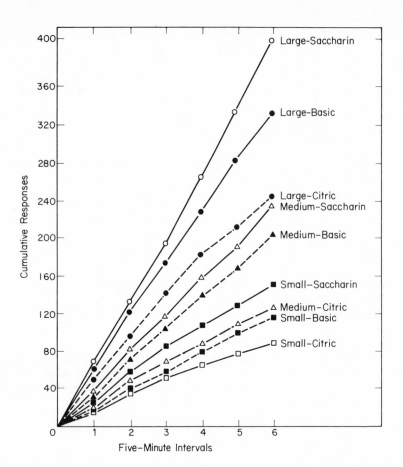

Fig. 23-16. *Mean cumulative response curves showing performance under various incentive conditions.* [Adapted from Hutt 1954.)

increasing function of the quantity or quality of the incentive units (bits of food reinforcement) received for instrumental responding (Crespi 1944; Schrier 1958) and of the quantity or concentration (quality) of a liquid sucrose solution used as the reinforcing agent (Collier 1962; Guttman 1953; Hutt 1954). This relationship is clearly shown in the results of Hutt's (1954) experiment. The animal subjects, 81 male rats, were trained on a fixed-interval (*FI-1* min) schedule to press a lever for liquid reinforcement. Three different taste values were produced by adding either saccharine, citric acid, or nothing to a basic mixture of flour, milk, and water. Each of nine groups received a different combination of the three taste values (saccharine, basic, or citric) and three incentive quantities (small, medium, or large). The cumulative number of responses made by each group during the final 30-min test session is illustrated in Figure 23-16. These functions clearly show that rate of lever pressing increased as a function of either quantity or quality of the incentive. The absence of a significant interaction suggests that incentive magnitude may have an additive effect upon performance strength rather than the multiplicative relationship proposed by Hull (1952).

Again, as when drive level is varied, it appears that the facilitating effect of an increase in incentive magnitude is more consistently demonstrated with the use of such time-dependent performance measures as latency of responding (Zeaman 1949), running speed (Hill and Spear 1962), or rate of lever pressing (Guttman 1953). Although the findings are not so consistent when the results of experiments using response probability measures are considered, most such investigations have revealed

some positive relationship between incentive magnitude and performance strength (Cofer and Appley 1964; Hall 1966).

It should be noted that two different experimental designs are commonly used for determining the effects of incentive magnitude. With a procedure referred to as a "between-subjects" design, each group of subjects experiences a different incentive magnitude. With the other method, called a "within-subjects" design, each subject repeatedly experiences all incentive magnitude conditions. In the latter case, since each subject becomes familiar with all incentive magnitude conditions, the relative difference ("contrast") among magnitudes could influence performance. Data indicate that the facilitating effect of incentive magnitude is greater when a within-subjects design is used. Results of the two experimental designs were compared in an experiment by Schrier (1958). There were four incentive quantity conditions (1, 2, 4, and 8 food pellets), and performance was measured throughout a series of 160 four-trial discrimination learning-set problems. In one group of primate subjects (the "shift" group), each animal experienced all incentive quantity conditions; a "non-shift" group was divided into four subgroups, each of which experienced only one incentive value. Figure 23–17 illustrates the relationship between performance strength and incentive magnitude under the two experimental conditions. Mean performance of the "shift" group was progressively better as a function of incentive quantity, whereas only the 8-pellet condition produced greater discrimination efficiency with the non-shift procedure. A number of investigations using rat subjects and other types of learning problems also have produced data indicating that the effect of incentive mag-

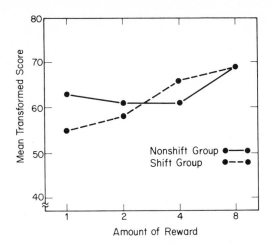

Fig. 23-17. *Mean arcsin-transformed percentage of correct responses as a function of number of pellets provided as reward. Each point on the curve for the nonshift condition represents a different subgroup, whereas each point on the curve for the shift condition represents the same Ss [Schrier 1958].*

nitude is more noticeable when each subject has an opportunity to experience all incentive conditions (Hall 1966).

Investigatory Behavior

In almost all of the previously described investigations of animal learning, some primary (or biological) reward such as food, water, or escape from aversive stimulation was used to reinforce some type of behavior. The many empirical demonstrations that such rewards acted as reliable and strong reinforcers led to a rather strict homeostatic model of animal learning. It was assumed that learning occurred when an animal was probed into action by some physiological drive and that the response pattern preceding drive reduction was automatically strengthened. Thus, most investigators tended to view all animal learning as the outcome of drive reduction reinforcement. Some investigators, however, recognized biological rewards as salient reinforcers but felt that a strictly homeostatic model of animal learning was too limited. There are data which apparently demonstrate learning in the absence of drive reduction reinforcement.

Results of a series of experiments by Montgomery (1952*a*, 1952*b*, 1953) showed that rat subjects were inclined to avoid recently visited areas in favor of investigating an unexplored area or stimulus. The subjects learned a simple two-choice maze with a procedure in which reinforcement consisted of the opportunity to explore a more complex environment (Montgomery 1954). While investigating the manipulatory behavior of rhesus monkeys, Harlow (1950) found that the animals learned to disassemble a simple "puzzle" composed of a pin, hook, and hasp when the only apparent reward was the opportunity to actively manipulate the puzzle components. Butler (1953) found that a rhesus monkey subject enclosed in an opaque box would repeatedly push aside a shutter to look through a small window. This visual exploratory behavior was very persistent and provided sufficient reinforcement for discrimination learning. Given a choice between two differently colored shutters, one

latched and one unlatched, the subjects soon learned to touch only the shutter which could be opened to permit visual exploration of the environment outside the box. The results of these and other similar experiments in which learning occurred in the absence of primary reward suggest that drive reduction may not be a necessary condition for animal learning.

When referring to such investigatory behavioral patterns initiated by an organism, some experimenters have proposed the existence of "intrinsic" motives or drives. Some of the behavioral patterns classified in this way include activity, manipulatory, visual exploratory, and curiosity drives (Butler and Harlow 1954; Harlow 1953; Hill 1956, Montgomery 1954). On the other hand, the postulation of some underlying drive or motive to account for this type of behavior has been viewed with scepticism by a number of psychologists (Brown 1953; Estes 1958, Mowrer 1960). Since there is no doubt that stimuli and responses associated with drive reduction acquire reinforcing properties, some investigators have preferred to incorporate most of the suggested "intrinsic" drives with a secondary reinforcement paradigm (Brown 1953; Mowrer 1960). This point of view assumes that investigatory behaviors such as manipulation, locomotion, and visual exploration occur because they result in some type of stimulation which has previously been associated with primary drive reduction.

Results of an experiment by Miles (1958), however, indicate that young cat subjects showed persistent manipulatory behavior which appeared to be reinforcing even though manipulation had never been obviously associated with drive reduction. So that the procurement of food would not be contingent upon manipulatory responses, eight kittens were fed a diet of soft food which could not be manipulated. After rearing under this feeding condition, the subjects were tested in a two-choice Y-maze. It was found that the opportunity to manipulate toys or to leave the maze and explore the test room for a brief period was sufficiently reinforcing to produce reliable learning functions. When given an opportunity in a free situation, the cats also were observed to actively manipulate hanging objects. Since there had been no direct association between manipulatory responses and drive reduction, it would appear that the manipulatory and exploratory behavior was rewarding in itself and that postulation of a secondary reward function is not necessary to account for the results of the experiment.

An overall review of investigations of exploratory and manipulatory behavior indicates that such activity is repeatedly and consistently exhibited by many animal species and that the opportunity to explore and manipulate serves as a mild but reliable reinforcer (Butler 1965; Fowler 1965). After preliminary research had established this type of activity as a significant behavioral phenomenon, subsequent investigations were designed to delineate relevant variables and systematic relationships.

A carefully conducted experiment by Welker (1956*a*) showed that young chimpanzees exhibited considerably more manipulatory behavior than did adult subjects. Results of another experiment (Welker 1956*b*) indicated that stimulus objects which differed with respect to both color and form induced more manipulatory behavior than did objects which were identical or differed only in color. Butler (1954) found that the frequency of visual exploratory responses emitted by rhesus monkeys was a function of the type of visual display. Response rate increased with the opportunity to observe an empty box, a food display, a moving electric train, and another monkey. In a later experiment (Butler and Woolpy 1963), rhesus monkeys could choose to look through one of two windows to observe a visual display projected on a screen. The subjects preferred to view pictures over a blank screen and moving pictures over slides. Viewing time was longest when the moving pictures were in color, brightly illuminated, moving at normal speed, and right side up. Rhesus monkeys also will observe a room much more frequently when it is illuminated than when it is dark (Rabedeau and Miles 1959), and the results of a study by Berlyne (1950) indicated that rat subjects chose to approach and observe relatively unfamiliar and more complicated visual displays.

Several experiments have shown higher than usual levels of general activity and exploratory behavior after an animal has been confined for a period of time. In investigations of activity in rats (Hill 1958) and cats (Miles 1962), results indicated a greater increase in activity as a function of length of the preceding confinement period. Butler (1957) and Fox (1962) found that frequency of a visual exploratory response followed by observation or light stimulation increased with an increase in the length of a preceding period of light deprivation. Results of a developmental study with rat subjects (Lockard 1963) indicated that adult preferences for certain levels of illumination were influenced by the illumination conditions experienced by the subjects during rearing. In general, when the behavior of subjects reared in a brightly illuminated environment was compared with that of animals reared in darkness or under a dim illumination conditions, the former group tended to turn on brighter light intensities and to leave the light on for longer periods. Berlyne et al. (1966) found that rat subjects reared in a noisy environment chose to press a lever which turned on novel light or buzzer stimulation, whereas subjects which had been reared in a quiet room preferred to turn on familiar stimulation.

The prevailing interpretation of investigatory behavior suggests that it is influenced by a number of different factors. Since there are no obvious eliciting stimuli, behavior such as manipulation, locomotion, and visual exploration would be classified as emitted responses. There is now considerable experimental evidence showing that novel or unexpected stimuli will "alert" an animal and temporarily raise its level of emitted behavior. For example, when a subject is placed in an unfamiliar room or suddenly confronted with an unanticipated stimulus, responses at first are emitted at a high rate which then decreases over time. This initial increase and subsequent decrease in response rate has been demonstrated in over a hundred species and apparently is a universal behavioral phenomenon. The phenomenon is clearly illustrated by the results of a comprehensive investigation (Glickman and Sroges 1966) in which orienting and contact responses of a variety of zoo inhabitants to a display of novel objects were recorded (Figure 23-18). Similar functions have been obtained with various behavioral measures in studies of general activity in cats (Miles 1962), rats (Hill 1956), squirrel monkeys (Miles and Blomquist 1960), and rhesus monkeys (French and Harlow 1955); of manipulatory responding in cats (Miles 1958) and chimpanzees (Welker 1956a); and of visual exploratory behavior in rhesus monkeys (Rabedeau and Miles 1959).

There are a variety of data showing that an underlying fear reaction has a significant influence upon exploratory behavior. Welker (1959) has shown that rat subjects which are actively

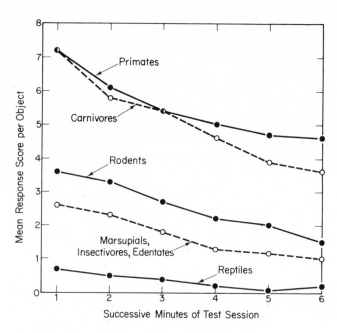

Fig. 23-18. *Mean reactivity to test objects during successive minutes of test sessions* [Glickman and Sroges 1966].

exploring an unfamiliar area will, when given the opportunity, escape from that area to a familiar chamber. In an experiment by Johnston (1964), rats were placed in an arena a short distance from their home cages so that exploratory sorties into an unfamiliar area would be in conflict with following a straight route to a familiar place. Results indicated that escape from the unfamiliar area was the dominant initial reaction to novelty and that fear dissipated as the subjects became familiar with the situation. In a similar investigation, Hebb and Mahut (1955) found that rat subjects were inclined to cease using a direct route to food in favor of a longer, indirect route after a period of exposure. Menzel et al. (1961) found that young chimpanzees were initially fearful of novel objects which moved in an erratic manner.

The above data provide general support for a behavioral "arousal" hypothesis proposed by Hebb (1955) and discussed in detail by Fiske and Maddi (1961). A rested animal in a familiar, unstimulating environment has a general arousal level sufficiently low as to constitute a mildly aversive state akin to "boredom." Almost any change or increase in stimulation will provide some reinforcement by raising the animal's level of activation, and the animal therefore will seek out new stimulation. If this new stimulation is highly novel or unusually stimulating, the arousal level increases from excitement to fear and the animal tends to either freeze, escape, or explore with extreme caution. As the stimulation becomes more familiar, the fear reaction subsides to the point where the animal will actively engage in exploratory and manipulatory behavior. Thus, it is assumed that there is some optimal level of arousal which induces further investigation of the environment. Dember et al. (1957) found that rat subjects, after a period of familiarization with one area, would move on to an area of greater stimulus novelty. A similar trend was reported by Sheldon (1969). When placed in a strange two-choice situation and given a choice between a familiar and a novel stimulus, rat subjects preferred the familiar stimulus at first and later chose the novel object. Subsequent exposure to another novel environment immediately before testing tended to change preference back to the familiar stimulus. Results of an experiment by Thomas (1969), in which cats were permitted to wander among three levels of stimulus complexity, showed that the subjects preferred more complex stimulation as they became familiar with the environment. Some experimental manipulations which were planned to induce higher than optimal arousal levels, such as the use of amphetamine (Stretch 1963), methamphetamine (Berlyne et al. 1966), shock (Thompson and Higgins 1958), and extreme hunger (Chapman and Levy 1957), reduced the inclination of rat subjects to explore novel stimulation.

Results of all these studies indicate that investigatory behavior occurs when an organism is aroused to a certain degree; a lower than optimal arousal level motivates the animal to seek new and more complex stimulation, while greater than optimal arousal induces retreat from novelty and a preference for more familiar and simpler stimuli. It would appear that these endogenous behavioral tendencies to leave a familiar area to explore new environmental regions and novel stimuli and to react with fear to unusually strange or intense stimulation have definite adaptive significance. Thorough exploration of surrounding areas would enable an animal to discover additional sources of food and water, to determine the relative safety of various regions, and to find hiding places and escape routes. The fear reaction is adaptive in that it leads to retreat from threatening situations and prevents bold and reckless exploration which would tend to expose the animal to predators and the possibility of injury. The fact that this behavioral pattern is exhibited by so many species attests to the importance of its role in providing an adaptive contact with the environment.

Summary

This general overview of animal learning begins with a brief historical sketch of early investigations and interpretations of animal learning. Descriptions of the basic types of learning common to most animals (classical conditioning, operant conditioning, and instrumental escape and avoidance learning) are followed by a discussion of reinforcement schedules, secondary reinforcement, and the phenomenon of habituation. The next section of the chapter includes descriptions and examples of several more complex learning procedures: extinction-reconditioning, successive reversals, temporal delay, double alternation, conditional discrimination, discrimination learning sets, and concept formation. These types of learning problems are discussed in order along an estimated difficulty dimension. Most of the methods were selected for inclusion because they are reasonable extensions of basic learning procedures which apparently have revealed the existence of more complicated learning processed in animals. These procedures have produced systematic and repeatable learning functions, and some of them have revealed differences among species commensurate with phylogenetic rank. The effects of motivational variables (drive level and incentive magnitude) and the adaptive significance of investigatory behavior were considered in the final sections of the chapter.

References

ANREP, G. V. The irradiation of conditioned reflexes. *Proceedings of the Royal Society*, 1923, *94B*, 404–26.

ARMUS, H. L. Drive level and habit reversal. *Psychological Reports*, 1958, *4*, 31–34.

BARRY, H., III. Effects of strength of drive on learning and on extinction. *Journal of Experimental Psychology*, 1958, *55*, 473–81.

BEACH, F. A. The descent of instinct. *Psychological Review*. 1955, *62*, 401–10.

BERLYNE, D. E. Novelty and curiosity as determinants of exploratory behavior. *British Journal of Psychology*, 1950, *41*, 68–80.

BERLYNE, D. E., KOENIG, I. D. V., and HIROTA, T. Novelty, arousal, and the reinforcement of diversive exploration in the rat. *Journal of Comparative and Physiological Psychology*, 1966, *62*, 222–26.

BERSH, P. J. The influence of two variables upon the establishment of a secondary reinforcer for operant responses. *Journal of Experimental Psychology*, 1951, *41*, 62–73.

BOLLES, R. C. *Theory of motivation.* New York: Harper & Row, 1967.

BROADHURST, P. L. Emotionality and the Yerkes-Dodson law. *Journal of Experimental Psychology*, 1957, *54*, 345–52.

BROGDEN, W. J., LIPMAN, E. A., and CULLER, F. The role of incentive in conditioning and extinction. *American Journal of Psychology*, 1938, *51*, 109–17.

BROWN, J. S. Problems presented by the concept of acquired drives. *In* M. R. JONES (ed .), *Current theory and research in motivation: A symposium.* Lincoln: University of Nebraska Press, 1953.

BROWN, T. S. Olfactory and visual discrimination in the monkey after selective lesions of the temporal lobe. *Journal of Comparative and Physiological Psychology*, 1963, *56*, 764–68.

BUCKWALD, A. M., and YAMAGUCHI, H. G. The effect of change in drive level on habit reversal. *Journal of Experimental Psychology*, 1955, *50*, 265–68.

BULLOCK, D. H., and SMITH, W. C. An effect of repeated conditioning-extinction upon operant strength. *Journal of Experimental Psychology*, 1953, *46*, 349–52.

BUTLER, R. A. Discrimination learning by rhesus monkeys to visual-exploration motivation. *Journal of Comparative and Physiological Psychology*, 1953, *46*, 95–98.

——— Incentive conditions which influence visual exploration. *Journal of Experimental Psychology*, 1954, *48*, 19–23.

——— The effect of deprivation of visual incentives on visual exploration motivation in monkeys. *Journal of Comparative and Physiological Psychology*, 1957, *50*, 177–79.

——— Investigative behavior. *In* M. A. SCHRIER, H. F. HARLOW, and F. STOLLMITZ (eds.), *Behavior of nonhuman primates*, vol. 2. New York: Academic Press, 1965.

BUTLER, R. A., and HARLOW, H. F. Persistence of visual exploration in monkeys. *Journal of Comparative and Physiological Psychology*, 1954, *47*, 258–63.

BUTLER, R. A., and WOOLPY, J. H. Visual attention in the rhesus monkey. *Journal of Comparative and Physiological Psychology*, 1963, *56*, 324–28.

CHAPMAN, R. M., and LEVY, H. Hunger drive and reinforcing effect of novel stimuli. *Journal of Comparative and Physiological Psychology*, 1957, *50*, 233–38.

CHOW, K. L. Effects of temporal neocortical ablation on visual discrimination learning sets in monkeys. *Journal of Comparative and Physiological Psychology*, 1954, *47*, 194–98.

COATE, W. B. Effect of deprivation on postdiscrimination stimulus generalization in the rat. *Journal of Comparative and Physiological Psychology*, 1964, *57*, 134–38.

COFER, C. N., and APPLEY, M. H. *Motivation: theory and research.* New York: John Wiley, 1964.

COLE, L. W. The relation of strength of stimulation to rate of learning in the chick. *Journal of Animal Behavior*, 1911, *1*, 111–24.

COLLIER, G. Some properties of saccharine as a reinforcer. *Journal of Experimental Psychology*, 1962, *64*, 184–91.

CORMAN, C. D., and MILES, R. C. Invariance of operant topography throughout changes in motivational conditions. *Journal of Comparative and Physiological Psychology*, 1966, *62*, 60–64.

CRESPI, L. P. Amount of reinforcement and level of performance. *Psychological Review*, 1944, *51*, 341–57.

DARWIN, C. *The descent of man.* New York: Appleton, 1871.

DEMBER, W. N., EARL, R. W., and PARADISE, N. Response by rats to differential stimulus complexity. *Journal of Comparative and Physiological Psychology*, 1957, *50*, 514–18.

DENENBERG, V. H., and KARAS, G. G. Supplementary report: The Yerkes-Dodson law and shift in task difficulty. *Journal of Experimental Psychology*, 1960, *59*, 429–30.

DODSON, J. D. The relation of strength of stimulus to rapidity of habit formation in the kitten. *Journal of Animal Behavior*, 1915, *5*, 330–36.

EISMAN, E. An investigation of the parameters defining drive (D). *Journal of Experimental Psychology*, 1956, *52*, 85–89.

EISMAN, E., ASIMOW, A., and MALTZMAN, I. Habit strength as a function of drive in a brightness discrimination problem. *Journal of Experimental Psychology*, 1956, *52*, 58–64.

ESTES, W. K. Comments on Dr. Bolles's paper. *In* M. R. JONES (ed.), *Nebraska symposium on motivation.* Lincoln: University of Nebraska Press, 1958.

FERSTER, C. B., and SKINNER, B. F. *Schedules of reinforcement.* New York: Appleton-Century-Crofts, 1957.

FISCHER, G. J. The formation of learning sets in young gorillas. *Journal of Comparative and Physiological Psychology*, 1962, *55*, 924–25.

FISKE, D. W., and MADDI, S. R. A conceptual framework. *In* D. W. FISKE and S. R. MADDI (eds.), *Functions of varied experience.* Homewood, Ill.: Dorsey, 1961.

FOWLER, H. *Curiosity and exploratory behavior.* New York: Macmillan, 1965.

FOX, S. S. Self-maintained sensory input and sensory deprivation in monkeys: A behavioral and neuropharmacological study. *Journal of Comparative and Physiological Psychology*, 1962, *55*, 438–44.

FRENCH, G. M. Associative problems. *In* A. M. SCHRIER, H. F. HARLOW, and F. STOLLNITZ (eds.), *Behavior of nonhuman primates*, vol. 1. New York: Academic Press, 1965.

FRENCH, G., and HARLOW, H. F. Locomotor reaction decrement in normal and brain-damaged monkeys. *Journal of Comparative and Physiological Psychology*, 1955, *48*, 496–501.

GLICKMAN, S. E., and SROGES, R. W. Curiosity in zoo animals. *Behaviour*, 1966, *26*, 151–88.

GRICE, G. R. The relation of secondary reinforcement to delayed reward in visual discrimination learning. *Journal of Experimental Psychology*, 1948, *38*, 1–16.

GRUENINGER, W. E., and PRIBRAM, K. H. Effects of spatial and nonspatial distractors on performance latency of monkeys with frontal lesions. *Journal of Comparative and Physiological Psychology*, 1969, *68*, 203–9.

GUTHRIE, E. *The psychology of learning.* New York: Harper, 1935.

GUTTMAN, N. Operant conditioning, extinction, and periodic reinforcement in relation to concentration of sucrose used as reinforcing agent. *Journal of Experimental Psychology*, 1953, *46*, 213–24.

HALL, J. F. *The psychology of learning.* Philadelphia: Lippincott, 1966.

HAMMES, J. A. Visual discrimination learning as a function of shock-fear and task difficulty. *Journal of Comparative and Physiological Psychology*, 1956, *49*, 481–84.

HARLOW, H. F. The formation of learning sets. *Psychological Review*, 1949, *56*, 51–65.

———— Analysis of discrimination learning by monkeys. *Journal of Experimental Psychology*, 1950a, *40*, 26–39.

———— Learning and satiation of response in intrinsically motivated complex puzzle performance by monkeys. *Journal of Comparative and Physiological Psychology*, 1950b, *43*, 289–94.

———— Motivation as a factor in the acquisition of new responses. *In* M. R. JONES (ed.), *Current theory and research in motivation: A symposium.* Lincoln: University of Nebraska Press, 1953.

HARLOW, H.F., HARLOW, M. K., RUEPING, R. R., and MASON, W. A. Performance of infant rhesus monkeys on discrimination learning, delayed response, and discrimination learning set. *Journal of Comparative and Physiological Psychology*, 1960, *53*, 113–21.

HARLOW, H. F., MEYER, D., and SETTLAGE, P. H. The effects of large cortical lesions on the solution of oddity problems by monkeys. *Journal of Comparative and Physiological Psychology*, 1951, *44*, 320–26.

HARLOW, H. F., and WOOLSEY, C. N. (eds.). *Biological and biochemical bases of behavior.* Madison: University of Wisconsin Press, 1958.

HARRIS, J. D. Habituatory response decrement in the intact organism. *Psychological Bulletin*, 1943, *40*, 385–422.

HEBB, D. O. Drives and the C.N.S. (Conceptual nervous system). *Psychological Review*, 1955, *62*, 243–54.

HEBB, D. O., and MAHUT, H. Motivation et recherche du changement perceptif chez le rat chez l'homme. *Journal de psychologie normale et pathologique*, 1955, *48*, 209–21.

HICKS, L. H. An analysis of number-concept formation in the rhesus monkey. *Journal of Comparative and Physiological Psychology*, 1956, *49*, 212–18.

HILL, W. F. Activity as an autonomous drive. *Journal of Comparative and Physiological Psychology*, 1956, *49*, 15–19.

———— The effect of varying periods of confinement on the activity in tilt cages. *Journal of Comparative and Physiological Psychology*, 1958, *51*, 570–74.

HILL, W. F., and SPEAR, N. F. Resistance to extinction as a joint function of reward magnitude and the spacing of extinction trials. *Journal of Experimental Psychology*, 1962, *64*, 636–39.

HILLMAN, B., HUNTER, W. S., and KIMBLE, G. A. The effect of drive level on the maze performance of the white rat. *Journal of Comparative and Physiological Psychology*, 1953, *46*, 87–89.

HOUSE, B. J., and ZEAMAN, D. Effects of practice on the delayed response of retardates. *Journal of Comparative and Physiological Psychology*, 1961, *54*, 255–60.

HULL, C. L. *Principles of behavior.* New York: Appleton-Century-Crofts, 1943.

———— *A behavior system.* New Haven, Conn.: Yale University Press, 1952.

HUNTER, W. S. The delayed reaction in animals and children. *Behavioral Monographs*, 1913, *2*, 1–86.

———— The temporal maze and kinaesthetic sensory processes in the white rat. *Phychobiology*, 1920, *2*, 1–18.

HUTT, P. J. Rate of bar pressing as a function of quality and quantity of food reward. *Journal of Comparative and Physiological Psychology*, 1954, *47*, 235–39.

JOHNSON, J. I. Double alternation by raccoons. *Journal of Comparative and Physiological Psychology*, 1961, *54*, 248–51.

JOHNSTON, W. A. Trends in escape and exploration. *Journal of Comparative and Physiological Psychology*, 1964, *58*, 431–35.

KIMBLE, G. A. *Hilgard and Marquis's conditioning and learning.* New York: Appleton-Century-Crofts, 1961.

LACHMAN, R. The influence of thirst and schedules of reinforcement-nonreinforcement ratios upon brightness discrimination. *Journal of Experimental Psychology*, 1961, *62*, 80–87.

LEARY, R. W., HARLOW, H. F., SETTLAGE, P. H., and GREENWOOD, D.D. Performance on double-alternation problems by normal and brain-injured monkeys. *Journal of Comparative and Physiological Psychology*, 1952, *45*, 576–84.

LEONARD, C., SCHNEIDER, G. E., and GROSS, C. G. Performance on learning set and delayed-response tasks by tree shrews (Tupaia glis). *Journal of Comparative and Physiological Psychology*, 1966, *62*, 501–4.

LEVINE, M. A model of hypothesis behavior in discrimination learning set. *Psychological Review*, 1959, *66*, 353–66.

LEVINE, M., and HARLOW, H. F. Learning sets with one- and twelve-trial oddity problems. *American Journal of Psychology*, 1959, *72*, 253–57.

LIVESEY, P. J. A note on double alternation by rabbits. *Journal of Comparative and Physiological Psychology*, 1964, *57*, 104–7.

———— Comparisons of double alternation performance of white rats, rabbits, and cats. *Journal of Comparative and Physiological Psychology*, 1965, *59*, 155–58.

———— Double- and single-alternation learning by rhesus monkeys. *Journal of Comparative and Physiological Psychology*, 1969, *67*, 526–30.

LOCKARD, R. B. Self-regulated exposure to light by albino rats as a function of rearing luminance and test luminance. *Journal of Comparative and Physiological Psychology*, 1963, *56*, 558–64.

MAIER, N. R. F., and SCHNEIRLA, T. C. *Principles of animal psychology.* New York: McGraw-Hill, 1935.

MCCLEARY, R. A. Response specificity in the behavioral effects of limbic system lesions in the cat. *Journal of Comparative and Physiological Psychology*, 1961, *54*, 605–13.

MENZEL, E. W., JR. The effects of stimulus size and proximity upon avoidance of complex objects in rhesus monkeys. *Journal of Comparative and Physiological Psychology*, 1962, *55*, 1044–46.

MENZEL, E. W., JR., DAVENPORT, R. K., and ROGERS, C. M. Some aspects of behavior toward novelty in young chimpanzees. *Journal of Comparative and Physiological Psychology*, 1961, *54*, 16–19.

MEYER, D. R. Food deprivation and discrimination reversal learning by monkeys. *Journal of Experimental Psychology*, 1951, *41*, 10–16.

——— Some psychological determinants of sparing and loss following damage to the brain. *In* H. F. HARLOW and C. N. WOOLSEY (eds.), *Biological and biochemical bases of behavior*. Madison: University of Wisconsin Press, 1958.

MEYER, D. R., and ANDERSON, R. A. Colour discrimination in cats. *In* WOLSTENHOLME and KNIGHT (eds.), *Ciba foundation symposium on physiology and experimental psychology of colour vision*. London: J. & A. Churchill, Ltd., 1965.

MEYERS, W. J., MCQUISTON, M. D., and MILES, R. C. Delayed-response and learning-set performance of cats. *Journal of Comparative and Physiological Psychology*, 1962, *55*, 515–17.

MILES, R. C. Delayed-response learning in the marmoset and the macaque. *Journal of Comparative and Physiological Psychology*, 1957a, *50*, 352–55.

——— Learning-set formation in the squirrel monkey. *Journal of Comparative and Physiological Psychology*, 1957b, *50*, 356–57.

——— Learning in kittens with manipulatory, exploratory, and food incentives. *Journal of Comparative and Physiological Psychology*, 1958, *51*, 39–42.

——— Discrimination in the squirrel monkey as a function of deprivation and problem difficulty. *Journal of Experimental Psychology*, 1959, *57*, 15–19.

——— Effect of food deprivation on manipulatory reactions in cat. *Journal of Comparative and Physiological Psychology*, 1962, *55*, 358–62.

——— Effectiveness of deprivation, incentive quality, and number of reinforcements after numerous reconditionings. *Journal of Comparative and Physiological Psychology*, 1965, *60*, 460–63.

MILES, R. C., and BLOMQUIST, A. J. Frontal lesions and behavioral deficits in the monkey. *Journal of Neurophysiology*, 1960, *23*, 471–84.

MILES, R. C., and MEYER, D. R. Learning sets in marmosets. *Journal of Comparative and Physiological Psychology*, 1956, *49*, 219–22.

MISHKIN, M. Visual discrimination performance following partial ablations of the temporal lobe: II. Ventral surface vs. hippocampus. *Journal of Comparative and Physiological Psychology*, 1954, *47*, 187–93.

MONTGOMERY, K. C. Exploratory behavior and its relation to spontaneous alternation in a series of maze exposures. *Journal of Comparative and Physiological Psychology*, 1952a, *45*, 50–57.

——— A test of two explanations of spontaneous alternation. *Journal of Comparative and Physiological Psychology*, 1952b, *45*, 287–93.

——— Exploratory behavior as a function of "similarity" of stimulus situations. *Journal of Comparative and Physiological Psychology*, 1953, *46*, 129–33.

——— The role of exploratory drive in learning. *Journal of Comparative and Physiological Psychology*, 1954, *47*, 60–64.

MOWRER, O. H. A stimulus-response analysis of anxiety and its role as a reinforcing agent. *Psychological Review*, 1939, *46*, 553–65.

——— *Learning theory and behavior*. New York: John Wiley, 1960.

NORTH, A. J., MALLER, O., and HUGHES, C. Conditional discrimination and stimulus patterning. *Journal of Comparative and Physiological Psychology*, 1958, *51*, 711–15.

PAVLOV, I. P. *Conditioned reflexes*. Oxford: Clarendon Press, 1927.

PERIN, C. T. Behavior potentiality as a joint function of training and the degree of hunger at the time of extinction. *Journal of Experimental Psychology*, 1942, *30*, 93–113.

PINTO-HAMUY, T., SANTIBANEZ, G., GONZALES, C., and VINCERIO, E. Changes in behavior and visual discrimination after selective ablations of the temporal lobe. *Journal of Comparative and Physiological Psychology*, 1957, *50*, 379–85.

PUBOLS, B. H., JR. Successive discrimination reversal learning in the white rat: A comparison of two procedures. *Journal of Comparative and Physiological Psychology*, 1957, *50*, 319–22.

——— Incentive magnitude, learning, and performance in animals. *Psychological Bulletin*, 1960, *57*, 89–115.

RABEDEAU, R., and MILES, R. C. Response decrement in visual exploratory behavior. *Journal of Comparative and Physiological Psychology*, 1959, *52*, 364–67.

RIOPELLE, A. J., ALPER, R. G., STRONG, P. N., and ADES, H. W. Multiple discrimination and patterned strong performance of normal and temporal-lobectomized monkeys. *Journal of Comparative and Physiological Psychology*, 1953, *46*, 145–49.

RIOPELLE, A. J., HARLOW, H. F., SETTLAGE, P. H., and ADES, H. W. Performance of normal and operated monkeys on visual learning tests. *Journal of Comparative and Physiological Psychology*, 1951, *44*, 283–89.

ROMANES, G. J. *Animal intelligence*. New York: Appleton, 1906.

RUMBAUGH, D. M. The learning and sensory capacities of the squirrel monkey in phylogenetic perspective. *In* L. A. ROSENBLUM and R. W. COOPER (eds.), *The squirrel monkey*. New York: Academic Press, 1968.

RUMBAUGH, D. M., and RICE, C. P. Learning-set formation in young great apes. *Journal of Comparative and Physiological Psychology*, 1962, *55*, 866–68 .

SCHRIER, A. M. Comparison of two methods of investigating the effect of amount of reward on performance. *Journal of Comparative and Physiological Psychology*, 1958, *51*, 725–31.

SHELDON, A. B. Preference for familiar versus novel stimuli as a function of the familiarity of the environment. *Journal of Comparative and Physiological Psychology*, 1969, *67*, 516–21.

SHELL, W. F., and RIOPELLE, A. J. Progressive discrimination learning in platyrrhine monkeys. *Journal of Comparative and Physiological Psychology*, 1958, *51*, 467–70.

SKINNER, B. F. *The behavior of organisms*. New York: Appleton-Century-Crofts, 1938.

——— *Science and human behavior*. New York: Macmillan, 1953.

SOKOLOV, E. N. Neuronal models and the orienting influence. *In* M. A. B. BRAZIER (ed.), *The central nervous system and behavior*. New York: Macy Foundation, 1960.

SOLOMON, R. L., and WYNNE, L. C. Traumatic avoidance learning: The principles of anxiety conservation and partial irreversibility. *Psychological Review*, 1954, *61*, 353–85.

SPENCE, K. W. The nature of discrimination learning in animals. *Psychological Review*, 1939, *43*, 427–49.

STRETCH, R. Effects of amphetamine and pentobarbitone on exploratory behavior in rats. *Nature*, 1963, *199*, 787–89.

TEEL, K. S. Habit strength as a function of motivation during learning. *Journal of Comparative and Physiological Psychology*, 1952, *45*, 188–91.

THOMAS, H. Unidirectional changes in preference for increasing visual complexity in the cat. *Journal of Comparative and Physiological Psychology*, 1969, *68*, 296–302.

THOMPSON, R. Approach-avoidance in an ambivalent object discrimination problem. *Journal of Experimental Psychology*, 1953, *45*, 341–44.

THOMPSON, R. A., and SPENCER, W. A. Habituation: A model phenomenon for the study of neuronal substrates of behavior. *Psychological Review*, 1966, *73*, 16–43.

THOMPSON, W. R., and HIGGINS, W. H. Emotion and organized behavior: Experimental data bearing on the Leeper-Young controversy. *Canadian Journal of Psychology*, 1958, *12*, 61–65.

THORNDIKE, E. L. *Animal intelligence*. New York: Macmillan, 1911.

TOLMAN, E. C. *Purposive behavior in animals and men*. New York: Appleton-Century-Crofts, 1932.

——— There is more than one kind of learning. *Psychological Review*, 1949, *56*, 144–55.

WADE, M. The effect of sedatives upon delayed response in monkeys following removal of the prefrontal lobes. *Journal of Neurophysiology*, 1947, *10*, 57–61.

WARDEN, C. J., JENKINS, T. N., and WARNER, L. H. *Comparative psychology*, vol. 3. New York: Ronald Press, 1936.

WARREN, J. M. Perceptual dominance in discrimination learning by monkeys. *Journal of Comparative and Physiological Psychology*, 1954, *47*, 290–92.

—— Individual differences in discrimination learning by cats. *Journal of Genetic Psychology*, 1961, *98*, 89–93.

—— Primate learning in comparative perspective. *In* A. M. SCHRIER, H. F. HARLOW, and F. STOLLNITZ (eds.), *Behavior of nonhuman primates*, vol. 1. New York: Academic Press, 1965.

WARREN, J. M., and AKERT, K. (eds.) *The frontal granular cortex and behavior*. New York: McGraw-Hill, 1964.

WARREN, J. M., and HARLOW, H. F. Discrimination learning by normal and brain operated monkeys. *Journal of Genetic Psychology*, 1952a, *81*, 45–52.

—— Learned discrimination performance by monkeys after prolonged postoperative recovery from large cortical lesions. *Journal of Comparative and Physiological Psychology*, 1952b, *45*, 119–26.

WARREN, J. M., and SINHA, M. M. Interactions between learning sets in monkeys. *Journal of Genetic Psychology*, 1959, *95*, 19–25.

WATSON, J. B. *Behavior: An introduction to comparative psychology*. New York: Holt, 1914.

WELKER, R. J. Escape, exploratory, and food-seeking responses of rats in a novel situation. *Journal of Comparative and Physiological Psychology*, 1959, *52*, 106–11.

WELKER, W. I. Effects of age and experience on play and exploration of young chimpanzees. *Journal of Comparative and Physiological Psychology*, 1956a, *49*, 223–26.

—— Some determinants of play and exploration in chimpanzees. *Journal of Comparative and Physiological Psychology*, 1956b, *49*, 84–89.

WICKENS, D. D., and MILES, R. C. Extinction changes during a series of reinforcement-extinction changes. *Journal of Comparative and Physiological Psychology*, 1954, *47*, 315–17.

YERKES, R. M., and DODSON, J. D. The relation of strength of stimulus to rapidity of habit-formation. *Journal of Comparative Neurology*, 1908, *18*, 459–82.

ZEAMAN, D. Response latency as a function of the amount of reinforcement. *Journal of Experimental Psychology*, 1949, *39*, 466–83.

Basic Processes and Definitions

Conditioning refers to a procedure and to a process. Its formal study is rapidly approaching 70 years of age. While we have learned a lot, there are many problems not satisfactorily answered. It is interesting that what appears on the surface to be such a simple phenomenon is, under the surface, so complex and difficult to solve. We might call this a classical example of the "iceberg" phenomenon.

Pavlov (1902), while studying digestive reflexes in dogs, noticed that they would often salivate at the sight of food. He considered this a "psychic reflex" resulting from the association formed through experience between the sight of food and the response of salivation originally produced by food in the mouth. This example of serendipity has resulted in the phenomenon being labeled synonomously classical conditioning and Pavlovian conditioning. However, Pavlov's contribution to the explication of the conditions affecting the formation and retention of these acquired associations between stimuli and responses was probably a greater contribution than his discovery of the phenomenon itself which, as a practical procedure, was known to animal trainers. Gypsies have been reported to train bears to dance to music by a simple conditioning procedure. The bear was chained to a surface under which a fire was built to heat the stone on which the bear stood. The gypsies played music while the bear moved about to relieve the pain in his feet. The music became a conditioned stimulus. After this experience, the sound of the music elicited foot movements that resembled dancing.

Unfortunately the term classical conditioning is more

The intent is to present here a coherent analysis of conditioning, not a comprehensive review of the literature. It also is an attempt to take seriously the generally accepted, but infrequently acted upon assumptions of the behaviorist: namely, that conditioning is: (a) the simplest form of learning; (b) able to provide the fundamental information to explain more complicated learning; and (c) sufficient to provide an information base for inferring the nature of the learning process in its more complex manifestations.

Lawrence M. Stolurow

Conditioning

24

established in its use than it is helpful as either a description or designation of a procedure. Further, the label is not coordinate with the frequently used contrasting term "instrumental" conditioning.

Based upon a functional analysis of the conditions involved and knowledge of the confluence of factors, B.F. Skinner (1935) suggested a set of distinctions which is gaining in use. He suggested the names "respondent" and "operant." This distinction represents a break with conventional stimulus-response psychology in reversing the usual argument. Skinner is response-rather than stimulus-oriented and assumes the presence of a stimulus whenever a response occurs, even though no stimulus is identifiable. This argument eliminates the possibility of "spontaneous" behavior; correspondingly he proposes two classes of responses, "elicited" and "emitted." Responses that are elicited are *respondents*; examples are the knee jerk, pupillary constriction to light, salivation to meat powder on the tongue. Emitted responses are *operants*. Primarily because operants are so common and their stimuli are unknown, Skinner uses rate of response as the primary measure of the strength of an association. An operant usually acquires a relationship with a stimulus that precedes it. When this happens, it is a discriminated operant, meaning that a stimulus has become the occasion for the operant behavior. Most human behavior is operant in character, according to Skinner.

CLASSICAL CONDITIONING

In the classical experimental arrangement a dog that has been operated upon is placed in a soundproof room, restrained in a stock, and exposed to a ticking metronome. The operation exposed a salivary gland at the external surface of his cheek so that it can be connected to a suction cup attached to a tube to collect the secretion as it is produced. This permits the measurement of salivary response in terms of quantity, time, and rate of flow. The experimenter, usually in another room, controls the stimulus events in rather precise ways. He not only chooses the stimuli but also pairs them. For example, a metronome is paired with the stimulus that produces a response in which he is interested such as that produced by placing meat powder in the dog's mouth. The experimenter observes and measures the salivation that results. After a few pairings of the two stimuli, provided other conditions are right, the salivation occurs when the metronome beats and before the meat powder is placed in the dog's mouth. When this happens, the salivary response is said to be conditioned. The dog's salivation to the metronome is a conditioned response (*CR*). The sound of the metronome itself is a conditioned stimulus (*CS*). The meat powder on the tongue is an unconditioned stimulus (*UCS*), and the salivation to the meat powder, which is a physiological, inherited, or native reflex is called the unconditioned response (*UCR*).

The paradigm is a paired presentation of a *CS* and a *UCS* for a series of trials followed by a test with the *CS* presented alone to determine if a *CR* occurs. Some logical variations of the paradigm are required as contrasting conditions if the inferences that have been drawn about the necessary and sufficient conditions and the nature of the process are to become more than hypotheses. For example, the behavior resulting from each of the following conditions needs to be compared with that resulting from the classical paradigm: (a) Presentation of *CS* alone; (b) presentation of *UCS* alone; (c) presentation of a random series of *CS* and *UCS* without pairing; (d) simultaneous presentation of *CS* and *UCS*; and (e) backward pairing of *CS* and *UCS*.

In classical conditioning the syntax is relatively simple. There is no necessary contingency between a particular *CS* and the presentation of a particular *UCS*. A large number of possibilities exist from which the experimenter has his choice. Either the experimenter, or natural circumstances, may determine: (a) what *CS* presentations will be used; (b) what *USC* will be paired with it; (c) whether the *CS–UCS* will be paired on every presentation of the *CS* or only on some. All of these decisions are made without regard to the occurrence or nonoccurrence of the *CR*. While there are options with regard to whether or not a *CS* and *UCS* occur together on a trial, the relationship between a particular *CS* and *CR* is established by the co-occurence of a *CS* and *UCS*. The *UCS* is the means by which a desired response can be made to occur with high reliability so that the *CS* can become associated with it. There is no real justification for using one *UCS* rather than another except for its existing control over a desired response. The response to be measured is the critical factor in the decision. In an important and useful sense the *UCS* serves two functions. First, it elicits the desired response and at an acceptable level of reliability. Second, it provides a reinforcement. This latter function follows the response but the former precedes the response. For example, food on the tongue elicits salivation and also reduces hunger which process follows salivation. The drive reduction theory of reinforcement, of which the reduction of hunger is an example, is one of a set of theories of reinforcement. While not the only one applicable in classical conditioning it is frequently used. (For further discussion, see Kimble 1961; Beecroft 1966.)

PSEUDOCONDITIONING

Effects that appear to be conditioning in that a response seems to be strengthened in its association with a previously neutral stimulus have been reported without the use of paired stimulation. This has been called pseudoconditioning by Grether (1938). The most extensive study has been reported by Harris (1941) who compared forward, backward, and pseudoconditioning with a random conditioning procedure making use of finger withdrawal. He found a higher proportion of *CR*s after pseudoconditioning than with the others. Earlier, Sears (1934) used separate stimulation and adapted fish to light before presenting them with electric shock while the illumination was held constant. He found responses to light. Grether (1938) frightened monkeys several times with a flash of light and then sounded a bell. He observed the fright response to the bell. Grant (1943a; 1943b), Harlow (1939), Harlow and Toltzien (1940) and Harris (1941) as well as Kimble, Mann, and Dufort (1955), Kimble and Dufort (1956), and Dufort and Kimble (1958) have all reported pseudoconditioning. One implication drawn by Kimble (1961) is that pseudoconditioning may be a part of all conditioning in which a noxious stimulus is used. However, Goodrich, Ross, and Wagner (1957) were unable to replicate the findings of Kimble, Mann, and Dufort (1955).

Further complications arise in that after an extinction series, the *UCS* presented alone, without the *CS*, for several times, may have the effect of producing an increment in the strength of the

CR. Usually conditioning is restored by reconditioning which is a few additional pairings of the *CS* and *UCS*.

Wickens and Wickens (1942) interpret the observations of pseudoconditioning as true conditioning. During training with a noxious stimulus, the organism acquires a transferable response to a neutral stimulus on test trials presumably because the stimuli are similar.

INSTRUMENTAL CONDITIONING

Implied by the use of the labels classical or Pavlovian conditioning is the fact that there are other types of conditioning as well. The most common label used to identify an alternative type is instrumental conditioning. Hilgard and Marquis (1940) formalized this distinction and it is now widely accepted terminology.

There have been many distinctions proposed and each has its terminology (see Kimble, 1961). Generally, the distinctions made go deeper than the identification of variations in training methods. The assumption often made is that different psychological processes are involved. Two sets of distinctions frequently used are: (a) that classical conditioning is association by contiguity, whereas instrumental conditioning is association by the law of effect; and (b) that classical conditioning is basically the association of autonomic nervous system responses whereas instrumental conditioning is central nervous system (*CNS*) reactions.

The taxonomy of instrumental paradigms is based upon Thorndike's dichotomy, a distinction between "satisfiers" and "annoyers," or "positive" and "negative" stimuli. It also can be considered from the response side in terms of approach and avoidance. Operationally, a satisfier is a stimulus or object which the organism does nothing to avoid and often does something to attain or preserve it. An annoyer is one which the organism commonly avoids or abandons.

Instrumental paradigms are dichotomized into *controlled* and *free* training paradigms. There are three controlled instrumental paradigms that provide for an increase in the response and two that provide for a decrease. Reward training, escape training, and avoidance training all result in increases in the response. Pseudo-extinction and punishment training, on the other hand, result in decreases in the response with practice. Free instrumental training refers to paradigms in which "trial and error" and "discovery" learning take place. These are operants in which a particular response or complex form of behavior is emitted and is then reinforced.

Several methods are associated with the label instrumental conditioning. Some of the paradigms are derived from the work of Bekhterev (1908; 1909; 1912; 1913*a*; 1913*b*; 1923*a*; 1923*b*; 1923*c*; 1928; 1932) and others, from C. Lloyd-Morgan (1894) and E. L. Thorndike (1898). Both of these men identified types of learning and problem solving situations that differ from classical conditioning but which have been considered since then as having a fundamental relationship with conditioning. The responses that are critical in these paradigms are instrumental to the production of a reward or to obtaining one, or they permit the learner to escape or avoid punishment.

In instrumental conditioning a contingent relationship is established between the occurrence of a particular response and the presentation or nonpresentation of a reinforcer. The nature of the *CS*—the conditioned or cue stimulus—the response, and the reinforcement are all independent variables in instrumental conditioning. As with classical conditioning, however, their relationship and the timing are critical factors.

In *reward* training, the paradigm can be traced to Lloyd-Morgan (1894) and Thorndike (1898) who described it as "trial, error, and accidental success." Either the animal is in an enclosure and the reward is not, or vice versa. Eventually, the organism performs the critical response or set of responses and achieves the reward. Some American psychologists have preferred to use simple T-mazes and even a straight runway (e.g., Graham and Gagne 1940); whereas others prefer the Heron-Skinner box (Heron 1933; Heron and Skinner 1939) in which a rat presses a bar to get food. In all cases, the learner receives a reward *after* making a response. But the response which precedes the reward need not be physically related in any way to the actual delivery of the reward. It may be a purely arbitrary relationship of simple convenience. The only essential aspect of instrumental training is that the reward follows the response in a systematic relationship.

Escape training is an instrumental paradigm in which the conditioned response is followed by the termination of a noxious stimulus such as electric shock. Mowrer (1940) placed a rat in a box with a metal grille floor used to deliver electric current as a shock. At one end of the box was a lever which, if pushed, could turn off the shock. The shock was turned off as long as the pedal was depressed, but if released the shock returned. By the tenth trial the rats pressed the lever as soon as they began to feel the shock. Many features of escape training are similar to reward training. In both, the correct response is not elicited by the reinforcing stimulus but must occur before the reinforcement is presented. The nature of the *CR* is not determined by the reinforcement. Reinforcement and elicitation are separated and are independent functions. Escape training should be distinguished from punishment training. In escape training, the critical response *increases* in its rate of appearance or probability. In escape training the noxious stimulus (e.g., shock) is presented *before* the critical response occurs. In punishment training the critical response *decreases* in its rate or probability; the noxious stimulus occurs *after* the critical response.

Avoidance training differs from the previously described paradigms in that the critical response *prevents* the noxious stimulus from appearing. Bekhterev's original paradigm is the reference experiment. The dog could lift its paw to prevent it from being shocked. Brogden, Lipman, and Culler (1938) put guinea pigs in a revolving cage and after a buzzer (*CS*) and shock (*UCS*) were presented, the animals ran (*UCR*). One group was shocked whether or not they ran; another group was not shocked if they ran (avoidance paradigm). Learning began at the same level but reached a higher level with the group trained under the avoidance paradigm.

Sidman (1953*a*, 1953*b*), unlike most investigators, has used avoidance training in a free-responding situation. At a fixed interval a shock appears unless a bar is pressed in the interval. No discrete exteroceptive signal is used. High rates of responding are developed with this paradigm.

A type of *pseudo extinction* or "omission" training (Sheffield in Kimble 1961) identifies another set of instrumental paradigms. The parent who withholds privileges for undesirable behavior represents one variety. Here the critical response has a high probability of occurrence and the intent is to reduce that to zero, but the *CS* is unknown. All "satisfiers" must be prevented from following the behavior that is undesirable at least within some contexts, e.g., the child is reinforced for undressing for bed but all reinforcers are withheld if she undresses in the living room with guests present.

Another variation is *punishment training* (e.g., Konorski 1948, chap. 2). In this paradigm, some noxious stimulus such as electric shock is made contingent upon the occurrence of a critical response. This is the opposite of avoidance training in which the noxious (painful) stimulus occurs only if the to-be-learned responses fail to occur. Also, in avoidance training the noxious stimulus occurs before the response whereas in punishment training the noxious stimulus occurs after the critical response. In punishment training, the interest is in the speed with which a response is abandoned. In avoidance training and in pseudo extinction the interest is in the development of an antagonistic response.

RESPONSE SYSTEMS AND VARIABLES

Most conditioning studies have been related to one or two basic processes: acquisition or extinction. However, a number of different response systems have been used in the study of these processes, e.g., *GSR*, heartbeat, pupillary, electroencephalographic, eyelid, and motor. The variations in the response systems and the species of organism used in conditioning studies give one the impression of an extensively investigated area. However, only a small number of independent variables have been studied in relation to the possible ones that could influence learning. Among the more extensively investigated variables are schedules of reinforcement, intervals between paired stimuli, the order in pairings, *CS* intensity, motivation, instructions, and set.

ACQUISITION

Acquisition is a generic term used to describe the basic process assumed to operate whenever learning takes place. The acquisition process and the learning process are used interchangeably to describe the internal changes that become apparent through modifications in response measures. Several different measures are used and their selection depends upon the nature of the learning task. Six different measures have become conventional indices in laboratory research: (a) probability of occurrence; (b) latency; (c) response speed; (d) rate of responding; (e) response magnitude; and (f) resistance to extinction. All of these measures are assumed to increase with practice; however, the form of the curve varies.

Form of the Curve. Spence (1956, pp. 61–76, 101–16) reviewed the data on conditioning curves for the classical paradigm most of which were from eyelid studies. He concluded:

In summary these findings suggest the generalization that frequency curves of classical conditioning are S-shaped, providing the complete course of conditioning is represented in the curve. *Frequency curves that do not exhibit an initial positively accel-*

erated phase do not do so either because the conditioning is so rapid that the period of initial acceleration is too brief to be revealed except by very small groups or blocks of trials." (pp. 69–70.)

See the following for curves that rise sharply and are negatively accelerated (Hovland 1937*d*; Moeller 1954; Champion and Jones 1961; Champion 1961; Jones 1961). For an S-shaped *GSR* curve, see Grings, Lovell, and Honnard (1961), Notterman, Schoenfeld, and Bersh (1952), and Gerall, Sampson, and Boslov (1957).

Continuous or "all-or-none" Process. A question of interest about the acquisition process is whether the strength of the *CR* is built up on a continuous or "all-or-none" basis. Voeks (1954) sought data to support Guthrie's all-or-none view. Grice and Davis (1958; 1960) identified a methodological problem with her approach. Kimble and Dufort (1956) and Spence (1956) failed to find support for "one trial" or "all-or-none" acquisition. Estes (1964) is the outstanding advocate of the noncontinuity interpretation. The issue is still alive, but the data argue more for the continuity of acquisition than for discontinuity. Further resolution of the measures used could help solve the problem.

Definitions. Acquisition and learning are broader terms than conditioning, at least as used by many psychologists. The broader concepts include both classical and instrumental conditioning as well as respondent and operant conditioning, but they also include a variety of other acquisition processes including problem solving. Many feel, however, that conditioning is the prototypical form of learning and use it as the basis for the analysis of the more complex forms of behavior (e.g., Skinner 1938, 1953; Hilgard and Marquis 1940; Ferster 1953; and Gagné 1965).

Acquisition is defined as a change in behavior potentiality that is developed by experience and demonstrated by a change in actual behavior. Through the learning process the organism acquires the capability to perform specific acts. Having acquired a set of capabilities the individual can be said to be competent in an area. Sometimes the acquired capability remains latent, however, and only becomes apparent later on. Also the learning may become apparent in a form that is known only indirectly.

Learning refers to long-term changes of the individual which are related to the opportunity to learn (past experience) including practice, rather than to physiological changes of the individual's state such as fatigue, adaptation, drug effects, motivation, maturation, or senescence.

Performance refers to a translation of learning into behavior; as such it depends upon the confluence of a variety of factors such as motivation and physiological changes. The upper limit of performance is set by the amount of learning that has occurred.

EXTINCTION

Pavlov defined extinction operationally as the repeated presentation of the conditioned stimulus (*CS*) unaccompanied by the usual reinforcement as provided by the unconditioned stimulus (*UCS*). Extinction becomes apparent by the decreasing occurrence of the *CR* when the *CS* is presented without the *UCS*. Changes due to extinction may be evident in the decreased frequency or amplitude of the *CR*.

A theory of extinction has to meet several tests. It must, at the same time, account for not only the *CR* decrement, but also spontaneous recovery of the *CR* following extinction, and the relatively more rapid rate of reconditioning than original conditioning.

Disinhibition is the inhibition of an inhibition and it is manifested by a rise in *CR* during extinction. Hovland (1936) reported that in four earlier studies there were larger responses on the second or third extinction trial than there was on the first. He interpreted this in the same way that Hilgard and Marquis did (1935), namely, that it was due to negative adaptation to continuous reinforcement. Hovland tested this interpretation and found support for it. Mednick and Wild (1962) also reported disinhibition in *GSR* conditioning to verbal stimuli.

External inhibition was described by Pavlov as a temporary reduction in the strength of a *CR* as a result of the occurrence of an extraneous stimulus. It can be contrasted with disinhibition in its effect, but it can be compared in terms of a stimulus similarity or generalization concept coupled with interference theory.

Theoretical Mechanisms. The *generalization decrement* hypothesis assumes that heightened resistance to extinction following partial reinforcement occurs because the training increases the similarity of the stimulus situation for learning and extinction with the result that there is less generalization decrement when extinction begins. In extinction there is less change in the stimulus situation if training has been with intermittent reinforcement than if it has been with continuous reinforcement. This position also makes the assumption that the stimulus traces of reinforcement and nonreinforcement dissipate in time. Therefore, with highly distributed training trials the superiority of partial reinforcement should disappear. Weinstock (1954) and Wilson, Weiss, and Amsel (1955), on the other hand, found that partial reinforcement during training always led to greater resistance to extinction, whatever the intertrial interval. The dissipation hypothesis does not seem to hold.

Interference theory assumes that extinction occurs when the *CS* elicits a response other than the conditioned response. The natural response evoked by the *CS* at the outset will decrease and disappear as learning proceeds if it is antagonistic to the newly developed *CR*. If no antagonism exists between the two responses, there will be no interference effect. Pavlov (1932*b*) in his description of the formation of a conditioned salivary response to a bell reported that the *CS* originally evoked listening movements—the dog turned its head and pricked up its ears. These listening movements gradually disappeared as the dog came to respond to the bell by licking its chops and turning toward the food pan. A similar example was reported by Erofeeva (1916). Hull (1934*b*) described another case, namely, one in which the interfering response was established in an earlier learning experience. Kellogg and Walker (1938*a*) also reported an example.

Combining the generalization concept, in which the altered

stimulus situation can be made a reasonable assumption, with the interference theory eliminates one of the classical objections to the interference theory, namely, that there was no basis for the appearance of the competing response during extinction. Another objection to interference theory remains, however, namely, the mechanism for reinforcing the competing response. In addition, this theory as it is stated runs into factual problems involving spontaneous recovery, distribution of practice and the influence of drugs. If extinction occurs through interference by a learned response, then spontaneous recovery would be expected to be just as slow as the forgetting of the newly acquired antagonistic response. A second objection comes from the finding that massing of trials produces more rapid extinction, but it retards conditioning. Finally, depressant drugs such as sodium bromide retard the rate of conditioning, but accelerate the rate of extinction.

Other two-factor theories have been proposed. Probably the most enthusiastically embraced was Hull's theory of conditioned inhibition. Its strongest claim is that it stimulated a number of studies designed to determine its usefulness. Still other single factor theories have proponents. One is the interference theory which maintains that every response elicited during extinction adds to the strength of an inhibitory tendency which opposes that response. The number of responses and their effort demands are considered important dimensions of the task determining the rate of extinction. Three effects which it does not handle sufficiently well are: (a) distribution of practice; (b) spontaneous recovery; and (c) resistance to extinction.

The basic assumption in the *frustration hypothesis* is that the omission of a positive reinforcer is frustrating, and the frustration it produces is a drive which (a) energizes behavior and (b) produces interfering responses.

Expectancy theory attempts to explain extinction in much the same way that interference theory does. However, the mechanism is cognitive. The learner develops an expectancy that reinforcement will no longer follow the *CS* or the occurrence of the instrumental response.

Summary. Extinction has turned out to be a phenomenon of much greater complexity than was originally thought. Not only do the variables appear to interact more than was anticipated, but also the research, while abundant, has been directed more at hypothesis testing than at the development of a useful data base. Also the variables that have figures most prominently are also variables that operate during acquisition—inhibition, frustration, alteration of the stimulus situation, interfering responses, and changes in secondary reinforcement. It seems that a simple explanation will not suffice, but the minimal combination also is not clearly identified. Extinction as a procedure is quite clear but as a set of internal processes it is not so clear.

The decrement in the *CR* is generally progressive and continues throughout extinction until it finally fails to occur. This decrement is not due to decay since it has been shown that *CR*s show only a very limited tendency to diminish with the passage of time. For example, the retention of *CR*s by sheep has been found to last two years (Liddell, James, and Anderson 1934); conditioned eyelid reactions in dogs for 16 months (Marquis and Hilgard 1936); conditioned eyelid reactions in man for 20 weeks (Hilgard and Campbell 1936); and for 19 months (Hilgard and Humphreys 1938); conditioned flexion reflexes in the dog for 30 months (Wendt 1937); conditioned salivation in man for 16 weeks (Razran 1939); a variety of responses in dogs for 6 months (Kellogg and Wolf 1939); and the impressive finding of pecking responses in pigeons for 4 years (Skinner 1950). These data leave little doubt that the reduction or elimination of a *CR* in a brief extinction session depends upon an active process or processes which are called extinction.

PRACTICE

Practice alone does not produce learning; it provides opportunities for the necessary and sufficient factors to actually produce learning. At least two factors seem to satisfy these conditions for conditioning. They are *temporal contiguity* among a set of basic elements and *reinforcement*. Contiguity theory states that for learning to occur, it is necessary only for two stimuli (*CS* and *UCS*) or a stimulus and a response to occur closely together in time. Effect theory states that for learning to occur it is necessary for the theoretical law of effect to operate or, in other words, for some satisfying or rewarding consequence to happen. This is usually coupled with the hypothesis that specific types of events are reinforcing. However, events are not invariant in their effect from person to person or time to time for the same person. In this sense objects and stimuli are not effective in an absolute sense but rather in a normative sense within a culture or for an individual. Independent operations can be used to determine the potential effect of reinforcers, however.

Models and Paradigms

Models of the conditioning paradigms are presented below and are based upon an analysis of the elements and relationships that are used in conditioning experiments. Four classes of elements are interrelated in these models. The symbolism adopted to represent them is: (a) *S* for explicit or manipulated stimulus; (b) *R* for overt (observable) response; (c) *rs* for the associative stimulus (the internal, covert, representation of the explicit stimulus); and *t* for the time interval. Numerical subscripts identify the sequential order, e.g., S_1 occurs before S_2.

CLASSICAL

There are five variations of classical conditioning: simultaneous, delayed, trace, backward, and temporal. The following diagram (Figure 24–1) places the basic elements in relation to one another.

VARIATIONS IN TIME INTERVALS

Examination of the "fine grain" of the various classical paradigms reveals that time intervals are critical. In fact, the names given to the various paradigms in the set called classical conditioning are based upon timing.

Simultaneous. S_1 and S_2 presented simultaneously:

$$\text{(CS)} \qquad\qquad\qquad\qquad\qquad \blacktriangleleft\text{-- On}$$
$$S_1 \qquad\qquad\qquad\qquad\qquad\quad \text{Off}$$

$$\text{(UCS)} \qquad S_2$$
$$\text{time}$$

$$t = 0$$

Delayed. S_1 while still on is followed after a definite interval by S_2.

$$\text{(CS)} \qquad\qquad\qquad\qquad\qquad \blacktriangleleft\text{---On}$$
$$S_1 \qquad\qquad\qquad\qquad\qquad \blacktriangleleft\text{---Off}$$

$$\text{(UCS)} \qquad S_2$$

$$t_1 \qquad\qquad\qquad t > 0$$

There are two variations of this paradigm:

short — $t_1 \leq .5$ sec

long — $t_1 > .5$ sec

Trace. S_1 goes on and off before S_2 goes on:

$$\text{(CS)} \qquad S_1$$

$$\text{(UCS)} \qquad S_2$$

$$t_1$$

There are two variations: (1) short and (2) long (see Wolfe, H. M. 1932).

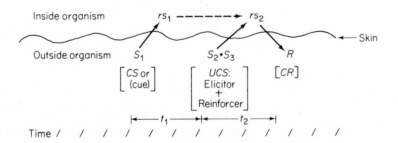

Fig. 24-1.

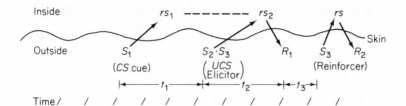

Fig. 24-2.

Backward. S_2 (CS) follows S_1 (UCS) so, in effect, the time relationship is reversed, or the time interval is a negative value.

(CS)　　S_2　　　　　　◄---On
　　　　　　　　　　　　◄---Off

(UCS)　　S_1

　　　　　◄--t_1

Conditioning seems to be impossible with this method.

Temporal. S_1 (CS) is a time interval between stimuli and not a sensory experience of the same kind as is employed in the previously described paradigms. S_2 (UCS) is presented at regular intervals. Then if the S_2 is omitted (no UCS), a CR may occur at approximately the interval used in training or at a time proportional to it. This paradigm should be related to pseudoconditioning.

The preceding illustrations reveal the ordering and temporal spacing of stimulus events in classical paradigms. In the typical paradigm the CS begins a brief time before the onset of the UCS. It may overlap the UCS in time, or terminate before the onset of the UCS. The time interval between the CS and the UCS may be short or long. The functional CS (rs_1) as contrasted with the manipulated CS, may be: (a) the onset; (b) the duration; or (c) the termination of the S_1. In *delayed conditioning* the CS appears prior to the UCS and lasts at least until the onset of the UCS. It may: (a) go off as the UCS comes on; (b) go off when the UCS does: or (c) persist beyond the offset of the UCS. In the *trace* paradigm the CS comes on briefly and goes off *before* the onset of the UCS In the backward paradigm the order is changed and the CS *follows* the UCS.

INSTRUMENTAL MODELS

There are two basic types of instrumental paradigms each of which permits variation. One is the controlled instrumental conditioning model. It is represented in Figure 24-2. Its variations are reward training, escape training, and avoidance training. These variations differ from one another in terms of the relation-

ship between R_1 and S_3 (reinforcement) as well as in the types of S_2 (UCS) used.

Free instrumental conditioning model is sometimes called a free operant. The cue stimulus may be either a continuous stimulus such as a bell or an internal one such as produced from a drive condition, or it may be intermittent and either internal or external. The S_3 event in the positive types of variation is a reinforcer, but in the negative variations it may be the witholding of reinforcement or punishment. Pseudoextinction and punishment training are examples of the latter variety. They are represented in Figure 24–3.

TIME RELATIONSHIPS IN THE CLASSICAL MODEL

Conditioning appears to occur only when the CS precedes the UCS by some interval, but the size of that interval which is optimal is not certain. It is also not established that the interval which is optimal for one organism is optimal for all or for all CS–UCS combinations. Related is the extent to which the CS–UCS interval that is used controls the latency of the CR.

Test-trial Procedure. To answer these questions the test-trial procedure is needed. It consists of the omission of the UCS when the critical data relating to the latency of the CR are obtained or when the existence of the CR is being determined. If the CS–UCS interval is too short and the test-trial procedure is not used, then the latency could not be measured since there would not be enough time for an anticipatory response to occur.

Optimal Interval. Fitzwater and Reisman (1952), White and Schlosberg (1952) Fitzwater and Thrush (1956) and Jones (1961) did not obtain motor conditioning with intervals under 100-msec. Pakovich (Asratyan, 1961) only obtained a motor CR when the CS preceded the UCS by 100 msec. Hansche and Grant (1960) found a 190-msec. interval insufficient. However, a 250-msec interval led to high levels of eyelid conditioning (Reynolds 1945a, 1945b; McAllister 1953a). For human adults at least 200-msec are needed; however, the optimal CS–UCS

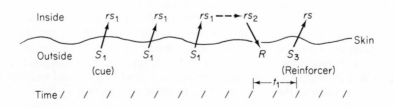

Fig. 24-3.

interval in *GSR*, eyelid and finger withdrawal, is approximately 500-msec for adult human learners.

The optimum interval seems to vary from organism to organism. McAdam, Knott, and Chiorini (1965) found 500-msec was effective for leg flexion in the cat; Noble and Adams (1963) found 4–8 sec for gross movements of pigs. Noble and Harding (1963) found 2 sec best for monkeys as did Boice and Denny (1965) for rats, and Noble, Gruender, and Meyer (1959) for fish. Klinman and Bitterman (1963) and Bitterman (1964*b*) found the latency for peak reaction to vary with interstimulus intervals from 1 to 9 sec. Black, Carlson, and Solomon (1962) found that heart rate in dogs was conditioned at intervals from 2.5 to 10 sec.

For skeletal *CR*s in human learners, latency is a positive increasing function of the *CS–UCS* interval; the shortest interval to produce substantial conditioning is 200 msec. For autonomic *CR*s, the minimum is usually under 2 sec, and it increases moderately with longer intervals.

Concepts

Concepts of the nature of the stimulus and response are fundamental to a great deal of the theoretical analysis of learning phenomena. Two levels of analysis figure in the account made of conditioning.

STIMULUS AND RESPONSE

Both stimuli and responses, as typically identified for simple descriptive purposes, e.g., electric shock (*UCS*) and withdrawal movements (*UCR*), are each a complex set of finer constituents. Both Guthrie (1935) and Hull (1930) recognized the existence of the finer grain of stimuli and responses in their theoretical conceptions of conditioning. An electric shock has an onset, a duration, an intensity, and a termination. Any of these features of the stimulus could acquire cue properties and if it did it, in effect, would be the *CS*. Similarly, molar responses, such as withdrawal movements, have a beginning, a quality, or topography (Skinner 1938), as well as intensive and temporal dimensions. Any of these components may become the stable element in an organism's performance that constitutes the *CR*.

The *unconditioned stimulus* (*UCS*) at the outset of an experiment evokes a replicable and measurable response. It is the *unconditioned response* (*UCR*). Any replicable and measurable response which the *UCS* evokes or elicits is a functional *UCR*. Its most critical property is its replicability. When the *UCS* is presented, the *UCR* should occur and the *UCS* relationship with the *UCR* should be reliable. The *UCR* does not have to be an unlearned reflex response to the *UCS*. It may be learned connection. Food placed on the tongue results in a *UCR* as a reflex, for example, but the salivation resulting from the sight and smell of food also can be very reliable. In fact, it was used by Pavlov as a *UCS*.

The *conditioned stimulus* (*CS*) has important functional properties that should be considered in deciding upon a particular one for a study or application. The following are useful functions to consider: (a) it does not evoke the *UCR* at the beginning of the conditioning series; (b) it is neutral but attachable to the

CR; (c) it can be paired with the *UCS* for associative purposes; (d) the response it evokes or elicits should not be incompatible with the *UCR*, produce a delay in the *UCR*, or alter the topography of the *UCR*. Ideally it should evoke an "attention" response to the *CS*. Pavlov called this an *orientation reflex*, what-is-it reflex, or *investigatory reflex*. In some conditioning, such as eyelid using a visual *CS*, the response to the *CS* may have the same topography as that to the *UCS* (e.g., a blink). When this condition exists, the response to the *CS* and to the *UCS* must be distinguishable in latency, form, or magnitude.

Any environmental change to which the learner is sensitive may serve as a *CS*. However, its effectiveness is determined by the context such as the motivational state of the learner and the *UCS* that is used, since the *UCR* and the response to the *CS* must not interfere with one another. Also, the effectiveness of a stimulus as a *CS* may depend on the rapidity of its onset, its summation, change in intensity, or termination. Unless a test is made, it is not clear which dimension of a molar stimulus is critical, i.e., the "subjective" or "effective stimulus"—as contrasted with the manipulated or "objective" stimulus (Wulf and Stolurow 1957). Once conditioning has taken place, the *CS* can be said to be "attached" to the *CR*.

The *conditioned response* (*CR*) occurs when on either a test trial with the *UCS* omitted or in anticipation of the *UCS* a response resembling the *UCR* follows the *CS*. It merely resembles the *UCR*; it is not identical with the *UCR*.

Generally it is assumed that the *CR* is either a fractional component of the *UCR* or that it is a preparation for the occurrence of the *UCS*. The *CR* appears to be weaker than the *UCR*. For example, the conditioned salivary response is often smaller in magnitude than the *UCR*. The fractional component idea was most developed by Hull (1952) and expanded upon by Osgood (1953). They pointed out that some fractional components of a *UCR* can occur in the absence of the *UCS* and at points remote from it in time or space. Thus this concept became the link with higher mental processes and symbolic behavior. The logical argument was made consistent by Hull's definition of the R_g or goal response and its components, some of which were called *fractional anticipatory goal response* (r_g). It was seen as the way the organism could relate to the "not here" and "not now" which, however, had to have been "here" previously. This analysis has been directly applied to the explanation of latent learning, delay of reinforcement, problem solving, and conflict behavior (Hull 1952; Osgood 1953). In this approach the r_g serves much the same function as the concept of expectancy; however, from a philosophy of science point of view, they are not the same. Whereas r_g represents a logical development, the expectancy concept represents an additional assumption. Thus the choice hinges on parsimony or preference.

Another line of reasoning is represented by the explanation of the *UCR*/*CR* difference in terms of function. From this position, the *CR* is viewed as a preparatory response; it prepares the organism for the *UCS*. From this point of view the *CR* need not resemble the *UCR* at all. Zener (1937) makes a strong case for this position.

The *CR* is probably an amalgam of these two components, the fractional anticipatory goal response and the preparatory. This suggests that some of the behavior, in the classical paradigm, is really instrumental. For example, readiness, or expectancy responses acquired in a classical situation can be thought of as being instrumental in nature.

REINFORCEMENT

There are two different meanings for the term reinforcement as it is used in learning: its empirical meaning and its theoretical meaning. Factually, it means a wide variety of conditions introduced into a learning situation that increase the probability that a given response will reoccur in the same situation. Theoretically, the meaning of reinforcement varies from one theorist to another. For example, Hull (1943) interprets it to mean drive reduction. Skinner (1938) and Tolman (1932) prefer to treat it in stimulus terms. For Thorndike (1911) it means either satisfiers or annoyers. Guthrie (1935) defined it most simply as anything that alters the stimulus situation for the learner. Sheffield (1948) and Denny and Adelman (1955) treat it as an elicitor of behavior. Each of these can be considered a special case of the general concept.

The strength of a conditioned response is increased by reinforcement and decreased by nonreinforcement. Two different properties of reinforcers are their quality and quantity. The quality of a reinforcer is obviously a subjective factor which, however, may be estimated on the basis of normative data obtained from similar learners. The quantity of a reinforcer is generally specified in terms of a physical measure such as weight or volume.

Amount. The amount of reinforcement appears to function as a performance factor. Performance increases as a negatively accelerated function in relation to increases in the amount of reinforcement. In support of this are such studies as Crespi (1942), Hutt (1954), and Zeaman (1949a). A similar relationship exists for quality of reinforcement and supporting studies include Guttman (1953), Hutt (1954), Collier and Marx (1959) Crespi (1944), Denny and King (1955), Dufort and Kimble (1956), Jenkins and Clayton (1949), Maher and Wickens (1954), and Nissen and Elder (1935).

Intensity. Fewer studies have been devoted to variations in the intensity of negative reinforcers, but the evidence that is available is rather consistent with the studies using positive reinforcement. Increasing intensities result in increasing amounts of conditioning (Boren, Sidman, Herrnstein 1959; Passey 1948; Prokasy, Grant, and Myers, 1958). Also the data suggest that the function is asymptotic beyond a particular intensity value.

Schedules. Reinforcement can be administered either consistently after every response or trial, or it may be administered only on some fraction of occasions. The former is referred to as 100 percent reinforcement schedule or continuous reinforcement. The other is partial, intermittent reinforcement. The latter is more characteristic of natural conditions; the former is typical of the laboratory. Intermittent reinforcement follows a schedule; reinforcement occurs either for the first response after a particular period of time (interval schedules) or after a specified number of responses (ratio schedules). In addition, the time interval or ratio may be constant from reinforcement to reinforcement (fixed) or haphazard changed (varied). This results in four basic types: fixed interval, variable interval, fixed ratio, and variable ratio. Each has a characteristic

effect on the performance of learners. One of the most significant effects of intermittent reinforcement is its ability to produce greater resistance to extinction (see Ferster and Skinner 1957).

DELAY IN REINFORCEMENT

The temporal and spatial proximity of reinforcement to an instrumental response affects the rate of learning. The quicker the reinforcement, the faster the conditioning. Support for this principle comes from a wide variety of different experiments with different paradigms and learners.

Examples of studies that support this conclusion are Tolman's (1943b) study using rats who were taught a discrimination; Montpellier's (1933) study of the backward order of elimination of blinds in a maze; Yoshioka's (1929) and Grice's (1942) study of the rats' selection of the shortest path to a goal; Hull's (1934c) study of locomotor gradients; and the Lambert and Solomon (1952) study of extinction.

The goal gradient, or performance rate in relation to proximity to the goal, and the delay-of-reinforcement gradient, was first formulated by Hull (1932, pp. 25–26). It has two related concepts: (a) the delay-of-reinforcement principle itself; and (b) the fine grain analysis of molar behavior into S-R elements that are chained into a serial sequence. Important in the explanation of chaining is the *response-produced* cue which refers to the fact that each overt response produces a characteristic proprioceptive stimulus. Learning consists in a strengthening of the tendency of the environmental and proprioceptive stimuli (as a distinctive pattern) to evoke the appropriate response. Time factors enter in two ways. The goal-gradient hypothesis deals with the relationship between each of these responses in the chain and the goal, and it says that the ones closest to the goal are associated first. The other interval is that which exists at each point in the task between the *CS* and *UCS*. The *UCS* may be a result of a drive in which case it is persistent throughout the series of overt responses.

Hull formulated the function for the delay-of-reinforcement gradient as a decelerated negative function of time, when the level of learning is expressed in terms of theoretical units of habit stength. This concept has been used to predict what would happen when the learner can take paths of different lengths to the goal. When applied to maze learning, it predicts a strict backward elimination of blinds so it has been combined with the principle of stimulus generalization to predict the pattern found for simple linear mazes. Existent data suggest that learning cannot take place if delays are greater than a few seconds, and this is true of both positive and negative reinforcers. When delays greater than this are not detrimental, there is evidence of immediate secondary reinforcement.

SECONDARY REINFORCEMENT

Some sources of reinforcement are learned. In general, any stimulus regularly associated with primary reinforcement takes on some of the characteristics of primary reinforcement. Saltzman (1949) trained rats to run a straight alley to obtain food in a distinctive goal box. He had a consecutive reinforcement group and a control group both of which were trained the same way. They received 25 rewarded trials in which food was paired with the distinctive goal box. A third group received 25 reinforced trials and 14 nonreinforced trials in the same goal box. A fourth group received the same number of reinforced and nonreinforced trials according to the same schedule but the goal box varied depending upon whether it was a reinforced trial or not. By placing the distinctive goal box at one end of a U and a different goal box at the end of the other. All groups chose the previously reinforced goal box sufficiently often to establish statistically that performance was not chance.

Stimuli that regularly precede a given reaction can come to elicit that reaction in an anticipatory fashion. Goal reactions can become antipatory in the same way; the learner can make fractional parts of the total goal response before the ultimate event takes place. The goal reactions can be divided into two parts: those that cannot be made without the goal object being present, and those that can be made when it is not present. In order for an initially neutral stimulus to acquire secondary motivating or reinforcing value, it must become associated with anticipatory goal reactions. Spence (1947) and Seward (1950) provide similar analyses and include the mechanism of generalization. The central argument is that certain stimuli, originally neutral with respect to motivational properties, come to have both motivating and reinforcing values by means of the eliciting fractional part.

Acquired Drive. The role of anxiety as both an acquired drive and reinforcing agent is one of the most highly developed examples. Shock is assumed to have three stimulus functions:

1. A *UCS*, in that it elicits certain reflexive and learned skeletal responses.
2. A painful stimulus that energizes all ongoing reaction systems, amplifying the vigor with which reactions are made.
3. An activator of the learner's autonomic nervous system (emotional state of fear).

Some of the fear reactions become associated with cue stimulus, such as a buzzer, and are elicited on subsequent occasions as fractional anticipatory responses. They are called anxiety. Accordingly, the reaction-produced stimulation is the secondary drive and its reduction is secondary reinforcement.

Most behavior in human adults is not motivated by primary biological drives. The mechanisms involved are called acquired drives and reinforcers. Although all the mechanism for their acquisition have not been identified, there has been enough theoretical and conceptual development to reveal the essential continuity of the argument.

GENERALIZATION

When an organism has been conditioned to respond to a particular stimulus, it can be shown that other similar stimuli also will elicit the response even though the substituted stimuli have not been used in training. The ability of other stimuli to evoke a conditioned response is called stimulus generalization. Its counterpart also has been described but studied less; response generalization is the ability of a stimulus that has acquired a response to elicit under some conditions a related response without special training.

Starting with Anrep (1923) and until the present time there have been a number of studies demonstrating the wide variety of stimuli and organisms that show stimulus generalization (see Kimble, 1961, pp. 329–30). Generalization has been observed with both the classical and instrumental paradigms.

It is important to realize that the graph of the magnitude of response to variations in stimuli generally produces a gradient. This is called the generalization gradient and its distinctive feature is that the modal frequency (or intensity) of response is at the point on the distribution represented by the conditioned stimulus. At all other points, on both sides, the response strength drops off (see Guttman and Kalish 1956; Hovland 1937a).

A number of factors appear to affect the nature of the generalization gradient, for example, the schedule of reinforcement during training, number of previous generalization tests, the dimension involved, and individual differences.

Hovland's (1937a) study using GSR along a pitch dimension is a reference experiment. He used four tones which were 25 just-noticeable-differences (j.n.d.'s) apart (frequencies of 153, 468, 1000, and 1967 cycles). The tones were equated for loudness. One group of learners was conditioned to the lowest tone and then tested, in extinction, on the others to determine the magnitude of the generalization responses. A second group was conditioned to the highest tone and then tested on the three lower tones. By using permutational orders of presentation, it was possible to pool the obtained results from all learners into a single curve. The curve showed that the degree of generalization decreases progressively with greater differences in pitch and that the gradient was concave.

Many early studies of generalization included tests for the generalization of extinction (Bass and Hull 1934; Hovland 1937a, 1937b). In the generalization study cited, Hovland (1937a) also carried out an extinction series for half the learners by presenting the highest tone without reinforcement. For the other half of the learners extinction was carried out with the lowest tone. The generalization of extinction was measured by the amount of reduction of response to the other frequencies. The curve was found to be similar to that obtained for generalization of conditioning. Kling (1952) studied the generalization of extinction in an instrumental situation. He found, as predicted from theory, that the more similar the two original stimuli the more generalization of extinction interfered with responding in the test.

There are two measures used in generalization studies: (a) absolute generalization or the response strength measured directly in the experiment, and (b) relative generalization or response strength measured as a percentage of the response strength to the *CS*. It has been found that generalization gradient varies with a number of factors. For example, generalization steepens during extinction (Hovland 1937d; Brown 1942; Wickens, Schroder, and Snide 1954). Guttman and Kalish (1956) used a variable-interval reinforcement schedule to develop a high level of response strength and then tested for generalization. They did not find that the range of generalization decreased with extinction. It remained about the same, but the gradient became flatter. They also looked at individual differences among pigeons in response rates and found that the range of generalization did not decrease in relation to the slowness of the rate. Humphreys (1939c) showed that the gradient of generalization is flatter following intermittent reinforcement than following continuous reinforcement. Bersh, Notterman, and Schoenfeld

(1956) showed that increased drive broadened the generalization gradient. This has been reported by Jenkins, Pascal, and Walker (1958) as well, but for a different *CR* and organism. Rosenbaum (1953) found that the threat of shock led to greater generalization of a voluntary response than threat of a weak shock. He reported data relating to individual differences in that his learners who were highly anxious showed broader generalization gradients than his less anxious learners.

Razran (1949) summarized the results of 54 Pavlovian studies in which stimulus intensity was manipulated. Since stimulus intensity alters the vigor of some *CR*s, this variable can complicate the generalization function. Razran's analysis corroborated Hovland's (1937*b*) study in which there is an increase in the magnitude of the *CR* as stimulus intensity increases. Studies using motor responses and instrumental paradigms usually report different results. In these studies generalization decrements occur both above and below the *CS* value. The amount of the decrement is typically greater with generalization tests based upon weaker stimuli than the *CS* than when based upon stronger stimuli (Grice and Saltz 1950; Miller and Greene 1954).

When more than one feature of the stimulus is changed, Fink and Patton (1953) found that varying the number led to progressively greater decrement in *CR*. The same was found by White (1958) and by Butter (1959) for children and pigeons, respectively.

The effect of discrimination training on generalization has been the source of considerable interest. Hull (1953) predicted a steepening of the gradient in the region between the reinforced and nonreinforced stimuli and a decrease in the total amount of generalized response strength. Contrary to the Lashley and Wade (1946, p. 74) view that the dimensions of a stimulus series do not exist for the learner until established by differential training, Grandine and Harlow (1948) and Grice (1948) report data to the contrary. Jenkins and Harrison (1958) report data that do, however, show that differential procedure results in the appearance of a gradient that is not otherwise apparent.

The ease with which generalized responses are extinguished is an important factor determining the rate at which a discrimination can be established (Hovland 1937*c*). It has been found that the *CR*s to the reinforced stimuli extinguish more slowly than the generalized *CR*s. The extinguished generalized responses appear to show greater spontaneous recovery so that after 24 hours following extinction, the difference between generalized and conditioned responses was no longer statistically significant. This is probably related to what Bindra and Cameron (1953) call the incubation effect and Perkins and Weyant (1958) the reminiscence of generalized responses.

The process of generalization was used by Hull (1943) to solve two logical problems relating to learning. If we are precise about it, it becomes clear that the same stimulus does not occur from trial to trial. How then do we learn? This is what Hull called the stimulus-learning paradox. While it presents no problem for the one-trial learning position, it does for the incremental learning position. But even the one-trial learning position has difficulty in explaining the fact that the learning is demonstrated at a later time when the cue stimulus can never be reinstated. This is the stimulus-evocation paradox. To solve these Hull theorized that habit strength, including generalized habit strength, summated. Bilodeau, Brown, and Meryman (1956) reported a small amount of summation. Kalish and Guttman

(1957) reported similar results. However, the amount seems to be much less than the theory suggests.

It is possible to look at the stimulus generalization data in two contrasting ways. One is that the dimension is an ordered set representing perceived similarities; the other is that the gradient is a result of a failure to perceive differences or a failure to discriminate (Guttman and Kalish 1956; Kalish 1958; Lashley and Wade 1946; Philips 1947; Schlosberg and Solomon 1943). Several investigators have taken the position that discriminability is simply a factor in stimulus generalization (Hull 1943; Shepard 1957, p. 1058).

SEMANTIC GENERALIZATION

Among various types of semantic generalization, the following are: (a) from object to sign; (b) from sign to sign; (c) from sign to object.

In the *object-to-sign* paradigm a reaction is conditioned to a nonverbal stimulus, such as a blue light, and then tests are made for generalization of the response to verbal signs (e.g., the words, "blue light") representing the original stimulus. Most of the standard *CR*s have been used, e.g., salivation, *PGR*, finger withdrawal, pupillary reflex. Some researchers (e.g., Osgood 1953) assume that there is a meaningful mediation process going on during the original conditioning of the reaction to the nonverbal stimulus, and that it is simultaneously conditioned to the new reaction. It is this process that provides the mechanism for mediated generalization. Most of the research has been reported by Russians who have used Pavlovian methods, e.g., Kapustnik (1930); Smolenskaya (1934); Kotliarevsky (1935); Metzner (1942); Taugott (1934); and Taugott and Fadeyeva (1934).

In the *sign-to-sign* paradigm, the response is conditioned to one sign and tested for with another. Here the role of a meaningful mediation process is more obviously implied. Razran (1939*a*) used his salivary conditioning procedure and flashed words and short sentences on a screen in random order at 2-min intervals while six adults were eating. Conditioning developed rapidly and in the second session, tests of transfer to new words and sentences were made. Generalization from the original (e.g., "poverty is degrading") to statements having total agreement in meaning was greatest. However, when the copulas were reversed (e.g, poverty is not uplifting), there was less generalization than when the entire meaning was reversed. With single words (e.g., "style" to "fashion") generalization is greater than to phonetically similar homonyms (e.g., "style" to "stile") suggesting that semantic factors are dominant over physical factors. Riess (1940; 1946), working on semantic generalization, studied it developmentally from 7 years 9 months through 18 years 6 months, using *GSR* to selected verbal stimuli associated with a buzzer whereas neutral words were not. He then tested for generalization to synonyms, antonyms, and homonyms, and found that synonyms increase in importance with development, whereas the hymonyms decrease. The course of antonyms in development is not clear from these data. This may or may not be due to the methodological problem of using different words at different age levels. Goodwin, Long, and Welch (1945) used species-genus relationships. In studies in which the *CS* and test stimuli were words there has been evidence of semantic generalization. Diven (1936), for example, reported that a *GSR* conditioned to the word *barn* generalized to other rural words, and his finding was verified by Lacey and Smith (1945) and by Lacey, Smith, and Green (1955) who used heart rate as their measure. However, Keller (1943) conditioned *PGR* to a boy scout hat picture and tested for generalization to a picture of a fireman's hat and to the word *hat*. As control stimuli she used words like *duck* and *ball*. While she found significant amounts of generalization to the fireman's hat, she did not find it to the word *hat*.

The relationships studied do not exhaust the logical possibilities. For example, generalization from sign-to-object, although the reverse of the developmental process, is of interest, not only because of verbal training for manual skills but also because of the frequently demonstrated finding that when *S-R* associations are formed, the learner also develops the ability to make the backward direction of association. Kapustnik (1930) demonstrated that salivary reactions to verbal signs representing visual and auditory stimuli transferred to these stimuli themselves. The existence of social or minority group prejudices among individuals who have not had personal experiences suggest that verbal associations transfer to individuals; however, data actually demonstrating the acquisition of these attitudes are not available. Still another interesting relationship is that between or among a physically dissimilar set of objects, e.g., objects belonging to a loved one. For this to happen, the stimuli need be similar only in that they had been conditioned to the same or similar response, e.g., a name. This analysis requires that the *same* mediating reaction be made to all of the objects. This explanation is easier to apply after the fact because of the methodological problem of specifying before the fact the degrees of similarity among mediating processes.

MEDIATED GENERALIZATION

Semantic generalization is really a special case of mediated generalization. The classical study of mediated generalization was conducted by Shipley (1933). His paradigm is diagrammed in three steps (Fig. 24–4):

Lumsdaine (1939) asked the question, "Did 'light flash' elicit the winking movement?" To obtain an answer, he repeated the study and found that the light did elicit a winking movement which was followed closely by finger withdrawal. However, in some cases the withdrawal reaction antedated eyelid movements. One possibility is that the eyelid movement is only an approximate, though overt, index of the internal mediation process. Using Osgood's extension of Hull as a response derived mediation theory, it could be argued that the observed *R* (e.g., eye wink) is a collection of smaller component responses some of which occur separately and anticipate the tap-on-the-cheek. In the Shipley study this would be S_2 as diagrammed. These fractional anticipatory responses (*rs*) are the mediators according to this theory. Each is assumed to have stimulus consequences which can be cues (*CS*) for other responses.

A reasonable question to ask is: "What kinds of events can serve as mediators?" The answer is that we do not know at this time; however, some inferences can be made from several experiments. One type are the responses associated with emotions or affective behavior, e.g., fear. (See Figure 24–5.)

A study reported by Miller (1948) fits the above description except for Step 3. His Step 3 is diagrammed below (see Fig. 24–6). Also in his study S_2 is a ratchet instead of a barrier (walled box) turning is a consequence of the running behavior, we call this R_2, mediated behavior. Here the mediator is mostly internal, presumed to be fear or anxiety; a visible index of the internal process is running, the overt *R*. The sequence goes like this: *A* (white-walled box) is associated with *B* (fear and running—a complex response). The *B* event (fear and running) is associated with *C* (ratchet turning). Now *A* is associated with *C*—white-walled box with ratchet turning. This illustrates how a fear reaction can mediate the transfer of another *R* to a cue stimulus with which it was not directly paired.

If we assume that fear is one instance of a class of events called emotions (construct validity) which are autonomic nervous system responses, then the above experiment could be considered as a basis for generalizing to all autonomic system events as possible mediators. In addition to emotion, the autonomic system operates when motivation is present; con-

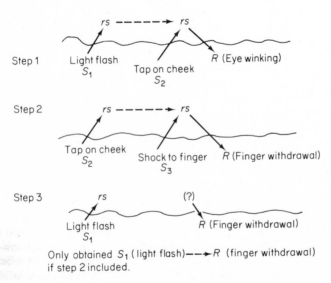

Only obtained S_1 (light flash)———▶ *R* (finger withdrawal) if step 2 included.

Fig. 24-4.

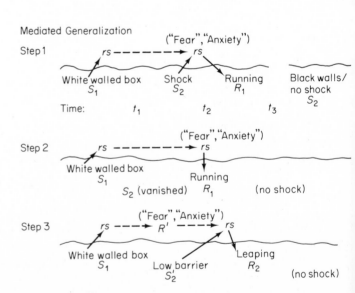

Fig. 24-5. *Diagram of a paradigm that involves anxiety.*

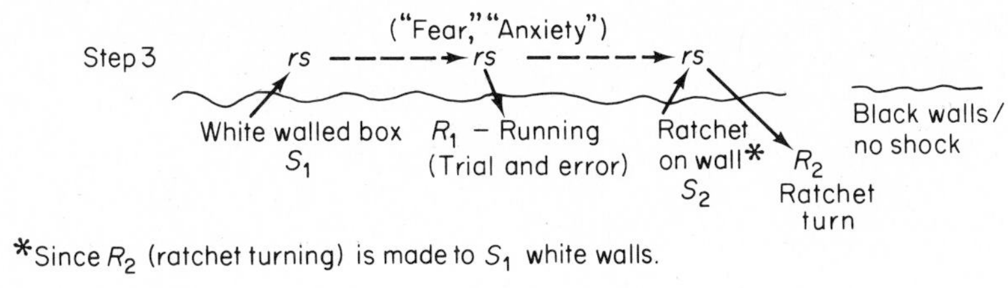

Step 3

rs ----→ rs ----→ rs ("Fear," "Anxiety")

White walled box S_1 R_1 – Running (Trial and error)   Ratchet on wall* S_2 R_2 Ratchet turn   Black walls/ no shock

*Since R_2 (ratchet turning) is made to S_1 white walls.

Fig. 24-6.

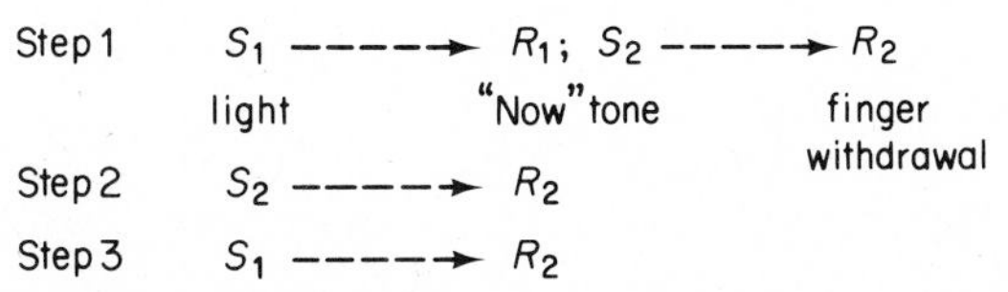

Step 1 S_1 ----→ R_1; S_2 ----→ R_2
          light   "Now"tone   finger withdrawal

Step 2 S_2 ----→ R_2

Step 3 S_1 ----→ R_2

Fig. 24-7. *Here a verbal response mediated the linkage, i.e. saying "Now." Step 1 established a many-to-one relationship, i.e., two stimuli each associated with a simple response. Also note that R_1 and R_2 are capable of occurring concurrently.*

sequently a potentially useful hypothesis is that these classes of behavior also could serve as mediators—emotions, motivations.

This added to the first example indicates that both skeletal and smooth muscle response systems and their cues can be mediators. Can any other system serve as a mediator?

PERCEPTUAL MEDIATION

Ellson (1941; 1942) produced hallucinations in human subjects by first pairing a light with a faint tone which was gradually intensified until it exceeded threshold. He tested with the light and asked Ss if they heard the tone. They reported hearing it when it was below threshold—a potential mediator.

Others have reported sensory-sensory conditioning or sensory preconditioning as it is sometimes called. Karn (1947), for example, obtained positive results even after a full day intervened between the original pairing of *light* (S_1) with buzzer (S_2) and the buzzer in conditioning. Then the light (S_1) when presented was followed by the conditioned response (R_1).

VERBAL MEDIATION

Wickens and Briggs (1951) went a step further. They showed how this type of result could be obtained without ever pairing the two sensory stimuli with each other. They had their Ss say. "Now" when either a light flashed or a tone sounded (Light— "now"; tone—"now"). Later on, the Ss responded to a *tone* in a typical finger-withdrawal study (tone—finger withdrawal). When light was presented, Ss responded to light as frequently as the sensory-sensory group.

Wickens and Briggs (1951) offer an explanation: Mediation through the verbal response: "Now." This response is the "built-in" common element acquired through training. Their paradigm was as follows (see Figure 24–7).

HIGHER-ORDER CONDITIONING

After a new association has been established between a cue and a response, the cue stimulus will function as an eliciting stimulus. This process can be continued for several steps, but

the limits have not yet been determined. The higher order association is usually more readily extinguished and requires continued reinforcement of the prior association to remain effective.

The problem in extending the length of the high order associations has been perceived as a problem in the maintenance of the motivation-reinforcement properties of the earlier associations upon which the later ones are built. No question seems to arise in connection with the continuation of the elicitation function. As previously indicated, the elicitation and reinforcement functions of stimuli may be aspects of the same stimulus or provided by different stimuli. In the instrumental paradigms the elicitation and reinforcement functions are provided by separate stimuli. Thus in higher order conditioning the practical problem is to *reinforce* the mediating behavior so that there is continuity of responses eventuating in the terminal overt R. The intermediate overt Rs may become extinguished because of lack of reinforcement causing the long sequences to break apart. We know that in serial learning the central part of the series is the least well learned, suggesting a critical problem.

It may be useful to examine higher order conditioning as a method in relation to the typical serial learning method. In higher order conditioning, the procedure is as shown in Figure 24–8, where Es is used instead of UCS.

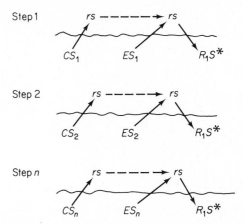

Step 1   rs ----→ rs

          CS_1 ES_1 R_1S*

Step 2   rs ----→ rs

          CS_2 ES_2 R_1S*

Step n rs ----→ rs

          CS_n ES_n R_1S*

Fig. 24-8. *Step 1 makes CS_1 an ES, here designated ES_2 in Step 2. Step 2 makes CS_2 an ES, etc.*

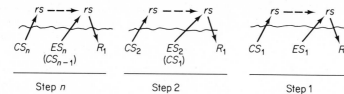

Fig. 24-9. *A set of steps in higher order conditioning. (Note that a new CS is added in taking each step, so that by Step 5, for example, CS_5 uses CS_4 as an ES, and it in turn used CS_3 as an ES, etc.*

In higher order conditioning, a phenomenon known to be limited in the number of steps that can be accomplished, we are dealing with a sequence of stimulus substitution steps. An analogy in verbal learning would be the substitution of different foreign language words as cues (e.g., first French, then German, then Swedish, etc.) for an English response. The limited number of substitutions observed with lower animals may not apply to the human learner, but this has not been studied. Also it may be that each of the preceding associations must be made in order for the learner to make R_1, once a number of cue substitutions have been made.

To make the relationship with serial learning clearer, let us place the individual steps in relation to one another, from *right* to left (the reverse of the order used). (See Figure 24–9.)

Thus the chain is CS_6—CS_5—CS_4—CS_3—CS_2—CS_1—R_1), a retrograde (from end to beginning) conditioning sequence might extend the chain.

Serial Learning

Serial learning is defined operationally in terms of a set of associations which has a definite time order to it. In other words, the cue stimuli and their responses are sequenced in an invariant order. Like higher order conditioning, there is a sequence of different cue stimuli. Unlike higher order conditioning, however, there is a set of different overt Rs, one per cue stimulus. A further difference is in the method of training typically employed. Whereas the higher order conditioning method is to add one new cue after another using the immediately preceding one as an eliciting stimulus, in serial learning a set of different S-R associations becomes chained. Furthermore, in higher order conditioning the last cue is expected to elicit the criterion response, R_1, immediately; whereas in serial learning the first cue is expected to set off a response sequence, each response being a cue for the next. Thus the higher order conditioning paradigm

is a progressive process of cue substitution, and serial learning, while it involves cue substitution, eventuates in the building of more and more complex responses.

We can diagram serial learning in the same way we used to describe the other paradigms. (See Figure 24–10.)

Osgood (1953) relies upon the "light weight" idea to account for the fractional anticipatory response cue as a mediator. This notion says that the inertia of the response is the critical factor. An alternative hypothesis described above is that the critical factor is the rapid extinction of higher order conditioned responses.

Hull-Osgood S-R Mediation Theory

Critical notions of Osgood's position will be outlined. General background of Hull's theory is assumed (Hilgard 1956). See Osgood (1953) for detailed description of the process.

A. First Step. Three stimuli S_1, S_2, and S_3 are dissimilar. Each is separately associated with an overt response. In establishing this connection mediation processes are generated which are common to all three stimuli since each was associated with the same overt response. $S_1 \rightarrow r_{m1} \rightarrow {}_{sm1} \rightarrow R_1$, $S_2 \rightarrow r_{m1} \rightarrow {}_{sm1} \rightarrow R_1$, $S_3 \rightarrow r_{m1} \rightarrow {}_{sm1} \rightarrow R_1$.

B. Second Step. One of the stimuli, S_1, is associated with a new response, R_2. This leads the same type of events sequence but produces new mediators since a new overt response is involved. $S_1 \rightarrow r_{m1} \rightarrow s_{m1} \rightarrow R_1$ $S_1 \rightarrow r_{m2} \rightarrow s_{m2} \rightarrow R_2$.

C. Third Step. S_1 is now attached to two separate overt responses each of which has its own mediating process. Consequently, when S_1 is presented both mediating processes are

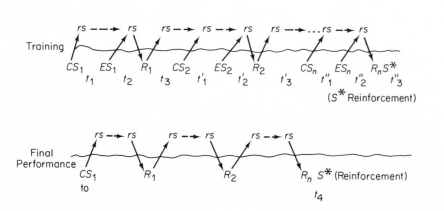

Fig. 24-10. *Stages in serial learning.*

elicited. The order in which the events occur permit the crossing over of each of these processes. Thus different mediating combinations may arise.

$$S_1 \quad \begin{matrix} r_{m1} \longrightarrow {}_{sm1} \longrightarrow R_1 \\ \\ r_{m2} \longrightarrow {}_{sm2} \longrightarrow R_2 \end{matrix}$$

D. Fourth Step. S_2, another stimulus not associated with R_2 could now elicit the R_2 response. This could come about because, as shown earlier, S_2 has been associated with r_{m1} when it was conditioned to R_1. r_{m1} as a mediating "perceptual reaction" could, as indicated in step 3 above, elicit the ${}_{sm2}$ ("stimulus effects") which in turn would cue R_2. Thus, while S_2 has never previously been associated with R_2, it could elicit this response through the mediation process described.

The above describes an acquired mediating situation. Osgood also states that "... the probability of two stimuli being associated with the same (perceptual) mediating process varies inversely with the physical differences between them" (p. 360).

Stimulus-objects typically elicit a complex pattern of reactions from the organism, some of which are dependent upon the sensory presence of the object for their occurrence and others of which can occur without the object being present. (p. 396)

When other stimuli occur in conjunction with the stimulus-object, they tend to be conditioned to the total pattern of reactions elicited by the object; when later presented without the support of the stimulus-object, these other stimuli elicit only the 'detachable' (light weight) reactions." (Osgood 1953, p. 396).

This latter statement identifies the so-called fractions of behavior which are elicited by objects and which come to serve as signs of these objects. Presumably they are limited only by sequences of events in the physical world and by the sensory capacities of the organism. Osgood goes on to say "of the total pattern of 'detachable' reactions conditioned to the sign, some fraction becomes the stable mediation process," (p. 397). Borrowing from Hull, he states, "... mediating reactions will tend to become as reduced as possible, while retaining their distinctive cue functions" (p. 397). In this connection he evokes three principles: (a) response interference; (b) energy expenditure; and (c) discriminatory capacity. The first principal says that mediating reactions that interfere with goal-oriented behavior will tend to be extinguished. The second says that the more energy expended in making a mediating reaction, the less likely it is to survive in the reduction process. The third says the greater the discriminatory capacity of an organism, the more reduced and implicit can become the "detachable" reactions finally included in the stable mediating process.

Whereas C. Morris links sign and object through partial identity of object-produced and disposition-produced behavior, Osgood links sign and object through partial identity of the "disposition" itself with the behavior elicited by the object. Words represent things because they produce some replica of the *actual behavior* toward these things. This is the crucial identification—the mechanism that ties signs to particular stimulus-objects and not to others. A formal statement of this follows:

... a pattern of stimulation which is not the object is a sign of the object if it evokes in an organism a mediating reaction, this (a) being some fractional part of the total behavior elicited by the object and (b) producing distinctive self-stimulation that mediates responses which would not occur without the previous association of non object and object patterns of stimulation. (Osgood 1953, pp. 695–96)

In this analysis the sign is r_m and the total behavior elicited by the object is $R_{t \cdot sm}$ is self-stimulation which occurs between the explicit stimulation and the overt response. The connection between ${}_{sm}$ and R is called the mediating relation. It is to be contrasted with the semantic relation—the relation between sign and its referent. The mediating relation is composed of hierarchies of habits associating intervening variables with overt behavior. The relative strengths of such habits depend upon momentary contextual conditions and pervasive cultural factors which have influenced the reward system in a particular society. The empathic relation is that between the response made to the sign (R_x) and that made to the object represented (R_t). At one extreme R_x is practically identical with R_t and the empathy is maximal—the learner responses to the sign exactly as he would to the object. An example is a fractional anticipatory goal response to a sign, salivation in the absence of food. Salivation is only part of the consumatory response involved in eating. These *rgs* and the stimuli they generate are what Hull meant as the mechanism which accounted for both knowledge and purpose. It is this same idea which Osgood employs in his mediation analysis of behavior.

The *rg*, or fractional goal response, since it comes between some external S and some goal response, *rg* can be considered an intervening variable hypothetical construct, depending upon how it is formulated by the particular theorist. Both Hull and Osgood consider it in terms of an intervening variable. But this is not always so apparent. The examples given suggest that it might also be a hypothetical construct in their thinking.

The *rg* is not limited to eating behavior. One can identify many anticipatory responses which do not require the manipulated objects associated with goal behavior for their occurrence.

References

ANREP, G. V. The irradiation of conditioned reflexes. *Proceedings of the Royal Society*, 1923, *94B*, 404–26.

ASRATYAN, E. A. Some aspects of the elaboration of conditioned connections and formation of their properties. *In* J. F. DELAFRESNAYE (ed.), *Brain mechanisms and learning*. Oxford: Blackwell, 1961.

BASS, M. J., and HULL, C. L. The irradiation of a tactile conditioned reflex in man. *Journal of Comparative Psychology*, 1934, *17*, 47–65.

BEECROFT, R. S. *Classical conditioning*. Goleta, Calif.: Psychonomic Press, 1966, p. 198.

BEKHTEREV, V. M. Die objective Untersuchung der neuropsychischen Tatigkeit. *Congrès International de Psychiatrie, de Neurologie, de Psychologie et de l'Assistance des Aliénés, 1st*, Amsterdam, 1904. Contes rendues des Travaux. Amsterdam: J. H. de Bus., 1908.

——— Die objektiv Untersuchung der neuropsychischen Sphare der Geisteskranken. *Zeitschrift für Psychotherapie und medizinische Psychologie*, 1909, *1*, 257–90.

——— Die Anwendung der Methode der motorischen Assoziationsreflexe zur Aufdeckung der Simulation. *Zeitschrift für die gesamte Neurologie und Psychiatrie*, 1912, *13*, 183–91.

——— *La psychologie objective*. Paris: Alcan, 1913a.

——— *Objective Psychologie oder Psychoreflexologie. Die Lehre von den Assoziationsreflexen.* Leipzig: Teubner, 1913*b*.

——— Die Perversitaten un Inversitaten vom Standpunkt der Reflexologie. *Archiv für Psychiatrie und Nervenkrankheiten,* 1923*a*, 68, 100–213.

——— Studium der Funktionen der Praefrontal und anderer Gebitete der Hirnrinde vermittelst der Associateivmotorischen Reflexe. *Schweiz. Archives of Neurology and Psychiatry,* 1923*b*, 13, 61–76.

——— Die Krankheiten der Personlichkeit vom Standpunkt der Reflexologie. *Zeitschrift für die gesamte Neurologie und Psychiatrie,* 1923*c*, 80, 265–309.

——— *General principles of human reflexology,* trans. E. and W. Murphy. New York: International, 1928.

——— *General principles of human reflexology.* New York: International, 1932.

BERSH, P. J., NOTTERMAN, J. M., and SCHOENFELD, W. N. Generalization to varying tone frequencies as a function of intensity of unconditioned stimulus. Air University, School of Aviation Medicine, U.S.A.F., Randolph AFB, Texas, 1956. 4 pp.

BINDRA, D., and CAMERON, LOIS. Changes in experimentally produced anxiety with the passage of time: Incubation effect. *Journal of Experimental Psychology,* 1953, 45, 197–203.

BITTERMAN, M. E. Classical conditioning in the goldfish as a function of the CS-US interval. *Journal of Comparative and Physiological Psychology,* 1964*b*, 58, 359–66.

BLACK, A. H., CAROLSON, N. J., and SOLOMON, R. L. Exploratory studies of the conditioning of autonomic responses in curarized dogs. *Psychological Monographs,* 1962, 76, no. 548.

BOICE, R., and DENNY, M. R. The conditioned licking response in rats as a function of the CS-UCS interval. *Psychonomic Science,* 1956, 3, 93–94.

BOREN, J. J., SIDMAN, M., and HERRNSTEIN, R. J. Avoidance, escape, and extinction as a function of shock intensity. *Journal of Comparative and Physiological Psychology,* 1959, 52, 420–25.

BRAUN, H. W., and GEISELHART, R. Age differences in the acquisition and extinction of the conditioned eyelid response. *Journal of Experimental Psychology,* 1959, 57, 386–88.

BROGDEN, W. J., LIPMAN, E. A., and CULLER, E. The role of incentive in conditioning and extinction. *American Journal of Psychology,* 1938, 51, 109–17.

BROWN, J. S. The generalization of approach responses as a function of stimulus intensity and strength of motivation. *Journal of Experimental Psychology,* 1942, 33, 209–26.

BUTTER, C. M. Stimulus generalization along the dimensions of wavelength and angular orientation. Ph. D. dissertation, Duke University, 1959.

CHAMPION, R. A. Interpolated UCS trials in GSR conditioning. *Journal of Experimental Psychology,* 1961, 62, 206–7.

CHAMPION, R. A., and JONES, J. E. Forward, backward, and pseudoconditioning of the GSR. *Journal of Experimental Psychology,* 1961, 62, 58–61.

COLLIER, G., and MARX, M. H. Changes in performance as a function of shifts in the magnitude of reinforcement. *Journal of Experimental Psychology,* 1959, 57, 305–9.

CRESPI, L. P. Quantitative variation of incentive and performance in the white rat. *American Journal of Psychology,* 1942, 55, 467–517.

——— Amount of reinforcement and level of performance. *Psychological Review,* 1944, 51, 341–57.

DENNY, M. R., and ADELMAN, H. M. Elicitation theory: I. An analysis of two typical learning situations. *Psychological Review,* 1955, 62, 290–96.

DENNY, M. R., and KING, G. F. Differential response learning on the basis of differential size of reward. *Journal of Genetic Psychology,* 1955, 87, 317–20.

DUFORT, R. H., and KIMBLE, G. A. Changes in response strength with changes in amount of reinforcement. *Journal of Experimental Psychology,* 1956, 51, 185–91.

——— Ready signals and the effect of UCS presentations in eyelid conditioning. *Journal of Experimental Psychology,* 1958, 56, 1–7.

EROFEEVA, M. Contributions a l'étude des reflexes conditionnels destructifs. *Comptes Rendus Hebdomodaires des Séances et Memoirs de la Sociète de Biologie,* 1916, 79, 239–40.

ESTES, W. K. All-or-none processes in learning and retention. *American Psychologist,* 1964, 19, 16–25.

FERSTER, C. B. Sustained behavior under delayed reinforcement. *Journal of Experimental Psychology,* 1953, 45, 219–24.

FERSTER, C. B., and SKINNER, B. F. *Schedules of reinforcement.* New York: Appleton-Century-Crofts, 1957.

FITZWATER, M. E., and REISMAN, M. N. Comparison of forward, simultaneous, backward, and pseudo-conditioning. *Journal of Experimental Psychology,* 1952, 44, 211–14.

FITZWATER, M. E., and THURSH, R. S. Acquisition of a conditioned response as a function of forward temporal contiguity. *Journal of Experimental Psychology,* 1956, 51, 59–61.

GAGNÉ, R. M. *Conditions of learning.* New York: Holt, Rinehart, & Winston, 1965.

GAKKEL, L. B., and ZININA, N. V. Changes of higher nerve function in people over 60 years of age. *Fiziologicheskii Zhurnal,* S.S.S.R. 1953, 39, 533–39.

GERALL, A. A., SAMPSON, P. B., and BOSLOV, G. L. Classical conditioning of human pupillary dilation. *Journal of Experimental Psychology,* 1957, 54, 467–74.

GOODRICH, K. P., ROSS, L. E., and WAGNER, A. R. Performance in eyelid conditioning following interpolated presentations of the UCS. *Journal of Experimental Psychology,* 1957, 53, 214–17.

GRAHAM, C. H., and GAGNÉ, R. M. The acquisition, extinction, and spontaneous recovery of a conditioned operant response. *Journal of Experimental Psychology,* 1940, 26, 251–80.

GRANDINE, L., and HARLOW, H. F. Generalization of the characteristics of a single learned stimulus by monkeys. *Journal of Comparative Physiology and Psychology,* 1948, 41, 327–38.

GRANT. D. A. The pseudo-conditioned eyelid response. *Journal of Experimental Psychology,* 1943*a*, 32, 139–49.

——— Sensitization and association in eyelid conditioning. *Journal of Experimental Psychology,* 1943*b*, 32, 201–12.

——— A sensitized eyelid reaction related to the conditioned eyelid response. *Journal of Experimental Psychology,* 1945, 35, 393–403.

GRANT, D. A., and NORRIS, E. B. Eyelid conditioning as influenced by the presence of sensitized beta-responses. *Journal of Experimental Psychology,* 1947, 37, 423–33.

GRETHER, W. F. Pseudo-conditioning without stimulation encountered in attempted backward conditioning. *Journal of Experimental Psychology,* 1938, 25, 91–96.

GRICE, G. R. An experimental study of the gradient of reinforcement in maze learning. *Journal of Experimental Psychology,* 1942, 30, 475–89.

GRICE, G. R., and DAVIS, J. D. Mediated stimulus equivalence and distinctiveness in human conditioning. *Journal of Experimental Psychology,* 1958, 55, 565–71.

——— Effect of concurrent responses on the evocation and generalization of the conditioned eyeblink. *Journal of Experimental Psychology,* 1960, 59, 391–95.

GRICE, G. R., and SALTZ, E. The generalization of an instrumental response to stimuli varying in the size dimension. *Journal of Experimental Psychology,* 1950, 40, 702–8.

GRINGS, W. W., LOVELL, E. L., and HONNARD, R. R. GSR conditioning with preschool-age deaf children. *Journal of Comparative Physiology and Psychology,* 1961, 54, 143–48.

GUTHRIE, E. R. *The psychology of learning.* New York: Harper & Row, 1935.

GUTTMAN, N. Operant conditioning, extinction, and periodic reinforcement in relation to concentration of sucrose used as reinforcing agent. *Journal of Experimental Psychology,* 1953, 46, 213–24.

GUTTMAN, N., and KALISH, H. I. Discriminability and stimulus generalization. *Journal of Experimental Psychology,* 1956, 51, 79–88.

——— Experiments in discrimination. *Scientific American,* 1958, 198, 77–82.

HANSCHE, W. J., and GRANT, D. A. Onset versus termination of a stimulus as the CS in eyelid conditioning. *Journal of Experimental Psychology,* 1960, 59, 19–26.

HARLOW, H. F. Forward conditioning, backward conditioning, and pseudoconditioning in the goldfish. *Journal of Genetic Psychology,* 1939, 55, 49–58.

HARLOW, H. F., and TOLTZIEN, F. Formation of pseudo-conditioned responses in the cat. *Journal of Genetic Psychology,* 1940, 23, 367–75.

HARRIS, J. D. Forward conditioning, backward conditioning, and pseudo-conditioning, and adaptation to the conditioned stimulus. *Journal of Experimental Psychology,* 1941, 28, 491–502.

HERON, W. T. An automatic recording device for use in animal psychology. *Journal of Experimental Psychology*, 1933, *16*, 149–58.

HERON, W. T., and SKINNER, B. F. An apparatus for the study of animal behavior. *Psychological Record*, 1939, *3*, 166–76.

HILGARD, E. R., and CAMPBELL, A. A. The course of acquisition and retention of conditioned eyelid responses in man. *Journal of Experimental Psychology*, 1936, *19*, 227–47.

HILGARD, E. R., and HUMPHREYS, L. G. The retention of conditioned discrimination in man. *Journal of Genetic Psychology*, 1938, *19*, 111–25.

HILGARD, E. R., and MARQUIS, D. G. Acquisition, extinction, and retention of conditioned lid responses to light in dogs. *Journal of Comparative Psychology*, 1935, *19*, 29–58.

———— Conditioned eyelid responses in monkeys, with a comparison of dog, monkey, and man. *Psychological Monographs*, 1936, *47*, no. 212, 186–98.

———— *Conditioning and learning.* New York: Appleton-Century-Crofts, 1940.

HOVLAND, C. I. "Inhibition of reinforcement" and phenomena of experimental extinction. *Proceedings of the National Academy of Sciences*, 1936, *22*, 430–33.

———— The generalization of conditioned responses. I. The sensory generalization of conditioned responses with varying frequencies of tone. *Journal of Genetic Psychology*, 1937a, 17, 125–48.

———— The generalization of conditioned responses. II. The sensory generalization of conditioned responses with varying intensities of tone. *Journal of Genetic Psychology*, 1937b, *51*, 279–91.

———— The generalization of conditioned responses. III. Extinction, spontaneous recovery, and disinhibition of conditioned and of generalized responses. *Journal of Experimental Psychology*, 1937c, *21*, 47–62.

———— The generalization of conditioned responses. IV. The effects of varying amounts of reinforcement upon the degree of generalization of conditioned responses. *Journal of Experimental Psychology*, 1937d, *21*, 261–76.

HUGHES, B., and SCHLOSBERG, H. Conditioning in the white rat. IV. The conditioned lid reflex. *Journal of Experimental Psychology*, 1939, *23*, 641–50.

HULL, C. L. Knowledge and purpose as habit mechanisms. *Psychological Review*, 1930, *37*, 511–25.

———— The goal-gradient hypothesis and maze learning. *Psychological Review*, 1932, *39*, 25–43.

———— The concept of the habit-family hierarchy and maze learning. *Psychological Review*, 1934a, *41*, 33–54, 134–52.

———— The rat's speed-of-locomotion gradient in the approach to food. *Journal of Comparative Psychology*, 1934b, *17*, 393–422.

———— Learning: II. The factor of the conditioned reflex. *In* C. MURCHISON (ed.), *A handbook of general experimental psychology.* Worcester, Mass.: Clark University Press, 1934c.

———— *Principles of behavior.* New York: Appleton-Century-Crofts, 1943.

———— *A behavior system.* New Haven, Conn.: Yale University Press, 1952.

HUMPHREYS, L. G. Generalization as a function of method of reinforcement. *Journal of Experimental Psychology*, 1939, *25*, 361–72.

HUNT, E. L. Establishment of conditioned responses in chick embryos. *Journal of Comparative Physiology and Psychology*, 1949, *42*, 107–17.

HUTT, P. J. Rate of bar pressing as a function of quality and quantity of food reward. *Journal of Comparative Physiology and Psychology*, 1954, *47*, 235–39.

JENKINS, H. M., and HARRISON, R. H. Auditory generalization in the pigeons. Washington: Air Research and Development Command. TN No. 58–443; Astia Document No. 158248, 1958.

JENKINS, W. O., and CLAYTON, FRANCES L. Rate of responding and amount of reinforcement. *Journal of Comparative Physiology and Psychology*, 1949, *42*, 174–81.

JENKINS, W. O., PASCAL, G. R., and WALKER, R. W., JR. Deprivation and generalization. *Journal of Experimental Psychology*, 1958, *56*, 274–77.

JONES, J. E. The CS-UCS interval in conditioning short- and long-latency responses. *Journal of Experimental Psychology*, 1961, *62*, 612–617.

KELLOGG, W. N., and WALKER, E. L. "Ambiguous conditioning," a phenomenon of bilateral transfer. *Journal of Comparative Psychology*, 1938, *26*, 63–77.

KELLOGG, W. N., and WOLF, I. S. The nature of the response retained after several varieties of conditioning in the same subjects. *Journal of Experimental Psychology*, 1939, *24*, 366–83.

KIMBLE, G. A. *Hilgard and Marquist conditioning and learning*, 2d ed. New York: Appleton-Century-Crofts, 1961.

KIMBLE, G. A. and DUFORT, R. H. The associative factor in eyelid conditioning. *Journal of Experimental Psychology*, 1956, *52*, 386–91.

KIMBLE, G. A., MANN, LUCIE I., and DUFORT, R. H. Classical and instrumental eyelid conditioning. *Journal of Experimental Psychology*, 1955, *49*, 407–17.

KLINMAN, C. S., and BITTERMAN, M. E. Classical conditioning in the fish: The *CS-US* interval. *Journal of Comparative Physiology and Psychology*, 1963, *56*, 578–83.

KONORSKI, J. *Conditioned reflexes and neuron organization.* New York: Cambridge University Press, 1948.

LAMBERT, W. W., and SOLOMON, R. L. Extinction of a running response as a function of distance of a block point from the goal. *Journal of Comparative Physiology and Psychology*, 1952, *45*, 269–79.

LASHLEY, K. S., and WADE, M. The Pavlovian theory of generalization. *Psychological Review*, 1946, *53*, 72–87.

LIDDELL, H. S., JAMES, W. T., and ANDERSON, O. D. The comparative physiology of the conditioned motor reflex: Based on experiments with the pig, dog, sheep, goat, and rabbit. *Comparative Psychological Monographs*, 1934, *11*, no. 51.

LLOYD-MORGAN, C. *An introduction to comparative psychology.* London: Scott, 1894.

MCADAM, D., KNOTT, J. R., and CHIRORINI, J. Classical conditioning in the cat as a function of the CS-US interval. *Psychonomic Science*, 1965, *3*, 89–90.

MCALLISTER, W. R. Eyelid conditioning as a function of the CS-USC interval. *Journal of Experimental Psychology*, 1953, *45*, 417–422.

MACDONALD, ANNETTE. The effect of adaptation to the unconditioned stimulus upon the formation of conditioned avoidance responses. *Journal of Experimental Psychology*, 1946, *36*, 1–12.

MAHER, WINIFRED, B., and WICKENS, D. D. Effect of differential quantity of reward on acquisition and performance of a maze habit. *Journal of Comparative Physiology and Psychology*, 1954, *47*, 44–46.

MARQUIS, D. G., and HILGARD, E. R. Conditioned lid responses to light in dogs after removal of the visual cortex. *Journal of Comparative Psychology*, 1936, *22*, 157–78.

MARQUIS, D. P. Can conditioned responses be established in the newborn infant? *Journal of Genetic Psychology*, 1931, *39*, 479–92.

MEDNICK, S. A., and WILD, C. Reciprocal augmentation of generalization and anxiety. *Journal of Experimental Psychology*, 1963, *63*, 621–26.

MILLER, W. C., and GREENE, J. E. Generalization of an avoidance response to various intensities of tone. *Journal of Comparative Physiology and Psychology*, 1954, *47*, 136–39.

MOELLER, G. The CS-UCS interval in GSR conditioning. *Journal of Experimental Psychology*, 1954, *48*, 162–66.

MONTPELLIER, G. DE. An experiment on the order of elimination of blind alleys in maze learning. *Journal of Genetic Psychology*, 1933, *43*, 123–39.

MORGAN, J. J. B., and MORGAN, S. S. Infant learning as a developmental index. *Journal of Genetic Psychology*, 1944, *65*, 281–89.

MOWRER, O. H. An experimental analogue of "regression" with incidental observations on "reaction formation." *Journal of Abnormal Social Psychology*, 1940, *35*, 56–87.

NISSEN, H. W., and ELDER, J. H. The influence of amount of incentive on delayed response performances of chimpanzees. *Journal of Genetic Psychology*, 1935, *47*, 49–72.

NOBLE, M., and ADAMS, C. K. Conditioning in pigs as a function of the interval between CS and US. *Journal of Comparative Physiology and Psychology*, 1963, *56*, 215–19.

NOBLE, M., GRUENDER, A., and MEYER, D. R. Conditioning in fish as a function of the interval between CS and US. *Journal of Comparative Physiology and Psychology*, 1959, *52*, 236–39.

NOBLE, M., and HARDING, G. E. Conditioning in rhesus monkeys as a function of the interval between CS and US. *Journal of Comparative Physiology and Psychology*, 1963, *56*, 220–34.

NOTTERMAN, J. M., SCHOENFELD, W. N., and BERSH, P. J. Partial reinforcement and conditioned heart rate response in human subjects. *Science*, 1952, *115*, 77–79.

OSGOOD, C. E. *Method and theory in experimental psychology.* New York: Oxford University Press, 1953.

PASSEY, G. E. The influence of intensity of unconditioned stimulus upon acquisition of a conditioned response. *Journal of Experimental Psychology*, 1948 *38*, 420–28.

PAVLOV, I. P. *The work of digestive glands.* Trans. W. H. Thompson. London: Charles Griffin, 1902.

————— The scientific investigation of the psychical faculties or processes in the higher animals. *Science*, 1906, *24*, 613–19. Also in *Lancet*, *2*, 911–15.

————— The reply to a physiologist to psychologists. *Psychological Review*, 1932, *39*, 91–127.

PERKINS, C. C., JR., and WEYANT, R. G. The interval between training and test trials as a determiner of the slope of generalization gradients. *Journal of Comparative Physiology and Psychology*, 1958, *51*, 596–600.

PROKASY, W. F., JR., GRANT, D. A., and MEYERS, N. A. Eyelid conditioning as a function of unconditioned stimulus intensity and intertrial interval. *Journal of Experimental Psychology*, 1958, *55*, 242–46.

RAZRAN, G. Stimulus generalization of conditioned responses. *Psychological Bulletin*, 1949, *46*, 337–65.

REYNOLDS, B. The acquisition of a trace conditioned response as a function of the magnitude of the stimulus trace. *Journal of Experimental Psychology*, 1945a, *35*, 15–30.

————— Extinction of trace conditioned responses as a function of the spacing of trials during the acquisition and extinction series. *Journal of Experimental Psychology*, 1945b, *35*, 81–95.

————— A repetition of the Blodgett experiment on 'latent learning.' *Journal of Experimental Psychology*, 1945c, *35*, 504–16.

ROSENBAUM, G. Stimulus generalization as a function of level of experimentally induced anxiety. *Journal of Experimental Psychology*, 1953, *45*, 35–43.

SALTZMAN, I. J. Maze learning in the absence of primary reinforcement: A study of secondary reinforcement. *Journal of Comparative Physiology and Psychology*, 1949, *42*, 161–73.

SEARS, R. R. Effect of optic lobe ablation on the visuo-motor behavior of goldfish. *Journal of Comparative Psychology*, 1934, *17*, 233–65.

SEWARD, J. P. Secondary reinforcement as tertiary motivation: A revision of Hull's revision. *Psychological Review*, 1950, *57*, 362–74.

SHEFFIELD, F. D. Avoidance training and the contiguity principle. *Journal of Comparative Physiology and Psychology*, 1948, *41*, 165–77.

SIDMAN, M. Avoidance conditioning with brief shock and no exteroceptive warning signal. *Science*, 1953a, *118*, 157–58.

————— Two temporal parameters of the maintenance of avoidance behavior by the white rat. *Journal of Comparative Physiology and Psychology*, 1953b, *46*, 253–61.

SKINNER, B. F. Two types of conditioned reflex and a pseudo type. *Journal of Genetic Psychology*, 1935, *12*, 66–77.

————— *The behavior of organisms; an experimental analysis.* New York: Appleton-Century, 1938.

————— Are theories of learning necessary? *Psychological Review*, 1950, *57*, 193–216.

————— *Science and human behavior.* New York: Macmillan, 1953.

SPELT, D. K. Conditioned responses in the human fetus *in utero*. *Psychological Bulletin*, 1938, *35*, 712–13.

————— The conditioning of the human fetus *in utero*. *Journal of Experimental Psychology*, 1948, *38*, 338–46.

SPENCE, K. W. The role of secondary reinforcement in delayed-reward learning. *Psychological Review*, 1947, *54*, 1–8.

————— *Behavior theory and conditioning.* New Haven, Conn.: Yale University Press, 1956.

THOMPSON, R., and MCCONNELL, J. Classical conditioning in the planarian, *dugesia dorotocephala*. *Journal of Comparative Physiology and Psychology*, 1955, *48*, 65–68.

THORNDIKE, E. L. Animal intelligence. An experimental study of the associative processes in animals. *Psychological Monographs*, 1898, *2*, no. 8.

————— *Animal intelligence.* New York: Macmillan, 1911.

TOLMAN, E. C. *Purposive behavior in animals and men.* New York: Appleton-Century, 1932.

VOEKS, V. W. Acquisition of S-R connections: A test of Hull's and Guthrie's theories. *Journal of Experimental Psychology*, 1954, *47*, 137–47.

WEINSTOCK, S. Resistance to extinction of a running response following partial reinforcement under widely spaced trials. *Journal of Comparative Physiology and Psychology*, 1954, *47*, 318–23.

WENDT, G. R. Two and one-half year retention of a conditioned response. *Journal of Genetic Psychology*, 1937, *17*, 178–80.

WHITE, C. T., and SCHLOSBERG, H. Degree of conditioning of the GSR as a function of the period of delay. *Journal of Experimental Psychology*, 1952, *43*, 357–62.

WHITE, S. H. Generalization of an instrumental response with variation in two attributes of the CS. *Journal of Experimental Psychology*, 1958, *56*, 339–43.

WICKENS, D. D., SCHRODER, H. M., and SNIDE, J. D. Primary stimulus generalization of the GSR under two conditions. *Journal of Experimental Psychology*, 1954, *47*, 52–56.

WICKENS, D. D., and WICKENS, C. D. Some factors related to pseudo-conditioning. *Journal of Experimental Psychology*, 1942, *31*, 518–26.

WILSON, W., WEISS, E. J., and AMSEL, A. Two tests of the Sheffield hypothesis concerning resistance to extinction, partial reinforcement, and distribution of practice. *Journal of Experimental Psychology*, 1955, *50*, 51–60.

WOLFE, HELEN M. Conditioning as a function of the interval between the conditioned and the original stimulus. *Journal of Genetic Psychology*, 1932, 7, 80–103.

WULFF, J. J., and STOLUROW, L. M. The role of class-descriptive cues in paired-associate learning. *Journal of Experimental Psychology*, 1957, *53*, 199–206.

YOSHIOKA, J. G. Weber's law in the discrimination of maze distance by the white rat. *University of California Publications in Psychology*, 1929, *4*, 155–84.

ZEAMAN, D. Response latency as a function of the amount of reinforcement. *Journal of Experimental Psychology*, 1949, *39*, 466–83.

ZENER, K. The significance of behavior accompanying conditioned salivary secretion for theories of the conditioned response. *American Journal of Psychology*, 1937, *50*, 384–403.

Historical Development

The history of operant conditioning begins with B. F. Skinner, then a graduate student in the Department of Psychology at Harvard. The atmosphere of the department in those days has recently been described by Keller (1970). In his autobiographical papers, however, Skinner (1956, 1967) has indicated that the members of the psychology faculty had relatively little effect on his basic orientation. The names to which he gives most frequent mention are: the biologists J. Loeb and W. J. Crozier who "talked about animal behavior without mentioning the nervous system" (1956, p. 223); C. S. Sherrington; I. P. Pavlov; the behaviorist, J. B. Watson; the antibehaviorist, B. R. Russell; and a fellow student, F. S. Keller.

The first part of his dissertation, published as a separate paper under the title of *The Concept of the Reflex in the Description of Behavior* (Skinner 1931), was a historical survey and an operational analysis of the concept of the reflex. Despite the fact that the concept had developed within the science of physiology, a careful inspection of the observations on which it was based showed that it involved nothing more than a functional relationship between two events, a stimulus and a response. Although Sherrington's synapse, for example, could be localized anatomically, in essence it was a hypothetical construct designed to account for a set of behavioral relationships. Moreover, Pavlov had shown that careful control of environmental conditions could be substituted for the surgical preparations normally employed by physiological investigators. This cleared the way for the adoption of the reflex as the basic unit of analysis for a science of behavior. To try to investigate the relationship between all of the subject's behavior and the total environment would overwhelm us with a mass of detail. Therefore, it was necessary to study something simpler, i.e., the relationship of a part of behavior (a response) to a part, or a modification of a part, of the environment (a stimulus).

The strength of such a reflex could be expressed or measured in terms of what he was later to call its "static properties": its threshold, its latency, the size and duration of the after-discharge,

James A. Dinsmoor

Operant Conditioning

25

and the ratio between the magnitude of the response and the intensity of the stimulus. Changes in these characteristics could therefore be used to study changes in reflex strength as a function of other variables, external to the original correlation between the stimulus and the response. Sherrington, for example, had shown that repeated elicitation of the response over a limited period of time produced an increase in latency and threshold and a decrease in the after-discharge and the magnitude of the response—a phenomenon known as "reflex fatigue." The effects of other variables, such as drive, emotion, and conditioning, could be studied in similar fashion. The resulting laws describing these changes in reflex strength would serve as the subject matter of the science of behavior.

In the meantime, as later described in *A Case History in Scientific Method* (1956), Skinner had been busy in the laboratory studying a variety of different reflexes in the rat. Finally he settled on that of eating. As his measure of reflex strength, he used the rate at which the rat ate successive pellets of food. By this time he had already discovered the cumulative recorder, and he used this device to trace the changes in rate as a function of continued ingestion (Skinner 1930). The results were summarized in a mathematical formula. The number of pellets (N) eaten by any time (t) during a period of continuous access to food was given by the equation $N = kt^n$.

For the empirical portion of his thesis, he offered two more studies of the effects of "drive" on the reflex of eating. In the first, he showed that interrupting the rat's access to food for a brief period of time led to a "compensatory" increase in rate, and in the second he showed that the form of his equation was independent of the particular reflex with which the behavior of eating was initiated. For the latter study, he added to his procedure a lever which the rat was required to depress before receiving his pellet. Naturally, he used the cumulative recorder once more to plot the acquisition of this new reflex, and soon he found himself in possession of a record of a change in reflex strength due to yet another type of variable, that of conditioning (Figure 25–1). This record he published in a paper entitled "On the Rate of Formation of a Conditioned Reflex" (1932).

In 1931, a few months after passing his orals, he moved his equipment into a laboratory in the basement of the new biology building. There he spent the next five years, first on a National Research Council Fellowship and later as a Junior Fellow in Harvard's Society of Fellows. His work on such problems as

extinction, discrimination, and chaining of the new reflex was first published in a series of papers in the *Proceedings of the National Academy of Sciences* and in the *Journal of General Psychology*; later it was collected, along with other work, in a single volume, *The Behavior of Organisms* (1938).

TWO TYPES OF CONDITIONING

By the time this work was completed, however, it had become obvious to Skinner that the procedure he was using to condition lever pressing did not conform to the paradigm employed by Pavlov to condition the secretion of the salivary glands. Since the change in reflex strength was produced by "presentation of a reinforcing stimulus in a certain temporal relation to behavior" (1937, p. 272), he did regard it as a type of conditioning. But in the procedure used by Pavlov the reinforcing stimulus (acid or meat powder) was paired or correlated with a *stimulus*; therefore, Skinner referred to this procedure as *Type S* conditioning. In his own procedure, however, the reinforcing stimulus (pellet of food) was temporally associated with a *response*; therefore, he called this *Type R*. A corresponding distinction was drawn between two types of behavior. "The kind of response that is made to specific stimulation," he called *respondent*, and "the kind of response which occurs spontaneously in the absence of any stimulation with which it may be specifically correlated" (p. 274) he called *operant*. Since by definition all conditioned reflexes of Type S were respondent and all conditioned reflexes of Type R were operant, it later become the custom to apply the labels for the two classes of behavior to the two types of conditioning. Also, since operant behavior did not conform to the historical connotations of the word "reflex," the latter term was eventually restricted to respondents (e.g., Skinner 1950, 1953).

MINNESOTA, INDIANA, AND BACK TO HARVARD

In the fall of 1936, Skinner obtained a job teaching small sections of the introductory psychology course at the University of Minnesota. It was there, in collaboration with one of his students, W. K. Estes, that he conducted the first study of what is now known as conditioned suppression, the effect on the rate

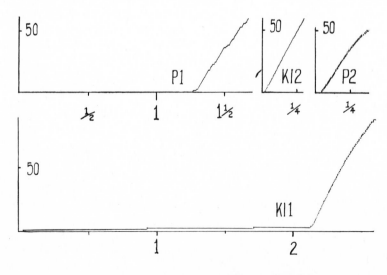

Fig. 25-1. *A reproduction of the first published records of the conditioning of bar pressing* [Skinner 1932].

of pressing of presenting a stimulus paired with shock (Estes and Skinner 1941). During the opening years of World War II he worked on a system for the visual guidance of missiles, using the pigeon as his pilot and an "aperiodic" (variable interval) schedule of reinforcement to maintain a stable and persistent performance (Skinner 1960).

In the fall of 1945 he assumed the chairmanship of the Department of Psychology at Indiana University. There he continued his research with the pigeon and wrote two important papers, one on the "superstititious" or noncontingent schedule of reinforcement (1948) and another which combined some comments on intervening variables and the testing of hypotheses as an experimental strategy with illustrative material from his work of the past decade (1950).

But in 1948 Skinner returned to Harvard, now as a member of its faculty. He was joined in 1950 by C. B. Ferster, fresh from Columbia, and together they launched a five-year program of research on the patterns of performance generated by various schedules of reinforcement. More than two billion responses were recorded as a part of this project, and more than 900 cumulative records were eventually published (Ferster and Skinner 1957). To the familiar interval and ratio schedules they added such combinations as mixed and multiple schedules, tandem and chained, concurrent, conjunctive, interlocking, and alternative schedules. It was during this period, too, that the Gerbrands recorder was perfected and that standardized modules for the electromagnetic (relay) programming of the experimental procedure were first constructed. Commercial versions of these modules were soon available from Grason-Stadler, Foringer, Scientific Prototype, Lehigh Valley, and other firms.

A SYSTEM OF BEHAVIOR

Although Skinner had made frequent reference throughout his writings to "a science of behavior" as the object of his efforts, his published work had remained forbiddingly technical. It was not until F. S. Keller and W. N. Schoenfeld reorganized the undergraduate curriculum at Columbia College, immediately following World War II, that an attempt was made to present the findings obtained in the animal conditioning laboratory to a nontechnical public as at least the beginnings of a general formulation for all behavior. Their aim, as stated in a subsequent report (Keller and Schoenfeld 1949), was to provide the student with a systematic treatment of behavior in terms of the variables of which it is a function. To introduce him to the experimental method, to train him in the use of a language based on observation, and perhaps to convince him of the reality of the phenomena with which he was asked to deal, they added four hours of laboratory per week to the introductory course. The student was provided with a rat, a lever, a cumulative recorder, and a series of instruction sheets and oral briefings for experiments ranging from the initial conditioning of the bar pressing response to an experimental prototype of masochism. To accompany these experiments, Keller and Schoenfeld prepared first a mimeographed and later a printed version of their *Principles of Psychology* (1950).

During the same period Skinner, too, was attempting to spell out some of the implications of conditioning principles for society at large. In the summer of 1945, he wrote the first draft of *Walden Two* (1948), a fictional description of a utopian community in which education and social regulation were based on positive reinforcement, rather than on the techniques of aversive control so prevalent in our society today. How, he argued, could society help but act in the interests of the individual if its control depended on giving the individual something that he wanted? But critics reared in the literary tradition took the innovation to be control itself, rather than a change in its techniques, and greeted the book with fear and dismay, as a threat to individual liberties and the spontaneity of action.

In 1948, on his arrival at Harvard, Skinner undertook to teach a course dealing specifically with human behavior. To provide suitable textual material to accompany his lectures, he wrote *Science and Human Behavior* (1953), which still remains an excellent exposition of his general point of view. The book did not cite experimental evidence but did summarize the basic principles arising from the laboratory before going on to apply them to more complex cases like thinking, private events, and self-control and to such areas of social concern as education, psychotherapy, and the design of cultures.

THE SPREAD OF OPERANT RESEARCH

By the middle forties, however, research using operant methods had become more than a one-man enterprise. At Minnesota, and again at Indiana, Skinner had attracted the interest and enlisted the assistance of some talented students. At Columbia, the postwar crop had been foundering in a morass of vague and fanciful theories accompanied by seemingly unrelated facts. But in Keller and Schoenfeld's program and text they found a solid ground combining unambiguous data, an objective language, and a systematic framework with relevance to the problems of man and his society. In stimulus discrimination, response differentiation, secondary reinforcement, drive, conflict, avoidance, and punishment they saw conceptual tools which could be used to bring order out of the chaos of traditional psychology. They were sure that publication of the text would launch a scientific revolution. Seizing their rats and their bars, they marched to the fray.

To facilitate the interchange of data and ideas between different laboratories, some medium of communication was needed. By 1946 there was enough activity in progress to justify calling together the first Conference on the Experimental Analysis of Behavior, a three-day talk-fest held in the upper reaches of Science Hall on the Indiana campus. A second conference was held at Indiana in 1948 and a third, attended by some forty or fifty people, at Columbia in 1949. After a hiatus in the early fifties, further conferences were held in conjunction with annual meetings of the American Psychological Association.

Skinner's return to Harvard and the establishment there of "the pigeon project" stirred up a new surge of student interest and activity. But the enthusiastic young investigators soon found themselves faced with a serious obstacle. To the reviewing editors for the established journals the primary criteria for sound design appeared to be the use of a substantial number of subjects, which ensured that a sufficient amount of work had been done, and the successful rout of the null hypothesis, which certified that the findings were trustworthy. Conclusions based on a small number of subjects and no statistics whatever were not readily accepted.

To make the data from each laboratory available to other

individuals across the country, it was decided at a small gathering held at the 1957 meeting of the Eastern Psychological Association to launch a new journal devoted to research based on the individual organism. Estimates of the potential circulation ran as high as 200. During the next few months an editorial board was assembled, composed mainly of recent graduates of the Harvard laboratory with a few assists from Columbia. The text of the first issue was typed by volunteer labor, the cumulative records were pasted on, and the final copy was shipped to Science Press for reproduction by a photo-offset process. Finally, in the fall of 1958, the January issue of the *Journal of the Experimental Analysis of Behavior* appeared. For an allegedly "narrow" journal it covered a surprising variety of topics, including not only some new schedules but also work with children, observing responses, the effects of drugs, the reception of Morse code, the development of ulcers, and animal psychophysics. By the end of the year, its circulation stood at 333, and by its twelfth birthday it had risen to 3538, rivaling that of its nearest competitor among the established journals.

A similar problem of differences in criteria arose with respect to the selection of papers to be presented at the annual convention of the American Psychological Association, and in 1964, at the Los Angeles meeting, Division 25, dedicated to the Experimental Analysis of Behavior, was formally inaugurated.

VERBAL BEHAVIOR

Before he turned to psychology, Skinner's primary interest had been in the field of literature (Skinner 1967). After he had completed his graduate studies and had embarked upon his research career, he returned once more to the same topic, but this time as an area of behavior to be subjected to a scientific analysis. His work began in the early thirties; a "final draft" was completed in 1946 and served as the basis for a summer course at Columbia in 1947 and for the William James Lectures at Harvard that fall. But other work intervened, and it was not until twenty-five years after he had begun his efforts that the book *Verbal Behavior* (1957) finally appeared in print.

A recurrent theme in Skinner's writings has been his objection to the use of inferences from behavior to explain that same behavior, and in this book he rejected the traditional interpretation of verbal behavior as an expression of the speaker's or writer's "ideas." Since there was virtually a one-to-one correspondence between the properties of these ideas and the properties of the original behavior, this form of explanation merely allowed the dependent variable to retreat into a hiding place where it became all but inaccessible. In its stead, Skinner proposed a functional analysis of verbal behavior itself in terms of its relationship to antecedent events. At a more concrete level, his thesis was a simple one: that verbal behavior and other behavior conform to the same principles, some of which have been revealed in the conditioning laboratory. Since the verbal behavior that develops within a natural environment is extremely complex, he collected a great variety of examples and showed how they could be analyzed within that framework. It is not necessary that all of these interpretations prove in their particulars to be correct; what is important is that he demonstrated the feasibility of such an undertaking.

Students of conditioning supposed that Skinner had successfully breached and probably overrun the last citadel of circular or mentalistic explanation. But within two years the book was met with an angry broadside by a prominent linguist (Chomsky 1959), attacking not only the details of Skinner's analysis but the very use of terms like "stimulus," "response," and "reinforcement" to analyze behavior. (For a reply, see MacCorquodale 1970.) This review has apparently been quite influential and has kept many linguists and even psycholinguists from reading the book.

Most of the early work stimulated by Skinner's views followed the general lines laid down in a dissertation by Greenspoon (published in 1955). The presentation of a stimulus such as "mm-hm" or "good" following words belonging to some grammatical or thematic category led to an increase in the frequency of such words relative to the total verbal production of the subject. During the next few years, more than a hundred studies appeared in which this "verbal conditioning" was studied as a function of a variety of parameters (Krasner 1958; Salzinger 1959). However, there have been indications that the phenomenon is more complex than was assumed by most of the early investigators. Perhaps a better illustration of the power of Skinner's analysis may be the work of Lovaas (1966) in building speech in autistic children. Beginning with prompts and selective reinforcement for the matching of sounds used in speech, he trained formerly mute children in progressive steps until they reached the point where they responded appropriately to such words as "under" and "beside" and responded with these words to the corresponding situations. Formerly echolalic children were carried all the way through simple mands and tacts (Keller and Schoenfeld 1950; Skinner 1957) to spontaneous, meaningful speech.

Skinner's conceptualization of knowledge as behavior also led him to propose an extension of the practices developed in the conditioning laboratory to the field of education. Earlier, in what might be considered a more primitive version of programmed instruction, Keller (1943) had designed a procedure for training Signal Corps recruits to receive Morse code. He broke the overall task down into smaller units in which the trainee learned to respond discriminatively to auditory signals, and he provided direct, immediate, and selective reinforcement of each correct response. Skinner's proposal included other features. The procedure of "successive approximation" used to focus the rat's behavior on the bar or the pigeon's behavior on the key led to the idea that the successive steps in the instructional program should be made sufficiently small so that a high density of reinforcement could be maintained, preventing extinction from setting in. The rate of reinforcement depended entirely on the individual's own rate of progress and not on the relation of his rate to that of other individuals. The techniques used to facilitate correct responding included formal and thematic prompts, taken from the analysis of verbal behavior, and "fading" or "vanishing," which permitted the transfer of control from highly effective to more subtle stimuli. The strategy of making the presentation of each new stimulus dependent upon the pupil's response to the previous item ensured that the learner was observing (or "attending to") each item in the sequence. (For a systematic review of programming techniques, see Taber, Glaser, and Schaefer 1965.)

OTHER APPLICATIONS

Beginning in the 1950s, elements of the operant methodology were also adopted for the study of sensory and physiological processes. Heise (1953), for example, used them to study auditory thresholds in the pigeon, and Blough to study dark adaptation (1956) and spectral sensitivity (1957). Olds and Milner (1954) used bar pressing to study the reinforcing effect of intracranial stimulation. Anliker and Mayer (1956) obtained differences in the pattern of eating associated with different types of obesity in mice. Blough (1966) has summarized the work on sensory processes, and Teitelbaum (1966) and Brady (1966) the work in the physiological area.

Since operant techniques included a number of behavioral baselines that could be continuously monitored and that remained relatively stable over extended periods of time, they seemed ideally suited for the detection and the analysis of the changes produced by various pharmacological agents. P. B. Dews organized an active program in the Department of Pharmacology at the Harvard Medical School, and J. V. Brady, who headed the Department of Experimental Psychology at the Walter Reed Army Institute of Research, persuaded such firms as Eli Lilly, Merck, Schering, Upjohn, and Smith, Kline and French to set up operant laboratories on their premises. Eventually it became clear that there was some conflict between the objectives of drug firms, which were interested primarily in the rough and ready screening of new compounds, and those of the operant workers, who were interested in more precise analyses of behavioral relationships. Nevertheless, behavioral pharmacology remained an active area of investigation and the operant technique continued to be well represented among the members of the Behavioral Pharmacology Society and later Division 28 (Psychopharmacology) of the American Psychological Association.

Operant techniques have also been used with increasing frequency to study behavioral processes in human subjects. The work on programmed instruction has already been mentioned. A major research and training program for the analysis and treatment of problem behaviors in preschool children was launched at the University of Washington, under the leadership of S. W. Bijou and D. M. Baer. (For a review of this area of research, see Sherman and Baer 1969.) During his stay at the Indiana University Medical Center, C. B. Ferster began a program of empirical and conceptual work on the problem of the autistic child. In 1954 an operant laboratory for the study of the behavior of psychotics was established at the Metropolitan State Hospital in Waltham, Massachusetts, under the immediate direction of O. R. Lindsley. At the state hospital at Anna, Illinois, procedures for managing the behavior of institutionalized patients were studied by T. Ayllon and N. H. Azrin. Therapeutic techniques for dealing with stuttering were developed by Goldiamond (1965). Most of the early papers in the modification of human behavior have been reprinted in collections by Eysenck (1964), Ullmann and Krasner (1965), or Ulrich, Stachnik, and Mabry (1966).

By the middle sixties, the volume of research literature dealing with the modification of human behavior in applied settings had become so great that it was apparent that a new journal was needed, not only to collect the data in one source but also to set a scientific standard. Accordingly, in the spring of 1967 the group which supervised the *Journal of the Experimental Analysis of Behavior* launched a sister publication, to be known as the *Journal of Applied Behavior Analysis*. The first issue appeared in the spring of the following year, and before long the new journal had a larger readership than that of its elder sibling.

Method of Research

LABORATORY INSTRUMENTATION

The first thing that comes to mind when someone mentions operant conditioning as a technology for the study of behavioral relationships is a box containing a rat and a lever or, more recently, a box containing a pigeon and a key. The box is important, since enclosing the animal insulates him both from haphazard fluctuations in the laboratory environment and also from more systematic biases that may be present, including the activities of the experimenter himself as an unintended stimulus. But the box is only one small feature of the total method.

To the visitor who tours the operant laboratory, the most impressive sight may be the large racks of electrical equipment, covered with an array of colored wires that link together the component modules controlling the logic and the timing of various experimental events. The popularity of this type of instrumentation may depend to some degree on considerations which are scientifically irrelevant. On the one hand, the availability of such equipment demands a substantial level of financial support and an understanding of the basic principles of switching circuitry, factors which often make it inaccessible to the beginning student. On the other hand, most psychologists probably find the construction and maintenance of programming circuits intellectually more stimulating than carrying a rat repeatedly back from the goal box to the start box or the home cage. More important from a technical point of view is the fact that a well-constructed circuit is faster, more accurate, and more reliable than the experimenter or his assistant can be, more objective, and capable of programming simultaneously a larger number of relationships. Even though it consumes more time than is sometimes realized, in the long run automated equipment is likely to increase the amount of data that can be collected.

In association with this circuitry, the instrumentation used in operant studies becomes extremely versatile. In most other types of apparatus the pattern of behavior and the attendant changes in stimulation within each trial are partly or wholly determined by the spatial characteristics of the apparatus and are relatively difficult to change. New procedures often require structural alterations or entirely different floor plans. But programming circuits are receptive both to responses and to time and are capable of great logical complexity; any relationship that is observed in the natural world between time, responses, and stimuli can be reproduced in the experimental environment.

Moreover, pressing a bar or pecking a key are units of behavior which are quickly executed and which do not involve locomotion through space. Repeated instances of these responses can therefore be used, in a variety of relationships to alternative or successive changes in stimulation, as basic components for the assembly of much larger and more complex patterns of interaction between the subject and his environment. In this way, behavioral relationships ranging from the very simple to the very complex can be studied, using the same constituent stimuli and responses in the same experimental setting. Furthermore, the component parts of the more complex patterns can still be individually monitored, since every press or peck is fed into the recording apparatus.

Many laboratories which do not subscribe to the operant tradition as a whole have nevertheless adopted such specific features as the bar-pressing response and automated programming equipment. A feature which is more distinctive, however, revealing greater familiarity and deeper involvement with the operant approach, is the cumulative recorder. This is not merely a device for the automatic recording of behavior in general but specifically for the representation in extremely condensed but highly readable form of the animal's rate of responding from one moment to the next throughout the experimental session. It reveals detailed changes which are not readily detected in any other way.

RATE AS A DEPENDENT VARIABLE

Although it has repeatedly been emphasized in various writings, there seems to be little awareness outside of operant circles of the central role that is played by frequency of responding as the basic datum in this type of research. Most discussions of the issue begin with a value judgment: What we would most like to know about behavior, it is argued, is not how the response is made but how likely it is to occur on a given occasion or how often it occurs on such occasions. Then it is pointed out that the number of responses per unit of time is closely related to this ultimate value.

But something more has been added, a feature of considerable technical importance. In natural settings, the occurrence of a specified response usually alters the situation in such a way that some other response becomes more appropriate. The original response is not repeated until the next time that the same situation or some similar situation is encountered. In laboratory work, however, the use of discrete trials would lead to a relatively slow accumulation of successive instances of the response. To obtain enough data for a reasonably reliable measure, it would be necessary to sum or average the data for successive periods of time or for several different subjects. Neither of these is entirely satisfactory as a general solution, since neither procedure provides an accurate assessment of the individual animal's behavior at a given point in time. When the bar or key is connected to a cumulative recorder, however, shifts in the rate of responding can often be detected in the form of changes in the slope of the record within a matter of seconds. This makes it possible not only to monitor but later to display rate of responding as virtually a continuous measure of the animal's behavior throughout a given period of time. Such an immediate and detailed feedback encourages the experimenter to concentrate his attention directly on the actual behavior of the individual subject rather than on some hypothetical quantity derived from a group average. If need be, he can even conduct a continuous interaction with his subject during the course of a single training session. Freedom from the need for group averaging makes it possible to conduct research with greater flexibility, economy, and efficiency than is possible with other measures (Dinsmoor 1966b; Sidman 1960).

In the conditioning laboratory, rate of responding is particularly useful because it is an absolute rather than a relative measure and because it does not suffer from the arbitrary limitations—floor and ceiling effects—which restrict the range and distort the relationships obtained with other measures. By comparison either with random variations or with the magnitude of change necessary to demonstrate a systematic effect, the range of values it can assume is quite large. With the pigeon, for example, local rates may range from zero to as many as fifteen responses per second (Ferster and Skinner 1957).

Rate of responding also appears to have a property which may prove extremely valuable in analyzing behavior. In at least some cases, the functional relationships into which it enters as a dependent variable remain invariant in their mathematical form under a variety of parametric conditions. All that is altered is a coefficient representing the particular parametric setting.

Since this point has not previously been discussed in the literature, it may be helpful to consider a concrete illustration. Butter (1963), for example, obtained gradients of generalization during test sessions as a joint function of two dimensions of his stimulus—the slope and the wave length of a narrow band of light projected on the pigeon's key. Three gradients were obtained expressing the rate of responding as a function of the slope of the stimulus, each at a different wave length. Butter found that there was a multiplicative relationship between these three gradients. In other words, the rates making up one gradient could be reproduced by multiplying the rates making up another gradient by a constant; this constant represented the difference between the two wave lengths at which these gradients were obtained. (For additional examples involving stimulus control, see Coate 1964; Dinsmoor 1952; Johnson 1970; Sidman 1961.)

The same type of relationship is illustrated in Figure 25–2, a family of curves taken from a study by Clark (1958). Three

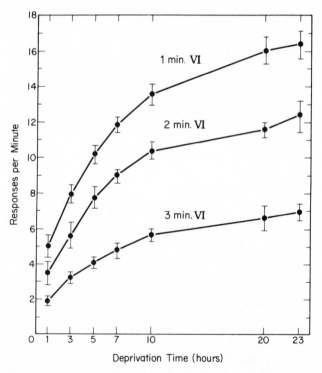

Fig. 25-2. *A family of curves showing rate of bar pressing as a joint function of mean interval between reinforcements and time since last feeding* [Clark, F. C., The effect of deprivation and frequency of reinforcement on variable-interval responding. *Journal of the Experimental Analysis of Behavior*, 1958, *1*, 221–28. Copyright 1958 by the Society for the Experimental Analysis of Behavior, Inc.].

groups of rats were used. In the first group, bar-pressing was reinforced on a variable-interval schedule averaging one reinforcement per minute. In the second group, reinforcement was available, on the average, once in every two minutes. For the third group, it was available once in every three minutes. After the performance had stabilized, Clark tested each of his animals at several different levels of deprivation (1, 3, 5, 7, 10, 20, and 23 hours since eating). The averaged results for each of the three groups are shown by the three curves in the figure. Again the relationship is multiplicative. For example, multiplying the rates for the three minute group (bottom curve) by 1.81 yielded a reasonable approximation to the rates for the two minute group (middle curve), and multiplying the same rates by 2.43 yielded a reasonable approximation to the rates for the one minute group (top curve).

Clark's data indicate that the function relating rate of responding to hours since eating is invariant at different frequencies of reinforcement. Also, since all of the values on one curve bear the same ratio to the corresponding values on one of the other curves, the function relating rate of responding to frequency of reinforcement is invariant at different levels of deprivation. All that is altered in either case is the numerical value of the coefficient by which the remainder of the mathematical expression is multiplied.

The importance of this multiplicative relationship can be made clear by considering the consequences that would ensue if such a relationship did not hold. Different experimenters typically employ different parametric settings—levels of deprivation, frequencies of reinforcement, intensities of stimulus, pressures required to operate the bar or key, species of subject, etc.—to investigate the same functional relationship. If differences in these background parameters altered the mathematical form of the relationship obtained, it would be extremely difficult to replicate prior data, to agree on the conclusions to be derived from these data, or to formulate general principles except in the grossest of terms. Furthermore, since equivalent physical specifications are not necessarily "behaviorally equivalent" for different individuals, it would be difficult even to obtain consistent results within the same experiment. It is possible, of course, that genuine interactions may be obtained, on occasion, between the effects of two different parameters; but the occurrence in a number of cases of simple linear transformations indicates that such interactions are not inherently characteristic of the measure employed.

Finally, rate of responding appears to be the nearest thing we have to a "universal" measure of behavior. Other measures commonly used in the conditioning laboratory apply only to special cases and do not provide a unified account of behavior in a variety of different situations. There are some problems, to be sure, that cannot be studied in terms of rate, but the restrictions seem less severe. Even changes in such dimensions of the individual response occurrence as speed or amplitude of movement, force, latency, or duration can be studied by dividing the range into class intervals and counting the number of instances that fall within each of these classifications. When we tabulate a frequency distribution in this manner, we lose many of the usual advantages of the rate measure, but we retain data that are systematically related to rate and which may provide a better picture of the processes at work than would a single measure of central tendency.

Rate of responding can be used to measure responses varying greatly in their physical dimensions. When we turn from an arbitrary response like that selected for use in the conditioning laboratory to responses selected for their ethological or applied interest, we find that many of them are difficult to specify, let alone to measure, in the conventional physical units of energy, wave length, or distance. Also, the target behaviors may be quite different in their physical dimensions in successive studies or even within the same study. In most cases a human observer is employed as the "recording instrument." Time and number are the most convenient dimensions. If instances of the target behavior can be quickly and reliably identified, even the human recorder can tally the number of occurrences; indeed, he often can tally several different responses simultaneously. Rate of responding is not only a dimension in terms of which a great variety of physically dissimilar responses can be quantified but also a relatively convenient measure to use in the applied setting (Bijou, Peterson, and Ault 1968).

INDIVIDUAL FUNCTIONS

One of the most important rules in operant research is that, whenever feasible, the investigator should obtain separate determinations of the relationship between the dependent and independent variable for each individual subject. Most of those working in the operant tradition have at one time or another employed data obtained by using a different group of subjects to determine each of the points on the function. But the emphasis that is placed on within-individual determinations may be indicated by the fact that since its inception each issue of the *Journal of the Experimental Analysis of Behavior* has carried inside its front cover the statement that it is "primarily for the original publication of experiments relevant to the behavior of individual organisms."

The characteristic design employed in this type of research begins with the establishment of a reasonably stable baseline performance under some specified set of conditions. This provides a reference point for within-subject comparisons; i.e., each subject serves as his own control. Then one of the conditions is altered and a new determination is made of the subject's performance. Several successive determinations may be obtained at different levels of the independent variable, including an occasional return to the baseline performance. Although this design raises certain problems of control which differ from those encountered in the conventional group design (Dinsmoor 1966b), it has important advantages.

First, it reduces what statisticians call the "error variance" by eliminating the usual confounding between variations in behavior associated with different values of the independent variable and variations in behavior associated with differences between individual subjects. Reliable determinations of the same function can often be obtained from each individual, and the replication of the same finding with successive individuals engenders considerable confidence in its validity. When the same finding can be replicated under different conditions, following different individual histories, or with different species, we also have increased confidence in the generality of the relationship.

Secondly, this design may be used with considerable effectiveness even in situations like those encountered in clinical practice in which the population is not necessarily homogeneous but in which each individual may represent a unique case, differing from others both in his past history and in his current behavior (e.g., see Dinsmoor 1966a; Wetzel 1966). Different therapeutic procedures may be required, but a fairly reliable determination can often be obtained of the effectiveness of the treatment for each individual. In some cases, one problem behavior is used as a dependent variable while another is used as a control.

In the third place, the within-subject design makes it possible to study differences between individuals in the characteristic way in which each of them reacts to changes in his environment or in the consequences of his actions. Individuals may differ in the form and even in the direction of the functional relationship between their behavior and some independent variable. By contrast, in the group design the term "individual differences" refers to a strictly one-dimensional effect—the variability in individual scores at some one point along the abscissa.

Finally, the functions which are apparent when the individual design is employed may be lost or distorted when averaged values are substituted, as required by the group design. For example, in my own laboratory we recently obtained data showing the frequency with which each pigeon pecked an "observing" key as a function of the proportion of occasions on which this led to the exposure of a favorable rather than of an unfavorable stimulus. One pigeon showed a consistent increase in the frequency of pecking as a function of increases in the percentage of times that the favorable stimulus appeared. But a second pigeon showed a decrease in the frequency of pecking as a function of the same variable. And a third pigeon pecked more often when the favorable stimulus was produced 50% of the time than when it was produced 10% of the time or 90% of the time. Each of these functions was replicable. But if we had no knowledge of the individual functions and were forced to rely on group averages, we would probably have concluded that the experimental variable produced great variability but no systematic effect.

Even when the individual relationships are the same in form and direction, their shape may be distorted by the averaging process (Sidman 1952). It is only with great circumspection, therefore, that the shape of the individual functions can be deduced from or tested by the shape of averaged data (Estes 1956).

ATTITUDE TOWARD THEORY

Psychologists who subscribe to the operant tradition are often thought to be "atheoretical" or even "antitheoretical" in their views. If this characterization is taken to mean that they are not interested in the formulation of general principles, it is obviously mistaken. The goal of most operant workers is the construction of a unified science of behavior within a common framework. Recognizing the complexity of this task, however, they attempt to exercise a stringent economy in their use of theoretical concepts; that is, they make every effort to restrict the number of new concepts which they accept and to account for as much of the data as possible with the concepts they already possess. This resistance to the admission of new concepts before they are clearly required, coupled with an emphasis on rigorous definition in terms of concrete observations, may account for their seemingly hostile attitude toward many theoretical endeav-

ors. Putting it colloquially, operant conditioners "try to stick close to the data."

The impression that operant workers reject theory seems also to be based in part on the title of Skinner's address to the Midwestern Psychological Association, "Are Theories of Learning Necessary?" (1950). But that title and that address can best be understood within the historical context of the period in which they were delivered. At that time, much of the research in conditioning or learning laboratories was dominated by comprehensive systems or theories of learning, such as those proposed by Hull and by Tolman, which consisted primarily of imaginary or hypothetical variables postulated in order to account for and to predict the relationships among observable events. It was hoped that these "intervening variables," as they were called, would serve to integrate the empirical data and to stimulate and give direction to further research. However, since the postulated variables were not directly observable, the only way in which their utility could be evaluated was to derive predictions from their assumed relationships and to subject these predictions to empirical test. There was no question concerning the scientific legitimacy of this procedure, if carefully conducted, but it was threatening to become the only accepted model for the conduct of behavioral research. It was the efficiency of this strategy and the exclusiveness of this model that Skinner was challenging.

The basic difficulty with these intervening variables, as Skinner saw it, was that they tended to serve as a substitute for, rather than as a summary of, the functional relationships between observable events. In popular accounts, there is often no evidence for the inner event other than the behavior it purports to explain. In scientific accounts, the need is usually acknowledged of specifying the relationship of the postulated variable to the events which precede it in the logical sequence as well as to those which follow it, but completion of this program is often left for the future. In the meantime, since there is nothing more solid available, the half-finished constructions find their way not only into research papers but also into reviews and textbooks. They provide considerable prestige for their authors and thereby lend authority to the model, but they may also serve as a source of distraction and confusion to the reader. Ultimately, most of these theories have proved to be incorrect.

There is also some question whether theoretical constructions of this sort provide the most effective strategy for the conduct of research. As Platt (1964) has emphasized, it is by the elimination of possible alternatives that science advances. A corollary of this viewpoint is that the alternatives to be compared should be as broad or as inclusive as possible within the confines of existing knowledge.

It is obvious that research can be generated without formulating any very formal or specific hypothesis, and in the early stages of exploring some set of relationships this may be the most effective strategy. A promising variable may be selected and may be manipulated through an extended range; the results will automatically exclude a host of possible interpretations, including some which may not as yet have been formulated and others which may already have been advanced. Some of the data reported in Skinner's address (1950), for example, raised considerable doubts concerning the viability, regardless of their details, of Hull's concepts of reactive and conditioned inhibition.

Later, when the range of alternative formulations has become somewhat narrower, it is helpful to focus one's attention on the remaining possibilities. Paradoxically, however, the attempt to leap ahead by "outguessing nature" and singling out an extremely specific hypothesis early in the game may be counterproductive. The probability of such a hypothesis being correct is extremely low, and its elimination adds relatively little to our stock of information. It is possible, of course, that other interpretations will be eliminated at the same time, as a by-product of the same experiment. But if a hypothesis deduced from some theoretical system is to have any function in directing research, it must generate a different experiment than would be generated by an attempt to distinguish among broader classes of alternatives. As a result, the data obtained from such an experiment are likely to bear primarily on that directing hypothesis and to lose much of their relevance when the theoretical system is modified or discarded.

Contingencies of Reinforcement

Perhaps the best way to characterize the concepts and the conclusions derived from operant research is to say that they describe the various contingencies of reinforcement and the effects of these contingencies on the subject's behavior (Evans 1968). In this context, it should be recognized that the word *reinforcement*, like other conditioning concepts, is defined in terms of its behavioral effects. To demonstrate that an event may be classified as a reinforcer, it is necessary to show: (a) that a response which is followed by this event increases in frequency, and (b) that the increase in frequency depends upon the temporal relationship or contingency between the response and this event. Attempts to specify what is reinforcing on other grounds (e.g., need reduction, change of situation, or behavior in the presence of the event) are not of primary interest and, in any case, have proved disappointing. The physiological mechanisms are little understood and are not a necessary part of a science of behavior.

The meaning of the word *contingency*, as used in operant research, can be illustrated by comparing two well-known schedules of reinforcement. In the first, known as *superstition* (Skinner 1948), grain is delivered to the pigeon at regular intervals, regardless of what the bird is doing. If the intervals are relatively short, the result, according to Skinner, is that many of the subjects learn idiosyncratic patterns of behavior which they repeat persistently throughout the experimental session. Adventitious pairings in which the behavior is followed by the grain apparently serve to maintain some behavior which happened to occur frequently or at the right time early in training. The grain has an effect on the frequency of responding even though that responding is not required for or responsible for the production of the grain. The only necessary condition for

the effect on responding is the temporal relationship—in this case, accidental—between the two events. On the other hand, there is no systematic contingency. Since the delivery of the grain is not dependent on any property of behavior, it does not regularly follow responses possessing any particular property. This means that no control is maintained over the form of the response. The experimenter cannot choose which response he will condition, and the form of the behavior is likely to drift or to degenerate completely over a period of time. The situation may be remedied by adding one further specification to the schedule: after the required interval of time has elapsed, a response of the form being recorded by the experimenter must occur before the grain is delivered. This specification, which changes the procedure from superstition to a fixed interval schedule of reinforcement, ensures that grain will be delivered immediately following instances of one class of behavior and of no other class of behavior. In other words, it establishes a systematic contingency between the response and the reinforcer. As a consequence, the fixed interval schedule is capable of maintaining a stable pattern of behavior for a period of time which is limited only by the health of the subject and the persistence of the experimenter.

In general, a contingency is a specification of what the reinforcer depends upon, or, more properly, what it follows. Some contingencies involve a relationship between the delivery of the reinforcer and the form of the response or the presence or absence of a given stimulus. Others depend only upon rules relating the delivery of the reinforcer to the passage of time and to the occurrence of instances of the class of responses which is being recorded. These rules are known as schedules of reinforcement. Since the effects of such rules are not readily studied with other types of apparatus, schedules of reinforcement are considered a relatively distinctive subject matter. The importance attached to this subject may be indicated by the fact that one of Skinner's two major research compilations (Ferster and Skinner 1957) was devoted wholly to this topic.

SCHEDULES DEPENDING ON NUMBER OF RESPONSES

The simplest schedule, in which each and every response is followed by the reinforcer, is known as regular or continuous reinforcement (*CRF*), or sometimes as fixed ratio one (*FR*1). In the latter expression, the word "ratio" refers to the number of responses required for each successive delivery of the reinforcer. If this number remains constant throughout some period of experimentation, the schedule is characterized as a fixed ratio, with a further specification added of the particular number that is required, as in *FR*5, *FR*10, etc. The procedure is a simple one, but the pattern of performance is more complex than might be

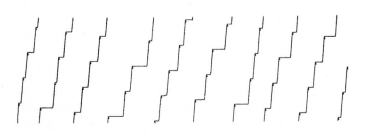

Fig. 25-3. *A cumulative record of one complete session of key pecking by a well-trained pigeon on a fixed ratio of 120 responses per reinforcement* [Dinsmoor 1970].

anticipated. For large ratios, the characteristic pattern that emerges following substantial training includes two phases. For some time after the delivery of the reinforcer, no responding occurs. Once responding begins, however, it continues at a rapid rate until the ratio is completed and another delivery of the reinforcer occurs. A variety of parameters have been shown to influence the mean length of the pause without having appreciable effect on the subsequent rate of responding.

In a similar but less common procedure, the number of responses required for each successive delivery of the reinforcer varies according to a predetermined pattern. This is known as a variable ratio schedule, and a number is appended specifying the mean value of the sequence of ratios, as in *VR5*, *VR10*, etc. A random ratio schedule may be generated by employing a very brief temporal cycle in which the probability of reinforcement is determined by the duration of the time segment in which a reinforcement is available divided by the total duration of the cycle. This is also sometimes known as a constant probability schedule and produces high and stable rates of responding.

SCHEDULES DEPENDING ON TIME SINCE REINFORCEMENT

As has been pointed out by Schoenfeld, Cumming, and Hearst (1956), varying the parameters of proportion and cycle length within the system just described enables it to incorporate other schedules of reinforcement. If, for example, the length of the cycle is increased substantially above the typical interresponse time of the subject and the time segment within which the (initial) response is reinforced occupies a large portion of the cycle, this temporally defined schedule becomes a fixed interval schedule.

In more conventional terms, the fixed interval (*FI*) schedule is usually defined by stating either: (a) that the first response following the completion of a specified interval of time since the last reinforcement is reinforced (timer stops at completion of interval and starts after reinforcement), or (b) that the first response within each interval timed from the beginning of the session is reinforced (timer runs continuously). The former procedure ensures that the interval between reinforcements is always at least as great as that specified; the latter procedure provides a more accurate specification of the mean interval between reinforcements. With extended exposure to a fixed interval schedule, the subject develops a pattern of performance characterized by a positive acceleration in the rate of responding within each interval between reinforcements.

This temporal discrimination may be avoided, however, by varying the length of each successive interval in an unpredictable sequence. The variable interval (*VI*) schedule, as it is called, maintains a stable and persistent rate of responding which is nevertheless sensitive to shifts in parametric values. Since this stable rate produces a straight line on the cumulative record, it provides a popular baseline for the study of temporary changes in performance, such as those induced by repeatedly presenting a neutral stimulus followed by a shock (conditioned suppression). The stability of the performance from session to session makes the *VI* schedule useful for the study of processes like discrimination, chaining, and concurrent schedules and as a baseline for the evaluation of parameters like frequency of reinforcement, level of deprivation, or intensity of punishment. Finally, the stability and the persistence of the behavior during extinction sessions, following reinforcement on a variable interval schedule, makes this schedule an especially useful one for the study of gradients of generalization or of any phenomenon that might be distorted by continued reinforcement. To make the rate of responding as uniform as possible between successive reinforcements, a random interval or constant probability *VI* may be preferred to other versions of this schedule (Catania and Reynolds 1968).

SCHEDULES DEPENDING ON TIME SINCE LAST RESPONSE

There are also schedules in which the delivery of the reinforcer depends directly on the rate of responding. For example, if the criterion is a period of specified duration without an occurrence of the response, the schedule is known as *DRO* (differential reinforcement of other behavior, or differential reinforcement of zero rate); this criterion can be combined with an additional temporal criterion, which must also be met, as in *VI DRO*. As might be expected, the *DRO* procedure leads to a rapid decrement from previous levels and to a near-zero terminal rate.

A procedure which is easily confused with *DRO* is *DRL* (differential reinforcement of low rates). In the usual form of this schedule, a pause of specified length is required, as in *DRO*, but a response must occur before the reinforcer is delivered. Despite the similarity in temporal criteria, it should be noted that what the reinforcer immediately follows is now a response rather than the absence of a response. This may generate conflicting behavioral tendencies. Under typical parametric values, the rat conforms fairly well to the temporal requirements but the pigeon produces far too many responses. Another procedure for the differential reinforcement of rates utilizes the number of responses occurring during a period of specified length as a criterion to determine whether the reinforcer is to be delivered. If the number is required to be less than some low value, the procedure is another version of the *DRL*; but if the number is required to be greater than some high value, the procedure is *DRH* (differential reinforcement of high rates).

COMBINED SCHEDULES

There are also a number of ways in which the basic schedules defined above may be combined in more complex schedules. If two or more schedules are presented successively to the subject, the combination is known as a mixed schedule; if each of the component schedules is accompanied by a discriminative stimulus, the same combination becomes a multiple schedule. Multiple schedules have been widely employed to examine the effects of various pharmacological agents, for example, since the effect on two or more patterns of performance can be compared in the same individual at the same point in the time course of the drug's action.

If completion of the requirements of one schedule leads merely to the subject's access to the next schedule, with no delivery of the primary reinforcer until the entire sequence of schedules has been completed, the combined schedule is known as a tandem schedule. Tandem schedules have frequently been used to manipulate the behavior immediately prior to the delivery of the reinforcer, in order to see what effect the terminal contingency may have on the overall pattern of responding. They have also been used as control schedules to examine the effects of the stimuli included in chained schedules; unfortunately, the discriminative and reinforcing effects of the chain stimuli are confounded in such a comparison.

RESPONSE VARIATION

Although these and other schedules of reinforcement have received considerable attention in the laboratory, the contingencies most frequently used in applied settings appear to be those making it possible to manipulate the form of the response or the circumstances under which it occurs. Space does not permit more than a brief sketch of such relationships, but for more extensive summaries the reader is referred to Dinsmoor (1970) or Reynolds (1968). For surveys of the research literature on selected topics, he is referred to the appropriate chapters in Honig (1966). A number of the more significant papers have been reproduced by Catania (1968) and Verhave (1966).

Variations in the topography of a response, like pressing the bar with the right paw, the left paw, or the nose, and variations along some dimension of the response, like its speed of execution, the extent of the movement, the force exerted, or the duration of the action, may, if we wish, be treated as if they were separate responses. That is, we may selectively reinforce or selectively extinguish one of these variants. But since the behavior is not inherently fragmented into natural units, it will be observed that some increment or decrement also occurs in the frequency of other, similar variants along any one of these dimensions. This process is known as response induction. Some of the data classified under this heading may reflect the similarity in the proprioceptive and other feedback stimulation (Notterman and Mintz 1965) which has selectively been associated with the delivery of the reinforcer. However, selective reinforcement of one variant and nonreinforcement of others does in time narrow the range of the behavior, a process known as response differentiation. Finally, by taking advantage of new variants produced by response induction, reinforcing these and withholding the reinforcer following earlier variants, it is possible to produce new forms of behavior not previously observed in the subject's repertoire. This process is known as successive approximation (Keller and Schoenfeld 1950) or shaping (Skinner 1953).

CONTINGENCIES INVOLVING BOTH STIMULUS AND RESPONSE

To understand stimulus control of behavior, we must consider the relationship between the environmental situation in which the response occurs and the delivery of the reinforcer. For convenience in exposition, it will be helpful to consider a simple stimulus, such as a light, a visual pattern, or a tone. Stimulus control is based on a dual contingency: the reinforcer follows the response only in the presence of the specified stimulus. It is observed, however, that the response increases in frequency not only in the presence of that particular stimulus but also in the presence of stimuli differing along such dimensions as shape or pattern, wave length, intensity, orientation, or location. This effect is called stimulus generalization. The increment in frequency tends to be maximal for precisely the stimulus which was present when the response was reinforced and to decline for

successive values along any dimension that can be ordered in physical terms. The slope of this function is known as the gradient of generalization. Repeated association in time between the presence or absence of the critical stimulus and the reinforcement or nonreinforcement of the response leads to increasingly steeper gradients, i.e., to more precise control of the response by the properties of the stimulus. It seems likely that at least part, if not all, of this improvement in stimulus control can be attributed to the establishment of more frequent and more accurate observing responses (Wyckoff 1969), which provide contact between the receptor organs and the stimulus energies that impinge upon them, or to comparable processes within the organism (attention). The organism also appears to observe and attend to the properties of the stimulus that accompanies nonreinforcement of the response, since independent gradients of generalization can be obtained for dimensions that are unique to this stimulus. In particular, the combined gradient along the dimension that distinguishes the positive (reinforcement) from the negative (nonreinforcement) stimulus becomes especially steep. The process of selective reinforcement by means of which the effects of the two stimuli are separated is known as discrimination training, and the resulting pattern of performance is known as a discrimination.

STIMULUS PAIRING

Stimuli may also be paired or correlated in time without any necessary or known mediation by the animal's behavior. Two basic forms of this relationship have been examined. In the first case, the initially neutral stimulus is presented shortly before the primary event, such as food or shock, as in Pavlovian conditioning, but not necessarily overlapping in time; to stress a detail, the primary event may arrive in the absence of the neutral stimulus. In the second case, the primary event is presented exclusively in the presence of the neutral stimulus or more frequently in its presence than in its absence. In either case, a stimulus which is associated with the delivery of food, for example, or some other primary reinforcer, becomes itself capable of serving as a reinforcer (conditioned reinforcer). A stimulus which is associated with the delivery of shock or some other aversive event becomes aversive to the subject (conditioned aversive stimulus). Responses which terminate this stimulus are reinforced. Furthermore, a stimulus which is paired with the termination of shock or which is inversely correlated with the delivery of shocks becomes a positive conditioned reinforcer. And there is some evidence to indicate that a stimulus which is inversely correlated with the delivery of food becomes a conditioned aversive stimulus.

COMPLEX CONTINGENCIES

The basic rules of discriminative control and of stimulus pairing also serve to explain or to integrate somewhat more complex patterns of interaction between stimulus and response. When a standard sequence of stimuli is produced by successive responses, we speak of the resulting pattern as a chain. If the same response class is operative at each point, the chain is described as homogeneous, but if different responses are required, the chain is considered to be heterogeneous. The successive stimuli serve both as discriminative stimuli for responding in their presence and as conditioned reinforcers for the responses that precede them. The observing response paradigm may be viewed as a special case of chaining.

Another complex pattern, which is based on conditioned aversive stimulation, is known as avoidance. In its most readily interpretable form, a neutral stimulus is presented which is either terminated by the response or followed by a primary aversive stimulus, such as shock. The pairings with the shock maintain the aversiveness of the stimulus and the termination of the stimulus reinforces the response. The stimulus in question also serves as a discriminative stimulus for the avoidance response, and a stimulus inversely correlated with shock may be presented following the response, as a reinforcer. Further elaborations of the same basic paradigm are found in cases in which a shock is delivered when a specified amount of time has passed since the last response (unsignalled avoidance) or in which a designated response is followed by shock but other behavior is not (punishment).

The Applicability of Conditioning Principles

Objection is frequently raised to the use of terms like stimulus, response, and reinforcement as conceptual tools for the analysis of behavior outside of the laboratory. Chomsky, for example, maintained that Skinner's interpretations of verbal behavior were.

Formulated in terms of a metaphoric extension of the technical vocabulary of the laboratory. . . .In fact the terms used in the description of real-life and of laboratory behavior may be mere homonyms, with at most a vague similarity of meaning (Chomsky 1959, pp. 30–31).

What bothered Chomsky was that in a natural setting the relationships between behavior and its controlling stimuli are extremely complex (not "lawful"). He argued, therefore, that concepts derived from situations in which these relationships have been clarified (by experimental manipulation) do not apply. But the problem lies in the difficulty of the material, not in the limitations of the concepts. To rule out conceptual terms based on experimental manipulation because the material to be analyzed is difficult is like ruling out biochemistry when one turns to the study of medicine.

Another objection which is frequently raised may be typified by the comments of Breger and McGaugh (1965) in their critique of "learning theory" approaches to psychotherapy: "Learning, as the behaviorist views it, is defined as the tendency to make a particular response in the presence of a particular stimulus" (p. 341). Objections of this type impute an atomistic bias to conditioning theorists and then proceed to refute it; they rest on a misconception of the way in which words like stimulus and response are used and of the way in which they are defined.

In laboratory practice, it is true that a particular instance of the class "stimulus" may be chosen which is easy to produce, easy to turn on and off by electrical means, and easy to specify in physical terms. This may mean a light of a certain wave length or a tone of a certain frequency. Specification in physical terms makes more precise replication possible and permits a check on the contribution that particular physical properties may have made to the results which were obtained. But in practice further work on the same problem may be conducted with a stimulus having quite different physical properties.

When stimuli are classified as discriminative, eliciting, aversive, or reinforcing, no mention is made of their physical characteristics; these categories are defined in terms of the temporal relationship of the stimulus to other events—i.e., the contingencies employed—and to the effects of this stimulus on the subject's behavior. That is, all such definitions are in functional or behavioral terms.

It is sometimes pointed out that the subject reacts consistently to patterns of stimulation, as distinguished from the elements making them up, or that he reacts in the same way to a variety of retinal patterns emanating from the same object. This, however, offers no difficulty to a functional analysis. If the subject reacts in the same way to different stimuli, as physically defined, they are functionally equivalent. If they are functionally equivalent, or to the extent that they are functionally equivalent, they may be treated as the same stimulus. If the same physical elements are sometimes equivalent and sometimes not, different levels of analysis may be required on different occasions. A conditioning terminology offers no magic wand by means of which these complexities may be abolished, but functional definition of the stimulus does offer a means by which established principles may be brought to bear on a concrete situation.

In a similar fashion, objection is sometimes raised to the use of the word "response" to deal with complex items of behavior. In their commentary Breger and McGaugh pointed out:

A learned response does not consist merely of a stereotyped pattern of muscular contraction or glandular secretion. . . .Anyone who has trained animals has recognized that animals can achieve the same general response, that is, make the same environmental change in a variety of different ways (1965, p. 342).

This is perfectly correct. The rat's response of depressing a bar, for example, can be carried out in a variety of ways—with the right paw, the left paw, both paws, the nose, the teeth, or even the tail. If the results are orderly—that is, if all of the topographical variants prove to be quantitatively interchangeable—no one is concerned. All of the different topographies, as physically specified, are classified and counted as variants of the same response.

Important questions may be raised as to which topographies are functionally equivalent and how they got that way, whether the equivalence can in some sense be explained at a more detailed level or must simply be accepted as an unanalyzable fact, but these are problems for further investigation, not for terminological reform.

The fact that the language emanating from the conditioning laboratory can be applied, without change of definition, to other events does not, of course, establish the conclusion that the functional relationships are the same. It does, however, mean that laboratory findings can be transferred to other situations and offered as a plausible interpretation of other patterns of behavior. The discrepancies, if any, between the results expected and those obtained can then be used to modify or to supplement the original analysis. Some of the objections to the early interpretations of experiments on "verbal conditioning," for example may be quite justified, since the data do not always fit the model that was proposed. It may be necessary to take the past history of the subject into account and to take a closer look at the way in which certain stimuli have been classified. The problem, however, does not appear to lie with the concepts but in the way in which they have initially been applied. There is nothing to be gained by trading in precision instruments for duller tools, i.e., for concepts which are so hazily defined that they encounter no difficulty with the subject matter.

References

ANLIKER, J., and MAYER, J. An operant conditioning technique for studying feeding-fasting patterns in normal and obese mice. *Journal of Applied Physiology*, 1956, 8, 667–70.

BIJOU, S. W., PETERSON, R. F., and AULT, M. H. A method to integrate descriptive and experimental field studies at the level of data and empirical concepts. *Journal of Applied Behavior Analysis*, 1968, 1, 175–91. Reprinted in W. C. BECKER (ed.), An empirical basis for change in education, pp. 99–126. Chicago: Science Research Associates, 1971.

BLOUGH, D. S. Dark adaptation in the pigeon. *Journal of Comparative and Physiological Psychology*, 1956, 49, 425–30.

———— Spectral sensitivity in the pigeon. *Journal of the Optical Society of America*, 1957, 47, 827–33.

———— The study of animal sensory processes by operant methods. In W. K. HONIG (ed.), *Operant behavior: Areas of research and application*, pp. 345–79. New York: Appleton-Century-Crofts, 1966.

BRADY, J. V. Operant methodology and the experimental production of altered physiological states. In W. K. HONIG (ed.), *Operant behavior: Areas of research and application*, pp. 609–33. New York: Appleton-Century-Crofts, 1966.

BREGER, L., and MCGAUGH, J. L. Critique and reformulation of "learning-theory" approaches to psychotherapy and neurosis. *Psychological Bulletin*, 1965, 63, 338–58.

BUTTER, C. M. Stimulus generalization along one and two dimensions in pigeons. *Journal of Experimental Psychology*, 1963, 65, 339–46.

CATANIA, A. C., ed. *Contemporary research in operant behavior*. Glenview, Ill.: Scott, Foresman, 1968.

————, and REYNOLDS, G. S. A quantitative analysis of the responding maintained by interval schedules of reinforcement. *Journal of the Experimental Analysis of Behavior*, 1968, 11, 327–83.

CHOMSKY, N. *Verbal behavior* by B. F. Skinner. In *Language*, 1959, 35, 26–58. Reprinted in Bobbs-Merrill Reprint Series in the Social Sciences. J. A. Fodor and J. J. Katz, eds. *The structure of language: Readings in the philosophy of language*, pp. 547–78. Englewood Cliffs, N.J.: Prentice-Hall, 1964. L. A. Jakobovits and M. S. Miron, eds. *Readings in the psychology of language*, pp. 142–71. Englewood Cliffs, N.J.: Prentice-Hall, 1967.

CLARK, F. C. The effect of deprivation and frequency of reinforcement on variable-interval responding. *Journal of the Experimental Analysis of Behavior*, 1958, 1, 221–28.

COATE, W. B. Effect of deprivation on postdiscrimination stimulus generalization in the rat. *Journal of Comparative and Physiological Psychology*, 1964, 57, 134–38.

DINSMOOR, J. A. The effect of hunger on discriminative responding. *Journal of Abnormal and Social Psychology*, 1952, 47, 67–72. Reprinted in T. Verhave (ed.), *The experimental analysis of behavior: Selected readings*, pp. 389–98. New York: Appleton-Century-Crofts, 1966.

———— Comments on Wetzel's treatment of a case of compulsive stealing. *Journal of Consulting Psychology*, 1966a, 30, 378–80. Reprinted in A. M. GRAZIANO (ed.), *Behavior therapy with children*, pp. 278–82. Chicago: Aldine-Atherton, 1971.

———— Operant conditioning. In J. B. SIDOWSKI (ed.), *Experimental methods and instrumentation in psychology*, pp. 421–49. New York: McGraw-Hill, 1966b.

———— *Operant conditioning: An experimental analysis of behavior*. Dubuque, Iowa: Wm. C. Brown, 1970.

ESTES, W. K. The problem of inference from curves based on group data. *Psychological Bulletin*, 1956, 53, 134–40.

————, and SKINNER, B. F. Some quantitative properties of anxiety. *Journal of Experimental Psychology*, 1941, 29, 390–400. Reprinted in B. F. Skinner, *Cumulative record*, pp. 393–404. New York: Appleton-Century-Crofts, 1959. A. C. Catania, ed., *Contemporary research in operant behavior*. Glenview, Ill.: Scott, Foresman, 1968.

EVANS, R. I. *B. F. Skinner: The man and his ideas*. New York: Dutton, 1968.

EYSENCK, H. J., ed. *Experiments in behaviour therapy*. New York: Macmillan, 1964.

FERSTER, C. B. Schedules of reinforcement with Skinner. In P. B. DEWS (ed.), *Festschrift for B. F. Skinner*, pp. 37–46. New York: Appleton-Century-Crofts, 1970.

————, and SKINNER, B. F. *Schedules of reinforcement*. New York: Appleton-Century-Crofts, 1957.

GOLDIAMOND, I. Stuttering and fluency as manipulatable operant response classes. In L. KRASNER and L. P. ULLMANN (eds.), *Research in behavior modification*, pp. 106–56. New York: Holt, Rinehart, & Winston, 1965.

GREENSPOON, J. The reinforcing effect of two spoken sounds on the frequency of two responses. *American Journal of Psychology*, 1955, 68, 409–16.

HEISE, G. A. Auditory thresholds in the pigeon. *American Journal of Psychology*, 1953, 66, 1–19.

HONIG, W. K., ed. *Operant behavior: Areas of research and application*. New York: Appleton-Century-Crofts, 1966.

JOHNSON, D. F. Determiners of selective stimulus control in the pigeon. *Journal of Comparative and Physiological Psychology*, 1970, 70, 298–307.

KELLER, F. S. Studies in International Morse code: I. A new method of teaching code reception. *Journal of Applied Psychology*, 1943, 27, 407–15.

———— Psychology at Harvard (1926–1931): A reminiscence. In P. B. DEWS (ed.), *Festschrift for B. F. Skinner*, pp. 29–36. New York: Appleton-Century-Crofts, 1970.

————, and SCHOENFELD, W. N. The psychology curriculum at Columbia College. *American Psychologist*, 1949, 4, 165–72.

———— *Principles of psychology*. New York: Appleton-Century-Crofts, 1950.

KRASNER, L. Studies of the conditioning of verbal behavior. *Psychological Bulletin*, 1958, 55, 148–70.

LOVAAS, O. I. A program for the establishment of speech in psychotic children. In J. K. WING (ed.), *Early childhood autism*. pp. 115–44. Oxford: Pergamon Press, 1966. Reprinted in H. N. Sloane and Barbara D. McAulay (eds.), *Operant procedures in remedial speech and language training*, pp. 125–54. Boston: Houghton-Mifflin, 1968.

MACCORQUODALE, K. On Chomsky's review of Skinner's *Verbal Behavior*. *Journal of the Experimental Analysis of Behavior*, 1970, 13, 83–99.

NOTTERMAN, J. M., and MINTZ, D. E. *Dynamics of response*. New York: John Wiley, 1965.

OLDS, J., and MILNER, P. Positive reinforcement produced by electrical stimulation of septal area and other regions of the rat brain. *Journal of Comparative and Physiological Psychology*, 1954, 47, 419–27.

PLATT, J. R. Strong inference. *Science*, 1964, 146, 347–52. Reprinted in W. C. BECKER (ed.), *An empirical basis for change in education*, pp. 84–98. Chicago: Science Research Associates, 1971.

REYNOLDS, G. S. *A primer of operant conditioning*. Glenview, Ill.: Scott, Foresman, 1968.

SALZINGER, K. Experimental manipulation of verbal behavior: A review. *Journal of Genetic Psychology*, 1959, 61, 65–95.

SCHAEFER, H. H., and MARTIN, P. L. *Behavioral therapy*. New York: McGraw-Hill, 1969.

SCHOENFELD, W. N., CUMMING, W. W., and HEARST, E. On the classification of reinforcement schedules. *Proceedings of the National Academy of Sciences*, 1956, 42, 563–70.

SHERMAN, J. A., and BAER, D. M. *Appraisal of operant therapy techniques with children and adults. In C. M. FRANKS (ed.), Behavior therapy: Appraisal and status*, pp. 192–219. New York: McGraw Hill, 1969.

SIDMAN, M. A note on functional relations obtained from group data. *Psychological Bulletin*, 1952, *49*, 263–69.

—— *Tactics of scientific research: Evaluating experimental data in psychology*. New York: Basic Books, 1960.

—— Stimulus generalization in an avoidance situation. *Journal of the Experimental Analysis of Behavior*, 1961, *4*, 157–69. Reprinted in T. VERHAVE (ed.), *The experimental analysis of behavior: Selected readings*, pp. 216–31. New York: Appleton-Century-Crofts, 1966.

SKINNER, B. F. On the conditions of elicitation of certain eating reflexes. *Proceedings of the National Academy of Sciences*, 1930, *16*, 433–38.

—— The concept of the reflex in the description of behavior. *Journal of General Psychology*, 1931, *5*, 427–58. Reprinted in B. F. Skinner, *Cumulative record*, pp. 319–46. New York: Appleton-Century-Crofts, 1959.

—— On the rate of formation of a conditioned reflex. *Journal of General Psychology*, 1932, *7*, 274–86. Reprinted in A. C. Catania (ed.), *Contemporary research in operant behavior*, pp. 48–52. Glenview, Ill.: Scott, Foresman, 1968.

—— Two types of conditioned reflex: A reply to Konorski and Miller. *Journal of General Psychology*, 1937, *16*, 272–79. Reprinted in B. F. Skinner, *Cumulative record*, pp. 376–83. New York: Appleton-Century-Crofts, 1959. A. C. Catania (ed.), *Contemporary research in operant behavior*, pp. 53–56. Glenview, Ill.: Scott, Foresman, 1968.

—— *The behavior of organisms: An experimental analysis*. New York: Appleton-Century-Crofts, 1938.

—— "Superstition" in the pigeon. *Journal of Experimental Psychology*, 1948, *38*, 168–72. Reprinted in A. C. Catania (ed.), *Contemporary research in operant behavior*, pp. 62–64. Glenview, Ill.: Scott, Foresman, 1968.

—— *Walden Two*. New York: Macmillan, 1948.

—— Are theories of learning necessary? *Psychological Review*, 1950, *57*, 193–216. Reprinted in A. C. Catania (ed.), *Contemporary research in operant behavior*, pp. 4–21. Glenview, Ill.: Scott, Foresman, 1968.

—— *Science and human behavior*. New York: Macmillan, 1953.

—— A case history in scientific method. *American Psychologist*, 1956, *11*, 221–33. Reprinted in S. Koch (ed.), *Psychology: A study of science*, vol. II. New York: McGraw-Hill, 1958. B. F. SKINNER, *Cumulative record*, pp. 77–100. New York: Appleton-Century-Crofts, 1959. A. C. Catania (ed.), *Contemporary research in operant behavior*, pp. 27–39. Glenview, Ill.: Scott, Foresman, 1968.

—— *Verbal behavior*. New York: Appleton-Century-Crofts, 1957.

—— Pigeons in a pelican. *American Psychologist*, 1960, *15*, 28–37.

—— *In* E. G. BORING and G. LINDZEY (eds.), *A history of psychology in autobiography*, vol. 5, pp. 387–413. New York: Appleton-Century-Crofts, 1967. Reprinted in P. B. DEWS (ed.), *Festschrift for B. F. Skinner*, pp. 1–21. New York: Appleton-Century-Crofts, 1970.

TABER, J. I., GLASER, R., and SCHAEFER, H. H. *Learning and programmed instruction*. Reading, Mass.: Addison-Wesley, 1965.

TEITELBAUM, P. The use of operant methods in the assessment and control of motivational states. *In* W. K. HONIG (ed.), *Operant behavior: Areas of research and application*, pp. 565–608. New York: Appleton-Century-Crofts, 1966.

ULLMANN, L. P., and KRASNER, L., eds. *Case studies in behavior modification*. New York: Holt, Rinehart & Winston, 1965.

ULRICH, R. E., STACHNIK, T. J., and MABRY, J., eds. *Control of human behavior*. Glenview, Ill.: Scott, Foresman, 1966.

VERHAVE, T., ed. *The experimental analysis of behavior: Selected readings*. New York: Appleton-Century-Crofts, 1966.

WETZEL, R. Use of behavioral techniques in a case of compulsive stealing. *Journal of Consulting Psychology*, 1966, *30*, 367–74. Reprinted in A. M. GRAZIANO (ed.), *Behavior therapy with children*, pp. 264–77. Chicago: Aldine-Atherton, 1971.

WYCKOFF, L. B., JR. The role of observing responses in discrimination learning. *In* D. P. HENDRY (ed.), *Conditioned reinforcement*, pp. 237–60. Homewood, Ill.: Dorsey Press, 1969.

The title of this chapter may be somewhat misleading to those who associate the term "human learning" with Ebbinghaus and nonsense syllables. This chapter will not attempt to bring together data in the verbal aspects of human learning since the time of the earlier valuable summaries and reviews by McGeoch (1942), McGeoch and Irion (1952), Hovland (1951), and the succession of *Annual Reviews*. An excellent summary has been provided in a little volume by Jung (1968). Specialized treatments of verbal and language learning are available in the work of Staats (1968) and collections of papers by Hall (1967), Cofer (1963), Dixon and Horton (1968), and Slamecka (1967); in fact, the field is flooded with reports of verbal learning, memory studies, and psycholinguistics. Anyone hoping to control this flood by personal assimilation is, at least, ambitious.

In the face of the flood we are in danger of overlooking basic and fundamental issues, problems, and principles, and I plan to map this area with suitable markers so that when the flood recedes we can make progress in some systematic fashion.

This chapter, then, will include:

1. An attempt to relate our present thinking to past endeavors that were, to a large extent, devoted to studies of animal learning and generated principles frequently and freely translated into the human realm. Whatever else man is, he is still an animal and we have no *a priori* reason to believe he does not learn as an animal learns. To ignore the contributions of students of animal learning may be to get lost in a maze of mentalism or computer transistors.
2. The basic variables of reinforcement and motivation, deriving largely from animal research, must be placed in appropriate settings and evaluated for application to human learning operations.
3. At the present time there is no widely accepted theory of human learning succinctly stated. What such a theory should be like must be described and perhaps ventured in a preliminary way.
4. Any such theory must be tested against the wide range of developments in the problem areas that have attracted

B. R. Bugelski

Human Learning

26

researchers in recent years (e.g., one-trial learning, mediation, meaning, imitation, free recall, etc., as well as such traditional problems of the human learning specialist as retroactive inhibition, transfer, the serial learning curve, etc.).

With full awareness of the scope of the problems and a recognition of the unlikelihood of successful attainment, this chapter will be an essay with these four objectives.

Part I. Human and Animal Learning

The title of this section, like that of the chapter itself, suggests a distinction that may be misleading and of little merit. The notion that human learning differs from that of nonhumans can begin to make sense only if different principles of learning apply in those realms of behavior wherein humans differ from other species. As far as we know, these differences, except for the obvious one of language and communication—i.e., interaction in verbal terms—are somewhat trivial; the opposable thumb and erect posture—both of which facilitate tool-using—do give man, compared to other species, great advantages in coping with the environment. What relevance they have for learning itself is largely unknown.

A difference between man and his animal relatives that may bear on learning is the relatively prolonged period of infancy when the human is carried about and does little, but where much is done to and for him. This language-less period may involve considerable learning that is not detectable by observation but can only be inferred through later experimentation. When such inferences are not correctly incorporated into analyses of learning, great errors may be made by learning theorists. The nature of the basic mechanisms underlying behavior may be seriously misinterpreted if theorists endow humans with various innate capacities, abilities, and functions that are not, in fact, inborn.

The difficulties of studying learning in the infant and the contrasting ease of observing captive adults in college classrooms have distorted the psychology of human learning into the analyses of college freshmen learning contrived verbal patterns in artificial and contrived circumstances. What has emerged, therefore, may be largely irrelevant to any basic analysis. For generations, we have studied college students learning lists of nonsense syllables (more recently, unrelated words, and, still more recently, related words [Lachman 1968]) in the standard arrangements of serial or paired-associate lists. What we now know applies to the learning by such subjects of such materials and to very little else. In some researches, humans have been studied in the acquisition of skills (pursuitrotor, tracking, mirror-drawing, dart-throwing, and card-sorting types of tasks) or in finding their way through pencil mazes. Again, whether student subjects observed in such situations' offer useful data for an analysis of human learning is questionable. Tracing a star in a mirror may provide information of some value if the subject has never seen a mirror before, but whether a college student provides pure learning data is dubious. Schultz (1969) has reviewed the problems inherent in the use of college student subjects; after consideration of the issues arising from experimenter bias and demand characteristics

research he is inclined to conclude that much of our voluminous data is of dubious value.

We are not much better off with the results of most studies of animal learning. To a considerable degree, energy has been expended on studies of instrumental behavior where there is a serious question as to what is being learned. We shall return to the question in Part II. For the present, we recognize that even with rats running a simple T-maze, psychologists were unable to agree on whether the rats were learning "about a place" or to make a response, and whether or not reinforcement was required. The great work of Pavlov, while honored by lip service, has been largely ignored by American psychologists because of their preoccupation with reinforcement, and although Watson and Guthrie did their best to make Pavlov popular, they fought a losing battle in the United States.

The post-World War II concern of psychologists with applications, clinical (and educational), and the collapse of traditional learning theory with the deaths of the giants of learning theory in the 1950s left a vacuum that has been filled by the sudden and explosive development of "human learning" research, which at once attempts to be practical, genuine, meaningful, and "cognitive." The modern human learning student has rejected not only Ebbinghaus, but also most—if not all—animal learning findings, including its basic orientation of the *S-R* approach. In some quarters this has become anathema.

A science of psychology without an *S-R* approach is in great danger of wandering off from its foundation in the biological sciences and its interest in behavior. It is not our present concern to support the *S-R* approach in its simple form or in its various modifications as two-phase or multiple stage *S-R* developments, but to recall to the enthusiastic human learning psychologist his need to come to terms with the animal nature of man, a creature with a nervous system and a chemically controlled brain.

While it is true that we cannot yet demonstrate the operations of stimulus traces, synapses, or the chemical reactions in learning and memory, there is a gradually accumulating body of data about the functions of the nervous system in behavior which may someday make the learning process understandable and perhaps controllable. Some longtime students of verbal behavior appreciate the need to keep the channels of communication with physiology open. Others, of course, couldn't care less. An approach that divorces itself from stimuli and responses and deals with some hypothetical entities (concepts, information processing, search, storage, retrieval strategy, plan testing, and organization), will find itself equally divorced from a deterministic science. It will begin (and has already started to do so) to endow the learner with capacities and operations without conceivable physiological underpinnings and with no hope of a unified science of behavior.

It is not the present intent to oppose the practice of postulating hypothetical constructs. Indeed, the concept of learning is itself a hypothetical construct based on inferences from observations of presumed indicants. Rather it is the intent here to restrict reference to such intervening hypothetical processes to those that may be demonstrated in physiological terms. A construct like "organization of information" may be incorporated in some computer program. At the moment it appears dubious that we will find a neurological equivalent. Computer analogues must be recognized for what they are—analogues. Before we proceed further, it is in order to clarify and come to grips with a definition of learning. In the Steven's *Handbook* (1951) such an attempt was made on five different occasions with the rather disappointing outcome that learning was something that remained after all changes in behavior that could be ascribed to fatigue, disease, growth, and drugs, were accounted for. Hilgard (1951) rather casually defined learning as what learning psychologists study or what the experiments in the field were about. I think we must do better and approach the issue positively. Many writers have been content to go along with the McGeoch (1942) attempt: "Learning is a change in performance as a result of practice." Some writers translate this into "The modification of behavior as a result of experience." Such definitions are probably adequate to get on with the job without getting mired in semantic quibbles even though they omit much (How much and what kind of changes? What is practice? What is exposure? What kind of experience? etc.).

I prefer to think of learning as an unconscious neural process (a physiological change) such that an organism, once having undergone such a process, is now able to (but need not) respond to a stimulus in a way not previously possible.

Consider the case of conditioning the cessation of an alpha rhythm of the brain. Here a tone can come to stop an alpha rhythm that formerly ceased only at the introduction of light stimulation. The subject is conditioned; learning has occurred; but the subject does not know this any more than he might know that he now gives a *GSR* to some stimulus that formerly did not elicit one.

How does such learning, as the conditioning of the alpha cessation, go on? Here we have no reinforcers in any serious sense of the Thorndike, Hull, Skinner variety: a few paired presentations and the new response tendency has been initiated. Things have gone on in the subject's head that he cannot describe. Should we take a case on another level and, say, speak to a subject using some such sounds as *zyk* or *vud* can we not assume that two neural (auditory) responses will occur in succession and that subsequently saying *zyk* will automatically arouse a neural response corresponding in some way to that originally aroused by *vud* as a spoken stimulus?

For another crude illustration, we might ask the normal preschool child for the cube root of 27. We are not surprised that he does not respond with "3". If we now suggest to him that when he hears the question again he should say "3" and he does so, he has learned. We need not presume he knows what a cube root is or anything beyond the fact that he says "3" on the appropriate occasion. He could not do this prior to the experience (learning); he can do it now (note that he need not) and, if he does, we can say he has learned. A more classical illustration is at hand from Pavlov's work: prior to paired stimulation of bell and food, the dog does not salivate to bell alone. Subsequent to this experience (learning) he salivates when the bell rings. He has learned. In neither case do we know precisely what has been learned while at the same time we do know that something has been learned. Another way of stating the case for a definition of learning is by using *antedating* as a criterion. If an organism responds to a stimulus in a way that differs from its natural response to this stimulus and does so *before* the natural stimulus for the response in question is presented, we can again state that learning has occurred. The stage actor in rehearsal who snaps his fingers and mutters "cue me" has not yet learned. When he recites his lines without cues, he has.

Part II. The Learning of Motivation

No function in behavior has so confounded the interpretation of understanding of learning as has that of motivation. The confounding arises from the multiple roles assigned to motivation in theoretical pronouncements where it has been described now as cause, now as effect, as general drive (*D*) or as specific incentive, as director or energizer. Motives have been described as first necessary for learning (to initiate behavior) to occur and then as having to be reduced or satisfied to make the learning occur or be strengthened.

Thorndike, the pioneer investigator in learning, did not concern himself with motivation in other than indirect ways. He used food as a reward and obviously knew that food was useful only to hungry cats. He also recognized some kind of escape motive operating in his caged animals, but primary focus was on rewards or satisfaction. In his later (Thorndike 1932) work with college students he was still concerned with rewards and assumed that to hear "Right" rather than "Wrong" was rewarding. The fact that it was also information did not affect him. Knowledge of results was only satisfying and a new reward, all-powerful and ubiquitous, was available to account for any learning where more tangible rewards could not be discerned.

The same orientation has characterized the important behavioral control work of Skinner. Skinner (1938) recognizes the need for having deprived, or "lean and hungry," rats and pigeons, but, again, deprivation is required only to make food rewards effective. There has never been any quarrel about the effectiveness of food in controlling some kinds of behavior of hungry organisms. Nor has there been any question that stimuli on the other side of the psychological fence, namely those related to punishment, have potency for controlling escape or avoidance. Controversies arose only when rewards and punishments were impressed into the service of learning, largely through the powerful influence of Clark Hull (1943).

It should be remembered that voices, and strong voices at that, had been raised by Watson, Guthrie, and Tolman—and we should not ignore Lashley and the entire Gestalt school—against the operation of making learning dependent upon reinforcement. Their demonstrations of latent learning and learning by insight were denied or explained away. The tour de force indulged in by Hull to account for latent learning by a sudden impact of incentive (*K*) now appears as a weak contrivance, as does his attempt to incorporate Pavlovian conditioning into reinforcement theory as a "special case" wherein the *US* serves as both response generator and reinforcer.

To a considerable degree the voices of critics were unheeded and the concepts of positive and negative reinforcement are now rather generally accepted (see most introductory texts and note the powerful teaching machine movement) as determining the course of instrumental or operant learning. Conditioning of the Pavlovian variety has largely been written off; even though everyone mentions Pavlov's dogs and bells, no one seems to do much more than that about it. Thorndike's dictum (see Woodworth 1938) that it was a laboratory curiosity has come into general acceptance.

The difficulties inherent to the reward-strengthens-learning principle became apparent to Hull (1952) and Spence (1954), and they began to restate the principle in various ways. Learning came to be a function of *N* (number of trials) but somehow *N* always seemed to mean effective trials or reinforced trials, or correct trials, where a reinforcement process could be assumed or understood. Rewards became *incentives* with a stimulus function implied, but not detailed, for the human level.

Through the forties and fifties psychologists struggled with the problem of reinforcement and the struggle is still continuing. It is now being demonstrated how physiological (cerebral) mechanisms can be excited to function as reinforcers for instrumental responses. The modern psychological research may be nothing more than a technologically more complex or sophisticated way of demonstrating what was done more crudely when sucrose solutions were injected into caudal veins of rats when they moved their heads to the left or right as the experimenter desired. The intellectual or scientific issue is not resolved by such research.

In 1960 O. Hobart Mowrer (1960*a*) suggested a way out. He perceived the issue clearly and recognized that the accumulated evidence dictated a sharp break with traditional reinforcement theory as far as learning is concerned while retaining a motivational function for reinforcement. Strongly influenced by the weight of the evidence for latent learning, Mowrer asserted bluntly and forcefully that learning not only can occur without reinforcement, but that all learning does indeed so occur.

Immediately Mowrer was faced with what by now was a formidable structure among learning psychologists. The view (which Mowrer had helped so greatly to generate) was that there are two kinds of learning: Pavlovian conditioning and so-called instrumental or operant learning. It should be noted also that in the academic circles the latter kind of learning was receiving far more attention as the really interesting kind, the more pervasive and human kind. With another bold stroke, Mowrer cut through this knot by asserting that we had been misled; that only one kind of learning occurs at any level; that this kind is a simple conditioning of what might be called the *S-S* or sensory-sensory variety; and that motor responses are not learned and never have been, nor are responses learned or conditioned to stimuli directly.[1]

The precise nature of the conditioning process was not spelled out by Mowrer in terms of any neural or other model. The entire case was put in terms of the assumption that certain stimuli (electric shock, food) would generate, in an unconditioned sense, some emotional condition, some primarily visceral reactions. The primary emotional state that calls for adjustment (in survival terms) is fear. The reality of fear is assumed. Fear and its opposite—a decrease in fear or a rise in hope—can be conditioned[2] to external or internal (primarily sensory feedback stimuli from some response mechanism) stimulation. Once the organism is in a state of fear, regardless of whether the stimulation was unconditioned or conditioned, the organism would engage in retreat, avoidance, and, if lucky, escape. The reduction of fear would result not in learning to make certain movements

(these movements were already available to the organism) but in what Mowrer loosely referred to as *wanting* to perform those movements or responses. Avoidance behavior becomes a matter of elimination of those movements that are not wanted.

The distinction between fear and hope is not clearly discriminated in Mowrer's presentation. Any painful (maladjusted nonhomeostatic) state (e.g., hunger) is described as having a fear component. The appearance or ingestion of food reduces not only hunger, but also hunger-fear. The anticipatory reduction of the fear component in hunger-fear generates the new state (hope). Stimuli associated with food (so-called secondary reinforcers) arouse hope. Under the influence of hope, the organism continues motion or movement in the same direction (this could also be reflected in continuing to stand still if that generated hope) or repeats activities if they are readily repeatable, as in the case of bar-pressing or pecking.

The function of reinforcers is then simple. They are of two kinds: *incremental* drive (negative emotion-arousing), and *decremental* (hope-arousing). They generate emotions (fear, hope, and their derivatives); emotions (natural or conditioned responses) guide and control behavior—i.e., they motivate. Some of Skinner's students have had remarkable successes in manipulating the behavior of schoolchildren and patients in mental hospitals. An example of the latter involved getting schizophrenics out of the ward and into a dining room at some reasonable pace after a dinner bell rang. By closing the dining room for late arrivers the patients were successfully "shaped up" to come to meals on time. What did they learn that they did not already know? Reinforcements control behavior, not learning. Reinforcers, in short, are motivators. They have nothing to do with learning *per se*. An illustration might be in order.

A youth on a basketball court for the first time is handed a basketball and told to "shoot a basket." We can presume that he has seen others try and need not concern ourselves about the galaxy of learnings that brought our youth to the foul line in a gymnasium.

The youth has already thrown some missiles at some targets and has no basic difficulty in throwing a basketball at some visible target. We can presume a miss on the first try. Mowrer would presume a conditioned negative emotional reaction to accompany such a failure. Mowrer would further presume that kinesthetic stimuli from arms, legs, body are pouring in at the moment of ball-release. A moment later the failure occurs and "fear" is generated. This fear is now conditioned to the pattern of kinesthetic feedback stimuli. On the next trial the youth begins the action and simultaneously experiences feedback from these preliminary movements. If the pattern is similar, fear will be generated and the youth will desist or alter his muscular posture. He tries again—another failure—and another kinesthetic pattern is conditioned to fear. In due course, many negative patterns will be conditioned to fear and will be replaced by alternate movements, some of which may result in success. In such instances the youth "feels hope" and he adjusts his limbs, hips, and torso. He "hopes" that he will make it on certain occasions. Eventually, with sufficient practice he should develop such "skill" that he will know without looking whether the effort was a success. He can shoot baskets while wearing a blindfold. His muscles will have told him as much as his eyes can.

The development of a skill is, then, a matter of conditioning certain kinesthetic feedbacks to a continuance of a set of ongoing

---

[1]There might be some retrenchment permitted here in connection with protective or emotional reflex responses, e.g., the eyelid blink or the *GSR*. One could postulate some primordial protective mechanism subject to conditioning in connection with vital organs or biological survival.

[2]No one has yet described a widely acceptable account of how fear itself could be learned on reinforcement principles. The problem is to find some drive or drive stimulus reduction feature generated by a state of fear. (Miller's [1959] effort cannot be described as having been well received. Miller's later efforts in this connection will be described shortly on p. 519.

movements. The learner has learned to want to do some things and not others which he is equally capable of doing, if not more so. It is presumed that informational types of learning are acquired in the same fashion; i.e., a person learns to want to say certain things under the control of fear and hope. He learns the information itself on an entirely different basis, namely, an *S-S* conditioning.

We may have arrived then at Mowrer's conclusion: that reinforcers are merely the unconditioned stimuli for fear or hope, and all that can be learned with their employment is to fear or be hopeful, when other (the conditioned) stimuli are present. All movements, responses, information, or knowledge are already available (from growth and development) or are acquired without the operation of reinforcers.

The controversy is by no means ended. Recently (1969) Miller has reopened the entire question by reporting on a series of experiments designed to demonstrate that all learning is instrumental; that is, reinforcement-developed. His approach consists of demonstrating that even the so-called autonomic responses are not autonomic at all but can be brought under control by reinforcement procedures. Thus, he reports the acquisition of responses like salivation, urine secretion, heart rate changes, blood pressure changes, and EEG alterations under reinforcement procedures. In much of this research animals are curarized and unable to move. This procedure, incidentally, might add weight to the argument that overt performance is unnecessary for learning. In essence Miller demonstrates to his satisfaction that a rat can learn to change its heart beat rate, for example—to make it beat more or less rapidly upon a signal. What Miller is asserting is that there is really only one kind of learning, and that is reward learning.

Careful attention must be paid to the extensive and systematic research reported by Miller. He may prove to be correct. He admits, as Katkin and Murray (1968) have pointed out, that there is no readily acceptable evidence that autonomic responses can be acquired through reinforcement operations in human subjects, but considers this a temporary weakness in research ingenuity. It may prove useful to review one of the studies cited by Miller (1969). With his colleague DiCara, Miller trained 12 curarized rats (6 per group) to increase the heart beat rate or to decrease it. The procedure involved a 10-sec. signal (light or tone) followed by a shock. The shock and signal continued until the heart beat changed in the desired direction. Over a series of trials the heart beats did begin to alter and significant differences were obtained between the responses to signals and the responses during "blank," and no signal periods. It is presumed here that termination of shock is reinforcing. Nothing, however, is said about the onset of shock and its effects. Considering the measure being used (heart rate) it is plausible that rats, after being shocked repeatedly, will react with fear to any prior signal. While we normally assume an acceleration of heart rate as a sign of fear there is no requirement that all rats respond in this fashion at all times and, in some instances, an inhibition of the heart might also occur. For those rats whose heart rates increased to the signal there would be no problem for Mowrer or Pavlov. They would judge that the rats merely learned to be frightened more and more effectively as training continued if the rise in heart rate is taken as a measure. The termination of the shock could well be irrelevant. The rats whose heart beat rate declined do present a problem. To interpret their declining heart rates as reflections of greater fear (rather than an adjustment which was instrumental in terminating the shock) is at first thought at least paradoxical if not unacceptable. However, it should be noted that Miller provides comparison rates for both groups in the "blank" periods. In both cases the blank period heart rate follows the pattern of rats under warning stimulus conditions; this could be interpreted to reflect an increasing fear response (whether measured by heart rate increase or decrease) to the general environmental and procedural stimuli. Furthermore, when Miller applied the "safe" stimulus, the heart rates in both instances show less change from what might be a normal heart rate and could be interpreted as indicating some state meriting a description like "relief" or "hope."

The experiments of Miller and his colleagues on autonomic instrumental learning call for rather complex and involved procedures and delicate measures. Replication calls for uncommon skills and facilities. Each of the experiments reported has its difficulties and while they may force a future conclusion that autonomic responses can be brought under control by rewards, they are not yet so conclusive and potent as to reverse the weight of the evidence that humans can and do learn without rewards. For the present, the conclusion can be maintained that the learning of autonomic responses is more or less directly a matter of Pavlovian conditioning, even though instrumental procedures can be employed to bring about some autonomic responses, perhaps through indirectly instituting the necessary conditions for Pavlovian conditioning to occur.

A recent study by Shapiro (1969) and his colleagues illustrates the difficulties of research of this kind on humans. An attempt was made to have human subjects control their blood pressure by raising it or lowering it at a given signal. The subjects did not know (although the use of an arm cuff might raise some question) what they were supposed to be doing. If their pressure followed the experimenter's purposes, a picture of a Playboy nude would be shown to the subjects. No evidence was supplied by any independent data that such pictures are, in fact, reinforcers. The subjects appeared to show some systematic effects in that the group that was supposed to lower the blood pressure did so. This could be the consequence of simple relaxation. No control group was described. The subjects who were to raise their pressure were not able to do so but more or less kept the original level. The subjects were all instructed to try to keep a light flashing. (This light was controlled by rises or falls in pressure.) How the effects were accomplished is not really clear from such a study and the role of the reinforcer is by no means established. Keeping the light flashing might itself have been the basic concern of the subjects and whatever efforts they were able to employ (tensing or relaxing), despite instructions to the contrary, might well have determined the results.

In the remainder of this chapter the position taken will be that the basic learning operation consists of an *S-S* association activity with the understanding that, like any other theoretical statement, it will be subject to change and correction by research results.

SECONDARY REINFORCERS AND SECONDARY DRIVES

The basic problem faced by reinforcement theoreticians was the obvious and simple fact that once you left the rat world with its electric shocks and food pellets and turned your attention to human learning, you had no convenient physiological drives or physical reinforcers to manipulate. Not only do humans learn without ostensible reinforcement and under aversive conditions, but they also learn things they do not want to learn. Now, all the talents for circumlocution that could be exploited were called on. What is the explanation for a human learning by himself while reading a book? How explain the learning of a student in a lecture class? How explain the complete mastery of an obnoxious television commercial (Church 1961)? New sources of motivation and/or reinforcement were now required. For Skinner, reinforcement could be the termination of aversive stimulation or, on the positive side, some immediate knowledge of results (shades of Thorndike!).

The heady and subjective ring of knowledge of results (more correctly, knowledge of being correct) as a reinforcing mechanism has not daunted the entire school of educational programmers even though research results indicate that equally successful performances can be expected when learners are not informed about their possible success. What is more important and immediately suggestive of the essential unsoundness of this principle is the simple fact that on a human verbal level a considerable amount of learning goes on without knowledge of results. Bugelski (1968a) has introduced a technique of studying mediation by mnemonic devices. Using such techniques, college students can memorize (in one trial) a large number of words heard once. Some subjects will remember 50 or more out of 60. The writer himself, using a mnemonic procedure, memorized 25 abstract words after one hearing and was able to report them in serial position order when words were called for at random; i.e., if asked for the 17th word he had no difficulty in responding correctly. The crucial point, however, is that after the list was read, and prior to the test, the writer had no knowledge of results. He certainly did not know that he knew all 25 words, or even one. He did not know what he knew. It can, of course, still be argued that each word was learned through some reinforcement operation, self-supplied; however, if there were any, the writer was not aware of it. All he felt was a growing concern, alarm, and panic as the word list was presented at an unvarying rate. To argue about some kind of momentary satisfactions or reductions of anxiety, elimination of aversive stimulation, appears not only contrary to the facts but leaves one out on the theoretical limb when there is a failure to recall some words that had equal probabilities of enjoying such reinforcement.

The use of knowledge of results as a reinforcement mechanism is an extension of the broader principle of secondary reinforcement. Clearly if humans are to learn much at all it would have to be on the basis of secondary rather than primary reinforcement. The words "good" and "bad" must have somehow acquired reinforcement value. There can be no question that such words and their synonyms are potent behavior controllers, but this only testifies to their function as conditioned stimuli for, according to Mowrer, emotional reactions which then serve as motivators for carrying on in the positive case or avoidance in the negative one.

The vast literature on secondary reinforcement (summarized by Wike 1966) becomes irrelevant to the issue of learning. To demonstrate that a click in a Skinner box occurring just prior to the pellet discharge prolongs bar-pressing extinction only proves that the animal is encouraged to persist in the now fruitless behavior. The click is a conditioned stimulus for hope, in Mowrer's view. Alternatively it can be considered a cue or signal that another signal (the rattle of food or its appearance)

is about to occur. In Hebb's (1949) terms, the click initiates a cell assembly associated with other assemblies (the totality making an "expectancy"). When all expectancies run off smoothly, including their motor components (seizing and ingesting food) the animal behaves in a routine pattern with one cue setting the stage for the next and motor patterns running off in a regular sequence. If the click is not presented in an extinction situation, the appropriate expectancies are not established and the behavior pattern will degenerate.

The suggestion that the click in the Skinner box is only a cue and not a reinforcer has recently received additional support. Schaub, Bugelski, and Horowitz (1968) introduced a light stimulus in a Skinner box as a secondary reinforcer (1 sec. prior to food discharge) at different stages in the training phase for three groups of rats. Each group was permitted 50 bar-presses with food reinforcement, but the light was presented only 25 times for each group. For one group the light occurred with the first 25 trials, for a second it occurred with the last 25 trials, for a third group if occurred at random 25 times. In extinction with the light, the first group exceeded the other two to a highly significant degree. The second group was superior to the third but the performances indicated that a so-called secondary reinforcer works only if it has a cue function. Introducing a stimulus to accompany a reinforcer after a pattern of stimulus sequences has been learned is of little value. The fundamental principle that a stimulus can acquire reinforcement potential if it accompanies a reinforcer is not strictly true. It depends upon the time period in training when it was introduced. The issue has been clearly stated by Mowrer (1960a). He analyzed Blodgett's (1929) experiment on latent learning as the prototype for all learning. All learning is latent. Skinner (1938) himself demonstrated this by showing that a typical extinction curve could be generated by a rat that had never pressed a bar but that had been presented food following a mechanical click. Pressing the bar in the extinction period was followed by the click but no food. The rat did not need to learn to press a bar. It already knew how. During extinction the rat pressed because the click aroused hope for a time. The decline in hope and rise in frustration ("disappointment" in Mowrer's language) eventually ceased to maintain bar pressing. Secondary reinforcers are only conditioned stimuli for emotions, not for overt behavior. To argue otherwise would be to say that while Skinner's rat was emitting the typical extinction curve he was also learning to press the bar. The paradox appears beyond resolution.

The inability to account for human learning by secondary reinforcers is matched by the failure to establish suitable secondary or learned drives to be reduced by the human learning. Despite the valiant effort of Neal Miller (1959) and Brown (1953) to establish anxiety as a base for curiosity and consequently for human learning it is again a case of trying to push one's luck too far. Spence's (1954) efforts to demonstrate that highly anxious rats or humans have more difficulty with complex problems and less difficulty with simple problems demonstrate only that too much stress or disturbance is disconcerting and ineffective in some situations. Again, humans learn too much in casual situations; they learn when they are not asked to or supposed to (see the section on "imitation," p. 526.) or when they do not want to (again the ubiquitous television commercial with its jingle); they also learn to be stressed and uncomfortable.

The approach through anxiety has had a positive and

valuable outcome, although not in the sense of confirming that a learned drive is reduced and thereby affects learning. It has turned investigations toward an appreciation of the arousal system and its role in the processing of incoming stimuli and outgoing motor impulses. On the psychological level it has developed concerns which resulted in such works as Berlyne's (1960) *Conflict, Arousal, and Curiosity*, and more recently, the detailed and systematic study of Trabasso and Bower (1968) on *Attention in Learning*.

Slowly the psychological world is coming back to the recognition of the concept of attention as a fundamental operation in learning. How this concept is treated will determine its survival in its current reincarnation. It will receive due attention later in this chapter. For the moment we will delay its consideration with the conclusion of this section by reasserting that it now appears that learning psychologists can dispense with the concepts of both motivation and reinforcement insofar as learning is concerned. And again, to repeat, these concepts are vital to accounts of behavior or performance, and they are by no means being dismissed. They are being assigned their proper functions. Finally, it might be profitable to consider Mowrer's suggestion that reinforcers are only unconditioned stimuli for emotions that guide behavior. Such a suggestion makes considerable sense and permits us to use learned motives, if we need to, by recognizing that fearful states and their opposites can be conditioned to originally neutral stimuli.

Part III. Theory

In the last decade there has been no serious effort to present a broad theoretical framework that accounts for all learning except that of Mowrer (1960*a*; 1960*b*). The Mowrer opus received less than enthusiastic reviews and if it has actually influenced many, this influence is largely hidden or obscured. References to Mowrer by other writers fail to cite his thinking seriously. Some writers (e.g., Staats 1968) cite Mowrer as support for their own views where it appears that support might be helpful, but many citations seem no more than casual recognition of what might as well be an unread work.

Leaving Mowrer aside, temporarily, it appears that since the passing of major theoretical writers like Hull, Spence, Guthrie, and Tolman, the theoretical field has been abandoned and learning problems have been left to Skinner and his followers, as one major influence group, and to a growing army of researchers in what might be called the "verbal learning" area. The "verbal learners" have revived interest in studies that had their origin in the pioneer work of Ebbinghaus and Müller and culminated in the work of McGeoch in the early forties. In the following two decades (1940–1960), psychologists were more concerned with rats and pigeons than with people. The rat and pigeon work has suffered a considerable decline (except among Skinnerians) with the revival of interest in verbal learning and memory processes now so actively being explored. Quite probably the need for applied psychology during World War II and the rise of the computer have led to the current enthusiasm for signal detection, information processing, simulation, short-term memory, free recall, and "subjective organization." All of these developments are post-World War II phenomena.

The preoccupation of verbal learning psychologists with lists of real words rather than nonsense syllables is another

marked change in orientation. Now psychologists are becoming more concerned with meaning and some verbal learning psychologists prefer to style themselves "cognitive psychologists" for somewhat obscure reasons. Cognitive psychologists have tried to incorporate the new field of psycholinguistics in their efforts but thus far no grand theories have developed to organize the widely scattered efforts that now enjoy some acceptance.

With the new concerns (memory, cognition, psycholinguistics) it is no longer feasible to theorize strictly from a rat psychology orientation. There is no room for concepts like reinforcement and motivation when a college student is asked to listen to a list of 40 words read once and to recite them in any order with no feedback or commentary from the experimenter. Lack of applicability of such popular learning principles of the past has led to an attack on *S-R* psychology generally, and the *S-R* formula has been denounced as not only useless, but harmful in the view which sometimes includes a favorable orientation toward what amount to innate ideas (Chomsky 1959).

Assuming the above description of the situation as a rough but generally correct, if not complete, account of the major trends in learning psychology over the past half-century,[3] it may be in order to take another look at the *S-R* case. It may not be as dead as it has been pronounced. In any event there has never been a proper autopsy or burial, and before the *S-R* approach is put away for good, it might be appropriate to attempt still another theoretical attack on the nature of learning along *S-R* lines, taking into account a rather extensive, if thus far unintegrated, body of factual information some of which was not even hinted at in the above crude and hasty history. What follows will be an effort to present in general terms an explanation of learning phenomena insofar as certain principles seem securely based on adequate data. The theoretical model to be described will not be strong on detail and may appear somewhat anemic, but it seems wiser at this stage to follow the folklore adage of "better safe than sorry."

We start, in keeping with hallowed tradition, with axioms, definitions, and postulates—as few as possible, and hopefully not of an *ad hoc* character. This is not done with any pretense of grandeur nor as some attempt at formal precision but only to make clear the assumptions that are taken for granted (the so-called axioms) and the assumptions that require some supportive argumentation. While some use will be made of symbols, they are only for shorthand purposes. The references to physiological processes are only such as are generally accepted and are not intended to suggest some detailed appreciation of their nature.

Axioms

1. *Living things (organisms) are motile.*[4] Being in an environment they must move toward or away from one aspect or another of this environment. Moving in one direction auto-

---

[3]George Mandler has described the changing scene most effectively in his review (1967) of current trends. Mandler presents a detailed account of an "information processing" treatment that he specifically describes as a non-theory.

[4]The need for this axiom is to avoid the problem of initiation of behavior. As long as an organism is alive it is in motion and there is no need to be concerned with the fact that it is moving. All that calls for explanation is a change in direction. Stimuli, including drive stimuli, can be called upon to account for such changes.

matically dictates a movement away from other directions. Such movements can be called *approach* and *avoidance* but these words should be used as neutral terms. Alternate terms such as *acceptance* and *rejection* can be substituted. The motility can also be interpreted as repetition of some activity (acceptance, getting more of) or inhibition (or failure to continue) without movement of the body in space. The motility may appear to subside from time to time (sleep, relaxation) but as long as life prevails there is activity—neural or visceral. From this point of view, a polio victim in an iron lung, or a curarized dog or human are all in motion, at least in part, and subject to the influence of external or internal stimulation.

2. *Causes are followed by effects.* In the area of learning phenomena we recognize certain events (e.g., stimuli) as preceding certain other events (responses). Behavior is continuous, with one event following another. In this sense there can be no uncaused events. In the situation where one behavioral event (a movement or response) follows another, the earlier movement or response is assumed to be the cause of (presumably, to generate stimuli for) the subsequent response.

3. *All behavior is determined.* The organism is to be considered as having been (and if alive, still being) programmed either by original, natural inheritance of certain structures (including dominant neural pathways for certain stimulus inputs) or by learning. All structures have (or have had and are now vestigial) some function developed in the course of evolution. Some behaviors must be taken as a given; e.g., human infant vocalization.

DEFINITIONS

1. *Environment stimulus.* A stimulus (S_E) is an environmental event or change (sound, light, physical impact) that activates a sensory structure and initiates an afferent neural process (NP_S). Note that no motor event or observable response or behavior is necessary or required to complete this definition; nor is anything said about "sensations" or awareness.

2. *Internal stimulus (S_I).* Internal organs due to pressure or other changes and contraction, and muscles, tendons, and joints, due to contraction or relaxation can also initiate neural processes (NP_S) of an afferent nature. Such stimuli (organic, kinesthetic) can also be called feedback stimuli.

3. *Responses.* Any activity of a muscle, group, or component thereof (smooth or striate), or gland can be considered a response. The distinction emphasized by Guthrie between movements and acts should be observed. Movements can be identified as R_M and acts as R_A when convenient. Otherwise R will refer to an overt, observable reaction such as making a vocal sound (e.g., pronouncing "yes", or pecking at a target), even though there might be an infinitude of potential movements which might accomplish the net result. In short, a characteristic, common or usual "act" will be considered a response. The fact that any response does indeed consist of movements of some kind should not be forgotten and will probably have to be accounted for in some ultimate analysis.

4. *Neural response (N_R).* It is assumed that an afferent process does not merely expire but that it frequently initiates directly (for practical purposes) some R_M as a reflex action.

On occasion, however, the afferent process arouses no observable R_M but does result in some sensory reaction (R_S) such as when an infant (or adult, for that matter) is exposed to a light in an otherwise dark environment. There may be some observable response (e.g., a pupillary contraction or eye movement), but the response may not be observed and is frequently ignored. The R_S may dissipate or lead to some other neural reaction or succession thereof which may, but need not, eventuate in an observable R_M or R_A. These nonobservable neural responses (e.g., the EEG) to afferent processes can be considered mediational (even though they do not eventuate in an R_M or R_A) and will be labeled $N_R$med.

Thus far nothing has been described that does violence to any existing knowledge of behavior or sensory, motor, or neural activities. A distinction, however, has been emphasized between overt responses (observable behavior) and internal neural processes that are reactions to S_E and S_I or to the consequences of such inputs. It is clear, therefore, that the present view will not be an *S-R* theory except in spirit, if that, and will instead be a multistage theory incorporating, where necessary, neural processes of an afferent and mediational variety similar to Hebb's postulations of cell assemblies and phase sequences. Three other definitions are necessary. The first two arise from a distinction between learning and performance. The third is an elaboration on the sensory reaction when it is aroused by other than a direct, natural stimulus.

5. *Performance* refers to any observable behavior, reflex or otherwise. It includes movements or acts and human vocal (verbal) responses. It is important to note that learning is generally inferred from behavior but failure of performance cannot be depended upon to deny learning; i.e., performance may be momentarily or even permanently inhibited even though learning has occurred. A curarized dog might have learned something but may also die before recovery. Latent learning is the prime example of learning without performance.

6. *Learning* is a hypothetical construct referring to a process of relatively permanent change in neural structures that mediate performance. For a wide range of situations learning can be asserted if an organism that previously did not respond to some S_E in a particular fashion comes to do so when the behavior is normally associated with some other S_E not now present. While there are complications, a simple illustration can clarify the definition: A young child normally will say "Thank you" only when told to do so by its mother in the presence of a gift. Later the gift situation is enough. Saying "Thank you" in such a situation is evidence of learning. In general, the feature of *antedating* is the criterion of learning. A response made in the absence of stimuli that will normally (naturally) evoke it and where it regularly follows some stimulus that originally did not evoke it, is a learned response.

7. *Imagery.* A neural response of a sensory nature (NR_S) can be aroused by stimuli (internal, external), or other neural responses which do not normally arouse that response. Such a response (a conditioned neural sensory-reaction) is called an *image*. Nothing is implied about awareness, although human subjects can frequently assert the presence of such reactions. The response referred to here is one that had previously been operative in the organism and not the original response (N_R) to some external stimulus.

I. *The stimulus trace.* When an S_E (or S_I) initiates an afferent process the said process will continue for some period of time. This is commonly referred to as a stimulus trace and whether an organism responds overtly or not, the trace is presumed to extend over some time span. If a stimulus trace represents (i.e., is initiated by) some unique (strong, strange, unusual) S_E or S_I, it may result in some structural change that will also be unique. Such a stimulus trace must persist over some period of time (unspecifiable, at present) for lasting effect, and if such lasting effect is generated, an organism will react to the same S_E or S_I in the future in about the same way. If an identical stimulus recurs, the same trace (more or less) will be reactivated (taking account of various physiological conditions like refractory phase, other inputs, status of the reticular activating system, etc.). Rapid repetition will result in habituation, adaptation, or saturation effects so that the stimulus may cease to be effective. A period free from stimulation seems necessary for effective rearousal of a trace.

II. *Generalization.* If a stimulus that is similar[5] to a previously effective stimulus impinges on the organism, the trace of the previous stimulus may be activated in whole or in part. The organism may respond (if overt movements are involved) in a way similar to that to the original stimulus. If the response can be considered the same, the stimulus can also be so considered. As far as the organism is concerned, it is the same stimulus even though an experimenter might have labeled it "different." The nominal stimulus must be differentiated from the "stimulus as coded" (*SAS*). In general, organisms respond in one way or in another. If the response differs, the stimulus must be considered different. Organisms do not differentiate or discriminate. They respond differently to different stimuli. If they do not, they are, in effect, responding to the *same* stimulus. This is generalization. There is no implication here that the organism "generalizes" or engages in any logical inferences. It merely responds to stimuli described by some other observer as different in the same way. See Martin (1967) for a more detailed account of this view.

COROLLARY 1.

Recognition and the Memory Trace. If the same (identical) or similar stimulus recurs and the same or similar stimulus trace is aroused, the organism will react as it did before. An observer can call this *"recognition"* if there is the same overt response. If the stimulus has been labeled "different," then the response may be described or judged as an error by the observer. Stimuli rarely occur in isolation and a specific stimulus may not evoke any observable response because other conditions may be eliciting other responses to more potent stimuli. A dog may not bark at the approach of his master, but may bark at strangers. In such a case it can be assumed that he has learned not to bark at his master (or is too busy with other affairs, such as sleeping) and has learned to bark at strangers (or not learned not to bark).

[5]Similarity is an undefined term. It may consist of identical elements or involve identical mediational reactions. In cold fact similarity of stimuli is inferred from the occurrence of similar responses.

With such differential behavior the observer can say: "The dog recognizes his master" simply from observation that the dog does nothing—a significant fact, it will be recalled, for Sherlock Holmes. Recognition, for nonverbal organisms, is differential behavior to stimuli with a prior history.

On the human/verbal level, stimuli and their traces are frequently labeled or otherwise responded to especially in some emotional pattern. Such patterns can also be labeled. If two stimuli are presented in succession and arouse the same label or emotional response the human can respond, after learning the appropriate words, with some verbal response such as "same," "alike," "similar," etc. to the second stimulus. If the stimuli differ (i.e., arouse different responses), the human may say "different," "not the same," etc. We have a simple sample in the Seashore Test of Musical Talent where successive patterns of tones are sounded and the subject is called on to label the second as "same" or "different."

If an extended time interval intervenes between two presentations of the same or similar stimuli, the human subject may be less accurate, from an observer's viewpoint, in his labeling behavior. The trace that was initially activated may no longer be available or may have been incorporated into other stimulus experiences. The subject can now state only something about the present stimulus and, if he has learned to use temporal terms, say that he has seen (heard, felt) such a stimulus before or that the stimulus is novel or that it belongs to such and such a class. The capacity of the human subject to label a stimulus as novel must be presumed. What the foundation for such a response is, is unknown. It may be that a novel stimulus (although nothing is likely to be completely novel), never having been translated into neural action of a precise or specific sort, arouses some stress or disturbance, whereas habitual stimuli encounter no obstacles or are readily processed. Assuming then the capacity to label a stimulus as novel or not, a human subject can be said to "recognize" in that he can deny novelty.

A special case of recognition involves the arousal of stimulus traces by other than the original stimulus. A previously experienced stimulus trace which has been labeled by the subject can be initiated by the label alone (a conditioned sensory reaction or image). Such an image can be generated by a variety of conditioned stimuli or, for that matter, by generalized stimuli. A picture or sketch of an object can arouse the traces originally activated by the stimulus itself; this is generalization. When holdup victims view photographs of known criminals the photographs systematically arouse stimulus traces. Most of these will be novel. Should a particular photograph arouse the traces developed at the time of the holdup, the subject can respond with "That's the one." He has pronounced a trace as not novel. In a complex recognition test of previously viewed objects now mixed in with a collection of "distractor" items, the human subject can dismiss most, if not all, of the distractors as novel and attain a positive score. It is easy to arrange such novel distractors as to guarantee success, or to make use of highly similar stimuli that prevent the subject from easy rejections because similar traces are being reactivated. If a Chinese ideograph is presented in a recognition test for standard English words, it will easily be dismissed as not one of the target series. Synonyms of the original list might prove troublesome.

In summary, it is being postulated that prior experience with a stimulus prepares or changes the organism in such a way as to facilitate its processing upon recurrence. Without prior experience with a stimulus, the organism may have no such processing "machinery" so that the stimulus evokes no regular response and may, in fact, arouse some degree of emotional disturbance, hesitation, inhibition of movement, or other irregular response pattern. On the basis of our private histories we are able to report that we have seen, felt, smelled, heard present stimuli before. Without specific prior experience we report stimuli to be new or novel. It should be recognized that we have easily moved from stimulus traces to memory traces. Stimulus traces that left no permanent aftereffect would preclude any learning. The memory trace is a necessary assumption.

Such memory traces as have been postulated here are considered as basic givens. They can be demonstrated by simple recall or recognition tests and presumably underlie any observations reported in tachistoscopic perception studies, intelligence test recall items, verbal learning operations involving random lists of words presented once. A recall test will normally be less productive of items from a long list than a recognition test because recall depends on still-active stimulus traces (recency effects). A recognition test involving distraction items may result in inflated scores because distractions are recognized as *not* having been experienced, either recently or at all, unless they have a high similarity or confusion value. A recall test suffers from the difficulty involved in attempting to label a declining trace. Studies of short term memory suggest something like an 18 sec. limit for single or simple items; e.g., a trigram heard once if some activity that prevents repetition is introduced (Peterson and Peterson 1959).

One issue involved in the necessity of this postulate is to identify a kind of learning where contiguity does not appear to be intimately relevant and where responses of an overt nature are not necessarily involved. For example, one might remember (recognize) a song heard once before but be unable to whistle or hum the tune prior to the reminder. Such simple recognition learning must be included in any theoretical conception and is here taken as a function of unique stimulation leading to a lasting (for some time) structural change if recognition can be demonstrated beyond a short-term memory span (less than a minute). Note Corollary 2 of Postulate III below.

POSTULATE III CONTIGUITY.

S-S *Conditioning.* When two or more stimulus traces are simultaneously operational they may (subject to as yet unknown limitations; e.g., of dominance, "belongingness," origin, cerebral localization) develop a structure-function relationship such that activation of one will tend to activate the other to some degree.

This is the traditional association postulate and as such it requires no extensive description. It is restricted here to afferent (i.e., S_E or S_I) stimulation sources and their neural consequences. Nothing is stated about overt responses R_M or R_A in this connection. This is a strictly S-S postulate. Nor is there any reference to any motivational or reinforcement principle.

COROLLARY I.

Backward Associations. If two sensory processes are labeled for convenience A and B, then A can initiate B or vice versa. It is possible to impose such orders of presentation that

A will normally initiate B but not the reverse. In ordinary behavior certain consequences of B may already be established at such strength that they will preclude A. Thus on a simple verbal level *table* might initiate *chair*, while *chair* initiates *sit* rather than *table*.

COROLLARY 2.

Generalization in Associations. Any S_E or S_I that can because of similarity in a variety of dimensions or parameters initiate the R_S that is normally aroused by S_E or S_I will also partially or wholly arouse R_S. This generalized R_S may in turn arouse any other R_S normally "associated" with S_E and/or S_I.

POSTULATE IV.

Conditioning of Responses. When some S_E or S_I has as one of its attributes or functions the arousal of some motor activity as in the simple "startle reflex" to a sudden loud sound, any S_E or S_I that accompanies such reflex activity will similarly tend to elicit or be followed by such reactions. The relative ease with which varying reflex responses can be so "conditioned" varies over a wide range. Certain vital processes related to personal or species survival (innate programming) such as generally activate changes in direction of behavior (approach, avoidance) will condition more or less readily. Thus visceral response patterns and their neural participants, commonly called emotions (especially "fear," or its opposite, "hope," according to Mowrer), appear to be readily instigated by some S_Es or S_Is and equally readily conditioned to other S_Es. That is, one S_E can come to substitute for another S_E, or at least in part, in connection with a certain limited (autonomic n.s. regulated) behavioral repetoire. It is assumed here that one S is associated with another S and not that an S is associated with an R although such direct connections with some responses may develop through neural short-circuiting, the nature of which is at present speculative.

COROLLARY 1.

Reinforcement as a Strengthener of Behavior or Performance. Emotional response patterns have the feature that they energize behavior or depress (decrease) it. To this extent they can strengthen or weaken ongoing behavior (not learning) or indeed, reverse the direction of ongoing behavior. The strengthening or weakening feature can be described as *reinforcement* or *weakening* [6] (for lack of a more descriptive word). Mowrer here uses the terms *incremental reinforcement* and *decremental reinforcement.* The former supports or increases avoidance or escape behavior; the latter supports or increases approach behavior. Thus, if fear is aroused, the organism flees with fervor. If pain or hunger is being reduced (hope is present), the organism continues doing what it is doing or staying where it is.

There is no direct role for reinforcement as far as learning is concerned and the use of the term in connection with learning should be abandoned. The term is too easily confused with the

[6] The term *inhibition* is not adopted because of its broad connotations.

introduction of external stimuli (e.g., electric shock or food) and these quickly become identified as *reinforcers*. Note that the reinforcers are functioning as unconditioned stimuli, for fear or hope, and are not directly affecting learning. Skinner's pigeons already know how to peck. Their pecking rates can be controlled by reinforcers but this means only that they have learned to want to peck faster or slower as the schedules dictate.

The presentation of reinforcers is of paramount importance in *controlling the behavior* of nonverbal organisms, as Skinner has so amply demonstrated, but the use of reinforcers only represents our inability to develop the circumstances on the animal level that we can easily set up on the human level to arrange for learning. What strong stimulation or deprivation and subsequent reinforcement do for animals is to catch their attention as effectively as can be done—never as well as desired—because the animal subject is still misdirected in its attention. It is attending to the food or pain rather than to what needs to be done to alleviate the situation, but at least it is not attending to stray and casual stimuli in the environment.

Postulate V.

Attention. Attention to pertinent stimuli or stimulus features is both necessary and sufficient for learning. Attention is defined as being affected by pertinent stimulation without interference from irrelevant stimuli. Attention, then, is a state of the organism, however arrived at (instructions, sets, deprivation, isolation) during which a stimulus (or stimuli) can have an impact (i.e., arouse a neural process) for some adequate (unspecified) time. Attention can be facilitated by an instructor or trainer by preliminary stimulation that may be described as leading to "arousal," vigilance, or "investigatory" reflexes. Attention presumably depends upon effective circumstances in the reticular activating system: the learner cannot be asleep or in a coma. If visual stimulation is being employed, the learner must have his eyes open, be looking in the right direction, and must not be otherwise concerned. He must, indeed, be somewhat concerned (worried, interested, anxious, fearful, curious—all equivalent terms) about the visual stimulation present or about to come. Such concern is facilitated or expressed by search activity, scanning, appropriate fixation, or tracking movements, etc. The learner, in short, must be "occupied,"—indeed, pre-occupied—by, or responding to the stimulation of concern to the teacher or trainer. If the preoccupation is aroused in the learner by circumstances of his own prior arrangement or history, a teacher is unnecessary, only the stimulation is required. It should be appreciated that some stimulus features (e.g., movement, pattern, etc.) might have effective attention-control aspects. If these are relevant, learning would be facilitated. Otherwise there would be inefficiency.

Corollary 1.

Time. Any learning requires time. The amount of time required varies with individuals and with learning content. The references to stimulus traces earlier reflect the significance of this corollary.

It is by now established that to learn (remember, recall, recognize) some content, the material (stimulation) must be present for an adequate time and some interval (trace period) must be relatively free thereafter from any interfering stimulation. To learn a nonsense syllable or a word it suffices to present it clearly for a brief interval (visually, a few milliseconds) or pronounce it distinctly. In an immediate test the learner responds correctly. If the learning called for involves more than one brief stimulus, more time is required during which the learner manifests his concern by occupying himself with the stimulation material if this is feasible. He may repeat it ("keep it in mind") or other neural processes representing past experiences (i.e., earlier sensory images) and emotional stimulation may be activated. Depending upon the nature of the content or task, the activities within the learner will determine the action on a subsequent test. The activities themselves, whether fruitful or not, take time. Luria (1968), for example, describes his remarkable mnemonist who could remember 30 numerals in 3 columns of 10 as being successful in this task if he could "work at it" for a minimum of a minute and a half (3 sec./numeral). It is argued then, that for this subject, learning numerals in this arrangement required a certain amount of time during which attention was "focused" on the content. Other learners might require more or less time. The differences might well be in degree of control of attention and what features of the content used up the time.

A subject looking at a central figure in a large painting would be unable to comment on background features that were not given adequate time. Depending upon the nature of the test, he might pass or fail. He would have learned what he spent the time on.

For the present state of the art or science of learning, it is held that the above listed postulates and corollaries are sufficient to account for the data accumulated in the laboratories over the past 80 years. If they are not sufficient, they must be amplified or ammended and this can be determined by application of the theory to the empirical findings. For the present purposes a theory is considered as an explanatory schema. It may, but need not, generate additional theorems. According to Russell (1927), such deductions are only extractions of what has already been introduced in the theory for the purpose of such deductions. The test of a theory is its capacity to account for empirical observations and not necessarily its fruitfulness for new applications. The ideas that scientists investigate may be sparked by theories, but are not generated by them. The notion that scientists work from theory to theorem is widely recognized as a pretty fantasy.

To test the theory presented above, it remains to array the facts from learning laboratories against it and determine the fit. For present purposes it might suffice to sample the broad field of learning research with a limited number of various data. An exhaustive compilation would call for an encyclopedic effort and knowledge beyond that available to the writer. The samples then will be chosen somewhat at random and as they occur to the writer, with only the guideline that the subject matter has received some regular and common treatment in surveys, symposia, and texts.

Part IV. Testing the Theory

It was stated earlier that a theory can be tested, at least in part, by its ability to account for the facts. In the field of human learning the facts themselves may be debatable, but over the years certain more or less stable findings have been accumulated and we can submit the theory incorporated in the five postulates to the test of accounting for the facts. It is assumed that the application of the theory to much of the data of verbal learning research is self-evident and requires no painstaking elaboration. Much has already been said about paired associate learning, at least by implication, and about recall and recognition. To explain or attempt to explain what may yet turn out to be controversial matters will not help the present theory. For example, the entire field of retroactive and proactive inhibition may prove to be only a matter of an experimental group being asked to remember more or learn more in a given amount of time than a control group (Slamecka 1969).

Instead of attempting explanations of all the data on serial lists, primacy, and recency effects, etc. where the application of the theory is quite clear, I will select four relatively new developments in the human learning area and attempt to determine the fit of the theory to fact. The four areas are: imitation, one-trial learning, mnemonics, and concept formation. We can begin with some somewhat dubious facts from the area of imitation.

IMITATION

For years psychologists were content to ignore the operation of imitation in learning. Thorndike had looked into the problem, found no imitation in his animals, and issued the edict: There is no learning by imitation; we must perform and be rewarded. It may well be that Thorndike's animals did not imitate one another, the popular adage about "monkey see, monkey do" notwithstanding. The great prestige of Thorndike (1913) was sufficient to carry the day, and it was not until Miller and Dollard's (1941) efforts that imitation was reinvestigated. The kind of imitation that interested Miller and Dollard, however, was more in the nature of leadership and followership and the conditioning of behavior to certain cues provided by the leader; thus the behavior itself only appeared to be imitation in the sense of "copying." It was not copying, however, but individual behavior conditioned to specific cues. Again, interest in imitation dropped and was revived for a second time by Bandura, Ross, and Ross (1961) and a succession of coworkers. The publication of the Bandura and Walters (1963) volume placed imitation in such a prominent position that it could no longer be neglected. Mowrer also revived interest in imitation by his paper on talking birds (1954), and in his 1960 volume on symbolic processes he again recognized the importance of imitation, especially in human learning.

There is no need here to review the literature on imitation. Flanders (1968) has already done this. It is sufficient for present purposes to examine the construct of imitation in the context of the theory presented earlier.

The facts of imitation are presumed to be sufficiently documented. Such facts, simply stated, are that some organisms, on occasion, witness another organism, the model (*M*), perform some act or emit some response in a given situation. The model may be reinforced or not—reinforcement is irrelevant. On a subsequent occasion the imitator (*I*) in the same situation performs in the same manner as *M*. In a typical Bandura instance, *M* kicks at a toy clown figure and knocks it down. *I* sees this but is removed from the situation. Later *I* returns, sees the clown in the same position and kicks it over. To account

for this behavior we assume (postulate) that when watching the *M* kick the clown, an S_1-S_2 association was formed such that with S_1 (appearance of clown), S_2 (*M* kicking clown) would be activated. The S_2 process would be in the form of an image, perhaps a succession of images including that of the clown falling, lying on the floor, etc. From here on we are past the point where learning is directly concerned and to explain or present *I*'s behavior becomes a secondary problem, presumably one involving motivation. Some *I*s will kick the clown, others might not. The old Jamesian (James 1890) theory of ideomotor action would account for positive instances as would a Hebbian phase sequence with motor elements. Mowrer would presume that (in the positive instances) *I* had been conditioned to experience hope in connection with stimuli generated by *M* if *M* were previously nurturant and positively reinforcing. It is assumed that watching *M* perform any act would arouse or maintain a hopeful state and that this would be conditioned to the sensory activity involved in observing *M* kick the clown. The imagery involved in now—seeing *M* kick the clown—would similarly generate a positive emotion-guiding behavior. The only behavior that could maintain the positive state would be that of kicking. *I* knows how to kick. Now, in addition, he *wants to*, and if Mowrer is correct, he will kick.

Note that the Mowrer explanation has the advantage of accounting for negative instances in cases where *M* is not admired or reinforcing.

The above account of imitative behavior involved a situation without reinforcement. Many researchers (see Flanders 1968) have studied situations where the *M* is reinforced and *I* is reinforced, if at all, vicariously. In such studies it is apparent that I_s can learn complicated and involved verbal and/or motor sequences without performance or reinforcement. In cases of vicarious reinforcement, according to Mowrer, the *I* imagines himself reinforced (positive or negative emotional reaction) and that this same reaction is generated in the test situation, again guiding, mediating, or controlling the subsequent behavior. In evaluating Aronfreed's (1968) adaptation of this interpretation as "the most sophisticated imitation viewpoint now available," Flanders notes that "far more evidence than is now available is needed to justify the major role assigned to affect." While this is correct enough, there is no other theory that does not regard imitation as some kind of unique behavioral mechanism that is only influenced by such other difficult-to-handle variables as knowledge about controlling stimulus incentives with "activating properties" [sic] and information about "probable reinforcement contingencies" (Bandura 1968).

CONCEPTS AND CONCEPT FORMATION

According to the theory outlined in Part III, concepts are internal responses aroused by any of a number of stimuli that may vary along many dimensions but which have some common element. The responses themselves consist of imaginal, emotional, and minor motoric components and, as such, can be considered as a generalized implementation or substitute for Hull's (1930) r_g, Osgood's (1952) r_m-s_m, and Hebb's (1949) "*t*."

It is assumed here, in common with Martin (1967) and Staats (1967) that stimuli of a given class or variety, say *animals*, will each arouse a specific perceptual-motor-emotional reaction and that part of this reaction will be common to all (or most) stimuli of the class; this partial common reaction will be the concept. To the extent that animals themselves are able to react to other animals with some common response they might merely be operating under the influence of generalization. If, however, the partial common component can be evoked by other stimuli, they could be said to have concepts. A dog that is trained to hunt small animals, e.g., rats, can be sent scurrying about looking for rats if the trainer merely says "Rats." Such a stimulus (a *CS*) can arouse only part of the response that a visible rat would and this partial component would be the concept of rats that the dog had acquired in his earlier training. Such training would of necessity involve the trainer saying "Rats" when the dog was looking at or otherwise involved with actual rats. Note that no specific motor acts would be required to acquire the concept.

On the human level it is assumed that just as a human being can learn to label toothaches, hunger, and other stimuli arousing conditions of a private nature, he can also learn to label such internal responses aroused by verbal or other stimuli. Concepts come before labels and can be enjoyed even by speechless individuals (e.g., deaf mutes) who demonstrate any number of concepts (see Furth 1966) without language to help them. A deaf child can and does sit on stools, chairs, sofas, etc., and clearly demonstrates a concept of objects to-be-sat-on.

Despite the common response feature of concepts, most of our reactions to specific labels or stimuli will be quite direct, concrete, and specific. Even though we have concepts of "animals" or "flowers," we are likely to respond to those terms in rather specific ways. Most college students will think of a dog or a rose when asked to react to those terms with the first thing they think of. What is more, it is likely to be a specific dog (their own) or a specific rose (a red one). The conceptual feature is hardly detectable save for a possible emotional response (some students dislike dogs). Similarly a concept of "crime" is likely to be represented by some emotionally toned imagery of police, muggers, or rioting in the streets. The notion that educated adult humans think in abstract terms and in some ephemeral machinery of a "concept" or ideational nature receives no support from such analyses as research on imagery (Bugelski 1968) has been able to provide. Subjects will report a series of images of such a specific, concrete, and idiosyncratic nature as to add considerable credence to Bishop Berkeley's ancient credo, and to cast considerable doubt on Wurzburgers.

It is suggested by the theory being exploited here that much research on concepts, facing college students with an odd assortment of colors, forms, and sizes, plus strange names, becomes not so much an exercise in concept formation but one of problem solving. The approach, introduced by Hull (1920), of going through processes of abstraction and generalization is not pertinent to the realities of concept formation in the growing human. Hull's (1930) later approach through the r_g permitted him to avoid the need for any such processes as abstraction and generalization and was a far more suitable approach.

One-Trial Learning

In 1957 Rock shook up the verbal learning world with his ingenious experiment in paired-associate learning wherein he dropped items not learned on the first trial and substituted new items which, in turn, were dropped if not learned on the next trial. In this way Rock established the empirical fact that subjects can learn a paired-associate on one trial and repetition is of little importance for learning (but useful for retention).

Rock's finding launched a barrage of researches calculated to prove him wrong but most of these studies missed the point. What was important to question was not the data but the meaning of a trial. In Rock's original study, 8 sec. were allowed per pair, and in all, it took 64 sec. to finish a trial. It should have been evident to everyone that if the subject chose to, he could spend all 64 sec. on one pair and learn a list of 8 pairs in 8 trials. Without a control over what the subject was actually doing during a so-called trial, no conclusions could be rigorously drawn.

The importance of Rock's results for the present theory is their relation to the postulate of attention and the corollary of time. It is obvious that anyone who can hear and speak can repeat a paired-associate unit as soon as he hears it. One trial is all that is required to learn that much. Psychologists have never studied the acquisition of a single pair for the simple reason that such study is only frustrating. It yields no data. In order to get data they complicate a subject's task by giving him more material to learn than he can retain for the given time period. In this way data are accumulated while our knowledge of learning decreases.

According to the present theory one-trial learning is readily accommodated granted that the time is long enough. Even tachistoscopic exposure permits learning of material if the material is sufficiently limited. A single pair of words or nonsense syllables can be learned virtually at once if at all seen and if the time for testing is not unduly delayed or if no other learning-type activity is interpolated. When a "trial" consists of several seconds a pair of items might be repeated by the subject as many as eight or nine times. There is some question as to the legitimacy of the term "trial" under such circumstances.

The general findings of primacy and recency can also be accommodated by the present theory if the issue involves the reading of a single list. It is common observation that when subjects are told to try to remember a 15-item word list they will indeed repeat the first three or four items, pay little or no attention to the middle and retain the last one or two for immediate delivery if this is permitted. The stimulus traces of the latter items are still active and those of the first three words have been amplified by repetition. The mysterious serial learning effect of the depressed middle can be accounted for, quite simply, as resulting from a failure to attend to the middle items for equal amounts of time.

Mnemonics

While memory has enjoyed considerable attention as a suitable subject of psychological inquiry, psychologists have largely ignored the rather remarkable performances of memory experts and have scoffed at the memory system salesmen. This might, indeed, be an appropriate attitude, yet much might be learned about learning by examining the operations of the "master mentalists." Recently, Luria (1968) mildly admonished the psychological researchers by his entertaining account of a mnemonist he had the good fortune to observe over a period of thirty years. In the course of his interviews he found that his subject employed, among others, a system of mnemonics that comes down to us from Ciceronian times. The publication in 64 A.D. of *Ad Herennium*, erroneously attributed to Cicero, has recently been given its belated recognition by Yates (1966) in her scholarly *The Art of Memory*. The system described in *Ad Herennium* amounts to visualizing (imaging) items to be remembered in sequence as placed in certain already well-learned places. The system can be labeled as one of "things and places," as Cicero called it. The orator or memorizer reviews the items to be recalled later by placing the first item at the entrance of a house or building he knows well. The second item goes into the hall or the hall closet, and so on. The writer has used a similar system in a number of studies (Bugelski 1968a; 1968b) with gratifying results. The fact that one can remember, with the use of a mnemonic system based on imagery, a large number of items thought about only briefly, is readily accounted for by the theory here proposed.

The assumption that subjects can conjure up images of well-known objects and can unite such images with those of other well-known objects has been amply supported. When comparable subjects try to learn lists of words by incorporating them into sentences as pure verbal exercises their success is modest. The same words mediated by images can be retained with far greater effectiveness in the same amount of time.

The failure of psychologists to concern themselves with imagery as a consequence of what now appears to be an ill-advised behavioristic attack on subjectivity has deprived the field of significant data. It is to the great credit of Hebb (1966) that he did not ignore the process of imagery in his physiological approach. The research into imagery is only beginning to enjoy a revival and has by no means begun to receive its due. The use of imagery by Mowrer in his account of imitation and in his model of a thermostat-like guide for behaviorial adjustments may prove to be of primary importance in the next decade.

For reasons of brevity these illustrations of the application of the theory described in Part III will have to suffice. There is no great difficulty about applications to other human learning operations. It is assumed that the selection of the four areas of application represent four of the more formidable problem areas and that other perennial questions might be approached with at least some modest degree of success.

It is perhaps unnecessary to restate that the theory is preliminary, cautious, and subject to amendment but if amendments are to come, they should be based on postulates that have some reasonable prospect of support and that amenders avoid the *deus ex machina* operations so commonly attempted by those who talk about plans, structures, and organizations. Before long they have planners, contractors and architects, and organizers neatly obscuring the problems that cry for explanation.

References

ARONFREED, J. *Conscience and conduct*. New York: Academic Press, 1968.

BANDURA, A. Social learning theory of identificatory processes. *In* D. A. GOSLIN (ed.), *Handbook of socialization theory and research*. Chicago: Rand-McNally, 1968.

———, ROSS, D., and ROSS, S. A. Transmission aggression through imitation of aggressive models. *Journal of Abnormal and Social Psychology*, 1961, *63*, 575–82.

BANDURA, A., and WALTERS, R. *Social learning and personality development*. New York: Holt, Rinehart & Winston, 1963.

BERLYNE, D. E. *Conflict, arousal, and curiosity*. New York: McGraw-Hill, 1960.

BLODGETT, H. C. The effect of the introduction of reward upon the maze performance of rats. *University of California Publications in Psychology*, 1929, *4*, 113–34.

BROWN, J. S. Problems presented by the concept of acquired drives. *In* M. R. JONES (ed.), *Current theory and research in motivation: A symposium*. Lincoln: University of Nebraska Press, 1953.

BUGELSKI, B. R. Images as mediators in one-trial paired-associate learning. II. Self-timing in successive lists. *Journal of Experimental Psychology*, 1968a, *77*, 328–34.

———, KIDD, E., and SEGMEN, J. The image as a mediator in one-trial paired-associate learning. *Journal of Experimental Psychology*, 1968b, *76*, 69–73.

CHOMSKY, N. Review of verbal behavior. *Language*, 1959, *35*, 26–58.

CHURCH, J. *Language and the discovery of reality*. New York: Vintage Books, 1961.

COFER, C. N., and MUSGRAVE, B. S., eds. *Verbal learning and behavior*. New York: McGraw-Hill, 1963.

DIXON, T. R., and HORTON, D. L. *Verbal behavior and general behavior theory*. Englewood Cliffs, N.J.: Prentice-Hall, 1968.

FLANDERS, J. P. A review of research on imitative behavior. *Psychological Bulletin*, 1968, *69*, 316–37.

FURTH, H. G. *Thinking without language*. New York: Free Press, 1966.

HALL, J. F. *Readings in the psychology of learning*. Philadelphia: Lippincott, 1967.

HEBB, D. O. *The organization of behavior*. New York: John Wiley, 1949.

——— *A textbook of psychology*. 2d ed. Philadelphia: Saunders, 1966.

HILGARD, E. Methods and procedures in the study of learning. *In* S. S. STEVENS (ed.), *Handbook of experimental psychology*. New York: John Wiley, 1951.

HOVLAND, C. I. Human learning and retention. *In* S. S. STEVENS (ed.), *Handbook of experimental psychology*. New York: John Wiley, 1951.

HULL, C. L. Quantitative aspects of the evolution of concepts. *Psychological Monographs*, 1920, *28*, no. 123.

——— Knowledge and purpose as habit mechanisms. *Psychological Review*, 1930, *37*, 511–25.

——— The principles of behavior. New York: Appleton-Century-Crofts, 1943.

——— *A behavior system*. New Haven, Conn.: Yale University Press, 1952.

JAMES, W. *Principles of psychology*. New York: Henry Holt, 1890.

JUNG, J. *Verbal learning*. New York: Holt, Rinehart & Winston, 1968.

KATKIN, E. S., and MURRAY, E. N. Instrumental conditioning of autonomically mediated behavior. *Psychological Bulletin*, 1968, *70*, 52–68.

LACHMAN, R., and DOOLING, D. J. Connected discourse and random strings: Effects of number of inputs on recognition and recall. *Journal of Experimental Psychology*, 1968, *77*, 517–22.

LURIA, A. R. *The mind of a mnemonist*. New York: Basic Books, Inc., 1968.

MCGEOCH, J. *The psychology of human learning*. New York: Longmans, Green, 1942.

———, and IRION, A. L. *The psychology of human learning*. New York: Longmans, Green, 1952.

MANDLER, G. Organization and memory. *In* KENNETH and JANET SPENCE (eds.), *Psychology of learning and motivation*. New York: Academic Press, 1967.

MARTIN, E. Formation of concepts. *In* B. KLEINMUTZ (ed.), *Concepts and the structure of memory*. New York: John Wiley, 1967.

MILLER, N. Liberalization of basic *S-R* concepts: Extensions to conflict behavior, motivation and social learning. *In* S. KOCH (ed.), *Psychology: A study of a science*, vol. 2. New York: McGraw-Hill, 1959.

——— Learning of visceral and glandular responses. *Science*, 1969, *163*, 434–45.

———, and DOLLARD, J. *Social learning and imitation*. New Haven Conn.: Yale University Press, 1941.

MOWRER, O. H. The psychologist looks at language. *American Psychologist*, 1954, *9*, 660–92.

——— *Learning theory and behavior*. New York: John Wiley, 1960a.

——— *Learning theory and the symbolic processes*. New York: John Wiley, 1960b.

OSGOOD, C. E., SUCI, G. J., and TANNENBAUM, P. H. *The measurement of meaning*. Urbana: University of Illinois Press, 1957.

PETERSON, L. R., and PETERSON, M. J. Short term retention of individual verbal items. *Journal of Experimental Psychology*, 1959, *58*, 193–98.

ROCK, I. The role of repetition in associative learning. *American Journal of Psychology*, 1957, *70*, 183–93.

RUSSELL, B. *Philosophy*. New York: W. W. Norton, 1927.

SCHAUB, R. E., BUGELSKI, B. R., and HOROWITZ, M. *Psychonomic Science*, 1968, *12*, 224.

SCHULTZ, D. The human subject in psychological research. *Psychological Bulletin*, 1969, *72*, 214–28.

SHAPIRO, D., TURSKY, B., GERSHON, E., and STERN, M. Effects of feedback and reinforcement on the control of human systolic blood pressure. *Science*, 1969, *163*, 588–89.

SKINNER, B. F. *The behavior of organisms*. New York: Appleton-Century-Crofts, 1938.

SLAMECKA, N. *Human learning and memory*. New York: Oxford University Press, 1967.

—— A temporal interpretation of some recall phenomena. *Psychological Review*, 1969, *76*, 492–503.

SPENCE, K. Current interpretations of learning data and some recent developments in stimulus-response theory. *In The Kentucky Symposium*. New York: John Wiley, 1954.

—— *Behavior theory and conditioning*. New Haven, Conn.: Yale University Press, 1956.

STAATS, A. *Learning, language, and cognition*. New York: Holt, Rinehart & Winston, 1968.

STEVENS, S. S. *Handbook of Experimental Psychology*. New York: John Wiley, 1951.

THORNDIKE, E. L. *Educational Psychology*. Vol. II: *The psychology of learning*. New York: Teachers College, Columbia University, 1913.

—— *The fundamentals of learning*. New York: Teachers College, Columbia University, 1932.

TRABASSO, T., and BOWER, G. *Attention in learning*. New York: John Wiley, 1968.

WIKE, E. L. *Secondary reinforcement*. New York: Harper & Row, 1966.

WOODWORTH, R. S. *Experimental psychology*. New York: Henry Holt, 1938.

YATES, F. A. *The art of memory*. Chicago: University of Chicago Press, 1966.

Remembering and forgetting are the two complementary processes of memory. Memory refers to the persistence of information over time. The to-be-remembered information must be presented to S in some form, and for memory to be demonstrated there must be registration, retention, and retrieval of the original information. The names given to these three processes may vary (e.g., an alternative nomenclature would be trace formation, trace storage, and trace utilization; see Melton 1963), but there seems to be consensus on both the need for and the nature of the distinction. Remembering can be demonstrated only to the extent that all three processes function correctly and that alternative explanations (e.g., guessing) can be ruled out; unsuccessful performance always poses the interpretive problem of where the breakdown occurred. Forgetting is a decrease in retention over time and remembering is its complement.

Most experimental work on memory has been conducted within an associationistic framework. Thus, if a rat learned an avoidance response in a shuttle box but with increasing difficulty the sooner a posttrial electro-convulsive shock was administered (Duncan 1949), it would commonly be assumed that some stimulus-response association was being formed and that the shock interfered with or disrupted the consolidation of this memory trace. Serial lists which have been used in studies of human learning since the time of Ebbinghaus would be considered a chain of such stimulus-response connections, with each item functioning successively as a response to the prior stimulus and then as a stimulus for the subsequent response. Paired-associate lists could then be considered as discrete stimulus-response associations, as though a number of the simple discriminations that are individually studied at the animal level were combined into many discriminations for study of memory at the human level.

Although the experimental analogues seem clear, it seems to be the case that "attempts to apply principles of classical conditioning to the phenomenon of verbal learning have been largely unsuccessful" (Keppel 1968, p. 194). Also in this same symposium Asch (1968) is very critical of what he considers to be the "doctrinal tyranny of associationism," and in quite a different

Bennet B. Murdock, Jr.

Remembering and Forgetting

27

connection Deese (1965) has questioned the wisdom of restricting study to associations based on temporal contiguity alone. However, regardless of one's theoretical orientation the experimental literature is based almost exclusively on research conducted in this tradition, and this by now extensive literature must provide the experimental data on which our theories of memory are based.

Forgetting is a decrease in retention over time; more precisely, it may be defined as the slope of the curve that shows the functional relationship between retention (y) and time (t). A number of simple and obvious assumptions as to what the basic process might be are shown in Table 27–1. According to a linear function, the rate of change of retention with respect to time is constant, or a plot of retention as a function of time should yield a straight line with slope of b and an intercept of y_0. The numerical value of y_0 would generally be assessed by performance on an immediate retention test.

Table 27-1. List of Possible Forgetting Functions. The Dependent Variable (y) Would be Performance as Measured by Some Test of Memory, and the Independent Variable (t) is Time.

Verbal Label	Derivative Form	Function
Linear	$dy/dt = -b$	$y = y_0 - bt$
Exponential	$dy/dt = -by$	$y = y_0 e^{-bt}$
Logarithmic	$dy/dt = -b/t$	$y = y_0 - b \log t$
Square root	$dy/dt = -b\sqrt{t}$	$y = y_0 - 2b\sqrt{t}$
Quadratic	$d^2y/dt^2 = -b$	$y = -(1/2)bt^2 + Bt + A$
	$Y(0) = A,\ Y'(0) = B$	

According to an exponential function, the rate of forgetting is proportional to the amount retained. This function, of course, is a very common one which is applicable to such diverse phenomena as radioactive decay, capacitor discharge in an RC circuit, even to the rate at which water drains from a bathtub. For obvious reasons it has received wide attention in terms of possible application to memory. A slight modification (see Murdock & Cook 1960) will yield an asymptote so the forgetting goes to some value greater than zero though still in exponential fashion.

According to a log function forgetting would be proportional to the reciprocal of time; for a square root function it would be inversely proportional to the square root of time. In all cases, the intercept is represented in Table 27–1 by y_0 (the value of y at $t = 0$) and b is the rate constant (the slope of the function when plotted in the appropriate manner). For the quadratic function a constant acceleration (second derivative of retention with respect to time) is assumed, and the constants A and B symbolize the value of the function and its first derivative, respectively, at $t = 0$.

On the basis of his empirical data Ebbinghaus reported a retention function such that savings (a reduction in number of relearning trials compared to the number of original learning trials) was "inversely proportional to a small power of the logarithm of . . . time" (Ebbinghaus 1964, p. 78). With typical modesty (and commendable scientific caution) he added, ". . . this statement . . . [has] no other value than that of a shorthand statement of the above results which have been found but once and under the circumstances described. Whether they possess a more general significance so that, under other circumstances or with other individuals, they might find expression in other

constants I cannot at the present time say" (p. 79). The particular retention function proposed by Ebbinghaus is not listed in Table 27–1, and it has not been much used by subsequent investigators.

A more widely accepted empirical finding has been the logarithmic function, where a plot of retention as a function of log time is linear (see Woodworth 1938, pp. 52–56). However, these measures are based on savings, which Luh (1922) found to be atypical as a retention measure (see Fig. 27–1, Postman & Rau 1957). This latter study also questioned the measure as they found ". . . savings are not strictly commensurate with the other measures since saving is a complex function of both recall and subsequent relearning" (Postman & Rau 1957, p. 266). This study is actually one of the very few systematic investigations of retention functions as reflected in different methods, but the authors conclude, "The shape of the retention curve varies with the nature of the material and the method of measurement" (p. 267).

Nowadays no one is seriously looking for *the* retention function, but perhaps more attention could be paid to quantitative description of the function under specified conditions. On theoretical grounds, certain of the functions in Table 27–1 are more plausible than others. As far as the writer knows, no one has seriously defended the linear function. The log and the square-root function may be unpalatable to some because the derivative form makes forgetting proportional to time. The role of time as an independent variable has long made memory theorists unhappy.

McGeoch (1932) argued that time as a causal factor was unsatisfactory; iron rusts in time, but the cause is oxidation. While this point of view has been widely espoused (e.g., Osgood 1953), recently Adams (1967) has demurred. He argues that, ". . . time is a perfectly respectable independent variable and has been throughout the history of science" (p. 25). Actually there are, as Adams seems to imply, two quite separate issues: (a) time as a causal factor, and (b) time as an independent variable. It would indeed be ludicrous to argue against the latter; in the physical sciences, theories often start with basic assumptions about underlying processes that are stated as differential equations with time as the independent variable. However, time provides a framework within which the process may occur, but the "cause" is indeed something else. Thus, in acoustics one can

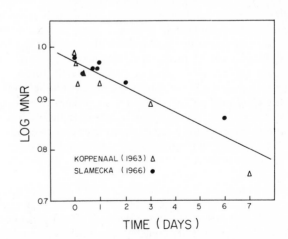

Fig. 27-1. *Log of mean number recalled (MNR) as a function of time* [data from Koppenaal 1963; and Slamecka 1966].

represent sound waves by waveform analysis which is a plot of amplitude as a function of time or by spectral analysis which is a plot of amplitude as a function of frequency (Hirsh 1952, p. 32), but the underlying equations are for simple harmonic motion.

Two recent studies have measured retention at enough different time intervals so one can with some confidence consider retention functions. Both studies dealt with the question of spontaneous recovery of associations over time, using short (10-item) paired-associate lists. The control group learned one list to a criterion, and there were different groups of Ss at each retention interval. Both for the data of Koppenaal (1963) and for the data of Slamecka (1966) semi-log plots showed that neither was well fit by the log function mentioned above. However, as shown in Figure 27.1, a simple exponential was not at all unreasonable, and both sets of data could be encompassed with the same straight line. Actually, the simple exponential listed in Table 27–1 seemed adequate; there was no need to assume an asymptote greater than zero. The half-life period (i.e., the length of time for retention to decrease by 50%) was approximately 12 days.

One final point in connection with retention curves: A current methodological problem in the measurement of memory which had been raised by Underwood (1964) and by Keppel (1965) is that of degree of original learning. That is, it is argued that one cannot assess the effects *on memory* of any particular independent variable which also has an effect on acquisition unless one can clearly and unambiguously assess the degree of original learning. Since the latter is often not easy to determine exactly (and the problem is exacerbated when overlearning is involved) the conclusion seems to be that any retention measures are of dubious value. However, if one obtains a retention *function* one is quite justified in drawing conclusions about memory from its slope, and of course slope is an independent parameter from intercept. One need not even measure "degree of original learning" in order to assess the effect of some independent variable upon the rate constant.

Methods

MEASURES

The four traditional measures of human memory have been recall, recognition, relearning, and rearrangement. In recall, the set of alternatives (number of possible answers) is not restricted by E. In recognition, the set of possible alternatives is provided by E. Three types of recognition tests may be distinguished (Murdock 1963d): (a) a yes-no procedure wherein single items are presented to S and the correct response would be "yes" to a target item but "no" to a lure; (b) an m-alternative forced-choice procedure wherein the one target is embedded among (m-1) lures (as in multiple-choice tests); and (c) a batch testing procedure wherein all targets and lures are randomly intermixed and presented in their entirety with instructions for S to select the targets.

Relearning is the method from which the measure of savings is derived. S learns the information at one point in time and relearns it at a later point in time; the fewer trials to relearn the more the savings and, presumably, the better the retention. Rearrangement is an attempt at a pure test of order information (Horowitz 1961); all items are presented to S with instructions to reconstruct the presentation order. As has been mentioned, the work of Luh (1922) and Postman and Rau (1957) suggest that the method of relearning is the most likely to yield atypical results.

Comparison of recall and recognition is of particular interest. It is commonly assumed that recall is a two-stage process whereas recognition is not (Kintsch & Morris 1965; Rosenberg & Cohen 1966). Recall may fail where recognition does not because of retrieval difficulties; that is, recall involves a search and then a decision but recognition only the decision, and recall may fail because the information is available but not accessible (Mandler 1967; Tulving & Pearlstone 1967). Acceptance of this point of view leads to a useful way of separating storage and retrieval effects in memory. Namely, an effect may be said to be a storage effect if it occurs under measures of recognition and recall but a retrieval effect if it occurs only under measures of recall (Lachman & Tuttle 1965; Murdock 1968).

The above point of view may be too simple. Even in a recognition task, S must "recognize" the stimulus. That is, the presented stimulus must be matched against the memory trace remaining from the prior presentation of this same stimulus so in this sense even a recognition test involves retrieval. This type of stimulus recognition is what is meant by the "Höffding problem"; for discussions see Asch (1968) and Rock and Ceraso (1964).

Davis, Sutherland, and Judd (1961) suggested that the superiority of recall to recognition could reflect merely the fact that each item recalled conveyed more information since the associated uncertainty (number of response alternatives) was far larger than under recognition conditions. Their Ss were given 15-item lists and, in the subsequent batch recognition test, had to recognize the targets (presented items) out of a list of 30, 60, 90, or recall the targets. With an information measure recall was not inferior to recognition. Dale (1967) found recall to be inferior to recognition only when the category could not be completely enumerated. Slamecka (1967) varied the *stimulus* uncertainty (size of the set from which the lists were selected) and found a large deterioration in performance as uncertainty increased. Dale and Baddeley (1962) questioned one of the assumptions of Davis et al. and showed that errors were not random (some lures were more seductive than others). Field and Lachman (1966) tried to determine the number of alternatives actually scanned by Ss in a recall task, and concluded that the relative standing of recognition and recall in terms of information-theory measures depended upon the assumptions about scanning made by E. Another factor is the unit of measurement, and McNulty (1965, 1966) has shown that differences between recall and recognition decrease when the recognition test makes selection on the basis of partial information difficult or impossible.

Other measures of memory (or, more accurately, modifications of the above measures) are currently in vogue. In MMFR (modified method of free recall) memory for competing associations is tested. Typically S has previously learned two lists A-B and A-C, where the nomenclature indicates that different responses have been associated to one stimulus term. Then, in MMFR (see Adams 1967) the stimulus (or A) terms are presented; S is to recall the B and C terms as he can, then assign them to lists (i.e., A-B or A-C). This method is often employed in the hope that it will eliminate response competition. List differentiation seems to be worst when the two lists have been equally well learned (Winograd 1968).

A recent development has been to apply methods of signal-detection analysis (TSD) to the measurement of memory (Egan 1958; Murdock 1965*b*; Norman 1966; Norman & Wickelgren 1965). From the point of TSD response probability (i.e., probability of a correct response) is unsatisfactory as a measure of associative strength in that it reflects the joint effect of sensitivity and criterion. That is, associative strength must be represented by some underlying distribution and incorrect associations as well. In a yes-no procedure large differences in the false alarm rate need not indicate any differences at all in the strengths of the memory trace (Donaldson & Murdock 1968); TSD provides a rational model and a method (making use of confidence judgments) by which criterion and sensitivity can be separated. An adequate presentation of these matters is impossible here; the interested reader could consult Egan and Clarke (1966) or Green and Swets (1966) for an exposition of TSD; see Bernbach (1967), Kintsch (1967), and Wickelgren and Norman (1966) for applications to memory.

Techniques

The measures discussed above are applied generally to the assessment of the dependent variable; in this section attention will be paid to the experimental conditions under which memories are formed and measured. Far more effort has been expended in developing and perfecting controlled conditions under which memory can be studied than in developing methods and techniques for careful and detailed response measurement. Thus, physiological psychologists have EEG's, plethysmagraphs, even CAT's; students of memory have paper and pencil with an occasional voice key. However, there is no assurance that more sophisticated measurement devices would materially increase our understanding of the underlying memorial processes.

Until recently the hallmark of the verbal-learning laboratory was the revered memory drum. It provided sequential presentation of lists of items under conditions where the duration of the presentation and (generally) anticipation periods were carefully controlled. In serial tasks presentation order was fixed (invariant) over trials but with free recall and paired associates the presentation order was deliberately randomized. As a consequence, particularly for paired associates the retention interval for any given item was a variable about which the average investigator

knew little and cared less. Since the typical verbal-learning task could be interpreted as a study of short-term memory where what is typically called "learning" is simply increased resistance to inter-trial forgetting (Bernbach 1965; Murdock 1963*c*), it seemed worthwhile to develop techniques whereby one could take a closer look at forgetting over short intervals of time.

The method that made psychologists aware of the possibilities of studying short-term memory was the distractor technique of Peterson and Peterson (1959). On a given trial a nonsense syllable was briefly presented, following which *S* was to count backward by threes (or fours) from some three-digit number. The nonsense syllable was assumed to constitute a single item, the interpolated activity (counting backward) was assumed to present rehearsal and thereby provide the necessary conditions under which forgetting could occur, and the duration of the interpolated activity determined the length of the retention interval. The efficacy of this technique was demonstrated by the striking effects obtained (see Fig. 27–2).

In fact, as noted by Adams (1967, p. 105), much earlier experiments on short-term memory had been done. In England in particular there were prior studies: Nixon (1946) performed some running memory span studies that were never published; Broadbent (1958) reported a number of studies using dichotic stimulation (split span with two-channel presentation), and John Brown (1958) did essentially the complementary study to the Petersons in which he varied the *amount* of material to be remembered (one to four consonant digrams) with a fixed retention interval (five two-digit numbers to be read aloud). The Petersons presented a single trigram and varied the *duration* of the distractor task over a range of 3–18 sec. However, it seemed to be the latter study that constituted the breakthrough and which led to a large number of further studies of memory.

By now there is a plethora of techniques for studying human memory, and no orthogonal taxonomy seems possible. However, a hierarchical classification can include the majority of current techniques for the study of short-term memory. In the following tree system, each terminal node is the address (reference) of an illustrative study. Tasks can be either *continuous* (where presentations and tests are intermixed) or *discrete* (presentations and tests alternate). Continuous tasks can employ *recall* (Lloyd, Reid, and Feallock 1960; Yntema and Muesser 1960) or *recognition*. Recognition tasks can test *whether* an item has been

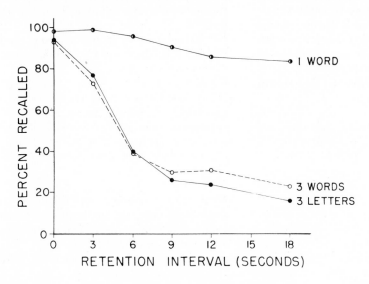

Fig. 27-2. *Performance in a Peterson and Peterson (1959) distractor task for trigrams and single words* [data from Murdock 1961a].

presented (Shepard & Teghtsoonian 1961) or *when* an item was presented (Yntema and Trask 1963).

Discrete tasks also can use either recognition or recall but, since most studies use recall, only the lower path will be followed here. One can ask for recall of *all* or *part* of the material. As suggested by Jung (1965), the former can be subdivided into *ROPE* (recall of presented items, exemplified by single-trial free recall; Binet & Henri 1894; Murdock 1960; Tulving 1968) and *ROME* (recall of missing items, which in the extreme becomes the missing scan of Buschke 1963). Partial recall can use the *distractor* technique (presentation of a sub-span item followed by rehearsal-preventing interpolated activity) or the *probe* technique (presentation of a list of items followed by a cue designating the to-be-remembered information). As pointed out by Broadbent (1965), distractor tasks can use *predictable* (Peterson & Peterson 1959) or *unpredictable* (Brown, 1958) interpolated activities. Probe techniques can use *serial* or *paired-associate* lists. Presentation of serial lists can be *single-channel* or *multichannel*. Single-channel presentation can use either a *sequential* probe (Waugh & Norman 1965) or a *positional* probe (Woodward & Murdock 1968). Multichannel presentation can have the items per channel *simultaneous* (Broadbent 1958; Moray, Bates, & Barnett 1965) or *staggered* (Moray 1960). In paired-associate lists one can probe *forward* associations (Murdock 1961a) or *backward* associations (Murdock 1966).

These techniques are used for the study of reproductive memory in the Ebbinghaus tradition; there is also reconstructive memory in the Bartlett (1932) tradition (see Hunter 1964). Also, studies of memory are certainly not restricted to those conducted in the human learning laboratory. Penfield quite literally has used a "probe" technique. He has found that in some fairly small proportion of cases direct stimulation of cortical areas elicits experiential records (Penfield & Perot 1963; Penfield & Roberts, 1959). Unfortunately, the reports of his patients are difficult to verify, and his findings have generally been considered more suggestive than conclusive. Also, it may be that experiential records can be obtained only from scarred cortex (cited in Pribram 1966).

Interest in the physiological basis of memory has led to use of electro-convulsive shock (ECS) and drug injections to study time-dependent processes in memory storage (McGaugh 1966; Miller 1967). It has been suggested (Coons & Miller 1960) that early studies using ECS may have found results due more to the punishment of the shock than to effects on memory. One solution to this confounding has been to use single-trial passive avoidance (McGaugh, 1966) where forgetting results in a *return* to the situation where the aversive stimulus had been administered. However, Weiskrantz (1966) has pointed out yet a further difficulty in that anterograde effects may also be present. For instance,

... ECS is generally acknowledged to bestow at least temporary benefits on emotionally disturbed patients, and it is difficult to accept that such benefits stem purely from the amnesic effects of the treatment. Since animal experiments commonly employ avoidance conditioning, the possibility exists that animals can remember but are not frightened (Weiskrantz, 1966, p. 8).

In contrast to the electrophysiological approach there is the biochemical approach, in which one looks for macromolecular processes underlying memory (Booth 1967; Hydén 1967).

Among others, there are the planaria experiments where transfer of memory was attempted in a startling fashion (Jacobsen, Fried, & Horowitz 1966; McConnell 1962). Still other techniques are spreading depression (Bureš & Burešová 1963; Schneider 1967) and split-brain techniques (Sperry 1964).

For abnormalities of memory, there is of course the Freudian work on repression, though satisfactory experimental analogues pose methodological problems (Zeller 1950). Studies of retrograde amnesia are, like Penfield's findings, difficult to verify. The work of Milner (1959, 1966) on hippocampal lesions has been noted by Atkinson and Shiffrin (1968) as the most convincing evidence for a dichotomy between short- and long-term memory. (For a recent review of hippocampal effects see Douglas 1967). Finally, there is the extensive work on the amnesic syndrome as studied in the chronic phase of Korsakoff's psychosis by Talland (1965).

Empirical Phenomena

The number of empirical effects (i.e., effects on memory of some experimental manipulation) which have been fairly reliably established is by now rather large. While clearly it would be preferable to start with a systematic theory and use it to integrate and discuss the experimental findings, data far outrun theory and such a presentation is unrealistic at the present time. In an attempt to avoid simple enumeration of effective variables (or, worse, of experimental studies) a classification scheme will be attempted. The risk is that certain factors will be slighted or omitted; the potential benefit is that the empirical status of the field may be brought into sharper focus.

Perhaps it should be pointed out that much experimental effort has been devoted to discovering variables which do or do not affect forgetting, presumably in the hopes that this approach would yield the greatest theoretical benefits. Many experiments have not sought to trace out a retention curve but instead made retention measures at a few (in the extreme case, one) retention intervals. Here the caveat of Underwood (1964, 1966) is indeed appropriate, and one might be completely wrong to attribute effects to *retention*. To reiterate the point made previously: If one has a retention *curve* one need know nothing about degree of original learning in order to draw conclusions about the slope of the function (i.e., forgetting); without knowledge of the functional relationship involved, inferences about *slopes* are hazardous.

Research on forgetting has been conducted on both the *animal* and on the *human* level. In the former, the strongest conclusion seems to be that,

... the long-lasting trace of an experience is not completely fixed, consolidated, or coded at the time of the experience. Consolidation requires time, and under at least some circumstances the processes of consolidation appear to be susceptible to a variety of influences ... for several hours after the experience (McGaugh 1966, p. 1357).

Manipulations have included ECS, drugs, spreading depression, and hypothermia; see the recent symposium on "Memory and Learning" of the American Philosophical Society (published as Vol. 3, no. 6, December 11, 1967).

In a general review of amnesiac effects (including both

retrograde and anterograde, naturally occurring or experimentally induced, reversible or irreversible) Weiskrantz (1966) suggests that two main conclusions clearly emerge from the data on retrograde amnesia: (a) ". . . the more recent the event the more likely it is to be affected retroactively by such treatments" [e.g., ECS, drugs, anoxia], and (b) ". . . the critical interval within which events are affected by treatments is extremely variable, even with a single type of treatment" (Weiskrantz 1966, p. 10). As mentioned earlier, this article very nicely brings out some of the interpractive problems in memory studies with animals and the difficulties in unambiguously ascribing performance effects to memory deficit.

Much of the work on memory at the animal level has been a search for the engram (Lashley 1950) or, if you wish, the underlying substrate of memory. Those interested in human memory have (perforce?) been less interested in this question, and this attitude may seem parochial to some. However, long ago McGeoch (1932) pointed out that the complex phenomena of human memory will not suddenly evaporate as soon as some basic storage mechanism or unit is found; the theoretical problems will still remain. In discussing the same issue, Neisser (1967) points out that the viewpoint of a cognitive psychologist is such that, in terms of a computer analogy, he is more interested in understanding the program than the hardware. For memory, "He wants to understand its utilization, not its incarnation" (p. 6).

Human memory can reflect *organismic* variation or *experimental* manipulation. Organismic variation can be either *normal* or *abnormal*. For the former, there are obviously individual differences among people. In general, experimentalists have shown little interest in this variation, though Underwood (1954) has concluded that there are no differences in forgetting as a function of fast vs. slow learners. However, this article seemed more motivated by the methodological issue of equating for degree of original learning than in individual differences per se. The other chief "normal" organismic variable is chronological (or mental) age. It has long been known that immediate memory span increases with a child's age (e.g., Woodworth 1938, p. 17). At the other end of the scale, Inglis and Caird (1963) found that, in a Broadbent-type dichotic (split-span) memory task the channel reported second showed a greater adverse effect due to age than the channel reported first. Thus, age particularly affects persistence in a short-term store. Broadbent and Heron (1962) found that a subsidiary task was particularly disrupting to memory for older people; they seemed to be quite unable to time-share in the face of two competing tasks. Laurence (1966) found age differences in free recall, also different differences in the subjective-organization measure of Tulving (1962).

Abnormal organismic variation in humans may result from cerebral accidents as in retrograde amnesia, but they are difficult to assess. The effect of hippocampal lesions on memory is striking to say the least; apparently the deficit is not one of initial registration (digit span is typically unaffected) nor is it a deficit in the long-term store (memory for preoperative events—disregarding the retrograde amnesiac period itself—is also unaffected). Rather there is complete amnesia for ongoing events; the patient will form no memory for (or be unable to retrieve) information which registered but from which his attention had been distracted (or rehearsal prevented). A recent summary of this evidence is given by Milner (1966), who suggested (both on the basis of the hippocampal data, amnesia after unilateral temporal lobectomy, and amnesia after intracarotid injection of sodium amytal) that, "It is possible that in normal learning, the hippocampal region acts to prime activity in cortical areas where storage is taking place, or that is has a downstream inhibitory effect on the activity of structures in the lower brainstream. . ." (Milner 1966, p. 130).

Extensive work on the Korsakoff syndrome has recently been reported by Talland (1965), which includes a clinical description of the characteristics of the patients, a very thorough historical review, experimental work on motor skills, perception, reasoning, learning, and remembering, and narrative reproduction in the Bartlett tradition, and a concluding theoretical interpretation. Any simple descriptive statement of the main findings would be a gross oversimplification of the wealth of empirical data and speculations presented; the interested reader should consult the monograph itself.

In contrast to what has been called organismic variation, the majority of work on human memory by experimental psychologists has involved experimental manipulation. The reasons are probably obvious; they permit standardization of conditions, experimental control over extraneous variables, lead to reproducible findings, and permit experimental tests of extant theories and models. There may be some "grey" areas of psychology where data are of questionable reproducibility and argument about the "facts" abounds; such is surely not the case in human memory. The results of experimental manipulation are generally large and highly reliable; disagreement in general is over the interpretation, not the phenomena.

Experimental effects may be divided into *extra-list* and *intra-list* effects. Extra-list effects may be *anterograde* or *retrograde* (i.e., experimental treatments introduced before or after presentation of the to-be-remembered [or target] information, also referred to as proactive and retroactive effects, respectively). The three main anterograde or proactive effects are number of prior lists (Keppel & Underwood 1962; Slamecka 1961; Underwood 1957), similarity of prior information to the target information (Wickens, Born, & Allen 1963) and the time interval between the prior experience and presentation of the target information. An example of the latter from short-term memory (Loess and Waugh 1967) showed that proactive effects from the previous trial decreased with spacing and, by two minutes, were neglible; also see Peterson and Gentile (1965). Conrad (1960b) has shown a similar effect for serial-order intrusions.

Retrograde or retroactive effects are concerned primarily with the nature, duration, and similarity of the interpolated activity. This is a classical problem of the interference theory of forgetting (McGeoch 1932; Melton & Irwin, 1940; Melton & von Lackum 1941; Slamecka and Ceraso 1960; Underwood 1966). In general, retention decreases with increases in the amount, duration, and similarity of the interpolated activity. There is of course comparable evidence from the field of short-term memory (Murdock 1963a; Peterson & Peterson 1959), though the role of similarity in short-term memory has been questioned (Broadbent 1963; Brown 1958). However, it now seems as if similarity effects also operate in short-term memory (Neimark, Greenhouse, Law, & Weinheimer 1965). Also, retention depends upon rehearsal and information-processing during the intervening time interval (Pollack 1963; Posner and Rossman 1965; Posner and Konick 1966; Sanders 1961).

Intra-list effects may be subdivided into those occurring

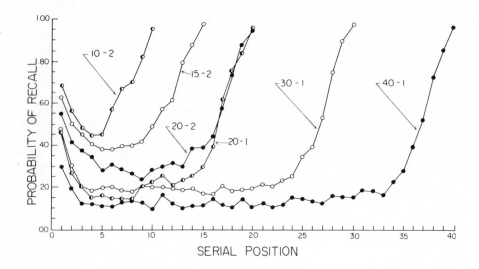

Fig. 27-3. *Series position curves for six different groups with lists of unrelated words varying in list length and presentation time* [data from Murdock 1962].

during presentation or at *input* and those occurring at retrieval or *output*. There are currently assumed to be a number of different input effects, and they will be briefly enumerated. There is obviously some duplication and overlap, and it seems likely that as our theoretical understanding progresses the list will shrink. Most of the evidence here comes from studies of short-term memory.

Serial position effects are ubiquitous and one of the most pervasive phenomena of human memory. Typical curves may be found in Woodworth (1938, Figure 27–5, p. 23) or Underwood (1966, Figure 11.4, p. 490); serial-position curves for free recall and serial lists are shown in Figures 27–3 and 27–4. The primacy effect is a gradient extending from the beginning of the list, the recency effect is a gradient extending from the end of the list, and while serial lists and free recall clearly differ both tasks show both effects. The free-recall curves characteristically show a level middle section or asymptote at some value greater than zero; this asymptote has been used by Waugh and Norman (1965) to estimate Secondary Memory.

Repetition effects are hardly surprising; a recent parametric study in short-term memory is that of Hellyer (1962). Perhaps more unexpected is the fact that repetition interacts with dis-

tribution of practice (Peterson Paradox); there is evidence that, for delayed retention tests, spaced repetition is better than massed (Greeno 1964; Melton 1967; Peterson 1966). List length and presentation rate also affect recall, but these effects may be subsumed under total presentation time (Murdock 1960, 1965a). At least in short-term memory number of words or pairs recalled following a single presentation is generally a linear function of total presentation time (Cohen 1963; Kolers 1966; Murdock, 1967; Tulving & Patterson 1968; Waugh 1967). The amount of material is an equally-obvious variable (Melton 1963; Murdock 1961a), though in studies with the distractor technique the size of the *n*-gram is generally confounded with rehearsal difficulty. The fact that it is more the number of items than their information value (in terms of the uncertainty measure) has led to the suggestion that the critical variable is chunks not bits (Miller 1956). Also, the fact that it is more the number of items rather than their presentation rate argues for interference rather than decay (Waugh & Norman 1965).

The effects of meaningfulness on memory are somewhat ambiguous. On the one hand, since association value of nonsense syllables and words does not affect retention given control over degree of original learning (e.g., Postman & Rau 1957)

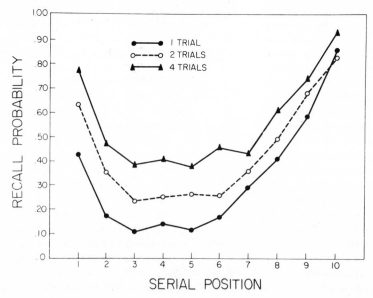

Fig. 27-4. *Serial position curves showing performance on a probe test following one, two, or four presentations* [data from Woodward 1968].

it could be argued (e.g., Underwood 1966) that meaningfulness affects acquisition not retention. On the other hand, it may be that retention (Lachman & Tuttle 1965) is dependent upon order of approximation to English (Miller & Selfridge 1950), sequential structure (Epstein 1961; Miller 1958), and amount and form of the internal constraint and organization (Bousfield 1953; Bousfield & Cohen 1956; Cofer 1959; Garner & Whitman 1965; Whitman & Garner 1962). Since the matter seems more a question of the definition of meaningfulness than anything else, perhaps it would be best not to phrase the issue in terms of meaningfulness at all but rather in terms of the defining measures.

Similarity effects in long-term memory have long been known (e.g., Underwood 1966) but only recently have they been demonstrated in short-term memory (Conrad 1964; Wickelgren 1965b). They seem to be of an acoustic or articulatory nature (Hintzman 1967; Levy & Murdock 1968; Murray 1965, 1967); since in long-term memory the relevant similarity dimension seems to be semantic this difference has been used as an argument for two different storage systems (e.g., Baddeley & Dale 1966). An alternate view would suggest that all four cases of this 2×2 classification could be filled; for acoustic similarity in long-term memory see Brown and McNeil (1966); for semantic (categorical) similarity in short-term memory see Murdock and vom Saal (1967).

Modality effects are pronounced at least over short intervals of time; auditory presentation of verbal material results in superior retention than visual presentation (Buschke 1962; McGhie, Chapman, & Lawson 1965; Murdock 1968). There is probably an interaction between modality and presentation rate such that speeding presentation helps auditory but hinders visually-presented information (Mackworth 1962, 1963, 1964). Natural-language mediators (Adams 1967) and recoding cues (Bower 1964; Laughery and Pinkus 1968; Lindley 1963; Schaub & Lindley 1964) also facilitate short-term memory. Finally, there is evidence (Broadbent & Heron 1962; Murdock 1965c; Rabbitt 1966) that introduction of a subsidiary task during input decreases retention. The general point of view is that the secondary task absorbs or uses up some of the information-processing capacity of the individual; this decreases the amount available for the memory task and so results in the observed decrement in retention.

Finally, there are three main intra-list output effects: order of report, alternatives in recognition memory, and retrieval cues (or context effects). The effects of order of report have long been known; as an example, reverse memory span (reporting the digits in a backward order relative to their presentation) yields a span appreciably shorter than a forward order of report (Woodworth 1938). Even forward memory span may depend upon the order of report (Posner 1964) and Broadbent (1958) obtains the same effect with dichotic presentation. With paired associates Murdock (1963b) and Tulving and Arbuckle (1963) find output interference (i.e., in some cases recall of a pair declines as other pairs are tested first). Another example is the prefix effect, wherein a redundant (known) digit interpolated between presentation and recall reduces number correctly recalled (Conrad 1960a; Crowder 1967; Dallett 1964), though not if the control condition uses lists one item longer.

Both the number and the similarity of the alternatives affect performance in recognition-memory tasks. For the former, the more alternatives the poorer the performance for both *m*-alternative tests and batch recognition testing (Davis, Sutherland, & Judd 1961; Kintsch 1968; Murdock 1963d; Postman 1950). The more similar the alternatives the more seductive they are as lures, by any of the three methods of testing recognition memory (Anisfeld & Knapp 1968; Dale & Baddeley 1966; Shepard & Chang 1963; Underwood 1965).

It has long been assumed that context effects are important in retrieval (McGeoch 1932; Melton 1963). That is, any information must be presented in some context, and failure to reinstate the contextual cues present at input may result in the inaccessibility of information at output. The operation of context cues may be inferred from transfer designs (McGovern 1964), or measured more directly by manipulation of retrieval cues (Tulving & Pearlstone 1966; Tulving & Osler 1968). With the latter method, these studies have shown that category names or weak associates of the target items facilitate recall "if and only if" the retrieval cue is presented at input (Tulving & Osler 1968).

Theory

In the previous section no particular distinction was drawn between short-term memory (STM) and long-term memory (LTM). The reason was the conviction that the similarities outweighted the differences. On the theoretical side, one cannot safely blur the distinction between STM and LTM since the major theoretical attempts have been oriented toward one or the other.

STM. From an information-processing point of view the most important and influential theoretical formulation has been that of Broadbent (1958). A block diagram of his model is shown in Figure 27–5. Stimuli impinge upon the sense organs and temporarily reside in a buffer or short-term store (S-system) from which decay is rapid. In his terms, stimuli change from line abreast (parallel) to line astern (serial) in passing through the limited-capacity channel (P-system); selection is effected by the filter. A rehearsal loop can recirculate information back through the S-system, or information can be stored in long-term or Secondary Memory (Waugh and Norman 1965). Among other things SM stores information about conditional probabilities (A-B associations) and time of arrival (for judgments of recency). Also it sets the filter (i.e., controls its selectivity).

The typical example is that of looking up an unfamiliar telephone number and holding it temporarily in the short-term store prior to dialing. If one has to walk across the room to the telephone the number may have to recirculate (the rehearsal loop) to avoid decay. The informational bottleneck is the P-system, and the limitation is on processing rate. Evidence for the single-channel hypothesis comes from studies of central intermittency where even very simple stimuli arriving close together in time (typically 150 msec. or less) cannot be processed simultaneously (Bertelson 1966; Welford 1960). Broadbent has argued for the necessity of a dual-storage model as similarity effects (semantic similarity in particular) affect SM but not, apparently, the buffer store (Broadbent 1963).

On the question of the distinction between STM and LTM, one argument in favor then is the similarity factor. Another is that an experimental separation can be achieved (Glanzer & Cunitz 1966). Thus, in studies of free recall temporal factors affect SM (or the asymptote; see Figure 27–4) while an inter-

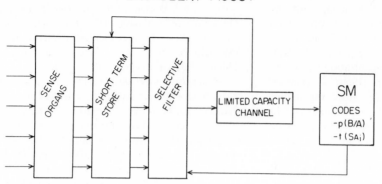

BROADBENT (1958)

Fig. 27-5. *Block diagram for the model of Broadbent* (*1958*). Reprinted with permission from Broadbent, D.E., *Perception and Communication*, 1958, Pergamon Press Ltd.

polated activity such as counting backward can eradicate PM (Primary Memory, or the short-term store) alone (Postman & Phillips 1965). A third argument (Atkinson & Shiffrin 1968) is the dramatic effects of hippocampal lesions which do not affect immediate registration or the long-term store, but apparently make it impossible to enter new information into LTM.

On the other hand, Melton (1963) has argued persuasively for a continuum rather than a dichotomy, suggesting that interference principles could apply to both. We now know that acoustic similarity does affect PM, and evidence that both acoustic and semantic effects operate in both STM and LTM has already been mentioned. As Milner (see Kimble 1967) has said, in the hippocampal cases the logical possibility of retrieval difficulties can not be excluded. Experimental separation of LTM and STM requires *failing* to find effects, which may reflect inadequate understanding of appropriate experimental conditions more than anything else. No sharp discontinuity (as in dark-adaptation curves in vision, for instance) has yet been demonstrated, and there is at least some evidence for a continuity of experimental manipulations (Melton 1963; Murdock 1963c, 1967). In other words, whether memory is dichotomous or continuous is not yet a settled issue.

Following the Broadbent model, Waugh and Norman (1965) were explicit in making the distinction between PM and SM and showing how a probe technique could yield useful information about PM. Their model (see Figure 27–6) says that items enter PM and may be copied or transferred into SM; they may also

be lost. The capacity of PM is sharply limited, and new items displace old items. There is both input and output interference, so probability of recall of an individual item decreases as number of intervening items (either presented or recalled) increases. Waugh and Norman were able to show essentially the same PM retention curve for probe-digit tests, single-trial free recall, paired associates, and single-item retention using the distractor technique of Peterson and Peterson (1959).

In the same tradition, a more extensive model is that of Atkinson and Shiffrin (see Atkinson & Shiffrin 1965; Phillips, Shiffrin, & Atkinson 1967). There is a short-term or memory buffer plus a long-term store. The distinction is both in terms of coding processes and length of stay. The two main processes are transfer from short-term to long-term (a copy process) and retrieval from long-term to the short-term store. The memory buffer probably holds a vector of information about the stimulus; but whatever it is S can report it back immediately if asked. Eventually all items are lost from the buffer, but they may have been copied into the long-term store first. The copy process is not destructive.

The main properties of the memory buffer are as follows:

1. It has constant size (capacity) for r items, though r can vary across experiments (largely a function of item difficulty).
2. There is temporal ordering in the buffer of a push-down nature; the most recent item is on top (in the rth position).
3. Once full the buffer stays full until attention wanders; it is at least partially cleared at the start of each new trial.
4. Each new item then displaces an old item. The displacement scheme is a geometric distribution starting with the 1st position; the oldest item is most likely to go (δ is the displacement parameter).
5. Coding in the buffer allows recall.
6. There is perfect recall given that the item is in the buffer.
7. The transfer (copy) process does not affect contents of the buffer.

There may be complete or partial transfer of one or more components of the buffer to the long-term store. The transfer parameter is θ which is a function of the number of items in the buffer, the ith item in the buffer, buffer size, input rate, and item complexity. Various alternatives for the long-term store are suggested; items may be represented once in all-or-none fashion, multiple or partial copies may be made depending upon time in buffer, or strength of an item may be proportional to time in buffer. When asked to recall information the retrieval process

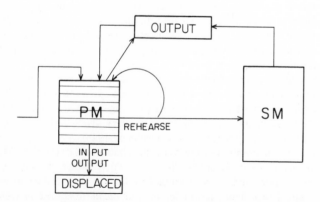

WAUGH & NORMAN (1965)

Fig. 27-6. *Block diagram for the model of Waugh and Norman* (*1965*).

becomes operative; imperfect retrieval from the long-term store could reflect interference (proactive, retroactive) or an imperfect search algorithm (destroy information or stop too soon). A later version of the model (Atkinson & Shiffrin 1968) distinguishes between permanent structures and control processes, and discusses many of the characteristics of each.

A forerunner to the Atkinson and Shiffrin model was a model suggested by Bower (1964) which may be described as a stochastic formalization of the Broadbent model. Assumptions regarding consolidation of memory traces were that rehearsal (recirculation) occurred n times per second, with each rehearsal there was some probability of transfer to the long-term store, and each second there is some probability of all-or-none loss. Also postulated was encoding in the short-term store, application of the Atkinson and Crothers (1964) long-term and short-term retention model to data, tests of other models, and application of a queuing model to generate the serial position curve of free recall.

An important step forward was the "multicomponent model" of Bower (1967) wherein the perceptual and mnemonic processes were explicitly interrelated (also see Aaronson 1967; Harcum 1967). This formulation dealt with the format of storage, and assumed that the stimulus input was processed through a pattern recognizer which then represented the stimulus in the short-term store in encoded form as a vector of information (ordered list of attributes). Forgetting then goes on at the level of item attributes. Two issues that this approach brings out are (a) whether attributes (components) are forgotten in hierarchical order or independently; (b) whether forgetting is uncertainty about the value of an attribute or replacement of its value by some other (erroneous) value. Evidence for forgetting at a more molecular level than the item itself comes from such studies as Anisfeld and Knapp (1968), Bregman and Chambers (1966), Conrad (1964), Underwood (1965), and Wickelgren (1965c, 1966b).

In a somewhat different vein, Brown (1959) has proposed that traces are stored with redundancy, that forgetting consists of a fall in the signal-to-noise ratio, and that there is not a one-to-one correspondence between trace decay and measured performance. Conrad (1967) is also sympathetic to the decay concept; elsewhere (Conrad 1965) he has suggested an "Event Storage" model (Buschke 1966) wherein items are deposited in bins during presentation and during recall these bins are scanned (Milner 1961) in some particular order. Items may decay within bins but rearrangement does not take place. Yntema and Trask (1963) have suggested what may be construed as a "Marker Storage" wherein presentation consists of tagging items already resident in the long-term store. A third type, "Address Storage," is essentially what has been proposed by Tulving in saying that "It is assumed that. . .information about the fact that the word occurred in the list is placed into a unitary store. . ." (Tulving and Patterson 1968, p. 246). Experimental tests of these alternatives have been done by Buschke (1963), Corballis (1967), and Wickelgren (1965a, 1966a).

LTM. In a different vein, interference theory (Keppel 1968; Postman 1961, 1963; Underwood & Ekstrand 1966) has concerned itself with long-term memory. According to interference theory, associations are formed during the course of original learning which both temporarily weaken or extinguish prior experimental associations to these stimuli and are themselves subsequently subject to later extinction or unlearning. Over time extinguished associations are presumed to recover, so for single-list retention studies the amount of forgetting must reflect recovery of prior associations. When a naive subject learns a single list and is tested for retention one day later retention is of the order of 75%; after perhaps 10 such cycles it is of the order of 25%. These dramatic findings and their implications were reported by Underwood (1957) in one of the classic papers in the field.

In a multi-list retention study the two major paradigms are the proactive and the retroactive inhibition paradigm (Underwood 1966). In both cases the experimental group learns two (or more) lists and the control one; in the proactive inhibition paradigm S recalls (after some retention interval) the second (or most recent) list, in the retroactive inhibition paradigm he recalls the first list. In the former, interference effects are presumed to occur because second-list learning results in extinction or unlearning of first-list responses (Barnes & Underwood 1959) which then spontaneously recover over the retention interval to produce the forgetting of the second list learned. In the latter (retroactive inhibition), there is simply the direct unlearning of the associations themselves.

It has been suggested (McGovern 1964) that there are both specific and nonspecific associations, the latter being contextual associations and the former subdivided into forward or A-B associations and backward or B-A associations. (For a dissenting view on forward and backward associations see Asch & Ebenholtz 1962). By assumptions on how these associations combined, the order of difficulty of various transfer paradigms could be predicted.

Interference theory postulates two factors which affect recall. The first is the unlearning which has already been discussed. The second is response competition which MMFR is presumed to eliminate. However, a recent critical assessment of interference theory by Postman (1967) has suggested that perhaps MMFR does not in fact eliminate response competition. Further, he questioned the long-term explanatory value of the distinction between specific and nonspecific associations. A transfer study with recall and recognition measures suggested that, in general, specific associations were highly resistant to interference and that retroactive inhibition was largely due to reduced response availability. This leads to the implausible conclusion that retroactive inhibition is essentially due to unlearning of contextual associations. It is implausible because the A-B, paradigm produces considerable negative transfer, and here it is the same responses simply paired with different stimulus terms. As Postman points out, some of the basic assumptions of interference theory are now undergoing reexamination, and the revision that seems inevitable may be quite different from its predecessor.

Finally, experiment and theory seems to be turning progressively more attention to the question of retrieval of information from memory. The Miller, Galanter, and Pribram (1960) TOTE mechanism was shown to be a plan which could organize and guide the retrieval process. Various experimental tests of retrieval factors (e.g., Kintsch 1969; Lachman and Tuttle 1965; Lockhart 1969; Peterson 1967; Slamecka 1968) have recently been reported. The use of retrieval cues (Tulving & Pearlstone 1966; Tulving & Osler 1968) seems to be a fruitful experimental technique with which to investigate these problems. Simulation of memory models (e.g., Hunt 1963) forces one to consider retrieval and retrieval processes. And for some provocative ideas on storage and retrieval of information from long-term memory, see Broadbent (1966).

In conclusion, this chapter has attempted to survey some of the methods, empirical phenomena, and theories of memory. Perhaps the reader has been bothered by the diversity and lack of agreement that seems to prevail. However, the field is active and robust in health, and better to have ardent dissention than disinterest or indifference. At the very least the important problems seem to be emerging, and one must ask the right questions in order to find the right answers.

Acknowledgment. Preparation of this paper was supported by research grants from the National Science Foundation, National Research Council, and Ontario Mental Health Foundation. The writer is indebted to Endel Tulving for a critical reading of the manuscript.

References

AARONSON, D. Temporal factors in perception and short-term memory. *Psychological Bulletin*, 1967, 67, 130–44.

ADAMS, J. A. *Human Memory.* New York: McGraw-Hill, 1967.

ANISFELD, M., and KNAPP, M. Association, synonymity, and directionality in false recognition. *Journal of Experimental Psychology*, 1968, 77, 171–79.

ASCH, S. E. The doctrinal tyranny of Associationism: Or what is wrong with rote learning. *In* T. R. DIXON and D. L. HORTON (eds.), *Verbal Learning and General Behavior Theory.* Englewood Cliffs, N.J.: Prentice-Hall, 1968, 214–28.

———, and EBENHOLTZ, S. M. The principle of associative symmetry. *Proceedings of the American Philosophical Society*, 1962, *106*, 135–63.

ATKINSON, R. C., and CROTHERS, E. J. A comparison of paired-associate learning models having different acquisition and retention axioms. *Journal of Mathematical Psychology*, 1964, *1*, 285–315.

ATKINSON, R. C., and SHIFFRIN, R. M. Mathematical models for memory and learning. *Technical Report Number 79*, Institute for Mathematical Studies in the Social Sciences, Stanford University, 1965.

——— Human memory: A proposed system and its control processes. *In* K. W. SPENCE and J. T. SPENCE (eds.), *The Psychology of Learning and Motivation: Advances in Research and Theory*, vol. 2. pp. 89–195. New York: Academic Press, 1968.

BADDELEY, A. D., and DALE, H. C. The effect of semantic similarity on retroactive interference in long- and short-term memory. *Journal of Verbal Learning and Verbal Behavior*, 1966, 5, 417–20.

BARTLETT, F. C. *Remembering: A study in Experimental and Social Psychology.* New York: Cambridge, 1932.

BERNBACH, H. A. A forgetting model for paired-associate learning. *Journal of Mathematical Psychology*, 1965, 2, 128–44.

——— Decision processes in memory. *Psychological Review*, 1967, 74, 462–80.

BERTELSON, P. Central intermittency twenty years later. *Quarterly Journal of Experimental Psychology*, 1966, 18, 153–63.

BINET, A., and HENRI, V. La mémoire des mots. *L'Année Psychologique*, 1894, *1*, 1–23.

BOOTH, D. A. Vertebrate brain ribonucleic acid and memory retention. *Psychological Bulletin*, 1967, 68, 149–77.

BOUSFIELD, W. A. The occurrence of clustering in the recall of randomly arranged associates. *Journal of General Psychology*, 1953, *49*, 229–40.

———, and COHEN, B. H. Clustering in recall as a function of the number of word-categories in stimulus-word lists. *Journal of General Psychology*, 1956, *54*, 95–106.

BOWER, G. H. Notes on a descriptive theory of memory. Paper presented at the Second Conference on Learning, Remembering, and Forgetting, Princeton, New Jersey, September, 1964.

——— A multicomponent theory of the memory trace. *In* K. W. SPENCE and J. T. SPENCE (eds.), *The psychology of learning and motivation: Advances in research and theory*, vol. 1, pp. 229–325. New York: Academic Press, 1967.

BREGMAN, A. S., and CHAMBERS, D. W. All-or-none learning of attributes. *Journal of Experimental Psychology*, 1966, 71, 785–93.

BROADBENT, D. E. *Perception and Communication.* New York: Pergamon Press, 1958.

——— Flow of information within the organism. *Journal of Verbal Learning and Verbal Behavior*, 1963, *2*, 34–39.

——— Techniques in the study of short term memory. *Acta Psychologica*, 1965, *24*, 220–33.

——— The well-ordered mind. *American Educational Research Journal*, 1966, *3*, 281–95.

———, and HERON, A. Effects of subsidiary task on performance involving immediate memory by younger and older men. *British Journal of Psychology*, 1962, *53*, 189–98.

BROWN, J. Some tests of the decay theory of immediate memory. *Quarterly Journal of Experimental Psychology*, 1958, 10, 12–21.

——— Information, redundancy and decay of the memory trace. In *The Mechanisation of Thought Processes.* National Physical Laboratory Symposium No. 10, H.M.S.O., 1959.

BROWN, R., and MCNEILL, D. The "tip of the tongue" phenomenon. *Journal of Verbal Learning and Verbal Behavior*, 1966, *5*, 325–37.

BUREŠ, J., and BUREŠOVÁ, O. Cortical spreading depression as a memory disturbing factor. *Journal of Comparative and Physiological Psychology*, 1963, *56*, 268–72.

BUSCHKE, H. Auditory and visual interaction in immediate memory. *Psychiatric Research*, 1962, *1*, 229–37.

——— Retention in immediate memory estimated without retrieval. *Science*, 1963, *140*, 56–57.

——— Types of immediate memory. *Journal of Verbal Learning and Verbal Behavior*, 1966, *5*, 275–78.

COFER, C. N. A study of clustering in free recall based on synonyms. *Journal of General Psychology*, 1959, *60*, 3–10.

COHEN, B. H. An investigation of recoding in free recall. *Journal of Experimenta Psychology*, 1963, 65, 368–76.

CONRAD, R. Very brief delay of immediate recall. *Quarterly Journal of Experimental Psychology*, 1960a, *12*, 45–47.

——— Serial order intrusions in immediate memory. *British Journal of Psychology*, 1960b, *51*, 45–48.

——— Acoustic confusions in immediate memory. *British Journal of Psychology*, 1964, *55*, 75–84.

——— Order error in immediate recall of sequences. *Journal of Verbal Learning and Verbal Behavior*, 1965, *4*, 161–69.

——— Interference or decay over short retention intervals? *Journal of Verbal Learning and Verbal Behavior*, 1967, *6*, 49–54.

COONS, E. E., and MILLER, N. E. Conflict versus consolidation of memory traces to explain "retrograde amnesia" produced by ECS. *Journal of Comparative and Physiological Psychology*, 1960, *53*, 524–31.

CORBALLIS, M. C. Serial order in recognition and recall. *Journal of Experimental Psychology*, 1967, *74*, 99–105.

CROWDER, R. G. Prefix effects in immediate memory. *Canadian Journal of Psychology*, 1967, *21*, 450–61.

DALE, H.C.A. Familiarity and free recall. *Quarterly Journal of Experimental Psychology*, 1967, *19*, 103–8.

———, and BADDELEY, A. D. Alternatives in testing recognition memory. *Nature*, 1962, *196*, 93–94.

——— Remembering a list of two-digit numbers. *Quarterly Journal of Experimental Psychology*, 1966, *18*, 212–19.

DALLETT, K. Effects of a redundant prefix on immediate recall. *Journal of Experimental Psychology*, 1964, *67*, 296–98.

DAVIS, R., SUTHERLAND, N. S., and JUDD, B. R. Information content in recognition and recall. *Journal of Experimental Psychology*, 1961, *61*, 422–29.

DEESE, J. *The Structure of Associations in Language and Thought.* Baltimore: The Johns Hopkins Press, 1965.

DONALDSON, W., and MURDOCK, B. B., JR. Criterion change in continuous recognition memory. *Journal of Experimental Psychology*, 1968, *76*, 325–30.

DOUGLAS, R. J. The hippocampus and behavior. *Psychological Bulletin*, 1967, *67*, 416–42.

DUNCAN, C. P. The retroactive effect of electroshock on learning.

Journal of Comparative and Physiological Psychology, 1949, *42*, 32–44.

EBBINGHAUS, H. *Memory: A contribution to experimental psychology.* New York: Dover, 1964.

EGAN, J. P. Recognition memory and the operating characteristic. Technical Note AFCRC–TN–58–51, 1958, Indiana University, Hearing and Communication Laboratory.

———, and CLARKE, F. R. Psychophysics and signal detection. *In* J. B. SIDOWSKI (ed.), *Experimental Methods and Instrumentation in Psychology*, pp. 211–46. New York: McGraw-Hill, 1966.

EPSTEIN, W. The influence of syntactical structure on learning. *American Journal of Psychology*, 1961, *74*, 80–85.

FIELD, W. H., and LACHMAN, R. Information transmission (*I*) in recognition and recall as a function of alternatives (*k*). *Journal of Experimental Psychology*, 1966, *72*, 785–91.

FLEXNER, L. B. Dissection of memory in mice with antibiotics. *Proceedings of the American Philosophical Society*, 1967, *111*, 343–46.

GARNER, W. R., and WHITMAN, J. R. Form and amount of internal structure as factors in free-recall learning of nonsense words. *Journal of Verbal Learning and Verbal Behavior*, 1965, *4*, 257–66.

GLANZER, M., and CUNITZ, A. R. Two storage mechanisms in free recall. *Journal of Verbal Learning and Verbal Behavior*, 1966, *5*, 351–60.

GREEN, D. M., and SWETS, J. A. *Signal Detection Theory and Psychophysics.* New York: John Wiley, 1966.

GREENO, J. G. Paired-associate learning with massed and distributed repetitions of items. *Journal of Experimental Psychology*, 1964, *67*, 286–95.

HARCUM, E. R. Parallel functions of serial learning and tachistoscopic pattern perception. *Psychological Review*, 1967, *74*, 51–62.

HELLYER, S. Frequency of stimulus presentation and short-term decrement in recall. *Journal of Experimental Psychology*, 1962, *64*, 650.

HINTZMAN, D. L. Articulatory coding in short-term memory. *Journal of Verbal Learning and Verbal Behavior*, 1967, *6*, 312–16.

HIRSH, I. J. *The Measurement of Hearing.* New York: McGraw-Hill, 1952.

HOROWITZ, L. M. Free recall and the ordering of trigrams. *Journal of Experimental Psychology*, 1961, *62*, 51–57.

HUNT, E. B. Simulation and analytic models of memory. *Journal of Verbal Learning and Verbal Behavior*, 1963, *2*, 49–59.

HUNTER, I. M. L. *Memory.* Middlesex: Penguin Books Ltd., 1964.

HYDÉN, H. Biochemical and molecular aspects of learning and memory. *Proceedings of the American Philosophical Society*, 1967, *111*, 326–42.

INGLIS, J., and CAIRD, W. K. Age differences in successive responses to simultaneous stimulation. *Canadian Journal of Psychology*, 1963, *17*, 98–105.

JACOBSON, A. L., FRIED, C., and HOROWITZ, S. D. Planarians and memory. *Nature*, 1966, *209*, 599–600.

JUNG, J. Recall of presented and missing elements of an exhaustive category as a function of percentage of elements presented. *Proceedings of the Convention of the American Psychological Association*, 1965, *1*, 55–56.

KEPPEL, G. Problems of method in the study of short-term memory. *Psychological Bulletin*, 1965, *63*, 1–13.

——— Retroactive and proactive inhibition. *In* T. R. DIXON and D. L. HORTON (eds.), *Verbal Learning and General Behavior Theory*, pp. 172–213. Englewood Cliffs, N.J.: Prentice-Hall, 1968.

———, and UNDERWOOD, B. J. Proactive inhibition in short-term retention of single items. *Journal of Verbal Learning and Verbal Behavior*, 1962, *1*, 153–61.

KIMBLE, D. P., ed. *Learning, Remembering, and Forgetting*, vol. 2. New York: New York Academy of Sciences, 1967.

KINTSCH, W. Memory and decision aspects of recognition learning. *Psychological Review*, 1967, *74*, 496–504.

——— An experimental analysis of single stimulus tests and multiple-choice tests of recognition memory. *Journal of Experimental Psychology*, 1968, *76*, 1–6.

——— Recognition and free recall of organized lists. *Journal of Experimental Psychology*, 1969, *78*, 481–87.

———, and MORRIS, C. J. Application of a Markov model to free recall and recognition. *Journal of Experimental Psychology*, 1965, *69*, 200–206.

KOLERS, P. A. Interlingual facilitation of short-term memory. *Journal of Verbal Learning and Verbal Behavior*, 1966, *5*, 314–19.

KOPPENAAL, R. J. Time changes in the strength of A-B, A-C lists: Spontaneous recovery? *Journal of Verbal Learning and Verbal Behavior*, 1963, *2*, 310–19.

LACHMAN, R., and TUTTLE, A. V. Approximations to English (AE) and short-term memory: Construction or storage? *Journal of Experimental Psychology*, 1965, *70*, 386–93.

LASHLEY, K. S. In search of the engram. *Symposium of the Society of Experimental Biology*, 1950, *4*, 454–82.

LAUGHERY, K. R., and PINKUS, A. L. Recoding and presentation rate in short-term memory. *Journal of Experimental Psychology*, 1968, *76*, 636–41.

LAURENCE, M. W. Age differences in performance and subjective organization in the free-recall learning of pictorial material. *Canadian Journal of Psychology*, 1966, *20*, 388–99.

LEVY, B. A., and MURDOCK, B. B., JR. The effects of delayed auditory feedback and intra-list similarity in short-term memory. *Journal of Verbal Learning and Verbal Behavior*, 1968, *7*, 887–94.

LINDLEY, R. H. Effects of controlled coding cues in short-term memory. *Journal of Experimental Psychology*, 1963, *66*, 580–87.

LLOYD, K. E., REID, L. S., and FEALLOCK, J. B. Short-term retention as a function of the average number of items presented. *Journal of Experimental Psychology*, 1960, *60*, 201–7.

LOCKHART, R. S. Retrieval asymmetry in the recall of adjectives and nouns. *Journal of Experimental Psychology*, 1969, *79*, 12–17.

LOESS, H., and WAUGH, N. C. Short-term memory and intertrial interval. *Journal of Verbal Learning and Verbal Behavior*, 1967, *6*, 455–60.

LUH, C. W. The conditions of retention. *Psychological Monographs*, 1922, *31*, no. 142.

MCCONNELL, J. V. Memory transfer through cannibalism in planarians. *Journal of Neuropsychiatry*, 1962, *3*, Supplement No. 1, 42–48.

MCGAUGH, J. L. Time-dependent processes in memory storage. *Science*, 1966, *153*, 1351–58.

——— Analysis of memory transfer and enhancement. *Proceedings of the American Philosophical Society*, 1967, *111*, 347–51.

MCGEOCH, J. A. Forgetting and the law of disuse. *Psychological Review*, 1932, *39*, 352–70.

MCGHIE, A., CHAPMAN, J., and LAWSON, J. S. Changes in immediate memory with age. *British Journal of Psychology*, 1965, *56*, 69–75.

MCNULTY, J. A. An analysis of recall and recognition processes in verbal learning. *Journal of Verbal Learning and Verbal Behavior*, 1965, *4*, 430–36.

——— A partial learning model of recognition memory. *Canadian Journal of Psychology*, 1966, *20*, 302–15.

MCGOVERN, J. B. Extinction of associations in four transfer paradigms. *Psychological Monographs*, 1964, *78*, no. 16.

MACKWORTH, J. F. Presentation rate and immediate memory. *Canadian Journal of Psychology*, 1962, *16*, 42–47.

——— The relation between the visual image and post-perceptual immediate memory. *Journal of Verbal Learning and Verbal Behavior*, 1963, *2*, 75–85.

——— Auditory short-term memory. *Canadian Journal of Psychology*, 1964, *18*, 292–303.

MANDLER, G. Organization and memory. *In* K. W. SPENCE and J. T. SPENCE (eds.), *The psychology of learning and motivation: Advances in research and theory*, vol. 1, pp. 327–72. New York: Academic Press, 1967.

MELTON, A. W. Implications of short-term memory for a general theory of memory. *Journal of Verbal Learning and Verbal Behavior*, 1963, *2*, 1–21.

——— Repetition and retrieval from memory. *Science*, 1967, *158*, 532.

———, and IRWIN, J. M. The influence of degree of interpolated learning on retroactive inhibition and the overt transfer of specific responses. *American Journal of Psychology*, 1940, *53*, 173–203.

MELTON, A. W., and VON LACKUM, W. J. Retroactive and proactive inhibition in retention: Evidence for a two-factor theory of retroactive inhibition. *American Journal of Psychology*, 1941, *54*, 157–73.

MILLER, G. A. The magical number seven, plus or minus two: Some limits on our capacity for processing information. *Psychological Review*, 1956, *63*, 81–96.

—— Free recall of redundant strings of letters. *Journal of Experimental Psychology*, 1958, *56*, 485–91.

——, GALANTER, E., and PRIBRAM, K. H. *Plans and the Structure of Behavior*. New York: Holt, Rinehart and Winston, 1960.

MILLER, G. A., and SELFRIDGE, J. A. Verbal context and the recall of meaningful material. *American Journal of Psychology*, 1950, *63*, 176–85.

MILLER, N. E. Laws of learning relevant to its biological basis. *Proceedings of the American Philosophical Society*, 1967, *111*, 315–25.

MILNER, B. The memory defect in bilateral hippocampal lesions. *Psychiatric Research Reports*, 1959, *11*, 43–58.

—— Amnesia following operation on the temporal lobes. *In* C.W.M. WHITTY and O. L. ZANGWILL (eds.), *Amnesia*, pp. 109–33. London: Butterworths, 1966.

MILNER, P. M. A neural mechanism for the immediate recall of sequences. *Kybernetik*, 1961, *1*, 76–81.

MORAY, N. Broadbent's filter theory: Postulate H and the problem of switching time. *Quarterly Journal of Experimental Psychology*, 1960, *12*, 214–20.

——, BATES, A., and BARNETT, T. Experiments on the four-eared man. *Journal of the Acoustical Society of America*, 1965, *38*, 196–201.

MURDOCK, B. B., JR. The immediate retention of unrelated words. *Journal of Experimental Psychology*, 1960, *60*, 222–34.

—— Short-term retention of single paired associates. *Psychological Reports*, 1961a, *8*, 280.

—— The retention of individual items. *Journal of Experimental Psychology*, 1961b, *62*, 618–25.

—— The serial position effect of free recall. *Journal of Experimental Psychology*, 1962, *64*, 482–88.

—— Short-term retention of single paired associates. *Journal of Experimental Psychology*, 1963a, *65*, 433–43.

—— Interpolated recall in short-term memory. *Journal of Experimental Psychology*, 1963b, *66*, 525–32.

—— Short-term memory and paired-associate learning. *Journal of Verbal Learning and Verbal Behavior*, 1963c, *2*, 320–28.

—— An analysis of the recognition process. *In* C. N. COFER and B. S. MUSGRAVE (eds.), *Verbal Behavior and Learning*, pp. 10–22. New York: McGraw-Hill, 1963d.

—— A test of the "limited capacity" hypothesis. *Journal of Experimental Psychology*, 1965a, *69*, 237–40.

—— Signal-detection theory and short-term memory. *Journal of Experimental Psychology*, 1965b, *70*, 443–47.

—— Effects of a subsidiary task on short-term memory. *British Journal of Psychology*, 1965c, *56*, 413–19.

—— Forward and backward associations in paired associates. *Journal of Experimental Psychology*, 1966, *71*, 732–37.

—— A fixed-point model for short-term memory. *Journal of Mathematical Psychology*, 1967, *4*, 501–6.

—— Modality effects in short-term memory: Storage or retrieval? *Journal of Experimental Psychology*, 1968, *77*, 79–86.

——, and COOK, C. D. On fitting the exponential. *Psychological Reports*, 1960, *6*, 63–69.

MURDOCK, B. B., JR., and VON SAAL, W. Transpositions in short-term memory. *Journal of Experimental Psychology*, 1967, *74*, 137–43.

MURRAY, D. J. Vocalization-at-presentation and immediate recall, with varying presentation-rates. *Quarterly Journal of Experimental Psychology*, 1965, *17*, 47–56.

—— The role of speech responses in short-term memory. *Canadian Journal of Psychology*, 1967, *21*, 263–76.

NEIMARK, E., GREENHOUSE, P., LAW, S., and WEINHEIMER, S. The effect of rehearsal-preventing task upon retention of CVC syllables. *Journal of Verbal Learning and Verbal Behavior*, 1965, *4*, 280–85.

NEISSER, U. *Cognitive Psychology*. New York: Appleton-Century-Crofts, 1967.

NIXON, S. R. Some experiments on immediate memory. Applied Psychology Research Unit, 1946, A.P.U. 39.

NORMAN, D. A. Acquisition and retention in short-term memory. *Journal of Experimental Psychology*, 1966, *72*, 369–81.

——, and WICKELGREN, W. A. Short-term recognition memory for single digits and pairs of digits. *Journal of Experimental Psychology*, 1965, *70*, 479–89.

PENFIELD, W., and PEROT, P. The brain's record of auditory and visual experience: A final summary and discussion. *Brain*, 1963, *86*, 595–696.

PENFIELD, W., and ROBERTS, L. *Speech and Brain Mechanisms*. Princeton, N.J.: Princeton University Press, 1959.

PETERSON, J. R. Short-term verbal memory and learning. *Psychological Review*, 1966, *73*, 193–207.

—— Search and judgment in memory. *In* B. KLEINMUNTZ (ed.), *Concepts and the Structure of Memory*, pp. 153–80. New York: John Wiley, 1967.

——, and GENTILE, A. Proactive interference as a function of time between tests. *Journal of Experimental Psychology*, 1965, *70*, 473–78.

PETERSON, L. R., and PETERSON, M. J. Short-term retention of individual items. *Journal of Experimental Psychology*, 1959, *58*, 193–98.

PHILLIPS, J. L., SHIFFRIN, R. M., and ATKINSON, R. C. The effects of list length on short-term memory. *Journal of Verbal Learning and Verbal Behavior*, 1967, *6*, 303–11.

POLLACK, I. Interference, rehearsal, and short-term retention of digits. *Canadian Journal of Psychology*, 1963, *17*, 380–92.

POSNER, M. I. Rate of presentation and order of recall in immediate memory. *British Journal of Psychology*, 1964, *55*, 303–6.

——, and KONICK, A. F. On the role of interference in short-term retention. *Journal of Experimental Psychology*, 1966, *72*, 221–31.

POSNER, M. I., and ROSSMAN, E. Effect of size and location of informational transforms upon short-term retention. *Journal of Experimental Psychology*, 1965, *70*, 496–505.

POSTMAN, L. Choice behavior and the process of recognition. *American Journal of Psychology*, 1950, *63*, 576–83.

—— The present status of interference theory. *In* C. N. COFER (ed.), *Verbal Learning and Verbal Behavior*, pp. 152–79. New York: McGraw-Hill, 1961.

—— Does interference theory predict too much forgetting? *Journal of Verbal Learning and Verbal Behavior*, 1963, *2*, 40–48.

—— Mechanisms of interference in forgetting. Vice-presidential address, American Association for the Advancement of Science, New York, December 30, 1967.

——, and PHILLIPS, L. W. Short-term temporal changes in free recall. *Quarterly Journal of Experimental Psychology*, 1965, *17*, 132–38.

POSTMAN, L., and RAU, L. Retention as a function of the method of measurement. *University of California Publications in Psychology*, 1957, *8*, 217–70.

PRIBRAM, K. H. Some dimensions of remembering: Steps toward a neuropsychological model of memory. *In* J. GAITO (ed.), *Macromolecules and Behavior*, pp. 165–87. New York: Appleton-Century-Crofts, 1966.

RABBITT, P. Recognition: Memory for words correctly heard in noise. *Psychonomic Science*, 1966, *6*, 383–84.

ROCK, I., and CERASO, J. Toward a cognitive theory of associative learning. *In* C. SCHEERER (ed.), *Cognition: Theory, Research, Promise*, pp. 110–46. New York: Harper & Row, 1964.

ROSENBERG, S., and COHEN, B. D. Referential processes of speakers and listeners. *Psychological Review*, 1966, *73*, 208–31.

SANDERS, A. F. Rehearsal and recall in immediate memory. *Ergonomics*, 1961, *4*, 25–34.

SCHAUB, G. R., and LINDLEY, R. H. Effects of subject-generated recoding cues on short-term memory. *Journal of Experimental Psychology*, 1964, *68*, 171–75.

SCHNEIDER, A. M. Control of memory by spreading cortical depression: A case for stimulus control. *Psychological Review*, 1967, *74*, 201–15.

SHEPARD, R. N., and CHANG, J. Forced-choice tests of recognition memory under steady-state conditions. *Journal of Verbal Learning and Verbal Behavior*, 1963, *2*, 93–101.

SHEPARD, R. N., and TEGHTSOONIAN, M. Retention of information under conditions approaching a steady state. *Journal of Experimental Psychology*, 1961, *62*, 302–9.

SLAMECKA, N. J. Proactive inhibition of connected discourse. *Journal of Experimental Psychology*, 1961, *62*, 295–301.

—— A search for spontaneous recovery of verbal associations. *Journal of Verbal Learning and Verbal Behavior*, 1966, *5*, 205–7.

—— An examination of trace storage in free recall. *Journal of Experimental Psychology*, 1968, *76*, 504–13.

——, and CERASO, J. Retroactive and proactive inhibition of verbal learning. *Psychological Bulletin*, 1960, *57*, 449–75.

SPERRY, R. W. The great cerebral commissure. *Scientific American*, 1964, *210*, 42–62.

TALLAND, G. A. *Deranged Memory*. New York: Academic Press, 1965.

TULVING, E. Subjective organization in free recall of "unrelated" words. *Psychological Review*, 1962, *69*, 344–54.

────── Theoretical issues in free recall. *In* T. R. DIXON and D. L. HORTON (eds.), *Verbal Learning and General Behavior Theory*, pp. 2–36. Englewood Cliffs, N.J.: Prentice-Hall, 1968.

──────, and ARBUCKLE, T. Y. Sources of intratrial interference in immediate recall of paired associates. *Journal of Verbal Learning and Verbal Behavior*, 1963, *1*, 321–34.

TULVING, E., and OSLER, S. Effectiveness of retrieval cues in memory for words. *Journal of Experimental Psychology*, 1968, *77*, 593–601.

TULVING, E., and PATTERSON, R. D. Functional units and retrieval processes in free recall. *Journal of Experimental Psychology*, 1968, *77*, 239–48.

TULVING, E., and PEARLSTONE, Z. Availability versus accessibility of information in memory for words. *Journal of Verbal Learning and Verbal Behavior*, 1966, *5*, 381–91.

UNDERWOOD, B. J. Speed of learning and amount retained: A consideration of methodology. *Psychological Bulletin*, 1954, *51*, 276–82.

────── Interference and forgetting. *Psychological Review*, 1957, *64*, 49–60.

────── Degree of learning and the measurement of forgetting. *Journal of Verbal Learning and Verbal Behavior*, 1964, *3*, 112–29.

────── False recognition by implicit verbal responses. *Journal of Experimental Psychology*, 1965, *70*, 122–29.

────── *Experimental Psychology*. 2d ed. New York: Appleton-Century-Crofts, 1966.

──────, and EKSTRAND, B. R. An analysis of some shortcomings in the interference theory of forgetting. *Psychological Review*, 1966, *73*, 540–49.

WAUGH, N. C. Presentation time and free recall. *Journal of Experimental Psychology*, 1967, *73*, 39–44.

──────, and NORMAN, D. A. Primary memory. *Psychological Review*, 1965, *72*, 89–104.

WEISKRANTZ, L. Experimental studies of amnesia. *In* C.W.M. WHITTY and O. L. ZANGWILL (eds.), *Amnesia*, pp. 1–35. London: Butterworths, 1966.

WELFORD, A. T. The measurement of sensory-motor performance: Survey and reappraisal of twelve years' progress. *Ergonomics*, 1960, *3*, 189–230.

WHITMAN, J. R., and GARNER, W. R. Free recall learning of visual figures as a function of form of internal structure. *Journal of Experimental Psychology*, 1962, *64*, 558–64.

WICKELGREN, W. A. Short-term memory for repeated and non-repeated items. *Quarterly Journal of Experimental Psychology*, 1965a, *17*, 14–25.

────── Acoustic similarity and retroactive interference in short-term memory. *Journal of Verbal Learning and Verbal Behavior*, 1965b, *4*, 53–61.

────── Distinctive features and errors in short-term memory for English vowels. *Journal of Acoustical Society of America*, 1965c, *38*, 583–88.

────── Phonemic similarity and interference in short-term memory for single letters. *Journal of Experimental Psychology*, 1966a, *71*, 396–404.

────── Distinctive features and errors in short-term memory for English consonants. *Journal of Acoustical Society of America*, 1966b, *39*, 388–98.

──────, and NORMAN, D. A. Strength models and serial position in short-term recognition memory. *Journal of Mathematical Psychology*, 1966, *3*, 316–47.

WICKENS, D. D., BORN, D. G., and ALLEN, C. K. Proactive inhibition and item similarity in short-term memory. *Journal of Verbal Learning and Verbal Behavior*, 1963, *2*, 440–45.

WINOGRAD, E. List differentiation as a function of frequency and retention interval. *Journal of Experimental Psychology Monograph Supplement*, part 2, (February 1968): 1–18.

WOODWARD, A. E., JR. A search for the stimulus in serial learning. Ph. D. dissertation, University of Toronto, 1968.

──────, and MURDOCK, B. B., JR. Positional and sequential probes in serial learning. *Canadian Journal of Psychology*, 1968, *22*, 131–38.

WOODWORTH, R. S. *Experimental Psychology*. New York: Holt, 1938.

YNTEMA, D. B., and MUESER, G. A. Remembering the present state of a number of variables. *Journal of Experimental Psychology*, 1960, *60*, 18–22.

YNTEMA, D. B., and TRASK, F. P. Recall as a search process. *Journal of Verbal Learning and Verbal Behavior*, 1963, *2*, 65–74.

ZELLER, A. F. An experimental analogue of repression: I. Historical summary. *Psychological Bulletin*, 1950, *47*, 39–51.

Language,
Thought,
and Intelligence

tional in nature. What the physiological properties (if any) of the symbolic analogue of overt behavior are, is left unspecified by Mandler.

HYPOTHESIS THEORY

Growing out of essentially nonassociational considerations is a conceptualization of thinking in terms of the symbolic manipulation and utilization of *hypotheses*. As in the case of mediational theory, there are many contemporary proponents of this point of view, not all of whom agree on all theoretical details. Prominent contributions to the recent literature have been made by Bruner, Goodnow, and Austin (1956), Restle (1962), Levine (1966), Dulany (1968), and others.

The general idea is that any situation encountered by a person will elicit within him one or more possibilities for action, i.e., hypotheses. If the situation requires action, one (or more) of these hypotheses will be selected and acted upon. The consequences of overt performance are what determine the person's next thought, decision, or hypothesis. For example, if what he does is completely successful, there is no need to change or revise the hypothesis. He may proceed directly to the next environmental encounter. If new information is generated by his response, some hypothesis revision might be indicated. If his response meets with environmental resistence, he might reject the hypothesis and select some new one (or more).

Hypothesis selection, test, and revision, according to prescribed rules, are the essential thought processes within this theoretical framework. The nature of hypotheses and the selection and revision rules vary among theorists, ranging from an essential random sampling process (Restle 1962), to the assumption of an integrated sequence of steps called a strategy (Bruner et al. 1956). In all cases, however, the hypotheses are said to be the basis for behavior, to provide a form of cognitive control of overt performance, and to be the stuff of mental life and thinking. Hypotheses are apparently accepted as primitive givens in these theories. They have, however, some critical features in common with Mandler's symbolic analogues, and might be assumed to originate in the same way, i.e., through learning. It has been suggested elsewhere (Bourne 1968) that the differences between hypothesis theory and general mediational theory are less substantive than semantic.

INFORMATION PROCESSING THEORY

A third, currently popular description of thinking conceptualizes the behaving organism as a complex information processing system (e.g., Hunt 1962; Newell, Shaw & Simon 1958). Generally, though not necessarily, it uses the computer (or computing program) as its model. People are said to behave, in a sense, like computers. The input to a computer is equivalent to the environmental stimulation of an organism. The output is analogous to its performance. The internal, programmed, information processing operations of a computing system are comparable to the inner thought processes of the organism. The general form of argument is that to the extent the actual performance of a human being or animal can be simulated in the output of a computer, the computing program is an adequate theory of his behavior. The processes and operations prescribed by the program are reasonable facsimiles of what actually goes on within a person before undertaking some overt performance.

Most human skills are programmable on a computer, although their time of execution is considerably more rapid. This follows, of course, from the fact that the computer is a contrivance of man *designed* to carry out his performances rapidly. These are performances, however, which could in principle (but much more inconveniently) be done without computing hardware. To be sure, as a tool, the computer has produced results which would otherwise be impossible because of the enormity of calculational labor involved. But the computer's substantive processing limitations are no less severe than those applying to man himself.

Information processing theory seems in general much more open and more broadly conceived than either the associational or hypothesis testing points of view. It admits to a much richer variety of skills and behavioral processes—any that can be represented within a computing program. Multiple characterizations of learning and problem solving are possible within the system and so the theory accommodates and accounts much more easily for the phenomena of individual differences than do other approaches. Newell et al., for example, have spelled out in detail a set of problem-solving procedures that might be useful in a number of different tasks, have described a manner of programming them, and have presented some examples of their application to real, logical problems.

More than merely removing the simplistic constraints that apply to other theories, the processing approach gives a more natural characterization of human behavior. Rather than couching all activity in the idiom of response (movement) elicitation by (physical or mediational) stimulation, the theory admits to complex and sensible functional units of behavior such as scanning arrays of data, comparing multiple sources of information, stepwise planning of solution attempts, and so on. One could analyze these operations perhaps to their "elementary" *S-R* constituents; but, as Hunt (1962) suggests, one might then have something comparable to a description of the functioning of an automobile in the language of atomic physics. It is always more useful and generally no less rigorous to work with a theoretical system which is coordinate with the phenomena to be explained.

Still there are troublesome problems to be solved within the processing approach. One particularly knotty question pertains to the origin of information processing operations. The theory seems merely to assume that thinkers have a repertoire of internal processes which carry on automatically. But, are they learned or inborn? How do we account for the different processes that different individuals presumably have or for the fact that some "thinking abilities" seem to be correlated with age? The theory, as currently stated, describes a relatively static organism insofar as his behavioral possibilities are concerned.

PIAGET'S THEORY

In contrast to the foregoing theoretical structures which took shape at the hands of many significant contributors, Piaget's system is almost exclusively a one-man product. It is an effort to plot the course of intellectual development, which takes the normal child through a metamorphosis from a newborn stage of overt, disconnected, primitive reflexes to an adult stage of thoughtful, well-controlled, skillful action. The system, as its supporting evidence, provides one kind of answer to questions about the origination of complex behaviors left open by contemporary information processing theory.

For Piaget, thinking and intelligent action are said to originate within a given biological substrate, a substrate beyond which it is rapidly extended according to a behavioral growth-like process paralleling in some ways biological growth or maturation. At the core of this process are two invariant functions, *organization* and *adaptation*. These have the status of given attributes of the human organism which guide its entire behavioral development. Thus, what a person *knows*, *can do*, *wants to do*, and *does*, at any stage of development tend to be well-organized and highly integrated. Furthermore, what he learns (comes to be able to do) is essentially a matter of adaptation to environmental circumstances. Note the strong connection implied here between psychological and biological processes. Organization and adaptation are the two main functional properties of living matter. Piaget has a bent toward reasoning through biological analogy—which is *not* to say that behavior, for him, is *strictly* a matter of maturation.

An individual's behavioral adaptation involves two interacting subfunctions: *assimilation* and *accommodation*. Assimilation is the process of changing new information, i.e., some aspect of the environment, so that it fits better with existing knowledge; accommodation, on the other hand, is an adjustment on the part of the organism itself so as to adapt better to existing circumstances. From this, it can be seen that intelligent behavior, while it is born of biological parentage, is considered by Piaget to develop mainly as an experiential process.

The product of assimilatory and accommodatory encounters over time with the environment are units of cognitive structure called *schemas*. Schemas are internalized representations of a class of similar actions or performances. They allow a person to do something "in his mind,"—i.e., a mental experiment—without committing himself to a course of overt action. They allow for operations on representations of reality so as to deduce problem solutions.

Schemas are not rigidly structured compartments of knowledge. They are, rather, specially organized, interlocking systems or networks of internalized information. They are not static, but adaptable, always open to new processes of assimilation and accommodation on new environmental situations. They represent the organism's preparation, at any point in time, to adapt to new circumstances and problems. One can then explain why it is that a person might accomplish with experience a goal which was formerly out of reach. The general principle of Piaget's theory which this illustrates is that a given period of behavioral development can be understood only in the context of earlier periods from which it arises.

Cognitive growth, according to Piaget, is an orderly developmental progression of cognitive forms emerging from a history of experiences. Its general features take shape universally in an invariant sequence of stages. Much empirical work within Piaget's system has been aimed at logging these ontogenetical changes. The general themes that characterize the development seem to be:

a. the progressive internalization of behavior (such that one might think out actions and consequences rather than overtly grope)

b. an increasing differentiation of schemas (thus expanding on the subject's range abilities)

c. the integration of schemas into hierarchies (adding to the stability and controllability of one's own behavior).

Piaget divides behavioral ontogenesis into three major periods, with a finer differentiation into subperiods, stages, and substages within each. Briefly, these epochs are described as:

a. the period of sensory-motor intelligence (0–2 years), taking the infant from a stage of primitive reflex to an objective understanding and differentiation of physical things, especially between the self and other objects

b. the period of concrete operations (2–11 years), covering the development of representational thinking and conceptualization and dimensionalization of the real world

c. the period of formal operations (11–15 years) which involves essentially the same process as (*B*), except applied recursively to symbolic structures rather than concrete or real world structures. In this stage, the subject is capable of truly mature, truly adult thinking. He can now deal with the general case, or the hypothetical; he can induce or make inferences; he can go beyond the information given.

What have been catalogued in other theories as internal information processing operations are learned (structured on prior knowledge of their components) during stage C. Piaget's descriptions of cognitive structures involved in this period bear remarkable resemblances to the processing operations accepted as givens in other theories.

Each period, note, is associated with a particular chronological age. Piaget's argument is that the periods themselves, and the order in which they occur, are invariant. The age at which each occurs, however, obviously is not.

NATIVISTIC THEORIES

All theories of behavior are to some extent nativistic. It is a simple, brute fact that human beings come biologically equipped with structures and functions that enter into any behavior description. Some theories are more nativistic than others, however, and classifying them is a little like the empirical problem of apportioning the variability in any behavioral characteristic into its genetic and experiential components (McClearn 1962). Associationism, including some of its mediational derivatives, can be thought of as an extreme emphasis on experience as a determiner of behavior. We consider briefly in this section the other extreme of emphasis on nonexperiential or nativistic determiners, using Gestalt theory as the main example.

As applied in this area, Gestalt theory is primarily a theory of problem solving, i.e., of goal-directed thinking. Its main tools of analysis are the apparently-innate laws of perception. Successful thinking involves a perception or an understanding of the structural and functional relationships within a problem context. To solve a problem one must grasp the "inner relationships" that bind that context into an organized whole. As a process, problem solving begins with a *centering* of attention on problem elements and their connection with the basic difficulty. A goal or solution is assumed to exist, and the subject is drawn to it by the most direct path. Solution attempts involve some active reorganization of elements by the individual with a resulting recentering of attention. Each recentering sets up a pattern of tensions toward the goal within the organism, which he seeks to resolve. These tensions vary according to a number of laws including those which pertain to figural qualities of the goal object and to subjects' geographical location relative to that object. Resolution or closure is achieved only by the attainment of the correct recentering, i.e., of a solution which is perceived as satisfactory. The resulting behavior change is often immediate, leading Gestalters to speak of *insight* as one of the fundamental phenomena of thinking (and learning).

Perception and thinking, for the Gestalt psychologists, are determined mainly by sensory data and the dynamics of forces toward organization and closure. There is a heavy emphasis on physiological mechanisms (e.g., organized stresses and tensions are commonly described as electrical field forces in the cerebral cortex) and on natural laws which are thought to apply automatically and invariantly to these mechanisms and to the behavior of all organisms. Every behavior—thoughtful, intelligent, or otherwise—is explained by some internal and innate structuring of the perceptual or cognitive (brain) field. The mechanisms and their functioning are under the essential control of biological maturation and of momentary physical field conditions. Thinking and problem solving are, then, essentially mechanical and largely indifferent to prior experience, learning, and other historical considerations. For these reasons Gestalt theory would have to be classified as nativistic, despite arguments to the contrary by Koffka (1928).

The newest of the nativistic theories is primarily the work of linguists, especially Chomsky (1965; see also McNeill 1968). As presently conceived, it is a theory of language and language development; but, because language is inextricably bound up with human behavior and thinking, it is easy to see how the theory might eventually be extended to a wider range of problems.

The idea can be summarized as follows: All children are endowed with a biologically based capacity for language. From birth, every child is in contact with the social behaviors of others. He hears them speak and from them receives and collects a corpus of speech. Based on this corpus, he formulates a grammatical system, i.e., a theory about the linguistic regularities that are present in the corpus. The theory represents abstractly the structure of sentences heard and allows the child to predict future and as-yet-unheard sentences. This theory constitutes the child's linguistic competence.

The formulation of a similar grammatical theory by each child is made possible by a biologically given internal structure, a machine for abstracting the essential features of speech. The process of abstraction is limited to the general and universal rules of language, which are the same no matter what particular language—English, German, etc.—the child might eventually speak and which constitute a sizeable component of speech behavior. Only the relatively minor, unique features of a particular language are learned through experience, and are not nativistically determined. An easy extension of this theory would exchange rules or principles of thought for rules of language, asserting that universal forms of thinking exist and are biologically derived. In fact, the assertion that all people embody a logical language analyzing and abstracting device is tantamount to conclusions about nativistic thought functions.

COMMENTS

Before passing to a review of empirical work, a few observations on the discussion so far might profitably be made. First of all, there is no pretension about completeness in the foregoing section. Only a selected, though hopefully representative array of theoretical systems has been presented. Within each system, moreover, only a bare minimum of contributors has been cited. An adequate review and statement of viable contemporary descriptions, explanations and interpretations of human thinking would constitute a considerable volume in itself.

Secondly, it is characteristic of theoretical work, and of the research that follows, to emphasize goal-directed or intentional thinking in contrast with its apparently more aimless forms. The theories outlined address problem solving behavior as the major issue, leaving aside such common experiences as day and night dreaming, fantasizing and much of what we call imagery. While there is some awareness of and concern about these phenomena (e.g., in associationistic [and mediational] accounts of free association [Jenkins & Palermo 1964]), they are clearly secondary, and perhaps epiphenomenal, aspects of thinking in most systems. The universal assumption seems to be that if one can account for intentional thinking, all other cases will fall out axiomatically.

Thirdly, there is an increasingly pronounced movement away from the behavioristic, physicalistic interpretation of thinking and behavior. This appears both in the current popularity of nonperformance concepts, such as analogic structure, hypothesis, schema, and internal structure, as ways and means of summarizing a variety of possible actions and in the attendant hierarchical as contrasted with linear ($S \longrightarrow R$) description of behavior. The formerly dominant conception of man as an inert object entirely at the mercy of "causative" factors of the "real world" has reluctantly given way in popularity to flexible concepts which are more appropriately descriptive of the complex achievements of man and which admit to non-physicalistic, i.e., abstract, determiners of performance.

Finally, in one form or another, all theories summarized describe thinking not as a behavior but as some nonbehavioral process or mechanism which in turn controls behavior. Typically the process is conceived as internal to the organism, having a physiological or quasi-physiological status. In many cases, the theories give the distinct impression of a man within a man, the inner man enabling and determining the performance of the outer man.

This form of argument has obvious logical difficulties and serious limitations. There is an alternative approach which might open up new possibilities without sacrificing any of the explanatory power and rigor identified with existing theoretical developments. The initial general goal of this approach is to develop an adequate descriptive system for behavior. It rejects the commonly accepted equation of behavior with movement (performance), on the argument that any complete and intelligible account of intentional behavior must include references to what the individual knows, knows how to do, and wants to do as well as what in fact he does (overt performance). *Knowledge*, *skill*, *intention*, and *activity* are logical parameters in rule-form descriptions of the *behavior* of organisms, not of internal nonbehavioral processes. This system—the rule-following model (Ossorio 1967)—recognizes thinking as a behavioral concept which provides a relatively noncommittal description of what a person is doing at certain times of minimal bodily movement, particularly those eventuating in direct action toward a goal. The rule-following approach represents a relatively new development in psychology, though its philosophical roots are familiar (e.g., Ryle 1949). As a consequence there is an unfortunately small literature to draw on (Ossorio 1966; Bourne, in press), making a detailed exposition of this promising alternative to classical psychological theory impossible.

Current Research in Thinking

The research literature in thinking is diverse and growing rapidly. Specifically delimiting what is to be designated as research in thinking seems unessential and probably fruitless at present. It is clear, for example, that much of the current work in verbal learning might really be classified in the area of thinking, e.g., the study of organization in free recall, research on coding processes in associative tasks, and mediation paradigm experiments. The relation of thinking and language would also justify some discussion of linguistic work, a topic considered elsewhere in this book.

Considerations of length and clarity simply demand that this chapter restrict the research reviewed to two general areas, problem solving and concept learning. These might be viewed as the traditional topics in thinking. Within each area, the literature is organized into three main topics: (a) variables concerned directly with the task, (b) variables concerned with the subject in the experiment, and (c) effects of previous training or experience on performance. Such a division is arbitrary and there are cases (e.g., memory in concept learning) where there is no clear basis for assigning research to one topic, or another. This system, it should be noted, is intended as nothing more than a convenience.

Concept Learning

While there are a variety of meanings of the term "concept" in everyday language, experimental psychologists have come to use the term in a special way. In this paper, "concept" is taken to refer to a principle for classifying objects or events into categories based on certain distinctive stimulus properties. Many such concepts in everyday life are associated with generic names, leading some psychologists to refer to concept learning as "learning the use of names" (Hunt 1962). It is not necessary, however, that the subject in a concept learning experiment have names for the categories employed. In general, it is not even necessary that he be able to describe the basis of classification. Learning the concept simply means that the subject can correctly classify stimuli in some set, although we can accept his verbal description as evidence that he knows how to do so.

In the usual task, the subject must learn to sort all stimulus patterns into two categories, those which are examples and those which are not examples of the concept; stimuli belonging in these categories are also sometimes called positive and negative instances. Stimuli differ typically in terms of a number of dimensions (using geometric designs as the stimulus population, the dimensions might be color, size, and form). Those dimensions which determine correct classification are called relevant dimensions, and the rest are called irrelevant dimensions. The specific

values (e.g., red) which are pertinent to classification are called relevant values or attributes.

The specification of all relevant attributes does not provide a sufficient description of any concept. As Haygood and Bourne (1965) have pointed out, every concept also involves some kind of rule which operates on the relevant dimension(s). One such rule is conjunction, the *and* rule, which specifies that only stimuli having all of the relevant attributes are examples of the concept. Another is inclusive disjunction, the *and/or* rule, for which any one or more of the relevant attributes must be present for the stimulus to be an example of the concept. Various other rules involving the same set of relevant attributes are possible, and, of course, generate different concepts.

Types of Problems

The attainment of some concept requires that the subject demonstrate knowledge of both the relevant attributes and the rule. Haygood and Bourne (1965) suggest that either of these aspects might be given to the subject at the beginning of the problem, thus simplifying the task for him. In most concept learning research, the rule has been given and the subject is required to learn or identify the relevant attributes; this task is called attribute identification. Haygood and Bourne proposed a task in which the attributes are given and the subject's task is to learn or identify the rule; this task is called rule learning.

Methods of Study

The methods used in the study of concept learning are numerous, but most can be considered as variations of two kinds of paradigms, which are distinguished in terms of whether the subject has an active role in the selection of the stimuli or not. Before describing the differences between these paradigms, certain communalities among nearly all methods can be noted. The subject sees several different stimuli; ordinarily, some of them are examples of the concept and some are not. He responds by categorizing these stimuli and/or by stating his verbal hypotheses concerning the concept. The experimenter provides feedback about the correctness of the categorizing response and/or the concept hypothesis. The subject continues to respond until he can categorize stimulus patterns correctly or until he can state the correct hypothesis.

Reception Paradigm. In this case, the subject has no control over the particular series of stimuli presented, the order being predetermined by the experimenter. The stimuli may be presented one at a time, the subject making one of two or more responses to each, or they may be presented two at a time, the subject choosing the positive instance of each pair. The most common measures of performance are number of errors and trials to solution for the series of categorizing responses.

Selection Paradigm. This paradigm permits the subject to select, from some set, each of the successive stimuli to be categorized. Generally, hypothesis statement is used as an index of solution attainment. Most important with this method is the relationship between stated hypotheses and the stimuli selected;

this relationship is used to infer strategies employed by the subject in attempting to solve the problem.

TASK-RELATED VARIABLES

Task-related variables, such as the selection of stimulus dimensions, the sequence of stimuli, the frequency of feedback, are those directly under the control of the experimenter. These variables have been the focus of a great deal of systematic experimentation, which is more completely reviewed by Bourne (1966).

Conceptual Rules. Most concept learning research has focused on problems which require the subject to identify the relevant attributes of some simple unidimensional or conjunctive concept. There are clear signs of interest in the very recent literature, however, in the processes of rule learning. Neisser and Weene (1962) compared a number of different conceptual rules in a series of problems in which neither the rule nor the attributes of the concept were known to the subject at the outset. Of the ten rules under investigation, the two unidimensionals—affirmation and negation—were by far the easiest; conjunctions and disjunctions in both positive and negative form were of intermediate difficulty; and the biconditional (e.g., Red if and only if Square) and exclusive disjunction (Red or Square but not both) were most difficult. The authors proposed a hierarchy of cognitive operations which might generate this particular order of rule difficulty. They assume that human beings work with conjunction (*and*), disjunction (*and/or*), and negation (*not*) as primitive operators. The difficulty of any concept is graduated in terms of the number of these primitive terms required to express it. This analysis generates three levels of logical difficulty corresponding to the levels of empirical difficulty observed in the experiment. Attractive though it might be on grounds of simplicity, this analysis leaves much to be desired. For one thing, there are within-level differences in difficulty among the rules which are ignored and, for another, it neglects possible transfer effects which might substantially change the order of rule difficulty.

Haygood and Bourne (1965) found essentially the same order of difficulty for three different types of problems, i.e., those (as Neisser and Weene) requiring the learning of both attributes and rules, those requiring only attribute identification, and those requiring only rule learning. They also found that rule learning was easier than attribute identification, although the relative difficulty of the two types of tasks must be in part related to the stimulus population. King (1966) has since found the same relative difficulty for the conjunctive and disjunctive rules with children as young as six years.

Laughlin and Jordan (1967), however, found the biconditional to be nearly as easy as the conjunction and considerably easier than the disjunction. Whether this unusual result reflects his use of two-valued dimensions, the selection paradigm, an hypothesis-criterion of solution, or some other variable in which their study differed from its predecessors is not known.

Inconsistent with the Neisser-Weene analysis, it has been found that differences in rule difficulty are virtually eliminated after the subject had solved several problems on each rule. Subjects apparently developed a general problem-solving strategy, called the truth-table strategy because of its resemblance to

that logical device, which converts all rules essentially to the same simple problem (Bourne 1967). Details of this strategy will be considered in a later section.

Stimulus Variables. Aspects of the stimulus have been extensively studied in concept learning research. Much of this work follows Hovland's (1952) informational analysis of concept learning which seems to have provided the impetus for considerable rigor and clarity in the study of the stimulus.

Variables related to the stimulus dimensions have produced results which generally fit an informational analysis. As the number of irrelevant dimensions increases, problem difficulty increases linearly (Bulgarella & Archer 1962). These results were recently extended by Haygood and Stevenson (1967) to rules other than conjunction and to the different type of conceptual problems, i.e., attribute identification and rule learning. In that study, increases in the number of irrelevant dimensions produced poorer attribute identification under all rules but had no significant effect on rule learning. This might be expected, since, in rule learning tasks, the subject is specifically instructed to watch the relevant dimensions and to ignore all others. Bower and King (1967), however, found that even rule learning performance on a biconditional rule was adversely affected by increasing the number of irrelevant dimensions, although the effect was limited to the first such problem. As the number of *relevant* dimensions increases, problem difficulty also increases (Bulgarella & Archer 1962; Schvaneveldt 1966); this trend is attributable to the increase in amount of information which the subject must identify and use to achieve problem solution.

Hovland's analysis helped to clarify the role of positive and negative instances in concept learning. Hovland pointed out that the distinction between (a) the informational values of positive and negative instances and (b) the subject's ability to utilize that information had not been recognized in previous research. Hovland and Weiss (1953) demonstrated that, even when the amount of information is equated in positive and negative instances, those subjects receiving positive instances perform better. Recently, Haygood and Devine (1967) proposed that these results at least partially reflect the nature of conjunctive concept problems. For the conjunctive rule, the only positive instances are those stimuli which have both of the relevant attributes. For other bidimensional rules, the proportion of instances with both attributes (say, x, y) can be manipulated independently of the proportion of positive instances. Thus, for the disjunctive rule, stimuli having only one of the relevant attributes (x, not $-y$ or not $-x$, y) are also positive. Haygood and Devine found that, for the disjunctive and biconditional rules, performance improved with increases in the proportion of x, y instances, even though the total proportion of positive instances was constant. They also found that varying the proportion of positive instances with the proportion of x, y instances constant produced little effect. These results argue that it is the occurrence of instances containing all relevant attributes rather than the occurrence of positive instances in general which is most significant in concept learning.

Informative Feedback. It is clear that the occurrence of some feedback is essential to solving concept problems. Information necessary to delineate the concept is spread over both the preresponse (object to be categorized) and postresponse (informative feedback) stimuli in these tasks. However, not all investigators are agreed as to the role feedback plays in learning, i.e., is it reinforcing or informing or both? Various studies have attempted to answer this question.

Omission of feedback on a certain percentage of all trials has been shown (Bourne & Pendleton 1958) to increase trials to solution more than could be accounted for by the simple number of trials without feedback. This effect is limited to very complex problems with many stimulus patterns varying in a large number of dimensions. As such, it seems likely to result from human memory limitations. When there are many stimuli to remember, those with no feedback interfere with memory for stimuli accompanied by feedback. While this interpretation is consistent with some theoretical work in the area (e.g., Underwood 1952), there seem to be no direct tests of it.

Considerable attention has been given to the comparison of feedback omitted on right versus wrong trials. Thus, Buss and Buss (1956) arranged conditions where feedback occurred (*Rn*) only after correct responses, (*nW*) only after incorrect responses, and (*RW*) on all trials. They found that *RW* and *nW* conditions produce approximately equivalent performance, which was superior to that of *Rn* subjects. They attribute these results to the greater *reinforcing* value of *W* feedback compared to *R* feedback. Bourne, Guy, and Wadsworth (1967) recently questioned this interpretation on the grounds that these conditions also vary in terms of the percentage of trials on which feedback occurs since, prior to solution, there are usually more wrong than right trials on the kind of (four-category) problem used. Bourne et al. varied the percentage of reinforcement after correct and after incorrect responses independently over several values from 0 to 100. Consistent with Buss and Buss, systematic effects for total trials to criterion were found; however, no significant effect or systematic trend existed when number of feedback trials to criterion was the measure. They suggested that trials on which feedback is omitted are essentially blank trials in these problems and that right feedback is apparently as important as wrong. This interpretation is not inconsistent with the results of Bourne and Pendleton in that the problems used in right versus wrong comparisons were typically quite simple.

A more disruptive effect is produced by providing erroneous feedback on some percentage of trials; this variable has been called misinformative, or probabilistic feedback, in concept learning. Suppose the concept is square, so that all squares belong in the positive category and all nonsquares in the negative category. But suppose that on some percentage of trials, just the opposite—squares negative, nonsquares positive—is signaled to the subject. It is not possible for the subject to match the feedback on every trial since the misinformation occurs on a random basis. Several experiments (e.g., Pishkin 1960) reported that subjects did learn to respond to the relevant dimension, even when confronted with up to 30% misinformation. In the later trials, subjects were found to match the probability of misinformative feedback; i.e., they would place squares in the negative category (and nonsquares in the positive category) on a percentage of trials about equal to the percentage of misinformation. While such matching surely reflects continued efforts by the subject to attain a complete solution to the problem, it is clearly not an optimal approach. The subject can maximize the percentage of feedback by always responding with the positive category to squares and with the negative category to nonsquares. Bourne (1963) extended the number of trials given to 600 and

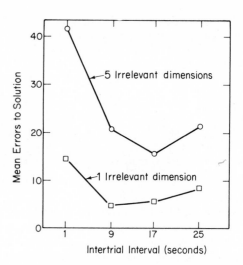

Fig. 28-1. *Performance in an attribute identification problem as a function of the length of the intertrial interval and the number of irrelevant stimulus dimensions.* [Bourne, L. E., Jr., Guy, D. C., Dodd, D. H., and Justesen, D. R. Concept identification: The effects of varying length and informational components of the intertrial interval. *Journal of Experimental Psychology*, 1965, *69*, 624-29. Copyright 1965 by the American Psychological Association and reprinted by permission.]

found that most subjects will reach this optimal solution with up to 30% misinformation. When transferred to a second problem with 15% misinformation, subjects originally trained on 0% *MF* showed considerably worse performance than those having a previous probabilistic problem.

Recent results by Saunders and Neimark (1967) seem to relate to Bourne's transfer findings. Some groups were informed prior to problem performance that misinformation might be given. The performance of these groups was much better than the performance of uninformed subjects. These findings, in conjunction with Bourne's transfer results, seem to argue that the subject considers the problem somewhat differently following knowledge, through training or instruction, that perfect performance is not possible.

Factors related to the timing of feedback have also been studied. Contrary to theoretical expectations, Bourne and Bunderson (1963), found that delay of the feedback (in the range 0 to 8 seconds) had little, if any, effect on performance. The delay between the feedback and the presentation of the stimulus for the next trial (the postfeedback or intertrial interval) is, however, quite important. This study, and another by Bourne, Guy, Dodd, and Justesen (1965), indicate that increases in the length of the intertrial interval are accompanied by better performance up to an asymptote determined by complexity of the problem. Further increases beyond the asymptote result in some decrement in performance. Figure 28–1 shows this relationship. The early part of this curve can be seen as reflecting the importance of additional time to process information about the stimulus and its correct category, a process which can be interrupted by the presentation of the next stimulus.

VARIABLES RELATED TO THE SUBJECT

The subject brings with him certain knowledge, skills, and motives to any problem-solving situation. These clearly are variables of potentially immense importance in the determination of his performance in the task. In many studies, concerted efforts are made by the experimenter to control and to minimize these variations among subjects; to the extent that he is unsuccessful there is "experimental error due to individual differences" in the data. This controlled approach, valuable though it is, ignores the interesting and informative possibilities that lie in the study of "individual differences" or subject-variables. Plainly, we stand to profit by a parallel and complementary research program focusing on what the subject brings to the task.

Unfortunately subject variables present more severe technical problems to the researcher than do task variables. For one thing, they are difficult and sometimes impossible to manipulate. Age and sex, for example, are fixed and one must sample subjects properly to determine their effects. Moreover, an experimenter can never be sure, despite detailed instructions and prolonged pretraining, that all subjects (in a particular experimental condition) have the same knowledge and skill. Even more disconcerting is the fact that researchers working on the same problem might not agree on what a particular subject-variable, such as creativity, is or on how to measure and control it.

So this is a vague area and difficult to work in. It will be some time before a substantial body of accepted fact is established. Nonetheless, a fair number of interesting experiments have been conducted, and provide a valuable beginning for this research enterprise.

Strategies. Bruner, Goodnow, and Austin (1956) described sets of ideal strategies that subjects might use in both selection and reception problems. A complete discussion of these strategies is impossible in the space allowed here. In their work, Bruner et al. inferred the strategies from hypotheses stated by subjects and categorizing responses or card selections.

For selection problems, four different ideal strategies applicable to conjunctive attribute identification problems were identified. The two *focusing* strategies both involve utilizing a single positive instance as a focus or standard. With each card selection, one or more stimulus dimensions are tested by comparison with the focus. The subject can thus infer the relevance of a dimension based on whether the new card is positive or negative. With a *conservative focusing* strategy, only one dimension is changed at a time, thus guaranteeing that the subject can determine the relevance of that dimension. With *focus gambling*, more than one dimension is tested at a time; this is a riskier approach, as the information gain might be either high (when the test instance is positive) or low (when it is negative). The other two strategies are variations of a *scanning* approach, in which the subject adopts one (*successive scanning*) or all (*simultaneous scanning*) of the possible hypotheses tenable, given existing information. Each trial provides information which is used to infirm incorrect hypotheses and select new ones. *Simultaneous scanning* is theoretically an optimal strategy. But the demands that both scanning strategies make on memory and inference are too great for either of them to be used with much success by most subjects. The focusing strategies, which entail fewer memory and inference requirements, are generally used more effectively.

Quantification of Strategies. Recently, several investigators (Bower & Trabasso 1964; Levine 1966; Restle 1962) have developed theories which assume that most or all subjects adopt a hypothesis-testing strategy to attribute identification (generally unidimensional) problems. These models are of particular interest because they have been formalized to the point of making numerous quantitative predictions about response characteristics in problem-solving situations.

Support for the hypothesis-testing models has been provided by the regular finding (e.g., Bower & Trabasso 1964) that presolution performance in concept identification problems is stationary, i.e., prior to the last error, the probability of a correct response is constant. Even more compelling support is the finding that repeatedly reversing the category assignment (Bower & Trabasso 1963) *or* repeatedly shifting the relevant dimensions (Trabasso & Bower 1964) prior to solution does not increase the total number of errors made, compared to groups performing on a standard concept problem.

Because these models have been relatively explicit in their assumptions and predictions, a number of experiments have been conducted to test them. Initially, Bower and Trabasso (see also Restle 1962) assumed that resampling of hypotheses on error trials occurred with replacement; in theory, the subject had essentially no memory for previous instances or hypotheses. However, it has been shown (Levine 1962; Holstein & Premack 1965) that a series of random reinforcements on the initial trials of a concept problem inhibits performance and that the amount of this inhibition is constant regardless of the number of random reinforcement trials. Because of these results and the evidence provided by some of their own experiments, Trabasso and Bower (1966) modified the sampling assumption so as to allow replacement of hypotheses in the sampling pool only after some number of trials has passed.

These models have also assumed that changes in hypothesis (and, consequently all information processing) occur only on error trials. The subject is considered to keep his hypothesis as long as it produces correct responses and to try something else when he makes an error. Erickson, Zajkowski, and Ehmann (1966) found indirect support for this argument in the fact that response latencies *after error trials* are greater than latencies after correct trials, but latencies *on error trials* and correct trials are not different. This evidence suggests the occurrence of more implicit problem-solving activity by the subject following an error than following a correct response. Other results (Bourne 1965; Suppes & Schlag-Rey 1965), however, clearly show changes of hypothesis after correct responses. Most recently, Rogers and Haygood (1968) found that, in a "concept" problem where feedback indicating right or wrong was actually noncontingent upon the subject's responses, hypothesis changes occurred during nearly half of five-trial blocks in which the subject was always correct and failed to occur on about half of five-trial blocks in which the subject was wrong at least once. Thus it does not seem to be correct to assume that subjects resample hypotheses if and only if they just made an error.

The all-or-none learning of many conceptual (and problem-solving) tasks seems to argue for the view that subjects use some strategy of the class proposed by these models. Whether the actual strategies are as simple as those proposed and whether all subjects employ the same strategy, however, are questions for future research to answer. Furthermore, the consideration of more complex conceptual problems and of the rule learning aspects of performance will require some additional attention by theorists. Analysis of strategy has made important contributions to a full account of conceptual behavior, and promises even further insights in the future.

Memory. Solving concept problems always entails the use of memory; even simple unidimensional concepts cannot generally be identified with the information provided on one or two trials. As noted above, certain strategies which have been taken to provide a theory of concept learning minimize memory requirements of the task. Nonetheless, the importance of memory has been demonstrated by a number of studies, many of them recently reviewed by Dominowski (1965).

Because more than one instance is required to provide sufficient information for solution, it might be expected that the sequence of stimuli would be of some importance. Underwood (1952) proposed that placing instances of a given concept closer together will result in more rapid acquisition of the concept. This hypothesis assumes that the subject must retain enough instances to abstract the relevant characteristics of the concept. While the studies of variation in time between instances have not been decisive, there is sound evidence that the interpolation of other stimuli between the positive instances of a particular concept produces interference. Kurtz and Hovland (1956), for example, presented instances of each of four concepts in either mixed or unmixed order. Subjects trained with the unmixed order gave more correct verbal descriptions of the concepts and made more correct test identification than did subjects trained with the mixed order. Bourne and Jennings (1963) studied four different degrees of contiguity among the instances of four different concepts and found that performance (i.e., total number of correct response) improved linearly with increased contiguity of instances of each concept.

Anderson and Guthrie (1966) showed that the effects of contiguity of instances are a function of the number of irrelevant dimensions varying on adjacent trials; they also found an exception to the contiguity hypothesis. All subjects received six training trials which provided enough information to solve the problem. During these trials, different groups received all positive instances or positive and negative instances on alternate trials. Within these groups, the number of dimensions which varied on any two adjacent trials was either one or three. During the test trials, the subject continued to categorize the stimuli which at that point were presented in a random sequence. The results showed that, if positive instances are contiguous, increasing variation in the irrelevant dimensions produces superior performance. On the other hand, if positive instances occur on alternate trials, holding all irrelevant dimensions constant produces superior performance. While the latter finding does not fit the contiguity hypothesis, it does demonstrate the importance of memory. Varying the relevant dimension and holding all other dimensions constant minimizes the memory requirements of the task since the problem can be logically solved in this case with the information provided on any two adjacent trials.

Other research has considered the effects of availability of previous information. Cahill and Hovland (1960) compared performance under a successive presentation condition, where no previous stimuli were available, with a condition of simultaneous presentation, where all previous stimuli were available. Not surprisingly, performance under the simultaneous condition was greatly superior. Cahill and Hovland defined two types of errors which might be made. The hypothesis stated by a subject in the successive condition on a particular trial might be inconsistent with information presented on a previous trial but no longer available. These *memory errors* showed increasing frequency as the information was more remote, i.e., as more trials intervened between the trial on which the hypothesis was stated and the trial on which the inconsistent information occurred. Hypotheses stated by subjects in the simultaneous condition could be inconsistent with presently available information. These perceptual-inference errors occurred quite infrequently, but a subject who was prone to make them was generally inferior in his overall performance on the problem. Bourne, Goldstein, and Link (1964) pointed out that the simultaneous and successive conditions are the endpoints of a continuum of availability. These experimenters studied availability over a range from 0 to 10 previous stimuli which were left for the subject's inspection. In general, increasing the availability of previous instances improve performance and the effect was more pronounced for more complex problems.

Intelligence. It seems hardly necessary to demonstrate empirically the positive relationship between intelligence and concept learning. More important questions concern the details underlying this relationship. Do people of high and low intelligence learn concepts in different ways? By different strategies? What aspects of intelligence are most important in concept learning? Does intelligence interact with other variables?

Osler and her associates have attempted to answer some of these questions in a series of experiments. Osler and Fivel (1961) compared normal (90–109) and high (over 110) IQ subjects at three different age levels (6, 10, and 14 years) and found that both increasing age and higher IQ were associated with better performance. Of special interest was the classification of subjects into sudden and gradual problem solvers. Gradual subjects show a continuous rise in percent correct responses prior to solution while sudden solvers perform at a chance level until solution is achieved. The analysis indicated that a higher percentage of high IQ subjects were sudden solvers at every age level. Osler and Fivel argue that the brighter subjects tend to adopt a more active, hypothesis-testing approach to the problem, while normals learn more often in a gradual, associational way.

In a subsequent experiment, Osler and Trautman (1961) sought to confirm their view of the difference between the two IQ groups. They argued that the high IQ subjects who use hypothesis-testing strategies should have great difficulty with relatively complex stimuli since the set of testable hypotheses would become very large. For normal subjects the process of conditioning of stimuli to response categories would not be affected by increasing complexity. This argument leads to the prediction of an interaction between stimulus complexity and intelligence. With relatively simple stimuli, the usual difference favoring bright subjects over normals would be expected. As complexity increases, the difference would diminish and, given sufficient complexity, the normals might even perform better. In their experiment, Osler and Trautman compared two levels of complexity within the age by intelligence design used in Osler and Fivel. All subjects learned the concept "twoness," i.e., all patterns containing two figures were positive and all others were negative. The less complex stimuli were black circles on a white background and varied only in terms of number. The more complex were pictures of common objects, varying in a large and unspecifiable number of ways. At every age level, the high IQ subjects performed better than the normals on the simple stimuli and worse than the normals on the complex stimuli. Performance by the normals was virtually unaffected by the complexity variable, but performance by the high IQ subjects was considerably better with the simple stimuli than with the complex stimuli.

Wolff (1967) recently questioned the Osler-Trautman conditioning analysis of learning and reported a failure to replicate this interaction of complexity and intelligence. Wolff argued that *S-R* theories, such as the Bourne and Restle (1959) model of conceptual behavior, *do* assume that stimulus complexity affects learning. Thus, the normals, assuming their learning follows such principles, should do worse on more complex problems, just as hypothesis testers do. Wolff's replication showed that both normals and high IQ subjects performed more poorly on the complex problems but that high IQ subjects were always better than normals. He found no hint of an interaction of the two variables. Wolff suggests that the critical difference between the two experiments may be that Osler and Trautman confounded complexity with variety of negative instances. Further experiments will be required to clarify this issue, however.

Of course some of the conclusions of Osler and associates were not disconfirmed. The sudden learning exhibited by brighter subjects and other evidence reported by them can still be taken to support the thesis that greater intelligence, knowledge, and experience tends to be associated with a more active, hypothesis-testing approach to solving conceptual problems.

TRANSFER

The influence of prior learning on a conceptual task may be facilitative (positive transfer), interfering (negative transfer), or without effect. Various transfer effects have been studied and discussed in the verbal learning literature (cf., Martin 1965) but the study of transfer in concept learning is neither extensive nor systematic. The bulk of the literature has been concerned with issues related to types of problem shifts, primarily with children. There is also some recent and preliminary work on transfer effects in rule learning.

Rule Learning. Haygood and Bourne (1965) found considerable positive interproblem transfer across a series of attribute identification and rule learning problems. Under rule learning, performance was virtually errorless by the sixth of a series of problems based on the same rule, regardless of the initial difficulty of the rule. Inter-rule effects have also been recently studied by Bourne and Guy (1968) who found that transfer to a biconditional (*x* if and only if *y*) rule learning problem was a function of the number of different training rules and of the particular training rules learned by the subject. Thus, experience with the largest number of rules (in this case, three) and specific experience with the conditional (if *x*, then *y*) rule produce maximal positive transfer to the biconditional problem. The authors account for these results in terms of the acquisition by subjects of a truth-table strategy, which involves coding the stimulus population into four types—patterns with both (*TT*), with one but not the other (*TF* and *FT*), and with neither (*FF*) relevant attribute and then learning the assignments of these four types to the two response categories—positive and negative instances. Acquisition of the strategy is facilitated by experience with a variety of rules and especially with the conditional.

In their paper, Haygood and Bourne also studied another kind of transfer problem called rule identification. Subjects were given experience with each of four bidimensional rules and were then required to identify which of the rules formed the solution to a new problem. The fact that most subjects were able to identify the rule after observing only four instances (one from each truth-table class) was taken as evidence that they come to use some version of the truth-table approach to the task. King (1966) recently studied rule identification with children. He found that, following rule learning on both conjunction and disjunction, many children as young as eight years could easily identify which of the two rules was in operation. Given a *TF* or an *FT* instance (either of which provides all the information needed to distinguish between the two rules), nearly all subjects could make the correct identification. Younger children showed less evidence of truth-table coding.

Hunt and Hovland (1960) have shown that subjects tend to choose a conjunctive over a disjunctive solution, if either is consistent with a particular grouping of some stimuli. Wells (1963) found that this effect is related in part to previous experience. Solving a series of disjunctive problems overcomes the subject's initial preference for conjunctions.

Attribute Learning. Both amount and variety of experience in attribute identification problems have received some systematic study. Grant and coworkers (e.g., Grant & Cost 1954) have considered the effects of overtraining in one problem on performance in a second problem with a different solution. As the number of trials beyond the subject's last error in the first problem increases (in this study the range was 5 to 40), performance after the solution shift improves. Also, the number of perseverative errors (i.e., errors on the second problem which would have been correct responses on the first) decreases as the number of overtraining trials increases. Neither of these results follows the principle that the persistence of a response increases with the number of reinforcements. Grant and Cost argue, rather, that with more criterion trials the subject is better able to discriminate the shift in feedback and the difference between problems.

Several studies have manipulated variety of experience. Morrissett and Hovland (1959) seem to have resolved discrepancies between several previous experiments and, therefore, only their study will be discussed. All subjects received 192 training trials prior to a transfer problem. Group I performed on the same problem for all 192 trials. Group II was trained on 24 different problems, eight trials on each. Finally, Group III was trained on three problems for 64 trials each. Thus Group I had the least variety of problem experience, Group II the greatest variety, and Group III an intermediate amount. All problems were based on the same principle which involved four different relative positional arrangements of two forms, the particular forms being varied from problem to problem. Following training, a new problem which also utilized the same principle was given as a transfer task. The results, shown in Figure 28-2, indicate best training performance by Group I, which performed throughout on the same problem, somewhat worse performance by Group III, and poorest performance by Group II, which had the greatest variety. Group III, which had a fairly high degree of learning within a problem and some variety of problems,

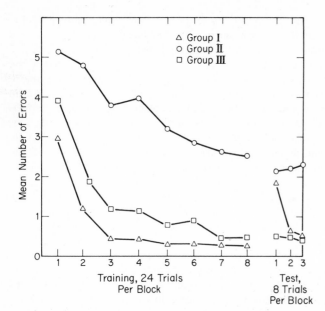

Fig. 28-2. *Performance in a series of concept problems. The three groups differ in terms of the conditions of training. All solved a common transfer test problem. See text for an explanation.* [From Morrisett, L., Jr., and Hovland, C. I. A comparison of three varieties of training in human problem solving. *Journal of Experimental Psychology*, 1959, *58*, 52-55. Copyright 1959 by the American Psychological Association and reprinted by permission.]

produced the best transfer performance. Group I, which had a high degree of training on a single problem, was inferior to Group III, but only on the first few trials of the transfer problem. Group II, which had low degrees of training on a large number of problems, was quite inferior. In short, these data indicate that both amount of training within a problem and variety of problems determine transfer, but that complete mastery of at least one problem is necessary. Solving a single problem thoroughly is of more transfer value than a minimal amount of experience with many problems. If sufficient learning on a particular problem is achieved, then positive transfer will increase with the number of different problems experienced. But if there is insufficient practice on each problem, then transfer is relatively poor.

Solution Shift Problems. The literature on various kinds of shifts in concept learning is vast; Wolff (1967) reviewed over 150 relevant studies in the current literature. Only a limited account of this work is possible here.

In conceptual shift experiments, the problem solution is changed, without warning. The subject must discover a new solution based on the previous relevant dimension (an intradimensional shift) or based on some other dimension (an extradimension shift). While there is more than one variation of each of these types of shift, the traditional intradimensional shift is one in which the two categories are reversed. Thus if red was positive and green negative during the original problem, then green is positive and red negative during the shift problems. This shift, in which the two categories are reversed, has been designated a reversal shift. The traditional extradimensional shift is called a nonreversal shift; with this shift, another dimension which was previously irrelevant, becomes relevant. Now the squares are positive instances and the triangles are negative,

regardless of their color. For a description of the various intra- and extradimensional procedures the interested reader may consult Wolff (1967).

A comparison of the reversal and nonreversal shifts has provided some interesting results. For rats and relatively young children (up to, say, 4 or 5 years of age) the nonreversal shift is easier than the reversal. This is generally taken to be consistent with a nonmediational, associationistic learning theory. The simple habit of responding to red as positive is more easily replaced by a relatively neutral association (squares are positive) than by the opposite response of red as negative. However, for older children and adults, the reversal shift is easier than the nonreversal (Kendler & Kendler 1962). Some variation of mediational, associationistic theory is often proposed to account for these latter results. Such views assume some kind of covert event between the observable *S* and *R*. The mediation may be a verbal label for the relevant dimension; the naming response "color" is produced covertly by the older, more verbal human subject. The Kendlers assume that such mediators (whether or not they are verbal) follow the conditioning principles like event responses. In the nonreversal shift, a new mediational link must be established. In the reversal shift, the mediation is unchanged. This argument is used to explain why the reversal shift is easier.

Problem Solving

One can scarcely disagree with the general conclusion of other reviewers that problem solving is one of the most chaotic research areas of psychology. This results in part from the wide diversity of experimental tasks which are designated as "problem solving." These tasks include virtually any complex learning situation not falling into a familiar category of learning, e.g., jigsaw puzzles, arithmetic problems, and anagrams. Further, even those falling into familiar categories are sometimes discussed as being essentially problem-solving tasks, e.g., verbal operant conditioning experiments (c.f., Dulany 1961).

The determination of what constitutes "problem solving" is not completely achieved by definition either. Gagné (1965) defined problem solving as behavior in situations in which the subject must achieve some goal by the use of a principle. He refers to a principle as a combination of or relationship between concepts, making "principle" sound like the definition of conceptual "rule" discussed in the previous section. A contrasting definition is offered by Staats (1968) who emphasizes the novelty of the required response(s) as the basis for defining problem solving.

The difficulties of determining what constitutes problem solving and what tasks are appropriate to its study are important ones, but there are no universally acceptable solutions. Consequently, we will proceed by dealing with those tasks conventionally designated as problem solving. Following description of these tasks and of the usual dependent measures, the various independent variables will be discussed under the general categories of task-related, subject-related, and transfer as in the concept learning section.

TYPES OF TASKS

No classification of problem solving tasks has been entirely satisfactory. It seems most appropriate here to list and briefly describe several of the most commonly used procedures before discussing suggested classificatory schemes.

Water-Jar Problems. These problems require the subject to determine how to obtain a certain volume of water by pouring between two or more jars holding known volumes (Luchins 1942). Generally, experimenters studying those tasks present a series of problems to study general transfer effects (rule learning).

Mental Arithmetic. The subject is asked to solve certain arithmetic problems or perform certain arithmetic operations (such as multiplication) in his head.

Anagrams. An anagram consists of several letters which the subject must rearrange to form a word. Generally (Johnson 1966) the solution word must use all the letters of the anagram.

Switch-Light Problems. A series of switches control, usually in a complex but lawful manner, a panel of lights (Duncan 1963). The subject must determine how to turn on a particular combination or pattern of lights.

Probability Learning. In the simplest kind of probability learning task, one of two or more feedback lamps is lighted, on a random basis, following the subject's choice of one of two or more response buttons (Humphreys 1939). Problem solution is generally held to be maximizing correctness by always pressing the button associated with the most frequent feedback signal. Complications in such a task are produced by making the feedback at least partially contingent upon (a) the subject's response, (b) preceding feedback signals, and/or (c) stimulus information. The latter problems may be classed as probabilistic or nondeterministic concept-learning problems.

"Insight" Problems. A large number of tasks have traditionally been designated "insight" problems, although this is a somewhat indiscriminate grouping. An example is Maier's (1930) pendulum problem in which the goal is to construct two pendulums which swing over designated places on the floor of a room. The best solutions, given the available materials, involved clamping two boards together to span from floor to ceiling and suspending the wires, with crayons attached, from a cross piece.

This listing does not pretend to be complete, but serves at least to illustrate the problems of organizing the area of problem solving.

A recent review by Davis (1966) has proposed a division into overt and covert tasks. He characterizes the overt task as one in which the subject does not know the outcomes of various response alternatives and is thus required to begin with overt trial and error. The covert task is one in which response alternatives are known and the subject can covertly test and reject the various possibilities.

This classification results in a reasonably clear separation of problem-solving tasks. However, it may more nearly characterize the propensities of researchers (perhaps for convenience) to use tasks in certain ways than it characterizes anything inherent in the task. It is clear, for example, that a covert task, such as mental multiplication, can be made relatively overt by having the subject recite each step. Similarly, a probability learning task, classified overt, might be made reasonably as covert by taking only a limited response sample. The effects of such changes between overt and covert forms of tasks are not really known, but the possibilities of change complicate the use of this classification scheme.

TASK VARIABLES

Thinking, as it occurs in a problem-solving situation, involves in some sense an operation by the subject on inputs or information from the environment to produce certain results. Structural characteristics of the problem no doubt have significant effects on these operations. While the study of variables related to the problem-solving task has not been as systematic as it has in concept learning some significant findings of this sort can be presented here.

Instructions to the Subject. The initial phase of any problem-solving experiment typically includes a set of instructions, the primary functions of which are (a) to specify the desired goal and (b) to outline the allowable approaches to it. While it is clear that instructions are a complex set of variables, it is difficult to specify and to characterize their significant properties. For this reason, research into their effects has been difficult to organize and conduct and has not followed any coherent line of development, theoretical or otherwise.

To illustrate the types of manipulation that have been investigated, two recent experiments on instructional variables can be noted. Duncan (1963) found that instructing subjects simply to "think" resulted in an increase in time to solve and a reduction in the number of overt "tries" at the solution of a switch-light problem. Instructions of this sort apparently induced more cognitive, nonovert, mental or "internal" problem-solving activity than is typical for this kind of problem task.

Providing the subject with "hints" about parts of the solution to an insight problem changes not only the likelihood of success but the types of attempted solutions as well (Burke, Maier, & Hoffman 1966). The implication of this result is that problem solving is hierarchically organized behavior, in that the occurrence of particular performances depends upon the availability of component knowledge and skills. Such knowledge can be provided either as "givens" in the instructions, as "hints" from the experimenter, or through extrinsic feedback after overt solution attempts.

Anagram Structure. The most frequently used task in research on problem solving is the anagram. Several different attempts have been made to account for the difficulty of anagrams in terms of their structural properties. Research in the area has confirmed the predictive utility of some of these approaches, but currently there is no compelling basis for selecting one view over another.

In the first of a long series of anagram studies, Mayzner and

Tresselt (1958) investigated the effects of the frequency of occurrence of solution words in natural language, as measured by Thorndike-Lorge counts. They proposed that higher frequency words are higher in the subject's repertoire of implicit solutions and are thus more likely to be selected than low frequency words. In accord with expectations, they found that anagrams constructed from high frequency words were more easily and more quickly solved.

Mayzner and Tresselt (1959) also explored the effect of the relative frequencies of occurrence in natural English language of all two-letter units (bigrams) in an anagram, which they call transition probability (TP). They argued that high TP anagrams (i.e., those with higher frequency bigrams) are harder to break up and rearrange into a word and therefore are more difficult to solve. Their data provided limited confirmation of this hypothesis. Not all results have agreed with this finding, however. Dominowski and Duncan (1964), for example, found no difference between high and low anagram TP in an experiment where both TP of the anagram and TP of the solution word were varied factorially. They did find an interaction between the two variables, however, such that the best performance occurred when a high TP anagram had a high TP word as a solution *or* a low TP anagram had a low TP word as a solution. They suggested that when the bigrams of the anagram were low frequency, the subject is more likely, through an associational process, to think of low-frequency bigrams in covert solution attempts, and vice versa.

More recently Dominowski (1966) proposed that letter moves (i.e., the number of letters whose position must be changed to attain solution) might be related to solution difficulty. Thus, for the word *camel*, the anagram *mceal* can be solved with a minimum of two moves; i.e., *c* to the first position and *a* to the second, while *mclae* requires three moves. Dominowski showed that variation in the number of letter moves, keeping bigram frequency relatively constant, has a considerable effect on the probability of solution and time to solution of five-letter anagrams. The fewer the moves, the better was performance. The major performance change was associated, however, with the difference between one- and two-letter moves, with some indication that three-move anagrams might even be easier than two. For five-letter words, a four-move anagram can be obtained only by completely inverting letter order of the word. The four-letter move condition was not used in this study, but one would intuitively guess it to be easier than problems with two- or three-letter moves. Dominowski's hypothesis seems at best only partially adequate.

Hebert and Rogers (1966) also studied letter moves, but in conjunction with the pronounceability (P) of the anagram. Using only anagrams with one- and two-letter moves, they found that P was inversely related to performance and that letter moves was an effective variable only for the low P condition. Thus when the anagram itself can be seen as a "cohesive" (pronounceable) unit, its resistance to rearrangement is increased and the significance of its likeness (in terms of letter order) to the solution is diminished.

An even more compelling example of the "cohesiveness" phenomena has been provided by presenting the subject with the problem of rearranging the letters of a word so as to construct another word. Beilin and Horn (1962) and Ekstrand and Dominowski (1965) both found that word (W) anagrams were more difficult than nonword (NW) anagrams. These studies controlled for some known sources of anagram difficulty, such as word frequency. Mayzner and Tresselt (1965), however, suggested that important, but unknown sources of problem difficulty might be uncontrolled when different words are used in the W and NW anagram conditions. Using the same solution for both W and NW anagrams, they repeated the study and found no difference between the two. It should be noted that, in this study, subjects who solved NW anagrams had two possible solutions—the one used as a word anagram for group W and the "appropriate" solution expected of both groups. Subjects in the NW condition might achieve the "appropriate" solution only after finding the other word, while subjects in condition W had only one possible solution. Requiring two solutions of some NW subjects might cancel the interfering effects of cohesiveness in condition W. In a replication of Mayzner and Tresselt, Beilin (1966) found that time to first solution (if correct) and time from first to second (if required) in condition NW were shorter than time to solution in condition W. Only for times from start to correct solution was there no difference between the conditions.

While there are persistent methodological problems, Beilin has concluded that W anagrams are more difficult primarily because a word is perceived as a whole, as a gestalt, and is not easily broken into letter parts. Ekstrand and Dominowski (1965) proposed a more explicit alternative interpretation to the effect that the word anagram produces implicit associates, generally other words, which are unlikely to include, and therefore will compete with, the solution word. There are obvious tests of this hypothesis, which no doubt will be reported in the near future.

Another aspect of the statistical structure of anagrams is what Ronning (1965) calls "rule out." His view assumes that a subject quickly and implicitly checks letter(s) as potential beginnings of words. Since certain consonant and consonant combinations seldom or never appear at the beginning of a word and since few words begin with vowels, the subject immediately "rules out" all possible recombinations of the letters which have those beginnings. Thus, of the $n!$ possible combination of n letters in an anagram, some proportion is eliminated as viable hypotheses. In an experiment, Ronning was able to show that the number of possibilities remaining after "rule-out" is significantly related to the difficulty of five-letter anagrams.

It is not certain how these analyses of the structure of the anagram and the solution word will be integrated to provide a useable theory of anagram problem solving. Johnson (1966) suggests that at least two stages are involved. In the first stage, wholistic solutions are attempted. Certain anagrams, (for example, *aewtr*) are solved immediately. If, however, initial attempts do not lead to solution, the subject begins to try various letter combinations. These combinations may be attempted by manipulating units of two and three letters and may involve selecting letters for beginnings of possible solutions. It may be that certain factors (e.g., pronounceability of the anagram, "word-ness" of the anagram) are most important in the wholistic stage and aspects of letter moves, bigram frequency, and the "rule out" factor might be significant in the later stage(s). Detailed empirical work to determine the validity of this and other multi-stage interpretations has yet to be reported.

Amount of Information. Most studies of informational variables in problem solving are compatible with similar research in concept identification. Two investigators, Lordahl (1967) with adults and Lubker and Spiker (1966) with children, have considered the effects of number of irrelevant dimensions on solutions of the oddity problem. In these problems the "odd" or correct stimulus was consistently different from the "non-odd" stimuli, with respect to some particular (relevant) dimension among several which were varied. Both studies found performance to be adversely affected by increases in the number of irrelevant dimensions, over the range from two to six in Lordahl and from zero to two in Lubker and Spiker.

Neimark and Wagner (1964) investigated the information-gathering activities of subjects in a sham trouble-shooting task. Subjects, by some process of elimination, had to narrow n possible solutions down to one on the basis of trial-by-trial information. Increases in n were matched, though not proportionately, by increases in information gathering moves and time to solution. Similar results were reported for the switch-light problem by Davis (1967), who found that the relation of mean number of responses to solution to the number of available switches was a negatively accelerated function. Pylyshyn (1963) earlier demonstrated that subjects' performance on switch-light problems is superior to that obtained by random scan algorithm; i.e., a procedure in which possible whole solutions are randomly sampled without replacement and tested on every trial. All of these results suggest that subjects acquire information from partial solutions, and that they can handle and evaluate several possible solutions at once. A specific description of strategies for the acquisition and utilization of information in these problems is impossible at the present time, however, for lack of sufficient detailed data.

Informative Feedback. The type and importance of informative feedback to the subject is related to the kind of problem-solving task employed. With some "insight" problems, for example, feedback is intrinsic to the task, consisting of the subject's perception and knowledge of a workable solution. With the more overt types of problems, explicit feedback is generally given by the experimenter on each of a series of discrete trials. In this case, information relevant to problem solution is contained both in a stimulus (or set of stimuli) and in the accompanying feedback signal. Neither is a sufficient source of information and the two must be properly integrated to effect an acceptable solution.

In these overt problems, as in the typical concept problems, feedback variables should take on considerable significance. There has been little systematic research, however. Donahoe (1960) demonstrated the importance of *form* as opposed to *amount* of information provided by the feedback. The subjects' task was to locate a predetermined point on a 7×7 grid. The subject made a guess on each trial, and the distance of his guess from the target was called "nearer than," "farther than," or "same as" on the previous trial. This information was given either for longitude and latitude separately or in combined form. Subjects who received the combined information solved faster even though the separate feedback logically provided more information and should on that basis have resulted in better performance. Hovland's (1952) analysis of concept learning tasks (see earlier discussion in concept section) drew attention to the distinction between amount of information provided *and* a subject's ability to utilize information. Such a distinction is appropriate to Donahoe's results, but there seems to be no further clarification of this outcome.

Research relating characteristics of the subject to his performance has been considerably more fragmentary than research on task variables. We review here only those few topics for which some reasonably consistent body of knowledge exists.

Age-Related Performance Changes. Recent research has indicated some important developmental changes in strategies for problem solving. A curvilinear relationship between efficiency of performance in a probability learning situation and age can be accounted for by strategy changes, according to Weir (1961). Young (3–4 years) and older (19 years) children performed better on a three-choice probability task than did those at several intermediate ages. Weir suggests that the behavior of young children can be described according to simple conditioning principles. The correct response is conditioned to the button response which is maximally rewarded, even though it does not continuously pay off. Somewhat older children, however, test hypotheses about the solution to such a problem, presumably in the hope of gaining reinforcement on every trial. Some such hypotheses might involve patterns of responses, e.g., press the right (R) button, the middle (M) one, then the left (L) one, an RML sequence. Weir observed that the frequency of patterned responses, such as RML, is highest for the middle-aged children. During these middle years, according to Weir, the child tries hypotheses but lacks the information processing skills which allow him to quickly test and infirm them. Only with increasing age does he achieve the skills necessary for efficient and accurate hypotheses selection and test. Adults, of course, have these skills, which lead them to the same solution (always press the button that pays off maximally) attained in another way by 3–4 year olds. While adults do reach a high level of performance on the problem, their performance curve rises more slowly to this level than does the performance curve of the youngest subjects. This, too, is consistent with the idea that adults tried out a variety of other possibilities before adopting the maximizing approach.

A more recent experiment (Weir 1967) provided related evidence in support of these views. Using the same three-choice probability learning task, Weir investigated the effects of memory aids, i.e., a record of which responses were followed by reinforcement and which by nonreinforcement. These aids were of no help to the oldest and were indeed a hindrance to the youngest subjects; they did, however, produce a considerable improvement in the performance of the "middle-aged" children. Weir argues that aids serve primarily to simplify the hypothesis testing routines attempted by these children.

Odom and Coon (1966) tested certain implications of Weir's analysis by reinforcing patterned responses of LMR and RML. They found that performance improved as age increased from 6 to 19 years, but that even many six-year-olds can learn complicated sequences. While Odom and Coon did show that fairly young children could "use hypotheses" about such sequences of responses, their youngest children were still older than the youngest (3–4 years) in Weir's experiments. Extension of the Odom-Coon procedure to these still younger children remains to be undertaken.

Neimark and Lewis (1967) examined the development of problem solving strategies using Neimark's information-gathering task. In the task, the subject may make a "safe" choice, which guarantees a moderate amount of information, or a "gambling" choice, which might provide either a high or a low amount of information. The outcome of each of a series of problems in this experiment was arranged so that a "safe" strategy always paid off. The investigators found no evidence that nine-year-old subjects could learn to follow a safe strategy; rather, they apparently continued across problems to make choices at random until a solution was obtained. More logical information-gathering was exhibited and more children were able to learn a "safe" strategy as age increased above 9 years.

Motivation. The study of motivational variables in human psychology has come to include certain personality measures (e.g., anxiety) as well as the effects of stressors, incentives, and the like on performance. Aspects of traditional *S-R* theory have been used (e.g., Spence 1958) in many cases to predict the effects of drive level, however measured or manipulated. These predictions are based on the notion that increases in drive will increase the strength of the dominant response(s) relative to weaker, nondominant habits. Thus, if the dominant response is the correct one for any particular problem, increases in drive will increase the likelihood that it will occur and performance will improve. If the correct response is not dominant, performance will be hindered since other responses are still more likely to occur. Much of the problem-solving research in the area of motivation has been primarily concerned with different aspects of these predictions.

The picture is none too clear with respect to paper-and-pencil tests of anxiety, which presumably reflect some chronic, generalized (the Manifest Anxiety Scale—MAS) or momentary (the Test Anxiety Questionnaire—TAQ) drive state. Sassenrath (1963*b*) used a task in which the problem solution was to respond to a word with the number of letters in the word minus one, for example, table—4, telephone—8, etc. The low TAQ subjects performed better than the high TAQ subjects on this task and a related transfer task. The MAS was not consistently related either to learning or transfer, however. Russell and Sarason (1965) found an interaction between anxiety and sex; high-anxiety female subjects performed worse on anagram problems than did low-anxiety females and all males. Harleston, Smith, and Arey (1965) reported the predicted effects of MAS on anagram performance of female subjects, but the results were statistically insignificant. Davis (1966), in his review of problem solving, simply concluded that the relationships predicted by Spence do "... not hold with anxiety-type drive as measured by TAQ or MAS" (p. 51). Certainly, these predicted relationships are not consistently found and, when found, are often marginal effects.

The predicted relationships were demonstrated by Glucksberg (1962, 1964) who manipulated motivation by incentives, offering subjects fairly large monetary rewards. Duncker's Candle Problem, an insight task which required the subject to figure out a way to mount a candle on the wall, was used in his first experiment. The box which was central to the solution was either (a) filled with matches, tacks, etc., emphasizing its primary function and presumably lowering other possible uses in the subject's response hierarchy, or (b) empty, which presumably allows alternative responses to remain relatively high in the hierarchy. High drive (incentive) was found to facili-

tate correct solution for those subjects in the "empty box" condition and to inhibit correct performance in the "filled box" condition. The same interaction of drive and task difficulty was found with a novel electrical wiring task in Glucksberg's later experiment. All of these results support Spence's predictions.

Kurz (1964) reported that different kinds of "stressors" have different effects on a mental arithmetic task. Specifically he found that pacing the subject results in better performance than a nonpaced control, whereas shock and listening to taped irrelevant materials results in nonsignificantly worse performance. These data imply important limitations on Spence's position, in that not all stressors (or motivators) can be counted on to have the same effect. Definite conclusions must wait until different "stressors" are manipulated over an extensive range of values and in conjunction with different levels of task difficulty.

The effects of drive on problem-solving performance have been studied in a number of experiments, but there are several unresolved issues. There seems to be no reason at present to doubt the conclusion that increased drive facilitates the emission of dominant responses. However, certain questions remain with respect to the measurement of drive as an anxiety state and with the universality of effects of various manipulations considered to be drive-producing.

Aptitudes. Various aptitude or skill measures have been used to attempt to predict problem-solving performance. While some of these have been successful, it is clear that predictors of problem-solving performance are likely to be useful only for particular kinds of problem-solving tasks.

Burke and Maier (1965) attempted to predict success on the hatrack problem, an insight task, with a variety of measures, including the verbal and mathematical subtests of the Scholastic Aptitude Test and several special tests produced by Guilford (e.g., Guilford & Christensen 1956). None of these tests correlated even moderately with performance (max. $r = .19$) on the problem-solving task. Gavurin (1967) demonstrated that spatial aptitude was related to anagram solving when the subject was not allowed to manipulate the letters of the anagram, but there was no evidence of a relationship when the subject was allowed to manipulate the letters. This could be taken to indicate that the two conditions elicit different problem-solving strategies, the non-manipulators trying visually to test various recombinations of the letters in an effort to attain solution.

The importance of vocabulary for anagram solving was demonstrated by Mendelsohn, Griswold, and Anderson (1966). The finding that vocabulary scores correlated weakly ($r = .29$) with anagram solving is an expected outcome. Of greater interest is the fact that vocabulary seems to be a limiting factor in anagram solving. As can be seen in Figure 28–3, low vocabulary scores are always associated with a low level of anagram performance, but high vocabulary may be associated with low or high anagram performance. Thus, an adequate level of vocabulary is presumably a necessary, but not sufficient, condition for good performance on anagrams.

Creativity. Mendelsohn and associates have explored the role of creativity, as measured primarily by the Remote Associates Test (RAT) in problem solving. Mendelsohn, Griswold and Anderson (1966) found a moderate ($r = .43$) correlation

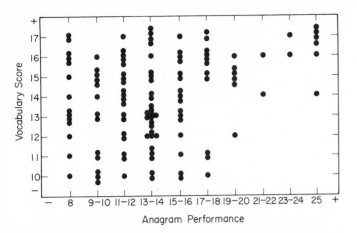

Fig. 28-3. *Scatter plot showing the relationship between vocabulary scores and number of anagrams solved within a fixed time interval. Subjects who score well on vocabulary might or might not perform well on anagrams, but subjects who are poor on vocabulary are also poor on anagrams. The product moment correlation reflected in this plot is .287.* [From Mendelsohn, G. A., Griswold, B. B., and Anderson, M. L. Individual differences in anagram-solving ability *Psychological Reports*, 1966, *19*, 799-809. Reprinted by permission of the author and publisher.]

between RAT and anagram performance. Together with the correlations of anagram performance with other tests, such as the Gottschaldt Test, a measure of ability to abstract embedded figures from complex visual patterns, the results are taken by them to demonstrate the importance of general fluidity and flexibility of thinking in problem solving.

In two other studies (Mendelsohn & Griswold 1964; 1966), high RAT subjects were observed to make better use of incidental stimuli provided in a preliminary task. The subjects first memorized a list of 25 words; during this learning a list of 25 extraneous distractor words was played by a tape recorder. Some of the subsequent anagram problems had words from both these lists as solutions; those from the learned list were considered to provide focal cues and those from the distracting list to provide incidental cues. The high RAT subjects were better at using both the focal and the incidental cues for solving anagrams.

Performance in a Group. Comparisons of subjects working alone, working *in the presence of* other subjects, and working *with* other subjects have been made in numerous problem-solving experiments. These studies have often had contradictory outcomes; of particular interest here are some recent attempts to integrate this literature.

Zajonc (1965) reported that the presence of others has been found both to facilitate and to inhibit performance in various studies. He concludes from these discrepant results that a primary effect of the presence of others is to arouse the subject. As was noted in the section on motivation, higher drive levels are held to enhance the emission of dominant responses. Thus the presence of other subjects or observers would be expected to facilitate performance on a task requiring well-learned responses and to inhibit performance on a task requiring new or less-than-dominant responses. There are apparently no deliberate efforts to test this view, but an experiment patterned after Glucksberg's (1964) might easily be conducted.

Other theoretical articles have been concerned with the

effects of a group of subjects working together on problem-solving tasks. Restle and Davis (1962) presented a mathematical model designed to predict success and speed of problem solving by individuals and groups. They assume that a problem-solving task is composed of independent stages each of which is solved in an all-or-none manner. In the cooperative group, contributions of the individuals involved are pooled so that the group achieves the solution to a stage as quickly as does the fastest member of the group. Results of empirical tests of this model indicate that it was necessary to assume that subjects who arrive at wrong solutions still consume an equal share of the groups' time.

Maier (1967) considered various assets and liabilities of groups for problem solving. Among the assets are a greater amount of knowledge and more alternative approaches to a problem. At the same time, there are certain liabilities, such as domination by one individual and efforts at winning arguments at the expense of the aim of solving the problem. The net loss or gain from group problem solving, Maier contends, will depend primarily on the skill of the leader, who can function most effectively as a coordinator of information and solution efforts.

TRANSFER

Considerable emphasis has been rightfully given to the concept of transfer of training in problem solving. According to Schulz (1960), for example, problem solving is primarily a transfer, not a learning phenomenon. Problem-solving performance is largely a product of the knowledge and skills the subject already has and not what he acquires in the task. Some of the research reviewed earlier illustrates this point. For example, the analysis of anagrams in terms of the transitional probabilities of pairs of letters is essentially a transfer analysis. That is, the subject's prior experience with letter sequences in words in his ordinary use of the language is assumed to affect his performance in the anagram problem. In most problems, specification of the prior learning, which is assumed to be effective in the task, is not straightforward and presents considerable difficulty for experimental analysis.

But not all studies have relied on extraexperimental habits to produce transfer effects. Some have tried to establish conditions of transfer in the context of the experiment itself. In this summary, the recent literature will be divided according to whether the learning which produces transfer occurred extraexperimentally or within the experiment itself.

Extraexperimental Sources of Transfer. "Functional fixedness" is a term applied to large negative transfer produced by previous experience with the use of certain stimulus materials. Many items have a particular single function, such that it is difficult to see them serving any other purpose. Thus, a pair of pliers is not likely to be used as a bob or weight for a solution requiring the construction of a pendulum because the subject's experience with pliers has involved their use in quite another way. In this situation it has been said that the subject suffers from functional fixedness with respect to the pliers.

Saugstad (e.g., Saugstad & Rascheim 1960) has attempted to demonstrate that functional fixedness is a direct result of the novel functions of objects being unavailable or unknown to the subject. If the necessary functions are taught to the subject in advance, by instruction or demonstrations, he will solve the problem without fixedness.

But there are several reasons to question the concept of "availability of functions." First of all, Saugstad's procedure might have done more than simply make novel functions available. It might have sensitized the subject to a solution already in his repertoire. In addition, there are some contrary experimental data. Glucksberg and Weisberg (1966) used the Candle Problem which requires the subject to mount a candle (given a limited amount of available materials) so that it will burn upright without dripping on the floor. The solution involves mounting the candle on a cardboard box and attaching the box to the wall. In the Glucksberg and Weisberg experiment, subjects were shown pictures of the experimental situation. In one group, all available materials—the box, the tacks in the box, the matches, and the candle—were labeled. In another group the only label was *tacks* on the side of the box. And in the control group, none of the materials was labelled. Providing the label *box* produced considerably better performance than did the control condition, whereas the label *tacks* resulted in only marginal improvement over the control. Glucksberg and Weisberg argued that the functionally fixed object (in this case, the box) is simply not available to the problem solver as an effective stimulus; he does not notice the box as part of solution materials when it is a container for tacks.

Sheerer's (1963) findings would also seem to support this view. Using an insight problem in which solution depended upon tying two sticks together with a piece of string, Sheerer found that if the piece of string was loose or holding an old calendar, it was likely to be used to solve the problem. If, however, the string was supporting a current calendar, subjects were less likely to solve. Thus the appropriate use of the string apparently made it unavailable as an effective stimulus.

Maier and Burke (1966) took issue with the concept of "availability of functions," but reached a somewhat different conclusions than Glucksberg or Sheerer about the causes of functional fixedness. In the Maier-Burke experiment, subjects were first given the Hatrack Problem and were grouped according to whether they solved without hints, solved with hints, or did not solve at all. In another room they were shown a construction quite similar to that required for problem solution and asked to list possible functions of this construction. Those who had solved the problem listed more functions than those who did not, but they did not list more functions pertinent to the problem-solving task. The nonsolvers were later returned to the problem-solving task and most were able to solve. But all of those who still could not solve had listed "coatrack" for the construction they had seen. Maier and Burke conclude that solvers and nonsolvers are not different in terms of the availability of relevant functions. Rather, they differ in terms of their selection of the proper functions in the task.

It is difficult to obtain definitive results on the issues of "functional fixedness" and "availability of functions" since little is known about the details of the subject's previous experience with the experimental materials. Perhaps, in accord with suggestions made by Schulz (1960), research related to such constructs would benefit from more direct manipulation in the laboratory. If "fixedness" were produced by direct controllable training, the issue of "availability of functions" could perhaps be more satisfactorily settled.

Transfer Within an Experiment. Much of the recent research on transfer within the experimental task has been concerned with the problem of *Einstellung* or set—two terms used more or less interchangeably. Both of these terms refer (in this context) to a relatively fixed and rigid approach to problem solving brought on by pretraining. A commonly used task in this type of study is the water-jar problem described earlier. The subject solves a series of problems having a similar solution, e.g., fill jar *B*, pour from it into *A* until it is full, and into *C* twice, symbolized *B-A-2C*. A test problem requires the subject either to solve (a) an optional-solution problem where he can use this method or an alternative, easier method, or (b) a problem by a different method. The series of training problems makes it likely that the subject will choose the old method on the optional task and that he will have great difficulty on a problem requiring a new method.

Some investigators have considered the Einstellung or set effect to be a learned response subject to the same principles which govern other learned responses. Gardner and Runquist (1958) found that subjects who had more training problems solved faster on the last training problem and showed greater resistance to extinction (as measured by time to solution on a problem requiring a new method). These investigators also predicted that postextinction performance on a problem of the type used in training would be the same for all groups, in accordance with other findings in associative learning. These results were equivocal, however, since those subjects receiving the most training performed (insignificantly) better than the other groups. Runquist and Sexton (1961) demonstrated that the problem solving set recovers spontaneously. As time increased between the extinction and postextinction problems, performance improved on the postextinction problem.

Whether the laws of associative learning can be satisfactorily applied to problem solving and the study of transfer in problem solving is not, however, settled by these results. What is significant about the "learning principle" approach is the effort it fosters to determine the effects of manipulated variables on problem-solving performance. While the theory might be wrong, it has been responsible for most of the knowledge that one currently has about problem solving.

Overview

While the topic has been with us throughout history, thinking, finally, in recent years, seems to have achieved maturity and scientific respectability in the community of psychologists. We have reviewed the contemporary theoretical and empirical work and find it clear and systematic. Although our understanding of various aspects of human thinking is still simplistic and fragmentary, new evidence and insights are being reported regularly and there is every reason to be confident about the future.

In this chapter, some currently popular theories about thinking were summarized. Two general comments seem appropriate. First, there is no shortage of theoretical ideas about thinking. Indeed, there is such a richness that it is sometimes difficult to agree that the various theorists are talking about the same phenomenon. Secondly, empirical research is more remote from theory in this area than in most others. For that reason, primarily, we found it difficult to relate the review of experiments to the preceding theoretical summary.

The literature review emphasized the topics of concept learning and problem solving, each of which was subdivided so as to consider separately the task, the performing subject, and intertask or transfer effects. Perhaps the most important thing to note about the study of task-related variables is its increasingly analytic nature. In concept learning much of this work followed Hovland's paper, outlining the application of informational analyses to conceptual problems. Performance can often be indexed with fair accuracy by considering the informational value of the stimuli, feedback, etc. Though many problem-solving tasks are not apparently amenable to informational measures, such analyses have been applied with some success to tasks which require overt performances (see Davis 1966).

Attributes of the performing subject (e.g., his motivation, his stage of development, etc.) are immensely important considerations in problem solving. Diversity of orientations, methods and results, however, makes it difficult to summarize relevant research. One predominant current theme is a concern with the subject's strategy, and other variables are often discussed in terms of their effect on strategies. Thus, we can note, for example, that younger and less intelligent subjects are described as exhibiting a more passive, associationistic strategy in their performance on conceptual and problem-solving tasks, while older and more intelligent subjects are described as actively testing hypotheses.

Finally, this review considered the effects of the subject's previous training and experience on his current performance. In problem solving, there is work which has had some success with applying conditioning principles to the study of *Einstellung*, or set. Much of the remaining literature might be described in terms of the learning of principles (cf. Gagné 1965) or rules. In concept learning the analysis of certain types of rules has received some theoretical discussion (Haygood & Bourne 1965). But in general, there has not been enough attention directed to describing the system of rules which is the basis of transfer within an experiment. As in other areas of research, there are large, unsettled difficulties in identifying and evaluating preexperimental sources of transfer. Perhaps, in accordance with the suggestions of Schulz (1960), the pertinent issues could best be resolved by designs which vary known conditions of training in the laboratory.

The study of thinking shows progress and promise. But few would claim that we have answered many of the interesting questions; such answers will not come easily. The development of new tasks will probably be required. In problem solving, for example, some recent technical developments, such as switchlight, have allowed more task-related research. At the same time, new types of measures and data analyses may be useful. For example, analyses of concept learning data trial by trial has shown that many concept learning problems are solved on an all-or-none basis. Finally, much of the new research may come to depend upon somewhat different notions of thinking. Such terms as strategy, rules, and principle seem to be replacing "stimulus" and "response." The study of thinking seems more appropriately linked to such terms; current progress would suggest that they are less restrictive and no less "scientific."

Acknowledgment. This review was supported in part by research grant MH-14314 from the National Institute of Mental Health and a faculty fellowship from the University of Colorado Council on Research and Creative Work.

References

ANDERSON, R. C., and GUTHRIE, J. T. Effects of some sequential manipulations of relevant and irrelevant stimulus dimensions on concept learning. *Journal of Experimental Psychology*, 1966, 72, 501–4.

BEILIN, H. Solving words as anagrams: A re-examined issue examined. *Psychonomic Science*, 1966, 6, 77–78.

———, and HORN, R. Transition probability effects in anagram problem solving. *Journal of Experimental Psychology*, 1962, 63, 514–18.

BOURNE, L. E., JR. Long-term effects of misinformation feedback upon concept identification. *Journal of Experimental Psychology*, 1963, 65, 139–47.

——— Hypotheses and hypothesis shifts in classification learning. *Journal of General Psychology*, 1965, 72, 251–61.

——— *Human Conceptual Behavior.* Boston: Allyn and Bacon, 1966.

——— Learning and utilization of conceptual rules. *In* B. KLEINMUNTZ (ed.), *Memory and the structure of concepts.* New York: John Wiley, 1967.

——— Concept attainment. *In* T. R. DIXON and D. L. HORTON (eds.), *Verbal behavior and general behavior theory.* Englewood Cliffs, N.J.: Prentice-Hall, 1968.

——— Concept learning and thought. *In* J. VOSS (ed.), *Approaches to thought.* Columbus, Ohio: Merrill Co., in press.

———, and BUNDERSON, C. V. Effects of delay of informative feedback and length of post feedback interval on concept identification. *Journal of Experimental Psychology*, 1963, 65, 1–5.

BOURNE, L. E., JR., GOLDSTEIN, S., and LINK, W. E. Concept learning as a function of availability of previously presented information. *Journal of Experimental Psychology*, 1964, 67, 439–48.

BOURNE, L. E., JR., and GUY, D. E. Learning conceptual rules: I. Some interrule transfer effects. *Journal of Experimental Psychology*, 1968, 76, 423–29.

———, DODD, D. H., and JUSTESEN, D. R. Concept identification: The effects of varying length and informational components of the intertrial interval. *Journal of Experimental Psychology*, 1965, 69, 624–29.

BOURNE, L. E., JR., GUY, D. E., and WADSWORTH, NANCY. Verbal-reinforcement combinations and the relative frequency of informative feedback in a card-sorting task. *Journal of Experimental Psychology*, 1967, 73, 220–26.

BOURNE, L. E., JR., and JENNINGS, P. C. The relationship between contiguity and classification learning. *Journal of General Psychology*, 1963, 69, 335–38.

BOURNE, L. E., JR., and PENDLETON, R. B. Concept identification as a function of completeness and probability of feedback. *Journal of Experimental Psychology*, 1958, 56, 413–20.

BOURNE, L. E., JR., and RESTLE, F. Mathematical theory of concept identification. *Psychological Review*, 1959, 66, 278–96.

BOWER, A. C., and KING, W. L. The effect of number of irrelevant stimulus dimensions, verbalizations, and sex on learning biconditional classification rules. *Psychonomic Science*, 1967, 8, 453–54.

BOWER, G., and TRABASSO, T. Reversals prior to solution in concept identification. *Journal of Experimental Psychology*, 1963, 66, 409–18.

——— Concept identification. *In* R. C. ATKINSON (ed.), *Studies in mathematical psychology.* Stanford: Stanford University Press, 1964.

BRUNER, J. S., GOODNOW, J. J., and AUSTIN, G. A. *A Study of Thinking.* New York: John Wiley, 1956.

BULGARELLA, ROSARIA, and ARCHER, E. J. Concept identification of auditory stimuli as a function of amount of relevant and irrelevant information. *Journal of Experimental Psychology*, 1962, 63, 254–57.

BURKE, R. J., and MAIER, N. R. Attempts to predict success on an insight problem. *Psychological Reports*, 1965, 17, 303–10.

———, and HOFFMAN, R. Functions of hints in individual problem solving. *American Journal of Psychology*, 1966, 79, 389–99.

BUSS, A. H., and BUSS, EDITH H. The effect of verbal reinforcement combinations on conceptual learning. *Journal of Experimental Psychology*, 1956, *52*, 282–87.

CAHILL, H. E., and HOVLAND, C. I. The role of memory in the acquisition of concepts. *Journal of Experimental Psychology*, 1960, *59*, 137–44.

CHOMSKY, N. *Aspects of the theory of Syntax*. Cambridge, Mass.: MIT Press, 1965.

DAVIS, G. A. Current status of research and theory in human problem solving. *Psychological Bulletin*, 1966, *66*, 36–54.

DAVIS, G. A. Detrimental effects of distraction, additional response alternatives, and longer response chains in solving switch-light problems. *Journal of Experimental Psychology*, 1967, *73*, 45–55.

DOMINOWSKI, R. L. Role of memory in concept learning. *Psychological Bulletin*, 1965, *63*, 271–80.

—— Anagram solving as a function of letter moves. *Journal of Verbal Learning and Verbal Behavior*, 1966, *5*, 107–11.

——, and DUNCAN, C. P. Anagram solving as a function of bigram frequency. *Journal of Verbal Learning and Verbal Behavior*, 1964, *3*, 321–25.

DONAHOE, J. W. The effect of variations in the form of feedback on the efficiency of problem solving. *Journal of Experimental Psychology*, 1960, *60*, 193–99.

DULANY, D. E., JR. Hypotheses and habits in verbal "operant conditioning." *Journal of Abnormal and Social Psychology*, 1961, *63*, 251–63.

—— Awareness, rules, and propositional control: A confrontation with *S-R* behavior theory. *In* T. R. DIXON and D. L. HORTON (eds.), *Verbal behavior and general behavior theory*. Englewood Cliffs, N.J.: Prentice-Hall, 1968.

DUNCAN, C. P. Effects of instructions and information on problem solving. *Journal of Experimental Psychology*, 1963, *65*, 321–27.

EKSTRAND, B. R., and DOMINOWSKI, R. L. Solving words as anagrams. *Psychonomic Science*, 1965, *2*, 239–40.

ERICKSON, J. R., ZAJKOWSKI, M. M., and EHMANN, E. D. All-or-none assumptions in concept identification: Analysis of latency data. *Journal of Experimental Psychology*, 1966, *72*, 690–97.

GAGNÉ, R. M. *The Conditions of Learning*, New York: Holt, Rinehart & Winston, 1965.

GARDNER, R. A., and RUNQUIST, W. N. Acquisition and extinction of problem solving set. *Journal of Experimental Psychology*, 1958, *55*, 274–77.

GAVURIN, E. I. Anagram solving and spatial aptitude. *Journal of Psychology*, 1967, *65*, 65–68.

GLUCKSBERG, S. The influence of strength of drive on functional fixedness and perceptual recognition. *Journal of Experimental Psychology*, 1962, *63*, 36–41.

—— Problem solving: Response competition and the influence of drive. *Psychological Reports*, 1964, *15*, 939–42.

——, and WEISBERG, R. W. Verbal behavior and problem solving: Some effects of labeling in a functional fixedness problem. *Journal of Experimental Psychology*, 1966, *71*, 659–64.

GRANT, D. A., and COST, J. R. Continuities and discontinuities in conceptual behavior in a card-sorting problem. *Journal of General Psychology*, 1954, *50*, 237–44.

GUILFORD, J. P., and CHRISTENSEN, P. R. A factor-analytic study of verbal fluency. *Report of the Psychological Laboratory*, University of Southern California, Los Angeles, 1956, no. 17.

HARLESTON, B. W., SMITH, M. G., and AREY, D. Test-anxiety level, heart rate, and anagram problem solving. *Journal of Personality and Social Psychology*, 1965, *1*, 551–57.

HAYGOOD, R. C., and BOURNE, L. E., JR. Attribute- and rule-learning aspects of conceptual behavior. *Psychological Review*, 1965, *72*, 175–95.

HAYGOOD, R. C., and DEVINE, J. V. Effects of composition of the positive category on concept learning. *Journal of Experimental Psychology*, 1967, *74*, 230–35.

HAYGOOD, R. C., and STEVENSON, M. Effects of number of irrelevant dimensions in nonconjunctive concept learning. *Journal of Experimental Psychology*, 1967, *74*, 302–4.

HEBERT, J. A., and ROGERS, C. A., JR. Anagram solution as a function of pronounceability and difficulty. *Psychonomic Science*, 1966, *4*, 359–60.

HOLSTEIN, S. B., and PREMACK, D. On the different effects of random reinforcement and presolution reversal on human concept identification. *Journal of Experimental Psychology*, 1965, *20*, 335–37.

HOVLAND, C. I. A "communication analysis" of concept learning. *Psychological Review*, 1952, *59*, 461–72.

——, and WEISS, W. Transmission of information concerning concepts through positive and negative instances. *Journal of Experimental Psychology*, 1953, *45*, 165–82.

HULL, C. L. Knowledge and purpose as habit mechanisms. *Psychological Review*, 1930, 57, 511–25.

HUMPHREYS, L. G. Acquisition and extinction of verbal expectations in a situation analogous to conditioning. *Journal of Experimental Psychology*, 1939, *25*, 294–301.

HUNT, E. B. *Concept Learning: An Information Processing Problem*. New York: John Wiley, 1962.

——, and HOVLAND, C. I. Order of consideration of different types of concepts. *Journal of Experimental Psychology*, 1960, *59*, 220–25.

JENKINS, J. J., and PALERMO, D. S. Mediation processes and the acquisition of linguistic structure. *In* U. BELLUGI and R. W. BROWN (eds.), *The acquisition of language. Monographs of the Society for Research in Child Development*, 1964, *29*, 79–92.

JOHNSON, D. M. Solution of anagrams. *Psychological Bulletin*, 1966, *66*, 371–84.

KENDLER, H. H. Some specific reactions to general *S-R* theory. *In* T. R. DIXON and D. L. HORTON (eds.), *Verbal behavior and general behavior theory*. Englewood Cliffs, N.J.: Prentice-Hall, 1968.

——, and KENDLER, T. S. Vertical and horizontal processes in problem solving. *Psychological Review*, 1962, *69*, 1–16.

KING, W. L. Learning and utilization of conjunctive and disjunctive rules: A developmental study. *Journal of Experimental Child Psychology*, 1966, *4*, 217–31.

KOFFKA, K. *The growth of the mind*. New York: Harcourt Brace, 1928.

KURTZ, K. H., and HOVLAND, C. I. Concept learning with different sequences of instances. *Journal of Experimental Psychology*, 1956, *51*, 239–43.

—— Effects of three kinds of stressors on human learning and performance. *Psychological Reports*, 1964, *14*, 161–62.

LAUGHLIN, P. R., and JORDAN, R. M. Selection strategies in conjunctive, disjunctive, and biconditional concept attainment. *Journal of Experimental Psychology*, 1967, *75*, 188–93.

LEVINE, M. Cue neutralization: The effects of random reinforcements upon discrimination learning. *Journal of Experimental Psychology*, 1962, *63*, 438–43.

—— Mediating processes in humans at the outset of discrimination learning. *Psychological Review*, 1963, *70*, 254–76.

—— Hypothesis behavior by humans during discrimination learning. *Journal of Experimental Psychology*, 1966, *71*, 331–36.

LORDAHL, D. S. The effect of irrelevant information in a multidimensional oddity task. *Psychonomic Science*, 1967, *7*, 141–42.

LUBKER, BONNIE J., and SPIKER, C. C. The effects of irrelevant stimulus dimensions on children's oddity-problem learning. *Journal of Experimental Child Psychology*, 1966, *3*, 207–15.

LUCHINS, A. S. Mechanization in problem solving: The effect of *Einstellung*. *Psychological Monographs*, 1942, *54*, (6, whole no. 248).

MCCLEARN, G. E. The inheritance of behavior. *In* L. POSTMAN (ed.), *Psychology in the making*. New York: Knopf, 1962.

MCNEILL, D. On theories of language acquisition. *In* T. R. DIXON and D. L. HORTON (eds.), *Verbal behavior and general behavior theory*. Englewood Cliffs, N.J.: Prentice-Hall, 1968.

MAIER, N. R. F. Reasoning in humans: I. On direction. *Journal of Comparative Psychology*, 1930, *10*, 115–43.

—— Assets and liabilities in group problem solving: The need for an integrative function. *Psychological Review*, 1967, *74*, 239–49.

——, and BURKE, R. J. Test of the concept of "availability of functions" in problem solving. *Psychological Reports*, 1966, *19*, 119–25.

MANDLER, G. From association to structure. *Psychological Review*, 1962, *69*, 415–27.

MARTIN, E. Transfer of verbal paired associates. *Psychological Review*, 1965, *72*, 327–43.

MAYZNER, M. S., and TRESSELT, M. E. Anagram solution times: A function of letter order and word frequency. *Journal of Psychology*, 1958, *56*, 376–79.

—— Anagram solution times: A function of transition probabilities. *Journal of Psychology*, 1959, *47*, 117–25.

—— Solving words as anagrams: An issue re-examined. *Psychonomic Science*, 1965, *3*, 363–64.

MENDELSOHN, G. A., and GRISWOLD, BARBARA B. Differential use of incidental stimuli in problem solving as a function of creativity. *Journal of Abnormal and Social Psychology*, 1964, *68*, 431–36.

—— Assessed creative potential, vocabulary level, and sex as predictors of the use of incidental cues in verbal problem solving. *Journal of Personality and Social Psychology*, 1966, *4*, 423–31.

——, and ANDERSON, M. L. Individual differences in anagram-solving ability. *Psychological Reports*, 1966, *19*, 799–809.

MORRISETT, L., JR., and HOVLAND, C. I. A comparison of three varieties of training in human problem solving. *Journal of Experimental Psychology*, 1959, *58*, 52–55.

NEIMARK, EDITH D., and LEWIS, NAN. The development of logical problem-solving strategies. *Child Development*, 1967, *38*, 107–17.

NEIMARK, EDITH D., and WAGNER, H. Information gathering in diagnostic problem solving as a function of number of alternative solutions. *Psychonomic Science*, 1964, *1*, 329–30.

NEISSER, U., and WEENE, P. Hierarchies in concept attainment. *Journal of Experimental Psychology*, 1962, *64*, 640–45.

NEWELL, A., SHAW, J. C., and SIMON, H. A. Elements of a theory of human problem solving. *Psychological Review*, 1958, *65*, 151–69.

ODOM, R. D., and COON, R. C. The development of hypothesis testing. *Journal of Experimental Child Psychology*, 1966, *4*, 285–91.

OSGOOD, C. E. *Method and Theory in Experimental Psychology*. New York: Oxford, 1953.

—— A behavioristic analysis of perception and language as cognitive phenomena. In *Contemporary approaches to cognition*. Cambridge, Mass.: Harvard University Press, 1957.

OSLER, SONIA F., and FIVEL, M. W. Concept attainment: I. The role of age and intelligence in concept attainment by induction. *Journal of Experimental Psychology*, 1961, *62*, 1–8.

OSLER, SONIA F., and TRAUTMAN, GRACE E. Concept attainment: II. Effect of stimulus complexity upon concept attainment at two levels of intelligence. *Journal of Experimental Psychology*, 1961, *62*, 9–13.

OSSORIO, P. G. *Persons*. Boulder, Colo.: Linguistic Research Institute Report, no. 3, 1966.

—— Explanation, falsifiability, and rule following. Symposium, Western Psychological Association, San Diego, 1968.

PIAGET, J. *Logic psychology*. New York: Basic Books, 1957.

PISHKIN, V. Effects of probability of misinformation and number of irrelevant dimensions upon concept identification. *Journal of Experimental Psychology*, 1960, *59*, 371–78.

PYLYSHYN, Z. W. Search strategy and problem structure in heuristic problem solving. *Canadian Journal of Psychology*, 1963, *17*, 291–301.

RESTLE, F. The selection of strategies in cue learning. *Psychological Review*, 1962, *69*, 329–43.

——, and DAVIS, J. H. Success and speed of problem solving by individuals and groups. *Psychological Review*, 1962, *69*, 520–36.

ROGERS, S. P., and HAYGOOD, R. C. Hypothesis behavior in a concept-learning task with probabilistic feedback. *Journal of Experimental Psychology*, 1968, *76*, 160–65.

RONNING, R. R. Anagram solution times: A function of the "ruleout" factor. *Journal of Experimental Psychology*, 1965, *69*, 35–39.

RUNQUIST, W. N., and SEXTON, B. Supplementary report: Spontaneous recovery of problem solving set. *Journal of Experimental Psychology*, 1961, *61*, 351–52.

RUSSELL, D. G., and SARASON, I. G. Test anxiety, sex, and experimental conditions in relation to anagram solution. *Journal of Personality and Social Psychology*, 1965, *1*, 493–96.

RYLE, G. *The concept of mind*. London: Hutchinson, 1949.

SASSENRATH, J. M. Test anxiety, manifest anxiety and concept learning without awareness. *Psychological Reports*, 1963, *12*, 71–81.

SAUGSTAD, P., and RAAHEIM, K. Problem solving, past experience and availability of functions. *British Journal of Psychology*, 1960, *51*, 97–104.

SAUNDERS, PATRICIA S., and NEIMARK, EDITH D. Effects of misinformative feedback and awareness of misinformation on concept attainment strategy. *Proceedings of the 75th Annual Convention of the American Psychological Association*, 1967, *2*, 49–50.

SCHULZ, R. W. Problem solving behavior and transfer. *Harvard Educational Review*, 1960, *30*, 61–77.

SCHVANEVELDT, R. W. Concept identification as a function of probability of positive instances and number of relevant dimensions. *Journal of Experimental Psychology*, 1966, *72*, 649–54.

SHEERER, M. Problem solving. *Scientific American*, 1963, *208*, no. 4, 118–28.

SLAMECKA, N. J. A methodological analysis of shift paradigms in human discrimination learning. *Psychological Bulletin*, 1968, *69*, 423–37.

SPENCE, K. W. A theory of emotionally based drive (*d*) and its relation to performance in simple learning situations. *American Psychologist*, 1958, *13*, 131–41.

STAATS, A. W. *Learning, language, and cognition*. New York: Holt, Rinehart & Winston, 1968.

SUPPES, P., and SCHLAG-REY, M. Observable changes of hypotheses under positive reinforcement. *Science*, 1965, *148*, 661–62.

TOLMAN, E. C. *Purposive behavior in animals and men*. New York: Century, 1932.

TRABASSO, T., and BOWER, G. Presolution reversal and dimensional shifts in concept identification. *Journal of Experimental Psychology*, 1964, *67*, 398–99.

—— Presolution dimensional shifts in concept identification: A test of the sampling with replacement axiom in all-or-none models. *Journal of Mathematical Psychology*, 1966, *3*, 163–76.

UNDERWOOD, B. J. An orientation for research on thinking. *Psychological Review*, 1952, *59*, 209–20.

WEIR, M. W. Developmental changes in problem-solving strategies. *Psychological Review*, 1964, *71*, 473–90.

—— Age and memory as factors in problem solving. *Journal of Experimental Psychology*, 1967, *73*, 78–84.

WELLS, H. Effects of transfer and problem structure in disjunctive concept formation. *Journal of Experimental Psychology*, 1963, *65*, 63–69.

WOLFF, J. L. Concept attainment, intelligence, and stimulus complexity: An attempt to replicate Gler and Trautman. *Journal of Experimental Psychology*, 1967, *73*, 488–90.

—— Concept-shift and discrimination-reversal learning in humans. *Psychological Bulletin*, 1967, *68*, 369–408.

ZAJONC, R. B. Social facilitation. *Science*, 1965, *149*, 269–74.

Language, including speech, is treated here as relationships of stimuli and the verbal responses of individual humans.[1] Verbal responses are actions of the vocal effectors or of other effectors that produce words or parts of words alone or in sequence. Verbal responses are also the words or parts of words, spoken or written, that these actions produce. The stimuli need not be, and often are not, words or parts of words. The stimuli may be words or parts of words. Therefore, some relationships are of words or parts of words as stimuli and as responses.

Words or parts of words are not defined further here. They are specified progressively, in part, by example, and, in part, by general criteria.

Two aspects of language thus conceived are considered. One is the present occurrence and prior learning of language on levels of: (a) speech sounds and their graphic representation; (b) words, morphemes; and (c) phrases and sentences. Pertinent methods of study, data, and theory on each level and on their interrelationships are examined in some detail.

The other aspect is uses of language in thought and action. Methods, data, and theory are noted but primarily as illustrative of the further significance of data and theory on the occurrence and learning of language.

The emphasis is current methods, and recent data and theory. Earlier contributions, relatively general in scope, are surveyed briefly in a separate initial section. Earlier contributions, more specific in scope, are cited as appropriate within the sections on occurrence and learning, and on use of language.

Among various limitations placed on the materials covered here, several warrant specific designation. Ignored or drawn on selectively are:

[1] More elaborate definitions of language by linguists, psychologists, and others abound (e.g., Hockett, 1958, pp. 141–42, 574–80; Robins, 1964, pp. 12–13; Sapir, 1921, pp. 6–7; Terwillinger, 1968, p. 4; Whatmough, 1956, pp. 7–17). Often, they include much that is to be explained, and even some explanatory concepts and principles. Thus, definition includes and often confounds conceptual analysis and generalizations about relationships among concepts.

Albert E. Goss

Speech and Language

29

(a) data on and principles of learning in general and of verbal learning in particular (Cofer, 1961, 1969; Cofer & Musgrave, 1963; Dixon & Horton, 1968; Ellis, 1969; Hall, 1966; Jung, 1968; Underwood, 1966)

(b) linguistics, except for some distinctions and classifications of structural linguistics, and for some data and theory on occurrence and acquisition of language (Abercombie, 1967; Fries, 1952; Gleason, 1961; Hall, 1964; Hockett, 1958; Lyons, 1968; Malmberg, 1963; Robins, 1964; Sebeok, 1966)

(c) language teaching and testing (Bennett, 1968; Davies, 1968; Dunkel, 1948; Lado, 1961, 1964; Mackey, 1965; Oliva, 1969; Rivers, 1964; Upshur & Fata, 1968) and second-language learning (Crothers & Suppes, 1967)

(d) phenomena of language in dyadic and more complex interaction situations (Hare, Borgatta, & Bales, 1961, pp. 353-67, 424–56), except some aspects of mother-child, teacher-child interactions

(e) data and theory on the structure and formation of attitudes, and of impressions of personality and persons (Fishbein 1967; Greenwald, Brock, & Ostrom, 1968)

(f) ethnolinguistics and sociolinguistics (Bright, 1966; Fishman, 1968; Greenberg, 1968; Hertzler, 1965; Hymes, 1964);

(g) neurological bases of language (Carterette, 1966; Lenneberg, 1967; Penfield & Roberts, 1959)

(h) reading, spelling, and writing, except for some analyses of general problems of assessment and acquisition (Anderson & Dearborn, 1952; Fries, 1962; Goodman, 1968; Gray, 1956; Robinson, 1968; Schick & May, 1969; Tinker, 1963, 1965)

(i) style of language either spoken or written (Sebeok, 1960; Ullman, 1964)

(j) pathologies of occurrence, learning, and use of language and of language users (Barbara, 1960; Furth, 1966; Hoch & Zubin, 1958, 1966; Johnson, 1959; Johnson & Leutenegger, 1955; Laffal, 1965; Rieber & Brubaker, 1966; Schiefelbusch et al., 1967; Spriestersbach & Sherman, 1968; Travis, 1957; Vetter, 1969; Wood, 1960)

(k) bilingualism (Vildomec, 1963)

(l) data and theory regarded as reflecting language and communication (Birdwhistell, 1970; Ruesch & Kees, 1956)

(m) sign languages of the deaf and for special purposes (Cissna, 1963; L. J. Fant, 1964)

(n) the philosophy of language (Hook, 1969; Katz, 1966; Quine, 1960)

(o) special, technical systems of notation, such as those for music, choreography, and "the computer."

The reasons for these limitations include treatment elsewhere in this volume, inadequate data, largely speculative theory, and specialties within other relatively independent disciplines.

Earlier Contributions, General in Scope

The period of interest is 1880 to 1957. Galton's (1879–1880) report of his own free associations marks the beginning. Skinner's *Verbal Behavior* (1957) marks the end.

During this period, general and more specific contributions to description and explanation of language phenomena appeared uninterruptedly. During this period, too, general and more specific contributions to the development of concepts and principles of verbal learning appeared uninterruptedly.

Scripture's *The Elements of Experimental Phonetics* (1902) serves as a convenient introduction to an account of early developments on occurrence, learning, and use of language that are relatively general in scope. It appeared relatively early. It reflects the confluence of psychology and several other disciplines from anatomy to phonology; and it reflects the confluence of several areas of psychology from Wundtian "experimental" psychology to Wundtian "folk" psychology (Wundt, 1900). It is both intensive and extensive in citation of original sources, most of which appeared after 1880.

The first section covers "curves of speech." Apparatus and associated techniques for recording and analyzing "vibratory movement" and for presenting such stimuli are described. The materials in this section are supplemented by those in Appendix E, which cover the "underlying principle" of Fourier Analysis, and in Appendix II which "is a condensed account of some work on the speech curves obtained as described in Chapter IV and analyzed as indicated in Chapter V" (p. 575).

In the second section, headed "perception of speech," chapters on "the organ of hearing," "perception of sounds," and "perception of speech elements" are followed by chapters on "speech ideas," "association of ideas," "habits of association," "special associations in speech," and "formation of speech associations." Except for relative scarcity of data on children's verbal behavior, and, perhaps, on sentence formation and transformation, these chapters, and those that follow in Parts III and IV, anticipate most of the topics that are treated here and elsewhere as language approached psychologically.

Parts III and IV contain detailed accounts of the "production of speech" and "factors of speech." The content of the chapters of Part III ranges from "voluntary action and the graphic method" to "vocal control." The content of the chapters of Part IV includes the "physical nature" of the vowels, liquids, and consonants; melody; auditory, motor, and speech rhythm.

Those desiring more detailed information about developments prior to 1900 can begin with Scripture. Esper (1968) provides a selective, more historically oriented account of "linguistics and psychology in 1900" (pp. 13–81). Also, he traces changes in Bloomfield's conception of language between 1914 and 1933 from the influence of Weiss back through Meyer to Geiger (1869).

Developments subsequent to Scripture that are relatively general in scope appeared in the form of whole books or monographs (B); chapters and sections of textbooks on general, social, developmental, and experimental psychology (ChB); chapters in handbooks (ChHB); and review articles (RA). Table 1 is a chronological list of some of these contributions, with a coded summary of their content. The code indicates appreciable presence of materials on previous contributions: history (H), method (M), data (D), and theory (T) regarding occurrence (0), learning (L), or use (U) of one or more among speech sounds (phones, phonemes, P), their graphic representation (G), words (W), or phrases and sentences (S) approached developmentally (Dev) or with little or no reference to development (nothing). Thus, M,D,T-L-P-Dev indicates method, data, theory on the learning of phonemes approached developmentally.

Although not exhaustive, the list contains many important

Table 29-1. Year, Author(s), Form, and Content of Representative Early Contributions to the Psychology of Language that are Relatively General in Scope; Abbreviations of Form, Coding of Content Explained in Text.

Year	Author	Form	Content
1903	Kirkpatrick	ChB	D–O–P,G,W,S–Dev.
1911	Meyer	ChB	T–L,U–P,W
1914	Watson	ChB	M,D,T–L,U–W–Dev.
1919	Watson	ChB	D,T–O,L–P,W
1921	Esper	RA	D,T–O,L–P,W,S
1922	Meyer	ChB	T–O,L,U–P,G,W
1924	Allport	ChB	D,T–O,L,U–P,W–Dev.
	Stern	ChB	D,T–O,L–P,W,S–Dev.
	Watson	ChB	M,D,T–O,L,U–P,W,S–Dev.
1927	De Laguna	B	H,T–O,L,U–P,W,S
1928	Bechterev	ChB	T–O,L,U–P,W
	Dashiell	ChB	M,D,T–O,L,U–P,W,S–Dev.
	Markey	B	H,M,D,T–O,L,U–W,S–Dev.
	Reed	ChB	M,D,T–O,L–G,W,S–Dev.
	Pillsbury & Meader	B	M,D,T–O,L,U–W,S
1929	Baldwin et al.	ChHB	M,D–O,L,U–P,W,S–Dev.
	Adams & Powers	RA	M,D,T–O,L,U–W
	McCarthy	RA	H,M,D–O–P,W–Dev.
	Metfessel	RA	M,D–O–P
	Powers	RA	M,D–O,L,U–W
	Weiss	ChB	T–L,U–W
1930	Bühler	ChB	D,T–O,L,U–W–Dev.
1932	Piaget	ChB	M,D,T–O,L,U–W,S–Dev.
1933	McCarthy	ChHB	H,D–O,U–P,W,S
1935	E. Dewey	ChB	D–O–P,W,S–Dev.
	Esper	ChHB	H,D,T–O,L,U–P,W,S–Dev.
1936	Kantor	B	H,T–O,W
	Lewis	B	H,M,D,T–O,L,U–P,W,S–Dev.
	McGranahan	RA	H,M,D,T–O,L,U–P,W,S–Dev.
1939	Judd	ChB	D,T–O,L,U–W,S
1942	Horn	ChHB	T–O,U–W
1946	Johnson	B	T–O,U–W,S
	McCarthy	ChHB	H,M,D,T–O,L,U–P,W,S–Dev.
	Morris	B	H,T–O,L,U–W,S
	Pronko	RA	H,M,D,T–O,L,U–P,W,S–Dev.
1951	Gardiner	B	T–O,L,U–W,S
1952	Osgood	RA	H,M,D,T–O,L–W
1953	Carroll	B	H,T–O,L,U–W–Dev.
	Osgood	ChB	H,M,D,T–O,L,U–P,W–Dev.
1954	McCarthy	ChHB	H,M,D,T–O,L,U–P,W,S–Dev.
1956	Révész	B	H,T–O,U–W,S

contributions and others that are representative of then contemporary orientation. Not included in Table 1 are some important books in French and German (Bühler, 1934; Decroly, 1930; Kainz, 1941, 1943, 1954, 1956; Marty, 1908; Stern & Stern, 1907; Stumpf; 1926; Wundt, 1901). Also not included, but of some influence on psychologists and important to anthropologists, linguists and sociologists, are Bloomfield's *An Introduction to the Study of Language* (1914), and *Language* (1933); Jesperson's *Language* (1922); and Sapir's *Language* (1921).

None of the contributions listed covers all topics of occurrence, learning, and use of language. But in one or another virtually no topic is ignored, and many cover a wide variety of topics.

For example, Dashiell (1928), in an introduction to general psychology, devotes one chapter to "language habits," within which he treats "the mechanisms of speech," "the learning of speech habits in the child," "the learning of speech habits in the race," and "reduction to implicit degree of activity." Data and theory pertinent to the learning of language are described in the chapter on "learning." In addition, he covers topics of use of language in parts of chapters on "Perceiving," "Social Behavior," "Discriminating and Generalizing," and "Thinking."

Phonology, morphology, syntax, and semantics constitute the content of only one of the three groupings of chapters in

Kantor's (1936) book. Developed in the first grouping is the need for and nature of "an objective psychology of grammar"; developed in the third grouping are "objective" analyses of "speech parts."

The ubiquitous opening phrase "a growing interest in," McGranahan (1936, p. 178) completes with "the psychology of language." He proceeds "to embrace all material having to do with the following topics: (a) the nature of language, so far as it is treated by psychological analysis; (b) the development of language, in both the phylogenetic and ontogenetic aspects; and (c) the significance of language for social psychology."

Ten years later, Pronko (1946) surveys the "Non-Psychological Study of Language." Included are the "anthropological study of language," "educational language problems," and "experimental phonetics." A survey of "Psychological Studies of Language" follows. Included are topics as wide-ranging as "experiments utilizing language-derived materials as stimuli," "gesture," and "studies in the perception of language." Finally, Pronko surveys "theory in psycho-linguistics." "Mentalistic" and "behavioristic-interbehavioral" theories are described.

The "emphasis" of McCarthy's (1946) handbook chapter is "the ontogenetic development of spoken language in normal children" (p. 476), as it was earlier (1929, 1933) and later (1954). Within this constraint, she covers topics from "developmental stages" to "the effect of various environmental factors." Her summary table (1946, pp. 482–85; 1954, pp. 459–502) on age of occurrence of various phenomena of language is particularly useful, as are Tables 4, 5, 6, and 7 (1946) and Tables 5, 6, 7 and 8 (1954) on sentence length and structure.

McCarthy's chapters (1946, 1954) are complemented by Miller's (1951) relatively catholic survey of method, data, and some theory on topics from "the phonetic approach" to "the social approach." These sources, perhaps with some supplementation by materials in Osgood (1953), provide reasonable bases for moving back to earlier contributions and forward to later contributions.

"Language" (pp. 680–727) is the pertinent chapter in Osgood. In addition to reiteration of much of "the nature and measurement of meaning" (Osgood, 1952), he outlines general theories and cites some data on "development of language in humans," and on "the statistical structure of language behavior." His chapter on "thinking" (pp. 638–79) was then and still is relatively unique in its emphasis on use of language in thought and action. Such use also enters some analyses of the chapter on "problem solving and insight" (pp. 603–37).

The product of the collaboration of psychologists and linguists, Osgood and Sebeok's (1954) monograph, *Psycholinguistics: A Survey of Theory and Research*, comprehends such topics as "models of the communication process"; linguistic, learning theory, and information theory approaches to language behavior; and "language, cognition, and culture." Perhaps because of relatively superficial and data-free treatment of most topics, its influence has been substantially popularization of "psycholinguistics," a term that has the merit of precise ambiguity of reference. However, "psycholinguistics," as a term, appeared earlier (e.g., Kantor, 1936, p. 55; Pronko, 1946).

The term "psycholinguistics" is ignored by Skinner (1957) and he prefers to replace "speech," "language," "linguistics" with "verbal behavior" (p. 2). Despite extensive coverage and despite "functional analyses" in terms of some concepts and principles of Skinner's own general account of behavior and learning, the *Verbal Behavior* is appropriate as the "end" of earlier contributions.

It is appropriate as the "end" because, like many prior "book length" contributions (e.g., DeLaguna, 1927; Markey, 1928; Kantor, 1936), Skinner essentially ignores details of method and data other than those obtained mostly through his own relatively informal observations. Some theoretical analyses not only begin but end with definition of classes of events. When carried beyond definition, the analyses are often so general and schematic that, without extensive and detailed suplementation, they do not generate further systematic observation and experimentation.[2]

Verbal Learning

Scripture's chapters whose headings include "association(s)" cover method, data, and theory on verbal learning. Through successive editions, Meuman provides a more detailed account of many experiments on *The Psychology of Learning* (1913) from 1885 to 1911. Strictly, the "learning" of the title should be qualified by "verbal."

Method, data, and theory on verbal learning comprise a substantial part of Thorndike's *The Psychology of Learning* (1913). The data and immediate focus of his later contributions (1928, 1931, 1932, 1935) are also verbal learning.

The salience of verbal learning in McGeoch's *The Psychology of Human Learning* (1942) reflects both his primary research interest and the nature of most research on human learning up to that time. Even with liberalization to include "conditioned response learning," the methods, data, and theory of verbal learning remain salient 10 years later (McGeoch & Irion, 1952).

Among textbooks of experimental psychology, Woodworth (1938, pp. 5–91, 156–233), Underwood (1949, pp. 384–554), Osgood (1953, pp. 495–595), and Woodworth and Schlosberg (1954, pp. 695–813) present comprehensive surveys of method, data, and theory on verbal learning within general treatments of human learning.

Hunter's (1934) handbook chapter, on "experimental studies of learning" is general in orientation as are Hilgard's (1951) and Hovland's (1951) later handbook chapters. All contain from some to considerable material on verbal learning.

Among these books and chapters, either the chapters in Underwood, or those in Osgood are satisfactory means both to obtain information about earlier developments in verbal learning and to provide background for understanding subsequent developments.

PRESENT OCCURRENCE AND PRIOR LEARNING

Phrases and sentences consist of morphemes, words in sequence. Morphemes, words are constituted of sequences of speech sounds, (phones, phonemes) or of their graphic representation (letters, graphemes). Despite these apparent interdependencies, method, data, and theory have been and continue to be

[2]Contributions of this kind do not end with Skinner. Later single- and multiple-author examples are Henle (1958), Hook (1969), Terwilliger (1968), and Thass-Thienemann (1968).

somewhat unique to each level. However, these levels share certain distinctions of units of observation and analysis, of kinds of stimulus-response relationships, of consideration of prior occurrence of units, of entry of age as a factor, and of pathologies. They also share certain general features of method.

The units of observation or analyses at each level may be observed or presumed relationships of stimuli and responses. They may be responses with little or no direct consideration of stimuli. The stimulus-response relationships may involve responses that are "recognitions" of the stimuli, "associations" to the stimuli, and "transformations" of the relationships.

Any of these three kinds of relationships can be considered in terms of their present occurrence. Any can be considered with reference both to their present occurrence and to their prior and possible subsequent occurrence with the same or similar stimuli, and responses. Consideration of prior and subsequent occurrence introduces phenomena of learning: acquisition, transfer, and retention.

In the observation of units and of phenomena involving these units, age of *S*s may or may not be a factor. When age is a factor, observation may be on the same *S*s at different ages (longitudinal). Observations may be on different *S*s of different ages (cross-sectional). Hopefully, the only differences among *S*s at different ages are their ages and age-related experiences and changes.

Phenomena observed in *S*s may be regarded as "normal" or as "pathological." The *S*s, on other grounds, may be considered "normal" or "pathological."

Among general features of method, investigations of stimulus-response relationships at each level involve: (a) specification, selection, and presentation of the stimuli of those relationships; (b) specification, selection, construction, presentation of instructional, motivational, and other stimuli that constitute the context of the stimulus-response relationships; (c) specification and recording, analysis, and ultimately presentation of the stimulus-response relationships; and (d) specification of *S*s. Investigations of occurrence of responses involve (c), except that relationships among responses are presented, (d), and possibly (b).

Speech Sounds and Their Graphic Representation

Speech sounds, phones and phonemes, are considered here. Their representation by letters, graphemes, and phoneme-grapheme correspondence are then noted, briefly.

Speech Sounds

Among speech sounds, phones are the initial elements of observation and manipulation. Phones, most generally, are distinguishable segments within the sequential vocal output of speakers of a language.[3] Some distinguishable intersegmental

[3]Distinguishable here refers to discrimination either by some general response (e.g., judgment of occurrence of successive "different" sounds, phones) or by more differentiated responses (e.g., repetition or "recognition" of successive sounds, phonemes).

Somewhat different criteria of distinguishability are required for segmentation of actions of vocal effectors and acoustic properties. Fant (1962, pp. 7–8) shows four different "concepts" of continuous-discrete views of speech.

changes in sounds might be included. Phonemes are the typical elements of summary or analysis of observation; they may be elements of manipulation.

Details of definition of phones and phonemes, and of phonetic and phonemic analysis of vocal output are described in various general and specialized linguistic sources (Chomsky & Halle, 1968, pp. 293–435; Gleason, 1961, pp. 257–85; Hall, 1964, pp. 36–40, 76–83, 119–23; Hockett, 1955, pp. 143–80; 1958, pp. 15–111; Jones, 1962, pp. 1–30; Kantner & West, 1960, pp. 13–39, 223–31; Robins, 1964, pp. 121–79).

Phonemes are determined by comparisons among phones that occur in the same or similar position within sequences of one or more phones that constitute words, morphemes. Those phones in the same or similar positions that are equivalent to each other, and distinct from other phones are a phoneme. Phonemes based on sound segments within sequences are segmental phonemes.

Durations of sounds that occur in one or more positions, their fundamental frequency (pitch), and their amplitude may be phonemic. Duration and degree of change in amplitude and, perhaps, of changes in duration and in pitch from one sound to the next (stress, juncture) may also be phonemic. Phonemes based upon these parameters are suprasegmental, plurisegmental.

The ultimate criteria of phonemes are behavioral, not anatomical-physiological, and not acoustic. Equivalence-distinctiveness of patterns is established by observation of relationships of some criterion response to different sounds in the same or similar positions within a word, morpheme. All other phones of the word, morpheme, are constant in form and position. The criterion response may be judgments of "same" or "yes," strictly, some arbitrary percentage or other cut off on these judgments. The criterion response may be some other, more differentiated response, such as a particular word or "meaning," or selection by pointing to or grasping some object, property, or relation in the environment. Phones that evoke one criterion response and not other criterion responses are grouped as members of one phoneme class. Equivalent phones are allophones. Henceforth, the phone, phoneme distinction is ignored; in general, only the latter term is used. Phonemes are considered first as responses with little or no explicit reference to stimuli. They are then considered as stimuli and as responses in stimulus-response relationships of recognition and association.

Phonemes as Responses. Description of motor and acoustic aspects of phonemes precedes discussion of their occurrence.

A. *Motor and acoustic aspects.* Of interest are phoneme transcription, anatomical-physiological bases of sound production, phonetic classification, acoustic parameters, and relationships among the latter three.

AI. *Phoneme transcription.* The phonemes of a language are not in one-to-one correspondence with the letters, graphemes or other forms in which a language is written. Required is some system of notation, an extended "alphabet," for transcribing phonemes. Then, occurrence of phonemes as responses or as stimuli can be recorded or specified more precisely.

The prototypical alphabet of phone, phoneme and symbol correspondence is the International Phonetic Alphabet (IPA, Gray & Wise, 1959, p. 237; IPA, 1949; Kantner & West, 1960, pp. *xviii-xix*, 10–11, 309–16; Robins, 1964, pp. 92–93).

The IPA and other alphabets (Carroll, 1964, pp. 14–15; Gleason, 1961, pp. 14–50; Trager & Smith, 1951) present the symbol used to represent each phone (strictly, with the symbols in brackets, [ ]), or each phoneme (strictly, with the symbols in virgules, / /) accompanied by a word or words containing a letter or letters that correspond to the phone, phoneme. Lists of illustrative equivalents are often only for some "standard" English (Van Riper & Smith, 1963). However, Wise (1957) and Gray and Wise (1959, pp. 264–320) provide lists for standard, substandard, and deviant forms of American and of British English. Wise also analyzes other dialects of these languages, and of other languages and dialects. *The Principles of the International Phonetic Association* (1949) provides phoneme-exemplar equivalences of 51 languages.

Phonetic alphabets typically involve classification into segmental and suprasegmental phonemes. Segmental phonemes are divided into, respectively, vowels and consonants, with further differentiation of each of these classes. Suprasegmental phonemes are divided into pitches, stresses, junctures (Carroll, 1964; Hockett, 1955, 1958); open transition, stresses, pitches, and clause terminals (Gleason, 1961, p. 50); or other comparable classes.

Other linguists and phoneticians use slightly different phonetic alphabets (Gleason, 1961, pp. 312–22). And dictionaries may use still different phonetic alphabets (Hanna et al., 1966, p. 16; Kantner & West, 1960, pp. 318–21).

A convenient phonetic alphabet for American English, particularly for representation of stimuli, is that of Hanna, et al. (1966, pp. 22–30). Their notation for each of 22 vowels and 30 consonants is an English capital sometimes followed by a single-digit Arabic number.

AII. *Physiological bases.* Following Kaplan (1960), speech production depends on structures, innervation, and resulting action of the: (a) respiratory (breathing) system—(1) skeletal framework, (2) muscles of the abdomen, diaphragm, back, thorax, (3) lungs; (b) laryngeal system—(1) trachea, (2) larynx, (3) laryngeal muscles, both extrinsic (one attachment outside larynx) and intrinsic (both attachments within larynx), particularly the *vocalis* muscles, the vibrating vocal folds, cords; (c) velopharyngeal system—(1) hard palate and alveolar or tooth ridge, (2) soft palate or velum and uvula, (3) pharynx; (d) nose and sinus; (e) mouth and associated structures, the articulators—(1) mouth, (2) tongue, (3) teeth, (4) lower jaw or mandible, (5) lips, cheeks, facial muscles (Fig. 29–1).

Their descriptive and developmental anatomy, innervation, and function are described in detail by Kaplan, and by Zemlin (1968). Valuable as a supplement of Kaplan are Heinberg's (1964) tables of location, origin, insertion, shape, and function of the respiratory muscles (pp. 58–59), the phonatory or laryngeal muscles (pp. 68–71), the resonatory muscles of the pharynx and soft palate (pp. 86–87), and the articulatory muscles (pp. 90–91). Zemlin (pp. 552–68) provides a similar summary.

Characteristics and actions of these structures enter into the processes or functions of phonation, resonance, and articulation.

AIIa. *Phonation.* Phonation involves the structures of (a) and (b). In phonation, the frequency spectrum of air expelled from the lungs is modified by opening-closing (abduction-adduction) or closing-opening-closing of the vocal cords. Described in greater detail when acoustic properties of speech sounds are considered, frequency spectra consist of (relative) amplitudes of component frequencies of complex sounds.

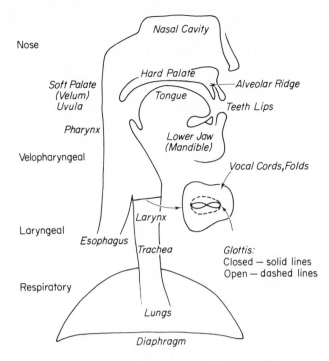

Fig. 29-1. *Some important structures of the vocal effectors.*

In cycles that begin with the vocal folds closed, pressure of air from the lungs (subglottal pressure) forces the cords open. With increasing abduction, increasing amounts of air pass through the opening, the glottis. Initial tension of the folds, elastic tension from abduction, reduction in subglottal air pressure by release of air, and decreased pressure due to increased rate of flow of air through the glottis (Bernoulli effect) combine to close the folds.

Techniques for observing and recording actions of the vocal folds are surveyed by Flanagan (1965, pp. 12–14), Kaplan, 1960, pp. 130–33), Lieberman (1967, pp. 8–13), van den Berg (1968), and Zemlin (1968, pp. 161–69). Among specific techniques, use of highspeed motion pictures is reviewed and described by Moore, White, and von Leden (1962). Soron's (1967) system provides motion pictures of cord activity and simultaneous wave forms as obtained from microphones at the mouth and throat.

Transillummation of the larynx by the technique described by Lisker, et al. (1969) provides "glottograms" of continuous speech rather than of single sounds produced with the mouth open. Another technique of continuous recording of activity of the vocal folds is based on ultrasonic Doppler frequency shift (Minifie, et al., 1968).

Techniques based on X-rays are reviewed by Subtelny and Subtelny (1962). Developments in X-ray laminography (sectional radiography) are described by Hollien (1964). Perkell (1969, pp. 3-12) covers apparatus and procedures of observation, recording, and analysis of "larynx height" by cineradiography (X-ray motion pictures). Techniques of cinefluorography are described by Moll (1960) and by Ramsey et al., (1960).

With recording by needle and surface electrodes, Cooper (1965) describes techniques and results of electromyographic (EMG) investigation of actions of muscles that affect subglottal and glottal changes. Determination of subglottal air pressure

from esophageal air pressure is described by Lieberman (1967, pp. 61–63) and by Lieberman et al. (1969). Both spectrograms and sound waves picked up directly by a contact microphone over the trachea are bases of von Leden's (1968, p. 57) determination of fundamental frequency.

Van den Berg (1968b) reviews prior use, and then describes methods and results of his own use of isolated human larynges. Ultrasonic Doppler frequency shift (Minifie et al., 1968) is also applicable.

Theories of action of the vocal folds in phonation are summarized by Kaplan (1960, pp. 133–38) and by Zemlin (1968, pp. 213–18), and presented more elaborately by Fant (1960). Lieberman's (1967, pp. 14–20) semiquantitive "myoelastic-aerodynamic" theory presumes interaction of aerostatic forces to open, and tissue and Bernoulli forces to close the vocal cords. A similar, somewhat more quantitative formulation is proposed by van den Berg (1968a).

Frequency of open-close or vibratory cycles per sec. substantially determines fundamental frequency ("pitch") of speakers' voices. Vocal pitch increases with increased tension and with increased length, decreased cross-section and decreased thickness of vocal folds as observed and recorded by laryngoscopic photography or laminography (Damste, Hollien, Moore, & Murray, 1968; Hollien, 1962; Hollien & Curtis, 1960; Hollien & Moore, 1960). Normal pitch of voices decreases with increases in size of the larynx (Hollien, 1960a), and in *normal* length, cross-section, and size of the vocal folds (Hollien, 1960b).

AIIb. *Resonance.* A tube or cavity of the same diameter throughout and closed at one end has a lowest natural or resonant frequency approximately equal to the frequency of a sound wave of length four times that of the tube. The additional resonant frequencies of the tube are odd whole number (3, 5, 7, etc.) multiples of its lowest resonant frequency. When sound waves of frequencies equal to resonant frequencies of a tube enter the tube, their amplitude increases. Amplitude of frequencies not equal to natural frequencies of the tube decreases. Resonance is the selective strengthening-weakening of amplitude.

Frequency spectra of postlaryngeal sounds consist of a lowest or fundamental frequency of greatest amplitude and higher frequencies of decreasing relative amplitude.

Resonatory modification of these spectra depends on their parameters and on parameters of the structures of c, d, and e. The latter include: (i) size and shape of the pharyngeal, nasal, and mouth cavities; (ii) size and shape of orifices from the pharyngeal cavity to nasal and to forward mouth cavities; (iii) presence and spacing of teeth, and size and shape of the dental opening; (iv) size and shape of the opening of the lips; and (v) size and shape of the sinuses. In turn, (i) and (ii) depend on extent-shape of the glottis, degree of elevation of the velum, and patterning of raising-lowering of the tip (apex), front, and back (dorsum) of the tongue. Changes in these parameters along with changes in (iii) and (iv) are the process or function of articulation.

AIIc. *Articulation.* Particular combinations of actions and results of action of the vocal folds, velum, tongue, lower jaw, and lips are the bases of the distinction between vowels and consonants, and of further differentiation of these classes of segmental phonemes. Changes in sizes and shapes of cavities and orifices of (a), (b), (c), and (d) above are additional bases of modification of postlaryngeal frequency spectra.

Some of the X-ray techniques (cinefluorography, cineradiology, laminography) for observing and recording action of the vocal folds are used to observe and record action of other articulators (Abramson & Cooper, 1963; Moll, 1960; Perkell, 1969, pp. 3–12; Ramsey et al., 1960; Subtelny & Subtelny, 1962). Strenger (1968) surveys techniques of radiography, palatography, and labiography.

In palatography, a false palate, dusted with powder or some other registering medium, is placed in the mouth. At places of contact by the tongue as in speaking some particular phone or phoneme, the powder is removed. The false palate is taken out of the mouth and points of contact noted (Kantner & West, 1960, p. 36; Moses, 1964, pp. 17–32; Strenger, 1968). An alternative technique is to paint the tongue or to coat the palate. Palatography can be continuous (Kydd & Belt, 1964).

In labiography, position of the lips is determined by photographs from front and side (profile), direct measurement with calipers, and X-ray techniques (Strenger).

Cooper (1965) describes use of EMG with electrode placement on the upper and lower lips, and at different velar and pharyngeal locations. Quantification of muscular action in speech by computer processing of EMG data is described by Fromkin and Ladefoged (1966). Electrodes have also been placed along the dorsal surface of the tongue (MacNeilage & Sholes, 1964). Harris, Rosov, Cooper and Lysaught (1964) describe working features of such systems of suction electrodes.

AIId. *Process interaction.* The speech sounds that emerge from the mouth or mouth-nostrils are products of characteristics (dimensions, features, parameters) of those structures and of their actions that contribute to phonation, resonance, and articulation.

Techniques, illustrative records, and analyses of simultaneous observation and recording of action of structures contributory to phonation, resonance, and articulation are described by Stetson (1951), Peterson (1957), Edfeldt (1960, pp. 31–74), Perkins and Yangihara (1968), and von Leden (1968). Fant (1968, pp. 176–77) summarizes these techniques.

From cineradiographs, Perkell (1969, pp. 10–11) obtained 35 measures of positions and relationships of the larynx, velum, tongue, mandible, teeth, and lips during pronunciation of two sentences and of 13 two-syllable (unstressed syllable, stressed consonant (C), vowel (V) syllable) utterances. Changes in 17 measures are plotted from 300 msec. before to 400 msec. after consonant release. From analysis and comparison of these changes, Perkell formulates generalizations about "physiological parameters" of "the vowel-producing system" (pp. 62–65), and the "consonant-producing system" (pp. 65–68).

X-ray photographs may also be used to estimate size and shape of cross-sections of cavities and orifices at successive, critical points of articulation from the pharynx to the lips (Fant, 1960; 1968, pp. 208–18). From these, profiles or curves of areas at each cross-section can be plotted for each phoneme, notably vowels.

MacNeilage, and DeClerk (1969) investigated differences in articulation of phonemes as revealed in five measurements of "vocal tract configurations" on cinefluorograms. These were supplemented by EMGs from four tongue positions and from five "peripheral" positions that reflected action of muscles of the larynx, velum, lips, and mandible.

Interaction of these processes may be simulated by electrical networks (e.g., Flanagan, 1965, pp. 38, 64) or represented by interconnecting cavities or tubes of simplified shape (Flanagan, 1965, pp. 22–23; Fant, 1960, 1968, pp. 191–223).

AIII. *Phonetic classification.* Phonetic classifications reflect observed and presumed patterns and consequences of actions of the vocal folds-glottis, velum, tongue, lower jaw, and lips. These classifications are divided into limited practical schemes, and into more comprehensive, theoretical schemes.

AIIIa. *Practical schemes.* In Bell's (1867) system of *Visible Speech* "each organ and each mode of organic action concerned in the production or modification of sound, has its appropriate Symbols; and all Sounds of the same nature produced at different parts of the mouth are represented by a Single Symbol turned in a direction corresponding to the organic position" (p. 35).[4] From one to four radical symbols that indicate actions or conditions of the glottis, velum, tongue, and lips are combined to show components of production of each consonant, vowel, glide, as well as modifier and tone. Vowels (pp. 37, 72, 77), consonants (pp. 37, 66), and glides (pp. 37, 70) are classified by manner and place of articulation.

Rather than compounds of elementary symbols, contemporary classification employs the IPA or some similar alphabet constituted of a single, unitary symbol for each phone, phoneme. The symbol for each phone or phoneme is presented in cells of tables whose rows and columns represent different places and manners of articulation. Thus, classification of vowels is typically in terms of location of the highest part of the tongue (front, central, back), degree of elevation (high, medium, low), and rounding of the lips (rounded, spread). For glides, movement of the tongue upward-downward, forward-backward is added.

Classification of consonants is typically in terms of manner of articulation, place of articulation, and voiced-voiceless (phonation present-absent during sound production). The scheme of the IPA (Robins, 1964, pp. 92–93) is eight specific combinations of manner of articulation and voiced-voiceless and nine places of articulation. Many of the 72 cells have more than one entry based on additional criteria.

Similar tables are presented and explained in Gleason (1961, p. 252), Hall (1964, pp. 48–50, 57), Hockett (1958, pp. 71, 78–79), Kantner and West (1960, pp. 196–98) and Wise (1957, pp. 46–47).

Kantner and West (1960) provide schematic cross-sections or profiles of the vocal tract along with word summaries and extended description of the particular patterns of articulation of most of the vowels (pp. 74–116, 179–86) and consonants (pp. 141–78).

AIIIb. *Comprehensive schemes.* The comprehensive schemes of Jakobson, Fant, and Halle (1963), Jakobson and Halle (1968), and Chomsky and Halle (1968) illustrate an approach in terms of many dimensions each binary or two-state. Thus, Jakobson and Halle propose "inherent distinctive features" of sonority (vocalic/nonvocalic, consonantal/nonconsonantal, nasalized/nonnasalized, compact/diffuse, abrupt/continuant, strident/nonstrident [mellow], checked/unchecked, voice/voiceless); of protensity (tense/lax); and of tonality (grave/acute, flat/nonflat, sharp/nonsharp).

The features (dimensions) distinguished by Chomsky and

[4]Earlier systems of classification are described by Abercrombie (1967, pp. 112–20) and, for vowels of English, by Chomsky and Halle (1968, pp. 259–89).

Halle (1968) are grouped within "headings" of major class, cavity, manner of articulation, source, and prosodic.

Another approach, that of Catford (1968), and of Peterson and Shoup (1966a), can be viewed as extension and refinement of various practical schemes. Peterson and Shoup divide place of articulation into horizontal place of articulation with 13 values, and vertical place of articulation also with 13 values. Eight values of manner of articulation are specified with *stop* covering *plosive, ejective, implosive,* and *click.* Their Figure 2 (p. 45) includes a table in which vowels and consonants are specified by combination of values of these three primary phonetic parameters. The 12 secondary phonetic parameters of this analysis also enter a figure in which vowels and consonants are specified by patterns of their values (p. 48). Completing the analysis are prosodic parameters of phonetic duration, average laryngeal frequency, and average speech production power.

AIV. *Acoustic parameters.* Values may be determined for speech at different points in the vocal tract from subglottal to emission from or as radiated from the lips or lips-nostrils.

Frequency spectra of speech sounds are described schematically. Techniques of analysis are noted, and then examples of classes of parameters.

AIVa. *Frequency spectra schematically.* In representations of frequency spectra, frequency in absolute or log values is on the *x*-axis or abscissa. Typically, relative amplitude in db below (and above) some reference amplitude is on the *y*-axis or ordinate. Amplitude of component frequencies may be represented by separate bars. Tops of the bars may be connected to yield an "envelope," curve, or profile that is usually smoothed. Only the curve may be used.

The frequency spectra of Figure 29–2 show speech sounds at two points in speech production: immediately after modification by conditions and action of the vocal folds and glottis (phonatory modification, postlaryngeal sound); and as emitted from lips or lips-nostrils (resonatory and articulatory modification). Postlaryngeal sound consists of a fundamental frequency of greatest amplitude and of higher-order partials and other frequencies whose relative amplitudes decrease in negatively accelerated fashion.

Resonatory and articulatory modification of postlaryngeal sound involves a shift upward in the frequency (frequency band) of greatest amplitude, and appearance of peaks of amplitude at higher frequencies. These peaks are called formants, abbreviated f_i for the *i*th formant. Formants are numbered successively upward from f_1 for the lowest frequency at which a peak occurs.

Relatively short, nontechnical treatments of frequency spectra and related topics are in Gray and Wise (1959, pp. 110–21), Heinberg (1964, pp. 125–29), and Malmberg (1963, pp. 37–66). Longer, more technical treatments are in Fant (1958, 1960, 1968), Flanagan (1965, pp. 22–70, 126–52), Fletcher (1953), Ladefoged (1962), and Pulgram (1959).

AIVb. *Techniques of analysis.* Frequency spectra are typically obtained by some version of the sound spectrograph or sonograph. Early versions of the sound spectrograph are described by Barney and Dunn (1957), Koenig, Dunn, and Lacy (1946), and Potter, Kopp, and Green (1947). Flanagan (1965, pp. 126–31) provides brief descriptions of early and later versions of the spectrograph and of techniques of "formant analysis of speech" (pp. 139–52). Fant (1968) reviews speech analysis

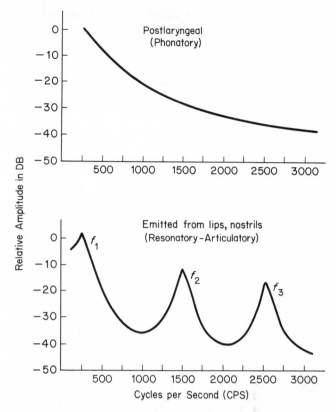

Fig. 29-2. *Idealized frequency spectra of speech sounds at points in speech production.*

techniques (pp. 175–91) and, later, "speech data analysis" (pp. 223–43). Detailed, analytical presentations can be found in Fant (1958, 1960).

The technique and results of computer analysis of frequency spectra are described by Bell, Fujisaki, Heinz, Stevens, and House (1961). Strong (1967) couples a terminal analog synthesizer and digital computer to obtain synthetic spectrograms of 2-sec. samples as well as fundamental frequency and frequency and amplitude of f_1, f_2, f_3, f_4 of natural speech.

For samples of speech of about 2.4 sec., the sound spectrograph analyzes speech sounds into: (a) component frequencies through time, with some indication of their relative amplitude (bar spectrograms); and (b) component frequencies at one or more points or sections in time, with some indication of their relative amplitudes (frequency spectrum, amplitude cross-section). In the visual representation of frequencies through time, time is the abscissa, frequency is the ordinate, and amplitude is shown by "density," "darkness," "blackness" of the record. Typically values for frequency are from 0–250 cps to 6000–10,000 cps in 300 cps or other bandwidths. In the usual representation of a point or section, frequency is the abscissa, relative amplitude the ordinate.

Potter, Kopp, and Green's (1947) *Visible Speech* is a compendium of spectrograms of vowels and consonants both alone and in words. Fant (1960, 1968) also presents spectrograms of diverse vowels and consonants.

Prestigiacomo (1957) describes a modified spectrograph that yields spectrograms from original tape. A later improvement (Presti, 1966) produces spectrograms of each successive or selected 2.4 sec. segments of original tape in 80 sec. Amplitude contours through time or "voiceprints" (Kersta, 1962) can also be obtained.

AIVc. *Classification.* Among comprehensive, analytical classifications of parameters of speech sounds, Fant (1962, p. 10) distinguishes nine parameters: segment duration (1); source (sound at vocal folds) intensity, energy, spectrum (2, 3, 4); voice fundamental frequency (5); F(formant)-pattern (6); and sound (after radiation at lips) intensity, energy, spectrum (7, 8, 9).

Peterson and Shoup (1966b, pp. 81–89) distinguish basic acoustic phonetic and prosodic parameters. The former include gap, voice bar, broadband continuous spectrum, frequencies of vowel and consonant formants, and formant amplitudes. The first three are included as primary phonetic parameters; the last three are replaced by frequencies of first three vowel and consonant formants, and first consonant antiresonance. The prosodic parameters are phonetic duration, average fundamental voice frequency, and average speech power. Each parameter is described, with accompanying quantitative definition by sound wave properties.

AV. *Relationships among physiological bases, classification, acoustic parameters.* Through organization of generalizations established by observation and experimentation (low-order laws, relationships), a system of generalizations or "theory" is evolving in which acoustic parameters are related to physiological parameters of speech. Ideally, the latter parameters are special cases of parameters of interconnected cavities and orifices as treated in physical acoustics. A system of generalizations about relationships of acoustic parameters and physiological parameters then becomes a special case, however complicated, within physical acoustics. The system of generalizations must be consistent with behavioral definition of phonemes by patterns of equivalence (generalization)-distinctiveness (discrimination) in relationships that involve acoustic parameters and criterion responses.

Peterson and Shoup (1966b) first present a table of "the relations of the acoustical speech parameters to the basic speech wave types" (p. 89). This table is the partial basis of cell entries in two subsequent tables. The upper symbol or symbols of each cell are basic or combined acoustical speech parameters; the lower are basic or combined wave types. The row categories of both tables are "various laryngeal actions." The column categories of the first table (p. 93) are manners of articulation, except stop manners, which are the column categories of the second table (p. 95). Together, the two tables represent presumed correspondences between combinations of laryngeal actions and manners of articulation, as physiological parameters, and acoustic parameters, both "speech wave types" and "acoustic phonetic parameters." Peterson and Shoup recognize that these tables "provide only part of the information required to identify specific phone types" (p. 96).

Peterson and Shoup also schematize "inverse transformation" from the acoustic phonetic parameters of $\log f_1$ and $\log f_2$ to physiological parameters of horizontal and vertical places of articulation of vowels produced by "rounded" and "unrounded" lip shape.

The Peterson and Shoup, and similar proposals (e.g., Catford, 1968; Chomsky & Halle, 1968, pp. 298–329, 400–435; Jakobson & Halle, 1968, pp. 428–32) are first steps in specifying relationships among physiological bases, classification, and acoustic parameters. At present, they are essentially more precise statements of objectives of theory rather than accomplished theory.

Analyses by Flanagan (1965, pp. 37–75) and Fant (1960, 1968) are examples of more limited but more precise and quantitative formulations of relationships that involve physiological parameters and acoustic parameters directly, and that can be extended to classification.

B. *Occurrence as responses.* Regardless of occurrence of phonemes as responses or in stimulus-response relationships, investigations of their occurrence may be ahistorical (synchronic) or historical (diachronic), descriptive or comparative, and nondifferential or differential with respect to individual differences.

Crosscutting these distinctions are implicit or explicit problems of sampling. Different periods, different broad languages or dialects, different categories or values of factors that distinguish groups may be sampled. Sampling can be used for assembly of individuals for group or individual comparison. When output of individuals is distinguished, it is sampled, and becomes the corpus of the investigation. When output of individuals is not distinguished, a larger output sampling is required to obtain the corpus.

Considered here as orientation are phonemic analyses of languages. Considered more specifically are frequency counts of phonemes both disregarding age and at different stages of development. Prosodic features are noted, briefly.

BI. *Phonemic analyses.* Phones and derivative phonemes of languages must be determined before they can be used as units or in units of observation of further investigations. Some general and specialized linguistic sources that describe phonetic analyses were noted previously.

Analyses of particular languages and dialects are too many and too varied to be cited here, even illustratively. Those planning studies of languages other than (standard American) English, but uncertain about which language, might begin with broad surveys such as those of Meillet and Cohen (1952) and Sebeok (1963, 1967, 1968). When the language(s) of interest are known or have been selected, appropriate phonetic and phonemic analyses are consulted in books, monographs, and journals.

BII. *Frequency counts.* Counts of phoneme frequency both illustrate the use of and constitute refinement of phonemic analyses. They are requisite to various quantitative comparisons among languages, and may aid in preparation of stimuli and interpretation of results of investigations of verbal behavior and verbal learning (Goss & Nodine, 1965; Underwood & Schulz, 1960).

Frequency counts involve decisions and procedures regarding: (a) selection of the target language(s); (b) use of spoken or written utterances; (c) general sources of utterances, (d) selection among, sampling of the particular general sources; (e) explicit criteria of inclusion-exclusion of sampled utterances; (f) use of one or some available, pertinent phonemic analyses; (g) an alphabet of symbols for phonemic transcription; (h) transcription of phonemes that identifies their source and prepares them for analysis. "Some preliminary decisions" by Hanna et al. (1966, p. 11–20) illustrate many of these decisions and procedures as does the description of method by Carterette and Jones (1968).

Preparations for analysis should include reduction to Hollerith or IBM cards for computer analysis. The analyses, both descriptive and inferential, should be substantially if not entirely by computer. General descriptions of appropriate programs are available (Hanna et al., 1966, pp. 17–20; Venezky, 1966).

For English, counts have been made of frequencies of single phonemes in social conversation (Carterette & Jones, 1968); in telephone conversations (French, Carter, & Koenig, 1930; Tobias, 1959); in more formal oral presentations (Hayden, 1956; Voelker, 1936); for words in the Oxford English dictionary (Trnka, 1935), for words in a phonetic reader (Fry, 1947) or readers (Denes, 1963); for words of a basic reading vocabulary (Atkin, 1926); for words of the Thorndike-Lorge count (Hanna et al., 1966); for words in newspapers (Dewey, 1923), and for words in modern prose and plays (Carroll, 1952, 1958; Fowler, 1957; Hultzén, Allen & Miron, 1964; Whitney, 1874); and for words in elementary grade readers, in books that "children like to read," and in previously analyzed passages (Carterette & Jones).

Wang and Crawford (1960) transform the consonants of 10 among these studies into IPA notation. The consonants are ranked for frequency, and listed by relative frequency. In the matrix of correlations of each count with every other count, 13, 28, and 37 rs exceeded .90, .80, and .70, respectively. In Hultzén, Allen, and Miron's (1964) matrix for seven consonant counts, 17 of 21 rs exceeded .90, and all 21 exceeded .80. Thus, for consonants, various counts agree reasonably well.

Frequencies obtained in separate counts of consonants in the natural speech of children in Grades 1, 3, and 5 and of adults enter Carterette and Jones's correlation matrix along with 10 Wang and Crawford counts and the Hultzén, Allen, and Miron count (redundant with Carroll's among the 10). The values of the correlation coefficients for the pairs of the former four are .93–.99; the values of pairs of one among these counts and each of the other 11 are, .60–.96, with 20 ≥ 90.

Data on phoneme sequences and transitional probabilities can be found in Carroll (1958), and in Hultzén, Allen, and Miron (1964). Denes reports frequencies of digrams (two phonemes) and of minimal pairs (to distinguish two words); and Carterette and Jones report frequencies of diphones and triphones.

Weir (1962) provides frequency counts on samples from among presleep monologues of her son at around 2 1/2 years. Relative percentage of occurrence were determined for individual vowels and nonvowels in initial, medial, and final positions in words. Absolute frequencies of all phonemes and all nonvowel phonemes are also reported.

For Herdan (1956, 1960, 1962, 1966), frequency counts on phonemes in diverse languages are substantially if not primarily means to illustrate descriptive and inferential application of both conventional and information-theory statistics. Both within presentations of frequency counts and elsewhere, he describes these statistics and their use. Attneave (1959), Garner (1962, pp. 19–28, 53–62, 98–112, 145–60, 213–42), and Hultzén, Allen and Miron (1964, pp. 26–41) describe and illustrate use of information statistics. Karlgren (1968) provides a summary introduction to statistical methods, and a guide to other references.

BIII. *Frequency counts developmentally.* Developmental data on occurrence of speech sounds in infancy and early child-hood have been obtained by observation and recording of their emission with no reference to immediate stimulus conditions. Data have also been obtained by use of words or pictures whose repetition or naming "correctly" entails production of phonemes of a language. In analyses of phonemes thus elicited, there is little or no reference to eliciting stimuli. Results of these investigations are described here. Considered, too, are various theories of occurrence of phonemes.

Method, data, and theory on occurrence of speech sounds in early infancy are reviewed by Brown and Berko (1960), Carroll (1960), Ervin-Tripp (1966), Ervin-Tripp and Slobin (1966), Esper (1935), Herzka (1967), Irwin (1941, 1952, 1957, 1960), Irwin and Chen (1943), McCarthy (1929, 1930, 1933, 1946, 1954, 1959), Rebulsky, Starr, and Luria (1967), and Winitz (1966, 1969). Leopold (1952) provides a bibliography. Observation and recording of frequencies of occurrence of speech sounds in infancy and early childhood involve decisions and procedures similar to those listed for frequency counts of spoken phonemes. An additional consideration is spectrographic analysis of taped records of infants vocalization (Fisichelli & Karelitz, 1966; Lynip, 1951; Murai, 1960; Winitz, 1960).

BIIIa. *Observation and recording of emission.* Conventionally, the cries of infants are distinguished from other vocalizations. The latter are often labeled babbling. Separate phones, phonemes are distinguishable even within the cries of infants. Fisichelli, et al. (1966) recorded the cries of different normal and brain-damaged infants at some time during days 1–8, 172–229, and 342–393. Within phonetic analysis by IPA, during days 1–8 eight and seven specific vowels occurred with some frequency in the cries of normal and brain-damaged infants, respectively.

In the first two months, Irwin and Chen (1946) distinguished an average of seven phoneme types within IPA which, during the 30 breaths sampled, occurred with a mean frequency of 61.8. Winitz (1961) observed repetitions in 7.4 of 30 breaths of infants of 0–2 months. Breaths with repetitions increase to about one year of age, and then decrease up to age two years.

Data obtained by Irwin and collaborators are too extensive for more than summary comment here. Irwin (1952, 1957) himself summarizes them. For normal children, number of types of all phonemes, of vowels, and of consonants increase during the first 30 months in negatively accelerated fashion (Irwin, 1952). Frequency of all phonemes (tokens) increases linearly, and then in positively accelerated fashion.

McCarthy (1954, pp. 507–11) describes and criticizes the methods and evaluates the results of many of the Irwin investigations. Her Table 2 (p. 510) is a useful "summary of basic data in seven Irwin studies."

Instead of Irwin's technique of observation of samples of infants' vocalizations and immediate transcription by IPA, Lynip (1951) proposes "objective analysis" by spectrogram. Winitz (1960) criticizes Lynip on both "acoustic and phonetic considerations" (pp. 172–77). Unlike Lynip, he finds reliable identification of vowels in infant vocalization. Frequencies of f_1, f_2 are displaced upwards in relationships like those for f_1, f_2 of vowels produced by men, women, and children (Peterson & Barney, 1952).

During parts of the first year of four Japanese infants, vocalizations were observed and recorded on tape and transcribed by IPA (Murai, 1960). Vowel patterns developed from middle vowels to front and back vowels. Consonant patterns went "from back gutteral sounds to front labial, dental sounds, and then back to gutteral consonants again" (p. 30).

BIIIb. *Elicitation, little or no reference to stimuli.* In an investigation with children of ages 2 to 6 years, Wellman et al. (1931) used 98 pictures of objects or persons, supplemented by "suggested conversations and questions," to elicit words or phrases constituted of one to five desired sounds among 26 consonants, 14 vowels, and 4 diphthongs in IPA. Tables are presented that, for each age, show number and percentage of children who produce each sound correctly; number of children who produce different groups of consonants correctly in initial, medial, and final position; and kinds of error in production of each sound.

Templin's (1957) assessment of articulatory and other language skills in young children is a guide to sampling of *S*s and to description of sample composition. Her words were to elicit 176 single and compound phonemes in different positions. Accuracy of articulation of these phonemes is described for the total sample by age, and for breakdowns by sex and socioeconomic status (SES).

For "relatively broad transcription" in IPA, articulation improves with age in negatively accelerated fashion. Up through age six, accuracy of articulation decreases in the order of diphthongs, vowels, consonants, double blends, triple blends. Boys lag behind girls and lower SES children lag behind upper SES children by about one year.

In these investigations, occurrence of phonemes was observed and transcribed immediately by IPA. Inadequacies of IPA and similar transcription are noted by Jones (1967). Instead he proposes a "phonotactic structure" based on "Jakobsonian distinctive features."

BIIIc. *Theories.* Theories have been proposed regarding origin of speech sounds differentiation of phonemes that are produced, and elicitation of phonemes by external stimuli.

BIIIc1. *Origins of speech sounds.* Beyond a prefatory demurral, Thorndike (1943) "glances at three time-honored and then dishonored theories . . . ding-dong theory, bow-wow theory, and pooh-pooh theory" (p. 1). He then describes Paget's theory and labels it "yum-yum" or "tongue-tied" (p. 3). For Thorndike, private language originates in prattling, with some object "syllable" relationships established by repetition and "confirming reactions" evoked by "enjoyment of man at play" (pp. 3–4). He proceeds from private language to establishment of one-way and then two-way speaker-hearer relationships (p. 5).

Because of origin in prattling and dependence on chance variation in object-syllable relationships, Thorndike labels his theory "babble-luck" (p. 5).

Thorndike assumes occurrence of prattling, or babbling. Its origins are obscure. Required are better data on immediate and more remote antecedents of infants' vocalizations than are now available. Speculative assumptions of neural mechanisms (Lenneberg, 1967, p. 221) are not a viable alternative to such data.

BIIIc2. *Differentiation.* Data obtained by Irwin and collaborators, and by others, suggest that, as infants become older, previously nondistinguished phonemes appear, and that relative frequencies of phones, phonemes change. Among theories of such differentiation, two different but possibly complementary approaches are distinguished.

One approach is application of the scheme of binary distinctive features as proposed by Jakobson (1941), although for early childhood rather than infancy. Leopold (1953–54) applied it to description of the speech development of primarily the older of his two daughters. During the first two months, Leopold noted low front and center vowels and high back vowels, the latter along with "all kinds of back consonants." Gleason (1961, pp. 258–59) describes his daughter's speech development in similar fashion. Jones' (1967) proposed refinement of the distinctive features has been noted; he provides an illustrative application.

More recently, Menyuk (1968) analyzed percentage usage of continuant/abrupt, diffuse/compact, grave/acute, nasal/oral, strident/nonstrident, voice(d)/voiceless in consonants produced by American children of ages 2,6 to 5 years. Consonants were transcribed from records of spontaneously generated sentences and some results with the Templin-Darley articulation test. Data permitting partial comparisons were available for Japanese children of ages 1–3 years.

Both for American and Japanese children, percentage usage of features decreased in the order nasal, grave, voiced, diffuse, continuant, strident with, however, little difference between the last two. Continuant and strident for American children excepted, all of the features were present in the consonants produced by the youngest children. For the Japanese children, particularly, the increases in percentage usage of features were negatively accelerated.

The other approach is application of concepts and principles of learning, primarily those for classical conditioning or for instrumental conditioning. Allport's (1924, p. 184) often-reproduced diagram of conditions that establish a circular reflex or response represents application of then-extant principles of classical conditioning. As Dennis (1954) notes, comparable analyses can be found in diverse presentations as far back as Hartley's (1749, pp. 105–7) associationistic account.

In a sequence of two or more repetitions of a phone or of a simple syllable like "da," the ith occurrence of a response produces stimuli, both auditory and kinesthetic, that are present for the $i+1$th occurrence of that response. Stimuli produced by the ith occurrence of the response can be considered conditioned stimuli (S_c); the $i+1$th occurrence of the response can be considered an unconditioned response (R_u). By principles of classical conditioning, S_c should come to elicit a response resembling R_u (R_c). The reflex becomes circular. By the particular principle of primary stimulus generalization, although this is typically implicit, responses of circular reflexes should be elicited by phonemes produced by others that resemble sounds produced by the child.

Details of conditions and principles that account for differentiation among phonemes are not clear. Miller and Dollard note another apparent defect: "The circular-reflex hypothesis does not clearly explain how crying (and presumably babbling) stops, if indeed it explains how crying starts at all" (p. 288).

Miller and Dollard's (1941) concepts and principles of "social learning and imitation" subsume classical and instrumental conditioning and also other simple learning situations. They apply these concepts and principles to crying and babbling in a manner analogous to their analyses of various instrumental conditioning situations. "The mother talks to the child while administering primary rewards, such as food" to a hungry infant. Therefore, "the sound of the human voice should acquire secondary reward value" that generalizes to sounds produced by the infant (p. 277). Beyond this suggestion, they are obscure on conditions and principles of differential strengthening-weakening of particular phonemes.

Mowrer (1950, pp. 707–10; 1960, pp. 70–74, 79–81), Jenkins and Osgood (Osgood & Sebeok, 1954, pp. 128–29), Staats and Staats (1963, pp. 118–19), Staats (1968, p. 118), and Winitz (1966, 1969) essentially repeat the Miller and Dollard analysis. Staats and Staats propose sounds produced by others as a possible other source of reinforcement (p. 118), and also such consequences as "a drink of water" and "presentation of the child's toy dog" (p. 119).

Skinner (1957, p. 31) has little to say. Olmstead's (1966) postulates that involve reinforcement are not used jointly with postulates on discriminability of acoustic components to generate theorems about differentiation of frequency as well as of forms of phonemes.

Circular-reflex and secondary-reward analyses are not necessarily incompatible. Miller and Dollard (1941, pp. 286–88) and Osgood (1953, p. 688) appear to use the latter to supplement the former. Whatever the exact form, these theories are not detailed, finished proposals; they are suggestions of direction and form of more detailed, systematic analyses.

Data available to guide and constrain more detailed, systematic analyses are inadequate. Only recently (Routh, 1969) have reasonably controlled observations been reported of increased frequency of occurrence of vowels, of consonants, and of vowels and consonants as a consequence of differential reinforcement ("A smile, three 'tsk' sounds, and concurrent light pressure on the abdomen" p. 220). However, the reinforcement used differs markedly from hypothesized secondary reinforcement by sounds produced either by infants or by others.

BIIIc3. *Elicitation by external stimuli.* Within the circular-reflex hypothesis, the principle of primary stimulus generalization accounts for eventual appearance of relationships between phonemes produced by others as stimuli and the child's production of phones resembling those phonemes as responses (R_cs). The circular-reflex hypothesis might be supplemented by reverse imitation (Watson, 1919, p. 319) in which the mother or others repeat some of the phones produced by the child as it continues to produce these phones. Phonemes of the mother or others are conditioned stimuli but in direct rather than generalized relationships with the child's responses that produce the reverse-imitated phones. Were reverse imitation more likely when the child produces phones resembling the phones of adult language, differential relationships might develop between phonemes of the language spoken by the mother and the child's production of those phones rather than of other phones.

Miller and Dollard essentially ignore analysis of elicitation by external stimuli. Mowrer (1950, pp. 686–87) describes reverse imitation but ignores it in his secondary-reinforcement analysis (1950, pp. 707–10; 1960, pp. 70–74, 79–81).

Skinner (1957, pp. 59–62) apparently assumes that external elicitation develops; and Staats and Staats (1965, p. 125) repeat this assumption. Staats (1968, p. 71) "explains" external elicitation of speech sounds by describing the manner of establishing "fine discriminative-stimulus control of bar-pressing by rats" (p. 71).

BIV. *Prosodic features.* Data are scarce on prosodic features of utterances comprised of a small number of phonemes. In her analysis of presleep monologues, Weir (1962, pp. 28–30) was able to distinguish four levels of pitch; falling, rising, and sustained contours in decreasing relative frequencies; and two levels of stress.

Tape recordings of vocalizations of two infants during the first 141 days were sampled to obtain the 108 95-sec. records analyzed by Shepard and Lane (1968). For a 100 msec. threshold of utterances, trends over days are plotted for various measures of central tendency and variation of prosodic features. Means of mean fundamental frequency decreased during the first month, later increased above the initial level, and stabilized at that level through 141 days. Duration of utterances became more uniform with increasing age.

Occurrence of Phonemes in Stimulus-Response Relationships. Phonemes may occur in stimulus-response relationships of "recognition" of stimuli, "associations" to them, or "transformation" of relationships. Because of lack of data on the latter, only the former two are considered here.

Phonemes of these relationships may be "real" or "synthetic." Real phonemes produced by one or more speakers are recorded with subsequent selection of stimuli at desired values of parameters. Devices for production of synthetic phonemes are treated in general by Fant (1958, 1960, 1968), and Flanagan (1965, pp. 166–209, 244–91). Strong's (1967) device has been noted; Rabiner (1968) describes an "improved digital-formant synthesizer."

Of particular importance is the "pattern playback" device described by Cooper and associates (Cooper, 1950; Cooper, Liberman, & Borst, 1951; Cooper et al., 1952). Spectrograms of real speech are reproduced on a transparent cellulose acetate base, or synthetic spectrograms are hand-painted on this base. Differences in frequencies on spectrograms become differences in reflected or transmitted light. These differences are transduced and amplified to occur as sounds whose frequency spectra reproduce those of the spectrograms. With sacrifice of some qualities of real voices, acoustic parameters of phonemes can be varied systematically and precisely. Rules for speech synthesis by pattern playback are summarized by Liberman et al. (1959).

A. *Recognition.* Recognition or identification of phones, phonemes involves n different stimuli and 2 to n different responses. The responses may be general criterion responses (same, different; yes; no; A, B in an ABX format; choice of push-buttons, switches on left, right). They may be more differentiated responses of producing (reproducing, echoing, repeating, saying, identifying) the phones, phonemes, or of selecting a corresponding or "correct" phone, phoneme from among members of a known set of responses, choices.

One focus or emphasis is acoustic parameters (acoustic phonetics), physiological or articulatory parameters (motor phonetics), or both of responses that are produced. Another focus is patterns of relationships between stimuli and responses, either produced or selected. The concern is discriminability, intelligibility, perception of differences among stimuli (perceptual phonetics).

AI. *Acoustic, physiological parameters.* Method and data on acoustic parameters and on physiological parameters of vowels and consonants produced in response to vowels and consonants in fixed and varied context are described illustratively rather than exhaustively. Theoretical analyses beyond those proposed for development of external elicitation are noted.

AIa. *Method and data.* Potter, Kopp, and Green (1947) reproduce spectrograms of production of vowels and consonants and present some generalizations on these data. Subsequently, Potter and Steinberg (1950) and then Peterson and Barney (1952) analyzed spectrograms of production of 10 vowels, first of 25 and then of 76 speakers. The vowels occurred between "h" and "d" in heed [i], hid [I], head [ɛ], had [æ], hod [a], hawed [ɔ], hood [ʊ], who'd [u], hud [ʌ], heard [ɝ]. The symbols are IPA, bracketed by Potter and Steinberg. Stimulus words appeared on cards; they were presented twice in two different orders. Speaker productions were recorded on tape from which spectrographs were made and analyzed. Representative spectrograms for each word with amplitude sections for vowels are reproduced.

Peterson and Barney report means of fundamental frequency, f_1, f_2, f_3 and amplitudes of f_1, f_2, f_3 for each vowel for men, women, and children separately.

They also present "scatter diagrams" of f_2 versus f_1 for all vowels for all speakers. Vowels between the same two consonants are spoken in ways that produce different combinations of f_1, f_2 for each vowel, with little overlap of f_1, f_2 of different vowels. Fundamental frequency, and f_1, f_2, f_3 increase in the order men, women, children, and infants (Winitz, 1960).

Holbrook and Fairbanks (1962) provide similar data on the diphthongs /ei/, /ai/, /ɔi/, /ou/, /au/, /ju/ (hay, high, hoy, hoe, Howe, and Hugh, respectively).

Lehiste and Peterson (1959a) describe 1263 English monosyllabic words of CNC (consonant, vowel or diphthong nucleus, consonant) sequence from the T-L list that comprise 359 different C—C contexts for sets of 1–10 different nuclei. Among determinations with these words are f_1, f_2, f_3 of their nuclei (Lehiste & Peterson, 1961), their duration (Lehiste & Peterson, 1961; Peterson & Lehiste, 1960), and their amplitude (Lehiste & Peterson, 1959b). Öhman (1966) presents f_1, f_2, f_3 and their transitions for Swedish, American English, and Russian vowels in VCV sequences.

The 72 combinations of 12 consonants and vowels prepared by House and Fairbanks (1953) were in wordlike huCVC sequences (e.g. hupeep). Duration, fundamental frequency, and relative power of vowels are modified by consonant context.

Lehiste (1960) determined f_1, f_2, f_3 for initial allophones of /l/ (*fee*lings) and /r/ (*r*am) in relation to subsequent syllable nuclei, for final allophones in relation to preceding syllable nuclei, and for diverse medial positions. Less extensive data are reported on f_1, f_2, f_3 of /y/ (*y*ip), /w/ (*w*e), /h/, and /ʍ/ (*wh*eat) in initial position.

These and other findings (Halle, Hughes & Radley, 1957; Stevens, 1960; Heinz & Stevens, 1961; Fujimara, 1962) indicate that each different vowel and consonant elicits responses that produce ranges of values of f_1, f_2, f_3 and of other parameters, one or more of which differ from ranges of values of f_1, f_2, f_3, and of other parameters of sounds produced by responses to other phonemes. Ranges of f_1, f_2, f_3 are influenced by position, and by class of preceding and succeeding phonemes.

Many investigations cited previously as sources of information about techniques of observation and recording of actions of verbal effectors provide data on physiological parameters of production. Among the more extensive of these investigations is MacNeilage and Sholes's (1964) determination of tongue movements in articulation of vowels.

Perkell (1969) presented seven vowels in a /hɔtV/ (hutV) context and six consonants in a /hɔCɛ/ context. A spectrogram, mid-phonetic tracing, and 17 measurements from cineradiographs are shown for each vowel and consonant (pp. 72–97).

Electrodes for EMGs were placed at the upper, corner, and lower lip, and at the tip, middle, and back of the tongue of the two normal and two deaf speakers of Huntington, Harris, and Sholes's (1968) study of articulation of 33 combinations of 11 consonants and three vowels in utterances of the form /hɔCVk/. Profiles of peak activity are shown for a normal speaker for combinations of the three vowels and two consonants and one vowel.

AIb. *Theoretical analysis.* Results of the various investigations of acoustic and physiological parameters of speech are typically discussed in terms of systems of generalizations or theory about action of component effectors of phonatory, resonatory, and articulatory processes, and of relationships between acoustic parameters and physiological or articulatory parameters (e.g., Chomsky & Halle, 1968; Fant, 1958, 1960, 1968; Flanagan, 1965; Perkell, 1969; Peterson & Shoup, 1966a, 1966b).

Of greater interest here are psychological theories of acquisition of articulations of phonemes, of production of distinguishable, stable vowels and consonants. Pertinent data are scarce, and available theories are vague and incomplete.

AIb1. *Data.* By a pretest of production of /srɔb/ (srub), Winitz and Preisler (1965) selected children who said /skr/ for /sr/. A total of 15 of these Ss were administered a discrimination task that involved pressing one bar to /srɔb/, and another bar to /skrɔb/ (scrub). Another 15 had /sliyp/ (sleep) and /sʃiyp/ (shleep) as discriminanda. Following discrimination training, Ss were tested again on production of /srɔb/. Acquisition of the /srɔb/-/skrɔb/ discrimination facilitated production of /srɔb/. With less tractable Ss, Winitz and Bellerose (1967) failed to obtain transfer to production of /r/ from training on easy-to-hard discriminations that ended with /riyb/ and /rwiyb/ as discriminanda.

Winitz and Bellerose (1965) investigated changes in articulation of /srɔb/ under conditions of its use as the name for a picture of a shrub, as the name for a cross-sectional view of cable wires, and as a stimulus to be repeated. Under these conditions, correct production of /sr/ by children in Grades 1 and 2 increased over trials. The condition in which /srɔb/ was the name for the cross-sectional view yielded a greater increase than the other two conditions. Presumably the former condition involved less interference from the previously acquired response of /shrɔb/ either as a name for the picture object or as a generalized response to hearing /srɔb/.

After 21 trials in which children's correct production of /viy/ was followed by E putting a peg in a hole, Ss had 21 more trials with /vowm/ as the stimulus to be produced (Baer & Winitz, 1968). Children with low, medium, and high errors in producing /v/ improved in the production of /v/ in /viy/ but not in /vowm/. The former group of children were better than the latter two groups.

AIb2. *Theory.* Winitz and Bellerose (1967) distinguish "a response production, availability or integration phase and a response association phase" in which respectively "new responses are acquired or made available . . . (and) available responses are associated or conditioned to appropriate stimuli" (p. 223). Effectiveness of discrimination pretraining is limited to the latter phase. Presumably concepts and principles of learning in general or of verbal learning are pertinent. None are mentioned explicity.

Miller and Dollard (1941), Mowrer (1950, 1960), Skinner (1957), Staats and Staats (1963), and Staats (1968) have little to say about acquisition of correct or incorrect forms of production of phonemes of a language. They either ignore the problem completely or treat it generally as, for example, a matter of differential reinforcement of "correct" and "incorrect" articulation of a phoneme or phoneme sequence.

AII. *Discrimination.* Discrimination used here includes both "absolute" discrimination of stimuli presented one at a time and relative discrimination between stimuli presented in close temporal succession. Methods and data are noted, and then theoretical analyses.

AIIa. *Methods and data.* Investigations of discrimination are conveniently divided into those with only a few (2, 3, 4) differentiated criterion responses, and those with larger numbers of criterion responses.

AIIa1. *Few criterion responses.* In the investigations mentioned here, the stimuli are synthetic. Initially, one or more reference set(s) of phones, phonemes (e.g. voiced [/b,d,g/], unvoiced [/p,t,k/] stop consonants or both) is specified, and particular members selected. Reference phonemes are usually presented in CV syllables, VC syllables, or combinations thereof.

Specification and selection of reference sets, and also of parameters to be manipulated, are guided by prior data and existing theory on those sets, and on parameters likely to influence discrimination of reference phonemes. The parameters varied are typically one or more among frequencies of f_1, f_2, f_3 of initial consonants or vowels, among frequencies of f_1, f_2, f_3 of terminal vowels or consonants, or both. Direction, degree, and form of transition from initial to terminal frequencies of f_1, f_2, f_3 constitute another important class of parameters.

Difference between and among reference sets of two or three phones, phonemes, at several values along one or more parameters, generate from fairly large (9–13) to quite large numbers (336) of stimuli. These stimuli may be presented in ABX or other formats for relative discrimination. In an ABX format, AB or BA occurs and then A or B for X; Ss indicate whether X is A or B. Frequencies or percentages of occurrence of reference phonemes as responses to each phoneme are determined and shown as stimulus-response functions or relationships. The value or range of values of one or more parameters that elicit a particular reference phoneme with maximum frequency or probability constitutes the cue for that phoneme. Experiments with consonants as reference phonemes are described, and then some with vowels as reference phonemes.

Identification of and discrimination between unvoiced (/p, t, k/) and voiced (/b, d, g/) stop consonants have been investigated extensively by Liberman and co-workers at the Haskins Laboratory. The parameters manipulated include f of bursts, schematic stops before vowels (Liberman et al. 1952); direction and steepness of f_2 and f_1 transition before vowels,

(Liberman et al., 1954); initial locus of f_1 and f_2, direction and steepness of their transition to steady state, and duration of initial silent inverval in transition of different lengths (Delattre et al., 1955); direction and steepness of f_2 and f_3 transition, (Liberman et al. 1957; Harris et al. 1958); direction and steepness of f_2 and f_3 transition, f of bursts (Hoffman, 1958); and delay of onset of f_1 (Liberman et al., 1961).

Among the findings of one or more of these experiments, bursts of high frequency and falling transitions are likely to elicit (are heard as) t; bursts of low frequency, rising transitions are likely to elicit p; and bursts of frequencies about equal to f_2 of the vowel, falling transitions are likely to elicit k. f_2 of 300 cps, 1800 cps, 720 cps elicit g, d, b, respectively, with g more likely to be elicited by a rising transition and d, b, by a falling transition. Observations of abrupt shifts from elicitation of b to elicitation of d, and from d to g, both in absolute discrimination and in relative discrimination in ABX format, have been replicated (Eimas, 1963).

In a preliminary experiment, Menyuk and Anderson (1969) observed "abrupt shifts" or "sharp boundaries" in identification by choice between /l-w/ (light-white), between /l-r/ (right), and between /w-r/ for five children from 3,11 to 7,2 years, and for five adults. In the main experiment, sharp boundaries were not found for preschool children, older children, or adults. Articulation of these consonantal semivowels may be more similar to articulation of vowels than of most consonants.

Identification of nasal consonants (/m, n, ŋ/) has been related to rising, falling f_2 (Liberman et al., 1954). Relationships have been determined for identification of initial liquids and semivowels (/w, j, r, l/) as functions of number of formats needed for synthesis; duration of onset of steady state; starting frequency of f_1, f_2, f_3; and duration of transition (O'Conner et al., 1957). Also investigated are absolute discrimination, relative discrimination, or both, of initial semivowels, (/w, r, l, y/) as influenced by frequency of f_1 and shape of f_1 transition (Ainsworth, 1968); of initial unvoiced fricatives (/f, θ, ʃ, s/) and voiced fricatives (/v, ð, z, ʒ/) as functions of friction and vocalic parts of members of each set of fricatives (Harris, 1958); and of initial voiced fricatives (/v/vs/ð/; /z/vs/ʒ/) as influenced by f_2, f_3 transition onset, and by frequency of f_2, f_3 (Delattre et al. 1964).

For vowels, Delattre et al. (1952) fixed f_1 at 250, 360, 510 and 720 cps and varied f_2 in ranges 480–3000, 500–2520, 840–2040, and 960–1800 cps, respectively. Results are presented as f_1, f_2 values that yield the "closest . . . approximation to the 16 cardinal vowels of IPA" (p. 198).

Among more recent experiments with vowels are those of Lindblom and Studdert-Kennedy (1967) who synthesized vowels along an [U]-[I] (*book-bit*) continuum, and Scholes (1967), who found different patterns of choices of vowels among native speakers of Spanish, Persian, Japanse, and American English.

AIIa2. *Larger number of criterion responses.* Fairly large number of different natural phonemes are presented for identification, typically by an equal number of responses. Thus, Peterson and Barney used 10 vowels as stimuli and as responses. The actual stimuli were the productions of 10 vowels in two words each by 76 speakers that had been recorded and also analyzed spectrographically. As each of these 1520 stimuli occurred in a word, listeners drew a line through the word heard from among the 10 words on each line.

Frequencies of each of the vowels recognized by listeners are shown for each of the vowels intended by speakers. Areas of frequencies of f_1, f_2 of vowels unanimously classified by listeners are presented in an f_2, f_1 plot. In general, confusions of listeners were choice of an adjacent vowel on an f_2, f_1 "loop." Intelligibility expressed as observer agreements decreased in the order [i], [ɜ·], [u], [ʊ], [æ], [I], [ɔ], [ʌ], [ɛ], [a].

The 16 consonants selected by Miller and Nicely (1955) constitute about 75% of all consonants and 40% of all phonemes that occur in normal speech. Five females served in turn as speaker and four listeners in saying and responding to nonsense syllables made up of the consonants followed by /a/ (father). For each of 17 conditions, 4000 written responses were obtained. The conditions were signal-to-noise (S/N) ratios of −18, −12, −6, 0, +6, +12 with "normal" filtering (200-6500 cps), and S/N = +12 with six low-pass bands and five high-pass bands.

In confusion matrices for each condition, consonants spoken and written are rows and columns, respectively.

With change in S/N from −18 to +12 and with change in high cutoff frequency from 300 to 5000 cps, correct responses and information transmitted increase. With change in low cutoff frequency from 200 to 4500 cps, correct responses and information transmitted decrease.

Similar data are available of unaspirated voiceless and voiced stop consonants (/p, t, k, b, d, g/) as discriminated by speakers of American English and Hindi (Singh, 1966).

Identifiability of phones, phonemes, particularly with masking or distortion of the speech signal or wave is sometimes called intelligibility. Thus, Miller and Nicely and Singh investigated intelligibility of phonemes. Earlier work on intelligibility is described in Fletcher (1953). Results of these experiments and of experiments by others (Black & Angello, 1964; Carterette, 1967; Williams & Hecker, 1968) indicate that intelligibility increases with increasing intensity of phonemes for any level of masking noise, and decreases with increasing intensity of masking noise for any level of intensity of phonemes. Deleting parts of the signal below an arbitrary level, eliminating frequencies above (low-pass filtering) or below (high-pass filtering) an arbitrary cutoff, and periodic interruption of signals reduce intelligibility. Intelligibility functions differ among speakers and types of test material (Williams & Hecker). Carterette found correct identification of Swedish vowels by individual listeners to be related linearly to "the weighted number of formants that remain after filtering" (p. 422).

Templin (1957, pp. 13–15, 61–73) reports that sound discrimination scores of 3- to 5-year-old children increase with age, do not differ between boys and girls, and are consistently and sometimes significantly better for high SES than for low SES children. Sound discrimination scores of 6- to 8-year-old children increase with age. Boys are consistently and sometimes significantly lower than girls, and high SES children are consistently and sometimes significantly above low SES children.

Thirty children, 15 males and 15 females, at each of ages 3.0–3.9, 4.0–4.9, and 5.0–5.9 responded twice to 22 consonants in different syllables with /d/ and with /ɛ/ (Bricker, 1967). Test-retest agreement of errors in pronunciation or recognition and intergroup correlations were high and enter significant correlations with frequency of occurrence of phonemes in infant and adult speech. Errors decreased with age, with fewer errors at the two younger ages for females than for males. Confusion matrices are presented for the 10 consonants that elicited the most errors. Mean percentage of specific attributes of speech sound that were pronounced correctly ("preserved-in-error") were highest for voiced-voiceless, slightly less high for manner of articulation, and markedly lower for place of articulation.

AIIb. *Theoretical analyses.* The system of generalizations about absolute and relative discrimination of stop consonants as functions of formant and other parameters described above exemplifies theoretical analyses of perception of phonemes. Liberman et al. (1967, pp. 434–44) describe this system of generalization in greater detail. They proceed to a less well developed system of generalizations about relationships between acoustic parameters of phonemes as stimuli and physiological or articulatory parameters of their production (pp. 449–51). Finally, "as a general rule" of "perception of the speech code," they propose: "there is typically a lack of correspondence between acoustic cue and perceived phoneme, and in all cases it appears that perception mirrors articulation more closely than sound" (p. 453).

Still general, but more precise statements of this analysis of speech perception can be reworded from Lane's classification of "evidence that favors a motor theory of speech perception" (1965, p. 277). The statements are: (a) acoustically similar phones, phonemes that consistently evoke different articulatory response will be discriminated both absolutely (identification) and relatively (discrimination); (b) acoustically dissimilar phones, phonemes that consistently evoke the same or similar articulatory responses will be discriminated poorly, if at all, both absolutely and relatively; and (c) with joint variation of acoustic parameters of phones, phonemes and of articulatory parameters, the latter are the more potent determinants of absolute and relative discrimination. Statements (a) and (b) are recognized, respectively, as notions similar to, if not special cases within, response-mediated dissimilarity (acquired distinctiveness of cues) and discrimination, and response-mediated similarity (acquired equivalence of cues) and generalization (Miller & Dollard, 1941, pp. 71–77; Dollard & Miller, 1950, pp. 101–3; Goss, 1955; Goss & Nodine, 1965, pp. 179–81).

After reviewing each kind of evidence, Lane criticizes the motor theory on several grounds, most generally that comparable "findings with nonlinguistic stimuli militate against the postulation of a special perceptual mechanism for speech" (1965, p. 292). Of importance, too, is Lane's comment that comparison of identification and discrimination of consonants and vowels is precluded by noncomparability of parameters of consonants and of vowels.

In contrast to Lane's view, Liberman et al. hold "that speech is, for the most part, a special code that must often make use of a special perceptual mechanism to serve as its decoder" (1967, p. 451). "Ordinary principles of psychophysics and discrimination learning" may have to be supplemented. Theories that allow for mediation by verbal and perhaps other effectors can accomodate complex patterns of relationships among multidimensional stimuli, mediating stimuli-response and criterion or terminating responses (Goss, 1961a).

The motor theory of speech perception, in its present form, is a theory of occurrence of absolute and relative discrimination of phonemes. Until more data are available on acquisition of relationships between acoustic parameters of phonemes and particularly their production, advocacy of special status for "perception of the speech code" seems premature.

B. *Association.* Responses of the stimulus-response relationships of association are formally or topographically different than response of recognition of phonemes either by production or selection. Associations to phonemes have been elicited under conditions to associations to words. Meaningfulness, and other attributes of phonemes such as familiarity, affectivity, and imagery might be obtained under conditions of such responses to words. Phonetic symbolism excepted, associations to phonemes have been of little interest. Accordingly, methods of investigation of associations, and of meaningfulness and other attributes, are considered subsequently for words rather than here.

Within a language, phonetic symbolism, as a possible phenomenon, is defined by occurrence of an association or set of associations significantly more often to some phonemes than to other phonemes. The latter may elicit other, often contrasting associations. Across languages, phonetic symbolism or "universal" phonetic symbolism, as a possible phenomenon, is defined in essentially the same way. The expectation is that phonemes of like class in each language compared elicit a common association or set of associations. Like class is typically specified as same or similar in place and manner of articulation.

In his distinction between referential and expressive symbolism, Sapir (1929) provides the general rationale for investigations of phonetic symbolism. In contrast to arbitrary referential symbolism, expressive symbolism might be association in such a proportion as:

phonetic entity "teeny": idea (or reference) "very small"
= phonetic entity "tiny": idea (or reference) "small"
(p. 225).

The relationship of size between "very small" and "small" as ideas or reference, he holds, is paralleled by the relationship between the phonetic entities, "teeny" and "tiny," more specifically between the phonemes *ee* (/i/) and *i* (/aI/). More generally, Sapir, asks: "Can it be shown, in other words, that symbolisms tend to work themselves out in vocalic and consonantal contrasts and scales in spite of the arbitrary allocations of these same vowels and consonants in the socialized field of reference?" (p. 226).

The phenomenon of phonetic symbolism has been extended to include the matching of words within and particularly between languages that have common reference (e.g., to small objects, to large objects). Thus, Tsura and Fries's (1933) stimuli were 36 pairs of antonyms in Japanese and corresponding pairs in English. Pairs were seen and heard by *S*s who matched members of Japanese pairs with those of English pairs. The 69 percent correct matches was taken as better than chance.

The words of word-pairs of these experiments do not differ phonemically in systematic fashion (Taylor, 1963, p. 203). Accordingly, although treated as phonetic symbolism (Brown, 1958, pp. 122–31; Weiss, 1964b; Siegal, Silverman & Markel, 1967; Gebels, 1969; Vetter, 1969, pp. 103–6), such investigations are excluded here.

Method and data on phonetic symbolism with phonemes are described, and then aspects of theoretical analysis.

BI. *Method and data.* For his first experiment, Sapir prepared 30 word-pairs that contrasted pairs of vowels familiar to those who speak English, and 30 word-pairs that contrasted unfamiliar vowels. Typically, one of the contrasting phonemes of pairs (e.g., /a/) was selected as symbolizing large more often

than the other phoneme (e.g., /i/). Similar results obtained in a second experiment with 100 word-pairs "involving every type of phonetic contrast" (p. 228) that were presented to a wide range of *S*s. Choices were apparently paralleled by acoustic differences, kinesthetic difference, or both. Thus, at the /a/ extreme of "the larger reference," the tongue is lower, retracted, with a larger resonance chamber at the front of the mouth; at the opposite, /i/ extreme "of the smaller reference," the tongue is higher, toward the front, with a smaller resonance chamber.

Newman (1933) transformed percentages of choice to values along small-large, bright-dark scales. Scale values of vowels on small-large paralleled front-back position of the tongue, high-low frequency of vocalic resonance, small-large size of oral cavity and, in a second experiment, short-long duration. Scale values of consonants on small-large varied with dental, labial, palatal positions, and with voiceless, voiced. In contrast, bright-dark varied with palatal, labial, dental, with voiceless consonants bright, voiced consonants dark.

On the basis of results of four experiments, Bentley and Varon suggest that simpler noises may have the same attributes as phonemes (1933). Furthermore, "these vocalic characteristics, and others like them in consonantal elements, pertain to the sounds as *sounds*. They attain a 'phonetic' or 'symbolic' signification only when we transfer them to other contexts" (p. 84). After a fifth experiment, they suggest possible acoustic and kinesthetic bases of differential responses to phonemes.

These are viewed "as a graded and labile system" without "any inherent power of specific symbolization" (p. 86).

Taylor (1963) suggests that, in pronouncing word-pairs, Sapir and Newman may have added difference in voice quality to intrinsic acoustic differences between contrasting phonemes. Among other limitations, she notes failure to vary the consonant context; use of only English speaking *S*s, a few Chinese excepted; restriction of dimensions to size or to size and darkness; and possible effects of judgments of size and darkness by the same *S*s.

The *S*s of Taylor and Taylor's (1962) third experiment spoke only one among the unrelated languages of English, Korean, Japanese, and Tamil. CVCs generated by permutation of six consonants and three vowels were rated on five-point scales for size, movement, pleasantness, and warmth. Written in each of the four languages, the CVCs were used in the native country. Either within a language or among languages, direction of ratings was not consistent.

Miron (1961) presented 50 CVCs to native speakers of American English and of Japanese for rating along three sets of five SD scales each. For both groups of speakers, low-high potency of vowels and consonants is paralled by front-back articulation. Low-high potency of vowels is paralled by decreasing frequency of f_2.

SD ratings have been used to determine consequences of associations to consonant sequences *gl*, *fl*, *sm*, *sp*, *st* combined with *ly* and *ah*, (Markel & Hamp, 1961). Weiss (1968) failed to find any relationship between fit of SD ratings along eight scales and sounds of verbs, nouns, and adjectives. Some evidence of high fit and strong connotation of verbs obtained.

The nonsense-word pairs of high and of low meaningfulness prepared by Weiss (1964a) included contrasting vowels and contrasting consonants. Each pair was accompanied by the name or picture of an object, and characterized as large or small, black or white, sharp or blunt. The most pronounced differential matching was for word-pairs presented with names of objects for response by black or white.

The proto-Polynesian words "oho" and "iti," and then six pairs of Sapir's CVCs contrasting *a* and *i* were pronounced both vocally and subvocally for college students to relate to size (Vetter & Tennant, 1967). With both vocal and subvocal pronunciation, "oho" and *a* were matched with larger, "iti" and "i" with smaller. Cues from articulation are the suggested bases of *S*s' differential associations.

BII. *Theoretical Analysis.* Within each of several languages, different vowels and different consonants presented in contrasting pairs or singly apparently elicit different associations. Congruent patterns to vowels and consonants of like class across languages may (Miron, 1961) or may not (Taylor & Taylor, 1962) occur.

Bentley and Varon's (1933) first experiment suggests that associations to phonemes that are produced rather than selected by *S*s do not typically refer to values along or to dimensions such as size.

Beyond apparent limitation to response by selection, the particular values along acoustic, kinesthetic and, on occasion, visual dimensions that elicit differential choice or rating are obscure. Speakers may provide acoustic and visual cues. In repeating stimuli, listeners may provide kinesthetic cues and, contingent on degree of overtness, acoustic cues. Locus (place) and perhaps height (manner) of tongue movement are among possible kinesthetic cues of articulation. Frequency of f_2, and possibly of other formants, are among possible acoustic cues.

Bentley and Varon suggest and provide evidence that these possible dimensions are not uniquely linguistic or symbolic. Solomon (1958, 1959a, 1959b) obtained differential responses to complex nonlinguistic sounds on SD scales, as have Kerrick et al. (1969) for various brief, nonlinguistic sounds.

Beyond problems of immediate cues of differential choice or rating are those of conditions and pertinent principles of development of observed relationships between phonemes and associations. Taylor (1963) suggests that a particular phoneme, and its grapheme, occur systematically in the same position within words that denote or connote a particular value (e.g., small, large) along some physical dimension (e.g., size). When this phoneme, or its grapheme, occurs in new contexts for choice between extremes or rating with reference to extremes of that dimension, *S*s choose or rate toward the name for that value, or a synonym.

Accordingly, she used Taylor and Taylor's results for initial G, K, N, T to reexamine Newman's (1933) list of words denoting large and small. G, K, which were the two consonants rated largest, occur more often in words that denote or connote large size than small. T, N, which were the consonants rated the two smallest, occur more often in words that denote or connote small size than large.

Taylor (p. 207) partly anticipates Weiss's (1964b) criticism of ignoring explanation of "how . . . unrelated words in a given language which share a common connotative meaning tend also to share structural components" (p. 456). She did not suggest that only initial consonants might become associated with some common response that labels an extreme on some dimension. Weiss's "theory" of phonetic symbolism (1964a, pp. 261–62) appears little different than Taylor's "language-habits" theory.

Johnson (1967) tested Newman's (1933) findings in a dif-

ferent way. Instead of by selection, words denoting largeness and smallness were obtained by having college students produce them. Other college students judged whether initial vowel phonemes that occurred five or more times in words were related to bigness or smallness. Frequency of occurrence of each vowel in words related to smallness (S) and to bigness (L) was expressed as an S-L ratio. The ratio decreased in the *i, e, a, u, o* order of Newman's paralogs and words. Johnson concludes that "degree of vowel symbolism is higher in the results of the production task than in Newman's thesaurus list" (p. 510). Johnson found no magnitude symbolism of initial and final consonants. Huang, Pratoomraj, and Johnson (1969) extend these findings to Mandarin Chinese and Thai.

GRAPHIC REPRESENTATION

Despite the importance of speech sounds, it is their graphic representation, "the alphabet," that Diringer (1948) subtitles "the key to the history of mankind." Analytical investigations of recognition of and associations to letters, graphemes are far less extensive than such investigations with phonemes.

Diringer (pp. 21–37) distinguishes embryo-writing from true writing. Embryo-writing includes undifferentiated picture-writing or iconography, mnemonic devices (e.g., knot devices, notched sticks), and "symbolic means of communication" (e.g., symbolical epistles, tokens).

True writing includes picture writing or pictography, in which pictures represent things; ideographic writing, in which pictures, symbols, arbitrary forms represent ideas; transitional scripts or word-syllabic systems (Gelb, 1963) that combine pictographs or ideographs and phonetic symbols; and phonetic writing. The visual symbols or forms of phonetic writing correspond to speech sounds. In syllabic writing, syllabaries, word-syllabic systems the correspondence is between single symbols and syllables or vowels. In alphabetic writing or alphabets the correspondence is between single symbols and segments of syllables, between letters, graphemes and phonemes. Only alphabetic writing is considered here and, more specifically, the alphabet of contemporary English.

Unlike speech, physiological bases of writing as arm-hand action have received little attention beyond treatment in general anatomy and neurology.

As stimuli, written letters might be classified by similarities-differences with respect to geometric parameters. As responses, they might be classified by similarities-dissimilarities along kinesiological parameters, geometric parameters, or both. As stimuli, printed letters might be distinguished by type face (Tinker, 1963) or, more analytically, along geometric parameters.

Analytical classifications of written and printed letters are rare. Handwriting has been scaled (e.g., Thorndike, 1910; Freeman, 1958). It can be scored on dimensions or features of heaviness, slant, . . ., formation of letters (Gray, 1956, p. 208). These scales and scoring are for general features, for style of handwriting. They do not provide for classifications of letters along several dimensions, features.

Gibson (1965, p. 1969) classifies 10 Roman capitals by geometric "features": straight segment (horizontal, vertical, oblique/, oblique\), intersection, redundancy (cyclic change, symmetry), discontinuity (vertical, horizontal). All 26 letters are classifiable (Gibson, 1968, p. 78).

Frequency counts of letters in printed text are surveyed, and then investigations with letters in stimulus-response relationships.

Frequency counts. Decisions, procedures, and statistics of counts of phoneme frequency also hold for counts of letter frequency.

However, frequency counts of phonemes and of letters even in the same corpus are not readily interchangeable. Contingent on context, several single letters, combinations of two or more letters, or both may be the graphemic option or equivalent of a single phoneme (Hanna et al., 1966).

Newman and Gerstman's (1952) count of letters in 10,000 words from the King James Bible has been expanded to three languages, and to words from other sources (Newman & Waugh 1960). Attneave (1953) presents counts of single letters in words or articles in a San Antonio newspaper and in popular magazines. An *r* of .98 holds for frequencies in the two sources.

Other estimates of frequency of occurrence of single letters can be found in Underwood and Schulz (1960, pp. 65–70). Rank-correlations for all pairs among four different counts are from .94 to .99.

Single letters have been counted for student names and single-word descriptors (e.g., optical; Bourne & Ford, 1961), for words from the London Times (Baddelay et al., 1960), and for 100 samples from various sources (Mayzner & Tresselt, 1962).

Proportions of letters in the natural speech of children in Grades 1, 3, and 5 and of adults, in the First, Third, and Fifth Ginn Basic Readers, and in adult text are available in Carterette and Jones (1968). The *r*s for all pairs among these eight counts are from .97 to .998.

Among sources of frequencies of two-letter sequences (bigrams) are Underwood and Schulz (1960, pp. 65–72, 333–35), Baddelay et al. (1960), Mayzner and Tresselt (1962, 1965), and Seibel (1963). Underwood and Schulz provide frequencies of trigrams (pp. 65–76, 336–69). Seibel extends the length of sequences to *n*-grams of up through 12 letters. Trigram, tetragram, and pentagram frequencies for combinations of word length and letter position are also available, (Mayzner, Tresselt, & Wolin, 1965a, b, c).

Stimulus-response relationships. Recognition of letters, and associations to them, are considered. Although usually presented visually, names of letters might be spoken, and letters might be shown and spoken simultaneously.

A. *Recognition.* Letters may be recognized by saying them or by writing them. They may be recognized by relative or absolute discrimination.

AI. *Production.* Data on production of individual letters by saying them or more importantly, by writing them, are scarce. Available data typically are for sets of letters as a whole rather than for each letter separately. Thus, Hildreth (1932) reports totals only of correct copying of 12 letters. Barrett (1966) notes other investigations that report only scores across letters.

Wilson and Flemming (1938) report numbers of correct responses and describe errors in giving letter sounds and in naming and writing each letter of different samples of eight capital or small letters by 4- and 5-year old kindergarten children, and by Grade 1 children. Subsequently, (1939) they report percentages of correct responses for all 26 letters.

Lewis and Lewis (1965) obtained samples of the manuscript handwriting of 354 first-grade children both at the beginning of the school year and after six months. Quality of postinstruction writing was placed along the Freeman (1958) scale. For both sessions combined, numbers of errors of each and all of 11 types are shown for each letter.

Theoretical analyses of conditions and principles of the occurrence and learning of letters are also uncommon. Miller and Dollard (1941) and Mowrer (1960) ignore handwriting. For Skinner "copying a text in a *familiar* alphabet differs from drawing in the size of the 'echoic' unit. The skilled copyist possesses a small number of standard responses (the ways in which he produces the letters of the alphabet) which are under the control of a series of stimuli (the letters in the text)" (1957, p. 70). Details of the nature of "standard response," and of occurrence and learning of such responses alone and in series are ignored.

Staats's initial statement is equally general: "the analysis of writing acquisition in learning terms follows very straight-forwardly from the previous general discussion of instrumental discrimination learning where a verbal stimulus comes to control a motor response" (1968, p. 216). But he does describe something of the conditions, presumed principles, and course of the learning of writing by his daughter Jennifer (pp. 293–98), and by other children (pp. 318–19; 328–37).

AII. *Discrimination.* Some data are available on discrimination of individual letters. These are described. Then theoretical analyses of the learning of discrimination are examined along with pertinent data.

AIIa. *Data.* Absolute discrimination or identification of letters was of concern to Cattell (1886a) and to Sanford (1888). Cattell presented Latin capitals and small letters at .001 sec. by a gravity chronometer. Correct recognition of capitals ranged from 241 of 270 for *W* down to 63/270 for *E*. Correct recognition of small letters ranged from 87/100 for *e* to 28/100 for *s*.

Sanford determined legibility of Snellen small letters at approximate fixed distance (1.5–3.2 meters). He also determined distance at which *S*s thought they recognized the letters, and were certain. Both Snellen small letters and letters in old type were presented tachistoscopically at .002–.006 sec. for recognition. Percentages of correct identification and type and number of confusions at fixed distance and duration are reported for each letter.

Among lower case letters, Smith (1928) found that *b, p, q, d* were the most difficult for first-grade children to match, and *a, e, w, o, m, s, g* the least difficult. Among capitals, *Q, B, D, J, Y, Z, R, U* were the most difficult to match and *A, C, F, H, I, O, S, X* were the least difficult. Matches of lowercase and capital letters varied markedly in difficulty with *Q, R, G, B, F, A, E, H, L* the most difficult, and *S, V, K, O, X* the least difficult.

Others have found discrimination between *b* and *d*, and between *p* and *q* to be difficult (Vernon, 1960, pp. 20–27). Barrett (1966) also summarizes investigations that have included discrimination of letters, and that have compared verbal and nonverbal discrimination. As with various investigations of production, these data are for all letters rather than individually.

Gibson (1965, p. 1068) obtained a confusion matrix of matching judgements of letters by four-year-old children. A confusion matrix is also being obtained for adults (1968, p. 78). "Percent feature difference" for letters proved somewhat related to confusions.

After kindergarten children were pretrained on a visual matching task, Popp (1964) obtained confusions in letter matching. For pairs of letters, the largest number of errors were with *p-q, b-d, b-q, d-p*; for single letters they were with *u, q, d, h, p, v, b, e, f, i, j, k.*

Gibson, Gibson, Pick, and Osser (1962) prepared letter-like forms which, like English letters, were transformed from line to curve, by rotation or reversal, in perspective, and by break and close. For children of ages 4 to 8 years, with some exceptions, decreasing percentages of errors occurred for perspective, rotation and reversal, line-to-curve, and break and close transformations.

In order to enhance discrimination between target and comparison letters, Dunn-Rankin (1968) presented each of 21 target letters with each of 210 possible pairs of 21 letters for children in Grades 2 and 3 to choose the letter of each comparison pair "most like the target letter" (p. 991). Similarity values on a 0–100 scale are presented for each comparison letter, including the target letter, with each target letter. The scalability value for each target letter indicates degree to which Ss were able to choose members of pairs most like the target letter.

AIIb. *Theoretical analyses.* Various general theories of discrimination learning (Reese, 1968, pp. 229–330), developed primarily or exclusively from data on discrimination of differences along one or a few simple physical dimensions might be extended to letter discrimination. With elaboration, perceptual enrichment, as proposed by Gibson and Gibson (1955; Gibson, 1968, pp. 100–102), might prove another general theory. It may differ little from a mediation theory that includes selection of more discriminable features of complex stimuli (Goss, 1955). Gibson's (1969) more recent analysis is noted later under theories of recognition of nonverbal, visual stimuli.

Extension of various theories of learning to discriminate along one or a few simple physical dimensions to occurrence and learning of letter discrimination are infrequent. Staats' (1968, pp. 66–71) proposed application is abortive: he presents no theory of discrimination learning. "What is learned in perceptual learning," as presented by Gibson (1968, pp. 66–71) describes selected data. But, the section on "learning principles" (pp. 72–74) is without learning principles.

Hively's (1966) "framework for the analysis of elementary reading behavior" classifies and give examples of possible relationships involving nonverbal, spoken, and written stimuli and nonlinguistic, written, and spoken responses. Even allowing for parallels within Skinner (1957), conditions and principles of discrimination learning are ignored.

Most recent investigations of bases of discrimination between and among letters have involved transfer from pretraining with letters or other stimuli to learning to read words. The broad theoretical orientation of various of these investigations is response-mediated similarity and generalization, dissimilarity and discrimination (Miller & Dollard, 1941, pp. 71–77; Dollard & Miller, 1950, pp. 101–3; Goss, 1955; Spiker, 1956; Arnoult, 1957; Cantor, 1965; Goss & Nodine, 1965, pp. 179–81).

Experiments by Muehl and coworkers indicate that kindergarten children: (a) learn to name or read words better with discriminative pretraining to match the same words than to match different words or geometric forms (Muehl, 1960); (b) learn names of pictures as responses to *b* or *d* better with discriminative pretraining on consistent or inconsistent orientations than on color patches (Hendrickson & Muehl, 1960); and (c) read better with discriminative pretraining with different meaningful than with different nonmeaningful words (King, 1960). Under some conditions, learning names for letters may interfere with discrimination between nonsense words that contain those letters as discriminative stimuli (Muehl, 1962).

The greater transfer from training with the same letters than with the same words also reported by King is not entirely consistent with prior findings of greater transfer from pretraining with words than with letters (Muehl, 1961; Staats et al., 1962). However, in the latter two experiments, S discriminated among letters in different words, while King's Ss discriminated among letters within words.

In an experiment by Levin et al. (1964), first-grade children traced initial, middle, or terminal graphemes of words in an artificial orthography. The control was going through a picture book. After Ss learned to associate names to words, they were tested on recognition of the words. Progressively lower means of correct associations and correct recognitions occurred in the order initial grapheme, control, terminal grapheme, middle grapheme. Differences between initial grapheme and control conditions were not significant.

Matching-to-sample discrimination training (Popp, 1967), training on discrimination between contrasting pairs (Wheelock & Silvaroli, 1967), and training with relevant orientation of line drawings (Caldwell & Hall, 1969) all lead to some improvement in letter discrimination.

Unfortunately, these findings are neither sufficiently comprehensive nor consistent to permit any but very general suggestions about conditions and principles of occurrence and learning of letter discrimination. Prior training in orientation toward distinctive parts of letters that are mirror images apparently facilitates. Whether pretraining with words or letters effects direction and degree of transfer apparently depends on particular further conditions such as discrimination among or within words.

Association. For upper-case and lower-case letters, Anderson (1965) obtained both single and continuous associations in 60 sec. by college students. For means of numbers of associations (*m*) to upper-case and lower-case letters, the rank-order correlation was .89. Primaries are reported for single-associations and first responses of continuous associations. In general, Ss responded with words whose initial letters were stimulus letters. Relatively high correlations occur for most pairs among frequencies of letters in initial position and in all positions in names and in words, *m* of both upper-case and lower-case letters, number of words per letter in the T-L count, vocal reaction time, and letter preference (Horton & Mecherikoff, 1960).

Underwood and Schulz (1960) obtained letter responses to single-letter stimuli (pp. 375–76), and also to all two-letter combinations (pp. 377–428). Comparable data are now available for second- and fifth-grade children (Amster & Keppel, 1966, 1968). Lachman and Laughery (1966) provide norms for letter-word relationships.

Instead of phonemes, Folkins and Lenbow (1966) used 43 grapheme equivalents, each of which was illustrated by five words. Rating by college students along the three sets of five SD scales used by Miron (1961) suggested differences on evaluation, potency, and activity that are associated with differences in articulation.

Replacement of deleted letters, a special case of letter association, varies directly with percentage deletion (Chapanis, 1954). Replacement is optimal with deletion of space and vowels (Miller & Friedman, 1957).

Theoretical analyses directed specifically at associations to letters, graphemes are essentially nonexistent. However, with sufficient time for responses, associations to letters, graphemes can be regarded as mediated initially by subvocal production of phonemes.

PHONEME-GRAPHEME CORRESPONDENCE

The imperfect correspondence between the 40 or more phonemes of English and their representation by graphemes comprised of 26 letters and combinations of those letters, as Downing (1967, pp. 1–31) notes, has been deplored from at least the mid-sixteenth century. Two aspects of phoneme-grapheme correspondence are considered. One is selected, recent general descriptions and analyses of phoneme-grapheme correspondence. The other is investigations of development and learning of phoneme-grapheme correspondence.

Description and Analysis. For a "basic writing vocabulary" of 10,000 words, Horn (1957) describes number and percent of occurrence of number of different and the most common spellings of diverse vowels, diphthongs, syllabic sounds, and consonants.

Hanna et al. (1966) describe frequency and percent occurrence of graphemes across all and in initial, medial, and final positions that correspond to 22 vowels and 30 consonants of American English. They also provide phonemic representation of words (pp. 137–416), and lists of words exemplifying each grapheme that corresponds to each sound in each position (pp. 426–1096). Particular phoneme-grapheme correspondences are analyzed as functions of phonological, morphological and, for homonyms, syntactic factors.

Venezky (1967) outlines and illustrates a two-step analysis of phoneme-grapheme correspondence.

Development and Learning. Age-related increases in achievement in reading and spelling serve as crude indices of development of phoneme-grapheme correspondence. From the same 10 sets of three letters, Gibson, Osser, and Pick (1963) constructed parallel words (W), pronounceable trigrams (PT), and unpronounceable trigrams (UT). When presented at 40 msec. to groups of 12 boys and 12 girls that had just finished first and third grades, correct recognitions by spelling increased in the order UT, PT, W for all but third-grade girls. The latter *S*s recognized the three kinds of stimuli equally well and consistently better than the former three groups. For three-letter sequences, third-grade girls excepted, saying the letter correctly apparently depends on prior exposure to them as words and on pronounceability. Regarded as concerned with "how the correspondence rules are learned," at best the experiment provides indirect evidence either of rules or of learning.

Bishop (1964) reports that training on letters of Arabic words produces better reading than word training or exposure to a quite different task. Transfer to reading two-grapheme words proved greater after single-phoneme or letter training than after double-phoneme or word training (Jeffrey & Samuels, 1967). Williams (1968) obtained better performance on responses to letterlike forms with concurrent than with successive training.

These experiments provide little data on either children's learning of phoneme-grapheme correspondence in a first language, or adult's learning of such correspondence in a second language. Unfortunately, classroom-based comparisons of effectiveness of different methods of initial instruction in reading (Bond & Dykstra, 1967; Downing, 1967) provide no direct data on the course of learning of phoneme-grapheme correspondence.

Words, Morphemes

Words as spoken, as a first approximation, are taken as recurrent sequences of the same phoneme before and after which "pausing is possible" (Hockett, 1958, p. 167). Words as written or printed, as a first approximation, are taken as recurrent sequence of the same letters before and after which spaces or punctuation (other than hyphens, single and double quotation marks, apostrophes) are possible.

Words and syllables, real or synthetic, are the units of observation and analysis of most of the investigations described here. Real words, loosely, are words that occur currently in a particular language. Synthetic words have phoneme, or letter, grapheme sequences homologous with those of real words. However, one or more of the phonemes or letters differ from those of real words.

Words and syllables have been the units of psychogical investigations. In contrast, for linguists, the morpheme is the unit of observation and analysis. Definition and classification of morphemes is discussed under morphemic analysis.

Occurrence of words is considered first simply as responses and then in stimulus-response relationships.

OCCURRENCE AS RESPONSES

Occurrence of words as responses essentially parallels occurrence of phonemes as responses. However, the distinction between auditory and visual modalities of the treatment of phonemes and graphemes is ignored. Data on words as spoken are too meager relative to data on words as written to warrant separate treatment.

Morphemic analysis is described, and then frequency counts both in general and developmentally. Discussion of theoretical analyses is deferred to treatment of recognition responses.

Morphemic analysis. Words consist of one or more morphemes. Morphemes are usually short sequences of phonemes, graphemes; they may be single phonemes, graphemes. Sequences of phonemes, of morphemes may form one syllable. They may form more than one syllable. Thus, morphemes and syllables are not identical.

Root morphemes are distinguished from affixes. An affix is a morpheme that is added before (prefix), inserted within (infix), or added after (suffix) one or more root morphemes. A stem is a morpheme or compound of morphemes that takes affixes. Affixes always occur with root morphemes: they are bound. Root morphemes typically can stand alone: they are free. However, some may be bound. In the word "sings," *sing* is a root morpheme that serves as the stem for the affix (suffix) *s*. Allomorphs are equivalent forms of the same root morphemes (*sing, sang, sung*) or the same affix (*s, es*). Morphemes that are part of words are segmental. Morphemes (e.g., intonation) not parts of words are suprasegmental.

Details of morphemic analysis, of morphology, are covered in various linguistic sources (Gleason, 1961, pp. 51–127, 220–38; Hall, 1964, pp. 130–67; Hockett, 1958, pp. 123–36; 147–82, 209–13, 240–45; Robins, pp. 201–14).

Frequency counts. Decisions and procedures of counts of word frequency are substantially those of counts of phoneme and grapheme frequency. Counts of words may precede and provide the corpus for counts of phonemes and graphemes. Recent studies by Howes (1966) and by Kučera and Francis (1967) illustrate the methodology of counts of word frequency.

Since the appearance of the 1944 T-L count (Thorndike & Lorge, 1944), it has been the primary source of word frequencies in written English. A brief history of word counts can be found in Harkin (1957) who lists counts in 16 different languages. Among more recent counts in other languages are those by Dabbs (1966) for newspaper Bengali, Landau (1959) for modern Arabic prose, and Van Berckel et al. (1965) for newspaper Dutch.

Horn (1926) reviews counts of writing vocabularies both "in" and "out" of school. Words obtained in children's free associations and drawn from diverse other counts of children's verbal output and of words in children's readers and spellers enter Buckingham and Dolch's (1936) list. Rinsland (1945) provides another list.

Semantic counts or counts of concepts in which different meanings of homonyms are available (Garvey, 1951; Lorge, 1949; Lorge & Thorndike, 1938; West, 1953). Inaccuracies occur in the latter three counts (Rosenzweig & McNeill, 1962).

For "present day American English," Kučera and Francis provide exact frequencies of occurrence of 50,406 "distinct graphic words (types)" that occur in the 1,014,232 words of 500 samples of about 2000 words each. The 500 samples consist of 6 to 80 samples from 15 different topical categories from "Press: Reportage" to "Humor." Words are presented in descending frequency and alphabetically.

Horn (1925) compiled a list of words that occurred with appreciable frequency in 270,000 words spoken by one- to six-year-old children. Other counts are based on smaller numbers of spoken words (French, Carter & Koenig, 1930; by H. Fairbanks in Johnson, 1944, pp. 19–38).

Word frequencies within a corpus of 250,000 words are reported by Howes (1966). A word count of spoken Russian is also available (Vakar, 1966).

Techniques of analysis and some data are covered by Herden (1956, 1960, 1962, 1966), Zipf (1935, pp. 20–48), Johnson (1944), Yule (1944), and Guiraud (1960).

Frequency counts developmentally. Criteria of and age of first word are considered, and then some data on frequency of occurrence of emitted words by young children. Theoretical analyses of word emission are noted.

A. *Age of first word.* Darley and Winitz (1961) review both general considerations of definition of the first word, and specific definitions. They conclude: "the use of operational definitions of the first word have been so consistently different from investigator to investigator as to be an important source of error in the reported age of appearance of the first word" (p. 283). Within this stricture, they summarize the results of 15 investigations of age of first word. The lower limit of reported onset of first words for normal children ranges from 4 to 9 months. Among their conclusions are: (a) little evidence of occurrence of first words earlier for girls than for boys, (b) occurrence of the first word of average children by 18 months, and (c) an inverse relationship between intelligence and age of first word.

B. *Emitted words.* The frequencies reported by Horn (1924) for one- to six-year-old children are neither specific for each word nor for ages separately. Such data, at least for English, apparently have not appeared subsequently. Weir (1962) does report word frequencies in the presleep monologues of her son (pp. 93–99). Various earlier assessments of vocabularies, largely of individual children, are reported or noted by Doran (1907), McCarthy (1930, pp. 14–16; 1946, pp. 504–5; 1954, pp. 526–27), Uhrbock (1936). Whipple (1915, pp. 316–17), and Whipple and Whipple (1909).

Vocabulary of use, as expressed by children in 50 utterances, has been analyzed by Templin (1957, pp. 114–17). Mean number of different words and mean total number of words increased through ages 3–8 years. No differences occurred between boys and girls but, at all ages, upper SES children used more different words than lower SES children.

Data on occurrence and modification of emitted verbal responses during infancy and early childhood are scarce. Some data are on nonverbal responses or on responses that are not yet words (Weisberg, 1963). Other data are on the verbal responses of children of kindergarten age and older (Salzinger et al., 1962), and hence of only indirect significance.

OCCURRENCE IN STIMULUS-RESPONSE RELATIONSHIPS

Syllables, words are recognized by producing them or selecting them. Forms and other nonverbal stimuli are recognized by producing their names or by selecting them. The responses of stimulus-response relationships of association typically are obtained under instructions that call for responses other than production of stimulus words or the names of nonverbal stimuli. Recognition responses may precede association responses. In general, the focus has been one or the other response, not both. Sequences of letters or words may be transformed into words or other words, respectively.

Relationships between recognition responses and association responses are discussed in greater detail by Goss (1963, pp. 128–33; 1969), and by Goss and Nodine (1965, pp. 113–14). Skinner (1957, pp. 55–69, 81–83) makes similar distinctions as echoic, textual, and tact behaviors. In Skinner's mand "the response has no specified relation to a prior stimulus" (p. 36).

Recognition. Recognition responses typically are obtained under conditions of stimulus presentation that are either considerably above threshold or "at" threshold. The stimuli may be verbal or nonverbal, are usually in auditory or visual modalities, and range from real to nonsensical, synthetic, ambiguous.

A. *Above threshold.* Selected data are noted, with particular interest in norms of frequencies of different responses to individual stimuli. Some theoretical analyses of immediate and more remote antecedents to those relationships are noted.

AI. *Data.* The stimuli may be syllables, words presented aurally or visually. They may be nonverbal, particularly presented visually.

AIa. *Verbal stimuli.* Suprathreshold aural presentation of syllables, words involves a high signal-to-noise ratio, extended or *S*-controlled signal duration, and no signal distortion. Required are *S*'s production (repetition, reproduction, imitation) of those syllables, words.

Middle-class and lower-class black and white children in Grade 3, 8 to 10 years old, listened to monosyllabic words spoken by educated and uneducated black and white speakers. Intelligibility was better with educated than noneducated speakers, with white than black speakers, for white than for black children, and for middle-class than for lower-class children (Eisenberg, Berlin, Dill & Frank, 1968). With these children's readings of monosyllabic words as stimuli for responses by teachers, intelligibility was better for speakers who were male, were white, and were middle class.

Data on pronunciation and mispronunciation of 40 synthetic words whose spelling patterns exemplify final *e*, initial and medial *c*, vowel digraphs, and miscellaneous combinations are reported by Calfee, Venezky, and Chapman (1969). The *S*s were children in third and sixth grades, high school and university students.

Data on pronunciation shade into data on articulation. Some of these data were noted previously under elicitation of phones, phonemes with little or no reference to stimuli (Templin, 1957). Relatively extensive data on misarticulation and on presumed antecedents and correlates of misarticulation are summarized elsewhere (Powers, 1957; Winitz, 1969, pp. 139–235).

Systematic norms for complete and incomplete recognition of words and for alternative pronunciations are uncommon and incomplete. Williams's Table 1, (1937, pp. 22–25) presents "erroneous speech sound substitutions of preschool children" of the Wellman et al. (1931) investigation. The stimuli were primarily pictures.

Words are also presented alone or in sentences for *S*s to read them. Thus, Cattell (1886*b*) obtained latencies of recognizing German and English words. Latency was shorter for short than for long words and for words in *S*'s native language than in the language foreign to him.

Typically, data on recognizing or reading words are obtained in tests of achievement in reading and spelling, and are presented as means of total scores or percentages of *S*s achieving some criterion (Bond & Dykstra, 1967; Downing, 1967, pp. 157–210; 267–91). However, Downing (pp. 164, 166–67, 242–43, 285–86) presents data on number and rank of but not kind of errors in reading words in traditional orthography after training on the initial teaching alphabet.

Woodworth surveys early experiments on "speed of reading" (1938, pp. 715–19). He also summarizes data on "cues in word perception" (pp. 737–45) as do Anderson and Dearborn (1952, pp. 176–202) and Tinker (1965) for both adults (pp. 9–24) and children (pp. 25–38). More recently, Smith (1969) found reading speed invariant over differences in case and size except for indiscriminability of relative size of lower-case letters which slowed reading speed.

Measurement of and patterns of occurrence of eye movements in reading are surveyed by Woodworth (1938, pp. 722–37), Anderson and Dearborn (1952, pp. 101–37), Woodworth and Schlosberg (1954, pp. 504–10), and Tinker (1965, pp. 53–112). Also pertinent are monographs by Buswell (1937) and by Morse, Ballantine, and Dixon (1951).

AIb. *Nonverbal stimuli.* Forms, colors, and forms and colors in combination may also be presented for recognition. Cattell (1886*b*) also reports latencies of naming pictures of objects from "anchor" to "watch." All objects were presumably named correctly.

In picture-vocabulary tests, three dimensional or, more often, two-dimensional forms that represent classes of objects are presented. These may be achromatic or chromatic. An example is identifying parts of the body in the 1960 revision of the Standford-Binet (Terman & Merrill, 1960). Normative frequencies of these responses are not provided.

The vocabulary test prepared by Williams and McFarland (1937) consists of two parallel sets of 42 pictures of objects, actions, and relations. Percentages of children who know these words range downward from 99.3 for "pocket" and "button" to 0.7 and 0.0 for "defeat" and "execute."

Other tests of picture vocabulary such as the "full-range" (Ammons & Ammons, 1948) and the Peabody (Dunn, 1965) require *S*s to select pictures of objects named by the examiner. Observed relationships are word-picture rather than picture-word.

In an investigation of "children's perceptions," Winch (1914) presented "the breakfast picture" for children from 3 to 13 years to say what they had seen in the picture. Examples of children's names of parts of the picture are presented.

Cattell (1886*b*) found shorter latencies for colors seen frequently (red, yellow, green, blue, black), than for those seen infrequently, (pink, violet, orange, gray, brown). Earlier investigations of the color naming of "primitive peoples" and of children are noted by Winch (1910). He presents tables of names of colors of worsted balls and of glass beads preferred by children of 3–4 years at seven different schools. Later, "confusions" of names for red, blue, green, and yellow stimuli are listed. "That color sensation is at first unitary, that it differentiates in the order red, blue, green, yellow, violet, orange" (p. 482) is Winch's suggestion.

"Rarely was anyone interested in what people meant by the color names they were using" (p. 328) is Chapanis's evaluation of earlier investigations of color naming. Using 1359 color chips as stimuli and 233 names as responses, his *S*s matched names with chips. His Figure 5 shows relationships between preferred names and strong Munsell hues.

Lenneberg (1967) describes three approaches to color naming and presents data on such color naming (pp. 340–43, 348–55). Anthropological data are in Berlin and Kay (1969).

Data on young children's names for colors can be found in Cook (1931) and Modreski and Goss (1969). Landar, Ervin, and Horowitz (1960) report the distribution of names for color chips used by Navaho. A study of Zuñi names for colors by Lenneberg and Roberts is described briefly by Brown and Lenneberg (1954, p. 461).

A special condition of color-naming is naming the color in which the name of another color is printed (e.g., name the blue color of the word "brown"), the Stroop (1935) test. In Klein's (1964) first experiment, nonsense syllables, rare English words, common English words unrelated to color names, words not color names that imply color names, words for colors different than the colors used, and words for colors the same as the colors used were combined with the colors red, green, yellow, and blue. The latter words and the colors were combined incongruently. Time to name the colors increased in order of listing from nonsense syllables to color names. In Klein's second experiment, a word-color sequence proved easier to read than a color-word sequence. Children in Grades 1, 2, 3, 5, and 8, and college freshmen served in Schiller's (1966) developmental partial replication and extension of Klein's first experiment.

On the "real-nonsensical, synthetic, ambiguous" dimension, the inkblots of the Rorschach and of various parallel and derived versions are presumably closer to the "latter" extreme than are pictures of picture-vocabulary tests. Instruction to adults may require Ss to "look at each card and tell the examiner what you see on each card, or everything that might be represented there" (Beck, Beck, Levitt, & Molish, 1961). Six-year-old children have been told to "look at these cards one at a time and tell me what they look like to you" (Ledwith, 1959).

Although not usually conceived as providing data on language, tables of names for wholes and parts of inkblot stimuli show relationships between names and form, form-color, and perhaps other variations in these nonverbal stimuli. Among investigators who supply some to complete data on frequencies of responses to wholes and parts of inkblots are Baughman (1959), Beck et al., (1950, 1961), Harrower-Erikson and Steiner (1945) for adults; Ames et al. (1954) for adults in old age; and Ames et al. (1952, 1959), Hertz (1961), and Ledwith (1959) for adolescents and children.

AII. *Theoretical analyses.* The theoretical analyses considered here are for verbal stimuli in aural and visual modalities, and for nonverbal stimuli in the visual modality.

AIIa. *Verbal: aural.* Some or all of the theoretical analyses of differentiation of production of phones, phonemes and of their elicitation by external stimuli (Miller & Dollard, 1941; Morris, 1946; Osgood, 1953; Skinner, 1957; Staats, 1968) noted previously cover differentiation of production of words and their elicitation by external stimuli. These analyses are no more satisfactory as theoretical analyses of relationships between spoken words and their recognition. The Winitz and Darley (1961) and Winitz (1968, 1969) contributions add little.

AIIb. *Verbal: visual.* Theoretical analyses of recognition responses to verbal stimuli presented visually are essentially equivalent to analyses of reading. For Anderson and Dearborn "reading is a controlled form of talking in which the words on the page are substituted for the usual stimuli for speech." The general theoretical approach is by the paradigm of classical or Pavlovian conditioning but without attendant concepts and principles. "Cues in the word perception of young children" (pp. 214–20) are considered but general concepts and principles of learning and perception are ignored.

Despite persisting interest in reading, more recent theoretical analyses are few. Typically, they are schematic and programmatic. Thus, Gibson (1965, 1969) divides reading skill into successive subskills of "learning to speak the language . . . learning to discriminate visually the letters of the alphabet . . . learning to read out in units of the spoken language what is directed by the graphic units . . . the skill of learning to read

in terms of higher order units . . . further superordinate skills" (1969, pp. 433–34).

Venezky, Calfee, and Chapman (1968) offer a slightly different list of skills. For Staats (1968), repertoire is substituted for skill. In the Hively (1966) "framework" noted previously, tasks rather than skills or repertoires are listed.

Important as these specifications of component skills or repertoires may be, they are preliminary to development of principles of learning to read. By and large such principles are applied in some detail only to relationships between "letters as stimuli" and their names (Staats, pp. 485–95). And the concepts and principles are more implied than stated explicitly.

Whatever their shortcomings, the Gibson and Staats analyses represent progress beyond listings of kinds of perception—visual, auditory, kinesthetic, multisensory—that presumably enter into learning to identify or recognize symbols (Russell & Fea, 1963, pp. 868–80).

Jenkins (1968), in a "summary" of a recent conference on reading, provides comments that characterize theoretical analyses of reading: "I don't think I learned what reading was. I don't think I learned how it ought to be characterized as a psychological process. I don't think I learned what the general scheme for the research ought to be" (p. 216). The plethora of models that appear in a subsequent compendium (Singer & Ruddell, 1970) may increase rather than decrease this confusion.

AIIc. *Nonverbal: visual.* Occurrence and learning of recognition responses to form, color, and form-color combinations might be placed within the general framework of discrimination learning and, particularly, visual discrimination learning (Gibson, 1969, pp. 19–117; Reese, 1968, pp. 229–330). For the most part, such theories are concerned with locomotion-manipulation of infra-human animals or with simple judgments, usually dichotomous, by humans. Therefore, these theories have only schematic or orientative pertinence.

Occurrence and learning of names for colors (Modreski & Goss, 1969) and for pictures can be accomodated within methods, data, and theory on paired-associates learning both 1 : 1 (Goss & Nodine, 1965; Nodine & Goss, 1969) and *n* : 1 (Goss, 1961a). However, data on acquisition of names for nonverbal stimuli presented visually are meager (Goss & Nodine, 1965, pp. 150–52).

Classical Gestalt theory (Wertheimer, 1923) offers little on occurrence and learning of relationships between forms and names. Gibson's (1969) apparent assumptions about detection of properties, patterns, and distinctive features are simply labels for "what is learned in perceptual learning" (pp. 77–91). She confuses principles and predictions from principles. Consequently, no principles are offered (pp. 95–117). Some factors that influence perceptual learning and their effects are noted but the focus is general rather than on occurrence and learning of names for forms.

For form-color stimuli like inkblots, beginning with Rorschach (1921), diverse theoretical analyses of, particularly, occurrence of responses have been advanced (Murstein, 1963, pp. 61–124; Shneidman, 1965, pp. 498–508).

Goss and Brownell (1957) analyze the occurrence and learning of relationships between form-color stimuli and names in terms of concepts and principles of general theories of learning. The analysis provides both for primary or nonmediated and for mediated generalization and discrimination. In less detail, Miller (1959, p. 220) notes implication of his conflict theory of displacement for responses to stimuli of projective tests. Moylan (1959) and Schrader and Goss (1964) explore possible factors in generalization of names for inkblot stimuli.

Various theories of perception that might contribute to an understanding of response to form-color stimuli like inkblots are reviewed by Zubin, Eron, and Schumer (1965, pp. 50–165).

B. *"At" threshold.*[5] Early data on recognition of letter sequences and words presented "at" threshold complement data noted previously on absolute discrimination or identification of letters. Thus, Cattell (1886a), before reporting data on recognition of letters, presents data on times at which individual observors identified correctly "half of" capital and small Latin and German letters, short and long English and German words.

Other experiments on recognition of letter sequences, words, and word sequences, presented tachistoscopically at relatively short durations, are noted by Woodworth (1938, pp. 737–45), Anderson and Dearborn (1952, pp. 176–202), and Tinker (1965, pp. 9–38). The general intent of most of these experiments was more precise specification of stimulus bases of S's recognition of words, of reading.

In contrast, many experiments on word recognition from the late 1940s have their ultimate origin in data described by and in the accompanying analysis of those data by Bruner and Postman (1947). An observed inverted-U relationship between associative reaction time and recognition time for 18 words is attributed to a negatively accelerated defense process combined additively with a skewed, inverted-U sensitization process. Familiarity is also invoked, but is regarded as unable to "account in entirety for the correlation between speed of association and speed of recognition" (p. 75). However, as experiments on "perceptual defense" have become more analytical, structure, location, sequence and other features of letters-words have reappeared as important variables, (Harcum, 1967, 1968; Hershenson, 1969). Moreover, processes such as perceptual defense have been substantially displaced by less dramatic perceptual and memory processes (Haber, 1969b, p. 1).

Considered briefly are methods of experiments on word recognition, data on effects of important classes of variables, and then some theories of recognition of words and forms. Data on recognition of words presented aurally, and on recognition of forms, are too scarce to warrant separation from data on words presented visually. Unless noted otherwise, the data considered are for words presented visually.

BI. *Method.* The common feature of experiments on recognition of words and forms is presentation of stimuli under conditions that assure recognition approximately "at" threshold. In visual presentation these conditions include one or more of the following: (a) relatively short duration of stimuli, sometimes from 4 or 5 msec. upward; (b) low illumination of stimuli or low contrast between stimuli and ground; (c) considerable distance between stimuli and S; and (d) presentation of homogeneous or patterned stimuli imposed simultaneously, before, or after target stimuli. The former three, W. P. Brown (1961, p. 45) classifies as negative "obscuration"; the latter as positive "obscuration." In addition, parts of words or forms might be deleted.

In aural presentation, signal-to-noise ratio may be varied

[5] Nancy J. Cobb provided an orienting bibliography of experiments on word recognition with classifications of their nature and outcome.

with "no" noise as a special case. Words may be altered by peak or center clipping of the signal, by changes in its fundamental frequency, and by delayed feedback.

W. P. Brown summarizes different specific procedures of combining stimuli, levels of the variable used to achieve recognition "at" threshold, and trials (p. 6). He also notes some among "criteria for correct recognition and recognition threshold [including] informational measures of recognition" (pp. 6–8). Signal-detection procedures and outcomes might also be used (Dandeliker & Dorfman, 1969; Dorfman, 1967; Price, 1966).

BII. *Data.* W. P. Brown also provides a useful, reasonably comprehensive summary of effects of various classes of variables on word and form recognition as suggested by experiments reported from 1947 through most of 1959. He divides the variables into "nonemotional influences" (pp. 9–20), and into emotional and value systems or emotional variables (pp. 21–61).

As bases for describing both prior and subsequent experiments and their results, Brown's categories have several shortcomings. Perhaps the most important of these is separation of familiarity and meaningfulness of stimuli from their emotionality. Also, frustration and ego-involvement are classified as nonemotional, and different kinds of "set" as "stimulus-tied."

The first distinction of the classification used here is between specific and less specific stimuli, responses, and stimulus-response relationships. The former are relatively localized or discrete in space-time; the latter are less localized and, particularly, persist through time. Specific stimuli and responses are distinguished with stimulus-response relationships noted within each category.

BIIa. *Specific stimuli, responses.* Specific stimuli are divided into target (criterion, reference) stimuli, and contextual (attendent, surrounding, ground) stimuli. Data for both classes of stimuli are considered, and then selected comparisons of specific responses.

BIIa1. *Target stimuli.* Effects of immediate or ahistorical parameters of target stimuli, and then of experiential or historical parameters are considered. Of concern among ahistorical parameters are emotionality, meaningfulness, and other attributes of verbal stimuli in relationships to different kinds of responses, and then physical attributes and dimensions of stimuli.

BIIa1a. *Emotionality.* Emotionality of stimuli is specified by attributes of relationships between the stimuli and such criterion responses as associations. For words matched for structure and frequency of occurrence, emotionality and length of associative reaction time are equated directly (Minard, 1965). Words of high and low or at different levels of emotionality, thus defined, may be selected across groups of Ss or for individual Ss (Inglis, 1961, pp. 270–73). Emotionality may also be defined by ratings along pleasant-unpleasant or good-bad scales, and by other criterion responses (Goss & Nodine, 1965, pp. 15, 46–48, 71–72).

Once words at two or more levels of emotionality are selected, response bias in recognition of these words may be determined by various measures of which the eight described by Minard (1965, pp. 78–82) are prototypical. With no significant difference in response bias for emotion-arousing and neutral words, Minard reports more correct recognitions of neutral than of emotion-arousing words by males, and the converse by females. For males, Sales and Haber (1968) also report greater clarity of frequent and very rare neutral words than of taboo words matched in length.

Until variables are discovered that account for the sex difference in direction, any generalizations about relationships between word recognition and emotionality are limited. Differences in method ignored, other findings for females suggest that direction of differences in probabilities of occurrence of neutral and taboo words both to blank intervals (response bias) and to word stimuli depends on a priori probability of a taboo word (Dorfman, 1967).

BIIa1b. *Meaningfulness and related attributes.* Diverse definitions of meaningfulness of stimuli are described subsequently under associations. In general, relatively high correlations obtain among different measures so that conclusions about relationships between recognition of stimuli and their meaningfulness should hold across measures.

Relatively early data suggest that recognition of CVCs does not vary with their meaningfulness (Goss & Nodine, 1965, p. 49). However, with frequency of words whose first three letters form a CVC as covariate, recognition threshold and Glaze association value were related inversely (Rodewald, 1968).

Recognition threshold and meaningfulness of words are apparently related inversely (Goss & Nodine, 1965, p. 49). More recently, with auditory presentation of pairs of words of high and low meaningfulness, Spreen, Borkowski, and Benton (1967) obtained more correct recognitions of words of high than of low meaningfulness. Similar findings are reported by Spreen, Borkowski, and Gordon (1966) for normal and mentally defective adults.

Data that suggest a direct relationship between recognition accuracy and pronounceability of verbal stimuli presented visually cannot be so interpreted unequivocally (Goss & Nodine, 1965, pp. 50–51; Lappin & Lowe, 1969; F. Smith, 1969). Data for aural presentation are also equivocal (Gibson, Pick, Osser & Hammond, 1962; Spreen et al., 1967).

Recognition accuracy apparently varies directly with familiarity as specified by various measures (Smith, 1967) and with degree of wordness or approximation to English (Hershenson, 1969; Reicher, 1969). Concreteness of words may not influence recognition accuracy with visual presentation (Winnick & Kressel, 1965) but may have direct influence with aural presentation (Spreen et al., 1966, 1967). Neutral words may be recognized better than affiliation words particularly by Ss low on production of affiliation words (Kaplan & Grier, 1968).

Exceptions to these generalizations exist. Moreover, some or all may be reducible to some common factor such as printed and spoken frequencies of component letters, bigrams, trigrams.

BIIa1c. *Physical attributes and dimensions.* Physical attributes and dimensions of stimuli often enter as dependent rather than independent variables. Thus, duration of stimuli presented visually, and amplitude of signals in signal-to-noise ratios, typically appear as dependent values of thresholds. They might be, and occasionally have been, treated as independent variables with percentage of correct recognitions or related measures as dependent variables (Miller, Heise, & Lichten, 1951; White, 1969a).

Other physical attributes such as size, face, and case of type have been of little interest. Kind of stimuli and their structural features have been of some interest. Thus, Hamid (1969) reports that symmetrical words and forms are recognized better than asymetrical words and forms. Symmetrical words excepted, descending structures are recognized better than ascending structures. For letter position independent of S's fixation,

Hershenson (1969) obtained an interaction of redundancy and position.

Physical attributes of stimuli such as letter position, are often specified in relation to S's visual field and fixation. Thus, Harcum (1966) presented 128 eight-letter English words equally often right or left of fixation under conditions of normal sequence and orientation of letters (BC), reversal of orientation and sequence (BR), reversal of sequence and normal orientation (SR), and normal sequence and reversal of orientation (LR). For positions left of fixation, errors were in the order BC < SR < BR = LR. For positions right of fixation, errors were in the same order but, for the same conditions, slightly less frequent. In general, the position curves were inverted-Us that differed among conditions in symmetry.

Symmetry or asymmetry of letters in normal and reversed order, position of letters in relation to point of fixation, and monocular or binocular viewing conditions combine, in ways still not completely determined, to influence recognition of letters in word and nonword sequences (Crovitz & Schiffman, 1965; Harcum, 1968; White, 1969a, b). Order-of-report may be an additional factor (White, 1969b).

BIIa1d. *Historical parameters.* Among historical parameters, the class of variables of greatest concern has been frequency of occurrence of words and of nonword letter sequences both prior to and within laboratory exposure. Recency of exposure, reward, and other historical parameters have been of some, but infrequent and sporadic concern; they are ignored here.

Frequency of occurrence preexperimentally is specified by various of the counts of frequencies of letters, letter sequences, and words mentioned earlier. Of these, the T-L counts, usually the general count or the magazine count, have been the most common estimates.

In general, recognition of words presented visually or aurally increases directly with counted frequency of words (Brown, 1961; Rosenzweig & Postman, 1958). However, recognition is jointly determined by frequency and length. With visual presentation, whether by method of limits or method of random series, the relationship between recognition and frequency becomes progressively steeper with increasing length. Poorest recognition is of infrequent, long words (McGinnies, Comer, & Lacey, 1952; Postman & Adis-Castro, 1957). With auditory presentation, the relationship between recognition and frequency became progressively steeper with decreasing length. Poorest recognition is of infrequent, short words (Howes, 1957).

More recent experiments on relationships between recognition and frequency attempt to specify the basis of these relationships more precisely. Thus, for words of low frequency or of low homogeneity of digram frequency, recognition and digram frequency are related directly (Biederman, 1966). In contrast, Broadbent and Gregory (1968) obtained an inverse relationship between recognition and digram frequency of low-frequency words.

Over five exposures in the experimental situation, Hershenson (1969) obtained improvement in recognition both of English words and of letter sequences of 0-, 1-, 2-, 3-order approximation to English words. However, frequency of occurrence prior to exposure has been of greater concern than frequency of exposure for recognition.

In the often-cited Goldiamond and Hawkins's (1958) experiment, two each of 10 CVCs of low association value were exposed 1, 2, 5, 10, or 25 times. With a "mottled gray section from Rorschach Plate I" instead of CVCs as the stimulus, average response frequency and percent of words "recognized" increased linearly with frequency of training. "Emission" of recognition responses, "response bias," varied directly with frequency of prior exposure. Because the CVCs were not presented, too, this experiment is a rare instance of one with a "control" condition but no "experimental" condition.

An experimental condition was present in Zajonc and Nieuwenhuyse's (1964) comparison of Dutch university students' recognition of Turkish words first presented 1, 2, 5, 10 and 25 times and then presented for recognition with the words present and with a blank interval. For a criterion of up through the "first response congruent with the word actually presented" (p. 278), words were recognized better than blanks across all five training frequencies. However, the curves were converging at 25 training exposures. Response bias influences recognition, presence of words also influences recognition.

Postman and Rosenzweig (1958) selected five pairs of trigrams whose members were of high or of low frequency of occurrence as syllables and as trigrams. These and filler stimuli were presented visually or aurally 0, 1, 2, 5, or 15 times. For four combinations of aural or visual training and aural or visual presentation for recognition, recognition of trigrams improved with frequency of prior exposures.

Frequency of words has also been manipulated experimentally by prior presentation as stimulus or response members of paired associates (Winnick & Nachbar, 1967). In Experiment I, the best recognition obtained for words of high or low T-L frequency that had been response members of paired associates.

In Experiment II, the words were pairs of adjectives of high or low rated similarity. Similarity had negligible influence. In Experiment III, amount of paired-associate learning was varied. Regardless of degree of learning, words that were stimulus members of response members were recognized better than control words. Recognition of words that had been response members was better than recognition of words that had been stimulus members at 100%, but not at 50% and 150% degree of learning.

BIIa2. *Contextual stimuli.* Contextual stimuli enter recognition in several ways. One way is one or more other stimuli that occur prior to or along with the target stimulus but under suprathreshold conditions. Another way is presentation of target words within all or part of a sentence, and still another way is masking stimuli.

BIIa2a. *Other stimuli; within sentences.* Rouse and Verinis (1963) presented pairs of words one of which appeared and was fixated before the second appeared at increasing durations. In Experiment I, second or target members of pairs were forward associates, backward associates, and nonassociates of the first or priming members. In Experiment II, backward associates were replaced by low-strength forward associates. Forward associates of high and low strength and backward associates were recognized better than nonassociates. Samuels (1969) added interfering associations and prior familiarization training. Recognition of target words decreased for familiarized forward associations, forward associations, familiarized target words alone, familiarized interfering associations, nonassociates with familiarized target words, and unfamiliarized target words alone.

Children in Grades 4, 8, and 12 saw primer-target pairs that represented forward (F), forward-backward (F-B), or no association (No) strength (Gallagher & Palermo, 1967). Recognition thresholds increased in the order FB < F < No, FB = F < No, and FB = F < No for children in Grades 4, 8, and 12 respectively.

Miller, Heise, and Lichten (1951) obtained better recognition of target words in sentences than alone. Eight-letter, three-syllable nouns presented in context of 0, 2, 4, or 8 words at exposure durations of 0, 20, 40, 60, 80, 100, 120, 140 msec. were recognized better as both context and exposure increased (Tulving, Mandler, & Baumal, 1964).

BIIa2b. *Masking.* Homogeneous or patterned stimuli may be imposed simultaneously with target stimuli. Metacontrast refers to occurrence of a masking stimulus after or before and after target stimuli; paracontrast refers to its occurrence before target stimuli (Kahneman, 1968). Other conventions of terminology are described by Kahneman, who proceeds to discuss "measurement of masking effects," "detection of target flashes under masking," "identification of forms under masking," and "theory." Within each of these general topics are subtopics that together constitute a comprehensive current assessment of method, data, and theory on visual masking. Accordingly, no further development is essayed here.

BIIa3. *Responses.* Stimulus words or forms may be without or with accompanying words that identify those stimuli. When presented without accompanying words or forms, for Ss to produce recognition responses, they may have from no to complete initial knowledge of sets of words necessary to identify the stimuli. When presented with accompanying words for Ss to select recognition responses, all or only parts of those words may appear, and these words may identify only some or all of the stimuli. Words that do not identify the stimuli may be introduced as distractors. Beyond these variations in verbal responses, responses of different topography and form may be observed and recorded.

Miller, Heise, and Lichten (1951) also prepared lists of 2, 4, 8, 16, 32, and 256 monosyllabic words known to Ss. These words and words not known to Ss were run under S/N ratios from −18 to +6. Percent words correct decreased with length of list, with only half of the words not known to Ss recognized correctly at S/N = +6.

Although prior investigations exist, Lazarus and McCleary (1951) initiated a period of comparison and interpretation of recognition by verbal responses, and by responses of different topography and form, notably the GSR. The final determination involved GSRs to five-letter nonsense syllables that had or had not been previously paired with shock and were or were not recognized correctly. For syllables not recognized correctly, GSRs in micromhos were greater for syllables that had been than for those that had not been accompanied by shock. The authors conclude: "In so far as autonomic activity can be regarded as a form of behavior, we believe that we may have an experimental instance of such an unconscious process" (p. 121).

Subsequently, Eriksen (1956) shows that apparent discrimination by GSR without "verbal awareness" might be an artifact of partial correlation involving the GSR and stimulus with the verbal recognition constant. Introduced, too, was lack of equivalence between continuous GSR and essentially discrete verbal responses. More generally, after reviewing data on "discrimination without awareness" obtained in various situations under diverse conditions, Eriksen (1960) asserts: "At present there is no convincing evidence that the human organism can discriminate or differentially respond to external stimuli that are at intensity level too low to elicit a discriminated verbal report" (p. 298).

BIIb. *Less specific stimuli, responses.* Among less specific stimuli, responses, stimulus-response relationships are instructional, motivational, situational, *E*, and *S* (individual-difference) variables. Set variables, either *E*-induced or *S*-induced, crosscut these variables.

None of these classes of variables has received the sustained attention accorded several of the classes of target variables. Often, too, in multi-variable experiments, these variables are secondary to target variables.

BIIb1. *Instructional.* Postman, Bronson, and Gropper (1953) presented neutral and taboo words to an uninformed group and to informed groups that only knew of the presence of taboo words (informed) or, in addition, were discouraged from (facilitate) witholding or encouraged to (inhibit) withold those words. Regardless of instructions, sex of *E*, and sex of *S*, taboo words were recognized better than neutral words. Recognition was in the order uninformed < inhibit < informed < facilitate for taboo words, and uninformed < informed = inhibit < facilitate for neutral words. However, Lacy, Lewinger, and Adamson (1953) and Cowen and Cowen (1953) describe interactions of information-foreknowledge and neutral-taboo or threat words that preclude simple generalizations about effects of knowledge on recognition.

BIIb2. *Motivational.* Among conventional motivational variables of hunger and thirst, Lazarus, Yousem, and Arenberg (1953) report better recognition of pictures of nonfood than of food objects at all levels of food deprivation.

Wispé and Drambarean's (1953) "need" words were not recognized as well as neutral words at 0 hours of food-water deprivation but were recognized better at 24 hours. However, Taylor (1956) presented neutral and both food and water need-related words to satiated and deprived *S*s, who were or were not informed about the need-related words. Satiation-deprivation did not influence recognition.

Bitterman and Kniffen (1953) found no effects of anxiety on recognition of taboo or of neutral words. Additional findings on anxiety and other affective processes that might be regarded as motivational are noted by Jenkin (1957), Inglis (1961), and Eriksen (1963).

BIIb3. *Situational, E, S.* Situational variables, independent of other classes of variables, have been essentially of no interest. Experimenter variables have been of interest primarily in combination with *S* variables. The typical design is a difference in stimuli, e.g., in their emotionality, combined with an *E* difference and an *S* difference. Thus, Whittaker, Gilchrist, and Fischer (1952) had a white and a Negro female *E* present positively valued, negatively valued, Negro-derogatory, and neutral words to groups of high anti-Negro whites, low anti-Negro whites, and Negroes. Existences of an interaction of *E*s, words, groups is reported, but without description. Postman, Bronson, and Gropper (1953), and also Cowen and Beier (1954), combined sex of *E* and sex of *S*. Neither alone nor in interaction did sex influence recognition.

Male-female differences in perceptual defense with response bias controlled were noted earlier (Minard, 1965). Messe, Chisena, and Shipley (1968) report better recognition of neutral words of

AA T-L frequency by males than by females both across and for individual words. But sex differences do not always occur (Cowen & Beier; Postman Bronson & Gropper).

Gibson, Osser, and Pick (1963) report some improvement in recognition with increasing age-grade in the early school years; Thomas (1968) found no difference. Across Grades 4, 8, and 12, at least for undirectional and nonassociated relationships between primer and target stimuli, recognition improves with age-grade (Gallagher & Palermo, 1967).

With a Negro female *E* and Negro-derogatory words, Whittaker, Gilchrist, and Fischer (1952) found no differences in recognition among white high anti-Negro, white low anti-Negro and Negro groups. Gilchrist, Ludeman and Lysak (1954) found no relationship between antisemitism and recognition of positively valued, neutral, and negatively valued words with "ink" and "Jew" as context words.

Often, variations in words recognition have been attributed to differences among *S*s in tendency to suppress or repress anxiety-arousing events. Thus, Hutt and Anderson (1967) selected the 20 lowest-(sensitizers) and 20 highest-(repressors) scoring students on the Byrne Repression-Sensitization scale. For the neutral condition, repressors had a slightly lower threshold than sensitizers. For the taboo condition, repressors had a significantly higher threshold than sensitizers. The mechanism suggested was contraction of pupils, and hence less light to the retina, in response to emotional stimuli. Because of differences in conditions for determining relationships between change in pupil size and emotionality of words, as well as inconsistent findings on such relationships (Paivio & Simpson, 1966; Peavler & McLaughlin, 1967; Polt & Hess, 1968), such explanation is premature.

Normals and retardates are compared by Spreen, Borkowski, and Gordon (1966). Similar zero-order and first-order partial correlations involving recognition of and meaningfulness, concreteness, and specificity held at both levels of intelligence. At 3-sec. exposure, a 2×2 array of letters was recognized better in the order retardates < equal MA normals < equal CA normals; at .01 sec. exposure, the groups did not differ (Winters & Gerjuoy, 1969).

BIII. *Theories.* Bruner and Postman (1947) emphasized defense and sensitization processes over familiarity. With demonstrations of consistent and pronounced effects of frequency, the issue was transformed into demonstration of perceptual defense (and, perhaps, sensitization) over and above variations in recognition not attributable to frequency and "error." Findings such as those by Minard (1965) and Zajonc and Nieuwenhuyse (1964) suggest that, most immediately, recognition is a joint function of strength of relationships between target stimuli and recognition responses and of relationships between these, and perhaps other stimuli, and a response or responses of inhibiting, suppressing, repressing, witholding overt recognition responses. All or parts of target stimuli may be immediate cues (Kempler & Weiner, 1963). Both sets of stimulus-response relationships may be functions of the same or substantially the same classes of observed and manipulated variables. Among these variables, frequency variables are usually potent.

Three kinds of theory often regarded as at least phenotypically different are considered. They are analyses by concepts and principles of changes in strengths of stimulus-response relationships, "information processing" models or analyses, and a variation on a signal-detection model or theory.

BIIIa. *Stimulus-response.* Eriksen's (1956, 1958, 1963) analyses and, more systematically, J. S. Brown's (1961, pp. 315–23) "competing response theory of perceptual defense" illustrate stimulus-response theories. Brown makes four assumptions about strength and summation of positive and negative tendencies to shocked or vulgar words (pp. 315–16). His illustrative deduction is "overt responses to 'dirty' words should have longer latency than responses to neutral words even when all are presented clearly" (p. 316).

Added are two assumptions about strength of positive and of negative tendencies as a function of exposure time (S/N ratio, etc.). With these, Brown deduces a longer exposure of a "very vulgar" word than of a "moderately vulgar" word (pp. 317–19). He comments: "Of especial significance, here, is the fact that neither emotion, nor drive, nor perceptual defense, nor differential familiarity has been invoked as a necessary adjunct to the deduction" (pp. 318–19).

Brown's assumptions concern largely ahistorical variables. Implicit in his analysis are classes of historical variables such as frequency and deprivation. Both frequency and deprivation variables presumably influence rate-slope of the positive and negative tendencies. Earlier, Brown presented a general treatment of possible manners of combination of frequency and deprivation variables through their "habit" and "drive" consequences (pp. 97–137). N. E. Miller (1959, pp. 204–20) provides another analysis. Response bias does not enter Brown's formulation explicitly, but can be accomodated as can accounts of perception based on "partial cues" (Kempler & Weiner, 1963; Weiner & Schiller, 1960).

BIIIb. *Information processing.* Hershenson's (1969) "ranch" model (1969) involves a sequence of stimulus, perceptual system, percept or visual image, memory system, response system, response. The special subclass of responses labelled "reports" are regarded as "isomorphic with the visual image" (p. 333). In the "split-level" model a sequence of stimulus, perceptual system, "splits" to percept or visual image and to memory system. Percept or visual image leads to "report" or memory system. Memory system leads back to perceptual system or to response system, response.

Unfortunately these and similar models and analyses (e.g., Haber, 1969) lack explicit ties to antecedent variables, precise criteria of specification of postulated component "systems" or operations, and quantification that permits even modest a priori prediction of order of experimental conditions. In a mathematically rigorous analysis of phenomena of metacontrast (Weisstein, 1968), phenomena presumably important to an information-processing analysis (Haber, 1969b), the "language" of information processing is irrelevant.

BIIIc. *Signal detection.* From patterns of high- and low-frequency errors to high- and low-frequency stimuli, and ratios of correct responses to errors, Broadbent (1967) concludes that a signal-detection model, as elaborated to accommodate "multiple choice situations with varying biases (pp. 7–10) . . . has been operative in all experiments on word frequency" (p. 13). Implied is "that the effect is due to a prior bias in favor of common words, which combines with sensory evidence favoring the objectively correct word" (p. 13).

However, Catlin (1969) shows that a sophisticated-guessing model also predicts independence between frequency of the stimulus word and the ratio of high-frequency errors to low-frequency errors. Also, this model accounts for the "structure of errors" while Broadbent's "signal detection" model does not (p. 506).

The actual systematic variables of Morton's (1969) "logogen" model are summarized in Table 1 (p. 168). Classes of stimuli that differ in frequency are identified and each (member of a) class $(1, \ldots i, \ldots n)$ is assigned four parameters: V_i, for threshold or effects of context; α_i for properties of the stimulus such as duration, contrast, S/N; M for number of stimuli in the class; and T_i, total of strengths. From one ratio, $\alpha_i V_i / T_i$ and another ratio, $(M-1)V_i/T_i$ he derives and tests a linear relationship between probability of correct recognition of stimulus i within a frequency class and probability of an incorrect recognition within that frequency class.

Association. Word association involves responses to verbal and nonverbal stimuli other than recognition of those stimuli. Goss and Nodine (1965, p. 17) classify situations that provide such relationships in terms of whether or not content of associations is considered, whether responses are produced or selected from among those provided by E, and whether single or multiple responses are required. In investigations of word association, content is considered. In investigations of meaningfulness and various other attributes of stimuli, content is usually ignored.

A. *Word association.*[6] Word associations may be to verbal or nonverbal stimuli. Among sources on early investigations of word association are Whipple (1915, pp. 43–119) and Jung (1918). Woodworth (1938, pp. 340–67) and Woodworth and Schlosberg (1954, pp. 43–72) provide convenient summaries of methods used and of some data obtained in both those early and subsequent investigations.

Data on children's word associations are reviewed by Palermo (1963). Jung (1965) covers experimental investigations of word association. Philosophical antecedents to and then investigations of word association are reviewed by Deese (1965) and also by Creelman (1965), the latter within a more general treatment of meaning. Pollio (1968) examines the nature and assessment of associative structure. Word associations of bilinguals are discussed by Riegel (1968).[7]

Osgood, Suci, and Tannenbaum (1957) describe the rationale for, the form of, and data on the special word association test they call the semantic differential (SD). Snider and Osgood's (1969) compendium of articles illustrates subsequent refinements in methods and findings with the SD.

Investigations with the SD largely excepted, Cramer (1968a) contributes a comprehensive review of investigations of word association reported between 1950 and 1965 in journals published in the United States. Exclusive of SD investigations, her account

---

[6] A survey of investigations of word association for 1966–1968 by Barry M. Loigman aided in development of the present description.

[7] Vocabulary tests or subtests of general tests of intelligence and of tests of school achievement can be considered word-association situations. Results with such tests are not considered here as, typically, they do not provide information about hierarchies of responses to individual stimuli, are not analyzed for relationships among different measures of association, or both. The Dale and Eicholz (1960) monograph is a useful exception to the former stricture. Listed are words whose meanings were selected correctly by 50% or more of children in Grades 4, 6, 8, 10, and 12.

Vocabulary development has been investigated extensively (Smith, 1941; McCarthy, 1946, 1954; Templin, 1957). Seashore and Eckerson (1940) discuss definition and sampling of words. A comprehensive bibliography of investigations of vocabulary up to about 1963 is available in Dale and Razik (1963).

obviates more than general consideration of contributions prior to 1966.

AI. *Method.* In her "Prologue," Cramer (1968a) discusses formats and methods of investigation of word association (pp. 10–21). She also treats quantitative, qualitative, and physiological response measures (pp. 25–30), and "measures of associative response overlap" (pp. 30–35). More explicit examples of computation of measures of associative overlap are provided by Deese (1962), Marshall and Cofer (1963), Goss and Nodine (1965, pp. 127–31), and Pollio (1968).

Four subsequent developments in method for produced associations are significant: additional techniques for specifying associative overlap; description of and rationale for word frequency distributions; optimization of elicitors; and identification of associative predictors.

Kiss (1968) describes representation of associative overlap or relationships between words by graph theory. Graph theory also enters Rappaport's (1967) tree-construction method.

Deese (1962, 1965) typically treats overlap among associates of relatively small sets of stimuli. Rotberg (1968) extends this data-base by using associates of those words as stimuli for further associates. For multiple associations, Szalay and Brent (1967) present an Index of Associative Affinity that reflects differences in position of responses within a sequence. Analyses of response to and with prepositions (Clark, 1968) illustrate use of cluster analysis (Johnson, 1967), analysis of proximities (Shepard, 1962), and multidimensional scaling (Kruskal, 1964).

Description of frequency distributions of word associations is often by frequency or percentage of occurrence of the most frequent response or primary, by number of different responses, or by both number of different responses and their relative frequency as reflected in the uncertainty statistic, H or U. Another approach—mentioned earlier for frequency distributions of phonemes and graphemes—is fitting some distribution function to observed frequencies. Thus, Carroll (1969) describes properties of and fit of two models of the asymptotic lognormal distribution.

On occasion, Es may wish to optimize elicitors of responses. Glanzer and Murphy (1968) describe and test a technique of identifications of single and multiple elicitors of responses. Rosenberg and Cohen (1966) develop theory and method and then provide data on speaker's production of a word to serve as a cue for listener's choice of one of two referents, and also on listener's use of the word to choose the referent.

Bilodeau and Howell (1968) develop eight predictors of free and simulated recall based on matrices of continued associations.

For the SD, Heise (1969) provides a comprehensive review of "methodological issues." These include the SD metric, sources of rating bias, structure of ratings, and ad hoc factor analysis.

AII. *Data.* Investigations of word associations are usually normative or correlational-experimental. The focus of the former is frequency distributions (repertoires, hierarchies) of associations to members of sets of words, individually or collectively, at some particular time, under fixed, usually standard conditions. The focus of the latter is relationship with or effects of ahistorical variables.

AIIa. *Normative.* Cramer's (1968a) bibliography lists a large number of investigations that provide norms for associations to different sets of different kinds of stimuli. Results of 20 normative investigations are summarized by Shapiro and Palermo (1968).

Among recent normative investigations, Entwisle's (1966) is the most extensive. It is also a good example of methodology in selection of stimuli, and in obtaining and analyzing word associations. For each of 96 words, she analyzes associations of males and females in kindergarten, in Grades 1, 3, and 5, and of adult age.

For 100 nouns, adjectives, adverbs, verbs, pronouns, and prepositions, Palermo and Jenkins (1966) provide norms for oral associations of male and female children in Grades 1, 2, 3, 4. Norms for associations to the Kent-Rosanoff (K-R) words by mentally retarded children who are in the public schools are also available (Hom & Prehm, 1967).

Among other sets of norms are those for 30 animal terms (Henley, 1969), 36 names for genera and species of bacteria (Loigman & Goss, 1969), 18 physical concepts (P. E. Johnson, 1964), and 40 quantifiers (Howe, 1966).

Noble's (1952) 96 word and nonword dissyllables were presented in print and aurally for undergraduates to write their associations (Schulz & Hopkins, 1968). Multiple associations to selected K-R words have been obtained and analyzed by Duncan and Wood (1966).

"For 1000 most frequent English words," Heise (1965) provides 50 values or profiles.

AIIb. *Correlational-experimental.* Data on word association are also organized within the distinction between specific and less specific stimuli, responses, and stimulus-response relationships. The former variables include Cramer's "task and environmental variables," "examples and instruction" and "stress" excluded. The latter variables subsume the excluded variables and Cramer's "subject variables."

AIIb1. *Specific stimuli, responses.* Data on target and contextual stimuli are examined in some detail. Response considerations are simply illustrated.

AIIb1a. *Target stimuli.* Cramer's (1968a) first class of task and environmental variables is "the stimulus word"; this corresponds to ahistorical parameters of target stimuli. She reviews findings on "stimulus affectivity" (pp. 56–63), "part of speech of a stimulus" (pp. 67–70), "semantic level of stimulus" (pp. 73–76), and "the stimulus defined in terms of the responses evoked" (pp. 77–80).

AIIb1a1. *Emotionality.* Emotionality of stimuli has been defined by attributes of word associations (Inglis, 1961; Minard, 1965). Emotionality has also been defined by values or ratings along scales such as good–bad. Ratings close to or at extremes of a scale, highly polarized ratings, define an emotional stimulus.

For emotionality defined by these and other criteria, independently of particular criterion measures of word association, Cramer (1968a) generalizes that direct relationships hold between emotionality of words and reaction time, response heterogeneity, association disturbances, number of emotional responses, psychophysiological disturbances, response on request, and errors in a modified reproduction test (p. 53). An inverse relationship holds between emotionality and response availability (meaningfulness). Results generally consistent with some of these generalizations are reported by Storms, Broen, and Levin (1967) for schizophrenics, neurotics, and normals.

Cramer also examines effects of different "types of affective stimuli" (pp. 47–50). These include food-related, water-related, and neutral words; hostile and neutral words; succourant, homosexual, and aggressive stimuli; and stimuli from various conflict areas.

AIIb1a2. *Meaningfulness and other attributes.* Among Cramer's generalizations on meaningfulness (pp. 71–81), familiarity including counted frequency (pp. 56–63), and concreteness (pp. 73–76), not always as she has phrased them, are: (a) an inverse relationship between meaningfulness and different associations (p. 80); (b) familarity and frequency of the primary and familiarity and number of different responses in direct and inverse relationships, respectively (p. 63); and (c) a direct relationship between degree of concreteness and number of continued or continuous associations (pp. 75, 77).

Data that generally agree with and extend these relationships are reported by Loigman and Goss (1969), Schönpflug and Vetter (1969), Schulz and Hopkins (1968), and Howe (1969).

Zippel (1967) computed two different measures of polarity of SD ratings (D_4, D^2) and a measure of agreement (A) of ratings of 84 words and nonwords of different structure. Correlations of .67, .76, and −.14 obtained between Noble's (1952) values of meaningfulness and D_4, D^2, and, A respectively.

AIIb1a3. *Grammatical function.* Grammatical function of words—either assigned to isolated words on the basis of their usual function or based on position within sentences—influences associative reaction time, number of different responses, strength of primary and of the first three responses, and both paradigmatic responses (same grammatical function as stimulus) and syntagmatic responses (presumed sequential stimuli; different grammatical function). Illustratively, the order for frequency of primaries is "adjective > noun > pronoun > adverb > preposition > verb > conjunction" (Cramer, 1968a, p. 71).

Loewenthal (1969) analyzes grammatical functions of associations to six sets of words: nouns; nominalisation of adjectives by adding a suffix; similar nominalisations of words of other grammatical function, usually a verb; adjectives; adjectivalization of adjectives by adding a suffix; and similar adjectivalization of words of other grammatical function.

AIIb1a4. *Physical attributes.* Physical attributes and dimensions of words are variables that have been of little interest. Among the relatively few investigations of effects of stimulus modality, Schulz and Hopkins (1968) found high agreement of primaries to the same word presented visually and aurally.

AIIb1a5. *Historical variables.* Among historical variables, frequency enters as repetition of word-association tests, and as prior exposure to target or related stimuli. Direct and indirect priming—conditions and phenomena treated here under contextual stimuli—might also be considered under prior exposure in the laboratory to stimuli related to target stimuli. Reinforcing or punishing consequences of responses to target or related stimuli have been of some interest.

Lists of stimuli may be presented two or more times, with no reinforcing or other consequences of responses to the stimuli. The general concern is stability change of associations through repetition; a particular concern is reliability of associations. Findings by Hall (1966), Brotsky and Linton (1967), Brotsky, Butler, and Linton (1967), Brotsky and Linton (1969), Breznitz (1968), and Shapiro (1966) indicate that, under usual instructions for word associations, Ss may make identical responses to reasonably high percentages of words in from two through as many as five repetitions.

However, the usual instructions may be replaced by instructions to Ss to make a different response to each repetition of a word (Maltzman, Bogartz, & Berger, 1958). Compared to controls, such instructions and experiences, sometimes called "originality training," increase number of idiosyncratic responses to words of the same list. Also, new words elicit more idiosyncratic responses (Cramer, 1968a, pp. 99–101, 107).

Prior exposure to target stimuli has also been varied in arrangements different from the word-association situation. One arrangement, that of experiments on semantic satiation or generation, involves exposure of words for Ss to repeat each one continuously through the same time interval or for a specified number of times. Another arrangement is presentation of words in diverse paired-associates situations.

A typical arrangement that involves repetition of words has two phases. The first is prerepetition assessment in which SD ratings along one or more scales or associations are obtained to each word of a relatively small list. The second is presentation of these (experimental) words or control words for their repetition, and then for postrepetition assessment by SD ratings or by associations.

For SD ratings, changes from pre- to postrepetition may be expressed as difference scores (post- minus prerepetition rating on a 7-point scale) or polarity scores (absolute values of deviations from the scale mean of "4"; prerepetition deviations are subtracted from postrepetition deviations). In general, the polarity score is preferable because occurrence of satiation or generation is independent of prerepetition rating above or below "4."

When no control words are used, comparison of difference or polarity scores for prerepetition and postrepetition ratings is against a hypothetical value of no or "0" change. A significant value of the statistic chosen is interpreted as evidence of semantic satiation (minus) or generation (plus).

For control of possible effects of intervening exposure and repetition of any stimulus, control words are exposed and repeated. Positive or negative changes in difference or polarity scores for experimental and control conditions are compared. A larger negative value for an experimental than for a control condition indicates semantic satiation; a larger positive value indicates semantic generation.

Amster (1964) notes both demonstrations and failures to demonstrate semantic or, as she prefers, connotative satiation and generation of SD ratings. In general, Jakobovist, Lambert, and collaborators (Jakobovits & Lambert, 1960; Messer, Jakobovits, Kanungo, & Lambert, 1964) find semantic satiation. So, too, have Amster (1964) and Amster and Glasman (1965), at least for words. Others report doubtful or no findings of one or both of semantic satiation and generation (Floyd, 1962; Reynierse & Barch, 1963; Schulz, Weaver & Radtke, 1965; Yelen & Schulz, 1963).

Among reasons for these outcomes are use of different measures, difference or polarity scores, and different, often uncontrolled prerepetition values of ratings. Kasschau (1969) presented words at initial values 0.77, 1.37, and 2.08 units from 4.00 on evaluation, potency, and activity scales either without repetition or for repetition at 2/sec. for 5, 10, 15, 30, 60, or 120 sec. For both mean difference and polarity difference scores, satiation increased with duration of repetitions in negatively accelerated fashion. For durations of 30 sec. and longer, satiation of mean difference scores tended to increase with increasing values of prerepetition ratings. Satiation of polarity difference scores was in the order $1.37 < 2.08 < .77$.

None of Kasschau's comparisons was against a comparable control condition. Regardless of meaningfulness of words, Ss' fluency, prerepetition polarity, or scale, polarity differences for S who had repeated experimental and control words did not differ (Hupka & Goss, 1969). Neither satiation nor generation occurred.

For associations that are produced, one criterion of occurrence of satiation is fewer relevant and more irrelevant associations (Kanungo & Lambert, 1963). A related criterion is fewer common and more uncommon responses (Fillenbaum, 1963; Smith & Raygor, 1956). Still other criteria are decreased strength of primaries (Cramer, 1968b), and increased latency of decision between pairs of words that differ in synonymity (Fillenbaum, 1964). Evidence of satiation by one or more of these criteria has and has not been obtained (Amster, 1964; Cramer, 1968a, pp. 103–6, 108–11; 1968b).

Esposito and Pelton (1969) partially repeated Fillenbaum's experiments with common-uncommon associations (1963) and decision latency (1964) as criteria of satiation. With *no* satiation, they obtained Fillenbaum's results of fewer common associations to synonyms than to identical or to unrelated words. With *no* satiation, they obtained Fillenbaum's order of decision time of close synonyms < far synonyms < unrelated.

In Cramer's (1968b) experiments, self-satiation, synonym-satiation, unrelated word-satiation, and no-satiation control were combined with three strengths of primary responses and two durations of satiation. Experimental and control conditions did not differ on number of primary responses, number of different responses, normative response rank, or associative response frequency. Thus, whether investigated by SD ratings or produced associations, semantic satiation and generation seem elusive. They occur; they do not occur.

Words have also been presented in diverse paired-associates situations with subsequent assessment of effects of such exposures on their meaning and meaningfulness as specified by SD ratings or by produced associations. Staats and Staats (1957) initiated a series of experiments that were concerned with the "classical conditioning" of meaning. Under the experimental condition, a CVC was presented as the functional equivalent of the CS of classical conditioning or the stimulus member of a paired-associate unit. Each time this CVC occurred, it was accompanied by a different one of 18 words. However, each of these words had the common property of ratings toward pleasant, active, or strong or toward unpleasant, passive, or weak. Presumably, they elicited a common covert response. Thus, the 18 words and the common response are the functional equivalent of the UCS-UCR or of response members. The control CVC was accompanied by words of heterogeneous values along the appropriate scale. The particular common response evoked by a set of 18 words is presumably conditioned to the CVC. On posttraining ratings of these stimuli along an SD scale, the CVCs that had been accompanied by words that elicited a common response toward an extreme might be rated closer to that extreme than control CVCs. This was the outcome reported by Staats and Staats.

Cohen (1964) essentially repeated the Staats and Staats experiment with words that had connotation toward pleasant or unpleasant. Differences between experimental and control words occurred for "aware" but not for "unaware" Ss. This complicates approaches to and interpretations of these and similar demonstrations of the classical conditioning of meaning. The Staats and Staats approach has further complications of the inferred status of the common response presumably conditioned to experimental CVCs or other stimuli, and of ambiguity of bases of transfer from formation of such relationships to subsequent rating.

McNeill (1963) tested the suggestion that paradigmatic associations arise, at least in part, from occurrence and use of words of the same grammatical class in the same speech context. For each of four triads of CVCs, 10 sentences were prepared of the form "word . . . word CVC_1 word . . . word CVC_2 (or CVC_3)." CVC_1, with adjectival function in these sentences, serves as the stimulus member. CVC_2 and CVC_3, with noun function, serve as alternative response members.

CVC_2-CVC_3 or CVC_3-CVC_2 associations from within a triad were classified as paradigmatic; CVC_2-CVC_1, or CVC_3-CVC_1 associations from within a triad were reversed syntagmatic. Regardless of training trials, reversed syntagmatic associations occurred more often than paradigmatic associations.

In two later experiments, McNeill (1966b) used the same materials but a somewhat different procedure. The results of both experiments together were interpreted as reflecting acquisition of specific associations involving CVC_2 and CVC_3 that also permitted Ss to use a rule of choice of syllables. McNeill concludes that paradigmatic associations do not arise from contiguity of an erroneous anticipation and the correct word.

The latter conclusion is based on results of McNeill's Experiment I in which paradigmatic associations did not differ significantly in relation to number of erroneous anticipations. Difference among conditions in anticipation errors, despite their statistical significance, may not have been sufficient to yield significant differences in paradigmatic associations.

McNeill's arrangement approximates the response-equivalence paradigm of experiments on mediated association (Deese, 1965, p. 33; Jenkins, 1963). Deese seemingly suggests mediation of paradigmatic associations by the common stimulus of the response-equivalence paradigm, or the common response of the stimulus equivalence paradigm (pp. 35, 62–63). McNeill's results do not preclude this interpretation.

Overlooked by McNeill is the possibility that many paradigmatic associations are the outcome of deliberate contiguity. The paired-associates situation that McNeill embedded in sentential context is the pattern of $1 : n$ or divergent pairing of stimulus members and response members. On some trials a stimulus member is accompanied by one response member; on other trials a stimulus member is accompanied by another response member. Relative percentage of occurrence of responses in simulated word-association tests is related directly to prior, actual relative percentages of occurrence of those responses as response members of paired associates in $1 : n$ pairing (Goss, 1969; Goss & Cobb, 1966, 1967; Osgood & Anderson, 1957; Rosenberg & Donner, 1968). Furthermore, Goss (1969) reports increasing polarity of SD ratings as a function of increasing percentage of occurrence of the response that designates one extreme of an SD scale.

Effects of positive reinforcement, of negative reinforcement, and of both together are covered by Cramer (1968a, pp. 115–23). Positive reinforcement of primary, secondary, and tertiary responses increase their frequency. Negative reinforcement after antonyms and after arbitrarily selected associations decreases their frequency.

AIIb1b. Contextual stimuli. Contextual stimuli, verbal or nonverbal, may be presented in a separate list prior to presentation of the list of target words. Contextual stimuli may also be presented in compounds with target words. Contextual stimuli may be other stimuli of a list. Contextual stimuli may be the remaining parts of a sentence or sentences from which words have been deleted. Finally, target stimuli may be at different (syntactic) positions within sentences.

AIIb1b1. Separate list. Contextual stimuli presented in a separate list may have some relation to target stimuli. For example, contextual stimuli may be primary or frequent responses to target stimuli, and target stimuli infrequent responses to contextual stimuli. An increase in frequency of contextual stimuli as responses to target stimuli under this condition is labelled direct priming (Cofer, 1967; Cramer, 1968a, pp. 82–84, 93–94).

Contextual stimuli presented in a separate list may elicit intended responses to target words; contextual stimuli and target words are unrelated. These conditions may also increase frequency of intended responses to target words, an effect labeled indirect or mediated priming (Cofer, 1967; Cramer, 1968a, pp. 84–86, 93–94).

The primed or contextual words of Segal's (1967) List S elicited the cue or target words as primaries; the target words elicited the contextual words with lower, often zero, probability. Some of the contextual words of her List 2 were related to target words in the same way; others of the contextual words were related in different ways, including the opposite pattern of a weaker association.

List S or List 2 were each presented under some of eight different combinations of pretask and recall conditions. Under all combinations of pretask and recall, more primed responses occurred than control responses. Also, priming generalized to nontarget stimuli. Pretask had differential effects on priming as had been observed earlier with other stimuli (Grand & Segal, 1966). Direct priming is a general phenomenon across but differentially influenced by pretask, by recall, and by association patterns. Differences in context reduce direct priming (Clifton, 1966).

AIIb1b2. Compounds. The contextual word(s) of one compound may vary in extent to which they enter an ordered, categorized, or quantitative relationship to those in other compounds that include the same or different target or other words. Responses may be to the compound "as a unit" (Cofer, 1967, p. 8). Responses may be to a designated target word, usually the last word. Cramer (1968a) includes this arrangement under indirect priming. However, as here, Cofer (1967) treats it as compounding.

For compounds "as a unit," with no ordered, categorized, or quantitative relationships among contextual stimuli of different compounds, and responses that are produced, longer reaction times, more different responses, and less frequent primaries occur to compounds than to words of the compounds separately (Cramer, p. 94).

In Musgrave, Cohen, and Robbins (1967) compounds, the second word elicited two synonymous responses, each with relatively low frequency, and the first word elicited one but not the other of those responses. Frequency of responses common to first and second words was higher for second words in compounds than alone. Also, fewer different responses occurred for second words in compounds than alone. Aural, *E*-paced, sequential occurrence of four-word compounds produced more criterion responses and fewer different responses than visual, *S*-paced, simultaneous occurrence (Musgrave & Cohen, 1967).

For compounds with a designated target word, frequency of criterion responses increases as a function of number of contextual stimuli, their proximity to the target stimulus, and T-L frequency of the target stimulus (Cramer, pp. 84–86, 94). Presumed is an association between contextual stimuli and criterion responses. Cramer's (1966) compounds consisted of two contextual words and a last, target word, each of which elicited the criterion response with probabilities of between .04 and .28. Target stimuli occurred immediately after contextual stimuli or after a 15 sec. interval that was unfilled, filled with crossing out *C*s among random letters, filled with reading-checking words to be recalled. Priming occurred under the former three but not under the latter condition.

In Howe's (1969) compounds, the contextual stimulus of one compound is in quantitative relationship with contextual stimuli of other compounds. The contextual stimuli of Study I were 10 probabilistic adverbs (e.g., "possibly"). The target stimuli were adjectives rated along an 11-point pleasantness-unpleasantness scale, both in isolation and in context. Values of the adjectives scaled by the successive intervals method were "multiplied" by the quantifiers to satisfy the equation $X_{ij} = C_i S_j + K$. X_{ij} is the scale value of the compound of the *i*th quantifier or contextual stimulus and the *j*th target stimulus, C_i is the multiplying value of the quantifier, S_j is the scale value of the target stimulus alone, and K is a constant difference between arbitrary and psychological zero.

Adjectives have also been in compounds with verb tenses negative forms, frequency and temporal proximity adverbs (Howe, 1966, 1969), and with intensive, probabilistic, and frequency adverbs (Cliff, 1959; Howe, 1962; Lilly, 1968a, 1968b).

AIIb1b3. Other words in list. Some evidence exists of a direct relationship between number of different continued associations to target stimuli and meaningfulness of contextual stimuli (Amster & Battig, 1965). An experiment (Wynne, Gerjuoy, Schiffman, & Wexler 1967), in part on effects of antonym-eliciting words early or late in a list of antonym and nonantonym associations, is described later.

AIIb1b4. Nondeleted words. The words that remain after other words or parts of words are deleted are the initial context for associations that replace the deleted words. Manipulation of context in this fashion, Taylor (1953) labeled the Cloze procedure. Subsequently, he discovered Ebbinghaus' (1897) earlier development of the manipulation.

In two pilot studies, Taylor (1953) deleted every fifth word (20%) or every tenth (10%); in Experiment 2 he deleted every seventh word (14.3%). Taylor's totals of correct replacements must be adjusted by number of *S*s and number of deletions. For three passages of increasing difficulty, mean correct replacements per opportunity for replacement were ordered 20% > 10% > 14.3%, 10% > 20% > 14.3%, 10% > 20% = 14.3%. In Experiment 1, correct placements per opportunity were greater for 10% random than 10% systematic deletion.

By deletion of every second, third, fourth, fifth, and sixth word, Fillenbaum, Jones, and Rapaport (1963) extended range and extent of deletion. Replacements were scored for correctness by form class (FC) and for correctness verbatim (V) both absolutely and conditional on correctness by FC. For all combinations of FC and V with deleted semantic (nouns, verbs, adjectives) and syntactic (articles, auxilliary verbs, prepositions, conjunctions) words, proportion correct increased with decreasing rate of deletion.

AIIb1b5. *Different syntactic positions.* In Johnson's (1967) sentences, six and then eight CVCs appeared around 12 transitive verbs (e.g., "'The NIJ hurt the GAQ'" p. 241). In Experiment I, the CVCs were subject or object; in Experiment II they were active or passive subject or object. In Experiment I, the subject position produced ratings of greater potency and activity than did the object position. Position made little difference in evaluation, one scale excepted. In Experiment II, ratings of animateness were active subject > passive subject > passive object > active object.

Gumenik and Dolinsky (1969) embedded CVCs as subjects of active, passive, question, or negative sentences with good-good, bad-bad, good-bad, or bad-good verb-object combinations. Sentences influenced values of both good-bad and active-passive ratings; combinations influenced only values of good-bad rating.

AIIb1c. *Responses.* Direct comparison of differences in format of responses to the same stimuli are too infrequent to warrant more than brief comment. Wynne, Gerjuoy, Schiffman, and Wexler (1967) found little or no difference between frequency of antonym responses by production or by selection from among five choices. Nonantonym responses were produced less frequently than they were selected.

AIIb2. *Less specific stimuli, responses.* As for recognition, less specific stimuli, responses subsume instructional, motivational, situational, E, and S variables. Originality training might also be considered instructional variables.

AIIb2a. *Instructional.* Cramer (1968a, pp. 91–93) generalizes that common or uncommon associations can be increased by S's exposure to examples of such associations just before the word-association test.

Among more specific instructions, those to respond like "most people" or to give opposites increase number of primaries; and those for original associations decrease commonality of responses. More recent investigations have been concerned with effects of instructions to repeat original responses (Braun, Constantini, Link, & Ehmer, 1967), to identify popular associates (Moran, 1967), and to give the same, different, or any response on successive tests (Jung, 1967).

Wynne, Gerjuoy, Schiffman, and Wexler (1967) combined two item orders (antonym-evoking words early or late) with six sequences of test conditions (standard, "most people" associations with production, and "most people" with selection among five choices). Both across and for most combinations of conditions separately, antonyms early led to more antonym and fewer nonantonym responses than antonyms late. Test conditions had little or no influence on antonyms late.

Specific instructions may be given that are designed to bring about particular characteristics of distributions of word associations, or changes in those characteristics. Alternatively, S's responses on a single administration or through two or more administrations of the same or different lists may be analyzed to determine the nature and extent of occurrence of one or more response patterns or styles. These may be unique or idiosyncratic to subgroups of Ss.

Under "response sets and cognitive styles," Cramer (1968a, pp. 174–75, 177–78) reviews findings on occurrence and some correlates of high or low commonality scores (number or percentage of associations by an individual S that correspond to primaries for words for that S's group or for the group against which that S is compared).

Moran, Mefferd, and Kimble (1964) began with 20 different sets of 25 words each. Within each set were 5 K-R words, 13 homonyms, 2 neutral words, and 5 K-R words repeated from a preceding set. Five sets or 125 words were administered on four successive days to 79 closely matched pairs of normal and schizophrenic men. Associations were characterized by their relationships to stimuli: synonym, contrast, logical coordinate, superordinate, subordinate, functional. Intercorrelations (rs) were obtained for these and other measures for the list of each day. Three orthogonal factors occurred through days and for normals and schizophrenics. They were "interpreted" as object-referent, conceptual-referent, and speed "idiodynamic" sets. Those Ss with one of these sets give more high commonality association to words eliciting compatible associations and exhibit more faults to words eliciting incompatible associations.

Moran (1966) reports additional data on occurrence and consequences of idiodynamic sets in diverse groups of college undergraduates.

Hypnosis, as exemplary of altered states of consciousness, might be subsumed under instructional variables. Cramer (1968a, pp. 105–6) reviews the scarce data.

AIIb2b. *Motivational.* Motivational variables, for Cramer (1968a), are "stress." Under "experimentally induced stress" (pp. 127–29) she includes food or food-water deprivation as well as situations such as preparation for parachuting or Kennedy's assassination (Mintz, 1969). These types of stress, time pressure to respond, and instruction-induced stress decrease frequency of primaries (pp. 129–32).

Stress as "high" scores on some measure of anxiety, Cramer's "stress as a subject variable," enters essentially no consistent relationships with frequency of the primary, response commonality, response heterogeneity, response availability, and response reproduction errors. However, associative reaction time and anxiety are related directly (pp. 124–26, 131–32). Cramer summarizes and discusses interactions involving two or more of these sources of stress (pp. 132–40).

Little is available on effects of drugs (Cramer, 1968a, p. 204).

AIIb2c. *Situational, E, S.* Situational and E variables have been of little interest. Age and sex are ubiquitous variables whose effects are reviewed by Palermo (1963), Entwisle (1966, pp. 103–32), and Cramer (1968a, pp. 141–55). Illustratively, frequency of primaries increases from age five to the thirties, and then declines. Entwisle describes commonality scores and paradigmatic responses by age, grade, and sex of children (pp. 51–56, 78–88).

Other data on relationships between word associations and age are reported by Dufilho, Mefferd, and Wieland (1969), Riegel and Birren (1966), Riegel and Riegel (1968), Rokosz and Correll (1966), and Wertham and Gerwitz (1966). Bright children of age six can be selected who exemplify predication, functional, synonym-superordinate, and contrast-coordinate idiodynamic sets (Sullivan & Moran, 1967).

Data on word-association by color or race are scarce. Cramer (1968a, pp. 154–55) notes some findings on effects of SES and educational level. In comparisons of two urban groups of average IQ, Entwisle (1966, pp. 88–89) found that SES was associated with only small differences in paradigmatic responses.

Somewhat more data exist for differences in intelligence and verbal ability, but they cannot be considered extensive (Cramer, 1968a, pp. 159–63). Entwisle (1966, pp. 75–86) obtains diverse differences attributable to intelligence that she summarizes as large enough to "distort or obscure age differences" (p. 85).

Semmel, Barrett, Bennett, and Perfetti (1968) compare paradigmatic associations of normal and mentally retarded Ss. Idiodynamic sets occur in the word-associations of both low-level and high-level retardates (Keilman & Moran, 1967). Common and uncommon associations of retarded and normal Ss can be modified by differential reinforcement of those responses (Seymore, Lotsof, & Bransky, 1966).

Among other classes of S variables considered by Cramer (1968a) are "values and interests" (pp. 164–68); various personality measures (pp. 168–73); "selected subject groups" that differ in creativity, occupation, study of physics, and other attributes (pp. 178–81); functional pathology, particularly schizophrenia, (pp. 191–203) and organic pathology, particularly brain damage (pp. 205–7).

Pavy (1968) reviews findings for schizophrenics with both conventional word association tests and the Cloze procedure. Illustrative of more recent investigations are those by Brenner (1967), Ries and Johnson (1967), and Storms, Broen, and Levin (1967).

Among other kinds of organic pathology, Nunnally and collaborators (Blanton, Nunnally & Odom, 1967; Koplin, Odom, Blanton & Nunnally, 1967; Nunnally & Blanton, 1966) have compared diverse aspects of word associations of deaf and normal Ss. Sefer and Henrikson (1966) compare associations to words of different grammatical classes by aphasics and normals.

Under cultural differences, Cramer (1968a) treats both "chronological changes" (pp. 217–21, 223–24) within the "same" culture and "cross-cultural studies" (pp. 221–25). Disregarding possible differences in composition of samples, data on samples of adults and children in the United States suggest that both frequency of primaries and commonality have increased from 1910–1930 to 1950–1965 (p. 223).

Moran (1966), Moran and Nunez (1967), and Riegel, Ramsey, and Riegel (1967) compare American and Spanish-speaking students. Among other cross-cultural comparisons are those involving American, Korean, and Columbian students (Szaly & Brent, 1967); American and Polish students (Kurcz, 1966); American and (European) French monolinguals, and Canadian monolinguals and bilinguals (Lambert & Moore, 1966); and Australian, American, English, and various Western European norms (Rosenzweig & Miller 1966). Moran and Murakawa (1968) compare the idiodynamic sets of Americans and Japanese.

Results of diverse cross-cultural comparisons by the SD can be found in Snider and Osgood (1969).

AIII. *Theory.* Explanation of word-associations are sometimes ahistorical and sometimes ahistorical-historical.

Theories of satiation of SD ratings or word associations are a special case within ahistorical-historical explanation. Because satiation and generation are doubtful phenomena, consideration of theories thereof is unnecessary beyond Amster's (1964) presentation of learning, inhibition, and adaptation-level "interpretations," and Cramer's (1968b) suggestion of selective activation of association networks.

AIIIa. *Ahistorical.* Analyses by Osgood, Suci, and Tannenbaum (1957), Carroll (1969), Flavell, Draguns, Feinberg, and Budin (1958), Moran (1966), Deese (1965), and Rosenberg and Cohen (1966) illustrate essentially ahistorical explanations of occurrence of word-associations.

The SD protocols described by Osgood, Suci, and Tannenbaum consist of ratings of one or more words along, typically, 15 or more scales. For a particular word, the ratings for each scale are correlated with those of every other scale. This matrix of correlations is then reduced by factor analysis which, for a wide variety of stimuli, yields three recurrent orthogonal factors of evaluation, potency, and activity. These three factors specify semantic space (p. 28). Osgood, Suci, and Tannenbaum interpret them "as a simultaneous hierarchy of representational reactions" (p. 27) whose intensity corresponds to length of each factor in semantic space.

Carroll's (1969) rationale for use of the asymptotic log-normal distribution to represent frequency distributions of word-associations entails a tree structure generated by successive binary decisions. He assumes that responses to words may be viewed as the outcome of a series of decisions of which four kinds are proposed: semantic interpretation, grammatical interpretation, grammatical processing, and further processing. Some of these nodes may correspond to idiodynamic sets (Moran, Mefferd & Kimble, 1964).

Flavell, Draguns, Feinberg, and Budin's (1958) "microgenetic approach to word association" assumes that: (a) "there are covert word responses that push for expression early in the associative process and that these early microgenetic forms are less logical, more 'paleological' . . . in character than later ones; . . . (and) (b) when normal individuals associate in a relatively unhurried fashion, their 'immature' responses are usually suppressed, the microgenetically later, more logical associations being the ones actually spoken" (p. 1). The more general orientation of this approach is developed by Flavell and Draguns (1957, pp. 200–211), who draw on an analysis by Rapaport, Gill, and Schafer (1946, pp. 22–24).

A related analysis is proposed by Moran (1966, pp. 20–33), whose "hierarchy of word-matching bases" becomes a developmental sequence of perceptual referent, object referent, concept referent. Parallels are drawn between this sequence and "Piaget's four periods in the development of thought" as summarized by Carroll (1964, pp. 78–81).

Deese (1965) suggests two associative laws: "(1) Elements are associatively related when they may be contrasted in some unique and unambiguous way, and (2) elements are associatively related when they may be grouped because they can be described by two or more characteristics in common" (p. 265). They are as much or more descriptive generalizations about Deese's data than they are independent principles with predictive function.

Rosenberg and Cohen (1966) focus on what they label "referential processes of speakers and listeners." Probabilistic models are developed for both the "speaker process" and the "listener process." The former is analyzed into sampling and comparison stages; the latter involves only comparison.

AIIIb. *Ahistorical-historical.* Among ahistorical-historical explanations of origins of word association are those summarized by Osgood including his own analysis (Osgood 1953, pp. 690–95). Osgood's analysis is a blend of paradigms of classical conditioning and, perhaps, of instrumental conditioning. The concepts and principles involved are presumably some version of those that have been identified as the Hull-Spence approach or theory (Goss, 1969; Hull, 1943; Spence, 1956).

Two other ahistorical-historical theories were described previously: Staats and Staats' (1957) "classical conditioning" account; and the more direct approach by the l:*n* paired-associates situation (Goss, 1969; Goss & Cobb, 1966, 1967; Osgood & Anderson, 1957; Rosenberg & Donner, 1968). Although Staats and Staats label their approach classical conditioning, the concepts and principles involved most immediately are also those of paired-associates learning (Goss, 1969; Goss & Nodine, 1965).

Among other ahistorical-historical approaches are the mediated generalization analysis of Cofer and Foley (1942), and paradigms of mediated association (Jenkins, 1963). The concepts and principles of paired-associates learning also hold for mediated association (Goss & Nodine, 1965, pp. 179–215).

Meaningfulness and other attributes. Goss and Nodine (1965, pp. 11–64) summarize methods and results of normative and correlational investigations of meaningfulness and related attributes up to mid-1964. Earlier reviews are in Underwood and Schulz (1960), Noble (1963), and Goss (1963). In diverse places, Cramer (1968a) examines some investigations covered in previous reviews and selected additional investigations.

One development in method is noted. Data on meaningfulness and other attributes since 1965 and then theoretical analyses are then examined.

BI. *Method.* Vicory and Asher (1966) propose and test a variation in method that "combines the advantages of the Glaze-Archer-Krueger type of measure with Noble's (1952) *m* scale" (p. 508). Instead of writing associations, in their AF technique *S*s tally each association to a word within 10 sec. In Study I, AF values of 24 nonword pronounceable CVCs enter *r*s of from .88 to .96 with values obtained in other calibrations or for other measures of meaningfulness. In Study II, CVCs, Japanese, Russian, Turkish, and Persian words were presented aurally and visually for *S*s to respond by the AF technique, Glaze's (1928) technique, and a combined Glaze-Archer-Krueger technique. High interrater reliabilities and high *r*s and correlation ratios involving values obtained by these techniques are reported.

BII. *Data.* The investigations considered here are divided into those that provide or utilize new values for single stimuli or for pairs of stimuli.

BIIa. *Single stimuli.* Investigations with single stimuli are concerned with essentially a single attribute or with multiple attributes. They involve new values for stimuli and, often, their comparison with old values for these stimuli along the same or other attributes.

BIIa1. *Single attributes.* For CCCs and CVCs, R. E. Johnson (1968) analyzes test-retest reliabilities. Reliability of values for all CVCs and, one excepted, for all *S*s was high. Reliability of values for individual CVCs and individual *S*s was not very high. Constantini and Blackwood (1968) found high retest reliability and an *r* of .79 with Witmer's (1935) values for 344 CCCs of low Witmer meaningfulness.

Lists of 50 CVCs, of 100 CVCs, and of 25 CVCs and 25 CCCs were administered to samples of children in Grades 4–5, 4–6, and 4–6, respectively. The values for CVCs enter high correlations with Archer's (1960) values; those for CCCs enter an *r* of .88 with Witmer's values.

An *r* of .61 held between values on "wordness" of 987 "Mexican" trigrams as judged by students at the National University of Mexico and Archer's (1960) values for the same trigrams (Young & Webber, 1968).

For nine-year-old children, Mickelson (1969a) contributes values for produced meaningfulness of 30 nouns each in four combinations of mass and count nouns with T-L A and T-L AA frequency. Subsequently, she reports (1969b) relatively more count (specific) nouns and relatively fewer mass (nonspecific) nouns in the upper quarters of meaningfulness. Meaningfulness was not related to frequency.

Brown and Ogle (1966) report biserial *r*s of .71, −.72, and −.47 between concreteness and, respectively, meaningfulness, reaction time in single association, and reaction time in continuous association.

Both multiple rank orders (MRO) and magnitude estimation (ME) were used to obtain estimates of frequency of words within lists of 16, 31, or 60 words by children in Grade 6, by adolescents in Grade 9, and by four different groups of adults, respectively (B. J. Shapiro, 1969).

All 2000 CVCs constituted of a, e, i, o, u, and nonduplicatory initial and terminal consonants have been scaled for latency of pronunciation or recognition (Nodine & Hardt, 1969). The *r* for latency of 144 of those CVCs and Gorfein's (1967) values for the same CVCs was .47. The *r*s for relationships to Archer (1960) meaningfulness and to association latency (R. C. Johnson, 1964) are −.37 and .27, respectively. Newman (1967) found that trigrams, mostly CVCs, rated easy to pronounce are spelled and pronounced faster than CCCs rated hard to pronounce.

Nodine and Hardt (1968) partial out differences in Archer (1960) meaningfulness of CVCs to obtain meaningfulness of consonants in initial, medial, and terminal positions. Rho's of .76 and .61 hold between generated meaningfulness of initial and final consonants and total letter frequency obtained by Mayzner and Tresselt (1965).

Anisfeld (1968) used two different groups of raters to obtain a list of 431 pleasant and 702 unpleasant words. Proportions of each letter in initial and any position were determined, and also guesses regarding origin in pleasant or unpleasant words, and estimates of relative frequency in pleasant and unpleasant words. Differences in the latter two measures were associated with occurrence of letters in initial position in unpleasant and pleasant words. Anisfeld explores implications of these findings for "at" threshold recognition of pleasant and unpleasant words.

Scott and Baddelay (1969) use confusion matrices for letters in immediate memory to generate values for acoustic confusibility of 1172 CCCs at Witmer (1935) association values from 0% to 100%.

Among nonverbal stimuli, rated numbers of associations are reported for 251 Munsell colors (Cochran, 1968).

BIIa2. *Multiple attributes.* Smith and Harleston (1966) obtained measures of association time, recall time, forgetting, response commonality, GSR, T-L frequency, and emotionality for 60 nouns.

Ratings of 329 high-frequency nouns on 7-point scales of concreteness, imagery, and pronounceability are available (Spreen & Schulz, 1966) as are ratings of 925 high-frequency nouns (Paivio, Yuille, & Madigan, 1968). Association value and pleasantness of 101 nouns were rated on a 5-point scale and on a 7-point "thermometer-type scale," respectively (Silverstein & Dienstbiet, 1968).

Including two scores for paired-associates learning and one for free recall, Paivio (1968) assessed 30 attributes of 96 nouns. The additional attributes were T-L frequency, verbal and imaginal reaction time, ease and vividness of imagery, meaningfulness, familiarity, three indices of associative variety, 16 SD scales, and polarity of SD ratings. Slightly less than 10% of the rs for pairs of measures were equal to or greater than .50.

Words used in a number of investigations of word associations, 650 in all, were presented to students in first-year psychology at Aberdeen University for ratings on 7-point scales of goodness, pleasantness, emotionality, concreteness, and associative difficulty (Brown & Ure, 1969).

Loigman and Goss (1969) report values for 36 bacteriological terms on diverse attributes: length, frequency of the primary of first associations, number of different first associations, meaningfulness, concreteness, familiarity, imagery, pronounceability, specificity, and noun function. Zechmeister (1969) obtained ratings of 150 words on 9-point scales of orthographic distinctiveness and pronounceability.

Results of these investigations indicate that values obtained for diverse attributes of words across Ss are reliable by both intra- and intergroup criteria. Reliability for individual words and individual Ss may be much lower.

Many of these attributes are interrelated, but in patterns that are not always reducible to simple generalizations. However, meaningfulness, rated frequency or familiarity, rated concreteness (concrete-abstract), and rated imagery appear frequently, if not always, in relatively high correlations with each other and with other attributes of various kinds of visual stimuli.

BIIb. *Pairs of stimuli.* Hakes (1966) selected 84 CVCs from among those with Noble (1961) m values less than 2.00. All possible pairs of different CVCs, 3486 in all, were rated along a 5-point scale of similarity.

Eleven rules for "letter-position identity in CVC pairs" provided classes of CVCs from which Runquist and Johnson (1968) prepared pairs for rating along a 100-point scale of similarity. Runquist (1968) provides similar data on nonword and word CVC trigrams of high Noble (1961) m, and on CCCs of low Witmer (1935) meaningfulness.

Eighteen pairs of words from Palermo and Jenkins (1964) norms and 52 other pairs of words were rated for relatedness along a symmetrical 7-point scale and along an asymmetrical 9-point scale without and with definition of the words (Gentile & Seibel, 1969). Levelt (1969) describes a technique for scaling syntactic relatedness of all pairs of a sentence. Values obtained for all pairs within three sample sentences are reported.

Montague and Kiess (1968) presented pairs of CVCs, under diverse conditions, for S to write the first "associative device" suggested by each pair. Associated values, as proportions of Ss reporting such devices, are given for each pair.

BIII. *Theories.* Two kinds of theories are offered of occurrence, origin, and use of meaningfulness and other attributes of verbal and nonverbal stimuli. One kind is a network of empirical generalizations on interrelationship of attributes. The other is reduction of such interrelationships to smaller numbers of concepts and principles.

Noble's (1963) summary of diverse, largely bivariate relationships exemplifies the former kind of theory. In successive figures he shows regression of one attribute upon another. General empirical equations are proposed for many of these relationships. An earlier schema (Noble, 1952) shows a stimulus eliciting up to n different responses with a value of Hull's (1943) habit strength ($_sH_r$) for each relationship. The $_sH_r$s link this schema to Hull-Spence (Hull, 1943; Spence, 1956) concepts and principles of behavior and learning-motivation.

Goss (1963) reviews some antecedent theoretical reductions of networks of empirical generalizations, particularly one by Sheffield (1946). The observed and inferred stimulus-response elements and relationships Goss proposes include covert and overt recognition (repetitions and naming) responses and responses of an association hierarchy (pp. 128–33). The fundamental or irreducible attributes or dimensions suggested are speed of evocation and completion of both recognition and association responses, nature and order of components of these responses, their stability, and order of occurrence of particular recognition and association responses. Diverse antecedents to and consequences of these properties of recognition and association responses are proposed (pp. 133–37).

For familiar nouns, their concreteness and imagery have proved strong predictors of acquisition with both paired-associates and other situations (Paivio, 1969). Accordingly, Paivio presents an analysis that combines concreteness, nonverbal imagery, and verbal responses.

Transformation. In transformation, changes occur in order-sequence of elements of a stimulus; in replacement, addition, or subtraction of elements; or both. Investigations involving two kinds of situations and phenomena are pertinent: the "verbal transformation effect" (Warren, 1968), and anagrams and their solution.

A. *Verbal transformation.* The condition of the verbal transformation effect is frequent repetition of the same stimulus within a period of several minutes. Any change in the stimulus heard is reported. The "effect" is one or more responses different than recognition of the stimulus, and one or more transitions between different forms. Warren (1968) provides a comprehensive description of the "nature of verbal transformation." He also summarizes effects of various classes of variables such as stimulus complexity, and intensity. Proposed as "mechanisms for verbal transformations . . . (are) first perceptual organization and then perceptual decay" (p. 268).

B. *Anagrams.* Anagrams are often viewed as a "problem solving" situation. However, they can be subsumed under transformation of words and of letter sequences. D. M. Johnson (1966) reviews research on anagrams by diverse investigators. Tressed (1968) notes some subsequent contributions, and summarizes the nature and outcome of an extensive program of research with Mayzner.

BI. *Method.* Nonword letter sequences or words are presented one at a time for *S*s to provide, usually by production, the response or responses specified by instructions. A single response or solution may be required; multiple responses or solutions may be required.

Single solution anagrams may be scored by time to reach the correct solution, number of correct solutions among *n* anagrams in some fixed time interval, or both. Multiple-solution anagrams may be scored by number of correct solutions within a fixed interval.

Regarding single-solution anagrams, Schwartz and Olson (1968) first question and then show that some of them have more than one solution. Investigators are invited to consult Schwartz and Olson's list of five-letter words, 12,870 in all, in *Webster's Third International Dictionary.*

BII. *Data.* The variables of investigations of anagram solution are also divided into specific and less specific stimuli, responses, stimulus-response relationships.

BIIa. *Specific stimuli, responses.* Attributes of initial words or nonwords, of anagrams, are considered specific stimuli. Contextual stimuli, as possible additional specific stimuli, have been of little interest. Attributes of solution words are considered specific responses. Relationships between anagrams and solution words combine specific stimuli, responses.

BIIa1. *Initial word, nonword.* Among ahistorical variables are word or nonword initial stimuli, their length, spacing of the letters, and number of letter moves required for solution. Because *S*s begin with anagrams, length is included here rather than under solution words. An additional special case is no initial word or nonword.

Faster solution of nonword than of word anagrams and no difference in solution time are reported (D. M. Johnson, 1966, p. 275). Beilin (1967) combined word, nonword with length. Solution of his 3-, 4- and 5-letter anagrams required a switch or change in only two letters. Words were solved less rapidly than nonwords with 5-letter but not with 3- and 4-letter anagrams, and by 12- and 14-year olds but not by 8- and 10-year olds.

Cumulative distributions of correct solutions up through 100 sec. are reported for words of 3, 4, 5, 6, 7, 8, 9, and 10 letters (Kaplan & Carvellas, 1968). Both limit of the curves and their rate of change decreased with increasing length.

Results on effects of spacing of letters are contradictory (Johnson, 1966, p. 275). In Dominowski's (1967) Experiment I, T-L words of relatively high frequency were the source of five-letter anagrams whose solution required 1, 2, and 3 letter moves. These anagrams were typed with one and 10 spaces between successive letters. Spacing had no effect on solution time.

Transitional probability is the class of historical variables of greatest importance in investigations of anagram solution. Transitional probability can be specified as frequency of successive letter pairs (digrams). They may be analyzed separately (1–2, 2–3, etc.) or summed as absolute values or ranks. Transitional probability can also be specified as frequency of trigrams and higher *n*-grams.

For two-solution anagrams, Mayzner and Tresselt (1966) obtained faster solutions with low than with high digram frequency totals of anagrams. Summed bigram rank was among Dominow-

ski's (1967) variables. In Experiment I, significantly more solutions occurred with anagrams of high than of low summed bigram rank. In Experiment II, faster solution occurred with anagrams of high than of low summed bigram rank, but the difference was not significant. Warren and Thompson (1969) also report faster solution of anagrams of low than of high transitional probability of component digrams.

The special case of no initial word or nonword has been called "word formation" (Battig, 1957). The underlying dimension is number of letters of *n*-letter solution words that are provided initially. Word formation and anagrams whose letters equal those of solution words are relatively extreme points on this dimension. There are *n*-2 intermediate values. Shouksmith's (1968) solution words were at two levels of difficulty in terms of guesses necessary to reach them. Vowel guessing early in the task and adherence to alphabetical order throughout were analyzed for *S*s distinguished as "good" and "poor" problem solvers.

BIIa2. *Solution words.* One historical variable of solution words is whether they are single-letter (e.g., cider) or double letter (e.g., label). Tresselt and Mayzner (1968) obtained faster solution of double- than of single-letter solution words of high and of low T-L frequency. Only the former difference was significant.

Mayzner and Tresselt (1966), Tresselt and Mayzner (1967), Dominowski (1968), Warren and Thompson (1969), and Edmonds and Mueller (1969) are among those who report faster and better solution of solution words of high than of low T-L frequency.

Mayzner and Tresselt (1966) consider seven aspects of digram position frequencies of solution words. In general, bigram frequencies specific to position were better predictors than digram frequency totals.

In Dominowski's (1967) Experiment I, a V-shaped relationship held between number of solutions and summed bigram rank of solution words of high and medium T-L frequency. Fewer anagrams of words of low T-L frequency were solved when of high than of medium or low summed bigram rank. In Experiment II, time to reach both high and low T-L solution words increased with summed bigram rank.

Harris and Loess (1968) also found an inverse relationship between solution time and digram frequencies. They failed to replicate Tresselt and Mayzner's (1965) finding of faster solution by *S*s with high than with low stored digram frequencies. Solutions of the more frequent CVC pattern are reached faster than solutions of the less frequent CVV, VVC, and VCV patterns (Schwartz, 1968).

After experimental exposure to 10-letter solutions words in a serial-anticipation situation, solution times paralleled the asymmetrical, inverted-U curve characteristic of errors in serial anticipation learning (Davis & Manske, 1968).

A suggestion by Underwood (1966, p. 590), led to Edmonds and Mueller's (1969) comparison of mean anagrams correct as a function of frequency of solution words and intervening experience with unmixed lists of high- or low-frequency solution words or with a mixed list of high- and low-frequency solution words. Experience with low-frequency words presumably constrained *S*s' guesses to low frequency words. Experience with mixed high- and low-frequency words presumably slowed or precluded such constraint.

Dominowski and Ekstrand's (1967) *S*s had five prior exposures to lists constituted of solution words (direct), of associates of solution words, and of inappropriate words or no prior exposure. Best solutions obtained for the first condition.

BIIa3. *Relationships between anagrams and solution words.* Among Mayzner and Tresselt's (1966) many conditions was a relationship of three letters within a nonword anagrama that appeared in one or the other of two solution words (e.g., HPE in AHSPE for SHAPE, and HSE in AHPSE for Phase). In general, *Ss* chose solution words consonant with order of letters of trigrams within anagrams. The five conditions used by Dominowski (1968) were no information and four kinds of information about relationships of letters in anagrams to their occurrence in solution words. Information about bigrams and their position, and about trigrams led to more solutions than did the other kinds of information.

BIIb. *Less specific stimuli, responses.* Among less specific stimuli, responses, instructional variables have been of greatest interest. D. M. Johnson (1966, pp. 372–74) reviews pertinent findings under "problem solving sets," and Tresselt (1968) does so under "set" and "letter order."

One group of Cozzolino's (1968) *Ss* read a passage designed to establish an artificial category set for solution words. Another group read a passage that included words unrelated to solution words. Significantly more solution words of the artificial category occurred with the former than with the latter condition.

Both Johnson (1966) and Tresselt (1968) consider effects of *S* variables. Johnson does so under "anagram-solving abilities" (pp. 379–80); Tresselt considers them "individual differences" (pp. 1115–18).

The interactions that involve *Ss*' age obtained by Beilin (1967) have been noted. Data across a wide range of grades-ages are reported by Stevenson, Klein, Hale, and Miller (1968).

BIII. *Theory.* Tresselt's (1968, pp. 1115–18) first mediational model postulates a sequence of anagram (input), "search of frequency hierarchy," "rearrangement of units," solution word (output). In order to allow for effects of word length and letter-position, a modified model is proposed. Anagrams may lead to search of a frequency hierarchy, re-arrangement of units, solution word. Alternately, they may lead to processing within "word-length, letter-position organization" with consequent "chunking" rearrangement of units, solution word. Johnson's (1966) "description of anagram solving processes" (pp. 380–383) can be assimilated within the modified model, as can Underwood's (1966) "spew law" (pp. 589–91, 600).

Phrases and Sentences

For Hockett (1958), "In English the independence of a grammatical form from those that precede and follow, if any, is often shown by intonation. Any intonation which ends with /31 ↓ / signals independence" (p. 199). The /31/ represents a combination of pitch levels as indicated by *3* and *1* and terminal contours as indicated by / ↓ /. Specifically, *3* is a relatively high level, *1* a relatively low level. The "positive characteristics of / ↓ / are a fading-away of the force of articulation, often with a drawling of the last few vowels and consonants" (p. 37).

Seemingly different conceptions abound (Chomsky, 1965, p. 131; Gleason, 1961, p. 149; Robins, 1964, p. 223). However, little is gained by explicit citation of instances that are manifestly different and whose possible reconciliation is likely to degenerate into definitional acrobatics.

Phrases and sentences as spoken by or for *E* and by *S*, as a first approximation, are a sequence of one to *n* words before and after which pausing is not only possible but usually occurs. The latter pause is usually the termination of /31 ↓ / intonation. Phrases and sentences as written by or for *E* and by *S*, as a first approximation, are a sequence of one to *n* words whose beginning and end is marked by some change in letter, grapheme form such as from lower to upper case, some change from letters such as space, punctuation or punctuation, space, or both.

Many investigators use more specific and detailed criteria of occurrence of phrases and sentences as developed by or for *E*, or as produced by *Ss*. When pertinent, these criteria are noted.

Phrases and sentences may be real, synthetic, or a mixture. The minimum requirement of a real sentence is occurrence of a real word as defined previously. Usually, this word or a sequence of *n* real words occurs within the criteria of intonation-pause or of changes in or from letters. The minimum requirement of a synthetic sentence is a synthetic word, usually within the same requirements.

Phrases and sentences as responses are considered, and then phrases and sentences in stimulus-response relationships.

OCCURRENCE AS RESPONSES

Diverse approaches to grammatical analysis are noted briefly. They are expanded as necessary for examination of data of some frequency counts and, later, on occurrence in stimulus-response relationships.

Grammatical Analysis. Grammatical analysis is often divided into morphology and syntax. Aspects of morphology have been considered under morphemic analysis. Beyond such analysis, and shading into syntax, are conditions of combination of root morphemes and affixes. Among apparent conditions are the nature and position of other words of a phrase or sentence. Syntax treats words, morphemes in relation to each other.

Three different treatments of grammatical analysis are pertinent. The first are general and some more specialized texts on linguistics (Cattell, 1969; Gleason, 1961, pp. 128–238; 1965, pp. 91–350; Hall, 1964, pp. 120–227; Hockett, 1958, pp. 137–267; Robins, 1964, pp. 223–70).

In more analytical treatments, the focus may be general (Chomsky, 1965; Chomsky & Miller, 1963; Harris, 1968), or it may be more restrictive, for example, for children's sentences (Menyuk, 1969) or for some "special construction" (Rosenbaum, 1967). Finally, special techniques may be treated. Thus, Hockett (1967) presents and illustrates the use of some mathematical techniques for representation of linguistic phenomena. Kontsoudas (1966) shows how to write transformational grammars.

Frequency Counts. Frequency counts on sentences of adults, almost exclusively written sentences, are noted. Frequency counts on sentences of children, usually spoken, are then examined.

A. *Adults.* Frequency counts on sentences of adults are primarily of relatively gross features such as means and other descriptive constants of length of sentences. "Sentence length" and also "styles in punctuation" and "verb-adjective ratio" are noted by Miller (1951) under "statistical indicators of style" (pp. 120–28). Herdan (1960) deals briefly with "sentence length as a style characteristic" (pp. 55–58).

Kučera and Francis (1967) include a study entitled "sentence-length distribution in the corpus" by Mackworth and Bell (pp. 368–405). They provide a useful example of criteria of a word ("generally regarded as any sequence of characters set off by spaces, although there were some exceptions to this rule," p. 369) and of "delimiter(s) of the graphic sentence boundary" (p. 365).

More analytical frequency counts have been essayed occasionally. For example, French, Carter, and Koenig (1930) count the frequency of occurrence of various "parts of speech" in telephonic conversations in American English.

Structures of real and synthetic sentences at "surface" levels, and of presumed structures of some of these sentences at "deeper" levels are cited frequently, often in development of linguistic analyses (e.g., Chomsky, 1965; Reibel & Schane, 1969). Examples do not substitute for analytical frequency counts on real sentences. It may be difficult to develop satisfactory general classes and subclasses of real sentences (Fries, 1952).

B. *Children.* Investigations of children's sentences up to about 1960 consider but do not particularly emphasize grammatical rules. Some important investigations after 1960 emphasize such rules.

BI. *Little emphasis on grammatical rules.* Templin (1957) first presents data on length of response, and compares her data to those reported previously by McCarthy (1930) and Davis (1937). Sentence length (words per remark) increases with age, from 4.1 for three-year olds to 7.6 for eight-year olds. Median number of one word remarks decreases from 4.8 for three-year olds to 0.6 for eight-year olds. Girls generally speak longer sentences but sex differences are small. Children of high SES produce longer sentences than those of low SES, seven-year olds excepted. Complexity of verbalizations, as expressed by diverse measures, is also analyzed.

BII. *Emphasis on grammatical rules.* One set of investigations focuses on children during the period from approximate first appearance of sequences or combination of two or more words, usually somewhat before age two years, to about 36 months of age. Another set focuses on sentence production from about 36 months mostly to ages five or six years.

BIIa. *First appearance to 36 months.* Observations by Braine (1963), Miller and Ervin (1964), Brown and Fraser (1964), Gruber (1967), and Menyuk (1969) overlap in method and findings but diverge somewhat in conclusions.

Braine's investigation begins at first observed occurrence of word combinations (an utterance of two or more words) in the speech of three children of 18, 19, 20 months. Number of combinations is described as few at first, increasing slowly during the first few months, and then increasing sharply.

In successive tables, Braine lists the word combinations of each child for the first four months of observation, for the first five months, and at the end of the fourth month. The majority were two-word utterances. These combinations Braine found primarily of two classes of words. One class consists of a few words that occur first or second in many combinations: pivot words. The other class consists of many words that occur in few combinations: X-words. Structural development is addition of pivot words. Vocabulary development is addition of X-words.

The words of primarily two-word sentences of two of Miller and Ervin's (1964) 25 children are summarized in a series of tables. Two classes of words are distinguished, operators and nonoperators. Operators, comparable to Braine's pivots, are few in number, occur frequently, and appear in a particular position. Nonoperators, comparable to Braine's X-words, are relatively many in number, and presumably occur less frequently. Relative frequencies of operators and nonoperators are not given.

Brown and Fraser (1964) present contexts of four words in the corpus of one child. They proceed to two-word utterances of another child that are analyzed as a contingency table of initial words and second words. The grammar proposed as descriptive of these combinations consists of a few initial words and classes of second words (C_i). The former correspond to Braine's pivots, Miller and Ervin's operators. The latter correspond to their X-words, nonoperators. Combination of two C_i words are listed, and various three-word utterances with accompanying grammers are noted.

Gruber's thesis is that utterances of a child just over two years, during the phase analyzed, are best described by a topic-comment construction. Among his examples for sentences with interrogative pronouns are "What do wheel?" "What does truck?" "Where went the wheel?" The adult parallel cited is "*Salt, I taste it in this food.*" In this construction, the topic is *salt*, the comment is *I . . . food.*

Gruber offers a set of eleven rules that generate observed topic-comment constructions. The topic-comment construction is considered "innately known." Utterances occur that can be approximately described and classified by a topic-comment construction, as they can by a pivot-open class construction. Such occurrence does not explain, and Gruber's appeal to similarity between topic-comment and *figure-ground* merely shifts the ambiguity. Figure-ground, too, must be explained.

Menyuk (1969, pp. 30–32) cites some two-word combinations. For these, she postulates an "underlying structure" whose observed aspects are a modifier and topic in either order. Modifier corresponds to open, nonoperator.

Because of McNeill's (1966a) analysis and extension, the former three observations particularly are cited widely. Therefore, it is important to recognize that, as they stand, these three and the Gruber and Menyuk observations have several shortcomings. First, the data presented are highly selected, being primarily combinations of two words. Second, even within the two-word constraint, frequencies often are not reported. Third, the rules that are proposed are empirical generalizations based on combinations and contingencies of first and second words; they are not explanations of those combinations and contingencies. Fourth, little or no information about either immediate or more remote antecedents of particular utterances is provided. Fifth, little use is made of information about relative frequencies of words in adult speech. Finally, analysis into more molecular syntactic classes is often ignored.

The latter stricture does not hold for a subsequent analysis by Brown, Fraser, and Bellugi (1964). They obtained a "sample lexicon" of 79 words. These words occurred often in diverse contexts of a 15-hour corpus of the speech of a 24-month-old boy. They were placed in 14 classes (definite articles, . . . count nouns, . . . qualifiers, . . . others), that became row and column headings of a matrix. Various ratios for assessing predictions from the 15-hour to an 11-hour corpus are explored.

Brown, Cazden, and Bellugi-Klima (1967) summarize features of development of the grammar(s) of the three children through what they designate as Points I, II, and III. At these points, they are writing generative grammars of the children's speech. Age spans of the three points differs among the children. They are 18–22, 27–34, and 27–36 months. Descriptive generalizations are offered of diverse facets of the children's grammars. Negation in these children's speech is described elsewhere (Klima & Bellugi, 1966), and Cazden (1968) provides a more detailed account of changes in inflection.

Regarding the role of training variables, the "telegraphic aspect" of the children's early sentences is ignored, as it had been covered before (Brown & Bellugi, 1964; Brown & Fraser, 1963). An experiment by Cazden (1965) is described briefly. Children from 28–38 months had 40 min. per day of either expansion of incomplete sentences into appropriate complete sentences or of exposure to well-formed sentences (modeling). There was a no-experience control. By each of six measures of language development separately and by a composite measure, modeling but not expansion aided acquisition of grammar.

On the basis of the Cazden results and of some additional analyses, Brown, Cazden, and Bellugi-Klima's conclusion is of a small amount of evidence of an influence of frequency of modeling on acquisition of grammatical knowledge. But frequency of expansion, occurrence of approval and disapproval, and occasional questions make no difference. These data, limited though they are, begin to contribute to an understanding of relationships between frequencies of particular sentence constructions in children's speech and specifiable antecedents in the speech of their parents.

Lee (1966) draws on McNeill's (1966a) analysis, and on many of the observations described above, to define and illustrate developmental sentence types. That the data used for 2-word constructions were not analyzed to reflect a distinction between surface and deep structure is one of Bloom's (1967) criticisms.

Relatively little information is available about development of phrases and sentences by children with first languages other than English. Data for acquisition of French are in Gregoire (1937, 1947). Data for children who are acquiring Russian are described by Slobin (1966a, pp. 132–35). Gruber (1967, p. 423) cites a Ph.D. dissertation on acquisition of Japanese (Kuroda, 1965). Kahane, Kahane, and Saporta (1958) provide some comparative data for English, French, and German on time and voice.

BIIb. *From 36 months.* Menyuk's (1969) observations were on cross-sectional samples of children of ages from about three to about seven years. Speech was obtained and recorded by tape in conditions of responses to pictures of the Blacky test, conversation with and questions by *E* in part regarding the test, and conversation with peers.

Following Chomsky (1965), Menyuk offers "a limited description of (syntactic classes) of base component structures" (p. 23). Some examples are listed of occurrences of noun phrases (p. 34), prepositional phrases, (p. 35) and pronouns (p. 36) in the speech of children both younger and older than three years. After presentation of examples of diverse transformations (pp. 67–104), assessment of grammatical competence and capacity of normal children is described (pp. 110–44). Data are then presented on occurrence of deviant forms in both normal and deviant (infantile language usage) speech groups (pp. 133, 137).

Goodenough (1938) obtained 50 consecutive free and controlled utterances from groups of children aged $2\frac{1}{2}$, $3\frac{1}{2}$, $4\frac{1}{2}$,

and $5\frac{1}{2}$ years. Frequency of occurrence of nine different classes of pronouns are reported for free and controlled utterances by boys and girls at each age level.

Carroll (1939) analyzed the same utterances of the first three groups of children for frequency of occurrence of definite (e.g., this) and indefinite (e.g., a(an), any) determining adjectives, numerating adjective (e.g., all), and words in these categories used as pronouns (class cleavage). Frequencies increase with age. Data on use of adverbials by five-year-old Australians are reported by Harwood (1959).

OCCURRENCE IN STIMULUS-RESPONSE RELATIONSHIPS

Phrases and sentences may occur in stimulus-response relationships of recognition, association, or transformation. Often intelligibility, comprehension, or understanding of sentences is investigated. These terms may be synonymous with association or transformation.

Some assessment of grammaticalness of sentences may be desirable. Among others, Coleman (1965) and Marks (1968) provide information on method and outcome of scalings of grammaticalness.

Complexity of sentences may also be pertinent. Miller and Coleman (1967) used the Cloze technique for scaling complexity.

Data on recognition, association, and transformation are considered. Separate theoretical analyses are not presented. Instead they are combined later in a single section.

Data. Recognition is limited to the stimuli presented. Association involves attempts at sentences beyond those presented. Transformation is overt change in relationships of words of sentences.

A. *Recognition.* Recognition of sentences is discussed, and then recognition of sentences-nonverbal stimuli and of nonverbal stimuli.

AI. *Sentences.* Experiments with sentences that represent different combinations of semantic and syntactic "sense" and "nonsense" are examined and then experiments with sentences in which surface or underlying structures are varied. The remaining experiments concern young children's imitation, and their reading errors.

AIa. *"Sense" and "nonsense."* Miller and Isard (1963) prepared sets of grammatical, semantically anomalous, and ungrammatical sentences. They were first presented in unsystematic order at S/N ratios of −5, 0, 5, 15, and "quiet." After hearing a sentence, Ss repeated it.

By sentences correct and principal words correct at each S/N, recognition decreased in the order grammatical, anomalous, ungrammatical. These results held for presentation of all sentences of each type in a block.

Most of Miller and Isard's "strings" were presented subsequently at S/N of 5, 8, and 10 with principal words spaced at .5-, 1-, and 2-sec. intervals (Martin, 1968a). At each interval, words and strings correct decreased in the order semantic (grammatical), grammatical (anomalous), scrambled (ungrammatical) strings. With semantic strings, words and strings correct decreased with greater spacing. With grammatical and scrambled strings, words correct increased and strings correct decreased and then increased.

In Martin's (1968b) next experiment, ordinary or grammatical, scrambled ordinary, anomalous, and scrambled anomalous (Marks & Miller, 1964) strings had 0, 1, 2, 3, or 4 function words. By words or strings correct, ordinary strings were recognized better than the other three types, which did not differ from each other. In general, recognition decreased with increasing numbers of function words.

The 4-, 5-, 6-, 7-, and 8-word strings prepared by Scholes (1969) were fully grammatical, meaningful (A); grammatical, anomalous (B); order of major constituents permuted (C); order of major constituents retained, word order within constituents permuted (D); both constituents and word order within constituents permuted (E). For children with 4-word strings, Type A + B/Type D + E error ratios were 39.5/38.5, 20.5/25.0, 18.5/29.5, and 8.0/16.5 for groups with median ages of 59.1, 56.3, 47.8, and 45.5 months, respectively. Adult performance was not markedly influenced by string length or type.

Martin's (1968a, b) results particularly suggest that, within the limitation of different metrics, differences in word recognition and in rated meaningfulness and grammaticality are due largely to semantic variables rather than to syntactic variables.

AIb. *Structures varied.* After preliminary experiments with paper-and-pencil tests, Miller and McKean (1964) moved to a situation in which Ss controlled duration of the process of matching active, affirmative sentences. Transformation to passive increased presentation time more than transformation to negative. Transformation to passive, negative increased presentation time by an amount about equal to the sum of increases due to single transformation.

Other experiments suggest that: (a) sets may be formed for particular types of surface or deep structures (Mehler & Carey 1967); (b) viewing time is influenced by position and type of error (Gladney & Krulee, 1967); and (c) reaction time to target words beginning with /b/ (*b*louse) is longer for low- than high-frequency target words and for target words early rather than late in sentences (Foss, 1969). Danks (1969) finds that ratings of comprehensibility of sentences, latencies of Ss understanding, and times to correct grammar and meaning varied with meaningfulness, and somewhat with grammaticalness. T-L frequency of words, interword associative strength, and sentence frame made no difference.

AIc. *Imitation.* Brown, Frazer, and Bellugi (1964) present, and Brown, Cazden, and Bellugi-Klima (1969) note some data on children's imitation of sentences. Earlier Fraser, Bellugi, and Brown (1963) had contrasted imitation, comprehension, and production of sentences by three-year-olds. For every one of ten different contrasts, scores for imitation and comprehension were higher (better) than for production. For nine of the ten, scores for imitation were higher than for comprehension.

AId. *Reading errors.* Counts of reading errors can be found in the literature on reading cited before. However, these are rarely within phonological, morphological, and syntactic considerations. Illustrative of use of such considerations is Clay's (1968) analysis of 10,525 reading errors made by 100 New Zealand children during their first year of school (5.2–5.5 to 6.0 years old). Three-fourths of these errors were substitution of which 72% involved an equivalent morpheme-class or morpheme-sequence. Only 41% of single-word substitutions indicated response on the basis of letters.

AII. *Sentence-nonverbal, nonverbal stimuli.* Verification of sentences has been investigated as functions of syntactic variables. Verbal-nonverbal stimuli have been used to determine children's use of rules of inflection. Also, nonverbal stimuli are presented for Ss to produce sentences that describe them.

AIIa. *Verification.* Gough (1965) assumed that time to verify sentences that describe pictures should vary with kind and number of transformations from kernel sentences. His 16 pictures represented the eight combinations of boy-girl, biting-kicking, boy-girl, and their mirror images. Kernels descriptive of the pictures, and their negative, passive, and negative-passive transformations were accompanied by pictures coincident with the last word of a sentence. Verification time was faster for active than for passive, for affirmative than for negative, and for true than for false sentences and sentence-picture relationships. However, syntactic interpretation is complicated by the effect involving the nonsyntactic, semantic truth-falsity variable. Also, syntactic variables are confounded with differential frequency of active-passive, affirmative-negative constructions.

Gough offers two explanations of the findings. One explanation of the findings of this and subsequent experiments is faster comparison of active sentence with active description than of passive sentence with active description. Alternatively, active construction and actor-victim description may be more congruent than passive construction and actor-victim description with consequent faster verification of sentences in active voice. In Herriot's (1968) Experiment 2, subject-object order produced more grammatically correct words than did object-subject order.

Data reported by Slobin (1966b) and Gaer (1969) suggest that children's verification of sentences varies with sentence structure.

AIIb. *Rules of inflection.* Berko (1958) constructed 28 stimuli that were nonsense forms accompanied by sentences read by adults or read to children by E. These stimuli covered diverse inflections of English. On the basis of percentages of children in preschool and Grade 1 who provided correct answers, Berko concludes that children "operate with clearly delimited morphological rules" (p. 171).

AIIc. *Produce descriptive sentences.* Pictures accompanied by model sentences were Hayhurst's (1967) stimuli. The model sentences were affirmation and negation without an expressed actor and with reversible and irreversible expressed actor. Percentage of correct constructions increased with age. Sentences without an expressed actor were easier to produce.

Eight children in kindergarten and each of Grades 1, 2, 3, and 4 were interviewed by Chomsky (1969). They responded to constructions described as easy to see, promise/tell, ask/tell, pronominalization.

The children's performances are illustrated by extensive protocols (pp. 24–105) and then summarized (pp. 112–19). Chomsky concludes: "Contrary to the commonly held view that a child has mastered the structures of his native language by the time he reaches the age of 6, . . . active syntactic acquisition is taking place up to the age of 9 and perhaps even beyond" (pp. 120–21).

Huttenlocher and Strauss (1968) used blocks and Huttenlocher, Eisenberg, and Strauss (1968) used a fixed and a mobile truck, respectively, to demonstrate influence of sentence subject and object on children's block placements and reaction times.

B. *Association.* On occasion, the distinction between or description under recognition and association is arbitrary; sentences produced or selected may contain or experiments may investigate relationships of recognition and association. Production of consistent second sentences (Foss, 1969) is best classified as association. For convenience, results for this type of response were juxtaposed with those for recognition. For the same reason, scalings of the grammaticality and meaningfulness of sentences (Danks, 1969) were noted under recognition. Associations may be to halves of sentences or to words that form a sentence frame. Associations may paraphrase some or all of real or synthetic words of sentences. Sentences may be produced as association around use of a word as a particular part-of-speech or around a topic word.

For brevity, investigations of sentence completion conceived as a test are not considered. Methods and results for sentences-completion lists are covered by Rotter (1951), Holsopple and Miale (1954), and Shneidman (1965, pp. 509–10).

BI. *Halves of sentences.* Drawing on Yngve (1960), Forster (1966) "deduces" that speakers of a predominately right-branching language such as English should complete right-deleted (RD) items better and faster than left-deleted (LD) items. For speakers of languages in which left-branching occurs, superiority of RD to LD should be reduced, if not reversed.

American students and Turkish students responded to RD and LD sentences in English and Turkish, respectively. Mean scores on completions per page were LD = 3.27 and RD = 5.49 for the English Ss, and LD = 3.53 and RD = 4.11 for Turkish Ss. The same pattern holds for German, a right-branching language, and Japanese, a left-branching language (Forster, 1968).

In order to equate encoding time, sentences of the second experiment had exactly the same phrase or phrases before RD or after LD. RD sentences were completed faster than LD sentences.

Subsequently, Forster (1967) tested the hypothesis that completion time varies directly with number of nodes of tree structures of sentences that traverse the cutting point (T-nodes). Positive zero-order and first-order partial correlations obtained between completion time for LD and number of T-nodes by four different determinations. Completion time for RD and number of T-nodes were related slightly, if at all.

BII. *Missing words in sentence frames.* Rosenberg (1965) presented 40 sentences of the structure "The _____ (Noun) _____ _____." In a second investigation (1966), the frame was a simple declarative ("The [Noun] _____ the _____."). Norms are presented for the blanks of these frames.

Fixed frames for active (The _____ _____ed the _____) and passive (The _____ was _____ed by the ———) constructions were completed by 120 high-school girls (Clark, 1965). In addition to active or passive frames, part given (no part; actor, verb, object) was varied, and the particular words were of high or low T-L frequency, and of high or low commonality. U (uncertainty) was computed for frequencies of response of each word type. Patterns of values of U differ between active and passive frames.

BIII. *Paraphrase.* From 16 sentences of the same structure (ordinary), Downey and Hakes (1968) derived one sentence each that violated rules of phrase-structure, strict subcategorization, and selection restriction. Strategies of paraphrasing these sentences are analyzed.

On the basis of Yngve's (1960) analysis, Herriot (1968) expected that "Ss would perform better when the predicate was longer than when the subject was longer . . ." Nonsense words in phrase-embedded (PE, phrase early) and phrase-suffixed (PS, phrase late) sentence frames were replaced by English words of the same function. For PS relative to PE, there were more correct substitutions, fewer overt errors, and more words correct within the qualifying phrase and in noun and verb phrases.

BIV. *Grammatical usage.* In Brown and Berko's (1960) Usage Test, pronounceable nonsense syllables are assigned to one of six "parts-of-speech": count noun, mass noun, transitive verb, intransitive verb, adjective, adverb. Sentences provide context that permits such assignment; each sentence is accompanied by a picture that represents its content. A sentence-picture pair is presented; Ss respond to a question designed to show their usage of the nonsense syllable.

For number of responses in the same class as the syllable of a sentence, differences occur among parts of speech (count nouns > adjectives > intransitive verbs > transitive verbs > mass nouns > adverbs), and among groups of Ss (adults > Grade 3 > Grade 2 > Grade 1).

BV. *Topic words.* The 120 topic words selected by Taylor (1969) were abstract and concrete nouns of high and low T-L frequencies. Twenty college students produced sentences around these words. Pauses and repetitions occurred more often with infrequent than with frequent words as topics. Frequent, concrete words appeared in the shortest sentences; the other three combinations did not influence sentence length consistently. Complexity of sentences and latencies also varied with concreteness and frequency of topic words.

In Bandura and Harris's (1966) experiment, children in Grade 2 read simple nouns and made up sentences with them. Their base rate was specified by presenting 20 nouns with no reinforcement beyond the first one or two responses. The experimental conditions were: control, reinforcement + set, modeling, modeling + reinforcement, and modeling + reinforcement + set.

Model + reinforcement + set and model + reinforcement increased production of passives. Reinforcement + set and model + reinforcement + set increased production of prepositional phrases. Thus, reinforcement + set + model had some general effectiveness.

In Odom, Liebert, and Hill's (1968) Experiment I, two of the conditions were like Bandura and Harris's model + reinforcement. These conditions applied to prepositional phrases of conventional form (ER; e.g., "at the door") or unconventional form (NR; e.g., "the door at"). The control was no model and no reinforcement.

Both ER and NR conditions led to more ER and fewer non-ER phrases than the control condition. Since the NR condition had effects similar to the ER condition, Experiment II was to decide between misperception and "active process" explanations. Modification of subject's verbatim reproduction of rewarded sentences by the model was added for new ER (ERR) and NR (NRR) conditions. Differences between ERR and NRR in means and medians of ÈR and non-ER scores were negligible.

Odom, Liebert, and Hill conclude: "Although Ss in the NR group apparently attended to the relevant unit in the rewarded productions of M (model), they performed the additional task of recoding the unit so that it conformed to an ER (grammatical) rather than an NR (ungrammatical) construction" (p. 138).

C. *Transformation.* The three experiments described here differ sufficiently to preclude grouping. Eight sentences like Gough's (1965) were the terminal strings that Morris, Rankine, and Reber (1968) presented in active (A), passive (P), negative (N) and negative-passive (NP) constructions. Response was by pressing keys labeled "boy," "girl," "nobody," "hit," "kick" to arrive at appropriate transformation to an active-declarative construction. With immediate and delayed transformation, order of latencies was A < P < N < NP. However, differences with delayed transformation were not significant, in contrast to Gough's (1966) results with delay of exposure of pictures after similar sentences.

Marks (1967) focused on interaction of left-to-right processing of sentences and type of sentence (active, passive, and infinitive). Sentences were derived from active and passive types that involved inversion of the first adjective-noun to noun-adjective, inversion of first noun-proximal verb to verb-noun, and inversion of verb-second adjective to adjective-verb. For infinitive sentences, the latter two inversions were replaced by first verb-noun phrase to noun phrase-verb, and second verb-noun phrase to noun phrase-verb.

For standard sentences and all inversion, latency measures were in the order active < passive. Differences between passive and infinitive were not as consistent. For active and passive sentences, latency measures were in the order normal < inversion of second adjective-noun < inversion of first adjective-noun < inversion of verb-second adjective < (or second verb-noun phrase) < inversion of first noun-verb (first noun phrase-verb). Regardless of syntactic structure, distortions early in the sentence increase latency more than distortions late in the sentence.

"The specific objective of . . . (Stolz's, 1967) experiment . . . was to see if Ss could properly decode sentences which contained a novel application of recursion to a grammatical construction which was obviously familiar in nonrecursive form" (p. 868).

In general, Ss had difficulty in dealing with about half of the sentences. The author concludes: "This study may contain a rather general lesson for psycholinguists who wish to base research on the dichotomy between linguistic competence and linguistic performance. It implies that one must be careful in his assumptions about what native speakers 'know' " (p. 872).

Theory. Many theories of occurrence of phrases and sentences do not distinguish among stimulus-response relationship of recognition, association, and transformation. Hence, these theories are described together.

The dichotomy of ahistorical and ahistorical-historical is useful here, too, for classification of theories of occurrence of phrases and sentences.

A. *Ahistorical.* Schemas by Miller (1962) and some suggestions by Chomsky (1965) are illustrative of ahistorical analyses of occurrence of phrases and sentences. Yngve's (1960) analysis and that of Brown and Bellugi (1964) are noted.

"The functional unit of speech perception," Miller argues, "is usually larger than a single word or a single morpheme and more nearly the size and shape of a syntactic constituent" (p. 754). His diagram of the "syntactic structure of the self-embedded sentence" illustrates this approach. Interesting and complex as a diagram, Miller does not show how it might explain occurrence of sentences even of the kind represented.

Miller proceeds to a "flow chart for strategy used in sentence matching test." The flow chart describes Ss' sequence of behavior in finding some sentence on the right that is the transformation of a sentence on the left (Miller & McKean, 1964).

Competence and performance, Chomsky (1965) characterizes, respectively, as "the speaker-hearer's knowledge of his language" and "the actual use of language in concrete situations" (p. 4). Regarding the former, Chomsky asserts: "Obviously, every speaker of a language has mastered and internalized a generative grammar that expresses his knowledge of his language" (p. 8). However, the "generative grammar is not a model for a speaker or a hearer."

Chomsky ultimately turns to "linguistic theory and language learning" (pp. 47–59). His apparent assumption about language acquisition is "that various formal and substantive universals are intrinsic properties of the language-acquisition system, these providing a schema that is applied to data and that determines in a highly restricted way the general form and, in part, even the substantive features of the grammar that may emerge upon presentation of appropriate data" (p. 53).

Presumably this and similar statements characterize a "language-acquisition system" or "device." However, the device is not developed in detail.

Chomsky proceeds to statements of "the speaker's ability to produce and understand instantly new sentences . . . (and of) a deep and abstract theory . . . many of the concepts and principles of which are only remotely related to experience by long and intricate chains of unconscious quasi-inferential steps" (pp. 57–58). However, apparent exceptions occur: even mature hearers do not always "understand instantly new sentences" (Stolz, 1967). "Understand" itself is not a notion that is immediately understood, and unambiguous (Goss, 1971, pp. 27–29), and Chomsky does not explicate the "long and intricate chains of unconscious quasi-inferential steps."

Among others, McNeill (1966) and possibly Brown, Cazden and Bellugi-Klima (1969) accept or apparently accept Chomsky's notion of a language-acquisition device. However, neither they nor Chomsky (1966) himself add anything of importance.

Some generative grammar is almost the entire substance of the preceding analyses. Accordingly, it is important to appreciate the nature and capabilities of such grammars. Postal (1964) comments: "It should be obvious at this point that a linguistic description as such which generates sentences, i.e., highly abstract triples of syntactic, semantic, and phonological properties, is neither a model of the speaker or of the hearer although it is often confused with these. *Generation* is not *production* or *recognition*" (p. 264).

Hockett (1967) comments in similar fashion. "Chomsky spoke from the beginning as though phrase structures, transformations, and the like are in the *language*, rather than merely useful descriptive devices . . . To achieve this peculiar state of affairs, he takes the language itself out of its speaker: that is, a language cannot in his view, be regarded as a set or system of *habits* of real people" (pp. 7–8). However, through the notion of "*competence, or knowledge of his language,* [Chomsky] puts the language back into its users in a different way . . . [but competence] is somehow to be distinguished from his actual *performance* and cannot even be identified with his regularities [habits] of actual performance" (p. 8).

Yngve's (1960) analysis is apparently intended to apply to sentence production. He assumes that a model of sentence production can be based on a "phrase-structure or immediate constituents framework" and that the model should allow for "left-to-right ordering according to conventional English orthography" (p. 445).

Elaboration of these assumptions involves a flow diagram of the mechanism that "gives precise meaning to the set of rules by providing explicitly the conventions for their application" (p. 445), and an outline of "the program that the mechanism uses" (p. 446).

Brown and Bellugi (1964) distinguish processes of "imitation and reduction," "imitation and expansion," and "induction of latent structure." On the whole, Brown and Bellugi simply describe some features of occurrence of phrases and sentences in young children's speech; they offer little of explanatory significance.

B. *Ahistorical-historical.* Ahistorical-historical theories include diverse ahistorical factors such as length of sentences expressed as morphemes, words or more elementary units, and physical similarity between and among these units. However, they also include historical variables usually those of some general theory of behaviour and learning-motivation-perception. Analyses of occurrence and acquisition of phrases, sentences within such theories typically begin with demonstration that some phenomena of occurrence and acquisition of language can be represented, at least approximately, by one or more relatively familiar paradigms of laboratory situations of experiments on learning. For example, Mowrer (1954), in his analysis of "what do sentences do?" (pp. 663–65), shows "how the sentence 'Tom is a thief' can be recast in the vernacular of conditioning theory" (p. 664).

Among sources of deceptive simplicity of such theories are use of didactic rather than analytical paradigms, and use of simple illustrations for expository purposes. Deceptive simplicity may arise from use of intermediate rather than fundamental explanatory concepts and principles. Thus, Bandura and Harris (1966) draw on some data and on conditions of modeling. For their purposes this was sufficient. But the background analyses of modeling are complex (e.g., Bandura, 1969, pp. 118–216; Bandura & Walters, 1963), and modeling or imitation itself has been treated as derived from more fundamental concepts and principles (Miller & Dollard, 1941; Osgood, 1956).

Absence of explicit presentation of those more fundamental concepts and principles is a further source of deceptive simplicity. Analysis of occurrence and acquisition of a sentence within a paradigm of simple conditioning and, more particularly, within some learning theory, ultimately entails all or most of the concepts and principles of that theory. Even ostensibly simple situations, such as classical conditioning, require theory of considerable complexity (Hull, 1943; Spence, 1956).

Within these caveats on deceptive simplicity, Osgood's (1963) ahistorical-historical analysis of "understanding and creating sentences" is described in some detail. Noted, too, are some suggestions by Jenkins and Palermo (1964), and an analysis by Braine (1963).

In his initial section on "the problem," Osgood describes and criticizes phrase-structure and transformational grammars. A jocular account of "a hypothetical sentence machine" follows.

The "components of a theory of the sentence" proposed by Osgood are word-form pool, semantic key sort, and cognitive mixer. The word-form pool is described with unnecessary virtuosity. The important notion is *the word is the characteristic unit of perceptual forms in language*" (p. 744). An approximate interpretation of the word pool is stimulus-response relationships of recognition.

Osgood eschews operation of the hypothetical semantic key sort. Instead, he assumes that "grammatical distinctions are at base semantic in nature" (p. 746) and assimilates semantic coding within his analysis of semantic space and his interpretation of "each bipolar factor with an independent reciprocally antagonistic reaction system" (p. 746). Presumably his own account of the origin of representative mediational processes is pertinent (Osgood, 1953, pp. 690–95).

Introduction of the "Cognitive Mixer,—but this, too, is really a process" (p. 747) is through brief criticism of Mowrer's conditioning analysis of "*Tom is a thief*," and description of Osgood and Tannenbaum's (1955) congruity hypothesis of attitude change.

Osgood considers phrase interpretation and then "cognitive resolution of sentences as wholes." The latter presumably involves "a series of phrase resolving interactions terminating in a final resolution of the basic kernel sentence, thereby yielding a uniquely modified meaning of the subject or 'topic' of the sentence" (p. 749). A "display" of such resolution follows (p. 750). The display includes input, operation, output.

Even with allowance for the caveats noted earlier, Osgood's analysis of understanding a sentence is unsatisfactory. He does not show the relationship between transformation to kernel sentences and components of the "input, operation, output" display. There is no rationale for the presumed sequence of inputs of the display.

Osgood's two- and three-stage mediational models appear as spatially near to rather than as integral aspects of "cognitive resolution of sentences as wholes." The same hiatus holds for such resolution and Osgood's tree diagram of "integration of sequential and simultaneous hierarchies" (p. 743).

Osgood fails to state what is meant by understanding a sentence. Nor does he deal explicitly with "creating" sentences.

Jenkins and Palermo (1964) "believe that associative correlates between verbal behaviors and events in the world around the beginning speaker rapidly appear through simple S-R laws and that labeling or naming in its broadest sense ought to be one of the earliest forms to appear" (p. 162). These relationships are those of recognition of nonverbal and verbal stimuli.

Existing labels plus "some sort of 'operator'" are the presumed components of "the simplest structure we have imagined" (pp. 162–63). Mediation principles, supplemented by reinforcement and primary stimulus generalization, are avowedly pertinent to the labels beginning to form a class. Class of "what" in relation to what stimuli is not clear, even after description and mediational interpretation of an experiment by Esper (1925).

Palermo and Jenkins then proceed to some quasi-descriptive generalizations about development of young children's language. Manners of application of mediation models to these phenomena are not elaborated. As the authors soon assert: "At the present time the evidence for the approach offered here is fragmentary and only suggestive; but we believe that it forms a pattern" (p. 166).

Braine (1963) summarizes: "'What is learned' are the locations of units, and associations between pairs of morphemes" (p. 348). Sentences are constituted of primary phrases; primary phrases are constituted of morphemes. Location of phrases within sentences is learned; location of morphemes within primary phrases is learned. Such learning is viewed as "perceptual learning—a process of becoming familiar with the sounds of units in temporal positions in which they recur" (p. 348).

Braine's supporting experiments on acquisition and contextual generalization of word position are primarily demonstrations rather than parametric determinations. Differences between visual and aural modalities disregarded, for supporting concepts and principles of learning, Braine could hardly have drawn on a more inadequate conception of perceptual learning (Gibson & Gibson, 1955). This particular conception is a description of, not an explanation of, occurrence of discrimination.

Bever, Fodor, and Weksel (1965a) criticize Braine's analysis on several grounds. Braine (1965) replies to each of their arguments. A reply by Bever, Fodor, and Weksel (1965b) follows. The inconclusiveness of this interchange emphasizes a simple general conclusion: no ahistorical or ahistorical-historical analysis that has been proposed thus far can be considered adequate. Each is inadequate for one or more reasons of remoteness from data, lack of explicit concepts and principles even at the level of the particular analysis, and tenuous or no apparent ties to presumed more general theory.

USES OF LANGUAGE

The uses of language in thought and action considered here are primarily those either explicitly under or readily subsumed under the general rubric of verbal mediation. The reasons for this limitation are several. First, experiments and theory on mediation are typically explicit on the presumed and observed patterns of relationships between verbal or nonverbal stimuli and verbal responses to those stimuli. Second, they are typically explicit on presumed and observed patterns of relationships between those verbal responses and subsequent verbal or motor responses. Third, they are typically explicit on meanings of thought and of action.

Noted briefly are various additional phenomena in which language is sometimes assigned an important role. Many of these analyses also involve verbal mediation.

Verbal Mediation

Use of language in thought and action is developed for paradigms and phenomena of mediation of increasing complexity. The simplest of these paradigms and phenomena are those that involve verbal or nonverbal stimuli that differ, actually or functionally, along what may be considered a single dimension. Of greater complexity are paradigms and phenomena that involve verbal or nonverbal stimuli that differ, actually or functionally, along two or more dimensions. Such complexity is increased further in paradigms and phenomena that presumably involve relatively complex sequences of mediating responses.

Differ Along Single Dimension

Use of language in the paradigms of acquired equivalence and acquired distinctiveness of cues is described. Use of language within additional paradigms of mediation is noted briefly.

Also noted briefly is use of information about word associations to specify initial states of verbal learning tasks.

Acquired Equivalence and Distinctiveness. In their chapter on the "higher mental processes," Miller and Dollard (1941) describe modes of adjustment they label "acquired cue value" and "acquired equivalence of cues." Within acquired cue value, they propose: "A cue which would otherwise not be distinctive can acquire greater distinctiveness in two ways: the individual may learn to direct his sense organs toward that cue, or he may learn to react to that obscure cue with a response, such as counting, which produces a more distinctive cue" (p. 74).

Regarding the acquired equivalence of cues, Miller and Dollard note the desirability of generalization from one situation to another despite a lack of common external cues. "Such generalization can be mediated by response-produced cues... [once] a common response [to different stimuli] is acquired through a number of separate learning situations, cues produced by this common response can serve as the common stimuli necessary for generalization" (p. 75).

Dollard and Miller (1950) refine these notions, and Goss (1955) provides a more general analysis.

Presupposed in these analyses are relationships between (external, initiating) stimuli and verbal recognition responses or verbal recognition and association responses. Presupposed, too, is influence of these relationships on acquisition or performance of stimulus-response relationships that involve additional verbal responses or motor responses. Whether the former stimulus-response relationship facilitates or retards acquisition or performance of the latter stimulus-response relationships depends on the particular patterns of relationships. Some patterns presumably facilitate, some presumably retard (Goss, 1955).

These analyses specify use or roles of recognition or of recognition and association responses in phenomena of generalization or discrimination of subsequent verbal or motor response. Specific methods used, results, refinements of theory, and criticisms thereof are found in Spiker (1956, 1963), Arnoult (1957), Goss and Greenfeld (1958), Cantor (1965), Reese (1968), Ellis (1969, pp. 408–16), Luria (1969, pp. 145–48), and Gibson (1969, pp. 63–79).

Acquired equivalence of cues, acquired distinctiveness of cues, or both enter diverse analyses of paired-associates learning. These begin with Gibson's (1940) analysis, proceed through Sheffield's (1946) analysis to analyses by Goss (1963), Goss and Nodine (1965) and Martin (1968). In these analyses, recognition responses to stimulus members and to response members of paired associates are regarded as significant determinants of acquisition and transfer. Association responses may also influence acquisition and transfer.

Semantic generalization and the related phenomenon of generalization between stimulus modalities are special cases of acquired equivalences of cues. Among analyses of semantic generalization are those of Cofer and Foley (1942), Osgood (1952), pp. 702–5), Jenkins (1963, pp. 215–16, 226–37), and Luria (1969, pp. 137–38). Osgood (1953, pp. 701–2) and Lifton and Goss (1962) discuss intermodal generalization.

Additional Paradigms. The paradigms or mechanisms of acquired equivalence and acquired distinctiveness of cues comprehend only some of the paradigms of mediation of generalization and discrimination with stimuli that differ along a single dimension. Goss and Nodine (1965, pp. 179–82) generate 16 paradigms based on similar-dissimilar initiating stimuli, similar-dissimilar mediating responses and stimuli, similar-dissimiliar terminating responses, and 0 or > 0 initial strength of association between mediating stimuli and terminating responses. They refer to acquired equivalence as response-mediated similarity, and to acquired distinctiveness as response-mediated dissimilarity.

Mediate or mediated association is another special case: initiating stimuli are dissimilar, mediating response-stimuli are dissimilar, terminating responses are dissimiliar, and initial associative strengths between mediating stimuli-terminating responses are > 0. The paradigms of mediated association that Jenkins (1963) labels chaining, stimulus equivalence, and response equivalence appear as further special cases of mediate association that are distinguished by stimulus-response relationships of antecedent tasks. Both Jenkins and, more recently, Kjeldergaard (1968) cover method and data on mediate association including use of word-association norms to specify initial strength of component stimulus-response relationships. Earhard and Mandler (1965) criticize data and theory on mediate association within concepts and principles of nonmediated transfer of paired-associates.

Initial States. Information about associations to verbal or nonverbal stimuli permit specification of strengths and derived of initial patterns relationships among stimulus members of paired-associates, among response members, and between and among stimulus members and response members (Goss, 1966; Goss & Nodine, 1965, pp. 101–10). Both associations between and among stimuli of categories and association of those stimuli to category names are variables that influence free recall (Cofer, 1965, 1969, pp. 324–35; Deese, 1965, pp. 59–60).

Meaningfulness and other attributes of stimuli also constitute specification of initial states of paired-associates, free-recall, serial-anticipation, and other learning situations. Methods, data, and theory on effects of these attributes on acquisition and other phenomena are covered extensively in diverse sources (Cofer, 1969, pp. 315–24; Goss, 1963; Goss & Nodine, 1965; Martin, 1968; Noble, 1963; Paivio, 1969; Underwood & Schulz, 1960).

Differ Along Two Dimensions

Investigations of concept formation or of conceptual behavior are often with stimuli constituted of different combinations of values along two or more physical dimensions (Goss, 1961a). Osgood (1952, pp. 668–72) applied the paradigm of acquired equivalence of cues to two, then-common, specific conceptual tasks. His application was anticipated by Watson and various other early behaviorists (Goss, 1961b), and by Miller and Dollard (1941), Cofer and Foley, (1942), and Dollard and Miller (1950).

Goss provides detailed analyses of use of verbal mediating responses, stimuli in concept-formation situations with stimuli that are or involve combinations of values along dimensions,

common elements or relations, and elicitation of common responses. Notions of abstract set, hypotheses, and strategies are incorporated within these analyses. These notions are treated as special cases of the use of language.

Attribute aspects of conceptual behavior can be regarded as relationships between stimuli and recognition responses (Haygood & Bourne, 1965). Various rules such as conjunction appear as particular patterns of occurrence of mediating responses in relation to initiating stimuli and terminating responses. Rules also appear as verbalizations that are designed to assure occurrence of such patterns or that are post hoc reports of occurrence of those patterns.

Method of investigating the occurrence of preexperimentally acquired recognition responses to multidimensional stimuli, and data on the role of these responses in conceptual sorting, are discussed by Goss (1964), Rosen and Goss (1965), and Goss and Gregory (1966). Other treatments of the use of language in conceptual behavior can be found in Kendler and Kendler (1962), and Vigotsky (1934).

Relatively Complex Sequences

Watson's and other early behaviorists' analyses of use of language in reasoning is described by Goss (1961b). Miller and Dollard (1941) and Dollard and Miller (1950) describe various uses of language in the "higher mental processes." Osgood's (1953) analyses of the use of language in problem solving and insight and in thinking were noted previously. Cofer (1957, 1960) and Kendler and Kendler (1962) develop their analyses of reasoning and problem solving substantially around verbal mediating responses. Subsequently, Clark (1969) outlines an account of "linguistic processes in deductive reasoning."

Goss (1961c) develops the role of verbal mediating responses in a number of complex situations including, under special conditions, production of sentences. Use of language in animistic thinking is also discussed (Goss, 1964, Looft & Bartz, 1969).

Additional Phenomena

Luria (1969, pp. 148–59) summarizes Russian experiments on the role of speech in voluntary attention, in imagination and thinking, and in regulation of action.

In diverse places, Dollard and Miller (1950), note the role of language in the psychoanalytic mechanism of suppression and repression, and in other phenomena of personality development and modification. Osgood (1956) offers an analysis of imitation that involves verbal mediation.

Rhine's (1958) treatment of attitudes as concepts involves verbal mediating responses. Use of language also enters Osgood and Tannenbaum's congruity hypothesis of attitude change (Osgood & Tannenbaum, 1955). Recognition responses to form have been conceived as important determinants of memory for form (Riley, 1962).

"Serial order in (speech) behaviour" has been analyzed in terms of recognition responses to phonemes and phoneme sequence as "context-sensitive associative memory" (Wickelgren 1969a). Wickelgren (1969b) also evaluates the possible role of recognition responses to phonemes in short-term memory.

Use of language in diverse kinds of "knowledge," but especially knowledge of classifications, is developed in Goss (1971). Musgrave and Cohen (1971) and Musgrave and Gerritz (1968) provide examples and data, respectively.

Gagné (1968) analyzes the acquisition and use of language in the Piagetian task of conservation of volume of liquids. Use of language in solution of some problems of physics is demonstrated by Johnson (1965).

These examples illustrate but do not exhaust instances of use of language in thought and action. Beyond diversity of use, the examples cited here were selected because they are relatively specific to and detailed in their treatment of the situations or phenomena of interest.

Acknowledgement. Preparation of this chapter was supported, in part, by Grant MH 13531 from the National Institute of Mental Health. Various suggestions by Nancy J. Cobb and Virginia L. Bernier have been used. Victoria P. Hart contributed in diverse ways to the final preparation of the manuscript; and Ilona K. Merel aided on the references.

References

ABERCROMBIE, D. *Elements of general phonetics.* Chicago: Aldine, 1967.

ABRAMSON, A. S., and COOPER, F. S. Slow motion X-ray pictures with stretched speech as a research tool. *Journal of the Acoustical Society of America*, 1963, *35*, 1888. (Abstract)

ADAMS, S., and POWERS, F. F. The psychology of language. *Psychological Bulletin*, 1929, *26*, 241–60.

AINSWORTH, W. A. First formant transitions and the perception of synthetic semivowels. *Journal of the Acoustical Society of America*, 1968, *44*, 689–94.

ALLPORT, F. H. *Social psychology.* Boston: Houghton-Mifflin, 1924.

AMES, L. B., LEARNED, J., MÉTRAUX, R., and WALKER, R. N. *Child Rorschach responses.* New York: Hoeber, 1952.

—— *Rorschach responses in old age.* New York: Hoeber, 1954.

AMMONS, R. B., and AMMONS, H. S. *Full range picture vocabulary.* Missoula, Montana: Psychological Test Specialists, 1958 (1948).

AMSTER, H. Semantic satiation and generation: Learning? adaptation? *Psychological Bulletin*, 1964, *62*, 273–86.

——, and BATTIG, W. F. Effect of contextual meaningfulness on rated association values (*m′*), number of associations (*m*), and free recall. *Psychonomic Science*, 1965, *3*, 569–70.

AMSTER, H., and GLASMAN, L. D. Verbal repetition and connotative change. *Journal of Experimental Psychology*, 1966, *71*, 389–98.

AMSTER, H., and KEPPEL, G. Letter association norms. *Psychonomic Monograph Supplements*, 1966, *1*(9), 211–38.

—— Letter sequence habits in children. *Journal of Verbal Learning and Verbal Behavior*, 1968, *7*, 326–32.

ANDERSON, I. H., and DEARBORN, W. F. *The psychology of teaching reading.* New York: Ronald, 1952.

ANDERSON, J. E. The development of spoken language. *Yearbook National Society for the Study of Education*, 1939, *38* (I), 211–24.

ANDERSON, N. S. Word associations to individual letters. *Journal of Verbal Learning and Verbal Behavior*, 1965, *4*, 541–45.

ANISFELD, M. Subjective approximation of relative letter incidence in pleasant and unpleasant words. *Journal of Verbal Learning and Verbal Behavior*, 1968, *7*, 33–40.

ARCHER, E. J. A re-evaluation of the meaningfulness of all possible CVC trigrams. *Psychological Monographs*, 1960, *74* (10, Whole No. 497).

ARNOLD, G. E. Morphology and physiology of the speech organs. *In* L. KAISER (ed.), *Manual of phonetics*, pp. 31–64. Amsterdam: North-Holland, 1957.

ARNOULT, M. D. Stimulus predifferentiation: Some generalizations and hypotheses. *Psychological Bulletin*, 1957, *54*, 339–50.

ATKINS, R. E. An analysis of the phonetic elements in a basal reading vocabulary. *The Elementary School Journal*, 1926, *26*, 595–606.

ATTNEAVE, F. Psychological probability as a function of experienced frequency. *Journal of Experimental Psychology*, 1953, *46*, 81–86.

—— *Applications of information theory to psychology.* New York: Holt, Rinehart & Winston, 1959.

——, and ARNOULT, M. D. The quantitative study of shape and pattern perception. *Psychological Bulletin*, 1956, *53*, 452–71.

BADDELAY, A. D., CONRAD, R., and THOMSON, W. E. Letter structure of the English language. *Nature*, 1960, *186*, 414–16.

BAER, W. P., and WINITZ, H. Acquisition of /v/ in "words" as a function of the consistency of /v/ errors. *Journal of Speech and Hearing Research*, 1968, *11*, 316–33.

BALDWIN, B. T. et al. Studies in language development. *Yearbook National Society for the Study of Education*, 1929, *28*, 495–568.

BANDURA, A. *Principles of behavior modification.* New York: Holt, Rinehart & Winston, 1969.

——, and HARRIS, M. B. Modification of syntactic style. *Journal of Experimental Child Psychology*, 1966, *4*, 341–52.

BANDURA, A., and WALTERS, R. H. *Social learning and personality development.* New York: Holt, Rinehart & Winston, 1963.

BARBARA, D. A. *Psychological and psychiatric aspects of speech and hearing.* Springfield, Ill.: Thomas, 1960.

BARNEY, H. L., and DUNN, H. K. Speech analysis. *In* L. KAISER (ed.), *Manual of phonetics*, pp. 180–201. Amsterdam: North-Holland, 1957.

BARRETT, T. C. The relationship between measures of prereading visual discrimination and first grade reading achievement: A review of the literature. *Reading Research Quarterly*, 1966, *1*, 51–76.

BATTIG, W. F. Some factors affecting performance on a word formation problem. *Journal of Experimental Psychology*, 1957, *54*, 96–104.

BAUGHMAN, E. E. An experimental analysis of the relationship between stimulus structure and behavior on the Rorschach. *Journal of Projective Techniques and Personality Assessment*, 1959, *23*, 134–83.

BECHTEREV, V. M. *General principles of human reflexology.* New York: International Publishers, 1928.

BECK, S. J., BECK, A. G., LEVITT, E. E., and MOLISH, H. B. *Rorschach's test:* 1. *Basic processes.* 3rd rev. ed. New York: Grune & Stratton, 1961.

BEIER, E. G., and COWEN, E. L. A further investigation of the influence of "threat expectancy" on perception. *Journal of Personality*, 1953, *22*, 254–57.

BEILIN, H. Developmental determinants of word and nonsense anagram solutions. *Journal of Verbal Learning and Verbal Behavior*, 1967, *6*, 523–27.

BELL, A. M. *Visible speech.* London: Simpkin, Marshall, 1867.

BELL, C. G., FUJISAKI, H., HEINZ, J. M., STEVENS, K. N., and HOUSE, A. S. Reduction of speech spectra by analysis-by-synthesis techniques. *Journal of the Acoustical Society of America*, 1961, *33*, 1725–36.

BENNETT, W. A. *Aspects of languages and language teaching.* Cambridge: Cambridge University Press, 1968.

BENTLEY, M., and VARON, E. An accessory study of "phonetic symbolism." *American Journal of Psychology*, 1933, *45*, 76–86.

BERKO, J. The child's learning of English morphology. *Word*, 1958, *14*, 150–77.

BERLIN, B., and KAY, P. *Basic color terms.* Berkeley: University of California Press, 1969.

BERRY, M. F., and EISENSON, J. *Speech disorders: Principles and practices of therapy.* New York: Appleton-Century-Crofts, 1956.

BEVER, T. G., FODOR, J. A., and WEKSEL, W. On the acquisition of syntax: A critique of "contextual generalization." *Psychological Review*, 1965a, *72*, 467–82.

—— Is linguistics empirical? *Psychological Review*, 1965b, *72*, 493–500.

BIEDERMAN, G. B. The recognition of tachistoscopically presented five-letter words as a function of digram frequency. *Journal of Verbal Learning and Verbal Behavior*, 1966, *5*, 208–9.

BILODEAU, E. A., and HOWELL, D. C. Association rules in the prediction of recall from free-association matrices. *Psychological Bulletin*, 1968, *70*, 201–9.

BIRDWHISTELL, R. L. *Kinesics and context,* Philadelphia: University of Pennsylvania Press, 1970.

BISHOP, C. H. Transfer effects of word and letter training in reading. *Journal of Verbal Learning and Verbal Behavior*, 1964, *3*, 215–21.

BITTERMAN, M. E., and KNIFFIN, C. W. Manifest anxiety and "perceptual defense." *Journal of Abnormal and Social Psychology*, 1953, *48*, 248–53.

BLACK, J. W., and AGNELLO, J. G. The prediction of effects of combined deterents to intelligibility. *Journal of Auditory Research*, 1964, *4*, 277–84.

BLANTON, R. L., NUNNALLY, J. C., and ODOM, P. B. Graphemic, phonetic, and associative factors in the verbal behavior of deaf and hearing subjects. *Journal of Speech and Hearing Disorders*, 1967, *10*, 225–31.

BLOOM, L. M. A comment on Lee's "Developmental sentence types: A method for comparing normal and deviant syntactic development." *Journal of Speech and Hearing Research*, 1967, *32*, 294–96.

BLOOMFIELD, L. *An introduction to the study of language.* New York: Holt, Rinehart & Winston, 1914.

———— *Language.* New York: Holt, Rinehart & Winston, 1933.

BOND, G. L., and DYKSTRA, R. The cooperative research program in first-grade reading instruction. *Reading Research Quarterly*, 1967, *2* (4), 1–42.

BOOTZIN, R. R., and NATSOULAS, T. Evidence of perceptual defense uncontaminated by response bias. *Journal of Personality and Social Psychology*, 1965, *1*, 461–68.

BOURNE, C. P., and FORD, D. F. A study of the statistics of letters in English words. *Information and Control*, 1961, *4*, 48–67.

BOUSFIELD, W. A. The problem of meaning in verbal learning. *In* C. N. COFER (ed.), *Verbal learning and verbal behavior*, pp. 81–91. New York: McGraw-Hill, 1961.

BRAINE, M. D. S. The ontogeny of English phrase structure: The first phase. *Language*, 1963a, *39*, 1–13.

———— On learning the grammatical order of words. *Psychological Review*, 1963b, *70*, 323–48.

———— On the basis of phrase structure: A reply to Bever, Fodor, and Weksel. *Psychological Review*, 1965, *72*, 483–92.

BRAUN, J. R., CONSTANTINI, W., LINK, J., and EHMER, B. J. Differential repetition of common versus uncommon word associations. *Psychonomic Science*, 1967, *9*, 463–64.

BRENNER, A. R. Effects of prior experimenter-subject relationships on responses to the Kent-Rosanoff word association list in schizophrenics. *Journal of Abnormal Psychology*, 1967, *72*, 273–76.

BREZNITZ, S. Analysis of reproductions in a word association task. *Journal of Verbal Learning and Verbal Behavior*, 1968, *7*, 510–15.

BRICKER, W. A. Errors in the echoic behavior of preschool children. *Journal of Speech and Hearing Research*, 1967, *10*, 67–76.

BRIGHT, W., ed. *Sociolinguistics.* The Hague: Mouton, 1966.

BROADBENT, D. E. Word frequency effect and response bias. *Psychological Review*, 1967, *74*, 1–15.

————, and GREGORY, M. Visual perception of words differing in letter digram frequency. *Journal of Verbal Learning and Verbal Behavior*, 1968, *7*, 569–71.

BROERSE, H. C., and ZWANN, E. J. The information value of initial letters in the identification of words. *Journal of Verbal Learning and Verbal Behavior*, 1966, *5*, 441–46.

BROTSKY, S. J., BUTLER, D. C., and LINTON, M. L. Association time, commonality, and the test-retest reliability of free association responses. *Psychonomic Science*, 1967, *9*, 319–20.

BROTSKY, S. J., and LINTON, M. L. The test-retest reliability of free association norms. *Psychonomic Science*, 1967, *8*, 425–26.

———— The test-retest reliability of free associations following successive associations. *Psychonomic Science*, 1969, *16*, 98–99.

BROWN, C. R., and RUBENSTEIN, H. Test of response bias explanation of word-frequency effect. *Science*, 1961, *133*, 280–81.

BROWN, J. S. *The motivation of behavior.* New York: McGraw-Hill, 1961.

BROWN, R. *Words and things.* Glencoe, Ill.: Free Press, 1958.

———— The development of Wh questions in child speech. *Journal of Verbal Learning and Verbal Behavior*, 1968, *7*, 279–90.

————, and BELLUGI, U. Three processes in the child's acquisition of syntax. *Harvard Educational Review*, 1964, *34*, 133–51.

BROWN, R. W., and BERKO, J. Psycholinguistic research methods. *In* P. H. MUSSEN (ed.), *Handbook of research methods in child development*, pp. 517–57. New York: John Wiley, 1960a.

———— Word association and the development of grammar. *Child Development*, 1960b, *31*, 1–14.

BROWN, R., CAZDEN, C., and BELLUGI-KLIMA, U. The child's grammar from I to III. *In* J. P. HILL (ed.), *Minnesota symposia on child psychology*, vol. 2. Minneapolis: University of Minnesota Press, 1969.

BROWN, R., and FRASER, C. The acquisition of syntax. *In* C. N. COFER and B. S. MUSGRAVE (eds.) *Verbal behavior and learning:* Problems and processes, pp. 158–97. New York: McGraw-Hill, 1963.

———— The acquisition of syntax. *Monographs of the Society for Research in Child Development*, 1964, *29*, (1, ser. no. 92), 43–79.

BROWN, R. W., and LENNEBERG, E. H. A study in language and cognition. *Journal of Abnormal and Social Psychology*, 1954, *49*, 454–62.

BROWN, W. P., and OGLE, W. C. Latencies in single word and continuous association. *Psychological Reports*, 1966, *19*, 172.

BROWN, W. P., and URE, D. M. J. Five rated characteristics of 650 word association stimuli. *British Journal of Psychology*, 1969, *60*, 233–49.

BRUBAKER, R. S. Experimental phonetics. *In* R. W. RIEBER and R. S. BRUBAKER (eds.), *Speech pathology*, pp. 77–99. Amsterdam: North-Holland, 1966.

BRUNER, J. S., and POSTMAN, L. Emotional selectivity in perception and reaction. *Journal of Personality*, 1947, *16*, 69–77.

BUCKINGHAM, B. R., and DOLCH, E. W. *A combined word list.* Boston: Ginn, 1936.

BÜHLER, K. *The mental development of the child.* New York: Harcourt Brace Jovanovich, 1930.

———— *Sprachtheorie.* Jena: Fischer, 1934.

BULLOWA, M., JONES, L. G., and BEVER, T. G. The development from vocal to verbal behavior in children. *Monographs of the Society for Research in Child Development*, 1964, *29*, (1, Ser. no. 92).

BUSWELL, G. T. *How adults read.* Chicago: University of Chicago Press, 1937.

CALDWELL, E. C., and HALL, V. C. The influence of concept training on letter discrimination. *Child Development*, 1969, *40*, 63–71.

CALFEE, R. C., VENEZKY, R. L., and CHAPMAN, R. S. Pronunciation of synthetic words with predictable and unpredictable letter-sound correspondences. Madison: Wisconsin Research and Development Center, University of Wisconsin, 1969.

CANTOR, J. H. Transfer of stimulus pretraining to motor paired-associate and discrimination learning tasks. *In* L. P. LIPSITT and C. C. SPIKER (eds.), *Advances in child development and behavior*, vol. 2, pp. 19–58. New York: Academic Press, 1965.

CARROLL, J. B. Determining and numerating adjectives in children's speech. *Child Development*, 1939, *10*, 215–29.

———— *The study of language.* Cambridge: Harvard University Press, 1953.

———— The assessment of phoneme cluster frequencies. *Language*, 1958, *34*, 267–78.

———— Language development of children. *In* C. W. HARRIS (ed.), *Encyclopedia of Educational Research.* New York: Macmillan, 1960.

———— Grapheme-phoneme correspondence in English orthography: A brief, chronologically arranged bibliography. Cambridge: Graduate School of Education, Harvard University, 1963.

———— *Language and thought.* Englewood Cliffs, N.J.: Prentice-Hall, 1964.

———— Word-frequency studies and the lognormal distribution. *In* E. M. ZALE (ed.), *Proceedings of the Conference on Language and Language Behavior*, pp. 213–35. New York: Appleton-Century-Crofts, 1968.

———— A rationale for an asymptotic lognormal form of word-frequency distributions. Princeton, N.J.: Unpublished Research Bulletin, Educational Testing Service, 1969.

CARTERETTE, E. C., ed. *Brain function*, vol. 3. Berkeley: University of California Press, 1966.

———— A simple linear model for vowel perception. *In* W. WATHERDUNN (ed.), *Models for the perception of speech and visual form.* Cambridge: M.I.T. Press, 1967.

————, and JONES, M. H. Phoneme and letter patterns in children's language. *In* K. S. GOODMAN (ed.), *The psycholinguistic nature of the reading process*, pp. 103–65. Detroit: Wayne State University Press, 1968.

CATFORD, J. C. The articulatory possibilities in man. *In* B. MALBERG (ed.), *Manual of Phonetics*, pp. 309–33. Rev. ed. Amsterdam: North-Holland, 1968.

CATLIN, J. On the word-frequency effect. *Psychological Review*, 1969, *76*, 504–6.

CATTELL, J. M. The inertia of the eye and brain. *Brain*, 1886a, *8*, 295–312.

—— The time taken up by cerebral operations. *Mind*, 1886b, *11*, 220–42, 377–87, 524–38.

CATTELL, M. R. *The new English grammar: A descriptive introduction.* Cambridge: M.I.T. Press, 1969.

CAVAGNA, G. A., and MARGARIA, R. Airflow rates and efficiency changes during phonation. *Annals of the New York Academy of Sciences.* 1968, *155* (art. 1), 152–64.

CAZDEN, C. B. Environmental assistance in the child's acquisition of grammar. Doctoral dissertation, Harvard University, 1965.

—— The acquisition of noun and verb inflections. *Child Development*, 1968, *39*, 433–48.

CHANANIE, J. D., and TIKOFSKY, R. S. Choice response time and distinctive features in speech discrimination. *Journal of Experimental Psychology.* 1969, *81*, 161–63.

CHAPANIS, A. The reconstruction of abbreviated printed messages. *Journal of Experimental Psychology*, 1954, *48*, 496–510.

—— Color names for color space. *American Scientist*, 1965, *53*, 327–46.

CHOMSKY, C. *The acquisition of syntax in children from 5 to 10.* Cambridge: M.I.T. Press, 1969.

CHOMSKY, N. *Aspects of the theory of syntax.* Cambridge: M.I.T. Press, 1965.

—— *Cartesian linguistics.* New York: Harper & Row, 1966.

——, and HALLE, M. *The sound pattern of English.* New York: Harper & Row, 1968.

——, and MILLER, G. A. Introduction to the formal analysis of natural languages, formal properties of grammars. *In* R. D. BUSH and G. GALANTER (eds.), *Handbook of mathematical psychology*, vol. 2, pp. 269–418. New York: John Wiley, 1963.

CISSNA, R. L. *Basic sign language.* Jefferson City, Mo.: Missouri Baptist Convention, 1963.

CLARK, H. H. Some structural properties of simple active and passive sentences. *Journal of Verbal Learning and Verbal Behavior*, 1965, *4*, 365–70.

—— On the use and meaning of prepositions. *Journal of Verbal Learning and Verbal Behavior*, 1968, *7*, 421–31.

—— Linguistic processes in deductive reasoning. *Psychological Review*, 1969, *76*, 387–404.

CLAY, M. M. A syntactic analysis of reading errors. *Journal of Verbal Learning and Verbal Behavior*, 1968, *7*, 434–38.

CLIFF, N. Adverbs as multipliers. *Psychological Review*, 1959, *66*, 27–44.

CLIFTON, C., JR. Some determinants of the effectiveness of priming word associates. *Journal of Verbal Learning and Verbal Behavior*, 1966, *5*, 167–71.

COCHRAN, S. W. Rated association values of 251 colors. *Journal of Verbal Learning and Verbal Behavior*, 1968, *7*, 14–15.

COFER, C. N. The mediation hypothesis in the analysis and description of behavior. *In* R. A. PATTON (ed.), *Current trends in the description and analysis of behavior.* Pittsburgh: University of Pittsburgh Press, 1957.

—— An experimental analysis of the role of context in verbal behavior. *Transactions of the New York Academy of Sciences*, ser. II, *22*, 341–47.

——, ed. *Verbal learning and verbal behavior.* New York: McGraw-Hill, 1961.

—— On some factors in the organizational characteristics of free recall. *American Psychologist*, 1965, *20*, 261–72.

—— Conditions for the use of verbal associations. *Psychological Bulletin*, 1967, *68*, 1–12.

—— Verbal learning. *In* M. H. MARX (ed.), *Learning: Processes*, pp. 301–78. New York: Macmillan, 1969.

——, and FOLEY, J. P. Mediated generalization and the interpretation of verbal behavior: I. Prolegomena. *Psychological Review*, 1942, *49*, 513–40.

COFER, C. N., and MUSGRAVE, B. S., eds. *Verbal behavior and learning:* Problems and processes. New York: McGraw-Hill, 1963.

COHEN, B. H. Role of awareness in meaning established by classical conditioning. *Journal of Experimental Psychology*, 1964, *67*, 373–78.

COLEMAN, E. B. Responses to a scale of grammaticalness. *Journal of Verbal Learning and Verbal Behavior*, 1965, *4*, 521–27.

CONTANTINI, A. F., and BLACKWOOD, R. O. CCC trigrams of low association value: A re-evaluation. *Psychonomic Science*, 1968, *12*, 67.

COOK, W. M. Ability of children in color discrimination. *Child Development*, 1931, *2*, 303–20.

COOPER, F. S. Spectrum analysis. *Journal of the Acoustical Society of America*, 1950, *22*, 761–62.

—— Research techniques and instrumentation: EMG. *Proceedings of the conference: Communicative problems in cleft palate.* American Speech and Hearing Association, 1965.

——, LIBERMAN, A. M., and BORST, J. M. The inter-conversions of audible and visible patterns as a basis for research on the perception of speech. *Proceedings of the National Academy of Sciences*, 1951, *37*, 318–25.

COOPER, F. S., DELATTRE, P. C., LIBERMAN, A. M., BORST, J. M., and GERSTMAN, L. J. Some experiments on the perception of synthetic speech sounds. *Journal of the Acoustical Society of America*, 1952, *24*, 597–606.

COWEN, E. L., and BEIER, E. G. The influence of "threat-expectancy" on perception. *Journal of Personality*, 1950, *19*, 85–94.

—— Threat expectancy, word frequencies, and perceptual precognition hypotheses. *Journal of Abnormal and Social Psychology*, 1954, *49*, 178–82.

COZZOLINO, J. P. Category set in anagram solutions. *Psychonomic Science*, 1968, *12*, 155–56.

CRAMER, P. Mediated priming of associative responses: The effect of time lapse and interpolated activity. *Journal of Verbal Learning and Verbal Behavior*, 1966, *5*, 163–66.

—— *Word association.* New York: Academic Press, 1968a.

—— Associative satiation or selective association? *Journal of Verbal Learning and Verbal Behavior*, 1968b, *7*, 1095–1105.

CREELMAN, M. B. *The experimental investigation of meaning.* New York: Springer, 1966.

CROTHERS, E., and SUPPES, P. *Experiments in second-language learning.* New York: Academic Press, 1967.

CROVITZ, H. F., and SCHIFFMAN, H. R. Visual field and the letter span. *Journal of Experimental Psychology*, 1965, *70*, 218–23.

DABBS, J. A. Word frequency in newspaper Bengali. College Station: Department of Modern Languages, Texas A & M University, 1966.

DALE, E., and EICHHOLZ, G. *Children's knowledge of words.* Columbus: Bureau of Educational Research, Ohio State University, 1960.

DALE, E., and RAZIK, T. *Bibliography of vocabulary studies.* 2d rev. ed. Columbus: Bureau of Educational Research, Ohio State University, 1963.

DAMSTÉ, P. H., HOLLIEN, H., MOORE, P., and MURRY, T. An X-ray study of vocal fold length. *Folia Phoniatrica*, 1968, *20*, 349–59.

DANKS, J. H. Grammaticalness and meaningfulness in the comprehension of sentences. *Journal of Verbal Learning and Verbal Behavior*, 1969, *8*, 687–96.

DANDELIKER, J., and DORFMAN, D. D. Receiver-operating characteristic curves for taboo and neutral words. *Psychonomic Science*, 1969, *17*, 201–2.

DARLEY, F. L., and WINITZ, H. Age of first word: Review of research. *Journal of Speech and Hearing Disorders*, 1961, *26*, 272–90.

DASHIELL, J. F. *Fundamentals of objective psychology.* Boston: Houghton Mifflin, 1928.

DAVIES, A., ed. *Language testing symposium: A psycholinguistic approach.* London: Oxford University Press, 1968.

DAVIS, B. J., and WERTHEIMER, M. Some determinants of associations to French and English words. *Journal of Verbal Learning and Verbal Behavior*, 1967, *6*, 574–81.

DAVIS, E. A. The development of linguistic skills in twins, singletons with siblings and only children from age five to ten years. *University of Minnesota Institute of Child Welfare Monograph*, no. 14. Minneapolis: University of Minnesota Press, 1937.

DAVIS, G. A., and MANSKE, M. E. Effects of prior serial learning of solution words upon anagram problem solving. *Journal of Experimental Psychology*, 1968, 77, 101–4.

DECROLY, O. *Le développement du langage parlé chez l'enfant.* Liège, Belgium: Edition Biblio, 1930.

DEESE, J. On the structure of associative meaning. *Psychological Review*, 1962, *59*, 161–75.

—— *The structure of associations in language and thought.* Baltimore: The Johns Hopkins University Press, 1965.

DE LAGUNA, G. *Speech: Its function and development.* New Haven, Conn.: Yale University Press, 1927.

DELATTRE, P. C., LIBERMAN, A. M., and COOPER, F. S. Formant transitions and loci as acoustic correlates of place of articulation in American fricatives. *Studia linguistica,* 1964, *18,* 104–21. Acoustic loci and transitional cues for consonants. *Journal of the Acoustical Society of America,* 1955, *27,* 769–73.

——, and GERSTMAN, L. J. An experimental study of the acoustic determinants of vowel color: Observations on one- and two-formant vowels synthesized from spectrographic patterns. *Word,* 1952, *8,* 195–210.

DENES, P. B. On the statistics of spoken English. *Journal of the Acoustical Society of America,* 1963, *35,* 892–904.

DENNIS, W. A note on the circular response hypothesis. *Psychological Review,* 1954, *61,* 334–38.

DEWEY, E. *Behavior development in infants.* New York: Columbia University Press, 1935.

DEWEY, G. *Relative frequency of English speech sounds.* Cambridge: Harvard University Press, 1923.

DIRINGER, D. *The alphabet.* New York: Philosophical Library, 1948.

DIXON, J. F., and SIMMONS, C. H. The impression value of verbs for children. *Child Development,* 1967, *37,* 861–66.

DIXON, T. R., and HORTON, D. L., eds. *Verbal behavior and general behavior theory.* Englewood Cliffs, N.J.: Prentice-Hall, 1968.

DOLLARD, J., and MILLER, N. E. *Personality and psychotherapy.* New York: McGraw-Hill, 1950.

DOMINOWSKI, R. L. Anagram solving as a function of letter moves. *Journal of Verbal Learning and Verbal Behavior,* 1966, *5,* 107–11.

—— Anagram solving as a function of bigram rank and word frequency. *Journal of Experimental Psychology,* 1967, *75,* 299–306.

—— Anagram solving as a function of letter-sequence information. *Journal of Experimental Psychology,* 1968, *76,* 78–83.

——, and EKSTRAND, B. R. Direct and associative priming in anagram solving. *Journal of Experimental Psychology,* 1967, *74,* 84–86.

DORAN, E. W. A study of vocabularies. *Pedagogical Seminary,* 1907, *14,* 401–38.

DORFMAN, D. D. Recognition of taboo words as a function of a priori probability. *Journal of Personality and Social Psychology,* 1967, *7,* 1–10.

DOWNEY, R. G., and HAKES, D. T. Some psychological effects of violating linguistic rules. *Journal of Verbal Learning and Verbal Behavior,* 1968, *7,* 158–61.

DOWNING, J. *Evaluating the initial teaching alphabet.* London: Cassell, 1967.

DUFILHO, J. H., MEFFERD, R. B., JR., and WIELAND, B. A. Influence of early formal reading training on commonality of word associations in children and adults. *Journal of Verbal Learning and Verbal Behavior,* 1969, *8,* 150–51.

DUNCAN, C. P., and WOOD, G. Norms for successive word associations. *Psychonomic Monograph Supplements,* 1966, *1* (7), 1–4.

DUNKEL, H. *Second-language learning.* Boston: Ginn, 1948.

DUNN, L. M. *Expanded manual for the Peabody picture vocabulary test.* Minneapolis: American Guidance Service, 1965.

DUNN-RANKIN, P. The similarity of lower-case letters of the English alphabet. *Journal of Verbal Learning and Verbal Behavior,* 1968, *7,* 990–95.

EARHARD, B., and MANDLER, G. Mediated associations: Paradigms, controls, and mechanisms. *Canadian Journal of Psychology,* 1965, *19,* 346–78.

EBBINGHAUS, H. Über eine neue methode zur prüfung geistiger fähigkeiten und ihre anwendung bei schulkindern. *Zeitschrift für Psychologie und Physiologie der Sinnesorgane,* 1897, *13,* 401–59.

EDFELDT, A. W. *Silent speech and silent reading.* Chicago: University of Chicago Press, 1960.

EDMONDS, EDM., and MUELLER, M. R. Effects of word frequency restriction on anagram solution. *Journal of Experimental Psychology,* 1969, *79,* 545–46.

EFRON, H. Y. Changes in recognition thresholds associated with chlorpromazine, promazine, and phenobarbitol. *Journal of Clinical Psychology,* 1959, *15,* 431–33.

EIMAS, P. D. The relation between identification and discrimination along speech and non-speech continua. *Language and Speech,* 1963, *6,* 206–17.

EISENBERG, L., BERLIN, C. I., DILL, A., and FRANK, S. Class and race effects on the intelligibility of monosyllables. *Child Development,* *39,* 1077–90, 1968.

ELLIS, H. C. Transfer and retention. *In* M. H. MARX (ed.) *Learning: Processes,* pp. 381–478. New York: Macmillan, 1969.

ENTWISLE, D. R. *Word associations of young children.* Baltimore: The Johns Hopkins Press, 1966.

ERIKSEN, C. W. Subception: Fact or artifact. *Psychological Review,* 1956, *63,* 74–80.

—— Unconscious processes. *In* M. R. JONES (ed.), *Nebraska symposium on motivation, 1958.* Lincoln: University of Nebraska Press, 1958.

—— Discrimination and learning without awareness: A methodological survey and evaluation. *Psychological Review,* 1960, *67,* 279–300.

—— Perception and personality. *In* J. W. WEPMAN and R. W. HEINE (eds.) *Concepts of personality.* Chicago: Aldine, 1963.

ERVIN, S. M. Changes with age in verbal determinants of word association. *American Journal of Psychology,* 1961, *74,* 361–72.

ERVIN-TRIPP, S. M. Language development. *In* L. W. HOFFMAN and M. L. HOFFMAN (eds.) *Review of child development research,* Vol. 2, pp. 55–105. New York: Russell Sage Foundation, 1966.

——, and SLOBIN, D. I. Psycholinguistics. *Annual Review of Psychology,* 1966, *17,* 435–74.

ESPER, A. *Mentalism and objectivism in linguistics.* New York: American Elsevier, 1968.

ESPER, E. A. The psychology of language. *Psychological Bulletin,* 1921, *18,* 490–96.

—— A technique for the experimental investigation of associative interference in artificial linguistic material. *Language Monographs,* 1925, (1).

—— Language. *In* C. MURCHISON (ed.) *A handbook of social psychology,* pp. 417–60. Worcester: Clark University Press, 1935.

ESPOSITO, N. J., and PELTON, L. H. A test of two measures of semantic satiation. *Journal of Verbal Learning and Verbal Behavior,* 1969, *8,* 637–44.

FANT, C. G. M. Modern instruments and methods for acoustic studies of speech. *Proceedings of the 8th International Congress of Linguists,* Oslo, 1958, pp. 282–358.

FANT, G. *Acoustic theory of speech production.* 's-Gravenhage, Netherlands: Mouton, 1960.

—— Descriptive analysis of the acoustic aspects of speech. *Logos,* 1962, *4,* 3–17.

—— Analysis and synthesis of speech processes. *In* B. MALMBERG (ed.). *Manual of phonetics,* pp. 171–277. Rev. ed. Amsterdam: North-Holland, 1968.

FANT, L. J. *Say it with hands.* Washington, D.C.: Gallaudet College, 1964.

FILLENBAUM, S. Verbal satiation and changes in meaning of related items. *Journal of Verbal Learning and Verbal Behavior,* 1963, *2,* 263–71.

—— Semantic satiation and decision latency. *Journal of Experimental Psychology,* 1964, *68,* 240–244.

——, JONES, L. V., and RAPAPORT, A. The predictability of words and their grammatical classes as a function of rate of deletion from a speech transcript. *Journal of Verbal Learning and Verbal Behavior,* 1963, *2,* 189–94.

FISICHELLI, V. R., and KARELITZ, S. Frequency spectra of the cries of normal infants and those with Down's syndrome. *Psychonomic Science,* 1966, *6,* 195–96.

FISHBEIN, M., ed. *Readings in attitude theory and measurement.* New York: John Wiley, 1967.

FISHMAN, J. A. *Readings in the sociology of language.* The Hague: Mouton, 1968.

FLANAGAN, J. L. *Speech analysis, synthesis and perception,* New York: Academic Press, 1965.

FLAVELL, J. H., and DRAGUNS, J. A microgenetic approach to perception and thought. *Psychological Bulletin,* 1957, *54,* 197–217.

——, FEINBERG, L. D., and RUDIN, W. A microgenetic approach to word association. *Journal of Abnormal and Social Psychology,* 1958, *57,* 1–7.

FLETCHER, H. *Speech and hearing in communication.* New York: Van Nostrand, 1953.

FLOYD, R. L. Semantic satiation: Replication and test of further implications. *Psychological Reports,* 1962, *11,* 274.

FOLKINS, C., and LEBOW, P. B. An investigation of the expressive value of graphemes. *Psychological Record,* 1966, *16,* 193–200.

FORSTER, K. I. Left-to-right processes in the construction of sentences. *Journal of Verbal Learning and Verbal Behavior,* 1966, *5,* 285–91.

——— Sentence completions latencies as a function of constituent structures. *Journal of Verbal Learning and Verbal Behavior,* 1967, *6,* 878–83.

——— Sentence completion in left and right-branching languages. *Journal of Verbal Learning and Verbal Behavior,* 1968, *7,* 296–99.

FOSS, D. J. Decision processes during sentence comprehension: Effects of lexical item difficulty and position upon decision times. *Journal of Verbal Learning and Verbal Behavior,* 1969, *8,* 457–62.

FOWLER, M. Herdan's statistical parameter and the frequency of English phonemes. *In* E. PULGRAM (ed.) *Studies presented to Joshua Whatmough,* pp. 47–52. 's-Gravenhage: Mouton, 1957.

FRANCIS-WILLIAMS, J. *Rorschach with children.* Oxford: Pergamon, 1968.

FRASER, C., BELLUGI, U., and BROWN, R. W. Control of grammar in imitation comprehension and production. *Journal of Verbal Learning and Verbal Behavior,* 1963, *2,* 121–35.

FREEMAN, F. N. *Evaluation scales for guiding growth in handwriting.* Columbus, Ohio: Zaner-Bloser, 1958.

FRENCH, N. R., CARTER, C. W., JR., and KOENIG, W., JR. The words and sounds of telephone conversation. *Bell System Technical Journal,* 1930, *9,* 290–324.

FRIES, C. C. *The structure of English.* New York: Harcourt Brace Jovanovich, 1952.

——— *Linguistics and reading.* New York: Holt, Rinehart & Winston, 1962.

FROMKIN, V., and LADEFOGED, P. Electromyography in speech research. *Phonetica,* 1966, *15,* 219–42.

FRY, D. B. The frequency of occurrence of speech sounds in Southern English. *Archives Néerlandaises de Phonétique Expérimentale,* 1947, *20,* 103–6.

———, ABRAMSON, A. S., EIMAS, P. D., and LIBERMAN, A. M. The identification and discrimination of synthetic vowels. *Language and Speech,* 1962, *5,* 171–89.

FUJIMARA, O. Analysis of nasal consonants. *Journal of the Acoustical Society of America,* 1962, *34,* 1865–75.

FURTH, H. *Thinking without language.* New York: Free Press, 1966.

GAER, E. P. Children's understanding and production of sentences. *Journal of Verbal Learning and Verbal Behavior,* 1969, *8,* 289–94.

GAETH, J. H., and ALLEN, D. V. Associated values for selected trigrams with children. *Journal of Verbal Learning and Verbal Behavior,* 1966, *8,* 473–77.

GAGNÉ, R. M. Contributions of learning to human development. *Psychological Review,* 1968, *75,* 177–91.

GALLAGHER, J. W., and PALERMO, D. S. The effect of type associative relation on word recognition times. *Child Development,* 1967, *38,* 849–55.

GALTON, F. Psychometric experiments. *Brain,* 1879–80, *2,* 149–62.

GARDINER, A. H. *The theory of speech and language,* 2d ed. New York: Oxford University Press, 1951.

GARNER, W. *Uncertainty and structure as psychological concepts.* New York: John Wiley, 1962.

GARVEY, A. M. *A vocabulary and concept study of recent primary readers.* Nashville, Tenn.: George Peabody College for Teachers, 1951.

GEBELS, G. An investigation of phonetic symbolism in different cultures. *Journal of Verbal Learning and Verbal Behavior,* 1969, *2,* 310–12.

GEIGER, L. *Der ursprung der sprache.* Stuttgart: Cotta, 1869.

GELB, I. V. *A study of writing.* Chicago: University of Chicago Press, 1963.

GENTILE, J. R., and SEIBEL, R. A rating scale measure of word relatedness. *Journal of Verbal Learning and Verbal Behavior,* 1969, *8,* 252–56.

GIBSON, E. J. A systematic application of the concepts of generalization and differentiation to verbal learning. *Psychological Review,* 1940, *47,* 196–229.

——— Learning to read. *Science,* 1965, *148,* 1066–72.

——— Perceptual learning in educational situations. *In* R. M. GAGNÉ and W. J. GEPHART (eds.). *Learning research and school subjects,* pp. 61–68. Ilasca, Ill: Peacock, 1968.

——— *Principles of perceptual learning and development.* New York: Appleton-Century Crofts, 1969.

———, PICK, A. D., and OSSER, H. H. A developmental study of the discrimination of letter-like forms. *Journal of Comparative and Physiological Psychology,* 1962, *58,* 897–906.

GIBSON, E. J., OSSER, H., and PICK, A. D. A study in the development of phoneme-grapheme correspondences. *Journal of Verbal Learning and Verbal Behavior,* 1963, *2,* 142–46.

———, and HAMMOND, M. The role of grapheme-phoneme correspondence in the perception of words. *American Journal of Psychology,* 1962, *75,* 554–70.

GIBSON, J. J., and GIBSON, E. J. Perceptual learning: Enrichment or differentiation. *Psychological Review,* 1955, *62,* 32–41.

GILCHRIST, J. C., LUDEMAN, J. F., and LYSAK, W. Values as determinants of word-recognition thresholds. *Journal of Abnormal and Social Psychology,* 1954, *49,* 423–26.

GLADNEY, T. A., and KRULEE, G. K. The influence of syntactic errors on sentence recognition. *Journal of Verbal Learning and Verbal Behavior,* 1967, *6,* 692–98.

GLANZER, M., and MURPHY, R. Estimating the elicitors of a word association response. *Journal of Verbal Learning and Verbal Behavior,* 1968, *7,* 746–49.

GLAZE, J. A. The association value of non-sense syllables. *Journal of Genetic Psychology,* 1928, *35,* 255–69.

GLEASON, H. A., JR. *An introduction to descriptive linguistics.* New York: Holt, Rinehart & Winston, 1961.

——— *Linguistics and English grammar.* New York: Holt, Rinehart & Winston, 1965.

GOLDIAMOND, I., and HAWKINS, W. F. Vexierversuch: The log relationship between word-frequency and recognition obtained in the absence of stimulus words. *Journal of Experimental Psychology,* 1958, *56,* 457–63.

GOODENOUGH, F. L. The use of pronouns by young children: A note on the development of self-awareness. *Journal of Genetic Psychology,* 1938, *52,* 333–46.

GOODMAN, K. S., ed. *The psycholinguistic nature of the reading process.* Detroit: Wayne University Press, 1968.

GORFEIN, D. S. Measurement of the pronunciability of CVC trigrams. *Psychological Reports,* 1967, *21,* 879–80.

GOSS, A. E. A stimulus-response analysis of the interaction of cue-producing and instrumental responses. *Psychological Review,* 1955, *62,* 20–31.

——— Verbal mediating responses and concept formation. *Psychological Review,* 1961a, *68,* 248–74.

——— Early behaviorism and verbal mediating responses. *American Psychologist,* 1961b, *16,* 285–98.

——— Acquisition and use of conceptual schemes. *In* C. N. COFER (ed.). *Verbal learning and verbal behavior,* pp. 42–69. New York: McGraw-Hill, 1961c.

——— Comments on Professor Noble's paper. *In* C. N. COFER and B. S. MUSGRAVE (eds.). *Verbal behavior and learning: Problems and processes,* pp. 119–55. New York: McGraw-Hill, 1963.

——— Verbal mediation. *Psychological Record,* 1964, *14,* 363–82.

——— Paired-associates learning by young children as functions of initial associative strength and percentage of occurrence of response members. *Journal of Experimental Child Psychology,* 1966, *4,* 398–407.

——— Comments on verbal mediating responses and concept formation. *In* L. A. JAKOBOBITS and M. S. MIRON (eds.), *Readings in the psychology of language,* pp. 604–11. Englewood Cliffs, N.J.: Prentice-Hall, 1957.

——— Frequency and meaning. *Transactions of the New York Academy of Sciences,* 1969, Ser. II, *31,* 975–91.

——— Paired associates and discourse in the acquisition of knowledge, *In* E. Z. Rothkopf and P. E. Johnson (eds.). *Verbal learning research and the technology of written instruction,* pp. 3–67. New York, Teachers' College Press, 1971.

———, and BROWNELL, M. H. Stimulus-response concepts and principles applied to projective test behavior. *Journal of Personality,* 1957, *25,* 505–23.

GOSS, A. E., and COBB, N. J. Formation, maintenance, generalization, and retention of response hierarchies. *Journal of Experimental Psychology*, 1966, *71*, 218–31.

—— Formation, maintenance, generalization and retention of response hierarchies: The role of meaningfulness of response members. *Journal of Experimental Psychology*, 1967, *74*, 272–81.

GOSS, A. E., and GREENFELD, N. Transfer to a motor task as influenced by conditions and degree of prior discrimination training. *Journal of Experimental Psychology*, 1958, *55*, 258–69.

GOSS, A. E., and GREGORY, B. N. Degree of mastery of experimentally acquired verbal responses and their use and influence in conceptual block sorting. *Journal of Genetic Psychology*, 1966, *74*, 279–87.

GOSS, A. E., and NODINE, C. F. *Paired-associates learning.* New York: Academic, 1965.

GOUGH, P. B. Grammatical transformation and speed of understanding. *Journal of Verbal Learning and Verbal Behavior*, 1965, *4*, 107–11.

—— The verification of sentences: The effects of delay of evidence and sentence length. *Journal of Verbal Learning and Verbal Behavior*, 1966, *5*, 492–96.

GRAND, S., and SEGAL, S. J. Recovery in the absence of recall: An investigation of color word priming. *Journal of Experimental Psychology*, 1966, *72*, 138–44.

GRAY, G. W., and WISE, C. M. *The bases of speech.* New York: Harper & Row, 1959.

GRAY, W. S. *The teaching of reading and writing.* Switzerland: Unesco, 1956.

GREEN, R. F., and GOLDFRIED, M. R. On the bipolarity of semantic space. *Psychological Monographs*, 1965, *79*, (6, whole no. 599).

GREENBERG, J. ed. *Anthropological linguistics.* New York: Random House, 1968.

GREENWALD, A. G., BROCK, T. C., and OSTROM, T. M., eds. *Psychological foundations of attitudes.* New York: Academic Press, 1968.

GREGOIRE, A. *L'apprentissage du langage: La troisieme année et les années suivantes*, vol. 2. Gembloux, France: Ducotot, 1947.

—— *L'apprentissage du langage: I. Les deux premières années*, vol. 1, Paris: Droz, 1937.

GRUBET, J. Topicalization in child language. *Foundations of Language*, 1967, *3*, 37–65.

GUIRAUD, P. *Problèmes et méthodes de la statistique linguistique.* Paris: Presses Universitaires de France, 1960.

GUMENICK, W. E., and DOLINSKY, R. Connotative meaning of sentence subjects as a function of verb and object meaning under different grammatical transformations. *Journal of Verbal Learning and Verbal Behavior*, 1969, *8*, 653–57.

HABER, R. N. Perception and thought: An information-processing analysis. *In* J. F. VOSS (ed.). *Approaches to thought*, pp. 1–26. Columbus, Ohio: Merrill, 1969a.

—— *Information-processing approaches to visual perception.* New York: Holt, Rinehart & Winston, 1969b.

HAKES, D. T. The assessment of phoneme similarity. Austin: Department of Psychology, University of Texas, 1964.

HALL, J. F. The reliability of free association responses. *Psychonomic Science*, 1966, *4*, 79–80.

—— *The psychology of learning.* Philadelphia: Lippincott, 1966.

HALL, R. A., JR. *Introductory linguistics.* Philadelphia: Chilton, 1964.

HALLE, M., HUGHES, G. W., and RADLEY, J. P. A. Acoustic properties of stop consonants. *Journal of the Acoustical Society of America*, 1957, *29*, 107–16.

HAMID, P. N. Symmetry and configurations in words and patterns of similar structure. *Psychonomic Science*, 1969, *14*, 281–82.

HANNA, P. R., HANNA, J. S., HODGES, R. E., and RUDORF, E. H., JR. *Phoneme-grapheme correspondence as cues to spelling improvement.* Washington, D.C.: U.S. Government Printing Office, 1966.

HARCUM, E. R. Visual hemifield differences as conflicts in direction of reading. *Journal of Experimental Psychology*, 1966, *72*, 479–80.

—— Hemifield differences in visual perception of redundant stimuli. *Canadian Journal of Psychology*, 1968, *22*, 199–211.

HARE, A. P., BORGOTTA, E. F., and BALES, R. F. *Small groups: Studies in social interaction.* New York: Knopf, 1961.

HARKIN, D. The history of word counts. *Babel*, 1957, *3*, 113–24.

HARRIS, K. S. Cues for the discrimination of American English fricatives in spoken syllables. *Language and Speech*, 1958, *1*, 1–7.

——, ROSOV, R., COOPER, F. S., and LYSAUGHT, G. F. A multiple reaction electrode system. *Electroencephalography and Clinical Neurophysiology*, 1964, *17*, 698–700.

HARRIS, K. S., HOFFMAN, H. S., LIBERMAN, A. M., DELATTRE, P. C., and COOPER, F. S. Effect of third-formant transitions on the perception of the voiced stop consonants. *Journal of the Acoustical Society of America*, 1958, *30*, 122–26.

HARRIS, R., and LOESS, H. Anagram solution times as a function of individual differences in stored digram frequencies. *Journal of Experimental Psychology*, 1968, *77*, 508–11.

HARRIS, Z. *Mathematical structures of language.* New York: John Wiley, 1968.

HARROWER-ERICKSON, M. R., and STEINER, M. E. *Large scale Rorschach techniques.* Springfield, Illinois: Thomas, 1945.

HARTLEY, D. *Observations on man, his frame, his duty, and his expectations*, part 1. Gainesville, Fla.: Scholars' Facsimiles and Reprints, 1966 (1749).

HARWOOD, F. W. Quantitative study of the syntax of the speech of Australian children. *Language and Speech*, 1959, *2*, 236–71.

HAYDEN, R. E. The relative frequency of phonemes in general-American English. *Word*, 1956, *6*, 217–23.

HAYGOOD, R. C., and BOURNE, L. E., JR. Attribute- and rule-learning aspects of conceptual behavior. *Psychological Review*, 1965, *72*, 175–95.

HAYHURST, H. Some errors of young children in producing passive sentences. *Journal of Verbal Learning and Verbal Behavior*, 1967, *6*, 634–39.

HEINBERG, P. *Voice training for speaking and reading aloud.* New York: Ronald, 1964.

HEINZ, J. M., and STEVENS, K. N. On the properties of voiceless fricative consonants. *Journal of the Acoustical Society of America*, 1961, *33*, 589–96.

HEISE, D. R. Semantic differential profiles for 1000 most frequent English words. *Psychological Monographs*, 1965, *79*, (8, whole no. 601).

—— Some methodological issues in semantic differential research. *Psychological Bulletin*, 1969, *72*, 406–22.

HENDRICKSON, L. H., and MUEHL, S. The effect of attention and motor response pretraining on learning to discriminate B and D in kindergarten children. *Journal of Educational Psychology*, 1962, *53*, 236–41.

HENLE, P., ed. *Language, thought, and culture.* Ann Arbor: University of Michigan Press, 1958.

HENLEY, N. M. A psychological study of the semantics of animal terms. *Journal of Verbal Learning and Verbal Behavior*, 1969, *8*, 176–84.

HERDAN, G. *Language as choice and chance.* Groningen: Noordhoff, 1956.

—— *Type-token mathematics.* 's-Gravenhage: Mouton, 1960.

—— *The calculus of linguistic observations.* 's-Gravenage: Mouton, 1962.

—— *The advanced theory of language as choice and chance.* New York: Springer Verlag, 1966.

HERRIOT, P. The comprehension of sentences as a function of grammatical depth and order. *Journal of Verbal Learning and Verbal Behavior*, 1968, *9*, 938–41.

—— The comprehension of active and passive sentences as a function of pragmatic expectations. *Journal of Verbal Learning and Verbal Behavior*, 1969, *8*, 166–69.

HERSHENSON, M. Stimulus structure, cognitive structure, and the perception of letter arrays. *Journal of Experimental Psychology*, 1969, *79*, 327–35.

HERTZ, M. R. *Frequency tables for scoring Rorschach responses.* 4th ed. Cleveland: The Press of Western Reserve University, 1961.

HERTZLER, J. O. *A sociology of language.* New York: Random House, 1965.

HERZKA, H. S. *Die sprache des säugling.* Basel: Schwake, 1967.

HILDRETH, G. The success of young children in number and letter construction. *Child Development*, 1932, *3*, 1–14.

HILGARD, E. R. Methods and procedures in the study of learning. *In* S. S. STEVENS (ed.) *Handbook of experimental psychology.* New York: John Wiley, 1951.

HIVELY, W. A framework for the analysis of elementary reading behavior. *American Education Research Journal*, 1966, *3*, 89–103.

HOCH, P., and ZUBIN, J., eds. *Psychopathology of communication.* New York: Grune & Stratton, 1958.

HOCKETT, C. F. *A manual of phonology.* Bloomington: Indiana University Publications in Anthropology and Linguistics, Mem. 11, 1955.

———— *A course in modern linguistics.* New York: The Macmillan Company, 1958.

———— *Language, mathematics, and linguistics.* The Hague: Mouton, 1967.

HOFFMAN, H. S. Study of some cues in the perception of the voiced stop consonants. *Journal of the Acoustical Society of America,* 1958, *30,* 1035–41.

HOLBROOK, A., and FAIRBANKS, G. Diphthong formants and their movements. *Journal of Speech and Hearing Research,* 1962, *5,* 38–58.

HOLLIEN, H. Some laryngeal correlates of vocal pitch. *Journal of Speech and Hearing Research,* 1960a, *3,* 52–58.

———— Vocal pitch variation related to changes in vocal fold length. *Journal of Speech and Hearing Research,* 1960b, *3,* 150–56.

———— Vocal fold thickness and fundamental frequency of phonation. *Journal of Speech and Hearing Research,* 1962, *5,* 237–43.

———— Laryngeal research by means of laminagraphy. *Archives of Otolaryngology,* 1964, *80,* 303–8.

————, and CURTIS, J. A laminagraphic study of vocal pitch. *Journal of Speech and Hearing Research,* 1960, *3,* 361–71.

HOLLIEN, H., and MOORE, P. Measurement of the vocal folds during changes in pitch. *Journal of Speech and Hearing Research,* 1960, *3,* 157–65.

HOLSOPPLE, J. Q., and MIALE, F. R. *Sentence completion: A projective method for the study of personality.* Springfield; Ill.: Thomas, 1954.

HOLT, E. B. *Animal drive and the learning process.* New York: Holt, Rinehart & Winston, 1931.

HOOK, SIDNEY, ed. *Language and philosophy: A symposium.* New York: New York University Press, 1969.

HORN, E. The commonest words in the spoken vocabulary of children up to and including six years of age. *Yearbook National Society for the Study of Education,* 1925, 24 (I), 186–98.

———— A basic writing vocabulary. *University of Iowa Monographs in Education,* Series 1, no. 4, 1926.

———— Language and meaning. In *Yearbook National Society for the Study of Education* 1942, (2), *41,* 377–413.

———— Phonetics and spelling. *Elementary School Journal,* 1957, *57,* 424–32.

HOMN, G. L., and PREHM, H. J. Oral word association norms for educable mentally retarded children in the public schools. *Psychological Reports,* 1967, *21,* 643–44.

HORTON, D. L., and MECHERIKOFF, M. Letter preferences. *Journal of Applied Psychology,* 1960, *44,* 252–53.

HOUSE, A. S., and FAIRBANKS, G. The influence of consonant environment upon the secondary acoustical characteristics of vowels. *Journal of the Acoustical Society of America,* 1953, *25,* 105–13.

HOVLAND, C. I. Human learning and retention. *In* S. S. STEVENS (ed.) *Handbook of experimental psychology,* pp. 613–89. New York: John Wiley, 1951.

HOWE, E. S. Probabilistic adverbial qualifications of adjectives. *Journal of Verbal Learning and Verbal Behavior,* 1962, *1,* 225–42.

———— Verb tense, negatives, and other determinants of the intensity of evaluative meaning. *Journal of Verbal Learning and Verbal Behavior,* 1966, *5,* 147–55.

———— Associative structure of quantifiers. *Journal of Verbal Learning and Verbal Behavior,* 1966, *5,* 156–62.

———— Effects of quantifiers on evaluative meaning: Replications using English subjects. *Journal of Verbal Learning and Verbal Behavior,* 1969a, *8,* 554–56.

———— Some quantitative free associative correlates of Noble's *m. Journal of Verbal Learning and Verbal Behavior,* 1969b, *8,* 597–603.

HOWES, D. On the relation between the intelligibility and frequency of occurrence of English words. *Journal of the Acoustical Society of America,* 1957, *29,* 296–305.

———— A word count of spoken English. *Journal of Verbal Learning and Verbal Behavior,* 1966, *5,* 572–604.

HUANG, Y-H, PRATOOMRAJ, S., and JOHNSON, R. C. Universal magnitude symbolism. *Journal of Verbal Learning and Verbal Behavior,* 1969, *8,* 155–56.

HULL, C. L. *Principles of behavior.* New York: Appleton-Century-Crofts, 1943.

HULTZÉN, L. S., ALLEN, J. H. D., JR., and MIRON, M. S. *Tables of transitional frequencies of English phonemes.* Urbana: University of Illinois Press, 1964.

HUNTER, W. S. *Learning: IV. Experimental studies of learning. In* C. MURCHISON (ed.). *A handbook of general experimental psychology,* pp. 497–570. Worcester: Clark University Press, 1934.

HUNTINGTON, D. A., HARRIS, K. S., and SCHOLES, G. H. An electromyographic study of consonant articulation in hearing impaired and normal speakers. *Journal of Speech and Hearing Research,* 1968, *11,* 147–58.

HUPKA, R. B., and GOSS, A. E. Initial polarity, semantic differential scale, meaningfulness, and subjects' associative fluency in semantic satiation and generation. *Journal of Experimental Psychology,* 1969, *79,* 308–11.

HUTT, L. D., and ANDERSON, J. P. Perceptual defense and vigilance: Predictions from the Bryne scale of repression-sensitization. *Psychonomic Science,* 1967, *9,* 473–74.

HUTTENLOCHER, J., and STRAUSS, S. Comprehension and a statement's relation to the situation it describes. *Journal of Verbal Learning and Verbal Behavior,* 1968, *7,* 300–304.

HUTTENLOCHER, J., EISENBERG, K., and STRAUSS, S. Comprehension: Relations between perceived action and logical subject. *Journal of Verbal Learning and Verbal Behavior,* 1968, *7,* 527–30.

HYMES, D., ed. *Language in culture and society,* New York: Harper & Row, 1964.

INGLIS, J. Abnormalities of motivation and "ego-functions." *In* H. J. EYSENCK (ed.). *Handbook of abnormal psychology.* New York: Basic Books, 1961.

International Phonetic Association. *The principles of the International Phonetic Association.* London: University College, 1949.

IRWIN, O. C. Research on speech sounds for the first six months of life. *Psychological Bulletin,* 1941, *38,* 277–85.

———— Development of speech during infancy: Curve of phonemic frequencies. *Journal of Experimental Psychology,* 1947, *37,* 187–93.

———— Speech development in the young child: 2. Some factors related to the speech development of the infant and young child. *Journal of Speech and Hearing Disorders,* 1952, *17,* 269–79.

———— Phonetical description of speech development in childhood. *In* L. KAISER (ed.) *Manual of phonetics,* pp. 403–25. Amsterdam: North-Holland, 1957.

———— Language and communication. *In* P. H. MUSSEN (ed.), *Handbook of research methods in child development,* pp. 487–516. New York: John Wiley, 1960.

————, and CHEN, H. P. Speech sound elements during the first year of life; a review of the literature. *Journal of Speech Disorders,* 1943, *8,* 109–21.

———— Development of speech during infancy: Curve of phonemic types. *Journal of Experimental Psychology,* 1946, *36,* 431–36.

JAKOBSON, R. *Kindersprache, aphasie und allgemeine lautgesetze.* Uppsala: Almquist & Wiksell, 1941. Reprinted in R. Jakobson, *Selected writings,* vol. I. 's-Gravenhage: Mouton, 1962, pp. 329–401.

————, FANT, G., and HALLE, M. *Preliminaries to speech analysis.* Cambridge: M.I.T. Press, 1963.

JAKOBSON, R., and HALLE, M. Phonology in relation to phonetics. *In* B. MALMBERG (ed.), pp. 411–63. *Manual of phonetics.* Rev. ed. Amsterdam: North-Holland, 1968.

JEFFREY, W. E., and SAMUELS, S. J. Effect of method of reading training on initial learning and transfer. *Journal of Verbal Learning and Verbal Behavior,* 1967, *6,* 354–58.

JENKIN, N. Affective processes in perception. *Psychological Bulletin,* 1957, *54,* 100–127.

JENKINS, J. J. Mediated associations: Paradigms and situations. *In* C. N. COFER and B. S. MUSGRAVE (eds.), pp. 210–45. *Verbal behavior and learning: Problems and processes.* New York: McGraw-Hill, 1963.

———— Summary. *In* J. F. KAVANAGH (ed.) *Communicating by language: The reading process,* pp. 215–22. Bethesda, Md.: U.S. Department of Health, Education, and Welfare, National Institute of Child Health and Development, 1968.

————, and PALERMO, D. S. Mediation processes and the acquisition of linguistic structure. *Monographs of the Society for Research in Child Development,* 1964, *29,* (1, Ser. No. 92), 141–69.

JENKINS, J. J., and RUSSELL, W. A. Systematic changes in word association norms: 1910–1952. *Journal of Abnormal and Social Psychology*, 1960, *60*, 293–304.

JESPERSON, O. *Language: Its nature, development, and origin.* New York: Holt, 1922.

JOHNSON, D. M. Solution of anagrams. *Psychological Bulletin*, 1966, *66*, 371–84.

JOHNSON, M. G. Syntactic position and rated meaning. *Journal of Verbal Learning and Verbal Behavior*, 1967, *6*, 240–46.

JOHNSON, P. E. Associative meaning of concepts in physics. *Journal of Educational Psychology*, 1964, *35*, 84–88.

——— Word relatedness and problem solving in high-school physics. *Journal of Educational Psychology*, 1965, *56*, 217–24.

JOHNSON, R. C. Mean associative latencies of 200 CVC trigrams. *Journal of Psychology*, 1964, *58*, 301–5.

——— Magnitude symbolism of English words. *Journal of Verbal Learning and Verbal Behavior*, 1967, *6*, 508–11.

JOHNSON, R. E. The reliability of associative norms. *Journal of Verbal Learning and Verbal Behavior*, 1968, *7*, 1084–89.

JOHNSON, S. G. Hierarchical clustering schemes. *Psychometrika*, 1967, *32*, 241–54.

JOHNSON, W. Studies in language behavior. *Psychological Monographs*, 1944, *56*, (2, whole no. 255), 1–111.

——— *People in quandaries.* New York: Harper, 1946.

——— *The onset of stuttering: Research findings and implications.* Minneapolis: University of Minnesota Press, 1959.

———, and LEUTENAGGER, R. R. *Stuttering in children and adults.* Minneapolis: University of Minnesota Press, 1955.

JONES, D. *The phoneme,* 2d ed. Cambridge, England: Heffer, 1962.

JONES, L. G. English phonotactic structure and first language acquisition. *Lingua*, 1967, *19*, 1–59.

JUDD, C. H. *Educational psychology.* Boston: Houghton Mifflin, 1939. Pp. 131–246.

JUNG, C. G. *Studies in word association.* London: Heineman, 1918.

JUNG, J. Experimental studies of factors affecting word association. *Psychological Bulletin*, 1966, *66*, 125–33.

——— Consistency of responding on a successive word association test. *Journal of Verbal Learning and Verbal Behavior*, 1967, *6*, 766–70.

——— *Verbal learning.* New York: Holt, Rinehart & Winston, 1968.

KAHANE, H., KAHANE, R., and SAPORTA, S. Development of verbal categories in child language. *International Journal of American Linguistics*, 1958, *24*, no. 4, part II.

KAHNEMAN, D. Method, findings, and theory in studies of visual masking. *Psychological Bulletin*, 1968, *70*, 404–25.

KAINZ, F. *Psychologie der sprache.* Books I-IV. Stuttgart: Verlag, 1941, 1943, 1954, 1956.

KANTNER, C. E., and WEST, R. *Phonetics.* Rev. ed. New York: Harper & Row, 1960.

KANTOR, J. R. *An objective psychology of grammar.* Bloomington, Indiana: Principia Press, 1952 (1936).

KANUNGO, R. N., and LAMBERT, W. E. Semantic satiation and meaningfulness. *American Journal of Psychology*, 1963, *76*, 421–28.

KAPLAN, H. M. *Anatomy and physiology of speech.* New York: McGraw-Hill, 1960.

KAPLAN, I. T., and CARVELLAS, T. Effect of word length on anagram solution time. *Journal of Verbal Learning and Verbal Behavior*, 1968, *7*, 201–8.

KAPLAN, M. F., and GRIER, J. B. Differences in auditory word recognition thresholds as a function of response hierarchy. *Psychonomic Science*, 1968, *12*, 43–44.

KARLGREN, H. Statistical methods in phonetics. *In* B. MALMBERG (ed.) *Manual of phonetics*, pp. 129–54. Rev. ed. Amsterdam: North-Holland, 1968.

KASSCHAU, R. A. Semantic satiation as a function of duration of repetition and initial meaning intensity. *Journal of Verbal Learning and Verbal Behavior*, 1969, *8*, 36–42.

KATZ, J. J. *The philosophy of language.* New York: Harper & Row, 1966.

KEILMAN, P. A., and MORAN, L. J. Association structures of mental retardates. *Multivariate Behavioral Research*, 1967, *2*, 35–45.

KEMPLER, B., and WIENER, M. Personality and perception in the recognition threshold paradigm. *Psychological Review*, 1963, *70*, 349–56.

KENDLER, H. H., and KENDLER, T. S. Vertical and horizontal processes in problem solving. *Psychological Review*, 1962, *69*, 1–16.

KENT, G. H., and ROSANOFF, A. J. A study of associations in insanity. *American Journal of Insanity*, 1910, *67*, 37–96, 317–90.

KENYON, J. S., and KNOTT, T. A. *A pronouncing dictionary of American English*, 2d ed. Springfield, Mass.: Merriam, 1953.

KERRICK, J. S., NAGEL, D. C., and BENNETT, R. L. Multiple ratings of sound stimuli. *Journal of the Acoustical Society of America*, 1969, *45*, 1014–21.

KERSTA, L. C. Voiceprint identification. *Nature*, 1962, *196*, 1253–57.

KIRKPATRICK, E. A. *Fundamentals of child study.* New York: Macmillan, 1903.

KISS, G. R. Words, associations, and networks. *Journal of Verbal Learning and Verbal Behavior*, 1968, *7*, 707–13.

KJELDERGAARD, P. M. Transfer and mediation in verbal learning. *In* T. R. DIXON and D. L. HORTON (eds.), pp. 67–96. *Verbal behavior and general behavior theory.* Englewood Cliffs, N.J.: Prentice-Hall, 1968.

KLEIN, G. S. Semantic power measured through the interference of words with color naming. *American Journal of Psychology*, 1964, *77*, 576–88.

KLIMA, E., and BELLUGI, U. Syntactic regularities in the speech of children. *In* J. LYONS and R. J. WALES (eds.) *Psycholinguistic papers*, pp. 183–208. Edinburgh: Edinburgh University Press, 1966.

KOENIG, W., DUNN, H. K., and LACY, L. Y. The sound spectrograph. *The Journal of the Acoustical Society of America*, 1946, *17*, 19–49.

KOUTSOUDAS, A. *Writing transformational grammars.* New York: McGraw-Hill, 1966.

KOPLIN, J. H., ODOM, P. B., BLANTON, R. L., and NUNNALLY, J. C. Word association test performance of deaf subjects. *Journal of Speech and Hearing Research*, 1967, *10*, 126–32.

KRUSKAL, J. B. Multidimensional scaling by optimizing goodness of fit to a nonmetric hypothesis. *Psychometrika*, 1964, *29*, 1–27.

KUČERA, H., and FRANCIS, W. N. *Computational analysis of present-day American English.* Providence, R. I.: Brown University Press, 1967.

KURCZ, I. Inter-language comparison of word association responses. *International Journal of Psychology*, 1966, *1*, 151–62.

KURODA, S-Y. Generative grammatical studies in the Japanese language. Ph. D. dissertation, M.I.T., 1965.

KYDD, W. L., and BELT, D. A. Continuous palatography. *Journal of Speech and Hearing Disorders*, 1964, *29*, 489–92.

LACHMAN, R., and LAUGHERY, K. R. Letter-word association: Lexical responses to alphabetic stimuli of 1180 college students. Buffalo: Research Program in Human Cognition and Information Processing, Department of Psychology, State University of New York, 1966.

LACY, O. W., LEWINGER, N., and ADAMSON, J. F. Foreknowledge as a factor affecting perceptual defense. *Journal of Experimental Psychology*, 1953, *45*, 169–74.

LADEFOGED, P. *Elements of acoustic phonetics.* Chicago: University of Chicago Press, 1962.

LADO, R. *Language testing.* London: Longmans, Green, 1961.

——— *Language teaching.* New York: McGraw-Hill, 1964.

LAFFAL, J. *Pathological and normal language.* New York: Atherton, 1965.

LAMBERT, W. E., and JAKOBOVITS, L. A. Verbal satiation and changes in the intensity of meaning. *Journal of Experimental Psychology*, 1960, *60*, 376–83.

LAMBERT, W. E., and MOORE, H. Word association responses: Comparisons of American and French monolinguals and bilinguals. *Journal of Personality and Social Psychology*, 1966, *3*, 313–20.

LANDAR, H. J., ERVIN, S. M., and HOROWITZ, A. E. Navaho color categories. *Language*, 1960, *36*, 368–82.

LANDAU, J. M. *A word count of modern Arabic prose.* New York: American Council of Learned Societies, 1959.

LANE, H. The motor theory of speech perception: A critical review. *Psychological Review*, 1965, *72*, 275–309.

LAPPIN, J. S., and LOWE, C. A. Meaningfulness and pronounceability in the coding of visually presented verbal materials. *Journal of Experimental Psychology*, 1969, *81*, 22–28.

LAZARUS, R. S. Subception: fact or artifact? A reply to Eriksen, *Psychological Review*, 1956, *63*, 343–47.

LAZARUS, R. S., and MCCLEARY, R. A. Autonomic discrimination without awareness: A study of subception. *Psychological Review*, 1951, *58*, 113–22.

LEDWITH, N. H. *Rorschach responses of elementary school children: A normative study.* Pittsburgh: University of Pittsburgh Press, 1959.

LEE, L. L. Developmental sentence types: A method for comparing normal and deviant syntactic development. *Journal of Speech and Hearing Disorders,* 1966, *31,* 311–30.

LEHISTE, I. *Acoustical characteristics of selected English consonants.* Bloomington: Indiana University Press, 1964.

———, and PETERSON, G. E. Linguistic considerations in the study of speech intelligibility. *Journal of the Acoustical Society of America,* 1959, *31,* 280–86.

——— Vowel amplitude and phonemic stress in American English. *Journal of the Acoustical Society of America,* 1959, *31,* 428–35.

——— Transitions, glides, and diphthongs. *Journal of the Acoustical Society of America,* 1961, *33,* 268–77.

LENNEBERG, E. H. *Biological foundations of language.* New York: John Wiley, 1967.

LEOPOLD, W. F. *Bibliography of child language.* Evanston, Ill.: Northwestern University Press, 1952.

——— Patterning in children's language learning. *Language Learning,* 1953–54, *5,* 1–14.

LEVELT, W. J. M. The scaling of syntactic relatedness: A new method in psycholinguistic research. *Psychonomic Science,* 1969, *17,* 381–82.

LEVIN, H., WATSON, J. S., and FELDMAN, M. Writing as pretraining for association learning. *Journal of Educational Psychology,* 1964, *55,* 181–84.

LEWIS, E. P., and LEWIS, H. An analysis of errors in the formation of manuscript letters by first-grade children. *American Educational Research Journal,* 1965, *2,* 25–36.

LEWIS, M. M. *Infant speech.* London: Kegan Paul, Trench, Trubner, 1936.

LIBERMAN, A. M. Some results of research on speech perception. *Journal of the Acoustical Society of America,* 1957, *29,* 117–23.

———, COOPER, F. S., HARRIS, K. S., and MACNEILAGE, P. F. A motor theory of speech perception. *Proceedings of the Speech Communication Seminar,* Stockholm, 1962. Stockholm: Royal Institute of Technology, 1963, D3.

LIBERMAN, A. M., COOPER, F. S., SHANKWEILER, D. P., and STUDDERT-KENNEDY, M. Perception of the speech code. *Psychological Review,* 1967, *6,* 431–62.

LIBERMAN, A. M., DELATTRE, P., and COOPER, F. S. The role of selected stimulus-variables in the perception of the unvoiced stop consonants. *American Journal of Psychology,* 1952, *65,* 497–516.

———, and GERSTMAN, L. J., The role of consonant-vowel transition in the perception of the stop and nasal consonants. *Psychological Monographs,* 1954, *68,* no. 8. (whole no. 379), 1–13.

LIBERMAN, A. M., HARRIS, K. S., HOFFMAN, H. S., and GRIFFITH, B. C. The discrimination of speech sounds within and across phoneme boundaries. *Journal of Experimental Psychology,* 1957, *54,* 358–68.

LIBERMAN, A. M., HARRIS, K. S., KINNEY, J. A., and LANE, H. The discrimination of relative onset time of the components of certain speech and nonspeech patterns. *Journal of Experimental Psychology,* 1961, *61,* 379–88.

LIBERMAN, A. M., INGEMANN, F., LISTER, L., DELATTRE, P., and COOPER, F. S. Minimal rules for synthesizing speech. *Journal of the Acoustical Society of America,* 1959, *31,* 1490–99.

LIEBERMAN, P. *Intonation, perception, and language.* Cambridge: M.I.T. Press, 1967.

———, KNUDSON, R., and MEAD, J. Determination of the rate of fundamental frequency with respect to subglottal air pressure during sustained phonation. *Journal of the Acoustical Society of America,* 1969, *45,* 1535–43.

LIFTON, H., and GOSS, A. E. Aural-visual transfer of paired-associates learning. *Journal of General Psychology,* 1962, *66,* 225–34.

LILLY, R. S. The qualification of evaluative adjectives by frequency adverbs. *Journal of Verbal Learning and Verbal Behavior,* 1968a, *7,* 333–36.

——— Multiplying values of intensive probabilistic and frequency adverbs when combined with potency adjectives. *Journal of Verbal Learning and Verbal Behavior,* 1968b, *7,* 854–59.

LINDBLOM, B. E. F., and STUDDERT-KENNEDY, M. On the role of formant transitions in vowel recognition. *Journal of the Acoustical Society of America,* 1967, *42,* 830–43.

LISKER, L., ABRAMSON, A. S., COOPER, F. S., and SCHVEY, M. A. Transillumination of the larynx in running speech. *Journal of the Acoustical Society of America,* 1969, *45,* 1544–46.

LLOYD, D. J., and WARFEL, H. R. *American English and its cultural setting.* New York: Knopf, 1956.

LOEWENTHAL, K. The form class of word associations to nominalizations and adjectivalizations. *Psychonomic Science,* 1969, *16,* 197–98.

LOIGMAN, B. M., and GOSS, A. E. Attributes of unfamiliar, long, scientific names. *Psychonomic Science,* 1969, *17,* 327–28.

LORGE, I. *The semantic count of the 570 commonest English words.* New York: Teachers College Press, 1949.

———, and THORNDIKE, E. L. *A semantic count of English words.* New York: Teachers College Press, 1938.

LOOFT, W. R., and BARTZ, W. H. Animism revived. *Psychological Bulletin,* 1969, *71,* 1–19.

LURIA, A. R. Speech development and the formation of mental processes. *In* M. COLE and I. MALTZMAN (eds.). *A handbook of contemporary Soviet psychology,* pp. 121–62. New York: Basic Books, 1969.

LYNIP, A. The use of magnetic devices in the collection and analysis of the preverbal utterances of an infant. *Genetic Psychology Monographs,* 1951, *44,* 221–62.

LYONS, J. *Introduction to theoretical linguistics.* Cambridge: Cambridge University Press, 1968.

MCCARTHY, D. The vocalization of infants. *Psychological Bulletin,* 1929, *26,* 625–51.

——— *The language development of the preschool child.* Minneapolis: University of Minnesota, 1930.

——— Language development. *In* C. MURCHISON (ed.) *A handbook of child psychology,* pp. 278–315. Worcester: Clark University Press, 1931.

——— Language development, *In* C. MURCHISON (ed.) *A handbook of child psychology,* pp. 329–73, 2d ed. rev. Worcester Mass.: Clark University Press, 1933.

——— *Language development in children. In* L. CARMICHAEL (ed.) *Manual of Child Psychology,* pp. 476–581. New York: John Wiley, 1946.

——— Language development in children. *In* L. CARMICHAEL (ed.), *Manual of child psychology,* 2d ed. New York: John Wiley, 1954.

——— Research in language development: Retrospect and prospect. *Monographs of the Society for Research in Child Development,* 1959, *24,* 5.

MCGEOCH, J. A. *The psychology of human learning.* New York: Longmans, Green, 1942.

———, and IRION, A. L. *The psychology of human learning,* 2d ed. New York: Longmans, Green, 1952.

MCGINNIES, E., COMER, P. B., and LACEY, O. L. Visual recognition threshold as a function of word length and word frequency. *Journal of Experimental Psychology,* 1952, *44,* 65–69.

MCGRANAHAN, D. V. The psychology of language. *Psychological Bulletin,* 1936, *33,* 178–216.

MCNEILL, D. The origin of associations within the same grammatical class. *Journal of Verbal Learning and Verbal Behavior,* 1963, *2,* 250–62.

——— A study of word association. *Journal of Verbal Learning and Verbal Behavior,* 1966a, *5,* 548–57.

——— Developmental psycholinguistics. *In* F. SMITH and G. A. MILLER (eds.) *The genesis of language,* pp. 15–84. Cambridge: M.I.T. Press, 1966b.

MACKEY, W. F. *Language teaching analysis.* Bloomington: Indiana University Press, 1965.

MACNEILAGE, P. F., and DECLERK, J. J. On the motor control of coarticulation in CVC monosyllables. *Journal of the Acoustical Society of America.* 1969, *45,* 1217–33.

———, and SHOLES, G. N. An electromyographic study of the tongue during vowel production. *Journal of Speech and Hearing Research,* 1964, *7,* 209–32.

MALMBERG, B. *Structural linguistics and human communication,* vol. 2. New York: Academic Press, 1963.

MALTZMAN, I., BOGARTZ, W., and BERGER, L. A procedure for increasing word association originality and its transfer effects. *Journal of Experimental Psychology,* 1958, *56,* 392–98.

MARKEL, N. M., and HAMP, E. P. Connotative meaning of certain phoneme sequences. *Studies in Linguistics*, 1961, *15*, 47–61.

MARKEY, J. F. *The symbolic process and its integration in children.* London: Kegan Paul, Trench, Trubner, 1928.

MARKS, L. E. Some structural and sequential factors in the processing of sentences. *Journal of Verbal Learning and Verbal Behavior*, 1967a, *6*, 707–13.

—— Judgements of grammaticalness of some English sentences and semi-sentences. *American Journal of Psychology*, 1967b, *80*, 196–204.

—— Scaling of grammaticalness of self-embedded English sentences. *Journal of Verbal Learning and Verbal Behavior*, 1968, 7, 965–67.

——, and MILLER, G. A. The role of semantic and syntactic constraints in the memorization of English sentences. *Journal of Verbal Learning and Verbal Behavior*, 1964, *3*, 1–5.

MARSHALL, G. R., and COFER, C. H. Associative indices as measures of word relatedness: A summary and comparison of ten methods. *Journal of Verbal Learning and Verbal Behavior*, 1963, *1*, 408–21.

MARTIN, E. Stimulus meaningfulness and paired associate transfer: An encoding variability hypothesis. *Psychological Review*, 1968, *75*, 421–41.

MARTIN, J. G. Temporal word spacing and the perception of ordinary, anomalous, and scrambled strings. *Journal of Verbal Learning and Verbal Behavior*, 1968a, 7, 154–57.

—— A comparison of ordinary, anomalous, and scrambled word strings. *Journal of Verbal Learning and Verbal Behavior*, 1968b, 7, 390–95.

MARTY, A. *Untersuchungen zur grundlegung der allgemeinen grammatik und sprachphilosophie.* Halle: Niemeyer, 1908.

MAYZNER, M. S., and TRESSELT, M. E. The ranking of letter pairs and single letters to match digram and single-letter frequency counts. *Journal of Verbal Learning and Verbal Behavior*, 1962, *1*, 203–7.

—— Tables of single-letter and digram frequency counts for various word-length and letter-position combinations. *Psychonomic Monograph Supplements*, 1965, *1*, 13–32.

—— Anagram solution times: A function of multiple solution anagrams. *Journal of Experimental Psychology*, 1966, *71*, 66–73.

——, and WOLIN, B. R. Tables of trigram frequency counts for various word-length and letter-position combinations. *Psychonomic Monograph Supplements*, 1965a, *1* (5), 33–78.

—— Tables of tetragram frequency counts for various word-length and letter-position combinations. *Psychonomic Monograph Supplements*, 1965b, *1* (5), 79–142.

—— Tables of pentagram frequency counts for various word-length and letter-position combinations. *Psychonomic Monograph Supplement*, 1965c, *1* (5), 145–85.

MEHLER, J., and CAREY, P. Role of surface and base structure in the perception of sentences. *Journal of Verbal Learning and Verbal Behavior*, 1967, *6*, 335–38.

MEILLET, A., and COHEN, M. (eds.) *Les langues du monde.* Paris: 1952.

MENYUK, P. Syntactic structure in the language of children. *Child Development*, 1963a, *34*, 407–27.

—— A preliminary evaluation of grammatical capacity in children. *Journal of Verbal Learning and Verbal Behavior*, 1963b, *2*, 429–39.

—— Comparison of grammar of children with functionally deviant and normal speech. *Journal of Speech and Hearing Research*, 1964a, 7, 109–21.

—— Syntactic rules used by children from preschool through first grade. *Child Development*, 1964b, *18*, 533–46.

—— The role of distinctive features in children's acquisition of phonology. *Journal of Speech and Hearing Research*, 1968, *11*, 138–46.

—— *Sentences children use.* Cambridge: M.I.T. Press, 1969.

——, and ANDERSON, S. Children's identification and reproduction of /w/, /r/, and /l/. *Journal of Speech and Hearing Research*, 1969, *12*, 39–52.

MESSÉ, L. A., CHISENA, P. R., JR., and SHIPLEY, R. H. A sex difference in the recognition level of words. *Psychonomic Science*, 1968, *11*, 131–32.

MESSER, S., JAKOBOVITS, L. A., KANUNGO, R. N., and LAMBERT, W. E. Semantic satiation of words and numbers. *British Journal of Psychology*, 1964, *55*, 155–63.

METFESSEL, M. Experimental phonetics. *Psychological Bulletin*, 1929, *26*, 305–23.

MÉTRAUX, R. W. Speech profiles of the preschool child 18 to 54 months. *Journal of Speech and Hearing Disorders*, 1950, *15*, 37–53.

MEUMANN, E. *The psychology of learning.* New York: D. Appleton, 1913.

MEWHORT, D. J. Sequential redundancy and letter spacing as determinants of tachistoscopic recognition. *Canadian Journal of Psychology*, 1966, *20*, 435–44.

MEYER, M. *The fundamental laws of human behavior.* Boston: Gotham, 1911.

—— *Psychology of the other-one*, 2d ed. rev. Columbia: Missouri Book Company, 1922.

MICHELS, K. M., and ZUSNE, L. Metrics of visual form. *Psychological Bulletin*, 1965, *63*, 74–86.

MICKELSON, N. I. Meaningfulness indices for 120 mass and count nouns for children aged nine years. *Journal of Verbal Learning and Verbal Behavior*, 1969, *8*, 80–82.

—— Meaningfulness (m): Its relation to frequency and specificity for children aged nine years. *Psychonomic Science*, 1969, *17*, 202.

MILLER, G. A. *Language and communication.* New York: McGraw-Hill, 1951.

—— Some psychological studies of grammar. *American Psychologist*, 1962, *17*, 748–62.

——, and FRIEDMAN, E. A. The reconstruction of mutilated English texts. *Information and Control*, 1957, *1*, 38–55.

MILLER, G. A., and MCKEAN, K. A chronometric study of some relations between sentences. *Quarterly Journal of Experimental Psychology*, 1964, *16*, 297–308.

MILLER, G. A., and NICELY, P. E. An analysis of perceptual confusions among some English consonants. *Journal of the Acoustical Society of America*, 1955, *27*, 338–52.

MILLER, G. A., HEISE, G. A., and LICHTEN, W. The intelligibility of speech as a function of the context of the test materials. *Journal of Experimental Psychology*, 1951, *41*, 329–35.

MILLER, G. R., and COLEMAN, E. B. A set of thirty-six prose passages calibrated for complexity. *Journal of Verbal Learning and Verbal Behavior*, 1967, *6*, 851–54.

MILLER, N. E. Liberalization of basic S-R concepts: Extension to conflict behavior, motivation, and social learning. *In* S. KOCH, (ed.) *Psychology: A study of a science*, vol. 2, pp. 196–292. New York: McGraw-Hill, 1959.

——, and DOLLARD, J. *Social learning and imitation.* New Haven, Conn.: Yale University Press, 1941.

MILLER, W., and ERVIN, S. The development of grammar in child language. *Monographs of the Society for Research in Child Development*, 1964, *29*, (1, Ser. No. 92), 9–34.

MINARD, J. G. Response bias interpretation of perceptual "defense": A selective review and an evaluation of recent research. *Psychological Review*, 1965, *72*, 74–88.

MINIFIE, F. D., KELSEY, C. A., and HIXON, T. J. Measurement of vocal fold motion using an ultrasonic Doppler velocity monitor. *Journal of the Acoustical Society of America*, 1968, *43*, 1165–69.

MINTZ, S. Effect of actual stress on word associations. *Journal of Abnormal Psychology*, 1969, *74*, 293–95.

MIRON, M. S. A cross-linguistic investigation of phonetic symbolism. *Journal of Abnormal and Social Psychology*, 1961, *62*, 623–30.

MODRESKI, R. A., and GOSS, A. E. Young children's initial and changed names for form-color stimuli. *Journal of Experimental Child Psychology*, 1969, *8*, 402–9.

MOLL, K. L. Cinefluorographic techniques in speech research. *Journal of Speech and Hearing Research*, 1960, *3*, 227–41.

—— Photographic and radiographic procedures in speech research. *American Speech and Hearing Association Reports*, 1965, *1*, 129–39.

MONTAGUE, W. E., and KIESS, H. O. The associability of CVC pairs. *Journal of Experimental Psychology Monograph Supplement*, 1968, *78*, no. 2, part 2.

MOORE, G. P., WHITE, F. D., and VONLEDEN, H. Ultra high speed photography in laryngeal physiology. *Journal of Speech and Hearing Disorders*, 1962, *27*, 165–71.

MORAN, L. J. Generality of word association response sets. *Psychological Monographs*, 1966, *80* (4, whole no. 612).

—— Objective approximations of idiodynamic associative sets. *Psychological Reports*, 1967, *20*, 827–33.

———, and MURAKAWA, N. Japanese and American association structures. *Journal of Verbal Learning and Verbal Behavior*, 1968, 7, 176–81.

MORAN, L. J., and NUNEZ, R. Cross-cultural similarities in association structures. *Revista Interamericana de Psicologia*, 1967, 1, 1–6.

MORAN, L. J., MEFFERD, R. B., and KIMBLE, J. P. Idiodynamic sets in word association. *Psychological Monographs*, 1964, 78 (2, whole no. 579).

MORRIS, G. *Signs, language, and behavior*. Englewood Cliffs, N.J.: Prentice-Hall, 1946.

MORRIS, V. A., RANKINE, F. C., and REBER, A. S. Sentence comprehension, grammatical transformations and response availability. *Journal of Verbal Learning and Verbal Behavior*, 1968, 7, 1113–15.

MORSE, W. C., BALLANTINE, F. A., and DIXON, W. R. *Studies in the psychology of reading*. Ann Arbor: University of Michigan Press, 1951.

MOSES, E. R., JR. *Phonetics: History and interpretation*. Englewood Cliffs, N.J.: Prentice-Hall, 1964.

MORTON, J. Interaction of information in word recognition. *Psychological Review*, 1969, 76, 165–78.

MOWRER, O. H. *Learning theory and personality dynamics*. New York: Ronald, 1950.

——— The psychologist looks at language. *American Psychologist*, 1954, 9, 660–94.

——— *Learning theory and the symbolic processes*, New York: John Wiley, 1960.

MOYLAN, J. J. Stimulus generalization in projective test (Rorschach) behavior. *Journal of Personality*, 1959, 27, 18–37.

MUEHL, S. The effects of visual discriminating training on learning to read a vocabulary list in kindergarten children. *Journal of Educational Psychology*, 1960, 51, 217–21.

——— The effects of visual discrimination pretraining with word and letter stimuli on learning to read a word list in kindergarten children. *Journal of Educational Psychology*, 1961, 52, 215–21.

——— The effects of letter-name knowledge on learning to read a word list in kindergarten children. *Journal of Educational Psychology*, 1962, 53, 181–86.

MUMA, J., and BROWN, B. B. Removing segments from a speech sample. *Journal of Speech and Hearing Disorders*, 1967, 32, 121–25.

MURAI, J. I. Speech development of infants. Analysis of speech sounds by sonograph. *Psychologia*, 1960, 3, 27–35.

MURSTEIN, B. I. *Theory and research in projective techniques*. New York: John Wiley, 1963.

MUSGRAVE, B. S., and COHEN, J. C. Word associations to compound stimuli under two associational methods. *Psychonomic Science*, 1967, 9, 315–16.

——— Relationships between prose and list learning, *In* E. Z. Rothkopf and P. E. Johnson (eds.), *Verbal learning research and the technology of written instruction*, pp. 73–109. New York: Teachers College Press 1971.

———, and ROBBINS, D. M. G. Convergent popular associations in a word association task. *Journal of Verbal Learning and Verbal Behavior*, 1967, 6, 540–43.

MUSGRAVE, B. S., and GERRITZ, K. Effects of form of internal structure on recall and matching with prose passages. *Journal of Verbal Learning and Verbal Behavior*, 1968, 7, 1088–94.

NEWMAN, E. B., and GERSTMAN, L. J. A new method for analyzing printed English. *Journal of Experimental Psychology*, 1952, 44, 114–25.

NEWMAN, E. B., and WAUGH, N. C. The redundancy of texts in three languages. *Information and Control*, 1960, 3, 141–53.

NEWMAN, S. S. Further experiments in phonetic symbolism. *American Journal of Psychology*, 1933, 45, 53–75.

NEWMAN, S. Response speeds for easy- and hard-to pronounce trigrams. *Journal of Verbal Learning and Verbal Behavior*, 1967, 6, 661–67.

NOBLE, C. E. An analysis of meaning. *Psychological Review*, 1952, 59, 421–430.

——— Measurements of association value (*a*), rated associations (*a′*), and scaled meaningfulness (*m′*) for the 2100 CVC combinations of the English alphabet. *Psychological Reports*, 1961, 8, 487–521.

——— Meaningfulness and familiarity. *In* C. M. COFER and B. S. MUSGRAVE (eds.), *Verbal behavior and learning:* Problems and processes, pp. 76–119. New York: McGraw-Hill, 1963.

NODINE, C. F., and GOSS, A. E. Temporal parameters in paired-associates learning. *Psychonomic Monograph Supplements*, 1969, 3, whole no. 33.

NODINE, C. F., and HARDT, J. V. Generated meaningfulness of single letters as a function of positions in CVC trigrams. *Psychonomic Science*, 1968, 10, 129.

——— A measure of pronunciability of CVC trigrams. *Behavior Research Methods and Instrumentation*, 1969, 1, 210–16.

NUNNALLY, J. C., and BLANTON, R. L. Patterns of word association in the deaf. *Psychological Reports*, 1966, 18, 87–92.

O'CONNER, J. D., GERSTMAN, L. J., LIBERMAN, A. M., DELATTRE, P. C., and COOPER, F. S. Acoustic cues for the perception of initial /w, j, k, l/ in English. *Word*, 1957, 13, 24–43.

ODOM, R. D., LIEBERT, R. M., and HILL, J. H. The effects of modeling cues, reward, and attentional set on the production of grammatical and ungrammatical syntactic constructions. *Journal of Experimental Child Psychology*, 1968, 6, 131–40.

ÖHMAN, S. E. G. Coarticulation in VCV utterances: Spectrographic measurements. *Journal of the Acoustical Society of America*, 1966, 39, 151–68.

OLIVA, P. F. *The teaching of foreign languages*. Englewood Cliffs, N.J.: Prentice-Hall, 1969.

OLMSTEAD, D. L. A theory of the child's learning of phonology. *Language*, 1966, 42, 531–35.

OSGOOD, C. E. The nature and measurement of meaning. *Psychological Bulletin*, 1952, 49, 197–237.

——— *Method and theory in experimental psychology*. New York: Oxford University Press, 1953.

——— Behavior theory and the social sciences. *Behavioral Science*, 1956, 1, 167–85.

——— Motivational dynamics of language behavior. *In* M. R. JONES (ed.), *Nebraska symposium on motivation: 1957*, pp. 348–424. Lincoln: University of Nebraska Press, 1957.

——— Comments on Professor Bousfield's paper. *In* C. N. COFER (ed.), *Verbal learning and verbal behavior*, pp. 91–106. New York: McGraw-Hill, 1961.

——— On understanding and creating sentences. *American Psychologist*, 1963, 18, 735–51.

———, and ANDERSON, L. Certain relations among experienced contingencies, associative structure, and contingencies in encoded messages. *American Journal of Psychology*, 1957, 70, 411–20.

OSGOOD, C. E., and MIRON, M. S., eds., *Approaches to the study of aphasia*. Urbana: University of Illinois Press, 1963.

OSGOOD, C. E., and SEBEOK, T. A., eds. Psycholinguistics. *Journal of Abnormal Social Psychology Monograph Supplement*, 1954, 49.

OSGOOD, C. E., SUCI, G. J., and TANNENBAUM, P. H. *The measurement of meaning*. Urbana: University of Illinois Press, 1957.

OSGOOD, C. E., and TANNENBAUM, P. H. The principle of congruity in the production of attitude change. *Psychological Review*, 1955, 62, 42–55.

PAIVIO, A. A factor analytic study of word attributes and verbal learning. *Journal of Verbal Learning and Verbal Behavior*, 1968, 7, 41–49.

——— Mental imagery in associative learning and memory. *Psychological Review*, 1969, 76, 241–63.

———, and SIMPSON, H. M. The effect of word abstractness and pleasantness on pupil size during an imagery task. *Psychonomic Science*, 1966, 5, 55–56.

PAIVIO, A., YUILLE, J. C., and MADIGAN, S. A. Concreteness, imagery, and meaningfulness values for 925 nouns. *Journal of Experimental Psychology Monograph Supplement*, 1968, 76, no. 1, part 2.

PALERMO, D. S. Word associations and children's verbal behavior. *In* L. P. LIPSITT and C. C. SPIKER (eds.), *Advances in child development and behavior*, vol. 2, pp. 31–68. New York: Academic Press, 1963.

———, and JENKINS, J. J. *Word association norms: Grade school through college*. Minneapolis: University of Minnesota Press, 1964.

——— Oral word association norms for children in grades one through four. *Research Bulletin No. 60*, University Park: Department of Psychology, Pennsylvania State University, 1966.

PAVY, D. Verbal behavior in schizophrenia. *Psychological Bulletin*, 1968, 70, 164–78.

PEAVLER, W. S., and MCLAUGHLIN, J. P. The question of stimulus content and pupil size. *Psychonomic Science*, 1967, 8, 505–6.

PENFIELD, W., and ROBERTS, L. *Speech and brain mechanisms.* Princeton, N.J.: Princeton University Press, 1959.

PERKELL, J. S. *Physiology of speech production: Results and implications of a quantitative cineradiographic study.* Cambridge: M.I.T. Press, 1969.

PERKINS, W. H., and YANGIHARA, H. Parameters of voice production: I. Some mechanisms for the regulation of pitch. *Journal of Speech and Hearing Research,* 1968, *11,* 246–67.

PETERSON, G. E. Breath stream dynamics, laryngeal vibrations, articulation. *In* L. KAISER (ed.) *Manual of phonetics,* pp. 139–65. Amsterdam: North-Holland, 1957.

————, and BARNEY, H. L. Control methods used in the study of vowels. *Journal of the Acoustical Society of America,* 1952, *24,* 175–84.

PETERSON, G. E., and LEHISTE, I. Duration of syllabic nuclei in English. *Journal of the Acoustical Society of America,* 1960, *32,* 693–703.

PETERSON, G. E., and SHOUP, J. E. A physiological theory of phonetics. *Journal of Speech and Hearing Research,* 1966a, *9,* 5–67.

———— The elements of an acoustic phonetic theory. *Journal of Speech and Hearing Research,* 1966b, *9,* 68–99.

PIAGET, J. *The language and thought of the child,* 2nd ed. London: Routledge & Kegan Paul, 1932.

PILLSBURY, W. B., and MEADER, C. L. *The psychology of language.* New York: Appleton, 1928.

PIOTROWSKI, Z. The Rorschach inkblot method. *In* B. B. WOLMAN (ed.), *Handbook of clinical psychology,* pp. 522–61. New York: McGraw-Hill, 1965.

POLLIO, H. R. Associative structure and verbal behavior. *In* T. R. DIXON and D. L. HORTON (eds.) *Verbal behavior and general behavior theory,* pp. 37–66. Englewood Cliffs, N.J.: Prentice-Hall, 1968.

POLT, J. M., and HESS, E. H. Changes in pupil size to visually presented words. *Psychonomic Science,* 1968, *12,* 389–90.

POPP, H. M. Visual discrimination of alphabet letters. *Reading Teacher,* 1964, *17,* 221–26.

———— The measurement and training of visual discrimination skills prior to reading instruction. *Journal of Experimental Education,* 1967, *35,* 15–26.

POSTAL, P. M. Underlying and superficial linguistic structure. *Harvard Educational Review,* 1964, *34,* 246–66.

POSTMAN, L., and ADIS-CASTRO, G. Psychophysical methods in the study of word recognition. *Science,* 1957, *125,* 193–94.

POSTMAN, L., BRONSON, W. C., and GROPPER, G. L. Is there a mechanism of perceptual defense? *Journal of Abnormal and Social Psychology,* 1953, *48,* 215–24.

POSTMAN, L., and ROSENZWEIG, M. R. Practice and transfer in visual and auditory recognition of verbal stimuli. *American Journal of Psychology,* 1956, *69,* 209–26.

POTTER, R. K., KOPP, G. A., and GREEN, H. C. *Visible speech.* New York: Van Nostrand, 1947.

POTTER, R. K., and PETERSON, G. E. The representation of vowels and their movements. *Journal of the Acoustical Society of America,* 1950, *22,* 528–35.

POTTER, R. K., and STEINBERG, J. C. Toward the specification of speech. *Journal of the Acoustical Society of America,* 1950, *22,* 807–20.

POWERS, F. F. The psychology of language learning. *Psychological Bulletin,* 1929, *26,* 261–74.

POWERS, M. H. Functional disorders of articulation—symptomology and etiology. *In* L. E. TRAVIS (ed.), *Handbook of speech pathology,* pp. 707–68. New York: Appleton-Century-Crofts, 1957.

PRESTI, A. High-speed sound spectrograph. *Journal of the Acoustical Society of America,* 1966, *40,* 628–34.

PRESTIGIACOMO, A. J. Plastic-tape sound spectrograph. *Journal of Speech and Hearing Disorders,* 1957, *22,* 321–37.

PRICE, R. H. Signal-detection methods in personality and perception. *Psychological Bulletin,* 1966, *66,* 55–62.

PRONKO, N. H. Language and psycholinguistics. *Psychological Bulletin,* 1946, *43,* 189–239.

PULGRAM, E. *Introduction to the spectrography of speech.* 's-Gravenhage: Mouton, 1959.

QUINE, W. V. *Word and object.* New York: John Wiley, 1960.

RABINER, L. S. Digital-formant synthesizer for speech-synthesis studies. *Journal of the Acoustical Society of America,* 1968, *43,* 822–29.

RAMSEY, G. H. S., WATSON, J. S., JR., TRISTAN, T. A., WEINBERG, S., and CORNWALL, W. S., eds. *Cinefluorography.* Springfield, Ill.: Thomas, 1960.

RAPAPORT, A. A comparison of two tree-construction methods for obtaining proximity measures among words. *Journal of Verbal Learning and Verbal Behavior,* 1967, *6,* 884–90.

RAPAPORT, D., GILL, M., and SCHAFER, R. *Diagnostic psychological testing,* vol. 2. Chicago: Year Book Publishers, 1946.

REBELSKY, F. G., STARR, R. H., JR., and LURIA, Z. Language development in the first four years. *In* Y. BRACKBILL (ed.), *Infancy and early childhood,* pp. 289–360. New York: The Free Press, 1967.

REED, H. B. *Psychology of elementary school subjects.* Boston: Ginn, 1927.

REESE, H. *The perception of stimulus relations: Discrimination learning and transposition.* New York: Academic Press, 1968.

REICHER, G. M. Perceptual recognition as a function of meaningfulness of stimulus material. *Journal of Experimental Psychology,* 1969, *81,* 275–80.

RÉVÉSZ, G. *Origins and prehistory of language.* New York: Philosophical Library, 1956.

REYNIERSE, J. H., and BARCH, A. M. Semantic satiation and generation. *Psychological Reports,* 1963, *13,* 700.

RHINE, R. J. A concept-formation approach to attitude acquisition. *Psychological Review,* 1958, *65,* 362–70.

REIBEL, D.A., and SCHANE, S. A. *Modern studies in English; readings in transformational grammar.* Englewood Cliffs, N. J.: Prentice-Hall, 1969.

RIEBER, R. W., and BRUBAKER, R. S. *Speech pathology.* Amsterdam: North-Holland, 1966.

RIEGEL, K. Some theoretical considerations of bilingual development. *Psychological Bulletin,* 1968, *70,* 647–70.

RIEGEL, K. F., and BIRREN, J. E. Age differences in verbal associations. *Journal of Genetic Psychology,* 1966, *108,* 153–70.

RIEGEL, K. F., RAMSEY, R. M., and RIEGEL, R. M. A comparison of the first and second languages of American and Spanish students. *Journal of Verbal Learning and Verbal Behavior,* 1967, *6,* 536–44.

RIEGEL, K. F., and RIEGEL, R. M. Developmental differences in word meaning and sentence structure. *Human Development,* 1968, *11,* 92–106.

RIES, H. A., and JOHNSON, M. H. Communality of word associations of good and poor premorbid schizophrenia. *Journal of Abnormal Psychology,* 1967, *72,* 487–88.

RILEY, D. A. Memory for form. *In* L. J. POSTMAN (ed.), *Psychology in the making,* pp. 402–65. New York: Knopf, 1962.

RINSLAND, H. D. *A basic vocabulary of elementary school children.* New York: Macmillan, 1945.

RIVERS, W. M. *The psychologist and the foreign-language teacher.* Chicago: University of Chicago Press, 1964.

ROBINS, R. H. *General linguistics.* Bloomington: Indiana University Press, 1964.

ROBINSON, H. M., ed. Innovation and change in reading instruction. *Yearbook National Society for the Study of Education,* 1968, *67.*

RODEWALD, H. K. Recognition thresholds as a function of association value of nonsense syllables. *Perceptual and Motor Skills,* 1968, *26,* 869–70.

ROKOSZ, S. F., and CORRELL, R. E. Free-association responses as a function of age and stimulus frequency. *Psychological Reports,* 1966, *18,* 195–99.

RORSCHACH, H. *Psychodiagnostics.* Berne, Switz.: Huber, 1942 (1921).

ROSEN, D. E., and GOSS, A. E. Pre-experimentally acquired verbal responses during acquisition and subsequent use of experimentally acquired verbal responses in conceptual block sorting. *Journal of Genetic Psychology,* 1965, *107,* 313–35.

ROSENBAUM, P. S. *The grammar of English predicate complement constructions.* Cambridge.: M.I.T. Press, 1967.

ROSENBERG, S. Associative sentence norms. Nashville, Tenn.: Department of Psychology, George Peabody College for Teachers, 1965.

———— Associative sentence norms II: Simple declarative sentence. Nashville, Tenn.: Department of Psychology, George Peabody College for Teachers, 1966.

————, and COHEN, B. D. Referential processes of speakers and listeners. *Psychological Review,* 1966, *73,* 208–31.

ROSENBERG, S., and DONNER, L. Choice behavior in a verbal recognition task as a function of induced associative strength. *Journal of Experimental Psychology,* 1968, *76,* 341–47.

ROSENZWEIG, M. R., and MCNEILL, D. Inaccuracies in the semantic count of Lorge and Thorndike. *American Journal of Psychology*, 1962, *75*, 316–19.

ROSENZWEIG, M. R., and MILLER, K. M. Comparisons of word association responses obtained in the United States, Australia, and England. *Journal of Verbal Learning and Verbal Behavior*, 1966, *5*, 35–41.

ROSENZWEIG, M. R., and POSTMAN, L. Frequency of usage and the perception of words. *Science*, 1958, *127*, 263–66.

ROTBERG, I. C. A method for developing comprehensive categories of meaning. *Journal of Verbal Learning and Verbal Behavior*, 1968, *7*, 589–92.

ROTHBERG, M. A. The effect of "social" instructions on word association behavior. *Journal of Verbal Learning and Verbal Behavior*, 1967, *6*, 298–300.

ROTTER, J. B. Word association and sentence completion methods. *In* H. H. ANDERSON and G. L. ANDERSON (eds.), *An introduction to projective techniques*, pp. 279–311. Englewood Cliffs, N.J.: Prentice-Hall, 1951.

ROUSE, R. O., and VERINIS, J. S. The effect of associative connections on the recognition of flashed cards. *Journal of Verbal Learning and Verbal Behavior*, 1963, *2*, 300–303.

ROUTH, D. K. Conditioning of vocal response differentiation in infants. *Developmental Psychology*, 1969, *1*, 219–26.

RUBENSTEIN, H., and POLLACK, I. Word predictability and intelligibility. *Journal of Verbal Learning and Verbal Behavior*, 1963, *2*, 147–58.

RUESCH, J., and KEES, W. *Nonverbal communication*. Berkeley: University of California Press, 1956.

RUNQUIST, W. N. Rated similarity of high *m* CVC trigrams and words and low *m* CCC trigrams. *Journal of Verbal Learning and Verbal Behavior*, 1968, *7*, 967–68.

———, and JOHNSON, P. A. Rated similarity of low association value CVC trigrams. *Journal of Verbal Learning and Verbal Behavior*, 1968, *7*, 317–20.

RUSSELL, D. H., and FEA, H. R. Research on teaching reading. *In* N. L. GAGE (ed.), *Handbook of research on teaching*, pp. 865–928. Chicago: Rand-McNally, 1963.

SALES, B. D., and HABER, R. N. A different look at perceptual defense for taboo words. *Perception and Psychophysics*, 1968, *3*, 156–60.

SALZINGER, K. S., SALZINGER, K., PORTNOY, S., ECKMAN, J., BACON, P. N., DEUTSCH, M., and ZUBIN, J. Operant conditioning of continuous speech in children. *Child Development*, 1962, *33*, 683–95.

SAMUELS, S. J. Effect of word associations on the recognition of flashed words. *Journal of Educational Psychology*, 1969, *60*, 97–102.

SANFORD, E. C. The relative legibility of the small letters. *American Journal of Psychology*, 1888, *1*, 402–35.

SAPIR, E. *Language*. New York: Harcourt Brace, 1921.

——— A study in phonetic symbolism. *Journal of Experimental Psychology*, 1929, *2*, 225–39.

SCHAFER, R. *Psychoanalytic interpretation of Rorschach testing*. New York: Grune & Stratton, 1954.

SCHICK, G. B., and MAY, M. M., eds. *The psychology of reading behavior*. Milwaukee, Wisc.: National Reading Conference, 1969.

SCHIEFELBUSCH, R. L., COPELAND, R. L., ROSS, H., and SMITH, J. O. *Language and mental retardation: Empirical and conceptual considerations*. New York: Holt, Rinehart & Winston, 1967.

SCHILLER, P. H. Developmental study of color-word interference. *Journal of Experimental Psychology*, 1966, *72*, 105–8.

SCHOLES, R. J. Phoneme categorization of synthetic vocalic stimuli by speakers of Japanese, Spanish, Persian, and American English. *Language and Speech*, 1967, *10*, 46–68.

——— Categorical responses to synthetic vocalic stimuli by speakers of various languages. *Language and Speech*, 1967, *10*, 252–82.

——— The role of grammaticality in the imitation of word strings by children and adults. *Journal of Verbal Learning and Verbal Behavior*, 1969, *8*, 225–28.

SCHÖNPFLUG, W., and VETTER, G. H. Relations among characteristics of CVC trigrams. *Journal of Verbal Learning and Verbal Behavior*, 1969, *8*, 157–58.

SCHROEDER, M. R. Period histogram and product spectrum: New methods for fundamental frequency measurement. *Journal of the Acoustical Society of America*, 1968, *43*, 829–34.

SCHULZ, R. W., and HOPKINS, R. H. Free-association responses to verbal stimuli of varying meaningfulness as a function of presentation mode. *Journal of Verbal Learning and Verbal Behavior*, 1968, *7*, 737–45.

SCHULZ, R. W., WEAVER, G. E., and RADTKE, R. C. Verbal satiation. *Psychonomic Science*, 1965, *2*, 43–44.

SCHWARTZ, R. Anagram solving: A function of the frequency of vowel consonant pattern. *Psychonomic Science*, 1968, *13*, 229–30.

———, and OLSON, R. Are alleged single-solution anagrams really single-solution? *Journal of Verbal Learning and Verbal Behavior*, 1968, *7*, 567–68.

SCOTT, D., and BADDELEY, A. D. Acoustic confusibility values for 1172 CCC trigrams. *Psychonomic Science*, 1969, *14*, 189–90, 192.

SCRIPTURE, E. W. *The elements of experimental phonetics*. New York: Charles Scribner's Sons, 1902.

SEASHORE, R. H., and ECKERSON, L. D. The measurement of individual differences in general English vocabularies. *Journal of Educational Psychology*, 1940, *31*, 14–38.

SEBEOK, T., ed. *Style in language*. New York: John Wiley, 1960.

———, ed. *Current trends in linguistics: Soviet and East European linguistics*, vol. 1. The Hague: Mouton, 1963.

———, ed. *Current trends in linguistics: Theoretical foundations*, vol. 3. The Hague: Mouton, 1966.

———, ed. *Current trends in linguistics: Linguistics in East Asia and South East Asia*, vol. 2. The Hague: Mouton, 1967.

———, ed. *Animal communication*. Bloomington: Indiana University Press, 1968a.

———, ed. *Current trends in linguistics, Ibero-American and Caribbean linguistics*, vol. 4. The Hague: Mouton, 1968b.

SEFER, J. W., and HENRIKSON, E. H. The relationship between word association and grammatical classes in aphasia. *Journal of Speech and Hearing Research*, 1966, *9*, 529–41.

SEGAL, S. J. The priming of association test responses: Generalizing the phenomenon. *Journal of Verbal Learning and Verbal Behavior*, 1967, *6*, 216–21.

SEIBEL, R. *Letter sequences (N-grams): I. Frequencies in samples of text from the (London) Times*. Yorktown Heights, N.Y.: IBM, 1963.

SEMMEL, M. I., BARRITT, L. S., BENNETT, S. W., and PERFETTI, C. A. A grammatical analysis of word associations of educable mentally retarded and normal children. *American Journal of Mental Deficiency*, 1968, *72*, 567–76.

SEYMORE, S., LOTSOF, E. J., and BRANSKY, M. Verbal conditioning of common word and uncommon word associations in retardates and normals. *Journal of Genetic Psychology*, 1966, *108*, 279–90.

SHAPIRO, B. J. The subjective estimation of relative word frequency. *Journal of Verbal Learning and Verbal Behavior*, 1969, *8*, 248–51.

SHAPIRO, S. I., and PALERMO, D. S. An atlas of normative free association data. *Psychonomic Monograph Supplements*, 1968, *2* (12, whole no. 28).

SHAPIRO, S. S. Word association norms: Stability of response and chains of associations. *Psychonomic Science*, 1966, *4*, 233–34.

SHEFFIELD, F. D. The role of meaningfulness of stimulus and response in verbal learning. Ph.D. dissertation, Yale University, 1946.

SHEPARD, R. N. The analysis of proximities: Multidimensional scaling with an unknown distance function I and II. *Psychometrika*, 1967, *27*, 125–39, 219–46.

SHEPPARD, W. C., and LANE, H. L. Development of the prosodic features of infant vocalizing. *Journal of Speech and Hearing Research*, 1968, *11*, 94–108.

SHIRLEY, M. M. Common content in the speech of preschool children. *Child Development*, 1938, *9*, 333–48.

SHNEIDMAN, E. S. Projective techniques. *In* B. B. WOLMAN (ed.), *Handbook of clinical psychology*, pp. 498–521. New York: McGraw-Hill, 1965.

SHOUKSMITH, G. Styles distinguishing "good" and "poor" performers in a word-formation game. *Journal of Verbal Learning and Verbal Behavior*, 1968, *7*, 1111–12.

SHRADER, W. K., and GOSS, A. E. The role of contextual cues in stimulus generalization with inkblot stimuli. *Journal of General Psychology*, 1964, *71*, 293–306.

SIEGEL, A., SILVERMAN, I., and MARKEL, N. M. On the effects of mode of presentation on phonetic symbolism. *Journal of Verbal Learning and Verbal Behavior*, 1967, *6*, 171–73.

SILVERSTEIN, A., and DIENSTBIER, R. A. Rated pleasantness and association value of 101 English nouns. *Journal of Verbal Learning and Verbal Behavior*, 1968, *7*, 81–86.

SINGER, H., and RUDDELL, R. B., (eds). *Theoretical models and processes of reading*. Newark, Delaware: International Reading Association, 1970.

SINGH, S. Cross-language study of perceptual confusion of plosive phonemes in two conditions of distortion. *Journal of the Acoustical Society of America*, 1960, *40*, 635–56.

SKINNER, B. F. *Science and human behavior*. New York: Macmillan, 1953.

———— *Verbal behavior*. New York: Appleton-Century-Crofts, 1957.

SLOBIN, D. I. The acquisition of Russian as a native language. *In* F. SMITH and G. A. MILLER (eds.) *The genesis of language*, pp. 129–48. Cambridge, Mass.: M.I.T. Press, 1966a.

———— Grammatical transformation and sentence comprehension in childhood and adulthood. *Journal of Verbal Learning and Verbal Behavior*, 1966b, *5*, 219–27.

SMITH, D. E. P., and RAYGOR, A. L. Verbal satiation and personality. *Journal of Abnormal and Social Psychology*, 1956, *52*, 323–26.

SMITH, E. E. Effect of familiarity on stimulus recognition and categorization. *Journal of Experimental Psychology*, 1967, *74*, 324–32.

SMITH, F. The use of featural dependencies across letters in the visual identification of words. *Journal of Verbal Learning and Verbal Behavior*, 1969, *8*, 215–18.

———— Familiarity of configuration vs. discriminability of features in the visual identification of words. *Psychonomic Science*, 1969, 261–62.

SMITH, M. G., and HARLESTON, B. W. Stimulus abstractness and emotionality as determinants of behavioral and physiological responses in a word-association task. *Journal of Verbal Learning and Verbal Behavior*, 1966, *5*, 309–13.

SMITH, M. K. Measurement of the size of general English vocabulary through the elementary grades and high school. *Genetic Psychology Monographs*, 1941, *24*, 311–45.

SMITH, N. B. Matching ability as a factor in first grade reading. *Journal of Educational Psychology*, 1928, *19*, 560–571.

SNIDER, J. G., and OSGOOD, C. E., eds. *Semantic differential techniques: A sourcebook*. Chicago: Aldine, 1969.

SOLOMON, L. N. Semantic approach to the perception of complex sounds. *Journal of the Acoustical Society of America*, 1958, *30*, 421–25.

———— Search for physical correlates to psychological dimensions of sounds. *Journal of the Acoustical Society of America*, 1959a, *31*, 492–97.

———— Semantic reactions to systematically varied sounds. *Journal of the Acoustical Society of America*, 1959b, *31*, 986–90.

SOMNAPAN, R. Development of sets of mutually equally discriminable random shapes. *Journal of Experimental Psychology*, 1968, *76*, 297–302.

SONESSON, B. The functional anatomy of the speech organs. *In* B. MALMBERG (ed.), *Manual of phonetics*, pp. 45–75. Rev. ed. Amsterdam: North-Holland, 1968.

SORON, H. I. High-speed photographs in speech research. *Journal of Speech and Hearing Research*, 1967, *10*, 768–76.

SPENCE, K. W. *Behavior theory and conditioning*. New Haven, Conn.: Yale University Press, 1956.

SPIKER, C. C. Experiments with children on the hypothesis of acquired distinctiveness and equivalence of cues. *Child Development*, 1956, *27*, 253–63.

———— Verbal factors in the discrimination learning of children. *Monographs of the Society for Research in Child Development*, 1963, *28*, (2, Serial no. 86).

SPREEN, O., and SCHULZ, R. W. Parameters of abstraction, meaningfulness, and pronunciability of 329 nouns. *Journal of Verbal Learning and Verbal Behavior*, 1966, *5*, 459–68.

SPREEN, O., BORKOWSKI, J. C., and BENTON, A. L. Auditory word recognition as a function of meaningfulness, abstractness, and phonetic similarity. *Journal of Verbal Learning and Verbal Behavior*, 1967, *6*, 101–5.

SPREEN, O., BORKOWSKI, J. G., and GORDON, A. M. Effects of abstractness, meaningfulness, and phonetic structure on auditory recognition of nouns. *Journal of Speech and Hearing Research*, 1966, *9*, 619–25.

SPRIESTERSBACH, D. C., and SHERMAN, D., eds. *Cleft palate and communication*. New York: Academic Press, 1968.

STAATS, A. W. *Learning, language, and cognition*. New York: Holt, Rinehart & Winston, 1968.

————, and STAATS, C. K. Meaning established by classical conditioning. *Journal of Experimental Psychology*, 1957, *54*, 74–80.

———— *Complex human behavior*. New York: Holt, Rinehart & Winston, 1963.

————, and SCHUTZ, R. E. The effects of discrimination pretraining on textual behavior. *Journal of Educational Psychology*, 1962, *53*, 32–37.

STERN, C., and STERN, W. *Die Kindersprache: Eine psychologische und sprach-theoretische Untersuchung*, 3rd. rev. ed. Leipzig: Barth 1922 (1907).

STERN, W. *Psychology of early childhood*, 3d ed. New York: Holt, 1924.

STETSON, R. H. *Motor phonetics*. Amsterdam: North-Holland, 1951.

STEVENSON, H. W., KLEIN, R. E., HALE, G. A., and MILLER, L. K. Solutions of anagrams: A developmental study. *Child Development*, 1968, *39*, 905–12.

STOLZ, W. S. A study of the ability to decode grammatically novel sentences. *Journal of Verbal Learning and Verbal Behavior*, 1967, *6*, 867–73.

STORMS, L. H., BROEN, W. S., and LEVIN, I. Verbal associative stability and communality as a function of stress in schizophrenics, neurotics, and normals. *Journal of Consulting Psychology*, 1967, *31*, 181–87.

STRENGER, F. Radiographic, palatographic, and labiographic methods in phonetics. *In* B. MALMBERG (ed.), *Manual of phonetics*, pp. 334–64. Rev. ed. Amsterdam: North-Holland, 1968.

STREVENS, P. Spectra of fricative noise in human speech. *Language and Speech*, 1960, *3*, 32–48.

STRONG, W. J. Machine-aided formant determination for speech synthesis. *Journal of the Acoustical Society of America*, 1967, *41*, 1434–42.

STROOP, J. R. Studies of interference in serial verbal reactions. *Journal of Experimental Psychology*, 1935, *18*, 643–61.

STUMPF, C. *Die sprachlaute: Experimentelle-phonetische untersuchungen*. Berlin: Springer, 1926.

SUBTELNY, J. D., and SUBTELNY, J. D. Roentgenographic techniques and phonetic research. *Proceedings 4th International Congress of Phonetic Science*, *1961*, The Hague: Mouton, 1962.

SULLIVAN, J. P., and MORAN, L. J. Association structures of bright children of age six. *Child Development*, 1967, *38*, 793–800.

SZALAY, L. B., and BRENT, J. E. The analysis of cultural meanings through free verbal associations. *Journal of Social Psychology*, 1967, *72*, 161–87.

TAYLOR, I. K. Phonetic symbolism reexamined. *Psychological Bulletin*, 1963, *60*, 200–209.

———— Content and structure in sentence production. *Journal of Verbal Learning and Verbal Behavior*, 1969, *8*, 170–75.

————, and TAYLOR, M. M. Phonetic symbolism in four unrelated languages. *Canadian Journal of Psychology*, 1962, *16*, 344–56.

TAYLOR, J. A. Physiological need, set, and visual duration threshold. *Journal of Abnormal and Social Psychology*, 1956, *52*, 96–99.

TAYLOR, W. L. "Cloze procedure": A new tool for measuring readability. *Journalism Quarterly*, 1953, *30*, 415–33.

TEMPLIN, M. C. *Certain language skills in children*. Minneapolis: University of Minnesota Press, 1957.

TERMAN, L. M., and MERRILL, M. A. *Stanford-Binet intelligence scale*, 3d rev. ed. Boston: Houghton Mifflin, 1960.

TERWILLIGER, R. F. *Meaning and mind*. New York: Oxford University Press, 1968.

THASS-THIENEMANN, T. *Symbolic behavior*. New York: Washington Square Press, 1968.

THOMAS, H. Children's tachistoscopic recognition of words and pseudo words varying in pronunciability and consonant-vowel sequence. *Journal of Experimental Psychology*, 1968, *77*, 511–13.

THORNDIKE, E. L. Handwriting. *Teachers' College Record*, 1910, *2*, 1–93.

———— *Educational psychology, Vol. II: The psychology of learning*. New York: Teachers' College, 1913.

———— *Handwriting*. New York: Teachers' College Press, 1917.

———— *Adult learning*. New York: Macmillan, 1928.

———— *Human learning*. New York: Century, 1931.

———— *The fundamentals of learning*. New York: Teachers' College Press, 1932.

———— *The psychology of wants, interests, and attitudes*. New York: Appleton-Century, 1935.

——— The origin of language. *Science*, 1943, *98*, 1–6.

———, and LORGE, I. *The teacher's word book of 30,000 words.* New York: Columbia University Press, 1944.

TIKOFSKY, R. S., and MCNISH, J. R. Consonant discrimination by seven year olds: A pilot study. *Psychonomic Science*, 1968, *10*, 61–62.

TINKER, M. A. *Legibility of print.* Ames: Iowa State University Press, 1963.

——— *Bases for effective reading.* Minneapolis: University of Minnesota Press, 1965.

——— Experimental studies on the legibility of print: An annotated bibliography. *Reading Research Quarterly*, 1966, *1*(4), 67–118.

TOBIAS, J. V. Relative occurrence of phonemes in American English. *Journal of the Acoustical Society of America*, 1959, *31*, 631.

TRAGER, G. L., and SMITH, H. L., JR. *Outline of English structure.* Norman, Okla.: Battenberg Press, 1951.

TRAVIS, L. E., ed. *Handbook of speech pathology.* New York: Appleton-Century-Crofts, 1957.

TRESSELT, M. E. A reexamination of anagram problem solving. *Transactions of the New York Academy of Sciences*, 1968, Ser. II, *30*, 1112–19.

———, and MAYZNER, M. S. Anagram solution times: A function of individual differences in stored digram frequencies. *Journal of Experimental Psychology*, 1965, *70*, 606–10.

——— Anagram solution times: A function of single- and double-letter solution words. *Journal of Verbal Learning and Verbal Behavior*, 1968, *7*, 128–32.

TRNKA, B. *A phonological analysis of present day standard English.* Prague: Charles University, 1935.

TSURU, S., and FRIES, H. S. A problem in meaning. *Journal of General Psychology*, 1933, *8*, 281–84.

TULVING, E., MANDLER, G., and BAUMAL, R. Interaction of two sources of information in tachistoscopic word recognition. *Canadian Journal of Psychology*, 1964, *18*, 62–71.

UHRBOCK, R. S. Words most frequently used by a five-year-old girl. *Journal of Educational Psychology*, 1936, *27*, 155–58.

ULLMAN, S. *Language and style.* New York: Barnes & Noble, 1964.

UNDERWOOD, B. J. *Experimental psychology.* New York: Appleton-Century-Crofts, 1949.

——— *Experimental psychology.* Rev. ed. New York: Appleton-Century-Crofts, 1966.

———, and SCHULZ, R. W. *Meaningfulness and verbal learning.* Philadelphia: Lippincott, 1960.

UPSHUR, J., and FATA, J., eds. *Problems in foreign language testing.* Ann Arbor: University of Michigan Press, 1968.

VAKAR, N. P. *A word count of spoken Russian: The Soviet usage.* Columbus: Ohio State University Press, 1966.

VAN BERCKEL, J. A. T., CORSTIUS, H. B., MOKKEN, R. J., and VAN WIJNGAARDEN. *Formal properties of newspaper Dutch.* Amsterdam: Mathematisch Centrum, 1965.

VAN DEN BERG, J. W. Mechanism of the larynx and the laryngeal vibrations. *In* B. MALMBERG (ed.), *Manual of phonetics*, pp. 278–308. Rev. ed. Amsterdam: North-Holland, 1968a.

——— Sound production in isolated human larynges. *Annals of the New York Academy of Sciences*, 1968b, *155*, Art. 1, 18–26.

VAN RIPER, C. G., and SMITH, D. E. *An introduction to general American phonetics*, 2d ed. New York: Harper & Row, 1963.

VENEZKY, R. L. Automatic spelling-to-sound conversion. *In* P. L. GARVIN and B. SPOLSKY, eds., *Computation in linguistics.* Bloomington: Indiana University Press, 1966.

———English orthography: Its graphical structure and its relation to sound. *Reading Research Quarterly*, 1967, *2* (3) 75–106.

———, CALFEE, R. C., and CHAPMAN, R. S. Skills required for learning to read; a preliminary analysis. Madison: Wisconsin Research and Development Center for Cognitive Learning, University of Wisconsin, 1968.

VERINIS, J. S., and COFER, C. N. Word recognition and set for association. *Psychonomic Science*, 1964, *1*, 179–80.

VERNON, M. D. *Backwardness in reading: A study of its nature and origin.* Cambridge: Cambridge University Press, 1960.

VETTER, H. J. *Language behavior and psychopathology.* Chicago: Rand McNally, 1969.

———, and TENNANT, J. A. Oral-gesture cues in sound symbolism. *Perceptual and Motor Skills*, 1967, *24*, 54.

VICORY, A. C., and ASHER, J. J. A simplified associative-frequency measure of meaningfulness in verbal learning. *Journal of Verbal Learning and Verbal Behavior*, 1966, *5*, 507–13.

VIGOTSKY, L. S. *Thought and language.* Cambridge, Mass.: M.I.T. Press, 1962 (1934).

VILDOMEC, V. *Multilingualism.* Leyden: Sythoff, 1963.

VOELKER, C. H. A sound count for the oral curriculum. *The Volta Review*, 1936, *25*, 55–56.

VON LEDEN, H. Objective measures of laryngeal function and phonation. *Annals of the New York Academy of Sciences*, 1968, *155*, Art. 1, 56–66.

VOSS, J. F., THOMPSON, C. P., and KEEGAN, J. H. Acquisition of probabilistic paired associates as a function of S-R$_1$, S-R$_2$ probability. *Journal of Experimental Psychology*, 1959, *58*, 390–99.

WANG, W. S-Y, and CRAWFORD, J. Frequency studies of English consonants. *Language and Speech*, 1960, *3*, 131–39.

WARREN, H. C. *A history of the association psychology.* New York: Scribner, 1921.

WARREN, M. W., and THOMSON, W. J. Anagram solution as a function of transition probabilities and solution word frequency. *Psychonomic Science*, 1969, *17*, 333–34.

WARREN, R. M. Verbal transformation effect and auditory perceptual mechanisms. *Psychological Bulletin*, 1968, *70*, 261–70.

WATSON, J. B. *Behavior: An introduction to comparative psychology.* New York: Holt, 1914.

——— *Psychology from the standpoint of a behaviorist.* Philadelphia: Lippincott, 1919.

——— *Behaviorism.* New York: Norton, 1924.

Webster's New International Dictionary, 2d ed. Springfield, Mass.: Merriam, 1934.

WEINER, M., and SCHILLER, P. H. Subliminal perception or perception of partial cues. *Journal of Abnormal and Social Psychology*, 1960, *61*, 124–37.

WEIR, R. H. *Language in the crib.* The Hague: Mouton, 1962.

WEISBERG, P. Social and non-social conditioning of infant vocalizations. *Child Development*, 1963, *34*, 377–88.

WEISS, A. P. *A theoretical basis of human behavior.* Rev. ed. Columbus, Ohio: Adams, 1929.

WEISS, J. H. The role of stimulus meaningfulness in the phonetic symbolism response. *The Journal of General Psychology*, 1964a, *70*, 255–63.

——— Phonetic symbolism re-examined. *Psychological Bulletin*, 1964b, *61*, 454–58.

——— Phonetic symbolism and perception of connotative meaning. *Journal of Verbal Learning and Verbal Behavior*, 1968, 7, 574–76.

WEISSTEIN, N. A Rashevsky-Landahl neural net: Simulations of metacontrast. *Psychological Review*, 1968, *75*, 494–521.

WELLMAN, B. L., CASE, I. M., MENGERT, I. G., and BRADBURY, D. E. Speech sounds of young children. *University of Iowa Studies in Child Welfare*, 1931, *5* (2), 1–82.

WERTHEIM, J., and GERWITZ, P. J. Free word associations of children and adults. *Psychonomic Science*, 1966, *4*, 57–58.

WERTHEIMER, M. Laws of organization in perceptual form. *In* W. D. ELLIS (ed. & trans.), *A sourcebook of Gestalt psychology*, pp. 136–48. New York: The Humanities Press, 1950 (1923).

WEST, M. *A general service list of English words.* New York: Longmans, Green, 1953.

WHEELOCK, W. H., and SILVAROLI, N. M. An investigation of visual discrimination training for beginning readers. *Journal of Typographical Research*, 1967, *1*, 147–56.

WHIPPLE, G. M. *Manual of mental and physical tests, Part II. Complex Processes.* Baltimore: Warwick & York, 1915.

———, and WHIPPLE (Mrs.), G. M. The vocabulary of a three-year-old boy with some interpretive comments. *Pedagogical Seminary*, 1909, *15*, 1–2.

WHITE, M. J. Identification and localization within digit and letter spans. *Psychonomic Science*, 1969a, *14*, 279–80.

——— Order of report and letter structure in tachistoscopic recognition. *Psychonomic Science*, 1969b, *17*, 364–65.

WHITNEY, W. D. The proportional elements of English utterances. *Proceedings of the American Philological Association*, 1874, *5*, 14–17.

WHITTAKER, E. M., GILCHRIST, J. C., and FISCHER, J. W. Perceptual defense or response suppression. *Journal of Abnormal and Social Psychology*, 1952, *47*, 732–33.

WICKELGREN, W. A. Context-sensitive coding, associative memory, and serial order in (speech) behavior. *Psychological Review*, 1969a, *76*, 1–15.

—— Auditory or articulatory coding in verbal short-term memory. *Psychological Review*, 1969b *76*, 332–35.

WILLIAMS, C. E., and HECKER, M. H. L. Relation between intelligibility scores for four test methods and three types of speech distortion. *Journal of the Acoustical Society of America*, 1968, *44*, 1002–6.

WILLIAMS, H. M. An analytical study of language achievement in preschool children; Part I: Development of language vocabulary in young children. *University of Iowa Studies in Child Welfare*, 1937, *13* (2), 9–18.

—— A qualitative analysis of the erroneous speech sound substitutions of preschool children; Part II: Development of language vocabulary in young children. *University of Iowa Studies in Child Welfare*, 1937, *13* (2), 21–32.

——, and MCFARLAND, M. L. A revision of the Smith vocabulary test for preschool children. *University of Iowa Studies in Child Welfare*, 1937, *13* (2), 33–46.

WILLIAMS, J. P. Successive versus concurrent presentation of multiple phoneme-grapheme correspondence. *Journal of Educational Psychology*, 1968, *59*, 309–14.

WILSON, F. T., and FLEMMING, C. W. Letter consciousness of beginners in reading. *Journal of Genetic Psychology*, 1938, *53*, 273–85.

—— Symbols scales for use in beginning reading. *Journal of Psychology*, 1939, *8*, 99–114.

WINCH, W. H. Colour-names of English school children. *American Journal of Psychology*, 1910, *21*, 453–82.

—— *Children's perceptions.* Baltimore: Warwick & York, 1914.

WINITZ, H. Spectrographic investigation of infant vowels. *Journal of Genetic Psychology*, 1960, *96*, 171–81.

—— Repetitions in the vocalizations and speech of children in the first two years of life. *Journal of Speech and Hearing Disorders Monograph Supplement*, 7, 1961.

—— The development of speech and language in the normal child. *In* R. W. RIEBERT and R. S. BRUBAKER (eds.), *Speech pathology*, pp. 42–76. Amsterdam: North-Holland, 1966.

—— *Articulatory acquisition and behavior.* New York: Appleton-Century-Crofts, 1969.

——, and BELLEROSE, B. Phoneme-cluster learning as a function of instructional method and age. *Journal of Verbal Learning and Verbal Behavior*, 1965, *4*, 98–102.

—— Relation between sound discrimination and sound learning. *Journal of Communication Disorders*, 1967, *1*, 215–35.

WINITZ, H., and PREISLER, L. Discrimination pretraining and sound learning. *Perceptual and Motor Skills*, 1965, *20*, 905–16.

—— Effect of distinctive feature pretraining in phoneme discrimination learning. *Journal of Speech and Hearing Research*, 1967, *10*, 515–30.

WINNICK, W. A., and KRESSEL, K. Tachistoscopic recognition thresholds, paired-associate learning, and free recall as a function of abstract-ness-concreteness and word frequency. *Journal of Experimental Psychology*, 1965, *70*, 163–68.

WINNICK, W. A., and NACHBAR, S. Tachistoscopic recognition thresholds following paired-associate learning. *Journal of Verbal Learning and Verbal Behavior*, 1967, *6*, 95–100.

WINTERS, J. J., and GERJUOY, I. R. Recognition of tachistoscopically exposed letters by normals and retardates. *Perception and Psychophysics*, 1969, *5*, 21–24.

WISE, C. M. *Applied phonetics.* Englewood Cliffs, N.J.: Prentice-Hall, 1957.

WISPÉ, L., and DRAMBAREAN, N. Physiological need, verbal frequency, and visual duration threshold. *Journal of Experimental Psychology*, 1953, *46*, 25–31.

WITMER, L. R. The association value of three-place consonant syllables. *Journal of Genetic Psychology*, 1935, *47*, 337–60.

WOOD, N. E., ed. *Language development and language disorders: A compendium of lectures.* Yellow Springs, Ohio: Antioch Press, 1960.

WOODWORTH, R. S. *Experimental psychology.* New York: Holt, 1938.

——, and H. SCHLOSBERG. *Experimental psychology.* Rev. ed. New York: Holt, 1954.

WUNDT, W. *Völkerpsychologie.* Leipzig: Engelmann, 1900.

—— *Sprachgeschichte und sprachpsychologie.* Leipzig: Engelmann, 1901.

WYNNE, R. D., GERJUOY, H., SCHIFFMAN, H., and WEXLER, N. Word association: Variables affecting popular response frequency. *Psychological Reports*, 1967, *20*, 423–32.

YELEN, D. R., and SCHULZ, R. W. Verbal satiation. *Journal of Verbal Learning and Verbal Behavior*, 1963, *1*, 373–77.

YNGVE, V. H. A model and an hypothesis for language structure. *Proceedings of the American Philosophical Association*, 1960, *104*, 444–66.

YOUNG, R. K., and WEBBER, A. Standardization of Mexican trigrams. *Psychonomic Science*, 1968, *11*, 354.

YULE, G. Y. *The statistical study of literary vocabulary.* London: Cambridge, 1944.

ZAJONC, R. B., and NIEUWENHUYSE, B. Relationship between word frequency and recognition. *Journal of Experimental Psychology*, 1964, *67*, 276–85.

ZALE, E. M., ed. *Proceedings of the conference on language and language behavior.* New York: Appleton-Century-Crofts, 1968.

ZECHMEISTER, E. B. Orthographic distinctiveness. *Journal of Verbal Learning and Verbal Behavior*, 1969, *8*, 754–61.

ZEMLEN, W. R. *Speech and hearing science: Anatomy and physiology.* Englewood Cliffs, N.J.: Prentice-Hall, 1968.

ZIPF, G. K. *The psycho-biology of language: An introduction to dynamic philology.* Boston: Houghton Mifflin, 1935.

ZIPPEL, B. Semantic differential measures of meaningfulness and agreement of meaning. *Journal of Verbal Learning and Verbal Behavior*, 1967, *6*, 222–25.

ZUBIN, J., ERON, L. D., and SCHUMER, F. *An experimental approach to projective techniques.* New York: John Wiley, 1965.

The concept of "intelligence" has never had a recognized position among the systematic constructs in any comprehensive psychological theory. One reason is probably the fact of its origin in the context of individual differences, whereas theorists have looked to studies of how individuals are alike for their empirical bases for system building. Psychologists who have pursued the one emphasis have had too little commerce with those who have pursued the other; communication between the two has been poor. Another reason may be that testing for the measurement of intelligence has usually been in applied contexts, another source naturally ignored by theorists. Recent events promise to change this general situation.

Historical Views of Intelligence

GALTON

The strong British interest in individual differences was a natural consequence of Darwin's evolutionary doctrines. The study of possible heredity of human mental qualities required instruments and techniques of assessment. In accordance with the British philosophical doctrine of associationism, Galton's attention was directed to simple sensory tests, including measures of sensory thresholds, both absolute and differential (Galton 1883). On the basis of that doctrine, Galton may have reasoned that since all we can know comes to us through the senses, good senses mean good intellect.

BINET

Alfred Binet came to the problems of assessing intellectual status of individuals from a unique background of experimental studies in the psychological laboratory, with no apparent philosophical bias to influence him. Having been focusing his attention on thinking and other so-called higher mental functions, he regarded Galton's tests as being too simple and not

J. P. Guilford

Theories of Intelligence

30

very relevant. Throughout the development of his successive scales of 1905, 1908 and 1911, Binet maintained and clearly stated his conviction that human intelligence is a very complex affair. For example, he believed that there is not just one general memory ability that is the same regardless of what is to be remembered, but that there are a number of memory abilities. Among the memory abilities Binet suggested different aptitudes for are: visual memory, memory for sentences, memory for musical tones, memory for colors, and memory for digits. Modern factor-analytic studies show him to be nearly correct so far as he went, but that there may be as many as 24 memory abilities when all are known. Eighteen have already been demonstrated.

In his general conceptions of the nature of intelligence, in which Binet made some changes as he gained more experience, he first emphasized traits of attention or adaptability to tasks, memory, judgment or common sense, and suggestibility. Later, when he saw the relevance of intelligence for problem solving, he came to emphasize four kinds of operation: taking a goal set, comprehension, solution finding (including invention of methods), and autocriticism (Binet & Simon 1909). To this day there is more or less common agreement upon such steps in complete problem solving, most explicitly set forth in the writer's general problem-solving model (Guilford 1967).

Terman

Terman was most impressed with the practical gains to be derived from the use of an intelligence scale like Binet's, and proceeded to adapt it to the U. S. with some enlargements. He was quite willing to accept Binet's conception that included the components of (1) tendency to take and maintain the direction toward an end, (2) finding means for reaching the goal, and (3) autocriticism. He wrongly assumed that Binet had rejected the type of thinking of faculty psychology, and that he believed in one master ability of "general intelligence" that operates in the different ways just specified (Terman 1916). He defended the thesis that one can measure a phenomenon without knowing its nature, as physicists had been measuring electricity before knowing about its fundamental nature. Binet may have misled Terman regarding his beliefs by his use of a single, mental-age score, which especially appealed to Terman.

E. L. Thorndike

While Terman was developing intelligence scales according to what Spearman (1927) called the "monarchic" view, E. L. Thorndike was developing a radically different view that Spearman later put in an "anarchic" category. It was a belief that intelligence is a conglomerate aggregation of a multitude of independent specific habits or skills, perhaps each as limited in scope as stimulus-response bonds. Thorndike undoubtedly came to this view of a completely unstructured intelligence for several reasons. One was his study, with Woodworth, of transfer of learning among skills in simple perceptual judgments. Another was awareness of Wissler's finding of such low intercorrelations of J. M. Cattell's adaptations of Galton's tests when administered to Columbia students. Still another was Thorn-

dike's developing theory of learning as being a matter of establishing specific stimulus-response bonds. His view of intelligence was naturally favored by many behaviorists, insofar as they were concerned with the concept at all.

Godfrey Thomson (Brown and Thomson 1925) held a similar view, which included the belief that psychological tests of any degree of complexity represent measurement of samplings of numerous independent, specific abilities. Correlations other than zero were taken to indicate the proportions of elements that were sampled in common by pairs of tests. From this point of view, even Spearman's g could be conceived as a broad, somewhat stable sampling of elementary abilities.

Spearman

In developing his famous revision of the Binet Scale, Terman was aware of Spearman's historical emphasis upon a "common central factor," demonstrated, as Spearman thought, by rigorous mathematical theory and operations, but he did not place much emphasis upon that finding (Terman 1916). Spearman maintained that all tests that could be regarded as being within the intellectual category, no matter how different they may look, measure in common the same universal ability that he called g. By 1927, he was ready to propose that g is a fund of mental energy that each person possesses. This energy could be directed into special channels or "engines" and the latter have some bearing upon scores in each test, each task having its own "specific" engine and determining a specific effect upon scores in that test.

In Spearman's view, the scores obtained in using any test in the intellectual domain is a function of both g and the specific component s. Spearman thought that his best evidence for g was his (erroneous) generalization that all intellectual tests intercorrelate positively. If two tests correlate positively they have something in common, and that something is g. The degree of correlation between the two tests is in proportion to their "saturations" with g. The s components of tests contribute nothing to intercorrelations, all being independent of g and of one another. Spearman was forced later to recognize that some correlation coefficients are larger than could be accounted for on the basis of their saturations with the universal factor g. The extra commonality sometimes occurred within a set of tests that are similar to one another in some rather obvious way (all tests of a set being numerical, spatial, or verbal) and this outcome was attributed to an additional common component in each set of tests. Such common features Spearman called "group" factors.

To state Spearman's theory rigorously, as he did, we can say that if no group factor is involved the score for person I in test J can be written:

$$z_{ij} = a_{jg}z_{ig} + a_{js}z_{is} \qquad [1]$$

in which z_{ij} is a test score in standard form. That is, any score

$$z_{ij} = (X_j - \bar{X}_j)/s_j,$$

where X_j is an obtained score on test J, $\bar{X}_j$ is the mean of the X_j scores, and s_j is their standard deviation. The term a_{jg} in Equation 1 is the saturation coefficient for g in test J, z_{ig} is the

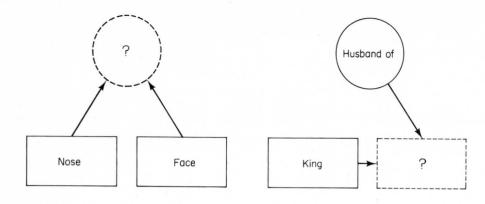

Fig. 30-1. *Graphic models representing Spearman's conception of eduction of relations (Item A) and eduction of correlates (Item B).*

amount of *g* possessed by person *I*, a_{js} is the weight to be given to the specific component *S*, and z_{is} measures *I*'s status in that component.

Psychologically, Spearman thought that his *g* component pertained to the manipulation of relations, and that the best tests for *g* involve relations, either by way of the examinee's seeing relations or using them in completing relationships or analogies. Two processes were defined: "eduction" of relations and eduction of correlates. Figure 30-1 illustrates these two operations. In the first case, two "fundaments" (items of information) are given in a test, with the examinee (*E*) to name the relation he sees between them. In the second case, *E* is given one fundament and a relation, to supply another fundament that is related to the given one as specified. In either case, it does not matter what kind of information is provided, verbal or nonverbal; *g* is the universal ability that takes care of all kinds of information.

Spearman must be given credit for introducing factor analysis into psychology, especially in its role of determining the component abilities in intelligence, and this has been extended to other areas—sensory, perceptual, and psychomotor. But subsequent experiences, as will be related in the next section, have shown that the "group" factors, which Spearman relegated to minor roles, are the most significant components of intelligence and the existence of a stable *g* component is extremely doubtful. The simple evidence for the last conclusion is that there are far too many zero correlations among tests of intellectual qualities, where one genuine zero correlation would be sufficient to justify rejecting the *universality* of *g*. In examining over 7000 correlation coefficients among numerous intellectual tests, the writer found that as many as 17 percent of them could be regarded as zero (Guilford 1964).

E. G. BORING

It cannot be said that psychology's outstanding historian provided a theory of intelligence, but he astutely offered an observation that would have naturally led to discovery of the basic variables in intelligence. Reacting to the seemingly hopeless efforts of others to achieve a satisfactory definition of "intelligence," Boring (1923) commented that it ". . . . . . must be defined as the capacity to do well in an intelligence test." This focuses attention where it belongs; on the nature of intelli-

gence tests. He suggested further that the natural route to understanding what intelligence tests measure is through information regarding their intercorrelations. Wissler (1901) had made a similar suggestion many years earlier. It remained for those who developed factor theory and factor-analytic theory to show how intercorrelations among tests could yield information about abilities underlying sets of tests, each set indicating how well different individuals are functioning psychologically in some recognizable, unique way. The next section will consider theories that have emerged from the psychometric approach that has employed the multivariate methods of factor analysis.

Psychometric Theories

In a real sense, a number of psychologists with a bent for measurement in their science followed the way that had been pointed out by Wissler and Boring, whether they were aware of the advice of those gentlemen or not, taking the additional step of factor analysis. Spearman belongs in this group, of course, but his views are considered now to have only historical significance. The major contemporary psychometric conceptions of intelligence will be treated here.

HOLZINGER'S BIFACTOR MODEL

There is one interesting link between Spearman's view of *g*, which is so simple that it needed no geometric model as a means of logically conceiving of intelligence, and later views that required structuring. This link was provided by Holzinger, who, as a student of Spearman, adopted *g* but also accepted the mounting evidence for the importance of group factors that were being found on both sides of the Atlantic. Holzinger's idea was that each test of an intellectual nature should have one group factor in addition to *g* (Holzinger & Swineford 1937). The common-factor pattern for a battery of tests was thought to exist such that each test had *g* in common with all other tests and one group factor in common to a select group of tests within the battery. The proposal was to factor analyze in such a way as to achieve that factor pattern. But analyses that have not imposed such a restriction upon the data find that tests may share relations to more than one group factor, thus spoiling the ideal bifactor picture.

Cyril Burt followed Spearman to the extent of accepting the existence of a universal ability for tests, but he preferred to call it "general intelligence." Unlike Spearman, he gave strong recognition to the group factors, of which he accepted an unusually large number, when he undertook a summarizing survey of intellectual abilities in 1949. In his view of intellectual operations, functions differ in complexity all the way from simple sensory processes and motor reactions to totally integrative events involving relations. Abilities, not only intellectual but also psychomotor, vary in degree of generality at different levels. Abilities of lower levels of generality bear subordinate relationships to those of higher levels. Four levels of generality were recognized, from highest to lowest: relational, associative, perceptual, and sensory, on the intellectual side of mental functioning.

Figure 30-2 shows the ideal kind of hierarchical model that Burt had in mind and toward which he believed the discovery of group factors and the growing acquaintance with their properties were leading. Although it seemed desirable to expect bifurcations into subcategories and sub-subcategories at each of the levels of generality, he did not succeed in placing the known group factors accordingly. The numbers of subsidary abilities within classes tended to exceed two.

From Burt's review of what he considered to be the acceptable group factors (Burt 1949), it is difficult to see how they would all go into a single hierarchical picture. Burt did not present the placement of all the abilities within a total hierarchy, nor could this writer do so, following Burt's discussions of their interrelationships. It is possible to give a few examples pertaining to limited areas of his total scheme. He accepts at the "sensation" level a factor of "general sensitivity." Under this are general abilities for each of the sense modalities—a visual ability, auditory ability, tactual-kinesthetic ability, and so on. Under the visual ability are two of more special nature—color sensitivity and form appreciation. Under color sensitivity are three sensitivities for the three primary colors of red, green, and blue. Under the general auditory ability he mentions discrimination abilities, of which there are five special ones: pitch, harmony, melody, loudness, and rhythm. Thus we see that even within the same general "level" of abilities there may be subhierarchies, each with additional levels.

In order to give further impressions of Burt's organization of abilities let us take an example at the "association" level. There is a general associative ability, according to Burt, under which are two groups of abilities, one in which abilities are distinguished in terms of their "formal" properties and the other in terms of "content" properties. There are two formal types of abilities: memory and productive association. There are two memory abilities distinguished as to kind, namely, short-term memory ability and long-term memory ability. Under productive-association ability there are fluency and cleverness. The content abilities in the association level are four: imagery, verbal, arithmetical, and practical. Imagery ability breaks down along sense-modality lines, as Galton had suggested in the preceding century. Verbal ability breaks down in terms of an ability dealing with single words, a general language ability, and a number of subsidiary abilities involved in speech.

At the highest, or "relational" level, at the apex of a subhierarchy is a general "thought-processes" ability. This subdivides into logical-thinking ability and aesthetic appreciation. Logical thinking has four subdivisions: verbal, productive association, apprehension of relations, and combination of relations. These four abilities do not seem to be fully coordinate, and, indeed, verbal and productive-association abilities were also mentioned at the associative level. Under aesthetic appreciation come appreciation for form and for relations.

It should be added that Burt points out at various places in the hierarchies that intellectual abilities have been found correlated with temperamental traits. It should also be said that parallel to the hierarchy coming under "logical processes," is another that is organized under the heading of "practical." At the higher levels in this hierarchy one finds spatial abilities and mechanical abilities; at the lower levels, the various psychomotor or manipulative abilities.

It would be possible to say that Burt's comprehensive scheme is essentially a writer's attempt to list abilities and other traits found by factor analysis in a reasonable, logical fashion, and nothing more than that, except for the fact that he cites factor-analytic data basic to many of his placements of abilities. His

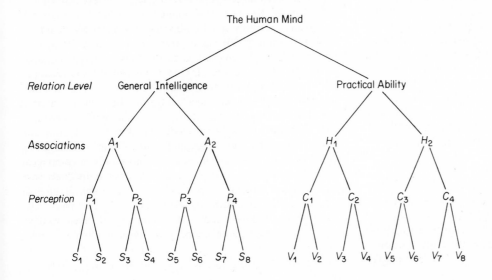

Fig. 30-2. *Diagram representing Burt's conception of an ideal hierarchical model for aptitude factors, with successive dichotomizations at different levels of generality.* [Reprinted by permission from Burt 1949.]

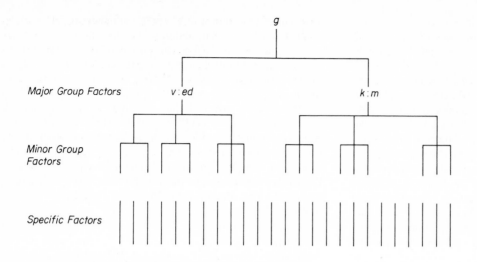

Major Group Factors $v:ed$ $k:m$

Minor Group
Factors

Specific Factors

Fig. 30-3. *A diagram representing the main features of Vernon's conception of the organization of aptitude factors.* [Adapted from Vernon 1950.]

general strategy in factor analysis has been first to extract a (or, the) universal factor, and from the residual correlations (the contributions of the universal factor having been removed) he extracts the next most general factors, removes their contributions, and so on as long as residual correlations appear to contain evidence of common factors. His partiality to the universal factor and the more general subsidiary factors would thus very likely attribute to them some proportions of total variance that properly belongs to factors of less generality.

VERNON'S HIERARCHICAL MODEL

P. E. Vernon's model for the intellectual abilities is very much like that of Burt. Vernon (1950) presents his basic model as shown in Figure 30-3. He is frank to say that this is an ideal pattern that gives only an approximate fit to all the known factors, the abilities and other traits.

The first major differentiation under g is between a very broad factor $v:ed$ (verbal-educational) and $k:m$ (spatial-mechanical), which corresponds to Burt's "practical" factor. This differentiation is regarded as primarily the result of education and experience in general. More searching analyses show that tests loaded on the $v:ed$ factor subdivide in analysis to give a verbal and a numerical factor, which Vernon regards as minor group factors. Further analysis of $k:m$ tests shows minor factors of spatial ability, mechanical knowledge, and some manual abilities. Any further breakdowns are along the lines of school subjects in the one major group and manipulative and athletic skills in the other. Vernon's primary interest in education leads him to reject factors that do not have potential value for education as he sees it. He presents more detailed models for the two broad categories of abilities, built around $v:ed$ in the one case $k:m$ in the other, with g central to both (Vernon 1950).

Evaluation of Hierarchical Models. The crux of a hierarchical model for intelligence is the belief in a g or g-like universal ability, and the fact that tests that presumably measure g can be further grouped, with the tests of each group measuring in common an ability of broad but not universal scope, on down to groups of one test each, at which point genuine specific abilities may be accepted.

Two important circumstances have favored the finding of evidence for such a state of affairs. One lies in the preferred methods of factoring, with insistence upon a g factor. It is possible to have a g among tests of intellectual functions if one insists upon it. It is also possible to have broad and narrow group factors if the methods of factoring favor such an outcome. With the same matrix of intercorrelations, however, if one is willing to let variances be distributed more evenly among the factors in the rotation of axes, this kind of result is not likely to occur. An exception would be the analysis in which resort is made to oblique rotations and one finds the more general factors as what Thurstone (1947) called higher-order factors, i.e., second order, third-order, and so on.[1] The finding of g, with additional factors of greater and lesser generality, then, is not necessarily an outcome compelled by the data. It can be attributed to predilections concerning the type of model expected.

The other circumstance favoring general factors is the use of samples of examinees from heterogeneous populations—populations in which individuals differ with respect to such variables as age, education, general experience, or sex. Tests that all correlate in the same direction with one or more of these extraneous variables will consequently show something in common in the factor analysis. But that "something in common" need not be anything intellectual, or even psychological. Truman Kelley (1928) pointed out many years ago that an apparent g ability could arise when such variables are uncontrolled. Vernon (1950) has expressed a preference for a wide-ranging population on the ground that it is more representative of human beings in general. One of his samples, for example, was made up of 1000 army recruits in which, evidently, only the variable of sex was fully controlled. In such a sample it would be possible to find nonzero correlations between even such disparate variables as vocabulary, numerical computations, mechanical knowledge, and motor dexterity, thus giving the impression that an all-encompassing g was a component in all these variables. In a population in which individuals have been equated for educational level, age, and other features of cultural background, there would probably be some zero correlations among those variables. In samples with even roughly equivalent ages and educational backgrounds, zero correla-

[1] For methods of extracting factors and rotating axes, see Harman (1967).

tions are often found, as pointed out earlier (Guilford 1964). The writer can see no reason to relax conditions of experimental control when the study is in the category of individual differences.

THE STRUCTURE-OF-INTELLECT THEORY

Multiple-Factor Theory. Before considering the structure-of-intellect (SI) model, it is important to have some acquaintance with multiple-factor theory and the methods of factoring that go naturally with it. The basic equation for this theory can be precisely expressed in terms of a linear equation, which states that an individual I's score in test J is a weighted sum of his status scores in each of q common factors, plus a weighted specific factor unique to test J, plus an error of measurement. The equation reads:

$$z_{ij} = a_{1j}z_{1i} + a_{2j}z_{2i} + a_{3j}z_{3i} + \cdots + a_{qj}z_{qi} \\ + a_{sj}z_{si} + e_{ij} \qquad [2]$$

where the zs are all standard scores, as in Equation 1 (p. 000) and the a terms are factor loadings or weights, i.e., a_{2j} is the loading for factor 2 in test J. There is no restriction on the degrees of generality of the factors and no restriction on the number of common factors each test can have. The only general assumption is that the factors are independent, i.e., uncorrelated in the population. In order to make the mathematical model even more general, we could change the equation so as not to require that the factors be orthogonal (uncorrelated). Essentially the same psychologically interpreted factors are most likely to come out of analyses under either assumption—orthogonal or oblique factor structure. This conclusion is based upon the assumption that correlations between factors are generally low, i.e., well below 0.7.

The equation just given applies to one particular score, made by one person in one test. The basic data for a factor analysis is a score matrix, a table of scores made by N individuals in n tests, where N is much larger than n. If these scores are arranged in n rows and N columns, we say that the matrix is of order n by N. If the scores are all in standard form, the elements of the matrix are called z_{ji}, where j is the number of the test and i is the number of the individual, and the entire matrix can be denoted by the single letter Z.

The intercorrelation of any two tests J and K by the Pearson product-moment method, when the scores in both J and K are in standard form, is given by the equation:

$$r_{jk} = \frac{\sum z_j z_k}{N} \qquad [3]$$

All such coefficients of correlation can be derived through applications of the matrix equation:

$$R = ZZ'/N \qquad [4]$$

where Z' is the transpose of Z. In the transpose of a matrix the rows of the original matrix become the columns of the transpose. Accordingly, the columns of Z become rows of Z'. Z' would have N rows and n columns, which is the more usual arrangement in tabulating scores from N people in n

tests, but this is arbitrary. R stands for the "reduced" correlation matrix, since it depends upon the common-factor loadings only. The specific and error components do not contribute to intercorrelations. A particular correlation coefficient r_{jk} is related to the factor loadings in tests J and K as in the equation

$$r_{jk} = a_{1j}a_{1k} + a_{2j}a_{2k} + a_{3j}a_{3k} + \cdots + a_{qj}a_{qk} \qquad [5]$$

It is this equation that makes possible the estimation of the common-factor loadings, the as, from knowledge of the empirically known matrix of rs. The end result of factoring is a matrix A. We can express all the equations of the form of Equation 5 within a selected set of n tests by the matrix equation

$$R = AA' \qquad [6]$$

Thus, the correlation matrix is also derivable from A and its transpose.[2] Both A and its transpose are unknown, of course, and are to be found from the information given by R, the procedures for which we cannot go into here.[3]

The Structure-of-Intellect Model. The writer's examination of the properties of the intellectual factors that had been found by application of multiple-factor-analytical procedures led to the inescapable conclusion that no clear hierarchical arrangement would take care of the situation and that, on the other hand, many of the factors could be paired off in parallel fashion on the basis of certain similarities and differences. For example, there was noted an ability to see or to grasp relations between pairs of figures and an ability to see relations between pairs of word meanings. Seeing that figure B is a mirror image of figure A or that figure K is an inversion of figure M would be items for a test of the one ability. Seeing that father and daughter are related as parent to child, as male to female, as large to small, or as old to young would be an item for the other ability. Two tests, one for each of these two kinds of items, were found to correlate close to zero.

The difference between these two abilities is only in the kind of information involved—visual figures in the one case, and concepts or meanings in the other. The abilities are alike in that both kinds of items require grasping or understanding, and also in that the kind of thing grasped is a relation. In this one example we see three bases for classifying the intellectual abilities; by kind of operation (cognition), kind of content (figural in the one case and semantic in the other), and product (relation in both cases). Each unique ability, then, is known in terms of its particular conjunction of a certain kind of operation, a certain kind of content, and a certain kind of product.[4]

---

[2] For further information on matrices and matrix multiplication, see Horst's book (1963).

[3] Much of the basic theory was developed by L. L. Thurstone (1947). For further treatment of theory and for methods of factor analysis, see Harman's book (1967).

[4] El-Koussy (1956) had apparently come to the same kind of conclusion after years of study of space tests. He remarked that every test could be regarded as having three aspects—content, form, and function. Suggested kinds of content were numbers, words, pictures, figures, symbols, and solids. Suggested kinds of form were classification, order, opposites, analogies, etc. Functions might be induction, deduction, memory, visualization, manipulation, etc. Some of these suggested categories can be translated into structure-of-intellect counterparts, but some cannot.

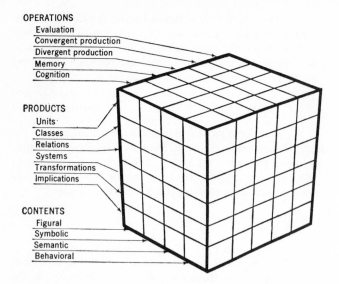

OPERATIONS
Evaluation
Convergent production
Divergent production
Memory
Cognition

PRODUCTS
Units
Classes
Relations
Systems
Transformations
Implications

CONTENTS
Figural
Symbolic
Semantic
Behavioral

Fig. 30-4. *The three-dimensional facet model representing the intellectual abilities, known as the structure of intellect.*

The rectangular, cross-classification type of model seen in Figure 30-4 represents five kinds of operation, four kinds of content, and six kinds of product, on the three dimensions of the model. Combining five kinds of operation, with four kinds of content, and six kinds of product yields 120 unique intersections, each standing for a potential ability. When the model was first conceived, nearly 40 abilities had been brought out by factor analysis, all of them being reinterpreted in terms of their structure-of-intellect (SI) properties. A few additional factor-analytically derived abilities in the literature fitted logically into other cells of the model. At the Aptitudes Research Project at the University of Southern California the model soon became the heuristic basis for hypotheses of intellectual abilities yet to be demonstrated by factor analysis, until, as this chapter was written, close to 100 abilities had been accounted for in terms of tests that were shown to represent them. Thus, the hypothetico-deductive value of the model has been repeatedly verified in a number of successive analyses.

Definitions of the SI Categories. Although the number of abilities projected by the theory is probably much larger than anyone had presupposed, considerable parsimony as well as psychological significance are provided by emphasis upon the 15 category concepts, which will now be defined and illustrated. Knowledge of these categories is sufficient for encompassing each and every ability. Each category will be given a formal definition, with additional informal comments to add to sharpening of the definition and to add connotative aspects to the concept. Definitions of the three parameters will also be given. In considering any of these concepts, it should be kept in mind that the definitions spring from the nature of the tests that represent the various abilities in each category. The tests provide the empirical referents for the abstract conceptions.

But first, we need a definition of "intellect." *Intellect is the information-processing aspect of the living organism, where "information" is that which organisms discriminate.* The having and using of discriminations, then, define intellectual function-ing. The term "intelligence" is best reserved for the level of goodness of individual intellectual functioning, which implies gradients of values and measurement. Since we have very little in the way of *absolute* scales for intellectual qualities, measurements are referred to scales of individual differences. Now for definitions of the categories, beginning each set with its parameter.

OPERATION: *Major kind of intellectual activity or process; something that the organism does with information.*

Cognition: *Immediate discovery, awareness, rediscovery, or recognition of information in various forms; comprehension or understanding.* Different tests that are known to measure cognition abilities emphasize variously the more specific kinds of activities mentioned in this definition. In general, an act of cognition is a decoding of information presented by a sensory inlet, and this decoding depends very heavily and rather directly upon relevant information that the organism has in memory storage. Another general description would be to say that cognition is the identification of particulars, where each "particular" is an item of information; a product of a certain kind.

It should be noted that the definition of "cognition" here is much more restricted than the somewhat common usage that makes the concept as broad as intellect itself. For this reason, in this chapter the expression "cognition ability" is preferred to "cognitive ability," to help maintain this discrimination.

Memory: *The fixation of information for storage purposes.* The operation of memory is to be clearly distinguished from the memory store, which is not an operation. Whether something more than "fixation" is concerned in the operation of memory is still to be determined.

The definition comes directly from the nature of memory tests. In them, after the instructions, a "study page" (if it is a printed test) is presented to E, who is to observe and to try to memorize, within a standard, limited time. Then E turns to a "test page," on which he must reproduce, recognize, or in some other way show how much he has fixated from his observation of the study page. The time interval between observation and test is very short in most cases, but most of the time it is sufficiently long to go beyond the condition for what most investigators would regard as "short-term memory."

In recent years, physiological studies involving the administration of drugs suggest that "fixation" is a recognizable brain process occurring during the early minutes following exposure to information. Much work needs to be done on abilities related to retentivity of fixed storage over longer periods of time.

Divergent Production: *Generation of information from given information, where the emphasis is upon variety and quantity of output from the same source.* A shorter statement would be: *the generation of logical alternatives.* Divergent production is likely to involve "transfer recall," i.e., the output has not been connected with the given information before in the previous operations of the individual. Thus, "remote associations" occur and new associations are formed without their being aroused by direct stimulation from the environment. Consequently, such activity is characteristic of much behavior that is recognized as being "creative," and divergent-production abilities in general play important roles in creative production.

Convergent Production: *Generation of information from given information, where the emphasis is upon achieving unique or conventionally accepted best outcomes.* It is likely that the given (cue) information fully determines the response. A shorter statement would be: *the generation of logical necessities.* The reference to "conventionally accepted" outcomes is included to take care of arbitrary, man-made rules, as in mathematics, logic, and in law, The "one right answer" specification that is sometimes stated with respect to convergent production is not sufficiently definitive, for tests of cognition, memory, and evaluation also often require one right answer without involving *production.*

The contrast between divergent and convergent production can be illustrated by two parallel tests. If asked to name sources of power commonly used in locomotion, one could say: gasoline, kerosene, electricity, steam, muscles, atomic energy, solar energy, and so on. This problem calls for alternatives and the door is opened fairly wide. But if the problem is to name the most commonly used source of power in automobiles, only the response "gasoline" qualifies; the restrictions placed upon the activity force convergence on a unique answer.

Evaluation: *Reaching decisions or making judgments concerning criterion satisfaction, for logical criteria such as identity, completeness, compatibility, congruency, and internal consistency.* Criteria of taste and other personal standards are apparently not relevant. This rules out judgments of aesthetic values and ethical values or any values that cannot be rigorously defined. There is also a large area of functioning in which there is sensitivity to error or awareness that something is wrong, which has been found to belong in the category of cognition, not evaluation.

CONTENTS: *Broad classes or types of information distinguished without regard to formal properties.* The differences among them are purely substantive.

Figural: *Information in concrete form, as perceived from sensory input or recalled in the form of images or other possible duplicates of perceived information.* The term "figural" minimally implies some degree of organization, as in figure-ground perceptual organization. The "possible duplicates" other than images might suggest the Würzburg conception of "imageless thoughts." If they can be regarded as such, they would still have clearly sensory references. The Würzburg imageless thoughts may be closer to the category of semantic content, in general, however.

Different sense modalities are involved, each with its own kind of figural information, depending upon the degrees of structuring that apply to each modality. Of the 30 potential visual-figural abilities of the *SI* model, 26 have been demonstrated. Possibly five of a parallel set of 30 auditory-figural abilities have been reported, and one kinesthetic-figural ability (Guilford 1967). These nonvisual abilities are mostly in the operation category of cognition, but some are in the memory area. There is a rich field for those who want to know much more than we do now concerning the abilities basic to music, speech, choreography, and athletics.

Symbolic: *Information in the form of denotative signs, having no significance in and of themselves, such as letters, numbers, musical notations, codes, and words, when meanings and form are not considered.* The qualification rules out semantic and figural affiliates of the signs, respectively, as being irrelevant when only symbolic information is under consideration. Printed words have visual form and they carry meanings, but it is only the combination and sequence of particular letters that characterizes the verbal-symbolic unit. Spoken words have auditory form and they carry meaning to those who have the required memory-store residuals. It is the stable sound pattern that constitutes the auditory sign or symbol. Products of symbolic information are like tokens or coins; they can be manipulated in ways we arbitrarily choose. Symbolic information is the substance with which the mathematician notably deals, also the logician and the cryptographer. It is the only kind of information with which electronic computers can deal directly. They can deal with other kinds of information only after translation into symbolic form.

The last statement can be generalized to say that it is possible to translate from one category of information to another, as if the content categories were different languages. This is a matter of recoding of information. An item of information in one "language" is an implication of, or is implied by, an item of information in some other.

Behavioral: *Information involved in interactions of individuals, where the attitudes, needs, desires, moods, intentions, perceptions, thoughts, etc. of other people and of ourselves are concerned.* The transmission of this information from one person to another comes through sensory cues in the form of expressive behavior, including bodily postures and movements, facial reactions, tones of voice, choice of words, and manner of speaking. Thus, the recipient of the behavioral information may skip or ignore the figural properties of face and voice and the semantic meanings that would obviously be carried by spoken or written words. He senses the mental disposition of the other person, he has empathic reactions to emotional signs, and "reads between the lines" of conversation.

PRODUCTS: *Forms that information takes in the organism's processing of it.*

Products are different kinds of mental constructs. The same products have been found applicable in all four general substantive areas, which have just been discussed, so that we have in prospect 24 basic categories of information. The writer has suggested (Guilford 1967) that this set of categories constitutes a basic psycho-epistemology, such as Piaget has been seeking. It is an empirically derived epistemology. Of the 24 kinds of information, 23 have been found differentiated in the operation category of cognition, and 22 of them in the divergent-production category, 18 of them in the memory category, 18 in the evaluation category, and 12 in the convergent-production category.

The six product categories (see Fig. 30-4, p. 636) are of interest in relation to logic. Classes, relations, and implications are obvious concepts familiar to all students of logic. Units of information are also implied in logic. Propositions are units; so are items of information that form classes and items of a pair, in which a relation exists. Logic has not yet formulated ways of dealing with systems and transformations, but mathematics has; for any complex expression can be a system, and transformations occur in the processes of simplifying, factoring, and transposing. The six product concepts thus provide a basis for a psychologic that could be adapted to psychological theory—a psychologic for which Piaget has also been searching (Piaget 1953).

Units: *Relatively segregated or circumscribed items of information having "thing" character.* This is essentially Gestalt psychology's definition of a "figure on a ground." The modifier "relatively" is used because there can be various degrees of separation of a unit from its surroundings as it occurs naturally. "Circumscribed" suggests closure from other informational substances; a "fenced-off" condition, as when a living cell acquires boundaries that interrupts continuity with other protoplasm.

Classes: *Conceptions underlying sets of items of information that are grouped by virtue of one or more attributes that they have in common.* Notice that it is the class idea that is intended, not the set of class members or exemplars. It can be added that not only units form classes; other kinds of products can also be classified. When we recognize or produce classes of classes, we have a hierarchical system. There can be classes of relations, of systems, and transformations, but it is not so clear that there are classes of implications, although that, too, might well be possible, as when the elements of one language imply elements in another language, and there are common features of sets of such translated elements.

Relations: *Connections between items of information based upon variables that they have in common or points of contact that apply to them.* Two things connected by a relation constitute a relationship. A relation is not merely a bond or association between two things; it is a definite item of information in its own right, as can be seen in Figure 30-1 (p. 632). When we say that a triangle is half of a diamond, the relation is part-whole, or more particularly, "half of." To say that K follows J injects a time or space relation between two letters. Bob is the son of William, and Gail is the daughter of Marie both illustrate parent-child relations, suggesting the property of transposibility. The fact that Mrs. Y dominates her husband illustrates a behavioral relation, which might be apparent when we see the two interacting at a party. There is no question about all these relations being different in kind and thus being something more than associative connections, which are so often assumed in theory to be alike in kind, differing only in strength.

Systems: *Organized or structured collections of items of information; complexes, of interrelated or interacting parts.* A layout of objects in space conceived visually would be a figural system. Spatial orientation is a matter of cognition of visual-figural systems. Each individual develops his personal "maps," all the way from his immediately-surrounding objects to his conceptions of geographical or even astronomical proportions. Each individual also develops with some degrees of detail and scope a reference frame for time. Experience with factoring tests show that sequences of events or of objects as conceived by an individual are semantic systems. Reference was made earlier to expressions in mathematics as being symbolic systems; this is also true of equations. Plans, strategies, and tactics are also systems. They might be semantic or behavioral, depending upon the emphasis. A social situation, with its interplay of perceptions, attitudes, and intentions, is a behavioral system, and, very largely, so is a story plot, especially in a "psychological" novel.

Transformations: *Changes of various kinds, such as redefinitions, shifts, and modifications in an existing item of information or in its function or use.* Moving an object in space is a figural transformation, whether it is a translation, a rotation, or some combination of the two. In a certain test the examinee is shown the initial position of an object such as a clock. He is informed as to what maneuvers are applied to the clock. Can he then select the correct alternative position the clock will have reached? This is a test of visualization, or in *SI* placement, cognition of visual-figural transformations.

A pun is a semantic transformation, for there is a shift in the meaning attached to the same sign, spoken or printed. In a test called Memory for Puns, E is given a statement on the study page containing a pun—for example, "The bird-loving bartender was arrested and charged with contributing to the delinquency of a mynah." The underlining is designed to call attention to the location of the pun, which is reasonably easy to see as "minor." On the test page, E is given an item with just the word MYNAH, to which he is to respond with "minor," to show that he does remember the transformation.

To illustrate the ability of convergent production of symbolic transformations, we may give a test such as Hidden-Word Production. In a sample item, E is to bury the word FORMER in as many different ways as he can in a number of phrases. For example, E might give the following responses, with "former" shown separated out:

Formerly one dollar
Uni form er rors
Yoursel f or Mer vin

These few examples will show not only some different transformation events, but how they can occur in different kinds of content and how different kinds of operations can be performed with respect to them. They also show how a unique combination of a kind of operation, a kind of content, and a kind of product converge to suggest a particular test idea for one particular ability in the *SI* model. This is one tactic for generating test ideas for particular suggested abilities. Another tactic is to look at successful tests for parallel abilities, where "successful" is indicated by high loadings of those tests on their factor. For example, having found that a good test for *DMU* (divergent production of semantic units) has items like "Name all the objects that you can that are both hard and round," we build a test for *EMU* (evaluation of semantic units) by giving items like: Which of these objects is best described by the words *round* and *hard*? The alternative answers, with E to choose the most descriptive might be: (a) revolver; (b) iron; (c) phonograph record; (d) tennis ball. In the first of these two tests, E has to *produce* the units; in the second, he has to *evaluate* the given units.

Before leaving the category of transformations, it should be pointed out that because of the flexibility that is obviously involved in the dealings with transformations, it is easy to conclude that this is surely one of the important categories for creative production. In creative production, things need not stay fixed as reality dictates. We can mold them more to our liking or to serve our purposes in problem solving. Genuine problem solving always has its creative aspects.

Implications: *Items of information suggested by other items of information.* Expected or predicted information is implied information. This is the category of inferences. In order that one item can suggest another, some kind of connection must be formed or must exist between the two. The connection may have arisen under the condition of contiguity, which is the case with what have been called "association." The product of implication is nearest to the common concept of "association," but as in the case of relations, as discussed earlier, an implication is something more than the "neutral bond" that Gestalt psychologists railed against. An implication is closer to E. L. Thorndike's concept of "belongingness." There is some reasonableness about one thing suggesting another, in spite of the circumstantial way in which implicational connections are often formed. In this respect, such connections are like relations, but there may be little or no definitive meaning attached in the case of the implications, whereas there always is in the case of relations. If one were to state adequately an implicational event or inference verbally, it would read like an implication in logic: If smoke, then fire. If heavy clouds, no sunshine. If I whistle, the girl will turn her head. If $X = Y$ and $Y = Z$, then $X = Z$.

The Question of Related Factors. The rectilinear model of Figure 30-4 (p. 636), with its sharply separated rows and columns and its right angles should not be taken to mean that the various abilities or functions that it represents operate in isolation in the going organism. Conceptually, the abilities are separate and they are parallel. But in the day-to-day transactions of the individual, in his tasks and his occupations, the chances are that more than one of these abilities is called into play and they function together toward a single end. If this were not so, the observation of these various functions as unique contributors to performances would have been much easier and perhaps should not have required the aid of factor analysis.

For many purposes it should be illuminating and useful to describe standardized tasks as functions of weighted combinations of *SI* abilities. Equation 2 should apply to ordinary tasks as it applies to tests, each of which is a kind of task. In fact, analyses of complex tasks have been done, and this kind of exercise has been applied to scores earned in successive trials in a task during the course of which learning occurs. Fleishman (1966) and others have done this for several kinds of tasks, and Dunham, Guilford, and Hoepfner (1966) have done it for concept-learning tasks, always with illuminating results. One general conclusion from such investigations is that as learning occurs there are some systematic changes of the importance of different abilities for individual differences in scores. Some factors are of greatest weight early in practice and diminish in importance for individual differences in scores as practice proceeds, others start low in weight and increase systematically, while still others have their greatest weights somewhere between earliest and latest practice trials.

The most reasonable hypothesis for these findings is that the way is that the strategy and tactics with which the subjects work on a task change with practice, and there are similarities in changes of this kind in large numbers of individuals within the sample. Each strategy or tactic may induce individuals to draw upon different resources in the way of *SI* abilities. In the complete theory of intellectual affairs, then, it is necessary to consider different kinds of strategies and tactics, and it may be of value to develop a catalog of them.

Another kind of relation that can occur among the abilities is correlation between them in the population. The general question of correlations among factors and their relations to possible higher-order, more general abilities and consequently to hierarchical patterns were discussed earlier in this chapter. It would be a good hypothesis that the nearer together two abilities are in the *SI* model the higher their correlation. Factors having two categories in common (i.e., those in the same row or column), might be expected to correlate more than those with only one category in common (those merely in the same slab or layer of the model), and the lowest correlations should be found where all three categories are different.

Thus far, the most common procedure for estimating correlations between factors has been to rotate axes obliquely, which means that at the end of the rotations the primary axes, each of which represents a factor, are free to stand at angles other than 90 degrees from one another. The correlation between any two factors is then the cosine of the angle of separation between the two axes. The intercorrelations of *r* factors provides a correlation matrix that is analyzed, with the expectation of finding second-order common factors in number less than *r*. The axes for these factors can also be rotated obliquely and their intercorrelations estimated to find the third-order factors, and so on.

The writer has consistently questioned the validity of such a procedure (Guilford & Zimmerman 1963). The main reason is that the location of oblique axes is so dependent upon the combination of tests that one happens to have in the battery for factor analysis. A change of battery would be likely to change angles between the primary axes, sometimes markedly. Another circumstance to be considered is that in constructing tests for two factors *A* and *B*, it is often difficult to control the conditions in the tests with the result that tests designed for factor *A* inadvertently also measure factor *B*, and tests designed for *B* inadvertently measure factor *A*. Factors *A* and *B* could actually be orthogonal (correlating zero) in the population and yet the data would make it appear that they are positively correlated, calling for an oblique solution with an angle of separation less than 90 degrees.

There are a few indirect indications about intercorrelations of factors in the *SI* model, suggesting a few generalizations. These indications come from apparent difficulties in separating pairs of factors when they are parallel, and when they have two categories in common. It has been found easiest to separate two factors in an orthogonal solution when the abilities differ only with respect to content. Next easiest to separate are factors whose abilities differ only in kind of operation. Most difficult to separate are some pairs of abilities differing only with respect to product, content and operation being the same. To give specific examples, there is some apparent sign of obliqueness between abilities dealing with units and systems, particularly when the categories in common are divergent production and visual-figural information. There is also some sign of obliqueness between abilities dealing with relations and implications, particularly in the memory area. One should not accept such generalization as final, however, for the difficulty may be in writing tests that permit the examinee to utilize the kind of product he is not supposed to employ and his strategy involves the use of the unintended kind of product. For example, it should be possible for him to memorize relations more easily than implications, so he may inject some relations into implication-memory test items. In memorizing in a relations test, he does not see or cognize some of the relations, so the task becomes for him, in part, the memorizing of probably less-meaningful implications. Thus, until we know that we have tests that measure their intended factors purely and simply, we are not ready to make good empirical estimates of interfactor correlations.

It can be naturally questioned whether two abilities can be completely independent when they have even one *SI* category in common. In a sense, this is a case of one common category out of three. It is also true that if we were to obtain a score for each of the 15 *SI* categories and if we combined these scores by threes to obtain composite scores for the various cells in the *SI* model, correlations would be substantial where there are categories in common. If there are 15 brain organs or mechanisms for the various *SI* categories, contributing to joint results when operating in conjunction, the goodness of each organ or mechanism in its own right would seem to ensure positive correlations among the factorial abilities. The obtained correlations among the factors are evidently much lower than such reasoning would lead us to expect. This is indicated by zero and near-zero correlations between tests representing pairs of factors, even when there is one, possibly when there are two, *SI* categories in common. The conclusion indicated is that there are certain interactions involved in the joint effects of triads of categories. Here we seem to have an inverse Gestalt effect: the whole is *less* than the sum (or product) of its parts!

There is evidence that when acceptable ways of determining correlations among factors become available, linear correlations will not tell the whole story. There are signs of some one-way dependencies between certain pairs of abilities (Guilford & Hoepfner 1966). Between mental age on an IQ test and tests of divergent-production (DP) abilities, scatter plots show almost no individuals who are high on a DP test if they are low on mental age. But there are numerous individuals who are high on mental age and low on the divergent-production test. The same kind of relationship appears when a vocabulary test is substituted for the IQ test. A vocabulary test measures the ability for cognition of semantic units rather uniquely, and the same factor dominates a verbal IQ test. A reasonable hypothesis can be suggested. Verbal IQ tests indicate how much basic, general information the individual has in his memory store and DP tests indicate how well he can produce information from his memory store. If the information is not there, naturally it cannot be produced. On the other hand, much information can be stored and yet it cannot be readily produced.

Another case of a relation with imbalance has just been reported (Hoepfner & O'Sullivan 1968). In relating scores from tests of behavioral cognition to IQ measures, it was found that while those who are high in IQ are also very likely to be high in behavioral-cognition abilities; those with relatively low IQ can be either high or low in behavioral cognition.

GUTTMAN'S FACET MODEL AND RADEX THEORY

Guttman (1958) has pointed out that the structure-of-intellect type of model is like R. A. Fisher's "factorial design," which is applied in analysis of variance. Each dimension in the Fisher model represents a variation of condition in some one respect, and is called a "facet." The *SI* model has three facets. Both models are known mathematically as "Cartesian products of sets." Each facet has a number of elements (categories) in the *SI* model; it represents a set of elements. The SI model's sets are operations (O), contents (C), and products (P). A facet, then, is defined as "a set involved in a Cartesian product" (Guttman 1958). Each ability in the model is an *ocp* product, where the lower-case letters are elements of the three facets O, C, and P, respectively. Incidentally, Guttman also relates facets mathematically to simple structure.

Guttman has thus given a mathematical basis for the SI model. He has different ideas regarding what some of the facets should be, however. In his choice of facets, he gives his attention to some of the obvious features of tests, which also helps him to relate facets to his radex theory, which has a radex type of model. Two facets that he recognizes are kinds of test items—numerical, verbal, and pictorial or geometrical—and degree of complexity. The first of these two facets is obviously in line with the content facet (C) of the SI model. Complexity has no obvious connection with operations and products, but Guttman (1958) suggests that those two other facets of the SI model may represent two kinds of complexity.

At any rate, to follow Guttman further, he has stated that if the facet of kind (content) is held constant and complexity varied, and these are the only variations in facet elements, the intercorrelations form a "simplex" pattern. This pattern has highest correlations along the principal diagonal of the correlation matrix, with the size of *r*s tapering off toward the upper-right and lower-left corners when the tests are put in order of complexity. The principle is that tests of similar complexity correlate higher than tests differing in degree of complexity. Guttman would expect to extract two factors by ordinary methods: a simple-function factor and a complex-function factor. If the test vectors are plotted in two-dimensional space, they would spread like a fan within a 90-degree angle.

On the other hand, if complexity is kept constant in a set of analyzed tests, with content varied, the resulting correlations should form a "circumplex" pattern. A circumplex of coefficients is like a simplex in having the largest coefficients along the principal diagonal but it differs by having a graded rise again going toward the two corners. Although tests neighboring in the sequence adopted in presenting the correlation matrix correlate higher than more remote ones, the tests at the two ends again correlate higher. An ordinary factor analysis would give three factors, but the striking thing for Guttman is that the test vectors would be arranged in space so as to form a cone, with the ends of the tests vectors forming a circle, hence the name "circumplex."

When two facets are allowed to vary in an analysis, a combination simplex and circumplex—a "radex" pattern—should result. Guttman (1964) illustrated this kind of situation with one facet being a contrast between "analytical" and "achievement" tests. In his conception, analytical tests call for discovery of a rule, as that of seeing a relation in an analogy item, and achievement tests call for applying a rule, as in adding 5 + 2 (the "rule" being indicated by the plus sign). Guttman (1964) displays graphically the results of analysis of large matrices by means of a two dimensional plot of the tests. Different kinds of content are illustrated by direction from a central point; the analytical-versus-achievement facet is represented by distance of the test from the center, the most analytical being in the center. Guttman regards the potential number of facets to be large, suggesting the difference between recall and recognition tests as another possible facet. In terms of variations in kinds of test items he is probably right. In terms of psychological variations, as in the *SI* model, three facets seem to be sufficient, with the possible need for the addition of an auditory facet and one or two other sensory facets. It can be said that the three facets of the *SI* model have been sufficient for very definitive sources of specification for constructing tests for any ability in the model.

In demonstrating a mathematical basis for the facet type of model for the intellectual abilities, Guttman has made a distinct contribution. His preferences for facets that pertain to more obvious features of tests, however, makes little contribution to psychological understanding. His choice of the facet of complexity leads to the difficulty of finding generally applicable criteria for that variable. His example is taken from tests of numerical operations for which he points out that tests of multiplication and division are more complex than tests of addition and subtraction (Guttman 1958). This is an unusually simple case.

It is doubtful whether Guttman's complexity facet is very useful. The SI model has ways of accounting for effects of complexity. For example, some of the more complex tests are likely to involve systems where less complex ones involve units, which are two elements from the *SI* facet of products. The recall-and-recognition facet that he suggested has already been demonstrated to be an unreal distinction for construction memory tests, for the two kinds measure the same abilities equally well (Guilford 1967). The distinction he makes between analytical versus achievement tests seems not to represent a single dimension of variation. Perhaps they are just poorly named, for his definitions of the elements as "discovery" and "use" of rules suggest the *SI* distinction between cognition and production (divergent or convergent). The use of his radex models, the simplex and circumplex, while interesting as models, apply only with special selections of appropriate sets of tests, which must be arranged in a certain order in each case. Their patterns of intercorrelations might be difficult to predict in advance.

CRYSTALLIZED AND FLUID INTELLIGENCE

A special kind of theory involves the distinction between a crystallized and a fluid intelligence. The theory was proposed by R. B. Cattell (1963) and has been investigated by Horn and Cattell (1966). The distinction was said to have been suggested by the fact that scores from certain classes of tests, representing different primary mental abilities, are commonly found to differ in relation to certain conditions. Certain abilities have seemed to be most affected when brain injuries occur early in life and others are most affected by brain injuries later in life. Certain abilities seem more affected than others by opportunities to acquire knowledge. Certain kinds of tests are more "culture-fair" than others. And some abilities tend to decline more rapidly than others with normal aging. Taking all these conditions together, it appears that certain abilities are determined more by cultural sources and therefore consitute a "crystallized intelligence." Those abilities less affected by cultural conditions constitute a "fluid intelligence." Roughly, the distinction is in accordance with hereditary versus environmental determination of abilities.

Horn and Cattell (1966) present empirical evidence, thought to support these two kinds of intelligence, in the form of a factor analysis. That analysis was very faulty, however, for a number of reasons. First, their selection of recognized primary abilities was quite limited, their assertion to the contrary. It was claimed that as many as 23 primary intellectual abilities were represented in their analysis, but about four times as many structure-of-intellect abilities were known at the time of their analysis, and no attempt was apparently made to sample structure-of-intellect abilities systematically. The sampling was therefore also biased. Second, eight variables from nonaptitude factors were included in the analysis. Since the latter are probably essentially orthogonal to the intellectual abilities, they could not help delineate the intellectual structure. They might rather tend to confuse the picture where chance variations were strong. Third, the primary factors were not well represented by tests. Of the 31 primary factors thought to be included, 13 were represented by only one test each. Even when two or more tests represented a factor, there was a hidden assumption that the variable score for a factor was colinear with the factor's vector in common-factor space. This assumption must be seriously questioned, especially where only one test represented a factor.

The sampling of experimental subjects was also seriously at fault. A condition needed for a good factor analysis is a relatively homogeneous sample. This is merely a matter of good experimental control. The sample used by these investigators ranged in age from 14 to 61. Thus, age-related tests, or tests similarly related to age, could generate an additional factor. There were also undoubtedly material differences in quantity and quality of education and in occupational experiences. Under these conditions, it is no wonder that a culture-dependent factor would appear for those variables that are most related to culture. Such, apparently, is the "crystallized-intelligence" factor in this study.

As an outcome from the analysis, not all the primary abilities could, by any means, be allotted to the two hypothesized higher-order factors supposedly under investigation. Eleven of the 23 primary intellectual abilities came out insignificantly and even negligibly loaded on both those "second-order" factors, where "insignificantly" means a loading below .30 and "negligibly" means a near-zero loading. The factor *Gf* (fluid intelligence) had only six significant loadings and factor *Gc* had only seven. Nine factors were rotated, three of which were singlets (only one loading of .30 or greater) and were therefore uninterpretable. That leaves four other common factors at the supposedly second-order level in addition to the "fluid" and "crystallized" factors. These factors were interpreted as "general visualization," "general speediness," "general fluency," and "carefulness." There may be some psychological sense in the speediness and carefulness factors, for which there is evidence from other sources. But it can be suggested that the general-visualization factor is rather a general-visual-figural ability, since it represents a number of tests none of which obviously involve visualizing but do have in common visual-figural content. It can also be suggested that the general-fluency factor is better interpreted as a higher-order divergent-production factor.

The general conclusion is that much better evidence is needed for the supposed entities of "fluid" and "crystallized" abilities. It may be that certain primary abilities are similarly involved in aging, in brain injury, and in "culture-fair" tests. Culture-fair tests, so-called, tend to be figural in content, involving a kind of information for which experiential opportunities have been more nearly equal in different ethnic and racial groups. Tests for which the scores tend to hold up in normally aging persons are apparently more dependent upon educational, and hence cultural, variables. The scores may be conceived as reflecting various degrees of overlearning, which persist with age.

In any case, it is more important to see how the primary abilities are affected by these various conditions, and to be concerned about similarity of effects on different factors after those effects become known. To bury abilities in large composites, even though these composites are not as broad as Spearman's g, would seem to be a big step backward in the general strategy of investigation of intelligence and its bases. Another general interpretation may be offered to take care of the distinction believed to have been found between "crystallized" and "fluid" type of tests. The former may be those for which differences in personal stored information are important. The cognition abilities in the structure of intellect reflect such differences most directly. The "fluid" tests may be measures of those abilities having to do with the *use* of stored information, as reflected more clearly in divergent-production and convergent-production abilities. In good tests of such abilities, we should like to have experimental control over the amount of stored information, in fact, to equate it for all individuals. A view of the Cattell-Horn distinction, such as this, may be less romantic, but it is definitely more operable.

Intelligence in General Psychological Theory

From Binet to the recent present, the findings regarding intellectual abilities have had little or no impact upon general theories in psychology. Writers on intelligence and intelligence tests have used terminology from experimental psychology but psychological theory has not drawn upon the findings of mental testers to any appreciable degree. Psychological theory has naturally drawn upon findings with respect to how individuals are alike and not how they differ. With the development of the structure-of-intellect theory, a new type of general-psychological theory has become available (Guilford 1967). It has been called an "informational-operational" theory, with the *SI* concepts applied to ongoing behavior. This theory regards the organism as an information-processing agent, where information is defined as that which the organism discriminates.

The many areas of behavior and the many traditional concepts that have arisen in psychology and that can be accounted for in terms of this informational-operational view have been treated previously (Guilford 1967). We can only take some very general looks at the applications of that view here. The facts of perception are envisaged under the figural category of information, although not all perception is thus accounted for, while facts of thinking pertain to symbolic, semantic, and behavioral information as well.

The facts of possession of information, knowing, and understanding belong in the category of cognition. Learning is acquisition of new items of information in any of its forms, involving new discriminations and their fixation and storage. Thinking is distinguished by its forms of production, divergent and convergent, and by evaluation, which includes judgment.

The conception of products of information is something quite new, and in time the products should replace the old but useful concept of "association," while adding a number of useful new concepts. The older conception of association is best equated to the product of implication, which can also replace the concept of "conditioned response," by regarding it as an expectation. "Association" never fully accounted for the products of units, systems, and transformations, although some weak efforts have been made in those directions.

The so-called higher mental processes, including problem solving, creative production, and decision making, can all be accounted for in terms of episodes involving many or all of the operations and the products of information, in whatever content area the occasion arises. A "structure-of-intellect problem-solving" (SIPS) model has been designed to provide a generic picture of the ongoing operations involved. The model applies to instances of creative production as well as instances of decision making. The model incorporates cybernetic principles, with evaluation supplying the step of matching output information with input information, with acceptance or rejection of information as conceived or produced.

Thus, by investigating the ways in which individuals differ from one another intellectually, we also discover how they are alike. Thus are differential psychology and general psychology brought together, with benefits to both. Thus, we see that an informational-operational view provides a very comprehensive theory, which can take into account numerous mental phenomena where a behavioristic view falls very far short.

Summary

The conceptions of intelligence for almost a century have grown up in connection with investigations of how individuals are functionally different from one another, hence they have stood very apart from those of general psychological theory, which has given rather strict attention to ways in which individuals function similarly. Similarities and differences are very much like views of the same thing seen from different directions, hence common conclusions should be expected. Only recently has a meeting of minds become possible with regard to the nature of human intellectual functioning.

Almost from the beginning, investigators who emphasized the differential view were little concerned with psychological theory, for they eventually found their tests working much to their satisfaction without the aid of that kind of theory. The few who were concerned with the psychological nature of abilities—particularly Spearman, Burt, and Thurstone—saw possibilities of understanding what variables exist in the realm of intellectual functioning through the application of factor analysis.

The psychometric approach, with its tool of factor analysis, led to the recognition of numerous different intellectual abilities, unique ways in which individuals differ from one another in performing on intellectual tasks. The first attempts at organizing these abilities systematically yielded the hierarchical type of model, with abilities at different levels of generality, a completely general one at the apex. The finding of a g factor has been ensured by the chosen method of analysis, but it is questionable whether such a factor has invariant relations to tests and has psychological meaning is very questionable. Broader, multiple-factor methods usually fail to find a g factor, and from such an approach the intellectual factors without a g component can be more reasonably organized in a morphological, or cross-classification scheme.

The structure-of-intellect (SI) model arranges all known and expected intellectual abilities within a three-dimensional rectangular block, like that which R. A. Fisher called a "Cartesian product of sets," with three dimensions, with five kinds of operations (on one dimension), four kinds of content, and six kinds of products. Any one ability, demonstrable as a factor, is uniquely defined in terms of its one kind of operation applied to one kind of content and one kind of product. Although the abilities are treated as if they were independent or uncorrelated in a given population, it is recognized that there may well be some nonzero correlations among the 120 abilities represented in the model.

When the concepts found in the structure-of-intellect theory are put to work in terms of the functioning organism, it is found that they provide the basis for a general point of view. Thus, we find the possibility of a psychological theory that applies both to general and differential psychology. The general view is described as "informational-operational." It regards the living organism as a processor of information. Information is of forms found in 24 categories, which arise as products of four times six content and product categories, respectively. Phenomena of perception, learning, memory, thinking, decision making, problem solving, and creative production can all be accounted for in terms of SI concepts when they are used in operational models.

References

BINET, A. *Les idées modernes sur les enfants.* Paris: Flammarion, 1909.

BORING, E. G. Intelligence as the tests test it. *New Republic,* 1923, *34,* 35–37.

BROWN, W., and THOMSON, G. H. *The essentials of mental measurement.* London: Cambridge Press, 1925.

BURT, C. The structure of the mind: A review of the results of factor analysis. *British Journal of Educational Psychology,* 1949, *19,* 100–111, 176–99.

CATTELL, R. B. Theory of fluid and crystallized intelligence. *Journal of Educational Psychology,* 1963, *54,* 1–22.

DUNHAM, J. L., GUILFORD, J. P., and HOEPFNER, R. Abilities pertaining to classes and the learning of concepts. *Reports from the Psychological Laboratory, University of Southern California,* no. 39, 1966.

EL-KOUSSY, M. A. H. Les directions de recherche dans le domain des aptitudes spatiales. *In* H. Laugier (ed.) *L'analyse factorielle et ses applications,* p. 327–51. Paris: Centre National de la Recherche Scientifique, 1966.

FLEISHMAN, E. A. *Human abilities and the acquisition of skills.* Washington, D. C.: American Institutes for Research, 1966.

GALTON, F. *Inquiries into human faculty and its development.* London: Macmillan, 1883.

GUILFORD, J. P. Zero intercorrelations among tests of intellectual abilities. *Psychological Bulletin,* 1964, *61,* 401–4.

———. *The Nature of Human Intelligence.* New York: McGraw-Hill, 1967.

———, and HOEPFNER, R. Creative potential as related to measures of IQ and verbal comprehension. *Indian Journal of Psychology,* 1966, *41,* 7–16.

GUILFORD, J. P., and ZIMMERMAN, W. S. Some variable-sampling problems in the rotation of axes in factor analysis. *Psychological Bulletin,* 1963, *60,* 289–301.

GUTTMAN, L. What lies ahead for factor analysis? *Educational and Psychological Measurement,* 1958, *18,* 497–515.

———. The structure of interrelations among intelligence tests. *In* C. W. Harris (ed.) *Invitational Conference on Testing Problems,* pp. 25–36. Princeton, N. J.: Educational Testing Service, 1965.

HARMAN, H. H. *Modern factor analysis.* Chicago: University of Chicago Press, 1967.

HOEPFNER, R., and O'SULLIVAN, MAUREEN. Social intelligence and the IQ. *Educational and Psychological Measurement,* 1968, *28,* 339–44.

HOLZINGER, K. J., and SWINEFORD, F. The bi-factor method. *Psychometrika,* 1937, *2,* 41–54.

HORN, J. L., and CATTELL, R. B. Refinement and test of the theory of fluid and crystallized general intelligence. *Journal of Educational Psychology,* 1966, *57,* 253–70.

HORST, P. *Matrix algebra for social scientists.* New York: Holt, Rinehart & Winston, 1963.

KELLEY, T. L. *Crossroads in the mind of man.* Stanford, Calif.: Stanford University Press, 1928.

PIAGET, J. *Logic and psychology.* Manchester: Manchester University Press, 1953.

SPEARMAN, C. *The abilities of man.* New York: Macmillan, 1927.

TERMAN, L. M. *The measurement of intelligence.* Boston: Houghton Mifflin, 1916.

THURSTONE, L. L. *Multiple factor analysis.* Chicago: University of Chicago Press, 1947.

VERNON, P. E. *The structure of human abilities.* New York: John Wiley, 1950.

WISSLER, C. The correlation of mental and physical tests. *Psychological Review Monograph Supplements,* 1901, *3,* no. 16.

The development of intelligence in man occurs over a prolonged period of time. Growth and observable changes in myelinization of the central nervous system continue from the fetal period to the ninth decade according to Yakovlev (1960). These maturational changes are continuously modified, modulated, and enriched by experience, resulting in the intelligent human being who responds with increasing complexity to what he feels, hears, sees, and thinks. The course of mental growth over the life span constitutes one of the most dramatic and exciting aspects of human development. Progress during this century in mental measurement, conceptualization, theory building, and understanding the changes in intellectual functioning is impressive. We shall attempt an overview of these changes in this chapter.

Historical Note

Individual differences in ability have been observed since the beginning of recorded history. But it was not until the present century that systematic methods were evolved which made it possible to assess an individual's progress along a continuum of mental growth from the first simple responses to the highly organized thought processes of the mature adult. Since in this chapter we are concerned with the growth of intelligence, we shall give brief mention of the tests which are most appropriate in the measurement of overall mental abilities from birth to senescence. In addition to the individual tests of intelligence, there are many other tests devised for specific purposes in research or in the assessment of the child by the educator and clinical psychologist (Anastasi 1961; Buros 1965; Freeman 1962).

TESTING CHILDREN

The greatest impetus for the intelligence testing of children came from the work of Alfred Binet of Paris who was asked to

Marjorie P. Honzik

The Development of Intelligence

31

devise tests that would differentiate children who could profit by school experience from those who could not (1905). Binet's efforts were highly successful and his test series has become the forerunner of the best tests available for the school-aged child. Herring (1922), Kuhlmann (1912, 1939), Terman (1916), and Yerkes (1915) were among those who revised and enlarged the Binet Tests for use in the United States. The Terman Revision was the most carefully standardized on a representative U.S. sampling of children and thus has become the intelligence test most frequently administered in the clinic and research laboratory. Terman's first revision of the Binet Scale appeared in 1916 and was widely used until superseded by two alternate Forms L and M in 1937. In 1960, the new L-M Form appeared with the test materials brought up to date, extension of the age range of usefulness from 2 years to adulthood, and an improved method of scoring and obtaining an IQ.

The Stanford-Binet in all its revisions yields a single score or mental age, which divided by or considered in relation to the child's chronological age gives an IQ, or Intelligence Quotient. This score is considered by psychologists and educators in the research laboratory, school, or clinic to yield the best single index of the child's intelligence at the time of the test. However, these scores depend on many abilities such as memory, problem solving, form discrimination, and language comprehension and facility that are measured with varying degrees of adequacy at successive ages. Wechsler, recognizing the need for continuity of measurement of these different mental abilities, standardized a series of tests for individuals ranging in age from the preschool years to old age. The Wechsler Scales (1944, 1949, 1955, 1958, 1967) measure eleven fairly specific abilities which are grouped into Verbal and Performance scales. These tests have permitted greater penetration into the components of intelligence functioning. For example, Money (1964) reports that girls with a missing X chromosome do relatively better than their peers on certain of the Verbal tests of the Wechsler and very poorly on the tests of Spatial Relations. The pattern of mental abilities shown by the Wechsler tests has significance both for the individual in his development and in assessing the effects of genetic and experiential factors on intelligence.

INFANT TESTS

Fortunately for our understanding of mental growth in the first two years of life, Arnold Gesell of Yale undertook extensive observations of the behavioral development of normal infants. Gesell's (1928, 1962) perceptive descriptions of the behavioral responses of infants during the first years of life constitute a classic. Gesell believed that the infant's behavior fell into four behavioral domains: adaptive behavior, motor, personal-social, and language. Within each of these four areas, the developmental sequence is shown to progress from very simple responses in the first month to the walking–talking problem solving child in the second year of life. Gesell's developmental schedules continue to be used by the pediatrician for diagnosis and evaluations. The psychologist is more likely to use one of the more traditionally standardized infant tests that have profited by Gesells' descriptions but also have considered normative placement of test items with respect to sampling, reliability, and validity. British psychologists use the infant test standardized by Ruth Griffiths (1954). This test considers six domains: eye-

hand, personal-social, hearing and speech, motor, locomotor, and adaptation. In the United States, Psyche Cattell's test of infant intelligence has proved valuable for diagnosis and research purposes (1960). A recent longitudinal study of infants born on the island of Kauai shows that the scores of over 600 children tested at 20 months on the Cattell test were relatively good predictors of IQ ($r = .49$) and achievement ($r = .44$) at age 10 years (Werner, Honzik & Smith 1968).

An infant test which has had long use in research on mental growth in infancy is Bayley's California First Year Mental Scale (1933). This test was constructed to test the longitudinally tested Berkeley Growth Study sample each month during the first year of life and at 3-month intervals thereafter. It was also the test used in the examinations of more than 15,000 infants at 8 months in the great Collaborative Study of infants born in 16 hospitals in various areas of the United States (Masland 1959). A well standardized version of the Bayley test was published in 1969 (Bayley 1969). This test has many advantages over previously published tests. It has almost twice as many items as the Cattell; and since the standardization is based on monthly testing of infants, age placement of test items is more accurate than is true for the other available tests.

This broad coverage of infant tests appears warranted in view of the extent to which mental growth occurs in the first few years of life.

Growth of Intelligence

Curves showing the growth and decline of mental ability with age are presented by Bayley (1949, 1968), Jones and Conrad (1933), and Miles and Miles (1932). These curves all show marked gains in intellect in the first years of life, but differ in their portrayal of the later years depending on whether the same or different cohorts of individuals are being tested.

The major difficulty in constructing curves for the first five years of life is the lack of absolute measures. The slope of the curve depends entirely on the test items used, as well as the method of presenting the scores, including the statistical analyses. Bloom (1964) concludes from both the correlational data and the attempts to construct "absolute scales of intelligence development" (Heinis 1924; Thorndike 1927; Thurstone 1928) that approximately 50 percent of mental development takes place between conception and age 4 years, about 30 percent between 4 and 8 years, and about 20 percent between 8 and 17 years. These can only be very rough approximations. Where absolute measures are available, as in height measurements, 50 percent of the total growth is achieved shortly before the end of the second year in females, and shortly after this age in males (Nicolson & Hanley 1953). Evidence is accruing that mental growth proceeds for a much longer time than growth in height. Until more is known about the total mental growth pattern in normal individuals, little can be said about the age at which a certain percent of individuals' intelligence has been achieved.

The nature of ability changes in maturity and old age has been the source of controversy for a number of years. Jones and Conrad (1933) tested all the inhabitants of certain villages and rural areas in Vermont. By plotting the average score for successive ages, they derived a curve which showed marked growth in mental ability during early childhood, with a peak performance at 19 years followed by a rather marked decline.

Similar results are reported by Miles and Miles (1932) and Wechsler (1939) for cohorts of varying ages, all tested during the same time period. More recent investigations of the same individuals studied over long periods of time show gains in measured ability at least until the fourth decade of life. Bayley (1957, 1966) finds increases in scores for a group of 33 cases tested on the Wechsler-Bellevue over the age period 16 to 21 years, and for the longer period 16 to 36 years. There were increases in this sample on all Verbal subtests except Arithmetic. For a larger group of 127 male college students, Owens (1953) reported significant gains over the age period 19 to 50 years on the Army Alpha. Greater increases in scores occurred on the Verbal subtests of Practical Judgment, Synonym-Antonym, Disarranged Sentences, and Information than on substets involving Following Directions, Arithmetic, and Number Series Completion. Both the Bayley and Owens samples are of above average ability. Baller (1967) and Charles (1953, 1964) have reported on the stability of mental test performance from the school years to the sixth decade for individuals of average mental test ability, and individuals classified as mentally deficient during their school years. Baller reports an average change for the most retarded group from IQs of 60 to "near 80," but nearly a third of "located" subjects were deceased; the change for the "middle" group was from an average of 80 IQ to 88; while the control group, with a mean IQ of 107 during the school years, maintained that score to middle age.

The fact that there is consistency within the findings for both cross-sectionally and longitudinally studied samples suggests that the difference in method accounts for the difference in results. The most likely reason for the discrepancy lies in the increasing level of education with each decade so that in any community, the oldsters have relatively less education than the more youthful members. Kuhlen (1968) notes that there is not only a secular trend in education but the distinct possibility that cooperation on the longitudinal studies is related to gains in scores. Since these gains occur at all ability levels and over age periods of from 20 to 40 years, the educational or opportunity difference is probably the more significant factor. Evidence to date suggests that the findings for the longitudinal samples of moderate gains in the mature years followed by declinations in certain abilities in older persons will be substantiated in future investigations.

Individual Differences in the Course of Mental Growth

The curve of mental growth is derived from the averaged scores of individuals of different ages. This is a composite of curves for individuals which are remarkable in their variation (Bayley 1949; Honzik et al. 1948; Sontag et al. 1958; Dearborn & Rothney 1941). One of the major contributions of the longitudinal studies has been the portrayal of the course of mental growth for normal individuals. The agreement in findings for

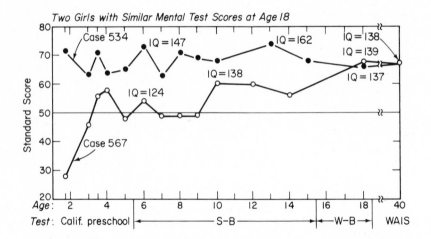

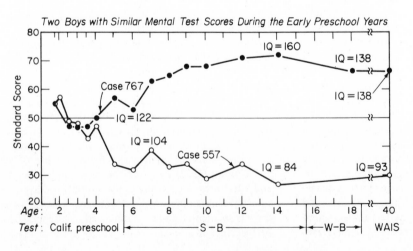

Fig. 31-1. *The mental test scores of four individuals between 21 months and 40 years.* [Honzik, M. P. Unpublished ms., University of California Institute of Human Development].

646   Language, Thought, and Intelligence

children tested by different investigators in different parts of the country is impressive. There are children of all abilities whose scores are relatively constant from early childhood to maturity in relation to the group (see Fig. 31-1). There are other individuals living in the same community, tested on the same tests by the same examiners, who show consistent gains or losses; and there are a few children whose scores fluctuate markedly in both directions. The extent of the changes is suggested by the fact that in two of the largest longitudinal studies (Honzik et al. 1948; Sontag et al. 1958), IQ changes on the Stanford-Binet during the age period 6 through 18 years were as great as 50 IQ points for 0.5 percent of the samples.

All studies agree in reporting an increasing constancy of test performance with age but there is a variation in the age at which this relative constancy is achieved. In Figure 31.1, we see the records of two boys whose scores are very similar in early childhood but later diverge to a marked degree. The school performance and later achievements of these boys are in line with these test scores. In contrast, the records of cases 534 and 567 show the opposite pattern of divergent scores in the preschool years but at 18 years they obtained the same IQ. It is of considerable interest that some children, like case 534, earn a high IQ on a first test given before the age of 2 years and maintain that position in relation to the group for the first 18 years of life; her score at age 40 years is still one of the highest in the sample. Relative constancy of intellectual functioning for individuals in the middle range of ability has been assumed.

A rather high degree of test constancy among children who are markedly handicapped or have limited ability is expected; but the fact that constancy can occur at all ability levels is only revealed by the repeated testing of these individuals.

The Constancy of Mental Test Performance

For many years, psychologists and educators believed that the IQ was a constant, like eye color. The basis for this belief was the high test-retest correlations always obtained for carefully tested school-aged children over short time periods, such as a year or less (Bayley 1949; Ebert & Simmons 1943; Honzik et al. 1948; Sontag et al. 1958). Only when results from the longitudinal studies began to appear was it shown that as the time span between tests lengthens, the correlations decrease. The matrices of interage correlations of mental test scores show a clear relation between the magnitude of the correlation and both the age of the child on the first test and the interval between tests. The younger the child on his first test, and the longer the time interval between test, the lower the prediction. Figure 31-2 shows the high agreement found in four different longitudinal studies in predicting 10-year IQs. This figure indicates that prediction of 10-year IQs from tests given during the first year of life is negligible, but that prediction increases markedly during the age period 1 to 8 years when the correlations reach 0.80 and higher. Although Bayley found no correlation between mental test scores earned in the first year and later scores, a factoring of age-at-first-passing these infant test items yielded a vocalization score based on test items in the 8-13 month age range, which is predictive of later test performance at all ages up to 28 years for girls, but not for boys (Cameron et al. 1967). This is a rather remarkable finding both in the predictive signifi-

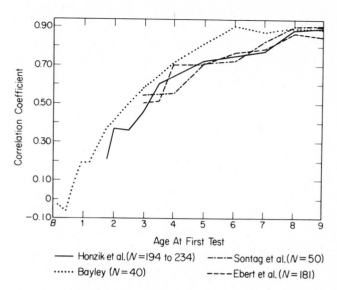

Fig. 31-2. *Prediction of IQ at 10 years from scores at earlier ages.* [Data from four longitudinal studies].

cance of these early scores and in the extent of the sex difference. One would suspect that this was a chance finding if Hindley (1965) had not reported for his longitudinal sample that girls' but not boys' scores on the Griffiths Scale at 6 months are predictive of later IQs. A somewhat similar finding of continuity in girls' vocalizations is reported by Kagan (1968) for infants observed during the first years of life.

Determinants of Mental Growth Patterns

Intellectual functioning, like height, depends on the potential for growth and a favorable environment at all stages of development. In the assessment of mental in contrast to physical growth, there is the additional problem of reliability and, even more important, the validity of the measurements. When tests are administered under near optimal conditions by perceptive and well trained examiners, high reliabilities are reported for individual mental tests at all age levels (Werner & Bayley 1966; Terman & Merrill 1960; and Buros 1965) but this does not preclude the possibility of individual tests being adversely affected by cultural and motivational factors. Vernon (1965) distinguishes three classes of determinants as A, B, and C. Intelligence A is determined by nonobservable and nonmeasurable genetic factors. Intelligence B refers to intellectual functioning as shaped and modified by experience; while Intelligence C refers to actual test results, that is, the particular sampling of Intelligence B that an intelligence test provides. Group C determinants include those characteristics of the test that frequently distort the results of unsophisticated testees, and which could be fairly effectively controlled by appropriate modifications of the form of the test and its administration. When Group C type determinants are well controlled, we can begin to evaluate the relevance of hereditary and experiential factors on mental growth. The decade of the nineteen sixties has seen an upsurge of interest in both behavior genetics and in the wide range of environmental factors which are related to mental test scores.

The relevance of inheritance to the individual's abilities is indicated by (1) the correlations between chromosomal variation and mental ability, and (2) intrafamily resemblance in test performance.

The advent of the hypotonic treatment of cells led to accurate counts of the number of chromosomes in the cells of normal human beings and the possibility of correlating abnormal counts with test abilities. One of the dramatic discoveries was that individuals with Down's syndrome, or mongolism, have an extra twenty-first chromosome. The devastating effect of this extra chromosome on growth and development, including mental growth, is well known. Although enriching experiences are beneficial to the language and social skills of these children, the limits are clearly set so that individuals with this chromosomal syndrome, tri-somy 21, rarely attain IQs above 50 (Bayley et al. 1966).

Another chromosomal aberration affecting intellectual development is Turner's syndrome. Girls with this anomaly have a missing X-chromosome. The effect of this absent chromosome is relative enhancement of verbal abilities but definitely poor visualization of space (Money 1964). In contrast to children with tri-somy 21, girls with the missing chromosome do not exhibit overall mental impairment but a distinctive pattern of abilities. It is to be expected that further correlations between aberrant chromosomal counts and patterns of mental ability will be discovered in the next few years.

The fact of resemblance in ability among family members has always been observed. In recent years, documentation has become more precise. Summarizing 52 different empirical studies yielding over 30,000 correlational pairings, Erlenmeyer-Kimling et al. (1963) report that, for most relationship categories, the *median* of the empirical correlations closely approaches the theoretical value predicted on the basis of the genetic relationship alone. The median parent-child correlations, and the correlations between children in the same family, is of the same order as height, 0.50 (Jones 1954). The median correlation for dizygotic twins, whether the same or opposite sex, is .53. When the relationship is closer as in identical twins, the correlation is higher: .87 for the twins brought up together and .75 for those brought up apart. The question of the effect of a similar environment is partially answered by comparing the resemblance of identical and same-sexed fraternal twins. The intra-pair correlation for fraternal twins is higher than for siblings (.53) but not as high as for identical twins (.87).

An extension of this finding is reported by Freedman and Keller (1963) who tested a group of same-sexed identical and fraternal twins each month during the first year of life. The examiners, and for the most part the parents, did not know until after the completion of the study whether a given pair was identical or fraternal. In this study, the intra-pair difference in mental, motor, and behavior scores was in nearly every instance less for the identical than the fraternal twins. A greater similarity in the Bayley Behavior Profile Scores of the identical than the fraternal pairs during the test situations was another finding of this study.

The above investigations may not be definitive since the more closely related family members may be living in more similar environments. This may even be true for twins. The identical twins' physical concordance may elicit more similar

reactions and experiences than is true for the fraternal twins. The crucial test of the effect of hereditary factors on resemblance between family members can only occur when they are living apart in different environments. Skodak and Skeels (1949) reported increasing correlations, for both IQs and number of years of schooling, between the mental test scores of a group of children adopted in early infancy and their true parents with whom they never lived. A negligible correlation was found between the education of the adopting parents and the children's scores. A fascinating aspect of this study was the similarity in the age changes in the correlations for the related-parent-and-children who never lived together as compared with the correlations for a group of children living with their parents (Honzik 1957). These relationships are low but clear in their implication of heredity as a factor determining an increasing amount of the variance in tested ability as children grow older (cf. Fig. 31-3). Confirmation of the finding of significant relationships between the abilities of children and their true parents but not

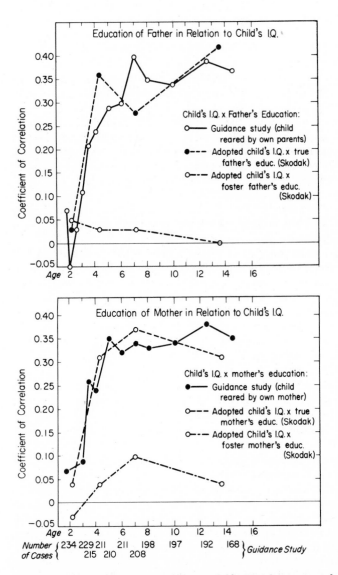

Fig. 31-3. *Parental education in relation to child's IQ: Comparison of results for adopted children and children reared by their own parents.* [Adapted from Honzik, M. P. 1957].

their adopting parents is also given in the earlier studies of Burks (1928) and Leahy (1935). These results do not imply that a favorable environment provided by adopting parents does not have a profound effect on the adopted children's mental development but rather that individual differences in the adopted children's abilities are only slightly related to the individual differences in the abilities of the adopting parents.

SPECIAL ABILITIES AND HEREDITY

In the majority of studies only IQs or total scores have been considered in the attempts to evaluate the effects of hereditary factors on mental development. Stafford (1961), however, reports that a specific ability, "visualization of space," in which males are usually superior, appears to be a sex-linked ability. All the correlations between scores on this ability for family members (father × mother, $r = .03$; father × son, $r = .02$; father × daughter, $r = .31$; mother × son, $r = .31$; and mother × daughter, $r = .14$) support the hypothesis that visual spatial ability is inherited as a recessive gene on the X chromosome.

SEX DIFFERENCES

Sex differences in tested intelligence are small but nevertheless exist. Differences in mean scores are seldom significant but the scores of girls are somewhat more predictive at an earlier age than is true for boys (Hindley 1960), and the onset of parent-child resemblance appears earlier in girls than boys (Hindley 1961; Honzik 1963). These facts taken in conjunction with the later physical maturation of boys suggests a somewhat earlier maturing of mental ability in girls than boys.

Bromley (1966) reports that "little is known about sex differences in mental abilities at the older age levels." He reports that there is some evidence of a differential decline with age on timed tests: younger men (30 years) are faster than younger women but older men (70 years) are slower than older women. Two of the factors which complicate the analysis of sex differences after the school years are differential experience and greater longevity in women.

Intelligence and Life Experience

Heredity sets the limits and is relevant to the child's intelligence as measured by his mental test performance but the correlations are low and suggest the effect that experiential factors may be having on the mental growth pattern.

Environmental factors do not begin with the birth of the child but at conception or before. Evidence is accruing which shows the marked effect of maternal nutrition during pregnancy on the child's later development (Zamenhof 1968). There is also concern that undernutrition during infancy may inhibit brain growth. The impairing effect of rubella, and possibly other virus infections, occurring at critical periods in the development of the embryo is well documented. Later in the gestation period, infections such as Western encephalitis may affect the developing fetus transplacentally with devastating effects on the developing brain. There is good evidence that the earlier in life the brain of the fetus or young infant suffers infection or trauma the

more likely that profound retardation will occur (Finley et al. 1967).

The developing brain's need for oxygen is not always met during the paranatal period. This may lead to later deficits. The impairment may be very slight and hardly noticeable or may be pervasive, leading to a condition of marked retardation. Graham et al. (1962) reported a significant difference between the mean test scores of three-year-olds who had been anoxic at birth as compared with a normal control group. There was not only a significant mean difference in IQs but also a generalized shift in the distribution of the anoxic group toward the lower end of the scale rather than a bimodality of low versus higher scores. A similar finding was reported by Honzik et al. (1965) for a group of infants who were "suspect" at birth of suffering anoxia. These infants and a control group of normal babies were tested at 8 months on the Bayley Scales. Significant differences in total test scores, and on individual test items, were obtained although the examiners, who were unaware of the diagnosis, judged most of these infants to be "normal." Corah et al. (1965) report, for the Graham sample, that the differences between the anoxic and normal groups were less marked on a test given at 7 years. Werner et al. (1967) report for the Kauai pregnancy study that, of the children who appeared handicapped at the end of the second year, those living in "good" environments were progressing well in school at 10 years but those living in "poor" environments tended to remain handicapped. We may conclude from these studies that paranatal anoxia has measurable deleterious effects on the cognitive abilities of infants and young children but that a supportive environment may help the child recover, cope, or overcome his difficulties. This finding highlights a more general one of the multifactor determination of patterns of mental growth.

A continuing search to pinpoint experiences which are related to and possibly affect intellectual development has taken place in recent years. In 1952, Bowlby published a monograph summarizing studies and observations on the ill effects of maternal deprivation. This monograph was the stimulus for a body of research which was reviewed in some detail by Ainsworth (1962), Casler (1961), and Yarrow (1961). These reviewers agreed that many children living in institutions are handicapped in their intellectual as well as their personality development. However, they reported that this deprivation was dependent on many factors, such as the previous experiences of the children, the care given in the institution, the age of the child, duration of his stay, and the constitution of the child himself. They agreed that the young infant and child need mothering but that multiple mothering, such as occurs in the Israeli Kibbutzim, had no ill effects on intelligence and personality. Casler concluded from his review that deprivation of maternal love is a significant variable after about the age of 6 months, but that before that age "malfunctioning must be due to perceptual deprivation." He believes that there is a lack, or relative absence, of tactile, vestibular, and other forms of stimulation in institutional care which accounts for some of the emotional, physical, and intellectual malfunctioning. In 1965 Casler undertook an investigation of the effects of extra tactile stimulation on infants living in an institution. He found that infants given tactile stimulation over a 10-week period did significantly better on the Gesell Developmental Schedules than did a matched control group.

The next question is how permanent are the ill effects of institutional care and the good effects of supplemental stimulation. Two investigations provide partial answers. Dennis and Najarian (1957) tested all the children in a Lebanese Crèche where health needs were met but the infants were minimally stimulated. They found that the children's IQs on the Cattell Infant Intelligence Scale were normal at age 2 months but fell to an average of 63 during the age period 3 to 12 months. When these children were tested at ages 4 and 5 years, they obtained IQs of "roughly 90" although they had spent their lives in the Crèche. These results suggest that the limited stimulation experienced during infancy did not lead to a marked deficit in intelligence in early childhood.

Rheingold and Bayley (1959) report transitory gains in social responsiveness in infants in an institution who were given "more attentive care" by one person from the sixth to the eighth month. However, these children performed no better on the Cattell Infant Intelligence Test a year later than did a control group who received no special attention.

In the studies by Casler and Rheingold, the programs of extra stimulation occurred during the first year. More recently intervention programs during the summer or year before school entrance have been provided for deprived children. These enrichment programs have met with varying success. Gray and Klaus (1965) reported the effects of an intensive educational experience during the preschool years in offsetting the progressive retardation which characterizes the culturally deprived child. The initial mean IQ of children in her program was 86 on the Stanford-Binet. After the nursery school experience, the children showed a gain of 9 points in contrast to the losses of 4 to 6 points in the control groups during the same time period. The later school performance of these children is not yet known but the IQ difference between the experimental and control groups is substantial and suggests that a good intervention program may have a fairly marked effect on highly deprived groups of preschool aged children.

Another approach to the problem of environmental influence is to relate parental attitudes, practices, and behavior to patterns of mental growth. Bayley and Schaefer (1964) report for the Berkeley Growth Study sample that boys but not girls who had loving mothers in the first years of life show accelerative mental growth patterns. They found that the girls' scores show little relation to maternal variables, except that the girls' IQs are negatively related to "maternal intrusiveness." Honzik (1967a) reports a similar finding for the longitudinally studied Berkeley Guidance Group. Boys but not girls who had a close relationship to their mothers at 21 months obtained high mental test scores in later childhood. Girls, on the other hand, living in homes where there was marital harmony showed accelerative mental growth patterns but this relationship did not hold for the boys. Moore (1968) found for a London sample that the "emotional atmosphere of the home" (where there is acceptance and love of the child) is significantly related to the IQs of both boys and girls at 8 years. The correlations at 3 years were positive but not significant. Still another study of the relation of early affectional relationships to later intellectual achievement is reported by Kagan and Moss (1962). They found that "maternal protection" of boys during the first three years correlated with the boys' intellectual achievement from 10 to 14 years. Intellectual achievement in girls during this age period was negatively related to "maternal acceleration" during the first three years. Other parental characteristics which are related to high mental test scores in their children are concern about

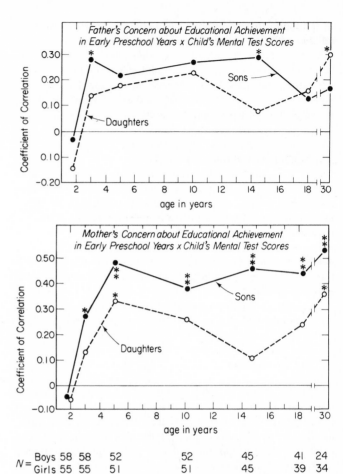

N = | Boys | 58 | 58 | 52 | | 52 | | 45 | | 41 | 24 |
    | Girls | 55 | 55 | 51 | | 51 | | 45 | | 39 | 34 |

*Significant at the 5% level **Significant at the 1% level

Fig. 31-4. *The relation of mental test scores of sons and daughters to parental concern about educational achievement* [Honzik, M. P. 1967a].

educational achievement. Figure 31-4 shows for the Guidance Group, increasing correlations between the father's and mother's concern about educational achievement and the son's and daughter's mental test scores (Honzik 1967a). The correlations are higher for the sons than the daughters but the trend is similar for both sexes. Moore (1968) reports a somewhat similar finding for the London sample. A rating of parental "example and encouragement" is positively related to the boy's and significantly related to the girl's vocabulary and IQ at 8 years.

A confounding factor in all studies of the relation of the home environment to the development of intelligence is the fact that the parents and children are related. There are a few reports of findings for adopted children. Yarrow (1962) reported for a sample of 40 adopted children that their 6-month IQs on the Cattell Infant Intelligence Scale were highly correlated with maternal care. Maternal variables correlating .50 or higher with the adopted children's IQs include stimulus adaptation ($r = .85$), achievement stimulation ($r = .72$), social stimulation ($r = .65$), communication ($r = .59$), and emotional involvement ($r = .55$). These correlations are in line with those found for older children but are. much higher. They suggest that positive experiences during the first year may have lasting although not always visible effects. Our hypothesis is that the favorable experiences of the first year may be slightly negatively related to the children's reactions to tests in the second and third years of life; but as the child gains greater control, he manifests again the good effects of his experiences during the first year.

The Environment and Specific Abilities

Thus far we have considered the effect of experience on only a single global overall measure of ability—the IQ. Specific mental abilities are intercorrelated but not so highly as to preclude different patterns of emergence, modified by different genetic and experiential determinants. Honzik (1967b) reports that verbal or language abilities are more closely related to early affectional ties in the family, or the warmth of the family members' interaction. Boys' memory for digits, information, vocabulary, comprehension, and similarities on the Wechsler-Bellevue at age 18 are correlated with closeness to his mother in early childhood; while the girls' verbal scores correlate with the father's affection for the mother (Fig. 31-5). Moore (1968) also reports that the boys' vocabulary at 8 years correlates significantly with the emotional atmosphere of the home but the correlation for the girls is only .25. In contrast to the findings for Verbal Abilities, Honzik (1967a) finds rather negative aspects of the early family environment correlated with the Performance items of the Wechsler Scale at 18 years. These negative aspects include irritability of the parent of the opposite sex and, for boys, a father who lacks confidence and does not show affection; and for girls, an energetic mother who provides good play facilities. We may hypothesize that small children who do not have much individual attention from their parents do not develop unusual verbal skill but turn rather to playing with objects and exploring the physical environment.

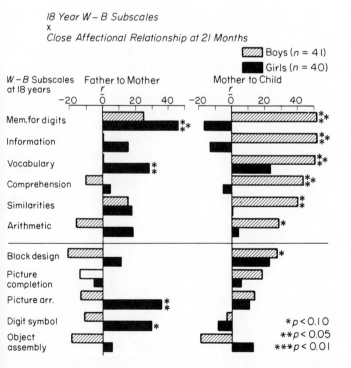

Fig. 31-5. *Close affectional relationships at 21 months × the Wechsler Bellevue subtests at 18 years* [Honzik, M. P. 1967b].

Theories of Cognitive Development

During the twentieth century, a number of significant trends occurred in the theories of the development of intelligence. One of these was an emphasis placed on the process of maturation; a second was concern with hereditary versus environmental determination; and a third trend involves the theories describing the process of mental growth. We shall describe these theories with brief accounts of the empirical bases described by their proponents.

Gesell (1928, 1962) concluded from his observations of the infant during the first years of life that the major explanatory principle was maturation. He spoke of the infant as a "growing action system, who comes by his mind in the same way that he comes by his body, through the process of development." Gesell believed that the developmental status of the infant and child can be determined by his behavior: "the body grows, behavior grows"; or more specifically, "as the nervous system undergoes growth differentiation the forms of behavior also differentiate." He cites as an example of the differentiation the fact that at one age the infant seizes with his whole hand, later with his third and index finger. Gesell states that "development yields to diagnosis, because the constitution of the action system on infant and child is determined by lawful growth forces." The example he gives of this process is that "at about the 18th fetal week, the hand grips as well as flexes; at about 40th postnatal week, the infant hand extends its finger to poke and pry." Since Gesell saw the developmental process as so orderly, he goes on to state that "diagnosis involves prognosis." This implies that prediction of mental growth is good. When Gesell found instances of poor prediction, he considered that a deviation in development had occurred due to "superior endowment," or "environmental retardation." Gesell's theory has been helpful in adding to our knowledge of the maturational process but it is not sensitive to the multiplicity of experiential factors affecting mental growth in normal populations of children. This theory becomes progressively less relevant after the first years of life as the growth rate begins to decelerate.

In contrast to Gesell's position, a major trend during the middle of the 20th century has been the emphasis on experience with little consideration of the biological organism who is growing in size and complexity. There have been a number of significant aspects of this trend including the contributions of the comparative psychologists, psychoanalysts, and learning theorists.

Harlow (1962) and Harlow et al. (1970) report on the infant monkey's favorable response to a feeding, rocking, tactually comforting surrogate "cloth mother." The infant monkey reared by a surrogate mother with favorable qualities is playful, explores his environment, and is free to learn about his surroundings; while the baby monkey with a cold wire surrogate mother is fearful and retreats to a corner of his cage. This later reaction resembles that of hospitalized infants (Bowlby et al. 1952). The need of the small mammal for a warm, supportive environment during early infancy is also included in Erikson's theory of stages (1950). His first stage is "Basic Trust." For good later adjustment, the infant must be able to trust his caretakers.

During the 1930s, a heated controversy took place between those who favored a hereditary point of view with respect to mental growth and the proponents of an environmental determination. The theorist responsible for the emphasis on the environment was probably John B. Watson (1928) who wrote in his book on the "Psychological Care of the Infant and Child" of the possibility of conditioning the child to behave or respond according to the desired standards. The research facility in this country which was then most environmentally oriented was the Iowa Child Welfare Research Station. Wellman published a series of reports on the favorable effects of nursery school experience (1946). These studies were criticized for their statistical naivete and inadequate use of control groups. From the vantage point of what we know today, we would probably conclude that the reports from Iowa were exaggerated but that the gains noted would probably be significant even if rigorous research and statistical standards had been followed. During the time that the Wellman studies were appearing, a more hereditarian point of view was prevalent among psychologists who were impressed by the research of Karl Pearson. He was reporting correlational studies of family members and finding that the closer the relationship, the higher the Pearsonian r. More than one psychologist has observed that if you wish to evaluate the effect of the environment, compute the difference between means for different subgroups, but if you wish to evaluate the effect of genetic factors, use correlations which reflect the individual differences.

Heinz Werner published his *Comparative Psychology of Mental Development* in 1957. According to his theory, the essence of development is increasing differentiation and centralization or hierarchic integration. He finds the following pairs of concepts useful in defining levels of mentality: syncretic–discrete; diffuse–articulated; indefinite–definite; rigid–flexible; and labile–stable.

In testing intelligence, we are measuring what a child or person can do at a particular moment in his life. What he can do today is the result of his integration of his life experiences and is varyingly predictive of what he can do in the future. The test results, however, tell us little about the process, or *how* this individual learned what he knows or came to be able to do what he does. Piaget's great contribution has been his descriptions of the *process* of how the individual acquires knowledge (1960). For Piaget, a central concept is the schema which may be described as a flexible mental structure, the primary unit of mental organization. The schemas of the neonate are a limited repertory of reflexes such as looking, listening, and grasping. These "schema" are modifiable by experience and are the bases for more complex learning. Piaget uses the terms *assimilation* and *accommodation* to describe the ways in which the organism takes in stimulations and is modified by it so as to adapt to the assimilated stimulation. Tuddenham (1969) points out that Piaget's theory differs from maturational accounts in that stimulation shapes inborn behavior patterns, according to Piaget; while stimulation is only needed to elicit behavior, according to maturational theory. Piaget writes that the organism always both experiences and acts upon the environment according to the individuals' adaptive organization or schema. This schema may be the simple "looking" of the newborn or a hypothetical analysis of the adult. Piaget describes the course of mental growth in terms of a series of stages which follow in an invariable sequence. These stages together constitute a hierarchical structure. There are four major stages which are only roughly related to chronological age: the first sensorimotor stage extends from birth to the end of the second year; the preoperational stage, from around 2 years to 6 or 7; the

stage of concrete operations extending from 6 or 7 to preadolescence; and the fourth stage that of formal operations. The first stage is further divided into six substages as follows;

1. *Exercising the ready-made schemata*, e.g., looking, sucking, listening (roughly birth to 1 month).
2. *Primary circular reactions* or coordination of the ready-made schemata so that things heard become something to look at, things seen become something to reach for and grasp, etc. (roughly 1 to $4\frac{1}{2}$ months).
3. *Secondary circular reactions*: coordination of motor habits and perceptions to form intentional acts (roughly 4 to 8 or 9 months).
4. *Coordination of secondary schemata*: Application of familiar schemata in new situations as means and ends: active search for vanished object and beginnings of imitation of auditory and visual models (age range roughly 8 or 9 months to 11 or 12 months).
5. *Tertiary circular reactions*: discovery of new means through active experimentation, interest in novelty, object permanence through sequences of visible displacements, systematic imitation of new models (age range 11 or 12 months to roughly 18 months).
6. *Internalization of sensorimotor schemata*: Invention of new means through mental combinations, object permanence through invisible sequences of displacements (roughly 18 months to 2 years).

Uzgiris and Hunt (1966) have constructed an Infant Psychological Development Scale based on Piaget's model of intellectual development. Wachs, Uzgiris, and Hunt (1967) used this scale in a study of the relation of home stimulation to development. They judged the amount of stimulation in the home by the noise, activity level in the home, chances of the child escaping excessive stimulation, and amount of interpersonal contact the child was exposed to. They found that at age levels 7, 11, 15, 18, and 22 months home stimulation was *negatively* related to intellectual development. Another home variable considered the amount and type of verbal interaction between the mother and child. This verbal interaction score was positively related to the children's scores at 15, 18, and 22 months. Another aspect of this study was a comparison of the test scores of a group of deprived and nondeprived children at these ages. Significant differences between the groups were obtained as early as 11 months and increase from 18 months on. Although this test was based on Piaget's model, the test items are similar to those used in other infant tests, such as the Bayley Scales, Cattell Infant Intelligence Scale, and the Gesell Developmental Schedules.

Bruner proposed a theory of cognitive growth during the 1960s. He believes that the development of human intellectual functions, from infancy to the adult's peak in performance, is shaped by a series of technological advances in the use of the mind (1964). Mental growth, then, depends on the mastery of techniques such as language. Bruner distinguishes three systems of processing information by which human beings construct models of their world: "through action, through imagery, and through the symbolism of language." A second concern of Bruner is with integration—"the means whereby acts are organized into higher order ensembles, making possible the use of larger and larger units of information for the solution of particular problems." In contrast to Gesell's definition of maturation in terms of neurological development, Bruner believes that "maturation consists of an orchestration of . . . components [simple acts] into an integrated sequence"; and that "integration depends upon patterns that come from the outside in—an internalization of the [environment]." Bruner states that the significant aspect of "memory" is not the storage of past experience but rather the "retrieval of what is relevant in some usable form." What the individual has to retrieve are previous "actions," "imagery" (of experiences), and "words." Bruner believes that what is significant about the growth of the mind is not "capacity for language or for imagery" but "upon the unlocking of capacity by techniques that come from exposure to the specialized environment of a culture."

Each theory contributes an ordering of certain of the facts of mental growth. No theory is complete. To a large extent they complement each other. In addition to the theories of the psychologists, anatomists and neurologists are contributing their observations about the developing brain. For example, the neuroanatomist Dodgson writes in 1962:

Man's slowly maturing brain is thus exceptional in being able to receive stimuli from the outside world for a considerable period of time against a changing background of cerebral maturation. . . . It seems probable that many of the inherited and more or less unalterable characteristics of behavior and attainment of a particular species can be related, not so much to final brain form, as to the temporal sequence according to which separate components of the central nervous system become functionally mature.

Increase in knowledge about the development of intelligence will continue to come from many sources. As the geneticist reports on chromosomal variations, the psychologist will note the accompanying distinctive patterns of abilities. As we provide more enriching programs for individuals from birth to senescence, we can measure the resulting patterns of abilities to see the extent of the plasticity of the human organism to develop its intellectual abilities. As we test more carefully the abilities of the middle aged and the aging individual, we will be able to determine more precisely the course of development of specific abilities through the life span.

References

AINSWORTH, M. D. The effects of maternal deprivation: A review of findings and controversy in the context of research strategy. *In Deprivation of maternal care: A reassessment of its effects*, pp. 97–165. Geneva, Switzerland: World Health Organization, 1962.

ANASTASI, A. *Psychological testing*. 2d ed. New York: Macmillan, 1961.

BALLER, W. R., CHARLES, D. C., and MILLER, E. K. Mid-life attainment of the mentally retarded: A longitudinal study. *Genetic Psychology Monographs*, 1967, 75, 234–329.

BAYLEY, N. *The California first-year mental scale*. Berkeley: University of California Press, Syllabus Series No. 243, 1933.

—— Consistency and variability in the growth of intelligence from birth to eighteen years. *Journal of Genetic Psychology*, 1949, 75, 165–96.

—— Data on the growth of intelligence between 16 and 21 years as measured by the Wechsler-Bellevue Scale. *Journal of Genetic Psychology*, 1957, 90, 3–15.

—— Age trends in mental scores: Ages sixteen to thirty-six years. Paper read at American Psychological Association, New York, 1966.

—— Cognition and aging, *In* K. W. Schaie (ed.) *Theory and methods of research on aging* pp. 97–119. Morgantown: West Virginia University, 1968.

—— *Bayley infant scales of development: Birth to two years*. New York: Psychological Corporation 1969.

——, RHODES, L., and GOOCH, B. A comparison of the growth and development of institutionalized and home-reared mongoloids: A follow-up study. Prepublication copy no. 356, California Department of Mental Hygiene, Bureau of Research, 1966.

BAYLEY, N., and SCHAEFER, E. S. Correlations of maternal and child behaviors with the development of mental abilities: Data from the Berkeley Growth Study. *Monographs of the Society for Research in Child Development*, 1964, 29 (6, whole no. 97).

BINET, A., and SIMON, T. Methodes nouvelles pour le diagnostic du niveau intellectuel des anormaux. *L'Année Psychologique*, 1905, 11, 191–244.

BLOOM, B. S. *Stability and change in human characteristics*. New York: John Wiley, 1964.

BOWLBY, J. *Maternal care and mental health*. Monograph Series no. 2, 2d edition. Geneva, Switzerland: World Health Organization, 1952.

——, ROBERTSON, J., and ROSENBLUTH, D. A two-year-old goes to the hospital. *In* R. S. Eissler et al. (eds.) *The psychoanalytic study of the child*, vol. 7, pp. 82–94. New York: International Universities Press, 1952.

BROMLEY, D. B. *The psychology of human aging*. Baltimore: Penguin, 1966.

BRUNER, J. The cause of cognitive growth. *American Psychologist*, 1964, 19, 1–15.

BURKS, B. S. The relative influence of nature and nurture upon mental development: A comparative study of foster parent-foster child resemblance and true parent-true child resemblance. *Yearbook of the National Society for the Study of Education*, 1928, 27, 219–316.

BUROS, O. K. *The sixth mental measurement yearbook*. Highland Park, N. J.: Gryphon Press, 1965.

CAMERON, J., LIVSON, N., and BAYLEY, N. Infant vocalizations and their relationship to mature intelligence. *Science*, 1967, 157, 331–33.

CASLER, L. Maternal deprivation: A critical review of the literature. *Monographs of the Society for Research in Child Development*, 1961, 26 (2, whole no. 80).

—— The effects of extra tactile stimulation on a group of institutionalized infants. *Genetic Psychology Monographs*, 1965, 71, 137–75.

CATTELL, P. *The measurement of intelligence of infants and young children*. New York: Science Press, 1940; Reprinted by Psychological Corporation, 1960.

CHARLES, D. C. Ability and accomplishment of persons earlier judged mentally deficient. *Genetic Psychology Monographs*, 1953, 47, 3–71.

——, and JAMES, S. T. Stability of average intelligence. *Journal of Genetic Psychology*, 1964, 105, 105–11.

CORAH, N. L., ANTHONY, E. J., PAINTER, P., STERN, J. A., and THURSTON, D. Effects of perinatal anoxia after seven years. *Psychological Monographs*, 1965, 79 (3, whole no. 596).

DEARBORN, W. F., and ROTHNEY, J. *Predicting the child's development*. Cambridge, Mass.: Science-Art Publications, 1941.

DENNIS, W., and NAJARIAN, P. Infant development under environmental handicap. *Psychological Monographs*, 1957, 71 (7, whole no. 436).

DODGSON, M. C. H. *The growing brain: An essay in developmental neurology*. Baltimore: Williams and Wilkins, 1962.

EBERT, E., and SIMMONS, K. The Brush Foundation study of child growth and development: I. Psychometric tests. *Monographs of the Society for Research in Child Development*, 1943, 8 (2, whole no. 35).

ERIKSON, E. H. *Childhood and society*. New York: Norton, 1950.

ERLENMEYER-KIMLING, L., and JARVIK, L. F. Genetics and intelligence: A review. *Science*, 1963, 142, 1477–79.

FINELY, K. H., FITZGERALD, L. F., RICHTER, R. W., RIGGS, N., and SHELTON, J. T. Western encephalitis and cerebral ontogenesis. *Archives of Neurology*, 1967, 16, 140–64.

FREEDMAN, D. G., and KELLER, B. Inheritance of behavior in infants. *Science*, 1963, 140, 196–98.

FREEMAN, F. S. *Theory and practice of psychological testing.* 3d ed. New York: Holt, Rinehart & Winston, 1962.

GESELL, A. *Infancy and human growth.* New York: Macmillan, 1928.

———, and AMATRUDA, C. *Developmental diagnosis: Normal and abnormal child development, clinical methods and practical applications,* 3d ed. New York: Harper & Row, 1962.

GRAHAM, F. K., ERNHART, C. B., THURSTON, D., and CRAFT, M. Development three years after perinatal anoxia and other potentially damaging newborn experiences. *Psychological Monographs,* 1962, *76* (3, whole no. 522).

GRAY, S. W., and KLAUS, R. A. An experimental preschool program for culturally deprived children. *Child Development,* 1965, *36,* 887–98.

GRIFFITHS, R. *The abilities of babies: A study in mental measurement.* New York: McGraw-Hill, 1954.

HARLOW, H. The development of learning in the Rhesus monkey. *In* W. R. Brode (ed.), *Science in progress: Twelfth series,* pp. 239–69. New Haven, Conn.: Yale University Press, 1962.

———, and SUOMI, S. J. Nature of love—simplified. *American Psychologist,* 1970, *25,* 161–68.

HEINIS, H. La loi developpement mental. *Archives de Psychologie,* 1924, *74,* 97–128.

HERRING, J. P. *Herring revision of the Binet-Simon tests.* Yonkers-on-Hudson, N. Y.: World Book, 1922.

HINDLEY, C. B. Social class differences in the development of ability in the first five years. *Proceedings of the XIV International Congress of Applied Psychology.* Copenhagen: Munksgaard, 1961.

——— Stability and change in abilities up to five years: Group trends. *Journal of Child Psychology and Psychiatry,* 1965, *6,* 85–99.

HONZIK, M. P. Developmental studies of parent-child resemblance in intelligence. *Child Development,* 1957, *28,* 215–28.

——— A sex difference in the age of onset of the parent-child resemblance in intelligence. *Journal of Educational Psychology,* 1963, *54,* 231–37.

——— Environmental correlates of mental growth: Predictions from the family setting at 21 months. *Child Development,* 1967a, *38,* 337–64.

——— Prediction of differential abilities at age 18 from the early family environment. *Proceedings, 75th Annual Convention of the American Psychological Association,* 1967b, 151–52.

———, HUTCHINGS, J. J., and BURNIP, S. R. Birth record assessments and test performance at eight months. *American Journal of Diseases of Children,* 1965, *109,* 416–26.

HONZIK, M. P., MACFARLANE, J. W., and ALLEN, L. The stability of mental test performance between two and eighteen years. *Journal of Experimental Education,* 1948, *4,* 309–24.

JONES, H. E. The environment and mental development. *In* L. Carmichael (ed.), *Manual of child psychology,* pp. 631–96. 2d ed. New York: John Wiley, 1954.

———, and CONRAD, H. S. The growth and decline of intelligence: A study of a homogeneous group between the ages of ten and sixty. *Genetic Psychology Monographs,* 1933, *13,* 223–98.

KAGAN, J. Stability of behavior during the first year. Unpublished manuscript, Harvard University, 1968.

———, and MOSS, H. A. *From birth to maturity: A study in psychological development.* New York: John Wiley, 1962.

KUHLEN, R. G. Age and intelligence: The significance of cultural change in longitudinal vs. cross-sectional findings. *In* B. Neugarten (ed.), *Middle age and aging,* pp. 552–57. Chicago: University of Chicago Press, 1968.

KUHLMANN, F. A revision of the Binet-Simon system for measuring the intelligence of children. *Journal of Psycho-Aesthenics,* Monograph Supplement 1912.

——— *Tests of mental development. A complete scale for individual examination.* Minneapolis: Educational Test Bureau, 1939.

LEAHY, A. M. Nature-nurture and intelligence. *Genetic Psychology Monographs,* 1935, *17,* 241–305.

MASLAND, R. The collaborative study. Paper given at Biennial Meeting of the Society for Research in Child Development, Bethesda, Maryland, 1959.

MILES, C. C., and MILES, W. R. The correlation of intelligence scores and chronological age from early to late maturity. *American Journal of Psychology,* 1932, *44,* 44–79.

MONEY, J. Two cytogenetic syndromes: Psychological comparison: I. Intelligence and specific factor quotients. *Journal of Psychiatric Research,* 1964, *2,* 223–31.

MOORE, T. Language and intelligence: A longitudinal study of the first eight years. Part II. Environmental correlates of mental growth. *Human Development,* 1968, *11,* 1–24.

NICOLSON, A. B., and HANLEY, C. Indices of physiological maturity: Derivation and interrelationships. *Child Development,* 1953, *24,* 3–38.

OWENS, W. A. Age and mental abilities: A longitudinal study. *Genetic Psychology Monographs,* 1953, *48,* 3–54.

PIAGET, J. *The psychology of intelligence.* Paterson, N. J.: Littlefield, Adams, 1960.

RHEINGOLD, H. L., and BAYLEY, N. The later effects of an experimental modification of mothering. *Child Development,* 1959, *30,* 363–72.

SKODAK, M., and SKEELS, H. M. A final follow-up study of 100 adopted children. *Journal of Genetic Psychology,* 1949, *75,* 85–125.

SONTAG, L. W., BAKER, C. T., and NELSON, V. L. Mental growth and personality development: A longitudinal study. *Monographs of the Society for Research in Child Development,* 1958, *23* (2, whole no. 68).

STAFFORD, R. E. Sex differences in spatial visualization as evidence of sex-linked inheritance. *Perceptual Motor Skills,* 1961, *13,* 428.

TERMAN, L. M. *The measurement of intelligence.* Boston: Houghton Mifflin, 1916.

———, and MERRILL, M. *Measuring intelligence: A guide to the new revised Stanford-Binet tests of intelligence.* Boston: Houghton Mifflin, 1937.

——— *Stanford-Binet intelligence scale. Manual for the third revision: Form L-M.* Boston: Houghton Mifflin, 1960.

THORNDIKE, E. L. *The measurement of intelligence.* New York: Bureau of Publications, Teachers College, Columbia University, 1927.

THURSTONE, L. L. The absolute zero in intelligence measurement. *Psychological Review,* 1928, *35,* 175–97.

TUDDENHAM, R. D. On growing intelligence: Implications of Piaget's theories. Paper presented at Conference of British Columbia School Superintendents, British Columbia, January, 1969.

UZGIRIS, I., and HUNT, J. M. An instrument for assessing infant psychological development. Paper presented at International Congress of Psychology, Moscow, 1966.

VERNON, P. E. Ability factors and environmental influences. *American Psychologist,* 1965, *20,* 723–33.

WACHS, T. D., UZGIRIS, I. C., and HUNT, J. M. Congitive development in infants of different age levels and from different environmental backgrounds. Paper presented at the Biennial Meeting of the Society for Research in Child Development, New York, March, 1967.

WATSON, J. B. *Psychological care of infant and child.* New York: Norton, 1928.

WECHSLER, D. *Measurement of adult intelligence.* Baltimore: Williams & Wilkins, 1939 (3rd ed. 1944).

——— *Wechsler intelligence scale for children, manual.* New York: Psychological Corporation, 1949.

——— *Wechsler adult intelligence scale, manual.* New York: Psychological Corporation, 1955.

——— *The measurement and appraisal of adult intelligence.* 4th ed. Baltimore: Williams & Wilkins, 1958.

———. *Wechsler preschool and primary scale of intelligence, manual.* New York: Psychological Corporation, 1967.

WELLMAN, B. L., and MCCANDLESS, B. R. Factors associated with Binet IQ changes of preschool children. *Psychological Monographs,* 1946, *60* (2, whole no. 278).

WERNER, E. E., and BAYLEY, N. The reliability of Bayley's revised scale of mental and motor development during the first year of life. *Child Development,* 1966, *37,* 39–50.

WERNER, E. E., SIMONIAN, K., BIERMAN, J. M., and FRENCH, F. Cumulative effect of perinatal complications and deprived environment on physical, intellectual and social development of preschool children. *Pediatrics,* 1967, *39,* 490–505.

WERNER, E. E., HONZIK, M. P., and SMITH, R. S. Prediction at ten years from twenty months pediatric and psychologic examinations. *Child Development,* 1968, *39,* 1063–75.

WERNER, H. *Comparative psychology of mental development.* New York: International Universities Press, 1957.

YAKOVLEV, P. I. Anatomy of the human brain and the problem of mental retardation. *In* P. W. Bowman and H. V. Mautner (eds.), *Proceedings of the First International Conference on Mental Retardation.* New York: Grune & Stratton, 1960.

YARROW, L. J. Maternal deprivation: Toward an empirical and conceptual re-evaluation. *Psychological Bulletin,* 1961, *58,* 459–90.

——— Research in dimensions of early maternal care. *Merrill-Palmer Quarterly of Behavior and Development,* 1963, *9,* 101–14.

YERKES, R. M., BRIDGES, J. W., and HARDWICK, R. S. *A point scale for measuring mental ability.* Baltimore: Warick & York, 1915.

ZAMENHOF, S., van MARTHENS, E., and MARGOLIS, F. L. DNA (cell number) and protein in neonatal brain: Alteration by maternal dietary protein restriction. *Science,* 1968, *160,* 322–23.

The methodology for measuring intelligence stands at the crossroads between the traditional clinical-empirical mode of development and the increasingly favored psychometric approach. At present the traditional clinical methods are serving as the basis and support for tests of single individuals while the statistical approach is being employed in progressively more group tests. We would be wise to pause at this point—as indeed we would at any confusing crossroads—and ponder the alternatives before proceeding. At this juncture we need to review our past course of development and to consider such important questions as these: Should we push forward with much the same attitudes and techniques, or are we now ready to work out a more precise plan of action for future work in the discipline? Can we detect a common thread linking past, present, and future methods of testing intelligence, or are they in fact mutually exclusive? The purpose of this chapter is to explain how each of the approaches operates and what it is contributing to our understanding of intelligence.

In the past, investigators developed certain tests to measure intelligence according to their preconceived notions of what, in functional terms, intelligence really meant. Those who defined intelligence as the ability to learn developed various tests to measure this quality. Similarly, those who regarded intelligence as synonymous with reasoning ability constructed reasoning problems and tasks to evaluate intelligence. In this way intelligence tests developed into a congeries of empirically assembled tasks organized according to various operational definitions of intelligence.

An intelligence test is a standardized procedure for objectively measuring what a person is able to do at the time he is being assessed and under the conditions of the assessment. Included in this concept is the realization that individual behavior, including mental processes, is neither consistent nor stable. Although scores for groups may be relatively stable, it does not follow that the individual scores within a group will be similarly stable. And the fact that a particular intelligence test may have high predictive validity does not mean that any individual taking this test may be accorded the same predictability as the

**Robert S. Morrow
& Selma Morrow**

The Measurement of Intelligence

32

group itself. Because intelligence is a product of nature as well as nurture, an individual's mental functioning will be influenced by many extrinsic factors such as cultural exposure, including quality and quantity of education, as well as intrinsic factors, such as personality characteristics. The most we may say for any intelligence test score is that it describes how the individual performs *here and now* and that, *all things being equal*, he will probably continue to function in a like manner.

Clinical-Empirical Individual Tests

The historical antecedents to modern intelligence testing derive from three sources, all of them empirically based. One source is a composite of Itard's (1801) work in mental retardation especially the techniques used in his study of "The Wild Boy of Aveyron" and Esquirol's (1838) investigations and their joint influence on the tests developed by Seguin (1866). The second antecedent derives from Sir Francis Galton's (1883) attempts to measure mental functions in his anthropometric laboratory in London. Here various individual tests, which were mainly sensory discrimination tasks, were utilized for assessing individual differences. Galton was also interested in investigating "hereditary faculties," with special focus on the study of "genius" (1892). He invented the notion of correlation which, with Pearson's improvement, became an important tool in the development and use of intelligence tests. The contributions of Cattell (1890) constitute the third source. It was he who first used the term "mental tests" in 1890. Essentially his series of tests represented a fusion of his earlier work under Wundt on reaction time, which the two considered a mental function, and his subsequent study with Galton on tests of discrimination and imagery. His work achieved a synthesis of objectivity and focus on individual differences.

While these three sources were the main forces shaping intelligence testing, other investigators contributed much of use. Peterson (1925) has noted the pioneering efforts of Kraepelin and his student Oehrn as well as the contributions of Ebbinghaus, Munsterberg, and J. A. Gilbert. Their efforts failed mainly because these investigators all tended to regard intelligence as a single entity that could be measured by a specific test or a few simple tasks; moreover, their standards were too subjective and arbitrary.

Binet and Henri (1896) criticized this simplistic approach. They conceptualized eleven mental faculties and specified tests for measuring each process. Binet, together with Simon, incorporated many of these tests into a scale that became the first successful attempt at measuring intelligence. The first version of the Binet-Simon scale, published in 1905, consisted of thirty assorted tasks. These covered such functions as memory, reasoning, attention, judgment, and discrimination. Because the scale was devised to distinguish between those who were mentally retarded and those who were not, it was organized to range from very simple to average or normal tasks. After the examiners determined the average number of items children at different age levels were able to complete correctly, their test could then determine whether a particular child was intellectually average for his age, and, if not, the extent to which he was retarded or accelerated.

On the basis of their initial findings Binet and Simon developed a revised test in 1908 and another in 1911. The tasks were now arranged into age groups based on which tasks could be performed by a majority of children in each age group. Through their work on this scale Binet and Simon made several valuable contributions to the measurement of intelligence. Their findings established (1) that intelligence could be studied objectively by standardized tasks; (2) a collection of tasks comprising a scale was a more effective measure than any single test or task; and (3) intelligence increases with age. The average seven-year-old, for instance, can do more complicated things than the average four-year-old, and with each year the child is able to do more and better. The average five-year-old will be able to copy a square but not a diamond, as can the average seven-year-old. The average four-year-old will be able to repeat only three digits, the average seven-year-old, five. From this developmental experience Binet and Simon fashioned their fourth important contribution, the concept of mental age.

A person's mental age is independent of his chronological age. In the 1908 revision mental age was determined as being the highest age level at which the subject failed only one test item. For example, a six-year-old who failed only one item at age seven and two at age eight was designated as mental age seven. However, an additional year of mental age could be earned for every five tasks he completed correctly beyond the seven-year level. In the 1911 revision every age level contained five items, each item having a value of two-tenths of a year. This value of .2 multiplied by the number of items passed beyond the base age created a product that when added to the basal year resulted in the mental age. Thus, in the illustration just given, the child's mental age would be exactly 7.4 years, since it represents the sum of 6 years basal plus .2 year for each of the four items passed at age seven and the three items at age eight. In the same year (1912) both Stern and Kuhlmann proposed the idea of an intelligence quotient that was based on the ratio of mental age to chronological age as follows:

$$IQ = \frac{\text{mental age}}{\text{chronological age}} \times 100$$

The Stanford-Binet Scale

The most successful of various revisions of the Binet-Simon scales was published in 1916 by Terman and became known as the Stanford-Binet (Terman 1916). It was a new test in every respect, with new items, administration procedures, and scoring techniques. One basic feature was that this scale was properly standardized on a large native-born white population of about one thousand children and four hundred adults carefully screened for age, geographic distribution, and education. It was also well standardized in the way it was to be administered so that it would be the same test for all. Terman stressed the need for rapport between examiners and subjects and strict adherence to procedures for giving and scoring the test; the latter included an insistence upon reading rather than memorizing directions, avoiding hints and suggestions, carefully recording responses, and starting from the basal age at which there were no failures and proceeding year by year to a ceiling at which there was no success. He set up guidelines for increased objectivity in scoring. The test started at year three and continued up to the adult level. At each age group up to year ten there were six items, each worth two months mental age if answered correctly. From age ten on up each of the items had a value of three or four months depending on the number of items in each group, with alternate years skipped. A significant feature was the expression of results as an intelligence quotient or IQ in addition to a mental age. Tables of IQ distribution and classification helped to popularize this measure as well as the test itself.

The need to have more than a single form of the test and the need to improve on some of its aspects led to an extensive revision of the Stanford-Binet in 1937 (Terman & Merrill 1937). Hundreds of items were pretested on about one thousand children and adults. The final standardization population consisted of about three thousand native-born white children and adults from typical rural and urban groupings in eleven representative states. The 1930 census was used to assure representative socioeconomic sampling. On the basis of this standardization two equivalent forms of the scales were developed, Form L and Form M. Each contained 129 items and could be administered to subjects ranging from age two through the superior adult level. The items in each form were different but equivalent in the sense that the median correlation between the two scales for the twenty-one age groupings was .91.

From ages two through five there were six items for each half-year level, with a value of one month mental age for each correct item. For this lowest age group the test was made more stimulating by including some colorful objects and putting less stress on verbal skills. The gaps that were present in the 1916 form for age levels eleven and thirteen were now filled so that the test now proceeded year by year from age six up to age fourteen, each of the six items per year assuming a value of two months mental age. Also, more top was contributed to each form by adding two additional superior adult levels. The average adult level, which followed age level fourteen, contained eight items, each with a two-month value. Superior Adult I had six tests worth four months apiece. Superior Adult II six items worth five months each, and Superior Adult III six that were worth six months apiece. The maximum possible mental age therefore was twenty-two years, ten months. Terman and Merrill had made empirical adjustments for the chronological age period thirteen to sixteen to conform to IQ distributions of younger subjects. On this basis fifteen years chronological age was utilized in computing IQs for all adults sixteen and over. Terman and Merrill included in their 1937 manual tables of computed IQs that included these chronological age adjustments and thereby reduced the possibility of arithmetic error. The distribution and classification of IQs for the 1937 standardization population are shown in Table 32-1 (Terman & Merrill 1960, p. 18).

We may note the absence of confusing terms like "genius" and "near-genius" from this table and the use of terms more generally accepted in the profession. Confusion in diagnosis frequently results when terms like "mental deficient" and "mental defective" are used interchangeably or when the diagnosis of feeblemindedness, mental defectiveness, or mental retardation—all of them synonymous—is based exclusively on the psychometric criterion of an IQ score below 70. Low IQ scores may be as much the result of physical defects (i.e., poor vision or hearing) or serious emotional disturbances (i.e., depression, schizophrenia, or autism in children) as the consequence of an actual defect in mental functioning. For this reason it is advisable to distinguish between dementia (mental deterioration) and amentia (mental insufficiency or lack of development). One

Table 32-1. Distribution of the 1937 Standardization Group

IQ	Percentage	Classification
160–169	0.03	Very superior
150–159	0.2	
140–149	1.1	
130–139	3.1	Superior
120–129	8.2	
110–119	18.1	High average
100–109	23.5	Normal or average
90–99	23.0	
80–89	14.5	Low average
70–79	5.6	Borderline defective
60–69	2.0	
50–59	0.4	Mentally defective
40–49	0.2	
30–39	0.03	

suffering from dementia, usually a transitory state, is capable of approaching his potential once the interfering psychopathology is corrected, whereas a victim of amentia has never functioned normally nor will he ever do so.

The term "pseudoretardation" may be applied most appropriately to inadequate scores resulting from disadvantaged sociocultural conditions. As a general rule a subject should not be classified as mentally retarded on the basis of his psychometric score alone if greater potential is revealed in even a few of the tests or subtests or by other signs, such as his academic performance including achievement test scores. Instead, the examiners should consider other possible causes—physical or emotional for the low IQ reading.

Still another revision of the Standford-Binet Scale, Form L-M, appeared in 1960 (Terman & Merrill), incorporating into a single scale the most discriminative items as determined by about forty-five hundred administrations of the 1937 Forms L and M. This is the revision most widely used at present. The essential features of the scale remain the same, and it continues to be, like its predecessors, an age scale. Greater precision and objectivity in administration and scoring have been introduced, however. The changes are mainly structural, with only slight changes in content. One significant modification is that IQ scores must be obtained from the tables only, and the scores are now "deviation IQs" that have been adjusted for variability (differences in standard deviation) at each level. This change makes the IQs more comparable from one age level to another since the IQ now becomes more truly a standard score with a mean of 100 and a standard deviation of 16. Another change extends the IQ tables to chronological age eighteen on the basis of research evidence that mental growth continues to improve beyond age sixteen on these scales.

With respect to reliability, the available evidence indicates a very high correlation of .90 (the coefficient of equivalence) between Forms L and M for various ages and IQ levels. A reliability coefficient of .90 with a standard deviation of 16 yields a standard error score of 5 IQ points, which means that the chances are about two to one (68 percent) that a given score will fluctuate less than 5 points between the two forms. In 99 percent of the cases the fluctuation should be no greater than 13 points (that is, 2.58×5) from any obtained IQ.

The validity of the Stanford-Binet is psychometrically high, judging by the traditional criteria. When examiners compared IQ scores with the usual measures of academic achievement, (i.e., grades, teachers' ratings, and scores on achievement tests) they usually find correlations ranging from .40 to .75. As for content validity, the biserial correlations of each subtest with scale L-M yield a mean correlation of .61. The highest correlations are for the verbal tests, revealing that the scale is rather heavily weighted for verbal ability. Construct validity, relative to the growth of intelligence as well as the division of the test into age levels, is demonstrated by the fact that the percentage of correct answers for successive items increases in tandem with chronological age. Furthermore, McNemar (1942) demonstrated that the scale had more or less the same factorial composition at the fourteen age levels he investigated. He found that a single verbal factor was common to the entire scale. The existence of a general verbal factor would tend to support the thesis that the scale is a measure of general intelligence.

Performance Scales

The high verbal loading is consistent with the criticism, empirically adduced, that the Stanford-Binet handicaps those who have language difficulties. Actually, the need for nonverbal tests was recognized before the Stanford-Binet was published. Healy and Fernold (1911) worked out a series of performance tests that they used in studying delinquent children. Soon afterward, Knox (1914) devised a group of rather crudely standardized nonverbal tests for the purpose of screening out mentally defective immigrants arriving in America. The Knox Cubes, which derive from this series, have been incorporated into other performance scales. Pintner and Paterson (1917) developed the first standardized battery of nonverbal tests, theirs consisting of ten parts.[1] This test was soon superseded by others, the two most popular being the Arthur Point Scale of Performance Tests (Arthur 1930)[2] and the Cornell-Coxe Performance Ability Scale (Cornell & Coxe 1934). All of these tests were administered individually, and they included such diverse tasks as the arrangement of form boards, the completion of missing parts, and the assembling of discrete parts into wholes. Scoring was based on the amount of time taken as well as the number of errors made.

In addition to tests involving a battery of tasks, some very effective single performance tests have been created. Among the most widely used of the individually administered ones are the Kohs Blocks (Kohs 1923), the Porteus Mazes (Porteus 1924), and the Goodenough Draw-A-Man Test (Goodenough 1926). The Kohs Blocks and some of the mazes are included in the more extensive performance batteries. In the Kohs Blocks[3] the subject is asked to match a series of designs with blocks containing different colors, proceeding from the simplest designs, which require four blocks, to the most complex, which require all

sixteen blocks. The Porteus Maze Test[4] consists of a series of pictures of mazes that become progressively more difficult, each maze having been solved correctly by a standardization population ranging from three years of age to the adult level. The subject has unlimited time to trace each maze, his mental age being determined by the relative difficulty of the last maze he is able to trace correctly. In the Goodenough Draw-A-Man Test the subject is asked to draw a man. The subject's score is based on the number of items involving body parts and clothing details that he draws, with additional points given for accuracy respecting number and location or perspective. The raw scores are then converted into MAs and IQs. This test was later revised by Harris as the Goodenough-Harris Test (Harris 1963) and now includes the drawing of a woman as well. The latter test has a better standardization than the original, and the raw or point score is directly converted into the IQ equivalent as a standard score based on a mean of 100 and a standard deviation of 15. Also the subject is asked to draw himself, but this drawing is used only as a projective personality test and does not enter into the scoring.

Other individual performance tests that are used for special clinical purposes are the Leiter International Performance Scale (1948) and the Columbia Mental Maturity Scale (Burgomeister, Blum, & Lorge 1953). The Leiter, which was intended as a culture-free test, is a mental age scale that ranges from age two to eighteen. It consists of sixty-eight test items, four at each age level. No time limits are imposed, and it can be administered by pantomime. It is reported to be especially suitable for children five to twelve years old. The MA is determined by the months of mental age earned, and from age thirteen up the chronological age is arbitrarily set at thirteen years. The scale attempts through performance to assess areas of competence that are normally verbal functions on the examinations; a typical sampling of tests might include the following: matching test that progresses from very simple objects and colors gradually to more complex designs and analogies; a test of abstract reasoning ability involving the classification of animals according to their native habitat; problems involving spatial relations; and problems testing recognition and retention abilities. The scale is particularly recommended for children who are handicapped—the culturally deprived and those with speech and hearing disorders, multiple disabilities, or brain damage. Tate (1952) reported a correlation of .81 between the Leiter and Form L, Stanford-Binet. Arthur (1952) has published her own adaptation of the Leiter for preschool children. The Columbia Mental Maturity Scale consists of 100 cards, each containing three to five drawings. The subject points out the one object that seems most inappropriate to the grouping or setting. Scores are expressed as MAs and ratio IQs. This scale seems well adapted for testing brain-damaged and physically handicapped children.

Infant and Preschool Tests

The testing of the intelligence of infants (usually defined psychometrically as persons below eighteen months of age)

---

[1] Although this test is no longer available in its entirety, portions of it have been incorporated into other performance scales, such as the Arthur Point Scale and the Merrill-Palmer Scale of Mental Tests.

[2] Form 1 of the Arthur Point Scale was assembled in 1925 by the Stoelting Company; Form II, which was revised in 1947, is sold by the Psychological Corporation.

[3] The Kohs Blocks are not sold by themselves but are available from the Psychological Corporation as parts of the Wechsler-Bellevue Block Design subtest. Western Psychological Services distributes the OHWAKI-KOHS Tactile Block Design Intelligence Test for use with blind persons six years of age and older. In this variation on Kohs's concept, touch is used to identify the designs.

[4] The Psychological Corporation sells the 1933 Vineland Revision as well as a Special Extension as a second form and a slightly more difficult supplement as a third form. They also stock the comprehensive 1965 manual entitled "Porteus Maze Tests: Fifty Years Application."

is normally achieved by means of developmental tests or scales that take into account the infant's rudimentary linguistic and muscular repertoire. The rationale for these tests is that sensory and motor development is concomitant with intellectual development. Two types of tests are employed for this age group: extensive preschool tests (including downward extensions of the Stanford-Binet) and scales developed specifically for infants.

Attempts to test the intelligence of infants began with Kuhlmann's revision of the Binet-Simon (Kuhlmann 1912), in which he extended the scale downward to the three-month level. Kuhlmann retained this starting point in a later revision of his own test (Kuhlmann 1939). The following excerpts from Kuhlmann's 1939 criteria demonstrate, as a typical developmental scale, the transition from purely sensory-motor functions to more verbal and finally more cognitive capabilities:

At Three Months: (*1*) *Child shows sufficient motor coordination to carry hand object to mouth more or less at will and not merely through random, chance movements;* (*2*) *Child reacts to sudden sound with start or wink;* (*3*) *Binocular coordination tested by moving bright object to left and right in front of child's face;* (*4*) *Child should be able to turn the eyes toward object without turning head;* (*5*) *Child should wink at a sudden pass toward the eyes.*
At Twelve Months: (*1*) *Child should stand up supported for 2 or 3 minutes or stand unsupported for about 5 seconds;* (*2*) *Child should be able to repeat such words as "dada", "mamma" and "nana" or give satisfactory evidence of combining 2 or 3 syllables with some success;* (*3*) *Child should be able to imitate such simple movements as shaking a rattle and nodding the head;* (*4*) *Child, after being interested and shown, can make simple strokes with a pencil or give evidence of voluntarily attempting to do so;* (*5*) *Child gives evidence of being able to discriminate between familiar objects, such as a bell, rattle, block or picture, by showing preference in his choice.*
At Two Years: (*1*) *Pointing out in picture such things as a hat, a man, or a dog;* (*2*) *Imitating such simple movements as clapping both hands or putting palms of hands on top of the head;* (*3*) *Obeying simple commands such as "catch the ball" and "throw it to me";* (*4*) *Copying a circle that has been shown to child who should reproduce it with at least partial success;* (*5*) *Removing wrapper from candy or sugar before taking it in its mouth.*

One of the most widely used developmental scales is the Gesell Developmental Schedules.[5] The schedules cover the period from four weeks to six years of age. In essence the test is a quantitative-qualitative assessment of a child's responses to standardized materials and situations, focusing in particular on motor and language development, adaptive behavior, and personal-social behavior. Items are scored plus or minus and have no numerical value. The developmental age (DA) is the highest age at which plus signs predominate, and the formula for the developmental quotient (DQ) is

$$DQ = \frac{\text{developmental age}}{\text{chronological age}} \times 100$$

[5] Although the Gesell Schedules, which is sold by the Psychological Corporation, comes with no accompanying manual, either *The First Five Years of Life* by Gesell and associates (1940) or *Developmental Diagnosis* by Gesell and Amatruda (1949) may be used to administer and interpret the test.

The DQ represents "the portion of normal development that is present at any age" and may be obtained for all of the broad functions named above upon which the scale is built. Richards and Nelson (1939) did a factor analysis of the Gesell Schedules at six-, twelve- and eighteen-month levels and found three factors present: a general factor, motor ability, and alertness. The items comprising the alertness factor correlated best with later tests of intelligence.

Another useful scale is the infant Intelligence Scale created by Psyche Cattell (1947). While it is primarily a downward extension of the 1937 Standford-Binet, Form L, it contains features of the Gesell and other infant tests as well. The scale covers the period from three to thirty months of age and passage of any item on the thirty month level leads to continued testing at the third-year level of the Stanford-Binet. The test correlated .83 at the thirty-month level with form L, Standford-Binet, but very low before age one (e.g., .10 for the three-month level). It proceeds from simple perceptual and motor tasks to more complex manipulatory and verbal functions, and uniquely it employs no time limits. Results are expressed as MAs and ratio IQs.

The Merrill-Palmer Scale of Mental Tests (Stutsman 1931) covers in six-month intervals the period from eighteen months to six years of age. It uses point scoring, from which MAs are computed, and is best suited for subjects twenty-four to sixty-three months old because subsequent IQs can be most accurately predicted among this group. The thirty-eight tests (which are colorful and interesting) are mostly of the performance type, but there are a few language tests as well. The functions tested include the opposition of thumb and fingers, standing on one foot, and the manipulation of scissors, pencil and paper, blocks, and puzzles. A unique feature of the Merrill-Palmer is that provision is made in the scoring for refused and omitted tasks, some of which are timed. Stutsman reported a correlation of .79 with Stanford-Binet.

Goodenough and co-workers developed the Minnesota Preschool Scale (Goodenough, Maurer, & Van Wagenen 1940), which is used with subjects eighteen months to six years old. There are two equivalent forms of the test, both containing nonverbal and verbal items, so that one may calculate separate verbal, nonverbal, and combined IQ scores for each. The results on this test have been used for longitudinal evaluation of intellectual stability by Goodenough and Maurer (1942). They followed a group of subjects twelve years who were initially tested on this scale at age two, subsequently retested after intervals of one and two years, and later given the Merrill-Palmer, Stanford-Binet, Arthur Point Scale, and American Council on Education College Entrance Examinations. While the correlations were, on the whole, positive, they were not high. Thus, the test-retest reliability for the Minnesota scale alone would have to be considered rather low, and the low correlations with the Merrill-Palmer and Arthur Point indicate that the test has little predictive validity; the correlations with Stanford-Binet were somewhat higher.

In her book *Mental Testing* Goodenough had this to say about the various infant tests. "None of these has shown an appreciable relationship to later mental standing for children tested before the age of 12 months. For tests given between the ages of 12 to 18 months, the correlations with the Stanford-Binet tests given to the same children at 3 years or older have generally been significantly positive but low, ranging from about .35 to .65" (1949, p. 310). Commenting about infant testing in his *Essentials of Psychological Testing*, Cronbach states: "Since tasks cannot be set for the child much below the age of 2, there is little hope of predicting the IQ from tests of infancy" (1960, p. 210).

The Scales of Infant Development by Nancy Bayley has just been made available by the Psychological Corporation. Bayley constructed these scales to measure the mental and motor development of infants and children whose age range is from two to thirty months. The scales yield both a Mental Development Index and a Psychomotor Development Index. According to Anastasi (1968) the new scales represent a revision of the California First-Year Mental Scale which Bayley developed in 1933 for use in the early stages of the Berkeley Growth Study. Of particular interest are Anastasi's comments regarding the predictive validity of Bayley's scale relative to her own longitudinal study and others: "In Bayley's longitudinal study with the California First-Year Mental Scale, correlations between tests administered under the age of one year and retests at 18 months were close to zero. . . . With subsequent retests, negative correlations as high as − .21 were obtained" (1968, p. 264). In a similar vein she further notes that the Cattell scale "had virtually no validity in predicting the 3-year Stanford-Binet IQ." She concludes that "pre-school tests have moderate validity in predicting subsequent intelligence test performance, but . . . infant tests have virtually none."

Two scales that enjoy a good reputation in England are the Griffiths Mental Development Scale (1954) and the Valentine Intelligence Tests for Children (1963). The Griffiths scale utilizes tasks involving the measurement of locomotion, personal-social, hearing-speech, hand-eye, and performance developments during the first two years. The Valentine, which combines items from many other well-known scales, is preferred as a preschool test, but it may be administered to persons ranging in age from eighteen months to fifteen years.

The low correlations between infant tests and subsequent tests of general intelligence may be variously interpreted. One interpretation suggests development is not concomitant with intellectual development. Another theorizes that we simply have yet to develop the right tools or approaches for assessing infant mentation. Both Bayley (1955) and Stott and Ball (1965) offer an explanation that implies that infant intelligence is qualitatively different from intelligence among school children— perhaps because of the greater impact of the sociocultural environment on the latter group. After surveying the broad scope of infant testing Stott and Ball conclude that "perhaps one of the reasons for the lack of 'predictive validity' of infant tests is that babies, as a result of wide variations in environmental stimulation, acquire varying degrees of ability within the limits of their developed capacity; tests measure the *acquisition* of the abilities rather than the capacity" (1965, p. 138).

Although these low correlations suggest that projecting future intelligence scores on the basis of infant test scores alone may be an exercise in futility, experimental and clinical findings by Escalona (1948) indicate that prediction is much improved when the testing is supplemented by other clinical data— specifically observations and personal histories of the infants. Using the Gesell Developmental Schedules and Cattell and Stanford-Binet tests Escalona found that test-retest scores were

higher (68 percent agreement) under "optimal" conditions than under nonoptimal conditions (19 percent agreement). Whether conditions were optimal and nonoptimal was a judgmental "field theory" decision based on the interaction between the clinical observations and the psychometric data (Escalona 1950). In a later study Escalona and Moriarty (1961) explored this area further with fifty-eight normal children who, between their third and thirty-third week received Cattell IQs, Gesell DQs, and a "clinical appraisal" "based on total test performance." These subjects were retested between ages six and nine, most of them on the Wechsler Intelligence Scale for Children. The researchers found practically no correlation between the two batteries of tests when their predictions were based on tests taken prior to twenty weeks of age. When the initial battery of tests was taken after twenty weeks, the correlations were low but positive (around .20). Results were much improved when the clinical appraisal based on the overall performance on both preschool tests was stated as a classification (low average, average, high average, or superior) rather than an actual IQ or DQ score. The correlations were even higher when the group was split into only two categories, namely, average (90–114 IQ) and superior (115 IQ or higher). On this basis 79 percent of the subjects who were past twenty weeks of age on initial testing remained in the same category on the retest six to nine years later. What should not be overlooked is that these tests may be very helpful in diagnosing and evaluating certain specific pathologies as well as general defects of development (Knobloch & Pasamanick 1960). The most recent of the preschool scales, the Wechsler Preschool and Primary Scale of Intelligence (WPPSI), is discussed as part of the Wechsler series of tests.

The Vineland Social Maturity Scale (Doll 1965) is a very broad spectrum scale that covers year-to-year development of eight functions related to activities of daily living, such as general self-help, self-help in eating and dressing, locomotion, communication, working, socializing, and self-direction from birth to adulthood. In this scale there are no formal tests at all, the evaluation information being obtained from observation and interviews. The scale yields a Social Age (SA) and Social Quotient (SQ). Correlations with Stanford-Binet scores are generally low, indicating that social maturity development is independent of general intelligence. The scale has clinical value in helping to confirm diagnoses of mental retardation on the basis of consistencies between low social maturation levels and psychometrically low IQs. The scale may also be of assistance in helping to determine how much care a retarded child will need.

With regard to infant and preschool tests in general, it is recommended that when important decisions about a child are contingent upon his intelligence classification, as in cases of adoption or placement, he should be tested several times at reasonably spaced periods, such as three- to six- month intervals.

The Wechsler Scales: W-B/WAIS

The next step in the development of individual intelligence tests was to design one scale that combined the most desirable features of both verbal and performance tests. This was accomplished by David Wechsler in his series of intelligence scales. Although this feature was initially introduced in Wechsler's test for adults, the idea of combining verbal and nonverbal components as well as other clinical features has since been carried over to his nonadult scales as well. The similarities in the organization as well as the overlap of the functions have the effect of welding Wechsler's three separate scales into a continuum that starts at age four and continues through the entire life-span.

The first of Wechsler's series was his test of adult intelligence, known originally as the Wechsler-Bellevue Intelligence Scale (Wechsler 1939). The scale evolved from the author's recognition of the need for a special test for adults that would answer the criticisms of the Stanford-Binet. Making full use of clinical and psychometric sophistication, Wechsler developed a series of tests not anchored to the mental age structure of the Stanford-Binet scales that proved to be more stimulating empirically. Most of the test items had not been standardized on adults. The scale also reflected Wechsler's criticism of the use of speed tests on the Stanford-Binet, which he believed handicapped older subjects unduly.

One of the key attributes of Wechsler's scales is their lack of dependence on the traditional IQ concept to evaluate general intelligence. Having been trained in Spearman's laboratory, Wechsler was influenced by Spearman's two-factor theory. His scale reflected this concept in that in addition to obtaining a *general* intelligence score (*g* factor) the examiner was able to assess *specific* functions (*s* factors) as well. The original Wechsler-Bellevue scale contained eleven subtests that yielded three IQs—Verbal IQ based on six verbal subtests, a Performance IQ based on five nonverbal tests, and a Full Scale or overall IQ. Each of the eleven subtests was designed to measure a specific facet of intelligence. Conscious of the high verbal emphasis of the Stanford-Binet, Wechsler devised a performance section so that persons with language handicaps could be evaluated mainly on the basis of the performance tasks (concomitantly, those with visual or motor disabilities could be evaluated primarily on the basis of the verbal tests). Wechsler's own personal experience with cultural deprivation contributed toward making his scale's performance section one of the earliest culture-fair tests.

Wechsler's clinical experience contributed to the development and organization of subtests that successfully tapped vital clinical functions such as memory, judgment, and planning ability. The test was so constructed that these special abilities could be compared with one another. Moreover, Wechsler's testing acumen enabled him to create questions that served the dual function of challenging the adult while at the same time revealing important clinical data. He recognized that nonintellective qualities, such as personality needs and conflicts, were so intertwined with intellective ones that the test might yield clinical hypotheses about the subject's personality in addition to mere raw scores.

Although the subtests contain different numbers of items, intertest comparisons are possible because the raw scores are transmuted to standard scores with a mean of 10 and a standard deviation of 3 for each subtest. The fact that each subtest contributes equal weight to the overall IQ permits the examiner to prorate for a subtest that was not given. This feature has been used to justify abbreviated versons of the scale. Also the fact that each subtest progresses from simple items to increasingly difficult ones makes clinical intertest analyses easier to conduct; that is, one may predict a subject's success with difficult items on the basis of his performance with easier ones. In addition, intertest comparisons may be used in clinical diagnosis to study patterns of dysfunction.

Wechsler considered the usual formula for IQ inappropriate in testing adults. As an alternative he introduced the revolutionary concept of the *deviation IQ*, in which all of the scores within each age group were scaled within the group itself. The mean for each group was transposed into a standard IQ score of 100 with a standard deviation of 15. In this technique each raw score is converted into a scaled score. The verbal scaled score, the performance scaled score, and both together are used to locate the subject's IQ in the tables for his age group. This technique permitted IQs to be obtained for persons aged anywhere from ten to sixty. For persons over sixty, extrapolation techniques were recommended.

The Wechsler-Bellevue was an instant success, as may be judged from the many commentaries and foreign translations that it has inspired. That the test is reasonably culture-fair is evidenced by the varity of modifications in its foreign adaptations. An alternate form of the Wechsler-Bellevue was published in 1946 as Form II of the test. This form was used mainly for retest purposes. Its standardization population consisted of males aged eighteen to forty, mainly armed forces personnel. The only difference between the two forms, according to Wechsler's statement in the manual (Wechsler 1946), is that "the Comprehension test is a little harder and the Object Assembly a little easier"; otherwise, the mean difference between Full Scale retest scores is less than 2 points and the subtest differences are similarly insignificant.

The name of the test has been changed in its most recent revision (Wechsler 1955) to Wechsler Adult Intelligence Scale (WAIS). Though similar in form and content to the "W-B," the WAIS has almost entirely supplanted the original because of its greater contemporareity and psychometric efficiency. It covers persons aged sixteen to seventy-five. A manual accompanies the test (Wechsler 1955), but Wechsler's new edition of his book on adult intelligence (Wechsler 1958) provides even more data on the tests. Much of the book is devoted to comparing WB-1 and WAIS as well as presenting extensive clinical and diagnostic findings. The WAIS, like its predecessor, yields Verbal, Performance, and Full Scale deviation IQs.

The six WAIS verbal subtests each attempt to measure something different. (1) The Information test taps a person's general knowledge by means of twenty-nine questions, ranging from easy ones like "What are the colors in the American flag?" and "What does rubber come from?" to moderately difficult ones like "Why are dark clothes warmer than light-colored clothes?" and on to the most difficult ones like "What is the Apocrypha?" (2) The Comprehension test measures judgment or common sense with fourteen questions ranging from "Why do we wash clothes?" to the interpretation of proverbs. Each items is scored 0, 1, or 2 depending upon the degree of understanding demonstrated, as typified by sample responses in the manual. (3) The Arithmetic test consists of fourteen items requiring arithmetic reasoning and alertness. The calculations are done mentally, and the problems proceed from simple computation to more complex exercises. (4) The Similarities test measures abstract and concrete thinking by asking the subject to specify what way a pair of items is alike, beginning with orange and banana and ending with fly and tree. The scoring of the thirteen items, by means of sample criteria and typical answers, ranges from 0 for a wrong answer to 1 for a typically concrete reponse to 2 for the more abstract response. (5) The Digit Span test measures the subject's ability to remember digits both forward and backward. (6) The Vocabulary test calls for definitions of a list of forty words progressing in difficulty from "bed" and "ship" to "hasten" and "sentence" and thence to "impale" and "travesty." The scoring (0, 1, or 2) is based on specified criteria.

The five performance tests similarly cover different areas. (1) The Digit Symbol test measures visual-motor coordination as well as speed of new learning by asking the subject to substitute symbols for the numbers they are associated with. The test results depend upon the subject's speed and accuracy since the scoring is based on the number of symbols he substitutes correctly within a ninety-second time limit. While a speed test of this kind doubtless handicaps older subjects, its main significance is in clinically detecting individuals who have difficulty in overall visual-motor coordination, such as brain-damaged subjects who become stimulus-bound and thus have difficulty shifting sets rapidly or those who become readily confused because of emotional disturbance. (2) In the Picture Completion test the subject states what important part is missing in each of twenty-one pictures depicting common settings or scenes, and here again the first few are much easier to detect than the last ones. In essence, this test of perceptual and conceptual sensitivity assesses the subject's awareness of his environment, and his ability to differentiate essential from nonessential details. This sense of awareness in a broader sense comprehends the ability to adapt to the existing world or environment. (3) The Block Design section measures the subject's ability to perceive, analyze, and integrate forms by putting together from four to nine multi-colored blocks according to specified designs. The subject's approach to each task yields much useful information about his personality and his methods of reasoning—i.e., whether he is impulsive or deliberate, whether he perceives fragments or "gestalts" (configurational wholes) more clearly, how he reacts to frustration, his degree of persistence and autocriticality, and so on. (4) The Picture Arrangement test consists of eight sets of cards, each presented in disarranged order and requiring rearrangement to tell a story, as in comic strips. The test measures the subject's ability to size up a total situation—his "social intelligence." On this test the examiner may obtain additional useful information by asking the subject to explain his chosen sequence, especially when the order of cards is unusual. (5) The Object Assembly test consists of four parts. Each part presents pieces of a common object that may be reassembled correctly. This type of form-board test measures the subject's ability to assemble discrete parts into meaningful wholes, which in turn reveals information about his perceptual style and his understanding of part-whole relationships.

The standardization of the WAIS was a model one, being based on a nationwide sample of 1700 adults aged sixteen to sixty-four chosen carefully in accordance with 1950 census data and including a proportionate number of nonwhites. The validity of the scale has been confirmed in several ways. The WAIS manual (1955, p. 21) revealed coefficients of correlation with Form L of the Stanford-Binet as .85 Full Scale, .86 Verbal, and .69 Performance. Wechsler (1955, p. 105) also believed that his scale was valid because he obtained significant IQ differences among certain educational and occupational groups. Reliability coefficients based on odd-even correlations for three age groups range from a low of .66 on Picture Arrangement and .68 on

Object Assembly to the area of .94–.99 for Full Scale, Verbal, and Performance IQs as well as for certain subtests like Vocabulary and Information.

Intertest correlations for three age groups are shown in the manual. They range from .37 to .86, with most clustering in the .50–.69 area. The highest correlations with the Full Scale IQ are for Information and Vocabulary, whereas the lowest correlations are for Object Assembly and Digit Span.

The calculation of adult norms for different age levels has made available valuable data about the growth and decline of intelligence. Contrary to former belief, which was based on Binet's view that intellectual growth reaches a plateau at age fifteen, Wechsler's findings have shown that intelligence continues to grow into the twenties and thirties. This period of growth is generally followed by a period of leveling-off or slow decline to about age sixty and a sharper decline thereafter. For well-learned functions, like vocabulary, the decline is negligible. The stability of the Vocabulary test plus the fact that it usually correlates highest with general intelligence makes it clinically useful as an index of intellectual potential. Results on the performance subtests decline at an earlier age and more rapidly.

In his book, *The Measurement and Appraisal of Adult Intelligence*, Wechsler (1958) has devoted an entire chapter to the factor-analytic studies of the W-B and the WAIS as well as the Wechsler Intelligence Scale for Children, which is described below. In almost all of these studies three main factors are present: "These are a broad verbal factor (verbal comprehension), a non-verbal organization factor (variously identified as performance, non-verbal, space and visual-motor organization) and *g* (sometimes referred to as the educative or general reasoning factor)" (p. 119).

Dr. Wechsler as well as many other clinical psychologists (Rapaport 1945 and Schafer 1948, among others) have used the Wechsler scales, especially the adult forms, as a psychodiagnostic tool in differential diagnosis. The relationships among the subtest scores are analyzed (this being known as "pattern analysis") for different diagnostic categories. This operation is based on a priori clinical reasoning that certain functions are interfered with under certain conditions. For example, the ability to absorb new knowledge or to think in abstract terms is diminished in brain-damaged subjects; similarly loss of judgment or loss of touch with reality is common among schizophrenics, and increased anxiety, which interferes with attention and concentration as measured by arithmetic reasoning and memory for digits, is common among neurotics. Wechsler and the others went beyond these observations to develop patterns among all the subtests for the most common conditions. Pattern analysis was based exclusively on psychometric patterns and did not utilize qualitative test information or other clinical data, such as the subject's behavior during testing or particularly pathognomonic or bizarre responses. Included in the clinical patterns was Wechsler's Mental Deterioration Index or Deterioration Quotient, which was based on the ratio of test scores that hold up despite structural brain pathology to those that do not.

In his chapter on "Diagnostic Use of Intelligence Tests" in Wolman's *Handbook of Clinical Psychology* Rabin (1965) reviews the extensive research on pattern analysis that Wechsler's claims stimulated and concludes that the findings are "contradictory and inconclusive." We should like to point out, however, that difficulties are inherent in research of this kind. In the first place, it is presumptuous to expect a single instrument alone, especially a test of intelligence, to serve as the basis for clinical diagnosis. This subject is a basic area of disagreement between psychometrician and clinician, as noted by Meehl (1954). Then, too, nosological categories overlap considerably and are not necessarily discrete. Disagreements over whether schizophrenia is a single disease or a more complex phenomenon, for example, further complicate the issue. In addition, the extent to which physiological or drug therapy for a schizophrenic or neurotic patient may cause changes in the brain is not yet clear. Lastly, the term "brain damage" is not so simple as it seems at first glance; it is too general, often including subcortical disturbances as well as failing to distinguish the precise location and the kind and amount of interference. Morrow and Mark (1955), taking all these factors into consideration, compared the Wechsler-Bellevue and autopsy findings on twenty-two patients whose deaths resulted from brain damage with those for twenty-two matched psychiatric patients. They report the existence of a typical Wechsler pattern of structural brain pathology in which the Verbal IQ is significantly higher than the Performance IQ and the scores inordinately low in the Digit Symbol, Block Design, Digit Span (especially digits backward), Arithmetic, and Similarities subtests.[6] Clinical confirmation is evident in the following WAIS pattern for a 32-year-old college graduate whose right cerebral cortex was removed: Full Scale IQ 100, Verbal 117, Performance 78; Information 14, Comprehension 16, Arithmetic 8, Similarities 12, Digit Span 14 (9 forward, but only 5 backward), Vocabulary 14, Digit Symbol 4, Picture Completion 9, Block Design 5, Picture Arrangement 9, Object Assembly 5. He was retested after six months, achieving much the same results.

Wechsler contributed yet another insight by emphasizing the interconnection between personality characteristics and intellectual functioning that is frequently evident in qualitative analyses of responses. The questions lend themselves to personalized answers. Rabin in emphasizing the "projective" value of Wechsler's tests, states that "there developed a shift in emphasis in diagnostic testing from the psychometric instrument—the test—to the human instrument—the tester." We offer some illustrations of personality projection from our testing experiences. On Information subtest question "How tall is the average American woman?" one patient with a homosexual history whose Full Scale score placed him at high average intelligence replied, "About six feet tall; no, check that, I'm six feet so that the average woman must be six-two or -three." It is not uncommon on the Comprehension question "What is the thing to do if you find an envelope in the street that is sealed, and addressed, and has a new stamp?" to get idiosyncratic responses such as the typical psychopathic suggestion "I know the correct thing is to mail it, but I'd first check for money" or the paranoid thinking implicit in "I'd ignore it because someone is trying to trap me." The Comprehension questions "Why does the state require people to get a license in order to be married?" and "Why should people pay taxes?" frequently evoke replies indicating dissatisfaction, frustration, or failure. A highly intelligent college graduate who stuttered badly revealed his exhibitionistic tendencies when he was asked in the Comprehension subtest "What should you do if while in the movies you were the first person to see smoke

and fire?" He stuttered and stammered for what seemed a time long enough for the movie house to burn down completely while answering that he would go up on the stage and tell the people that there's a fire, not to panic, and to choose the nearest exit. These are but a few examples showing how nonintellective factors might influence cognitive functioning.

The Wechsler Scales: WISC

The need for a scale for children comparable to Wechsler's adult scale led to the construction of the Wechsler Intelligence Scale for Children (Wechsler 1949). The WISC taps the same functions as the WAIS; despite the overlap in materials, however, the tests are separate and independently standardized. The WISC covers ages five through fifteen, thereby extending the Wechsler battery down to preschool age. The scale consists of ten subtests, which, as in the W-B/WAIS, yield Full Scale, Verbal, and Performance IQs. The five Verbal tests are General Information, General Comprehension, Arithmetic, Similarities, and Vocabulary. The Digit Span is given as either a supplementary or alternative test. The Performance tests are Picture Completion, Picture Arrangement, Block Design, Object Assembly, and Coding, with the Maze test as supplementary or alternative.

The MA is not used,[7] the IQ scores being deviation IQs resulting from the comparison of scores among peers. The mean for each group is equivalent to 100 IQ, with a standard deviation of 15. The IQ is obtained from the tables for each age group and thus represents a person's relative intelligence rating within his own age group. As with the W-B/WAIS, subtest scores are converted in each case to standard or scaled scores with a mean of 10 and a standard deviation of 3. Intertest correlations and split-half reliabilities are satisfactory but not as high as on the WAIS.

In a study of 332 New York City school children Krugman et al. (1951) correlated Stanford-Binet and WISC scores and calculated coefficients of .82 for Full Scale, .74 for Verbal, and .64 for Performance. The mean IQs for this group were Stanford-Binet 108, WISC Full Scale 101, Verbal 103, and Performance 98. The discrepancy in favor of the Binet was greater for brighter and younger subjects. For example, for WISC IQs above 130, Stanford-Binet IQs were on the average 19 points higher. For the least bright, the WISC more frequently yielded a higher mean IQ than the Binet.

The Wechsler Scales: WPPSI

The third scale in the series, the Wechsler Preschool and Primary Scale of Intelligence (Wechsler 1967), covers ages four to 6½. Though similar to the WISC in form and content, the WPPSI is a distinctively separate test. While the intellectual process is continuous and amenable to testing at different ages, the need for special assessment at critical periods, such as the preschool stage, makes the WPPSI an integral part of a viable process. Wechsler claims that the main difference between his scale and other preschool tests is that we are able to discern

---

[6] We are in the process of replicating this study with patients autopsied since 1955 who had been given the WAIS. On the basis of our initial findings the same pattern appears to prevail.

[7] Although Wechsler is critical of the concept of MA, he has nevertheless worked out a system of obtaining the MA from the scores on his scales (Wechsler 1951).

in his a "metric of moreness or lessness" rather than the mere presence or absence of correct answers, which the others measure.

Unlike the WISC, the WPPSI is administered with the verbal and performance tests intermixed in order to hold interest. Eight of its eleven subtests are borrowed directly from the WISC. The three that are new are Animal House, Geometric Design, and Sentences, which is a supplementary subtest. These tests tap abilities contributing to early school performance more successfully than the four they replaced (Digit Span, Picture Arrangement, Object Assembly, and Coding). In this scale, too, the scores are presented as deviation IQs, and in the manual there is a table for converting scores into MA equivalents. The IQ equivalents on all three Wechsler scales range from about 45 to 155, with the 2 percent at 130 and higher labeled "very superior" and the 2 percent below 70 designated "mental defective."

Almost everything we said about the adult scales respecting personality clues, diagnostic possibilities, and culture-fair features applies equally to the WPPSI. What is of major importance is that these tests measure different abilities as well as global intelligence so that one may see how and to what extent the child's assets and shortcomings may influence his overall functioning.

Group Intelligence Tests

Group tests of intelligence are used much more extensively than individual tests. They are valuable and economical because many people can be tested at one time. The examiner does not need special skills in administration, scoring, or evaluation. As a matter of fact, machine scoring nowadays takes care of most of his functions. A matter of importance, frequently overlooked, is that group testing gives information about how an individual functions within a peer setting, in contrast to the one-to-one confrontation of individual testing. Some individuals perform better in group competition or in the protective anonymity of the group while others need the stimulation and encouragement of the tester, which is lacking in the group setting. For children, the group examination more typically approximates the classroom situation than does the individual test.

By the time the United States entered World War I in 1917, two perceptions about testing had gained widespread acceptance. The first was the common agreement on the usefulness and legitimacy of intelligence tests; the second was the obvious need for testing programs that could be administered to many subjects at a time. A committee of American psychologists under R.M. Yerkes responded to the military need and developed first the Army Alpha and then the nonverbal Army Beta (Yoakum & Yerkes 1920; Yerkes 1921) as group intelligence tests.

Whereas individual testing was first developed for children in response to an educational need and the children's ready availability in schools, the earliest group tests were developed for adults because of the military need and the ready availability of an ideally large population for standardization. The immediate success of the Army tests served to stimulate further group testing that later progressed beyond intelligence testing. Testimony to the effectiveness of both Army Alpha and Beta may be seen in the fact that updated versions of these tests are still in wide use.

The Army Alpha was an attempt to measure for group members what the Stanford-Binet measured for the individual; that is, it yielded a single score based on eight empirically determined functions, such as following directions, arithmetic reasoning, general information, vocabulary, and analogies. The current form, Alpha Examination, Modified Form 9, now yields Numerical and Verbal ability subscores in addition to the total score. The Beta examination was created for use with those who had language handicaps, e.g., foreigners and illiterates, primarily. It contained six subtests, each requiring little verbal knowledge, and could even be administered in pantomime. Some of the tests attempted to adapt Stanford-Binet items, such as picture completion and absurdities, to group test use; others represented the adaptation of performance scale items, such as mazes and form boards, to group paper-pencil use. The present Beta revision utilizes the scoring procedure devised by Wechsler for his scales; the examiner converts raw scores into a profile of weighted scores and converts the total weighted score into a deviation IQ (called Beta IQ) from tables for the subject's own age group.

The success of the Army tests resulted in a proliferation of postwar civilian editions and new tests and eventually the creation of a thriving industry devoted to intelligence testing. Group testing has been employed most widely in secondary schools and colleges, where the tests have been helpful in evaluation, placement, and prediction. Widespread utilization of these tests led to further developments and refinements, such as the construction of multilevel batteries that comprise a series of overlapping tests covering the entire educational process from kindergarten through college. The overall single score gave way to separate scores and factor-analyzed group or unit scores. Individual descriptions of some of the more wisely used tests follow.

Among the oldest of the multilevel tests still in current use are the Kuhlmann-Anderson Intelligence Tests and the Otis Quick Scoring Mental Ability Tests. Each has been revised several times. The Kuhlmann-Anderson (published by Personnel Press of Princeton, N. J.) covers kindergarten through high school years, with separate tests for each grade through grade 6, one for 7–8, and another for 9–12. Each test consists of several timed subtests, such as understanding and following directions, counting and number series, and opposites and similarities, from which a single IQ is obtained. From the fourth grade on, one may compute verbal, quantitative, and full-test IQs. The Otis scales consist of Form Alpha for grades 1–4, which requires no reading, and Forms Beta for grades 4–9 and Gamma for grades 9–16. The single overall IQ is effective in predicting school achievement. The first form of the Otis was published in 1920 by the World Book Company, which also published several revisions. The latest version has been adapted by Lennon for Harcourt Brace Jovanovich.

Others tests have been created for one special reason or another. The Lorge-Thorndike Intelligence Tests (published by Houghton Mifflin) range from kindergarten to college freshman levels and include an adult form as well. In the kindergarten–grade 1 and grade 2–3 forms questions are read by an examiner, and the pupils respond by making pictures. From grade 4 on (i.e., in the forms for grades 4–6, 7–9, and 9–13 as well as the form for adults) separate verbal and nonverbal tests are available. The Henmon-Nelson Tests of Mental Ability (published by Houghton Mifflin) date back to 1931 and presently cover grades 3–6, 6–9, 9–12 and 13–17. The test emphasizes verbal skills and yields only a single score. At the college level the score is given in percentile ranks instead of deviation IQs, as in the other forms. The Henmon-Nelson is a typical "spiral-omnibus" test in which different problems, analogies, and tasks are rotated in increasing difficulty; this type of test is in contrast to the "omnibus" examination (e.g., the Kuhlmann-Anderson), which tests specific abilities and then combines the subscores into an overall total. In contrast to both types is the so-called homogeneous test, which measures intelligence by means of a single function only (e.g., the Porteus Maze Test, the Raven Progressive Matrices Test, and the Miller Analogies Test).

Science Research Associates has published two sets of tests, the Tests of Educational Ability (TEA) for grades 4–6, 6–9, and 9–12 and the Short Test of Educational Ability (STEA) for kindergarten–grade 1, and grades 2–3, 7–8, and 9–12. The tests measure three subject areas that bear directly on scholastic aptitude, namely, language and quantitative and reasoning skills. These subtest scores and a total score may be converted to IQs. McNemar has revised a test that has enjoyed a good reputation, the Terman Group Intelligence Test, as the Terman-McNemar Test of Mental Ability (published by Harcourt, Brace & World) for grades 7–12. It stresses verbal skills and yields a single IQ.

The Pintner General Ability Tests (published by Harcourt Brace Jovanovich) includes both a verbal and a nonlanguage series, the latter being used frequently by children with hearing and reading difficulties. The Chicago Non-Verbal Examination (published by the Psychological Corporation) has been standardized for both verbal and pantomime directions, with separate norms for each. It may be used in testing anyone from age six to the adult level who is handicapped in English language usage, including deaf people.

One of the most widely used nonverbal tests is the Raven Progressive Matrices Test (distributed by the Psychological Corporation). This is a homogeneous test in that only the two-dimensional analogies are used as an index of intelligence. The test measures problem-solving ability through the use of figures that are altered from left to right according to an unstated but deducible principle. The subject selects the design that completes the pattern. Norms are for established English children and adults, including mental defectives. This description applies mainly to the 1938 and 1947 forms, both of which are untimed. The 1962 form is more abstract and was designed for intellectually above-average adolescents and adults. A so-called culture-free test, it was effective in Great Britain during World War II for selection and placement of military personnel, but, more important, Cronbach (1960) shows its applicability in testing backward groups such as largely uneducated African tribes (p. 217). Hall (1957), using patients in a U.S. veterans hospital who were neither brain-damaged nor psychotic, found that the Raven Progressive Matrices correlated .721 with the Full Scale Wechsler Adult Intelligence Scale IQ, .705 with the Performance IQ, and .584 with the Verbal IQ. Block Design showed the highest subtest correlation of .642.

The Raven Progressive Matrices Test was developed under the strong influence of Spearman's two-factor theory. It is heavily saturated with the g (general ability) factor in that it contains many abstract reasoning problems, which are considered the best measure of g. A Vocabulary test is also available to accompany the Raven Matrices.

Science Research Associates publishes two nonverbal tests that are highly recommended. One is the SRA Non-Verbal Form, which tests for reasoning ability through the utilization of drawings and designs. The other is the SRA Tests of General Ability, which John Flanagan devised. The scores give both IQs and grade expectancies, although few school-learned skills are checked in the test. An important feature of this test is the availability of a Spanish Edition. The Psychological Corporation also has a verbal intelligence test in Spanish intended for use with Latin Americans called the Test Rapido Barranquilla or the Barranquilla Rapid Survey Intelligence Test (BARSIT). It contains both verbal and numerical problems and is recommended for third-graders on up to adults with elementary school education.

Intelligence tests have been constructed for school selection and placement purposes as well as for prediction of academic success. One of the earliest of these was the American Council Psychological Examination (ACE) by Thurstone and Thurstone, which dates back to 1924. It yielded Quantitative proficiency (Q) and Language proficiency (L) scores in addition to a total score. The Educational Testing Service has replaced the ACE with the improved Cooperative School and College Ability Tests (SCAT), which now extends from the fourth grade to the college level. A favorable feature of the SCAT is the conversion of scores into a *percentile band* rather than a single percentile. The percentile band covers one standard error of measurement on either side of the corresponding percentiles and thereby represents the score as a range or "confidence interval" within which the "true" score probably lies rather than as a single point that is variable and in reality is *never more than a relative measure.*

There are three college selection tests that are used for that purpose only. One is the American College Testing Program (ACT), which was devised by Lindquist and is used mainly in state universities. Its four parts consist of English Usage, Social Studies Reading, Math Usage, and Natural Science Reading. Another widely used test is the Scholastic Aptitude Test (SAT), which is published each year by the College Entrance Examination Board (CEEB). The test results are in the form of separate Verbal and Mathematics scores. A comparable shorter form called the Preliminary Scholastic Aptitude Test (PSAT) is also available. The third major test used for college selection is the College Qualification Tests (CQT) produced by the Psychological Corporation for high school and college students. There are three forms of the test; each form consists of three parts— the CQT-Verbal, CQT-Numerical, and CQT-Information; the last, in turn, yields a Science subscore and a Social Studies subscore in addition to the total CQT-Information score. A special form of this test (Form A) is not restricted to college selection uses and is available to qualified professionals for special testing and guidance purposes.

Three tests that graduate schools have found particularly useful are the Concept Mastery Test and the Miller Analogies Test (both distributed by the Psychological Corporation) and the Graduate Record Examination (GRE). The Concept Mastery Test is a reasoning test focusing on ideas and concepts through verbal problems involving either synonyms and antonyms or analogies. It is one of the few tests for college students that is not timed. The norms are percentile ranks for graduate students and college seniors applying for graduate fellowships as well as special professional and administrative types. The Miller Analogies Test consists of 100 very difficult verbal analogies based on the content of academic subjects. It has a high predictive validity for subsequent success in graduate school. The test is restricted to use solely by graduate schools. The most widely used test for graduate school selection is the Graduate Record Examination, which is given under the control of the Educational Testing Service. The GRE is made up of an intelligence test called the Aptitude Test as well numerous Advanced Tests, which are achievement tests in specific fields of interest. The GRE Aptitude Test scores are separated into Verbal and Quantitative components and given as standard scores with a mean of 500 and a standard deviation of 100.

Most group intelligence tests are timed or speed tests in which time is called at a prescribed point irrespective of the number of items completed. Tests that have time limits that allow the average subject to complete most items are not technically speed tests, but simply timed tests. Tests that have no time limit at all are called power tests. An example of a well-regarded college entrance power test is the Ohio State University Psychological Test (OSUPT). It is entirely verbal in content and commercially available to qualified professionals through Science Research Associates. As earlier noted, the Concept Mastery Test is also a power test. The relative advantages of speed versus power are well summarized by Cronbach:

When the criterion task does not demand speed or demands a type of speed not involved in the test, speeding the test introduces an irrelevant variable. For general academic criteria, a measure of power independent of speed is more relevant than a speeded score. With a long testing time, an unspeeded test is more valid than a speed test covering the same material. If only a short time is available for testing, however, a speeded test will be more reliable than an unspeeded test containing very few items. As a result, the short speeded test has greater predictive validity than the even briefer tests that everyone can finish in the same time (F.M. Lord, 1953). The trend in recent American tests is to provide ample time for nearly everyone to finish. This point of view is not universally accepted. Eysenck (1953) and Furneaux, in England, argue that the speed with which the mind produces hypotheses is the essence of good problem solving, and that a speeded test is therefore the best measure of mental ability.
[1960, pp. 222–23]

Because general intelligence tests have often been used for personnel selection, several tests have been specifically designed for this purpose. One of these is the Psychological Corporation's Personnel Test for Industry, which contains three short tests: PTI-Verbal (short vocabulary), PTI-Numerical (shop computing and measurement), and PTI-Oral (for language-handicapped subjects). At a higher level the Psychological Corporation offers the Wesman Personnel Classification Test. The Wonderlic Personnel Test is a twelve-minute test that has been used extensively. The California Test Bureau has developed two thirty-minute tests, the California Capacity Questionnaire and the Survey of Mental Maturity, for use in business and industrial personnel programs.

The special need for a group test of intelligence during the World War II period resulted in the creation of the Army General Classification Test (AGCT). It is a spiral-omnibus test containing an equal number of vocabulary, block-counting (estimating the number of blocks in a series of piles), and arithmetic items. The standardization population was greater than twelve million men. The single score is a transmuted standard score equivalent to the IQ, with a mean of 100 and a standard deviation of 20. A civilian version of the AGCT is available through Science Research Associates. At present the Armed Forces Qualification Test (AFQT) has replaced the AGCT. The AFQT is constantly revised from time to time, but in its original form it closely resembled the AGCT, except that spatial relations items replaced the block-counting exercises.

Factor-Analyzed Intelligence Tests

The existence of interrelationships and correlations among the various tests and subtests was mentioned earlier. This possibility suggested to Carl Spearman that there was something basic or common in all tests, leading him to distinguish between general and specific factors: "All branches of intellectual activity have in common one fundamental function (or group of functions) whereas the remaining or specific elements of the activity seem in every case to be wholly different from that in all the others" (Spearman 1904). According to this two-factor theory, as described in Spearman's classic book *The Abilities of Man* (1927), intelligence tests combine a factor of general intelligence (g), accounting for the usually positive relationships among tests, with factors describing specific abilities (s's); in other words, the s factors comprehend such specific abilities as word knowledge, verbal reasoning, number conceptualization, arithmetic ability, memory, and abstract thinking ability—and these in varying amounts contribute to the overall g. Functions that manifest a high positive correlation with overall intelligence scores (e.g., vocabulary), are considered to be more saturated with g than functions that have a low correlation with overall intelligence (e.g., visual-motor letter-cancelling tests). Spearman referred to overlapping specific factors as "group factors."

We have already described two tests that were influenced by the Spearman two-factor theory, namely, the entire series of Wechsler scales and the Raven Progressive Matrices. In the Wechsler scales g was represented in the overall or Full Scale IQ and the s's in the subtests. The Raven Progressive Matrices was constructed around the concept that abstract reasoning was the best measure of g.

The techniques of factor analysis developed from attempts to study these group factors, or clusters of highly intercorrelated groups of tests. In studying a correlation matrix the observer could discern that certain tests correlated more highly among themselves than with other tests, leading him to conclude that the highly correlated set of tests must be measuring like aspects of intelligence. Using the factor analysis technique he devised, Thurstone posited the theory that group or multiple factors were basic to intelligence testing rather than the single g. In his first important publication, *Vectors of Mind* (Thurstone 1935), Thurstone isolated three primary group factors on the basis of fifteen tests and identified these as Verbal, Numerical, and Visual Imagery factors. Subsequently Thurstone increased the number of factors to six based on fifty-six tests (Thurstone 1938), and later to seven, based on sixty group intelligence tests (Thurstone & Thurstone 1941; Thurstone 1947).

Thurstone identified the primary factors as V (verbal meaning) in vocabulary exercises and disarranged sentences, W (word fluency) in anagrams and word naming, N (number ability) in computations, M (memory) in rote learning, S (spatial relations) in forms and designs, P (perceptual speed) in visual similarities and differences, and R (reasoning ability) in induction exercises and syllogisms. The Thurstones utilized these factors in constructing the Chicago Tests of Primary Mental Abilities (published by Science Research Associates) and its subsequent revisions. The revised version is given at five levels from kindergarten through twelfth grade. Each battery yields a total intelligence score as well as four or five primary factor scores, as described above. The California Test Bureau publishes the California Test of Mental Maturity for various grade levels, which, in addition to Language, Non-language and Total scores, also features factor scores for Logical Reasoning, Spatial Relations, Numerical Reasoning, Verbal Concepts, and Memory. A short form of the test gives somewhat similar scores.[8]

The existence of these group factors does not rule out the presence of a general factor since the intercorrelations among the primary factors are usually positive and they all show rather high correlations with g (Bischof 1954). Moreover, Morrow (1941), in a factor-analytic study of intelligence and aptitude tests, reported finding a basic integrating factor that appears to transpose ability into a meaningful entity. Vernon (1960, 1965) has formulated a hierarchical model of factors with g at the top level followed by two broad group factors labeled Verbal-Educational and Practical-Mechanical. These group factors are further subdivided into minor group factors such as Verbal, Number, Spatial, and Manual, and at the fourth or lowest level the specific factors are enumerated.

J. P. Guilford (1959, 1967) has spent many years attempting to discover the structure of cognitive functioning through the technique of factor analysis. He has isolated 120 specific and group factors that are interrelated in his three-dimensional "Structure of Intellect" model. "Each dimension represents one of the modes of variation of the factors" (1959, p. 471). One dimension of his cube is called Operations, which covers the kinds of processes or operations performed or what the respondent actually does. The five possible operations are Evaluation, Convergent Thinking, Divergent Thinking, Memory, and Cognition. Along the second dimension are Contents, i.e., the specification of the material or information on which operations are being performed. The four kinds of Contest are Figural, Symbolic, Semantic, and Behavioral. The third dimension defines the Products that result when a certain operation is applied to a certain kind of content. This dimension describes the form in which information occurs or is conceived by the respondent. According to Guilford, "There is enough evidence available to suggest that, regardless of the combinations of operations and content, the same six kinds of products may be found associated" (1959, p. 470). The six fundamental kinds of products "into which one might fit all kinds of information psychologically" are Units, Classes, Relations, Systems, Transformations, and Implications. This three-dimensional relationship results in a matrix of 120 cells ($5 \times 4 \times 6$), each containing at least one factor. Thus, each factor is described in terms of its three dimensions, and attempts are being made to develop tests for each homogeneous cell. About fifty of these cells have already been matched with tests.

The important question remains whether the best evaluation of intellect requires such refined specificity, as advocated by Guilford, or whether it can be understood better in terms of a more simplistic, holistic conceptualization, as advocated by Cattell, Vernon, and Wechsler.

[8] A desirable feature of these California tests is the availability at all levels of special Pre-Tests of Vision, Hearing, and Motor Coordination to identify those for whom group tests may not be valid.

Culture-Fair Intelligence Tests

For many years psychologists, cognizant of the fact that environmental conditions influence intelligence test results, sought to develop tests that would be relatively independent of cultural influence, calling these culture-free tests. At length, recognizing that while cultural influence might be reduced it certainly could not be eliminated completely, psychologists came to prefer the term "culture-fair" to "culture-free." In essence what has happened all along is that socioculturally deprived minority groups have been consistently handicapped on tests in which they were not proportionately represented in the standardization population and on tests stressing language facility and reading ability. Many of the performance and nonverbal group tests discussed earlier were intended to be culture-free or -fair. The critical need for culture-fair tests was highlighted several years ago when the New York City Board of Education abandoned the use of group intelligence tests in its schools because of their imputed unfairness to large numbers of disadvantaged pupils, substituting group achievement tests in their place.

We are unable to review here the growing literature on cross-cultural and socioanthropological aspects of intelligence testing. We can, however, discuss some of the culture-fair tests currently in use.

The Progressive Matrices Test by Raven has been widely debated as a culture-fair instrument. Those who regard it as culture-fair note that it is nonverbal and has been used in different parts of the world. As one would expect, it is not entirely culture-free since the results have been shown to be influenced by environmental factors such as the quantity and quality of education and practice in relevant skills.

A test that is received more favorably for this purpose is R. B. Cattell's Culture-Fair Intelligence Test. It is published by the Institute for Personality and Ability Testing (IPAT), and from its inception in 1933 through the many revisions to date this group test has focused on using items that are considered reasonably free of cultural influences. It relies mostly on nonverbal and nonreading tasks for content and comes in three forms for different age groups; the first covers those aged four to eight and retardates, the second those aged eight to thirteen and average adults, and the third high school and college subjects and superior adults. Actually only four of the eight subtests fall into the culture-fair category and by themselves represent an abbreviated culture-fair scale. These are the Series Completion, Matrices, Classification, and Conditions subtests, most of which involve reasoning through the use of designs.

Cattell has been strongly influenced by the two-factor theory of Spearman and has developed his test on this basis. In his factor-analytic research Cattell (1963) has isolated two gs rather than one. One he calls g_c or Crystallized General Ability, which is highly verbal and acquired by cultural experience; it also includes numerical skills, memory, and mechanical knowledge. The other he calls g_f or Fluid Ability, which is more evident in culturally fair perceptual and performance tests involving spatial judgment and inductive reasoning.

In essence Cattell, through factor analysis, seems to support the empirically-clinically determined rationale of the Wechsler scales, since, with minor exceptions, his g_c is akin to Wechsler's Verbal Component and his g_f to Wechsler's Performance element. What is more important, however, is that—so far as intelligence tests and culture are concerned—no test can be completely independent of educational and other environmental factors until all societies become homogeneous in every way. Short of that millennium, we will have to either devise an infinite variety of tests for different cultural and subcultural groups or settle for the more feasible alternative of utilizing reasonably fair tests. Of course, a test that gives only a single IQ score for underprivileged subjects is inevitably inadequate because it fails to give the individual the analysis he needs of his relative capabilities and limitations on verbal-cultural functions as opposed to nonverbal-cultural functions.

Summary Analysis and Future Trends

Looking back at the development of intelligence testing, we can see that it did not develop in topsy-turvy fashion with no semblance of cause or direction, as some critics of testing techniques maintain. Rather, for the most part a definable clinical or scientific rationale has brought it to its present state. As Wechsler and other investigators have shown, both empirical-clinical and scientific-psychometric approaches are contributing to coherent theory and improved techniques for measuring intelligence. Theory may differ regarding the complex structure of intelligence, but the differences now focus less on the number and identification of significant factors than on how best to measure and understand them. The likelihood for the future is that by utilizing several scores in place of composite scores examiners will be able to interpret intellectual functioning more adequately. Moreover, even the composite scores will have greater meaning to the subject because their constituent factors will be better defined and understood. Present trends in group testing will likely result eventually in a computerized psychometric arrangement of numerous scores into discrete patterns that have valuable clinical, educational, and commercial implications. In individual testing, similarly, clinical enrichment will likely result from increasingly rigorous qualitative analysis.

References

ANASTASI, A. *Psychological testing*, 3rd ed. New York: Macmillan, 1968.

ARTHUR, G. *A Point scale of performance tests: I. Clinical manual.* New York: The Commonwealth Fund, 1930.

—— *The Arthur adaptation of the Leiter International Performance Scale.* Washington, D. C.; Psychological Service Center Press, 1952.

BAYLEY, N. On the growth of intelligence. *American Psychologist*, 1955, *10*, 805–18.

BINET, A., and HENRI, V. La psychologie individuelle. *L'Année Psychologique*, 1896, *2*, 411–65.

BINET, A., and SIMON, T. Sur la necessité d'établir un diagnostic scientifique des etats inferieurs de l'intelligence. *L'Année Psychologique*, 1905, *11*, 163–90.

—— Application des méthodes nouvelles au diagnostic du niveau intellectuel chez des enfants normaux et anormaux d'hospice et d'ecole primaire. *L'Année Psychologique*, 1905, *11*, 245–66.

—— Le développement de l'intelligence chez les enfants. *L'Année Psychologique*, 1908, *14*, 1–94.

—— La mesure du développement de l'intelligence chez les jeunes enfants. *Bulletin de la Société Libre pour l'Etude Psychologique de l'Enfant*, 1911 (trans. by Clara Harrison Town, A method of measuring the development of the intelligence of young children, 1915).

BISCHOF, L. J. *Intelligence: statistical concepts of its nature.* Garden City, N. Y.: Doubleday, 1954. (This is a pamphlet in the Doubleday Papers in Psychology series which is now out of print).

BURGEMEISTER, B., BLUM, L. H., and LORGE, I. *Columbia Mental Maturity Scale.* N. Y.: Harcourt Brace Jovanovich, 1953.

CATTELL, J. M. Mental tests and measurements. *Mind*, 1890, *15*, 373–80.

CATTELL, P. *The measurement of intelligence of infants and young children.* N. Y.: Psychological Corporation, 1947.

CATTELL, R. B. Theory of fluid and crystallized intelligence: a critical experiment. *Journal of Educational Psychology*, 1963, *54*, 1–22.

CORNELL, E. L., and COXE, W. W. *Cornell-Coxe Performance Ability Scale: Manual of directions.* Yonkers, N. Y.: World Book Co., 1934.

CRONBACH, L. J. *Essentials of psychological testing*, 2d ed. N. Y.: Harper & Row, 1960.

DOLL, E. A. *Vineland Social Maturity Scale: manual of directions.* Rev. ed. Minneapolis: Educational Test Bureau (Now American Guidance Service), 1965.

ESCALONA, S. K. The predictive value of psychological tests in infancy: A report on clinical findings. *American Psychologist*, 1948, *3*, 281.

—— The use of infant tests for predictive purposes. *Bulletin of the Meninger Clinic*, 1950, *14*, 117–28.

——, and MORIARTY, A. Prediction of school age intelligence from infant tests. *Child Development*, 1961, *32*, 597–605.

ESQUIROL, J. E. D. *Des maladies mentales considerées sous les rapports médical, hygiénique, et médico-légal.* 2 vols. Paris: Baillière, 1838.

GALTON, F. *Inquiries into human faculty and its development.* London: Macmillan, 1883.

—— *Hereditary genius.* 2d ed. London: Macmillan, 1892.

GESELL, A., and Associates. *The first five years of life.* New York: Harper & Row, 1940.

GESELL, A., and AMATRUDA, C. *Developmental diagnosis.* New York: Harper & Row, 1949.

GOODENOUGH, F. L. *The measurement of intelligence by drawings.* Yonkers, N. Y.: World Book Co., 1926.

—— *Mental testing: its history, principles and applications.* New York: Holt, Rinehart & Winston, 1949.

——, and MAURER, K. M. The mental growth of children from two to fourteen years, a study of the predictive value of the Minnesota Preschool Scales. *Univ. Minnesota Institute Child Welfare Monographs. No. 19*, 1942.

——, and VAN WAGENEN, M. J. *Minnesota Preschool Scales.* Minneapolis: University of Minnesota Press, 1942.

GRIFFITHS, R. *The abilities of babies.* London: University of London Press, 1954.

GUILFORD, J. P. Three faces of intellect. *American Psychologist*, 1959, *14*, 469–79.

—— *The nature of human intelligence.* New York: McGraw-Hill, 1967.

HALL, J. Correlation of a modified form of Raven's Progressive Matrices (1938) with the Wechsler Adult Intelligence Scale. *Journal of Consulting Psychology*, 1957, *21*, 23–28.

HARRIS, D. B. *Children's drawings as measures of intellectual maturity: a revision and extension of the Goodenough Draw-A-Man Test.* New York: Harcourt Brace Jovanovich, 1963.

HEALY, W., and FERNALD, G. M. Tests for practical mental classification. *Psychological Monographs*, 1911, *13*, no. 2.

ITARD, J. M. G. *The wild boy of Aveyron.* 1801, trans. George and Muriel Humphrey. New York: Appleton-Century-Crofts, 1932.

KNOBLOCH, H., and PASSAMANICK, B. An evaluation of the consistency and predictive value of the 40 week Gesell Developmental Schedule. *Psychiatric Research Reports*, 1960, *13*, 10–41.

KNOX, H. A. A scale based on the work at Ellis Island for estimating mental defect. *Journal of the American Medical Association*, 1914, *62*, 741–47.

KOHS, S. C. *Intelligence measurement: a psychological and statistical study based upon the Block-Design Tests.* New York: Macmillan, 1923.

KRUGMAN, J. I., JUSTMAN, J., WRIGHTSTONE, J. W., and KRUGMAN, M. Pupil functioning on the Stanford-Binet and the Wechsler Intelligence Scale for Children. *Journal of Consulting Psychology*, 1951, *15*, 475–83.

KUHLMANN, F. A revision of the Binet-Simon system for measuring the intelligence of children. *Journal of Psycho-Asthenics, Monograph Supplement*, 1912, *1*, 1–41.

——— *Tests of mental development*. Minneapolis: Educational Test Bureau, 1939.

LEITER, R. G. *Leiter International Performance Scale*. Chicago: C. H. Stoelting Co., 1948.

MCNEMAR, Q. *The revision of the Stanford-Binet Scale: An analysis of the standardization data*. Boston: Houghton Mifflin, 1942.

MEEHL, P. E. *Clinical vs. statistical prediction: a theoretical analysis and a review of the evidence*. Minneapolis: Univ. of Minnesota Press, 1954.

MORROW, R. S. An experimental analysis of the theory of independent abilities. *Journal of Educational Psychology*, 1941, *32*, 495–512.

———, and MARK, J. The correlation of intelligence and neurological findings on twenty-two patients autopsied for brain damage. *Journal of Consulting Psychology*, 1955, *19*, 283–389.

PETERSON, J. *Early conceptions and tests of intelligence*. Yonkers, N. Y.: World Book Co., 1925.

PINTNER, R., and PATERSON, D. G. *A Scale of Performance Tests*. New York: Appleton-Century-Crofts, 1917.

PORTEUS, S. D. *Guide to Porteus Maze Test*. Vineland, N. J.: The Training School, 1924. (The 1965 manual *Porteus Maze Tests: Fifty years application* is sold by the Psychological Corporation in New York).

RABIN, A. I. Diagnostic use of intelligence tests. *In* B. B. Wolman (ed.) *Handbook of clinical psychology*. New York: McGraw-Hill, 1965, p. 477–97.

RAPAPORT, D. *Diagnostic psychological testing*, vol. 1. Chicago: Year Book Medical Publishers, 1945.

RICHARDS, T. W., and NELSON, V. L. Abilities of infants during the first eighteen months. *Journal of Genetic Psychology*, 1939, *55*, 299–318.

SCHAFER, R. *The clinical application of psychological tests*. New York: International Universities Press, 1948.

SEGUIN, E. *Idiocy: Its treatment by the physiological method*. (Reprinted from original ed. of 1866). New York: Bureau of Publications, Teachers College, Columbia University, 1907.

SPEARMAN, C. "General intelligence" objectively determined and measured. *American Journal of Psychology*, 1904, *15*, 201–93.

——— *The abilities of man*. New York: Macmillan, 1927.

STERN, W. *The psychological methods of testing intelligence* (trans. Whipple, 1914). Baltimore, Md: Warwick & York Inc., 1912.

STOTT, C. H., and BALL, R. S. Infant and preschool mental tests: Review and evaluation. *Monographs of the Society for Research in Child Development*, 1965, *30*, no. 3.

STUTSMAN, R. *Mental measurement of preschool children with a guide for the administration of the Merrill-Palmer Scale of Mental Tests*. Yonkers, N. Y.: World Book Co., 1931.

TATE, N. E. The influence of cultural factors on the Leiter International Performance Scale. *Journal of Abnormal and Social Psychology*, 1952, *47*, 497–501.

TERMAN, L. M. *The measurement of intelligence*. Boston: Houghton Mifflin, 1916.

———, and Merrill, M. A. *Measuring intelligence*. Boston: Houghton Mifflin, 1937.

——— *Stanford-Binet Intelligence Scale: Manual for the third revision, Form L-M*. Boston: Houghton Mifflin, 1960.

THURSTONE, L. L. *The vectors of mind: Multiple-factor analysis for the isolation of primary traits*. Chicago: University of Chicago Press, 1935.

——— Primary mental abilities. *Psychometric Monographs*, 1939, no. 1.

——— *Multiple-factor analysis*. Chicago: University of Chicago Press, 1947.

———, and THURSTONE, T. G. Factorial studies of intelligence. *Psychometric Monographs*, 1941, no. 2.

VALENTINE, C. W. *Valentine Intelligence Tests for Children*, 6th ed. New York: Barnes & Noble, 1963.

VERNON, P. E. *The structure of human abilities*. Rev. ed. London: Methuen, 1960.

——— Ability factors and environmental influences. *American Psychologist*, 1965, *20*, 723–33.

WECHSLER, D. *The measurement of adult intelligence*. Baltimore: Williams & Wilkins, 1939.

——— *The Wechsler-Bellevue Intelligence Scale, Form II*. New York: The Psychological Corporation, 1946.

——— *Manual for the Wechsler Intelligence Scale for Children*. N. Y.: Psychological Corporation, 1949.

——— Equivalent test and mental ages for the WISC. *Journal of Consulting Psychology*, 1951, *15*, 381–84.

——— *Manual for the Wechsler Adult Intelligence Scale*. New York: Psychological Corporation, 1955.

——— *The measurement and appraisal of adult intelligence*. (4th ed.) Baltimore: Williams & Wilkins, 1958.

——— *Manual for the Wechsler Preschool and Primary Scale of Intelligence*. New York: Psychological Corporation, 1967.

YERKES, R. M. ed. Psychological examining in the United States Army. *Memoirs of the National Academy of Sciences*, 1921, *15*.

YOAKUM, C., and YERKES, R. M. *Army mental tests*. New York: Holt, Rinehart & Winston, 1920.

Motivation and Emotion

"Motivation" has played an increasingly important role in psychological theories in this century. Motivational concepts and hypotheses have been integral parts of many theories of learning and of personality, and during the last three decades more special theories of motivation have been formulated. This production of theories has, of course, been connected with an increased amount of experimental activity, but, since the empirical research methods and results obtained in the field of motivation are dealt with in other chapters of this book, we may concentrate here on theories of motivation.

We have not used any formal criteria in selecting theories of motivation, but we have tried to study all psychological discourses which contain explanations of motivational phenomena or explanations of other phenomena based on motivational concepts. We shall leave the more formal properties of theories until the last part of this chapter.

In accordance with a pioneer in the field—P. Thomas Young —we shall start with a conception of motivation as a common term for "all determinants of behavior" (cf. the subtitle of Young's latest book, 1961). We shall thus postpone the presentation of a more precise definition until the second main part of this chapter. We have, therefore, selected from among all discourses those which contain explanatory terms like *motivation, motive, drive, need, instinct, force, incentive, valence*, etc., and we hope that we have succeeded in selecting those discourses which have influenced psychological research and theoretical development during the last three or four decades.

The reader who wants deeper or broader information about theories of motivation is referred to surveys which also have proved valuable sources for the present author: Atkinson (1964), Bolles (1967), Cofer and Appley (1964), Hilgard (1963), Kich (1959), Madsen (1959), Thomae (1965), and Young (1961), besides all the other books and papers listed in the bibliography. From this list we should especially like to mention the extremely valuable sourcebook: *Nebraska Symposium on Motivation*, edited annually by Marshall R. Jones since 1953 and more recently by David Levine.

K. B. Madsen

Theories of Motivation

33

We have decided not to present all the most important theories of motivation one by one, but instead to present the results of a comparative study of theories[1] of motivation under the following section headings:

1. Historical survey.
2. Concepts of motivation.
3. Categories of motivation.
4. Hypotheses of motivation.
5. Theories of motivation.

Historical Survey

INTRODUCTION

It has been said (by Ebbinghaus) of psychology—and it could have been said especially about the psychology of motivation—that "it has a long past but a short history." Motivational concepts and hypotheses have formed an important part of philosophy and psychology throughout their whole history since the time of the Greek philosophers. But the first book completely devoted to motivation appeared in 1936 (Young 1936), and the first textbooks—as well as bigger "Handbooks" —covering the field of motivational psychology have appeared only in the last decade. The first was written by another old pioneer in the field, R.S. Woodworth (1958). It was soon followed by others: Bindra (1959), Madsen (1959), Hall (1961), Brown (1961), Young (1961), Rethlingshafer (1963), Atkinson (1964), Cofer and Appley (1964), Thomae (1965), Bolles (1967) and several others. The first review-survey of the field appeared in "Annual Review of Psychology," 1952, and was written by O. H. Mowrer.

In the light of the space available to us in this survey we have chosen to deal with motivation in the history of experimental psychology and to leave out its roots in the history of philosophy. The reader is referred to other historical surveys which the present author has also found useful: Atkinson (1964), Bolles (1967), Cofer and Appler (1964), Misiak and Sexton (1966), Murphy (1949), Thomae (1965), Watson (1963), and Woodworth and Sheehan (1964). In my opinion the most extensive and profound historical treatment of motivational psychology to date is the one presented by Bolles (1967).

CLASSICAL PSYCHOLOGY

When psychology was born as an independent science it was as a result of "cross-breeding" between philosophy and experimental physiology. In this "classical" experimental psychology—created by Fechner, Wund, Ebbinghaus and other German psychologists—there was no room or use for motivational concepts or hypotheses. Possible reasons for this historical fact are that the classical experimental psychologists concentrated exclusively on cognitive processes–especially sensation and perception. In addition, the classical experimental

---

[1] The comparative study of theories constitutes a special meta-scientific discipline, which the present author suggests calling "systematology" (Madsen 1968 and the introductory chapters of Madsen forthcoming).

psychologists employed exclusively the introspective method, which later psychologists have demonstrated to be a rather fruitless procedure. It is also possible that a German *Zeitund Ortgeist* contributed to the lack of motivational concepts and hypotheses in classical experimental psychology. There was in any event quite another trend developing at the same time in the Anglo-Saxon countries.

THE PSYCHOLOGY OF INSTINCT

While experimental psychology was developing in Germany a more significant scientific revolution was launched in England with the publication of Darwin's *The Origin of Species* (1859), a book which influenced psychology profoundly. Darwin's theory of biological evolution made it possible to explain human behavior by the application of the same principles which had long been used in explaining animal behavior. Since the dawn of history the principal concept used in explaining animal behavior had been *instinct*. This term was used for the "driving forces" as well as the "steering mechanisms" in animal behavior. After Darwin's theory was published the instinct concept also became popular among psychologists, especially in the more "functionalistic" Anglo-Saxon countries. Thus, the first important American psychologist, William James, introduced several instincts in explaining human behavior, but it was as a parallel to other explanatory concepts such as "habits," "emotions," and "volition."

It was the British-American psychologist W. McDougall (1908) who regarded "instinct" as the main concept in the explanation of human behavior. In his very influential *Introduction to Social Psychology*, more than 30 editions of which have been published since 1908, he defined "instinct" in this way:

We may, then, define an instinct as an inherited or innate psycho-physical disposition which determines its possessor to perceive, and to pay attention to, objects of a certain class, to experience an emotional excitement of particular quality upon perceiving such an object, and to act in regard to it in a particular manner, or, at least, to experience an impulse to such action (p. 25).

It is clear form this quote that "instinct" in McDougall's theory was an all-inclusive explanatory term containing both directing cognitive components ("to perceive," "to pay attention to") as well as dynamic energizing components ("emotional excitement," "to experience an impulse," "to act"). And as these directing and dynamic functions were determined by an inherited disposition, McDougall's instinct-concept could have become a completely pseudoexplanatory concept, if he had not resisted the temptation to "invent" too many instincts. In his *Social Psychology* (1908) he only introduced twelve instincts, later extending this number to fourteen and ending with the eighteen so-called propensities. This shift of term was the result of the long critical polemics which occupied psychologists in the 1920s. The so-called instinct-controversy had its center in the psychologist, John B. Watson. Watson and other behaviorists saw the pseudoexplanatory character of the instinct concept, which had become obvious after many psychologists and anthropologists had made free, uninhibited and uncritical use of inventing a new instinct every time they needed an explanatory concept. McDougall retained in his propensity concept only the more dymamic components of his former instinct concept, which can be seen in this definition:

A propensity is a disposition, a functional unit of the mind's total organization, and it is one which, when it is excited, generates an active tendency, a striving, an impulse or drive towards some goal (1932, p. 118).

He later designated the term instinct in this way:

An instinct is that special part of the creature's organization (a functional unit) which expresses itself in a train of instinctive action (p. 49).

By the last definition of instinct McDougall is more in accord with the use of the term among modern ethologists who have resolved the old vague, all-inclusive instinct concept into several components with more precise meanings.

The main representatives of the ethologists are the "founder," K. Lorenz, and the systematical theorist, N. Tinbergen. The latter summarizes his theory of instinct in this definition:

I will tentatively define an instinct as an hierarchically organized nervous mechanism which is susceptible to certain priming, releasing and directing impulses of internal as well as of external origin, and which responds to these impulses by co-ordinated movements that contribute to the maintenance of the individual and the species (1951, p. 112).

As this citation demonstrates, Tinbergen has defined instinct as a mechanism which is activated by impulses. These impulses are in other connections defined in these terms:

The effect of these internal factors determines the motivation of an animal, the activation of its instincts (p. 57).

This distinction between mechanism and motivation is also found in other theories which have been developed in this century parallel to the ethological theories.

OTHER THEORIES OF MOTIVATION: A PREVIEW

After having followed the development of instinct-theory within ethology, we are going back in time to the turn of the century and make a broad survey of the development of motivational psychology or motivology.[2]

At the time when McDougall was elaborating his theory of instincts, two other trends in psychology appeared, both of which were influenced more by Darwin than by Wundt.

These two trends were the embryonic development of two new disciplines in psychology: the psychology of learning or manthanology[3] and the psychology of personality or personology.[4]

---

[2] This term was suggested by R. S. Woodworth (1918).
[3] This term is derived from a suggestion presented by Clyde E. Noble in a review in *Contemporary Psychology*, 1968, *13*, p. 10.
[4] This term was suggested by H. A. Murray (1938).

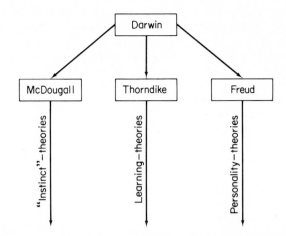

Fig. 33-1. *A rough overview of the theoretical developments relevant motivational psychology.* [More detailed overview in Fig. 33-2.]

Motivational psychology is still connected strongly to these two fields of psychology, and many contemporary conceptions and hypotheses about motivation can only be understood in relation to this historical background. We shall, therefore, in the following two paragraphs describe the development of motivational psychology within these two disciplines. Later, we shall describe other independent theoretical developments, and, finally, we shall describe the status quo in motivational psychology today. These main trends in motivational psychology are illustrated in Figure 33-1.

Before we begin this exposition the present author proposes an historical hypothesis to explain the fact that motivational psychology has been mainly connected to the psychology of learning and personality.

The classical, experimental psychologists made no use of motivational concepts because they worked exclusively with students as experimental subjects, and they were always motivated to do what their professor required. Thus motivation was a rather constant variable in their experiments, and they consequently had no opportunity to become aware of the importance of motivation.

In contradiction to this the first experiments in learning were performed on animals, who did not have the same respect for the professors as the students, and, therefore, psychologists such as Thorndike were forced to motivate the experimental subjects, and, by doing so, had an opportunity to observe the importance of motivation.

A similar explantation can be given for the fact that Freud made use of motivation in his theory: he was working with patients whose behavior could not be explained or changed by therapy without noticing and dealing with the "driving forces" behind the symptoms.

MOTIVATION AND LEARNING

Inspired by Darwin's theory of evolution a growing interest in animal learning manifested itself in the last decades of the nineteenth century. Among those inspired by Darwin's efforts was the American psychologist, Edward Lee Thorndike, who was the great pioneer in the creation of an experimental psychology of learning. As early as 1898 he reported about his famous experiments with cats in a puzzle-box. In this he described the learning as "Trial-and-Error" or "selective learning." In order to explain learning he proposed several laws of learning, among which was the famous "Law-of-Effect":

Of several responses made to the same situation, those which are accompanied or closely followed by satisfaction to the animal will, other things being equal, be more firmly connected with the situation, so that, when it recurs, they will be more likely to recur; those which are accompanied or closely followed by discomfort to the animal will, other things being equal, have their connections with that situation weakened, so that, when it recurs, they will be less likely to occur. The greater the satisfaction or discomfort, the greater the strengthening or weakening of the bond (1898, 1911).

This "Law of Effect" made reinforcement the central theme in the psychology of learning for two-thirds of a century. By introducing the concepts *satisfaction* and *discomfort* as positive and negative reinforcers, Thorndike made motivational variables the most important factors in the psychology of learning, just as reduction of motivation (satisfaction) and nonreduction of motivation (discomfort) became the most important conditions for learning (at least in Thorndike's post-1929 work).

As a designation for the main motivational variable, Thorndike used the popular term "instinct." But when the "instinct controversy" was over, the term *instinct* was replaced in learning theories by other terms for primary motivational variables, such as "drives," "needs," "appetites," "aversions," "demands," etc.

It was R. S. Woodworth (1918) who introduced the term *drive* to designate the dynamic variable which energizes or activates the mechanisms of behavior. But the most important introduction of motivational variables into the psychology of learning was made by Edward C. Tolman. His famous book, *Purposive Behavior in Animals and Men* (1932) introduced motivational variables such as drives and demands as the most important behavior determinants or intervening variables alongside the cognitive variables "means-end-readiness" and "-expectations". Tolman was not a reinforcement theorist, but motivation played an important role for him as the determinant of performance, which is directed or guided purposively by the cognitive determinants.

Tolman never laid stress on the formal development of his theory, and he changed his terminology considerably over the years. Starting with "demands" and "drives," he changed to "need" and finally returned to "drive."[5]

But Tolman influenced the important learning theorist, Clark L. Hull, whose main works, dating from 1943 and 1952, represent the most formally developed of any general behavior-theory. In these books (1943, 1952), Hull developed Thorndike's Law-of-Effect into a systematic and precise reinforcement-theory. In this theory Thorndike's "satisfaction" was replaced by "need-reduction" and later by "drive-reduction." The two important motivational terms, "need" and "drive," were defined in this way:

When a condition arises for which action on the part of the organism is a prerequisite to optimum probability of survival of either the individual or the species, a state of need is said to exist. Since a need, either actual or potential, usually precedes and accompanies the action of an organism, the need is often said to motivate or drive the associated activity. Because of this motivational characteristic of needs they are regarded as producing primary animal drives.

It is important to note in this connection that the general concept of drive (D) tends strongly to have the systematic status of an intervening variable or X, never directly observable (Hull 1943, p. 57).

Thus "need" is an independent variable which determines the intervening variable "drive," which in turn combines with other intervening variables in determining behavior.

Among the most important intervening variables are, in addition to drive (*D*), the incentive-motivation variable (*K*), which is determined by the amount and quality of the reward and the habit-strength (*sHr*). These intervening variables combine multiplicatively into the reaction-evocation-potential (*sEr*) in this way:

$$\text{Behavior} = f(sEr) = f(D \times K \times sHr)^6$$

Hull's theory influenced the development of learning theory very significantly. Among his most influential coworkers and students were K. W. Spence, N. E. Miller, O. H. Mowrer and, J.S. Brown.[7]

K. W. Spence's special contribution was the development of the "incentive-concept" among the motivational variables. He has changed his concept from a drive-reduction-reinforcement theory to the so-called Empirical Law-of-Effect, in which motivation and motivation-reduction only play a role in performance, while learning is conceived of as classical conditioning following a "contiguity-principle" (1956, 1960).

N. E. Miller has, in cooperation with J. Dollard, applied a simplified version of Hull's theory to social learning (Miller & Dollard 1941) and to personality theory and psychotherapy (Dollard & Miller 1950). Besides this he has developed a rather formal theory of conflict-behavior (Miller 1959). The most important concepts in Miller's theory are "drive," "cue," "reward," and "response." "Drive" is defined as "a strong stimulus." Every strong stimulus has a "drive-function" which activates responses. In addition to this, stimuli can have a "cue-function" which directs behavior. Reward is something which produces "drive-reduction," which in turn reinforces the responses to the stimulus. There are many advantages in defining a drive as a sort of stimulus. First, the law of generalization (and other laws of learning) may be applied to a drive. Second, "the basic mechanism of motivation (strong stimulation) is the same for primary and learned drives, and the basic mechanism of reinforcement (a reduction in strong stimulation) is the same for primary and learned rewards." (Miller 1959, p.440) Miller has in recent years performed many important experiments dealing with motivation and learning.

[5] See the main works of Tolman from 1942, 1951, and 1959; also an analysis of Tolman's theories in Madsen (1968).

[6] This is, of course, a very brief representation of Hull's theory. The reader is referred to S. Koch's thorough analysis in Estes et al. (1954) and in Madsen (1968).

[7] Another theory that is influenced to some extent by Hull is presented by J. A. Deutsch (1960).

O. H. Mowrer (in collaboration with Miller) has, on the basis of their experiments, introduced "fear" as an acquired drive, which perhaps is the basis for many other acquired drives (Mowrer 1950). Mowrer has in the course of time changed his theory from the one-factor *reinforcement-theory* to a so-called two-factor-theory and later back again to a revised two-factor-theory, which is, in reality, a one-factor-theory with *contiguity* as the main factor in learning—not so different from K. W. Spence's theory. The difference is, perhaps, that in Spence's theory *incentive* motivation is the main motivational variable, while in Mowrer's theory *fear* is the main motivational variable.

J. S. Brown has brought about a crystallization of the motivation-theory immanent in Hull's general behavior theory (1961). He has made it clear that the most important motivational variable, "drive" (*D*), is a general activating and non-directing, intervening variable. This clearly distinguishes Hull's and Brown's drive concept from other drive concepts (e.g., those of Tolman and Freud). Furthermore, Brown has the most clear, systematic and empirically testable theory about *secondary motivation*: there are no acquired or learned "drives," but there are "learned sources" of drive, which in the same manner as primary sources (needs) all determine or influence the same general drive. Brown, like Mowrer and Miller, points to fear as the basis for all "secondary motivational systems" (1968). Furthermore, Brown accepts the possibility of identifying "drive" with "arousal" in the reticular arousal system.

With this physiological interpretation of drive we touch upon another line of development to which we shall now give our attention.

We have followed the main line of development in the psychology of learning starting with Thorndike, but there is another important parallel trend beginning with Pavlov.

There were apparently no motivational concepts in his original theory (as presented in Pavlov 1927). Perhaps the reason is that he conducted his experiments with animals under rather passive, constrained conditions. With no free actions from the animals, there was no need for an activating variable in the theory. But this, of course, constitutes a rather superficial interpretation of Pavlov. If we look more closely at his theory we find that the process of conditioning and the behavior of the animal in the experimental situation are determined by a complicated, dynamic interaction between two fundamental processes: "excitation" and "inhibition." And between these two, "excitation," at least, is an activating, energizing process, and thus a motivational variable in the traditional meaning of motivation. Furthermore, there is some connection with motivation in the unconditioned stimulus (*US*) which reinforces the conditioning if it follows the conditioned stimulus (*CS*). The *US* is often connected with something which, in the Hullian meaning of the words, is either drive-reducing (e.g., food) or drive-inducing (e.g., electric shock). In addition, Pavlov pointed to the so-called Orienting Reflex (*OR*) as an important factor in the formation of every conditioned reaction (*CR*). The problems of the *OR* have been investigated intensively in the last two decades in the Soviet Union. Some of the results of this research are presented in the English translation of a work edited by L. G. Voronin, A. N. Leontiev, A. R. Luria, E. N. Sokolov, and O. S. Vinogradova (Voronin et al. 1965). Following this line of research the Soviet psychologists have very nearly approached the research carried out during the same period by Western psychologists. Thus, there is a high degree of similarity between the theories of the Soviet psychologist, E. N. Sokolov (1963), and the Canadian psychologist, D. E. Berlyne (1960, 1967). Both these theories emphasize the role of the Reticular Arousal System (*RAS*) in exploratory behavior.[8]

Berlyne has been influenced by Soviet psychologists and Jean Piaget with whom he has worked, but especially by D. O. Hebb. It was especially Hebb who, in his main work (1949), connected Western psychology with the original Pavlovian tradition and was responsible for creating a renaissance in physiological theorizing in the field of psychology. In the first edition of his theory (1949), Hebb revealed a very special conception of motivation, as he postulated that the brain was always active, and no special concepts were needed to explain the activation of behavior, only concepts for the directing and organization of behavior, which was determined by the so-called cell-assemblies and phases-sequences. Later Hebb changed his theory motivation and laid stress on the role of the Reticular Arousal System (*RAS*) in motivation. Hebb (1959) further elaborated his theory in a paper and in a textbook (1966). Besides Berlyne, whom we have already mentioned, Hebb has also influenced James Olds (1956) who has been a pioneer in experiments with intracranial stimulation, through which he discovered the reinforcing function of the septum (1955).

The important role of the Reticular Arousal System for behavior generally, and especially for motivation, has been acknowledged since the physiologists Moruzzi and Magoun discovered the function of the *RAS* (first presented in Moruzzi & Magoun [1949], and elaborated in Magoun [1954]). This research has been made available to psychologists especially by the work of Donald B. Lindsley (1957). And the role of the *RAS* has been integrated in a theory of motivation by Elisabeth Duffy (1962) who, as early as the 1930s, stressed the role of two main concepts in the description (and explanation) of behavior: *activation* and *direction*. Before the investigation of the function of the *RAS*, this motivating function was assumed to be the result of the activity of the Autonomic Nervous System (*ANS*), which is now regarded as being subsidiary and of secondary importance compared to the *RAS*.

The role of the *RAS* is also stressed in the theory of Dalbir Bindra (1959) who states that he has combined the approaches of Hebb and Skinner.

B. F. Skinner has not been mentioned before because his theory—or, rather, descriptive system—does *not* contain any explanatory terms referring to intervening variables or hypothetical constructs. Skinner's system, therefore, includes no motivational variables in the traditional sense—even fewer than Pavlov's. But Skinner makes use of terms for empirical, independent variables, which are connected to the motivational variables in the more traditional sense. The most important of these motivation-related variables in Skinner's system are *deprivation* and *reinforcement*. Deprivation determines the general degree of activation, and reinforcement determines the response-strength or probability of the occurrence of response.

---

[8] Among other early physiological theories of motivation we can also mention Clifford T. Morgan's theory of the "Central Motive State" (1957, 1959). A theory stressing the importance of "excitatory" and "inhibitory" centers in the hypothalamus is presented by Elliot Stellar (1954).

Skinner presently has one of the most influential positions in the modern psychology of learning, and his experimentally based system has been applied to very general and broad problems (1953). His research results have been applied to behavior-therapy and especially to teaching (1968). A very convincing critique of Skinner's antitheoretical orientation was made by Miller (1959), who pointed to the "economical" utility of introducing intervening variables in cases where more than two independent and dependent variables are under observation in an experiment.

Finally, I think we should mention one of the pioneers in motivational psychology, P. T. Young, whose orientation is closer to the psychology of learning and the psychophysiological approach to motivation than it is to the psychology of personality. Young has conducted many experiments with animals about the problems of food preference. On the basis of these experiments, Young has constructed an objective hedonistic theory of motivation. The main postulate of this theory is that incentives (like food) determine affective arousal, and this process determines behavior and influences learning. Young does not neglect other sources of motivation (such as needs and aversive stimuli), but he emphasizes that the positive-hedonic affects have been neglected in the modern experi-

mental psychology of motivation. Young (1961) organizes the whole spectrum of research results in modern motivational psychology in his provocative descriptive system or frame of reference, which is called the "multi-perspective," "attitudinal," or "relativistic" approach. This is a modern version of his earlier pioneering works (Young 1936, 1943).

After having surveyed the *biotropic* area of motivational psychology which took place within physiological and learning psychology, we now turn to the *sociotripic* area, concerning developments within the psychology of personality. The interaction of these two branches appears in Figure 33-2.

PERSONALITY DYNAMICS

We turn once again to the beginning of the century. At the same time that Pavlov, Thorndike and McDougall were creating their theories, Sigmund Freud was laying the foundation of psychoanalysis. He had, after trying to construct a physiological theory (1896), written his first main work about dreams (1900). His theories, from the very beginning, had been dynamic in the sense that they stressed psychological "energies," "forces," and the "intrapsychic conflicts" as determinants of normal and

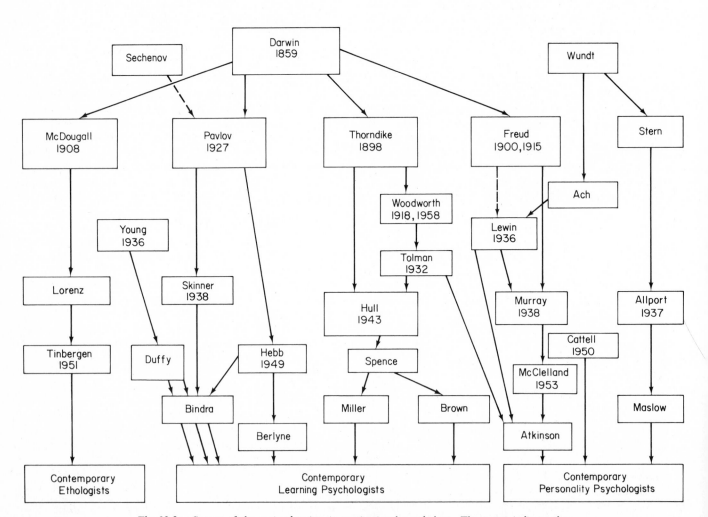

Fig. 33-2. *Survey of the main theorists in motivational psychology. The years indicate the publication of main works.*

pathological behavior. In 1915, however, Freud first made a more systematic formulation of a motivational theory in the more traditional sense (Freud 1915). In this paper he defined his main motivational variable: instinct or rather, drive.[9] In this paper he formulates several basic postulates and definitions, such as:

The task of the nervous system is—broadly speaking—to master stimuli. . . .

We may probably conclude that instincts and not external stimuli are the true motive forces in the progress that has raised the nervous system with all its incomparable efficiency, to its present high level of development. . . .

We find further that the activity of even the most highly developed mental apparatus is subject to the pleasure-pain principle. . . .

If we now apply ourselves to considering mental life from a biological point of view, an "instinct" appears to us as a borderland concept between the mental and the physical, being both the mental representative of the stimuli emanating from within the organism and penetrating to the mind, and at the same time a measure of the demand upon the energy of the latter in consequence of its connection with the body.

We are now in a position to discuss certain terms used in reference to the concept of an instinct, for example, its impetus, its aim, its object and its source.

By the impetus *of an instinct we understand its motor element, the amount of force or the demand upon energy which it represents.*

The aim *of an instinct is in every instance satisfaction, which can only be obtained by abolishing the condition of stimulation in the source of the instinct.*

The object *of an instinct is that in or through which it can achieve its aim. It is the most variable thing about an instinct and is not originally connected with it, but becomes attached to it only in consequence of being peculiarly fitted to provide satisfaction.*

By the source *of an instinct is meant that somatic process in an organ or part of the body from which there results a stimulus represented in mental life by an instinct (Freud 1915).*

After presenting these basic postulates and definitions, Freud goes on to discuss the important problem concerning the number and the different kinds of instinctual drives:

Now what instincts and how many should be postulated? There is obviously a great opportunity here for arbitrary choice.

I have proposed that two groups of such primal instincts be distinguished: the self-preservative *or* ego-*instincts and the* sexual *instincts. But this proposition has not the weight of a necessary postulate, such as, for instance, our assumption about the biological "purpose" in the mental apparatus (v. supra); it is merely an auxiliary construction, to be retained only so long as it proves useful, and it will make little difference to the results of our work of description and classification if we replace it by another (Freud 1915).*

[9] As several authors have pointed out, the most correct translation of the German word *Trieb* would have been "drive" and not "instinct," as it infortunately was translated. We follow Rapaport's (1960) suggestion to call Freud's motivational concept "instinctive drive."

This last comment was very wise, as Freud himself changed his classification of instinctual drives twice: From the two mentioned to one (libido) and back to two again, "Eros" (or life-instinct) and Thanatos (or death-instinct). But we cannot make a detailed study of Freud's theory in this chapter. Instead, we must let the passages quoted speak for themselves to characterize the basic postulates and definitions of the first and the most original and fruitful dynamic theory in psychology.

The psychoanalytic theory of motivation has, of course, been changed and developed considerably since Freud's death. In this chapter we can only comment on a few of the main theorists. Kenneth M. Colby (1955) has made a very profound analysis of the psychoanalytic theory of motivation and made it very clear that "energy" and "structure" are the two basic and complementary concepts in the psychoanalytic (perhaps in every) theory of motivation. He has further proposed "a cyclic-circular structural model" to replace Freud's old tripartite model of id, ego, and superego.

Walter Toman has also elaborated the psychoanalytic theory of motivation. He has particularly stressed the importance of the *periodicity* of motivation (1960a), and he has also emphasized the necessity of a *genetic* explanation of motivation. In addition, he has demonstrated the application of the psychoanalytic theory to the different phases of the life-cycle (1960b).

One of the most comprehensive and systematic reconstructions of the psychoanalytic theory was made by David Rapaport (1959). He has also made an analysis specifically concerned with the psychoanalytic theory of motivation. In this profound analysis (1960) he points to the difference between causes and motivation, the latter being a special kind of cause. He also distinguishes between "instinctual drives" and other types of motives. Rapaport, like Colby, emphasizes the important interaction between drives and structures (defense mechanisms, etc.). Furthermore, Rapaport makes some very valuable comparisons between psychoanalytic theory in general and J. Piaget's developmental theory and learning theory (in the version of Miller and Dollard).[10]

The present author regards these comparative studies as valuable contributions to a future integration of all the major theories in psychology.

Finally, we should mention Benjamin B. Wolman as a psychoanalytical theorist who has revised the psychoanalytical theory of motivation and pointed towards an integration with other psychological theories (especially those of Pavlov and his students). Wolman has presented his proposals for revisions of Freud's theory in several papers, and he has summarized his theory in the two last chapters (Wolman 1968), from which we quote:

The neonate is endowed with two instinctual forces, Eros and Ares, both serving initially protection and preservation of the organism, both capable of cathexis of the mental energies at their disposal, the libido and destrudo respectively. (p. 544)

Ares, like Eros, has impetus, source, object, and aim. Its impetus is the amount of destrudo energy at its disposal. Its source, we believe, is the feeling of danger, of a threat to life. Its object can be any living or inanimate thing (inclusive of one's own

[10] Among modern psychoanalytical theories we can also include the theory of Thomas M. French (1952). For a further analysis the reader is referred to Madsen (1968).

organism) *which represents the threat. Ares' energy, destrudo, can be cathected in any object. Its aim can be complete or partial destruction depending upon the degree of fusion with the libido and upon the inhibiting actions of the ego and superego (p. 542).*

To this postulation of two life-preserving drives Wolman has added a hypothesis about the development of "inter-individual cathexes":

Children normally enter every social relationship with an "instrumental attitude," i.e., the attitude adopted towards other people when they are treated as instruments for satisfaction. In the course of life the child develops a "mutual acceptance" of give-and-take relationships with other people. Later, as parents themselves, they develop a "vectorial attitude," i.e., the willingness to *give* without taking.

This social development is correlated with the balance of *libido cathexis* as described in Freud's theory. But in opposition to the Eros, Wolman writes that:

The Ares and destrudo have no developmental line. Ares is always archaic, primitive, and primordial. It is always indicative of aggression. Libido is love, and there are many stages in love. Destrudo is hate; it is regression to aggression, to wilderness, to savagery, to bestiality. There is no progress in hate (p. 543).

Wolman has also supplemented Freud's pleasure and reality principles with a so-called Antigone-principle. This principle is a statement of the fact that human beings express a willingness to sacrifice their own satisfaction—and sometimes even their own lives—for other people or for an ideal.

This Antigone principle is integrated with a hypothesis advanced by G. Razran into a new hypothesis of three levels of behavior:

1. The *prehedonic level*:
   The motivation of behavior follows Freud's "pleasure-principle," and learning is sheer classical *conditioning* by contiguity.
2. The *hedonic level*:
   The motivation of behavior here follows Freud's "reality-principle," and learning is *instrumental* learning reinforced by tension-reduction.
3. The *post-hedonic level*:
   The motivation of behavior in this case follows the Antigone principle, and learning is *cognitive* learning.

In conclusion we should mention Wolman's "principles of monistic *transitionism*," which are elaborated in Wolman (1965). This is a theory about the mind-body or rather the soma-psyche-problem, to which this theory suggests a monistic solution. This is achieved by postulating a continuity in the biological evolution from the lowest to the highest forms of life-processes, including a transition from somatic to mental processes through the unconscious mental processes. Thus Wolman bridges the gap between soma and psyche without sacrificing the methodological independence of psychology.

It would take us too far from motivational theory if we should go deeper into Wolman's "socio-psycho-somatic" theory of schizophrenia (Wolman 1967), and his classification of mental disorders (Wolman 1966), so we now turn from psychoanalytical theories to other theories of motivation.

Let us now look at the original theory of motivation of Kurt Lewin. This theory is the only theory of motivation which is in any way connected with classical, experimental psychology. While studying with the founder of the Gestalt school, Wertheimer, together with Köhler and Koffka, the young Kurt Lewin was inspired to perform his first experimental work about "determining tendencies," which proved to be a criticism of the wirk of N. Ach, who worked with the problem of volition within a classical, associationistic frame of reference (Ach 1905). Lewin (1922) demonstrated that other determining tendencies existed besides associations, and that these determining factors were the primary driving forces behind the "associative mechanisms." Lewin, together with collaborators, continued his experimental work and his very penetrating conceptual analysis of these determining tendencies, or "needs" (*Bedürfnis*) as he later called them (1928). Lewin was not as interested in the biological needs as in the so-called quasi-needs, which are tendencies determined by decisions (*Vorsatz*) and other sets (*Einstellungen*). He and his coworkers elaborated the experimental foundations for a theory of human motivation (as distinguished from the theory of animal motivation, which was elaborated by the learning theorists). This work encompassed such classical problems as "level-of-aspiration," "substitute-activity," "retention of uncompleted tasks" (the *Zeigernik* effects), etc. The results of this work done in Lewin's German period have been collected and translated into English (1935).

In his American period Lewin elaborated a complete, so-called topological, system for describing the structure of the person (*P*) and the (perceived) environment (*E*). This descriptive system (1936) was later (1938) supplemented by an explanatory system, in which behavior (*B*) was explained as a function of the person and the environment: $B = f(P, E)$. The most important motivational variable was psychological force. This explanatory construct was determined by a state of tension in the person (correlated with a state of need in the organism) and by a valence of some object or activity in the (perceived) environment (*E*).

Lewin's "field theory" is very exact and systematic, but it has been criticized for being too loosely connected to observable events (i.e., too few operational definitions). In spite of this, Lewin's theory has furnished inspiration for several experimental works, both in child psychology and (especially) in social psychology. His main theoretical papers (Lewin 1952) were collected after his death. Besides these works, Lewin has influenced learning theory through Tolman and personality theory through Henry A. Murray. Murray conceives his own theory as a modern version of a psychoanalytic theory of motivation and acknowledges his debt to both McDougall and Lewin. One of the most fruitful trends in Murray's (and coworkers') very intensive *Explorations in Personality* (1938a) is the integration of experimental and clinical methods used in one of the first real examples of teamwork in psychology. While the empirical and methodological results are the work of the whole team, it is fair to say that the theory is Murray's own work. The main feature of this theory is that an attempt is made to integrate something valuable from learning theory with the fundamentals of psychoanalytic theory. Thus Murray creates a very precise taxonomy for describing behavior, but in his explanations of behavior he stresses the genesis of the personality—especially the importance of early childhood events and the "dynamics of personality." With this definition and summary of his main hypothesis, Murray introduced the motivational variable "need."

A need is a construct (a convenient fiction or hypothetical concept) which stands for a force (the physico-chemical nature of which is unknown) in the brain region, a force which organizes perception, apperception, intellection, conation and action in such a way as to transform in a certain direction an existing, unsatisfying situation. A need is sometimes provoked directly by internal processes of a certain kind (viscerogenic, endocrinogenic, thalamicogenic) arising in the course of vital sequences, but, more frequently (when in a state of readiness) by the occurrence of one of a few commonly effective press (or by anticipatory images of such press). Thus, it manifests itself by leading the organism to search for or to avoid encountering or, when encountered, to attend and respond to certain kinds of press. It may even engender illusory perceptions and delusory apperceptions (projections of its imaged press into unsuitable objects). Each need is characteristically accompanied by a particular feeling or emotion and tends to use certain modes (sub-needs and actones) to further its trend. It may be weak or intense, momentary or enduring. But usually it persists and gives rise to a certain course of overt behavior (or fantasy), which (if the organism is competent and external opposition not insurmountable) changes the initiating circumstance in such a way as to bring about an end situation which stills (appeases or satisfies) the organism (Murray 1938, pp. 123–24).

It is obvious from this quotation that Murray's "need" is very different from Hull's and the learning theorists' "need," which is confined to a state of deprivation in some peripheral organs (or in the "viscera"). Murray's "need," on the other hand, is a (hypothetical) central state. It is more encompassing than Hull's "drive"—rather similar in fact to his *sEr*—than Freud's "instinctive drive." But instead of Freud's two basic "instinctual drives," Murray's theory contains approximately forty needs, divided into "viscerogenic needs" (thirteen) and "psychogenic needs" (at least twenty). This wealth of motivational as well as other explanatory variables, represents both the strength and the weakness of Murray's theory. The strength lies in the possibility afforded of making very differentiated descriptions of individual personalities, and the weakness lies in the risk of pseudo-explanations which may appear when less critical psychologists than Murray himself apply his theory. We shall return to this problem in a later section of this chapter, but at this time we shall only point to the fact that Murray himself has revised his theory several times (e.g., Murray 1951, 1953, 1959), and he has now replaced the "need" concept by a narrower and more precise concept called "thematic dispositions":

It has become more and more apparent to one that the energetic components of personality can be better defined as thematic dispositions than as general actional dispositions (1959, p. 34).

Murray has continued to invent new descriptive and explanatory concepts, and he has influenced the psychology of personality enormously through his theory, his methodological inventions (among these the well-known Thematic Apperception Test)

and by the results he has obtained in his experiments. The present author thinks that it is fair to characterize Murray as a driving force in personality theory, where he is perhaps second only to Freud.

Following close behind Murray is David McClelland, who has continued empirical research with the TAT and the development of a theory of motivation. Thus he has made a group-test version of the TAT, which he and his coworkers have tried out in validation experiments. They measure the content of fantasies in the TAT-stories made by subjects in several different situations, where different motivations may be created (motivations such as hunger, sex, aggression, fear, affiliation, power, and achievement). In this work McClelland and his coworkers have exhibited very imaginative inventiveness in combining experimental and field-observational methods. McClelland and his coworkers have also made a sort of standardization of the procedure of content-analysis of the TAT-stories, which has been developed to such an extent that it can be done by an electronic computer. It is also symptomatic for modern psychology that McClelland's group has concentrated its research and theoretical development mainly on one motivational variable, the so-called achievement-motive (McClelland et al. 1953). Through this research they have demonstrated that individual differences in the strength of the achievement-motive as measured by the TAT are dependent on the environment —especially when child-rearing practices favor independence and self-reliance. In later works McClelland's group has also demonstrated the value of the TAT in measuring other motives (McClelland 1955 and Atkinson 1958). McClelland himself has investigated the achievement-motive's influence on economical growth in contemporary and ancient societies (1961).

On the theoretical side, McClelland has made a significant contribution by shifting from a need-determined to a hedonistic, expectation-determined conception of motivation (which is influenced by, or is at least parallel to, Young's and Tolman's theories). This is apparent from McClelland's first formulation of his theory.

A motive becomes a strong affective association, characterized by an anticipatory goal reaction and based on past association of certain cues with pleasure and pain (1951, p. 446).

Later McClelland defines and summarizes the basic postulates of his theory in this way:

Our definition of a motive is this: A motive is the redintegration by a cue of a change in an affective situation. The word redintegration in this definition is meant to imply previous learning. In our system, all motives are learned. The basic idea is simply this: Certain stimuli or situations involving discrepancies between expectations (adaption level) and perception are sources of primary, unlearned affect, either positive or negative in nature. Cues which are paired with these affective states, changes in these affective states, and the conditions producing them become capable of redintegrating a state (A) derived from the original affective situation (A), but not identical with. it (McClelland et al. 1953, p. 28).

It is apparent from this that McClelland's conception of motivation deviates to some extent from that of his predecessors.

This trend in the direction of an "expectation × value" theory is further developed by John W. Atkinson, one of McClelland's closest associates. Atkinson has been especially concerned with risk-taking behavior and its dependence on achievement motivation. In recent years he has developed the theory of achievement motivation into a very fruitful paradigm for a theory of human motivation (1964). In addition to McClelland, Atkinson has been strongly influenced by Lewin and Tolman, and he has also incorporated something from modern decision-theory.

The most important motivational variables and their interactions are presented in Atkinson's formula:

$$T_s = M_s \times E_s \times I_s$$

where T_s is the tendency to approach success, which is a function of a stable inherited or acquired disposition, called the "motive" to achieve success (M_s), combined with an "expectation" of success (E_s) and the "incentive-value" of the task (I_s). Expectation—or subjective probability (P_s)—is interrelated with incentive in achievement situations in this way:

$$I_s = 1 \div P_s$$

Parallel with this positive motive to approach success, Atkinson also postulates a negative "fear of failure" or "motive to avoid failure":

$$T_{+f} = M_{AF} \times E_f \times I_f$$

One of the basic postulates of Atkinson's theory is that behavior is a result of interaction between at least two motives. In achievement-arousing situations the behavior (R) is a product of the two conflicting motives:

$$R = T_s \div T_{+f}$$

Thus Atkinson also includes some hypotheses borrowed from N. E. Miller's theory of conflict behavior.

During the most recent period Atkinson has worked with Norman T. Feather, and they have collected some of their own and coworkers' research in a new volume (Atkinson & Feather 1966). In this book they demonstrate the value of their "miniature-theory" of achievement motivation and touch upon the possibility of extending the theory into a general theory of human motivation, which combines the two disciplines of scientific psychology: differential (test-) psychology of personality and general (experimental) psychology.

Feather (1967) has described the application of the "expectation × value" model to information-seeking behavior and has thus approached the field of research formerly occupied by the more "biotropic," physiological psychologists and learning-psychologists (e.g., Berlyne).

Atkinson has also criticized the "Law of Effect" for not being applicable to achievement-behavior (Atkinson & Feather 1966) and points to the fact that this same criticism was made by Allport more than twenty years ago.

We thus turn from this very recent research back to the theory of Gordon W. Allport, who represents another trend in the psychology of personality. In his important book about personality (1937), he proposed a theory—or rather a descriptive system—of personality which was to some extent in contradiction with the more dynamic mainline of personality theory as represented by Freud, Lewin, Murray, etc. Allport denied the importance of biological needs or drives as well as the importance of childhood development for the adult personality. As an alternative he formulated a hypothesis about the functional autonomy of adult motivation (originally proposed by Woodworth 1918). In a revision of his theory he states:

From this point of view functional autonomy is merely a way of stating that men's motives change and grow in the course of life, because it is the nature of man that they should do so (Allport 1968, p. 252).

In another connection he declares that his hypothesis about functional autonomy "frankly depends upon certain philosophical assumptions regarding the nature of human personality" (p. 230). The "philosophical assumption" to which Allport refers is a philosophy of man which is developed in the direction of existentialism.

Allport is joined in this existentialistic philosophy of man by another contemporary personality theorist, Abraham H. Maslow, who has been one of the most influential leaders in this humanistic trend in personality theory. Maslow has criticized the psychoanalytic theory for being onesided, stressing deficiency-motivation and completely neglecting growth-motivation. Maslow postulates that this "growth-motivation" manifested as a need for self-realization can only manifest itself in behavior when the other, more deficiency-determined-needs are satisfied. He proposes a hierarchical relationship between the needs (1954). The basic needs are the physiological needs (hunger, thirst, etc.). The next level consists of the safety needs. When these needs are satisfied the person's behavior is determined by the social needs for affection and approval. The upper level of motivation consists of the growth-needs: the need for knowledge, aesthetic experience and self-realization. This pyramid model of needs has been very influential in applied psychology (e.g., in educational psychology and industrial psychology). In recent years Maslow has been working on the formulation of his view about the relationship between the psychology of personality and the philosophy of man (especially in Maslow 1959; also see 1962, 1966, 1967, and 1968).

Before concluding this picture of personality theory today, we must mention the Anglo-American psychologist, Raymond B. Cattell. It is not easy to classify Cattell as belonging to any school or tradition in the psychology of personality; rather he is the founder and leader of a new school that is characterized by the use of factor-analysis, a mathematical technique of theory-building created within the psychology of intelligence. Cattell has created several personality tests by which he and his coworkers have collected a great deal of data about personality. This data is incorporated in his theory of personality in which "dynamic traits" or motivational variables play an important role. Cattell has borrowed some of these concepts from McDougall and Freud, but he has restructured them into a more precise and systematic theory. The main motivational variables in his *dynamic lattice*, which is a model of the dynamic structure of the personality, are "erg," "sentiment," and "attitude." An erg is introduced in this way:

It seems that we are so constructed that our final satisfactions have to be instinctive ones, or ergic *ones. The term* erg, *from the Greek* ergon *for work or energy, is used in the dynamic calculus for a structure which has hitherto been called, at once too vaguely and elaborately, an instinct or drive, which is the energy source behind behavior. As we shall see in a moment an erg (hard "g") can be precisely factor-analytically located and defined, whereas instinct, need, drive, etc., have become all things to all men and can no longer be used with scientific precision (Cattell 1965, pp. 185–86).*

Thus we see a new term suggested for the basic motivational variables of which Cattell has identified at least eleven. These constitutional sources of energy are channelled through learned structures called "attitudes" and "sentiments"—concepts also known from other personality theories.

It would take us too far to go more deeply into Cattell's theory here because of the size of his production. In addition to a great many papers he has written several books (1946, 1950, 1957, and 1965), and has been coauthor and editor of a number of works. Therefore, he is dealt with in a special section in the survey chapter about "Personality Structure" written by J. S. Wiggins for the *Annual Review of Psychology* (1958).

Another leader in the field of factor-analytical personality theory is the British psychologist, H. J. Eysenck. He has been especially interested in the application of the factor-analytical theory and methods in clinical psychology or "behavior-therapy" (See Eysenck 1964).

The present author thinks that in the future personality theory may be more and more dominated by factor-analytical methods and theory—a parallel to the role of mathematical models in learning theory.

Concepts of Motivation

INTRODUCTION: THE FRAME OF REFERENCE

We now turn to the task of studying the many different motivational concepts presented in our historical survey. It is not an easy task, because the same terms (e.g., drive) are used in different ways by different psychologists, and similar variables are designated by different terms in the various theories.[11] It is extremely difficult to sort out the apparent similarities and differences. But many psychologists are undoubtedly interested in a deeper understanding and a comprehensive overview of psychological theories. Therefore, they must create and use a neutral terminology or taxonomy, which makes it possible to describe both precisely and systematically the results of a comparative study of different theories. Such a taxonomy of concepts and theories belongs to a metascientific discipline which the present author suggests calling *systematology* (i.e., the comparative study of scientific "systems," models, etc.). This discipline constitutes, together with epistemology and methodology, the broader field: philosophy of science. And this broader

footnote:
[11] Previously we have used the words "term," "concept," and "variable" rather loosely as interchangeable designations. It is now time to introduce more precise definitions: "term" will be used for the words in the psychological texts, while "concept" will be used for that cognitive structure which is supposed to be functioning in the head texts of the writer (and the reader) as he uses the terms. "Variable" will be used to designate the psychological processes, states, and structures that the term designates.

field, together with the history of science, the sociology of science, and the psychology of scientists and scientific activity, constitutes the all-inclusive science of sciences or "meta-science" (see Table 33-1).

Table 33-1. A Survey of the disciplines of "Meta-Science" or the "Science of Sciences."

Meta-Science
1. Philosophy of Science
a. Epistemology
b. Methodology
c. Systematology
2. History of Science
3. Sociology of Science
4. Psychology of Scientists and Scientific Activity

Thus, this whole chapter may be considered as a special example of a field of study belonging to meta-science: the first part belongs to the history of science (especially the history of psychology), and the following sections of the chapter all belong to systematology (especially the systematology of psychological theories).[12]

We shall now present and apply some classifications developed in connection with a systematological study of theories of motivation (Madsen 1968, forthcoming).

EMPIRICAL AND HYPOTHETICAL TERMS

Motivational concepts and theories are created to explain behavior. But we do not need motivational concepts for all types or aspects of behavior. Simple reflexive reactions (inborn reflexes) may be explained exclusively by a stimulus acting on an inborn structure, the "reflex-arc." But complex behavior (actions or behavior-acts) are often described as purposive or goal-directed, and such behavior can be explained by motivational theories. The terms "purposive" or "goal-directed" behavior are descriptive terms of a very complex and abstract nature. These terms may be used for describing or designating behavior which exhibits a complex of several observable traits. McDougall (1908) was the first to analyze and describe the criteria for purposive behavior. He counted seven criteria in all. Tolman referred to these criteria when, in his famous book, he defined purposive behavior (1932). Later Bindra (1959), in a very penetrating analysis, reduced the criteria to three: appropriateness, persistence, and searching. He also suggested the term "goal-directed" instead of purposive, and he uses goal-directed as a synonym for motivated behavior.

The simplest and most precise descriptive terminology is perhaps that presented by Elisabeth Duffy. She introduced it as early as the 1930s and elaborated it later (1962). In Duffy's terminology, all behavior can be described by the combination of two descriptive terms: intensity and direction. It is these two aspects of behavior which are supposed to be explained by motivational theories.

In a psychological explanation we often use two categories of terms: empirical terms and hypothetical terms.

footnote:
[12] An analysis of the concepts and the main theories of motivation made upon another philosophical basis is presented by R. S. Peters (1958).

The *empirical* terms designate those *independent variables* which are supposed to be the ultimate causes of behavior (which is the dependent variable). These independent variables may include both external stimuli from the environment as well as internal stimuli from the different organs and tissues of the organism. These internal stimuli must be observable if they are to be conceived of as independent variables describable by empirical terms. As the independent variables may be described in terms of (external and internal) stimuli, we may call them "*S*-variables."

Some psychologists, e.g., Skinner, would prefer to concentrate exclusively on the description of the observed relationships between *S*-variables and behavior. Such descriptions are sometimes formulated into general propositions about frequent and regularly observed relationships between types of *S*-variables and types of behavior or *R*-variables. These general propositions are often called "laws" (or *S-R*-relationships). Skinner regards the formulation and application of such "laws" as the only (scientific) explanation. But most psychologists prefer to suppose the existence of some "mediating" or "intervening" variables between the *S*-variables and the *R*-variables (behavior). As such intervening variables are not directly observable, but inferred or hypothesized; we may call them *Hypothetical variables* or "*H*-variables."[13]

It was especially for the explanation of purposive behavior that Tolman introduced such "intervening variables" as "drive" and "cognition."

On the basis of Tolman's *S-H-R*-paradigm we can introduce a basic classification of psychological variables and apply it to motivational variables from the most important theories we have studied (see Table 33-2).

It is obvious from this table that a very inconsistent and confusing use of terms exists in psychology. It is especially evident in the very different interpretations placed on the two important terms "need" and "drive." Thus Hull and Tolman (1951) use the two terms in opposite ways, and Murray used "need" in still another way. The confusion is in fact greater than this table shows, which will become clear after we introduce other classifications.

DISPOSITIONS AND FUNCTIONS

Tolman also made another classification of psychological variables. It is a classification according to the duration of the existence of the variables: Some psychological variables exist for a long time, perhaps for the whole life of the individual, from birth to death. They are the *inherited dispositions.*[14] Others are acquired by a learning process at one time or another in the life of the individual, and they exist for a shorter or longer time, but after they are acquired they play the same role as the inherited dispositions. Therefore, we may use the term "dispositions" or "disposition-variables" about inherited as well as acquired variables. Instead of "disposition" one may prefer the terms "factor" or perhaps "structure."

---

[13]We shall delay the discussion of the distinction between "intervening variables" and "hypothetical constructs" (both covered by the term "*H*-variables") until the last part of our chapter.

[14] As these dispositions are constant throughout life it seems a little strange to call them "variables," but the term may also be justified in this case, as they *vary* from one individual to another.

In opposition to these variables there is another class of psychological variables possessing shorter duration of existence. This class contains two subclasses: the processes, which perhaps only exist for seconds or minutes; and the states,[15] which may exist for hours and even days. As it may be difficult to distinguish between shorter processes and longer states, we may use the common term "functions" (or "function variables").

Different psychologists give greater attention to one of these categories of variables than to the other.

The disposition variables are mainly studied by the use of test methods in differential psychology, including the psychology of personality and intelligence. (The term "factor-analysis" indicates an interest in "factors" or dispositions.) On the other hand, the function-variables are mainly studied by the use of experimental methods in general psychology, including learning, cognition, and motivation.

There is, however, an intimate relationship between dispositions and functions, as the dispositions influence the course of the functions and create the individual differences in behavior which are directly determined by the functions. Therefore, the same term is often used as a designation for both a disposition and the related function. Sometimes this may create confusion and misunderstanding among psychologists. Thus the term "need" in the psychology of learning often designates a function (more presisely, a state). In personality theory, on the other hand, "need" is often used to cover both a function motivating behavior and the disposition that determines the individual differences in strength, duration, etc., in these functions. Murray has understood this and changed his main concept by replacing the term "need" with the new term "thematic dispositions."

This confusing use of terms for dispositions and functions can be seen from our next table of classification (see Table 33-3).

These are not all the sources of confusion, however. There is another conceptual dimension in psychology which creates confusion if it is not clearly expressed in appropriate terms.

DYNAMIC AND DIRECTIVE VARIABLES

This conceptual dimension which we are now going to analyze and express in a classification is the most important for motivational theory, because this conceptual distinction is intimately connected with the *R*-variable: "goal-directed behavior."

So far as the present author knows, the first who made a penetrating analysis of the motivational concepts was K. Lewin, especially in *Psychological Forces*, which appeared in 1938. In this he makes a distinction between forces and valences.

Forces are characterized as to both strength *and* direction; therefore, they may be represented mathematically by vectors. In opposition to this, we have valences which are only definable as to their strength, and therefore may be presented mathematically by scalars.

Lewin is not the only one who has conceived such a conceptual distinction. Woodworth, as early as 1918, made the distinction between drive and mechanism (which perhaps con-

---

[15] Cattell and his coworkers have demonstrated that factor-analysis may be useful in measuring and dealing with changing states such as anxiety, stress, excitement, regression, and elation-depression (Cattell 1969).

Table 33-2. S-, H- and R-variables in some Theories of Motivation

Name of the psychologist	S-variables Independent variables	H-variables Intervening variables	R-variables Dependent variables
McDougall	(External) Stimuli	Instinct (1908) Propensity Tendency (1932)	Purposive behavior
Freud	Somatic Sources of drives and stimuli	Instinctive drives, cathexes, ps.energy Id, Ego, Super-ego	Free associations Dream reports Neurotic symptoms and other behavior
Tolman	Initiating physiological state (1932) Drive (1951) Stimuli	Demand (1932) Need-system (1951) Belief-value matrix (1951)	Purposive behavior
Young	Needs Stimuli	Drive, set Attitude, desire	Behavior
Allport	Drives Stimuli	Motivational and instrumental traits	Expressive and instrumental behavior
Lewin	Needs Stimuli (especially from goal-objects)	Force, tension, valence	Behavior
Murray	Alpha-Press (1938) and other stimuli. Internal sources of needs	Needs (1938) Beta-Press (1938) Cathexes Thematic dispositions (1959)	Actones 1. Verbones 2. Motones
Hull	C_D (= Need) External stimuli	Drive (D) Incentive-Motivation (K) Reaction-potential (sEr) Habit-strength (sHr)	$R \begin{cases} t \\ n \\ p \\ A \end{cases}$
Hebb	External and internal stimuli	Cell-assemblies and Phase-Sequences (1949) Cue-function and Arousal (1955)	Organized behavior
Tinbergen	Releasing stimuli Motivational factors	Innate releasing mechanisms Instinct-mechanisms Motivation	Appetitive behavior Consummatory acts
McClelland	Cues Deviations from adaption level	Motive Affective arousal	TAT-responses and other behavior
Cattell	Stimuli Physiological State	Erg Attitude Sentiment	Test-responses and other behavior
Skinner	Deprivation Reinforcers Aversive stimuli	Response-strength or -probability?	Respondent and operant behavior
Atkinson	Stimuli	Tendency Motive Expectation Incentive-Value	TAT-responses and other behavior
Berlyne	Collative variables Arousal-potential	Arousal (RAS) Curiosity	Exploratory and epistemic behavior

tained some confusion with the other distinction into dispositions and functions). The pioneer in motivational psychology proper, P. T. Young, also makes a similar distinction in his definition: "Motivational psychology may be defined as the study of all conditions which *arouse* and *regulate* the behavior of organisms" (1936, p. 45). (Italics added here.)

At the same time (in the 1930s), Elisabeth Duffy set forth her distinction between intensity and direction as the main descriptive concepts in psychology (elaborated in Duffy 1962).

Still later, J. E. Farber suggested a distinction between "dynamogenic" and "directive" aspects of psychological variables (1955), and he discusses this distinction with J. S. Brown in the first two volumes of the *Nebraska Symposium* (1953, 1954).

It was on the basis of these different suggestions that the present author (Madsen 1959, first ed.) proposed a new classification of psychological variables which should supplement the former classifications (which were mainly based on Tolman). This classification is based upon a distinction between the different effects on behavior:

1. *Dynamogenic* variables, which are energizing or activating, and thus have an *intensity effect* on behavior.
2. *Directive* variables, which are directing, guiding, regulating, or "organizing," and thus have a directive effect on behavior.
3. *Vector* variables, which are both intensity- and direction-determining variables.

Table 33-3. Disposition and Functions. A Classification According to the Duration of the Existence of Psychological Variables

Name of the psychologist	Disposition-variables "Factors" or "Structures"	Function-variables States and Processes
McDougall	Instinct Propensity Sentiment	Tendency
Fured	Id, Ego and Super-ego Defense mechanisms	Primary and secondary processes Drives and energy
Tolman	Capacities and temperamental traits (1932) Means-end-readiness (1932) Belief-value-matrix (1951)	Expectations Demands (1932) Needs (1951) Drives (1959)
Young	Attitude	Drive, need Set, desire
Allport	Motivational and instrumental traits	Motivational and instrumental traits
Lewin	Structures of personality and environment	Tension, Valence Force
Murray	Need (1938) Thematic dispositions (1959) Cathexis (1959)	Need (1938) Press and cathexes (1938)
Hull	Habit-strength (sHr)	Drive (D) Reaction-potential (sEr) Incentive-motivation (K)
Hebb	Cell-assemblies	Phase-sequences (1949) Cue-function and arousal (1955)
Tinbergen	Instinct-mechanisms Innate-releasing-mechanisms	Motivation Motivational factors
McClelland	Adaptation level	Motive Affective arousal
Cattell	Erg Sentiment Attitude	Activation of ergs, sentiments and attitudes
Skinner	Reaction-probability or response-strength	Deprivation Reinforcing Aversive stimulation
Atkinson	Motive	Incentive value Expectation Tendency
Berlyne	Reticular arousal system and other neural structures	Collative variables Arousal, curiosity

This classification is applied to the theories of motivation previously presented, and the results appear in the next table (see Table 33-4).[16]

As it clearly appears from an inspection of this classification, we once again have a source of confusion in psychological theories. Thus the term "drive" is used as a purely dynamogenic variable in Hull's and coworkers' theory (clearly defended in Brown 1961). But in Freud's theory, "drive" is used as a vector variable. The same is true for the term "need," which is used as a dynamogenic variable in Hull's theory, but as a vector variable in Murray's early theory (1938) and in many other personality theories.

Furthermore, there are differences between vector variables, such as McDougall's "instinct" and Freud's "drive" on the one hand, and Hull's *sEr* and Atkinson's "tendency" on the other hand. Thus McDougall's "instinct" is a vague and all-inclusive concept (and therefore must be classified as a vector

variable), while Hull's *sEr* is clearly defined as a combination of a dynamogenic variable ("drive") and a directive variable ("habit-strength"); thus:

$$sEr = f(D \times sHr).$$

But unfortunately Hull and the "Hullians" have blended—or at least not clearly distinguished between—the two conceptual dimensions, "disposition versus function" and "dynamogenic versus directive." Thus *sEr* and *D* are functions, while *sHr* is in reality a disposition (activated by *D* and so also a function; but Hull and the Hullians have no term for the *sHr* as a function). The reason for this very frequent confusion is, perhaps, that dispositions are often directive (as is *sHr*), and functions are often dynamogenic (as is *D*). But there are dispositions which are dynamogenic (e.g., temperamental factors) and functions which are directive (e.g., perception and other cognitive processes). Thus Atkinson's formula $T = f(M \times E \times I)$ contains a distinction between both dimensions. *T* (tendency) and *E* (expectation) as well as *I* (incentive-value) are all functions, with *T* as a vectorial, *E* as a directive and *I* as a dynamogenic function. *M* (motive) is in Atkinson's theory (1964) clearly defined as a disposition—but not clearly according to its effects on behav-

[16] Hans Thomae, in his very penetrating analysis of motivation variables (Thomae 1965, Chapters 1 and 2), uses some similar concepts, which can be found in the heading of the sections in the second chapter: *Gerichtetkeit als Grundmerkmal, Motivationsgeschehnisse als "energetiserende" Phänomene*, and *Motivation und Orientierung* (i.e., *Zielorientierung, Mittelorientierung*, and *Normorientierung*).

Table 33-4. Dynamic, Directive and Vector-variables, A Classification of Variables in Accordance with Their Effects on Behavior

Name of the psychologist	Dynamogenic Variables	Directive Variables	Vector-variables
McDougall	Propensity Tendency		Instinct Sentiment
Freud	Cathexes*	Ego, Super-Ego Primary and secondary processes	Drives Id
Tolman	Demand (1932) Drive (1951) Need (1951) Drive (1959)	Means-end-readiness and -expectations (1932) Belief-value Matrix (1951) Beliefs (1959)	Drive (1932) Immediate Behavior space (1951)
Young	Need Drive	Set Attitude	Desire (1936) Motive (1961)
Allport	Drive Motivational traits	Instrumental traits	
Lewin	Need Tension Valence		Force
Murray	Press Cathexes		Need (1938) Thematic dispositions (1959)
Hull	Need (or C_D) Drive (D) Incentive motivation (K)	Antedating goal Reaction (r_G-s_G) Drive-Stimulus (S_D) Habit-Strength (sHr)	Reaction-potential (sEr)
Hebb	Arousal (1955)	Phase-sequence (1949) Cell-assemblies (1949) Cue-function (1955)	
Tinbergen	Releasing stimuli Motivational factors Motivation	Innate releasing mechanisms Instinct-mechanisms	
McClelland	Affective arousal	Cues	Motive
Cattell	Erg		Attitude Sentiment
Skinner	Deprivation		Aversive stimuli Reinforcer Response-strength
Atkinson	Incentive-value Motive	Expectation	Tendency
Berlyne	Arousal	Thinking and other cognitive processes	Collative variables Curiosity

* The author has had some doubt about the classification of "cathexes," "valence," "incentive-value," etc. They may have been placed as vector-variables, as they have *some* directive function, but this function is only dependent on the spatial localization of the "valence," etc., in relation to the individual and not dependent on the valued object itself.

ior—and therefore it may be classified as a vector disposition as well as a dynamic dispositon.

The significance of the distinction between these two conceptual dimensions may be more clearly illustrated if we combine these two dimensions in one classification.[17] In our next table of classification (Table 33-5), we have only included the most representative or typical examples from motivational theories.

If we examine this classification thoroughly we can see why the old instinct concept (e.g., McDougall's "instinct") was so scientifically barren. The old instinct concept made no distinctions at all between the conceptual dimensions. Instinct was a term designating both a disposition and functions, and the functions were unspecified vector functions.

The course of development in theories of motivation is characterized by an increasing conceptual differentiation between different conceptual dimensions. This conceptual development

[17] For the moment we can disregard the first *S-H-R* classification.

is, of course, in intimate interaction with the experimental development.

Perhaps we could use the classification "dynamic versus directive" to give a very rough description of theories of motivation: the older theories (McDougall's, Freud's, and to some extent Murray's and Tolman's first versions) were theories using vectorial concepts. The newer theories are divided into two groups: those which stress the dynamogenic variables (especially Hull's and followers'), and those which stress the directive variables (especially McClelland's and Atkinson's and coworkers').

An important result of an analytical and comparative study such as we have presented in the foregoing pages could be an increasing tendency among psychologists to use different terms for the different conceptual aspects of the psychological variables they deal with in their theories.

A further step in the development of psychological theorizing would be an acceptance of a common terminology as long as it is common concepts the psychologists express with their terms. (Of course there must be room for using new and different

Table 33-5. Classification of Hypothetical Variables: a Combined Classification*

Effect: *Existence:*	*Directive variables:*	*Dynamic variables:*	*Vectorial variables:*
Dispositions:	Freud's "Ego" and "Super Ego" Hull's "sHr"	Atkinson's "Motive"	Freud's "Id" Murray's "Need" (=Personality factor)
Functions:	Atkinson's "Expectation" Young's "set"	Atkinson's "Value" Freud's "energy" Lewin's "tension" Hull's "drive"	Atkinson's "Tendency" Freud's "drive" Lewin's "force" Hull's "sEr" Murray's "Need" (=drive)

* The two classifications from Table 3 and Table 4 combined in one classification. Only a few representative variables are placed in the scheme.

terms when a theorist has created a new concept or discovered a variable.)

As a contribution to such a common terminology the present author has suggested some definitions of terms (Madsen 1959, first ed.). We shall recapitulate them here (see Table 33-6) in a modified version including theories advanced since 1959. The principles upon which the suggestions are based may still be valid, and the interested reader is referred to the original proposals (Madsen 1968a, 4th ed., Chap. 18).

Categories of Motivation

THE PROBLEM

In this part of the chapter we shall deal with the problem of defining the number and main classes of motivational vari-

ables. These are really two interrelated problems. We shall deal with the problem of defining the number first.

THE NUMBER OF MOTIVATIONAL VARIABLES

There would be no problem about defining the number of motivational variables if they were all empirical. But the historical fact that motivational variables were introduced into psychology for the purpose of explanation of (goal-directed) behavior created the following problem: How many different *hypothetical*, motivational variables must we postulate to explain behavior?

This problem is really a part or version of a more general problem in the philosophy of science: the problem of the fruitfulness, validity, or "explanatory power" of hypothetical constructs.

Table 33-6. Proposed Definitions of Motivational Variables

The terms proposed	Definitions in systematological terms	Possible neural bases	Hull	Cattell	Lewin	Atkinson
1. "Motivation"	Generic term including *all* dynamic and vector variables					
2. "Central Motive State" or "Motive"	Vector-functions, H-variables consisting of 2a, 2b, 2c	Sub-cortical brain processes or -states	sEr	"E" Ergic tension level	Force	Tendency
2a. "Central sensitization processes" or "Sensitization"	Specific-dynamic* functions, H-variables	Activation of hypothalamic and limbic centers	S_D	P Physiological component		
2b. "Central incentive processes" or "Incentive-motive"	Specific-dynamic functions, H-variables	Activation of acquired cortico-sub-cortical structures	K		Valence	Incentive-value
2c. "Central activating processes" or "Arousal"	General-dynamic* functions, H-variables	Arousal of Reticular Formation	D		Tension	
3. "Motivational Dispositions"	Dynamic and Vector dispositions, H-variables	Individual differences in neural centers or acquired neural structures		Constitution and *H*istory	Structural differences in "P" and "E"	Motive
4. "Motivational Stimuli"	*Dynamic* functions, S-variables	Stimuli with inborn releasing *or* with acquired dynamic effect		$S + K$		
5. "Motivational Impulses"	Dynamic functions, S-variables	Neural impulses and humoral influences on sub-cortical centers	C_D (*Need*)	G Gratification	Need	
6. "Informational processes" or "Cognition"	Directive functions, S- and H-variables	Sensoric and cortical processes	sHr $r_G - s_G$			Expectation

* We have introduced a distinction between "*specific*-dynamic" and *general*-dynamic functions, which refers to specific, selective activation and unspecific, general activation respectively.

The subdivision of "Motive" into "incentive" "sensitization" and "arousal" is inspired by Cofer and Appley (1964).

The term "Central Motive State" was originally proposed by Clifford T. Morgan, who has developed a very consistent "physiological theory" of motivation (Morgan 1957; 1959).

The problem can be conceived of as a question of avoiding two dangerous extremes. One extreme is the explanatory approach which involves the construction of so many hypothetical variables that we have one for every fact we wish to explain. This is the "pseudoexplanatory" approach. Thus in this case we have just as many motivational variables as there are goal-directed behavior-acts to be explained. It is easy to see that this approach leads to a pseudoexplanation with a superfluous duplicity of all terms: a set of descriptive terms and a parallel set of hypothetical terms. This was the chief failure of the old "instinct" theories, that they deprived their hypothetical constructs of any explanatory power or predictive validity by creating too many constructs.

The other extreme explanatory approach is the one which tries to explain everything by one or a very few hypothetical constructs. This is the "speculative-philosophical approach." The most well-known case in the history of psychology is Freud's "life-instinct" and "death-instinct."

Perhaps it is not so easy to see the shortcomings in this speculative-philosophical approach, because the purpose of theories always is to reduce the number of data by organizing or systematizing them into fewer categories. And further the number of abstract descriptive categories may be organized into a coherent system by introducing a few hypothetical constructs. So it seems to be a consequence of this general scientific approach that we try to reduce as often as possible by introducing the fewest possible hypothetical variables—perhaps only one. But the danger of this approach is that it may be very difficult—even impossible—to connect such an abstract hypothetical variable to empirical variables with operational definitions.

Thus the solution of the problem is to construct the optimal number of hypothetical variables: enough variables to avoid speculative-philosophical vagueness by making operational definitions possible, and not so many variables that they become pseudoexplanatory.

N. E. Miller (1959) has demonstrated clearly that the introduction of an intervening or hypothetical variable is justified by the old epistemological principle of economy if—and only if—the hypothetical variable is connected with at least three S-variables on one side and three R-variables on the other. This may be conceived of as a rule for avoiding the pseudo-explanatory fallacy. Unfortunately we do not know a similar simple rule for avoiding the speculative-philosophical fallacy. Psychologists, in this case, have to make use of their scientific self-control.

Fortunately most modern theories of motivation demonstrate that most psychologists of today have avoided the two extreme explanatory approaches and instead have used what we could call "a moderate parsimonious reduction" or, perhaps better: an "optimal explanatory conceptual system." These terms were selected because the history of science demonstrates—as strongly emphasized by the provocative theory of Thomas Kuhn (1962)—that scientists prefer the most parsimonious theories with the most explanatory "power" and avoid the oversimplified philosophical approach as well as the pseudo-explanatory theories.

Thus in most modern theories of motivation parsimonious reduction is obtained by assuming the existence of an optimal system of basic motivational variables or primary motives. These primary motives (also called "biogenic," "viscerogenic," "organical," "instinctive," "inborn," or "unlearned" motiva-

tional variables) are often estimated to number about ten to fifteen. In addition to this, most—but not all—theories presuppose the existence of an indeterminate number of secondary motives (also called "psychogenic," "learned," or "acquired" motivational variables). Furthermore, many theories of motivation presuppose the existence of certain principles for combinations of motivational variables into motivational systems (such as "sentiments," etc.). By this addition the explanatory power of the theories is increased without sacrificing the parsimonious number of basic, explanatory concepts.

But this categorizing into primary and secondary motives has raised at least two problems:

1. What criteria should be used in defining a system of primary motives?
2. How is the development of secondary motives explained?

We shall deal with these two problems in the following two sections of this chapter.

CRITERIA FOR THE DEFINITIONS OF PRIMARY MOTIVES

In a comparative study of twenty theories of motivation the present author found (Madsen 1968) that three different criteria for defining primary motives are used.

The most commonly used criterion may be called the physiological criterion. According to this rule the definition of primary motives is accomplished by selecting those motivational variables which are known to be functionally related to observable physiological states or processes (outside the central nervous system). Thus primary motives are organically determined motivational variables.

At the present time psychologists using this physiological criterion can agree about the existence of a dozen primary motives, such as hunger, thirst or, sex. They are known to be mainly determined—but not necessarily exclusively—by organic states or processes outside the CNS. In most instances it is possible to determine the central location of motivational centers in the hypothalamus or other parts of the brain using electro-physiological or other methods.

The physiological criterion has two advantages: it results in maximum agreement among psychologists and it facilitates cooperation between psychologists and physiologists.

Another widely used criterion for defining primary motives may be called the comparative-psychological criterion (or, by H. Thomae [1965], the "universal behavior-repertoire"—*universelles Verhaltensinventar*). According to this principle, primary motives are selected from among the motivational variables that are supposed to determine universal classes of behavior—or at least species-specific behavior. In other words, primary motives are motivational variables which determine universal behavior-acts. If we apply this criterion we arrive at almost the same set of primary motives as that established by the psychological criterion. But the comparative-psychological criterion has the disadvantage that only a few species-specific or common human behavior acts exist. Most human behavior is learned and consequently varies among individuals.

A third criterion for the definition of primary motives Thomae (1965) calls "the cue-criterion" (*Schlüsselreiz*-criterion). According to this criterion, primary motives are selected from

Table 33-7. Primary Motivational Variables in Some Theories

McDougall's "Propensities" 1932	Young's "Primary Drives" 1936	Murray's "Viscerogenic Needs" 1938	Cattell's "Ergs" 1950	Madsen's "Primary Motives" 1959
1. Food seeking p	1. Hunger	1. n Inspiration	1. Escape	1. Hunger motive
2. Disgust p	2. Nausea	2. n Water	2. Appeal	2. Thirst motive
3. Sex p	3. Thirst	3. n Food	3. Acquisitiveness	3. Sex motive
4. Fear p	4. Sex	4. n Sentience	4. Laughter	4. Nursing motive
5. Curiosity p	5. Nursing	5. n Sex	5. Pugnacity	5. Temperature motives
6. Protective and parental p	6. Urinating	6. n Lactation	6. Self-assertion	6. Pain-avoidance motive
7. Gregarious p	7. Defecating	7. n Expiration	7. Sleep	7. Excretory motives
8. Self-assertive	8. Avoiding heat	8. n Urination	8. Play	8. Oxygen motive
9. Submissive p	9. Avoiding cold	9. n Defecation	9. Self-abasement	9. Rest and sleep motive[18]
10. Anger p	10. Avoiding pain	10. n Noxavoidance	10. Mating	10. Activity motives[19]
11. Appeal p	11. Air hunger	11. n Heatavoidance	11. Gregariousness	11. Security motive (or fear)
12. Constructive p	12. Fear and anger	12. n Coldavoidance	12. Parental drive	12. Aggression motive
13. Acquisitive p	13. Fatigue	13. n Harmavoidance	13. Curiosity	
14. Laughter p	14. Sleep		14. Construction	
15. Comfort p	15. Curiosity		15. Disgust	
16. Rest or sleep p	16. Social instinct		16. Hunger	
17. Migratory p	17. Tickle			
18. Coughing, sneezing, breathing, etc.				

among motivational variables which are known to be determined by a species-specific releasing stimulus which presupposes the existence of IRM (Innate Releasing Mechanisms, as defined by Tinbergen 1951). In other words: Primary motives are motivational variables determined by innate "cues."

The cue-criterion has the same disadvantage as the criterion of universal behavior: we know about very few innate cues in man.

With these three criteria we have exhausted all the possibilities for directly operational definitions: the hypothetical motivational variables (called "primary motives") are defined either by their causes (organic processes or innate cues) or by their consequences (species-specific or universal behavior).

We shall only discuss one more criterion which McDougall, among others, applied. It may be called the "psycho-pathological criterion" as it defines primary motives as motivational variables that the organism must have satisfied or reduced in order to retain health and life; therefore, it may also be called the "survival criterion." If we apply this criterion, we arrive at approximately the same, or perhaps a fewer, number of primary motives.

In concluding this discussion of criteria for the definition of primary motives, we may propose that *maximum agreement about definitions of primary motives may be accomplished by using all the criteria in combination* and only selecting those as primary motives which are so defined by all the criteria. The most useful criterion, as mentioned earlier, is the physiological criterion. By using this criterion we arrive at the following list of primary motives (see Table 33-7). Alongside these we have placed those established by Cattell, McDougall, and Murray.

SECONDARY MOTIVATION

This important problem has been studied intensively during the past few decades. A very extensive and penetrating review of research and theories has been made by J. S. Brown and I. F.

[18] A very elaborate theory concerning "sleep" as a primary motive is presented by Edward J. Murray. This theory has important consequences for motivational theory in general (Murray 1965).
[19] A need (drive) for sensory variation, "sensoristasis," is postulated in Duane O. Schultz, *Sensory Restriction* (New York, Academic Press, 1965).

Farber (1968). In addition, Brown has proposed one of the clearest and most consistent theories concerning secondary motivation (1961). Therefore, in the following pages we shall draw considerably on these sources.

The earlier theories of motivation—such as Tolman's and Murray's—introduced the notion of acquired drives or psychogenic needs, but they did not possess any explanatory hypotheses with experimental support concerning the origins of secondary motivation.

The first experimental investigation of the origins of secondary motivation was carried out by O. H. Mowrer (1930). This was supplemented by N. E. Miller (1941, 1948), who later made extensive use of the concept of secondary motivation in his and Dollard's book about *Social Learning* (1941). In these early experiments and theories *fear* (or anxiety) was regarded as the basis for secondary motivation. In their classic experiments they first demonstrated that fear as an unconditioned reaction to noxious stimuli could be conditioned to a previously neutral stimulus. Next, they demonstrated that this conditioned fear could motivate the learning of a new instrumental reaction. This first experimental establishment of fear as an acquirable drive was followed up by many experiments. Many of these have been conducted to disprove the original notions of Mowrer and Miller, but in spite of this, Brown and Farber conclude their critical survey with these words:

It is worth noting that the concept of conditioned fear as a secondary motivational system has proved unusually robust (Brown & Faber 1968, p. 110).

The present author believes that Brown's own theory (1961) is based on convincing experimental evidence. In his theory Brown proposes the hypothesis that fear is the basis for (almost) all secondary motivations.

In their review Brown and Farber further emphasize the possibility that Hull's and Spence's incentive motivation (K) may be another important source of secondary motivation. Brown and Farber survey the numerous experimental investigations and theoretical discussions concerning this concept. They seem to be inclined to accept a sort of "frustration interpretation" of the motivating function of "K" (or $r_g - s_g$) with these words:

This view implies that it is the lack of an incentive or goal object, in the presence of cues previously associated with that incentive that is motivating. Anticipatory motivation is thus transformed into deficit motivation with aversive properties and the conditions leading to this sequence of events are indistinguishable from those that produce frustration (Brown & Farber 1968, p. 115).

Thus Brown and Farber have reduced all (secondary) motivation to the same formula: "deficit or aversive motivation." Brown and Farber further discuss, and seem to accept, the possibility of an "incentive-motivation-interpretation" of sensory reinforcements from novel stimuli, etc. This interpretation seems to be close to that proposed by Harry Fowler (1967) but contrary to D. E. Berlyne's drive-interpretation of curiosity (1960).

Brown and Farber conclude that other primary need-states, such as hunger and thirst, do not seem to be conditionable.

We can thus conclude this discussion of secondary motivation in this way: Secondary motivation seems to be based on—or

perhaps is identical with—conditioned fear and incentive-motivation. Both sources of secondary motivation may be interpreted as types of aversive or deficit motivation. We can thus see a clear similarity to primary motivation as conceived by Hull and his followers.

But there are, of course, other explanations of primary and secondary motivation, and, therefore, we shall analyze and compare the basic hypotheses of motivation in the following section. (See Fig. 33-3.)

Basic Hypotheses of Motivation

DEFINITION OF "HYPOTHESIS"

In the earlier sections of this chapter we have mentioned that there are many different conceptions concerning the working of motivational variables. Such conceptions may to some

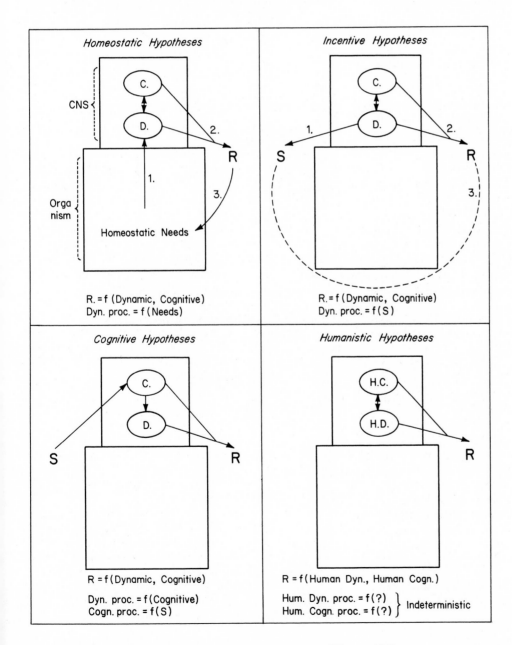

Fig. 33-3. *Models of motivation.*

degree be included in definitions of the motivational variables. But they may also be formulated into general propositions concerning the functional relationships between S-variables, H-variables and R-variables. Such general propositions designating a functional relationship we call "hypotheses." Thus, a hypothesis may be an $S \rightarrow H \rightarrow R$ relationship *or* an $S \rightarrow H$, an $H \rightarrow H$, *or* an $H \rightarrow R$ relationship. If a general proposition is only concerned with functional relationships between S-variables and R-variables we call it a "law" (an $S \rightarrow R$-relationship). Thus we do not differentiate between different degrees of verification ("laws" are no more reliable or plausible than "hypotheses" according to our terminology). Nor do we distinguish between kinds of functional relationships, such as causal relationships and probability relationships. Hypotheses may be formulated in words or in logical or mathematical symbols. If there are several hypotheses, they may be loosely connected, or they can be related to each other in a logical system of hypotheses, a so-called deductive system consisting of some primary hypotheses (axioms, postulates) and several secondary derivative hypotheses (theorems).

In the following paragraphs we shall only be concerned with the content of the hypotheses of motivation, and we shall leave the discussion of the form of the system of hypotheses until the last part of the chapter, which deals with theories of motivation. We now turn to a consideration of the basic hypotheses of several theories. These basic hypotheses may be the only, or the most important, hypotheses in the theory; but, of course, the basic hypotheses may also be axioms or postulates in deductive systems.

"HOMEOSTASIS" HYPOTHESES

One of the first and most widely accepted basic hypotheses of motivation was the "homeostasis hypothesis" formulated by Walter B. Cannon (1915), but having its origins in Claude Benard's conception of the "internal milieu." Thus, "homeostasis" denotes the optimal conditions of equilibrium in the organism. The main point of this basic hypothesis is, that all biological processes (including behavior) are determined by a disturbance of homeostasis, and that the processes go on until homeostasis is regained (or the organism is dead). Thus behavior fullfills an important function as a homeostasis-regulating process.

This conception of motivation has several advantages, which explains its popularity among psychologists: it was a simple hypothesis, which is always important for scientists; and it was a biological hypothesis, which was important for psychologists in the post-Darwinian era. Many theories of motivation contain a basic hypothesis about homeostasis in different forms. We shall take up the most typical and later collect them in a table of classification.

Hull's (1943) original theory is one of the most influential cases of a homeostasis hypothesis. "Need" is conceived of as a disturbance of homeostasis and the functional relationship may be presented in this way:

$$\text{Need} \rightarrow \text{Drive} \rightarrow \text{Behavior} \rightarrow \text{Need-reduction}$$

As "need-reduction" in this version of the theory was the reinforcing event, Hull's theory thus explained learning (as well as motivation) on the basis of homeostasis.

Freud's theory also contained a version of a homeostasis, or equilibrium-hypothesis, even though it was developed before Cannon's construction of the homeostasis concept. Thus Freud's conception of the mental apparatus "as possessing a stimulus-reducing function," together with his definition of drive, may be regarded as forming a homeostasis conception.

K. Lewin's theory is a little more difficult to classify as containing a homeostasis hypothesis. Lewin is not especially biologically oriented, but on the other hand his concepts of "tension" and "force" are not unlike a homeostasis conception.

Murray's first theory (1938) may also be said to contain a homeostasis hypothesis, but in his later writings he emphasized that not only "tension-reduction" but "tension-induction" as well characterize motivation and behavior.

Freeman's theory (1948) is perhaps the clearest and most consistent elaboration of a homeostasis conception.[20]

R. S. Stagner's and T. F. Karwoski's theory (1952) is a typical example of the widening, and loosening, of the homeostasis conception, so that it also includes social equilibrium. Thus they write:

The key concept which is used in this volume to tie the various aspects of psychology together is homeostasis [p. 116]. . . . [that homeostasis] appears to function on the social as well as the biological level. (Stagner & Karwoski 1952, p. 18)

Too much use of an explanatory principle may cause its destruction, as it may become too vague, possibly even pseudo-explaining.

At the time of the culmination of the popularity of the homeostasis hypothesis, it was already on its way out and was soon replaced—to some extent at least—by other basic hypotheses of motivation.[21]

INCENTIVE HYPOTHESES

The "homeostasis period" lasted from approximately 1915 (the year of Cannon's first formulation) until about 1953 (the year of the first Nebraska Symposium). During this whole period there had, of course, been ample criticism from the more humanistic and sociotrope psychologists such as Allport and Maslow. But the most important and convincing criticism came from the biotropes themselves. Thus H. F. Harlow in the first Nebraska Symposium in 1953 criticized the homeostasis hypothesis as being too narrow. He pointed out that there were other biological primary motivations than homeostasis drive. Thus Harlow supported the existence of visual exploratory drive and concluded:

Now we have presented a series of researches which indicate that exteroceptive stimuli may motivate a monkey as strongly

[20] Freeman's theory is interesting, among other things, because it anticipated the concept of "arousal" before the discovery of the function of the reticular formation or Reticular Arousal System (*RAS*). For a more detailed analysis of Freeman's theory the reader is referred to Madsen (1968).

[21] As another example of theories based upon the homeostasis hypothesis, we could mention the theories of N.R.F. Mairer (1949) and Jules H. Masserman (1966, 2nd ed.) These theories, together with Stagner's and Karwoski's theory, are analyzed in Madsen (1968).

and at least as persistently as any described source of internal stimuli (Harlow 1953, p. 45).

Later, it was demonstrated by many experiments that even the so-called homeostatic drives (especially hunger, thirst, and sex) cannot be completely explained by the use of a homeostasis hypothesis.

The earliest and strongest experimentally based attack on a narrow homeostasis conception was made by P. T. Young. As early as the beginning of the 1940s, Young presented evidence gathered from animal experiments concerning the existence of food preferences which were *not* based on homeostasis (1941). Throughout the following years Young collected an important mass of experimental data which he interpreted through the application of his "hedonic theory." Some of the basic hypotheses in this theory are formulated thus:

Stimulation has affective as well as sensory consequences.

An affective arousal orients the organism toward or against the stimulus object. . . .

The laws of conditioning apply to affective processes. . . .

Affective processes regulate behavior by influencing choice. . . .

Neuro-behavioral patterns are organized according to the hedonic principle of maximizing the positive and minimizing the negative affective arousal (1961, pp. 198–201).

The present author believes that Young's hedonic theory is that which is best supported by experimental evidence and the most explicit and consistent formulation we have of a hedonic theory. Furthermore, it is *not* one-sided, as Young conceives of the hedonic hypothesis as supplementing a homeostatic hypothesis.

The main ideas to be found in the hedonic hypothesis are very old. The can be traced back to the ancient philosophers (among others, Epicurus) and to the Utilitarians (e.g., J. Bentham) in the 1700s. The hedonic conception is also inherent in Thorndike's Law of Effect and Freud's pleasure-principle. But Young was the first to formulate the hedonic conception explicitly and to build his formulation upon experimental evidence.

Other modern psychologists have followed in Young's footsteps. McClelland's and coworkers' theory (1953) is explicitly a hedonic theory. In opposition to Young, McClelland makes a hedonic hypothesis serve as the sole basis for his motivational theory. We also find a hedonic hypothesis in Hebb's early theory (1949). This conception is strongly supported by Olds' and coworkers' experiments with intracranial stimulation in "reward- and punishment-centers" of the brain. Atkinson has elaborated McClelland's theory, but he has not done so much about the hedonic basis as about the incentive concept.

The value- or incentive-concept is inherent in a hedonic theory, but it is not based exclusively on a hedonic hypothesis. An incentive is an *S*-variable which has a dynamogenic effect on behavior through an intervening *H*-variable called "incentive-motivation." If this dynamogenic effect is inherited it may be explained by a hedonic hypothesis, but the inborn dynamogenic effect may also be explained by Lorenz's and Tinbergen's hypothesis about inborn releasing mechanisms (IRM).

Furthermore, the dynamogenic effect of an incentive may be learned (by contiguity or by reinforcement). In that case, the incentive motivation may be based on a general learning or behavior theory like Hull's.

Thus the incentive conception of motivation is broader than the hedonic hypothesis, which is only *one* possible explanation of incentive motivation.

Incentive motivation may be traced back in the history of psychology to such concepts as Thorndike's "satisfiers" and "annoyers" and to Freud's "cathexis." Perhaps K. Lewin's theory was the first motivational theory in which incentive-motivation played an important role, although it did so under the name "valence." It seems fair to say that valence was more important than "need" in determining "psychological forces" in Lewin's theory.

Atkinson has combined Lewin's incentive concept with Tolman's (and McClelland's) expectation concept. Thus Atkinson's theory is the most explicit expectation × value theory.

With "expectation" we move to another kind of basic hypothesis of motivation, the cognitive hypothesis. But before we make a deeper analysis of this matter, we shall conclude this section with a discussion of the development of incentive-motivation within learning theory.

As mentioned earlier it is possible to include an incentive concept in a learning theory. This was clearly illustrated by K. W. Spence, who motivated Hull to include an incentive motivation variable in his theory. This concept was based on Hull's earlier concept, "fractional antedating goal response" (r_g) and the related concept, "goal-stimulus" (s_g). These two variables were in Hull's earliest formulations from the 1930s and were brought together in the $r_g - s_g$-mechanism. Hull treated this *H*-variable exclusively as a directive variable, which played a similar role in his theory to "expectation" in Tolman's. But Spence pointed to the dynamogenic effect of the $r_g - s_g$-mechanism. This dynamogenic effect may—according to Brown (1968)—be explained as based upon the aversive effect of the frustration of the consummatory reaction (R_g). This frustration-determined dynamogenic effect is connected to the antedating goal response (r_g) and its connection with S_g. In order to separate the dynamogenic effect of the antedating or "anticipatory goal-reaction" from the directive effect, Hull used the letter *K* as a symbol for this *H*-variable.[22] In the 1951 version of Hull's theory incentive motivation (*K*) was combined multiplicatively with drive (*D*) and habit (*sHr*)—and some other variables—to determine "reaction-evocation-potential" (*sEr*).

In Spence's later theories (e.g., Spence 1960) incentive-motivation (*K*) played a greater role than drive. *K* was assumed to be learned by reinforcement (drive-reduction), while habit (*sHr*) was assumed to be learned by classical conditioning (contiguity).

Incentive-motivation was further elaborated experimentally and theoretically by Hull's student, Frank A. Logan, in his book *Incentive* (1960).

Later R. C. Bolles (1967) analyzed the development of motivational theories, especially the theories of motivation relating to learning. On the basis of his own experiments, supplemented by an intensive review of the results of many other experiments, Bolles emphasizes the importance of incentive motivation as compared to drive.

---

[22] According to Brown (1968) the letter *K* was used to honor Kenneth W. Spence.

He concludes with an explanation of incentive motivation based on reinforcement. Finally, he explicitly supports Skinner's "theory" (or descriptive laws of reinforcement).

We thus have the growth of motivational concepts and basic hypotheses within learning theory, which stretches from the old vague instinct concept combined with Thorndike's Law of Effect via the need-drive conception in Hullian theory to an incentive conception based upon reinforcement (as already conceived by Thorndike!).

Through this development—especially as manifested in Spence's theory—this trend in learning theory has come rather close becoming a cognitive hypothesis of motivation, to which we now turn.

"COGNITIVE" HYPOTHESES

As pointed out by Fritz Heider (1960), there was a motivational hypothesis contained in the classic Gestalt theory. The "tendency to closure" or "to create the good figure" was treated by the classic Gestalt psychologists as a dynamic factor or force. This conception was never elaborated into an explicit motivational hypothesis, and the "tendency to closure" was perhaps only intended to explain the motivation of cognitive processes. Fritz Heider, on the basis of Gestalt conceptions, has elaborated a "theory of balance" to explain the motivation of social behavior.

A similar theory has been proposed by Leon Festinger under the title *Cognitive dissonance theory* (1957). The concept "cognitive dissonance" is defined by Festinger as a discrepancy between perception and expectation, or a discrepancy between percepts and concepts. This conception is rather similar to Berlyne's concept of perceptual and conceptual conflicts which determine curiosity (1960). But Festinger's cognitive dissonance is assumed to motivate cognitive processes, defense mechanisms and behavior generally.

The most highly developed and influential cognitive hypothesis is included in Tolman's theory. Besides drives and needs Tolman assumes the existence of cognitive determinants of behavior such as "expectations." And these cognitive determinants play the most important role in performance and learning. According to Tolman's theory it is neither "reinforcement" ("drive-reduction", etc.) nor S-R-associations through contiguity that are the critical factors in learning, but rather the individual's cognitive organizing of guiding structures ("cognitive maps"). Besides these variables, in his 1932 version of the theory Tolman includes a kind of mixed variable called "sign-gestalt-readiness." This variable is such a peculiar and intimate combination or rather total blending of cognitive (directive) and motivational (dynamic) aspects in *one* variable, that the present author has never seen its like in any theory of motivation. We may conclude thus: In Tolman's theory cognitive variables are the most important both as determiners of behavior and of learning. In addition, they intimately influence the other "purely" motivational variables.

A modern version of a cognitive hypothesis of motivation is presented in J. McV. Hunt's theory of "intrinsic motivation" (e.g., Hunt 1965). Hunt defines this term as:

a motivation inherent in the organism's informational interaction with circumstances through the distance receptors and in its intentional goal-anticipating actions (Hunt 1965).

This theory is based on the assumption that behavior is directed by a complex information process analogous to those going on in electronic computers. Hunt furthermore assumes that those directive, cognitive processes have their own intrinsic motivation or inherited dynamic forces. The basis for this intrinsic, cognitive motivation is incongruence between the informational feedback and the inborn and learned standards (similar to adaption levels).

A very significant feature about Hunt's theory is the possibility of integrating it with other well-established theories. One of his greatest accomplishments has been to demonstrate that Piaget's theory of cognitive development implicitly contains a basic hypothesis about intrinsic motivation. Furthermore, Hunt shows that this theory is consistent with modern neuropsychological theory, especially the one proposed by K. H. Pribam (1958). Finally, Hunt's theory of intrinsic motivation at certain points comes close to the modern Soviet psychologists' tendency to elaborate the role of the "orienting reflex" in learning (Sokolov 1964), and therefore also close to Berlyne's theory of curiosity (1960).

Hunt points to the similarity between his cognitive, intrinsic motivational theory and the old philosophical view of man as a "rational and free-deciding being".[23]

We now approach the last basic hypothesis about motivation, which we shall discuss in the next section, "The humanistic hypothesis of motivation." But before doing that, we shall complete this section with some comments on other intrinsic motivational theories. So far as the author knows, Sigmund Koch first used the term and proposed an outline of such a theory. Koch (1956) criticized contemporary theories of motivation and suggested an "intrinsic" motivational theory as an alternative.

The most highly elaborated theory of this kind was proposed by one of the pioneers in motivational theory, the late Robert S. Woodworth (1958), in his revision of his 1918 work *Dynamic Psychology*, which appeared forty years later. In this book, Woodworth formulates what he calls a behavior-primacy theory which he contrasts with the more traditional theories of Freud, Murray, and Hull collected under the label, "need-primacy theories." Woodworth's basic hypothesis of motivation is found in this passage:

The behavior-primacy theory regards the tendency to deal with the environment as a primary drive, and indeed as the primary drive in behavior. The various capacities for dealing with the environment afford outlets for the general behavior drive and give it different forms—given the necessary environmental opportunities. So the manifold human interests are predictable from the combination (Woodworth 1958, p. 133).

The similarity between this behavior-primacy theory and Hunt's intrinsic motivation is very marked. The only difference is, perhaps, that Woodworth's theory is broader and more general than Hunt's. In Woodworth's theory, it is not only cognitive processes that possess their own intrinsic motivation, but all behavior is *intrinsically* as well as extrinsically motivated by needs and incentives.

If needs and incentives were still not accepted as extrinsic

[23] Another cybernetic model is presented very convincingly by J. P. Guilford (1965).

sources of motivation, one would have been tempted to conclude that the long development of motivational theories had ended with intrinsically motivated behavior. That is almost the same as saying that explanatory concepts and hypotheses about motivation were replaced by the very fact of motivation: activation of behavior.[24]

HUMANISTIC HYPOTHESES

The last group of basic hypotheses of motivation represents the modern version of an old tradition going back to the ancient philosophers. This traditional view conceives of man as a being completely different from all other organisms. The distinguishing —almost defining—human traits, according to this conception, are rational thinking and free will. Despite the developments in the natural sciences—especially of Darwin's theory—there are still thinkers, scholars, and philosophers who adhere to this ancient, humanistic conception of man.

In other branches of psychology, such as cognitive psychology, it has been easier to defend the existence of a fundamental difference between Man and animals. The ability to use language and to think abstractly, for example, are specifically human traits. But in motivational psychology it has been very difficult to continue believing in a fundamental difference between man and animals—at least after Freud demonstrated that not even in his own personality was man the "master of his own house," as the rational ego was determined by unconscious forces of sexual and aggressive origin.

Despite the testimony of Freud there remain psychologists —even American psychologists—who believe that the motivation of man is fundamentally different from that of animals.

Among these psychologists who have expressed belief in a humanistic conception of man are two who have defended their theories so completely that they cannot be neglected in a survey of theories of motivation. These two psychologists, who deserve respect even from nonbelievers, are Allport and Maslow.

Gordon W. Allport proposed his humanistic theory of personality and motivation in his famous book, first published in 1937. (Revised edition 1961). As mentioned in the historical survey, Allport's basic hypothesis about motivation is called functional autonomy. Allport postulates functional autonomy as regards motivation in adult human beings. By this hypothesis

he preserved the special humanistic trend concerning the motivation of adults. This had two consequences for Allport: (1) the results of experiments in motivation with animals had no bearing on human motivation, and (2) Freud's theories of instinctive drives had no relationship to normal, adult human beings, because they were founded on material concerning neurotic patients who were more infantile in their motivation than normal adults. It was in this way that Allport justified his standpoint that human motivation was of a special humanistic nature. But this justification depended on the hypothesis of functional autonomy, and this hypothesis has the status of a postulate which is mainly defended on philosophical, not empirical, grounds. Thus, Allport's philosophy of man has determined his basic hypothesis of motivation.[25]

We remember from the historical survey that Abraham H. Maslow has written extensively about motivation and personality (see especially Maslow 1954). Maslow defends the basic humanistic hypothesis in this way: Freud's—and the animal learning theorists' hypotheses of motivation are only valid for what he calls "deficiency-motivation." This kind of motivation (the basic physiological needs, the need for safety, the social needs) is the determiner of behavior in animals and neurotic human beings. But the behavior of normal, healthy adults, whose deficiency needs are satisfied, is determined by a different kind of motivation called "growth motivation" (later, "meta-motivation" [1967]). This type of motivation includes the need for self-realization, for creative work, for altruistic actions, etc.

Maslow's hypothesis is supported by empirical evidence, especially that drawn from his investigations of many well-known, creative persons (artists, scientists, etc.). Maslow also finds support for his hypothesis in his description of so-called peak-experience, to which belong the religous mystic's experience of transcendental phenomena.

But besides this empirical evidence Maslow also bases his hypothesis upon his philosophy of man. Maslow has defended the view[26] that psychologists must have a philosophy of man before they carry out any empirical, psychological research. Maslow points to the fact that psychologists always have an implicit philosophy of man, which unconsciously determines their scientific methodology. Therefore, it would be better for psychologists to state their philosophy of man explicitly before they plan their research and formulate their hypotheses.[27]

In concluding our discussion of the basic hypotheses of motivation, we should like to draw the reader's attention to the line of discourse we have followed:

From the strongly biological hypotheses of homeostasis and incentives we moved to the less biological hypotheses of cognitive and intrinsic motivation and ended with the humanistic hypotheses.

Although there seems to be a difference in degree between Hunt's view of the rational, free-deciding, information-processing man and Maslow's and Allport's "human man," there cer-

---

[24] Another presentation of a theory which comes quite close to Woodworth's is that presented by Robert W. White, who deals with competance or effectance motivation. He regards this sort of motivation as neurogenic, rather than viscerogenic, in origin (White 1959). A third representative of the intrinsic-motivation conception is the Belgian psychologist Joseph Nuttin. However, Nuttin's theory is very complex and therefore not easy to classify according to basic hypotheses. Nuttin takes his starting point in Freud's theory, which he elaborates in several places (Nuttin 1956, 1957, 1963, 1966). Thus Nuttin's theory bears some resemblance to both Woodworth's and Allport's theory, the latter belonging to the next group.

Finally we should mention the work of Robert W. Leeper. For many years in numerous publications he has proposed a so-called motivational theory of emotion. In his latest presentation (Leeper 1965) he further elaborates this theory. Leeper subsumes all sorts of motivation (emotional as well as physiological) under the broader concept representative processes, which also includes perception and cognitive processes. Therefore, we think it is fair to place Leeper in this category.

[25] Allport has admitted that this theory has a special philosophical basis in a personal communication to the author.

[26] Among other places, in a discussion with the author.

[27] A sort of humanistic—or rather "Thomistic"—theory of motivation is presented by Thomas V. Moore (1948). For a more detailed analysis of this theory, the reader is referred to Madsen (1968). Other representatives of the humanistic approach are Victor E. Frankel (1963) and Charlotte Bühler (1959).

Table 33-8. Classification of Basic Motivational Hypotheses

Basic Hypotheses	Homeostatic Hypotheses	Incentive Hypotheses	Cognitive Hypotheses	Humanistic Hypotheses
Names of Psychologists	Pavlov? Freud Hull Murray (1938) Freeman Duffy	Lewin Young Tinbergen Hebb Murray (1959) McClelland Atkinson Miller Spence Brown Logan Berlyne Skinner Bindra Bolles	Tolman Woodworth Koch Festinger McV. Hunt White Nuttin Leeper	Allport Maslow Bühler

tainly is a fundamental difference in the philosophy of science behind these two theories: the cognitive and intrinsic motivational hypotheses are based upon a naturalistic philosophy of science, while the humanistic hypothesis is based upon a quite different philosophy of science and man.[28] It is important to notice that the adoption of these different philosophies of science depends largely upon the scientists' personal choice. The justification of this choice may only be based upon which of the philosophies is of greatest scientific utility to science in the long run. So, ultimately, it may be the future historians of psychology who may judge which philosophy of science is the most fruitful at a given time.

With these comments we approach the problems of theories-as-wholes, which we shall deal with in the next section of the chapter, but first let us summarize this section.

SUMMARY OF HYPOTHESES

We shall conclude this section about the basic hypotheses of motivation in two steps: A classification and an attempt to synthesize.

First, we shall look at a table of classification based on the dimension of classification we have used and including some typical examples of theories (Table 33-8).

Second, we shall look at two syntheses which attempt to integrate most of the basic hypotheses of motivation.

Cofer and Appley, in the last chapter of their great book present an excellent synthesis of all the literature (encompassing almost 100 pages of bibliography) about theories and research in motivation which they have dealt with in their research work (1964). In their general summary, they write:

We wished to point out that the drive concept is without utility... and we have made arousal, *we think, an attractive alternative... we have therefore attempted to anchor it (arousal) to internal and situational stimuli by means of* sensitization *and* anticipation *(p. 837, italics added).*

[28] As far as the author knows the only exposition and critical evaluation of *both* these traditions or schools of metascience written by one person is that of Gerard Radnitzky in *Contemporary Schools of Meta-Science* (Göteborg: Scandinavian University Press, 1968).

Cofer and Appley have postulated two mechanisms for determining arousal or invigoration (the latter term is preferred by Cofer and Appley because "arousal" may imply emotional arousal). The two mechanisms are a "sensitization-invigoration mechanism" (*SIM*), which is assumed to be inborn, and an "anticipation-invigoration mechanism" (*AIM*), which is assumed to be acquired. Their functions are summarized in the following passage:

In any case, arousal is the key factor, so far as motivation is concerned, in behavioral events in which sensitization is critical. We may speak of a sensitization-arousal *or* sensitization-invigoration mechanism (*SIM*) which parallels the anticipation-arousal *or* anticipation-invigoration-mechanism.

When the behavior energized either by anticipation-arousal *or by* sensitization-arousal *occurs and leads to consummatory behavior, the aroused state must be affected in some way. The feedback from consummatory behavior, sometimes described as reinforcing, evidently permits given arousal episode to be terminated* (Cofer & Appley 1964, p. 824).

The two authors convincingly demonstrate how nicely their two mechanisms replace drive (substituted by SIM) and incentive (substituted by AIM), and how these mechanisms are able to explain the main part of motivational psychology. The present author has also tried to suggest a synthesis of his comparative study of twenty theories (and some additional theories), which originally appeared in 1959 (see fourth edition of Madsen 1968a). This synthesis is formulated as a deductive system consisting of: a meta-theory, some definitions (a modified version is presented in Table 33-6 in this chapter), plus five axioms and twenty-six theorems.

Space permits us to present only the five axioms, which, however, may give the reader an impression of the main content of this deductive system. The theory includes the following axioms:

Axiom 1. Behavior is a function of interacting motives (Mc), central cognitive processes (Cc), plus dynamogenic (*dyd*) and directive (*did*) dispositions; thus

$$B = f([Mc \times dyd] \times [Cc \times did]). \tag{1}$$

or $\quad B = f(P_B), \tag{1a}$

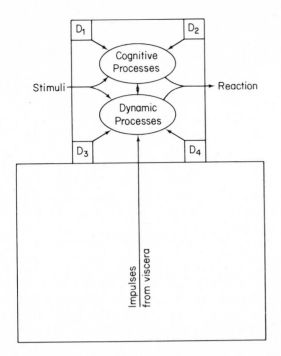

Fig. 33-4. *The diagram illustrates that reaction is determined by cognitive and dynamic processes in interaction. These processes are determined by external stimuli and internal impulses from the viscera, and the processes are also influenced by dispositions, which cause individual differences.*

D = dispositions

D_1 *and* D_2 *are acquired and constitutional intellectual dispositions (intelligence factors, etc.).*

D_3 *and* D_4 *are constitutional and acquired dynamic dispositions (personality factors).*

as P_{BD} equals the probability of the existence of an action, defined in formula [1].[29]

Axiom 2. Motives (Mc) are a function of interacting motivating impulses (Mi), motivating stimuli (Ms), plus central cognitive processes (Cc) and dynamogenic and directive dispositions; thus

$$Mc = f([Mi \times dyd] \times [Ms \times dyd] \times [Cc \times did]). \qquad [2]$$

Axiom 3. Motivating impulses (Mi) are a function of organic conditions (O) which deviate from the organism's normal level of adjustment[30], and the latter is determined by both innate (id) and acquired (ad) dispositions; thus

$$Mi = f(O \times id \times ad). \qquad [3]$$

[29] Thus P_B is a vector variable corresponding to, e.g., Hull's sEr, with the difference, however, that P is only a logical symbol for formula (1).

[30] Axiom 3 is thus a revision of the principle of homeostasis as "the level of adjustment" (an expression taken from McClelland) is a more practical term than homeostasis, biological balance, deprivation, etc.

Axiom 4. The dynamogenic function of motivating stimuli (Ms) is a function of the intensity of the stimulus (S) and of innate ($idyd$) or acquired ($adyd$) dynamogenic dispositions; thus

$$Ms = f(S \times idyd \times adyd). \qquad [4]$$

Axiom 5. Central cognitive processes (Cc) are a function of external directive stimuli (S) and directive dispositions (did) and simultaneously existing motives (Mc); thus

$$Cc = f([S \times did] \times Mc). \qquad [5]$$

These axioms may be physiologically interpreted (cf. also the definitions in Table 33-6). But they may also be conceived of as genuine constructions—a so-called black-box model. Such an interpretation is reproduced in the following diagram (Fig. 33-4).

Another black-box interpretation of these five axioms, together with the twenty-six theorems, can be found in the Danish economist Erik Johnsen's "multi-objective" decision-model (1968). In this model, the axioms and theorems are "translated" into symbolic-logic formulas, which are used in computer-simulation research concerned with a decision model.

Thus, a synthetic theory of motivation may be of some utility for other fields of research.

Theories of Motivation: the Formal Properties

INTRODUCTION: DEFINITION OF "THEORY"

In the earlier sections of this chapter we have successively analyzed and compared the elements (or components) of various theories of motivation: the concepts, the categories, and the basic hypotheses. In this last section we shall make a comparative study of the theories as whole structures. While in the preceding sections we concentrated mainly on the contents of the theories, we shall now concentrate on their formal properties.

Before we begin our description of theories we must define "theory." It is a word which has been used in many different ways, but I suggest a very broad definition: *A theory is a scientific text or discourse.* A scientific text contains descriptions of facts and relationships between facts, and it also contains explanations of the described facts and their relationships, and perhaps predictions of new facts. It is also possible that the text contains some "meta-propositions"; that is, sentences about basic (epistemological) problems, about preferred (empirical) methods, and about the type of explanation and description. But a scientific text rarely contains evaluative or normative meta-propositions or prescriptions. Therefore, we might define a "scientific text" as being able to contain descriptions, explanations, predictions, and metapropositions alone or in combination.

THE STRATA OF A THEORY

We can use this definition to distinguish between different strata in a scientific text or theory (see Fig. 33-5).

Meta-Stratum:

    Epistemological

    Systematological and Methodological propositions

Explanatory-Stratum:

    Explanatory propositions ("hypotheses") and expl. terms ("intervening variables" and "hypothetical constructs")

Descriptive-Stratum:

    General, empirical propositions ("laws" or S - R - relationships) and particular "protocol-sentences" in the data-language

Fig. 33-5. *The strata of a theory (a scientific discourse).*

The basic stratum is the descriptive stratum, which contains descriptions both of single facts and relationships between facts. Some of the descriptive terms aud sentences are very concrete and specific, others are more general and abstract. There can be several strata in the descriptive stratum or, rather, a whole continuum from the most concrete to the most abstract. The same holds true for the next stratum, which we might call the explanatory stratum.

This stratum of the theory contains hypothetical terms and sentences which are used as explanations as well as predictions (which, from a systematological point of view, are identical). Some of the hypothetical terms can be operationally defined by relating them directly to the descriptive terms and sentences. Other hypothetical terms are more remote from the descriptive stratum and can only be indirectly related to it. Many of these abstract hypothetical terms stand for hypo-

thetical constructs related to each other in an "explanatory system."

The formal development of the explanatory system varies from a very informal explanatory "sketch" to a highly formal "deductive system." A mathematical calculus and possibly a concrete "model"[31] can be contained in the explanatory system. The relationships between the hypotheses, the model, and the mathematical calculus are formulated in coordinating rules, which belong to the next stratum, the *meta-stratum*.

This stratum of the theory or scientific text contains the propositions about fundamental epistemological problems, about the empirical methods and the coordinating rules concerning the relationships between the explanatory system, the model, and the mathematical calculus.

PSYCHOLOGICAL THEORIES

If we apply this description of a scientific text to psychological texts, we get a diagram representing a psychological theory (Fig. 33-6).

At the descriptive stratum we have descriptions of stimuli (S-variables) and reactions (R-variables). We have made a rough division between two substrata: the most concrete and particular descriptions formulated in the so-called data language or (protocol language), and the more general and abstract descriptions formulated in special descriptive terms, which are related to the data language by operational definitions. Of course we could have made divisions into several substrata. The most abstract descriptive terms can prove difficult to distinguish from the explanatory terms at the lowest substratum. These explanatory terms, which can be related to the descriptive level by operational definitions, have been called "intervening vari-

[31] A mathematical calculus is frequently called a (mathematical) model, but we prefer to confine the term "model" to concrete representations (two- or three-dimensional).

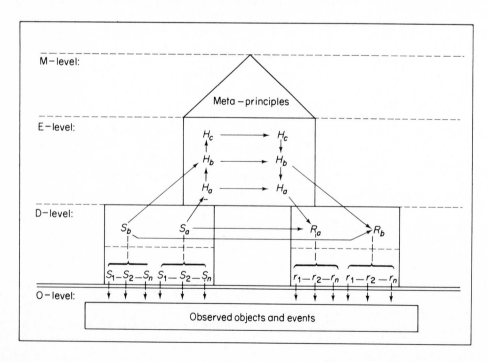

Fig. 33-6. *The strata of a scientific discourse: diagram representing a psychological theory. There are four levels (from below):*

O-level ("Object-level"): Observed objects and events.

D-level ("Descriptive level"): Descriptions of the observations. $S_1 \ldots S_n$ and $r_1 \ldots r_n$ represent basic terms for constituting protocol statements. S_a, S_b, and R_a, R_b represent generalized terms and empirical generalizations ($S_a \longrightarrow R_a$, $S_b \longrightarrow R_b$).

E-level ("Explanatory level"): The explanatory system containing explanatory terms (or H-variables) and explanatory sentences ("hypotheses": $H \longrightarrow H$ relationships). $H_c \longrightarrow H_c$ represents variables and hypotheses without direct connection with the empirical level.

M-level ("Meta-level"): Meta-principles about epistemological, methodological, and systematological problems.

ables" by psychologists, because they intervene between *S*- and *R*-variables.

At the higher substrata of the explanatory stratum we have the terms standing for hypothetical constructs. There has been a lively discussion in psychology, as in other sciences, about the meaning and use of these constructs. The most important problem is: Can hypothetical constructs be allowed to have some "surplus meaning," added to the operationally defined meaning which they have in common with the intervening variables? The solution of this problem has divided psychologists into several groups. Some psychologists (e.g., Skinner) prefer to do without any sort of intervening variables or hypothetical constructs and, therefore, produce theories that contain only the descriptive stratum (and perhaps some meta-propositions). Other psychologists (e.g., N. E. Miller) permit the use of operationally defined intervening variables, but exclude inclusion of any surplus meaning. Those who permit and perhaps find surplus meaning useful are divided concerning the kind of surplus meaning they prefer and argue for.

One group of psychologists (e.g., Pavlov and Hebb) add a physiological surplus meaning to their hypothetical constructs, which they conceive as ultimately identifiable with brain processes and structures.

Other psychologists (e.g., many Gestalt psychologists) add a mentalistic surplus meaning to their hypothetical constructs, which they conceive of as identical or analogous to conscious processes and states known from their own introspection.

The last group of psychologists (e.g., Freud, Tolman, Lewin, Hull, and many others) allow for free use of hypothetical constructs with surplus meaning borrowed from many sources: mathematics, cybernetics, information theory, General System Theory, etc. These psychologists often consider the hypothetical constructs conventional, fictive, or heuristic "models" or conceptual "constructs" (in the original meaning of the term). These constructs possess only explanatory and predictive functions and do not refer to any sort of ultimate reality. For these psychologists there are no major differences between hypothetical constructs and intervening variables. Thus Tolman, who invented the concept intervening variable, declared, at a later date, that for him there was no real difference—perhaps only a difference in degree of abstraction—between "intervening variables" and "hypothetical constructs." It is for these reasons that the author has formulated the term "hypothetical variable" (*H*-variable) as a common designation for both "intervening variable" and "hypothetical construct."[32]

The categories of *H*-variables discussed above may be denoted in this way:

1. *Organismic* or *neurophysiological H*-variables, which are the *H*-variables with surplus meaning borrowed from neurophysiology.
2. *Neutral-formal H*-variables, which include both hypothetical constructs (with neutral or no surplus meaning) and the purely formal intervening variables.
3. *Mentalistic* or *phenomenological H*-variables, which are the *H*-variables with surplus meaning borrowed from introspective or phenomenological observation.

[32] Other psychologists use the term "mediating variables" as the common term (= *H*-variable in this terminology).

This classification of *H*-variables may be combined with the classification of psychological variables presented in the earlier sections of this chapter. This complex combination of classifications has been applied to motivational variables taken from twenty theories and analyzed and compared in Madsen 1968. The classification scheme used is presented here as Table 33-9.

THE PHILOSOPHICAL BACKGROUND

Which of these interpretations of hypothetical variables a psychologist prefers depends, among other things, on his philosophical background or orientation, which is expressed in his meta-propositions. Therefore, we shall now take a closer look at the meta-stratum of the psychological texts.

An important philosophical problem is the epistemological question about the choice of data language: behavioristic or phenomenological? Most contemporary psychologists have found it convenient to select a behavioristic data language as the best suited for communication between psychologists and other scientists.

Another problem is the methodological question about selection of empirical methods. Independent of choice of data-language, the psychologists may select behavioristic and/or introspective (or phenomenological) methods. In general, modern psychologists are rather liberal and tolerant concerning this question.

The third important problem is the systematological question about which type of explanatory term is more useful: the *H*-variable with physiological surplus meaning, or those with mentalistic surplus meaning, or perhaps those with neutral surplus meaning? This choice depends on the psychologist's attitude toward or theory about the old mind-body problem. Only a few modern psychologists are explicit in their texts or theories about the problem, but their choice of *H*-variable type may be largely determined by their implicit (or explicit) theory about this problem. For the purpose of this chapter, the theories concerning the mind-body, or, in modern terms, psychosomatic relationship may be roughly divided into three categories:

1. The *materialistic theories*
2. the *neutral-monistic theories*[33]
3. the *dualistic* theories.

Those psychologists who have adopted one of the many versions of materialistic theories about the psychosomatic relationship often choose the type of *H*-variable with physiological surplus meaning, or like Skinner, they may not use any *H*-variable.

The psychologists who have adopted one of the many versions of a neutral-monistic theory about the psychosomatic relationship will often choose the type of *H*-variable with a neutral surplus meaning, or, in other words: the genuine hypothetical constructs. Perhaps they will prefer to use only the purely formal "intervening variables" with operationally defined meaning.

[33] To this category belong the theories of L. von Bertalanffy, Gustav Bergman, Rudolf Carnap, Herbert Feigl, Bertrand Russel, Gilbert Ryle, Benjamin Wolman, and many other modern psychologists. An excellent analysis of these problems is presented in M.B. Turner (1967).

Table 33-9. Classifications of Psychological Variables

		Empirical Variables (Independent, antecedent Variables)	Hypothetical Variables			Behavior Variables (Dependent, consequent variables)
			Neutral-formal	Neurophysiological	Phenomenological	
Disposition Variables	Directive — Vector		4 variables (e.g., Murray's Need)			
			3 variables (e.g., Young's Attitude)	Tinbergen's "Instinct"		
	Dynamogenic		4 variables (e.g., McDougall's Propensity Cattell's Erg)			
Function Variables	Directive — Vector	2 variables (e.g., Masserman's Need)	7 variables (e.g., Murray's Need) Tolman's Drive (1932)	3 variables (e.g., Stagner's Drive)	Young's Desire	
	Directive	2 variables (e.g., Hull's Drive stimulus)	5 variables (e.g., Young's Set)	2 variables (e.g., Freeman's Set)		
	Dynamogenic	11 variables (e.g., Tolman's Drive [1951]) Young's Need Hull's Need (CD)	8 variables (e.g., Hull's Drive Tolman's Need [1951] Lewin's Tension)	3 variables (e.g., Young's Drive)	2 variables (e.g., Moore's Impulse)	

The psychologists employing one of the many versions of the dualistic theories of the psychosomatic relationship will often choose an *H*-variable with a mentalistic surplus meaning. Perhaps they will develop a type of theory which we have not mentioned.

I am thinking about one of the versions of the so-called *Geisteswissenschaftliche* or *Verstehen-Psychologie*. In America they are often labeled "humanistic," "phenomenological," or "existential." In the following pages I shall call them *Verstehen Psychologie*," because they are often based upon intuition, empathy, or *Verstehen*. This is a sort of subjectivistic understanding, which is different from the scientific explanation (and prediction) that is based upon intersubjective methods and data language. The author must admit that he is not very familiar with this type of psychological theory. But it seems that until now this kind of psychology has had more success among psychotherapists than among theoretical psychologists.[34]

TYPES OF THEORIES

We can summarize the preceding paragraphs with a classification of psychological theories into the following types:

1. *The S-R theories*, which include all purely descriptive theories with a behavioristic data language.[35] These theories may include descriptions of law-like relationships between *S*- and *R*-variables, but no further explanation of these laws based on fundamental hypotheses.

2. *The S-O-R theories*, which include all theories that explain the described *S-R* relationships by use of *H*-variables with physiological surplus meaning. (*O* stands for "organism".)[36]

3. *The S-H-R theories*, which include all theories that explain the described *S-R*-relationships by the use of *H*-variables possessing a "neutral" surplus meaning not referring to any ultimate form of reality or substance (in other words, the "genuine" constructs). This type of theory also includes all the theories that explain by use of the formal type of "intervening variables" (e.g., mathematical models). But as mentioned earlier, the present author doesn't think there is any fundamental difference between hypothetical constructs of the "neutral" type and "intervening variables." (Therefore, *H* stands for *H*-variable.)

4. *The S-M-R theories*, which include all theories that explain the described *S-R* relationships by the use of *H*-variables having a mentalistic surplus meaning. (*M* stands for "mental" or "mind".)

5. *The M-theories* include theories that express an understanding or *Verstehen* that is not based upon an exact and objective description in behavioristic data language. These *Verstehen*-theories may be based upon a phenomenological data language, but *Verstehen* psychologists are not so explicit

---

[34] The only book the author knows about which deals with both the naturalistic (explanatory) and humanistic (understanding) philosophies of science is that of Gerard Radnitzky (1968).

[35] Purely descriptive theories with a phenomenological data language are very rare in the history of psychology. The reason is probably that when an attempt is made to develop such a theory, it is implicitly changed into a theory of the fourth or fifth type.

[36] We can distinguish the genuine reductive theories from this type of theory because they explain behavior through physiological data (not hypothetical constructs). But such theories exist only "programs." The theories which come nearest to these "programs" are the *S-O-R* theories.

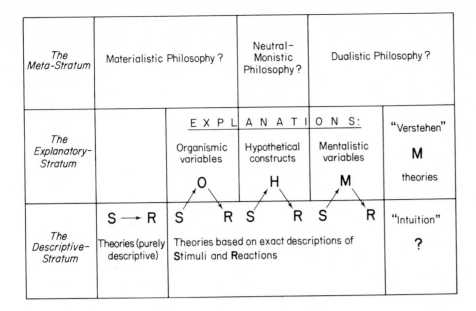

The Meta-Stratum	Materialistic Philosophy?		Neutral–Monistic Philosophy?	Dualistic Philosophy?	

Fig. 33-7. *Types of theories.*

about this as they are about their philosophy of man. We have summarized this classification in two schemes of classification, which are presented here as Figures 33-7 and 33-8.

We can now apply this new classification of theories to the theories of motivation which are presented in this chapter. We shall only select the most typical theories and present them in Table 33-10.[37]

Table 33-10. Types of Theories of Motivation

Types of Theories:	S-R-theories	S-O-R-theories	S-H-R-theories	S-M-R-theories
	Skinner	Pavlov	Freud	Allport
	Bolles	Young	Woodworth	Maslow
		Hebb	Lewin	
		Tinbergen	Tolman	
		Duffy	Hull	
		Freeman	Miller	
		Berlyne	Spence	
		Bindra	Brown	
		Morgan	Murray	
		Stellar	Cattell	
		Konorski	McClelland	
			Atkinson	
			McV. Hunt	
			Koch	
			Festinger	
			Pribram	

(Names of Psychologists)

We may go a step further and combine the classification into types of theories with the classification of basic hypotheses, which we have previously presented in Table 33-8. This combined classification is presented in a classification scheme as Table 33-11.

A FINAL CLASSIFICATION

Before concluding this chapter on the structure of psychological theories, we shall introduce one more classification

[37] We have left out the frame with *M*-theories, as there are no theories of this type in our sample.

Table 33-11. Combined Classification of Theories of Motivation

Types of Theories / Basic Hypotheses	S-R-theories	S-O-R-theories	S-H-R-theories	S-W-R-theories
Homeostatic Hypotheses		Pavlov? Duffy Freeman	Freud Hull Murray (1938)	
Incentive Hypotheses	Skinner Bolles	Young Tinbergen Hebb Berlyne Bindra	Murray (1959) Lewin McClelland Atkinson Cattell Miller Spence	
Cognitive Hypotheses			Brown Tolman Woodworth McV. Hunt Koch Festinger	
Humanistic Hypotheses				Allport Maslow

of theories. This is a classification which may be developed into a description along a dimension that perhaps can be expressed numerically. This dimension corresponds to a classification into more or less speculative and more or less empirical theories. In his *Theories of Motivation* the author has developed a method for a more precise evaluation or measurement of a theory's "degree of speculativeness." We simply count the number of theoretical hypotheses which exclusively contain *H*-variables. We call them *H-H*-hypotheses. Then we count the number of partly empirical hypotheses which contain at least one empirical variable (*S*- or *R*-variable). We call these hypotheses *S-H*- and *H-R*-hypotheses. After counting all the hypotheses in the theory, we relate them to each other in a

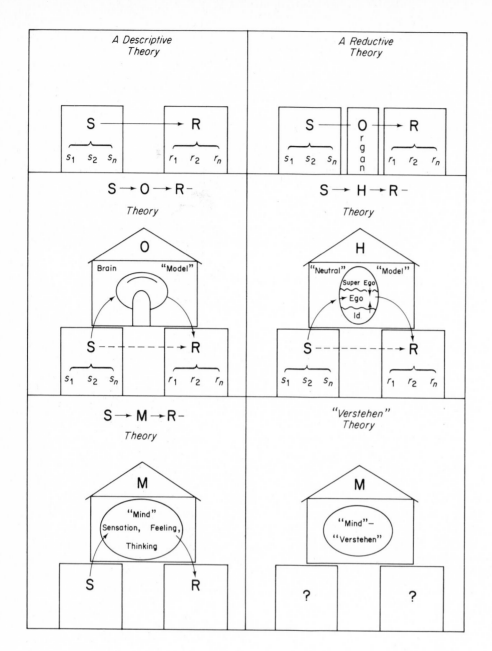

Fig. 33-8. *Types of theories.*

t/e ratio or "hypotheses-quotient," which is defined in this way:

$$HQ = \frac{(H \longrightarrow H)}{(S \longrightarrow H) + (H \longrightarrow R)}$$

We have calculated the HQ for several theories. The variations extend from 0.19 (which is the HQ for Cattell's theory) to 1.43 (the HQ for Tolman's theory).[38]

[38] The HQ of the theories analyzed in *Theories of Motivation* (1959): Tinbergen: 0.11; Hebb: 0.13; McClelland: 0.14; Hull: 0.30; McDougall: 0.43; Lewin: 0.50; Murray: 0.71; Young: 0.82; Allport: 1.00; Tolman: 1.43.
The HQ of the theories analyzed in *Modern Theories of Motivation* (forthcoming): Cattel: 0.09; Maslow: 0.13; Duffy: 0.14; Miller: 0.20 (and 0.60); Fowler: 0.25; Brown: 0.29; Pribram: 0.2); Bindra: 0.30; Berlyne: 0.38; Sokolov: 0.38; Eysenck: 0.43; Irwin: 0.50; Konorski: 0.54; Woodworth: 0.57; Luria: 0.75; Festinger: 0.84; Atkinson: 0.86; (Atkinson and Birch: 0.43); Rogers: 1.25.

We have illustrated the HQ by means of a diagram which depicts the two extreme examples of theories in Figure 33-9. A very important aspect of all scientific theories is expressed in the t/e ratio or HQ. It is that aspect which is expressed in one of the oldest and most universally supported epistemological principles: the principle of parsimony or Occam's razor. This principle can be formulated thus: If other things are equal, then among several theories about the same phenomena scientists normally choose the simplest one—the one that explains the most phenomena with the fewest explanatory constructs. The HQ thus gives us an opportunity to make an exact estimation of which theory really is the most simple or economical.

While it is certain that the HQ measures an important aspect of theories, it is not certain that the method of calculation is good enough. One important weakness of the method is that only a few theories are so formally developed that it is

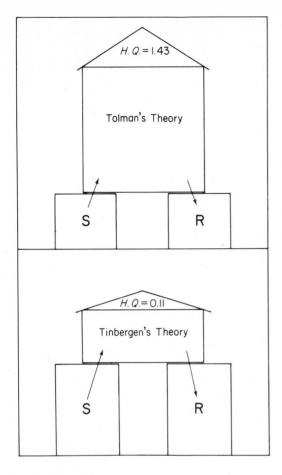

Fig. 33-9. *Some theories' HQ.*

$$\text{Hypotheses-Quotient} = \frac{(H \longrightarrow H)}{(S \longrightarrow H) + (H \longrightarrow R)}$$

possible to count the number of hypotheses. For many of the psychological theories, it was first necessary to make a systematic reconstruction before the hypotheses could be counted. This, of course, introduces a personal, subjective factor. We are working on the possibility of constructing a computer program that would count all words in a scientific text and make a classification into descriptive and hypothetical terms. Then it should be easy for the computer to calculate the *HQ* for any scientific discourse. Such a computer program might be a valuable tool for the development of systematology as a metascientific discipline.

Acknowledgment:. The author's English manuscript has been carefully corrected and improved by John T. Bruce, M. A.

References

ACH, N. *Über die Willenstatigheit und das Denken.* Göttingen: Vandenhoech und Ruprecht, 1905.

ALEXANDER, F. Three fundamental dynamic principles. *Dialectica,* 1951, *5,* 239–45.

ALLPORT, G. W. *Personality: a psychological interpretation.* New York: Holt, Rinehart & Winston, 1937.

———— *Pattern and growth in personality.* New York: Holt, Rinehart & Winston, 1961.

ATKINSON, J. W. *An introduction to motivation.* Princeton, N.J.: Van Nostrand, 1964.

———— (ed.) *Motives in fantasy, action, and society.* Princeton, N.J.: Van Nostrand, 1958.

———— and BIRCH, D. *The dynamics of action.* New York; Wiley, 1970.

———— and FEATHER, N. T. (eds.) *A theory of achievement motivation.* New York: John Wiley, 1966.

BEACH, F. A. Characteristics of masculine "sex drive." *In* M.R. Jones (ed.), *Nebraska symposium on motivation.* Lincoln: Nebraska University Press, 1956.

BERKOWITZ, L. *The development of motives and values in the child.* New York and London: Basic Books, 1964.

———— *Aggression.* New York: McGraw-Hill, 1962.

BERLYNE, D. E. *Conflict, arousal, and curiosity.* New York: McGraw-Hill, 1960.

———— Motivation problems raised by exploratory and epistemic behavior. *In* S. Koch (ed.), *Psychology—a study of a science,* vol. 5. New York: McGraw-Hill, 1963.

———— Reinforcement and arousal. *In* David Levine (ed.), *Nebraska symposium on motivation.* Lincoln: Nebraska University Press, 1967.

BINDRA, D. *Motivation: a systematic reinterpretation.* New York: Ronald Press, 1959.

BOLLES, R. C. *Theory of motivation.* New York and London: Harper & Row, 1967.

BORING, E. G. *A history of experimental psychology,* 2d ed. New York: Appleton-Century-Crofts, 1950.

BROWN, J. S. *The motivation of behavior.* New York: McGraw-Hill, 1961.

———— and FARBER, J. E. Secondary motivational systems. *In* P. R. Farnsworth (ed.), *Annual review of psychology.* Palo Alto, Calif.: Annual Reviews, Inc., 1968.

BÜHLER, C. Maturation and motivation. *Dialectica,* 1951, *5,* 312–61.

———— Theoretical observations about life's basic tendencies. *American Journal of Psychotherapy,* 1959, *13,* 561.

BÜHLER, C. and MASSARIK, F. *The course of human life.* New York: Springer, 1968.

CANON, W. B. *Bodily changes in pain, hunger, fear and rage.* New York: Appleton-Century-Crofts, 1915.

CATTELL, R. B. *Description and measurement of personality.* New York: Harcourt, 1946.

———— *Personality: a systematic theoretical and factual study.* New York: McGraw-Hill, 1950.

———— *Personality and motivation structure and measurement.* New York: World Book Co., 1957.

———— *The scientific analysis of personality.* Baltimore: Penguin, 1965.

———— (ed.) *Handbook of modern personality theory.* Chicago: Aldine, forthcoming.

COFER, C. N., and APPLEY, M. H. *Motivation: theory and research.* New York: John Wiley, 1964.

COLBY, K. M. *Energy and structure in psychoanalysis.* New York: Ronald Press, 1955.

DEUTSCH, J. A. *The structural basis of behavior.* Chicago: University of Chicago Press, 1960.

DIEL, P. *Psychologie de la motivation.* Paris: Presses Universitaires de France, 1948.

DOLLARD, J., and MILLER, N. E. *Personality and psychotherapy.* New York: McGraw-Hill, 1950.

DUFFY, ELISABETH. *Activation and behavior.* New York: John Wiley, 1962.

EPSTEIN, S. The measurement of drive and conflict in humans. *In* M. R. Jones (ed.), *Nebraska symposium on motivation.* Lincoln: Nebraska University Press, 1962.

ESTES, W. K. Stimulus–response theory of drive. *In* M.R. Jones (ed.), *Nebraska symposium on motivation.* Lincoln: Nebraska University Press, 1954.

———— et al. *Modern learning theory.* New York: Appleton-Century-Crofts, 1954.

EYSENCK, H. J. *The biological basis of personality.* Springfield, Ill.: Charles C Thomas, 1967.

EYSENCK, H. J. (ed.) *Experiments in motivation.* Oxford: Pergamon Press, 1964.

FARBER, I. E. Anxiety as a drive state. *In* M.R. Jones (ed.), *Nebraska symposium on motivation*. Lincoln: Nebraska University Press, 1954.

―――― The role of motivation in verbal learning and performance. *Psychological Bulletin*, 1955, *52*, 311–27.

FEATHER, N. T. An expectancy-volve model of information-seeking behavior. *Psychological-Review*, 1967, *5* (74), 342–60.

FESTINGER, L. *A theory of cognitive dissonance*. Evanston, Ill.: Row, Peterson, 1957.

FOWLER, H. *Curiosity and exploratory behavior*. New York and London: Macmillan, 1965.

―――― Satiation and curiosity. *In* K. W. Spence and Janet Taylor (eds.), *The psychology of learning and motivation*, vol. 1. New York and London: Academic.

FRANKEL, V. E. *Man's search for meaning: an introduction to logotherapy*. New York: Washington Square Press, 1963.

FREEMAN, G. L. *The energetics of human behavior*. Ithaca, N. Y.: Cornell University Press, 1948.

FRENCH, T. M. *The integration of behavior*. Chicago: University of Chicago Press, 1952.

FRENKEL-BRUNSWIK, E. Motivation and behavior. *Genetic Psychological Monograph*, 1942, *26*, 121–264.

FREUD, S. The projects for a scientific psychology. *In* Marie Bonaparte et al. (eds.), *The origins of psychoanalysis*. London: Imago, 1954.

―――― *Die Traumdeutung*. Vienna, 1900.

―――― Instincts and their vicissitudes. *In* S. Freud, *The collected papers*. New York: Collier Books, 1915 (paperback edition).

GUILFORD, J. P. Motivation in an informational psychology. *In* David Levine (ed.), *Nebraska symposium on motivation*. Lincoln: Nebraska University Press, 1965.

HALL, J. F. *Psychology of motivation*. Philadelphia: Lippincott, 1961.

HARLOW, H. F. Motivations as a factor in the acquisition of responses. *In* M.R. Jones (ed.), *Nebraska symposium on motivation*. Lincoln: Nebraska University Press, 1953.

HEBB, D. O. *Organisation of behavior*. New York: John Wiley, 1949.

―――― Drives and the CNS (conceptual nervous system). *Psychological Review*, 1955, *62*, 243–54.

―――― A neurophysiological theory. *In* S. Koch, *Psychology—a study of a science*, vol. 1. New York: McGraw-Hill, 1959.

―――― *A textbook of psychology*. Philadelphia: Saunders, 1966.

HECKHAUSEN, H. *The anatomy of achievement motivation*. New York: Academic, 1967.

HEIDER, F. The Gestalt theory of motivation. *In* M. R. Jones (ed.), *Nebraska symposium on motivation*. Lincoln: Nebraska University Press, 1960.

HELSON, H. Some problems in motivation from the point of view of the theory of adaptation level. *In* David Levine (ed.), *Nebraska symposium on motivation*. Lincoln: Nebraska University Press, 1966.

HILGARD, E. R. Motivation in learning theory. *In* S. Koch (ed.), *Psychology—a study of a science*, vol. 5. New York: McGraw-Hill, 1963.

HOLT-HANSEN, KR. *After-effects in the behaviour of mice*. Copenhagen: Munksgaard, 1965.

HULL, C. L. *Principles of behavior*. New York: Appleton-Century-Crofts, 1943.

―――― *A behavior system*. New Haven: Yale University Press, 1952.

HUNT, MCV. Incentive motivation and its role in psychological development. *In* David Levine (ed.) *Nebraska symposium on motivation*. Lincoln: Nebraska University Press, 1965.

IFF, V. La motivation à l'avancement professional. Paris: *Monographies françaises de Psychologie*, *IX*, 1962.

IRVING, F. *Motivation and intention behavior*. (Forthcoming).

JOHNSEN, E. *Studies in multi-objective decision models*. Lund: Student Litteratur, 1968.

JONES, M. R. (ed.) *Nebraska symposium on motivation*. Lincoln: Nebraska University Press, 1953–1963.

KENDLER, H. Motivation and behavior. *In* David Levine (ed.), *Nebraska symposium on motivation*. Lincoln: Nebraska University Press, 1965.

KOCH, S. Behavior as "intrinsically" regulated. *In* M. R. Jones (ed.), *Nebraska symposium on motivation*. Lincoln: Nebraska University Press, 1956.

―――― (ed.) *Psychology—a study of a science*. New York: McGraw-Hill, vols. 1–6, 1959–1963.

KONORSKI, J. *The integrative action of the brain*. Chicago: Chicago University Press, 1967.

KRECH, D. Cognition and motivation in psychological theory. *In* W. Dennis (ed.), *Current trends in psychological theory*. Pittsburgh: University of Pittsburgh Press, 1951.

KUHN, TH. S. *The structure of scientific revolutions*. Chicago and London: University of Chicago Press, 1962.

LANGKJAER, A. *Contribution to a general normology or theory of purpose setting*. Copenhagen: Dansk Videnskabs Forlag, 1961.

LEEPER, R. W. Some needed developments in the motivational theory of emotions. *In* David Levine (ed.), *Nebraska symposium on motivation*. Lincoln: Nebraska University Press, 1965.

LÉONTIEV, A. N. Les besoins, les motifs, et la conscience. *Proceedings of the XVIII International Congress of Psychology*. Moscow: Symposium No. 13, 1966.

LEVINE, D. (ed.) *Nebraska symposium on motivation*. Lincoln: Nebraska University Press, 1964.

LEWIN, K. Das Problem der Willenmessung der Assoziation. *Psychologische Forschung*, 1921, *1*, 191–302; 1922, *2*, 65–141.

―――― Vorsatz, Wille, und Bedürfnis. *Psychologische Forschung*, 1928, *7*, 330–85.

―――― *A dynamic theory of personality*. New York: McGraw-Hill, 1935.

―――― *Principles of topological psychology*. New York: McGraw-Hill, 1936.

―――― *The conceptual representation and the measurement of psychological forces*. Durham N.C.: Duke University Press, 1938.

―――― *Field theory in social science*. D. Cartwright (ed.). New York: Harper & Row, 1952.

LINDSLEY, D. B. Psychophysiology and motivation. *In* M.R. Jones (ed.), *Nebraska symposium on motivation*. Lincoln: Nebraska University Press, 1957.

LINDZEY, G. (ed.) *Assessment of human motives*. New York: Grove Press, 1958.

LOGAN, F. A. *Incentive*. New Haven, Conn.: Yale University Press, 1960.

LURIA, A. R. *Human brain and psychological processes*. New York: Harper, 1966.

LYNN, R. *Attention, arousal, and orientation reaction*. Oxford: Pergamon Press, 1966.

MCCLELLAND, DAVID C. *Personality*. New York: Dryden Press, 1951.

―――― *The achieving society*. Princeton, N.J.: Van Nostrand Reinhold, 1961.

―――― (ed.) *Studies in motivation*. New York: Appleton-Century-Crofts, 1955.

――――, ATKINSON, JOHN W., CLARK, RUSSELL A., and LOWELL, L. *The achievement motive*. New York: Appleton-Century-Crofts, 1953.

MCCLELLAND, D. and WINTER, D. *Motivating economic achievement*. New York: Free Press, 1969.

MCDOUGALL, W. *An introduction to social psychology*. London: Methuen, 1908. The 1960 edition is used here.

―――― *The energies of men*. London: Methuen, 1932.

MADSEN, K. B. *Theories of motivation*, 4th ed. Copenhagen: Munksgaard, 1959. 4th ed., 1968.

―――― Integration through meta-science. Exemplified by a comparative study of psychological theories. *Proceedings of the XIV International Congress of Philosophy*, Vienna, 1968b.

―――― *Modern theories of motivation*. Copenhagen: Munksgaard, forthcoming.

MAGOUN, H. W. The ascending reticular system and wakefulness. In *Brain mechanisms and consciousness*. Oxford: Blackwell, 1954.

MAIER, NORMAN R. F. *Frustration—the study of behavior without a goal*. New York: McGraw-Hill, 1949.

MALMO, R. B. Measurement of drive: an unsolved problem in psychology. *In* M.R. Jones (ed.), *Nebraska symposium on motivation*. Lincoln: Nebraska University Press, 1958.

MASLOW, A. H. *Motivation and personality*. New York: Harper & Row, 1954.

―――― *New knowledge in human values*. New York: Harper & Row, 1959.

―――― *Toward a psychology of being*. Princeton, N.J.: Van Nostrand Reinhold, 1962.

——— *The psychology of science.* New York: Harper & Row, 1966.

——— A theory of meta-motivation: The biological rooting of the value-life. *Journal of Humanistic Psychology*, 1967, 93–127.

——— Farther reaches of human nature. *Journal of Transhumanistic Psychology*, I, 1968.

MASSERMANN, J. H. *Principles of dynamic psychiatry*, 2d ed. Philadelphia and London: Saunders, 1961.

MILLER, N. E. An experimental investigation of acquired drives. *Psychological Bulletin*, 1941, *38*, 534–35.

——— Studies of fear as an acquirable drive. *Journal of Experimental Psychology*, 1948, *38*, 89–101.

——— Learnable drives and rewards. *In* S.S. Stevens (ed.), *Handbook of experimental psychology.* New York: John Wiley, 1951.

——— Liberalization of basic S-R-concepts: extension to conflict-behavior, motivation, and social learning. *In* S. Koch (ed.), *Psychology—A study of a science*, vol. 2. New York: McGraw-Hill, 1959.

——— Some reflections of the law of effect produce a new alternative to drive reduction. *In* M. R. Jones (ed.), *Nebraska symposium on motivation.* Lincoln: Nebraska University Press, 1963.

——— and DOLLARD, J. *Social learning and imitation.* New Haven, Conn: Yale University Press, 1941.

MISIAK, H. and SEXTON, V. S. *History of psychology.* New York and London: Grune & Stratton, 1966.

MOORE, T. V. *The driving forces of human nature.* New York: Grune & Stratton, 1948.

MORGAN C. T. *Physiological mechanisms of motivation. In* M. R. Jones (ed.), *Nebraska symposium on motivation.* Lincoln: Nebraska University Press, 1957.

——— Physiological theory of drive. *In* S. Koch (ed.), *Psychology —a study of a science.* vol. 1. New York: McGraw-Hill, 1959.

MORUZZI, G., and MAGOUN, H. W. Brain stem reticular formation and activation of EEG. *EEG Clinical Neurophysiology*, 1949, *1*, 455–73.

MOWRER, O. H. A stimulus-response analysis of anxiety and its role as a reinforcing agent. *Psychological Review*, 1939, *46*, 553–65.

——— *Learning theory and personality dynamics.* New York: Ronald Press, 1950.

——— Motivation. *Annual Review of Psychology*, 1952, *3*, 419–32.

——— *Learning theory and behavior.* New York and London: John Wiley, 1960a.

——— *Learning theory and the symbolic processes.* New York and London: John Wiley, 1960b.

MURPHY, G. *Historical introduction to modern psychology.* New York: Harcourt, 1949.

MURRAY, E. J. *Sleep, dreams, and arousal.* New York: Appleton-Century-Crofts, 1965.

MURRAY, H. A. *Explorations in personality.* New York: Oxford University Press, 1938.

——— Toward a classification of interaction. *In* T. Parson and E. A. Shill (eds.), *Towards a general theory of action.* Cambridge, Mass.: Harvard University Press, 1951.

——— Preparations for the scaffold of a comprehensive system. *In* S. Koch (ed.) *Psychology—a study of a science*, vol. 3. New York: McGraw-Hill, 1959.

Nebraska Symposium on Motivation. M. R. Jones (ed.) 1953–1963. D. Levine (ed.) 1964–. Lincoln: Nebraska University Press.

NUTTIN, J. Human motivation and Freud's theory of energy discharge. *Canadian Journal of Psychology*, 1956, *10*, 1967–68.

——— Personality dynamics. *In* H. P. David and H. von Bracken (eds.), *Perspectives in personality theory.* New York: Basic Books, 1957.

——— Time perspective in human motivation and learning. *Proceedings of XVII International Congress of Psychology*, Washington, D.C., 1963.

——— Motivation et fonction cognitives dans le comportement humain. *In Proceedings of the XVIII International Congress of Psychology.* Moscow: Symposium No. 13, 1966.

——— *Punishment and reward in human learning.* New York: Academic, 1968.

OLDS, J. Physiological mechanisms of reward. *In* M. R. Jones (ed.), *Nebraska symposium on motivation.* Lincoln: Nebraska University Press, 1955.

——— *The growth on structures of motives.* Glencoe, Ill.: Free Press, 1956.

PAVLOV, I. P. *Conditioned reflexes.* London: Oxford University Press, 1927.

PETERS, R. S. *The concept of motivation.* London: Routledge & Kegan Paul, 1958.

PRIBAM, K. H. Neocortical function in behavior. *In* H.F. Harlow and C.N. Wolsey (eds.), *Biological and biochemical bases of behavior.* Madison: University of Wisconsin Press, 1958.

——— *Languages of the brain.* Englewood Cliffs, N. J.: Prentice-Hall, 1971.

RADNIZKY, G. *Contemporary Schools of meta-science.* Göteborg, Sweden: Scandinavian University Books, 1968.

RAPAPORT, D. The structure of psychoanalytic theory: a systematic attempt. *In* S. Koch (ed.), *Psychology—a study of a science*, vol. 3. New York: McGraw-Hill, 1959.

——— On the psychoanalytic theory of motivation. *In* M.R. Jones (ed.) *Nebraska symposium on motivation.* Lincoln: Nebraska University Press, 1960.

RASMUSSEN, E. Tranekjær: *Dynamisk psykologi og dens grundlag.* Copenhagen: Munksgaard, 1960.

RETHLINGSHOFER, D. *Motivation as related to personality.* New York: McGraw-Hill, 1963.

SCHACHTER, S. *The psychology of affiliation.* Stanford, Calif.: Stanford University Press, 1959.

SCHULZ, D. P. *Sensory restriction.* New York: Academic, 1965.

SKINNER, B. F. *Science and human behavior.* New York: Macmillan, 1953.

——— *Technology of teaching.* New York: Appleton-Century-Crofts, 1968.

SOKOLOV, E. N. *Perception and the conditioned reflex.* Oxford: Pergamon Press, 1963.

SPENCE, K. W. *Behavior theory and conditioning.* New Haven, Conn.: Yale University Press, 1956.

——— *Behavior theory and learning.* Englewood Cliffs, N. J.: Prentice-Hall, 1960.

——— and JANET TAYLOR SPENCE (eds.) *The psychology of learning and motivation.* New York and London: Academic Press.

STAGNER, R., and KARWOSKI, T. F. *Psychology.* New York: McGraw-Hill, 1952.

STELLAR, E. The physiology of motivation. *Psychological Review*, 1954, *61*, 5–221.

STOCKFELT, T. *Motivation, learning, and performance.* Stockholm: Svenska Bokförlaget, 1963.

THOMAE, H. (ed.) *Allgemeine Psychologie II: Motivation.* Göttingen: Hogrefe's Verlag für Psychologie, 1965.

THORNDIKE, E. L. Animal intelligence. *Psychological Review*, 1898, Monograph Supplement *2*, 8.

——— *Animal intelligence.* New York: Macmillan, 1911.

TINBERGEN, N. *The study of instinct.* Oxford: Oxford University Press, 1951.

TOLMAN, E. C. *Purposive behavior in animals and men.* New York: Appleton-Century-Crofts, 1932.

——— *Drives toward war.* New York: Appleton-Century-Crofts, 1942.

——— A psychological model. *In* T. Parson and E. A. Shill (eds.), *Toward a general theory of action.* Cambridge, Mass.: Harvard University Press, 1951.

——— Principles of purposive behavior. *In* S. Koch (ed.), *Psychology —A study of a science*, vol. 2. New York: McGraw-Hill, 1959.

TOMAN, W. On the periodicity of motivation. *In* M. R. Jones (ed.), *Nebraska symposium on motivation.* Lincoln: Nebraska University Press, 1960a.

——— *An introduction to psychoanalytic theory of motivation.* New York: Pergamon Press, 1960b.

TURNER, M. B. *Philosophy and the science of behavior.* New York: Appleton-Century-Crofts, 1967.

WALKER, E. L. Psychological complexity as a basis for a theory of motivation and choice. *In* D. Levine (ed.), *Nebraska symposium on motivation.* Lincoln: Nebraska University Press, 1964.

WATSON, I. R. *The great psychologists.* Philadelphia and New York: Lippincott, 1963.

WHILE, R. W. Motivation reconsidered: the concept of competence. *Psychological Review*, 1959, *66*, 297–333.

———— Competence and the psycho–sexual stages of development. *In* M. R. Jones (ed.), *Nebraska symposium on motivation*. Lincoln: Nebraska University Press, 1960.

WIGGINS, J. S. Personality structure. *Annual Review of Psychology, 19.* Palo Alto, Calif.: Annual Reviews, Inc.

WOLMAN, B. *Contemporary theories and systems in psychology.* New York: Harper & Row, 1960.

———— Principles of monistic transitionism. *In* B. B. Wolman and E. Nagel (eds.), *Scientific psychology.* New York: Basic Books, 1965.

———— Classification of mental disorders. *Psychotherapy, Psychosom,* 1966, *14,* 50–65.

———— The socio-psycho-somatic theory of schizophrenia. *Psychotherapy, Psychosom,* 1967, *15,* 375–87.

WOODWORTH, R. S. *Dynamic psychology.* New York: Columbia University Press, 1918.

———— *Dynamics of behavior.* New York: Holt, Rinehart & Winston, 1958.

———— and SHEEHAN, M. R. *Contemporary schools of psychology,* 3rd ed. New York: Ronald Press, 1964.

VOROGIN, L. E. et al. Orienting reflex and exploratory behavior. *Russian Monographs on Brain and Behavior,* no. 3. Washington, D.C.: American Institute of Biological Sciences, 1965.

YOUNG, P. T. *Motivation of behavior.* New York: John Wiley, 1936.

———— The experimental analysis of appetite. *Psychological Bulletin,* 1941, *38,* 129–64.

———— *Emotion in man and animal.* New York: John Wiley, 1943.

———— *Motivation and emotion.* New York: John Wiley, 1961.

Hostile behavior is a common term for some of the activities that comprise social fighting and the general system of agonistic behavior. Rather than trying to define hostility itself, with all the extra meaning that this word has accumulated over the period of centuries, I shall define agonistic behavior, a relatively new scientific term which still carries with it a precise meaning. Essentially, it is adaptive behavior which arises out of conflict between two members of the same species. It is manifested in a group of behavior patterns, each of which may be useful under certain circumstances, either alone or in combination with other patterns.

Each species has its own peculiar patterns of agonistic behavior, but most of them fall into four or five general categories. To take a specific example, when two male house mice are placed together, one of them may attack the other, particularly if he has previously been trained to attack. In this attack he chases or pursues the other mouse. When he has caught up, he strikes at it with his teeth, usually around the back or the base of the tail. The second mouse responds with defensive fighting, using the same patterns of biting and scratching as the attacker; and soon the two are rolling over and over each other in a ball, biting and scratching each other. This may be repeated time after time, until eventually one of the mice is badly hurt and uses another behavior pattern, that of escape. If he is unable to escape, he will soon begin to adopt a defensive posture, standing up straight and holding his forelimbs out toward the other mouse as if to hold him off. In many cases the victorious mouse will approach as if to attack, but stops as soon as the loser assumes the defensive posture. This abortive attack constitutes another behavior pattern, the threat. Still another pattern occurs when the losing mouse is attacked. He is very likely to squeak in response to either an attack or a threat. This vocalization is a reaction to pain or distress and to some extent has the effect of inhibiting the attack by the first mouse. A final pattern of behavior occurs when a mouse is caught in a situation from which he cannot escape. In this case he may become completely passive or show freezing behavior. This is very similar to the "death feigning" seen in animals like opossums in response to

J. P. Scott

Hostility and Aggression

34

an attack by a predator. Freezing has adaptive value in that a completely quiet animal is not as stimulating as an active one.

The use of the various patterns of agonistic behavior in the mouse does not always occur in the above order, and numerous variations are possible. Fighting may be preceded by hair fluffing and tail rattling, in which the mouse whips his tail rapidly from side to side with a rattling noise as it touches the side of the cage. In many species of birds and fish, actual fighting may be preceded by elaborate displays of feathers or fins and special postures which communicate threat. In any case, patterns of communication are a regular part of agonistic behavior.

Distribution and Evolutionary History of Agonistic Behavior

SOCIAL FIGHTING IN THE ANIMAL KINGDOM

With the exception of Porifera or sponges, all major phyla in the animal kingdom show some forms of behavior, the most primitive kinds being ingestive behavior (the taking in of nourishment, in solid or liquid form), sexual behavior, exploratory behavior, and shelter seeking. Also universal is some form of escape behavior from injury. This last may be considered the predecessor of agonistic behavior. However, we find social fighting developed only in the highest phylum of invertebrates, the arthropods, and in the vertebrates themselves.

There are two major factors which limit the distribution of social fighting. First, in order for fighting to be adaptive, individuals must be able to discriminate between other individuals of the same species, as indiscriminate attacks on all species mates would be completely nonadaptive and should be strongly selected against. In order to make this discrimination, a species must have sense organs adequate for making social discriminations and with this must show enough polymorphism or individual variation so that individuals can be recognized (Caspari 1967). A second major prerequisite for adaptive social fighting is the possession of motor organs which can inflict pain or damage on a species mate. Among vertebrates, the order Amphibia has neither teeth nor claws, and social fighting is almost nonexistent, although some species of frogs show mild forms of agonistic behavior as one frog wrestles with or jumps on another. Aside from this, agonistic behavior has been commonly observed in all other major classes of vertebrates, including fish, reptiles, birds, and mammals. Among the arthropods, agonistic behavior occurs rather commonly among the decapods (crustaceans such as crabs, lobsters, and crayfish) and in a few orders of insects, particularly in the orthopterans (grasshoppers and crickets), and less commonly in the more highly social insects such as ants, belonging to the order Hymenoptera. Social fighting is, then, relatively new in evolutionary history and reaches its highest development in the vertebrates.

EVOLUTIONARY HISTORY OF AGONISTIC BEHAVIOR

Unlike the evolution of anatomical form, whose history can often be reconstructed rather precisely by the use of fossils, the evolution of behavior can only be hypothesized on the basis of the behavior of living forms and can never be verified. This makes it doubly important that speculation should be soundly based.

Assuming that behavior is most likely to be evolved from preexisting behavior, the most likely precursors of fighting are the escape behavior and defensive threats which are almost universal in all animals. Escape is, of course, adaptive in response to injury, whether it is caused by physical forces, by predators, or by species mates. This applies equally to animals which are completely defenseless and to those that have motor organs capable of inflicting damage. In the latter, behavior patterns of defensive threat or defensive attack become adaptive and occur commonly. Attacks and threats are not adaptive against pain produced by such physical forces as falling rocks, but they are effective against both predators and species mates. Since animals living together are likely to accidentally jostle or injure each other by their movements, this should inevitably elicit any pattern of defensive attack which had been evolved in connection with reactions to predators. From this it is only a step to social fighting, since a defensive attack on an animal which had accidentally hurt another would in turn elicit a similar reaction, and both would be fighting.

Once social fighting occurs, selective forces should guide the evolution of social fighting in various directions. Patterns of offensive attack could easily be evolved from defensive attack. Vocalization in response to injury is adaptive as a warning signal to species mates in case of attack by predators, and could evolve readily into a part of social conflict in any species that regularly protects and cares for its young. In many such species a defensive attack by a parent is a regular part of agonistic behavior.

The hypothesis that social fighting has generally evolved from predation is very unlikely. In the first place, agonistic behavior is just as common in nonpredatory animals as it is in predators. Second, predation against a member of the same species is in most cases strongly maladaptive. Finally, predators have defensive reactions from which social fighting could have been evolved more effectively. Contrary to popular thinking, the typical predator is not bloodthirsty in his reactions to his own species and, in fact, agonistic behavior is likely to be highly ritualized and controlled (Eibl-Eibesfeldt 1967).

The Functions of Agonistic Behavior

Agonistic behavior has evolved independently in every species of animals in which it occurs. As it has done so, it has taken on a variety of social functions. As indicated above, the avoidance of injury is almost a universal function of this type of behavior. Likewise, in almost every case, it has the effect of keeping the individuals spaced out from each other at greater or lesser distances (McBride 1964). In addition to these, agonistic behavior may have a variety of other functions.

AGONISTIC BEHAVIOR IN FISH

Many species of freshwater fish set up nesting territories in which the eggs are laid by the female and sometimes guarded by the male. In the three-spined stickleback, a small fish extensively studied by Tinbergen (1953), the adults live much of the year in schools in which no agonistic behavior occurs. During the breeding season, the males leave the school and each selects a small area in which he builds an elaborate nest mound, making a tunnel through it in which he stays. If another male approaches, the resident drives him away. Females swim by and the male goes toward them in a courtship dance. If one of the females is ready to lay eggs, she returns with him to the nest and lays the eggs, which are immediately fertilized by the male. He then drives the female away and remains to guard the nest. The young hatch in approximately a week, and the male continues to guard them, even picking them up in his mouth and returning them to the nest if they wander away. After a few weeks he leaves the nest territory and the young fry go off together in a school.

Such behavior may have a very ancient origin, as it is seen in the river dogfish, *Amia calva*, one of the most primitive of modern bony fishes. In the stickleback, agonistic behavior has the effect of dividing up favorable breeding areas and keeping the nests spaced out so that there is enough food for the offspring in each nest. The behavior has the further effect of protecting the eggs and young fry in their most vulnerable stages, as most fish do not distinguish between the young of their own species and that of others.

In the stickleback no fighting takes place while the fish are swimming in schools, and other species, such as the herring and mackerel, have evolved in the direction of greater emphasis on schooling. These fish spend almost all their lives in groups, even while spawning. At the opposite extreme are certain tropical fish, such as the so-called Jack Dempsey, *Cichlasoma biocellatum*. These common aquarium fish attack each other on sight, whether males or females (Gottier 1968). If they are forced to stay close together, they develop a dominance order in which each fish avoids the threats and attacks of those fish superior to him. If allowed to move apart, they do so, with the result that they seldom come into contact. In this species the effect of agonistic behavior is to keep individuals spaced out and apart from each other. In spite of the great amount of fighting, the fish are rarely severely hurt. In fighting, two fish lock jaws and pull away at each other until they become tired, the most severe injury being bruising of the jaws.

These two species illustrate most of what is known about the functions of agonistic behavior in fish. In general, social fighting in these animals facilitates reproduction and regulates spacing.

Reptiles

Among reptiles agonistic behavior has been studied most thoroughly in lizards, many of which live in desert areas and are active in daylight and hence readily available for observation. These are solitary predators on insects and other small animals, and agonistic behavior has the effect of keeping them spaced out from each other and hence more likely to have an adequate food supply. Some species also guard their nests (Ferguson 1966).

Birds

Many different species of birds have evolved agonistic behavior in relation to breeding territories. Of these, the red-winged blackbird (similar in habits to the English reed bunting on which Elliot Howard [1920] made his original studies on song and territory in birds) is a classical example. During the winter season the redwinged blackbirds live in flocks in the southern part of the United States. In the late winter, the males begin

to move northward in flocks, eventually stopping off in the areas in which they have previously lived. The flocks break up, and each male establishes a territory, usually in the middle of a cattail swamp, and sits on top of a tall cattail or small tree and sings a warning song. If other males approach, he attacks them and pursues them until they reach a boundary, so precisely defined that each bird seems to recognize a line drawn in midair. Later the female flock arrives, and a female stops off with each male and eventually mates and rears a brood or two of young. In this species fighting has the function of providing an adequate breeding area and food supply for the young and probably also has an indirect effect of limiting the total population size.

The occurrence and function of social fighting varies from species to species. Unlike redwings, starlings continue to show agonistic behavior during the nonbreeding season, in their case chiefly over the possession of nesting holes (Davis 1959). Size and function of territories may vary a great deal. Gulls, which normally nest on small islands in crowded colonies, have territories which are only as large as the distance which a nesting gull can reach with its beak, and which have no relation to food supply.

Agonistic behavior has quite different forms and functions in the gallinaceous birds. In the sage grouse, males gather each year in a mating area and through a series of fights and scuffles form a dominance order. The result is that the most dominant cock occupies the center of the ground with others spaced out around him at intervals. When females arrive, they wander through the mating ground and about 80 percent of them are mated by the most dominant animal or master cock. In this case fighting has the function of determining which animal will do the majority of mating and has little to do with the rearing and protection of the young. It is noteworthy that in this species, in which agonistic behavior and mating are so highly organized, the amount and severity of fighting is much less than in related species of grouse which do not have such highly organized mating grounds (Scott 1950).

In feral domestic fowl (McBride 1968) observed on an island off Australia, the dominant males guard definite territorial boundaries during the breeding season. In each territory, subordinate males occupy smaller subterritories. Both are accompanied by nonbroody females, and the hens show a peck order at feeding places. Certain low-ranking cocks are excluded from all territories and hence from contact with females and from access to the best feeding places. Broody females with chicks become solitary, wandering and feeding near a nest and attacking or threatening all birds who came close to the chicks. In this highly complex social organization agonistic behavior has many functions: determining access to feeding sites and females, maintaining spatial relationships, defense of the young, and division of food. Further, the functions of agonistic behavior differ between the two sexes.

Mammals

One of the most successful groups of mammals in terms of numbers of species, worldwide distribution, and density of population, is the order Rodentia. Of these only a few species have been thoroughly studied with respect to social behavior. In the house mouse, as we have seen above, fighting is largely confined to males, and the chief eliciting stimulus is pain; an adult male will invariably respond to an attack by another mouse. They do not fight over females, and while under certain circumstances they will struggle over the possession of food, such fighting is never severe. They are capable of developing small territories around their nests if the boundaries are such that only two or three places need to be defended, but this function is relatively unimportant. Mice normally tolerate the individuals with whom they grow up and only fight strangers. The general effect is to permit familiar animals to live in high densities where there is a concentrated food supply, but to prevent strange animals from coming in. Mice are incapable of developing dominance orders which would permit them to use agonistic behavior in close social groups in a relatively harmless way. The general function of agonistic behavior in mice is, therefore, to keep the animals dispersed (Scott 1966).

A more drastic dispersive effect is seen in the common woodchuck. These animals are intolerant of each other except for brief periods during the mating season and while the females care for their young. At other times woodchucks attack or threaten each other on sight. Dominance is developed after brief encounters, and thereafter the dominant animal forces the subordinate one to stay at a maximum distance. The result is that woodchucks maintain a distance between each other which is approximately equal to that from which one woodchuck can see another. No territorial boundaries are involved, and the mutual pressure generated by agonistic behavior results in any empty living space being filled almost immediately (Bronson 1964).

The highly organized agonistic behavior of prairie dogs, large ground squirrels which live close together in enormous numbers, contrasts greatly with that of the woodchuck. A male and several females live constantly together in the same burrow system, around which there is a definite territorial boundary that is defended by the resident animals. However, this is done in a highly ritualized fashion, with little or no injury, the resident always stopping at the boundary and signaling by reversing his body and raising his tail. New territories are established by the older animals, who move to the edge of the colony and leave the old burrow system to the young raised in the previous year. The general effect of agonistic behavior in this species is to give exclusive use of a burrow system and the surrounding foraging area to a particular group of animals, but still permitting them to remain in close visual and auditory contact (King 1955).

While male deer mice of the species *Peromyscus maniculatus bairdii* will get into severe fights when caged in laboratory situations, they are likely to show mutual avoidance in the field, even when a resident male finds his burrow occupied by another (Terman 1962). In many situations large numbers of animals will peacefully occupy the same burrows. Females of this species, like many other rodents, will attempt to defend their young against either predators or members of the same species.

All of the rodents are relatively small in size. The most successful group of large herbivorous animals are the Artiodactyla, or even-toed ungulates. The social behavior of only a few of these has been studied in detail. In mountain sheep, males and females move in separate flocks except during the rutting season in the autumn of the year. At this time the males take part in ritualized fights in which two males back off at a considerable distance and run together headlong, clashing their heavy horns together. After a few encounters the male that is either tired or shaken up will retire from the field, leaving the oppor-

tunity for mating with the females to the victor. Fighting is always done in pairs, and groups of males never make combined attacks on a single individual. At other seasons of the year agonistic behavior in the male flocks is confined to one male pushing or butting another out of the way in order to occupy more room or a particular spot in which to lie down. This kind of fighting is never prolonged and is apparently governed by a dominance order. There is ordinarily no fighting over food and no territorial boundaries are defended (Scott 1945).

Domestic goats will readily form dominance orders involving both males and females. In most situations fighting is reduced to brief threats or single butts by dominant animals against subordinates, which have the effect of keeping the flock spaced out a foot or two apart. Under natural feeding conditions there is no fighting over food, but goats can readily be trained to butt each other out of the way to obtain small amounts of favored food placed so that only one animal has access to it. As with sheep, prolonged and serious fighting takes place only in the presence of females in estrus. Again, such fighting takes place in ritualized pair combats, and the victorious animal attempts to keep all other males away from the females (Hafez & Scott 1962).

In the American elk, or wapiti, male and female herds only come together in the rutting season, at which time the antlers of the males have reached their full size and are used in the pushing contests. These weapons are potentially dangerous, but in most cases two males simply push against each other's antlers until one becomes exhausted and runs away. The victorious male attempts to keep females in a tight group and mates with each in turn as each comes into estrus. After a few days he may become exhausted by his efforts to defend his position and give way to another. There is little fighting at other seasons of the year. The antlers, which occur only in males and are discarded after the rutting season, are not used against predators, defense being achieved by striking with the forefeet.

In general, agonistic behavior in the hoofed animals has the primary function of determining which males shall do the mating. In these animals, which live in large herds and wander about to obtain their relatively abundant plant food, there is no effect of dispersion. In the vast majority no territorial boundaries are defended, although in one curious case of an African antelope, the Uganda Kob, males have evolved breeding grounds on which they show behavior similar to that of the sage grouse. Each male patrols a circular area about 100 yards in diameter, keeping out all other males. Females in estrus may enter such an area and be mated but the male does not attempt to keep them inside or follow them when they leave (Buechner 1963).

Agonistic behavior in the order Carnivora is unusually interesting in that these animals are usually equipped with physical strength and weapons which could permit them to do serious harm. Some carnivora are highly social and others are largely solitary, and these are well exemplified by the domestic dog and cat. In the latter, individuals usually live in a solitary fashion, attached to a particular spot which is normally a human dwelling. Each cat wanders around his home, hunting small animals and birds. No territory is guarded, but if two strange cats meet, they will fight. As a result of fighting dominance is established, and as a result the subordinate cat simply keeps out of the way when the two meet. This behavior has the effect of insuring that no two animals will hunt in the same area in close succession, which of course would be likely to be unsuccessful for the second animal. Fighting between males also takes place at the time when a female is in estrus, but the choice of mates is usually determined by the female. Agonistic behavior in this species therefore has the primary function of dispersion (Leyhausen 1965).

A more elaborate system of control of hunting behavior is seen in the African cheetah. These hunting cats travel in small groups looking for prey. As they move, they repeatedly mark places with urine. When a second group of cheetahs happens to cross the path of the first, they stop and follow its trail for a distance, apparently until they can determine in which direction the group was going, and then take off in a different direction, avoiding the area which has already been hunted over. The marking has no relationship to a permanent territory (Eaton 1970).

Wolves, the wild ancestors of our domestic dog, are highly social pack animals and have an elaborately developed system of agonistic behavior. They defend a small area around the den as a territory, but hunt over a much larger range. As they go, they mark scent posts with urine and feces. How other packs react to these has never been determined, but in the domestic dog a newcomer simply adds his scent to that which has been left before and shows no sign of avoidance. Scent posts do inform males of visits from females in estrus, which results in the gatherings of males around such a female (Scott & Fuller 1965).

Both wolves and dogs develop dominance orders within their social groups. Dominance determines the possession of food and may also affect the choice of mates, although this is still not well understood. In a group of dogs reared together since puppyhood, serious fighting is likely to break out at the time the first females come into estrus, and occurs in both males and females, although not ordinarily between the two sexes. In a captive pack of wolves studied by Rabb et al. (1967) the most dominant male did no mating at all, but the most dominant female prevented other females from mating, with the result that only one litter was usually born each year. Whether or not this takes place under natural conditions is unknown.

Thus in a solitary carnivore agonistic behavior regulates the process of hunting. In a more social one it has the chief effect of regulating the distribution of food but also the occurrence of mating. In addition, carnivores will defend their young against other predators. One of the most interesting findings is that the patterns of behavior employed in social fighting are quite distinct from the more injurious patterns used in predation and are ordinarily unlikely to produce serious injury. For example, in wolves and dogs, the usual pattern of predation is to dash toward the rear of the prey animal and attempt to hamstring it and at the same time avoid injury. On the other hand, when two wolves fight, they meet each other head on and each attempts to seize the other by the back of the neck and force him to the ground.

Even in this brief survey of nonprimate mammals it is evident that agonistic behavior has evolved in a great variety of ways and may have several different functions, none of which are universal. The most basic and general effect of agonistic behavior is dispersion, that is, fighting is most useful in driving another individual away, but even this is not necessarily true in highly social species that are capable of developing dominance orders. The function of dispersal is integrated with specific areas (producing the phenomenon of territoriality) only in certain special cases. Territoriality is important only where it is practical, that is, where animals live in close contact and can constantly observe each other in adjacent areas, as in the case of the colonial

prairie dogs that are active in daylight. Where large areas are required for living, as in most ungulates, or where animals are nocturnal, as in most small rodents, territoriality is usually unimportant. Fighting over food depends upon the distribution of food, being important only when it is highly concentrated, as in the prey of carnivores. The importance of agonistic behavior with respect to mating behavior depends on the species involved, and seems to be general only in the large herbivorous animals. It is also possible that fighting between like-sexed individuals has the effect of preventing the sterile sexual behavior involved in homosexual approaches, as fighting is a common reaction to such behavior among males. Females also react defensively toward males when not in estrus.

The order Primata, to which man belongs, is distinctly different from any of the other groups of mammals, and its members have evolved in many different ways. Primates have specialized in manipulative ability, all of them having well-developed fingers, some having toes which are almost equally useful, and some having prehensile tails as well. Probably for this reason, primates, with the exception of man, live almost entirely in tropical regions, for without protective gloves fingers stiffen and become useless in cold weather. With respect to food, primates tend to be omnivorous food gatherers with a largely vegetarian diet. Gorillas have become entirely herbivorous, and at the opposite extreme, the galagos, or bush babies, are almost entirely insectivorous; but in no case are primates primarily adapted as predators on other vertebrates, as are some of the carnivores.

The first primate species to be thoroughly studied under conditions of natural social organization was the howling monkey (Carpenter 1934). These animals move in groups of a few adult males, a larger number of females, and assorted young, in the treetops of the Central American forests, eating fruits and leaves. Agonistic behavior is almost entirely expressed in vocalization. When two troops come close to each other, the males roar and the two troops avoid each other. Each troop has an area within which it lives and wanders, but this overlaps that of other troops and no territorial boundaries are defended. When females come into estrus they may pass from male to male as one becomes satiated, without fighting between the males. The reaction of the troop to a potential predator such as man is to run around in the treetops vocalizing and showering down twigs and excrement.

When first reported, it was thought that this behavior represented a highly specialized form of social life, but since then many of its features have been found to be widespread in other primate social groups. The common living pattern for such species as rhesus monkeys, langurs, and others is a troop occupying a small core area exclusively but wandering out to find food in a larger home range which overlaps with that of other troops. As might be expected of animals that have to wander over large areas to gather widely distributed food, no territorial boundaries are defended, but the troops are spaced out by reactions of mutual threat and avoidance. However, a few cases of true territoriality have been recently reported in some of the smaller species of monkeys (Bernstein 1967).

In the vast majority of primates females show only brief periods of sexual receptivity, and while they are likely to mate with the most dominant male in a group, this is not always true (Jay 1965). No permanent consortships are formed, and females pass from one male to another without fighting. One exception is the hamadryas baboon, in which each male guards a small group of females (Kummer 1968).

Food ordinarily causes no fighting, as the natural food of primates is widely distributed. However, artificially concentrating the food given captive rhesus monkeys will increase the amount of fighting (Southwick 1969), and rhesus bands may occasionally fight each other when attracted by the free food supplied in Indian temples.

Perhaps the most interesting primates from a human viewpoint are savannah baboons. Like human beings, these are adapted for life as plains-living primates in relatively large groups, although in physique they are much less similar than the more closely related anthropoid apes. Males develop a strong dominance order which has the effect of keeping males spaced out from each other in the troop, with the most dominant male in the center and the youngest and less dominant individuals on the edges. Females and their young are likely to be concentrated in the center of the group, which of course represents the area of greatest safety. This organization is highly adaptive with respect to defense against predators, as the youngest and presumably the most alert males are on the outside edges where they are likely to make the first contact. When a predator is seen a baboon gives a warning bark, and the other males rush over to him and attack or threaten the predator as a group. In this way the baboons are able to protect themselves against any predator except the lion. Young baboons learn their place in the dominance order through play with each other. If one is hurt and cries out, an older male immediately rushes over and threatens the playing animals. If a younger male teases an older one, the latter retaliates by chasing it until it becomes terrorized, but seldom inflicts any physical injury (DeVore 1965).

In general, the most characteristic expression of agonistic behavior in primates is through a dominance order within groups of males, which results in the males within a group remaining spaced out from each other. Territorial fighting is rare, but antagonism between males of adjacent groups tends to keep the groups apart. Fighting over the possession of females is likewise a rare phenomenon. Far from being predators themselves, one of the principal problems of primates is dealing with large predators, and they meet this very effectively by living in groups which make possible the efficient discovery of predators, by using vocal signals to warn the rest of the group, and finally by group threats against predators. These largely consist of vocalization and other annoying behavior rather than outright attacks.

From this information it is not possible to draw the conclusion that there are general trends in the evolution of agonistic behavior in primates and that these culminate in human behavior. Rather, each primate species has evolved independently and diverged in numerous ways. We must therefore examine human behavior directly to determine what forms agonistic behavior may take, remembering that even in the nonhuman primates agonistic behavior is developed as an adaptation to meet particular situations and can vary considerably even in the same species. Human beings may have evolved, any, or all, or even new, potentialities for agonistic behavior as compared with those of other primate species. We can, however, draw certain negative conclusions. The most important of these is that man is not descended from a predatory primate, or "killer ape." The prehuman fossils that have been discovered in South Africa are all of relatively small individuals with weak teeth, very much like modern man (Leakey 1967). Man has become a predator only

secondarily, through the use of tools. How he has used these tools is obviously not the result of a previously developed "killer instinct." Further, one of the consequences of the evolution toward manipulative ability in the primates has been the realization of general adaptive capacities rather than special ones, and such adaptive capacities have been enormously amplified by the evolution of language. Consequently the heredity of man neither forces the emission of certain kinds of behavior nor limits its expression to the extent that may occur in certain nonhuman animals. Rather, hereditary changes have evolved toward a capacity for greatly increased variation in adaptive behavior.

Ritualization and Dominance

As we have seen above, much of the agonistic behavior in natural groups of animals is relatively harmless in nature. In the great majority of cases, fights only take place between individual pairs, and fighting stops before either animal is seriously injured. The evolutionary tendency for behavior to evolve toward a symbolic form is called ritualization. The theoretical reasons why agonistic behavior frequently becomes ritualized are as follows.

SOCIAL EVOLUTION

Selection, while it is not the sole moving force in evolution, is its major guiding force. Selection pressures come from a variety of forces which can be included under the general headings of the physical environment, the biotic environment (including predation and disease) and the social environment. These pressures can affect both group and individual survival. As we have seen above, defensive agonistic behavior promotes individual survival and also the survival of a group, provided it is directed against members of another species. When directed against the same species, the result depends upon the vigor and magnitude of the behavior. If it is of a mild sort, it promotes the survival of the individual showing it and has no effect on the other individual. However, if the defense reaction is very strong, it can result in serious injury to the other individual and hence work against the survival of the group. Finally, unrestricted strong attacks on other members of the same species should have no survival value for either the group or the individual, and such behavior should be strongly selected against. Consequently, there is a tendency in most animal species for agonistic behavior to evolve into relatively harmless forms, i.e., for agonistic behavior to become ritualized.

The degree to which this occurs varies a great deal. Semisolitary animals like woodchucks can survive simply by keeping apart despite a capacity for developing a great deal of violent agonistic behavior, whereas similar tendencies would result in wholesale slaughter if they occurred in a colony-living rodent like the prairie dog. Consequently, the greater the degree of close social contact and social organization, the greater the degree of ritualization of agonistic behavior.

DOMINANCE

The reduction of agonistic behavior to symbolic forms is a developmental process as well as an evolutionary one. Domestic chickens of both sexes are capable of inflicting serious injuries on each other. When females live in large flocks, a great deal of threatening and pecking goes on, but when individuals are identified it is seen that the threats are always delivered in a precise relationship. If two strange hens are brought together for the first time, they will ordinarily get into a fight, as a result of which one wins and the other loses. At each subsequent encounter the issue is settled more quickly, until finally the winner, or dominant hen, has merely to threaten the subordinate one to make it stay away.

The phenomenon of dominance organization is widespread among mammals as well as birds and may show a great deal of variation both between and within species. In a flock of goats dominance appears in many degrees, ranging from complete dominance, in which the subordinate goat always avoids coming near the dominant one and hence no fighting occurs, through conditions in which the dominant animal butts but no retaliation occurs, to conditions in which the subordinate animal never initiates fighting but always returns an attack. There are also cases of individuals that are completely peaceful (Scott 1948).

Similar varieties of dominance occur in groups of dogs. There can be complete dominance, where one individual always takes precedence, or other pairs in which the relationship is one of mutual threat, with neither animal being dominant. In still other cases, the first animal to possess a bone or other desired object becomes temporarily dominant. Dominance relationships develop among young puppies in a litter as an outcome of playful fighting, with the result that the dominance order in such a naturally formed group is fixed before the capacity for severe fighting appears. Among female puppies the dominance order is ususally settled by threats and vocalizations rather than by overt fighting (Scott & Fuller 1965).

Social animals are capable of developing dominance with members of other species, and in the dog–human relationship the human being usually becomes dominant. This relationship can be established without the use of overt violence. In one experiment involving several hundred puppies we never punished the animals. However, from birth onward we picked them up and carried them from place to place on a daily and weekly routine. These animals all became unusually submissive, and if we wished to control them all we had to do was to pick them up. Dominance can thus take many forms and also be achieved as a result of restraint rather than punishment or violent attacks. It is probable that dominance in human societies is achieved largely in such subtle ways as these.

Human Aggression

EVOLUTIONARY BASIS

As indicated above, agonistic behavior has evolved in many diverse ways in different members of the animal kingdom, even within the order of primates to which man belongs. Because of the extraordinary degree of cultural diversity in modern human societies it is impossible to state with any degree of certainty what the agonistic behavior of precultural man may have been. The latest fossil evidence indicates that man developed on the South African plains and was in physique very similar to modern man. The closest living models are the Australian aborigines, who up until recently lived on the Australian deserts

under similar conditions (although this probably represents a secondary return to such conditions by men who had lived in other environments before they emigrated to Australia), and the South African bushmen, who may have lived continuously in the same environment. At any rate, these are small groups of individuals, containing perhaps a few dozen at the most because of the liminations of their food supply. They obtain most of their food while wandering around in a familiar area. Food gathering supplemented by hunting occupies most of their time.

Hunting in precultural man would have been less important because of the lack of tools, and territoriality would have been unimportant because of the impossibility of defending the relatively large area needed to supply food under these conditions. The life of our remote ancestors with respect to agonistic behavior may well have been much like that of the savannah baboons, with a dominance order among the adults which was learned by the children through play. One would expect proto-human children to cry out when hurt just as they do today and to be rescued by their parents. One would also expect them to tease their elders and to learn to be subordinate from the resulting retaliation. It is also likely that the adult males cooperated in attacking or threatening predators that approached the group. If, like modern females, our prehistoric ancestors did not have definite estrus periods but were almost constantly receptive, we can surmise that there may have been more tendency to develop permanent consortships than in other primates, and along with this some tendency toward sexual jealousy.

Once language was developed, those social groups which used it most effectively must have had an enormous advantage for survival, because learned ways of adapting to new situations could be passed along so much more effectively. Among the things that can be transmitted culturally are tools, and among the first tools must have been those that were used for getting food: digging sticks for getting food out of the ground, cutting stones, and sticks and stones that could be used for killing small animals at a distance.

Once such tools for hunting were developed, it must have been immediately obvious that these could be used in agonistic behavior. For example, an individual with a club or stone has an obvious advantage in achieving dominance over an individual who has no such tools. One would also expect that cultural regulation of the use of tools was soon begun, keeping them out of the hands of children and other individuals low in the dominance order. At any rate, with the invention of tools for hunting, there must have begun the prehistory of the use of tools in agonistic behavior, one result of which is an enormous increase in the potentiality for damage.

THE KINDS OF HUMAN AGGRESSION

As one observes behavior in a well-organized human society, it is obvious that there is very little overt fighting, and that the small amount that does occur is highly regulated. If one wants to study fighting in human societies, one is almost forced to look primarily at the playful fighting seen in young children, or to watch the closely related mock fighting bouts seen in various organized sports, such as wrestling and boxing. Or, one can set up various mock fighting situations as is often done in experimental social psychology. When fighting is overtly expressed among adults, it very often consists of a great deal of vocalization and threats and relatively little actual violence. Other than this, there are the cases in which social control has broken down. In spite of ominous crime statistics, such unlawful acts are so rare that it is possible to study them only in retrospect.

When human fighting does occur, it is very likely to involve fighting between groups. In this respect human behavior is very different from that of the nonhuman animals. Among the latter, fighting between groups of the same species is extremely rare. While groups may occasionally attack a single individual, as when a pack of wolves attacks a single outsider, or occasionally the males of two bands of rhesus monkeys attack each other when they unexpectedly come into contact, there is nothing like the coordinated and organized fighting between groups that occurs within and between human societies. Warfare and similar intergroup conflicts within a society are therefore a human biological or cultural invention (Scott 1969).

The motivational systems involved in intergroup fighting are very different from those that are important in fights between pairs of individuals, although there may be some overlap. Allelomimetic behavior and all the emotional and motivational factors associated with it are a prominent part of group fighting. Especially in modern warfare where hand-to-hand combat is very uncommon, group fighting has a decidedly different emotional basis, as Bourne (1969) points out. The situation in modern warfare is very different from that in individual conflicts, both psychologically and physiologically, although there may be a common element in that soldiers taking part in modern warfare may be subjected to the same sort of physiological stress and fear to which an animal which is being constantly defeated may be subjected.

All fighting, whether between groups or between individuals, is "instrumental" in the sense that it has an effect, or function. As we have seen above, the form and quality of fighting varies tremendously with respect to the function involved. Furthermore, there are great differences between species. For example, food as a cause of fighting is very important to dogs and relatively unimportant to mice, which can be induced to fight over food only under very special circumstances. In man, determining which kinds of fighting are most important is very much a matter of guesswork, partly because so little overt fighting can be observed, and partly because fighting is so highly regulated by culture, both in a positive and negative way. As we have indicated above, many of the kinds of fighting that are important in nonhuman animals could also be important in man, but not necessarily so; and furthermore, there may be certain unique kinds of fighting in human beings. Fighting produced by pain and fear is probably highly important in man, simply because this kind of defensive fighting has almost universal usefulness and is the probable basic kind of behavior from which all other social fighting has evolved. As might be expected in a highly social species, this kind of defensive fighting has been extended to the defense of others: the defense of species mates, particularly of females by males, and the defense of children by parents of both sexes.

As a group-living animal, one would expect that space would not be a highly important cause of fighting in man; and indeed, most people seem to be highly tolerant of the nearness of others, even permitting actual physical contact under many circumstances. There is nothing like the spacing reactions seen in a flock of goats, and most people prefer to walk shoulder to shoulder. While fighting can produce dispersion between human individuals, this is by no means a regular reaction.

Territoriality (particularly, group territoriality) has been alleged to be a major cause of fighting among men (Tinbergen 1968). Wars have, of course, been fought over the possession of land, and there are many cases of boundary quarrels between individuals. However, there are many human societies in which territoriality is relatively unimportant, as it is among man's closest relatives, the primates. Like warfare, territoriality in man may be either a cultural or a biological invention, and as such does not share the basic importance of defensive fighting caused by pain and fear.

A common cause of quarreling and fighting between human beings is social jealously, defined as an attempt by one individual to obtain exclusive possession of the companionship and attention of another. This phenomenon is much broader than the attempts of various nonhuman animals to obtain exclusive possession of females, and is consequently much broader than sexual jealousy. A child will attempt, for example, to monopolize the attention of his mother, or of a favorite friend. Such competition is likely to develop in any triangular situation.

Food is probably relatively unimportant as a motivating force for fighting in human beings. While children frequently become quarrelsome when hungry, food sharing is almost a universal phenomenon in human societies, being usually restricted in our own society to members of the nuclear family, but extended to whole tribes in many primitive societies. Food sharing is probably an extension of parental behavior and, except among young children, who will struggle for favorite bits of food, fighting over food is probably relatively unimportant in human individuals.

In addition to the above, there are relatively rare cases of individuals who periodically become extremely irritable or who show violent outbursts of temper which are not associated with external causes and for which the individual himself has no explanation. In most cases these can be traced back to pathological conditions of the nervous system, resulting from lesions or other malfunctioning as indicated by abnormal electroencephalograms.

Finally, there is a peculiarly human kind of fighting associated with the human characteristic of highly developed language. Human beings will fight over disagreements in ideas, and particularly ideas which describe how human behavior should be. Whatever the biological basis of this trait may be, it is a fact that both individuals and groups have fought long and violently over disagreements on matters of alleged truth and doctrines. Human beings are comfortable when their ideas agree logically and do not contradict each other. One way to solve the problem of contradiction is to drive away or eliminate those individuals with whom one disagrees.

Internal Stimulation

There is no doubt that internal conditions have an important effect upon the occurrence of fighting and other forms of agonistic behavior. As with all other forms of behavior, feelings, emotions, and internal sensations have important effects. These internal states can be studied both introspectively and objectively, but in either case one of the basic theoretical problems is to trace the causes of internal activity.

THE SOURCES OF INTERNAL STIMULATION

Agonistic behavior is unlike sexual and ingestive behavior in that the sensation of internal organs in activity is a relatively unimportant factor. Cannon (1929) demonstrated that the emotion of anger consists principally of activity within that portion of the brain known as the hypothalamus. Subsequent physiological work with lesions and implanted electrodes has confirmed this finding for a variety of animals. The peripheral sensations of high blood pressure and other changes in the circulatory system can be duplicated by injections of adrenalin, but both clinical experience and the experiments of Schachter (1962) indicate that these sensations are not identical with anger. In the case of fear there is a more important peripheral element, since the gastrointestinal system is affected, producing sensations of nausea and even the symptoms of diarrhea, but experiments with implanted electrodes indicate that the major component of even this emotion is produced by the activity of particular parts of the hypothalamus.

The next step in tracing the source of internal stimulation is to discover how the emotional mechanisms in the hypothalamus are activated. The classical view of this problem was to postulate endogenous stimulation having a cumulative effect and leading to a "hydraulic" theory of behavior. From a physiological viewpoint this is nonsense, as there is no mechanism in the nervous system which permits pressure to build up like steam in a boiler or water in a tank. Nor is there any way in which any appreciable amount of energy can be stored in the nervous system. The hydraulic model has value only in that it describes what it feels like to become angry or afraid under certain conditions.

On the other hand, as indicated above, agonistic behavior and the emotional sensations accompanying it can be readily elicited by a variety of external stimuli. We can therefore postulate a theory which is in much better accordance with both physiology and objectively observed behavior: namely that the emotional mechanisms of the hypothalamus have the effect of magnifying and prolonging the effects of external stimulation but do not themselves originate stimulation. This theory is also consistent with the evolutionary viewpoint of agonistic behavior as adaptive behavior. Obviously it is nonadaptive for an animal to be afraid when there is nothing to fear and, since social fighting is potentially dangerous, it would be equally nonadaptive for an individual to build up endogenous stimulation which would lead unnecessarily into danger. The internal mechanisms concerned with agonistic behavior are always ready to be activated by external stimulation but, with certain exceptions noted below, they are quiescent in the absence of such stimulation.

CUMULATIVE EFFECTS

The emotional reactions of the hypothalamus are a mechanism which keeps the effect of external stimulation from dying out immediately. Experiments with fighting mice indicate that the measurable physiological effects of fighting persist as long as 24 hours and perhaps longer (Bronson & Eleftheriou 1965). In such a length of time it is obvious that added and repeated external stimulation could take place and have a cumulative effect. A series of rather weak stimuli could eventually produce a high degree of emotional arousal. This, of course, is related to the well-known physiological effect of summation of stimuli.

A second mechanism by which cumulative effects could be produced is through the process of reinforcement. While the process of learning has still not been reduced to a set of physiological processes, it is one of the basic principles of learning that repeated reinforcement produces an increase in motivation. Since both external and internal activities are affected by conditioning, it would be expected that the emotional reactions of either anger or fear could be strengthened in a particular situation by repeated reinforcement.

Finally, there are possible situations in which motivation from other systems of behavior can be associated with that of fighting. For example, endogenous stimulation is a well-known phenomenon in connection with hunger or thirst. One would expect that if there is a tendency to fight over food, then endogenous stimulation arising in the hunger mechanism would lead to an increasing probability that an individual would fight, provided food and another competing individual were present. It is also possible, since emotional conditions are often not readily identifiable in human beings, that a hungry individual might associate his unpleasant emotion with the presence of another person and react as if the other had caused the emotion by attempting to drive him away.

IRRITABILITY

In addition to the above, there are a number of well-known physiological conditions which can produce a state of irritability, which is essentially one of a lowered threshold to external stimulation. One of the classical cases is that of "sham rage" in cats, which is produced either by removing the cerebral cortex or by electrical stimulation of certain areas (Gunne 1969). Such cats will react violently to the merest touch. Introducing certain chemical substances into the bloodstream will produce a similar effect, as will altering the concentration of serum proteins in the brain (Everett & Wiegand 1962). Chronic states of irritability have been associated with brain lesions and with abnormal EEGs in human subjects. One of the most promising leads for controlling internal states affecting agonistic behavior is research in both the production and reduction of irritability states.

Controlling Mechanisms of Agonistic Behavior

As indicated above, actual overt violence is relatively rare in a well-organized human society. The mechanisms of social control operate very successfully and we can postulate that most of the mechanisms concerned are essentially similar to those seen in animal societies.

PASSIVE INHIBITION

The most effective and least spectacular way of controlling destructive violence is based on an important but little noticed principle discovered by Pavlov, namely that an animal can develop an inhibition in a particular situation simply by not doing anything in this situation. In Pavlov's case this was produced by lack of stimulation or reinforcement, but the same effect can be produced even more effectively by forming habits of productive, or at least harmless, activity in particular situations. In short, an individual forms habits of not fighting simply by not fighting in particular situations. Since internal as well as external activities are affected by conditioning, one would predict that this method would lead to an inhibition of emotional reactions such as anger or fear as well as overt behavior. This method is by far the most general and the most effective of any means for the social control of fighting.

MOCK-FIGHTING: GAMES AND SPORTS

Closely related to the principle of passive inhibition is deliberate training in the recognition and control of strong emotions such as are produced by many competitive sports. In a sport such as football, for example, the game is so organized that the players are repeatedly hurt and are almost continually frustrated from reaching the goal by the other team. This is a situation calculated to produce the emotion of anger, but the game is so organized that any expression of this in violence, beyond that permitted by the rules, results in penalties. Furthermore, the individual who becomes angry loses his skill and cannot perform as well. This and similar games are thus effective training grounds for the control of violence, and this as much as anything may account for the fact that trained athletes are relatively unlikely to become involved in socially disapproved forms of violence.

DOMINANCE AND SUBORDINATION

One of the common methods for the control of violence seen in group-living animals is that of the dominance hierarchy, in which certain individuals give way to others and thus avoid overt fighting. Such a dominance relationship can result from a fight but, as we found in our experiments with dogs, it can also result from carrying young individuals around, starting at an early age. Thus the young animal forms a habit of being helpless in relation to certain individuals, and this persists into adult life. It is obvious that this is one of the characteristic ways of controlling human infants, and it is probable that much of the dominance seen in human relationship is established in such subtle ways as these, in addition to the rarer cases when it results from outright struggle.

PUNISHMENT

This is one of the least effective ways of controlling overt fighting behavior. While it will inhibit fighting if sufficiently severe, it also has the effect of stimulating the individual to retaliate in a situation in which he cannot express such behavior. One of the common results is that the violent behavior is passed along to other less dominant individuals as displaced aggression. And, of course, the parent or other individual who is doing the punishing is presenting a model of violent behavior rather than peacefulness, and this example is likely to be followed in other situations. Where force must be used, physical restraint is much more effective than punishment.

TERRITORIALITY

In any human society which emphasizes private property, territoriality is obviously an important way of avoiding agonistic behavior. If individuals stay within their own boundaries, they necessarily avoid engaging in conflicting activities. Boundary disputes of course can be a cause of quarrels, but the principal significance of territoriality is its use as a controlling system against fighting rather than as its cause. In the ordinary suburban or village situation in the U. S., it is interesting that house lot boundaries are respected almost completely by adults, but violations by children and juveniles are usually tolerated.

NO MAGIC CUTOFF SIGNALS

Lorenz (1966) has popularized the notion that a beaten or subordinate wolf can stop the attack of the aggressor by "exposing the jugular vein." This was based on an erroneous bit of observation (Schenkel 1967). The dominant wolf is the only member of the pair that can voluntarily break off the quarrel, and he sometimes signals this by turning his head aside and moving off in a different direction. The subordinate animal can reduce the severity of attack and punishment by reacting defensively with snapping teeth and being passive except when threatened. However, he cannot turn off the attack, and in many such encounters the subordinate animal is badly injured or even killed.

SOCIAL CODES

One human controlling device which does not exist in the lower animals is the existence of verbal codes of behavior defining the sorts of behavior that are permissable or appropriate to given situations. In every human society there are codes regulating the expression of violent behavior. These can vary from those of the Hopi Indians which not only forbid overt violence but also even feelings of anger, to those of the various plains Indians which glorified the expression of violence in intergroup conflicts. In our own society there are a number of such codes which tend to be confusing in number and conflicting in application. For example, the code of Christianity, strictly applied, is one of complete nonviolence, but physical punishment of children is tolerated. Except for the death penalty, physical punishment of adults is now not permitted in most cases. In general, there is a tendency toward less tolerance of violent behavior in social codes as they gradually change throughout the years.

THE EFFECT OF REPRESSION OF FIGHTING ON EMOTION

Enough has been said to indicate that fighting is, in a society like our own, under strong controls. Part of this control results from a structuring of situations so that stimuli such as pain are avoided. However, it is inevitable in any practical situation that a certain amount of stimulation to fight may occur. When such stimulation does occur, an individual will attempt to react in accordance with the general law of stimulation, trying out a variety of responses until one of them produces some form of satisfactory adaptation. In the case of agonistic behavior, the most satisfactory form of response is overt physical activity directed toward the individual who produced the stimulus. The attack may range from an actual blow to verbal abuse. If both of these responses are blocked by training, the individual may make an imaginary attack or, if this reaction is suppressed, he may react unconsciously, the response only emerging in the form of dreams. Any of these responses may be displaced onto other individuals or objects than the person who instigated the aggression, even including self-inflicted attacks. Obviously, the most satisfactory response is direct reprisal against the individual who stimulated the aggression. The least satisfactory are imaginary or unconscious reactions against other individuals or objects (Scott 1958).

The most effective methods of the control of overt fighting are based on physical restraint and training methods which follow the general rules of conditioning. Since internal reactions as well as external ones can be conditioned, it would follow that the internal reactions following stimulation, including emotional responses, should be as readily suppressed as external responses. If this is indeed the case, overt behavior can be suppressed without producing the chain of events described above. It is probable that this does happen in some cases, but by no means all.

Why do overt and emotional responses react differently to training techniques? There are several possible answers. In the first place, the emotional responses of agonistic behavior form a mechanism which has the function of magnifying and prolonging the effects of external stimulation. While external stimulation may be momentary, emotional reactions may continue for many hours. Time relationships with external events are therefore quite different in overt reactions and emotional ones. Further, emotional reactions are not subject to voluntary control and can only be inhibited in indirect ways. At any rate, if overt behavior is repressed, but emotional reactions are not, the result may be very unsatisfactory for the individual concerned, particularly if the same situation is repeated over and over again. This should lead to an intensification of the emotional response, which may eventually reach almost unbearable levels.

In our society women are particularly susceptible to this kind of effect. Having on the average a higher threshold of stimulation than males, they are as young children particularly easy to train to be completely nonaggressive in both word and deed. They can nevertheless be stimulated to anger or fear, and long exposure to this kind of emotion may lead to various psychosomatic symptoms.

Similarly, men in certain occupations may be called upon to suppress overt expressions of agonistic behavior. This is particularly true in some business occupations where it would be disastrous to offend a customer or employer. The results may be high blood pressure, ulcers, or other psychosomatic symptoms. On the whole, however, men are more likely than women in our culture to have developed some successful method of dealing with emotions of this sort.

Some Problems of Contemporary American Culture

Because overt violence is so effectively controlled in our society, there are relatively few places in which it can be studied either by observation or experiment. Most of the observational studies have been made on young children of nursery-school age, who are still in the process of learning how to control aggressive behavior. Some experimental studies are possible through the use of dolls, either small ones which represent familiar figures and which can be punished with impunity, or life-sized doll figures that can be attacked. Other than this, experimental studies are limited to somewhat artificial and contrived situations with college students. One favorite device is the "aggression machine" (Buss 1961), a device by which an experimental subject supposedly punishes another person who is being "trained" to perform a certain task. Various social stimuli are given the subject before he attempts to do the training, and the results on the severity and length of the punishment given can thus be measured with great accuracy. The result is an objective rather than a subjective measure of hostility toward another person.

CATHARSIS

One of the theories arising from the hydraulic model of motivation for aggression is that of catharsis; that is, once the drive for aggression has been released by activity of some sort, the pressure will be reduced and it will take considerable time for it to build up again. In general, the experimental evidence does not support this idea strongly. When aggressive behavior is sanctioned, the result is generally to build up a habit of being aggressive on subsequent similar occasions. Buss (1961) has suggested that an effect of catharsis is produced only when it is preceded by a strong feeling of anger. Once some overt activity has taken place, anger will be reduced, and a feeling of relief may follow. However, such behavior still has the effect of forming a habit of aggressive activity in that particular situation.

A much better case can be made for the usefulness of any form of violent exercise, whether it includes agonistic behavior or not. One of the effects of the prolonged emotion of anger or fear is that it puts the body in readiness for strong physical effort. Hard exercise has the effect of restoring homeostatic balance, and along with this induces relaxation.

THE EFFECT OF ENTERTAINMENT DEPICTING VIOLENCE

Another controversial question is the effect which violence such as is depicted commonly on television shows has on the subsequent behavior of the viewers (Comstock et al. 1972). In some of Berkowitz's (1967) experiments he showed subjects two types of movies, one depicting a great deal of violence, such as a boxing match, and the other an equally exciting event such as a race, but not including violence. The experimental subjects were subsequently more likely to inflict pain on others if they had seen the moving picture containing violence. It is probable, however, that the emotions aroused in this way are of relatively short duration and are likely to affect only the behavior which occurs immediately after watching the performance.

It has sometimes been argued that watching a TV Western in which people shoot each other and roll around in their own blood is unlikely to induce normal individuals to go out and imitate them, and that only persons who were ready to commit violence in any case would be much affected. The fact remains that such theatrical productions do provide models of violent behavior. The person who is about to commit a crime is thus provided with the techniques for accomplishing it, and there is a chance that otherwise his behavior might have taken an equally violent but less fatal form.

Another interesting question is why television programs containing violence are so popular. One possibility is that spectators at any form of entertainment quickly become habituated or bored, and particularly by the unending stream of talk and pictures that comes out of the television tube. One way to overcome this habituation is to present scenes which are uncommon, as are scenes of violence in everyday life. However, once these have been repeatedly presented in the form of entertainment, they too become boring. One way to overcome boredom is to step up the level of violence. This, in effect, is what has been happening in recent years with television entertainment.

Another possibility arises from the limitations of the form of presentation. The entertainer has only a few minutes between commercials in which to arouse interest and emotion, and it is very difficult to do this with some of the milder emotions or those which need to be built up over long periods of time. It is perhaps only the emotions related to violence that can be aroused within these short periods. These, however, are simple problems compared with the more general one of managing the feelings of hostility which are destructive to the individual rather than to others.

The Nature of Hostility

As we have seen earlier in this chapter, fighting is an almost universal reaction to painful stimulation. This defensive reaction is the most probable base from which all varieties of social fighting have evolved. A recent experimental paper by Plotnik and Delgado (1971) lends strong support to this finding and leads to some very interesting general conclusions. They were able, with rhesus monkeys, to produce fighting in social situations by stimulation with intracranial electrodes. They found that only those areas of the brain which produced noxious stimulation would cause one monkey to attack another when the two were together. The basic adaptive function of agonistic behavior is to drive another individual away and keep him at a distance. We can therefore conclude that any feeling of discomfort or unpleasantness that occurs at the time another individual is present will be associated with that particular individual and will therefore produce either overt aggression or a wish to express it which can be labeled a feeling of hostility. The unpleasant, or noxious, feeling need not be actually caused by another individual but only to appear so. A good example is the occurrence of fighting in children when they are hungry. Quarreling does not get them food (although it might through physiological means actually diminish the sensation of hunger if they become angry enough). The child acts as if the unpleasant sensation in his stomach had been produced by his companion, just as a rat standing on an electric grid will respond to footshock as if the other rat had bitten him.

Thus it is possible to set up a relatively simple theory of the dynamics of hostility and aggression. The basic mechanism is that of driving away another individual who has either produced, or appears to have produced, painful external stimulation or an internal emotion of a noxious and unpleasant nature. Since a wide variety of social stimuli and social conditions can produce unpleasant sensations, this mechanism will account for the wide variety of causes that may be associated with aggressive behavior and hostile feelings. Whatever behavioral and emotional responses are elicited, they will be organized by the processes of learning in accordance with the principles of either classical or operant conditioning.

AGGRESSION AS A TOOL

The above general theory will account for the genesis and subsequent amplification of most feelings of hostility, as well as for much of the overt violence which sometimes accompanies such emotions. However, it will not account for the cases in which violence and threats of violence are purposefully used to attain ends which are quite different from the primitive biological functions of protection against pain and maintenance of distance relationships.

That force and violence can be used as tools is obvious even to young children. It is a rare child who has not at some time taken candy or toys away from a younger and weaker one. Others learn that aggression can be used to obtain desired changes in behavior, as when a child kicks its mother in order to obtain attention. Older individuals may use force to obtain money, as in armed robbery, or sexual satisfaction in the case of rape. The case of group aggression used as a tool is particularly serious, as this is the most universal explanation of war—its use as a tool for obtaining land, loot, slaves, power, religious conversion, and a variety of other real and imagined results (Scott 1969).

It is obvious that a great variety of emotions and other sorts of motivation are involved in the use of aggression as a tool, whether on the individual or group level. Attempting to solve the problem by eliminating all possible causes would be an exercise in futility because unexpected situations where force appears to be useful can arise momentarily. In a positive way, we can attempt to set up social organization which satisfies the basic needs of most individuals in a reasonably adequate fashion. In a modern civilized society, there is no reason other than poor social organization that leads to individuals going without food, clothing, and shelter.

In a negative way, we can set up social organization in such a way that aggression as a tool does not work. In the case of the child who takes candy from his baby brother, the parents immediately stop it and show their displeasure. An efficient police force catches the bank robber before he has time to spend the loot. And we need to develop the kind of international organization that will effectively preclude the use of warfare as a tool by preventing any possible payoff.

Conclusion

Now that we are beginning to understand the behavioral and physiological mechanisms that underlie agonistic behavior, it is no longer necessary to account for social fighting as "an instinct." While the concept of instinct was a very useful one in an earlier period of scientific thought, it was in fact a collective name for a whole array of unknown evolutionary, developmental, physiological, and behavioral mechanisms. Simply because it represented the unknown, the concept of instinct led to that of powerful and uncontrollable forces. Our knowledge of more detailed principles and mechanisms makes agonistic behavior understandable, predictable, and avoidable.

References

BOOKS

BERKOWITZ, L. Experiments on automatism and intent in human aggression. *In* C. D. Clemente and D. B. Lindsley (eds.), *Aggression and defense: neural mechanisms and social patterns*. Los Angeles: University of California Press, 1967, pp. 243–66.

BOURNE, P. Altered adrenal function in two combat situations in Viet Nam. *In* B. E. Eleftheriou and J. P. Scott (eds.), *The physiology of aggression and defeat*. New York: Plenum Press, 1971, pp. 265–90.

BUSS, A. H. *The psychology of aggression*. New York: John Wiley, 1961.

CANNON, W. B. *Bodily changes in pain, hunger, fear, and rage*. Boston: Branford, 1929, 1953.

CASPARI, E. W. Behavioral consequences of genetic differences in man: a summary. *In* J. N. Spuhler (ed.), *Genetic diversity and human behavior*. Chicago: Aldine, 1967, pp. 269–78.

COMSTOCK, G. A., RUBENSTEIN, E. A., and MURRAY, J. P. (eds.) *Television and social behavior: A technical report to the Surgeon General's Scientific Advisory Committee on Television and Social Behavior*. Department of Health, Education, and Welfare Publication No. HSM 72–90957. 5 vols. Washington, D.C.: U.S. Government Printing Office, 1972.

DEVORE, I. (ed.) *Primate behavior*. New York: Holt, Rinehart & Winston, 1965.

EIBL-EIBESFELDT, I. Ontogenetic and maturational studies of aggressive behavior. *In* C. D. Clemente and D. B. Lindsley (eds.), *Aggression and defense: neural mechanisms and social patterns*. Los Angeles: University of California Press, 1967, pp. 57–94.

GOTTIER, R. F. The effects of social disorganization in *Cichlasoma biocellatum*. Unpublished Ph.D. thesis, Bowling Green State University, 1968.

GUNNE, L. Brain catecholamines in the rage response evoked by intracerebral stimulation and ablation. *In* S. Garattini and E. B. Sigg (eds.), *Biology of Aggressive Behavior*. New York: John Wiley, 1969, pp. 238–42.

HAFEZ, E. S. E. and SCOTT, J. P. The behaviour of sheep and goats. *In* E. S. E. HAFEZ (ed.), *The behaviour of domestic animals*. London: Ballière, Tindall & Cox, 1962, pp. 297–333.

HOWARD, E. *Territoriality in bird life*. London: John Murray, 1920; Collins, 1948.

JAY, P. The common langur of North India. *In* I. DeVore (ed.), *Primate behavior*. New York: Holt, Rinehart & Winston, 1965, pp. 197–249.

KUMMER, H. *The social organization of hamadryas baboons*. Chicago: University of Chicago Press, 1968.

LEAKEY, L. S. B. Development of aggression as a factor in early human and pre-human evolution. *In* C. D. Clemente and D. B. Lindsley (eds.), *Aggression and defense: neural mechanisms and social patterns*. Los Angeles: University of California Press, 1967, pp. 1–34.

LORENZ, K. *On aggression*. New York: Harcourt, Brace & World, 1966.

MCBRIDE, G. Theories of animal spacing: the role of flight, fight, and social distance. *In* A. Esser (ed.), *The use of space by animals and men*. New York: Plenum Press, 1971, pp. 53–60.

PLOTNIK, R. and DELGADO, J. M. R. Aggression and pain in restrained rhesus monkeys. *In* B. E. Eleftheriou and J. P. Scott (eds.), *The physiology of aggression and defeat*. New York: Plenum Press, 1971, pp. 143–221.

SCOTT, J. P. *Aggression*. Chicago: University of Chicago Press, 1958.

—— The biological basis of human warfare. *In* M. Sherif (ed.), *Interdisciplinary relationships in the social sciences*. Chicago: Aldine, 1969. pp. 121-36.

—— and FULLER, J. L. *Genetics and the social behavior of the dog*. Chicago: University of Chicago Press, 1965.

SOUTHWICK, C. H. Aggressive behavior of rhesus monkeys in natural and captive groups. *In* S. Garattini and E. B. Sigg (eds.), *Biology of Aggressive Behavior*. New York: John Wiley, 1969, pp. 32–43.

TINBERGEN, N. *Social behaviour in animals*. London: Methuen, 1953.

JOURNAL ARTICLES

BERNSTEIN, I. S. Territoriality and the lutong (*Presbytis cristatus*): A field study. *American Zoologist*, 1967, 7, 803.

BRONSON, F. H. Agonistic behavior in woodchucks. *Animal Behaviour*, 1964, 12, 470–78.

—— and ELEFTHERIOU, B. E. Relative effects of fighting on bound and unbound corticosterone in mice. *Proceedings Society for Experimental Biology and Medicine*, 1965, 118, 146–49.

BUECHNER, H. K. Territoriality as a behavioral adaptation to environment in the Uganda Kob. *Proceedings XVI International Congress of Zoology*, 1963, 3, 59–63.

CARPENTER, C. R. A field study of the behavior and social relations of howling monkeys. *Comparative Psychology Monographs*, 1934, 10, (2), 1–168.

DAVIS, D. E. Territorial rank in starlings. *Animal Behaviour*, 1959, 7, 214–21.

EATON, R. L. Group interactions, spacing, and territoriality in cheetahs. *Zeitschrift für Tierpsychologie*, 1970, 10, 1–88.

EVERETT, G. M., and WIEGAND, R. G. Central amines and behavioral states; a critique and new data. *Proceedings First International Pharmacological Meeting*, 1962, 8, 85–92.

FERGUSON, G. W. Releasers of courtship and territorial behavior in the side-blotched lizard (*Uta stansburiana*). *Animal Behaviour*, 1966, 14, 89–92.

KING, J. A. Social behavior, social organization, and population dynamics in a black-tailed prairiedog town in the Black Hills of South Dakota. *Contributions from the Laboratory of Vertebrate Biology*, University of Michigan, Ann Arbor, 1955.

LEYHAUSEN, P. The communal organization of solitary mammals. *Symposia Zoological Society of London*, 1965, 14, 249–63.

MCBRIDE, G. A general theory of social organization and behaviour. *University of Queensland Papers: Faculty of Veterinary Science*, 1964, 1(2), 75–110.

RABB, G. B., WOOLPY, J. H. and GINSBURG, B. E. Social relationships in a group of captive wolves. *American Zoologist*, 1967, 7, 305–11.

SCHACHTER, S. and SINGER, J. Cognitive, social, and physiological determinants of emotional state. *Psychological Review*, 1962, 69, 379–99.

SCHENKEL, R. Submission: its features and functions in the wolf and dog. *American Zoologist*, 1967, 7, 319–30.

SCOTT, J. P. Social behavior, organization, and leadership in a small flock of domestic sheep. *Comparative Psychology Monographs*, 1945, 18, (4), 1–29.

—— Dominance and the frustration-aggression hypothesis. *Physiological Zoology*, 1948, 21, 31–39.

—— Agonistic behavior of mice and rats; a review. *American Zoologist*, 1966, 6, 683–701.

SCOTT, J. W. A study of the phylogenetic or comparative behavior of three species of grouse. *Annals New York Academy of Sciences*, 1950, 51, 1062–73.

SOUTHWICK, C. H. Experimental studies of intragroup aggression in rhesus monkeys. *American Zoologist*, 1966, 6, 301.

TERMAN, C. R. Spatial and homing consequences of the introduction of aliens into semi-natural populations of prairie deermice. *Ecology*, 1962, 43, 216–23.

TINBERGEN, N. On war and peace in animals and man. *Science*, 1968, 160, 1411–18.

Fundamental Organic Drives

Certain behaviors are closely associated with basic physiological requirements and together form the conditions prerequisite to the survival and well-being of the individual. Adaptation in terms of internal regulation has continued to constitute an area of elementary motivational significance with the increasing awareness of salient behavioral components inherent in the maintenance of delicate balances characteristic of organ systems. The initiation and processing of these behaviors are associated with energizing and appetitive influences which function in concert to provide optimal internal conditions for essential metabolic activities. Although the mechanisms by which these drives become manifest in specific behaviors are manifold, and not all well-understood, progress is now being made not only in the isolation of central mechanisms of drives such as thirst and hunger, but also in the understanding of the relationships of these states to each other, and to their role in the still more complex motivational states so characteristic of man and higher animals.

HUNGER

Feeding behaviors vary with the variety of organic requirements, with palatability, and with other factors, but a generalized hunger drive is a useful classification, and can be seen in states of food deprivation. The competition for food, and thus hunger, appears to be an important factor in the evolution of life forms, and may form a basis on which to study speciation and animal distributions. The close relationship of food and motivated behavior is further emphasized through consideration of prime solar energy and its restricted availability to higher animals within the environment. Behavior is the essential feature of this acquisition of energy as plants or plant-eaters must be sought out and consumed. It is difficult to imagine a more basic factor to the life processes of energy exchange than food metabolism, and it is not surprising that a large number of bodily activities

Lowell T. Crow

Other Drives

35

have evolved which are directly related to hunger, food seeking behaviors, eating, and satiation.

Physiological signaling systems of impending depletion of energy stores are closely associated with, if not the essence of, the sensations of hunger. These systems are set off by changes in internal conditions of which no one has been shown crucial, but of which several appear to be important. The early work by Cannon (1929) on local sensations of hunger from gastric activity has led to a great deal of experimental research revealing the inadequacy of any single localized factor as *the* basis of hunger. Denervation or removal of the stomach does not eliminate feeding or the maintenance of body weight, and although gastric stimuli may be of importance in feeding and in satiation under certain conditions, such sensations are not essential in food regulation.

The level and utilization of blood sugar has been related to hunger by Mayer (1955). Lowering of blood sugar level by insulin induces feeding in rats, and Mayer postulated central detectors of blood glucose which might instigate hunger or satiety. Direct injections of sugar into the blood may diminish hunger, although the extent of this diminution may be limited. In support of this *glucostatic* hunger theory, mice injected with goldthioglucose develop hyperhagia (overeating) and show a build-up of the toxic metallic particles within the ventromedial nuclei of the hypothalamus, the site of the postulated glucoreceptors, and changes in electrical activity of these central regions have been reported as a result of blood sugar level (Liebelt & Perry 1957; Anand et al. 1962).

The importance of temperature in the energy exchanges involved in food regulation has been stressed by Brobeck (1960). Animals in cold environments eat more than normal, hot environments and fever decrease feeding, and animal diets may conform as a whole to the food's metabolic activity production (*specific dynamic action*). An important factor of such temperature changes appears to be the interrelation of heat changes and feeding behavior with other bodily processes such as activity, estrus, and fluid levels (Brobeck 1965).

Although there are other peripheral systems at work in the production of hunger (probably many of the bodily changes associated with an ultimate inanition contribute to the need to feed and hunger sensations), the central aspects of food regulation appear more closely related to food seeking behaviors and have received a large share of the research attention. Early clinical descriptions of obesity as the result of brain damage in man led directly to the localization of the regions responsible by the use of stereotaxically placed lesions in the brains of animals (Hetherington & Ranson 1942). *Hyperphagia* (overeating) was observed only when the lesions involved the ventromedial areas of the hypothalamus, this being true even though the closely approximate pituitary gland was spared. Brobeck, Tepperman, and Long (1943) went on to show that the obesity was indeed a result of overeating (not a general metabolic dysfunction) the food intake becoming as much as three times the normal amount. Animals displaying hypothalamic hyperphagia were seen to eat large amounts of food, greatly increasing their bodyweight, then to plateau in terms of bodyweight and remain at this obese level. This initial "dynamic" phase of the lesion effects was contrasted to the subsequent "static" phase in which the elevated bodyweight remained at a relatively stable level. That the effects were chronic was shown by the fact that starvation subsequent to the achievement of the static phase would again be followed by overeating and a return to the obese condition.

Kennedy (1950) studied the whole of the hypothalamic hyperphagia syndrome in great detail including the effects of diets of different quality on the eating patterns during the dynamic and static phases of the disorder. It was noted that while the quality or kind of food was not an important factor in the dynamic or developmental stage of the obesity, the static phase was associated with more discriminative taste preference and certain foods were chosen over others. Less palatable foods (for example dry foods) led to a reduction of food intake in obese animals, but not in the earlier stages of the pronounced hyperphagia. The early stages of the disorder appear to represent the effects of a basic hunger, while the later stage of obesity is characterized by a more discriminative hunger, and these may represent a fundamental dichotomy in food regulation. Teitelbaum (1955) replicated many of Kennedy's findings and noted especially the sensitivity to different kinds of foods in the obese or static phase of the disorder.

Several investigators have observed that the hyperphagic phase following the ventromedial hypothalamic lesion does not appear to be associated with a correspondingly high "motive" to eat, and that although food will be taken in great quantities if freely available, the animals will not work on high schedules of reinforcement for their food (Miller et al. 1950). These findings are complicated, however, by the general decrease in activity which appears to accompany the dynamic phase, and some evidence exists that food motivated responses are increased in the dynamic phase (Falk 1961).

The ventromedial areas of the hypothalamus have been considered as "satiety centers" for hunger, and that the basic deficit involved is a failure of a cutoff mechanism for eating. A reciprocal "feeding center" has been conceptualized in the closely adjacent lateral hypothalamic regions of the diencephalon. Anand and Brobeck (1951) were able to show that lesions of these lateral areas would result in the hypophagia or a complete failure to eat (aphagia). Animals with lateral hypothalamic damage may accept no food or water even in the case of *ad libitum* accessability. That this is not simply a general debilitation or sensory-motor deficit, but in addition a specific impairment in food regulation is supported by evidence that stimulation of these regions by electrical or chemical means may initiate feeding responses (see Smith 1961). Some return of function is possible in the case of the destruction of the lateral hypothalamic regions, and stages of recovery under intensive nursing care have been described by Teitelbaum and Epstein (1962) who stressed the importance of the nature of the diet in the postoperative care of the animals.

The generality of the concept of an "on-off" reciprocity of feeding functions between the ventromedial and lateral hypothalamic areas has been brought to test by several recent investigations (see also section on ICSS below). If both the ventromedial and lateral areas are electrocoagulated, the result will be a failure to eat suggesting an "on" primacy within the systems, and suggestions have been that one need consider only effects on the lateral fiber tracts to account for the findings if ventromedial lesions in some way stimulate or irritate the "feeding center" (Reynolds 1965). Many of the studies previously cited have utilized high amperage direct current for the electrocoagulation with a resulting deposit of metallic particles in the region of the lateral tracts, and there is evidence that the presence of these particles (which may be present in radio frequency lesions as well) is correlated with the existence and extent of hyperphagia (Rabin & Smith 1968; Dahl & Ursin 1969). In this connection hypothalamic hyperphagia does not appear to be a syndrome easily prepared in the laboratory; its incidence not always being correlated with bilateral ventromedial hypothalamic damage. It appears that among rats, females are more likely to exhibit the syndrome (Cox et al. 1969). That the ventromedial hypothalamic areas do exert inhibitory influences on other diencephalic and limbic systems appears, however, to be well established. Electrical stimulation of these ventromedial areas will inhibit feeding, even in the hungry animal (Morgane & Jacobs 1969).

An examination of the anatomy of the lateral hypothalamic areas under discussion reveals a system of fiber tracts which (unlike the well defined ventromedial nuclei) do not afford a convenient reference nomenclature. Lesions of the "lateral hypothalamus" may differ in extent of damage and locus among investigators and there is evidence that different placements of the ablations may produce different effects (Morgane 1961, 1969). Most of the lateral hypothalamic effects (including ICSS effects, see below) involve the medial forebrain bundle, a longitudinally oriented structure which acts in a "bridge-like" fashion in association and coordination of integrative neural activity with closely related areas of the brain. The limbic and rhinen-

cephalic regions of the brain have been related to eating, drinking, and other motivated behaviors and appear to constitute neural *systems* extremely important to conceptualizations of drive and drive states. Of these structures, the amygdala has received perhaps the greatest amount of attention in studies of food regulation. A number of investigators including Morgane and Kosman (1960) have found increases in food intake as a result of specific manipulations of the amygdala and inhibitory influences on feeding have been postulated as one aspect of amygdaloid function. Other related structures which have been associated with eating include the globus pallidus of the basal cerebral ganglia, certain ablations of which may lead to aphagia (Morgane 1961).

The tying of the limbic and rhinencephalic systems, which have long been associated with arousal and emotion to the fundamental systems of feeding, makes more difficult a simplistic neural model of a feeding center located autonomously within the hypothalamus and suggests a complexity of interactions of various drives in hunger- and food-motivated responses. Morgane (1969) has related both the ventromedial hypothalamic influences and the medial forebrain bundle to the limbic lidbrain systems including the reticular formation. Electrical stimulation of the ventromedial area produced electroencephalographic sleep activity ("satiation sleep"), while electrical stimulation of the lateral hypothalamic regions resulted in a cortical dysynchroniza-

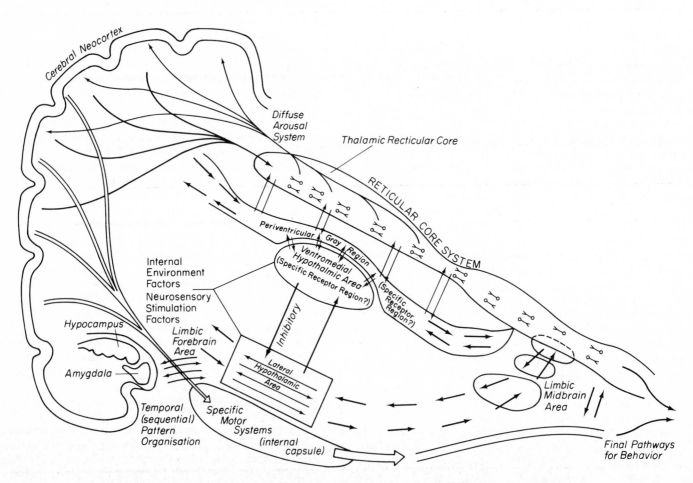

Fig. 35-1. *Schematic relations of some of the principal central nervous factors involved in food and water intake.* [Morgane 1966]

tion of electrical activity. This latter effect is similar to that obtained by direct reticular stimulation. It is becoming clearer that the diencephalic systems of food regulation are closely associated with the diffuse activating mechanisms of the midbrain, and that hunger and satiety are functions which may be partly described in terms of nonspecific arousal of the cerebral cortex. Discrimination of specific foods has been mentioned in connection with the static phase of hypothalamic hyperphagia, and other brain lesions have been shown to change food preferences. Amygdala lesions have been found to enhance meat choices in the feeding patterns of monkeys as orbitofrontal (Ursin et al. 1969) and spetal lesions in rats may increase preferences for saline solutions (Chiaraviglio 1969). The affective arousal of specific food substances in terms of hedonic tone and palatability have been studied intensively by Paul T. Young (1966), and perhaps the field is now in the position to begin the assimilation of these findings into the study of central mechanisms of hunger. Proposals have been made by Malmo (1959) and by Ax (1964) to attempt a further integration of motivational states, like hunger, to the physiology of specific patterns of autonomic and central nervous arousal, and it would appear that the studies of the central mechanisms of hunger are now coming to bear on these issues. Further evidence on the relation of specific arousal patterns and hunger will be noted in the "approach behavior and reinforcement" section of the present paper.

Thirst

The metabolism of water is, of course, closely tied with that of food, but the intake of water in a relatively pure form is essential to most land animals and must match the output of water in the various losses from respiration, perspiration, urination, and defecation so that a balance or homeostatic state is to some degree constantly in existence. A deficit in water level would appear to be the basis of thirst, as indeed it may be, but the picture is complicated by the nature of organic make-up. First, the bodily water is compartmentalized into water within the cell and that which is extracellular, the former constituting the major proportion of the total body water. Secondly, these fluids vary in terms of ionic concentration and are subject to osmotic forces due to the separations imposed by the cellular memberanes. Dehydration of the extracellular fluids may lead to cellular dehydration by means of the flow of water into the more concentrated extracellular fluids. During this process the sensation of thirst and thirst drives may be initiated, and although factors of absolute water volume are extremely important, thirst is also bound to ionic and osmotic regulation.

Early work on thirst involved the drying of the mouth and throat due to decreased activity of the salivary glands. The "dry mouth" thirst factor may be an important one, especially in the sensation thirst, but subsequent research has shown that water balance may be maintained in the absence of such local sensations and that other detectors of water deficit must surely exist (Adolph et al. 1954). Hypertonic sodium chloride solutions injected into the blood will elicit drinking in an amount roughly proportional to the concentration (Holmes & Gregersen 1950); this thirst occurs in the presence of an adequate level of bodily water in an absolute sense. Hypertonic blood concentrations of salt, however, cause a redistribution of cellular and extracellular

water, the former being diminished through osmotic factors. It appears the blood concentration per se is not the crucial factor as hypertonic concentrations of urea, which do not produce an osmotic transfer of water from out of the cell, do not produce thirst. The direct hypothesis of cellular dehydration as the prime thirst element is not without conflicting evidence, but has a great deal of supporting data.

The reduction of extracellular fluid volume (*hypovolemia*) is known to produce thirst (as in hemorrhage), and drinking can also be observed following the artificial reduction of plasma volume without changes in intracellular hydration. Subcutaneous injection of polyethylene glycol will produce such physiological effects, and initiate drinking in proportion to the concentration administered (Fitzsimons 1961). Stricker (1968) was able to show the existence of thirst motivated behavior by requiring lever pressing on various reinforcement schedules. The polythylene glycol injection was found to increase hematacrit (cells to plasma ratio), decrease plasma water, and increase plasma protein without affecting water within the cells.

Corbit (1969) observed the amount of water intake in rats after various concentrations of hypertonic sodium chloride had been injected intraperitoneally, and compared these intakes to those expected from a *perfect osmometer hypothesis*. Thus, accounting for water losses, the amount drunk should equal the amount of water necessary to restore isotonic equilibrium between intra- and extracellular fluid systems. It was found that rats will closely approximate this amount of intake, this being true regardless of the animal weight, and correctable for water losses (assumed as a function of time after injection). Corbit was unable to find a drinking "threshold" in terms of extent of disruption of the isotonic state by extremely small volumes of injected hypertonic saline, the amount drunk being a continuous function of the volume of the injected salt solution throughout the values tested.

Undoubtedly the peripheral bodily changes involved in dehydration, like those in food deprivation, are complexly represented throughout the intra- and extracellular systems, and no one signaling device easily accounts for the experimental observations. The work on the central mechanisms of water balance, like that of hunger, was developed from early clinical observations and followed closely the invention of the stereotaxic instrument by which lesions could be accurately placed within the brains of animal subjects. It was Fisher, Ingram, and Ranson (1938) who showed that lesions of the *supraoptic hypophysial* system of the hypothalamus would produce the clinical disorder, *diabetes insipidus*, in which large volumes are drunk (*polydipsia*). The supraoptic hypophysial system constitutes a series of nuclei and nerve tracts which extend from the anterior hypothalamus ventrally to the posterior pituitary gland. This system was shown to be composed of neurosecretory cells which produced hormones (ultimately to be liberated at the pituitary gland) including an *antidiuretic hormone* (ADH), a principle which normally functioned to facilitate water reabsorption into the blood at the distal renal tubules, and, in effect, increase water loss via urination. In diabetes insipidus, the polydipsia appears to be a concomitant condition to the excessive water loss through copious urination. But the importance of the role of ADH in water was clearly established and it was by way of ADH that Verney (1947) was able to show the rather sensitive bodily reaction to increases in blood osmolality. Water deprivation will result in an increased ADH activity *as will stress and noxious stimuli* (Bargman 1957;

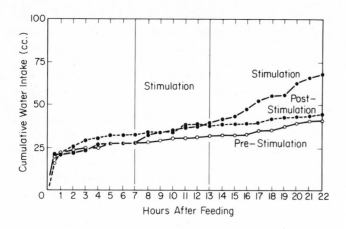

Fig. 35-2. *The effect of bilateral lateral hypothalamic electrical stimulation on free drinking behavior. Intake is shown on days preceding, following, and during stimulation which occurred during the seventh through thirteenth hour. Note the "stimulus bound" as well as long-term effect.* [Crow 1967]

Verney 1947). It is quite interesting to note that some of the same mechanisms are instigated by thirst and by "threat and alarm" external stimulation. The similarities here in water balance with the findings of Morgane (1969) in food regulation in which the central systems of hunger so closely associated with sleep and arousal. That thirst is associated with cortical dysynchrony was demonstrated by Steiner (1962). The relationship of pituitary functioning to avoidance conditioning and reactions to noxious stimuli will be noted in the following section. In any case the relationship of urinary water loss to the maintenance of an adequate fluid level is an important consideration in thirst, as a certain water loss is obligatory and is limited by the extent to which the urine can be concentrated.

The anterior and lateral hypothalamus have been noted as containing a "drinking center," although an autonomous thirst mechanism has been as difficult to find as has been a "feeding center." It is possible to instigate drinking by the direct injection of salt into the hypothalamus (Andersson 1953), and electrical stimulation of the lateral hypothalamus may lead to an increased water intake (Crow 1967). It was previously mentioned that ablation of the lateral areas of the hypothalamus results in aphagia, but these lesions produce an impairment in drinking as well, and a *hypodipsia* or *adipsia* induced by lateral hypothalamic damage results in a more persistent effect than the lack of eating.

As with the central areas of hunger, those of thirst are surely not encompassed in their entirety within the hypothalamus, rather the hypothalamus, especially the lateral areas, is made up of fiber tracts, as well as nuclei, which link extrahypothalamic regions of the brain, and it is likely that these *systems* are those involved in thirst and in hunger. In this connection it is interesting to note that complete circumsection of the hypothalamus severing all connections save those of the pituitary gland produces adipsia and aphagia, although the syndrome is described as unlike that found with lateral hypothalamic lesions (Ellison 1968). The specificity of these lateral hypothalamic tracts in terms of function is also of interest in the light of the apparent multiplicity of functions associated with this region. The same electrode can be used sequentially to instigate drinking behavior and to ablate lateral hypothalamic areas producing adipsia (Crow 1967). In addition to the adipsia produced by the ablations, it was noted that urinary volume (in proportion to stomach tubing of water in nursing) was *increased*, thus suggesting that this region has some effect on water losses by urinary excretion as well. Evidence supporting this latter finding were obtained in subsequent studies in which it was found that lateral hypothalamic ablation had some of the same effects as ablation of the supraoptic hypophysial systems (Crow 1968b).

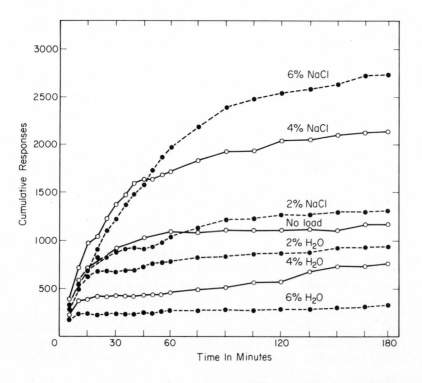

Fig. 35-3. *Effects of salt and water preloading on performance under a fixed ratio (FR-5) schedule of water reinforcement. The salt concentrations are percent NaCl, the water loads are expressed in units of volume (percent of body weight in cc).* [O'Kelly, Crow, Tapp & Hatton 1966]

Septal area lesions may result in a polydipsia as well as a polyuria, this occuring even after water deprivation (Donovick & Burright 1968). Other parts of the brain have been associated with water balance, including the globus pallidus, amygdala, and the dorsal longitudinal fasciculus (Morgane 1969; Crow 1967).

Thirst can be induced in rats by the stomach tubing of hypertonic sodium chloride solutions, the water intake being proportional to the concentration of the solution. By means of the use of thirsty rats ($23\frac{1}{2}$-hour deprivation schedules) and appropriate preloading of water and salt solutions of varying concentrations, the intensity of thirst motivated behavior can be quantified for experimental designs utilizing drive variables (O'Kelly & Beck 1960). A wide range of drive intensity is possible and is applicable to operant conditioning situations involving water reinforcement under a variety of reinforcement schedules (O'Kelly & Falk 1958; O'Kelly et al. 1966). Since the establishment of these techniques several studies involving thirst drive variables have been carried out using salt and water loading apparently equivalent to, but more easily quantified than, water deprivation alone (Beck & McLean 1967; Hatton 1965; O'Kelly et al. 1965; Goldstein et al. 1966).

THERMOREGULATION AND OXYGEN BALANCE

The mode of heat regulation and temperature preference have been shown to be important limiting factors in species ecology both in cold and in warm blooded animals (Mayr 1966). Animals are greatly influenced by temperature changes, for example in circadian rhythms (Marler & Hamilton 1966), but they may also control their own bodily temperature by various mechanisms. In higher animals this control or regulation of bodily temperature is a function of cardiovascular and respiratory changes, sweating, shivering, as well as through behaving in specific ways. Basic autonomic activity in heat regulation appears to be under the direct influence of the hypothalamus, the anterior areas acting in heat stress and the posterior areas mediating reactions in both heat loss and heat conservation. The temperature of the hypothalamus itself as well as peripheral temperature (especially skin temperature) appears to be an important factor in thermoregulation. Sweating seems to be controlled by central temperatures as is the inhibition of shivering, although the initiation of shivering may be due to changes in skin temperature alone (Brengelmann & Brown 1965).

Behavioral thermoregulation has become an area of increasing interest as it has been shown that animals in a cold environment will acquire a response leading to exposure to a heat source (Carlton & Marks 1958). Weiss and Laties (1961) were able to show that the gradual fall in subcutaneous temperature within a cold environment (2 degrees centigrade) was rather suddenly reversed by heat contingency responding, and that the higher subcutaneous temperature was maintained by this process. Greater amounts of heat per reinforcement produced a proportionately lower reinforcement rate. The relative contributions of decreasing peripheral (local detectors of heat loss) versus central temperature changes are now being investigated, but are not yet well understood. In a study by Carlisle (1968) rats were shorn of their fur and the unclipped animals were subjected to a zero degree centigrade environment which included a lever pressing device for heat reinforcement. Measures were made of the incidence of lever pressing as related to skin and hypothalamic temperature. The unclipped rats failed to learn the pressing response, maintaining a rather constant central temperature in the face of a falling peripheral temperature. Clipped animals usually did learn the response after a fall of hypothalamic temperature to below 37 degrees centigrade, but this was not the case in all animals. In some cases a decrease in skin temperature alone was sufficient to instigate lever pressing, and the author concludes that a decrease in skin temperature may be a sufficient, but not a necessary condition for behavioral thermoregulation under these conditions. The extension of these findings on operant control of environmental temperature have been extended to include the consideration of schedules of reinforcement (Carlisle 1969) and

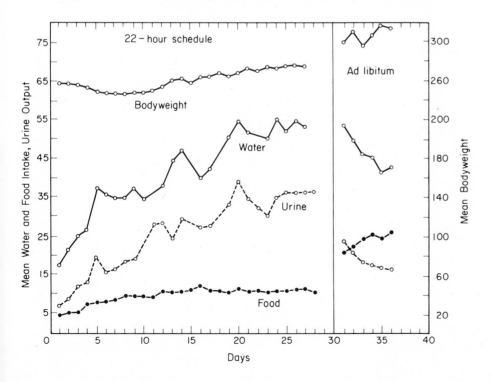

Fig. 35-4. *The rat's adaptation to a 22-hour food deprivation schedule, and the subsequent reinstatement of* ad libitum *feeding conditions. Note the increased water intake and urinary excretion which is associated with food deprivation.* [Crow 1968; reprinted by permission of the publisher.]

situations involving more complex manipulanda for temperature control. Professor Merle E. Meyer and John Wright (1971) have developed a thermal preference box for rats in which there are two levels, for "warmer" and for "colder", this accomplished by means of differentially heated water flowing through the compartment in which the animal is partially submerged. In this way clipped rats will readily learn to maintain an optimal temperature within narrow limits (see Figure 35-4).

The regulation of oxygen is generally autonomic as chemical changes, especially oxygen-decrease and carbon dioxide build-up, produce increased ventilation through neural control of the respiratory systems (Young 1965). In addition to this respiratory control of oxygen intake, behavioral regulation within the gaseous environment is now receiving experimental research attention. It has been shown that rats, mice, and birds will press a switch to remove carbon dioxide from their surroundings (Weinstein 1963, 1966). Carbon dioxide concentrations as low as 3 percent can be detected, and above this level, changes as small as $\frac{1}{2}$ percent can be discriminated. It appears, however, that the detection of oxygen in this way is difficult, and animals who have mastered the carbon dioxide increment task may die under conditions of changes in oxygen concentration response contingencies.

INTERRELATIONS OF DRIVES

Although many distinct drives have been conceptualized independently, the interrelation of bodily activities is such that a thorough investigation of one drive to the exclusion of others is difficult if not impossible. Hunger, thirst, and temperature and oxygen regulation interact in a variety of ways so that changes in one may have repercussions on the others, and a "control" of "extraneous" factors is, at the least, difficult. Such relations between hunger and thirst have received the greatest amount of attention, and appear extremely complex even when disregarding other effects such as temperature, but the importance of research acknowledgement of the far reaching physiological effects of the manipulation of a single drive is becoming apparent.

Under *ad libitum* conditions of food and water availability, a close association exists between eating dry food and drinking, in that meals appear to be invariably followed by fluid ingestion (Fitzsimons & LeMagnen 1969). When either food or water is withheld, however, the resultant behavior may or may not be a simple complementary inhibition. Deprivation of water generally leads to a decrease in food consumption in most animals. That water economy may be responsible for the feeding change appears likely in that food metabolism requires water uptake and loss from the body. McFarland and Wright (1969) found with the Barbary Dove that fecal water loss varies directly with amount of food intake. In this connection it is interesting to note that hypertonic saline injections which produce thirst will lead to a reduction of food intake, as will subcutaneous injections of polyethylene glycol (hypovolemic thirst induction), whereas isotonic saline injection may increase feeding activity (Gutman & Krausz 1969). Deprivation of food may not lead to a decrease in water intake, but rather to increased drinking. In the gerbil a pronounced polydipsia may develop after 2 to 5 days of food deprivation (Kutscher 1968), and in the rat starvation may produce a relative increase in water consumption

compared to *ad libitum* levels (Morrison 1967). In addition, food deprivation schedules of various kinds may produce enhanced drinking. Water intake may reach levels comparable to those seen in diabetes insipidus with a "schedules indiced polydipsia" (Falk 1961). Rats maintained on an approximate 21-hour food deprivation schedule (with water always available) will drink large amounts during three hours per day of an intermittantly reinforced food rewarded operant responding situation. Rats will also consume relatively large quantities of water put on a 22-hour food deprivation schedule if water is not allowed during the feeding period (Crow 1968c). In this instance prolonging the "meal period" appears to prolong the drinking period following the feeding, whereas in the situation developed by Falk the meals themselves are "shortened" providing a higher incidence of subsequent draughts of water. It has been shown that feeding schedules which restrict water during the feeding period result in dramatic variations of blood osmolarity before and after feeding. With a 23-hour food deprivation schedule of this sort for a duration of two weeks, the osmolarity (mOsm/kg) changed from 298 before feeding to 318 immediately after as compared to a normal value of approximately 307 (Gutman & Krausz 1969).

Interrelations of temperature and energy regulation with feeding have been mentioned, and while further work is being carried out in the clarification of these interactions, generalizations at this time are difficult to make. Several studies have demonstrated that thermoregulatory behavior is influenced by food availability. The length of time that a self-demand heat source was turned on, the number of reinforcements, and the response rate for heat have been found greater for animals which were food deprived (Weiss 1957; Hamilton 1959; Baldwin & Ingram 1968). Andersson and Larsson (1961) found that temperature changes within the hypothalamus (direct heating or cooling) produced either eating or drinking in goats, and related these findings to a theory of hunger and thirst. Fluctuations of temperature within the hypothalamus are known to occur which may not be directly related to thermoregulation.

Interactions are known to exist between thermoregulation and oxygen intake, as exposure to cold environments increases metabolic rate and oxygen consumption. In the case of behavioral thermoregulation, oxygen intake may be maintained at a constant level (Baldwin & Ingram 1967).

The effects of temperature on energy expenditure and water loss are important considerations in studies involving hunger and thirst as temperature directly affects feeding, and water loss is in part a function of heat regulation. Lipton and Morotto (1969) have shown that behavioral thermoregulation is influenced by desalivation of male rats. Oxygen levels may also influence hunger and thirst, but such effects, as well as those of temperature have only recently been adequately accounted for in behavioral studies, and are not yet clear.

Environmental Tolerance of Organic Drives

The approach to or avoidance of specific environmental conditions related to physiological requirements is complicated by the extent of disperal of these materials or conditions and by the changes which occur in external conditions. Changes in external conditions will, if sensed by the animal, generally lead

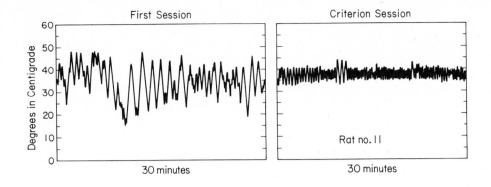

Fig. 35-5. *Thermal preference of the rat. Two levers, one for "warmer" and one for "colder," are operated by the rat to maintain environmental temperature. Through successive training the animal learns to produce an optimal temperature range within the limits shown in the criterion session.* [Meyer & Wright 1971]

to behavioral modifications. These behavioral modifications appear to be dependent upon their consequences in terms of reinforcement, and an important part of the physiological basis of drives has been in the nature of specific reinforcements both positive and negative, both primary and secondary. It should be noted that not all redirections of appetitive activities are due to changing environmental conditions, many arise internally, but physiological processes are closely bound to the nature of the environment, and are to some extent limited by prevailing conditions. In this way and to this extent, the tolerance of the environment to the pressures of drives determines the resultant observables of behavioral change. Whereas we have been concerned primarily with specific organic systems and general environmental conditions, we now turn to particular environmental conditions and their effects upon more general organic systems. Motivational states do not appear to be discretely present or absent, but rather the arousal or excitation of animals constitutes a continuum from states of extremely low activity, as in sleep, to the heightened activity of certain wakeful states. Along this continuum lie intermediate states which vary from moment to moment, as well as diurally. In addition, differential patterns of various aspects of central and peripheral physiological activity may emerge which are at the same time stimulus specific to certain environmental effects and unique to the individual. Such arousal may be indexed by a number of psychophysiological changes, notably cardiovascular activity, electrodermal and skin temperature activity, respiration, gastrointestinal processes, and central nervous activity as recorded through electroencephalography (EEG). The peripheral autonomic nervous system appears to be under the influence of neural activities associated primarily with the diencephalon and midbrain, especially the hypothalamus and the diffuse cortical projection systems. The complex of autonomic balancing is greatly influenced by the hypothalamus, and patterns of arousal of the cerebral cortex are closely associated with the reticular formation of the brain stem. Although the role of the patterning of autonomic and central neural activities in basic drives seems to be both relevant and significant, it does not appear to be a simple one. Autonomic nervous system changes occur with certain external stimuli characterized by novelty and uniqueness (orienting responses), and specific emotions may be associated with particular autonomic response patterns, especially in the case of noxious stimuli. But the part played by these neural changes in behavioral modification and their relationship to traditional concepts of reinforcement, while perhaps now emerging, is not yet clear.

APPROACH BEHAVIOR AND REINFORCEMENT

A large number of researchers have attempted to correlate peripheral neural physiology, especially functions related to autonomically influenced organs, to approach behavior and reinforcement. The cardiovascular systems as they are influenced by autonomic neural processes have been particularly singled out in this regard. Although the complexity of cardiovascular reflexes and adjustments make difficult the assessment of short term effects of experimental stimulus presentations (Katcher et al. 1969), data is being amassed on specific heart changes as a result of particular stimulus situations. A dominant parasympathetic effect of deceleration of heart rate has been associated with the anticipation of stimuli both aversive and nonaversive in man (Wood & Obrist 1964; Obrist, Webb & Sutterer 1969). Such anticipatory reactions have been associated by Obrist and his associates with an inhibition of somatic motor activity, and found not to be due to respiratory or baroreceptor reflexes. The stimulus situations producing such deceleration of heart rate have been of an attentional or anticipatory character, such as the foreperiod in a simple reaction time task (Obrist et al. 1969). It has also been found that activity, especially consummatory activities associated with reinforcement, may result in increases in heart activity. Both food reward (Ehrlich & Malmo 1967) and water reward (Goldstein, Stern, & Rothenberg 1966) have been associated with an increase in heart rate and with an arousal or incentive effect. Seward, Cosmides, and Humphrey (1969) presented rats with both positive and negative reinforcements, and observed heart rate changes to reinforcement and to light signals preceding reinforcement. It was found that an increase in heart rate accompanied reinforcement consummatory activity, but that a decrease in heart rate was found with the presentation of the signals. This decrease persisted in the case of the negative signal, but dropped out during the acquisition of the positively signaled reinforcement.

The discovery of the rewarding effects of intracranial electrical stimulation and the phenomena of intracranial self-stimulation (ICSS) (Olds & Milner 1954), has led to a series of investigations attempting to delineate regions of the brain involved in certain kinds of reinforcement. Positive sites for ICSS (those for which the animal would press a lever) were found by Olds and his associates to include the hypothalamus, rhinecephalon, and tegmentum of the midbrain. Lateral hypothalamic and adjacent areas are associated with feeding and drinking, as previously noted, and these same areas are positive sites for ICSS. Olds

(1958) noted higher response rates in these areas as a result of food deprivation and these findings have been confirmed by other investigators, some of which have suggested that ICSS reward at this site may be like that of the reward of eating (Gibson et al. 1965; Hoebel 1968) and of drinking sugar and water (Poschel 1968). The notion of the reciprocal relation of the ventromedial nuclei in satiety and the lateral hypothalamus in the initiation of feeding is supported by reports that stimulation of the ventromedial nuclei decreases feeding as well as ICSS in the lateral region, while lesions of the ventromedial nuclei increase eating and rate of ICSS in the lateral area (Hoebel & Teitelbaum 1962). The interpretation of these findings in terms of subjective "pleasures", "gratifications", etc. have been appropriately questioned by Morgane and Jacobs (1969) who pointed out the difficulties involved in such psychic equations of electrical stimulation of the brain and eating. These findings have been verified by subsequent investigations which have been extended to include other parts of the brain as well as other drives. Morgane (1969) has shown that lateral hypothalamic ICSS is inhibited by both ventromedial hypothalamic stimulation and amygdaloid stimulation, there being a stimulus bound supressant effect on the rate of ICSS responding. Mogenson and Stevenson (1966, 1967) have studied ICSS phenomena and thirst and found that positive ICSS sites and sites at which passive stimulation would produce drinking exhibited considerable overlap. The drink-eliciting sites were generally positive ICSS sites and involved the dorso-lateral perifornical areas of the lateral hypothalamus.

The coincidence of ICSS positive sites and the brain regions involved in hunger and thirst, especially the hypothalamus and septal area, has been apparent. The question of the nature of these mechanisms in terms of specificity of drive and the relation of drive and motivating factors to these approach behaviors has been of particular interest. Olds (1955) pointed out that while drives are commonly associated with physiological need, the two are not necessarily interdependent as exemplified by ICSS in which rewarding and reinforcing effects can be seen in the absence of apparent need. ICSS, however, is an arbitrary contrivance and differs in important respects from the more ordinary processes of reinforcement. The central effects of ICSS may not merely cut off peripheral stimulation, but may diminish or augment such neural and hormonal effects in some complex manner. Centrally derived efferent peripheral effects may also be disrupted. Deutsch (1966) distinguishes a motivational and a reinforcement component of ICSS, and explains the relatively rapid rate of extinction of ICSS in terms of differential drive decay. This notion is supported by data showing that hungry animals display greater resistance to extinction than do sated ones in ICSS responding. Routtenberg (1968) views the limbic forebrain structures as part of a second arousal system (in addition to the brain stem reticular activating system) which mediates positive incentive. Reward is distinguished from reinforcement and is seen as positive incentive which may or may not be followed by an increase in the probability of response depending on the activity of other systems. That positive ICSS sites involve structures closely associated with rather specific arousal and motivational phenomena is supported by findings of differential effects of brain stimulation depending upon the specific environment (Mendelson 1969). Rats will choose longer durations of lateral hypothalamic stimulation if feeding and drinking is allowed during the period. The results were interpreted by Mendelson as evidence that lateral hypothalamic stimulation becomes aversive due to excessive buildup of drive in the experimental situation devoid of food or water.

AVOIDANCE AND ORGANIC REACTIONS TO NOXIOUS STIMULI

The role of noxious stimuli in the general order of psychological phenomena, and the extent of its influence on drive variables has long been enigmatic and has contributed to controversy within motivational and learning theories. The issue may be crucial to a point of view, but common to most viewpoints is a consideration of the basic biological and neurophysiological consequences or reactions to stimuli actively avoided by the individual. The pioneer work in this country of Walter Cannon (1929) established the importance of the autonomic nervous system in general physiology. Sympathetic arousal was shown to produce a multitude of gastrointestinal and cardiovascular effects, and environmentally related physiological changes were linked to these "emergency" reactions. Largely on the basis of Cannon's influence, the significance of these effects on the psychophysiological systems of various environmental factors were to be acknowledged by a large segment of the scientific community producing farreaching effects on interdisciplinary theory and research. The processes of the bodily *general adaptation syndrome* in stress were noted by Seyle (1950) who has continued to relate tissue trauma and disease to a host of specific physiological defense systems including the release of adrenalcorticotropic hormone (ACTH), changes in sodium metabolism and other hormonal influences. Much of the contemporary work in psychophysiology, psychobiology, and physiological psychology as well as that in psychopharmacology, neuropharmacology, endocrinology, and related disciplines is directly relevant to reactions of neural and hormonal systems to noxious stimulation and to avoidance behavior. Within the psychology of motivation the acquisition of drives through aversive stimulation was demonstrated and the theoretical and empirical considerations of the role of fear in such conditioning has been explored (Miller 1948; Mowrer 1960).

The conditioned emotional response (CER) and the conditioned avoidance response (CAR) are typical behavioral situations used in the study of aversive stimuli. The CER relates to the suppression of an ongoing response to a signal which has been previously paired with an aversive stimulus, such as an electric shock. Avoidance may be either active or passive. Active avoidance involves an anticipatory movement by the animal on a signal previously paired with a noxious stimulus; this movement may be stepping off a grid floor associated with impending shock. Passive avoidance may be described as "not responding" in order to avoid an impending noxious stimulation. In addition, avoidance responding may be seen in an operant conditioning situation in which no external stimuli signal impending shock, but shock will be forthcoming unless the avoidance operant occurs (Sidman 1953). In this way a stable rate of avoidance responding may be established in a lever pressing task, and a "free operant avoidance" or "Sidman avoidance" situation explored.

While noxious stimuli with attending fear can be used to promote drive and learning, the associated physiological events are not well understood although a great deal of research has been directed toward this end. Sympathectomy may slow CAR acquisition as may demedullation of the adrenals (Wynne &

Solomon 1955; Levine & Soliday 1962) although this effect is not always evident. Injection of adrenalin may facilitate CAR acquisition (Latane & Schacter 1962), but negative results have also been reported (Stewart & Broodshire 1968). The lack of unanimity in results of studies of this kind certainly may be due to species, methodological, and individual differences, but an important aspect of the CAR is the host of dysfunctions which may slow acquisition, including a basic debilitation of the animal which is compounded with specific functional changes. Anterior lobectomy of the hypophysis may slow CAR acquisition, but the retardation may be due to a general debilitation including sensory and motor impairment as the simple escape from a noxious stimulus in a runway situation was also slowed (De Wied 1964).

A role of ACTH and adrenal corticosteroids in avoidance behavior now appears to be established, although the relative importance of these principles to the various phases of acquisition and extinction of these responses is far from settled. Since anterior lobectomy does not prevent CAR acquisition, ACTH does not appear essential to the response, but replacement therapy was found to reverse the debilitating effects of the adenohypophysectomy (De Wied 1964). ACTH may increase the strength of an incompletely learned avoidance response (either active or passive) and may enhance performance in the Sidman avoidance situation (Levine & Brush 1967; Levine & Jones 1965; Wertheim et al. 1967). Wertheim, Conner, and Levine (1969) have demonstrated a direct relation between plasma levels of corticosteroids and the attainment of proficiency in the Sidman avoidance condition. Injection of ACTH may not influence the rate of CAR acquisition in normal animals (Murphy & Miller 1955), but may influence its rate of extinction (Miller & Ogawa 1962). The measurement of extinction in the study of system impairments on CAR appears to be a most sensitive and promising one. Bohus and De Wied (1966) have discovered inhibitory as well as facilitatory effects on CAR extinction depending upon changes in ACTH molecular structure.

The relation of ADH to noxious stimulation was noted by Verney (1947) and has since been confirmed by other investigators (Mirsky et al. 1954; De Wied 1960). De Wied (1965) found no effect on acquisition of a CAR with posterior lobectomy of the hypophysis, but did note faster extinction in these animals which was reversed with replacement therapy of ADH and ACTH. Levine and Soliday (1960) found a facilitation of CAR with lesions of the median eminence producing diabetes insipidus, however, and Crow (1966) found a facilitation of conditioned avoidance responding with dosages of alcohol producing a maximal short term diuresis. Heavy dosages of ethyl alcohol invariably produce sensory and motor impairment and thus will produce a decrement in any performance if a severe enough ataxia is induced but at certain dose levels performance may be "stimulated" or enhanced especially in situations involving some degree of noxicity. The "stimulation" effect of alcohol has been attributed to depression of inhibiting neural systems associated with emotionality and fear (Barry, Wagner, & Miller 1962). It is interesting to note that although the depressant effects of alcohol are widespread throughout the cerebral cortex and higher brain systems, the hypothalamic regions are also affected. The diuresis which accompanies alcohol ingestion has been related to inhibition of ADH release by the supraoptic hypophysial system (van Dyke & Ames 1951; Crow 1968b).

While these data on autonomic and endocrine systems may be consistent in many respects with models of avoidance behavior based on fear and attendant organic reactions, the work on central processes are also of interest in this respect. The limbic and rhinencephalic systems are particularly relevant as are the diencephalic regions of the hypothalamus.

It was the neuroanatomist Papez (1937) who on the basis of the work of Cannon, Ranson, and others explored the relationship of the hypothalamus to closely related brain systems, and proposed a mechanism of emotion, "Papez circuit", which included the hypothalamic connections throughout the visceral brain (hypothalamus, anterior thalamic nuclei, cingulate gyrus, hippocampus, and their interconnections). More recently MacKay (1959), acknowledging the importance of Papez's work and of affect in more general motivational phenomena, has proposed a neurological model of motivation which delineates interrelations between the visceral brain, the neocortex, the ascending reticular activating system, and the sensorium and effector systems, and brings together in terms compatable with scientific inquiry much of the psychology of motivation in terms of its neurological basis.

A role for affect in general and specific parts of Papez circuit in avoidance behavior has been clearly demonstrated, but not as yet precisely defined. Septal lesions which produce heightened emotionality and hyperresponsivity may facilitate CAR acquisition (King 1958; Kriekhaus et al. 1964), but hinder passive avoidance responding (Slotnick & Jarvik 1966). Septal self-stimulation parameters of brain shock administered noncontingently or passively by a repeat cycle timer during the course of training also facilitates CAR acquisition (Goldstein 1966b). Septal ICSS has been shown to interfere with CER acquisition (Brady & Conrad 1960), the disruption apparently due to the spetal stimulation per se as noncontingent septal stimulation during an operant for water reinforcement produces a similar effect (Goldstein 1966a). It is interesting to note that neither septal nor amygdala lesions greatly impair the orienting response in terms of general autonomic activity, the amygdala lesion producing the only disruption, and that in terms of the galvanic skin response (Holdstock 1969). In anesthetized animals, septal stimulation decreases heart rate by way of vagal inhibition (Bromley & Holdstock 1969). Both anterior and posterior hippocampal lesions facilitate CAR acquisition (Rabe & Haddad 1969); lesions of the mammillothalamic tract are found to disrupt the CAR in a shuttle box situation (Kriekhaus 1965). Lesions of the ventromedial hypothalamus are found to interfere with a passive avoidance reaction (Kaada, Rasmussen, & Kveim 1962), and it has been theorized that this area may mediate suppressant effects of punishment as well as satiety, although two systems appear to exist (Margules & Stein 1969). Recently Greidanus and De Wied (1969) have found that corticosteroids which facilitate CAR extinction when injected subcutaneously, will produce the same effects when implanted within the median and posterior thalamus or lateral ventricles.

The difficulty of a clear organization of these data on emotion and affect, their measureable physiological manifestations, and their role in avoidance behaviors is apparent. Virtually every study of this nature here cited has been questioned either by the presentation of contradictory results or by criticism in terms of methodological or theoretical predispositions of the various scientists involved. Two problems in this definition of the place of noxious stimuli in behavioral events seem paramount: (1) individual differences in animals of the same species, especially

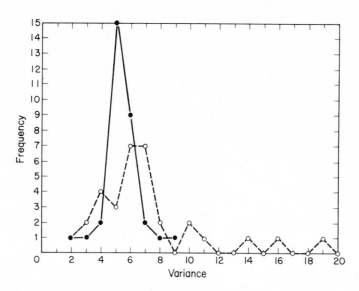

Fig. 35-6. *Frequency distribution of variances of latency scores in conditioned avoidance responding early in training (solid line) and late in training* [broken line].

in pretreatment reactivity to standard stimuli, and (2) behavioral measures of avoidance responding.

With notable exceptions, the field of avoidance and reactions to aversive stimuli has almost entirely neglected to account for the rather striking individuality of affective reactivity which is known to exist. In man such uniqueness has been shown by Malmo and Shagass (1949) and in a series of remarkable studies by Lacey and his associates (see Lacey & Lacey 1958) in the principle of autonomic response stereotypy. The strain studies of rats (see Broadhurst & Levine 1963) are also cases in point. The arguments for attending to such factors have been made convincingly by Hirsch (1963). Studies are beginning to appear more frequently which account for individuality, especially in the case of drugs (Rech 1967) and one can only hope that this trend is further developed in the field of avoidance conditioning. The nature of the task is a second problem area. The several ways of instituting avoidance responding in animals have been sketched earlier, and, of course, there are many variations of these basic procedures. There is ample evidence that different procedures may yield different results, especially in the assessment of central nervous ablations, and the interpretation of such differences in conflict situations, one-way and two-way avoidance, and the extinction of these responses is at least very difficult. These differences in the measurement of avoidance and the ubiquity of new procedures of avoidance conditioning may, of course, simply reveal the true complexity of such behavior, but it is possible that many of the contradictory findings in this literature are due to such procedural characteristics of the researcher.

One approach to the acknowledgement of these difficulties is to utilize more fully the data collected in studies of this kind. With the present ease of access to high-speed electronic data processing equipment more information on individuality might be presented as well as elaborations of group data summaries. Comparisons of studies with "differing results" made in this way might be revealing. In addition to a more thorough coverage of individualized data, it is suggested that more of the group data be reported than is presently the case. Information on the distribution of data may be especially valuable and the presentation of frequency distributions of dependent variables would add a great deal of information with little increase in journal space.

With this added information measures may be derived from avoidance conditioning more meaningful in terms of adaptation on the animal's part than those measures presently employed. One such adaptation in the face of noxious stimulation from the viewpoint of the species may lie in individual differences of responding to a given situation. Another may be *intraindividual differences* in responding within the same animal over the period of the exposure to a stressful situation, the within subjects variance. Figure 35-6 shows the results of a shuttle box avoidance responding situation for 32 animals each of which received 100 trials. Latency measures for the first 50 trials, and for the last 50 trials have been converted to variance scores and cast into the frequency distribution shown. The differences in variance scores are highly reliable for animals who acquired the CAR quickly as well as for those who elicited no avoidance responses throughout the 100 trials. This diminution in variability of response with stress may be correlated with changes in the mean response or may not be so correlated. Changes in variability of the response may occur when the mean remains unchanged. Such an effect was found by Crow (1968a) in the case of heart rate changes as a result of alcohol intoxication, and it would be interesting to extend this sort of "analysis of variability" to the various experimental situations involving noxious stimulus elements.

References

ADOLPH, E. F., BARKER, J. P., and HOY, P. A. Multiple factors in thirst. *American Journal of Physiology*, 1954, *178*, 538–62.

ANAND, B. K., and BROBECK, J. R. Localization of a feeding center in the hypothalamus of the rat. *Proceedings of the Society of Experimental Biology and Medicine*, 1951, 77, 323–24.

ANAND, B. V., CHHINA, G. S, and SINGH, B. Effect of glucose on the activity of hypothalamic "feeding centers." *Science*, 1962, 597–98.

ANDERSSON, B. The effect of injections of hypertonic NaCl-solutions into different parts of the hypothalamus of goats. *Acta Physiologica Scandanavica*, 1953, *28*, 188–201.

―――― and LARSSON, S. The influence of local temperature changes in the preoptic area and rostral hypothalamus on regulation of food and water intake. *Acta Physiologica Scandanavica*, 1961, *52*, 75–89.

AX, A. F. Goals and methods in psychophysiology. *Psychophysiology*, 1964, *1*, 8–25.

BALDWIN, B. A., and INGRAM, D. L. Behavioral thermoregulation in pigs. *Physiology and Behavior*, 1967, *2*, 15–21.

—— The effects of food intake and acclimatization to temperature on behavioral thermoregulation in pigs and mice. *Physiology and Behavior*, 1968, *3*, 395–400.

BARGMANN, W. Relationship between neurohypophysial structure and function. *In* H. Heller (ed.), *The Neurohypophysis*. London: Butterworth, 1957.

BARRY, H. B. III, WAGNER, A. R., and MILLER, N. E. Effects of alcohol and amobarbital on performance inhibited by experimental extinction. *Journal of Comparative and Physiological Psychology*, 1962, *55*, 464–68.

BECK, R. C., and MCLEAN, J. F. Effect of schedule of reinforcement and stomach loads on bar pressing by thirsty rats. *Journal of Comparative and Physiological Psychology*, 1967, *63*, 530–33.

BOHUS, B., and DE WIED, D. Inhibitory and facilitatory effect of two related peptides on extinction of avoidance behavior. *Science*, 1966, *153*, 318–20.

BRADY, J. V., and CONRAD, D. B. Some effects of limbic system self-stimulation upon conditioned emotional behavior. *Journal of Comparative and Physiological Psychology*, 1960, *53*, 128–37.

BRENGELMANN, G., and BROWN, A. C. Temperature regulation, *In* T. C. Ruch and H. D. Patton (eds.), *Physiology and biophysics*. Philadelphia: Saunders, 1965.

BROADHURST, P. L., and LEVINE, S. Behavioral consistency in strains of rats selectively bred for emotional elimination. *British Journal of Psychology*, 1963, *54*, 121–25.

BROBECK, J. R. Regulation of feeding and drinking. *In* J. Field, H. W. Magoun, and V. E. Hall, *Handbook of physiology*, vol. 2. Baltimore: Williams & Wilkins, 1960.

—— Regulation of energy exchange. *In* R. C. Ruch and H. D. Patton (eds.), *Physiology and biophysics*. Philadelphia: Saunders, 1965.

—— TEPPERMAN, J., and LONG, C. N. H. Experimental hyperphagia in the albino rat. *Yale Journal of Biology and Medicine*, 1943, *15*, 831–53.

BROMLEY, D. V., and HOLDSTOCK, T. L. Effects of septal stimulation on heart rate in vagotomized rats. *Physiology and Behavior*, 1969, *4*, 399–401.

CANNON, W. B. *Bodily changes in pain, hunger, fear and rage*. New York: Appleton-Century-Crofts, 1929.

CARLISLE, H. Initiation of behavior responding for heat in a cold environment. *Physiology and Behavior*, 1968, *3*, 827–30.

—— Effect of fixed-ratio thermal reinforcement on thermoregulatory behavior. *Physiology and Behavior*, 1969, *4*, 23–28.

CARLTON, P. L., and MARKS, R. Cold exposure and heat: Reinforced operant behavior. *Science*, 1958, *128*, 1344.

CHIARAVIGLIO, E. Effects of lesions in the septal area and olfactory bulbs on sodium chloride intake. *Physiology and Behavior*, 1969, *4*, 693–97.

CORBIT, J. Osmotic thirst: Theoretical and experimental analysis. *Journal of Comparative and Physiological Psychology*, 1969, *67*, 3–14.

COX, V., KAKOLEWSKI, J., and VALENSTEIN, E. Ventromedial hypothalamic lesions and changes in body weight and food consumption in male and female rats. *Journal of Comparative and Physiological Psychology*, 1969, *67*, 320–26.

CROW, L. T. Effects of alcohol on conditioned avoidance responding. *Physiology and Behavior*, 1966, *1*, 89–91.

—— Subcommissural organ, lateral hypothalamus and dorsal longitudinal fasciculus in water and salt metabolism. *Anatomical Record*, 1967, *157*, 457–64.

—— Effects of alcohol on heart rate. *Physiology and Behavior*, 1968a, *3*, 71–73.

—— Diencephalic influence in alcohol diuresis. *Physiology and Behavior*, 1968b, *3*, 319–22.

—— Maintenance and measurement of water-regulatory variables through controlled feeding. *Psychological Reports*, 1968c, *22*, 1125–28.

DAHL, E., and URSIN, H. Obesity produced by iron and tissue destruction in the ventromedial hypothalamus. *Physiology and Behavior*, 1969, 315–17.

DEUTSCH, J. A. *The structural basis of behavior*. Chicago: University of Chicago Press, 1966.

DE WIED, D. A simple and sensitive method for the assay of antidiuretic hormone with notes on the potency of plasma under different experimental conditions. *Acta Physiologica Pharmacologica Neerlandica*, 1960, *9*, 69–81.

—— The influence of the anterior pituitary on avoidance learning and escape behavior. *American Journal of Physiology*, 1964, *207*, 255–59.

—— The influence of the posterior and intermediate lobe of the pituitary and pituitary peptides on the maintenance of a conditioned avoidance response in rats. *International Journal of Neuropharmacology*, 1965, *4*, 157–67.

DONOVICK, P. J., and BURRIGHT, R. G. Water consumption of rats with septal lesions following two days of water deprivation. *Physiology and Behavior*, 1968, *3*, 285–88.

DYKE, VAN H. B., and AMES, R. G. Alcohol diuresis. *Acta Endocrinology*, 1951, *7*, 110–21.

EHRLICH, D. J., and MALMO, R. B. Electrophysiological concomitants of simple operant conditioning in the rat. *Neuropsychologia*, 1967, *5*, 219–36.

ELLISON, G. D. Appetitive behavior in rats after circumsection of the hypothalamus. *Physiology and Behavior*, 1968, *3*, 221–26.

FALK, J. L. Production of polydipsia in normal rats by an intermittant food schedule. *Science*, 1961, *133*, 195–96.

—— Comments on Dr. Teitelbaum's paper. *In* M. Jones (ed.), *Nebraska Symposium on Motivation*, 1961, *9*, 65–68.

FISHER, C., INGRAM, W. B., and RANSON, S. W. *Diabetes insipidus and the neurohumoral control of water balance*. Ann Arbor, Mich.: Edwards, 1938.

FITZSIMONS, J. T. Drinking by rats depleted of body fluid without increase in osmotic pressure. *Journal of Physiology* (London), 1961, *159*, 297–309.

FITZSIMONS, T., and LE MAGNEN, J. Eating as a regulatory control of drinking in the rat. *Journal of Comparative and Physiological Psychology*, 1969, *67*, 273–83.

GIBSON, W. E., REID, L. D., SOKAI, M., and PORTER, P. B. Intercranial reinforcement compared with sugar-water reinforcement. *Science*, 1965, *148*, 1357–58.

GOLDSTEIN, R. Effects of noncontingent septal stimulation on the CER in the rat. *Journal of Comparative and Physiological Psychology*, 1966a, *61*, 132–35.

—— Facilitation of active avoidance behavior by reinforcing septal stimulation in the rat. *Physiology and Behavior*, 1966b, *1*, 335–39.

—— STERN, J. A., and ROTHENBERG, S. J. Effect of water deprivation and cues associated with water on the heart rate of the rat. *Physiology and Behavior*, 1966, *1*, 199–203.

GREIDANUS van WIMERSMA TJ. B., and DE WIED, D. Effects of intracerebral implantation of cortiocosteroids on extinction of an avoidance response in rats. *Physiology and Behavior*, 1969, *4*, 365–70.

GUTMAN, Y., and KRAUSZ, M. Regulation of food and water intake in rats as related to plasma osmolarity and volume. *Physiology and Behavior*, 1969, *4*, 311–13.

HAMILTON, C. L. Effect of food deprivation on thermal behavior of the rat. *Proceedings of the Society of Experimental Biology*, 1959, *100*, 354–56.

HATTON, G. I. Drive shifts during extinction: Effects on extinction and spontaneous recovery of bar-pressing behavior. *Journal of Comparative and Physiological Psychology*, 1965, *59*, 385–91.

HETHERINGTON, A. W., and RANSON, S. W. The relation of various hypothalamic lesions to adiposity in the rat. *Journal of Comparative Neurology*, 1942, *76*, 475–99.

HIRSCH, J. Behavior genetics and individuality understood. *Science*, 1963, *142*, 1436–42.

HOLDSTOCK, T. L. Autonomic reactivity following septal and amygdaloid lesions in white rats. *Physiology and Behavior*, 1969, *4*, 603–7.

HOEBEL, B. G. Inhibition and disinhibition of self-stimulation and feeding. *Journal of Comparative and Physiological Psychology*, 1968, *66*, 89–100.

—— and TEITELBAUM, P. Hypothalamic control of feeding and self-stimulation. *Science*, 1962, *135*, 375–77.

HOLMES, J. H., and GREGERSEN, M. I. Observations on drinking induced by hypertonic solutions. *American Journal of Physiology*, 1950, *162*, 326–37.

KAADA, B. R., RASMUSSEN, E. W., and KVEIM, O. Impaired acquisition of passive avoidance behavior by subcallosal, septal, hypothalamic, and insular lesions in rats. *Journal of Comparative and Physiological Psychology*, 1962, *55*, 661–70.

KATCHER, A. H., SOLOMON, R., TURNER, L. H., LOLORDO, V., OVERMIER, J., and RESCORLA, R. Heart rate and blood pressure responses to signaled and unsignaled shocks: Effects of cardiac sympathectomy. *Journal of Comparative and Physiological Psychology*, 1969, *68*, 163–74.

KEENEDY, G. C. The hypothalamic control of food intake in rats. *Proceedings of the Royal Society*, 1950, *137*, 535–49.

KING, F. A. Effects of septal and amygdaloid lesions on emotional behavior and conditioned avoidance response in the rat. *Journal of Nervous and Mental Disease*, 1958, *126*, 57–63.

KREIKHAUS, E. E. Decrements in avoidance behavior following mammillothalamic tractotomy in rats and subsequent recovery with D-amphetamine. *Journal of Comparative and Physiological Psychology*, 1965, *60*, 31–35.

—— SIMMONS, H. J., THOMAS, G. J., THOMAS, G. J., and KENYON, J. Septal lesions enhance shock avoidance behavior in the rat. *Experimental Neurology*, 1964, *9*, 107–13.

KUTSCHER, C., STILLMAN, R., and WEISS, I. Food deprivation polydipsia in gerbils (Meriones unguiculatus). *Physiology and Behavior*, 1968, *3*, 667–71.

LACEY, J. I., and LACEY, B. C. Verification and extension of the principle of autonomic response-stereotypy. *American Journal of Psychology*, 1958, *71*, 50–73.

LATANE, B., and SCHACTER, S. Adrenaline and avoidance learning. *Journal of Comparative and Physiological Psychology*, 1962, *55*, 214–16.

LEVINE, S., and SOLIDAY, S. The effects of hypothalamic lesions on conditioned avoidance learning. *Journal of Comparative and Physiological Psychology*, 1960, *53*, 497–501.

—— An effect of adrenal demedullation on the acquisition of conditioned avoidance response. *Journal of Comparative and Physiological Psychology*, 1962, *55*, 214–16.

LEVINE, S., and BRUSH, F. R. Adrenocortical activity and avoidance as a function of time after avoidance training. *Physiology and Behavior*, 1967, *3*, 385–88.

LEVINE, S., and JONES, L. Adrenocorticotropic hormone (ACTH) and passive avoidance learning. *Journal of Comparative and Physiological Psychology*, 1965, *59*, 357–60.

LIEBELT, R. A., and PERRY, J. H. Hypothalamic lesions associated with goldthioglucose-induced obesity. *Proceedings of the Society of Experimental Biology and Medicine*, 1957, *95*, 774–77.

LIPTON, J. M., and MOROTTO, D. R. Effects of desalivation on behavioral thermoregulation against heat. *Physiology and Behavior*, 1969, *4*, 723–27.

MACKAY, R. P. The neurology of motivation. *Archives of Neurology*, 1959, *1*, 535–43.

MALMO, R. B. Activation: A neuropsychological dimension. *Psychological Review*, 1959, *66*, 367–86.

—— and SHAGASS, C. Physiologic study symptom mechanisms in psychiatric patients under stress. *Psychosomatic Medicine*, 1949, *12*, 362–76.

MARGULES, D. L., and STEIN, L. Cholinerigic synapses in the ventromedial hypothalamus for the suppression of operant behavior by punishment and satiety. *Journal of Comparative and Physiological Psychology*, 1969, *3*, 327–35.

MARLER, P., and HAMILTON, W. J. *Mechanisms of animal behavior.* New York: John Wiley, 1966.

MAYER, J. Regulation of energy intake and the body weight. The glucostatic theory and the lipostatic hypothesis. *Annals of the New York Academy of Science*, 1955, *63*, 15–43.

MAYR, E. *Animal species and evolution.* Cambridge, Mass.: Harvard University Press, 1966.

MCFARLAND, D., and WRIGHT, P. Water conservation by inhibition of food intake. *Physiology and Behavior*, 1969, *4*, 95–99.

MENDELSON, J. Lateral hypothalamic stimulation: Inhibition of aversive effects by feeding, drinking, and gnawing. *Science*, 1969, *166*, 1431–33.

MEYER, M., and WRIGHT, J. Thermoregulatory behavior in normal and hypophysectomozed rats. *Communications in Behavioral Biology*, 1971, *6*, 71–77.

MILLER, N. E. Studies of fear as an acquirable drive. I. Fear as motivation and fear reduction as reinforcement in the learning of new responses. *Journal of Experimental Psychology*, 1948, *38*, 89–100.

—— BAILEY, C. J., and STEVENSON, J. A. F. Decreased "hunger" but increased food intake resulting from hypothalamic lesions. *Science*, 1950, *112*, 256–59.

MILLER, R. E., and OGAWA, N. The effect of adrenocorticotrophic hormone (ACTH) on avoidance conditioning in the adrenalectomized rat. *Journal of Comparative and Physiological Psychology*, 1962, *55*, 211–13.

MIRSKY, I., STEIN, M., and PAULISCH, G. The secretion of antidiuretic substance into the circulation of rats exposed to noxious stimuli. *Endocrinology*, 1954, *54*, 491–505.

MOGENSON, G. J., and STEVENSON, J. A. F. Drinking and self-stimulation with electrical stimulation of the lateral hypothalamus. *Physiology and Behavior*, 1966, *1*, 251–54.

—— Drinking induced by electrical stimulation of the lateral hypothalamus. *Experimental Neurology*, 1967, *17*, 119–27.

MORGANE, P. J. Alterations in feeding and drinking behavior of rats with lesions in globi pallidi. *American Journal of Physiology*, 1961, *201*, 420–28.

—— The Role of the limbic-midbrain circuit, reticular formation, and hypothalamus in regulating food and water intake. *Proceedings of the Seventh International Congress of Nutrition*, 1966, *2*, 1–16.

—— The function of the limbic and rhinic forebrain-limbic midbrain systems and reticular formation in the regulation of food and water intake. *Annals of the New York Academy of Science*, 1969, *157*, 806–48.

—— and KOSMAN, A. J. Relationship of the middle hypothalamus to amygdalar hyperphagia. *American Journal of Physiology*, 1960, *198*, 1315–18.

MORGANE, P., and JACOBS, H. Hunger and satiety. *World Review of Nutrition and Dietetics*, 1969, *10*, 100–213.

MORRISON, S. D. The adrenal cortex and the regulation of water exchange during food deprivation. *Endocrinology*, 1967, *80*, 835–39.

MOWER, O. H. *Learning theory and behavior.* New York: John Wiley, 1960.

MURPHY, J. V., and MILLER, R. E. The effect of adrenocorticotrophic hormone (ACTH) on avoidance conditioning in the rat. *Journal of Comparative and Physiological Psychology*, 1955, *48*, 47–49.

OBRIST, P. A., WEBB, R. A., and SUTTERER, J. R. Heart rate and somatic changes during aversive conditioning and a simple reaction time task. *Psychophysiology*, 1969, *5*, 696–723.

O'KELLY, L. I., and BECK, R. C. Water regulation in the rat: III. The artificial control of thirst with stomach loads of water and sodium chloride. *Psychological Monographs*, 1960, *74* (whole number).

—— CROW, L. T, TAPP, J. T., and HATTON, G. I. Water regulation in the rat: Drive intensity and fixed ratio responding. *Journal of Comparative and Physiological Psychology*, 1966, *61*, 194–97.

O'KELLY, L. I., and FALK, J. L. Water regulation in the rat. II. The effects of preloads of water and sodium chloride on the bar-pressing performance of thirsty rats. *Journal of Comparative and Physiological Psychology*, 1958, *51*, 22–25.

O'KELLY, L. I., CROW, L. T., TAPP, J. T., and HATTON, G. I. Water regulation in the rat: Drive intensity and fixed ratio responding. *Journal of Comparative and Physiological Psychology*, 1966, *61*, 194–97.

O'KELLY, L. I., HATTTON, G. I., TUCKER, L., and WESTALL, D. Water regulation in the rat: Heart rate as a function of hydration, anesthesia, and association with reinforcement. *Journal of Comparative and Physiological Psychology*, 1965, *59*, 159–65.

OLDS, J. Physiological mechanisms of reward. *In* M. R. Jones (ed.), *Nebraska symposium on motivation.* Lincoln: University of Nebraska Press, 1955.

—— Self-stimulation of the brain. *Science*, 1958, *127*, 315–24.

—— Approach-avoidance dissociations in rat brain. *American Journal of Physiology*, 1960, *199*, 965–68.

—— and MILNER, P. Positive reinforcement produced by electrical stimulation of the septal area and other regions of the rat brain. *Journal of Comparative and Physiological Psychology*, 1954, *47*, 419–27.

PAPEZ, J. W. A proposed mechanism of emotion. *Archives of Neurology and Psychiatry*, 1937, *38*, 725–44.

POSCHEL, B. P. H. Do biological reinforcers act via the self-stimulation areas of the brain? *Physiology and Behavior*, 1968, *3*, 53–60.

RABE, A., and HADDAD, R. Acquisition of two-way shuttle-box avoidance after selective hippocampal lesions. *Physiology and Behavior*, 1969, *4*, 319–23.

RABIN, B., and SMITH, C. Behavioral comparison of the effectiveness of irritative and non-irritative lesions in producing hypothalamic hyperphagia. *Physiology and Behavior*, 1968, *3*, 417–20.

RECH, R. H. Effects of drugs on the behavior of rats which perform poorly in a conditioned avoidance situation. Paper presented at the American Psychological Association, Washington, D. C., 1967.

REYNOLDS, R. W. An irritative hypothesis concerning the hypothalamic regulation of food intake. *Psychological Review*, 1965, *72*, 104–16.

ROUTTENBERG, A. The two-arousal hypothesis: Reticular formation and limbic system. *Psychological Review*, 1968, *75*, 51–80.

SELYE, H. *The physiology and pathology of exposure to stress*. Montreal: Acta, 1950.

SEWARD, J. P., COSMIDES, R. A., and HUMPHREY, G. L. Changes in heart rate during discriminative reward training and extinction in the rat. *Journal of Comparative and Physiological Psychology*, 1969, *67*, 358–63.

SIDMAN, M. Avoidance conditioning with brief shock and no exteroceptive warning signal. *Science*, 1953, *118*, 157–58.

SLOTNICK, B. M., and JARVIK, M. E. Deficits in passive avoidance and fear conditioning in mice with septal lesions. *Science*, 1966, *154*, 1207–08.

SMITH, O. A. Food intake and HT stimulation. *In* D. E. Sheer (ed.), *Electrical Stimulation of the Brain*. Austin: University of Texas Press, 1961.

STEINER, W. G. Electrical activity of rat brain as a correlate of primary drive. *Electroencephalography and Clinical Neurophysiology*, 1962, *14*, 233–43.

STEWARD, C., and BROOKSHIRE, K. Effect of epinephrine on acquisition of conditioned fear. *Physiology and Behavior*, 1968, *3*, 601–4.

STRICKER, F. Some physiological and motivational properties of the hypovolamic stimulus for thirst. *Physiology and Behavior*, 1968, *3*, 379–85.

TEITELBAUM, P. Sensory control of hypothalamic hyperphagia. *Journal of Comparative and Physiological Psychology*, 1955, *48*, 156–63.

—— and EPSTEIN, A. The lateral hypothalamic syndrome: recovery of feeding and drinking after lateral hypothalamic lesions. *Psychological Review*, 1962, *69*, 74–90.

URSIN, H., ROSVOLD, H. E., and VEST, B. Food preferences in brain lesioned monkeys. *Physiology and Behavior*, 1969, *4*, 609–12.

VERNEY, E. The anidiuretic hormone and the factors which determine its release. *Proceedings of the Royal Society of London*, 1947, *135*, 25–101.

WEINSTEIN, S. O_2 and CO_2 as reinforcers in conditioning. *Federation Proceedings*, 1963, *22*, 222.

—— The effect of hypoxia upon learned escape from carbon dioxide. *Psychonomic Science*, 1966, *6*, 91–92.

WEISS, B. Thermal behavior of the subnourished and pantothenic-acid-deprived rat. *Journal of Comparative and Physiological Psychology*, 1957, *50*, 481–85.

—— and LATIES, V. Behavioral thermoregulation. *Science*, 1961, *133*, 1338–44.

WERTHEIM, G. A., CONNER, R. L., and LEVINE, S. Adrenocortical influences on free-operant avoidance behavior. *Journal of Experimental Analysis of Behavior*, 1967, *10*, 555–63.

—— Avoidance conditioning and adreno-cortical function in the rat. *Physiology and Behavior*, 1969, *4*, 41–44.

WOOD, D. M., and OBRIST, P. A. The effects of controlled and uncontrolled respiration on the conditioned heart rate in human beings. *Journal of Experimental Psychology*, 1964, *68*, 221–29.

WYNNE, L. C., and SOLOMON, R. E. Traumatic avoidance learning: Acquisition and extinction in dogs deprived of normal peripheral autonomic function. *Genetic and Psychological Monograph*, 1955, *52*, 241–81.

YOUNG, A. C. Neural control of respiration. *In* T. C. Ruch and H. D. Patton (eds.), *Physiology and Biophysics*. Philadelphia: Saunders, 1965.

YOUNG, P. T. Hedonic organization and regulation of behavior. *Psychological Review*, 1966, *73*, 1–15.

Introduction

This chapter is prefaced with several *caveat lector* statements. The first one is that the data cannot be presented at the level of certainty or sophistication possible in many of the chapters of this volume. Until the late 1950s sleep research was a sleeping giant. Prior to that time only two systematic books had been written on the topic: Pieron's (1913) and Kleitman's (1939). Research in the area was intermittent and scattered across the peripheries of a wide variety of disciplines. Since the late 1950s, however, there has been a massive output of research and writing. An indication of this is the publication of at least 15 books within the space of six years concerned exclusively with sleep.

Wolstenholme & O'Connor	*1961*
Oswald	*1962*
Kleitman	*1963*
Murray	*1965*
Akert, Bally & Schade	*1965*
Jouvet	*1965*
Luce & Segal	*1966*
Foulkes	*1966*
Hartmann	*1967*
Koella	*1967*
Witkin & Lewis	*1967*
Kety, Evarts & Williams	*1967*
Webb	*1968*
Abt & Reisman	*1968*
Kales	*1969*

With such a research outburst, perspective is difficult to find; new findings are daily events; tentative conclusions emerge, they are modified, and they are often destroyed. What is presented here is where we are now, in the midst of building a body of knowledge about sleep. We cannot even guarantee that these are foundations, they may merely represent a site clearance.

Secondly, sleep and dream research extends from the biochemical bases through neurophysiology, physiology, ecology,

Wilse B. Webb

Sleep and Dreams

36

psychology, and psychopathology. We have concentrated our efforts on reviewing the psychology of the sleep of human subjects. This has been at the expense of other areas. Since these areas are of relevance to an understanding of the sleep process, a section citing critical resources on these other areas has been included at the end of this chapter.

Measurement of Sleep

The measurement of sleep as a process is an unusually formidable one. In the adult human it is a prolonged response which typically occupies a period of seven to eight hours in every twenty-four hours. Since time between sleep periods in humans poorly predicts the probability of sleep, and there are no certain stimulus conditions which elicit sleep, it is under limited stimulus control; it cannot be readily defined by its antecedents as, for example, thirst or hunger. As a response, sleep involves numerous and complex physiological, neurological and behavioral aspects of the total organism. Furthermore the physiological changes are rarely of an on-off type but are generally slow changing, unstable, and present in varying complexes within other states. From a psychological point of view, two characteristics are most frustrating. It is the very absence of behavior rather than its unique form which typifies sleep. Similarly, in terms of consciousness, awareness, or self-reports, the response is defined in the null. Malcolm (1959) spends forty-eight pages establishing the epistemological meaninglessness of the statement, "I am asleep."

Indeed even defining sleep is a difficult task. Crudely, sleep may be defined as a state characterized by a supine position, muscular relaxation, heightened threshold, reduced physiological activation, and an unconsciousness or unawareness of one's environmental surroundings. This, however, is a crude definition. A supine position is not a requirement; muscular relaxation is not continuous; the threshold is quite variable and is often no higher than that found in many waking states; physiological activation is high rather than low during at least 20 percent of the sleep period; the unconsciousness and unawareness are only relative and are far more profound in such conditions as anesthesia.

In spite of these difficulties, efforts to measure sleep have gone forward. The usual approach has been to take one of the above aspects of sleep and attempt to measure that dimension as an index of the total process. As such, sleep has been measured in terms of length (time supine), muscular relaxation (motility), threshold, a variety of physiological measures such as temperature, heart rate, etc., and brain states (consciousness) by means of the electroencephalogram (EEG). These measures have been reviewed in some detail elsewhere (Webb & Agnew 1968a). However, a few summary comments are in order, as is a slightly more extended description of the EEG measures because of their current prominence in research and their place in the succeeding sections of this paper.

THRESHOLD

The earliest attempt to systematically measure the sleep process involved threshold measures. In a medical doctorate thesis completed in 1862, Kohlschutter, a student of Fechner, presented a "depth of sleep" curve derived from the level of sound required to awaken subjects throughout the night (reported in Wohlisch 1957). Because depth of sleep is a critical variable, threshold experiments have continued into the present. The difficulties associated with such studies are summarized elsewhere (Webb & Agnew 1968a). Currently, rather than being attempts to describe the total sleep process, threshold measures are more particularly directed toward the studies of the depth of particular phases of sleep as identified by the EEG (cf., Williams et al. 1966).

MOTILITY

Motility as an index of the "quality" of sleep was also introduced early in sleep research. The pioneer work in activity measurement was done by Syzmanski (1914). Extensive work on motility and sleep was done by Johnson in the 1920s (Johnson & Swan 1930). A detailed study of children's sleep was published in 1933 (Renshaw et al.) using motility as the primary dependent variable. This technique of measurement was widely used in Russia under the title of "actography" and continued in use into the 1950s (cf., Andreev 1951). This is an easily obtained measure which does not interact with the sleep process. Furthermore, it reflects individual differences and is sensitive to experimental variables. As a measure of the "quality" of sleep, however, motility has generally been replaced by the more continuous EEG measures. Current interests relating to motility are centered around the relation of body movements to dream episodes (Dement & Wolpert 1958) and to other stages of sleep (Oswald et al. 1963).

PHYSIOLOGICAL MEASURES

A wide variety of physiological measures relative to sleep have been assessed. Of most interest have been those which have been peripherally accessible. An excellent summary of the autonomic measures (electrodermal, respiration, circulation, and penile erections) may be found in Snyder et al. (1964). The temperature variable, which has received considerable attention since Pieron's early work, is reviewed in detail by Kleitman (1963). In general, these measures have not been effective in the description of the overall sleep process because they are slow changing, with wide individual differences in base rates. Furthermore, they have characteristically shown little discernible relationship to the functional character of sleep. More recent work, however, has closely tied the autonomic responses to the REM period (Johnson & Lubin 1966; McDonald et al. 1967).

THE EEG

The landmark paper of Loomis, Harvey, and Hobart (1937) presents a systematization of five identifiable electroencephalographic "stages" (A through E) which occur during sleep. This made the changing and complex intrasleep process continuously available to observation. Aserinsky and Kleitman (1953) subsequently noted that, in conjunction with rapid eye movements (REM's), one of the sleep categories (Stage 1, below) was systematically related to dreaming. Dement and Kleitman (1957a)

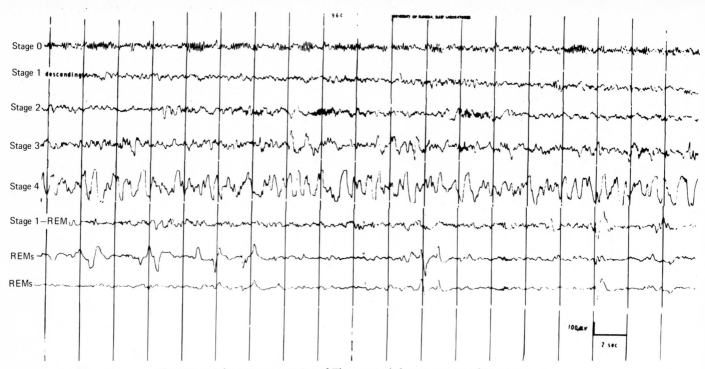

Fig. 36-1. *Schematic presentation of Electroencephalogram tracing of Sleep Stages.*

included this finding into a scoring system comprised of four non-REM stages of sleep (1 through 4) and Stage 1-REM. Currently this system, presented below, is the one most commonly used in describing the intrasleep process (Rechtshaffen & Kales 1968).

Figure 36-1 schematizes these EEG stages of sleep. Descriptively the criteria for these stages of sleep are as follows:

Stage 0: This stage is seen in the record of an awake, eyes-closed subject, as a rhythmic 8–12 cps activity in the occipital area with a minimum amplitude of 40 microvolts (peak to peak). This is the alpha rhythm.

Stage 1: This is a low voltage, desynchronized record. The record is generally indistinguishable from a highly alert subject whose eyes are open.

Stage 2: This stage is identified by "spindling" (rhythmic "bursts" of waves which are typically 12–15 cps but show individual variations) or by K-complexes typified by a brief, sharp, small wave and a sharp, high voltage, slower wave followed by a "tail" of faster waves. This K-complex is a "burst" type activity which follows sensory stimulation but occurs spontaneously during sleep.

Stage 3: This stage is marked by the appearance of the Stage 4 "slow waves" (.5–2 cps) of high amplitude (greater than 40 microvolts) as well as the continuation of the Stage 2 characteristics.

Stage 4: This stage is dominated by high voltage slow waves between .5 and 2 cps.

Stage 1-REM: This stage has a typical Stage 1 EEG accompanied by Rapid Eye Movements (which are usually monitored by an electrooculogram recorded on the EEG machine). A sharp decrease in electromygram (EM) taken from the hyoid region (Berger 1961) and the onset of penile erections (Fisher et al. 1965) are also typical. The Stage 1-REM sleep is usually

an "ascending Stage 1" emerging from Stage 2, in contrast to the "descending Stage 1" associated with sleep onset.

The characteristics of sleep associated with these measures will be presented in the section on intrasleep characteristics. Generally, Stages 1 through 4 represent a sleep depth continuum and Stage 1-REM is closely identified, in the human subject, with visual dreaming.

The scoring of EEG sleep records requires considerable training and care in order to achieve satisfactory reliability and validity (Webb & Agnew 1968a). For this reason and because of the likelihood that the stages are refinable, attempts are being made to use more sophisticated electronic techniques. Amplitude analysis was explored as early as 1935 (Kornmueller 1935) and frequency analysis as early as 1942 (Knott, Gibbs & Henry 1942). A recent report on amplitude analysis is that of Agnew et al. (1967a). More recent and refined frequency analyses are those of period analysis (Burch 1959) and spectral analysis using digital computers (Walter & Shipton 1951). The use of the average computer transient (CAT) responses to programmed inputs has also been explored (Williams et al., 1962).

SLEEP LENGTH

Length is one of the most obvious measures of sleep. The data which emerge from such a measure are reported in the following section. Although reliable self-reports can be obtained (Webb & Stone 1963), the grossness of this measure has limited it to early studies or broad group comparisons.

Patterns of Sleep and Waking

With a binary process within a set time period, such as sleep and waking in a twenty-four hour interval, there are a limited number of dimensions of variation. There is the total time occupied by the two elements, in this case, the total sleep and

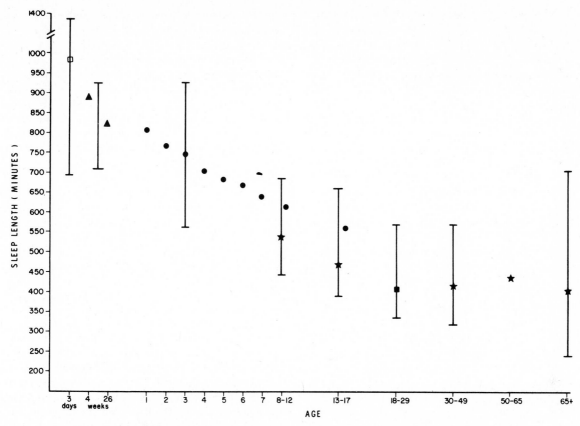

Fig. 36-2. *Hours of sleep per twenty-four hours for various age groups derived from six studies* [*see text*].

the total waking time. There are the number of events, i.e., the number of sleep periods and reciprocally the number of wake periods. There is the "density" or position of the events temporally, i.e., diurnal patterning of the amounts of sleep and waking within the twenty-four hours.

LENGTH OF SLEEP

The length of time asleep relative to the length of time awake has been reviewed elsewhere (Webb & Agnew 1968*a*). Figure 36-2 summarizes the data from this review. These data were derived from the following studies: Chant and Blatz (1928); Faegre and Anderson (1929); Flemming (1925); O'Connor (1964); Reynolds and Malloy (1933); Terman and Hocking (1913); Wagner (1933).

Besides the obvious age-linked character of the curve, two points are of particular interest in this figure. First, there is the considerable discrepancy of more than one hour between the two data points in the 8-12 and the 13-17 age groups. These data were collected more than fifty years apart in time (Terman 1913–O'Connor, 1964). Both sets of data are self-reports. It is likely that both data points are equally valid and reflect real culturally determined differences of sleep length. Terman noted in his paper discrepancies between his figures and those obtained in industrial settings in Germany and England. His data were collected in a small western community; the data from Florida were collected in a middle-sized community.

Secondly, there is a persistent range of sleep within the age

groupings. This is a particularly challenging problem for which there is little data. The sources of these differences are likely to be complex, e.g., genetics, early training, chronic physiological characteristics, environmental demands. Relevant studies such as those of Monroe (1967) on the characteristics of chronic insomniacs or Baekeland and Lasky (1966) on the sleep patterns of athletes have only recently begun to emerge. Although the question of the effects of these differences in sleep length received some attention in the 1920s, their results yielded quite conflicting findings (Moore 1922; Terman 1925; Fortune 1926). More recent studies relative to sleep length have been concerned with the effects of part-time reduction of sleep (see "partial deprivation"). Two recent studies concerning chronic "long" and "short" sleepers are also discussed in this section.

Positioning of Sleep

The typical human sleep pattern of the adult is a monophasic period of sleep during the night. The primary exception is the biphasic "siesta" pattern of the tropics and the semitropics, with an afternoon period of sleep in addition to the nocturnal period. There are no known studies of the prevalence or precise character of this pattern.

The organization of this adult pattern begins quite early. The systematic reorganization of the sleep process was studied by Kleitman and Engelmann (1953). In the third week nearly 57 percent of the sleep obtained was placed in the hours from 9:00 P.M. to 8:00 A.M.; by the twenty-sixth week, sleep during this time period constituted 73 percent of the total sleep. By the twenty-sixth week the daytime sleep had also become organized around two periods of time (from 10:00 A.M. to noon and 2:00 P.M. to 4:00 P.M.). By the end of the first year these daytime naps have typically consolidated into a single afternoon nap. Reynolds and Malloy (1933) report that afternoon naps, about 12 percent of the total sleep between the ages of 1 to 2, have decreased to 5 percent by the age of 4, and have dropped out entirely for 98 percent of their subjects by the age of 5. In addition, the night sleep period shows signs of consolidation. Moore and Ucko (1957) report 30 percent of the subjects awakening once between midnight and 5:00 A.M. at the age of 3 months, 17 percent at 6 months, and 10 percent at the end of one year.

There is evidence that the stability of this pattern of positioning begins to deteriorate with aging. Electroencephalographic studies (Agnew et al. 1967c; Feinberg et al. 1967; Kales et al. 1967) and questionnaire studies (McGhie 1962; O'Connor 1964) give clear indication that the nocturnal sleep pattern becomes "frayed" by increasingly frequent awakening (Table 36-1 below). Reports of increased "napping" in the elderly are common (Liberson 1945). On the other hand there is little evidence that the absolute amount of sleep increases (Figure 36-2), and the proportion of REM sleep appears relatively constant (Table 36-1).

Table 36-1. Average percentage of sleep stages for three nights of sleep for various age groups.

Age	Stage					
	0	1	2	3	4	REM
21–31 mo.	2	8	43	—	18	29
8–11 yr.	2	6	44	6	18	24
16–19 yr.	1	5	47	6	18	23
20–29 (male)	1	5	50	7	13	24
20–29 (female)	1	6	48	7	16	22
30–39	2	8	53	5	10	22
50–59	4	11	51	8	3	23
60–69	9	12	51	5	3	20
Stan. Dev.						
20–29 (female)	.9	2.7	8.7	3.5	4.6	3.1

Source: Webb & Agnew 1968a

Perhaps the primary question posed by the data on sleep positioning and sleep length is this: To what extent is this patterning and length a cultural pattern, and to what extent is it a naturalistic one? Edges of evidence support the role of both determinants. Sleep in the Arctic regions seems to result in a maintenance of a sleep length of about 7½ hours but shows signs of redistribution (Lewis & Masterson 1957). The studies of Kleitman in Trondheim, Norway, indicate a significant difference between sleep length during full dark and full light periods (Kleitman & Kleitman 1953). Sleep in sensory isolation results in a rapid fragmentation of the sleep patterning (Kato et al. 1968).

One final group of studies relevant to sleep positioning should be noted: those concerning displacement of sleep into different temporal periods. The jet age of today and the increasing use of "round-the-clock" shift work schedules have raised the questions about shifting of sleep from one period of time (e.g., 11:00 P.M. to 7:00 A.M.) to a different period (e.g., 8:00 A.M. to 4:00 P.M.). There is clear evidence that a performance decrement during the previous sleep period is present and persis-

tent (Wilkinson, R.T., personal communication). However, it is only recently that several studies have looked at the displaced sleep process (Kripke 1968; Weitzman et al. 1967; Webb and Agnew 1967). The findings of these studies are in agreement and somewhat surprising. In general the same percentages of sleep stages occur (with some evidence of "lightening" of sleep); however, the temporal distribution of these stages is clearly different from typical intrasleep cycling. The most striking tendency is for Stage 4 and REM sleep to be less clearly associated with the beginning and the end of the wake-sleep cycle respectively (see temporal distribution of sleep below).

Intrasleep Patterns

Figure 36-3 represents diagrammatically three nights of sleep of a single subject which have been scored for the six EEG stages of sleep and waking. Narratively and superficially, it is difficult to detect a patterning in this complex of changing events. On the first night, for example, the subject quickly went to sleep and during thirty minutes moved through equal stage lengths into Stage 4. Sleep onset is considerably more abrupt on the second night, and presents a still different pattern on the third night. On the first night, the first episode of Stage 4 is interrupted by a movement of some ten minutes through Stage 3 into Stage 2 and back into Stage 4. On the second night there is a brief return to Stage 3, and on the third night, the first Stage 4 episode is uninterrupted. On the first night the subject briefly wakened after about two and a half hours, there was no awakening on the second night, and an awakening occurred after about three and three-quarter hours on the third night. Although there are five REM episodes each night, their temporal placement differs from night to night.

Even in this single subject, however, the shape of a number of program characteristics of human sleep can be seen. These will be noted in our example as we discuss the programs below.

Sleep Stage Bands

First, it is clear that our subject did not simply sleep in one stage of sleep one night, another stage on the second night, and still a third on the third night. He shifted instead across all stages of sleep each night. Further he did not divide the night equally among these stages. Stage 2, in fact, occupied approximately 50 percent of each night, whereas REM sleep approximated 20 percent.

Table 36-1 presents data collected in our laboratories which show the average percentage slept in each stage for a wide age range of subjects. The standard deviation of the female 20–29 year group is also given in Table 36-1. The Stage 0 of this table is that occurring after the onset of the first Stage 1 period.

This table indicates that there are "bands" of sleep which are characteristic of human subjects and that these "bands" have different "weights" or "amounts" associated with them. The standard deviations shown for the 20–29 year females is typical across the age range for these sleep "bands." There is, however, an increase in range within stages at the extremes of the age distribution.

It is interesting that, although Stage 1-REM is remarkably stable from the age of 8–11 into the sixties, the overall tendency

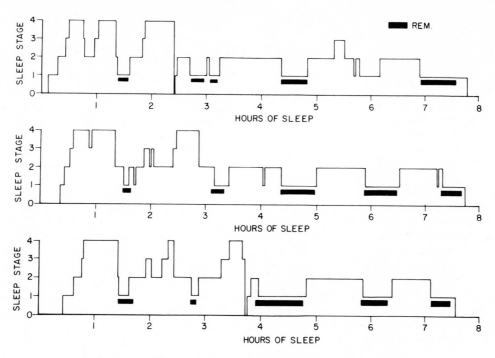

Fig. 36-3. *Sleep stages of a single subject over three nights of sleep.*

resulting from aging is toward a "lighter" sleep, a reduction in Stage 4, and an increase in Stage 0 and 1. A recent summary of the relationships between sleep and aging has found suggestions of a Stage 1-REM decrement in subjects beyond the age of 70 (Kahn & Fisher 1969).

INTRA-SUBJECT AND INTER-SUBJECT DIFFERENCES

In considering the overall percentages of sleep stages across the night without regard to precise point of temporal emergence, an interesting and critical question arises: Is there consistency in stage programming from night to night in terms of individual subjects? Our example in Figure 36-3 suggests such a possibility. This subject showed the following Stage 1-REM amounts across the three nights: 22 percent, 28 percent, 28 percent. Stage 4 percentages were 15, 16, and 14. To evaluate this possibility, intrastage subject correlations across three nights of recordings were obtained on the data appearing in Table 36-1. These are given in Table 36-2. These data are the average correlations between nights 2 and 3 and nights 3 and 4 from four nights of experimentally uninterrupted sleep periods. These, then, amount to correlations between two nights.

Table 36-2. Average night-to-night correlations of sleep stage amounts across three nights for various age groups.

Age	Stage					
	0	*1*	*2*	*3*	*4*	*REM*
8–11	.1	.4	.4	.7	.8	.5
16–19	.2	.3	.6	.2	.5	.3
20–29	.0	.4	.6	.7	.7	.5
30–39	.4	.4	.8	.3	.8	.4
50–59	.4	.6	.8	.7	.7	.6

Source: Webb & Agnew 1968a

Clearly the correlations are substantial. The lower correlations in the cases of Stage 0 and 1 are probably due both to the restricted amount of these stages and transient arousals resulting from external sources. In the older groups, where these stages are greater in amount, the correlations are higher (Table 36-1). In the case of Stage 1-REM, the generally lower correlations can be attributed to the restriction of range between subjects which is associated with this stage (Table 36-1).

SEQUENCING OF STAGES

A further reference to our example suggests another underlying pattern of events. The stages do not emerge at random; e.g., 1, 3, 2, 4, 1, etc. Rather, they seem to show an ordinal interrelationship to each other as noted in the onset of sleep. Table 36-3 attests to this. Basically, this table illustrates that the highest

Table 36-3. Ordinal interrelations between sleep stages. The stages of the horizontal columns are followed by the stages of the vertical columns.

		This sleep stage . . .				
		0	*1*	*2*	*3*	*4*
. . . is followed	0	—	9	3	—	1
by this stage	1	83%	—	50	5	11
	2	17%	91	—	37	37
	3	—	—	47	—	50
	4	—	—	—	57	—

probability of the next stage of sleep is the adjacent stage in the ordinal sequence of 1 through 4. REM sleep is preceded by and followed by Stage 2 with the few exceptions of Stage 1 without REM or brief awakenings (Stage 0).

In our example, it is difficult to predict the stage of sleep at any given time point after retiring. For example, at the second hour the subject was respectively in Stage 4, Stage 3, and Stage 2 on the three nights. However, considering the overall pattern of the night, two temporal characteristics emerge. First, Stage 4 seems to appear predominantly in the early part of the night, and Stage 1-REM toward the latter part. Secondly, there appears to be some consistency of spacing in the Stage 1-REM appearances. As we consider these trends across subjects and nights, we see evidence of such a systematic temporal programming of sleep. Figure 36-4 presents the data from thirty-two young male subjects recorded for three nights each, showing the mean hourly minutes spent in Stage 4 and Stage 1-REM. In addition, REM data from a study by Verdone (1968) are included. This has been found to be an exceedingly stable pattern within sleep. Evidence of this stability is discussed under the topic of "differential deprivation."

Evidence for a systematic cycling of onset times for REM was first presented by Dement and Kleitman (1957a) who noted that REM episodes tend to occur in regularly spaced intervals of about ninety minutes. Further evidence of this fixed interval cycling of REM has been presented by Hartmann (1968) and Webb and Agnew (1968a). This characteristic of REM sleep is also found in lower animals but with different episode intervals. The rat, for example, shows a stable interval of about seven minutes (Van Twyver 1969). Clearly then, the increase in REM, as a function of sleep time (Figure 36-4), results from increasing lengths of REM "bursts." Stage 4 is episodic as well but does not show a clear-cut fixed interval. The descending amount of Stage 4 as a function of time appears to be a function of two factors: variations in number of episodes (all nights having one episode with a few showing as many as six) and decreasing length of episodes.

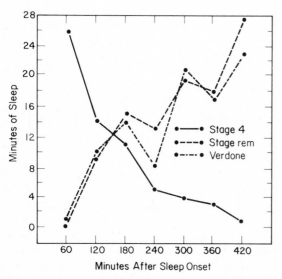

Fig. 36-4. *Minutes of Stage 4 and Stage 1-REM sleep by hours during the night of sleep.*

Dreams

The observation of Aserinsky and Kleitman (1953) that rapid eye movements during a Stage 1 EEG stage were closely associated with visual dreaming, and the explication of that relationship by Dement and Kleitman (1957b) initiated a massive new interest in dreams. This era of the experimental analysis of dreams has been called the "new" dream research to contrast with the earlier psychoanalytical research of dream content. This new research, which can be dated from 1957, has been indeed explosive. For example, in a recent supplement of *Experimental Neurology* (1957), "Physiological Correlates of Dreams," contains a bibliography of 221 items. Some 90 percent of these date from 1957. Hartmann's recent book (1967), *The Biology of Dreaming*, has a bibliography of 656 items, 85 percent of these dating from 1957.

This recent research ranges from biochemistry to content. It is impossible to summarize in detail this extensive literature. In this section we have selected for review three predominantly psychological questions: Stage 1-REM and non-REM content; dream recall; and the function of dreaming. We will consider dream deprivation in a later section.

REM and Non-REM Content

In a musical, *Man of La Mancha*, there is a song that states a most challenging task, ". . . to dream the impossible dream." This is the formidable challenge of the cognitive aspect of dream research. How does one "dream the impossible dream"? The content of dreams exists in the secret, silent world of each individual's sleep. It cannot be seen or heard at its time of occurrence, nor can it be reproduced. The person gives or does not give a verbal report of mental events which he could not have reported during the event and which neither he nor anyone else can recapture or objectify. Freud called dreams (and he could have only meant the recall of dreams) "the royal road to the unconsciousness." New dream research has found this a most rugged path.

Perhaps the best demonstration of the difficulty of the problem can be seen in the attempt to answer the question, Do dreams only occur during Stage 1-REM? In the original and elegantly systematic analysis of this question by Dement and Kleitman (1957b) dreams were noted upon awakening from Stage 1-REM sleep 84 percent of the time, and from non-REM sleep (Stage 1 without REM and Stages 2, 3, and 4) 7 percent of the time. The nature of these figures suggested that dreaming was associated only with the Stage 1-REM period and that the limited recall during the non-REM period and the lack of recall during the REM period were perhaps experimental errors.

Subsequent research has not let the problem stand in such neat simplicity. Foulkes (1967) in his review of non-REM mentation cites studies which range from 23 percent to 74 percent of recall of mental activity on awakening. Hartmann (1967) in reviewing recall from Stage 1-REM cites studies which range from 60 percent to 88 percent recall on awakening.

One of the prime difficulties lies in the problem of the definition of the dream. One study, for example, defines the dream as a "coherent, fairly detailed description of dream content"

(Dement & Kleitman 1957b). In this study subjects who had dreamed without recalling the content or who reported vague fragments of content were counted in the negative. Another study defined the dream as "any occurrence with visual, auditory, or kinesthetic imagery or any phenomenon lacking such imagery but in which the subject either assumed another identity than his own or felt he was thinking in a physical setting other than that in which he actually was" (Foulkes 1962). Clearly, with such a range of definitions, findings are likely to vary.

The problems of sleep mentation, however, extend well beyond definitional ones. Foulkes, who has most intensively explored the non-REM mentation phenomena, notes three theoretical assumptions which create bases of reluctance for accepting non-REM mentations:

(a) while the low-voltage, random EEG or REM sleep is compatible with the existence of ongoing thought processes, the high-voltage, low frequency EEG of non-REM sleep is not; (b) a report of a mental experience is not credible unless supported by public behavioral or physiological observation; and (c) REM sleep is so vastly different physiologically from non-REM sleep that there must also be a vast psychological difference between the two, such as vivid dreaming versus little or no mental activity (Foulkes 1967 p. 31).

In defending the status of mentation during non-REM sleep, Foulkes accepts the fact that non-REM reports can be distinguished from Stage 1-REM reports (Foulkes 1962; Rechtshaffen et al. 1963) and that the former are relatively less "dream like" and more "thought like." However, he points out that these same studies describe the "modal" non-REM report as a "dream"; that discrimination is not a simple task (Monroe et al. 1965); and that there is a content interrelationship within subjects between the two forms (Foulkes 1962; Rechtshaffen et al. 1963). In short, Foulkes concludes the non-REM reports are "functionally similar to, rather than radically different from, those obtained from REM sleep" (Foulkes 1967, p. 38).

The most recent research in this area has been focused on a "phasic" and "non-phasic" dichotomy within the Stage 1-REM period. It is increasingly evident that Stage 1-REM period is not a homogeneous condition but characterized by "phasic" periods in which eye movements and other physiological states are highly active and other periods during which only the Stage 1-EEG is present. Molinari and Foulkes (1969) have recently demonstrated that recall characteristics during non-phasic Stage 1-REM more closely resemble recall from non-REM periods than "phasic" Stage 1-REM periods. When to this is added the presence in the non-REM period of lateral geniculate spiking activity which is closely associated with the phasic Stage 1-REM periods (Dement 1967), we may see the breakdown of the "classical" non-REM–Stage 1-REM dichotomy in the near future.

The persistent overlap found between Stage 1-REM and non-REM mentation, and the difficulties of defining dreaming by either the EEG or verbal reports have led Stoyva and Kamiya (1968) to propose that dreaming be defined "as a hypothetical construct, not directly accessible to public observation. This hypothetical construct is indexed, but indexed in an imperfect way, by both REM's and verbal report" (p. 199).

THE RECALL OF DREAMS

As noted above, some 80 percent or more of the awakenings from REM sleep result in a dream recall. We may infer from this that, during a great part of the typical ninety minutes or more of REM sleep which occurs each night, the person is experiencing the often vivid state of dreams. In spite of these facts there is often no recall of dreaming on awakening in the morning. Moreover, the recall that does occur is often quite limited and certainly not a recall of some eighty minutes of dreams.

It may be noted that the amount of morning dream recall closely approximates the amount that would be predicted from laboratory dream research. When asked during the day, 37.5 percent of a large group of subjects reported that they had recalled a dream that morning. An analysis of the last hour of sleep records of thirty-two subjects over three nights showed that the probability of awakening during a Stage 1-REM state during that hour was 45 percent. Recall of a dream upon arousal from a REM state would be expected to occur about 84 percent of the time. Hence the 37.5 percent recall of dreams on arousal would have been predicted ($.84 \times .45 = 37.8$) (Webb & Kersey 1967).

These overall figures, however, do not relate to at least two major points of interest in dream recall: individual differences in recall and the nonrecall of the extensive amounts of dreaming which occur prior to arousal.

INDIVIDUAL DIFFERENCES

Many individuals report almost no dreams and others often recall dreams. It is less difficult to account for the high recallers than the nonrecallers. One may suggest that high recallers are "set" or learn to awaken during REM episodes. The study above, for example, reported that 20 of 32 subjects had a Stage 1-REM episode on all 3 nights studied in their last half hour of sleep (Webb & Kersey 1967). Or there is the possibility that S's are "set" or learn to "recapture" the dream on arousal. The method of arousal may be different for high recallers and favor dream recall; e.g., abrupt arousals result in higher dreamlike recall (Foulkes 1966, Chap. 2).

It is more difficult, however, to account for nonrecall, and perhaps because of this problem, nonrecallers have been more often studied. It should be noted that nonrecallers, defined by morning recall reports, do indeed recall less on awakening from Stage 1-REM. In fact they recall dreams on only about one-half the number of occasions of arousal when compared with controls (Goodenough et al. 1959). For nonrecallers the *amount* of Stage 1-REM time is only slightly reduced; however, the characteristics of Stage 1-REM are different (Antrobus et al. 1964). Surprisingly, the nonrecaller's REM periods are characterized by both a higher alpha percentage and a higher number of eye movements per unit time. There are also differences in personality characteristics of nonrecallers. Using personality tests, several studies have found the nonrecallers to have the tendency to deny anxieties, and show signs of repression, inhibition, and defensiveness (Schonbar 1959; Singer & Schonbar 1961; Tart 1962). However, Lachman et al. (1962) did not find nonrecallers to be "repressors."

The most elaborate recent discussion of this problem of individual differences may be found in Goodenough (1967).

There is, however, the more general problem of nonrecall beyond the question of the relatively low level of recall by certain subjects. How may one account for the general absence of recall for the one and a half hours of mental activity which occur each night? Four general notions have been suggested: (1) repression; (2) conditions for poor learning and retention; (3) "consolidation" difficulties; and (4) limiting neurophysiological conditions.

The repression of dreams as an explanation of nonrecall clearly stems from orthodox Freudian theory. Dreams represent the emergence of the repressed in the lower resistance state of sleep, and awakening reinstitutes the state of repression. Two studies are directly relevant to this issue. One study found that the more intense dreams reported on REM awakening were better remembered than less intense dreams on the following morning (Meier et al. 1968). The authors inferred that this supports the prediction of classical memory theory and was contrary to the psychoanalytic theory. Whitman et al. (1963) studied dreams of patients reported to an experimenter on REM awakening and later reported to their therapist. They concluded, on the basis of a few dreams which were reported to either the experimenter or the therapist but not both, that the crucial variable seems to be ". . . the current and/or transference relationship between the dreamer and listener and the fantasy of how the listener will receive the content" (p. 281).

Meier et al. (above) would favor an explanation of forgetting based on classical memory theory. Studying 198 Stage 1-REM awakenings of a single subject and their reported content in their relationship to morning recall, they found that recency, intensity, amount of material, and intraserial interference influenced the morning recall of dreams in a fashion predictable from classical memory theory. Several other aspects of dream recall which would predict poor recall can also be cited: low set to recall or learn (analogous to incidental learning paradigms); limited feedback and/or response level; difficulties of encoding and storing unfamiliar or bizarre material; nonrepetitive presentation; effects of retroactive inhibition on poorly learned material.

A third explanatory candidate is a variant of classical memory theories. It proposes that poor conditions for "consolidation" are responsible for nonrecall. A most impressive study in support of this position is the study of Portnoff et al. (1966). Subjects were awakened from non-REM sleep and presented verbal learning materials. The latency of the subsequent non-REM onset was varied. Material presented immediately prior to non-REM onset was more poorly retained than material followed by a period of wakefulness. The authors concluded that non-REM sleep may be a state which impedes consolidation of memory traces.

Finally, there is the suggestion that the neurophysiological state of the brain during sleep is not one in which learning or retention can effectively occur. We would note here the earlier work on sleep learning by Simon and Emmons (1955) which suggested that retention of material presented during the sleep period could only occur in the presence of alpha rhythms and that alpha rhythms are absent almost continuously throughout the night. We would further refer to a paper by Brazier (1967) which specifically analyzes this "brain state" hypothesis relative to the more recent findings of the neurophysiologist and memory.

The Function of Dream Sleep

In a recent book the complaint was voiced ". . . that sleep research has been almost exclusively atheoretical in its general approach and has been diligently devoted to the collection of empirical facts" (Webb 1968, p. 56). In regard to sleep, per se, this statement continues to be accurate. Little in the way of theorizing regarding the role and function of sleep can be found beyond the summary statements of Kleitman (1963). In contrast, there is a plethora of speculation, hypotheses, and theorizing regarding the function of Stage 1-REM sleep. These speculations range from attempts to specify or organize the neurophysiological bases of dreaming, statements regarding the function of dreams in physiological or psychological terms, and "models" to account for various groupings of data. The more elaborate considerations frequently blend all of these elements. Because of this overlap, the grouping of the hypotheses into the three categories below of physiological, functional, and psychic can represent only emphasis rather than effective coding.

PHYSIOLOGICAL HYPOTHESES

Pontine. The work of Jouvet (Jouvet & Jouvet 1963) established a critical role for the caudal-pontine area in REM activation. As a result, this area has been conceptualized as a "dream center". The fact that the pontine is in the "old" or rhombencephalic part of the brain has led to much speculation about the "primitive" character of dreaming. Little has been done to elaborate the functional aspects of this dream center.

Geniculate-Cortical. The presence of high voltage spike waves focused in the lateral geniculate body during Stage 1-REM sleep has been suggested as a potential candidate for accounting for the visual imagery aspects of dreaming (Moruzzi 1963). Dement (1967) has recently elaborated the role of lateral geniculate activity in dream recall.

Cortical-Limbic. The most elaborate attempt to relate the neurophysiological complex and the dream state has been that of Hernandez-Peon (1967). In a paper published shortly before his recent death he outlined a complex inhibitory-facilitory system to account for dreams. He hypothesized that there would be a disinhibition of the cortical and limbic neurons associated with muscle and motivation systems. This would be consecutive to the inhibition of vigilance neurons by the "hypnogenic neurons of the sleep system." The neo- and paleocortical neurons associated with recent and remote memory would underlie the manifest content of dreams, and the limbic neurons would interact giving rise to the latent content. The subjective experience itself would be accomplished by the specialized integrative center that Hernandez-Peon has hypothesized as being in the rostral part of the brain stem. As with many of his contributions, Hernandez-Peon elaborately supports these complex notions with phylogenetic considerations as well as electrophysiological and biochemical data.

Metabolic. The function attributed to the Stage 1-REM state has been that of clearing the nervous system of some form of endogenous metabolite built up within the nervous system (Dement 1966).

Endogenous Stimulation. There have been two suggestions that the REM period serves as a form of endogenous stimulation. The first of these (Roffwarg et al. 1966) emphasized the role that such stimulation may play in the developing cortex of the infant. The second of these viewed the Stage 1-REM period as a homeostatic, endogenous stimulation to offset the within sleep reduced exogenous stimulation which is ordinarily present in the waking state (Ephron & Carrington 1966).

Evolutionary. This hypothesis suggests that Stage 1-REM sleep has an evolutionary and biological function, functioning as an activation within the unprotected sleep period which reorients the animal for protection (Snyder 1963).

Psychic. The psychoanalytical theories proposed, primarily, that dreams were forms of wish fulfillment (Freud), or problem solving (Adler). Generally these theories also viewed the dream as protecting the sleeper from awakening. A recent elaboration of this psychoanalytical position suggested that dreams discharge drives (Fisher 1965). In an extensive review of the Freudian dream theory, Breger (1967) critiques and reanalyzes the psychoanalytical theory and hypothesizes that the dream plays a role in the "assimilation and mastery of arousal material into 'solutions' embodied in existing arousary systems."

Computer. A number of recent theories, using the analogy of the computer, have suggested that the dream state is a period during which irrelevant and unneeded information is "cleared" (Evans & Newman 1964; Gaarder 1966), memories are transferred from short term to long term storage systems, or that the dream period permits a playback and sorting of sensory experiences (Shapiro 1967).

Sleep Deprivation

Perhaps the most embarrassing unanswered question about sleep research is the fundamental one: What is the need for sleep? The classical approach has been to deprive the subject of the need in question and then examine the consequences. We shall review sleep deprivation in terms of three paradigms of deprivation: total, partial, and differential.

The earliest systematic work on total deprivation of sleep by Manaceine (1897) established death as its ultimate consequence. Puppies died after from 92 to 143 hours of total deprivation. Patrick and Gilbert in 1896 initiated the research on sleep deprivation in performance. The succeeding experiments have

resulted in promising leads, paradoxical failures of replication, and an emerging clarification of the performance decrements associated with sleep deprivation. Little has emerged to inform us about the fundamental core need for sleep.

Although early workers reported death and the appearance of postmortem damage, Legendre and Pieron (1907, 1908) found that their animals were in good physical condition after 500 hours of sleep deprivation. Although they noted neurological change, particularly in the Nissl structure of the prefrontal cortex, these changes were reversible (1907). Kleitman (1927), similarly working with puppies and deprivation periods of from one to seven days, states that neurological examinations and autonomic measures were within the limits exhibited by control animals.

The results of prolonged deprivation in human subjects vary from reports of protracted psychiatric disturbances (West et al. 1962) to a report of a subject deprived of sleep for 264 hours who, ". . . aside from quite evident mental and physical fatigue, showed no significant abnormalities" (Ross 1965). Indeed, recently we have indication of at least a partial recovery of autonomic and electroencephalographic measures during deprivation (Naitoh et al. 1967).

There are, of course, behavioral effects of deprivation. One of the most adequate descriptions of these effects is found in Kleitman:

While there were differences in the subjective experiences of the many sleep-evading persons, there were several features common to most . . . during the first night the subject did not feel very tired or sleepy. He could read or study or do laboratory work, without much attention from the watcher, but usually felt an attack of drowsiness between 3: 00 A.M. and 6: 00 A.M. The drowsiness was accompanied by an unpleasant itching of the eyes. Next morning the subject felt well, except for a slight malaise which always appeared on sitting down and resting for any length of time. However, if he occupied himself with his ordinary daily tasks, he was likely to forget having spent a sleepless night. During the second night the individual's condition was entirely different. His eyes not only itched but felt dry, and he could abolish that sensation only by closing his eyes, which made it extremely hard to remain fully awake, even if walking. Reading or study was next to impossible because sitting quietly was conducive to even greater sleepiness. As during the first night, there came a 2-3 hour period in the early hours of the morning when the desire for sleep was almost overpowering. At this time the subject often saw double. Later in the morning the sleepiness diminished once more, and the subject could perform routine laboratory work, as usual. It was not safe for him to sit down, however, without the danger of falling asleep, particularly if he attended lectures. . . . All efforts could be sustained for only a short time. An example of this failure was the repeated inability of the subject to count his own pulse for as long as a minute. After counting to 15 or 20, he invariably lost track of the numbers and would find himself dozing off.

The third night resembled the second, and the fourth day was like the third. . . . At the end of that time the individual was as sleepy as he was likely to be. Those who continued to stay awake experienced the wavelike increase and decrease in sleepiness with the greatest drowsiness at about the same time every night (Kleitman 1963, p. 220).

A recent extensive review of the research on behavioral

effects of total deprivation (Naitoh 1969) can be summarized as follows:

Factors which increase the likelihood of deprivation effects are: time of testing within the 24-hour cycle (midnight to 8:00 A.M.); longer task duration; increased work; work-paced tasks; increasing complexity; and short term memory demands.

Factors which offset deprivation effects are: time of testing within the 24-hour cycle (8:00 A.M. to noon); short term tasks; automatic skills; self-paced tasks; knowledge of results; moderate physical exercise; drugs; and personal motivation.

One of the most viable interpretations of the behavior effects has used a "lapse" model in which performance capacity is not conceived of as "running down" but rather being subjected to intermittent performance "lapses" which increase with continuing deprivation (Williams et al. 1959). To this model must be added the components of "motivational" or "compensational" or "mobilizational" responses on the part of the subject.

Total deprivation has thus left us with a most puzzling picture. On one hand, we have our own clear subjective evidence of total sleep loss effects and substantial reports of devastating effects in both animals and humans in both physiological and psychological measures. Yet there are the reported instances in which these effects are far less than were expected and often surprizingly negligible. Naitoh (1968) in an attempt to resolve this problem has recently suggested that perhaps total sleep deprivation does not occur but rather that subjects are being sustained physiologically by Stage 1 sleep, i.e., that total sleep deprivation is in essence a form of differential sleep deprivation in Stages 2, 3, 4, and Stage 1-REM. Certainly this hypothesis deserves further consideration.

PARTIAL DEPRIVATION

Three factors make the question of partial sleep deprivation (a jargonized expression for not getting enough sleep) of particular interest. First, it is the most natural and prevalent modification of sleep. Secondly, it is probably the most practical aspect of sleep to study. If sleep could be reduced by ten to twenty percent without significant consequences, man's living existence could be markedly enhanced. If a person who sleeps seven hours per day, for example, slept only six hours beginning at the age of twenty, he would be existentially present in this world between the ages of twenty and seventy a total of 18,250 hours more. Since his waking days would ordinarily have been seventeen hours long, he would have added some 1,073 days to his existence. Finally, for the sleep researcher, partial deprivation is an interesting methodological situation; partial deprivation which results from early awakening is in fact differential deprivation. This follows from Figure 36.4 where it will be noted that reduction of sleep by eliminating the last part of the sleep cycle results in little or no Stage 4 deprivation but significant Stage 1-REM deprivation.

There have been four recent studies concerned with experimentally restricting sleep regimes (Webb & Agnew 1965; Sampson 1965; Dement & Greenberg 1966; Rush et al. 1968). These studies are in good agreement. When sleep is reduced by about two hours, there is little increase in Stage 4 on subsequent nights. When there is an increase in deprivation time, however, there is an increase in Stage 4 sleep within the restricted period. There is, as expected, a marked Stage 1-REM depriva-

tion and an associated Stage 1-REM "oversleep" on recovery nights, and there is evidence that Stage 1-REM "moves" forward into the restricted period if that period is prolonged. This move forward, however, is slow and by no means effectively accomplished in seven days.

Two recent studies have been concerned with the behavioral consequences of restricted sleep. Both of these studies focused on performance measures, although the Wilkinson studies (1968) were interpreted in motivational terms. Webb and Agnew (1965) found a deterioration of performance on three short term tasks on the seventh and eighth nights of a three hour per twenty-four hour regime, although these decrements ". . . were neither uniform nor fully consistent." Wilkinson assessed the effects of restricted regimes of one, two, three, and five hours of sleep per twenty-four hours by using day-long testing on a vigilance task and an addition task. He found evidence of performance decrements under all four conditions. In interpreting his results by using signal detection theory he found evidence that the different regimes and their associated differential deprivations resulted in different basis of performance decrements. In brief, the more limited deprivation had little or no effect on "capacity to perform" but affected the "willingness or motivation to perform." These would represent the effect of REM deprivation but limited Stage 4 deprivation. Regimes of three hours or less affected "capacity to perform." He concluded that ". . . the impression was gained that Stage 4 sleep and Stage 1-REM sleep may influence respectively the capacity and willingness to carry out sensory decrements. . . ." These studies have their unfortunate limitations in that the longest lasted seven nights and these regimes were imposed on already established patterns of longer sleep.

Two studies have recently been reported on sleep characteristics of chronically restricted regimes. One study analyzed the sleep patterns of high-school students who chronically slept less than six and a half hours per night (Webb & Agnew 1968b). It was found that these "short sleepers" obtained the same amounts of Stage 1-REM sleep as an unselected population (who averaged an hour more sleep per night). This would indicate that REM sleep can and does "adjust" forward in time. Jones and Oswald (1968) have reported on the sleep of two subjects who averaged three hours of sleep per twenty-four hours within one sleep period each day. For the two subjects it was found that approximately fifty percent of this sleep was Stage 3–4 type sleep (80–90 percent of sleep periods averaging 165 minutes). On the other hand Stage 1-REM sleep occupied only about forty minutes of the sleep periods. During the twenty-four hours this, of course, represents a severe Stage 1-REM deprivation. If Stage 1-REM is considered as intrasleep process which is related to increased amount of sleep, it is possible to interpret the Jones and Oswald data in other than deprivation terms.

DIFFERENTIAL SLEEP DEPRIVATION

As we have noted, partial sleep deprivation is a form of differential sleep deprivation. It is experimentally feasible, however, to specifically deprive subjects of Stage 1-REM or Stage 4 sleep throughout the night.

Dement reported the first of the studies (Dement 1960). Subjects' sleep was monitored by the EEG and they were awakened from sleep upon the appearance of each Stage 1-REM episode. Over successive nights the number of arousals required increased markedly and, following nights of uninterrupted sleep, there was a statistically significant increase in Stage 1-REM sleep over preexperimental baseline amounts. Dement further noted the presence of mild to moderate psychological disturbances. Subsequent studies have invariably confirmed the necessity of an increased number of arousals as a function of increased deprivation and the recovery effects of Stage 1-REM "rebound" on the uninterrupted nights following deprivation. The findings of psychological disturbances have been more equivocal. Kales, et al. (1964), and Snyder (1962), noted no substantial psychic changes. Sampson (1965) found no significant changes on limited psychological testing. However, he noted certain behavioral changes similar to those reported by Dement and Fisher (1963): increased appetite, disturbances in reality relationships, instances of childish behavior, and aggressiveness. More recently three experiments, using psychological tests, have reported discernible Stage 1-REM deprivation effects. Clemes and Dement (1967) reported an increase in "need and feeling intensity with a drop in certain ego control functions." Greenberg et al. (1966), using projective tests, noted the emergence of "that which seemed well defended against." Agnew et al. (1967b), found indications ". . . that subjects became less well-integrated and less interpersonally effective."

These trends receive considerable support from animal studies involving Stage 1-REM deprivation. Jouvet (1967) reported "hallucinatory" behavior, hyperactivity, and increased appetitive behavior in cats operatively deprived of Stage 1-REM sleep by lesions. Such cats ultimately died in "manic delirium" if Stage 1-REM sleep did not reappear. Dement (1966) and his coworkers have reported a wide variety of "heightened drive" behavior resulting from REM deprivation; hypersexuality, increased grooming, individual fighting, increased spontaneous activity, and more rapid acquisition of avoidance behavior.

Stage 4 deprivation has received less attention, perhaps because of its lack of a psychic penumbra of dreams. Shortly after the initial Stage 1-REM deprivation experiment, a Stage 4 deprivation for four days demonstrated a similar increased requirement in the number of stimulations required to prevent appearance of Stage 4 and a small but significant rebound or recovery effect on subsequent, uninterrupted nights of sleep (Agnew et al. 1964). A second study (reported below) confirmed these findings and noted from psychological test results the fact that ". . . subjects became physically uncomfortable, withdrawn, less aggressive and manifested concern over vague physical complaints . . ." (Agnew et al. 1967b).

More recently, a comparative study of the two forms of differential deprivation has been reported (Agnew et al. 1967b). After four nights of baseline recording, two groups of six subjects each were treated identically except that one group was Stage 1-REM deprived and the other group, Stage 4 deprived. A brief but strong electric shock was administered on the appearance of the specific stage of sleep and continued until the indices of this stage had disappeared.[1] The three recovery nights were recorded. Results of this comparison strongly suggest these differential deprivations have different effects. At the beginning of the experiment almost six times the number of stimulations were required to eliminate Stage 4 from sleep when compared

---

[1] It is interesting to note that after the first night there were few actual awakenings.

with Stage 1-REM, and by the seventh night the amount of stimulation required was still some three times that for Stage 1-REM, although Stage 1-REM stimulus requirements had increased almost threefold during the experiment. In terms of rebound, however, Stage 4 showed a recovery within one night, whereas the rebound effects of Stage 1-REM continued to persist throughout the recorded three nights. As noted above, different psychological responses were noted in this comparative study. On one hand the REM deprivation subjects appeared to have lowered ego control and high sensitivity to stimulation, whereas the Stage 4 resulted in hypoactivity and a lowered response base.

Other Relevant Research Areas

Because of space limitations and/or less direct psychological relevance, a considerable portion of the research on sleep has been omitted or given only passing reference. To somewhat amend these limitations, this section lists some of these areas with recent relevant sources for further reading.

1. *Neurophysiology and physiology of sleep and dreams:* Jouvet (1967); Akert et al. (1965); Hartmann (1967, Chaps. 4–5); Koella (1967, Chaps. 1 and 7); Kety, Evarts, and Williams (1967, Chaps. 1, 8, 9, and 12); Jouvet (1965).
2. *Phylogeny and comparative aspects of sleep and dreams:* Hartmann (1967, Chap. 2); Snyder (1963); Kales (1969).
3. *Ontogeny of dreams:* Roffwarg et al. (1966); Hartmann (1967, Chap. 3).
4. *Psychopathology of sleep and dreams:* Hartmann (1967, Chaps. 9 and 10); Murray (1965, Chap. 8); Broughton (1968); Kety, Evarts, and Williams (1967, Chaps. 10, 18, and 21); Feinberg, 1967; Hawkins et al. (1967).
5. *Biochemistry of sleep and dreams:* Hartmann (1967, Chap. 7); Koella (1967); Kety, Evarts, and Williams (1967, Chaps. 4–7); Jouvet (1965, Sec. 1).
6. *Dream content:* Foulkes (1964); Domhoff and Kamiya (1964); Witkin and Lewis (1967, Chaps. 2 and 4).
7. *Dreams and hypnosis:* Tart (1965).

References

ABT, L. A., and RIESS, B. F. (eds.) *Progress in clinical psychology*, vol. 7. New York: Grune & Stratton, 1968.

AGNEW, H. W., JR., PARKER, J. C., WEBB, W. B., and WILLIAMS. R. L. Amplitude measurement of the sleep electroencephalogram. *Electroencephalography and Clinical Neurophysiology*, 1967a, 22, 84–86.

AGNEW, H. W., JR., WEBB, W. B., and WILLIAMS, R. L. The effects of stage four sleep deprivation. *Electroencephalography and Clinical Neurophysiology*, 1964, 17, 68–70.

———. Comparison of stage four and 1-REM sleep deprivation. *Perceptual and Motor Skills*, 1967b, 24, 851–58.

———. Sleep patterns in late middle age males: An EEG study. *Electroencephalography and Clinical Neurophysiology*, 1967c, 23, 168–71.

AKERT, K., BALLY, C., AND SCHADE, J. P., eds. *Sleep mechanisms* (Progress in Brain Research, vol. 18). Amsterdam: Elsevier, 1965.

ANDREEV, B. V. Actograph applicable in the clinic for the objective study of sleep. *Klinicheskaia Meditsina* (Moscow), 1951, 29, 81–82.

ANTROBUS, J., DEMENT, W., and FISHER, C. Patterns of dreaming and dream recall: An EEG study. *Journal of Abnormal and Social Psychology*, 1964, 69, 341–44.

ASERINSKY, E., and KLEITMAN, N. Regularly occurring periods of eye motility and concomitant phenomena during sleep. *Science*, 1953, *118*, 273–74.

BAEKELAND, F., and LASKY, R. Exercise and sleep patterns in college athletes. *Perceptual and Motor Skills*, 1966, *23*, 1203–7.

BERGER, R. J. Tonus of extrinsic laryngeal muscles during sleep and dreaming. *Science*, 1961, *134*, 840.

BRAZIER, M. A. B. Absence of dreaming or failure to recall? *Experimental Neurology Supplement*, 1967, *4*, 91–98.

BREGER, L. Function of dreams. *Journal of Abnormal Psychology*, 1967, *72*, 1–28.

BROUGHTON, R. J. Sleep disorders: Disorders of arousal? *Science*, 1968, *159*, 1070–78.

BURCH, N. R. Automatic analysis of the electroencephalogram: A review and classification of systems. *Electroencephalography and Clinical Neurophysiology*, 1959, *11*, 827–34.

CHANT, N., and BLATZ, W. A study of sleeping habits of children. *Genetic and Psychological Monographs*, 1928, *4*, 13–43.

CLEMES, S. R., and DEMENT, W. C. Effect of REM sleep deprivation on psychological functioning. *Journal of Nervous and Mental Disorders*, 1967, *144*, 485–91.

DEMENT, W. C. The effect of dream deprivation. *Science*, 1960, *131*, 1705–7.

———. Psychophysiology of sleep and dreams. *In* S. Arieti (ed.) *American Handbook of Psychiatry*, vol. 3. New York: Basic Books, 1966.

———. Possible physiological determinants of a possible dream intensity cycle. *Experimental Neurological Supplement*, 1967, *4*, 38–55.

———, and FISHER, C. Experimental interference with the sleep cycle. *Canadian Psychiatric Association Journal*, 1963, *8*, 400–405.

DEMENT, W. C., and GREENBERG, S. Changes in total amount of stage four sleep as a function of partial sleep deprivation. *Electroencephalography and Clinical Neurophysiology*, 1966, *20*, 523–26.

DEMENT, W. C., and KLEITMAN, N. Cyclic variations in EEG during sleep and their relation to eye movements, body motility, and dreaming. *Electroencephalography and Clinical Neurophysiology*, 1957a, *9*, 673–90.

———. The relation of eye movements during sleep to dream activity. *Journal of Experimental Psychology*, 1957b, *53*, 339–46.

DEMENT, W. C., and WOLPERT, E. A. The relation of eye movements, body motility, and external stimuli to dream content. *Journal of Experimental Psychology*, 1958, *55*, 543–53.

DOMHOFF, B., and KAMIYA, J. Problems in dream content study with objective indicators: 1. A comparison of home and laboratory dream reports. 2. Appearance of experimental situation in laboratory dream narratives. 3. Changes in dream content throughout the night. *Archives of General Psychiatry*, 1964, *11*, 519–24; 525–28; 529–32.

EPHRON, H. S., and CARRINGTON, P. Rapid eye movement sleep and cortical homeostasis. *Psychological Review*, 1966, *73*, 500–526.

EVANS, C. R., and NEWMAN, E. A. Dreaming: An analogy from computers. *New Science*, 1964, *24*, 577–79.

FAEGRE, M. L., and ANDERSON, J. F. *Child Care and Training*. Minneapolis: University of Minnesota Press, 1929.

FEINBERG, I. Sleep electroencephalographic and eye-movement patterns in patients with schizophrenia and with chronic brain syndrome. *In* S. S. Kety, E. V. Evarts, and H. L. Williams (eds.) *Sleep and altered states of consciousness*. Baltimore: Williams & Wilkins, 1967.

———, KORENSKO, R. L., and HELLER, N. EEG sleep patterns as a function of normal and pathological aging in man. *Journal of Psychiatric Research*, 1967, *5*, 107–44.

FISHER, C. Psychoanalytic implications of recent research on sleep and dreaming. 1. Empirical findings. 2. The relationship of instinctual drives to physiological processes. *Journal of the American Psychoanalytic Association*, 1965, *13*, 197–270; 271–303.

———, GROSS, J., and ZUCH, J. Cycle of penile erection synchronous with dreaming (REM) sleep. *Archives of General Psychiatry*, 1965, *12*, 29–45.

FLEMMING, B. M. A study of the sleep of young children. *Journal of the American Association of University Women*, 1925, *19*, 25–27.

FORTUNE, R. F. Sleep and muscular work. The effect of sleep on the ability to perform muscular work. *Australian Journal of Psychology*, 1926, *4*, 36–40.

FOULKES, W. D. Dream reports from different stages of sleep. *Journal of Abnormal Social Psychology*, 1962, *65*, 14–25.

———. Theories of dream formation and recent studies of sleep consciousness. *Psychological Bulletin*, 1964, *62*, 236–47.

———. *The psychology of sleep*. New York: Scribner's, 1966.

———. NREM mentation. *Experimental Neurology*, 1967, Supplement 4, 28–38.

GAARDER, K. R. A conceptual model of sleep. *Archives of General Psychiatry*, 1966, *14*, 253–60.

GOODENOUGH, D. R. Some recent studies of dream recall. *In* H. A. Witkin and H. B. Lewis (eds.), *Experimental Studies of Dreaming*. New York: Random House, 1967.

———, SHAPIRO, A., HOLDEN, M., and STEINSCHRIBER, L. A. A comparison of "dreamers" and "nondreamers": eye movements, electroencephalograms, and the recall of dreams. *Journal of Abnormal Social Psychology*, 1959, *59*, 295–302.

GREENBERG, R., KAWLICHE, S., and PEARLMAN, C. Dream deprivation study. Report to the Association for the Psychophysiological Study of Sleep, Gainesville, March, 1966.

HARTMANN, E. L. *The biology of dreaming*. Springfield, Ill.: Charles C Thomas, 1967.

———. The 90-Minute Sleep-Dream Cycle. *Archives of General Psychiatry*, 1968, *18*, 280–86.

HAWKINS, D. R., MENDELS, J., SCOTT, J., BENSCH, G., and TEACHEY, W. The psychophysiology of sleep in psychotic depression: A longitudinal study. *Psychosomatic Medicine*, 1967, *29*, 329–44.

HERNANDEZ-PEON, R. Neurophysiology, phylogeny, and functional significance of dreaming. *Experimental Neurology Supplement*, 1967, *4*, 106–25.

JONSON, H. M., and SWAN, T. H. Sleep. *Psychological Bulletin*, 1930, *27*, 1–39.

JOHNSON, L. C., and LUBIN, A. Spontaneous electrodermal activity during waking and sleeping. *Psychophysiology*, 1966, *3*, 8–17.

JONES, H. S., and OSWALD, I. Two cases of healthy insomnia. *Electroencephalography and Clinical Neurophysiology*, 1968, *24*, 378–80.

JOUVET, M. *Aspects anatomo-fonctionnels de la physiologie du sommeil* (Lyon Symposium). Paris: Editions Du Centre National De La Recherche Scientifique, 1965.

———. Neurophysiology of the states of sleep. *Physiological Review*, 1967, *47*, 117–77.

———, and JOUVET, D. A study of the neurophysiological mechanisms of dreaming. *Electroencephalography and Clinical Neurophysiology*, 1963, Supplement 24, 133–57.

KAHN, E., and FISHER, C. The sleep characteristics of the normal aged male. *Journal of Nervous Mental Disorders*, 1969, *148*, 477–94.

KALES, A. (ed.) *Sleep: Physiology and psychopathology*. New York: Lippincott, 1969.

KALES, A., HOEDEMAKER, F. S., JACOBSEN, A., and LICHTENSTEIN, E. L. Dream deprivation: An experimental reappraisal. *Nature*, 1964, *204*, 1337–38.

KALES, A., WILSON, T., KALES, J. D., JACOBSON, A., PAULSON, M. J., KOLLAR, E., and WALTER, R. D. Measurements of all-night sleep in normal elderly persons: Effects of aging. *Journal of the American Geriatric Society*, 1967, *15*, 405–14.

KATO, T., TANAKA, H., TADA, H., and YAHATAYAMA, T. Studies in sensory deprivation. Part I. General methods and results of polygraphic records, behavioral observations and interviews. *Tohoku Psychological Folia*, 1968, *26*, 1–11.

KETY, S. S., EVARTS, E. V., and WILLIAMS, H. D. (eds.) *Sleep and altered states of consciousness*. Baltimore: Williams & Wilkins, 1967.

KLEITMAN, N. Studies on the physiology of sleep. 5. Some experiments on puppies. *American Journal of Physiology*, 1927, *84*, 386–95.

———. *Sleep and wakefulness*. Chicago: University of Chicago Press, 1939; 2nd ed., 1963.

———, and ENGELMANN, T. G. Sleep characteristics of infants. *Journal of Applied Physiology*, 1953, *6*, 269–82.

———, and KLEITMAN, E. Effect of non-twenty-four-hour routines of living on oral temperature and heart rate. *Journal of Applied Physiology*, 1953, *6*, 283–91.

KNOTT, J. R., GIBBS, F. A., and HENRY, C. E. Fourier transforms of electroencephalogram during sleep. *Journal of Experimental Psychology*, 1942, *31*, 465–77.

KOELLA, W. P. *Sleep—its nature and physiological organization*. Springfield, Ill.: Charles C Thomas, 1967.

KORNMUELLER, A. E. Der mechanismus des epileptischen anfalles auf grand bioelektrischer unterschungen am zentralnervensystem. *Fortschritte der Neurologie, Psychiatrie und Ihrer Grenzgebiete*, 1935, *7*, 391–400.

KRIPKE, D. F. Sleep in night workers. Presented to the American Psychiatric Association, Boston, May, 1968.

LACHMANN, T. M., LAPKIN, B., and HANDELMANN, N. S. The recall of dreams: Its relation to repression and cognitive control. *Journal of Abnormal Social Psychology*, 1962, *64*, 160–62.

LEGENDRE, R., and PIERON, H. Retour a l'état normal des cellules nerveuses après les modifications provoquées par l'insomnie experimentale. *Comptes Rendus Societé de Biologie*, 1907, *62*, 1007–8.

———. Distribution des alterations cellulaires du systeme nerveux dans l'insomnie experimentale. *Comptes Rendus Societe de Biologie*, 1908, *64*, 1102–4.

LEWIS, H. E., and MASTERSON, J. P. Sleep and wakefulness in the Arctic. *Lancet*, 1957, *1*, 1262–66.

LIBERSON, W. T. Problem of sleep and mental disease. *Digest of Neurological Psychiatry*, 1945, *13*, 93–108.

LOOMIS, A. L., HARVEY, E. N., and HOBART, G. A. Cerebral states during sleep, as studies by human brain potentials. *Journal of Experimental Psychology*, 1937, *21*, 127–44.

LUCE, G. G., and SEGAL, J. *Sleep*. New York: Coward-McCann, 1966.

MCDONALD, D. G., SHALLENBERGER, H., and CARPENTER, F. A. Spontaneous autonomic responses during sleep and wakefulness. Report to the Association for the Psychophysiological Study of Sleep, Santa Monica, March, 1967.

MCGHIE, A., and RUSSELL, S. M. The subjective assessment of normal sleep patterns. *Journal of Mental Science*, 1962, *108*, 642–54.

MALCOLM, N. *Dreaming*. New York: Humanities Press, 1959.

MANACEINE, M. DE. *Sleep: Its physiology, pathology, hygiene, and psychology*. London: Walter Scott, 1897.

MEIER, C. A., RUEF, H., and ZIEGLER, A. Forgetting of dreams in the laboratory. *Perceptual and Motor Skills*, 1968, *26*, 551–57.

MOLINARI, S. and FOULKES, D. Tonic and phasic events during sleeppsychological correlates and implications. *Perceptual and Motor Skills*, 1969, 343–68.

MONROE, L. J. Psychological and physiological differences between good and poor sleepers. *Journal of Abnormal Social Psychology*, 1967, *72*, 255–64.

———, RECHTSCHAFFEN, A., FOULKES, D., and JENSEN, J. Discriminability of REM and NREM reports. *Journal of Personality and Social Psychology*, 1965, *2*, 456–60.

MOORE, L. M., JENKINS, M., and BARKER, L. Relation of number of hours of sleep to muscular efficiency. *American Journal of Physiology*, 1922, *59*, 471.

MOORE, T., and UCKO, L. E. Night waking in early infancy. *Archives of Disease in Childhood*, 1957, *32*, 333–42.

MORUZZI, G. Active processes in the brain stem during sleep. *Harvey Lecture Series*, 1963, *58*, 233–97.

MURRAY, E. J. *Sleep, dreams, and arousal*. New York: Appleton-Century-Crofts, 1965.

NAITOH, P. Sleep loss and its effect on performance. U. S. Navy Medical Neuropsychiatric Unit, Report No. 68–3, 1969.

———. Sleep loss and its effect on task performance. American Psychological Association Symposium on Sleep Deprivation, 1968.

———, KALES, A., KOLLAR, E. J., and JACOBSON, A. Interpretation of non-sleep EEG and sleep EEG pattern in recovery nights after 204 hours of prolonged wakefulness. Report to the Association for the Psychophysiological Study of Sleep, Santa Monica, March, 1967.

O'CONNOR, A. L. Questionnaire response about sleep. Unpublished M. A. thesis. Gainesville, University of Florida: 1964.

OSWALD. L. *Sleeping and waking: Physiology and psychology*. New York: Elsevier, 1962.

———, BERGER, R. J., JARAMILLO, R. A., KEDDIE, K. M. G.; OLLEY, P. D., and PLUNKETT, G. B. Melancholia and barbiturates: A controlled EEG, body and eye movement study of sleep. *British Journal of Psychiatry.*, 1963, *109*, 66–78.

PATRICK, G. T. W., and GILBERT, J. A. On the effects of loss of sleep. *Psychological Review*, 1896, *3*, 469–83.

PIERON, H. *Le probleme physiologique du sommeil*. Paris: Masson and Cie, 1913.

PORTNOFF, G., BAEKELAND, G., GOODENOUGH, D. R., KARACAN, I., and SHAPIRO, A. Retention of verbal materials perceived immediately prior to onset of non-REM sleep. *Perceptual and Motor Skills*, 1966, *22*, 751–58.

RECHTSCHAFFEN, A., and KALES, A. (eds.) *A manual of standardized terminology, techniques and scoring system for sleep stages of human subjects*. Washington, D.C.: Public Health Service, Government Printing Office, 1968.

RECHTSCHAFFEN, A., VERDONE, P., and WHEATON, J. Reports of mental activity during sleep. *Canadian Psychiatric Association Journal*, 1963, *8*, 409–14.

RENSHAW, S., MILLER, V. L., and MARQUIS, D. P. *Children's sleep*. New York: Macmillan, 1933.

REYNOLDS, N. M., and MALLOY, H. The sleep of children in a 24-hour nursery school. *Journal of Genetic Psychology*, 1933, *43*, 322–51.

ROFFWARG, H. P., MUZIO, J. N., and DEMENT, W. C. Ontogenetic development of the human sleep dream cycle. *Science*, 1966, *152*, 604–19.

ROSS, J. J. Neurological findings after prolonged sleep deprivation. *Archives of Neurology*, 1965, *12*, 399–403.

RUSH, A. J., ROFFWARG, H. P., and MUZIO, J. N. Sleep limitation—its effect on sleep stage organization. Presented to the American Psychiatric Association, Boston, May, 1968.

SAMPSON, H. Deprivation of dreaming by two methods. 1. Compensatory REM time. *Archives of General Psychiatry*, 1965, *13*, 79–86.

SCHONBAR, R. A. Some manifest characteristics of recallers and non-recallers of dreams. *Journal of Consulting Psychology*, 1959, *23*, 414–18.

SHAPIRO, A. Dreaming and the physiology of sleep. A critical review of some empirical data and a proposal for a theoretical model of sleep and dreaming. *Experimental Neurology Supplement*, 1967, *4*, 56–81.

SIMON, C. W., and EMMONS, W. H. Learning during sleep? *Psychological Bulletin*, 1955, *52*, 328–42.

SINGER, J. L., and SCHONBAR, R. A. Correlates of day dreaming: A dimension of self-awareness. *Journal of Consulting Psychology*, 1961, *25*, 1–6.

SNYDER, F. Theoretical comment on the significance of the "dream deprivation" findings. Report to the Association for the Psychophysiological Study of Sleep, Chicago, March, 1962.

———. The new biology of dreaming. *Archives of General Psychiatry*, 1963, *8*, 381–91.

———, HOBSON, J. A., MORRISON, D. F., and GOLDFRANK, F. Changes in respiration, heart rate, and systolic blood pressure in human sleep. *Journal of Applied Physiology*, 1964, *19*, 417–22.

STOYVA, J., and KAMIYA, J. Electrophysiological studies of dreaming as the prototype of a new strategy in the study of consciousness. *Psychological Review*, 1968, *75*, 192–205.

SYZMANSKI, J. S. Eine methode zur untersuchung der rühe und activitaetsperioden bei tieren. *Pfluegers Archiv für die Gesamte Physiologie des Menschen und der Tiere*, 1914, *158*, 343–85.

TART, C. T. Frequency of dream recall and some personality measures. *Journal of Consulting Psychology*, 1962, *26*, 467–70.

———. The hypnotic dream: Methodological problems and a review of the literature. *Psychological Bulletin*, 1965, *63*, 87–99.

TERMAN, L. M. *Genetic studies of genius. Mental and physical traits of 1000 gifted children*. Stanford, California: Stanford University Press, 1925.

———, and HOCKING, A. The sleep of school children; its distribution according to age and its relation to physical and mental efficiency. *Journal of Educational Psychology*, 1913, *4*, 138–47.

WAGNER, M. A. Day and night sleep in a group of young orphanage children. *Journal of Genetic Psychology*, 1933, *42*, 442–59.

WALTER, W. G., and SHIPTON, H. W. A new toposcopic display system. *Electroencephalography and Clinical Neurophysiology*, 1951, *3*, 281–92.

WEBB, W. B. *Sleep: An experimental approach*. New York: Macmillan, 1968.

——— Twenty-four-hour sleep cycling. *In* A. Kales (ed.) *Sleep: Physiology and psychopathology*, New York: Lippincott, 1969.

——— and AGNEW, H. W., JR. Sleep: Effects of a restricted regime. *Science*, 1965, *150*, 1745–47.

——— Sleep cycling within twenty-four-hour periods. *Journal of Experimental Psychology*, 1967, *74*, 158–60.

——— Measurement and characteristics of nocturnal sleep. *In* L. A. Abt and B. F. Riess (eds.), *Progress in clinical psychology*, vol. 7. New York: Grune & Stratton, 1968*a*.

——— Sleep patterns of long and short sleepers. Report to the Association for the Psychophysiological Study of Sleep, Denver, March, 1968*b*.

WEBB, W. B., and KERSEY, J. Recall of dreams and the probability of Stage 1-REM sleep. *Perceptual and Motor Skills*, 1967, *24*, 627–30.

WEBB, W. B., and STONE, W. A note on the sleep responses of young college adults. *Perceptual and Motor Skills*, 1963, *16*, 162.

WEITZMAN, E. D., GOLDMACHER, D., KRIPKE, D., MACGREGOR, P., KREAM, J., and HELLMAN, L. Reversal of sleep-waking cycle effect on sleep stage pattern and certain neuro-endocrine rhythms. Report to the Association for the Psychophysiological Study of Sleep, Santa Monica, March, 1967.

WEST, L. J., JANSZEN, H. H., LESTER, B. K., and CORNELISOON, F. S. The psychosis of sleep deprivation. *Annals of the New York Academy of Science*, 1962, *96*, 66–70.

WHITMAN, R. M., KRAMER, M., and BALDRIDGE, B. Which dream does the patient tell? *Archives of General Psychiatry*, 1963, *8*, 277–82.

WILKINSON, R. T. Sleep deprivation: Performance tests for partial and selective sleep deprivation. *In* L. A. Abt and B. F. Riess (eds.), *Progress in clinical psychology*, vol. 7. New York: Grune & Stratton, 1968.

WILLIAMS, H. L., LUBIN, A., and GOODNOW, J. J. Impaired performance with acute sleep loss. *Psychological Monograph*, 1959, *73*, 1–26.

WILLIAMS, H. L., MORLOCK, H. C., JR., and MORLOCK, J. V. V. Instrumental behavior during sleep. *Psychophysiology*, 1966, *2*, 208–16.

WILLIAMS, H. L., TEPAS, D. I., and MORLOCK, H. C., JR. Evoked responses to clicks and electroencephalographic stages of sleep in man. *Science*, 1962, *138*, 685–86.

WITKIN, H. A., and LEWIS, H. B. (eds.) *Experimental studies in dreaming.* New York: Random House, 1967.

WOHLISCH, E. Der schlaftiefenverlauf und sein erholungs-aequivalent. *Klinische Wochenschrift*, 1957, *35*, 705–14.

WOLSTENHOLME, G. E. W., and O'CONNOR, M. (eds.) *Ciba foundation symposium on the nature of sleep.* Boston: Little, Brown, 1961.

VAN TWYVER, H. B. Sleep patterns in five rodent species. *Physiology and Behavior*, 1969, *4*, 901–5.

VERDONE, P. Sleep satiation: Extended sleep in normal adults. *Electroencephalography and Clinical Neurophysiology*, 1968, *24*, 417–23.

Almost everyone except the psychologist knows what an emotion is. Fear, terror, anger, rage, horror, lust, embarrassment, agony, excitement, disgust, grief, jealousy, shame, humiliation, amusement, laughter, joy, sorrow, weeping, *are* emotions. The trouble with the psychologist is that emotional processes and states are complex and can be analyzed from so many points of view that a complete picture is virtually impossible. It is necessary, therefore, to examine emotional events piecemeal and in different systematic contexts.

Relative to the concept of emotion, Sheer (1961) writes:

The concept of emotion has had a much-maligned but ever-present place in the history of psychology. There is an extensive literature to indicate that emotion, both subjectively in its experiential or feeling aspect and objectively in its expressive or behavioral aspect, involves the organism at many levels of psychological and physiological integration. It is primarily because of this widespread influence and interactions with other psychological processes (before emotion finds expression in behavior) that the concept has been so difficult to deal with. Also, its close association with the clinic in the various forms of anxiety, frustration, hostility, and so forth, has served to complicate matters further. Everyone knows something of what is meant by emotion but not precisely what (p. 433).

In the following account I have considered emotions in the broader context of affective processes. The literature on feeling and emotion is so vast and complex that I cannot presume to review it.

A few references to pertinent sources are the following: Cofer and Appley (1964, pp. 357–411) discussed hedonic and activation theories of emotion. Young (1961, pp. 344–410) considered the nature and bodily mechanisms of emotion in the context of motivation. Arnold (1960, vol. I) examined the nature and role of feeling and emotion in broad historical and theoretical perspective. Early discussions of human passions are reviewed in a scholarly work by Gardiner, Metcalf, and Beebe-Center (1937). Experimental studies of the galvanic skin response,

Paul Thomas Young

Feeling and Emotion

37

facial expression, and other topics, are reviewed by Woodworth and Schlosberg (1954). Lindsley (1951) discussed the autonomic nervous system, the bodily changes of emotion, the brainstem reticular activating system, and presented his well known activation theory of emotion. Current physiological and neuropsychological research on emotion and self-stimulation effects is reviewed in two excellent chapters by Grossman (1967, pp. 498–595). The work of Olds and Milner (1954) upon self-stimulation with implanted electrodes is historically important. Routtenberg (1968) has proposed a two-arousal hypothesis. The volume edited by D. C. Glass (1968), entitled *Neurophysiology and emotion*, contains important papers by Brady, Kety, Mandler, Pribram, Schachter, and others, all of which have references to the literature. Advanced biochemical research has been reviewed by Schildkraut and Kety (1967). The volume by Izard (1971) contains material on the universal nature of certain facial expressions and important theoretical discussions of emotion. Young (1973) has published a revised edition of *Emotion in man and animal*, which contains early and current references to the literature.

The Nature of Emotion

HISTORY OF THE WORD EMOTION AND EARLY CONCEPTS

Aristotle (384–322 B.C.) used the word *passion* ($\pi\acute{\alpha}\theta\eta$) to include appetite, anger, fear, confidence, envy, joy, love, hate, longing, emulation, pity, and, in general, various states accompanied by pleasure and pain. Incidentally, this Greek root appears in words designating physical disorder (*pathology*) as well as passion (*sympathy*, *apathy*). The passions were roughly equivalent to what psychologists today call affective processes. Ludovicus Vives (1492–1540), however, used the term *passiones* as appropriate only to violent emotions. Thus rage, terror, horror, agony, ecstasy, are among the passions. The modern word *emotion* is sometimes used in Aristotle's sense to include the whole gamut of affective processes and sometimes in the more restricted sense of Vives to designate affective processes that are intense, disruptive, disorganized, violent (Gardiner, Metcalf & Beebe-Center 1937, pp. 42, 123).

According to Murray's (1888) dictionary, the word *emotion* is derived from the Latin *e* (out) and *movere* (to move). Originally the word meant a moving out of one place into another, in the sense of a migration. Thus: "The divers emotions of that people [the Turks]" (1603). "Some accidental Emotion . . . of the Center of Gravity" (1965). The word came to mean a moving, stirring, agitation, perturbation, and was so used in a strictly physical sense. Thus: "Thunder . . . caused so great an Emotion in the air" (1708). "The waters continuing in the caverns . . . caused the emotion or earthquake" (1758). This physical meaning was gradually transferred to political and social agitation; the word came to mean tumult, popular disturbance. Thus: "There were . . . great stirres and emocions in Lombardye" (1579). "Accounts of Public Emotions, occasioned by the Want of Corn" (1709). Finally the word came to be used to designate any agitated, vehement, or excited mental state of the individual. Thus: "The joy of gratification is properly called an emotion" (1762).

In the nineteenth and early twentieth centuries, three basic attributes of the mind were categorized as cognition, affection, conation. Affection referred to the way something *affects* the individual in consciousness and outward expression. Affection includes the entire range of feelings and emotions.

The popular term *feeling* has many meanings. It refers to tactual perception, cognitive belief, emotion, and the simple experiences of pleasantness and unpleasantness. In technical psychology Wundt, in his tridimensional theory of feeling, included pleasantness and unpleasantness, excitement and calm, strain and relaxation. Titchener restricted the concept of affective process to experiences of pleasantness and unpleasantness. Both Wundt and Titchener distinguished between feelings and emotions.

To clarify the picture consider the following classes of affective processes:

1. *Simple feelings* of pleasantness and unpleasantness associated with odors, tastes, tactual stimuli, tones, colors, and other sensory excitations.
2. Negative *organic feelings* of hunger, thirst, pain, fatigue; and positive organic feelings of dietary satisfaction, relief, physical well-being, sex.
3. *Activity feelings* including appetitive states such as hunger, thirst, sexual desire, eliminative urges and also including activity feelings of interest, aversion, enthusiasm, commitment, boredom, ennui, disinterest, resentment.
4. Moral, esthetic, religious, intellectual, social *sentiments and attitudes* which are based upon previous experience, education, training.
5. Persisting *moods* of cheerfulness, elation, excitement, depression, anxiety, grief.
6. Pathological *affects* of deep depression, mania, apathy, anxiety, hostility.
7. *Emotions* of fear, anger, laughing, weeping, sexual excitement, agony, shame, humiliation, embarrassment.
8. *Temperaments* of individuals are cheerful, vivacious, phlegmatic, sanguine, depressed, apathetic, moody. Temperaments are stable though they are known to change with age, health, and environmental circumstances.

The above categories of affective processes overlap. Emotion is only one variety. I suggest that emotion be defined as *an acutely disturbed affective process or state which originates in the psychological situation and which is revealed by marked bodily changes in smooth muscles, glands, and gross behavior.* According to this definition an emotion is a disturbance—a departure from the normal state of composure. Emotions are affective in that they are characteristically pleasant, unpleasant, or indifferently excited. Emotions differ from simple feelings of pleasantness and unpleasantness in that they originate in perception and memory rather than receptor stimulation. Emotions differ from intraorganic feelings in that they arise from a psychological situation which always includes an environmental factor, present or past. Emotions differ from activity feelings in that they are disruptive, whereas highly motivated activity commonly results from emotional upsets. Emotions are briefer and more intense than moods. Emotions are normal although they appear during pathological affects and in persons with different temperaments.

There are two aspects of all affective processes: (1) an acute, temporary event and (2) a chronic, persisting state. The first aspect is revealed in experience and behavior. The second aspect is actually assumed. When we speak of "an emotionally disturbed child," "emotional development," "emotional maturity," "emotional balance," "emotional instability," we imply a persisting state of maladjustment, conflict, frustration, or a stable attitude or disposition.

SUBJECTIVE AND OBJECTIVE VIEWS OF AFFECTIVE PROCESSES

The criticism has been made that subjective data have no place in scientific psychology. The criticism implies that psychology is strictly an objective science—a branch of biology and, possibly, of objective social science.

I will point out, however, that there are two views of objectivity: (1) objective experience, and (2) objective inference or interpretation. Although feelings of pleasantness and unpleasantness are *not* objectively observed, they are none the less reported as valid components of conscious experience. All the empirical data of conscious experience (including facts of perception, memory, thought, feeling, and emotion) can be objectively interpreted. An objective interpretation in terms of bodily mechanisms is precisely what the physiological psychologist aims to accomplish in his research upon feeling and emotion.

The primary data of neuropsychology are: (1) objectively observed neural structures, and (2) facts of human conscious experience and animal (including human) behavior. When one examines the brain objectively it appears as a physical object like other objects of perception. The brain is a piece of meat! One does not find flags, loyalty oaths, feelings of pleasantness, and emotions of anger in the brain. The neuropsychologist, therefore, must start his analysis from psychological facts as well as the data of neurology and biology.

Whether one starts from the facts of conscious experience and behavior or from physiological and biological data, one ends inevitably with inferences, hypotheses, and theories. At this point one encounters the classical mind-body problem. Are there two realities—mind and body—or a single conscious organism? My answer is that we need to postulate only one psychobiological organism. That organism, however, is fully adequate as a substrate to account for all the facts of conscious experience and behavior.

In the practical disciplines of clinical psychology, psychiatry, psychosomatic medicine, counseling, and other psychotechnologies, human feelings and emotions play a dominant role. The total facts must be considered in their own right regardless of one's point of view and regardless of one's scientific and philosophical biases.

Bodily Changes in Feeling and Emotion

Early writers referred the passions to bodily changes in the heart, liver, muscles, stomach, sex organs, brain, nerves, blood vessels, lungs, viscera, and other bodily parts. In the Bible one reads the phrase "bowels of mercy". Shakespeare in *Lucrece* writes: "To quench the coale that in his liver glowes." In the record from Waltham Abbey dated 1554 are these words: "This bishop was bloody Bonner, that corpulent tyrant, full (as one said) of guts and empty of bowels." Modern slang contains similar phrases: "He has plenty of gall"; "He got his spleen up"; "He could not stomach it"; "Have a heart"; "He lacked the guts"; "Es ist ihm etwas über die Leber gelaufen [He is peeved]" (Murray's dictionary, 1888).

Despite an ancient emphasis on bodily changes of feeling and emotion, modern attempts to define and distinguish the passions in terms of bodily changes have been disappointing. At the turn of the century experiments had been made with the so-called method of expression. Physiological measures of heart beat, respiration, blood pressure, electrical changes at the skin, etc., were made while the subjects were calm and affectively aroused. Correlations between introspective reports of feeling and associated bodily changes showed some functional relations. For example, reports of pleasantness were associated with vasodilation and unpleasantness with vasoconstriction but the relationship was not perfect; no bodily sine qua non of these affective processes was discovered. The failure to find a one-to-one relation was blamed on the introspective method. Perhaps this is fair since many subjects do confuse cognitive judgments (statements of meaning) with immediate reports of actually felt experience. Probably, however, a better explanation is that no one-to-one relation in fact exists between felt pleasantness (or unpleasantness) and any peripheral change. Current evidence indicates that the physiological basis of affective processes lies deeply buried in subcortical neural stations. Since the work of Olds and Milner (1954), it has for the first time become possible to probe into the bodily substrate of pleasantness and unpleasantness.

DARWIN'S PRINCIPLES OF EMOTIONAL EXPRESSION

In his classical work, *The Expression of Emotions in Man and Animal*, Darwin (1872) brought together a mass of accurate observations, some anecdotal material, and an interpretation of the materials in terms of three principles of emotional expression.

Darwin's first principle, which he called *serviceable associated habits*, states that adaptive behavior, at first performed voluntarily, became habitual and the habit, in some way, was transmitted from generation to generation. This Lamarckian concept, we know today, is unsound but Darwin's main emphasis was on the biological utility of emotional behavior in the struggle for existence. In man, many expressions of emotion are components of biologically useful acts or vestiges of acts that were useful in an earlier stage of evolution. Thus when an angry man bares the canine teeth by curling his lips he does not intend to bite but the expression is a vestige of a biologically useful act. Emotional expressions have, or at one stage of evolution had, utility for survival.

Darwin's second principle of *antithesis* recognizes that some emotional expressions are directly opposed, or antithetical, to biologically useful acts. One of Darwin's examples of antithetical behavior is illustrated in Figure 37-1. Figure 37-1a shows the bodily posture of a hostile cat, an animal ready to spring and attack an enemy. The body is extended; the tail, or just the tip of it, is lashed or curled from side to side; the hair, especially

Fig. 37-1. *Emotional expressions of the cat. 1a, Cat prepared for attack. 1b, Friendly, pleasant, cat. 1c, Cat terrified by a barking dog.* [Redrawn from Darwin 1872]

cat stands upright with back slightly arched; the tail is rigid and stands straight up; the hair, instead of bristling, is smooth; the ears are erect and pointed; the mouth is closed and relaxed; the claws are withdrawn; instead of a growl the vocalization is a purr. The friendly animal rubs against the leg of her master. In a word, friendly behavior is the antithesis, the negation, of hostility. The expression of terror is different but more akin to hostility than to friendliness. Figure 37.1c shows the posture of a cat terrified by a barking dog. The emotional arousal is complete. As in hostility the hair bristles; the pupils are dilated; the ears are pressed back; the teeth are bared, the claws protrude. But there is a difference. The terrified animal hisses or spits. The back is arched which makes a formidable appearance to her enemy. The animal is poised so that either attack or flight is possible. What happens next will depend upon the external situation but for the moment the emotional state of terror persists.

Darwin's third principle, *direct action of the nervous system*, frankly recognizes limitations of the first two principles: Emotional expressions which cannot be explained by the first two principles Darwin explained in terms of neural structure. Thus the structure of the nervous system explains certain expressions such as writhing in agony and crying out during emotional excitement. There is an overflow of nervous excitation in highly excited emotions which produces physiological changes that are outwardly expressed.

Darwin's work was the most influential study of emotions during the nineteenth century. The work has been criticized. For example, Arnold (1960, vol. 1, pp. 100–105) argues that Darwin's work is "prescientific" because Darwin accepted the Lamarckian doctrine of inheritance of acquired characters and because some of his evidence is anecdotal and because he failed to consider the inner nature of emotion which is outwardly expressed. But in defense of Darwin it can be said that he dealt objectively with the manifestations of emotion while avoiding speculations about the mind-body problem; he emphasized the biological utility of many emotional expressions; he recognized that perception of the situation is an important determinant of emotional behavior; and, importantly, in his third principle he pointed to the structural organization of the nervous system as the basis for explaining many emotional expressions. When Darwin's work is viewed in the light of the psychology and biology of his day the work must be considered as a major scientific advance.

FACIAL EXPERSSIONS OF FEELING AND EMOTION

Landis (1924) aroused genuine emotions in human subjects and then photographed their facial expressions. He evoked emotions with these situations: listening to music, reading the Bible, smelling ammonia, hearing a loud noise, writing out a faux pas, viewing pictures of skin diseases, pornographic material, reading sex case histories, art studies, handling live frogs, decapitating a rat, experiencing electric shocks, and relief from these ordeals. As an aid in analyzing the subject's facial expressions dark marks were placed upon the subject's face. Measurements of distances between these marks on photographs revealed the degree to which different groups of facial muscles were involved in the expressions.

From a study of the measurements and the verbal reports

that on the tail, bristles; the ears are pressed backward into a position that protects them during a fight; the mouth is open baring the teeth; the forefeet are prepared to strike with claws protruding; the animal utters a growl. The overall picture is that of an animal prepared to fight. Now consider Figure 37-1b, the friendly, pleasant, cat. Instead of crouching the friendly

Fig. 37-2. *Crying and laughing in the infant.* [Courtesy of Dr. Nancy Bayley]

of the subjects Landis concluded that emotion, as expressed in the face, is not a true reflexive response as is, for example, the wink reflex. He suggested that common names for emotions usually refer to inducing situations rather than to reflexive facial patterns. He found that individuals tended to use particular groups of facial muscles habitually to the exclusion of others in expressing various emotions. Also the degree of general disturbance is a factor in recognizing human emotions.

Landis drew an important distinction between social and emotional expressions. Facial expressions are used in communication much as spoken words are employed. The expressions posed by actors are conventional and are not true reflexive patterns of response. This conclusion needs to be qualified.

The subjects in Landis's experiments were sophisticated adults and the situations he employed were weak on the positive side of joy, smiling, and laughter. There can be no doubt that certain facial expressions are universally recognized. Crying and laughing, for example, are human expressions that are observed the world over in all societies and cultures. See Figure 37-2. Crying expresses a negative affective state and laughing a positive reaction. Parents and others instantly recognize crying and screaming as signs of distress and smiling and laughing as signs of delight. Different levels of neutral excitement are also universal in infants. During the early stages of infant development crying appears earlier than smiling and laughing.

Schlosberg (1952) made a careful study of the recognition of emotions from photographs of facial expressions. He concluded that expressions can be classified by reference to two perpendicular scales. The vertical scale is hedonic with gradations from pleasantness to unpleasantness. The horizontal scale extends from rejection through neutrality to positive attention. This scale implies that some expressions indicate rejection and avoidance, others are neutral, and still others indicate attentive observation and interest.

How are Emotions Recognized and Named?

Although the bodily expressions of feeling and emotion provide some reliable cues for recognizing and naming affective processes, these cues are not sufficient for identification of all the shades of emotion distinguished in everyday life. The above experiments of Landis (1924) and others by Sherman (1927) prove the point.

Sherman took motion pictures of the emotional behavior of infants and presented the pictures for identification to groups of competent judges. He found that when the judges were ignorant of the inducing situations there was little agreement in naming emotions. In agreement with Landis he concluded that knowledge of the inducing circumstances is a major factor in identifying and naming emotions but Sherman also failed to include expressions of joy, smiling, and laughing.

Hebb (1946) studied the diary records of thirty chimpanzees to discover how emotions are recognized by persons who had firsthand dealings with the animals. Observations had been made by persons who observed the chimpanzees repeatedly for periods of time varying from six to twelve years; many of the records were based on intimate knowledge of the subjects. The diary contained numerous references to emotional outbursts. Hebb explained that temperamental traits and specific emotions are recognized as deviations from a normal base of behavior rather than as momentary patterns of response. For example, a long acquaintance with the animals is necessary to distinguish between such states as rage and hate.

Apart from long acquaintance with a subject and knowledge of his habitual manner of reacting, an important factor in recognizing and naming emotions is the observer's understanding of the specific situation that induces a response. This point was demonstrated in an important study by Schachter and Singer (1962) who varied separately the environmental situation and the physiological state.

To control the physiological state Schachter and Singer injected epinephrine—a drug known to produce tremor, increase in rate and strength of heart beat, accelerated breathing, vasodilation, and other bodily changes. To control the subject's understanding of the situation, subjects were misinformed concerning the real purpose and conditions of the experiment. Some subjects were given correct information about the physiological effects of epinephrine; some were given no information; others were told incorrectly, "Your feet will feel numb, you will have an itching sensation over parts of your body, and you may get a slight headache." After injection the subject was placed in a room and a stooge entered. The stooge acted either in a euphoric or in an angry manner. The social environment was thus controlled. There were self-ratings of emotional behavior and ratings by observers hidden from the view of the subject. Schachter and Singer concluded that emotional states are a function of (1) the physiological state, and (2) the subject's understanding or knowledge of the inducing situation. Further, if an individual has no immediate explanation for his bodily state, he will describe his feelings in terms of whatever cognitions are available to him. He may label an emotion "joy" or "anger" according to his understanding of the situation.

It is theoretically important that a pattern of bodily changes, produced by an injection of epinephrine, can be present in emotional states as diverse as euphoria and anger.

The importance of situational cues in recognizing and naming emotions was again underscored in studies by Hunt, Cole, and Reis (1958). They assumed that most unpleasant emotions arise from frustration. Fear is present when the subject (S) perceives a threat to his goal and the uncertainty of achieving it; in fear there is a reference to future time. Anger occurs when a frustrating agent or obstacle is present and central in S's perception. Sorrow arises when S perceives the goal as irretrievably lost and his concern is limited to the loss of the goal; in sorrow the reference is to the past. In the first study Hunt, Cole, and Reis described thirty situations designed to arouse anger or fear or sorrow and asked Ss to name the emotion appropriate to the situation. In the second study ten additional situations were described and four groups of one hundred college and high school students were instructed to read the descriptive paragraphs and name the appropriate emotions. The studies showed clearly that there is a cognitive basis for naming and distinguishing anger, fear, and sorrow. In these studies the perception of bodily changes was not a factor in naming the emotions.

In the light of the above experiments it is clear that the awareness of an inducing situation plays a dominant role in recognizing and naming emotions. Tolman (1923), in a behavioristic account, stressed the situation-response relationship. It is not the stimulus-situation as such, he wrote, nor the response as such which can serve to define emotion. Rather it is the response as affecting or calculated to affect the stimulus-situation. Thus, in fear it is escape from the stimulus-object, in anger the destruction of it, and in love the encouragement or enticement of the stimulus-object which objectively characterize the specific emotions. It is the "response as back-acting upon the stimulus" which distinguishes emotions. According to Tolman, each emotion is characterized by a tendency toward its own particular type of adaptive behavior. An emotion, therefore, is motivating.

Tolman was concerned with purposive behavior. McDougall (1926) defined emotion as a conscious experience associated with purposive behavior. According to McDougall, conscious emotions are correlated with specific instincts. Thus fear is associated with instinctive flight; anger, with pugnacity; lust, with sexual behavior; tender emotion, with parental behavior; elation, with self-assertion; disgust, with repulsion, etc.

McDougall made a mistake in correlating emotions with specific instincts. Quite apart from the vigorous objections that were raised against his instinct doctrine, the doctrine disregards the dynamic mechanisms of frustration, conflict, relief, satisfaction, etc., that underlie emotional disturbances.

In general, the above discussion indicates that identifying specific feelings and emotions is a complex process. Involved are the internal physiological state, the outward manifestations in behavior including reflexive, and posed facial expressions, the environmental situation and, especially, the individual's perception or understanding of the inducing situation and his reaction to that situation as he understands it. The complexity of emotion is clearly apparent!

Dynamic Determinants of Feeling and Emotion

Rapaport (1950) wrote that a good deal of confusion concerning the definition of emotion has been due to failure of investigators to distinguish between the phenomena of emotions and the underlying dynamic mechanisms. The phenomena of emotion are complex but can be observed and analyzed from several points of view. In particular, the phenomena include:

1. The consciously experienced emotion or feeling.
2. The emotional behavior of animals and men.
3. The physiological processes, especially neural, that occur during emotional disturbances.

The phenomena of emotion are observed contemporary events. The underlying mechanisms, contrastingly, are always inferred or postulated.

A discussion of the dynamic conditions that elicit emotion follows.

INTENSE STIMULATION

For every task there is an optimal level of incentive. If the incentive is stimulation by electric shock, there is a strength of shock that yields optimal performance. Strengths of shock above the optimum lead to impaired performance and emotional disorganization. According to the Yerkes-Dodson law, the optimal level of shock is lower for a difficult than for an easy task. With human subjects a painful electric shock can disturb a smooth performance. The subject may "lose his head," "go to pieces," "become emotionally upset."

FRUSTRATION AND INTERRUPTION

It is the thesis of Dollard et al. (1939) that whenever aggressive behavior appears the aggressor is frustrated. In other words, aggressive behavior is determined by frustration. The converse of this proposition is not necessarily true, however, for frustration can lead to emotional upset without aggression. Frustration can also lead to resignation or to passive acceptance of a frustrating situation. Further, frustration can lead to regression—a return to an earlier and less effective way of reacting.

The most direct form of aggressive behavior is physical attack upon the frustrating object to destroy, injure, remove it, or to change the frustrating situation. If direct attack is impossible, displaced aggression may appear. Thus a man, frustrated by his boss in the office, puts on a smile and says nothing but when he comes home at night he kicks the cat, spanks his child, and complains about the food. The blame and hostility can readily be directed from one victim to another.

Mandler (1964) prefers to speak of the *interruption* of behavior, rather than frustration, as a principal cause of emotional behavior. When a behavioral sequence is interrupted, Mandler states, the organism tends to complete the sequence directly or through substitution. It is not necessary to invoke some drive to account for the completion of interrupted acts. As long as the psychobiological machine stays alive, it must continue to execute successive steps of some plan. If the planned action is controlled within specific limits, it can be organized and integrated with other sequences; but if there is no relevant behavior, an interruption will be disruptive. Mandler recognizes both organized and disorganized forms of emotional behavior.

CONFLICT

Perhaps conflict is a special form of frustration. According to Dewey's conflict theory of emotion, as reformulated by Angier (1927), an emotion is a state of conflict. Thus (to use Dewey's example) a man riding a bicycle is hurrying to an important engagement. He passes a friend and waves a hearty greeting. Waving does not interfere with bicycle riding and there is no emotion. But if the friend stops the rider and engages him in a lengthy conversation, the cyclist, concerned over reaching his destination on time, is thrown into conflict and becomes emotionally disturbed by the delay. It is the conflict, or interference, Dewey argues, that produces emotion. "*Without* a conflict, there is no emotion; *with* it, there is." Dewey's conflict theory of emotion was an attempt to reconcile the historical views of Darwin and James.

It should be added that in addition to acute dynamic conflicts there are also chronic, persisting, states of conflict that repeatedly lead to emotional disturbances.

RELEASE OF TENSION

The above conditions—intense and painful stimulation, frustration and interruption, and conflict—tend to build up unpleasant excited feelings and a state of tension. Feelings and emotions are also produced by conditions that release tension. Smiling, laughing, joy, weeping, and sadness are often caused by release of a tension that has been built up.

Why do we weep? Lund (1930) argues that weeping occurs in complex, typically social situations. It is not merely a loss or bereavement which brings tears. Lund's investigation showed that it is the presence of some alleviating or redeeming feature in an otherwise distressing situation that is the immediate occasion for tears. For example, at a funeral the tears flow when the speaker eulogizes the deceased by saying that he was a wonderful father, a great-hearted citizen, well loved in the community, etc. An emphasis upon the goodness of the lost loved one brings the tears. This emphasis accentuates a conflict and weeping is the release. Incidentally, Lund found, contrary to common belief, that a deep depressive psychosis is tearless.

Why do we laugh? Philosophers, psychologists, and others, have attempted to answer the question but there is no agreement. Hayworth (1928) argued that laughter has a social origin and function. According to his theory, laughter developed as a form of communication. In a tense situation in which there is impending danger or strain, laughter is the signal that all is well. Through a smile or laugh one flashes the meaning, "Have no fear; I will not hurt you."

Hayworth summarized conditions which are said to elicit laughter:

1. *Triumph or victory*, whether in battle or in a game of cards, brings a feeling of superiority and laughter.
2. *Surprise* which brings a feeling of superiority as in the practical joke, an easy victory, an unexpected reward, brings joy, smiling, and laughter.
3. *Tickling*, especially in children, induces laughter. The tickler assumes the role of attacker and then stimulates in a light playful way thus releasing tension.
4. A *funny story* builds up tension and then suddenly releases the tension with an unexpected turn.
5. Laughter is aroused by *incongruous situations*. Incongruity covers a considerable range of humor, e.g., a dignified man slipping and falling on the ice.
6. Laughter is associated with a *sense of well-being, good health, social safety*.
7. Finally, *an individual sometimes laughs voluntarily* to hide shyness or embarrassment, to show contempt or to conceal thought. Some persons laugh to appear cheerful and agreeable in social situations. Such laughter, of course, is voluntary and not a reflexive expression of emotion.

In general, I think one can conclude that in both laughing and weeping there is frequently a release of tension with an effect that may be pleasant or unpleasant depending on circumstances. Many kinds of situations provide tension release.

SUPPRESSED MOTIVATIONS

In his theory of wit Freud referred to an endopsychic censorship which suppresses mention of certain words in polite society. Words referring to sexual and eliminative functions are censored. The smutty joke avoids the censorship and causes a smile or laugh. Some such mechanism is implied in experiments performed by McGinnies.

McGinnies (1949) exposed single words in a tachistoscope with exposure times too brief to permit complete recognition. In preliminary trials he determined the threshold recognition time for each subject by exposing stimulus words for 0.01 second, 0.02 second, etc. Then in the main experiment he exposed eighteen words one at a time. Of these words eleven were neutral and acceptable but seven were loaded or taboo words: *raped, belly, whore, kotex, penis, filth, bitch*. The subjects were instructed to report what they saw on each exposure, regardless of what it was. Reports were delayed six seconds so that galvanic skin responses could develop and be recorded. McGinnies obtained two kinds of data for each exposed word: the recognition time in fractions of a second and the magnitude of galvanic skin response.

McGinnies found that thresholds of recognition were consistently higher for taboo words than for neutral controls such as: *apple, dance, child*. Also the magnitude of the galvanic skin response was greater for taboo words than for the controls. He interpreted the result as "perceptual defense" against recognition of certain words. The interpretation does not reveal the mechanism involved. There is a question whether the delay is a suppression of sensory inputs or a blocking of motor outputs. Possibly a careful introspective study would throw light on the psychological aspect of suppressed taboo words.

Predisposing Conditions of Feeling and Emotion

In addition to dynamic determinants of feeling and emotion there are predisposing conditions both psychological and physical. Among the physical conditions that influence moods are the weather (temperature and humidity), the intraorganic state of depletion (hunger, thirst, fatigue, deprivation of sleep, etc.), physiological processes (endocrine balance, elimination, etc.), and the state of health. Some of these predisposing conditions are considered below.

BIOCHEMICAL DETERMINANTS

Pribram (1967) referred to the ancient doctrine that circulating humors are the cause of moods and emotions. The doctrine needs to be modified for it is known that circulating humors come up against a blood-brain barrier which often makes them ineffective centrally. Further, some humors are synthesized by the brain itself: norepinephrine, serotonin, histamine, dopamine, and others. It is known that unidentified chemical "releasers" are secreted into the venous portal system which bathes the base of the brain where it joins the pituitary—the master endocrine gland which controls the secretion of other endocrine glands.

Pribram pointed out that core structures in the diencephalon and mesencephalon are sensitive to a variety of chemical agents. Receptor sites have been identified that are sensitive to estrogenic steroids, circulating glucose, some acids or derivatives, osmotic equilibrium of electrolytes, androgenic and adrenal steroids, acetylcholine, epinephrine, and the partial pressure of CO_2. These chemical agents play an important role in the regulation of internal homeostasis. The chemical agents are circulated in the blood stream to and from certain target organs.

Schildkraut and Kety (1967) reviewed the extensive literature on biochemical factors in emotion. They pointed out that psychological and situational factors can affect differentially the relative excretion of epinephrine and norepinephrine. Increased epinephrine excretion occurs in states of anxiety that involve a threat or that are unpredictable in outcome. Norepinephrine excretion occurs in states of anger or aggression or in situations that present a challenge. The increase of either epinephrine or norepinephrine or both is specifically adaptive in the inducing situation.

We are just beginning to get an understanding of the role of these biochemical factors in behavior and conscious experience but enough is known to indicate their great importance in the regulation of motivational and emotional processes.

THE INFLUENCE OF DRUGS UPON MOODS

Nowlis and Nowlis (1956), working with G. R. Wendt and others, made a careful study of conditions that influence moods. They examined the effects of moderate dosages of commonly used drugs such as amphetamines, antihistamines, and barbiturates on the social, emotional, and motivational behavior of college men. Over a five-year period, 95 men were observed in approximately 2400 hours of controlled social observation and in about 4800 hours of relatively free activity in group work. There were self-ratings and objective behavior ratings by partners and other observers. In this work the S's did not know whether they were taking a drug or a placebo. They did not know what the behavioral effects of a drug might be. Although several methods of testing moods were tried, the most

successful method was a check list of 100–200 adjectives. In making a rating S read the list rapidly, checking words that described his feeling, double checking words that indicated strong feeling, ignoring words that did not apply, and crossing out words that definitely did not apply. See Nowlis (1953).

The check list gave a clear picture of the prevailing mood. For example, dramamine usually produced a definite increase in checking *tired, drowsy, detached, sluggish, disinterested, dull, lazy, retiring, withdrawn;* and a decrease in *businesslike, general, industrious, talkative, cheerful, energetic.* Benzedrine gave an increase in *businesslike, talkative, capable, enterprising, independent,* and sometimes *nervous, jittery;* and a decrease in *lazy, languid, nonchalant.* The ratings of partners and observers strongly confirmed the self-ratings.

Nowlis and Nowlis reported a social influence of seconal. In one experiment a group of four men were tested together. The main hypothesis of the study, namely, that a subject on seconal is more influenced by the mood of his partners than a subject on dramamine, received strong support. The mood of companions as well as the nature of the task and the drug itself influenced the ratings.

SOCIAL CONDITIONS AND HAPPINESS

In an early study (Young 1937) of laughing, weeping, and moods, I found that college students attributed the causes of weeping to factors in the social environment in 80 to 90 percent of the records; and the causes of laughter were referred to the social environment in 98 percent of the records. Moods of cheerfulness were reported 4.6 times as frequently as moods of depression. Organic influences like fatigue, nervousness, bodily injury, illness, and the weather, were largely ignored by the Ss. This finding, of course, is a function of the test conditions and does not minimize the importance of nonsocial factors that are known to influence moods.

Wilson (1967) reviewed the literature dealing with avowed happiness. In summarizing he described the happy individual as follows:

The happy person emerges as a young, healthy, well-educated, well-paid, extroverted, optimistic, worry-free, religious, married person with high self-esteem, high job morale, modest aspirations, of either sex and of a wide range of intelligence.

The statement indicates some general conditions associated with avowed happiness. Wilson does not tell us what percent of the population meet all the conditions of happiness!

PREVIOUS EXPERIENCES

A final word should be added about an obvious and important group of conditions that predispose the individual to feelings and emotions—previous experiences. Memories of unrequited love, accident, injury, embarrassing incidents, unresolved conflicts, and the like, persist. When a situational cue recalls a past emotional experience the feeling tends to be reintegrated.

As a single example consider the phobia. A phobia is a latent liability to fear of a specific object or situation. Some persons show intense fears of enclosed spaces, open spaces, high places, running water, insects, etc. Phobias have been given high-sounding names which give an air of profundity to the discussion but explain nothing: *pyrophobia* (fear of fire), *doraphobia* (fear of fur), *thanatophobia* (fear of death), *claustrophobia* (fear of enclosed places), *odontophobia* (fear of teeth), etc. Phobias orginate in a previous fright which the subject may or may not be able to recall. Often the fright is associated with a sense of guilt. Through aided recall a phobia can sometimes be reduced or removed.

Psychological Theories of Emotion

It is possible to deal with the phenomena of feeling and emotion descriptively without theory, but to bring law and order into the mass of data it is almost necessary to go beyond the facts and to make some postulates. Several of the more important psychological theories of emotion are considered below.

THEORIES OF JAMES, LANGE, WENGER

William James's paper, "What is an emotion?" appeared in *Mind* in 1884. He stated his theory in the first (1890) edition of his well-known text and in subsequent editions. James (1913) pointed out that profound bodily changes occur during emotional states and that our awareness of these changes *as they are occurring* is what distinguishes emotional from nonemotional consciousness.

In a widely quoted paragraph James wrote:

Our natural way of thinking about these coarser emotions is that the mental perception of some fact excites the mental affection called the emotion, and that this latter state of mind gives rise to the bodily expression. My theory, on the contrary, is that the bodily changes follow directly the perception of the exciting fact, and that our feeling of the same changes as they occur IS the emotion. *Common-sense says, we lose our fortune, are sorry and weep; we meet a bear, are frightened and run; we are insulted by a rival, are angry and strike. The hypothesis here to be defended says that this order of sequence is incorrect, that the one mental state is not immediately induced by the other, that the bodily manifestations must first be interposed between, and that the more rational statement is that we feel sorry because we cry, angry because we strike, afraid because we tremble, and not that we cry, strike, or tremble, because we are sorry, angry, or fearful, as the case may be. Without the bodily states following on the perception, the latter would be purely cognitive in form, pale, colorless, destitute of emotional warmth. We might then see the bear, and judge it best to run, receive the insult and deem it right to strike, but we should not actually* feel *afraid or angry (pp. 449–450).*

Three main features of James's theory will be noted. First, emotion is assumed to be a consciously felt experience. Second, the theory deals with the sequence of (a) perception of the exciting fact, and (b) perception of involuntary bodily changes. Third, there is an implication of causation. Do we run *because* we feel afraid? Or do we feel afraid *because* we tremble, have an impulse to run, etc.? Taken literally, this implies psychophysical interaction between conscious experience and physical reaction.

James's theory is commonly referred to as the James-Lange theory of emotion but Wenger (1950) pointed out that the theory is really that of James. Textbook discussions of the theory usually follow James's striking presentation.

The Danish physiologist, C. G. Lange, in 1885 published a paper in which he emphasized the vasomotor disturbances as real outcomes of affective experience. The vascular innervations, Lange wrote, produced secondary disturbances such as motor abnormalities, sensations of paralysis, subjective sensations, disturbances of secretion, and intelligence. Lange viewed emotion as a visceral reaction.

Wenger extended Lange's view. For Wenger an emotion *is* a visceral reaction and not a conscious experience of bodily changes. Wenger does not speak of visceral changes *induced* by emotion, since the visceral response *is* the emotion itself. Wenger writes:

. . . Emotion would be continuous, because autonomic activity is continuous, while the state of homeostasis would be regarded as a state of emotion, and we would speak of increased or decreased emotion from this basic pattern. We would distinguish between emotions per se only insofar as we can differentiate patterns of visceral change, and we no longer would speak of visceral changes induced by emotion. Furthermore, all other reactions would be regarded as correlates or noncorrelates of emotional response (p. 5).

There are indeed visceral patterns, Wenger explains. Perhaps the best example of unique visceral patterning is the specific emotional complex found in sexual excitement. Three or four visceral patterns can be detected in sexual excitement. Wenger would accept the observed visceral patterns *as* emotions. He criticizes James, Cannon, and others, who define emotion as a conscious experience.

WATSON'S PATTERN-REACTION THEORY OF EMOTION

Watson, in his polemic against subjectivism and the introspective method, defined emotion as a pattern of response. Although he recognized at least three other formulations, Watson (1919) explicitly defined emotion as a pattern-reaction: "*An emotion is an hereditary pattern-reaction involving profound changes of the bodily mechanism as a whole, but particularly of the visceral and glandular systems.*"

In practice, the pattern-reactions described by Watson (fear, rage, love) are complex behavioral responses to such inducing situations as loss of support, a loud noise, restraint of free movements, stroking sensitive zones. Watson claimed that pattern-reactions can be described in terms of stimulus and response. The pattern-reaction theory is in line with Pavlovian reflexology and current S-R theories of behavior. Watson's behavioristic approach has been influential.

The pattern-reaction definition of emotion has definite advantages and makes a strong appeal to physiological psychologists:

1. Patterns of response are observed objectively and the conditions of their occurrence can be controlled.
2. Patterns of response are, in fact, prominent components in emotional behavior. See, for example, Figures 37-1 and 37-2.

3. Emotional patterns are similar to reflexes in that they can be conditioned and extinguished.
4. The patterns can be analyzed from the stimulus-response point of view.
5. The neural mechanisms that integrate some of the emotional patterns can be accurately described.

There are, however, difficulties with the theory:

1. The pattern-reaction definition of emotion does not provide a criterion for distinguishing between emotional and non-emotional patterns. Simple reflexes and the instincts described by ethologists are well-integrated patterns. How does emotion differ from other patterns?
2. The pattern-reaction definition ignores the acute affective disorganization that is present in strong emotions. In fairness to Watson it should be said that he called attention to the disruptive effect of emotions.
3. It has proved difficult to determine precisely what elements of response constitute a pattern. For example, Watson claimed that "fear" is a primary innate pattern of emotion; but his description of "fear" includes more elementary components: crying, catching the breath, startle, possibly the Moro reflex, an impulse to crawl away, etc.

The analytical description of patterned reactions is a straightforward and important task quite apart from the problem of defining emotion. The patterns are worthy of study for their own sake. No bias concerning the nature of emotion should interfere with the task of describing emotional patterns and the conditions of their occurrence. For further discussion see Young (1961), pp. 383–401.

Ax (1953) claimed that fear and anger can be distinguished in terms of the pattern of bodily changes. He aroused fear and anger with forty-three Ss while recording heart rate, ballistocardiogram (index of stroke volume), respiration rate, face temperature, skin conductance, and integrated muscle potential. Of fourteen physiological scores, seven showed a significant discrimination between fear and anger. The intercorrelations among measures demonstrated a greater physiological integration during anger than during fear.

ARNOLD'S APPRAISAL-EXCITATORY THEORY

Arnold (1960) defines emotion as: *The felt tendency toward anything intuitively appraised as good (beneficial), or away from anything intuitively appraised as bad (harmful). This attraction or aversion is accompanied by a pattern of physiological changes organized toward approach or withdrawal. The patterns differ for different emotions* (vol. I, p. 182).

The essential feature of Arnold's definition is an emphasis on appraisal, estimation, and evaluation. Pleasantness and unpleasantness, Arnold states, are rudimentary appraisals based upon sensory stimulations. There are also cognitive appraisals that rest upon perception and knowledge of the situation that induces emotion. For example, perception of a bear in the woods elicits fear but perception of a caged bear in the zoo does not elicit fear. The difference is obviously one of cognition and estimation of the situation. Something must be known

(actually or in imagination) before it can be feared, hated, or wanted.

The emotional response involves involuntary changes in viscera and skeletal muscles. The feedback from these peripheral changes, Arnold states, is evaluated in terms of, "How I feel in this situation." According to the James-Lange theory, this feedback is the basis of the conscious emotion; the sequence is

Situation $\longrightarrow$ *Expression* $\longrightarrow$ *Emotion*

But it would be better, Arnold states, to consider the sequence

Situation $\longrightarrow$ *Appraisal* $\longrightarrow$ *Emotion.*

It is the appraisal, or estimation, of a situation that elicits emotion.

When the situation is appraised and an emotion aroused, the subject is motivated for action. There is a desire to flee from danger, to attack an enemy, to entice a mate, or to make some other response that is appropriate to the situation. The desire (Nina Bull's "attitude") is an essential component of normal emotions. Emotions are thus motivating. The emotional individual becomes integrated, organized, for some form of adaptive behavior. Emotional disorganization (which Arnold carefully considers) is a secondary phenomenon.

In Arnold's theory the main emphasis is upon cognitive appraisal of the situation as the source of emotion. This cognitive appraisal is a cerebral process. Hence cerebral excitation is the main cause of emotional behavior. The excitatory aspect of her theory will be considered in a later section.

LEEPER'S PERCEPTUAL-MOTIVATIONAL THEORY

Closely akin to Arnold's theory is that of Leeper (1965) which places a dual emphasis on cognition and motivation. Leeper asked: How are emotions distinguished from each other? He rejected as not fully adequate the views that emotions are distinguished on the basis of conscious experiences or as perceived patterns of bodily reactions or by their disruptive effects or by the lack of adequate adjustment. These views, he said, are partially correct but there must be some more basic means of recognizing and distinguishing emotions. Leeper wrote that emotional processes are distinguished from each other, and from other types of processes, on the basis of their motivational effects. Thus in fear one flees, in anger one strikes, in love one entices, etc. We recognize and distinguish emotion by their dynamic effects, by what the individual does while in an emotional state. Emotions *are* motives and akin to traditional motives and drives.

With this emphasis on motivation Leeper considers the relation between emotional motives and cognitive events. He points to the important role of perception in the arousal and regulation of emotional behavior. Perception and emotion are commonly regarded as separate processes but actually perception and emotion are most intimately related.

Darwin (1872) recognized this long ago. Darwin described the hostile behavior of a dog approaching a stranger. When the animal *perceived* that the stranger was actually his beloved master the hostile behavior instantly vanished and the dog became friendly. The change from hostile to friendly behavior depended on perception.

Physiological Theories of Emotion

Current physiological theories of emotion tend to stress the central neural mechanisms. Some of the more important contemporary theories are described below.

CANNON'S THALAMIC THEORY OF EMOTION

According to the James-Lange theory of emotion, the peripheral changes in viscera and skeletal musculature follow directly the perception of the exciting fact and the awareness of these changes as they occur *is* the emotion. Cannon (1927, 1931) criticized this theory and proposed an alternate interpretation.

Cannon's interpretation will be made clear by reference to Figure 37-3. According to Cannon, the excitations of receptors (R) are relayed through the thalamus (Th) to the cerebral cortex (C) over neural pathways 1 and 1′. When an emotional pattern (P) in the thalamus, is excited there is a reflex discharge over pathway 2 to viscera (V) and skeletal musculature (Sk M). Cannon assumed that the cerebral cortex constantly inhibits emotional expressions that are integrated in the thalamus. This continuous inhibitory action is represented by pathway 3. Perception of an emotion-including situation produces cortical disinhibition and thus frees the thalamic centers from their normal restraint. When disinhibition occurs the emotional expressions automatically appear. Incoming sensory impulses from viscera and skeletal musculature arrive at the thalamus and are relayed to the cerebral cortex over pathway 4. These incoming impulses, according to Cannon, give an emotional *quale* to conscious experience.

In arguing for his theory Cannon made five points:

1. Total separation of viscera from the central nervous system does not alter emotional expression and behavior. Hence incoming excitations from the viscera are not essential in emotion.
2. The same visceral changes occur in different emotional states and under nonemotional conditions. The response of the viscera is too uniform to account for the variety of conscious emotions.
3. The viscera are relatively insensitive structures and hence could not serve to distinguish among conscious emotions as implied by James and Lange.
4. Visceral changes are too slow to be a source of emotional feeling. They do not occur soon enough to account for affective tone.
5. Artificial induction of the visceral changes typical of strong emotion does not produce them. Cannon referred to the experiments of Marañon upon the effects of injecting adrenin.

Cannon goes on to consider postural factors in emotion. He cites the experiments of Bechterev, Woodworth and Sherrington, and Bard to show that "sham rage" is present after ablation of all brain structures anterior to the diencephalon. These results point to the thalamus, Cannon states, as a region from which, in the absence of cortical government, impulses are discharged which evoke an extreme degree of emotional activity, both visceral and muscular.

Cannon cites the work of Head to show that human subjects with unilateral lesions in the thalamic region react excessively to emotional stimuli; the reactions are both pleasant and unpleasant. Head attributed this to release from cortical inhibition. Also if the lower centers are released from cortical dominance by nitrous oxide ("laughing gas"), the subject laughs and weeps. The drug weakens cortical inhibition. Hence there is clinical evidence suggesting that James's section, entitled "No Special Brain Centers for Emotion," must be modified.

Cannon's theory of emotion is supported by the surgical studies of Bard (1934a, 1934b, 1950). Bard demonstrated, by successive operations, that after bilateral removal of the entire cerebral cortex the cat and dog are capable of displaying behavior that closely resembles rage in normal animals. The decerebrate animals are hypersensitive. Stroking the fur, which is indifferent or pleasurable to normal animals, evokes displays of intense rage in decerebrate subjects. Transsections below the level of the caudal hypothalamus abolish the pattern of rage.

The emotional reactions of decorticate animals are poorly directed with respect to provoking stimuli. A normal animal exhibits better coordination and precision, in fighting, than does a decerebrate preparation. The intact animal responds with rage to visually perceived situations, such as the approach of a familiar enemy, but decerebrate animals are not aroused in this way. The telencephalon thus widens the range of conditions that are effective in producing rage and renders behavior more effective in combat.

Decorticate cats have been observed to purr and show the usual pleasure reactions of normal animals, as well as rage. Sherrington (1911) reported that decorticate dogs show rage and also disgust. When presented with dog flesh for food the animals showed a normal disgust. Sherrington called these reactions *pseudoaffective* assuming that conscious emotion is a cortical process and that decorticate animals could not *feel* rage. This raises a moot question. Since the subcortical mechan-

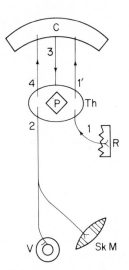

Fig. 37-3. *Diagram of connections postulated by the thalamic theory of emotion.* [From Cannon 1931, p. 282]

isms in man and other animals are illiterate, there is no way of knowing whether primitive consciousness accompanies the emotional behavior. In any event the studies of Bard and Sherrington support Cannon's contention that emotional reactions are coordinated at subcortical levels.

Critique of Cannon's Theory. In criticizing Cannon's theory Grossman (1967) raised several factual objections:

1. Complete removal of the thalamus has no effect on rage reactions of decorticate animals. The emotional responses disappear only when the posterior and ventral portions of the *hypothalamus* are removed. The hypothalamus, however, has neither the specific sensory inputs nor the sensory projections to the cortex which Cannon's thalamic theory requires.

2. If rage were elicited by the release of thalamic mechanisms from cortical inhibition, removal of the source of inhibition should produce a continuous, permanent rage but this does not occur. Some (not all) stimuli elicit rage in decorticate subjects. The stimuli elicit rage from occasion to occasion, not continuously.

3. Rage responses have been elicited by stimulation of the hypothalamus, the cerebral cortex, and even the cerebellum. Such facts cannot be explained in terms of the release of cortical inhibition.

In his book, *Bodily Change in Pain, Hunger, Fear and Rage,* Cannon (1929) emphasized the utility of the bodily changes of emotion in the struggle for existence. He claimed that the secretion of the adrenal gland prepares the organism for vigorous activity as in a fight or a race for one's life. Grossman has summarized the evidence to show that the effects of epinephrine are quite different from those mentioned by Cannon in support of his emergency theory of emotion.

Epinephrine depletes liver glycogen but also decreases glycogen stores in muscle even when the concentration is too low to produce a rise in blood pressure. Also epinephrine tends to inhibit utilization of glucose by slowing its transfer from extracellular fluids to tissue cells. Far from aiding the reconversion of lactic acid to glycogen, epinephrine seems to break down muscular glycogen and thus hinders rather than helps the emergency reaction. The cardiovascular effects of epinephrine are complex but do not seem to be designed to "prepare the organism for a struggle." Epinephrine decreases the blood flow in muscles at rest and has similar effects on active muscle. Epinephrine accelerates the heart beat but this does not necessarily imply improved circulation since stroke volume may decrease with high acceleration. Hence Cannon's view of the emergency function of adrenin is probably incorrect.

ARNOLD'S EXCITATORY THEORY OF EMOTION

Arnold's appraisal-excitatory theory of emotion was discussed above but the physiological aspect was not considered. Arnold (1950) formulated an excitatory theory which is tied in with her emphasis on the cerebral processes of cognition and appraisal. Details of the theory can be understood by inspecting Figure 37-4.

Stimulation of receptors (*R*) sends afferent impulses through

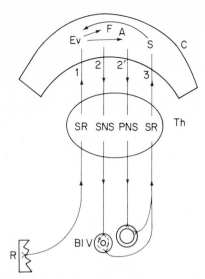

Fig. 37-4. *Diagram of connections postulated by Arnold's excitatory theory of emotion.* [From Arnold 1950; © 1950 by McGraw-Hill Book Company, Inc., used by permission of McGraw-Hill Book Company.]

sensory relay stations (*SR*) in the thalamus (*Th*) over pathway 1 to the cerebral cortex (*C*). At the cortical level the situation is evaluated (*Ev*) and a specific attitude such as fear (*F*) or anger (*A*) is formed. The cortical attitude sends a pattern of impulses over pathway 2 to the sympathetic nervous system relay station (*SNS*) or over pathway 2′ to the parasympathetic nervous system relay station (*PNS*) or to both of these thalamic centers. The excitation then discharges to blood vessels (*Bl V*) and visceral structures. Afferent impulses from the peripheral structures are sent through sensory relay stations (*SR*) in the thalamus to the cortex where there is sensation (*S*) from visceral changes. This sensory feedback from the periphery is evaluated at the cortical level. The feedback, as James postulated, transforms the purely cognitive experience into an emotion which is felt.

Grossman (1967) has raised several objections to Arnold's theory: First, the cortical control over lower centers is both inhibitory (as emphasized by Cannon) and excitatory (as emphasized by Arnold). Each view is partial and incomplete. Moreover, some cortical areas are excitatory with respect to specific emotional targets and inhibitory with respect to other targets. Again, Arnold's postulate that specific cortical areas regulate particular types of emotions, such as fear and anger, is gratuitous; there is lack of evidence for this assumption. Finally, Arnold and others have proposed a classification of emotional reactions in terms of their sympathetic-parasympathetic components. But since autonomic changes are essential neither to the experience nor the expression of emotion, it is unlikely that such changes can determine the site of cortical representation of specific emotions.

Despite Grossman's criticisms of the theories of Cannon and Arnold these theories have made important contributions to our understanding of emotional behavior.

LINDSLEY'S ACTIVATION THEORY OF EMOTION AND MOTIVATION

Lindsley (1951) formulated an activation theory of emotion based largely on his researches in electroencephalography.

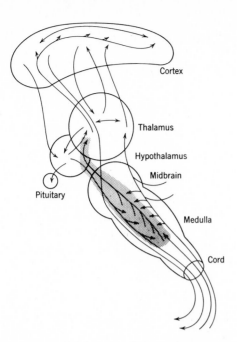

Fig. 37-5. *Schematic representation to show location of neural structures and probable projection pathways in the reticular formation. The approximate location of the reticular network is indicated by crosshatched markings.* [Modified from D.B. Lindsley, "Emotion" in *Handbook of Experimental Psychology*, ed. Stevens; ©1951 by John Wiley & Sons, Inc., New York.]

The theory takes account not only of excited emotions such as rage, fear, terror but also states which are not ordinarily regarded as emotional: drowsiness, sleep, coma. For this reason Lindsley's theory is more accurately described as a theory of activation than a general theory of emotion.

Activation is a central neural process within the brainstem reticular formation and the diffuse corticothalamic projection systems. See Figure 37-5. The activating mechanism is composed of two interrelated systems: the brainstem reticular formation and a system of fibers that project diffusely through thalamic nuclei to the cerebral cortex. The reticular network is located at the levels of the medulla, midbrain, hypothalamus, and lower thalamus. The system is a network that contains many synapses and small neural systems.

It is known that sensory pathways from all sense organs, including those from viscera and somatic structures, send collaterals into the reticular activating system. Impulses are then integrated and distributed to the hypothalamus where they excite the diencephalic waking center as well as nonspecific thalamic nuclei through which they activate all parts of the cerebral cortex—sensory and nonsensory. Excitation of the diffuse projection system tones up the cortex as a whole.

Arrows in Figure 37-5 indicate two-way conduction. There is conduction of neural impulses into the reticulum and upward, through diffuse projection tracts, to the cerebral cortex. There is also conduction downward from the cortex to the reticulum and outward to peripheral effectors, as shown by other arrows. The descending reticular system regulates spinal motor activity. It has a persisting influence in providing tonus for posture and motor responses.

Lindsley describes different levels of activation which can

be represented upon a vertical continuum. At the highest level are excited emotional states. Below, in descending order, are alert attentiveness, relaxed wakefulness, drowsiness, light sleep, deep sleep, coma, and death. These levels of activation can be described in different ways: in terms of brain waves, in terms of the level of general activity, in terms of performance, and in terms of conscious awareness. For further discussion see Young (1961, pp. 181–91).

In developing the activation theory, Lindsley (1957) considered the motivational aspect. The process of motivation, he stated, has two main aspects: (1) There is a general alerting and arousing process which is dynamic and energizing, and (2) there is a sharpening or focusing of activity upon stimulus cues associated with a goal or with the satisfaction of a need. The second aspect is important in relation to attention.

Attention involves the selective awareness of certain sensory messages with simultaneous suppression of others. During the attentive state the brain integrates for consciousness a limited amount of sensory information, specifically, the inputs concerned with the object of attention. The peripheral inputs from receptors are controlled by central processes; some inputs are facilitated while others are blocked. A centrifugal regulation of afferent influx has been demonstrated in all sense departments.

Lindsley's activation theory has had a great impact on discussions of motivation. The impact is shown in studies by Hebb (1955), Duffy (1957), Brown (1961), and others. I will consider only Duffy.

Duffy (1957) pointed out that the term *activation* has a wide range of applicability within the psychology of motivation and emotion. In Lindsley's sense, the term is closely related to *excitatory level, level of energy mobilization, intensity of drive, degree of arousal,* and other dynamic concepts. According to the dictionary, however, the term *activate* also means *to make active* or *to render capable of reacting* or *to promote reaction.* In this last sense, activation is almost synonymous with motivation.

In one meaning of activation (which must not be confused with Lindsley's usage) a psychological determinant can be said to be latent or activated. When a latent emotional conflict is activated there can be acute affective disturbance—a manifest feeling or emotion. The popular phrase, "Let sleeping dogs lie," implies that emotional dispositions can be dormant or activated. Psychologists well know that music, words, odors, and other kinds of stimulation, can activate memories that are emotionally disturbing.

THE CIRCUIT OF PAPEZ

After thorough review of the physiological literature on emotion, Papez (1937) formulated a psychoneural theory. He described a complex neural structure, known as the Papez circuit, which mediates emotional behavior (including expression) and also emotional consciousness.

The emotive process, according to Papez, is built up in the hippocampus. When the hippocampus is excited, impulses are relayed via the fornix to the mammillary bodies of the hypothalamus. From the hypothalamus excitations are sent to the anterior thalamic nuclei and onward to the cingulate gyrus of the cerebrum. Completing the circuit are fibers that conduct excitations from the cingulate gyrus to the hippocampus and amygdala.

These structures, located in the mesocortex and archicortex, influence the cerebral cortex through excitations in the cingulate gyrus and in this way add emotional coloring to conscious experience. Papez describes this circuit as a harmonious mechanism, a reverberating circuit, which elaborates the central emotion and participates in both emotional consciousness and emotional expression.

The circuit is closely related to the midbrain reticular formation and to the limbic system. The circuit receives impulses from the reticular formation by way of the olfactory tubercle. The reticular formation (considered above) is a primitive diffuse system of interlacing nerve cells and fibers which form the central core of each half of the brainstem. It occupies the central part of the medulla, pons, and midbrain tegmentum; and continues upward into the intralaminar and reticular nuclei of the thalamus and ventral thalamus. The reticular formation sends specific fibers to circumscribed areas of the cortex and also nonspecific fibers, by means of side branches, to several cortical regions.

The Papez circuit receives fibers from the limbic system which, in turn, receives excitations from the auditory, visual, gustatory, olfactory, somato- and viscero-receptor systems. The circuit is believed to integrate information from the limbic system. Possibly it provides a basis for the integration of positive and negative hedonic effects.

The limbic lobe is situated bilaterally at the base of the forebrain and is so called because it forms a "limbus," or border, around the brainstem. The limbic lobe runs practically the entire length of the cerebrum. Together with its nuclear structures and interconnections the limbic system is functionally integrated. This system includes the cingulate and hippocampal gyri, the orbitoinsulotemporal region and the subcortical cell stations: amygdala, septal nuclei, hypothalamus, epithalamus, anterior thalamic nuclei, and parts of the basal ganglia. Papez includes the habenular and pituitary structures in the limbic system.

The limbic system, superimposed on the hypothalamus, serves as a regulatory system for autonomic functions. These structures integrate and coordinate visceral and bodily needs with sensory, including peripheral, events. The structures regulate innate activities concerned with searching, feeding, attack, flight, sex, and environmental situations that provoke emotion. (Papez does not define emotion assuming, perhaps, that everyone knows what an emotion is.)

In a paragraph reminiscent of William James' "stream of consciousness" and the time-honored tripartite distinctions among action, thought, and feeling, Papez writes:

It is thus evident that the afferent pathways from the receptor organs split at the thalamic level into three routes, each conducting a stream of impulses of special importance, One route conducts impulses through the dorsal thalamus and the internal capsule to the corpus striatum. This route represents "the stream of movement." The second conducts impulses from the thalamus through the internal capsule to the lateral cerebral cortex. This route represents "the stream of thought." The third conducts a set of concomitant impulses through the ventral thalamus to the hypothalamus and by way of the mammillary body and the anterior thalamic nuclei to the gyrus cinguli, in the medial wall of the cerebral hemisphere. This route represents "the stream of feeling." In this way, the sensory excitations which reach the lateral cortex through the internal capsule receive their emotional coloring from the concurrent processes of hypothalamic origin which irradiate them from the gyrus cinguli (p. 729).

In general, Papez argues that the cingulate gyrus is the seat of that dynamic vigilance by which experiences are endowed with emotional consciousness. The theory also proposes that the hypothalamus, the anterior thalamic nucleui, the gyrus cinguli, the hippocampus and their interconnections constitute a circuitous mechanism for elaborating the functions of central emotion, as well as participating in emotional behavior and expression. Papez's theory is thus much more extensive and inclusive than the previous theories of emotion.

MacLean's Concept of a "Visceral Brain"

MacLean (1949) has elaborated and extended Papez's theory of emotion. MacLean writes:

The problem pertaining to emotional mechanisms is basically one of communication in the central nervous system. It may be assumed that messages from both without and within the organism are relayed to the brain by nervous impulses traveling along nerve fibers and possibly by humoral agents carried in the blood stream. Ultimately, however, any correlation of these messages must be a function of a highly integrated body of neurones capable of sorting, selecting and acting upon various patterns of bioelectric activity. . . (p. 338).

The rhinencephalon, which MacLean refers to as the "visceral brain," is strategically situated so that it can correlate every form of internal and external perception. In the "visceral brain" there is the possibility of bringing into association not only oral and visceral sensations, but also impressions from the sex organs, body wall, eye, and ear. In contrast to the neopallium, the "visceral brain" has many strong connections with the hypothalamus. MacLean regards the hypothalamus as the head ganglion of the autonomic nervous system. The "visceral brain" (mesopallium) coordinates impressions from all sense organs, intraorganic and peripheral, and through the hypothalamus regulates visceral responses along with skeletal responses shown in fear, rage, and other emotions.

The mesopallium is transitional between phylogenetically old and new brains. The mesopallium contributes the affective component of awareness by relaying impulses to the cerebral cortex. Evidence indicates that only the cerebral cortex is capable of appreciating all the affective qualities of experience and combining them into such states of feeling as fear, anger, love, and hate. The cerebral cortex is involved in *experiencing* emotion; the hypothalamus in *expressing* emotion.

The "visceral brain," MacLean states, is not at all unconscious (possibly not even in certain stages of sleep), but rather eludes the grasp of the intellect because it cannot communicate in verbal terms. Perhaps one should say that the "visceral brain" is animalistic, illiterate, primitive. It does, however, have a kind of "organic language."

MacLean's view agrees with a generally accepted proposition that the affective, including emotional, processes are mediated by subcortical mechanisms and that cognitive, intellectual, evaluative, processes are functions of the cerebral cortex. The anatomy of the central nervous system provides a clue to understanding the difference between what we *feel* and what we *know*.

Maclean has a practical interest in emotions. In psychosomatic illnesses such as asthma, ulcerative colitis, peptic ulcer, and hypertension, an emotional state of rage, fear, hostility, grief, resentment, or other, is definitely involved. From a therapeutic point of view, therefore, it is important to understand the neural mechanisms of emotion.

Pribram's Comprehensive Account of Emotion

Pribram (1967, 1968) has presented an exceedingly broad and comprehensive account of emotion based upon a thorough analysis of the physiological and neuropsychological facts. In summary, Pribram states that his theory differs from most currently-held views of emotion in five respects:

1. The proposed theory is *memory-based* rather than drive- or viscerally based. This means that to understand emotion one must take account of previous experience and the present emotion-including situation. This also implies that the cerebral cortex has an important role in instigating emotion. Emotion is relative to some plan or program that is under way rather than to level of activation as in Lindsley's theory.
2. The proposed theory regards *organized stability as the baseline* from which perturbations occur. Inputs that are incongruous with the baseline produce a disturbance. An important part of the baseline is continuing activity of viscera, regulated through the autonomic nervous system. A mismatch between expected and actual bodily changes in heart rate, sweating, "butterflies," etc., is sensed as a discrepancy which is the basis of visceral theories of James and Lange.
3. The theory makes explicit the relation between motivation and emotion by linking both to ongoing, prebehavioral organization, i.e., to a plan, program or disposition. Emotion is a *perturbation*, an interruption, a disruption, of normal ongoing activity. Pribram's theory implies an extension of the homeostasis doctrine from intraorganic events to the total organism-environment relation.
4. The proposal defines emotion as *e*-motion, *a process that takes the organisms temporarily out of motion* and effects control through the regulation of sensory inputs. The processes that occur when an organism is "out of" or "away from" motion are just as important and interesting scientifically as the normal activities of organisms carrying out plans.
5. There is *central control through the regulation of peripheral inputs.* The proposed theory identifies two forms of regulation of sensory inputs. One form inhibits peripheral inputs while the organism determines what to do, what plan to follow. The other form enhances inputs thus making the organism attentive to critical aspects of the situation. Pribram gives details of this dual process.

In general, Pribram's theory takes account of the total organism and its experiences (memories, plans, etc.) as well as the environmental situation. In this respect the theory is an advance over the peripheral theories of James and Lange, the thalamic theory of Cannon, and the psychoneural theories of Papez and MacLean. The history of theories of emotion shows a steady advance from theories that do not involve the nervous system through those that involve peripheral structures and the autonomic nervous system to theories that involve the central nervous system, and finally the organism as a whole living within an environment, present and past.

Pribram's theory is closely related to equilibrium-disequilibrium theories of motivation. Emotion, for him, is a state of disequilibrium, a perturbation, disturbance. Pribram is not clear, however, as to how emotional perturbation differs specifically from nonemotional disturbance but neither is any one else very clear on this matter.

The Neural Substrate of Emotion

The role of the autonomic nervous system in regulating peripheral manifestations of emotion has been extensively studied. There is a vast experimental literature dealing with physiological correlates of emotion: electrical properties of the skin; circulatory changes; changes in respiration; muscle tension; skin temperature; gastrointestinal activity; metabolic rate; pilomotor responses; measures of biochemical processes, etc. For references to the literature and discussion of the autonomic nervous system see Lindsley (1951). Dunbar (1935) reviewed early studies of emotion from the point of view of psychosomatic medicine. Woodworth and Schlosberg (1954) give many references to experimental studies, especially to work on the galvanic skin response.

Current emphasis, however, is upon the regulatory role of neural centers in the diencephalon and mesencephalon rather than peripheral changes and the autonomic nervous system. Pribram and Kruger (1954) reviewed an extensive literature dealing with the structure and function of the rhinencephalon. Originally the rhinencephalon was thought to be exclusively concerned with smell and was described as an "olfactory brain." It is now known that only one part of this structure (the olfactory bulb and closely connected neural structures) is concerned exclusively with olfaction. Other parts regulate emotional and social behavior.

The rhinencephalon, in fact, contains three structural systems. The first of these systems is concerned with olfactory discrimination. The second and third systems are implicated in emotional and social behavior. The second system has a variety of functions. It mediates visceral functions but cannot, according to Pribram, be regarded exclusively as a "visceral brain" because it is implicated in olfactory and gustatory reactions as well as social and emotional behavior. Hence one cannot assign any single function to this system. The third system, designated by Pribram and Kruger as the "allo- and juxtallocortical system," also has several interrelated functions. It is not exclusively concerned with emotion.

In general, there are diffuse excitations within these three structural systems. The diffuseness contrasts with the discreteness of organization of the afferent and efferent projection systems. Pribram and Kruger suggest that the affective and motivational aspects of psychological processes may *require* a diffuse rather than a specific neural substrate, but evidence for this is sparce. Physiological psychologists appear to agree that the limbic and related systems provide a neural substrate for motivational and affective (including emotional) processes but little is known regarding the interrelations of functions of different parts of the limbic system and the relation between limbic structures and other portions of the brain. The limbic system is a group of structures and regions in the forebrain that are anatomically interconnected with each other and with the hypothalamus. The major structures of the limbic system include the *amygdala*, a large nuclear mass embedded deeply in the temporal lobe; the *hippocampus*, a long tubelike structure of cortical tissue embedded in the cerebrum; the *septum*, a nuclear region in the anterior medial depths of the forebrain; the *olfactory projection fields*, regions which receive direct anatomical projections from the olfactory bulb; and several areas called the "old cortex" because they are more primitive in appearance than the neocortex.

Affective Arousal and Reinforcement

Human beings are able to experience and report simple feelings and moods of pleasantness and unpleasantness. Is it possible to study these affective processes objectively?

Long ago (Young 1922) I found that simple feelings of pleasantness are not always expressed by movements of pursuit; there is a relaxed form of pleasantness during which the subject does nothing actively. Although unpleasantness was usually associated with movements of avoidance, there were situations in which avoidance was impossible; unpleasantness was simply endured. I recommended that the traditional hedonistic doctrine be abandoned. Subsequent objective studies have changed my mind about hedonism.

AFFECTIVE AROUSAL AND BEHAVIOR

In a series of studies of food preferences with rats, I observed that some substances (sucrose solutions) are immediately accepted and others (quinine solutions) are rejected. If an animal is given a choice between a sugar solution and a quinine solution, he will continue drinking the sugar and avoid the quinine. Young and Madsen (1963) relied on this principle to define preference objectively. Immediately after forced preliminary sampling of two test fluids the animal was given a free choice. When one fluid was accepted for 5-10 seconds continuously, both fluids were removed and a preference recorded for the fluid that first elicited sustained drinking. Continuing acceptance, therefore, was the criterion of preference. The preference method, in one form or another, has been utilized in psychophysical studies of hedonic processes (Young 1967a).

The positive and negative aspects of behavior have long been recognized. Today the contrast is between *Go-Stop*, *Approach-Withdraw*, *Accept-Reject*, *Continue-Terminate*. There is a genuine difference between the positive and negative forms of behavior.

It is not possible, however, to identify a positive affective arousal with positive behavior and a negative affective arousal with negative behavior. The reason for this is that positive and negative reactions can proceed habitually without any affective arousal. Consider, for example, the reactions to red and green traffic lights. It is obvious that the *Go* when the light turns green and the *Stop* when a red light appears, are not marks of *felt* pleasantness and unpleasantness.

Within subjective experience pleasantness is equivalent to a go-approach-accept-continue type of reaction and unpleasantness to a stop-withdraw-reject-terminate reaction. Some stimulations innately, without learning, elicit one type of reaction and other stimulations elicit the other type. On the basis of the innate processes human and animal subjects *learn* positive and negative behaviors. The learned behaviors eventually proceed automatically without any affective arousal. It is for this reason that positive and negative reactions do not infallibly indicate genuine affective arousal.

The difficulty of objective definition arises in tests of preference. Preference is evaluative choice. Evaluation can rest on immediate affective arousals or evaluation can be a habit of choice based on previous experience. There are two closely related bases of preferential discrimination. Correspondingly there are two criteria of preference. The first criterion (utilized in psychophysical studies) rests upon the tendency to continue or terminate a reaction. A preferential discrimination reveals relative hedonic intensities. The second criterion (utilized in experiments with serial presentations) is *learning* which implies reinforcement. Within wide limits these two criteria yield consistent results.

In numerous studies of taste preferences of rats I have relied on the *development* of a consistent choice (the preferential trend) as a dependable criterion of relative preference. The criterion implies that along with affective arousal there is a reinforcing effect. A habit of choice, in fact, can become so strong that it functions as an independent determinant in the selection of foodstuffs.

REWARD AND PUNISHMENT

In everyday life parents, teachers, animal trainers, and others, utilize rewards and punishments to control behavior and the process of learning. Rewards are bestowed and punishments inflicted to guide behavior of children and pets, and to force social conformity upon adults.

In numerous experiments the intracranial self-stimulation (through implanted electrodes) is referred to as "rewarding" or "punishing." These terms are generally understood because the *S*'s behavior, in fact, is a form of self-reward or self-punishment. But internal neural processes are not directly observed as "rewards" or "punishments." I had to smile when a physiological psychologist, reading a paper at a meeting of the American Psychological Association, referred to the injection of an "anti-punishment" drug!

Underlying rewards and punishments is a basic physiological principle of positive and negative arousal. Some receptor stimulations have a positive, facilitating, influence; others have a negative, inhibiting, effect. There are also excitations which are neutral—neither hedonically positive nor negative. In nature some stimulus-situations elicit a positive and others a negative effect. This is true whether or not the situations are interpreted as "reward" or "punishment."

REINFORCEMENT AND AFFECTIVE AROUSAL

Reinforcement is a phenomenon of learning. Reinforcement is shown by the enhanced probability that a response will recur in a repeated stimulus-situation. Reinforcement does not necessarily depend on affective arousal. For example, in numerous human experiments the instruction to memorize is sufficient to produce learning, regardless of whether the task is pleasant, unpleasant, or neutral. An intent to learn plus the active participation of S is sufficient to produce associative learning. But can affective arousal occur without reinforcement? There is some evidence that it can.

Roberts (1958), in experiments with self-stimulation through electrodes implanted in the hypothalamus, demonstrated an important distinction between escape and avoidance. He found that cats will escape rapidly from a noxious motivational state elicited by hypothalamic stimulation; there were signs of the strongest flight and escape from the stimulating situation. Yet the animals did not *learn* to avoid the situation in as many as 270 trials. This observation implies that the neural mechanism mediating immediate escape from a noxious stimulation is different from the neural mechanism that leads to avoidance learning. There were thus signs of affective arousal without learning.

Other studies, however, have demonstrated that animals can learn to anticipate both positive and negative effects produced by intracranial stimulation. Brady (1961) gave a lucid account of effects obtained by self-stimulations through electrodes implanted in the brains of rat, cat, and monkey. Brady reports that the rate of self-stimulation is influenced by the schedule of self-stimulations. A schedule allows the animal to anticipate impending positive and negative effects. In a "joy" experiment the rate of barpressing increased just prior to the onset of positive self-stimulation. If a signal warned of an impending negative effect, the rate of barpressing decreased. In human terms, the experimental results suggest that animals can learn to anticipate pleasant and unpleasant effects.

Glickman and Schiff (1967) argued that reinforcement is based upon the facilitation of consummatory acts that are specific to a species. Species have evolved diverse patterns of behavior that are adaptive in various habitats. Wild and laboratory rats, for example, exhibit well-integrated patterns of feeding, drinking, gnawing, fighting, running, nesting, sexual and maternal behavior, and other adaptive patterns. Such patterns can be categorized biologically in two ways: (1) Patterns that bring the organism into contact with stimuli that are relevant to survival of individual and species, and (2) Patterns that remove the organism from stimuli that threaten survival. There are built-in neural mechanisms which regulate these adaptive patterns. Glickman and Schiff argue that whatever facilitates the action of species-specific neural mechanisms, whether by natural means or by implanted electrodes, is reinforcing.

This view makes good sense but it does not explain how the adaptive (including emotional) patterns came into existence nor does it explain the exact nature of reinforcement. Some patterns associated with injury and pain are negative. Others associated with sex are positive. Still others associated with the smell and taste of foodstuffs are sometimes positive and sometimes negative. The suggestion is ancient that pleasure is associated with biological utility and pain with biological harm. But precisely what neural mechanisms control pleasure and pain? There is much to learn before one can answer.

SOME FACTS TO BE EXPLAINED

Experimental studies of the food preferences of rats have brought to light the following facts which must be explained by any complete theory of behavior:

1. Rats that are nondeprived and free from every known metabolic need develop remarkably stable and consistent preferences when offered a choice between solid or fluid foods (Young 1967a, 1967b).
2. Naive rats that have been depleted upon some dietary essential prior to testing develop (when tested with foods widely separated as in a T- or Y-maze) preferences that are wise in the sense that their selections tend to meet metabolic needs. For example, naive water-deprived rats develop a preference of water to dry solid food; food-deprived animals develop a preference for food. Again, protein-starved rats develop a preference of casein to sucrose; need-free (nondeprived) animals prefer sucrose (Young 1968).
3. A habit of preferential discrimination, whether established in need-free or depleted Ss, tends to become an independent determinant of food selection which may lead to selections directly opposed to known metabolic needs and to prior conditions of palatability.
4. Some teste solutions (sucrose) are innately accepted by normal rats. Others (quinine hydrochloride) are innately rejected. Still others (sodium chloride, sodium saccharin) are accepted at low concentrations and rejected at high concentrations. These reactions are remarkably uniform and stable for the species.
5. The sensory and hedonic properties of foods are distinct. Foods that differ greatly in appearance, taste, smell, texture, and other sensory properties, may be isohedonic, and foods that have the same sensory quality (sweet or salty) differ in hedonic sign and intensity with changes in the concentration of a taste solution.
6. Preferential habits develop with repeated choices between a pair of test foods. Some preferences appear immediately; others develop gradually with a series of repeated choices. The rate of development depends upon the *difference* of hedonic intensity between the test foods.
7. If a compound taste solution containing a positive solute (sucrose) and a negative solute (quinine) is presented to rats, the separate hedonic intensities summate algebraically. This demonstrates hedonic integration (Young & Trafton 1964).
8. Hedonic integration occurs across sense departments. The palatability level of a test food depends upon smell, taste, temperature, touch, and surrounding environment. Hedonic integration was demonstrated in some unpublished observations of Dr. Clinton L. Trafton. He found that preferences can be changed by giving rats a shock on the feet every time they taste a preferred fluid. Normal rats developed this preference:

$$8 \text{ CHO} > 8 \text{ CHO} + .01 \text{ QHCl}$$

in which CHO = sucrose; QHCl = quinine hydrochloride; numbers indicate grams of solute per 100 cc. of solution.

When the rats were given a shock every time they touched 8 CHO they developed this preference:

$$8 \text{ CHO} + .01 \text{ QHCl} > 8 \text{ CHO} + \text{footshock}$$

The shock had the same influence upon choice as a quinine solution of high intensity.

9. Rats learn preferential discriminations that maximize positive and minimize negative hedonic intensity. After a preferential habit has been established it can be extinguished by removing the preferred solution and substituting a fluid of lower hedonic value. Extinction is a form of learning.

10. Hedonic evaluations can be chained or linked together in time. For example, rats often smell a food before tasting it. If the olfactory reaction is positive, the food is tasted; if the taste reaction is positive, the food is swallowed. There are thus successive evaluations (Young 1968).

THE NEURAL SUBSTRATE OF AFFECTIVE AROUSAL

Routtenberg (1968) has reviewed neuropsychological literature on affective arousal, particularly researches stemming from the work of Olds and his associates. On the basis of experimental evidence Routtenberg postulated two arousal systems. Arousal System I includes the reticular activating system of the brainstem; this system maintains arousal of the organism and provides for organization of responses. Arousal System II includes the limbic system; it provides control of responses elicited through incentive-related stimuli. Evidence indicates that the two arousal systems are mutually inhibitory and reciprocally related. It is necessary to postulate reciprocal relations between the two systems to explain the facts. At present, however, anatomical and physiological details are far from clear.

Grossman (1967, pp. 564–95) reviewed current research on the rewarding and aversive effects of self-stimulation. Evidence indicates that reward-aversion mechanisms are widely distributed in the limbic and related systems and are not localized with any single structure. Grossman believes that experimental evidence favors a hedonic theory of motivation.

There are many unsolved problems regarding the specificity of hedonic effects. Are hedonic effects bound up with specific patterns of behavior such as feeding, sex, and temperature regulation? Or is the mechanism diffuse and general? Or are both specific and diffuse systems involved in hedonic evaluation? How can one explain hedonic integration?

Olds and Olds (1963), in self-stimulation experiments with implanted electrodes, found that large portions of the brain are inert. About sixty percent of implants in the neocortex and in most of the thalamus produced neither positive nor negative effects. The positive system includes large portions of the rhinencephalon and hypothalamus, and some portions of the thalamus and tegmentum. The highest rates of responding were with implants in the posterior hypothalamus and medial tegmentum, the preoptic and septal area, and some placements in the posterior rhinencephalon. Aversive effects were observed from only a few sites in the posterior and lateral diencephalon and lateral tegmental regions. Negative points were located in the immediate vicinity of the most effective positive sites. Both systems can be affected by electrical stimulation of the posterior hypothalamus.

The amygdaloid complex contains two distinct arousal systems. The central and medial nuclei of the corticomedial division of the amygdala are parts of a positive system; animals will self-stimulate at high rates when electrodes are implanted in these parts. The lateral and basolateral nuclei of the basolateral division appear to be part of a purely negative system. Intervening portions of the amygdaloid complex are ambivalent. For details see Olds and Olds (1963, 1964), Grossman (1967), and Routtenberg (1968).

Emotion and Motivation

Do we need two concepts: emotion and motivation? Duffy (1941) argued that the term *emotion* is superfluous. Emotional behavior, she said, differs only in degree from other forms of behavior. Duffy wrote:

I am aware of no evidence for the existence of a special condition called "emotion" which follows different principles of action from other conditions of the organism. I can therefore see no reason for a psychological study of "emotion" as such. Emotion has no distinguishing characteristics. It represents merely an extreme *manifestation of characteristics found in some degree in all responses.*

Duffy goes on to point out some of the characteristics common to all responses. First, there is the degree of energy mobilization—a variable closely related to level of activation. Second, there is the degree of disorganization or organization. Third, there is pleasantness and unpleasantness. No one of these variables, she states, distinguishes emotion as such.

MOTIVATIONAL DIMENSIONS

The concept of dimensions of affectivity is not new. One recalls the tridimensional theory of feeling proposed by Wundt. His dimensions were excitement-calm, tension-relaxation, pleasantness-unpleasantness. Titchener reduced the system to a single variable—pleasantness-unpleasantness—and finally abandoned that for a pure sensationism.

After a careful analysis of moods Nowlis and Nowlis (1956) postulated four dimensions of affectivity:

1. The level of activation or arousal.
2. The level of control. This dimension is similar to the traditional dimension of organization-disorganization since a high level of control implies integration and a low level disintegration.
3. Social orientation. This dimension refers to an aspect of mood in which there is readiness for interaction with other persons or readiness to hurt, reject, ignore others.
4. Hedonic tone. This is the classic dimension of pleasantness-unpleasantness which relates to all moods.

The proposed dimensions of variability differ from investigator to investigator but there is considerable agreement and overlap. Most students of the problem of motivational dimensions recognize activation, or arousal. And I think all recognize the hedonic dimension.

A dimensional analysis of feelings and emotions is very different from the analysis in terms of patterns of response.

Duffy's critique raises some fundamental questions: Does a dimensional analysis prove that a concept of emotion is unnecessary? Do we need both concepts—emotion and motivation? If so, how can emotion and motivation be distinguished?

Organized and Disorganized Activity

A common distinction between emotional and nonemotional activity is based upon the difference between organized and disorganized behavior. Nearly everyone, in describing emotion, uses such terms as *stirred-up state*, *disturbance*, *disruption*, *upset*, *turbulence*, *perturbation*, and similar words that imply disorganization. During an emotion the organism is for a time "out of" or "away from" integrated, purposive, planned action.

The state of disorganization may be acute—brief, intense, disruptive—or it may be chronic and of long duration. Psychiatrists, clinical psychologists, and others, speak of persisting emotional conflicts, emotional disturbances and maladjustments, affects of anxiety, hostility, depression, euphoria, and the like. These are more or less persisting states of disorganization within the individual. The clinical aim is to restore composure, complacency, and peace of mind.

Acute emotional upsets are produced by such dynamic conditions as frustration, insult, failure, bereavement, unexpected news (good or bad), etc. The animal is emotionally excited by the appearance of an enemy, a threat to his security, invasion of his territory, infliction of pain, enticement by a mate, and other conditions. Now it is true that emotional disturbances frequently lead to highly energized, integrated behavior such as a flight from danger or attack upon an enemy or pursuit of a mate. Well-integrated built-in patterns of attack and defense may appear during emotional disturbance. Well-organized goal-oriented behavior may be the immediate outcome of emotional upset. The emotional behavior may be biologically useful and highly adaptive.

Leeper (1948) challenged the view that emotion is disorganized response. Young (1949) defended the view that emotion is acute affective disturbance of psychological origin. Further critical studies were made.

Bindra (1955) wrote that disorganization and organization are successive stages in the development of all behavior. Consider, for example, the behavior of a rat in a maze. At first the naive animal is highly motivated when placed in a strange environment. He explores, urinates, defecates. With successive runs the behavior becomes increasingly goal-oriented, smooth, organized and the signs of disturbance (emotional defecation) disappear. Smith (1958) slightly changed Bindra's interpretation. Smith took a broader view of motivation. If all behavior is motivated (in the sense of being causally determined), then behavior is emotional to the degree that it is (*a*) highly motivated, and (*b*) poorly organized. The degree of organization can be defined in terms of the strength of habit that develops out of an initially disorganized state. The thoroughly habituated rat is not emotionally disturbed.

But emotion is not necessary for the development of a habit. In acquisition of a human skill, such as typewriting, there is increasing integration with practice; words, then phrases become the units of response. The entire process of learning can be free of emotional disorganization. Duffy (1941) would certainly agree.

Neural integration occurs at different levels. Sherrington (1911) demonstrated integration in the spinal reflexes of the dog. Hedonic integration (considered above) occurs at the level of the limbic and related systems, and can be tested by methods that reveal immediate preference. Total integration of the organism involves the cerebral cortex. If there is conflict or blocking at the cortical level, reflex patterns organized at a lower level may appear. Possibly this is what occurs during emotional upsets.

The Definition of Emotion

In the light of the foregoing discussion I will define emotion as *an affectively disturbed state of psychological origin*. To clarify this definition a few comments will be helpful.

Emotional processes are mediated by neural centers and mechanisms in the limbic and related systems including the hypothalamus. An emotion involves the arousal of the subcortical structures. There are, of course, psychological processes that do not excite emotional patterns of response. As an example consider Sokolov's theory of the "neuronal model."

Sokolov (1960) postulated a "neuronal model" which is a kind of biological filter or sieve that acts selectively upon sensory inputs. The "neuronal model" senses differences between current inputs and inputs to which the organism has been habituated. For example, if a dog, in a laboratory situation, has become conditioned to a signal tone of 1000 cps, another tone will arouse an alerting reflex. The alerting reflex appears as a tonic change in skeletal musculature which is immediately followed by an orienting reflex. The difference in sensory input may be one of frequency, intensity, duration, or some other parameter; even the failure of a tone to occur is sensed as a difference. The "neuronal model" is a mechanism, established by habituation, which senses differences between present and previous inputs and provides a stable background against which incoming patterns of excitation are matched, tested, and responded to. The mechanism underlies expectation, anticipation, and recognition of differences. A novel pattern of stimulation elicits the alerting and orienting reflexes but does not necessarily produce an emotional pattern. And habituated action is free from emotion. Sokolov's "neuronal model" is quite similar to the Test-Operate-Test-Exit (TOTE) mechanism described by Miller, Galanter, and Pribram (1960).

Pribram's comprehensive account of emotion considers the affective component of emotional disturbances. His view is almost identical with my own. For Pribram an emotion is an affective perturbation, or disturbance, during which the organism is temporarily "out of" or "away from" planned action. An organism becomes emotional when there is a sufficient discrepancy between present situation and a baseline developed through previous experience. The discrepancy is felt as a mismatch between expected and actual visceral processes. See the above discussion of Pribram's theory of emotion.

In the above definition an emotion was defined as an affectively disturbed state of psychological origin. What is meant by psychological origin? Emotion originates in perception, memory, and knowledge, as distinct from intraorganic physiological processes. Hunger, fatigue, headache, and other internal conditions, are commonly called *feelings* and *moods* but not emotions. In contrast with these intraorganic conditions are emotions of fear, anger, love, embarrassment, etc., which originate in some environmental event and depend upon an individual's understanding, memory, attitudes, and motives. The psychological situation as distinct from internal physiological processes involves the entire organism-environment relationship, present and past.

The contrast between psychological and physiological determinants of behavior is recognized in the distinction between homeostatic and nonhomeostatic drives. Grossman (1967, pp. 596–617) reviewed the psychophysiological theories of Lashley, Beach, Morgan, Stellar, and Lindsley, and then described his own view as a "contemporary two-factor theory of motivation." The two factors are homeostatic and nonhomeostatic. Homeostatic drives such as hunger, thirst, sleep, elimination, are elicited and reduced by changes in the internal environment. The homeostatic drives are controlled by specific needs, specific homeostats, specific messenger systems, and chemical regulators. The nonhomeostatic drives such as attack, flight, sexual and maternal behavior, are controlled by environmental events and situations. Nonhomeostatic drives utilize diffuse structures within the nervous system. The nonhomeostatic drives are released by perception of complex sensory inputs. For example, monkeys respond with a specific pattern of fear when they encounter a snake. Since the fear response is unlearned, one must assume that it is regulated by some built-in mechanism.

The physiological theory of homeostasis has led to the assumption that animals must be deprived in some way to create a need and make them work. But there is now abundant evidence that animals explore, manipulate objects, observe, ingest foods, play, and move about when there is no known intraorganic deprivation. Also many affective reactions to sensory stimulation are not dependent upon the internal metabolic state. It should be added, however, that there is a close relation between affective arousals and the weal and woe of an organism. For example, the extremes of heat and cold are unpleasant and the organism withdraws from such damaging temperatures. If one is heated, coolness is pleasing; if one is cold, warmth is agreeable.

Simple affective processes like the more disruptive emotions, originate within the psychological situation.

MOTIVATION AND EMOTION

It is clear from the above discussion that emotion and motivation are closely related. The question whether we need both concepts is a reasonable one. The answer depends on how one views motivation. There are both narrow and broad definitions of motivation.

According to Webster's dictionary, a motive is "that within the individual, rather than without, which inclines him to action: any idea, need, emotion, or organic state that promotes to an action." This definition includes conscious intents, unconscious motives, emotions, organic states of hunger, drowsiness, drunkenness, and other internal determinants of action. The definition excludes environmental stimuli.

Some psychologists restrict the study of motivation to analysis of behavior which is purposive, goal-oriented, need-related, and organized. Such behavior is explained by postulating a set intention, desire, plan, drive, incentive, or other determinant. This is a narrow view. Since emotional upsets, such as

uproarious laughter, are disorganized and lack a goal, they are *not* (according to this view) motivated. Other examples of non-motivated behavior include physical movement (such as falling out of a window), uncoordinated movements during an epileptic seizure, physiological reflexes such as the knee jerk, and abnormal stereotyped behavior that lacks a goal.

A broader view equates motivation with all the *psychological* determinants of activity. According to this view, motivational psychology includes an analysis of attitudes, traits of personality, habits, associations, and all determinants of behavior whether dynamic or nondynamic. In this broader view, emotional upsets are motivated in the sense that they are *psychologically* determined even though they lack a goal. This broader view has an advantage: with it one can trace out the development of organized behavior all the way from unorganized responses and innate reflexive patterns to integrated, goal-oriented behavior.

Still broader is the view that all behavior is motivated in the sense of being causally determined. A search for determinants, however, leads beyond psychology into the fields of physics, biochemistry, physiology, and all the biological and social sciences. With this broadest of definitions the study of motivation becomes a problem for all of the sciences and motivation is almost equivalent to explanation.

At present psychologists do not agree upon the definition and scope of motivational psychology. Some would restrict motivation to processes of activation, or arousal, of activity. Since neurons are always active, even in dreamless sleep, the problems of motivation are concerned with *changes* in the level of energy release and expenditure. I think, however, that the process of activation cannot be divorced from the mechanisms that sustain, direct, regulate, and control behavior; nor can direction and regulation be divorced from reinforcement and development. The basic aspects of activation, direction, development, are interrelated even in the simplest sensory stimulations. Gustatory stimulations, for example, yield sensory information; they are activating; they are regulating in that they produce a positive or negative hedonic effect; and they are reinforcing in that they promote learning.

Practical Considerations

Although current research on feeling and emotion is characterized by empirical investigation and theorizing, down through the centuries there has been a practical, moral interest in the topic. Eighteenth century discussions of egoism and altruism, hedonism and standards of conduct, preserve the ethical tradition. Current psychiatry and clinical psychology emphasize the therapeutic importance of emotional release in psychosomatic disorders.

EMOTION AND MENTAL HEALTH

Dr. George M. Beard, in 1876, read a paper before the American Neurological Association in New York City entitled "The Influence of Mind in the Causation and Cure of Disease and the Potency of Definite Expectations." Dr. Beard maintained that disease might appear and disappear without influence of any other agent than some form of emotion. Fear, terror, anxiety, grief, anger, wonder, or a definite expectation he regarded as mental conditions likely to produce disease. Dr. Beard argued that certain emotional states could neutralize therapeutics and increase the effects of drugs. At the time, his ideas were new and startling; later the ideas were recognized in a movement now known as psychosomatic medicine.

Today it is widely accepted that persisting emotional disturbances constitute an important factor in certain disorders: peptic ulcer, essential hypertension, rheumatoid arthritis, ulcerative colitis, bronchial asthma, hyperthyroidism, neurodermatitis, and other disorders. The health of the patient is strongly influenced by conditions of living which produce emotional traumata —such as financial failure, bereavement, insult, injury, unrequited love, threatened divorce, loss of self-esteem, guilt, chronic physical disease, and various other factors of stress. Today psychogenic disorders are well recognized in the medical and psychological professions.

Emotional expression plays an important role in psychotherapy. Psychotherapy is not merely an intellectual process. It has wrongly been said that the way to bring about readjustment is to help the patient gain an intellectual understanding of his problems. A cognitive understanding of one's life-situation is helpful but not sufficient to effect a cure. Psychotherapy operates in the sphere of emotion. The aim of psychotherapy is to provide corrective emotional experience by relaxing the subject's defenses and permitting him to reappraise the situations that produced anxiety. In the major methods of psychotherapy the subject is encouraged to *feel*, to express his emotions. The emotional expressions are of primary importance. They can, of course, be supplemented by rational suggestions, arguments, and persuasions.

Psychoanalysts have long recognized the importance of emotion in the etiology and therapy of neuroses. Unresolved conflicts, anxieties, phobias, repressed hostility, loss of confidence and self-esteem, and similar conditions, underlie neurotic symptoms. To reveal unconscious motivations and alleviate mental disorder psychoanalysts resort to free verbal association, aided recall, and interpretation of dreams, all the while observing emotional expressions. The clinical aim is to elicit thoughts that accompany the emotional reactions. A dominant emotion is associated with something important to the patient, something that affects him deeply. Just why it is important can be learned only by getting the patient to talk, to express his thoughts.

EMOTION AND SOCIAL PROBLEMS

The contrast between cognition and emotion is widely recognized. One hears such phrases as "intellect and emotion," "reason and emotion," "mind and emotion." The implication is that intellect, reason and mind are rational; emotion is non-rational. A man with a towering rage and uncontrolled impulses is said to be temporarily "out of his mind," "irrational," "unreasonable." Feelings of hunger, pain, fear, and the like, simply exist; they are not the results of logical reasoning.

One must remember that man like other animals has a limbic system and a hypothalamus! These subcortical structures are products of eons of evolution; they preserve the structural basis for primitive, semiautonomous, animalistic, illiterate behavior that appears in flight from danger, aggressive attack, sexual advance, maternal behavior, selection of foods, and other basic activities. Exhortations cannot change the biological facts.

Sociologists and cultural anthropologists emphasize the wide diversity in human behavior and the relativity of behavior to culture and social experience. The point is well taken but it is equally true that there is a common denominator to human behavior which rests upon an anatomical and physiological basis. In all societies and at all times men have common needs. All men know hunger, thirst, satiation, pain, suffocation, heat and cold, good health and sickness, sleep and wakefulness, eliminative urges, fatigue and restedness, sexual excitement, and protective urges. On the level of emotional behavior all men smile, laugh, cry, weep; all are aware of love and hate, fear and anxiety, anger and lasting hostility, pleasantness and unpleasantness. Men crave security, freedom to work and play and think. Man shares many of these behaviors and experiences with other animals.

Man is a social animal. Interpersonal and intergroup relations are of tremendous importance. Equally basic is an individual's feeling of self-esteem based on his relations to other persons. Saving face, being accepted by the group, and being recognized as competent and worthwhile are important matters. The social attitudes, motives, and habits formed within the group are fundamental factors in any study of interpersonal and intergroup relations.

In every society the developing child *learns* but *what* he learns differs from group to group with culture, place, and time. If we compare different groups, we find that adults differ in religious beliefs, political practices, methods in agriculture, medicine, education, and in other ways. Individuals differ in skills, knowledge, moral and esthetic values, loyalties, goals, interests, intelligence, personality traits, and in other characteristics. Despite these individual and group differences there is a common psychobiological denominator.

The student of motivation and emotion can make an important contribution to our understanding of human nature. We are in the midst of a profound social revolution. No one can foresee the outcome. To some it looks as if the survival of *homo sapiens* upon the earth is at stake. There are many aspects of the revolution: biological, psychological, sociological, economic, political, moral, religious, historical, aesthetic, technological, scientific, and others. The task of the behavioral scientist is to give a true account of the nature of man and the factors that influence action.

EMOTION AND THE CONTROL OF HUMAN BEHAVIOR

The idea that human action can be controlled by reasoning and logic has a limitation because man is only in part a rational creature. Emotional appeals are more effective than logic in creating loyalties, commitments, motives, attitudes, and ideals. This fact is frankly recognized in the fields of advertising, evangelism, political propaganda, oratory, salesmanship, and other practices concerned with action. To get action one needs to create a feeling that the action is right and reasonable. This is not always easy but the principle should be kept in mind while considering social changes in such important areas as war and peace, population control, eugenics, race relations, industrial and international relations, health, government, education, and religion.

On college and university campuses today it appears that present-day students intend to act rather than merely to learn and think. In education there is a growing emphasis on activation. This is a revolutionary departure from traditional intellectualism. In considering the matter one should remember that the same psychological laws govern student behavior on and off the campus. The activation movement among students changes the entire character of education and the relation of education to political life and government. Student behavior is like that of other human beings in that it can be controlled by emotional appeals as well as by logic, argument, and information. From a practical point of view emotional appeal (affective arousal) appears to be more effective in promoting action than argument. But feeling and reason must go hand in hand. Man is in part a rational creature.

Conclusion

The study of feeling and emotion is complex and presents many problems. The complexity is due to the fact that affective processes are related to almost everything that is psychological—perception, memory, learning, reasoning, and action.

There are different views concerning the nature of emotion. According to one view, emotion is a pattern of response that is elicited reflexively by a stimulating situation. According to another view, emotion is a disturbed affective state that is elicited by an environmental situation rather than by intraorganic conditions. Broadly viewed, emotion is both an acute affective upset and a chronic affectively toned state of disorganization.

One can study affective processes experimentally as facts of experience, facts of behavior, and as physiological (especially neural) events. One can describe the dimensions along which affective processes vary.

Although there are many views concerning the nature of affective processes, there is general agreement upon the basic importance of feelings and emotions in behavior, in conscious experience, in individual development, and in social life. Affective disturbances are practically important in relation to mental health, education, social welfare, and to human adjustment and happiness.

References

ANGIER, R. P. The conflict theory of emotion. *American Journal of Psychology*, 1927, *39*, 390–401.

ARNOLD, MAGDA B. An excitatory theory of emotion. *In* M. L. Reymert (ed.) *Feelings and emotions.* New York: McGraw-Hill, 1950, pp. 11–33.

⸻ *Emotion and personality:* vol. 1, *Psychological aspects;* vol. 2, *Neurological and physiological aspects.* New York: Columbia University Press, 1960.

AX, A. F. The physiological differentiation between fear and anger in humans. *Psychosomatic Medicine*, 1953, *15*, 433–42.

BARD, P. The neurohumoral basis of emotional reactions. *In* C. Murchison (ed.), *A handbook of general experimental psychology.* Worcester, Mass.: Clark University Press, 1934a.

⸻ An emotional expression after decortication with some remarks on certain theoretical views. *Psychological Review*, 1934b, *41*, 309–29.

⸻ Central nervous mechanisms for the expression of anger in animals. *In* M. L. Reymert (ed.), *Feelings and emotions.* New York: McGraw-Hill, 1950.

BINDRA, D. Organization in emotional and motivated behaviour. *Canadian Journal of Psychology*, 1955, *9*, 161–67.

BRADY, J. V. Motivational–emotional factors and intracranial self-stimulation. *In* D. E. Sheer (ed.), *Electrical stimulation of the brain: an interdisciplinary survey of neurobehavioral integrative systems.* Austin: University of Texas Press, 1961.

BROWN, J. S. *The motivation of behavior.* New York: McGraw-Hill, 1961.

CANNON, W. B. The James–Lange theory of emotions: A critical examination and an alternative theory. *American Journal of Psychology*, 1927, *39*, 106–24.

⸻ *Bodily changes in pain, hunger, fear, and rage: An account of recent researches into the function of emotional excitement*, 2nd ed. New York: Appleton-Century-Crofts, 1929.

⸻ Again the James–Lange and the thalamic theories of emotion. *Psychological Review*, 1931, *38*, 281–95.

COFER, C. N., and APPLEY, M. H. *Motivation: Theory and research.* New York: John Wiley, 1964.

DARWIN, C. *The expression of the emotions in man and animals.* London: John Murray, 1872.

DOLLARD, J., DOOB, L. W., MILLER, N. E., MOWRER, O. H., and SEARS, R. R. *Frustration and aggression.* New Haven, Conn.: Yale University Press, 1939.

DUFFY, ELIZABETH. An explanation of "emotional" phenomena without the use of the concept "emotion." *Journal of General Psychology*, 1941, *25*, 283–93.

⸻ The psychological significance of the concept of "arousal" or "activation." *Psychological Review*, 1957, *64*, 265–75.

DUNBAR, HELEN F. *Emotions and bodily changes: A survey of literature on psychosomatic interrelationships, 1910–1933.* New York: Columbia University Press, 1935.

GARDINER, H. M., METCALF, R. C., and BEEBE–CENTER, J. G. *Feeling and emotion: A history of theories.* New York: American Book, 1937.

GLASS, D. C. (ed.) *Neurophysiology and emotion: Proceedings of a conference under the auspices of Russell Sage Foundation and The Rockefeller University.* New York: Rockefeller University Press, 1968.

GLICKMAN, S. E., and SCHIFF, B. B. A biological theory of reinforcement. *Psychological Review*, 1967, *74*, 81–109.

GROSSMAN, S. P. *A textbook of physiological psychology.* New York: John Wiley, 1967.

HAYWORTH, D. The social origin and function of laughter. *Psychological Review*, 1928, *35*, 367–84.

HEBB, D. O. On the nature of fear. *Psychological Review*, 1946, *53*, 259–76.

⸻ Drives and the C. N. S. (Conceptual Nervous System). *Psychological Review*, 1955, *62*, 243–54.

HUNT, J. MCV., COLE, MARIE-LOUISE W., and REIS, EVA E. S. Situational cues distinguishing anger, fear, and sorrow. *American Journal of Psychology*, 1958, *71*, 136–51.

IZARD, C. E. *The face of emotion.* New York: Appleton-Century-Crofts, 1971.

JAMES, W. *The principles of psychology*, vol. 2. New York: Holt, 1913, chapter 25.

LANDIS, C. Studies of emotional reactions: II. General behavior and facial expression. *Journal of Comparative Psychology*, 1924, *4*, 447–501.

LEEPER, R. W. A motivational theory of emotion to replace "emotion as disorganized response." *Psychological Review*, 1948, *55*, 5–21.

⸻ Some needed developments in the motivational theory of emotion. *In* D. Levine (ed.), *Nebraska Symposium on Motivation, 1965.* Lincoln: University of Nebraska Press, 1965.

LINDSLEY, D. B. Emotion. *In* S. S. Stevens (ed.) *Handbook of experimental psychology.* New York: John Wiley, 1951.

⸻ Psychophysiology and motivation. *In* M. R. Jones (ed.), *Nebraska Symposium on Motivation, 1957.* Lincoln: University of Nebraska Press, 1957.

LUND, F. H. Why do we weep? *Journal of Social Psychology*, 1930, *1*, 136–51.

MCDOUGALL, W. The principal instincts and the primary emotions of man. *An introduction to social psychology*, Chap. 3. Boston: Luce, 1926.

MCGINNIES, E. Emotionality and perceptual defense. *Psychological Review*, 1949, *56*, 244–51.

MACLEAN, P. D. Psychosomatic disease and the "visceral brain": Recent developments bearing on the Papez theory of emotion. *Psychosomatic Medicine*, 1949, *11*, 338–53.

MANDLER, G. The interruption of behavior. *In* D. Levine (ed.) *Nebraska Symposium on Motivation, 1964.* Lincoln: University of Nebraska Press, 1964.

MILLER, G. A., GALANTER, E. H., and PRIBRAM, K. H. *Plans and the structure of behavior.* New York: Holt, 1960.

MURRAY, J. A. H. *Emotion. A New English dictionary on historical principles, founded mainly on the materials collected by the philosophical society.* Oxford and New York: Macmillan, 1888.

NOWLIS, V. The development and modification of motivational systems in personality. *In* M. R. Jones (ed.), *Current theory and research in motivation.* Lincoln: University of Nebraska Press, 1953.

———, and NOWLIS, H. H. The description and analysis of mood. *Annals of the New York Academy of Sciences*, 1956, *65*, 345–55.

OLDS, J., and MILNER, P. Positive reinforcement produced by electrical stimulation of septal area and other regions of rat brain. *Journal of Comparative and Physiological Psychology*, 1954, *47*, 419–27.

OLDS, J., and OLDS, M. E. The mechanism of voluntary behavior. *In* R. G. Heath (ed.), *The role of pleasure in behavior—A symposium by 22 authors.* New York: Hoeber, 1964.

OLDS, M. E., and OLDS, J. Approach-avoidance analysis of rat diencephalon. *The Journal of Comparative Neurology*, 1963, *120*, 259–95.

PAPEZ, J. W. A proposed mechanism of emotion. *Archives of Neurology and Psychiatry*, 1937, *38*, 725–43.

PRIBRAM, K. H. The new neurology and the biology of emotion. *American Psychologist*, 1967, *22*, 830–38.

——— Emotion: Steps toward a neuropsychological theory. *In* D. C. Glass (ed.), *Neurophysiology and emotion.* New York: Rockefeller University Press, 1968.

———, and KRUGER, L. Functions of the "Olfactory Brain." *Annals of the New York Academy of Sciences*, 1954, *58*, 109–38.

RAPAPORT, D. *Emotions and memory.* New York: International Universities Press, 1950.

ROBERTS, W. W. Rapid escape learning without avoidance learning motivated by hypothalamic stimulation in cats. *Journal of Comparative and Physiological Psychology*, 1958, *51*, 391–99.

ROUTTENBERG, A. The two-arousal hypothesis: Reticular formation and limbic system. *Psychological Review*, 1968, *75*, 51–80.

SCHACHTER, S., and SINGER, J. E. Cognitive, social, and physiological determinants of emotional state. *Psychological Review*, 1962, *69*, 379–99.

SCHILDKRAUT, J. J., and KETY, S. S. Biogenic amines and emotion. *Science*, 1967, *156*, 21–30.

SCHLOSBERG, H. The description of facial expressions in terms of two dimensions. *Journal of Experimental Psychology*, 1952, *44*, 229–37.

SHEER, D. E. Emotional facilitation in learning situations with subcortical stimulation. *In* D. E. Sheer (ed.), *Electrical stimulation of the brain: An interdisciplinary survey of neurobehavioral integrative systems.* Austin: University of Texas Press, 1961.

SHERMAN, M. The differentiation of emotional responses in infants-I. Judgments of emotional responses from motion picture views and from actual observation; II. The ability of observers to judge the emotional characteristics of the crying of infants, and of the voice of an adult. *Journal of Comparative Psychology*, 1927, *7*, 265–84; 335–51.

SHERRINGTON, C. S. *The integrative action of the nervous system.* New Haven, Conn.: Yale University Press, 1911.

SMITH, K. On the inter-relationships among organization, motivation, and emotion. *Canadian Journal of Psychology*, 1958, *12*, 69–73.

SOKOLOV, E. N. Neuronal models and the orienting reflex. *In* M. A. B. Brazier (ed.), *The central nervous system and behavior*, Transactions of the third conference, Josiah Macy, Jr., Foundation, 1960.

TOLMAN, E. C. A behavioristic account of the emotions. *Psychological Review*, 1923, *30*, 217–27.

WATSON, J. B. A schematic outline of the emotions. *Psychological Review*, 1919, *26*, 165–96.

WENGER, M. A. Emotion as visceral action: An extension of Lange's theory. *In* M. L. Reymert (ed.), *Feelings and emotions.* New York: McGraw-Hill, 1950, pp. 3–10.

WILSON, W. Correlates of avowed happiness. *Psychological Bulletin*, 1967, *67*, 294–306.

WOODWORTH, R. S., and SCHLOSBERG, H. *Experimental psychology.* New York: Holt, Rinehart & Winston, 1954.

YOUNG, P. T. Movements of pursuit and avoidance as expressions of simple feeling. *American Journal of Psychology*, 1922, *33*, 511–26.

——— Laughing and weeping, cheerfulness and depression: A study of moods among college students. *Journal of Social Psychology*, 1937, *8*, 311–34.

——— Emotion as disorganized response—A reply to Professor Leeper. *Psychological Review*, 1949, *56*, 184–91.

——— *Motivation and emotion: A survey of the determinants of human and animal activity.* New York: John Wiley, 1961.

——— Affective arousal: Some implications. *American Psychologist*, 1967a, *22*, 32–40.

——— Palatability: The hedonic response to foodstuffs. *In* C. F. Code et al. (eds.), *Handbook of physiology*, section 6, *Alimentary canal*, vol. 1. Baltimore: Williams & Wilkins, 1967b.

——— Evaluation and preference in behavioral development. *Psychological Review*, 1968, *75*, 222–41.

——— *Emotion in man and animal: Its nature and dynamic basis.* Revised edition. Huntington, N. Y.: Krieger, 1973.

———, and MADSEN, C. H., JR. Individual isohedons in sucrose–sodium chloride and sucrose–saccharin gustatory areas. *Journal of Comparative and Physiological Psychology*, 1963, *56*, 903–9.

YOUNG, P. T., and TRAFTON, C. L. Activity contour maps as related to preference in four gustatory stimulus areas of the rat. *Journal of Comparative and Physiological Psychology*, 1964, *58*, 68–75.

Personality

This section surveys the broad range of topics encompassed under the area of structured personality assessment. In the course of this review a number of related issues will be touched upon, including those relevant to conceptions of the process of measurement and to conceptions of the nature of personality. Issues of historical concern as well as those arising out of contemporary research will be introduced where appropriate. The focus will be more contemporary than historical, however, because the area of personality measurement has benefitted considerably from the influence of a great deal of recent research. This research, facilitated by the modern digital computer, has given rise to fresh conceptions and new insights.

From an early struggling growth in the construction of personality inventories to the present, one can discern a series of cumulative developments. At first these early primitive steps represented attempts at gaining footholds for deriving scientifically solid generalizations and measurements. To many observers, these efforts too often met with failure, leading to a great deal of skepticism regarding even the possibility of valid and reliable measurement in personality. But the contemporary situation is one rich in potential and diversity. Many innovations have been introduced, both in the methodology of assessment and in the statistical treatment of data. It is possible for the personality assessment specialist to perceive an enormous amount of progress, not only in data analysis, but in the theory of the test response. As a price for progress, however, the field has become more specialized, more quantitative, with the result that for the casual observer, it has become increasingly more difficult to resolve controversial issues without an understanding of the details of studies, and of alternative methods for analyzing data. Research in this area, as in others in psychology, increasingly requires a blending of the substantive with the methodological. Both theoretical and quantitative skills are necessary, and neither is sufficient in itself to do justice to problems of assessment.

With the variety of methods available for observing personality, the question arises, why focus on the structured approach to personality measurement? There are at least three

Douglas N. Jackson

Structured Personality Assessment

38

good reasons for emphasizing structured approaches to assessment.

First of all, structured assessment derives from, and is dependent upon, what perhaps may be considered one of the most important discoveries of modern psychology: the psychological test item. At first glance this statement might appear to have been made partially in jest, but it was not. The ability to sample and to analyze a discrete unit of behavior allows the psychologist to utilize a variety of conceptions derived from statistics and formal test theory (Gulliksen 1950; Lord & Novick 1968), such as the concept of reliability. Implicit in the idea that a personality item represents a sample of behavior is the requirement that distinct samples so constituted be representative and distinguishable units in a way that casual observation of behavior may not allow. For example, three different naive judges viewing the behavior of a group of adults at work might each focus on different facets of behavior, one on verbal communication, a second on nonverbal aspects of interaction, and a third on inferred intrapsychic states. The personality item, on the other hand, does not permit this kind of diversity. Usually responses to a well-selected personality item are made in terms of one determinant or a small set of determinants.

A second advantage of structured approaches to personality assessment is objectivity and replicability. Objectivity in the present context has reference to the degree to which tests may be scored without an individual judgment or evaluation of each response. The use of highly standardized procedures is one of the important contributions of the discipline of psychological measurement of the past half century. Using objective scoring, it is possible to avoid the often considerable source of unreliability associated with the application of divergent judgmental criteria for evaluating a unit of behavior, while contributing substantially to ease and economy of scoring and quantification. Indeed, one may adopt a number of concepts from formal test theory, including those related to the item operating characteristic, true score, error of measurement, and reliability (Gulliksen 1950; Lord & Novick 1968).

A third reason for favoring structured approaches to personality assessment, particularly those employing the printed statement, is a very pragmatic one. In general, structured personality tests have proved to be more valid than alternative approaches. The reasons for this are becoming progressively more apparent. First, the segmenting of a questionnaire into a number of small units or items permits a broader sampling of behavior than do techniques employing grosser units. Secondly, it is possible to apply any one of a number of analytical procedures for maximizing or optimizing the utility of a set of items for some intended purpose. Thirdly, much of what is termed personality can appropriately be considered in terms of a person's verbal behavior. While not denying the possible value of other approaches in certain situations, linguistic stimuli and response modes on the average will often provide a sample of behavior superior to other approaches in terms of the degree to which they correspond to such widely employed criteria as behavior ratings and situational tests.

It would not be accurate to conclude from this outline of the advantages of the personality questionnaire that knowledge of personality items is by any means complete, nor is there a completely adequate basis for selecting on a priori grounds those which will provide an optimal level of validity. But by the very nature of the personality item, it is more amenable to analysis and evaluation, more amenable to the successive small steps that characterize cumulative science, than are many other approaches using grosser and less clearly defined units of analysis. Thus, one can have confidence that, given the already respectable levels of fidelity and validity attained and the potential for progress, questionnaires will continue to be the method of choice for most assessment decisions.

Assessment Implications of Alternative Definitions of Personality

Some theorists have defined personality extremely broadly so that it encompasses almost everything that a person does, ranging from much of what is considered homeostatic physiological functioning, to cognitive performance. While this is possible, personality is usually thought of in a narrower, more focused way. Personality, for most psychologists, refers to a unique organization of traits characterizing an individual, and influencing his interaction with his environment, social and nonsocial (cf. Kleinmuntz 1967). Thus, the emphasis is upon motives and behavioral patterns serving to differentiate people, particularly in a social context. This is still a rather broad definition, but there might be some risk in too great a definitional restriction. For example, there have been some unfortunate consequences from implicitly equating personality with psychopathology, particularly for assessment decisions. For example, the use of tests of psychopathology like the Minnesota Multiphasic Personality Inventory (MMPI) for applications like industrial selection has been criticized (Whyte 1956) because the presence or absence of minor forms of psychopathology had little bearing upon what was at issue, namely, human potential. Those who view personality as simple or fairly narrow may be led into the trap of believing that various personality tests are more or less interchangeable. This erroneous belief often leads to the assessment of traits having little relevance to the practical decision to be made.

The scope and nature of one's definition of personality will be related to theoretical proclivities. For example, a preference for psychoanalytic theory might cause an investigator to emphasize certain kinds of psychopathology, as well as "primary process" activities, their derivatives, and defense mechanisms. Those influenced by Skinnerian learning theory would tend to avoid postulating inferred states or hypothetical constructs, and even might not wish to make a sharp distinction between psychopathology and other forms of behavior (Ullman & Krasner 1969). An investigator influenced by Rotter's (1954) social learning theory would be prone to emphasize situational determinants of personality (Mischel 1968), possibly at the expense of other determinants. Each theoretical vantage point involves a focusing, an abstraction of certain facets of personality and an exclusion of others. Whatever advantage this may have for theory, from an assessment standpoint it results in a wide diversity of measures of personality, which are by no means interchangeable.

Usually, there is a tendency to think of personality as very culture-bound, and very much related to the context in which it occurs. Cultural anthropologists are quite prone to emphasize the diversity of behavioral patterns that may be observed in different cultures, and they would have us believe that personality is highly dependent upon the broader culture and particular context in which it occurs. There is a great deal of evidence consistent with this point of view. It is possible, on the other hand, to carry this argument too far, and to overlook the broad areas of behavior where there are important cultural constraints. Most cultures would discourage many types of psychopathology and of aggression. A series of studies of the stability of mean social desirability judgments of personality items across different cultures would suggest that there is considerably more than a trivial relationship between the way in which people in quite widely varying cultures and subcultures evaluate the content of personality items (Cowen & Frankel 1964; Edwards 1957; Iwawaki & Cowen 1964).

Situationism and Change

The role of situational determinants in personality theory and assessment has had a long history. Murphy (1947) devoted a chapter to situationism, the doctrine that the primary source of behavioral consistency is not a constellation of traits, nor a set of internally defined motives, but, rather, springs out of forces derived from the environment in which the person finds himself. This is a position preferred by a majority of sociologists. Within psychology, this position has recently been effectively championed by those interested in applying behavioristic learning theory to behavior therapy and change.

Mischel (1968), in an influential book, has advocated the point of view that behavior is regulated by highly specific stimulus variables and response contingencies, rather than by broad constructs or traits. Consistent with this viewpoint is the belief that both personality assessment and psychotherapy need to be more focused and less global than is usually the case. According to Mischel (1968),

Global estimates of the overall strength or frequency of broad response dispositions, as in trait-state descriptions of people as generally "hostile," "aggressive," "passive-dependent," "neurotic," or "anxious," have turned out to have little utility beyond gross screening. Instead, a more useful type of assessment would have to deal with behavior in relation to specific contingencies and discriminative conditions (p. 193).

For Mischel, it is not enough to know that a person is "anxious." He would want to know the specific conditions that triggered the behavior characterized as "anxious," what the history of the acquisition of this behavior was, and how the response varies with specific changes in the situation. By understanding the conditions affecting behavior, it is the hope of the behaviorist-situationist psychologist, to establish contingencies so that undesirable behavior may be extinguished, and more advantageous behavior substituted. This results in a shift in focus. The goal of assessment is not the assignment of a person to a diagnostic category, not the prediction of behavior in an unknown situation, nor is it the attempt to impute the presence of traits or personality dynamics. Rather, the focus is upon designing treatments to change a client's behavior so that it is in line with his expectations.

There is much merit in this position, in that it demands of assessment a utility that it may not possess under other circumstances. The behavior therapist is quite properly critical of those who perform psychiatric diagnostic functions in a vacuum, apart from the assignment of a treatment. Like Cronbach and Gleser (1964), the focus of the behavior therapist is not upon the sheer identification of the person's location on a trait dimension, but what decision is likely to result from an assessment, and the resulting utility of such a decision. This focus has resulted in a remarkably prolific series of investigations in such diverse areas as the manner in which certain types of behavior are acquired during childhood, and the types of reinforcements appropriate to different kinds of behavior change. While it is the author's view that the rejection of the concept of broad personality constructs is extreme, and may leave the investigator with inadequate conceptual tools with which to understand behavior change, it is nevertheless true that the challenge to traditional thinking in assessment afforded by this approach has been a healthy one.

A different view of the situation as it affects behavior is presented by McClelland et al. (1953). A situation serves to define a motive. In order to measure a motive (i.e., achievement need, sex need, affiliation need, power need), it must be aroused properly under suitable environmental conditions. Thus, achievement fantasy is assessed by first arousing, through competitively oriented instructions, an appropriate level of motivation, and then providing the respondent with stimulus pictures similar to those used in the Thematic Apperception Test. Thus, McClelland does not disclaim the reality of general motivational variables, but insists that they do not exist in a vacuum. In order that they be meaningfully assessed, they must emerge in the right situation, interacting with appropriate situational variables.

There is indeed evidence that achievement and sex-related fantasy, for example, can be demonstrated to vary with the situation. But it would be uneconomical and unfortunate to base all of assessment upon the prior arousal of a motive, especially if the situation depended upon the effectiveness of deception, as in some of the studies cited by McClelland. While it is possible to fool some subjects some of the time (e.g., by reading contrived achievement related instructions), repeated use of such procedures fail to be effective (cf. Stricker, Messick, & Jackson 1969), and, indeed, result in measures of very low reliability. Subjects can report on their typical preferences and activities even when not aroused by the relevant situation. A person need not be angry to outline situations which arouse his ire. Such reports of typical behavior are more likely to be stable over time and to be predictive of generalized response dispositions than are procedures bound by the degree to which a person rises to a particular stimulating situation.

Milestones

Jane Loevinger (1968) and Ruth Wessler (1968) have proposed a unique kind of measure, one which is sensitive to the stages through which personality passes in development. While most assessment views the individual as represented by a series of traits or states, not on a time dimension, but at a fixed time, Loevinger and Wessler have sought to capture what they consider to be the dimension of ego development. Citing psychoanalytic theory, and the writings of Adler, Sullivan, and Fingarette, the authors have conceptualized a series of stages or milestones through which an individual passes during development. Not everyone achieves the higher states, but there is a fixed order of passage. The earliest stage is *presocial*, not itself measurable, but is retained for theoretical completeness. The other stages in order are: the *impulsive*, the *opportunistic*, the *conformist*, the *conscientious*, the *autonomous*, and the *integrated*. For each level there is a unique type of impulse control and character development, style of interpersonal relations, conscious preoccupations, and self-concept. This dimension is measured by a sentence completion test in which a response in every case is classified according to one of the levels. A response can thus be assigned to only one level, and an individual's score is related to the average score assigned to each response. Scores obtained with this procedure have been shown to be reliable, to correlate with chronological age (0.74 for boys and 0.69 for girls), and to be associated with ratings, by interviewers, of ego development in the range of 0.58 to 0.61.

The interesting innovation in the approach of Loevinger and Wessler is the conceptualization of personality as passing through stages of personality development. Like Harvey, Hunt, and Schroder (1961) before them, personality is seen as unfolding in terms of levels of complexity. One might have preferred that a number of dimensions of ego development had been postulated, rather than only a single one. However, a developmental approach to personality, common in personality theory, is a welcome addition to thinking in the assessment area.

Traits and Types

Characterizing individuals in terms of traits or types is much older than assessment methodology; but, even within formal psychological theorizing, this way of thinking has a long and distinguished history. Four decades ago, Gordon W. Allport (1931) presented a paper entitled "What is a trait of personality?" Traits, for Allport, represented a cornerstone for the personality theorist. Returning to this theme on the occasion of his receipt of the 1964 Distinguished Scientific Contribution Award of the American Psychological Association, Allport reexamined the concept of trait in the light of more recent thinking. In the face of the advances of positivism, situationism, and a variety of other intellectual forces, Allport conceded that a theory of traits could not be as simple as it once was, but nevertheless argued eloquently for not sweeping aside the trait conception.

Traits, according to Allport (1966), are generic terms, covering all the general "permanent possibilities for action."

Traits are cortical, subcortical, or postural dispositions having the capacity to gate or guide specific phasic reactions. It is only the phasic aspect that is visible; the tonic is carried somehow in the still mysterious realm of neurodynamic structure. Traits . . . include long-range sets and attitudes, as well as such variables as "perceptual response dispositions," "personal constructs," and "cognitive styles" (p. 3).

Traits are viewed as more or less discrete characteristics which involve a particular level or a particular quantity of a propensity or probability for behaving in a certain way. They are conceived of as being possessed by every individual to a greater or lesser extent so that even when it is said that an individual is a very unaggressive individual, the trait, "aggression," is still relevant to him. A type, on the other hand, does not focus upon single attributes, but upon a syndrome of characteristics which are assumed to go together. The diagnoses used in psychiatry are examples of types, rather than traits. The implicit assumption is that a knowledge of the diagnosis of an individual provides broad information about many more specific characteristics. A trait or a type conception has, of course, important implications for the kinds of measures that are used to characterize personality. Traits are usually assumed to be continuous, and varying in quantity, so there is usually an attempt to draw some sort of isomorphic relationship between the individual's behavior in a situation and the presence of a certain degree of the trait.

A typology, on the other hand, requires different kinds of evidence. A typology may be reflected by the presence of certain "signs" as in the identification of psychiatric diagnosis of paranoia on the basis of systematic delusions, or it may be reflected in the individual manifesting an extreme level of one or more traits. Murray (1938) suggested, for example, that the Jungian conception of the extrovert type should rather be considered in terms of a combination of a number of traits that were actually more descriptive of personality than this type. The important thing to note is that the measurement implications for a type are different than those for a trait conception.

A type is difficult to deal with from the standpoint of measurement. One must define some rule for establishing discrete nonoverlapping categories. A number of statistical procedures are available for approaching this problem from different directions (Cooley & Lohnes 1962) but each of these techniques must cope with the difficulty that test scores are distributed continuously. Groups of test scores usually can be represented as a multivariate normal distribution, with points representing individual test scores or profiles distributed more or less uniformly throughout a geometric space. Empirical and theoretical work by Lorr (1966) and his associates comparing alternative grouping or typing methods has advanced our knowledge, but there are as yet no universally accepted, definitive procedures for establishing types.

The trait approach, on the other hand, is fundamental to most measurement in personality. In general, an underlying assumption is that there is homogeneity in the *trait*, homogeneity in the *measure*, and *isomorphism* between the distribution of scores and the underlying trait or attribute being reflected. It is also assumed that both traits and scores vary continuously, that increasing scores reflect increasing amounts of a single attribute to which all of the items share a relation, and that other irrelevant attributes measured by items are uncorrelated from one item to the next. Upon these assumptions rests almost all of formal test theory (Gulliksen 1950; Rozeboom 1966; Lord & Novick 1968) and more than 95 per cent of the attempts to measure personality. Factor analysis similarly is based on the assumption of homogeneous, continuous scores, which can be partitioned into error variance, specific variance, and common factor variance (Harman 1967; Horst 1965). Without the convenience of these assumptions, little of the vast structure of formal test and reliability theory could have been adopted in personality measurement, and little of the cumulative progress apparent at present would have been possible.

Whatever else one considers relevant to the definition of personality, the assessment of personality can be viewed as a form of communication. The subject is attempting to communicate certain states, certain emotions, certain values, motives, or wishes, or to report certain past behavior to another individual. The vehicle within which the communication takes place is important, to be sure. There have been differences observed between the interview and the printed questionnaire, and, undoubtedly, there will be further differences uncovered between the printed questionnaire and interactional computer approaches. But the notion of communication is essential in assessment. Thus, assessment might be viewed in field theoretic terms (Murphy 1947) as that aspect of the individual's behavior oriented toward a certain situation. The goal of personality assessment is ordinarily a generalization about the nature of some broader set of behavioral consistencies than contained in the test stimuli. In evaluating this attempt at generalization, the assessment specialist is quite aware that the respondent may have certain constraints acting upon him—that in attempting to communicate he may suffer from self-deception and a need for social approval—and that he may refuse to communicate certain aspects of behavior altogether. The study of such response biases or response styles has formed an important part of the assessment literature over the past decade, and has developed into a diverse and sometimes controversial body of knowledge. In a later section, these issues are considered in some detail.

The Evolution of Concepts in Personality Assessment

Like the evolution of knowledge in other areas, there is evidence of both a *Zeitgeist* of prevailing opinion, and an episodic quality to the singular achievements of particular individuals (cf. Boring 1950). One might be tempted to characterize the changes in intellectual climate as having the tempo of a slow pendulum, swinging from theory and intuition to empiricism, and returning to theory. But it will probably be more accurate to liken the changes in thinking to a spiral, in which fresh approaches are integrated in such a manner that a return to theory or empiricism is not to the same mode of thought as prevailed previously.

Modern structured personality assessment is just about a half century old. It was in 1920 that Woodworth published the *Personal Data Sheet* based on work done to meet the exigencies of World War I for the psychiatric screening of large numbers of military personnel. This work ushered in the first phase of largely intuitively based and, by modern standards, crude personality assessment devices. The second phase may be traced to the publication of the MMPI (Hathaway & McKinley 1940, 1942) and Meehl's (1945) incisive and lucid account of the method of empirical item selection against external criteria. The third phase, extending to the present, is marked by a widely cited paper on the importance of theory in personality assessment (Cronbach & Meehl 1955) and by a great production of both new ideas and empirical findings.

Woodworth's *Personal Data Sheet* served as a prototype of other personality tests developed in its wake, based largely on the author's idea of how a particular type of person, such as a neurotic, might respond. Woodworth's test contained items requiring a "yes" or "no" response to such questions as "Did you have a happy childhood?" and "Does it make you uneasy to cross a bridge over a river?" The lineage of many of these items can be traced from the Woodworth personality test through Thurstone's *Personality Schedule* (1929), *The Bernreuter Personality Inventory* (1931), to the MMPI, the CPI, down to the present. The important contribution of Woodworth and other authors (e.g., Allport 1928) in this early phase was that they

demonstrated that it was possible to approach personality testing in a manner similar to the approach used in achievement or aptitude testing; items could be added to yield a total score, which in turn could be analyzed for reliability and validity. The measurement of personality was not, however, as simple as the measurement of aptitudes, and early personality tests were subject to so many problems that critical reviews (Ellis 1946; Ellis & Conrad 1948; Vernon 1953) saw little justification for placing confidence in the whole approach. The tests were transparent, rested on the untested assumption that the author used good judgment regarding the relevance of the item to the dimension, and suffered from a notable lack of validity (Ellis 1946).

One of the first multiscore personality inventories was Bernreuter's (1931, 1933), which purported to measure Self-Sufficiency, Dominance-Submission, Introversion-Extraversion, and Neurotic Tendency. Item scoring weights were based on the degree to which each item correlated with total scores of other personality scales bearing similar names, a criterion far from free of systematic error. The resulting scale scores proved to correlate so highly (range − .32 to + .93) as to raise questions regarding their distinctiveness. Two factors identified by Flanagan (1935) from his analysis of Bernreuter scales were incorporated into the regular scoring of the Bernreuter, even though the Flanagan results implied that the other four scales were largely redundant, and from a modern perspective, largely due to response bias. While factor-analytically based tests having their roots in this era (Cattell 1950; Guilford & Martin 1945), showed somewhat lower interscale correlations, the scales were still too redundant to permit sufficient distinctiveness for individual trait measurement. In general, item pools were too small, and insufficiently refined to yield scales of high quality. The skepticism quite legitimately growing out of this early experience has carried down to the present, and has been overgeneralized to skepticism regarding even the possibility of valid assessment in personality.

With the publication of MMPI (Hathaway & McKinley 1942) a new era in personality assessment began. Based to a large extent on the rationale used in the development of the Strong Vocational Interest Blank, introduced by Strong some years before, the authors did not put their faith in their judgment regarding the keying of the items. Rather, they sought to identify criterion groups of diagnosed psychiatric patients, and determine which items distinguished these patients from normals. Thus, the rationale was based on the ability of scales to *predict* an empirical criterion, rather than to *measure* a latent trait or dimension. Neither did the authors have faith in the truthfulness or accuracy of self-reports. Meehl (1945) argued that the "projective" qualities or the biases in self-report elicited by items might contribute to item and scale validity. By utilizing items empirically keyed for predicting status in a criterion group, with little obvious content relevance to the criterion, the authors of the MMPI hypothesized that subtle and therefore unfakeable scales might be generated. But this approach assumes that items have been selected without measurement error. It has proved to be the case that items bearing little substantive relation to a criterion generally do not hold up well under cross-validation; i.e., they do not continue to correlate with the criterion when re-administered to a new sample of respondents.

The MMPI continues to be the most widely used personality test. It was originally devised to predict psychiatric diagnosis, and the scales were given labels based on the criterion groups which they discriminated. Thus, the clinical scales were named Hypochondriasis, Depression, Hysteria, Psychopathic Deviate, Masculinity-Femininity, Paranoia, Schizophrenia, Mania, and Social Introversion. Texts and handbooks on the MMPI rarely mention these names anymore. Either abbreviations (e.g., *Pd* for Psychopathic Deviate) or merely numerals are substituted for the original names. This change occurred for several reasons: (a) medical psychologists moved away from the psychiatric diagnostic scheme and the underlying *class* or *typological* model implicit in the use of these names; (b) the MMPI proved not to be highly valid for the specific purpose of differentially predicting psychiatric diagnosis; and (c) the scales took on different interpretations based on a kind of "bootstraps" (Cronbach & Meehl 1955) operation, in which new theoretical and empirical links were discovered. Thus, the "surplus meaning" of the *Pd* scale was enriched by findings that persons causing hunting accidents had elevated *Pd* scale scores, as did college women rated by peers as more talkative. The MMPI thus has been modified from its original conception as a predictive device to one purporting to measure basic constructs or traits. It has generated a truly remarkable diversity of research. Representative earlier studies are contained in Welsh and Dahlstrom (1956). There are over one thousand references in *An MMPI Handbook* (Dahlstrom & Welsh 1960); since that time probably twice that number of articles on the MMPI have appeared. These studies often bear on particular populations, such as psychiatric populations or alcoholics. Perhaps 300 special MMPI scales have been developed using empirical selection of items with a wide range of criteria and populations. Although the pace of such scale proliferation has slowed somewhat, one may choose "scales" derived for diverse criteria, even though many of these scales are not very reliable, nor do they manifest a distinctive pattern of correlations. One interpretation for their lack of distinctiveness is that MMPI scales to a large extent measure only two factors. Although the degree to which these scales measure content or style is controversial (Block 1965, 1967; Edwards 1967; Jackson 1967*c*, 1967*d*), the unchallenged assertion that two factors will predict the major portion of the common variance is a basis for skepticism regarding the usefulness of dozens or even hundreds of empirically derived scales generated from the same item pool.

Because the largest component of MMPI scales is an elevation component, related to the tendency to endorse pathological and/or undesirable content, many MMPI users have focused upon the *pattern* of the profile. Most use a coding system originally devised by Hathaway, and modified by Welsh (1948). In general, approaches based on profile interpretation, such as that advanced by Marks and Seeman (1963), seek to link certain types of patients or other persons to a pattern of high and low MMPI scores. Because the relative elevation of standardized scores is used, rather than their absolute value, the elevation component tends to be reduced. This type of profile analysis has been used for generating computer-based narrative interpretation in the form of a report of testing. The profile pattern interpretation is favored over the traditional method of single score interpretation because it is believed that a combination of scores will be more accurate than the same scores used singly. But it should be recognized that any pattern-based system rests upon the psychometric properties of individual scales, such as their reliability. If scales can vary due to measurement error,

or because the same score is obtained for different reasons, the interpretability of the pattern of scores will be confounded. Ideally, the reliability of the difference between two scores is a function of their respective reliabilities and their mutual correlation. MMPI scales are substantially correlated; therefore, it is hazardous to make a great deal out of minor differences in scale elevation. Nevertheless, the analysis of profile patterns rather than the simple interpretation of scores offers an alternative which may indeed prove superior for characterizing personality variables in typological terms.

The modern era, heralded by the introduction of the importance of theory in assessment (Cronbach & Meehl 1955; Loevinger 1957), has resulted in a number of fresh approaches. If structured tests are to play an important role in psychological assessment, they must be developed on the basis of sound theory, and be validated, not only by purely empirical means, but by the degree to which they reflect the theoretical construct that they were designed to measure. Ideally, an item pool is generated from theory and tested for substantive cogency, termed the *substantive component of validity* by Loevinger. There should be an isomorphism between theoretical linkages in a "nomological net" of constructs and the empirical effects to be expected. An explicit conception of the nature of a trait or a construct is formulated. This conception should imply a structural model, to which item responses should conform. Thus, postulating a single homogeneous continuous dimension should result in items eliciting responses conforming to this postulated structure. Similarly, postulating a typology would involve a class model of structure as in the initial formulation of the MMPI rationale. Stricker and Ross (1964) evaluated test structure in relation to the theory of Jungian typology, finding little support for the latter in the structuring of item responses. The degree to which the observed structure fits the postulated structure is termed the *structural component of validity* by Loevinger. The *external component of validity*, traditionally evaluated in terms of the degree to which a test correlates with an empirical criterion, has been broadened to include a number of diverse kinds of evaluations. Among these are experimental treatments, and the assessment of relations not only with criteria to be predicted, but with those bearing a direct link with the theoretical construct of interest. The understanding of the nature and the surplus value of the construct is thereby enhanced. Not only is the test validated, but the construct as well.

Campbell and Fiske (1959) made an important methodological contribution to the validation process by pointing out that every psychological measure can be conceived of as consisting of both *trait* and *method* variance. These are logically distinct, although confounded in measurement. Tests of distinct traits can be invalidated by too high a correlation with irrelevant traits, as well as by too low a correlation with a relevant trait. A crucial requirement for evaluating the validity of a putative measure of a trait is the demonstration of *convergent* and *discriminant validity*. A test should be associated with relevant traits and substantially independent of irrelevant traits. This is done in the context of a *multitrait-multimethod matrix*, in which several traits are evaluated by correlating them with the same traits measured by additional methods. Recently, Jackson (1969) has proposed a technique termed *multimethod factor analysis*, which focuses upon the analysis of structure in heteromethod correlations, for the evaluation of convergent and discriminant validity. Jackson showed that factor analysis, as traditionally employed, often led to erroneous conclusions regarding the degree of heteromethod validity because of the similar structure of trait and method variance often encountered in practice. When traditional factor analytic methods have been compared with multimethod factor analysis (Kusyszyn & Jackson 1968), the results have indicated that substantial heteromethod convergent and discriminant validity could be demonstrated using multimethod factor analysis, even though traditional methods yielded misleading method-specific factors.

Cronbach and Gleser (1964) have departed from traditional thinking in test theory by introducing concepts derived from statistical decision theory. They argue that whereas traditional test theory has focused upon the reliability and validity of single tests, a more fitting emphasis is upon the *utility* of decisional outcomes, taking into account cost of testing, relative test validity, selection ratio, and the importance of the various decisions to be made. Cronbach and Gleser explicate a *bandwidth-fidelity dilemma*, in which, given finite testing time, one may allocate testing resources so as to concentrate upon reliable assessment of a characteristic relevant to a single outcome, or upon the less reliable assessment of several characteristics relevant to several decisions. It is shown that under conditions of equivalent cost, validity, and importance of decisions, it is better to sacrifice some fidelity for bandwidth. Such analyses can be used to justify the application of techniques, such as the interview, which, while relatively unreliable, might provide information relevant to a wide array of decisions.

It would be inappropriate to ignore the very real impact of the modern computer on advances in assessment methodology. Factor analytic techniques, for example, which were totally impractical with a desk computer, are now routinely performed in seconds on a high speed computer with far more accuracy than previously attainable (Horst 1965). Similarly, multivariate methods for classifying individuals, for evaluating cutting scores, and for assessing the structure of underlying processes (Cooley & Lohnes 1962) have been enormously facilitated by the availability of the computer. The computer has served as an impetus, not only to analyses of data, but as a device for explicating structural and mathematical models using simulation methods (Cliff & Hamburger 1967; Tomkins & Messick 1963). Finally, more sophisticated test construction has been possible by employing computer optimization techniques to item selection and scale construction (Jackson 1967*b*, 1970; Neill & Jackson 1970).

The Problem of Response Bias and Method Variance

A number of years ago, a distinction was made (Jackson & Messick 1958) between the interpretation of behavior in terms of *content* and of *style*. The assessment implications of this distinction are important, in that, although the focus of assessment is usually upon a substantive trait, need state, or motive, an individual's response is also determined by his preferred mode or style of responding. The particular form in which the assessment is cast or the particular method of measurement will often interact with an individual's preferred style of responding to affect his response, quite apart from his location on the trait dimension of interest or the content of the item. Thus, a subject motivated to present himself in a desirable light will seek to do this over a variety of categories of content. While such a tendency to respond desirably may itself be indica-

tive of a broad disposition of personality (Jackson & Messick 1958; Block 1965), the interpretation of the particular attribute or trait being assessed is inevitably complicated by the presence of such a pervasive stylistic dimension.

Jackson and Messick (1962*a*) expanded upon this distinction as follows:

... variance associated with content *is considered to refer to response consistencies in certain defined assessment situations which reflect a particular set of broader behavioral tendencies, relatively enduring over time, having as their basis some unitary personality trait, need state, attitudinal or belief disposition, or psychopathological syndrome. The* item content *used to elicit such behavioral predispositions may be developed initially on theoretical or a* priori *grounds, may be obvious or subtle, may be direct or indirect, and may be highly relevant or only slightly relevant to some particular prediction criterion; the initial defining property of content assessment is some form of* response consistency. ...*variance associated with* response style *has reference to expressive consistencies in the behavior of respondents which are relatively enduring over time, with some degree of generality beyond a particular test performance to responses both in other tests and in non-test behavior, and usually reflected in assessment situations by consistencies in response to item characteristics other than specific content* (*p. 134*).

The reliability of a number of response biases on personality and attitude questionnaires has been demonstrated repeatedly (Barnes 1956; Bendig 1962; Berg 1967; Cronbach 1946, 1950; Crowne & Marlowe 1960; Damarin & Messick 1965; Edwards 1967; Jackson 1967*a*; Jackson & Messick 1962*b*; Martin 1964; Stricker 1963; Wiggins 1962). Some of the most frequently encountered forms of response bias include tendencies to:

1. respond *desirably* (Boe & Kogan 1963; Edwards 1967; Hanley 1956; Jackson & Messick 1961, 1962*a*, 1962*b*, 1969; Taylor 1959)
2. respond *defensively*, related to a tendency to fake on personality items (Crowne & Marlow 1964; Kogan & Wallach 1964)
3. respond in a *true-keyed direction* (Couch & Keniston 1960; Cronbach 1946, 1950; Jackson & Messick 1957, 1958; Martin 1964; Mitzell, Rabinowitz, & Ostreicher 1956; Rundquist 1966; Rundquist & Sletto 1936)
4. *endorse many traits or items as self-descriptive* (Fulkerson 1958; Jackson 1967*a*; Jackson & Messick 1965; Messick 1967; Morf & Jackson 1969; Trott & Jackson 1967)
5. *be evasive* (Mitzell et al. 1956)
6. use *extreme categories* on rating scales (Berg 1953; Kusyszyn & Jackson 1968; Osgood 1941; Rundquist 1950)
7. *prefer sweeping generalizations* vs. cautiously worded statements on attitude questionnaires (Jackson & Messick 1958; Clayton & Jackson 1961)
8. respond *deviantly or randomly* (Berg 1959, 1967; Sechrest & Jackson 1963).

Other response styles, like *criticalness* (Frederiksen & Messick 1959) and *risk taking* (Kogan & Wallach 1964), are more cognitive in nature, and have been developed in broader contexts even though they are related to performance on a personality questionnaire.

All of the literature about each of these response styles will not be discussed here. Rather, the focus of this section is upon those which are prominent in personality questionnaires. Research will be reviewed in the light of recent evidence and critiques of the response style conception, with the aim of seeking clarification of what may appear to be a large and sometimes contradictory literature.

Ever since the first personality inventories were published, there was some awareness that respondents might be other than completely frank in their responses. Edwards (1953b) following an earlier paper by Gordon (1951), who in turn acknowledged through personal communication the priority of Wherry and Horst, demonstrated that there was a relation between an item's desirability scale value and the proportion of people endorsing the item. Of course, this is a generalization about items, not people per se. The linear relation that has been observed to occur repeatedly—with a correlation in the vicinity of 0.88—has been misinterpreted as indicating various generalizations about individual differences in people, a distinction clarified by Norman (1967), but can more reasonably be viewed in part as reflecting the fact that more frequently occurring behavior is generally considered to be desirable, and rarer behavior undesirable (Jackson & Messick, 1969).

The identification of desirability as a judged attribute of an item apart from its denotative content (Messick & Jackson 1961) introduced a wide variety of studies into the assessment area, and, in particular, resulted in the hypothesis that desirability response style accounted for a major portion of the response variance on published personality tests. This was the import of a series of studies conducted by Edwards (1967) and by Jackson and Messick (1961, 1962a, 1962b). Jackson and Messick reported that the largest factor in three separate factor analyses of the MMPI was highly associated with the average judged desirability scale value of items on each of 40 MMPI subscales. Many additional studies proceeded to establish variations on this theme. But questions immediately arose as to the interpretation of this finding. For example, Messick (1960) reported that it was possible to identify separate dimensions of judged desirability, as distinct from the general dimension originally reported by Edwards. Similarly, Jackson and Singer (1967) reported that desirability could be distinguished in terms of at least five dimensions: desirable in oneself, desirable in others, what others consider desirable, harmfulness, and frequency. Each of these dimensions tended to interact differentially with scale content and with subject characteristics.

The interpretation of desirability response bias has been a matter of dispute. A number of investigators have quite appropriately pointed out that pathological content and undesirability are inevitably confounded in an inventory such as the MMPI. However, it is now established beyond a reasonable doubt that responding in terms of the desirability of an item, especially when the item is extreme in this property, is an ubiquitous confounding source of variance in personality questionnaires requiring the attention of serious investigators. If it is desired to measure personality traits as distinct from such a general characteristic, it is necessary to make allowance for desirability bias. This has been attempted in a number of ways. In the construction of the *Edwards Personal Preference Schedule* (Edwards 1953a), for example, an attempt was made to pair items similar in desirability level to avoid the problem of desirability bias. While to some extent effective, this technique unfor-

tunately tends to heighten the contrast inevitable in items not precisely identical in desirability scale value (LaPointe & Auclair 1961) and to introduce a variety of problems of a statistical nature traceable to an ipsative format, i.e., one in which individual statements in forced-choice form are ranked by a subject. These statistical problems (Clemans 1966; Radcliffe 1963) include a built-in negative correlation among the scale scores and interscale dependencies, making a factor analysis inappropriate. Moreover, by virtue of the fact that scale scores must sum to a constant, attempts to compare the score of one subject with another are inappropriate. A more effective technique for controlling for desirability bias is to measure it separately, removing that portion of the content scale variance related to the desirability scale from the content scale by partial regression techniques. An even better procedure is to select items with a low level of association with desirability responding. Using scales constructed in this way, Jackson and Lay (1968) demonstrated that it was possible to identify content factors entirely distinct from a desirability factor, and from other sources of response bias.

The desirability factor referred to in the above paragraph is to be distinguished from a tendency to manifest *defensiveness*, and to dissimulate or fake. While the desirability and defensiveness would appear to be similar, and, indeed, they are to some extent related, a variety of studies have demonstrated that a second factor is required to account for dissimulation. When subjects are requested or instructed to fake a desirable protocol, items showing low endorsement frequencies but high desirability scale values tend to shift in the direction of a higher endorsement frequency. Thus, under instructions to fake, more subjects respond "true" to the item "I never become angry," than they do under standard instructions. Because these items are uniquely sensitive to faking instructions, and because they can be selected on purely judgmental criteria in terms of the discrepancy between judged desirability and judged frequency of endorsement (Jackson & Messick 1969), it is appropriate to consider dissimulation as a further manifestation of a type of response style, and as distinct from desirability responding. Actually, many subjects manifest defensiveness without consciously attempting to fake a personality test.

In a notable series of studies, Crowne and Marlowe (1964) conceptualized defensiveness as the *need for social approval*, and demonstrated that individuals who consistently responded atypically to items low in endorsement frequency and high in desirability showed a variety of predictable tendencies in different experimental situations. For example, such subjects showed greater conformity and greater sensitivity to the demand characteristics of experiments, as in a verbal learning task. They also tended not to express aggression outwardly when instigated to aggression in an experimental situation, but, rather, showed repression and displacement (Conn & Crowne 1964). The Crowne and Marlowe studies perhaps best illustrate the manner in which a stylistic variable may have broad implications for personality functioning. While beginning with an analysis of the test response, their studies drew them into a variety of areas, calling forth a great deal of insight both into the nature of experimental situations and into personality theory.

Ever since the early studies reviewed by Cronbach (1946, 1950), *acquiescence response bias*, originally identified as a tendency to respond "true" or "like," has elicited a great deal of research. It has also been the center of a fair degree of controversy in recent years. Acquiescence was identified as a major source of variance on the California Authoritarian Scale; Jackson and Messick (1961, 1962a, 1962b) and others (e.g., Fulkerson 1958) implicitly assumed that this same form of acquiescence was operative in the MMPI. Jackson and Messick uncovered a factor which completely separated true- from false-keyed MMPI subscales in three separate large factor analyses, a finding replicated in every single instance in which it has been sought not only on the MMPI but on a variety of other personality inventories as well (e.g., Trott & Jackson 1967). However, a number of investigators (e.g., McGee 1962) reported that there was only moderate to low agreement between different types of acquiescence scales drawn from different inventories. Furthermore, a series of item reversal studies with the MMPI, in which the same items were reversed in direction, indicated that original and reversed scales correlated in what appeared to be the content direction. This caused Bock, Dicken, and Van Pelt (1969) to conclude that although acquiescence was present on the MMPI, its role was small. Rorer (1965), having first reinterpreted response style as restricted to this phenomenon, concluded that response style was a "myth." But scrutiny of the results of these item reversal studies indicates that however comforting it might be in personality assessment to believe that response styles were nonexistent, there is little ground for such a belief. A factor analysis of the Rorer and Goldberg (1965) reversed and unreversed MMPI scales (Jackson & Messick 1965) revealed that two large factors accounted for almost all of the consistency between original and reversed scales. One of these was the familiar one associated with desirability. The second factor was associated with a tendency to describe oneself in terms of many or few traits. While controversy still remains about the interpretation of these and other findings a recent factor analytic study undertaken by Morf and Jackson (1969) has shown that what had been considered a single process of "acquiescence" could be distinguished as two separate uncorrelated factors. The first of these, particularly associated with attitude items in the tradition of the California Authoritarian Scale, was characterized by a tendency to respond "true," regardless of the direction of wording; the second factor, marked in particular by personality scales, involved the tendency to endorse many items as self-descriptive, even when a double negation was involved, as in responding "false" to the statement "It is not true that my eyes frequently hurt." The hypothesis of two distinct acquiescence processes of true responding and item endorsement was first advanced by Jackson and Messick (1965) in collaboration with Bentler, and was elaborated by Campbell, Seigman, and Rees (1967). Morf and Jackson also reported two further response style factors, one involving the tendency to check many adjectives as self-descriptive, and the other the familiar desirability factor. In addition to response style factors, four trait factors each defined by eight content-specific scales were uncovered by Morf and Jackson. This illustrates that content can be measured apart from response style, and that these two sources of variance often exist side by side in the same inventory.

Minimizing the Role of Response Biases

Although the relative importance of various response styles has been controversial, it is a matter settled beyond any reason-able doubt that personality questionnaires are subject to various forms of confounded bias and distortion. The question then arises as to whether and to what extent explicit steps may be taken to avoid as much as possible this form of distortion. Essentially there are six important methods for controlling for response biases in personality assessment. These include the use of *statistical corrections*, the use of a *forced-choice format*, the use of *indirect* or disguised methods of assessment, the introduction of *validity keys*, the use of objective or *maximum performance* tests, and, finally, the use of careful *item selection techniques*.

Ever since Horst (1941) identified the suppressor variable as one which, while wholly uncorrelated with the criterion, contributed to predictive validity by virtue of its removing invalid variance, psychologists held hope that biases might be removed statistically, without interfering with the validity of the test. While the original Horst rationale is correct in principle, few psychologists today develop personality tests for purely predictive purposes. The implication that a test is being employed to predict an empirical criterion is usually unwarranted. This rationale, incorporated, for example, in the development of the MMPI K scale, often yields some rather illogical results. The use of K-corrected scales essentially involves adding a component to the original scale score which is correlated negatively with it and which may drastically change the interpretation of the score. What interpretation can be placed upon an individual who has only answered three of the original psychopathological items in the keyed direction, but achieved a score deviant in the pathological direction only because he has scored very high on the K scale? Ordinarily, when a scale score is interpreted, we wish to impute a trait characteristic to the individual, rather than predict a criterion. In practice, as with the K scale, it has been exceedingly rare to find an investigator who has gone to the trouble of reassessing the validity of the corrected score. Rather, the empirical prediction rationale is often misapplied in a context in which basic psychological measurement of a latent construct is involved.

If correction of a statistical nature is to be imposed upon a set of psychological measures, it would make more sense to apply these using a somewhat different rationale from the suppressor variable approach. This approach might well involve partial regression techniques, or their factor analytic analogues, in which an unwanted factor or an irrelevant source of variance is subtracted from the original standardized score. This is done with the intent of purifying the measure, regardless of its effect upon empirical validity. Thus, a research worker might decide that the role of general desirability bias should be removed statistically from an aggression scale by measuring it separately and by computing a new standardized raw score based on the subtraction of the desirability factor. The validity might go up or it might go down. However, the important thing is that the assessment specialist is now more confident that the attributes being assigned to the respondent on the basis of his test score are due to what the scale is putatively measuring, rather than some irrelevant component. It should be emphasized, however, that this approach would be more appropriate in a research setting than in a practical decision-making situation with an individual subject. This is true because the calculation of the appropriate regression weight or the factor score to be removed should be based upon a relevant set of data on subjects drawn from the same population. In general, statistical correction for individuals in a counseling or other individual assessment situation is impractical.

The use of a *forced-choice methodology* has already been considered in the context of the discussion of the *Edwards Personal Preference Schedule*. It was pointed out that its liabilities are tied to the ipsative nature of these scores. These disadvantages include the inappropriateness of comparing one subject with another when he has essentially been asked to rank responses with respect to his own standing on them. In spite of the statistical difficulties, however, forced-choice methodology does have some important advantages. First of all, there are times when it is appropriate to make ipsative decisions rather than normative decisions. That is, one may wish to rank attributes within subjects rather than between subjects. An excellent example of this is when one is interested in vocational interest measurement with the aim of aiding individuals in their choice of a career. Here, it makes little difference from the assessee's point of view how his own responses related to those of other people. Rather, he is more interested in how he should choose between two or more occupations, such as physician or physical scientist. Traditionally, when individuals are asked to indicate a liking or a disliking for various activities related to vocational interests, some subjects will endorse many activities, and some very few. The first subject would receive a generally elevated profile, while the second would receive one with hardly any or perhaps no areas of expressed interest. For this reason, Kuder (1966), as well as other vocational interest test authors, has opted for a forced-choice technique. A second advantage of the forced-choice procedures is that it completely eliminates other possible forms of acquiescence, like true responding. One technique, advocated by a variety of authors, is to pair the relevant items with irrelevant items matched for desirability or for response frequency. This was an approach used by Heineman (1953), Jackson and Minton (1963), Jackson and Payne (1963), and by Loevinger and her associate (Ernhart & Loevinger 1969). In the Payne and Jackson study a scale for measuring shallow affect was found to increase in reliability from 0.81 to 0.96 when a forced-choice form was introduced. This increase in reliability was due to the increased item variance caused by the greater range of scores possible when unpopular items are paired with other unpopular items. Of course, pairing two unpopular items can create rapport problems. For example, a subject might be asked to choose between two alternatives such as the following: (a) "There is something wrong with my sex organs"; (b) "Accidents, even if serious, never bother me." Some of these rapport problems can be circumvented by the use of a third more popular item of the type: "I like to read historical novels." The individual's response to the latter item is disregarded, but the manner in which he ranks the key item in relation to the third item is considered important (Heineman 1953; Jackson & Payne 1963). It is possible, however, that neither of the alternative unpopular items are true of the subject, but this does not necessarily prevent him from ranking them reliably. In general, the forced-choice method extracts a price for whatever value it may have in reducing response bias. It may eliminate certain forms of bias, but by virtue of the irrelevant member of each pair, may introduce a source of unreliability in that the subject may check the non-keyed response not because the keyed response was unattractive, but because the irrelevant member is more attractive. The interested reader is referred to recent reviews of the literature by Berkshire (1958), Scott (1968a, 1968b), and Zavala (1965).

It is perhaps appropriate to introduce parenthetically into the discussion of forced-choice methodology the question of the possibility of using other types of formats. The great majority of personality questionnaires use a true-false or agree-disagree format. There are a number of reasons why such dichotomous formats are favored over multicategory formats, in which, for example, sets of adverbs might be used to indicate how strongly each alternative indicated the presence of a trait. In a recent paper, Jones (1968) reported a comparison of items using two options and response categories scored in terms of ten alternatives. Jones's reason for undertaking the study was to evaluate these two alternatives, not so much in terms of response biases, but in terms of their reliability and their acceptability to subjects. Jones found, surprisingly, no differences in mean response consistency between single and multicategory response formats. However, he did find a very clear preference on the part of subjects for multiple category formats over single category formats. The former were judged as more accurate, reliable, interesting, and less ambiguous than were dichotomous formats. Thus, under circumstances in which the efficiency of the simpler dichotomous format is not an issue, such as when a computer might be used to score the subject's responses, there is some advantage in using the more differentiated response. Although there is no clear evidence that a multicategory response will reduce bias, the fact that it seems to contribute to greater rapport might yield some beneficial payoff in terms of better test-taking attitudes.

Maximum performance measures of personality and the dimension of directness-indirectness. One of the ways in which bias may be reduced is by using what Cattell (1957) and Campbell (1957) call "objective" measures of performance. In these situations, the subject is led to believe that there is a single correct answer, and that his task is to strive to find it. From an assessment standpoint, the focus is not primarily upon the subject's ability to attain a right answer, but upon some other aspect of performance. For example, in the assessment of social attitudes, Campbell describes the *error-choice* technique in which a subject is given what is putatively an information test which has equally incorrect alternatives biased in different directions. For example, attitudes toward water fluoridation might be reflected in a willingness to endorse, in an information test format, an alternative indicating the harmful effects of fluoridation. Messick and Hills (1960) developed an ingenious kind of maximum performance test. These authors were interested in the dimension of cautiousness versus impulsivity, and utilized a test in which a number of very difficult vocabulary and figural items were placed in a form where a subject could lift tabs to obtain clues as to the right answer. These clues gave different amounts of information about the right answer. For example, for the word *bairn* the first clue was that the bairn was small. The giving of a clue as to the size tended to make certain alternatives less likely. The next clue was that the bairn was not very healthy. This ruled out "barn" as an alternative. The last clue was "The hunters found the murdered bairn." This fairly conclusively identified bairn as a child. The subject could obtain extra points by guessing correctly on the basis of limited clues, or could manifest a degree of intolerance of ambiguity and a need for certainty by requiring more information before guessing. The test thus yielded a knowledge score and a score for cautiousness or intolerance of ambiguity. Since the subjects were motivated to give maximum performance, it would be relatively difficult to fake on such a task.

There are a variety of other such tasks mentioned by Campbell (1957). Many of these objective measures of performance have as a key element the fact that the *purpose of testing is concealed from the subject*. Campbell refers to such tests as indirect measures, in that the subject believes that he is being tested for one purpose and is actually being tested for another. Ordinarily, disguise carries a price, although concealing the exact nature of the purposes of assessment and the interpretation of items is one of the most widely used practices to foster validity in personality assessment. There is very good evidence that if respondents know precisely the dimensions being measured, or if items are grouped in such a way that it is easy for them to discover this by inspecting the item content, it is relatively easier for them to fake. Therefore, most personality tests do not give away the exact titles of the dimensions being measured in the title of the test. Furthermore, it is a common practice to randomize or otherwise assemble the items so that similar types of content are not all grouped together, as they are, for example, in achievement and ability tests. In general, if there is any reason to believe that subjects may show marked favorability bias or other evidence of motivated distortion, it is quite advisable to avoid calling explicit attention to the precise nature of the dimensions being assessed.

SPECIAL VALIDITY KEYS

The use of validity keys to detect faking and other forms of test-taking bias has been popular over a considerable period of time. Perhaps the most widely used validity keys are those contained in the MMPI. Although the authors originally included a "cannot say" score in the four MMPI validity scales, the latter is rarely used now. The remaining validity scales, however, are widely interpreted as indicating something about the subject's test-taking attitudes. These include the F scale, the K scale, and the Lie scale. The F scale was constructed empirically on the basis of items which were endorsed by fewer than approximately 5 per cent of the normative samples of the MMPI. It was designed to identify individuals who were careless or otherwise unable to understand the questions and answer purposefully. Unfortunately, however, many of the F scale items are also indicative of severe psychopathology, so that F scale scores are often elevated for subjects who have answered the tests purposefully, such as groups of chronic schizophrenics who actually possess the psychopathology reflected in the item. The MMPI K scale was developed, as indicated previously, as a device for distinguishing empirically individuals in the pathological range who gave apparently normal profiles from individuals who actually were within the normal range. It was based on a suppressor variable rationale, with the focus upon maximizing the ability of the clinical scales to discriminate and the validity of the test as a whole. Unfortunately, empirical validity will often depend upon a number of local conditions, including base rates (Meehl & Rosen 1955) and other specific factors, which may not generalize to other samples. The author is aware of no studies which have sought to cross-validate the use of the

MMPI K scale as a suppressor variable. While the K scale may be useful in identifying tests which have been answered invalidly, the rationale of adding this score, or any correction scale, to another scale score to obtain a meaningful assessment is open to considerable question.

The MMPI Lie scale is another good example of a validity key. It has been shown to be quite effective in identifying individuals who consciously fake or distort their protocols. There are, however, other reasons why the Lie scale may be elevated. As has been mentioned, Crowne and Marlowe (1964) have demonstrated that individuals scoring high on a similar scale show a variety of other personality traits which are consistent with this pattern of responses. Thus, if the Lie scale is elevated, it *may* indicate that the individual is consciously faking or distorting his responses, or it may be indicative of a more subtle form of bias in self-regard, one which ought to be considered in the overall interpretation of the test, but which does not require throwing out the entire protocol as invalid.

The Infrequency Scale of the Personality Research Form (Jackson 1967*b*) is similar in rationale to the MMPI F scale, but consists of items so rare that it is hardly possible that the subject would respond purposefully to the content. Thus, a subject who reports that he has visited the Republic of Samoa during the past year, he has never seen an apple, or he has never driven in an automobile, raises the suspicion that he might have answered randomly. One interesting aspect of the Infrequency Scale score is that it is predictive of the degree of test-retest reliability manifested on the PRF (Bentler 1964) and is quite useful in identifying not only errors of responding, but errors of scoring as well.

In general, verification or validity keys are useful in personality assessment in that they call attention to invalid records. They do not completely solve the problem of errors in responding, faking, or distortion, but they do tend to call attention to this problem where it exists. The point is that it is difficult to know what to do with records that have elevated validity scores. Probably the best thing to assume is that the results should not be included in a regular sample and to base the assessment on some different method. Further research is required to investigate the effects of various instructional sets upon purposefulness in responding. It is possible, for example, that enlightening a subject about the presence of validity keys may be a safeguard against simplistic faking. Thus, validity keys point to individuals who have not taken the test seriously, but do not always tell us what to do about them other than to disregard or partially disregard their responses.

Methods for Constructing Personality Tests

While there has been a diversity of different approaches to developing multiscale personality tests, in general these can be categorized under three major headings (cf. Hase & Goldberg 1967). The first, and oldest, kind of personality test (Woodworth 1920) involves a rational or intuitive strategy. Here the author of the test postulates implicitly or explicitly a dimension of personality to be assessed and seeks to identify items meeting his criterion. The rational strategy fell into some disrepute (Meehl 1945) because, in an age of radical empiricism, the intuition of an experimenter was often suspect as a source of hypotheses about the nature of personality. The argument was that little was actually known about the complexities of personality, and that sole reliance on a single investigator's intuition about the link between a trait and an item might be hazardous. A refinement of the rational approach involves the use of a carefully prepared, explicitly devised definition of appropriate variables of personality. Murray (1938), for example, believed that the taxonomic task of defining variables of personality was an essential first step in the science of personality. It has more recently proved to be possible to devise large item pools on the basis of explicit theory in such a way that the item content can be evaluated as to the degree to which it reflects the underlying definition.

A second general strategy in personality scale construction involves the use of one or another form of internal consistency analysis. Most commonly, factor analysis has been employed to identify item sharing a common structural bond, and this strategy has been said to underlie the personality inventories developed by such authors as Eysenck (1947), Guilford and Zimmerman (1956), and Cattell and his collaborators (1957). Basic to the approach of factor analysis is the idea that items sharing consistent responses will define a single common factor, and that the number of common factors within an item pool is somehow a reflection of the important dimensions in the domain of personality being considered. Of course, the adequacy of the dimensions which emerge is very much a function of the adequacy of the original item pool. Similarly, whether or not the personality scales so derived will be relevant for a given prediction or assessment problem will rest upon the degree of relevance of the content contained in the item pool and the criterion situation.

Because of the enormous labor involved, prior to the advent of the modern computer, in undertaking a factor analysis, most studies of personality inventories which purported to be based upon factor analysis were actually not based upon analyses of the intercorrelations among single items. It simply was not feasible until very recently to intercorrelate 200 or more items and to uncover their factor analytic structure. Thus, even though the Cattell 16-Personality Factor Questionnaire was developed within the context of a factor analytic rationale, nowhere has Cattell ever published a set of inter-item correlations. Rather, he has sought to demonstrate the factorial validity of the device by reporting factor analyses based on scores derived from sets of items. Computers are now available which are equal to this task (e.g., Comrey 1961), but as of this date (1973) only a very small number of published personality inventories (e.g., Edwards 1966) are based on a factor analysis of a large pool of items. However, perhaps too much emphasis has been placed upon the factor analytic method as opposed to other methods of internal consistency analysis. Henrysson (1962), for example, has shown that the first centroid factor loading of a set of items can be expressed as a function of the point biserial correlation of the item with the total scale. In an empirical analysis of some 15 different methods of item selection, Neill and Jackson (1970) demonstrated a very close correspondence between first principal component factor loadings and the point biserial, biserial, and other indices of item-total scale correlation, such that items selected using each of these strategies would have yielded extremely similar scales. Actually, the important findings from this comparison of item selection indices were that (a) purposeful selection strategies were all superior to random strategy, and

(b) it was possible to preserve scale homogeneity substantially while suppressing extraneous response style variance. Although factor analysis is one device for evaluating convergent and discriminant properties for items, its distinctiveness and advantages over alternative methods have probably been overemphasized. Without an a priori conception of the appropriate level of abstraction of the trait to be measured, purely empirical means to select scales based upon factors may lead to scales either too broad or too specific. Eysenck, for example, has described two major dimensions using factor analysis, while Edwards, also with the aid of factor analysis, defines scores for 53 scales! In the Neill and Jackson study, although the total scale of Evaluation Sensitivity yielded a reliability of 0.93, eight distinct factors could be identified among the items.

The use of other statistical procedures such as homogeneity keying to obtain scales has been advocated by some investigators (Loevinger, Gleser, & DuBois 1953). Generally, these procedures involved rules for clustering items which empirically meet some criterion of internal consistency, such as the requirement that a certain coefficient of homogeneity not be decreased by the addition of a new item. Such procedures can be very useful as exploratory or hypothesis-generating aids when entering a new domain of personality about which little is known. But the blind empirical application of such procedures, without clearly formulated conceptions of what dimensions are to be measured, can lead to a clustering of items based on response biases (Meehl & Hathaway 1946). Ernhart and Loevinger (1969), for example, used such a technique in an attempt to isolate attitudinal dimensions of family ideology, but found that under cross-validation, four of the five dimensions obtained failed to be replicated. The fifth appeared to be a dimension related to response bias. Clearly, substantive as well as empirical homogeneity is required if measures of broad construct validity are to be developed.

A third major strategy of test construction involves the use of an external criterion. Here, the focus is not upon the characteristics measured by a clustering of items, but rather, an attempt is made to capture the psychological characteristics defined by some criterion situation. The criterion may well be the individual's status, as, for example, his psychiatric diagnosis. One may attempt to identify a psychological dimension by looking for items which distinguish very different kinds of criterion groups. For example, Gough (1952, 1957) in the development of the California Psychological Inventory Femininity Scale administered a large number of items to males and females and identified those which, on cross-validation, separated the two groups. He was not attempting here to find a personality scale effective in separating males from females —self-report usually serves reasonably well for this purpose— but rather, he was seeking to measure psychological femininity within each sex by a scale constructed to distinguish males from females. In the construction of the MMPI, Hathaway and McKinley hoped that it would be possible to predict psychiatric status by finding items distinguishing patients from normals. In the original rationale for the test, there was an implicit adoption of a *class model*. The authors implied that psychiatric diagnostic categories represented a discretely different type of person from normal individuals. As with the CPI, users of the MMPI have sought to expand upon the original narrow, criterion-oriented, predictive-validity rationale on which the scales were based, and have attempted to place greater emphasis upon the scales as trait measures. There may, however, be considerable hazard in this departure from strict empiricism. The rationale for empirically predicting a criterion, although developed in a philosophically more naive era, has a certain consistency. To be sure, it is sometimes dangerous to assume that one's criterion has not changed over time, or to assume that antecedent probability and base rates will have no effect upon validity or upon item selection (cf. Meehl & Rosen 1955). There is, nevertheless, a certain logic to this approach. However, when test authors and users argue that scales so derived can be generalized across a wide variety of situations to measure traits of general import, they are departing from the logic of strict empiricism. It becomes necessary at every stage to evaluate, either empirically or theoretically, the degree to which a scale, originally having few or no foundations in theory, can be generalized to measure traits of universal import, or to predict criteria quite different from those upon which the scale was based.

Hase and Goldberg (1967) undertook a systematic study of the efficacy of the different strategies of scale construction in predicting a number of diverse criteria. They used four major strategies of test construction: (a) factor analytic, (b) group discriminative or empirical, (c) intuitive-theoretical, and (d) intuitive-rational. Using the factor analytic strategy, Hase and Goldberg constructed eleven scales (e.g., extroversion-introversion, serenity-depression, harmonious childhood, etc.), based on each item's factor loading. Their empirically derived, or group discriminative, scales were based on the original empirical item selection used by Gough in the construction of the California Psychological Inventory. The intuitive-theoretical scales were based upon judgments of CPI items by three advanced graduate students in terms of their relevance to the definitions of personality for the Murray (1938) variables of personality. The fourth strategy used by Hase and Goldberg (i.e., the rational strategy) involved the development of initial pools of items judged in terms of their criterion relevance, and the subsequent refinement of these scales using item analyses designed to maximize internal consistency.

The major findings of Hase and Goldberg were that the four primary strategies of scale construction were equivalent in average validity. Each strategy yielded scales which contributed to a multiple correlation with each of several criteria at about the same magnitude. The authors content that "strategies make little difference," and suggest that this finding has "profound implications for personality assessment." While it is indeed of some interest to note that one strategy of scale construction was not clearly superior to other strategies in this particular situation, certain cautions should be noted both in the design of the study and in the interpretation of the results. First of all, the comparison among the various strategies was based on an extant item pool, namely, that of the CPI. Any deficiencies in this item pool in terms of nondiscriminating or irrelevant items would inevitably limit the validity of scales derived by any strategy. Secondly, scales were constructed without regard to their length and to their reliability. Thirdly, the authors based their analysis entirely upon the ability of all scales to predict a particular criterion in a multiple prediction equation. It would have been very fruitful, alternatively, to compare strategies of scale construction in terms of their convergent and discriminant validity. This might have yielded quite different results. Hase and Goldberg suggest that it is entirely possible that scale strategies more novel than those employed in their study might

yield higher validities than those they recorded, but they add that it would be up to the proponents of such strategies to prove their relative superiority. The validities reported by Hase and Goldberg, while typical of many such studies, certainly do not lend much encouragement to any of the strategies of scale construction used by these authors. The median validity of the "best" scale constructed by each strategy proved to be 0.32 for the factor approach, 0.24 for the empirical approach, 0.26 for the theoretical approach, and 0.29 for the rational approach. Since none of these validity coefficients is significantly different from the others, such findings do indeed lend a note of caution to those who argue that there is only one viable method of scale construction. However, in the present, more sophisticated world of psychological assessment, where the theoretical framework of psychology is blended with methodological achievements, it hardly seems justifiable to argue for the anachronism of a single strategy of scale construction.

A Modern Approach to Assessment

As noted in the previous section, until recently authors have selected a single approach to the construction of multi-scale personality tests, arguing for its efficacy on theoretical grounds or, in the case of Hase and Goldberg (1967), evaluating alternatives on empirical grounds. A basic assumption underlying this sort of comparison is that alternative strategies of scale construction are, in one or another sense, mutually exclusive. A test constructor either had to be in one assessment strategy camp or another. Either he accepted the value of factor analysis, or the power of theory in generating items. The two were somehow conceived of as mutually contradictory approaches.

This sort of ideological posturing makes for interesting reading—most people enjoy a good debate. However, when one considers the possibility that several approaches to personality scale construction are by no means mutually exclusive and, indeed, may be combined in a single sequential strategy, these debates, and even empirical comparisons of different assessment approaches, become unnecessary, and even fatuous. An inkling of this possibility was provided by the consideration of the Hase and Goldberg study. A careful scrutiny of the bases for comparison of the alternative strategies of scale construction indicated that it was very difficult to separate unequivocally one strategy from the others. How much theoretical definition should be permitted in the applications of the factor analytic approach, or how much internal consistency analysis is appropriate where the primary focus is upon intuitive selection of items? Clearly, it is possible to view virtually any method of scale construction as a step in a sequential series of hurdles which each item must surmount prior to its being added to a scale.

THE DEVELOPMENT OF THE PERSONALITY RESEARCH FORM

The Personality Research Form was recently developed (Jackson 1967b) as an attempt to evaluate the degree to which a sequential strategy might overcome some of the traditional difficulties encountered in personality scale construction. Many of the procedures employed in the development of the PRF involved unique criteria for item selection, as well as more traditional strategies used in unique combinations. It will be seen that this approach involved elements of all of the major strategies outlined above, with the exception of the method of empirical keying, but in addition involved a number of steps not incorporated into the development of any previously published personality inventory. As noted, the major distinguishing characteristic of this more modern approach is the use of a *combination* of steps in a *sequential* series. Each of these steps is viewed as a necessary, but not sufficient, basis for the construction of personality measures possessing the properties of construct and of convergent and discriminant validity. These successive steps are reviewed in detail in this section to illustrate how a modern personality inventory is constructed.

First of all, a necessary precondition for measuring a personality variable was the development of a careful, theoretical definition of each relevant construct. According to Hempel (1952), a sufficiently complete definition of a construct will incorporate an understanding of both its theoretical and empirical properties. Thus, the defining of a trait involves an attempt, always subject to revision, to determine its salient properties and to explicate the conditions under which certain consequences may be expected. In the case of a personality variable, this involves a statement of its manifestations in a variety of situational and organismic contexts. For the Personality Research Form a decision was made to utilize the variables of personality first defined by Murray (1938) and his colleagues, primarily because careful definitions of these variables had already been prepared. These definitions were subject to some modification, particularly with respect to their mutual distinctiveness. A guiding principle in this prior conceptual analysis was that the Campbell-Fiske (1959) criteria for the *evaluation* of multitrait-multimethod matrices should be extended so as to be applicable to a program of test construction. Variables should be defined in such a way as to be exclusive and nonredundant. That is, if one is to strive for the property of convergent and discriminant validity in a test's correlations with external criteria, it is reasonable to expect that definitions of traits, prior to measurement and prior to item writing, be sufficiently distinct so as to permit the categorization of items in a set of mutually exclusive item sets serving to define each variable. Thus, the preparation of items for the PRF item pool was preceded by careful and explicit definitions of traits to be measured. This definition included the development of a grid of events and occasions so that manifestations of a trait could be understood across a variety of representative situations in an individual's characteristic activity. This kind of explicit formulation of the nature of a trait to be measured is in sharp contrast to the traditional method of empirical item selection (Meehl 1945) in which, at the extreme, sole reliance is placed on an item's ability to distinguish empirically an external criterion, and in which conceptual analysis is viewed with some considerable suspicion. It should be noted, however, in fairness to Meehl, that his eloquent 1945 statement of the empiricist tradition has been superseded by an equally forthright statement about the importance of theoretical constructs in measurement (Cronbach & Meehl 1955). Because this kind of definitional explication of the constructs to be measured is based on a number of implicit judgmental criteria, it is not easy to discuss in a precise manner all of the considerations leading to the definition of a trait. However, both formal and informal psychological theory, as well as available empirical research, is most helpful in this task.

Following conceptual analysis, the development of the PRF proceeded by the construction of substantial item pools for each dimension to be measured. Here the major tasks were: to relate each item with a definition; to avoid systematic biases in the saturation of one facet of a trait over another; and to avoid biases in item wording and sampling favoring one subgroup, such as males, over another. It proved to be particularly difficult for an item writer to focus on the discriminant, distinctive features of items, particularly when as many as 140 items had to be written for one scale. Nevertheless, in spite of potential difficulties, it is recommended in the light of experience with the PRF that for any assessment task it will ordinarily be advantageous to write new items rather than to cull items from any available and convenient source. For each of the large pools of items representing each of the 20 substantive variables in the development of the PRF, a thorough editorial review was undertaken to evaluate items for their distinctive and representative reflection of the trait in question. Items not acceptable were either rejected or salvaged by subjecting them to a rewriting and reevaluation process.

This process places a great deal of emphasis upon human judgment in the theoretical explication of the nature of a trait. Although it is entirely understandable that a good deal of skepticism attends what might appear to be a highly intuitive, subjective evaluation of item properties, there is recent empirical evidence (Boyd & Jackson 1966) that judges can indeed relate hypothetical people to item content in a way that reflects remarkably reliable and refined distinctions between personality traits. In the study cited, three distinct hypothesized dimensions were defined and related to relevant person descriptions by independent sets of judges performing a multidimensional scaling task. For each of the three dimensions, substantial agreement between judges was evidenced by correlations between independently obtained dimensions consistently in excess of 0.95.

The PRF item pools derived in this way were administered to a number of samples of subjects totalling in excess of 1000. A number of item and scale statistics were computed on these samples of subjects. First of all, the long provisional scales (ranging from 100 to 140 items) were evaluated for internal consistency using the Kuder-Richardson formula 20. The median reliability of the long scales was in excess of 0.92, indicating that personality variables can be measured with as much fidelity as is typically found in achievement tests of comparable length. Of course, had any of the PRF scales shown an unacceptably low level of reliability, the scale would have been discarded as failing to meet a minimum criterion for the structural component of validity (Loevinger 1957). After scale statistics were calculated and evaluated, each item was subjected to a number of analytic steps which can be thought of as hurdles. In every case if the item was successful in meeting the criterion, it passed in turn to the next hurdle. Needless to say, a necessary condition for such strategy was a large item pool of sufficient content saturation that enough items would remain at the end of the screening to form a scale. These successive hurdles included:

1. The requirement that an item show an endorsement proportion not so extreme as to preclude its discrimination between subjects. For example, the amount of information contained in an item with an endorsement proportion of 0.01 is essentially yielding information on only one percent of the people, whereas an item with an endorsement

proportion of 0.50 yields approximately 25 times more useful information as estimated from the respective item variances;

2. Biserial correlations were computed between each scale and the scale for which it was written, and for a number of irrelevant scales. Items correlating more highly with an irrelevant scale than with their own scale were discarded. Again, this involved a requirement that items show convergent and discriminant properties in the process of test development, a necessary precondition to the requirement that a test, after construction is completed, will show these properties against external criteria;

3. Items were also rejected which showed a higher correlation with a specially constructed desirability scale in relation to their own total score. Again, a set of items correlating more highly with a scale reflecting desirability bias inevitably would tend not to show discriminant validity and sufficient distinctiveness to permit its use as a valid indicator of distinctive traits;

4. A further step in the suppression of response style variance in scale construction was the use of a differential reliability index. This technique, developed by the author in collaboration with Samuel Messick, involves the calculation of an index based on squaring the item's biserial correlation with its own scale and subtracting from that the item's biserial correlation with a desirability scale and then calculating the square root of this difference. This index represents the reliable portion of the item variance associated with its own content dimension as distinct from a desirability dimension. Ranking items on this basis, as was done with the Personality Research Form items, yields a set of items with relatively higher levels of content saturation and with desirability variance suppressed. The resulting scales thus tended to show substantial levels of reliability but were free from the high levels of correlation with desirability marker scales characteristically found in tests such as the MMPI (Jackson & Messick 1961) and the CPI (Jackson & Pacine 1961);

5. An iterative computer program was designed to minimize the statistical differences between pairs of parallel forms representing the same traits;

6. The scales were again edited to evaluate them for the important property of *generalizability* (Cronbach, Rajaratnam, & Gleser 1963). Essentially, this involved reviewing scales to determine whether or not they were sufficiently representative of the trait that they were designed to measure;

7. Scales were evaluated for convergent and discriminant validity, as indicated in the studies cited below.

For readers interested in the details of the effects of such a procedure on characteristics of scales, including convergent and discriminant properties, reference is made to a recent article (Jackson 1970) describing these in detail. In general, each of the successive item selection hurdles resulted in a particular scale property. The elimination of items correlating too highly with irrelevant scales contributed to discriminant validity, as did the suppression of desirability variance. Reliability is influenced by focusing upon the content saturation of items in the item selection process. The statistical procedures designed to maximize the similarity between parallel forms had the effect of yielding scales which, when subjected to a multimethod factor analysis, defined 22 factors each with high loadings for the pair

or relevant scales and negligible loadings for irrelevant scales (Jackson 1969). The focus upon convergent and discriminant properties of scales and items resulted in the demonstration of substantial convergent and discriminant validity as demonstrated by a multimethod factor analysis in one study (Jackson & Guthrie 1968) of peer ratings, self-ratings, and PRF scale scores for some 202 subjects; and in a second study of convergent and discriminant validity for peer ratings on relevant traits, PRF endorsements, and certain other indirect criteria (Kusyszyn & Jackson 1968). In general, the results based on the PRF indicate that certain worthwhile properties of personality scales are fostered, not by using only a single strategy of scale construction or even a small number of procedures; but by basing one's development of personality scales upon a variety of procedures, both theoretical and empirical, which have been demonstrated to yield scales with optimal properties.

References

ALLPORT, G. W. A test for ascendance-submission. *Journal of Abnormal and Social Psychology*, 1928, 23, 118–36.
——— What is a trait of personality? *Journal of Abnormal and Social Psychology*, 1931, 25, 368–72.
——— Traits revisited. *American Psychologist*, 1966, 21, 1–10.
BARNES, E. H. Response bias and the MMPI. *Journal of Consulting Psychology*, 1956, 20, 371–74.
BENDIG, A. W. A factor analysis of "social desirability," "defensiveness," and "acquiescence" scales. *Journal of Genetic Psychology*, 1962, 66, 129–36.
BENTLER, P. M. Response variability: Fact or artifact? (Unpublished doctoral dissertation, Stanford University, 1964.)
——— Review of J. Block, The challenge of response sets. *American Scientist*, 1966, 54, 495A–96A.
——— Semantic space is (approximately) bipolar. *Journal of Psychology*, 1969, 71, 33–40.
BERG, I. A. The reliability of extreme position response sets in two tests. *Journal of Psychology*, 1953, 36, 3–9.
——— The unimportance of test item content. *In* B. M. Bass and I. A. Berg (eds.), *Objective approaches to personality assessment.* New York: Van Nostrand Reinhold, 1959.
———, ed. *Response set in personality assessment.* Chicago: Aldine, 1967.
BERKSHIRE, J. R. Comparisons of five forced-choice indices. *Educational and Psychological Measurement*, 1958, 23, 553–61.
BERNREUTER, R. G. *The personality inventory.* Stanford, Calif.: Stanford University Press, 1931.
——— The theory and construction of the personality inventory. *Journal of Social Psychology*, 1933, 4, 387–405.
BLOCK, J. *The challenge of response sets.* New York: Appleton-Century-Crofts, 1965.
——— Remarks on Jackson's "Review" of Block's "Challenge of response sets." *Educational and Psychological Measurement*, 1967, 27, 499–502.
BOCK, R. D., DICKEN, C., and VAN PELT, J. Methodological implications of content-acquiescence correlation in the MMPI. *Psychological Bulletin*, 1969, 71, 127–39.
BOE, E. E., and KOGAN, W. S. Social desirability response set in the individual. *Journal of Consulting Psychology*, 1963, 27, 369.
BORING, E. G. *A history of experimental psychology*, 2d ed. New York: Appleton-Century-Crofts, 1950.
BOYD, J. E., and JACKSON, D. N. An empirical evaluation of judgment and response methods in multivariate attitude scaling. *American Psychologist* (abstract), 1966, 21, 718.
CAMPBELL, D. T. The indirect assessment of social attitudes. *Psychological Bulletin*, 1950, 47, 15–38.
——— A typology of tests, projective and otherwise. *Journal of Consulting Psychology*, 1957, 21, 207–10. Reprinted in D. N. Jackson and S. Messick (eds.), *Problems in human assessment.* New York: McGraw-Hill, 1967.

————, and FISKE, D. W. Convergent and discriminant validation by the multitrait-multimethod matrix. *Psychological Bulletin*, 1959, *56*, 81–105.

CAMPBELL, D. T., and O'CONNELL, E. J. Method factors in multitrait-multimethod matrices: Multiplicative rather than additive? *Multivariate Behavioral Research*, 1967, *2*, 409–26.

CAMPBELL, D. T., SEIGMAN, C. R., and REES, M. B. Direction-of-wording effects in the relationships between scales. *Psychological Bulletin*, 1967, *68*, 293–303.

CATTELL, R. B. *Personality: A systematic theoretical and factual study.* New York: McGraw-Hill, 1950.

———— *Personality and motivation structure and measurement.* Yonkers-on-Hudson, N. Y.: World Book, 1957.

————, EBER, H. W., and TATSUOKA, M. M. *Sixteen Personality Factor Questionnaire.* Champaign, Ill.: Institute for Personality and Ability Testing, 1967.

CLAYTON, M. B., and JACKSON, D. N. Equivalence range, acquiescence, and overgeneralization. *Educational and Psychological Measurement*, 1961, *21*, 371–82.

CLEMANS, W. V. An analytical and empirical examination of some properties of ipsative measures. *Psychometric Monographs*, 1966, no. 14.

CLIFF, N., and HAMBURGER, C. D. The study of sampling errors in factor analysis by means of artificial experiments. *Psychological Bulletin*, 1967, *68*, 430–45.

COMREY, A. L. Factored homogeneous dimensions in personality research. *Educational and Psychological Measurement*, 1961, *21*, 417–31.

CONN, L. K., and CROWNE, D. P. Instigation to aggression, emotional arousal, and defensive emulation. *Journal of Personality*, 1964, *32*, 163–79.

COOLEY, W. W., and LOHNES, P. R. *Multivariate procedures for the behavioral sciences.* New York: John Wiley, 1962.

COUCH, A., and KENISTON, K. Yeasayers and naysayers: Agreeing response set as a personality variable. *Journal of Abnormal and Social Psychology*, 1960, *60*, 151–74.

COWEN, E. L., and FRANKEL, G. The social desirability of trait-descriptive terms: Application to a French sample. *Journal of Social Psychology*, 1964, *63*, 233–39.

CRONBACH, L. J. Response set and test validity. *Educational and Psychological Measurement*, 1946, *6*, 475–94.

———— Further evidence on response sets and test design. *Educational and Psychological Measurement*, 1950, *10*, 3–31.

————, and GLESER, G. *Psychological tests and personal decisions,* 2d ed. Urbana: University of Illinois Press, 1964.

CRONBACH, L. J., and MEEHL, P. E. Construct validity in psychological testing. *Psychological Bulletin*, 1955, *52*, 281–302.

CRONBACH, L. J., RAJARATNAM, N., and GLESER, G. C. Theory of generalizability: A liberalization of reliability theory. *British Journal of Statistical Psychology*, 1963, *16*, 137–63.

CROWNE, D. P., and MARLOWE, D. A new scale of social desirability independent of psychopathology. *Journal of Consulting Psychology*, 1960, *24*, 349–54.

———— *The approval motive.* New York: John Wiley, 1964.

DAHLSTROM, W. G., and WELSH, G. S. *An MMPI handbook.* Minneapolis: The University of Minnesota Press, 1960.

DAMARIN, F. L., and MESSICK, S. Response styles as personality variables: Evidence from published multivariate research. Princeton, N. J.: Educational Testing Service Research Bulletin, 1965.

EDWARDS, A. L. *Edwards Personal Preference Schedule.* New York: Psychological Corporation, 1953a.

———— The relationship between the judged desirability of a trait and the probability that the trait will be endorsed. *Journal of Applied Psychology*, 1953b, *37*, 90–93.

———— *The social desirability variable in personality assessment and research.* New York: Dryden, 1957.

———— *Edwards Personality Inventory.* Chicago: Science Research Associates, 1966.

———— The social desirability variable: A broad statement. *In* I. A. Berg (ed.), *Response set in personality assessment.* Chicago: Aldine, 1967.

ELLIS, A. The validity of personality questionnaires. *Psychological Bulletin*, 1946, *43*, 385–440.

————, and CONRAD, H. S. The validity of personality inventories in military practice. *Psychological Bulletin*, 1948, *45*, 385–426.

ERNHART, C. B., and LOEVINGER, J. Authoritarian family ideology: A measure, its correlates, and its robustness. *Multivariate Behavioral Research Monograph*, 1969 (69–1).

EYSENCK, H. J. *Dimensions of personality.* London: Kegan Paul, 1947.

FLANAGAN, J. C. *Factor analysis in the study of personality.* Stanford, Calif.: Stanford University Press, 1935.

FREDERIKSEN, N., and MESSICK, S. Response set as a measure of personality. *Educational and Psychological Measurement*, 1959, *19*, 137–57.

FULKERSON, S. C. An acquiescence key for the MMPI. *USAF School of Aviation Medicine Report*, no. 58–71, July 1958.

GORDON, L. V. Validation of forced-choice and questionnaire methods of personality measurement. *Journal of Applied Psychology*, 1951, *35*, 407–12.

GOUGH, H. G. Identifying psychological femininity. *Educational and Psychological Measurement*, 1952, *12*, 427–39.

———— *Manual for the California Psychological Inventory.* Palo Alto, Calif.: Consulting Psychologists Press, 1957.

GREEN, B. F. Attitude measurement. In G. Lindzey (ed.), *Handbook of social psychology*, vol. 1. Reading, Mass.: Addison-Wesley, 1954. Reprinted in D. N. Jackson and S. Messick (eds.), *Problems in human assessment.* New York: McGraw-Hill, 1967, pp. 725–36.

GUILFORD, J. P., and MARTIN, H. G. *The Guilford-Martin Personnel Inventory.* Beverly Hills, Calif.: Sheridan Psychological Services, 1945.

GUILFORD, J. P., and ZIMMERMAN, W. S. *The Guilford-Zimmerman Aptitude Survey*, 2d ed. Beverly Hills, Calif.: Sheridan Psychological Services, 1956.

GULLIKSEN, H. *Theory of mental tests.* New York: John Wiley, 1950.

HANLEY, C. Social desirability and responses to items from three MMPI scales: *D*, *Sc*, and *K. Journal of Applied Psychology*, 1956, *40*, 324–28.

HARMAN, H. H. *Modern factor analysis*, 2d ed. Chicago: The University of Chicago Press, 1967.

HARVEY, O. J., HUNT, D. E., and SCHRODER, H. U. *Conceptual systems and personality organization.* New York: John Wiley, 1961.

HASE, H. D., and GOLDBERG, L. R. Comparative validity of different strategies of constructing personality inventory scales. *Psychological Bulletin*, 1967, *67*, 231–48.

HATHAWAY, S. R., and MCKINLEY, J. C. A multiphasic personality schedule (Minnesota): I. Construction of the schedule. *Journal of Psychology*, 1940, *10*, 249–54.

———— *Minnesota Multiphasic Personality Inventory.* Minneapolis: University of Minnesota Press, 1942.

———— *The Minnesota Multiphasic Personality Inventory* (Manual). New York: Psychological Corp., 1943. (Revised, 1951).

HEINEMAN, C. E. A forced-choice form of the Taylor Anxiety Scale. *Journal of Consulting Psychology*, 1953, *17*, 447–54.

HEMPEL, C. G. *Fundamentals of concept formation in empirical science.* Chicago: University of Chicago Press, 1952.

HENRYSSON, S. The relation between factor loadings and biserial correlations in item analysis. *Psychometrika*, 1962, *27*, 419–24.

HORST P., ed. The prediction of personal adjustment. *Bulletin no. 48.* New York: Social Science Research Council, 1941.

HORST, P. *Factor analysis of data matrices.* New York: Holt, Rinehart & Winston, 1965.

IWAWAKI, S., and COWEN, E. L. The social desirability of trait-descriptive terms: Applications to a Japanese sample. *Journal of Social Psychology*, 1964, *63*, 199–205.

JACKSON, D. N. Assessing conformity with desirability judgments. *American Psychologist* (abstract), 1961, *16*, 446.

———— Desirability judgments as a method of personality assessment. *Educational and Psychological Measurement*, 1964, *24*, 223–38.

———— Acquiescence response styles: Problems of identification and control. *In* I. A. Berg (ed.), *Response set in personality assessment.* Chicago: Aldine, 1967a.

———— *Manual for the Personality Research Form.* Goshen, New York: Research Psychologists Press, 1967b.

———— Review of J. Block, The challenge of response sets. *Educational and Psychological Measurement*, 1967c, *27*, 207–19.

—— Balanced scales, item overlap, and the stables of Augeas. *Educational and Psychological Measurement*, 1967d, *27*, 502–7.

—— Multimethod factor analysis in the evaluation of convergent and discriminant validity. *Psychological Bulletin*, 1969, *72*, 30–49.

—— A sequential system for personality scale development. *In* C. D. Spielberg (ed.), *Current topics in clinical and community psychology*, vol. 2. New York: Academic Press, 1970.

——, and GUTHRIE, G. M. Multitrait-multimethod evaluating of Personality Research Form. *Proceedings of the 76th Annual Convention of the American Psychological Association*, 1968, 177–78.

JACKSON, D. N., and LAY, C. H. Homogeneous dimensions of personality scale content. *Multivariate Behavioral Research*, 1968, *3*, 321–38.

JACKSON, D. N., and MESSICK, S. J. A note on ethnocentrism and acquiescent response sets. *Journal of Abnormal and Social Psychology*, 1957, *54*, 132–34.

—— Content and style in personality assessment. *Psychological Bulletin*, 1958, *55*, 243–52.

—— Acquiescence and desirability as response determinants on the MMPI. *Educational and Psychological Measurement*, 1961, *21*, 771–90.

—— Response styles and the assessment of psychopathology. *In* S. Messick and J. Ross (eds.), *Measurement in personality and cognition*. New York: John Wiley, 1962a.

—— Response styles on the MMPI: Comparison of clinical and normal samples. *Journal of Abnormal and Social Psychology*, 1962b, *65*, 285–99.

—— Acquiescence: The nonvanishing variance component. *American Psychologist* (abstract), 1965, *20*, 498.

——, eds. *Problems in human assessment*. New York: McGraw-Hill, 1967.

—— A distinction between judgments of frequency and of desirability as determinants of response. *Educational and Psychological Measurement*, 1969, *29*, 273–93.

JACKSON, D. N., and MINTON, H. L. A forced-choice adjective preference scale for personality assessment. *Psychological Reports*, 1963, *12*, 515–20.

JACKSON, D. N., and PACINE, L. Response styles and academic achievement. *Educational and Psychological Measurement*, 1961, *21*, 1015–27.

JACKSON, D. N., and PAYNE, I. R. Personality scale for shallow affect. *Psychological Reports*, 1963, *13*, 687–98.

JACKSON, D. N., and SINGER, J. E. Judgments, items, and personality. *Journal of Experimental Research in Personality*, 1967, *2*, 70–79.

JONES, R. R. Differences in response consistency and subjects' preferences for three personality inventory response formats. *Proceedings of the 76th Annual Convention of the American Psychological Association*, 1968, 247–48.

KLEINMUNTZ, B. *Personality measurement: An introduction*. Homewood, Ill.: Dorsey, 1967.

KOGAN, N., and WALLACH, M. A. *Risk taking: A study in cognition and personality*. New York: Holt, Rinehart & Winston, 1964.

KUDER, G. F. *Occupational interest survey: General manual*. Chicago: Science Research Associates, 1966.

KUSYSZYN, I., and JACKSON, D. N. A multimethod factor analytic appraisal of endorsement and judgment methods in personality assessment. *Educational and Psychological Measurement*, 1968, *28*, 1047–61.

LAPOINTE, R. E., and AUCLAIRE, G. A. The use of social desirability in forced-choice methodology. *American Psychologist* (abstract), 1961, *16*, 446.

LAY, C. H., and JACKSON, D. N. Analysis of the generality of trait-inferential relationships. *Journal of Personality and Social Psychology*, 1969, *12*, 12–21.

LICHTENSTEIN, E., and BRYAN, S. H. Acquiescence and the MMPI: An item reversal approach. *Journal of Abnormal Psychology*, 1965, *70*, 290–94.

LOEVINGER, J. Objective tests as instruments of psychological theory. *Psychological Reports* (Monograph Supplement 9), 1957, *3*, 635–94.

—— Measuring ego development by sentence completion. *Proceedings of the 76th Annual Convention of the American Psychological Association*, 1968, 747.

——, GLESER, G., and DUBOIS, P. H. Maximizing the discriminating power of a multiple-score test. *Psychometrika*, 1953, *18*, 309–17.

LORD, F. M., and NOVICK, M. R. *Statistical theories of mental test scores*. Reading, Mass.: Addison-Wesley, 1968.

LORR, M. *Explorations in typing psychotics*. New York: Pergamon Press, 1966.

MARKS, P. A., and SEEMAN, W. *The actuarial description of abnormal personality—an atlas for use with the MMPI*. Baltimore: Williams & Wilkins, 1963.

MARTIN, J. Acquiescence—measurement and theory. *British Journal of Clinical Psychology*, 1964, *3*, 216–25.

MCCLELLAND, D. C., ATKINSON, J. W., CLARK, R. A., and LOWELL, E. L. *The achievement motive*. New York: Appleton-Century-Crofts, 1953.

MCGEE, R. K. Response as a personality variable: By what criterion? *Psychological Bulletin*, 1962, *59*, 284–95.

MEEHL, P. E. The dynamics of "structured" personality tests. *Journal of Clinical Psychology*, 1945, *1*, 296–303.

——, and HATHAWAY, S. R. The K factor as a suppressor variable in the MMPI. *Journal of Applied Psychology*, 1946, *30*, 525–64.

MEEHL, P. E., and ROSEN, A. Antecedent probability and the efficiency of psychometric signs, patterns, or cutting scores. *Psychological Bulletin*, 1955, *52*, 194–216.

MESSICK, S. Dimensions of social desirability. *Journal of Consulting Psychology*, 1960, *24*, 279–87.

—— The psychology of acquiescence: An interpretation of research evidence. *In* I. A. Berg (ed.), *Response set in personality assessment*. Chicago: Aldine, 1967.

——, and HILLS, J. R. Objective measurement of personality: Cautiousness and intolerance of ambiguity. *Educational and Psychological Measurement*, 1960, *20*, 685–98.

MESSICK, S., and JACKSON, D. N. Acquiescence and the factorial interpretation of the MMPI. *Psychological Bulletin*, 1961, *58*, 299–304.

MISCHEL, W. *Personality and assessment*. New York: John Wiley, 1968.

MITZELL, H. E., RABINOWITZ, W., and OSTREICHER, L. M. The effects of response sets on the validity of the Minnesota Teacher Attitude Inventory. *Educational and Psychological Measurement*, 1956, *16*, 501–15.

MORF, M. E., and JACKSON, D. N. An analysis of two response styles: True responding and item endorsement. *University of Western Ontario Research Bulletin* no. 98 (London, Canada), November, 1969.

MURPHY, G. *Personality*. New York: Harper & Row, 1947.

MURRAY, H. A. et al. *Explorations in personality*. New York: Oxford University Press, 1938.

NEILL, J. A., and JACKSON, D. N. An evaluation of item selection strategies in personality scale construction. *Educational and Psychological Measurement*, 1970, *30*.

NORMAN, W. T. On estimating psychological relationships: Social desirability and self-report. *Psychological Bulletin*, 1967, *67*, 273–93.

OSGOOD, C. E. Ease of individual judgment processes in relation to polarization of attitudes in the culture. *Journal of Social Psychology*, 1941, *14*, 403–18.

RADCLIFFE, J. A. Some properties of ipsative score matrices and their relevance for some current interest tests. *Australian Journal of Psychology*, 1963, *15*, 1–11.

RORER, L. G. The great response style myth. *Psychological Bulletin*, 1965, *63*, 129–56.

——, and GOLDBERG, L. R. Acquiescence in the MMPI? *Educational and Psychological Measurement*, 1965, *25*, 801–17.

ROSEN, E. Self-appraisal and perceived desirability of MMPI personality traits. *Journal of Counseling Psychology*, 1956, *3*, 44–51.

—— Self-appraisal, personal desirability, and perceived social desirability of personality traits. *Journal of Abnormal and Social Psychology*, 1956, *52*, 151–58.

ROTTER, J. B. *Social learning and clinical psychology*. Englewood Cliffs, N. J.: Prentice-Hall, 1954.

ROZEBOOM, W. W. *Foundations of the theory of prediction*. Homewood, Ill.: Dorsey, 1966.

RUNDQUIST, E. A. Response sets: A note on consistency in taking extreme positions. *Educational and Psychological Measurement*, 1950, *10*, 97–99.

—— Item and response characteristics in attitude and personality assessment: A reaction to L. G. Rorer's "The great response style myth." *Psychological Bulletin*, 1966, *66*, 166–77.

——, and SLETTO, R. F. *Personality in the depression*. Minneapolis: University of Minnesota Press, 1936.

SCOTT, W. A. Social desirability and individual conceptions of the desirable. *Journal of Abnormal and Social Psychology*, 1963, *67*, 574–85.

—— Attitude measurement. *In* G. Lindzey and E. Aronson (eds.), *The handbook of social psychology*, 2d ed. Reading, Mass.: Addison-Wesley, 1968a, pp. 204–73.

—— Comparative validities of forced-choice and single-stimulus tests. *Psychological Bulletin*, 1968b, *70*, 231–44.

SECHREST, L., and JACKSON, D. N. Deviant response tendencies: Their measurement and interpretation. *Educational and Psychological Measurement*, 1963, *23*, 33–53.

STRICKER, L. J. Acquiescence and social desirability response styles, item characteristics, and conformity. *Psychological Reports* (Monograph Supplement 2–12), 1963, *12*, 319–41.

—— "Test-wiseness" on personality scales. *Journal of Applied Psychology Monograph*, 1969, *53*, 1–18.

——, MESSICK, S., and JACKSON, D. N. Evaluating deception in psychological research. *Psychological Bulletin*, 1969, *71*, 343–51.

STRICKER, L. J., and ROSS, J. Some correlates of a Jungian personality inventory. *Psychological Reports*, 1964, *14*, 623–43.

TAYLOR, J. B. Social desirability and MMPI performance: The individual case. *Journal of Consulting Psychology*, 1959, *23*, 514–17.

THURSTONE, L. L. *Personality Schedule*. Chicago: University of Chicago Press, 1929.

TOMKINS, S. S., and MESSICK, S., eds. *Computer simulation of personality*. New York: John Wiley, 1963.

TROTT, D. M., and JACKSON, D. N. An experimental analysis of acquiescence. *Journal of Experimental Research in Personality*, 1967, *2*, 278–88.

ULLMAN, L. P., and KRASNER, L. *A psychological approach to abnormal behavior*. Englewood Cliffs, N. J.: Prentice-Hall, 1969.

VERNON, P. E. *Personality tests and assessments*. New York: Holt, Rinehart & Winston 1953.

WELSH, G. S. An extension of Hathaway's MMPI profile coding system. *Journal of Consulting Psychology*, 1948, *12*, 343–44.

——, and DAHLSTROM, W. G., eds. *Basic readings on the MMPI in psychology and medicine*. Minneapolis: University of Minnesota Press, 1956.

WESSLER, R. Empirical evaluation of manual for rating level of ego development from sentence completion. *Proceedings of the 76th Annual Convention of the American Psychological Association*, 1968, 748.

WHYTE, W. H. *The organization man*. New York: Simon & Schuster, 1956.

WIGGINS, J. S. Strategic, method, and stylistic variance in the MMPI. *Psychological Bulletin*, 1962, *59*, 224–42.

—— Substantive dimensions of self-report in the MMPI item pool. *Psychological Monographs*, 1966, *80* (22, whole no. 620).

WOODWORTH, R. S. *Personal Data Sheet*. Chicago: Stoelting, 1920.

ZAVALA, A. Development of the forced-choice rating scale technique. *Psychological Bulletin*, 1965, *63*, 117–24.

E. Howarth

& R. B. Cattell

On the Importance of Multivariate Experiment (and on the Necessity for Prior Multivariate Operational Definition)

Any penetration into the problems of psychology requires the understanding of the concepts of psychology. Having said this, we must ask: What are these, where are the laws of psychology, how are the facts ordered, under which hypothesis are observations and predictions made? Elsewhere, (Howarth in Dreger 1972) it was stated that bivariate experimental psychologists have succumbed to *the error of commonsense*, and by this we mean the assumption that we know what we are measuring from a single, or restricted group of measures. Let us take an example. Suppose we carry out the dermographia measure. One way this can be done is to exert a pressure on the inner surface of the upper arm where the pigmentation is reduced. The pressure is exerted by an instrument which gives x kg, and the pressure lines, of y cm, are crossed at right angles. After a short time, the reddening becomes apparent and finally, after times ranging from several minutes upwards, disappears. We believe we are measuring a local autonomic response to a stressor but this is, in the first instance, subject to autonomic balancing. Secondly, it is a single personality measure, i.e. the dermographic latency is highly correlated with a "personality factor." But it is of no use whatever to think of, or to specify, a personality dimension by one measure, however "good," that measures probably only a small fraction of its variance. The factor is located by several measures, and the factor has "meaning" only from a group of measures. Similarly, one can measure an aspect of learning, or reaction time, or threshold by one measure but we are only taking a small corner of the performance. When we ask, "What does this measure?" we should be careful not to fall into the error of commonsense. Suppose that one wished to measure the effect of drug A on concept formation. How then are we to tap "concept formation"? If we choose test B as our operational definition, how do we know that we are adequately penetrating the space of concept formation? Another example

The Multivariate Experimental Contribution to Personality Research

39

is anxiety. Suppose we wish to test the effect of anxiety level on learning. Here we have two "ends" of our bivariate design, and both the dependent and the independent variable must be subject to prior evaluation. Each, in fact, merits a giant prior study so that we can specify the composition of the anxiety measure *and* the learning measure. Then, preferably, we could multipli-specify anxiety on the one hand and learning on the other. In the end we would need (a) a prior factorial study for battery establishment, and operational definition of "anxiety," and "learning," (b) a multivariate design to study the interactions between the operational components. Naturally, this research strategy is time consuming and it is of interest to observe how often (1) the impatient clinician says, "*This* is what I mean by anxiety," and (2) the impatient experimenter similarly is prone to say, "*That* is what I mean by anxiety (or learning)."

Both suffer from a false conception of operationism; how is it possible to satisfactorily establish a relationship with the "ends" loosely or carelessly defined? Such a procedure is analogous to a physicist measuring the resistance of impure metals, using a defective battery and a worn galvanometer. Another way of looking at the matter is to say they lack the sense of "concept (or construct) validity" possessed by the psychometrist in the concept, "How much does the test correlate with the pure factor?" The problem is that without such a foundation any X psychologists can provide Y definitions of, for example, intelligence (Y usually being greater than X!). Suppose we wish to study the relation between intelligence and learning. Very well, we measure all our S's on the Stanford Binet, then we subject them to paired-associate learning. We would correlate the "ends" or segregate the S's by intelligence groups. We could then vary the difficulty level of the P/A learning in the design. Note that a truly adequate definition of "intelligence" is wanting, and the measure of learning is restricted to a very specific example of learning. How much more valuable would be a broad factorial operational definition of intelligence and a broad factorial operational definition of learning, where other factors such as motivational components would need to be controlled or adequately cared for in the design.

If we measure restricted aspects of our operational field we are leaving a great deal to choice. Let us say we wish to measure the fusion of two brief light pulses presented close together in time. We can build a complex apparatus for stimulus control and then choose, say, 6 S's out of the world's population. This is the *error of individual differences* (Howarth in Dreger 1972). We assume that by random choice we can measure the performance of the "normal eye"; why not, instead, find *what we are measuring* in multivariate terms? Does the fusion experiment have any embedded relation to a personality factor? Indeed, it does, and so do many other perceptual measures such as the Poggendorf illusion, or the Muller-Lyer. Even various measures derived from the classical reaction time experiment have an embedded (factorial) relationship and can well serve as personality measures. In choosing 6 S's out of the world's population, it is surely of value to investigate the S parameters and at least ensure that the S is in the middle or "safe" range on the personality dimensions which have been shown to influence or bias the measure. In other words, to overcome the error of individual differences, we must relate the S and M parameters instead of blithely assuming that the relationship either does not exist, or is unconnected with the purpose of the experiment. Another excellent example

is the massing or spacing of trials in learning experiments using paired-associate or serial learning.[1]

The importance of multivariate experiment does not then consist as an alternative to bivariate experimentation but is rather a necessary condition for effective bivariate experiment and is a precondition for adequate operational definition. Somehow this point does not seem to have penetrated far into the practice of experimental psychology. Consequently, the concepts, laws, and relationships have not progressed as far as they might, possibly due to conflicting results (and hence theories) obtained from what we may term *quasi-operationalism*.

In Chapter 3 of the *Handbook of Multivariate Experimental Psychology*, Cattell discusses the Data Box. This concept can be extended into that of prior multivariate operational definition (PMOD) of concepts. What this implies is the ordering of the relationship among the data by multivariate means at an *early* not a *late* stage, so that the definition can be erected not on a commonsense basis but on a pattern of measurements basis. It is as though, in psychology, we had a collection of insect hunters each busily capturing and labelling isolated specimens. In order to establish classifications these have to be brought together so that overlaps can be reduced and the general lines of classification established.

In the absence of this prior multivariate operational definition, there is *no reason why psychology should not proceed for many years wandering in the desert of isolated instances*. With X isolated measures of Y, and A isolated measures of B, there are XA possible doctoral investigations of the Y-B relationship! If there are, for example, 200 measures of anxiety and 100 measures of learning, then 20,000 Ph.D. theses are made possible! As there must be over a hundred problems of this kind 2,000,000 theses are possible. It is perhaps relevant to calculate that at the rate of 500 per year this will occupy psychology for the next 4,000 years. A better strategy would be for group research in the 100 areas which would discover the operationally natural existing response patterns (in the case of anxiety), growth patterns, and individual difference structure patterns, which could be done in a much shorter time. On this basis the next half century could be profitably spent relating these constructs, with the likely establishment of the "laws and concepts of psychology."

The material in Table 39-1 summarizes the comparison between the clinical, multivariate-experimental, and bivariate-experimental approaches. The accentuation in the latter is in terms of prediction within a limited parameter framework and this results in the generation of miniature laws without regard to individual differences.

Sociohistorical Considerations in the Impact of Experimental Methods upon Personality Research

Personality research and personality concepts may be thought of as having gone through three main phases: (1)

[1] See e.g., E. Howarth, "Learning and Personality: II. Memory and Interference in Verbal Learning," *Proceedings XIXth International Congress of Psychology* (London: British Psychological Society, 1971); and E. Howarth, "Personality Differences in Serial Learning Under Distraction," *Perceptual and Motor Skills* 28 (1969): 379–82 and E. Howarth, "Extraversion and Increased Interference in Paired-Associate Learning," *Perceptual and Motor Skills* 29 (1969): 403–6.

Table 39-1.

AREA	Clinical-qualitative	Multivariate-experimental	Bivariate-experimental
General characteristic	qualitative	quantitative	quantitative
Statistic	Elementary categorization	Correlations, factor analysis, etc.	Significance tests, etc.
Analysis	Historical	Structural	Dependency
Method	Proto-clinical	"R-R"	"S-R"
Uses	Qualitative categorization	Prediction on basis of broad scope	Prediction within parameter framework
Aim	Idiographic description	Nomothetic description and explanation	Miniature laws without regard to individual differences
Potential	Theoretical suggestion, e.g., Kretschmer	Future—both applied and theoretical	No broad "psychological" laws as yet—possibility remains
Application	Service	Both theory and practical practical	Interscience, e.g., physiology-psychology-
Coverage	Abnormal with "normal" implication	I.D. range and explanation	Restricted problems in learning, perception, etc.
Setup	Person/person observation plus case history	Test, group conditions	Apparatus, design

a general literary and observational stage, from antiquity until modern times; (2) a clinical observational phase, in which observations are more systematic and disciplined than in the first phase, and in which the objectives are entirely scientific, not partly aesthetic—this phase may be said to have grown out of general medicine around the 18th century and come to its finest fruition in Freud, Jung, Adler and others since— and (3) the experimental phase which did not properly begin till the turn of the present century and did not gather any real momentum until twenty years ago.

By "experimental," however, we would by no means restrict ourselves to the narrow "brass instrument" concept. An experiment properly defined, as Cattell has pointed out in the *Handbook of Multivariate Experimental Psychology* (1967), is *an organized system of gathering data with an organized analysis to follow, in terms of fitting some prescribed model*. Such an experiment includes *both* multivariate experiment, in which many variables are allowed to vary, *and* bivariate experiment in which one arbitrarily takes something called an independent variable and, on manipulatively varying it, observes what happens to a dependent variable. Manipulation is *not* the criterion of an experiment. Both bivariate and multivariate experimental designs have important roles in personality research, but their respective roles have by no means been profitably perceived and applied. The contempt of the clinician—it can scarcely be described by anything less—for much of personality research is based on the misunderstanding that experiment is a brass instrument experiment, with two variables at a time, and only on the relatively trivial aspects of personality that can be imported into a laboratory setting. Actually, multivariate experiment can deal with the same wholistic concepts as the clinician uses, but deal with them much more quantitatively, exactly, and in terms of more complex laws and models. Indeed, the ordinary bivariate experiment has been objected to on the grounds that it cannot deal with broad and vital features of personality, because it is not ethically possible to manipulate powerful stimuli affecting the basic emotions and personality development of children and others. The multivariate methods, by contrast, lend themselves far better to nonmanipulative methods, though not confined thereto. In these the planful psychologist chooses situations in which life inevitably does its own experiments, and then teases out the exact relationships of "this to that" by sophisticated statistical methods, e.g., factor analysis.

Some false antitheses have from time to time been drawn between experimental and other approaches. For example, it is sometimes said that there is "a clinical method" as distinct from "a scientific method," but, although there may be a clinical approach, there is in the last resort no fundamental difference in scientific method which is applicable. All science requires the working out "of laws which subsist as relations between the elements of phenomena," (to quote Mach) and whether we do this with the clinician's unaided eye or with a measuring instrument on the one hand, or with the help of instruments and a computer to investigate the relationships on the other, is a secondary matter. Another false antithesis has shown itself in the tendency of some experimentalists, particularly of the reflexological and brass instrument schools, to decline immediately all psychoanalytic concepts and terms. It so happens that the factor analytic method finds structures in personality which are undoubtedly close to—and the hidden core of—the notions to which clinicians have applied the terms of superego and ego structure. There seems no reason to deliberately break continuity by declining to use these terms when, in fact, they represent the clinician's perception of a structure which can be more reliably demonstrated by experimental measurement and computer analyses.

At the same time an awareness of the conceptual differences between clinical and multivariate experimental methods remains very important. For example, occasionally clinicians have said that the conception of ego strength and of superego strength exemplified by the items in the scales (C and G) of the 16 PF for these dimensions do not entirely correspond to their conceptions of ego strength, etc. In a situation such as this, the clinician either has to demonstrate by correlational methods that something more closely corresponding to his conception exists or, alternatively, he has to adapt his conceptions to the best that experimental work can show regarding the mode of expression of such structures.

As a general strategy for the experimental investigation of personality, it has been systematically argued by Cattell, that cross-sectional investigations of structure by factor analytic and allied methods should proceed experiment in the more bivariate sense (e.g., see the first section of this chapter). That is to say, it is important to find out what the central structures are in personality at the various ages before one begins experiment on the relation of these entities to various influences, and to various effects. In pursuit of this ideal such researchers as Burt, Cattell, Damarin, Eysenck, Guilford, Hundleby, Nesselroade, Pawlik, Sweney, Warburton and others have worked over the last 20 years to establish the principle normal and abnormal structures, in terms of precise factor analytic concepts, in various (e.g., Q, L, and T) media of observation.

Considerable success has attended the mapping of personality structure by these researches, though much still remains to be done. The three possible media of observation are usually called L-data, Q-data, and T-data. L-data refers to observations in the life situation, i.e., ratings, records, and other evidence (often called "criterion" evidence among psychometrists) on behavior in the real situations of everyday life in the culture. Q-data might be called consulting room or questionnaire data, since it involves statements made by the individual about his own behavior, and thus perceived by introspection. T-data refers to objective, nonfakeable laboratory-type tests or miniature situations, in which the person is placed in a standard situation and allowed to respond, his behavior being scored on aspects of his behavior (as measured variables) of which he is not aware, so that the "self-report" of the questionnaire is superseded.

In the following sections the particular qualities of each of these media will be dealt with in a separate section devoted to the methods and findings of each. After that we shall discuss integration of findings and proceed to further, more theoretical, analysis.

To anticipate the nature of this further analysis and experiment, it may be said that most of it is concerned with theoretical and conceptual issues emerging from the coordinated, programmatic work by Cattell, Eysenck, Scheier, Hundleby, Howarth, Nesselroade, and others. The issues which it pursues are the following.

First, it aims at conceptual interpretation of the factor patterns now repeatedly replicated. Before launching hypotheses that are specifically of a genetic and physiological nature, or specifically of an environmental and learning nature, it seems best, in terms of an economic strategy, to launch a research to find out how much of the origins of a particular personality source trait is genetic and how much environmental. This can be handled by well-known methods, such as the twin methods or the multiple abstract variance analysis (MAVA) methods; these have already made a good deal of advance.

Second, as part of the process of interpretation, one needs to know as much as possible about the natural history of the personality factor or source trait; namely, what the typical age change curve in culture is. For example, it has been shown that some factors, such as UI 23 (Cattell's mobilization vs. regression, Eysenck's neuroticism), follow a curve of maturation much like that of intelligence, whereas others, e.g., UI 21 (exuberance), actually decline from early childhood onward. Part of this natural history investigation also concerns the distribution of the trait in the population and so on.

Third, one looks for criterion relations of the personality factors in everyday life performances in school and occupation, in leadership, in clinical phenomena, etc. A rich harvest of results has been gathered in the last decade in this respect. For example, in the High School Personality Questionnaire and the 16 PF test,[2] the first and second order factors of which can be scored, significant correlations with criteria in a great range of real life situations have been shown. This, incidentally, is reassuring evidence that the personality factors are not "mathematical abstractions" or products of some narrow corner of the laboratory with little relevance to the total personality.

Fourth, we seek to manipulate the level of some of the factors in the typical classical bivariate experiment where these factors are used as independent variables to be related to the particular dependent variables in which we are interested (or, conversely, as single dependent variables).

Although this whole approach has been very successful and has led to all kinds of positive information and significant relationships where previously little had been found through the use of ad hoc questionnaire scales or through narrow bivariate experiments, the grasp among the general body of psychologists of its practical implications has been weak. In passing on structural and dynamic concepts from multivariate experiments to clinicians and general personality theorists, the ball has somehow been fumbled. This appears to be due to a teaching situation from which the social historian of science will draw some interesting and valuable conclusions. The statistical and analytical techniques required in the multivariate approach are intrinsically complex. Until recently they were not taught at all in quite a number of psychology graduate departments, and the assumption in most places still seems to be that they cannot be incorporated into undergraduate instruction. For example, in physics and engineering it is assumed that the undergraduate student must master the mathematics that the subject requires. But the overwhelming undergraduate tradition of teaching psychology merely as part of the humanities has the unfortunate result that even the student going on to graduate work has to make do with those superficial views of personality structure and dynamics that can be put into the language of the novel or, to be more precise, the language of the novel put into an artificial jargon.

Thus both the available research and the available teaching personnel in this area have been very limited, and the available audience in terms of persons capable of participating in the conceptual unraveling of the results has covered perhaps one in twenty of alleged degree-qualified psychologists. In particular the paradox has existed that the clinician, for whom this approach could be most helpful, has avoided it most because his teachers typically have left him the least trained of psychologists in these statistical areas. However, at the same time, the traditional experimental psychologist, in the bivariate or brass instrument tradition, has also been unable to participate, since multivariate training was also remote from many laboratories which stayed essentially in a projection of the Wundtian or Pavlovian tradition.

The foundation in 1960 of the *Society of Multivariate Experimental Psychology*, has done much to remedy the situation. But meanwhile, the outcome has been that the necessary combination of experimental and research skills with multivariate statistical training has been sufficiently uncommon so that most of the work in this field has been carried forward by probably less

[2] For the results of the first thorough item-factor-analysis of the 16PF test (187 items), see E. Howarth and J. A. Browne, "An Item-Factor-Analysis of the 16PF," *Personality* 2 (1971): 117–39. Also see E. Howarth and J. A. Browne, "Investigation of Personality Factors in a Canadian Context: I. Market Structure in Personality Questionnaire Items," *Canadian Journal of Behavioral Science* 3 (1971): 161–73.

than one hundred psychologists which creates problems of adequate replication since much of this work has to be done on an adequate scale in regard to population samples if it is to be any real contribution. (This means either somewhat unusual grant resources or a quite unusual degree of dedication to hard work!)

However, with the degree of replication of factor structures over different ages and cross cultures the situation regarding wider cooperation in this field has become greatly improved. Many investigators are now able to proceed with the use of these batteries in their particular experimental, clinical, or social fields. They may also employ the associated precise source trait concepts having facilities for factor analysis per se in their own circle. For with this available definition, factor analysis is unnecessary and the requisite instrumental measurement concepts are available for limited bivariate experimental designs in which particular postulated relationships can be studied more closely. That is to say, research has now moved into a new phase in which the second, third, and fourth programmatic phases above can be pursued using the test measurements generated in the first phase, in designs less complicated and extensive than were required in the first (overall defining) phase. Thus, in effect, the first stage has constituted a sort of bottleneck, which cut off certain developing concepts from many psychologists who wished to investigate personality, e.g., developmentally, physiologically, or in learning contexts by more traditional designs and who, consequently, have meanwhile used other devices (although theoretically far less satisfactory than others available to them from multivariate sources).

Some Central Methodological and Conceptual Issues

Although our arguments have been as forcefully presented as we believe they should be for the strategic advantages of concentrating *first* on the discovery of personality structures and the development of suitable batteries for their measurement, and *then* on the manipulative and applied research, such research can now, as just indicated, be effectively pursued in the classical bivariate experimental framework with the new facilities.

It may be desirable to illustrate the methodological and conceptual points made somewhat abstractly above in terms of some actual personality research issues. Let us consider, for example, the bulk of the research done on anxiety prior to its factor analytic definition in replicated, simple structure multivariate researches. Actually the chief investigators did not proceed with any naive use of concepts without adequate representation, but stated an "operational" position in which they would say, for example, that what they meant by anxiety was low electrical skin resistance, and what was meant by strength of the hunger drive was the number of hours of deprivation of food, or what they meant by ego strength was the tendency to be insuggestible in the Sway Suggestibility Test, etc. The contention of Cattell, Eysenck, Guilford, Scheier, and other multivariate experimentalists is that the bivariate experimenter merely washes his hands of responsibility in this kind of statement. But since, if the general structure of behavior is what everything points to its being, no single variable will adequately represent a concept, and the result should be a generally poor predictive power, together with mutual confusion of concepts. Anyone who compares the literature over the last 20 years of the bivariate and

the multivariate approaches in this area will surely have to conclude that both of these predictions have come true.

Any abstract concept, such as anxiety, drive, ego strength, schizothyme temperament, etc., is likely to show itself in a whole pattern of behavior manifestations. If we are unusually lucky we may, after many years of multivariate research, be able to land on a particular variable which correlates quite highly with the source trait factor, but in general we have to depend upon a whole pattern. For example, the anxiety factor turns out to express itself in low electrical skin resistance, unwillingness to venture in a miniature risk-taking situation, underestimation of one's capacities, high irritability, large pulse-rate response to the cold pressor test, and several other verbal and other behaviors (see Cattell & Scheier 1961, pp. 86–91). Any one of these measures has a correlation around 0.3 to 0.4 with the factor, and thus succeeds in accounting for only something from 10 to 20 percent of its variance. Consequently, in the investigation of the relationship of anxiety to some other concept, e.g., drive strength, which uses only one of these variables "operationally" to represent anxiety, one risks missing significant relationships where they exist. What is worse, it has the reciprocal danger of finding significant relationships where they *do not* exist. For perhaps 85 percent of the variance for that particular variable is not due to the anxiety factor, and any number of relationships might be found with this 85 percent of the variance and ascribed to the anxiety factor. This has actually happened, for example, in regard to the stress response and the anxiety response, which have a number of variables in common in their loading pattern. Therefore results due to one, e.g., high cholesterol in the blood stream, have been assigned to the other.

Probably the greater danger from false leads in research by the bivariate method arises, however, not from Type 1 errors concluding that there is no relationship where with good pattern measurement one would be found, but from Type 2 errors associated particularly with the impotence of bivariate methodology to separate one concept clearly from another. For example, in this same anxiety area, the concept of repressors versus sensitizers has been developed by Ericson and others, as a distinct a priori concept from anxiety, and quite a number of researches have been done on repressors versus sensitizers apparently with the belief that this is a different concept from anxiety. Factor analytic research, however, shows that when the variance due to the general anxiety factor has been taken out of the measurements supposed to distinguish repressors from sensitizers, no specific variance remains. In other words, a factor analytic approach from the beginning, in accordance with the strategy outlined above, would have led to clearer results and to an integration of these findings with the general findings on the anxiety factor.

Another widely used method of measuring "anxiety" has been by the use of self-evaluative verbal measures such as the neuroticism scales harking back to Woodworth's World War I scale and, more recently, the Taylor Manifest Anxiety Scale. When this was factored it was found to measure aspects of both extraversion and neuroticism and not solely the latter. Consequently correlations obtained between WAS and learning measures (in some cases positive and in others negative) would be due to the extraversion aspect of the measure and was not necessarily due to the explanation in terms of "anxiety as a drive" offered by Taylor and Spence.

A less extreme and at first sight safer position than that of setting up a single operation for a concept is that in which the investigator has perceived that there is a correlation among some *cluster* of variables, and sets up his concept on this basis. Witkin's idea of field independence is an example of this approach.

The examples are interesting because they lead us up to an important concept in the personality area, namely, the difference between a surface trait and a source trait. A surface trait is operationally defined as the central aid of a bunch of intercorrelating variables, whereas a source trait is defined as an independent factor dimension defined as to position by simple structure based on the appearance of a definite hyperplane. The latter is called a source trait because, by a broader scientific model, it can be argued that a simple structured factor is a source of influence or variance upon behavior; i.e., it is a determiner. In a domain where there are two or three source traits operative there may be as many as a dozen surface traits operative because the factors can combine their influences in various ways to produce these sheaves of variables constituting a correlation cluster. The surface trait has always had a peculiar attraction to the psychologist who "wants to keep his feet on the ground," for it can be shown that correlation clusters cannot be clearly separated from one another and that they have a changing and largely subjective definition. Consequently, all further discussion here will hinge on the source trait concept.

While we are on the subject of methodology of structure, it should be pointed out that the structural analyses on which the substantive psychological conclusions are based in the following sections are not merely the classical *R*-technique in factor analysis, i.e., correlations having to do with individual differences. Correlations are also done across time as in *P*-technique and differential *R*-technique, and they are also carried out with and without manipulated conditions, in what Cattell and Scheier have called the condition-response research design. An example of the meaning of simple structure is shown in Figure 39-1.

The conditions for recognizing source traits as such are that they should show significant simple structure, indicating a single influence at work, and that they should be replicable across samples. Just how replicable they should be is a matter for discussion. For example, we know that intelligence shows itself in a somewhat changing pattern as we go from seven years of age to seventeen years of age. Similarly, across cultures we would expect some modification of the mode of expression of the personality factor. Nevertheless, using congruence coefficients and the *s*-index of salient variable similarities to check objectively the replication of a factor pattern, it has been possible to show a fairly high degree of consistency of the factor patterns across ages and across cultures.

However, progress in this area would be clearer if we distinguished definitely between a factor as a replicable pattern on the one hand, and our interpretation of it on the other. Indeed, in a good deal of work the investigator deceives both himself and other people by adopting too soon a conceptual interpretation of what results he has obtained. For this reason Cattell has suggested that a standard index should be used, whereby investigators can refer to factor patterns dependably, by numbers or letters, in the period which normally elapses between

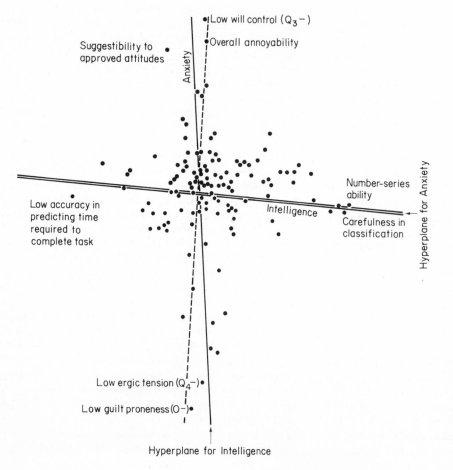

Fig. 39-1. *This shows the appearance of simple structures as defined by a hyperplane. The latter are formed by the intersection of planes, each of which is defined by a pair of factors, in N space. As a practical matter the latter is treated by taking factors by pairs, e.g., in a ten factor solution there are 45 different plots to be considered. The criterion of simple structure was developed initially by Thurstone but it now resolves into the counting of the number of variables in a given study which appear in the hyperplane. Essentially (and paradoxically) a factor is defined by the variables which do not load on it, the factor is a "normal" to the plane. When factors are rotated they may be thought of as a handle to manipulate the disc (or ellipsoid) which is the hyperplane. Computer programs have been written to count the variables in the hyperplane [see Cattell 1957, for a concise and readable description].*

the sure identification of a pattern and its reliable interpretation theoretically. This same technique was used successfully in the field of item research, and in several other fields of science. Accordingly, universal index (UI) numbers have been assigned in the surveys of the Cattell group.

A technical problem which arises here is that of factor order or stratum. When factors have been obtained, they are typically systematically correlated one with another, as would be expected in an interacting maneuver, and so they can in turn be factored and second-order factors obtained. This can be repeated leading to third- or even higher-order factors. However, a distinction can be drawn between order and stratum: order is simply referring to an operation of sequence of factoring, and stratum corresponding to a conceptual generality of level of action, which is derived not only from factor order evidence but from other sources of evidence.

In this framework, most personality factors have been pursued into the second- and third-orders, with quite consistent results. For example, it appears that the work of Eysenck can be brought into line with the work of Cattell, Guilford, and others only by recognizing that Eysenck has operated at the second-stratum level. The meaning of stratum is tied to a concept of *density of sampling of variables*, for which Cattell's *personality sphere* concept has provided a practical basis. Granted that the proper sampling of variables is made, we can arrive at reasonably good maps of the different strata and their relations one to another. Thus, anxiety has repeatedly been found as a very replicable pattern at the second-order in regard to the primary personality factors in the 16 PF or the High School Personality Questionnaire, etc. Furthermore, it has been noted that patterns which appear at the second-order in questionnaires are likely to appear at the first-order in objective tests or *T*-data. Thus, *T*-data factors numbers I and II, called extraversion and anxiety, in the questionnaire domain, turn out as UI 32 and UI 24 in the *T*-data domain, which is the index for primaries in that medium of observation. The basic model for explanation of behavior in terms of source traits is, of course, the linear specification equation, in which any particular piece of behavior has assigned to it weights on particular factors as shown in the following equation:

$$a_{hij} = b_{hj1} T_{1i} + \ldots b_{hjk} T_{ki} + b_{hj} T_{hji}$$

where *a* is the magnitude of the act *j* in the stimulus situation h_i. T_1 through T_k are *k* broad personality source traits, at the level possessed by individual *i*, and T_{hj} is some trait specific to situation and act *hj*. The *b*s are, statistically, factor loadings, and psychologically, behavioral indices, saying how much the factor is involved in that behavior.

Alternatively, we can express a whole series of behaviors (*a*s) in matrix form, thus:

$$Z_a = Z_T V_{fp}$$

where Z_a are the standard scores of *N* people on *n* variables, Z_T are the scores of *N* people on *k* factors (and *n* specifics) and V_{fp} is the factor pattern matrix (loadings of *n* variables by *k* factors).

The factor source traits (*T*s) in this equation can be abilities or personality factors or motivation factors. The present chapter is going to be concerned only with the factors found in personality and in motivational behavior, but the ability realm will

probably be well known to the reader from other sources. He will recognize Thurstone's primary abilities as primaries and Spearman's *G* as a higher order factor.

In this equation, the weights or *behavioral indices* as they would be better described for the psychologists—the *b*'s in the equation—show the degree to which each personality factor is involved for that response, *j*, in the situation, *h*. The pattern of behavioral indices (*b*s) for a particular stimulus response situation is therefore a description of the *meaning* of the situation, i.e., they are parameters by which the situation may be described. Thus, the general formulation in this area takes account both of the personality and of the situation and incorporates them in a total model from which the response behavior is predicted. A number of refinements on this model should be read elsewhere, but essentially it is an elaboration of the standard stimulus-response-organism model:

$$R = f(O.S)$$

in which the *T*s give the pattern of the organism, *O*, and the *b*s give the pattern of the stimulus situation, *S*.

With this necessarily very brief outline of the model for the systematic experimental attack on personality, and of the results, we shall proceed to examine the findings in each of three media of observation and each of the three modalities of traits; namely, general *personality, temperament,* and *motivation.* It should be understood in following this work that the terms for describing source traits are intended to be descriptive until such time as reliable interpretive labels can be introduced. Thus, UI 20 has been called *comention,* indicating that the whole pattern is one of tending to think the same as other people in the group, whereas UI 24, anxiety, uses the interpretive and familiar label of anxiety. This needs to be mentioned because a certain fretfulness is shown by those who encounter new labels for new factor analytic concepts for the first time. Such labels sometimes can be made to correspond to familiar concepts, e.g., in clinical psychology. (As indicated at the outset, they *do* sometimes correspond to familiar concepts, in which case the familiar title is used.) However, it is the objective of factor analysis, as in any scientific method, to find out something *new,* and when something new is found it is given a new name, as new elements were when they appeared in chemistry from year to year. The non-committal assigned *universal index number* is actually meant to be the firm "handle" by which to hold these concepts, but the terms are an attempt, tentative and perhaps temporary, to remind the psychologists what the descriptive nature of a factor is.

What is Personality?

We may now turn, as an introduction to the consideration of substantive research findings, to the definition of personality. We can say that, for our immediate purposes, personality consists of those behavioral characteristics which differentiate a man from his fellows. More precisely, and consistently with the above equations, the definition has been proposed by Cattell: *Personality is that which enables us to predict what a person will do in a given, defined situation.* This prediction involves both intraspecies and interspecies weights. Thus, it is equally true to say that on the one hand we (meaning by this the human species) are all essentially alike, while on the other hand we differ from each other in many respects. This is the "paradox of personality," that of concomitant sameness and difference. For our ultimate purposes the mere definition as "that which differentiates" is too vague, if only because we must immediately ask, "which characteristics are you talking about?" Some characteristics we carry, not so much behaviorally, as evidentially. True, some of these have behavioral consequences, e.g., "Bill Smith is a tall boy," or "Mary Jones is a well built girl." In the same way the color of a person's skin can be an evidential characteristic which can have behavioral consequences. Imagine for the moment that we are all alike. Your IQ would be 100, but you would not know this, just as you are not aware of being compressed at the rate of 14 pounds per square inch, or just as we tend to take gravity for granted. Indeed, there would be no *relative* differences, and no normal distribution of abilities. Similarly, if these were personality dimensions of comparable importance to the intelligence dimension we could only detect, and nomothetically[3] study, those on which there was a spread of differences.

From the multivariate point of view, as seen above, it is possible, indeed quite necessary, to treat personality differences in the same way as psychologists have long treated intelligence differences, and as we shall see as we proceed in this discussion, intelligence differences are found to be naturally embedded in the framework of personality differences.

Personality, then, may be defined in terms of discoverable, measurable *common* dimensions, replicable within a given culture, and also across cultures and subcultures. It may also deal with dimensions unique to an individual, as found by *P*-technique (Cattell 1957). Some of these dimensions will be seen to have a large genetic determination—these, one would expect, would be more stable across cultures. Others have a large environmental determination and we would not expect these to be so traceable across cultures and subcultures (patterns of aggression, for example, vary). It is the framework of these dimensions which is the framework of personality.

A reader who has not grasped the factoring of *behavior* may comment at this point that personality is dynamic rather than static, that it is a series of tendencies or readinesses to respond rather than an inert framework. This is quite true, and it should be noted that the framework is a measurement framework from which "something in the person" remains to be inferred. Each dimension of the framework represents the *S–O–R* conceptualization, and each is definable in terms of *S* and *R*. It is the inferences which we make about *O* (the interpersonal variables, traits, states, drives and so forth) which form a "theory of personality," because the *S* and *R* aspects of the model, or paradigm, are observable and controllable. The *S* represents the stimulus, which in the present context means the test situation which places the person in "an artificially contrived standardized test situation." The *R* represents what the person does in that situation, or some particular aspect of what he does. To take an instance, we place a child in a small chair and ask him to sit quietly for awhile. Unknown to the child a series of microswitches record the movements of the chair. (Many examples of tests of a nonfakeable kind will be given later in this chapter.)

[3] Parenthetically, in contrast, say to Allport, we would argue that science is nomothetic and art is idiographic. The single, uncompared case (and this excludes comparison over time) does not belong to science, but to aesthetics or religion.

In the light of the foregoing, we will define personality in *S–R* terms as:

1. In any situation in which an individual is placed and to which he reacts in a manner different from his fellows, then that reaction reveals his personality.
2. Personality is the individual departure from the norms (i.e. the norms appertaining in a given culture, subculture, or socioeconomic level); it is the "profile" of departures along factorially separable dimensions.
3. It is thus that "individuality" can be operationally described in factor-trait form and given more precise description by the operational and mathematical measurement of trait differences.

Perhaps we can say that personality study, as is the case for science in general, is a two-way process in which ideas for scientific study (behavior *B*) are generated by commonsense real life observation (behavior *A*), and in which, following fruitful and replicable discovery in the *B*-realm, general principles applicable to the *A*-realm are generated. On both sides precautions must clearly be observed. In the *A*-realm we must beware of too facile judgments, while in the *B*-realm we must avoid overabstraction and a tendency to artificialization.

Multivariate Experimental Findings in Rating and Questionnaire

STUDIES (Note: This section begins with a brief discussion of surface traits pointing to the need for the more precise factorial definition of source traits.)

There are several issues which should be delineated before we may list the phenomenal clusters (a term to be explained shortly) which have been discovered by research, in order to compare them with the commonsense differences discussed above.

1. As in psychology generally the *S–R* model seems to be applicable here, because when we rate another person on a given quality (e.g. "leadership potential") the other person is the stimulus to which we are giving a response. Thus, it is some "quality" of that person's response characteristics which becomes a recurrent stimulus, enabling us to make a response judgment or rating. For this process to be valid (i.e. connectable or related to a criterion) or reliable (i.e. reproducible beyond the specific occasion), there must be controls above and beyond those of everyday or commonsense personality judgment. Cattell (1957) lists several methodological requirements:
   a. The rater should have ample opportunity for time sampling the behavior of the other person, for instance the ratee may live in the same fraternity house as the rater.
   b. The ratee must be observed in several roles and stimulus conditions, so that his acts (R, above) are not atypical, and that judgment is made on a consensus of acts, true generalization and correct appreciation of the one situation (S, above) being dependant thereon.
   c. Implied in (a) and (b) but worthy of separate note, is time length, for the rater and ratee must be in close proximity for at least three months.

d. The trait to be used for rating must be clearly defined. "Leadership potential" is, for example, an insufficient designation for a rating scale because of its many possible meanings. Preferably the rater should have some experience with each scale so that not only the meaning of the scale as a whole is clear, but also the points on the scale. It is important that, where ratings are to be combined, the scales are in comparable units, remembering that a "behavioral scale" can become a "psychological scale" in the interpretive process. The more clearly the scale points are defined behaviorally, the less possibility of subjective distortion or bias.

e. Special role relations between the rater and ratee are to be avoided, especially those likely to produce "halo" effects. Obviously a close friendship will tend to produce effects of this kind.

f. Combinations of ratings on each scale are desirable in order to overcome the possible effects in (e) above, and each subject should be rated on a given scale by ten to twenty judges. In this process independent evaluation is required and the raters should not be given opportunity to discuss the subject's qualities among themselves.

Cattell (1946)[4] describes (in Chapters 8 and 9) the method by which the main surface (cluster analysis) and source (factor analysis) rating traits were discovered, beginning by condensing Allport and Odbert's list of about 2,000 trait terms down to a total of 171. This was done by first eliminating synonyms and then adding to these terms from (i) type classifications both normal and abnormal, (ii) unitary abilities found in psychometric research, (iii) interest categories, (iv) special psychological concepts such as frustration tolerance, level of aspiration, and disposition rigidity. Cattell was surprised to find, however, that most of these were already included in the common language list of about 160 terms and that "the interest categories turned out to be the only real addition, for the trait lists of the dictionary are, for some reason, short on interests."

The aim of all this preliminary work in the *L*-data field was to provide a foundation for trait analysis in the form of a comprehensive *personality sphere*. (Too many researches had begun with arbitrary sets of variables.) From a surface trait treatment, i.e., clustering of the 160 variables according to correlation clusters, a standard list of 45 variables was set out (Cattell 1957) which has since been used as a basis of comparison and collation in various factor analytic studies. Surface traits, incidentally, are of little use in personality *in themselves*, because they run vaguely one into another, lacking the precise definition that a hyperplane gives to a factor.

2. It seems desirable to indicate in a little more detail why "clusters", i.e., surface traits, are insufficient for defining unitary traits. Consider, for example, that height, weight, and physical strength measures correlate together and form a cluster. This forms a poor unity and any such cluster is vague for the following reasons:

a. There had to be an arbitrary decision as to the size of the correlation coefficient which will admit a given measure to the cluster. The lower we set this limit, of course, the larger the cluster.

b. At the same time, lowering the cluster boundary reduces the clarity of the groupings, and measures appear which now appear to belong equally well to several clusters.

c. There is no clear way of segregating clusters. They are like "clouds in the sky" which run into each other.

For these reasons, statistical psychologists, such as Spearman, Burt, and Thurstone, have developed the method known as factor analysis and while there is no requirement, for our purposes, to present details of how this is carried out, several concepts are vital to understand the remainder of this chapter.

If we think of the correlation between any two measures as an angle between two vectors (the test vectors), we can visualize a large correlation matrix as a whole series of lines, diverging from a common point. These lines will form close groupings here and there, as tests correlate with each other, and it is the function of factor analysis to place lines through these groups of vectors.

Once the factor lines (or vectors) have been established, the projections of the test vectors on the factors can be calculated. This gives the "factor loading" of a given test, and typically, a given measure will load on several factors. In intelligence measures we might find one test loaded highly on the numerical factor and only a small amount on the verbal factor, while in another case the reverse might apply. A "factor loading" expresses how much a test is correlated with a factor. Factors are thus a means of analyzing and summarizing large batteries of tests, e.g., in the case of Thurstone's factorial study of intelligence the following tests loaded on the numerical and verbal factors:

Number code	.63	Reading	.55
Addition	.76	Word grouping	.46
Subtraction	.67	Opposites	.64
Multiplication	.81	Synonyms	.50

(The factor loadings are shown in each case)

Clearly, the nature of the factors discovered cannot go beyond the material put into the original test battery. But if sufficient measures are used then factor analysis may reveal the presence of functional unities within a domain of measurement and hypotheses can then be set up going beyond the immediate pattern in the data. Both cluster and factor analysis depend on certain assumptions, principally that the correlation groupings will reveal functional unities or influences which show as a conjoint effect on the bias of two or more measures. (A surface trait is usually an overlap of the effects of several influences, but a source trait [factor] is a single influence.) In the intelligence measurements, above, for example, "something," some quality of performance, has biased performance in the verbal measures, so that a person low in one is generally low in the others. This quality is presumably inherent in the person, i.e., in the way in which he processes or handles the given kind of situation to produce that avenue of response bias.

Later we shall see how factor analysis, along with other approaches, enables us also to decide positively on the dynamic unities, and on their connections in the *dynamic lattice*. This involves studying multivariate relationships *over time* and in

[4] R. B. Cattell, *The Description and Measurement of Personality* (New York: World Publishing Co., 1946).

relation to incentives. However, in the rating field nothing of this kind has been done because ratings are not precise enough for the dynamic analysis formulae.

SOURCE TRAITS

Having mentioned the surface traits discovered using cluster analysis (surface inspection of groups of correlations) let us proceed to give source traits the greater attention which they justify. A number of studies have revealed factors in both behavior and ratings which are roughly comparable so that, in order to save time, we will present the factors in order of importance, meaning by this the order of size of variance contribution to the personality sphere of variables. Remembering that the population tested was often "normal" it is worthy of note that the first factor to emerge is:

A. Affectothymia versus Sizothymia. Easygoing, adaptable, warmhearted, impulsive, cooperative versus obstructive, secretive, reserved, suspicious, hostile, impersonal. There is evidence of substantial hereditary determination for this factor. Cyclothymes are typically successful in dealing with people whereas schizothymes are good at dealing with ideas and things. There is a high proportion of A + persons among managers or salesmen, whereas A − persons are found among physicists and foresters. Academics in general, and outstanding researchers in particular, are more schizothyme than the general population.

It is interesting to note that this factor with the largest variance has been outstanding in the field of psychiatric classification and Kretschmer's detailed descriptions describe the factor very well.

Let it be said at this point, so that examples of behavior may be given for each factor from both rater-observed (*T*-data) and self-observed (questionnaire, *Q*-data) variables, that essentially the same (roughly twenty) primary source traits have appeared in both media. This has been debated (Becker 1960)[5] and several factor analytic technicalities would have to be discussed, but both Cattell and Eysenck find this parallelism at the second-order level, and Cattell, Coan, Digman, Scheier, and others at the primary source trait level. "Instrument factors" have to be set aside to bring out the fact that *Q*- and *L*-data factors are essentially the same structures in different dress. Accordingly, the affectothyme pattern can also be illustrated as a dimension in questionnaire response, by the following:[6]

1. Would you rather work as
    a. engineer
    b. *a social science teacher*
2. At a picnic would you rather spend some time
    a. exploring the woods alone?
    b. *playing around the campfire with the crowd*?
3. When you are asked to write an essay about your private thoughts and emotions, do you
    a. *enjoy expressing yourself*?

[5] W. C. Becker, "The Matching of Behavior Rating and Questionnaire Personality Factors," *Psychological Bulletin*, 57 (1960): 201–12.
[6] This and other items, the copyright of the Institute for Personality and Ability Testing, Champaign, Illinois, are separated from the 16 PF Questionnaire, by kind permission of IPAT.

b. prefer to keep your feelings to yourself?
4. Do you feel hurt if people borrow your things without asking you?
    a. Yes
    b. *No*

The A + person says he would rather vacation at a populous resort, likes to sell things, will listen happily to people's complaints, has no difficulty in starting a conversation with strangers, is well aware of what is going on around him, tends to be quick in expressing ideas in words, and would rather join a debating society than a photographic club.

B. Intelligence. In personality studies, in both rating and questionnaire data, we find intelligence appearing as the factor of second largest variance associated with indications of being thoughtful, cultured, conscientious, versus unreflective, boorish, quitting, and conscienceless. The criteria associated with high loadings on this factor are more skilled occupation, less frequent unemployment, less frequent delinquency, and more frequent membership in social, recreational, and political groups.

C. Ego Strength versus General Emotionality. Emotionally stable, free of neurotic symptoms, not hypochondriacal, realistic about life, unworried, steadfast, self-controlled, calm, patient, persevering and thorough, loyal, dependable, versus emotional, dissatisfied, showing a variety of neurotic symptoms, hypochondriacal, plaintive, evasive, immature, autistic, worrying, anxious, changeable, excitable, impatient, quitting, careless, and undependable.

In questionnaires, illustrative questions are as follows:

1. Is your health unpredictable, forcing you frequently to alter your plans? *No*.
2. Do you often make big plans and get excited about them, only to find they just won't work out?
    a. Yes
    b. *No*
3. When you do a foolish thing, do you generally feel so bad that you wish the earth would swallow you up?
    a. Yes
    b. *No*
4. Are you satisfied that you do well enough what most people expect of someone your age?
    a. *Yes*
    b. No

The C + person says he does not walk or talk in his sleep, he does not feel critical of other people's work, does not avoid exciting situations because they are too fatiguing, does not indulge in self-pity, and keeps emotions under control.

❦

D. Excitability versus Insecurity. Demanding, impatient, attention-getting, exhibitionistic, overactive, prone to jealousy, self-assertive, egotistical, versus emotionally mature, self-sufficient, not easily jealous, self-effacing, self-controlled.

In L-Data: This pattern occurs most clearly in abnormal clinical names and in young children who are fatigued, over-excited, and insecure. There is a pattern of demandingness, dependence, excitability, assertion, and changeability. The D+ person is attention-getting, exhibitionistic and prone to jealousy. The D− person is self-effacing, deliberate, self-controlled, and emotionally mature. This factor has not been found clearly enough in adult data to justify inclusion in the 16 PF Questionnaire.

In Q-Data: The similarity to the rating data factor *D* is marked. The D+ person says his mind wanders when reading something difficult, feels bad if people differ with him or play jokes on him, and gets impatient with people who cannot decide quickly. Such a person has a tendency to imaginative overreaction when reading stories or at the movies.

E. Dominance–Submission. Conceited, willful, pugnacious, insensitive to social disapproval, boastful versus submissive, modest, retaining, tactful. The E+ person is sure of himself, sarcastic about rules, unconventional, grave, sometimes haughty, and not cooperative except to try to dominate others.

Q-Data items:

1. Have people sometimes told you that you are a proud, stuck-up person?
   a. *Yes*
   b. No
2. Can you deliberately lie to a friend and keep a straight face?
   a. *Yes*
   b. No

The E+ person says he does not believe in censorship of movies and books, does not try to be polite to waiters, likes people to listen rather than talk, heckles a public speaker, and upbraids poor workmen.

F. Surgency–Desurgency. Cheerful, joyous, energetic, humorous, talkative, resourceful, adaptable, trustful, versus pessimistic, seclusive, retiring, subdued, languid, dull, phlegmatic, unable to relax, obsessional, slow to accept a situation, bound by habit, and rigid.

In L-Data: The following pattern is based on seven studies: Cheerful, sociable, energetic, humorous, talkative, adaptable, trustful, versus pessimistic, taciturn, anxious, unadaptable, suspicious.

In Q-Data: Surgency is an important but distinct component in extraversion. The surgent person is superficially clever, tells a good story, wants to be liked, is rapid at mental work, and recovers readily from anger. Surgency has been found to be associated with being chosen as a leader of new groups *before* the person is known well whereas desurgency (F−) had been found to correlate with officer potential in the army. Generally F+ goes along with sociometric popularity in an immediate group but leads to poorer long term performance in serious undertakings. Academically successful men, and particularly researchers, are markedly desurgent. Surgency shows a steep downward trend between the ages of twenty and thirty but declines more slowly thereafter.

G. Superego Strength. Persevering, determined, responsible, attentive to people, versus quitting, fickle, immature, indolent, unscrupulous, neglectful of social chores, changeable.

In L-Data: Responsible, conscientious, persevering, versus quitting, fickle, frivolous, and immature. The G+ person shows honesty in schoolwork, regard for property, public concern, hard work in assigned tasks, personal and professional integrity, physical and moral courage. This factor had a high correlation with success in Officer Candidate School and later correlated with rating by superiors on military effectiveness.

In Q-Data:

1. Should any job be done thoroughly or can some jobs be done less well than others?
   a. *Yes*
   b. No

The G+ person likes to anticipate difficulties ahead of time and to plan in advance; he believes most people could make a success of their lives if they would only try, and values a person with a sense of duty above a brilliant person.

H. Parmia (Parasympathetic Immunity to Threat) versus Threctia or Threat Reactivity. Adventurous, likes meeting people, shows strong interest in opposite sex, gregarious, genial, responsive, kindly, friendly, frank, impulsive (but no inner tension), self-confident, versus shy, timid, withdrawn, little interest in opposite sex, aloof, cold, self-contained, hostile, secretive, inhibited, recoils from life.

In L-Data: Adventurous, genial, responsive, frank, self-confident, versus shy, little interest in opposite sex, self-contained, recoils from life, lacking confidence.

The H+ person tends to be bold, talkative with marked overemotional expression, trustful, composed, well liked but not socially adept, aesthetically sensitive, tolerant, and attentive to people. "Dating" counts show that both A+ and H+ go with greater sex interest, with H− the most prominent factor association.

In Q-Data:

1. Do you find that you have little difficulty talking to people?
   a. *Yes*
   b. No
2. Are you easily embarrassed?
   a. Yes
   b. *No*
3. When talking in front of several people, do you sometimes stammer a bit, and find it hard to say what you want?
   a. Yes
   b. *No*

The H− person, i.e., the threctic individual, is shy, easily gives up a difficult problem, and is troubled with a sense of inferiority. Cattell believes this factor to be identical with Thurstone's Ascendance Factor and to be a combination of Guilford's Ascendance. He also points to some discovered association with physical signs of emotionality at the threctic pole, e.g., with greater disturbance of pulse rate by threats (hence threctia).

I. Premsia versus Harria. Demanding, impatient, immature, aesthetically fastidious, introspective, imaginative, intuitive, versus emotionally mature, independent minded, hardheaded, lacking artistic feeling, unaffected by "fancies," practical, logical.

In L-Data: Demanding, dependent, introspective, intuitive, versus mature, hard, lacking artistic feeling, practical, self-sufficient. The I+ person has a general neurotic tendency, is hypochondriacal, shows effort, intolerance, and anxiety. The hypothesis about I+, which seems well supported, is that it represents effects of parental overprotection and an oversensitive family atmosphere.

In Q-Data:

1. Do you enjoy dangerous and exciting things like going on a roller coaster as much as your friends seem to?
   a. Yes
   b. *No*
2. In a stage play would you rather act the part of
   a. *a kindly and famous teacher*
   b. a bold pirate (or pirate's lady)
3. When you see something very sad in a play do you
   a. *find it hard to keep the tears away*?
   b. say, "Oh, this is just a lot of make-believe"?

The next four factors have smaller variance, both in the rating field and in the questionnaire field. In consequence, some investigators using comparative coarse factors analytic techniques have failed to locate them. However, even as early as 1945 various investigators had located L and O, while M and N are quite clear in ratings.

L. Protension. Suspicious, jealous, self-sufficient, withdrawn, versus trustful, understanding, composed, socially comfortable.

L-Data: Fault-finding, tyrannical, jealous, "never in the wrong."

Q-Data: The items show what is sometimes popularly labelled "paranoid" aggressiveness, but actually the whole factor seems to be an habitual tendency to use the defense mechanism of projection, in tense situations, hence the interpretive label "protension."

M. Autia. Unconventional, eccentric, aesthetically fastidious, sensitively imaginative, "a law unto himself," occasional hysterical emotional upsets, intellectual, cultured interests, versus conventional, uninterested in art, practical and logical, conscientious, worrying, anxious, alert, poised, tough control, narrower interests.

L-Data: Bohemian, subjective, impractical, wrapped up in inner ideas.

Q-Data: The items fit the theory that this is a generalized autistic tendency, in which the individual is more concerned with his inner life than external demands. The criterion relations of M in the 16 PF are with artistic creativity and accident-proneness.

N. Shrewdness. Polished, socially skillful, exact mind, cool, aloof, aesthetically fastidious, insightful regarding self, insightful regarding others, versus socially clumsy, awkward, vague and sentimental mind, company seeking, lacking independence of taste, lacking self-insight, naive.

In L-Data: The rating loadings are on for shrewd, sophisticated, realistic, cold, as opposed to warm, natural, and simplehearted.

In Q-Data: The questions and answers agree with the *L*-data picture of an unsentimental, objective, disciplined, socially skillful, "groomed" individual, alert to necessities and possibly to immediate exigencies more than principles.

O. Guilt Proneness or Timidity. Worrying, lonely, suspicious, sensitive, discouraged, versus self-confident, self-sufficient, accepting, tough, spirited.

In L-Data: Easily guilty and worried, self-abasing, easily upset.

In Q-Data: The items indicate a feeling of worthlessness easily turning to depression and guilt. The factor is high in anxiety neurotics and other clinical cases.

1. When you talk with your teachers, do you feel
   a. *as if you are not as good as they had hoped*?
   b. quite at ease?
2. Do you wish you could learn to be more carefree and lighthearted about your school work?
   a. *Yes*
   b. Not particularly
3. Do you find it easy to go up and introduce yourself to an important person?
   a. Yes
   b. *No*

There are a total of fourteen personality factors discoverable in observers' behavior ratings by factor analysis and these account for two-thirds of the variance, meaning by this that further factor extraction reveals factors of doubtful size and identity which account for little of the remaining variance. Correlations and factor loadings associated with such factors are small and the factors are difficult to identify as to meaning.

However, questionnaires seem somewhat more sensitive and reveal more information than ratings. At least four factors have been found in the questionnaire assessment of personality which are not clearly replicable in rating studies. These factors are as follows:

Q_1. *Radicalism versus Conservatism.*

1. Would you rather
   a. see a good historical movie
   b. *read a book by H.G. Wells*
2. Do you think that more difficulties arise in society today through
   a. lack of religious ideals
   b. *ignorance concerning scientific discoveries*

The Q+ person believes in evolution rather than Genesis and thinks things out for himself rather than accepting conventional rules. The hypothesis is that this is a general personality factor associated with willingness to try the new, not just a politico-social "left-wing" set of attitudes, though Thurstone's first discovery of the factor was probably compounded with cultural attitudes per se.

Q_2. *Self-sufficiency.*

In Q-Data: This factor has been confirmed in adults but does not appear in child Q-data. It shows a person who prefers reading to classes, does not like to work in committees, does not avoid doing things which might make him seem odd. Becomes absorbed in creative work, believes "he travels fastest who travels alone."

This factor has rather marked correlations with other introvert factors in second order. The Q_2 individual avoids society because it wastes his time, not because of any emotional rejection, and because experience has told him his thinking is well enough organized to solve problems for himself.

Q_3. *Self-sentiment Control*

In Q-Data: Is well organized, attends to responsibilities to others, does not spend time thinking about what might have been, does not have fantastic impossible dreams at night, interests do not change rapidly, persists in the face of distraction, is not considered childish, does not doubt other people have a good opinion of him, does not get rattled, does not mind having to work in a team.

This factor is attributed to a harmonious and well-disciplined upbringing and is largely environmentally determined. It is *negatively* associated with anxiety (UI 24) in the *T*-data realm. The most promising hypothesis is that it represents the degree to which the person has achieved integration of the self-sentiment (note similarity to McDougall's supposition that "will power is the self-regarding sentiment in action").

Q_4. *Ergic Tension.*

In Q-Data: The Q_4+ person often wakes up at night, feels moody without reason, has anxiety, feels depressed, has lapses of memory, is unduly upset by small happenings, doodles when inactive, fidgets a great deal, is more disheartened than helped by criticism.

The pattern is very clear down the age range. An 11-year-old child reports he feels scared, sweats, and shakes for no reason; worries, gets tense and excited thinking over the day's events; is easily annoyed over small things; gets discouraged if others do not think enough of him.

This factor is prominent in the second order factor differing from the factor O type of anxious depression in being a resultant of id pressure or ergic demand which is unsatisfied. It fits the Freudian view that undischarged ergic tension turns to anxiety, as in the typical transference neurosis called anxiety hysteria.

SECOND ORDER FACTORS

If factor analysis aims at a unique solution, as it must for scientific purposes, by carefully maximizing simple structure it is in general found that the source traits are oblique at that position. (There is no reason why influences in the same universe should ever be precisely uncorrelated, i.e., orthogonal.) Consequently, one can work out correlations among the primaries and factor-analyze these to find broader "second-stratum" factors operating upon the primaries. It would be a mistake to consider these "more important." In factors one can predict less of criteria from them than from the primaries; they are simply acting at a different level.

Repeated factors have consistently yielded eight second-stratum personality factors. Of these, the first two are of special note and should be compared to Eysenck's factors, "extraversion" and "neuroticism."

I. Exvia-Invia. This shows a loading on A, F, H, and Q_2 (see descriptions above). The factor obtained by Eysenck by underfactoring at the item level (which cannot be so precise a definition) matches this pretty closely and both form the core of what has popularly been called extraversion.

II. Anxiety. This shows a second order among C−, L, H, O, and Q_4. It appears to fit the Freudian theory that anxiety is associated with low ego strength, neuroticism, paranoid tension, high undischarged ergic tension, and poor self-sentiment control.

III. Corticalertia versus Pathemia. This loads factors A−, I, and N+. Just as exvia aligns as a factor with UI 32 (exvia) in objective tests (see below) and anxiety with UI 24 (anxiety) in objective tests, so this pattern aligns, though less confirmedly, with UI 22 (corticalertia). It seems to represent the typical level of arousal at which the individual operates.

IV. Independence. This loads E, M, Q_1, and Q_2, and shows alignment with UI 19 (independence) in objective tests.

Faced with what may seem to him rather abstract mathematical procedures for locating structure, the student—especially the clinical student—may wonder how "practical" these results are. Of course, in scientific methodology they actually carry out that search for covarying features that the clinician does with the unaided eye, with the new resources of measurement and the computer. There is really no contradiction. And when one looks to the criterion associations of these factors the validation of the tests for these is shown in terms of (a) Table 39-2 which shows scores for various occupational groups, and (b) Table 39-3, showing clinical profiles. The kind of standard scores used in Tables 39-2 and 39-3 are stens.[7] They divide the range of scores up into ten equal subparts with a mean of 5.5 and one sten equivalent to one SD unit. Standardization of the scores is necessary because the different distributions along the separate dimensions A, B, C, etc. are not alike and must be made comparable.

We will now proceed to illustrative instances referring to Table 39.2.

1. A sample of 245 airmen showed significant departures from the norm (above or below) on factors C, E, H, Q (p < .01),

[7] *Stens* was a term suggested by Cattell in the handbook for the 1949 (first) edition of the 16 PF (to distinguish the ten-range unit from the nine-range unit, the *stanine* popularized by Guiford and Air Force psychologists during World War II. At that time, he pointed out certain advantages of sten over stanine and it was adopted by various writers during the next two or three years.

Table 39-2. Typical 16 PF Occupational Profiles

Description of Occupational Group	N	A	B	C	E	F	G	H	I	L	M	N	O	Q₁	Q₂	Q₃	Q₄
Airmen	245	6.4	6.0	7.5	9.2	5.4	4.2	9.0	4.0	6.7	5.0	6.6	4.6	5.6	7.9	6.1	6.6
Athletes (Olympic Champions)	41	5.6	6.0	7.6	7.8	6.4	3.9	7.5	6.5	4.7	5.6	5.0	3.3	4.9	5.1	5.9	6.1
Farmers	84	5.9	2.9	3.0	3.6	2.8	5.0	4.5	6.9	6.7	6.9	5.9	7.7	4.9	6.4	5.7	7.0
Midshipmen (Seniors)	110	6.0	6.0	6.4	6.0	6.1	6.3	5.9	4.0	5.1	5.3	7.6	3.3	4.9	5.2	6.1	5.9
Professors, University	81	5.0	8.0	4.5	3.5	2.6	3.1	4.7	7.1	6.1	6.9	5.3	5.2	7.5	7.8	6.2	5.2
Scientists, Research	144	3.4	6.8	6.9	7.2	3.5	3.4	6.5	7.1	4.1	5.6	5.5	3.6	6.2	6.5	6.8	5.1

Table 39-3. Typical 16 PF Clinical Profiles (in stens)

Description of Clinical Group	N	A	B	C	E	F	G	H	I	L	M	N	O	Q₁	Q₂	Q₃	Q₄
Neurotics (all types in population proportions)	272	5.8	5.0	3.1	4.3	3.5	4.8	4.1	7.0	6.9	6.5	5.2	8.1	5.0	6.2	4.5	7.9
Alcoholics M	696	5.7	4.2	3.5	4.2	3.8	4.8	4.4	6.4	6.4	6.9	4.9	7.8	4.5	6.0	4.9	7.9
Homosexuals M	136	6.5	3.5	2.6	5.0	4.9	3.6	4.5	7.6	7.3	7.7	5.3	7.8	6.1	6.6	4.9	7.3

G, L, N, Q (p < .05). The significance levels (5 and 1 percent) are statistically conventional, the 1 percent level being stricter and expressing the probability that such a sample would appear, by chance, only once in a hundred samples.

2. The sample of 41 Olympic athletes also shows C, E, and H at the 1 percent level. Like the airmen, they are evidently high in ego strength, dominance, and show parasympathetic immunity.

3. Farmers are high on ego strength (C), warmhearted outgoingness (F), and low on guilt proneness (O).

4. University professors are highly intelligent (B), low on dominance (E), and outgoingness (F), low on superego strength (G), high on radicalism (Q), and self-sufficiency (Q₂).

As compared with the above normal groups we now turn to Table 39.3 which shows that:

5. Neurotics are low in ego strength (C), rather cold (F), high on guilt proneness (O), and ergic tension (Q₄).

6. Alcoholics are low on ego strength (C), and, like neurotics, high on guilt proneness (O), and ergic tension (Q₄).

7. Homosexuals are highly intelligent (B), low on ego strength (C), high on premsia (protected oversensitivity) (I), high on bohemian tendency (M), and on timidity (O).

As an illustrative example, we can look at an individual profile (Fig. 39-2), and see whether the salients on his profile match those of the given occupation. (Salients are profile emergents, traits which emerge significantly in a given occupation.) It will become clear (from an inspection of Fig. 39-2) for vocational guidance and industrial selection, what is needed is "the two file system." The job profiles are kept in one file and the individual profiles in another (or in corresponding tape storage for the computer). In this way, we can go into the *I* file looking for profiles suitable for certain jobs in the *J* file, or we can have the computer (or card sorter) select the best people for the given job. Also we can, in the high school situation, advise an individual student as to the recommended occupations suitable to his aptitudes, personality characteristics, and interests.

As an illustration of the need for personality measurement in augmentation of the conventional aptitude measurement, let us take the recent research findings of Cattell and Butcher (1968) concerning school achievement.

It will be seen that the factors which influence school achievement, in addition to intelligence, are G+ (superego strength), Q₂+ (self-sufficiency), E− (submission), A+ (affectothymia), Q₃+ (strength of self-sentiment), D− (phlegmatic temperament).

We find an achievement specification equation for high school achievement loaded as follows (Note: Positive loading means that the trait aids achievement with the weighting as noted, negative, the reverse):

$$\text{High School Achievement}: .15A + .50B + .10C - .10D - .15E + .10F + .25C + .10H - .10I + .15J + .20Q_2 + .20Q_3 + .10Q_4$$

The pattern of G₁, Q₂, E(−) makes good sense. In other words where intelligence is equal, conscientiousness (G), self-sufficiency or resourcefulness (Q₂), and docility toward authority (E−), will aid school achievement. The opposite of Q₂ (group dependency) does not favor school achievement; this carries the implication that studying is incompatible with "going around with the gang." The dominance aspect is reversed at the university graduate level, i.e., it helps to be nondominant prior to graduation, but when later work requires independence of mind rather than docile absorption dominance helps achievement in postgraduate studies.

The point which Table 39-4 makes is that much more accurate predictions can be made by adding personality measures, e.g., the behavior record is poorly predicted by (a) but more than twice as accurately predicted by (b). Incidentally, when one gets to such calculations of multiple correlations it quickly becomes apparent that using the main primary source traits as defined above gives better, closer predictions, than using the broader, vaguer, popularly discussed secondaries, such as "extraversion." For example, on the primaries partly involved in extraversion (A, F, H, Q₂), leading scientists are "extravert" on H but "introvert" on A, F, and Q₂. Thus an extraversion measure fails in its purpose in this instance.

The neurotic profile, to which we now turn, shows values which significantly depart from the norm on:

Lower than normal
C − Ego strength

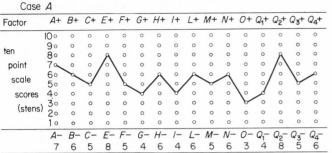

Case A

Airmen (pilot cadets in training) 245 Cases

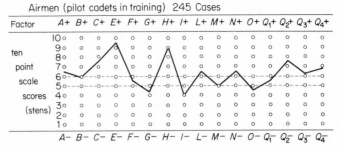

Case B

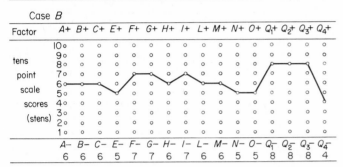

Priests 40 Cases

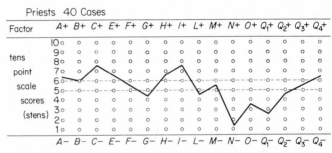

Executives and Directors (business managerial) 63 Cases

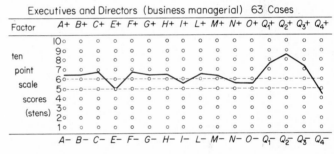

Fig. 39-2. *This is self-explanatory and illustrates the need for a two-file system in schools and industry for matching individual and job profiles. A statistical index has been developed for more precise matching and the process can be fully automated by appropriate sorting and computer methods. The entire process of test scoring and matching can be automated.*

Table 39-4.   Prediction of Achievement and Adjustment Measures (correlations)
(adapted from Cattell and Butcher, 1968)

	Intelligence Measure	Intelligence plus personality (H.S.P.Q.)	Significance level
Leadership	.62	.69	.05
Behavior record	.23	.50	.01
Adjustment	.45	.56	.05
Stanford achievement	.72	.79	.01

E — Dominance
F — Surgency (outgoingness)
H — Resistance to threat
Higher than normal
I + Emotional sensitivity
L + Paranoid tension
O + Guilt process
Q + Ergic tension

(This 16 PF profile emergent is obtained by combining ten studies, summing to 201 clinically judged neurotic cases.)

Before considering the objective test (*T*-data) patterns of the main personality factors it seems desirable to complete the general picture by adding the motivation structure findings to those on general personality factors.

The Measurement of Motivation Components, Ergs and Sentiments

Obviously, general temperament-disposition traits and abilities do not cover the whole realm of personality. There is also the extremely important dynamic motivational modality. (Aristotle recognized *cognition* [ability modality], *affection* [perhaps the general temperament modality], and *conation*, unquestionably what psychology now calls the dynamic modality.) In the late 1940s Cattell and a series of gifted coworkers—Horn, Sweeney, Heist, Scheier, Radcliffe, Sealy, Butcher, Krug, Cross, Miller and others—turned upon dynamic structure the multivariate experimental methods and objective measurements that had now been shown to work as well for personality as ability variables and concepts. However, the challenge of the more changeable and subtle dynamic structural phenomena was greater, and there were not lacking those, in the psychoanalytic school particularly, who predicted failure.

Whereas the general personality domain had been attacked by factor analytic methods by Guilford and Guilford (1938),[8] the attack by objective tests on the domain of dynamic modality has been, in the main, an undertaking of the Illinois group. Its first products were the concepts of motivation components, of erg and sentiment structures, of the dynamic lattice, etc. Cattell's definitions of an erg (Cattell 1950, p. 199) was an innate psychophysical disposition which permits its possessor to acquire reactivity to certain classes of objects more readily than others, to experience a specific emotion in regard to them, and to start on a course of action which ceases more completely at a certain specific goal activity. The pattern (of an erg) also includes preferred behavior subsidiation paths to the preferred goal.

Obviously we can see that by erg, Cattell means what McDougall at first called an instinct and later a propensity.

[8] J. P. Guilford and R. B. Guilford "An analysis of the Factors in a Typical Test of Intraversion-Extraversion," *Journal of Abnormal and Social Psychology* 28 (1934) 377–99.

In fact Cattell's theory owes much to McDougall with a large dash of Freud and a hint of Murray here and there (e.g., in the notion of subsidation). The radical difference between ergs and these earlier concepts, such as Murray's needs, however, lies in the fact that they are operationally defined also as the factors which emerge when the domain of objectively measured interest —attitudes covering the dynamic personality sphere—is factored. The expression of ergs, the direction they take, the amount of energy dissipated, and the gradual modification of ergic expression occurs at various dynamic crossroads. Here the expression of the erg can meet satisfaction, deprivation, modification, or supercession by provocation of more powerful drive, or frustration by a barrier. Ways which are found around barriers are referred to as *long-circuiting*. This network of crossroads and pathways has been illustrated elsewhere (Cattell 1957) as a dynamic "flow chart" (Fig. 39-3) in which the various outcomes of each confrontation between goal path and barrier have been assessed.

The basic method by which the particular expressions of innate ergs are modified is therefore the law of effect. Failing satisfaction, behavior becomes more varied and dispersed, rage or displacement or apathy intervenes, or some partially satisfying response may be made which modifies the expression of the erg. If satisfaction or partial satisfaction later accompanies some part of the varied behavior not immediately satisfied then the person begins to build up a sentiment. Thus, a sentiment may be considered a pattern of acquired interests reflecting the particular learning and reinforcement history of the organism. The primary interests from which sentiment structures emerge are, of course, the ergs. The dynamic interconnections and subsidation among ergs and sentiments have been shown in the purposive sequences of Cattell's *dynamic lattice*.

Here we see an ergic level at one end and an attitude level at the other. Various ergs express themselves in a learned sentiment structure clustered around various goals or centers of expression for socially modified ergs.

Let us now look at the latest research in this area. It presents quite a simple and straightforward picture. The first step was to

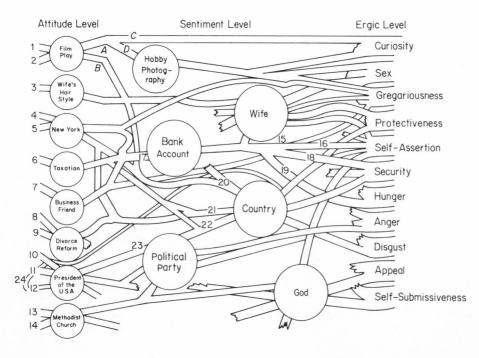

Fig. 39-3. *The diagram shows the overt grouping of attitudes on one side and the hidden ergs and sentiments on the other side. Appropriate analysis by the MAT (Motivation Analysis Test) enables the strength of ergs, sentiments, and attitudes to be examined in a given subject. Use of the MAT is recommended in research into clinical, educational, and industrial behaviors as a necessary addition to presently available methods such as the Strong Inventory and Kuder Preference.*

Between the attitudes (overt) and the hidden ergs and sentiments are strongly held general feelings about (e.g.) politics and religion. These are dynamic foci in what is called the subsidation lattice. The figure illustrates this lattice.

discover the components of attitude strength. With these preliminary notions clear about the history and development of interest strength we can proceed to a more detailed examination of the primary concepts of this theory and a presentation of the firm research foundations on which they rest.

As mentioned above, the radical difference between this present conception of motivation and earlier theories (i.e., McDougall, Murray), lies in the fact that the former begins, not in the armchair, but in the laboratory. In this sense, it is thoroughly empirical. It has attempted, through accurate assessment and rigorous mathematical formulation to isolate and quantify major dimensions of motivation which exist and are demonstrably replicable.

The primary unit of observation for the "dynamic calculus," as the present theory has been called, is the attitude defined in the following paradigm:

In these circumstances (stimulus situation) to do this (direction)	I want (organism) (need) with that (object)	so much (intensity)

It should be immediately apparent that this differs in complexity from a fairly common conception of an attitude as expressing a simple interest "for" or "against" a particular object.

In order to keep matters simple we need only take one representative attitude, measure it by a whole host of devices, and see how these devices measure or reflect various types of motive strength. Let us say we measure two hundred male subjects on a single attitude such as interest in taking part in athletics. This was actually done by Cattell and Baggalley who developed over seventy motivational measurement devices and actually used fifty-five on the one attitude (see Cattell 1957, pp. 465–71).

Students will be interested to hear how the motivational measurement devices were developed. We should mention at this point that these devices have now been tried out on a variety of attitudes and not just one as in the initial study and that a clear replicable structuring or grouping has appeared. Several devices were developed on the basis of the argument that where the interest in an area has been strong, a high level of information and/or skill will have been attained in the given area. Other devices come from selective memory for items in the interest area. So far we have (a) information and (b) memory. Another test is selective attention; we can then test fluency of ideas or associations to words taken either in or out of the given area. Again, physiological measures are used and in most of these response "insult to the attitude" proved more effective in practice than "stimulus to the attitude."

Sample measures are:

1. Information (several devices in each category)
2. Memory (see SMAT examples)
3. Fluency
4. Autonomic responses (measures of muscle tension, metabolic rate changes, peripheral circulation, etc.)
5. Dynamisms (fantasy, misperception, autism, rationalization, distortion of reasoning)

In a first study, the attitude tested on all these measures was to athletics. A later study sampled five different attitudes. The results of these studies agreed in showing five factors or components of motivation strength:

Motivation Factor Alpha Id Component

Test devices with high loading	Rationalization	.99
	Autism	.93
	Distortion of reasoning	.85

Beta: Ego

	Memory for words	.99
	Information	.68

Gamma: Superego

	Choice of fantasy topic	.85
	Easy memory path	.73
	Decision time	.42

Delta: Unconscious physiological

Systolic, diastolic and area of heart wave to threat	1.00

Epsilon: Repressed complexes

	Reminiscence by recall	−1.00
	Memory for incomplete question	− .85

Cattell points out that the demonstration and replication of these five components shows that previous approaches to attitude measurement have been too simple. For example, he finds that only one-tenth of the variance is typically accounted for by the direct question type of attitude assessment.

A careful determining of the angles between the five factors yielded two major second-order factors which showed a division into conscious integrated interest strength (factors beta and gamma) versus unconscious, unintegrated interest strength (factors alpha, delta and epsilon).

In practice, it was found possible to add the strength of scores on these two second-order factors with equal weight for a single individual. One can then say that his total strength of interest in a given course of action springs from a summation of integrated (I) and unintegrated (U) sources.

INVESTIGATION OF DYNAMIC STRUCTURE

With this clarification of what is done when we measure any *single* attitude interest, the stage is set for the second phase of investigation, in which a large variety of attitudes or motives are measured and correlated to determine the dynamic structure residing in them. Attempts to measure structure among attitudes by correlation have previously been made but the measurements have usually been made only in terms of conscious, opinionaire-type evaluations which have low validities and measure only a small part of the variance. Furthermore, the choice of attitudes, as in studies by Gallup, Cantril, Guttman, and Eysenck has been dictated by practical, industrial, or political interests. In the present study only 5–10 percent have been variables of this kind, whereas the remainder consists of a wide spectrum of attitudes concerning wife and home, children, career, health, hobbies, religion, and so on.

The investigation of attitude structure can proceed in two ways. The first approach, analogous to the procedure used in isolating the motivational components, is to take a variety of attitudes measured on a single device. In this way the covariance among devices is held constant and it is the covariance among attitudes which provides the basis for the resulting structure. The second approach is to use several devices (thus avoiding the problems arising from reliance on a single technique) and add the scores for a single attitude together across the various devices on which it has been measured.

Such analyses have resulted in at least nine clear ergic drive structures and as many as twenty sentiment structures. The five most replicable of each have been brought together in the Motivation Analysis Test (MAT; Cattell, Horn, Sweeney, & Radcliffe 1964) and are presented below along with attitudes which are known to define the particular structure.

ERGS
1. Mating
   a. I want to fall in love with a beautiful woman/handsome man.
   b. I want to satisfy my sexual needs.
2. Assertiveness
   a. I want to be smartly dressed with an appearance that commands admiration.
   b. I want to increase my salary and social status.
3. Fear
   a. I want my home better protected against the terror of an atomic bomb attack.
   b. I want to see the danger of death from disease and accidents reduced.
4. Narcism–comfort
   a. I want to lie in bed in the mornings and have a very easy time of life.
   b. I want to enjoy fine foods, fine drinks, candies, and delicacies.
5. Pugnacity–sadism
   a. I want my country to go all out to destroy the enemy.
   b. I want to see movies or plays showing gangster fights and violence, where many people are injured or slain.

From this deeper investigation of attitudes and dynamic structure we may now propose a somewhat tighter definition of an erg as "a pattern found among dynamic manifestations by factor analysis, and hypothesized to be an innately determined, goal-directed unity." An erg is a source of reactivity or energy; it is definitely a better term for general use than "drive," "need," or "tension," as it refers to definable structures in behavior. The attitudes defining an erg all have a common emotional quality in spite of diverse cultural content, e.g., the escape of fear responses all found clustered together refer now to a fear of war, now to a fear of anxiety, to fears of loss of job, death, disease, etc.

The "Five Sentiment Structures" are as follows:

1. Sentiment to self-concept
   a. I want to maintain a good reputation and command respect in my community.
   b. I want to keep my impulses under sufficient and proper control.
2. The superego sentiment to socio-parental sanctions (the moral-ethical "ideal self")
   a. I want to satisfy a sense of duty to my community, my country, and my God.
   b. I want to see an end to gambling, idleness, excessive drinking, prostitution, and all other forms of vice.

3. Career-profession
   a. I want to learn more about the technical skills in my job or job-to-be.
   b. I want to stick with my job or chosen career.
4. Sweetheart-spouse
   a. I want to spend time with my sweetheart, enjoying our common interests.
   b. I want to bring gifts to my sweetheart, to share in his or her delight in them.
5. Home-parental
   a. I am proud of my parents and want them to be proud of me.
   b. I want to turn to my parents for affection, comradeship, and guidance.

As we inspect the attitudes brought together in these non-ergic patterns it becomes clear that they represent common learning and, indeed, environmental mould traits. Typically, one can see as the central focus a single social institution such as the family, a career, or a particular form of organized recreation. A sentiment is thus a pattern of common variance in attitudes, presumably acquired by the ordinary rules of learning, involving repeated common reward for the attitudes involved. For example, attending church may reinforce diverse ergs but their expression coalesces into a given institution and a given sentiment pattern.

In this present section we have only touched on the major points of the dynamic calculus. The value of a theory, however, lies not only in its intricate network of structural concepts but also in the applicability of these concepts (i.e., ergs, sentiments, unintegrated and integrated interest strength) to the prediction and understanding of behavior. In this respect, the dynamic calculus is in an early stage of development.

Personality Structure as it Emerged in Objective Tests (*T*-Data)

If we have identified the factors representing a usable abstract of the vast area of language descriptions of personality characteristics and everyday life behavior in *Q*-data, why should we feel a need also to proceed with the investigation of *T*-data factors? The reason for this is that in the first instance we cannot be sure that language has captured all the aspects of behavior, and we suspect this possibility because it did not do so in the case of intelligence. When the latter was explored by multivariate means it became possible to measure, compare, and specify the relevant individual differences in a way which everyday language had not done. The concepts of the normal distribution are not contained in the language, which simply embodies common assumptions, and is essentially unscientific. The language of the common man, or even of the scholar, embodies the limitations of his senses, and it does not, for example, understand the workings of nature. The language of science, on the other hand, takes us below the surface screen of language and into the forces and causes involved in the macrocosm and the microcosm. Science extends man's senses, and correlates and "makes sense" of these in the form of laws which are not revealed by common sense. The myopic Pavlov could see more in his way than Bernard Shaw. The rich descriptions of Shakespeare were of less import for science than the condensed formulae of Newton. Wordsworth's poems are an evocation of sensitive man peering out into the world of nature, but Darwin's prose has given us greater enlightenment as to the meaning of nature and the place of man in the world of living objects.

L- and Q-data may be regarded as a first broad encompassing of common sense but now we wish to go beyond common sense into a realm of "transportable artificial" situations. These tests are essentially S–R measures. We provide the standardized stimulus situation and observe the response under these conditions. We may thus discover

S–O–R

major factors in this realm and attempt inferences about the nature of these factors. Going further, we can attempt inferences about the processes going on within *O*.

The study of the *T*-data realm actually encompasses all the other realms, for it is possible to envisage a total sphere of possible observations in which the person is made to respond in all possible ways. These would range from physiological measures to tests of his modes of apperception, and of the nature of his logic and epistemology. Thus, the approach to *T*-data should be made in the realization that it is a long term process of discovery, which will encompass aptitude and intelligence factors, physical factors, physiological factors, and state as well as trait factors. The whole realm of behavior is the area of *T*-data; genetics and learning are to be found, as well as conscious integrated dynamic traits, and also the area of individual difference traits.

In this section we present what is, although based on a number of extremely large researches, actually but the beginning of a penetration into an unknown sea. Herein we will find many paradoxes and many questions begging for further enquiry into trait names in the English language than those from which Cattell (1946)[9] obtained the original clusters and thence the *L*-data factors.

PERSONALITY SPHERE: DEFINITION

The personality sphere, in its most comprehensive form, includes all possible personality differences which are reliable, replicable and valid. It thus includes intelligence, aptitude, interest, motivation, *L*- and *Q*-data, and nonfakeable factor measures. It thus encompasses physiological, self-evaluative, behavioral, drug or instruction instigated, fatigue effected, arousal influenced measures and even special state measures, related to hypnotism and suggestibility effects, group dependent or group affected measures. It extends from primary-physiological and primary-genetic measures to those affected by development and aging measures.

A tremendous amount of invention, linked to intuitive and to explicit theoretical insights, went into the four hundred different objective tests, and one thousand behavioral measures derivable from them, on which thirty years of progress in this field have now been built. The reader will find them, indexed and discussed, in Cattell and Warburton (1967).[10] This list is not a final list, for the operational definition of the personality sphere

[9] Cattel, *The Description and Measurement of Personality*.
[10] R. B. Cattell, and F. W. Warburton, *Objective Personality and Motivation Tests* (Champaign-Urbana: University of Illinois Press, 1967).

is a matter of ongoing concern for all psychologists. It is an inventive progression requiring factor hypothesis, clinical insight, mathematical ingenuity, in short, a combination of the most difficult skills in the armamentarium of the modern psychologist. Only by an iterative procedure, in which the same marker variables have been carried on from experiment to experiment over these thirty years, has it been possible to check results, systematically extend dimensions, and create measures ever closer to the inferred nature of the emerging source traits.

Today, the field of personality research is crowded by questionnaires and inventories of one kind or another. Many of these are unfactorized and actually measure mixtures of various major traits with supposedly "pure" scales, e.g., the MMPI, the Taylor MAS, the California scale, the TAT, and so forth. To the basic researcher it is evident that if criterion relations are to be helpful in personality theory the applied psychologist must redirect his subjective thinking from this "patent medicine" stage into (1) the area of factored instruments, and beyond the (2) use of non-fakeable measures. One can believe that progress is inevitable, but it is, at the same time, regrettably slow. It is as though a few prospectors were aware of, and were beginning to work, a rich metallic mother lode, while nearby, and quite unheeding, others are spending much time on a far poorer one. For the findings—some twenty replicated primary dimensions—have indeed been rich. Yet progress must be slow until more researchers become available with full training in all the required areas.

In what follows, we will refer to "objective" tests as non-fakeable tests and will use the abbreviation NF. The reason for adopting the new nomenclature is that the term "objective" has been widely used both in regard to objective examinations and objective scoring. As these are a new venture, or rather a new penetration into the personality sphere, and as their advantage is that they are nonfakeable (or, in some instances, relatively nonfakeable), it has seemed more suitable, at this juncture, to introduce the term NF to categorize these tests. (Another perfectly acceptable term, *in relation to findings*, is *T*-data, although there is a possible confusion with the term "t-test.")

Although the largest portion of this chapter has already been devoted to *L*-data, *Q*-data, and motivation measurement devices, there is an as yet untapped potential inherent in NF tests. In the first place, the factors appearing in *T*-data are of broader scope than in *L*- and *Q*-data. Thus, for example, UI 24 anxiety is a first-order factor in *T*-data, and is a second-order factor in *Q*-data. The primaries in *T*-data are as broad as the secondaries in *Q*-data. Three of the second-order in the latter—UI 32 extraversion, UI 24 anxiety, and UI 22 corticalertia—are found as primaries in *T*-data.

In considering NF tests, we will use three divisions to organize our description:

1. We will first describe generally a typical NF battery using as our illustration Howarth's 1969 APT (Advanced Personality Test) Battery.
2. We will then turn to tables for five *T*-data factors which have been shown to discriminate normals from neurotics at the 1 percent level of confidence.
3. We will then close the section by giving illustrations of:
   a. Second-orders among NF factors.
   b. Relations to electroencephalograph frequencies.
   c. General comments and theoretical interpretations.
   d. State (as compared to trait) measurement.

A Typical Nonfakeable (NF) Test Battery

It will be apparent from an inspection of Tables 39-5–39-9 that many of the factor marker tests have reappeared in from six to ten studies. Six of the markers for UI 16 have appeared in at least six researches, and two measures (T35 and T10) have appeared in as many as ten studies. Perhaps the remaining factors shown (*n.b.* the entire series goes from UI 16–UI 35) are not as well marked or replicated but even UI 28 shows two measures (T124 and T20) which have appeared in at least four researches.

Each of the researches represents a large investment of time and money. For example, the R15 study tested 198 subjects in five schools using about twenty hours of school time in each school. Prior to testing, the assembly of the battery is a logistic exercise worthy of the D-Day invasion, and the succeeding data analysis is sufficiently enormous and prolonged to tax the resources of a large computer.

One of the disadvantages of previous NF batteries has been removed in the 1969 APT Battery assembled by the junior author. This is composed entirely of group tests so that no transportation of apparatus (e.g., the reaction time apparatus) is required, and about one hour per subject of individual testing is avoided. (This is not to say that suitable instrument batteries for, e.g., extraversion and anxiety will not be evolved in the course of time.)

The APT Battery includes (samples and descriptions are now given):

Maze Test.   This consists of four mazes, two are broad and two are more difficult narrow trail mazes. The subject is scored on aspiration, errors, distance travelled.

Symbol Cancellation.   This uses computer generated sequences and the subject has to cross out a different subset of symbols on each row.

Working Fast.   This is a group form of the cursive miniature situation, originally devised by Cattell on the basis of McDougall's apparatus. The group form uses patterns which *S* follows checking certain shapes but not others and working under speeded conditions.

Hidden Objects.   A revised and redrawn form of an older test (O-A 1955) which is a form of misperception test in which the subject structures an ambiguous or partly structured perceptual field.

Humor List.   A greatly revised version of Cattell's Humor Test (Form A). Many of the jokes have been modernized.

Set Change.   Adapted from Howarth's 1963 test battery for extraversion. This tests the subject's ability to change set from one task to another (e.g., division, multiplication, addition).

What will Happen?   Derived from the R15 (Cattell and Howarth) battery. A series of pictures display two possible outcomes, e.g., a man is shown swimming in the water followed by a shark. The item asks: will he (a) get caught? (b) escape the shark?

Best Words.   This gives alternatives to test rhyming or alliterative skidding (psychotic).

In this particular battery there are about 60 tests, providing about 300 measures for subsequent data analysis. On a rule of thumb basis it would be desirable to give the battery to 900 subjects. At the present state of research, some 450 NF tests have been invented (see Cattell & Warburton 1967).[11] Twenty-three hundred sixty-six derived measures are listed in the compendium. About ten factors have been reasonably well replicated, and lists for five of these (UI 16, 19, 21, 23, and 28) are given in Tables 39.5, .6, .7, .8, and .9 respectively. *All* of these have been shown to differentiate at the 1 percent level between neurotics and normals.

Some NF Factor Descriptions

Operationally, one identifies factors by means of the pattern of measures which load the factor after sufficient rotation has been carried out.

One then has to face the task of "intuitively abstracting" what might be the common element(s) among the variables loaded on the factor. In the case of UI 16, which typically carries the largest proportion of the variance (squares of factor loadings summed by columns) in these studies, we see self-assertiveness combined with a general competence, efficiency, and assertive-

---

[11] Cattell and Warburton, *Objective Personality and Motivation Tests.*

Table 39-5.   UI 16 Assertive Ego VS. Disciplined Ego

Description of Variable	Average Corr.	No. of Researches
Greater accuracy of mazes (distance travelled correctly)	+.27	6
Faster speed of letter comparison	+.51	8
Higher total score in C.M.S.	+.46	8
Greater number of objects seen in unstructured drawings	+.27	9
Faster ideomotor speed	+.58	2
More acceptance of unqualified statements	+.19	4
Greater numerical ability	+.50	10
Faster speed of number comparison	+.80	1
More "highbrow" tastes	+.30	5
More immaturity of opinion	+.14	10
Faster ideomotor tempo	+.43	4
Faster tempo of tapping	+.46	3

ness. It correlates with Guilford-Zimmermin's activity, ascendance and sociability, with MMPI schizophrenia and with the Harria factor in *Q*-data (16 PF). Criterion indications include a positive relation to the Aviation Qualification Test (but a *negative* relation to peer ratings of pilot proficiency). It shows a marked environmental determination.

Table 39-6. UI 19 Promethean Will vs. Subduedness

Description of Variable	Average Corr.	No. of Researches
Greater accuracy in Gottschaldt figures	.23	8
Greater accuracy in searching task	.33	8
Less regression toward real objects in memory or designs	.33	6
Culture fair subtest 1	.46	3
Fewer number of obvious objects given as hidden	.26	2
Faster speed of checking under complex instructions	.37	2
Faster speed of tapping (group paper and pencil)	.17	6
Higher score: Index of carefulness	.14	9

UI 19 has been identified in factor studies (thirteen adult, five child). It aligns somewhat with Thurstone's *E* factor-"suppressive manipulation of configurations." Cross media alignments are with parmia (adventurous, thick skinned), schizothymia and possibly shrewdness. Normals score higher on 19 than do neurotics. As in the case of UI 16, it shows competence measures but this factor (UI 19) shows an ability to concentrate, even in the face of distraction. It is the kind of quality useful to scientific researchers or to writers of chapters in handbooks (and may even prove useful to readers of chapters in handbooks). There is a certain corticalness of others while maintaining a rather more complacent view of oneself, in this factor.

UI 21 fourteen factor studies support this general picture,

pilot proficiency. It has not yet been discovered in *P*-technique (state) studies, or in incremental *R*-technique. There is an absence of, or resistance to, social suggestibility in this factor, and a lack of concern for, or involvement with, social issues. Body build measures indicate smaller shoulder width, less mesomorphy, and a lower score on a muscular index.

UI 23 has been relatively easy to identify as the NF measure of general neuroticism, but readers should note carefully that, as might be expected from "common sense," this factor is neither alone, nor is it the most efficient, in differentiating neurotics from normals. It is regarded as "an inner security, coherence, and capacity to mobilize as opposed to overwrought, distracted, inaccurate reactions to many outside stimuli, along with indications of ergic regressions from adaptive interests." The factor is regarded as similar to Eysenck's neuroticism factor. A predominant characteristic is flexibility versus rigidity, and the capacity to change responses. Rigidity is especially shown by poor performance in such tests as: "Where do the lines cross?", "Where do you land?", upside-down drawings, doing arithmetic, and logical

Table 39-7. UI 21 Exuberance vs. Suppressibility

Description of Variable	Average Corr.	No. of Researches
Better immediate memory for statements	.32	8
Larger number of hidden objects seen	.58	8
Faster speed of line length judgment	.35	9
Higher total score on C.M.S.	.21	9
More correctness of drawing completion (more real life objects drawn)	.39	5
Perceptual speed of design; faster speed of Gestalt completion	.60	3
Better memory for designs	.18	3
Hardheaded decisiveness: Faster speed of judgment	.52	4
Fluency: Higher total verbal fluency on topics	.38	8

especially at the adult level where it has been shown to have a high hereditary determination, and to characterize a person who is enthusiastic, energetic, dominant, and excitable. As in the case of UI 16, it loads negatively on peer ratings of helicopter

problems in one's head. More preference for color over form has appeared consistently in this factor. Cattell and Scheier have shown that UI 23 increases during stress or immediate anticipation of stress.

Table 39-8. UI 23 High Mobilization vs. Neurotic Regressive Debility (or Regression)

Description of Variable	Average Corr.	No. of Researches
Higher rigidity	−.20	6
More accuracy in partial judgment	+.23	6
Higher ratio of accuracy to speed	+.13	3
Higher ratio considered possible for self *vs.* others	−.37	2
More preference for competitive *vs.* non-competitive work	−.33	2
Greater personal relations to institution value	+.67	1
Higher speed of reading to one's self	+.37	3
Higher speed of coding	+.29	6
Dynamometer: more persistence	+.54	2
Two-hand coordination: greater accuracy relative to speed	−.19	11
More body sway suggestibility		

Table 39-9. UI 28 Dependent, Negativistic Asthenic vs. Undisciplined Self-Assuredness

Description of Variable	Average Corr.	No. of Researches
Auditory hallucinations: fewer attempted items	.22	2
Lower score on Subtest 4	.33	1
Myokinesis: greater size	.21	5
Drawing: fewer number of threatening objects seen in unstructured drawing	.28	4
Lower ratio of accuracy to speed in picture completion	.21	3
Fewer "highbrow" tastes	.31	1
Criticalness in humor	.30	2
Longer time interval estimates	.34	1
More considered possible in given time	.44	1
Less fluctuation of attitudes	.36	1
Higher estimate of time required for others	.47	1

UI 28—possibly not so well marked as the factors previously described, and as its number indicates, appearing later in the factor series (although not so late as UI 32 Exvia-Invia), UI 28 is included because of its neurotic-normal discriminatory power, as being of interest, therefore, to clinicians. With only three replicated marks (in Table 39-9) the description must be tentative but in R9 neurotics scored higher on this factor, whereas in study R10 both delinquents and drug addicts scored lower than nondelinquent normals. Two main attributes can be commented on: low psychophysical momentum and lack of self-confidence. A person low on UI 28 shows strong physique and low autonomic activation level, so that there may be certain parallels here to the dichotomy between hysteria and dysthymia drawn by Eysenck. (The factor may measure across extraversion and neuroticism.) Cattell (1964) has suggested an early parental repressiveness hypothesis for the "authoritarian" personality factor: UI 28.

We may now turn from the specific descriptions of certain T-data factors to more general considerations of:

1. Second-order factors have been discovered among the oblique factor primaries in T-data (Pawlik & Cattell 1964). These are as follows:

    I. Tied Socialization
        UI 20, UI 28, UI 19, UI 25, UI 35, UI 32
    II. Expansive Ego
        UI 16, UI 19, UI 23, UI 36, UI 18
    III. Temperamental Ardor
        UI 21, UI 20, UI 19, UI 27, UI 32
    IV. High Educated Self-Consciousness
        UI 22, UI 18, UI 25, UI 36, UI 30, UI 29, UI 33

2. Certain relationships to EEG measures have appeared (Pawlik & Cattell 1964):
    Alpha index, frequency, phase length, amplitude are related to UI 22 and UI 16 (all negative except frequency positive).

3. Some general comments illustrate the urgent need for further research. For example, there is a need for better NF definition of UI 32 exvia, and work is proceeding in order to mark the factor more clearly and to "bring it forward" in prominence in the NF factor listing. For some strange reason, this factor so prominent in Cattell's Q- and L-data, and in the work of Eysenck and his coworkers, has not yet been prominent in T-data. Another example is the relative failure of UI 24 (anxiety) to differentiate between neurotics and normals, although it is a "neurotic contributory factor" What is needed now is research concentration on particular factors and this is being done.

4. State measurements. Factors listed as P(U 1) refer to those discovered by P-technique which entails repeating a group of measurements on a given subject over repeated occasions in order to discover which measures covary together and thus identify (or result in) a state, rather than a trait factor. We may compare the data from an incremental-R technique study of questionnaires with the T-data P-technique. In the former the 16 PF is given on two different occasions to the same group of Ss and the differences are measured. Such a study revealed second-order factors corresponding to Q-data R-technique, viz.:

I	II	III	IV
Exvia-Invia	Anxiety	Corticalertia	Promethean Will

(compare with T-data UI 32, 24, 22, and 19, respectively)

Typically in P-technique some 40 to 60 measures are taken on one individual over 80 to 100 days. A number of NF state factors have been identified in this way, some of which are well marked by physiological indicators, e.g.:

Cortical alertness (PUI 2), effort stress (PUI 4), Regression versus mobilization (PUI 8), Promethean Will (PUI 11). These align with UI 22, 26, 23, and 19, respectively. Greater research is needed on several of these, although anxiety has been well studied and its operational measurement has been made more precise by factorial assessment of putative variables. PUI 8 mobilization is an intriguing state dimension, for (on the organized pole) it shows reality readiness, mental organization, and "a state of being braced and ready to cope." At its negative pole it shows a neurotic sense of failure, inability to react adequately, higher emotionality of comment (outbursts), muscle tension, and heart rate variability.

Summary

1. In this chapter we have outlined a particular approach to personality.[12] We have covered that approach of a broad

[12] The aim of this chapter is to present the reader with a distillation of Cattell's system, which has been presented and developed in more than 20 books and 250 articles. The chapter is, therefore, written in an uncritical manner. Readers who wish to pursue a more critical evaluation of Cattell's system should begin by consulting the following references:

Howarth, E., and Browne, J. A. An item-factor-analysis of the 16 PF. *Personality* 1971, *2*, 117–39.

Howarth, E., Browne, J. A., and Marceau, R. An item analysis of Cattell's 16 PF. *Canadian Journal of Behavioral Science*, 1972, *4*, 85–90.

group of investigators using the multivariate experimental approach and the chapter began by explaining both, (a) the meaning of "multivariate experimental," and (b) the absolute necessity for it in psychology for the provision of prior multivariate operational definition of concept (PMOD).

2. Then followed a socio-historical discussion of why certain narrow, restricted and unsatisfactory effects, which were standing in the path of progress, were being made in psychology. Indications were given of desirable changes in training and attitudes especially as related to the multivariate methods. It was pointed out that the state of affairs vis-à-vis adequately training personality researchers was, overall, far from satisfactory.

3. Some substantive discoveries in questionnaire and rating data were described by outlining the meaning (factor meaning) of a dozen or so replicated primary factors. Second-order factors were then described. These factors can be measured at the adult level by means of the 16 PF (Forms A and B) or at the younger age levels by the HSPQ and CPQ. A description of practical applications (profiles) was given, and the value of a "two-file" (an individual file and a job file) system for matching person to job was outlined.

4. Although it has been demonstrated that the addition of personality measures increases the predictive power of test batteries in relation to scholastic achievement and adjustment in the school situation, it is likely that even greater accuracy will ensue from the addition of, first, motivational measurement, and second, nonfakeable test measurement. Thus, after describing Q-data, we proceeded to describe, first, motivational devices, then T-data. The motivational device now available for research is the M.A.T. (Motivational Analysis Test) which uses four devices—two integrated or conscious, two unintegrated or only partly conscious—to measure a number of ergs and sentiments as described in the body of the chapter.

5. Finally, we described some of the fruits of research into nonfakeable (formerly called "objective tests" but to avoid confusion now called *NF* tests) measurements, which represent the work of 25 years in which over 3,000 actual measures and almost 500 different miniature situations have been invented (Cattell & Warburton 1967).[13] As 6 of these factors differentiate significantly between neurotics and normals, we organized the discussion about a group of these and provided criterion illustrations along with, (a) a general description of the present consensus of meaning of each factor, (b) a listing of the number of confirmatory studies

and the average correlation across the studies of marker variables for the factor.

Acknowledgments. Acknowledgments for the defining studies underlying the contents of this chapter are due to the following researchers (specific references to their work should be sought in the bibliographies of the books cited).: A. R. Baggeley, John and Halla Beloff, Ake Bjerstadt, Duncan Blewett, John Butcher, M. Choynowski, Richard Coan, Eugene Cogan, Fred Damarin, Karl Delhees, Kern Dickman, Ted Dielman, Samuel S. Dubin, Merle Foster, Cecil Gibb, Dick Gorsuch, Walter Gruen, John Horn, Wolfgang Horn, Edgar Haverland, P. A. Heist, John Hundleby, Akira Ishikawa, Tor Meeland, Gerald M. Meredith, John Nesselroade, Kurt Pawlik, Richard Peterson, John Radcliffe, Karl Rickels, David Saunders, Ivan Scheier, Klaus Schneewind, Jim Schuerger, Peter Schunemann, A. P. Sealey, Laura Specht, Glen Stice, Arthur Sweney, Donald Tollefson, Ben Tsujioka, Karl Uberla, Frank Warburton, Joseph Williams, Alvin Winder.

Reference Guidance

Rather than providing an unstructured listing of references, we have attempted to guide the reader into what is an enormously complicated area, e.g., Cattell's references span forty years and include more than twenty books, twenty-five chapters in books, and over 200 references in journal articles. The reader is advised to begin by reading Cattell, R. B., *Scientific Analysis of Personality* (Pelican, 1965). There are also three tapes by Professor Cattell (McGraw-Hill, 1962) which can be used by teachers to illustrate this text: (1) Theory and method in personality research, (2) Measuring personality by structurally defined factors, (3) The dynamic calculus of personality. After this, there are certain key sections of books, e.g.:

CATTELL, R. B. *Personality and motivation theory and measurement.* New York: World Books, 1957, chaps. 1–7.

CATTELL, R. B., and SCHEIER, I. H. *The meaning and measurement of neuroticism and anxiety.* New York: Ronald Press, 1961, chaps. 4–5.

CATTELL, R. B., and BUTCHER, H. J. *The prediction of achievement and creativity.* New York: Bobbs-Merrill, 1968, chaps. 9, 10, 13.

The following are key references covering particular topics:

GENETIC COMPONENTS OF TRAITS

(a) CATTELL, R. B., BLEWETT, D. B., and BELOFF, J. R. The inheritance of personality. *American Journal of Human Genetics,* 1955, 7, 122–46.

SECOND ORDERS

(b) CATTELL, R. B. Higher order factor structures and reticular *vs.* hierarchical formulae for their interpretation. *In* C. Banks and P. L. Broadhurst (eds.), *Studies in psychology in honor of Sir Cyril Burt.* London: University of London Press, 1965.

ILLUSTRATIVE FACTOR ANALYTIC MODELS

(c) CATTELL, R. B., and SULLIVAN, W. The scientific nature of factors: A demonstration by cups of coffee. *Behavioral Science,* 1962, 7, 184–93.

Skinner, N. F., and Howarth, E. Cross-media independence of questionnaire and objective-test personality factors. *Multivariate Behavioral Research,* 1972 (in press).

Howarth, E. A factor analysis of selected markers for objective personality factors. *Multivariate Behavioral Research,* 1973 (in press).

Howarth, E. and Browne, J. A. Investigation of personality factors in a Canadian context I. Marks structure in personality questionnaire items. *Canadian Journal of Behavioral Science,* 1971, *3,* 161–73.

Howarth, E., and Browne, J. A. Investigation of personality factors in a Canadian context. II. Standards of decision regarding personality factors in questionnaires. *Canadian Journal of Behavioral Science,* 1972 (in press).

[13] *Objective Personality and Motivation Tests.*

DYNAMIC MEASUREMENTS

(d) CATTELL, R. B., and HORN, J. L. An integrating study of the factor structure of adult attitude interests. *Genetic Psychology Monographs*, 1963, *67*, 89–149.

STUDIES OF BROAD GENERAL IMPLICATION

(e) CATTELL, R. B., and NESSELROADE, J. R. Likeness and completeness theories examined by sixteen personality factor measures on stably and unstably married couples. *Journal of Personality and Social Psychology*, 1967, *7*, 351–61.

P-TECHNIQUE (STATE MEASUREMENT)

(f) CATTELL, R. B., CATTELL, A. K. S., and RHYMER, R. M. P-technique demonstrated in determining psycho-physiological source traits in a normal individual. *Psychometrika*, 1947, *12*, 267–88.

FACTOR HYPOTHESIS GENERATION

(g) CATTELL, R. B., and HOWARTH, E. Hypotheses on the principal personality dimensions in children and tests constructed for them. *Journal of Genetic Psychology*, 1962, *101*, 145–63.

SAMPLE R-TECHNIQUE STUDY

(h) CATTELL, R. B., and HOWARTH, E. Verification of objective test personality factor patterns in middle childhood. *Journal of Genetic Psychology*, 1964, *104*, 331–49.

COMPARISON OF CATTELL AND EYSENCK

(i) HOWARTH, E. A source of independent verification: convergencies and divergencies in the work of Cattell and Eysenck. *In* R. M. Dreger (ed.), *Multivariate personality research*. Baton Rouge, La.: Claitor, 1972.

CLINICAL APPLICATIONS

(j) CATTELL, R. B., and TATRO, D. F. The personality factors, objectively measured, which distinguish psychotics from normals. *Behavior Research and Therapy*, 1966, *4*, 39–51.

The following test handbooks should be consulted for relevant validation studies:

(k) Handbook for the Culture Fair Intelligence Test Scale 3, Forms A and B (prepared by Cattell, R. B., and Cattell, A.K.S.) IPAT, 1959.
(l) Handbook for the Motivational Analysis Test ("MAT") (prepared by Cattell, R.B., Horn, J.L., Sweney, A.B., and Radcliffe, J.A.) IPAT, 1964.
(m) Handbook for the Music Preference Test (prepared by Cattell, R.B., and Eber, H.W.) IPAT, 1954.
(n) Handbook for the Anxiety Scale Questionnaire (prepared by Cattell, R. B., and Scheier, I.H.) IPAT, 1963.
(o) Handbook for the Contact Personality Questionnaire (prepared by Cattell, R. B., King, J. E., and Schuettler, A.K.) IPAT, 1954.
(p) Handbook for the 16 P.F. (prepared by Cattell, R. B., and Associates), IPAT, 1968.
(q) Handbook for the O-A battery (prepared by Cattell, R.B., and Associates), IPAT, 1955, 1964.
(r) Handbook for the High School Personality Questionnaire (H.S.P.Q.) (prepared by Cattell and Associates), IPAT, 1956.
(s) Manual for the 16 PF IPAT, 1971.

The humanistic approach is relatively new and less well formulated than many other theories of personality. Like all of humanistic psychology, it has come to the fore only in the 1960s. Before defining and examining the humanistic approach in detail, let us consider briefly the major viewpoints which have paved the way for its emergence as a thesis of personality.

The social and cultural orientation has been taken up in an earlier chapter of this book. Of the various personality theorists in this group, probably Erich Fromm comes closest to a humanistic interpretation. The breadth of his social emphasis is shown in *Escape from Freedom*. (15) In later books he has espoused a "sane society" which would be more suited to man's human condition and not frustrating to his basic social needs. (16) Such a society, Fromm suggests, might be called "humanistic communitarian socialism." It is a society

in which man relates to man lovingly, in which he is rooted in bonds of brotherliness and solidarity, rather than in the ties of blood and soil; a society which gives him the possibility of transcending nature by creating rather than destroying, in which everyone gains a sense of self by experiencing himself as the subject of his powers rather than by conformity, in which a system of orientation and devotion exists without man's needing to distort reality. . . (17, p. 314)

Fromm also spoke of man's urge for transcendence, his need to rise above his animal nature. He wrote *The Art of Loving* in order to show "that love is not a sentiment that can be easily indulged in by anyone, regardlesss of the level of maturity reached by him." (17) He sought to convince the reader "that all his attempts for love are bound to fail, unless he tries most actively to develop his total personality, so as to achieve a productive orientation." (17, p. vii)

The pioneering of Freud and his early collaborators in dynamic psychology was marked by breadth as well as depth. Freud not only plumbed the unconscious but drew upon man's history and institutional life—all at a time long before much had been done which could be called anthropological or so-

S. Stansfeld Sargent

The Humanistic Approach to Personality

40

ciological research. His grasp of history, art, literature, and religion was remarkable; his contributions to the humanities (e.g., Leonardo, Moses) are classic. His work in social psychology has been considered to cover five areas: socialization of the individual, family structure and dynamics, group psychology, the origin of society, and the nature of human culture. (19, p. 165)

Jung was even broader than Freud; he was both one of the most mystical and one of the most experimental psychologists of personality. He delved into history, mythology, classics, archaeology, anthropology, and religion. His spiritual aspirations are expressed in *Modern Man in Search of a Soul*, which is in large part a protest against what he considered to be negative and oversexualized trends in Freudian theory. (26)

Less historically and philosophically oriented than Freud or Jung, Alfred Adler showed great awareness of social and economic conditions—so much so that Murphy called Adler's system the first that developed in a social science direction. (37, p. 341) Furthermore, he stressed man's primarily social motivation, notably his social interest and style of life in relation to others. Another focus of Adler's "individual psychology" is phenomenological, with its emphasis on self and consciousness. His predominantly humanistic trend has been characterized as follows:

By endowing man with altruism, humanitarianism, co-operation, creativity, uniqueness, and awareness, he restored to man a sense of dignity and worth that psychoanalysis had pretty largely destroyed...Adler offered a portrait of man which was more satisfying, more hopeful, and far more complimentary to man. (20, p. 125)

Another forerunner of the humanistic approach to personality is the existential philosophy and the psychotherapy which developed from it. Deriving from the ideas of Kierkegaard and Nietzsche, as expressed by Heidegger and Binswanger, existentialism differed sharply from logical positivism and behaviorism in its stress on the significance of values and meanings in personality. "Existentialism," says Rollo May, "is the endeavor to understand man by cutting below the cleavage between subject and object which has bedeviled Western thought and science since shortly after the Renaissance." (33, p. 11) Both existentialism and Eastern philosophies like Zen Buddhism are concerned with ontology, the study of being. They hold that Western man's absorption in gaining power over nature results in the estrangement of man from nature and even from himself. May continues:

Existentialism is immersed in and arises directly out of Western man's anxiety, estrangement and conflicts. . . Like psychoanalysis, existentialism seeks not to bring in answers from other cultures but to utilize these very conflicts in contemporary personality as avenues to the more profound self-understanding of Western man and to find solutions to our problems in direct relation to the historical and cultural crises which gave the problems birth. (33, p. 19)

Rollo May and Victor Frankl are two existential psychotherapists whose theories contribute to the humanistic psychology of personality. According to May, part of the problem of Western man comes from resistance, avoidance, and repression of concern with "being," to the extent that he may even lose the sense of being, a situation which is related to collectivist and conformist trends in our culture. He sees part of the solution in "intentionality," a factor in all psychotherapy and also at the heart of consciousness and key to the problem of wish and will. "It is in intentionality and will that the human being experiences his identity." (32, p. 209) Victor Frankl speaks of the "existential neurosis" deriving from a person's inability to find meaning in life. The goal of his "logotherapy" is to help the individual achieve a more authentic system of values, and to become aware of his responsibilities and his need to make choices. (13) Another idea of Frankl's is that human existence is characterized by man's capacity for self-detachment and self-transcendence. The latter is especially important since self-actualization "if made an end in itself, contradicts the self-transcending quality of human existence." (14, p. 99)

The Gestalt psychologist, Kurt Lewin, developed his "field theory" and applied it in the areas of personality and social psychology. He emphasized the pattern of present influences acting upon a person at a given time, as perceived or interpreted by the individual. He drew diagrams of the "life space" of the individual, with symbols to represent all the significant regions, forces, and barriers present—i.e., the persons and events which might influence the behavior of the person. (27) Among the concepts of special interest to humanists are goal seeking, and the "valence" of a region, which is very close to the concept of value. Furthermore, the "level of aspiration" concept, developed by Lewin and his students, has become very important in clinical and counseling psychology as well as in personality theory.

The following comments by Hall and Lindzey not only furnish an excellent summary of Lewin's contribution to the psychology of personality, but also suggest its significance for humanistic psychology:

Lewin's theory was one of those that helped to revive the conception of man as a complex energy field, motivated by psychological forces, and behaving selectively and creatively. The hollow man was replenished with psychological needs, intentions, hopes, and aspirations. The robot was transformed into a living human being. The crass and dreary materialism of behaviorism was replaced by a more humanistic picture of man. While "objective" psychology tailored many of its empirical propositions to be tested on dogs, cats, and rats, Lewin's theory led to research on human behavior as expressed in more or less natural settings. Children at play, adolescents in group activities, housewives planning meals, these were some of the natural life situations in which hypotheses derived from Lewin's field theory were empirically tested. With such vital research being done under the persuasive aegis of field theory, it is not surprising that Lewin's viewpoint became widely popular. . . (20, pp. 253–54)

At this point the reader may be asking: "Can't we spell out more specifically the features of a thoroughly humanistic approach to personality? And let's hear from some of the more contemporary writers in the field." Let us start by quoting a statement made by the American Association for Humanistic Psychology at the time the organization was founded, in 1962:*

Humanistic psychology may be defined as the third main branch of the general field of psychology (the two already in

---

* Its name was changed in 1969 to the Association for Humanistic Psychology.

existence being the psychoanalytic and the behaviorist) and as such, is primarily concerned with those human capacities and potentialities that have little or no systematic place, either in positivist or behaviorist theory or in classical psychoanalytic theory: e.g., love, creativity, self, growth, organism, basic need-gratification, self-actualization, higher values, being, becoming, spontaneity, play, humor, affection, naturalness, warmth, ego-transcendence, objectivity, autonomy, responsibility, meaning, fair-play, transcendental experience, psychological health, and related concepts. This approach can also be characterized by the writing of Allport, Angyal, Asch, Bühler, Fromm, Goldstein, Horney, Maslow, May, Moustakas, Rogers, Wertheimer, etc., as well as by certain aspects of the writings of Jung, Adler, and the psychoanalytic ego-psychologists, existential and phenomenological psychologists. (48)

Bugental, first president of the American Association for Humanistic Psychology, lists five basic postulates for humanistic psychology:

Man, as man, supersedes the sum of his parts. He must be recognized as something other than an additive product of various part functions.

Man has his being in a human context. The unique nature of man is expressed through his always being in relationship with his fellows.

Man is aware. All aspects of his experience are not equally available to man, but awareness is an essential part of man's being.

Man has choice. When man is aware, he is aware that his choices make a difference, that he is not a bystander but a participant in experience.

Man is intentional. Man intends through having purpose, through valuing, and through creating and recognizing meaning. Man's intentionality is the basis on which he builds his identity, and it distinguishes him from other species. (6, pp. 23–24)

Bugental goes on to specify some of the characteristics of the humanistic orientation in psychology. Humanistic psychology cares about man, values meaning more than procedure, looks for human rather than nonhuman validations, and accepts the relativism of all knowledge. It relies heavily upon the phenomenological orientation, and it does not deny the contributions of other views, but tries to supplement them and give them a setting within a broader conception of the human experience. (6, pp. 24–25)

Focusing more upon the approach to personality and social psychology, Sargent suggests the following important humanistic criteria:

Breadth and inclusiveness. To what extent does the viewpoint under consideration encompass man in relation to his world, his philosophy of life, his past and future, his present cultural frame of reference?

Social orientation and sensitivity. How clearly spelled out is man's relation to his fellow men and his interaction with them? Are people regarded as ends rather than as means?

Focus on the experiencing person. Does the theory have regard for subjective reactions, particularly feelings? This would include concepts like the self-image, self-esteem, and the unity or integrity of the personality.

Concern with higher human qualities. These are often neglected through involvement with problems of adjustment. Such qualities would include love, creativity, spontaneity, autonomy, sympathy, empathy, openness to stimuli, transcendence, and the like.

Consideration of values, goals, and purposes. Is man regarded as "proactive" or future-seeking, rather than as merely "reactive"? Is he thought to be capable of self-actualization?

Methodology. Is the theory or research problem-oriented rather than technique-oriented? Is the method well-adapted to the problem or task? (44)

Let us turn now to contemporary contributors to the humanistic psychology of personality. We shall describe and discuss only the relevant aspects of their work. Gardner Murphy's contribution is called the "biosocial theory of personality" because it was designed to integrate the biological, psychological, and social approaches. (36) He sought to study the whole man, as a biological creature, as a psychological organism, and as a personality enmeshed in an environment which is significantly social. Murphy's background fitted him well for the task, since he has contributed to general and experimental psychology, historical, social, educational, and para-psychology as well as the psychology of personality. His is a field theory, but broader and more eclectic than Lewin's. He traced the development of personality from physiological dispositions through early "canalizations" and conditioned responses to the habits, concepts, and attitudes and values which are the components of adult personality. The scope of his approach is aptly described by Hall and Lindzey:

Since Murphy's view of motivation holds that there is an almost infinite number of needs and tensions, limited only by the number of tissues and the permutations and combinations of tensions arising from these tissues, the number of canalizations that a person is capable of forming during his lifetime is virtually limitless. Perhaps no other theory of personality has given a more satisfactory explanation for the versatility of man than has Murphy's. . . (20, p. 515)

In 1958 Murphy extended his views of personality in his *Human Potentialities,* where he spoke of three kinds of human nature: (38)

1. A modifiable biological individuality;
2. The mold of culture—i.e., devices transmissible to future generations, but in danger of becoming rigidified;
3. A creative thrust of understanding, an urge toward discovery and intellectual adventure, which is the force in man fighting against tradition and making possible the freeing of his own potentialities.

Thus Murphy calls for freeing intelligence through breaking the mold of custom and culture, as we strive creatively to bring about emergence of new forms of organization. Here is a basis in personality theory for the positive qualities emphasized so strongly by the humanistic psychologists.

A towering figure among theorists of personality is Gordon

W. Allport. (2) Above all he has stressed the uniqueness of the individual, by championing the idiographic method (study of the individual case) as compared to the nomothetic (universal or statistical). He has been very interested in the self or ego as *a* central, if not *the* central, component of personality. He has stressed traits and attitudes and also values, as crucial factors in personality. Following Spranger, he worked out a test of values designed to indicate whether the theoretical, economic, esthetic, social, political, or religious values dominated in a given personality.

One feature of Allportian theory is of particular interest to humanistic psychologists—the theory of functional autonomy. This theory maintains, in a word, that behaviors once acquired in order to serve another purpose become an end in themselves and act as motives. That is, purposive activities come to proceed under their own steam, no matter how they originated. In Allport's words, adult motives are "infinitely varied . . . self-sustaining, *contemporary* systems, growing out of antecedent systems, but functionally independent of them." (2, p. 228) The ex-sailor yearns for the sea, or the businessman "long since secure economically works himself into ill-health, and sometimes even back into poverty, for the sake of carrying on his plans. What was once an instrumental technique becomes a master motive." (2, p. 196)

Perhaps Allport is the most eclectic of personality theorists. His wide philosophical, scholarly, social, and international interests make him strongly interdisciplinary in his approach. It has been said that his stress upon the uniqueness of the individual makes him pessimistic as to the possibility of unraveling the mystery of human behavior. (20, p. 260) Part of this discouragement derives from the current focus upon pathology rather than health and strength and man's higher powers. As he says, many theories

are based largely upon the behavior of sick and anxious people or upon the antics of captive and desperate rats. Fewer theories have derived from the study of healthy human beings, those who strive not so much to preserve life as to make it worth living. Thus we find today studies of criminals, few of law-abiders; many of fear, few of courage; more on hostility than on affiliation; much on the blindness in man, little on his vision; much on his past, little on his outreaching into the future. (1, p. 18)

As we shall see, this view has been stressed even more by Maslow, and has become one of the cardinal emphases of humanistic psychology.

Another noted personality theorist and colleague of Allport at Harvard is Henry A. Murray, known for his treatment of "lives-as-wholes." With a background in medicine, biochemistry, Jungian analysis, philosophy, anthropology, and literature, he explored all aspects of human experience. His organismic and field-theory approach has been called "personology," meaning the full understanding of the individual case, but always in the field, the environmental context. Unlike Lewin, past history is important to Murray, and like the psychoanalysts, unconscious motivation.

Murray's list of approximately twenty basic needs (e.g., abasement, harm-avoidance, succorance) is well-known; his classification of items of "press" (external influences) is also important, as is his elaboration of vectors and values, and of "themas" (the total sequence). All these concepts are illustrated in the construction and interpretation of the Thematic Apperception Test, worked out by Murray and several colleagues in the 1930s. (39) He later placed increasing emphasis on aims or goals which might serve to fulfill several needs. (3, p. 163)

Asked recently in an interview to describe his "personological system," Murray responded as follows:

To oversimplify everything, one might say that waking life from birth to death consists of a long procession of proceedings of different classes, one after another. The two major largest classes are external and internal proceedings: external when you're physically or verbally interacting with the environment in some way, and internal when you're physically and verbally inactive, but involved in your own feelings, dreams, fantasies, ideas, thoughts, or plans for the future. These make up the heart and mind of a person which the behaviorists leave out. (21, p. 62)

Murray and Allport have been lumped together as humanistic psychologists because they both seek to encompass the entire personality, to see man as proactive, psychologically unique, future-oriented, and concerned with normal rather than pathological people. (28) In his recent interview, Murray noted that he and Allport differed greatly: "He was antipathetic to most of the notions that absorbed me: hedonism, instinctual drives, violent emotions, process, unconscious fantasies, change and creativity, social roles, situational determinants, and so forth." On the other hand, "we were among the very few in academic psychology who were advocating the ideal notion of a personality as a differentiated whole—a real live human being as a going concern. That made us both humanists—rare birds 20 years ago." (21, p. 63)

Kurt Goldstein, a neurologist and psychiatrist, is often called the founder of organismic or holistic psychology, both being closely related to Gestalt. The central theme is that personality is organized, unified, integrated, although differentiation into figure and ground occurs. The only real motive in a person's behavior is self-actualization, which Goldstein considers the fulfilling of one's capacities or potentialities in the best possible way under a given condition. Self-actualization is the theme or trend which regulates the interaction between organism and environment. (18)

A normal, healthy organism is one in which the "tendency toward self-actualization is acting from within, and overcomes the disturbance arising from the clash with the world, not out of anxiety but out of the joy of conquest." (18, p. 305) What seem to be different needs or drives, said Goldstein, are really aspects of the same master motive, self-actualization or self-realization. He believed that people can be helped to discover their potentialities and to overcome environmental threats and the anxiety they may engender, including feelings of failure.

A. H. Maslow's "holistic-dynamic" or "holistic-integrative" theory of personality draws heavily upon Goldstein, Allport, and others. He felt that only an organismic approach could avoid the pitfalls of reductionism and overanalysis, and he objected to the negative and pessimistic conception of man implied by many psychologists. He noted their:

limited conception of the full height to which the human being can attain, their totally inadequate conception of his level of aspiration in life, and their setting of his psychological limits at too low a level. As things stand now in psychology, the science as a whole too often pursues limited or trivial goals with limited methods and techniques and under the guidance of limited vocabulary and concepts.

The science of psychology has been far more successful on the negative than on the positive side; it has revealed to us much about man's shortcomings, his illnesses, his sins, but little about his potentialities, his virtues, his achievable aspirations, or his full psychological height. It is as if psychology had voluntarily restricted itself to only half its rightful jurisdiction, and that the darker, meaner half. . . (29, pp. 353–54)

Maslow made a real contribution to motivational theory by proposing a hierarchy of needs or drives, in order of decreasing priority or potency:

1. Physiological needs
2. Safety needs
3. Belongingness and love
4. Esteem needs
5. Self-actualization

When a person is hungry, thirsty, or in danger, he is taken up with satisfying these needs. But "what happens to man's desires," asks Maslow, "when there *is* plenty of bread and when his belly is chronically filled?"

[At once other (and higher) needs emerge] *and these, rather than physiological hungers, dominate the organism. And when these in turn are satisfied, again new (and still higher) needs emerge, and so on. This is what we mean by saying that the basic human needs are organized into a hierarchy of relative prepotency.* (29, p. 83)

Psychologists and personality theorists, in their studies of animals and neurotics, have been overconcerned with physiological and safety needs, Maslow maintains, so they overlook the role of higher motives in man. Actually, the list of motives is not only a series of increasing need-gratifications, but also a series of increasing degrees of psychological health. It is clear

that, other things being equal, a man who is safe and belongs and is loved will be healthier (by any reasonable definition) than a man who is safe and belongs, but who is rejected and unloved. And if in addition, he wins respect and admiration, and because of this, develops his self-respect, then he is still more healthy. (29, p. 115)

Maslow presented evidence for his views in a study of "self-actualizing people"—i.e., a group of normal, successful, and superior people. Some were famous, like Lincoln, Whitman, Thoreau, Eleanor Roosevelt, Einstein, and Schweitzer; others were chosen from among Maslow's own friends and acquaintances. The criterion was that they were judged to have realized their potentialities. The question was: in what ways did they differ from ordinary persons? Briefly, he found that the self-actualizing people showed superior perception of reality; greater acceptance of self, others, and nature; increased spontaneity; stronger focus on problems outside themselves; greater detachment and need for privacy; more autonomy and independence of culture and environment. He also discovered in the self-

actualizers greater freshness of appreciation and richness of feeling, more frequent mystic or transcendent experience, presence of *Gemeinschaftsgefühl* (a term used by Alfred Adler to describe a deep feeling of identification with mankind), more profound interpersonal relations, more democratic character structure, less confusion of means with ends, a philosophical and whimsical rather than a hostile sense of humor, greater creativeness, and resistance to cultural conformity. (29)

More recently Maslow has elaborated his theories contrasting deficiency and growth motivation, or "metamotivation," which is best shown in self-actualizing people. He investigated also the "cognition of Being" he finds in their creative activities and "peak experiences"—those moments of the highest happiness and fulfillment which are almost mystical in quality. (30)

Neurosis is considered by Maslow a failure of personal growth, an interference with the process of self-actualization. He dislikes the terms "therapy," "psychotherapy," and "patient" in connection with counseling. This is part of the medical model, and it suggests that "the person who comes to the counselor is a sick person, beset by disease and illness, seeking a cure." The psychologist or counselor should rather "help his particular client to unfold, to break through the defenses against his own self-knowledge, to recover himself, and to get to know himself." (31, p. 285.) Throughout, Maslow rejects as inadequate the concept of health as *adjustment* to reality or to environment. We must go beyond this, he insists, "to the clear recognition of transcendence of the environment, independence of it, ability to stand against it, to fight it, to neglect it, or to turn one's back on it. . . For a theory of mental health, extra-psychic success is not enough; we must also include intra-psychic health." (31, p. 169)

Another growth-oriented humanistic psychologist is Anthony J. Sutich. As early as 1949, he defined a growth experience as "the direct achievement of a significantly improved level or quality of integrating action and reaction tendencies in the emotional, attitudinal, and other related aspects of an individual's general interpersonal behavior." A growth experience is also "a significant step forward in the process of attaining emotional liberation." Sutich assumed that there is both a need and a capacity for continuous emotional growth in every individual, though individuals vary in their level of emotional development at any given time. (47, pp. 156–57) He reported that when he adopted a growth-centered approach with his clients "a de-emphasis on therapy tends to occur and is replaced by a fuller awareness of and interest in the achievement of higher levels of personality and character growth." (47, p. 161).

Sutich saw clearly that psychiatrists and clinical psychologists are therapy-oriented and would need reeducation to become growth oriented—a point which has been coming to the fore some fifteen to twenty years later, largely in connection with criticisms of the "medical model." After founding and editing the *Journal of Humanistic Psychology* for eight years, Sutich has turned to spearhead "a fourth force in psychology—Transpersonal Psychology," which is to supplement humanistic psychology. Transpersonal psychology is the title given to an emerging force in the psychology field by a group of psychologists and professional men and women from other fields who are interested in those *ultimate* human capacities and potentialities which have been somewhat neglected—e.g., becoming, metaneeds, ultimate values, peak experiences, ecstasy, mystical experience, awe, bliss, wonder, transcendence of the self, cosmic awareness and many other concepts, experiences and activities. (49, pp. 77–78)

Though Carl Rogers is primarily a psychotherapist, he presented in 1947 a theory of personality. (40) This has come to be called his "self-theory" or "self-centered theory," and is of course related to his client-centered therapy. It has been suggested that Rogers's main theme is the self as an experiencing mechanism, with the three subsidiary themes of self-actualization, self-maintenance, and self-enhancement. (3. p. 428)

Drawing on phenomenological, organismic, interpersonal, and already existing self theory, Rogers stated and elaborated almost two dozen propositions about personality. (40), (43) Each individual is at the center of a continually changing world of experience; he reacts to his perceptual field as reality, and as an organized whole, as he seeks to actualize, maintain, and enhance himself. "Behavior is basically the goal-directed attempt of the organism to satisfy its needs as experienced, in the field as perceived." A self-structure is formed, "particularly as a result of evaluational interaction with others," and values develop— from the self and from experiences. "Most of the ways of behaving which are adopted by the organism are those which are consistent with the concept of self."

Psychological tension exists, says Rogers, when the organism denies to awareness significant experiences which are then not symbolized and organized into the self-structure; experience inconsistent with the self may be perceived as threat, "and the more of these perceptions there are, the more rigidly the self-structure is organized to maintain itself." On the other hand, adjustment exists when experiences of the organism are assimilated "into a consistent relationship with the concept of self," and the individual is more understanding and accepting of others. Rogers later added that the above may be overruled by socially generated desires for social esteem and self-esteem, out of which may develop an attitude of self-worthiness.

Rogers's three themes of self-actualization (to become oneself), self-maintenance (to keep on being oneself), and self-enhancement (to transcend the status quo), are important both in personality development and in psychotherapy. Rogers has spelled out in detail the nature of the interpersonal relations underlying successful therapy: the therapist must be genuinely himself, must freely accept the client, must be sensitively and empathically aware of the client's experiences, and must be able to communicate to the client that he understands his feelings and experiences. (42, pp. 95ff, also 41)

Charlotte Bühler, well-known for her work in child and developmental psychology, has become an outstanding contributor to humanistic psychology. The central subject of humanistic psychology, she states, is the study of human life as a whole. She sees the self as a core system within which certain basic tendencies are integrated: need-satisfaction, self-limiting adaptation, creative expansion, and upholding the internal order. "This core system's thrust into life is that *intentionality* with which the individual strives toward a hoped-for *fulfillment*. In the ideal case this is identical with the realization of the individual's best potentials." (10. p, 87)

Bühler has been particularly interested in the role of goals and values in personality theory, and has studied the values found in normal and neurotic development. She has also explored the significance of values in psychotherapy, including the interoperation of their differing value systems as the therapist helps the patient to achieve new or modified values. (9) She concludes:

"A valid impact of the therapist's personality and value orientation will not be expected before the patient is free enough to see himself and his therapist realistically and to make choices of directions for himself." (10, p. 90)

James F. T. Bugental has been one of the most active and articulate leaders in humanistic psychology; he was first president of the American Association for Humanistic Psychology, and he edited the comprehensive *Challenges of Humanistic Psychology*. (8) In his writing he has insisted on the primacy of the subjective, both in theory and practice. He sees the task of humanistic psychology as broader than a theory of personality. Humanistic psychology, he says

has as its ultimate goal the preparation of a complete description of what it means to be alive as a human being. This is, of course, not a goal which is likely ever to be fully attained; yet it is important to recognize the nature of the task. Such a complete description would necessarily include an inventory of man's native endowment; his potentialities of feeling, thought, and action; his growth, evolution, and decline; his interaction with various environing conditions. . . ; the range and variety of experience possible to him; and his meaningful place in the universe. (8, p. 7)

Authenticity, says Bugental, means "a way of being in the world in which one's being is in harmony with the being of the world itself." He believes that authenticity amounts to the resolution of the subject–object split, the self-world dichotomy. In his book, *The Search for Authenticity*, which he calls an "existential-analytic approach to psychotherapy," Bugental proposes using the term "ontogogy" instead of "therapy." By ontogogy he means "a creative effort to help a person toward greater realization of life's potential." Ontogogy is set in contrast to the reparative perspective implicit in the term "psychotherapy." (7)

Sidney M. Jourard stresses the importance of self-disclosure or openness in healthy personality development and in preventing misunderstanding and sickness. He deflates such poses as role-playing and the "bedside manner," and invites the reader to be an "authentic" being—particularly if he is a psychologist! (22) Jourard reports studies showing that the usual "impersonal" experimenter–subject relationship is mystifying and manipulative and fails because it is not a genuine encounter. He has written an imaginary letter from Subject to Experimenter showing how students feel who have been frequent subjects in experiments; an excerpt is the following:

I wonder who you are, what you are really up to. I wonder what you are going to do with the "behavior" I give you. Who are you going to show my answers to? Who is going to see the marks I leave on your response-recorders? Do you have any interest at all in what I think, feel, and imagine as I make the marks you are so eager to study and analyze? Certainly, you never ask me what I mean by them. If you asked, I'd be glad to tell you. . . (24, p. 10)

Jourard and his students have turned their efforts to studying the person authentically, as a "collaborator in our enterprise." Preliminary findings suggest that experimental validity is increased. (23)

Hubert Bonner has been primarily concerned with intentionality and "proaction." Proactive psychology, he says, contrasts sharply with both psychoanalysis and behaviorism, which present us with one-sided views of man. "One described man as a blind victim of his past, the other, as a driven creature of habits." (4, p. 6) He later quotes Allport in the same vein: "People, it seems are busy leading their lives into the future, whereas psychology, for the most part, is busy tracing them into the past." (4, p. 37)

Bonner's proactive man reminds one of Maslow's self-actualizing people. The proactive person, he concludes,

like every healthy and creative individual, resists engulfment by custom and rigid habits, the impairing force of narrow enculturation, and all barriers to a free and active forward movement of his personality. He has both the will and the capacity to resist external pressures toward conformity and to transform himself in the light of his personal goals and values. He is that individual who strives to attain a more free and creative state for himself and his fellow human beings. He exemplifies in his style of living the belief that the future of man is largely of his own making. He validates the view that man is possessed of a creative selfhood.

In fine, proactive man is that being who more than any other human being strives to make of himself a work of art. (5, pp. 65–66)

Clark Moustakas has dealt with major problems in self-psychology, notably the effects of loneliness on behavior. He makes a distinction betweeen "existential loneliness," an inevitable part of human experience, and "the loneliness of self-alienation and self-rejection," which is a vague and disturbing anxiety. The first can be a source of creative activity and deepened sensitivity. (34) Moustakas also explored the nature of his study of loneliness in order to clarify research philosophy and perspective. His findings help to point up the contrast between humanistic and more orthodox research methods. For example:

My way of studying loneliness, in its essential form, was to put myself into an open, ready state, into the lonely experiences of hospitalized children, and to let these experiences become the focus of my world. I listened. I watched. I stood by. In dialogue with the child, I tried to put into words the deep regions of his experience. Sometimes my words touched the child in the interior of his feelings, and he began to weep; sometimes the child formed words in response to my presence, and thus he began to break through his numbness and the dehumanizing impact of the hospital atmosphere and practice. At this point, loneliness became my existence. It entered into every facet of my world—into my teaching, my interviews in therapy, my conversations with friends, my home life. Without reference to time or place or structure, somehow (more intentionally than accidentally) the theme came up. I was clearly aware that exhaustively and fully, and in careful manner, I was searching for, studying, and inquiring into the nature and impact of loneliness. I was totally involved and immersed in this search for a pattern and meaning which would reveal the various dimensions of loneliness in modern life. This was research in the sense of a close searching and inquiring into the nature of a reality of human experience. (35, pp. 103–4)

Franklin J. Shaw, an earthy and practical humanistic psychologist, makes this observation:

Man's emancipation from his animal heritage has been purchased at the price of ease of acting. In exchange, man has gained potentialities for becoming that are beyond the reach of his infrahuman fellows. Infrahuman conflict over following or opposing the herd is more easily resolved in straightforward action than human ambivalence over conformity versus nonconformity. Man, though, can become something other than a simple creature of conformity or rebellion through reconciling the opposition between them by means of a concept of responsibility, one which allows for both possibilities. (46, p. 66)

However, adds Shaw, one has to go through the experience of reconciling the contradictions himself. He evolved a theory of reconciliation as an integrating concept for psychology—that "organisms seek dilemmas as persistently as they seek release from overwhelming 'challenge.'" This he finds basic to psychological growth and self-actualization. (25)

Herbert Fingarette notes three contrasting concepts of self-transformation in contemporary psychotherapeutic theory: (1) the (Freudian) notion of *self-discovery*, (2) the (existentialist) notion of *self-creation*, and (3) the (Aristotelian) notion of *self-realization*. (11, p. 75) After discussing the three approaches, he concludes:

It is well for us to explore intensively each of these aspects of the therapeutic experience, and it is natural and effective to use the language which fits that aspect best. Need we suppose that one perspective is the *most correct or profound? There are an indefinite number of ways of talking about the same event; the important question is: which ones are profitable or illuminating, and under what sorts of circumstances and for what investigative purposes are they so? All this cannot be decided a priori. . . We need to devise maps showing how each road leads in a genuinely different and interesting direction, though perhaps all happen to intersect at certain places, one of these places being in the region of dynamic insight in psychotherapy. (11, p. 89)*

Fingarette has been very interested in exploring self-transformation from the standpoint of both Western and Eastern thought. For example, he finds parallels between the *karmic* doctrine of reincarnation and psychoanalysis, both of which are concerned with the "community of selves." (12)

Another apostle of rapprochement between Eastern and Western concepts of man is Alan Watts, perhaps the best-known American student of Zen. He has summed up the "Oriental and Occidental approaches to the nature of man" as follows:

there are two views of man which are not contradictory, but which should stand to each other in a hierarchical order. (1) The Eastern view of man as a node in a unified field of behavior, because, after all, this so-called mystical experience is nothing other than a direct sensation of man-and-the-universe as a single pattern of behavior. That's all it is. You don't need to invoke any spooky business whatsoever. (2) The Western view, which stresses the special value of each organism and its unique character.

These two views of man go together in a hierarchical pattern. They are not mutually exclusive. I have sometimes said that it is characteristic of maturity to be able to distinguish what is more important from what is less important, without making what is less important unimportant. I feel that it is quite basic that we need a conception of man coupled with a sensation of man as really belonging in his natural and cosmic environment. (50, p. 109)

In this paper we have taken up the theories and findings on personality of leading humanistic psychologists. On the basis of this survey, is it possible—and reasonable—to say there is a "humanistic approach to personality"? Certainly all the humanistic psychologists do not agree in their conceptualizations, theories, research methods, and conclusions. (Note, for example, the variety of views expressed in Frank Severin's *Humanistic Viewpoints in Psychology* (45) or Bugental's *Challenges of Humanistic Psychology* [8].) Nonetheless many believe there are enough features in common to justify our speaking of a humanistic approach. Its main features appear to be as follows:

A focus upon the whole person, in all his relationships and involvements, internal and external, including the existential, spiritual, and mystical;

An intense caring for people; persons are regarded as ends in themselves and not merely as means to a scientific, political, religious, or other end.

A phenomenological emphasis; the subjective aspect is crucial— i.e., man as he sees, feels, interprets, and is aware of himself and his world;

Similarly, values and meanings are of central significance as experiential data;

Intentionality, purpose, and choice are of primary concern; man is "proactive" as well as "reactive";

Emphasis on the positive: personality study should not be so largely involved with pathology, or even with "adjustment," but increasingly with self-actualization and the cultivation of higher human qualities;

A growing interest in transcendence and the transpersonal rather than being limited to the immediate, the given, the here-and-now;

Less concern with causative factors in personality, involving the past, than with Being (present) and Becoming (future);

Flexibility as to research methods and techniques, but with emphasis on the study of whole personalities of normal or outstanding people, rather than part processes of sick people or of animals. Increasing criticism of the limited, deceptive, or exploitive trends found in many laboratory psychological experiments.

Humanistic psychologists are a relatively new, young, and enthusiastic group; we may confidently expect from them a continuing, broadening, and augmented contribution to the psychology of personality.

References

1 ALLPORT, G. W. *Becoming.* New Haven, Conn.: Yale University Press, 1955.

2 ———, *Pattern and growth in personality.* New York: Holt, Rinehart & Winston, 1961.

3 BISCHOF, L. J. *Interpreting personality theories.* New York: Harper & Row, 1964. 2nd ed., 1970.

4 BONNER, H. *On being mindful of man.* Boston: Houghton Mifflin, 1965.

5 ———, The proactive personality. *In* J. F. T. Bugental (ed.), *Challenges of humanistic psychology.* New York: McGraw-Hill, 1967.

6 BUGENTAL, J. F. T. The third force in psychology. *Journal of Humanistic Psychology,* 1964, *4*, 19–26.

7 ———, *The search for authenticity.* New York: Holt, Rinehart & Winston, 1965.

8 ———, ed. *Challenges of humanistic psychology.* New York: McGraw-Hill, 1967.

9 BÜHLER, C. *Values in psychotherapy.* New York: Free Press, 1962.

10 ———, Human life as a whole as a central subject of humanistic psychology. *In* J. F. T. Bugental (ed.), *Challenges of humanistic psychology.* New York: McGraw-Hill, 1967.

11 FINGARETTE, H. A fresh perspective on a familiar landscape. *Journal of Humanistic Psychology,* 1962, *2*, 75–89.

12 ———, *The self in transformation.* New York: Basic Books, 1963.

13 FRANKL, V. *The doctor and the soul.* New York: Knopf, 1957.

14 ———, Self-transcendence as a human phenomenon. *Journal of Humanistic Psychology,* 1966, *6*, 97–106.

15 FROMM, E. *Escape from freedom.* New York: Holt, Rinehart & Winston, 1941.

16 ———, *The sane society.* New York: Holt, Rinehart & Winston, 1955.

17 ———, *The art of loving.* New York: Harper & Row, 1956.

18 GOLDSTEIN, K. *The organism.* New York: American Book, 1939.

19 HALL, C. S., and LINDZEY, G. Psychoanalytic theory and its applications to the social sciences. *In* G. Lindzey (ed.), *Handbook of social psychology.* Reading, Mass.: Addison-Wesley, 1954.

20 ———, *Theories of personality.* New York: John Wiley, 1957. 2nd ed., 1970.

21 HALL, M. H. The psychology of personality—a conversation with Henry A. Murray, *Psychology Today,* 1968, *2*, (4), 56–63.

22 JOURARD, S. M. *The transparent self.* New York: Van Nostrand Reinhold, 1964.

23 ———, Experimenter–subject dialogue: a paradigm for a humanistic science of psychology. *In* J. F. T. Bugental (ed.), *Challenges of humanistic psychology.* New York: McGraw-Hill, 1967.

24 ———, *Disclosing man to himself.* New York: Van Nostrand Reinhold, 1968.

25 ———, and OVERLADE, D. C. (eds.) *Reconciliation: a theory of man transcending.* New York: Van Nostrand Reinhold, 1966.

26 JUNG, C. G. *Modern man in search of a soul.* New York: Harcourt Brace Jovanovich, 1933.

27 LEWIN, K. *Dynamic theory of personality.* New York: McGraw-Hill, 1935.

28 MADDI, S. R. Humanistic psychology: Allport and Murray. *In* J. M. Wepman and R. W. Heine (eds.), *Concepts of personality.* Chicago: Aldine, 1963.

29 MASLOW, A. H. *Motivation and personality.* New York: Harper & Row, 1954.

30 ———, *Toward a psychology of being.* New York: Van Nostrand Reinhold, 1962. 2nd ed., 1968.

31 ———, Self-actualization and beyond. *In* J. F. T. Bugental (ed.), *Challenges of humanistic psychology.* New York: McGraw-Hill, 1967.

32 MAY, R. Intentionality, the heart of human will. *Journal of Humanistic Psychology,* 1965, *5*, 202–9.

33 ———, ENGEL, E., and ELLENBERGER, H. F. (eds.) *Existence—a new dimension in psychiatry and psychology.* New York: Basic Books, 1958.

34 MOUSTAKAS, C. *Loneliness.* Englewood Cliffs, N.J.: Prentice-Hall, 1961.

35 ———, Heuristic research. *In* J. F. T. Bugental (ed.), *Challenges of humanistic psychology.* New York: McGraw-Hill, 1967.

36 MURPHY, G. *Personality: a biosocial approach to origins and structure.* New York: Harper & Row, 1947.

37 ———, *Historical introduction to modern psychology.* New York: Harcourt Brace Jovanovich, 1949.

38 ———, *Human potentialities.* New York: Basic Books, 1958.

39 MURRAY, H. A. *Explorations in personality.* New York: Oxford University Press, 1938.

40 ROGERS, C. R. Some observations on the organization of personality. *American Psychologist,* 1947, *2*, 358–68.

41 ———, *Client-centered therapy.* Boston: Houghton Mifflin, 1951.

42 ———, The necessary and sufficient conditions of therapeutic personality change. *Journal of Consulting Psychology,* 1957, *21*, 95–103.

43 ———, A theory of therapy, personality, and interpersonal relationships as developed in a client-centered framework, *In* S. Koch (ed.), *Psychology: a study of a science,* vol. 3. New York: McGraw-Hill, 1959.

44 SARGENT, S. S. Humanistic methodology in personality and social psychology. *In* J. F. T. Bugental (ed.), *Challenges of humanistic psychology*. New York: McGraw-Hill, 1967.

45 SEVERIN, F. T. (ed.) *Humanistic viewpoints in psychology*. New York: McGraw-Hill, 1965.

46 SHAW, F. J. The problem of acting and the problem of becoming. *Journal of Humanistic Psychology*, 1961, *1*, 64–69.

47 SUTICH, A. J. The growth experience and the growth-centered attitude. *Journal of Psychology*, 1949, *28*, 293–301. (Reprinted in *Journal of Humanistic Psychology*, 1967, 7, 155–62.)

48 ———, American Association for Humanistic Psychology: Progress Report, 1962 (mineo). (Reprinted in part in *Journal of Humanistic Psychology*, 1964, *4*, 22.)

49 ———, Transpersonal psychology. *Journal of Humanistic Psychology*, 1968, *8*, 77–78.

50 WATTS, A. W. Oriental and occidental approaches to the nature of man. *Journal of Humanistic Psychology*, 1962, *2*, 107–9.

The idea that what a man perceives may depend as much upon who he is or what he is feeling as upon what is "out there" is hardly a new one. Shakespeare, for example, in *Midsummer Night's Dream*, says:

> *Such tricks hath strong imagination,*
> *That, if it would but apprehend some joy,*
> *It comprehends some bringer of that joy;*
> *Or in the night, imagining some fear,*
> *How easy is a bush supposed a bear.*

In the past two decades, however, under the impetus of the postwar emergence of clinical psychology, and concomitant concern with projective techniques and Freudian ideas about unconscious motivation, a great deal of research has been conducted in an attempt to turn this intuitive generalization into a system of precise and scientifically documented statements about the relation between personality variables and perceptual processes. The present chapter will examine the main trends of research in this area—an area marked by intense controversy, provocative findings, and intriguing unanswered questions, but perhaps most notable for the degree to which it has aroused efforts to integrate the insights and viewpoints of clinical workers and the methodological and theoretical perspectives of experimentalists.

The common meeting ground in this area for workers from a variety of backgrounds and orientations has been a broadly functional view of perception. According to this view, man learns not only to modify his overt behavior, his muscular movements or verbal comments; he learns also to modify his looking and hearing so as to be able to notice what he needs to notice in order to survive, or sometimes to avoid noticing what it hurts to notice, even at the price of survival value.

Eriksen (1963), in an earlier review, suggested that research in personality and perception can conveniently be divided into investigations which stress some general phenomenon, such as the selective emphasis in perception on drive-related stimuli, and those which focus on individual differences. His own work,

David L. Wolitzky
& Paul L. Wachtel

Personality and Perception

41

however, as well as that of many other investigators, points to the need for taking into account both aspects of the personality-perception relationship. The general laws are only partially understood if the occurrence of individual differences is not accounted for, and the web of correlations yielded by studying individual differences can be fully understood only if the relevant processes and stimulus conditions are understood. Differences in the perceptual approaches of different people reflect differences in their experience of the world, and hence not only in how they go about the task of adaptation but also in what kind of perceived world they are adapting to.

Studies of Need in Perception

As in most good marriages, the wedding of perceptual research and personality theory, consummated in the late 1940s after a long engagement, found each partner bringing to the match qualities needed by the other. Workers in perception had behind them a long tradition of methodological sophistication and laboratory precision. Students of personality brought with them recognition of the importance of motivation in all aspects of behavior. Not surprisingly, among the first fruits of the marriage were efforts to demonstrate, in tightly controlled laboratory experiments, the role of needs or motives in perception.

That needs do influence perception has long been an almost unquestioned assumption of many clinical workers. The nature of this influence, however, has been recognized by sophisticated workers with projective techniques as being extraordinarily complex. Will a person characterized by strong repressed hostility see many implements of destruction or aggressive creatures on the Rorschach test? He is as likely to evidence excessively benign percepts, highly filtered or disguised aggressive connotations, or any of several other possible expressions of his unique style. Furthermore, at least as important as what he sees is how he sees it—whether he sees it accurately, what part of the blot he uses to form the percept, whether the color and shading of the blot play a role, etc.

Early laboratory studies stressed the direct expression of drive in what is seen. For example, in a pioneering series of studies, Sanford (1936, 1937) found that by and large the greater the number of hours since S's last meal, the more food interpretations he gave to a series of ambiguous pictures. A new wrinkle was introduced, however, with the suggestion that in certain circumstances food imagery might be "suppressed." In a later study along similar lines, Levine, Chein, and Murphy (1942) found evidence that with an increase in the number of hours of food deprivation, the amount of food imagery seen *decreased*. These and other findings were the forerunners of a huge number of studies, beginning shortly after World War II, in which such processes as perceptual vigilance, perceptual defense, and perceptual accentuation were proposed and debated. As we shall see, these studies pointed to the need for greater precision and clarity in the use of the term "perception," which was used as a referent for processes at quite different levels; they led as well to considerable work on the role of unconscious factors in perception and to investigations of the individual differences responsible for the complexity of findings in this area.

In a study which become a controversial classic, Bruner and Goodman (1947) investigated the effect of value upon perceived size. Ten-year-olds from rich and poor backgrounds were asked to adjust a variable circle of light to the size of a coin (experimental group) or a gray cardboard disc (control group) held in their hands. Coins from a penny to a half dollar in value were judged for size, and the cardboard discs used by the control group were of the same sizes as the various coins.

The size judgments made for the coins were consistently larger than for the same sized cardboard discs, and (with a slight exception for the fifty-cent piece) the greater the value of the coin, the greater the deviation of apparent size from actual size. Furthermore, when the results for rich and poor children were looked at separately, it was found that the poor children overestimated the sizes of the coins more than the rich children and also showed a greater tendency toward increasingly accentuating the size with greater coin value.

In a study that slightly varied this design, however, Carter and Schooler (1949) reported findings somewhat at odds with the interpretation that valuing a stimulus highly leads to its being perceived as larger. Comparing the size judgments of rich and poor children, they report that

when judgments are being made with the physical object present as a standard of reference there are no significant differences in judgment between the rich and the poor subjects, but when the judgments are made from memory the poor children imagine the coins to be larger than do the rich subjects (p. 203).

They suggest that their findings "raise doubt as to the general importance of value systems as organizing factors in the presence of clear, physically present objects" but that "needs and values may play a role when the stimulus object is equivocal or not present as in the case of judgments made from memory." They further suggest that some of the findings in the Bruner and Goodman study were questionable because of the small size of the sample employed.

In an effort to reconcile the Bruner-Goodman and the Carter-Schooler findings, Bruner and Rodrigues (1953) performed a study having features of both of the two previous investigations. They concluded that the value of an object does not necessarily influence its judged *absolute* magnitude, but that the *relative* value of an array of objects accentuates the *relative* differences in the apparent size of the objects. A somewhat similar, though more detailed, conclusion was reached by Tajfel (1957) in a review of the work in this area. Attempting to integrate disparate findings, Tajfel suggested that in a series of stimuli varying concomitantly in value and in some physical dimension, perceived differences among the stimuli of the value series are greater than in a comparable neutral series. He postulated as well that the perceived differences in magnitude among stimuli of the value series and of the neutral series are greater than corresponding differences among neutral stimuli. According to Tajfel's scheme, overestimation of valued stimuli results from these two processes only when, in the value series, increase in value and increase in magnitude are positively correlated.

In addition to size estimation, studies of the influence of value and need upon the perception of phenomenal attributes have included, for example, judgments of weight (Dukes & Bevan 1952) and brightness (Atkinson & Walker 1956). The work in this area during the period of most active interest is well reviewed by Jenkin (1957). Recent studies have attempted to consider the complex interaction of variables influencing such phenomenal judgments (Dorfman & Zajonc 1963). It seems, however, that interest in personality-perception relationships has shifted in recent years; of the lines of research on attributive perception stemming from the Bruner-Goodman study, it is the work on individual differences by Klein and his co-workers (Klein 1954; Klein, Schlesinger, & Meister 1951), discussed below, which has generated the most sustained interest. The latter work has made it clear that without consideration of individual differences, confusing and contradictory experimental results are likely.

MOTIVATION AND PERCEPTUAL THRESHOLD

Although the studies discussed above were of major importance in the development of the "new look" in perception, the largest number of "new look" studies has probably been concerned with the effects of need upon *thresholds* for perceptual recognition. Such studies have been the major battlefield upon which different views of the relation between need and perception have clashed, and the tachistoscope has been the major weapon in these encounters. The unique strengths and weaknesses of this instrument have shaped much of the research in this area.[1]

The tachistoscope satisfies one of the main requirements for studying motivational effects upon perception: by flashing the stimulus for very brief periods of time, the experimenter can insure that it is a marginal one (Pine 1964), lacking clarity and providing limited information. It has generally been assumed by workers in this area that such an impoverished stimulus is necessary to demonstrate motivational effects upon perception; were it not assumed that motivational effects are quite limited in the perception of more definite stimuli, experimenters would seem to be postulating a solipsistic trend in perception which would make it difficult to account for the degree of adaptive, reality-attuned behavior which is readily observable.[2] It is important to note that the degree to which a stimulus is in fact ambiguous depends in part upon the response set induced by the question which *S* is asked. As Hochberg (1956) has pointed out, Rorschach inkblots are hardly ambiguous if one is aiming to elicit from *S* the response "inkblot," but may be highly ambiguous when the standard instructions are given.

The paradigmatic tachistoscopic experiment in the area

---

[1] Other approaches to the study of motivational influences upon perceptual threshold have been used as well, e.g., presentation of auditory stimuli at low volume (Kurland 1954) or against a background of white noise (Lazarus, Eriksen, and Fonda 1951), presentation of unclear carbon copies of written words (Carpenter, Wiener, & Carpenter 1956; Wiener 1955). Where these methodologies have different implications than has tachistoscopic exposure, they will be discussed separately. In general, the discussion which follows in the text applies to them as well.

[2] Most observations of the effects of need on perception, both in psychological experiments and in more literary and naturalistic sources, do refer to instances where full scrutiny of the stimulus is prevented by brevity of exposure, darkness, fuzziness, etc. The work on cognitive controls, however, discussed below, provides a means of examining personal selectivity in *all* perceptual situations without the danger of postulating solipsism.

of need and perception involves comparison of the levels of stimulation required for correct report of stimuli with varying motivational implications for the subject. Early findings included: words consonant with a subject's values as assessed by the Allport-Vernon Scale of Values were correctly reported at shorter durations than words not as consonant (Postman, Bruner, & McGinnies 1948); socially taboo words (e.g., whore, bitch) required longer exposure times for correct reporting than non-taboo words (McGinnies 1949); words having long association times on the word association test required either much longer or much shorter durations for recognition than words with medium or short association times (Bruner & Postman 1947).

Other means of providing neutral and emotionally charged stimuli for recognition experiments have included the association of stimuli with shock (McNamara, Solley, & Long 1958; Phares 1962; Pustell 1957; Reece 1954; Rosen 1954), the use of stimuli judged beforehand to be emotional or not on a priori grounds (Kurland 1954; Lazarus, Eriksen, & Fonda 1951; Smock 1956), stimuli previously associated with successful or unsuccessful performance on a task (Bootzin & Stephens 1967; Brown & Yandell 1966; Eriksen & Browne 1956; Miller 1954; Spence 1957a; 1957b), stimuli with varying degrees of interracial connotations (Loiselle & Williamson 1966), and pictures of disabled and nondisabled people (Lipp, Kolstoe, James, & Randell 1968). An interesting procedure was employed by Wiener (1955). He looked at thresholds for recognition of several words of ambiguous meaning in contexts which tended to emphasize either their "neutral" or their "threatening" meanings. The word "fairy," for example, was included in the series story-angel-*fairy*-godmother for the neutral group, and in the series queer-village-*fairy*-homosexual for the threat group. In such a procedure the critical stimuli are clearly of equal familiarity for threat and neutral conditions; the difference lies in meaning.

The body of findings of such studies has been interpreted by many authors (Blum 1954, 1955; Eriksen 1951a, 1951b, 1954; Lazarus & McLeary 1951) as reflecting the operation of defensive processes akin to those postulated by dynamic personality theories. According to this view, the avoidance of perception or anxiety-provoking stimuli is but one instance of the general process of avoiding awareness of anything that arouses anxiety or other unpleasant affects. But, as we shall see, such a view has not gone unchallenged.

Studies using taboo words have been particularly subject to criticism. McGinnies (1949) assumed that the higher threshold for taboo words in his study was a function of their emotion-arousing quality, leading to a process of perceptual defense. Howes and Solomon (1950), however, stated that the "taboo" words were also words less frequently seen in print and advanced the notion that the lesser familiarity of the taboo words (along with the reluctance to say them noted below) accounted for the threshold differences. Considerable debate then followed over the appropriateness of Thorndike-Lorge lists as a measure of the familiarity of these words to college students, the role of *relative* frequency in the recognition of words of high and low *absolute* frequency, and similar issues (see Howes 1954; Solomon & Postman 1952; Howes & Solomon 1951; McGinnies 1950; Solomon & Howes 1951).

Another difficulty with taboo-word studies stems from the emphasis in most of the studies on *correct reporting* of the stimulus as the critical dependent variable. *S*'s may be quite reluctant to *say* taboo words to an experimenter if they are at all uncertain about what has been flashed on the tachistoscope. Comparable levels of uncertainty about nontaboo words may not be accompanied by similar reluctance. (It is far less uncomfortable to tell the experimenter you saw "table" when you are unsure about what was really flashed than to say you saw "whore"). Hence a raising of the *perceptual* threshold for taboo words may be erroneously assumed when in fact it is merely a *response* threshold that is involved. Continued efforts have been made to clarify the effect of taboo words on perceptual threshold (e.g., Bitterman & Kniffen 1953; Dorfman, Grossberg, & Kroeker 1965; Forrest, Gordon, & Taylor 1965; Goldstein 1966; McGinnies & Sherman 1952; Postman, Bronson, & Gropper 1953; Sales & Haber 1968; Taylor & Forrest 1966; Walters & Pilipec 1964; Zajonc 1964), but as Brown (1961) has noted, the evaluation of studies using the taboo-word approach is often quite difficult.

The criterion of correct reporting of the stimulus in perceptual defense studies has presented problems even where taboo words have not been used, for *S* may be required to *say* something other than what he *sees*. Eriksen (1956), for example, has illustrated how a correct or incorrect report of a briefly flashed stimulus may be a result of the constraints which *E*'s instructions place upon the verbal categories available to *S* for indicating what he has seen.

While we tend to act as though the perceptual stimulus presented to a subject in a tachistoscopic exposure of a nonsense syllable was the nonsense syllable itself, this is not the stimulus perceived by the subject. If it were, there would be no point in using the tachistoscope. When the nonsense syllable SIDAK is tachistoscopically exposed for a short duration and the subject is instructed to report just what he perceives (and is allowed the freedom of the English language for responses), we tend to get responses such as "I saw an S followed by what seemed to be two blurred letters, then an a and a k." If, however, the subject is instructed implicitly or explicitly to respond in terms of nonsense syllables, we obtain the response "sidak" or some other nonsense syllable . . . that has the correct sequence of letters (Eriksen 1956, p. 78).

Such a description of the events in a tachistoscopic threshold experiment is one of several which can be described as "part-cue theories" (Kempler & Wiener 1963). "Perceptual avoidance theory" is the term used by Kempler and Wiener to describe the position of Allport (1955), Eriksen (1954), and Osgood (1957). This theory posits that perceptual defense is a result of learned avoidance of certain perceptual responses and that this avoidance is conditioned to fractional elements of the presented stimulus. Kempler and Wiener agree with Eriksen (1958) and Wiener and Schiller (1960) that such a position is untenable because the meaning of the stimulus is carried only by the whole and cannot be inferred by the structural characteristics of the partial cues. They illustrate their position by pointing out that words like "whore" and "where" differ in connotation and emotionality only when the whole stimulus is perceived; structurally they are very similar. Perceptual avoidance theory has much in common with the reinforcement explanations of perceptual defense phenomena reviewed by Brown (1961), in which perception is treated as a response and perceptual responses that reduce anxiety are seen as more likely to occur than those that are

followed by punishment (Dulany 1957; Newton 1956; Reece 1954; Rigby & Rigby 1956; Rosen 1954). Brown commented that these explanations are useful as attempts to relate perceptual defense phenomena to behavior theory in general, but failed to account adequately for the lowering of thresholds for stimuli of high emotionality.

Another part-cue theory which gained considerable prominence is the "hypothesis theory" of Bruner and Postman (Bruner 1951; Postman 1951, 1953). The primary explanatory concept in this framework is the hypothesis: "a predisposition of the perceiver to organize stimulus cues in specific ways" (Postman 1953, p. 300). The stronger a hypothesis, the more likely it is to be aroused, the less stimulus support is needed to confirm it, and the more stimulus support is needed to *dis*confirm it. Motivational variables are viewed as influencing the strength of hypotheses, and hence the emotionality of a stimulus is a relevant factor in the likelihood of its being perceived. Perceptual defense is explained as resulting from "the dominance of strong alternative hypotheses rather than from active repression of the inimical or dangerous" (Postman 1953, p. 300). Perceptual vigilance is explained as the result of strong hypotheses related to the negative stimulus. Brown (1961), however, has argued that although this theory can accommodate the data of perceptual defense studies, it is of limited usefulness because its explanations are somewhat ex post facto and its terms vague enough to accommodate exactly opposite data; thus it has limited predictive value. Blum has criticized hypothesis theory on more substantive grounds, claiming that the theory cannot account for the results of his experiment (Blum 1955) and that perceptual defense must be conceived of as an active avoidance reaction to threatening stimuli, which are discriminated unconsciously.

Kempler and Wiener (1963) criticized hypothesis theory on the grounds that it implies that the subject distorts the stimulus presented according to his predisposition. Their theory, which they call a "part-cue response-characteristic" theory, implies no such distortion, but asserts that the difference between the subject's response and the "correct" response is strictly a result of the subject's responding to a limited sample of the information input. "The part-cue response-characteristic model leads to the general reformulation that differences in recognition threshold for different words (or for different subjects for the same word) can be considered a function of differential response characteristics of a subject (or between subjects) *to the specific seen part-cues*" (Kempler & Wiener 1963, p. 352). Blum's criticism of hypothesis theory, if correct, applies to this theory as well in that it too does not include a conception of active avoidance of perception.

Still another part-cue formulation is the response-avoidance model of Eriksen and Browne (1956). These authors advance a behavior theory model of perceptual defense in many ways similar to Kempler and Weiner's model discussed above. The two positions differ mainly in the former's emphasis on the effects of anxiety upon the genesis of response hierarchies. Brown (1961) claimed that this formulation also failed to explain the inverted-U function which, according to him, expresses the empirically derived relation between recognition threshold and stimulus emotionality.

The part-cue theories noted above were efforts to account for the results of perceptual defense studies without postulating a homunculuslike preperceiver which, without accompanying awareness, scans perceptual input and allows only some of it to enter consciousness.[3] A more radical attempt to deal with this problem was made by Goldiamond (1958), who suggested that the differential thresholds obtained in these studies have nothing to do with perception at all and were exclusively a function of response bias. Goldiamond's position seems to imply that the immediate stimulus has less influence upon behavior than is commonly assumed. Thus, in one experiment (Goldiamond & Hawkins 1958), differences were reported in "recognition thresholds" (number of trials necessary to name the "correct" stimulus) for various stimuli when in fact the stimuli were never presented in the tachistoscope. The experimenters had arbitrarily assigned a different nonsense syllable as correct for each series of trials, and the results were interpreted as reflecting response bias in the absence of differences in perceptual recognition. The implication of the study to its authors seems to be that such response biases account for the results of perceptual-defense studies. As Kempler and Wiener (1963) have pointed out, however, it is one thing to suggest that response biases account for most of the variance in the absence of cues to guide responding and quite another to suggest the same when the subject is responding to varied stimulation. The Goldiamond and Hawkins study demonstrates the existence of response biases. It does not demonstrate that they alone account for the results of the perceptual defense studies.

In its various forms, the controversy over a response versus a perceptual interpretation of the perceptual-defense studies has been one of the most persistent and most confusing in this area (Bootzin & Natsoulas 1965; Goldiamond 1962; Goldstein 1962, 1964; Goldstein, Himmelfarb, & Feder 1962; Matthews & Wertheimer 1958; Minard 1965; Minard, Bailey, & Wertheimer 1965; Nothman 1962). Designing experiments which contain the necessary converging operations (Garner, Hake, & Eriksen 1956) to rule out nonperceptual interpretations of the data is extremely difficult. Recently, Natsoulas (1965) has pointed out that even in studies like Blum's (1955), which critics (e.g., Eriksen 1958) have cited as containing the necessary converging operations (though questioning the reproducibility of the data), a perceptual interpretation is not unequivocal. Natsoulas notes that differential effects in stimulus-present and stimulus-absent conditions may reflect the fact that S has different response tendencies in different stimulus situations without implying that S does not see emotional stimuli as well as neutral ones.

What exactly is meant by "see" in such a statement is not easy to conceptualize. Natsoulas (1965) has noted that distinguishing perception from categorization or even immediate memory is a knotty conceptual problem, and several authors (e.g., Bruner 1957; Swets, Tanner, & Birdsall 1961) have placed categorization and decision processes at the center of their definitions of perception. Indeed, as Hochberg (1956) points out, classical definitions distinguished between sensation and perception, emphasizing that the latter is determined by both sensation and the arousal of associated memory images. Hochberg notes that between the extreme of complete psychophysical correspondence, where variance in response is completely determined by variance in stimulus, and the extreme

of complete independence of present stimuli (e.g., imagery) "lies an important domain (corresponding to some extent to the classical area of *perception*) in which the stimulus accounts for some but not all of the response variance, and here it may be fruitful to inquire as to how much of the residual variance may be sought in factors of motivation and habit" (Hochberg 1956, p. 404).

Much of the debate between clinicians and experimenters about perceptual defense seems to be a pseudodebate deriving from lack of attention to these differing definitions of perception. The clinician or personality theorist who insists that motives and defenses do influence perception generally means something different by perception than do authors like Garner, Hake, and Eriksen, or Natsoulas. For the former, it is the perceptual *experience* which is altered. This experience includes not only the microscopic inferred perceptual process, but also memory and associative processes, and possibly even responses, for how one responds to an ambiguous stimulus plays an important role in how one experiences it. The shadow seen out of the corner of one's eye is a different perceptual experience to the frightened man who (at least for the moment) labels it an assailant than it is to his calmer comrade who sees "just a shadow." The *experience* is perceptual even though finer analysis might yield an understanding of the event in terms of response processes. The functional relations described by personality theorists tend to be in terms of the antecedents and consequences of the perceptual experience rather than in terms of the perceptual process, but the term perception (with its particular connotations in the history of psychology) obscures the phenomenological links in the theory.

The use of the tachistoscope, or similar means of presenting a single impoverished stimulus to be identified or not, contributes to the obscurity. Tachistoscopic studies do not readily lend themselves to the study of the continual selection of features from a complex stimulus array, yet such continual selection is what is postulated by dynamic personality theories. In everyday life it is rare to encounter the demand simply to name a stimulus upon brief exposure. Rather, one selects continuously from and responds continuously to an ever-changing pattern of stimulation. Further, and most important for the study of personality functioning, the selection of cues and concomitant selective response itself changes the stimulus array which the person confronts. For example, if Mr. A selects a few indicators of hostility from the total pattern presented by Mr. B and responds on the basis of the hostility he perceived, then A's angry response is likely to lead B to become in fact more hostile, thereby presenting to A a stimulus configuration which "confirms" A's original perception. The complex topic of "person perception" (see Cline 1964; Tagiuri & Petrullo 1958) is beyond the scope of the present chapter, but it seems appropriate to note how examples such as the above help to clarify the limits and implications of tachistoscopic studies. For investigating the perception-personality relationship, such studies are likely to provide data closer to the concerns of the perceptual theorist than to those of the personality theorist.

Individual Differences in Perceptual Defense. It is a common clinical observation that some persons deal with anxiety by avoiding what threatens them whereas others attempt to search

---

[3] A fuller discussion of the issues involved in discrimination without awareness and subliminal stimulation follows below (see also Lazarus & McLeary 1951).

out and confront dangers in order to deal with them. A similar distinction has frequently emerged in studies of thresholds for neutral and emotional stimuli, and many investigators have postulated contrasting processes of perceptual vigilance and defense and have studied persons primarily manifesting one or the other of these approaches. In an important early series of studies, Eriksen (1951a, 1951b, 1952a, 1952b, 1954b; Lazarus, Eriksen, & Fonda 1951) demonstrated the value of viewing perceptual defense data as reflecting individual consistencies in defensive strategies which were manifested in perception,[4] memory, and learning. He emphasized the need to assess independently the person's defensive style and the relevance of the "emotional" or "threatening" stimuli to the particular subject. These sentiments have been echoed repeatedly in the course of research in this area, but seem to represent an insight which is easily submerged; in a review written more than a decade after these initial studies, it was necessary for Minard (1965) to remind his readers that to average across persons differing in sex or personality and across stimuli differing in emotionality may obscure and mislead. It is necessary to note, however, that despite continuing reports of the usefulness of considering individual differences in recognition threshold differentials (e.g., Brown & Yandell 1966; Dodwell 1964) a number of studies have questioned the generality of individual styles in this regard (Bootzin & Stephens 1967; Palmer 1968; Spence 1957a).

Brown (1961), in his extensive review of research on perceptual defense, also noted that the data point compellingly to the occurrence of *both* raising and lowering of thresholds for emotional stimuli. He differs, however, in accounting for this variation from those who postulate modes of defense. Brown suggests that the recognition threshold initially rises with increases in the emotionality of the stimulus, but then reaches a peak and declines with further increases in emotionality. According to Brown's scheme, all persons exhibit such an inverted U-curve, and individual differences lie in the point along the continuum of stimulus emotionality where the peak of the curve occurs. If the more emotionally arousing of two stimuli is still before the peak of the curve for a person, his threshold for the emotional stimulus will be higher and he will be classified as a repressor; if the emotional stimulus is beyond his peak, in the range where increases in emotionality lead to *lowered* thresholds, he will appear to be a sensitizor. Brown claims that his conception, which treats stimulus emotionality as a continuous variable, better accounts for the fact that, despite general personal tendencies, persons who primarily repress are sometimes hypervigilant and vice versa.

Brown's warning about the dangers of typological thinking notwithstanding, extensive efforts have been made recently to develop measures and examine the correlates of individual differences in the tendency to exhibit repressive or sensitizing defenses in perceptual and other situations. Paper and pencil scales bearing on this dimension have been developed by Byrne (1961) and Ullmann (1962). The work in this area has been reviewed in some detail by Byrne (1964).

In a recent study, Minard and Mooney (1969) reported that

[4] In a recent review of his own and others' work in this area, Eriksen (1963) has claimed that the effects earlier attributed to perception are response phenomena, but has reaffirmed his view that the behavior manifested in these experiments reflects important individual differences in ego-defensive mechanisms.

field-dependent subjects exhibited a greater tendency toward perceptual defense than did field-independent subjects. They attribute these results to a greater ability of field-independent persons (see below) to separate emotion from perception.

Coping and Perceptual Defense. Among the many studies which have examined perceptual thresholds for neutral and threatening stimuli, relatively few have considered whether the perceiver has available means of coping with the "threat." There are many indications, however, that this variable may be an extremely important one. In a different aspect of perceptual functioning, for example, it was found that the narrowing of attention which accompanied threat did not occur when the threat was one which the person had a chance to avert through his own efforts (Wachtel 1968b). Considerable research on the implications of structuring a situation as one in which a person can or cannot control his fate and on individual differences in the tendency to perceive situations as possible or not possible to control has been reviewed by Lefcourt (1966) and Rotter (1965).

Reece (1954) presented his Ss with a learning task in which for some subjects a shock associated with the presentation of a nonsense syllable was terminated by pronouncing the syllable (escape-shock group). For others the shock occurred throughout the time the stimulus was exposed and could not be terminated by S (nonescape-shock). Ss in the escape-shock group showed lower tachistoscopic thresholds for these syllables than did Ss in the nonescape shock group. In a somewhat similarly conceived study, Rosen (1954) found that when shocks were administered only after wrong responses, subsequent tachistoscopic recognition improved, whereas when no avoidance of shock was possible, subjects showed poorer recognition. McNamara, Solley, and Long (1958) suggested that alerting to a punished percept is more likely when escape is possible than when it is not. In a study which attempted to control for amount of shock received, and varied only the definition of the situation as one in which the subject's skill was or was not relevant, Phares (1962) found that subjects told they could avert a shock by learning the proper contingencies subsequently had lower thresholds for shock-associated words than Ss who thought their possibility of ending shock was completely random. The latter group had higher thresholds than a nonshock control group. These and other similar findings suggest that it may prove fruitful to pay greater attention to the person's view of a threatening situation as one with which it is or is not possible to cope, whether that view reflects the structure of the situation or is an aspect of the person's personality. In general, it seems that research attempting to "prove" that perceptual defense does or does not occur is of limited value for personality researchers by now, but that the perceptual-defense paradigm may still be useful for examining a number of specific issues regarding the implications of individual differences of various sorts, the conditions under which different defensive strategies are adopted, etc.

Subliminal Perception

A central objection to the conception of perceptual defense proposed by workers with a psychoanalytic orientation was the apparent postulation of a preperceiver. It appeared to many (e.g., Eriksen 1958) that in order for perception of anxiety-provoking stimuli to be actively avoided, the stimulus must first be perceived and identified as "something not-to-be-perceived." It was in order to avoid this seeming paradox that the partial-cue theories noted above were developed.

An alternative resolution of the preperceiver paradox was the suggestion that "perception" could occur without awareness. According to this hypothesis, stimuli might be "perceived" at levels below the threshold of recognition, and knowledge of their "safe" or "dangerous" nature might then play a role in determining their threshold for perception *with* awareness (Lazarus & McCleary 1951). Spurred in part by the controversy over how to account for "perceptual defense," but also from other sources (see, e.g., the discussion below of the Pötzl phenomenon [Pötzl 1917]), investigation of "perception" without awareness became an active research area in its own right.[5]

Spence (1967) has suggested that perceptual defense and subliminal perception can be considered as part of a single continuum. In both cases, a stimulus is presumed to have "registered" outside of awareness. In the case of perceptual defense the result is an alteration of perceptual sensitivity. In studies of "subliminal perception," the way the stimulus is presented precludes the possibility of recognition and its influence is sought not in a threshold for the stimulus, but in some other response indicator. Here, the failure to recognize the identity of the stimulus is not due to its aversive quality or to personal characteristics of the subject. Nonrecognition shifts from being a dependent variable to being an independent variable.

It is possible to discern three main lines of research in the voluminous, periodically reviewed literature on subliminal perception (Miller 1942; Adams 1957; Eriksen 1958, 1960, 1962; Goldiamond 1958; McConnell, Cutler, & McNeil 1958; Klein 1956, 1959a, 1959b, 1970; Klein & Holt 1960; Bevan 1964: Pine 1964). One line of studies, usually undertaken within the orientation of psychophysics or signal detection theories, is designed to determine the information-processing limits of the perceptual apparatus (e.g., Bevan 1964). A second line, examining verbal conditioning without awareness, has focused largely on establishing experimental analogues of therapeutically effective learning (Greenspoon 1955; Krasner 1958; Dulany 1962; Kimble 1962; Spielberger 1962; Verplanck 1962).

It is the third[6] major line of research in this area, reflecting a joint interest in perception and personality (see Klein 1970), that will be discussed below.[7] This research was guided by

[5] Subliminal research can be traced back at least a century, to Suslowa's 1863 report of an increase in the two-point discrimination threshold as a function of subliminal electrical stimulation (Baker 1937; Miller 1939). In 1942, Miller presented more than a dozen definitions of the term "unconscious," reviewed the then substantial literature on subliminal effects, and concluded that there was positive evidence for the existence of the phenomenon. There was a hiatus in research in this area until the onset of the perceptual defense studies and the studies of subliminal effects to be reviewed below.

[6] The advertising industry was briefly excited by the commercial potential of subliminal stimulation (McConnell et al. 1958).

[7] No attempt will be made here at an exhaustive review of the literature on subliminal perception and the claims and counterclaims that abound in it. The reviews cited above can be consulted for that purpose. The present aim is to focus on a large body of research, with important implications for personality theory, which has largely been ignored in previous reviews.

the desire to make the phenomena of preconscious and unconscious thinking, described by Freud, amenable to systematic study in the laboratory. Before considering this literature in detail, it will be useful first to review the techniques, criteria of awareness, and response indicators used in these studies.

TECHNIQUES OF SUBLIMINAL STIMULATION

Three main methods have been used to present stimuli without S's awareness.

1. *Incidental stimulation.* An above-threshold stimulus is presented, but the subject's attention is diverted from it by a separate focal task (Bach 1960; Pine 1960, 1961). This has been the least frequently used method. Though it is closest to a "real-life" situation, the status of the incidental stimulus with respect to awareness cannot be independently or precisely assessed since the measures of awareness used rely on memory rather than perception.
2. *Backward masking.* Developed by Werner (1935) and Cheatham (1952), and referred to as the masking or *A-B* technique (Klein et al. 1958; Eagle 1959; it is also called metacontrast by some), this method involves the tachistoscopic exposure of one (*A*) stimulus immediately followed by exposure of a second (*B*) stimulus. The first stimulus is presented at an exposure long enough for it to be fully recognized were it not obliterated or masked by the second stimulus, which is clearly supraliminal. The influence of the *A* stimulus is sought in S's response to the *B* stimulus.
3. *Impoverished direct stimulation.* One stimulus is exposed tachistoscopically very briefly one or more times and its influence is sought on a subsequent task (e.g., Spence & Holland 1962). This method has been the one most frequently used.

In methods 2 and 3, independent threshold determinations of subliminality are made, usually after the experiment proper, using the exposure level at which the critical stimuli were exposed. A subliminal effect is claimed if there is a discrepancy between response indicators, i.e., no awareness as measured by verbal report and discrimination or detection thresholds, but an effect inferred from a detectable influence on some *other* response. The specific criteria of subliminality vary from study to study and are described in the next section.

CRITERIA OF AWARENESS AND UNAWARENESS

Hilgard (1962) has presented a useful descriptive categorization of subliminal stimuli, presented below with slight modifications.

1. The stimulus is *below the level of registration*. The input is so minimal that there is no physiological effect.
2. Above the level of registration, but below the *level of detection*. In this range S cannot discriminate between the stimulus and a blank field. In the event of negative results, it is impossible to say that the stimulus has, in fact, been registered.

3. Above the detection level, but below the *level of stimulus discrimination*. Hilgard (1962) does not include this level. It often happens, however, that a stimulus can be reliably discriminated from a blank field, but not from another stimulus (Wolitzky 1961).

4. Above detection and discrimination level, but below the *level of identification*. In this range, *S* can achieve a "something-nothing" and a "something-something" discrimination, but the partial cues are not enough for him to make a correct identification of the stimulus.

5. Below the identification level only because of a defensive reaction. This refers to a raised recognition threshold in the perceptual-defense kind of experiment.

While these criteria of subliminality are presented in terms of the threshold measures used, levels 1–4 should probably be considered as a continuum of information input, with eventual recognition reflecting a qualitative change in perceptual experience because of the introduction of *meaning*.

As will become apparent later, much of the controversy in this area is definitional, centered on the meaning of such terms as "subliminal," "awareness," and "perception" (e.g., Schwartz & Shagass 1961; also Libet 1965).

DEMONSTRATIONS OF SUBLIMINAL INFLUENCES ON BEHAVIOR

Pötzl (1960 [1917]) published a study, cited by Freud (1953 [1900], p. 181, footnote) as an important contribution to knowledge about the role of the day residue in dream formation. Pötzl exposed pictures of landscapes tachistoscopically for about 1/100 of a second and asked *S*s to draw and describe what they had seen. They were asked to return the following day and to report any dreams they had had in the interim. Parts of the stimulus that were unnoticed following the tachistoscopic exposure frequently appeared in the manifest content of the dreams. Confirmatory findings were reported by Malamud and Linder (1931), and by Allers and Teler (1960 [1924]), who used a free-association and imagery task (see also Hilgard 1958).

A revival of interest in what has come to be called "the Pötzl phenomenon" was sparked by Fisher's research. Beginning with an essentially intuitive approach which involved ad hoc data analyses (Fisher 1954), and becoming increasingly rigorous in matters of threshold measurement, scoring criteria, and statistical analysis (Fisher & Paul 1959; Paul & Fisher 1959), Fisher showed that subliminal stimuli can influence the content of both dreams and images (see also Fisher 1956, 1957, 1960*a*; Friedman & Fisher 1960). Other investigators reported supporting evidence (Luborsky & Shevrin 1956; Shevrin & Luborsky 1958). Johnson and Eriksen (1961), however, failed to replicate the effect.

Eriksen (1960) argued that the issue of the base rates for appearance of ideas in fantasy had been neglected, and suggested that an artificial subliminal effect could occur if one perceived element in a cohesive picture led to related associations (see also Hilgard 1962). Moreover, *S*s might not report items they were unsure of in intentional recall, but such content might emerge during imagery when *S*s might employ more relaxed criteria. Johnson and Eriksen (1961) replicated the Shevrin and

Luborsky (1958) study and controlled[8] for base-rate production of stimulus-related ideas; no subliminal effect was found.[9]

In a carefully controlled study which seems to have adequately met Eriksen's (1960) criticisms, Haber and Erdelyi (1967) obtained positive findings. The experimental group received a brief exposure of a relatively unfamiliar, complex, cohesive picture. After describing and drawing what they saw, they were asked to free associate, keeping the picture in mind. The first 12 words elicited were each used as stimuli for 10 further associations. After this procedure, *S* was again asked to draw and describe the initial picture. Two control groups were run: a "dart-control" group played darts instead of free associating; a "yoked-control" group never saw the original stimulus, but redrew the initial drawing of an experimental *S* before associating and then did another drawing and description. Comparisons of the first and second drawings revealed that only the experimental group showed a significant recovery of initially unreported stimulus elements. Thus, the free associations had a facilitative or priming effect on recovery (see also Giddan 1967).

The influence of subliminal stimuli has been demonstrated on a variety of other behaviors in addition to dreams, images, and word associations: trait attributions (Klein, Spence, Holt, & Gourevitch 1958; Eagle 1959; Smith, Spence & Klein 1959), drawings (Klein et al. 1958), guessing (Spence 1961*b*), reaction time (Spence & Bressler 1962), problem solving[10] (Kolers 1957), visual illusions (Smith & Henriksson 1955), bias in intentional recall (Spence & Holland 1962; Spence 1964*a*), TAT-like stories (Pine 1960, 1961), Rorschach content (Silverman & Silverman 1964), and formal aspects of thought (Silverman 1967).

Klein et al. (1958), for example, used the *A-B* masking technique: the subliminal *A* stimuli were line drawings of male or female genitals or symbols thereof, and the supraliminal *B* stimulus was a drawing of a person of ambiguous gender. Both the drawing and ratings (of the *B* stimulus) were biased according to the gender of the subliminal *A* stimulus. Eagle (1959), using the same technique, reported that *A* stimuli depicting a person engaged in a benevolent or aggressive act differentially affected *S*'s responses to a picture of the same person in a neutral pose (*B* stimulus), as indicated by *S*'s drawings and ratings of trait-descriptive adjectives. Smith et al. (1959) found that descriptions of supposed changes in the facial expression of a *B* stimulus were influenced by the preceding *A* stimulus (e.g., the word "happy").

The studies cited thus far provide examples of influences of a subliminal stimulus upon the content of subsequent cognition. Such measurable influences have been referred to variously as *activation*, *recovery*, or *emergence* (Klein 1959*a*, 1959*b*; Hilgard 1962). These studies, as well as Silverman's (1967) on subliminal influences on ego functioning, have as an important feature in common the fact that *S* is not asked to make an inten-

[8] Shevrin and Luborsky (1958) used an indirect control for base rates, based on *S*s' guesses of unseen objects (Taves 1945) and found that infrequent items showed up significantly in their measure of preconscious recall.

[9] In many studies, illumination levels, stimulus size and contrast, length of dark adaptation, and other relevant details are, unfortunately, not reported.

[10] Gerard (1960), however, did not find a positive effect.

tional, direct response to the subliminal stimulus, of which he is unaware. He is, therefore, also unaware of its influence on a subsequent task. This facet of the procedure is considered to parallel the unintentional influence of a preconscious or unconscious idea (Pine 1964). In contrast, the perceptual-defense studies generally require an intentional, discriminative response to the critical stimulus.

CONTROVERSIAL ISSUES IN SUBLIMINAL RESEARCH

Before discussing studies of the conditions which govern the appearance of subliminal effects, it must be noted that several writers seriously question, on a variety of grounds, the validity of subliminal effects (see, e.g., Eriksen 1960; Goldiamond 1958; Wiener & Schiller 1960).

The major controversies have concerned whether cognition is influenced by stimuli that are "really" outside awareness, and whether a "preperceiver" is being posited. In discussing these issues, it will be convenient to follow the lines of division drawn by Wiener and Schiller (1960), who speak of a "two-process" versus a "one-process" view of perception. Briefly stated, the two-process view holds that a "critical stimulus not perceived via the supraliminal process (consciously) may be perceived via the subliminal process (not consciously); the subliminal process may then set off the appropriate need-related or defense-related responses" (Wiener & Schiller 1960, p. 124).[11]

The "one-process" theorists posit "a single perceptual process to account for the phenomena in question as well as for perceptual behavior in general" (Wiener & Schiller 1960, p. 124). In this latter view, the basic process is described by a monotonic relationship between stimulus intensity or duration and response strength (generally discriminative accuracy). By implication, the quality of response is assumed to be essentially the same at any point on the stimulus-intensity continuum, though it may be impoverished as a result of low-level inputs. Thus, awareness is conceived of in degrees, and it is argued that in purported demonstrations of cognition without awareness, refined threshold procedures will reveal the presence of partial cues or indicate that the subject was potentially aware of the stimulus input. Eriksen (1960) and Goldiamond (1958) have been particularly prominent in arguing that so-called subliminal effects are attributable to such artifacts. Since proponents of subliminal effects generally admit that the effects are often subtle and elusive, there is ample room for both ambiguous findings and conflicting interpretations.

The so-called two-process view is stated somewhat differently by Klein (1959a, 1959b) who referred to *registration* without awareness as usually defined rather than *perception* without awareness. In his preference for the term "registration," Klein recognizes that the term subliminal "perception" is a misnomer, as he includes in his definition of perception an awareness of the meaning or identity of the stimulus. It is not two different *perceptual* processes that are being posited. The distinction between registration and perception points to the possibility that a stimulus which is not discriminated percep-

tually can nonetheless exert an influence on other modes of experience, such as imagery (see the related studies of Goldberg & Fiss 1959; Fiss, Goldberg, & Klein 1963). The use of the more conservative term *marginal* stimuli suggests that the issue of partial cues is irrelevant, except for a theory of perception.[12] (Klein 1959a, 1959b; Klein & Holt 1960).

It seems, then, as in the related area of perceptual defense, that much of the ambiguity and controversy in this area stems from differing theoretical and experimental predilections of different researchers. This in turn leads to different definitions of the terms "subliminal" and "awareness," as well as to different experimental methods, which, in turn, make it difficult to compare studies using different stimuli, different response measures, and different threshold procedures.

From the standpoint of the aims and theoretical perspectives developed by Klein (1956, 1958, 1959a, 1959b, 1962), the controversy over methodological issues has deflected subliminal research from a potentially valuable direction. The programmatic interest of Klein's work was the interaction of central and peripheral trains of thought. In this view, it is more important to ask how far "up" in awareness (associated with what intention) must a stimulus be before it produces a qualitative change in behavior, than to ask how far "down" we can go in stimulus intensity and still get an influence on behavior. The latter question leads to a preoccupation with sensory thresholds and straight to ESP; the former raises essentially the same issues as do studies of incidental learning. For example, under what conditions will peripheral ideation intrude upon or become incorporated into conscious, intentional thinking? How does intentional, reality-oriented thinking persist in the face of ideational systems that are active but irrelevant to a person's executive intentions (Klein 1962, 1967)? This perspective was intended to guide research on two related major issues: (1) the functional importance of awareness, and (2) the specification of conditions which determine behavioral effects of peripherally aroused trains of thought. The strategy involves comparing effects of "incidental" stimuli (related to the peripheral arousal of an intention) with those of focal stimuli (related to the dominant train of intentional thought).

In this schema, subliminal stimulation was intended to be only a methodological entry into the problem, a means of insuring "incidentalness" of stimulation under controlled conditions. This strategy was perhaps an unfortunate one, in the light of the complexity of issues which have ensnared the subliminal stimulation paradigm itself. As a result, generalizations from

---

[11] Evidence from studies of the effects of subliminal anchors on judgment of magnitude (Bevan 1964) and from other studies (e.g., Eagle, Wolitzky, & Klein 1966) indicates that the response in the two-process view need not necessarily be defense-related or need-related.

[12] Though several studies have responded to the criticisms of Goldiamond (1958) and Eriksen (1960) and employed more refined threshold procedures, the controversy continues (e.g., Guthrie & Wiener 1966; Silverman & Spiro 1967b; Wiener & Kleespies 1968; Silverman 1968). Since the threshold is a statistical concept, it is impossible to obtain absolute *proof* that partial cues were not present. It may be noted that there are neurophysiological findings which appear to be consonant with the assumption of registration without awareness, i.e., that there are independent sensory mechanisms specific for sensory transmission, and others responsible for awareness (e.g., Samuels 1959; Libet 1965, 1966, 1967; Shevrin & Rennick 1967; Shevrin & Fritzler 1968; Shevrin, Smith, & Fritzler 1969). Libet et al. (1967), for example, recorded directly from the cortex of awake human *S*s and obtained evoked potentials in the absence of conscious experience. It has also been increasingly acknowledged that awareness is no mere epiphenomenon and that conscious experience has an organizing and directing causal influence on brain processes and behavior (Sperry 1969; see Dixon 1971 for a thoughtful review).

studies of peripheral trains of thought are equivocal to the extent that the subliminal stimulation method is central in them. While this method permits control over stimulus input, what is frequently lost sight of is the central issue referred to, i.e., that the issue of "subliminality" belongs in the larger context of the differential effects of peripheral (marginal) versus focal awareness of stimuli (and ideas) (Klein 1959a, 1959b, 1967, 1970).

However, since the methods used in both the Pötzl-type studies and in more recent studies involve (with rare exceptions) the tachistoscopic presentation of impoverished, low-level stimuli, the studies will be discussed in terms of "subliminal" and "supraliminal" influences on behavior.

Subliminal Versus Supraliminal Influences on Behavior

The experimental demonstrations that cognition can be affected by stimuli outside of awareness promised to make possible an experimental psychology of unconscious phenomena and to provide an answer to the related issue of the contribution of consciousness to cognitive processes (Klein 1959a, 1959b; Klein & Holt 1960). The theoretical basis for these issues rests in a general way on Freud's distinction between primary-process and secondary-process thinking (Hilgard 1962). It has been assumed that the absence of focal awareness precludes the opportunity to scrutinize, categorize, and evaluate the stimuli and, therefore, to respond in an intentional, secondary-process way that may be adaptive and/or defensive (Klein 1959a, 1959b; Pine 1964; Silverman & Spiro 1968). The early subliminal studies seem to have assumed that a stimulus outside anyone's awareness is, by virtue of this status, less subject to his critical judgment and inhibitory control, and is more likely to have a direct, automatic impact on behavior which bears the imprint of primary-process thinking (Klein 1959a, 1959b; Klein & Holt 1960).

An examination of studies which include subliminal versus supraliminal comparisons does not permit a clear-cut answer to the question of whether perceived, compared with unperceived, stimuli lead to different degrees and kinds of influence. For example, Pötzl's (1917) finding that conscious percepts are less likely to appear in dreams than are "unperceived" stimuli (the "law of exclusion") is refuted by both everyday observation and empirical studies (e.g., Shevrin & Luborsky 1958; Fisher 1960b). While only an exploratory study, Fisher's (1960a) results indicate the extreme difficulty of drawing any general conclusion that does not require extensive qualification. He used both subliminal and supraliminal stimuli (pictures of a snake and a swastika) and suggested that the likelihood and manner of incorporation into the dream was a complex interaction of awareness versus nonawareness of the stimulus, the meaning of the stimulus to S, and S's conflicts and defenses.[13]

Another indication of the complexity of this issue comes from the work of Spence. Spence and Holland (1962) reported that a subliminal stimulus ("cheese") produced a greater bias in recall than a blank or a supraliminal exposure. The experiment was designed so that access to a wider network of associations

would produce a scoreable positive effect.[14] In a subsequent study, however, food deprivation emerged as a key variable; deprived Ss showed a preferential recall effect, whether the stimulus was subliminal or supraliminal, provided that S rated his subjective hunger before the stimulus presentation (Spence & Ehrenberg 1964).

The only consistent indication that subliminal stimuli produce a greater impact on behavior than do supraliminal stimuli comes from the series of studies by Silverman (1967) to be described more fully below. The studies of Silverman (1967) and others (Pine 1960; Shevrin & Luborsky 1961) suggest that the differential effects of subliminal and supraliminal stimuli may be evident not only in the amount of effect but in the kind of effect obtained as well. The difference in the kinds of effect can be characterized as direct versus indirect (Pine 1964). Direct effects are those that, although connotative variants rather than literal replicas of the stimulus (Klein & Holt 1960), nonetheless show a relatively close link or logical relation to the subliminal stimulus (e.g., the subliminal stimulus "don't write" leading to shorter TAT stories, Zuckerman 1960; see also Smith et al. 1959; Spence & Holland 1962). Indirect effects refer to a *transformation* of the original subliminal input often suggestive of primary-process thinking (symbolization, condensation, displacement). Pine (1960) had Ss read a passage (the focal stimulus) while, as an incidental stimulus, they "heard" someone reading a passage about a cow. The Ss' subsequent TAT stories were influenced by the incidental cow passage as reflected in an emphasis on themes indicative of nurturant, passive interpersonal relationships. The focal stimulus, when it influenced the story, was not distorted. (In a similar study, a more affect-laden incidental stimulus led to an inhibitory effect [Pine 1961].)[15]

The kinds of indirect effects described above seem to depend on both a subliminal stimulus (particularly a drive-relevant one) *and* the inclusion of an open-ended response task to capture the effect. It appears that whereas indirect effects are less likely with supraliminal stimuli, subliminal stimuli can give rise to *both* direct and indirect effects if the same study includes the appropriate response measures (as in Spence 1961; Spence & Bressler 1962). In other words, subliminal stimuli can affect secondary-process thinking, though under certain conditions, they can also set off reverberations over a wider range of associations than do supraliminal stimuli (Spence & Holland 1962; Shevrin & Luborsky 1961; Shevrin & Fisher 1967).

In the studies cited above, indirect effects are seen in transformations of stimulus content. Silverman's (1967, 1970) studies

---

[13] However, in a further discussion of this study, Fisher (1960b, p. 23) draws the generalization that subliminal stimuli are more susceptible to primary-process transformations.

[14] Worthy of mention here is the apparent paradox of an *inverse* correlation between level of stimulus input, as indicated by a postexperimental threshold procedure, and degree of subliminal effect (e.g., Bach 1960; Klein et al. 1958; Eagle 1959; Paul & Fisher 1959; Spence & Holland 1962). Apparently, structural or partial cues can interfere with the sought-after effect (e.g., Spence & Holland 1962), although other studies (e.g., Wiener & Schiller 1960) report a positive correlation. When a "something-nothing" discrimination threshold is obtained, it is difficult to understand the inverse relationship other than by the assumption that Ss within the range of chance discrimination were in fact getting partial cues (e.g., Spence & Holland 1962). When a recognition threshold is obtained, it may be that Ss with a perceptual-defense reaction show an inhibited effect (Klein et al. 1958).

[15] Other indications of indirect effects are the numerous reports of symbolic transformations of subliminal stimuli in dreams (Fisher 1954), free associations (Dixon 1956, 1958), and images (Arey 1960), and condensation in thinking, e.g., the "rebus effect" found by Shevrin & Luborsky (1961).

reveal another kind of indirect effect. The dependent variable is not recovery of content, but fluctuations in aspects of ego functioning set in motion by particular subliminal inputs. His focus has been on the "psychodynamic effects" of subliminally presented conflict-related stimuli (Silverman 1965, 1966; Silverman & Spiro 1967a, 1968).

The replicated findings reported by Silverman and his co-workers include the following:

1. In several groups of schizophrenics, subliminal aggressive stimuli intensify regressive thinking and/or regressive non-verbal behavior (Silverman 1966; Silverman & Spiro 1967a, 1968; Silverman et al. 1969).
2. The subliminal activation of conflicts does not necessarily always lead to impaired ego functioning. In three experiments with relatively differentiated schizophrenics, the subliminal presentation of a stimulus depicting symbiotic union with the mother *reduced* psychopathological expressions, compared with behavior following subliminal exposure of neutral stimuli (Silverman et al. 1969; Silverman & Candell 1970).
3. Central to the present discussion is Silverman's report that in four studies which involved comparisons based on subliminal and supraliminal exposure of the same conflict-related stimulus, *supraliminal* stimuli *failed* to affect in any way the psychopathological behavior studied (Silverman & Goldweber 1966; Silverman & Spiro 1968; Silverman et al. 1969; Silverman et al. 1970). (See Silverman 1967, 1970 for details of the methods and procedures used in his studies and for a theoretical overview of the findings.)[16]

FACTORS AFFECTING SUBLIMINAL INFLUENCES ON BEHAVIOR

The effect typically sought in subliminal studies is a delayed and indirect one; that is, it appears as a variant of the initial stimulus reflected in a subsequent cognitive response. The stimulus input is minimal, S has no conscious intention to respond directly to it, and response is delayed (often for several hours, as in the Pötzl experiment); not surprisingly, the effects are not robust. In fact, subliminal effects are sometimes not easily replicated (e.g., Bruel, Ginsberg, Lukomnik, & Schmeidler 1966; Jung 1966; Worell & Worell 1966) and are frequently weak, subtle, or ambiguous (Hilgard 1962). Recent investigations have therefore devoted more attention to a consideration of the factors that facilitate or inhibit subliminal effects.

Stimulus and Task Variables. Subliminal effects have been obtained with verbal (Spence & Holland 1962), auditory (Pine 1960, 1961; Dixon 1956), and pictorial (Klein et al. 1958) stimuli, and with explicit and symbolic drive-related stimuli (Klein et al. 1958; Eagle 1959). There are, however, no systematic findings concerning the probability of a subliminal effect on the

content of thought as a function of stimulus form or sensory modality.

With regard to task variables and response measures, it appears that tasks ambiguous and open-ended are most conducive to a subliminal recovery effect. For example, Goldstein and Barthol (1960) found that stories given after subliminal stimuli were superimposed on ambiguous (out-of-focus) TAT cards showed an effect which was not produced with in-focus exposure (see also Allison 1963).

State of Consciousness. The recovery of subliminal stimuli may depend on the particular state of consciousness of the subject. Just as an open-ended task, an ambiguous stimulus, and appropriate instructions may encourage S to suspend critical judgment, so, too, a less alert person may be *more inclined* to abandon a strict reality orientation, especially in an ambiguous task, to deploy attention more broadly, and to be more responsive to inner stimuli (Klein 1959). Following this rationale, Fiss (1966) tested the hypothesis that Ss would be more responsive to subliminal stimuli in a nonalert than in an alert state of consciousness (as indexed by continuous monitoring of basal skin resistance [BSR] level). A greater subliminal effect was associated with greater nonalertness (BSR and self-ratings) during the recovery task (imagery); variations in alertness at the moment of stimulation, however, were uncorrelated with the effect.

Spence, Fiss, and Varga (1968) found sensitivity to minimal cues negatively correlated with a GSR orienting response and positively correlated with a drop in BSR during a task in which S attempted to detect minimal cues. Consistent with these findings are the reports of a greater subliminal influence upon imagery when S was in a supine rather than a seated position (Fisher & Paul 1959), or under the influence of LSD, compared with the normal waking state (Friedman & Fisher 1960).

These studies support the idea that a relaxed state enhances the probability that a wider range of thoughts, images, and cues will be activated. If at the same time there is a greater reliance on or attention to inner experience, this will tend to facilitate the incorporation and use of marginal inputs (see also Lapkin 1962; Fox 1960).

State of consciousness also appears to be related to the kind of subliminal effect obtained. Shevrin and Fisher (1967), for example, tracked the effects of a subliminal rebus stimulus (a picture of a pen and a knee) exposed before S went to sleep. Free associations elicited upon awakenings from sleep were scored (see Shevrin & Luborsky 1961) for conceptual effects (e.g., associations like ink, leg, etc.) and rebus effects (associations based on a combination of the two stimuli, e.g., penny, coin, etc.). Stage II sleep awakenings led to more conceptual than rebus associations; the converse was found for Stage I sleep awakenings. These results suggest that a more dreamlike state of consciousness is associated with a shift from secondary- to primary-process thinking; other findings in the study suggest that sleep may enhance the overall subliminal effect (see also Stross & Shevrin 1968, 1969).

Needs, Motives, Drives. Klein and Holt (1960) suggested that a "marginal stimulus seems to have an advantage for recovery if it makes contact with an active drive-schema"

---

[16] In the experiments cited above, the major interest has not been on *demonstrating* subliminal effects—rather, Silverman assumes the validity of the phenomenon and attempts to use it to study psychodynamic relationships. However, his findings are in keeping with the idea of subliminal registration (Silverman & Spiro 1967b), and he argues that it would be very difficult to account for them in any other way (e.g., partial cues).

(p. 81). Several studies support (Fisher 1956, 1957) and have been guided (Spence & Ehrenberg 1964; Spence 1964b; Silverman 1965, 1967) by this proposition. Drive-relevance can be established by exposing a manifestly drive-related subliminal stimulus (Eagle 1959; Silverman 1967) or by tailoring the stimulus to an existing (Spence & Ehrenberg 1964; Silverman 1967) or induced (Spence & Gordon 1967) drive state.

Spence and Ehrenberg (1964) thought that their failure to obtain a clear-cut replication of the original finding of Spence and Holland (1962, p. 167, footnote 3) of a subliminal effect of "cheese" on selective recall might have occurred because the replication group was not as hungry as the original sample. The basic experiment was repeated, using several indices of oral deprivation as independent variables. Under conditions of food deprivation, *both* subliminal and supraliminal exposures of the word "cheese" led to a preferential recall of cheese associates, as compared with a blank (control) condition. Drive state was more critical than degree of awareness, but a stimulus was necessary for the effect.

Spence and Gordon (1967) hypothesized that experimental induction of strong personal rejection (by their peers and by E) would activate an unconscious fantasy of being fed, especially in "high oral" Ss (those who acknowledge eating as a response to frustration or rejection). "Rejected" and "accepted," "high-oral" and "low-oral" groups were exposed to a blank slide or a subliminal stimulus (the word "milk") and then asked to learn a list of words containing "regressive" (e.g., "suck," "mother") and conceptual (e.g., "dairy," "butter") milk-associates, plus a group of control words. The rejected, high-oral, *subliminal* group showed a significantly greater mean number of importations (i.e., words not on the word list) or oral-regressive words in their attempt to recall the word list than any of the other groups. No differential effect was found in importations of oral nonregressive words. A similar though nonsignificant result was found with regard to actual recall.

There is some indication that, in contrast to neutral or symbolically drive-related stimuli, explicit drive-related stimuli may inhibit a subliminal recovery effect (Pine 1961; Klein et al. 1958), especially in Ss with particular defensive needs and defensive styles (e.g., Silverman & Silverman 1964). However, focusing on ego functioning rather than recovery of content, Silverman (1967), as noted earlier, has consistently found that aggressive subliminal stimuli lead to significantly greater pathological thinking and other kinds of ego disturbance than do neutral subliminal stimuli (or supraliminal aggressive stimuli), especially in schizophrenics in whom aggressive conflict and inadequate defenses are assumed to be characteristic. However, under certain conditions subliminal drive-related stimuli have been found to raise the level of perceptual-cognitive functioning. In a schizophrenic group, a subliminal stimulus which connotes "merging" (a picture of a man and a woman merged with the words "Mommy and I are one"), compared with a neutral stimulus, leads to decreases in psychopathological thinking, the particular effect being determined by additional factors. Also, Antell (1969) found an increase in creative responses (on the Remote Associates Test) following both an aggressive and a sexual subliminal stimulus, but not after a neutral stimulus.

The work of Orne (1962) and Rosenthal (1966), among others, has forced upon us an explicit recognition of the importance for experimental outcomes of the needs and motives activated by subject-experimenter relationships and expectan-cies. While not systematically investigated, it appears that interpersonal needs (to cooperate, to please, etc.) and transference reactions may well influence reactions to subliminal stimuli (Fisher 1954). Luborsky and Shevrin (1956) emphasize the special importance of the relationship with the experimenter; Ss with whom they had no prior contact were less likely to dream and, of course, less likely to show a subliminal effect. Fisher (1954, 1957) reports that even when good rapport was established, many Ss did not report dreams unless the suggestion to dream was given. As Fisher put it (1954, p. 429):

The experimental situation, procedure and instructions activate unconscious wishes in relation to the experimenter, which. . . organize the preconsciously perceived [percepts]. . .later. . .included in the dream. . .

Kaley (1969) presents a thoughtful review of the role of transference in the Pötzl experiment.

Prevailing Set. A number of studies suggest that a subliminal stimulus is more likely to be incorporated into and bias a stream of conscious thought if it is congruent with it. One way of enhancing the effect of a subliminal stimulus is to prime or prepare the S for it. A drive state, for example, may play a greater role if it is cognitively coded.

The subliminal effect obtained by Spence and Ehrenberg (1964) was strongest in Ss who rated their state of hunger before the subliminal exposure, suggesting that attention to a need state may facilitate a subliminal effect. Gordon and Spence (1966) pursued this line of reasoning more directly. They found a significant triple interaction among set, stimulus, and food deprivation. Set was varied by having Ss read and rate for literary style either a paragraph about pumpkin pie (food set) or a control passage. The greatest preferential recall of cheese-associates was found in food-deprived Ss who received the subliminal "cheese" stimulus *and* who had read the passage proclaiming the pleasures of eating pumpkin pie. A separate analysis indicated that the subliminal effect was greatest in Ss who had poor recall of the food passage, suggesting that some optimal intensity of set facilitates the subliminal effect (see also Gadlin & Fiss 1967).

In studies on the effects of aggressive subliminal stimuli in normals (Silverman 1965; Silverman & Goldweber 1966), Silverman studied the role of "priming." Reading or recalling a drive-related passage congruent in content with the subsequently exposed "aggressive" subliminal stimulus was a necessary condition for a subliminal effect (on Rorschach content and regressive thinking) in nonpsychiatric Ss who responded to the priming with blatant aggressive imagery.

Although the variable of set has been systematically investigated only in more recent subliminal studies, it seems always to have been assumed to be a factor likely to enhance the effect. For example, when an outline of a duck was presented subliminally as a concealed, background form, the recovery task required S to draw an image of a *nature scene* (Eagle, Wolitzky, & Klein 1966; Eagle 1959).

These studies, taken together, support the idea that the presentation of a subliminal stimulus while S is simultaneously engaged in thoughts congruent with those evoked by the stimulus is likely to enhance the effect and, at times, may be a precondition for it.

Personality Characteristics. Under this heading we will consider subliminal effects in relation to individual differences in general personality traits, in defensive patterns, and in specific attributes (e.g., recognition threshold differences). As in the perceptual defense studies, these variables have attracted research attention in an effort to account for marked interindividual variations in the degree and kind of subliminal effects which are obtained within the context of generally significant experimental-control differences. Some of the psychological characteristics that are positively correlated with a subliminal effect have been induced in unselected Ss by manipulation of task variables or organismic state (e.g., a relaxed, noncritical attitude).

In the Bach and Klein (1957) study, Ss who showed a greater subliminal effect (describing a neutral face in accord with the content of the subliminal stimulus: "happy" or "angry") could be characterized, on the basis of their TAT stories, as more passive-receptive, psychologically minded, empathic, and better able to cope with unstructured situations. Subjects who showed minimal effects tended to give glib, highly structured, conventional TAT stories. Comparable results were obtained in a similar study (Smith et al. 1959); greater subliminal sensitivity was associated with a more flexible approach and a greater tolerance of passive attitudes, as reflected in TAT stories. Klein et al. (1958) found that self-image (especially in regard to masculinity-femininity) and recognition threshold for a picture of the male genital were related to subliminal sensitivity to that stimulus, but the relationships are too complex to describe in detail here.

A study by Eagle (1962) supports and extends the above findings. His data came largely from his earlier study in which subliminal aggressive and benevolent A-stimuli had significant differential effects on ratings of a neutral B-figure. Available personality data about these Ss consisted primarily of Q-sort ratings made by clinical judges on the basis of Ss' TAT, Rorschach, Wechsler-Bellevue scale, interviews, autobiography, and pencil-and-paper tests. Eagle found a number of significant correlations between rated personality traits and subliminal sensitivity. For example, greater subliminal sensitivity was associated with a stronger interpersonal orientation (e.g., gregariousness, need for affiliation), a greater receptivity to inner cues (e.g., intuitive, insightful, capable of vivid imagery and fantasy), and a greater cognitive and affective openness. In a sensory-deprivation situation (see Goldberger & Holt 1958), the more subliminally sensitive Ss tended more readily to suspend a strict reality orientation, to experience more pleasant affect, and, in general, to cope more adaptively with the situation (see also Spence & Paul 1959).

Some studies have focused on more specific personality traits or defenses as predictive of the amount and kind of subliminal effect. For example, with male Ss Silverman and Silverman (1964) used a drive-related subliminal stimulus (picture of a female torso) and a recognition threshold measure of denial. Subjects low in denial showed an increase in heterosexual ideas in their Rorschach percepts, whereas Ss high in denial showed a decrease in such content, but an increase in responses denoting phallic preoccupation. Shevrin, Smith and Fritzler (1969) attempted to determine whether repressiveness might play a role in subliminal sensitivity to a manifestly *neutral* stimulus. Subjects assessed for repression (using an index based on their Rorschach responses) were asked

to free associate following the exposure of a subliminal rebus stimulus shown previously to yield subliminal effects (Shevrin & Luborsky 1961; Shevrin & Fisher 1967; Stross & Shevrin 1968). Repressive Ss showed less verbal responsiveness to the subliminal stimulus as well as a lesser average evoked potential, leading the authors to hypothesize an extremely rapid interaction between "complex subliminal inputs and psychological processes" (Shevrin et al. 1969, p. 261; see also Luborsky & Shevrin 1962).

Relevant here are two of Silverman's findings: (1) that normals who were deficient in "neutralizing" aggression showed an increase in regressive thinking following subliminal aggressive stimuli, whereas Ss free of such an impairment did not (Silverman 1965; Silverman & Goldweber 1966); (2) that stutterers, assumed to have conflicts centering on "anal" issues, showed increased speech difficulties following subliminal exposure of a picture of a dog defecating (Silverman et al. 1970).

The results of the studies cited in this section point to the general conclusion that an absence of defensiveness and conflict and an openness to experience are positively associated with a subliminal influence on the content of cognition[17] and negatively correlated with disturbance in formal aspects of ego functioning.

Overview and Theoretical Accounts of Subliminal Effects

Several general conclusions can be drawn from this research literature. First, given failures of replication and unknown instances of negative results, there are, nonetheless, numerous demonstrations that stimulus input in the absence of awareness (as usually defined) can measurably influence a variety of S's subsequent behaviors. That is, registration and perception are independent, and meanings can therefore be activated without awareness. Second, the same kinds of variables (set, drive, state, personality traits, etc.) that govern the selection of and behavioral response to consciously perceived stimuli are at least as important when the stimulus is marginal with respect to awareness. Lacking, however, is sufficient *systematic* consideration of these variables—e.g., their relative importance in subliminal studies and in comparison with supraliminal stimuli. Third, subliminal stimuli can, under certain conditions, lead to effects distinctively different from those obtained with supraliminal stimuli: for example, the greater likelihood of indirect effects, the apparently greater impact of drive-related stimuli, particularly the disruptive effects of subliminal aggressive stimuli on perceptual-cognitive functioning in schizophrenics. Such differences appear to be related to the fact that in subliminal studies the effects are gauged indirectly and S is unaware of the stimulus and unaware that it influences his response, thus precluding certain adaptive and defensive reactions (Silverman & Spiro 1968). Nonetheless, under some conditions subliminal and supraliminal stimuli can elicit comparable effects. It is not clear what variables, other than the nature of the response measure used, contribute to the similarities or differences in subliminal and supraliminal effects.

[17] See also Fox (1960), Lapkin (1962), Smith and Henriksson (1955, 1956), Shevrin and Luborsky (1959), Spence and Paul (1959), Shevrin and Stross (1968, 1969).

The available evidence suggests that recovery of subliminal stimuli, especially in indirect form, is facilitated by an open-ended response task, a relaxed state of consciousness, a relevant need state, a mental set congruent with the stimulus, and a lack of defensiveness. Many reported subliminal effects on formal aspects of ego functioning appear to depend on stirring up a drive and/or conflict and using a response measure which allows for the intensification of S's characteristic mode of dealing with the conflict. Enhancement of adaptive functioning is, however, also possible.

An examination of the subliminal studies, excluding those concerned with sensory thresholds, reveals a reliance on three related theoretical models which are aspects of the psychoanalytic theory of cognition.

First, there is the "day-residue" model. One kind of day residue is the recent, indifferent, barely noticed, unassimilated impression. According to psychoanalytic theory, such material is "selected" for dreams precisely because of its manifest lack of psychic significance; it resonates with unconscious, infantile wishes and emerges in dreams as a derivative cognitive representation of the drive, owing to the requirements of censorship and the nature of unconscious thinking. The Pötzl experiment and its variants (e.g., Pine 1960) are based on this model, but depart from it in several ways.

The second model is that of Freud's view of preconscious thinking, in which he assumed that such thinking tends to spread out over a wider network of associations than is the case in conscious thought. The direction of preconscious thinking can be biased by unconscious motives and sets ("guiding ideas"). The studies of Spence et al. are based on this model. The subliminal stimulus is expected to bias the preconscious stream of thought, especially if there is a boost from unconscious or conscious motives.

The third model, evident mainly in Silverman's (1967) work, is Freud's conception of unconscious motivation, conflict and defense. This model assumes that a subliminal input raises the activation level of existing unconscious motives and that it can therefore be considered analogous to an internally generated increase in the intensity of unconscious motives.

Several of the studies reviewed fail to make explicit which of the three related models is the basis for the investigation, and at times refer to one model when in fact the design is closer to another. These three models are combined in the concept of "schema" activation proposed by Klein and Holt (1960). They assume that memory schemata are activated by sets, by relevant incoming stimuli, and by drives. Under appropriate conditions, marginal inputs are likely to activate drive-related ideas and lead to an effect.[18] This conceptualization is elaborated by Klein (1956, 1970) in terms of a model of motivation in perception which stresses the interplay of executive and concurrently active peripheral motives in relation to their accessibility to awareness, and as determinants of what is focal versus subsidiary in perceptual experience. If subliminal stimuli are considered as a special case of incidental or peripheral activation, then this model constitutes a promising way to understand the interaction of the variables studied in subliminal research.

Starting from a somewhat different framework, Hilgard (1962) arrives at a similar view. He suggests that incidental stimuli act in the same way as unnoticed aspects of supraliminal stimuli. Some unperceived information is lost or dissipated, while some may remain in a state of "...readiness for assimilation to cognitive structure" (p. 66). This information can then become incorporated into a cognitive structure that is in the process of becoming formed (e.g., a TAT story). Hilgard (1962) arrives, then, at a twofold process in perception: (a) immediate assimilation of stimulus input to cognitive structure, via secondary-process thinking (categorizing, etc.), and (b) unassimilated fragments which persist in time and are available for assimilation to cognitive structures. These fragments are most suitable for inclusion in fantasy productions, following the rules of primary-process thinking.

Recovery of subliminal inputs has been interpreted by some (Holt 1959; Pine 1964) in the light of Lewin's (1935) concept of "quasi needs" and the Zeigarnik effect (1927). The assumption is that an experimentally presented unreportable stimulus arouses tension because it is "unfinished business" (Holt 1959) and that this tension provides the impetus for its emergence into a cognitive product. While from a phenomenological standpoint there may be no experience of incompleted activity, it can be seen as analogous to preconscious thinking about an unsolved problem.

SUMMARY OF METHODOLOGICAL PROBLEMS

Many of the subliminal studies reviewed above were summarized uncritically since a detailed analysis of each study would have prevented the reader from forming an overall picture of the research in this area. It therefore needs to be clearly stated that the majority of findings should be regarded as tentative. Perhaps the most serious problems are small sample size, weak effects, and rare attempts at exact replication. The sequence of subliminal studies suggests that investigators are made unhappy by weak results, think of an uncontrolled variable that might be relevant, include it in the next experiment, and get results, which, however, in turn are not subjected to replication. The outcome is a proliferation of seemingly relevant variables. The issue of the reliability of earlier results is obscured and creates doubt about the solidity of the overall findings.

Neisser (1967) quickly dismisses the possibility of subliminal effects. He claims that such an effect is suspect for one or more of the following reasons: it does not make sense from the standpoint of evolution;[19] the results are tenuous; partial cues were available; The results are artifacts based on the "demand characteristics" (Orne 1962) of the experiment. Neisser cites several studies to which these criticisms are applicable and have the virtue of greater parsimony; nevertheless, in many instances one would have trouble applying them. For example, Guthrie and Wiener (1966) claim that Eagle's (1959) findings are attributable to partial cues (e.g., cues of angularity connot-

---

[18] Implied here is the idea that the stimulus has to be relevant to the S and maintained over time, factors stressed by Spence (1967) reviewing his own work, and considered more critical than awareness per se.

[19] This comment applies specifically to the A-B masking technique: "In view of the very specialized nature of backward masking, which is almost impossible to produce without tachistoscopic control of the stimuli, it seems unlikely that evolution would have equipped us with sophisticated unconscious mechanisms for dealing with it." And, "... they could hardly be an aid to survival" (Neisser 1967, p. 30).

ing aggression), but Silverman and Spiro (1967b) present data that provide a convincing counterargument.

A few additional methodological comments are in order. First, the subliminal input is often expected to emerge in transformed ways, and it is at times difficult to be certain that a scored recovery is actually a variant of the stimulus (e.g., Fisher 1954), even when criteria are specified a priori (e.g., Paul & Fisher 1959). Part of the problem is that there is no independent way of knowing exactly what is activated by the stimulus. Second, procedural flaws, such as the use of difference scores, make some studies suspect. Spence and Holland (1962), for example, use a difference score between recall of "cheese" and control associates as the index of subliminal effect. In experimental-control comparisons, it is not clear whether there is increased recall of cheese associates or decreased recall of control words. Lastly, in comparing group means we of course never know which Ss are "really" showing the effect.

An alternative research strategy might more clearly elucidate the role of personality in this kind of perceptual experiment. Subjects could be selected on the basis of a careful assessment of relevant personality attributes. They would then be run repeatedly in a series of subliminal, blank, and supraliminal conditions where the stimulus, task, and organismic variables discussed above would be systematically manipulated. Such an approach might provide reliable information of the following kind: which (if any) kind of S is consistently sensitive to subliminal stimuli? If a "loose" cognitive structure facilitates a subliminal effect (Allison 1963), is this "looseness" as an attribute of the S interchangeable with "looseness" induced via experimental manipulation? Other complex interactions could be examined and perhaps integrated with studies of perceptual defense in the same Ss. Such an ambitious undertaking, on the model of Murray et al.'s (1938) approach to personality investigation, holds the promise of providing the kind of information needed.

The theories and explanations advanced to account for the subliminal effect have thus far been unable to specify clearly the mechanisms involved or the necessary conditions for its appearance in a way that would allow accurate prediction. The accounts are essentially descriptive generalizations focused on the nature of perceptual-cognitive processes and awareness; in this regard, greater efforts might be made to integrate this work with that on information processing (Gaito 1964; Haber 1969) and attention (Egeth & Bevan 1970; Swets & Kristofferson 1970).

So far, the promise of a clinical-experimental psychology of unconscious phenomena has not been fulfilled; the theoretical and empirical yield has been disappointing. Perhaps a major reason for this outcome is that the emphasis on subliminality obscured the potential of experimental designs involving the use of peripheral (incidental) stimuli. Such "above threshold" stimuli that escape focal attention are clearly more characteristic of everyday behavior and might lead to more substantial effects. The subliminal studies have not contributed much beyond demonstrating under controlled conditions what is well established on the basis of clinical observation; viz., that conscious thinking can be influenced by ideas outside of awareness. The exceptions to this conclusion are the suggestion that subliminal inputs may undergo almost immediate transformation (Fisher 1954; Shevrin et al. 1969) and Silverman's (1967, 1970) findings concerning the effects of subliminal stimuli on ego functioning.

It is undoubtedly implausible to many that the *meaning* of a less than ten millisecond subliminal blip like "Mommy and I are one" could indeed register and lead to a measurable effect. Such highly provocative findings in a number of experiments (Silverman et al. 1969; Silverman & Candell 1970) are not readily accommodated within current perceptual or information-processing models (Neisser 1967). Independent replication[20] is therefore important, especially since Silverman's (1967, 1970) very promising work goes beyond demonstrating subliminal effects to tests of specific, controversial psychoanalytic propositions.

Cognitive Controls and Cognitive Style

In many respects, the work on cognitive style, to be discussed next, can be viewed as the culmination of the effort to bring research on personality and on perception into fruitful cross-fertilization. Workers on cognitive style have continued to exhibit interest in reflections of motivational and defensive processes in perception and in the role of conscious and unconscious factors in perception. They have gone beyond the original ways of framing such questions, however, and made possible a consideration of broadly based individual differences and of processes leading to reality-attuned perception as well as to distortion.

Much of the work on cognitive style grew rather directly out of efforts to come to terms more productively with understanding the role of motivation in perception (e.g., Klein 1958). Interest in the dimension of field dependence-field independence, however, which is perhaps the most studied of all the cognitive style dimensions, had somewhat different origins. We shall consider first the work done on this aspect of cognitive style, and then consider a broader approach which treats field dependence-independence as but one of several dimensions that contribute to a person's cognitive style.

FIELD DEPENDENCE AND PSYCHOLOGICAL DIFFERENTIATION

The concept of field dependence-independence grew out of efforts by Witkin and others (e.g., Witkin 1949, 1950, 1952; Witkin & Asch 1948a, 1948b; Asch & Witkin 1948a, 1948b) in the late 1940s to explore the factors involved in perception of the vertical.

Among the instruments used was the rod and frame test (RFT), which consists of a movable rod surrounded by a rectangular frame tilted at an angle from the vertical. In a darkened room, with only the rod and frame illuminated, the subject is required to set the rod to the upright. Highly consistent individual differences were found. Some subjects view the rod as vertical when it is aligned with the tilted frame around it, even if this means that the rod is actually markedly deviating from the vertical. Others are able to avoid the influence of the surrounding frame and readily set the rod to the true vertical.

Another test used by Witkin, the body adjustment test

[20] Work of this kind has begun. In a recent doctoral dissertation, Lomangino (1969) reported results in accord with Silverman's (1967) findings that subliminal aggressive stimuli (words or pictures) intensify pathological thinking in schizophrenics (see also Buchholz 1968).

(BAT), also yielded large and consistent individual differences. Here the subject sits in a movable chair, initially tilted to the left or right, within a room which is itself tilted to the left or right. Subjects are asked to position the chair so that they are sitting in an upright position. Again, some subjects consistently align themselves with the walls of the tilted room, although they are then considerably tilted, and others readily adjust the seat to the true vertical. In both tests, without the distorting influence of the surrounding field, the task is easy for all subjects. If no frame is present, all can easily set the rod accurately to the vertical; with their eyes closed, subjects who said that they were vertical when aligned with the room readily sense that they are tilted and can accurately set themselves upright.

Consistent correlations have been found between performance on these two tests and between performance on each and on the embedded figures test (EFT), in which subjects must find a simple geometric figure which is disguised by being embedded in a larger, more complex configuration (Witkin, Lewis, Hertzman, Machover, Meissner, & Wapner 1954; Witkin, Dyk, Faterson, Goodenough, & Karp 1962). In all of these procedures, successful performance requires the subject to perceive an item independently of the field or context which surrounds it. For this reason, the dimension of individual consistency tapped by these tests was designated as field dependence versus field independence.

Developmentally, there is a clear trend toward increasing field independence from about age 5 to age 15, with a leveling off until the early 40s and a subsequent trend toward greater field dependence with increasing age. Throughout this development, however, individual differences remain quite stable; that is, although absolute levels change with time, the person's position relative to his age group remains the same (Witkin, Goodenough, & Karp 1967). Small but consistent sex differences have repeatedly been found, boys tending to be more field independent than girls.

Witkin et al. (1962) have suggested that these tests of perceptual field dependence tap a broader aspect of personality functioning, designated by Witkin as psychological differentiation and linked by him to conceptions of Werner (1948) and Lewin (1935). In this scheme, development moves from a global organization to a more structured and articulated organization, and individual personality organizations are viewed as consistent in the degree of differentiation manifested. Perceptually, this means that field-independent persons are able to perceive parts of the field as discrete and the field as structured, whereas the perception of field-dependent persons is strongly dominated by the overall organization of the field and they are unable to break it up into its parts. In other aspects of cognitive functioning, the degree to which cognition is articulated and differentiated is reflected, for example, in performance on the Einstellung problems and on the Duncker problems, which require for their solution that S break the set which usually organizes his conceptualizations. Ss who are perceptually field independent on tests like the EFT and RFT tend to be more able to reorganize their conceptual frameworks, to overcome the embedding context of their old ideas (Guilford 1957; Karp 1963; Fenchel 1958; Zaks 1954; Guetzkow 1951; Goodman 1960; Witkin et al. 1962).

Field dependence or psychological differentiation also shows strong relationships to other aspects of personality. Witkin et al. (1962) report, for example, that field-dependent subjects draw the human figure in a far less articulated fashion than do field-independent subjects. They interpret this well-replicated finding as reflecting a less articulated body concept in the field dependent. Witkin et al. have also reported a variety of other findings in accord with their view that field-dependent persons experience the self (including one's body, one's needs and characteristics, and one's frame of reference) as less separate and structured than do field independents. Thus, field-dependent subjects, more than field independents, asked for guidance and definition when taking the TAT, answered personality questionnaires in ways indicative of social dependency, conformism, and need for others' approval, and changed their judgments in the autokinetic situation when under the social influence of a planted confederate.

In the area of controls and defenses, a variety of findings suggest that field-dependent subjects are more likely to use such defenses as denial and repression, whereas field-independent subjects, with a greater tendency to keep things discrete and separate, rely upon intellectualization and isolation (e.g., Witkin et al. 1962; Zukmann 1957; Bertini 1960; Schimek 1968).

Such a defense preference is also suggested by the kinds of psychopathology likely to be evident in extremely field-dependent and field-independent persons. Degree of field dependence per se does not seem related to frequency of psychological disorder, although there are suggestions of greater psychopathology in persons of either extreme than in intermediates. The types of disorders among the extreme groups, however, differ in quite consistent fashion. Among field-dependent persons, common kinds of psychopathology include identity problems, excessive dependency, inadequate controls, problems of passivity and helplessness, alcoholism, ulcers, obesity, and hysterical disorders. Among schizophrenic patients, catatonics and patients who hallucinate tend to be field dependent. Psychopathology among the field independent is more likely to include delusions, expansive and euphoric ideas of grandeur, outward direction of aggression, overideation, and obsessive-compulsive disorders. Among schizophrenics, paranoids and ambulatory schizophrenics with a well-developed defensive structure are the most field independent (Witkin 1965).

There can be little question that the concept of field dependence-independence as a reflection of a pervasive trend in personal functioning has helped to generate and organize an imposing array of findings. Several unresolved theoretical difficulties exist, however, which are relevant to our consideration of cognitive style research in general. First of all, there is some ambiguity about whether the field dependence-independence dimension reflects differences in capacity or in stylistic preferences or strategies (Wachtel 1968a). Witkin et al. (1962) refer in several places to divergent *directions* of development and seem to imply "separate but equal" strategies for coping with the task of being a human being. Yet examination of the procedures used to assess a person's position on this "style" dimension reveals that they *require* him to function field-independently. The person who fails to position the rod accurately, or to find the hidden figures rapidly, shows himself to have a *deficit*. The theoretical conception of differentiation, too, implies a deficit among the field dependent—these people have developed and matured less completely.

Witkin et al. (1962) do point out that a successful (i.e., nonpathological) adaptation can be made at any level of development, that many aspects of personality must be assessed in evaluating a person, and that extreme field independence may also be associated with negative attributes such as coldness and isolation. There is nonetheless an acknowledged (1962, p. 21) implication that, other things being equal, the field-independent person has richer, more diversified resources for coping with life than the field dependent. The field-dependent person's "style," even when it leads him to develop valuable traits (such as empathy or the capacity for interpersonal cooperation), seems, in this view, to be essentially the expression of his developmental deficit and his efforts to cope with or live with that deficit.

It must be noted, however, that although tests like the RFT and EFT measure a particular ability, it is still possible that they indicate different *directions* of development and not just different degrees. For as is often suggested by proponents of scatter analysis of intelligence tests (Rapaport et al., 1968), particular skills and capacities may be purchased at the price of lesser development in other areas. As persons develop in their own characteristic fashion, they are likely to place great emphasis on some modes of adaptation and to inhibit others, perhaps even actively. Thus, many of the persons who are field dependent on the Witkin perceptual tests may be so because early in their development they put their eggs in another basket. For them, field dependence is part of a larger style of adaptation, a reflection of a particular individual strategy. Others may be field dependent because of a general truncation of personal development. Only by assessing a wide range of capacities and modes of adaptation can these two types of "field-dependent" persons be distinguished (Wachtel 1972). The work to be discussed next represents an effort to encompass the field dependence-independence dimension within a general conception of stylistic strategies.

Cognitive Controls: A Multidimensional Approach

Early in the history of the "New Look" in perception, Klein and Schlesinger (1949) raised the question: "Where is the perceiver in perceptual theory?" This question has guided a large body of research which has attempted to integrate psychoanalytic and other conceptions of personality structure and functioning with the ideas and methods of perceptual and cognitive psychologists.

Many early studies of the influence of need on perception suffered from a naive attempt to find uniform effects across all Ss. In time it became apparent that different kinds of people can react in diametrically opposed ways. Contradictory findings, inhibitory effects following prolonged deprivation, and the realization that perception is, after all, usually free from significant distortion, combined to further the search for laws of *perceivers*, i.e., how persons are organized to cope with motives and needs (Klein, Schlesinger, & Meister 1951; Klein 1951, 1954, 1956, 1958).

Over the past twenty years, there has been an increasing tendency toward such a view of motivation and personality. This trend, traced in detail by Sanford (1963), has two aspects. First, motivational aspects of behavior have been conceptualized in terms of general cognitive processes and functions; for example, Festinger's (1957) theory of cognitive dissonance, Schachter's (1964) work on cognitive determinants of emotional states, Lazarus's (1966) studies of cognitive appraisal in coping with stress, and Zimbardo's (1969) investigations of the cognitive

control of pain. Second, dimensions of personality were seen in terms of individual differences in perceptual cognitive behavior. The studies by Witkin, discussed above, and by Klein (1951) provided the major impetus for this approach.

The development of Klein's conception of cognitive controls can be traced (Gardner, Holzman, Klein, Linton, & Spence 1959) to his studies of personality theory (Klein 1951), motivation (Klein 1954, 1958), defense (Klein 1954), psychophysics and Gestalt theory (Holzman & Klein 1954), and psychoanalytically oriented inquiries concerning the adaptive significance of perception (Klein 1958, 1959a). The observation of consistent individual differences in psychophysical tasks and the idea that motivational and environmental forces operate within structural constraints were central to the development of the concept of perceptual and cognitive "attitudes" or *Anschauungen* (Klein 1951, 1953), terms which were later replaced by the word "control" to emphasize the hypothesized regulative aspect of these behaviors.

According to Klein (1958), cognitive controls ". . .have the status of intervening variables and define rules by which perception, memory, and other basic qualitative forms of experience are shaped" (p. 107). The underlying premise of investigations of cognitive controls is that a wide range of adaptive efforts can be understood as variants of relatively few basic dimensions of perceptual-cognitive organization.[21] Cognitive controls are conceptualized by Gardner et al. (1959) as:

. . .slow-changing, developmentally stabilized structures: (a) they are relatively invariant over a given class of situations and intentions; (b) they are operational despite the shifts in situational and behavioral contexts typical of cognitive activity from moment to moment. Cognitive controls refer to a level of organization that is more general than the specific structural components underlying perception, recall, and judgment. The invariant which defines a control has to do with the manner of coordination between a class of environmental situations. They are the individual's means of programming the properties, relations, and constraints of events and objects in such a way as to provide an adaptively adequate resolution of the intentions which brought him into an encounter with reality (Gardner et al. 1959, pp. 5-6).

Efforts have been made to place this conception of cognitive control and cognitive style[22] within the framework of psychoanalytic theory (Klein 1958; Gardner et al. 1959; Gardner, Jackson, & Messick 1960). Cognitive controls are considered to be analogous to defenses, but are activated by and serve adaptive rather than conflictual aims; they are seen as relatively "conflict-free," secondary-process, controlling structures which regulate drive expression.

Research based on this conceptualization of cognitive controls has focused on identifying control dimensions, developing tests that reflect them, specifying the perceptual processes

[21] This approach has a long history in psychology and in personality theory (see Helson's [1964] discussion of Brentano, Benussi, and Frenkel-Brunswik). Also relevant are the early studies of expressive movement (Allport & Vernon 1933) and Thurstone's (1944) pioneering factorial study of perception.

[22] The arrangements of cognitive controls within a person are referred to as "cognitive styles"; little systematic work has been conducted on styles as such, however. Many authors tend to use the terms as loosely synonymous. See Wachtel (1972).

presumed to be involved in performance, determining their stability and generality, and exploring the relations among controls and between controls and motivational variables such as drives and defenses (see Gardner et al. 1959; Gardner, Jackson, & Messick 1960; Gardner 1962). More recently, cognitive controls have been studied in relation to development (e.g., Gardner 1964a; Gardner & Moriarty 1968), genetic and cultural variables (Gardner 1965), physical maturation (Broverman, Broverman, Vogel, Palmer, & Klaiber 1964), physiological correlates (e.g., Israel 1966; Witkin & Oltman 1967), sensory feedback (Holzman & Rousey 1971), attention and consciousness (Gardner 1969; Silverman 1964a), and psychopathology (Israel 1966; Silverman 1964a, 1964b; Witkin 1965; Shapiro 1965).

The studies cited above have involved primarily the cognitive control principles originally hypothesized by Klein and isolated by Gardner et al. (1959) in their factor-analytic study. They are: field-articulation (i.e., field dependence-independence), leveling-sharpening, scanning, equivalence range (later called "conceptual differentiation" [Gardner & Schoen 1962]), constricted-flexible control, and tolerance for unrealistic experiences. These dimensions (to be discussed below) are not of course thought to exhaust the number of dimensions that might be significant for ego functioning and adaptation. There has, in fact, been a proliferation of proposed perceptual-cognitive controls or styles: "ego-closeness-ego-distance" (Voth & Mayman 1963; Mayman & Voth 1969), automatization (Broverman 1964), complexity-simplicity (Bieri 1961), conceptual systems (Harvey, Hunt, & Schroder 1961), importing (Paul 1959), augmenting-reducing (Petrie 1967), analytic and reflective attitudes (Kagan, Rosman, Day, Albert, & Phillips 1964), and tolerance for ambiguity (Frenkel-Brunswik 1949), among others. These dimensions have not been studied in relation to one another or in relation to the dimensions proposed by Gardner et al. (1959). Nor do we know where any of these dimensions, or Witkin's, are located in the factor-analytic space of Cattell (1970), Guilford (1967), or Eysenck (1967). The dimensions are typically studied one at a time and in relation to one or two dependent variables. Absent as of now is an integrated theory which would specify a hierarchical organization of regulative principles clearly linking perception and personality.

A number of logical, theoretical, and methodological problems (Gardner et al. 1959; Postman 1955; Vernon 1964; Mischel 1968) are involved in the research on cognitive controls. Since most of the problems are common to all the control dimensions studied they will, with a few exceptions, be discussed after a review of the empirical work.

Leveling-Sharpening. This control dimension describes variations in "...modes of organizing a *sequence* of stimuli" (Gardner et al. 1959, pp. 22-23). Leveling refers to "maximal assimilation effects, and ... memory organizations in which the fine shades of distinctions among individual elements are lost" (Gardner et al. 1959). Sharpening refers to minimal assimilation effects between new percepts and related memories of previous percepts. These terms had been used in a somewhat different sense by Wulf (1922), Carmichael, Hogan, and Walter (1932), and Allport and Postman (1947).

The main task used to assess leveling-sharpening tendencies is the Schematizing Test, adapted from Hollingsworth (1913).

This test consists of a series of squares, shown in sets of five, with a gradual increase in size as the series progresses. The S is required to judge the size of each square. The degree to which S's judgments fail to keep pace with the general increase in size is considered to result from the assimilation of current perceptual experience to the aggregate of memories of the previous, smaller squares. The measures derived from this procedure are ranking accuracy (for each set of five squares), increment error, and log lag. The properties of and relationships among these measures have themselves been studied, since they vary in predictive power and in their behavioral correlates (see Gardner & Long 1960b, 1960e; Israel 1966; Kratwohl & Cronbach 1956; Vick & Jackson 1967).

The process rationale for the Schematizing Test was developed in a series of studies which showed leveling-sharpening tendencies to be related to visual, auditory, and kinesthetic time-error (Holzman 1954; Holzman & Klein 1954; Klein & Holzman 1950).[23] The leveling-sharpening dimension is a relevant factor in proactive and retroactive inhibition (Paul 1959), in accuracy of recall in measures of serial learning (Gardner & Long 1960b), in the serial reproduction of a story (Gardner & Lohrenz 1961), in the recall of a childhood story (Holzman & Gardner 1960), and in other tasks involving memory organization (see Gardner et al. 1959). Sharpeners showed a general superiority in these studies. Efforts have been made to relate leveling-sharpening, as well as other control principles, to defenses. Gardner et al. (1959) found that repressors (as classified by Rorschach scores) tend to be levelers, although levelers are not necessarily repressors. Similar findings were reported by Holzman and Gardner (1960).[24] They suggest that repression relies, in part, on leveling, but note that alternative interpretations are possible (e.g., that leveling is a consequence of repression; that leveling and repression refer to the same mental processes viewed from two perspectives—adaptation and defense).

The idea that extreme defensive or psychopathological characteristics are associated with extreme reliance on a given perceptual-cognitive strategy has been proposed by others (Silverman 1964a; Witkin 1965; Israel 1966). In an effort to extend the rationale of leveling-sharpening and investigate its defensive aspects, Israel (1966) studied some physiological correlates of leveling-sharpening in both normals and schizophrenics. She found support for the hypothesis that sharpeners would show slower rates of habituation (indexed by the orienting reflex [OR] component of the GSR) than levelers to a sequence of visual stimuli varying in size. The result was significant for the schizophrenic group; sharpeners showed extreme OR reactivity, and levelers extreme inactivity. Israel (1966) suggested that "...extreme leveling may exemplify a form of perceptual defense involving the dampening of attentional and arousal mechanisms..." (p. 88). In a subsequent study, sharpeners showed consistent anticipatory cardiac deceleration to a sequence of visual stimuli regardless of variations in attitude toward the expected stimulus; levelers showed cardiac acceleration when

[23] Gardner and Lohrenz (1961) found that investment of attention seems to stabilize percepts and renders them less susceptible to assimilative interaction in the course of memory formation.

[24] The Rorschach measure of repression was indirect, i.e., it was assumed that certain indicators (e.g., notable lack of specificity, little variety in content, etc.) were consequences of repression. It is primarily a measure of hysterical defensive style.

anxiety-arousing stimuli were anticipated, no cardiac change when bored or uninterested in the stimuli, and anticipatory deceleration prior to stimuli judged to be interesting (Israel 1969). According to Lacey et al. (1963), cardiac deceleration is assumed to correspond to active attention to the environment, and acceleration is associated with rejection of external input.

Scanning. Originally termed focusing (Schlesinger 1954), the scanning control principle, as reformulated by Gardner et al. (1959), refers to individual consistencies in attention deployment: Scanners sample stimulus fields extensively, whereas nonscanners restrict their attention to limited aspects of a stimulus field.[25]

Scanning emerged as a factor, though for men only, in the Gardner et al. (1959) study. The main measure used was the average error on a size-estimation task in which *S* adjusts a variable circle of light to match the size of a standard disc. Overestimation is asumed to be a function of relative centration (see Piaget 1961) on the standard stimulus and is taken as an indication of limited scanning; a low average error of overestimation defines the (broadly ranging) scanner.

Gardner and his associates explored the generality of scanning strategies in a series of studies on the role of selective attention (the EFT measure of field-articulation was also used) in size judgments and visual illusion effects (Gardner 1959, 1961; Gardner & Long 1960a, 1960b, 1962a, 1962b). The main findings in these studies, which were guided by Piaget's (1961) centration hypothesis, were that large overestimation of the standard disc in the size-estimation test was related to greater errors of the standard in inverted-T and reversed-L illusions, and that there are individual consistencies in centration effects, size-estimation performances, and in other indices of actual eye-movement behavior.

In view of the fact that the size-estimation measure of scanning is *indirect*, Gardner and Long (1962a, 1962b) obtained direct recordings of actual eye movements while *S* was performing in a series of size-estimation tasks. While several eye movement measures were positively correlated across conditions, the correlations between size estimation and eye-movement behavior were low. This outcome calls into question findings that are based only on the size-estimation measures (e.g., Silverman's [1964b] finding that paranoid schizophrenics tend to be extensive scanners, whereas nonparanoid schizophrenics tend to be limited scanners). McKinnon and Singer (1969) focus on this issue. Paranoid and nonparanoid schizophrenics, psychotic depressives, and control *S*s were studied in free-search and size-estimation conditions, with concomitant recording of actual eye movements (movement rate and fixation rate). While paranoid schizophrenics receiving medication (phenothiazine drugs) showed greater underestimation than medicated nonparanoid schizophrenics (as Silverman [1964b] found), opposite results were found for nonmedicated paranoid and nonparanoid groups. Furthermore, psychiatric classification was not related to eye-movement behavior.[26]

[25] It might be noted here that several cognitive-control dimensions have been conceptualized in attentional terms (e.g., Gardner 1959, 1961; Silverman 1964a). However, the different meanings that can be assigned to the terms broad and narrow attention have not always been distinguished (see Wachtel [1967] for clarification of this point).

[26] Medicated *S*s produced significantly fewer eye movements and lower fixation rates.

either during free-search conditions or during the size judgment tasks (prior to a training and extinction procedure), nor was there any relationship between size judgments and eye-movement scores (see, however, Silverman & Gaarder 1967).

It is clear that direct measures of scanning strategies are required. Direct recordings show stable, individual consistencies in saccadic eye movements over a wide range of experimental situations. Rate of visual scanning is unrelated to binocular coordination, fixation steadiness, and tracking efficiency (McKinnon 1966). Performance on scanning tasks that allow free inspection of the visual field (e.g., Luborsky, Blinder, & Schimek 1965) may have different implications than does the Gardner et al. (1959) measure of scanning, which requires a size judgment about the relation between two stimuli. For example, the latter task calls for an adaptive response—there is a right answer. This task seems bound to have variance due to ability, as is suggested by the studies of visual illusions (Gardner & Long 1960a, 1960b, 1962a, 1962b).

Several studies have explored links between scanning and defenses. Gardner et al. (1959) reported that extreme reliance on the defense of isolation, as judged from the Rorschach, is associated with extreme scanning, although extreme scanners are not necessarily isolators. Gardner and Long (1962b) found that extreme, versus limited, scanners were judged, by Rorschach indices, to be higher in isolation, projection, and generalized delay. Neither of these studies, however, presents the full range of scores of all *S*s on both the scanning and defense measures. A more clear-cut link between scanning and isolation is provided by Luborsky et al. (1965). They exposed pictures of neutral, sexual, or aggressive content and simultaneously recorded eye-movement behavior. They found positive correlations between the degree of isolation (again, based on Rorschach indices) and the degree of looking around. Repression was negatively correlated with looking around (and with isolation). Recall of the sexual stimuli was positively correlated with isolation scores and negatively with repression scores. While these results accord well with a clinical view of defenses, the precise nature of the isolation-scanning link is not clear (see Gardner et al. [1959, pp. 127-28] for a general discussion of different ways to think about control-defense relationships).

Tolerance for Unrealistic Experiences. This dimension, originally proposed by Klein and Schlesinger (1951),[27] refers to the extent to which *S* departs from a strict reality orientation and accepts perceptual experiences which he knows are not real. The main tasks used for assessment are an apparent movement (*phi*-phenomenon) task and an aniseikonic lenses task. In the apparent movement test, stimuli in two fields are presented in sequences in such a way that one can experience alternation, movement, and simultaneity. The instructions inform *S* that *real* movement never occurs. The scores used are mean movement threshold and/or mean range of apparent movement. In the aniseikonic lenses test, developed by Ames (1946), special glasses make things look tilted and the time to recognize the tilt and the degree of perceived tilt are recorded (Gardner et al. 1959).

Klein and Schlesinger (1951), using apparent movement and the Rorschach, tested the generality of a perceptual attitude

[27] A similar dimension, "tolerance for ambiguity," was earlier proposed by Frenkel-Brunswik (1949).

of tolerance for instability versus clinging to reliable familiar perceptual experience. Subjects who were characterized as "form-labile," versus "form-bound," on the basis of various Rorschach criteria (for example, $F + \%$), showed a wider range of *phi* experience. (Jeffreys [1953] reported comparable results.) In a subsequent study, Klein, Gardner, and Schlesinger (1962) found that the range of apparent movement was related to a greater number of experienced reversals of a reversible figure; the length of time the more conventional phase of the figure was experienced; the amount of distortion induced by aniseikonic lenses and time taken to recognize the distortion; and the ability to accept an imaginative and relaxed approach to the Rorschach test as judged qualitatively by clinicians. Factor analysis of the two criterion measures along with other tests gives further support for a dimension of tolerance for unrealistic experiences (see Gardner et al. 1959). Findings from other studies are consistent with these. For example, Kaplan (1952) found that subjects who tended to resist the distortion brought about by wearing the lenses also tended to recall fewer loosely related story elements (see also Martin 1954; Segal 1968).

Feirstein (1967) investigated the relationship between tolerance for unrealistic experiences and certain personality factors, guided by psychoanalytic concepts, particularly Kris's (1952) concept of regression in the service of the ego. Several measures of tolerance for unrealistic experiences (including the *phi*-phenomenon and aniseikonic lenses) were used. Measures of amount and integration of unrealistic thinking were derived from the Rorschach test by Holt's (Holt & Havel 1960; Holt 1966) method, an art preference test, and a word-association test. Feirstein found, in support of his hypothesis, that an overall measure of the amount of tolerance for unrealistic experiences was significantly correlated with the degree of *integrated* unrealistic thinking on the Rorschach ("adaptive regression"), but not with the sheer amount of unrealistic thinking. On the basis of these and other findings, Feirstein concludes that the inability to achieve integrated drive-related and unrealistic thinking is associated with an avoidance of the conflict involved in the measures of tolerance for unrealistic experiences (TUE). The implication is that subjects with low TUE scores attempt to keep a firm grasp on reality and try to avoid becoming disrupted and confused by drive-related and unrealistic thoughts.

A cognitive control dimension proposed by Voth and Mayman (1963, 1966; Mayman & Voth 1969), ego-closeness-ego-distance, appears to be similar to tolerance for unrealistic experiences, although the two do not seem to have been studied together. This dimension is based on the idea that "persons habitually differ with respect to their closeness to or distance from their concrete stimulus fields" (1969, p. 635). The major measure is the degree of autokinetic movement (the degree of experienced movement of a steadily fixated pinpoint of light in an absolutely dark room). The ego-close person (the person who experiences relatively little autokinetic movement) is less likely to become oblivious to his concrete surroundings in the test situation and is less likely to embellish the autokinetic experience with fantasy and imagery. In previous studies (Voth & Mayman 1963, 1966, 1968), normal persons with low autokinetic scores could be characterized as outgoing and responsive in contrast to those with high autokinetic scores, who tended to be detached and unlikely to experience strong impulses and feelings. Among the emotionally disturbed subjects, high autokinetic scores gave evidence of excessive rumination and schizoid fantasy whereas

low-scoring emotionally disturbed subjects tended to be emotionally labile and prone to acting out. It should be noted that this dimension is orthogonal to Witkin's field dependence-independence dimension (Cancro & Voth 1969).

Equivalence Range. This control principle, also called "conceptual differentiation" (Gardner & Schoen 1962), refers to individual consistencies in categorizing behavior (Gardner 1953). A *narrow* equivalence range implies detailed categorization of stimuli, whereas a *broad* equivalence range reflects coarser differentiation in tasks involving judgments, rather than perception (see Marrs 1955), of similarities and differences. Individual variations in equivalence range do not seem to be based on varying awareness of stimulus differences but rather on a preference to act on or ignore the differences (Gardner et al. 1959). The preference for broad, versus narrow, categorizing appears to be independent of capacity for abstraction (Gardner & Schoen 1962) and inductive and deductive reasoning abilities (Gardner et al. 1960).

The most commonly used measure of this dimension is an object sorting task (Gardner 1953). In this task, a heterogeneous array of objects is presented to S with instructions to group together those objects which seem to belong together for a particular reason. The instructions emphasize that there are no right and wrong answers. The score used is the number of groups; each object put by itself is considered an additional group (Gardner et al. 1959; Gardner, Jackson, & Messick 1960).

Several studies have shown that a paper-and-pencil form of this test gives comparable results (Sloane, Gorlow, & Jackson 1936; Clayton & Jackson 1961; Gardner, Lohrenz, & Schoen 1968). Sorting tasks involving objects, descriptive statements of everyday behaviors, Chinese ideographs (Marrs 1955), drawings of objects, names of objects, photographs of human faces, and descriptions of people (Sloane 1959) reveal a fair degree of individual consistency.

In his initial study of this dimension, Gardner (1953) explored the limits of its generality. He found that Ss with narrow as opposed to those with broad equivalence range were more accurate in matching the brightness of light patches, and in matching shapes in a size-constancy situation. These relationships, however, were not reliably replicated (Gardner et al. 1959; Gardner, Jackson, & Messick 1960; Sloane 1959).

The evidence for the generality and unidimensionality of equivalence range is not clear-cut. Fillenbaum (1959) obtained significant but moderate correlations among several tests (e.g., similarity of rectangles, synonyms substituted in a sentence, etc.) and suggested that there was a consistency in the "fineness" or "coarseness" of categorizing behavior. Sloane, Gorlow, and Jackson (1963) conducted a factor-analytic study using 23 measures which included several sorting tasks, Pettigrew's (1958) category width test, size constancy and brightness judgment measures, etc. The first and largest factor (called sorting equivalence range) included the sorting measures but none of the other tasks (see also Forehand 1962; Gardner & Schoen 1962). The findings of Gardner, Lohrenz, and Schoen (1968) further attest to the complexity and multidimensionality of categorizing behavior (see also Glixman 1965; Wyer 1964).

There appears to be some conceptual overlap among "psychological differentiation" (Witkin et al. 1962), "conceptual differentiation" (Gardner & Schoen 1962), "cognitive complexity" (Bieri 1961), and "conceptual systems" (Harvey, Hunt, & Schroder 1961). All seem to involve the articulation of judgment and experience. Gardner et al. (1968) factor-analyzed several relevant measures; among the factors extracted were Person and Object Differentiation, Conceptual Differentiation in Categorizing, and Object Differentiation. (The object sorting task loaded on the last two factors as well as on a Leveling-Sharpening factor.)

A measure analogous to Bieri's (1961) index of cognitive complexity loaded on the first factor and, as in other instances, it would be of interest to know something concrete about the similarity of the two concepts. The concept of cognitive complexity-simplicity (Bieri 1961) refers to the "relative differentiation of a person's system of dimensions for construing behavior" (Bieri, Atkins, Briar, Leaman, Miller, & Tripodi 1966, p. 185). A person's standing on this proposed dimension is determined by his performance on a variation of the Role Construct Repertory (Rep) Test devised by Kelly (1955). In the Rep Test, S is asked to rate a group of 10 people (e.g., self, father, boss, etc.) on descriptive traits (e.g., calm-excitable, outgoing-shy, etc.), using a six-step Likert scale. The greater the disparity of ratings across the 10 people, the greater the cognitive complexity of the S. Cognitive complexity has proved to be a predictor of differences in social and clinical judgments. For example, more complex judges seem to tune in more on inner states in their judgments, discriminate better among incongruent stimuli (Leventhal & Singer 1964). In a similar vein, Blatt, Allison, and Feirstein (1969) found that the capacity to cope with cognitive complexity was associated with adaptive regression and defense effectiveness, Rorschach indices based on Holt's (1970) system of scoring primary-processing thinking.[28]

Constricted-Flexible Control. The constricted-flexible control principle, first proposed by Klein (1954), refers to differences in the degree of susceptibility to interference from compelling but task-irrelevant stimuli (Gardner et al. 1959). The major measure of this dimension is the Color-Word Test (Jaensch et al. 1929; Stroop 1935; Thurstone 1944). The critical part of the Color-Word Test (CWT), as used by Gardner et al. (1959), consists of a series of color names printed in incongruent colors (e.g., the word "red" printed in blue ink, the word "green" printed in yellow ink, etc.). The S is instructed to *ignore* the words and call aloud the names of the colors in which they are printed as quickly and as accurately as he can. Constricted Ss are defined by slow performance (high interference) and flexible Ss are defined by rapid performance (low interference), relative to their invariably faster reading time for strips of colors alone. The difficulty of the color-word interference task is assumed to be due to the necessity for actively inhibiting the overlearned tendency to read words and for restricting attention to the colors. Klein (1964) provides convincing evidence of the role of competing response tendencies in the CWT. In one condition, allowing S to read the word and then name the color resulted in markedly faster reading time than when S named the color and then read the word.

As yet, the factorial composition of Klein's (1954) constricted-flexible control dimension is unclear; color-word interference[29] loaded on the field-articulation factor in the Gardner et al. (1959) study, but not in the Gardner, Jackson, and Messick (1960) study.[30]

The assumption that cognitive controls regulate the impact of needs and motives underlies Klein's (1954) study of the influence of thirst upon perceptual and cognitive behavior. Klein used groups of Ss who were extremely high or low on color-word interference. Half of each group was given a thirst-inducing meal. A series of size-estimation, tachistoscopic recognition, free association, and incidental recognition tasks, which included neutral and thirst-related stimuli, was administered to all Ss. Thirst seemed to exaggerate the coping modes typical of constricted and flexible Ss under nonthirsty conditions. For example, constricted (high-interference) thirsty Ss increased their tendency to underestimate sizes of discs containing both neutral and need-related stimuli, whereas flexible (low-interference) thirsty Ss increased their tendency to overestimate size, leading to a significant group X condition interaction (see also Klein, Schlesinger, & Meister 1951). The critical point is that if the question of a need effect were posed without reference to the control dimension, the results would be negative. It was on the basis of observed consistencies of response across the task situations that Klein (1954) proposed the terms constricted and flexible control to connote the greater facility of flexible Ss in handling needs and affects.

Several subsequent studies yielded results in accord with Klein's (1954) formulation and findings. For example, constricted Ss have been found to be less able than flexible Ss to integrate contradictory elements in a series of ambiguous tasks, more vulnerable to performance decrement under stress or need conditions (Hardison & Purcell 1959; Lazarus, Baker, Broverman, & Mayer 1957; Segal 1968), and less able to modulate drive expression (Holt 1960) or deny dissonance-arousing ideas (Wolitzky 1967a). In most of these studies, a failure to consider interference proneness as a regulative or mediating factor would have led to the conclusion of "no effect" in comparisons of neutral and motive-arousing conditions (Wolitzky 1967b). The concept of constricted-flexible control has been questioned, however, by Lipton, Kaden, and Phillips (1958) and Levine (1968).

---

[28] Primary-process Rorschach indices are related, though in complex ways, to aspects of reasoning and personality organization (Heath 1965; Holt 1966) and creativity (Pine & Holt 1960; Holt 1970). Klein (1958) has suggested that they may be regarded as measures of cognitive style.

[29] Apart from its use in assessing individual differences, the phenomenon of color-word interference has received a considerable amount of research interest, e.g., in relation to studies of psychological development (Rand, Werner, Wapner, & McFarland 1963) and attention (Santos & Montgomery 1962). Jensen and Rohwer (1966) present a thorough review of studies using the CWT (see Jensen [1965] for a discussion of the relative merits of different scoring formulas).

[30] Karp (1963) found that tests tapping the ability to overcome embeddedness and the ability to resist distraction (apparently a determinant of color-word interference) loaded on separate factors. Gardner et al. (1960) noted that CWT is different in a critical way from EFT and seems to involve different aspects of ego organization (pp. 39–40, 47). Broverman (1964), using ipsative scoring techniques, identified a major factor (which he called "automatization"), defined at the positive pole by the CWT (and a letter cancellation test, among others) and at the negative pole by the Thurstone and Witkin EFT measures. Thus, weak automatizers are adept, not at novel tasks per se, but on tasks where the relevant stimulus is not immediately apparent and has to be searched for (e.g., the EFT).

Evidence about the relationship of color-word interference to content aspects of personality is limited. A series of studies by Smith (Smith & Nyman 1962; Smith & Johnson 1964) indicates that the CWT, scored serially (Smith & Klein 1953), is related to aspects of psychiatric status. Stein and Langer (1966) developed an interesting variant of the CWT, using phonetic symbols which had been matched with particular colors by a normative group. Subjects high on this measure of covert interference tended, on a self-report inventory, to be more anxious, to experience greater conflict about aggressive impulses, and generally to function less effectively.

Broverman and his co-workers conducted a series of studies (Broverman & Lazarus 1958; Broverman 1960a, 1964; Broverman, Broverman, Vogel, Palmer, & Klaiber 1964) in which they explored the correlates of two stylistic dimensions derived from the CWT, "automatization" (also based on color-word interference scores) and "conceptual versus perceptual-motor dominance" (based on the relative speed of reading color names versus naming color patches). Strong automatizers are less vulnerable than weak automatizers to distraction while performing simple addition problems (an automatized, i.e., highly practiced conceptual task) or tracing a straight line (automatized perceptual-motor task); no differences were found for non-repetitive, relatively novel tasks (Broverman 1960a). Other studies have considered automatization and conceptual versus perceptual-motor dominance in terms of intraindividual variation in abilities (Broverman 1960b, 1964). Positive relationships have been reported between automatization and occupational and socioeconomic levels, maturation of physical characteristics, abilities, etc. (Broverman 1964; Broverman et al. 1964).

There appears to be some commonality, perhaps indicative of a higher-order dimension, in the findings that less color-word interference is associated with greater flexibility (Klein 1954; Lazarus et al. 1957), greater assertiveness and effectiveness (Broverman 1960b), less psychological disturbance (Stein & Langer 1966; Langer, Stein, & Rosenberg 1969), and superior academic achievement (Silverman, Davids, & Andrews 1963).

Problems and Issues in Cognitive Control Research

We have presented a fairly representative sample[31] of cognitive control studies in an effort to convey the nature of some hypothesized controls and the variables studied in relation to these controls. As noted earlier, these controls clearly do not exhaust the possible dimensions of organization. They do, however, appear to constitute important aspects of adaptation: that is, in the process of functioning, people vary in the extent to which they scan inner and outer stimuli, extract information from embedding contexts, inhibit responses to irrelevant stimuli, distinguish between current and past experience, categorize stimuli, and adhere to and at times suspend a strict reality-orientation.

Several trends emerge from the work on cognitive controls. First, the scores derived from the tasks used to assess controls are generally reliable and stable over time (e.g., Gardner & Long 1960a; Witkin et al. 1967). Second, individual differences

in cognitive controls enable one to organize and account for findings regarding performances on a variety of perceptual-cognitive tasks. Third, there is some evidence of a link between certain controls and defenses. Fourth, some controls regulate and modify the impact of motives.

However, an overall theoretical interpretation which would integrate the complex and varied empirical findings is difficult to make at this point.[32] A major reason for this is to be found in certain persistent, unresolved methodological and conceptual issues that are evident in this area of research. These issues, some of which have already been mentioned, will be summarized below.

1. There is need for a more precise specification of what is measured by the particular tests most commonly used in cognitive control research. A final score can be obtained by a variety of perceptual and decision processes (e.g., Vick & Jackson 1967). In general, the psychometric properties of the tasks require further clarification; the intercorrelations of tasks sometimes vary considerably from one study to the next as populations and test batteries change.

2. Too many investigators rely on *one* task to assign Ss to positions along a particular cognitive control dimension. One reason may be the lack of information on whether there are stable, replicable factor-analytic structures; nonetheless, the consequence is that measurement error, test-specific variance, and construct variance are mixed together, making the use of the term cognitive control invalid. For example, criticalness and carefulness account for considerable variance on the Schematizing Test (Frederiksen & Messick 1959; Vick & Jackson 1967). These attributes are not central to the conception of leveling-sharpening, yet the Schematizing Test is almost always used as the sole measure of this dimension. It might also be noted that the constructs themselves are quite complex, as seen, for example, when many measures of categorizing behavior are studied together (Sloane, Gorlow, & Jackson 1963; Gardner, Lohrenz, & Schoen 1968; Gardner & Lohrenz 1969).

   One also finds variations across studies in the scores derived from the same test as well as in the test used to locate S on a given control dimension. Investigators sometimes devise their own tests without checking to see if they correlate with previously developed tests of a proposed cognitive control dimension. Olson, Goldstein, Neuringer, and Shelly (1969) used two measures of "equivalence range," neither of which was in the battery used by Gardner (Gardner & Schoen 1962). Bochner (1965 p. 394), in discussing intolerance of ambiguity, states the problem well: "...usually one or another of the criteria is seized on as *the* measure of intolerance of ambiguity, a test is constructed which may or may not be compatible with *other* implications of the theory, and then this test is related to some 'criterion' variable" (see also Bochner's [1965] discussion of procedures for validating a control dimension).

3. Further information about the relations among cognitive control dimensions is surely needed. The Gardner et al. (1959) factor-analytic study has been one of the few attempts to deal with several hypothesized controls at the same time.

---

[31] The number of published papers and unpublished doctoral dissertations on cognitive controls in the last 20 years is probably well over 1,000.

[32] But see the model developed by Klein (1970) as a framework in which these findings could be accommodated.

However, the sample size was extremely inadequate and the results were complex. Although, with the exception of constricted-flexible control, the hypothesized dimensions did emerge as independent factors, not all appeared for each sex: field-articulation, leveling-sharpening, and equivalence range for women, and scanning and tolerance for unrealistic experiences for men. Furthermore, tests expected to load on a given factor at times appeared as part of another factor (e.g., the log recognition measure derived from the aniseikonic lenses test loaded 0.65 on the leveling-sharpening factor).

4. Assessments of *cognitive style* and predictions on the basis of such configurations of several control dimensions, while rarely attempted, seem necessary to bring this approach to greater fruition. A promising start in this direction is the multidimensional assessment of cognitive controls, defenses, and other personality variables in a recent study of preadolescents by Gardner and Moriarty (1968; see also Santostefano 1969). Such efforts may permit some specification of the hierarchical organization of the controls themselves as well as their place within the overall context of personality development. This approach is needed both to find a home for the already postulated controls and as a means of deducing others.

5. The relationship of cognitive controls to intellectual abilities is not clear, nor is it clear how such relationships are best conceptualized. In a preliminary response to these problems, Gardner, Jackson, and Messick (1960) conducted a factor-analytic study of measures from these two classes of variables. They administered (to 63 college females) a battery of control-principle tests for field-articulation, constricted-flexible control, leveling-sharpening, and equivalence range. The intellectual abilities tests (see French 1954) included measures of verbal knowledge (vocabulary), flexibility of closure, spatial relations and orientation, inductive and deductive reasoning, associative memory, etc. Their main findings were that the correlations among the controls were low and that, as anticipated, only the field-articulation control was related to ability (mainly the measures of flexibility of closure and spatial relations and orientation). They note that pairs of tests designed to sample the same ability frequently failed to cluster together, although each was linked to the field-articulation control principle. Findings such as this are used in support of a major assumption guiding the study, namely that controls and abilities ". . . can be conceptualized within a single set of principles of personality organization. . ." (Gardner et al. 1960). Alternatively, one might hold that essentially the same test is merely being given different labels. For example, the EFT is used as a measure of field-articulation and the Concealed Figures test is used as a measure of flexibility of closure. Both are modifications of the original Gottschaldt figures and have the highest correlation in the matrix of the 8 control and 16 ability scores. This seems simply an instance of alternate-form reliability. However, since Gardner, Jackson, and Messick (1960) clearly acknowledge the similarity between some of the control and ability tests, it would appear that they want to stress an understanding of cognitive processes in terms of individual consistencies in attentional strategies.

6. Some of the current cognitive control dimensions seem to deal more readily with stylistic preferences (e.g., equivalence range); others, as currently assessed, seem to be primarily matters of ability. It would be useful to explore how readily dimensions such as field dependence-field independence could be assessed in free-choice situations which have no "right" answer and which permit observation of how the person *prefers* to organize stimulus information. Eagle, Goldberger, and Breitman (1969), for example, have attempted to approach this dimension in a way which would avoid the "good guy" versus "bad guy" connotation which is typically evident.[33] A somewhat different strategy with a similar aim has been suggested by Broverman (1964), who uses ipsative scoring to examine the pattern of abilities.

7. Cognitive control tasks vary in the degree of conscious intentionality involved. In sorting objects into groups, Ss make active, deliberate, voluntary decisions. In contrast, the number of fixations on the standard in a size-estimation task appears to be less directly under Ss' conscious control. The implications of this difference are not clear.

8. A continuum or dimensional approach to cognitive controls runs into certain difficulties. What does it mean to be in the middle of the range of scores when the intent is to describe distinctive modes of organizing experience (e.g., what can be said about Ss who are neither levelers nor sharpeners?)?

9. The plasticity versus rigidity of controls, especially in relation to psychopathology, is an interesting issue that merits further scrutiny (see Witkin 1965; Haronian & Sugerman 1967). Under what conditions will S intensify his characteristic modes of responding and under what conditions will he abandon his preferred strategy (see Silverman 1964a, 1964b, 1967)?

10. Even if the foregoing issues are resolved, there would remain a central issue in cognitive style research, and in personality research generally, viz., the assumption of broad dimensions of personality which possess substantial generality across situations. Klein's (1958) comment, made more than ten years ago, still holds: ". . .the empirical limits of the assumed generality of cognitive attitudes and styles are at present by no means clear" (p. 107). It appears that as one departs from simple laboratory-type tasks, predictive power suffers, especially if extreme groups are not used (for a detailed critique see Mischel 1968). A major reason for this drop in predictive efficiency may be the fact that while the adaptive requirements and situational characteristics which evoke a cognitive control are analyzed in the original test situation, there is a frequent failure similarly to analyze the range of life situations in which the control is expected to exert an influence (see, e.g., the study by Levine [1968]). What is indicated, then, is a careful analysis and scaling of situations in terms of the probability that a given behavioral disposition (e.g., a cognitive control) will be evoked (see Yinger 1963, 1965).

In a critique of personality studies of trait generality, Hunt (1965, p. 181) claimed that the amount of variance attributable to persons seems to be only about 4 to 25 percent. With regard to research on cognitive controls, it appears that the variance due to individual differences is typically

[33] But see Wachtel (1972) for a discussion of some of the difficulties in this approach.

15 to 25 percent. This is a major reason why theorists such as Mischel (1968) argue for an interpretation of behavior based on situational determinants and social learning processes. There is no quarrel with the argument that analysis and control of situational and stimulus variables are essential for understanding individual differences in personality and predicting behavior; e.g., even slight changes in cognitive control tests can drastically reduce a correlation (Mischel 1968, p. 18). It is impressive, however, that, in the absence of detailed situational analysis, scaling and systematic sampling of situations, the correlations between cognitive control scores and other variables often do extend into the 0.40 to 0.50 range.[34]

Despite the problems outlined above (for other examples see Wallach 1962), cognitive control conceptions, by stressing the regulative and stylistic aspects of ego adaptation as reflected in perceptual-cognitive behaviors, continue to promise to be a major component of an eventual unified theory of personality and perception. It is necessary to emphasize once more that in order to possess predictive utility, such a theory will have to show an appreciation for the complexity of motivation (Klein 1956, 1958; Vinacke 1962) and for the essential interrelatedness of situational, dynamic, and structural determinants of perceptual selection and organization. Furthermore, an approach to the study of cognitive controls which considers the interrelated development of controls, defenses, conflicts, abilities, and other facets of personality is likely to yield crucial information about the hierarchical organization of personality and its relation to perception (Gardner 1964a, 1964b, 1965).

Most of the theorizing in the area of personality and perception has been either piecemeal, i.e., concerned with small segments of behavior, or guided in only a *general* way by theory, mainly psychoanalytic. It is therefore difficult to impose order on the array of findings discussed in this chapter and to specify lawful perception-personality relationships which would have generality within a comprehensive model of organismic functioning. However, given the increasing methodological sophistication and the growing realization that the complexity of behavior demands a multivariate approach, further empirical investigation will hopefully lead to a more definitive psychology of personality and perception.

Acknowledgment: Preparation of this chapter was supported by a United States Public Health Service Research Scientist Development Award (Number 5-KO1-MH-17450) to David L. Wolitzky, Research Grant (Number 5-RO1-MH-06733) to Robert R. Holt and George S. Klein, and Research Grant (Number 1-PO1-MH-17545) to George S. Klein from the National Institute of Mental Health. The authors wish to thank Drs. Hartvig Dahl, Leo Goldberger, Nancy R. Israel, Lloyd Silverman, Donald P. Spence, and, especially, Robert R. Holt and George S. Klein for their helpful comments on this paper. We are grateful to Suzette Annin for her valuable editorial assistance. Although this entire chapter was a product of the joint effort of the two coauthors, the sections on need in per-

[34] The problem of the generality versus specificity of behavior also needs to be considered in relation to the issue that underneath "... 'phenotypic' diversities ... there exist underlying 'genotypic' unities of personality" (Mischel [1968, p. 181] discusses this question).

ception, perceptual defense, and field dependence were the particular responsibility of Paul L. Wachtel and those on subliminal stimulation and on the other dimensions of cognitive style the particular responsibility of David L. Wolitzky.

This review of the literature was completed in January 1970.

References

ADAMS, J. K. Laboratory studies of behavior without awareness. *Psychological Bulletin*, 1957, *54*, 383–405.

ALLERS, R., and TELER, J. (1924). On the utilization of unnoticed impressions in associations. *In* Preconscious stimulation in dreams, associations, and images: Classical studies. *Psychological Issues*, 1960, *2* (3), Monograph 7, pp. 121–50.

ALLISON, J. Cognitive structure and receptivity to low intensity stimulation. *Journal of Abnormal and Social Psychology*, 1963, *67*, 132–38.

ALLPORT, F. *Theories of perception and the concept of structure.* New York: John Wiley, 1955.

ALLPORT, G. W., and POSTMAN, L. *The psychology of rumor.* New York: Holt, Rinehart & Winston, 1947.

ALLPORT, G. W., and VERNON, P. E. *Studies in expressive movement.* New York: Macmillan, 1933.

AMES, A., JR. Binocular vision as affected by relations between uniocular stimulus-patterns in commonplace environments. *American Journal of Psychology*, 1946, *59*, 333–57.

ANTELL, M. The effect of subliminal activation of sexual and aggressive drive derivatives on literary creativity. Doctoral dissertation, New York University, 1969.

AREY, L. B. The indirect representation of sexual stimuli by schizophrenic and normal subjects. *Journal of Abnormal and Social Psychology*, 1960, *61*, 424–31.

ASCH, S. E., and WITKIN, H. A. Studies in space orientation: 1. Perception of the upright with displaced visual fields. *Journal of Experimental Psychology*, 1948a, *38*, 325–37.

——— Studies in space orientation: 2. Perception of the upright with displaced visual fields and with body tilted. *Journal of Experimental Psychology*, 1948b, *38*, 455–77.

ATKINSON, J. W., and WALKER, E. L. The affiliation motive and perceptual sensitivity to faces. *Journal of Abnormal and Social Psychology*, 1956, *53*, 38–41.

BACH, S. Symbolic associations to stimulus words in subliminal, supraliminal, and incidental presentation. Doctoral dissertation, New York University, 1960.

——— and KLEIN, G. S. The effects of prolonged subliminal exposures of words. *American Psychologist*, 1957, *12*, 397–98.

BAKER, L. E. The influence of subliminal stimuli upon verbal behavior. *Journal of Experimental Psychology*, 1937, *20*, 84–100.

BENFARI, R. Defense and control: Further indications. *Perceptual and Motor Skills*, 1966a, *22*, 736–38.

——— Scanning control principle and its relationship to affect manipulation. *Perceptual and Motor Skills*, 1966b, *22*, 203–16.

BERTINI, M. Traits somatiques aptitude perceptives et traits superieurs de personalité. Paper read at International Psychological Congress, Bonn, Germany, 1960.

BEVAN, W. Subliminal stimulation: A pervasive problem for psychology. *Psychological Bulletin*, 1964, *61*, 81–99.

BIERI, J. Complexity-simplicity as a personality variable in cognitive and preferential behavior. *In* D. W. Fiske and S. R. Maddi (eds.), *Functions of varied experience.* Homewood, Ill.: Dorsey, 1961.

——— ATKINS, A. L., BRIAR, S., LEAMAN, R. L., MILLER, H., and TRIPODI, T. *Clinical and social judgment: The discrimination of behavioral information.* New York: John Wiley, 1966.

BITTERMAN, M., and KNIFFEN, C. Manifest anxiety and "perceptual defense." *Journal of Abnormal and Social Psychology*, 1953, *48*, 248–52.

BLATT, S. J., ALLISON, J., and FEIRSTEIN, A. The capacity to cope with cognitive complexity. *Journal of Personality*, 1969, *37*, 269–88.

BLUM, G. An experimental reunion of psychoanalytic theory with vigilance and defense. *Journal of Abnormal and Social Psychology*, 1954, *49*, 94–97.

—— Perceptual defense revisited. *Journal of Abnormal and Social Psychology*, 1955, *51*, 24–29.

BOCHNER, S. Defining intolerance of ambiguity. *Psychological Record*, 1965, *15*, 393–400.

BOOTZIN, R., and NATSOULAS, T. Evidence for perceptual defense uncontaminated by response bias. *Journal of Personality and Social Psychology*, 1965, *1*, 461–68.

BOOTZIN, R., and STEPHENS, M. Individual differences and perceptual defense in the absence of response bias. *Journal of Personality and Social Psychology*, 1967, *6*, 408–12.

BROVERMAN, D. M. Dimensions of cognitive style. *Journal of Personality*, 1960a, *28*, 167–85.

—— Cognitive style and intra-individual variation in abilities. *Journal of Personality*, 1960b, *28*, 240–56.

—— Generality and behavioral correlates of cognitive styles. *Journal of Consulting Psychology*, 1964, *28*, 487–500.

—— Ability to automatize and automatization cognitive style. *Perceptual and Motor Skills*, 1966, *23*, 419–37.

—— BROVERMAN, I. K., VOGEL, W., PALMER, R. D., and KLAIBER, E. L. The automatization cognitive style and physical development. *Child Development*, 1964, *35*, 1343–59.

BROVERMAN, D. M., and LAZARUS, R. S. Individual differences in task performance under conditions of cognitive interference. *Journal of Personality*, 1958, *26*, 94–105.

BROWN, W. Conceptions of perceptual defense. *British Journal of Psychology*, 1961, Monograph Supplement No. 35.

—— and YANDELL, R. Individual perception styles following induced failure. *Journal of Personality and Social Psychology*, 1966, *3*, 359–62.

BRUEL, I., GINSBERG, S., LUKOMNIK, M., and SCHMEIDLER, G. R. An unsuccessful attempt to replicate Spence's experiment on the restricting effects of awareness. *Journal of Personality and Social Psychology*, 1966, *3*, 128–30.

BRUNER, J. Personality dynamics and the process of perceiving. *In* R. R. Blake & G. V. Ramsay (eds.) *Perception: An approach to personality*. New York: Ronald Press, 1951.

—— On perceptual readiness. *Psychological Review*, 1957, *64*, 123–52.

—— and GOODMAN, C. Value and need as organizing factors in perception. *Journal of Abnormal and Social Psychology*, 1947, *42*, 33–44.

BRUNER, J., and POSTMAN, L. Emotional selectivity in perception and reaction. *Journal of Personality*, 1947, *56*, 66–77.

BRUNER, J., and RODRIGUES, J. Some determinants of apparent size. *Journal of Abnormal and Social Psychology*, 1953, *48*, 17–24.

BUCHHOLZ, E. S. A study in the management of aggression by schizophrenics: The effects of aggressive stimuli on cognition in schizophrenics and normals. Doctoral dissertation, New York University, 1968.

BYRNE, D. The repression-sensitization scale: Rationale, reliability, and validity. *Journal of Personality*, 1961, *29*, 334–49.

—— Repression-sensitization as a dimension of personality. *In* B. Maher (ed.) *Progress in experimental personality research*, vol. 1. New York: Academic Press, 1964, pp. 169–220.

CANCRO, R., and VOTH, H. M. Autokinesis and psychological differentiation. *Perceptual and Motor Skills*, 1969, *28*, 99–103.

CARMICHAEL, L., HOGAN, H. P., and WALTER, A. A. An experimental study of the effect of language on the reproduction of visually perceived forms. *Journal of Experimental Psychology*, 1932, *15*, 73–86.

CARPENTER, B., WIENER, M., and CARPENTER, J. Predictability of perceptual defense behavior. *Journal of Abnormal and Social Psychology*, 1956, *52*, 380–83.

CARTER, L., and SCHOOLER, E. Value, need, and other factors in perception. *Psychological Review*, 1949, *56*, 200–208.

CATTELL, R. B. (ed.) *Handbook of modern personality theory*. Chicago: Aldine, 1970.

CHEATHAM, P. G. Visual perceptual latency as a function of stimulus brightness and contour shape. *Journal of Experimental Psychology*, 1952, *43*, 369–80.

CLAYTON, M., and JACKSON, D. N. Equivalence range, acquiescence, and overgeneralization. *Educational and Psychological Measurement*, 1961, *21*, 371–82.

CLINE, V. B. Interpersonal perception. *In* B. Maher (ed.), *Progress in*

experimental personality research, vol. 1. New York: Academic Press, 1964, pp. 221–84.

DIXON, N. F. Symbolic associations following subliminal stimulation. *International Journal of Psycho-Analysis*, 1956, *37*, 159–70.

—— The effect of subliminal stimulation upon autonomic and verbal behavior. *Journal of Abnormal and Social Psychology*, 1958, *57*, 29–36.

—— *Subliminal perception: The nature of a controversy*. London: McGraw-Hill, 1971.

DODWELL, P. Some factors affecting the hearing of words presented dichotically. *Canadian Journal of Psychology*, 1964, *18*, 72–91.

DORFMAN, D., GROSSBERG, J., and KROEKER, L. Recognition of taboo words as a function of exposure time. *Journal of Personality and Social Psychology*, 1965, *2*, 552–62.

DORFMAN, D., and ZAJONC, R. Some effects of sound, background brightness, and economic status on the perceived size of coins and discs. *Journal of Abnormal and Social Psychology*, 1963, *66*, 89–90.

DUKES, W. F., and BEVAN, W. Accentuation and response variability in the perception of personally relevant objects. *Journal of Personality*, 1952, *20*, 457–65.

DULANY, D. E. Avoidance learning of perceptual defense and vigilance. *Journal of Abnormal and Social Psychology*, 1957, *55*, 333–38.

—— The place of hypotheses and intentions: An analysis of verbal control in verbal conditioning. *In* C. W. Eriksen (ed.), *Behavior and awareness*. Durham, N. C.: Duke University Press, 1962, pp. 102–29.

EAGLE, M. The effects of subliminal stimuli of aggressive content upon conscious cognition. *Journal of Personality*, 1959, *27*, 578–600.

—— Personality correlates of sensitivity to subliminal stimulation. *Journal of Nervous and Mental Disease*, 1962, *134*, 1–17.

—— GOLDBERGER, L., and BREITMAN, M. Field dependence and memory for social vs. neutral and relevant vs. irrelevant incidental stimuli. *Perceptual and Motor Skills*, 1969, *29*, 903–10.

EAGLE, M., WOLITZKY, D. L., and KLEIN, G. S. Imagery: Effect of a concealed figure in a stimulus. *Science*, 1966, *151*, 837–39.

EGETH, H., and BEVAN, W. Attention. *In* B. Wolman (ed.), *Handbook of general psychology*. Englewood Cliffs, N. J.: Prentice-Hall, 1973.

ERIKSEN, C. W. Perceptual defense as a function of unacceptable needs. *Journal of Abnormal and Social Psychology*, 1951a, *46*, 557–64.

—— Some implications for TAT interpretation arising from need and perception experiments. *Journal of Personality*, 1951b, *19*, 283–88.

—— Defense against ego-threat in memory and perception. *Journal of Abnormal and Social Psychology*, 1952a, *47*, 230–35.

—— Individual differences in defensive forgetting. *Journal of Experimental Psychology*, 1952b, *44*, 442–46.

—— The case for perceptual defense. *Psychological Review*, 1954a, *61*, 175–82.

—— Psychological defense and "ego strength" in the recall of completed tasks. *Journal of Abnormal and Social Psychology*, 1954b, *49*, 45–50.

—— Subception: Fact or artifact? *Psychological Review*, 1956, *63*, 74–80.

—— Unconscious processes. *In* M. R. Jones (ed.) *Nebraska symposium on motivation*. Lincoln, Nebraska: University of Nebraska Press, 1958, pp. 169–226.

—— Discrimination and learning without awareness. *Psychological Review*, 1960, *67*, 279–300.

—— Figments, fantasies, and follies: A search for the subconscious mind. *In* C. W. Eriksen, *Behavior and awareness*. Durham, N. C.: Duke University Press, 1962, pp. 3–26.

—— Perception and personality. *In* S. M. Wepman and R. W. Heine (eds.) *Concept of Personality*. Chicago: Aldine, 1963, pp. 31–62.

—— and BROWNE, C. An experimental analysis of perceptual defense. *Journal of Abnormal and Social Psychology*, 1956, *52*, 224–50.

EYSENCK, H. J. *The biological basis of personality*. Springfield, Ill.: Charles C Thomas, 1967.

FEIRSTEIN, A. Personality correlates of tolerance for unrealistic experiences. *Journal of Consulting and Clinical Psychology*, 1967, *31*, 387–95.

FENCHEL, G. H. Cognitive rigidity as a behavioral variable manifested in intellectual and perceptual tasks by an outpatient population. Doctoral dissertation, New York University, 1958.

FESTINGER, L. *A theory of cognitive dissonance.* Evanston, Ill.: Row, Peterson, 1957.

FILLENBAUM, S. Some stylistic aspects of categorizing behavior. *Journal of Personality,* 1969, *27,* 187–95.

FISHER, C. Dreams and perception. *Journal of the American Psychoanalytic Association,* 1954, *2,* 389–445.

————— Dreams, images and perception: A study of unconscious-preconscious relationships. *Journal of the American Psychoanalytic Association,* 1956, *4,* 5–48.

————— A study of the preliminary stages of the construction of dreams and images. *Journal of the American Psychoanalytic Association,* 1957, *6,* 5–60.

————— Subliminal and supraliminal influences on dreams. *American Journal of Psychiatry,* 1960a, *116,* 1009–17.

————— (1924) Introduction to O. Pötzl, R. Allers, and J. Teler, Preconscious stimulation in dreams, associations, and images; Classical studies. *Psychological Issues,* 1960b, *2* (3), Monograph 7, pp. 1–40.

————— and PAUL, I. H. The effect of subliminal visual stimulation on images and dreams: A validation study. *Journal of the American Psychoanalytic Association,* 1959, *7,* 35–83.

FISS, H. The effects of experimentally induced changes in alertness on response to subliminal stimulation. *Journal of Personality,* 1966, *34,* 577–95.

————— GOLDBERG, F. H., and KLEIN, G. S. Effects of subliminal stimulation on imagery and discrimination. *Perceptual and Motor Skills,* 1963, *17,* 31–44.

FOREHAND, G. A. Relationships among response sets and cognitive behavior. *Educational and Psychological Measurement,* 1962, *22,* 287–302.

FORREST, D., GORDON, N., and TAYLOR, A. Generalization of perceptual defense: An interpretation in terms of set. *Journal of Personality and Social Psychology,* 1965, *2,* 137–41.

FOX, M. Regression as an aid to subliminal sensitivity. *American Psychologist,* 1960, *15,* 429.

FREDERIKSEN, N., and MESSICK, S. Response set as a measure of personality. *Educational and Psychological Measurement,* 1959, *19,* 137–57.

FRENCH, J. W. *Manual for kit of selected tests for reference aptitude and achievement factors.* Princeton: Educational Testing Service, 1954.

FRENKEL-BRUNSWIK, E. Intolerance of ambiguity as an emotional and perceptual personality variable. *Journal of Personality,* 1949, *18,* 108–43.

FRIEDMAN, S., and FISHER, C. Further observation on primary modes of perception: The use of a masking technique for subliminal visual stimulation. *Journal of the American Psychoanalytic Association,* 1960, *8,* 100–29.

FREUD, S. (1900). The interpretation of dreams. *Standard Edition,* vols. 4–5. London: Hogarth, 1953.

GADLIN, W., and FISS, H. Odor as a facilitator of the effects of subliminal stimulation. *Journal of Personality and Social Psychology,* 1967, *7,* 95–100.

GAITO, J. Stages of perception, unconscious processes, and information extraction. *Journal of General Psychology,* 1964, *70,* 183–97.

GARDNER, R. W. Cognitive styles in categorizing behavior. *Journal of Personality,* 1953, *22,* 214–33.

————— Cognitive control principles and perceptual behavior. *Bulletin of the Menninger Clinic,* 1959, *23,* 241–48.

————— Cognitive controls of attention deployment as determinants of visual illusions. *Journal of Abnormal and Social Psychology,* 1961, *62,* 120–29.

————— Cognitive controls in adaptation: Research and measurement. *In* S. Messick and J. Ross (eds.) *Measurement in personality and cognition.* New York: John Wiley, 1962, pp. 83–198.

————— The development of cognitive structures. *In* C. Scheere (ed.) *Cognition: Theory, research, promise.* New York: Harper & Row, 1964a.

————— The Menninger Foundation study of twins and their parents. Paper given at the American Psychological Association meeting, Los Angeles, 1964b.

————— Genetics and personality theory. *In* S. G. Vandenberg (ed.) *Methods and goals in human behavior genetics.* New York: Academic Press, 1965.

————— Organismic equilibration and the energy-structure duality in psychoanalytic theory: An attempt at theoretical refinement. *Journal of the American Psychoanalytic Association,* 1969, *17,* 3–67.

————— Individuality in development. Presented at a regional meeting of the American Association of Psychiatric Clinics for Children, Topeka, Kansas, 1969.

—————, HOLZMAN, P. S., KLEIN, G. S., LINTON, H. B., and SPENCE, D. P. Cognitive control: A study of individual consistencies in cognitive behavior. *Psychological Issues,* 1959, *1* (4), Monograph 4.

GARDNER, R. W., JACKSON, D. N., and MESSICK, S. J. Personality organization in cognitive controls and intellectual ability. *Psychological Issues,* 1960, *2* (4), Monograph 8.

GARDNER, R. W., and LOHRENZ, L. J. Leveling-sharpening and serial reproduction of a story. *Bulletin of the Menninger Clinic,* 1960, *24,* 295–304.

————— Attention and assimilation. *American Journal of Psychology,* 1961, *74,* 607–11.

————— Some old and new group tests for the study of cognitive controls and intellectual abilities. *Perceptual and Motor Skills,* 1969, *29,* 935–50.

————— and SCHOEN, R. A. Cognitive control of differentiation in the perception of persons and objects. *Perceptual and Motor Skills,* 1968, *26,* 311–30.

GARDNER, R. W., and LONG, R. I. The stability of cognitive controls. *Journal of Abnormal and Social Psychology,* 1960a, *61,* 485–87.

————— Leveling-sharpening and serial learning. *Perceptual and Motor Skills,* 1960b, *10,* 179–85.

————— Errors of the standard and illusion effects with the inverted-T. *Perceptual and Motor Skills,* 1960c, *10,* 47–54.

————— Errors of the standard and illusion effects with L-shaped figures. *Perceptual and Motor Skills,* 1060d, *10,* 107–9.

————— Cognitive controls as determinants of learning and remembering. *Psychologia,* 1960e, *3,* 165–71.

————— Control, defense, and centration effect: A study of scanning behaviour. *British Journal of Psychology,* 1962a, *53,* 129–40.

————— Cognitive controls of attention and inhibition: A study of individual consistencies. *British Journal of Psychology,* 1962b, *53,* 381–88.

GARDNER, R. W., and MORIARTY, A. *Personality development at preadolescence: Explorations of structure formations.* Seattle: University of Washington Press, 1968.

GARDNER, R. W., and SCHOEN, R. A. Differentiation and abstraction in concept formation. *Psychological Monographs,* 1962, *76,* (No. 41 [Whole No. 560]).

GARNER, W., HAKE, H., and ERIKSEN, C. Operationism and the concept of perception. *Psychological Review,* 1956, *63,* 149–59.

GERARD, F. O. Subliminal stimulation in problem solving. *American Journal of Psychology,* 1960, *73,* 121–26.

GIDDAN, N. S. Recovery through images of briefly flashed stimuli. *Journal of Personality,* 1967, *35,* 1–19.

GLIXMAN, A. T. Categorizing behavior as a function of the meaning domain. *Journal of Personality and Social Psychology,* 1965, *2,* 370–77.

GOLDBERG, F. H., and FISS, H. Partial cues and the phenomenon of "discrimination without awareness." *Perceptual and Motor Skills,* 1959, *9,* 243–51.

GOLDBERGER, L., and HOLT, R. R. Experimental interference with reality contact (perceptual isolation): Method and group results. *Journal of Nervous and Mental Disease,* 1958, *127,* 99–112.

————— Experimental interference with reality contact: Individual differences. *In* P. Solomon et al. (eds.) *Sensory deprivation.* Cambridge, Mass.: Harvard University Press, 1961, pp. 130–42.

GOLDIAMOND, I. Indicators of perception: I. Subliminal perception, subception, unconscious perception: An analysis in terms of psychophysical indicator methodology. *Psychological Bulletin,* 1958, *55,* 373–411.

————— Perception. *In* A. Bachrach (ed.) *Experimental foundations of clinical psychology.* New York: Basic Books, 1962, pp. 280–340.

————— and HAWKINS, W. Vexierversuch: The log relationship between word-frequency and recognition obtained in the absence of stimulus words. *Journal of Experimental Psychology,* 1958, *56,* 457–63.

GOLDSTEIN, M. J. A test of the response probability theory of perceptual defense. *Journal of Experimental Psychology*, 1962, *63*, 23–28.

—— Perceptual reactions to threat under varying conditions of measurement. *Journal of Abnormal and Social Psychology*, 1964, *69*, 563–67.

—— Relationship between perceptual defense and exposure duration. *Journal of Personality and Social Psychology*, 1966, *3*, 608–10.

—— and BARTHOL, R. P. Fantasy responses to subliminal stimuli. *Journal of Abnormal and Social Psychology*, 1960, *60*, 22–26.

GOLDSTEIN, M. J., HIMMELFARB, S., and FEDER, W. A further study of the relationship between response bias and perceptual defense. *Journal of Abnormal and Social Psychology*, 1962, *64*, 56–62.

GOODMAN, B. Field dependence and the closure factors. Unpublished study, 1960.

GORDON, C. M., and SPENCE, D. P. The facilitating effects of food set and food deprivation on responses to a subliminal food stimulus. *Journal of Personality*, 1966, *34*, 406–15.

GREENSPOON, J. The reinforcing effect of two responses. *American Journal of Psychology*, 1955, *68*, 409–16.

GUETZKOW, H. An analysis of the operation of set in problem-solving behavior. *Journal of Genetic Psychology*, 1951, *45*, 219–44.

GUILFORD, J. P. A revised structure of intellect. *Reports of the Psychological Laboratory*, 1957, no. 19. Los Angeles: University of Southern California.

—— The nature of human intelligence. New York: McGraw-Hill, 1967.

GUTHRIE, G., and WIENER, M. Subliminal perception or perception of partial cue with pictorial stimuli. *Journal of Personality and Social Psychology*, 1966, *3*, 619–28.

HABER, R. N. Perception and thought: An information-processing analysis. *In* J. F. Voss (ed.) *Approaches to thought.* Columbus, Ohio: Charles E. Merrill, 1969, pp. 1–26.

—— and ERDELYI, M. H. Emergence and recovery of initially unavailable perceptual material. *Journal of Verbal Learning and Verbal Behavior*, 1967, *6*, 618–28.

HARDISON, J., and PURCELL, K. The effects of psychological stress as a function of need and cognitive control. *Journal of Personality*, 1959, *27*, 250–58.

HARONIAN, F., and SUGERMAN, A. A. Fixed and mobile field independence: A review of studies relevant to Werner's dimension. *Psychological Reports*, 1967, *21*, 41–57.

HARVEY, O. J., HUNT, D. E., and SCHRODER, H. M. *Conceptual systems and personality organization.* New York: John Wiley, 1961.

HEATH, D. H. *Explorations of maturity.* New York: Appleton-Century-Crofts, 1965.

HELSON, H. *Adaptation-level theory.* New York: Harper & Row, 1964.

HILGARD, E. R. *Unconscious processes and man's rationality.* Urbana, Ill.: University of Illinois Press, 1958.

—— What becomes of the input from the stimulus? *In* C. W. Eriksen (ed.) *Behavior and awareness: A symposium of research and interpretation.* Durham, N. C.: Duke University Press, 1962, 46–72.

HOCHBERG, J. Perception: Toward the recovery of a definition. *Psychological Review*, 1956, *63*, 400–405.

HOLLINGWORTH, H. Experimental studies of judgment. *Archives of Psychology*, 1913, *29*, 44–52.

HOLT, R. R. Discussion of "Further observations on the Pötzl phenomenon: A study of day residues," by Charles Fisher. *Psychoanalytic Quarterly*, 1959, *28*, 442.

—— Cognitive controls and primary processes. *Journal of Psychological Researches*, Madras, 1960, *4*, 105–12.

—— A clinical experimental strategy for research in personality. *In* S. Messick and J. Ross (eds.), *Measurement in personality and cognition.* New York: John Wiley, 1962.

—— Measuring libidinal and aggressive motives and their controls by means of the Rorschach test. *In* D. Levine (ed.) *Nebraska symposium on motivation, 1966.* Lincoln, Neb.: University of Nebraska Press, 1966, pp. 1–47.

—— Artistic creativity and Rorschach measures of adaptive regression. *In* B. Klopfer, M. Meyer, and B. Brawer (eds.) *Developments in the Rorschach technique*, vol. 3. New York: Harcourt Brace Jovanovich, 1970.

—— and HAVEL, J. A method for assessing primary and secondary

process in the Rorschach. *In* M. A. Rickers-Ovsiankina (ed.) *Rorschach psychology.* New York: John Wiley, 1960, pp. 263–315.

HOLZMAN, P. S. The relationship of assimilation tendencies in visual, auditory, and kinesthetic time-error to cognitive attitudes of leveling and sharpening. *Journal of Personality*, 1954, *22*, 375–94.

—— and GARDNER, R. W. Leveling and repression. *Journal of Abnormal and Social Psychology*, 1959, *59*, 151–55.

—— Leveling-sharpening and memory organization. *Journal of Abnormal and Social Psychology*, 1960, *61*, 176–80.

HOLZMAN, P. S., and KLEIN, G. S. Cognitive system principles of leveling and sharpening: Individual differences in assimilation effects in visual time-error. *Journal of Personality*, 1954, *37*, 105–22.

HOLZMAN, P. S., and ROUSEY, C. Disinhibition of communicated thought: Generality and role of cognitive style. *Journal of Abnormal Psychology*, 1971, *77*, 263–74.

HOWES, D. On the interpretation of word frequency as a variable affecting speed of recognition. *Journal of Experimental Psychology*, 1954, *48*, 106–12.

—— and SOLOMON, R. L. A note on McGinnies' "Emotionality and perceptual defense." *Psychological Review*, 1950, *57*, 235–40.

—— Visual duration threshold as a function of word probability. *Journal of Experimental Psychology*, 1951, *41*, 101–11.

HUNT, J. McV. Traditional personality theory in the light of recent evidence. *American Scientist*, 1965, *53*, 80–96.

HUSTMYER, F. E., JR., and KARNES, E. Background autonomic activity and "analytic perception." *Journal of Abnormal and Social Psychology*, 1964, *68*, 467–68.

ISRAEL, N. R. Individual differences in GSR orienting response and cognitive control. *Journal of Experimental Research and Personality*, 1966, *1*, 244.

—— Leveling-sharpening and anticipatory cardiac response. *Psychosomatic Medicine*, 1969, *31*, (6).

JACKSON, D. N., MESSICK, S., and MYERS, T. Evaluation of group and individual forms of embedded-figures measures of field independence. *Educational and Psychological Measurement*, 1966, *24*, 177–92.

JAENSCH, E., and collaborators. *Grundformers menschlichen Seins.* Berlin: Otto Eisner, 1929.

JEFFREYS, A. W., JR. An exploratory study of perceptual attitudes. Doctoral dissertation, University of Houston, 1953.

JENKIN, N. Affective processes in perception. *Psychological Bulletin*, 1957, *54*, 100–127.

JENSEN, A. R. Scoring the Stroop Test. *Acta Psychologica*, Amsterdam, 1965, *24*, 398–408.

—— and ROHWER, W. D., JR. The Stroop color-word test: A review. *Acta Psychologica*, Amsterdam, 1966, *25*, 36–93.

JOHNSON, H., and ERIKSEN, C. W. Preconscious perception: A re-examination of the Pötzl phenomenon. *Journal of Abnormal and Social Psychology*, 1961, *62*, 497–503.

JUNG, J. Restricting effects of awareness? Serial position bias in Spence's study. *Journal of Personality and Social Psychology*, 1966, *3*, 124–28.

KAGAN, J., ROSMAN, B. L., DAY, D., ALBERT, J., and PHILLIPS, W. Information processing in the child: Significance of analytic and reflective attitudes. *Psychological Monographs*, 1964, *78*, (1).

KALEY, HARRIETTE W. The effects of subliminal stimuli and drive on verbal responses and dreams. Doctoral dissertation, New York University, 1969.

KAPLAN, J. M. Predicting memory behavior from cognitive attitudes toward instability. *American Psychologist*, 1952, *7*, 322.

KARP, S. A. Field dependence and overcoming embeddedness. *Journal of Consulting Psychology*, 1963, *27*, 294–302.

—— POSTER, D. C., and GODMAN, A. Differentiation in alcoholic women. *Journal of Personality*, 1966, *31*, 386–93.

KELLY, G. A. *The psychology of personal constructs.* New York: Norton, 1955.

KEMPLER, B., and WIENER, M. Personality and perception in the recognition threshold paradigm. *Psychological Review*, 1963, *70*, 349–56.

KIMBLE, G. A. Classical conditioning and the problem of awareness. *In* C. W. Eriksen (ed.) *Behavior and awareness.* Durham, N.C.: Duke University Press, 1962, pp. 27–45.

KLEIN, G. S. The personal world through perception. *In* R. R. Blake and G. V. Ramsey (eds.) *Perception: An approach to personality.* New York: Ronald Press, 1951, pp. 328–55.

——— The Menninger Foundation research on perception and personality. *Bulletin of the Menninger Clinic*, 1953, *17*, 93–99.

——— Need and Regulation. *In* M. R. Jones (ed.) *Nebraska symposium on motivation, 1954.* Lincoln: University of Nebraska Press, 1954, pp. 224–74.

——— Perception, motives and personality: A clinical perspective. *In* J. L. McCary (ed.) *Psychology of personality.* New York: Logos, 1956, pp. 121–99.

——— Discussion remarks on Charles Fisher's "A study of the preliminary stages of the construction of dreams and images." *Psychoanalytic Quarterly*, 1957, *26*, 155–56.

——— Cognitive control and motivation. *In* G. Lindzey (ed.) *Assessment of human motives.* New York: Rinehart, 1958, pp. 87–118.

——— Consciousness in psychoanalytic theory: Some implications for current research in perception. *Journal of the American Psychoanalytic Association*, 1959a, 7, 5–34.

——— On subliminal activation. *Journal of Nervous and Mental Disease*, 1959b, *128*, 293–301.

——— On inhibition, disinhibition, and "primary process" in thinking. *In* G. Nielson (ed.) *Proceedings of the XIV International Congress of Applied Psychology*, vol. 4, *Clinical psychology.* Copenhagen: Munksgaard, 1962, pp. 179–98.

——— Semantic power measured through the interference of words with color-naming. *American Journal of Psychology*, 1964, *77*, 576–88.

——— Peremptory ideation: Structure and force in motivated ideas. *In* R. R. Holt (ed.), Motives and thought: Psychoanalytic essays in honor of David Rapaport. *Psychological Issues*, 1967, *5* (2–3), Monograph 18/19, pp. 80–128.

——— *Perception, motives, and personality.* New York: Knopf, 1970.

KLEIN, G. S., BARR, H. L., and WOLITZKY, D. L. Personality. *In* P. A. Farnsworth (ed.) *Annual Review of Psychology*, 1967, *18*, 467–560.

KLEIN, G. S., GARDNER, R. W., and SCHLESINGER, H. J. Tolerance for unrealistic experiences: A study of the generality of cognitive control. *British Journal of Psychology*, 1962, *53*, 41–55.

KLEIN, G. S., and HOLT, R. R. Problems and issues in current studies of subliminal activation. *In* J. G. Peatman and E. L. Hartley (eds.) *Festschrift for Gardner Murphy.* New York: Harper & Row, 1960, pp. 75–93.

KLEIN, G. S., and HOLZMAN, P. S. The "schematizing" process: Personality qualities and perceptual attitudes in sensitivity to change. *American Psychologist*, 1950, *5*, 312.

——— and LASKIN, D. The perception project: Progress report for 1953–54. *Bulletin of the Menninger Clinic*, 1954, *18*, 260–66.

KLEIN, G. S., and SCHLESINGER, H. J. Where is the perceiver in perceptual theory? *Journal of Personality*, 1949, *18*, 32–47.

——— Perceptual attitudes toward instability: Prediction of apparent movement experiences from Rorschach responses. *Journal of Personality*, 1951, *19*, 289–302.

——— and MEISTER, D. E. The effect of personal values on perception: An experimental critique. *Psychological Review*, 1951, *58*, 96–112.

KLEIN, G. S., SPENCE, D. P., HOLT, R. R., and GOUREVITCH, S. Cognition without awareness: Subliminal influences upon conscious thought. *Journal of Abnormal and Social Psychology*, 1958, *57*, 255–66.

KOLERS, P. A. Subliminal stimulation in problem solving. *American Journal of Psychology*, 1957, *70*, 437–41.

KRASNER, L. Studies of the conditioning of verbal behavior. *Psychological Bulletin*, 1958, *55*, 148–70.

KRATWOHL, D., and CRONBACH, L. Suggestions regarding a possible measure of personality: The squares test. *Educational and Psychological Measurement*, 1956, *16*, 305–16.

KRIS, E. *Psychoanalytic explorations in art.* New York: International Universities Press, 1952.

KURLAND, S. The lack of generality of defense mechanisms as indicated in auditory perception. *Journal of Abnormal and Social Psychology*, 1954, *49*, 173–77.

LACEY, J. I., KAGAN, J., LACEY, B. C., and MOSS, H. A. The visceral level: Situational determinants and behavioral correlates of autonomic response patterns. *In* P. Knapp (ed.) *Expression of the emotions in man.* New York: International Universities Press, 1963, pp. 161–96.

LANGER, J., STEIN, K., and ROSENBERG, B. G. Cognitive interference by nonverbal symbols in schizophrenics. *Journal of Abnormal Psychology*, 1969, *74*, 474–76.

LAPKIN, B. The relation of primary-process thinking to the recovery of subliminal material. *Journal of Nervous and Mental Disease*, 1962, *135*, 10–25.

LAZARUS, R. S. *Psychological stress and the coping process.* New York: McGraw-Hill, 1966.

——— and ALFERT, E. Short-circuiting of threat by experimentally altering cognitive appraisal. *Journal of Abnormal and Social Psychology*, 1964, *69*, 195–205.

LAZARUS, R. S., BAKER, R. W., BROVERMAN, D. M., and MAYER, J. Personality and psychological stress. *Journal of Personality*, 1957, *25*, 559–77.

LAZARUS, R. S., ERIKSEN, C. W., and FONDA, C. Personality dynamics and auditory perceptual recognition. *Journal of Personality*, 1951, *19*, 471–82.

LAZARUS, R. S., and MCCLEARY, R. A. Autonomic discrimination without awareness: A study of subception. *Psychological Review*, 1951, *58*, 113–22.

LAZARUS, R. S., and OPTON, E. M., JR. The study of psychological stress. *In* C. D. Speilberger (ed.), *Anxiety and behavior.* New York: Academic Press, 1966, pp. 225–62.

LEFCOURT, H. M. Internal versus external control of reinforcement: A review. *Psychological Bulletin*, 1966, *65*, 206–20.

LEVENTHAL, H., and SINGER, D. L. Cognitive complexity, impression formation and impression change. *Journal of Personality*, 1964, *32*, 210–36.

LEVINE, F. J. Color-word test performance and drive regulation in three vocational groups. *Journal of Consulting and Clinical Psychology*, 1968, *32*, 642–47.

LEVINE, R., CHEIN, I., and MURPHY, G. The relation of the intensity of a need to the amount of perceptual distortion: A preliminary report. *Journal of Psychology*, 1942, *13*, 283–93.

LEWIN, K. *A dynamic theory of personality.* New York: McGraw-Hill, 1935.

LIBET, B. Cortical activation in conscious and unconscious experience. *Perspectives in Biological Medicine*, 1965, *9*, 77–86.

——— Brain stimulation and the threshold of conscious experience. *In* John C. Eccles (ed.) *Brain and conscious experience.* New York: Springer-Verlag, 1966, pp. 165–81.

——— ALBERTS, W. W., WRIGHT, E. W., and FEINSTEIN, B. Responses of human somatosensory cortex stimuli below threshold for conscious sensation. *Science*, 1967, *158*, 1597–1600.

LIPP, L., KOLSTOE, R., JAMES, W., and RANDALL, H. Denial of disability and internal control of reinforcement: A study using a perceptual defense paradigm. *Journal of Consulting Psychology*, 1968, *32*, 72–75.

LIPTON, H., KADEN, S., and PHILLIPS, L. Rorschach scores and decontextualization: A developmental view. *Journal of Personality*, 1958, *26*, 291–302.

LOISELLE, R., and WILLIAMSON, L. Perceptual defense to racially significant stimuli. *Perceptual and Motor Skills*, 1966, *23*, 730.

LOMANGINO, L. The depiction of subliminally and supraliminally presented aggressive stimuli and its effect on the cognitive functioning of schizophrenics. Doctoral dissertation, Fordham University, 1969.

LOOMIS, H. K., and MOSKOWITZ, S. Cognitive style and stimulus ambiguity. *Journal of Personality*, 1958, *26*, 349–64.

LUBORSKY, L., BLINDER, B., and SCHIMEK, J. G. Looking, recalling and GSR as a function of defense. *Journal of Abnormal Psychology*, 1965, *70*, 270–80.

LUBORSKY, L., and SHEVRIN, H. Dreams and day residues: A study of the Pötzl observation. *Bulletin of the Menninger Clinic*, 1956, *20*, 135–48.

——— Forgetting of tachistoscopic exposures as a function of repression. *Perceptual and Motor Skills*, 1962, *14*, 189–90.

MALAMUD, W. Dream analysis: Its application in therapy and research in mental diseases. *Archives of Neurology and Psychiatry*, 1934, *31*, 356–72.

——— and LINDER, F. E. Dreams and their relationship to recent impressions. *Archives of Neurology and Psychiatry*, 1931, *25*, 1081–99.

MARRS, C. L. Categorizing behavior as elicited by a variety of stimuli. Master's thesis, on file, University of Kansas Library, 1955.

MARTIN, B. Intolerance of ambiguity in interpersonal and perceptual behavior. *Journal of Personality*, 1954, *22*, 494–503.

MATTHEWS, A., and WERTHEIMER, M. A "pure" measure of perceptual defense uncontaminated by response suppression. *Journal of Abnormal and Social Psychology*, 1958, *57*, 373–76.

MAYMAN, M., and VOTH, H. Reality closeness, phantasy, and autokinesis: A dimension of cognitive style. *Journal of Abnormal Psychology*, 1969, *74*, 635–41.

MCCONNELL, J. V., CUTLER, R. L., and MCNEIL, E. B. Subliminal stimulation: An overview. *American Psychologist*, 1958, *13*, 229–42.

MCGINNIES, E. Emotionality and perceptual defense. *Psychological Review*, 1949, *56*, 244–51.

———— Discussion of Howes' and Solomon's note on "emotionality and perceptual defense." *Psychological Review*, 1950, *57*, 235–41.

———— and SHERMAN, H. Generalization of perceptual defense. *Journal of Abnormal and Social Psychology*, 1952, *47*, 81–85.

MCKINNON, T. A. Individual differences in visual scanning behavior. Master's thesis, University of Sydney, 1966.

———— and SINGER, G. Schizophrenia and the scanning cognitive control: A re-evaluation. *Journal of Abnormal Psychology*, 1969, *74*, 242–48.

MCNAMARA, H., SOLLEY, C., and LONG, J. The effects of punishment (electric shock) on perceptual learning. *Journal of Abnormal and Social Psychology*, 1958, *57*, 91–98.

MESSICK, S., and DAMARIN, F. Cognitive styles and memory for faces. *Journal of Abnormal and Social Psychology*, 1964, *69*, 313–18.

MESSICK, S., and FRITZKY, F. J. Dimensions of analytic attitude in cognition and personality. *Journal of Personality*, 1963, *31*, 346–70.

MESSICK, S., and KOGAN, N. Category width and quantitative aptitude. *Perceptual and Motor Skills*, 1965, *20*, 493–97.

MESSICK, S., and ROSS, J. (eds.) *Measurement in personality and cognition.* New York: John Wiley, 1962.

MILLER, C. Consistency of cognitive behavior as a function of personality characteristics. *Journal of Personality*, 1954, *23*, 233–49.

MILLER, J. G. Discrimination without awareness. *American Journal of Psychology*, 1939, *52*, 562–78.

———— *Unconsciousness.* New York: John Wiley, 1942.

MINARD, J. Response-bias interpretation of "perceptual defense": A selective review and evaluation of recent research. *Psychological Review*, 1965, *72*, 74–88.

———— BAILEY, D., and WERTHEIMER, M. Measurement and conditioning of perceptual defense, response bias, and emotionally biased recognition. *Journal of Personality and Social Psychology*, 1965, *2*, 661–68.

MINARD, J., and MOONEY, W. Psychological differentiation and perceptual defense: Studies of the separation of perception from emotion. *Journal of Abnormal Psychology*, 1969, *64*, 131–39.

MISCHEL, W. (ed.) *Personality and assessment.* New York: John Wiley, 1968.

MURRAY, H. A. et al. *Explorations in personality.* New York: Oxford, 1938.

NATSOULAS, T. Converging operations for perceptual defense. *Psychological Bulletin*, 1965, *64*, 393–401.

NEISSER, U. *Cognitive psychology.* New York: Appleton-Century-Crofts, 1967.

NEWTON, K. Visual recognition thresholds and learning. *Perceptual and Motor Skills*, 1956, *6*, 81–87.

NOTHMAN, E. H. The influence of response conditions on recognition thresholds for tabu words. *Journal of Abnormal and Social Psychology*, 1952, *65*, 154–61.

OLSON, J. L., GOLDSTEIN, G., NEURINGER, C., and SHELLY, C. H. Relation between equivalence range and concept formation ability in brain-damaged patients. *Perceptual and Motor Skills*, 1969, *28*, 743–49.

ORNE, M. T. On the social psychology of the psychological experiment: With particular reference to demand characteristics and their implications. *American Psychologist*, 1962, *17*, 776–83.

OSGOOD, C. Motivational dynamics of language behavior. *In* M. R. Jones (ed.) *Nebraska symposium on motivation, 1957.* Lincoln: University of Nebraska Press, 1957, pp. 348–424.

PALMER, R. Patterns of defensive response to threatening stimuli: Antecedent and consistency. *Journal of Abnormal Psychology*, 1968, *73*, 30–36.

PAUL I. H., and FISHER, C. Subliminal visual stimulation: A study of its influence on subsequent images and dreams. *Journal of Nervous and Mental Disease*, 1959, *129*, 315–40.

PAUL, I. H., and KLEIN, G. S. The effects of subliminal cueing on retention. Paper read at the Eastern Psychological Association annual meeting, Philadelphia, 1961.

PETRIE, A. *Individuality in pain and suffering.* Chicago, Ill.: University of Chicago Press, 1967.

PETTIGREW, T. F. The measurement and correlates of category width as a cognitive variable. *Journal of Personality*, 1958, *26*, 532–44.

PHARES, E. J. Perceptual threshold decrements as a function of skill and chance expectancies. *Journal of Psychology*, 1962, *53*, 399–408.

PIAGET, J. *Les mecanismes perceptifs.* Paris: Presses Universitaires de France, 1961.

PINE, F. Incidental stimulation: A study of preconscious transformations. *Journal of Abnormal and Social Psychology*, 1960, *60*, 68–75.

———— Incidental versus focal presentation of drive related stimuli. *Journal of Abnormal and Social Psychology*, 1961, *62*, 482–90.

———— The bearing of psychoanalytic theory on selected issues in research on marginal stimuli. *Journal of Nervous and Mental Disease*, 1964, *138*, 205–22.

———— and HOLT, R. R. Creativity and primary process: a study of adaptive regression. *Journal of Abnormal and Social Psychology*, 1960, *61*, 370–79.

POSTMAN, L. Towards a general theory of cognition. *In* J. H. Rohrer and M. Sherif (eds.), *Social psychology at the crossroads.* New York: Harper & Row, 1951.

———— On the problem of perceptual defense. *Psychological Review*, 1953, *60*, 298–306.

———— Review of Witkin, Lewis, Hertzman, Machover, Meissner and Wapner's *Personality through perception. Psychological Bulletin*, 1955, *52*, 79–83.

POSTMAN, L., BRONSON, W., and GROPPER, G. Is there a mechanism of perceptual defense? *Journal of Abnormal and Social Psychology*, 1953, *48*, 215–44.

POSTMAN, L., BRUNER, J., and MCGINNIES, E. Personal values as selective factors in perception. *Journal of Abnormal and Social Psychology*, 1948, *42*, 143–54.

PÖTZL, O. (1917). The relationship between experimentally induced dream images and indirect vision. *Psychological Issues*, 1960, *2* (3), Monograph 7, pp. 41–120.

PUSTELL, T. The experimental induction of perceptual vigilance and defense. *Journal of Personality*, 1957, *25*, 425–38.

RAND G., WAPNER, S., WERNER, H., and MCFARLAND, J. Age differences in performance on the Stroop color-word test. *Journal of Personality*, 1963, *31*, 534–58.

RAPAPORT, D., GILL, M. M., and SCHAFER, R. *Diagnostic Psychological Testing.* rev. ed. R. R. Holt. New York: International Universities Press, 1968.

REECE, M. The effect of shock on recognition thresholds. *Journal of Abnormal and Social Psychology*, 1954, *49*, 165–72.

RIGBY, W., and RIGBY, M. Reinforcement and frequency as factors in tachistoscopic thresholds. *Perceptual and Motor Skills*, 1956, *6*, 29–35.

ROSEN, A. Changes in perceptual thresholds as a protective function of the organism. *Journal of Personality*, 1954, *23*, 182–94.

ROSENTHAL, R. The effects of the experimenter on the result of psychological research. *In* B. A. Maher (ed.), *Progress in experimental personality research.* New York: Academic Press, 1964, pp. 80–114.

———— *Experimenter effects in behavioral research.* New York: Appleton-Century-Crofts, 1966.

ROTTER, J. B. Generalized expectancies for internal vs. external control of reinforcement. *Psychological Monographs: General and Applied*, 1966, *80*, (1).

SALES, B., and HABER, R. N. A different look at perceptual defense for taboo words. *Perception and Psychophysics*, 1968, *3*, 156–60.

SAMUELS, I. Reticular mechanisms and behavior. *Psychological Bulletin*, 1959, *56*, 1–25.

SANFORD, R. N. The effects of abstinence from food upon imaginal processes: A preliminary experiment. *Journal of Psychology*, 1936, *2*, 129–36.

———— The effects of abstinence from food on imaginal processes: A further experiment. *Journal of Psychology*, 1937, *3*, 145–59.

———— Personality: its place in psychology. *In* S. Koch (ed.), *Psy-*

chology: A study of a science, vol. 5. New York: McGraw-Hill, 1963, pp. 488–592.

SANTOS, J. F., and MONTGOMERY, J. R. Stability of performance on the color-word test. *Perceptual and Motor Skills,* 1962, *15,* 397–98.

SANTOSTEFANO, S. Cognitive controls and exceptional states in children. *Journal of Clinical Psychology,* 1964, *20,* 213–18.

——— Cognitive controls vs. cognitive styles: An approach to diagnosing and treating cognitive disabilities in children. *Seminars in Psychiatry,* 1969, *1,* (3).

SCHACHTER, S. The interaction of cognitive and physiological determinants of emotional states. *In* P. H. Leiderman and D. Shapiro (eds.), *Psychobiological approaches to social behavior.* Stanford: Stanford University Press, 1964.

SCHIMEK, J. G. Cognitive style and defenses: A longitudinal study of intellectualization and field independence. *Journal of Abnormal Psychology,* 1968, *73,* 575–80.

SCHLESINGER, H. J. Cognitive attitudes in relation to susceptibility to interference. *Journal of Personality,* 1954, *22,* 354–74.

SCHWARTZ, M., and SHAGASS, C. Physiological limits for "subliminal" perception. *Science,* 1961, *133,* 1017–18.

SEGAL, S. J. Patterns of response to thirst in an imaging task (Perky technique) as a function of cognitive style. *Journal of Personality,* 1968, *36,* 574–88.

SHAPIRO, D. *Neurotic styles.* New York: Basic Books, 1965.

SHEVRIN, H., and FISHER, C. Changes in the effects of a waking subliminal stimulus as a function of dreaming and nondreaming sleep. *Journal of Abnormal Psychology,* 1967, *72,* 362–68.

SHEVRIN, H., and FRITZLER, D. E. Visual evoked response correlates of unconscious mental processes. *Science,* 1968, *161,* 295–98.

SHEVRIN, H., and LUBORSKY, L. The measurement of preconscious perception in dreams and images: An investigation of the Pötzl phenomenon. *Journal of Abnormal and Social Psychology,* 1958, *56,* 284–94.

——— The disappearance of fleeting impressions as a function of repression. Presented at Joint Meeting of American Psychological Association and American Psychoanalytic Association, April, 1959.

——— The rebus technique: A method for studying primary-process transformations of briefly exposed pictures. *Journal of Nervous and Mental Disease,* 1961, *133,* 479–88.

SHEVRIN, H., and RENNICK, P. Cortical response to a tactile stimulus during attention, mental arithmetic and free associations. *Psychophysiology,* 1967, *3,* 381–88.

SHEVRIN, H., SMITH, W. H., and FRITZLER, D. Repressiveness as a factor in the subliminal activation of brain and verbal responses. *Journal of Nervous and Mental Disease,* 1969, *149,* 261–69.

SILVERMAN, J. The problem of attention in research and theory in schizophrenia. *Psychological Review,* 1964a, *71,* 352–79.

——— Scanning-control mechanism and "cognitive filtering" in paranoid and nonparanoid schizophrenia. *Journal of Consulting Psychology,* 1964b, *28,* 385–93.

——— Perceptual control of stimulus intensity in paranoid and nonparanoid schizophrenia. *Journal of Nervous and Mental Disease,* 1964c, *139,* 545–49.

——— and GAARDER, K. Rates of saccadic eye movement and size judgments of normals and schizophrenics. *Perceptual and Motor Skills,* 1967, *25,* 661–67.

SILVERMAN, L. H. On the relationship between aggressive imagery and thought disturbance in Rorschach responses. *Journal of Projective Techniques,* 1963, *27,* 336–44.

——— Ego disturbance in TAT stories as a function of aggression-arousing stimulus properties. *Journal of Nervous and Mental Disease,* 1964, *38,* 248–54.

——— A study of the effects of subliminally presented aggressive stimuli on the production of pathological thinking in a nonpsychiatric population. *Journal of Nervous and Mental Disease,* 1965, *141,* 443–55.

——— A technique for the study of psychodynamic relationships: The effects of subliminally presented aggressive stimuli on the production of pathological thinking in a schizophrenic population. *Journal of Consulting Psychology,* 1966, *30,* 103–11.

——— An experimental approach to the study of dynamic propositions in psychoanalysis: The relationship between the aggressive drive and ego regression. *Journal of the American Psychoanalytic Association,* 1967, *15,* 376–403.

——— Further comments on matters relevant to investigations of subliminal phenomena: A reply. *Perceptual and Motor Skills,* 1968, *27,* 1343–50.

——— Further experimental studies of dynamic propositions in psychoanalysis: On the function and meaning of regressive thinking. *Journal of the American Psychoanalytic Association,* 1970, *18,* 102–24.

——— and CANDELL, P. On the relationship between aggressive activation, symbiotic merging, intactness of body boundaries and manifest pathology in schizophrenics. *Journal of Nervous and Mental Disease,* 1970, *150,* 387–99.

SILVERMAN, L. H., and GOLDWEBER, A. A further study of the effects of subliminal aggressive stimulation on thinking. *Journal of Nervous and Mental Disease,* 1966, *143,* 463–72.

SILVERMAN, L. H., and SILVERMAN, D. K. A clinical-experimental approach to the study of subliminal stimulation: The effects of a drive-related stimulus upon Rorschach responses. *Journal of Abnormal and Social Psychology,* 1964, *69,* 158–72.

SILVERMAN, L. H., and SILVERMAN, S. E. The effects of subliminally presented drive stimuli on the cognitive functioning of schizophrenics. *Journals of Projective Techniques and Personality Assessment,* 1967, *31,* 78–85.

SILVERMAN, L. H., and SPIRO, R. H. A further investigation of the effects of subliminal aggressive stimulation on the ego functioning of schizophrenics. *Journal of Consulting Psychology,* 1967a, *31,* 225–32.

——— Some comments on the partial cue controversy and other matters relevant to investigations of subliminal phenomena. *Perceptual and Motor Skills,* 1967b, *25,* 325–38.

——— The effects of subliminal, supraliminal, and vocalized aggression on the ego functioning of schizophrenics. *Journal of Nervous and Mental Disease,* 1968, *146,* 50–61.

——— WEISBERG, J. S., and CANDELL, P. The effects of aggressive activation and the need to merge on pathological thinking in schizophrenics. *Journal of Nervous and Mental Disease,* 1969, *148,* 39–51.

SILVERMAN, L. H., KLINGER, H., LUSTBADER, L., and FARRELL, J. The effects of subliminal drive stimulation on the speech of stutterers. Unpublished manuscript, New York Veterans Administration Hospital, 1970.

SILVERMAN, M., DAVIDS, A., and ANDREWS, J. M. Powers of attention and academic achievement. *Perceptual and Motor Skills,* 1963, *17,* 243–49.

SILVERMAN, S. E. The effects of subliminally induced drive derivatives on ego functioning in schizophrenia. Doctoral dissertation, New York University, 1969.

SLOANE, H. N. The generality and construct validity of equivalence range. Unpublished doctoral dissertation, Pennsylvania State University, 1959.

——— GORLOW, L., and JACKSON, D. N. Cognitive styles in equivalence range. *Perceptual and Motor Skills,* 1963, *16,* 389–404.

SMITH, G. J. W., and HENRIKSSON, M. The effect on an established percept of a perceptual process beyond awareness. *Acta Psychologica,* 1955, *11,* 346–55.

SMITH, G. J. W., and JOHNSON, G. Experimental description of a group of psychiatric patients before and after therapy by means of MCT (the metacontrast technique) and CWT (the serial color-word test). *Psychological Research Bulletin,* 1964, 4, (7).

SMITH, G. J. W., and KLEIN, G. S. Cognitive controls in serial behavior patterns. *Journal of Personality,* 1953, *22,* 188–213.

SMITH, G. J. W., and NYMAN, G. E. The serial color-word test: A summary of results. *Psychological Research Bulletin,* 1962, *2,* (6).

SMITH, G. J. W., SPENCE, D. P., and KLEIN, G. S. Subliminal effects of verbal stimuli. *Journal of Abnormal and Social Psychology,* 1959, *59,* 167–76.

SMOCK, C. Replication and comments: "An experimental reunion of psychoanalytic theory with perceptual vigilance and defense." *Journal of Abnormal Psychology,* 1956, *53,* 68–73.

SOLOMON, R., and HOWES, D. Word frequency, personal values, and visual duration thresholds. *Psychological Review,* 1951, *58,* 256–70.

SOLOMON, R., and POSTMAN, L. Frequency of usage as a determinant of recognition thresholds for words. *Journal of Experimental Psychology*, 1952, *43*, 195–210.

SPENCE, D. P. A new look at vigilance and defense. *Journal of Abnormal and Social Psychology*, 1957a, *54*, 103–8.

—— Success, failure, and recognition thresholds. *Journal of Personality*, 1957b, *25*, 712–20.

—— An experimental test of schema interaction. *Journal of Abnormal and Social Psychology*, 1961a, *62*, 611–15.

—— The multiple effects of subliminal stimuli. *Journal of Personality*, 1961b, *29*, 40–53.

—— Conscious and preconscious influence on recall. *Journal of Abnormal and Social Psychology*, 1964a, *68*, 92–99.

—— Effects of a continuously flashing subliminal verbal food stimulus on subjective hunger ratings. *Psychological Reports*, 1964b, *15*, 993–94.

—— Subliminal perception and perceptual defense: Two sides of a single problem. *Behavioral Science*, 1967, *12*, 183–93.

—— and BRESSLER, J. Subliminal activation of conceptual associates: A study of "rational" preconscious thinking. *Journal of Personality*, 1962, *30*, 89–105.

SPENCE, D. P., and EHRENBERG, B. The effects of oral deprivation on responses to subliminal and supraliminal verbal food stimuli. *Journal of Abnormal and Social Psychology*, 1964, *69*, 10–18.

SPENCE, D. P., FISS, H., and VARGA, M. Sensitivity to latent cues as a function of 2 changes in skin resistance: Orienting response and basal drop. *Psychosomatic Medicine*, 1968, *30*, 311–23.

SPENCE, D. P., and GORDON, C. Activation and measurement of an early oral fantasy: An exploratory study. *Journal of the American Psychoanalytic Association*, 1967, *15*, 99–129.

SPENCE, D. P., and HOLLAND, B. The restricting effects of awareness: A paradox and an explanation. *Journal of Abnormal and Social Psychology*, 1962, *64*, 163–74.

SPENCE, D. P., and PAUL, I. H. Importation above and below awareness (Abs.). Read at the meetings of the American Psychological Association, Cincinnati, Ohio, 1959.

SPERRY, R. W. A modified concept of consciousness. *Psychological Review*, 1969, *76*, 532–36.

SPIELBERGER, C. D. The role of awareness in verbal conditioning. *In* C. W. Eriksen (ed.) *Behavior and awareness*. Durham, N. C.: Duke University Press, 1962.

SPIRO, R. H., and SILVERMAN, L. H. The effects of body awareness and aggressive activation on the cognitive functioning of schizophrenics. Unpublished manuscript, Manhattan Veterans Administration Hospital, 1967.

STEIN, K. B., and LANGER, J. The relation of covert cognitive interference in the color-phonetic symbol test to personality characteristics and adjustment. *Journal of Personality*, 1966, *34*, 241–51.

STROOP, H. R. Studies in interference in serial verbal reaction. *Journal of Experimental Psychology*, 1935, *18*, 643–61.

STROSS, L., and SHEVRIN, H. Thought organization in hypnosis and the waking state: The effects of subliminal stimulation in different states of consciousness. *Journal of Nervous and Mental Disease*, 1968, *147*, 272–88.

—— Hypnosis as a method for investigating unconscious thought processes. *Journal of the American Psychoanalytic Association*, 1969, *17*, 100–135.

SUSLOWA, M. Veranderungen der Hautgefühle unter dem Einflusse electrischer Reizung. *Zeitschrift Rationeller Medizine*, 1863, *18*, 155–60.

SWETS, J. A., and KRISTOFFERSON, A. B. Attention. *Annual Review of Psychology*, 1970, *21*, 339–66.

SWETS, J., TANNER, W., and BIRDSALL, T. Decision processes in perception. *Psychological Review*, 1961, *68*, 301–40.

TAGIURI, R., and PETRULLO, L. (eds.) *Person perception and interpersonal behavior*. Stanford, Calif.: Stanford University Press, 1958.

TAJFEL, H. Value and the perceptual judgment of magnitude. *Psychological Review*, 1957, *64*, 192–204.

TAVES, E. The construction of an American catalogue. *Journal of American Social Psychology and Research*, 1945, *39*, 151–56.

TAYLOR, A., and FORREST, D. Two types of set and the generalization of perceptual defense. *British Journal of Psychology*, 1966, *57*, 255–61.

THURSTONE, L. L. *A factorial study of perception*. Chicago, Ill.: University of Chicago Press, 1944, pp. 5–148.

TRIPODI, T. Cognitive complexity, perceived conflict and certainty. *Journal of Personality*, 1966, *34*, 144–53.

—— and BIERI, J. Information transmission in clinical judgments as a function of stimulus dimensionality and cognitive complexity. *Journal of Personality*, 1964, *32*, 119–37.

UHLMAN, F. W., and SALTZ, E. Retention of anxiety material. *Journal of Personality and Social Psychology*, 1965, *1*, 55–62.

ULLMANN, L. P. An empirically derived MMPI scale which measures facilitation-inhibition of recognition of threatening stimuli. *Journal of Clinical Psychology*, 1962, *18*, 127–32.

VERNON, P. E. *Personality assessment: A critical survey*. New York: John Wiley, 1964.

VERPLANCK, W. S. Unaware of where's awareness: Some verbal operants—notates, monents, and notants. *In* C. W. Eriksen (ed.) *Behavior and awareness*. Durham, N. C.: Duke University Press, 1962, pp. 130–58.

VICK, O. C., and JACKSON, D. N. Cognitive styles in the schematizing process: A critical evaluation. *Educational and Psychological Measurement*, 1967, *21*, 267–86.

VINACKE, E. W. Motivation as a complex problem. *In* M. R. Jones (ed.), *Nebraska symposium on motivation, 1962*. Lincoln: University of Nebraska Press, pp. 1–46.

VOTH, H. M., and MAYMAN, M. A dimension of personality organization. *Archives of General Psychiatry*, 1963, *8*, 366–80.

—— The psychotherapy process: Its relation to ego-closeness-ego-distance: Part I. *Journal of Nervous and Mental Disease*, 1966, *143*, 324–37.

—— The psychotherapy process and its relation to ego closeness-ego distance. II. *Journal of Nervous and Mental Disease*, 1968, *147*, 308–15.

WACHTEL, P. L. Conceptions of broad and narrow attention. *Psychological Bulletin*, 1967, *68*, 417–29.

—— Style and capacity in analytic functioning. *Journal of Personality*, 1968a, *36*, 202–12.

—— Anxiety, attention and coping with threat. *Journal of Abnormal Psychology*, 1968b, *73*, 137–43.

—— Field dependence and psychological differentiation: A re-examination. *Perceptual and Motor Skills*, 1972.

WALLACH, M. A. Active analytic vs. passive global cognitive functioning. *In* S. Messick and J. Ross (eds.), *Measurement in Personality and Cognition*. New York: John Wiley, 1962, pp. 199–215.

WALTERS, R., and PILIPEC, N. Perceptual defense: A replication with improved controls. *Perceptual and Motor Skills*, 1964, *18*, 864.

WERNER, H. Studies on contour: I. Qualitative analysis. *American Journal of Psychology*, 1935, *47*, 40–46.

—— *Comparative psychology of mental development*. Rev. ed. Chicago: Follett, 1948.

WIENER, M. Word frequency or motivation in perceptual defense. *Journal of Abnormal and Social Psychology*, 1955, *51*, 214–17.

—— and KLEESPIES, P. Some comments and data on partial cue controversy and other matters relevant to investigations of subliminal phenomena: A rejoinder. *Perceptual and Motor Skills*, 1968, *27*, 847–61.

WIENER, M., and SCHILLER, P. Subliminal perception or perception of partial cues. *Journal of Abnormal and Social Psychology*, 1960, *61*, 124–37.

WITKIN, H. A. Perception of body position and the position of the visual field. *Psychological Monographs*, 1949, *63*, (Whole No. 302).

—— Perception of the upright when the direction of force acting on the body is changed. *Journal of Experimental Psychology*, 1950, *40*, 93–106.

—— Further studies of perception of the upright when the direction of the force acting on the body is changed. *Journal of Experimental Psychology*, 1952, *43*, 9–20.

—— Psychological differentiation and forms of pathology. *Journal of Abnormal Psychology*, 1965, *70*, 317–36.

—— and ASCH, S. E. Studies in space orientation: III. Perception of the upright in the absence of a visual field. *Journal of Experimental Psychology*, 1948a, *38*, 603–14.

—— Studies in space orientation: IV. Further experiments on perception of the upright with displaced visual fields. *Journal of Experimental Psychology*, 1948b, *38*, 762–82.

WITKIN, H. A., DYK, R. B., FATERSON, H. F., GOODENOUGH, D. R., and KARP, S. A. *Psychological differentiation*. New York: John Wiley, 1962.

WITKIN, H. A., GOODENOUGH, D. R., and KARP, S. A. Stability of cognitive style from childhood to young adulthood. *Journal of Personality and Social Psychology*, 1967, 7, 291–300.

WITKIN, H. A., LEWIS, H. B., HERTZMAN, M., MACHOVER, K., MEISSNER, P., and WAPNER, S. *Personality through perception*. New York: Harper & Row, 1954.

────── Relation of pre-sleep experiences to dreams. *Journal of the American Psychoanalytic Association*, 1965, *13*, 819–49.

WITKIN, H. A., and OLTMAN, P. K. Cognitive Style. *International Journal of Neurology*, 1967, *6*, 119–37.

WOLITZKY, D. L. Sexually symbolic responses as a function of low-level stimulation with sexual stimuli. Doctoral dissertation, University of Rochester, 1961.

────── Cognitive control and cognitive dissonance. *Journal of Personality and Social Psychology*, 1967a, *5*, 486–90.

────── Effect of food deprivation on perception-cognition. *Psychological Bulletin*, 1967b, *68*, 342–44.

WORRELL, L., and WORRELL, J. An experimental and theoretical note on "conscious and preconscious influences on recall." *Journal of Personality and Social Psychology*, 1966, *3*, 119–23.

WULF, F. Über die veränderung von vorstellungun (gedächtnis und gestalt). *Psychologishe Forschung*, 1922, *1*, 333–73.

WYER, R. S., JR. Assessment and correlates of cognitive differentiation and integration. *Journal of Personality*, 1964, *32*, 495–509.

YINGER, J. M. Research implications of a field view of personality. *American Journal of Sociology*, 1963, *68*, 580–92.

────── *Toward a field theory of behavior*. New York: McGraw-Hill, 1965.

ZAJONC, R. Response suppression in perceptual defense: A replication with improved controls. *Perceptual and Motor Skills*, 1964, *18*, 864.

ZAKS, M. S. Perseveration of set, a determinant in problem-solving rigidity. Master's thesis, Roosevelt College, Chicago, Illinois, 1954.

ZEIGARNIK, B. Über das behalten von erledigten und unerledigten handlungen. *Psychologische Forschung*, 1927, *9*, 1–85.

ZIMBARDO, P. G. *The cognitive control of motivation: The consequences of choice and dissonance*. Glenview, Ill.: Scott, Foresman, 1969.

ZUKMANN, L. Hysteric compulsive factors in perceptual organization. Doctoral dissertation, New School for Social Research, New York, 1957.

ZUCKERMAN, M. The effects of subliminal and supraliminal suggestion on verbal productivity. *Journal of Abnormal and Social Psychology*, 1960, *60*, 404–11.

Selected
Areas

Developmental psychology has been characterized as the study of biological, psychological, and behavioral capabilities as they change from simple to more complex systems. Developmental psychology has also been characterized as the study of the above capabilities as they shift from diffuse to differentiated patterns, from disconnected to integrated patterns or from one pattern of organization to another. Many have approached developmental psychology as the study and identification of sequential stages or levels through which, normatively speaking, the organism passes in a specific order. Others have been primarily interested in observing or manipulating behavior or other functions of immature organisms and making comparisons to later levels of functioning. Thus, although the foci may differ somewhat, the general interest of the developmental psychologist is in the transformations organisms undergo as they move forward in time.

How developmental psychology is actually studied depends in large part on other considerations about which there is still widespread disagreement.[1] For example, does the agent of transformation or change lie within the organism (inherent and internal tendencies) or without the organism (environmental impact and modifications based on experience and learning)? Many have taken the position of the co-determination of biological and experiential factors in development, and the disentanglement of maturational processes (i.e., the appearance of characteristics in specific sequential order which are relatively unaffected by environmental conditions) and learned behavior has received much study.

Another dimension on which researchers and theorists differ is the alignment with physical growth processes or with the emergence of personality and life-goal attainment. Those defining development primarily in terms of characteristics correlating with physical change would tend to focus their interest on the period of maximum extrauterine physical expansion (i.e., birth through late childhood or adolescence) and perhaps

[1] For a detailed account of specific developmental theories and theoretical issues see Baldwin (1968) and Stone & Church (1968, Chap. 4).

Charlotte Bühler,

Patricia Keith-Spiegel,

& Karla Thomas

Developmental Psychology

42

pick it up again when the growth curve droops in old age after the long, relatively level period of adulthood or physical maturity. Those concerned with personality and life-goal development are more likely to view the curve of development as a linear one extending into, and through, the adulthood period.

Next is the question of how growth progresses. Is it a smooth and gradually accruing process, or a series of stages or levels, each with its unique or dominant characteristics? Although a stage-based framework is most prevalent, the criteria for defining stages and the number of stages in the life cycle vary. Regarding the latter, some have divided the life cycle whenever a characteristic behavior or ability normally appears and others have characterized but three periods separated off by puberty and the climacteric. (The theoretical framework of C. Bühler will be presented later in the chapter.)

The great breadth of the area of developmental psychology has led to many subspecialties. As Stevenson (1967) stated, "The day of the generalist in developmental psychology seems to have passed" (p. 87). Hence, the field is fragmented and unfortunately lacking the integration which the very definition of the area itself implies. It is currently common to specialize in studying development in specific organisms (or concentrate on animals *or* humans), or to concentrate on a specific chronological age period, or to study exclusively the development of a specific part-function such as cognition, sensory functions, or language acquisition. Thus, though Birren (1968), Bühler (1966), and others have proposed the need to study development over the entire life cycle, and to relate the physiological, psychological, and social aspects of development to each other, we have a long way to go before this integrative goal is fulfilled.

The purpose of this chapter is to provide a general overview of the field of developmental psychology by presenting the major methodological orientations in the area, some contributions from animal research, and finally, summaries of the normal developmental process in the various stages of the human life cycle.[2] Due to the limited space allotted, and the extraordinary stockpile of material relevant to behavioral and psychological development of organisms, we have necessarily had to select a relatively small number of works to include in our illustrations. Also subject matter pertinent to other chapters in this volume was generally excluded (e.g., intellectual and somatological development).

Overview of Study Approaches

HISTORICAL PERSPECTIVE

Interest in children, particularly concerning their training and education, can be found in the writing of ancient scholars.

[2] In the human development sections, an attempt was made to integrate two diverse approaches to the study of psychological phenomena. Patricia Keith-Spiegel described the human being at the various developmental stages by assembling many separate research study findings. Charlotte Bühler attempted to integrate from her developmental studies as well as biographical and clinical experience, the humanistically oriented global picture of the "person." The animal development section was contributed by Karla Thomas who has attempted to summarize the experimental research on vertebrate animal development as well as some descriptive studies of normal development of the commonly studied laboratory animals. She has stressed early stages of development, since most animal research in this area is on immature organisms.

An interest in development of children as a scientific discipline, however, is relatively recent. The eternal search for a "fountain of youth" prompted similar historical interests in aging, but again, scientific study of aging processes is quite recent.

The philosophy of education as forwarded by the Moravian Bishop Comenius in the seventeenth century is cited as a major influence on European developmental psychology. Comenius believed that teaching should follow according to the nature of the child's developmental process. Subsequent early educators, such as Pestalozzi, Rousseau, Froebel, Herbart, and later Dewey, also asserted that child-training methods should proceed according to the principles of children's nature.

The associationists, during the same era, asserted that knowledge is based on experience. The mind, blank at birth, soon responds to stimuli coming in from the environment, and thus begins experiencing—hence *learning*. However, child study did not immediately catch on during this era, even though it could have been legitimized on theoretical grounds.

Darwin (1877) thought perhaps the young child was the "missing link" between higher animals and human adults. He made observations of the development of his child and shared notes with the philosopher Taine who was making similar observations on his child's developmental progress. Other early direct observations of children using the diary description method were done by Pestalozzi (1774), Preyer (1882), Shinn (1900), Scupin and Scupin (1907), and Stern (1914).

The diary method was subsequently replaced by experimental studies on children. The interest was on specific aspects of children's behavior, such as speech, play, fantasy, psychopathology, and sensory capacities. Much of this work by such investigators as D. Katz and Wilhelm and Clara Stern, has been expanded by Karl Bühler (1918). The study of the total behavior of the child in a laboratory setting began with Charlotte Bühler in Vienna during the mid 1920s. Using both observation techniques and instrumentations devised especially for use with children, Bühler and her students studied such behaviors as social interaction, sucking behavior and mealtime situations, and learning in infants (Bühler 1927b).

The testing of the mental abilities of school children had been done early (e.g., Bolton 1892 and Gilbert 1894) but received major prominence with the work of Binet (1903) and Binet and Simon (1905) in France. This approach was brought to the United States and applied by Goddard (1910) and revised by Terman (1916). The theoretical and research contributions of Piaget on cognitive development began in the 1920s at the University of Geneva (e.g., Piaget 1926, 1928, 1929, 1930, 1932). The observation and interview techniques he devised to study how the child comes to understand the world around him, and his elaborate theoretical concepts, have received major attention in the United States only in recent years.

Although there are numerous important historical American figures in child and developmental psychology, G. S. Hall deserves special mention. In 1891 he founded the *Pedagogical Seminary*, the first journal devoted to child study. The interview studies with young children (Hall 1891) and works on adolescence (Hall 1905) are among his well-known writings. Other early American developmentalists will be cited as their work applies to other sections of the chapter.

Freud's psychoanalytic concepts set the stage for a different kind of developmental study in which dynamic and life-shaping forces were attributed to the young child. Freud did not himself do research in the scientific sense of the term, nor did he work directly with children. His conclusions were based on analyses of adult neurotic patients in which he traced the symptoms to childhood experiences. The effects of early experience on later behavior has become a prominent area of study for psychologists studying human and animal development. The techniques for exploring unconscious motivation were prototypes for other methods adopted for use with young children. For example, through free-play observations, or associations to unstructured stimuli, child and developmental psychologists have sought to gain information that the subject cannot or will not express directly or verbally.[3]

METHODOLOGICAL ISSUES

The earlier methodological orientations are still in use today. However, developmental psychology has become so diverse in its orientations that nearly every method devised to study behavior has also been used to study aspects of development (Stevenson 1967). For this reason, only a cursory overview of some of the basic methodological issues and approaches can be presented here.[4]

Basic vs. Complex Research. Probably no one would disagree with the statement that the process of development, particularly in humans, depends on a complexity of interrelated factors taking place around and within the organism. But what this fact means in terms of how to go about investigating development has met with a variety of opinions and approaches. Terrell (1958) has lucidly argued the viewpoint that developmental designs should remain basic and simple due to the vast methodology problems of the more all-encompassing "study" approach. Though not discounting the value of all research on complex human behavior, he concluded that "... the great preponderance of the research which is now being done at a more complicated level will have to be redone in the light of the results of the more basic research in child psychology" (p. 309). In a similar vein, Werboff (1963) suggested that biological-psychological events occurring very early in the life cycle should receive careful study, since these may well be related in a direct and *causal* fashion to later development, behavior, and adjustment. Others would disagree with the necessity or even the validity of using simple or basic designs. The major argument would be that development is not a simple phenomenon, and to research it as if it were would result in a great loss of meaningful data and spurious conclusions. And although the information bearing directly on development from the biological, physiological, and behavioral genetic researchers will be of great value, can we afford to wait for it? Many would speculate that much relevant information will not ultimately be strongly linked to physiological or hereditary factors. Research utilizing multiple measures to identify relationships and studies of the whole person, whole families, and environmental impact will, no doubt, continue to flourish. *The Study of Lives* (White 1969) is an impressive compilation of essays reflecting whole dynamic personalities. This work was written to honor H. A. Murray whose own orientation stressed the study of the entire person as the legitimate method of learning about human behavior (Murray 1938).

Degree of Scientific Rigor. What amount of scientific rigor is desirable or practical in developmental-psychology research? The developmentalists using animal subjects are in the best position to follow strict scientific experimental procedures, since many controls can be incorporated into their studies (e.g., genotype, nutrition, environmental situation, and exposure to experience or training). Much rigor must be sacrificed by the researchers using human subjects, not because they are unaware of the principles of control, but because to follow many such principles would be impossible or, as Smith (1967) discussed, ethically indefensible. We cannot raise humans in cages or vary their experiences in strict and systematic ways. Rather we must remain content to match groups as best we can on certain variables of interest, collect as much information as possible about the factors which may account for the person's behavior or performance, use the best sampling techniques we can, or locate a population or situation which is occurring *naturally* and affords the possibility of study.

Specific Life Phase vs. Life-cycle Study. Many laboratories or institutions are set up to study individuals at particular life stages. Concentrating on one specific life phase, with its biological, psychological, and social components, may well be a full time commitment. Others have been interested in learning about the life cycle in its totality. Such researchers may be forced to spread their talents thinly, and the methods may be less scientific (such as biography analysis). But accounts of the *continuity* of a person's life is seen to be of great value. Some of the major longitudinal project programs have become life cycle studies because their subjects have grown to adulthood and continue to be evaluated.

Individual vs. Group Data. The focus on the development of a single individual vs. studies involving large numbers of subjects calls for different methods. The standard statistical procedures cannot so easily be applied to a single case, hence many reports of individuals are descriptive accounts. A quotation from Shinn (cited by Wright 1960) reflects the advantage of studying a single individual. "If I should find out that a thousand babies learned to stand at an average age of forty-six weeks and two days, I should not know as much that is important about standing, as a stage in human progress, as I should after watching a single baby carefully through the whole process" (Shinn 1900, p. 11)." Studies utilizing many subjects, however, have the advantage of using inferential statistics. Though sampling procedures must be adequate, generalizations about developmental processes are more valid when a number of subjects are tested. It should be noted that longitudinal studies may simultaneously use both approaches since, in a very real sense, they are accounts of individual development on a number of subjects.

---

[3] For more detailed overviews of child study in historical perspective, see Bradbury 1937; Dennis 1949; Murphy 1949, Ch. 26; McNeill 1966, Ch. 1; and Glatt 1967.

[4] Papers delving into methodological considerations in developmental research include Bell (1960a); Gump and Kounin (1960), and Bijou (1968).

Descriptive vs. Experimental Studies. Finally, there is the issue of descriptive vs. experimental studies of child development. The methodologies used in both approaches may be quite different. The most common method used in descriptive studies consists of a variety of *observational techniques*. This approach is briefly outlined below.

The earliest method in developmental psychology was an observation technique called the "diary description." Infants were observed, usually by their own parent, over a period of time and their behavior was recorded. Although observations were often made at irregular intervals, unusual or atypical behavior may have been more likely to be noted, and the observers were no doubt biased in that their own offspring was the subject, these accounts are the prototypes of the more refined observation techniques and the longitudinal method. The basic diary approach is still used (e.g., Scott 1961).

The situation in which the child is observed may be contrived or in a natural setting. Most often the situation is not an unfamiliar or unusual one allowing for the recording of spontaneous and uninhibited behavior. Since children are generally impervious to a nonintrusive adult when in familiar surroundings, the method is especially suited to them.

Observation techniques generally fall into two categories; open and closed. In the former, running accounts of behavior are recorded as in the diary and specimen description methods. The closed techniques allow for the quantification of data in that the observer is concerned with limited aspects of behavior and can often "count" their occurrence rather than recording all behavior in detail. The time-sampling, event-sampling, and trait-rating techniques are examples of closed methods of observation. The quality of observational data depends on the ability of the observer to record and interpret behavior accurately. For a detailed discussion of these methods, the reader is referred to Wright (1960).

A highly evolved observation technique of *psychological ecology* has been established by two midwestern psychologists (Wright & Barker 1949; Barker & Wright 1954; Wright 1956). A field station was set up in a small community for the purpose of studying human behavior as it occurs naturally. With the use of trained observers, behavior settings and behavior episodes of children have been carefully recorded. The result has been a wealth of data which presents children as they actually behave and interact in their environment. In a recent book, Barker (1968) presents a theory of behavior settings in which the relationship between environmental situations and behavioral inputs and reactions are examined. With a dominant general theme of the 1970s promising to be "ecology," perhaps an increasing interest in this method and theory will also ensue.

Research which involves systematic manipulation of variables in a controlled situation, and the observation of what occurs, is termed *experimental*. Many have argued that artificial laboratory experiments are not conducive to eliciting any organism's natural behavior. One often loses the spontaneity, breadth, and depth of a child's behavior when he is placed in an unfamiliar environment with a "strange" experimenter. Being able to hold the attention of a child long enough to complete the task, even if he is initially responsive, calls for special skills in research design and technique.

It is likely that to do adequate experimental research on children, one needs to have observed them in a variety of natural situations or as "whole persons." A quote from Smith and Stone's review succinctly illustrates the problem which can arise here. "To require a human being to spin a web or peck at corn would be hardly less appropriate than some of the tasks carried over directly from, say, rats or pigeons, which have been set for children. Some of these seem more like studies of how to limit conditions so children cannot learn than attempts to determine the true dimension of capability" (Smith & Stone 1961, pp. 1–2).

Fifteen years ago, McCandless and Spiker (1956) pointed to the need for child psychologists to engage in more experimental research. They offered some speculations as to why experimental approaches had been avoided. It is true that in the 1950s developmental psychology seemed to be falling behind other areas in psychology in using rigorous experimental procedures. However, many current studies in child and developmental psychology reflect a high level of experimental sophistication and ingenuity.

DESIGN ORIENTATIONS TO THE MEASUREMENT OF DEVELOPMENT

Kessen (1960) gives a very lucid account of the meaning of developmental psychology and how research proceeds. Though the field can be summarized as the study of responses which are a function of age, he warns against the use of age by itself as being the *explanation* of behavioral change.

Time, as a pure variable, is impossible to isolate, since something is happening within and without the organism which modifies it as time passes. And it is these influences and processes which are of major interest to developmentalists rather than time passage per se.

Three common approaches are the longitudinal, cross-sectional, and clinical methods. Each will be briefly described.

Longitudinal Approach. The longitudinal method consists of measuring the same individuals at different intervals over a period of time. Some longitudinal studies are relatively short-term, whereas others are impressively long-term: thirty or more years. Longitudinal studies vary in their scope with some concentrating on specific techniques, abilities, or behaviors, and others encompassing a variety of techniques with the interest on multiple facets of development.

Perhaps the major asset of the longitudinal method is that it remains the most true to the concept of developmental psychology; emerging characteristics and changes are assessed. As Kagan has stated, "It is obvious that longitudinal investigations are mandatory if we are to ascertain the permanence—or lack of permanence—of various response tendencies" (Kagan 1964, p. 1). Continuity can be plotted without having to worry about differential sampling among age groups (as may occur in cross-sectional investigations). Individual growth increments and patterns can be presented. Cause, effect, and prediction statements can be advanced with more certainty than when other designs are utilized. (Cross-sectional investigations usually present data in the form of central tendency descriptions, since wide individual variations cannot be accounted for meaningfully.)

Aside from the valuable assets of the longitudinal method, there are some shortcomings and inherent difficulties which must be mentioned. The monetary expense of the long-term studies is tremendous. Large numbers of highly trained administrative, professional, and clerical personnel are involved in even the moderate-scale projects. Turnover in personnel, in the longer-term projects, may necessitate various types of readjustments. Since the same subjects must be retested, it is necessary to maintain cooperation as well as locating them again and again. Samples may become increasingly biased due to "dropouts." This problem is especially notable in longitudinal studies of aged populations where subjects may begin to die off. With some evidence suggesting that more able individuals live longer (Riegel, Riegel and Meyer 1967a, 1967b) the interpretation of trend data, on a diminishing sample, becomes difficult and, unfortunately, unresolvable.

The design and statistical problems involved in handling longitudinal data include both the task of dealing with mounds of measurement scores (the high-speed computer becoming of increasing assistance here) and with properly analyzing them. Longitudinal developmental studies are not true experiments because one cannot order the time variable. In the true repeated measurement design, order effects are balanced among subjects. But it is impossible to arrange for, say, two groups to be tested at two time periods in two different orders. Pinneau and Newhouse (1964) and Pinneau, Dillehay, and Sassenrath (1966) have described an interesting method and its application, using Institute of Human Development longitudinal data. This multivariate approach describes how variables change in interrelationships over time. Factor structures on measures of the same subjects at different ages are compared.

The longitudinal researcher cannot control the environment of the subjects between testing. These history effects which correlate with measures of developmental processes cannot be parceled out even if they can be identified. Carryover or sequence effects (i.e., any aspect of one testing situation which may affect the next testing session) may be operating in some longitudinal-research projects, especially if the testing periods are close together and the task performance is one which could be affected by practice or exposure.

Finally, there is the problem of "finding out tomorrow what are the relevant variables one should have taken into account yesterday" (Meyers 1966, p. 14). Once a design is set in motion, it is difficult to alter in the light of newer techniques. When innovations are added, it is impossible to recapture data using the new or revised method with subjects at previous age stages.

It is perhaps unfortunate that this chapter was structured in such a way as to preclude the presentation of long-term longitudinal research. The reader is referred to Kagan (1964) for an excellent summary of the major long-term longitudinal research programs. Abstracts of longitudinal studies through 1955 have been presented by Stone and Onqué (1959). More detailed considerations of longitudinal methodology may be found in Kodlin and Thompson (1958), Baldwin (1960), Schaie (1965), and Meyers (1966).

Cross-sectional Approach. By simultaneously measuring groups of individuals from different age populations, and comparing them on specific variables, a composite picture of development is constructed. This widely used technique has the advantage of saving a great deal of time, since the researcher need not wait for his subject pool to progress to the next age level to be retested. Further, it is not necessary to "keep finding" the same subjects to be tested again.

Most normative studies, that is the charting of age periods at which certain functions or characteristics appear, are based on data from cross-sectional investigations.

But because different subjects are used at different age levels, certain information is lost or unavailable. The continuity of development as it occurs in a single person is lost. The comparability of groups can only be assumed. The reasons for individual differences at each age level cannot be ascertained. Baldwin (1960) has suggested the use of the cross-sectional technique as a first step in locating the needs for future longitudinal research.

A method proposed by Bell (1953, 1954) incorporated some of the advantages of both the longitudinal and cross-sectional methods. This *convergence* approach is, simply stated, a series of shorter-term longitudinal studies using age ranges which overlap. For example, one group may be tested at ages 2, 3, and 4, another group at ages 4, 5, and 6, another at 6, 7, and 8, etc. This method cuts down on the time necessary to run a study and also provides "check points" to compare different subjects at the same ages.

Clinical Approach. Originally the clinical approach was used exclusively as a means of understanding and evaluating those who were emotionally disturbed. Since Freud's theory and psychoanalytic procedures connected mental illness to the early years of life, the clinical approach is concerned with development. The individual usually presents his own history complemented by the therapist's explorative questions regarding specific experiences. The techniques of exploration vary, even as they did when Freud and his successors experimented with several approaches. An important point is that the clinician is *not* interested in developmental facts as such, but primarily as they relate to emotional impacts on the person. The Freudian school speaks, in this connection, of the emotional dynamics of a person's development.

The method of case history study, with or without the use of depth analysis, has been extended to other study areas concerned with human development. It represents, for example, one of the main tools of the social worker. Most important, however, is the recent extension of the clinical approach to the study of the development in healthy persons. This method is particularly prevalent among the humanistic psychologists.

One of the main problems of the clinical approach as a research tool is the question of the scientific validity of such data collected on an individual. This approach yields no numbers to manipulate and little possibility of systematically comparing people, since the purpose is to understand each individual as a unique person. However, several writers have convincingly argued the point that to truly describe a person, one must first have a meaningful relationship with that person as well as an understanding of the meaningful relationships in his life (Polanyi 1958; Matson 1964; Bühler 1967b).

Study Techniques. Besides the observation and experimental methods discussed earlier, a variety of other techniques have been used to collect data reflecting development. Space allows for only a listing of some of these methods, but references which cover the material in substantial detail are cited: interviews (Yarrow 1960); case histories (Anderson 1954); projective tech-

Bühler, Keith-Spiegel, & Thomas

niques (Henry 1960); children's productions such as paintings, drawings, or constructions with other materials (Goodenough 1926; Altschuler & Hattwick 1947; Goodenough & Harris 1950; Smith & Appelfeld 1965; Richards & Ross 1967); analysis of biographical account and life histories (Bühler 1928; Allport 1942, 1961a, 1962; Pikunas 1969); psychometric measures such as tests of ability (Anastasi 1960); doll play (Levin & Wardwell 1962) and responses to other toys and materials (Bühler, Lumry & Carroll 1951; Murphy 1956; Sutton-Smith 1968; Bowyer 1970); and mode of play activity (Getzels & Jackson 1962; Wallach & Kogan 1965; Leiberman 1965, 1967). Another specialized technique is the study of twins (Vandenberg 1966).

No single technique is appropriate for all age levels or for all forms of behavior (Hurlock 1964). For this reason, many investigators, studying people at different ages or attempting to describe the "whole person" have utilized data gleaned from many techniques. For example, Murphy and her collaborators (1962) used pediatric examination reports, psychiatric interviews, psychometric and projective tests, interviews with mothers, and observation records from many settings in their study of the child's coping behavior development. Escalona (1968) made use of an even larger array of measures and descriptive techniques in the accounts of her work on the development of infants during the first half year of life. The sheer weight of such data is at once impressive and bewildering leaving the burden of adequate presentation, integration, and interpretation to skillful investigators.[5]

Animal Studies

The development of animal behavior has become a specialized area of developmental psychology. Several reviews covered the work done prior to 1950: Cruikshank's (1954) chapter on the sensory-motor, emotional, social, and cognitive responses of young animals; Beach & Jaynes's (1954) review of the effects of early experience on behavior; Carmichael's (1954) review of prenatal development; and Sperry's (1951) discussion of neural maturation and its implications for behavior. Two recent reviews of developmental psychology included sections on animal development (Campbell & Thompson 1968; Kagan & Henker 1966), and several recent books summarized some of the major findings in the area (Scott 1968; Stevenson, Hess & Rheingold 1966; Sluckin 1965). The basic data and theories of animal development are provided not only by developmental psychologists but also by comparative and physiological psychologists and the behaviorally oriented zoologists, especially the ethologists. The zoological approach appears in the work of Ewer (1968), Hinde (1966), Manning (1967), Marler and Hamilton (1966), and Thorpe (1963), while the traditional developmental psychological approach is evident in the work of Cruikshank (1954) and Munn (1965). Today the area is interdisciplinary, and no single volume has summarized all the data and theories.

The following discussion is based on the development of vertebrate behavior. Invertebrate behavioral development is ignored here, as it is by most psychologists.

[5] For a detailed account of many techniques of developmental psychology see Anderson 1954 and Mussen 1960.

DEVELOPMENT OF BEHAVIOR IN THE EMBRYO

Behavior, however defined, does not begin at birth or at hatching, but in the embryo. The exact age at which behavior begins is unknown. Carmichael (1954) defined behavior as "true receptor-initiated neuromuscular activity," that is, activity involving sensory and nervous systems as well as the muscles. Working with amphibian embryos, Coghill (1929) described the first behavior as slight "C-flexure" of the entire embryo produced by light touch on any part of it. As the animal matures, the "C" becomes tighter and frequently reverses, finally producing an "S" response which eventually undergoes repeated reversals and results in swimming in the larval stage of development. From this work came Coghill's principle of *individuation*, whereby more precise movements differentiate from the global organization present in the earliest stages. Though this generalization may be valid for lower vertebrates such as amphibians, Carmichael (1954) believed that mammalian development does not proceed in this manner. In the guinea pig and other mammals, discrete sensory-motor patterns occur before some of the more generalized responses, and whole-body mass movements are more likely to occur just before death than during prenatal or neonatal stages (Marler & Hamilton 1966). Growth gradients were observed by Coghill as well as by other workers (Carmichael 1954): in many vertebrate embryos development proceeds *cephalocaudally* (head-to-tail, with the anterior end dominant) and *proximodistally* (from the center to the extremities).

A major question is whether or not sensory stimulation is essential to normal development. Arguing against the traditional nativistic maturational theory, Kuo (1932a, 1932b) reported that the opportunity for self-stimulation by the duck embryo is present at early stages of development. He hypothesized that movement-produced sensory feedback is necessary for normal neuromuscular activity to develop (Kuo 1967; see also Schneirla 1965). However, Hamburger, Wenger, and Oppenheim (1966) found that leg movements in the chick embryo develop normally in spite of early differentiation of the leg. Whether sensory feedback is necessary for the development of other responses is not known.

Can embryos learn? The fetal guinea pig and other mammals possess clear, well-coordinated sensory-motor reflexes at later stages of prenatal development (Carmichael 1954). Such reflexes may be amenable to classical conditioning, though expression of conditioned or unconditioned responses normally may be inhibited *in utero* because of spatial or mechanical constraints. Whether mammalian fetuses can be classically conditioned is disputed; however, Gottlieb (1968) has discussed several successful attempts to condition avian embryos. In addition, Grier, Counter, and Shearer (1967) were able to imprint ducklings before they hatched, by exposing the eggs to an auditory stimulus. If imprinting is a rapid form of early learning (Klopfer 1961; Moltz 1963), this experiment produced prenatal learning.

Although learning, either in the form of classical or operant conditioning or in terms of sensory-motor feedback, is not well described in mammalian fetuses, there is evidence that environmental changes *in utero* can affect postnatal behavior. A wide variety of environmental agents, ranging from drugs to natural alterations in maternal metabolism, has been implicated in the behavioral deficiencies observed in young mammals whose mothers were subjected in pregnancy to such environmental changes. Although many of the studies have been criticized on methodological grounds, the weight of the evidence points toward deleterious effects produced by several tranquilizing and sedative drugs (Joffe 1969). In rats, prenatal maternal stress reduced later activity of the offspring (Thompson 1957). However, De Fries, Weir, and Hegmann (1967) have shown that in laboratory mice the effect of prenatal maternal stress varies not only with the genetic background of the mother but also with that of the embryo. Nevertheless, it is clear that the embryo is not fully protected from exogenous stimuli, but the pathway from stimulus to effect is probably indirect and the effects themselves are not clearly understood.

POSTNATAL DEVELOPMENT: DESCRIPTIVE STUDIES

Research on the developmental psychology of animals has been based more often on hypothesis testing than is the case in human developmental psychology. The emphasis on predictive experiments has resulted in failure to gather basic descriptive developmental data for most species. The importance of the few descriptive studies that do exist cannot be exaggerated. Those of special interest to psychologists are summarized in this section. Most studies cover only limited periods of development instead of the entire lifespan; and description has been most intensive in the early postnatal stages of development. Scott (1962) classified altricial avian and mammalian development into four postnatal phases: neonatal, transitional, primary socialization, and juvenile. These terms are useful as shorthand expressions, but the end of each phase tends to blend gradually into the beginning of the next, and the characteristic behaviors of each phase vary considerably among species.

Primates. The development of infrahuman primates has been observed in the laboratory and field. Similarities and differences in the development of a human and a chimpanzee infant reared together were described by Kellogg and Kellogg (1933). Recently, Rumbaugh and Riesen[6] produced a cinematographic study of gorilla development, in which comparisons to human and chimpanzee infancy were drawn. In these three groups, neonates show similar groping, grasping, and sucking reflexes. In each, the neonate is highly dependent on the attention of an adult caretaker and will die unless fed and supported. However, behavioral differences are apparent from birth. The human infant is more visually oriented than the gorilla, while the apes have greater motor abilities. Kellogg and Kellogg (1933) found that in many activities the chimpanzee, Gua, was superior to the human, Donald, up to the age of about three years. At that age, Donald's language ability was well developed and he began to perform consistently better than Gua on problems which did not require great skill or strength.

Communication skills have been studied in the chimpanzee in two ways. Early attempts to teach infant chimpanzees to voice English words had very limited success (Kellogg 1968). However, chimpanzees in natural conditions communicate through gestures (Nissen 1931; von Lawick-Goodall 1968);

and Kellogg and Kellogg (1933) noted that Gua and Donald used similar gestures to gain adult attention (e.g., tugging at the mother's skirts). Gardner and Gardner (1969) have verified the use of both spontaneous and trained gestures by an infant chimpanzee, Washoe, learning the American Sign Language.

The affectional development of the primates shows many similarities from group to group, at least within monkeys and apes. A strong attachment of infant to mother develops early. Harlow (1961) has investigated this attachment in rhesus monkeys; his work will be discussed in a later section. In some, but not all, primates, older infants receive paternal care (Mitchell 1969). For example, De Vore (1963) reported that adult male baboons are protective of infants and remain near juvenile play groups.

Readers interested in primate behavior development will find of value the reports of Hinde and Spencer-Booth (1967) on a group of rhesus monkey infants, Jay (1965) on the langur, Rosenblum and Kaufman (1967) on comparisons between pigtail and bonnet macaques, Berkson (1966) on a captive gibbon infant, Vandenburgh (1966) on an infant squirrel monkey, and Anthoney (1968) on the development of social skills in captive baboons, in addition to the works mentioned in the preceding paragraphs. Kellogg (1969) has summarized the results of six studies in which chimpanzees were reared in human homes.

Carnivores. In carnivores, the most widely studied group with respect to development is the domestic dog. The available data stem primarily from the efforts of workers at the Jackson Laboratory, Bar Harbor, Maine, who did a longitudinal study of five breeds (Scott & Fuller 1965). Although extensive breed differences in physical and behavioral maturation were found, Scott and Fuller identified stages through which all puppies pass.[7] In the neonatal phase, which lasts for approximately twelve days, the eyes and ears are closed and most sensory systems are "off." Neonatal puppies respond to temperature changes by wriggling until they reach a warm spot. They respond to taste stimulation by sucking, licking, or rejecting the substance. Contrary to popular opinion, neonatal puppies are relatively insensitive to odors. They require maternal care even to eliminate wastes. The neonate is adapted to a life of helplessness in which the mother provides most of its stimulation. Stimuli received by the pup are primarily tactile; as Scott and Fuller put it, "The puppy is in touch with only that part of the environment which actually touches him" (p. 87).

Following the neonatal phase is a transition period in which sensory and motor capacities change and develop. The eyes and ears open and motor behavior improves; the pup begins to walk more often than to belly-crawl. Though it still receives most of its nourishment from the mother, the pup begins to lap and eat from a bowl.

The third stage of canine development is of special interest to Scott, who calls it the period of primary socialization. At about three to four weeks of age the pup begins to be weaned by the mother and begins to form an attachment to the pack. If reared with dogs alone, the pup would become a pack animal. Domesticated dogs usually are reared with humans and at the

---

[6] *Primate growth and development: a gorilla's first year.* New York: Appleton-Century-Crofts. 16 mm film in color with sound and narration.

[7] Reflexive behavior in the dog was described by Fox (1964), who found that neurological developmental stages slightly precede Scott's behavioral stages.

stage of primary socialization form bonds with both dogs and humans. In this period, play patterns, forerunners of adult social behavior patterns, are prominent.

The juvenile period occurs during approximately three to six months of age and is characterized by increases in the strength and skill of established behavior patterns. By the end of this period, the dog is sexually mature and forms adult sexual relationships.

Similar observations have been made on wild dogs. Fentress (1967) observed the development of a hand-reared male timber wolf, Lupey, obtained from a zoo at the age of four weeks. Lupey showed primary socialization to both dogs and humans, but did not become "tame" in the sense that the term is applied to domestic dogs. Wolf development has also been discussed by Ginsburg (1965) and Murie (1944).

Behavioral development has been studied in other carnivores, but none has received the attention that has been given the dog. The development of domestic cats was described in articles by Rosenblatt, Turkewitz, and Schneirla (1961), Rosenblatt and Schneirla (1962), and Schneirla, Rosenblatt, and Tobach (1963). Sucking behavior in kittens was investigated by Kovach and Kling (1967). Schenkel (1966) and Forbes (1963) reported the behavior of wild and captive lion cubs. Eibl-Eibesfeldt (1961) observed the development of behavior patterns in captive polecats, and Heidt, Petersen, and Kirkland (1968) made similar observations on weasels.

Rodents. The postnatal behavioral development of laboratory rats was described by Bolles and Woods (1964), Baenninger (1967), and Rosenblatt and Lehrman (1963). Rats are born hairless, with closed eyes and ears. Little is known of their capacity to taste and smell at birth. The development of laboratory mice is similar to that of rats (Williams & Scott 1953). Neonatal rats and mice produce high-frequency squeaks, some of which are ultrasonic (Noirot 1966, 1968), which elicit retrieving and licking responses by the mother to varying degrees depending on the age of the pups (Noirot & Pye 1969). The infant rat or mouse is weaned by its mother by approximately 24 days of age. Scott (1968) has commented that standard laboratory practice results in premature weaning, since laboratories customarily wean rats at 18–20 days. Thus, most psychological studies of rat behavior probably are studies of the behavior of rats which have experienced maternal deprivation in late infancy.

King (1969) compared the development of two species of deer mice (*Peromyscus*), and Scudder, Karczmar, and Lockett (1967) compared the development of several genera and strains of mice. Both studies noted differences in behavior that were qualitative as well as quantitative in nature. For example, Scudder et al. found that social development was more rapid in the grain-eating mouse, *Microtus*, than in the carnivorous grasshopper mouse, *Onychomys*. During its slower development, *Onychomys* showed play patterns reminiscent of the chase-and-pounce play of domestic kittens. These authors suggest that the predatory way of life requires longer prepubertal development so that the predatory patterns can be shaped. The house mouse, *Mus musculus*, was the slowest genus to mature. The authors concluded that *Mus* is "neither a placid herbivorous animal like *Microtus*, nor a specialized predator like *Onychomys*, but an exploring, omnivorous, aggressive animal" (Scudder et al. 1967, p. 362).

Other Animals. Research in behavior development in other mammals is rare. Early filial behavior in some hoofed mammals will be discussed later in this section. Early development has been described for the big brown bat, *Eptesicus fuscus* (Davis, Barbour, & Hassell 1968), and the tree shrew, *Tupaia belangeri* (Martin 1968).

The following list of references will guide the reader who wants information about the early development of some non-mammalian vertebrates. The list is incomplete, but works of special interest to psychologists are included. Kruijt (1964) described the development of Burmese red jungle fowl; and Nice (1937, 1943) wrote a complete description of the life history and early development of the song sparrow, *Melospiza melodia*. Though some of the earliest work in developmental biology was done with amphibians and fish (see Carmichael 1954; Kuo 1967), little information on postembryonic development of behavior has been added. Shaw (1960, 1961) studied the development of schooling behavior in the fishes known as "silversides" (genus *Menidia*). The development of behavior in reptiles has rarely been studied. Even the adult behavior of this group is not well known. A few investigators have studied visual determinants of orientation to the sea in hatchling sea turtles (Ehrenfeld & Carr 1967; Mrosovsky & Shettleworth 1968) and prey attack in newborn snakes (Burghardt 1967; Burghardt & Hess 1968).

POSTNATAL DEVELOPMENT: HYPOTHESIS TESTING OR PREDICTIVE APPROACH

Early development is the focus of most research in comparative developmental psychology. This section summarizes some of the major experimental approaches to the development of social, perceptual, and cognitive responses in animals.

The Concept of the Critical Period. The concept of the critical or sensitive period in the development of a given behavior is an elaboration of the embryological generalization of critical periods. Morphological and physiological systems are most sensitive to modification by external stimuli during the time of the most rapid organization and growth. After organization is complete or well underway, the system resists reorganization (Lorenz 1957; Scott 1962). For example, it is commonly known that human embryos are sensitive to *Rubella* (German measles) virus during the first trimester of pregnancy. Applied to behavior, the critical period hypothesis can be stated in "strong" form as follows: a given response or set of responses must be acquired during a specific stage of development if it is to be expressed normally. If not acquired then, the response will be absent or abnormal. The hypothesis can be stated in a weaker form: a given response or set of responses is most easily acquired at a specific stage of organismic development. This concept, in one or the other of its forms, is central to experiments on imprinting and the effects of early experience on later behavior.

Imprinting. Bateson (1966) and Sluckin (1965) have written complete reviews of the research on imprinting. Imprinting was first described as the approach of a young precocial bird (e.g., duckling, gosling, chick) toward the first object it encounters, and the subsequent preference of the bird for that object or one similar to it (Lorenz 1937). Through this process, the young bird learns the identity of its parent and later of its species.

Imprinting can be considered a rapid form of learning occurring early in life (Lorenz 1955; Klopfer 1961; Moltz 1963). Birds can be imprinted to a variety of stimulus objects, ranging from humans to inanimate objects or flickering lights (e.g., Sluckin & Salzen 1961; Klopfer 1967; Hoffman, Schiff, Adams, & Searle 1966). The imprinting object need not move. However, some objects elicit approach more easily than others. Gottlieb (1965) found that the parental call of the species is preferred to that of another species, and Klopfer (1967), using visual stimuli, found that some preferences could be modified by training while others could not. Imprinting occurs in the absence of conventional reinforcement and without apparent practice. However, the imprinting stimulus itself can serve as a reinforcer (Hoffman et al. 1966). Ramsay & Hess (1954) found imprinting to occur within a critical period in the posthatching development of mallard ducklings, but other investigators have been able to vary the period and to extend it (Sluckin 1965). Although Lorenz (1955) believes that imprinting is irreversible, Salzen & Meyer (1967) established reversal in domestic chicks, and Moltz & Rosenblum (1958) showed habituation of the following response in Peking ducklings. Furthermore, sexual behavior need not be restricted to the species of the imprinting object (Fabricius 1962).

Although most imprinting experiments have been done with precocial birds, Shipley (1963) and Sluckin (1968) reported imprinting-like behavior in guinea pigs. Newborn lambs and moose, and older goat kids and elk calves, follow moving objects, usually the mother, and later transfer affiliative responses to the entire flock or herd (Scott 1960; Hersher, Richmond, & Moore 1963; Altmann 1963). If orphaned lambs or kids are reared by humans, the adult sheep or goats remain aloof from others of their species, preferring human company (Scott 1945). Filial attachments in these hoofed mammals appear similar to those observed in precocial birds, but in these mammals the mother plays a major role in the development of the filial bond. If a newborn lamb is separated from its mother for more than 4 hours, the mother no longer accepts her offspring, but butts it away (Collias 1956). It has been suggested that this behavior is a kind of imprinting in the mother, occurring during a sensitive period following parturition. Again, the effect is not irreversible; it has been possible to force rejecting ewes and dams to accept alien lambs and kids (Hersher, Richmond, & Moore 1963). The imprintinglike responses may be merely analogous, rather than based on common physiological mechanisms, and caution should be taken against the premature assumption that filial responses occur for the same physiological reasons in all vertebrates.

Effects of Variations in Maternal Care. Harlow and his coworkers have carried out a series of investigations on the development of affectional responses in rhesus monkeys reared with various types of mother surrogates (Harlow 1961). Rhesus infants prefer cloth surrogates which provide tactual stimulation but not nourishment to wire surrogates which provide milk but not "contact comfort" (Harlow 1958). The presence of a cloth surrogate reduces infant "fear" responses to novel objects (Harlow & Zimmermann 1959). However, the cloth surrogate is an adequate mother only for young infants; older ones require interaction with real monkeys if normal behavior

is to develop. The monkey reared without other monkeys is usually reluctant to mate, and males may be incapable of effective mating behavior (Harlow & Harlow 1965). If they have offspring, females reared by surrogate mothers are poor mothers, ignoring or mistreating their infants (Seay, Alexander, & Harlow 1964). The infants of cruel mothers neverthelesss develop normal attachments to their mothers, a phenomenon which has been observed also in human "battered children."

Variations in maternal behavior have been studied in other mammals. Denenberg, Hudgens, and Zarrow (1964) fostered mice to albino rat mothers and found that the mice formed social attachments to rats. Mainardi, Marsan, and Pasquali (1965) reared mice with perfumed or normal parents. When tested for preference between normal or perfumed sexual partners, male mice showed no preference, but females preferred mates which resembled the parents with which they had been reared. Furchtgott, Lazar, and Deitchman (1969) found that offspring of multiparous female mice, as compared with offspring of primiparous mothers, were less active in an open field, emerged more readily from the home cage, and learned an avoidance response more slowly. The authors interpreted these differences as indicating less "fear" in the offspring of multiparous mothers. Mitchell, Ruppenthal, Raymond, and Harlow (1966) found offspring of multiparous rhesus monkeys to be more hostile to strangers but more playful and relaxed with their cagemates than were offspring of primiparous mothers. Parental handling was observed directly by Ressler (1962), who found that BALB/c mice handle their offspring more than do C57BL/10 mice. Offspring fostered to these strains differed in that BALB/c mothering resulted in heavier offspring at weaning, increased viability to weaning, and more visual exploration. Greater weight at weaning and faster growth also occurs in mice reared in a communal nursing situation (Sayler & Salmon 1969).

In rhesus monkeys the social status of a mother is directly related to the dominance status of her male offspring (Koford 1963); aggressiveness in the son can be increased by artificial elevation of the mother's status (Marsden 1968).

Maternal deprivation generally results in abnormal behavior of the offspring. Male rats reared in incubators did not achieve appropriate mounting of females (Gruendel & Arnold 1969). However, another rodent, the guinea pig, showed no aberrant sexual behavior (Harper 1968). In the goat, maternal deprivation results in increased heartrate and respiration rate, more "emotionality," and less social dominance. However, maternally deprived female kids, unlike rhesus monkeys (Seay et al. 1964) become normal mothers (Hersher 1969).

Schneirla, Rosenblatt, and Tobach (1963), found that maternally deprived kittens could not nurse easily upon their return to the mother and litter. These authors believe that the effects of maternal deprivation are not due to simple lack of stimulation but to the inability of the separated kitten to develop appropriate responses to changes in maternal responsiveness to the changing behavior of the litter. The responses which develop in isolation are maladaptive when the kitten returns to the social situation. Maladaptive responses of this type were also seen in the surrogate-reared rat (Thoman, Wetzel, & Levine 1968).

Effects of Littermates and Social Companions on Later Behavior. In the rhesus monkey, infants reared in social isolation for six or twelve months become autistic and incapable of normal social behavior. Such monkeys retain abnormal behavior patterns to adulthood. Motherless infants reared with other young monkeys escape these ill effects (Harlow 1969). The play patterns of infant monkeys have been described by Harlow (1969), who stresses their significance in the development of adult social patterns.

Young mammals which are reared with cagemates of a different species often develop social attachments which prevent interspecific attack behavior. Kuo (1930) found that cats reared with rats did not kill rats, but each cat developed an attachment to its rat companion. If more than one kitten shared the cage with the rats, attachment did not develop (Kuo 1938), but the cats still would not kill adult rats. However, they did kill and eat rat pups. Denenberg, Paschke, & Zarrow (1968) produced a similar effect, a decrease of mouse-killing behavior in rats reared with mice.

Early Sensory Deprivation. Many experiments in which infant animals are isolated from their mothers or littermates confound social deprivation with sensory deprivation. When a young animal experiences no social contacts and receives nourishment from an inanimate surrogate, the animal probably is deprived of much of the sensory stimulation it would normally receive.

Severe stimulus and social deprivation has been studied in domestic dogs (Thompson, Melzack, & Scott 1956; Lessac & Solomon 1969; Lessac, cited by Zubek 1969; Thompson & Heron 1954). Such deprivation often has devastating effects; when the animals are removed from restriction they behave in bizarre fashion. Fuller (1967) has discussed this "postisolation" syndrome in light of three theoretical interpretations: Hebb's theory that restriction prohibits perceptual learning, Lessac's theory that restriction destroys neural organization, and the theory of Fuller and Clark that sudden postisolational exposure to massive stimulation produces massive emotional responsivity.

Deprivation of visual stimuli in infancy produces different effects in different vertebrate animals. Chow, Riesen, and Newell (1957) reported that chimpanzees light deprived from birth not only were unable to see as juveniles but also experienced retinal ganglion cell degeneration. Unresponsivity of cells in the visual cortex was found in kittens reared not in total darkness but with monocular visual pattern deprivation (Wiesel & Hubel 1963). However, rats reared in darkness showed neither impairment of ability to perform visual pattern discriminations (Woodruff & Slovak 1965) nor impairment of depth perception (Walk 1965). Rearing in darkness interferes with the visual cliff performance of cats and rabbits, but not that of chicks, sheep, or goats (Walk 1965). Light deprivation may impair the ability of young chicks to peck accurately at objects (Padilla 1935), but Kovach (1969) recently failed to replicate this result.

Held and Hein (1967) believe that it is not pattern deprivation itself that produces visual deficits, but the lack of feedback that the normally stimulated animal produces by moving about in the visual environment. They have shown that in the kitten, movement-produced stimulation results in better performance on visual tests than does passive exposure to moving stimuli (Held & Hein 1963; 1967).

Tactual deprivation was investigated by Nissen, Chow, and Semmes (1951), who reared a young chimpanzee in limb restraints which prevented it from grooming and from manipulating objects in its environment. After 31 months, this animal was deficient in many types of tactual discrimination and locomotor ability and could not localize stimulation on various parts of its body.

Analogous experiments in the auditory modality are done primarily with songbirds, whose adult behavior depends heavily on auditory stimuli. Male chaffinches (*Fringilla coelebs*) do not sing until the spring after they hatch. If hatchlings are removed from the nest before hearing the adult male song, they develop only a rudimentary, simplified song which resembles the normal adult form only in approximate length and number of notes. If exposed in adulthood to the adult song, these isolated birds do not learn it. If the infant chaffinch is allowed to hear the adult song but is then isolated, the bird in its first spring of adulthood sings a chaffinch-like song which lacks the embellishments of the complete song. Thus, in the chaffinch, development of the complete song depends not only on hearing the adult song in infancy, but also on exposure in young adulthood to the complete song. Furthermore, once the complete song is learned, it cannot be modified by exposure to new variants of the song (Thorpe 1965). The development of singing is similar, but not identical, in some other songbirds, such as the white-crowned sparrow, *Zonotrichia leucophrys* (Marler & Tamura 1964). Not all songbirds require modeling of this type, however (Nottebohm 1970).

Enrichment of the Environment. The definitive experiment on the effect of enriched environment probably has not been run, since the normal environment of the laboratory rat is restricted in comparison to the normal environment of the wild rat. With that reservation in mind, we turn to the effects of enriched environments on later behavior. Typically, the experimental group is given extra stimulation not available to the control animals. As is the case in deprivation experiments, the stimuli may be unimodal, but multimodal enrichment is usually employed.

The effects of enrichment on both physiological and behavioral development have been studied in a series of experiments by Rosenzweig, Krech, and Bennett and their students (Rosenzweig 1966). Rats reared in enriched cages, with toys and cagemates, show at puberty greater cortical brain weights than do isolated rats (Bennett, Krech, & Rosenzweig 1964). Enrichment in adulthood has produced similar effects (Rosenzweig, Bennett, & Krech 1964); thus no narrow critical period exists for the effects of enrichment on brain weight. However, Forgays and Read (1962) reported such an effect on the ability of rats to perform in the Hebb-Williams maze test; rats which experienced enrichment during the period of 21 days to 3 months of age performed better than those experiencing enrichment at later ages. Rats reared as house pets also performed better on the Hebb-Williams maze than did normally reared laboratory rats (Hebb 1947) and rats reared in a room learned mazes faster than rats reared in a small cage (Bingham & Griffiths 1952). Unfortunately, experimentation on the question of environmental enrichment in infancy is still sparse, and since enrichment usually consists of both inanimate and social objects, the effective stimuli are unknown. However, these studies have provided empirical support for environmental enrichment programs for human children.

Beneficial effects on later behavior have also been obtained when animals were handled or even given mild electric shocks in infancy (e.g., R. W. Bell 1964; Denenberg & Grota 1964; Meyers 1965; Wilson, Warren, & Abbott 1965). Various effects of early stimulation have been reviewed by Bovard (1958), Levine (1960; 1962), and Denenberg (1962; 1964), who have put forward physiological and psychological theories of early stimulation.

Age Changes in Learning. Scott (1967) has noted that most investigators of learning in animals do not study developmental changes, but are "content to show that some sort of modification of behavior takes place in young animals." Two studies from Harlow's laboratory are among those reporting age changes. Mason and Harlow (1961) found that young monkeys improved with age in ability to solve a crossed-string problem. Harlow, Blazek, and McClearn (1956) showed that infant monkeys would learn to solve manipulatory puzzles in the absence of conventional reinforcement and that this manipulative behavior increased with age.

Campbell (1967) has reviewed the literature on the development of learning abilities in infraprimate mammals, and has investigated age changes in avoidance conditioning in rats. He has concluded that simple learning ability does not change significantly from youth to adulthood, but that retention differences do exist: "memory develops with age." This type of research, which analyzes one type of learning in detail, may open the way toward a true developmental psychology of animal learning.

Studies on Aging in Animals. Since few experimental animals are allowed to die of old age, experiments on the effects of aging on animal behavior are rare. Jerome (1959) summarized the results of a group of experiments done by C. P. Stone and others, who tested rats of various ages, including senescents. In many of the learning tasks there were no age differences. However, where differences did occur, the aged rats were slower to learn. Birren and Kay (1958) found that older rats (aged 22 to 27 months) were slower swimmers in a water runway than were younger rats. Older animals also fatigued more easily, but, like younger rats, increased their tolerance to fatigue when given practice (Kay & Birren 1958). Reaction time of the rat to a loud noise and to electric shock was also slower in older animals (Birren 1955). Older rats (15 to 24 months old) also showed a decrease in locomotor activity and exploration as compared with younger ones (Goodrick 1965). Lagerspetz and Portin (1968) came to the same conclusion about older laboratory mice.

In mice, longevity is associated with genotype (Russell 1966) and increases with litter size (Roderick & Storer 1961). To test one of the major theories of aging, the "wear and tear theory" that each stressful agent takes its toll of a limited amount of life material, Curtis (1963) exposed a long-lived and a short-lived strain of mice to repeated massive but nonlethal physiological stressors (e.g., nitrogen mustard, tetanus toxoid). These experimental mice lived as long as did controls.

Two conclusions can be drawn from this survey of the development of animal behavior. First, the course of the normal development of most animals is unknown. The data for comparative developmental psychology have yet to be gathered. Second, young organisms are the most frequently studied and adulthood as a developmental period is ignored. In this respect, animal and human developmental studies are similar. Furthermore, old age receives a minor share of the attention in human studies and practically none in animals.

Human Studies

The organization of the presentation of human studies in developmental psychology is based on the life-cycle stages as proposed by Charlotte Bühler. Before detailing some of the research findings relevant to each stage, Bühler's life-cycle developmental theory is briefly outlined. Central to the theory are the emphases on studying the whole person and changing goals during the course of life.

In the study of the human life cycle, the individual is seen as a psychobiological system which progresses through a series of changes. Under normal circumstances, the biological growth and decline processes (*maturation*) follow a sequential and irreversible order. The sequence of psychological developmental stages is determined only in part by the underlying biological process. Environmental influences from the beginning are effective in the timing and structuralization of the individual's development. Both factors are merged in the actual psychological development.

There are different theories regarding the subdivision of the life-cycle development into *phases* according to different assumptions about the relevant determinants of a phase. These subdivisions are, of course, arbitrary, since the developmental process represents a continuity. They serve primarily the practical purpose of organizing the unifying characteristics of a person at any time of his life. The variation of these views is not as great as one might expect. The basic stages distinguished have been *infancy, childhood, adolescence, adulthood,* and *old age.* These subdivisions have remained more or less the same throughout the centuries and in different cultures.

Though, on first sight, these distinctions of phases appear obvious, a complexity of factors is involved. More recent subdivisions of the life cycle have been based on various specific considerations. One is the question of how the *unit of a person* is to be conceived. This indeed is one of the basic problems of all psychology as well as specifically for developmental psychology per se. Gordon Allport lists the "bewildering array" of current proposals. "Besides instincts, drives, needs, value-vectors, and sentiments, we encounter habits, attitudes, syndromes, regions, ergs, personal constructs, preferred patterns, dimensions, factors, schemata, traits, and trends" (Allport 1961, p. 314). No single one of these applied concepts would suffice to define the unit of, say, Don Smith, a 35-year-old ambitious lawyer with a wife and family. Being aware of this multiplicity of individualizing characteristics, one cannot hope to give an adequate description of a person by singling out one specific unifying trait or trend. There are any number of normative data which distinguish, say, a child from an adolescent, not to speak of a specific individual person. But in order to organize our material, we have to choose some organizing principles.

A first organizing principle is the directional trend of the biological developmental process which has a certain psychological parallel. It is the basic scheme of *growth* and *decline* used by Charlotte Bühler (1933) as representing processes of *expansion* and *restriction*. The biological expansion is seen in the generative growth process from birth to about 21 years of age; the biological restriction is seen in the decline process from around 50 years of age on. In between, growth and decline processes are more or less in balance. There are considerable individual variations in the timing of these processes, especially in the decline process.

The interpretation of growth and decline as processes of expansion and restriction suggests the inclusion of *reproductive ability* under this consideration. If simultaneously the ability to reproduce is taken into consideration as an indirect means of expansion through one's biological product, a five-phase scheme can be devised. The ages from birth to puberty (0 to about 11–15) comprise a first period of growth which precedes reproductivity. The period of the onset of reproductive abilities in puberty until the end of generative growth (approximately 15 or earlier to 21 or sooner) is biologically speaking the most expansive in that there is not only physical growth, but also the ability of self-multiplication. This second is followed by a third phase in which generative growth has ceased but reproductive abilities continue, thus allowing for further expansive possibilities (from approximately 21 to 45–50). The fourth period may entail the beginning of decline as well as the loss of reproductive abilities for the female (approximately 45–50 to about 55–65). The fifth period (after 65) is one of great variation among individuals. Biological losses may be slow and delayed or fast and accelerated before life processes cease altogether. And while in the individual's life cycle the biological expansion comes to a standstill, one might say that in reproducing the individual transfers his expansive tendencies to his offspring. In this sense, expansion might be designated a basic tendency of life.

The reflection of both the dominant expansive trend of life and the restrictive tendency in the aging can be found in each individual's motivation patterns. There is, as will be illustrated in the more detailed study of life phases, considerable evidence to support this theoretical contention. However, the manifold environmental influences on a person's experiential, mental, emotional, and behavioral development modify the biological process in an individualizing way. Emerging is the personality with its singular traits and trends. If among these we look for a characteristic which might contribute most to the unit of a person, *motivation* plays perhaps the most decisive role. Although motives may change or even conflict during the course of a person's life, it is widely assumed that there is a single unifying end goal. Two theories on the nature of the end goal prevail: *homeostasis* and *self-realization* (or *self-actualization*). The first has its main representative in psychoanalytically and other drive-reduction oriented psychologists, and the second is accepted by a wide range of thinkers who belong more or less directly to the new school of humanistic psychology. In his circumspect foregoing chapter on *Theories of Motivation*, K. B. Madsen distinguishes "incentive hypotheses" and "cognitive hypotheses" besides "homeostatic" and "humanistic hypotheses." While the first two types of theories describe important implementary processes of behavior, they do not specify the end goals which are emphasized in dynamic psychologies.

Motivational changes represent a second organizing principle of the course of human development. Motivational development, in Freudian terms, progresses through the stages of the id (defined as the instinctual drive to satisfy basic needs), the ego (representing the individual's ability and willingness to cope with reality), and the superego (reflecting the infusion of societal demands). Since all three processes develop in childhood, the original Freudian scheme does not foresee new contributing motivational factors during further stages of the life cycle. E. Erikson's (1959) scheme of development parallels that of the Freudian libido development, but continues on to span the whole life cycle. Successful adjustment to life depends on the ability of the individual to coordinate his inborn needs with the expectations of society and various stages of his life.

Bühler (1933a) describes motivational development in stages of self-determination to goals towards self-fulfillment. Childhood is the *first* phase before self-determination to long-range goals is realized. The *second*, or adolescent, phase is characterized by preliminary and experimental approaches to self-determination of life goals. In early adulthood, the *third* phase, self-determination becomes more definite. In the *fourth* phase of late adulthood, self-evaluation of the past and of future potentials becomes predominant and often crucial, invoking changes in direction. The *fifth* and final phase is characterized by an active or a restful fulfillment or else depression and/or despair may be the end.

Bühler has distinguished four *basic tendencies* which are instrumental to a person's goal setting. These are the *tendency to need satisfaction*, predominating in infancy and early childhood; the *tendency to self-limiting adaptation*, predominating in later childhood; the *tendency to creative expansion*, predominating in adolescence and adulthood; and the *tendency to upholding and restoring the internal order*, predominating in late adulthood and old age. All tendencies are assumed to be in operation during all phases of life, but each is ascendant in different developmental phases and there may be variations within different individuals. During the fifth phase (old age), any of the tendencies may prevail but need satisfaction and adaptation are the most frequent.

Because the individual's motivational changes are codetermined by the demands of the environment, the *sequence of social requirements* represents a third organizing principle. An extensive description of "developmental tasks" representing the expectations and demands society makes on the individual during his lifetime has been done by R. Havighurst (1952, 1953).

While the amount of research studies devoted to the development in childhood and adolescence is impressive, considerably less work has been devoted to the later stages of life. However, the real paucity of studies is in the area of the *life cycle* as a whole. Few textbooks in developmental psychology include chapters beyond the late childhood or adolescent stages (exceptions include Hurlock 1968 and Pikunas 1969) or present their material in total life-cycle perspectives (exceptions include Zubeck & Solberg 1954, and Pressey & Kuhlen 1957). The life-cycle studies which have been done may be grouped into five categories. In historical order they are: *developmental-biographical* accounts, *psychoanalytically* oriented life-history cases, *sociologically* oriented studies, *behavioristic-statistical* studies, and *humanistic-psychological* studies. The main differences among these descriptions lie in the basic orientations from which the person's life is seen. Only the behavioristic-statistical approach limits itself to assembling data covering different age groups without an overall theory of life as a whole (Bühler & Ekstein 1970).

We now turn to a consideration of each life phase.

Phase I: Childhood

THE NEONATE

The period of the neonate is traditionally designated as the first month of postnatal life, during which the baby must adjust to a new environment as well as to his newly activated physiological equipment.[8]

The tiny red and wrinkled newborn, flailing erratically about, may appear on cursory observation to be the epitomy of incompetence. States Escalona (1968), "Until fairly recently the human neonate was described in textbooks as a functionally decorticate organism, imperfectly equipped to discriminate (or even receive) sensory stimulation, and essentially passive and vulnerable in its relationship to the physical and social environment" (p. 3). However, Eiduson stated recently in an excellent chapter on the nature of the newborn, "The relevant literature is now replete with data which show the persistence, vigor, and selectivity with which an infant pursues external stimuli" (Eiduson 1968, p. 107).

Although some disorganization may be experienced during the first day or two after birth (Brazelton 1961), the newborn is capable of making a variety of responses and adjustments to his new environment, and these become more integrated and perfected during the first month of life. The ability of the newborn to attend to stimuli progresses rapidly during the first weeks of life (Carpenter & Stechler 1967). But aside from the adjustive and reactive behaviors, there is evidence that the neonate is an active seeker of experience and capable of internally elicited coping behavior (Bühler & Massarik 1968).

The Europeans saw internally initiative behavior in so-called spontaneous movements which differed from mass activity and reactions to stimuli (e.g., Preyer 1882). Turning away from, as well as turning toward, stimuli is observable from 10 to 14 days following birth (Bühler & Hetzer 1928; Ripin & Hetzer 1930). Murphy (1962) noting the necessity of the neonate to manage incoming stimulation states, "We believe that some of these earliest coping efforts are seen in the use of sleep, turning away, spitting out, etc., to avoid or get rid of unpleasant stimuli" (p. 308).

Thus, along with the primary needs of the infant (food, warmth, sleep, etc.) are other such important needs as tactile contact and search for arousal or stimulation. This has necessitated the reevaluation of the tension-reduction or pleasure-pain conception of neonatal behavior (Eiduson 1968).

Physiological and Sensory Capacities. Aspects of postnatal life to which the newborn must adjust include: temperature change, autorespiration, sucking and swallowing, elimination, internal self-propelled blood, digestion, and maintenance of the acid-alkaline balance in the body (McNeil 1966; Hurlock 1968). Thus, the first task of life is to achieve adequate integration of physiological functioning (Ribble 1943; Greenacre 1952)

[8] For a detailed review of the neonate, see Pratt 1946, 1954.

or as Stone and Church (1968) put it, "If the neonate is to grow and flourish, his first order of business is to stay alive" (p. 6).

The newborn is prepared to digest food. There is evidence for preliminary alimentation activity during the fetal period (Bersot 1920). Elimination begins shortly after birth (Halverson 1940). Because the musculature involved in breathing is not completely coordinated for the first few weeks of life, respiration is irregular (Smith 1963). The heart beats rapidly because the heart is small in relation to the arteries (Grossman & Greenberg 1957). The range is 124 beats per minute during deep sleep to 218 beats per minute during crying (Halverson 1941). In general, body temperature is higher and more variable in the neonate than in the average adult (Pratt 1954). The newborn is sensitive to thermal stimuli (Pratt, Nelson & Sun 1930; Bridger & Reiser 1959; Birns, Blank & Bridger 1966). Newborns are more active when environmental temperature is cool and less active when it is warm (Pratt 1930; Stirniman 1939).

The newborn baby is sensitive to differences in light intensity (Pratt 1934), can discriminate between colors (Chase 1937), and within about two weeks he can track a moving horizontal visual stimulus (McGinnis 1930). The newborn can also discriminate patterns and spends more time fixating on black and white figures than color areas, and on stimuli resembling the human face than on random arrangements of human facial features (Fantz 1963). Soon after birth, the baby will spend different amounts of time looking at stimuli of different brightness levels (Hershenson 1964).

Although the newborn's hearing may be impaired due to the presence of fluid in the middle ear, studies have demonstrated reflex responses to auditory stimuli right after birth (Wedenberg 1956; Hardy, Dougherty & Hardy 1959; Suzuki, Kamijo & Kiuchi 1964). Newborns react differentially to sounds of varying frequencies and pitch (Pratt, Nelson & Sun 1930; Ewing & Ewing 1944; Eisenberg, Griffin, Coursin & Hunter 1964). The neonate can discriminate between tones, but the differences must be quite disparate (Leventhal & Lipsitt 1964). Lower tones are more soothing to a newborn than are high tones (Birns, Blank, Bridger & Escalona 1965). Positive reactions (smiling and cooing) to the sound of a human voice were found as early as 14 days (Hetzer & Tudor-Hart 1927). Wertheimer (1961) found that a newborn turned to look toward the sound made by a toy cricket within a few minutes after birth. Leventhal and Lipsitt (1964) found that neonates could discriminate the location of sound within the first five days of life. Other studies, however, did not demonstrate sound localization until the infant was several months old (Gesell 1925; Ewing & Ewing 1944; Chun, Pawsat & Forster 1960).

Although findings suggest that there is little or no taste sensitivity at birth, the ability to differentiate gustatory stimuli increases quite rapidly (Pratt, Nelson & Sun 1930; Peiper 1963).

Thresholds of sensitivity to smell change considerably during the first days of life (Engen, Lipsitt, & Kaye 1963). Other studies have demonstrated the neonate's ability to discriminate odors (Disher 1934; Engen, Lipsitt & Kaye 1963; Lipsitt, Engen, & Kaye 1963) and to adapt or accommodate to odors (Lipsitt 1966).

Newborns are sensitive to tactile stimuli (Bell 1964; Lipsitt & Levy 1959). The areas of greatest sensitivity are the face, hands, and soles of the feet (Peiper 1928). At birth, the human is relatively insensitive to pain. But sensitivity increases rapidly (Sherman & Sherman 1925; Lipsitt & Levy 1959).

Behavior and Learning. Dennis (1932), Delman (1935), Bell (1960b), Peiper (1963) and Wolff (1966) conclude from their observations that a number of organized behavioral systems exist in the newborn baby. What the newborn does do, behaviors usually assumed to be unlearned, has been documented (e.g., Watson 1963; Desmond et al. 1963).

Most of the behavioral responses to incoming stimuli made by the newborn are believed to be reflex actions in that they can be rather consistently elicited. Some reflexes disappear within a short time and similar activities appear later but in a more sophisticated form. These include the swimming movements of the neonate when he is supported in a horizontal belly-down position, stepping movements when the neonate is held vertically with his feet lightly touching a surface, and strong grasping response when a rod or other object is placed in the palm.

The so-called mass activity of the newborn has been attributed to neurological immaturity (Irwin 1943) rather than reflexive behavior. Although, as has been mentioned, closer analysis of mass activity has revealed more patterned and self-initiated behavior than earlier findings had suggested, yet—because the voluntary muscles are not completely under control until the end of the first year (Thompson 1954)—motor development proceeds more slowly than sensory capacities.

The newborn's major "activity" is sleeping. Eighteen or more hours per day are spent asleep, though it is lighter than that of the adult and is broken by brief waking periods (Bühler 1930). Rapid eye movements (REM sleep) have been confirmed as occurring during a large portion of the newborn's sleep (Roffwarg, Muzio, & Dement 1966; Parmelee et al. 1967). The whole question of "state" of the neonate (that is, level of arousal on a sleep-awake-active dimension) has become a very important factor in evaluating infant reactivity and responsiveness (Graham 1956; Levy 1958; Bridger 1961; Gordon & Bell 1961; Escalona 1962; and Rovee & Levin 1966). "States" of neonates have been described by several researchers (Fries & Wolff 1953; Wolff 1959; Bell 1960b; Brazelton 1962; Brown 1964; and Wolff 1966). When the newborn is in a state of physiological equilibrium, he sleeps or stares blankly (Strang 1959). This state of satisfaction, however, is the one from which positive spontaneous exploratory behavior can then arise. High activity is seen as a rough index of discomfort and such activity is often present just before feeding (Irwin 1932a) and subsides when the hunger is appeased. Yet some recent research has found that neonate arousal and activity states are not necessarily linked up to nutritive drives (Bridger 1962; Hendry & Kessen 1964). Rather, the neonate can be observed from two weeks on engaging in self-initiated movement of the limbs and especially the fingers. By three weeks the baby watches his own bodily movements. This behavior is seen as the beginning of exploratory behavior (Bühler 1930). The neonate's activity level can be influenced by outside stimuli (Pratt, Nelson & Sun 1930; Weiss 1934; Bartoshuk 1962; and Birns, Blank, Bridger & Escalona 1965). Differences in activity level have been related to such factors as breast-feeding vs. bottle-feeding (Davis, Sears, Miller & Brodbeck 1948; Newton & Newton 1951) and whether or not there were complications in delivery (Prechtl 1964).

Sucking responses rapidly become more efficient as the days progress following birth (Gesell & Ilg 1937). This extremely important behavior capacity is described by Murphy (1962) as ". . . the first effort to earn a living, or to work, and for some involves considerable struggle or requires considerable en-

couragement. . ." (p. 308). The great individual differences among newborns in rate and intensity of sucking have been described by Kron, Stein, and Goddard (1963). Characteristics of the intraoral stimuli (Lipsitt & Kaye 1965) and whether or not the sucking response was accompanied by the intake of nutritive substance have been demonstrated to affect sucking behavior (Kaye 1966; Dubignon & Campbell 1969). Introduction of competing stimuli (e.g., light movement) can reduce sucking rate (Haith 1966). Sucking has also been proposed to be an innate pacifier in that it inhibits movement and calms the newborn (Kessen & Leutzendorff 1963; Kessen, Leutzendorff & Stoutsenberger 1967). Changes in the newborn's sucking behavior at feeding time, toward being more accommodating (e.g., removing hands from mouth, opening mouth) have been observed within the first few feedings following birth (Ripin & Hetzer 1930) which Bühler interprets as evidence of "self-limiting" adaptation.

Although the first vocalization is the "birth cry," the respiratory and vocal organs are capable of functioning well before full-term birth (Hooker 1943). Strong stimuli, loud noises, or rough handling will cause the neonate to cry (Dennis 1939). Aldrich, Sung, and Knop (1945a, 1945b) concluded that hunger and "being wet" were the major apparent causes of spontaneous crying in the neonate. But approximately one-third of the cries could not be "diagnosed" as to precipitating factors. The motor correlates of crying have been described by Ames (1941).

Because of the limited sensory and motor abilities of the neonate, many experimenters believe that learning ability is quite limited (Scott 1968), or has not been conclusively demonstrated (Bijou & Baer 1965), or may be due to inadequate techniques (Watson 1967).

The failure of many early American studies to establish conditioned responses in the neonate (Marinesco & Kreindler 1933; Kasatkin 1936; Kasatkin & Levikova 1935), and the partial or tentative success reported by some (Wickens & Wickens 1940; Wenger 1936; and Marquis 1931) led Pratt (1954) to summarize, "There is some evidence that certain responses may be conditioned to experimental stimuli during the neonatal period. The responses are difficult to establish, highly unstable, and cannot be set up in all infants" (p. 270). More recent American studies have demonstrated evidence of learning in the neonate (Lipsitt 1966). Lipsitt and his co-workers have presented evidence for conditioning of responses involving mouth stimulation (Lipsitt & Kaye 1964) and the strengthening of head-turning responses through the use of reinforcement contingencies (Siqueland & Lipsitt 1966, and Siqueland 1968).

Emotional and Social Responsiveness. Bühler (1968d) notes that the controversies surrounding the attribution of covert processes to infants are due to the fact that all theory is based on interpretation. This state of affairs is particularly noticeable in the writings on the emotional make-up of the neonate. The designation of a particular response to a particular stimulation as evidence of a specific "emotion" has led to many disagreements over the emotional make-up of the neonate. The ability of the newborn to respond "emotionally," however, is considered to be an unlearned process (Bakwin 1947).

The psychoanalysts saw reason to presume that the human being is capable of profound and intense feelings at birth (Freud 1936; Issacs 1936). Jersild (1946) points to the work of John B.

Watson (Watson 1919; Watson & Morgan 1917) as precipitating much of the research in this area. Watson described the original emotions of the newborn as *fear* (evidenced by the startled reaction to loud sounds or the trembling, crying, whimpering, and catching of breath when there is a sudden loss of support), *rage* (evidenced by the stiffening reaction to restriction of movement or other reactions such as "slashing" movements of hands and legs, holding the breath, or screaming), and *love* (evidenced by the "expansive" relaxation to gentle patting or stroking, or other reactions such as spreading fingers and toes, cooing and gurgling).

Subsequent studies have been unable to substantiate Watson's differentiation of initial emotions (Pratt, Nelson & Sun 1930; Taylor 1934). Irwin (1932a) dropped neonates "free-fall" style for a distance of two feet, and only two of his 85 subjects cried, while some made no overt response at all.

Any intense stimulation will cause the newborn to react with what might appear to be "fear" (startle response, squirming, crying, etc.). But as Jersild (1960) notes, other forms of stimulation, not considered at all fearful by adult standards, can cause identical reactions. Sherman's (1927) study demonstrated that adult observers, who had no knowledge of the precipitating stimuli (hunger, sudden loss of support, restraint of the head and face, and pricking with a needle) could not agree on the emotions being expressed by neonates or what might have caused the reactions.

Bridges (1932) and Bühler (1930) concluded from their observations that the most common reaction in the newborn to stimulating situations was a diffuse agitation or excitement and that more specific emotions did not differentiate for several weeks. Bühler and Hetzer (1928) and Sherman (1928) differentiated the newborn's emotional response capabilities into general positive and negative reactions. Similarly Jersild (1960) groups the neonate's expressive emotional reactions into those of apparent withdrawal and those of apparent acceptance, quiescence, passivity, and a rudimentary form of pursuit (e.g., turning the head and opening mouth to suckle when an object is placed near his lips).

Pratt (1946) notes that the evidence for lack of differentiation of emotional response in the neonate has led many to abandon the term "emotion" as applied to this age level. "In its place they advocate a purely descriptive account of the extent of organismic involvement in a response under definite conditions or stimulation, age of the organism, and so on" (p. 236).

Although we do not speak of the neonate having a "personality" as the term is generally used, the existence of primary individuality is assumed to exist (Bühler 1968d) and will receive further discussion below. Further, it might be reasonable to expect that certain prenatal influences affecting the fetus, thus causing a modification of its newborn behavior pattern, could affect personality development (Peckos 1957; Sontag 1966).

It may be more feasible to discuss social responsiveness, which is assumed, of course, to reflect and contribute strongly to personality development. The first weeks of life are considered crucial because the basic attitude of "trust" will emerge if the neonate's needs of comfort, nutrition, etc., are satisfied (Erikson 1959; Strang 1959).

Because the attitudes and behavior of the parents directly affect the social development of the baby, it is no wonder that many investigators have discovered differences, even at a very early age, in infants where there were distortions from the onset (or before) of maternal behavior (Yarrow 1961; Levy & Hess 1952; Waldrop & Bell 1966; Carithers 1951; Newton 1955; Escalona 1945; Lakin 1957; Stewart et al. 1954).

Hertzer and Tudor-Hart (1927) and Bühler (1930) found smiling in the neonate and smiles could be elicited by an adult's glance or voice. Wolff (1963) discovered that within hours after birth, neonates grimaced with their mouths in a way that morphologically suggested a smile while the rest of the face remained "relaxed." (Much earlier Preyer [1882] designated this as a "mouth smile" which he explained in terms of muscular action rather than a social reaction.) As early as the third week, Wolff confirmed Bühler's (1930) finding of clear indications of social smiling in that specifically human stimuli elicited smiles more consistently than other stimulus configurations.

Other evidences of social behavior in the neonate include responding to the human voice with some vocalization, and being quieted when picked up. Of course, it is obvious that social responsiveness (that is, conscious and purposive interaction with others) depends to a large extent on perceptual ability. Social behavior will, then, play an increasingly prominant role in the individual's life.

Individual Differences. No two newborn babies are exactly identical in appearance or behavior patterns (Bell 1960b). Differences may be due primarily to genetic determinants, but although we start computing age at birth, the neonate has existed in an environment which has influenced him for many months. Complications arising from the birth process itself can affect postnatal behavior (Graham, Matarazzo, & Caldwell 1956).

Not all babies are equally mature at birth. Newborns differ in their ability to maintain homeostasis (Grossman & Greenberg 1957), in their capacities to deal with incoming stimulation (Brazelton 1962), and in psychological reactivity (Lipton, Steinschneider, & Richmond 1961; Lipton & Steinschneider 1964).

Numerous studies have substantiated the variability among newborn babies on activity-level dimensions (Irwin 1930; Sontag 1946; Fries & Wolff 1953; Wolff 1959; Bridger & Reiser 1959; Gordon & Bell 1961; Kessen, Hendry & Leutzendorff 1961; Escalona 1965; Wolff 1966). Differences among newborns have also been documented in sleeping patterns (Irwin 1930; Reynard & Dockeray 1939; Wolff 1959), crying behavior (Aldrich, Sung & Knop 1945b), oral behaviors such as mouthing and finger sucking (Korner, Chuck & Dontchos 1968; Kessen, Williams, & Williams 1961), and attention span and alertness (Cobb, Grimm, Dawson & Amsterdam 1967).

Is the neonate a *person*? The answer depends on how one defines a person, and this has been done in several ways. G. Allport (1961a) concludes his famous book, *Patterns and Growth in Personality*, by saying, "we study the human person most fully when we take him as an individual" (p. 573). Obviously the neonate is an individual, and therefore a person. He is a person with a potential personality beginning with a great many individual differences: greatly varying degrees of activity vs. passivity, alertness vs. lack of responsiveness, sensitivity degrees, varying responses to food and the mealtime situation, varying behavior during sleep, and varying emotionality in kind and degree. From an open receptiveness which soon will develop to curiosity and active exploration of the environment, to a passive lethargy and dull unresponsiveness or much crying and expression of discomfort, we find many variations which from the first day on are being influenced by the attending mother and other persons and circumstances.

The Infant

For the first two years of life, the baby is incapable of caring for almost all of his own needs from an adult standpoint. He needs to be fed and cleaned and demands careful supervision. His cognitive impressions and communications are basically prelingual. But because the individual is helpless in the sense of self-sustaining abilities, this does not lead to the erroneous conclusion that the baby is passive and unmotivated. The infancy stage is, rather, characterized by tremendous advances in all aspects of development which serve as the foundation for his future behavior patterns, emotional makeup, intellectual and other abilities, and attitudes toward himself and others.

In the discussion of the neonate, we noted some of the abilities which developed and became perfected before the individual was one month old. Before the end of the second year, the baby will have progressed from a horizontal to a vertical being capable of sitting, standing, walking, and running. He will have made great advances in his ability to communicate his needs and feelings to others. He will have moved from a mostly reactive organism to an active manipulator of his environment and a laughing, game-playing, social being (Hurlock 1968; Stone & Church 1968). He will be expected to learn and perform various tasks, including taking solid foods, developing various types of physical controls and coordinations over muscles and organs of elimination, achieving reasonable physiological stability such as in hunger and sleep rhythm, learning the foundations of speech, relating to others, and discovering and promoting his own individuality (Havighurst 1953; Pikunas 1969).

Evidence for the existence of self-initiated goal-striving behavior in the infant has replaced the outmoded view of the baby as a creature who passively waits to have his bodily needs cared for by others (Anderson 1948; White 1959; Hunt 1960; Martin 1960; Bühler 1962a; Murphy 1962; Kessen 1963). The healthy baby is active and curious and seeks stimulation from the environment (Bühler 1930, 1968; Stirniman 1940; Berlyne 1960; Murphy 1962; Brown 1963; Scott 1963; Eiduson 1968; Hurlock 1968; Pikunas 1969). The baby derives much pleasure from his emerging abilities to be increasingly active in the world (Mittleman 1954). The striving toward "competence," which displays itself in all forms of behavior and activities which promote effective ways of interacting with the environment, has been put forth by White (1959) as the primary motivating force in human development even during early life. Bühler (1962a) also spoke of "selective responsiveness" on the part of the infant, since in early life the baby shows certain preferences and dislikes for foods, colors, sounds, persons, and objects. The baby also develops patterns of approaching, screening, and handling his environment which become highly individualized (Bühler 1930; Murphy 1962).

Although the great individual differences in behavior among infants may be genetically determined (Sontag 1950; Freedman & Keller 1963), there is wide support for the notion that infantile experiences are crucial in determining the directions of the development of individuality (Bernstein 1955; Escalona 1965; Spitz 1965; Frank 1966; Freedman, Loring & Martin 1967).

For impressive and extensive accounts of individual patterns of behavior during the infancy period, the reader is referred to Thomas, Birch, Chess, Hertzig, & Korn (1963) and Escalona (1968).

Already during the period of infancy we feel the futility of describing various aspects of development (such as perception, motor skills, language, and social awareness) as if they were distinct or even separable systems. All aspects of physical, psychological, and social development are so interrelated and dependent upon each other that discussing each one in turn is highly artificial and perhaps even misleading. For example, exploration and curiosity depend in great measure on the level of physical development. Social attachments are dependent on the functioning of the perceptual processes. The rate of language acquisition depends on external models and reinforcements for vocalizations. Thus the task of outlining human development—an everchanging integration-reintegration process among a multitude of factors unique to each individual depending on his genetic and experiential background—is virtually impossible to describe adequately or succinctly even at this early stage of life.

Growth, Physical and Perceptual Changes. Growth continues at a rapid rate during the first year and slows down during the second. The baby gains around 15 pounds and 9 or 10 inches during the first year, and about 5 pounds and 4 inches during the second year (Watson & Lowrey 1967), though there are marked variations among individuals in growth patterns (Krogman 1957; Bayley 1965).

The daily cycles of routine behavior change considerably during the first year of life. At one month, the baby spends two-thirds of his time sleeping and the other third is divided among dozing, having "negative" reactions, taking food, with a small portion of time spent in impulsive movement (Bühler 1930). By three months, a diurnal sleep-wake cycle is established in most infants (Parmelee, Wenner & Schultz 1964; Breckenridge & Vincent 1965). By about six months, the baby's eyes are open almost half of the time, which remains constant through the first year (Bühler 1930; Dittrichová & Lapáčková 1964) and about the same during the second year (Kleitman 1963). The waking activities by one year consist of much experimentation and play activity and the baby has considerably less "negative" reactions than during the early months (Bühler 1930). Babies differ widely in activity levels (Thomas, Birch, Chess, Hertzig & Korn 1960; Escalona 1968) and such differences present even during the fetal period have been related to the level of postnatal test performance (Walters 1965).

The period of infancy is characterized by rapid development in musculature coordination and motor abilities. Muscles in the head region are the first to be voluntarily controlled, those in the legs being last (Richmond 1964), with the orderly sequence of motor control following the same directions (Shirley 1933). Walking alone is among the last of the basic motor skills to appear (Shapiro 1962). Space limitations preclude the presentation of the stages of motor development and control, which include lifting parts of the body through reaching, sitting, crawling, standing, and finally walking alone in the beginning months of the second year. The sequence of development, which is highly dependent on maturation, has been described by Bühler (1930), Shirley (1931), McGraw (1935, 1946), Gesell and Amatruda (1941), Gesell (1946, 1954), Illingworth (1960), Vincent and

Martin (1961), Bayley (1965), Breckenridge and Vincent (1965), Werner and Bayley (1966), and Pickler (1968).

Although it is necessary for the young infant to receive liquid foods, sucking is a need that demands gratification in its own right (Freud 1905; Levy 1928; Kunst 1948; Yarrow 1954; Traisman & Traisman 1958; Stone & Church 1968). Finger sucking later on has been related to too brief feeding periods in early infancy (Roberts 1944; Levine & Bell 1950). Infants use their mouths actively to further explore objects they pick up with their hands.

During the second year, the child is quite skillful with the use of his hands, though "handedness" may shift around during infancy (Gesell & Ames 1947). Before 5 months the baby grasps objects he sees (White, Castle, & Held 1964), and displays primitive forms of hand manipulations with objects (Gesell 1954). The infant rapidly progresses in his attempts to reach out (Halverson 1933, 1937; White, Castle, & Held 1964) and to touch, handle, and explore the properties of objects and may repeat experimenting with them over and over again as if willfully practicing his emerging skills (Bühler 1930). Before the second year, the baby can manage complex feats involving the hands, such as feeding himself (Gesell & Ilg 1937) and taking off clothing (Ryan 1966).

Most of the work on perceptual processes in infancy is specifically in the area of vision. As was noted earlier, the senses are quite well developed very early in life, though, of course, preferences and discriminations become more acute with learning. For a review of sensory and perceptual processes in infancy, the reader is referred to Spears & Hohle (1967).

Brightness discrimination develops rapidly in the first months of life (Doris & Cooper 1966; Doris, Casper & Poresky 1967). Sustained visual fixation peaks during the first months of life (Ling 1942). Visual acuity progresses markedly during the first two years (Evans 1946), and by the fourth month accommodation is extremely efficient (Haynes, White & Held 1965). Color discrimination is present in early infancy (Chase 1937), and by the fourth month there are color preferences (Spears 1964).

In the early months, infants prefer to attend to stimuli representing the human face as compared to other stimulus configurations (Kagan & Lewis 1965; Thomas 1965; Lewis 1969). There is increasing attention to patterns with contour (Karmel 1969), and novel or more complex stimuli (Fantz 1958, 1961; Saayman, Ames & Hoffett 1964; Wilcox 1969). The average infant discriminates depth as soon as, and perhaps before, it can crawl (Walk & Gibson 1961; Walk 1966). In fact, recent evidence suggests that the abilities to discriminate depth, orientation, and size and shape constancy is present during the third month (Bower 1966). It has been suggested that the development of visual ability parallels curiosity behavior (McReynold, Acker & Pietila 1961) and, indeed, for much of the infancy period, a major form of curiosity behavior is visual exploration (Gesell 1950). The complex process of integrating perceptual data with thought processes resulting in the understanding of the relationship between visual perception and the object and its function has been described by Piaget (1954), Frankl (1963), and Schaffer & Parry (1969).

The social implications of visual processes are important during the prespeech years, since mutual visual regard between the infant and another person is among the earliest channels of communication (Greenman 1963; Robson 1967; Moss & Robson 1968).

Learning, Intellectual, and Cognitive Development. The development of learning, intellectual, and cognitive abilities can only be treated here in a cursory manner. For detailed accounts of learning and cognition during early life, the reader is referred to Piaget (1926, 1928, 1930, 1952, 1954), Bijou & Baer (1961), Fowler (1962), Sigel (1964), and Elkind (1967).

During infancy, the individual begins to organize sensory input which affects his perceptions, activity, and feelings. Learning occurs as the processing and interpretation of what is perceived increases (Bruner, Olver & Greenfield 1966; Pikunas 1969). At about 4 months, when the baby becomes capable of making perceptual discriminations, we see an increasing amount of differentiation of behavior (Escalona 1968). And as simple reactions and impulsive movements become integrated into continuous activities and actions during the first year, a significant increase in mentally directed actions is observed (Bühler 1930). During infancy, behavior organization has been described as "pre-logical" (Piaget 1954), and yet there is evidence of memory for earlier events (Levy 1960), recognition of familiar objects and persons (Eiduson 1968; Hurlock 1968), cognitive organization (Ricciuti 1965), and ability to solve problems (Richardson 1932, 1934).

The majority of studies on learning during the first year use conditioning procedures (Escalona 1968). Rapid and stable conditioning becomes possible during the early months (Scott 1968) and has been demonstrated in many studies (e.g., Brackbill 1958; Siqueland 1964; Caron 1967; Levison & Levison 1967; Wahler 1969). An extensive review of conditioning in infancy may be found in Brackbill & Koltsova (1967).

Though learning development is regulated to a large extent by maturational processes, the exposure to experiences and opportunity is also considered to be of major importance for both learning as well as intellectual development (Pinneau & Jones 1958; Hunt 1961; Fowler 1962). Training has been found to improve ability even during the first year (Welch 1939; Ling 1941), and, conversely, deprivation experiences (institutionalization) have been related to atypical or inferior cognitive and intellectual development (Bowlby 1951; Flint 1966; Taylor 1968a).

Much importance has also been attached to the notion that the baby seeks out his own opportunities for learning independent of primary needs (White 1959; Hunt 1960; Escalona 1968; Eiduson 1968). Murphy (1967) has outlined many ways the infant spontaneously learns: orienting and attending to stimuli, exploring the environment, intentionally combining things to observe results, mastering bodily functions, learning what evokes rewards and punishments, trial-and-error behavior, imitating, and learning how to amuse himself.

Tests to assess the intellectual level of infants have been devised (e.g., Bühler & Hetzer 1935; Cattell 1940; Gesell 1949; Griffiths 1954). These measures have numerous limitations in regard to predictions of later ability (Anderson 1939; Stott & Ball 1965), though they have been used successfully along with clinical assessments to diagnose atypical functioning (Escalona 1954; Honzik, Hutchings & Burnip 1965).

Vocalization and Language Development. The period of infancy is an active one in terms of vocalization and language development. Whereas the newborn's earliest sounds are monosyllabic cries, by the age of two he may have a vocabulary of 250 words (Smith 1926; lrwin 1949).

The transformation of spontaneous vocalizations into words which the child uses and understands is dependent on a variety of factors including maturation of the organs and control of the mouth parts involved in speech, cognitive development, opportunity to imitate external sounds, and reinforcement for vocalizations (Keppel 1964). Recent experts in the area of psycholinguistics have pointed to the inadequacies of a maturation-learning model as *the* explanation of speech development and have suggested additional possibilities such as a language generator, represented in the brain, which contains information-processing potentials (Brown & Bellugi 1964; Lennenberg 1964).

We see much self-initiated activity in language acquisition. By the fourth week of life, crying is used as an attention-getting device, and the tones of the cries can be differentiated according to what is being signified by the baby (McCarthy 1960). Whereas crying may be the mechanism for communicating negative states, vocalizations of positive states start as early as the first month when the child utters a single sound while in a quiet position of comfort. At two months he utters sounds of pleasure to accompany his perceptions of objects and people, and he is cooing happily by 6 months. By 7 months he makes shouts of joy, clicks his tongue, and squeaks and sighs when satisfied. Before the end of the first year the frequency of positive vocalizations exceeds that of negative ones (Bühler 1930). Very early in life, the baby actively attempts to imitate sounds that suggest already the rudiments of understanding, sociability, and identification (Guillaume 1925; Bühler 1931; Lewis 1951; Piaget 1951; Stone & Church 1968).

Though the infant's first word is usually uttered at about the age of one year (K. Bühler 1918; Stern & Stern 1929; McCarthy 1946; Darley & Winitz 1961), the prelinguistic phase of life is characterized by active changes in vocalizations. The baby develops through states of grunting and other noises, reacting to other's voices, cooing and babbling, social vocalizations, imitating sounds, "talking" to others, "singing" sounds, expressive sounds, differentiating words of others, and understanding commands well before he can actually speak himself. (Bühler 1930; Bayley 1933; Shirley 1933; Gesell & Thompson 1934; Gesell, Thompson & Amatruda 1938. A comparison of normative data from these and other studies may be found in McCarthy 1946.)

By the third month, vocal responses can be conditioned or modified by social reinforcements provided by adults (Rheingold, Gewirtz & Ross 1959; Weisberg 1963). Human presence may not be a necessary factor in conditioning infant vocalizations, but it functions to increase the effectiveness of the human voice as a reinforcer (Todd & Palmer 1968).

Babbling, the vocal activity most similar to meaningful speech, begins during the early weeks (Jesperson 1922) and reaches a peak during the later portion of the first year (Tischler 1957). The infant derives pleasure for its own sake in attending to his own babbles and experiments actively with the sounds he can make. This form of vocalization is the basis for true speech and will decline as language is developed (Irwin 1949; Dittrichová & Lapáčková 1964).

During the latter part of the first year, infants prefer the voice of the mother, can discriminate between mother's and stranger's voices, and begin to shift preferences toward more complex speech inflections and vocabulary (Friedlander 1968). Reactions to the quality of the mother's voice may begin early

in life and affect the baby's behavior patterns (Milmoe, Novey, Kagan & Rosenthal 1968).

First words are usually labels for objects or persons, and perhaps action verbs (K. Bühler 1918; Stern & Stern 1929). Encouragement provided through exposing the baby to experiences with an object while repeating its name may facilitate the learning of names of objects (Mallitskaya 1960). Early sentences, starting at about 18 months, are simple and abbreviated and consist of two words or even just a single word which functions as several (Hetzer & Riendorf 1927; McCarthy 1954; Braine 1963; Ervin & Miller 1963).

Deprivation experiences during the infancy period, such as institutionalization, have been reported to retard language development (Hetzer & Riendorf 1927; Gesell & Amatruda 1941; Goldfarb 1943, 1945; Brodbeck & Irwin 1946; Rheingold & Bayley 1959; Koch 1961; Provence & Lipton 1962).

Detailed accounts and reviews of language acquisition in early life may be found in McCarthy (1946, 1959, 1960), Ervin-Tripp (1966), Rebelsky, Starr & Luria (1967), and Friedlander (1970).

Emotional and Social Behavior. Bridges's (1932) scheme of emotional development illustrates rapid differentiation from the "diffuse excitement" of the neonate. Around three months, distress and delight appear. By six months, fear and disgust are present, and elation and affection are added at one year. Jealousy and joy are differentiated out during the second year. As babies become more adept and discriminating among persons and situations, their emotional displays also become more selective (Pikunas 1969). They further become a means of self-expression, and toward the end of the first year positive emotional reactions exceed negative ones (Bühler 1930). Crying as an emotional expression generally decreases during infancy and the cause of crying changes from internal to environmental reasons (Bühler 1930; Bayley 1932).

Jersild and Holmes (1935) and Jersild (1943) have studied age trends in children's fears. During earlier infancy, fear is associated with specific situations and intense stimuli or unexpected and strange occurrences. In the second year, some of the earlier fears drop out while new ones, such as being left alone or in the dark, appear. The patterns of fear objects are dependent on the baby's perceptual development and the attached meaning and understanding he has of them. The young infant cannot realistically perceive danger or differentiate well among familiar or strange types of stimuli. Intangible fears, such as being afraid of imaginary creatures, develop only when the individual has advanced to the point of comprehending such possibilities. Thus these more "sophisticated" fears are largely absent in infancy. Fears can be conditioned and exhibit generalization properties in infancy (Watson & Watson 1923).

Evidence of positive social behavior toward others appears early in the infant's life. Between the second and third month, an interest in people manifests itself through crying when left alone or reacting with displeasure when persons in close proximity are ignoring him (Schaffer & Emerson 1964; Stone & Church 1968). A general increase in outgoing activity is apparent by four months (Banham 1950).

Though there may be basic temperamental differences among children in regard to social responsiveness and enjoyment of affection bestowed by others (Bühler 1931; Schaffer & Emerson

1964; Ferguson 1970), the level of responsiveness in social and other types of behavior development has been linked to the amount of attentiveness given by the mother (Walters, Pearce & Dahms 1957; Rubenstein 1967; Moss 1967; Bronfenbrenner 1968), the opportunity to interact with other persons besides the mother (Schaffer & Emerson 1964; Ainsworth 1964), the role of perceptual processes and outside sensory stimulation (Rheingold 1961; Ainsworth 1964; Kistiakovskaia 1965; Walters & Parke 1965; Robson 1967), opportunity to imitate (Bandura & Walters, 1963) and the amount of affection received from others (Alexander 1951).

The development of attachment to others is a two-way process between the baby and another person. The secondary-drive theory of attachment, which holds that the infant becomes attached to the person who is instrumental in satisfying the primary hunger drive, has come under criticism (Bühler 1927; Bowlby 1958; Schaffer & Emerson 1964; Walters & Parke 1965). The baby takes his own initiative in forming attachments, and not only with the mother who feeds him but with others who interact and play with him (Ainsworth 1964).

In the beginning weeks of life, the baby makes "striving toward" relationships to others and is not selective in regard to which person pays attention to him (Ainsworth 1964). Once a clearly differentiated attachment to one person has developed, however, mothering from anyone else is not acceptable (Bowlby 1951). Fear of strangers, not present during the early months, peaks from the seventh to the ninth month (Schaffer 1963) and the stronger the attachment to the mother, or very few other persons, the more intense is stranger anxiety (Schaffer & Emerson 1964; Collard 1968). Fear of strangers generally terminates at around the fifteenth month (Tennes & Lampl 1964), though play and speech decrease when the baby of this age is placed in an unfamiliar environment without his mother (Cox & Campbell 1968).

The development of affection is primarily directed to relationships with people rather than things (Bossard & Boll 1966). Early the infant maintains contact with the mother by eliciting her attention through vocalizations and postural movements and visually tracking her movements (Ferguson 1970). After 4 months he will reach out toward the loved one to be picked up, and still later, when he is able, will approach the person through locomotion (Ainsworth 1964; Stone & Church 1968).

The smile is an important form of social behavior which, once acquired, will have the lifelong function of indicating a friendly attitude (J. P. Scott 1968). Social smiling occurs during early months (Jones 1926; Bühler 1928; Gesell & Thompson 1934; Spitz & Wolf 1946; Wolff 1963; Gewirtz 1965). Bühler (1928) and Wolff (1963) report social smiling when there is eye-to-eye contact or to a human voice during the second month. Soon afterwards, smiling becomes a predictable and repeatable response to a number of stimuli. It becomes more selective and more differentiated from organismic states. At 2 months, babies were observed grinning in the absence of perceiving other persons as they were visually exploring the environment or regarding their own bodies or movements. Laughter also occurs in the early months of life (Bühler 1930; Bridges 1932) and is primarily elicited during social activity (Brackett 1933).

Early play activities are more solitary than social and are confined to playing with one's own body (Bühler 1928). Genital play is common in infants, especially males, producing a soothing effect during early infancy and actual pleasure later on (Spitz 1949; Stone & Church 1968). But during the early months infants become coordinated enough to enjoy experimenting with toy objects as well as social games with others such as "peek-a-boo," and passing toys back and forth (Maurer 1967; Stone & Church 1968). The baby derives what K. Bühler (1918) has called "function pleasure" from repeating movements or actions over and over again. Without direct purpose or awareness, the baby is, then, learning and perfecting skills in play. Playing becomes more sophisticated with time, and during the early years of life it will be the activity that dominates most of the child's waking hours.

Babies show an active interest in each other by as early as 5 months. One baby may touch the other, they smile at each other, and a little later they may exchange toys (Bühler 1927). Later in infancy, the baby's interest shifts from play materials to his playmates and cooperative play, rather than fighting for toy possession (Maudry & Nekula 1939).

During the second year, the baby has developed to the point where language use becomes a major vehicle for social interaction. A period of "negativism" may ensue where the baby resists requests of adults (Hurlock 1968). This does not indicate that attachments and affections have subsided in strength, but rather that the baby is striving for autonomy and is interested in exploring and manipulating the environment on his own (Erikson 1959; Ferguson 1970). Resistance during the second year may also be partially explained by the fact that the child is now constantly confronted with new situations which he does not fully understand and is expected to do things for which he has not yet acquired complete skills (Strang 1959).

Among the more difficult tasks others will demand of the infant is that he control his bowels and bladder in a prescribed manner. This feat depends in part on maturational readiness, but the baby must also learn to sense internal cues and make appropriate reactions. Social factors relating to bladder and bowel training, many of which may lead to deleterious effects when training is severe, have been studied by Despert (1944), Macfarlane, Allen and Honzik (1954), Sears, Maccoby, and Levin (1957), and Stein and Susser (1967).

Child-rearing techniques during the infancy period have been reviewed by Wolfenstein (1953) and Caldwell (1964). Though there is evidence to suggest that what parents do, or do not do, affects the child's immediate behavior, long-range effects have been less clearly demonstrated except in cases of severe deprivation experiences (Escalona 1968).

Erikson (1959) has proposed that the healthy personality must develop on a foundation of "basic trust." This attitude relates both to the individual's concept of himself as well as his orientation to the outside world. Trust develops during the first year of life and is dependent on the satisfaction of needs which, initially, must be met by others. Though the satisfaction of psychophysical needs is recognized as a basic goal from the beginning of life, the emotional climate in which they are administered is also considered to be of primary importance (Spitz 1965). The first two years of life are considered by many to be critical ones in the development of behavior, abilities, personality, and social responsiveness (Spitz 1945, 1946; Spitz & Wolf 1946a; Stendler 1952; Casler 1961; Ambrose 1963).

When the baby's needs for care, affection, and environmental stimulation are not met or improperly administered due to various circumstances, evidence suggests that development of many behaviors and abilities may be retarded, progress abnormally, or even be irreversibly affected (Goldfarb 1945a, b; Spitz 1949; Bowlby 1951; Gerard 1956; Dennis & Majarian 1957; Schaffer & Callender 1959; Dennis 1960; Casler 1961; Provence & Lipton 1962; Richmond 1964; Gewirtz 1965; Flint 1966). "Deprivation" is not a simple or single variable (Casler 1961; Yarrow 1968). Major types of deprivation experiences include social isolation, cruelty and neglect, economic and cultural deprivation, adverse child rearing practices or distortions in the quality of mothering, separation experiences, institutional upbringing, and sensory or perceptual privation (Clarke & Clarke 1960; Yarrow 1961). Early nutritional deficiencies may irreversibly affect the development of adaptive behavior (Cravioto 1968).

The effects of deprivation experiences depend on such factors as duration of the experience, intensity of the experience, age of occurrence, experiences previous to and/or following the deprivation period, and the makeup of the individual involved (Clarke & Clarke 1960; Yarrow 1964). Not all studies have concluded that irregular situations—that is, where the child is raised by other than his own mother—are damaging to normal infant development (Rabin 1957, 1958; Gardner & Swiger 1958; Rheingold 1961). Others have shown that intervention, in terms of increasing stimulation or amount and quality of caretaking, can have positive effects on subsequent development (Rheingold 1956; Casler 1965; Sayegh & Dennis 1965; Taylor 1968a; Denenberg 1967). And it must be mentioned that a child raised by its *own* mother can manifest adverse behavior patterns or be retarded in development as, for instance, in the case of extreme overprotectiveness (Levy 1943; Davids, Holden & Gray 1963).

THE CHILD

The childhood period, ranging from the beginning of the third year to age ten or so, is characterized by size expansion and shape changes, but not by the marked maturational landmarks noted in the earlier phases. The dramatic or impressive physical changes will not appear again until the adolescent years are approached. However, development during the childhood years in the realm of emerging skills, self-identity and personality formation, social relationships, language, and concept attainment are so extensive that within the confines of a few pages the directions can only be mentioned.

Physical Growth and Skill Development. Growth is slower during the childhood years (as compared to the infancy period) and proceeds at a uniform rate (Wallis 1931). There is a high correlation between height and weight increments (Meredith 1965) and other aspects of growth as well (Olson & Hughes 1944). The child gains four or five pounds per year and grows two to three inches in height (Thompson 1954; Bayley 1965; Watson & Lowrey 1967), though these increments decrease in rate during later childhood (Harris, Jackson, Paterson & Scammon 1930; Pressey & Robinson 1944). Girls and boys differ only slightly in height and weight during the childhood years. There are individual variations from the norm in body size due to such factors as body build (Massler & Suher 1951). These differences may be particularly striking, as was documented in Meredith's (1968) comparisons of many samples of preschool children in various parts of the world.

A noticeable change in bodily proportions occurs during the early childhood years. The individual loses his top-heavy sack-like appearance and begins to approximate adult proportions. Head growth is slowest, the torso lengthens, and the most rapid growth is in the limbs (Meredith & Knott 1938; Thompson 1954). Later the body and appendages continue to elongate and the individual may have the "spindly" look characteristic of the older child (Meredith 1937; Watson & Lowrey 1967; Hurlock 1968).

The amount of sleep needed decreases slightly during the early childhood years to about eleven hours a day (Despert 1949; Roffwarg, Muzio & Dement 1966). At this age, there are several conditions that may affect the amount of sleep the child gets, such as excitement or overstimulation, teething pain, fear of the dark, or worries and tensions (Strang 1959). Nighttime bladder control is achieved by most children during the early childhood years (Macfarlane, Allen & Honzik 1954; Muellner 1960). Children relish and need opportunities to be physically active (Mittleman 1955; Hartley & Goldenson, 1957; Strang 1959).

During the early childhood years the child advances markedly in motor-performance skills and coordination in terms of what he can do with his own body (Jenkins 1930; Bayley 1935; Goodenough 1935; Goodenough & Smart 1935; McCaskill & Wellman 1938; Gutteridge 1939; Gesell, Halverson, Thompson, Ilg, Castner, Ames & Armatruda 1940; Connolly, Brown & Bassett 1968) and how he manipulates and perceives possibilities in materials such as wheel toys (Jones 1939), building blocks (Johnson 1933; Slater 1939) and buttons and buttonholes (Wagoner & Armstrong 1928). Motor skills become increasingly incorporated into more elaborate projects that combine with social and intellectual abilities (Jersild 1960) and aesthetic pursuits such as artwork and rhythm (Strang 1959). During the preschool years the individual is not yet able to perform highly refined complex, fine-detailed psychomotor skills, but these abilities emerge during the school years (Gutteridge 1939). The preschool child, however, heartily manipulates tools suited to him (such as blunt-edged scissors) and enjoys drawing and painting (W. Wolff 1946; Strang 1959; Stone & Church 1968). Dominant handedness is usually completed by the third or fourth year (Hildreth 1949).

The development of motor abilities is not only significant in terms of improvement in coordination, but contributes to psychological development as well. The child's self-concept is intimately related to how he feels about his level of bodily control, and how others react to his level of motor skill (Gardner 1964). The awkward child may be rejected by other children, thus negatively affecting his social development and self-esteem (Ausubel 1957; Strang 1959; Hawkes & Pease 1962; Hurlock 1968).

Personality and Social Changes. Early childhood, the preschool years from after two to the fifth or sixth year, is characterized by an expanding sense of awareness of self and others, effective self-expression and communication through the medium of language, the establishment of defensive behavior patterns with which to react in anxiety-provoking situations, perfection of physical skills, increasing autonomy, independence, and achievement. The young child discovers that he can say "yes" and "no" to requests from other people. He also discovers his ability to create things out of materials and his imagination

(Bühler 1928). The young child must learn to relate emotionally to parents, siblings, and others in a more mature and giving manner than when he was a baby. He is expected to learn sex differences, sexual modesty, and to identify with his own sex role. He also learns to identify with parental models and incorporate standards of right and wrong (Havighurst 1952; Fraiberg 1968; Longstreth 1968; Muller 1969; Mussen, Conger & Kagan 1969; Ferguson 1970). The young child is still impulsive, self-centered, and expresses his emotions honestly, now using language rather than positive or negative behavioral reactions (Strang 1959; Stone & Church 1968; Pikunas 1969). A crisis in emotional development occurs during this period. Although the child's strongest emotional attachment is to his parents, he must now cope with disapproval from these persons whose love he needs so much. From the process of learning to conform so that parental love can be retained, identification and the conscience emerge (Bühler 1962a). From a developing sense of self-control without loss of self-esteem, a lasting sense of autonomy and pride develop in the healthy child (Erikson 1959). The young child is especially curious both in terms of actively exploring the environment through vigorous locomotor skills, and by asking numerous questions now that cognitive and language skills are rapidly developing. An especially notable characteristic is the persistent attempt of the child to do things for himself (Erikson 1959; White 1959; Strang 1959; Bühler 1962a).

Around the fifth or sixth year, our culture introduces a regime which will have tremendous impact on all areas of the child's psychological development. A life centered and shaped primarily in the home by family members expands to include the influence of the school setting. The teacher becomes a new, important, and controlling adult influence on the child's behavior and attitudes. He will be around many children and is expected to successfully relate to them, and their influence on him will be strong as well. He begins to "rank himself" alongside other children. He is also expected to learn the rudiments of knowledge in the manner prescribed by the educational system. Havighurst (1952) identifies three outward pushes of the older child: the thrust out of the home into a world of peers, a physical thrust into the world of games and work requiring real muscular skills, and a mental thrust into the realm of adultlike concepts and communications. In order to adequately meet these challenges, there are certain tasks the child must accomplish. These include taking responsibilities, learning skills necessary for games, building a wholesome self-concept, learning to get along with persons of his own age, learning appropriate sex roles, developing a set of personal values, achieving some personal independence from peer and parental control so that some choices and decisions can be made autonomously when new opportunities and challenges present themselves, and discovering workable ways to control energies and emotions in order to maintain effective relationships with others (Bühler 1928; Havighurst 1952; Pikunas 1969). Though the primary responsibility of achieving success in the developmental tasks of this period rests with the child's own motivations and abilities, the teacher and the child's age-mates affect this process, whereas before the parents represented the primary outside influence (Erikson 1959; Hurlock 1968; Ferguson 1970).

The healthy school-aged child will now strive to do things of his own. Bühler (1928) discussed the voluntary achievement of tasks as the most important aspect of development from early to middle childhood. As Erikson (1959) stated, "The child now wants to be shown how to get busy with something and how to be busy with others" (p. 82). Erikson (1959) later spoke of learning to win recognition by achievement and the attendant pleasure derived from steady attention and diligence until a task is completed. He called it the "sense of industry." The danger associated with this stage of identity development is that the child may, because of incomplete development up to this stage or because he is not encouraged by others, feel useless and inferior. Here is where the elementary-school teacher can become a crucial determinant, one way or the other, on the development of the child's approach to mastery. The older child may be difficult to handle because he has a tendency to want more independence than his parents may be willing to give. He becomes secretive, as opposed to the open if not overfrank expressions of his feelings as a preschool child. He is expected to behave in a mature manner and his babyish antics, tolerated and perhaps even encouraged during the years he was at home, are no longer acceptable. He may reject adult demands and turn away from the family in favor of being with his peers (Stone & Church 1968; Hurlock 1968).

The older childhood years are considered to be of crucial importance for the individuation of personality. In many ways the child is on his own to make his way in the world and the methods he uses are likely to be the ones he will continue to follow into adulthood. By viewing the behavioral strategies of the school-aged child, one may obtain a moderately accurate picture of what the individual will be like as an adult (Kagan & Moss 1962; Ferguson 1970).

The older childhood years are indeed complex to trace from a developmental standpoint because of the variety of situations affecting the growing person and his emerging abilities and stable self-concept. The reader is referred to Gesell and Ilg (1946) and Hawkes and Pease (1962) for a thorough outline of characteristics of the middle childhood years of life.

Language and Cognitive Development.   The childhood period is a time for rapid expansion in language and cognitive abilities. During the school years, the individual will undergo structured training in perfecting both of these intimately related abilities but, as will be stressed, the preschool years are characterized by rapid self-initiated advances in speech and mental functioning. The young person is imaginative and actively interested in learning and solving problems for himself.

During the childhood years, the attainment of speech, and how it functions as an integral part of the child's total development, is among the most crucial and impressive aspects of this life phase. There is an increasing interest in the development of the acquisition, processing, and improvement of speech competence (Bellugi & Brown 1964; Ervin & Miller 1963).

Speech becomes a valuable means of self-expression during the preschool years. It also becomes the means by which the environment and cultural demands are understood (Gesell & Ilg 1949). It allows the child to initiate and maintain social interaction and assists in establishing his own self-identity (Gardner 1964). Yet, perhaps the most important aspect is the intimate relationship between language and thought (McCarthy 1946; Mussen, Conger & Kagan 1969). Whereas physical exploration of the environment becomes possible with expanding motor capabilities, the development of language skills provides opportunities for symbolic exploration and mastery (Ferguson

1970). Early speech accompanies activity as if the child is thinking through his actions aloud (Luria 1957; Bereiter 1961). Flavell & Hill (1969) have described the intrapersonal role of verbalization as the means of attaching labels to perceptual, attentional, and other processes involved in communicating with oneself, i.e., thinking.

The greatest feat in regard to language development is the combination of words into grammatically meaningful sentences (Irwin 1949). The child has mastered many of the grammatical rules at a very early age (Brown & Fraser 1964). Sentence structures of the young child tend to be simple and complete, though not as complex as those of the adult (Stalnaker 1933; Fisher 1934; McCarthy 1954; Rebelesky, Starr & Luria 1967). The child may continue to use infantile pronunciations through the fourth year (McCarthy 1960; Bellugi & Brown 1964) and grammatical errors, particularly the use of pronouns, verbs, and verb tenses, are common (Hurlock 1968; Stone & Church 1968). The young child has a tendency to ramble on in a loose-jointed fashion and may omit or bury key information in the transmission of abounding detail (Stone & Church 1968).

The rate of acquiring a vocabulary takes a tremendous upsurge during the third and fourth years (Templin 1957) and then tapers off (McCarthy 1930, 1946). At two years the child understands about 900 words. By four he understands over 1500 words, by five almost 2100 and by six, he understands almost 2600 words (Smith 1926). There are wide individual differences in language ability at any age. For example, by age five the average child is using 4- to 5-word sentences (McCarthy 1946), though gifted children may use 9- to 10-word sentences by the same age or even earlier (Fisher 1934). Other factors contributing to individual differences in linguistic skills include sex of the child, intelligence, family size, the ordinal position of the child in the family, number of children in the home, parental attitudes toward and encouragement of the child's speech, and the quality of speech models available (Gardner 1964; Cazden, 1966; Rebelesky, Starr & Luria 1967; Johnson & Medinnus 1969). There is evidence to suggest that nowadays children are becoming linguistically skilled at earlier ages than previously because of such factors as increased stimulation from mass media and nursery or preschool experiences (McCarthy 1959).

Early speech of the three- to five-year-old has been called by Piaget (1926) "egocentric" as compared to the more socialized speech of the older child. The needs of the "audience" may not be considered by the small child when he communicates to them (Glucksberg & Krauss 1967). Several researchers, however, have reported that the flow of speech, as an agent of communication with others, is highly characteristic of children even at very young ages (McCarthy 1930; Johnson & Josey 1931; Bühler 1931; Huang & Chu 1936; Williams & Mattson 1942).

The child asks many questions (Gesell & Ilg 1949; Vernon 1960). Questioning accounts for 10 to 15 percent of the preschool child's conversation (Fahey 1942). Questioning increases with age in novel or incongruous situations as the child becomes more motivated to fill in gaps in his knowledge (Berlyne & Frommer 1966). The development of *wh* questions in children has been studied by Bellugi (1965) and Brown (1968).

Numerous researchers have presented data which indicated that girls excel boys in various aspects of language ability (Doran 1907; Stern & Stern 1929; M. E. Smith 1926, 1933 McCarthy 1930, 1946, 1954; Valentine 1930; Fisher 1932; Poole 1934; Williams, McFarland & Little 1937; Jersild & Ritzman 1938;

Young, 1941; Templin 1953 & 1957). However, whether girls actually do have the advantage is still controversial (Ervin-Tripp 1966) as studies have shown virtually no sex differences (Templin 1957) or boys as more advanced (Anastasi & D'Angelo 1952). Johnson & Medinnus (1969) cited a study by Cowan, Weber, Hoddinott, and Klein (1967), which demonstrated that the sex of the experimenter influenced language tests, and suggested girls may have performed better in the earlier language studies since most of the testers were women. McCarthy (1953) has also discussed possible explanations for sex differences in language development.

The very young child is verbal, highly active, and enjoys solving problems, though he is unable to verbalize his solutions. With increased language ability, his conceptual world expands as he finds that all things have names (Elkind 1967). Objects come to mean what they can be used for as well as how the child "feels" about them (K. Bühler 1918; Fisher 1934; Vernon 1960). Around age five, learning and problem-solving behavior in experimental situations increases markedly (Suppes & Ginsberg 1962; N. H. White 1965).

Young children still classify objects according to their appearance and broad general impressions rather than considering details or specific and significant qualities. The ability to distinguish similarities and differences among stimuli increases steadily with age (Ames 1953; Allen 1955; Gibson & Gibson 1955; Elkind, Van Doorninck, & Schwarz 1967). Qualities such as color, size, and weight are not noticed or understood apart from the objects to which they belong for the younger child (Piaget 1952; Vernon 1960). Relationships among parts of a whole are not grasped before the sixth or seventh year (Gesell & Ames 1946; Ghent 1956; Piaget & Inhelder 1956). The young child perceives events according to what implications they have for him, rather than approaching the world more objectively and logically as the older child is capable of doing (Piaget 1926). Abstract thought, possessed by the older child, depends on increased assimilation of knowledge and modification of existing concepts to conform to external reality (Piaget 1929; Hunt 1961; Flavell 1963).

Because maturation is involved in processes affecting learning ability, it has been asserted that there is an optimal time for introducing the child to learning situations (Hilgard 1932; Vernon 1960). Yet ways of enhancing cognitive development through the use of appropriate pre- or early-school experiences has been a popular interest in recent years (Gray & Klaus 1965; Almy 1966; Bereiter & Engelmann 1966; Schermann 1966, 1967; Kamii & Radin 1967; Schwartz, Deutsch & Weissmann 1957; Speeth 1967; Wohlwill 1967; Kohlberg 1968; Datta 1969; Grotberg 1969).

Reviews of research in cognitive development and learning in children may be found in Munn (1946), Fowler (1962), Sigel (1964), Stevenson (1965), Bruner et al. (1966), Lovell (1968), and Greenfield and Bruner (1969).

Phase II: Adolescence

Adolescence is the pivotal point of life for individuals in our culture. Not yet adults, but not still children, adolescents are in the period of transition which is often comprised of both forward and backward movements (Jersild 1963; Schulhofer 1965).

The adolescent phase of development can be defined in several ways. The use of physical developmental indicators, starting with a growth spurt and the appearance of primary and secondary sex characteristics and terminating when physical growth is essentially completed, is one definition. Another is defining adolescence simply by assigning it an age span. A third involves the use of sociocultural concepts such as a period of transition from child to adult roles and status, or the period of becoming an independent and self-sustaining person (Rogers 1962). These three approaches can be combined or interrelated. Medinnus and Johnson (1969) for example, defined adolescence as beginning with sexual maturity and ending when the individual is independent of parental control. It is further noted that the number of years separating these two points in time is widening in Western civilizations, since evidence suggests that the onset of sexual maturity is earlier and dependency continues longer as compared to earlier times.

Despite the attempts to adequately define the adolescent phase of development, and to put forth theories explaining phenomena characteristic of this period (see Muuss 1969), the individuals confined within this stage occupy an ambiguous position with respect to assigned roles and position (Hess & Goldblatt 1957; Maier 1965). Yet there is wide agreement that the understanding of adolescents is crucial, since they are on the brink of inheriting the society toward which they persistently, if often confusingly, strive to enter (Rogers 1962; Otto & Otto 1967).

Perhaps the most unfortunate aspect of the adolescent period is the pervasive attitudes many adults have about "teenagers." As Hess and Goldblatt (1957) noted, with the possible exception of old age, no other period of development is marked by so many negative connotations and lack of positive sanctions. These views, by themselves, no doubt have a deleterious effect on the adolescent (Otto & Otto 1967). Positive attributes of adolescents are rarely discussed, though Otto and Healy (1966) list several features of contemporary adolescents which may be *more* positive than those of adults. These include energy and vitality, concern about the future of the country and the world, heightened sensory awareness and perceptivity, a sense of fairness and dislike of intolerance, flexibility, frankness, optimistic outlook on life, and engagement in a sincere ongoing search for identity.

Nixon (1966) has suggested that many of the characteristics of the adolescent group should be viewed as normal, and perhaps even adaptive, in the process of attaining maturity. He stated that the high degree of self-regard, the conscious recognition of anxiety as a symptom of the coping process, and the questioning of principles accepted heretofore as invariant, are all aspects of psychological normality.

Adolescents may, however, shrink from facing the pressures which arise during this transitional phase of life by avoiding conflict and limiting or constricting their goals (Adelson 1964; Shainberg 1966). They may feel alone and friendless (Bühler 1922), and become extremely depressed (Remmers & Radler 1957; Poinsard 1967). Integrating sex with love, and one's own interests with society's demands, are among the more critical and difficult aspects of adolescent development. Though the life adjustments an adolescent is making cannot truly be evaluated until he settles into adulthood (Kuhlen 1960), there is general agreement that many adolescents are in need of guidance based on a thorough understanding of this unique life phase (Gardner

1959; Brosin 1967; Schonfeld 1967). Psychiatric treatments designed especially for adolescents have been put forward by many therapists (e.g., Gitelson 1948; Balser 1957; Stranaham, Schwartzman, & Atkin 1957; Hulse 1960; Lorand & Schneer 1961; Falstein & Offer 1963). Parents, likewise, may need assistance in dealing with their adolescent children (Helfat 1967).

CENTRAL ASPECTS OF ADOLESCENT STRIVINGS

Havighurst (1952) has outlined the major tasks which must be mastered by the adolescent if his transition into adulthood is to be successful. These include achieving new and more mature relations with age mates of both sexes, identifying and achieving a masculine or feminine social role, accepting one's body, achieving emotional independence from parents and other adults, selecting and preparing for an occupation and eventual economic independence, desiring and achieving socially responsible behavior, acquiring an internal ethical system to serve as a guide to acceptable behavior, and preparing for marriage and family life.

Adolescent maturation is a highly personal phase of development, and each individual must answer for himself the question, "Who am I?" (Pikunas 1969). In the striving for mature status, the adolescent is confronted with the necessity of establishing a sense of personal identity (Jones 1943; Erikson 1963; Kahn 1969). As Stone and Church (1968) stated, "The central theme of adolescence is that of *identity*, coming to know who one is, what one believes in and values, and what one wants to accomplish and get out of life" (p. 437). The adolescent who realistically appraises and accepts himself is extremely fortunate (Jersild 1963). But all too often the quest for identity is hindered and frustrated when society offers no clear guidelines to assist the person with this task (Friedenberg 1959; Rogers 1962).

Achieving maturity also involves becoming autonomous through developing emotional independence and mature patterns of interdependence (Gardner 1959; Whitehorn 1962; Bettelheim 1963). However, adolescents frequently rebel against restrictions imposed by parents or other adult authorities only to replace these hard-fought victories with submission to peer group standards (Coleman 1961b; Rogers 1962; Stone & Church 1968).

Integrated with the process of identity is a process of elaborate self-evaluation. Though adolescents may often be characterized by an extreme self-consciousness, the evaluation procedure ultimately contributes to the beginnings of long-range goal-setting if the person discovers in himself the potentials which relate him to society (Bühler 1967).

Pikunas (1969) adapted from Cole (1964) a variety of goals toward which the individual moves during the adolescent period. These include *social and emotional maturation* (social awkwardness to social poise, imitation of peers to interdependence and self-esteem, feelings of uncertainty about oneself and others to feelings of acceptance and sociability, and lack of emotional control to constructive and creative expressions), *growth in heterosexuality* (acute awareness of sexual changes to genuine acceptance of sex, and identification with members of the same sex to interest and association with peers of the opposite sex), *cognitive maturation* (desire for final answers to need for explanation of facts and theories, acceptance of truth on the basis of authority to demand for substantial evidence before acceptance, and many interests and concerns to a few stable and genuine concerns), and, finally, *development of a philosophy of life* (from behavior motivated by pleasure to behavior based on duty and conscience, and behavior dependent on reinforcements to behavior guided by moral responsibility and ideals).

GROWTH AND SEXUAL MATURATION

Virtually every treatise on adolescent development points to the physical changes as the most dramatic observable aspect of this life phase. This "physical rebellion," as Erikson (1963) called it, is perhaps best represented in terms of its significance by Jersild's (1963) statement, "Before these changes occur the adolescent *is* a child; after they have occurred the young person can *have* a child" (p. 45). The bodily changes during adolescence have such strong implications for personality, social, and self-concept development that a discussion of physical development at this life phase is hardly complete without considering other direct effects on the individual. Similarly, it is difficult to separate "standard" growth changes from the maturation of sexual functions and capacities, as the process of both growth changes is highly correlated in the individual (Shuttleworth 1949; Olson & Hughes 1943; Simmons 1944; Greulich 1950; Mussen, Conger & Kagan 1969).

Although the adolescent undergoes a physical revision, there is a consistency or pattern within each individual which remains discernable as he moves from childhood into adulthood (Medinnus & Johnson 1969; Sheldon, Stevens & Tucker 1940). There are also considerable individual differences in the onset of the adolescent "growth spurt" and the rate at which one becomes physically mature (Mussen, Conger & Kagan 1969; Medinnus & Johnson 1969). A standard growth curve for adolescents cannot be constructed, since development proceeds asynchronously, i.e., different organs and parts of the body are proceeding at different rates and times (Horrocks 1954; Jersild 1963; Stone & Church 1968). Sex differences in growth acceleration have been noted (Baldwin, Busby & Garside 1928; Bayley 1943a, 1943b), with girls commencing the growth acceleration earlier (Shuttleworth 1949; Tanner 1955; Maresh 1964). Environmental factors, such as nutrition and illness, affect, to some degree, physical development during the adolescent period (Greulich 1944), though hereditary factors are important determinants as well (Bayley 1954; Jersild 1963).

Characteristics of Adolescent Growth. The status of the individual's maturity has been ascertained by several approaches including skeletal growth indices (Todd 1937), ossification indices such as in the hand and wrist (Greulich & Pyle 1959), changes in dentition (Carlos & Gittelsohn 1965), and degree of sexual maturity such as the onset of the menarche in girls (Rogers 1962) or maturity of pubic hair in males (Crampton 1908). Using a variety of indices for assessing an individual's developmental status has included the ones mentioned above and others such as weight, height, and mental ages (Olson 1949).

The variety of physical changes actually starts in late childhood, though the term "pubescence" has been used to designate this life phase, which overlaps childhood and adolescence (Hurlock 1968). The characteristic changes associated with pubescence include a rapid increase in the rate of physical growth, the matur-

ing of primary (the sex organs) and secondary (breast development, voice changes, skin composition and appearance of hair on the pubes, face, and axillae) sex characteristics, changes in bodily proportions with the extremities and neck growing faster than the head and trunk, and changes in facial proportions with the chin and nose becoming more prominent (Stone & Church 1968). In boys, the growth spurt in terms of height and weight begins at about 13 years of age and begins to decline after 15. In girls, the growth spurt begins earlier, at about 11, and declines at about age 13, though individuals of both sexes continue to grow some until about age 21. Within these general trends are great individual differences (Shuttleworth 1949; Pressey & Robinson 1944; Stolz & Stolz 1951; Tanner 1955; Maresh 1964). For a time in adolescence, average girls are heavier and taller than boys, but the curves cross at about age 13 and boys gain considerably as the profile for girls tapers off (Pressey & Robinson 1944). The development of adipose tissue differs between the sexes with girls gaining in the thickness of fat layers during the ages of about 12 to 15, whereas boys show a drop during the same period. Though boys gain in the volume of fat during later adolescence, girls maintain a higher ratio into the late teen-age years (Reynolds 1951).

"Puberty" is the term referring to the time at which the individual becomes sexually mature and capable of reproducing his kind (Horrocks 1954). The menarche (the appearance of the first menses) is usually the criterion used for females. The presence of live spermatozoa and other chemicals in the urine, nocturnal emissions, and time of first ejaculation are among the criteria used for males (Kinsey, Pomeroy & Martin 1948; Hurlock 1968).

Evidence suggests that the average age at menarche is lowering in the Western civilization to slightly under 13 years (Tanner 1968). Hereditary factors (Gould & Gould 1932) and social factors such as family size and intellectual abilities (Poppleton 1968) may also be related to the onset of puberty in girls. There is much variation among girls with respect to the age of puberty (McCammon 1965), as well as among boys (Schonfeld 1943). Actual reproductive ability may not correspond exactly with the appearance of pubertal signs (Mills & Ogle 1936; Greulick 1944; Stuart 1946; Montagu 1950).

An important determinant of the accelerated physical growth as well as the onset of sex characteristics is the activity associated with endocrine glands (Harris, Jackson, Paterson & Scammon 1930; Nathanson 1941; Shock 1944; Tanner 1955). Though directions of behavior are not affected by hormonal activity, the range, depth, and tone of feelings accompanying emotions are no doubt influenced (Rogers 1962).

In boys, physical strength doubles between the ages of 12 and 16, whereas the greatest increase in strength among girls appears about the time of the menarche (Hurlock 1968). Boys surpass girls in physical strength (Brooks & Shaffer 1937; Jones 1944, 1949); yet maximum strength is not reached until early adulthood for males, whereas girls attain their level of maximum strength in late adolescence (Martin & Vincent 1960).

Differences in strength between the sexes is due to differences in musculature, weight, and skeletal structure, but environmental and cultural differences (e.g., boys engaging in more physical activity while girls are concerned with entering less active "feminine" pursuits) also influence the disparity (Horrocks 1954). Yet as Havighurst (1952) has noted, though women definitely become the "weaker sex" during adolescence, they are, at the same time, becoming physically attractive to males, thus gaining one kind of power while losing another.

Quickness or speed of response increases sharply in adolescence, but increments in ability continue into the early adulthood years (Fisher & Birren 1947). General motor performance reaches its peak during adolescence. For girls, the age of peak ability is about 15 and in boys about 18 (Rogers 1962). For males, motor ability is of special importance, since athletic prowess is associated with "masculinity" and popularity (Jones 1949; Horrocks 1954; Rogers 1962).

Factors Related to Physical Changes.   The course of physical development of the adolescent's body has major implications for his personality development as well. Problems can arise with self-concept formation based on real, exaggerated, or imagined deviations in maturational status (Havighurst 1952; Schonfeld 1969). A teen-age boy cannot imagine that his physical or athletic prowess will be of lesser importance later on. Nor can the homely teen-age girl be convinced that glamour is not the major criterion for personal worth in adulthood (Rogers 1962).

Concern and self-consciousness over facial complexion is common among adolescents (Remmers & Radler 1957). Causation of blemishes has been attributed to hormonal secretion imbalance (Lawrence & Werthessen 1942; Hamilton 1941) and increased sebaceous gland activity (Greulick 1944). Although skin problems usually clear up by early adulthood, the tension and anxiety related to the presence of acne, blackheads, and pimples may only aggravate the physical condition (Hornick 1967). Concern over bodily odors, related to both physiological changes in sweat glands and incomplete aptitudes in grooming skills, is another problem of adolescents (Rogers 1962).

Along with skin problems, Frazier and Lisonbee (1950) found common adolescent bodily concerns to be irregular teeth, wearing glasses, face and nose shape, and being homely. A large proportion of teenagers want to improve their appearance, and weight (i.e., being too heavy or too thin) was a major expressed concern (Remmers & Radler 1957). When height varies from the norm, there exists a proportional concern, though height deviations are especially difficult for the short boys and tall girls (Rogers 1962).

Physical appearance does count in interpersonal choice situations among adolescents (Perrin 1921; Ohmann 1942; Roff & Brody 1953). Girls judge the physical *maturity* of boys by the status of their beard and extent of voice change. Boys judge girls by their figure, especially breast development (Rogers 1962). There is evidence to suggest that adolescents who mature physically early are more socially accepted and psychologically adjusted than late physical maturers (Tryon 1939; Jones 1957; Jones & Mussen 1958; Weatherly 1964). Boys retarded in their physical development may feel personal inadequacy (Mussen & Jones 1957) and though sociable, it may take the form of clowning or childish attention-getting behavior (Jones & Bayley 1950). Early-maturing girls may lack prestige in the elementary-school years, but ratings excel late-maturing girls in junior high school (Faust 1960). Greater physical maturity has been associated with more mature interests among girls (Stone & Barker 1939).

Sexual Attraction and Behavior.   In adolescence, sexual attraction becomes an increasingly dominant force in the indi-

vidual's life (Hildreth 1933; Blos 1941; Kuhlen & Lee 1943; Havighurst 1952; Broderick & Weaver 1968). This phenomenon is related in part to approaching biological maturity (Stone & Church 1968) but also related to social pressures (Hurlock 1968). About the time of puberty or before, there is an increased intellectual curiosity about the "facts of life" (Lantagne 1958; Calderwood 1965; Brown & Lynn 1966; Stone & Church 1968).

Girls are less sexually active than boys (Kinsey, Pomeroy, Martin & Gebhart 1953; Reevy 1961). In fact, the male is more active during the mid-teen years than he will ever be again in terms of frequency of sexual climax. The sexual activity in adolescent males, however, is more likely to be in the form of masturbation or perhaps homosexual outlets than in heterosexual relations (Ramsey 1943; Kinsey, Pomeroy & Martin 1948). By age 17, almost all boys have experienced orgasm as compared with about 35 percent of the girls (Kinsey, Pomeroy, Martin & Gebhart 1953). The incidence of petting behavior (physical contact motivated to arouse but not involving genital union) is common among adolescents of both sexes (Smith 1924; Kinsey, Pomeroy & Martin 1948; Kinsey, Pomeroy, Martin & Gebhart 1953).

The reason for earlier and heightened sexual activity in males is because the sex drive is highly specific, centered in the penis, and demands discharge (Douvan & Adelson 1966; Stone & Church 1968). Boys are easily aroused by a variety of stimuli, and erections, often at embarrassing times, are frequent. As Jersild (1963) stated, ". . . Often the organ behaves as though it had a will and personality of its own" (p. 83). Other possible reasons for the differences between the sexes include a biologically determined difference in the onset of the sex drive, the fact that the sex organs of the female are less prominent, the culturally induced "double standard" which condemns girls for engaging in sexual behavior, and differences in forms of sexual expression.

For girls, sexual impulses are generally of lower intensity, less specific, and less differentiated from other feelings. Although there is a wide range of individual differences among girls in time of onset and form of sexual expression, Stone and Church (1968) stated, "For most adolescent girls, . . . 'desire' or 'lust' is not the correct description, and we might do better to speak of 'sexual stirrings'" (p. 484). Whereas young teen-age boys find sexual gratification and love to be easily separable, girls tend to view the two as related. In fact, love takes priority over sex for girls, and the "boy-crazy" girl may only have a negligible interest in sexual contact (Douvan & Adelson 1966; Stone & Church 1968).

When it comes to social heterosexual interest, evidence suggests that girls precede boys during early adolescence (Stolz, Jones & Chaffey 1937; Gesell, Ilg & Ames 1956; Jones 1960) and the result is often a dissatisfaction with boys of the same age (Havighurst 1952).

Dating begins as early as 10 to 11 (Bernard 1961). Often these dates are in groups (Hurlock 1968). By the middle teen-age years serious dating and "going steady" are common (Scheinfeld 1965). Since asking for a date is the male prerogative, girls must make themselves attractive so they will be selected, though both sexes use a variety of techniques (dress, mannerisms, etc.) to attract the attention of the opposite sex (Hurlock 1968; Coleman 1961a).

The transition from an "asexual" being to a "sexual" one is not without intense and complicated conflicts in our culture. As Mussen, Conger, and Kagan (1969) have pointed out, one problem is that our society tells children to relate to sex with anxiety when they are growing up but turns around and demands that they react to it *without* anxiety after they marry. The intense emotionality characteristic of the adolescent period may frighten teenagers because of the sexual implications which they do not yet fully understand. The sources of conflict in males include the already mentioned fear of and embarrassment resulting from "unplanned erections," fear that the illicit thoughts which are often with them will somehow slip out, ignorance of how girls feel about sexual advances (often complicated by their apparent "come on" followed by rejection if advances are actually made), sensitivity to the size of the penis (especially if it is small), the ambivalence about sexual relations when pleasure is followed by feelings of guilt, the fear of getting a girl pregnant, the fear of contracting a venereal disease, and conflicts about masturbatory activity (Blum 1953; Jersild 1963; Stone & Church 1968). The sources of conflict in females include the fear of becoming pregnant, and the pressures by society to remain "pure" until marriage. Both sexes are fearful of public disapproval or disgrace, and yet may feel the need to prove their masculinity or femininity (Jersild 1963). Further, there appears to be confusion and lack of adequate preparation about sex issues in general (Couch 1967).

Though the sex code in the United States has been characterized as a highly restrictive one (Ford & Beach 1951), there appears to be an increasing liberalization in attitudes about sex which is usually referred to as "the new morality." Greater openness and honesty about sex, and the tendency to view sexual behavior as a personal rather than public matter are the major aspects of newer attitudes (Mussen, Conger & Kagan 1969). Acceptance of engagement in heterosexual behavior prior to marriage is dependent on the degree of closeness of the relationship between partners (Reiss 1964). The area of the acceptability of premarital sex is still the issue on which there is least agreement between parents and teenagers (Reiss 1960). However, Bell (1970) has postulated that there may be a decrease in the conflict between the adolescent and his parents with regards to premarital sexual intimacy due to the emergence of a more liberal view of the functions of sexual satisfaction as an end in itself.

In Bühler's (1922) analyses of 150 adolescent diaries, deep expressions of struggling with sex and love needs were highly characteristic. A central theme was an intense longing to belong with one person. Often the object of adolescent love is not a person of the same age or opposite sex. "Crushes" on teachers or heroes, often much older people, are common, and the desire for physical contact may be absent (Bühler 1932). Objects of love can be so absorbing that dwelling about them dominates the adolescents' thoughts (Hobart 1958). Crushes, however, reach their peak of incidence at about age 14, after which there is a decline in this form of attachment (Hurlock 1968).

The phases of sexual love have been described as starting with physical desires in early adolescence, moving to emotional needs not generally related to physical desire, to companionship seeking, with sexual contact being secondary to interpersonal social contact, and finally an integrated mature relationship uniting physical sex with caring deeply for another person (Lazarsfeld, quoted in Bühler 1928).

In conclusion, attainment of psychosexual maturity implies not only the ability to make adequate heterosexual adjustments, but healthy attitudes towards sex, the forming of appropriate relations with one's own sex, and a healthy identification with one's own sex role (Hurlock 1968).

Adolescence is a time for intellectual expansion and involvement in the academic experience (Horrocks 1954). The adolescent has increased abilities to generalize, to deal with abstractions, to deal with the concept of time, to deal with ideas without immediate personal involvement, to engage in logical thought, and to communicate with others (Jersild 1963).

Intellectual Development. Many investigations have reported data indicating that intellectual growth reaches its highest potential during the mid- to late-teenage years (Hart 1924; Sudweeks 1927; Woodrow 1928; Burks, Jensen, & Terman 1930; Dearborn & Cattell 1930; Jones & Conrad 1933). (As will be discussed in later sections of this chapter, others have reported continuing development of some aspects of intelligence into later years.)

The transition from concrete to abstract thought processes occurring during late childhood and early adolescence has been substantiated (Koch 1913; Habrich 1914; Ormian 1926; Bühler 1928; Piaget 1952b; Yudin & Kates 1963; Weir 1964; Elkind 1966; Yudin 1966; Elkind, Barocas & Johnsen 1969). The observed qualitative differences in child and adolescent cognitive abilities have been related to personality changes in adolescence (Yudin 1967; Elkind 1968b). In fact, it has been suggested that a major *task* of early adolescence is the conquest of thought (Elkind 1967b). The level of cognitive ability reached during adolescence has implications for the efficiency with which the individual meets many of the tasks of this life phase (e.g., academic performance and preparing for a vocation) as well as how he copes with directing his own life (Elkind 1968a; Mussen, Conger & Kagan 1969).

Creativity. The high value placed on creative, gifted, and achieving individuals in our society has necessarily led to the question of the identification of such individuals during earlier phases of life and characteristics of their backgrounds which may have shaped their behavior (Guilford 1962; Torrance 1962; Arasteh 1968).

Creative adolescents have been characterized as more independent and self-directing and less conforming and socially oriented than less creative adolescents (Pepinsky 1960; Warren & Heist 1960; Holland 1961; Getzels & Jackson 1962; Garwood 1964; Trowbridge & Charles 1966). The relationship between creativity and academic aptitude may be negligible (Holland 1961).

Authoritarian child-rearing practices may not hamper academic performance in adolescence, but may stifle originality (Nichols 1964). The family of the highly creative adolescent has also been characterized as one permitting individual divergence and risks (Getzels & Jackson 1962). Families who want their sons to achieve allow independent behavior (Strodtbeck 1958). Studies of creative adults have shown different family-background patterns for different types of creative endeavor. Roe (1960), for example, described the salient features of the background of eminent social scientists as characterized by overprotective and firm parental behavior which was often responded to with rebelliousness. Her description of the backgrounds of eminent biologists and physicists tended toward a pattern of self-direction with little personal interaction with, or rebellion against, the parents. In Eiduson's (1962) study of creative chemists, the father was often the less influential personality, while the mother was characterized as ambitious. Goertzel and Goertzel (1962) also described the presence of a father who relinquished power because of weaknesss or out of principle and a mother with strong ideas about achievement to be favorable to the son's development of talent. A strong father influence, however, has been noted by others as contributing to the shaping of creative individuals such as in the autobiography of J. S. Mill (1908).

It is possible that much of the creative production of adolescents goes unnoticed or is generally unavailable for study. A common form of creative endeavor by adolescents is the personal diary (Spiegel 1951). Beautiful and deeply expressive poems, stories, and musical productions are common, but are often strictly private expressions of the joy and pain of the adolescent experience (Bühler 1922).

Achievement. The family background of achievement strivings in adolescents is likely to be related to a variety of factors such as social class, family size, and birth order (Rosen 1961). However, high-achieving adolescents are more likely to report that their parents warmly encouraged achievement, shared in their activities, and allowed them more autonomy than are underachieving adolescents (Morrow & Wilson 1961). The high achieving adolescent also has a high commitment to academic values (Sugarman 1967) and engagement in intellectual activities is highly related to achievement behavior in adulthood (Moss & Kagan 1961). The superior achiever has been characterized as mature, planful in orientation to tasks and problems, willing to postpone immediate gratifications, and positively oriented to master his circumstances (Hummel & Sprinthall 1965).

The "underachiever" is considered to be a tragedy because such a person represents a drain on the reservoir of talent available in the society (McClelland, Baldwin, Bronfenbrenner, & Strodtbeck 1958; Miller 1961). Factors related to the underachieving adolescent include parental disinterest, inadequacies in the educational system, personality maladjustments, cultural impoverishment, and failure to accept or gain acceptance into a social group (Goodman 1956; Havighurst & Neugarten 1957; Friedenberg 1959; Thorndike 1963; Hummel & Sprinthall 1965).

Interests. The interests and activities of adolescents are extremely diverse, and the "turnover" rate in specific types of interests may be quite rapid. Because the adolescent is, for the first time, experimenting with experiences and situations which reflect an adultlike rather than childlike flavor, the involvement in a wide variety of interests and activities is of positive value to his future development. In the next phase of life, the mature person will, by necessity, have to restrict his activity choices due to the obligations and demands of adult life. The choice of interests in adolescence is dependent on many factors among which are sex, intelligence, family setting, prestige value of different interests, interests of peer groups, and opportunities available for forming and engaging in interests (Hurlock 1968). The types of activities engaged in most often are those which bring the adolescent into contact with others of the same age and serve as a basis for companionship (Jersild 1963).

Among the major interests of boys are organized outdoor sports, hobbies (such as working on cars), radio listening and TV watching, playing musical instruments, and being "with the group." The interests of girls include the same sedentary interests as listed above for boys plus reading and listening to records. Boys tend to pursue more active interests, perhaps because society offers more such pursuits for them than for girls (Coleman 1961a). The skill in activities involving athletics or strength carries with it social acceptance value for boys (Thrasher 1927; Cowell 1935).

One of the more recent interests involves cars. Automobiles can serve many adolescent needs and purposes, e.g., giving him a status symbol, increasing mobility, and providing privacy, excitement, etc. (Coleman 1961b; Bernard 1961; Jersild 1963).

A major aspect of the adolescent period is the choice of an occupational identity (Bradley 1943; Cawley 1947; Super & Bachrach 1957; Super 1957; Erikson 1963; Tyler, Sundberg & Rohila 1968). Vocational interests and choices are related to a variety of factors including social class (Hollingshead 1949; Caro 1966), parental and family influence (Seward 1945; Kahl 1953; Lipset & Bendix 1959; White 1959; Dansereau 1961; Simpson 1962; Bell 1963; Green & Parker 1965; Werts 1966), peer and school influences (Bell 1963; Day 1966; Seward & Williamson 1969), and personality characteristics (Holland 1963; Burnstein 1963; Sinha 1964). There are also differences between the sexes in regard to vocational choices and aspirations, with boys showing interest in high-prestige jobs and girls preferring those of a less prestigious and service-oriented nature (Witty 1961; Smelser 1963; Ulrich, Hecklik & Roeber 1966; Seward & Williamson 1969).

Adolescents tend to overestimate their ability in terms of vocational aspirations (Douvan & Adelson 1966) or make unrealistic choices (Myers 1947). Young people tend to aspire to higher-level jobs than those of their parents (Kroger & Louttit 1935). There is often considerable fluctuation in vocational interests (Norton 1953a, 1953b) which lessens and becomes more realistic with increasing age (Horrocks 1954). The lure of money as a cure-all may lead some adolescents to leave school and take a job (Dentler 1964; Elliott 1966), though later they may sadly realize the penalties of their shortsightedness (Lazersfeld 1931). Nowadays, with the variety of opportunities for part-time work and volunteer positions, young people are able to sample occupations without having to leave school.

DEVELOPMENT OF VALUE ORIENTATIONS

Adolescence is the decisive period in moving from externally imposed conduct patterns to an internally controlled set of personal values and moral standards (Douvan & Adelson 1966). Piaget (1932) described the course of moral development as moving from a rigid sense of justice to a more flexible consideration of appropriate standards, which takes mitigating circumstances into account.

The values of the child are shaped primarily by the family (Peck & Havighurst 1960; Riley & Moore 1961). Even though there may be rebellion from parental values during early adolescence, values tend to converge toward those of the parents later on (Bath & Lewis 1962; Perrone 1967). Pacella (1967) noted that adolescents may appear to move away from parental values in an attempt to deny or repress their feelings of dependency, but that ethical and moral guidelines should continue to be provided by their elders while understanding that the adolescent needs to feel that he is developing his own value system. Allport (1961b) pointed, however, to the problems of guiding youth in a rapidly advancing technological society, since the world in which they will reside is quite unlike the one in which our stockpile of wisdom is based. Medinnus and Johnson (1969) have characterized many present-day younger people as accepting the expressed values of the culture, but they have tended to react actively to the discrepancy between accepted values and actual behavior practices by society's members.

In establishing a set of values, the pattern of development may differ between the sexes. Girls tend to move from an acceptance of the views of parental authority to identifying with them. Boys, on the other hand, are more characterized by a period of defiance (Crane 1958; Douvan & Adelson 1966; Perrone 1967). A "negative phase" between the ages of 11 to 13 for girls has been described (Bühler 1922; Hetzer 1926) in which there is a rebellion against the parents. Open defiance, particularly directed at the mother, is common as well as having negative feelings about many aspects of life.

Positive values held by adolescents include honesty, politeness, kindness, cooperation, and friendliness. Blameworthy behavior includes dishonesty, having a bad character, carelessness, and disloyalty. These values maintain a rather marked consistency from late elementary-school years through high school (Thompson 1949). Lying, if it is socially justified, becomes more acceptable as age increases (Tudor-Hart 1926).

What are the current values held by adolescents? Mussen, Conger & Kagan (1969) suggested an emphasis on being natural and honest in interpersonal relationships, increased concern with issues relating to civil rights, and faith in some of society's institutions such as medicine, science, and higher education. These authors also noted that "materialistic values" are often vigorously decried by adolescents, but the level of affluence and actual or desired possessions of objects is extremely high. Perhaps this discrepancy indicates that possessions are desirable but not considered to be *the* vehicle of self-fulfillment in life.

Adolescence is often characterized by a high degree of idealism, which may reveal itself in a variety of ways depending on the individual, through religion (Stone & Church 1968). Evidence suggests that adolescents become less dogmatic during the teen-age years (Kuhlen & Arnold 1944; Anderson 1962) and previous religious beliefs are often questioned (Remmers & Radler 1957; Landis 1960; Middleton & Putney 1962) and reevaluated (Hurlock 1968). Some adolescents may, on the other hand, become deeply involved in religion and mysticism (Bühler 1922). Religious beliefs move from the childish fanciful stage to a realistic or secure stage based on acceptance of authority to an individualistic stage where the person selects from religion what reflects his own needs (Harms 1944; Hirschberg 1956).

Though church function attendance may continue, or rituals in sororities and fraternities remain an integral part of the group functioning, the reasons may be less related to spiritual efficacy than to social approval and maintenance of group cohesiveness (Williams 1967; Eberly 1967). Attitudes about religion vary according to sex, religious denomination, cultural expectations, and personality differences (Elkind & Elkind 1962).

The Peer Group. Among the most noticeable tendencies of today's adolescent is the importance he attaches to, and the degree he is influenced by, his age mates (Horrocks 1954; Remmers & Radler 1957; Bernard 1961; Symonds 1961; Ginsberg 1962; Smith 1963; Sherif & Sherif 1964). The time spent away from home and the family, usually to be with people of the same age, is higher during adolescence than any other phase of life (Wright 1956). The peer group comes to have more influence on the adolescent's interests, attitudes, and values than does the family (Bowerman & Kinch 1959).

The adolescent is between two worlds, yet needs to share his strong and confusing emotions, doubts, and dreams with others (Mussen, Conger, & Kagan 1969). His own age mates, who are in the same predicament, provide the opportunity to share ideas and feelings, help him to find out who he is, broaden his values and interests beyond those held by the family, allow him to form a social identity that society at large denies to him, and imposes order to an ambiguous and stressful period of life (Tryon 1944; Rogers 1962; Jersild 1963; Schwartz & Merton 1967).

The negative aspects of the peer-group influence relate to the consequences submission to authority has on the development of the individual's own personal goals and quest for self-fulfillment. It will be remembered that the development of self-identity has been put forth as a major aspect of the adolescent period, yet the young person may temporarily overidentify with his crowd, thus losing his own (Erikson 1963). The requirements for conformity within his own subculture are extremely strong (Bell 1963) and distinctive evaluative standards are imposed (Schwartz & Merton 1967). An unfortunate aspect of this situation is that the elusive "authority" is composed of individuals who themselves are attempting to cope with a host of confusing unknowns.

A "popularity neurosis" characterizes many adolescents, perhaps because they cannot realistically evaluate their own worth and thus need others to assure them that they are acceptable and worthy individuals (Stone & Church 1968). The desire for popularity permeates all social class levels (Remmers & Radler 1957).

Several writers have described the phenomenon of the "teen-age culture" which emphasizes fun, popularity, fads and teen paraphernalia, characteristic dating patterns, activities, language, and songs (Coleman 1961a, 1961b; Bernard 1961). Social-class distinctions are extremely pervasive in teen-age cultures (Hollingshead 1949). Perhaps this is presently changing.

Although school may be the focal point of gripes during adolescence (Hurlock 1968), it also encompasses the adolescent community. However, how popular one is, how well one does in sports and other activities, the social contacts one makes, etc., are more important than the learning opportunities the school provides or how well one does in intellectual pursuits (Bernard 1961; Coleman 1961a, 1961b; Jersild 1963; Coleman 1965; McDill & Coleman 1965; Stone & Church 1968).

Up to now, peer-group relationships have been portrayed in rather desperate terms, with the adolescent submitting and conforming out of a need to fit in somehow. However, the development of true friendships characterized by individually determined shared frames of reference, is also a part of the adolescent period, and when an adolescent finds a *real* friend, he has found something very precious (Jersild 1963). Friendship stability and social responsibility increase markedly as the individual moves from childhood into adolescence (Horrocks & Thompson 1946; Thompson & Horrocks 1947; Horrocks & Buker 1951; Harris 1957; Skorepa, Horrocks & Thompson 1963; McKinney 1968).

Even though adolescence is characterized as a period of intense sociability, it is often a time of intense loneliness (Bernard 1961; Mussen, Conger & Kagan 1969). A substantial number of teenagers feel left out and unwanted (Remmers & Radler 1957) which suggests that part of the striving to belong to a group is partially determined by the desire to escape from loneliness.

Parents and Society. There has always been a "generation gap." Yet it appears to be widening in our society, possibly because our young people are becoming increasingly sophisticated and powerful and feel more free to express themselves openly.

Despite the fact that parents from all walks of life want their children to be happy (Kohn 1959), friction between the adolescent and his parents is common and can lead to misery and frustration for both sides. A "substantial part of the time the adolescent spends with his family is likely to be colored by feelings—on both sides—of frustration, outrage, humiliation, sullenness, resentment, and dramatic (or melodramatic) despair" (Stone & Church 1968, p. 445).

Medinnus and Johnson (1969) have suggested that adolescence comes at a particularly poor time for the parent. Most parents, now in their forties and fifties, are having some crucial life adjustments of their own to make. Facing "middle age" may be difficult enough, especially for the mother who may feel her life function of bearing and rearing children is coming to an end. Parents who have tended to relive their lives through their children, or parents who have used their children as emotional supports, may find "letting go" extremely difficult (Jersild 1963). Parents must adjust to no longer being the "ideal persons" (Havighurst, Robinson & Dorr 1946) and losing the status of being the child's primary love objects (Jersild 1963).

Common sources of irritation and disagreement among adolescents and their parents include the limits and types of parental control and discipline techniques, sexual values, choice of friends and social activities, money matters, nagging and criticism (Stott 1935, 1940a, 1940b; Block 1937; Punke 1943; Heath & Gregory 1946; Lloyd 1952; Remmers, Horton & Scarborough 1952; Connor, Johannis & Walters 1954; Elder 1963; Meissner 1965; Bell 1970). Specific incidents and confrontations are only intensified by the fact that adolescents and their parents tend to distrust each other (Hess & Goldblatt 1957) and have difficulty in communicating, possibly because their mutual feelings are often mixed and unclear (Jersild 1963).

Many of the battles center around adolescents' quest for independence and emancipation from the parents. In general, boys have fewer conflicts with the family (Block 1937; Stott 1940a; Punke 1943), probably because parents restrict girls more than they do boys (Komarovsky 1950; Powell 1955).

Too much or too little parental involvement in the lives of adolescents may hamper the successful achievement of autonomy (Douvan & Adelson 1966). Adolescents making good adjustments report family relationships characterized by warmth, trust, and shared activities (Warnath 1955; Peck 1958).

The attainment of independent status within the family may not necessarily be frought with turmoil, and once the adolescent achieves autonomy he may move rather easily into a place in the society. However, recently many authors are describing the alienation that increasing numbers of young people are experiencing in their relationships with society-at-large (Keniston 1960, 1967; Flacks 1967; Brown 1967). Although the causes of the alienation and the forms that reactions to it might take are complex and varied, we are faced with a refusal to accept society and its institutions by many of our most competent young people (Baumrind 1968).

Phase III and IV: Young and Middle Adulthood

The middle years of life are the ones in which the person *should* come to the fullest development in all phases of life activities as well as reach the plateau of physical expansion. Generally speaking, during adulthood the individual exercises his widest range of potentials, and he remembers the adulthood years (particularly the earlier ones) as the "happiest" (Landis 1942; Morgan 1937; Pressey & Kuhlen 1957; Lehr 1964; Meltzer & Ludwig 1967). Yet many find these years torn by frustration and feelings of failure because of the difficulties of coping with the necessary integration of so many different aspects of life. Development in adulthood might even be defined as the crucial phase of the integrational process of the person to a more or less unified entity.

However, research study of the mature years, as a developmental phase of life, is disappointingly sparse.[10] This is unfortunate, since adulthood represents the culmination of the effects of development in earlier phases of life (Hahn 1962; Bromley 1966; Bühler 1967b; Bischof 1969).

There are several reasons for the underemphasis of the adulthood developmental phase in research. Only a few writers have outlined theoretical statements of adult development (Bortner 1966; Bühler 1967b; Bischof 1969). Further, whereas early and very late stages of human development are replete with physical and physiological changes which provide strong "handles" to underpin psychological or behavioral change, the adulthood period is not characterized by marked upward or downward biologically determined shifts. In fact, the physical development and decline in adults shows tremendous individual variation (Selye 1956) and proceeds unevenly (Morgan 1968). Adulthood is characterized by a bewildering complexity of interrelationships in psychological, social, and cultural spheres, which must be known in order to fully understand the continuity of development in the adult (Bühler & Massarik 1968). Because each adult is a unique entity as a result of his own past, his own motives and goals, and the situation in which he finds himself, it would seem that the result has been to concentrate on presenting individual case analyses or studying "bit parts" of adulthood functioning (e.g., learning ability, occupational choices, etc.) without facing the methodological difficulties of measuring changes in large numbers of "whole" adults.

[10] For more detailed presentations of development in adulthood see Pressey & Kuhlen 1957; Bühler & Massarik 1968; Hurlock 1968, Chaps. 10–14; Bischof 1969.

MOTIVATIONAL AND GOAL DEVELOPMENT

The psychologists who see the adulthood phase of human life as an important phase of human development tend to be those who view life as having a continuing directionality and purpose. Bühler has used the term "intentionality" to refer to the integrated direction fulfilled person's exhibit.

As indicated earlier, development throughout the life cycle has been conceived of in various ways by different authors and schools. Regardless of how the stages of the process are conceptualized, there is agreement on the fact that some time during the middle period of life maturity should be reached.

This implies and requires the taking up and mastering of new areas of life (which the adolescent just began to become aware of), namely sex, love, higher education, marriage, family, home, careers and professional roles, social groups, status and possessions, and political, community, and world affairs. How these areas of life are met by the individual, what they mean to him in terms of his own personal development, and how he copes with the integration of these activities of life have basically gone unnoticed by developmental psychologists. Much of the data available is, rather, from the field of sociology.

Many psychologists have outlined the criteria designating the mature personality (e.g., Bühler 1933a; Maslow 1954; Erikson 1959; Allport 1961a; Pikunas 1969). Among the characteristics cited by these authors are the ability to integrate one's experiences into a relatively stable identity, the ability to participate fully in life, the ability to use one's knowledge and skills effectively, the ability to relate to others in a significant and sensitive manner, the ability to make positive and constructive responses to the situations of life, the willingness to assume responsibility, emotional security, acceptance of the self, and perhaps most significantly, a development and maintenance of a directedness in life leading to self-fulfillment or self-actualization.

PHYSICAL CHANGES IN ADULTHOOD

In general, the middle phase of life (21 to 45–50) is characterized by optimal bodily functioning. The "prime of life," in the physical sense, occurs during the twenties. The fourth phase of life (45–50 to 55–65) is characterized by slowly diminishing vitality, which decreases at an accelerated rate as the old-age period is reached. In women there exists the more noticeable delineation between young and middle adulthood in that reproductive abilities cease. The psychological significance of the menopause is perhaps best revealed through the more popular term "change of life."

Some accounts of physical change during adulthood cited in Zubek and Solberg (1954), Pressey and Kuhlen (1957), and Bischof (1969) are briefly presented here. There are processes which change systematically over the whole life span, such as vision where loss of accommodation abilities increases slowly from childhood and then more rapidly after 40. Changes in the skin, due to decreases in regenerative capacities and degenerative changes in skin tissue, cause wrinkles and dryness. This process, which has great psychological implications due to the value placed on youthful appearance, actually starts in adolescence with various facial and neck lines appearing in a fairly definite sequence. Changes in hair color (eventually turning grey) and

balding progress slowly from young adulthood to become most pronounced and noticeable after 40.

Changes which are most pronounced in the later adulthood phase (aside from the female menopause) include general health factors, particularly susceptibility to heart disease in males, and the ability to maintain bodily homeostasis. Lowered metabolic rates, loss of muscular vigor, and the increasing inability to dissipate heat through the skin make bodily temperature more difficult to maintain. The susceptibility to illness and death changes with age which, according to Pressey and Kuhlen (1957), provides strong evidence of the rise and fall in the organism's vitality and constitutional changes.

Among the functions remaining fairly stable during both adulthood phases are pituitary functioning, blood pressure (although systolic blood pressure increases noticeably after age 60), digestive system functioning, and taste sensitivity. Once adult stature is reached, height remains constant into old age (with a slight loss due to shrinkage of cartilage and joint ligaments and poor posture due to loss of muscle tonus). Other physical processes, such as respiratory vital capacity, muscle growth (though maximum strength is reached at about 30), and hearing of higher-pitched tones, maintain a steady rate up to about 50 and then slowly decline up to the old-age period when the deceleration is more rapid. Weight begins to increase slowly, then more rapidly in middle-adulthood, and decreases again in old age.

CHANGES IN SEXUAL PROCESSES AND ACTIVITY

The output of sex hormones changes during the adult years. Androgen secretion peaks in output for both males and females in the twenties, though the level is much higher for males. A decrease then progresses steadily for both sexes, though the sex-difference curves converge in later years. The maximum output of estrogen is from 17 to 29 in both sexes and for males there is no subsequent decline. Yet for females the output is considerably higher than for males during the reproductive years; but after the menopause (at about 47 years of age) it drops sharply to below the level of the male and remains constant (Zubek & Solberg 1954).

It has been asserted that the sharp drop in the estrogen level of women coincides with depression, energy loss, nervousness, and "hot flashes" (Kirk 1951). However, many feel the correlated symptoms may be a result of emotional stress and anxiety over the loss of reproductive ability (Zubek & Solberg 1954; Parker 1960; Bischof 1969). Sexual potency decreases slowly but steadily with age. In males, the total sexual outlet per week drops from 3.4 during the twenties to 2.4 in the thirties, 1.8 in the forties, and 1.2 in the sixties (Kinsey, Pomeroy, & Martin 1948). A climacteric also occurs in males, though it begins later, usually in the sixties, and proceeds more gradually. The male climacteric is characterized by a decrease in sexual potency and desire (Freeman 1961). Sexual expression in later life depends on the complex interplay of physical changes, psychological reactions, and the social context (Butler 1967). In one longitudinal study, Pfeiffer, Verwerdt, and Wang (1968) discovered that a sizable percentage of aged individuals showed rising patterns of sexual interest and activity as compared with previous years. Of those couples who had ceased activity, the man and wife agreed that the husband was the determining factor in the cessation of intercourse.

CHANGES IN ABILITIES

The shifts in intellectual ability and performance on various other learning and motor tasks during the adult years is difficult to assess, since a multitude of factors appear to greatly influence test performance. Although abilities generally tend to peak in the twenties, some studies have reported a general increment in mental functioning over the years (Bayley & Oden 1955; Bentz 1953; Nisbet 1957). Verbal and general information scores are particularly resistant to change with age (Jones & Conrad 1933; Bayley 1968). Yet individual variation is great and has been linked to such factors as initial ability, amount of education, living setting, amount of participation in hobbies and other activities, earned income, the nature and intensity of environmental stimulation (Birren 1964; Owens 1966; Schaie & Strother 1968).

Although many studies of motor abilities show a slow decline after the twenties (Thorndike 1928; Ruch 1934; Smith 1938; Zubek & Solberg 1954; Hodgkins 1962), several writers speak of motivation and attitudinal determinants accounting for age differences (Surwillo & Quilter 1964; Bromley 1966; Bischof 1969). Other studies have not found significant decreases with age (Wetherick 1964; Collins 1964), but as Bischof (1969) points out, data do not exist regarding how well single individuals solve problems throughout their life span.

CREATIVITY IN ADULTHOOD

Effort has been extended in the search for variables identifying and producing talented or creative adults (McClelland, Baldwin, Bronfenbrenner & Strodtbeck 1958; Stein & Heinze 1960; Goertzel & Goertzel 1962; Taylor & Barron 1963). Often the focus is on studying characteristics of persons possessing certain specific skills or aptitudes, such as architects (MacKinnon 1962), musicians (Willman 1944), biologists (Roe 1949, 1951), chemists (Eiduson 1962), psychologists and anthropologists (Roe 1952, 1953), inventors (Rossman 1964), and writers (Barron 1965). Though identifying characteristics vary depending on the area of creativity or skill, in general the creative person is characterized as self-stimulating, independent, sensitive, goal-oriented, and capable of integrating and giving direction to his life (Eiduson 1962; Bühler 1968b; Arasteh 1968).

Specific creative persons have been analyzed, such as Goethe (Eissler 1963) and Leonardo da Vinci (Freud 1947) and autobiographies of creative persons are often cited (e.g., J. S. Mill 1908; N. Wiener 1953).

In 1933, Bühler presented in her first "Course of Human Life" book some of the findings of the distribution and the curves of an individual's productions in life on about one thousand biographies assembled under the direction of Frenkel and Brunswik. Their survey of many types of work productions and products, including laborers, sportsmen, engineers, traveling missionaries, lawyers, business men, surgeons, scientists, artists, composers, diplomats, and philosophers, shows four curves of production. The output of people, quantitatively as well as qualitatively speaking, may culminate in the various life phases (i.e., early, middle, or late) or it may spread in irregular fashion over the life cycle. Bühler proposed the prevalence of factors called "vitality" and "mentality" as responsible for these distributions.

Lehman (1953) continued these studies by quantifying the output of groups, rather than individuals as the Viennese psychologists had done. Some of his major findings on age groupings and types of peak outstanding performance are: *the twenties* (chemistry, some types of poetry, top "box office" female acting, and athletics of the more physically demanding sort), *the thirties* (physical sciences with the exception of chemistry, mathematics, inventions of a practical and medical nature, biological sciences, most types of musical composition, movie directing, top "box office" male acting, and athletics of the less physically demanding sort such as golf and billiards), *the forties* (some types of musical composition, many types of writing such as best sellers and novels, metaphysics, and modern architecture), *the fifties* (leadership such as college presidents and U.S. presidents), *the sixties* (military leadership, outstanding commercial and industrial leadership, and earned annual incomes in excess of fifty thousand dollars per year), and *the seventies* (Supreme Court Justices, religious leaders, and annual income in excess of one million dollars per year).

CHANGES IN INTERESTS

In young adulthood, interests may shift as the focus of life moves from the school group to one's own family and the community (Donald & Havighurst 1959; Hurlock 1968) but the lifelong interests are established early in adulthood (Strong 1958) and further aging may have an insignificant influence on the person's recreational patterns and preferences. Factors influencing the choice of interests include marital status, socioeconomic class, the sex of the person, and the family composition (Hurlock 1968), but they also reflect the internal needs of the person (Bühler 1961b; Pressey & Kuhlen 1957). Interest pattern change over the years reflects changes in abilities, energy, sex orientation, personality, and cultural expectations (Pressey & Kuhlen 1957). In general, there is a shift from more active and competitive interests to more passive and "feminine" interests (Strong 1931; Shuttleworth 1949; Havighurst 1957), though persons with high achievement in power positions may become even more domineering in later years (Lehman 1953). There is generally a narrowing of interest choices (Pressey & Kuhlen 1957), though Youmans (1968) found that few of his middle-adult sample expected to give up any of their present hobbies and a substantial number of males rejected the idea of ever retiring. With middle-adulthood, participation in formal organization is at its highest (Pressey & Kuhlen 1957). Pikunas (1969) stated that the utilization of time with creative, constructive, and noncompetitive activities was the major task of the later-adulthood years.

LIFE CHANGES IN ADULTHOOD

In several writings Bühler has outlined the basic tendencies in the development of the self in adulthood. Much of this theory has been based on case history and biographical analyses. During very early adulthood, the individual makes a tentative self-determination of his role in society, he still works through his sexual needs and sexual identity, and experiments with occupational and love object choices. From 25–30 to 45–50 the person's goals are more definite and specified. Self-realization in one's occupation, marriage, and the family, as well as acceptance of these roles, become the crucial factors in self-development. Persons coming for psychotherapy when in their 30s are often those who feel it is not yet too late to lead a complete and adequate life, but are aware of "failure areas" in their sexual, work, or interpersonal lives. The climacteric years, 45–50 to 65–70 mark a renewed period of self-assessment. Life goals and aspirations must be tempered with the reality of the situation in which the individual finds himself. The person may still continue to expand his horizons and find new avenues of expression, though these may be affected by health problems, obligations to the family or community, or difficulties in life patterns or situations accruing from previous stages of life (Bühler 1962*b*, 1968*a*).

Erikson (1959) defines two stages of early- and middle-adulthood. First, the young adult must have attained a reasonable sense of self-identity so that true intimacy with another person can be established. Sexual intimacy is only part of the ability to develop a sensitive, mutual relationship with another person. If the young adult isolates himself, the relationships he has with others will be highly formal and lacking in deep warmth and spontaneity. Individuals who find true-love relations with a partner may move on to the next stage which he calls "generativity." Though this developmental stage, which involves the wish to establish and guide successive generations, is most often realized through bearing a common offspring, other forms of activity such as creative productions relate to this phase.

Characteristics and Tasks of Early Adulthood. Some regard the short period of time immediately following adolescence as a significant and separate phase of human development. Wittenberg (1968), for example, sees postadolescence as characterized by a self-image crisis which he describes as a sharp vascillation between superego and ego ideals, the necessity of giving up all adolescent role playing, the necessity to cope fully with time continuity, and the neccessity of choosing the right partner, which is often bypassed by an escape into an early marriage. He also discusses economic difficulties of this phase in terms of the young adult's need to be self-supporting but often finding society reluctant to absorb him into the marketplace.

Havighurst (1952) designated young adulthood (20–30) the most individualistic period of life, but also the loneliest, since one individual, or two at most, must make a life without much assistance from others or society. The developmental tasks of this period are: selecting a mate, learning to live with a marriage partner, starting a family, rearing children, managing a home, getting started in an occupation, taking on civic responsibilities, and finding a congenial social group.

Characteristics and Tasks of Middle-Adulthood. The middle-adult period involves a time of critical self-assessment (Bühler 1962*a*). The high aspirations which had been set in earlier years probably have not yet been realized, at least in their fullest sense,

and doubts enter as to whether they ever will be, now that many facets of life have begun to decline. Defenses may become apparent, such as blaming others or trying desperately to recapture youth, or anxiety may magnify the problem (Pikunas 1969). The environment may be viewed as complex and overwhelming as the individual moves from a position of "active" to "passive" mastery (Neugarten et al. 1964).

The developmental tasks of this period are achieving adult civic and social responsibility, establishing and maintaining an economic standard of living, assisting the teen-age children to become happy and responsible adults, developing adult leisure-time activities, relating oneself to one's spouse as a person accepting and adjusting to the physiological changes of middle-age, and adjusting to aging parents (Havighurst 1952).

Marmor (1968) discussed the four "crises" of middle adulthood. The first is the moment when somatic evidences of aging, particularly those relating to appearance changes, can no longer be ignored. The second is the cultural stress occurring in our society. When youth and vigor subside, so does one's social value and attraction level. The third is increased economic stress. Many middle-aged persons have trouble being hired into a new job and may have financial burdens due to higher-education training for their children and/or the necessity of supporting aged parents. Finally come the various psychological stresses such as separation losses (children leaving, death of parents, loss of love in a "tired" marriage), loss of the fantasy hopes of youth, and confronting the fact of mortality. Women may feel these stresses more strongly than men, since their identity with the child-bearing and child-raising function is no longer tenable.

Changes in Vocational Life from Young to Middle-Adulthood. Vocational choice is a crucial decision in the life of a person because one's work can be the source of pleasure, esteem, and goal-fulfillment, or it can contribute to disappointment and feelings of failure. The choice of life work is a complex process involving an interplay of personal values and self-image, the social-cultural situation, capabilities, personality traits, aspiration level, economic conditions, and sexual and religious factors (Friedman, Havighurst & Harlan 1954; Lyman 1955; Holland 1959; Lockwood 1958; Chown 1959; Froehlich & Wolins 1960; Stephenson 1961; Levinson 1964; Friedman & Wallace 1968). The type of job a person chooses depends on his educational background and is influenced by the educational level of his parents (Miller & Form 1951). The work situation will necessarily bring the person into a situation and context which will greatly affect numerous other aspects of the person's adult life (Pressey & Kuhlen 1957).

Normally, the peak of vocational status and income comes during middle-adulthood (Hurlock 1968) and job satisfaction reaches a summit in the mid-fifties before it drops off abruptly (Salen & Otis 1964). Reasons for working reveal different motivations. Friedman, Havighurst, and Harlan (1954) found, for example, that laborers stated they were primarily interested in monetary rewards, whereas white-collar and professional workers felt their jobs allowed self-expression.

While the first half of life reveals a striving for self-development and self-improvement in both the private and vocational life, around forty years of age a self-assessment takes place which may lead to a reorientation in thinking about one's job. People may be less interested in ever changing jobs or the possibility of promotion and view ultimate retirement more favorably or, more rarely, make drastic changes in occupations (Kuhlen & Johnson 1952; Bühler 1933a; Frenkel 1936).

In the late-adulthood phase, workers may have difficulties, especially when a change of jobs is involved (Belbin 1953; Cavan 1959; Ross & Ross 1965) but older workers have received job-performance ratings which are competitive with those of younger workers and in the areas of attendance, steadiness, and conscientiousness may even exceed their younger counterparts (Bowers 1952).

Marriage and Divorce

We are indebted to the sociologists for most existing data on courtship and marriage relationships, a sample of which is presented here.

Dating begins very early in our culture and by the mid-teens becomes particularly emotionally significant. "Going steady" is increasing and often leads to early marriage (Williamson 1966).

The age of marriage has been declining over the years (to approximately 21 for women and 23 for men) and the age difference between the husband and wife is decreasing, possibly due to a trend toward the "companionship" marriage (Burgess, Locke & Thomes 1963). It has been estimated, however, that one in five marriages in the United States is preceded by conception (Williamson 1966). In general, the closer the couple in chronological age, the higher the ratings of adjustment to, and satisfaction with, the marriage (Blood & Wolfe 1960).

The selection of a marriage partner is one of the crucial choice points of life, and whether or not the decision was a good one may not be known until a few years after the marriage takes place (Kephart 1967; Parke & Glick 1967). Factors affecting marital happiness and adjustment have been studied, such as communication patterns between husband and wife, sexual compatibility, relationships with other family members and outsiders, assignment of task responsibility, personality-trait compatibility, maturity of the couple, the amount of preparation for the marriage, the perception of marital roles, and whether the couple can adjust to the reality that the adolescent conception of romantic love and fun is only part of what is involved in married life (Hurlock 1968; Fishbein & Kennedy 1957; Tharp 1965; Pickford, Signori & Rempel 1966; Rabkin 1967; Luckey 1966; Paris & Luckey 1966; Dean 1966).

About 8 percent of the adult population never marries for reasons ranging from personal choice to lack of opportunity due to such circumstances as responsibilities to other family members precluding the possibility of planning a life of one's own (Hurlock 1968). There is evidence to suggest that single people are less well-adjusted than marrieds (Rallings 1966; Knupfer, Clark & Room 1966; Lowe 1967; Klemer 1954; Martinson 1955).

Approximately one of four marriages end in divorce (Hurlock 1968). When people marry between the ages of 35 and 39 years, over 60 percent are for the second time (Williamson 1966) and remarriage within two years after divorce is common, especially among younger people (Goode 1956). What divorce *means* to the person is the crucial factor in self-development, and to a substantial number of people, especially those over 30, divorce is a traumatic experience (Goode 1956). The deleterious effects of family disorganization caused by divorce have been substantiated by much research (Despert 1953; Jacobson 1959; Landis 1960, 1963). However, parents staying together, though extremely unhappy, may lead to even more severe emotional reactions in their children than if they had separated (Nye 1957; Goode 1964).

Parenthood and the Family

Although Handel (1965) has stressed the need for the psychological study of interrelationships in whole families, most research utilizing parents focuses on their children or the effects of parental behavior, attitudes, or rearing techniques on children (Medinnus 1967).

Some noteworthy research along these lines are studies on parent-child relationships (Schaefer & Baley 1963; Hess & Shipman 1965; Hatfield, Ferguson & Alpert 1967; Spitz 1965; Brody 1956; Bowlby 1951), the effects of maternal employment on the child (Despert 1953; Siegel & Haas 1963; Nye & Hoffman 1963; Heer 1958; Douvan & Adelson 1966; Hoffman 1961; Stoltz 1960), and parental attitudes (Sears, Maccoby & Levin 1957; Symonds 1939, 1949; Baldwin, Kalhorn & Breese 1945).

Some research has been done dealing with the age of the mother. Age was not found to be an important factor affecting the attitude of the mother toward her pregnancy. Rather, the number of children already in the family was a more important factor (Sears, Maccoby & Levin 1957). Older parents are more anxious and concerned about their responsibilities to the child (Bossard & Boll 1966) and may be overly protective towards them, causing personality disturbances in the children (Stone & Rowley 1965, 1966).

Again, the meaning of parenthood to the individual and the dynamics of family living tend to be most prevalent in the field of sociology (Blood & Wolfe 1960; Anshen 1949; Kirkpatrick 1955; Williamson 1966; Burgess, Locke & Thomes 1963; Goode 1964; Frazier 1948; Glick 1957; Burgess & Wallin 1953).

Phase V: Old Age

The definitions of aging, or what defines an "old" person, show much variation. Aging may be defined as commencing with birth (or even before with the process of differentiation), since the individual is growing older with each minute of life. Aging has also been defined as the progressive loss of functions and capacities after the organism has reached maturity.[11] Aging, or the reaching of old age, has also been defined legally (usually 65 years) when retirement and the onset of government benefits take place. Others hold that a definition of reaching old age based on chronological age alone is not meaningful due to the great individual differences in the onset of aging "signs."

The biologists have advanced many theories as to the causes of aging and have been pondering such intriguing questions as, "why do cells cease functioning after the passage of a certain amount of time?" Many theories, some with evidence to support them, have been advanced but none has been firmly accepted.

[11] Freidman (1966) describes aging as retrogression or involution (the obverse of "development") as characterizing *normal* senescent functioning.

Proposals as to the causes of aging include effects of the accumulation of stress over time (Selye & Prioreschi 1960), progressive cell death (Heilbrunn 1943), disorganization of the system due to progressive slowing of the rate of neural impulse transmission (Still 1956), enzyme deterioration (Bjorksten 1966), autoimmunity reactions (Blumenthal & Bernes 1964), mutations of somatic cells causing development of inferior cells (Failla 1958), and the cross-linkage or bonding together of cells creating a less mobile aggregate with new properties (Bjorksten 1968).[12]

Shock (1960, 1968) reviews some attempts to alter longevity lengths through environmental means, such as manipulating temperature, food supply, radiation exposure, etc., but stresses the major role of genetic determinants as programming general longevity limits among the various species of organisms. Rose (1964) summarizes possible social factors which correlate with longevity in humans. These include: parental longevity; senior birth order in a large family; triad of intelligence, education, and satisfying occupation; status-group membership; small number of children to raise; maintenance of "with spouse" status; and a maintenance of occupational role or its surrogate into elderly years. These factors contribute to assuring good health maintenance, psychological well-being, and the minimization of life stresses.

The aging process can be differentiated into two separate declines in function. *Primary* aging, apparently rooted in heredity, refers to the inherent and inevitable changes which take place over time. *Secondary* aging results from acquired disabilities related to trauma and chronic disease (Busse 1967). The study of these two types of aging are primarily the province of biology, physiology, and medicine. Perhaps a *third* level should be included which deals with the *effects* of primary and secondary aging of the human as a psychological and social being. The changes in behavior capacities, life style, productivity, self-concept, sources of support, etc., are the main interest and concern to the social scientists and social-service professions. Pincus (1967), for example, discusses aging as a "social disease." A major problem in researching aging phenomena is the difficulty in disentangling effects of disease, physical losses, social and other environmental changes, and preexisting personality patterns, from changes which are purely *age-specific* (Butler 1963*a*).

Changes in Physiological Processes with Aging

Any discussion of chronic illnesses which often accompany old age is beyond the scope of this chapter except to note the enormity of this problem. In people over 65 years of age, 78.7 percent have chronic disorders with 45.1 percent of these being disabling (Busse 1967). The relationships between the physiological and the psychological have been well documented (Birren, Imus, & Windle 1959; Blumenthal 1962; Tibbits & Donahue 1962; Birren, Butler, Greenhouse, Sokoloff & Yarrow 1963; Williams, Tibbits, and Donahue 1963; Welford & Birren 1965). The human is conscious of the changes in his mind and body which accompany increasing age and reacts psychologically to these irretrievable losses (Reichenbach & Mathers 1959; Birren 1965).

Sense organs function less efficiently as the individual grows

[12] For very readable reviews of the current biological theories of aging, see Bjorksten 1969; Shock 1960, 1966.

older (Charles 1965). Excellent and extensive reviews of the sensory and perceptual changes which accompany the aging process appear in Birren's *Handbook of Aging and the Individual* (1959). Weiss's chapter on sensory functions describes impairment as affecting the organism's ability to interact with its external or internal environment. "If the impairment is not too severe, the organism may be able to compensate for the deficit by a variety of means, such as using a different modality, either in addition to or in lieu of the impaired modality, or by intensifying the stimulus or prolonging its time of action" (Weiss 1959, p. 503). Weiss categorizes sensory decrements into "non-neural" (e.g., reduction of the pupillary aperture and increased rigidity of the middle-ear structures) and "neural" (such as reduction in nerve-cell populations and the resulting reduction in the capacity of the nerves to transmit information). Braun's (1959) chapter on perceptual processes also presents the data which shows reduced perceptual abilities in the elderly as well as data indicating that many sensory phenomena have *not* been related to aging (e.g., light adaptation, after-images, and color contrast). Braun also reviews studies which suggest that the poorer performance by aged individuals may reflect a change in a "general speed factor" underlying many perceptual processes. The increasing inability to perceive stimuli has an obvious effect on the person aside from physical loss, since an attendant loss is communication with the world around him.

Welford (1959) concluded that psychomotor-performance abilities decrease with age, primarily due to limitations of the central mechanisms (e.g., perception, translation from perception to action, shaping and initiating of reaction), though peripheral organs may set limits in tasks requiring fine sensory discriminations or strenuous muscular activity. Welford suggested industrial implications of psychomotor studies. Jobs requiring lower rapidity of actions and less extremely complex series tasks could be handled well by older people. Finally, Botwinick and Thompson (1968) implied the difficulties in labeling old people as a group in ability level. In their study, though their older subjects were significantly slower in a reaction-time task than "young athletes," they did not differ significantly from young "non-athletes."

Senility, the pathologic entity frequently occurring in late senescence, has been linked with physiological processes. (Linden & Courtney [1953], stress that this term should not be confused with normal predeath deterioration). In most psychiatric institutions in the United States, more than 35 percent of the patients are over 60 years of age (Wolff 1963). Busse (1959) has summarized and discussed the major psychopathological states frequently appearing in older patients. These include disorders caused by or associated with impairment of brain-tissue function, disorders associated with disturbances of metabolism, growth, or nutrition, and disorders of psychogenic origin with no clearly associated physical cause or structural alteration.

Intelligence and Achievement

More controversial than the area of physiological changes in old age is the area of intelligence and ability to perform, particularly when there are mental requirements.

A decline in total intelligence test scores, as age progresses, has been established by many (Miles & Miles 1932; Jones & Conrad 1933; Wechsler 1944). After reviewing several I.Q. test studies, Chown and Heron (1965) report that the verbal-subtest scores do *not* decline (and may even increase) until very late in life, whereas performance-test scores decline early and continuously. Owens (1953) found more gains than losses in Army Alpha subtest performance when a group of Iowa State College students who were freshmen in 1919 were retested in 1950.

Thomae (1968) reviewed several recent studies which reflected a high degree of stability of important intellectual functioning as people became older. For example, in a population of octogenarians and nonagenarians, Klonoff and Kennedy (1965) found no significant performance differences on the Wechsler-memory scale as compared with 65-year-old subjects. Heron and Chown (1967) found high age stability in linguistically bound capacities.

Test performance involving learning and memory processes demonstrate in general decreasing abilities with age (e.g., Kay 1951; Botwinick, Brinley & Robbin 1959; Ruch 1934; Korchin & Basowitz 1957; Bromley 1958; Eisdorfer, Axelrod & Wilkie 1963; Inglis, Ankus, & Sykes 1968). It has been pointed out by Jerome (1959), however, that a number of factors related to human aging may favor younger subjects, such as motivation level, speed of performance, and physiological status. Similarly, Butler (1963a, 1963b) discussed the "ego function" in memory by suggesting that the "here and now" may be painful or dull for oldsters and therefore motivation to remember is low. Remote memories ("reminiscences") may, on the other hand, remain vivid. McNulty and Caird (1966, 1967) hypothesized that elderly people have difficulty in the capacity to "store" memory, whereas Schonfield (1965, 1967a) proposed that the difficulty lies in retrieving memories from storage.

Memory loss, a component in many senile psychoses, may result from a feeling of uselessness and retreat or withdrawal into the past in attempt to escape coping with death (Morgan 1965). Others support the notion that memory disorders exhibited by some senile patients result from disturbances in learning ability (Inglis 1958; Caird 1966).

Butler (1965) found that a "senile quality" sample and a "nonsenile quality" sample did not differ significantly in chronological age, which again reminds us of the great variability within aged populations.

There are obviously great *individual differences* in old people's memory abilities. Beard (1967), for example, found mentally alert subjects with abilities to remember past events in her sample of centenarians.

In a review of reaction and movement time, Chown and Heron (1965) summarize evidence which suggests that latency time increases with time. Learned skills and very simple movements may not be affected, however, until very late in life.

The great individual differences are also found in the display of interests and in the accomplishments of older people. Hobby participation may increase with age up to a point (Cavan et al. 1949), especially right after retirement (Briggs 1938), but drops off as very old age is reached. In studying some 200 biographies, Frenkel and Brunswik established with Bühler (1933a) the occurrence of performance peaks in certain types of creative persons at late ages. Persons whose creativity is based more on what Bühler has called "mentality" rather than on "vitality" are associated with those whose productions may culminate in late years. Immanuel Kant's most important works were written in his sixties and seventies. Grandma Moses, who began to paint at 67, and created pictures into her nineties, is a popular example.

"Even now," she said at 90, "I don't feel old." Accounts of oldsters past 80 who have made substantial and distinctive contributions exist as impressive reminders that aging does not necessarily imply diminished usefulness (Pressey 1958; Pressey & Pressey 1967). Lehman (1953) gives accounts of some 100 persons past 70 years of age who made brilliant discoveries or created other notable works. He also found high income levels and many types of important leadership positions in late adulthood extending into old age.

PSYCHOLOGICAL AND SOCIAL ADJUSTMENTS TO OLD AGE

Aside from physical declines and illnesses, most aging persons must contend with making many other readjustments (Havighurst 1953). These include retirement from work, economic and financial decrements, new living quarters, filling leisure time, forced abdication of more active hobbies and interests, the role of one's children, depression, dependency, deaths of marriage partners and other family members and close friends, and coping with the imminent possibility of death. These factors often result in the necessity of changing one's self-concept. Some of these situations will be discussed in more detail in this section.

Retirement. Retirement, particularly if it is involuntary and set at a predetermined time, is traumatic for many aging people (McConnell 1960). Though the loss or lowering of income may be a disadvantage, Havighurst (1960) suggested that the *major* disadvantage of retirement is a moral or spiritual one, since the meanings attached to one's work have numerous noneconomic significances, such as basis for sense of worth and locus of social participation. Bühler (1968a) has described the loss of status accompanying retirement through case history material.

Reichard, Livson, and Peterson (1962) describe five types of retirees based on styles which have developed through their lifetimes: (1) the mature individual who accepts himself and life realistically and without regret; (2) the "rocking chair" individual who, because of passivity in the past welcomes a chance to be free from responsibility and dependent; (3) the "armored" individual whose well-developed defenses continue to serve him in old age; (4) the "angry" individual who continues to blame his own weaknesses on others; and (5) the "self-hater" who was disappointed with his life and continues to look back in disappointment and self-resentment.

Havighurst (1960) described advantages of retirement as including freedom from the irksome restraints of work and the opportunity to do the things time had not permitted before. Yet, one of the principal problems facing the aging person, with no definite tasks, is to learn how to organize his time (Bühler 1968b).

Because the life expectancy in the United States continues to rise, with some speculations that the general expected life span will reach the mid-seventies or above in the not-too-distant future (Shock 1968), retirement and leisure-time use become crucial areas of study. Implementations of policies and programs to assist the older person in adjusting to retirement might include allowing the individual maximum choice concerning the age and circumstance of his retirement, establishing retirement counseling programs, assuring reasonable financial support in old age, and finding ways to realistically assure the retired person that there is still a place for him (Havighurst 1960; Chen 1968).

Living Arrangements and Institutionalization. Older people must often find new living arrangements due to such factors as financial decrements, the inability to maintain a home and grounds which had previously accommodated a larger family, and decreased health levels requiring special care.

It has been asserted that living congregations of old people may facilitate satisfactory adjustment due to greater opportunities for social interaction and the provision of a normative system to which older people are capable of adapting (Hoyt 1954; Weil 1955; Roscow 1964; Anderson 1965; Messer 1967, 1968). The fact that most programs for the elderly have been based on the assumption that radical environmental changes are essential has been criticized (Banay 1964; Schwartz & Papas 1967). However, carefully planned environments to assist the older person with his needs have demonstrated success (Weil 1966; Carp 1967).

Institutionalized older people generally make poorer adjustments to old age than those who live outside institutions (Davidson & Kruglov 1952). Yet as Busse (1967) points out, declining physical health often brings about the decision to enter an institution. Elderly people forced to live in institutions tend to deteriorate (Bennett & Nahemow 1965; Davidson & Kruglov 1952) as opposed to more satisfactory adjustments of those accepting institutional living (Pam 1954; Bennett 1963).

Dependency. Becoming dependent on others after a long period of independency is a situation in which many aging persons find themselves. Kalish (1967) points out how painful this may be, since our culture shows little indulgence for dependent behavior. Further, dependency may be accelerated by the treatment received from families or hospital personnel (Bennett 1963). The feelings of helplessness that follow may take the form of lowered pride, dignity and loss of purpose and identity (Goldfarb 1969). Blenkner (1969) lists four types of dependency: economic, physical, mental, and social. Clark (1969) adds neurotic dependency as a culturally conditioned character trait.

Depression. Among the severe emotional difficulties in old people, depressive disorders are the most common (Levin 1963; Davies 1965). Even in the "normal" aged, depressive periods are common (Busse 1965). Zung (1967) found the major causes of depression in his normal aged population relating to apathy, disinterest, feelings of inferiority, and loss of self-esteem. Butler (1967) also links depression to physical change, hospitalization, and surgery, but warns against linking any psychiatric disorders as being *caused* by physical change. Chen (1968) blames the cultural pattern on overemphasizing youth and devaluating age as leading to the self-rejection and inner-directed hostility that results in depression so commonly characteristic of the aged. The suicide rate, when old age advances, takes a notable trend upwards (Busse 1959).

Attitudes and Self-Concept. There is evidence to suggest that older people are more dogmatic and rigid in their attitudes

than younger people (Riegel & Riegel 1960; Wier 1961; Chown 1961). Neugarten et al. (1964) described intrapsychic personality changes in old age. Some general conclusions were the change of active to passive mastery in old age, an increasing preoccupation with one's own inner life, and a constriction in the ability to deal with complicated or challenging situations. In the socioadaptive spheres of personality, however, these researchers found that such factors as work status, health, financial resources, and marital status were more decisive than chronological age in influencing degrees of adjustment.

There is also evidence to suggest that as a person grows older, he has a less positive regard for himself (Kuhlen 1959). Perlin and Butler (1963) speak of an "identity crisis" occurring in many aged persons. More knowledge is needed, however, about the processes whereby a person changes his attitudes and feelings about himself as his social and situation contexts change around him (Bortner 1967). With the cultural accent on youth in our American culture and the increasing futility in trying to look and act and *be* youthful as time passes, it is no wonder that old people may suffer from deflating self-concepts and depression. To be designated as "old" or "aged" or "elderly," though not meant as unkind labels, contains an element of despair as we have come to think of the terms. Studies have shown that many elderly people refuse to identify themselves as "old" or "elderly" (Kutner, Fanshell, Togo & Langer 1956; Kuhlen 1959; Zola 1962). Butler (1967) found many aged people refusing to even look at themselves in a mirror.

Schonfield (1967b) has come up with a possible "antedote" to the negative label connotations which, in a "self-fulfilling prophecy" sort of way, may have positive affects. He proposes calling the process of living enjoyably through the later adult years "geronting." The "geronters" can teach all of us how to be successful in our later years and hence attain a high-status teaching obligation as well as giving younger people something to possibly look forward to! Schonfield and Trimble (1967) interviewed subjects in various age groups, including older people, and report that there are advantages to aging which rarely get incorporated into the stereotypes of the aged population. Freedom to engage in activities for their own sake (rather than as a means to some pressured ends) and freedom to be self-directed were among the advantages younger people rarely have.

Orientations to Death. The problem of death is one central theme of the final stage in the life cycle (Butler 1968; Bühler 1968b). The study of attitudes towards one's imminent death in old age has recently received attention (Kastenbaum 1966). How a person feels about death is most probably related to how his entire life span has been patterned (Erikson 1963; Wolff 1966). Many aging people begin to fear death (Morgan 1965) but may not have previously discussed death with others (Christ 1961). Birren et al. (1963) found a reasonable adjustment to the concept of death in slightly over half of their healthy-aged sample. About one-third expressed fear and the remainder used denial defenses. Williams and Wirth (1965) reported that the majority of their healthy-aging sample feared becoming disabled and burdensome more than they feared death. Munnichs (1969) suggests that different attitudes toward death exist depending on whether the person is growing old or has reached very old age, though others stress personality and situational variables as more important determinants of death attitudes (Rhudick & Dibner 1961; Swenson 1961).

People with strong religious beliefs are less likely to fear death (Jeffers, Nichols & Eisdorfer 1961; Swenson 1961; Feifel 1956). How to handle the concept of death with old and dying persons is another problem which has received attention (Verwoerdt 1966; Hinton 1967; Butler 1968).

Bühler (1961b, 1962a) discussed the process of "autobiographical retrospect" in which the individual may find feelings of fulfillment in looking over the whole of his life and hopefully finding in this survey that he contributed something that gave happiness or was of help to others. Leaving something of value behind is many peoples' motive through the ages, but increasingly so toward the end of life. Butler (1963b) also discussed the "life review" process in old age which may account for the increased reminiscences in older people. It can contribute to depression or other mental disorders (such as feelings of failure, panic, excessive rumination, and suicide) or the evolution of candor, serenity, or personality integration.

"Successful" and "Unsuccessful" Aging. An aspect of gerontology which has attracted large numbers of social scientists is factors affecting "successful" and "unsuccessful" patterns of adjusting to the later years of life. Currently one out of every eleven persons in the United States is over 65 years old (18.5 million) and an increase to 25 million is expected within the next twenty years. Thus, information bearing on successful aging patterns is more than mere scientific curiosity, it is a crucial social issue! And it is, at this point, where the paucity of material dealing with the entire life span constitutes a tragedy, as we may well be too late to step in when people are 65 and become concerned with their development and adjustments. As Allport (1961a) has stated, "All of what one was bears directly on what each individual will be in old age." This simple but wise statement indicates that more attention should be given to the developmental aspects of that great gap of time—*middle-adulthood*.

Erikson's writings extended psychoanalytic theory past the stage of maturity. At the last of his three stages of adulthood, the person with a healthy personality stands ready to defend the dignity of his life. The ego has consolidated from all of the previous stages and life finally has an order and meaning. Erikson calls this outcome "ego integrity" and considers this state to be the goal of human development. In contrast, another outcome of the final life crisis can be "despair" and is characterized by lack of ego integration with resultant fears of death, disappointment or disgust with the previous years of life, and a grim realization that time is now too short to try out life again. This despair is often disguised as misanthropy or a chronic contemptuous dislike of certain institutions or people (Erikson 1959, 1963).

Peck (1956) noted that Erikson's final stage extended over a very long period of time—some forty or more years. He further subdivided Erikson's final life stage into "ego differentiation vs. work-role preoccupation" (dealing with the person's ability to make role shifts following retirement), "body transcendence vs. body preoccupation" (dealing with the ability of the person to accept and cope with failing health and loss of function), and "ego transcendence vs. ego preoccupation" (dealing with the person's ability to take pleasure in the constructive and meaningful effect his own life has had on others who will continue to live after he has gone).

Bühler (1968a) notes that one hardly ever finds a completely fulfilled life. "Denials, losses, and failures seem unavoidable but many lives are at least partially, or even essentially, fulfilled" (p. 402). Successful experiences in sex, love, and accomplishments are among the major life areas she feels lead to self-realization and subsequently fulfillment.

Cumming and Henry (1961) are the major proponents of the "disengagement" theory of successful or "adjusted" aging. "The theory of disengagement holds that intrinsic to aging is a process of mutual severing of ties between the individual and the social system in which he lives, reduced normative control by his social system, and reduced obligations to it" (p. 3). Their extensive work, from the Kansas City Study of Adult Life project, set out to identify the patterns of healthy and economically secure old people.

The concept of disengagement and the theoretical formulations generated have come under critical review by the original proponents (Cumming 1963; Henry 1964). Havighurst, Neugarten, and Tobin (1964) and Tobin and Neugarten (1961) found greater life satisfaction with *less* disengagement. Continuing active interaction with the social environment has been found to contribute to the aging individual's morale (Cavan, Burges, Havighurst & Goldhamer 1949; Havighurst & Albrecht 1953; Maddox & Eisendorfer 1962).

Havighurst (1963) has contrasted the disengagement theory of successful aging with what he terms the "activity" theory of successful aging. The activity theory asserts that successful aging means maintaining, to the fullest possible, the activities and attitudes of middle age.

The encouragement of continued activity in older persons has been studied by several authors. Using institutionalized veterans, Kaiman and his associates have concluded that activity is "good" for old people and that any decline found in activity in the aged is an artifact based on variables, such as poor health, other than aging per se (Kaiman, Desroches & Ballard 1965, 1966; Kaiman 1969). Factors such as physical disability, psychological adjustment, social class education, and loss of peers have been related to declining activities—none of which need be related to the aging process itself (Kaplan 1960; De Grazia 1961; Jeffers & Nichols 1961; Veld 1962; Zborowski & Eyde 1962; Butler 1963a; Roscow 1963; Tallmer & Kutner 1969).

May (1966) supported the encouragement of elderly persons participating in purposeful activities. He found, using home-resident subjects, that many participating in the activity program showed improvement in physical functioning, emotional and mental health, and socializing abilities as compared to a control group which was matched on the variables of age and physical characteristics. Other studies have also demonstrated improvements in adjustment of aged patients following activity program participation (Donahue 1963; Filer & O'Connell 1962; Filer & O'Connell 1964).

Williams and Wirth (1965), using the Kansas City Study of Adult Life sample, presented a wealth of extended case-history material describing characteristics of successful and unsuccessful agers. Factors which seem to characterize successful aging subjects according to their criteria were "autonomy," "persistance," "clarity and saliency of style," "good use of action energy," "flexibility," "life satisfaction," and "keeping active." These authors concluded that aging *should* be a period of attaining new social goals and of receiving new kinds and levels of rewards.

Bühler (1961a) suggested, on the basis of interviews, that there are four groups of older people: those who wish to rest and relax; those who wish to remain active; those who are dissatisfied with the past but resigned to old age; and those who felt their lives had been meaningless and are frustrated and guilty in old age. A later study (Bühler, Brind & Horner 1968) found clusters of older respondents on Bühler's life goal inventory which generally paralleled the above four groupings.

When one realizes that the old age situation means different things to different people, depending on their individual life styles, environmental pressures, and biological deteriorations or disabilities, the prescription of *a* successful pattern of aging seems unrealistic (Bühler 1961b; Jones 1961; Havighurst 1961; Reichard, Livson, & Peterson 1962; Perlin & Butler 1963; Butler 1967; Pincus 1967).

It follows from the previously reported studies that in the fifth phase, towards the end of life, the picture of the individual person may be a varying one. It may be that of a person who like one patient said when near death, "I am glad it is all over," or else as a well-known Swiss woman physician, Marie Heim-Vögtleim, said shortly before she died, "There is nothing in my life that I wish had been different. Nothing. I am satisfied."

References

ADELSON, J. The mystique of adolescence. *Psychiatry*, 1964, *27*, 1–8.

AINSWORTH, M. D. Patterns of attachment behavior shown by the infant in interaction with his mother. *Merrill-Palmer Quarterly*, 1964, *10*, 51–58.

ALDRICH, C. A., SUNG, C., and KNOP, C. The crying of newly born babies: I. Community phase. *Journal of Pediatrics*, 1945a, *26*, 313–26.

—— The crying of newly born babies: II. The individual phase. *Journal of Pediatrics*, 1945b, *27*, 89–96.

ALEXANDER, P. Certain characteristics of the self as related to affection. *Child Development*, 1951, *22*, 285–90.

ALLEN, R. M. Nine quarterly Rorschach records of a young girl. *Child Development*, 1955, *26*, 63–69.

ALLPORT, G. W. *The use of personal documents in psychological science.* New York: Social Science Research Council, 1942.

—— *Pattern and growth in personality.* New York: Holt, Rinehart & Winston, 1961a.

—— Values and our youth. *Teachers College Record*, 1961b, *63*, 211–19.

—— The general and unique in psychological science. *Journal of Personality*, 1962, *30*, 405–22.

—— (ed.) *Letters from Jenny.* New York: Harcourt, Brace & World, 1965.

ALMY, M. Spontaneous play: an avenue for intellectual development. *Child Study*, 1966, *28*, 2–15.

ALTMANN, M. Naturalistic studies of maternal care in moose and elk. *In* H. R. Rheingold (ed.), *Maternal behavior in mammals.* New York: John Wiley, 1963.

ALTSCHULER, R. H., and HATTWICK, L. B. W. *Painting and personality: a study of young children*, vols. 1 & 2. Chicago: University of Chicago Press, 1947.

AMBROSE, J. A. The concept of a critical period for the development of social responsiveness in early human infancy. *In* B. M. Foss, *Determinants of infant behavior, II.* New York: John Wiley, 1963.

AMES, L. B. Motor correlates of infant crying. *Journal of Genetic Psychology*, 1941, *59*, 239–47.

—— Development of perception in the young child as observed in responses to the Rorschach Test blots. *Journal of Genetic Psychology*, 1953, *82*, 183–204.

ANASTASI, A. Standardized ability testing. *In* P. H. Mussen (ed.), *Handbook of research methods in child development.* New York: John Wiley, 1960.

—— and D'ANGELO, R. Y. A comparison of Negro and white preschool children in language development and Goodenough Draw-a-man I. Q. *Journal of Genetic Psychology*, 1952, *81*, 147–65.

ANDERSON, C. G. A developmental study of dogmatism during adolescence with reference to sex differences. *Journal of Abnormal and Social Psychology*, 1962, *65*, 132–35.

ANDERSON, J. E. The limitations of infant and preschool tests in the measurement of intelligence. *Journal of Psychology*, 1939, *8*, 351–79.

—— Personality organization in children. *American Psychologist*, 1948, *3*, 409–16.

—— Methods of child psychology. *In* L. Carmichael (ed.), *Manual of child psychology.* New York: John Wiley, 1954.

ANDERSON, N. N. Institutionalization, interaction and self-conception in aging. *In* A. M. Rose and W. A. Peterson (eds.), *Older people and their social world.* Philadelphia: Davis, 1965.

ANSHEN, R. N. (ed.) *The family: Its function and destiny.* New York: Harper, 1949.

ANTHONEY, T. R. The ontogeny of greeting, grooming, and sexual motor patterns in captive baboons (Superspecies *Papio cynocephalus*). *Behaviour*, 1968, *31*, (3–4), 358–72.

ARASTEH, A. R. *Creativity in the life cycle*, vol. 2. Leiden, Netherlands: E. J. Brill, 1968.

AUSUBEL, D. *Theory and problems of child development.* New York: Grune & Stratton, 1957.

BAENNINGER, L. P. Comparison of behavioural development in socially isolated and grouped rats. *Animal Behaviour*, 1957, *15*, 312–23.

BAKWIN, H. The emotional status at birth. *American Journal of Diseases in Children*, 1947, *74*, 373–76.

BALDWIN, A. L. The study of child behavior and development. *In* P. H. Mussen (ed.), *Handbook of research methods in child development.* New York: John Wiley, 1960.

—— *Theories of child development*, New York: John Wiley, 1968.

—— KALHORN, J., and BREESE, F. Patterns of parent behavior. *Psychological Monographs*, 1945, *58* (3.).

BALDWIN, B. T., BUSBY, L. M., and GARSIDE, H. V. A study of some bones of the hand, wrist, and lower forearm by means of roentgenograms. *University of Iowa Studies in Child Welfare*, 1928, no. 4.

BALSER, B. H. (ed.) *Psychotherapy of the adolescent.* New York: International Universities Press, 1957.

BANAY, I. Social services for the aged: A reconsideration. *In* R. Kastenbaum (ed.), *New thoughts on old age.* New York: Springer-Verlag, 1964.

BANDURA, A., and WALTERS, R. H. *Social learning and personality development.* New York: Holt, 1963.

BANHAM, A. The development of affectionate behavior in infancy. *Journal of Genetic Psychology.* 1950, *76*, 283–89.

BARKER, R. G. *Ecological psychology.* Stanford, Calif.: Stanford University Press, 1968.

—— and WRIGHT, H. F. *Midwest and its children.* Evanston, Ill.: Row, Peterson, 1954.

BARRON, F. The psychology of the creative writer. Paper presented at the American Psychological Association meeting, Chicago, 1965.

BARTOSHUK, A. K. Response decrement with repeated elicitation of human neonatal cardiac acceleration to sound. *Journal of Comparative and Physiological Psychology*, 1962, *55*, 9–13.

BATESON, P. P. G. The characteristics and context of imprinting. *Biological Review*, 1966, *41*, 177–220.

BATH, J. A., and LEWIS, E. C. Attitudes of young female adults toward some areas of parent-adolescent conflict. *Journal of Genetic Psychology*, 1962, *100*, 241–53.

BAUMRIND, D. Authoritarian vs. authoritative parental control. *Adolescence*, 1968, *3*, 255–72.

BAYLEY, N. A study of crying in infants during mental and physical tests. *Journal of Genetic Psychology*, 1932, *40*, 306–29.

—— Mental growth during the first three years. *Genetic Psychology Monographs*, 1933, *14* (1).

—— The development of motor abilities during the first three years. *Monographs of the Society for Research in Child Development*, 1943a *14*, 47–90.

—— Size and body build of adolescents in relation to rate of skeletal maturing. *Child Development*, 1943a, *14*, 47–90.

——— Skeletal maturing in adolescence as a basis for determining percentage of completed growth. *Child Development*, 1943*b*, *14*, 1–46.

——— Some increasing parent-child similarities during the growth of children. *Journal of Educational Psychology*, 1954, *45*, 1–21.

——— Research in child development: A longitudinal perspective. *Merrill-Palmer Quarterly*, 1965, *11*, 183–208.

——— Behavioral correlates of mental growth: Birth to thirty-six years. *American Psychologist*, 1968, *23*, 1–17.

——— and ODEN, M. The maintenance of intellectual ability in gifted adults. *Journal of Gerontology*, 1955, *10*, 91–107.

BEACH, F. A., and JAYNES, J. Effects of early experience upon the behavior of animals. *Psychological Bulletin*, 1954, *51*, 239–63.

BEARD, B. B. Social and psychological correlates of residual memory in centenarians. *Gerontologist*, 1967, 7, 120–24.

BELBIN, R. M. Difficulties of older workers in industry. *Occupational Psychology*, 1953, *27*, 177–90.

BELL, G. D. Processes in the formation of adolescent's aspirations. *Social Forces*, 1963, *42*, 179–95.

BELL, R. Q. Convergence: An accelerated longitudinal approach. *Child Development*, 1953, *24*, 145–52.

——— An experimental test of the accelerated longitudinal approach. *Child Development*, 1954, *25*, 281–86.

——— Retrospective and prospective views of early personality development. *Merrill-Palmer Quarterly*, 1960*a*, *6*, 131–44.

——— Relations between behavior manifestations in the human neonate. *Child Development*, 1960*b*, *31*, 463–77.

——— Three tests for sex differences in tactile sensitivity in the newborn. *Biology of the Neonate*, 1964, 7 335–47.

BELL, R. R. *Marriage and family interaction*. Homewood, Ill.: Dorsey, 1963.

——— Parent-child conflict in sexual values. *In* P. H. Mussen, J. J. Conger, and J. Kagan (eds.), *Readings in child development and Personality*. New York: Harper & Row, 1970.

BELL, R. W. Note: emotionality after mild, chronic stress as a function of infantile handling. *Psychological Reports*, 1964, *14*, 657–58.

BELLUGI, U. The development of interrogative structures in children's speech. *In* K. Riegel (ed.) *The development of language functions*. Ann Arbor: Michigan Language Development Program, 1965, no. 8.

——— and BROWN, R. (eds.) The acquisition of language. *Monographs of the Society for Research in Child Development*, 1964, *29*, (1).

BENNETT, E. L., KRECH, D., and ROSENZWEIG, M. R. Reliability and regional specificity of cerebral effects of environmental complexity and training. *Journal of Comparative and Physiological Psychology*, 1964, *57*, 440–41.

BENNETT, R. The meaning of institutional life. *Gerontologist*, 1963, *3*, 117–25.

——— and NAHEMOW, L. The relations between social isolation, socialization, and adjustment in residents of a home for the aged. *In* M. P. Lawton, and F. G. Lawton (eds.), *Mental impairment of the aged*. Philadelphia: Philadelphia Geriatric Center, 1965.

BENTZ, V. J. A. A test-retest experiment on the relationship between age and mental ability. *American Psychologist*, 1953, *8*, 319–20.

BEREITER, C. Fluency ability of pre-school children. *Journal of Genetic Psychology*, 1961, *98*, 47–48.

——— and ENGELMANN, S. *Teaching disadvantaged children in the preschool*. Englewood Cliffs, N. J.: Prentice-Hall, 1966.

BERKSON, G. Development of an infant in a captive gibbon group. *Journal of Genetic Psychology*, 1966, *108*, 311–25.

BERLYNE, D. E. *Conflict, arousal and curiosity*. New York: McGraw-Hill, 1960.

——— and FROMMER, F. D. Some determinants of the incidence and content of children's questions. *Child Development*, 1966, *37*, 177–89.

BERNARD, J. (ed.) Teen-age culture. *Annals of the Academy of Political and Social Science*, 1961, no. 338.

BERNSTEIN, A. Some relations between techniques of feeding and training during infancy and certain behavior in childhood. *Genetic Psychology Monographs*, 1955, *51*, 3–44.

BERSOT, H. Développement réactionnel et réflexe plantaire du bébé né avant terme à celui de deux ans. *Schweizer Archiv für Neurologie und Psychiatrie*, 1920, 7, 212–39.

BETTLEHEIM, B. The problem of generations. *In* E. H. Erikson (ed.) *The challenge of youth*. New York: Doubleday, 1963.

BIJOU, S. W. Ages, stages, and the naturalization of human development. *American Psychologist*, 1968, *23*, 419–27.

——— and BAER, D. M. *Child development*, vol. I. *A systematic and empirical theory*. New York: Appleton-Century-Crofts, 1961.

——— *Child development*, vol. II. *Universal stage of infancy*. New York: Appleton-Century-Crofts, 1965.

BINET, A. *L'étude expérimentale de l'intelligence*. Paris: Ancienne Librairie Schleicher, 1903.

——— and SIMON, T. Méthodes nouvelles pour le diagnostic du niveau intellectuel des anormaux. *Année Psychologie*, 1905, *11*, 191–244.

BINGHAM, W. E., and GRIFFITHS, W. J., JR. The effect of different environments during infancy on adult behavior in the rats. *Journal of Comparative and Physiological Psychology*, 1952, *45*, 307–12.

BIRNS, B., BLANK, M., and BRIDGER, W. H. The effectiveness of various soothing techniques on human neonates. *Psychosomatic Medicine*, 1966, *28*, 313–22.

——— and ESCALONA, S. K. Behavioral inhibition in neonates produced by auditory stimuli. *Child Development*, 1965, *36*, 639–45.

BIRREN, J. E. Age differences in startle reaction time of the rat to noise and electric shock. *Journal of Gerontology*, 1955, *10*, 437–40.

——— Reactions to loss and the process of aging: interrelations of environmental changes, psychological capacities, and physiological status. *In* M. A. Berezin and S. H. Cath (eds.), *Geriatric Psychiatry*. New York: International Universities Press, 1965.

——— Research on aging: A frontier of science and social gain. *Gerontologist*, 1968, *8*, 7–13.

——— (ed.) *Handbook of aging and the individual*. Chicago: University of Chicago Press, 1959.

——— (ed.). *Relations of development and aging*. Springfield, Ill.: Charles C Thomas, 1964.

——— BUTLER, R. N., GREENHOUSE, S. W., SOKOLOFF, L., and YARROW, M. R. (eds.) *Human aging: A biological and behavioral study*. Bethesda, Md.: U. S. Department of Health, Education & Welfare, 1963.

BIRREN, J. E., IMUS, H. A., and WINDLE, W. F. (eds.) *The process of aging in the nervous system*. Springfield, Ill.: Charles C Thomas, 1959.

BIRREN, J. E., and KAY, H. Swimming speed of the albino rat: I. Age and sex differences. *Journal of Gerontology*, 1958, *13*, 374–77.

BISCHOF, L. J. *Adult psychology*. New York: Harper & Row, 1969.

BJORKSTEN, J. Enzymes in aging. *In Enzymes in mental health*. New York: Neuberg Society, Third Symposium on Progress in Biochemistry and Therapeutics, 1966, pp. 84–94.

——— The crosslinkage theory of aging. *Journal of the American Geriatric Society*, 1968, *23*, 408–27.

——— Theories. *In* S. Bakerman (ed.), *Aging life processes*. Springfield, Ill.: Charles C Thomas, 1969.

BLENKNER, M. The normal dependencies of aging. *In* R. A. Kalish (ed.), *The dependencies of old people*. Ann Arbor, Mich.: Institute of Gerontology, 1969.

BLOCK, V. L. Conflicts of adolescents with their mothers. *Journal of Abnormal and Social Psychology*, 1937, *32*, 193–206.

BLOOD, R. O., and WOLFE, D. M. *Husbands and wives*. Glencoe, Ill.: Free Press, 1960.

BLOS, P. *The adolescent personality*. New York: Appleton-Century-Crofts, 1941.

BLUM, G. S. Prepuberty and adolescence. *Psychoanalytic theories of personality*. New York: McGraw-Hill, 1953.

BLUM, L. H. The discotheque and the phenomenon of alone-togetherness: A study of the young person's response to the frug and comparable current dances. *Adolescence*, 1967, *1*, 351–66.

BLUMENTHAL, H. T. *Aging around the world: Medical and clinical aspects of aging*. New York: Columbia University Press, 1962.

——— and BERNES, A. W. Autoimmunity and aging. *In* B. L. Strehler (ed.), *Advances in gerontological research*, vol. I, New York: Academic Press, 1964.

BOLLES, R. C., and WOODS, P. J. The ontogeny of behaviour in the albino rat. *Animal Behaviour*, 1964, *12*, 427–41.

BOLTON, T. L. The growth of memory in school children. *American Journal of Psychology*, 1892, *4*, 362–80.

BORTNER, R. W. Adult development or idiosyncratic change? A plea for the developmental approach. *Gerontologist*, 1966, *6*, 159–64.

——— Personality and social psychology in the study of aging. *Gerontologist*, 1967, 7, 23–36.

BOSSARD, J. H. S., and BOLL, E. S. *The sociology of child development*, 4th ed. New York: Harper & Row, 1966.

BOTWINICK, J., BRINLEY, J. F., and ROBBIN, J. S. Further results concerning the effect of motivation by electric shocks on reaction-time in relation to age. *American Journal of Psychology*, 1959, 72, 140.

BOTWINICK, J., and THOMPSON, L. W. Age difference in reaction time: an artifact? *Gerontologist*, 1968, 8, 25–28.

BOVARD, E. W. The effects of early handling on viability of the albino rat. *Psychological Review*, 1958, 65, 257–71.

BOWER, T. G. R. The visual world of infants. *Scientific American*, 1966, 215, 80–92.

BOWERMAN, C. E., and KINCH, J. W. Changes in family and peer orientation of children between the fourth and tenth grades. *Social Forces*, 1959, 37, 205–11.

BOWERS, W. H. An appraisal of worker characteristics as related to age. *Journal of Applied Psychology*, 1952, 36, 296–300.

BOWLBY, J. *Maternal care and mental health*. Geneva: World Health Organization, 1951.

——— The nature of the child's tie to his mother. *International Journal of Psychoanalysis*, 1958, 39, 1–34.

BOWYER, L. R. *The Lowenfeld World Technique*. Oxford: Pergamon Press, 1970.

BRADLEY, W. H. Correlates of vocational preferences. *Genetic Psychology Monographs*, 1943, 28, 99–169.

BRACKBILL, Y. Extinction of the smiling response in infants as a function of reinforcement schedule. *Child Development*, 1958, 29, 114–24.

——— and KOLTSOVA, M. M. Conditioning and learning. *In* Y. Brackbill (ed.) *Infancy and early childhood*. New York: Free Press, 1967.

BRACKETT, C. S. Laughing and crying of preschool children. *Journal of Experimental Education*, 1933, 2, 119–26.

BRADBURY, D. E. The contribution of the child study movement in child psychology. *Psychological Bulletin*, 1937, 34, 21–38.

BRAINE, M. D. S. The ontogeny of English phrase structure: the first phase. *Language*, 1963, 39, 1–13.

BRAUN, H. W. Perceptual processes. *In* J. Birren (ed.), *Handbook of aging and the individual*. Chicago: University of Chicago Press, 1959.

BRAZELTON, T. B. Psychophysiologic reactions in the neonate. *Journal of Pediatrics*, 1961, 58, 508–12.

——— Observations of the neonate. *Journal of the American Academy of Child Psychiatry*, 1962, 1, 38–58.

BRECKENRIDGE, M. E., and VINCENT, E. L. *Child Development*, 5th ed. Philadelphia: Saunders, 1965.

BRIDGER, W. H. Sensory habituation and discrimination in the newborn. *American Journal of Psychiatry*, 1961, 117, 991–96.

——— Ethological concepts and human development. *In* J. Wortes (ed.), *Recent advances in biological psychiatry*. New York: Plenum Press, 1962.

——— and REISER, M. F. Psychophysiological studies of the neonate: an approach toward the methodological and theoretical problems involved. *Psychosomatic Medicine*, 1959, 21, 265–76.

BRIDGES, K. M. Emotional development in early infancy. *Child Development*, 1932, 3, 324–34.

BRIGGS, E. S. How adults in Missouri use their leisure time. *School and Society*, 1938, 47, 805–8.

BRODBECK, A. J., and IRWIN, O. C. The speech behavior of infants without families. *Child Development*, 1946, 17, 145–56.

BRODERICK, C. B., and WEAVER, J. The perceptual context of boy-girl communication. *Journal of Marriage and the Family*, 1968, 30, 618–27.

BRODY, S. *Patterns of mothering*. New York: International Universities Press, 1956.

BROMLEY, D. B. Some effects of age on short-term learning and remembering. *Journal of Gerontology*, 1958, 13, 398–406.

——— *The psychology of human aging*. Baltimore, Md.: Penguin, 1966.

BRONFENBRENNER, U. When is infant stimulation effective? *In* D. C. Glass (ed.), *Biology and behavior: Environmental influences*. New York: Russell Sage Foundation, 1968.

BROOKS, F. D., and SHAFFER, L. F. *Child psychology*. Boston: Houghton Mifflin, 1937.

BROSIN, H. W. Adolescent crises. *New York State Journal of Medicine*, 1967, 67, 2003–11.

BROWN, D. G., and LYNN, D. B. Human sexual development: An outline of components and concepts. *Journal of Marriage and the Family*, 1966, 28, 155–62.

BROWN, J. D. (ed.) *The hippies*. New York: Time-Life, 1967.

BROWN, J. L. Social play of infants. *Proceedings, Society for Research on Child Development*, 1963.

——— States in newborn infants. *Merrill-Palmer Quarterly*, 1964, 10, 313–27.

BROWN, R. The development of Wh questions in child speech. *Journal of Verbal Learning and Verbal Behavior*, 1968, 7, 279–90.

——— and BELLUGI, U. Three processes in the child's acquisition of syntax. *Harvard Educational Review*, 1964, 34, 133–51.

BROWN, R., and FRASER, C. The acquisition of syntax. *In* U. Bellugi and R. Brown (eds.) The acquisition of language. *Monographs of the Society for Research in Child Development*, 1964, 29 (1).

BRUNER, J., OLVER, R., GREENFIELD, P. M., and others. *Studies in cognitive growth*. New York: John Wiley, 1966.

BÜHLER, C. *Das Seelenleben des Jugendlichen*. Jena: Gustav Fischer, 1922.

——— Soziologische und psychologische studien über das erste Lebensjahr. *Quellen und Studien zur Jugendkunde*, 1927a, no. 5.

——— The first reactions of infants. *Quellen und Studien zur Jugendkunde*, 1927b, no. 5.

——— *Kindheit und Jugend*. Jena: Gustav Fischer, 1928.

——— *The first year of life*. New York: Day, 1930.

——— The social behavior of children. *In* C. Murchison (ed.), *Handbook of child psychology*, 2d ed. Worcester, Mass.: Clark University Press, 1931.

——— *Jugendtagebuch und Lebenslauf*. Jena: Gustav Fischer, 1932.

——— *Der menschliche Lebenslauf als psychologisches Problem*. Leipzig: S. Hirzel, 1933a.

——— The social behavior of children. *In* C. Murchison (ed.), *A handbook of child psychology*. 2d ed. Worcester, Mass.: Clark University Press, 1933b.

——— Old age and fulfillment of life with considerations of the use of time in old age. *Acta Psychology*, 1961a, 19, 126–48.

——— Meaningful living in the mature years. *In* R. W. Kleemeier (ed.), *Aging and leisure*. New York: Oxford University Press, 1961b.

——— Genetic aspects of the self. *New York Academy of Sciences Monographs*, 1962a, 96, 730–64.

——— *Values in psychotherapy*. New York: Free Press, 1962b.

——— The life cycle: Structural determinants of goal-setting. *Journal of Humanistic Psychology*, 1966, 6, 37–52.

——— Human life goals in the humanistic perspective. *Journal of Humanistic Psychology*, 1967a, 6, 1–17.

——— Human life as a whole as a central subject of humanistic psychology. *In* J. F. T. Bugental (ed.), *Challenges of humanistic psychology*. New York: McGraw-Hill, 1967b.

——— Fulfillment and failure of life. *In* C. Bühler, and F. Massarik (eds.), *The course of human life*. New York: Springer, 1968a.

——— *Psychology for contemporary living*. New York: Hawthorn, 1968b.

——— The developmental structure of goal setting in group and individual studies. In C. Bühler, and F. Massarik (eds.), *The course of human life*. New York: Springer-Verlag, 1968c.

——— The course of human life as a psychological problem. *Human Development*, 1968d, 11, 184–200.

——— BRIND, A., and HORNER, A. Old age as a phase of human life. *Human Development*, 1968, 11. 53–63.

BÜHLER, C., and EKSTEIN, R. Anthropologische Resultate aus biographischer Forschung. *In* H. Gadamer (ed.), *Eine neue Anthropologie*. Stuttgart: Georg Thieme Verlag, 1973.

BÜHLER, C., and HETZER, H. First understanding of expression in the first year of life. *Psychologie Zeitschrift*, 1928, 107, 50–61.

——— *Testing children's development from birth to school age*. London: Allen & Unwin, 1935.

BÜHLER, C., LUMRY, G. K., and CARROLL, H. The World Test, a projective technique. *Journal of Child Psychiatry*, 1951, 2, 1–81.

BÜHLER, C., and MASSARIK, F. *The course of human life.* New York: Springer-Verlag, 1968.

BÜHLER, K. *Die geistige Entwicklung des Kindes.* Jena: Verlag von Gustav Fischer, 1918.

BURGESS, E. Q., and WALLIN, P. *Engagement and marriage.* Philadelphia: Lippincott, 1953.

BURGESS, E. W., LOCKE, H. J., and THOMES, M. M. *The family from institution to companionship.* New York: American Book Company, 1963.

BURGHARDT, G. M. Chemical-cue preferences of inexperienced snakes: comparative aspects. *Science,* 1967, *157,* 718–21.

―――― and HESS, E. H. Factors influencing the chemical release of prey attack in newborn snakes. *Journal of Comparative and Physiological Psychology,* 1968, *66,* 289–95.

BURKS, B. S., JENSEN, D. W., and TERMAN, L. M. The promise of youth. *In Genetic Studies of Genius,* No. 3, Palo Alto, Calif.: Stanford University Press, 1930.

BURNSTEIN, E. Fear of failure, achievement motivation, and aspiring to prestigeful occupations. *Journal of Abnormal and Social Psychology,* 1963, *67,* 189–93.

BUSSE, E. W. Psychopathology. *In* J. E. Birren (ed.), *Handbook of aging.* Chicago: University of Chicago Press, 1959.

―――― Treatment of the nonhospitalized emotionally disturbed elderly person. *Geriatrics,* 1965, *11,* 173–79.

―――― Geriatrics today—an overview. *American Journal of Psychiatry,* 1967, *123,* 1226–33.

BUTLER, R. N. The facade of chronological age: An interpretative summary. *American Journal of Psychiatry,* 1963a, *119,* 721–28.

―――― The life review: An interpretation of reminiscence in the aged. *Psychiatry,* 1963b, *26,* 65–76.

―――― Recall in retrospection. *Journal of the American Geriatrics Society,* 1963c, *11,* 523–29.

―――― Research and clinical observations on the psychologic reactions to physical changes with age. *Mayo Clinic Proceedings,* 1967, *42,* 596–619.

―――― Toward a psychiatry of the life-cycle: Implications of sociopsychologic studies of the aging process for the psychotherapeutic situation. *Psychiatric Research Report,* 1968, *23,* 233–48.

―――― DASTUR, D. K., and PERLIN, S. Relationships of senile manifestations and chronic brain syndromes to cerebral circulation and metabolism. *Journal of Psychiatric Research,* 1965, *3,* 229–38.

CAIRD, W. K. Memory loss in the senile psychoses: Organic or psychogenic? *Psychological Reports,* 1966, *18,* 788–90.

CALDERWOOD, D. Adolescent's views on sex education. *Journal of Marriage and the Family,* 1965, *27,* 291–98.

CALDWELL, B. M. The effects of infant care. *In* M. L. Hoffman, and L. W. Hoffman (eds.), *Review of child development research, I.* New York: Russell Sage Foundation, 1964.

CAMPBELL, B. A. Development studies of learning and motivation in infra-primate mammals. *In* H. W. Stevenson; E. H. Hess; and H. L. Rheingold (eds.), *Early behavior: comparative and developmental approaches.* New York: John Wiley, 1967.

CAMPBELL, D., and THOMPSON, W. R. Developmental psychology. *Annual Review of Psychology,* 1968, *19,* 251–92.

CARITHERS, H. A. Mother-pediatrician relationship in the neonatal period. *Journal of Pediatrics,* 1951, *38,* 654–60.

CARLOS, J. P., and GITTELSOHN, A. M. Longitudinal studies of the natural history of caries. I. Eruption patterns of the permanent teeth. *Journal of Dental Research,* 1965, *44,* 509–16.

CARMICHAEL, L. The onset and early development of behavior. *In* L. Carmichael (ed.), *Manual of child psychology.* New York: John Wiley, 1954.

CARO, F. G. Social class and attitudes of youth relevant for the realization of adult goals. *Social Forces,* 1966, *44,* 492–98.

CARON, R. F. Visual reinforcement of head-turning in young infants. *Journal of Experimental Child Psychology,* 1967, *5,* 489–511.

CARP, F. M. The impact of environment on old people. *Gerontologist,* 1967, *7,* 106–9.

CARPENTER, G. C., and STECHLER, G. Selective attention to mother's face from week 1 through week 8. *Proceedings, 75th Annual Convention APA,* 1967, 153–54.

CASLER, L. Maternal deprivation: A critical review of literature. *Monographs of the Society for Research in Child Development,* 1961, *26,* 1–64.

―――― The effects of extra tactile stimulation on a group of institutionalized infants. *Genetic Psychology Monographs,* 1965, *71,* 137–75.

CATTELL, P. *The measurement of intelligence of infants and young children.* New York: Psychological Corporation, 1940.

CAVAN, R. S. Unemployment—crisis of the common man. *Marriage and Family Living,* 1959, *21,* 139–46.

―――― BURGESS, E., HAVIGHURST, R., and GOLDHAMER, H. *Personal adjustment in old age.* Chicago: Science Research Associates, 1949.

CAWLEY, A. M. A study of the vocational interests trends of secondary school and college women. *Genetic Psychology Monographs,* 1947, *35,* 166–75.

CAZDEN, C. B. Subcultural differences in child language: An interdisciplinary review. *Merrill-Palmer Quarterly,* 1966, *12,* 185–219.

CHARLES, D. C. Outstanding characteristics of older patients. *In* C. B. Vedder and A. S. Lefkowitz (eds.), *Problems of the aged.* Springfield, Ill.: Charles C Thomas, 1965.

CHASE, W. P. Color vision in infants. *Journal of Experimental Psychology,* 1937, *20,* 203–22.

CHEN, R. The emotional problems of retirement. *Journal of the American Geriatrics Society,* 1968, *16,* 290–95.

CHOW, K. L., RIESEN, A. H., and NEWELL, F. W. Degeneration of retinal ganglion cells in infant chimpanzees reared in darkness. *Journal of Comparative Neurology,* 1957, *107,* 27–42.

CHOWN, S. M. Personality factors in the formation of occupational choice. *British Journal of Educational Psychology,* 1959, *29,* 23–33.

―――― Age and the rigidities. *Journal of Gerontology,* 1961, *16,* 353–62.

―――― and HERON, A. Psychological aspects of aging in man. *Annual Review of Psychology,* 1965, 417–50.

CHRIST, A. E. Attitudes toward death among a group of acute geriatric psychiatric patients. *Journal of Gerontology,* 1961, *16,* 56–59.

CHUN, R. W. M., PAWSAT, R., and FORSTER, F. M. Sound localization in infancy. *Journal of Nervous and Mental Disease,* 1960, *130,* 472–76.

CLARK, M. Cultural values and dependency in later life. *In* R. A. Kalish (ed.), *The dependencies of old people.* Ann Arbor, Mich.: Institute of Gerontology, 1969.

CLARKE, A. D. B., and CLARKE, A. M. Some recent advances in a study of early deprivation. *Child Psychology and Psychiatry,* 1960, *1,* 26–36.

CLOWARD, R. A., and OHLIN, L. *Delinquency and opportunity: A theory of delinquent groups.* Glencoe, Ill.: Free Press, 1960.

COBB, K., GRIMM, E. R., DAWSON, B., and AMSTERDAM, B. Reliability of global observations of newborn infants. *Journal of Genetic Psychology,* 1967, *110,* 253–67.

COGHILL, G. E. *Anatomy and the problem of behaviour.* London: Cambridge University Press, 1929.

COLE, L. *Goals of the adolescent period.* New York: Holt, 1964.

COLEMAN, J. S. *Social climates in high schools.* Washington, D. C.: Office of Education, U. S. Department of Health, Education, and Welfare, 1961a.

―――― *The adolescent society.* Glencoe, Ill.: Free Press, 1961b.

―――― *Adolescents and the school.* New York: Basic Books, 1965.

COLLARD, R. R. Social and play responses of first-born and later-born infants in an unfamiliar situation. *Child Development,* 1968, *39,* 325–34.

COLLIAS, N. E. The analysis of socialization in sheep and goats. *Ecology,* 1956, *37,* 228–39.

COLLINS, G. R. Changes in optional level of complexity as a function of age. *Dissertation Abstracts,* 1964, *24,* 5538.

CONNOLLY, K., BROWN, K., and BASSETT, E. Developmental changes in some components of a motor skill. *British Journal of Psychology,* 1968, *59,* 305–14.

CONNOR, R., JOHANNIS, T. B., and WALTERS, J. Parent-adolescent relationships. I. Parent-adolescent conflicts. *Journal of Home Economics,* 1954, *46,* 183–86.

COUCH, G. B. Youth looks at sex. *Adolescence,* 1967, *2,* 255–66.

COWAN, P. A., WEBER, J., HODDINOTT, B. A., and KLEIN, T. Mean length of a spoken response as a function of stimulus, experimenter, and subject. *Child Development*, 1967, *38*, 191–203.

COWELL, C. C. An abstract of a study of differentials in junior high school boys based on the observation of physical education activities. *Research Quarterly*, 1935, *6*, 129–36.

COX, F. N., and CAMPBELL, D. Young children in a new situation with and without their mothers. *Child Development*, 1968, *39*, No. 1, 123–31.

CRAMPTON, C. W. Anatomical or physiological age versus chronological age. *Pedagogical Seminary*, 1908, *15*, 23–237.

CRANE, A. R. The development of moral values in children: Pre-adolescent gangs and the moral development of children. *British Journal of Educational Psychology*, 1958, *28*, 201–8.

CRAVIOTO, J. Nutritional deficiencies and mental performance in childhood. *In* D. C. Glass (ed.), *Biology and behavior: Environmental influences.* New York: Russell Sage Foundation, 1968.

CRUIKSHANK, R. Animal infancy. *In* L. Carmichael (ed.), *Manual of child psychology.* New York: John Wiley, 1954.

CUMMING, E. Further thoughts on the theory of disengagement. *International Social Science Journal*, 1963, *15*, 377–93.

——— New thoughts on the theory of disengagement. *In* R. Kastenbaum (ed.), *New thoughts on old age.* New York: Springer-Verlag, 1964.

——— and HENRY, W. E. *Growing old.* New York: Basic Books, 1961.

CURTIS, H. J. Biological mechanism underlying the aging process. *Science*, 1963, *141*, 686–94.

DANSEREAU, H. K. Work and the teenager. *Annals of the American Academy of Political and Social Science*, 1961, *338*, 44–52.

DARLEY, F. L., and WINITZ, H. Age of first word: review of research. *Journal of Speech and Hearing Disorders*, 1961, *26*, 272–90.

DARWIN, C. R. A biographical sketch of an infant. *Mind*, 1877, *2*, 285–94.

DATTA, L. *A report on evaluation studies of Project Head Start.* Washington, D. C.: Office of Child Development, Department of Health, Education, and Welfare, 1969.

DAVIDS, A., HOLDEN, R. H., and GRAY, G. B. Maternal anxiety during pregnancy and adequacy of mother and child adjustment eight months following child birth. *Child Development*, 1963, *34*, 993–1002.

DAVIDSON, H. H., and KRUGLOV, L. P. Personality characteristics of the institutionalized aged. *Journal of Consulting Psychology*, 1952, *16*, 5–10.

DAVIES, B. Problems of aging. *Postgraduate Medicine*, 1965, *38*, 314–20.

DAVIS, H., SEARS, R. R., MILLER, H. C., and BRODBECK, A. J. Effects of cup, bottle, and breast feeding on oral activities of newborn infants. *Pediatrics*, 1948, *2*, 549–58.

DAVIS, H., BARBOUR, R. W., and HASSELL, M. D. Colonial behavior of *Eptesicus fuscus. Journal of Mammalogy*, 1968, *49*, 44–50.

DAY, S. R. Teacher influence on the occupational preferences of high school students. *Vocational Guidance Quarterly*, 1966, *14*, 215–19.

DEAN, D. G. Emotional maturity and marital adjustment. *Journal of Marriage and the Family*, 1966, *28*, 454–57.

DEARBORN, W. F., and CATTELL, P. The intelligence and achievement of private school pupils. *Journal of Educational Psychology*, 1930, *21*, 197–211.

DEFRIES, J. C., WEIR, M. W., and HEGMANN, J. P. Differential effects of prenatal maternal stress on offspring behavior in mice as a function of genotype and stress. *Journal of Comparative and Physiological Psychology*, 1967, *63*, 332–34.

DEGRAZIA, S. The uses of time. *In* R. W. Kleemeier (ed.), *Aging and leisure.* New York: Oxford University Press, 1961.

DELMAN, L. The order of participation of limbs in response to tactual stimulation of the newborn infant. *Child Development*, 1935, *6*, 98–109.

DENENBERG, V. H. The effects of early experience. *In* E. S. E. Hafez (ed.), *The behaviour of domestic animals.* London: Bailliere, Tindal & Cox, 1962.

——— Critical periods, stimulus input, and emotional reactivity: a theory of infantile stimulation. *Psychological Review*, 1964, *71*, 335–51.

——— Stimulation in infancy, emotional reactivity, and exploratory behavior. *Biology and behavior: Neuro-physiology and emotion.* New York: Russell Sage Foundation, 1967.

——— and GROTA, L. J. Social-seeking and novelty-seeking behavior as a function of differential rearing histories. *Journal of Abnormal and Social Psychology*, 1964, *69*, 453–56.

DENENBERG, V. H., HUDGENS, G. A., and ZARROW, M. X. Mice reared with rats: Modification of behavior by early experience with another species. *Science*, 1964, *143*, 380–81.

DENENBERG, V. H., PASCHKE, R. E., and ZARROW, M. H. Killing of mice by rats prevented by early interaction between the two species. *Psychonomic Science*, 1968, *11*, 39.

DENNIS, W. The role of mass activity in the development of infant behavior. *Psychological Review*, 1932, *39*, 593–95.

——— Infant reaction to restraint: An evaluation of Watson's theory. *Transactions of the New York Academy of Sciences*, 1939, Series II, *2*, 202–19.

——— Historical beginnings of child psychology. *Psychological Bulletin*, 1949, *46*, 224–35.

——— Causes of retardation among institutional children: Iran. *Journal of Genetic Psychology*, 1960, *96*, 47–59.

——— and NAJARIAN, P. Infant development under environmental handicaps. *Psychological Monographs*, 1957, *71*, No. 7.

DENTLER, R. A. Dropouts, automation, and the schools. *Teachers College Record*, 1964, *65*, 475–83.

DESMOND, M. M., FRANKLIN, R. R., VALLBONA, C., HILT, R. H., PLUMB, R., ARNOLD, H., and WATTS, J. The clinical behavior of the newly born: I. *Journal of Pediatrics*, 1963, *62*, 307–25.

DESPERT, J. L. Urinary control and enuresis. *Psychosomatic Medicine*, 1944, *6*, 294–307.

——— Sleep in preschool children: A preliminary study. *Nervous Child*, 1949, *8*, 8–27.

——— *Children of divorce.* New York: Doubleday, 1953.

DEVORE, I. Mother-infant relations in free-ranging baboons. *In* H. L. Rheingold, (ed.), *Maternal behavior in mammals.* New York: John Wiley, 1963.

DISHER, D. R. The reactions of newborn infants to chemical stimuli administered nasally. *Ohio State University Studies Contributions in Psychology*, 1934, No. 12, 1–52.

DITTRICHOVÁ, J. and LAPÁCKOVA, V. Development of the waking state in the young child. *Child Development*, 1964, *35*, 365–70.

DONAHUE, W. Rehabilitation of long-term aged patients. *In* R. H. Williams, C. Tibitts, and W. Donahue (eds.), *Process of aging:* vol. I. New York: Atherton, 1963.

DONALD, M. N., and HAVIGHURST, R. J. The meaning of leisure. *Social Forces*, 1959, *37*, 355–60.

DORAN, E. W. A study of vocabularies. *Pedagogical Seminary*, 1907, *14*, 401–38.

DORIS, J., CASPER, M., and PORESKY, R. Differential brightness thresholds in infancy. *Journal of Experimental Child Psychology*, 1967, *5*, 522–35.

DORIS, J., and COOPER, L. Brightness discrimination in infancy. *Journal of Experimental Child Psychology*, 1966, *3*, 31–39.

DOUVAN, E., and ADELSON, J. *The adolescent experience.* New York: John Wiley, 1966.

DUBIGNON, J. and CAMPBELL, D. Sucking in the newborn during a feed. *Journal of Experimental Child Psychology*, 1969, *7*, 282–98.

EBERLY, C. G. The influence of the fraternity ritual. *College Student Survey*, 1967, *1*, 9–10.

EHRENFELD, D. W., and CARR, A. The role of vision in the sea-finding orientation of the green turtle (*Chelonia mydas*). *Animal Behaviour*, 1967, *15*, 25–36.

EIBL-EIBESFELDT, I. The interactions of unlearned behaviour patterns and learning in mammals. *In* J. F. Delafresnaye (ed.) *Brain mechanisms and learning.* Springfield, Ill.: Charles C Thomas, 1961.

EIDUSON, B. T. *Scientists,* New York: Basic Books, 1962.

——— Infancy and goal-setting behavior. *In* C. Bühler and F. Massarik (eds.), *The course of human life.* New York: Springer-Verlag, 1968.

EISDORFER, C., AXELROD, S., and WILKIE, F. L. Stimulus exposure time as a factor in serial learning in an aged sample. *Journal of Abnormal and Social Psychology*, 1963, *67*, 594–600.

EISENBERG, R. B., GRIFFIN, E. H., COURSIN, D. B., and HUNTER, M. Auditory behavior in the human neonate: a preliminary report. *Journal of Speech and Hearing Research*, 1964, 7, 245–69.

EISSLER, K. R. *Goethe: a psychoanalytic study.* Detroit, Mich.: Wayne State University Press, 1963, 2 vols.

ELDER, G. H. Parental power legitimation and its effect on the adolescent. *Sociometry*, 1963, *26*, 50–65.

ELKIND, D. Conceptual orientation shifts in children and adolescents. *Child Development*, 1966, *37*, 493–98.

———— Cognition in infancy and early childhood. *In* Y. Brackbill (ed.), *Infancy and early childhood.* New York: Free Press, 1967a.

———— Egocentrism in adolescence. *Child Development*, 1967b, *38*, 1025–34.

———— Cognitive development in adolescence. *In* J. F. Adams (ed.), *Understanding adolescence.* Boston: Allyn & Bacon, 1968a.

———— Cognitive structure and adolescent experience, 1968b, *2*, 427–34.

———— BAROCAS, R., and JOHNSEN, P. Concept production in children and adolescents. *Human Development*, 1969, *12*, 10–21.

ELKIND, D., and ELKIND, S. Varieties of religious experience in young adolescents. *Journal for the Scientific Study of Religion*, 1962, *2*, 102–12.

ELKIND, D., VAN DOORNINCK, W., and SCHWARZ, C. Perceptual activity and concept attainment. *Child Development*, 1967, *38*, 1153–61.

ELLIOTT, D. S. Delinquency, school attendance, and dropout. *Social Problems*, 1966, *13*, 307–14.

ENGEN, T., LIPSITT, L. P., and KAYE, H. Olfactory responses and adaptation in the human neonate. *Journal of Comparative and Physiological Psychology*, 1963, *56*, 73–77.

ERIKSON, E. H. Identity and the life cycle, *Psychological Issues*, 1959, No. 1.

———— *Childhood and Society* (2nd ed.). New York: Norton, 1963.

ERVIN, S. M., and MILLER, W. R. Language development. *In* H. W. Stevenson (ed.) *Child psychology: The sixty-second yearbook of the National Society for the Study of Education; Part 1.* Chicago: University of Chicago Press, 1963.

ERVIN-TRIPP, S. Language development. *In* L. W. Hoffman and M. L. Hoffman (eds.), *Review of child development research, Vol. II.* New York: Russell Sage Foundation, 1966.

ESCALONA, S. K. Feeding disturbances in very young children. *American Journal of Orthopsychiatry*, 1945, *15*, 76–80.

———— The use of infant tests for predictive purposes. *In* W. E. Martin and C. B. Stendler (eds.), *Readings in child development.* New York: Harcourt, Brace & World, 1954.

———— The study of individual difference and the problem of state. *Child Psychiatry*, 1962, *1*, (1), 1962.

———— Some determinants of individual differences in early ego development. *Transactions of the New York Academy of Sciences*, 1965, *27*, 802–17.

———— *The roots of individuality.* Chicago: Aldine, 1968.

EVANS, J. N. A visual test for infants. *American Journal of Ophthalmology*, 1946, *29*, 73–75.

EWER, R. F. *Ethology of mammals.* New York: Plenum Press, 1968.

EWING, I. R., and EWING, A. W. G. The ascertainment of deafness in infancy and early childhood. *Journal of Laryngology, Rhinology, and Otology*, 1944, *59*, 309–33.

FABRICIUS, E. Some aspects of imprinting in birds. *Symposia of the Zoological Society of London*, 1962, *8*, 139–48.

FAHEY, G. L. The questioning activity of children. *Journal of Genetic Psychology*, 1942, *60*, 337–57.

FAILLA, G. The aging process and cancerogenesis. *Annals of the New York Academy of Science*, 1958, *71*, 1124–40.

FALSTEIN, E. I., and OFFER, D. Adolescent therapy. *In* L. E. Abt and B. F. Riess (eds.), *Progress in clinical psychology*, vol. V. New York: Grune & Stratton, 1963.

FANTZ, R. L. Pattern vision in young infants. *Psychological Record*, 1958, *8*, 43–47.

———— Origin of form perception. *Scientific American*, 1961, *204*, 66–72.

———— Pattern vision in newborn infants. *Science*, 1963, *140*, 296–97.

FAUST, M. W. Developmental maturity as a determinant in prestige of adolescent girls. *Child Development*, 1960, *31*, 173–84.

FEIFEL, H. Older persons look at death. *Geriatrics*, 1956, *11*, 127–30.

FENTRESS, J. C. Observations on the behavioral development of a hand-reared timber wolf. *American Zoologist*, 1967, *7*, 339–51.

FERGUSON, L. R. *Personality development*, Belmont, Calif.: Brooks-Cole, 1970.

FILER, R. N., and O'CONNELL, D. D. A useful contribution climate for the aging. *Journal of Gerontology*, 1962, *17*, 51–57.

———— Motivation of aging persons. *Journal of Gerontology*, 1964, *19*, 51–52.

FISHBEIN, M., and KENNEDY, R. J. (eds.) *Modern marriage and family living.* Fair Lawn, New Jersey: Oxford University Press, 1957.

FISHER, M. B., and BIRREN, J. E. Changes with age in strength and quickness. *Journal of Applied Psychology*, 1947, *31*, 490–97.

FISHER, M. S. Language patterns of preschool children. *Journal of Experimental Education*, 1932, *1*, 70–85.

———— Language patterns of preschool children. *Child Development Monographs*, 1934, No. 15.

FLACKS, R. The liberated generation: An exploration of the roots of student protest. *Journal of Social Issues*, 1967, *22*, 52–75.

FLAVELL, J. H. *The developmental psychology of Jean Piaget.* Princeton, N. J.: Van Nostrand, 1963.

———— and HILL, J. P. Developmental psychology. *Annual Review of Psychology*, 1969, *20*, 1–56.

FLINT, B. *The child and the institution.* Toronto: University of Toronto Press, 1966.

FORBES, R. B. Care and early behavioral development of a lion cub. *Journal of Mammalogy*, 1963, *44*, 110–11.

FORD, C. S., and BEACH, F. A. *Patterns of Sexual Behavior.* New York: Harper, 1951.

FORGAYS, D. G., and READ, J. M. Crucial periods for free-environmental experience in the rat. *Journal of Comparative and Physiological Psychology*, 1962, *55*, 816–18.

FOWLER, W. Cognitive learning in infancy and early childhood. *Psychological Bulletin*, 1962, *59*, 116–52.

FOX, M. W. The ontogeny of behavior and neurologic responses in the dog. *Animal Behaviour*, 1964, *12*, 301–10.

FRAIBERG, S. The origins of identity. *Smith College Studies in Social Work*, 1968, *38*, 79–101.

FRANK, L. K. *On the importance of infancy.* New York: Random House, 1966.

FRANKL, L. Development of object constancy: Stages in the recognition of the baby's feeding bottle. *Journal of Humanistic Psychology*, 1963, *3*, 60–72.

FRAZIER, A., and LISONBEE, L. K. Adolescent concerns with physique. *School Review*, 1950, *58*, 397–405.

FRAZIER, E. F. *The Negro family in the United States.* New York: Dryden, 1948.

FREEDMAN, D. G., and KELLER, B. Inheritance of behavior in infants. *Science*, 1963, *140*, 196–98.

FREEDMAN, D. G., LORING, C. B., and MARTIN, R. M. Emotional behavior and personality development. *In* Y. Brackbill (ed.), *Infancy and early childhood.* New York: Free Press, 1967.

FREEMAN, J. T. Sexual capacities in the aging male. *Geriatrics*, 1961, *16*, 37–43.

FRENKEL, E. Studies in biographical psychology. *Character and personality*, 1936, *5*, 1–34.

FREUD, S. *The problem of anxiety.* New York: Norton, 1936.

———— *Leonardo da Vinci: a study in psychosexuality.* Trans. A. A. Brill. New York: Random House, 1947.

———— *Three essays on sexuality: II. Infantile sexuality* (1905). *Collected works.* London: Hogarth, 1957.

FRIEDENBERG, E. Z. *The vanishing adolescent* Boston: Beacon Press, 1959.

FRIEDLANDER, B. Z. The effect of speaker identity, voice inflection, vocabulary, and message redundancy on infants' selection of vocal reinforcement. *Journal of Experimental Child Psychology*, 1968, *6*, (3), 443–59.

———— Receptive language development in infancy: Issues and problems. *Merrill-Palmer Quarterly*, 1970.

FRIEDMAN, H. Memory organization in the aged. *Journal of Genetic Psychology*, 1966, *109*, 3–8.

FRIEDMAN, R., and WALLACE, M. Vocational choice and life goals. *In* C. Bühler and F. Massarik (eds.) *The course of human life.* New York: Springer-Verlag, 1968.

FRIEDMANN, E. A., HAVIGHURST, R. J., and HARLAN, W. H. *The meaning of work and retirement.* Chicago: University of Chicago Press, 1954.

FRIES, M., and WOLFF, P. Some hypotheses on the role of the congenital activity type in personality development. *Psychoanalytic Study of the Child*, 1953, *8*, 46–62.

FROEHLICH, H. P., and WOLINS, L. Job satisfaction as need satisfaction. *Personnel Psychology*, 1960, *13*, 407–20.

FULLER, J. L. Experiential deprivation and later behavior. *Science*, 1967, *158*, 1645–52.

FURCHTGOTT, E., LAZAR, J. W., and DEITCHMAN, R. Maternal parity and offspring behavior in the domestic mouse. *Developmental Psychology*, 1969, *1*, 227–30.

GARDNER, D. B. *Development in early childhood*. New York: Harper & Row, 1964.

GARDNER, D. B., and SWIGER, M. K. Developmental status of two groups of infants released for adoption. *Child Development*, 1958, *29*, 521–30.

GARDNER, G. E. Psychiatric problems of adolescence. *In* S. Arieti (Ed.), *Handbook of American Psychiatry*. New York: Basic Books, 1959.

GARDNER, R. A., and GARDNER, B. T. Teaching sign language to a chimpanzee. *Science*, 1969, *165*, 664–72.

GARWOOD, D. Personality factors related to creativity in young scientists. *Journal of Abnormal and Social Psychology*, 1964, *68*, 413–19.

GERALL, H. D. Effect of social isolation and physical confinement on motor and sexual behavior of guinea pigs. *Journal of Personality and Social Psychology*, 1965, *2*, 460–64.

GERARD, M. *The emotionally disturbed child*. New York: Child Welfare League, 1956.

GESELL, A. *The mental growth of the preschool child*. New York: Macmillan, 1925.

—— The ontogenesis of infant behavior. *In* L. Carmichael (ed.), *Manual of child psychology*. New York: John Wiley, 1946.

—— *Developmental schedules*. New York: Psychological Corporation, 1949.

—— Infant vision. *Scientific American*, February, 1950.

—— The ontogenesis of infant behavior. *In* L. Carmichael (ed.), *Manual of child psychology*, 2nd ed., New York: John Wiley, 1954.

—— and AMATRUDA, C. S. *Developmental diagnosis*. New York: Hoeber, 1941.

GESELL, A., and AMES, L. B. The development of directionality in drawing. *Journal of Genetic Psychology*, 1946, *68*, 45–61.

—— The development of handedness. *Journal of Genetic Psychology*, 1947, *70*, 155–75.

GESELL, A., HALVERSON, H. M., THOMPSON, H., ILG, F. L., CASTNER, B. M., AMES, L. B., and AMATRUDA, C. S. *The first five years of life: A guide to the study of the preschool child*. New York: Harper & Row, 1940.

GESELL, A., and ILG, F. L. *Feeding behavior of infants*. Philadelphia: Lippincott, 1937.

—— *The child from five to ten*. New York: Harper & Row, 1946.

—— *Child development: An introduction to the study of human growth*. New York: Harper & Row, 1949.

—— and AMES, L. B. *Youth: The years from ten to sixteen*. New York: Harper & Row, 1956.

GESELL, A., and THOMPSON, H. *Infant behavior: Its genesis and growth*. New York: McGraw-Hill, 1934.

—— and AMATRUDA, C. S. *The psychology of early growth*. New York: Macmillan, 1938.

GETZELS, J. W., and JACKSON, P. W. *Creativity and intelligence: Explorations with gifted students*. New York: John Wiley, 1962.

GEWIRTZ, J. L. The course of infant smiling in four child-rearing environments in Israel. *In* B. M. Foss (ed.), *Determinants of infant behaviour, III*. London: Methuen, 1965.

GHENT, L. Perception of overlapping and embedded figures by children of different ages. *American Journal of Psychology*, 1956, *69*, 575–81.

GIBSON, J. J., and GIBSON, E. J. Perceptual learning: Differentiation or enrichment? *Psychological Review*, 1955, *62*, 32–41.

GILBERT, J. A. Researches on the mental and physical development of school children. *Studies from the Yale Psychological Laboratory*, 1894, *2*, 40–100.

GINSBERG, E. *Values and ideals of American youth*. New York: Columbia University Press, 1962.

GINSBURG, B. E. Coaction of genetical and non-genetical factors influencing sexual behavior. *In* F. A. Beach (ed.), *Sex and behavior*. New York: John Wiley, 1965.

GITELSON, M. Character synthesis: The psychotherapeutic problem of adolescence. *American Journal of Orthopsychiatry*, 1948, *18*, 422–31.

GLATT, C. A. European antecedents of the scientific study of children. *Child Study Center Bulletin* (State University College at Buffalo), 1967, *3*, 93–98.

GLICK, P. C. *American families*. New York: John Wiley, 1957.

GLUCKSBERG, S., and KRAUSS, R. M. What do people say after they have learned how to talk? Studies of the development of referential communication. *Merrill-Palmer Quarterly*, 1967, *13*, 309–16.

GODDARD, H. H. A measuring scale for intelligence. *Training School*, 1910, *6*, 146–54.

GOERTZEL, V., and GOERTZEL, M. G. *Cradles of eminence*. Boston: Little Brown, 1962.

GOLDFARB, A. I. The psychodynamics of dependency and the search for aid. *In* R. A. Kalish (ed.), *The dependencies of old people*. Ann Arbor, Mich.: Institute of Gerontology, 1969.

GOLDFARB, W. Infant rearing and problem behavior. *American Journal of Orthopsychiatry*, 1943, *13*, 249–65.

—— Effects of psychological deprivation in infancy and subsequent stimulation. *American Journal of Psychiatry*, 1945a, *102*, 18–33.

—— Psychological privation in infancy and subsequent adjustment. *American Journal of Orthopsychiatry*, 1945b, *15*, 247–55.

GOODE, W. J. *After divorce*. Glencoe, Ill.: Free Press, 1956.

—— *The family*. Englewood Cliffs, N. J.: Prentice-Hall, 1964.

GOODENOUGH, F. L. *Measurement of intelligence by drawings*. New York: World Publishing, 1926.

—— A further study of speed of tapping in early childhood. *Journal of Applied Psychology*, 1935, *19*, 309–15.

—— and HARRIS, D. B. Studies in the psychology of children's drawings, II, 1928–1949. *Psychological Bulletin*, 1950, *47*, 369–443.

GOODENOUGH, F. L. and SMART, R. C. Interrelationships of motor abilities in young children. *Child Development*, 1935, *6*, 141–53.

GOODMAN, P. *Growing up absurd*. New York: Random House, 1956.

GOODRICK, C. L. Social interactions and exploration of young, mature, and senescent male albino rats. *Journal of Gerontology*, 1965, *20*, 215–18.

GORDON, N. S., and BELL, R. Q. Activity in the human newborn. *Psychological Reports*, 1961, *9*, 103–16.

GOTTLIEB, D., and RAMSEY, C. *The American adolescent*. Homewood, Ill.: Dorsey, 1964.

GOTTLIEB, G. Imprinting in relation to parental and species identification by avian neonates. *Journal of Comparative and Physiological Psychology*, 1965, *59*, 345–56.

—— Prenatal behavior of birds. *Quarterly Review of Biology*, 1968, *43*, 148–74.

GOULD, H. N., and GOULD, M. R. Age of first menstruation in mothers and daughters. *Journal of the American Medical Association*, 1932, *98*, 1349–52.

GRAHAM, F. K. Behavioral differences between normal and traumatized newborns: I. The test procedures. *Psychological Monographs*, 1956, *70* (20).

GRAHAM, F. K., MATARAZZO, R. G., and CALDWELL, B. M. Behavioral differences between normals and traumatized newborns: II. Standardization, reliability, and validity. *Psychological Monographs*, 1956, *70*, (21).

GRAY, S. W., and KLAUS, R. A. An experimental preschool program for culturally deprived children. *Child Development*, 1965, *36*, 884–98.

GREEN, L. B., and PARKER, H. J. Parental influence upon adolescents' occupational choice: A test of an aspect of Roe's theory. *Journal of Counseling Psychology*, 1965, *12*, 379–83.

GREENACRE, P. *Trauma, growth and personality*. New York: Norton, 1952.

GREENFIELD, P. M., and BRUNER, J. S. Culture and cognitive growth. *In* D. A. Goslin (ed.), *Handbook of socialization theory and research*. New York: Rand McNally, 1969.

GREENMAN, G. W. Visual behaviour of newborn infants. *In* A. Solnit and S. Provence (eds.), *Modern perspectives in child development*. New York: International Universities Press, 1963.

GREULICH, W. W. Physical changes in adolescence. *In Adolescence, 43rd Yearbook*. Chicago: University of Chicago Press, 1944.

—— The rationale of assessing the developmental status of children from roentgenograms of the hand and wrist. *Child Development*, 1950, *21*, 33–44.

—— and PYLE, S. I. *Radiographic atlas of skeletal development of the hand and wrist* (2nd ed.) Stanford, Calif.: Stanford University Press, 1959.

GRIER, J. B., COUNTER, S. A., and SHEARER, W. M. Prenatal auditory imprinting in chickens. *Science*, 1967, *155*, 1692–93.

GRIFFITHS, R. *The abilities of babies: A study of mental measurement.* New York: McGraw-Hill, 1954.

GROSSMAN, H. J., and GREENBERG, N. H. Psychosomatic differentiation in infancy. *Psychosomatic Medicine*, 1957, *19*, 293–306.

GROTBERG, E. H. *Review of Research, 1965 to 1969: Project Head Start.* Washington, D. C.: Office of Economic Opportunity, 1969.

GRUENDEL, A. D., and ARNOLD, W. J. Effects of early social deprivation on reproductive behavior of male rats. *Journal of Comparative and Physiological Psychology*, 1969, *67*, 123–28.

GUILFORD, J. P. Factors that aid and hinder creativity. *Teachers College Record*, 1962, *63*, 380–92.

GUILLAUME, P. *Imitation in children.* Paris: Alcan, 1925.

GUMP, P. V., and KOUNIN, J. S. Issues raised by ecological and "classical" research efforts. *Merrill-Palmer Quarterly*, 1960, *6*, 145–52.

GUTTERIDGE, M. A study of motor achievement of young childern. *Archives of Psychology* (New York), 1939, *244*.

HABRICH, J. Ueber die Entwicklung der Abstraktionsfähigkeit von Schülerinnen, *Zeitschrift für angewandte Psychologie*, 1914, No. 9.

HAHN, M. E. Forgotten people: The normal individual and, and in, professional psychology. *American Psychologist*, 1962, *17*, 700–705.

HAITH, M. M. The response of the human newborn to visual movement. *Journal of Experimental Child Psychology*, 1966, *3*, 235–43.

HALL, G. S. The contents of children's minds on entering school. *Pedagogical Seminary*, 1891, *1*, 139–73.

—— *Adolescence*, vol. I & II. New York: Appleton-Century-Crofts, 1905.

HALVERSON, H. M. The acquisition of skill in infancy. *Journal of Genetic Psychology*, 1933, *43*, 3–48.

—— Studies of the grasping reflex of early infancy. *Journal of Genetic Psychology*, 1937, *51*, 371–449.

—— Genital and sphincter behavior of the male infant. *Journal of Genetic Psychology*, 1940, *56*, 95–136.

—— Variations in pulse and respiration during different phases of infant behavior. *Journal of Genetic Psychology*, 1941, *59*, 259–330.

HAMBURGER, V., WENGER, E., and OPPENHEIM, R. Motility in the chick embryo in the absence of sensory input. *Journal of Experimental Zoology*, 1966, *162*, 133–60.

HAMILTON, J. B. Male hormone substance: A prime factor in acne. *Journal of Clinical Endocrinology*, 1941, *1*, 570–92.

HANDEL, G. Psychological study of whole families. *Psychological Bulletin*, 1965, *63*, 19–41.

HARDY, J. B., DOUGHERTY, A., and HARDY, W. G. Hearing responses and audiologic screening in infants. *Journal of Pediatrics*, 1959, *55*, 382–90.

HARLOW, H. F. The nature of love. *American Psychologist*, 1958, *13*, 673–85.

—— The development of affectional patterns in infant monkeys. *In* B. M. Foss (ed.), *Determinants of infant behavior*. London: Methuen, 1961.

—— Age-mate or peer affectional system. *In* D. S. Lehrman, R. A. Hinde, and E. Shaw (eds.), *Advances in the study of behavior*, vol. 2, New York: Academic Press, 1969.

HARLOW, H. F., BLAZEK, N. C., and MCCLEARN, G. E. Manipulatory motivation in the infant rhesus monkey. *Journal of Comparative and Physiological Psychology*, 1956, *49*, 444–48.

HARLOW, H. F., and HARLOW, M. K. The affectional systems. *In* A. M. Schrier, H. F. Harlow, and F. Stollnitz, *Behavior of nonhuman primates*, vol. II. New York: Academic Press, 1965.

HARLOW, H. F., and ZIMMERMANN, R. R. Affectional responses in the infant monkey. *Science*, 1959, *130*, 421–32.

HARMS, E. The development of religious experiences in children. *American Journal of Sociology*, 1944, *50*, 112–22.

HARPER, L. V. The effects of isolation from birth on the social behaviour of guinea pigs in adulthood. *Animal Behaviour*, 1968, *16*, 58–64.

HARRIS, D. B. A scale for measuring attitudes of social responsibility in children. *Journal of Abnormal and Social Psychology*, 1957, *55*, 322–26.

HARRIS, J. A., JACKSON, C. M., PATERSON, D. G., and SCAMMON, R. E. *The measurement of man.* Minneapolis: University of Minnesota Press, 1930.

HART, H. The slowing-up of growth in mental test ability. *School and Society* 1924, *20*, 573–74.

HARTLEY, R. E., and GOLDENSON, R. M. *The complete book of children's play.* New York: Thomas Y. Crowell, 1957.

HATFIELD, J., FERGUSON, L., and ALPERT, R. Mother-child interaction and the socialization process. *Child Development*, 1967, *38*, 365–414.

HAVIGHURST, R. J. *Developmental tasks and education.* New York: Longmans, Green, 1952.

—— *Human development and education.* New York: McKay, 1953.

—— The leisure activities of the middle-aged. *American Journal of Sociology*, 1957, *63*, 152–62.

—— Work and retirement. *In* N. W. Shock (ed.), *Aging: Some social and biological aspects.* Washington, D. C.: American Association for the Advancement of Science, 1960.

—— Successful aging. *Gerontologist*, 1961, *1*, 8–13.

—— Successful aging. *In* R. H. Williams; C. Tibbetts, and W. Donahue (eds.), *Process of Aging*, vol. I. New York: Atherton, 1963.

—— and ALBRECHT, R. *Older people.* New York: Longmans, 1953.

HAVIGHURST, R. J., and NEUGARTEN, B. L. *Society and education.* Boston: Allyn & Bacon, 1957.

—— and TOBIN, S. Disengagement, personality, and life satisfaction in the later years. *In* P. F. Hansen (ed.), *Age with a future.* Philadelphia: Davis, 1964.

HAVIGHURST, R. J., ROBINSON, M., and DORR, M. The development of the ideal self in childhood and adolescence. *Journal of Educational Research*, 1946, *40*, 241–57.

HAWKES, G. R., and PEASE, D. *Behavior and development from 5 to 12.* New York: Harper & Row, 1962.

HAYNES, H., WHITE, B. L., and HELD, R. Visual accommodation in human infants. *Science*, 1965, *148*, 528–30.

HEATH, C. W., and GREGORY, L. W. Problems of normal college students and their families. *School and Society*, 1946, *63*, 355–58.

HEBB, D. O. The effects of early experience on problem solving at maturity. *American Psychologist*, 1947, *2*, 306–7.

HEER, D. M. Dominance and the working wife. *Social Forces*, 1958, *36*, 341–47.

HEIDT, G. A., PETERSEN, M. K., and KIRKLAND, G. L., JR. Mating behavior and development of least weasels (*Mustela nivalis*) in captivity. *Journal of Mammalogy*, 1968, *49*, 413–19.

HEILBRUNN, L. V. *Outline of general physiology* (2nd ed.). Philadelphia: Saunders, 1943.

HELD, R., and HEIN, A. Movement-produced stimulation in the development of visually guided behavior. *Journal of Comparative and Physiological Psychology*, 1963, *56*, 872–76.

—— On the modifiability of form perception. *In* W. Wathen-Dunn (ed.), *Models for the perception of speech and visual form.* Cambridge, Mass.: The M. I. T. Press, 1967.

HELFAT, L. Parents of adolescents need help too. *New York State Journal of Medicine*, 1967, *67*, 2764–68.

HENDRY, L. S., and KESSEN, W. Oral behavior of newborn infants as a function of age and time since feeding. *Child Development*, 1964, *35*, 201–8.

HENRY, W. E. Projective techniques. *In* P. H. Mussen (ed.), *Handbook of research methods in child development.* New York: John Wiley, 1960.

—— The theory of intrinsic disengagement. *In* P. F. Hansen (ed.), *Age with a future.* Philadelphia: Davis, 1964.

HERON, A., and CHOWN, S. M. *Age and function.* London: J. & A. Churchill, 1967.

HERSHENSON, M. Visual discrimination in the human newborn. *Journal of Comparative and Physiological Psychology*, 1964, *58*, 270–76.

HERSHER, L. Maternal deprivation in goats. *Developmental Psychology*, 1969, *1*, 95–101.

HERSHER, L., RICHMOND, J. B., and MOORE, A. U. Maternal behavior in sheep and goats. *In* H. R. Rheingold (ed.), *Maternal behavior in mammals*. New York: John Wiley, 1963.

HESS, R., and GOLDBLATT, I. The status of adolescents in American society: A problem in social identity. *Child Development*, 1957, *28*, 459–68.

HESS, R., and SHIPMAN, V. Early experience and the socialization of cognitive modes in children. *Child Development*, 1965, *36*, 869–86.

HETZER, H. Der Einfluss der negativen Phase auf soziales Verhalten und literarische Produktion pubertierender Mädchen. *Quellen und Studien zur Jugendkunde*, 1926, no. 4.

—— and RIENDORF, G. Sprachentwicklung und soziales Milieu. *Zeitschrift Angewandte Psychologie*, 1927, *29*.

HETZER, H., and TUDOR-HART, B. H. Die frühesten Reaktionen auf die menschliche Stimme. *In* C. Bühler (ed.), *Quellen und Studien zur Jugendkunde*, 1927, *5*, 194–24.

HILDRETH, G. Adolescent interests and abilities. *Journal of Genetic Psychology*, 1933, *43*, 65–93.

—— Development and training of hand dominance: III. Developmental tendencies in handedness. *Journal of Genetic Psychology*, 1949, *75*, 221–54.

HILGARD, J. R. Learning and maturation in preschool children. *Journal of Genetic Psychology*, 1932, *41*, 36–56.

HINDE, R. A. *Animal behaviour*. New York: McGraw-Hill, 1966.

—— and SPENCER-BOOTH, Y. The behaviour of socially living rhesus monkeys in their first two and a half years. *Animal Behaviour*, 1967, *15*, 169–96.

HINTON, J. *Dying*. Baltimore: Penguin, 1967.

HIRSCHBERG, J. C. Religion and childhood. *Menninger Quarterly*, 1956, *10*, 22–24.

HOBART, C. W. Some effects of romanticism during courtship on marriage role opinions. *Sociology and Social Research*, 1958, *42*, 336–43.

HODGKINS, J. Influence of age on the speed of reaction and movement in females. *Journal of Gerontology*, 1962, *17*, 385–89.

HOFFMAN, H. S.; SCHIFF, D., ADAMS, J., and SEARLE, J. L. Enhanced distress vocalization through selective reinforcement. *Science*, 1966, *151*, 352–54.

HOFFMAN, L. W. Mother's enjoyment of work and effects on the child. *Child Development*, 1961, *32*, 187–97.

HOLLAND, J. L. A theory of vocational choice. *Journal of Counseling Psychology*, 1959, *6*, 35–44.

—— Creative and academic performance among talented adolescents. *Journal of Educational Psychology*, 1961, *52*, 136–47.

—— Explorations of a theory of vocational choice: II. Self descriptions and vocational preferences. *Vocational Guidance Quarterly*, 1963, *12*, 17–24.

HOLLINGSHEAD, A. B. *Elmtown's youth*. New York: John Wiley, 1949.

HONZIK, M. P., HUTCHINGS, J. J., and BURNIP, S. R. Birth record assessment and test performance at eight months. *American Journal of Diseases of Childhood*, 1965, *109*, 416–26.

HOOKER, D. Reflex activities in the human fetus. *In* R. G. Barker, J. S. Kounin, and H. F. Wright (eds.), *Child behavior and development*. New York: McGraw-Hill, 1943.

HORNICK, E. J. Emergencies, anxiety, and adolescence. *New York State Journal of Medicine*, 1967, *67*, 1979–81.

HORROCKS, J. E. The adolescent. *In* L. Carmichael (ed.), *Manual of child psychology*. New York: John Wiley, 1954.

—— and BUKER, M. E. A study of friendship fluctuations of preadolescents. *Journal of Genetic Psychology*, 1951, *78*, 131–44.

HORROCKS, J. E., and THOMPSON, G. G. A study of the friendship fluctuations of rural boys and girls. *Journal of Genetic Psychology*, 1946, *69*, 189–98.

HOYT, G. C. The life of the retired in a trailer park. *American Journal of Sociology*, 1954, *59*, 361–70.

HUANG, U., and CHU, Y. J. The social function of children's language. *Chung Hua Educational Review*, 1936, *23*, 69–94.

HULSE, W. C. Psychiatric aspects of group counseling with adolescents. *Psychiatric Quarterly Supplement*, 1960, *2*, 1–7.

HUMMEL, R. H., and SPRINTHALL, N. Underachievement related to interests, attitudes, and values. *Personnel and Guidance Journal*, 1965, *44*, 388–95.

HUNT, J. M. Experience and the development of motivation: some reinterpretations. *Child Development*, 1960, *31*, 489–504.

—— *Intelligence and experience*. New York: Ronald, 1961.

HURLOCK, E. B. *Child development*. 4th ed. New York: McGraw-Hill, 1964.

—— *Developmental psychology*. 3rd ed. New York: McGraw-Hill, 1968.

ILLINGWORTH, R. S. *The development of the infant and young child, normal and abnormal*. London: Livingstone, 1960.

INGLIS, J. Psychological investigations of cognitive deficit in elderly psychiatric patients. *Psychological Bulletin*, 1958, *54*, 197–214.

——, ANKUS, M. N., and SYKES, D. H. Age-related differences in learning and short-term-memory from childhood to the senium. *Human Development*, 1968, *11*, 42–52.

IRWIN, O. C. The amount and nature of activities of newborn infants under constant external stimulating conditions during the first ten days of life. *Genetic Psychology Monographs*, 1930, *8*, 1–92.

—— The distribution of the amount of motility in young infants between two nursing periods. *Journal of Comparative Psychology*, 1932a, *14*, 429–45.

—— Infant responses to vertical movements. *Child Development*, 1932b, *2*, 167–69.

—— The activities of newborn infants. *In* R. G. Barker, J. S. Kounin, and H. F. Wright (eds.), *Child behavior and development*. New York: McGraw-Hill, 1943.

—— Infant speech. *Scientific American*, 1949, *18*, 22–24.

ISSACS, S. *The nursery years*. New York: Vanguard, 1936.

JACOBSON, P. H. *American marriage after divorce*. New York: Holt, 1959.

JAY, P. Field studies. *In* A. M. Schrier, H. F. Harlow, and F. Stollnitz (eds.), *Behavior of non-human primates*, vol. II. New York: Academic Press, 1965.

JEFFERS, F. C., and NICHOLS, C. R. The relationship of activities and attitudes to physical well-being in older people. *Journal of Gerontology*, 1961, *16*, 67–70.

—— and EISDORFER, C. Attitudes of older persons toward death: A preliminary study. *Journal of Gerontology*, 1961, *16*, 53–56.

JENKINS, L. M. A comparative study of motor achievement of children of five, six, and seven years of age. *Contributions to Education*, 1930, *414*, 16–17.

JEROME, E. A. Age and learning: Experimental studies. *In* J. E. Birren (ed.), *Handbook of aging and the individual*. Chicago: University of Chicago Press, 1959.

JERSILD, A. T. Studies of children's fears. *In* R. G. Barker, J. S. Kounin, and H. F. Wright (eds.), *Child behavior and development*. New York: McGraw-Hill, 1943.

—— Emotional Development. *In* L. Carmichael (ed.), *Manual of child psychology*, New York: John Wiley, 1946.

—— *Child psychology*. Englewood Cliffs, N. J.: Prentice-Hall, 1960.

—— *The psychology of adolescence*. 2d ed. London: Macmillan, 1963.

—— and HOLMES, F. B. Children's fears. *Child Development Monographs*, 1935, No. 20.

JERSILD, A. T., and RITZMAN, R. Aspects of language development: The growth of loquacity and vocabulary. *Child Development*, 1938, *9*, 243–59.

JESPERSEN, O. *Language: Its nature, development, and origin*. London: Allen & Unwin, 1922.

JOFFE, J. M. *Prenatal determinants of behavior*. New York: Pergamon, 1969.

JOHNSON, E. C., and JOSEY, C. C. A note on the development of the thought forms of children as described by Piaget. *Journal of Abnormal and Social Psychology*, 1931, *26*, 338–39.

JOHNSON, H. M. *The art of block building*. New York: John Day, 1933.

JOHNSON, R. C., and MEDINNUS, G. R. *Child psychology: Behavior and development*. New York: John Wiley, 1969.

JONES, H. E. *Development in adolescence*. New York: Appleton-Century-Crofts, 1943.

—— The development of physical abilities. *National Society for the Study of Education Yearbook*, 1944, *43*, (1).

—— *Motor performance and growth*. Berkeley: University of California Press, 1949.

—— The age-relative study of personality. *Acta Psychology*, 1961, *19*, 140–42.

—— and CONRAD, H. S. The growth and decline of intelligence: A study of a homogeneous group between the ages of ten and sixty. *Genetic Psychology Monographs*, 1933, *13*, 223–98.

JONES, M. C. The development of early behavior patterns in young children. *Pedagogical Seminary*, 1926, *33*, 537–85.

—— The later careers of boys who were early or late maturing. *Child Development*, 1957, *28*, 113–28.

—— A comparison of the attitudes and interests of ninth grade students over two decades. *Journal of Educational Psychology*, 1960, *51*, 175–86.

—— and BAYLEY, N. Physical maturing among boys as related to behavior. *Journal of Educational Psychology*, 1950, *41*, 129–48.

JONES, M. C., and MUSSEN, P. H. Self conceptions, motivations, and interpersonal attitudes of early- and late-maturing girls. *Child Development*, 1958, *29*, 491–501.

JONES, T. D. The development of certain motor skills and play activities in young children. *Child Development Monographs*, 1939, No. 26.

KAGAN, J. American longitudinal research on psychological development. *Child Development*, 1964, *35*, 1–32.

—— and HENKER, B. A. Developmental psychology. *Annual Review of Psychology*, 1966, *17*, 1–50.

KAGAN, J., and LEWIS, N. Studies of attention in the human infant. *Merrill-Palmer Quarterly*, 1965, *11*, 95–128.

KAGAN, J., and MOSS, H. A. *Birth to maturity: A study in psychological development.* New York: John Wiley, 1962.

KAHL, J. A. Educational and occupational aspirations of "common-man" boys. *Harvard Educational Review*, 1953, *23*, 186–203.

KAHN, M. D. The adolescent struggle with identity as a force in psychotherapy. *Adolescence*, 1969, *3*, 395–424.

KAHN, R. L., GOLDFARB, A. I., POLLACK, M., and GERBER, I. E. The relationship of mental and physical status in institutionalized aged persons. *American Journal of Psychiatry*, 1960, *117*, 120–24.

KAIMAN, B. D. Age and activity. Paper presented at the 8th international Congress of Gerontology, 1969.

—— DESROCHES, H. F., and BALLARD, H. T. Activity preferences of older people. *In* H. F. Desroches and B. D. Kaiman (eds.), *Report of Psychological Research* no. 11. Mountain Home, Tenn.: VA Center, 1965.

—— Therapeutic effectiveness of minimal activity in an aged population. *Psychological Reports*, 1966, *19*, 439–43.

KALISH, R. A. Of children and grandfathers: A speculative essay on dependency. *Gerontologist*, 1967, *7*, 67–70.

KAMII, C. K., and RADIN, N. L. A framework for a preschool curriculum based on some Piagetian concepts. *Journal of Creative Behavior*, 1967, *1*, 314–23.

KAPLAN, M. The use of leisure. *In* C. Tibbitts (ed.), *Handbook of Social Gerontology*. Chicago: University of Chicago Press, 1960.

KARMEL, B. Z. The effect of age, complexity, and amount of contour on pattern preferences in human infants. *Journal of Experimental Child Psychology*, 1969, *7*, 339–54.

KASATKIN, N. I. The development of visual and acoustic conditioned reflexes and their differentiation in infants. *Psychological Abstracts*, 1936, No. 1756.

—— and LEVIKOVA, A. M. On the development of early conditioned reflexes and differentiations of auditory stimuli in infants. *Journal of Experimental Psychology*, 1935, *18*, 1–19.

KASTENBAUM, R. Death as a research problem in social gerontology: An overview. *Gerontologist*, 1966, *6*, 67–69.

KAY, H. Learning of a serial task by different age groups. *Quarterly Journal of Experimental Psychology*, 1951, *3*, 166–83.

—— and BIRREN, J. E. Swimming speed of the albino rat: II. Fatigue, practice, and drug effects on age and sex differences. *Journal of Gerontology*, 1958, *13*, 378–85.

KAYE, H. The effects of feeding and total stimulation on non-nutritive sucking in the human newborn. *Journal of Experimental Child Psychology*, 1966, *3*, 131–45.

KELLOGG, W. N. Communication and language in the home-raised chimpanzee. *Science*, 1968, *162*, 423–27.

—— Research on the home-raised chimpanzee. *In* G. H. Bourne (ed.), *Anatomy, behavior, and diseases of chimpanzees*. Basel and New York: S. Karger, 1969.

—— and KELLOGG, L. A. *The ape and the child: A study of environmental influence on later behavior.* New York: McGraw-Hill, 1933.

KENISTON, K. *The uncommitted: Alienated youth in American society.* New York: Dell, 1960.

—— The sources of student dissent. *Journal of Social Issues*, 1967, *23*, 108–37.

KEPHART, W. M. Some correlates of romantic love. *Journal of Marriage and the Family*, 1967, *29*, 494–99.

KEPPEL, G. Verbal learning in children. *Psychological Bulletin*, 1964, *61*, 63–80.

KESSEN, W. Research design in the study of developmental problems. *In* P. H. Mussen (ed.), *Handbook of research methods in child development*. New York: John Wiley, 1960.

—— Research in the psychological development of infants: An overview. *Merrill-Palmer Quarterly*, 1963, *9*, 83–94.

——, HENDRY, L. S., and LEUTZENDORFF, A. M. Measurement of movement in the human newborn: A new technique. *Child Development*, 1961, *32*, 95–105.

KESSEN, W., and LEUTZENDORFF, A. M. The effect of nonnutritive sucking on movement in the human newborn. *Journal of Comparative and Physiological Psychology*, 1963, *56*, 69–72.

—— and STOUTSENBERGER, U. Age, food-deprivation, non-nutritive sucking and movement in the human newborn. *Journal of Comparative and Physiological Psychology*, 1967, *63*, 82–86.

KESSEN, W., WILLIAMS, E. J., and WILLIAMS, J. P. Selection and test of response measures in the study of the human newborn. *Child Development*, 1961, *32*, 7–24.

KING, J. A. A comparison of longitudinal and cross-sectional groups in the development of behavior of deer mice. *Annals of the New York Academy of Science*, 1969, *159*, 696–709.

KINSEY, A. C., POMEROY, W. B., and MARTIN, C. E. *Sexual behavior in the human male.* Philadelphia: Saunders, 1948.

—— and GEBHART, P. H. *Sexual behavior in the human female.* Philadelphia: Saunders, 1953.

KIRK, J. E. Steroid hormones and aging: a review. *Journal of Gerontology*, 1951, *6*, 253–62.

KIRKPATRICK, C. *The family as process and institution.* New York: Ronald Press, 1955.

KISTIAKOVSKAIA, M. I. Stimuli evoking positive emotions in infants in the first month of life. *Soviet Psychology and Psychiatry*, 1965, *3*, 39–48.

KLEEMEIER, R. W. Leisure and disengagement in retirement. *Gerontologist*, 1964, *4*, 180–84.

KLEITMAN, N. *Sleep and wakefulness.* Chicago: University of Chicago Press, 1963.

KLEMER, R. H. Factors of personality and experience which differentiate single from married women. *Marriage and Family Living*, 1954, *16*, 41–44.

KLONOFF, H., and KENNEDY, M. Memory and perceptual functioning in octogenarians and nonagenarians in the community. *Journal of Gerontology*, 1965, *20*, 328–33.

KLOPFER, P. H. Imprinting, *Science*, 1961, *133*, 923–24.

—— Stimulus preferences and imprinting. *Science*, 1967, *156*, 1394–96.

KNUPFER, G., CLARK, W., and ROOM, R. The mental health of the unmarried. *American Journal of Psychiatry*, 1966, *122*, 841–51.

KOCH, A. Experimentelle Untersuchungen über die Abstraktionsfähigkeit von Volksschulkindern. *Zeitschrift für angewandte Psychologie*, 1913, No. 7.

KOCH, J. An attempt to analyze the influence of the environment of children's homes on the neuropsychic development of 4- to 12-month-old children. *Ceskoslovenska Pediatric*, 1961, *16*, 322–30.

KODLIN, D., and THOMPSON, D. J. An appraisal of the longitudinal approach to studies of growth and development. *Monographs of the Society for Research in Child Development*, 1958, *23*, No. 1.

KOFORD, C. B. Rank of mothers and sons in bands of rhesus monkeys. *Science*, 1963, *141*, 356–57.

KOHLBERG, L. Early education: A cognitive-developmental view. *Child Development*, 1968, *39*, 1013–62.

KOHN, M. L. Social class and parental values. *American Journal of Sociology*, 1959, *64*, 377–51.

KOMAROVSKY, M. Functional analysis of sex roles. *American Sociological Review*, 1950, *15*, 508–16.

KORCHIN, S. H., and BASOWITZ, H. Age differences in verbal learning. *Journal of Abnormal and Social Psychology*, 1957, *54*, 64–69.

KORNER, A. F., CHUCK, B., and DONTCHOS, S. Organismic determinants of spontaneous oral behavior in neonates. *Child Development*, 1968, *39*, 1145–57.

KOVACH, J. K. Development of pecking behavior in chicks: Recovery after deprivation. *Journal of Comparative and Physiological Psychology*, 1969, *68*, 516–23.

——— and KLING, A. Mechanisms of neonate sucking behavior in kittens. *Animal Behaviour*, 1967, *15*, 91–101.

KROGER, R., and LOUTTIT, C. M. The influence of father's occupation on the vocational choices of high school boys. *Journal of Applied Psychology*, 1935, *19*, 203–12.

KROGMAN, W. M. The physical growth of the child. *In* M. Fishbein and R. J. R. Kennedy (eds.), *Modern marriage and family living*. Fairlawn, N. J.: Oxford, 1957.

KRON, R. E., STEIN, M., and GODDARD, K. E. A method of measuring sucking behavior in newborn infants. *Psychosomatic Medicine*, 1963, *25*, 181–91.

KRUIJT, J. P. *Ontogeny of social behavior in Burmese Red jungle-fowl.* Brill, The Netherlands: Leiden, 1964.

KUHLEN, R. G. Aging and life adjustment. *In* J. E. Birren (ed.), *Handbook of aging and the individual*. Chicago: University of Chicago Press, 1959.

——— Adolescence. *In* C. W. Harris (ed.), *Encyclopedia of educational research*. New York: Macmillan, 1960.

——— and ARNOLD, M. Age differences in religious beliefs and problems during adolescence. *Journal of Genetic Psychology*, 1944, *65*, 291–300.

KUHLEN, R. G. and JOHNSON, G. H. Changes in goals with adult increasing age. *Journal of Consulting Psychology*, 1952, *16*, 1–4.

KUHLEN, R. G., and LEE, B. J. Personality characteristics and social acceptability in adolescence. *Journal of Educational Psychology*, 1943, *34*, 321–40.

KUNST, M. S. A study of thumb and finger sucking in infants. *Psychological Monographs*, 1948, *62*, No. 3.

KUO, Z. Y. The genesis of the cat's responses to the rat. *Journal of Comparative Psychology*, 1930, *11*, 1–35.

——— Ontogeny of embryonic behavior in Aves: III. The structural and environmental factors in embryonic behavior. *Journal of Comparative Psychology*, 1932a, *13*, 245–71.

——— Ontogeny of embryonic behavior in Aves: IV. The influence of embryonic movements upon the behavior after hatching. *Journal of Comparative Psychology*, 1932b, *14*, 109–22.

——— Further study on the behavior of the cat toward the rat. *Journal of Comparative Psychology*, 1938, *25*, 1–8.

——— *The dynamics of behavior development: An epigenetic view.* New York: Random House, 1967.

KUTNER, B. D., FANSHELL, A. M., TOGO, and LANGER, T. S. *Five hundred over sixty*. New York: Russell Sage Foundation, 1956.

LAGERSPETZ, K., and PORTIN, R. Simulation of cues eliciting aggressive responses in mice at two age levels. *Journal of Genetic Psychology*, 1968, *113*, 53–63.

LAKIN, M. Personality factors in mothers of excessively crying (colicky) infants. *Monographs of the Society for Research in Child Development*, 1957, *22*, No. 1.

LANDIS, B. Y. Religion and youth. *In* E. Ginzberg (ed.), *The nation's children*, vol. 2. *Development and education*. New York: Columbia University Press, 1960.

LANDIS, J. T. What is the happiest period of life? *School and Society*, 1942, *55*, 643–45.

——— The trauma of children when parents divorce. *Marriage and Family Living*, 1960, *22*, 7–13.

——— Social correlates of divorce or nondivorce among the unhappy married. *Marriage and Family Living*, 1963, *25*, 178–80.

LANTAGNE, J. E. Interests of 4,000 high school pupils in problems of marriage and parenthood. *Research Quarterly of the American Association for Health, Physical Education and Recreation*, 1958, *28*, 407–16.

LAWRENCE, C. H., and WERTHESSSEN, N. T. Treatment of acne with orally administered estrogens. *Journal of Clinical Endocrinology*, 1942, *2*, 636–38.

LAZARSFELD, P. Jugend und Beruf. *Quellen und Studien zur Jugendkunde*, 1931, No. 8.

LEHMAN, H. C. *Age and achievement*. Princeton, N. J.: Princeton University Press, 1953.

LEHR, U. Positive and negative attitudes toward different ages, *Vita Humana*, 1964, 7, 201–27.

LENNENBERG, E. H. (ed.). *New directions in the study of language*. Cambridge, Mass: M. I. T., 1964.

LESSAC, M. S., and SOLOMON, R. L. Effects of early isolation on the later adaptive behavior of beagles: A methodological demonstration. *Developmental Psychology*, 1969, *1*, 14–25.

LEVENTHAL, A. S., and LIPSITT, L. P. Adaptation, pitch discrimination, and sound localization in the neonate. *Child Development*, 1964, *35*, 759–67.

LEVIN, H., and WARDWELL, E. The research uses of doll play. *Psychological Bulletin*, 1962, *59*, 27–56.

LEVIN, S. Depression in the aged: a study of the salient external factors. *Geriatrics*, 1963, *18*, 302–7.

LEVINE, M. L., and BELL, A. I. The treatment of colic in infancy by use of the pacifier. *Journal of Pediatrics*, 1950, *37*, 750–55.

LEVINE, S. Stimulation in infancy. *Scientific American*, No. 436. San Francisco: W. H. Freeman, 1960.

——— The psychophysiological effects of early stimulation. *In* E. Bliss (ed.), *Roots of behavior*. New York: Harper and Row, 1962.

LEVINSON, H. What work means to a man. *Menninger Quarterly*, 1964, *18*, 1–11.

LEVISON, C. A., and LEVISON, P. K. Operant conditioning of head turning for visual reinforcement in three-month infants. *Psychonomic Science*, 1967, *8*, 529–30.

LEVY, D. M. Finger sucking and accessory movements in early infancy: An etiologic study. *American Journal of Psychiatry*, 1928, *7*, 881–918.

——— *Maternal overprotection*. New York: Columbia University Press, 1943.

——— *Behavioral analysis*. Springfield, Ill.: Charles C Thomas, 1958.

——— The infant's early memory of innoculation: a contribution to public health procedures. *Journal of Genetic Psychology*, 1960, *96*, 3–46.

——— and HESS, A. Problems in determining maternal attitudes toward newborn infants. *Psychiatry*, 1952, *15*, 273–86.

LEWIS, M. M. *Infant speech* (2nd ed.). New York: Humanities Press, 1951.

——— Infants' responses to facial stimuli during the first year of life. *Developmental Psychology*, 1969, *1*, 75–86.

LIEBERMAN, J. N. The relationship between playfulness and divergent thinking at the kindergarten level. *Journal of Genetic Psychology*, 1965, *107*, 219–24.

——— A developmental analysis of playfulness as a clue to cognitive style. *Journal of Creative Behavior*, 1967, *1*, 391–97.

LINDEN, M. E., and COURTNEY, D. The human life cycle and its interruptions: a psychologic hypothesis. *American Journal of Psychiatry*, 1953, *109*, 906–15.

LING, B. C. Form discrimination as a learning cue in infants. *Comparative Psychology Monographs*, 1941, *17*, No. 86.

——— A genetic study of sustained visual fixation and associated behavior in the human infant from birth to six months. *Journal of Genetic Psychology*, 1942, *61*, 227–77.

LIPSET, S. M., and BENDIX, R. *Social mobility in industrial society*. Berkeley: University of California Press, 1959.

LIPSITT, L. P. Learning processes of human newborns. *Merrill-Palmer Quarterly*, 1966, *12*, 45–71.

——— ENGEN, T., and KAYE, H. Developmental changes in the olfactory threshold of the neonate. *Child Development*, 1963, *34*, 371–76.

LIPSITT, L. P., and KAYE, H. Conditioned sucking in the human newborn. *Psychonomic Science*, 1964, *1*, 29–30.

——— Change in neonatal response to optimizing and non-optimizing sucking stimulation. *Psychonomic Science*, 1965, *2*, 221–22.

LIPSITT, L. P. and LEVY, N. Electrotactual threshold in the neonate. *Child Development*, 1959, *30*, 547–54.

LIPTON, E. L., and STEINSCHNEIDER, A. Studies on the psychophysiology of infancy. *Merrill-Palmer Quarterly*, 1964, *10*, 103–17.

——— and RICHMOND, J. B. Autonomic function in the neonate, IV. Individual differences in cardiac reactivity. *Psychosomatic Medicine*, 1961, *23*, 472–84.

LLOYD, R. C. Parent-youth conflicts of college students. *Sociology and Social Research*, 1952, *36*, 227–30.

LOCKWOOD, W. V. Realism of vocational preference. *Personnel Guidance Journal*, 1958, *37*, 98–106.

LONGSTRETH, L. E. *Psychological development of the child.* New York: Ronald Press, 1968.

LORAND, S., and SCHNEER, H. I. (eds.) *Adolescents: Psychoanalytic approach to problems and therapy.* New York: Paul B. Hoeber, 1961.

LORENZ, K. The companion in the bird's world. *Auk*, 1937, *54*, 245–73.

——— Morphology and behavior patterns in closely allied species. *In* B. Schaffner (ed.), *Group Processes.* New York: Macy Foundation, 1955.

——— Companionship in bird life: Fellow members of the species as releasers of social behavior. *In* C. H. Schiller (ed.), *Instinctive behavior.* New York: International University Press, 1957.

LOVELL, K. Some recent studies in cognitive and language development. *Merrill-Palmer Quarterly*, 1968, *14*, 123–38.

LOWE, C. M. The relationship between marital and socioeconomic status and in-patient impairment. *Journal of Clinical Psychology*, 1967, *23*, 315–18.

LUCKEY, E. B. Number of years married as related to personality perception and marital satisfaction. *Journal of Marriage and the Family*, 1966, *28*, 44–48.

LURIA, A. R. The role of language in the formation of temporary connections. *In* B. Simon (ed.), *Psychology in the Soviet Union.* Stanford, Calif.: Stanford University Press, 1957.

LYMAN, E. L. Occupational differences in the value attached to work. *American Journal of Sociology*, 1955, *61*, 138–44.

MCCAMMON, R. W. Are boys and girls maturing physically at earlier ages? *American Journal of Public Health*, 1965, *55*, 103–6.

MCCANDLESS, B., and SPIKER, C. C. Experimental research in child psychology. *Child Development*, 1956, *27*, 75–80.

MCCARTHY, D. The language development of the preschool child. *Institute of Child Welfare Monographs*, 1930, no. 4.

——— Language development in children. *In* L. Carmichael (ed.), *Manual of child psychology.* New York: John Wiley, 1946.

——— Some possible explanations of sex differences in language development and disorders. *Journal of Psychology*, 1953, *35*, 155–60.

——— Language development in children. *In* L. Carmichael (ed.), *Manual of child psychology.* 2d ed. New York: John Wiley, 1954.

——— Research in language development: Retrospect and prospect. *Monographs of the Society for Research in Child Development*, 1959, *24*, No. 5.

——— Language development. *Monographs of the Society for Research in Child Development*, 1960, *25*, No. 3.

MCCASKILL, C. L., and WELLMAN, B. L. A study of common motor achievements at the preschool ages. *Child Development*, 1938, *9*, 141–50.

MCCLELLAND, D. C., BALDWIN, A. L., BRONFENBRENNER, U., and STRODTBECK, F. L. *Talent and society.* New York: Van Nostrand Reinhold 1958.

MCCONNELL, J. W. Economic aspects. *In* N. W. Shock (ed.), *Aging: Some social and biological aspects.* Washington, D. C.: American Association for the Advancement of Science, Publication 65, 1960.

MCDILL, E. L., and COLEMAN, J. Family and peer influences in college plans of high school students. *Sociology and Education*, 1965, *38*, 112–26.

MCGINNIS, J. M. Eye-movements and optic nystagmus in early infancy. *Genetic Psychology Monographs*, 1930, *8*, 321–430.

MCGRAW, M. B. *Growth: A study of Johnny and Jimmy.* New York: Appleton-Century-Crofts, 1935.

——— Maturation of behavior. *In* L. Carmichael (ed.), *Manual of child psychology.* New York: John Wiley, 1946.

MCKINNEY, J. P. The development of choice stability in children and adolescents. *Journal of Genetic Psychology*, 1968, *113*, 79–83.

MACKINNON, D. W. The personality correlates of creativity: A study of American architects. *In* S. Coppersmith (ed.), *International Association of Applied Psychology Proceedings. Vol. II: Personality Research.* Copenhagen: Munksgaard, 1962.

MCNELL, E. B. *The concept of human development.* Belmont, Calif.: Wadsworth, 1966.

MCNULTY, J. A., and CAIRD, W. Memory loss with age: Retrieval or storage. *Psychological Reports*, 1966, *19*, 229–30.

——— Memory loss with age: An unsolved problem. *Psychological Reports*, 1967, *20*, 283–88.

MCREYNOLD, P., ACKER, M., and PIETILA, C. Relation of object curiosity to psychological adjustment in children. *Child Development*, 1961, *32*, 393–400.

MACFARLANE, J. W., ALLEN, L., and HONZIK, M. P. *A developmental study of the behavior problems of normal children between twenty-two months and fourteen years.* Berkeley: University of California Press, 1954.

MADDOX, G. L. Disengagement theory: A critical evaluation. *Gerontologist*, 1964, *4*, 80–82.

——— and EISENDORFER, C. Some correlates of activity and morale among the elderly. *Social Forces*, 1962, *40*, 254–60.

MAIER, H. W. Adolescenthood. *Social Casework*, 1965, *46*, 3–6.

MAINARDI, D., MARSAN, M., and PASQUALI, A. Causation of sexual preferences in the house mouse. The behavior of mice reared by parents whose odour was artificially altered. *Società Italiana di scienza naturale (Milan)* 1965, *104*, 325–38.

MALLITSKAYA, M. K. A method for using pictures to develop speech comprehension in children at the end of the first and in the second year of life. *Voprosy Psikhiatrii i Nevropatologii*, 1960, *3*, 122–26.

MANNING, A. *An introduction to animal behavior.* Reading, Mass.: Addison-Wesley, 1967.

MARESH, M. M. Variations in patterns of linear growth and skeletal maturation. *Journal of the American Physical Therapy Association*, 1964, *44*, 881–90.

MARINESCO, G., and KREINDLER, A. Des réflexes conditionnels: I. L'organisation des réflexes conditionnels chez l'enfant. *Journal de Psychologie Normale et Pathologigue*, 1933, *30*, 855–86.

MARLER, P. R., and HAMILTON, W. J. *Mechanisms of animal behavior.* New York: John Wiley, 1966.

MARLER, P. R., and TAMURA, M. Culturally transmitted patterns of vocal behavior in sparrows. *Science* 1964, *146*, 148–86.

MARMOR, J. The crisis of middle age. *Psychiatry Digest*, 1968, *29*, 17–21.

MARQUIS, D. P. Can conditioned responses be established in the newborn infant? *Journal of Genetic Psychology*, 1931, *39*, 479–92.

MARSDEN, H. M. Agonistic behaviour of young rhesus monkeys after changes induced in social rank of their mothers. *Animal Behaviour*, 1968, *16*, 38–44.

MARTIN, P. C. and VINCENT, E. L. *Human development.* New York: Ronald Press, 1960.

MARTIN, R. D. Reproduction and ontogeny in tree-shrews (*Tupaia belangeri*) with reference to their general behavior and taxonomic relationship. *Zeitschrift für Tierpsychologie*, 1968, *25*, 409–95.

MARTIN, W. E. Rediscovering the mind of the child: A significant trend in research in child development. *Merrill-Palmer Quarterly*, 1960, *6*, 67–76.

MARTINSON, F. M. Ego deficiency as a factor in marriage. *American Sociological Review*, 1955, *20*, 161–64.

MASON, W. A., and HARLOW, H. F. The effects of age and previous training on patterned-string performance of rhesus monkeys. *Journal of Comparative and Physiological Psychology*, 1961, *54*, 704–9.

MASSLER, M., and SUHER, T. Calculation of "normal" weight in children. *Child Development*, 1951, *22*, 75–94.

MATSON, F. *The broken image.* New York: Braziller, 1964.

MAUDRY, M., and NEKULA, M. Social relations between children of the same age during the first two years of life. *Journal of Genetic Psychology*, 1939, *54*, 193–215.

MAURER, A. The game of peek-a-boo. *Diseases of the Nervous System*, 1967, *28*, 118–21.

MAY, S. H. Purposeful mass activity. *Geriatrics*, 1966, *21*, 193–200.

MEDINNUS, G. R. (ed.) *Readings in psychology of parent-child relations.* New York: John Wiley, 1967.

——— and JOHNSON, R. C. *Child and adolescent psychology*, New York: John Wiley, 1969.

MEISSNER, W. W. Parental interaction of the adolescent boy. *Journal of Genetic Psychology*, 1965, *107*, 225–33.

MELTZER, H., and LUDWIG, D. Age differences in memory optimism and pessimism in workers. *Journal of Genetic Psychology*, 1967, *110*, 17–30.

MEREDITH, H. V. The prediction of stature of North European males throughout the elementary school years. *Human Biology*, 1937, *8*, 279–83.

—— Selected anatomic variables analyzed for interage relationships of the size-size, size-gain, and gain-gain varieties. *In* L. P. Lipsitt and C. C. Spiker (eds.), *Advances in child development and behavior*, vol. 2. New York: Academic Press, 1965.

—— Body size of contemporary groups of pre-school children studied in different parts of the world. *Child Development*, 1968, *39*, 335–77.

—— and KNOTT, V. B. Changes in body proportions during infancy and the preschool years: III. The skelic index. *Child Development*, 1938, *9*, 49–62.

MESSER, M. The possibility of an age-concentrated environment becoming a normative system. *Gerontologist*, 1967, *51*, 247–51.

—— Age grouping and the family status of the elderly. *Sociology and Social Research*, 1968, *52*, 271–79.

MEYERS, C. E. New trends in child study. *Child Study*, 1966, *28*, (3).

MEYERS, W. J. Effects of different intensities of postweaning shock and handling in the albino rat. *Journal of Genetic Psychology*, 1965, *106*, 51–58.

MIDDLETON, R., and PUTNEY, S. Religion, normative standards, and behavior. *Sociometry*, 1962, *25*, 141–52.

MILES, C. C. and MILES, W. R. The correlation of intelligence scores and chronological age from early to late maturity. *American Journal of Psychology*, 1932, *44*, 44–78.

MILL, J. S. *Autobiography*. London: Longmans, Green, 1908.

MILLER, D. C., and FORM, W. H. *Industrial sociology*. New York: Harper & Row, 1951.

MILLER, H. H. (ed.) *Guidance for the underachiever with superior ability*. Washington, D. C.: United States Department of Health, Education, and Welfare, 1961.

MILLS, C. A., and OGLE, C. Physiologic sterility of adolescence. *Human Biology*, 1936, *8*, 607–15.

MILMOE, S.; NOVEY, M. S., KAGAN, J., and ROSENTHAL, R. The mother's voice: Postdictor of aspects of her baby's behavior. *Proceedings, 76th Annual Convention, American Psychological Association*, 1968.

MITCHELL, G. D. Paternalistic behavior in primates. *Psychological Bulletin*, 1969, *71*, 399–417.

—— RUPPENTHAL, G. C., RAYMOND, E. J., and HARLOW, H. F. Long-term effects of multiparous and primiparous monkey mother rearing. *Child Development*, 1966, *37*, 781–91.

MITTELMAN, B. Motility in infants. *Psychoanalytic Studies of the Child*, 1954, *9*, 142–77.

—— Motor patterns and genital behavior: Fetishism. *Psychoanalytic Studies of the Child*, 1955, *10*, 241–63.

MOLTZ, H. Imprinting: An epigenetic approach. *Psychological Review*, 1963, *70*, 123–38.

—— and ROSENBLUM, L. A. The relation between habituation and the stability of the following response. *Journal of Comparative and Physiological Psychology*, 1958, *51*, 658–61.

MONTAGU, M. F. A. The existence of a sterile phase in female adolescence. *Complex*, 1950, *1*, 27–30.

MORGAN, M. The attitudes and adjustments of recipients of old-age assistance in upstate and metropolitan New York. *Archives of Psychology*, 1937, *30*, (214).

MORGAN, R. F. Note on the psychopathology of senility: Senescent defense against threat of death. *Psychological Reports*, 1965, *16*, 305–6.

—— The adult growth examination: Preliminary comparisons of physical aging in adults by sex and race. *Perceptual and Motor Skills*, 1968, *27*, 595–99.

MORROW, W. R., and WILSON, R. R. Family relations of bright high-achieving and under-achieving high school boys. *Child Development*, 1961, *32*, 501–10.

MOSS, H. A. Sex, age, and state as determinants of mother-infant interaction. *Merrill-Palmer Quarterly*, 1967, *13*, 19–36.

—— and KAGAN, J. Stability of achievement and recognition seeking behaviors from early childhood through adulthood. *Journal of Abnormal and Social Psychology*, 1961, *62*, 504–13.

MOSS, H. A., and ROBSON, K. S. Maternal influences in early social visual behavior. *Child Development*, 1968, *39*, 401–8.

MROSOVSKY, N., and SHETTLEWORTH, S. J. Wavelength preferences and brightness cues in the water finding behavior of sea turtles. *Behaviour*, 1968, *32*, 211–57.

MUELLNER, S. R. Development of urinary control in children. *Journal of the American Medical Association*, 1960, *172*, 1256–61.

MULLER, P. *The tasks of childhood*. New York: McGraw-Hill, 1969.

MUNN, N. L. Learning in children. *In* L. Carmichael (ed.) *Manual of child psychology*. New York: John Wiley, 1946.

—— *The evolution and growth of human behavior*. 2d ed. Boston: Houghton Mifflin, 1965.

MUNNICHS, J. M. A. Death and dying. Paper presented at the 8th international Congress of Gerontology, 1969.

MURIE, A. *The wolves of Mt. McKinley*. Fauna Series No. 5, U. S. Department of the Interior, 1944.

MURPHY, G. *Historical introduction to modern psychology*. New York: Harcourt Brace Jovanovich, 1949.

MURPHY, L. B. *Personality in young children*. 2 vols. New York: Basic Books, 1956.

—— *The widening world of childhood*. New York: Basic Books, 1962.

—— Spontaneous ways of learning in young children. *Children*, 1967, *14*, 210–16.

MURRAY, H. A. *Explorations in personality*. New York: Oxford University Press, 1938.

MUSSEN, P. H. (ed.) *Handbook of research methods in child development*. New York: John Wiley, 1960.

—— CONGER, J. J., and KAGAN, J. *Child development and personality*. New York: Harper & Row, 1969.

MUSSEN, P. H., and JONES, M. C. Self-conceptions, motivations, and interpersonal attitudes of late- and early-maturing boys, *Child Development*, 1957, *28*, 243–56.

MUUSS, R. E. *Theories of adolescence*. New York: Random House, 1969.

MYERS, W. E. High school graduates choose vocations unrealistically. *Occupations*, 1947, *25*, 332–33.

NATHANSON, I. I., TOWNE, L. E., and AUB, J. C. Normal excretion of sex hormones in childhood. *Endocrinology*, 1941, *23*, 851–65.

NEUGARTEN, B. L., BERKOWITZ, H., CROTTY, W. J., GRUEN, W., GUTMANN, D. L., LUBIN, M. I., MILLER, R., PECK, F., ROSEN, J. L., SHUKIN, A., TOBIN, S. S., and FALK, M. (eds.), *Personality in middle and late life*. New York: Atherton, 1964.

NEWTON, N. *Maternal emotions*. New York: Hoeber-Harper, 1955.

—— and NEWTON, M. Recent trends in breast feeding: A review. *American Journal of Medical Science*, 1951, *221*, 691–98.

NICE, M. M. Studies on the life-history of the song sparrow: I. *Transactions of the Linnaean Society, New York*, 1937, *4*, 1–247.

—— Studies on the life-history of the song sparrow: II. *Transactions of the Linnaean Society, New York*, 1943, *4*, 1–328.

NICHOLS, R. C. Parental attitudes of mothers of intelligent adolescents and creativity of their children. *Child Development*, 1964, *35*, 1041–50.

NISBET, J. D. Intelligence and age: Retesting with twenty-four years' interval. *British Journal of Educational Psychology*, 1957, *27*, 190–98.

NISSEN, H. W. A field study of the chimpanzee. *Comparative Psychology Monographs*, 1931, *8*, 1–122.

—— CHOW, K. L., and SEMMES, J. Effects of restricted opportunity for tactual, kinesthetic, and manipulative experience on the behavior of a chimpanzee. *American Journal of Psychology*, 1951, *64*, 485–507.

NIXON, R. E. Psychological normality in adolescence. *Adolescence*, 1966, *1*, 211–23.

NOIROT, E. Ultrasounds in young rodents: I. Changes with age in albino mice. *Animal Behaviour*, 1966, *14*, 459–62.

—— Ultrasounds in young rodents: II. Changes with age in albino rats. *Animal Behaviour*, 1968, *16*, 129–34.

—— and PYE, D. Sound analysis of ultrasonic distress calls of mouse pups as a function of their age. *Animal Behaviour*, 1969, *17*, 340–49.

NORTON, J. L. Patterns of vocational interest development and actual job choice. *Journal of Genetic Psychology*, 1953a, *82*, 235–62.

—— General motives and influences in vocational development. *Journal of Genetic Psychology*, 1954b, *82*, 263–78.

NOTTEBOHM, F. Ontogeny of bird song. *Science*, 1970, *167*, 950–56.

NYE, F. I. Child adjustment in broken and in unhappy homes. *Marriage and Family Living*, 1957, *19*, 356–61.

—— and HOFFMAN, L. (eds.). *The employed mother in America.* Chicago: Rand McNally, 1963.

OHMANN, O. The psychology of attraction. *In* H. M. Jordan (ed.) *You and marriage.* New York: John Wiley, 1942.

OLSON, W. C. *Child development.* Boston: Heath, 1949.

—— and HUGHES, B. O. Growth of the child as a whole. *In* R. G., Barker, J. S. Kounin, and H. F. Wright (eds.), *Child behavior and development.* New York: McGraw-Hill, 1943, 199–208.

—— Concepts of growth—their significance to teachers. *Childhood Education*, 1944, *21*, 53–63.

ORMIAN, H. Das schlussfolgernde Denken des Kindes. *Wiener Arbeiten zur pädagogischer Psychologie*, 1926, No. 4.

OTTO, H. A., and HEALY, S. L. Adolescents' self-perception of personality strengths. *Journal of Human Relations*, 1966, *14*, 483–91.

OTTO, H. A., and OTTO, S. T. A new perspective of the adolescent. *Psychology in the Schools*, 1967, *4*, 76–81.

OWENS, W. A. Age and mental abilities: A longitudinal study. *Genetic Psychology Monographs*, 1953, *48*, 3–54.

—— Age and mental abilities. *Journal of Educational Psychology*, 1966, *57*, 311–25.

PACELLA, B. L. Morals, ethics, and religion. *New York State Journal of Medicine*, 1967, *67*, 1975–78.

PADILLA, S. Further studies on the delayed pecking of chicks. *Journal of Comparative Psychology*, 1935, *20*, 413–43.

PAM, J. S. Institutional and personal adjustment in old age. *Journal of Genetic Psychology*, 1954, *85*, 155–58.

PARIS, B. L., and LUCKEY, F. B. A longitudinal study in marital satisfaction. *Sociology and Social Research*, 1966, *50*, 212–22.

PARKE, R., and GLICK, P. C. Prospective changes in marriage and the family. *Journal of Marriage and the Family*, 1967, *29*, 249–56.

PARKER, E. *The seven ages of woman.* Baltimore: Johns Hopkins, 1960.

PARMELEE, A. H., SCHULTZ, M. A., AKUJAMA, Y., WENNER, W. H., and STERN, E. A fundamental periodicity in sleep in infants. Paper presented at the Association for the Psychophysiological Study of Sleep Conference, 1967.

PARMELEE, A. H., WENNER, W. H., and SCHULTZ, H. R. Infant sleep patterns: From birth to 16 weeks of age. *Journal of Pediatrics*, 1964, *65*, 576–82.

PECK, R. Psychological developments in the second half of life. *In* J. E. Anderson, (ed.), *Psychological aspects of aging.* Washington, D.C.: American Psychological Association, 1956.

—— Family patterns correlated with adolescent personality structure. *Journal of Abnormal and Social Psychology*, 1958, *57*, 347–50.

—— and HAVIGHURST, R. *The psychology of character development.* New York: John Wiley, 1960.

PECKOS, P. S. Nutrition during growth and development. *Child Development*, 1957, *28*, 273–85.

PEIPER, A. *Die Hirntätigkeit des Säuglings.* Berlin: Springer, 1928.

—— *Cerebral function in infancy and childhood.* New York: Consultants Bureau, 1963.

PEPINSKY, P. N. A study of productive non-conformity. *Gifted Child Quarterly*, 1960, *4*, 81–85.

PERLIN, S., and BUTLER, R. N. Psychiatric aspects of adaptation to the aging experience. *In* J. E. Birren, R. N. Butler, S. W. Greenhouse, L. Sokoloff, and M. R. Yarrow (eds.), *Human aging.* Washington, D. C.: U. S. Government Printing Office, 1963.

PERRIN, A. C. Physical attractiveness and repulsiveness. *Journal of Experimental Psychology*, 1921, *4*, 203–17.

PERRONE, P. A. Stability of values of junior high school pupils and their parents over two years. *Personnel and Guidance Journal*, Nov., 1967, 268–74.

PESTALOZZI, J. A father's diary, 1774. *Cited in* R. De Guimps, *Pestalozzi, his life and work.* New York: Appleton, 1906.

PFEIFFER, E., VERWOERDT, A., WANG, H-S., and DURHAM, N. C. Sexual behavior in aged men and women. *Archives of General Psychiatry*, 1968, *19*, 753–58.

PIAGET, J. *The language and thought of the child.* New York: Harcourt Brace Jovanovich, 1926.

—— *Judgment and reasoning in the child.* New York: Harcourt Brace Jovanovich, 1928.

—— *The child's conception of the world.* New York: Harcourt Brace Jovanovich, 1929.

—— *The child's conception of physical causality.* New York: Harcourt Brace Jovanovich, 1930.

—— *The moral judgement of the child.* New York: Harcourt Brace Jovanovich, 1932.

—— *Play, dreams, and imitation in childhood.* New York: Norton, 1951.

—— *The child's conception of number.* London: Routledge & Kegan Paul, 1952a.

—— *The origins of intelligence in children.* New York: International Universities Press, 1952b.

—— *The construction of reality in the child.* New York: Basic Books, 1954.

—— and INHELDER, B. *The child's conception of space.* London: Routledge & Kegan Paul, 1956.

PICKFORD, J. H.; SIGNORI, E. I., and REMPEL, H. Similar or related personality traits as a factor in marital happiness. *Journal of Marriage and the Family*, 1966, *28*, 190–92.

PIKLER, E. Some contributions to the study of the gross motor development of children. *Journal of Genetic Psychology*, 1968, *113*, 27–39.

PIKUNAS, J. *Human development: A science of growth.* New York: McGraw-Hill, 1969.

PINCUS, A. Toward a developmental view of aging for social work. *Social Work*, 1967, *12*, 33–41.

PINNEAU, S. R., DILLEHAY, R. C., and SASSENRATH, J. M. *Behavior patterns of normal children.* Office of Education, U. S. Government Printing Office, 1966.

PINNEAU, S. R., and JONES, H. E. Development of mental abilities. *Review of Educational Research*, 1958, *28*, 392–400.

PINNEAU, S. R., and NEWHOUSE, A. Measures of invariance and comparability in factor analysis for fixed variables. *Psychometrika*, 1964, *29*, 271–81.

POINSARD, P. J. Psychiatric problems of adolescence. *Annals of the New York Academy of Sciences*, 1967, *143*, 820–23.

POLANYI, M. *Personal knowledge.* Chicago: University of Chicago. Press, 1958.

POOLE, I. Genetic development of articulation of consonant sounds in speech. *Elementary English Review*, 1934, *11*, 159–61.

POPPLETON, P. K. Puberty, family size and the educational progress of girls. *British Journal of Educational Psychology*, 1968, *38*, 286–92.

POWELL, M. Age and sex differences in degree of conflict within certain areas of psychological adjustment. *Psychological Monographs*, 1955, *69*, No. 2.

PRATT, K. C. Note on the relation of temperature and humidity to the activity of young infants. *Journal of Genetic Psychology*, 1930, *38*, 480–84.

—— The effects of repeated visual stimulation upon the activity of newborn infants. *Journal of Genetic Psychology*, 1934, *44*, 117–26.

—— The neonate. *In* L. Carmichael (ed.), *Manual of child psychology.* New York: John Wiley, 1946.

—— The neonate. *In* L. Carmichael (ed.), *Manual of child psychology.* 2d ed. New York: John Wiley, 1954.

—— NELSON, A. K., and SUN, K. H. The behavior of the newborn infant. *Ohio State University Studies Contributions in Psychology*, 1930, no. 10.

PRECHTL, M. F. R. *The neurological examination of the full term newborn infant.* London: Heinemann Medical Books, 1964.

PRESSEY, S. L. Jobs at 80. *Geriatrics*, 1958, *13*, 678–81.

—— and KUHLEN, R. G. *Psychological development through the life span.* New York: Harper & Row, 1957.

PRESSEY, S. L., and PRESSEY, A. D. Genius at 80, and other oldsters. *Gerontologist*, 1967, *183–87.*

PRESSEY, S. L., and ROBINSON, F. P. *Psychology and the new education.* New York: Harper, 1944.

PREYER, W. *The mind of the child.* Leipzig: Fernau, 1882.

PROVENCE, S. and LIPTON, R. C. *Infants in institutions: A comparison of their development with family-reared infants during the first year of life.* New York: International Universities Press, 1962.

PUNKE, H. H. High-school youth and family quarrels. *School and Society* 1943, *58*, 507–11.

QUARTERMAN, C. J., and RIEGEL, K. F. Age differences in the identification of concepts of the natural language. *Journal of Experimental Child Psychology*, 1968, *6*, 501–9.

Bühler, Keith-Spiegel, & Thomas

RABIN, A. I. Personality maturity of kibbutz (Israeli collective settlement) and non-kibbutz children as reflected in Rorschach findings. *Journal of Projective Techniques*, 1957, *31*, 148–53.

—— Behavior research in collective settlements in Israel: infant and children under conditions of "intermittent" mothering in the kibbutz. *American Journal of Orthopsychiatry*, 1958, *28*, 577–86.

RABKIN, R. Uncoordinated communication between marriage partners. *Family Process*, 1967, *6*, 10–15.

RALLINGS, E. M. Family situations of married and never-married males. *Journal of Marriage and the Family*, 1966, *28*, 485–90.

RAMSAY, A. O., and HESS, E. H. A laboratory approach to the study of imprinting. *Wilson Bulletin*, 1954, *66*, 196–206.

RAMSEY, G. V. The sexual development of boys. *American Journal of Psychology*, 1943, *56*, 217–33.

REBELSKY, F. G., STARR, R. H., and LURIA, Z. Language development: The first four years. *In* Y. Brackbill (ed.), *Infancy and early childhood*. New York: Free Press, 1967.

REEVY, W. R. Adolescent sexuality. *In* A. Ellis (ed.),*The encyclopedia of sexual behavior*. New York: Hawthorn, 1961.

REICHARD, S., LIVSON, F., and PETERSON, P. G. *Aging and personality*. New York: John Wiley, 1962.

REICHENBACH, M., and MATHERS, R. A. The place of time and aging in the natural sciences and scientific philosophy. *In* J. Birren (ed.), *Handbook of aging and the individual*. Chicago: University of Chicago Press, 1959.

REISS, I. L. *Premarital sexual standards in America*. Glencoe, Ill.: Free Press, 1960.

—— The scaling of premarital sexual permissiveness. *Journal of Marriage and the Family*, 1964, *26*, 188–99.

REMMERS, H. H., HORTON, R. E., and SCARBOROUGH, B. B. Youth views, purposes, practices, and procedures in education. *Purdue Opinion Panel, Purdue University*, 1952, *11* (31).

REMMERS, H. H., and RADLER, D. H. *The American teenager*. Indianapolis: Bobbs-Merrill, 1957.

RESSLER, R. H. Parental handling in two strains of mice reared by foster parents. *Science*, 1962, *137*, 129–30.

REYNARD, M. C., and DOCKERAY, F. C. The comparison of temporal intervals in judging depth of sleep in newborn infants. *Journal of Genetic Psychology*, 1939, *55*, 103–20.

REYNOLDS, E. L. The distribution of subcutaneous fat in childhood and adolescence. *Monographs of the Society for Research in Child Development*, 1951, *15*, no. 2.

RHEINGOLD, H. L. The modification of social responsiveness in institutional babies. *Monographs of the Society for Research in Child Development*, 1956, *21*, 5–48.

—— The effective environmental stimulation upon social and exploratory behavior in the human infant. *In* B. M. Foss (ed.), *Determinants of infant behavior: I*. New York: John Wiley, 1961.

—— and BAYLEY, N. The later effects of an experimental modification of mothering. *Child Development*, 1959, *30*, 363–72.

RHEINGOLD, H. L.; GEWIRTZ, J. L., and ROSS, H. W. Social conditioning of vocalizations. *Journal of Comparative and Physiological Psychology*, 1959, *52*, 68–73.

RHUDICK, P. J., and DIBNER, A. S. Age, personality and health correlates of death concerns in normal aged individuals. *Journal of Gerontology*, 1961, *16*, 44–49.

RIBBLE, M. *Rights of infants*. New York: Columbia University Press, 1943.

RICCIUTI, H. N. Object grouping and selective ordering behavior in infants twelve to twenty four months old. *Merrill-Palmer Quarterly*, 1965, *11*, 129–48.

RICHARDS, M. P. M., and ROSS, H. E. Developmental changes in children's drawings. *British Journal of Educational Psychology*, 1967, *37*, 73–80.

RICHARDSON, H. M. The growth of adaptive behavior in infants: An experimental study of seven age levels. *Genetic Psychology Monographs*, 1932, *12*, 195–359.

—— The adaptive behavior of infants in the utilization of the lever as a tool: A developmental and experimental study. *Journal of Genetic Psychology*, 1934, *44*, 352–77.

RICHMOND, J. B. Observations of infant development: Clinical and psychological aspects. *Merrill-Palmer Quarterly*, 1964, *10*, 95–101.

RIEGEL, K. F., and RIEGEL, R. M. A study on changes of attitudes and interests during later years of life. *Vita Humana*, 1960, *3*, 177–206.

—— and MEYER, G. Socio-psychological factors of aging: A cohort-sequential analysis. *Human Development*, 1967a, *10*, 27–56.

—— A study of the dropout rates in longitudinal research on aging and the prediction of death. *Journal of Personality and Social Psychology*, 1967b, *5*, 342–48.

RILEY, M. W., and MOORE, M. E. Adolescent values and the Riesmann typology: An empirical analysis. *In* S. M. Lipset, and L. Lowenthal (eds.), *Culture and social character*. New York: Free Press, 1961.

RIPIN, R., and HETZER, H. Früheste Lernen des Säuglings in der Ernährungssituation. *Zeitschrift für Psychologie*, 1930, *118*, 83–127.

ROBERTS, E. Thumb and finger sucking in relation to feeding in early infancy. *American Journal of Diseases of Childhood*, 1944, *68*, 7–8.

ROBSON, K. The role of eye-to-eye contact in maternal-infant attachment. *Journal of Child Psychology and Psychiatry*, 1967, *8*, 13–25.

RODERICK, T. H., and STORER, J. B. Correlation between mean litter size and mean life span among 12 inbred strains of mice. *Science*, 1961, *134*, 48–49.

ROE, A. Analysis of group Rorschachs of biologists. *Rorschach Exchange and Journal of Projective Techniques*, 1949, *13*, 25–43.

—— A psychological study of eminent biologists, *Psychological Monographs*, 1961, *65*, no. 14.

—— Analysis of group Rorschachs of psychologists and anthropologists. *Journal of Projective Techniques*, 1952, *16*, 212–14.

—— A psychological study of eminent psychologists and anthropologists and a comparison with biological and physiological scientists. *Psychological Monographs*, 1953, *67*, no. 2.

—— Crucial life experiences in the development of scientists. *In* E. P. Torrance (ed.), *Talent and education*. Minneapolis: University of Minnesota Press, 1960.

ROFF, M., and BRODY, D. Appearance and choice during adolescence. *Journal of Psychology*, 1953, *36*, 347–56.

ROFFWARG, H. P., MUZIO, J. N., and DEMENT, W. C. Ontogenetic development of the human sleep-dream cycle. *Science*, 1966, *152*, 604–18.

ROGERS, D. *The psychology of adolescence*. New York: Appleton-Century-Crofts, 1962.

ROSCOW, I. Adjustment of the normal aged. *In* R. H. Williams, C. Tibbitts, and W. Donahue (eds.), *Processes of aging*, vol. II. New York: Atherton, 1963.

—— Local concentrations of the aged and intergenerational relations. *In* P. F. Hansen (ed.), *Age with a future*, Philadelphia: Davis, 1964.

ROSE, C. L. Social correlates of longevity. *In* R. Kastenbaum (ed.), *New thoughts on old age*. New York: Springer-Verlag, 1964.

ROSEN, B. C. Family structure and achievement motivation. *American Sociological Review*, 1961, *26*, 574–85.

ROSENBLATT, J. S., and LEHRMAN, D. S. Maternal behavior of the laboratory rat. *In* H. L. Rheingold (ed.), *Maternal behavior of mammals*. New York: John Wiley, 1963.

ROSENBLATT, J. S., and SCHNEIRLA, T. C. The behaviour of cats. *In* E. S. E. Hafez (ed.), *The behaviour of domestic animals*. Baltimore: Williams & Wilkins, 1962.

ROSENBLATT, J. S., TURKEWITZ, G., and SCHNEIRLA, T. C. Early socialization in the domestic cat as based on feeding and other relationships between female and young. *In* B. M. Foss (ed.), *Determinants of infant behaviour*, vol. I. London: Methuen, 1961.

ROSENBLUM, L. A., and KAUFMAN, C. Laboratory observations of early mother-infant relations in pig-tail and bonnet macaques. *In* S. A. Altman (ed.), *Social communication among primates*. Chicago: University of Chicago Press, 1967.

ROSENZWEIG, M. R. Environmental complexity, cerebral change, and behavior. *American Psychologist*, 1966, *21*, 321–32.

ROSENZWEIG, M. R.; BENNETT, E. L., and KRECH, D. Cerebral effects of environmental complexity and training among adult rats. *Journal of Comparative and Physiological Psychology*, 1964, *57*, 438–39.

ROSS, A. M., and ROSS, J. N. Employment problems of older workers. *In* C. B. Vedder (ed.), *Problems of the middle-aged*. Springfield, Ill.: Charles C Thomas, 1965.

ROSSMAN, J. *Industrial creativity: The psychology of the inventor*. 3d ed. New York: University Books, 1964.

ROVEE, C. K., and LEVIN, G. R. Oral "pacification" and arousal in the human newborn. *Journal of Experimental Child Psychology*, 1966, *3*, 1–17.

RUBENSTEIN, J. Maternal attentiveness and subsequent exploratory behavior in the infant. *Child Development*, 1967, *38*, 1089–1100.

RUCH, F. L. The differentiative effects of age upon human learning. *Journal of Genetic Psychology*. 1934, *11*, 261–86.

RUSSELL, E. S. Lifespan and aging patterns. *In* E. L. Green (ed.), *Biology of the laboratory mouse*, New York: McGraw-Hill, 1966.

RYAN, M. S. *Clothing: a study in human behavior.* New York: Holt, Rinehart & Winston, 1966.

SAAYMAN, G., AMES, E. W., and MOFFETT, A. The response to novelty as an indicator of visual discrimination in the human infant. *Journal of Experimental Child Psychology*, 1964, *1*, 189–98.

SALEH, S. D., and OTIS, J. L. Age and level of job satisfaction. *Personnel Psychology*, 1964, *17*, 425–30.

SALZEN, E. A., and MEYER, C. C. Imprinting: Reversal of a preference established during the critical period. *Nature*, 1967, *215*, 785–86.

SAYEGH, Y., and DENNIS, W. The effect of supplementary experiences upon the behavioral development of infants in institutions. *Child Development*, 1965, *36*, 81–90.

SAYLER, A., and SALMON, M. Communal nursing in mice: Influence of multiple mothers on the growth of the young. *Science*, 1969, *164*, 1309–10.

SCHAEFER, E., and BAYLEY, N. Maternal behavior, child behavior, and their intercorrelations from infancy through adolescence. *Monographs of the Society for Research in Child Development*, 1963, *28*, no. 3.

SCHAFFER, H. R. Some issues for research in the study of attachment behavior. *In* B. M. Foss (ed.) *Determinants of infant behavior, II.* New York: John Wiley, 1963.

—— and CALLENDER, W. S. Psychological effects of hospitalization in infancy. *Pediatrics*, 1959; *24*, 528–39.

SCHAFFER, H. R., and EMERSON, P. E. Development of social attachment in infancy. *Monographs of the Society for Research in Child Development*, 1964, *29*, 1–77.

SCHAFFER, H. R., and PARRY, M. H. Perceptual-motor behaviour in infancy as a function of age and stimulus familiarity. *British Journal of Psychology*, 1969, *60*, 1–9.

SCHALE, K. W. A general model for the study of developmental problems. *Psychological Bulletin*, 1965, *64*, 92–107.

—— and STROTHER, C. K. A cross-sequential study of age changes in cognitive behavior. *Psychological Bulletin*, 1968, *70*, 671–80.

SCHEINFELD, A. *Your heredity and environment.* Philadelphia: Lippincott, 1965.

SCHENKEL, R. Play, exploration and territoriality in the wild lion. *In* P. A. Jewell and C. Loizos (eds.), *Play, exploration, and territory in mammals. Symposia of the Zoological Society of London*, No. 18, London: Academic Press, 1966.

SCHERMANN, A. Cognitive goals in the nursery school. *Child Study*, 1966, *28*.

—— Cognitive goals in the nursery school: Criteria for evaluating material. *Child Study*, 1967, *29*.

SCHNEIRLA, T. C. Aspects of stimulation and organization in approach-withdrawal processes underlying vertebrate development. *In* D. S. Lehrman, R. A. Hinde, and E. Shaw (eds.), *Advances in the study of behavior*, vol. 1. New York: Academic Press, 1965.

—— ROSENBLATT, J. S., and TOBACH, E. Maternal behavior in the cat. *In* H. L. Rheingold (ed.), *Maternal behavior in mammals.* New York: John Wiley, 1963.

SCHONFELD, W. A. Primary and secondary sexual characteristics: Study of their development in males from birth through maturity, with biometric study of penis and testes. *American Journal of Diseases of Children*, 1943, *65*, 535–49.

—— Adolescent psychiatry. *Archives of General Psychiatry*, 1967, *16*, 713–19.

—— The body and the body-image in adolescents. *In* G. Caplan and S. Lebovici (eds.) *Adolescence: Psychosocial perspectives.* New York: Basic Books, 1969.

SCHONFIELD, D. Memory changes with age. *Nature*, 1965, *208*, 918.

—— Memory loss with age: Acquisition and retrieval. *Psychological Reports*, 1967a, *20*, 223–26.

—— Geronting: Reflections on successful aging. *Gerontologist*, 1967b, *7*, 270–73.

—— and TRIMBLE, J. Advantages of aging. Paper presented at the Gerontological Society, 1967.

SCHULHOFER, E. The crises of adolescence: The opportunities and the hazards for growth and maturation. *Tulane Studies in Social Welfare*, 1965, *8*, 36–42.

SCHWARTZ, G., and MERTEN, D. The language of adolescence: An anthropological approach to the youth culture. *American Journal of Sociology*, 1967, *72*, 453–68.

SCHWARTZ, S., DEUTSCH, C. P., and WEISSMANN, A. Language development in two groups of socially disadvantaged young children. *Psychological Reports*, 1967, *21*, 169–78.

SCHWARTZ, W., and PAPAS, A. T. Geriatric hazards. *Journal of the American Geriatrics Society*, 1967, *15*, 936–40.

SCOTT, D. H. An empirical approach to motivation based on the behaviour of a young child. *Journal of Child Psychology and Psychiatry*, 1961, *2*, 97–117.

SCOTT, J. P. Social behavior, organization and leadership in a small flock of domestic sheep. *Comparative Psychology Monographs*, 1945, *18*, 1–29.

—— Comparative social behavior. *In* R. H. Waters, D. A. Rethlingshafer, and W. E. Caldwell (eds.),*Principles of Comparative Psychology*, New York: McGraw-Hill, 1960.

—— Critical periods in behavior development. *Science*, 1962, *138*, 949–58.

—— The process of primary socialization in canine and human infants. *Monographs of the Society for Research in Child Development*, 1963, *28*, 1–47.

—— Comparative psychology and ethology. *Annual Review of Psychology*, 1967, *18*, 65–86.

—— *Early experience and the organization of behavior.* Belmont, Calif.: Brooks-Cole, 1968.

—— and FULLER, J. L. *Genetics and the social behavior of the dog.* Chicago: University of Chicago Press, 1965.

SCUDDER, C. L., KARCZMAR, A. G., and LOCKETT, L. Behavioural developmental studies on four genera and several strains of mice. *Animal Behaviour*, 1967, *15*, 353–63.

SCUPIN, E., and SCUPIN, G. *Bubi's erste Kindheit.* Leipzig: Grieben, 1907.

SEARS, R. R., MACCOBY, E. E., and LEVIN, H. *Patterns of childrearing.* Evanston, Ill.: Row & Peterson, 1957.

SEAY, B., ALEXANDER, B. K., and HARLOW, H. F. Maternal behavior of socially deprived rhesus monkeys. *Journal of Abnormal and Social Psychology*, 1964, *69*, 345–54.

SELYE, H. *The stress of life.* New York: McGraw-Hill, 1956.

—— and PRIORESCHI, P. Stress theory of aging. *In* N. W. Shock (ed.), *Aging: Some social and biological aspects.* Washington, D. C.: American Association for the Advancement of Science, 1960.

SEWARD, G. H. Cultural conflict and the feminine role: An experimental study. *Journal of Social Psychology*, 1945, *22*, 177–94.

—— and WILLIAMSON, R. C. A cross-national study of adolescent professional goals. *Human Development*, 1969, *12*, 248–54.

SHAINBERG, D. Personality restriction in adolescents. *Psychiatric Quarterly*, 1966, *40*, 258–70.

SHAPIRO, H. The development of walking in a child. *Journal of Genetic Psychology*, 1962, *100*, 221–34.

SHAW, E. The development of schooling behavior in fishes. *Physiological Zoology*, 1960, *33*, 79–86.

—— The development of schooling in fishes, II. *Physiological Zoology*, 1961, *34*, 263–72.

SHELDON, W. H., STEVENS, S. S., and TUCKER, W. B. *The varieties of human physique: An introduction to constitutional psychology.* New York: Harper & Row, 1940.

SHARIF, M., and SHERIF, C. W. *Reference groups: Exploration into conformity and deviation of adolescents.* New York: Harper & Row, 1964.

SHERMAN, M. The differentiation of emotional responses. *Journal of Comparative Psychology*, 1927, 7, 265–84.

—— The differentiation of emotional responses in infants: III. A proposed theory of the development of emotional responses in infants. *Journal of Comparative Psychology*, 1928, 8, 385–94.

—— and SHERMAN, I. C. Sensori-motor responses in infants. *Journal of Comparative Psychology*, 1925, *5*, 53–68.

SHINN, M. W. *The biography of a baby.* Boston: Houghton Mifflin, 1900.

SHIPLEY, W. U. The demonstration in the domestic guinea pig of a process resembling classical imprinting. *Animal Behaviour*, 1963, *11*, 470–74.

SHIRLEY, M. M. The first two years: A study of twenty-five babies: I. Postural and locomotor development. *Institute of Child Welfare Monographs Series no. 6.* Minneapolis: University of Minnesota Press, 1931.

—— The first two years: A study of twenty-five babies: II. Intellectual development. *Institute of Child Welfare Monographs Series no. 7.* Minneapolis: University of Minnesota Press, 1933.

SHOCK, N. W. Physiological changes in adolescence. *In Adolescence, 43rd Yearbook.* Chicago: University of Chicago Press, 1944.

—— Some of the facts of aging. *In* N. W. Shock (ed.), *Aging: Some social and biological aspects.* Washington, D. C.; American Association for the Advancement of Science, 1960.

—— Age with a future. *Gerontologist*, 1968, *8*, 147–52.

—— *Perspectives in experimental gerontology.* Springfield, Ill.: Charles C. Thomas, 1966.

SHUTTLEWORTH, F. K. The physical and mental growth of girls and boys, age six to nineteen, in relation to age at maximum growth. *Monographs of the Society for Research in Child Development*, 1944, *9*, no. 1.

—— The adolescent period: A graphic atlas. *Monographs of the Society for Research on Child Development*, 1949, *14*, no. 1.

SIEGEL, A. E., and HAAS, M. B. The working mother: A review of research. *Child Development*, 1963, *34*, 513–42.

SIGEL, I. E. The attainment of concepts. *In* M. L. Hoffman, and L. W. Hoffman (eds.), *Review of child development research*, vol. I. New York: Russell Sage Foundation, 1964.

SIMMONS, K. The Brush Foundation study of child growth and development: II. Physical growth and development. *Monographs of the Society for Research in Child Development*, 1944, *9*, no. 1.

SIMPSON, R. L. Parental influence, anticipatory socialization, and social mobility. *American Sociological Review*, 1962, *27*, 517–22.

SINHA, A. K., PRASAA, M. S., and MADHUKAR, R. P. Extraversion-introversion and rigidity of vocational aspirations. *Guidance Review*, 1964, *2*, 88–94.

SIQUELAND, E. R. Operant conditioning of head turning in 4-month infants. *Psychonomic Science*, 1964, *1*, 223–24.

—— Reinforcement patterns and extinction in human newborns. *Journal of Experimental Child Psychology*, 1968, *6*, 431–42.

—— and LIPSITT, L. P. Conditioned head-turning in human newborns. *Journal of Experimental Child Psychology*, 1966, *3*, 356–76.

SKOREPA, C. A., HORROCKS, J. E., and THOMPSON, G. G. A study of friendship fluctuations of college students. *Journal of Genetic Psychology*, 1963, *102*, 151–57.

SLATER, E. Types, levels, and irregularities of response to a nursery school situation of forty children observed with special reference to the home environment. *Monographs of the Society for Research in Child Development*, 1939, No. 2.

SLUCKIN, W. *Imprinting and early learning.* Chicago: Aldine, 1965.

—— Imprinting in guinea-pigs. *Nature*, 1968, *220*, 1148.

—— and SALZEN, E. Z. Imprinting and perceptual learning. *Quarterly Journal of Experimental Psychology*, 1961, *13*, 65–77.

SMELSER, W. T. Adolescent and adult occupational choice as a function of family socioeconomic history. *Sociometry*, 1963, *26*, 393–409.

SMITH, C. A. The first breath. *Scientific American*, 1963, *209*, 27–35.

SMITH, E. A. *American youth culture.* New York: Free Press, 1963.

SMITH, G. F. Certain aspects of the sex life of the adolescent girl. *Journal of Applied Psychology*, 1924, *8*, 347–49.

SMITH, H. P., and APPELFELD, S. W. Children's paintings and the projective expression of personality: An experimental investigation. *Journal of Genetic Psychology*, 1965, *107*, 289–93.

SMITH, H. T. and STONE, L. J. Developmental psychology. *Annual Review of Psychology*, 1961, *12*, 1–26.

SMITH, K. R. Age and performance on a repetitive manual task. *Journal of Applied Psychology*, 1938, *22*, 295–306.

SMITH, M. B. Conflicting values affecting behavioral research with children. *American Psychologist*, 1967, *22*, 377–82.

SMITH, M. E. An investigation of the development of the sentence and the extent of vocabulary in young children. *University of Iowa Studies in Child Welfare*, 1926, *3* (5).

—— Grammatical errors in the speech of preschool children. *Child Development*, 1933, *4*, 183–90.

SONTAG, L. W. Some psychosomatic aspects of childhood. *Nervous Child*, 1946, *5*, 296–304.

—— The genetics of differences in psychosomatic patterns in childhood. *American Journal of Orthopsychiatry*. 1950, *20*, 3.

—— Implications of fetal behavior and environment for adult personalities. *Annals of the New York Academy of Sciences*, 1966, *132*, 782–86.

SPEARS, W. C. Assessment of visual preference and discrimination in the 4-month-old infant. *Journal of Comparative and Physiological Psychology*, 1964, *57*, 381–86.

—— and HOHLE, R. H. Sensory and perceptual processes in infants. *In* Y. Brackbill (ed.), *Infancy and early childhood.* New York: Free Press, 1967.

SPEETH, S. D. The rational design of toys. *Journal of Creative Behavior*, 1967, *1*, 398–410.

SPERRY, R. W. Mechanisms of neural maturation. *In* S. S. Stevens (ed.), *Handbook of experimental psychology.* New York: John Wiley, 1951.

SPIEGEL, L. A. A review of contributions to a psychoanalytic theory of adolescence. *Psychoanalytic Study of the Child*, 1951, *6*, 375–93.

SPITZ, R. A. Hospitalism: An inquiry into the genesis of psychiatric conditions in early childhood. *In* A. Freud (ed.), *The psychoanalytic study of the child*, vol. I. New York: International Universities Press, 1945.

—— Hospitalism: A follow-up report on investigations described in Vol. I. *In* A. Freud (ed.), *The psychoanalytic study of the child*, vol. II. New York: International Universities Press, 1946.

—— The role of ecological factors in emotional development in infancy. *Child Development*, 1949a, *20*, 145–55.

—— Autoeroticism: Some empirical findings and hypotheses on three of its manifestations in the first year of life. *In* A. Freud (ed.), *The psychoanalytic study of the child*, vol. III, IV. New York: International Universities Press, 1949b.

—— *The first year of life.* New York: International Universities Press, 1965.

—— and WOLF, K. M. Anaclytic depression: An inquiry into the genesis of psychiatric conditions in early childhood. *In* A. Freud (ed.), *The psychoanalytic study of the child*, vol. II. New York: International Universities Press, 1946a.

—— The smiling response: A contribution to the ontogenesis of social relationships. *Genetic Psychology Monographs*, 1946b, *34*, 57–125.

STALNAKER, E. Language of the preschool child. *Child Development*, 1933, *4*, 229–36.

STEIN, M. I., and HEINZE, S. J. *Creativity and the individual: Summaries of selected literature in psychology and psychiatry.* Chicago: University of Chicago Press, 1960.

STEIN, Z., and SUSSER, M. Social factors in the development of sphincter control. *Developmental Medicine and Child Neurology*, 1967, *9*, 692–706.

STENDLER, C. B. Critical periods in socialization and overdependency. *Child Development*, 1952, *23*, 3–12.

STEPHENSON, R. M. Occupational choice as a crystallized self concept. *Journal of Counseling Psychology*, 1961, *8*, 211–16.

STERN, W. *Psychologie der frühen Kindheit.* Leipzig: J. A. Barth, 1914.

—— and STERN, C. *Die Kindersprache* (4th ed.). Leipzig: J. A. Barth, 1928.

STEVENSON, H. W. Social reinforcement of children's behavior. *In* L. P. Lipsitt and C. C. Spiker (eds.), *Advances in child development and behavior*, vol. II. New York: Academic Press, 1965.

—— Developmental psychology. *Annual Review of Psychology*, 1967, *18*, 87–128.

—— HESS, E. H., and RHEINGOLD, H. L. *Early behavior: Comparative and ethological approaches.* New York: John Wiley, 1966.

STEWART, A. H., WELLAND, I. H., LEIDER, A. R., MANGHAM, C. A., HOLMES, T. H., and RIPLEY, H. S. Excessive infant crying (colic) in relation to parent behavior. *American Journal of Psychiatry*, 1954, *110*, 687–94.

STILL, J. Are organismal aging and aging death necessarily the result of death of vital cells in the organism? (A cybernetic theory of aging.) *Medical Annals of the District of Columbia*, 1956, *25*, 199–203.

STIRNIMAN, F. Versuche über die Reaktionen Neugeborener auf Wärme- und Kältereize. *Zeitschrift für Kinderpsychiatrie*, 1939, *5*, 143–50.

—— *Psychologie des neugeborenen Kindes.* Zürich: Räscher, 1950.

STOLZ, H. R., JONES, M. C., and CHAFFEY, J. The junior high school age. *University High School Journal*, 1937, *15*, 63–72.

STOLZ, H. R., and STOLZ, L. M. *Somatic development of adolescent boys.* New York: Macmillan, 1951.

STOLZ, L. M. Effects of maternal employment on children: Evidence from research. *Child Development.* 1960, *31*, 749–82.

STONE, A. A., and ONQUÉ, G. C. *Longitudinal studies of child personality abstracts with index.* Cambridge, Mass.: Harvard University Press, 1959.

STONE, C. P., and BARKER, R. G. The attitudes and interests of premenarcheal and postmenarcheal girls. *Journal of Genetic Psychology*, 1939, *54*, 27–71.

STONE, F. B., and ROWLEY, V. N. Children's behavior problems and parental attitudes. *Journal of Genetic Psychology*, 1965, *107*, 281–87.

——— Children's behavior problems and mother's age. *Journal of Psychology*, 1966, *63*, 229–33.

STONE, L. J. and CHURCH, J. *Childhood and adolescence.* 2d ed. New York: Random House, 1968.

STOTT, L. H. Adolescents' dislikes regarding parental behavior and their significance. *Journal of Genetic Psychology*, 1935, *26*, 169–76.

——— Adolescents' dislikes regarding parental behavior and their significance. *Journal of Genetic Psychology*, 1940a, *57*, 393–414.

——— Home punishment of adolescents. *Journal of Genetic Psychology*, 1940b, *57*, 415–28.

——— and BALL, R. S. Infant and pre-school mental tests: Review and evaluation. *Monographs of the Society for Research in Child Development*, 1965, *30*, No. 101.

STRANAHAM, M., SCHWARTZMAN, C., and ATKIN, E. Activity group therapy with emotionally disturbed delinquent adolescents. *International Journal of Group Psychotherapy*, 1957, 7, 425–36.

STRANG, R. *An Introduction to child study.* New York: Macmillan, 1959.

STRODTBECK, F. L. Family interaction, values, and achievement. *In* D. C. McClelland; A. L. Baldwin; U. Brofenbrenner; and F. L. Strodtbeck (eds.), *Talent and Society*, New York: Van Nostrand Reinhold 1958.

STRONG, E. K. *Changes of interests with age.* Stanford, Calif.: Stanford University Press, 1931.

——— Satisfactions and interests. *American Psychologist*, 1958, *13*, 449–56.

STUART, H. C. Normal growth and development during adolescence. *New England Journal of Medicine*, 1946, *234*, 666–72; 693–700; 732–38.

SUDWEEKS, J. Intelligence of the continuation school pupils of Wisconsin. *Journal of Educational Psychology*, 1927, *18*, 601–10.

SUGARMAN, B. Involvement in youth culture, academic achievement and conformity in school: An empirical study of London Schoolboys. *British Journal of Sociology*, 1967, *18*, 151–64.

SUPER, D. E. *Vocational development: A framework for research.* New York: Bureau of Publications, Teachers College, Columbia University, 1957.

——— and BACHRACH, P. B. *Scientific careers and vocational development theory.* New York: Bureau of Publications, Teachers College, Columbia University, 1957.

SUPPES, P., and GINSBERG, R. Experimental studies of mathematical concept formation in young children. *Science Education*, 1962, *46*, 230–40.

SURWILLO, W. W., and OUILTER, R. Vigilance age, and response-time. *American Journal of Psychology*, 1964, 77, 614–20.

SUTTON-SMITH, B. Novel responses to toys. *Merrill-Palmer Quarterly*, 1968, *14*, 151–58.

SUZUKI, T., KAMIJO, Y., and KIUCHI, S. Auditory tests of newborn infants. *Annals of Otology, Rhinology and Laryngology*, 1964, *73*, 914–23.

SWENSON, W. M. Attitudes toward death in an aged population. *Journal of Gerontology*, 1961, *16*, 49–52.

SYMONDS, P. M. *The psychology of parent-child relationships.* New York: Appleton-Century-Crofts, 1939.

——— *The dynamics of parent-child relationships.* New York: Appleton-Century-Crofts, 1949.

——— *From adolescent to adult.* New York: Columbia University Press, 1961.

TALLMER, M., and KUTNER, B. Disengagement and the stresses of aging. *Journal of Gerontology*, 1969, *24*, 70–75.

TANNER, J. M. *Growth at adolescence.* Springfield, Ill.: Charles C Thomas, 1955.

——— Earlier maturation in man. *Scientific American*, 1968, *218*, 21–28.

TAYLOR, A. Institutionalized infants' concept formation ability. *American Journal of Orthopsychiatry*, 1968a, *38*, 110–15.

——— Deprived infants: Potential for affective adjustment. *American Journal of Orthopsychiatry*, 1968b, *38*, 835–45.

TAYLOR, C. W., and BARRON, F. (eds.), *Scientific creativity: Its recognition and development.* New York: John Wiley, 1963.

TAYLOR, J. H. Innate emotional responses in infants. *Ohio State University Studies, Contributions in Psychology*, 1934, *12*, 69–81.

TEMPLIN, M. C. Norms on a screening test of articulation for ages three through eight. *Journal of Speech and Hearing Disorders*, 1953, *18*, 323–31.

——— *Certain language skills in children: Their development and interrelationships.* Minneapolis: University of Minnesota Press, 1957.

TENNES, K. H., and LAMPL, E. E. Stranger and separation anxiety in infancy. *Journal of Nervous and Mental Disease*, 1964, *139*, 247–54.

TERMAN, L. *The measurement of intelligence.* Boston: Houghton, 1916.

TERRELL, G. The need for simplicity in research in child psychology. *Child Development*, 1958, *29*, 303–10.

THARP, R. G. Marriage roles, child development and family treatment. *American Journal of Orthopsychiatry*, 1965, *35*, 531–38.

THOMAE, H. *Das Individuum und seine Welt.* Göttingen: Verlag für Psychologie, 1968.

THOMAN, E., WETZEL, A., and LEVINE, S. Learning in the neonatal rat. *Animal Behaviour*, 1968, *16*, 54–57.

THOMAS, A., BIRCH, H. C., CHESS, S, HERTZIG, M. E., and KORN, S. *Behavioral individuality in early childhood.* New York: New York University Press, 1963.

THOMAS, H. Visual-fixation responses of infants to stimuli of varying complexity. *Child Development*, 1965, *36*, 629–38.

THOMPSON, G. G. Age trends in social values during the adolescent years. *American Psychologist*, 1949, *4*, 250.

——— and HORROCKS, J. E. A study of friendship fluctuations of urban boys and girls. *Journal of Genetic Psychology*, 1947, *70*, 53–63.

THOMPSON, H. Physical growth. *In* L. Carmichael, (ed.), *Manual of child psychology.* 2d ed. New York: John Wiley, 1954.

THOMPSON, W. R. Influence of prenatal maternal anxiety on emotionality in young rats. *Science*, 1957, *125*, 698–99.

——— and HERON, H. The effects of restricting early experience on the problem solving capacity of dogs. *Canadian Journal of Psychology*, 1954, *8*, 17–31.

THOMPSON, W. R., MELZACK, R., and SCOTT, T. H. "Whirling behavior" in dogs as related to early experience. *Science*, 1956, *123*, 939.

THORNDIKE, E. L. *Adult learning.* New York: Macmillan, 1928.

THORNDIKE, R. L. *The concepts of over- and underachievement.* New York: Bureau of Publication, Teachers College, Columbia University, 1963.

THORPE, W. H. *Learning and instinct in animals* (2nd ed.). London: Methuen, 1963.

——— The ontogeny of behavior. *In* J. A. Moore (ed.), *Ideas in modern biology.* New York: Natural History Press, 1965.

THRASHER, F. M. *The gang.* Chicago: University of Chicago Press, 1927.

TIBBITS, C. and DONAHUE, W. *Aging around the world: social and psychological aspects of aging.* New York: Columbia University Press, 1962.

TIEDEMANN, D. *Beobachutungen über die Entwicklung der Seeltenfähigkeiten bei Kindern.* C. Ufer (ed.), Alternburg: Bonde, 1897.

TISCHLER, H., Schreien, Lallen und erstes Sprechen in der Entwicklung des Säuglings. *Zeitschrift für Psychologie*, 1957, *160*, 210–63.

TOBIN, S. S., and NEUGARTEN, B. L. Life satisfaction and social interaction with aging. *Journal of Gerontology*, 1961, *16*, 344–46.

TODD, A. G., and PALMER, B. Social reinforcement of infant babbling. *Child Development*, 1968, *39*, 591–96.

TODD, T. W. *Atlas of skeletal maturation.* St. Louis: Mosby, 1937.

TORRANCE, E. P. Education and creativity. *In* C. W. Taylor (ed.), *Creativity: Progress and potential.* Englewood Cliffs, N. J.: Prentice-Hall, 1962.

TRAISMAN, A. S., and TRAISMAN, H. S. Thumb and finger-sucking: A study of 2,650 infants and children. *Journal of Pediatrics*, 1958, *52*, 566–672.

TROWBRIDGE, N., and CHARLES, D. C. Creativity in art students. *Journal of Genetic Psychology*, 1966, *109*, 281–89.

TRYON, C. M. Evaluations of adolescent personality by adolescents. *Monographs of the Society for Research of Child Development*, 1939, *4*, No. 4.

———— The adolescent peer culture. *Yearbook, National Society for the Study of Education*, 1944, *43*, 217–39.

TUDOR-HART, B. E. Are there cases in which lies are necessary? *Journal of Genetic Psychology*, 1926, *33*, 586–641.

TYLER, L. E., SUNDBERG, N. D., and ROHILA, P. K. Patterns of choices in Dutch, American, and Indian adolescents. *Journal of Counseling Psychology*, 1968, *15*, 522–29.

ULRICH, G., HECKLIK, J., and ROEBER, E. C. Occupational stereotypes of high school students. *Vocational Guidance Quarterly*, 1966, *14*, 169–74.

VALENTINE, C. W. The psychology of imitation with special reference to early childhood. *British Journal of Psychology*, 1930, *21*, 105–32.

VANDENBERG, S. G. Contributions of twin research to psychology. *Psychological Bulletin*, 1966, *66*, 327–52.

VANDENBERGH, J. G. Behavior observations of an infant squirrel monkey. *Psychological Reports*, 1966, *18*, 683–88.

VELD, J. T. Patterns of leisure-time behavior of the aged in the Netherlands. *In* J. Kaplan and G. J. Aldridge (eds.). *Aging around the world*, vol. II. *Social welfare of the aging*. New York: Columbia University Press, 1962.

VERNON, M. D. The development of perception in children. *Educational Research*, 1960, *3*, 2–11.

VERWOERDT, A. *Communication with the fatally ill*. Springfield, Ill.: Charles C Thomas, 1966.

VINCENT, E. L., and MARTIN, P. C. *Human psychological development*. New York: Ronald Press, 1961.

VON LAWICK-GOODALL, J. The behavior of free-living chimpanzees in the Gombe Stream Reserve. *Animal Behaviours Monographs*, 1968, *1*, 161–311.

WAGONER, L. C., and ARMSTRONG, E. M. The motor control of children as involved in the dressing process. *Pedogogical Seminary*, 1928, *35*, 84–97.

WAHLER, R. G. Infant social development: Some experimental analyses of an infant-mother interaction during the first year of life. *Journal of Experimental Child Psychology*, 1969, *7*, 101–13.

WALDROP, M. E., and BELL, R. G. Effects of family size and density on newborn characteristics. *American Journal of Orthopsychiatry*, 1966, *36*, 544–50.

WALK, R. D. The study of visual depth and distance perception in animals. *In* D. S. Lehrman, R. A. Hinde, and E. Shaw (eds.), *Advances in the study of behavior*, vol. I. New York: Academic Press, 1965.

———— The development of depth perception in animals and human infants. *Monographs of the Society for Research in Child Development*, 1966, *31*, 82–108.

———— and GIBSON, E. J. Visual depth perception in infants. *Psychological Monographs*, 1961, No. 57.

WALLACH, M. A., and KOGAN, N. *Modes of thinking in young children: A study of the creativity-intelligence distinction*. New York: Holt, Rinehart & Winston, 1965.

WALLIS, R. W. How children grow: an anthropometric study of private school children from two to eight years of age. *University of Iowa Studies in Child Welfare*, 1931, *5*, (1).

WALTERS, C. E. Prediction of postnatal development from fetal activity. *Child Development*, 1965, *36*, 801–8.

WALTERS, J., PEARCE, D., and DAHMS, L. Affectional and aggressive behavior of pre-school children. *Child Development*, 1967, *28*, 15–26.

WALTERS, R. H. and PARKE, R. D. The role of the distance receptors in the development of social responsiveness. *In* L. P. Lipsitt and C. C. Spiker (eds.), *Advances in child development and behavior*, II. New York: Academic Press, 1965, 59–96.

WARNATH, C. F. The relation of family cohesiveness and adolescent independence to social effectiveness. *Marriage and Family Living*, 1955, *17*, 346–48.

WARREN, J. R., and HEIST, P. A. Personality attributes of gifted college students, *Science*, 1960, *132*, 330–37.

WATSON, E. H., and LOWREY, G. H. *Growth and development of children*. 5th ed. Chicago: Year Book Publishers, 1967.

WATSON, J. B. *Psychology from the standpoint of a behaviorist*. Philadelphia: Lippincott, 1919.

———— The birth equipment of the human being. *In* W. Dennis (ed.), *Readings in child psychology*. 2d ed. Englewood Cliffs, N. J.: Prentice-Hall, 1963.

———— and MORGAN, J. J. B. Emotional reactions and psychological experimentation. *American Journal of Psychology*, 1917, *28*, 163–74.

WATSON, J. B., and WATSON, R. R. Conditioned emotional reactions. *Journal of Experimental Psychology*, 1923, 1–14.

WATSON, J. S. Memory and "contingency analysis" in infant learning. *Merrill-Palmer Quarterly*, 1967, *13*, 55–76.

WEATHERLEY, D. Self-perceived rate of physical maturation and personality in late adolescence. *Child Development*, 1964, *35*, 1197–1210.

WECHSLER, D. *The measurement of adult intelligence*, 3d ed. Baltimore: Williams & Wilkins, 1944.

WEDENBERG, E. Determination of the hearing acuity in the newborn. *Nordisk Medicin*, 1956, *50*, 1022–24.

WEIL, J. C. The effects of work on the physical and mental health of older citizens in a home for the aged. In *Old age in the modern world*. London: Livingston, 1955.

———— Special program for the senile in a home for the aged. *Geriatrics*, 1966, *21*, 197–202.

WEIR, M. W. Developmental changes in problem-solving strategies. *Psychological Review*, 1964, *71*, 472–90.

WEISBERG, P. Social and nonsocial conditioning of infant vocalization. *Child Development*, 1963, *34*, 377–88.

WEISS, A. D. Sensory functions. *In* J. Birren (ed.), *Handbook of aging and the individual*. Chicago: University of Chicago Press, 1959.

WEISS, L. A. Differential variations in the amount of activity of newborn infants under continuous light and sound stimulation. *University of Iowa Studies of Child Welfare*, 1934, *9*, 1–74.

WELCH, L. The development of size discrimination between the ages of 12 and 40 months. *Journal of Genetic Psychology*, 1939, *55*, 243–68.

WELFORD, A. T. Psychomotor performance. *In* J. Birren (ed.), *Handbook of aging and the individual*. Chicago: University of Chicago Press, 1959.

———— and BIRREN, J. E. (eds.). *Behavior, aging, and the nervous system*. Springfield. Ill.: Charles C Thomas, 1965.

WENGER, M. A. An investigation of conditioned responses in human infants. *University of Iowa Studies of Child Welfare*, 1936, *12*, 1–90.

WERBOFF, J. Research related to the origins of behavior, *Merrill-Palmer Quarterly*, 1963, *9*, 115–22.

WERNER, E. E., and BAYLEY, N. The reliability of Bayley's revised scale of mental and mode of development during the first year of life. *Child Development*, 1966, *37*, 39–50.

WERTHEIMER, M. Psychomotor coordination of auditory and visual space at birth. *Science*, 1961, *134*, 1692.

WERTS, C. E. Social class and initial career choice of college freshmen. *Sociology and Education*, 1966, *39*, 74–85.

WETHERICK, N. E. A comparison of the problem-solving ability of the young, middle-aged and old subjects. *Gerontologia*, 1964, *9*, 164–78.

WHITE, B. J. The relationship of self concept and parental identification to women's vocational interests. *Journal of Counseling Psychology*, 1959, *6*, 202–6.

WHITE, B. L., CASTLE, P., and HELD, R. Observations on the development of visually-directed reaching. *Child Development*, 1964, *35*, 349–64.

WHITE, N. H. Evidence for a hierarchical arrangement of learning processes. *In* L. P. Lipsitt and C. C. Spiker (eds.), *Advances in child development and behavior*, vol. 2. New York: Academic Press, 1965.

WHITE, R. W. Motivation reconsidered: The concept of competence. *Psychological Review*, 1959, *66*, 297–333.

———— (ed.). *The study of lives*. New York: Atherton, 1969.

WHITEHORN, J. C. A working concept of maturity of personality. *American Journal of Psychiatry*, 1962, *119*, 197–202.

WICKENS, D. D., and WICKENS, C. A study of conditioning in the neonate. *Journal of Experimental Psychology*, 1940, *26*, 94–102.

WIENER, N. *Ex-prodigy: My childhood and youth.* New York: Simon & Schuster, 1953.

WIER, A. Value judgments and personality in old age. *Acta Psychology*, 1961, *19*, 148–49.

WIESEL, T., and HUBEL, D. Single-cell responses in striate cortex of kittens deprived of vision in one eye. *Journal of Neurophysiology*, 1963, *26*, 1003–17.

WILCOX, B. M. Visual preferences of human infants for representation of the human face, *Journal of Experimental Child Psychology*, 1969, *7*, 10–20.

WILLIAMS, E., and SCOTT, J. P. The development of social behavior patterns in the mouse, in relation to natural periods. *Behaviour*, 1953, *6*, 35–65.

WILLIAMS, H. M., MCFARLAND, M. L., and LITTLE, M. F. Development of language and vocabulary in young children. *University of Iowa Studies in Child Welfare*, 1937, *13*, (2).

WILLIAMS, R. H., and WIRTH, C. G. *Lives through the years: Styles of life and successful aging.* New York: Atherton, 1965.

WILLIAMS, R. H., TIBBITS, C., and DONAHUE, W. (eds.) *Process of aging: Social and psychological perspectives.* vols. I & II. New York: Atherton, 1963.

WILLIAMS, R. L. Psychological efficacy of religiosity in late adolescence. *Psychological Reports*, 1967, *20*, 926.

WILLIAMS, R. M., and MATTSON, M. L. The effect of social grouping upon the language of preschool children. *Child Development*, 1942, *13*, 233–45.

WILLIAMSON, R. C. *Marriage and family relations.* New York: John Wiley, 1966.

WILLMAN, R. H. An experimental investigation of the creative process in music. *Psychological Monographs*, 1944, *57*, no. 1.

WILSON, M., WARREN, J. M., and ABBOTT, L. Infantile stimulation, activity and learning by cats. *Child Development*, 1965, *36*, 843–53.

WITTENBERG, R. *Postadolescence: Theoretical and clinical aspects of psychoanalytic therapy.* New York: Grune & Stratton, 1968.

WITTY, P. H. A study of pupil's interests, grades 9, 10, 11, 12. *Education*, 1961, *82*, 39–45, 100–10, 169–74.

WOHLWILL, J. F. Developmental studies of perception. *Psychological Bulletin*, 1960, *57*, 249–88.

——— The mystery of the pre-logical child. *Psychology Today.* July, 1967, 25–34.

WOLFENSTEIN, M. Trends in infant care. *American Journal of Orthopsychiatry*, 1953, *23*, 120–30.

WOLFF, K. *Geriatric Psychiatry.* Springfield, Ill.: Charles C Thomas, 1963.

——— Personality type and reaction toward aging and death: A clinical study. *Geriatrics*, 1966, *21*, 189–92.

WOLFF, P. H. Observations on newborn infants. *Psychosomatic Medicine*, 1959, *21*, 110–18.

——— Observations on the early development of smiling. *In* B. M. Foss (ed.) *Determinants of infant behaviour*, vol. 2. New York: John Wiley, 1963.

——— The causes, controls, and organization of behavior in the neonate. *Psychological Issues*, 1966, *5* (17), 1–105.

WOLFF, W. *The personality of the preschool child.* New York: Grune & Stratton, 1946.

WOLMAN, B. B. The social development of Israeli youth. *Jewish Social Studies*, 1949, *50*, 283–306; 343–72.

——— Spontaneous groups in childhood and adolescence. *Journal of Social Psychology*, 1951, *34*, 171–82.

WOODROW, H. Mental unevenness and brightness. *Journal of Educational Psychology*, 1928, *9*, 289–302.

WOODRUFF, A. B., and SLÖVAK, M. L. The effects of severely restricted visual experience on the perception of "identity." *Psychonomic Science*, 1965, *2*, 41–42.

WRIGHT, H. F. Psychological development in the Midwest. *Child Development*, 1956, *27*, 265–86.

——— Observational child study. *In* P. H. Mussen (ed.), *Handbook of research methods in child development.* New York: John Wiley 1960.

——— and BARKER, R. G. Psychological ecology and the problem of psychosocial development. *Child Development*, 1949, *20*, 131–43.

YARROW, L. J. The relationship between nutritive sucking experiences in infancy and non-nutritive sucking in childhood. *Journal of Genetic Psychology*, 1954, *84*, 149–62.

——— Interviewing children. *In* P. H. Mussen (ed.), *Handbook of research methods in child development.* New York: John Wiley, 1960.

——— Maternal deprivation: Toward an empirical and conceptual re-evaluation. *Psychological Bulletin*, 1961, *58*, 459–90.

——— Separation from parents during early childhood. *In* M. L. Hoffman and L. W. Hoffman (eds.), *Review of child development research*, vol. I. New York: Russell Sage Foundation, 1964.

——— The crucial nature of early experience. *In* D. C. Glass, (ed.), *Biology and behavior: Environmental influences.* New York: Russell Sage Foundation, 1968.

YOUMANS, E. G. Orientations to old age. *Gerontologist*, 1968, *8*, 153–58.

YOUNG, F. M. An analysis of certain variables in a developmental study of language. *Genetic Psychology Monographs*, 1941, *23*, 3–141.

YUDIN, L. W. Formal thought in adolescence as a function of intelligence. *Child Development*, 1966, *37*, 697–708.

——— The nature of adolescent thought. *Adolescence*, 1967, *2*, 137–51.

——— and KATES, I. S. Concept attainment and adolescent development. *Journal of Educational Psychology*, 1963, *55*, 1–9.

ZBOROWSKI, M., and EYDE, L. D. Aging and social participation. *Journal of Gerontology*, 1962, *17*, 424–30.

ZOLA, I. L. Feelings about age among older people. *Journal of Gerontology*, 1962, *17*, 65–68.

ZUBEK, J. P. (ed.), *Sensory deprivation: Fifteen years of research.* New York: Appleton-Century-Crofts, 1969.

——— and SOLBERG, P. A. *Human development.* New York: McGraw-Hill, 1954.

ZUNG, W. W. K. Depression in the normal aged. *Psychosomatics*, 1967, *8*, 287–92.

Social psychology is the study of individual behavior as it is influenced by the behavior of other persons or groups within some cultural context. It involves the scientific study of persons interacting with and adapting to others in situations defined and limited by the social system of which they are a part. When individuals interact, their behavior can be analyzed not only as responses to others but also as stimuli for others.

Many social psychologists attempt to relate individual psychological variables to social-cultural variables and, as a consequence of this, the field has been the concern of both psychologists and sociologists, each group tending to approach the subject matter from its own special vantage point, and sometimes minimizing the content and variables of the other discipline. For example, "psychological social psychologists" emphasize such individual processes as motivation and learning, relevant to social behavior, and tend to study face-to-face interaction within small groups of individuals, while "sociological social psychologists" tend to focus on the structure (formal and informal) and dynamics of large organizations (e.g., industrial, military) with less emphasis on the personalities or individual characteristics of the people making up the organizations. Symbolic of the dual orientation to the subject matter of social psychology is the fact that the first two textbooks in the field, published in the same year (1908), were written by McDougall, a psychologist, and by Ross, a sociologist.

There is an extensive and fascinating literature on the social behaviors of infrahuman organisms (e.g., Thompson & Hebb 1968; Scott 1969; Zajonc 1969) with which this chapter will not deal. While this work on lower animals provides information on phylogenetic continuity and a comparative baseline for the study of human social psychology, the present chapter can concentrate only on a few dominant trends within contemporary social psychology and these are trends directly concerned with human beings.

An attempt will be made here to present a general view of the field by reviewing theory and research within some broad and active subareas. To this end socialization, attitudes, and groups have been chosen as illustrative areas for discussion.

Albert J. Lott

Social Psychology

43

A final section will comment on some general methodological and ethical issues which have been raised by social psychological research but which are having a far-reaching influence on the understanding, planning, and design of investigations in other areas within psychology as well as in the other social sciences.

Socialization

It is through development and learning in a social context that an individual acquires his social behaviors. The question of how children are raised is, therefore, of importance in understanding their early and later behaviors and, for this reason, the topic of socialization is a major concern of many social psychologists. In fact, Gerard (1968) has suggested that social psychology can be regarded broadly as the study of socialization and its products—how people learn the beliefs and attitudes of their groups and how they internalize group expectations for their behavior.

Zigler and Child (1969) conceive of socialization as the "whole process by which an individual develops, through transaction with other people, his specific patterns of socially relevant behavior and experience" (p. 474). Given the wide range of behaviors potentially available to a newborn infant, the socialization process may be assumed to exert pressure on the organism to learn and display actual behaviors that are much more circumscribed and narrow than what it is capable of at birth (Child 1954). The range of actual behaviors learned is determined by what is customary and acceptable according to the standards of the groups of which he is a part.

BIRTH ORDER

The primary aim of social psychologists concerned with socialization variables has been to identify and study child-rearing practices and other conditions that are antecedents of the behavior of a socialized adult or of an individual in the process of being socialized. Thus, for example, Schachter (1959) and others (Helmreich & Collins 1967; Nisbett & Schachter 1966; Wrightsman 1960) have found that first-borns report more fear and are more anxious than later-borns under certain kinds of stress (anticipated pain) and seek out companionship with others as a means of anxiety reduction. In general, firstborns not only prefer being in the presence of others when they are personally threatened, i.e., exhibit strong affiliative tendencies in anxiety-provoking situations, but they tend to conform more to group pressures and situational standards, i.e., are more susceptible to social influence when frightened (Walters & Park 1964). It has also been shown that ordinal position is related to academic achievement, with first-borns excelling later-borns in years of schooling completed, measured intellectual endowment, and the achievement of eminence (Altus 1966; Bradley 1968; Roe 1953; Sampson 1962, 1965; Warren 1966).

The social and familial dynamics leading to birth order effects still need to be experimentally tested. Among other things, the consistency across families of differential treatment of first-borns as opposed to later-borns, which may give rise to behaviors associated with ordinal position, need to be looked at (Burton 1968). The most recent attempt to explain known birth order phenomena has been made by Kagan (1969). Concentrating on childhood socialization, Kagan sees three influences on first-born or only children that he regards as "advantages" and that are perhaps sources of the achievement efficiency of these individuals. First, the only child or first-born is more likely to have adults provide reference points for his standards. His major experience is with adults and he will therefore set high standards of competency for himself in those areas that are positively valued by his parents and directly reinforced by them. Later-born children, however, may develop more realistic standards of performance because they have children as well as adults setting standards for them. A second influence has to do with identification dynamics. The first-born has primarily adult models available to him. Since older persons are usually more competent than children, the first-born, through identification with adults, is internalizing more stringent performance goals for himself than the later-born, who can use child models to modify, dilute, or counteract any standards adopted from adults. Third, Kagan believes that the first-born is likely to experience the world as more orderly because parents are likely to give him consistent, rational answers to his questions, whereas later-born children will experience less order because they will tend to get their answers from other children who will not be as consistent or rational in their explanation of events and will confuse the younger child.

While the influences enumerated above may help explain the first-born's subsequent striving for high-level competence and rationality, Kagan postulates two counter influences that suggest the roots of the less positive characteristics of heightened anxiety, affiliation, dependence on groups, and conformity. Because the first-born becomes accustomed to the excessive affection of the parents, he is more subject to anxiety over loss of affection when the next child is born. Also, since the first-born is accustomed to nurturance from adults, he more easily turns to adults when he is anxious. The later-born child shares parental affection from birth. Finally, the first-born child is more predisposed to guilt over the hostility and jealousy he feels for his siblings. Since he is taught by his parents that a new baby needs extra attention he cannot justify his hostility and thus feels guilty. Kagan feels that the guilt may even lead to self-derogation.

Obviously the precise mechanisms and antecedents of social behaviors based on the order of birth are yet to be discovered, but descriptive and normative data are at hand to document the durability of certain birth-order phenomena, and broad theoretical schemes are available for guiding the study of this aspect of socialization.

SOCIAL CLASS AND CHILD-REARING PRACTICES

Perhaps a more dynamic, analytic use of socialization variables in social psychological work has been the study of the different child-rearing practices of different social classes and the consequent behavioral differences exhibited by persons of these classes. This represents an area of cooperative interdisciplinary research with sociologists and developmental psychologists contributing valuable theories, techniques, and data to social psychology. While the literature on social class differences in behavior and child-rearing practices is voluminous, a brief sketch can perhaps illustrate some of the major findings and problems. (See Zigler & Child 1969 for a comprehensive treatment of this topic.)

Cavan (1964) has reviewed evidence showing social class

variations in family structure and roles (as well as class-related demographic background variables such as religion, affiliation, type of dwelling, ethnic background, etc.). Two related behaviors, independence and achievement striving, have been found to be handled differently in the generalized or typical middle-class and working-class homes. Middle-class parents push for independence earlier and more consistently than working-class parents (Bronfenbrenner 1965; Rosen 1956). At the same time the middle-class parent is communicating to his child higher expectations for school performance as well as a general, overall concern with competence, mastery and achievement, i.e., striving for standards of excellence in whatever activity the child undertakes (McClelland et al. 1953). Because of these and other research findings (e.g., Winterbottom 1958), it has been assumed that training for independence is one of the antecedents to the acquisition of achievement as a motive and that, therefore, achievement is inversely related to dependence. While many studies do find a correlation between independence training and later achievement motivation, there are cogent reasons for assuming that a simple view of the dependence–independence dimension is not adequate to understanding the achievement situation. For example, Zigler and Child (1969) argue that if achievement efforts are rewarded by social recognition or approval by others, then the outcome of such behaviors is a kind of dependency, although it may be regarded as mature, as opposed to inappropriate infantile dependency. Also, Bronfenbrenner (1965) noted that middle-class parents who reward independence in their children may not, at the same time, punish dependency behaviors. One therefore gets the picture of certain behaviors (independence and achievement) being pushed and rewarded and other behaviors (dependence) being tolerated. Indeed, it may be the case that because the middle-class parent tends to permit, or even foster, infantile dependency and does not brusquely attempt to extinguish it in later childhood he is able to push with such vigor and such success the training for independence or whatever other behavior he values (McCandless 1961). Bronfenbrenner (1965) has also suggested that the love-oriented or psychological disciplinary techniques which are used more typically in the middle-class home are potentially more powerful molders of the child's behavior than physical punishment or ridicule, which are used more frequently in working-class homes.

An additional interesting conception of the independence-achievement relationship has been presented by Rosen (1959) who distinguishes two socialization practices: training for independence, i.e., training that "seeks to teach the child . . . to do things on his own," and training for achievement, i.e., "getting the child to do things well." A study by Rosen and D'Andrade (1959) found support for the importance of the second process. By observing children perform experimental tasks while parents were present the investigators found that the mothers of high-achievement boys emphasized direct achievement behavior rather than independence or autonomy, rewarded success with approval, and communicated to their children high standards and expectations for success. The results relevant to the fathers of high- as compared with low-achievement boys, were less clear-cut, although tending in the same direction as the mothers' data. In a recent extension of his work, Rosen (1962) finds that knowledge of intrafamilial values, attitudes, and structure surrounding independence, indulgence, dependence, and achievement combine to give the best account of the development of achievement motivation. Thus, it appears that a focus on total family dynam-

ics represents the best bet for understanding many socialization processes and that future research in this area could fruitfully concentrate on studies of whole families (Frank 1965; Handel 1965; Zuckerman 1966).

A cautionary note must be introduced into any serious discussion of social class differences in child-rearing techniques. Studies based on actual observation of maternal behavior toward the child in the home suggest that interclass differences are not as great as one would assume by looking at studies based on interviews with parents (see Waters & Crandall 1964; Zigler & Child 1969). This is still another reason to encourage the study of whole families with regard to broad dimensions of organization and structure. In other words, the contemporary state of affairs seems to be something like this: observed differences in behavior of individuals from different social classes have been documented but the precise intrafamilial socialization techniques have not been sufficiently identified across classes to adequately account for these differences. Perhaps the approach of Miller and Swanson (1958, 1960) provides a useful model. They characterized broad life styles within families as entrepreneurial or bureaucratic and were able to find some class-related differences (i.e., use of different defense mechanisms, broad expressive styles, etc.) in combination with life style or family organizational structure (i.e., middle class perhaps more entrepreneurial and lower class more bureaucratic).

The socialization of aggression represents yet another highly active area of study by social psychologists. The reader interested in reviewing some of this work can consult Bandura and Walters (1963); Becker (1964); Berkowitz (1962, 1965); Feshbach (1964); and Zigler and Child (1969).

ADULT SOCIALIZATION

A relatively recent research development in the area of socialization is work on continuing socialization throughout the individual's life history, i.e., where the focus is on the adult in contrast to the traditional emphasis on the infant and child. Some of these adult-oriented studies have centered on the learning of role behaviors associated with adult statuses (e.g., Brim 1960), the assumption being that childhood socialization is not fully adequate for the training of task requirements of later life. Brim (1968) has delineated three types of adult socialization: *legitimate*, where the individual was not expected to have learned the role behaviors before; *illegitimate*, where he should have learned the role or basic aspects of the role earlier; and *resocialization*, representing a kind of reversal of previous, incorrect learning or knowledge about a particular role. Learning of occupational-appropriate behavior is an example of legitimate adult socialization (e.g., Moore 1969); the lack of adequate "apprenticeship" for parental and marital roles in one's original family would be an example of illegitimate adult socialization (e.g., Hill & Aldous 1969); and rehabilitation of an accused criminal would be an example of resocialization.

Political socialization is an example of a specific continuing process which has received explicit attention (especially since Hyman 1959). Greenstein (1968) defines political socialization as ". . . all political learning . . . at every stage of the life cycle . . . such as the learning of politically relevant social attitudes and the acquisition of politically relevant personality characteristics." Both Hyman (1959) and Greenstein (1965) have found the family to be an important source of political beliefs about party preference and participation in politics. By about age nine children are as likely to have attachments to one of the major political parties as are young adults of voting age, and these attachments are most likely to be the same as those of their parents. Political attachments are developed before broad political or ideological orientations, and little awareness of general political issues is present before adolescence.

In spite of the fact that a number of socialization variables have been identified as important for subsequent behavior and the research literature on socialization is extensive, Zigler and Child (1969), in evaluating the state of knowledge in the area, note that researchers are still not able to choose among alternative theoretical explanations for their results, nor are practitioners able to construct a manual for parents on how to raise their children to produce reliably certain end results.

Attitudes

The study of attitudes has been the major concern of social psychologists and can be said to be the identifying activity of social psychology as a branch of inquiry within the total field. Gordon Allport's classic article on attitudes in the first *Handbook of Social Psychology* (1935) not only reviewed the status of the concept up to that time but contributed valuable insights regarding the acquisition and dynamics of attitude phenomena. A simple indication of the continuing importance of attitudes to the field is the fact that in the 1968–1969 *Handbook of Social Psychology* three chapters are devoted to attitudes: one on their nature and change (McGuire 1969), one on measurement (Scott 1968), and one on the effects of the mass media of communication on attitudes (Weiss 1969).

The utility and durability of the attitude concept in social psychology comes from several sources. First, since people are presumed to have attitudes about socially relevant objects or events, the concept provides a mechanism for coordinating psychological representations of societal phenomena with the social phenomena themselves. The early sociologists Thomas and Znaniecki (1918) called an attitude a "state of mind of the individual toward a value," and values were social in nature and defined by agreement among members of a social group. Second, personality descriptions almost always involve some account of the individual's major attitudes, including especially those toward the self. Third, social psychologists approaching the field from different theoretical orientations have found it useful to translate the concept into their own theoretical language as a heuristic device for guiding empirical work.

Definition of Attitude

Katz and Stotland (1959) present a general characterization of attitude which conforms to traditional commonly-accepted definitions: "a tendency or predisposition to evaluate an object or symbol of that object in a certain way." They thus stress evaluation as a basic aspect of attitude. Rokeach (1968a) would add that in addition to evaluation the predisposition to respond in some preferential way must be relatively enduring and stable through time. Responding in some preferential manner refers to a general approach-avoidance, pro-con, desirable-undesirable,

favorable-unfavorable dimension that is the crux of the attitude concept. Campbell's (1947) definition emphasizes responses ("An individual's social attitude is a syndrome of response consistency with regard to social objects."), while Asch's (1948, 1952) emphasizes perception ("Attitudes are particularly enduring sets formed by past experience.")

The most popular general model of attitudes is what McGuire (1969) has labeled mediationalist. Within this model an attitude is viewed as a hypothetical or latent variable (Green 1954) that is inferred from a large number of related responses which are made consistently to a set of stimuli that have something in common. The latent variable is viewed as organizing the diverse responses (contributing to parsimony), mediating between stimuli and responses, and providing a basis for prediction of individual behavior in known or new situations that can be rationally related to the class of stimuli that has called forth the consistent responses in the past. The present author's approach to interpersonal attitudes illustrates the use of a mediational model within the wider context of general behavior theory.

Employing a reinforcement theory model, a positive attitude is defined as an implicit anticipatory goal response and a negative attitude is defined as an implicit anticipatory pain or frustration response. Once an attitude toward a person has been acquired, as a result, primarily, of relatively consistent association between that person and satisfying or aversive events, the attitude should function as a mediator which can evoke a variety of both unlearned and learned responses. Such responses may cover a broad spectrum from autonomic to perceptual to overt physical and evaluative (Lott & Lott 1970).

Attitude Structure

Most theorists view attitude structure as being composed of three components. The affective or emotional component refers to the feelings of good or bad, like or dislike, for the object of the attitude. For some theorists it is this emotional loading that provides the motivational energy of attitudes (although there is some disagreement as to whether attitudes are both driving as well as directive or only directive, with the energy coming from some other motivational source). The affective loading of an attitude is also assumed to vary in degree, providing one basis for differentiating strong from weak attitudes.

A cognitive component is viewed as the information, knowledge, and beliefs which the individual has about the attitudinal object. The work of Osgood, Suci, and Tannenbaum (1957) and Osgood (1962), however, has shown that most concepts have a factorial loading on an evaluative dimension, suggesting that the information making up the cognitive component is rarely neutral or cold. For this reason, Rokeach (1968b) has recently objected to the usual conceptual distinction drawn between belief and attitude. Katz and Stotland (1959) maintain, nevertheless, that attention to a cognitive aspect of attitudes is useful in determining how much information an individual has about an attitudinal object, regardless of the evaluative loading of the information. The separation of the affective and cognitive components provides Katz and Stotland with a basis for suggesting different processes of attitude change, which will be discussed below.

The behavioral or action component describes the response predisposition associated with attitude. Different attitudes may have different thresholds at which they are elicited, providing a way of conceptualizing attitude strength based on the behavioral component. Doob (1947) views the consequences to the behavior which is mediated by an attitude as the major determinant of the attitude's strength and persistence.

Katz and Stotland (1959) and others assume that the components of attitude are related to one another in a lawful way, that there is a trend toward consistency (high intercorrelations) among the three components. In general the research literature supports such a contention. D. Campbell (1947) has shown consistency among components of attitudes toward minority groups. The cognitive component of ethnic attitudes (measured by the self-report California E scale) has been related to the affective component (GSR changes in the presence of Negroes or their photographs), thus supporting the consistency principle (Porier & Lott 1967; Westie & DeFleur 1959). Examples of the relations between the cognitive and behavioral components can be found in a study by DeFleur and Westie (1958), in which degree of public commitment by white subjects relevant to posing for photographs with Negroes was related to paper and pencil measures of attitudes toward Negroes, and in an investigation by A. Campbell et al. (1960) showing a significant correlation between voting behavior and political attitudes. The greatest strain or pressure toward consistency is presumably found within the single attitude because the three components are focused on a single object, making inconsistencies among the behavioral, cognitive, or emotional elements more apparent if they exist. Behind this notion is the assumption that individuals find inconsistency, imbalance, dissonance, or incongruity upsetting (Zajonc 1960) and will adjust their psychological functioning in such a way as to achieve balance.

In addition to intra-attitude consistency, there is the question of the consistency characteristics of the person's attitude system, i.e., the degree of conflict among different attitudes. While the basic assumption of a strain toward consistency may serve as a starting point, it seems clear that interattitude conflict is not as disturbing to individuals as is intra-attitude inconsistency. Discrepancies among attitudes can be tolerated because people can move from group to group expressing different attitudes in the various groups and thus behave appropriately within different social contexts. Katz and Stotland (1959) argue that the extent of interattitude inconsistency may be governed by the self-concept, i.e., that individuals with a stable self-concept will tend to have stable and consistent attitudes across social situations, especially with respect to self-related attitudes.

McGuire (1969) identifies a more complex type of consistency pattern that takes into account both components and objects. Thus an investigator might be interested in the cognitive component of one attitude as coordinate with the emotional component of another, but related, attitude. Traditional attitude study has neglected this type of consistency, but within the field of personality this approach is typically taken without explicit reference necessarily being made to attitudes or their components in the explanations employed.

Another consequence growing out of the trilogy of attitudinal components is a suggestion for classifying attitudes or constructing a typology (Katz 1960; Katz & Stotland 1959). This requires the additional assumption that attitudes serve a variety of functions for the individual and that information

about the motivational substrate of these functions is therefore useful in classification (Smith 1968; Smith, Bruner, & White 1956). The attitude typology presented below, and the explanation of each type, is based on the work of the above theorists, in addition to that of McGuire (1969).

Intellectualized attitudes are so classified because the cognitive component is highly developed and dominant, with behavioral tendencies and emotional loading present at only minimal levels. The principal motivational base for such attitudes is a need for feeling competent (White 1959) with regard to objects and events in the external world that have meaning for individual motives and goals. Perhaps at the broadest level it is curiosity (Berlyne 1960) or stimulation management (Fisk & Maddi 1961) or mastery of the environment (Hartmann 1958) that lies at the heart of intellectualized attitudes. These should be amenable to change on the basis of new information presented to the person. Given the highly developed cognitive component, change attempts based on cognitive appeals should be potentially successful.

Action-oriented attitudes are conceived as mediating behavior toward important objects without much cognitive or emotional involvement on the part of the individual. Such attitudes may be expressed easily in familiar groups where role relations are stable and where the social structure does not impede easy expression of them. Only when the habitual behavior is blocked or when it is followed by atypical consequences will these attitudes change or will the emotional and cognitive components take on added importance. Experimental work on attitude change through role playing (e.g., Scott 1959) demonstrates that reinforcement of a subject's behavior that is contrary to his expressed attitude will lead to a change in the attitude. Attitude change techniques most effective with this type of attitude should be those that shape the attitude-mediated behavior in some way and a cognitive-informational assault on action-oriented attitudes should have little effect on changing them. However, recalling the principle of consistency or balance, it is to be expected that, for attitudes in general, a change in one component will tend to induce pressures or strains on the other components to change also. If the attitude-based behavior is changed, an individual may generate the appropriate cognitive and emotional support to balance with the new behavior. It is on this point that both dissonance theorists (Brehm & Cohen 1962; Festinger 1957) and learning theorists (Doob 1947; Lott & Lott 1968) would seem to agree: the implicit and explicit consequences of behavior have a profound effect on a person's attitudes. Rosenberg (1960) showed that by changing the emotional component of attitudes the cognitive components fell in line, i.e., changed also without any additional, new information. Through posthypnotic suggestion, Rosenberg experimentally reversed, for individual subjects, the emotional component of several attitudes and then demonstrated that cognitive reorganization took place in the direction of balance with the newly acquired emotional component.

The work of Hovland and his associates on changing attitudes through communication, information, and persuasion represents the most comprehensive approach to changing the cognitive component of attitudes and then looking for other aspects of change (Hovland, Janis, & Kelley 1953; Hovland 1957; Hovland & Janis 1959; Hovland & Rosenberg 1960). Hovland's work dissects the communication situation thoroughly and has called attention to variables other than the content of the information itself, such as source credibility, information organization, emotional appeals, audience characteristics, etc., which must be understood before an adequate account of attitude change (and development) can be constructed.

Katz and Stotland (1959) include the notion of a balanced attitude, in which each of the three components is about equally developed. They suggest that such attitudes most typically have economic or political objects. Given a common cultural setting, such attitudes help an individual in his social adjustment with significant others and reference groups. These attitudes are assumed to be stable and, therefore, significant affiliative and self-other relations are mediated by them.

Ego-defensive attitudes, still another suggested type, are said to develop from internal conflicts. The motivational base is a defensive reaction. Thus the behaviors directed toward the attitudinal object are less related to the characteristics of the object itself than to the defensive needs of the individual holding such an attitude. The study of authoritarianism, with its concomitant anti-Semitic and anti-Negro attitudes, offers an excellent example of ego-defensive attitudes (Adorno et al. 1950; Kirscht & Dillehay 1967).

Because the characteristics of the objects of ego-defensive attitudes are of little value in the resolution of the inner conflict, new information about them should make little difference in terms of attitude change. The individual "needs" such attitudes to maintain his psychological equilibrium and comfort and they will, therefore, change only when self-insight about the internal conflict is achieved. Some experimental work has provided information about the influence of self-insight and cathartic techniques in changing ethnic attitudes (Katz, Sarnoff, & McClintock 1956; Katz, McClintock, & Sarnoff 1957).

While the above typology may serve to clarify aspects of attitude change, provide suggested criteria for labeling different kinds of attitudes, and be heuristically interesting, little direct empirical work has been undertaken to demonstrate how some attitudes become intellectualized while others become action-oriented, for example. The typology suggests possible differences in the conditions of their acquisition but these have not been adequately studied. Post hoc interpretations of experimental findings can reasonably relate results to typologies, but few predictive or developmental studies have been carried out.

ATTITUDES AND VALUES

Over the years there has been continuing interest in comparing attitudes and values, either to show how they are different or to show how they articulate with one another. Allport (1935) saw values as simply enduring attitudes about a class of objects (as opposed to a single object) held by a mature individual—one who had thought about and organized the attitudes into a comprehensive system. A quarter of a century later, Katz and Stotland (1959) have restated, somewhat more elaborately, the Allport position. They state that individual attitudes are "frequently organized into larger structures called value systems which are integrated about some abstractions concerning a general class of objects." The value system is based on the individual's own organization of his attitudes. This latter fact serves to distinguish ideology from values: an ideology is presumed to be more impersonal whereas the value system is more idiosyncratic. Katz and Stotland thus extend their separation of concept (purely cognitive, intellectual appraisal) and attitude (affective

evaluation) to the broader variables of ideology and values. As was noted earlier, it may be virtually impossible to appraise a concept without some evaluative reaction being involved, although Rhine (1958) has suggested how some concepts may be operationally analyzed as descriptive and others as evaluative.

In essence, then, a value is thought to be a kind of super attitude at a higher level of abstraction. Commonalities among a person's attitudes can be identified and grouped around a smaller number of broad themes which provide the labels for the values. A single attitude may be part of one or several values and it is, therefore, possible to consider how isolated or integrated an attitude is within the value system. Integrated attitudes should be harder to change because they can gain additional support from the larger value system of which they are a part. Finally, what gives coherence and stability to the value system is the self-concept. The extent to which an individual's image of himself is reflected in his values will determine his (emotional) reaction to attempts to change his values or the attitudes on which the values are based.

Rokeach (1968a, 1968b) has recently presented an interesting contrasting view of values and attitudes. Considering the functional basis for attitudes, he argues that the value-expressive function is superordinate to all other functions, i.e., all of a person's organized attitudes serve, at base, his values. And the value system is designed to enhance self-regard. Rokeach proposes that the knowledge, adjustive, and ego-defensive functions served by attitudes can be reduced to the major, special function of value-expression. By placing special emphasis on values, interdisciplinary relevance may be increased because of the importance of the concept of value to such areas as philosophy, sociology, and political science. Rokeach, in suggesting that value expression is the major source of self-realization, notes that he is building on the earlier ideas of McDougall (1908) who viewed the master sentiment (attitude) as that of self-regard.

ATTITUDES AND BEHAVIOR

A major question is how knowledge of a person's attitudes can lead to accurate predictions of his behavior. From the perspective of attitude measurement, Green (1954), for example, has noted that inferences about behavior should not be made from the sample of verbal responses that make up the typical attitude questionnaire. Whether such verbal responses are or are not predictive of responses in nonverbal situations, however, must be determined.

Perhaps the area that best illustrates the difficulties and nuances of predicting behavior from verbal attitude measures is that of relating intergroup behavior to ethnic attitudes. For example, La Pierre (1934), Kutner, Wilkins, and Yarrow (1952) and Minard (1952) all demonstrated in various field contexts that there were inconsistencies between nonverbal behavior toward individual members of minority groups and verbal expressions of attitudes toward the general minority group. The basic finding was that interpersonal behavior in specific situations was generally less indicative of prejudice than were responses made by the same individuals to paper and pencil tests of prejudice.

Two recent attempts have been made to interpret findings such as these. Campbell (1963) has argued that the inconsistency is a pseudophenomenon that has been exaggerated. Rather, he suggests, verbal discrimination and behavioral discrimination are associated with different thresholds of elicitation. Apparently there is a higher threshold for acting out prejudice in a face to face encounter with an individual member of the disliked group than for verbally admitting to holding a group prejudice. Campbell has concluded that most of the subjects in the intergroup studies mentioned above had middling attitudes toward the ethnic groups involved and behaved consistently if the assumed differential thresholds in the behavioral context and verbal context are taken into account.

Rokeach (1968a) has proposed a different resolution of the apparent phenomenon of inconsistency by suggesting that a person's social behavior is always mediated by at least two attitudes—"one activated by the object and the other activated by the situation." Traditional attitude study has focused primarily on the object of the attitude across situations rather than on the measurement of attitudes toward situations across objects. Since an attitude is almost always encountered in some social context (even in the wording of a questionnaire item), Rokeach argues that the two kinds of attitudes must be assessed before a behavioral prediction can be confidently made. Assuming, further, that the two attitudes cognitively interact, it is recognized that some attitude-based behaviors are more determined by a powerful attitude toward the object while other behaviors are more determined by a strong attitude toward the situation.

Rephrasing the Rokeach position, it might be said that the situation can also be called an attitudinal object and that behavioral predictions in complex situations must take into account several attitudes operating simultaneously (e.g., Porier & Lott 1967). It has been noted by others, such as Cook and Selltiz (1964), that knowledge of an individual's attitudinal disposition toward an object is not sufficient for predicting his behavior in a particular situation. In addition to the attitude, other characteristics of the individual (his motivational state, expressive style, his disposition toward other objects in the situation, and so on) and other characteristics of the situation (cultural prescriptions for appropriate behavior, expectations of others, probable consequences of certain acts, and so on) must be known. Cook and Selltiz also propose that multiple measures of the same attitudes will provide a better basis for behavioral expectations than just a single measure. They suggest five types of measuring techniques ranging from self-reports about the attitudinal object to information drawn from physiological responses not under conscious control of the individual.

Groups

Contemporary scientific concentration on face to face interacting groups began during the decade from 1930 to 1940. Although before this time experimental work by the psychologist Floyd Allport (1920, 1924) on co-acting groups had explored the phenomenon of social facilitation (see also Dashiell 1935; Zajonc 1965) and the theorizing of sociologists like Charles Cooley (1909) and Georg Simmel (see Wolff 1950) had pointed to the importance of primary groups and the significance of numbers in social living, it was in the 1930s that the potential richness, vigor, and range of scientific work on groups became clear.

In a classic field study, Newcomb (1943) demonstrated the feasibility and value of studying the influence of reference groups on the development and change of individual attitudes. His longitudinal study examined changes in the attitudes of girls who came from conservative families into a liberal college community and provided evidence for the impact of group identifications on these changes. He found that those students who continued to anchor their political attitudes in the home and family remained conservative while those who used the college community as their major reference group became less conservative. In an interesting follow-up study conducted more than twenty years after his original work, Newcomb (1963a) found that the attitude changes in the direction of liberalism seemed to persist. In the early 1960s his subjects were more nonconservative than a comparable group from the same upper-middle social class. The major mediating factor seemed to be the kinds of husbands the girls chose. After acquiring more liberal economic-political attitudes during their college years, these graduates chose (or were chosen by) husbands who were more nonconservative than was typical for girls in general from a similar socioeconomic level.

The experimental work of Sherif (1936) on the development and persistence of social norms showed not only that such phenomena could be studied in a controlled laboratory setting but also demonstrated empirically that group norms could become internalized as individual standards. When Sherif's subjects were first asked to make their own judgments of an ambiguous stimulus (apparent movement of light in an autokinetic situation) they quickly structured the situation by creating individual norms for themselves. When these same subjects moved into a group context and heard other subjects giving their judgments verbally, a new group norm of judgment emerged which was a rough average of the norms of the individuals present. A final individual phase of the experiment revealed that the norm adopted in the group context was the one that persisted. In other words, once the individuals had changed their personal standards in a group context, the group-based standard became their subsequent individual one. Sherif was also able to show the influence of prestige suggestion and other individual and group variables by employing variations of this basic laboratory procedure.

Perhaps the most dramatic, elaborate, and influential studies undertaken during this early period were those investigating the effects of leadership styles on group atmosphere and individual behavior, the famous field experiments of Lewin and his colleagues (Lewin, Lippitt, & White 1939; White & Lippitt 1960). These experiments not only examined task and social-emotional outcomes (dependent measures) under autocratic, democratic, and laissez-faire leader styles but also charted the quantity and quality of interaction within the groups as well as relating certain extra-experimental personality characteristics of the individual subjects to their within-group behavior. In addition to providing a wealth of information about leadership and resulting group reactions, Lewin's work demonstrated that the complex phenomena of face-to-face interaction, leadership, morale, group productivity, etc. could be subjected to creative and rigorous experimental investigation.

Three other influential group studies in the 1930s, carried out within more anthropological and sociological traditions, will be mentioned briefly before turning to the contemporary scene. W. F. Whyte (1943) spent several years living in the slum areas of Boston as a participant observer of gang behavior, recording in rich detail the dynamics of group processes and interaction among individuals. The care with which he observed and described such phenomena as leadership, group cohesiveness, and status relationships provided a vivid source for hypotheses to be explored in future more-controlled research. The work of Elton Mayo and his associates in the Hawthorne plant of the Western Electric Company (Roethlisberger & Dixon 1939) also involved observation of a natural group. In this case, the effects of human factors on productivity were examined by manipulating human relations and quantifying interaction. In addition to producing a comprehensive account of the functioning of task-oriented groups, the so-called Hawthorne effect was discovered. It was found that group productivity increased whenever special attention was paid to the individuals under study regardless of whether the experimental interventions were of a positive or negative character (for some recent discussion of this work see Carey 1967; and Sommer 1968). A final influential study in the same decade was that of Moreno (1934) and Jennings (1950) at the New York State Training School for Girls. By eliciting measures of interpersonal acceptance and rejection from the girls at the school, a picture of the social structure of the school population, as seen by the subjects themselves, was obtained. The very simple questionnaire used was called a sociometric test and, in one form or another, has remained a useful measuring device for innumerable studies of interpersonal relations (see, for example, Lindzey & Byrne 1968). Besides developing a measuring technique, Moreno and Jennings pointed to the importance of interpersonal liking and disliking as particularly significant and pervasive elements in social life. Since Moreno, interest in interpersonal attraction has greatly increased (Berscheid & Walster 1969; Bramel 1969; Byrne 1969; Lott & Lott 1965; Pepitone 1964), although much of the contemporary work is concerned with testing hypotheses from more elaborate theoretical models and employs other measuring devices in addition to the sociometric test (see, for example, Lott & Lott 1970).

Wolman (1956, 1958) has distinguished three types of face-to-face groups, namely instrumental, mutual and vectorial. When people join a group in order to satisfy their own needs, the group is instrumental for them; when they intend to satisfy their own needs and the needs of others, it is a mutual group; and when they join a group in order to help others it is a vectorial group. Wolman developed an experimental technique that measures social relations within a group in terms of power (ability to satisfy needs) and acceptance (the willingness to do so). The division into the three types of social relationships was applied to the study of families (Wolman 1965a) and to a sociogenic classification of mental disorders (Wolman 1965b).

Group Formation

A group is made up of two or more persons who recognize their interdependence in the pursuit of common or individual goals, who interact with one another in the group context, and who are cognizant of each other and of the fact that they form a social unit. Long term groups develop norms and role relationships in order to stabilize their functioning with regard to matters of importance relating to task performance and group maintenance.

One of the best accounts of the dynamics of group formation is available in the data obtained by the Sherifs (1964, 1969) from field experiments. Bion (1961) also has presented a detailed (psychoanalytically oriented) description of group development in the therapy context. The four essentials of group formation proposed and identified by the Sherifs will provide the basis for the present discussion.

Sherif and Sherif suggest that the first essential ingredient conducive to group formation is a motivational factor. When persons believe that they cannot effectively reach some commonly held goal through individual efforts, the situation is ripe for joining together, communicating, and sharing, in order to deal with the goal-striving in a collective manner. If the initial interactions are rewarded by success, the group can become a stable, long-term social unit, and new motives and goals based on intragroup activities can develop among the group members. At this time a second essential feature of group formation, a stable organization or structure, emerges. That is to say, intermember expectations for the behaviors of one another assume a certain degree of patterned regularity (see Collins & Raven 1969 for an extensive discussion of group structure). The Sherifs believe that the fine grain of group structure can be defined in terms of role and status relations (see also Hare 1962), where role denotes expected behavior relevant to the group, especially intermember rights and obligations, and where status refers to a member's position in the power structure (that is, his ability to control or initiate activities). The rate of organization varies depending on both intragroup (e.g., member characteristics) and extragroup (e.g., intergroup competition) conditions, but, typically, a leader position stabilizes before other positions. The third essential of group formation is the development of group norms. Norms delineate the range of behaviors that are acceptable and valued by the group. Norms are identified by noting similarities in the behaviors of individual group members over time (latitude of acceptance) and by observing the behaviors that result in negative sanctions (latitude of rejection). Ultimately the important norms of the group become internalized which means that the individual group member regulates his own behavior in terms of group standards without explicit reaction or surveillance from the group.

Group Behavior

Only a small sample of the research concerned with relationships among variables in small, face-to-face groups can be mentioned here. Deutsch (1968) has estimated that since 1960 articles on groups have been appearing at the rate of more than 250 per year, and before 1960, too, there exists a voluminous literature on group processes. Hare (1962), and McGrath and Altman (1966) have compiled extensive summaries of the literature while Collins and Raven (1969) and Kelley and Thibaut (1969) have recently provided evaluative-analytic discussions of a broad range of group phenomena.

Most of the research to be discussed here has been performed on artificial ad hoc groups brought together for some experimental purpose. This reflects the state of the field (Golembiewski 1962) and not a selection bias on the part of the writer.

Ever since the studies of Lewin (1947) on the changing of food habits, one question that has continued to be raised is that of the relative superiority of individually oriented change techniques (lectures) as opposed to group discussion as a means of altering individual attitudes, opinions, and behaviors. Lewin found, for example, that group discussion was superior to individual instruction in inducing housewives and mothers to adopt new feeding practices for their families. Bennett (1955) refined the Lewin results by showing that reaching a decision about the behavior in question and perceiving consensus in the group for follow-through on the group decision were major factors in the typically found superiority of the group method. Apparently people are more likely to reach a personal decision during group discussion, especially if they see others as having reached consensus about what they are going to do outside of the group situation. This then served to mediate actual carryover from the group context to the agreed-upon postgroup behavior.

One of the liveliest current research topics is that of the "risky-shift" phenomenon in discussion groups (Kogan & Wallach 1967). Simply put, it has been rather consistently found that, after group discussion of a variety of lifelike problems posing dilemmas to be resolved (Kogan & Wallach 1964), the group average of risk-taking agreed upon is significantly more risky than that of the average individual group member before discussion. At least three interpretations have been offered for this phenomenon. Brown (1965) suggests that there is a cultural value associated with risk taking in America. He noted a kind of "rhetoric regularity" in this direction in recorded group discussions he listened to. The group discussion serves, apparently, to inform the members of the greater risk preference on the part of most of their fellows. This, in combination with the presumed greater valuation of risk in the society at large, serves to displace the modal group standard in a riskier direction. A recent study by Levinger and Schneider (1969) demonstrated that, while risky positions are generally admired by undergraduate college students, this is not equally the case for all life areas (e.g., those, according to Brown, that involve the vital interests of others). Another reason for the usually observed shift toward riskiness is that the initially risky individual is personally more persuasive during the group discussion and therefore influences his fellow group members more. Some current research supports this contention (Wallach, Kogan, & Bem 1962; Wallach, Kogan, & Burt 1965). Rim (1963, 1964) has attempted to relate greater risk preferences to the personality characteristics of extraversion and need for achievement. Kelley and Thibaut (1969) propose that, in addition to cultural standards and individual personality factors, diffusion of responsibility through group discussion contributes to a risky shift. If responsibility for risk taking is shared, no one individual may be pinpointed as "causing" the mistake if the risky choice leads to negative outcomes. [For a discussion of diffusion of responsibility in a different context see Darley and Latané (1968) and Latané and Darley (1968).]

Current laboratory study of the risky shift phenomenon is extensive. (See special issue of the *Journal of Personality and Social Psychology*, December 1971, Vol. 20, No. 3 for an extensive and intensive analysis of the risky shift.) What would seem to be of great relevance is further exploration of this process in the study of natural groups who actually have to follow through after making decisions on a course of action.

Another area in which groups and individuals have been compared is problem-solving efficiency. Kelley and Thibaut (1954) noted that early in the study of groups the relative superiority of individuals or groups was a salient concern. Although the level of experimental and theoretical sophistication has changed, the question has remained an important one for contemporary investigators (Kelley & Thibaut 1969). In general, research has shown groups to be equal, or superior, to individuals

on problems where information distribution is an essential feature of the problem-solving process. In the typical experimental paradigm for work in this area, individuals solve some problems while alone and subsequently discuss and solve the same or similar problems in a group. Group accuracy is then compared to individual accuracy. Group solutions may be superior for a variety of reasons: members may compare individual solutions for correctness; members may together be able to assemble more information about a problem than any one member alone can contribute; the more correct group member may also be more confident about his solution and more actively influence fellow group members; and/or identification and recognition of the correct answer may be enhanced through social processes.

Some studies show group performance below the level of the best group members (e.g., Davis & Restle 1963). The particular problems to be solved, in such cases, seem to be ones which might be called individually-oriented, i.e., where the solution is gained through a careful sequence of ideas that must be pursued only in a certain order for a correct solution to be reached. In other words, a division of labor with respect to such problems would be difficult to achieve and may even prove detrimental to problem solution if it were attempted. Thibaut and Kelley's (1959) characterization of two major types of group tasks helps to clarify the group performance picture. They designate a task as conjunctive if more than one group member has to make a certain response in order for a group to solve a problem or receive a reward. Disjunctive tasks can be solved independently by any group member without the strict necessity of communication with other group members or any explicit coordination of intermember efforts. Conjunctive tasks force more concern with group coordination and organization than do disjunctive tasks (e.g., Deutsch 1949). Partially because of this need for intermember coordination, groups tend to be slower than individuals in solving problems (e.g., Davis & Restle 1963; Taylor & Faust 1952). Thus it may be that, in the group context, speed is sacrificed for accuracy.

One group problem-solving technique that was contrived to be different from the usual ones is called brainstorming (Osborn 1957). During a brainstorming session group members throw out ideas spontaneously without regard to their apparent value and other group members build on these ideas without evaluating or criticizing them; in a way, the group forces itself to remain at the orientation level of a problem-solving sequence [defined by Bales (1950) and demonstrated by Bales and Strodtbeck (1951)]. The belief is that brainstorming can lead to creative solutions because typical constraints are held in abeyance permitting group members to be as free and open as possible in suggesting ideas. In general, the research carried out on this technique does not support the basic contention that such groups are, in fact, more creative than individuals operating under similar instructions (Taylor, Berry, & Block 1958; Dunnette, Campbell & Jaastad 1963). From the laboratory studies, the data obtained suggest that instructions for spontaneity are not sufficient to elicit the desired outcomes. It may be that training in the brainstorming technique is necessary before it can operate as originally intended. In other words, it may be an accurate observation that groups typically and prematurely engage in evaluation and criticism of suggested problem solutions, and that the other extreme of no evaluation appears to be difficult to achieve.

Social psychologists studying groups have been struck by the fact that some group processes seem not to be easily associated with the individual characteristics of the group members nor with random relationships among the members. The study of group structure has emerged from observations that individuals behave in certain ways in groups because of the internal organization of the group and their place in this organization. Group structure refers to stable relationships among group members with regard to some dimension like communication, power, or attraction. Once a structural dimension has been identified, the position of each member may be determined. For example, in the communication structure members may be characterized as being in a central or peripheral position (Bavelas 1950; Leavitt 1951; Shaw 1964) depending upon the number of communication links to which they have access. Each member can not only be characterized by the number of such links but also different degrees of centrality can be related to individual morale, leadership potential, and relative contribution to group problem-solving efficiency. Cartwright and Zander (1968) have described the roots of group structure as being efficient group performance and a way of capitalizing on different abilities and motivations of the individual group members. With organization, work proceeds more smoothly and individual members have an opportunity to stress those activities that are most in keeping with their abilities and preferences.

Much of the work by social psychologists on group structure has involved the interpersonal relations among group members as opposed to the role or status structure of the group. Brief examples of two kinds of interpersonal structure will be presented: the sociometric structure (intermember attraction, or group cohesiveness) and the power structure.

The patterning of likes and dislikes within groups may be analyzed on an interpersonal level (attraction) as well as on a group level (cohesiveness). The antecedents of interpersonal attraction have been broadly related to satisfactions experienced through achieving various kinds of interpersonal balance (e.g., Festinger & Aronson 1968; Heider 1958; Newcomb 1963b) or to rewards received from, mediated by, or experienced in contiguity with other individuals (e.g., Homans 1961; Lott & Lott 1960, 1968; Newcomb 1960; Thibaut & Kelley 1959). When attraction variables are organized into a group pattern they form a major aspect of group cohesiveness. Lott and Lott (1965) have pointed out that most researchers operationalize group cohesiveness through manipulating intermember attraction in some fashion and measuring cohesiveness as a dependent variable by measuring interpersonal attitudes. Tagiuri (1958) has noted, too, that factor analytic studies of groups point to the special importance of the like-dislike factor as a determinant of interaction. Other nominal definitions of group cohesiveness, however, continue to appear. Cartwright (1968), in a recent critical analysis of the concept, sticks with and amplifies the earlier conception of Festinger (1950) who defined cohesiveness as "the resultant of all forces acting on members to remain in the group." Cartwright identifies the two major forces as the attractiveness of the group and the attractiveness of alternative group memberships. At the operational level, Collins and Raven (1969) concentrate on interpersonal attraction by defining cohesiveness as the ratio of ingroup to outgroup choices. While disagreements exist on the most meaningful nominal definition of cohesiveness and the most

accurate operational definition, the above articles in combination present a wealth of information about the consequences of varying amounts of cohesiveness on group morale, conformity, communication, intermember evaluation, task performance, and so on.

There is an extensive literature on the power structure of groups. Cartwright (1959, 1965), Collins and Raven (1969), and Schopler (1965) present fine reviews and analyses. For the purpose of illustration here, we will focus on the work of French and Raven (1959). They see social power in terms of the ability of some influencing agent, O, to change the cognitions, attitudes, behaviors, or emotions of another person, P. In other words, when changes in P can be attributed to influences of O, this signifies O's power over P. From the perspective of an interpersonal basis of group structure, French and Raven delineate five sources of social power that derive from different types of relationships between P and O.

Reward power has as its base the ability of O to administer positive reinforcements and decrease negative reinforcements for P. Through time, the exercise of this type of power should lead to increased attraction of P toward O. Coercive power, on the other hand, stems from the fact that O will punish P if he fails to conform to O's influence attempts, and this will eventually lead to decreased attraction of O for P. Schopler (1965) has pointed to some of the potential difficulties of distinguishing between reward and coercive power in terms of certain group outcomes like conformity (Zipf 1960). It may be that the interpersonal by-products of these two types of reward become the major differentiating characteristics. Reward power, with its potential for increasing attraction, may lead P to internalize O's standards (referent power—see below) so that eventually P is behaving as O would like without O explicitly exerting his influence. Coercive power, however, will require continual surveillance of P by O if it is to continue to operate effectively. It would thus appear to be more effortful for O.

Referent power is based on identification of P with O, the desire of P to be similar to O. The stronger the identification, the stronger the referent power. Collins and Raven (1969) have attempted to interpret various phenomena like social-comparison processes, uniformity pressures, personality factors as determinants of reactions to group pressures, and so on, in terms of referent power.

A type of power based on O's greater knowledge in a given area relative to P is called expert power. P will presumably follow O's leadership only in the area of expertise and only as long as he perceives O to be trustworthy and not attempting to deceive him. Expert power can lead to dependence of P on O to the extent that P cannot gain similar expertness or to the extent that O will not or cannot communicate the basis of his knowledge to P.

Legitimate power is, according to French and Raven (1959), the most complex type of all. It stems from the fact that cultural standards or group structure prescribe one individual as a legitimate source of influence over another. When P and O have accepted these standards, P then is obligated to accept O's influence attempts. The range of legitimate power may be wide (parents' power over their children) or narrow (college professor's power over students) and thus this type of power is hypothesized to operate only within the range prescribed by the social norm. Collins and Raven (1969) and Schopler (1965) present critiques of the research on the various kinds of power described above as well as interesting detailed comparisons of the nuances associated with each.

The Social Psychology of the Psychological Experiment

At the national meetings of the American Psychological Association in 1961 a symposium examined aspects of the typical psychological experiment in terms of the social relationships involved when human experimenters gather data from, and about, human subjects. With the subsequent publication of papers by the symposium participants (McGuigan 1963; Orne 1962; Rosenthal 1963; Riecken 1962) an active concern was generated about the subtle (covert) interpersonal relationships between experimenters and subjects and how they might affect the results of the experiment. Orne (1962) coined the term "demand characteristics" to designate those extraneous aspects of an experimental procedure or setting that might convey to a subject some suggested or desirable behavior within the context of the experiment. If demand characteristics determine the results of an experiment, and not the independent variables, then the validity and generalizability of the experimental findings are, of course, seriously limited. Orne described some techniques which could be utilized in psychological experimentation to assess the potential presence of demand characteristics or to minimize their effects.

Rosenthal (1964, 1966) has written extensively on what he calls the experimental "outcome-orientation" (bias) of human experimenters. He has shown that there is a tendency on the part of some experimenters to unintentionally influence their subjects in such a way as to evoke from them data that support the research hypotheses. A detailed exploration and criticism of the work on experimenter bias effects is contained in an exchange of articles between Barber and Silver (1968a, 1968b) and Rosenthal (1968) where Barber and Silver conclude that the bias phenomenon is not as well established as generally assumed. As with Orne's analysis, Rosenthal's work has led to suggestions about how researchers might do things differently so as to reduce, eliminate, or assess the potential effects of unintentional biasing.

An interesting look at authority relations in social research is provided by Argyris (1968) who likens the relationship between experimenter and subject to that between manager and employee. He then proceeds to show how organization theory can provide a useful framework for understanding some of the implicit and unexpected negative consequences of rigorous research. Like lower level employees reacting to their managers, experimental subjects may feel put-upon by their experimenters. As a consequence of this they may respond in a variety of ways, from physical and psychological withdrawal to an emphasis on monetary rewards for participation, or even unionization. (Argyris reports that some of his colleagues reacted to the thought of a student organization which would provide subjects for a price in a very similar manner to a businessman who hears for the first time that his employees are contemplating the formation of a union!)

The results of empirical investigations may also have limited generalizability if they are gathered in a highly authoritarian context. This is to say, they may be relevant primarily to other authoritarian settings. Argyris suggests that elaborate preplanning for experiments, in direct consultation with representatives of the subjects who will be in the experiment (or a similar group

that will not actually provide the experimental subjects), will not only improve the effectiveness and relevance of research techniques, but will elicit a stronger commitment and interest on the part of participating subjects to take their job seriously with a high level of motivation.

With interest focused on the social psychology of the psychological experiment, it was inevitable that the use of deception (Stricker 1967) would come under scrutiny. Kelman (1966, 1967, 1968) has considered this phenomenon in detail. He is critical of the use of deception on three counts: the ethical implications of deceiving human subjects; methodological considerations (as word gets around, subjects will be diverted from their experimental tasks to trying to identify the deception); and the future of social psychology (i.e., can a scientific discipline be built on a foundation of data gathered through deception?). While recognizing the difficulties associated with eliminating all types of deception from experiments, Kelman suggests that the use of gross, negative types of deception should be stopped and that new experimental techniques should be developed. Two possible alternatives to deceiving subjects are the use of role playing subjects, and asking subjects to withold judgement and evaluation of the experiment until it is completed, at which time they are given a full description of what it was all about.

In the present context, role playing refers to an experimenter describing the situation to a subject and having the subject describe how he would behave in the situation if he were actually in it. The pros and cons of studies utilizing this technique have been discussed by Freedman (1969) who concludes that data gathered through role playing provide only people's opinions about their behavior and not a true indication of their actual behavior (see also Greenberg 1967). Aronson and Carlsmith (1968) also argue that role playing is not the answer. In their interesting chapter on all phases of experimentation in social psychology, they opt for an artfully created realism in the construction of experimental settings, while keeping in mind broad ethical implications of what is done to subjects. They assume that if the experimental process is realistic and involving for the subject, the data he provides through his spontaneous responses will be accurate and meaningful.

McGuire (1967) describes the full extent of variety and creativity available to social psychological investigators. While noting a past overemphasis on laboratory research (with its various advantages and disadvantages) he sees new methodological progress being made in theory-oriented research in natural environments (work by Milgram, Bickman & Berkowitz 1969; Piliavin, Rodin & Piliavin 1969; and Wrightsman 1969, represents good examples of this approach). He also proposes that social psychologists become acquainted with already accumulated nationwide surveys of public opinion as a source of hypothesis testing. All the above techniques (see also Willems & Raush 1969), together with archival data, computer simulation of psychological and social situations, content analysis, etc., can provide a new breadth and quality to social psychological knowledge.

Concluding Comment

This chapter has attempted to convey some of the flavor of what is currently happening in social psychology. It has been selective in its coverage and has obviously omitted a great deal. The reader interested in pursuing at greater depth and complexity theoretical and experimental issues being explored today in this branch of psychology can do no better than turn to the five volumes of the second edition of the *Handbook of Social Psychology* (Lindzey & Aronson 1968, 1969). If this chapter has succeeded in stimulating such a pursuit, it will have served its primary function.

Acknowledgement. Preparation of this chapter was partially supported by a grant (GS-1438) from the National Science Foundation, Division of Social Sciences.

References

ADORNO, T. W., FRENKEL-BRUNSWIK, E., LEVINSON, D. J., and SANFORD, R. N. *The authoritarian personality.* New York: Harper & Row, 1950.

ALLPORT, F. H. The influence of the group upon association and thought. *Journal of Experimental Psychology*, 1920, *3*, 159–82.

———— *Social psychology.* Boston: Houghton Mifflin, 1924.

ALLPORT, G. W. Attitudes. *In* C. Murchison (ed.), *A handbook of social psychology.* Worcester, Mass.: Clark University Press, 1935.

ALTUS, W. D. Birth order and its sequellae. *Science*, 1966, *151*, 44–49.

ARGYRIS, C. Some unintended consequences of rigorous research. *Psychological Bulletin*, 1968, *70*, 185–97.

ARONSON, E., and CARLSMITH, J. M. Experimentation in social psychology. *In* G. Lindzey and E. Aronson (eds.), *Handbook of social psychology*, 2d ed., vol. 2. Reading, Mass.: Addison-Wesley, 1968.

ASCH, S. E. The doctrine of suggestion, prestige, and imitation in social psychology. *Psychological Review*, 1948, *55*, 250–76.

———— *Social psychology.* Englewood Cliffs, N. J.: Prentice-Hall, 1952.

BALES, R. F. *Interaction process analysis: A method for the study of small groups.* Cambridge, Mass.: Addison-Wesley, 1950.

————, and STRODTBECK, F. L. Phases in group problem-solving. *Journal of Abnormal and Social Psychology*, 1951, *46*, 485–95.

BANDURA, A., and WALTERS, R. H. *Social learning and personality development.* New York: Holt, Rinehart & Winston, 1963.

BARBER, T. X., and SILVER, W. J. Fact, fiction, and the experimenter bias effect. *Psychological Bulletin Monograph Supplement*, 1968*a*, *70*, 1–29.

———— Pitfalls in data analysis and interpretation: A reply to Rosenthal. *Psychological Bulletin Monograph Supplement*, 1968*b*, *70*, 48–62.

BAVELAS, A. Communication patterns in task-oriented groups. *Journal of the Acoustical Society of America*, 1950, *22*, 725–30.

BECKER, W. C. Consequences of different kinds of parental discipline. *In* M. L. Hoffman and L. W. Hoffman (eds.), *Review of child development research*, vol. 1. New York: Russell Sage Foundation, 1964.

BENNETT, E. B. Discussion, decision, commitment, and consensus in "group decision." *Human Relations*, 1955, *8*, 251–73.

BERKOWITZ, L. *Aggression: A social psychological analysis.* New York: McGraw-Hill, 1962.

———— The concept of aggressive drive: Some additional considerations. *In* L. Berkowitz (ed.), *Advances in experimental social psychology*, vol. 2. New York: Academic Press, 1965.

BERLYNE, D. E. *Conflict, arousal, and curiosity.* New York: McGraw-Hill, 1960.

BERSCHEID, E., and WALSTER, E. H. Interpersonal attraction. Reading, Mass.: Addison-Wesley, 1969.

BION, W. R. *Experiences in groups and other papers.* New York: Basic Books, 1961.

BRADLEY, R. W. Birth-order and school related behavior: A heuristic review. *Psychological Bulletin*, 1968, *70*, 45–51.

BRAMEL, D. Interpersonal attraction, hostility, and perception. *In* J. Mills (ed.), *Experimental social psychology.* New York: Macmillan, 1969.

BREHM, J. W., and COHEN, A. R. *Explorations in cognitive dissonance.* New York: John Wiley, 1962.

BRIM, O. G., JR. Personality development as role-learning. *In* I. Iscoe and H. Stevenson (eds.), *Personality development in children.* Austin: University of Texas Press, 1960.

———— Adult socialization. *In* D. L. Sills (ed.), *International encyclopedia of the social sciences*, vol. 14. New York: Crowell Collier and Macmillan, 1968.

BRONFENBRENNER, U. Socialization and social class through time and space. *In* H. Proshansky and B. Seidenberg (eds.), *Basic studies in social psychology.* New York: Holt, Rinehart & Winston, 1965.

BROWN, R. *Social psychology.* New York: Free Press, 1965.

BURTON, R. V. Socialization: Psychological aspects. *In* D. L. Sills (ed.), *International encyclopedia of the social sciences*, vol. 14. New York: Crowell Collier and Macmillan, 1968.

BYRNE, D. Attitudes and attraction. *In* L. Berkowitz (ed.), *Advances in experimental social psychology*, vol. 4. New York: Academic Press, 1969.

CAMPBELL, A., CONVERSE, P. E., MILLER, W. E., and STOKES, D. E. *The American voter.* New York: John Wiley, 1960.

CAMPBELL, D. T. The generality of social attitudes. Doctoral dissertation, University of California, Berkeley, 1947.

———— Attitudes and other acquired behavioral dispositions. *In* S. Koch (ed.), *Psychology: A study of a science*, vol. 6. New York: McGraw-Hill, 1963.

CAREY, A. The Hawthorne studies: A radical criticism. *American Sociological Review*, 1967, *32*, 403–16.

CARTWRIGHT, D. Influence, leadership, and control. *In* J. G. March (ed.), *Handbook of organizations.* Chicago: Rand McNally, 1965.

———— The nature of group cohesiveness. *In* D. Cartwright and A. Zander (eds.), *Group dynamics: Research and theory.* 3d ed. New York: Harper & Row, 1968.

————, (ed.), *Studies in social power.* Ann Arbor: University of Michigan Press, 1959.

———— and ZANDER, A. Structural properties of groups. *In* D. Cartwright and A. Zander (eds.), *Group dynamics: Research and theory.* 3d ed. New York: Harper & Row, 1968.

CAVAN, R. S. Subculture variations and mobility. *In* H. T. Christensen (ed.), *Handbook of marriage and the family.* Chicago: Rand McNally, 1964.

CHILD, I. L. Socialization. *In* G. Lindzey (ed.), *Handbook of social psychology*, vol. 2. Cambridge, Mass.: Addison-Wesley, 1954.

COLLINS, B. E., and RAVEN, B. H. Group structure: Attraction, coalitions, communication, and power. *In* G. Lindzey and E. Aronson (eds.), *Handbook of social psychology*, vol. 4. 2d ed. Reading, Mass.: Addison-Wesley, 1969.

COOK, S. W., and SELLTIZ, C. A multiple-indicator approach to attitude measurement. *Psychological Bulletin*, 1964, *62*, 36–55.

COOLEY, C. H. *Social organization.* New York: Scribners, 1909.

DARLEY, J., and LATANÉ, B. Bystander intervention in emergencies: Diffusion of responsibility. *Journal of Personality and Social Psychology*, 1968, *8*, 377–83.

DASHIELL, J. F. Experimental studies of the influence of social situations on the behavior of individual human adults. *In* C. C. Murchison (ed.), *Handbook of social psychology.* Worcester, Mass.: Clark University Press, 1935.

DAVIS, J. H., and RESTLE, F. The analysis of problems and prediction of group problem solving. *Journal of Abnormal and Social Psychology*, 1963, *66*, 103–16.

DEFLEUR, M. L., and WESTIE, F. R. Verbal attitudes and overt acts: An experiment on the salience of attitudes. *American Sociological Review*, 1958, *23*, 667–73.

DEUTSCH, M. An experimental study of the effects of cooperation and competition upon group process. *Human Relations*, 1949, *2*, 199–232.

———— Group behavior. *In* D. L. Sills (ed.), *International encyclopedia of the social sciences*, vol. 6. New York: Crowell Collier and Macmillan, 1968.

DOOB, L. W. The behavior of attitudes. *Psychological Review*, 1947, *54*, 135–56.

DUNNETTE, M. D., CAMPBELL, J., and JAASTAD, K. The effect of group participation on brainstorming effectiveness for two industrial samples. *Journal of Applied Psychology*, 1963, *47*, 30–37.

FESHBACK, S. The function of aggression and the regulation of aggressive drive. *Psychological Review*, 1964, *71*, 257–72.

FESTINGER, L. Informal social communication. *Psychological Review*, 1950, *57*, 271–82.

———— A theory of cognitive dissonance. Stanford, Calif.: Stanford University Press, 1957.

————, and ARONSON, E. Arousal and reduction of dissonance in social contexts. *In* D. Cartwright and A. Zander (eds.), *Group dynamics: Research and theory*. 3d ed. New York: Harper & Row, 1968.

FISK, D. W., and MADDI, S. R. *Functions of varied experience*. Homewood, Ill.: Dorsey, 1961.

FRANK, G. H. Role of the family in the development of psychopathology. *Psychological Bulletin*, 1965, *64*, 191–205.

FREEDMAN, J. L. Role playing: Psychology by consensus. *Journal of Personality and Social Psychology*, 1969, *13*, 107–14.

FRENCH, J. R. P., JR., and RAVEN, B. H. The bases of social power. *In* D. Cartwright (ed.), *Studies in social power*. Ann Arbor: University of Michigan Press, 1959.

GERARD, H. B. Social psychology. *In* D. L. Sills (ed.), *International encyclopedia of the social sciences*, vol. 14. New York: Crowell Collier and Macmillan, 1968.

GOLEMBIEWSKI, R. T. *The small group: An analysis of research concepts and operations*. Chicago: University of Chicago Press, 1962.

GREEN, B. F. Attitude measurement. *In* G. Lindzey (ed.), *Handbook of social psychology*, vol. 1. Cambridge, Mass.: Addison-Wesley, 1954.

GREENBERG, M. S. Role playing: An alternative to deception? *Journal of Personality and Social Psychology*, 1967, *7*, 152–57.

GREENSTEIN, F. I. *Children and politics*. New Haven, Conn.: Yale University Press, 1965.

———— Political socialization. *In* D. L. Sills (ed.), *International encyclopedia of the social sciences*, vol. 14. New York: Crowell Collier and Macmillan, 1968.

HANDEL, G. Psychological studies of whole families. *Psychological Bulletin*, 1965, *63*, 19–41.

HARE, A. P. *Handbook of small group research*. New York: Free Press, 1962.

HARTMAN, H. *Ego psychology and the problem of adaptation*. New York: International Universities Press, 1958.

HEBB, D. O., and THOMPSON, W. R. The social significance of animal studies. *In* G. Lindzey and E. Aronson (eds.), *Handbook of social psychology*, vol. 2. 2d ed. Reading, Mass.: Addison-Wesley, 1968, pp. 729–74.

HEIDER, F. *The psychology of interpersonal relations*. New York: John Wiley, 1958.

HELMREICH, R. L., and COLLINS, B. E. Situational determinants of affiliative preference under stress. *Journal of Personality and Social Psychology*, 1967, *6*, 79–85.

HILL, R., and ALDOUS, J. Socialization for marriage and parenthood. *In* D. A. Goslin (ed.), *Handbook of socialization theory and research*. Skokie. Ill.: Rand McNally, 1969.

HOMANS, G. C. *Social behavior: Its elementary forms*. New York: Harcourt Brace Jovanovich, 1961.

HOVLAND, C. I. (ed.), *Order of presentation in persuasion*. New Haven, Conn.: Yale University Press, 1957.

————, and JANIS, I. L. (eds.), *Personality and persuasion*. New Haven, Conn.: Yale University Press, 1959.

————, and KELLEY, H. H. *Communication and persuasion*. New Haven, Conn.: Yale University Press, 1953.

HOVLAND, C. I., and ROSENBERG, M. J. (eds.), *Attitude organization and change*. New Haven, Conn.: Yale University Press, 1960.

HYMAN, H. H. *Political socialization: A study in the psychology of political behavior*. Glencoe, Ill.: Free Press, 1959.

JENNINGS, H. H. *Leadership and isolation*, 2d ed. New York: Longmans, Green, 1950.

KAGAN, J. Personality development. *In* I. Janis, G. F. Mahl, J. Kagan, and R. R. Holt, *Personality: Dynamics, development and assessment*. New York: Harcourt Brace Jovanovich, 1969.

KATZ, D. The functional approach to the study of attitude. *Public Opinion Quarterly*, 1960, *24*, 163–204.

————, MCCLINTOCK, C., and SARNOFF, I. The measurement of ego defense as related to attitude change. *Journal of Personality*, 1957, *25*, 465–74.

————, SARNOFF, I., and MCCLINTOCK, C. Ego defense and attitude change. *Human Relations*, 1956, *9*, 27–46.

KATZ, D., and STOTLAND, E. A preliminary statement to a theory of attitude structure and change. *In* S. Koch (ed.), *Psychology: A study of a science*, vol. 3. New York: McGraw-Hill, 1959.

KELLEY, H. H., and THIBAUT, J. W. Experimental studies of group problem solving and process. *In* G. Lindzey (ed.), *Handbook of social psychology*, vol. 2. Cambridge, Mass.: Addison-Wesley, 1954.

———— Group problem solving. *In* G. Lindzey and E. Aronson (eds.), *Handbook of social psychology*, vol. 4, 2d ed. Reading, Mass.: Addison-Wesley, 1969.

KELMAN, H. C. Deception in social research. *Transaction*, 1966, *3*, 20–24.

———— Human use of human subjects: The problem of deception in social psychological experiments. *Psychological Bulletin*, 1967, *67*, 1–11.

———— *A time to speak: On human values and social research*. San Francisco: Jossey-Bass, 1968.

KIRSCHT, J. P., and DILLEHAY, R. C. *Dimensions of authoritarianism*. Lexington: University of Kentucky Press, 1967.

KOGAN, N., and WALLACH, M. A. *Risk taking: A study of cognition and personality*. New York: Holt, Rinehart & Winston, 1964.

———— Risk taking as a function of the situation, the person, and the group. *In* G. Mandler et al. (eds.), *New Directions in Psychology No. 3*. Rinehart & Winston, 1967.

KUTNER, B., WILKINS, C., and YARROW, P. R. Verbal attitudes and overt behavior involving racial prejudice. *Journal of Abnormal and Social Psychology*, 1952, *47*, 647–52.

LAPIERRE, R. T. Attitudes vs. actions. *Social Forces*, 1934, *13*, 230–37.

LATANÉ, B., and DARLEY, J. Group inhibition of bystander intervention in emergencies. *Journal of Personality and Social Psychology*, 1968, *10*, 215–21.

LEAVITT, H. J. Some effects of certain communication patterns on group performance. *Journal of Abnormal and Social Psychology*, 1951, *46*, 38–50.

LEVINGER, G., and SCHNEIDER, D. J. Test of the "risk is a value" hypothesis. *Journal of Personality and Social Psychology*, 1969, *2*, 165–69.

LEWIN, K. Group decision and social change. *In* T. M. Newcomb and E. L. Hartley (eds.), *Readings in social psychology*. New York: Holt, Rinehart & Winston, 1947.

————, LIPPITT, R., and WHITE, R. Patterns of aggressive behavior in experimentally created "social climates." *Journal of Social Psychology*, 1939, *10*, 271–99.

LINDZEY, G., and ARONSON, E. (eds.), *Handbook of social psychology*, vols. 1–4. 2d ed. Reading, Mass.: Addison-Wesley, 1968, 1969.

————, and BYRNE, D. Measurement of social choice and interpersonal attraction. *In* G. Lindzey and E. Aronson (eds.), *Handbook of social psychology*, vol. 2. 2d ed. Reading. Mass.: Addison-Wesley, 1968.

LOTT, A. J., and LOTT, B. E. Group cohesiveness as interpersonal attraction: A review of relationships with antecedent and consequent variables. *Psychological Bulletin*, 1965, *64*, 259–309.

———— A learning theory approach to interpersonal attitudes. *In* A. G. Greenwald, T. C. Brock, and T. M. Ostrom (eds.), *Psychological foundations of attitudes*. New York: Academic Press, 1968.

———— Some indirect measures of interpersonal attraction among children. *Journal of Educational Psychology*, 1970, *61*, 124–35.

LOTT, B. E., and LOTT, A. J. The formation of positive attitudes toward group members. *Journal of Abnormal and Social Psychology*, 1960, *61*, 297–300.

MCCANDLESS, B. R. *Children and adolescents*. New York: Holt, Rinehart & Winston, 1961.

MCCLELLAND, D. C., ATKINSON, J. W., CLARK, R. A., and LOWELL, E. L. *The achievement motive*. New York: Appleton-Century-Crofts, 1953.

MCDOUGALL, W. *Introduction to social psychology*. London: Methuen, 1908.

MCGUIGAN, F. J. The experimenter: A neglected stimulus object. *Psychological Bulletin*, 1963, *60*, 421–28.

MCGUIRE, W. J. Some impending reorientations in social psychology: Some thoughts provoked by Kenneth Ring. *Journal of Experimental Social Psychology*, 1967, *3*, 124–39.

—— The nature of attitudes and attitude change. *In* G. Lindzey and E. Aronson (eds.), *Handbook of social psychology*, vol. 3, 2d ed. Reading, Mass.: Addison-Wesley, 1969.

MCGRATH, J. E., and ALTMAN, I. *Small group research: A synthesis and critique of the field.* New York: Holt, Rinehart & Winston, 1966.

MILLER, D. R., and SWANSON, G. E. *The changing American parent.* New York: John Wiley, 1958.

—— *Inner conflict and defense.* New York: Holt, Rinehart & Winston, 1960.

MILRAM, S., BICKMAN, L., and BERKOWITZ, L. Note on the drawing power of crowds of different size. *Journal of Personality and Social Psychology*, 1969, *2*, 79–82.

MINARD, R. D. Race relationships in the Pocahontas coal field. *Journal of Social Issues*, 1952, *8*, 29–44.

MOORE, W. E. Occupational socialization. *In* D. A. Goslin (ed.), *Handbook of socialization theory and research.* Chicago: Rand McNally, 1969.

MORENO, J. L. *Who shall survive?* Nervous and Mental Disease Monograph no. 58. Washington, D. C., 1934.

NEWCOMB, T. M. *Personality and social change.* New York: Dryden Press, 1943.

—— Varieties of interpersonal attraction. *In* D. Cartwright and A. Zander (eds.), *Group dynamics: Research and theory.* 2d ed. Evanston, Ill.: Row, Peterson, 1960.

—— Persistence and regression of changed attitudes: Long range studies. *Journal of Social Issues*, 1963a, *19*, 3–14.

—— Stabilities underlying changes in interpersonal attraction. *Journal of Abnormal and Social Psychology*, 1963b, *66*, 376–86.

NISBETT, R. E., and SCHACHTER, S. S. Cognitive manipulation of pain. *Journal of Experimental Social Psychology*, 1966, *2*, 227–36.

ORNE, M. T. On the social psychology of the psychological experiment. *American Psychologist*, 1962, *17*, 776–83.

OSBORN, A. F. *Applied imagination.* New York: Scribner's, 1957.

OSGOOD, C. E. Studies on the generality of affective meaning systems. *American Psychologist*, 1962, *17*, 10–28.

——, SUCI, G. J., and TANNENBAUM, P. H. *The measurement of meaning.* Urbana: University of Illinois Press, 1957.

PEPITONE, A. *Attraction and hostility.* New York: Atherton, 1964.

PILIAVIN, I. M., RODIN, J., and PILIAVIN, J. A. Good samaritanism: An underground phenomenon? *Journal of Personality and Social Psychology*, 1969, *13*, 289–99.

PORIER, G., and LOTT, A. J. Galvanic skin responses and prejudice. *Journal of Personality and Social Psychology*, 1967, *5*, 253–59.

RHINE, R. J. A concept-formation approach to attitude acquisition. *Psychological Review*, 1958, *65*, 362–70.

RIECKEN, H. W. A program for research on experiments in social psychology. *In* N. F. Washburn (ed.), *Decisions, values, and groups*, vol. 2. New York: Pergamon Press, 1962.

RIM, Y. Risk taking and need for achievement. *Acta Psychologica.* 1963, *21*, 108–15.

—— Personality and group decisions involving risk. *Psychological Record*, 1964, *14*, 37–45.

ROE, A. A psychological study of eminent psychologists and anthropologists and a comparison with biological and physical scientists. *Psychological Monographs*, 1953, *67*, no. 2.

ROETHLISBERGER, F. J., and DICKSON, W. J. *Management and the worker.* Cambridge, Mass.: Harvard University Press, 1939.

ROKEACH, M. Attitudes. *In* D. L. Sills (ed.), *International encyclopedia of the social sciences*, vol. 1. New York: Crowell Collier and Macmillan, 1968a.

—— *Beliefs, attitudes, and values.* San Francisco: Jossey-Bass, 1968b.

ROSEN, B. C. The achievement syndrome: A psycho-cultural dimension of social stratification. *American Sociological Review*, 1956, *21*, 203–11.

—— Race, ethnicity, and the achievement syndrome. *American Sociological Review*, 1959, *24*, 47–60.

—— Socialization and achievement motivation in Brazil. *Sociological Review*, 1962, *27*, 611–24.

——, and D'ANDRADE, R. The psychosocial origins of achievement motivation. *Sociometry*, 1959, *22*, 185–218.

ROSENBERG, M. J. Cognitive reorganization in response to hypnotic reversal of attitudinal affect. *Journal of Personality*, 1960, *28*, 39–63.

ROSENTHAL, R. On the social psychology of the psychological experiment: The experimenter's hypothesis as unintended determinant of experimental results. *American Scientist*, 1963, *51*, 268–83.

—— The effect of the experimenter on the results of psychological research. *In* B. A. Maher (ed.), *Progress in experimental personality research*, vol. 1. New York: Academic Press, 1964.

—— *Experimenter effects in behavioral research.* New York: Appleton-Century-Crofts, 1966.

—— Experimenter expectancy and the reassuring nature of the null hypothesis decision procedure. *Psychological Bulletin Monograph Supplement*, 1968, *70*, 30–47.

ROSS, E. A. *Social psychology: An outline and source book.* New York: Macmillan, 1908.

SAMPSON, E. E. Birth order, need achievement, and conformity. *Journal of Abnormal and Social Psychology*, 1962, *64*, 155–59.

—— The study of ordinal position: Antecedents and outcomes. *In* B. A. Maher (ed.), *Progress in experimental personality research*, vol. 2. New York: Academic Press, 1965.

SCHACHTER, S. *The psychology of affiliation: Experimental studies of the sources of gregariousness.* Stanford, Calif.: Stanford University Press, 1959.

SCHOPLER, J. Social power. *In* L. Berkowitz (ed.), *Advances in experimental social psychology*, vol. 2. New York: Academic Press, 1965.

SCOTT, J. P. The social psychology of infrahuman animals. *In* G. Lindzey and E. Aronson (eds.), *Handbook of social psychology*, vol. 4. 2d ed. Reading, Mass.: Addison-Wesley, 1969, pp. 611–42.

SCOTT, W. A. Attitude change by response reinforcement: Replication and extension. *Sociometry*, 1959, *22*, 328–35.

—— Attitude measurement. *In* G. Lindzey and E. Aronson (eds.), *Handbook of social psychology*, vol. 2. 2d ed. Reading, Mass.: Addison-Wesley, 1968.

SHAW, M. E. Communication networks. *In* L. Berkowitz (ed.), *Advances in experimental social psychology*, vol. 1. New York: Academic Press, 1964.

SHERIF, M. *The psychology of social norms.* New York: Harper & Row, 1936.

——, and SHERIF, C. *Reference groups: Exploration into conformity and deviation of adolescents.* New York: Harper & Row, 1964.

—— *Social psychology.* New York: Harper & Row, 1969.

SMITH, M. B. Attitude change. *In* D. L. Sills (ed.), *International encyclopedia of the social sciences*, vol. 1. New York: Crowell Collier and Macmillan, 1968.

——, BRUNER, J. S., and WHITE, R. W. *Opinions and personality.* New York: John Wiley, 1956.

SOMMER, R. Hawthorne dogma. *Psychological Bulletin*, 1968, *70*, 592–95.

STRICKER, L. J. The true deceiver. *Psychological Bulletin*, 1967, *68*, 13–20.

TAGIURI, R. Social preference and its perception. *In* R. Taguiri and L. Petrullo (eds.), *Person perception and interpersonal behavior.* Stanford, Calif.: Stanford University Press, 1958.

TAYLOR, D. W., BERRY, P. C., and BLOCK, C. H. Does group participation when using brainstorming facilitate or inhibit creative thinking? *Administrative Science Quarterly*, 1958, *3*, 23–47.

——, and FAUST, W. L. Twenty questions: Efficiency in problem solving as a function of size of group. *Journal of Experimental Psychology*, 1952, *44*, 360–68.

THIBAUT, J. W., and KELLEY, H. H. *The social psychology of groups.* New York: John Wiley, 1959.

THOMAS, W. I., and ZNANIECKI, F. *The Polish peasant in Europe and America.* Boston: Badger, 1918.

WALLACH, M. A., KOGAN, N., and BEM, D. J. Group influence on individual risk taking. *Journal of Abnormal and Social Psychology*, 1962, *65*, 75–86.

——, KOGAN, N., and BURT, R. B. Can group members recognize the effects of group discussion upon risk taking? *Journal of Experimental Social Psychology*, 1965, *1*, 379–95.

WALTERS, R. H., and PARKE, R. D. Social motivation, dependency, and susceptibility to social influence. *In* L. Berkowitz (ed.), *Advances in experimental social psychology*, vol. 1. New York: Academic Press, 1964.

WARREN, J. R. Birth order and social behavior. *Psychological Bulletin*, 1966, *65*, 38–49.

WATERS, E., and CRANDALL, V. J. Social class and observed maternal behavior from 1940–1960. *Child Development*, 1964, *35*, 1021–32.

WEISS, W. The effects of the mass media of communication. *In* G. Lindzey and E. Aronson (eds.), *Handbook of social psychology*, vol. 5. 2d ed. Reading, Mass.: Addison-Wesley, 1969.

WESTIE, F. R., and DEFLEUR, M. L. Autonomic responses and their relation to race attitudes. *Journal of Abnormal and Social Psychology*, 1959, *58*, 340–47.

WHITE, R. W. Motivation reconsidered: The concept of competence. *Psychological Review*, 1959, *66*, 297–334.

WHITE, R., and LIPPITT, R. *Autocracy and democracy*. New York: Harper, 1960.

WHYTE, W. F., JR. *Street corner society*. Chicago: University of Chicago Press, 1943.

WILLEMS, E. P., and RAUSH, H. L. (eds.), *Naturalistic viewpoints in psychological research*. New York: Holt, Rinehart & Winston, 1969.

WINTERBOTTOM, M. The relation of need for achievement and learning experiences in independence and mastery. *In* J. W. Atkinson (ed.), *Motives in fantasy, action, and society*. Princeton, N. J.: Van Nostrand, 1958.

WOLFF, K. H. *The sociology of Georg Simmel*. Glencoe, Ill.: Free Press, 1950.

WOLMAN, B. B. Leadership and group dynamics. *Journal of Social Psychology*, 1956, *43*, 11–25.

———— Instrumental, mutual acceptance and vectorial groups. *Acta Sociologica*, 1958, *3*, 19–28.

———— Family dynamics and schizophrenia. *Journal of Health and Human Behavior*, 1965a, *6*, 147–55.

———— Mental health and mental disorders. *In* B. B. Wolman (ed.), *Handbook of clinical psychology*. New York: McGraw-Hill, 1965b.

WRIGHTSMAN, L. S., JR. Effects of waiting with others on changes in level of felt anxiety. *Journal of Abnormal and Social Psychology*, 1960, *61*, 216–22.

———— Wallace supporters and adherence to "law and order." *Journal of Personality and Social Psychology*, 1969, *1*, 17–22.

ZAJONC, R. B. The concepts of balance, congruity, and dissonance. *Public Opinion Quarterly*, 1960, *24*, 280–96.

———— Social facilitation. *Science*, 1965, *149*, 269–74.

———— *Animal social psychology: A reader of experimental studies*. New York: John Wiley, 1969.

ZIGLER, E., and CHILD, I. L. Socialization. *In* G. Lindzey and E. Aronson (eds.), *Handbook of social psychology*, vol. 3. 2d ed. Reading, Mass.: Addison-Wesley, 1969.

ZIPF, S. G. Resistance and conformity under reward and punishment. *Journal of Abnormal and Social Psychology*, 1960, *61*, 102–9.

ZUCKERMAN, M. Save the pieces! A note on "The role of the family in the development of psycho-pathology." *Psychological Bulletin*, 1966, *66*, 78–80.

Introduction

Industrial psychology is essentially the application of many areas of psychology to the industrial scene. Over the years it has deepened and broadened its scope to include more complex aspects of human behavior in a greater variety of industrial-social settings. Haire (1959) distinguishes three "traditions" within the field of industrial psychology: industrial-social psychology, personnel psychology, and human engineering. Each is relatively independent in its development and encompasses a different conceptual foundation. Most authors and practitioners also conceptualize such a tripartite division. More recently, however, the term organizational psychology has been replacing industrial-social psychology and human factors engineering taking the place of human engineering.

Organizational psychology is concerned with the study of men within organizations for purposes of implementing effective coordination and control. Its origins may be found within social psychology and sociology. Personnel psychology revolves around the study of individual differences and the comparative analysis of job candidates for purposes of identifying those best suited for a given position. Its roots stem from applied personality theory, learning theory, psychometrics, and educational psychology. Human factors engineering assumes a somewhat opposite approach. In human factors the working environment is manipulated to achieve compatibility with the individual while in personnel the individual is selected to be compatible with the environment. The lineage of human factors is traceable to applied psychology and psychophysiology.

Personnel Psychology

SELECTION AND PLACEMENT

The process of selection attempts to optimize the number of successful employees hired by an organization. It was perhaps the earliest function performed by the industrially employed

Benjamin Balinsky

& Jay M. Finkelman

Industrial Psychology

44

psychologist, commencing with the work of Münsterberg in the first decade of this century. Selection is the process of choosing a group of workers from the population of workers seeking employment, while placement involves the differential assignment of new employees to the available jobs within a firm.

Two basic models may be used in the selection process. The prediction model attempts to derive the predictors manifesting the highest correlation with the criteria established for job success. It may yield a single predictor or multiple predictors, in which relevant factors are optimally combined through statistical methods or through clinically evaluated judgments.

The concurrent model obviates the delay inherent in the collection of criteria data by obtaining such data concurrently with the predictor measures. Aside from this expediency the concurrent model is identical to the prediction model. The prediction model yields a measure of predictive validity of future performance while the concurrent model yields a measure of concurrent validity of present performance.

Miner (1969) furnishes a description of the operation of each of these models as well as a discussion of the modern trends in selection. One such trend is represented by the synthetic validity model which was developed for use where small sample sizes or economic considerations preclude the use of the predictive or concurrent models. This model has some weaknesses. In effect it uses the predictors gained from one set of job predictions to predict performance on another, but similar job. A second trend is found in the decision model which is based upon the utility concept of mathematical decision theory. "Utility is defined by the benefits that accrue from a given set of decisions less the total costs incurred in the decision-making process," (Miner 1969, pp. 135–36). The approach is restricted, however, in that viable measures of the relevant utilities are not generally available for most decisions.

The inability to derive satisfactory measures and performance criteria is a perennial problem in selection. There are also other problems. Existing predictors may not isolate relevant characteristics indicative of actual behavior in an organization and the most valid predictors may be too costly to justify their use. In today's changing labor markets, the varying numbers of job applicants can either enhance the selection process, or reduce it to a frustrating exercise. Standards have to be adjusted to the changing conditions.

The functional value of any selection instrument is dependent upon the selection ratio which can be defined as the ratio of the number of available jobs to the number of applicants. Today, as indicated, the selection ratio approaches 1.00 in many industries, obfuscating the effectiveness of a selection instrument. There are almost as many jobs as applicants. In such a seller's market a firm cannot afford to be too selective in hiring its work force. There is, however, a method of retaining some of the utility of the selection ratio concept. Assuming there are at least two different job types to be filled and assuming each has its own set of predictors it is still possible to place selectively even if all job applicants must be hired. Thus, to a degree, differential placement can mediate an unfavorable labor situation and boost the effective selection ratio.

Selection is theoretically an attempt to remove from a large group a smaller group higher than the average on a given trait. The personnel director engages in a trade-off in which he can accept on the basis of test results a few individuals who will perform poorly and eliminate a few who might have succeeded,

"*if on the whole his percentage of successful placements is higher with the tests than it is without them*" (Tiffin & McCormick 1965, p. 131).

In typical group testing selection programs, a further trade-off is possible between the validity of the test and the selection ratio. If one can afford to be more selective and thus reduce the selection ratio, a test of lower validity can be utilized as effectively as one of higher validity. However, for cases of individual counseling and prediction, it is only the validity of the test which will determine its effectiveness and, in the current seller's market, one would be well advised to rely upon tests of relatively substantial validity for group as well as individual predictions.

There is yet another determinant of the effectiveness of a selection instrument. Holding selection ratio and validity constant, the smaller the percentage of present employees thought satisfactory, the greater the percentage of satisfactory employees that can be hired using that selection test. The precise interaction of test validity, selection ratio, and percentage of present employees thought satisfactory, can be derived from the Taylor-Russell (1939) tables, which then yield an expression of the expected future level of satisfactory employees. Blum and Naylor (1968) suggest the substitution of the Naylor-Shine tables for those of Taylor-Russell because they are thought to yield a more meaningful measure of test validity.

Both tables assumed a linear relationship between test scores and the criterion. In addition, because of the gradual termination of unsatisfactory employees, over a period of time there will be a disparity in the validity measure by the concurrent method as compared with the predictive method. Since the concurrent method entails immediate prediction, it will become less representative with the passage of time and its coefficient will be lower. This disparity tends to underestimate the increase in the expected "percentage of present employees thought satisfactory" when concurrent validity is used in placed of predictive validity. Further discussion of the limitations of such tables may be found in Smith (1948). However, the reader may also wish to consult the work of Tiffin and Vincent (1960) who compared empirical and theoretical expectancies and found the assumption of linearity to be generally justified.

Training and Development

The current need for workers, especially qualified workers, is encouraging industry to accept responsibility for the education and training of workers. Perhaps industrial psychology has too long been emphasizing selection of the most capable workers when it should also have been considering the development of workers within the labor force. Training and development is fast becoming an important part of industrial psychology. Where the labor pool is limited, training takes on even greater significance. Where selection of different ethnic groups is concerned, selection standards may have to be revised and training utilized in accordance with present level of development.

Kirkpatrick, Ewen, Barrett, and Katzell (1968) undertook an extensive experimental evaluation of the fairness and validity of selection tests for different ethnic groups. They explain that unfair discrimination occurs only when applicants who are equally likely to succeed if hired do not have the same chance of being selected. A person may not achieve an acceptable score on a test and yet perform satisfactorily on the job.

The results of the studies revealed instances in which tests differ in their validity for different ethnic groups. They also failed to substantiate the often reputed statements that nonverbal tests show higher validity for certain ethnic groups. It was found that job training could be expected to improve the test scores of all ethnic groups and thus could be applied to the particular needs of each group. On the basis of their investigation, the authors recommend the separate validation and standardization of tests for each ethnic group so as to keep the advantages of objective testing while eliminating the chance of accidental discrimination.

Recently, industrial psychologists have been attacking the problems of labor shortages and minority group pressures with considerable ingenuity and creativity. Segments of industry have already responded selfishly and selflessly to both the limited labor pool and legitimate aspirations of minority groups.

M. Finkelman (1969) reported recent successful efforts by both large and small firms to integrate these goals through hiring and training of disadvantaged workers. First National City Bank, for example, has fabricated a branch bank for training purposes, where nothing is simulated save the currency. Day care centers for disadvantaged mothers of young children are no longer atypical of a major thrust coming from industry. KLH, among others, has refused to accept rejection of their job offer by disadvantaged mothers on the basis of the need to care for children. Not only have they made day care centers available, but there is tremendous flexibility and tolerance to absenteeism, tardiness, inappropriate attire, and lack of discipline while adjustment is taking place. The offender, the handicapped, the disturbed, and the retarded are not barred. With patience and persistent training, this firm is meeting both its own needs and society's goals.

Other firms are adopting these concepts to yield discrete results, including American Telephone and Telegraph, Geigy Chemical, Hardware Design, Liggett and Myers, and General Motors. BFS Psychological Associates has consulted and developed similar programs with such firms as Chase Manhattan Bank. The contemporary psychologist has already accepted his newer and more difficult role in selection and placement. In-service training programs are now typical of a large segment of industry, with hiring predicated upon potential rather than experience. The activity that has been described is clearly not a transient phenomenon and the trend of industrial psychology foretells its progress and expansion.

Executive Appraisal

A specialty which straddles the fields of clinical and industrial psychology had its inception about the time of World War II, when, according to Glaser (1958) some clinically oriented industrial psychologists began to concentrate on developmental counseling with high level management. These psychologists believed that difficulties with personnel and with organizational functioning could be traced to the orientation and behavior of the managers. The trend toward developmental counseling came as much from the needs of the professional managers as from the psychologists who were involved in studying the qualities of performance within an organization.

The appraisal of executive personnel began to grow separately as part of selection and was also linked with developmental counseling. Studies of military officers were made during World War I on a limited scale and increased greatly during World War II. The work of the OSS Assessment staff (Murray, MacKinnon, Miller, Fiske, & Hanfmann 1948) is particularly relevant to the processes, procedures, and problems in appraising executive level personnel.

Executive appraisal is an individualized process requiring a high degree of sophistication on the part of the practitioner. There are also important criterion problems. Success of executive personnel varies with the company size, its hierarchical structure, area of operations and the like. To reduce the criterion problem, the consultant usually tries to learn all he can about the individual. He can thus respond to questions which management may pose with respect to an individual's organizational fit and executive potential. Management makes the final decision to hire the individual after conferences with the consultant and comparison with other candidates.

The individualized selection process develops rigor as the psychologist gains experience with what constitutes success in general as well as within a particular company. This allows him to develop models for predicting job success which he can then evaluate and revise based upon the actual performance of the executives. The fittings are not absolute and can vary from company to company depending upon the organizational setup and interaction with other key personnel. In executive appraisal there is a close tie-in between the success of the executive, the interpersonal climate, and opportunities for development.

Testing in the appraisal process may be deceptive in that most tests do not show the specific behavior about which a psychologist may be ultimately concerned. Instead, behavior must be inferred from such measures as interest, attitude, and personality. Of course, many variables intervene between the test measures and the behavior. Personality tests, especially, have been criticized for isolating characteristics of an individual that may never appear in behavior. Behavioral inferences from test results is thus a crucial problem.

Standard procedures of a more "elementaristic" variety, such as paper and pencil questionnaires, are more efficient in screening out and eliminating those who may not be suitable for the job (Murray et al. 1948). However, for higher level people there is a need to describe how they might behave under a variety of circumstances. Leadership potential is an important characteristic of executive personnel and is often associated with the ability for appropriate self-assertiveness. Projective techniques may aid in obtaining relevant data.

In an early study, Balinsky (1944) utilized the Rorschach in the selection of a plant superintendent. He found it valuable in the measurement of such characteristics as basic attitude, drive, relation to authority, and relation to subordinates. Piotrowski and Rock (1963) utilized the Rorschach to describe the behavior of successful and unsuccessful executives. These descriptions were closely associated with their actual job success. Grant, Katkovsky, and Bray (1967) found that the Rotter Incomplete Sentences, the Management Incomplete Sentences, and the Thematic Apperception Test made significant contributions to the measurement of leadership role, achievement motivation, and dependence.

It must be stressed that the predictive power to be derived from a projective instrument is dependent upon the experience and training of the practitioner. It is usually inadvisable to utilize a projective technique exclusively. Rather, both objective and projective tests have a role in selection and their data must be integrated into an organismic whole. Balinsky (1964) suggests the interview as a matrix which can facilitate this integration. The interviewer is in a unique position to both elicit information and evaluate the individual in an actual behavioral sampling.

The most widely used test in industrial psychology, and in fact, in all of psychology, is the intelligence test. Such tests are reputed to measure the more fundamental intellectual factors, including the general ability to learn. In a study of the contribution of the Wechsler Adult Intelligence Scale (WAIS) to management appraisal, Balinsky and Shaw (1956) found the arithmetic reasoning subtest and the verbal intelligence score to correlate highly with the performance of executive personnel. Intelligence has also been shown to correlate well with occupational rank as given by the Census Bureau.

Intelligence, though crucial, is unable to account for all of the variance in the executive prediction process. Personality factors are clearly relevant to leadership and managerial ability. Ghiselli (1963) reports that beyond a certain level of intelligence, factors of personality become more important. In fact, the usual executive range in intelligence is probably restricted to the upper 15 % of the total population, and in such a superior subgroup, intelligence is less able to discriminate managerial potential (Balinsky 1966).

Organizational Psychology

Selection and training must be considered in a total context. The positions for which individuals are selected and the kinds of training they receive are linked to the organizational structure, which constitutes the human and physical characteristics of the work environment. There are human relations training programs as well as skills training programs. Human relations programs have been offered predominantly to supervisory and executive personnel. They vary markedly in depth and complexity. Fryer, Feinberg and Zalkind (1956) include a relevant description of psychological principles underlying supervisory training procedures. A tremendous amount of research is being conducted in the complex human relations program commonly referred to as sensitivity training.

Sensitivity Training

Sensitivity training, also known as T-Group or Laboratory Training, after originating in the late 1940s, has grown steadily and has become one of the more controversial areas of industrial psychology. The present discussion of sensitivity training must be limited to a consideration of its accompanying behavioral learning and change and their organizational implications. Competent and detailed reviews of this and other aspects of sensitivity training, including greater individual and group perspectives, may be found in such sources as House (1967), Bradford, Gibb and Benne (1964), Schein and Bennis (1965), Argyris (1968), and Dunnette and Campbell (1968).

The learning derived from sensitivity training should enhance the individual's awareness of group processes, as well as the perception of his behavior so that he is better able to function within the group. It is the learning that can be transferred and applied to the organization that is of concern here. Responding to this issue, Stock (1964) reviewed the relevant literature and concluded that the question was highly complex and confounded by many factors. What are the criteria for successful learning and change? How are they to be evaluated? Must there be visible change? If not, how much information can be derived from self-reports, with their multiple sources of contamination? Stock compiled a partial list of factors shown to be affected by sensitivity training such as: self-perception, self-insight, interpersonal sensitivity, role flexibility, diagnostic ability, self-confidence, and behavioral skills. He cautions, however, that changes in these factors have been observed only "for some people, under certain conditions" (p. 434).

What determines which individuals manifest behavioral change after sensitivity training? J. Finkelman (1969) has developed a model for the prediction of such change based upon a multiplicative combination of individual and organizational factors. While Stock concludes from the literature that organizational factors may be "less potent" than supposed, it is probable that the organizational factors considered with moderating individual variables may manifest valuable significance in the predictive process.

Fruitful experimental efforts toward the substantiation of certain variables potentially relevant for such a model have just been completed by Steele, Zand and Zalkind (1970). They found "moderate support" for their hypothesized relationship between prelaboratory expectations and pressures, and later involvement and learning; and greater support for the relationship between prelaboratory set and laboratory experience with involvement in the change activities of an organizational program.

House (1968) addresses himself to the highly relevant problem of the possible dysfunctional consequences of sensitivity training within the organization. Even if the experience is successful in creating desirable behavioral changes, the changes may nonetheless conflict with the prevailing organizational environment, especially when sensitivity training is not uniformly practiced throughout the organization. There is also a possibility that there will be an increase in the role conflict for the trainee, an increase in grievances and turnover, a decrease in job performance, and an increase in interpersonal stress between the trainees and other individuals in the organization.

A Laboratory Training Symposium, published in 1968, contains positions by Dunnette and Campbell and by Argyris dealing with fundamental issues in the evaluation of the effectiveness of sensitivity training. Dunnette and Campbell are concerned with the organizationally relevant behavioral outcome of sensitivity training and object to the traditionally poor means of evaluating that difficult issue because of the societal assumption that such training must be "inherently good."

They suggest the following standards which they believe to be necessary for proper scientific investigation of training experience but which have seldom been applied. Measures of the participants' behavior must be taken both before and after training. The change in such measures should be compared with any occurring in a "control group" with a similar, though untrained population. The degree of interaction between the evaluation measures and trainee behavior must somehow be estimated, possibly through an additional control group taking part in the training but subjected only to the "after measures."

Reviewing those investigations which sought to isolate

change in job behavior, Dunnette and Campbell acknowledge that the associates of individuals who have undergone sensitivity training most often report observable change in the job behavior of their colleagues. However, the authors question whether the reported changes in fact reflect real changes in job behavior or rather the multiplicative sources of contamination and bias. They further note that even if job behavior did change, no study has as yet demonstrated a favorable effect on performance effectiveness.

In response to the criticism of Dunnette and Campbell, Argyris draws a distinction between research geared to scientific understanding and that geared to evaluation of "social action activities" such as sensitivity training. The objective of scientific research is the compilation of factual knowledge through maximum rigor and objectivity. Sensitivity training research, if it is to be responsive to its objectives, "*includes, but goes beyond,* the rules used to gain knowledge for the sake of knowledge" (p. 28).

The work of Zand, Steele, and Zalkind (1969) reveals that variables such as trust and openness, as evaluated by the individual, actually decreased after sensitivity training, especially on a short term basis. Such a phenomenon was thought by Argyris to account for some of the "no-change" results of training studies which in fact represented actual learning, because "interviews with the laboratory participants would reveal that many learned how inaccurate they were about their capacity to trust and be open" (p. 40).

Argyris implies that the evaluation of sensitivity training through the criterion of behavioral change in the organization is not a fair one because of lack of consonance between organizational and laboratory values. He points out that even its advocates are "cautious" about the carry-over of successful sensitivity training to the organization. On the other hand, the individual may profit personally by the training experience.

DETERMINANTS OF JOB SATISFACTION

In industrial psychology, the mention of job satisfaction brings to mind the Two-Factor Theory of Herzberg, Mausner, and Snyderman (1959), not because of its validity as a model, but rather because it is clearly the most heuristic as well as controversial theory ever to emerge in explanation of job satisfaction. In brief, the theory attributes job satisfaction and job dissatisfaction to different and distinct sets of variables in the work situation. The "satisfiers" or "motivators" may result only in overall job satisfaction; their absence should not lead to dissatisfaction. The "dissatisfiers" or "hygienes" may result only in job dissatisfaction; their optimization should not lead to satisfaction.

The Two-Factor Theory emerged from the use of a "critical incident technique" to investigate the causes of job satisfaction and dissatisfaction among engineers and accountants. Satisfying factors were found to be associated with the basic job context, such as achievement, responsibility, recognition, and advancement, the "intrinsic" factors. Dissatisfying factors were found to be associated with the context or environment in which the job was performed, such as working conditions, supervision, hours, and vacations, the "extrinsic" factors. Thus, the two factors were thought to be unidimensional and independent.

The Herzberg theory is in clear contrast to traditional job satisfaction theories in which any relevant variable can be responsible for satisfaction or dissatisfaction, arrayed along a continuum. House and Wigdor (1967) summarize the criticism of the theory on the grounds that it is methodologically bound, built upon a faulty research foundation, and inconsistent with previous evidence.

Vroom (1964, 1966) concludes that the findings of the theory are methodologically bound in the critical incident technique. It is ego-enhancing for a worker to attribute satisfaction to intrinsic job achievement factors and ego-defensive to attribute dissatisfaction to extrinsic environmental factors over which he has no control. The results are also criticized because of their faulty research foundations. The intrinsic-extrinsic classification of job dimensions must be interpreted by the rater, possibly contaminating the coding. The operational definitions for motivator and hygiene factors are inadequate in that they do not always allow for a clear dichotomous distinction. Ewen (1964) notes that there is a lack of an overall measure of job satisfaction. This makes it difficult to determine the precise contribution of the motivators and hygienes to either job satisfaction or dissatisfaction.

It is especially noteworthy that an investigation conducted by Hinton (1968), which included two separate collections of data utilizing the Herzberg methodology, was unable to support either the two-factor theory or the reliability of its methodology as a measure of job satisfaction. Differences between two motivator sequence comparisons and between two hygiene sequence comparisons prove greater than those found between the motivator-hygiene comparisons. Clearly, if there are greater differences within experimental groups than there are between, the use of a motivator-hygiene criterion cannot be justified.

Whitsett and Winslow (1967) published an analysis of studies critical of the Herzberg theory in an attempt to defend the theory against its critics and their alleged "misinterpretation." They conclude that "the studies reviewed offer little empirical evidence for doubting the validity of the theory" (p. 411). However, it must be indicated that an analysis of all the current literature favors the critics of the Herzberg theory.

JOB SATISFACTION AND PERFORMANCE

The development of job satisfaction is a worthy organizational objective but does not automatically insure optimal job performance. Motivational incentives have been found to vary as a function of an array of individual characteristics. It is thus unrealistic to expect maximum motivation under any given set of organizational conditions. Maximal motivation would require congruent goals and objectives on the part of labor and management. Thus, maximum satisfaction may be inconsistent with optimal production and the former will be sacrificed should the latter be demanded. A useful distinction is drawn between short-term and long-term goals in that long-term production may be sabotaged in the service of short-term expediency. Cooperation, compromise, and mutual honesty can do much to maximize the long-term outcome for both labor and management.

Research in industrial psychology has established that there exists an optimal range of intelligence for most job categories. The implication is that to insure maximum satisfaction and optimum performance, upper as well as lower intelligence boundaries must be considered in the selection process. Interests congruent with job demands have also been found to be positively correlated with job satisfaction and to a somewhat different degree with performance. It need not necessarily follow that job satisfaction is linked with high productivity. It is, in fact, more likely to be linked to such behavioral manifestations as less lateness, absenteeism, turnover, and industrial conflict.

It is conceivable, however, that the worker manifesting high job satisfaction is the same type of worker who is more likely to exhibit the aforementioned behaviors, but not specifically because he is satisfied. Thus, although there may be a significant correlation, the lack of an established causal relationship should caution against the belief that organizationally induced change in job satisfaction will result in a concomitant change in job behavior (Tiffin & McCormick 1965).

Individual differences in personality may, of course, mediate any observed relationships with job satisfaction. In fact, job satisfaction is probably the result of the interactive influence of personality and environmental factors. Fruitful personnel research is currently being undertaken in the direction of the moderating effects of "self-esteem." Korman (1967) determined that need satisfaction was correlated to overall satisfaction only for high-self-esteem individuals, and in a like vein, found task success related to task satisfaction only for these same persons (1968).

Reviewing the research relating job satisfaction to its behavioral manifestations, Vroom (1964) concluded that there was a consistent inverse relationship between satisfaction and absences, a slight inverse relationship between satisfaction and accidents, but no "simple relationship between job satisfaction and job performance" (p. 186). Some researchers have maintained that good performance results from job satisfaction while others argue that such performance results in satisfaction. Vroom believes that the latter logic is the more defensible especially "when effective performance brings with it greater rewards, at not appreciably greater costs than ineffective performance" (p. 187). Effective performance might then influence job satisfaction. While predominantly supporting the rationale of Vroom one can also envision circumstances in which job satisfaction results in better performance.

Korman (1970a) derives a relevant, though as yet only partially substantiated, formulation which may well aid in the resolution of the job satisfaction-performance dilemma: ". . . we could wind up with what might be an intriguing moderating effect of self-esteem, i.e., at high levels of self-esteem performance predicts satisfaction whereas at low levels of self-esteem satisfaction predicts performance."

Weitz and Nuckols (1955) investigated the relationship between specific job satisfaction and dissatisfaction and the performance of life insurance agents. They found attitudes pertaining to job training, immediate supervision, and to a lesser degree, the insecurity of new agents, to be related to the criterion of termination of employment. It is interesting that the predictive items clustered only into specific categories suggesting "that the decision to quit is at least not portrayed by general dissatisfaction with the job" (p. 299).

Katzell, Barrett, and Parker (1961) studied the relationship between job satisfaction and performance. They considered job satisfaction and performance as outputs, with work situation characteristics as the inputs. Among their findings they noted the lack of homogeneity of job performance and the basic independence of different performance measures. Job satisfaction was found linked to quantity of production per man-hour and to profits but not to quality of production or to turnover. The authors' interpretation of the role of situational variables "regards the situational characteristics as independent variables, with job satisfaction and performance as dependent variables which are correlated because each is a function of the same situational characteristic; employee needs and expectations are postulated as variables intervening between the situational and both the satisfaction and performance variables" (p. 72).

Likert and Bowers (1969) state that the interactions between employee attitudes and productivity are too complex to be accurately investigated at any single point in time. They show that relations that are not immediately apparent may in fact eventually manifest themselves. In a study of managerial behavior and employee productivity, they found no significant correlations in the short run, but after one year managerial behavior proved significantly related to employee productivity. It apparently takes time for the effects of such behavior to become manifest. This finding should caution against the investigation of complex behavioral variables over short periods of time. Clearly, there is need for more longitudinal studies.

It is becoming increasingly apparent that traditional organizational and leadership models are no longer capable of coping with modern society. "An organization which is based on the principle of surveillance theory where one individual monitors the activities of another for conformity to some norm can be effective only to the extent that the monitoring agent is able to reward or punish appropriately. Increasingly, however, this is not the case in today's world. . ." (Korman 1970b). Such models are debilitating because they lessen performance motivation by providing consistently negative evaluation of the work force. Korman suggests a conducive developmental environment which expects more from the workers than simply high production, permits more internal activities control, and encourages independent thinking and creativity.

It is appropriate to consider the motivational implications of a bold new concept in office planning, that of the office landscape. This system views the office as an information processing center designed to facilitate efficient decision making by enhancing the effectiveness of intraoffice communication and information exchange. The actual informal organization serves as the basis for the physical design rather than the formally charted structure. The office is most often constructed without fixed partitions or walls, with its inhabitants working in the open, though separated by free standing screens so as to create the sensation of visual privacy where necessary. "The layout represents a trade-off between the organizational needs for communication and the individual's desire for privacy, between the freedom of circulation and the minimization of distraction, between the optimization of function and the preservation of structure" (Zeitlin 1969).

Zeitlin evaluated the motivational value and acceptability of the office landscape concept through attitudinal measurements of employees. While demonstrating the test installation to be a "qualified success," the study also revealed that the physical design of an office cannot by itself induce motivation within its workforce. This is especially true for professional workers thought to be predominantly motivated through intrinsic job characteristics. Although it may furnish some satisfaction for workers at a lower occupational level, one must not assume that this gain is inherent within its physical makeup.

WAGE INCENTIVES AND PRODUCTIVITY

A prime "classical" function of wage payment was to motivate the worker to attain the maximum productivity of which he is capable. March and Simon (1958) note, however, that incentive payment plans predicated upon traditional "time study" encompass overly simplified and sometimes erroneous motivational assumptions. They conclude that wages constitute only one of the possible organizational rewards, that their effectiveness may not be linearly related to their magnitude, and that this relationship may vary with change in aspirations over time. A major incentive system consists of flat hourly, weekly, or yearly payments independent of productivity. Other systems base the pay upon individual or group production or some combination of the two. March and Simon note that the closer the relationship between monetary rewards and performance, the more readily will management be able to implement a decision to raise production. Thus, incentive wage plans have in general been found to increase production over that of a flat rate.

Andrews (1967) investigated the relationship between "wage inequality" and job performance and found that underpaid subjects compensated for this inequality by raising work output at the expense of its quality. In contrast, overpaid subjects actually reduced work output and raised its quality in order to feel they were earning their pay. Thus, work quality is positively correlated to wage rate. Andrews also found partial support for his hypothesis that a small underpayment has as much a negative effect on performance as a large overpayment has a positive effect. Workers apparently manifest greater sensitivity to underpayment than to overpayment. One would also expect rather serious consequences to result from external and visible inequality, such as the violation of "equal treatment of all employees" (Adams 1963).

Haire (1964), after exhaustively reviewing productivity as related to wage payment plans, concluded that we are not really paying for more than physical attendance and a minimum level of production. Productivity is clearly influenced by factors other than pay and the relationship between the two is sometimes rather tenuous.

Human Factors Engineering

The earliest scientific investigation of work was probably the study of muscular fatigue undertaken by the Italians Mosso and Maggiora in 1890, which considered work decrement and recovery following rest. The actual merger of engineering with psychology can probably be traced to Taylor who attempted to increase industrial productivity through the use of job analysis to improve work methods and who is responsible for the scientific management movement which originated early in this century. The new field advanced with the husband and wife team, Frank and Lillian Gilbreth, management specialist and psychologist, respectively. "This pair symbolizes the joint interest in work methods that has since been manifested by industrial engineers and psychologists, although in the United States today the former are more actively doing such work in industry" (Katzell 1962, p. 192).

Haire (1959) comments that the human engineering approach in psychology can probably be traced to the early interest in working conditions. The environment was the prime concern in the investigation of such factors as fatigue, lighting, and music. "The plant tended to be the unit of variation and the work group the unit of response" (p. 171). The Hawthorne studies followed this approach into the 1930s, when the individual finally became the focus of concern. Virtually all modern design work in human factors retains the individual as the central focus of attention and the unit of response for whatever variable is being investigated.

Human factors engineering, also known as psychological engineering, is in a phase of rapid growth and development, due in large measure to the current emphasis on space and undersea exploration, sophisticated military weapons, communications systems, and complex industrial processes. Today it is intolerable that equipment be designed and not include relevant human factors. The design deficiencies uncovered during World War II which made equipment incompatible with its operator and thereby resulted in costly and sometimes fatal errors must not be repeated. The modern systems approach to equipment design attempts to optimize both the engineering and the human aspects of man-machine systems.

A man-machine system combines a human operator with the equipment necessary to achieve certain objectives given certain inputs. The system may be closed loop, incorporating feedback which facilitates a continuous control process, or it may be open loop, lacking relevant feedback. The system may incorporate displays to present properly coded information to the operator, through appropriate sensory modalities, most frequently visual, and second most frequently auditory. It will contain controls, which in contrast to displays, remove information from the operator and transmit it to the machine. McCormick (1964) reports a series of studies which collectively indicate that the type, design, and location of controls influence their precision, speed of response, and potential human force capabilities.

Much of the fundamental research pertaining to the interaction of man and machine has incorporated tracking tasks in which the operator corrects for the discrepancy between an actual and a desired output in a continuous closed loop system. The dynamics of the system determines the order of control; that is, whether the operator is to control position, as in a zero order system, velocity, as in a first order system, or acceleration, as in a second order system, and so on. When a system is "aided," part of the control process such as differentiation and integration, is undertaken by the machine. When a system is "quickened," the information presented to the operator is altered such that it tends to facilitate an appropriate response. Control-display compatibility is crucial for optimal system efficiency.

Information theory is the science of the transmission and measurement of information, the basic measure being the "bit." Weiner (1948) is usually credited with having formulated some of the early constructs of information theory, while Shannon and Weaver (1949) developed some of the mathematical expressions. In information theory, channel capacity refers to the limit of information that can be handled by any communications channel, and by analogy, human channel capacity refers to the maximum limit of the information that can be received by a human through all sensory modalities.

Information theory can be applied to a problem often faced by the human factors engineer, that of determining the perceptual load imposed upon an operator by a sensorimotor task. It may surprise one to learn that when dealing with a task such as driving, which normally permits an operator to function well within his limits, greater driver loading, perhaps due to inexperience or fatigue, may fail to produce an increase in overt errors. The theoretically poorer or stressed driver is still able to perform without error by increasing the percentage of his channel capacity that he allocates to the primary task of driving until he reaches the limits of his capacity. Thus, the driver restricts his attention to only the most vital sources of information and he may drop out nonessential activities, such as conversation, in an effort to maintain his level of performance. Of course, the poorer driver will reach his limit earlier, and consequently be less capable of coping with high load emergency situations or a hostile driving environment.

How then can the human factors engineer determine the load imposed during normal operation of a man-machine system? He could introduce a second task to load down the operator, and note the level at which errors occur. But among the limitations of this procedure is the obvious danger of forcing the operator to commit errors in such situations as high speed driving. What is needed is a technique for determining operator loading on tasks such as driving, which are performed substantially without error under normal operating conditions. The measure must be sensitive to gradations in information processing load as task difficulty increases.

Such a technique may be the measurement of "spare capacity" in which the operator is regarded as a communications channel capable of processing a fixed amount of information characterized by his channel capacity. Spare capacity may be inferred by observing performance degradation on a subsidiary task while the operator attempts to hold his primary task performance (i.e., driving) constant. Degradation in subsidiary task performance is indicative of increasing primary task demands upon the operator, thus facilitating the determination of information processing load before precipitating primary task error. Further discussion of spare capacity measurement may be found in the thorough explorations of such investigators as Brown and Poulton (1961) and Brown (1962, 1964). Some of the most recent research in this area has been conducted by Zeitlin and J. Finkelman (1969b, 1971) who utilized a delayed digit recall subsidiary task as a refinement of their original random digit generation task (Zeitlin & J. Finkelman 1969a) to investigate the perceptual loading imposed in vehicular control simulation.

In system design and development, it may be useful to employ simulation for purposes of research and evaluation. Simulation varies markedly in complexity and fidelity, and the more sophisticated systems now incorporate computer assistance. Operational problems can thus be isolated and solved in advance of actual system construction. The optimal division of tasks between man and machine, utilizing the maximum potential of both, can be experimentally evaluated. Should the simulator also be used for purposes of training, consideration must be given to the amount of transfer that can be expected to occur from the simulator to the real world environment. The fidelity of simulation is crucial to transfer of training although the relationship "is not clear and unequivocal" (Biel 1965, p. 373).

Noise control is today a significant human factors problem, although research dates back many years. Prolonged exposure to intense noise levels (above 80–90 db.) is thought to precipitate hearing loss. High level impact and impulse noise is probably even more dangerous than that of a continuous duration. Further discussion of these issues may be found in Glass and Singer (1972), Kryter (1970), McCord, Teal, and Witheridge (1938), and Machle (1945).

Research on the effect of noise on performance has been inconclusive and inconsistent. Kryter has criticized the experimental procedures of most industrial noise studies that manifested performance degradation. However, there is evidence to indicate that certain task characteristics are usually associated with performance degradation. Such degradation most often occurs when high total information processing demands are placed upon the individual. J. Finkelman and Glass (1970, 1971) found that unpredictable, as opposed to predictable noise, resulted in performance degradation on a subsidiary task measure of information processing load, although no degradation was observed on a primary task. They concluded that earlier research may have failed to detect performance degradation because the measurement techniques lacked sensitivity with respect to total information processing load.

It is hoped that relevant research in areas such as these will eventually result in solutions to the many perennial problems plaguing mankind.

References

ADAMS, J. S. Wage inequities, productivity, and work quality. *Industrial Relations*, 1963, *3*, 9–16.

ANDREWS, I. R. Wage inequity and job performance: An experimental study. *Journal of Applied Psychology*, 1967, *51*, 39–45.

ARGYRIS, C. Issues in evaluating laboratory education. *Industrial Relations*, 1968, *8*, 28–40.

BALINSKY, B. A note on the use of the Rorschach in the selection of supervisory personnel. *Rorschach Research Exchange*, 1944, *8*, 184–88.

———— Some experiences and problems in appraising executive personnel. *In* M. R. Feinberg, Outside consultants to industry: Strengths, problems and pitfalls (a symposium). *Personnel Psychology*, 1964, *17*, 107–33.

———— The relevance of personality to job performance: Objective techniques as an aid in predicting executive performance. Symposium presented at the American Psychological Association, New York, September 1966.

————, and SHAW, W. The contribution of the WAIS to a management appraisal program. *Personnel Psychology*, 1956, *9*, 207–9.

BIEL, W. C. Training programs and devices. *In* R. M. Gagné (ed.), *Psychological principles in system development*. New York: Holt, Rinehart & Winston, 1965, pp. 343–84.

BLUM, M. L., and NAYLOR, J. C. *Industrial psychology: Its theoretical and social foundations*. New York: Harper & Row, 1968.

BRADFORD, L. P., GIBB, J. R., and BENNE, K. D. *T-Group theory and laboratory method*. New York: John Wiley, 1964.

BROWN, I. D. Studies of component movement, consistency, and spare capacity of car drivers. *Annals of Occupational Hygiene*, 1962, *5*, 131–43.

———— The measurement of perceptual load and reserve capacity. *The Transactions of the Association of Industrial Medical Officers*, 1964, *14*, 44–49.

————, and POULTON, E. C. Measuring the "spare mental capacity" of car drivers by a subsidiary task. *Ergonomics*, 1961, *4*, 35–40.

DUNNETTE, M. D., and CAMPBELL, J. P. Laboratory education: Impact on people and organizations. *Industrial Relations*, 1968, *8*, 1–27.

EWEN, R. B. Some determinants of job satisfaction: A study of the generality of Herzberg's theory. *Journal of Applied Psychology*, 1964, *48*, 161–63.

FINKELMAN, J. M. A multiplicative model for the prediction of personal and organizational change following sensitivity training. Unpublished manuscript, New York University, 1969.

———, and GLASS, D. G. Reappraisal of the relationship between noise and human performance by means of a subsidiary task measure. *Journal of Applied Psychology*, 1970, *54*, 211–13.

——— An information processing evaluation of the effect of environmental noise upon human performance. Paper presented before the annual meeting of the Human Factors Society, New York, October 21, 1971.

FINKELMAN, M. The placement of the disadvantaged in industry. Counselor Training Symposium presented under auspices of Community Mental Health Board. Westchester, New York, May 6, 1969.

FRYER, D. H.; FEINBERG, M. R., and ZALKIND, S. S. *Developing people in industry*. New York: Harper & Row, 1956.

GHISELLI, E. E. Managerial talent. *American Psychologist*, 1964, *18*, 631–42.

GLASER, E. M. Psychological consultation with executives: A clinical approach. *American Psychologist*, 1958, *13*, 486–89.

GLASS, D. G., and SINGER, J. E. *Urban stress: Experiments on noise and social stressors*. New York: Academic Press, 1972.

GRANT, D. L., KATKOVSKY, W., and BRAY, D. W. Contributions of projective techniques to assessment of management potential. *Journal of Applied Psychology*, 1967, *51*, 226–32.

HAIRE, M. Psychological problems relevant to business and industry. *Psychological Bulletin*, 1959, *56*, 169–94.

——— *Psychology in Management*. 2d ed. New York: McGraw-Hill, 1964.

HERZBERG, F., MAUSNER, B., and SNYDERMAN, B. *The motivation to work*. New York: John Wiley, 1959.

HINTON, B. L. An empirical investigation of the Herzberg methodology and two-factor theory. *Organizational Behavior and Human Performance*, 1968, *3*, 286–309.

HOUSE, R. J. T-group education and leadership effectiveness: A review of the empirical literature and a critical evaluation. *Personnel Psychology*, 1967, *20*, 1–32.

——— Leadership training: Some dysfunctional consequences. *Administrative Science Quarterly*, 1968, *12*, 556–71.

———, and WIGDOR, L. A. Herzberg's dual-factor theory of job satisfaction and motivation: A review of the evidence and criticism. *Personnel Psychology*, 1967, *20*, 369–89.

KATZELL, R. A. Psychologists in industry. *In* W. B. Webb (ed.), *The profession of psychology*. New York: Holt, Rinehart & Winston, 1962, pp. 180–211.

———, BARRETT, R. S., and PARKER, T. C. Job satisfaction, job performance, and situational characteristics. *Journal of Applied Psychology*, 1961, *45*, 65–72.

KIRKPATRICK, J. J., EWEN, R. B., BARRETT, R. S., and KATZELL, R. A. *Testing and fair employment: Fairness and validity of personnel tests for different ethnic groups*. New York: New York University Press, 1968.

KORMAN, A. K. Relevance of personal need satisfaction for overall satisfaction as a function self-esteem. *Journal of Applied Psychology*, 1967, *51*, 533–38.

——— Task success, task popularity, and self-esteem as influences on task liking. *Journal of Applied Psychology*, 1968, *52*, 484–90.

——— Toward a hypothesis of work behavior. *Journal of Applied Psychology*, 1970a, *54*, 31–41.

——— Industrial and organizational psychology: An overview of the field. Unpublished manuscript, New York University, 1970b.

KRYTER, K. D. *The effects of noise on man*. New York: Academic Press, 1970.

LIKERT, R., and BOWERS, D. G. Organizational theory and human resource accounting. *American Psychologist*, 1969, *24*, 585–92.

MCCORD, C. P., TEAL, E. E., and WITHERIDGE, W. N. Noise and its effect on human beings. *Journal of the American Medical Association*, 1938, *110*, 1553–60.

MCCORMICK, E. J. *Human factors engineering*. New York: McGraw-Hill, 1964.

MACHLE, W. The effects of gun blast on hearing. *Archives of Otolaryngology*, 1945, *42*, 164–68.

MARCH, J. G., and SIMON, H. A. *Organizations*. New York: John Wiley, 1958.

MINER, J. B. *Personnel Psychology*. New York: Macmillan, 1969.

MURRAY, H. A., MACKINNON, D. W., MILLER, J. G., FISKE, D. W., and HANFMANN, E. *Assessment of men*. New York: Holt, Rinehart & Winston, 1948.

PIOTROWSKI, Z. A., and ROCK, M. R. *The perceptanalytic executive scale*. New York: Grune & Stratton, 1963.

SCHEIN, E. H., and BENNIS, W. G. *Personal and organizational change through group methods: The laboratory approach*. New York: John Wiley, 1965.

SHANNON, C. E., and WEAVER, W. *The mathematical theory of communication*, Urbana: University of Illinois Press. 1949.

SMITH, M. Cautions concerning the use of the Taylor-Russell tables in employee selection. *Journal of Applied Psychology*, 1948, *32*, 595–600.

STEELE, F. I., ZAND, D. E., and ZALKIND, S. S. Managerial behavior and participation in a laboratory training process: A study of prior expectations and later involvement in organizational change efforts. *Personnel Psychology*, 1970, *23*, 77–91.

STOCK, D. A survey of research on T-Groups. *In* L. P. Bradford, J. R. Gibb; and K. D. Benne (eds.), *T-Group theory and laboratory method*. New York: John Wiley, 1964.

TAYLOR, H. D., and RUSSELL, J. T. The relationship of validity coefficients to the practical effectiveness of tests in selection: Discussion and tables. *Journal of Applied Psychology*, 1939, *23*, 565–78.

TIFFIN, J., and MCCORMICK, E. J. *Industrial psychology*. 5th ed. Englewood Cliffs, N. J.: Prentice-Hall, 1965.

———, and VINCENT, N. L. Comparisons of empirical and theoretical expectancies. *Personnel Psychology*, 1960, *13*, 59–64.

VROOM, V. H. *Work and motivation*. New York: John Wiley, 1964.

——— A comparison of static and dynamic correlational methods in the study of organizations. *Organizational Behavior and Human Performance*, 1966, *1*, 55–70.

WEITZ, J., and NUCKOLS, R. C. Job satisfaction and job survival. *Journal of Applied Psychology*, 1955, *39*, 294–300.

WHITSETT, D. A., and WINSLOW, E. K. An analysis of studies critical of the motivator-hygiene theory. *Personnel Psychology*, 1967, *20*, 391–415.

WIENER, N. *Cybernetics*. New York: John Wiley, 1948.

ZAND, D. E., STEELE, F. I., and ZALKIND, S. S. The impact of an organizational development program on perceptions of interpersonal, group, and organization functioning. *Journal of Applied Behavioral Science*, 1969, *5*, 393–410.

ZEITLIN, L. R. A comparison of employee attitudes toward the conventional office and the landscaped office. *Administrative Management*. New York: Port of New York Authority, 1969.

———, and FINKELMAN, J. M. A "random digit" generation subsidiary task measure of operator perceptual-motor loading. *Experimental Publication System*, no. 1 (Manuscript No. 035B), 1969a.

——— Subsidiary task measures of operator loading in vehicle control. Paper presented before the annual meeting of the Human Factors Society, Philadelphia, October 8, 1969b.

——— A comparative evaluation of the subsidiary task techniques of "random digit generation" and "delayed digit recall" as measures of loading in man-machine systems. Paper presented before the annual meeting of the Human Factors Society, New York, October 21, 1971.

More experimental investigations have been conducted on hypnotism during the past dozen years than during its previous 200-year history. This recent research has shown that many traditional notions on this topic are invalid. Major revisions and new conceptions in this area, which will be reviewed in turn in this paper, include the following:

1. The notion that the hypnotist places his subjects in a somnambulistic-like trance is now known to be fallacious.
2. The notion that hypnotic subjects are able to have experiences and to perform feats that are very difficult if not impossible to perform under other conditions is also invalid.
3. Responsiveness to suggestions of limb rigidity, hallucination, age-regression, time-distortion, analgesia, amnesia, etc. *under base-level or control conditions* is much higher than has been commonly assumed.
4. Motivational factors are now known to play an important role in eliciting *hypnotic behaviors*, that is, in eliciting a high level of overt and subjective responses to suggestions of limb or body rigidity, hallucination, analgesia, age-regression, amnesia, etc.
5. An important factor in eliciting hypnotic behaviors is simply that the situation is defined to the subject as hypnosis and this definition of the situation carries the implication that a high level of response to suggestions is not only possible but is desired and expected.
6. Subtle changes in the experimental situation produce marked changes in the subjects' propensity to manifest hypnotic behaviors.
7. Despite traditional notions to the contrary, good hypnotic subjects do not appear to possess distinct personality traits or characteristics that set them apart from poor hypnotic subjects.
8. Whether or not a subject manifests a high or low level of response to suggestions of limb rigidity, hallucination, analgesia, age-regression, amnesia, etc. depends, to an important degree, on his attitudes, motivations, and

Theodore Xenophon Barber

Experimental Hypnosis

45

expectancies with respect to the specific test-situation. Stated otherwise, the mediating variables which intervene between the stimulus conditions and the subject's response can be fruitfully conceptualized in terms of specific kinds of attitudes, motivations, and expectancies.

The Traditional Somnambulistic Model of the Hypnotic Subject

A small proportion of individuals (around 5 percent) at times walk in their sleep. Many earlier notions concerning these sleepwalkers or somnambulists have been generally confirmed by recent studies (Jacobson, Kales, Lehmann, & Zweizig 1965; Kales, Jacobson, Paulson, Kales, & Walter 1966; Pai 1946) which indicate the following:

1. When sleepwalkers arise from their bed, the electroencephalogram (EEG) indicates that they are sleeping (stages 3 or 4 of sleep). When the sleepwalking episode is short in duration, the EEG continues to show waves indicative of sleep; however, during longer sleepwalking episodes, the EEG begins to resemble that found during light sleep or very relaxed wakefulness.
2. It is reasonable to infer that the somnambulist is in an altered state of consciousness or in a trance since he shows a blank stare, rigid or shuffling movements, a low level of motor skill, a markedly reduced awareness of the environment, and a fixation of purpose with attention fixed mechanically on whatever he is doing. Furthermore, if spoken to, the sleepwalker usually does not reply; if he replies, he tends to mumble or to speak in a vague and detached manner.
3. The sleepwalker does not awaken when he is simply told to wake up. Persistent measures are necessary to awaken him; for instance, it may be necessary to repeat his name over and over, each time more loudly.
4. When the somnambulist awakens in the morning, or if he is awakened during his sleepwalking, he appears to be completely amnesic for the episode.

The sleepwalker has traditionally served as the implicit model for conceptualizing the state and characteristics of the person who is said to be in deep hypnosis or to be deeply hypnotized. In former years, subjects who were judged to be deeply hypnotized (that is, who showed a high level of response to suggestions of analgesia, hallucination, amnesia, etc. and who were thought to be in an altered state of consciousness or in a trance) were termed somnambulists or somnambules with the clearcut implication that they resembled the natural sleepwalker. In the same way as the sleepwalker, the subject who was judged to be deeply hypnotized was thought to be in a stage between sleep and waking, to have a low level of awareness, to be detached from his surroundings, to have a fixation of purpose, to be in a trance, and to show amnesia on awakening.

It is crystal clear, to all sophisticated present-day researchers in this area, that the traditional somnambulistic model of the hypnotic subject is fallacious. In fact, it is clear that the "deeply

hypnotized" subject[1] differs from the sleepwalker in every respect that they were once thought to be similar:

1. The EEG of the "deeply hypnotized" subject does not resemble the EEG of the sleepwalker. Judging from EEG criteria, the sleepwalker is typically asleep whereas the "deeply hypnotized" subject is typically awake. More precisely: (a) "deeply hypnotized" subjects do not show characteristic patterns on the EEG that might clearly distinguish them from nonhypnotized subjects and (b) the EEG of the "deeply hypnotized" subject varies continually, in the same way as in the waking subject, with whatever instructions or suggestions he is given or with whatever activities he is engaged in (Barber 1961b; Chertok & Kramarz 1959).[2]
2. Some "deeply hypnotized" subjects at times seem to resemble the sleepwalker in that they manifest trancelike characteristics such as blank stare, rigid facial expression, lack of spontaneity, disinclination to talk, lack of humor, and literal-mindedness (Erickson, Hershman, & Secter 1961, pp. 55-58; Gill & Brenman 1959, pp. 38-39; Pattie 1956a, p. 21; Weitzenhoffer 1957, pp. 211-12). However, this apparent resemblance between some "deeply hypnotized" subjects and the sleepwalker is superficial and misleading. The following points apply to the "deeply hypnotized" subject but *not* to the sleepwalker:

    a) Such trancelike characteristics can be removed, by explicitly or implicitly suggesting to the "deeply hypnotized" subject that he no longer show them, and many subjects will continue to respond overtly and subjectively to suggestions of analgesia, hallucination, amnesia, etc. without manifesting trancelike characteristics (Barber 1958, 1962b; Gill & Brenman 1959, p. 36; Fisher 1954).

    b) Some subjects who have been exposed to a hypnotic-induction procedure (that is, to repeated suggestions of relaxation, drowsiness, and sleep) and who manifest high response to suggestions do not show trancelike characteristics (Erickson 1962). Also, some subjects who have not been exposed to a hypnotic-induction procedure manifest a high level of overt and subjective responses to suggestions of analgesia, age-regression, hallucination, etc. without manifesting trancelike characteristics (Barber 1969b; Klopp 1961).

---

[1] Since the traditional somnambulistic-trance implications of the terms *deep hypnosis*, *deeply hypnotized*, *hypnotic trance*, and re-

lated terms will be subjected to critical analysis in the remainder of this chapter, the terms will henceforth be surrounded by quotation marks.

[2] Other physiological measures also vary in "deeply hypnotized" subjects in the same way as in waking control subjects. Depending on the suggestions or instructions that the subject receives, both the "deeply hypnotized" subject and the control subject may show high, medium, or low levels of skin resistance or conductance, basal metabolic rate, heart rate, blood pressure, respiration, peripheral blood flow, blood clotting time, oral temperature, and so forth (Barber 1961b; Crasilneck & Hall 1959; Levitt & Brady 1963; Timney & Barber 1969). Furthermore, when specific types of suggestions, such as suggestions of analgesia, blindness, deafness, or age regression, produce autonomic changes or other types of physiological changes in "deeply hypnotized" subjects, the suggestions also produce very similar physiological changes in control subjects (Barber 1961b, 1965c). For instance, in both "deeply hypnotized" subjects and in control subjects suggestions of analgesia or anesthesia at times reduce electromyographic and respiratory responses to noxious stimuli (Barber & Hahn 1962).

c) Some hypnotic subjects who manifest trancelike characteristics show very little response to suggestions of analgesia, hallucination, amnesia, etc. (Barber 1957, 1963).

d) When hypnotic subjects show trancelike characteristics, these characteristics have been explicitly or implicitly suggested. That is, the hypnotist repeatedly suggests to the subject (or has repeatedly suggested to him in a previous session) that he is becoming relaxed, drowsy, and sleepy with the implication that he is to inhibit spontaneity, he is not to initiate conversation, and he is to behave in a relaxed, drowsy, or sleepy manner. Since these characteristics have been explicitly or implicitly suggested, they can also be removed by suggestions. As stated above, the hypnotist can tell the subject to be alert and awake but to continue responding to suggestions. Furthermore, there is no compelling reason for the hypnotist to suggest either explicitly or implicitly to his subject that he manifest a trancelike appearance. As Wells (1924) pointed out many years ago, a procedure of "waking hypnosis" can be used in which the subject is given direct suggestions of analgesia, hallucination, amnesia, etc. but is *not* given suggestions of relaxation, drowsiness, and sleep, or any other suggestions that might produce a trancelike appearance.

3. Although the sleepwalker is not brought back to normality when he is simply told to wake up, practically all "deeply hypnotized" subjects open their eyes and "wake up" when the experimenter simply states, "The experiment is over," or "Wake up." In those very rare instances when a "deeply hypnotized" subject does not open his eyes when told that the experiment is over, it can be shown that the subject either (a) desires to remain a little longer in a relaxed or passive condition, (b) has been given a posthypnotic suggestion that he does not want to carry out, (c) is resisting the hypnotist or is testing the hypnotist's ability to control him, or (d) is manifesting spite toward the hypnotist or is attempting to frighten him by refusing to "wake up" (Weitzenhoffer 1957, pp. 226-29; Williams 1953).[3]

4. Sleepwalkers are amnesic for their somnambulistic episodes. Contrariwise, if suggestions for amnesia are not given during the hypnotic session, practically all "deeply hypnotized" subjects state on awakening that they remember what occurred (Barber & Calverley 1966b; Hilgard 1966).[4]

[3] In those very rare instances in which a "deeply hypnotized" subject does not open his eyes when told that the experiment is over, experienced hypnotists recommend the following: "The simplest way of proceeding is to ask him why he does not wake up. Most subjects are quite willing to explain why. If the subject is uncooperative you may have to request an answer more forcefully. Usually the answer tells the hypnotist what to do ... An excellent way to dehypnotize an intractable subject is simply to say to him in a final tone: 'Very well then, if you will not wake up I will just have to leave you as you are.' You then ignore the subject entirely and go on to other things ... but frequent checks of the subject's condition should be made ..." (Weitzenhoffer 1957, p. 228). Although there are a few anecdotal reports of subjects who remained "deeply hypnotized" for several days, there are no documented cases in which a hypnotic subject did not "wake up" after the hypnotist had proceeded in the manner described above.

[4] In very rare instances, hypnotic subjects who are not given suggestions for amnesia state postexperimentally that they do not remember what occurred. There are several reasons why we cannot conclude that the apparent forgetting in these instances was spontaneous: (a) In many of these instances, the subjects had received suggestions for amnesia in previous hypnotic sessions and they may have

Furthermore, it appears that *no* subject has ever forgotten the events occurring during "deep hypnosis" when told during the hypnotic session that the events were to be remembered (Barber 1962b; Orne 1966; Watkins 1966).

Although some present-day researchers still use the old terminology and refer to the very responsive hypnotic subject as a somnambulist or somnambule and as being in a somnambulistic trance or hypnotic trance, they do not mean by these terms that the subject's condition is the same as or even similar to that of the sleepwalker. To illustrate this contention, let us look closely at how these terms are used by Milton H. Erickson, who has written very extensively on both clinical and experimental hypnosis (Erickson 1967):

1. Erickson often judges hypnotic subjects to be in a somnambulistic trance when they appear normal and awake. For instance, he writes: "In the well-trained subject, the [somnambulistic trance] is that type of trance in which the subject is seemingly awake and functioning adequately, freely, and well in the total hypnotic situation, in a manner similar to that of a nonhypnotized person operating at the waking level" (Erickson 1967, p. 13).

2. Erickson's subjects often disagree with him; when he says they were in a somnambulistic trance or deep trance, they deny it. For instance, in a report presented by Secter (1960), Erickson judged eight subjects to be in a deep trance; one subject agreed with him, and the other seven denied that they were in a deep trance.

3. Erickson has noted that other experienced hypnotists cannot easily tell whether his subjects are in a somnambulistic trance or are normally awake. For instance, he writes as follows: "An illustrative example is the instance in which the author, as a teaching device for the audience, had a subject in a profound somnambulistic trance conduct a lecture and demonstration of hypnosis (unaided by the author) before a group of psychiatrists and psychologists. Although many in the audience had had experience with hypnosis, none detected that she was in a trance" (Erickson 1967, p. 14).

In brief, the subjects that Erickson labels as being in a somnambulistic trance very often appear normally awake, almost always deny that they were in a deep trance, and are often judged by other investigators as being awake. It is quite clear that, when Erickson states that a hypnotic subject is in a somnambulistic trance, he does *not* mean that the subject's condition is at all similar to that of the sleepwalker. What then does the term *somnambulistic trance* mean in Erickson's papers? A close reading of Erickson's work provides the following answer. Whenever Erickson states that a hypnotic subject was in a somnambulistic trance, he almost always states on the same page that the subject was highly responsive to suggestions.

generalized these suggestions to apply to subsequent sessions. (b) Suggestions to sleep are almost always given in hypnosis sessions. Since sleep is followed by amnesia, the suggestions to sleep include the implicit suggestion that the subject is expected to show amnesia on awakening. (c) Some subjects seem to believe that good hypnotic subjects manifest amnesia (London 1961) and that the experimenter will consider them poor subjects and the experiment will be spoiled if they state on awakening that they remember what occurred.

In fact, it appears that quite often Erickson first observes that the subject is very responsive to suggestions of age-regression, hallucination, anesthesia, amnesia, etc. and then infers that, since he is so responsive, he must be in a somnambulistic trance. As pointed out elsewhere (Barber 1964a), it is difficult to avoid circular reasoning here because "trance" is said to give rise to a high level of response to suggestions and a subject is said to be in "trance" when he manifests a high level of response to suggestions.

There is another possible way of understanding the terms *somnambulistic trance*, *deep trance*, or *deep hypnosis*, as used by Erickson and other present-day investigators. It may be that these terms are being used to refer to whatever change has occurred within the subject that has made him highly responsive to suggestions. From this viewpoint, the terms can be construed as referring to *whatever* variables or factors mediate between the experimenter's manipulations (independent variables) and the subject's high level of response to suggestions (dependent variables).

In brief, present-day investigators clearly do not use the terms *somnambulistic trance*, *hypnotic trance*, etc. to refer to a state which resembles the condition of the sleepwalker and they might be using these terms to refer to the mediating variables or intervening variables between the stimulus situation and the subject's high level of responsiveness. What are these mediating variables? Although very few investigators have attempted to specify them clearly, recent experimental data indicate that the mediating variables can be fruitfully conceptualized as including a change in the subject's motivations, attitudes, and expectancies toward the test situation. These mediating variables will be discussed again in the last section of this chapter.

Hypnotic Phenomena

It has been commonly believed both by laymen and by earlier investigators in this area that "deeply hypnotized" subjects are able to have experiences and to carry out feats which are very difficult if not impossible under other conditions. The traditional view was that if "deeply hypnotized" subjects were given appropriate suggestions, they could (a) experience analgesia and undergo surgical operations painlessly, (b) regress to childhood and perform on psychophysiological tests and on tests of recall in the same way as children, (c) see and hear things that were not actually present, (d) forget the experimental events, (e) experience sensory-perceptual alterations such as deafness, color-blindness, and blindness, and (f) manifest remarkable physiological effects such as removal of warts and production of blisters. Research conducted during recent years has shown that some of these notions are misleading and others are fallacious. Let us look in turn at each of the aforementioned phenomena.

Analgesia

It has been claimed that some "deeply hypnotized" subjects are able to undergo surgery painlessly. This claim has been typically documented (e.g., Kroger 1963, chap. 32) by referring to a series of surgical operations carried out by Esdaile in India from 1845 to 1851, prior to the discovery of ether and other anesthetic drugs. Although Esdaile's cases are used to support the claim that painless surgery can be performed under "hypnotic trance," a close reading of the original report (Esdaile 1850) indicates that Esdaile's "entranced" patients often manifested anxiety or pain, e.g., "About the middle of the operation he gave a cry" (p. 222) and "He awoke, and cried out before the operation was finished" (p. 232). Furthermore, Esdaile contended that many of his operations were successful, not because the patients failed to experience pain, but because they forgot the pain that they experienced, e.g., ". . . he has only been disturbed by a night-mare, of which on waking he retains no recollection" (p. 146).

In 1846 a committee of physicians and judges evaluated Esdaile's procedures. Esdaile carefully selected nine patients to undergo surgery before the committee. Three of these were dismissed when it was found that they could not be placed in a satisfactory "trance" after repeated attempts extending up to eleven days. Esdaile removed scrotal tumors from the remaining six carefully selected patients who were finally placed in a "trance" after they were exposed to "mesmeric" or hypnotic procedures extending over a period of about eight hours. The committee reported that, during the surgery, at least 2 of the 6 selected patients showed marked elevation in pulse rate on the order of 40 beats per minute and at least 3 of the remaining 4 showed "convulsive movements of the upper limbs, writhing of the body, distortions of the features, giving the face a hideous expression of suppressed agony; the respiration became heaving, with deep sighs" (Braid 1847). Esdaile also performed surgery (without anesthetic drugs) upon a series of patients who could not be placed in "trance"; a small percentage (the exact percentage is not clear) of these "non-mesmerized" patients showed no more and no less anxiety or pain than those who were said to be in deep trance (Esdaile 1850, pp. 214-15). In short, it seems unlikely that Esdaile's "deep trance" patients were free of anxiety or pain during surgery. The data appear to justify a much more limited conclusion, namely, the mesmeric or hypnotic procedures used by Esdaile (which extended over many days or hours) were apparently effective in some cases in producing a more passive and quiet surgical patient and were apparently effective in some cases in producing some degree of reduction in anxiety or pain.

More recent investigations, reviewed in detail elsewhere (Barber 1970), also indicate that surgery performed in a hypnosis situation may not be as free of anxiety and pain as has been supposed. In most cases, sedative and analgesic drugs were used together with the hypnotic procedures and the most that was claimed was that hypnotism reduced the drug dose that was needed (Marmer 1959; Owen-Flood 1959; Tinterow 1960). In those few instances in which patients underwent surgery with "hypnoanalgesia" alone (without any drugs), they characteristically manifested autonomic reactions, such as increased heart rate and irregular respiration, that were indicative of anxiety or pain (Finer & Nylen 1961; Kroger & DeLee 1957; Taugher 1958) and, in many cases, chemical analgesics or anesthetics had to be given to the patients before the surgery was completed (Anderson 1957; Butler 1954). In sum, the data available at present (Barber 1963; Hilgard 1969; Hilgard, Cooper, Lenox, Morgan, & Voevodsky 1967; Kaplan 1960; McGlashan, Evans, & Orne 1969; Nichols 1968) are harmonious with the conclusions reached many years ago that "hypnotism only rarely succeeded as an anesthetic" (Bernheim 1886, p. 116) and "a complete analgesia is extremely rare in hypnotism, although authors, copying from one another, assert that it is common" (Moll 1889, p. 105).

Although it is questionable that hypnotic procedures obliterate severe pain, various types of suggestions or instructions (given either in a hypnotic situation *or in a control situation*) can often produce some reduction and, at times, a marked reduction in less severe types of pain:

1. Pain is at times reduced when placebos are administered with the implication (or the explicit statement) that they are pain-relieving drugs (Barber 1959; Beecher 1959).

2. Pain is at times reduced by instructions intended to alleviate anxiety and anticipation of pain (Hill, Kornetsky, Flanary, & Wikler 1952*a*, 1952*b*; Kornetsky 1954; Shor 1967).

3. Instructions or suggestions intended to produce relaxation are at times effective with hypnotic subjects and also with control subjects in reducing physiological and subjective responses to pain (Barber & Calverley 1969*a*; Jacobson 1938, 1954; Hilgard et al., 1967).

4. Suggestions of analgesia or anesthesia are effective in reducing subjective reports of pain in a substantial number of subjects who have been randomly assigned to a hypnotic group and in an equal number of subjects who have been randomly assigned to a control group (Barber & Calverley 1969*a*; Spanos, Barber, & Lang 1969).

5. Subjective and physiological responses to pain-producing stimulation can be reduced by instructing control subjects to try to think about and to imagine vividly a pleasant situation during the stimulation (Barber & Hahn 1962). Also, pain is reduced to an equal degree in hypnotic and control subjects when both types of subjects are distracted during the pain-producing stimulation by having them listen to and try to remember the details of an interesting story presented on a tape recording (Barber & Calverley 1969*a*). Other studies (e.g., Kanfer & Goldfoot 1966) also showed that subjective reports of pain are reduced in a nonhypnotic situation when the subjects are distracted while exposed to noxious stimulation. In fact, many years ago, Liébeault (1885) concluded from wide experience that, if and when suggestions of analgesia are effective in reducing pain in "deeply hypnotized" subjects, the mediating processes can be described simply as the focusing of attention on ideas other than those concerning pain. Similarly, a large-scale investigation with 1000 patients (August 1961, p. 62) indicated that hypnotic procedures are effective in reducing pain during childbirth to the extent that they direct "attention away from pain responses toward pleasant ideas."

AGE REGRESSION

It has been claimed that suggestions to regress to childhood are effective with at least some "deeply hypnotized" subjects in reinstating behaviors and psychophysiological processes that were actually present during childhood. Investigations presented by Gidro-Frank and Bowersbuch (1948), True (1949), and Parrish, Lundy, and Leibowitz (1968) appear to support this claim. Let us look at each of these investigations in turn.

Gidro-Frank and Bowersbuch (1948) reported that three selected "deep trance" subjects who were hypnotically regressed to four months of age showed a Babinski toe response, that is, stimulation of the sole of the foot produced dorsiflexion of the large toe and fanning of the other toes. Since a number of neurology texts stated that the Babinski toe response is present in early infancy but is not present after six months of age, it appeared that Gidro-Frank and Bowersbuch had demonstrated that hypnotic regression to early infancy reinstates a physiological reflex that is characteristic of early infancy. However, the neurology texts were mistaken. Investigators who have actually looked at infants have observed that the characteristic response of the four-month-old infant to stimulation of the sole of the foot is sudden withdrawal of the limb with variability in response of the toes. In fact, the Babinski toe response is rarely if ever observed in early infancy (Burr 1921; McGraw 1941; Wolff 1930).[5]

True (1949) reported that adult subjects who were hypnotically regressed to ages eleven, seven and four recalled the exact day of the week on which their birthday and Christmas fell on the particular year involved. However, six subsequent investigations failed to confirm these results (Barber 1961*a*; Best & Michaels 1954; Fisher 1962; Leonard 1963; Mesel & Ledford 1959; Reiff & Scheerer 1959). In a series of attempts to validate True's results made by the present writer, one subject was finally found who named the exact day of the week at each regressed chronological birthdate. However, this subject stated, after the hypnotic session, that she was able to perform this feat simply because (a) she knew that the days of the week go backward one day each year and two on leap years and (b), knowing the day of the week on which her birthdate fell in a recent year, she could easily and quickly (within 20 seconds) figure out the day of the week it must have fallen in an earlier year (cf., Sutcliffe 1960; Yates 1960).

Parrish, Lundy, and Leibowitz (1968) reported that good hypnotic subjects who were hypnotically regressed to the ages of nine and five performed on two optical illusions—the Ponzo and Poggendorff illusions—in a manner which closely approximated the performance of children of ages nine and five. However, the results of this investigation could not be confirmed in two subsequent experiments carried out by Ascher and Barber (1968) and Spanos and Barber (1969). Ascher and Barber (1968) closely replicated the experimental procedures employed by Parrish et al. When the good hypnotic subjects were hypnotically regressed to ages nine and five their performance on the Ponzo and Poggendorff illusions was virtually the same as their adult performance and was not at all similar to the performance of children who are actually nine or five. Spanos and Barber (1969) also replicated the experimental procedures of Parrish et al. and, in addition, used only exceptionally good hypnotic subjects who had previously passed a large number of test-suggestions including negative hallucination, deafness, anosmia,

---

[5] There are a number of possible reasons why the three "deep trance" subjects who were hypnotically regressed to early infancy in the Gidro-Frank and Bowersbuch experiment showed a Babinski toe response which is *not* characteristic of early infancy. For instance, the Babinski toe response is often found during profound relaxation and the subjects may have become very relaxed when they assumed the "sleeping posture of the infant"; or, the subjects may have become aware of the response that was desired by the experimenters and may have voluntarily given that response (Barber 1962*a*; Sarbin 1956).

auditory and visual hallucination, analgesia, and amnesia. Again, under hypnotic regression to ages nine and five, these exceptionally good hypnotic subjects performed on the Ponzo and Poggendorff illusions in a manner which was practically the same as their adult performance and which did not remotely resemble the performance of children of ages nine and five.

Other studies in this area yielded results as follows:

1. "Deep trance" subjects who are hypnotically regressed to childhood manifest some childlike responses (on intelligence tests, the Rorschach, the House-Tree-Person test, the Bender-Gestalt, and on other tasks) but their performance is generally at a level which is superior to the norms for the specified age or to the subject's own actual performance at the earlier age (Crasilneck & Michael 1957; Hoskovec & Horvai 1963; Leonard 1965; Orne 1951; Sarbin 1950b; Sarbin & Farberow 1952; Taylor 1950; Troffer 1966; Young 1940).
2. When subjects who have been randomly assigned to a control group or a hypnotic group are given suggestions to go back or to regress to an earlier time, the same proportion of subjects in the control group as in the hypnotic group report that they imagined, felt, or believed that they had returned to the earlier time (Barber & Calverley 1966a).
3. Instructions to play the role of a child or to simulate a childlike performance given to control subjects (or to hypnotic subjects) are generally as effective as hypnotic regression in eliciting a childlike performance (Gordon & Freston 1964; Greenleaf 1969; Hoskovec & Horvai 1963; Staples & Wilensky 1968; Troffer 1966).
4. Subjects who give a childlike performance when hypnotically regressed to childhood also give an equally convincing portrayal of an older individual or a senile individual when hypnotically "progressed" to the age of 70, 80, or 90 (Kline 1951; Rubenstein & Newman 1954). Also, some subjects who give a childlike performance when hypnotically regressed to childhood also give a good performance when hypnotically regressed to prenatal life in the womb or to a time which preceded their present life (the "Bridey Murphy" phenomenon) (Bernstein 1956; Kelsey 1953).

Although various theoretical formulations might possibly account for the above data, one formulation that can parsimoniously explain the findings is as follows: When it is suggested to subjects in a hypnotic situation or in a control situation that they are in the past or in the future (a) some subjects in both the hypnotic group and the control group try to the best of their ability to imagine, fantasy, or think that they are in the past or in the future, (b) some of these subjects succeed in imagining or fantasying vividly, and (c) when vividly imagining or fantasying themselves in an earlier time or in a future time, some subjects feel as if they are in the past or in the future and behave to a certain limited extent as if they are in the past or future.

HALLUCINATIONS

Practically all earlier texts on hypnotism asserted that hallucinations can be produced in "deeply hypnotized" subjects by appropriate suggestions. Since these texts used the word *hallucinate*, not the words *imagine* or *visualize*, they strongly implied that "deeply hypnotized" subjects perceived an object (that was not present) and believed that their perception had objective reference. Recent research indicates that these implications are misleading.

"Deeply hypnotized" subjects are said to "hallucinate" when they report that they clearly hear and clearly see those things that are suggested to them. However, three recent experiments (Barber & Calverley 1964a; Bowers 1967; Spanos & Barber 1968) demonstrated that such reports are much easier to elicit *in a control situation* than has been commonly assumed. In each of these three experiments, direct suggestions to hear a record playing a specified song and to see a certain object in the room were given to unselected subjects under a control or base-level condition (without any special preliminaries, hypnotic or otherwise). In each experiment, about 50 percent of the control subjects reported that they clearly heard the suggested song and about 33 percent reported that they clearly saw the suggested object. Furthermore, the most recent of these experiments (Spanos & Barber 1968) also showed that about half of the control subjects reported "auditory hallucinations" (clearly hearing a suggested song) and about one-third reported "visual hallucinations" (clearly seeing a suggested object) when they were interviewed by a person other than the experimenter who demanded that they give honest reports. The last-mentioned study also showed that, when honest reports are explicitly requested, a hypnotic-induction procedure (consisting of repeated suggestions of relaxation, drowsiness, and sleep) produces a few more reports that the suggested object was clearly perceived but fails to enhance the reported clarity of the suggested "auditory hallucination" above the already high base-level.

A wide variety of methods and techniques have been used to ascertain whether suggested "hallucinations" give rise to objective effects that resemble those found during auditory or visual perception. The results indicate the following:

1. In the great majority of studies, "hypnotic hallucinations" did not give rise to objective effects (Barber 1964e). For instance, Sutcliffe (1961) conducted a study based on the following consideration: When subjects are actually exposed to delayed auditory feedback (in which their ongoing speech is momentarily delayed and returned to their ears through headphones), they typically stutter, mispronounce words, and speak more loudly and more slowly. Sutcliffe showed that when "deep trance" subjects "hallucinate" delayed auditory feedback, they do not show any of the objective effects that are produced by actual exposure to delayed auditory feedback, that is, they neither stutter, nor mispronounce words, nor speak more loudly or more slowly. Similarly, a series of studies with subjects who did not have prior knowledge of complementary color phenomena indicated that "hypnotically hallucinated" colors differ from actual colors in that they do not give rise to complementary colored after-images (Barber 1964b; Bernheim 1886; Dorcus 1937; Elsea 1961; Hibler 1935; Naruse 1962; Sidis 1906).
2. In a few instances, "hypnotic hallucinations" gave rise to objective effects; however, the same effects were also elicited in a control situation by instructions to imagine vividly. For instance, two recent experiments were designed to ascertain whether a suggested visual hallucination of an

optokinetic drum (a revolving drum with alternate black and white vertical stripes) gives rise to involuntary nystagmoidlike eye movements which resemble those found when an individual actually looks at an optokinetic drum. The results were that (a) a small percentage of "deep trance" subjects manifested nystagmoidlike eye movements when they were given suggestions to hallucinate the optokinetic drum (Brady & Levitt 1966) and (b) an equally small percentage of unselected subjects under a control or base-level condition manifested nystagmoidlike eye movements when they were instructed to imagine vividly the optokinetic drum (Hahn & Barber 1966). Along similar lines, studies by Underwood (1960) and by Sarbin and Andersen (1963) showed that a small percentage of selected "deep trance" subjects and an equally small percentage of unselected control subjects report a few effects which are similar to those produced by an optical illusion when they are instructed to hallucinate or to vividly imagine the optical illusion.

A parsimonious conceptualization of the above data, and also of related data reviewed elsewhere (Barber 1964e; Thorne 1967a), can be attained by postulating the following: (a) When "deep trance" subjects are given suggestions to hallucinate and also when control subjects are asked to imagine vividly, both types of subjects typically try to imagine or visualize to the best of their ability. (b) Some hypnotic subjects and also some control subjects succeed in imagining or visualizing vividly. (c) The process of vividly imagining or visualizing sounds or objects is at times associated with objective effects (e.g., nystagmoidlike eye movements) which resemble the effects that are produced by actually perceiving the sounds or objects.

Amnesia

Although *no* hypnotic subject has ever manifested amnesia on awakening when told during the hypnotic session to remember the events (Barber 1962b; Orne 1966; Watkins 1966), a substantial number of hypnotic subjects manifest apparent amnesia on awakening when told during the hypnotic session to forget the events. Let us look carefully at this suggested amnesia:

1. When subjects who have been randomly assigned either to a control group or a hypnotic group are given peremptory suggestions for amnesia ("You will forget"), an equal number of subjects in both groups report postexperimentally that they do not remember what occurred (Barber & Calverley 1966b). When control and hypnotic subjects are given permissive suggestions for amnesia ("Try to the best of your ability to forget"), a greater number of subjects *in the control group* rather than in the hypnotic group state postexperimentally that they have forgotten what occurred (Barber & Calverley 1966b; Thorne 1967b). Furthermore, when given either peremptory or permissive suggestions for amnesia, subjects in the control group and those in the hypnotic group perform in the same way on tests of recognition (recognizing the "forgotten" material *more readily* than neutral material) (Barber & Calverley 1966b; Williamsen, Johnson, & Erikson 1965).

2. Amnesic hypnotic subjects remember the "forgotten" material when they are given explicit or implicit permission to do so. Explicit permission is given by telling the subject, "Now you remember," and implicit permission is given, for example, by asking the subject "Do you remember?" with the intonation that he is permitted to do so (Barber 1962b).

3. When the apparent amnesia is assessed by more objective methods, for example, by assessment of practice effects or of retroactive inhibition effects, hypnotic subjects who claim that they have forgotten the events perform in the same way as hypnotic or control subjects who state that they remember the events perfectly well (Graham & Patton 1968; Life 1929; Mitchell 1932; Patten 1932; Sturrock 1966).

4. Hypnotic subjects typically refer to their apparent amnesia in motivational terms: "My mind doesn't want to think"; "I could remember without being able to say it"; "I know what it is but I just kind of stop myself before I think of it"; "I put the material out of mind by thinking of other things" (Barber & Calverley 1962; Blum 1961; White 1941). Also, as Hilgard (1966) has pointed out, "An 'almost' recall is very common, as though something is there but inaccessible . . . Sometimes the events are seen clearly in imagery, but *S* is unable to bring himself to describe verbally what he sees."

In brief, it appears that the apparent amnesia which can be elicited by suggestions in a hypnotic situation and also in a control situation differs in several important respects from actual forgetting (e.g., the "forgotten" material is recalled on command and it affects performance in the same way as material that is remembered). Finally, it appears that the data briefly summarized above and other pertinent data reviewed elsewhere (Barber 1962b, 1969b) can be parsimoniously conceptualized by postulating that suggested "amnesia" involves an "effortful, motivated inattention . . . deverbalization . . . [or] suppression of . . . content" (Rosenberg 1959) or "an unwillingness to remember, an attempt to occupy oneself with other things than an effort to recall" (Pattie, 1956b, p. 8).

Sensory-Perceptual Alterations (Deafness, Color-blindness, and Blindness)

Not too many years ago, Erickson (1938a, 1938b, 1939) claimed to have demonstrated that suggestions of deafness, colorblindness, or blindness, given to "deeply hypnotized" subjects, produce conditions which are indistinguishable from neurologically based deafness, colorblindness, and blindness. These claims do not hold up under close scrutiny. Let us look first at hypnotic deafness.

Erickson (1938a) gave repeated emphatic suggestions of deafness to thirty highly selected "deep trance" subjects. Twenty-four of the thirty subjects (80 percent) did not show signs of deafness. However, Erickson judged the remaining six subjects to have become deaf as indicated by such signs as failure to react to unexpected sounds, "failure to raise voice when reading aloud while an irrelevant continuous extraneous noise becomes increasingly disturbing," and "failure to show any response to deliberately embarrassing remarks." Erickson concluded from these and similar data that "there was produced a condition not distinguishable from neurological deafness by any of the ordinarily competent tests employed."

Erickson's conclusion does not clearly follow from the data he presented. For instance, failure to react to unexpected sounds does not demonstrate that the sounds were not heard. In a study carried out by Dynes (1932), three selected "deep trance" subjects, who had received suggestions of deafness, did not become noticeably startled when a pistol was fired unexpectedly; however, each subject testified postexperimentally that he had heard the pistol shot. Similarly, lack of response to a disturbing noise or to embarrassing remarks does not demonstrate that the subject cannot hear since these responses can be rather easily inhibited voluntarily.

In another study, Erickson (1938b) found that two selected hypnotic deaf subjects did not manifest a hand-withdrawal response that had been conditioned to a sound. He interpreted this outcome as demonstrating that the subjects were "unconcious of the sound." This interpretation is invalid; it has been repeatedly demonstrated that subjects can *voluntarily* inhibit hand-withdrawal responses that have been conditioned to a sound (Hamel 1919; Hilgard & Marquis 1940, pp. 269-70).

Several decades after the publication of Erickson's studies, five experiments were conducted which used the technique of delayed auditory feedback to assess hypnotic deafness objectively (Barber & Calverley 1964d; Kline, Guze & Haggerty 1954; Kramer & Tucker 1967; Scheibe, Gray & Keim 1968; Sutcliffe 1961). Each of the five experiments showed that the so-called hypnotic deaf subject is affected by auditory stimuli in essentially the same way as the person with normal hearing; that is, when exposed to delayed auditory feedback, the hypnotic deaf subject and the person with normal hearing (but not the person who is actually deaf) typically stutter, mispronounce words, and speak more loudly and more slowly.

Although the hypnotic deaf subject may be trying not to hear, he simply does not succeed in blocking out sounds. The fact that the subject can hear is often obvious. For instance, hypnotists typically remove the hypnotic deafness by stating, "Now you can hear again." Since the subject now responds again to sound stimuli, it is obvious that he could hear all along.

The same considerations that apply to hypnotic deafness also apply to other supposed sensory-perceptual alterations that have been said to be produced under "deep hypnosis" such as "hypnotic colorblindness" and "hypnotic blindness." The research in these areas can be subsumed under two general principles:

1. Whatever overt performances and verbal reports are elicited by suggestions of deafness, colorblindness, and blindness given to selected "deep trance" subjects in a hypnotic situation can also be elicited from unselected subjects in a control situation by instructions to try to ignore auditory stimuli, specific colors, or visual stimuli (Barber 1964c; Barber & Deeley 1961; Bravin 1959; Rock & Shipley 1961).
2. Suggestions of deafness, colorblindness, or blindness, given either in a hypnotic situation or in a control situation, do *not* obliterate responses to sounds, colors, or visual stimuli, although at times (depending primarily on what techniques are used for assessment) they may give rise to some changes in response (Barber 1964c; Malmo,

Boag & Raginsky 1954; McPeake 1968; Pattie 1950). For instance, although suggestions of colorblindness, given to hypnotic subjects or to control subjects, at times elicit some responses to the Ishihara which seem to resemble the responses of colorblind individuals, this resemblance is superficial; the responses under suggested colorblindness differ qualitatively from the responses of individuals who are actually colorblind (Grether 1940). Similarly, although suggestions of blindness or suggestions to ignore visual stimuli, given in a hypnotic situation or in a control situation, at times prevent the alpha desynchronization (alpha block) that normally follows visual stimulation (Gerard 1951, p. 94; Loomis & Harvey; Hobart 1936; Yeager & Larson 1957), it does not follow that the subjects cannot see; when the subjects are tested in other ways, they respond to visual stimuli in the normal manner (Deckert & West 1963a; Pattie 1935; Sutcliffe 1960; Underwood 1960).

PHYSIOLOGICAL EFFECTS

Suggestions are at times effective in (a) reducing or removing warts (Dudek 1967; Sinclair-Gieben & Chalmers 1959; Ullman & Dudek 1960), (b) producing cardiac acceleration or deceleration (Klemme 1963), (c) improving visual acuity in some myopic subjects (Kelley 1958, 1961), (d) inhibiting or augmenting allergic responses (Ikemi & Nakagawa 1962), (e) reducing the degree of inflammatory reaction and tissue damage produced by intense heat (Chapman, Goodell & Wolff 1959), (f) inhibiting gastric hunger contractions and increasing gastric acid secretions (Ikemi 1959; Lewis & Sarbin 1943; Luckhardt & Johnston 1924), (g) inducing and also inhibiting labor contractions in some women at term (Carter 1963; Logan 1963; Rice 1961; Schwartz 1963), and (h) mitigating ichthyosis (fish-skin disease) (Mason 1952; Wink 1961). We can place these effects in perspective by noting the following:

1. In the studies cited above, the suggested physiological effects were produced in some individuals but not in others. From the data available at present, we cannot specify the physiological propensities or other characteristics of those individuals who showed positive results. Clearly, much further research is needed in this area.
2. In general, when the study included a control group that received the same suggestions as the hypnotic group, about the same number of subjects in both groups showed the suggested effects (Barber 1965c). For instance, suggestions that the heart was accelerating and also suggestions that it was decelerating were as effective with a control group as with a hypnotic group in producing the suggested change in heart rate (Klemme 1963); suggestions intended to produce heightened visual acuity were equally effective with a control group and a hypnotic group in improving vision in myopic subjects (Kelley 1958, 1961); and suggestions intended to inhibit and also to augment allergic responses were as effective with controls as with hypnotic subjects in altering allergic responses (Ikemi & Nakagawa 1962). Similarly, although suggestions of eating a delicious meal are at times effective in evoking gastric secretions in some subjects who are said to be in "deep trance," it is not uncom-

mon for subjects in a nonhypnotic situation to show similar effects when they think about savory foods (Luckhardt & Johnston 1924; Miller, Bergeim, Rehfuss & Hawk 1920; Wolf & Wolff 1947). Furthermore, although suggestions for wart removal are at times effective when they are given in a hypnotic situation, they are also at times effective when they are given in a control situation. Bloch (1927), Sulzberger and Wolf (1934), and Vollmer (1946) reported that warts at times disappear when they are simply painted with an innocuous dye and the subjects are told that the placebo-dye is a powerful wart-curing drug. Furthermore, in those instances in which suggestions for wart removal were effective, there is evidence that the warts may have been of the "labile" type, that is, of the type that would have gone away "spontaneously" within a reasonably short period of time (Memmescheimer & Eisenlohr 1931).

Another physiological effect that has been traditionally associated with suggestions given under "deep hypnosis"—production of blisters—requires more extended comment.

Raising "Blisters." During the past century a rather large number of investigators have suggested to "deeply hypnotized" subjects that a blister would form in a localized area on the skin. In the great majority of instances, *no* dermatological changes whatsoever were observed. However, in about a dozen instances, the investigators reported that the suggestions gave rise to various skin changes and some of these alterations were labeled as *blisters.* The positive results can be placed in context by noting the following points which have been delineated in a series of reviews (Barber 1961b; Gorton 1949; Paul 1963; Pattie 1941; Sarbin 1956; Weitzenhoffer 1953):

1. With few exceptions, the positive results were obtained prior to the advent of rigorous controls in this area, namely, during the period between 1886 and 1927.
2. Very few investigations in this area used careful controls to exclude the possibility that subjects may deliberately injure their skin in an attempt to produce dermatological changes. Furthermore, one subject rubbed poison ivy leaves where the dermatological change was supposed to appear (Wolberg 1948, p. 49), another attempted to injure his skin by vigorously rubbing it and pricking it with a needle (Schrenck-Notzing 1896), and another vigorously rubbed snow on the area in which the blister was supposed to form (Ullman 1947).
3. With a few possible exceptions, the positive results were obtained with patients who were either classified as hysterics (hystero-epilepsy, hysterical hemianesthesia, hysterical aphonia, and hysterical blindness) or as suffering from various skin ailments (wheals, neurotic skin gangrene, hysterical ecchymoses, and neurodermatitis).
4. With few exceptions, it is not clear from the studies reporting positive results whether the cutaneous alterations that were observed were blisters, or wheals, or dermographism. A study which carefully considered this problem (Borelli 1953) showed definitely that the alteration was dermographism, not a blister. It is noteworthy that dermographism (wheal formation in response to a single moderately strong strok-

ing of the skin) is not as uncommon as is generally supposed. Testing eighty-four apparently normal young men, Lewis (1927) found a detectable swelling of the skin as a reaction to a single firm stroke in 25 percent and in 5 percent a full wheal developed. Also, some individuals show wheal formation at sites of mild pressure stimulation, such as around a wristwatch strap, a belt, or a collar (Graham & Wolf 1950). These data are relevant to understanding the positive results obtained in the studies mentioned above because in all but one of the successful experiments tactual stimulation was employed to localize the place where the blister was to form and in many of these studies the stimulus object was a small piece of metal.

5. All of the aforementioned studies lack an important control: suggestions for blister formation were not given in a nonhypnotic situation. Apparently, it was assumed, without any clear justification, that hypnotic procedures were necessary to obtain positive results.

SUMMARY

The discussion in this section can be summarized as follows:

1. The performances observed in a hypnosis situation are quite different from what they might at first appear to be. The "analgesia" that can be produced by suggestions in a hypnotic situation (or in a control situation) is by no means the same as the analgesia that is produced in surgical patients by the anesthesiologist. Similarly, the term *deafness* has quite different meanings when it refers to two individuals who report that they cannot hear but one has been given suggestions of deafness in a hypnotic experiment and the other is enrolled in a school for the deaf. Other labels that are used to describe the overt and verbal performances observed in hypnotic experiments—e.g., age-regression, hallucination, amnesia, colorblindness, and blindness—are similarly misleading.
2. Suggestions given in a hypnosis experiment are at times effective in producing physiological effects such as alterations in gastric secretions, inhibition of gastric hunger contractions, inhibition or augmentation of allergic responses, reduction of warts, and production of skin changes which resemble wheals or dermographism. However, when experiments included a control group that received the same suggestions as the hypnotic group, the physiological effects were usually produced in an equal number of subjects in both groups.

Base-Level Response to Suggestions

Not too many years ago, studies in this area rarely used a control group that was tested for response to suggestions of analgesia, age-regression, hallucination, etc. without receiving a hypnotic-induction procedure. Apparently, it was assumed that control subjects would not respond to suggestions of this type. This assumption is now known to be fallacious. Beginning in the 1950s, many experiments have been published which used a control group; these experiments have demonstrated that, under control or base-level conditions, response to suggestions is much higher than has been commonly assumed.

In the preceding section of this chapter, it was stated or implied that:

a. Suggestions of analgesia or anesthesia are effective in producing a reduction in verbally reported pain in most control subjects (Barber & Calverley 1969a; Spanos, Barber, & Lang 1969).

b. Suggestions to regress to an earlier time are effective in about 10 percent of control subjects in eliciting postexperimental testimony that they "thoroughly felt" and "thoroughly believed" they had returned to the earlier time (Barber & Calverley 1966a).

c. Suggestions to see an object (that is not present) are effective with about 33 percent of control subjects in eliciting reports that they clearly saw (the suggested) object ("visual hallucination") and suggestions to hear a phonograph record playing are effective with about 50 percent of control subjects in eliciting reports that they clearly heard (the nonexistent) record ("auditory hallucination") (Barber & Calverley 1964a; Bowers 1967; Spanos & Barber 1968).

d. Suggestions to forget the experimental events are effective in producing "total amnesia" (postexperimental testimony that the events have been completely forgotten) in about 6 percent of control subjects and in eliciting "partial amnesia" (testimony that some of the events have been forgotten) in about 28 percent of control subjects (Barber & Calverley 1966b).

e. Suggestions that the heart is accelerating, or is decelerating, are effective with most control subjects in eliciting a significant increase or decrease in heart rate, respectively (Klemme 1963).

f. Suggestions intended to produce heightened visual acuity produce a significant increase in apparent acuity in a substantial proportion of myopes who are assigned to a control group (Kelley 1958, 1961).

g. Suggestions intended to inhibit allergic responses, and also suggestions intended to augment allergic responses, produce a significant inhibition or augmentation of allergic responses, respectively, in most allergic subjects assigned to a control group (Ikemi & Nakagawa 1962).

Furthermore, recent studies indicate that:

h. Most control subjects proceed to carry out ostensibly antisocial or harmful acts when given direct suggestions to do so (Milgram 1963; Orne & Evans 1965).

i. The majority of unselected control subjects who receive direct suggestions that time is slowing down report that they experienced "time-distortion," that is, they experienced a short period as a long period of time (Barber & Calverley 1964f; Casey 1966).

Surprisingly high levels of response were also obtained in a series of studies in which the standardized test-suggestions of the Stanford Hypnotic Susceptibility Scale or the Barber Suggestibility Scale were administered to unselected college students without special preliminaries—under a base-level, control

condition (Andersen & Sarbin 1964; Barber 1965a; Barber & Glass 1962; Weitzenhoffer & Sjoberg 1961). For instance, three studies with the Barber Suggestibility Scale (Barber 1965b) showed the following: about half of the control subjects passed the Hand Lock item (failing to take their hands apart, when told they could not do so, and testifying that they did not compliantly keep their hands together but actually felt they could not unclasp them); about half of the control subjects also passed the Thirst "Hallucination" item; about one-fourth of the control subjects passed the Arm Lowering, Arm Levitation, Body Immobility, and Verbal Inhibition items; and at least one-eighth of the control subjects passed the "Posthypnotic-Like" Response and Selective Amnesia items. The study by Andersen and Sarbin (1964), which employed the Stanford Hypnotic Susceptibility Scale, yielded results such as the following: 14 percent of the control subjects could not bend their arm when given suggestions of arm rigidity, 19 percent could not say their name when given suggestions of verbal inhibition, and 17 percent could not move their arm when given suggestions of arm immobilization.

The same "surprisingly" high level of responsiveness is found under base-level, control conditions if the tasks are of the type that are traditionally used by the stage-hypnotist. For example, let us look at the human-plank feat which is part of the repertoire of many stage-hypnotists. The stage-hypnotist suggests to his selected subject, who has ostensibly been placed in a "deep trance," that his body is stiff and rigid. He repeats the suggestions of total body rigidity until the subject appears rigid and then suspends the subject between two chairs, one chair below the subject's head and the other at his ankles. The subject remains suspended between the two chairs for several minutes while the orchestra plays a crescendo and the audience gasps in astonishment. Although it is commonly believed that this human-plank feat is difficult to perform, recent studies indicate that it can be easily elicited by suggestions given to a control group. Barber (1969b) found that at least 80 percent of unselected male and female control subjects are able to perform the feat when they are given suggestions to make their body rigid. Collins (1961) obtained similar results in an earlier study; when given suggestions to become and to stay rigid, subjects in a control group (and also subjects in a hypnotic group) remained suspended for two to four minutes. In postexperimental interviews, most of the control subjects (and also most of the hypnotic subjects) stated that they were amazed at their own performance since they did not believe initially that they had the ability to become human-planks.[6]

---

[6] At times, stage-hypnotists place a rock on the chest of the human-plank and break it with a sledge hammer. Also, stage hypnotists may ask one or more men to stand on the human-plank. Both of these feats are much easier to perform than is commonly believed (Meeker & Barber 1969). The rock that is placed on the human-plank's chest is made of sandstone and breaks easily. When a person is to stand on him, the human-plank is given additional support by placing one chair underneath his shoulders and the other chair beneath the calves of his legs. No weight is placed directly on the human-plank's stomach, which might cause him to collapse. Instead, the weight of the standing person is distributed over the human-plank's chest and over the lower part of his legs which are almost directly above the supporting chairs.

Motivational Factors

Motivational factors appear to play an important role in eliciting the type of responsiveness that has been historically associated with the word *hypnotism*. Let us look at a few examples.

Working with nine "deeply hypnotized" male subjects, Orne (1959) administered suggestions that the subjects would not experience fatigue and other suggestions intended to produce heightened physical endurance. When the subjects were next asked to hold a heavy weight, they held it for a very long time, manifesting the type of endurance that has been traditionally associated with the effects of suggestions given under "deep hypnosis." Subsequently, the same male subjects were given motivational instructions under a control condition; for example, they were told that they should try to surpass the performance of females and the "female performance" was defined to each subject as equal to whatever period of time he had held the weight during the preceding hypnotic trial. All subjects showed greater endurance under the motivated control condition as compared to their previous hypnotic performance. With one exception (Slotnick & London 1965), all other experiments in this area similarly demonstrated that motivational instructions given to control subjects are sufficient to produce the type of heightened physical endurance that has been associated with hypnotism (Barber 1966; Barber & Calverley 1964*h*; Evans & Orne 1965; Levitt & Brady 1964; London & Fuhrer 1961).

A series of experiments, reviewed in detail elsewhere (Barber 1965*a*, 1965*b*, 1969*a*), indicate that motivational instructions raise responsiveness to a series of standardized test-suggestions above the already high level that is obtained under base-level control conditions. Each of these experiments included at least two random groups. Subjects in a control group were assessed individually on the Barber Suggestibility Scale. Subjects in another group were tested individually on the same suggestibility scale after receiving motivational instructions; that is, each subject in this group was told that his performance would depend on his willingness to try to imagine vividly and to experience those things that would be described to him, previous subjects were able to imagine and to experience the effects, and if he tried to imagine to the best of his ability he would experience interesting things and would not be wasting either his own or the experimenter's time. These motivational instructions generally produced a clear-cut rise in suggestibility. For instance, although nearly half of the subjects passed the Hand Lock and Thirst "Hallucination" items under the base-level control condition, more than 75 percent passed these items under the motivational condition. Furthermore, twice as many subjects under the motivational condition, as compared to the base-level control condition, passed the remaining six test-suggestions on the scale (Arm Lowering, Arm Levitation, Verbal Inhibition, Body Immobility, "Posthypnotic-Like" Response, and Selective Amnesia).

In addition to those subjects who were randomly assigned either to the base-level control condition or to the motivational condition, the above experiments also included a third group of subjects who were randomly assigned to a hypnotic-induction condition. These experiments generally showed that (a) subjects who were exposed either to a standardized hypnotic-induction procedure or to motivational instructions were significantly more responsive to test-suggestions than subjects who were tested under the base-level control condition and (b) responsiveness to suggestions was generally as high in subjects who received motivational instructions as in those who received the hypnotic-induction procedure (Barber & Calverley 1962, 1963*a*, 1963*b*, 1965*a*). These results led to a debate concerning whether and under what conditions hypnotic-induction procedures raise subjects' responsiveness to test-suggestions above the level found under a motivational treatment (Barber 1965*a*; Hilgard 1965). This debate was resolved by subsequent experiments (Barber & Calverley 1968; Edmonston & Robertson 1967; Hilgard & Tart 1966) which indicated the following: (a) Motivational instructions produce a relatively high level of suggestibility and this high level generally approximates the level found with a hypnotic-induction procedure. (b) However, if sensitive experimental designs or a large number of subjects are used, a hypnotic-induction procedure can be shown to produce a small but significant increase in responsiveness to test-suggestions above the level found under a motivational condition.

The disagreements in the debate mentioned above are tiny compared to the broad areas of agreement. All participants appear to agree that, when subjects are randomly assigned either to a hypnotic treatment or to a motivational treatment, (a) a hypnotic-induction procedure does *not* produce a markedly higher level of response to test-suggestions of arm levitation, limb immobility, hallucination, amnesia, etc., (b) a hypnotic-induction procedure, at best, produces a small increment in response, and (c) sensitive experimental designs or large number of subjects are needed to detect the small increment. Furthermore, the reason why the overall suggestibility-enhancing effect of hypnotic procedures is "surprisingly" small is that (a) most subjects show a rather constant level of suggestibility when they are tested under a hypnotic treatment and under a motivational treatment, (b) a small proportion of subjects (possibly around 5–10 percent) are *less* responsive to suggestions under a hypnotic treatment as compared to a motivational treatment, and (c) only a slightly greater proportion of subjects (possibly around 20 percent) show a higher level of response after a hypnotic-induction as compared to a motivational condition.

Since hypnotic-induction procedures generally appear to raise suggestibility in a group of subjects to a small degree above motivational instructions, the next question that arises is, What factors in a hypnotic-induction procedure give rise to this small increment? One factor in a hypnotic-induction procedure that might produce the overall small gain in suggestibility is that the situation is defined to the subjects as hypnosis. Let us now turn to this factor.

Definition of the Situation as Hypnosis

The word *hypnosis*, by itself, is sufficient to produce a small but significant gain in response to test-suggestions. In recent experiments (Barber & Calverley 1964*g*, 1965*a*) subjects were randomly assigned to one of two groups. One group was told that it was participating in a hypnosis experiment and the other group was simply told that it was to be tested for ability to imagine. Subjects in both groups were then treated *identically*; that is, they were tested individually on response to the standardized test suggestions of the Barber Suggestibility Scale. Subjects told they were participating in a hypnosis experiment were slightly but significantly more responsive to the test suggestions than those told they were being tested for imaginative ability.

These experiments raise an important question: When other variables are held constant, why are subjects significantly more responsive to suggestions if the situation is defined to them as hypnosis rather than as a test of imagination? One possible explanation is based on the following considerations: For more than a century it has been commonly believed that subjects in a hypnosis situation show a high level of response to suggestions. Subjects used in present-day experiments (e.g., college students and nursing students) also believe that this notion is valid (Dorcus, Brintnall & Case 1941; London 1961). Consequently, when subjects are told that they are in a hypnosis experiment, they typically construe this to mean that they are in an unusual situation in which high response to test-suggestions and "unprecedented kinds of experiences" are to be expected (Gill & Brenman 1959, p. 10), whereas when subjects are told simply that they are to be tested for imaginative ability, they are being told by implication that they are not necessarily expected to show a high level of response to test-suggestions of the type traditionally associated with the word *hypnosis*.

RELAXATION-DROWSINESS-SLEEP SUGGESTIONS

In three experiments (Barber & Calverley 1965a, Exp. 3; 1965b, Exp. 1 and 2) subjects assigned at random to experimental groups were tested on response to the Barber Suggestibility Scale after they were either simply told that they were participating in a hypnosis experiment or, in addition, were told repeatedly that they were becoming relaxed, drowsy, and sleepy. Each of these three experiments showed that, when other variables are held constant, repeated relaxation-drowsiness-sleep suggestions produce a small but significant gain in suggestibility above that found when subjects are told only that they are participating in a hypnosis experiment. However, the suggestibility-enhancing effect of relaxation-drowsiness-sleep suggestions might be due to their special effectiveness in defining the situation to the subject as hypnosis. There are five interrelated aspects to this interpretation: (a) Present-day subjects are aware that repeated suggestions of relaxation, drowsiness, and sleep are administered in a hypnosis experiment. (b) When subjects are told that they are participating in a hypnosis experiment, but are *not* then given repeated suggestions that they are becoming relaxed, drowsy, and sleepy, they are not always convinced that the situation is truly hypnosis or that the experimenter is an effective hypnotist. (c) However, practically all present-day subjects believe that they are truly participating in a hypnotic experiment and the experimenter is a competent hypnotist if the experimenter goes on to suggest to them repeatedly that they are becoming more relaxed, drowsy, and sleepy. (d) When the situation is *effectively* defined as hypnosis to present-day subjects, it is being implicitly defined as one in which a high level of response to test-suggestions of hallucination, amnesia, etc. is not only possible but is also desired and expected. (e) Finally, when the experimenter defines the situation as hypnosis and then goes on to suggest repeatedly that the subject is becoming relaxed, drowsy, and sleepy, it is clear to present-day subjects that, if they are *not* responsive to suggestions, they are negating the purpose of the experiment, they will be considered as poor or uncooperative subjects, the experimenter's time and effort will be wasted, and the experimenter will be disappointed.

This "definition of the situation" interpretation of the suggestibility-enhancing effects of relaxation-drowsiness-sleep suggestions can account for the following experimental results that are otherwise difficult to explain: (a) Relaxation-drowsiness-sleep suggestions facilitate responsiveness to suggestions of analgesia, hallucination, amnesia, etc. even in those subjects who become alert and activated when they receive such suggestions (Barber 1969b). (b) Subjects who become relaxed when they are receiving relaxation-drowsiness-sleep suggestions do not remain relaxed, but become rather highly activated, when they are assessed on response to test-suggestions (Barber & Coules 1959).

Importance of Subtle Factors

Ostensibly subtle factors can make a rather dramatic difference in the degree to which subjects will manifest hypnotic behaviors and report hypnotic experiences. Let us look at a few examples.

HOW THE SUBJECT DEFINES THE SITUATION TO HIMSELF

If subjects are told, immediately prior to the experiment, that they are to be tested for gullibility, and then are tested for response to suggestions of limb rigidity, hallucination, amnesia, posthypnotic-like response, etc., they show very little if any response to the suggestions. However, if a comparable group of subjects are told that they are to be tested for ability to imagine, they show a markedly higher level of response to the same suggestions (Barber & Calverley 1964e). The introduction of one word—either *gullibility* or *imagination*—can thus make a rather dramatic difference in the subjects' propensity to manifest hypnotic behaviors. Although hypnotists do not define the situation to their subjects as a test of gullibility, it appears that some subjects who show a very low level of response to test-suggestions *define the situation to themselves in this way* and it can be surmised that their low level of response is functionally related to their belief that they are being evaluated for an undesirable characteristic (gullibility).

As previously stated, (a) when the situation is defined to subjects as hypnosis they are slightly but significantly more responsive to suggestions than when the situation is defined as a test of imagination and (b) it appears that the increment in response produced by introducing the word *hypnosis* into the experimental setting is due to the subject's perceiving the situation as one in which high response to suggestions is not only possible but is also desired and expected. We can also surmise that when the connotationally rich term *hypnosis* is introduced into an experimental situation, there are many additional subtle variations among subjects in their conceptions of what is involved in the experiment. Further studies are clearly needed to delineate more precisely how subjects define the situation to themselves and how their own definition of the situation is related to their response.

Subtle Factors Determing Subjects' Reports that They Were or Were Not Hypnotized

Whether or not subjects testify postexperimentally that they were hypnotized depends on a series of relatively subtle variables that have been commonly neglected:

1. Subjects' testimony that they were or were not hypnotized depends, in part, on their preconceptions of what hypnosis is supposed to involve. Subjects differing in their preconceptions of hypnosis give markedly different testimony *even when there is every indication that they had very similar experiences.* For instance, subject *A* believes that a person is hypnotized if he forgets what occurred whereas subject *B* believes that a person is hypnotized if he becomes very relaxed. When both subjects have the same experiences during the hypnotic session, for instance, when both become very relaxed and respond well to all suggestions but do not forget what occurred, subject *A* will testify postexperimentally that he was not hypnotized whereas subject *B* will testify that he was hypnotized.
2. Subjects' testimony pertaining to whether or not they were hypnotized is also dependent, in part, on the wording and tone of the questions that are used to elicit their testimony (Barber, Dalal & Calverley 1968). This important point will be amplified in the next section of the chapter.
3. Subjects' testimony pertaining to whether or not they were hypnotized is also dependent, in part, on whether the experimenter states or implies that *he* believes they were hypnotized (Barber, Dalal & Calverley 1968).

   In brief, whether or not subjects report that they were hypnotized appears to depend, in part, on rather subtle variables such as their preconceptions of what hypnosis is supposed to involve, the wording and tone of the questions that are used to elicit their testimony, and cues given by the experimenter pertaining to whether he believes they were or were not hypnotized.

Wording and Tone of Inquiry

It appears that subtle factors influence not only the subjects' testimony pertaining to whether or not they were hypnotized but also a wide range of other testimony given by hypnotic subjects. Let us look closely at an experiment by Barber, Dalal, and Calverley (1968) which demonstrated that the hypnotic subject's reports of his experiences is dependent, in part, on a rather subtle variable, namely, on the wording and tone of the questions he is asked. The rationale and design of the experiment were as follows:

An earlier paper by Orne (1959) had concluded that the "essense of hypnosis" will be found in the subject's "report of alterations in his experience" as indicated, for example, by his report of "an inability to resist a cue [a suggestion] given by the hypnotist" and of having experienced the "[hypnotic] state as basically different from the normal one." The experiment by Barber et al. was designed to ascertain to what extent subjective reports of this type are influenced by the wording of the questions that are submitted to the subjects. Fifty-three student nurses were exposed individually to the Stanford Hypnotic Sucseptibility Scale (Form A) which includes repeated relaxation-drowsiness-sleep suggestions followed by a series of standardized test-suggestions. After the subjects were told that the experiment was over, they were randomly allocated to three experimental groups and each group was asked questions that differed "slightly" in wording. Let us look at the results obtained with two of the random groups.

Subjects in Group A were asked individually, "Did you feel you could resist the suggestions?", whereas those in Group B were asked individually, "Did you feel you could not resist the suggestions?" The two questions elicited markedly different subjective reports: 22 percent of the subjects in Group A and 83 percent in Group B reported that they could not resist the suggestions. A separate analysis was performed for the very good subjects in each group (who had either or both judged themselves as "deeply hypnotized" and had passed all of the test suggestions). Only *half* of the very good subjects in Group A and *all* of the very good subjects in Group B reported that they could not resist.

Next, subjects in Group A were asked, "Did you experience the hypnotic state as basically similar to the waking state?", and those in Group B were asked, "Did you experience the hypnotic state as basically different from the waking state?" Only a minority of the subjects in Group A (17 percent of all subjects in the group and 33 percent of the very good subjects) reported that they experienced the two states as different whereas the great majority of subjects in Group B (72 percent of all subjects and 75 percent of the very good subjects) reported that they experienced the two states as different.

These results, and the results obtained with a third experimental group that was asked questions worded differently, strongly indicated that the subjective reports of hypnotic subjects are *markedly affected* by ostensibly subtle variations in the wording of the questions that are submitted to them. The term *markedly affected* is used advisedly here because the wording of the questions accounted for 42 percent of the variance in subjects' reports of "ability to resist suggestions" and for 31 percent of the variance in their reports of "having experienced the hypnotic state as similar to the waking state."

There is also evidence to indicate that the *tone* and *inflections* of the questions submitted to hypnotic subjects also influence their testimony. For instance, subjects can be asked, "Do you remember what occurred?", with a tone of voice and with inflections implying that they can and should remember or with a tone and inflections implying that they cannot and should not. More subjects will state that they do not remember (will manifest "amnesia") when the question is asked in the latter rather than in the former way (Barber 1962b).

The inconsistencies in the hypnotic subjects' experiential reports that are produced by ostensibly minor variations in the wording or tone of the questions may be due to one or both of the following:

1. The subjects may be misreporting their experiences in order to comply with the desires of the experimenter as indicated by the wording and tone of his questions.
2. The subjects may accept the categories for classifying their experiences (that are implicitly offered to them by the specific wording and tone of the experimenter's questions) because their experiences were vague and they do not know how to categorize them. For instance, subjects may give inconsistent testimony when asked if they experi-

enced the hypnotic state as similar to the waking state or as different from the waking state, because their experiences were ambiguous and difficult to classify. They may feel that their state during the hypnotic session was somewhat different from the waking state because they experienced various suggested effects that they had not previously experienced; however, they might simultaneously feel that their state was similar to the waking state because they were aware of what was going on and were continuously thinking about their role in the situation.

Further studies are needed to determine to what extent the variability in hypnotic subjects' experiential reports that is associated with changes in the wording and tone of the questions is due to each of the foregoing possibilities and to other possibilities.

THE EFFECTS OF OTHER RELATIVELY SUBTLE FACTORS

Recent research indicates that other ostensibly subtle factors play a role in determining whether and to what extent subjects will manifest hypnotic behaviors. These variables, which were generally neglected by previous generations of workers in this area, include the following: (a) whether or not the subject was acquainted with or had formed a special relationship with the hypnotist prior to the first attempted hypnotic induction (Kramer 1969; Richman 1965); (b) whether or not the subject had prior practice or training in hypnotic experiment (Barber & Calverley 1966c; Cooper, Banford, Schubot & Tart 1967); (c) whether the subject was or was not proficient in role-taking ability or dramatic ability (Coe & Sarbin 1966; Sarbin & Lim 1963); (d) whether the subject volunteered or was coerced to participate in the experiment (Boucher & Hilgard 1962); (e) whether the subject was unselected or was selected as high or low in suggestibility or hypnotic susceptibility (London, Conant & Davison 1966; London & Fuhrer 1961; Rosenhan & London 1963); (f) whether the subject was tested individually or in a group session (Sarbin 1964, p. 201); (g) whether or not the subject's performance was observed by an audience (Coe 1966); (h) whether or not the subject received verbal reinforcement for desired responses (Giles 1962; Sachs & Anderson 1967); (i) whether the test suggestions were presented in a firm tone of voice or in a less firm or more lackadaisical tone (Barber & Calverley 1964b); (j) whether or not honest subjective reports were requested or demanded during the postexperimental inquiry; and (k) whether the postexperimental inquiry was conducted by the hypnotist or by another person (Bowers 1967; Spanos & Barber 1968).[7]

In brief, it appears that (a) hypnotic behaviors are *multi-determined* in that *many* variables influence the subject's overt performance and subjective reports in a hypnotic situation, (b)

some of these variables, which were missed by earlier researchers in this area, must be rather subtle, and (c) the hypnotic situation appears to be at least as complex as any social-psychological situation that has thus far been subjected to experimental analysis.

Personality and Hypnotic Susceptibility

It has been commonly assumed that good hypnotic subjects possess a set of personality traits or characteristics that set them apart from poor hypnotic subjects. This notion has been found not only among laymen but also among earlier professional workers in this area: during the long history of hypnotism, one or more investigators has asserted that good hypnotic subjects differ from poor subjects in gullibility, neuroticism, tendency to repression, hysterical traits, dependency, ego strength, sociability, or various other characteristics of personality. Recent research indicates that this notion is misleading. If good hypnotic subjects differ in any personality traits or characteristics from poor hypnotic subjects, these characteristics are by no means obvious or easily specified.

A large number of attempts have been made to relate personality traits to responsiveness to test-suggestions in a hypnotic situation (hypnotic susceptibility) or to responsiveness to the same test-suggestions in a nonhypnotic or control situation (suggestibility). These studies, which have been reviewed elsewhere (Barber 1964d; Deckert & West 1963b; Hilgard 1965), generally yielded either negative or conflicting results. For instance, one study found a positive correlation between neuroticism and hypnotic susceptibility or suggestibility, another found a negative correlation, and a series of studies found no relationship between these variables (Cooper & Dana 1964; Eysenck 1947; Furneaux & Gibson 1961; Heilizer 1960; Hilgard & Bentler 1963; Ingham 1954, 1955; Lang & Lazovik 1962; Thorn 1961). Similarly, although some investigators (As 1962; Shor, Orne. & O'Connell 1962) reported that responsiveness to test-suggestions was correlated with propensity to have natural hypnoticlike experiences such as vivid daydreams, other investigators failed to find this relationship (Barber & Calverley 1965c; Dermen 1964; London, Cooper, & Johnson 1962; Wilson 1967). Furthermore, investigators working in different laboratories have failed to confirm the results previously obtained in other laboratories which indicated that hypnotic susceptibility may be related to some aspect of personality as measured by the Rorschach, the Thematic Apperception Test, the California Psychological Inventory, the Minnesota Multiphasic Personality Inventory, the Maudsley Personality Inventory, the Guilford-Zimmerman Temperament Survey, the Cattell 16 PF Questionnaire, the Edwards Personal Preference Schedule, the Marlowe-Crowne Social Desirability Scale, the Jourard Self-Disclosure Scale, the Leary Interpersonal Check List, and many other personality instruments (Barber 1964d; Deckert & West 1963b; Hilgard 1965). Not only have investigators failed to confirm the results of other investigators, but the same investigators typically find one relationship between hypnotic susceptibility and personality in one sample of subjects and then fail to find the relationship when they test a new sample (Barber 1964d; Barber & Glass 1962; Rhoades & Edmonston 1969).

In brief, a large number of studies in this area have failed to demonstrate that susceptibility is clearly related to any of a

---

[7] Rosenhan (1967) has hypothesized that another factor, namely, the experimenter's expectancies or biases concerning the subject's performance, also plays a subtle role in influencing the behavior of the hypnotic subject. This hypothesis has not as yet been confirmed in hypnosis research. In other areas of psychology, however, there are some experimental data which suggest that the experimenter's expectancies or biases may in rare instances play a subtle role in influencing the subject's performance (Barber & Silver 1968a, 1968b; Rosenthal 1968).

large number of personality characteristics (including gullibility, neuroticism, hysteria, extroversion, dominance, ego strength, sociability, general cooperativeness, deference, abasement, dependency, impunitiveness, tendency to repression, "basic trust," tendency to give socially desirable responses, willingness for self-disclosure, and field-dependency). This failure to find clear-cut relations between personality characteristics and hypnotic susceptibility or suggestibility has several important implications that are discussed in the next section.

Attitudes, Motivations, and Expectancies

The notion that some enduring personality characteristics must be related to hypnotic susceptibility is based on the underlying assumption that susceptibility is very stable over time and in various situations, that is, good hypnotic subjects remain good subjects and poor hypnotic subjects remain poor subjects when tested in a variety of situations by different hypnotists. Recent research has uncovered serious problems with respect to the underlying assumption:

1. Most good hypnotic subjects remain good subjects, and most poor hypnotic subjects remain poor subjects *when they are tested in the same way twice* (test-retest correlations, which are usually around .72 to .82, account for about one-half to two-thirds of the variance) (Barber 1965b; Hilgard 1965). Although most subjects show a relatively stable level of responsiveness in two sessions, some subjects perform as poor subjects when tested by one experimenter and then perform as good subjects when tested in another session by the same or by a different experimenter and, vice versa, some subjects first perform as good subjects and later perform as poor subjects (Barber 1957; Dorcus 1963; Meares 1960; Pattie 1956a; Sarbin 1950a; Shaffer 1962; Shor & Schatz 1960; White 1941). Furthermore, subjects may show marked variability in their hypnotic susceptibility when they are tested in exactly the same way by the same experimenter five or more times (correlations between subjects' first day performance and their fifth day performance may drop to around .18 to .22) (Barber & Calverley 1966c).

2. When subjects show variability in their responsiveness, this can usually be shown to be closely related to changes in their attitudes, motivations, and expectancies toward the test-situation. For example, the study mentioned above (Barber & Calverley 1966c) which found marked changes in subjects' hypnotic susceptibility when they were tested in exactly the same way several times includes very cogent evidence that good subjects may become poor subjects when they lose interest or become bored with the experimental situation. Similarly, another study (Barber & Calverley 1964c) showed that when a prestigeful person other than the experimenter attempts to induce unfavorable attitudes and negative motivations toward the test situation in experimental subjects, subjects who had previously shown high levels of susceptibility or suggestibility now show a very low level of response. Similar data have been presented by other investigators. Pattie (1956a) referred to subjects who performed well in the first hypnotic session but not in a second session and presented data

indicating that such changes are correlated with changes in the subjects' attitudes toward the hypnotic situation. Sarbin (1950a) observed that some subjects were refractory to suggestions in a first hypnotic session and very responsive in a second session and offered presumptive evidence that such changes were due to alterations in subjects' attitudes and motivations with respect to the test-situation. Similarly, White (1941) referred to drastic alterations in hypnotic susceptibility observed by himself and by other investigators and concluded that some subjects "who at first are insusceptible become excellent subjects when changes are made in the pattern of motives."

3. A series of experiments cited earlier in this chapter indicate that motivational factors play a role in determining subjects' susceptibility or suggestibility: when an attempt is made to motivate subjects to try to experience the suggested effects, they generally show a significant elevation in their responsiveness to suggestions of hallucination, verbal inhibition, selective amnesia, etc. Also, as stated previously in this chapter, subjects' responsiveness varies with ostensibly subtle changes in the experimental situation, for example, with variations in the words used by the experimenter to describe the purpose of the experiment or with variations in the experimenter's tone of voice when he is administering the test suggestions. These changes in hypnotic susceptibility or suggestibility with variations in the situation cannot be attributed to changes in the subjects' personality traits (since such traits remain constant) but can be attributed to changes in the subjects' attitudes, motivations, and expectancies with respect to the test situation.

Other experiments also indicate that specific kinds of attitudes and expectancies play an important role in determining subjects' hypnotic susceptibility or suggestibility. These experiments were *not* concerned with undifferentiated or general attitudes and expectancies but with delimited, specific kinds of attitudes and expectancies that can be labeled as (a) attitudes and expectancies with regard to hypnotism or to tests of suggestibility, (b) task-expectancy, and (c) expectancy of appropriate behavior. Let us look in turn at the empirical data which indicate the importance of each of these specific types of attitudes and expectancies.

ATTITUDES AND EXPECTANCIES WITH REGARD TO
HYPNOTISM OR TO TESTS OF SUGGESTIBILITY

Andersen (1963) obtained a significant correlation of .47 between hypnotic susceptibility and scores on a preexperimental scale measuring attitudes toward hypnotism (e.g., "There are things that would worry me about being hypnotized," and "I would feel uneasy or uncomfortable as a subject"). In another study (Barber & Calverley 1966c) hypnotic susceptibility was significantly correlated with subjects' preexperimental expectations (self-predictions) of their own hypnotic depth (average $r = .41$) and with a preexperimental attitude toward hypnosis measure (perceiving hypnotism as interesting) (average $r = .55$). Similarly, other studies (Barber & Calverley 1969b; Dermen & London 1965; London, Cooper & Johnson 1962; Melei & Hilgard 1964; Rosenhan & Tomkins 1964;

Shor, Orne, & O'Connell 1966) generally yielded small positive correlations (which were more often significant for females than for males) between subjects' hypnotic susceptibility and their preexperimental attitudes toward hypnotism and their preexperimental expectations (self-predictions) of their own hypnotic depth. Another study (Barber & Calverlery 1964c), in which attitudes toward the test situation were manipulated experimentally, indicated that negative attitudes toward the test situation (which involved a test of suggestibility) preclude responsiveness to test-suggestions; or, stated in a different way, to manifest some degree of response to suggestions of body immobility, arm heaviness, arm levitation, verbal inhibition, selective amnesia, and posthypnotic-like response, it is necessary for the subject to hold at least neutral if not positive attitudes toward the test-situation.

TASK-EXPECTANCY

Several experiments mentioned in the preceding paragraph showed that hypnotic susceptibility or suggestibility is affected by one specific type of expectancy, namely, subjects' expectancy pertaining to the depth of hypnosis they will attain. Three recent experiments demonstrated that another type of expectancy also plays a role, namely, an expectancy that the tasks or those things that will be suggested will be rather easy to perform or to experience (task-expectancy).

The first experiment (Barber & Calverley 1964g) showed that subjects are significantly more responsive to standardized test suggestions when they are told that the tests are easy rather than difficult to pass. In a second experiment (Klinger 1968) subjects were individually assessed on response to the standardized test suggestions of the Barber Suggestibility Scale after they had observed another subject (who was actually a stooge) responding to the suggestions. Prior to the experiment, the stooge had been secretly instructed to role-play a very suggestible person half of the time and a very unsuggestible person the other half of the time. Subjects who had observed the responsive stooge (who performed as if it was very easy to respond to suggestions) obtained a mean score of 6.0 whereas those who had observed the unresponsive stooge obtained a significantly lower mean score of 2.6 on the 8-point suggestibility scale.

In a third experiment (Wilson 1967) the following procedure was used to lead subjects to expect that the suggested effects were easy to experience: the subjects were asked to imagine various suggested effects while ingenious methods were employed to help them experience the effects without their knowing that they were receiving such aid. For instance, the subject was asked to imagine that the room was red while a tiny bulb was lit secretly which provided a very faint red tinge to the room. Following these procedures, the subjects were assessed on the Barber Suggestibility Scale. Another random group of subjects (controls) were tested on the same suggestibility scale but were not exposed to the preliminary procedures used with the experimental group. The experimental group, which had apparently been led to expect that the suggested effects were easy to experience, obtained a mean score of 5 whereas the control group obtained a significantly lower mean score of 3 on the 8-point suggestibility scale.

In brief, three experiments, which employed different methods to induce an expectancy that the suggested tasks are easy to perform and the suggested effects are easy to experience, indicate that positive task-expectancy plays an important role in eliciting hypnotic behaviors.

EXPECTANCY OF APPROPRIATE BEHAVIOR

A study by Orne (1959) demonstrated that the performance of hypnotic subjects is also affected by another type of expectancy, namely, their expectancy of what type of behaviors are appropriate in a hypnotic situation. An experimental group was told in a class lecture that hypnotic subjects typically manifest catalepsy of the dominant hand whereas a control group was not told anything about catalepsy. Subsequently, subjects in both groups were tested individually in a hypnotic session on response to various test-suggestions and on response to a test for catalepsy. Since 55 percent of the subjects in the experimental group and none in the control group showed catalepsy of the dominant hand, it appears that the subjects' expectations concerning what behaviors are appropriate in a hypnotic experiment play an important role in determing their performance.

In summary, the data indicate that whether or not and to what degree subjects manifest hypnotic behaviors such as suggested body immobility, hallucination, amnesia, etc. is determined, at least in part, by their attitudes toward hypnotism, their expectations of their own performance, and their expectations of what behaviors are appropriate in a hypnotic situation. Furthermore, three studies indicate that subjects manifest more hypnotic behaviors when an attempt is made to produce an expectancy that the tasks are easy to perform.

ATTITUDES, MOTIVATIONS, AND EXPECTANCIES AS MEDIATING VARIABLES IN HYPNOTIC BEHAVIOR

The data presented above, and also the data presented previously in this chapter pertaining to the effects of motivational factors, can be considered from another viewpoint. The data can be interpreted as indicating that attitudinal, motivational, and expectancy variables mediate or intervene between the antecedent variables in a hypnotic situation (e.g., the experimenter's statements and manipulations) and the dependent or consequent variables (e.g., the subject's responses to test-suggestions of analgesia, hallucination, age regression, amnesia, etc.). The data allow us to postulate that subjects manifest behaviors of the type historically associated with the word *hypnotism* to the extent that the following mediating variables are present: the subjects have (a) positive attitudes toward the hypnotic or suggestion situation, (b) positive motivations to try to perform well on the suggested tasks and to try to experience those things that are suggested, (c) positive expectancies that the tasks and suggested effects will be rather easy to perform and to experience, (d) positive expectancies that various types of unusual behaviors are appropriate in a hypnotic or suggestion situation, and (e) positive expectancies that they themselves will be "hypnotized."

The mediating variables listed above can be conceived as similar to those that operate in many types of interpersonal test situations. For instance, when an examiner tests an individual on any one of various types of tasks (e.g., a learning task, a psychomotor task, or a physical endurance task), it appears likely that the individual's performance is mediated, in part, by his attitudes toward the test situation, his motivation to perform maximally on the task, his expectancies pertaining to the difficulty of the task, and his expectancies of his own performance. These mediating variables can also be viewed as overlapping with those that play a role in a variety of interpersonal situations in which a person in the more dominant role, such as a teacher or a psychotherapist, attempts to influence the behavior and experiences of a person in a less dominant role. For instance, the effective teacher presumably attempts to induce in the pupil positive attitudes, motivations, and expectancies toward the school situation and toward the learning tasks. There is also evidence indicating that mediating variables of this type play an important role in psychotherapy (Goldstein, Heller & Sechrest 1966).

Theoreticians in the area of hypnotism are now faced with an important question: What mediating variables, in addition to changes in subjects' attitudes, motivations, and expectancies, need to be postulated in order to account for hypnotic behavior? As stated earlier in this chapter, it appears that the mediating variables in hypnotic behavior have been traditionally subsumed under such umbrella constructs as *altered state of consciousness*, *hypnotic state*, or *trance state*. However, it has never been clear what these states might involve; for instance, it has never been clear whether they might be conceptualized in terms of changes in subjects' attitudes, motivations, and expectancies toward the specific test-situation. Furthermore, as pointed out elsewhere (Barber 1964a; Chaves 1968; Dalal 1966), writers in this area have traditionally used the term *hypnotic state* or *trance state* in a circular fashion; that is, a subject was said to be in a hypnotic trance state when he manifested a high level of response to suggestions of age regression, analgesia, hallucination, amnesia, etc., and he was said to manifest a high level of response to these suggestions because he was in a hypnotic trance state. It appears to the present writer that (a) the mediating variables in hypnotic behavior can be fruitfully conceptualized in terms of specific kinds of attitudinal, motivational, and expectancy factors, (b) these attitudinal, motivational, and expectancy variables are on a continuum with similar variables that play an important role when subjects perform well in various types of test situations, (c) it is misleading to label these variables as an *altered state of consciousness* or as a *hypnotic trance state*, and (d) it is now incumbent upon those who wish to continue using such terms as *altered state of consciousness* or *hypnotic trance state* to specify the referents for these terms unambiguously and to show clearly when and how these terms might be useful in conceptualizing the factors involved in hypnotic behavior.

Acknowledgment. Work on this chapter was supported by a research grant (MH-11521) from the National Institute of Mental Health, U. S. Public Health Service.

References

ANDERSEN, M. L. Correlates of hypnotic performance: an historical and role-theoretical analysis. Unpublished doctoral dissertation. University of California, Berkeley, 1963.

—— and SARBIN, T. R. Base rate expectancies and motoric alterations in hypnosis. *International Journal of Clinical and Experimental Hypnosis*, 1964, *12*, 147–58.

ANDERSON, M. N. Hypnosis in anesthesia. *Journal of the Medical Association of Alabama*, 1957, *27*, 121–25.

AS, A. Non-hypnotic experiences related to hypnotizability in male and female college students. *Scandinavian Journal of Psychology*, 1962, *3*, 112–21.

ASCHER, L. M., and BARBER, T. X. An attempted replication of the Parrish-Lundy-Leibowitz study on hypnotic age regression. Harding, Mass.: Medfield Foundation, 1968.

AUGUST, R. V. *Hypnosis in obstetrics*. New York: McGraw-Hill, 1961.

BARBER, T. X. Hypnosis as perceptual-cognitive restructuring: III. From somnambulism to autohypnosis. *Journal of Psychology*, 1957, *44*, 299–304.

—— Hypnosis as perceptual-cognitive restructuring: II. "Post"-hypnotic behavior. *Journal of Clinical and Experimental Hypnosis*, 1958, *6*, 10–20.

—— Toward a theory of pain: Relief of chronic pain by prefrontal leucotomy, opiates, placebos, and hypnosis. *Psychological Bulletin*, 1959, *56*, 430–60.

—— Experimental evidence for a theory of hypnotic behavior: II. Experimental controls in hypnotic age-regression. *International Journal of Clinical and Experimental Hypnosis*, 1961a, *9*, 181–93.

—— Physiological effects of "hypnosis." *Psychological Bulletin*, 1961b, *58*, 390–419.

—— Hypnotic age regression: A critical review. *Psychosomatic Medicine*, 1962a, *24*, 286–99.

—— Toward a theory of hypnosis: Posthypnotic behavior. *Archives of General Psychiatry*, 1962b, *7*, 321–42.

—— The effect of "hypnosis" on pain: A critical review of experimental and clinical findings. *Psychosomatic Medicine*, 1963, *25*, 303–33.

—— "Hypnosis" as a causal variable in present-day psychology: A critical analysis. *Psychological Reports*, 1964a, *14*, 839–42.

—— Hypnotically hallucinated colors and their negative afterimages. *American Journal of Psychology*, 1964b, *77*, 313–18.

—— Hypnotic "colorblindness," "blindness," and "deafness." *Diseases of the Nervous System*, 1964c, *25*, 529–37.

—— Hypnotizability, suggestibility, and personality: V. A critical review of research findings. *Psychological Reports*, 1964d, *14*, 299–320.

—— Toward a theory of "hypnotic" behavior: Positive visual and auditory hallucinations. *Psychological Record*, 1964e, *14*, 197–210.

—— Experimental analysis of "hypnotic" behavior: A review of recent empirical findings. *Journal of Abnormal Psychology*, 1965a, *70*, 132–54.

—— Measuring "hypnotic-like" suggestibility with and without "hypnotic induction": Psychometric properties, norms, and variables influencing response to the Barber Suggestibility Scale (BSS). *Psychological Reports*, 1965b, *16*, 809–44.

—— Physiological effects of "hypnotic suggestions": A critical review of recent research (1960–64). *Psychological Bulletin*, 1965c, *63*, 201–22.

—— The effects of hypnosis and suggestions on strength and endurance: A critical review of research studies. *British Journal of Social and Clinical Psychology*, 1966, *5*, 42–50.

—— An empirically based formulation of hypnotism. *American Journal of Clinical Hypnosis*, 1969a, *12*, 100–130.

—— *Hypnosis: A scientific approach*. New York: Van Nostrand Reinhold, 1969b.

—— *LSD, marihuana, yoga, and hypnosis*. Chicago: Aldine, 1970.

BARBER, T. X., and CALVERLEY, D. S. "Hypnotic" behavior as a function of task motivation. *Journal of Psychology*, 1962, *54*, 363–89.

—— The relative effectiveness of task-motivating instructions and trance induction procedure in the production of "hypnotic-like" behaviors. *Journal of Nervous and Mental Disease*, 1963a, *137*, 107–16.

—— Toward a theory of hypnotic behavior: Effects on suggestibility of task motivating instructions and attitude toward hypnosis. *Journal of Abnormal and Social Psychology*, 1963b, *67*, 557–65.

—— An experimental study of "hypnotic" (auditory and visual) hallucinations. *Journal of Abnormal and Social Psychology*, 1964a, *63*, 13–20.

—— Effect of E's tone of voice on "hypnotic-like" suggestibility. *Psychological Reports*, 1964b, *15*, 139–44.

——— Empirical evidence for a theory of "hypnotic" behavior: Effects of pretest instructions on response to primary suggestions. *Psychological Record*, 1964c, *14*, 457–67.

——— Experimental studies in "hypnotic" behavior: Suggested deafness evaluated by delayed auditory feedback. *British Journal of Psychology*, 1964d, *55*, 439–46.

——— The definition of the situation as a variable affecting "hypnotic-like" suggestibility. *Journal of Clinical Psychology*, 1964e, *20*, 438–40.

——— Toward a theory of "hypnotic" behavior: An experimental study of "hypnotic time distortion." *Archives of General Psychiatry*, 1964f, *10*, 209–16.

——— Toward a theory of hypnotic behavior: Effects on suggestibility of defining the situation as hypnosis and defining response to suggestions as easy. *Journal of Abnormal and Social Psychology*, 1964g, *68*, 585–92.

——— Toward a theory of "hypnotic" behavior: Enhancement of strength and endurance. *Canadian Journal of Psychology*, 1964h, *18*, 156–67.

——— Empirical evidence for a theory of "hypnotic" behavior: Effects on suggestibility of five variables typically included in hypnotic induction procedures. *Journal of Consulting Psychology*, 1965a, *29*, 98–107.

——— Empirical evidence for a theory of "hypnotic" behavior: The suggestibility-enhancing effects of motivational suggestions, relaxation-sleep suggestions, and suggestions that the subject will be effectively "hypnotized." *Journal of Personality*, 1965b, *33*, 256–70.

——— Hypnotizability, suggestibility, and personality: II. Assessment of previous imaginative-fantasy experiences by the As, Barber-Glass, and Shor questionnaires. *Journal of Clinical Psychology*, 1965c, *21*, 57–58.

——— Effects on recall of hypnotic induction, motivational suggestions, and suggested regression: A methodological and experimental analysis. *Journal of Abnormal Psychology*, 1966a, *71*, 169–80.

——— Toward a theory of "hypnotic" behavior: Experimental analyses of suggested amnesia. *Journal of Abnormal Psychology*, 1966b, *71*, 79–107.

——— Toward a theory of hypnotic behavior: Experimental evaluation of Hull's postulate that hypnotic susceptibility is a habit phenomenon. *Journal of Personality*, 1966c, *34*, 416–33.

——— Toward a theory of "hypnotic" behavior: Replication and extension of experiments by Barber and co-workers (1962–1965) and Hilgard and Tart (1966). *International Journal of Clinical and Experimental Hypnosis*, 1968, *16*, 179–95.

——— Effects of hypnotic induction, suggestions of anesthesia, and distraction on subjective and physiological responses to pain. Paper presented at Eastern Psychological Association, Annual Meeting, Philadelphia, April 10, 1969a.

——— Multidimensional analysis of "hypnotic" behavior. *Journal of Abnormal Psychology*, 1969b, *74*, 209–20.

BARBER, T. X., and COULES, J. Electrical skin conductance and galvanic skin response during "hypnosis." *International Journal of Clinical and Experimental Hypnosis*, 1959, *7*, 79–92.

BARBER, T. X., DALAL, A. S., and CALVERLEY, D. S. The subjective reports of hypnotic subjects. *American Journal of Clinical Hypnosis*, 1968, *11*, 74–88.

BARBER, T. X., and DEELEY, D. C. Experimental evidence for a theory of hypnotic behavior: I. "Hypnotic" color-blindness without "hypnosis." *International Journal of Clinical and Experimental Hypnosis*, 1961, *9*, 79–86.

BARBER, T. X., and GLASS, L. B. Significant factors in hypnotic behavior. *Journal of Abnormal and Social Psychology*, 1962, *64*, 222–28.

BARBER, T. X., and HAHN, K. W., JR. Physiological and subjective responses to pain producing stimulation under hypnotically suggested and waking-imagined "analgesia." *Journal of Abnormal and Social Psychology*, 1962, *65*, 411–18.

BARBER, T. X,. and SILVER, M. J. Fact, fiction, and the experimenter bias effect. *Psychological Bulletin*, 1968a, *70* (6, pt. 2), 1–29.

——— Pitfalls in data analysis and interpretation: A reply to Rosenthal. *Psychological Bulletin*, 1968b, *70* (6, pt. 2), 48–62.

BEECHER, H. K. *Measurement of subjective responses*. New York: Oxford University Press, 1959.

BERNHEIM, H. *Suggestive therapeutics*. Westport, Conn.: Associated Booksellers, 1957. (Original date of publication: 1886.)

BERNSTEIN, M. *The search for Bridey Murphy*. New York: Doubleday, 1956.

BEST, H. L., and MICHAELS, R. M. Living out "future" experience under hypnosis. *Science*, 1954, *120*, 1077.

BLOCH, B. Ueber die Heilung der Warzen durch Suggestion. *Klinische Wochenschrift*, 1927, *6*, 2271–75, 2320–25.

BLUM, G. S. *A model of the mind*. New York: John Wiley, 1961.

BORELLI, S. Psychische Einflüsse und reactive Hauterscheinungen. *Münch. med. Wochenschrift*, 1953, *95*, 1078–82.

BOUCHER, R. G., and HILGARD, E. R. Volunteer bias in hypnotic experimentation. *American Journal of Clinical Hypnosis*, 1962, *5*, 49–51.

BOWERS, K. S. The effect of demands for honesty on reports of visual and auditory hallucinations. *International Journal of Clinical and Experimental Hypnosis*, 1967, *15*, 31–36.

BRADY, J. P., and LEVITT, E. E. Hypnotically induced visual hallucinations. *Psychosomatic Medicine*, 1966, *28*, 351–63.

BRAID, J. Facts and observations as to the relative value of mesmeric and hypnotic coma, and ethereal narcotism, for the mitigation or entire prevention of pain during surgical operation. *Medical Times*, 1847, *15*, 381–82.

BRAVIN, M. Role-play and direct suggestion in hypnotically induced color blindness. Unpublished doctoral dissertation, University of Denver, 1959.

BURR, C. W. The reflexes of early infancy. *British Journal of Childhood Diseases*, 1921, *18*, 152–53.

BUTLER, B. The use of hypnosis in the care of the cancer patient. *Cancer*, 1954, 7, 1–14.

CARTER, J. E. Hypnotic induction of labor: A review and report of cases. *American Journal of Clinical Hypnosis*, 1963, *5*, 322–25.

CASEY, G. A. Hypnotic time distortion and learning. Unpublished doctoral dissertation. Michigan State University, 1966.

CHAPMAN, L. F., GOODELL, H., and WOLFF, H. G. Increased inflammatory reaction induced by central nervous system activity. *Transactions of the Association of American Physicians*, 1959, *72*, 84–109.

CHAVES, J. F. Hypnosis reconceptualized: An overview of Barber's theoretical and empirical work. *Psychological Reports*, 1968, *22*, 587–608.

CHERTOK, L., and KRAMARZ, P. Hypnosis, sleep, and electro-encephalography. *Journal of Nervous and Mental Disease*, 1959, *128*, 227–38.

COE, W. C. Hypnosis as role enactment: The role demand variable. *American Journal of Clinical Hypnosis*, 1966, 8, 189–91.

——— and SARBIN, T. R. An experimental demonstration of hypnosis as role enactment. *Journal of Abnormal Psychology*, 1966, *71*, 400–406.

COLLINS, J. K. Muscular endurance in normal and hypnotic states: A study of suggested catalepsy. Honors thesis, Dept. of Psychology, University of Sydney, 1961.

COOPER, G. W., JR., and DANA, R. H. Hypnotizability and the Maudsley Personality Inventory. *International Journal of Clinical and Experimental Hypnosis*, 1964, *12*, 28–33.

COOPER, L. M., BANFORD, S. A., SCHUBOT, E., and TART, C. T. A further attempt to modify hypnotic susceptibility through repeated individualized experience. *International Journal of Clinical and Experimental Hypnosis*, 1967, *15*, 118–24.

CRASILNECK, H. B., and HALL, J. A. Physiological changes associated with hypnosis: A review of the literature since 1948. *International Journal of Clinical and Experimental Hypnosis*, 1959, *7*, 9–50.

CRASILNECK, H. B., and MICHAEL, C. M. Performance on the Bender under hypnotic age regression. *Journal of Abnormal and Social Psychology*, 1957, *54*, 319–22.

DALAL, A. S. An empirical approach to hypnosis. *Archives of General Psychiatry*, 1966, *15*, 151–57.

DECKERT, G. H. and WEST, L. J. Hypnosis and experimental psychopathology. *American Journal of Clinical Hypnosis*, 1963a, *5*, 256–76.

——— The problem of hypnotizability: A review. *International Journal of Clinical and Experimental Hypnosis*, 1963b, *11*, 205–235.

DERMEN, D. Correlates of hypnotic susceptibility. Masters thesis, University of Illinois, 1964.

——— and LONDON, P. Correlates of hypnotic susceptibility. *Journal of Consulting Psychology*, 1965, *29*, 537–45.

DORCUS, R. M. Modification by suggestion of some vestibular and visual responses. *American Journal of Psychology*, 1937, *49*, 82–87.

——— Fallacies in predictions of susceptibility to hypnosis based upon personality characteristics. *American Journal of Clinical Hypnosis*, 1963, *5*, 163–70.

——— BRINTNALL, A. K., and CASE, H. W. Control experiments and their relation to theories of hypnotism. *Journal of General Psychology*, 1941, *24*, 217–21.

DUDEK, S. Z. Suggestion and play therapy in the cure of warts in children: A pilot study. *Journal of Nervous and Mental Disease*, 1967, *145*, 37–42.

DYNES, J. B. An experimental study of hypnotic anesthesia. *Journal of Abnormal and Social Psychology*, 1932, *27*, 79–88.

EDMONSTON, W. E., JR., and ROBERTSON, T. G., JR. A comparison of the effects of task motivational and hypnotic induction instructions on responsiveness to hypnotic suggestibility scales. *American Journal of Clinical Hypnosis*, 1967, *9*, 184–87.

ELSEA, O. C., JR. A study of the effect of hypnotic suggestion on color perception. Unpublished doctoral dissertation, University of Oklahoma, 1961.

ERICKSON, M. H. A study of clinical and experimental findings on hypnotic deafness: I. Clinical experimentation and findings. *Journal of General Psychology*, 1938a, *19*, 127–50.

——— A study of clinical and experimental findings on hypnotic deafness: II. Experimental findings with a conditioned response technique. *Journal of General Psychology*, 1938b, *19*, 151–67.

——— The induction of color blindness by a technique of hypnotic suggestion. *Journal of General Psychology*, 1939, *20*, 61–89.

——— Basic psychological problems in hypnotic research (and panel discussion). *In* G. H. Estabrooks (ed.), *Hypnosis: Current problems*. New York: Harper & Row, 1962, pp. 207–23, 238–72.

——— *Advanced techniques of hypnosis and therapy.* New York: Grune & Stratton, 1967.

——— HERSHMAN, S., AND SECTER, I. I. *The practical application of medical and dental hypnosis.* New York: Julian Press, 1961.

ESDAILE, J. *Hypnosis in medicine and surgery.* New York: Julian Press, 1957. (Original date of publication: 1850.)

EVANS, F. J., and ORNE, M. T. Motivation, performance, and hypnosis. *International Journal of Clinical and Experimental Hypnosis*, 1965, *13*, 103–16.

EYSENCK, H. J. *Dimensions of personality.* London: Routledge & Kegan Paul, 1947.

FINER, B. L., and NYLEN, B. O. Cardiac arrest in the treatment of burns, and report on hypnosis as a substitute for anesthesia. *Plastic and Reconstructive Surgery*, 1961, *27*, 49–55.

FISHER, S. The role of expectancy in the performance of post-hypnotic behavior. *Journal of Abnormal and Social Psychology*, 1954, *49*, 503–7.

——— Problems of interpretation and controls in hypnotic research. *In* G. H. Estabrooks (ed.), *Hypnosis: Current problems*, New York: Harper & Row, 1962, pp. 109–26.

FURNEAUX, W. D., and GIBSON, H. G. The Maudsley Personality Inventory as a predictor of susceptibility to hypnosis. *International Journal of Clinical and Experimental Hypnosis*, 1961, *9*, 167–76.

GERARD, R. W. General discussion of symposium. *In* L. A. Jeffress (ed.), *Cerebral mechanisms in behavior: The Hixon symposium.* New York: John Wiley, 1951, p. 94.

GIDRO-FRANK, L., and BOWERSBUCH, M. K. A study of the plantar response in hypnotic age regression. *Journal of Nervous and Mental Disease*, 1948, *107*, 443–58.

GILES, E. A cross-validation study of the Pascal technique of hypnotic induction. *International Journal of Clinical and Experimental Hypnosis*, 1962, *10*, 101–8.

GILL, M. M., and BRENMAN, M. *Hypnosis and related states.* New York: International Universities Press, 1959.

GOLDSTEIN, A. P., HELLER, K., and SECHREST, L. B. *Psychotherapy and the psychology of behavior change.* New York: John Wiley, 1966.

GORDON, J. E., and FRESTON, M. Role-playing and age regression in hypnotized and nonhypnotized subjects. *Journal of Personality*, 1964, *32*, 411–19.

GORTON, B. E. The physiology of hypnosis. *Psychiatric Quarterly*, 1949, *23*, 317–43, 457–85.

GRAHAM, K. R., and PATTON, A. Retroactive inhibition, hypnosis, and hypnotic amnesia. *International Journal of Clinical and Experimental Hypnosis*, 1968, *16*, 68–74.

GRAHAM, D. T., and WOLF, S. Pathogenesis of urticaria: Experimental study of life situations, emotions, and cutaneous vascular reactions. *Journal of the American Medical Association*, 1950, *143*, 1396–1402.

GREENLEAF, E. Developmental-stage regression through hypnosis. *American Journal of Clinical Hypnosis*, 1969, *12*, 20–36.

GRETHER, W. F. A comment on "The induction of color blindness by a technique of hypnotic suggestion." *Journal of General Psychology*, 1940, *23*, 207–10.

HAHN, K. W., JR., and BARBER, T. X. Hallucinations with and without hypnotic induction: An extension of the Brady and Levitt study. Harding, Mass.: Medfield Foundation, 1966. (Mimeo)

HAMEL, I. A. A study and analysis of the conditioned reflex. *Psychological Monographs*, 1919, *27*, (118).

HEILIZER, R. An exploration of the relationship between hypnotizability and anxiety and/or neuroticism. *Journal of Consulting Psychology*, 1960, *24*, 432–36.

HIBLER, F. W. An experimental study of positive visual hallucinations in hypnosis. Unpublished doctoral dissertation, Ohio State University, 1935.

HILGARD, E. R. *Hypnotic susceptibility.* New York: Harcourt, Brace & World, 1965.

——— Posthypnotic amnesia: Experiments and theory. *International Journal of Clinical and Experimental Hypnosis*, 1966, *14*, 104–11.

——— Pain as a puzzle for psychology and physiology. *American Psychologist*, 1969, *24*, 103–13.

——— and BENTLER, P. M. Predicting hypnotizability from the Maudsley Personality Inventory. *British Journal of Psychology*, 1963, *54*, 63–69.

HILGARD, E. R., COOPER, L. M., LENOX, J., MORGAN, A. H., and VOEVODSKY, J. The use of pain-state reports in the study of hypnotic analgesia to the pain of ice water. *Journal of Nervous and Mental Disease*, 1967, *144*, 506–13.

HILGARD, E. R.. and MARQUIS, D. G. *Conditioning and learning.* New York: Appleton-Century, 1940.

HILGARD, E. R., and TART, C. T. Responsiveness to suggestions following waking and imagination instructions and following induction of hypnosis. *Journal of Abnormal Psychology*, 1966, *71*, 196–208.

HILL, H. E., KORNETSKY, C. H.; FLANARY, H. G., and WIKLER, A. Effects of anxiety and morphine on discrimination of intensities of painful stimuli. *Journal of Clinical Investigation*, 1952a, *31*, 473–80.

——— Studies on anxiety associated with anticipation of pain: I. Effects of morphine. *Archives of Neurology and Psychiatry*, 1952b, *67*, 612–19.

HOSKOVEC, J., and HORVAI, I. Speech manifestations in hypnotic age regression. *Activitas nervosa superior*, 1963, *5*, 13–21.

IKEMI, Y. Hypnotic experiments on the psychosomatic aspects of gastrointestinal disorders. *International Journal of Clinical and Experimental Hypnosis*, 1959, *7*, 139–50.

——— and NAKAGAWA, S. A psychosomatic study of contagious dermatitis. *Kyushu Journal of Medical Science*, 1962, *13*, 335–50.

INGHAM, J. G. Body-sway suggestibility and neurosis. *Journal of Mental Science*, 1954, *100*, 432–41.

——— Psychoneurosis and suggestibility. *Journal of Abnormal and Social Psychology*, 1955, *51*, 600–603.

JACOBSON, A., KALES, A., LEHMANN, D., and ZWEIZIG, J. R. Somnambulism: All-night electroencephalographic studies. *Science*, 1965, *148*, 975–77.

JACOBSON, E. *Progressive relaxation.* Chicago: University of Chicago Press, 1938.

——— Relaxation methods in labor: A critique of current techniques in natural childbirth. *American Journal of Obstetrics and Gynecology*, 1954, *67*, 1035–48.

KALES, A., JACOBSON, A.; PAULSON, M. J., KALES, J. D., and WALTER, R. D. Somnambulism: Psychophysiological correlates: I. All-night EEG studies. *Archives of General Psychiatry*, 1966, *14*, 586–94.

KANFER, F. H., and GOLDFOOT, D. A. Self-control and tolerance of noxious stimulation. *Psychological Reports*, 1966, *18*, 79–85.

KAPLAN, E. A. Hypnosis and pain. *Archives of General Psychiatry*, 1960, 2, 567–68.

KELLEY, C. R. Psychological factors in myopia. Unpublished doctoral dissertation, New School for Social Research, 1958.

—— Psychological factors in myopia. Paper presented at American Psychological Association, Annual Meeting, New York, August 31, 1961.

KELSEY, D. E. R. Phantasies of birth and prenatal experiences recovered from patients undergoing hypnoanalysis. *Journal of Mental Science*, 1953, *99*, 216–23.

KLEMME, H. L. Heart rate response to suggestion in hypnosis. Topeka, Kansas: Veterans Administration Hospital, 1963. (Mimeo)

KLINE, M. V. Hypnosis and age progression: A case report. *Journal of Genetic Psychology*, 1951, *78*, 195–206.

——, GUZE, H., and HAGGERTY, A. D. An experimental study of the nature of hypnotic deafness: Effects of delayed speech feedback. *Journal of Clinical and Experimental Hypnosis*, 1954, *2*, 145–56.

KLINGER, B. I. The effects of peer model responsiveness and length of induction procedure on hypnotic responsiveness. Paper presented at Eastern Psychological Association, Annual Meeting, Washington, D. C., April 18, 1968.

KLOPP, K. K. Production of local anesthesia using waking suggestion with the child patient. *International Journal of Clinical and Experimental Hypnosis*, 1961, *9*, 59–62.

KORNETSKY, C. Effects of anxiety and morphine in the anticipation and perception of painful radiant heat stimuli. *Journal of Comparative and Physiological Psychology*, 1954, *47*, 130–32.

KRAMER, E. Hypnotic susceptibility and previous relationship with the hypnotist. *American Journal of Clinical Hypnosis*, 1969, *11*, 175–77.

—— and TUCKER, G. R. Hypnotically suggested deafness and delayed auditory feedback. *International Journal of Clinical and Experimental Hypnosis*, 1967, *15*, 37–43.

KROGER, W. S. *Clinical and experimental hypnosis.* Philadelphia: Lippincott, 1963.

—— and DELEE, S. T. Use of hypnoanesthesia for caesarean section and hysterectomy. *Journal of the American Medical Association*, 1957, *163*, 442–44.

LANG, P. J., and LAZOVIK, A. D. Personality and hypnotic susceptibility. *Journal of Consulting Psychology*, 1962, *26*, 317–22.

LEONARD, J. R. An investigation of hypnotic age-regression. Unpublished doctoral dissertation, University of Kentucky, 1963.

—— Hypnotic age regression: A test of the functional ablation hypothesis. *Journal of Abnormal Psychology*, 1965, *70*, 266–69.

LEVITT, E. E., and BRADY, J. P. Psychophysiology of hypnosis. *In* J. M. Schneck (ed.), *Hypnosis in modern medicine* (3d ed.). Springfield, Ill.: Charles C Thomas, 1963, pp. 314–62.

—— Muscular endurance under hypnosis and in the motivated waking state. *International Journal of Clinical and Experimental Hypnosis*, 1964, *12*, 21–27.

LEWIS, J. H., and SARBIN, T. R. Studies in psychosomatics: I. The influence of hypnotic stimulation on gastric hunger contractions. *Psychosomatic Medicine*, 1943, *5*, 125–31.

LEWIS, T. *The blood vessels of the human skin and their responses.* London: Shaw, 1927.

LIEBEAULT, A. A. Anesthesie par suggestion. *Journal Magnestisme*, 1885, 64–67.

LIFE, C. The effects of practice in the trance upon learning in the normal waking state. Bachelor's thesis, University of Wisconsin, 1929.

LOGAN, W. G. Delay of premature labor by the use of hypnosis. *American Journal of Clinical Hypnosis*, 1963, *5*, 209–11.

LONDON, P. Subject characteristics in hypnosis research: I. A survey of experience, interest, and opinion. *International Journal of Clinical and Experimental Hypnosis*, 1961, *9*, 151–61.

——, CONANT, M., and DAVISON, G. C. More hypnosis in the unhypnotizable: Effects of hypnosis and exhortation on rote learning. *Journal of Personality*, 1966, *34*, 71–79.

LONDON, P., COOPER, L. M., and JOHNSON, H. J. Subject characteristics in hypnosis research: II. Attitudes toward hypnosis, volunteer status, and personality measures. III. Some correlates of hypnotic susceptibility. *International Journal of Clinical and Experimental Hypnosis*, 1962, *10*, 13–21.

LONDON, P., and FUHRER, M. Hypnosis, motivation, and performance. *Journal of Personality*, 1961, *29*, 321–33.

LOOMIS, A. L., HARVEY, E. N., and HOBART, G. Electrical potentials of the human brain. *Journal of Experimental Psychology*, 1936, *19*, 249–79.

LUCKHARDT, A. B., and JOHNSTON, R. L. Studies in gastric secretions: I. The psychic secretion of gastric juice under hypnosis. *American Journal of Physiology*, 1924, *70*, 174–82.

MCGLASHAN, T. H., EVANS, F. J., and ORNE, M. T. The nature of hypnotic analgesia and placebo response to experimental pain. *Psychosomatic Medicine*, 1969, *31*, 227–46.

MCGRAW, M. B. Development of the plantar response in young infants. *American Journal Diseases of Children*, 1941, *61*, 1215–21.

MCPEAKE, J. D. Hypnosis, suggestions, and psychosomatics. *Diseases of the Nervous System*, 1968, *29*, 536–44.

MALMO, R. B., BOAG, T. J., and RAGINSKY, B. B. Electromyographic study of hypnotic deafness. *Journal of Clinical and Experimental Hypnosis*, 1954, *2*, 305–17.

MARMER, M. J. *Hypnosis in anesthesiology.* Springfield, Ill.: Charles C Thomas, 1959.

MASON, A. A. A case of congenital ichthyosiform erythrodermia of Brocq treated by hypnosis. *British Medical Journal*, 1952, *2*, 422–23.

MEARES, A. *A system of medical hypnosis.* Philadelphia: Saunders, 1960.

MEEKER, W. B., and BARBER, T. X. Stage hypnosis: Fact and fiction. Harding, Mass.: Medfield Foundation, 1969. (Mimeo)

MELEI, J. P., and HILGARD, E. R. Attitudes toward hypnosis, self-predictions, and hypnotic susceptibility. *International Journal of Clinical and Experimental Hypnosis*, 1964, *12*, 99–108.

MEMMESCHEIMER, A. M., and EISENLOHR, E. Untersuchungen über die Suggestivebehandlung der Warzen. *Dermatologie Zeitschrift*, 1931, *62*, 63–68.

MESEL, E., and LEDFORD, F. F., JR. The electroencephalogram during hypnotic age regression (to infancy) in epileptic patients. *Archives of Neurology*, 1959, *1*, 516–21.

MILGRAM, S. Behavioral study of obedience. *Journal of Abnormal and Social Psychology*, 1963, *67*, 371–78.

MILLER, R. J., BERGEIM, O., REHFUSS, M. E., and HAWK, P. B. Gastric response to food: X. The psychic secretion of gastric juice in normal men. *American Journal of Physiology*, 1920, *52*, 1–27.

MITCHELL, M. B. Retroactive inhibition and hypnosis. *Journal of General Psychology*, 1932, *7*, 343–58.

MOLL, A. *The study of hypnotism.* New York: Julian Press, 1958. (Orginal date of publication: 1889.)

NARUSE, G. Hypnosis as a state of meditative concentration and its relationship to the perceptual process. *In* M. V. Kline (ed.), *The nature of hypnosis.* New York: Institute for Research in Hypnosis, 1962, pp. 37–55.

NICHOLS, D. C. A reconceptualization of the concept of hypnosis. *In* S. Lesse (ed.), *An evaluation of the results of the psychotherapies.* Springfield, Ill.: Charles C. Thomas, 1968, chap. 11.

ORNE, M. T. The mechanism of hypnotic age regression: An experimental study. *Journal of Abnormal and Social Psychology*, 1951, *46*, 213–25.

—— The nature of hypnosis: Artifact and essence. *Journal of Abnormal and Social Psychology*, 1959, *58*, 277–99.

—— On the mechanisms of posthypnotic amnesia. *International Journal of Clinical and Experimental Hypnosis*, 1966, *14*, 121–34.

—— and EVANS, F. J. Social control in the psychological experiment: Antisocial behavior and hypnosis. *Journal of Personality and Social Psychology*, 1965, *1*, 189–200.

OWEN-FLOOD, A. Hypnosis in anesthesiology. *In* J. M. Schneck (ed.), *Hypnosis in modern medicine* (2nd ed.), Springfield, Ill.: Charles C Thomas, 1959, pp. 89–100.

PAI, M. N. Sleep-walking and sleep activities. *Journal of Mental Science*, 1946, *92*, 756–62.

PARRISH, M., LUNDY, R. M., and LEIBOWITZ, H. W. Hypnotic age regression and magnitudes of the Ponzo and Poggendorff illusions. *Science*, 1968, *159*, 1375–76.

PATTEN, E. F. Does post-hypnotic amnesia apply to practice effects? *Journal of General Psychology*, 1932, *7*, 196–201.

PATTIE, F. A. A report of attempts to produce uniocular blindness by hypnotic suggestion. *British Journal of Medical Psychology*, 1935, *15*, 230–41.

—— The production of blisters by hypnotic suggestions: A review. *Journal of Abnormal and Social Psychology*, 1941, *36*, 62–72.

—— The genuineness of unilateral deafness produced by hypnosis. *American Journal of Psychology*, 1950, *63*, 84–86.

—— Methods of induction, susceptibility of subjects, and criteria of hypnosis. *In* R. M. Dorcus (ed.), *Hypnosis and its therapeutic applications*. New York: McGraw-Hill, 1956*a*, chap. 2.

—— Theories of hypnosis. *In* R. M. Dorcus (ed.), *Hypnosis and its therapeutic applications*. New York: McGraw-Hill, 1956*b*, chap. 1.

PAUL, G. L. The production of blisters by hypnotic suggestion: Another look. *Psychosomatic Medicine*, 1963, *25*, 233–44.

REIFF, R., and SCHEERER, M. *Memory and hypnotic age regression*. New York: International Universities Press, 1959.

RHOADES, C. D., and EDMONSTON, W. E., JR. Personality correlates of hypnotizability: A study using the Harvard Group Scale of Hypnotic Susceptibility, the 16-PF, and the IPAT. *American Journal of Clinical Hypnosis*, 1969, *11*, 228–33.

RICE, F. G. The hypnotic induction of labor: Six cases. *American Journal of Clinical Hypnosis*, 1961, *4*, 119–22.

RICHMAN, D. N. A critique of two recent theories of hypnosis: The psychoanalytic theory of Gill and Brenman contrasted with the behavioral theory of Barber. *Psychiatric Quarterly*, 1965, *39*, 278–92.

ROCK, N. L., and SHIPLEY, T. Ability to "fake" color blindness in the waking state: A control for suggested color blindness under hypnosis. Philadelphia: Dept. of Psychiatry, Temple University Medical Center, 1961. (Mimeo)

ROSENBERG, M. J. A disconfirmation of the description of hypnosis as a dissociated state. *International Journal of Clinical and Experimental Hypnosis*, 1959, *7*, 187–204.

ROSENHAN, D. On the social psychology of hypnosis research. *In* J. E. Gordon (ed.), *Handbook of clinical and experimental hypnosis*. New York: Macmillan, 1967, pp. 481–510.

—— and LONDON, P. Hypnosis: expectation, susceptibility, and performance. *Journal of Abnormal and Social Psychology*, 1963, *66*, 77–81.

ROSENHAN, D. L., and TOMKINS, S. S. On preference for hypnosis and hypnotizability. *International Journal of Clinical and Experimental Hypnosis*, 1964, *12*, 109–14.

ROSENTHAL, R. Experimenter expectancy and the reassuring nature of the null hypothesis decision procedure. *Psychological Bulletin*, 1968, *70*, (6, pt. 2), 30–47.

RUBENSTEIN, R., and NEWMAN, R. The living out of "future" experiences under hypnosis. *Science*, 1954, *119*, 472–73.

SACHS, L. B., and ANDERSON, W. L. Modification of hypnotic susceptibility. *International Journal of Clinical and Experimental Hypnosis*, 1967, *15*, 172–80.

SARBIN, T. R. Contributions to role-taking theory: I. Hypnotic behavior. *Psychological Review*, 1950*a*, *57*, 255–70.

—— Mental changes in experimental regression. *Journal of Personality*, 1950*b*, *19*, 221–28.

—— Physiological effects of hypnotic stimulation. *In* R. M. Dorcus (ed.), *Hypnosis and its therapeutic applications*. New York: McGraw-Hill, 1956, chap. 4.

—— Role theoretical interpretation of psychological change. *In* P. Worchel and D. Byrne (eds.), *Personality change*. New York: John Wiley, 1964, pp. 176–219.

—— and ANDERSEN, M. L. Base-rate expectancies and perceptual alterations in hypnosis. *British Journal of Social and Clinical Psychology*, 1963, *2*, 112–21.

SARBIN, T. R., and FARBEROW, N. L. Contributions to role-taking theory: A clinical study of self and role. *Journal of Abnormal and Social Psychology*, 1952, *47*, 117–25.

SARBIN, T. R., and LIM, D. T. Some evidence in support of the role-taking hypothesis in hypnosis. *International Journal of Clinical and Experimental Hypnosis*, 1963, *11*, 98–103.

SCHEIBE, K. E., GRAY, A. L., and KEIM, C. S. Hypnotically induced deafness and delayed auditory feedback: A comparison of real and simulating subjects. *International Journal of Clinical and Experimental Hypnosis*, 1968, *16*, 158–64.

SCHRENCK-NOTZING, A. F. Ein experimenteller und kritischer Beitrag zur Frage des suggestiven Hervorrufung circumscripter vasomo-torischer Veränderungen auf der aüsseren Haut. *Zeitschrift Hypnotismus*, 1896, *4*, 209.

SCHWARTZ, M. M. The cessation of labor using hypnotic techniques. *American Journal of Clinical Hypnosis*, 1963, *5*, 211–13.

SECTER, I. I. An investigation of hypnotizability as a function of attitude toward hypnosis. *American Journal of Clinical Hypnosis*, 1960, *3*, 75–89.

SHAFFER, G. W. Discussion of paper by W. D. Furneaux. *In* M. V. Kline (ed.), *The nature of hypnosis*. New York: Institute for Research in Hypnosis, 1962, pp. 15–17.

SHOR, R. E. Physiological effects of painful stimulation during hypnotic analgesia. *In* J. E. Gordon (ed.), *Handbook of clinical and experimental hypnosis*. New York: Macmillan, 1967, pp. 511–49.

——, ORNE, M. T., and O'CONNELL, D. N. Validation and cross-validation of a scale of self-reported personal experiences which predicts hypnotizability. *Journal of Psychology*, 1962, *53*, 55–75.

—— Psychological correlates of plateau hypnotizability in a special volunteer sample. *Journal of Personality and Social Psychology*, 1966, *3*, 80–95.

SHOR, R. E., and SCHATZ, J. A critical note on Barber's case-study of "Subject J." *Journal of Psychology*, 1960, *50*, 253–56.

SIDIS, B. Are there hypnotic hallucinations? *Psychological Review*, 1906, *13*, 239–57.

SINCLAIR-GIEBEN, A. H. C., and CHALMERS, D. Evaluation of treatment of warts by hypnosis. *Lancet*, 1959, *2*, 480–82.

SLOTNICK, R., and LONDON, P. Influence of instructions on hypnotic and nonhypnotic performance. *Journal of Abnormal Psychology*, 1965, *70*, 38–46.

SPANOS, N. P., and BARBER, T. X. "Hypnotic" experiences as inferred from subjective reports: auditory and visual hallucinations. *Journal of Experimental Research in Personality*, 1968, *3*, 136–50.

—— A second attempted replication of the Parrish-Lundy-Leibowitz study on hypnotic age regression. Harding, Mass.: Medfield Foundation, 1969. (Mimeo)

—— and LANG, G. Effects of hypnotic induction, suggestions of analgesia, and demands for honesty on subjective reports of pain. Department of Sociology, Boston University, 1969. (Mimeo)

STAPLES, E. A., and WILENSKY, H. A controlled Rorschach investigation of hypnotic age regression. *Journal of Projective Techniques and Personality Assessment*, 1968, *32*, 246–52.

STURROCK, J. B. Objective assessment of hypnotic amnesia. Paper presented at Eastern Psychological Association, Annual Meeting, New York, April 15, 1966.

SULZBERGER, M. B., and WOLF, J. The treatment of warts by suggestion. *Medical Record*, 1934, *140*, 552–57.

SUTCLIFFE, J. P. "Credulous" and "sceptical" views of hypnotic phenomena: A review of certain evidence and methodology. *International Journal of Clinical and Experimental Hypnosis*, 1960, *8*, 73–101.

—— "Credulous" and "skeptical" views of hypnotic phenomena: experiments in esthesia, hallucination, and delusion. *Journal of Abnormal and Social Psychology*, 1961, *62*, 189–200.

TAUGHER, V. J. Hypno-anesthesia. *Wisconsin Medical Journal*, 1958, *57*, 95–96.

TAYLOR, A. The differentiation between simulated and true hypnotic regression by figure drawings. Masters thesis, College of the City of New York, 1950.

THORN, W. A. F. A study of the correlates of dissociation as measured by post-hypnotic amnesia. Paper presented at British Psychological Society, Australian Overseas Branch, Sydney, August, 1961.

THORNE, D. E. Is the hypnotic trance necessary for performance of hypnotic phenomena? *Journal of Abnormal Psychology*, 1967*a*, *72*, 233–39.

—— Memory as related to hypnotic suggestion, procedure, and susceptibility. Unpublished doctoral dissertation, University of Utah, 1967*b*.

TIMNEY, B. N., and BARBER, T. X. Hypnotic induction and oral temperature. *International Journal of Clinical and Experimental Hypnosis*, 1969, *17*, 121–32.

TINTEROW, M. M. The use of hypnoanalgesia in the relief of intractable pain. *American Surgeon*, 1960, *26*, 30–34.

TROFFER, S. A. H. Hypnotic age regression and cognitive functioning. Unpublished doctoral dissertation, Stanford University, 1966.

TRUE, R. M. Experimental control in hypnotic age regression states. *Science*, 1949, *110*, 583–84.

ULLMAN, M. Herpes simplex and second degree burn induced under hypnosis. *American Journal of Psychiatry*, 1947, *103*, 828–30.

—— and DUDEK, S. On the psyche and warts: II. Hypnotic suggestion and warts. *Psychosomatic Medicine*, 1960, *22*, 68–76.

UNDERWOOD, H. W. The validity of hypnotically induced visual hallucinations. *Journal of Abnormal and Social Psychology*, 1960, *61*, 39–46.

VOLLMER, H. Treatment of warts by suggestion. *Psychosomatic Medicine*, 1946, *8*, 138–42.

WATKINS, J. G. Symposium on posthypnotic amnesia: discussion. *International Journal of Clinical and Experimental Hypnosis*, 1966, *14*, 139–49.

WEITZENHOFFER, A. M. *Hypnotism: An objective study in suggestibility.* New York: John Wiley, 1953.

—— *General techniques of hypnotism.* New York: Grune & Stratton, 1957.

—— and SJOBERG, B. M., JR. Suggestibility with and without "induction of hypnosis." *Journal of Nervous and Mental Disease*, 1961, *132*, 204–20.

WELLS, W. R. Experiments in waking hypnosis for instructional purposes. *Journal of Abnormal and Social Psychology*, 1924, *18*, 389–404.

WHITE, R. W. A preface to the theory of hypnotism. *Journal of Abnormal and Social Psychology*, 1941, *36*, 477–505.

WILLIAMS, G. W. Difficulty in dehypnotizing. *Journal of Clinical and Experimental Hypnosis*, 1953, *1*, 3–12.

WILLIAMSEN, J. A., JOHNSON, H. J., and ERIKSEN, C. W. Some characteristics of posthypnotic amnesia. *Journal of Abnormal Psychology*, 1965, *70*, 123–31.

WILSON, D. L. The role of confirmation of expectancies in hypnotic induction. Unpublished doctoral dissertation, University of North Carolina, 1967.

WINK, C. A. S. Congenital ichthyosiform erythrodermia treated by hypnosis: Report of two cases. *British Medical Journal*, 1961, *2*, 741–43.

WOLBERG, L. R. *Medical hypnosis*, vol. 1: *The principles of hypnotherapy.* New York: Grune & Stratton, 1948.

WOLF, S. and WOLFF, H. G. *Human gastric function: An experimental study of a man and his stomach* (2nd ed.). New York: Oxford University Press, 1947.

WOLFF, L. V. The response to plantar stimulation in infancy. *American Journal Diseases of Children*, 1930, *39*, 1176–85.

YATES, A. J. Simulation and hypnotic age regression. *International Journal of Clinical and Experimental Hypnosis*, 1960, *8*, 243–49.

YEAGER, C. L. and LARSON, A. L. A study of alpha desynchronization in the electroencephalogram utilizing hypnosis. Paper presented at American Electroencephalographic Society, Annual Meeting, Santa Fe, October, 1957.

YOUNG, P. C. Hypnotic regression—fact or artifact? *Journal of Abnormal and Social Psychology*, 1940, *35*, 273–78.

Indexes

Author Index

NOTE: References to authors' articles are in **boldface,** bibliographical references are in *italics.*

Eguchi, S., 300, *305*
Egyházi, E., 181, *186*
Ehmann, E. D., 555, *566*
Ehmer, B, J., 600, *615*
Ehrenberg, B., 835, 837, *856*
Ehrenfeld, D. W., 868, *902*
Ehrenfels, C. von, 421, 422, *445*
Ehrlich, D. J., 727, *731*
Eibl-Eibesfeldt, I., 708, *719*, 868, *902*
Eichelman, W. H., 406, *418*
Eicholz, G., 595n, *616*
Eiduson, B. T., 873, 876, 877, 887, 891, *902*
Eijkman, Ē., 72, *87*
Eimas, P. D., 581, *617*
Einstein, A., 11, 24, 25, 28, 29, 31, 34, 35, 41, 42, 44, 46, 454, 821
Eisdorfer, C., 895, 897, *902, 906, 909*
Eisenberg, K., 608, *620*
Eisenberg, L., 489, *617*
Eisenberg, R. B., 873, *902*
Eisenhower, D. D., 139
Eisenlohr, E., 950, *961*
Eisler, H., 71, 72, *87*
Eisman, Z., 474, *480*
Eissler, K. R., 891, *903*
Ekman, G., 72, 74, *87*, 281, 284, *305, 370, 377*
Ekstein, R., 873, *900*
Ekstrand, B. R., 560, *566*, 604, 605, *617*
Ekstrand, R. D., 539, *543*
Elashoff, J. D., 100, *106*
Elder, G. H., 889, *903*
Elder, J. H., 491, *499*
Eldredge, D. H., 358, 359, *377, 380*
Eleftheriou, B. E., 715, *719*
Elias, P., 290, *305*
Elkind, D., 877, 882, 886, 888, *903*
Elkind, J. I., 191, *202*
Elkind, S., 888, *903*
El-Koussy, M. A. H., 635n, *643*
Ellenberger, H. F., 824
Elliott, D. S., 887, *903*
Elliott, K. A. C., 166, *186*
Elliott, L. L., 364, *377*
Elliott, P. B., 298, *305*
Ellis, A., 779, *790*
Ellis, B., 68, 74, *87*
Ellis, F. W., 261, *267*
Ellis, H. C., 569, 612, *617*
Ellis, M. J., 196, *202, 203*
Ellison, G. D., 193, *203*, 724, *731*
Ellson, D. G., 191, *203*, 495
Elsea, O. C., Jr., 947, *960*
Emerson, P. E., 878, 879, *913*
Emery, N., 171, 172, *186*
Emmerich, 292
Emmons, W. H., 742, *747*
Engebretson, A. M., 359, *377*
Engel, B. T., 253, *271*
Engel, E., 432, 433, *445*, 824
Engel, G. L., 246, 248, 252, 253, 257, 264, *268*
Engelmann, S., 882, *899*
Engelmann, T. G., 737, *746*
Engen, T., 72, *87*, 284, *305*, 873, *903*
Enterline, P. E., 264, *271*
Entwisle, D. R., 596, 600, 601, *617*
Ephron, H. S., 743, *746*
Epicurus, 6, 693
Epstein, A., 372, *377*, 721, *733*
Epstein, L. H., 410, *418*
Epstein, S., 389, *393, 703*
Epstein, W., 406, *416*, 537, *541*
Erdelyi, M. H., 833, *852*
Ericksen, C. W., 151, *161*, 403, *416*, 427, *445*, 593–95, *617*, 826, 828, 829, 831–34, *850, 852, 853*
Erickson, J. R., 555, *566*

Erickson, M. H., 943–45, 948–49, *960*
Erickson, R. P., 384
Ericson, R. A., 797
Eriksen, C., 830, *851*
Erikson, A. W., 221, *226*
Erikson, C. W., 948, *963*
Erikson, E. H., 651, *653*, 872, 875, 879, 881, 883, 884, 887, 888, 890, 892, 896, 897, *903*
Erlenmeyer-Kimling, L., 221, *226*, 648, *653*
Ernest, E., 233, *239*
Ernhart, C. B., 649, *654*, 784, 786, 790
Erofeeva, M., 487, *498*
Eren, L. D., 591, *629*
Ervin, S., 606, *623*
Ervin, S. M., 589, *617, 621*, 878, 881, *903*
Ervin-Tripp, S. M., 577, *617*, 882, *903*
Escalona, S. K., 661, 669, 873–77, 879, *899, 903*
Esdaile, J., 945, *960*
Esper, A., 569, *617*
Esper, E. A., 570, 577, 611, *617*
Esposito, N. J., 598, *617*
Esquirol, J. E. D., 657, *669*
Essen-Möller, E., 219, *226*
Estes, W. K., 12, 14, *20*, 43, 44, *46*, 129, 139, 143, 151–53, *161*, 456, *460*, 477, *480*, 486, *498*, 502, 503, 508, *513*, 676n, *703*
Estess, B. D., 391, *393*
Evans, C. R., 743, *746*
Evans, E. F., 360, *377*, 407, *416*
Evans, F. J., 945, 951, 952, *961*
Evans, J. N., 877, *903*
Evans, R. I., 509, *513*
Evans, W. O., 412, *417*
Evarts, E. V., 734, *746*
Everett, G. M., 715, *719*
Ewen, R. B., 934, 937, *941*
Ewer, R. F., 866, *903*
Ewing, A. W. G., 873, *903*
Ewing, I. R., 873, *903*
Ewing, J. A., 263, *270*
Eyde, L. D., 897, *917*
Eysenck, H. J., 216, 218, 220–22, *226, 269*, 390, 408, *416, 417*, 505, *513*, 667, 683, 702n, *703*, 786, *790*, 796, 797, 799, 805, 809, 814, 843, *850, 855, 960*

Fabricus, E., 869, *903*
Fadeyeva, 493
Faegre, M. L., 737, *746*
Fagot, R. F., 74, *86*
Fahey, G. L., 882, *903*
Failla, G., 894, *903*
Fain, M., 260, *268*
Fairbanks, G., 580, *620*
Fairbanks, H., 588
Falconer, D. S., *226*
Falek, A., 222, *226*
Falk, J. L., 721, 725, 726, *731, 732*
Falk, M., 892, 896, *910*
Falkner, F., 236, 237, *239*
Falstein, E. I., 883, *903*
Fanning, E. A., 237, *239*
Fanshell, A. M., 896, *908*
Fant, C. G. M., 575, 579, 580, *617*
Fant, G., 571n, 573–76, 579, 580, *617, 620*
Fant, L. H., 569, *617*
Fantz, R. L., 873, 877, *903*
Faraday, M., 454
Farber, I. E., 690, *704*
Farber, J. E., 685, 691, *703*
Farberow, N. L., 947, *962*
Farley, B. G., 118, *121*

Faroqi, M. A., 366, *377*
Farrell, J., 855
Farrow, J. T., 181–82, *187*
Fata, J., 569, *628*
Faterson, H. F., 841, *857*
Faulkner, W., 139
Faust, M. W., 885, *903*
Faust, W. L., 926, *931*
Fea, H. R., 590, *626*
Feallock, J. B., 533, *541*
Feather, N. T., 682, *703, 704*
Fechner, G. T., 69, 71, 72, 275–78, 282, 283, *305*, 674, 735
Feder, W., 445, 526, 830, *852*
Fehrer, E. V., 445, 446, 522
Feider, A., 172, *186*
Feifel, H., 897, *903*
Feigenbaum, E. A., 119, 120, *121*, 455, *460*
Feigl, H., 23, 27. 34, 37, 43–45, *46, 48*, 431, *445*, 699n
Feinberg, I., 738, *746*
Feinberg, L. D., 601, *617*
Feinberg. M. R., 936, *941*
Feinstein, B., 853
Feirstein, A., 845, 846, 849, 850
Feldberg, W., 171, 173, *185*
Feldman, A. S., 354, *377*
Feldman, J., 119, 120, *121*, 455, *460*
Feldman, M., 586, *622*
Feldman, S. M., 253, *267*
Feldstein, A., 180, *186*
Feldtkeller, R., 365, *377*
Feller, W., 56, *65*
Fellman, J., 221, *226*
Fellows, E. J., 182, *185*
Fenchel, G. H., 841, *850, 851*
Fender, D., 326, 327, *328*
Fendrick, P., 408, *416*
Fenichel, O., 244
Fenress, J. C., 868, *903*
Feré, C. S., *416*
Ferenczi, S., 246, *268*
Ferguson, 78
Ferguson, G. W., 709, *719*
Ferguson, L. R., 879, 881–82, 893, *903, 905*
Fernandez, C., 357, 359, *377*
Fernold, G. M., 659, *669*
Ferris, E. B., 217
Ferster, C. B., 465, *480*, 486, *491*, 503, 505, 506, 509, *513*
Feshbach, S., 391, 392, *393*, 920, *930*
Festinger, L., *20*, 200, *203*, 694, 701, 702n, *704*, 842, *851*, 922, 927, *930*
Feyerabend, P. K., 24, *46*
Fex, J., 289, *305*
Ficks, L., 368, *379*
Field, J., 40, 41, *46*
Field, S., 455, *460*
Field, W. H., 532, *541*
Fieandt, K. V., 430, *445*
Figge, F. H. J., 353, *380*
Filer, R. N., 897, *903*
Fillenbaum, S., 598, 599, *617, 851*
Finer, B. L., 945, *960*
Fingarette, H. A., 777, 823, *824*
Fink, M., *185*, 493
Finkelman, J. M., **933–41**
Finkelman, M., 935, *941*
Finley, K. H., 649, *653*
Finn, J. D., 101, *106*, 117, *121*
Fiorentini, A., 289, *305*
Firestone, F. A., 363, *376*
Fisch, U., 354, *377*
Fischer, G. J., 473, *480*
Fischer, J. W., 594, *628*
Fishbein, M., 569, *617*, 893, *903*
Fisher, A. E., 172, *185*

Fisher, C., *268*, 723, *731*, 739, 743, 745, 746, 833, 835–38, 840, *851, 854, 855*
Fisher, H. G., 352, *377*
Fisher, M. B., 885, *903*
Fisher, M. S., 882, *903*
Fisher, R. A., 97, 105, *106*, 207, 640, 643
Fisher, S., 943, 946, *960*
Fishman, J. A., 569, *617*
Fisichelli, V. R., 577, *617*
Fiske, D. W., 79, *86*, 478, *480*, 780, *790*, 922, *930*, 935, *941*
Fiss, H., 834, 836, 837, *851, 856*
Fitts, P. M., 188, 189, 191, 192, 194, 195, 197–201, *202, 203, 205*, 400, 401, *416*
Fitzgerald, L. F., 649, *653*
Fitzhugh, R., 290, *305*, 325, *329*
Fitzsimons, J. T., 723, *731*
Fitzsimons, T., 726, *731*
Fitzwater, M. E., 489, *498*
Fivel, M. W., 556, *567*
Flacks, R., 889, *903*
Flagg, W., 260, *267*
Flanagan, J., 666
Flanagan, J. C. 779, *790*
Flanagan, J. L., 357, *377*, 573–76, 579, 580, *617*
Flanary, H. G., 946, *960*
Flanders, J. P., 526, *528*
Flavell, J. H., 10, *20*, 601, *617*, 882, *903*
Fleck, F. S., 426, *447*
Fleishman, E. A., 190–94, 199, *203*, 204, 639, *643*
Fleming, C. W., 585, *629*
Fleming, R. M., 169, *185*
Flemming, B. M., 737, *746*
Fletcher, H., *305*, 364, *377*, 575, 582, *618*
Flexner, J. B., 183, 184, *185*
Flexner, L. B., 183, 184, *185, 541*
Flint, B., 877, 880, *903*
Flory, C. D., 238, *239*
Flottorp, G., 364, 365, *381*
Floyd, R. L., 497, *618*
Fodor, J. A., 612, *614*
Foley, J. P., 602, 612, 613, *616*
Folkins, C., 586, *618*
Foll, C. V., 233, 238, *239*
Fonda, C., 828, 831, *853*
Forbes, A., 435, *445*
Forbes, B. G., 232, *239*
Forbes, R. B., 868, *903*
Ford, A., 408, *416*
Ford, C. S., 886, *903*
Ford, D. F., 585, *615*
Forehand, G. A., 845, *851*
Forgays, D. G., 870, *903*
Form, W. H., 892, *910*
Forrest, D., 829, *851, 856*
Forrin, B., 400, *417*
Forsmann, H., 216, *226*
Forster, F. M., 873, *901*
Forster, K. I., 609, *618*
Fortune, R. F., 737, *746*
Foss, D. J., *618*
Foss, M., 9n, *20*, 258
Foulkes, D., 741, *747*
Foulkes, W. D., 734, 741, *746*
Fourier, 318
Fowler, H., 195, 477, *480*, 691, 702n, *704*
Fowler, M., 577, *618*
Fowler, W., 877, 882, *903*
Fox, H. M., 262, *268*
Fox, M., 836, 838n, *851*
Fox, M. W., 867n, *903*
Fox, S. S., 478, *480*
Fox, W. C., 71, *88*, 290, *305*
Fraiberg, S., 881, *903*
Franchi, C. M., 176, *185*

Francis, W. N., 588, 606, *621*
Francis-Williams, J., *618*
Frank, G. H., 920, *930*
Frank, L. K., 876, *903*
Frank, P., 27–29, 34, *46*
Frank, S., 589, *617*
Frankel, G., 777, *790*
Frankel, V. E., 695n, *704*
Frankenhaeuser, M., 170, 172, *187*
Frankl, L., 877, *903*
Frankl, V., 818, *824*
Franklin, R. R., 874, *902*
Frankmann, S., 411, *416*
Franks, J. A., 295, 296, *306*
Fraser, C., 582, 606, 607, 608, *615*, *618*, *900*
Frazier, A., 885, *903*
Frazier, E. F., 893, *903*
Frederiksen, N., 781, *790*, 847, *851*
Freedman, D. G., 648, *653*, 876, *903*
Freedman, J. L., 928, *930*
Freedman, S. J., 352, *377*
Freedy, A. F., 411, *417*
Freeman, E. H., 265, *268*
Freeman, F. N., 190, 201, *203*, 210, 221, *228*, 407, *416*, 584, 585, *618*
Freeman, F. S., 644, *654*
Freeman, G. L., 692, 696, 700, 701, *704*
Freeman, J. T., 890, *903*
Freeman, W. H., 356, 357, *377*
French, G. M., 474, 478, *480*
French, J. P., 250, *268*
French, J. R. P., Jr., 927, *930*
French, J. W., 848, *851*
French, N. R., 577, 588, 606, *618*
French, T. M., 260, *269*, 679n, *704*
Frenkel, E., 891, 893, 895, *903*
Frenkel-Brunswik, E., 14, *20*, 304, 424, 427–31, *444*, *704*, 842n, 843, 844n, *851*, 929
Freston, M., 947, *960*
Freud, S., 6, 24, 36, 37, 39–45, *46*, 242, 244, 246, 255, 256, 259, 260, 387, 391, *393*, 677–80, 682, 685–89, 692–96, 699, 701, *704*, 728, *731*, 795, 817, 818, 833, 839, *851*, 862–63, 874, 877, 891, *903*
Freyberger, H., *269*
Frick, 13
Fricke, J., E. 363, *377*
Fried, C., 407, *416*, 534, *541*
Fried, R. L., 238, *239*
Friedenberg, E. Z., 883, 887, *903*
Friedlander, B. Z., 878, *903*
Friedman, E. A., 587, *623*
Friedman, H., *903*
Friedman, M. P. *161*, 288, 289, *304*, 363, *376*
Friedman, R., 892, *903*
Friedman, S., 833, 836, *851*
Friedman, S. B., 253, 260, 263, *268*
Friedmann, E. A., 892, *903*
Fries, C. C., 569, 606, *618*
Fries, H. S., 583, *628*
Fries, M., 874, 875, *903*
Fritzky, F. J., *854*
Fritzler, D., 834n, 838, *855*
Froebel, F., 862
Froehlich, H. P., 892, *904*
Fromkin, V., 574, *618*
Fromm, E., 39, 817, 819, *824*
Frommer, F. D., 882, *899*
Fry, A., 341, *347*
Fry, C., 257, *269*
Fry, D. B., 577, *618*
Fry, E. I., 236, *239*
Fry, G. A., 383, *384*

Fryer, D. H., 936, *941*
Fuchs, A. H., 191, *204*
Fuhrer, M., 952, 955, *961*
Fujimara, O., 580, *618*
Fujisaki, H., 575, *614*
Fulkerson, S. C., 781, 783, *790*
Fuller, F. F., 113, *121*
Fuller, J. L., 206, 207, 209, 210, 212–15 *226*, *228*, *229*, 711, 713, *719*, 867, 870, *904*, *913*
Furchtgott, E., 869, *904*
Furneaux, W. D., 955, *960*
Furth, H. G., 527, *528*, 568, *618*
Fuxe, K., 169, 176, *186*

Gaarder, K., 743, *746*, 844, *855*
Gadlin, W., 837, *851*
Gaier, E. P., 608, *618*
Gaeth, J. H., *618*
Gagné, R. M., 485, 486, *498*, 558, 565, *566*, 613, *618*
Gaito, J., 180, 181, 184, *185*, 840 *851*
Gaitonde, M. R., 265, *268*
Gakkel, L. B., *498*
Galambos, R., 289, *305*, 359, 360, *377*, *378*
Galanter, E. H., 10, 15, *21*, 72 87, *162*, 190, 200, *204*, 393, 539, *542*, 767, *771*
Galen, 242
Galileo, 4, 5, 7, 16, 22, 24, 25
Galin, D., 252, *268*
Gallagher, J. W., 593, 594, *618*
Gallup, G., 809
Galton, F., 6, 207, 569, *618*, 630–31, *643*, 657, *669*
Gannon, R. P., 359, *378*, *379*
Gardiner, A. H., 570, *618*
Gardiner, H. M., 749, 750, *770*
Gardner, B. T., 867, *904*
Gardner, D. B., 880–82, *904*
Gardner, G. E., 883, *904*
Gardner, L. L., *46*
Gardner, R. A., 564, *566*, 567, *904*
Gardner, R. W., 390, *394*, 414, 842–49, *851*, *852*, *853*
Garma, A., 246, *268*
Garn, S. M., 237, *239*
Garner, W. R., 284, *305*, 362, 368, 376, *378*, *379*, 400, 401, 407, *416*, *418*, 422, 427, *445*, 537, *541*, *543*, 577, *618*, 830, *851*
Garside, H. V., 884, *898*
Garvey, A. M., *618*
Garvey, W. D., 191, *204*, 406, *417*
Garwood, D., 886, *904*
Gautier, M., 216, *227*
Gavurin, E. I., 563, *566*
Gebels, G., 583, *618*
Gebhart, P. H., 885, *907*
Gebsattel, V. E. von, 246, 249, *268*
Gedda, L., 219, *226*
Geiger, L., 569, *618*
Geiselhart, R., *498*
Gelb, I. V., 584, *618*
Gellerman, L. W., 436, *445*
Gentile, A., 535, *542*
Gentile, J. R., 603, *618*
Gephart, W. J., 586, *618*
Gerall, A. A., 486, *498*
Gerall, H. D., *904*
Gerard, F. O., 833n, *851*
Gerard, H. B., 919, *930*
Gerard, M., 880, *904*
Gerard, R. W., 180, *185*, 949, *960*
Gerber, I. E., *907*
Gerjuoy, H., 599, 600, *629*
Gerjuoy, I. R., *629*
Gerritz, K., 613, *624*
Gershon, E., 519, *529*

Gerstman, L. J., 581, 585, *622*, *624*
Gerwitz, P. J., 600, *628*
Gesell, A., 600n, 645, 651, 653, *654*, *669*, 873, 874, 876–82, 885, *904*
Getzels, J. W., 866, 886, *904*
Gewirtz, J. L., 878–80, *904*, *912*
Ghent, L., 882, *904*
Ghiselli, E. E., 76, 87, 936, *941*
Ghosh, S., 233, *239*
Giacomelli, F., 354, *378*
Giarman, J. J., 173, *185*
Gibb, J. D., 936, *940*
Gibbons, J. L., 263, *270*
Gibbs, C. G., 199, *202*, *203*
Gibbs, F. A., 736, *746*
Gibson, E. J., 294, *305*, 437, *445*, *447*, 584–87, 590, 592, 594, 612, *618*, 877, 882, *904*, *916*
Gibson, H. G., 955, *960*
Gibson, J. J., 12, *20*, 41, *46*, 294, *305*, 426, 434–39, *444*, *445*, 586, 612, *618*, 882, *904*
Gibson, W. E., 728, *731*
Giddan, N. S., 833, *851*
Gidro-Frank, L., 946, *960*
Gilbert, D. S., 326, 327, *328*
Gilbert, J. A., 657, 743, *747*, 862, *904*
Gilbreth, F., 939
Gilbreth, L., 939
Gilchrist, J. C., 594, *618*, *628*
Giles, E., 955, *960*
Giles, N. B., 237, *239*
Gill, M. M., 601, *625*, *854*, 843, 953, *960*
Ginsberg, B. E., 206, 215, *226*, 711, *719*
Ginsberg, E., 888, *904*
Ginsberg, R., 882, *915*
Ginsberg, S., 836, *850*
Ginsborg, B. L., 327, *328*
Ginsburg, B. E., 868, *904*
Girshick, M. A., 234, *240*
Gitelson, M., 883, *904*
Gittelsohn, A. M., 884, *901*
Gladney, T. A., 608, *618*
Glanville, A. D., 407, *416*
Glanzer, M., 537 *541*, 596, *618*
Glaser, E. M., 935, *941*
Glaser, R., 504, *514*
Glasgow, L. A., *268*
Glasman, L. D., 597, *614*
Glasman, E., 181, *187*
Glass, D. C., 750, *770*
Glass, D. G., 940, *941*
Glass, G. V., 94n, 95n, 97, 100, 105, *106*
Glass, L. B., 951, 955, *959*
Glaze, J. A., 602, *618*
Gleason, H. A., Jr., 569, 572, 574, 588, 605, *618*
Gleitman, H., 424, 427, *446*
Glen, J. S., 406, *416*
Gleser, G., 777, 781, 786, *790*, *791*
Gleser, G. C., 78, 79, *87*
Glick, P. C., 893, *904*, *911*
Glickman, S. E., 478, *480*, 765, *770*
Glixman, A. T., 845, *851*
Glorig, A., 354, 360, 361, 372, *378*, *379*, *380*
Glow, P. H., 169, 170, 173, 175, *185*
Glowinski, J., 169, 177, *185*
Glucksberg, S., 562–64, *566*, 882, *904*
Goddard, H. H., 862, *904*
Goddard, K. E., 874, *908*
Godman, A., *852*
Goedel, K., 27, 30, *47*
Goertzel, M. G., 887, 891, *904*

Goertzel, V., 887, 891, *904*
Goethe, J. W. von, 6, 17, 891
Golby, C. W., 201, *202*
Goldberg, F. H., 834, *851*
Goldberg, J. P., 366, *379*
Goldberg, L. R., 114, *121*, 783, 785, 787, *790*, *791*
Goldberg, R., 238, *241*
Goldberger, L., 388, *393*, 838, 848, 850, *851*
Goldblatt, I., 883, 889, *906*
Golden, J. T., 117, *121*
Goldenson, R. M., 880, *905*
Goldfarb, A. I., 896, *904*, *907*
Goldfarb, J., 196, *203*
Goldfarb, W., 878, 880, *904*
Goldfoot, D. A., 946, *961*
Goldfrank, P., 747
Goldfried, M. R., *619*
Goldhamer, H., 895, 897, *901*
Goldiamond, I., 505, *513*, 592, *618*, 830, 832, 834, 847, *851*, *854*
Golding, W., 17–19, *20*
Goldmacher, D., 748
Goldstein, 392
Goldstein, A. P., 958, *960*
Goldstein, E. B., 342, *347*
Goldstein, G., 847, *854*
Goldstein, H., 451, *460*
Goldstein, I. L., 409, *416*
Goldstein, K., 819, 820, *824*
Goldstein, M. J., 426, *445*, 829, 830, 836, *852*
Goldstein, R., 362, 372, *378*, *380*, 725, 727, *731*, *732*
Goldstone, S., 196, *203*, 443, *444*, 556, *565*
Goldweber, A., 836, 837, 838, *855*
Golembiewski, R. T., 925, *930*
Gollob, H. F., 81, *87*
Gonzales, C., 473, *481*
Gooch, B., *653*
Goode, W. J., 893, *904*
Goodell, H., 949, *959*
Goodenough, D. R., 741, *746*, *747*, 841, *857*
Goodenough, F. L., 607, *618*, 659, 660, *669*, 866, 880, *904*
Goodman, B., 841, *852*
Goodman, C. C., 426, *444*, 827, *850*
Goodman, K. S., 569, *618*
Goodman, P., 887, *904*
Goodnow, J. J., 549, 555, *565*, 748
Goodrich, K. P., 484, *498*
Goodrick, C. L., 871, *904*
Goodwin, 493
Gordon, R. E., 258
Gordon, A. M., 592, 594, *627*
Gordon, C., 837, *856*
Gordon, C. M., 837, *852*
Gordon, J. E., 947, *960*
Gordon, L. V., 782, *790*
Gordon, N., 829, *851*, 874, 875, *904*
Gorfein, D. S., 602, *618*
Gorlow, L., 845, 847, *855*
Görres, 259
Gorton, B. E., 950, *960*
Goss, A. E., **568–629**
Gottesman, I. I., 216, 218–23, *226*
Gottesman, K. S., 171, 172, *186*
Gottier, R. F., 709, *719*
Gottlieb, D., *904*
Gottlieb, G., 866, 869, *904*
Gottlieb, S., 390, *393*
Gottschaldt, K., 425, 427, *445*
Gottschalk, L. A., 262, 263, *268*
Gough, H. G., 786, 787, *790*
Gough, P. B., 608, 610, *619*
Gould, H. N., 884, *904*
Gould, J. D., 410, *416*
Gould, M. R., 884, *904*
Gourevitch, S., 833, 838, *853*

Katzell, R. A., 934, 938, 939, *941*
Kaufman, C., 867, *912*
Kaufman, E. L., 407, *417*
Kaufman, I. C., 257, 260, *269*
Kaufman, R. M., 267, *269*
Kawliche, S., *746*
Kay, H., 871, 895, *899, 907*
Kay, J., 201, *202*
Kay, P., 589, *614*
Kay, R. E., 383, *384*
Kaye, H., 873, 874, *903, 907, 908*
Keats, J. A., 78, 79, *88*
Keddie, K. M. G., *747*
Keegan, J. H., *628*
Keele, S. W., 197, 199–201, *203*
Kees, W., 569, *626*
Keesey, Ü. T., **307–29**
Kehoe, M., 264, *269*
Keilman, P. A., 601, *621*
Keim, C. S., 949, *962*
Keith-Spiegel, P., **861–917**
Kelleher, R. T., *178*
Keller, B., 648, *653, 876, 903*
Keller, F. S., 190, *203*, 494, 501, 503, 504, 511, *513*
Keller, L., *161*
Kelley, C. R., 949, 951, *961*
Kelley, H. H., 922, 925–27, *930, 931*
Kelley, T. L., 634, *643*
Kellogg, L. A., 867, *907*
Kellogg, W. N., 487, 488, *499*, 867, *907*
Kelly, D. H., 319, *329*
Kelly, G. A., 846, *852*
Kelman, H. C., 928, *930*
Kelsey, C. A., 573, *623*
Kelsey, D. E. R., 947, *961*
Kelsey, E., 359, *378*
Kemeny, J. G., 15n, *21*
Kemp, E. H., 160, *161*, 322, *328*
Kempler, B., 594, 595, *621*, 829, 830, *852*
Kendall, M. G., 77, *88*
Kendler, H. H., 548, 558, *566*, 613, *621*
Kendler, T. S., 558, *566*, 613, *621*
Keniston, K., 781, *790*, 889, *907*
Kennedy, G. C., 721, *732*
Kennedy, J. A., 262, *269*
Kennedy, M., 895, *907*
Kennedy, R. J., 893, *903*
Kenny, D. T., 391, *393*
Kenshalo, D., 383, *384*
Kent, G. H., *621*
Kent, M., 441, *444*
Kenyon, J., 729, *732*
Kenyon, J. S., *621*
Kephart, W. M., 893, *907*
Keppel, G., 530, 532, 535, 539, *541*, 586, *614*, 878, *907*
Kerrick, J. S., 584, *621*
Kersey, J., 741, *748*
Kersta, L. C., 576, *621*
Kerstin, S., 408, *417*
Kessel, F. S., 24, *47*
Kessen, W., 864, 874–76, *905, 907*
Kety, S. S., 166, 179, *186, 187*, 218, *228*, 734, *746, 750, 756, 771*
Keyfitz, N., 233, *240*
Khanna, S. M., 353, 354, 358, *379, 380*
Khavari, K. A., 171, 172, 175, *186*
Kibuchi, Y., 296, *305*
Kidd, E., *528*
Kidd, J. S., 410, *417*
Kiell, N., 19, *21*
Kientzle, M. J., 190, 192, *204*
Kierkegaard, S., *818*
Kiess, H. O., 603, *623*
Kilpatrick, F. P., 431, 432, *446*
Kimball, C. P., 262, *269*

Kimble, D. P., 455, 456, *460*, 538, *541*
Kimble, G. A., 35, 456, *460*, 462, 474, *480*, 484–86, 491, 492, 498, 499, 832, *852*
Kimble, J. P., 600, 601, *624*
Kimura, R. S., 356, 359, *378, 379*
Kinch, J. W., 888, *900*
King, P. J., *586*
King, F. A., 729, *732*
King, G. F., 788, *394*, 481, 492, *498*
King, J. A., 710, *719*, 868, *907*
King, J. E., *816*
King, J. H., 361, *377*
King, W. L., 553, 557, *565, 566*
Kinney, J. A., 581, *622*
Kinsbourne, M., 407, *418*
Kinsey, A. C., 884, 885, 890, *907*
Kintsch, W., 133–35, 151, *162*, 532, 533, 537, 539, *541*
Kirchner, F. R., 356, *378*
Kirk, J. E., 890, *907*
Kirk, R. E., 94n, 98, 101, 105, *106*, 411, 412, *416*
Kirkland, G. L., Jr., 868, *905*
Kirkpatrick, C., 893, *907*
Kirkpatrick, E. A., 570, *621*
Kirkpatrick, J. J., 934, *941*
Kirscht, J. P., 923, *930*
Kiss, G. R., 596, *621*
Kissen, D. M., 260, *269*
Kistiakovskaia, M. I., 879, *907*
Kitto, G. B., 184, *185*
Kiuchi, S., 873, *915*
Kjeldergaard, P. M., 613, *621*
Klaiber, E. L., 843, 847, *850*
Klatt, D. H., 357, *378*
Klaus, R. A., 650, *654*, 882, *904*
Kleemeier, R. W., *907*
Kleespies, P., 834n, *856*
Klein, G. S., 390, 391, 393, 394, 400, 414, *417*, 423, 433, *446*, 489, 590, *621*, 828, 832–39, 842–49, *849, 850, 851, 852, 853, 854, 855*
Klein, H., 237, *240*
Klein, I. C., 412, *415*
Klein, M., 246, *269*
Klein, R. E., 605, *627*
Klein, T., 882, *902*
Klenmuntz, B., 119, *121*, 776, *790*
Kleitman, E., 738, *746*
Kleitman, N., 734, 735, 737, 738, 740, 742, 743, *746*, 876, *907*
Klemer, R. H., 893, *907*
Klemme, H. L., 949, 951, *961*
Kline, M. V., 947, 949, *961*
Kling, A., 868, *908*
Klinger, B. I., 857, *961*
Klinger, E., 387, *394*
Klinger, H., *855*
Klinman, C. S., 490, *499*
Klonoff, H., 895, *907*
Klopfer, B., *388*
Klopfer, P. H., 866, 869, *907*
Klopp, K. K., 943, *961*
Kmietowicz-Zukowska, A., 238, *241*
Knaff, P. R., 410, *418*
Knapp, M., 537, 539, *540*
Knapp, P. H., 265, *270*
Kniffen, C. W., 534, *615*, 829, *849*
Knight, J., *185*
Knobloch, H., 661, *669*
Knop, C., 874, 875, *898*
Knott, J. R., 490, *499*, 736, *746*
Knott, T. A., *621*
Knott, V. B., 236, 237, 239, *240*, 880, *910*
Knox, C., 217, *227*, 361, *378*
Knox, H. A., 659, *669*

Knudson, R., 573, *622*
Knupfer, G., 893, *907*
Koch, A., 886, *907*
Koch, H., 221, 222, *227*
Koch, J., 878, *907*
Koch, S., 15, *20, 21*, 34, 44, *47*, 673, 676n, 694, 701, *704*
Kodlin, D., 865, *907*
Kodman, R., Jr., 292, *306*
Koella, W. P., 180, *186*, 734, *746*
Koenig, I. D. V., 478, *479*
Koenig, W., 575, *621*
Koenig, W., Jr., 577, 588, 606, *618*
Koffka, K., 422, 424, 434, 443, *446*, 551, *566*, 680
Koford, C. B., 869, *907*
Kogan, N., 781, *791*, 854, 866, *916*, 926, *930, 931*
Kogan, W. S., 781, *789*
Kohlberg, L., 882, *907*
Köhler, W., 13, *21*, 422, 434, 442, *446*, 680
Kohlschutter, *735*
Kohn, M. L., 889, *907*
Kohs, S. C., 659, *669*
Kolers, P. A., 536, *541*, 833, *853*
Kollar, E. J., *746, 747*
Kolstoe, R., 828, *853*
Koltsova, M. M., 877, *900*
Komarovsky, M., 889, *908*
Knock, A. F., 191, *204*, 535, *542*
König, A., 320, 321, *329*
Konochi, T., 359, *378*
Konorski, J., 455, *460*, 486, *499*, 701, 702n, *704*
Kopin, I., 168, 178, *185*
Koplin, J. H., 601, *621*
Kopp, A., 575, 580, *625*
Koppenaal, R. J., 531, 532, *541*
Korchin, S. H., 895, *908*
Korensko, R. L., *746*
Korman, A. K., 938, *941*
Korn, S., 222, 228, 876, *915*
Korner, A. F., 875, *908*
Kornetsky, C. H., 946, 960, *961*
Kornmueller, A. E., 736, *747*
Kosman, A. J., 722, *732*
Kotarbinski, T., 23, 27, 30, 42, *47*
Kotliarevsky, L. I., *493*
Kotlaff, D. H., *853*
Kounin, J. S., 863n, *905*
Koutsoudas, A., 605, *621*
Kovach, J. K., 868, 870, *908*
Kovaly, J. J., 292, *306*
Kowal, S. J., 261, *269*
Kozaki, A., 440, *446*
Kozaki, T., 439, 440, 442, *446*
Kraepelin, E., *657*
Kral, T. P., 441, *444*
Kramarz, P., 943, *959*
Kramer, E., 949, 955, *961*
Kramer, J., 362, *378*
Kramer, M., *748*
Krantz, D. H., 75, *88*, 147, 149, 155, 156, *162*, 427, *447*
Krantz, D. L., 451, *460*
Krantz, J. C., 166, *186*
Kranz, F., 295, 298, *305*, 362, *377*
Kranz, H., 219, *227*
Krasner, L., 504, 505, *513, 514*, 776, 792, 832, *853*
Kratwohl, D., *853*
Krauskopf, J., 324, *329*, 337, *347*, 436, *446*
Krauss, R. M., 882, *904*
Krausz, M., 726, *731*
Kream, J., *748*
Krech, D., 12, 13, 169, 170, 176, *186*, 423, 424, 430, 431, *446*, 704, 899
Krech, E. S., 870, *899, 912*
Kreikhaus, E. E., 729, *732*
Kremer, S. J., 193, *203*
Krendal, E. S., 191, *204*

Kreps, *191*
Kressel, K., 592, *629*
Kriendler, A., 874, *909*
Kringlen, E., 219, *227*
Kripke, D. F., 738, *747, 748*
Kris, E., 845, *853*
Kristofferson, A. B., 303, *306*, 840, *856*
Kristy, N. F., 218, *226*
Kroeker, L., 829, *850*
Kroger, R., 887, *908*
Kroger, W. S., 945, *961*
Krogman, W. M., 235, 240, 876, *908*
Kron, R. E., 874, *908*
Krug, R. S., *808*
Kruger, L., 763, *771*
Kruglov, L. P., 896, *902*
Krugman, J. I., *669*
Krugman, M., *669*
Kruijt, J. P., 868, *908*
Krulee, G. K., 608, *618*
Krus, D. M., 434, *446, 447*
Krushinski, L. V., 215, *227*
Kruskal, J. B., 83, *88*, 284, *305*, 596, *621*
Kryter, K. D., 282, *305*, 373, *378*, 940, *941*
Kubie, L. S., 247–48, *269*, 391, *394*
Kubitschek, P. E., 238, *240*
Kučera, H., 588, 606, *621*
Kuder, G. F., 76, 874, *791*
Kuffler, S. W., 325, *329*
Kuhlen, R. G., 646, *654*, 872, 883, 885, 888–93, 896, *908, 911*
Kuhlmann, F., 645, *654*, 660, *670*
Kuhn, T. S., 689, *704*
Kulka, A. M., 257, *269*
Külpe, O., 396, 397, 402, *417*
Kummer, H., 712, *719*
Künnapas, T., 72, *88*
Kunst, M. S., 877, *908*
Kuo, Z. Y., 866, 868, 870, *908*
Kuppuusawny, B., 212, *227*
Kurcz, I., 601, *621*
Kurland, S., 828, *853*
Kuroda, S-Y., 607, *621*
Kurtz, K. H., 556, 562, *566*
Kusano, K., 383, *384*
Krusyszyn, I., 781, 789, *791*
Kutner, B. D., 896, 897, *908, 915*, 923, *930*
Kutscher, C., 726, *732*
Kveim, O., 729, *732*
Kydd, W. L., 574, *621*

La Barba, R. C., 261, *269*
LaBenz, P., 373, *378*
La Berge, D. L., 397–99
Lacey, B. C., 730, *732, 853*
Lacey, J. I., 252–54, *269*, 494, 730, *732*, 844, *853*
Lacey, L. Y., 575, *621*
Lacey, O. L., 592, *622*
Lachman, H., 44, *47*, 474, *480*, 516, *528*, 532, 533, 537, 539, *541*, 586, *621*
Lachman, T. M., 741, *747*
Lackum, W. J., von, 535, *541*
Lacy, O. W., 594, *621*
Ladd-Franklin, *330*
Ladefoged, P., 574, 575, *618, 621*
Lado, R., 569, *621*
Laffal, J., 569, *621*
Lagerspetz, K., 871, *908*
Lahja, A., 171, 182, *186*
Laing, W. A. D., 261, *272*
Laird, D. A., 408, *417*
Lakin, M., 875, *908*
Lamarck, C. de, *6*
Lamb, S. I., 169, 176, *186*
Lambert, W. E., 597, 598, 601, *621, 623*

Maurer, A., 879, *909*
Maurer, K. M., 660, *669*
Mausner, B., 937, *941*
Maxwell, 330
Maxwell, A. E., 82, *88*
Maxwell, G., 23, *46*
May, M. M., 569, *626*
May, R., 17, *21*, 818, 819
May, S. H., *909*
Mayer, J., 505, *513*, 721, *732*, 846, *853*
Mayman, M., 390, *394*, 843, 844, *854, 856*
Mayo, E., 925
Mayr, E., 725, *732*
Mayzner, M. S., 559–60, *566*, 585, 602, 604, 605, *623, 628*
Mazel, A., 260, *270*
Mead, J., 573, *622*
Mead, M., 246, 249, *270*
Meader, C. L., 570, *625*
Meares, A., 956, *961*
Mecherikoff, M., 586, *620*
Medawar, P. B., 231, *240*
Medinnus, G. R., 882–84, 888, 889, 893, *905, 909*
Mednick, S. A., 456, *460*, 487, *499*
Meehan, J. P., 250, 266, *269*
Meehl, P. E., *9n, 21*, 44, *47*, 79, 87, 114, *121*, *305*, 456, 458, *460*, 664, *670*, 779, 780, 785–88, *790*
Meeker, W. B., 951*n, 961*
Meerloo, J. A. M., 261, *270*
Mefferd, R. B., 600, 601, *624*
Mefferd, R. B., Jr, 600, *617*
Mehler, J., 608, *623*
Meier, C. A., 742, *747*
Meighan, T. W., 410, *416*
Meillet, A., 576, *623*
Meinong, 421, 422
Meissner, P., 841, *857*
Meissner, W. W., 889, *909*
Meister, D. E., 828, 842, 846, *853*
Mei-Tal, V., 260, *271*
Melei, J. P., 956, *961*
Melkumova, G. G., 361, *379*
Melrose, J., 292, *306*
Melton, A. W., 190, *204*, 431, 451, *460*, 535–38, *541*
Meltzer, H., 889, *910*
Melzack, R., 870, *915*
Memmescheimer, A. M., 950, *961*
Menaker, S. L., 114, 115, 119, *122*
Mendel, G., 39, 207
Mendels, J., 263, *270, 746*
Mendelsohn, G. A., 562–63, *567*
Mendelson, H. H., 262, *270*
Mendelson, J., 728, *733*
Méndez, J., 233, 238, *240, 241*
Menduke, H., 373, *379*
Mengert, I. G., 589, *628*
Menyuk, P., 578, 581, 605–7, *623*
Menzel, E. W., Jr., 471, 478, *481*
Meredith, H. V., **230–41**, 880, *910*
Meredith, W., 77, *88*
Merrill, M. A., 589, *627*, 647, *654*, 658, *670*
Merryman, C. T., 440, 441, *447* 493
Merton, D., 888, *913*
Merton, R. K., 24, 42, *47*
Mesel, E., 946, *961*
Messé, L. A., 594, *623*
Messer, M., 896, *910*
Messer, S., 597, *623*
Messick, S. J., 70, 73, 79, 85, 87, 88, 89, 119, 120, *122*, 777, 781–84, 789, *790, 791, 792*, 842, 843, 845–48, *851, 852, 854*
Metcalf, R. C., 749, 750, *770*
Metcalfe, M., 260, *268*
Metfessel, M., *623*
Métraux, R., 590, *614*

Metzner, 493
Meuman, E., 571, *623*
Mewhort, D. J., *623*
Meyer, C. C., 869, *913*
Meyer, D. R., 472–74, *481*, 490, *499*
Meyer, G., 865, *912*
Meyer, M., 292, *305*, 569, 570, *623*
Meyer, M. E., 726, 727, *732*
Meyers, C. E., 865, *910*
Meyers, E. S. A., 233, *240*
Meyers, W. J., 469, 472, *481*, 871, *910*
Miale, F. R., 609, *620*
Michael, C. M., 947, *959*
Michaels, R. M., 946, *959*
Michels, K. M., 423, *446, 623*
Michels, W. C., 440, *446*
Michelson, A. A., 31
Michelson, N., 238, *240*
Michelson, R. P., 376, *379*
Michon, J. A., 196, *205*, 367, *379*
Mickelson, N. I., 602, *623*
Micocci, A., 410, *417*
Middleton, R., 888, *910*
Midlo, C., 218, *226*
Mikhail, A. A., 264, *270*
Miles, C. C., 645, 646, *654*, 894, *910*
Miles, G. H., 191, *204*
Miles, R. C., **461–82**
Miles, W. R., 645, 646, *654*, 894, *910*
Milgram, S., 222, *228*, 928, *931*, 951, *961*
Mill, J. S., 34, 167, 887, 891, *910*
Miller, 607, 808
Miller, A. L., 407, *417*
Miller, C., 828, *854*
Miller, D. C., 892, *910*
Miller, D. R., 920, *931*
Miller, D. S., 215, *226*
Miller, E., 252, 253, 266, *268*
Miller, E. K., 646, *653*
Miller, F. R., 260, *270*
Miller, G., 362, *378*
Miller, G. A., *9n*, 10, *21*, 113, *121*, 190, 200, *204*, 293, *305*, 367, *379*, 393, 407, *417*, 456, *460*, 537, 539, *541, 542*, 570, 582, 587, 592, 593, 605, 609, 610, *616, 623, 767, 771*
Miller, G. R., 607, 608, *623*
Miller, H., 846, *849*
Miller, H. C., 874, *902*
Miller, H. H., 887, *910*
Miller, J. D., 301–2, *305*
Miller, J. G., 12, 13, 832, *854*, 935, *941*
Miller, K. M., 601, *626*
Miller, L. K., 605, *627*
Miller, N. E., 35, 40, *46, 47*, 169, 171, 172, *186*, 391, *394*, 456, *460*, 518*n*, 519, 520, 526, *528*, 534, *542*, 578–79, 581, 582, 585, 586, 590–91, 595, 611, 612, 613, *617, 623*, 676–79, 682, 689, 690, 694, 699, 701, 702*n*, 703, 704, 705, 721, 728, 729, 731, *732*, 754, *770*
Miller, R., 892, 896, *910*
Miller, R. E., 729, *732*
Miller, R. J., 950, *961*
Miller, V. L., *747*
Miller, W. C., 493, 494, *499*
Miller, W. R., 606, *623*, 878, 881, *903*
Millis, J., 233, *240*
Millman, J., 100, *106*
Mills, C. A., 238, *240*, 884, *910*
Millward, R. B., *161*
Milmoe, S., 878, *910*
Milner, B., 534, 535, *542*

Milner, P., 505, *513*, 727, *732*, 750, 751, *771*
Milner, P. M., 434, 435, *447*, 538, 539, *542*
Milton, J., 17
Miminoshvili, D. I., 253, *270*
Minard, J. G., 591, 594, 596, *623*, 830, 831, *854*
Minard, R. D., 923, *931*
Miner, J. B., 436, *447*, 934, *941*
Minifie, F. D., 573, *623*
Minres, 82
Minton, H. L., 784, *791*
Minturn, A. L., 396, 407, *415, 417*
Mintz, D. E., 511, *513*
Mintz, E. U., 325–27, *328*
Mintz, S., 600, *623*
Miron, M. S., 577, 583, 584, 586–87, *620, 623*
Mirsky, I. A., 246, 252, 254, 264, *270*, 729, *732*
Mischel, W., 776, 777, *791*, 843, 848, *854*
Mises, R. von, 27, 28, *47*
Mishkin, M., 473, *481*
Misiak, H., 674, *705*
Miskolczy-Fodor, F., 362, *379*
Mitchell, G. D., 867, 869, *910*
Mitchell, M. B., 948, *961*
Mitnick, L. L., 191, *204*
Mitscherlich, 246
Mittleman, B., 876, 880, *910*
Mitzell, H. E., 781, *791*
Modreski, R. A., 589, 590, *623*
Moeller, G., 486, *499*
Møhl, B., 361, *379*
Mohrman, K., 430, *447*
Mokken, R. J., 588, *628*
Molière, 24
Molinari, S., 741, *747*
Molish, H. B., 590, *614*
Moll, A., 946, *961*
Moll, K. L., 573, 574, *623*
Moltz, H., 866, 869, *910*
Moncrieff, A., 217, *228*
Money, J., 645, 648, *654*
Monroe, L. J., 737, 741, *747*
Montagu, M. F. A., 237, 238, *240*, 884, *910*
Montague, W. E., 400, 411, *417*, 603, *623*
Montague, W. P., *9n, 21*
Montgomery, J. R., 846*n, 855*
Montgomery, K. C., 477, *481*
Montpellier, G. de, 491, *499*
Mood, A. M., 63, 64, *65*
Mooney, W., 831, *854*
Moore, A. U., 869, *906*
Moore, G. P., 573, *623*
Moore, H., 601, *621*
Moore, K. E., 178, *186*
Moore, L. M., 737, 738, *747*
Moore, M. E., 887, *912*
Moore, P., 573, *616, 620*
Moore, T., 650, 651, *654*
Moore, T. V., 695*n*, 700, *705*
Moore, W. E., 920, 922, 929, *931*
Morales, S., 238, *241*
Moran, L. J., 600, 601, *621, 623* 627
Morant, R. B., 433, *447*
Moray, N., 368, *379*, 402, 403, *417*, 534, *542*
Mordkoff, A., 265, *270*
Moreno, J. L., 925, *931*
Morf, M. E., 781, 783, *791*
Morgan, 768
Morgan, A. H., 945, 946, *960*
Morgan, B. B., Jr., 400, 401, *417*
Morgan, C. T., 290, *306*, 677*n*, 688*n*, 701, *705*
Morgan, J. J. B., 407, *417*, 875, *916*
Morgan, M., 889, *910*

Morgan, R. F., 895, 896, *910*
Morgane, P. J., 722, 724, 725, 728, *732*
Morgenbesser, E., 47
Moriarty, A., 661, *669*, 843, 848, *851*
Morin, R. E., 400, *417*
Morita, 259
Morkkonen, L., 210, *228*
Morley, E. W., 31
Morlock, H. C., Jr., *748*
Morlock, J. V. V., *748*
Morotto, D. R., 726, *732*
Morris, C. J., 133, 134, 135, *162*, 497, 532, *541*
Morris, G., 570, 590, *624*
Morris, J. H., *121*
Morris, V. A., 610, *624*
Morrissett, L., Jr., 557, 558, *567*
Morrison, D. F., *747*
Morrison, H. W., 69, *89*
Morrison, S. D., 726, *732*
Morrow, R. S., **656–70**
Morrow, S., **656–70**
Morrow, W. R., 887, *910*
Morse, W. C., 589, *624*
Morton, J., 427, *445*, 595, *624*
Moruzzi, G., *417*, 677, *705*, 742, *747*
Moscona, A. A., 231, *240*
Moscovitch, D. H., 359, *378, 379*
Moses, 818
Moses, E. R., Jr., 574, *624*
Moses, G., 895
Moses, L. E., 64, *65*
Mosier, C. I., 81, *88*
Moskowitz, S., *853*
Moss, H. A., 650, *654, 853*, 877, 879, 881, 887, *907, 910*
Mosso, 939
Mosteller, F., 14, 15*n*, 20, 43, *46*, 65, 71, *88*, 455, *460*
Mote, F. A., **307–29**
Moulin, L. K., 372, *376*
Moulin, L. L., 304
Moustakas, C., 819, 823, *824*
Mowatt, M. H., 422, *447*
Mowrer, O. H., *9n*, 15*n, 21*, 35, *46*, 413, *417*, 465, 477, *481*, 485, *499*, 518–21, 524, 526, 528, 579, 581, 585, 611, *624*, 674, 676, 677, 690, *705*, 728, *732*, 754, *770*
Moylan, J. J., 591, *624*
Mozell, M. M., 383
Mozzo, W., 354, *378*
Mrosovsky, N., 868, *910*
Mudd, S. A., 369, *379*
Muehl, S., 586, *619, 624*
Mueller, C. G., 308, 322, *329*
Mueller, J., 36
Mueller, M. R., 604, *617*
Muellner, S. R., 880, *910*
Muerle, J. L., 84, *86*
Muesser, G. A., 533, *543*
Müller, 275, 276, 521
Muller, P., 881, *910*
Müller-Lyer, 440, 441
Mulligan, B. D., 363, *379*
Munn, N. L., 866, 882, *910*
Munnichs, J. M. A., 896, *910*
Munro, T. A., 217, 221, *228*
Munroe, P., 193, *203*
Munsell, 74
Munson, W. A., *305*
Munsterberg, 657, 934
Murai, J. I., 577, *624*
Murakawa, N., 601, *623, 624*
Murchison, C., 275, *305*
Murdock, B. B., 442, *447*
Murdock, B. B., Jr., **530–43**
Murie, A., 868, *910*
Murphy, D. B., 412, *418*

General Index

Anticipation, timing and, effects on motor skills of, 194–97
Anticipation-invigoration mechanism of motivation (AIM), 696
Antidiuretic hormone (ADH), 723, 972
Antigone principle of motivation, 680
Antisocial behavior, chromosomal aberration and, 216
Antithesis, principle of, emotional expressions and, 751–52
Anxiety:
    human learning and, 520–21
    multivariate experimental research on, 805
    paradigm involving, 494 (*figure*)
    problem solving and, 562
    as reinforcer, 492
    word associations and, 600
AP (Nerve Action Potentials), 358, 359
APL (A Programming Language), 116
Appraisal-excitatory theory of emotion, 758
Approach behavior to organic drives, 727–28
APT (Advanced Personality Test), 811, 812
Aptitudes, defined, 192 (*see also* Abilities)
Archetypal characters in drama, 17–18
"Are Theories of Learning Necessary" (Skinner), 508
Area theories, 13 (*table*)
Aristotelian conception of soul, 4
Arm-hand steadiness, defined, 193–94
Armed Forces Qualification Test (AFQT), 667
Army Alpha Test, 646, 665
Army General Classification Test (AGCT), 667
Arousal (central activating processes). *See also* Stimuli
    behavioral arousal hypothesis, 478
    defined, 688
    emotion and affective, 764–66
Art of Loving, The (Fromm), 817
Art of Memory, The (Yates), 528
Arthur Point Scale of Performance Tests, 659
Articulation:
    manners of, 575
    process interaction between phonation, resonance and, 574
    of speech sounds, 573–74
Artists, cognitive processes of, 9–10
ASA (American Standards Association), 281, 291, 361, 362
ASA curves, defined, 295
Assertive ego, disciplined vs., 812 (*table*)
Assessment capability of computers, 114–15, 119
Assimilation:
    during cognitive development, 652
    thinking and, 550
Association:
    backward, 534, 534
    doctrine of memory by, criticized, 530–31
    forward, 534
    phonemes produced by, 583–84
        graphic representation of, 586–87
    sentences formed by, 609
    of words, 595–602
Association for Humanistic Psychology (American Association for Humanistic Psychology), 818–19, 822
Assumptions of statistical hypotheses, 61
Asthmatic personality, 265
Astronomy, 4–5
"At" threshold recognition of words, 591–95
Attention, 395–418
    in human learning, 521, 525
    intensive properties of, 406–14
        as long-term phenomena, 408–11
        as short-term phenomena, 406–8
    perception and, 436 (*see also* Perception)
    selective, 396–406
        hearing and, 401–3
        distraction and, 400–401
        factors affecting, 399–400
        mediated by meaning, 404–6
        vision and, 396–99
Attitude questionnaires, latent structure analysis of responses to, 77

Attitudes, 921–24
    cognitive, 842
    defined, 921
    toward hypnosis, 956–58
    instrumental, 680
    as motivational variables, 683
    of old people, 896
    social, 750
    structure of, 921–23
        investigation of, 809–10
Attribute learning, transfer effects and, 557–58
Attributes:
    of auditory perception, 368–71
    identification of, 554 (*figure*)
    of sensations, 280–82
    of word associations, 602–3
Attributive perception, 827–28
Audibility, thresholds of, 360, 361 (*figure*), 362
Audiometers, reference level for, 361, 362 (*figure*)
Audiometry, 371–72
Auditory cortex, neural pathways and, 359, 360 (*figure*)
Auditory perception, attributes of, 368–71
Auditory stimuli, duration of, 366–67
Auditory system. *See also* Hearing
    anatomy and physiology of, 352–60
        external ear, 352, 353 (*figure*)
        inner ear (*see* Inner ear)
        middle ear, 352, 353 (*figure*), 354–55
Aural stimuli, verbal learning and, 590
Authenticity, defined, 822
Authoritarianism, as way of knowing, 10n
Autia, 804
Automatic audiometry, 372
Autonomic nervous system (ANS):
    control behavior and, 250–58
    emotion and, 677, 763–64
Autonomous stage of personality development, 778
Availability:
    of functions, 563–64
    of responses, motor skills and, 189
Aversive conditioning, 157
Avoidance:
    as aspect of motility of organisms, 522
    of noxious stimuli, 728–30
Avoidance conditioning, 157
Avoidance learning, 464–65
Avoidance training, 485
Axes in factor analysis, criteria for determining location of, 83
Axiomatic systems of measurement theory, 75
Awareness (*Bewusstein*), 32, 832–34 (*see also* Consciousness)

Back reactions in brightness discrimination, 321
Backward association, 524, 534
Backward masking (*A–B* masking):
    experiments with, 153 (*figure*)
    subliminal stimulation and, 832, 839n
Balanced attitudes, 923
Balanced incomplete block designs, 101
Ballistic movements, 190
Bandwidth-fidelity dilemma in administration of personality tests, 781
Bandwidths, critical, 364 (*figure*), 365
Bar pressing:
    conditioning for, 502
    curves showing rates of, 506 (*figure*)
Barber Suggestibility Scale, 951–53
Barranquilla Rapid Survey Intelligence Test (BARSIT), 666
Basal skin resistance level (BSR level), subliminal stimulation and, 836
Basic Trust stage of cognitive development, 651
BAT (Body Adjustment Test), 840–41
Bayes estimators, 63
Bayes Theorem, 144, 145 (*figure*)
Bayesian inference, 64–65
Bayley Behavior Profile Scores, 648
Bayley's California First-Year Mental Scale, 645, 652, 661

BCTRY system (computer system), 116
Bees, genetic studies of, 211 (*figure*)
Behavior. *See also* Agonistic behavior; Animal behavior; Behavior genetics; Human behavior; Social behavior
    antisocial, 216
    atomism of units of, 6
    attitudes and, 923–24
    biochemical substrates of, 167–87
        cerebral monoamines and, 176–80
        cholinergic mechanisms in, 172–76
        history of biochemistry, 166–67
        protein synthesis, 180–84
        research methods in, 167–72
    control of:
        by autonomic nervous system, 250–58
        emotion and, 769–70 (*see also* Emotion)
    disorganized, 767
    group, 925–26
    of neonates, 874
    observable, 42–43
    pathological, heritability of, 219–20 (*figure*)
    patterns of, 169
        selective or differential effects of, 170
    reinforcement as strengthener of, 524–25 (*see also* Reinforcement)
    social-organizational, 120
    theory of:
        consolidation of, 15n
        influence of logical positivism on, 34
Behavior-genetic Analysis (Hirsch), 207
Behavior genetics, 206–29
    animal studies in, 211–15
    basic methods used in, 208–11
    history of, 207–8
    human studies, 215–25
        anomalies associated with chromosomal aberrations, 216–17
        heritability of abnormal and normal trait, 217–21, 223–25
        of identical and fraternal twins, 221–23
Behavior Genetics (Fuller and Thompson), 206, 207
Behavioral information, defined, 637
Behavior of Organisms, The (Skinner), 12, 503
Behavioral arousal hypothesis of animal learning, 478
Behavioral pharmacology, 505
Behavioral Science (magazine), 116
Behavioral psychology, 5
Behavioral threshold, defined, 280
Behavioristic hypothesis of psychosomatic disorders, 257–58
Beneficial anticipation, defined, 195
Berkeley Growth Study, 645, 650
Bernreuter Personality Inventory, 779
Bifactor model of intelligence, 632
BIMED programs (computer program), 116
Binaural phenomena, 367
Binet-Simon scale, 657, 660
Binet Scale of intelligence, 645
Biochemical determinants of emotion, 756
Biochemical substrates of behavior, 165–87
    cerebral monoamines and, 176–80
    cholinergic mechanisms in, 172–76
    history of biochemistry, 166–67
    protein synthesis, 180–84
    research methods in, 167–72
Biochemical variables, 167–70
Biochemistry, 166–67
Biological expansion and restriction processes, 872
Biological growth and decline processes, 871, 872
Biological needs, 425
Biological sciences, 5–6
Biology of Dreaming, The (Hartmann), 740
Biometrics (magazine), 105
Biometrika (magazine), 105
Biosocial theory of personality, 819
Biotropic area of motivation, 678
Birds, agonistic behavior of, 709
Birth order, socialization and, 919

Dentistry, 263
Deoxyribonucleic acid (DNA), 167 (*figure*), 184
Dependency of old people, 896
Dependent variables (*R*-variables), 93, 684, 685 (*table*)
Depression:
  of old people, 896
  role of hormones in, 263
Deprivation:
  adaptation to food, 725 (*figure*)
  motivation through, 677
  sensory:
    animal development and, 890
    psychosomatic research in, 262
  sleep, 743–45
Derived sampling distributions, defined, 57
Description and Measurement of Personality, The (Cattell), 801*n*
Descriptive statistics, defined, 51
Desurgency, as personality trait, 803
Detection. *See also* Signal Detectability, Theory of
  criterion of, 410
  theories of, 145–50
Determination of behavior, defined, 522
Determinism, methodological, 453
Deuteranopes, defined, 338
Development. *See* Adolescent development; Adult development; Animal development; Childhood development; Cognitive development; Infant development; Human development; Intelligence—development of; Language development; Personality development; Somatological development
Developmental Diagnosis (Gesell and Amatruda), 660*n*
Developmental psychology:
  characterized, 861–62
  design orientation toward measurement of development, 864–66
  historical perspective on, 862–63
  methodological problems of, 863–64
Deviation IQ, 662
Diagnosis by computers, 114–15
Diallel table, 209 (*table*)
Dichromat, defined, 338
Differential reinforcement of high rates (DRH) 510
Differential reinforcement of low rates (DRL), 510
Differential reinforcement of other behavior (DRO; differential reinforcement of zero rate), 510
Differential sleep deprivation, effects of, 744–45
Differential thresholds (DL determination):
  defined, 70–71
  of hearing, 365–66
Differentiation of phonemes, 578–79
Diffuse-articulated level of mentality, 652
Digital computers:
  analog vs., 107–9
  defined, 107
Digital Computers in Research (Green), 120
Digital-formant synthesizers for production of phonemes, 599
Dign an sich, defined, 25
Direct stimulation, impoverished, 832
Directive variables, 684–88
Directly observable behavior, synthetic propositions describing, 42
Disciplined ego, assertive vs., 812 (*table*)
Discomfort, as factor in learning, 676
Discourse on Method (Descartes), 5
Discrete sample spaces, 52–53
Discrete-state models used in psychophysics, 284–86
Discrete tasks in memory studies, 533
Discriminability:
  defined, 278
  index of (d′), 302–3
Discriminal dispersions, defined, 278
Discriminant validity in personality assessment, 980

Discrimination:
  auditory, 362–63
  brightness, 320–23
  frequency, 365 (*figure*)
  intensity, 365, 366 (*figure*)
  signal, 362–65
  something-nothing threshold of, 835*n*
  of speech sounds, 581–82, 585–86
Discrimination learning:
  animal, 158–60
  conditional, 470–71
  curves of, 472 (*figure*)
Discrimination training, effects of, 493
Disengagement theory of successful aging, 897
Disinhibition, defined, 487
Disorders. *See also* Psychosomatic disorders
  hearing, 371–75
    aging and, 374–75 (*figures*)
    audiometry and, 371–72
    noise exposure and, 372, 373–74 (*figures*)
Disordinal interactions, defined, 94
Disorganized behavior, 767
Disruption of responses, 426
Distal focus, generality of, 429–30
Distance, as variable, 68
Distraction:
  causes of, 400–401
  intensive properties of attention and, 407–8
Distractor technique used in studies of memory, 534
Divergent-production abilities, defined, 636
Divorce, 893
DL determination. *See* Differential thresholds
DNA (deoxyribonucleic acid), 167 (*figure*), 184
Dominance:
  agonistic behavior controlled by, 716
  dominance responses, 426
  ritualization of agonistic behavior and, 712–13
  submission and, 803
Doraphobia, defined, 757
Dose-response relations in use of drugs, 172
Double alternation learning, 470
Down's syndrome (mongolism), 216, 648
Drama, as most behavioral art form, 17–19
Dream sleep, function of, 742–43
Dreams, 740–42
DRH (differential reinforcment of high rates), 510
Drinking:
  effects of, on choline activity, 176 (*figure*)
  genes and, 220
Drives:
  acquired, 492
  affects, daydreaming and, 391–92
  defined, 676
  instinctive, 679, 681
  level of, animal learning influenced by, 474–75
  organic, 720–33
    environmental tolerance of, 726–30
    hunger as (*see* Hunger)
    thermoregulation and oxygen balance and, 725–26
    thirst, 723–25
  primary, 690 (*table*)
  reduction of:
    fantasy and, 391
    reinforcement as, 491
  secondary, 519–21
  Skinner's definition of, 43
DRL (differential reinforcement of low rates), 510
DRO (differential reinforcement of other behavior; differential reinforcement of zero rate), 510
Drugs:
  antibiotic, hearing disorders and, 375–76
  characteristics of, 171
  dose-response relations and, 172
  influence of, on moods, 756
  inhibiting protein synthesis, 183
  as stimuli, 166
Dualistic theories of motivation, 699
Duplicity theory, 308
Dynamic facts. *See* Constructs

Dynamic lattice, 801, 808 (*figure*)
Dynamic motivation, 697 (*figure*), 808
Dynamic motivational modality, components of, 808
Dynamic Psychology (Woodworth), 694
Dynamic theories of visual acuity, 327
Dynamic variables, 684–86, 687 (*table*), 688
Dynamogenic variables, 685, 687 (*table*)
Dysacusis, varieties of, 371

Ear, the. *See* Auditory system; Hearing
Early adulthood, characteristics and tasks of, 892–93
Eastern Psychological Association, 504
Education:
  computers in, 115
  operant techniques used in, 504, 505
  parental, child's IQ and, 648 (*figure*)
  parental concern about, child's intelligence and, 650 (*figure*)
Educational Ability, Tests of (TEA), 666
Educational and Psychological Measurement, 105, 106
Educational Testing Service, 666, 667
Eduction of relations and correlates, 632 (*figure*)
Edwards Personal Preference Schedule, 782, 784, 955
EEA (electroencephalic audiometry), 372
EEG. *See* Electroencephalograph
Effect, Law of, 458, 676, 682, 693
Effectance motivation (competance motivation), 695*n*
Effective stimuli (subjective stimuli), 490
Effector anticipation, defined, 195
Efferent fibers of organ of Corti, 357
Efferent neural pathways, auditory cortex and, 359–60
Efficient estimators, defined, 59
EFT (embedded figures test), 841, 842, 846*n*
Ego-closeness, ego-distance dimension of daydreaming, 390
Ego-defensive attitudes, 923
Ego strength, as personality trait, 802
Eight-response display, 137 (*figure*)
Ejective articulation, 575
Electrical potentials, generation of, in inner ear, 355–59
Electroencephalic audiometry (EEA), 372
Electroencephalograph (EEG):
  in sleep measurement, 735–36
  of somnambulistic subjects, 943
Electronic brain, shortcomings of, 15
Electroretinogram (ERG):
  components of, 340 (*figure*)
  effects of stimulus contrast on, 324
  in physiology of color vision, 340–41
Elementary Perceiver and Memorizer (EPAM), 119
Elemente der Psychophysik (Fechner), 276
Elements of Experimental Phonetics, The (Scripture), 569
Elicitation of speech sounds, 578
  external stimuli and, 579
Eliciting stimuli, defined, 463
Embedded figures test (EFT), 841, 842, 846*n*
Embryos, development of animal, 866–68
Emission of phonemes, 577–78
Emotion, 749–71
  of adolescents, 883
  affective processes of, 750–51, 764–66
  autonomic nervous system and, 677, 763–64
  bodily changes and, 751–54
  defined, 749–51, 767–68
  description of, 437
  dynamic determinants of, 754–55
  effects of repressed agonistic behavior on, 716–17
  of infants, 878–80
  mental health and, 768–69
  motivation and, 766–68
    suppressed motivation as determinant of emotion, 755

Psychosexual stage of development, 256
Psychosocial field situations, 41
Psychosomatic disorders:
  behavioristic hypothesis of, 257–58
  conditioning and, 256–57
  defined, 244
  necessary conditions for, 245
  psychosomatic and neurological explanations
    of, 255–56
  sociocultural factors in, 263–64
  specificity of, 245–46
Psychosomatic medicine, 242–72
  autonomic nervous system in, 250–58
  emergence of, 243
  importance of, 244–45
  models of, 246–50
  from 1935 to present, 258–60
  research literature on, 260–67
  tools of research in, 243–44
Psychosomatic Specificity (Alexander et al.), 260
Psycho-pathological criterion, primary motives
    determined by, 690
Puberty, defined, 884
Pubescence, defined, 884
Punishment:
  agonistic behavior controlled by, 716
  emotion and, 764
Punishment training, defined, 486
Pure-tone audiometry, 371–72
Pure-tone masking, 362–63
Pure tones, 349–50, 351 (*figure*)
  equal loudness contours for, 370 (*figure*)
Purposive Behavior in Animals and Men (Tolman),
    676
Pyrophobia, defined, 757
Pythagorean conception of numbers, 4

Q technique of factor analysis, 80
Quantification of strategies of concept learning,
    555
Quantitative variables in psychometrics, 68
Quantum theory, 41
Quartimax, defined, 84
Quasi-experiments, defined, 91
Quasi-needs, 839

R conditioning, defined, 502
R technique of factor analysis, 80
R-variables (dependent variables), 93, 684, 685
    (*table*)
Radex theory of intelligence, 640–41
Radical reductionism, 36–37
Radiant energy, responses to, 309 (*figure*)
Radicalism, as personality trait, 804–5
Rage, as emotion of neonates, 875
Random-effects factor, defined, 96
Randomization, 93–94, 96–97
Randomized-block designs, defined, 97–98
Random variables in statistical inference, 56
Ranking of heritability, 222
Rapid Eye Movements sleep. See REM sleep
RAS (Reticular Arousal System), 677, 692*n*
RAT (Remote Associates Test), 562–63
Rate control, as ability, 193
Rating scale method of scaling, 72
Ratio class method of scaling, 72
Rationalism:
  empiricism vs., 25
  logical consistency and, 9
  as way of knowing, 8
Raven Progressive Matrices Test, 666–68
Reaction time, defined, 193
Reactive effects of experimental arrangements,
    defined, 104
Reading errors, nature of, 608
Reading speed, mean scores of, 95 (*figure*)
Real phonemes, defined, 579
Real-time applications of computers, 113
Real-Time Computers (Uttal), 120
Rearrangement, as measure of memory, 532
Rebirth, as theme in literature, 17

Recall:
  defined, 437
  of dreams, 741
  as measure of memory, 532, 533 (*see also*
    Memory)
Receiver-operating characteristic curve (ROC
    curve), 286, 291 (*figures*), 412–13
Recency principle in animal learning, 462
Recent Advances in Psychosomatic Medicine
    (Wittkower and Cleghorn), 260
Reception paradigms of concept learning, 552
Receptor anticipation, defined, 195
Receptor potentials of color vision, 342
Recognition, 145–56
  as measure of memory, 532, 533
  memory trace and, 523–24
  pattern:
    simulation and, 118
    temporal variables in, 151–54
  perception and, mathematical models for, 145–56
  of phonemes, 579
    graphic representation of, 585
  of response incongruity, 426
  of sentences, 607
  stimulus magnitude and, 154–56
  of words, 588–95
Reductionism, 36–40
  methodological, 33
  observation and, 39–40
  theoretical, 36–38
Reflection densitometry, defined, 345
Reflex:
  defined, 463
  orientation and investigatory, 490
Reflex actions, physiologically conditioned, 5–6
Reflexes of the Brain, The (Sechenov), 260
Reflexive behavior of dogs, 867*n*
Regression:
  age, 946–47
  high mobilization vs., 813 (*table*)
Regular reinforcement (continuous
    reinforcement; *CRF*), 509
Reimorphism of causation, 42
Reinforcement:
  affective arousal and, 764–65
  cognitive, 437
  contingencies of, in operant conditioning,
    509–12
  decremental function of, 518, 524
  defined, 456–59
  delays in, 491
  incremental and decremental, 518, 524
  in learning theories, 455–56, 677
  motivation through, 677 (*see also* Motivation)
  negative, 425
  of organic drives, 727–28
  schedules of, 491
    in animal learning, 465
    combined schedules, 510–11
    depending on number of responses, 509–10
  secondary:
    in animal learning, 465–66
    described, 491–92
    in human learning, 518–21
  as strengthener of performance, 524–25
  temporal contiguity and, 488
  vigilance and, 410–11
Reinforcers:
  defined, 458
  synthesizing new, 459
Relativity theory, 41
Relaxation-drowsiness-sleep suggestions, effects
    of, 953
Relearning, as measure of memory, 532
Reliabilty estimates, 76
Religion, 19
REM (rapid eye movements) sleep, 738–45
  deprivation of, 744–45
  dreams in, 740–42
  functions of, 742–43
  minutes of sleep stages in, 740 (*figure*)
  of neonates, 874
  sleep stage bands in, 738–39

Remembering. *See also* Memory
  defined, 530
  time and, 531 (*figure*), 532
Remote Associates Test (RAT), 562–63
Rep Test (Construct Repertory Test), 846
Repetitions, memory and, 536
Representativeness of experiments (external
    validity of experiments), 104–5
Reproductive ability, cycle of, 872
Reptiles, agonistic behavior of, 709
Republic (Plato), 32
Resocialization, defined, 920
Resolution acuity, 327
Resonance:
  principle of, 423–24
  process interaction between phonation,
    articulation and, 574
  of speech sounds, 573
Respondents, defined, 484
Response orientation, defined, 193
Response-produced cues, defined, 491
Responses, *See also* Stimuli; Stimulus-response
    relationships
  in animal discrimination learning, 160 (*figure*)
  animal patterns of, 211–12
  base-level, 950–51
  biases of, 781–85
  cognitive control of, 251
  competing response theory:
    of perceptual defense, 595
    selective attention and, 401
  conditioned:
    defined, 464, 484
    conditioned emotional responses, 728
    in human learning, 524
    occurence of, 490
  conditioned avoidance, 728–30
    frequency distribution of, 730 (*figure*)
  criterion, 581–82
  defined, 522
  as effects of perception, 831*n*
  eight-response display, 137 (*figure*)
  Human Movement, 388, 390
  internal response continuum, 69
  mean latency of positive and negative, 153
    (*figure*)
  Method of Free Response, 302
  motor skills and, 188–89
  neural, 522
  occurrence of sentences as, 605–7
  occurrence of words as, 587–88
  to operant conditioning:
    rate of responses, 506–7
    variations of responses, 511
  performance and, 293, 294 (*figure*)
  phonemes as, 572–79
  precognition, 426
  proclivities of, 276
    methods of study for, 296–97
    sensory capability and, 278, 279 (*table*), 280
  of single receptor cells, 288 (*figure*)
  strength of, hypothetical distributions of, 138
    (*figure*)
  somatic, 253
  unconditioned, 463, 484, 490
  in word transformation, 604, 605
Restricted randomization, 93
Reticular Arousal System (*RAS*), 677, 692*n*
Reticular formation, projection pathways of,
    761 (*figure*)
Retina:
  funtion of, 307–9
  structure of, 308 (*figure*)
Retinal illuminance, relation of visual acuity to,
    325 (*figure*)
Retinex theory of color, 339–40
Retirement, adjusting to, 895–96
Retrograde extra-list effects, defined, 535
Review of Educational Research (magazine), 105
Reward analysis of phoneme differentiation,
    578–79
Reward thresholds, theory of, 179–80
Reward training, 485

monoaminergic theories of, 180
non-REM, 736, 740–42
patterns of waking and, 736–37
positioning of, 737–38
REM, 738–45
    deprivation of, 744–45
    dreams in, 740–42
    functions of, 742–43
    minutes of sleep stages in, 740 (*figures*)
    of neonates, 874
    sleep stage bands in, 738–39
    stages of, 736 (*figure*), 738 (*table*), 739 (*tables*), 740
Sleepwalkers, amnesia of, 944
Slow tension movements, 190
Small rank hypotheses, defined, 81
S-M-R theories of motivation, 700, 701 (*table*)
Social Age (SA), 661
Social attitudes, defined, 750
Social behavior:
    of adolescents, 883
    of animals, 213–14
    of children, 880–81
    of infants, 878–80
    of neonates, 874–85
    theory of, 13
Social class, child-rearing practices and, 919–20
Social codes, agonistic behavior controlled by, 716
Social conditions, emotion and, 756, 769.
        See also Emotion
Social fighting, as instinct, 718
Social Learning (Dollard), 690
Social objects, perception of, 430
Social-organizational behavior, simulation of, 120
Social psychology, 918–32
    attitudes (*see* Attitudes)
    defined, 918
    development of, 6–7
    of groups, 88–89, 924–27
    socialization, 919–21
Social Quotient (SQ), 661
Socialization, 919–21
Society:
    adolescent relations to, 889
    body-mind-society interaction, 266–67
    20th-century Western, 11
Society of Multivariate Experimental Psychology, 796
Sociocultural factors in psychosomatic disorders, 263–64
Sociotropic area of motivation, 678
Solipsism, defined, 36
Solution shifts, transfer effects and, 558
Solution words, 604–5
Somatic responses, 253
Somatological development, 230–41
    anatomical ontogenesis, 230–32
    puberal changes in, 237–39
    size and form of body segments, 235–36
    tooth agenesis, eruption and loss, 236–37
    weight of fetus, child, and adolescent, 232–35
Somesthesis, components of, 382
Something-nothing discrimination threshold, 835*n*
Somnambulistic model of hypnotic subjects, 943–45
Somnambulistic trance (deep trance; deep hypnosis), 944–45
Sone, defined, 281, 282
Sonic frequency, absolute threshold of audibility and, 360
S-O-R theories of motivation, 700, 701 (*table*)
Soul, conceptions of, 4
Sound, 365–70. *See also* Phonemes
    hearing levels and, 374, 375 (*figures*)
    intensity of, 351
        discrimination of, 365–66
    localization of, 367
    loudness of, 281, 369–70
    pitch of, 368–70
    pressure of, 281, 351
    variables of, 349–52

Sound-produced convulsions, susceptibility to, 214, 215 (*figure*)
Source personality traits, multivariate research on, 802–5
SP (summating potentials), 359
Space-time relationship, 68
Span of attention, 407
Spare capacities, 940
Specific-dynamic functions, defined, 688*n*
Specific life phase studies of developmental psychology, 863
Spectral distribution curves of monochromatic primary colors, 336 (*figure*)
Spectral sensitivity:
    in color vision, 331–33
    curves of, 333
        for erythrolabe and chlorolabe, 345 (*figure*)
        photopic and scotopic, 331 (*figure*)
Spectrum of sounds, 349, 350
Speculative philosophy, 25
Speech, defined, 350. *See also* Phonemes
Speech audiometry, 372
Speech sounds. *See* Phonemes
Spew law of word transformation, 605
Sports, agonistic behavior controlled by, 716
SQ (Social Quotient), 661
S-R theories:
    of mediation, 496–97
    of motivation, 700, 701 (*table*)
SRA Non-Verbal Form (test), 666
SRA Tests of General Ability, 666
S-S conditioning (sensory-sensory conditioning), 518, 519, 524
Stanford-Binet Scale, 645, 647, 657–62, 664, 665
Stanford Hypnotic Susceptibility Scale, 951
Stanines, as unit of measurement, 805*n*
Static theories of visual acuity, 327
Statistical decision theory, 63–64
Statistical estimation, defined, 51
Statistical hypotheses:
    defined, 51
    testing, 61–63
Statistical inference, 56–65
    Bayesian, 64–65
    defined, 51
    interval estimation in, 60
    point estimation in, 58–60
    populations, parent and sampling distributions in, 57–58
    probability distributions in, 56–57
    statistical decision theory in, 63–64
    testing statistical hypotheses in, 61–63
Statistical method, 49–66. *See also* Probability theory
    developed by computers, 115–18
    empiricism and, 51–52
    place of psychological investigations in, 50
    realtionship of, to psychometrics, 68
    scaling and, 69–75
        measurement theory in, 74–75
        models and, 69–70
        multidimensional, 73–74
        psychophysical laws of, 72–73
        sensitivity determined by, 70–71
    statistical inference in, 56–65
        Bayesian, 64–65
        defined, 51
        interval estimation in, 60
        point estimation in, 58–60
        populations, parent and sampling distributions in, 57–58
        probability distributions in, 56–57
        statistical decision theory in, 63–64
        testing statistical hypotheses in, 61–63
    survey of statistics, 50–51
Statistical regression in psychological experiments, 104
Statistical routines, 116–17
Status studies, experiments vs., 93
Stem, defined, 587–88
Stens, as unit of measurement, 805
Stevens' law, 72

Stimuli. *See also* Responses; Stimulus-response relationships
    acoustic:
        physical basis for, 349
        by waveform and spectrum, 350 (*figure*)
    auditory, duration of, 366–67
    aural, verbal learning and, 590
    in concept learning, 553, 554 (*figure*)
    conditioned and unconditioned:
        defined, 463, 484
        functional properties of, 490
    constant, 292 (*figure*)
    contextual:
        word associations and, 599–600
        word recognition and, 593
    continuum of, 69
    contrasts of, 324
    direct, impoverished, 832
    discriminability between 278
    drugs as, 166
    emotionality of:
        word associations and, 596–97
        word recognition and, 591–92
    emotionally loaded, perception and, 425–26
    endogenous, 743
    environment, 522
    external, 578
        elicitation of speech sounds by, 579
        physical external stimuli, 41
    generalization, transposition and equivalence of, 441–42, 463
    generation of, for computer use, 113
    ideal observer derived from nature of, 290–92
    information available to, 438–39
    instructional:
        word association and, 600
        word recognition and, 594
    intense, 754
    intermittent flicker and, 317–20
    internal, 522, 714–15
    intracranial electrical, 727–28
    j.n.d. in, 282
    magnitude of, 154–56
        psychological magnitude and, 283 (*table*)
    motivational:
        defined, 688
        word associations and, 600
        word recognition and, 594
    natural and simple sources of, 382–83
    nonverbal, recognition of words and, 589–90
    noxious, 728–30
    pairing of, 511
    parameters of, signal detection and, 362–63
    performance and, 293, 294 (*figure*)
    shock as source of, 492
    specificity of, 252
    subliminal, 832–40
        controversies over, 834–35
        influence of, 833–34, 836–39
        problems in studies, 839–40
        supraliminal vs., 835–36
        techniques, 832
    trace of, defined, 523
    verbal, 589
        verbal-nonverbal, 608
    visual, 590–91
    in word transformation, 604, 605
Stimulus-independent mentation, defined, 387.
        See also Daydreaming
Stimulus-response relationships:
    occurrence of phonemes in, 579–85
    occurrence of sentences in, 607–12
    occurrence of words in, 588–605
Stored-program digital information-processing system. *See* Computers
Storm and stress movement (*Sturm und Drang*), 7
Strategies of concept learning, 555
Stratification (ordinal-scale classificatory factors), 98
Stress:
    ADH activity under, 723
    general adaptation syndrome in situations of, 728

influence of, on perception, 425
psychosomatic research on, 262
word association under, 600
Strong True Score Theory, 76–78
Strong Vocational Interest Blank, 779, 808
Structural precognition responses, defined, 426
Structuralism, perception in, 420–21
Structure-of-intellect problem-solving model (SIPS), 642
Structure-of-intellect theory of intelligence (SI theory of intelligence), 635–40
Structure of Science, The (Nagel), 31
Structured personality assessment. *See* Personality assessment
Study of Lives, The (White), 863
Subduedness, will vs., 813 (*table*)
Subjective probability, inferred, 143 (*figure*)
Subjective stimuli (effective stimuli), 490
Subjectively expected utility model of choice (SEU model of choice), 142
Subliminal perception, 831–40
Subliminal registration, 836n
Subliminal stimulation, 832–40
controversies over, 834–35
effects of, 833–34, 836–39
problems in studies of, 839–40
supraliminal stimulation vs., 835–36
techniques of, 832
Subroutine libraries for computer programs, 112
Substantive component of validity in personality assessment, 780
Successive approximation, defined, 504
Successive reversal learning, 467
Successive scanning approach to concept learning, 555
Sufficient estimators, defined, 59
Summating potentials (SP), 359
Superego strength, multivariate research on, 803
Suppressibility, exuberance vs., 813 (*table*)
Supraoptic hypophysical system of hypothalamus, 723
Surface personality traits, multivariate research on, 800–802
Surgency, as personality trait, 803
Surgery, 262
Sway Suggestibility Test, 797
Switch-light problems, solving, 559
Syllables, morphemes compared with, 587
Symbolic analogue theory of thinking, 548–49
Symbolic information, defined, 637
Symbolism, as way of knowing, 9n, 16
Symbols:
in formal science, 23
in humanistic psychology, 16–17
Syncretic-discrete level of mentality, 652
Synthetic phonemes, defined, 579
Synthetic propositions:
of empirical sciences, 23–24
generalizations conveyed by, 43
psychological, 42–43
Systematic model of behavior, 109
Systematology, defined, 683
Systems:
defined, 108
of information, defined, 638

T-data tests (NF tests), 801, 812–14 (*tables*)
T-Group training (sensitivity training; Laboratory Training), 936–37
Tachistoscopic recognition, 152 (*figure*), 153 (*figure*)
Talbot-Plateau law, 317
TAQ (Test Anxiety Questionnaire), 562
Target populations, 95–96
Target stimuli, word associations and, 596
Targets of visual acuity, 323–24
Tasks:
complexity of, 408–9
discrete, in memory studies, 533
of early adulthood, 892–93
predictable distractor, 534
in problem solving, 558–61

variables of, 553–54, 559–61, 836
TAT (Thematic Apperception Test), 387–89, 391–92, 681, 777, 811, 820, 836, 838, 839, 841, 935, 955
Tautologies, defined, 24
Taylor Manifest Anxiety Scale, 797
TEA (Tests of Educational Ability), 666
Technometrics (magazine), 105
Teeth, agenesis, eruption and loss of, 236–37
Temperaments:
of animals, 213–14
defined, 750
Templin-Darley articulation test, 578
Temporal bone of ear, 353 (*figure*)
Temporal contiguity theory, 488
Temporal delayed learning, 468–70
Temporal forced-choice method for study of capability, 297
Temporal integration, role of, in hearing, 362
Temporal uncertainty in psychophysical research, 302–3
Temporal variables in pattern recognition, 151–54
Temporary threshold shift (TTS), 372
Tension:
ergic, 805
release of, as determinant of emotion, 755
Terman Group Intelligence Test, 666
Terman-McNemar Test of Mental Ability, 666
Terms, hypothetical and empirical, 683–84. *See also* Words
Territoriality, agonistic behavior and, 709–11, 714, 716
Test Anxiety Questionnaire (TAQ), 562
Test-Operate-Test-Exit mechanism (TOTE), 767
Test theory, 75–80
classical, 75–76
further developments in, 76–78
generalizability theory and, 78–79
mathematical models used in, 14
nature of measurement of the individual in, 79–80
Testing in psychological experiments, 104
Test-trial procedure applied to classical model of conditioning, 489
Thalamic theory of emotion, 759 (*figure*), 760
Thanatophobia, defined, 757
Thematic Apperception Test (TAT), 387–89, 391–92, 681, 777, 811, 820, 836, 838, 839, 841, 935, 955
Theorem, defined, 35
Theoretical physics, 42
logical positivism and, 30–31, 34
Theoretical reductionism, 36–38
Theories of Motivation (Madsen), 701
Theorists of motivation, listed, 678 (*figure*)
Theory:
defined, 697
formation of, 34–35, 43–44
operant attitude toward, 508–9
strata of, 697–98
Thermoregulation:
oxygen balance and, 725–26
thermal preference of rats, 725 (*figure*)
Thinking, 547–67
concept learning and (*see* Concept learning)
contemporary theory of, 548–52
errors of, 9
preconscious, 839
problem solving and, 124–29, 558–64
age and, 561–62
anagrams, 559–60, 563 (*figure*), 603–4
concept identification in, 124–27
motivation in, 562
multistage problems of, 127–29
transfer in, 563–64
variables in, 558–59, 561–63
Thirst, 723–25
Thomistic theory of motivation, 695n
Thought, *Zeitgeist* and, 4
Threctia, defined, 803
Three-ness concept in concept formation by animals, 474

Threshold:
above threshold recognition of words, 588–91
absolute:
of audibility, 360–61
determination of, 70–71
of human vision, 310
"at" threshold recognition of words, 591–95
behavioral, 280
differential:
defined, 70–71
of hearing, 365–66
incremental, of spectral sensitivity, 331–32
level above:
defined, 281
intensity discrimination and, 365
perceptual, 828–31
sensory, 147–48
of sleep, 735
something-nothing discrimination, 835n
theory of reward, 179–80
Threshold shift. *See* Tones
Thurstone Personality Schedule, 779
Thurstone Temperament Survey, 220
Thurstone Primary Abilities Test, 220
Timbre of sounds, defined, 370–71
Time:
as factor in human learning, 525
memory and, 531 (*figures*), 532
predicted and obtained portions of, 140 (*table*)
space-time relationship, 68
theoretical and empirical cumulative distributions of, 128 (*figure*)
Time-response relations of drugs, 172
Time-shared systems of computers, 110
Timidity, as personality trait, 804
Tones (threshold shift):
defined, 372
masking of, 289 (*figure*)
pure-tone masking, 362–63
pure, 349–50, 351 (*figure*)
equal loudness contours of, 370 (*figure*)
used in hypnosis, 954–55
TOTE mechanism (Test-Operate-Test-Exit mechanism), 767
Traceline Theories, 76–78
Tractatus Logico-Philosophicus (Wittgenstein), 27
Training:
avoidance, 485
sensitivity, 936–37
transfer of, memorizing and, 132–33
Training and development, psychology of, 934–35
Transaction, perception as, 431–33
Transcendent truth:
in causation, 41
defined, 24
modified, 30
theory formation and, 44
Transcription of phonemes, 572
Transcultural psychosomatics, defined, 249–50
Transfer:
effects of, on concept learning, 557–58
experiments in:
paired-associate items in, 133 (*figure*)
protein synthesis, 181–82
in problem solving, 563–64
Transformable significant interactions, defined, 95
Transformation, occurrence of sentences by, 610
Transformative abilities of intellect, 638
Transgeneration, defined, 116
Transitionism:
principles of monistic, 680
in psychology, 38
Transitional states, reinforcement in, 458–59
Transpersonal psychology, 821–22
Treatise on the Chemical Composition of the Brain, A (Thudichum), 166
Treatment, defined, 92
Trend analysis, 98
Trends, characterization of, 4
Trichromatic theory of color, 339
Trichomats, defined, 338